리얼오리지널

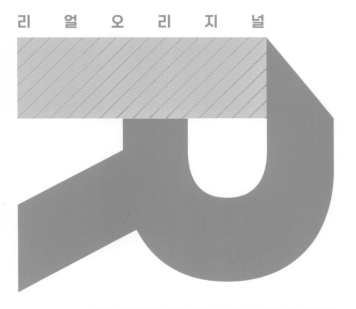
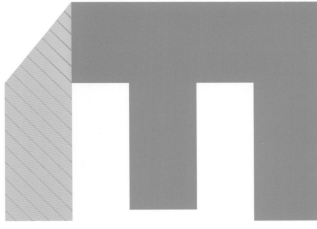
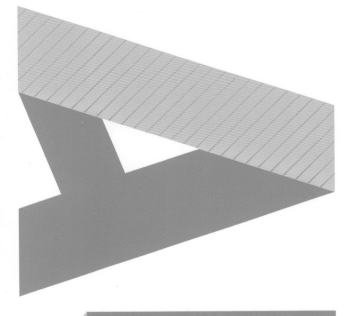

REAL

575만권
베스트셀러
리얼 오리지널 시리즈 누적 판매
2006~2024

2025 학력평가 + 내신대비

전국연합 학력평가
5개년 기출문제집

20회 ⌈ 3월·6월·9월·11월 학력평가 기출 20회 ⌋

• 2020~2024 최신 5개년 [고1] 전국연합 학력평가 20회
• 영어 [독해 28문항]을 회차별로 구성한 [유형별] 모의고사
• 학교시험 [중간·기말고사]를 대비한 내신 필수 문제집
• 매회 어휘를 복습할 수 있는 [어휘 리뷰 TEST] 20회
• 친절한 입체적 해설 [직독직해·구문 풀이·고난도 꿀팁]
• 회차별 [SPEED 정답 체크표·STUDY 플래너·정답률]
• [특별 부록] 회차별 영단어

고1 영어 독해

모바일로 학습하는
회차별 영단어 QR 코드 제공

● 문 제 편 ●

수능 모의고사 전문 출판
ipfly 입시플라이

REAL

REAL ORIGINAL

입시플라이

전국연합학력평가
5개년 기출 문제집

고1 영어 독해

Contents

독해는 18번부터 45번까지 일정한 흐름과 출제 패턴이 고정되어 있기 때문에 「유형별로 푸는 것도 중요」하지만 독해 28문항을 「한 세트로 풀어보는 훈련」이 매우 중요합니다.

수능 모의고사 전문 출판
입시플라이

실전은 연습처럼! 연습은 실전처럼! 「리얼 오리지널」

수능 시험장에 가면 낯선 환경과 긴장감 때문에 실력을 제대로 발휘 못하는 경우가 많습니다. 실전 연습은 여러분의 실력이 됩니다.

01

실제 시험지와 똑같은 문제지

고1 영어 독해는 **전국연합 학력평가 영어 [독해 28문항]**을 회차별로 20회를 구성한 모의고사입니다.

❶ 실제 시험지의 크기와 느낌을 그대로 살려 **실전과 동일한 조건** 속에서 영어 영역 독해 문제만 풀어 볼 수 있습니다.

❷ 문제를 풀기 전에 먼저 학습 체크 표에 학습 날짜와 시간을 기록 하고, [45분] 타이머를 작동해 실전처럼 풀어 보십시오.

02

하루 28문항 · 20일 완성

영어 영역에서 듣기 문항을 제외한 영어 [독해 문항]만 집중 학습할 수 있도록 만든 [20일 완성] 교재입니다.

❶ 독해 [18번~45번] 문제만 수록했으며, 영어 독해는 전체 유형의 문제를 [통으로 푸는 훈련]을 해야 점수가 올라갑니다.

❷ 독해 문제만 하루 [28문항 · 20일] 완성 교재이며, 독해 파트만 집중해 학습할 수 있는 효율적인 교재입니다.

03

회차별 [VOCA LIST]

회차별로 쉬운 단어부터 어려운 단어까지 모든 단어를 정리한 [VOCA LIST]를 제공합니다.

❶ 회차별, 문항별로 단어를 정리하여 매회 문제편 뒤에 제공되며 출제된 모든 핵심 단어를 수록했습니다.

❷ 빠른 독해와 영어의 생명은 어휘입니다. 회차별 단어를 문항별로 정리한 VOCA LIST로 어휘를 복습해 보세요.

※ 모바일로 영단어를 학습할 수 있도록 VOCA 상단에 QR 코드를 제공합니다.

★ 해설편 앞 부분에 「SPEED 정답 체크 표」가 있습니다.
오려서 정답을 확인하거나 책갈피로 사용하시면 됩니다.

04

회차별 [어휘 리뷰 TEST]

어휘와 독해력까지 동시에 잡을 수 있도록 [어휘 리뷰 TEST]를
총 20회 부록으로 제공합니다.

❶ VOCA LIST와 함께 매회 문제편 뒤에 제공되며 단어를 복습할
수 있도록 [어휘 리뷰 TEST]를 수록했습니다.

❷ 먼저 VOCA LIST로 학습하고 [어휘 리뷰 TEST]로 복습을
하시면 어휘력도, 독해력도 쑥~쑥 올라갑니다.

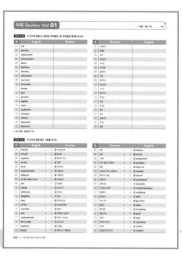

05

입체적 해설 & 문제 해결 꿀 팁

혼자서도 학습이 충분하도록 자세한 [입체적 해설]과 함께
고난도 문제는 문제 해결 꿀~팁까지 수록을 했습니다.

❶ 입체적 해설로 직독직해, 구문 풀이가 수록되어 있으며 혼자서도
학습이 충분하도록 자세한 해설을 수록했습니다.

❷ 등급을 가르는 고난도 문제는 많이 틀린 이유와 함께 문제 해결
꿀 팁까지 명쾌한 해설을 수록했습니다.

06

정답률 & SPEED 정답 체크 표

문제를 푼 후 빠르게 정답을 확인할 수 있는 SPEED 정답
체크 표와, 문항별 정답률까지 제공합니다.

❶ 문제를 푼 후 빠르게 정답을 확인할 수 있는 SPEED 정답 체크
표를 제공하며, 오려서 책갈피로도 사용할 수 있습니다.

❷ 문항별로 정답률을 제공하므로 문제의 난이도를 파악할 수 있어
문제 풀이에 답답함이 없습니다.

STUDY 플래너

① 문제를 풀기 전 먼저 〈학습 체크표〉에 학습 날짜와 시간을 기록하세요.
② 회분별 기출 문제는 영역별로 정해진 시간 안에 푸는 습관을 기르세요.
③ 정답 확인 후 점수와 등급을 적고 성적 변화를 체크하면서 학습 계획을 세우세요.
④ **리얼 오리지널**은 실제 수능 시험과 똑같이 학습하는 교재이므로 실전을 연습하는 것처럼 문제를 풀어 보세요.

● 영어 [독해] | 시험 개요

문항 수	문항당 배점	문항별 점수 표기	원점수 만점	학습 시간	문항 형태
28문항	2점, 3점	•3점 문항에 점수 표시 •점수 표시 없는 문항 모두 2점	63점	45분	5지 선다형

● 영어 [독해] | 학습 체크

회분	학습 날짜	학습 시간	채점 결과	틀린 문제	시간 부족 문제
01회 2024학년도 3월	월 일	시 분~ 시 분			
02회 2023학년도 3월	월 일	시 분~ 시 분			
03회 2022학년도 3월	월 일	시 분~ 시 분			
04회 2021학년도 3월	월 일	시 분~ 시 분			
05회 2020학년도 3월	월 일	시 분~ 시 분			
06회 2024학년도 6월	월 일	시 분~ 시 분			
07회 2023학년도 6월	월 일	시 분~ 시 분			
08회 2022학년도 6월	월 일	시 분~ 시 분			
09회 2021학년도 6월	월 일	시 분~ 시 분			
10회 2020학년도 6월	월 일	시 분~ 시 분			
11회 2024학년도 9월	월 일	시 분~ 시 분			
12회 2023학년도 9월	월 일	시 분~ 시 분			
13회 2022학년도 9월	월 일	시 분~ 시 분			
14회 2021학년도 9월	월 일	시 분~ 시 분			
15회 2020학년도 9월	월 일	시 분~ 시 분			
16회 2023학년도 11월	월 일	시 분~ 시 분			
17회 2022학년도 11월	월 일	시 분~ 시 분			
18회 2021학년도 11월	월 일	시 분~ 시 분			
19회 2020학년도 11월	월 일	시 분~ 시 분			
20회 2019학년도 11월	월 일	시 분~ 시 분			

18. 다음 글의 목적으로 가장 적절한 것은?

Dear Ms. Jane Watson,

I am John Austin, a science teacher at Crestville High School. Recently I was impressed by the latest book you wrote about the environment. Also my students read your book and had a class discussion about it. They are big fans of your book, so I'd like to ask you to visit our school and give a special lecture. We can set the date and time to suit your schedule. Having you at our school would be a fantastic experience for the students. We would be very grateful if you could come.

Best regards,
John Austin

① 환경 보호의 중요성을 강조하려고
② 글쓰기에서 주의할 점을 알려 주려고
③ 특강 강사로 작가의 방문을 요청하려고
④ 작가의 팬 사인회 일정 변경을 공지하려고
⑤ 작가가 쓴 책의 내용에 관하여 문의하려고

19. 다음 글에 드러난 Sarah의 심경 변화로 가장 적절한 것은?

Marilyn and her three-year-old daughter, Sarah, took a trip to the beach, where Sarah built her first sandcastle. Moments later, an enormous wave destroyed Sarah's castle. In response to the loss of her sandcastle, tears streamed down Sarah's cheeks and her heart was broken. She ran to Marilyn, saying she would never build a sandcastle again. Marilyn said, "Part of the joy of building a sandcastle is that, in the end, we give it as a gift to the ocean." Sarah loved this idea and responded with enthusiasm to the idea of building another castle—this time, even closer to the water so the ocean would get its gift sooner!

① sad → excited
② envious → anxious
③ bored → joyful
④ relaxed → regretful
⑤ nervous → surprised

20. 다음 글에서 필자가 주장하는 바로 가장 적절한 것은?

Magic is what we all wish for to happen in our life. Do you love the movie *Cinderella* like me? Well, in real life, you can also create magic. Here's the trick. Write down all the real-time challenges that you face and deal with. Just change the challenge statement into positive statements. Let me give you an example here. If you struggle with getting up early in the morning, then write a positive statement such as "I get up early in the morning at 5:00 am every day." Once you write these statements, get ready to witness magic and confidence. You will be surprised that just by writing these statements, there is a shift in the way you think and act. Suddenly you feel more powerful and positive.

① 목표한 바를 꼭 이루려면 생각을 곧바로 행동으로 옮겨라.
② 자신감을 얻으려면 어려움을 긍정적인 진술로 바꿔 써라.
③ 어려운 일을 해결하려면 주변 사람에게 도움을 청하라.
④ 일상에서 자신감을 향상하려면 틈틈이 마술을 배워라.
⑤ 실생활에서 마주하는 도전을 피하지 말고 견뎌 내라.

21. 밑줄 친 push animal senses into Aristotelian buckets가 다음 글에서 의미하는 바로 가장 적절한 것은? [3점]

Consider the seemingly simple question *How many senses are there?* Around 2,370 years ago, Aristotle wrote that there are five, in both humans and animals — sight, hearing, smell, taste, and touch. However, according to the philosopher Fiona Macpherson, there are reasons to doubt it. For a start, Aristotle missed a few in humans: the perception of your own body which is different from touch and the sense of balance which has links to both touch and vision. Other animals have senses that are even harder to categorize. Many vertebrates have a different sense system for detecting odors. Some snakes can detect the body heat of their prey. These examples tell us that "senses cannot be clearly divided into a limited number of specific kinds," Macpherson wrote in *The Senses*. Instead of trying to push animal senses into Aristotelian buckets, we should study them for what they are.

*vertebrate: 척추동물 **odor: 냄새

① sort various animal senses into fixed categories
② keep a balanced view to understand real senses
③ doubt the traditional way of dividing all senses
④ ignore the lessons on senses from Aristotle
⑤ analyze more animals to find real senses

22. 다음 글의 요지로 가장 적절한 것은?

When we think of leaders, we may think of people such as Abraham Lincoln or Martin Luther King, Jr. If you consider the historical importance and far-reaching influence of these individuals, leadership might seem like a noble and high goal. But like all of us, these people started out as students, workers, and citizens who possessed ideas about how some aspect of daily life could be improved on a larger scale. Through diligence and experience, they improved upon their ideas by sharing them with others, seeking their opinions and feedback and constantly looking for the best way to accomplish goals for a group. Thus we all have the potential to be leaders at school, in our communities, and at work, regardless of age or experience.

*diligence: 근면

① 훌륭한 리더는 고귀한 목표를 위해 희생적인 삶을 산다.
② 위대한 인물은 위기의 순간에 뛰어난 결단력을 발휘한다.
③ 공동체를 위한 아이디어를 발전시키는 누구나 리더가 될 수 있다.
④ 다른 사람의 의견을 경청하는 자세는 목표 달성에 가장 중요하다.
⑤ 근면하고 경험이 풍부한 사람들은 경제적으로 성공할 수 있다.

23. 다음 글의 주제로 가장 적절한 것은?

Crop rotation is the process in which farmers change the crops they grow in their fields in a special order. For example, if a farmer has three fields, he or she may grow carrots in the first field, green beans in the second, and tomatoes in the third. The next year, green beans will be in the first field, tomatoes in the second field, and carrots will be in the third. In year three, the crops will rotate again. By the fourth year, the crops will go back to their original order. Each crop enriches the soil for the next crop. This type of farming is sustainable because the soil stays healthy.

*sustainable: 지속 가능한

① advantage of crop rotation in maintaining soil health
② influence of purchasing organic food on farmers
③ ways to choose three important crops for rich soil
④ danger of growing diverse crops in small spaces
⑤ negative impact of crop rotation on the environment

24. 다음 글의 제목으로 가장 적절한 것은?

Working around the whole painting, rather than concentrating on one area at a time, will mean you can stop at any point and the painting can be considered "finished." Artists often find it difficult to know when to stop painting, and it can be tempting to keep on adding more to your work. It is important to take a few steps back from the painting from time to time to assess your progress. Putting too much into a painting can spoil its impact and leave it looking overworked. If you find yourself struggling to decide whether you have finished, take a break and come back to it later with fresh eyes. Then you can decide whether any areas of your painting would benefit from further refinement.

*tempting: 유혹하는 **refinement: 정교하게 꾸밈

① Drawing Inspiration from Diverse Artists
② Don't Spoil Your Painting by Leaving It Incomplete
③ Art Interpretation: Discover Meanings in a Painting
④ Do Not Put Down Your Brush: The More, the Better
⑤ Avoid Overwork and Find the Right Moment to Finish

25. 다음 도표의 내용과 일치하지 <u>않는</u> 것은?

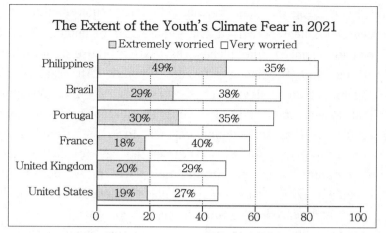

The Extent of the Youth's Climate Fear in 2021
☐ Extremely worried ☐ Very worried

	Extremely worried	Very worried
Philippines	49%	35%
Brazil	29%	38%
Portugal	30%	35%
France	18%	40%
United Kingdom	20%	29%
United States	19%	27%

    The above graph shows the extent to which young people aged 16−25 in six countries had fear about climate change in 2021. ① The Philippines had the highest percentage of young people who said they were extremely or very worried, at 84 percent, followed by 67 percent in Brazil. ② More than 60 percent of young people in Portugal said they were extremely worried or very worried. ③ In France, the percentage of young people who were extremely worried was higher than that of young people who were very worried. ④ In the United Kingdom, the percentage of young generation who said that they were very worried was 29 percent. ⑤ In the United States, the total percentage of extremely worried and very worried youth was the smallest among the six countries.

26. Jaroslav Heyrovsky에 관한 다음 글의 내용과 일치하지 <u>않는</u> 것은?

    Jaroslav Heyrovsky was born in Prague on December 20, 1890, as the fifth child of Leopold Heyrovsky. In 1901 Jaroslav went to a secondary school called the Akademicke Gymnasium. Rather than Latin and Greek, he showed a strong interest in the natural sciences. At Czech University in Prague he studied chemistry, physics, and mathematics. From 1910 to 1914 he continued his studies at University College, London. Throughout the First World War, Jaroslav served in a military hospital. In 1926, Jaroslav became the first Professor of Physical Chemistry at Charles University in Prague. He won the Nobel Prize in chemistry in 1959.

① 라틴어와 그리스어보다 자연 과학에 강한 흥미를 보였다.
② Czech University에서 화학, 물리학 및 수학을 공부했다.
③ 1910년부터 1914년까지 런던에서 학업을 이어 나갔다.
④ 제1차 세계 대전이 끝난 후 군 병원에 복무했다.
⑤ 1959년에 노벨 화학상을 수상했다.

27. Spring Tea Class for Young People에 관한 다음 안내문의 내용과 일치하지 <u>않는</u> 것은?

Spring Tea Class for Young People

    Join us for a delightful Spring Tea Class for young people, where you'll experience the taste of tea from various cultures around the world.

Class Schedule
• Friday, April 5 (4:30 p.m. − 6:00 p.m.)
• Saturday, April 6 (9:30 a.m. − 11:00 a.m.)

Details
• We will give you tea and snacks.
• We offer special tips for hosting a tea party.

Participation Fee
• Age 13 − 15: $25 per person
• Age 16 − 18: $30 per person

Note
    If you have any food allergy, you should email us in advance at youth@seasonteaclass.com.

---

① 수강생은 전 세계 다양한 문화권의 차를 경험할 수 있다.
② 금요일 수업은 오후에 1시간 30분 동안 진행된다.
③ 수강생에게 차와 간식을 제공할 것이다.
④ 15세 이하의 수강생은 30달러의 참가비를 내야 한다.
⑤ 음식 알레르기가 있는 수강생은 이메일을 미리 보내야 한다.

28. Clothes Upcycling Contest 2024에 관한 다음 안내문의 내용과 일치하는 것은?

Clothes Upcycling Contest 2024

    Are you passionate about fashion and the environment? Then we have a contest for you!

• **Participants**
 − Anyone living in Lakewood, aged 11 to 18

• **How to participate**
 − Take before and after photos of your upcycled clothes.
 − Email the photos at lovelw@lwplus.com.
 − Send in the photos from April 14 to May 12.

• **Winning Prize**
 − A $100 gift card to use at local shops
 − The winner will be announced on our website on May 30.
For more details, visit our website www.lovelwplus.com.

---

① Lakewood에 사는 사람이면 누구든지 참가할 수 있다.
② 참가자는 출품 사진을 직접 방문하여 제출해야 한다.
③ 참가자는 5월 14일까지 출품 사진을 제출할 수 있다.
④ 우승 상품은 지역 상점에서 쓸 수 있는 기프트 카드이다.
⑤ 지역 신문을 통해 우승자를 발표한다.

29. 다음 글의 밑줄 친 부분 중, 어법상 <u>틀린</u> 것은? [3점]

It would be hard to overstate how important meaningful work is to human beings — work ①that provides a sense of fulfillment and empowerment. Those who have found deeper meaning in their careers find their days much more energizing and satisfying, and ②to count their employment as one of their greatest sources of joy and pride. Sonya Lyubomirsky, professor of psychology at the University of California, has conducted numerous workplace studies ③showing that when people are more fulfilled on the job, they not only produce higher quality work and a greater output, but also generally earn higher incomes. Those most satisfied with their work ④are also much more likely to be happier with their lives overall. For her book *Happiness at Work*, researcher Jessica Pryce-Jones conducted a study of 3,000 workers in seventy-nine countries, ⑤finding that those who took greater satisfaction from their work were 150 percent more likely to have a happier life overall.

* numerous: 수많은

30. 다음 글의 밑줄 친 부분 중, 문맥상 낱말의 쓰임이 적절하지 <u>않은</u> 것은? [3점]

The rate of speed at which one is traveling will greatly determine the ability to process detail in the environment. In evolutionary terms, human senses are adapted to the ①speed at which humans move through space under their own power while walking. Our ability to distinguish detail in the environment is therefore ideally ②suited to movement at speeds of perhaps five miles per hour and under. The fastest users of the street, motorists, therefore have a much more limited ability to process details along the street — a motorist simply has ③enough time or ability to appreciate design details. On the other hand, pedestrian travel, being much slower, allows for the ④appreciation of environmental detail. Joggers and bicyclists fall somewhere in between these polar opposites; while they travel faster than pedestrians, their rate of speed is ordinarily much ⑤slower than that of the typical motorist.

* distinguish: 구별하다 ** pedestrian: 보행자

[31 ~ 34] 다음 빈칸에 들어갈 말로 가장 적절한 것을 고르시오.

31. Every species has certain climatic requirements — what degree of heat or cold it can endure, for example. When the climate changes, the places that satisfy those requirements change, too. Species are forced to follow. All creatures are capable of some degree of _____. Even creatures that appear immobile, like trees and barnacles, are capable of dispersal at some stage of their life — as a seed, in the case of the tree, or as a larva, in the case of the barnacle. A creature must get from the place it is born — often occupied by its parent — to a place where it can survive, grow, and reproduce. From fossils, scientists know that even creatures like trees moved with surprising speed during past periods of climate change.

* barnacle: 따개비 ** dispersal: 분산
*** fossil: 화석

① endurance
② movement
③ development
④ transformation
⑤ communication

32. No respectable boss would say, "I make it a point to discourage my staff from speaking up, and I maintain a culture that prevents disagreeing viewpoints from ever getting aired." If anything, most bosses even say that they are pro-dissent. This idea can be found throughout the series of conversations with corporate, university, and nonprofit leaders, published weekly in the business sections of newspapers. In the interviews, the featured leaders are asked about their management techniques, and regularly claim to continually encourage _____ from more junior staffers. As Bot Pittman remarked in one of these conversations: "I want us to listen to these dissenters because they may intend to tell you why we can't do something, but if you listen hard, what they're really telling you is what you must do to get something done." [3점]

* dissent: 반대

① unconditional loyalty
② positive attitude
③ internal protest
④ competitive atmosphere
⑤ outstanding performance

33. One of the most striking characteristics of a sleeping animal or person is that they do not respond normally to environmental stimuli. If you open the eyelids of a sleeping mammal the eyes will not see normally—they _____. Some visual information apparently gets in, but it is not normally processed as it is shortened or weakened; same with the other sensing systems. Stimuli are registered but not processed normally and they fail to wake the individual. Perceptual disengagement probably serves the function of protecting sleep, so some authors do not count it as part of the definition of sleep itself. But as sleep would be impossible without it, it seems essential to its definition. Nevertheless, many animals (including humans) use the intermediate state of drowsiness to derive some benefits of sleep without total perceptual disengagement. [3점]

* stimuli: 자극   ** disengagement: 이탈
*** drowsiness: 졸음

① get recovered easily
② will see much better
③ are functionally blind
④ are completely activated
⑤ process visual information

34. A number of research studies have shown how experts in a field often experience difficulties when introducing newcomers to that field. For example, in a genuine training situation, Dr Pamela Hinds found that people expert in using mobile phones were remarkably less accurate than novice phone users in judging how long it takes people to learn to use the phones. Experts can become insensitive to how hard a task is for the beginner, an effect referred to as the 'curse of knowledge'. Dr Hinds was able to show that as people acquired the skill, they then began to underestimate the level of difficulty of that skill. Her participants even underestimated how long it had taken themselves to acquire that skill in an earlier session. Knowing that experts forget how hard it was for them to learn, we can understand the need to _____, rather than making assumptions about how students 'should be' learning. [3점]

* novice: 초보

① focus on the new functions of digital devices
② apply new learning theories recently released
③ develop varieties of methods to test students
④ forget the difficulties that we have had as students
⑤ look at the learning process through students' eyes

35. 다음 글에서 전체 흐름과 관계 없는 문장은?

A group of psychologists studied individuals with severe mental illness who experienced weekly group music therapy, including singing familiar songs and composing original songs. ① The results showed that the group music therapy improved the quality of participants' life, with those participating in a greater number of sessions experiencing the greatest benefits. ② Focusing on singing, another group of psychologists reviewed articles on the efficacy of group singing as a mental health treatment for individuals living with a mental health condition in a community setting. ③ The findings showed that, when people with mental health conditions participated in a choir, their mental health and wellbeing significantly improved. ④ The negative effects of music were greater than the psychologists expected. ⑤ Group singing provided enjoyment, improved emotional states, developed a sense of belonging and enhanced self-confidence.

* therapy: 치료   ** efficacy: 효능

[36 ~ 37] 주어진 글 다음에 이어질 글의 순서로 가장 적절한 것을 고르시오.

36.

In many sports, people realized the difficulties and even impossibilities of young children participating fully in many adult sport environments.

(A) As examples, baseball has T ball, football has flag football and junior soccer uses a smaller and lighter ball and (sometimes) a smaller field. All have junior competitive structures where children play for shorter time periods and often in smaller teams.

(B) In a similar way, tennis has adapted the court areas, balls and rackets to make them more appropriate for children under 10. The adaptations are progressive and relate to the age of the child.

(C) They found the road to success for young children is unlikely if they play on adult fields, courts or arenas with equipment that is too large, too heavy or too fast for them to handle while trying to compete in adult-style competition. Common sense has prevailed: different sports have made adaptations for children.

* prevail: 널리 퍼지다

① (A) − (C) − (B)   ② (B) − (A) − (C)
③ (B) − (C) − (A)   ④ (C) − (A) − (B)
⑤ (C) − (B) − (A)

37.

> With no horses available, the Inca empire excelled at delivering messages on foot.

(A) When a messenger neared the next hut, he began to call out and repeated the message three or four times to the one who was running out to meet him. The Inca empire could relay messages 1,000 miles (1,610 km) in three or four days under good conditions.

(B) The messengers were stationed on the royal roads to deliver the Inca king's orders and reports coming from his lands. Called Chasquis, they lived in groups of four to six in huts, placed from one to two miles apart along the roads.

(C) They were all young men and especially good runners who watched the road in both directions. If they caught sight of another messenger coming, they hurried out to meet them. The Inca built the huts on high ground, in sight of one another. [3점]

　　　　　　　　　　　　　* excel: 탁월하다　** messenger: 전령

① (A) － (C) － (B)　　　② (B) － (A) － (C)
③ (B) － (C) － (A)　　　④ (C) － (A) － (B)
⑤ (C) － (B) － (A)

[38 ~ 39] 글의 흐름으로 보아, 주어진 문장이 들어가기에 가장 적절한 곳을 고르시오.

38.

> Research in the 1980s and 1990s, however, demonstrated that the "tongue map" explanation of how we taste was, in fact, totally wrong.

The tongue was mapped into separate areas where certain tastes were registered: sweetness at the tip, sourness on the sides, and bitterness at the back of the mouth. (①) As it turns out, the map was a misinterpretation and mistranslation of research conducted in Germany at the turn of the twentieth century. (②) Today, leading taste researchers believe that taste buds are not grouped according to specialty. (③) Sweetness, saltiness, bitterness, and sourness can be tasted everywhere in the mouth, although they may be perceived at a little different intensities at different sites. (④) Moreover, the mechanism at work is not place, but time. (⑤) It's not that you taste sweetness at the tip of your tongue, but rather that you register that perception *first*.

　　　　　　　　　　　　　　　　　* taste bud: 미뢰

39.

> Environmental factors can also determine how the animal will respond during the treatment.

No two animals are alike. (①) Animals from the same litter will display some of the same features, but will not be exactly the same as each other; therefore, they may not respond in entirely the same way during a healing session. (②) For instance, a cat in a rescue center will respond very differently than a cat within a domestic home environment. (③) In addition, animals that experience healing for physical illness will react differently than those accepting healing for emotional confusion. (④) With this in mind, every healing session needs to be explored differently, and each healing treatment should be adjusted to suit the specific needs of the animal. (⑤) You will learn as you go; healing is a constant learning process.

　　　　　　　　　　* litter: (한 배에서 태어난) 새끼들

40. 다음 글의 내용을 한 문장으로 요약하고자 한다. 빈칸 (A), (B)에 들어갈 말로 가장 적절한 것은?

> The mind has parts that are known as the conscious mind and the subconscious mind. The subconscious mind is very fast to act and doesn't deal with emotions. It deals with memories of your responses to life, your memories and recognition. However, the conscious mind is the one that you have more control over. You think. You can choose whether to carry on a thought or to add emotion to it and this is the part of your mind that lets you down frequently because — fueled by emotions — you make the wrong decisions time and time again. When your judgment is clouded by emotions, this puts in biases and all kinds of other negativities that hold you back. Scared of spiders? Scared of the dark? There are reasons for all of these fears, but they originate in the conscious mind. They only become real fears when the subconscious mind records your reactions.

↓

> While the controllable conscious mind deals with thoughts and ___(A)___, the fast-acting subconscious mind stores your responses, ___(B)___ real fears.

　　(A)　　　　　　　(B)
① emotions　　‥‥‥　forming
② actions　　 ‥‥‥　overcoming
③ emotions　　‥‥‥　overcoming
④ actions　　 ‥‥‥　avoiding
⑤ moralities　‥‥‥　forming

[41 ~ 42] 다음 글을 읽고, 물음에 답하시오.

Norms are everywhere, defining what is "normal" and guiding our interpretations of social life at every turn. As a simple example, there is a norm in Anglo society to say *Thank you* to strangers who have just done something to (a) help, such as open a door for you, point out that you've just dropped something, or give you directions. There is no law that forces you to say *Thank you*. But if people don't say *Thank you* in these cases it is marked. People expect that you will say it. You become responsible. (b) Failing to say it will be both surprising and worthy of criticism. Not knowing the norms of another community is the (c) central problem of cross-cultural communication. To continue the *Thank you* example, even though another culture may have an expression that appears translatable (many don't), there may be (d) similar norms for its usage, for example, such that you should say *Thank you* only when the cost someone has caused is considerable. In such a case it would sound ridiculous (i.e., unexpected, surprising, and worthy of criticism) if you were to thank someone for something so (e) minor as holding a door open for you.

41. 윗글의 제목으로 가장 적절한 것은?

① Norms: For Social Life and Cultural Communication
② Don't Forget to Say "Thank you" at Any Time
③ How to Be Responsible for Your Behaviors
④ Accept Criticism Without Hurting Yourself
⑤ How Did Diverse Languages Develop?

42. 밑줄 친 (a)~(e) 중에서 문맥상 낱말의 쓰임이 적절하지 <u>않은</u> 것은?

① (a)   ② (b)   ③ (c)   ④ (d)   ⑤ (e)

[43 ~ 45] 다음 글을 읽고, 물음에 답하시오.

(A)

Long ago, when the world was young, an old Native American spiritual leader Odawa had a dream on a high mountain. In his dream, Iktomi, the great spirit and searcher of wisdom, appeared to (a) him in the form of a spider. Iktomi spoke to him in a holy language.

(B)

Odawa shared Iktomi's lesson with (b) his people. Today, many Native Americans have dream catchers hanging above their beds. Dream catchers are believed to filter out bad dreams. The good dreams are captured in the web of life and carried with the people. The bad dreams pass through the hole in the web and are no longer a part of their lives.

(C)

When Iktomi finished speaking, he spun a web and gave it to Odawa. He said to Odawa, "The web is a perfect circle with a hole in the center. Use the web to help your people reach their goals. Make good use of their ideas, dreams, and visions. If (c) you believe in the great spirit, the web will catch your good ideas and the bad ones will go through the hole." Right after Odawa woke up, he went back to his village.

(D)

Iktomi told Odawa about the cycles of life. (d) He said, "We all begin our lives as babies, move on to childhood, and then to adulthood. Finally, we come to old age, where we must be taken care of as babies again." Iktomi also told (e) him that there are good and bad forces in each stage of life. "If we listen to the good forces, they will guide us in the right direction. But if we listen to the bad forces, they will lead us the wrong way and may harm us," Iktomi said.

43. 주어진 글 (A)에 이어질 내용을 순서에 맞게 배열한 것으로 가장 적절한 것은?

① (B) - (D) - (C)   ② (C) - (B) - (D)
③ (C) - (D) - (B)   ④ (D) - (B) - (C)
⑤ (D) - (C) - (B)

44. 밑줄 친 (a)~(e) 중에서 가리키는 대상이 나머지 넷과 <u>다른</u> 것은?

① (a)   ② (b)   ③ (c)   ④ (d)   ⑤ (e)

45. 윗글에 관한 내용으로 적절하지 <u>않은</u> 것은?

① Odawa는 높은 산에서 꿈을 꾸었다.
② 많은 미국 원주민은 드림캐처를 현관 위에 건다.
③ Iktomi는 Odawa에게 거미집을 짜서 주었다.
④ Odawa는 잠에서 깨자마자 자신의 마을로 돌아갔다.
⑤ Iktomi는 Odawa에게 삶의 순환에 대해 알려 주었다.

＊ 확인 사항

◦ 답안지의 해당란에 필요한 내용을 정확히 기입(표기)했는지 확인하시오.

18
001 □ science ⓝ 과학
002 □ recently ⓪ 최근에
003 □ impressed ⓐ 감명을 받은
004 □ latest ⓐ 최신의, 최근의
005 □ discussion ⓝ 토론
006 □ special ⓐ 특별한
007 □ lecture ⓝ 강의
008 □ suit ⓥ 맞추다
009 □ schedule ⓝ 일정
010 □ fantastic ⓐ 굉장한, 멋진
011 □ experience ⓝ 경험
012 □ grateful ⓐ 감사한

19
013 □ daughter ⓝ 딸, 여식
014 □ sandcastle ⓝ 모래성
015 □ enormous ⓐ 거대한
016 □ wave ⓝ 파도, 물결
017 □ destroy ⓥ 부수다
018 □ response ⓝ 반응, 대응, 부응
019 □ stream ⓥ 흐르다
020 □ break ⓥ 깨어지다, 부서지다
021 □ ocean ⓝ 바다
022 □ respond ⓥ 반응하다
023 □ enthusiasm ⓝ 열정

20
024 □ magic ⓝ 마법, 마술
025 □ in real life 실제로
026 □ create ⓥ 창조하다
027 □ trick ⓝ 비결, 요령, 묘책
028 □ challenge ⓝ 어려움, 도전
029 □ deal ⓥ 다루다, 처리하다, 취급하다
030 □ statement ⓝ 진술
031 □ positive ⓐ 긍정적인
032 □ struggle ⓥ 어려움을 겪다
033 □ witness ⓥ 목격하다
034 □ confidence ⓝ 자신감
035 □ surprise ⓥ 놀라게 하다
036 □ shift ⓝ 변화
037 □ act ⓥ 행동하다
038 □ powerful ⓐ 강력한

21
039 □ consider ⓥ 고려하다
040 □ seemingly ⓪ 외견상으로, 겉보기에는
041 □ sense ⓝ 감각
042 □ sight ⓝ 시각
043 □ hearing ⓝ 청각
044 □ smell ⓝ 후각
045 □ taste ⓝ 미각
046 □ touch ⓝ 촉각
047 □ according to ~에 따르면
048 □ philosopher ⓝ 철학자
049 □ doubt ⓥ 의심하다
050 □ miss ⓥ 빠뜨리다, 빼놓다
051 □ perception ⓝ 인식
052 □ balance ⓝ 균형
053 □ link ⓝ 연결
054 □ categorize ⓥ 분류하다
055 □ vertebrates ⓝ 척추동물

056 □ detect ⓥ 감지하다
057 □ odor ⓝ 냄새
058 □ snake ⓝ 뱀
059 □ prey ⓝ 먹잇감
060 □ divide ⓥ 나누다
061 □ instead ⓪ 대신에
062 □ bucket ⓝ 양동이
063 □ category ⓝ 범주
064 □ traditional ⓐ 전통의, 전통적인

22
065 □ historical ⓐ 역사적인
066 □ importance ⓝ 중요성
067 □ far-reaching ⓐ 광범위한
068 □ influence ⓝ 영향력
069 □ noble ⓐ 고귀한
070 □ goal ⓝ 목표
071 □ worker ⓝ 노동자
072 □ citizen ⓝ 시민
073 □ possess ⓥ 가지다, 소유하다
074 □ aspect ⓝ 측면
075 □ improve ⓥ 개선하다
076 □ scale ⓝ 규모
077 □ diligence ⓝ 근면
078 □ share ⓥ 함께 쓰다, 공유하다
079 □ opinion ⓝ 의견
080 □ feedback ⓝ 피드백
081 □ constantly ⓪ 끊임없이
082 □ accomplish ⓥ 성취하다
083 □ potential ⓝ 잠재력
084 □ community ⓝ 공동체
085 □ regardless of ~와 관계없이

23
086 □ crop rotation ⓝ 윤작
087 □ farmer ⓝ 농부, 농장주, 농장 경영자
088 □ crop ⓝ 농작물, 수확물
089 □ field ⓝ 밭
090 □ order ⓝ 순서
091 □ carrot ⓝ 당근
092 □ bean ⓝ 콩
093 □ rotate ⓥ 순환하다
094 □ go back (앞에 있었던 일로) 돌아가다
095 □ original ⓐ 원래의
096 □ enrich ⓥ 비옥하게 하다
097 □ soil ⓝ 토양
098 □ sustainable ⓐ 지속 가능한
099 □ organic ⓐ 유기농의

24
100 □ painting ⓝ 그림
101 □ rather ⓪ 오히려, 차라리
102 □ concentrate ⓥ 집중하다
103 □ area ⓝ 범위, 영역
104 □ often ⓪ 흔히, 종종, 자주
105 □ important ⓐ 중요한
106 □ step ⓝ 걸음
107 □ back ⓥ 뒤로 물러서다
108 □ assess ⓥ 평가하다
109 □ spoil ⓥ 망쳐 놓다
110 □ impact ⓝ 영향(력)
111 □ overwork ⓥ 과하게 작업하다

112 □ decide ⓥ 결정하다
113 □ fresh ⓐ 새로운
114 □ benefit ⓥ 득을 보다

25
115 □ above ⓪ 위에
116 □ extent ⓝ 정도
117 □ fear ⓝ 공포, 두려움, 무서움
118 □ climate ⓝ 기후
119 □ extremely ⓪ 극도로
120 □ worry ⓥ 걱정하다
121 □ follow ⓥ 뒤를 잇다, 뒤따르다
122 □ generation ⓝ 세대

26
123 □ secondary school ⓝ 중등학교
124 □ natural science 자연 과학
125 □ chemistry ⓝ 화학
126 □ physics ⓝ 물리학
127 □ mathematics ⓝ 수학
128 □ continue ⓥ 계속하다, 지속하다
129 □ throughout ⓟⓡⓔⓟ 내내
130 □ served ⓥ 일하다, 복무하다
131 □ military ⓐ 군대의

27
132 □ delightful ⓐ 즐거운
133 □ experience ⓥ 경험하다
134 □ various ⓐ 다양한
135 □ culture ⓝ 문화
136 □ host ⓥ (파티 등을) 주최하다
137 □ in advance 미리

28
138 □ passionate ⓐ 열정적인
139 □ fashion ⓝ 패션, 의류
140 □ environment ⓝ 환경
141 □ contest ⓝ 대회
142 □ upcycled ⓐ 업사이클된
143 □ local ⓐ 지역의
144 □ announce ⓥ 발표하다

29
145 □ overstate ⓥ 과장해서 말하다
146 □ meaningful ⓐ 의미 있는, 중요한
147 □ provide ⓥ 제공하다
148 □ fulfillment ⓝ 성취감
149 □ empowerment ⓝ 권한
150 □ career ⓝ 직업, 경력
151 □ energizing ⓐ 활기찬
152 □ satisfying ⓐ 만족감을 주는
153 □ employment ⓝ 직업, 고용
154 □ source ⓝ 원천
155 □ pride ⓝ 자부심, 긍지
156 □ psychology ⓝ 심리
157 □ numerous ⓐ 수많은
158 □ workplace ⓝ 업무 현장, 직장
159 □ fulfilled ⓐ 성취감을 느끼는
160 □ quality ⓝ 질
161 □ output ⓝ 성과
162 □ generally ⓪ 일반적으로
163 □ earn ⓥ (돈을) 벌다

164 □ income ⓝ 수입
165 □ overall ⓪ 전반적으로
166 □ satisfaction ⓝ 만족(감)

30
167 □ rate ⓝ 빠르기
168 □ traveling ⓐ 이동하는, 움직이는
169 □ determine ⓥ 결정하다
170 □ ability ⓝ 능력
171 □ evolutionary ⓐ 진화의, 진화론적인
172 □ adapted ⓐ 맞추어진, 적응된
173 □ distinguish ⓥ 구별하다
174 □ ideally ⓪ 이상적으로
175 □ suited ⓐ 적합한
176 □ perhaps ⓪ 아마도
177 □ motorist ⓝ 운전자
178 □ limited ⓐ 제한된
179 □ appreciate ⓥ 감상하다, 제대로 인식하다
180 □ on the other hand 반면에
181 □ pedestrian ⓝ 보행자
182 □ allow for 가능하게 하다, 허락하다
183 □ appreciation ⓝ 감상
184 □ polar ⓐ 극과 극의
185 □ opposite ⓝ 반대의 것
186 □ ordinarily ⓪ 보통
187 □ typical ⓐ 전형적인

31
188 □ certain ⓐ 확실한, 틀림없는, 특정한
189 □ climatic ⓐ 기후의
190 □ requirement ⓝ 요건
191 □ degree ⓝ 정도
192 □ endure ⓥ 견디다
193 □ satisfy ⓥ 충족시키다
194 □ creature ⓝ 생명체
195 □ capable ⓐ ~을 할 수 있는
196 □ dispersal ⓝ 해산, 분산
197 □ appear ⓥ ~인 것 같다
198 □ immobile ⓐ 움직이지 않는
199 □ barnacle ⓝ 따개비
200 □ seed ⓝ 씨앗
201 □ larva ⓝ 유충
202 □ occupy ⓥ 점유하다
203 □ survive ⓥ 생존하다
204 □ reproduce ⓥ 번식하다
205 □ fossil ⓝ 화석

32
206 □ respectable ⓐ 존경할 만한
207 □ make it a point 반드시 ~하도록 하다
208 □ discourage ⓥ 못하게 하다
209 □ speak up 자유롭게 의견을 내다
210 □ maintain ⓥ 유지하다
211 □ prevent ⓥ 막다
212 □ disagree ⓥ 동의하지 않다
213 □ viewpoint ⓝ 관점
214 □ get aired 공공연히 알려지다
215 □ if anything 오히려
216 □ boss ⓝ (직장의) 상관, 상사
217 □ conversation ⓝ 대담, 대화
218 □ corporate ⓐ 기업
219 □ nonprofit ⓐ 비영리인

220 □ publish ⓥ 발행하다, 출판하다
221 □ section ⓝ (신문의) 난
222 □ feature ⓥ (기사로) 다루다
223 □ management ⓝ 경영
224 □ technique ⓝ 기법
225 □ regularly ad 어김없이, 규칙적으로
226 □ claim ⓥ 주장하다
227 □ continually ad 계속해서, 끊임없이
228 □ encourage ⓥ 격려하다, 장려하다
229 □ remark ⓥ 말하다
230 □ dissenter ⓝ 반대자
231 □ unconditional ⓐ 무조건의, 무제한의, 절대적인
232 □ loyalty ⓝ 충성
233 □ attitude ⓝ 태도, 사고방식
234 □ protest ⓝ 항의
235 □ atmosphere ⓝ 분위기, 기운

33
236 □ striking ⓐ 두드러진
237 □ characteristic ⓝ 특징
238 □ normally ad 정상적으로
239 □ environmental ⓐ 환경의
240 □ stimulus ⓝ 자극 (pl. stimuli)
241 □ eyelid ⓝ 눈꺼풀
242 □ mammal ⓝ 포유류
243 □ functionally ad 기능상
244 □ apparently ad 분명히
245 □ process ⓥ 처리하다
246 □ shorten ⓥ 짧아지다
247 □ weaken ⓥ 약해지다
248 □ fail ⓥ 실패하다
249 □ perceptual ad 지각의
250 □ disengagement ⓝ 이탈
251 □ probably ad 아마
252 □ function ⓝ 기능
253 □ protect ⓥ 보호하다, 지키다
254 □ definition ⓝ (어떤 개념의) 정의
255 □ impossible ⓐ 불가능한
256 □ essential ⓐ 필수적인
257 □ intermediate ⓐ 중간의
258 □ derive ⓥ 얻다

34
259 □ research ⓝ 연구
260 □ expert ⓝ 전문가
261 □ difficulty ⓝ 어려움
262 □ introduce ⓥ 처음으로 경험하게 하다, 입문시키다
263 □ newcomer ⓝ 초보
264 □ genuine ⓐ 실제
265 □ situation ⓝ 상황, 처지, 환경
266 □ remarkably ad 놀랍게
267 □ accurate ⓐ 정확한
268 □ novice ⓝ 초보자
269 □ judge ⓥ 판단하다
270 □ insensitive ⓐ 무감각한
271 □ effect ⓝ 결과, 효과
272 □ acquire ⓥ 습득하다
273 □ underestimate ⓥ 과소평가하다
274 □ participant ⓝ 참가자
275 □ session ⓝ 기간, 시간

276 □ assumption ⓝ 추정, 가정

35
277 □ psychologist ⓝ 심리학자
278 □ severe ⓐ 심각한
279 □ therapy ⓝ 치료, 요법
280 □ familiar ⓐ 익숙한, 친숙한
281 □ compose ⓥ 작곡하다
282 □ result ⓝ 결과
283 □ review ⓥ 검토하다
284 □ article ⓝ 기사, 논문
285 □ efficacy ⓝ 효능, 효험
286 □ mental health 정신 건강
287 □ treatment ⓝ 치료
288 □ finding ⓝ 결과
289 □ choir ⓝ 합창단
290 □ wellbeing ⓝ 행복
291 □ significantly ad 상당히
292 □ enhance ⓥ 강화하다

36
293 □ realize ⓥ 깨닫다
294 □ impossibility ⓝ 불가능
295 □ competitive ⓐ 경쟁적인
296 □ structure ⓝ 구조
297 □ period ⓝ 기간
298 □ similar ⓐ 비슷한, 유사한
299 □ racket ⓝ 라켓
300 □ appropriate ⓐ 적절한
301 □ progressive ⓐ 점진적인
302 □ relate to ~와 관련되다
303 □ unlikely ⓐ ~할 것 같지 않은
304 □ arena ⓝ 경기장
305 □ equipment ⓝ 장비
306 □ handle ⓥ 다루다
307 □ compete ⓥ 경쟁하다
308 □ common sense ⓝ (일반인들의) 공통된 견해, 상식
309 □ adaptation ⓝ 조정

37
310 □ available ⓐ 구할 수 있는
311 □ empire ⓝ 제국
312 □ excel ⓥ 뛰어나다, 탁월하다
313 □ deliver ⓥ 전달하다
314 □ on foot 걸어서, 도보로
315 □ near ⓥ 다가가다
316 □ hut ⓝ 오두막, 막사
317 □ repeat ⓥ 반복하다
318 □ relay ⓥ 이어가다
319 □ condition ⓝ 사정, 상황
320 □ messenger ⓝ 전달자, 전령
321 □ station ⓥ 배치하다
322 □ royal ⓐ 왕의, 왕실의
323 □ report ⓥ 보고
324 □ apart ad 떨어진
325 □ especially ad 특히, 특별히
326 □ direction ⓝ 방향
327 □ hurry out 서둘러 나오다

38
328 □ demonstrate ⓥ 보여 주다

329 □ tongue ⓝ 혀
330 □ explanation ⓝ 설명
331 □ in fact 사실은
332 □ totally ad 완전히, 전적으로
333 □ separate ⓐ 분리된, 독립된, 개별적인
334 □ register ⓥ 등록하다
335 □ sweetness ⓝ 단맛
336 □ tip ⓝ 끝
337 □ sourness ⓝ 신맛
338 □ bitterness ⓝ 쓴맛
339 □ turn out ~인 것으로 밝혀지다
340 □ map ⓥ (지도에) 구획하다
341 □ misinterpretation ⓝ 오해
342 □ mistranslation ⓝ 오역
343 □ conduct ⓥ 수행하다
344 □ taste bud (혀의) 미뢰
345 □ specialty ⓝ 특화된 분야
346 □ perceive ⓥ 지각하다
347 □ intensity ⓝ 강도
348 □ site ⓝ 위치
349 □ moreover ad 게다가, 더욱이
350 □ mechanism ⓝ 기제

39
351 □ factor ⓝ 요인, 인자
352 □ alike ⓐ 서로 같은, 비슷한
353 □ litter ⓝ (개·돼지 등의) 한 배에서 난 새끼들
354 □ display ⓥ 보이다
355 □ feature ⓝ 특징, 특색
356 □ exactly ad 정확히, 꼭, 틀림없이
357 □ each other 서로
358 □ therefore ad 그런 까닭에
359 □ entirely ad 완전히, 전부
360 □ healing ⓝ 치료
361 □ rescue ⓥ 구조하다
362 □ differently ad 다르게, 같지 않게
363 □ domestic ⓐ 가정의
364 □ in addition (~에) 덧붙여, 게다가
365 □ illness ⓝ 질병
366 □ react ⓥ 반응하다
367 □ confusion ⓝ 동요, 혼란
368 □ explore ⓥ 탐구하다
369 □ specific ⓐ 특정한, 구체적인
370 □ constant ⓐ 끊임없는
371 □ process ⓝ 과정

40
372 □ conscious ⓐ 의식적
373 □ subconscious ⓐ 잠재의식(적)
374 □ emotion ⓝ 감정, 정서
375 □ recognition ⓝ 인식
376 □ control ⓝ 통제력
377 □ carry on 계속 가다
378 □ frequently ad 자주, 빈번히
379 □ fuel ⓥ (감정 등을) 부채질하다
380 □ judgment ⓝ 판단(력)
381 □ cloud ⓥ (기억력, 판단력 등을) 흐리게 하다
382 □ bias ⓝ 편견
383 □ negativity ⓝ 부정성
384 □ hold ⓥ 억누르다, 억제하다
385 □ scare ⓥ 무서워하다
386 □ originate ⓥ 비롯되다

41~42
387 □ norm ⓝ 규범
388 □ define ⓥ 규정하다
389 □ interpretation ⓝ 해석
390 □ society ⓝ 사회
391 □ stranger ⓝ 낯선 사람
392 □ drop ⓥ 떨어뜨리다
393 □ force ⓥ 강요하다
394 □ marked ⓐ 눈에 띄는
395 □ expect ⓥ 기대하다
396 □ responsible ⓐ 책임이 있는
397 □ worthy ⓐ 받을 만한
398 □ criticism ⓝ 비난
399 □ expression ⓝ 표현, 표출
400 □ central ⓐ 중심적인
401 □ translatable ⓐ 번역할 수 있는
402 □ cost ⓝ 대가, 비용
403 □ considerable ⓐ 상당한
404 □ ridiculous ⓐ 우스꽝스러운
405 □ unexpected ⓐ 예상치 못한
406 □ minor ⓐ 사소한

43~45
407 □ Native American ⓝ 미국 원주민
408 □ spiritual ⓐ 영적인
409 □ spirit ⓝ 정신, 영혼
410 □ wisdom ⓝ 지혜, 슬기, 현명함
411 □ holy ⓐ 성스러운
412 □ filter ⓥ 여과하다, 거르다
413 □ spin ⓥ 짜다 (과거형 spun)
414 □ cycle ⓝ 순환

● 채점 : 맞은 개수 _____ / 80

TEST A-B 각 단어의 뜻을 [A] 영어는 우리말로, [B] 우리말은 영어로 쓰시오.

A	English	Korean
01	suit	
02	possess	
03	requirement	
04	interpretation	
05	detect	
06	definition	
07	intensity	
08	enthusiasm	
09	overwork	
10	newcomer	
11	endure	
12	bias	
13	perceive	
14	register	
15	noble	
16	equipment	
17	compose	
18	military	
19	frequently	
20	statement	

B	Korean	English
01	구조하다	
02	특정한	
03	강의	
04	규정하다	
05	극도로	
06	구조(물)	
07	습득하다	
08	수입	
09	배치하다	
10	무감각한	
11	나누다	
12	평가하다	
13	먹잇감	
14	규범	
15	경기장	
16	성과	
17	치료	
18	순환하다	
19	부수다	
20	질병	

▶ A-D 정답 : 해설편 011쪽

TEST C-D 각 단어의 뜻을 골라 기호를 쓰시오.

C	English			Korean
01	witness	(	)	ⓐ 이상적으로
02	remark	(	)	ⓑ 말하다
03	separate	(	)	ⓒ 못하게 하다
04	on foot	(	)	ⓓ 권한
05	excel	(	)	ⓔ 목격하다
06	empowerment	(	)	ⓕ 검토하다
07	diligence	(	)	ⓖ 개별적인
08	on the other hand	(	)	ⓗ 비롯되다
09	rate	(	)	ⓘ 반면에
10	overall	(	)	ⓙ 이어가다
11	fulfillment	(	)	ⓚ 즐거운
12	delightful	(	)	ⓛ 근면
13	relay	(	)	ⓜ 전반적으로
14	review	(	)	ⓝ 과소평가하다
15	overstate	(	)	ⓞ 빠르기
16	holy	(	)	ⓟ 과장해서 말하다
17	underestimate	(	)	ⓠ 걸어서, 도보로
18	discourage	(	)	ⓡ 성스러운
19	originate	(	)	ⓢ 성취감
20	ideally	(	)	ⓣ 빼어나다, 탁월하다

D	Korean			English
01	변화	(	)	ⓐ feature
02	오해	(	)	ⓑ enrich
03	가정의	(	)	ⓒ progressive
04	(파티 등을) 주최하다	(	)	ⓓ domestic
05	행복	(	)	ⓔ allow for
06	가능하게 하다, 허락하다	(	)	ⓕ marked
07	움직이지 않는	(	)	ⓖ stream
08	약해지다	(	)	ⓗ concentrate
09	눈에 띄는	(	)	ⓘ immobile
10	(기사로) 다루다	(	)	ⓙ misinterpretation
11	집중하다	(	)	ⓚ wellbeing
12	번식하다	(	)	ⓛ shift
13	극과 극의	(	)	ⓜ get aired
14	떨어진	(	)	ⓝ apart
15	점진적인	(	)	ⓞ if anything
16	받을 만한	(	)	ⓟ polar
17	흐르다	(	)	ⓠ host
18	비옥하게 하다	(	)	ⓡ reproduce
19	오히려	(	)	ⓢ worthy
20	공공연히 알려지다	(	)	ⓣ weaken

※ 영어 [독해] 파트만 수록한 문제지이므로 18번부터 시작합니다. ● 점수 표시가 없는 문항은 모두 2점 ● 문항수 28개 | 배점 63점 | 제한 시간 45분

18. 다음 글의 목적으로 가장 적절한 것은?

> To whom it may concern,
>
> I am a resident of the Blue Sky Apartment. Recently I observed that the kid zone is in need of repairs. I want you to pay attention to the poor condition of the playground equipment in the zone. The swings are damaged, the paint is falling off, and some of the bolts on the slide are missing. The facilities have been in this terrible condition since we moved here. They are dangerous to the children playing there. Would you please have them repaired? I would appreciate your immediate attention to solve this matter.
>
> Yours sincerely,
> Nina Davis

① 아파트의 첨단 보안 설비를 홍보하려고
② 아파트 놀이터의 임시 폐쇄를 공지하려고
③ 아파트 놀이터 시설의 수리를 요청하려고
④ 아파트 놀이터 사고의 피해 보상을 촉구하려고
⑤ 아파트 공용 시설 사용 시 유의 사항을 안내하려고

19. 다음 글에 드러난 'I'의 심경 변화로 가장 적절한 것은?

On a two-week trip in the Rocky Mountains, I saw a grizzly bear in its native habitat. At first, I felt joy as I watched the bear walk across the land. He stopped every once in a while to turn his head about, sniffing deeply. He was following the scent of something, and slowly I began to realize that this giant animal was smelling me! I froze. This was no longer a wonderful experience; it was now an issue of survival. The bear's motivation was to find meat to eat, and I was clearly on his menu.

* scent: 냄새

① sad → angry
② delighted → scared
③ satisfied → jealous
④ worried → relieved
⑤ frustrated → excited

20. 다음 글에서 필자가 주장하는 바로 가장 적절한 것은?

It is difficult for any of us to maintain a constant level of attention throughout our working day. We all have body rhythms characterised by peaks and valleys of energy and alertness. You will achieve more, and feel confident as a benefit, if you schedule your most demanding tasks at times when you are best able to cope with them. If you haven't thought about energy peaks before, take a few days to observe yourself. Try to note the times when you are at your best. We are all different. For some, the peak will come first thing in the morning, but for others it may take a while to warm up.

* alertness: 기민함

① 부정적인 감정에 에너지를 낭비하지 말라.
② 자신의 신체 능력에 맞게 운동량을 조절하라.
③ 자기 성찰을 위한 아침 명상 시간을 확보하라.
④ 생산적인 하루를 보내려면 일을 균등하게 배분하라.
⑤ 자신의 에너지가 가장 높은 시간을 파악하여 활용하라.

21. 밑줄 친 The divorce of the hands from the head가 다음 글에서 의미하는 바로 가장 적절한 것은? [3점]

If we adopt technology, we need to pay its costs. Thousands of traditional livelihoods have been pushed aside by progress, and the lifestyles around those jobs removed. Hundreds of millions of humans today work at jobs they hate, producing things they have no love for. Sometimes these jobs cause physical pain, disability, or chronic disease. Technology creates many new jobs that are certainly dangerous. At the same time, mass education and media train humans to avoid low-tech physical work, to seek jobs working in the digital world. The divorce of the hands from the head puts a stress on the human mind. Indeed, the sedentary nature of the best-paying jobs is a health risk — for body and mind.

* chronic: 만성의 ** sedentary: 주로 앉아서 하는

① ignorance of modern technology
② endless competition in the labor market
③ not getting along well with our coworkers
④ working without any realistic goals for our career
⑤ our increasing use of high technology in the workplace

22. 다음 글의 요지로 가장 적절한 것은?

When students are starting their college life, they may approach every course, test, or learning task the same way, using what we like to call "the rubber-stamp approach." Think about it this way: Would you wear a tuxedo to a baseball game? A colorful dress to a funeral? A bathing suit to religious services? Probably not. You know there's appropriate dress for different occasions and settings. Skillful learners know that "putting on the same clothes" won't work for every class. They are flexible learners. They have different strategies and know when to use them. They know that you study for multiple-choice tests differently than you study for essay tests. And they not only know what to do, but they also know how to do it.

① 숙련된 학습자는 상황에 맞는 학습 전략을 사용할 줄 안다.
② 선다형 시험과 논술 시험은 평가의 형태와 목적이 다르다.
③ 문화마다 특정 행사와 상황에 맞는 복장 규정이 있다.
④ 학습의 양보다는 학습의 질이 학업 성과를 좌우한다.
⑤ 학습 목표가 명확할수록 성취 수준이 높아진다.

23. 다음 글의 주제로 가장 적절한 것은?

As the social and economic situation of countries got better, wage levels and working conditions improved. Gradually people were given more time off. At the same time, forms of transport improved and it became faster and cheaper to get to places. England's industrial revolution led to many of these changes. Railways, in the nineteenth century, opened up now famous seaside resorts such as Blackpool and Brighton. With the railways came many large hotels. In Canada, for example, the new coast-to-coast railway system made possible the building of such famous hotels as Banff Springs and Chateau Lake Louise in the Rockies. Later, the arrival of air transport opened up more of the world and led to tourism growth.

① factors that caused tourism expansion
② discomfort at a popular tourist destination
③ importance of tourism in society and economy
④ negative impacts of tourism on the environment
⑤ various types of tourism and their characteristics

24. 다음 글의 제목으로 가장 적절한 것은?

Success can lead you off your intended path and into a comfortable rut. If you are good at something and are well rewarded for doing it, you may want to keep doing it even if you stop enjoying it. The danger is that one day you look around and realize you're so deep in this comfortable rut that you can no longer see the sun or breathe fresh air; the sides of the rut have become so slippery that it would take a superhuman effort to climb out; and, effectively, you're stuck. And it's a situation that many working people worry they're in now. The poor employment market has left them feeling locked in what may be a secure, or even well-paying — but ultimately unsatisfying — job.

* rut: 틀에 박힌 생활

① Don't Compete with Yourself
② A Trap of a Successful Career
③ Create More Jobs for Young People
④ What Difficult Jobs Have in Common
⑤ A Road Map for an Influential Employer

25. 다음 도표의 내용과 일치하지 <u>않는</u> 것은?

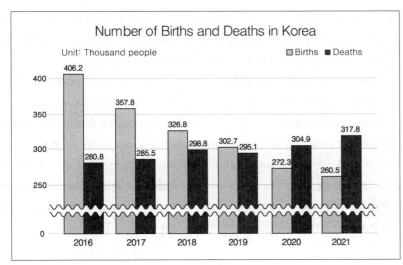

The above graph shows the number of births and deaths in Korea from 2016 to 2021. ① The number of births continued to decrease throughout the whole period. ② The gap between the number of births and deaths was the largest in 2016. ③ In 2019, the gap between the number of births and deaths was the smallest, with the number of births slightly larger than that of deaths. ④ The number of deaths increased steadily during the whole period, except the period from 2018 to 2019. ⑤ In 2021, the number of deaths was larger than that of births for the first time.

26. Lilian Bland에 관한 다음 글의 내용과 일치하지 <u>않는</u> 것은?

Lilian Bland was born in Kent, England in 1878. Unlike most other girls at the time she wore trousers and spent her time enjoying adventurous activities like horse riding and hunting. Lilian began her career as a sports and wildlife photographer for British newspapers. In 1910 she became the first woman to design, build, and fly her own airplane. In order to persuade her to try a slightly safer activity, Lilian's dad bought her a car. Soon Lilian was a master driver and ended up working as a car dealer. She never went back to flying but lived a long and exciting life nonetheless. She married, moved to Canada, and had a kid. Eventually, she moved back to England, and lived there for the rest of her life.

① 승마와 사냥 같은 모험적인 활동을 즐겼다.
② 스포츠와 야생 동물 사진작가로 경력을 시작했다.
③ 자신의 비행기를 설계하고 제작했다.
④ 자동차 판매원으로 일하기도 했다.
⑤ 캐나다에서 생의 마지막 기간을 보냈다.

27. Call for Articles에 관한 다음 안내문의 내용과 일치하지 <u>않는</u> 것은?

> ### Call for Articles
>
> Do you want to get your stories published? *New Dream Magazine* is looking for future writers! This event is open to anyone aged 13 to 18.
>
> **Articles**
> • Length of writing: 300−325 words
> • Articles should also include high-quality color photos.
>
> **Rewards**
> • Five cents per word
> • Five dollars per photo
>
> **Notes**
> • You should send us your phone number together with your writing.
> • Please email your writing to us at article@ndmag.com.

① 13세에서 18세까지의 누구나 참여할 수 있다.
② 기사는 고화질 컬러 사진을 포함해야 한다.
③ 사진 한 장에 5센트씩 지급한다.
④ 전화번호를 원고와 함께 보내야 한다.
⑤ 원고를 이메일로 제출해야 한다.

28. Greenhill Roller Skating에 관한 다음 안내문의 내용과 일치하는 것은?

> ### Greenhill Roller Skating
>
> Join us for your chance to enjoy roller skating!
>
> • Place: Greenhill Park, 351 Cypress Avenue
> • Dates: Friday, April 7 − Sunday, April 9
> • Time: 9 a.m. − 6 p.m.
> • Fee: $8 per person for a 50-minute session
>
> **Details**
> − Admission will be on a first-come, first-served basis with no reservations.
> − Children under the age of 10 must be accompanied by an adult.
> − We will lend you our roller skates for free.
>
> Contact the Community Center for more information at 013-234-6114.

① 오전 9시부터 오후 9시까지 운영한다.
② 이용료는 시간 제한 없이 1인당 8달러이다.
③ 입장하려면 예약이 필요하다.
④ 10세 미만 어린이는 어른과 동행해야 한다.
⑤ 추가 요금을 내면 롤러스케이트를 빌려준다.

29. 다음 글의 밑줄 친 부분 중, 어법상 틀린 것은? [3점]

The most noticeable human characteristic projected onto animals is ① that they can talk in human language. Physically, animal cartoon characters and toys ② made after animals are also most often deformed in such a way as to resemble humans. This is achieved by ③ showing them with humanlike facial features and deformed front legs to resemble human hands. In more recent animated movies the trend has been to show the animals in a more "natural" way. However, they still use their front legs ④ like human hands (for example, lions can pick up and lift small objects with one paw), and they still talk with an appropriate facial expression. A general strategy that is used to make the animal characters more emotionally appealing, both to children and adults, ⑤ are to give them enlarged and deformed childlike features.

* deform: 변형하다 ** paw: (동물의) 발

30. 다음 글의 밑줄 친 부분 중, 문맥상 낱말의 쓰임이 적절하지 않은 것은? [3점]

The major philosophical shift in the idea of selling came when industrial societies became more affluent, more competitive, and more geographically spread out during the 1940s and 1950s. This forced business to develop ① closer relations with buyers and clients, which in turn made business realize that it was not enough to produce a quality product at a reasonable price. In fact, it was equally ② essential to deliver products that customers actually wanted. Henry Ford produced his best-selling T-model Ford in one color only (black) in 1908, but in modern societies this was no longer ③ possible. The modernization of society led to a marketing revolution that ④ strengthened the view that production would create its own demand. Customers, and the desire to ⑤ meet their diverse and often complex needs, became the focus of business.

* affluent: 부유한

[31~34] 다음 빈칸에 들어갈 말로 가장 적절한 것을 고르시오.

31. People differ in how quickly they can reset their biological clocks to overcome jet lag, and the speed of recovery depends on the _____ of travel. Generally, it's easier to fly westward and lengthen your day than it is to fly eastward and shorten it. This east-west difference in jet lag is sizable enough to have an impact on the performance of sports teams. Studies have found that teams flying westward perform significantly better than teams flying eastward in professional baseball and college football. A more recent study of more than 46,000 Major League Baseball games found additional evidence that eastward travel is tougher than westward travel.

* jet lag: 시차로 인한 피로감

① direction
② purpose
③ season
④ length
⑤ cost

32. If you want the confidence that comes from achieving what you set out to do each day, then it's important to understand _____. Over-optimism about what can be achieved within a certain time frame is a problem. So work on it. Make a practice of estimating the amount of time needed alongside items on your 'things to do' list, and learn by experience when tasks take a greater or lesser time than expected. Give attention also to fitting the task to the available time. There are some tasks that you can only set about if you have a significant amount of time available. There is no point in trying to gear up for such a task when you only have a short period available. So schedule the time you need for the longer tasks and put the short tasks into the spare moments in between.

* gear up: 준비를 갖추다, 대비하다

① what benefits you can get
② how practical your tasks are
③ how long things are going to take
④ why failures are meaningful in life
⑤ why your leisure time should come first

[해설편 p.015]

33. In Lewis Carroll's *Through the Looking-Glass*, the Red Queen takes Alice on a race through the countryside. They run and they run, but then Alice discovers that they're still under the same tree that they started from. The Red Queen explains to Alice: "*here*, you see, it takes all the running you can do, to keep in the same place." Biologists sometimes use this Red Queen Effect to explain an evolutionary principle. If foxes evolve to run faster so they can catch more rabbits, then only the fastest rabbits will live long enough to make a new generation of bunnies that run even faster — in which case, of course, only the fastest foxes will catch enough rabbits to thrive and pass on their genes. Even though they might run, the two species _____. [3점]

* thrive: 번성하다

① just stay in place
② end up walking slowly
③ never run into each other
④ won't be able to adapt to changes
⑤ cannot run faster than their parents

34. Everything in the world around us was finished in the mind of its creator before it was started. The houses we live in, the cars we drive, and our clothing — all of these began with an idea. Each idea was then studied, refined and perfected before the first nail was driven or the first piece of cloth was cut. Long before the idea was turned into a physical reality, the mind had clearly pictured the finished product. The human being designs his or her own future through much the same process. We begin with an idea about how the future will be. Over a period of time we refine and perfect the vision. Before long, our every thought, decision and activity are all working in harmony to bring into existence what we _____. [3점]

* refine: 다듬다

① didn't even have the potential to accomplish
② have mentally concluded about the future
③ haven't been able to picture in our mind
④ considered careless and irresponsible
⑤ have observed in some professionals

35. 다음 글에서 전체 흐름과 관계 <u>없는</u> 문장은?

Whose story it is affects *what* the story is. Change the main character, and the focus of the story must also change. If we look at the events through another character's eyes, we will interpret them differently. ① We'll place our sympathies with someone new. ② When the conflict arises that is the heart of the story, we will be praying for a different outcome. ③ Consider, for example, how the tale of Cinderella would shift if told from the viewpoint of an evil stepsister. ④ We know Cinderella's kingdom does not exist, but we willingly go there anyway. ⑤ *Gone with the Wind* is Scarlett O'Hara's story, but what if we were shown the same events from the viewpoint of Rhett Butler or Melanie Wilkes?

* sympathy: 공감

[36 ~ 37] 주어진 글 다음에 이어질 글의 순서로 가장 적절한 것을 고르시오.

36.

In the Old Stone Age, small bands of 20 to 60 people wandered from place to place in search of food. Once people began farming, they could settle down near their farms.

(A) While some workers grew crops, others built new houses and made tools. Village dwellers also learned to work together to do a task faster.

(B) For example, toolmakers could share the work of making stone axes and knives. By working together, they could make more tools in the same amount of time.

(C) As a result, towns and villages grew larger. Living in communities allowed people to organize themselves more efficiently. They could divide up the work of producing food and other things they needed.

* dweller: 거주자

① (A) − (C) − (B)　　② (B) − (A) − (C)
③ (B) − (C) − (A)　　④ (C) − (A) − (B)
⑤ (C) − (B) − (A)

37.

Natural processes form minerals in many ways. For example, hot melted rock material, called magma, cools when it reaches the Earth's surface, or even if it's trapped below the surface. As magma cools, its atoms lose heat energy, move closer together, and begin to combine into compounds.

(A) Also, the size of the crystals that form depends partly on how rapidly the magma cools. When magma cools slowly, the crystals that form are generally large enough to see with the unaided eye.

(B) During this process, atoms of the different compounds arrange themselves into orderly, repeating patterns. The type and amount of elements present in a magma partly determine which minerals will form.

(C) This is because the atoms have enough time to move together and form into larger crystals. When magma cools rapidly, the crystals that form will be small. In such cases, you can't easily see individual mineral crystals. [3점]

* compound: 화합물

① (A) － (C) － (B)   ② (B) － (A) － (C)
③ (B) － (C) － (A)   ④ (C) － (A) － (B)
⑤ (C) － (B) － (A)

[38~39] 글의 흐름으로 보아, 주어진 문장이 들어가기에 가장 적절한 곳을 고르시오.

38.

Bad carbohydrates, on the other hand, are simple sugars.

All carbohydrates are basically sugars. (①) Complex carbohydrates are the good carbohydrates for your body. (②) These complex sugar compounds are very difficult to break down and can trap other nutrients like vitamins and minerals in their chains. (③) As they slowly break down, the other nutrients are also released into your body, and can provide you with fuel for a number of hours. (④) Because their structure is not complex, they are easy to break down and hold few nutrients for your body other than the sugars from which they are made. (⑤) Your body breaks down these carbohydrates rather quickly and what it cannot use is converted to fat and stored in the body.

* carbohydrate: 탄수화물 ** convert: 바꾸다

39.

It was also found that those students who expected the lecturer to be warm tended to interact with him more.

People commonly make the mistaken assumption that because a person has one type of characteristic, then they automatically have other characteristics which go with it. (①) In one study, university students were given descriptions of a guest lecturer before he spoke to the group. (②) Half the students received a description containing the word 'warm', the other half were told the speaker was 'cold'. (③) The guest lecturer then led a discussion, after which the students were asked to give their impressions of him. (④) As expected, there were large differences between the impressions formed by the students, depending upon their original information of the lecturer. (⑤) This shows that different expectations not only affect the impressions we form but also our behaviour and the relationship which is formed. [3점]

40. 다음 글의 내용을 한 문장으로 요약하고자 한다. 빈칸 (A), (B)에 들어갈 말로 가장 적절한 것은?

To help decide what's risky and what's safe, who's trustworthy and who's not, we look for *social evidence*. From an evolutionary view, following the group is almost always positive for our prospects of survival. "If everyone's doing it, it must be a sensible thing to do," explains famous psychologist and best selling writer of *Influence*, Robert Cialdini. While we can frequently see this today in product reviews, even subtler cues within the environment can signal trustworthiness. Consider this: when you visit a local restaurant, are they busy? Is there a line outside or is it easy to find a seat? It is a hassle to wait, but a line can be a powerful cue that the food's tasty, and these seats are in demand. More often than not, it's good to adopt the practices of those around you.

* subtle: 미묘한 ** hassle: 성가신 일

↓

We tend to feel safe and secure in ___(A)___ when we decide how to act, particularly when faced with ___(B)___ conditions.

	(A)		(B)
①	numbers	······	uncertain
②	numbers	······	unrealistic
③	experiences	······	unrealistic
④	rules	······	uncertain
⑤	rules	······	unpleasant

[41 ~ 42] 다음 글을 읽고, 물음에 답하시오.

Chess masters shown a chess board in the middle of a game for 5 seconds with 20 to 30 pieces still in play can immediately reproduce the position of the pieces from memory. Beginners, of course, are able to place only a few. Now take the same pieces and place them on the board randomly and the (a) difference is much reduced. The expert's advantage is only for familiar patterns — those previously stored in memory. Faced with unfamiliar patterns, even when it involves the same familiar domain, the expert's advantage (b) disappears.

The beneficial effects of familiar structure on memory have been observed for many types of expertise, including music. People with musical training can reproduce short sequences of musical notation more accurately than those with no musical training when notes follow (c) unusual sequences, but the advantage is much reduced when the notes are ordered randomly. Expertise also improves memory for sequences of (d) movements. Experienced ballet dancers are able to repeat longer sequences of steps than less experienced dancers, and they can repeat a sequence of steps making up a routine better than steps ordered randomly. In each case, memory range is (e) increased by the ability to recognize familiar sequences and patterns.

* expertise: 전문 지식 ** sequence: 연속, 순서
*** musical notation: 악보

41. 윗글의 제목으로 가장 적절한 것은?

① How Can We Build Good Routines?
② Familiar Structures Help Us Remember
③ Intelligence Does Not Guarantee Expertise
④ Does Playing Chess Improve Your Memory?
⑤ Creative Art Performance Starts from Practice

42. 밑줄 친 (a) ~ (e) 중에서 문맥상 낱말의 쓰임이 적절하지 <u>않은</u> 것은?

① (a) ② (b) ③ (c) ④ (d) ⑤ (e)

[43 ~ 45] 다음 글을 읽고, 물음에 답하시오.

(A)

Once upon a time, there was a king who lived in a beautiful palace. While the king was away, a monster approached the gates of the palace. The monster was so ugly and smelly that the guards froze in shock. He passed the guards and sat on the king's throne. The guards soon came to their senses, went in, and shouted at the monster, demanding that (a) he get off the throne.

* throne: 왕좌

(B)

Eventually the king returned. He was wise and kind and saw what was happening. He knew what to do. He smiled and said to the monster, "Welcome to my palace!" He asked the monster if (b) he wanted a cup of coffee. The monster began to grow smaller as he drank the coffee.

(C)

The king offered (c) him some take-out pizza and fries. The guards immediately called for pizza. The monster continued to get smaller with the king's kind gestures. (d) He then offered the monster a full body massage. As the guards helped with the relaxing massage, the monster became tiny. With another act of kindness to the monster, he just disappeared.

(D)

With each bad word the guards used, the monster grew more ugly and smelly. The guards got even angrier — they began to brandish their swords to scare the monster away from the palace. But (e) he just grew bigger and bigger, eventually taking up the whole room. He grew more ugly and smelly than ever.

* brandish: 휘두르다

43. 주어진 글 (A)에 이어질 내용을 순서에 맞게 배열한 것으로 가장 적절한 것은?

① (B) − (D) − (C)   ② (C) − (B) − (D)
③ (C) − (D) − (B)   ④ (D) − (B) − (C)
⑤ (D) − (C) − (B)

44. 밑줄 친 (a) ~ (e) 중에서 가리키는 대상이 나머지 넷과 <u>다른</u> 것은?

① (a) ② (b) ③ (c) ④ (d) ⑤ (e)

45. 윗글에 관한 내용으로 적절하지 <u>않은</u> 것은?

① 왕이 없는 동안 괴물이 궁전 문으로 접근했다.
② 왕은 미소를 지으며 괴물에게 환영한다고 말했다.
③ 왕의 친절한 행동에 괴물의 몸이 계속 더 작아졌다.
④ 경비병들은 괴물을 마사지해 주기를 거부했다.
⑤ 경비병들은 겁을 주어 괴물을 쫓아내려 했다.

* 확인 사항
○ 답안지의 해당란에 필요한 내용을 정확히 기입(표기)했는지 확인하시오.

18

001 □ to whom it may concern 담당자 귀하, 관계자 귀하
002 □ resident ⓝ 주민
003 □ observe ⓥ (보고) 알다, 관찰하다
004 □ in need of ~이 필요한
005 □ repair ⓝ 보수, 수리
006 □ pay attention to ~에 주의를 기울이다
007 □ condition ⓝ 상태
008 □ playground ⓝ 놀이터
009 □ equipment ⓝ 장비
010 □ swing ⓝ 그네
011 □ damaged ⓐ 손상된
012 □ fall off 벗겨지다, 떨어져 나가다
013 □ slide ⓝ 미끄럼틀
014 □ missing ⓐ 없어진, 실종된
015 □ facility ⓝ 시설
016 □ terrible ⓐ 끔찍한
017 □ immediate ⓐ 즉각적인
018 □ matter ⓝ 문제

19

019 □ grizzly bear (북미·러시아 일부 지역에 사는) 회색곰
020 □ native ⓐ 토착의, 토종의
021 □ habitat ⓝ 서식지
022 □ at first 처음에
023 □ joy ⓝ 기쁨, 즐거움
024 □ walk across ~을 횡단하다
025 □ every once in a while 이따금
026 □ turn about 뒤돌아보다, 방향을 바꾸다
027 □ sniff ⓥ 킁킁거리다
028 □ deeply ⓐⓓ 깊게
029 □ scent ⓝ 냄새
030 □ slowly ⓐⓓ 천천히
031 □ giant ⓐ 거대한
032 □ smell ⓥ 냄새 맡다
033 □ freeze ⓥ 얼어붙다
034 □ no longer 더 이상 ~않다
035 □ issue ⓝ 문제, 이슈
036 □ survival ⓝ 생존
037 □ motivation ⓝ (행동의) 이유, 동기 (부여)
038 □ clearly ⓐⓓ 분명히
039 □ jealous ⓐ 질투하는
040 □ frustrated ⓐ 좌절한

20

041 □ maintain ⓥ 유지하다
042 □ constant ⓐ 지속적인
043 □ attention ⓝ 주의, 집중
044 □ throughout prep ~ 내내
045 □ working day 근무 시간대
046 □ characterise ⓥ ~을 특징으로 하다
047 □ peaks and valleys 정점과 저점, 부침, 성쇠
048 □ alertness ⓝ 기민함
049 □ achieve ⓥ 성취하다
050 □ confident ⓐ 자신감 있는
051 □ benefit ⓝ 이득
052 □ demanding ⓐ 까다로운, 힘든
053 □ cope with ~을 처리하다
054 □ warm up 준비가 되다, 몸을 풀다

21

055 □ adopt ⓥ 수용하다, 받아들이다
056 □ cost ⓝ 비용 ⓥ (~의 비용을) 치르게 하다
057 □ livelihood ⓝ 생계
058 □ push aside 밀어치우다
059 □ progress ⓝ 진보
060 □ remove ⓥ 제거하다
061 □ million ⓝ 100만
062 □ produce ⓥ 만들어내다
063 □ physical ⓐ 신체적인
064 □ disability ⓝ 장애
065 □ chronic ⓐ 만성의
066 □ certainly ⓐⓓ 분명히, 확실히
067 □ mass ⓝ (일반) 대중 ⓐ 대중의, 대량의
068 □ seek ⓥ 찾다, 추구하다
069 □ divorce A from B A와 B의 분리, A를 B로부터 분리시키다
070 □ put a stress on ~에 스트레스[부담]를 주다
071 □ sedentary ⓐ 주로 앉아서 하는
072 □ nature ⓝ 본성, 특성
073 □ health risk 건강상 위험
074 □ ignorance ⓝ 무지
075 □ endless ⓐ 끝없는
076 □ competition ⓝ 경쟁
077 □ labor market 노동 시장
078 □ get along (well) with ~와 잘 지내다
079 □ realistic ⓐ 현실적인

22

080 □ course ⓝ 수업, 강좌
081 □ rubber-stamp ⓝ 고무도장, 잘 살펴보지도 않고 무조건 허가하는 사람
082 □ colorful ⓐ 화려한, 색색의
083 □ funeral ⓝ 장례식
084 □ bathing suit 수영복
085 □ religious service 종교 의식
086 □ appropriate ⓐ 적절한
087 □ occasion ⓝ 상황, 경우
088 □ setting ⓝ 환경, 배경
089 □ skillful ⓐ 숙련된
090 □ flexible ⓐ 융통성 있는
091 □ strategy ⓝ 전략
092 □ multiple-choice test 객관식 시험, 선다형 시험

23

093 □ social ⓐ 사회적인
094 □ get better 나아지다, 개선되다
095 □ wage ⓝ 임금
096 □ working condition 근무 조건
097 □ improve ⓥ 향상되다
098 □ gradually ⓐⓓ 점차, 점점
099 □ time off 휴가
100 □ at the same time 동시에, 한편
101 □ transport ⓥ 운송, 이동
102 □ industrial revolution 산업 혁명
103 □ lead to ~을 초래하다
104 □ railway ⓝ 철도
105 □ seaside ⓝ 해변
106 □ arrival ⓝ 도래, 도착
107 □ tourism ⓝ 관광(업)

24 (continued)

108 □ growth ⓝ 성장
109 □ factor ⓝ 요인
110 □ expansion ⓝ 확장
111 □ discomfort ⓝ 불편
112 □ tourist destination 관광지
113 □ impact ⓝ 영향, 여파
114 □ characteristic ⓝ 특징

24

115 □ intended ⓐ 의도된
116 □ path ⓝ 길
117 □ rut ⓝ 틀에 박힌 생활
118 □ be good at ~을 잘하다
119 □ be rewarded for ~에 대해 보상받다
120 □ look around 둘러보다
121 □ deep ⓐ 깊은
122 □ breathe ⓥ 호흡하다
123 □ slippery ⓐ 미끄러운
124 □ take effort to ~하는 데 (…한) 노력이 들다
125 □ superhuman ⓐ 초인적인
126 □ effectively ⓐⓓ 실질적으로, 사실상
127 □ be stuck 꼼짝 못하다
128 □ employment ⓝ 고용
129 □ well-paying ⓐ 보수가 좋은
130 □ ultimately ⓐⓓ 궁극적으로
131 □ unsatisfying ⓐ 불만족스러운
132 □ compete with ~와 경쟁하다
133 □ have ~ in common ~을 공통적으로 지니다
134 □ influential ⓐ 영향력 있는

25

135 □ the number of ~의 수
136 □ decrease ⓥ 감소하다
137 □ period ⓝ 기간
138 □ gap between A and B A와 B 사이의 격차
139 □ slightly ⓐⓓ 약간
140 □ steadily ⓐⓓ 꾸준히
141 □ except prep ~을 제외하고
142 □ for the first time 처음으로

26

143 □ unlike prep ~와 달리
144 □ at the time (과거) 당시에
145 □ trousers ⓝ 바지
146 □ spend time ~ing ~하면서 시간을 보내다
147 □ adventurous ⓐ 모험적인
148 □ horse riding 승마
149 □ hunting ⓝ 사냥
150 □ wildlife ⓝ 야생 동물
151 □ photographer ⓝ 사진 작가
152 □ design ⓥ 설계하다
153 □ persuade ⓥ 설득하다
154 □ safe ⓐ 안전한
155 □ end up ~ing 결국 ~하다
156 □ work as ~로서 일하다
157 □ car dealer 자동차 판매상
158 □ go back to ~로 되돌아가다
159 □ nonetheless ⓐⓓ 그럼에도 불구하고
160 □ have a kid 자식을 낳다
161 □ the rest of ~의 나머지

27

162 □ publish ⓥ 출간하다
163 □ be open to ~을 대상으로 하다
164 □ article ⓝ 기사
165 □ length ⓝ 길이
166 □ high-quality ⓐ 고품질의

28

167 □ session ⓝ (특정한 활동을 위한) 시간
168 □ admission ⓝ 입장
169 □ first-come, first-served 선착순
170 □ accompany ⓥ 동반하다
171 □ for free 공짜로

29

172 □ noticeable ⓐ 눈에 띄는, 두드러지는
173 □ characteristic ⓝ 특징
174 □ project onto ~에게 투영시키다
175 □ cartoon character 만화 캐릭터
176 □ deform ⓥ 변형하다
177 □ in such a way as to ~한 방식으로
178 □ resemble ⓥ ~와 닮다
179 □ humanlike ⓐ 인간 같은
180 □ animated movie 만화 영화
181 □ natural ⓐ 자연스러운
182 □ lift ⓥ 들어올리다
183 □ paw ⓝ (동물의) 발
184 □ facial expression 얼굴 표정
185 □ emotionally ⓐⓓ 정서적으로
186 □ appealing ⓐ 매력적인
187 □ enlarge ⓥ 확대하다
188 □ feature ⓝ 특징, 이목구비

30

189 □ major ⓐ 주요한, 큰
190 □ philosophical ⓐ 철학적인
191 □ shift ⓝ 변화, 전환 ⓥ 바뀌다
192 □ industrial ⓐ 산업의
193 □ affluent ⓐ 부유한
194 □ competitive ⓐ 경쟁적인
195 □ geographically ⓐⓓ 지리적으로
196 □ spread ⓥ 퍼지다
197 □ force ⓥ (~이) 어쩔 수 없이 …하게 하다
198 □ in turn 결과적으로
199 □ reasonable ⓐ 합리적인, 적당한
200 □ essential ⓐ 매우 중요한
201 □ best-selling ⓐ 가장 많이 팔리는, 베스트셀러인
202 □ modernization ⓝ 현대화
203 □ revolution ⓝ 혁명
204 □ strengthen ⓥ 강화하다
205 □ demand ⓝ 수요
206 □ complex ⓐ 복잡한

31

207 □ differ in ~에 관해 다르다
208 □ reset ⓥ 재설정하다
209 □ biological clock 체내 시계
210 □ overcome ⓥ 극복하다
211 □ jet lag 시차로 인한 피로감
212 □ recovery ⓝ 회복
213 □ depend on ~에 좌우되다

214 ☐ **westward** ⓐⓓ 서쪽으로
215 ☐ **lengthen** ⓥ 연장하다
216 ☐ **eastward** ⓐⓓ 동쪽으로
217 ☐ **shorten** ⓥ 단축하다
218 ☐ **sizable** ⓐ 꽤 큰, 상당한
219 ☐ **have an impact on** ~에 영향을 주다
220 ☐ **performance** ⓝ (선수의) 경기력, 수행, 성과
221 ☐ **significantly** ⓐⓓ 상당히, 현저히
222 ☐ **additional** ⓐ 추가적인
223 ☐ **tough** ⓐ 어려운, 힘든

32
224 ☐ **confidence** ⓝ 자신감
225 ☐ **set out** 착수하다
226 ☐ **each day** 매일
227 ☐ **over-optimism** ⓝ 지나친 낙관주의
228 ☐ **time frame** (어떤 일에 쓸 수 있는) 시간(대)
229 ☐ **work on** ~에 공을 들이다
230 ☐ **make a practice of** ~을 습관으로 하다
231 ☐ **estimate** ⓥ 추산하다
232 ☐ **alongside** ⓟⓡⓔⓟ ~와 함께
233 ☐ **learn by experience** 경험을 통해 배우다
234 ☐ **than expected** 예상보다
235 ☐ **fit** ⓥ ~에 맞추다
236 ☐ **available** ⓐ 이용 가능한
237 ☐ **set about** ~을 시작하다
238 ☐ **there is no point in** ~하는 것은 의미가 없다
239 ☐ **gear up** 준비를 갖추다, 대비하다
240 ☐ **spare** ⓐ 여분의
241 ☐ **in between** 사이에
242 ☐ **practical** ⓐ 현실성 있는, 타당한
243 ☐ **come first** 가장 중요하다, 최우선 고려 사항이다

33
244 ☐ **countryside** ⓝ 시골 지역
245 ☐ **discover** ⓥ 발견하다
246 ☐ **explain** ⓥ 설명하다
247 ☐ **biologist** ⓝ 생물학자
248 ☐ **evolutionary** ⓐ 진화적인
249 ☐ **principle** ⓝ 원리
250 ☐ **evolve** ⓥ 진화하다, 발전하다
251 ☐ **generation** ⓝ 세대
252 ☐ **thrive** ⓥ 번성하다
253 ☐ **pass on** 물려주다
254 ☐ **gene** ⓝ 유전자
255 ☐ **species** ⓝ (생물) 종
256 ☐ **run into** ~을 우연히 만나다
257 ☐ **adapt to** ~에 적응하다

34
258 ☐ **creator** ⓝ 창조자
259 ☐ **clothing** ⓝ 옷, 의복
260 ☐ **begin with** ~로 시작되다
261 ☐ **refine** ⓥ 다듬다
262 ☐ **perfect** ⓥ 완성하다, 완벽하게 하다
263 ☐ **nail** ⓝ 못
264 ☐ **turn A into B** A를 B로 바꾸다
265 ☐ **picture** ⓥ 상상하다, 그리다
266 ☐ **finished product** 완제품

267 ☐ **process** ⓝ 과정
268 ☐ **over a period of time** 일정 기간에 걸쳐서
269 ☐ **before long** 머지않아
270 ☐ **in harmony** 조화롭게
271 ☐ **bring into existence** ~을 생겨나게 하다
272 ☐ **mentally** ⓐⓓ 머릿속에, 마음속으로
273 ☐ **careless** ⓐ 조심성 없는
274 ☐ **irresponsible** ⓐ 무책임한
275 ☐ **professional** ⓝ 전문가 ⓐ 전문적인

35
276 ☐ **affect** ⓥ 영향을 미치다
277 ☐ **main character** 주인공
278 ☐ **look through** ~을 통해서 보다
279 ☐ **interpret** ⓥ 해석하다, 이해하다
280 ☐ **differently** ⓐⓓ 다르게
281 ☐ **sympathy** ⓝ 공감
282 ☐ **conflict** ⓝ 갈등
283 ☐ **arise** ⓥ 발생하다
284 ☐ **pray for** ~을 위해 기도하다
285 ☐ **outcome** ⓝ 결과
286 ☐ **tale** ⓝ 이야기
287 ☐ **shift** ⓥ 바꾸다
288 ☐ **viewpoint** ⓝ 관점
289 ☐ **evil** ⓐ 사악한 ⓝ 악
290 ☐ **stepsister** ⓝ 의붓자매
291 ☐ **kingdom** ⓝ 왕국
292 ☐ **exist** ⓥ 존재하다
293 ☐ **willingly** ⓐⓓ 기꺼이
294 ☐ **what if** ~라면 어떨까

36
295 ☐ **Old Stone Age** 구석기 시대
296 ☐ **band** ⓝ (소규모) 무리
297 ☐ **wander** ⓥ 돌아다니다, 배회하다
298 ☐ **from place to place** 여기저기
299 ☐ **in search of** ~을 찾아서
300 ☐ **settle down** 정착하다
301 ☐ **crop** ⓝ 작물
302 ☐ **dweller** ⓝ 거주자
303 ☐ **work together** 함께 일하다, 협력하다
304 ☐ **share** ⓥ 나누다, 공유하다
305 ☐ **axe** ⓝ 도끼
306 ☐ **as a result** 그 결과
307 ☐ **community** ⓝ 공동체, 지역사회
308 ☐ **organize** ⓥ 조직하다, 정리하다
309 ☐ **efficiently** ⓐⓓ 효율적으로
310 ☐ **divide up** ~을 나누다

37
311 ☐ **form** ⓥ 형성하다
312 ☐ **mineral** ⓝ 광물
313 ☐ **in many ways** 많은 방법으로
314 ☐ **melt** ⓥ 녹이다, 녹다
315 ☐ **surface** ⓝ 표면
316 ☐ **trap** ⓥ 가두다
317 ☐ **below** ⓟⓡⓔⓟ ~의 아래에
318 ☐ **atom** ⓝ 원자
319 ☐ **combine into** ~로 결합되다
320 ☐ **compound** ⓝ 화합물
321 ☐ **crystal** ⓝ 결정체, 수정

322 ☐ **partly** ⓐⓓ 부분적으로
323 ☐ **rapidly** ⓐⓓ 빠르게
324 ☐ **with the unaided eye** 육안으로
325 ☐ **arrange** ⓥ 배열하다
326 ☐ **orderly** ⓐ 질서 있는
327 ☐ **element** ⓝ 원소, 구성요소
328 ☐ **in such cases** 이런 경우에

38
329 ☐ **carbohydrate** ⓝ 탄수화물
330 ☐ **simple sugar** 단당류
331 ☐ **basically** ⓐⓓ 기본적으로
332 ☐ **break down** 분해하다
333 ☐ **nutrient** ⓝ 영양소
334 ☐ **chain** ⓝ 사슬
335 ☐ **release** ⓥ 방출하다
336 ☐ **provide A with B** A에게 B를 공급하다
337 ☐ **a number of** 많은
338 ☐ **structure** ⓝ 구조
339 ☐ **other than** ~ 외에
340 ☐ **be made from** ~로 구성되다
341 ☐ **rather** ⓐⓓ 다소, 상당히, 꽤
342 ☐ **convert** ⓥ 바꾸다
343 ☐ **store** ⓥ 저장하다, 보유하다

39
344 ☐ **lecturer** ⓝ 강사, 강연자
345 ☐ **interact with** ~와 상호작용하다
346 ☐ **commonly** ⓐⓓ 흔히
347 ☐ **mistaken** ⓐ 잘못된, 틀린
348 ☐ **assumption** ⓝ 가정, 추정
349 ☐ **characteristic** ⓝ 특성
350 ☐ **automatically** ⓐⓓ 자동으로, 저절로
351 ☐ **go with** ~와 어울리다
352 ☐ **description** ⓝ 설명
353 ☐ **speak to** ~에게 말하다, 이야기를 걸다
354 ☐ **receive** ⓥ 받다
355 ☐ **contain** ⓥ 포함하다, (~이) 들어 있다
356 ☐ **be told** ~을 듣다
357 ☐ **discussion** ⓝ 토론, 논의
358 ☐ **impression** ⓝ 인상
359 ☐ **as expected** 예상된 대로
360 ☐ **original** ⓐ 최초의, 원래의
361 ☐ **expectation** ⓝ 기대, 예상
362 ☐ **relationship** ⓝ 관계

40
363 ☐ **risky** ⓐ 위험한
364 ☐ **trustworthy** ⓐ 신뢰할 만한
365 ☐ **evidence** ⓝ 근거, 증거
366 ☐ **almost** ⓐⓓ 거의
367 ☐ **prospect** ⓝ 예상, 가망성
368 ☐ **sensible** ⓐ 분별 있는, 현명한
369 ☐ **frequently** ⓐⓓ 자주, 빈번히
370 ☐ **product review** 상품평
371 ☐ **subtle** ⓐ 미묘한
372 ☐ **cue** ⓝ 단서, 신호
373 ☐ **signal** ⓥ 알리다 ⓝ 신호
374 ☐ **local** ⓐ 지역의, 현지의
375 ☐ **hassle** ⓝ 성가신 일
376 ☐ **tasty** ⓐ 맛있는
377 ☐ **in demand** 수요가 많은

378 ☐ **more often than not** 대개
379 ☐ **practice** ⓝ 관례, 실행
380 ☐ **particularly** ⓐⓓ 특히
381 ☐ **faced with** ~와 직면한
382 ☐ **uncertain** ⓐ 불확실한
383 ☐ **unrealistic** ⓐ 비현실적인
384 ☐ **rule** ⓝ 규칙 ⓥ 지배하다
385 ☐ **unpleasant** ⓐ 불쾌한

41~42
386 ☐ **master** ⓝ 달인, 고수
387 ☐ **chess board** 체스판
388 ☐ **in the middle of** ~의 한가운데에
389 ☐ **in play** 시합 중인
390 ☐ **reproduce** ⓥ 재현하다
391 ☐ **position** ⓝ 위치
392 ☐ **from memory** 외워서, 기억하여
393 ☐ **beginner** ⓝ 초심자
394 ☐ **only a few** 몇 안 되는 (것)
395 ☐ **place** ⓥ 놓다, 배치하다
396 ☐ **randomly** ⓐⓓ 무작위로
397 ☐ **reduce** ⓥ 줄이다, 감소시키다
398 ☐ **advantage** ⓝ 유리함, 이점
399 ☐ **familiar** ⓐ 익숙한, 친숙한
400 ☐ **previously** ⓐⓓ 이전에, 사전에
401 ☐ **unfamiliar** ⓐ 익숙지 않은, 낯선
402 ☐ **domain** ⓝ 영역, 분야
403 ☐ **disappear** ⓥ 사라지다
404 ☐ **beneficial** ⓐ 유익한, 이로운
405 ☐ **expertise** ⓝ 전문 지식
406 ☐ **sequence** ⓝ 연속, 순서
407 ☐ **musical notation** 악보
408 ☐ **accurately** ⓐⓓ 정확하게
409 ☐ **unusual** ⓐ 특이한
410 ☐ **movement** ⓝ 동작, 움직임
411 ☐ **experienced** ⓐ 숙련된, 경험 많은
412 ☐ **routine** ⓝ 습관, (정해진) 춤 동작, 루틴
413 ☐ **guarantee** ⓥ 보장하다

43~45
414 ☐ **once upon a time** 옛날 옛적에
415 ☐ **palace** ⓝ 궁전
416 ☐ **approach** ⓥ 다가오다, 접근하다
417 ☐ **gate** ⓝ 문
418 ☐ **ugly** ⓐ 추한
419 ☐ **smelly** ⓐ 냄새 나는, 악취가 나는
420 ☐ **in shock** 충격을 받아
421 ☐ **throne** ⓝ 왕좌
422 ☐ **come to one's senses** 정신을 차리다
423 ☐ **shout at** ~을 향해 소리치다
424 ☐ **get off** ~을 떠나다
425 ☐ **wise** ⓐ 현명한
426 ☐ **if** ⓒⓞⓝⓙ ~인지 아닌지
427 ☐ **take-out** ⓐ 사서 가지고 가는
428 ☐ **call for** ~을 시키다, ~을 요구하다
429 ☐ **gesture** ⓝ 몸짓, (감정의) 표시, 표현
430 ☐ **massage** ⓝ 마사지
431 ☐ **tiny** ⓐ 아주 작은
432 ☐ **brandish** ⓥ 휘두르다
433 ☐ **scare away** ~을 겁주어 쫓아버리다
434 ☐ **take up** ~을 차지하다
435 ☐ **than ever** 그 어느 때보다

TEST A-B 각 단어의 뜻을 [A] 영어는 우리말로, [B] 우리말은 영어로 쓰시오.

A	English	Korean
01	conflict	
02	mineral	
03	carbohydrate	
04	discussion	
05	unpleasant	
06	approach	
07	guarantee	
08	take up	
09	willingly	
10	release	
11	scent	
12	frustrated	
13	confident	
14	arise	
15	combine into	
16	cope with	
17	adopt	
18	adapt to	
19	maintain	
20	call for	

B	Korean	English
01	정착하다	
02	효율적으로	
03	포함하다	
04	~을 겁주어 쫓아버리다	
05	발견하다	
06	유전자	
07	무작위로	
08	지속적인	
09	(생물) 종	
10	조직하다, 정리하다	
11	질투하는	
12	이유, 동기부여	
13	추산하다	
14	돌아다니다, 배회하다	
15	원리	
16	인상	
17	공감	
18	서식지	
19	기대, 예상	
20	구조	

▶ A-D 정답 : 해설편 021쪽

TEST C-D 각 단어의 뜻을 골라 기호를 쓰시오.

C	English		Korean
01	picture	( )	ⓐ 화합물
02	warm up	( )	ⓑ 규칙, 지배하다
03	rule	( )	ⓒ 상상하다, 그리다
04	expertise	( )	ⓓ 영양소
05	refine	( )	ⓔ 유익한, 이로운
06	compound	( )	ⓕ 왕좌
07	faced with	( )	ⓖ ~내내
08	alertness	( )	ⓗ 준비가 되다, 몸을 풀다
09	run into	( )	ⓘ 다듬다
10	thrive	( )	ⓙ 우연히 만나다
11	bring into existence	( )	ⓚ 결과
12	nutrient	( )	ⓛ 미묘한
13	outcome	( )	ⓜ 전문지식
14	dweller	( )	ⓝ 이야기
15	beneficial	( )	ⓞ 번성하다
16	throne	( )	ⓟ 거주자
17	tale	( )	ⓠ ~을 생겨나게 하다
18	assumption	( )	ⓡ 기민함
19	throughout	( )	ⓢ 가정
20	subtle	( )	ⓣ ~와 직면한

D	Korean		English
01	질서 있는	( )	ⓐ stepsister
02	영역, 분야	( )	ⓑ no longer
03	원소, 구성요소	( )	ⓒ careless
04	무책임한	( )	ⓓ prospect
05	근거, 증거	( )	ⓔ element
06	위험한	( )	ⓕ interpret
07	현실성 있는, 타당한	( )	ⓖ practice
08	해석하다, 이해하다	( )	ⓗ orderly
09	수요가 많은	( )	ⓘ familiar
10	더 이상~ 않다	( )	ⓙ band
11	의붓자매	( )	ⓚ in demand
12	조심성 없는	( )	ⓛ from memory
13	예상, 가망성	( )	ⓜ irresponsible
14	익숙한, 친숙한	( )	ⓝ accurately
15	관례, 실행	( )	ⓞ practical
16	(소규모) 무리	( )	ⓟ sequence
17	외워서, 기억하여	( )	ⓠ gesture
18	연속, 순서	( )	ⓡ evidence
19	몸짓	( )	ⓢ domain
20	정확하게	( )	ⓣ risky

18. 다음 글의 목적으로 가장 적절한 것은?

Dear Ms. Robinson,
　The Warblers Choir is happy to announce that we are invited to compete in the International Young Choir Competition. The competition takes place in London on May 20. Though we wish to participate in the event, we do not have the necessary funds to travel to London. So we are kindly asking you to support us by coming to our fundraising concert. It will be held on March 26. In this concert, we shall be able to show you how big our passion for music is. Thank you in advance for your kind support and help.
Sincerely,
Arnold Reynolds

① 합창 대회 결과를 공지하려고
② 모금 음악회 참석을 요청하려고
③ 음악회 개최 장소를 예약하려고
④ 합창곡 선정에 조언을 구하려고
⑤ 기부금 사용 내역을 보고하려고

19. 다음 글에 드러난 Zoe의 심경 변화로 가장 적절한 것은?

　The principal stepped on stage. "Now, I present this year's top academic award to the student who has achieved the highest placing." He smiled at the row of seats where twelve finalists had gathered. Zoe wiped a sweaty hand on her handkerchief and glanced at the other finalists. They all looked as pale and uneasy as herself. Zoe and one of the other finalists had won first placing in four subjects so it came down to how teachers ranked their hard work and confidence. "The Trophy for General Excellence is awarded to Miss Zoe Perry," the principal declared. "Could Zoe step this way, please?" Zoe felt as if she were in heaven. She walked into the thunder of applause with a big smile.

① hopeful → disappointed　② guilty → confident
③ nervous → delighted　④ angry → calm
⑤ relaxed → proud

20. 다음 글에서 필자가 주장하는 바로 가장 적절한 것은?

　When I was in the army, my instructors would show up in my barracks room, and the first thing they would inspect was our bed. It was a simple task, but every morning we were required to make our bed to perfection. It seemed a little ridiculous at the time, but the wisdom of this simple act has been proven to me many times over. If you make your bed every morning, you will have accomplished the first task of the day. It will give you a small sense of pride and it will encourage you to do another task and another. By the end of the day, that one task completed will have turned into many tasks completed. If you can't do little things right, you will never do the big things right.

　　　* barracks room: (병영의) 생활관　** accomplish: 성취하다

① 숙면을 위해서는 침대를 깔끔하게 관리해야 한다.
② 일의 효율성을 높이려면 협동심을 발휘해야 한다.
③ 올바른 습관을 기르려면 정해진 규칙을 따라야 한다.
④ 건강을 유지하기 위해서는 기상 시간이 일정해야 한다.
⑤ 큰일을 잘 이루려면 작은 일부터 제대로 수행해야 한다.

21. 밑줄 친 Leave those activities to the rest of the sheep이 다음 글에서 의미하는 바로 가장 적절한 것은? [3점]

A job search is not a passive task. When you are searching, you are not browsing, nor are you "just looking". Browsing is not an effective way to reach a goal you claim to want to reach. If you are acting with purpose, if you are serious about anything you chose to do, then you need to be direct, focused and whenever possible, clever. Everyone else searching for a job has the same goal, competing for the same jobs. You must do more than the rest of the herd. Regardless of how long it may take you to find and get the job you want, being proactive will logically get you results faster than if you rely only on browsing online job boards and emailing an occasional resume. Leave those activities to the rest of the sheep.

① Try to understand other job-seekers' feelings.
② Keep calm and stick to your present position.
③ Don't be scared of the job-seeking competition.
④ Send occasional emails to your future employers.
⑤ Be more active to stand out from other job-seekers.

22. 다음 글의 요지로 가장 적절한 것은?

Many people view sleep as merely a "down time" when their brain shuts off and their body rests. In a rush to meet work, school, family, or household responsibilities, people cut back on their sleep, thinking it won't be a problem, because all of these other activities seem much more important. But research reveals that a number of vital tasks carried out during sleep help to maintain good health and enable people to function at their best. While you sleep, your brain is hard at work forming the pathways necessary for learning and creating memories and new insights. Without enough sleep, you can't focus and pay attention or respond quickly. A lack of sleep may even cause mood problems. In addition, growing evidence shows that a continuous lack of sleep increases the risk for developing serious diseases.

* vital: 매우 중요한

① 수면은 건강 유지와 최상의 기능 발휘에 도움이 된다.
② 업무량이 증가하면 필요한 수면 시간도 증가한다.
③ 균형 잡힌 식단을 유지하면 뇌 기능이 향상된다.
④ 불면증은 주위 사람들에게 부정적인 영향을 미친다.
⑤ 꿈의 내용은 깨어 있는 시간 동안의 경험을 반영한다.

23. 다음 글의 주제로 가장 적절한 것은? [3점]

The whole of human society operates on knowing the future weather. For example, farmers in India know when the monsoon rains will come next year and so they know when to plant the crops. Farmers in Indonesia know there are two monsoon rains each year, so next year they can have two harvests. This is based on their knowledge of the past, as the monsoons have always come at about the same time each year in living memory. But the need to predict goes deeper than this; it influences every part of our lives. Our houses, roads, railways, airports, offices, and so on are all designed for the local climate. For example, in England all the houses have central heating, as the outside temperature is usually below 20°C, but no air-conditioning, as temperatures rarely go beyond 26°C, while in Australia the opposite is true: most houses have air-conditioning but rarely central heating.

① new technologies dealing with climate change
② difficulties in predicting the weather correctly
③ weather patterns influenced by rising temperatures
④ knowledge of the climate widely affecting our lives
⑤ traditional wisdom helping our survival in harsh climates

24. 다음 글의 제목으로 가장 적절한 것은?

Our ability to accurately recognize and label emotions is often referred to as *emotional granularity*. In the words of Harvard psychologist Susan David, "Learning to label emotions with a more nuanced vocabulary can be absolutely transformative." David explains that if we don't have a rich emotional vocabulary, it is difficult to communicate our needs and to get the support that we need from others. But those who are able to distinguish between a range of various emotions "do much, much better at managing the ups and downs of ordinary existence than those who see everything in black and white." In fact, research shows that the process of labeling emotional experience is related to greater emotion regulation and psychosocial well-being.

* nuanced: 미묘한 차이가 있는

① True Friendship Endures Emotional Arguments
② Detailed Labeling of Emotions Is Beneficial
③ Labeling Emotions: Easier Said Than Done
④ Categorize and Label Tasks for Efficiency
⑤ Be Brave and Communicate Your Needs

25. 다음 도표의 내용과 일치하지 <u>않는</u> 것은?

Percentage of UK People
Who Used Online Course and Online Learning Material
(in 2020, by age group)

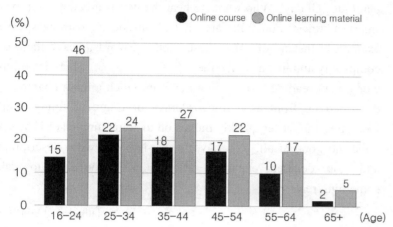

● Online course ● Online learning material

The above graph shows the percentage of people in the UK who used online courses and online learning materials, by age group in 2020. ① In each age group, the percentage of people who used online learning materials was higher than that of people who used online courses. ② The 25−34 age group had the highest percentage of people who used online courses in all the age groups. ③ Those aged 65 and older were the least likely to use online courses among the six age groups. ④ Among the six age groups, the gap between the percentage of people who used online courses and that of people who used online learning materials was the greatest in the 16−24 age group. ⑤ In each of the 35−44, 45−54, and 55−64 age groups, more than one in five people used online learning materials.

26. Antonie van Leeuwenhoek에 관한 다음 글의 내용과 일치하지 <u>않는</u> 것은?

Antonie van Leeuwenhoek was a scientist well known for his cell research. He was born in Delft, the Netherlands, on October 24, 1632. At the age of 16, he began to learn job skills in Amsterdam. At the age of 22, Leeuwenhoek returned to Delft. It wasn't easy for Leeuwenhoek to become a scientist. He knew only one language — Dutch — which was quite unusual for scientists of his time. But his curiosity was endless, and he worked hard. He had an important skill. He knew how to make things out of glass. This skill came in handy when he made lenses for his simple microscope. He saw tiny veins with blood flowing through them. He also saw living bacteria in pond water. He paid close attention to the things he saw and wrote down his observations. Since he couldn't draw well, he hired an artist to draw pictures of what he described.

* cell: 세포 ** vein: 혈관

① 세포 연구로 잘 알려진 과학자였다.
② 22살에 Delft로 돌아왔다.
③ 여러 개의 언어를 알았다.
④ 유리로 물건을 만드는 방법을 알고 있었다.
⑤ 화가를 고용하여 설명하는 것을 그리게 했다.

27. Rachel's Flower Class에 관한 다음 안내문의 내용과 일치하지 <u>않는</u> 것은?

Rachel's Flower Class
Make Your Life More Beautiful!

Class Schedule (Every Monday to Friday)

| Flower Arrangement | 11 a.m. − 12 p.m. |
| Flower Box Making | 1 p.m. − 2 p.m. |

Price
- $50 for each class
  (flowers and other materials included)
- Bring your own scissors and a bag.

Other Info.
- You can sign up for classes either online or by phone.
- No refund for cancellations on the day of your class

To contact, visit www.rfclass.com or call 03−221−2131.

① 플라워 박스 만들기 수업은 오후 1시에 시작된다.
② 수강료에 꽃값과 다른 재료비가 포함된다.
③ 수강생은 가위와 가방을 가져와야 한다.
④ 수업 등록은 전화로만 할 수 있다.
⑤ 수업 당일 취소 시 환불을 받을 수 없다.

28. Nighttime Palace Tour에 관한 다음 안내문의 내용과 일치하는 것은?

Nighttime Palace Tour

Date: Friday, April 29−Sunday, May 15

Time

Friday	7 p.m. − 8:30 p.m.
Saturday & Sunday	6 p.m. − 7:30 p.m.
	8 p.m. − 9:30 p.m.

Tickets & Booking
- $15 per person (free for kids under 8)
- Bookings will be accepted up to 2 hours before the tour starts.

Program Activities
- Group tour with a tour guide (1 hour)
- Trying traditional foods and drinks (30 minutes)

※ You can try on traditional clothes with no extra charge.
※ For more information, please visit our website, www.palacenighttour.com.

① 금요일에는 하루에 두 번 투어가 운영된다.
② 8세 미만 어린이의 티켓은 5달러이다.
③ 예약은 투어 하루 전까지만 가능하다.
④ 투어 가이드의 안내 없이 궁궐을 둘러본다.
⑤ 추가 비용 없이 전통 의상을 입어 볼 수 있다.

29. 다음 글의 밑줄 친 부분 중, 어법상 틀린 것은?

We usually get along best with people who we think are like us. In fact, we seek them out. It's why places like Little Italy, Chinatown, and Koreatown ① <u>exist</u>. But I'm not just talking about race, skin color, or religion. I'm talking about people who share our values and look at the world the same way we ② <u>do</u>. As the saying goes, birds of a feather flock together. This is a very common human tendency ③ <u>what</u> is rooted in how our species developed. Imagine you are walking out in a forest. You would be conditioned to avoid something unfamiliar or foreign because there is a high likelihood that ④ <u>it</u> would be interested in killing you. Similarities make us ⑤ <u>relate</u> better to other people because we think they'll understand us on a deeper level than other people.

* species: 종(생물 분류의 기초 단위)

30. 다음 글의 밑줄 친 부분 중, 문맥상 낱말의 쓰임이 적절하지 <u>않은</u> 것은? [3점]

Rejection is an everyday part of our lives, yet most people can't handle it well. For many, it's so painful that they'd rather not ask for something at all than ask and ① <u>risk</u> rejection. Yet, as the old saying goes, if you don't ask, the answer is always no. Avoiding rejection ② <u>negatively</u> affects many aspects of your life. All of that happens only because you're not ③ <u>tough</u> enough to handle it. For this reason, consider rejection therapy. Come up with a ④ <u>request</u> or an activity that usually results in a rejection. Working in sales is one such example. Asking for discounts at the stores will also work. By deliberately getting yourself ⑤ <u>welcomed</u> you'll grow a thicker skin that will allow you to take on much more in life, thus making you more successful at dealing with unfavorable circumstances.

* deliberately: 의도적으로

[31 ~ 34] 다음 빈칸에 들어갈 말로 가장 적절한 것을 고르시오.

31. Generalization without specific examples that humanize writing is boring to the listener and to the reader. Who wants to read platitudes all day? Who wants to hear the words great, greater, best, smartest, finest, humanitarian, on and on and on without specific examples? Instead of using these 'nothing words,' leave them out completely and just describe the _____. There is nothing worse than reading a scene in a novel in which a main character is described up front as heroic or brave or tragic or funny, while thereafter, the writer quickly moves on to something else. That's no good, no good at all. You have to use less one word descriptions and more detailed, engaging descriptions if you want to make something real.

* platitude: 상투적인 말

① similarities
② particulars
③ fantasies
④ boredom
⑤ wisdom

32. Face-to-face interaction is a uniquely powerful — and sometimes the only — way to share many kinds of knowledge, from the simplest to the most complex. It is one of the best ways to stimulate new thinking and ideas, too. Most of us would have had difficulty learning how to tie a shoelace only from pictures, or how to do arithmetic from a book. Psychologist Mihàly Csikszentmihàlyi found, while studying high achievers, that a large number of Nobel Prize winners were the students of previous winners: they had access to the same literature as everyone else, but _____ made a crucial difference to their creativity. Within organisations this makes conversation both a crucial factor for high-level professional skills and the most important way of sharing everyday information.

* arithmetic: 계산 ** literature: (연구) 문헌

① natural talent
② regular practice
③ personal contact
④ complex knowledge
⑤ powerful motivation

33. Most times a foreign language is spoken in film, subtitles are used to translate the dialogue for the viewer. However, there are occasions when foreign dialogue is left unsubtitled (and thus incomprehensible to most of the target audience). This is often done if the movie is seen mainly from the viewpoint of a particular character who does not speak the language. Such absence of subtitles allows the audience to feel a similar sense of incomprehension and alienation that the character feels. An example of this is seen in *Not Without My Daughter*. The Persian language dialogue spoken by the Iranian characters is not subtitled because the main character Betty Mahmoody does not speak Persian and the audience is _____. [3점]

* subtitle: 자막(을 넣다) ** incomprehensible: 이해할 수 없는
*** alienation: 소외

① seeing the film from her viewpoint
② impressed by her language skills
③ attracted to her beautiful voice
④ participating in a heated debate
⑤ learning the language used in the film

34. One dynamic that can change dramatically in sport is the concept of the home-field advantage, in which perceived demands and resources seem to play a role. Under normal circumstances, the home ground would appear to provide greater perceived resources (fans, home field, and so on). However, researchers Roy Baumeister and Andrew Steinhilber were among the first to point out that these competitive factors can change; for example, the success percentage for home teams in the final games of a playoff or World Series seems to drop. Fans can become part of the perceived demands rather than resources under those circumstances. This change in perception can also explain why a team that's struggling at the start of the year will _____ to reduce perceived demands and pressures. [3점]

* perceive: 인식하다 ** playoff: 우승 결정전

① often welcome a road trip
② avoid international matches
③ focus on increasing ticket sales
④ want to have an eco-friendly stadium
⑤ try to advertise their upcoming games

35. 다음 글에서 전체 흐름과 관계 <u>없는</u> 문장은?

Who hasn't used a cup of coffee to help themselves stay awake while studying? Mild stimulants commonly found in tea, coffee, or sodas possibly make you more attentive and, thus, better able to remember. ① However, you should know that stimulants are as likely to have negative effects on memory as they are to be beneficial. ② Even if they could improve performance at some level, the ideal doses are currently unknown. ③ If you are wide awake and well-rested, mild stimulation from caffeine can do little to further improve your memory performance. ④ In contrast, many studies have shown that drinking tea is healthier than drinking coffee. ⑤ Indeed, if you have too much of a stimulant, you will become nervous, find it difficult to sleep, and your memory performance will suffer.

* stimulant: 자극제 ** dose: 복용량

[36 ~ 37] 주어진 글 다음에 이어질 글의 순서로 가장 적절한 것을 고르시오.

36.

Toward the end of the 19th century, a new architectural attitude emerged. Industrial architecture, the argument went, was ugly and inhuman; past styles had more to do with pretension than what people needed in their homes.

(A) But they supplied people's needs perfectly and, at their best, had a beauty that came from the craftsman's skill and the rootedness of the house in its locality.

(B) Instead of these approaches, why not look at the way ordinary country builders worked in the past? They developed their craft skills over generations, demonstrating mastery of both tools and materials.

(C) Those materials were local, and used with simplicity — houses built this way had plain wooden floors and whitewashed walls inside.

* pretension: 허세, 가식

① (A) - (C) - (B)　　② (B) - (A) - (C)
③ (B) - (C) - (A)　　④ (C) - (A) - (B)
⑤ (C) - (B) - (A)

37.

> Robert Schumann once said, "The laws of morals are those of art." What the great man is saying here is that there is good music and bad music.

(A) It's the same with performances: a bad performance isn't necessarily the result of incompetence. Some of the worst performances occur when the performers, no matter how accomplished, are thinking more of themselves than of the music they're playing.

(B) The greatest music, even if it's tragic in nature, takes us to a world higher than ours; somehow the beauty uplifts us. Bad music, on the other hand, degrades us.

(C) These doubtful characters aren't really listening to what the composer is saying—they're just showing off, hoping that they'll have a great 'success' with the public. The performer's basic task is to try to understand the meaning of the music, and then to communicate it honestly to others. [3점]

* incompetence: 무능 ** degrade: 격하시키다

① (A) − (C) − (B) ② (B) − (A) − (C)
③ (B) − (C) − (A) ④ (C) − (A) − (B)
⑤ (C) − (B) − (A)

[38 ~ 39] 글의 흐름으로 보아, 주어진 문장이 들어가기에 가장 적절한 곳을 고르시오.

38.

> But, when there is biodiversity, the effects of a sudden change are not so dramatic.

When an ecosystem is biodiverse, wildlife have more opportunities to obtain food and shelter. Different species react and respond to changes in their environment differently. (①) For example, imagine a forest with only one type of plant in it, which is the only source of food and habitat for the entire forest food web. (②) Now, there is a sudden dry season and this plant dies. (③) Plant-eating animals completely lose their food source and die out, and so do the animals that prey upon them. (④) Different species of plants respond to the drought differently, and many can survive a dry season. (⑤) Many animals have a variety of food sources and don't just rely on one plant; now our forest ecosystem is no longer at the death! [3점]

* biodiversity: (생물학적) 종 다양성 ** habitat: 서식지

39.

> Since the dawn of civilization, our ancestors created myths and told legendary stories about the night sky.

We are connected to the night sky in many ways. (①) It has always inspired people to wonder and to imagine. (②) Elements of those narratives became embedded in the social and cultural identities of many generations. (③) On a practical level, the night sky helped past generations to keep track of time and create calendars — essential to developing societies as aids to farming and seasonal gathering. (④) For many centuries, it also provided a useful navigation tool, vital for commerce and for exploring new worlds. (⑤) Even in modern times, many people in remote areas of the planet observe the night sky for such practical purposes.

* embed: 깊이 새겨 두다 ** commerce: 무역

40. 다음 글의 내용을 한 문장으로 요약하고자 한다. 빈칸 (A), (B)에 들어갈 말로 가장 적절한 것은?

> The common blackberry (*Rubus allegheniensis*) has an amazing ability to move manganese from one layer of soil to another using its roots. This may seem like a funny talent for a plant to have, but it all becomes clear when you realize the effect it has on nearby plants. Manganese can be very harmful to plants, especially at high concentrations. Common blackberry is unaffected by damaging effects of this metal and has evolved two different ways of using manganese to its advantage. First, it redistributes manganese from deeper soil layers to shallow soil layers using its roots as a small pipe. Second, it absorbs manganese as it grows, concentrating the metal in its leaves. When the leaves drop and decay, their concentrated manganese deposits further poison the soil around the plant. For plants that are not immune to the toxic effects of manganese, this is very bad news. Essentially, the common blackberry eliminates competition by poisoning its neighbors with heavy metals.

* manganese: 망가니즈(금속 원소) ** deposit: 축적물

↓

> The common blackberry has an ability to __(A)__ the amount of manganese in the surrounding upper soil, which makes the nearby soil quite __(B)__ for other plants.

	(A)		(B)
①	increase	⋯⋯	deadly
②	increase	⋯⋯	advantageous
③	indicate	⋯⋯	nutritious
④	reduce	⋯⋯	dry
⑤	reduce	⋯⋯	warm

[41 ~ 42] 다음 글을 읽고, 물음에 답하시오.

The longest journey we will make is the eighteen inches between our head and heart. If we take this journey, it can shorten our (a) misery in the world. Impatience, judgment, frustration, and anger reside in our heads. When we live in that place too long, it makes us (b) unhappy. But when we take the journey from our heads to our hearts, something shifts (c) inside. What if we were able to love everything that gets in our way? What if we tried loving the shopper who unknowingly steps in front of us in line, the driver who cuts us off in traffic, the swimmer who splashes us with water during a belly dive, or the reader who pens a bad online review of our writing?

Every person who makes us miserable is (d) like us — a human being, most likely doing the best they can, deeply loved by their parents, a child, or a friend. And how many times have we unknowingly stepped in front of someone in line? Cut someone off in traffic? Splashed someone in a pool? Or made a negative statement about something we've read? It helps to (e) deny that a piece of us resides in every person we meet.

* reside: (어떤 장소에) 있다

41. 윗글의 제목으로 가장 적절한 것은?

① Why It Is So Difficult to Forgive Others
② Even Acts of Kindness Can Hurt Somebody
③ Time Is the Best Healer for a Broken Heart
④ Celebrate the Happy Moments in Your Everyday Life
⑤ Understand Others to Save Yourself from Unhappiness

42. 밑줄 친 (a) ~ (e) 중에서 문맥상 낱말의 쓰임이 적절하지 <u>않은</u> 것은?

① (a)　　② (b)　　③ (c)　　④ (d)　　⑤ (e)

[43 ~ 45] 다음 글을 읽고, 물음에 답하시오.

(A)

One day a young man was walking along a road on his journey from one village to another. As he walked he noticed a monk working in the fields. The young man turned to the monk and said, "Excuse me. Do you mind if I ask (a) you a question?" "Not at all," replied the monk.

* monk: 수도승

(B)

A while later a middle-aged man journeyed down the same road and came upon the monk. "I am going to the village in the valley," said the man. "Do you know what it is like?" "I do," replied the monk, "but first tell (b) me about the village where you came from." "I've come from the village in the mountains," said the man. "It was a wonderful experience. I felt as though I was a member of the family in the village."

(C)

"I am traveling from the village in the mountains to the village in the valley and I was wondering if (c) you knew what it is like in the village in the valley." "Tell me," said the monk, "what was your experience of the village in the mountains?" "Terrible," replied the young man. "I am glad to be away from there. I found the people most unwelcoming. So tell (d) me, what can I expect in the village in the valley?" "I am sorry to tell you," said the monk, "but I think your experience will be much the same there." The young man lowered his head helplessly and walked on.

(D)

"Why did you feel like that?" asked the monk. "The elders gave me much advice, and people were kind and generous. I am sad to have left there. And what is the village in the valley like?" he asked again. "(e) I think you will find it much the same," replied the monk. "I'm glad to hear that," the middle-aged man said smiling and journeyed on.

43. 주어진 글 (A)에 이어질 내용을 순서에 맞게 배열한 것으로 가장 적절한 것은?

① (B) − (D) − (C)　　② (C) − (B) − (D)
③ (C) − (D) − (B)　　④ (D) − (B) − (C)
⑤ (D) − (C) − (B)

44. 밑줄 친 (a) ~ (e) 중에서 가리키는 대상이 나머지 넷과 <u>다른</u> 것은?

① (a)　　② (b)　　③ (c)　　④ (d)　　⑤ (e)

45. 윗글에 관한 내용으로 적절하지 <u>않은</u> 것은?

① 한 수도승이 들판에서 일하고 있었다.
② 중년 남자는 골짜기에 있는 마을로 가는 중이었다.
③ 수도승은 골짜기에 있는 마을에 대해 질문받았다.
④ 수도승의 말을 듣고 젊은이는 고개를 숙였다.
⑤ 중년 남자는 산속에 있는 마을을 떠나서 기쁘다고 말했다.

★ 확인 사항
○ 답안지의 해당란에 필요한 내용을 정확히 기입(표기)했는지 확인하시오.

18
001 □ choir ⓝ 합창단
002 □ announce ⓥ 발표하다, 알리다
003 □ compete in ~에서 경쟁하다
004 □ takes place 열리다
005 □ participate in ~에 참가하다
006 □ support ⓥ 후원하다
007 □ fundraising ⓝ 모금
008 □ passion ⓝ 열정
009 □ in advance 미리, 앞서

19
010 □ present ⓥ 수여하다
011 □ academic ⓐ 학업의
012 □ row ⓝ 열, 횡렬
013 □ finalist ⓝ 최종 후보자, 결승 진출자
014 □ gather ⓥ 모이다
015 □ wipe ⓥ 닦다
016 □ sweaty ⓐ 땀에 젖은
017 □ handkerchief ⓝ 손수건
018 □ glance at ~을 흘긋 보다
019 □ pale ⓐ 창백한
020 □ uneasy ⓐ 불안한
021 □ subject ⓝ 과목
022 □ rank ⓥ 평가하다, 순위를 매기다
023 □ confidence ⓝ 자신감
024 □ declare ⓥ 선언[포고]하다, 공표하다
025 □ this way 이리로
026 □ applause ⓝ 박수갈채
027 □ guilty ⓐ 죄책감이 드는, 가책을 느끼는

20
028 □ instructor ⓝ 교사, 교관, 강사
029 □ barrack ⓝ 막사, 병영
030 □ inspect ⓥ 조사하다
031 □ task ⓝ 일, 과업, 과제
032 □ require ⓥ 필요[요구]하다
033 □ make the bed 잠자리를 정돈하다
034 □ perfection ⓝ 완벽, 완전
035 □ ridiculous ⓐ 우스꽝스러운
036 □ wisdom ⓝ 지혜
037 □ prove ⓥ 입증[증명]하다
038 □ accomplish ⓥ 완수하다, 성취하다
039 □ encourage ⓥ 용기를 북돋우다
040 □ complete ⓥ 완수하다
041 □ turn into ~로 바뀌다

21
042 □ job search 구직 활동
043 □ passive ⓐ 수동적인
044 □ browse ⓥ 훑어보다
045 □ reach ⓥ ~에 이르다, ~에 도착[도달]하다
046 □ goal ⓥ 목표
047 □ claim ⓥ 주장하다
048 □ purpose ⓝ 목적
049 □ serious ⓐ 진지한
050 □ clever ⓐ 영리한
051 □ else ⓐ 다른
052 □ rest ⓝ (어떤 것의) 나머지
053 □ herd ⓝ 무리
054 □ regardless of ~와 상관없이
055 □ proactive ⓐ 상황을 앞서서 주도하는

056 □ logically ⓐ 논리적으로
057 □ result ⓝ 결과
058 □ occasional ⓐ 가끔씩의
059 □ resume ⓝ 이력서
060 □ stand out from ~에서 두드러지다
061 □ sheep ⓝ 양, 어리석은 사람

22
062 □ view A as B A를 B로 보다
063 □ merely ⓐ 그저, 단순히
064 □ down time 정지 시간, 휴식 시간
065 □ shut off 멈추다
066 □ in a rush 서둘러
067 □ household ⓝ (한 집에 사는 사람들을 일컫는) 가정
068 □ responsibility ⓝ 책임
069 □ cut back on ~을 줄이다
070 □ activity ⓝ 활동
071 □ reveal ⓥ 밝히다
072 □ a number of 많은
073 □ vital ⓐ 매우 중요한
074 □ carry out ~을 수행하다
075 □ during ⓟⓡⓔⓟ 동안
076 □ maintain ⓥ 유지하다
077 □ enable ~을 할 수 있게 하다
078 □ function ⓥ 기능하다
079 □ at one's best 최상의 수준으로
080 □ form ⓥ 형성하다
081 □ pathway ⓝ 경로
082 □ memory ⓝ 기억
083 □ insight ⓝ 통찰력
084 □ focus ⓥ 정신을 집중하다
085 □ pay attention 주의를 기울이다
086 □ respond ⓥ 반응하다
087 □ lack ⓝ 부족
088 □ cause ⓥ 일으키다
089 □ mood ⓝ 기분, 감정
090 □ in addition 게다가
091 □ grow ⓥ 커지다, 증대하다
092 □ evidence ⓝ 증거
093 □ risk ⓝ 위험
094 □ develop a disease 병을 키우다

23
095 □ whole ⓝ 전체
096 □ human society 인간 사회
097 □ operate ⓥ 운영되다, 돌아가다
098 □ monsoon ⓝ (동남아 여름철의) 몬순, 우기, 장마
099 □ plant ⓥ 심다
100 □ crop ⓝ 작물
101 □ harvest ⓝ 수확
102 □ knowledge ⓝ 지식
103 □ past ⓝ 과거
104 □ predict ⓥ 예측하다
105 □ influence ⓥ 영향을 미치다
106 □ railway ⓝ 철도
107 □ climate ⓝ 기후
108 □ central heating 중앙난방
109 □ temperature ⓝ 기온
110 □ below ⓟⓡⓔⓟ ~보다 아래에
111 □ air-conditioning ⓝ 냉방(기)

112 □ rarely ⓐ 거의 없게
113 □ beyond ⓟⓡⓔⓟ 위로
114 □ opposite ⓝ 정반대
115 □ technology ⓝ 과학기술
116 □ deal ⓥ 처리하다, 다루다
117 □ correctly ⓐ 정확하게
118 □ affect ⓥ 영향을 미치다
119 □ harsh ⓐ 혹독한

24
120 □ accurately ⓐ 정확하게
121 □ recognize ⓥ 인식하다
122 □ label ⓥ 이름을 붙이다
123 □ refer to A as B A를 B라고 부르다
124 □ granularity ⓝ 낟알 모양, 입상(粒狀)
125 □ psychologist ⓝ 심리학자
126 □ vocabulary ⓝ 어휘
127 □ absolutely ⓐ 절대적으로
128 □ transformative ⓐ 변화시키는
129 □ explain ⓥ 설명하다
130 □ communicate ⓥ 전달하다
131 □ support ⓝ 지지
132 □ distinguish ⓥ 구별하다
133 □ a range of 광범위한
134 □ various ⓐ 다양한
135 □ ups and downs 좋은 일과 궂은 일, 오르락내리락
136 □ ordinary ⓐ 평범한
137 □ existence ⓝ 존재
138 □ process ⓝ 과정
139 □ related to ~에 관련된
140 □ regulation ⓝ 통제
141 □ psychosocial ⓐ 심리사회적인
142 □ well-being ⓝ 행복
143 □ friendship ⓝ 우정, 교우관계
144 □ endure ⓥ 견디다, 참다, 인내하다
145 □ argument ⓝ 논쟁, 논의
146 □ beneficial ⓐ 유익한, 이로운
147 □ categorize ⓥ 분류하다
148 □ efficiency ⓝ 효율, 능률

25
149 □ course ⓝ 강의
150 □ learning material 학습 자료
151 □ age group 연령 집단
152 □ be the least likely to ~할 가능성이 가장 낮다

26
153 □ known for ~으로 알려진
154 □ job skill 직무 기술
155 □ Dutch ⓝ 네덜란드어
156 □ unusual ⓐ 드문
157 □ curiosity ⓝ 호기심
158 □ endless ⓐ 끝없는
159 □ make A out of B B로 A를 만들다
160 □ come in handy 도움이 되다
161 □ microscope ⓝ 현미경
162 □ vein ⓝ 정맥
163 □ flow ⓥ 흐르다
164 □ pond ⓝ 연못
165 □ pay attention to ~에 주의를 기울이다

166 □ observation ⓝ 관찰
167 □ hire ⓥ 고용하다
168 □ describe ⓥ 설명하다, 서술하다, 묘사하다

27
169 □ flower arrangement 꽃꽂이
170 □ material ⓝ 재료
171 □ scissor ⓝ 가위
172 □ sign up for ~에 등록하다
173 □ refund ⓝ 환불
174 □ cancellation ⓝ 취소
175 □ contact ⓥ 연락하다

28
176 □ palace ⓝ 궁전
177 □ book ⓥ 예약하다
178 □ traditional ⓐ 전통적인
179 □ extra charge 추가 비용, 할증요금
180 □ visit ⓝ 접촉 ⓥ 방문하다

29
181 □ get along with ~와 잘 지내다, 어울리다
182 □ seek out (오랫동안 공들여) 찾아다니다
183 □ exist ⓥ 존재하다
184 □ race ⓝ 인종
185 □ religion ⓝ 종교
186 □ value ⓝ 가치관
187 □ way ⓝ 방식
188 □ as the saying goes 속담에서 말하듯이, 옛말처럼
189 □ feather ⓝ 깃털
190 □ flock ⓥ 모이다, 무리 짓다
191 □ common ⓐ 흔한
192 □ tendency ⓝ 경향, 경향성
193 □ be rooted in ~에 뿌리박고 있다, ~에 원인이 있다
194 □ species ⓝ 종(생물 분류의 기초 단위)
195 □ be conditioned to ~에 조건화되어 있다
196 □ avoid ⓥ 피하다
197 □ unfamiliar ⓐ 친숙하지 않은
198 □ likelihood ⓝ 가능성
199 □ similarity ⓝ 유사점
200 □ relate to ~을 이해하다, ~에 공감하다

30
201 □ rejection ⓝ 거절
202 □ handle ⓥ 감당하다
203 □ painful ⓐ 고통스러운
204 □ rather ⓐ 오히려, 차라리
205 □ negative ⓐ 부정적인
206 □ tough ⓐ 강한
207 □ reason ⓝ 이유
208 □ consider ⓥ 고려하다
209 □ therapy ⓝ 요법
210 □ come up with ~을 생각해내다, 떠올리다
211 □ request ⓝ 요청
212 □ deliberately ⓐ 고의로, 의도적으로
213 □ grow a thick skin 무덤덤해지다, 둔감해지다
214 □ thus ⓐ 따라서, 그러므로
215 □ unfavorable ⓐ 호의적이지 않은
216 □ circumstance ⓝ 상황, 환경

31

217 □ generalization ⓝ 일반화
218 □ specific ⓐ 구체적인, 명확한
219 □ humanize ⓥ 인간적으로 만들다
220 □ platitude ⓝ 진부한 말, 상투적인 문구
221 □ finest ⓐ 가장 훌륭한
222 □ humanitarian ⓐ 인도주의적인
223 □ leave out ~을 빼다
224 □ completely ⓐⓓ 완전히, 전적으로
225 □ novel ⓝ 소설
226 □ main character 주인공
227 □ up front 대놓고
228 □ heroic ⓐ 대담한, 영웅적인
229 □ brave ⓐ 용감한
230 □ tragic ⓐ 비극적인
231 □ thereafter ⓐⓓ 그 후에
232 □ description ⓝ 묘사
233 □ at all 전혀
234 □ detailed ⓐ 세밀한
235 □ engaging ⓐ 마음을 끄는, 몰입시키는
236 □ boredom ⓝ 지루함

32

237 □ interaction ⓝ 상호 작용
238 □ uniquely ⓐⓓ 유례없이
239 □ powerful ⓐ 영향력 있는, 강력한
240 □ simplest ⓐ 가장 간단한
241 □ complex ⓐ 복잡한
242 □ stimulate ⓥ 자극하다
243 □ difficulty ⓝ 어려움
244 □ tie ⓥ 묶다
245 □ shoelace ⓝ 신발 끈
246 □ arithmetic ⓝ 산수
247 □ achiever 성취도를 보이는 사람
248 □ previous ⓐ 이전의
249 □ crucial ⓐ 아주 중요한, 중대한, 경쟁적인
250 □ organization ⓝ 조직, 단체
251 □ conversation ⓝ 대화
252 □ factor ⓝ 요소

33

253 □ foreign ⓐ 외국의, 낯선
254 □ subtitle ⓝ (영화·텔레비전 화면의) 자막
255 □ translate ⓥ 번역하다, 통역하다
256 □ dialogue ⓝ 대화
257 □ viewer ⓝ 관객
258 □ occasion ⓝ 경우, 때
259 □ incomprehensible ⓐ 이해할 수 없는
260 □ target audience 주요 대상 관객
261 □ mainly ⓐⓓ 주로
262 □ viewpoint ⓝ 관점, 시점
263 □ particular ⓐ 특정한
264 □ absence ⓝ 부재
265 □ alienation ⓝ 소외
266 □ impressed ⓐ 감명[감동]을 받은
267 □ attract ⓥ 끌어당기다
268 □ participate ⓥ 참여하다

34

269 □ dynamic ⓝ 역학
270 □ dramatically ⓐⓓ 극적으로
271 □ concept ⓝ 개념

272 □ home-field advantage 홈 이점
273 □ perceive ⓥ 인지하다
274 □ demand ⓝ 부담, 요구
275 □ play a role in ~에 역할을 하다, 일조하다
276 □ provide ⓥ 제공하다
277 □ researcher ⓝ 연구원
278 □ point out 지적하다
279 □ competitive ⓐ 경쟁력 있는
280 □ appear ⓥ ~인 것같이 보이다
281 □ perception ⓝ 인식
282 □ struggling ⓐ 고전하는
283 □ reduce ⓥ 줄이다
284 □ road trip 장거리 자동차 여행
285 □ increase ⓥ 증가하다
286 □ advertise ⓥ (상품이나 서비스를) 광고하다
287 □ upcoming ⓐ 다가오는, 곧 있을

35

288 □ mild ⓐ 가벼운
289 □ stimulant ⓝ 자극제, 흥분제
290 □ commonly ⓐⓓ 흔히, 보통
291 □ attentive ⓐ 주의 깊은
292 □ likely ⓐ ~ 할 것 같은
293 □ have an effect on ~에 영향을 미치다
294 □ ideal ⓐ 이상적인
295 □ currently ⓐⓓ 현재
296 □ unknown ⓐ 알려지지 않은
297 □ wide awake 아주 잠이 깨어
298 □ well-rested 잘 쉰
299 □ further ⓐⓓ 더욱
300 □ in contrast 반면에
301 □ indeed ⓐⓓ 실제로
302 □ nervous ⓐ 신경이 과민한
303 □ suffer ⓥ 악화되다

36

304 □ architectural ⓐ 건축의
305 □ attitude ⓝ 사고방식
306 □ emerge ⓥ 나타나다, 출현하다
307 □ industrial ⓐ 산업의
308 □ inhuman ⓐ 비인간적인
309 □ pretension ⓝ 허세, 가식
310 □ supply ⓥ 공급하다
311 □ perfectly ⓐⓓ 완벽하게
312 □ craftsman ⓝ 장인
313 □ rootedness ⓝ 뿌리내림, 고착, 정착
314 □ locality ⓝ (~이 존재하는) 지역, 곳
315 □ instead ⓐⓓ 대신에
316 □ approach ⓝ 접근
317 □ craft ⓝ 공예
318 □ generation ⓝ 세대
319 □ demonstrate ⓥ 입증하다
320 □ mastery ⓝ 숙달된 기술
321 □ simplicity ⓝ 단순함
322 □ plain ⓐ 평범한, 단순한

37

323 □ moral ⓐ 도덕의
324 □ necessarily ⓐⓓ 반드시
325 □ incompetence ⓝ 무능
326 □ occur ⓥ 일어나다, 발생하다
327 □ accomplished ⓐ 숙달된, 기량이 뛰어난

328 □ in nature 사실상
329 □ somehow ⓐⓓ 어떻게든지
330 □ uplift ⓥ 고양시키다, 들어올리다
331 □ on the other hand 반면에
332 □ degrade ⓥ 격하시키다
333 □ doubtful ⓐ 미심쩍은
334 □ character ⓝ 사람, 등장인물
335 □ composer ⓝ 작곡가
336 □ show off 과시하다, 뽐내다
337 □ honestly ⓐⓓ 정직하게

38

338 □ biodiversity ⓝ 생물의 다양성
339 □ sudden ⓐ 갑작스러운
340 □ ecosystem ⓝ 생태계
341 □ wildlife ⓝ 야생 생물
342 □ opportunity ⓝ 기회
343 □ obtain ⓥ 얻다
344 □ shelter ⓝ 서식지
345 □ react ⓥ 작용하다
346 □ entire ⓐ 전체의
347 □ food web 먹이 그물, 먹이 사슬 체계
348 □ dry season 건기(乾期)
349 □ die out 멸종되다, 자취를 감추다
350 □ prey upon ~을 잡아먹다, 괴롭히다
351 □ drought ⓝ 가뭄
352 □ survive ⓥ 살아남다
353 □ rely ⓥ 의지하다
354 □ at the death 종말에 처한

39

355 □ dawn ⓝ 시작, 새벽
356 □ civilization ⓝ 문명
357 □ ancestor ⓝ 선조
358 □ myth ⓝ 신화
359 □ legendary ⓐ 전설의
360 □ connect ⓥ 연결되다
361 □ inspire ⓥ 영감을 주다
362 □ wonder ⓥ 궁금하다
363 □ element ⓝ 요소
364 □ narrative ⓝ 이야기
365 □ embed ⓥ ~을 깊이 새겨 두다, 끼워 넣다
366 □ identity ⓝ 정체성
367 □ practical ⓐ 실용적인
368 □ keep track of ~을 기록하다
369 □ calendar ⓝ 달력
370 □ aid ⓝ 보조 도구
371 □ farming ⓝ 농업
372 □ seasonal ⓐ 계절에 따른
373 □ gathering ⓝ 수집, 수확
374 □ navigation ⓝ 항해
375 □ commerce ⓝ 무역, 상업
376 □ explore ⓥ 탐험하다
377 □ remote ⓐ 멀리 떨어진
378 □ planet ⓝ 지구
379 □ observe ⓥ 관찰하다

40

380 □ layer ⓝ 층
381 □ soil ⓝ 토양
382 □ root ⓝ 뿌리
383 □ funny ⓐ 기이한

384 □ talent ⓝ 재능
385 □ nearby ⓐ 근처
386 □ manganese ⓝ 망가니즈(금속 원소)
387 □ harmful ⓐ 해로운, 유해한
388 □ concentration ⓝ 농도, 농축
389 □ unaffected ⓐ 영향을 받지 않은
390 □ damaging ⓐ 해로운
391 □ evolve ⓥ 발달시키다
392 □ redistribute ⓥ 재분배하다
393 □ shallow ⓐ 얕은
394 □ absorb ⓥ 흡수하다
395 □ concentrate ⓥ 모으다, 농축시키다
396 □ decay ⓥ 썩다
397 □ deposit ⓝ 축적물, 퇴적물
398 □ poison ⓥ (독성 물질로) 오염시키다, 중독시키다
399 □ be immune to ~에 면역이 있다
400 □ toxic ⓐ 유독한
401 □ essentially ⓐⓓ 본질적으로
402 □ eliminate ⓥ 제거하다
403 □ competition ⓝ 경쟁자
404 □ poisoning ⓝ 중독
405 □ neighbor ⓝ 이웃
406 □ surrounding ⓐ 주변의

41~42

407 □ shorten ⓥ 줄이다
408 □ misery ⓝ 불행, 비참함
409 □ impatience ⓝ 조급함
410 □ judgment ⓝ 비난
411 □ frustration ⓝ 좌절
412 □ anger ⓝ 분노
413 □ reside ⓥ 존재하다
414 □ shift ⓥ 바뀌다
415 □ get in one's way ~을 방해하다
416 □ unknowingly ⓐⓓ 무심코
417 □ cut off ~을 가로막다
418 □ in traffic 차량 흐름에서
419 □ splash ⓥ (물을) 튀기다, 끼얹다
420 □ pen ⓥ (글을) 쓰다
421 □ review ⓝ 후기
422 □ miserable ⓐ 비참한
423 □ human being 인간
424 □ child ⓝ 자녀
425 □ statement ⓝ 진술
426 □ deny ⓥ 부인하다
427 □ forgive ⓥ 용서하다

43~45

428 □ journey ⓝ 여정, 여행 ⓥ 여행하다
429 □ village ⓝ 마을
430 □ monk ⓝ 수도승
431 □ field ⓝ 들판
432 □ reply ⓥ 대답하다
433 □ middle-aged ⓐ 중년의
434 □ come upon ~을 우연히 만나다
435 □ valley ⓝ 골짜기
436 □ unwelcoming ⓐ 불친절한, 환영하지 않는
437 □ expect ⓥ 예상하다
438 □ helplessly ⓐⓓ 힘없이, 무기력하게
439 □ elder ⓐ 원로들, 어른들
440 □ generous ⓐ 관대한

● 채점 : 맞은 개수 _____ / 80

TEST A-B 각 단어의 뜻을 [A] 영어는 우리말로, [B] 우리말은 영어로 쓰시오.

A	English	Korean
01	announce	
02	responsibility	
03	passion	
04	gather	
05	task	
06	complete	
07	serious	
08	insight	
09	temperature	
10	recognize	
11	curiosity	
12	handle	
13	specific	
14	previous	
15	viewpoint	
16	reduce	
17	emerge	
18	ecosystem	
19	survive	
20	eliminate	

B	Korean	English
01	유지하다	
02	전달하다	
03	통제	
04	흐르다	
05	낯선	
06	마음을 끄는, 몰입시키는	
07	경쟁력 있는	
08	반드시	
09	재료	
10	영향을 미치다	
11	전통적인	
12	대답하다	
13	실제로	
14	관찰하다	
15	문명	
16	현재	
17	주장하다	
18	요소	
19	평범한, 단순한	
20	주로	

▶ A-D 정답 : 해설편 031쪽

TEST C-D 각 단어의 뜻을 골라 기호를 쓰시오.

C	English		Korean
01	harsh	( )	ⓐ 인종
02	misery	( )	ⓑ 환불
03	ridiculous	( )	ⓒ 정반대
04	support	( )	ⓓ 좌절
05	craftsman	( )	ⓔ 기후
06	confidence	( )	ⓕ 혹독한
07	distinguish	( )	ⓖ 고려하다
08	climate	( )	ⓗ 조급함
09	race	( )	ⓘ 얻다
10	existence	( )	ⓙ 얕은
11	shallow	( )	ⓚ 우스꽝스러운
12	obtain	( )	ⓛ 장인
13	opposite	( )	ⓜ 자신감
14	frustration	( )	ⓝ 존재
15	wisdom	( )	ⓞ 구별하다
16	consider	( )	ⓟ 불행, 비참함
17	wipe	( )	ⓠ 농도, 농축
18	refund	( )	ⓡ 후원하다
19	impatience	( )	ⓢ 닦다
20	concentration	( )	ⓣ 지혜

D	Korean		English
01	거절	( )	ⓐ suffer
02	입증하다	( )	ⓑ perception
03	구성	( )	ⓒ accomplished
04	이력서	( )	ⓓ element
05	번역하다, 통역하다	( )	ⓔ occasional
06	수확	( )	ⓕ fundraising
07	사고방식	( )	ⓖ stimulate
08	가끔씩의	( )	ⓗ resume
09	고양시키다, 들어 올리다	( )	ⓘ construction
10	조사하다	( )	ⓙ demonstrate
11	용감한	( )	ⓚ instructor
12	모금	( )	ⓛ harvest
13	악화되다	( )	ⓜ generalization
14	숙달된, 기량이 뛰어난	( )	ⓝ uplift
15	교사, 교관, 강사	( )	ⓞ operate
16	요소	( )	ⓟ rejection
17	자극하다	( )	ⓠ inspect
18	인식	( )	ⓡ translate
19	운영되다, 돌아가다	( )	ⓢ brave
20	일반화	( )	ⓣ attitude

※ 영어 [독해] 파트만 수록한 문제지이므로 18번부터 시작합니다.　　● 점수 표시가 없는 문항은 모두 2점　● 문항수 28개 | 배점 63점 | 제한 시간 45분

18. 다음 글의 목적으로 가장 적절한 것은?

Dear members of Eastwood Library,

Thanks to the Friends of Literature group, we've successfully raised enough money to remodel the library building. John Baker, our local builder, has volunteered to help us with the remodelling but he needs assistance. By grabbing a hammer or a paint brush and donating your time, you can help with the construction. Join Mr. Baker in his volunteering team and become a part of making Eastwood Library a better place! Please call 541-567-1234 for more information.

Sincerely,
Mark Anderson

① 도서관 임시 휴관의 이유를 설명하려고
② 도서관 자원봉사자 교육 일정을 안내하려고
③ 도서관 보수를 위한 모금 행사를 제안하려고
④ 도서관 공사에 참여할 자원봉사자를 모집하려고
⑤ 도서관에서 개최하는 글쓰기 대회를 홍보하려고

19. 다음 글에 드러난 Shirley의 심경으로 가장 적절한 것은?

On the way home, Shirley noticed a truck parked in front of the house across the street. New neighbors! Shirley was dying to know about them. "Do you know anything about the new neighbors?" she asked Pa at dinner. He said, "Yes, and there's one thing that may be interesting to you." Shirley had a billion more questions. Pa said joyfully, "They have a girl just your age. Maybe she wants to be your playmate." Shirley nearly dropped her fork on the floor. How many times had she prayed for a friend? Finally, her prayers were answered! She and the new girl could go to school together, play together, and become best friends.

① curious and excited
② sorry and upset
③ jealous and annoyed
④ calm and relaxed
⑤ disappointed and unhappy

20. 다음 글에서 필자가 주장하는 바로 가장 적절한 것은?

At a publishing house and at a newspaper you learn the following: *It's not a mistake if it doesn't end up in print*. It's the same for email. Nothing bad can happen if you haven't hit the Send key. What you've written can have misspellings, errors of fact, rude comments, obvious lies, but it doesn't matter. If you haven't sent it, you still have time to fix it. You can correct any mistake and nobody will ever know the difference. This is easier said than done, of course. Send is your computer's most attractive command. But before you hit the Send key, make sure that you read your document carefully one last time.

① 중요한 이메일은 출력하여 보관해야 한다.
② 글을 쓸 때에는 개요 작성부터 시작해야 한다.
③ 이메일을 전송하기 전에 반드시 검토해야 한다.
④ 업무와 관련된 컴퓨터 기능을 우선 익혀야 한다.
⑤ 업무상 중요한 내용은 이메일보다는 직접 전달해야 한다.

21. 밑줄 친 translate it from the past tense to the future tense가 다음 글에서 의미하는 바로 가장 적절한 것은? [3점]

Get past the 'I wish I hadn't done that!' reaction. If the disappointment you're feeling is linked to an exam you didn't pass because you didn't study for it, or a job you didn't get because you said silly things at the interview, or a person you didn't impress because you took entirely the wrong approach, accept that it's *happened* now. The only value of 'I wish I hadn't done that!' is that you'll know better what to do next time. The learning pay-off is useful and significant. This 'if only I ...' agenda is virtual. Once you have worked that out, it's time to translate it from the past tense to the future tense: 'Next time I'm in this situation, I'm going to try to ...'.

* agenda: 의제 ** tense: 시제

① look for a job linked to your interest
② get over regrets and plan for next time
③ surround yourself with supportive people
④ study grammar and write clear sentences
⑤ examine your way of speaking and apologize

22. 다음 글의 요지로 가장 적절한 것은?

If you care deeply about something, you may place greater value on your ability to succeed in that area of concern. The internal pressure you place on yourself to achieve or do well socially is normal and useful, but when you doubt your ability to succeed in areas that are important to you, your self-worth suffers. Situations are uniquely stressful for each of us based on whether or not they activate our doubt. It's not the pressure to perform that creates your stress. Rather, it's the self-doubt that bothers you. Doubt causes you to see positive, neutral, and even genuinely negative experiences more negatively and as a reflection of your own shortcomings. When you see situations and your strengths more objectively, you are less likely to have doubt as the source of your distress.

* distress: 괴로움

① 비판적인 시각은 객관적인 문제 분석에 도움이 된다.
② 성취 욕구는 스트레스를 이겨 낼 원동력이 될 수 있다.
③ 적절한 수준의 스트레스는 과제 수행의 효율을 높인다.
④ 실패의 경험은 자존감을 낮추고, 타인에 의존하게 한다.
⑤ 자기 의심은 스트레스를 유발하고, 객관적 판단을 흐린다.

23. 다음 글의 주제로 가장 적절한 것은?

When two people are involved in an honest and open conversation, there is a back and forth flow of information. It is a smooth exchange. Since each one is drawing on their past personal experiences, the pace of the exchange is as fast as memory. When one person lies, their responses will come more slowly because the brain needs more time to process the details of a new invention than to recall stored facts. As they say, "Timing is everything." You will notice the time lag when you are having a conversation with someone who is making things up as they go. Don't forget that the other person may be reading your body language as well, and if you seem to be disbelieving their story, they will have to pause to process that information, too.

* lag: 지연

① delayed responses as a sign of lying
② ways listeners encourage the speaker
③ difficulties in finding useful information
④ necessity of white lies in social settings
⑤ shared experiences as conversation topics

24. 다음 글의 제목으로 가장 적절한 것은?

Think, for a moment, about something you bought that you never ended up using. An item of clothing you never ended up wearing? A book you never read? Some piece of electronic equipment that never even made it out of the box? It is estimated that Australians alone spend on average $10.8 billion AUD (approximately $9.99 billion USD) every year on goods they do not use — more than the total government spending on universities and roads. That is an average of $1,250 AUD (approximately $1,156 USD) for each household. All the things we buy that then just sit there gathering dust are waste — a waste of money, a waste of time, and waste in the sense of pure rubbish. As the author Clive Hamilton observes, 'The difference between the stuff we buy and what we use is waste.'

① Spending Enables the Economy
② Money Management: Dos and Don'ts
③ Too Much Shopping: A Sign of Loneliness
④ 3R's of Waste: Reduce, Reuse, and Recycle
⑤ What You Buy Is Waste Unless You Use It

25. 다음 도표의 내용과 일치하지 <u>않는</u> 것은?

Devices Students Used to Access Digital Content

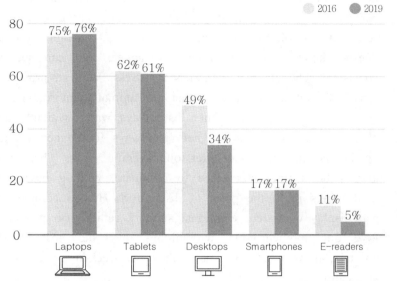

The above graph shows the percentage of students from kindergarten to 12th grade who used devices to access digital educational content in 2016 and in 2019. ① Laptops were the most used device for students to access digital content in both years. ② Both in 2016 and in 2019, more than 6 out of 10 students used tablets. ③ More than half the students used desktops to access digital content in 2016, and more than a third used desktops in 2019. ④ The percentage of smartphones in 2016 was the same as that in 2019. ⑤ E-readers ranked the lowest in both years, with 11 percent in 2016 and 5 percent in 2019.

26. Elizabeth Catlett에 관한 다음 글의 내용과 일치하지 <u>않는</u> 것은?

Elizabeth Catlett was born in Washington, D.C. in 1915. As a granddaughter of slaves, Catlett heard the stories of slaves from her grandmother. After being disallowed entrance from the Carnegie Institute of Technology because she was black, Catlett studied design and drawing at Howard University. She became one of the first three students to earn a master's degree in fine arts at the University of Iowa. Throughout her life, she created art representing the voices of people suffering from social injustice. She was recognized with many prizes and honors both in the United States and in Mexico. She spent over fifty years in Mexico, and she took Mexican citizenship in 1962. Catlett died in 2012 at her home in Mexico.

① 할머니로부터 노예 이야기를 들었다.
② Carnegie Institute of Technology로부터 입학을 거절당했다.
③ University of Iowa에서 석사 학위를 취득했다.
④ 미국과 멕시코에서 많은 상을 받았다.
⑤ 멕시코 시민권을 결국 받지 못했다.

27. Spring Farm Camp에 관한 다음 안내문의 내용과 일치하지 <u>않는</u> 것은?

Spring Farm Camp

Our one-day spring farm camp gives your kids true, hands-on farm experience.

When: Monday, April 19 — Friday, May 14
Time: 9 a.m. — 4 p.m.
Ages: 6 — 10
Participation Fee: $70 per person
(lunch and snacks included)
Activities:
- making cheese from goat's milk
- picking strawberries
- making strawberry jam to take home

We are open rain or shine.
For more information, go to www.b_orchard.com.

① 6세 ~ 10세 어린이가 참가할 수 있다.
② 참가비에 점심과 간식이 포함되어 있다.
③ 염소젖으로 치즈를 만드는 활동을 한다.
④ 딸기잼을 만들어 집으로 가져갈 수 있다.
⑤ 비가 오면 운영하지 않는다.

28. Great Aquarium에 관한 다음 안내문의 내용과 일치하는 것은?

Great Aquarium

Opening Hours: 10 a.m. — 6 p.m., daily
Last entry is at 5 p.m.

Events

Fish Feeding	10 a.m. — 11 a.m.
Penguin Feeding	1 p.m. — 2 p.m.

Ticket Prices

Age	Price
Kids (12 and under)	$25
Adults (20 — 59)	$33
Teens (13 — 19) Seniors (60 and above)	$30

* Ticket holders will receive a free drink coupon.

Booking Tickets
- ALL visitors are required to book online.
- Booking will be accepted up to 1 hour before entry.

① 마지막 입장 시간은 오후 6시이다.
② 물고기 먹이 주기는 오후 1시에 시작한다.
③ 60세 이상의 티켓 가격은 33달러이다.
④ 티켓 소지자는 무료 음료 쿠폰을 받는다.
⑤ 예약은 입장 30분 전까지 가능하다.

29. 다음 글의 밑줄 친 부분 중, 어법상 <u>틀린</u> 것은? [3점]

Although there is usually a correct way of holding and playing musical instruments, the most important instruction to begin with is ① <u>that</u> they are not toys and that they must be looked after. ② <u>Allow</u> children time to explore ways of handling and playing the instruments for themselves before showing them. Finding different ways to produce sounds ③ <u>are</u> an important stage of musical exploration. Correct playing comes from the desire ④ <u>to find</u> the most appropriate sound quality and find the most comfortable playing position so that one can play with control over time. As instruments and music become more complex, learning appropriate playing techniques becomes ⑤ <u>increasingly</u> relevant.

30. 다음 글의 밑줄 친 부분 중, 문맥상 낱말의 쓰임이 적절하지 <u>않은</u> 것은? [3점]

When the price of something fundamental drops greatly, the whole world can change. Consider light. Chances are you are reading this sentence under some kind of artificial light. Moreover, you probably never thought about whether using artificial light for reading was worth it. Light is so ① <u>cheap</u> that you use it without thinking. But in the early 1800s, it would have cost you four hundred times what you are paying now for the same amount of light. At that price, you would ② <u>notice</u> the cost and would think twice before using artificial light to read a book. The ③ <u>increase</u> in the price of light lit up the world. Not only did it turn night into day, but it allowed us to live and work in big buildings that ④ <u>natural</u> light could not enter. Nearly nothing we have today would be ⑤ <u>possible</u> if the cost of artificial light had not dropped to almost nothing.

* artificial: 인공의

[31 ~ 34] 다음 빈칸에 들어갈 말로 가장 적절한 것을 고르시오.

31. One of the most important aspects of providing good care is making sure that an animal's needs are being met consistently and predictably. Like humans, animals need a sense of control. So an animal who may get enough food but doesn't know when the food will appear and can see no consistent schedule may experience distress. We can provide a sense of control by ensuring that our animal's environment is _____: there is always water available and always in the same place. There is always food when we get up in the morning and after our evening walk. There will always be a time and place to eliminate, without having to hold things in to the point of discomfort. Human companions can display consistent emotional support, rather than providing love one moment and withholding love the next. When animals know what to expect, they can feel more confident and calm.

* eliminate: 배설하다

① silent
② natural
③ isolated
④ dynamic
⑤ predictable

32. When a child is upset, the easiest and quickest way to calm them down is to give them food. This acts as a distraction from the feelings they are having, gives them something to do with their hands and mouth and shifts their attention from whatever was upsetting them. If the food chosen is also seen as a treat such as sweets or a biscuit, then the child will feel 'treated' and happier. In the shorter term using food like this is effective. But in the longer term it can be harmful as we quickly learn that food is a good way to _____. Then as we go through life, whenever we feel annoyed, anxious or even just bored, we turn to food to make ourselves feel better.

① make friends
② learn etiquettes
③ improve memory
④ manage emotions
⑤ celebrate achievements

33. Scientists believe that the frogs' ancestors were water-dwelling, fishlike animals. The first frogs and their relatives gained the ability to come out on land and enjoy the opportunities for food and shelter there. But they _____. A frog's lungs do not work very well, and it gets part of its oxygen by breathing through its skin. But for this kind of "breathing" to work properly, the frog's skin must stay moist. And so the frog must remain near the water where it can take a dip every now and then to keep from drying out. Frogs must also lay their eggs in water, as their fishlike ancestors did. And eggs laid in the water must develop into water creatures, if they are to survive. For frogs, metamorphosis thus provides the bridge between the water-dwelling young forms and the land-dwelling adults. [3점]

* metamorphosis: 탈바꿈

① still kept many ties to the water
② had almost all the necessary organs
③ had to develop an appetite for new foods
④ often competed with land-dwelling species
⑤ suffered from rapid changes in temperature

34. It is important to distinguish between being legally allowed to do something, and actually being able to go and do it. A law could be passed allowing everyone, if they so wish, to run a mile in two minutes. That would not, however, increase their *effective* freedom, because, although allowed to do so, they are physically incapable of it. Having a minimum of restrictions and a maximum of possibilities is fine. But in the real world most people will never have the opportunity either to become all that they are allowed to become, or to need to be restrained from doing everything that is possible for them to do. Their effective freedom depends on actually _____. [3점]

* restriction: 제약 ** restrain: 저지하다

① respecting others' rights to freedom
② protecting and providing for the needy
③ learning what socially acceptable behaviors are
④ determining how much they can expect from others
⑤ having the means and ability to do what they choose

35. 다음 글에서 전체 흐름과 관계 <u>없는</u> 문장은?

Today's music business has allowed musicians to take matters into their own hands. ① Gone are the days of musicians waiting for a gatekeeper (someone who holds power and prevents you from being let in) at a label or TV show to say they are worthy of the spotlight. ② In today's music business, you don't need to ask for permission to build a fanbase and you no longer need to pay thousands of dollars to a company to do it. ③ There are rising concerns over the marketing of child musicians using TV auditions. ④ Every day, musicians are getting their music out to thousands of listeners without any outside help. ⑤ They simply deliver it to the fans directly, without asking for permission or outside help to receive exposure or connect with thousands of listeners.

[36~37] 주어진 글 다음에 이어질 글의 순서로 가장 적절한 것을 고르시오.

36.

> Almost all major sporting activities are played with a ball.

(A) A ball might have the correct size and weight but if it is made as a hollow ball of steel it will be too stiff and if it is made from light foam rubber with a heavy center it will be too soft.

(B) The rules of the game always include rules about the type of ball that is allowed, starting with the size and weight of the ball. The ball must also have a certain stiffness.

(C) Similarly, along with stiffness, a ball needs to bounce properly. A solid rubber ball would be too bouncy for most sports, and a solid ball made of clay would not bounce at all.

* stiffness: 단단함

① (A) − (C) − (B)   ② (B) − (A) − (C)
③ (B) − (C) − (A)   ④ (C) − (A) − (B)
⑤ (C) − (B) − (A)

37.

> If you had to write a math equation, you probably wouldn't write, "Twenty-eight plus fourteen equals forty-two." It would take too long to write and it would be hard to read quickly.

(A) For example, the chemical formula for water is H_2O. That tells us that a water molecule is made up of two hydrogen ("H" and "2") atoms and one oxygen ("O") atom.

(B) You would write, "$28 + 14 = 42$." Chemistry is the same way. Chemists have to write chemical equations all the time, and it would take too long to write and read if they had to spell everything out.

(C) So chemists use symbols, just like we do in math. A chemical formula lists all the elements that form each molecule and uses a small number to the bottom right of an element's symbol to stand for the number of atoms of that element. [3점]

* chemical formula: 화학식   ** molecule: 분자

① (A) − (C) − (B)
② (B) − (A) − (C)
③ (B) − (C) − (A)
④ (C) − (A) − (B)
⑤ (C) − (B) − (A)

[38 ~ 39] 글의 흐름으로 보아, 주어진 문장이 들어가기에 가장 적절한 곳을 고르시오.

38.

> Meanwhile, improving by 1 percent isn't particularly notable, but it can be far more meaningful in the long run.

It is so easy to overestimate the importance of one defining moment and underestimate the value of making small improvements on a daily basis. Too often, we convince ourselves that massive success requires massive action. (①) Whether it is losing weight, winning a championship, or achieving any other goal, we put pressure on ourselves to make some earthshaking improvement that everyone will talk about. (②) The difference this tiny improvement can make over time is surprising. (③) Here's how the math works out: if you can get 1 percent better each day for one year, you'll end up thirty-seven times better by the time you're done. (④) Conversely, if you get 1 percent worse each day for one year, you'll decline nearly down to zero. (⑤) What starts as a small win or a minor failure adds up to something much more.

39.

> Before a trip, research how the native inhabitants dress, work, and eat.

The continued survival of the human race can be explained by our ability to adapt to our environment. (①) While we may have lost some of our ancient ancestors' survival skills, we have learned new skills as they have become necessary. (②) Today, the gap between the skills we once had and the skills we now have grows ever wider as we rely more heavily on modern technology. (③) Therefore, when you head off into the wilderness, it is important to fully prepare for the environment. (④) How they have adapted to their way of life will help you to understand the environment and allow you to select the best gear and learn the correct skills. (⑤) This is crucial because most survival situations arise as a result of a series of events that could have been avoided. [3점]

* inhabitant: 주민

40. 다음 글의 내용을 한 문장으로 요약하고자 한다. 빈칸 (A), (B)에 들어갈 말로 가장 적절한 것은?

> In one study, researchers asked pairs of strangers to sit down in a room and chat. In half of the rooms, a cell phone was placed on a nearby table; in the other half, no phone was present. After the conversations had ended, the researchers asked the participants what they thought of each other. Here's what they learned: when a cell phone was present in the room, the participants reported the quality of their relationship was worse than those who'd talked in a cell phone-free room. The pairs who talked in the rooms with cell phones thought their partners showed less empathy. Think of all the times you've sat down to have lunch with a friend and set your phone on the table. You might have felt good about yourself because you didn't pick it up to check your messages, but your unchecked messages were still hurting your connection with the person sitting across from you.
>
> * empathy: 공감

↓

> The presence of a cell phone ____(A)____ the connection between people involved in conversations, even when the phone is being ____(B)____.

	(A)		(B)
①	weakens	......	answered
②	weakens	......	ignored
③	renews	......	answered
④	maintains	......	ignored
⑤	maintains	......	updated

[41 ~ 42] 다음 글을 읽고, 물음에 답하시오.

As kids, we worked hard at learning to ride a bike; when we fell off, we got back on again, until it became second nature to us. But when we try something new in our adult lives we'll usually make just one attempt before judging whether it's (a) worked. If we don't succeed the first time, or if it feels a little awkward, we'll tell ourselves it wasn't a success rather than giving it (b) another shot.

That's a shame, because repetition is central to the process of rewiring our brains. Consider the idea that your brain has a network of neurons. They will (c) connect with each other whenever you remember to use a brain-friendly feedback technique. Those connections aren't very (d) reliable at first, which may make your first efforts a little hit-and-miss. You might remember one of the steps involved, and not the others. But scientists have a saying: "neurons that fire together, wire together." In other words, repetition of an action (e) blocks the connections between the neurons involved in that action. That means the more times you try using that new feedback technique, the more easily it will come to you when you need it.

41. 윗글의 제목으로 가장 적절한 것은?

① Repeat and You Will Succeed
② Be More Curious, Be Smarter
③ Play Is What Makes Us Human
④ Stop and Think Before You Act
⑤ Growth Is All About Keeping Balance

42. 밑줄 친 (a)~(e) 중에서 문맥상 낱말의 쓰임이 적절하지 않은 것은?

① (a)　　② (b)　　③ (c)　　④ (d)　　⑤ (e)

[43 ~ 45] 다음 글을 읽고, 물음에 답하시오.

(A)

Once upon a time, there lived a young king who had a great passion for hunting. His kingdom was located at the foot of the Himalayas. Once every year, he would go hunting in the nearby forests. (a) He would make all the necessary preparations, and then set out for his hunting trip.

(B)

Seasons changed. A year passed by. And it was time to go hunting once again. The king went to the same forest as the previous year. (b) He used his beautiful deerskin drum to round up animals. But none came. All the animals ran for safety, except one doe. She came closer and closer to the drummer. Suddenly, she started fearlessly licking the deerskin drum.

* round up: ~을 몰다　** doe: 암사슴

(C)

Like all other years, the hunting season had arrived. Preparations began in the palace and the king got ready for (c) his hunting trip. Deep in the forest, he spotted a beautiful wild deer. It was a large stag. His aim was perfect. When he killed the deer with just one shot of his arrow, the king was filled with pride. (d) The proud hunter ordered a hunting drum to be made out of the skin of the deer.

* stag: 수사슴

(D)

The king was surprised by this sight. An old servant had an answer to this strange behavior. "The deerskin used to make this drum belonged to her mate, the deer who we hunted last year. This doe is mourning the death of her mate," (e) the man said. Upon hearing this, the king had a change of heart. He had never realized that an animal, too, felt the pain of loss. He made a promise, from that day on, to never again hunt wild animals.

* mourn: 애도하다

43. 주어진 글 (A)에 이어질 내용을 순서에 맞게 배열한 것으로 가장 적절한 것은?

① (B) − (D) − (C)　　② (C) − (B) − (D)
③ (C) − (D) − (B)　　④ (D) − (B) − (C)
⑤ (D) − (C) − (B)

44. 밑줄 친 (a)~(e) 중에서 가리키는 대상이 나머지 넷과 다른 것은?

① (a)　　② (b)　　③ (c)　　④ (d)　　⑤ (e)

45. 윗글에 관한 내용으로 적절하지 않은 것은?

① 왕은 매년 근처의 숲으로 사냥 여행을 갔다.
② 암사슴은 북 치는 사람으로부터 도망갔다.
③ 왕은 화살로 단번에 수사슴을 맞혔다.
④ 한 나이 든 신하가 암사슴의 행동의 이유를 알고 있었다.
⑤ 왕은 다시는 야생 동물을 사냥하지 않겠다고 약속했다.

★ 확인 사항

○ 답안지의 해당란에 필요한 내용을 정확히 기입(표기)했는지 확인하시오.

18

001 successfully [ad] 성공적으로
002 raise (v) (돈을) 모으다
003 remodel (v) 개조하다, 리모델링하다
004 local (a) 지역의
005 builder (n) 건축업자
006 volunteer (v) 자원하다
007 assistance (n) 도움
008 grab (v) 쥐다
009 hammer (n) 망치
010 donate (v) 기부하다
011 construction (n) 공사, 건설
012 become (v) …(해)지다, …이 되다

19

013 notice (v) 알아차리다
014 park (v) 주차하다
015 across the street 길 건너에
016 neighbor (n) 이웃
017 be dying to 간절히 ~하고 싶어 하다
018 interesting (a) 흥미를 끄는
019 joyfully [ad] 즐겁게
020 playmate (n) 놀이 친구
021 pray (v) 기도하다
022 curious (a) 호기심이 많은
023 jealous (a) 질투 나는
024 disappointed (a) 실망한

20

025 publishing house 출판사
026 following (a) 다음에[아래]에 나오는[언급되는]
027 end up 결국 ~이 되다
028 in print 출간되는, 발표되는
029 misspelling (n) 오탈자
030 rude (a) 무례한
031 comment (n) 말
032 obvious (a) 명백한
033 matter (v) 문제가 되다
034 fix (v) 고치다
035 correct (v) 수정하다
036 easier said than done 행동보다 말이 쉽다
037 attractive (a) 매력적인
038 command (n) 명령(어) (v) 명령하다
039 make sure that 반드시 ~을 하다
040 document (n) 문서, 서류
041 carefully [ad] 주의 깊게

21

042 get past 지나가다, 추월하다
043 reaction (n) 반응
044 disappointment (n) 실망
045 be linked to ~과 연관되다
046 impress (v) 인상을 주다
047 entirely [ad] 완전히, 전적으로
048 wrong (a) 잘못된
049 approach (n) 접근 방법
050 accept (v) 받아들이다
051 value (n) 가치
052 pay-off (n) 이득, 보상
053 useful (a) 유용한
054 significant (a) 의미가 있는, 중요한

055 virtual (a) 가상의
056 work ~ out ~을 파악하다
057 translate (v) 바꾸다, 번역하다
058 situation (n) 상황
059 get over ~을 극복하다
060 surround (v) 둘러싸다
061 supportive (a) 힘이 되는, 지지를 주는
062 sentence (n) 문장
063 examine (v) 검토하다, 조사하다
064 apologize (v) 사과하다

22

065 place value on ~에 가치를 두다
066 concern (n) 관심, 걱정
067 internal (a) 내적인
068 achieve (v) 성취하다
069 do well 성공하다
070 normal (a) 정상적인, 일반적인
071 doubt (n) 의심 (v) 의심하다
072 self-worth (n) 자아 존중감, 자기 가치감
073 suffer (v) 상처를 입다, 괴로워하다
074 uniquely [ad] 특유의 방법으로, 독특하게
075 activate (v) 활성화하다
076 self-doubt (n) 자기 의심
077 bother (v) 괴롭히다
078 neutral (a) 중립적인
079 genuinely [ad] 진정으로
080 reflection (n) 반영
081 shortcoming (n) 단점
082 strength (n) 강점
083 objectively [ad] 객관적으로
084 source (n) 원천, 근원

23

085 be involved in ~에 참여하다, ~과 관련되다
086 back and forth 왔다 갔다하는
087 smooth (a) 순조로운, 원활히 진행되는
088 exchange (n) 대화, 주고받음, 교환
089 draw on ~에 의존하다, ~을 이용하다
090 pace (n) 속도
091 response (n) 반응
092 process (v) 처리하다
093 invention (n) 꾸며 낸 이야기, 창작
094 recall (v) 회상하다
095 stored (a) 저장된
096 make up 만들어내다, 꾸며내다
097 disbelieve (v) 불신하다, 믿지 않다
098 pause (v) 잠시 멈추다
099 delay (v) 지연하다
100 encourage (v) 격려하다
101 necessity (n) 필요성

24

102 electronic (a) 전자의
103 equipment (n) 기기, 장비
104 estimate (v) 추산하다
105 average (n) 평균
106 billion (n) 십 억
107 approximately [ad] 대략
108 goods (n) 물건, 제품, 상품
109 household (n) 가구, 세대

110 gather (v) 모으다
111 dust (n) 먼지
112 waste (n) 낭비, 쓰레기
113 in the sense of ~이라는 의미에서
114 pure (a) 순전한, 순수한
115 rubbish (n) 쓰레기
116 observe (v) 말하다, 관찰하다
117 difference (n) 뺀 것, (양의) 차이
118 stuff (n) 물건

25

119 device (n) 기기, 장치
120 access (v) 이용하다, 접근하다, 접속하다
121 laptop (n) 노트북 (컴퓨터)
122 e-reader (n) 전자책 단말기
123 kindergarten (n) 유치원
124 educational (a) 교육의
125 rank (v) 순위를 차지하다

26

126 slave (n) 노예
127 disallow (v) (공식적으로) 거절하다, 인정하지 않다
128 entrance (n) 입학, 입장
129 earn (v) 얻다, 취득하다
130 master's degree 석사 학위
131 fine arts 순수 미술
132 represent (v) 대표하다, 나타내다
133 suffer from ~으로 고통받다
134 injustice (n) 불평등, 부당함
135 recognize (v) 인정하다
136 honor (n) 표창, 명예
137 citizenship (n) 시민권

27

138 hands-on (a) 직접 해 보는, 체험의
139 participation fee 참가비
140 include (v) 포함하다
141 goat (n) 염소
142 rain or shine 날씨에 상관없이

28

143 aquarium (n) 수족관
144 entry (n) 입장
145 feeding (n) 먹이 주기
146 senior (n) 노인
147 holder (n) 소지자
148 receive (v) 받다, 받아들이다
149 booking (n) 예약
150 up to ~까지

29

151 correct (a) 맞는, 정확한
152 instrument (n) 악기, 도구
153 instruction (n) 지침, 가르침
154 look after ~을 관리하다, 돌보다
155 explore (v) 탐구하다
156 handle (v) 다루다
157 stage (n) 단계
158 desire (n) 욕구, 욕망
159 appropriate (a) 적절한
160 quality (n) 질, 품질

161 complex (a) 복잡한
162 increasingly [ad] 점점 더
163 relevant (a) 유의미한, 적절한, 관련 있는

30

164 fundamental (a) 기본적인
165 drop (v) 하락하다, 떨어지다 (n) 하락
166 consider (v) 생각하다
167 chances are 아마 ~일 것이다
168 artificial (a) 인공의
169 probably [ad] 아마
170 worth (a) ~의 가치가 있는
171 cheap (a) 값이 싼
172 cost (n) 비용 (v) (~에게 …의 비용을) 요하다, 치르게 하다
173 amount (n) 총액, 총계
174 light up (불을) 밝히다
175 turn ~ into ... ~을 …으로 바꾸다
176 nearly [ad] 거의
177 possible (a) 가능한

31

178 aspect (n) 측면
179 need (n) 욕구
180 consistently [ad] 일관적으로
181 predictably [ad] 예측 가능하게
182 sense of control 통제감
183 appear (v) 보이게 되다
184 schedule (n) 일정
185 distress (n) 괴로움
186 ensure (v) 반드시 ~하다, 보장하다
187 environment (n) 환경
188 get up 일어나다
189 walk (n) 산책
190 hold ~ in ~을 참다
191 to the point of ~할 수 있을 정도로
192 discomfort (n) 불편함
193 display (v) 보이다, 나타내다
194 emotional (a) 정서적인
195 support (n) 지지, 뒷받침
196 moment (n) 순간
197 withhold (v) 주지 않다
198 expect (v) 기대하다
199 confident (a) 자신감 있는
200 calm (a) 차분한, 온화한
201 isolated (a) 고립된

32

202 upset (a) 화난 (v) 화나게 하다
203 quick (a) 빠른
204 calm ~ down ~을 진정시키다
205 act as ~으로 작용하다
206 distraction (n) 정신을 분산시키는 것, 주의를 돌리는 것
207 shift (v) 돌리다, 바꾸다
208 upsetting (a) 속상하게 하는
209 attention (n) 주의
210 see A as B A를 B로 간주하다
211 treat (n) 간식 (v) 대접하다
212 effective (a) 효과적인
213 harmful (a) 해로운
214 annoyed (a) 짜증 난

04회

215 ☐ anxious ⓐ 불안한
216 ☐ turn to ~에 의지하다
217 ☐ etiquettes ⓝ 예의[에티켓]
218 ☐ improve ⓥ 개선하다, 향상시키다
219 ☐ emotion ⓝ 감정, 정서
220 ☐ celebrate ⓥ 축하하다
221 ☐ achievement ⓝ 성취

33
222 ☐ ancestor ⓝ 조상
223 ☐ dwell ⓥ 거주하다, 살다
224 ☐ water-dwelling ⓐ 물에 사는
225 ☐ fishlike ⓐ 물고기와 같은
226 ☐ relative ⓝ 친척
227 ☐ gain ⓥ 얻다
228 ☐ opportunity ⓝ 기회, 가능성
229 ☐ shelter ⓝ 살 곳, 쉼터, 은신처
230 ☐ lung ⓝ 폐
231 ☐ oxygen ⓝ 산소
232 ☐ breathe ⓥ 호흡하다
233 ☐ skin ⓝ 피부
234 ☐ properly ⓐⓓ 적절히
235 ☐ moist ⓐ 촉촉한
236 ☐ take a dip 잠깐 수영을 하다
237 ☐ every now and then 이따금
238 ☐ dry out 건조하다, 바짝 마르다
239 ☐ lay ⓥ (알을) 낳다
240 ☐ develop ⓥ 발달하다, 성장하다
241 ☐ creature ⓝ 생물
242 ☐ bridge ⓝ 다리
243 ☐ land-dwelling ⓐ 육지에 사는
244 ☐ adult ⓝ 성체
245 ☐ tie ⓝ 관계, 연결
246 ☐ necessary ⓐ 필요한
247 ☐ organ ⓝ (신체) 기관
248 ☐ appetite ⓝ 식욕
249 ☐ compete with ~와 경쟁하다
250 ☐ rapid ⓐ 빠른
251 ☐ temperature ⓝ 온도, 기온, 체온

34
252 ☐ distinguish ⓥ 구별하다
253 ☐ legally ⓐⓓ 법적으로
254 ☐ allowed ⓐ 허가받은, 허용된
255 ☐ actually ⓐⓓ 실제로, 사실
256 ☐ be able to ~을 할 수 있다
257 ☐ freedom ⓝ 자유
258 ☐ physically ⓐⓓ 신체적으로, 물리적으로
259 ☐ be incapable of ~을 할 수 없다
260 ☐ minimum ⓐ 최소한
261 ☐ maximum ⓐ 최대한
262 ☐ possibility ⓝ 가능성
263 ☐ restrain ⓥ 저지[제지]하다
264 ☐ depend on ~에 좌우되다
265 ☐ needy ⓐ (경제적으로) 어려운, 궁핍한
266 ☐ acceptable ⓐ 허용 가능한, 수용 가능한
267 ☐ means ⓝ 수단

35
268 ☐ business ⓝ 사업
269 ☐ take matters into one's own hands
　　스스로 일을 추진하다, 일을 독자적으로 하다

270 ☐ gone ⓐ (특정한 상황이) 끝난
271 ☐ gatekeeper ⓝ 문지기, 수위
272 ☐ prevent ⓥ 막다
273 ☐ let in ~을 들여 보내다
274 ☐ label ⓝ 음반사
275 ☐ be worthy of ~을 받을 만하다
276 ☐ spotlight ⓝ 주목
277 ☐ ask for ~을 요청하다
278 ☐ permission ⓝ 허락, 허가
279 ☐ fanbase ⓝ 팬층
280 ☐ rising ⓐ 증가하는
281 ☐ concern ⓝ 우려
282 ☐ outside ⓐ 바깥쪽의, 외부의
283 ☐ simply ⓐⓓ 간단히, 단순히
284 ☐ deliver ⓥ 전달하다
285 ☐ directly ⓐⓓ 직접, 곧장
286 ☐ exposure ⓝ 노출, 매스컴 출연
287 ☐ connect ⓥ 잇다, 연결하다

36
288 ☐ major ⓐ 주요한
289 ☐ hollow ⓐ (속이) 빈
290 ☐ steel ⓝ 강철
291 ☐ stiff ⓐ 단단한
292 ☐ light ⓐ 가벼운
293 ☐ foam rubber 발포 고무
294 ☐ center ⓝ 중심부, 중앙
295 ☐ type ⓝ 유형
296 ☐ weight ⓝ 무게
297 ☐ certain ⓐ 확실한, 틀림없는
298 ☐ bounce ⓥ 튀어오르다
299 ☐ solid ⓐ 순수한(다른 물질이 섞이지 않은)
300 ☐ rubber ⓝ 고무
301 ☐ clay ⓝ 점토

37
302 ☐ equation ⓝ 방정식, 등식
303 ☐ equal ⓥ 같다
304 ☐ be made up of ~으로 구성되다, 이루어지다
305 ☐ hydrogen ⓝ 수소
306 ☐ atom ⓝ 원자
307 ☐ chemistry ⓝ 화학
308 ☐ chemist ⓝ 화학자
309 ☐ all the time 항상
310 ☐ spell out 상세히 말하다
311 ☐ symbol ⓝ 기호
312 ☐ list ⓥ 나열하다, 열거하다
313 ☐ element ⓝ 원소, 요소
314 ☐ bottom ⓝ 아래
315 ☐ stand for ~을 나타내다[대표하다]

38
316 ☐ meanwhile ⓐⓓ 한편
317 ☐ particularly ⓐⓓ 특별히
318 ☐ notable ⓐ 눈에 띄는, 두드러지는
319 ☐ meaningful ⓐ 의미 있는
320 ☐ in the long run 장기적으로
321 ☐ overestimate ⓥ 과대평가하다
322 ☐ defining ⓐ 결정적인, 정의하는
323 ☐ underestimate ⓥ 과소평가하다
324 ☐ on a daily basis 매일

325 ☐ convince ⓥ 납득시키다, 설득하다
326 ☐ massive ⓐ 거대한
327 ☐ success ⓝ 성공
328 ☐ require ⓥ 필요로 하다
329 ☐ action ⓝ 행동, 조치
330 ☐ lose weight 체중을 줄이다
331 ☐ win a championship 결승전에서 이기다
332 ☐ put pressure on ~에 압박을 가하다
333 ☐ earthshaking ⓐ 극히 중대한, 세상을 떠들썩하게 하는
334 ☐ tiny ⓐ 극히 작은
335 ☐ over time 시간이 지남에 따라
336 ☐ conversely ⓐⓓ 역으로
337 ☐ decline ⓥ 떨어지다, 감소하다
338 ☐ minor ⓐ 사소한
339 ☐ failure ⓝ 패배

39
340 ☐ research ⓥ 조사하다, 연구하다
341 ☐ native ⓐ 토착의, 지방 고유의
342 ☐ survival ⓝ 생존
343 ☐ human race ⓝ 인류
344 ☐ adapt to ~에 적응하다
345 ☐ ancient ⓐ 고대의
346 ☐ skill ⓝ 기술
347 ☐ gap ⓝ 간극, 격차
348 ☐ rely on ~에 의존하다
349 ☐ heavily ⓐⓓ 심하게, 많이
350 ☐ modern ⓐ 현대의
351 ☐ technology ⓝ 기술
352 ☐ head off ~로 향하다
353 ☐ wilderness ⓝ 황무지
354 ☐ prepare ⓥ 준비하다, 대비하다
355 ☐ gear ⓝ 장비
356 ☐ crucial ⓐ 매우 중요한
357 ☐ arise ⓥ 발생하다, 일어나다
358 ☐ as a result of ~의 결과로
359 ☐ event ⓝ 사건
360 ☐ avoid ⓥ 피하다

40
361 ☐ study ⓝ 공부[연구], 학습, 학문
362 ☐ researcher ⓝ 연구원, 조사원, 탐색자
363 ☐ pair ⓝ 짝
364 ☐ stranger ⓝ 모르는 사람, 낯선 사람
365 ☐ chat ⓥ 이야기하다
366 ☐ cell phone 휴대폰
367 ☐ place ⓥ 놓다, 두다
368 ☐ nearby ⓐ 근처의
369 ☐ present ⓐ 존재하는
370 ☐ participant ⓝ 참가자
371 ☐ report ⓥ 말하다, 전하다
372 ☐ relationship ⓝ 관계
373 ☐ partner ⓝ 상대
374 ☐ empathy ⓝ 감정이입, 공감
375 ☐ unchecked ⓐ 확인되지 않은
376 ☐ hurt ⓥ 손상시키다, 다치게 하다
377 ☐ connection ⓝ 관계, 연결
378 ☐ involved ⓐ 관여하는, 관련된, 연루된
379 ☐ weaken ⓥ 약화시키다
380 ☐ answer ⓥ 대답하다, 대응하다
381 ☐ ignore ⓥ 무시하다

382 ☐ renew ⓥ 새롭게 하다, 갱신하다, 재개하다
383 ☐ maintain ⓥ 유지하다

41~42
384 ☐ work hard at ~을 들이파다, 열심히 하다
385 ☐ fall off 넘어지다
386 ☐ nature ⓝ 본성, 천성
387 ☐ make an attempt 시도하다
388 ☐ judge ⓥ 판단하다, 판정하다
389 ☐ awkward ⓐ (기분이) 어색한, 불편한
390 ☐ ourselves ⓟⓡⓞⓝ 우리 자신[스스로/직접]
391 ☐ rather than ~하기보다는
392 ☐ give it a shot 시도하다
393 ☐ shame ⓝ 애석한 일, 딱한 일
394 ☐ repetition ⓝ 반복
395 ☐ central ⓐ 핵심적인
396 ☐ process ⓝ 과정
397 ☐ rewire ⓥ 재연결하다, 전선을 다시 배치하다
398 ☐ network ⓝ 연결망, 네트워크
399 ☐ neuron ⓝ 뉴런, 신경 세포
400 ☐ technique ⓝ 기술
401 ☐ reliable ⓐ 신뢰할 만한
402 ☐ hit-and-miss ⓐ 되는 대로 하는, 마구잡이로 하는
403 ☐ remember ⓥ 기억하다, 기억나다
404 ☐ involve ⓥ 연관시키다
405 ☐ block ⓥ 차단하다
406 ☐ easily ⓐⓓ 쉽게
407 ☐ growth ⓝ 성장
408 ☐ keep ⓥ 유지하다[유지하게 하다]
409 ☐ balance ⓝ 균형[평형]

43~45
410 ☐ passion ⓝ 열정
411 ☐ kingdom ⓝ 왕국
412 ☐ locate ⓥ 위치시키다
413 ☐ at the foot of ~의 기슭에, 하단부에
414 ☐ forest ⓝ 숲
415 ☐ preparation ⓝ 준비, 채비
416 ☐ set out for ~을 향해 나서다
417 ☐ season ⓝ 계절
418 ☐ pass by (시간이) 지나가다
419 ☐ previous ⓐ 이전의
420 ☐ deerskin ⓝ 사슴 가죽
421 ☐ fearlessly ⓐⓓ 겁 없이, 대담하게
422 ☐ lick ⓥ 핥다
423 ☐ palace ⓝ 궁궐
424 ☐ spot ⓥ 알아채다, 발견하다
425 ☐ aim ⓝ 겨냥, 목표 ⓥ 겨누다
426 ☐ arrow ⓝ 화살
427 ☐ order ⓥ 명령하다
428 ☐ sight ⓝ 광경
429 ☐ servant ⓝ 신하
430 ☐ behavior ⓝ 행동
431 ☐ belong to ~의 것이다
432 ☐ mate ⓝ 짝
433 ☐ have a change of heart 마음을 바꾸다, 심경의 변화가 생기다
434 ☐ realize ⓥ 깨닫다
435 ☐ pain ⓝ 고통
436 ☐ loss ⓝ 상실
437 ☐ promise ⓝ 약속

● 채점 : 맞은 개수 _____ / 80

TEST A-B 각 단어의 뜻을 [A] 영어는 우리말로, [B] 우리말은 영어로 쓰시오.

A	English	Korean
01	harmful	
02	massive	
03	rude	
04	translate	
05	aspect	
06	confident	
07	gather	
08	approximately	
09	meanwhile	
10	worth	
11	fix	
12	properly	
13	arise	
14	joyfully	
15	instrument	
16	complex	
17	increasingly	
18	entry	
19	organ	
20	adapt to	

B	Korean	English
01	실망한	
02	식욕	
03	수용하다, 허용하다	
04	성취	
05	납득시키다, 설득하다	
06	전달하다	
07	처리하다	
08	괴로움	
09	방정식, 등식	
10	이전의	
11	불편함	
12	포함하다	
13	눈에 띄는, 두드러지는	
14	핵심적인	
15	유지하다	
16	허용 가능한, 수용 가능한	
17	거주하다, 살다	
18	입학, 입장	
19	법적으로	
20	지나가다, 추월하다	

▶ A-D 정답 : 해설편 041쪽

TEST C-D 각 단어의 뜻을 골라 기호를 쓰시오.

C	English			Korean
01	observe	(	)	ⓐ ~에 좌우되다
02	anxious	(	)	ⓑ 인정하다
03	overestimate	(	)	ⓒ 과대평가하다
04	obvious	(	)	ⓓ 겨냥, 목표
05	impress	(	)	ⓔ 불안한
06	recognize	(	)	ⓕ 돌리다, 바꾸다
07	appropriate	(	)	ⓖ 적절한
08	genuinely	(	)	ⓗ 말하다, 관찰하다
09	internal	(	)	ⓘ 애석한 일, 딱한 일
10	artificial	(	)	ⓙ 내적인
11	spell out	(	)	ⓚ 진정으로
12	shame	(	)	ⓛ 인상을 주다
13	ignore	(	)	ⓜ 상세히 말하다
14	command	(	)	ⓝ 준비, 채비
15	depend on	(	)	ⓞ 무시하다
16	present	(	)	ⓟ 명령(어)
17	arise	(	)	ⓠ 인공의
18	preparation	(	)	ⓡ 존재하는
19	aim	(	)	ⓢ 발생하다, 일어나다
20	shift	(	)	ⓣ 명백한

D	Korean			English
01	역으로	(	)	ⓐ unchecked
02	떨어지다, 감소하다	(	)	ⓑ amount
03	확인되지 않은	(	)	ⓒ repetition
04	~을 극복하다	(	)	ⓓ distinguish
05	완전히, 전적으로	(	)	ⓔ permission
06	탐구하다	(	)	ⓕ necessity
07	대표하다, 나타내다	(	)	ⓖ means
08	불평등, 부당함	(	)	ⓗ instruction
09	지침, 가르침	(	)	ⓘ injustice
10	수단	(	)	ⓙ get over
11	실질적인, 효과적인	(	)	ⓚ explore
12	구별하다	(	)	ⓛ conversely
13	허락	(	)	ⓜ entirely
14	총액, 총계	(	)	ⓝ effective
15	필요성	(	)	ⓞ drop
16	기기, 장비	(	)	ⓟ equipment
17	반복	(	)	ⓠ decline
18	(기분이) 어색한, 불편한	(	)	ⓡ remodel
19	하락하다, 떨어지다	(	)	ⓢ awkward
20	개조하다	(	)	ⓣ represent

※ 영어 [독해] 파트만 수록한 문제지이므로 18번부터 시작합니다.

● 점수 표시가 없는 문항은 모두 2점 ● 문항수 28개 | 배점 63점 | 제한 시간 45분

18. 다음 글의 목적으로 가장 적절한 것은?

Dear Ms. Spadler,

You've written to our company complaining that your toaster, which you bought only three weeks earlier, doesn't work. You were asking for a new toaster or a refund. Since the toaster has a year's warranty, our company is happy to replace your faulty toaster with a new toaster. To get your new toaster, simply take your receipt and the faulty toaster to the dealer from whom you bought it. The dealer will give you a new toaster on the spot. Nothing is more important to us than the satisfaction of our customers. If there is anything else we can do for you, please do not hesitate to ask.

Yours sincerely,
Betty Swan

* warranty: 품질 보증(서)

① 새로 출시한 제품을 홍보하려고
② 흔히 생기는 고장 사례를 알려주려고
③ 품질 보증서 보관의 중요성을 강조하려고
④ 고장 난 제품을 교환하는 방법을 안내하려고
⑤ 제품 만족도 조사에 참여해줄 것을 요청하려고

19. 다음 글에 드러난 'I'의 심경 변화로 가장 적절한 것은?

I was diving alone in about 40 feet of water when I got a terrible stomachache. I was sinking and hardly able to move. I could see my watch and knew there was only a little more time on the tank before I would be out of air. It was hard for me to remove my weight belt. Suddenly I felt a prodding from behind me under the armpit. My arm was being lifted forcibly. Around into my field of vision came an eye. It seemed to be smiling. It was the eye of a big dolphin. Looking into that eye, I knew I was safe. I felt that the animal was protecting me, lifting me toward the surface.

* prodding: 쿡 찌르기

① excited → bored
② pleased → angry
③ jealous → thankful
④ proud → embarrassed
⑤ frightened → relieved

20. 다음 글에서 필자가 주장하는 바로 가장 적절한 것은?

Keeping good ideas floating around in your head is a great way to ensure that they won't happen. Take a tip from writers, who know that the only good ideas that come to life are the ones that get written down. Take out a piece of paper and record everything you'd love to do someday — aim to hit one hundred dreams. You'll have a reminder and motivator to get going on those things that are calling you, and you also won't have the burden of remembering all of them. When you put your dreams into words you begin putting them into action.

① 친구의 꿈을 응원하라.
② 하고 싶은 일을 적으라.
③ 신중히 생각한 후 행동하라.
④ 효과적인 기억법을 개발하라.
⑤ 실현 가능한 목표에 집중하라.

21. 밑줄 친 "rise to the bait"가 다음 글에서 의미하는 바로 가장 적절한 것은? [3점]

We all know that tempers are one of the first things lost in many arguments. It's easy to say one should keep cool, but how do you do it? The point to remember is that sometimes in arguments the other person is trying to get you to be angry. They may be saying things that are intentionally designed to annoy you. They know that if they get you to lose your cool you'll say something that sounds foolish; you'll simply get angry and then it will be impossible for you to win the argument. So don't fall for it. A remark may be made to cause your anger, but responding with a cool answer that focuses on the issue raised is likely to be most effective. Indeed, any attentive listener will admire the fact that you didn't "rise to the bait."

① stay calm
② blame yourself
③ lose your temper
④ listen to the audience
⑤ apologize for your behavior

22. 다음 글의 요지로 가장 적절한 것은?

Practically anything of value requires that we take a risk of failure or being rejected. This is the price we all must pay for achieving the greater rewards lying ahead of us. To take risks means you will succeed sometime but never to take a risk means that you will never succeed. Life is filled with a lot of risks and challenges and if you want to get away from all these, you will be left behind in the race of life. A person who can never take a risk can't learn anything. For example, if you never take the risk to drive a car, you can never learn to drive. If you never take the risk of being rejected, you can never have a friend or partner. Similarly, by not taking the risk of attending an interview, you will never get a job.

① 위험을 무릅쓰지 않으면 아무 것도 얻지 못한다.
② 자신이 잘하는 일에 집중하는 것이 효율적이다.
③ 잦은 실패 경험은 도전할 의지를 잃게 한다.
④ 위험 요소가 있으면 미리 피하는 것이 좋다.
⑤ 부탁을 자주 거절하면 신뢰를 잃는다.

23. 다음 글의 주제로 가장 적절한 것은?

Although individual preferences vary, touch (both what we touch with our fingers and the way things feel as they come in contact with our skin) is an important aspect of many products. Consumers like some products because of their feel. Some consumers buy skin creams and baby products for their soothing effect on the skin. In fact, consumers who have a high need for touch tend to like products that provide this opportunity. When considering products with material properties, such as clothing or carpeting, consumers like goods they can touch in stores more than products they only see and read about online or in catalogs.

* property: 속성

① benefits of using online shopping malls
② touch as an important factor for consumers
③ importance of sharing information among consumers
④ necessity of getting feedback from consumers
⑤ popularity of products in the latest styles

24. 다음 글의 제목으로 가장 적절한 것은?

In life, they say that too much of anything is not good for you. In fact, too much of certain things in life can kill you. For example, they say that water has no enemy, because water is essential to all life. But if you take in too much water, like one who is drowning, it could kill you. Education is the exception to this rule. You can never have too much education or knowledge. The reality is that most people will never have enough education in their lifetime. I am yet to find that one person who has been hurt in life by too much education. Rather, we see lots of casualties every day, worldwide, resulting from the lack of education. You must keep in mind that education is a long-term investment of time, money, and effort into humans.

* casualty: 피해자

① All Play and No Work Makes Jack a Smart Boy
② Too Much Education Won't Hurt You
③ Too Heads Are Worse than One
④ Don't Think Twice Before You Act
⑤ Learn from the Future, Not from the Past

25. 다음 도표의 내용과 일치하지 <u>않는</u> 것은?

The Most Spoken Languages Worldwide in 2015

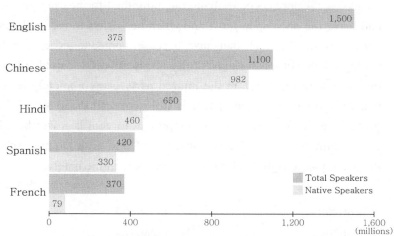

- Note: Total Speakers = Native Speakers + Non-native Speakers

The above graph shows the numbers of total speakers and native speakers of the five most spoken languages worldwide in 2015. ① English is the most spoken language worldwide, with 1,500 million total speakers. ② Chinese is second on the list with 1,100 million total speakers. ③ In terms of the number of native speakers, however, Chinese is the most spoken language worldwide, followed by Hindi. ④ The number of native speakers of English is smaller than that of Spanish. ⑤ French is the least spoken language among the five in terms of the number of native speakers.

26. Ellen Church에 관한 다음 글의 내용과 일치하지 <u>않는</u> 것은?

Ellen Church was born in Iowa in 1904. After graduating from Cresco High School, she studied nursing and worked as a nurse in San Francisco. She suggested to Boeing Air Transport that nurses should take care of passengers during flights because most people were frightened of flying. In 1930, she became the first female flight attendant in the U.S. and worked on a Boeing 80A from Oakland, California to Chicago, Illinois. Unfortunately, a car accident injury forced her to end her career after only eighteen months. Church started nursing again at Milwaukee County Hospital after she graduated from the University of Minnesota with a degree in nursing education. During World War II, she served as a captain in the Army Nurse Corps and received an Air Medal. Ellen Church Field Airport in her hometown, Cresco, was named after her.

① San Francisco에서 간호사로 일했다.
② 간호사가 비행 중에 승객을 돌봐야 한다고 제안했다.
③ 미국 최초의 여성 비행기 승무원이 되었다.
④ 자동차 사고로 다쳤지만 비행기 승무원 생활을 계속했다.
⑤ 고향인 Cresco에 그녀의 이름을 따서 붙인 공항이 있다.

27. Science Selfie Competition에 관한 다음 안내문의 내용과 일치하지 <u>않는</u> 것은?

Science Selfie Competition

For a chance to win science goodies, just submit a selfie of yourself enjoying science outside of school!

Deadline: Friday, March 20, 2020, 6 p.m.

Details:
- Your selfie should include a visit to any science museum or a science activity at home.
- Be as creative as you like, and write one short sentence about the selfie.
- Only one entry per person!
- Email your selfie with your name and class to mclara@oldfold.edu.

Winners will be announced on March 27, 2020.

Please visit www.oldfold.edu to learn more about the competition.

① 학교 밖에서 과학을 즐기는 셀카 사진을 출품한다.
② 셀카 사진에 관한 하나의 짧은 문장을 써야 한다.
③ 1인당 사진 여러 장을 출품할 수 있다.
④ 셀카 사진을 이름 및 소속 학급과 함께 이메일로 보내야 한다.
⑤ 수상자는 2020년 3월 27일에 발표될 것이다.

28. Toy & Gift Warehouse Sale에 관한 다음 안내문의 내용과 일치하는 것은?

Toy & Gift Warehouse Sale

at Wilson Square
from April 3 to April 16

We carry items that are in stock at bigger retailers for a cheaper price. You can expect to find toys for children from birth to teens. Ten toy companies will participate in the sale.

Wednesday – Friday: 10 a.m. – 6 p.m.
Saturday & Sunday: 11 a.m. – 5 p.m.
Closed on Monday & Tuesday

Returns must be made within one week of purchase.

For more information, please visit us at www.poptoy.com.

① 4월 16일부터 시작된다.
② 십 대를 위한 장난감은 판매하지 않는다.
③ 스무 개의 장난감 회사가 참여한다.
④ 월요일과 화요일에는 운영되지 않는다.
⑤ 반품은 구입 후 2주간 가능하다.

29. 다음 글의 밑줄 친 부분 중, 어법상 <u>틀린</u> 것은? [3점]

"You are what you eat." That phrase is often used to ① <u>show</u> the relationship between the foods you eat and your physical health. But do you really know what you are eating when you buy processed foods, canned foods, and packaged goods? Many of the manufactured products made today contain so many chemicals and artificial ingredients ② <u>which</u> it is sometimes difficult to know exactly what is inside them. Fortunately, now there are food labels. Food labels are a good way ③ <u>to find</u> the information about the foods you eat. Labels on food are ④ <u>like</u> the table of contents found in books. The main purpose of food labels ⑤ <u>is</u> to inform you what is inside the food you are purchasing.

* manufactured: (공장에서) 제조된
** table of contents: (책 등의) 목차

30. 다음 글의 밑줄 친 부분 중, 문맥상 낱말의 쓰임이 적절하지 <u>않은</u> 것은? [3점]

We often ignore small changes because they don't seem to ① <u>matter</u> very much in the moment. If you save a little money now, you're still not a millionaire. If you study Spanish for an hour tonight, you still haven't learned the language. We make a few changes, but the results never seem to come ② <u>quickly</u> and so we slide back into our previous routines. The slow pace of transformation also makes it ③ <u>easy</u> to break a bad habit. If you eat an unhealthy meal today, the scale doesn't move much. A single decision is easy to ignore. But when we ④ <u>repeat</u> small errors, day after day, by following poor decisions again and again, our small choices add up to bad results. Many missteps eventually lead to a ⑤ <u>problem</u>.

[31~34] 다음 빈칸에 들어갈 말로 가장 적절한 것을 고르시오.

31. Remember that _____ is always of the essence. If an apology is not accepted, thank the individual for hearing you out and leave the door open for if and when he wishes to reconcile. Be conscious of the fact that just because someone accepts your apology does not mean she has fully forgiven you. It can take time, maybe a long time, before the injured party can completely let go and fully trust you again. There is little you can do to speed this process up. If the person is truly important to you, it is worthwhile to give him or her the time and space needed to heal. Do not expect the person to go right back to acting normally immediately.

* reconcile: 화해하다

① curiosity ② independence
③ patience ④ creativity
⑤ honesty

32. Although many small businesses have excellent websites, they typically can't afford aggressive online campaigns. One way to get the word out is through an advertising exchange, in which advertisers place banners on each other's websites for free. For example, a company selling beauty products could place its banner on a site that sells women's shoes, and in turn, the shoe company could put a banner on the beauty product site. Neither company charges the other; they simply exchange ad space. Advertising exchanges are gaining in popularity, especially among marketers who do not have much money and who don't have a large sales team. By _____, advertisers find new outlets that reach their target audiences that they would not otherwise be able to afford.

* aggressive: 매우 적극적인 ** outlet: 출구

① trading space
② getting funded
③ sharing reviews
④ renting factory facilities
⑤ increasing TV commercials

33. Motivation may come from several sources. It may be the respect I give every student, the daily greeting I give at my classroom door, the undivided attention when I listen to a student, a pat on the shoulder whether the job was done well or not, an accepting smile, or simply "I love you" when it is most needed. It may simply be asking how things are at home. For one student considering dropping out of school, it was a note from me after one of his frequent absences saying that he made my day when I saw him in school. He came to me with the note with tears in his eyes and thanked me. He will graduate this year. Whatever technique is used, the students must know that you _____.
But the concern must be genuine — the students can't be fooled.

① care about them
② keep your words
③ differ from them
④ evaluate their performance
⑤ communicate with their parents

34. Say you normally go to a park to walk or work out. Maybe today you should choose a different park. Why? Well, who knows? Maybe it's because you need the connection to the different energy in the other park. Maybe you'll run into people there that you've never met before. You could make a new best friend simply by visiting a different park. You never know what great things will happen to you until you step outside the zone where you feel comfortable. If you're staying in your comfort zone and you're not pushing yourself past that same old energy, then you're not going to move forward on your path. By forcing yourself to do something different, you're awakening yourself on a spiritual level and you're forcing yourself to do something that will benefit you in the long run. As they say, _____. [3점]

① variety is the spice of life
② fantasy is the mirror of reality
③ failure teaches more than success
④ laziness is the mother of invention
⑤ conflict strengthens the relationship

[35 ~ 36] 주어진 글 다음에 이어질 글의 순서로 가장 적절한 것을 고르시오.

35.

> Ideas about how much disclosure is appropriate vary among cultures.

(A) On the other hand, Japanese tend to do little disclosing about themselves to others except to the few people with whom they are very close. In general, Asians do not reach out to strangers.

(B) Those born in the United States tend to be high disclosers, even showing a willingness to disclose information about themselves to strangers. This may explain why Americans seem particularly easy to meet and are good at cocktail-party conversation.

(C) They do, however, show great care for each other, since they view harmony as essential to relationship improvement. They work hard to prevent those they view as outsiders from getting information they believe to be unfavorable. [3점]

* disclosure: (정보의) 공개

① (A) − (C) − (B)   ② (B) − (A) − (C)
③ (B) − (C) − (A)   ④ (C) − (A) − (B)
⑤ (C) − (B) − (A)

36.

> A god called Moinee was defeated by a rival god called Dromerdeener in a terrible battle up in the stars. Moinee fell out of the stars down to Tasmania to die.

(A) He took pity on the people, gave them bendable knees and cut off their inconvenient kangaroo tails so they could all sit down at last. Then they lived happily ever after.

(B) Then he died. The people hated having kangaroo tails and no knees, and they cried out to the heavens for help. Dromerdeener heard their cry and came down to Tasmania to see what the matter was.

(C) Before he died, he wanted to give a last blessing to his final resting place, so he decided to create humans. But he was in such a hurry, knowing he was dying, that he forgot to give them knees; and he absent-mindedly gave them big tails like kangaroos, which meant they couldn't sit down.

① (A) − (C) − (B)   ② (B) − (A) − (C)
③ (B) − (C) − (A)   ④ (C) − (A) − (B)
⑤ (C) − (B) − (A)

[37~38] 글의 흐름으로 보아, 주어진 문장이 들어가기에 가장 적절한 곳을 고르시오.

37.

In the U.S. we have so many metaphors for time and its passing that we think of time as "a thing," that is "the weekend is almost gone," or "I haven't got the time."

There are some cultures that can be referred to as "people who live outside of time." The Amondawa tribe, living in Brazil, does not have a concept of time that can be measured or counted. (①) Rather they live in a world of serial events, rather than seeing events as being rooted in time. (②) Researchers also found that no one had an age. (③) Instead, they change their names to reflect their stage of life and position within their society, so a little child will give up their name to a newborn sibling and take on a new one. (④) We think such statements are objective, but they aren't. (⑤) We create these metaphors, but the Amondawa don't talk or think in metaphors for time. [3점]

* metaphor: 은유 ** sibling: 형제자매

38.

Of course, within cultures individual attitudes can vary dramatically.

The natural world provides a rich source of symbols used in art and literature. (①) Plants and animals are central to mythology, dance, song, poetry, rituals, festivals, and holidays around the world. (②) Different cultures can exhibit opposite attitudes toward a given species. (③) Snakes, for example, are honored by some cultures and hated by others. (④) Rats are considered pests in much of Europe and North America and greatly respected in some parts of India. (⑤) For instance, in Britain many people dislike rodents, and yet there are several associations devoted to breeding them, including the National Mouse Club and the National Fancy Rat Club.

* pest: 유해 동물 ** rodent: (쥐, 다람쥐 등이 속한) 설치류

39. 다음 글에서 전체 흐름과 관계 없는 문장은?

Paying attention to some people and not others doesn't mean you're being dismissive or arrogant. ① It just reflects a hard fact: there are limits on the number of people we can possibly pay attention to or develop a relationship with. ② Some scientists even believe that the number of people with whom we can continue stable social relationships might be limited naturally by our brains. ③ The more people you know of different backgrounds, the more colorful your life becomes. ④ Professor Robin Dunbar has explained that our minds are only really capable of forming meaningful relationships with a maximum of about a hundred and fifty people. ⑤ Whether that's true or not, it's safe to assume that we can't be real friends with everyone.

* dismissive: 무시하는 ** arrogant: 거만한

40. 다음 글의 내용을 한 문장으로 요약하고자 한다. 빈칸 (A), (B)에 들어갈 말로 가장 적절한 것은?

While there are many evolutionary or cultural reasons for cooperation, the eyes are one of the most important means of cooperation, and eye contact may be the most powerful human force we lose in traffic. It is, arguably, the reason why humans, normally a quite cooperative species, can become so noncooperative on the road. Most of the time we are moving too fast — we begin to lose the ability to keep eye contact around 20 miles per hour — or it is not safe to look. Maybe our view is blocked. Often other drivers are wearing sunglasses, or their car may have tinted windows. (And do you really want to make eye contact with those drivers?) Sometimes we make eye contact through the rearview mirror, but it feels weak, not quite believable at first, as it is not "face-to-face."

* tinted: 색이 옅게 들어간

↓

While driving, people become _____(A)_____, because they make _____(B)_____ eye contact.

	(A)		(B)
①	uncooperative	······	little
②	careful	······	direct
③	confident	······	regular
④	uncooperative	······	direct
⑤	careful	······	little

[41 ~ 42] 다음 글을 읽고, 물음에 답하시오.

Many high school students study and learn inefficiently because they insist on doing their homework while watching TV or listening to loud music. These same students also typically (a) interrupt their studying with repeated phone calls, trips to the kitchen, video games, and Internet surfing. Ironically, students with the greatest need to concentrate when studying are often the ones who surround themselves with the most distractions. These teenagers argue that they can study *better* with the TV or radio (b) playing. Some professionals actually (c) oppose their position. They argue that many teenagers can actually study productively under less-than-ideal conditions because they've been exposed repeatedly to "background noise" since early childhood. These educators argue that children have become (d) used to the sounds of the TV, video games, and loud music. They also argue that insisting students turn off the TV or radio when doing homework will not necessarily improve their academic performance. This position is certainly not generally shared, however. Many teachers and learning experts are (e) convinced by their own experiences that students who study in a noisy environment often learn inefficiently.

41. 윗글의 제목으로 가장 적절한 것은?

① Successful Students Plan Ahead
② Studying with Distractions: Is It Okay?
③ Smart Devices as Good Learning Tools
④ Parents & Teachers: Partners in Education
⑤ Good Habits: Hard to Form, Easy to Break

42. 밑줄 친 (a) ~ (e) 중에서 문맥상 낱말의 쓰임이 적절하지 않은 것은? [3점]

① (a)   ② (b)   ③ (c)   ④ (d)   ⑤ (e)

[43 ~ 45] 다음 글을 읽고, 물음에 답하시오.

(A)

Dorothy was home alone. She was busy with a school project, and suddenly wanted to eat French fries. She peeled two potatoes, sliced them up and put a pot with cooking oil on the stove. Then the telephone rang. It was her best friend Samantha. While chatting away on the phone, Dorothy noticed a strange light shining from the kitchen, and then (a) she remembered about the pot of oil on the stove!

(B)

A while later, after the wound had been treated, the family sat around the kitchen table and talked. "I learned a big lesson today," Dorothy said. Her parents expected (b) her to say something about the fire. But she talked about something different. "I have decided to use kind words more just like you." Her parents were very grateful, because Dorothy had quite a temper.

(C)

Dorothy dropped the phone and rushed to the kitchen. The oil was on fire. "Chill! Take a deep breath," (c) she said to herself. *What did they teach us not to do in a situation like this? Don't try to put it out by throwing water on it, because it will cause an explosion*, she remembered. She picked up the pot's lid and covered the pot with it to put out the flames. In the process she burned her hands. Dorothy felt dizzy and sat down at the kitchen table.

(D)

A couple of minutes later, her parents came rushing into the house. Samantha had suspected that something might be wrong after Dorothy dropped the phone just like that, and (d) she had phoned Dorothy's parents. Dorothy started to cry. Her mother hugged her tightly and looked at the wound. "Tell me what happened," she said. Dorothy told her, sobbing and sniffing. "Aren't you going to yell at me?" (e) she asked them through the tears. Her father answered with a smile, "I also put my lid on to keep me from exploding." Dorothy looked at him, relieved. "But be careful not to be so irresponsible again."

* sob: 흐느껴 울다 ** sniff: 코를 훌쩍거리다

43. 주어진 글 (A)에 이어질 내용을 순서에 맞게 배열한 것으로 가장 적절한 것은?

① (B) − (D) − (C)   ② (C) − (B) − (D)
③ (C) − (D) − (B)   ④ (D) − (B) − (C)
⑤ (D) − (C) − (B)

44. 밑줄 친 (a) ~ (e) 중에서 가리키는 대상이 나머지 넷과 다른 것은?

① (a)   ② (b)   ③ (c)   ④ (d)   ⑤ (e)

45. 윗글의 Dorothy에 관한 내용으로 적절하지 않은 것은?

① 프렌치프라이를 만들려고 감자 두 개를 깎았다.
② 친절한 말을 더 많이 쓰겠다고 다짐했다.
③ 불붙은 기름에 물을 끼얹지 말아야 한다는 것을 기억했다.
④ 뚜껑으로 냄비를 덮어 불을 끄다가 손을 데었다.
⑤ 아버지의 말을 듣고 화를 냈다.

★ 확인 사항
○ 답안지의 해당란에 필요한 내용을 정확히 기입(표기)했는지 확인하시오.

18

001 complain ⓥ 불평하다
002 work ⓥ 작동되다[기능하다]
003 refund ⓝ 환불
004 warranty ⓝ 보증기간
005 replace A with B A를 B로 교환[교체]하다
006 faulty ⓐ 결함이 있는
007 receipt ⓝ 영수증
008 dealer ⓝ 판매자
009 on the spot 현장에서
010 satisfaction ⓝ 만족
011 customer ⓝ 고객
012 hesitate ⓥ 망설이다

19

013 dive ⓥ 잠수하다
014 terrible ⓐ 심한
015 stomachache ⓝ 복통
016 sink ⓥ 가라앉다
017 hardly ⓐⓓ 거의 ~ 않다
018 remove ⓥ 벗다, 제거하다
019 weight belt 웨이트 벨트 (잠수, 운동 때 무게를 더하기 위해 착용하는 벨트, 재킷)
020 suddenly ⓐⓓ 갑자기
021 behind ⓐⓓ 뒤에, 뒤떨어져
022 armpit ⓝ 겨드랑이
023 lift ⓥ 들어 올리다, 들리다
024 forcibly ⓐⓓ 강제로, 강력히
025 field of vision 시야, 가시 범위
026 smiling ⓐ 미소짓는
027 dolphin ⓝ 돌고래
028 protecting ⓐ 지키는, 보호하는, 방어하는
029 toward ⓟⓡⓔⓟ …쪽으로, …을 향하여
030 surface ⓝ 표면
031 excited ⓐ 신이 난, 들뜬, 흥분한
032 bored ⓐ 지루해하는
033 pleased ⓐ 기쁜
034 angry ⓐ 화난, 성난
035 jealous ⓐ 질투하는, 질투나 나는
036 thankful ⓐ 감사하는
037 proud ⓐ 자랑스러워하는, 자랑스러운
038 embarrassed ⓐ 당황한
039 frightened ⓐ 겁먹은, 무서워하는
040 relieved ⓐ 안도하는, 다행으로 여기는

20

041 float ⓥ 뜨다
042 ensure ⓥ 보장하다
043 happen ⓥ (무엇의 결과로) 일어나다[되다]
044 writer ⓝ 작가, 문인, 저술가
045 come to life (사물이) 생명력을 얻다, 살아 움직이다
046 take out 꺼내다
047 a piece of paper 한 장의 종이
048 record ⓥ 기록하다
049 aim ⓥ 반드시 ~하다, 목표로 하다
050 hit ⓥ (특정 수량·수준에) 이르다
051 reminder ⓝ 상기시키는 것
052 motivator ⓝ 동기 요인, 동기를 부여하는 것
053 get going 시작하다, 착수하다
054 remember ⓥ 기억하다
055 burden ⓝ 부담

056 put A into words A를 글 [말]로 적대[하다]
057 put into action 실행에 옮기다

21

058 temper ⓝ (걸핏하면 화를 내는) 성질
059 argument ⓝ 논쟁
060 keep ⓥ 유지하다
061 cool ⓐ 차분한, 침착한
062 intentionally ⓐⓓ 일부러, 의도적으로
063 design ⓥ 고안하다
064 annoy ⓥ 화나게 하다
065 lose one's cool 침착함을 잃다
066 foolish ⓐ 어리석은
067 simply ⓐⓓ 그냥 (간단히), 그저 (단순히)
068 impossible ⓐ 불가능한
069 fall for ~에 속아넘어가다
070 make a remark 말을 하다
071 respond ⓥ 대응하다
072 answer ⓝ 대답, 회신, 대응
073 focus ⓝ 초점, 주목
074 raise ⓥ (문제 등을) 제기하다
075 effective ⓐ 효과적인
076 indeed ⓐⓓ 정말로
077 attentive ⓐ 주의 깊은
078 admire ⓥ 감탄하다
079 rise to the bait 미끼를 물다
080 stay calm 차분함, 침착함을 유지하다
081 blame oneself 자신을 책망하다
082 lose one's temper 화를 내다
083 apologize for ~에 대해 사과하다
084 behavior ⓝ 행동, 태도

22

085 practically ⓐⓓ 사실상, 거의
086 value ⓝ 가치
087 require ⓥ 요구하다
088 take a risk 위험을 무릅쓰다
089 failure ⓝ 실패
090 reject ⓥ 거절하다
091 price ⓝ (치러야 할) 대가
092 achieve ⓥ 성취하다
093 greater ⓐ ~보다 큰
094 reward ⓝ 보상
095 lie ⓥ 있다, 놓여 있다
096 ahead of (공간·시간상으로) ~ 앞에
097 mean ⓥ …라는 뜻[의미]이다, …을 뜻하다 [의미하다]
098 succeed ⓥ 성공하다
099 sometime ⓐⓓ 언젠가
100 filled with ~로 가득 찬
101 challenge ⓝ 도전
102 get away from ~에서 벗어나다[피하다]
103 be left behind 뒤처지다
104 race ⓝ 경주, 레이스
105 for example 예를 들어
106 similarly ⓐⓓ 마찬가지로
107 attend ⓥ 참석하다

23

108 individual ⓐ 개인의
109 preference ⓝ 선호
110 vary ⓥ 다양하다

111 touch ⓝ 촉감, 감촉 ⓥ 만지다
112 come in contact with ~와 접촉하다
113 aspect ⓝ 측면
114 consumer ⓝ 소비자
115 feel ⓝ 촉감, 감촉
116 soothing ⓐ 진정시키는
117 opportunity ⓝ 기회
118 considering ⓟⓡⓔⓟ …을 고려[감안]하면
119 material ⓝ 재료, 직물
120 property ⓝ 특성, 속성
121 clothing ⓝ 옷[의복]
122 carpeting ⓝ 카펫류, 카펫천
123 benefit ⓝ 혜택, 이득
124 factor ⓝ 요인
125 among ⓟⓡⓔⓟ …중[사이]에
126 necessity ⓝ 필요성
127 latest ⓐ (가장) 최근의[최신의]

24

128 be good for ~에 좋다
129 enemy ⓝ 적
130 essential ⓐ 필수적인
131 take in ~을 섭취하다
132 drown ⓥ 물에 빠지다, 익사하다
133 education ⓝ 교육
134 exception ⓝ 예외
135 knowledge ⓝ 지식
136 in one's lifetime 평생
137 be yet to- 아직 ~하지 못하다
138 hurt ⓥ 피해를 보다
139 worldwide ⓐⓓ 전 세계에서
140 result from ~로 인해 생기다
141 lack ⓝ 부족, 결여
142 keep in mind ~을 명심하다, 염두에 두다
143 long-term ⓐ 장기적인
144 investment ⓝ 투자
145 effort ⓝ 노력, 공
146 worse ⓐ 더 나쁜[못한/엉망인]

25

147 native speaker 원어민
148 in terms of ~의 면에서
149 follow ⓥ ~의 뒤를 잇다
150 least ⓐⓓ 가장 적게
151 term ⓝ 용어, 말

26

152 graduate from ~을 졸업하다
153 nursing ⓝ 간호(학)
154 suggest ⓥ 제안하다
155 take care of ~을 돌보다
156 passenger ⓝ 승객
157 female ⓐ 여성[여자]인
158 flight attendant 항공 승무원
159 injury ⓝ 부상
160 force ⓥ 어쩔 수 없이 ~하게 하다, 강요하다
161 end one's career 일을 그만두다
162 degree ⓝ 학위
163 serve as ~로 복무하다, ~의 역할을 하다
164 captain ⓝ 대위
165 hometown ⓝ 고향
166 name after ~의 이름을 따서 짓다

27

167 selfie ⓝ 셀카 사진
168 goody ⓝ 매력적인 것, 갖고 싶은 것
169 submit ⓥ 출품하다, 제출하다
170 outside of …의 바깥쪽에, 밖에[으로]
171 deadline ⓝ 마감 기한
172 detail ⓝ 세부 사항
173 include ⓥ 포함하다
174 activity ⓝ (취미나 특별한 목적을 위한) 활동
175 creative ⓐ 창의적인
176 sentence ⓝ 문장
177 entry ⓝ 출품작
178 announce ⓥ 발표하다, 안내하다

28

179 warehouse ⓝ 창고
180 carry ⓥ (상점이 상품을) 취급하다
181 item ⓝ 품목
182 in stock 재고로 있는
183 retailer ⓝ 소매상
184 participate ⓥ 참가[참여]하다
185 return ⓝ 반품
186 purchase ⓝ 구입

29

187 phrase ⓝ 구절
188 relationship ⓝ 관계
189 physical ⓐ 신체적인, 물리적인
190 processed ⓐ 가공된
191 canned ⓐ 통조림으로 된
192 packaged ⓐ 포장된
193 contain ⓥ 함유하다
194 chemical ⓝ 화학 물질
195 artificial ⓐ 인공의
196 ingredient ⓝ 재료
197 food label 식품 (영양 성분) 라벨
198 fortunately ⓐⓓ 다행스럽게도, 운 좋게도
199 main ⓐ 주된, 가장 중요한
200 purpose ⓝ 목적
201 inform ⓥ 알리다, 통지하다
202 inside ⓟⓡⓔⓟ …의 안[속/내부]에[으로]
203 purchasing ⓝ 구매 (행위)

30

204 ignore ⓥ 무시하다
205 matter ⓥ 중요하다
206 in the moment 당장, 지금
207 millionaire ⓝ 백만장자
208 slide back into ~로 돌아가다, 복귀하다
209 previous ⓐ 이전의
210 routine ⓝ 일상
211 pace ⓝ 속도
212 transformation ⓝ 변화
213 break a bad habit 나쁜 습관을 버리다
214 unhealthy ⓐ 몸에 좋지 않은, 건강하지 않은
215 scale ⓝ 체중계, 저울
216 decision ⓝ 결정
217 add up to (합이) 결국 ~이 되다
218 misstep ⓝ 실수, 잘못된 조치
219 eventually ⓐⓓ 결국

05회

31
220 □ be of the essence 가장 중요하다
221 □ apology ⓝ 사과
222 □ accept ⓥ 받아들이다
223 □ hear ~ out ~의 말을 끝까지 들어주다
224 □ conscious ⓐ 알고 있는, 의식하는
225 □ fully ⓐ 완전히, 충분히
226 □ forgive ⓥ 용서하다
227 □ take time 시간이 걸리다
228 □ injured ⓐ 상처받은, 부상 당한
229 □ party ⓝ 당사자, 상대방
230 □ completely ⓐ 완전히
231 □ let go (걱정·근심 등을) 떨쳐 버리다
232 □ speed up 빨라지게 하다
233 □ process ⓝ 과정
234 □ be worthwhile to- ~하는 것이 가치가 있다
235 □ heal ⓥ 치유되다
236 □ go back to (이전 상황·상태로) 돌아가다
237 □ normally ⓐ 정상적으로
238 □ immediately ⓐ 즉시, 곧
239 □ curiosity ⓝ 호기심
240 □ independence ⓝ 자립, 독립
241 □ patience ⓝ 인내

32
242 □ business ⓝ 사업체
243 □ typically ⓐ 보통, 전형적으로
244 □ afford ⓥ ~할 여유가 있다
245 □ aggressive ⓐ 매우 적극적인
246 □ get the word out 말을 퍼뜨리다
247 □ place ⓥ (광고를) 게시하다[내다]
248 □ for free 공짜로, 무료로
249 □ in turn 차례로, 결국
250 □ charge ⓥ (요금을) 청구하다, 부과하다
251 □ gain in popularity 인기를 얻다
252 □ marketer ⓝ 마케팅 담당자
253 □ reach ⓥ ~와 접촉하다
254 □ target audience 목표 접속자
255 □ otherwise ⓐ 그러지 않으면
256 □ fund ⓥ 기금을 지원하다 ⓝ 기금
257 □ facility ⓝ 시설
258 □ commercial ⓝ 광고 ⓐ 상업적인

33
259 □ motivation ⓝ 동기 부여
260 □ several ⓐ 여러 가지의, 몇몇의
261 □ source ⓝ 공급원
262 □ respect ⓝ 존중
263 □ undivided ⓐ 완전한, 전적인
264 □ attention ⓝ 집중, 주의
265 □ a pat on the shoulder (격려의 의미로) 어깨를 토닥임
266 □ accepting ⓐ 포용적인, 수용적인
267 □ drop out of school 학교를 중퇴하다
268 □ frequent ⓐ 잦은, 빈번한
269 □ absence ⓝ 결석
270 □ make one's day ~을 행복하게 만들다
271 □ technique ⓝ 기법, 기술
272 □ concern ⓝ 관심, 걱정
273 □ genuine ⓐ 진실한, 진짜의
274 □ fool ⓥ 속이다

275 □ keep one's words 약속을 지키다
276 □ differ from ~와 다르다
277 □ evaluate ⓥ 평가하다

34
278 □ work out 운동하다
279 □ connection ⓝ 연결
280 □ run into ~을 우연히 만나다
281 □ never A until B B하고 나서야 비로소 A하다
282 □ comfort zone 안락 지대
283 □ move forward 앞으로 나아가다
284 □ path ⓝ 진로
285 □ awaken ⓥ 깨우다
286 □ spiritual ⓐ 영적인, 정신적인
287 □ benefit ⓥ 이롭게 하다
288 □ in the long run 결국에는, 장기적으로
289 □ spice ⓝ 묘미, 향신료
290 □ laziness ⓝ 게으름
291 □ invention ⓝ 발명
292 □ conflict ⓝ 갈등
293 □ strengthen ⓥ 강화하다

35
294 □ appropriate ⓐ 적절한
295 □ vary ⓥ 다르다
296 □ tend to- ~하는 경향이 있다
297 □ except to ~을 제외하고
298 □ close ⓐ 친한, 가까운
299 □ in general 일반적으로
300 □ reach out to ~에게 관심을 보이다
301 □ stranger ⓝ 낯선[모르는] 사람
302 □ willingness ⓝ 기꺼이 ~하려는 마음
303 □ be good at ~에 능숙하다
304 □ view A as B A를 B로 간주하다
305 □ harmony ⓝ 조화
306 □ improvement ⓝ 발전, 개선
307 □ prevent A from ~ing A가 ~하지 못하게 막다
308 □ outsider ⓝ 외부인
309 □ unfavorable ⓐ 불리한, 호의적이 아닌

36
310 □ defeat ⓥ 패배시키다
311 □ rival ⓐ 경쟁하는
312 □ fall out of ~에서 떨어지다
313 □ take pity on ~을 불쌍히 여기다
314 □ bendable ⓐ 구부릴 수 있는
315 □ cut off ~을 잘라 내다
316 □ inconvenient ⓐ 불편한
317 □ at last 마침내
318 □ cry out for ~을 얻고자 외치다
319 □ matter ⓝ 문제
320 □ blessing ⓝ 축복
321 □ resting place 안식처
322 □ be in a hurry 서두르다
323 □ absent-mindedly ⓐ 아무 생각 없이

37
324 □ passing ⓝ (시간의) 흐름, 경과
325 □ think of A as B A를 B라고 간주하다
326 □ that is 즉, 다시 말해서

327 □ refer to A as B A를 B라고 부르다, 언급하다
328 □ tribe ⓝ 부족
329 □ concept ⓝ 개념
330 □ measure ⓥ 측정하다
331 □ serial ⓐ 연속되는
332 □ rooted in ~에 뿌리를 둔
333 □ reflect ⓥ 반영하다
334 □ stage ⓝ (발달상의) 단계
335 □ give up ~을 넘겨주다
336 □ newborn ⓐ 갓 태어난
337 □ take on ~을 갖게 되다, ~을 맡다
338 □ statement ⓝ 말, 진술
339 □ objective ⓐ 객관적인

38
340 □ attitude ⓝ 태도
341 □ dramatically ⓐ 극적으로
342 □ symbol ⓝ 상징
343 □ literature ⓝ 문학
344 □ central ⓐ 중심인, 중심의
345 □ mythology ⓝ 신화
346 □ poetry ⓝ 시
347 □ ritual ⓝ 의식
348 □ holiday ⓝ 기념일
349 □ exhibit ⓥ 보여주다, 전시하다
350 □ opposite ⓐ 정반대의
351 □ given ⓐ (이미)정해진; 특정한
352 □ species ⓝ 종(種)
353 □ honor ⓥ 존경하다
354 □ association ⓝ 협회, 연관
355 □ devoted to ~에 전념하는
356 □ breed ⓥ 기르다, 낳다

39
357 □ pay attention to ~에 주의를 기울이다
358 □ hard fact 명백한 사실
359 □ limit ⓝ 한계 ⓥ 제한하다
360 □ the number of 수(數)
361 □ possibly ⓐ 아마
362 □ develop ⓥ 발전하다
363 □ stable ⓐ 안정적인
364 □ social relationship 사회적 관계
365 □ background ⓝ 배경
366 □ colorful ⓐ 다채로운
367 □ be capable of doing ~할 수 있다
368 □ form ⓥ 형성하다
369 □ meaningful ⓐ 유의미한
370 □ assume ⓥ 가정하다

40
371 □ evolutionary ⓐ 진화적인
372 □ cooperation ⓝ 협동, 협력
373 □ means ⓝ 수단
374 □ eye contact 시선의 마주침
375 □ force ⓝ 힘
376 □ traffic ⓝ (차량) 운행, 교통
377 □ arguably ⓐ 주장컨대
378 □ cooperative ⓐ 협동하는, 협조하는
379 □ noncooperative ⓐ 비협조적인
380 □ most of ~의 대부분
381 □ block ⓥ 차단하다

382 □ rearview mirror 백미러
383 □ believable ⓐ 믿을 수 있는
384 □ confident ⓐ 자신감 있는

41~42
385 □ inefficiently ⓐ 비효율적으로
386 □ insist on ~을 고집하다, 주장하다
387 □ interrupt ⓥ 방해하다
388 □ trip ⓝ (어디까지의) 이동
389 □ surf ⓥ (인터넷을) 서핑하다 [검색하다]
390 □ ironically ⓐ 모순적이게도
391 □ concentrate ⓥ 집중하다
392 □ surround ⓥ 에워싸다
393 □ distraction ⓝ 주의를 산만하게 하는 것
394 □ argue ⓥ 주장하다
395 □ professional ⓝ 전문가
396 □ actually ⓐ 실제로
397 □ oppose ⓥ 반대하다
398 □ position ⓝ 견해
399 □ productively ⓐ 생산적으로
400 □ less-than-ideal ⓐ 결코 이상적이지 않은
401 □ condition ⓝ 상황, 조건
402 □ expose ⓥ 노출시키다
403 □ repeatedly ⓐ 반복적으로
404 □ background noise 배경 소음
405 □ educator ⓝ 교육 전문가
406 □ used to ~에 익숙한
407 □ not necessarily 반드시 ~인 것은 아니다
408 □ improve ⓥ 높이다, 향상시키다
409 □ academic performance 학업 성적
410 □ generally ⓐ 일반적으로
411 □ convinced ⓐ 확신하는
412 □ noisy ⓐ 시끄러운
413 □ successful ⓐ 성공한, 성공적인
414 □ plan ahead 미리 계획하다, 장래의 계획을 세우다

43~45
415 □ busy with ~로 바쁜
416 □ peel ⓥ 깎다, 껍질을 벗기다
417 □ slice up ~을 얇게 자르다
418 □ chat away 수다 떨다
419 □ notice ⓥ 알아차리다
420 □ wound ⓝ 상처
421 □ treat ⓥ 치료하다
422 □ grateful ⓐ 감사해하는
423 □ have quite a temper 성질이 보통이 아니다
424 □ chill ⓥ 진정하다
425 □ deep breath 심호흡
426 □ put out 불을 끄다
427 □ explosion ⓝ 폭발
428 □ lid ⓝ 뚜껑
429 □ flame ⓝ 불길
430 □ burn ⓥ 불에 데다
431 □ dizzy ⓐ 어지러운
432 □ rush into 급하게[무모하게] ···하다
433 □ suspect ⓥ 의심하다
434 □ tightly ⓐ (쥐거나 안는 방식이) 꼭
435 □ yell at ~에게 고함지르다
436 □ explode ⓥ 폭발하다
437 □ irresponsible ⓐ 무책임한

TEST A-B 각 단어의 뜻을 [A] 영어는 우리말로, [B] 우리말은 영어로 쓰시오.

A	English	Korean
01	lose one's temper	
02	soothing	
03	keep in mind	
04	armpit	
05	scale	
06	genuine	
07	breed	
08	independence	
09	inefficiently	
10	in terms of	
11	run into	
12	grateful	
13	bendable	
14	vary	
15	convinced	
16	motivator	
17	routine	
18	conflict	
19	association	
20	assume	

B	Korean	English
01	결함이 있는	
02	인공의	
03	(문제 등을) 제기하다	
04	중요하다	
05	패배시키다	
06	요인	
07	인내	
08	구절	
09	거절하다	
10	잦은, 빈번한	
11	부상	
12	안정적인	
13	강화하다	
14	의식	
15	평가하다	
16	신체적인, 물리적인	
17	관심, 걱정	
18	완전한, 전적인	
19	결국에는, 장기적으로	
20	알리다, 통지하다	

▶ A-D 정답 : 해설편 051쪽

TEST C-D 각 단어의 뜻을 골라 기호를 쓰시오.

C	English		Korean
01	interrupt	( )	ⓐ 투자
02	investment	( )	ⓑ 재료
03	suspect	( )	ⓒ 방해하다
04	in turn	( )	ⓓ 차례로, 결국
05	evolutionary	( )	ⓔ 약속을 지키다
06	float	( )	ⓕ 강요하다
07	force	( )	ⓖ (합이) 결국 ~이 되다
08	on the spot	( )	ⓗ 의심하다
09	keep one's words	( )	ⓘ 현장에서
10	add up to	( )	ⓙ ~을 고집하다, 주장하다
11	selfie	( )	ⓚ 진화적인
12	insist on	( )	ⓛ 불리한, 호의적이 아닌
13	unfavorable	( )	ⓜ 셀카 사진
14	reminder	( )	ⓝ 상기시키는 것
15	ingredient	( )	ⓞ 뜨다
16	reflect	( )	ⓟ 모순적이게도
17	ironically	( )	ⓠ 보장하다
18	filled with	( )	ⓡ ~로 가득 찬
19	ensure	( )	ⓢ 반영하다
20	conscious	( )	ⓣ 알고 있는, 의식하는

D	Korean		English
01	광고; 상업적인	( )	ⓐ spiritual
02	재고로 있는	( )	ⓑ in stock
03	객관적인	( )	ⓒ eventually
04	~할 여유가 있다	( )	ⓓ hesitate
05	차단하다	( )	ⓔ block
06	표면	( )	ⓕ surface
07	집중하다	( )	ⓖ commercial
08	폭발	( )	ⓗ aspect
09	~에 주의를 기울이다	( )	ⓘ concentrate
10	뒤처지다	( )	ⓙ objective
11	결국	( )	ⓚ pay attention to
12	측면	( )	ⓛ afford
13	영적인, 정신적인	( )	ⓜ explosion
14	망설이다	( )	ⓝ be left behind
15	고안하다	( )	ⓞ design
16	안식처	( )	ⓟ arguably
17	주장컨대	( )	ⓠ yell at
18	~할 수 있다	( )	ⓡ resting place
19	높이다, 향상시키다	( )	ⓢ be capable of doing
20	~에게 고함지르다	( )	ⓣ improve

※ 영어 [독해] 파트만 수록한 문제지이므로 18번부터 시작합니다.　　　● 점수 표시가 없는 문항은 모두 **2점**　　● 문항수 **28개** | 배점 **63점** | 제한 시간 **45분**

18. 다음 글의 목적으로 가장 적절한 것은?

Dear Reader,

We always appreciate your support. As you know, our service is now available through an app. There has never been a better time to switch to an online membership of *TourTide Magazine*. At a 50% discount off your current print subscription, you can access a full year of online reading. Get new issues and daily web pieces at TourTide.com, read or listen to *TourTide Magazine* via the app, and get our members-only newsletter. You'll also gain access to our editors' selections of the best articles. Join today!

Yours,
TourTide Team

① 여행 일정 지연에 대해 사과하려고
② 잡지 온라인 구독을 권유하려고
③ 무료 잡지 신청을 홍보하려고
④ 여행 후기 모집을 안내하려고
⑤ 기사에 대한 독자 의견에 답변하려고

19. 다음 글에 드러난 'I'의 심경 변화로 가장 적절한 것은?

As I walked from the mailbox, my heart was beating rapidly. In my hands, I held the letter from the university I had applied to. I thought my grades were good enough to cross the line and my application letter was well-written, but was it enough? I hadn't slept a wink for days. As I carefully tore into the paper of the envelope, the letter slowly emerged with the opening phrase, "It is our great pleasure..." I shouted with joy, "I am in!" As I held the letter, I began to make a fantasy about my college life in a faraway city.

① relaxed → upset
② anxious → delighted
③ guilty → confident
④ angry → grateful
⑤ hopeful → disappointed

20. 다음 글에서 필자가 주장하는 바로 가장 적절한 것은?

Having a messy room can add up to negative feelings and destructive thinking. Psychologists say that having a disorderly room can indicate a disorganized mental state. One of the professional tidying experts says that the moment you start cleaning your room, you also start changing your life and gaining new perspective. When you clean your surroundings, positive and good atmosphere follows. You can do more things efficiently and neatly. So, clean up your closets, organize your drawers, and arrange your things first, then peace of mind will follow.

① 자신의 공간을 정돈하여 긍정적 변화를 도모하라.
② 오랜 시간 고민하기보다는 일단 행동으로 옮겨라.
③ 무질서한 환경에서 창의적인 생각을 시도하라.
④ 장기 목표를 위해 단기 목표를 먼저 설정하라.
⑤ 반복되는 일상을 새로운 관점으로 관찰하라.

21. 밑줄 친 luxury real estate가 다음 글에서 의미하는 바로 가장 적절한 것은? [3점]

The soil of a farm field is forced to be the perfect environment for monoculture growth. This is achieved by adding nutrients in the form of fertilizer and water by way of irrigation. During the last fifty years, engineers and crop scientists have helped farmers become much more efficient at supplying exactly the right amount of both. World usage of fertilizer has tripled since 1969, and the global capacity for irrigation has almost doubled; we are feeding and watering our fields more than ever, and our crops are loving it. Unfortunately, these luxurious conditions have also excited the attention of certain agricultural undesirables. Because farm fields are loaded with nutrients and water relative to the natural land that surrounds them, they are desired as luxury real estate by every random weed in the area.

*monoculture: 단일 작물 재배   **irrigation: (논,밭에) 물을 댐; 관개

① a farm where a scientist's aid is highly required
② a field abundant with necessities for plants
③ a district accessible only for the rich
④ a place that is conserved for ecology
⑤ a region with higher economic value

22. 다음 글의 요지로 가장 적절한 것은?

When it comes to helping out, you don't have to do much. All you have to do is come around and show that you care. If you notice someone who is lonely, you could go and sit with them. If you work with someone who eats lunch all by themselves, and you go and sit down with them, they will begin to be more social after a while, and they will owe it all to you. A person's happiness comes from attention. There are too many people out in the world who feel like everyone has forgotten them or ignored them. Even if you say hi to someone passing by, they will begin to feel better about themselves, like someone cares.

① 사소한 관심이 타인에게 도움이 될 수 있다.
② 사람마다 행복의 기준이 제각기 다르다.
③ 선행을 통해 자신을 되돌아볼 수 있다.
④ 원만한 대인 관계는 경청에서 비롯된다.
⑤ 현재에 대한 만족이 행복의 필수조건이다.

23. 다음 글의 주제로 가장 적절한 것은?

We often try to make cuts in our challenges and take the easy route. When taking the quick exit, we fail to acquire the strength to compete. We often take the easy route to improve our skills. Many of us never really work to achieve mastery in the key areas of life. These skills are key tools that can be useful to our career, health, and prosperity. Highly successful athletes don't win because of better equipment; they win by facing hardship to gain strength and skill. They win through preparation. It's the mental preparation, winning mindset, strategy, and skill that set them apart. Strength comes from struggle, not from taking the path of least resistance. Hardship is not just a lesson for the next time in front of us. Hardship will be the greatest teacher we will ever have in life.

① characteristics of well-equipped athletes
② difficulties in overcoming life's sudden challenges
③ relationship between personal habit and competence
④ risks of enduring hardship without any preparation
⑤ importance of confronting hardship in one's life

24. 다음 글의 제목으로 가장 적절한 것은?

Your behaviors are usually a reflection of your identity. What you do is an indication of the type of person you believe that you are — either consciously or nonconsciously. Research has shown that once a person believes in a particular aspect of their identity, they are more likely to act according to that belief. For example, people who identified as "being a voter" were more likely to vote than those who simply claimed "voting" was an action they wanted to perform. Similarly, the person who accepts exercise as the part of their identity doesn't have to convince themselves to train. Doing the right thing is easy. After all, when your behavior and your identity perfectly match, you are no longer pursuing behavior change. You are simply acting like the type of person you already believe yourself to be.

① Action Comes from Who You Think You Are
② The Best Practices for Gaining More Voters
③ Stop Pursuing Undesirable Behavior Change!
④ What to Do When Your Exercise Bores You
⑤ Your Actions Speak Louder than Your Words

25. 다음 도표의 내용과 일치하지 <u>않는</u> 것은?

Electronic Waste Collection and Recycling Rate
by Region in 2016 and 2019

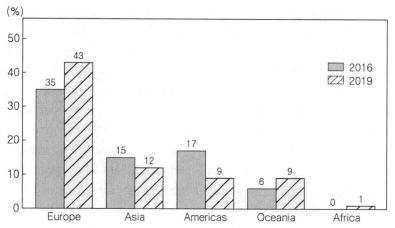

The above graph shows the electronic waste collection and recycling rate by region in 2016 and 2019. ① In both years, Europe showed the highest electronic waste collection and recycling rates. ② The electronic waste collection and recycling rate of Asia in 2019 was lower than in 2016. ③ The Americas ranked third both in 2016 and in 2019, with 17 percent and 9 percent respectively. ④ In both years, the electronic waste collection and recycling rates in Oceania remained under 10 percent. ⑤ Africa had the lowest electronic waste collection and recycling rates in both 2016 and 2019, showing the smallest gap between 2016 and 2019.

26. Fritz Zwicky에 관한 다음 글의 내용과 일치하지 <u>않는</u> 것은?

Fritz Zwicky, a memorable astrophysicist who coined the term 'supernova', was born in Varna, Bulgaria to a Swiss father and a Czech mother. At the age of six, he was sent to his grandparents who looked after him for most of his childhood in Switzerland. There, he received an advanced education in mathematics and physics. In 1925, he emigrated to the United States and continued his physics research at California Institute of Technology (Caltech). He developed numerous theories that have had a profound influence on the understanding of our universe in the early 21st century. After being appointed as a professor of astronomy at Caltech in 1942, he developed some of the earliest jet engines and holds more than 50 patents, many in jet propulsion.

* patent: 특허(권) ** propulsion: 추진(력)

① 불가리아의 Varna에서 태어났다.
② 스위스에서 수학과 물리학 교육을 받았다.
③ 미국으로 이주하여 연구를 이어갔다.
④ 우주 이해에 영향을 미친 수많은 이론을 발전시켰다.
⑤ 초창기 제트 엔진을 개발한 후 교수로 임용되었다.

27. Gourmet Baking Competition에 관한 다음 안내문의 내용과 일치하지 <u>않는</u> 것은?

Gourmet Baking Competition

Get out your cookbooks and dust off your greatest baking recipes.

When & Where
- 5 p.m. – 7 p.m. Saturday, August 3rd
- Gourmet Baking Studio

Registration
- Register online at www.bakeoff.org by July 25th.
- Anyone can participate in the competition.

Categories
- Pies, Cakes, and Cookies
- Each person can only enter one category.

Prizes & Gifts
- Prizes will be given to the top three in each category.
- Souvenirs will be given to every participant.

① 8월 3일 토요일에 개최된다.
② 온라인으로 참가 신청이 가능하다.
③ 누구나 참가할 수 있다.
④ 참가자 한 명이 여러 부문에 참여할 수 있다.
⑤ 모든 참가자에게 기념품이 제공될 것이다.

28. Winter Sports Program에 관한 다음 안내문의 내용과 일치하는 것은?

Winter Sports Program
Winter is coming! Let's have some fun together!

Time & Location
- Every Sunday in December from 1 p.m. to 3 p.m.
- Grand Blue Ice Rink

Lesson Details
- Ice Hockey, Speed Skating, and Figure Skating
- Participants must be 8 years of age or older.

Fee
- Ice Hockey: $200
- Speed Skating / Figure Skating: $150

Notice
- Skates and helmets will be provided for free.
- You should bring your own gloves.

※ For more information, visit www.wintersports.com.

① 오후 2시에서 4시 사이에 실시된다.
② 네 종목의 강좌가 개설된다.
③ 참가 연령에 제한은 없다.
④ 모든 종목 강좌의 수강료는 같다.
⑤ 장갑은 각자 가져와야 한다.

29. 다음 글의 밑줄 친 부분 중, 어법상 틀린 것은? [3점]

The hunter-gatherer lifestyle, which can ① be described as "natural" to human beings, appears to have had much to recommend it. Examination of human remains from early hunter-gatherer societies ② has suggested that our ancestors enjoyed abundant food, obtainable without excessive effort, and suffered very few diseases. If this is true, it is not clear why so many humans settled in permanent villages and developed agriculture, growing crops and domesticating animals: cultivating fields was hard work, and it was in farming villages ③ what epidemic diseases first took root. Whatever its immediate effect on the lives of humans, the development of settlements and agriculture ④ undoubtedly led to a high increase in population density. This period, known as the New Stone Age, was a major turning point in human development, ⑤ opening the way to the growth of the first towns and cities, and eventually leading to settled "civilizations."

＊remains: 유적, 유해 ＊＊epidemic: 전염병의

30. 다음 글의 밑줄 친 부분 중, 문맥상 낱말의 쓰임이 적절하지 않은 것은? [3점]

Many human and non-human animals save commodities or money for future consumption. This behavior seems to reveal a preference of a ① delayed reward over an immediate one: the agent gives up some immediate pleasure in exchange for a future one. Thus the discounted value of the future reward should be ② greater than the un-discounted value of the present one. However, in some cases the agent does not wait for the envisioned occasion but uses their savings ③ prematurely. For example, early in the year an employee might set aside money to buy Christmas presents but then spend it on a summer vacation instead. Such cases could be examples of ④ weakness of will. That is, the agents may judge or resolve to spend their savings in a certain way for the greatest benefit but then act differently when temptation for immediate pleasure ⑤ disappears.

＊envision: 계획하다

[31~34] 다음 빈칸에 들어갈 말로 가장 적절한 것을 고르시오.

31. The costs of _____ are well-documented. Martin Luther King Jr. lamented them when he described "that lovely poem that didn't get written because someone knocked on the door." Perhaps the most famous literary example happened in 1797 when Samuel Taylor Coleridge started writing his poem *Kubla Khan* from a dream he had but then was visited by an unexpected guest. For Coleridge, by coincidence, the untimely visitor came at a particularly bad time. He forgot his inspiration and left the work unfinished. While there are many documented cases of sudden disruptions that have had significant consequences for professionals in critical roles such as doctors, nurses, control room operators, stock traders, and pilots, they also impact most of us in our everyday lives, slowing down work productivity and generally increasing stress levels.

＊lament: 슬퍼하다

① misunderstandings   ② interruptions
③ inequalities   ④ regulations
⑤ arguments

32. There's a lot of scientific evidence demonstrating that focused attention leads to _____. In animals rewarded for noticing sound (to hunt or to avoid being hunted for example), we find much larger auditory centers in the brain. In animals rewarded for sharp eyesight, the visual areas are larger. Brain scans of violinists provide more evidence, showing dramatic growth and expansion in regions of the cortex that represent the left hand, which has to finger the strings precisely, often at very high speed. Other studies have shown that the hippocampus, which is vital for spatial memory, is enlarged in taxi drivers. The point is that the physical architecture of the brain changes according to where we direct our attention and what we practice doing.

＊cortex: (대뇌) 피질(皮質) ＊＊hippocampus: (대뇌 측두엽의) 해마

① improved decision making
② the reshaping of the brain
③ long-term mental tiredness
④ the development of hand skills
⑤ increased levels of self-control

33. How did the human mind evolve? One possibility is that _____ caused our brains to evolve the way they did. A human tribe that could out-think its enemies, even slightly, possessed a vital advantage. The ability of your tribe to imagine and predict where and when a hostile enemy tribe might strike, and plan accordingly, gives your tribe a significant military advantage. The human mind became a weapon in the struggle for survival, a weapon far more decisive than any before it. And this mental advantage was applied, over and over, within each succeeding generation. The tribe that could out-think its opponents was more likely to succeed in battle and would then pass on the genes responsible for this mental advantage to its offspring. You and I are the descendants of the winners. [3점]

① physical power to easily hunt prey
② individual responsibility in one's inner circle
③ instinctive tendency to avoid natural disasters
④ superiority in the number of one's descendants
⑤ competition and conflicts with other human tribes

34. To find the hidden potential in teams, instead of brainstorming, we're better off shifting to a process called brainwriting. The initial steps are solo. You start by asking everyone to generate ideas separately. Next, you pool them and share them anonymously among the group. To preserve independent judgment, each member evaluates them on their own. Only then does the team come together to select and refine the most promising options. By _____ before choosing and elaborating them, teams can surface and advance possibilities that might not get attention otherwise. This brainwriting process makes sure that all ideas are brought to the table and all voices are brought into the conversation. It is especially effective in groups that struggle to achieve collective intelligence. [3점]

* anonymously: 익명으로 ** surface: 드러내다

① developing and assessing ideas individually
② presenting and discussing ideas out loud
③ assigning different roles to each member
④ coming to an agreement on these options
⑤ skipping the step of judging these options

35. 다음 글에서 전체 흐름과 관계 <u>없는</u> 문장은?

Simply giving employees a sense of agency—a feeling that they are in control, that they have genuine decision-making authority—can radically increase how much energy and focus they bring to their jobs. ① One 2010 study at a manufacturing plant in Ohio, for instance, carefully examined assembly-line workers who were empowered to make small decisions about their schedules and work environment. ② They designed their own uniforms and had authority over shifts while all the manufacturing processes and pay scales stayed the same. ③ It led to decreased efficiency because their decisions were not uniform or focused on meeting organizational goals. ④ Within two months, productivity at the plant increased by 20 percent, with workers taking shorter breaks and making fewer mistakes. ⑤ Giving employees a sense of control improved how much self-discipline they brought to their jobs.

* radically: 급격하게 ** shift: (근무) 교대

[36~37] 주어진 글 다음에 이어질 글의 순서로 가장 적절한 것을 고르시오.

36.

As businesses shift some core business activities to digital, such as sales, marketing, or archiving, it is assumed that the impact on the environment will be less negative.

(A) When we store bigger data on clouds, increased carbon emissions make our green clouds gray. The carbon footprint of an email is smaller than mail sent via a post office, but still, it causes four grams of CO_2, and it can be as much as 50 grams if the attachment is big.

(B) However, digital business activities can still threaten the environment. In some cases, the harm of digital businesses can be even more hazardous. A few decades ago, offices used to have much more paper waste since all documents were paper based.

(C) When workplaces shifted from paper to digital documents, invoices, and emails, it was a promising step to save trees. However, the cost of the Internet and electricity for the environment is neglected. A recent *Wired* report declared that most data centers' energy source is fossil fuels. [3점]

① (A) – (C) – (B)   ② (B) – (A) – (C)
③ (B) – (C) – (A)   ④ (C) – (A) – (B)
⑤ (C) – (B) – (A)

37.

> Problems often arise if an exotic species is suddenly introduced to an ecosystem.

(A) The grey had the edge because it can adapt its diet; it is able, for instance, to eat green acorns, while the red can only digest mature acorns. Within the same area of forest, grey squirrels can destroy the food supply before red squirrels even have a bite.

(B) Britain's red and grey squirrels provide a clear example. When the grey arrived from America in the 1870s, both squirrel species competed for the same food and habitat, which put the native red squirrel populations under pressure.

(C) Greys can also live more densely and in varied habitats, so have survived more easily when woodland has been destroyed. As a result, the red squirrel has come close to extinction in England.

* edge: 우위 ** acorn: 도토리

① (A) − (C) − (B)
② (B) − (A) − (C)
③ (B) − (C) − (A)
④ (C) − (A) − (B)
⑤ (C) − (B) − (A)

[38~39] 글의 흐름으로 보아, 주어진 문장이 들어가기에 가장 적절한 곳을 고르시오.

38.

> Farmers, on the other hand, could live in the same place year after year and did not have to worry about transporting young children long distances.

Growing crops forced people to stay in one place. Hunter−gatherers typically moved around frequently, and they had to be able to carry all their possessions with them every time they moved. (①) In particular, mothers had to carry their young children. (②) As a result, hunter−gatherer mothers could have only one baby every four years or so, spacing their births so that they never had to carry more than one child at a time. (③) Societies that settled down in one place were able to shorten their birth intervals from four years to about two. (④) This meant that each woman could have more children than her hunter−gatherer counterpart, which in turn resulted in rapid population growth among farming communities. (⑤) An increased population was actually an advantage to agricultural societies, because farming required large amounts of human labor.

* counterpart: (대응 관계에 있는) 상대

39.

> By comparison, birds with the longest childhoods, and those that migrate with their parents, tend to have the most efficient migration routes.

Spending time as children allows animals to learn about their environment. Without childhood, animals must rely more fully on hardware, and therefore be less flexible. (①) Among migratory bird species, those that are born knowing how, when, and where to migrate — those that are migrating entirely with instructions they were born with — sometimes have very inefficient migration routes. (②) These birds, born knowing how to migrate, don't adapt easily. (③) So when lakes dry up, forest becomes farmland, or climate change pushes breeding grounds farther north, those birds that are born knowing how to migrate keep flying by the old rules and maps. (④) Childhood facilitates the passing on of cultural information, and culture can evolve faster than genes. (⑤) Childhood gives flexibility in a changing world. [3점]

40. 다음 글의 내용을 한 문장으로 요약하고자 한다. 빈칸 (A), (B)에 들어갈 말로 가장 적절한 것은?

> Over the last several decades, scholars have developed standards for how best to create, organize, present, and preserve digital information for future generations. What has remained neglected for the most part, however, are the needs of people with disabilities. As a result, many of the otherwise most valuable digital resources are useless for people who are deaf or hard of hearing, as well as for people who are blind, have low vision, or have difficulty distinguishing particular colors. While professionals working in educational technology and commercial web design have made significant progress in meeting the needs of such users, some scholars creating digital projects all too often fail to take these needs into account. This situation would be much improved if more projects embraced the idea that we should always keep the largest possible audience in mind as we make design decisions, ensuring that our final product serves the needs of those with disabilities as well as those without.

↓

> The needs of people with disabilities have often been ____(A)____ in digital projects, which could be changed by adopting a(n) ____(B)____ design.

	(A)		(B)
①	overlooked	......	inclusive
②	accepted	......	practical
③	considered	......	inclusive
④	accepted	......	abstract
⑤	overlooked	......	abstract

[41~42] 다음 글을 읽고, 물음에 답하시오.

All humans, to an extent, seek activities that cause a degree of pain in order to experience pleasure, whether this is found in spicy food, strong massages, or stepping into a too-cold or too-hot bath. The key is that it is a 'safe threat'. The brain perceives the stimulus to be painful but ultimately (a) non-threatening. Interestingly, this could be similar to the way humor works: a 'safe threat' that causes pleasure by playfully violating norms. We feel uncomfortable, but safe. In this context, where (b) survival is clearly not in danger, the desire for pain is actually the desire for a reward, not suffering or punishment. This reward-like effect comes from the feeling of mastery over the pain. The closer you look at your chilli-eating habit, the more remarkable it seems. When the active ingredient of chillies—capsaicin—touches the tongue, it stimulates exactly the same receptor that is activated when any of these tissues are burned. Knowing that our body is firing off danger signals, but that we are actually completely safe, (c) produces pleasure. All children start off hating chilli, but many learn to derive pleasure from it through repeated exposure and knowing that they will never experience any real (d) joy. Interestingly, seeking pain for the pain itself appears to be (e) uniquely human. The only way scientists have trained animals to have a preference for chilli or to self-harm is to have the pain always directly associated with a pleasurable reward.

41. 윗글의 제목으로 가장 적절한 것은?

① The Secret Behind Painful Pleasures
② How 'Safe Threat' Changes into Real Pain
③ What Makes You Stronger, Pleasure or Pain?
④ How Does Your Body Detect Danger Signals?
⑤ Recipes to Change Picky Children's Eating Habits

42. 밑줄 친 (a)~(e) 중에서 문맥상 낱말의 쓰임이 적절하지 않은 것은?

① (a)　② (b)　③ (c)　④ (d)　⑤ (e)

[43~45] 다음 글을 읽고, 물음에 답하시오.

(A)

An airplane flew high above the deep blue seas far from any land. Flying the small plane was a student pilot who was sitting alongside an experienced flight instructor. As the student looked out the window, (a) she was filled with wonder and appreciation for the beauty of the world. Her instructor, meanwhile, waited patiently for the right time to start a surprise flight emergency training exercise.

(B)

Then, the student carefully flew low enough to see if she could find any ships making their way across the surface of the ocean. Now the instructor and the student could see some ships. Although the ships were far apart, they were all sailing in a line. With the line of ships in view, the student could see the way to home and safety. The student looked at (b) her in relief, who smiled proudly back at her student.

(C)

When the student began to panic, the instructor said, "Stay calm and steady. (c) You can do it." Calm as ever, the instructor told her student, "Difficult times always happen during flight. The most important thing is to focus on your flight in those situations." Those words encouraged the student to focus on flying the aircraft first. "Thank you, I think (d) I can make it," she said, "As I've been trained, I should search for visual markers."

(D)

When the plane hit a bit of turbulence, the instructor pushed a hidden button. Suddenly, all the monitors inside the plane flashed several times then went out completely! Now the student was in control of an airplane that was flying well, but (e) she had no indication of where she was or where she should go. She did have a map, but no other instruments. She was at a loss and then the plane shook again.

* turbulence: 난(亂)기류

43. 주어진 글 (A)에 이어질 내용을 순서에 맞게 배열한 것으로 가장 적절한 것은?

① (B) − (D) − (C)　② (C) − (B) − (D)
③ (C) − (D) − (B)　④ (D) − (B) − (C)
⑤ (D) − (C) − (B)

44. 밑줄 친 (a)~(e) 중에서 가리키는 대상이 나머지 넷과 다른 것은?

① (a)　② (b)　③ (c)　④ (d)　⑤ (e)

45. 윗글에 관한 내용으로 적절하지 않은 것은?

① 교관과 교육생이 소형 비행기에 타고 있었다.
② 배들은 서로 떨어져 있었지만 한 줄을 이루고 있었다.
③ 교관은 어려운 상황에서는 집중이 가장 중요하다고 말했다.
④ 비행기 내부의 모니터가 깜박이다가 다시 정상 작동했다.
⑤ 교육생은 지도 이외의 다른 도구는 가지고 있지 않았다.

* 확인 사항

○ 답안지의 해당란에 필요한 내용을 정확히 기입(표기)했는지 확인 하시오.

18
001 appreciate ⓥ 감사하다
002 support ⓥ 지원
003 available ⓐ 가능한
004 switch ⓥ 전환하다
005 discount ⓝ 할인
006 current ⓐ 현재의
007 subscription ⓝ 구독료
008 access ⓥ 접근하다
009 a full year 만 1년
010 piece ⓝ (신문·잡지에 실린 한 편의) 기사
011 editor ⓝ 편집자
012 article ⓝ 기사

19
013 mailbox ⓝ 우편함
014 beat ⓥ 뛰다
015 rapidly ⓐⓓ 빠르게
016 hold ⓥ 잡다, 쥐다
017 university ⓝ 대학교
018 apply ⓥ 지원하다
019 grade ⓝ 성적, 학점
020 good enough 만족스러운
021 application ⓝ 지원서
022 carefully ⓐⓓ 조심스럽게, 신중히
023 envelope ⓝ 봉투
024 emerge ⓥ 나오다, 나타나다
025 faraway ⓐ 멀리 떨어진, 먼

20
026 messy ⓐ 지저분한
027 negative ⓐ 부정적인
028 feeling ⓝ 감정
029 destructive ⓐ 파괴적인
030 psychologist ⓝ 심리학자
031 disorderly ⓐ 무질서한, 난잡한, 어질러진
032 indicate ⓥ 가리키다
033 disorganized ⓐ 체계적이지 못한
034 expert ⓝ 전문가
035 moment ⓝ 순간
036 perspective ⓝ 관점, 시각
037 surrounding ⓐ 주변
038 positive ⓐ 긍정적인
039 atmosphere ⓝ 분위기
040 follow ⓥ 따라오다
041 efficiently ⓐⓓ 효과적으로
042 neatly ⓐⓓ 깔끔하게
043 closet ⓝ 벽장
044 drawer ⓝ 서랍
045 arrange ⓥ 정리하다, 배열하다

21
046 soil ⓝ 토양, 흙
047 farm ⓝ 농장
048 perfect ⓐ 완벽한
049 monoculture ⓝ 단일 작물 재배
050 achieve ⓥ 달성하다
051 nutrient ⓝ 영양소, 영양분
052 fertilizer ⓝ 비료
053 irrigation ⓝ 관개, 물 대기
054 crop ⓝ 작물
055 efficient ⓐ 효과적인

056 supply ⓥ 제공하다
057 amount ⓝ 양
058 capacity ⓝ 능력
059 luxurious ⓐ 사치스러운, 호화로운
060 agricultural ⓐ 농업의
061 undesirable ⓐ 바람직스럽지 못한, 달갑지 않은
062 relative ⓐ 비교상의
063 surround ⓥ 둘러싸다, 에워싸다
064 real estate 부동산

22
065 care ⓥ 관심을 가지다
066 notice ⓥ 알아차리다
067 lonely ⓐ 외로운
068 social ⓐ 사회적인
069 owe ⓥ 빚지다
070 attention ⓝ 관심
071 ignore ⓥ 무시하다
072 pass by 지나가다

23
073 often ⓐⓓ 흔히, 종종, 자주
074 cut ⓝ 지름길
075 challenge ⓝ 도전
076 route ⓝ 길
077 fail ⓥ 실패하다
078 acquire ⓥ 얻다, 획득하다
079 strength ⓝ 힘, 기운
080 compete ⓥ 경쟁하다
081 mastery ⓝ 숙달
082 area ⓝ 영역
083 tool ⓝ 도구
084 useful ⓐ 유용한
085 prosperity ⓝ 번영
086 successful ⓐ 성공한, 성공적인
087 hardship ⓝ 고난
088 preparation ⓝ 준비
089 strategy ⓝ 계획, 전략
090 lesson ⓝ 교훈
091

24
092 usually ⓐⓓ 보통, 대개
093 reflection ⓝ 반영
094 identity ⓝ 정체성
095 indication ⓝ 지시, 암시
096 type ⓝ 유형, 종류
097 consciously ⓐⓓ 의식적으로
098 research ⓝ 연구
099 particular ⓐ 특정한
100 aspect ⓝ 측면
101 according to (지시·합의 등에) 따라
102 belief ⓝ 믿음, 확신, 신념
103 voter ⓝ 투표자, 유권자
104 similarly ⓐⓓ 비슷하게
105 accept ⓥ 받아들이다
106 convince ⓥ 설득하다
107 train ⓥ 훈련하다
108 pursue ⓥ 추구하다

25
109 electronic ⓐ 전자의

110 collection ⓝ 수집, 수거
111 recycling ⓝ 재활용
112 rate ⓝ 비율, -율
113 region ⓝ 지역
114 rank ⓥ (등급·등위·순위) 차지하다
115 respectively ⓐⓓ 각각
116 remain ⓥ 남다

26
117 memorable ⓐ 기억할만한
118 astrophysicist ⓝ 천체물리학자
119 coin ⓥ (단어를) 발명하다
120 term ⓝ 말, 전문어, 용어
121 supernova ⓝ 초신성
122 emigrate ⓥ 이주하다, 이민을 가다
123 develop ⓥ 발달시키다
124 numerous ⓐ 수많은
125 theory ⓝ 이론
126 astronomy ⓝ 천문학
127 patent ⓝ 특허권
128 propulsion ⓝ 추진력

27
129 gourmet ⓝ 미식가
130 competition ⓝ 경쟁
131 cookbook ⓝ 요리책
132 dust ⓝ 먼지
133 participate ⓥ 참여하다
134 category ⓝ 분류
135 enter ⓥ 응시하다, 출전하다
136 souvenir ⓝ 기념품

28
137 provide ⓥ 제공하다
138 bring ⓥ 가져오다
139 glove ⓝ 장갑
140 information ⓝ 정보

29
141 hunter-gatherer 수렵·채집인
142 lifestyle ⓝ 생활 방식
143 natural ⓐ 자연적인
144 appear ⓥ ~인 것같이 보이다
145 recommend ⓥ 추천하다
146 examination ⓝ 조사
147 remains ⓝ 유적, 유해
148 ancestor ⓝ 조상, 선조
149 abundant ⓐ 풍부한
150 obtainable ⓐ 얻을 수 있는
151 excessive ⓐ 지나친, 과도한
152 effort ⓝ 노력
153 suffer ⓥ 겪다
154 disease ⓝ 질병, 질환
155 settle ⓥ 정착하다
156 permanent ⓐ 영구적인
157 village ⓝ 마을
158 agriculture ⓝ 농업
159 domesticate ⓥ 길들이다
160 cultivate ⓥ 경작하다, 일구다
161 epidemic ⓝ 전염병
162 settlement ⓝ 정착지
163 increase ⓝ 증가

164 population density 인구 밀도
165 period ⓝ 시기
166 New Stone Age 신석기 시대
167 turning point 전환점
168 eventually ⓐⓓ 결국, 드디어
169 civilization ⓝ 문명

30
170 commodity ⓝ 상품
171 consumption ⓝ 소비
172 behavior ⓝ 행동
173 reveal ⓥ 드러내다
174 preference ⓝ 선호
175 reward ⓝ 보상
176 immediate ⓐ 즉각적인
177 agent ⓝ 행위자
178 exchange ⓥ 교환하다
179 discounted ⓐ 할인된
180 value ⓝ 가치
181 case ⓝ 경우, 사례
182 wait ⓥ 기다리다
183 envision ⓥ 계획하다
184 occasion ⓝ 기회
185 instead ⓐⓓ 대신에
186 judge ⓥ 판단하다
187 resolve ⓥ 결심하다
188 benefit ⓝ 이익
189 temptation ⓝ 유혹

31
190 cost ⓝ 비용
191 interruption ⓝ 방해
192 lament ⓥ 애통하다, 슬퍼하다
193 describe ⓥ 묘사하다
194 poem ⓝ 시(詩)
195 famous ⓐ 유명한
196 literary ⓐ 문학적인
197 unexpected ⓐ 예기치 않은, 뜻밖의
198 guest ⓝ 손님
199 untimely ⓐⓓ 때에 맞지 않게
200 visitor ⓝ 방문객
201 particularly ⓐⓓ 특히, 특별히
202 inspiration ⓝ 영감

32
203 scientific ⓐ 과학적인
204 evidence ⓝ 증거
205 demonstrate ⓥ 입증하다
206 attention ⓝ 집중
207 auditory ⓐ 청각의
208 sharp ⓐ 예리한, 날카로운
209 eyesight ⓝ 시력
210 visual ⓐ 시각의
211 dramatic ⓐ 극적인
212 growth ⓝ 성장
213 expansion ⓝ 확장
214 cortex ⓝ 대뇌피질
215 represent ⓥ 나타내다
216 string ⓝ (악기의) 현(絃), 끈, 줄
217 precisely ⓐⓓ 정확하게
218 hippocampus ⓝ 해마
219 vital ⓐ 필수적인

220 □ spatial ⓐ 공간의, 공간적인
221 □ enlarge ⓥ 확대되다
222 □ physical ⓐ 물리적인
223 □ architecture ⓝ 구조, 구성
224 □ practice ⓥ 연습하다

33

225 □ evolve ⓥ 진화하다
226 □ possibility ⓝ 가능성
227 □ conflict ⓝ 갈등
228 □ tribe ⓝ 부족
229 □ enemy ⓝ 적
230 □ slightly [ad] 약간, 조금
231 □ possess ⓥ 점유하다, 소유하다, 가지다
232 □ advantage ⓝ 장점
233 □ imagine ⓥ 상상하다
234 □ predict ⓥ 예측하다
235 □ hostile ⓐ 적대적인
236 □ strike ⓥ 공격하다
237 □ accordingly [ad] (상황에) 부응해서, 그에 맞춰
238 □ significant ⓐ 중요한
239 □ military ⓐ 군사의
240 □ weapon ⓝ 무기
241 □ decisive ⓐ 결정적인
242 □ mental ⓐ 정신적인
243 □ over and over 반복해서
244 □ generation ⓝ 세대
245 □ opponent ⓝ 상대
246 □ battle ⓝ 전투
247 □ gene ⓝ 유전자
248 □ responsible ⓐ 책임지고 있는, 책임이 있는
249 □ offspring ⓝ 자식, 자손
250 □ descendant ⓝ 후손

34

251 □ hidden ⓐ 숨겨진
252 □ potential ⓝ 가능성
253 □ shift ⓥ 바꾸다
254 □ generate ⓥ 만들어 내다
255 □ separately [ad] 개별적으로
256 □ pool ⓥ 모으다
257 □ anonymously [ad] 익명으로
258 □ independent ⓐ 독립적인, 독립된
259 □ judgment ⓝ 판단
260 □ evaluate ⓥ 평가하다
261 □ select ⓥ 고르다, 선택하다
262 □ refine ⓥ 다듬다, 정제하다
263 □ promising ⓐ 유망한
264 □ elaborate ⓥ 잘 다듬다
265 □ surface ⓥ 드러내다
266 □ conversation ⓝ 대화
267 □ struggle ⓥ 다투다
268 □ collective ⓐ 집단의
269 □ intelligence ⓝ 지성

35

270 □ employee ⓝ 직원
271 □ agency ⓝ 주인
272 □ control ⓥ 통제하다
273 □ genuine ⓐ 진짜의
274 □ decision-making 의사 결정
275 □ authority ⓝ 권한
276 □ radically [ad] 급진적으로
277 □ plant ⓝ 공장
278 □ examine ⓥ 검사하다
279 □ assembly-line ⓐ 조립 라인의
280 □ empower ⓥ 권한을 주다
281 □ decision ⓝ 결정
282 □ schedule ⓝ 일정, 스케줄
283 □ work environment 작업환경
284 □ manufacturing processes 제조 공정
285 □ pay scale 급여 체계
286 □ stay ⓥ 머무르다, 그대로 있다
287 □ decrease ⓥ 줄다, 감소하다
288 □ efficiency ⓝ 효율성, 능률
289 □ organizational ⓐ 조직의
290 □ goal ⓝ 목표
291 □ productivity ⓝ 생산성
292 □ break ⓝ 휴식
293 □ mistake ⓝ 실수, 잘못

36

294 □ core ⓐ 핵심적인, 가장 중요한
295 □ activity ⓝ 활동
296 □ archiving ⓝ 파일 보관
297 □ environment ⓝ 환경
298 □ emission ⓝ 배출
299 □ carbon footprint 탄소 발자국
300 □ attachment ⓝ (이메일의) 첨부 파일
301 □ threaten ⓥ 위협하다
302 □ hazardous ⓐ 위험한
303 □ decade ⓝ 10년
304 □ waste ⓝ 쓰레기
305 □ document ⓝ 자료
306 □ workplace ⓝ 직장
307 □ invoice ⓝ 청구서
308 □ electricity ⓝ 전기
309 □ neglect ⓥ 방치하다, 간과하다
310 □ declare ⓥ 발표하다, 밝히다

37

311 □ exotic species 외래종
312 □ suddenly [ad] 갑자기
313 □ introduce ⓥ 소개하다
314 □ edge ⓝ 우위
315 □ for instance 예를 들어
316 □ ecosystem ⓝ 생태계
317 □ acorn ⓝ 도토리
318 □ digest ⓥ 소화하다, 소화시키다
319 □ mature ⓐ 익은, 성숙한
320 □ forest ⓝ 숲, 삼림
321 □ destroy ⓥ 파괴하다, 말살하다
322 □ supply ⓝ 공급
323 □ bite ⓥ 베어 물다
324 □ survive ⓥ 살아남다
325 □ woodland ⓝ 삼림 지대
326 □ as a result 결과적으로
327 □ extinction ⓝ 멸종

38

328 □ on the other hand 반면에, 다른 한편으로는
329 □ year after year 해마다, 매년
330 □ transport ⓥ 이송하다
331 □ distance ⓝ 거리
332 □ typically [ad] 일반적으로
333 □ frequently [ad] 자주
334 □ carry ⓥ 휴대하다, 가지고 다니다
335 □ possession ⓝ 소유물, 소지품
336 □ spacing ⓝ 간격
337 □ birth ⓝ 출산
338 □ at a time 한 번에
339 □ settled ⓐ 정착한
340 □ interval ⓝ 간격
341 □ counterpart ⓝ 상대
342 □ rapid ⓐ 빠른
343 □ population ⓝ 인구
344 □ agricultural society 농경 사회, 농업사회
345 □ labor ⓝ 노동

39

346 □ comparison ⓝ 비교
347 □ childhood ⓝ 유년기
348 □ migrate ⓥ 이주하다
349 □ migration ⓝ 이주
350 □ flexible ⓐ 유연한
351 □ migratory bird 철새
352 □ entirely [ad] 전적으로
353 □ instruction ⓝ 지시, 명령
354 □ inefficient ⓐ 비효율적인
355 □ adapt ⓥ 적응하다
356 □ dry up (강·호수 등이) 바싹 마르다
357 □ climate change 기후 변화
358 □ breeding ground (야생 동물의) 번식지
359 □ facilitate ⓥ 촉진하다
360 □ flexibility ⓝ 유연성

40

361 □ scholar ⓝ 학자
362 □ organize ⓥ 정리하다
363 □ present ⓥ 제공하다
364 □ preserve ⓥ 보존하다
365 □ disability ⓝ 장애
366 □ valuable ⓐ 가치가 큰, 소중한
367 □ resource ⓝ 원천
368 □ useless ⓐ 소용없는, 쓸모없는
369 □ distinguish ⓥ 구별하다
370 □ situation ⓝ 상황
371 □ improve ⓥ 개선되다, 나아지다
372 □ embrace ⓥ 받아들이다, 포옹하다
373 □ audience ⓝ 청중

41~42

374 □ extent ⓝ 정도
375 □ seek ⓥ 찾다
376 □ degree ⓝ 정도
377 □ pain ⓝ 고통
378 □ pleasure ⓝ 즐거움
379 □ spicy ⓐ 매운
380 □ step ⓥ 움직이다
381 □ threat ⓝ 협박, 위협
382 □ perceive ⓥ 인지하다
383 □ stimulus ⓝ 자극
384 □ painful ⓐ 고통스러운, 아픈
385 □ ultimately [ad] 궁극적으로, 결국
386 □ interestingly [ad] 흥미있게, 재미있게
387 □ similar ⓐ 비슷한, 유사한
388 □ playfully [ad] 장난삼아, 재미있게
389 □ violate ⓥ 위반하다, 침해하다
390 □ norm ⓝ 규범
391 □ uncomfortable ⓐ 불편한, 불쾌한
392 □ context ⓝ (어떤 일의) 정황, 배경, 환경
393 □ desire ⓝ 욕구, 갈망
394 □ suffering ⓝ 고통
395 □ punishment ⓝ 처벌, 형벌
396 □ remarkable ⓐ 놀랄 만한, 놀라운
397 □ ingredient ⓝ 성분
398 □ receptor ⓝ 수용체
399 □ tissue ⓝ 조직
400 □ burn ⓥ 태우다
401 □ completely [ad] 완전히

43~45

402 □ alongside [prep] ~옆에, 나란히
403 □ experienced ⓐ 경험이 있는, 능숙한
404 □ instructor ⓝ 교관
405 □ wonder ⓝ 궁금증
406 □ appreciation ⓝ 감사
407 □ meanwhile [ad] 그 동안에
408 □ patiently [ad] 침착하게
409 □ emergency ⓝ 긴급 상황
410 □ relief ⓝ 안도
411 □ panic ⓥ 당황하다, 공포에 질리다
412 □ aircraft ⓝ 비행기
413 □ turbulence ⓝ 난기류

● 채점 : 맞은 개수 _____ / 80

TEST A-B 각 단어의 뜻을 [A] 영어는 우리말로, [B] 우리말은 영어로 쓰시오.

A	English	Korean	B	Korean	English
01	envision		01	부족	
02	article		02	전환하다	
03	indication		03	증거	
04	emission		04	안도	
05	patent		05	간격	
06	declare		06	지원하다	
07	atmosphere		07	비교	
08	beat		08	능력	
09	distinguish		09	이주하다	
10	auditory		10	다투다	
11	inspiration		11	빠른	
12	describe		12	노동	
13	reveal		13	생태계	
14	route		14	파괴적인	
15	emergency		15	처벌, 형벌	
16	rapidly		16	자료	
17	preference		17	보존하다	
18	appreciate		18	기념품	
19	surrounding		19	제공하다	
20	examine		20	고난	

▶ A-D 정답 : 해설편 061쪽

TEST C-D 각 단어의 뜻을 골라 기호를 쓰시오.

C	English			Korean	D	Korean			English
01	pass by	(	)	ⓐ 지저분한	01	정착한	(	)	ⓐ coin
02	scholar	(	)	ⓑ 확장	02	위험한	(	)	ⓑ threat
03	descendant	(	)	ⓒ 번영	03	궁금증	(	)	ⓒ dry up
04	gourmet	(	)	ⓓ 미식가	04	침착하게	(	)	ⓓ facilitate
05	interruption	(	)	ⓔ 비슷하게	05	가져오다	(	)	ⓔ wonder
06	hostile	(	)	ⓕ 입증하다	06	권한	(	)	ⓕ epidemic
07	mastery	(	)	ⓖ 방해	07	(단어를) 발명하다	(	)	ⓖ seek
08	similarly	(	)	ⓗ 소화하다, 소화시키다	08	비행기	(	)	ⓗ patiently
09	digest	(	)	ⓘ 영구적인	09	찾다	(	)	ⓘ owe
10	demonstrate	(	)	ⓙ 결심하다	10	즉각적인	(	)	ⓙ settled
11	permanent	(	)	ⓚ 후손	11	촉진하다	(	)	ⓚ enlarge
12	opponent	(	)	ⓛ 숙달	12	추진력	(	)	ⓛ bring
13	lament	(	)	ⓜ 지나가다	13	조직	(	)	ⓜ disability
14	prosperity	(	)	ⓝ 주인	14	빚지다	(	)	ⓝ tissue
15	expansion	(	)	ⓞ 슬퍼하다	15	확대되다	(	)	ⓞ hazardous
16	bite	(	)	ⓟ 적대적인	16	각각	(	)	ⓟ immediate
17	resolve	(	)	ⓠ 핵심적인, 가장 중요한	17	협박, 위협	(	)	ⓠ authority
18	messy	(	)	ⓡ 베어 물다	18	장애	(	)	ⓡ propulsion
19	core	(	)	ⓢ 상대	19	전염병의	(	)	ⓢ aircraft
20	agency	(	)	ⓣ 학자	20	바싹 마르다	(	)	ⓣ respectively

※ 영어 [독해] 파트만 수록한 문제지이므로 18번부터 시작합니다.　　● 점수 표시가 없는 문항은 모두 **2점**　● 문항수 **28개** | 배점 **63점** | 제한 시간 **45분**

18. 다음 글의 목적으로 가장 적절한 것은?

ACC Travel Agency Customers:

Have you ever wanted to enjoy a holiday in nature? This summer is the best time to turn your dream into reality. We have a perfect travel package for you. This travel package includes special trips to Lake Madison as well as massage and meditation to help you relax. Also, we provide yoga lessons taught by experienced instructors. If you book this package, you will enjoy all this at a reasonable price. We are sure that it will be an unforgettable experience for you. If you call us, we will be happy to give you more details.

① 여행 일정 변경을 안내하려고
② 패키지 여행 상품을 홍보하려고
③ 여행 상품 불만족에 대해 사과하려고
④ 여행 만족도 조사 참여를 부탁하려고
⑤ 패키지 여행 업무 담당자를 모집하려고

19. 다음 글에 드러난 'I'의 심경 변화로 가장 적절한 것은?

When I woke up in our hotel room, it was almost midnight. I didn't see my husband nor daughter. I called them, but I heard their phones ringing in the room. Feeling worried, I went outside and walked down the street, but they were nowhere to be found. When I decided I should ask someone for help, a crowd nearby caught my attention. I approached, hoping to find my husband and daughter, and suddenly I saw two familiar faces. I smiled, feeling calm. Just then, my daughter saw me and called, "Mom!" They were watching the magic show. Finally, I felt all my worries disappear.

① anxious　　　 → relieved　　② delighted → unhappy
③ indifferent　 → excited　　　④ relaxed　　 → upset
⑤ embarrassed → proud

20. 다음 글에서 필자가 주장하는 바로 가장 적절한 것은?

Research shows that people who work have two calendars: one for work and one for their personal lives. Although it may seem sensible, having two separate calendars for work and personal life can lead to distractions. To check if something is missing, you will find yourself checking your to-do lists multiple times. Instead, organize all of your tasks in one place. It doesn't matter if you use digital or paper media. It's okay to keep your professional and personal tasks in one place. This will give you a good idea of how time is divided between work and home. This will allow you to make informed decisions about which tasks are most important.

① 결정한 것은 반드시 실행하도록 노력하라.
② 자신이 담당한 업무에 관한 전문성을 확보하라.
③ 업무 집중도를 높이기 위해 책상 위를 정돈하라.
④ 좋은 아이디어를 메모하는 습관을 길러라.
⑤ 업무와 개인 용무를 한 곳에 정리하라.

21. 밑줄 친 become unpaid ambassadors가 다음 글에서 의미하는 바로 가장 적절한 것은?

Why do you care how a customer reacts to a purchase? Good question. By understanding post-purchase behavior, you can understand the influence and the likelihood of whether a buyer will repurchase the product (and whether she will keep it or return it). You'll also determine whether the buyer will encourage others to purchase the product from you. Satisfied customers can become unpaid ambassadors for your business, so customer satisfaction should be on the top of your to-do list. People tend to believe the opinions of people they know. People trust friends over advertisements any day. They know that advertisements are paid to tell the "good side" and that they're used to persuade them to purchase products and services. By continually monitoring your customer's satisfaction after the sale, you have the ability to avoid negative word-of-mouth advertising.

① recommend products to others for no gain
② offer manufacturers feedback on products
③ become people who don't trust others' words
④ get rewards for advertising products overseas
⑤ buy products without worrying about the price

22. 다음 글의 요지로 가장 적절한 것은?

The promise of a computerized society, we were told, was that it would pass to machines all of the repetitive drudgery of work, allowing us humans to pursue higher purposes and to have more leisure time. It didn't work out this way. Instead of more time, most of us have less. Companies large and small have off-loaded work onto the backs of consumers. Things that used to be done for us, as part of the value-added service of working with a company, we are now expected to do ourselves. With air travel, we're now expected to complete our own reservations and check-in, jobs that used to be done by airline employees or travel agents. At the grocery store, we're expected to bag our own groceries and, in some supermarkets, to scan our own purchases.

* drudgery: 고된 일

① 컴퓨터 기반 사회에서는 여가 시간이 더 늘어난다.
② 회사 업무의 전산화는 업무 능률을 향상시킨다.
③ 컴퓨터화된 사회에서 소비자는 더 많은 일을 하게 된다.
④ 온라인 거래가 모든 소비자들을 만족시키기에는 한계가 있다.
⑤ 산업의 발전으로 인해 기계가 인간의 일자리를 대신하고 있다.

23. 다음 글의 주제로 가장 적절한 것은?

We tend to believe that we possess a host of socially desirable characteristics, and that we are free of most of those that are socially undesirable. For example, a large majority of the general public thinks that they are more intelligent, more fair-minded, less prejudiced, and more skilled behind the wheel of an automobile than the average person. This phenomenon is so reliable and ubiquitous that it has come to be known as the "Lake Wobegon effect," after Garrison Keillor's fictional community where "the women are strong, the men are good-looking, and all the children are above average." A survey of one million high school seniors found that 70% thought they were above average in leadership ability, and only 2% thought they were below average. In terms of ability to get along with others, *all* students thought they were above average, 60% thought they were in the top 10%, and 25% thought they were in the top 1%!

* ubiquitous: 도처에 있는

① importance of having a positive self-image as a leader
② our common belief that we are better than average
③ our tendency to think others are superior to us
④ reasons why we always try to be above average
⑤ danger of prejudice in building healthy social networks

24. 다음 글의 제목으로 가장 적절한 것은?

Few people will be surprised to hear that poverty tends to create stress: a 2006 study published in the American journal *Psychosomatic Medicine*, for example, noted that a lower socioeconomic status was associated with higher levels of stress hormones in the body. However, richer economies have their own distinct stresses. The key issue is time pressure. A 1999 study of 31 countries by American psychologist Robert Levine and Canadian psychologist Ara Norenzayan found that wealthier, more industrialized nations had a faster pace of life — which led to a higher standard of living, but at the same time left the population feeling a constant sense of urgency, as well as being more prone to heart disease. In effect, fast-paced productivity creates wealth, but it also leads people to feel time-poor when they lack the time to relax and enjoy themselves.

* prone: 걸리기 쉬운

① Why Are Even Wealthy Countries Not Free from Stress?
② In Search of the Path to Escaping the Poverty Trap
③ Time Management: Everything You Need to Know
④ How Does Stress Affect Human Bodies?
⑤ Sound Mind Wins the Game of Life!

25. 다음 도표의 내용과 일치하지 <u>않는</u> 것은?

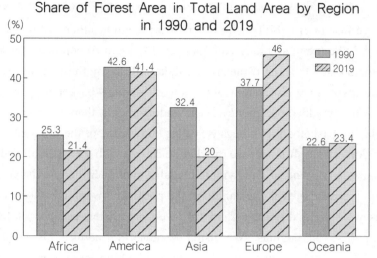

Share of Forest Area in Total Land Area by Region in 1990 and 2019

(%)

Africa: 25.3 (1990), 21.4 (2019)
America: 42.6 (1990), 41.4 (2019)
Asia: 32.4 (1990), 20 (2019)
Europe: 37.7 (1990), 46 (2019)
Oceania: 22.6 (1990), 23.4 (2019)

The above graph shows the share of forest area in total land area by region in 1990 and 2019. ① Africa's share of forest area in total land area was over 20% in both 1990 and 2019. ② The share of forest area in America was 42.6% in 1990, which was larger than that in 2019. ③ The share of forest area in Asia declined from 1990 to 2019 by more than 10 percentage points. ④ In 2019, the share of forest area in Europe was the largest among the five regions, more than three times that in Asia in the same year. ⑤ Oceania showed the smallest gap between 1990 and 2019 in terms of the share of forest area in total land area.

26. Gary Becker에 관한 다음 글의 내용과 일치하지 <u>않는</u> 것은?

Gary Becker was born in Pottsville, Pennsylvania in 1930 and grew up in Brooklyn, New York City. His father, who was not well educated, had a deep interest in financial and political issues. After graduating from high school, Becker went to Princeton University, where he majored in economics. He was dissatisfied with his economic education at Princeton University because "it didn't seem to be handling real problems." He earned a doctor's degree in economics from the University of Chicago in 1955. His doctoral paper on the economics of discrimination was mentioned by the Nobel Prize Committee as an important contribution to economics. Since 1985, Becker had written a regular economics column in *Business Week*, explaining economic analysis and ideas to the general public. In 1992, he was awarded the Nobel Prize in economic science.

* discrimination: 차별

① New York City의 Brooklyn에서 자랐다.
② 아버지는 금융과 정치 문제에 깊은 관심이 있었다.
③ Princeton University에서의 경제학 교육에 만족했다.
④ 1955년에 경제학 박사 학위를 취득했다.
⑤ *Business Week*에 경제학 칼럼을 기고했다.

27. 2023 Drone Racing Championship에 관한 다음 안내문의 내용과 일치하지 <u>않는</u> 것은?

2023 Drone Racing Championship

Are you the best drone racer? Then take the opportunity to prove you are the one!

When & Where
- 6 p.m. — 8 p.m., Sunday, July 9
- Lakeside Community Center

Requirements
- Participants: High school students only
- Bring your own drone for the race.

Prize
- $500 and a medal will be awarded to the winner.

Note
- The first 10 participants will get souvenirs.

For more details, please visit www.droneracing.com or call 313 - 6745 - 1189.

① 7월 9일 일요일에 개최된다.
② 고등학생만 참가할 수 있다.
③ 자신의 드론을 가져와야 한다.
④ 상금과 메달이 우승자에게 수여될 것이다.
⑤ 20명의 참가자가 기념품을 받을 것이다.

28. Summer Scuba Diving One-day Class에 관한 다음 안내문의 내용과 일치하는 것은?

Summer Scuba Diving One-day Class

Join our summer scuba diving lesson for beginners, and become an underwater explorer!

Schedule
- 10:00 - 12:00 Learning the basics
- 13:00 - 16:00 Practicing diving skills in a pool

Price
- Private lesson: $150
- Group lesson (up to 3 people): $100 per person
- Participants can rent our diving equipment for free.

Notice
- Participants must be 10 years old or over.
- Participants must register at least 5 days before the class begins.

For more information, please go to www.ssdiver.com.

① 오후 시간에 바다에서 다이빙 기술을 연습한다.
② 그룹 수업의 최대 정원은 4명이다.
③ 다이빙 장비를 유료로 대여할 수 있다.
④ 연령에 관계없이 참가할 수 있다.
⑤ 적어도 수업 시작 5일 전까지 등록해야 한다.

29. 다음 글의 밑줄 친 부분 중, 어법상 틀린 것은? [3점]

Although praise is one of the most powerful tools available for improving young children's behavior, it is equally powerful for improving your child's self-esteem. Preschoolers believe what their parents tell ① them in a very profound way. They do not yet have the cognitive sophistication to reason ② analytically and reject false information. If a preschool boy consistently hears from his mother ③ that he is smart and a good helper, he is likely to incorporate that information into his self-image. Thinking of himself as a boy who is smart and knows how to do things ④ being likely to make him endure longer in problem-solving efforts and increase his confidence in trying new and difficult tasks. Similarly, thinking of himself as the kind of boy who is a good helper will make him more likely to volunteer ⑤ to help with tasks at home and at preschool.

* profound: 뜻 깊은 ** sophistication: 정교화(함)

30. 다음 글의 밑줄 친 부분 중, 문맥상 낱말의 쓰임이 적절하지 않은 것은?

Advertisers often displayed considerable facility in ① adapting their claims to the market status of the goods they promoted. Fleischmann's yeast, for instance, was used as an ingredient for cooking homemade bread. Yet more and more people in the early 20th century were buying their bread from stores or bakeries, so consumer demand for yeast ② increased. The producer of Fleischmann's yeast hired the J. Walter Thompson advertising agency to come up with a different marketing strategy to ③ boost sales. No longer the "Soul of Bread," the Thompson agency first turned yeast into an important source of vitamins with significant health ④ benefits. Shortly thereafter, the advertising agency transformed yeast into a natural laxative. ⑤ Repositioning yeast helped increase sales.

* laxative: 완하제(배변을 쉽게 하는 약·음식·음료)

[31~34] 다음 빈칸에 들어갈 말로 가장 적절한 것을 고르시오.

31. Individuals who perform at a high level in their profession often have instant credibility with others. People admire them, they want to be like them, and they feel connected to them. When they speak, others listen — even if the area of their skill has nothing to do with the advice they give. Think about a world-famous basketball player. He has made more money from endorsements than he ever did playing basketball. Is it because of his knowledge of the products he endorses? No. It's because of what he can do with a basketball. The same can be said of an Olympic medalist swimmer. People listen to him because of what he can do in the pool. And when an actor tells us we should drive a certain car, we don't listen because of his expertise on engines. We listen because we admire his talent. _____ connects. If you possess a high level of ability in an area, others may desire to connect with you because of it.

* endorsement: (유명인의 텔레비전 등에서의 상품) 보증 선전

① Patience
② Sacrifice
③ Honesty
④ Excellence
⑤ Creativity

32. Think of the brain as a city. If you were to look out over a city and ask "where is the economy located?" you'd see there's no good answer to the question. Instead, the economy emerges from the interaction of all the elements — from the stores and the banks to the merchants and the customers. And so it is with the brain's operation: it doesn't happen in one spot. Just as in a city, no neighborhood of the brain _____. In brains and in cities, everything emerges from the interaction between residents, at all scales, locally and distantly. Just as trains bring materials and textiles into a city, which become processed into the economy, so the raw electrochemical signals from sensory organs are transported along superhighways of neurons. There the signals undergo processing and transformation into our conscious reality.

[3점]

* electrochemical: 전기화학의

① operates in isolation
② suffers from rapid changes
③ resembles economic elements
④ works in a systematic way
⑤ interacts with another

33. Someone else's body language affects our own body, which then creates an emotional echo that makes us feel accordingly. As Louis Armstrong sang, "When you're smiling, the whole world smiles with you." If copying another's smile makes us feel happy, the emotion of the smiler has been transmitted via our body. Strange as it may sound, this theory states that _____. For example, our mood can be improved by simply lifting up the corners of our mouth. If people are asked to bite down on a pencil lengthwise, taking care not to let the pencil touch their lips (thus forcing the mouth into a smile-like shape), they judge cartoons funnier than if they have been asked to frown. The primacy of the body is sometimes summarized in the phrase "I must be afraid, because I'm running." [3점]

* lengthwise: 길게 ** frown: 얼굴을 찡그리다

① language guides our actions
② emotions arise from our bodies
③ body language hides our feelings
④ what others say affects our mood
⑤ negative emotions easily disappear

34. _____ boosts sales. Brian Wansink, Professor of Marketing at Cornell University, investigated the effectiveness of this tactic in 1998. He persuaded three supermarkets in Sioux City, Iowa, to offer Campbell's soup at a small discount: 79 cents rather than 89 cents. The discounted soup was sold in one of three conditions: a control, where there was no limit on the volume of purchases, or two tests, where customers were limited to either four or twelve cans. In the unlimited condition shoppers bought 3.3 cans on average, whereas in the scarce condition, when there was a limit, they bought 5.3 on average. This suggests scarcity encourages sales. The findings are particularly strong because the test took place in a supermarket with genuine shoppers. It didn't rely on claimed data, nor was it held in a laboratory where consumers might behave differently. [3점]

* tactic: 전략

① Promoting products through social media
② Reducing the risk of producing poor quality items
③ Restricting the number of items customers can buy
④ Offering several options that customers find attractive
⑤ Emphasizing the safety of products with research data

35. 다음 글에서 전체 흐름과 관계 <u>없는</u> 문장은?

Although technology has the potential to increase productivity, it can also have a negative impact on productivity. For example, in many office environments workers sit at desks with computers and have access to the internet. ① They are able to check their personal e-mails and use social media whenever they want to. ② This can stop them from doing their work and make them less productive. ③ Introducing new technology can also have a negative impact on production when it causes a change to the production process or requires workers to learn a new system. ④ Using technology can enable businesses to produce more goods and to get more out of the other factors of production. ⑤ Learning to use new technology can be time consuming and stressful for workers and this can cause a decline in productivity.

[36~37] 주어진 글 다음에 이어질 글의 순서로 가장 적절한 것을 고르시오.

36.

Up until about 6,000 years ago, most people were farmers. Many lived in different places throughout the year, hunting for food or moving their livestock to areas with enough food.

(A) For example, priests wanted to know when to carry out religious ceremonies. This was when people first invented clocks — devices that show, measure, and keep track of passing time.

(B) There was no need to tell the time because life depended on natural cycles, such as the changing seasons or sunrise and sunset. Gradually more people started to live in larger settlements, and some needed to tell the time.

(C) Clocks have been important ever since. Today, clocks are used for important things such as setting busy airport timetables — if the time is incorrect, aeroplanes might crash into each other when taking off or landing! [3점]

① (A) − (C) − (B)   ② (B) − (A) − (C)
③ (B) − (C) − (A)   ④ (C) − (A) − (B)
⑤ (C) − (B) − (A)

37.

> Managers are always looking for ways to increase productivity, which is the ratio of costs to output in production. Adam Smith, writing when the manufacturing industry was new, described a way that production could be made more efficient, known as the "division of labor."

(A) Because each worker specializes in one job, he or she can work much faster without changing from one task to another. Now 10 workers can produce thousands of pins in a day — a huge increase in productivity from the 200 they would have produced before.

(B) One worker could do all these tasks, and make 20 pins in a day. But this work can be divided into its separate processes, with a number of workers each performing one task.

(C) Making most manufactured goods involves several different processes using different skills. Smith's example was the manufacture of pins: the wire is straightened, sharpened, a head is put on, and then it is polished.

* ratio: 비율

① (A) − (C) − (B)　　② (B) − (A) − (C)
③ (B) − (C) − (A)　　④ (C) − (A) − (B)
⑤ (C) − (B) − (A)

[38~39] 글의 흐름으로 보아, 주어진 문장이 들어가기에 가장 적절한 곳을 고르시오.

38.

> Yet we know that the face that stares back at us from the glass is not the same, cannot be the same, as it was 10 minutes ago.

Sometimes the pace of change is far slower. (①) The face you saw reflected in your mirror this morning probably appeared no different from the face you saw the day before — or a week or a month ago. (②) The proof is in your photo album: Look at a photograph taken of yourself 5 or 10 years ago and you see clear differences between the face in the snapshot and the face in your mirror. (③) If you lived in a world without mirrors for a year and then saw your reflection, you might be surprised by the change. (④) After an interval of 10 years without seeing yourself, you might not at first recognize the person peering from the mirror. (⑤) Even something as basic as our own face changes from moment to moment.

* peer: 응시하다

39.

> As children absorb more evidence from the world around them, certain possibilities become much more likely and more useful and harden into knowledge or beliefs.

According to educational psychologist Susan Engel, curiosity begins to decrease as young as four years old. By the time we are adults, we have fewer questions and more default settings. As Henry James put it, "Disinterested curiosity is past, the mental grooves and channels set." (①) The decline in curiosity can be traced in the development of the brain through childhood. (②) Though smaller than the adult brain, the infant brain contains millions more neural connections. (③) The wiring, however, is a mess; the lines of communication between infant neurons are far less efficient than between those in the adult brain. (④) The baby's perception of the world is consequently both intensely rich and wildly disordered. (⑤) The neural pathways that enable those beliefs become faster and more automatic, while the ones that the child doesn't use regularly are pruned away. [3점]

* default setting: 기본값 ** groove: 고랑 *** prune: 가지치기하다

40. 다음 글의 내용을 한 문장으로 요약하고자 한다. 빈칸 (A), (B)에 들어갈 말로 가장 적절한 것은?

> Nearly eight of ten U.S. adults believe there are "good foods" and "bad foods." Unless we're talking about spoiled stew, poison mushrooms, or something similar, however, no foods can be labeled as either good or bad. There are, however, combinations of foods that add up to a healthful or unhealthful diet. Consider the case of an adult who eats only foods thought of as "good" — for example, raw broccoli, apples, orange juice, boiled tofu, and carrots. Although all these foods are nutrient-dense, they do not add up to a healthy diet because they don't supply a wide enough variety of the nutrients we need. Or take the case of the teenager who occasionally eats fried chicken, but otherwise stays away from fried foods. The occasional fried chicken isn't going to knock his or her diet off track. But the person who eats fried foods every day, with few vegetables or fruits, and loads up on supersized soft drinks, candy, and chips for snacks has a bad diet.

↓

> Unlike the common belief, defining foods as good or bad is not ___(A)___ ; in fact, a healthy diet is determined largely by what the diet is ___(B)___ .

	(A)		(B)
①	incorrect	……	limited to
②	appropriate	……	composed of
③	wrong	……	aimed at
④	appropriate	……	tested on
⑤	incorrect	……	adjusted to

[41~42] 다음 글을 읽고, 물음에 답하시오.

Early hunter-gatherer societies had (a) minimal structure. A chief or group of elders usually led the camp or village. Most of these leaders had to hunt and gather along with the other members because the surpluses of food and other vital resources were seldom (b) sufficient to support a full-time chief or village council. The development of agriculture changed work patterns. Early farmers could reap 3-10 kg of grain from each 1 kg of seed planted. Part of this food/energy surplus was returned to the community and (c) limited support for nonfarmers such as chieftains, village councils, men who practice medicine, priests, and warriors. In return, the nonfarmers provided leadership and security for the farming population, enabling it to continue to increase food/energy yields and provide ever larger surpluses.

With improved technology and favorable conditions, agriculture produced consistent surpluses of the basic necessities, and population groups grew in size. These groups concentrated in towns and cities, and human tasks (d) specialized further. Specialists such as carpenters, blacksmiths, merchants, traders, and sailors developed their skills and became more efficient in their use of time and energy. The goods and services they provided brought about an (e) improved quality of life, a higher standard of living, and, for most societies, increased stability.

* reap: (농작물을) 베어들이다 ** chieftain: 수령, 두목

41. 윗글의 제목으로 가장 적절한 것은?

① How Agriculture Transformed Human Society
② The Dark Shadow of Agriculture: Repetition
③ How Can We Share Extra Food with the Poor?
④ Why Were Early Societies Destroyed by Agriculture?
⑤ The Advantages of Large Groups Over Small Groups in Farming

42. 밑줄 친 (a)~(e) 중에서 문맥상 낱말의 쓰임이 적절하지 않은 것은? [3점]

① (a)　② (b)　③ (c)　④ (d)　⑤ (e)

[43~45] 다음 글을 읽고, 물음에 답하시오.

(A)

A nurse took a tired, anxious soldier to the bedside. "Jack, your son is here," the nurse said to an old man lying on the bed. She had to repeat the words several times before the old man's eyes opened. Suffering from the severe pain because of heart disease, he barely saw the young uniformed soldier standing next to him. (a) He reached out his hand to the soldier.

(B)

Whenever the nurse came into the room, she heard the soldier say a few gentle words. The old man said nothing, only held tightly to (b) him all through the night. Just before dawn, the old man died. The soldier released the old man's hand and left the room to find the nurse. After she was told what happened, she went back to the room with him. The soldier hesitated for a while and asked, "Who was this man?"

(C)

She was surprised and asked, "Wasn't he your father?" "No, he wasn't. I've never met him before," the soldier replied. She asked, "Then why didn't you say something when I took you to (c) him?" He said, "I knew there had been a mistake, but when I realized that he was too sick to tell whether or not I was his son, I could see how much (d) he needed me. So, I stayed."

(D)

The soldier gently wrapped his fingers around the weak hand of the old man. The nurse brought a chair so that the soldier could sit beside the bed. All through the night the young soldier sat there, holding the old man's hand and offering (e) him words of support and comfort. Occasionally, she suggested that the soldier take a rest for a while. He politely said no.

43. 주어진 글 (A)에 이어질 내용을 순서에 맞게 배열한 것으로 가장 적절한 것은?

① (B) − (D) − (C)　② (C) − (B) − (D)
③ (C) − (D) − (B)　④ (D) − (B) − (C)
⑤ (D) − (C) − (B)

44. 밑줄 친 (a)~(e) 중에서 가리키는 대상이 나머지 넷과 다른 것은?

① (a)　② (b)　③ (c)　④ (d)　⑤ (e)

45. 윗글에 관한 내용으로 적절하지 않은 것은?

① 노인은 심장병으로 극심한 고통을 겪고 있었다.
② 군인은 간호사를 찾기 위해 병실을 나갔다.
③ 군인은 노인과 이전에 만난 적이 있다고 말했다.
④ 간호사는 군인이 앉을 수 있도록 의자를 가져왔다.
⑤ 군인은 잠시 쉬라는 간호사의 제안을 정중히 거절하였다.

＊ 확인 사항
○ 답안지의 해당란에 필요한 내용을 정확히 기입(표기)했는지 확인하시오.

18
001 travel agency 여행사
002 turn A into B A를 B로 바꾸다
003 reality ⓝ 현실
004 A as well as B B뿐 아니라 A도
005 meditation ⓝ 명상
006 experienced ⓐ 경험 많은, 숙련된
007 instructor ⓝ 강사
008 reasonable ⓐ 적당한
009 unforgettable ⓐ 잊지 못할

19
010 midnight ⓝ 자정
011 ring ⓥ 울리다
012 worried ⓐ 걱정한
013 decide ⓥ 결심하다, 정하다
014 ask for help 도움을 요청하다
015 catch one's attention 관심을 끌다
016 approach ⓥ 다가가다
017 suddenly ⓐⓓ 문득, 갑자기
018 familiar ⓐ 익숙한
019 disappear ⓥ 사라지다
020 anxious ⓐ 불안한
021 delighted ⓐ 기쁜
022 embarrassed ⓐ 당황한

20
023 personal life 사생활
024 sensible ⓐ 분별 있는, 현명한
025 separate ⓐ 별개의
026 lead to ~로 이어지다
027 distraction ⓝ 주의 분산, 정신을 흩뜨리는 것
028 missing ⓐ 빠진, 실종된
029 to-do list 할 일 목록
030 multiple ⓐ 여럿의, 다수의
031 organize ⓥ 정리하다
032 task ⓝ 일, 과업
033 professional ⓐ 직업의, 전문적인
034 divide ⓥ 나누다, 분배하다
035 make an informed decision 잘 알고 결정하다

21
036 react to ~에 반응하다
037 purchase ⓝ 구매 ⓥ 사다
038 likelihood ⓝ 가능성, 확률
039 whether ⓒⓞⓝⓙ ~인지 아닌지
040 buyer ⓝ 구매자
041 return ⓥ 반품하다
042 encourage ⓥ 격려하다
043 satisfied ⓐ 만족한
044 unpaid ⓐ 무급의
045 ambassador ⓝ (외교 시 나라를 대표하는) 대사, 사절
046 on the top of ~의 맨 위에
047 opinion ⓝ 의견, 생각
048 advertisement ⓝ 광고
049 be paid to 돈을 받고 ~하다
050 continually ⓐⓓ 지속적으로
051 word-of-mouth ⓐ 구전의
052 for no gain 대가 없이
053 overseas ⓐⓓ 해외에

22
054 computerize ⓥ 컴퓨터화하다
055 repetitive ⓥ 반복되는
056 drudgery ⓝ 고된 일
057 pursue ⓥ 추구하다
058 off-load ⓥ 짐을 내리다, 떠넘기다
059 as part of ~의 일환으로
060 be expected to ~하도록 기대되다
061 complete ⓥ 완수하다 ⓐ 완전한
062 reservation ⓝ 예약
063 grocery store 슈퍼, 식료품 가게
064 scan ⓥ 스캔하다, 찍다, 훑다

23
065 possess ⓥ 지니다, 소유하다
066 a host of 여러, 다수의
067 socially ⓐⓓ 사회적으로
068 desirable ⓐ 바람직한
069 characteristic ⓝ 특성
070 be free of ~가 없는
071 general public 일반 대중
072 intelligent ⓐ 지적인
073 fair-minded ⓐ 공정한
074 prejudiced ⓐ 고정 관념이 있는
075 skilled ⓐ 능숙한
076 behind the wheel 운전할 때, 핸들을 잡은
077 automobile ⓝ 자동차
078 phenomenon ⓝ 현상
079 reliable ⓐ 믿을 만한
080 ubiquitous ⓐ 도처에 있는
081 fictional ⓐ 허구의
082 good-looking ⓐ 잘생긴
083 million ⓝ 100만
084 high school senior 고교 졸업반
085 in terms of ~의 면에서
086 get along with ~와 어울리다
087 self-image ⓝ 자아상(사람이 자기 자신에 대해 가진 이미지)
088 superior to ~보다 우월한
089 social network 사회적 네트워크

24
090 poverty ⓝ 가난
091 publish ⓥ 출판하다
092 socioeconomic ⓐ 사회경제적인
093 status ⓝ 지위
094 be associated with ~와 연관되다
095 distinct ⓐ 특유의, 독특한, 뚜렷한
096 time pressure 시간 압박
097 psychologist ⓝ 심리학자
098 wealthy ⓐ 부유한
099 industrialize ⓥ 산업화하다
100 nation ⓝ 나라
101 pace ⓝ 속도
102 standard of life 생활 수준
103 constant ⓐ 지속적인
104 urgency ⓝ 다급함
105 prone to ~에 걸리기 쉬운
106 productivity ⓝ 생산성
107 in search of ~을 찾아서
108 escape ⓥ 탈출하다, 빠져나가다
109 sound ⓐ 건전한

25
110 share ⓝ 점유율, 몫
111 region ⓝ 지역
112 decline ⓥ 감소하다, 줄어들다
113 percentage point 퍼센트포인트(백분율 간 격차)
114 more than ~ 이상
115 gap ⓝ 격차, 차이

26
116 well educated 교육을 많이 받은
117 financial ⓐ 재정적인
118 political ⓐ 정치적인
119 graduate from ~을 졸업하다
120 major in ~을 전공하다
121 handle ⓥ 다루다, 대처하다
122 earn ⓥ 얻다, 취득하다
123 doctor's degree 박사 학위
124 doctoral paper 박사 논문
125 discrimination ⓝ 차별
126 mention ⓥ 언급하다
127 contribution ⓝ 기여, 이바지
128 analysis ⓝ 분석
129 award ⓝ 상을 주다, 수여하다

27
130 drone ⓝ 드론, 무인 항공기
131 championship ⓝ 선수권
132 take an opportunity 기회를 잡다
133 prove ⓥ 증명하다
134 community center 주민센터
135 requirement ⓝ 필수 요건
136 bring ⓥ 가져오다, 지참하다
137 souvenir ⓝ 기념품

28
138 one-day class 일일 수업
139 underwater ⓐ 물속의, 수중의
140 explorer ⓝ 탐험가
141 basics ⓝ 기본, 필수적인 것들
142 private lesson 개인 레슨
143 equipment ⓝ 장비

29
144 praise ⓝ 칭찬
145 available ⓐ 이용할 수 있는
146 improve ⓥ 개선하다, 향상시키다
147 self-esteem ⓝ 자존감
148 preschooler ⓝ 미취학 아동
149 profound ⓐ 뜻 깊은
150 cognitive ⓐ 인지적인
151 sophistication ⓝ 정교화(함)
152 reason ⓥ 추론하다
153 analytically ⓐⓓ 분석적으로
154 reject ⓥ 거부하다
155 consistently ⓐⓓ 지속적으로
156 be likely to ~할 가능성이 크다
157 incorporate A into B A를 B로 통합시키다
158 endure ⓥ 지속하다, 참다
159 problem-solving ⓝ 문제 해결
160 confidence ⓝ 자신감

30
161 display ⓥ 보이다, 전시하다
162 considerable ⓐ 상당한
163 facility ⓝ 능력, 재능
164 claim ⓥ 주장
165 goods ⓝ 상품, 재화
166 yeast ⓝ (반죽 발효에 쓰는) 효모, 이스트
167 ingredient ⓝ 재료
168 century ⓝ 100년, 세기
169 demand ⓝ 수요 ⓥ 요구하다
170 hire ⓥ 고용하다
171 come up with 떠올리다, 고안하다
172 strategy ⓝ 전략
173 boost ⓥ 촉진하다, 증진하다
174 sale ⓝ 매출, 판매
175 significant ⓐ 상당한, 중요한
176 shortly thereafter 그 후 얼마 안 되어
177 transform ⓥ 변모시키다
178 laxative ⓝ 완하제(배변을 쉽게 하는 약·음식·음료)
179 reposition ⓥ (제품의) 이미지를 바꾸다

31
180 perform ⓥ 수행하다
181 profession ⓝ 직업
182 instant ⓐ 즉각적인
183 credibility ⓝ 신뢰
184 admire ⓥ 존경하다
185 connected to ~에 연결된
186 even if 설령 ~일지라도
187 have nothing to do with ~와 관련이 없다
188 advice ⓝ 조언
189 world-famous ⓐ 세계적으로 유명한
190 make money 돈을 벌다
191 endorsement ⓝ (유명인의 텔레비전 등에서의 상품) 보증 선전
192 knowledge ⓝ 지식
193 endorse ⓥ (유명인이 광고에 나와 특정 상품을) 보증하다, 홍보하다
194 medalist ⓝ 메달리스트
195 certain ⓐ 특정한
196 expertise ⓝ 전문 지식
197 desire ⓥ 바라다, 열망하다
198 patience ⓝ 인내심
199 sacrifice ⓝ 희생
200 honesty ⓝ 정직

32
201 think of A as B A를 B로 여기다
202 look out ~을 내다보다
203 instead ⓐⓓ 대신에
204 emerge ⓥ 나타나다, 생겨나다
205 element ⓝ 요소
206 merchant ⓝ 상인
207 operation ⓝ 작동, 작용
208 spot ⓝ 지점
209 neighborhood ⓝ 근방, 이웃, 지역
210 resident ⓝ 주민
211 scale ⓝ 규모
212 locally ⓐⓓ 국지적으로
213 distantly ⓐⓓ 멀리, 원거리로

214 textile ⓝ 직물	35	
215 process ⓥ 가공하다, 처리하다	270 potential ⓝ 잠재력	324 appear ~인 것처럼 보이다
216 raw ⓐ 원재료의, 날것의	271 negative ⓐ 부정적인	325 proof ⓝ 증거
217 electrochemical ⓐ 전기화학의	272 impact ⓝ 영향, 충격	326 clear ⓐ 명확한
218 sensory organ 감각 기관	273 have access to ~에 접근하다, ~을 이용하다	327 snapshot ⓝ 스냅사진, 짧은 묘사
219 transport ⓥ 수송하다, 실어 나르다	274 whenever ⓒⓞⓝⓙ ~할 때마다	328 reflection ⓝ (물이나 거울에 비친) 그림자
220 undergo ⓥ 거치다, 겪다	275 stop A from B A가 B하지 못하게 막다	329 surprised ⓐ 놀란
221 transformation ⓝ 변화, 변모	276 production ⓝ 생산, 제조	330 interval ⓝ 간격
222 conscious ⓐ 의식적인	277 cause ⓥ 야기하다	331 at first 처음에
223 in isolation 고립되어	278 require ⓥ 요구하다	332 peer ⓥ 응시하다
224 resemble ⓥ ~와 닮다	279 enable ⓥ ~할 수 있게 하다	333 basic ⓐ 기본적인
225 systematic ⓐ 체계적인	280 get A out of B B에게서 A를 얻어내다	334 from moment to moment 시시각각
33	281 factor ⓝ 요인, 요소	39
226 body language 신체 언어, 몸짓 언어	282 time-consuming ⓐ 시간이 많이 걸리는	335 absorb ⓥ (정보를) 받아들이다
227 affect ⓥ 영향을 미치다	36	336 possibility ⓝ 가능성
228 emotional ⓐ 정서적인	283 up until ~에 이르기까지	337 harden ⓥ 굳어지다
229 echo ⓝ 메아리	284 throughout ⓟⓡⓔⓟ ~ 내내	338 belief ⓝ 믿음, 신념
230 accordingly ⓐⓓ 그에 따라	285 hunt for ~을 사냥하다	339 educational ⓐ 교육의
231 copy ⓥ 복사하다	286 livestock ⓝ 가축	340 curiosity ⓝ 호기심
232 transmit ⓥ 전달하다	287 carry out 수행하다	341 decrease ⓥ 감소하다
233 via ⓟⓡⓔⓟ ~을 통해서	288 religious ⓐ 종교적인	342 default setting 기본값
234 strange ⓐ 이상한	289 invent ⓥ 발명하다	343 disinterested ⓐ 무관심한
235 theory ⓝ 이론	290 device ⓝ 장치	344 groove ⓝ 고랑
236 state ⓥ 진술하다	291 measure ⓥ 측정하다	345 channel ⓝ 경로
237 mood ⓝ 기분, 분위기	292 keep track of ~을 추적하다, 기록하다	346 development ⓝ 발달
238 lift up ~을 들어올리다	293 natural cycle 자연적 주기	347 childhood ⓝ 어린 시절
239 be asked to ~하도록 요청받다	294 sunrise ⓝ 일출, 해돋이	348 infant ⓝ 유아
240 bite down on ~을 깨물다	295 sunset ⓝ 일몰, 해넘이	349 neural ⓐ 신경의
241 lengthwise ⓐⓓ 길게	296 gradually ⓐⓓ 점차	350 mess ⓝ 엉망
242 take care (not) to ~해지 않도록 주의하다	297 settlement ⓝ 정착(지)	351 perception ⓝ 지각, 인식
243 touch ⓥ 닿다, 만지다	298 tell the time 시간을 알다	352 consequently ⓐⓓ 그 결과
244 judge ⓥ 판단하다	299 ever since 그 이후로	353 intensely ⓐⓓ 대단히, 강렬하게
245 frown ⓥ 얼굴을 찡그리다	300 timetable ⓝ 시간표	354 disordered ⓐ 무질서한
246 primacy ⓝ 우선함	301 crash into ~에 충돌하다	355 pathway ⓝ 경로
247 summarize ⓥ 요약하다	302 take off 이륙하다	356 automatic ⓐ 자동적인
248 arise from ~에서 생겨나다	303 land ⓥ 착륙하다	357 prune ⓥ 가지치기하다
249 hide ⓥ 숨기다	37	40
34	304 ratio ⓝ 비율	358 nearly ⓐⓓ 거의
250 investigate ⓥ 조사하다	305 cost ⓝ 비용	359 unless ⓒⓞⓝⓙ ~하지 않는 한
251 effectiveness ⓝ 유효성, 효과 있음	306 output ⓝ 산출	360 spoiled ⓐ 상한
252 tactic ⓝ 전략	307 manufacturing industry 제조업	361 poison mushroom 독버섯
253 persuade ⓥ 설득하다	308 describe ⓥ 설명하다	362 label A as B A를 B라고 분류하다
254 discount ⓝ 할인	309 efficient ⓐ 효율적인	363 either A or B A 또는 B
255 rather than ~ 대신에	310 known as ~라고 알려진	364 combination ⓝ 조합
256 condition ⓝ 조건	311 division of labor 분업	365 add up to 결국 ~이 되다
257 control ⓝ 통제 집단(실험에서 처치를 가하지 않고 둔 집단)	312 specialize in ~에 특화되다	366 healthful ⓐ 건강에 좋은
258 limit ⓝ 제한 ⓥ 제한하다	313 thousands of 수천의	367 broccoli ⓝ 브로콜리
259 volume ⓝ 양	314 a number of 많은	368 tofu ⓝ 두부
260 unlimited ⓐ 제한되지 않은, 무제한의	315 involve ⓥ 포함하다, 수반하다	369 nutrient-dense ⓐ 영양이 풍부한
261 on average 평균적으로	316 straighten ⓥ 곧게 펴다	370 supply ⓥ 공급하다
262 scarcity ⓝ 희소성	317 sharpen ⓥ 뾰족하게 하다	371 a wide variety of 매우 다양한
263 genuine ⓐ 진짜의	318 put on 끼우다, 달다, 입다, 착용하다	372 nutrient ⓝ 영양분
264 rely on ~에 의존하다	319 polish ⓥ 다듬다	373 occasionally ⓐⓓ 가끔
265 laboratory ⓝ 실험실	38	374 otherwise ⓐⓓ 그렇지 않으면, 다른 경우에는
266 behave ⓥ 행동하다	320 stare back at ~을 마주 보다	375 stay away from ~을 멀리하다
267 differently ⓐⓓ 다르게	321 far ⓐⓓ (비교급 앞에서) 훨씬	376 off track 제 길에서 벗어난
268 attractive ⓐ 매력적인	322 reflect ⓥ 반사하다	377 load up on ~로 배를 가득 채우다
269 emphasize ⓥ 강조하다	323 probably ⓐⓓ 아마도	378 unlike ⓟⓡⓔⓟ ~와 달리

379 largely ⓐⓓ 대체로, 주로
380 composed of ~로 구성된

41~42	
381 hunter-gatherer ⓝ 수렵 채집인	409 carpenter ⓝ 목수
382 minimal ⓐ 최소한의	410 blacksmith ⓝ 대장장이
383 structure ⓝ 구조	411 sailor ⓝ 선원
384 chief ⓝ 추장, 족장, 우두머리	412 bring about ~을 야기하다, 초래하다, 가져오다
385 along with ~와 함께	413 quality of life 삶의 질
386 surplus ⓝ 잉여, 흑자	414 stability ⓝ 안정성
387 vital ⓐ 필수적인, 매우 중요한	415 shadow ⓝ 그림자
388 resource ⓝ 자원	43~45
389 seldom ⓐⓓ ~할 때가 드물다, 좀처럼 ~하지 않다	416 anxious ⓐ 불안한, 걱정하는
390 sufficient ⓐ 충분한	417 bedside ⓝ 침대 옆, 머리맡
391 support ⓥ 지원하다, 부양하다	418 lie on ~에 눕다
392 full-time ⓐ 전임의, 정규직의	419 repeat ⓥ 반복하다
393 agriculture ⓝ 농업	420 several ⓐ 몇몇의, 여럿의
394 reap ⓥ (농작물을) 베어들이다	421 severe ⓐ 극심한
395 grain ⓝ 곡물	422 heart disease 심장병
396 plant ⓥ (식물을) 심다	423 barely ⓐⓓ 간신히 ~하다, 거의 못 ~하다
397 community ⓝ 지역 사회	424 uniformed ⓐ 유니폼을 입은
398 chieftain ⓝ 수령, 두목	425 reach out one's hand 손을 뻗다
399 practice medicine 의사로 개업하다, 의술을 행하다	426 gentle ⓐ 부드러운, 다정한
400 priest ⓝ 성직자	427 tightly ⓐⓓ 꽉
401 warrior ⓝ 전사	428 through the night 밤새
402 security ⓝ 안보	429 dawn ⓝ 새벽
403 yield ⓝ 수확량	430 release ⓥ 놓다, 해방시키다
404 favorable ⓐ 우호적인	431 hesitate ⓥ 주저하다
405 basic necessity 기본 필수품	432 for a while 잠시
406 grow in size 규모가 커지다	433 take A to B A를 B에게 데려가다
407 concentrate ⓥ 집중되다	434 wrap ⓥ 감싸다
408 further ⓐⓓ 더욱	435 take a rest 쉬다
	436 politely ⓐⓓ 정중하게

● 채점 : 맞은 개수 _____ / 80

TEST A-B 각 단어의 뜻을 [A] 영어는 우리말로, [B] 우리말은 영어로 쓰시오.

A	English	Korean
01	meditation	
02	anxious	
03	likelihood	
04	superior to	
05	fictional	
06	status	
07	consistently	
08	ask for help	
09	facility	
10	emerge	
11	peer	
12	surplus	
13	hesitate	
14	endure	
15	region	
16	distinct	
17	phenomenon	
18	desirable	
19	pursue	
20	distraction	

B	Korean	English
01	익숙한	
02	지니다, 소유하다	
03	생산성	
04	경험 많은, 숙련된	
05	무급의	
06	감소하다, 줄어들다	
07	상을 주다, 수여하다	
08	고용하다	
09	진술하다	
10	강조하다	
11	호기심	
12	간신히 ~하다, 거의 ~ 못하다	
13	필수적인, 매우 중요한	
14	안정성	
15	기여	
16	당황한	
17	상당한	
18	~로 구성된	
19	~하지 않는 한	
20	반사하다	

▶ A-D 정답 : 해설편 071쪽

TEST C-D 각 단어의 뜻을 골라 기호를 쓰시오.

C	English		Korean
01	instructor	( )	ⓐ 관심을 끌다
02	word-of-mouth	( )	ⓑ 분별 있는, 현명한
03	drudgery	( )	ⓒ 잘 알고 결정하다
04	prejudiced	( )	ⓓ 직업
05	industrialize	( )	ⓔ 거치다, 겪다
06	financial	( )	ⓕ 초래하다, 야기하다
07	strategy	( )	ⓖ (정보를) 받아들이다
08	profession	( )	ⓗ 강사
09	undergo	( )	ⓘ 얼굴을 찡그리다
10	frown	( )	ⓙ 무질서한
11	have access to	( )	ⓚ 전략
12	bring about	( )	ⓛ 극심한
13	severe	( )	ⓜ 미취학 아동
14	preschooler	( )	ⓝ 재정적인
15	catch one's attention	( )	ⓞ 구전의
16	sensible	( )	ⓟ ~에 접근하다, ~을 이용하다
17	make an informed decision	( )	ⓠ 산업화하다
18	absorb	( )	ⓡ 상한
19	spoiled	( )	ⓢ 고정 관념이 있는
20	disordered	( )	ⓣ 고된 일

D	Korean		English
01	기쁜	( )	ⓐ prone to
02	많은	( )	ⓑ analysis
03	자동차	( )	ⓒ self-esteem
04	기념품	( )	ⓓ ingredient
05	뜻깊은	( )	ⓔ livestock
06	비율	( )	ⓕ automobile
07	~에 걸리기 쉬운	( )	ⓖ delighted
08	분석	( )	ⓗ sophistication
09	인지적인	( )	ⓘ sacrifice
10	요약하다	( )	ⓙ genuine
11	차별	( )	ⓚ ratio
12	자존감	( )	ⓛ neural
13	재료	( )	ⓜ summarize
14	변모시키다	( )	ⓝ carry out
15	희생	( )	ⓞ transform
16	진짜의	( )	ⓟ cognitive
17	가축	( )	ⓠ profound
18	신경의	( )	ⓡ souvenir
19	수행하다	( )	ⓢ discrimination
20	정교화	( )	ⓣ a host of

18. 다음 글의 목적으로 가장 적절한 것은?

Dear Boat Tour Manager,

On March 15, my family was on one of your Glass Bottom Boat Tours. When we returned to our hotel, I discovered that I left behind my cell phone case. The case must have fallen off my lap and onto the floor when I took it off my phone to clean it. I would like to ask you to check if it is on your boat. Its color is black and it has my name on the inside. If you find the case, I would appreciate it if you would let me know.

Sincerely,
Sam Roberts

① 제품의 고장 원인을 문의하려고
② 분실물 발견 시 연락을 부탁하려고
③ 시설물의 철저한 관리를 당부하려고
④ 여행자 보험 가입 절차를 확인하려고
⑤ 분실물 센터 확장의 필요성을 건의하려고

19. 다음 글에 드러난 Matthew의 심경 변화로 가장 적절한 것은?

One Saturday morning, Matthew's mother told Matthew that she was going to take him to the park. A big smile came across his face. As he loved to play outside, he ate his breakfast and got dressed quickly so they could go. When they got to the park, Matthew ran all the way over to the swing set. That was his favorite thing to do at the park. But the swings were all being used. His mother explained that he could use the slide until a swing became available, but it was broken. Suddenly, his mother got a phone call and she told Matthew they had to leave. His heart sank.

① embarrassed → indifferent
② excited → disappointed
③ cheerful → ashamed
④ nervous → touched
⑤ scared → relaxed

20. 다음 글에서 필자가 주장하는 바로 가장 적절한 것은?

Meetings encourage creative thinking and can give you ideas that you may never have thought of on your own. However, on average, meeting participants consider about one third of meeting time to be unproductive. But you can make your meetings more productive and more useful by preparing well in advance. You should create a list of items to be discussed and share your list with other participants before a meeting. It allows them to know what to expect in your meeting and prepare to participate.

① 회의 결과는 빠짐없이 작성해서 공개해야 한다.
② 중요한 정보는 공식 회의를 통해 전달해야 한다.
③ 생산성 향상을 위해 정기적인 평가회가 필요하다.
④ 모든 참석자의 동의를 받아서 회의를 열어야 한다.
⑤ 회의에서 다룰 사항은 미리 작성해서 공유해야 한다.

21. 밑줄 친 put the glass down이 다음 글에서 의미하는 바로 가장 적절한 것은? [3점]

A psychology professor raised a glass of water while teaching stress management principles to her students, and asked them, "How heavy is this glass of water I'm holding?" Students shouted out various answers. The professor replied, "The absolute weight of this glass doesn't matter. It depends on how long I hold it. If I hold it for a minute, it's quite light. But, if I hold it for a day straight, it will cause severe pain in my arm, forcing me to drop the glass to the floor. In each case, the weight of the glass is the same, but the longer I hold it, the heavier it feels to me." As the class nodded their heads in agreement, she continued, "Your stresses in life are like this glass of water. If you still feel the weight of yesterday's stress, it's a strong sign that it's time to put the glass down."

① pour more water into the glass
② set a plan not to make mistakes
③ let go of the stress in your mind
④ think about the cause of your stress
⑤ learn to accept the opinions of others

22. 다음 글의 요지로 가장 적절한 것은?

Your emotions deserve attention and give you important pieces of information. However, they can also sometimes be an unreliable, inaccurate source of information. You may feel a certain way, but that does not mean those feelings are reflections of the truth. You may feel sad and conclude that your friend is angry with you when her behavior simply reflects that she's having a bad day. You may feel depressed and decide that you did poorly in an interview when you did just fine. Your feelings can mislead you into thinking things that are not supported by facts.

① 자신의 감정으로 인해 상황을 오해할 수 있다.
② 자신의 생각을 타인에게 강요해서는 안 된다.
③ 인간관계가 우리의 감정에 영향을 미친다.
④ 타인의 감정에 공감하는 자세가 필요하다.
⑤ 공동체를 위한 선택에는 보상이 따른다.

23. 다음 글의 주제로 가장 적절한 것은?

Every day, children explore and construct relationships among objects. Frequently, these relationships focus on how much or how many of something exists. Thus, children count — "One cookie, two shoes, three candles on the birthday cake, four children in the sandbox." Children compare — "Which has more? Which has fewer? Will there be enough?" Children calculate — "How many will fit? Now, I have five. I need one more." In all of these instances, children are developing a notion of quantity. Children reveal and investigate mathematical concepts through their own activities or experiences, such as figuring out how many crackers to take at snack time or sorting shells into piles.

① difficulties of children in learning how to count
② how children build mathematical understanding
③ why fingers are used in counting objects
④ importance of early childhood education
⑤ advantages of singing number songs

24. 다음 글의 제목으로 가장 적절한 것은?

Only a generation or two ago, mentioning the word *algorithms* would have drawn a blank from most people. Today, algorithms appear in every part of civilization. They are connected to everyday life. They're not just in your cell phone or your laptop but in your car, your house, your appliances, and your toys. Your bank is a huge web of algorithms, with humans turning the switches here and there. Algorithms schedule flights and then fly the airplanes. Algorithms run factories, trade goods, and keep records. If every algorithm suddenly stopped working, it would be the end of the world as we know it.

① We Live in an Age of Algorithms
② Mysteries of Ancient Civilizations
③ Dangers of Online Banking Algorithms
④ How Algorithms Decrease Human Creativity
⑤ Transportation: A Driving Force of Industry

25. 다음 도표의 내용과 일치하지 <u>않는</u> 것은?

Percent of U.S. Households with Pets

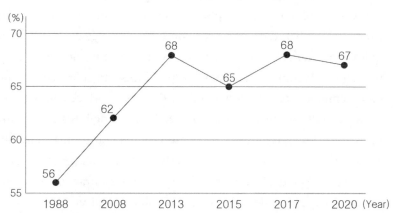

The graph above shows the percent of households with pets in the United States (U.S.) from 1988 to 2020. ① In 1988, more than half of U.S. households owned pets, and more than 6 out of 10 U.S. households owned pets from 2008 to 2020. ② In the period between 1988 and 2008, pet ownership increased among U.S. households by 6 percentage points. ③ From 2008 to 2013, pet ownership rose an additional 6 percentage points. ④ The percent of U.S. households with pets in 2013 was the same as that in 2017, which was 68 percent. ⑤ In 2015, the rate of U.S. households with pets was 3 percentage points lower than in 2020.

26. Claude Bolling에 관한 다음 글의 내용과 일치하지 <u>않는</u> 것은?

Pianist, composer, and big band leader, Claude Bolling, was born on April 10, 1930, in Cannes, France, but spent most of his life in Paris. He began studying classical music as a youth. He was introduced to the world of jazz by a schoolmate. Later, Bolling became interested in the music of Fats Waller, one of the most excellent jazz musicians. Bolling became famous as a teenager by winning the Best Piano Player prize at an amateur contest in France. He was also a successful film music composer, writing the music for more than one hundred films. In 1975, he collaborated with flutist Rampal and published *Suite for Flute and Jazz Piano Trio*, which he became most well-known for. He died in 2020, leaving two sons, David and Alexandre.

① 1930년에 프랑스에서 태어났다.
② 학교 친구를 통해 재즈를 소개받았다.
③ 20대에 Best Piano Player 상을 받았다.
④ 성공적인 영화 음악 작곡가였다.
⑤ 1975년에 플루트 연주자와 협업했다.

27. Kids Taekwondo Program에 관한 다음 안내문의 내용과 일치하지 <u>않는</u> 것은?

Kids Taekwondo Program
Enjoy our taekwondo program this summer vacation.

□ **Schedule**
- Dates: August 8th − August 10th
- Time: 9:00 a.m. − 11:00 a.m.

□ **Participants**
- Any child aged 5 and up

□ **Activities**
- Self-defense training
- Team building games to develop social skills

□ **Participation Fee**
- $50 per child (includes snacks)

□ **Notice**
- What to bring: water bottle, towel
- What not to bring: chewing gum, expensive items

① 8월 8일부터 3일간 운영한다.
② 5세 이상의 어린이가 참가할 수 있다.
③ 자기 방어 훈련 활동을 한다.
④ 참가비에 간식비는 포함되지 않는다.
⑤ 물병과 수건을 가져와야 한다.

28. Moonlight Chocolate Factory Tour에 관한 다음 안내문의 내용과 일치하는 것은?

Moonlight Chocolate Factory Tour
Take this special tour and have a chance to enjoy our most popular chocolate bars.

□ **Operating Hours**
- Monday − Friday, 2:00p.m. − 5:00 p.m.

□ **Activities**
- Watching our chocolate-making process
- Tasting 3 types of chocolate (dark, milk, and mint chocolate)

□ **Notice**
- Ticket price: $30
- Wearing a face mask is required.
- Taking pictures is not allowed inside the factory.

① 주말 오후 시간에 운영한다.
② 초콜릿 제조 과정을 볼 수 있다.
③ 네 가지 종류의 초콜릿을 시식한다.
④ 마스크 착용은 참여자의 선택 사항이다.
⑤ 공장 내부에서 사진 촬영이 가능하다.

29. 다음 글의 밑줄 친 부분 중, 어법상 틀린 것은?

Despite all the high-tech devices that seem to deny the need for paper, paper use in the United States ① has nearly doubled recently. We now consume more paper than ever: 400 million tons globally and growing. Paper is not the only resource ② that we are using more of. Technological advances often come with the promise of ③ using fewer materials. However, the reality is that they have historically caused more materials use, making us ④ dependently on more natural resources. The world now consumes far more "stuff" than it ever has. We use twenty-seven times more industrial minerals, such as gold, copper, and rare metals, than we ⑤ did just over a century ago. We also each individually use more resources. Much of that is due to our high-tech lifestyle.

* copper: 구리

30. 다음 글의 밑줄 친 부분 중, 문맥상 낱말의 쓰임이 적절하지 않은 것은? [3점]

Do you sometimes feel like you don't love your life? Like, deep inside, something is missing? That's because we are living someone else's life. We allow other people to ① influence our choices. We are trying to meet their expectations. Social pressure is deceiving — we are all impacted without noticing it. Before we realize we are losing ownership of our lives, we end up ② ignoring how other people live. Then, we can only see the greener grass — ours is never good enough. To regain that passion for the life you want, you must ③ recover control of your choices. No one but yourself can choose how you live. But, how? The first step to getting rid of expectations is to treat yourself ④ kindly. You can't truly love other people if you don't love yourself first. When we accept who we are, there's no room for other's ⑤ expectations.

[31~34] 다음 빈칸에 들어갈 말로 가장 적절한 것을 고르시오.

31. One of the big questions faced this past year was how to keep innovation rolling when people were working entirely virtually. But experts say that digital work didn't have a negative effect on innovation and creativity. Working within limits pushes us to solve problems. Overall, virtual meeting platforms put more constraints on communication and collaboration than face-to-face settings. For instance, with the press of a button, virtual meeting hosts can control the size of breakout groups and enforce time constraints; only one person can speak at a time; nonverbal signals, particularly those below the shoulders, are diminished; "seating arrangements" are assigned by the platform, not by individuals; and visual access to others may be limited by the size of each participant's screen. Such _____ are likely to stretch participants beyond their usual ways of thinking, boosting creativity.

① restrictions　　　　② responsibilities
③ memories　　　　　④ coincidences
⑤ traditions

32. The law of demand is that the demand for goods and services increases as prices fall, and the demand falls as prices increase. *Giffen goods* are special types of products for which the traditional law of demand does not apply. Instead of switching to cheaper replacements, consumers demand more of giffen goods when the price increases and less of them when the price decreases. Taking an example, rice in China is a giffen good because people tend to purchase less of it when the price falls. The reason for this is, when the price of rice falls, people have more money to spend on other types of products such as meat and dairy and, therefore, change their spending pattern. On the other hand, as rice prices increase, people _____. [3점]

① order more meat
② consume more rice
③ try to get new jobs
④ increase their savings
⑤ start to invest overseas

33. In a study at Princeton University in 1992, research scientists looked at two different groups of mice. One group was made intellectually superior by modifying the gene for the glutamate receptor. Glutamate is a brain chemical that is necessary in learning. The other group was genetically manipulated to be intellectually inferior, also done by modifying the gene for the glutamate receptor. The smart mice were then raised in standard cages, while the inferior mice were raised in large cages with toys and exercise wheels and with lots of social interaction. At the end of the study, although the intellectually inferior mice were genetically handicapped, they were able to perform just as well as their genetic superiors. This was a real triumph for nurture over nature. Genes are turned on or off _____. [3점]

* glutamate: 글루타민산염   ** manipulate: 조작하다

① by themselves for survival
② free from social interaction
③ based on what is around you
④ depending on genetic superiority
⑤ so as to keep ourselves entertained

34. Researchers are working on a project that asks coastal towns how they are preparing for rising sea levels. Some towns have risk assessments; some towns even have a plan. But it's a rare town that is actually carrying out a plan. One reason we've failed to act on climate change is the common belief that _____.
For decades, climate change was a prediction about the future, so scientists talked about it in the future tense. This became a habit — so that even today many scientists still use the future tense, even though we know that a climate crisis is ongoing. Scientists also often focus on regions most affected by the crisis, such as Bangladesh or the West Antarctic Ice Sheet, which for most Americans are physically remote. [3점]

① it is not related to science
② it is far away in time and space
③ energy efficiency matters the most
④ careful planning can fix the problem
⑤ it is too late to prevent it from happening

35. 다음 글에서 전체 흐름과 관계 <u>없는</u> 문장은?

According to Marguerite La Caze, fashion contributes to our lives and provides a medium for us to develop and exhibit important social virtues. ① Fashion may be beautiful, innovative, and useful; we can display creativity and good taste in our fashion choices. ② And in dressing with taste and care, we represent both self-respect and a concern for the pleasure of others. ③ There is no doubt that fashion can be a source of interest and pleasure which links us to each other. ④ Although the fashion industry developed first in Europe and America, today it is an international and highly globalized industry. ⑤ That is, fashion provides a sociable aspect along with opportunities to imagine oneself differently — to try on different identities.

* virtue: 가치

[36~37] 주어진 글 다음에 이어질 글의 순서로 가장 적절한 것을 고르시오.

36.

Mrs. Klein told her first graders to draw a picture of something to be thankful for. She thought that most of the class would draw turkeys or Thanksgiving tables. But Douglas drew something different.

(A) The class was so responsive that Mrs. Klein had almost forgotten about Douglas. After she had the others at work on another project, she asked Douglas whose hand it was. He answered softly, "It's yours. Thank you, Mrs. Klein."

(B) Douglas was a boy who usually spent time alone and stayed around her while his classmates went outside together during break time. What the boy drew was a hand. But whose hand? His image immediately attracted the other students' interest.

(C) So, everyone rushed to talk about whose hand it was. "It must be the hand of God that brings us food," said one student. "A farmer's," said a second student, "because they raise the turkeys." "It looks more like a police officer's," added another, "they protect us."

① (A) - (C) - (B)   ② (B) - (A) - (C)
③ (B) - (C) - (A)   ④ (C) - (A) - (B)
⑤ (C) - (B) - (A)

37.

According to legend, once a vampire bites a person, that person turns into a vampire who seeks the blood of others. A researcher came up with some simple math, which proves that these highly popular creatures can't exist.

(A) In just two-and-a-half years, the original human population would all have become vampires with no humans left. But look around you. Have vampires taken over the world? No, because there's no such thing.

(B) If the first vampire came into existence that day and bit one person a month, there would have been two vampires by February 1st, 1600. A month later there would have been four, the next month eight, then sixteen, and so on.

(C) University of Central Florida physics professor Costas Efthimiou's work breaks down the myth. Suppose that on January 1st, 1600, the human population was just over five hundred million. [3점]

① (A) − (C) − (B)   ② (B) − (A) − (C)
③ (B) − (C) − (A)   ④ (C) − (A) − (B)
⑤ (C) − (B) − (A)

[38~39] 글의 흐름으로 보아, 주어진 문장이 들어가기에 가장 적절한 곳을 고르시오.

38.

For example, if you rub your hands together quickly, they will get warmer.

Friction is a force between two surfaces that are sliding, or trying to slide, across each other. For example, when you try to push a book along the floor, friction makes this difficult. Friction always works in the direction opposite to the direction in which the object is moving, or trying to move. So, friction always slows a moving object down. (①) The amount of friction depends on the surface materials. (②) The rougher the surface is, the more friction is produced. (③) Friction also produces heat. (④) Friction can be a useful force because it prevents our shoes slipping on the floor when we walk and stops car tires skidding on the road. (⑤) When you walk, friction is caused between the tread on your shoes and the ground, acting to grip the ground and prevent sliding.

       * skid: 미끄러지다 ** tread: 접지면, 바닥

39.

But, a blind person will associate the same friend with a unique combination of experiences from their non-visual senses that act to represent that friend.

Humans born without sight are not able to collect visual experiences, so they understand the world entirely through their other senses. (①) As a result, people with blindness at birth develop an amazing ability to understand the world through the collection of experiences and memories that come from these non-visual senses. (②) The dreams of a person who has been without sight since birth can be just as vivid and imaginative as those of someone with normal vision. (③) They are unique, however, because their dreams are constructed from the non-visual experiences and memories they have collected. (④) A person with normal vision will dream about a familiar friend using visual memories of shape, lighting, and colour. (⑤) In other words, people blind at birth have similar overall dreaming experiences even though they do not dream in pictures.

40. 다음 글의 내용을 한 문장으로 요약하고자 한다. 빈칸 (A), (B)에 들어갈 말로 가장 적절한 것은? [3점]

According to a study of Swedish adolescents, an important factor of adolescents' academic success is how they respond to challenges. The study reports that when facing difficulties, adolescents exposed to an authoritative parenting style are less likely to be passive, helpless, and afraid to fail. Another study of nine high schools in Wisconsin and northern California indicates that children of authoritative parents do well in school, because these parents put a lot of effort into getting involved in their children's school activities. That is, authoritative parents are significantly more likely to help their children with homework, to attend school programs, to watch their children in sports, and to help students select courses. Moreover, these parents are more aware of what their children do and how they perform in school. Finally, authoritative parents praise academic excellence and the importance of working hard more than other parents do.

↓

The studies above show that the children of authoritative parents often succeed academically, since they are more (A) to deal with their difficulties and are affected by their parents' (B) involvement.

   (A)   (B)
① likely ······ random
② willing ······ minimal
③ willing ······ active
④ hesitant ······ unwanted
⑤ hesitant ······ constant

[41~42] 다음 글을 읽고, 물음에 답하시오.

U.K. researchers say a bedtime of between 10 p.m. and 11 p.m. is best. They say people who go to sleep between these times have a (a) lower risk of heart disease. Six years ago, the researchers collected data on the sleep patterns of 80,000 volunteers. The volunteers had to wear a special watch for seven days so the researchers could collect data on their sleeping and waking times. The scientists then monitored the health of the volunteers. Around 3,000 volunteers later showed heart problems. They went to bed earlier or later than the (b) ideal 10 p.m. to 11 p.m. timeframe.

One of the authors of the study, Dr. David Plans, commented on his research and the (c) effects of bedtimes on the health of our heart. He said the study could not give a certain cause for their results, but it suggests that early or late bedtimes may be more likely to disrupt the body clock, with (d) positive consequences for cardiovascular health. He said that it was important for our body to wake up to the morning light, and that the worst time to go to bed was after midnight because it may (e) reduce the likelihood of seeing morning light which resets the body clock. He added that we risk cardiovascular disease if our body clock is not reset properly.

* disrupt: 혼란케 하다 ** cardiovascular: 심장 혈관의

41. 윗글의 제목으로 가장 적절한 것은?

① The Best Bedtime for Your Heart
② Late Bedtimes Are a Matter of Age
③ For Sound Sleep: Turn Off the Light
④ Sleeping Patterns Reflect Personalities
⑤ Regular Exercise: A Miracle for Good Sleep

42. 밑줄 친 (a)~(e) 중에서 문맥상 낱말의 쓰임이 적절하지 <u>않은</u> 것은?

① (a)   ② (b)   ③ (c)   ④ (d)   ⑤ (e)

[43~45] 다음 글을 읽고, 물음에 답하시오.

(A)

Once, a farmer lost his precious watch while working in his barn. It may have appeared to be an ordinary watch to others, but it brought a lot of happy childhood memories to him. It was one of the most important things to (a) him. After searching for it for a long time, the old farmer became exhausted.

* barn: 헛간(곡물·건초 따위를 두는 곳)

(B)

The number of children looking for the watch slowly decreased and only a few tired children were left. The farmer gave up all hope of finding it and called off the search. Just when the farmer was closing the barn door, a little boy came up to him and asked the farmer to give him another chance. The farmer did not want to lose out on any chance of finding the watch so let (b) him in the barn.

(C)

After a little while the boy came out with the farmer's watch in his hand. (c) He was happily surprised and asked how he had succeeded to find the watch while everyone else had failed. He replied "I just sat there and tried listening for the sound of the watch. In silence, it was much easier to hear it and follow the direction of the sound." (d) He was delighted to get his watch back and rewarded the little boy as promised.

(D)

However, the tired farmer did not want to give up on the search for his watch and asked a group of children playing outside to help him. (e) He promised an attractive reward for the person who could find it. After hearing about the reward, the children hurried inside the barn and went through and round the entire pile of hay looking for the watch. After a long time searching for it, some of the children got tired and gave up.

43. 주어진 글 (A)에 이어질 내용을 순서에 맞게 배열한 것으로 가장 적절한 것은?

① (B) − (D) − (C)   ② (C) − (B) − (D)
③ (C) − (D) − (B)   ④ (D) − (B) − (C)
⑤ (D) − (C) − (B)

44. 밑줄 친 (a) ~ (e) 중에서 가리키는 대상이 나머지 넷과 <u>다른</u> 것은?

① (a)   ② (b)   ③ (c)   ④ (d)   ⑤ (e)

45. 윗글에 관한 내용으로 적절하지 <u>않은</u> 것은?

① 농부의 시계는 어린 시절의 행복한 기억을 불러일으켰다.
② 한 어린 소년이 농부에게 또 한 번의 기회를 달라고 요청했다.
③ 소년이 한 손에 농부의 시계를 들고 나왔다.
④ 아이들은 시계를 찾기 위해 헛간을 뛰쳐나왔다.
⑤ 아이들 중 일부는 지쳐서 시계 찾기를 포기했다.

* 확인 사항
○ 답안지의 해당란에 필요한 내용을 정확히 기입(표기)했는지 확인하시오.

18

001 □ return ⓥ 돌아오다
002 □ leave behind ~을 남겨놓고 오다
003 □ lap ⓝ 무릎
004 □ clean ⓥ 닦다
005 □ inside ⓐⓓ 안에
006 □ appreciate ⓥ 감사하다

19

007 □ take ⓥ 데리고 가다
008 □ dress ⓥ 옷을 입다
009 □ swing ⓝ 그네
010 □ favorite ⓐ 매우 좋아하는
011 □ available ⓐ 이용할 수 있는
012 □ sink ⓥ 가라앉다
013 □ embarrassed ⓐ 당황한
014 □ indifferent ⓐ 무관심한
015 □ disappointed ⓐ 실망한
016 □ ashamed ⓐ 수치스러운
017 □ nervous ⓐ 긴장한
018 □ touched ⓐ 감동한
019 □ scared ⓐ 겁에 질린
020 □ relaxed ⓐ 느긋한

20

021 □ encourage ⓥ 촉진하다, 격려하다
022 □ creative ⓐ 창의적인
023 □ on average 평균적으로
024 □ participant ⓝ 참가자
025 □ consider ⓥ 여기다
026 □ meeting time 회의 시간
027 □ unproductive ⓐ 비생산적인
028 □ productive ⓐ 생산적인
029 □ discuss ⓥ 논의하다
030 □ expect ⓥ 기대하다

21

031 □ psychology ⓝ 심리학
032 □ raise ⓥ (무엇을 위로) 들어 올리다
033 □ management ⓝ 관리
034 □ principle ⓝ 원칙, 원리
035 □ heavy ⓐ 무거운
036 □ shout ⓥ 외치다
037 □ various ⓐ 다양한
038 □ reply ⓥ 대답하다
039 □ absolute ⓐ (상대적이 아닌) 절대적인
040 □ matter ⓥ 중요하다
041 □ depend ⓥ ~에 달려 있다, 좌우되다
042 □ quite ⓐⓓ 꽤
043 □ straight ⓐⓓ 계속해서
044 □ severe ⓐ 심각한
045 □ pain ⓝ 아픔, 통증, 고통
046 □ case ⓝ 사례
047 □ nod ⓥ 끄덕이다
048 □ in agreement 동의하며
049 □ continue ⓥ 계속하다, 이어서 말하다
050 □ sign ⓝ 신호
051 □ put down ~을 내려놓다
052 □ pour ⓥ 쏟다, 붓다
053 □ mistake ⓝ 실수
054 □ let go of ~을 내려놓다, 버리다, 포기하다
055 □ opinion ⓝ 의견

22

056 □ deserve ⓥ ~을 받을 만하다
057 □ attention ⓝ 주목
058 □ unreliable ⓐ 믿을 만하지 않은
059 □ inaccurate ⓐ 부정확한
060 □ source of information 정보 출처
061 □ reflection ⓝ 반영
062 □ conclude ⓥ 결론을 내리다
063 □ behavior ⓝ 행동, 태도
064 □ depressed ⓐ 우울한
065 □ decide ⓥ 결정하다
066 □ poorly ⓐⓓ 좋지 못하게
067 □ interview ⓝ 면접
068 □ mislead A into B A를 속여 B하게 하다
069 □ support ⓥ 뒷받침하다, 지지하다

23

070 □ explore ⓥ 탐구하다
071 □ construct ⓥ 구성하다
072 □ relationship ⓝ 관계
073 □ object ⓝ 사물
074 □ frequently ⓐⓓ 자주, 종종, 빈번히
075 □ exist ⓥ 존재하다
076 □ thus ⓐⓓ 따라서
077 □ sandbox ⓝ (어린이가 안에서 노는) 모래 놀이 통
078 □ compare ⓥ 비교하다
079 □ calculate ⓥ 계산하다
080 □ instance ⓝ 예시, 사례
081 □ notion ⓝ 개념
082 □ quantity ⓝ (측정 가능한) 양, 수량
083 □ reveal ⓥ 밝히다, 드러내다
084 □ investigate ⓥ 연구하다, 조사하다
085 □ concept ⓝ 개념
086 □ such as 예를 들어
087 □ sort A into B A를 B로 분류하다
088 □ shell ⓝ (조개 등의) 껍데기
089 □ advantage ⓝ 이점

24

090 □ generation ⓝ 세대
091 □ mention ⓥ 말하다, 언급하다
092 □ algorithm ⓝ 알고리즘, 연산
093 □ draw a blank 아무 반응을 얻지 못하다
094 □ civilization ⓝ 문명
095 □ connect ⓥ 이어지다, 연결되다
096 □ everyday life 일상생활
097 □ appliance ⓝ 가전 (제품)
098 □ here and there 여기저기에
099 □ fly an airplane 비행기를 운항하다
100 □ run ⓥ (사업체 등을) 운영하다
101 □ factory ⓝ 공장
102 □ trade ⓥ 거래하다, 교역하다
103 □ ancient ⓐ 고대의
104 □ decrease ⓥ 줄다, 감소하다
105 □ driving force 원동력

25

106 □ household ⓝ 가정, 가구
107 □ own ⓥ 보유하다, 소유하다
108 □ period ⓝ 기간, 시기
109 □ ownership ⓝ 보유, 소유(권)

110 □ rise ⓥ 오르다
111 □ additional ⓐ 추가의

26

112 □ composer ⓝ 작곡가
113 □ big band (재즈의) 빅 밴드
114 □ classical music 고전 음악
115 □ youth ⓝ 젊은 시절, 청춘
116 □ introduce ⓥ 소개하다
117 □ musician ⓝ 음악가
118 □ film music 영화 음악
119 □ collaborate with ~와 협업하다
120 □ flutist ⓝ 플루티스트
121 □ publish ⓥ 발매하다, 출간하다
122 □ well-known ⓐ 잘 알려진, 유명한

27

123 □ self-defense ⓝ 자기 방어
124 □ training ⓝ 교육, 훈련, 연수
125 □ social skill 사교성
126 □ water bottle 물병
127 □ expensive ⓐ 비싼

28

128 □ have a chance to ~할 기회를 갖다
129 □ operating hour 운영 시간
130 □ process ⓝ 과정
131 □ require ⓥ 필요로 하다

29

132 □ despite ⓟⓡⓔⓟ ~에도 불구하고
133 □ high-tech ⓐ 첨단 기술의
134 □ device ⓝ 장치, 기기
135 □ deny ⓥ 부인[부정]하다
136 □ nearly ⓐⓓ 거의
137 □ recently ⓐⓓ 최근에
138 □ consume ⓥ 소비하다
139 □ globally ⓐⓓ 전 세계적으로
140 □ grow ⓥ 커지다, 늘다, 많아지다
141 □ resource ⓝ 자원
142 □ advance ⓝ 발전
143 □ promise ⓝ 가능성
144 □ material ⓝ 물질, 자재, 재료
145 □ historically ⓐⓓ 역사적으로
146 □ dependently ⓐⓓ 의존적으로, 남에게 의지하여
147 □ natural resources 천연자원
148 □ stuff ⓝ 재료
149 □ industrial ⓐ 산업의
150 □ mineral ⓝ 광물
151 □ copper ⓝ 구리
152 □ rare ⓐ 희귀한, 드문
153 □ ago ⓐⓓ (얼마의 시간) 전에
154 □ individually ⓐⓓ 개별적으로, 각각 따로
155 □ lifestyle ⓝ 생활 방식

30

156 □ sometimes ⓐⓓ 때때로, 가끔
157 □ missing ⓐ 빠진, 실종된
158 □ else ⓐⓓ 다른
159 □ meet the expectation 기대를 충족하다
160 □ pressure ⓝ 압박, 압력

161 □ deceiving ⓐ 현혹시키는, 속이는
162 □ impact ⓥ 영향을 미치다
163 □ realize ⓥ 깨닫다, 알아차리다
164 □ lose ⓥ 잃어버리다
165 □ ignore ⓥ 무시하다
166 □ regain ⓥ 되찾다
167 □ recover ⓥ 회복하다
168 □ get rid of ~을 없애다
169 □ expectation ⓝ 예상, 기대
170 □ treat ⓥ 대하다
171 □ accept ⓥ 받아들이다

31

172 □ face ⓥ 직면하다
173 □ innovation ⓝ 혁신
174 □ entirely ⓐⓓ 완전히
175 □ virtually ⓐⓓ (컴퓨터를 이용해) 가상으로
176 □ expert ⓝ 전문가
177 □ have a negative effect on ~에 부정적 영향을 미치다
178 □ solve ⓥ 해결하다
179 □ overall ⓐⓓ 전반적으로, 대체로
180 □ constraint ⓝ 제한, 한계, 통제
181 □ collaboration ⓝ 공동 작업, 협업
182 □ face-to-face ⓐ 대면하는
183 □ setting ⓝ 설정
184 □ for instance 예를 들어
185 □ press ⓥ 누르다
186 □ control ⓥ 제어하다
187 □ breakout group (전체에서 나누어진) 소집단
188 □ enforce ⓥ 시행하다
189 □ at a time 한 번에
190 □ nonverbal ⓐ 비언어적인
191 □ particularly ⓐⓓ 특히
192 □ shoulder ⓝ 어깨
193 □ diminish ⓥ 줄이다
194 □ seating arrangement 좌석 배치
195 □ assign ⓥ 배정하다, 할당하다
196 □ access ⓝ 접근
197 □ stretch ⓥ 늘이다, 확장하다
198 □ restriction ⓝ 제한점
199 □ responsibility ⓝ 책임
200 □ coincidence ⓝ 우연의 일치, 동시 발생
201 □ tradition ⓝ 전통
202 □ boost ⓥ 증진시키다

32

203 □ law ⓝ 법칙
204 □ demand ⓝ 수요 ⓥ 필요로 하다, 요구하다
205 □ increase ⓥ 증가하다
206 □ fall ⓥ (값이) 떨어지다
207 □ type ⓝ 유형
208 □ apply for ~에 적용되다
209 □ instead ⓐⓓ 대신에
210 □ switch to ~로 바꾸다
211 □ cheaper ⓐ 값이 더 싼
212 □ replacement ⓝ 대체(품)
213 □ consumer ⓝ 소비자
214 □ decrease ⓥ 내리다
215 □ tend ⓥ 경향이 있다
216 □ purchase ⓥ 구입하다

217 □ reason [n] 이유
218 □ dairy [n] 유제품
219 □ pattern [n] (정형화된) 양식, 패턴
220 □ on the other hand 다른 한편으로는, 반면에
221 □ invest [v] 투자하다
222 □ overseas [ad] 해외에

33

223 □ study [n] 연구
224 □ look [v] ~ 을 조사하다, 관찰하다
225 □ different [a] 다른
226 □ intellectually [ad] 지적으로
227 □ superior [a] 우수한
228 □ modify [v] 수정하다, 바꾸다
229 □ gene [n] 유전자
230 □ glutamate [n] 글루타민산염
231 □ receptor [n] 수용체
232 □ chemical [n] 화학 물질
233 □ necessary [a] 필요한
234 □ genetically [ad] 유전적으로
235 □ manipulate [v] 다루다, 조작하다
236 □ inferior [a] 열등한
237 □ cage [n] 우리
238 □ wheel [n] 바퀴
239 □ handicapped [a] 장애가 있는, 불리한 입장인
240 □ perform [v] 수행하다
241 □ as well as ~ 과 마찬가지로 잘
242 □ triumph [n] 승리
243 □ nurture [n] 양육
244 □ survival [n] 생존
245 □ free from ~ 없이, ~을 면하여
246 □ entertain [v] 즐겁게 해 주다

34

247 □ researcher [n] 연구원
248 □ coastal [a] 해안의
249 □ prepare [v] 준비하다
250 □ sea level 해수면
251 □ assessment [n] 평가
252 □ actually [ad] 실제로
253 □ carry out ~을 수행[이행]하다
254 □ climate change 기후 변화
255 □ belief [n] 믿음, 신념
256 □ decade [n] 10년간
257 □ prediction [n] 예측
258 □ tense [n] (문법) 시제
259 □ future tense 미래 시제
260 □ ongoing [a] 진행 중인
261 □ region [n] 지방, 지역
262 □ affect [v] 영향을 미치다
263 □ crisis [n] 위기
264 □ Antarctic [a] 남극의
265 □ ice sheet 빙상
266 □ physically [ad] 물리적으로, 신체적으로
267 □ remote [a] 멀리 떨어진
268 □ relate [v] 관련시키다
269 □ far away 멀리
270 □ energy efficiency 에너지 효율
271 □ careful [a] 신중한
272 □ prevent [v] 막다

35

273 □ contribute to ~에 기여하다, ~의 원인이 되다
274 □ provide [v] 제공하다
275 □ medium [n] 수단
276 □ exhibit [v] 보여주다, 드러내다
277 □ virtue [n] 가치
278 □ innovative [a] 혁신적인
279 □ useful [a] 유용한
280 □ display [v] 드러내다
281 □ taste [n] 취향
282 □ care [n] 관심
283 □ represent [v] 나타내다, 표현하다
284 □ self-respect [n] 자기 존중, 자존심
285 □ concern [n] 관심, 우려
286 □ pleasure [n] 기쁨, 즐거움
287 □ link A to B A와 B를 연결하다
288 □ highly [ad] 매우
289 □ sociable [a] 사교적인, 사람들과 어울리기 좋아하는
290 □ along with ~와 더불어
291 □ opportunity [n] 기회
292 □ identity [n] 정체성

36

293 □ thankful [a] 고맙게 생각하는, 감사하는
294 □ turkey [n] 칠면조
295 □ thanksgiving [n] 추수감사절
296 □ responsive [a] 즉각 반응하는, 관심을 보이는
297 □ forget [v] 잊다
298 □ softly [ad] 부드럽게
299 □ stay [v] 머무르다
300 □ classmate [n] 반 친구
301 □ break time 휴식 시간
302 □ immediately [ad] 즉시
303 □ attract one's interest ~의 관심을 끌다
304 □ raise [v] 기르다, 키우다
305 □ police officer 경찰관
306 □ protect [v] 보호하다, 지키다

37

307 □ according [ad] ~에 의하면
308 □ legend [n] 전설
309 □ vampire [n] 흡혈귀
310 □ turn [v] (…한 상태로) 변하다
311 □ seek [v] 구하다
312 □ prove [v] 입증[증명]하다
313 □ popular [a] 인기 있는, 대중적인
314 □ creature [n] 생명이 있는 존재, 생물
315 □ human [n] 인류
316 □ look around 둘러보다
317 □ take over ~을 지배하다, 장악하다
318 □ no such thing 그런 일은 없다
319 □ come into existence 생기다, 나타나다
320 □ break down 무너뜨리다
321 □ myth [n] 미신, (잘못된) 통념

38

322 □ rub [v] 문지르다
323 □ friction [n] 마찰
324 □ force [n] 힘
325 □ surface [n] 표면
326 □ slide [v] 미끄러지다
327 □ each other 서로
328 □ direction [n] 방향
329 □ opposite [a] 반대의
330 □ slow down ~을 느려지게 하다
331 □ amount [n] 양
332 □ rough [a] 거친
333 □ slip [v] (넘어지거나 넘어질 뻔하게) 미끄러지다
334 □ slip [v] 미끄러지다
335 □ skid [v] 미끄러지다
336 □ tread [n] 접지면
337 □ act [v] 역할을 하다
338 □ grip [v] 붙잡다

39

339 □ blind person 맹인, 시각 장애인
340 □ associate A with B A와 B를 연결 짓다, 연상하다
341 □ unique [a] 독특한
342 □ combination [n] 조합
343 □ experience [n] 경험
344 □ non-visual 비시각적
345 □ sense [n] 감각
346 □ sight [n] 시력
347 □ collect [v] 모으다, 수집하다
348 □ understand [v] 이해하다
349 □ entirely [ad] 전적으로
350 □ result [n] 결과
351 □ amazing [a] 놀라운
352 □ ability [n] 능력
353 □ collection [n] 수집
354 □ dream [n] 꿈
355 □ vivid [a] 생생한
356 □ imaginative [a] 상상력이 풍부한
357 □ normal [a] 정상적인
358 □ vision [n] 시력
359 □ familiar [a] 익숙한, 친숙한
360 □ shape [n] 모양, 형태
361 □ in other words 다시 말해서
362 □ similar [a] 비슷한, 유사한

40

363 □ adolescent [n] 청소년
364 □ important [a] 중요한
365 □ factor [n] 요인
366 □ success [n] 성공
367 □ respond [v] 반응을 보이다
368 □ authoritative [a] 권위적인
369 □ parenting [n] 육아
370 □ passive [a] 수동적인, 소극적인
371 □ afraid [a] 두려워하는, 겁내는
372 □ indicate [v] 나타내다
373 □ involve [v] 관련시키다, 참여시키다
374 □ helpless [a] 무기력한
375 □ put effort into ~에 노력을 쏟다
376 □ significantly [ad] 상당히
377 □ homework [n] 숙제, 과제
378 □ attend [v] 참석하다, 참여하다
379 □ watch [v] 지켜보다
380 □ select [v] 선택하다
381 □ course [n] 강의, 과목
382 □ moreover [ad] 게다가, 더욱이
383 □ aware [a] 알고 있는
384 □ praise [v] 칭찬하다
385 □ random [a] 무작위적인
386 □ hesitant [a] 망설이는
387 □ constant [a] 지속적인

41~42

388 □ bedtime [n] 취침 시간
389 □ heart disease 심장병
390 □ volunteer [n] 지원자
391 □ monitor [v] 추적 관찰하다
392 □ health [n] 건강
393 □ go to bed 자다, 취침하다
394 □ ideal [a] 이상적인
395 □ timeframe [n] 기간, 시간
396 □ author [n] 저자
397 □ comment [v] 언급하다, 의견을 말하다
398 □ effect [n] 영향
399 □ certain [a] 확실한
400 □ cause [n] 원인
401 □ suggest [v] 암시하다, 시사하다
402 □ late [a] 늦은
403 □ disrupt [v] 혼란케 하다
404 □ body clock 생체 시계
405 □ consequence [n] 결과, 영향
406 □ cardiovascular [a] 심장 혈관의
407 □ midnight [n] 자정
408 □ likelihood [n] 가능성, 공산
409 □ reset [v] 다시 맞추다, 재설정하다
410 □ disease [n] 질환
411 □ properly [ad] 적절하게
412 □ sound [a] 좋은, 건전한
413 □ personality [n] 성격

43~45

414 □ farmer [n] 농부
415 □ watch [n] 시계
416 □ while [conj] ~하는 동안
417 □ barn [n] 헛간(곡물·건초 따위를 두는 곳)
418 □ ordinary [a] 평범한
419 □ others [n] 다른 사람들
420 □ bring [v] 가져다주다
421 □ childhood [n] 어린 시절
422 □ search [v] 찾아보다
423 □ for a long time 오랫동안
424 □ exhaust [v] 기진맥진하게 만들다
425 □ slowly [ad] 천천히, 서서히
426 □ tired [a] 지친
427 □ give up 포기하다
428 □ hope [n] 희망
429 □ precious [a] 소중한, 귀중한
430 □ call off ~을 중단하다, 멈추다
431 □ chance [n] 기회
432 □ lose out on ~을 놓치다, ~에게 지다
433 □ delight [v] 매우 기뻐하다
434 □ reward [v] 보상하다
435 □ promise [v] 약속하다
436 □ attractive [a] 매력적인
437 □ pile [n] 더미
438 □ hay [n] 건초

● 채점 : 맞은 개수 _____ / 80

TEST A-B 각 단어의 뜻을 [A] 영어는 우리말로, [B] 우리말은 영어로 쓰시오.

A	English	Korean
01	deceiving	
02	attractive	
03	principle	
04	self-defense	
05	discuss	
06	explore	
07	physically	
08	grip	
09	reflection	
10	unreliable	
11	coincidence	
12	prediction	
13	genetically	
14	unique	
15	ownership	
16	quantity	
17	consequence	
18	nurture	
19	touched	
20	publish	

B	Korean	English
01	과정	
02	해외에	
03	소비하다	
04	참가자	
05	표면	
06	수정하다, 바꾸다	
07	기르다, 키우다	
08	우수한	
09	가정, 가구	
10	구성하다	
11	회복하다	
12	부정확한	
13	평가	
14	가라앉다	
15	역사적으로	
16	소개하다	
17	소중한, 귀중한	
18	제한, 한계	
19	언급하다, 의견을 말하다	
20	관심, 우려	

▶ A-D 정답 : 해설편 080쪽

TEST C-D 각 단어의 뜻을 골라 기호를 쓰시오.

C	English		Korean
01	missing	( )	ⓐ 즉각 반응하는, 관심을 보이는
02	embarrassed	( )	ⓑ 개념
03	deserve	( )	ⓒ 계산하다
04	responsive	( )	ⓓ 청소년
05	pour	( )	ⓔ 생생한
06	material	( )	ⓕ 심각한
07	combination	( )	ⓖ 거래하다, 교역하다
08	trade	( )	ⓗ 문지르다
09	vivid	( )	ⓘ 늘이다, 확장하다
10	investigate	( )	ⓙ 빠진, 실종된
11	replacement	( )	ⓚ 가전제품
12	notion	( )	ⓛ ~을 받을 만하다
13	authoritative	( )	ⓜ 쏟다, 붓다
14	adolescent	( )	ⓝ 당황한
15	rub	( )	ⓞ 열등한
16	appliance	( )	ⓟ 물질, 자재, 재료
17	severe	( )	ⓠ 연구하다, 조사하다
18	inferior	( )	ⓡ 조합
19	calculate	( )	ⓢ 권위적인
20	stretch	( )	ⓣ 대체품

D	Korean		English
01	상상력이 풍부한	( )	ⓐ reveal
02	사교적인	( )	ⓑ immediately
03	줄이다	( )	ⓒ support
04	미신, (잘못된) 통념	( )	ⓓ imaginative
05	준비하다	( )	ⓔ taste
06	산업의	( )	ⓕ enforce
07	세대	( )	ⓖ industrial
08	비생산적인	( )	ⓗ dairy
09	가능성, 공산	( )	ⓘ sociable
10	즉시	( )	ⓙ slide
11	안에	( )	ⓚ represent
12	유제품	( )	ⓛ unproductive
13	미끄러지다	( )	ⓜ author
14	나타내다, 표현하다	( )	ⓝ prepare
15	취향	( )	ⓞ diminish
16	밝히다, 드러내다	( )	ⓟ creature
17	시행하다	( )	ⓠ inside
18	저자	( )	ⓡ likelihood
19	생명이 있는 존재, 생물	( )	ⓢ generation
20	뒷받침하다, 지지하다	( )	ⓣ myth

※ 영어 [독해] 파트만 수록한 문제지이므로 18번부터 시작합니다.
● 점수 표시가 없는 문항은 모두 2점 ● 문항수 28개 | 배점 63점 | 제한 시간 45분

18. 다음 글의 목적으로 가장 적절한 것은?

Dear Mr. Jones,

I am James Arkady, PR Director of KHJ Corporation. We are planning to redesign our brand identity and launch a new logo to celebrate our 10th anniversary. We request you to create a logo that best suits our company's core vision, 'To inspire humanity.' I hope the new logo will convey our brand message and capture the values of KHJ. Please send us your logo design proposal once you are done with it. Thank you.

Best regards,
James Arkady

① 회사 로고 제작을 의뢰하려고
② 변경된 회사 로고를 홍보하려고
③ 회사 비전에 대한 컨설팅을 요청하려고
④ 회사 창립 10주년 기념품을 주문하려고
⑤ 회사 로고 제작 일정 변경을 공지하려고

19. 다음 글에 드러난 Cindy의 심경 변화로 가장 적절한 것은?

One day, Cindy happened to sit next to a famous artist in a café, and she was thrilled to see him in person. He was drawing on a used napkin over coffee. She was looking on in awe. After a few moments, the man finished his coffee and was about to throw away the napkin as he left. Cindy stopped him. "Can I have that napkin you drew on?", she asked. "Sure," he replied. "Twenty thousand dollars." She said, with her eyes wide-open, "What? It took you like two minutes to draw that." "No," he said. "It took me over sixty years to draw this." Being at a loss, she stood still rooted to the ground.

① relieved → worried
② indifferent → embarrassed
③ excited → surprised
④ disappointed → satisfied
⑤ jealous → confident

20. 다음 글에서 필자가 주장하는 바로 가장 적절한 것은?

Sometimes, you feel the need to avoid something that will lead to success out of discomfort. Maybe you are avoiding extra work because you are tired. You are actively shutting out success because you want to avoid being uncomfortable. Therefore, overcoming your instinct to avoid uncomfortable things at first is essential. Try doing new things outside of your comfort zone. Change is always uncomfortable, but it is key to doing things differently in order to find that magical formula for success.

① 불편할지라도 성공하기 위해서는 새로운 것을 시도해야 한다.
② 일과 생활의 균형을 맞추는 성공적인 삶을 추구해야 한다.
③ 갈등 해소를 위해 불편함의 원인을 찾아 개선해야 한다.
④ 단계별 목표를 설정하여 익숙한 것부터 도전해야 한다.
⑤ 변화에 적응하기 위해 직관적으로 문제를 해결해야 한다.

21. 밑줄 친 <u>want to use a hammer</u>가 다음 글에서 의미하는 바로 가장 적절한 것은? [3점]

We have a tendency to interpret events selectively. If we want things to be "this way" or "that way" we can most certainly select, stack, or arrange evidence in a way that supports such a viewpoint. Selective perception is based on what seems to us to stand out. However, what seems to us to be standing out may very well be related to our goals, interests, expectations, past experiences, or current demands of the situation — "with a hammer in hand, everything looks like a nail." This quote highlights the phenomenon of selective perception. If we <u>want to use a hammer</u>, then the world around us may begin to look as though it is full of nails!

① are unwilling to stand out
② make our effort meaningless
③ intend to do something in a certain way
④ hope others have a viewpoint similar to ours
⑤ have a way of thinking that is accepted by others

22. 다음 글의 요지로 가장 적절한 것은?

Rather than attempting to punish students with a low grade or mark in the hope it will encourage them to give greater effort in the future, teachers can better motivate students by considering their work as incomplete and then requiring additional effort. Teachers at Beachwood Middle School in Beachwood, Ohio, record students' grades as *A*, *B*, *C*, or *I* (Incomplete). Students who receive an *I* grade are required to do additional work in order to bring their performance up to an acceptable level. This policy is based on the belief that students perform at a failure level or submit failing work in large part because teachers accept it. The Beachwood teachers reason that if they no longer accept substandard work, students will not submit it. And with appropriate support, they believe students will continue to work until their performance is satisfactory.

① 학생에게 평가 결과를 공개하는 것은 학습 동기를 떨어뜨린다.
② 학생에게 추가 과제를 부여하는 것은 학업 부담을 가중시킨다.
③ 지속적인 보상은 학업 성취도에 장기적으로 부정적인 영향을 준다.
④ 학생의 자기주도적 학습 능력은 정서적으로 안정된 학습 환경에서 향상된다.
⑤ 학생의 과제가 일정 수준에 도달하도록 개선 기회를 주면 동기부여에 도움이 된다.

23. 다음 글의 주제로 가장 적절한 것은?

Curiosity makes us much more likely to view a tough problem as an interesting challenge to take on. A stressful meeting with our boss becomes an opportunity to learn. A nervous first date becomes an exciting night out with a new person. A colander becomes a hat. In general, curiosity motivates us to view stressful situations as challenges rather than threats, to talk about difficulties more openly, and to try new approaches to solving problems. In fact, curiosity is associated with a less defensive reaction to stress and, as a result, less aggression when we respond to irritation.

* colander: (음식 재료의 물을 빼는 데 쓰는) 체

① importance of defensive reactions in a tough situation
② curiosity as the hidden force of positive reframes
③ difficulties of coping with stress at work
④ potential threats caused by curiosity
⑤ factors that reduce human curiosity

24. 다음 글의 제목으로 가장 적절한 것은?

When people think about the development of cities, rarely do they consider the critical role of vertical transportation. In fact, each day, more than 7 billion elevator journeys are taken in tall buildings all over the world. Efficient vertical transportation can expand our ability to build taller and taller skyscrapers. Antony Wood, a Professor of Architecture at the Illinois Institute of Technology, explains that advances in elevators over the past 20 years are probably the greatest advances we have seen in tall buildings. For example, elevators in the Jeddah Tower in Jeddah, Saudi Arabia, under construction, will reach a height record of 660m.

① Elevators Bring Buildings Closer to the Sky
② The Higher You Climb, the Better the View
③ How to Construct an Elevator Cheap and Fast
④ The Function of the Ancient and the Modern City
⑤ The Evolution of Architecture: Solutions for Overpopulation

25. 다음 도표의 내용과 일치하지 <u>않는</u> 것은?

Health Spending as a Share of GDP for Selected OECD Countries [2018]

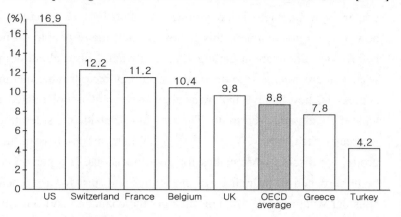

The above graph shows health spending as a share of GDP for selected OECD countries in 2018. ① On average, OECD countries were estimated to have spent 8.8 percent of their GDP on health care. ② Among the given countries above, the US had the highest share, with 16.9 percent, followed by Switzerland at 12.2 percent. ③ France spent more than 11 percent of its GDP, while Turkey spent less than 5 percent of its GDP on health care. ④ Belgium's health spending as a share of GDP sat between that of France and the UK. ⑤ There was a 3 percentage point difference in the share of GDP spent on health care between the UK and Greece.

26. Lithops에 관한 다음 글의 내용과 일치하지 <u>않는</u> 것은?

Lithops are plants that are often called 'living stones' on account of their unique rock-like appearance. They are native to the deserts of South Africa but commonly sold in garden centers and nurseries. Lithops grow well in compacted, sandy soil with little water and extreme hot temperatures. Lithops are small plants, rarely getting more than an inch above the soil surface and usually with only two leaves. The thick leaves resemble the cleft in an animal's foot or just a pair of grayish brown stones gathered together. The plants have no true stem and much of the plant is underground. Their appearance has the effect of conserving moisture.

* cleft: 갈라진 틈

① 살아있는 돌로 불리는 식물이다.
② 원산지는 남아프리카 사막 지역이다.
③ 토양의 표면 위로 대개 1인치 이상 자란다.
④ 줄기가 없으며 땅속에 대부분 묻혀 있다.
⑤ 겉모양은 수분 보존 효과를 갖고 있다.

27. "Go Green" Writing Contest에 관한 다음 안내문의 내용과 일치하지 <u>않는</u> 것은?

"Go Green" Writing Contest
Share your talents & conserve the environment

□ **Main Topic:** Save the Environment
□ **Writing Categories**
   • Slogan   • Poem   • Essay
□ **Requirements:**
• Participants: High school students
• Participate in one of the above categories
  (only one entry per participant)
□ **Deadline: July 5th, 2021**
• Email your work to apply@gogreen.com.
□ **Prize for Each Category**
   • 1st place: $80   • 2nd place: $60   • 3rd place: $40
□ The winners will be announced only on the website on July 15th, 2021. No personal contact will be made.
□ For more information, visit www.gogreen.com.

---

① 대회 주제는 환경 보호이다.
② 참가자는 한 부문에만 참가해야 한다.
③ 마감 기한은 7월 5일이다.
④ 작품은 이메일로 제출해야 한다.
⑤ 수상자는 개별적으로 연락받는다.

28. Virtual Idea Exchange에 관한 다음 안내문의 내용과 일치하는 것은?

Virtual Idea Exchange

Connect in real time and have discussions about the upcoming school festival.

□ **Goal**
• Plan the school festival and share ideas for it.
□ **Participants:** Club leaders only
□ **What to Discuss**
• Themes   • Ticket sales   • Budget
□ **Date & Time:** 5 to 7 p.m. on Friday, June 25th, 2021
□ **Notes**
• Get the access link by text message 10 minutes before the meeting and click it.
• Type your real name when you enter the chatroom.

---

① 동아리 회원이라면 누구나 참여 가능하다.
② 티켓 판매는 논의 대상에서 제외된다.
③ 회의는 3시간 동안 열린다.
④ 접속 링크를 문자로 받는다.
⑤ 채팅방 입장 시 동아리명으로 참여해야 한다.

29. 다음 글의 밑줄 친 부분 중, 어법상 틀린 것은? [3점]

There have been occasions ① in which you have observed a smile and you could sense it was not genuine. The most obvious way of identifying a genuine smile from an insincere ② one is that a fake smile primarily only affects the lower half of the face, mainly with the mouth alone. The eyes don't really get involved. Take the opportunity to look in the mirror and manufacture a smile ③ using the lower half your face only. When you do this, judge ④ how happy your face really looks — is it genuine? A genuine smile will impact on the muscles and wrinkles around the eyes and less noticeably, the skin between the eyebrow and upper eyelid ⑤ are lowered slightly with true enjoyment. The genuine smile can impact on the entire face.

30. 다음 글의 밑줄 친 부분 중, 문맥상 낱말의 쓰임이 적절하지 않은 것은? [3점]

Detailed study over the past two or three decades is showing that the complex forms of natural systems are essential to their functioning. The attempt to ① straighten rivers and give them regular cross-sections is perhaps the most disastrous example of this form-and-function relationship. The natural river has a very ② irregular form: it curves a lot, spills across floodplains, and leaks into wetlands, giving it an ever-changing and incredibly complex shoreline. This allows the river to ③ prevent variations in water level and speed. Pushing the river into tidy geometry ④ destroys functional capacity and results in disasters like the Mississippi floods of 1927 and 1993 and, more recently, the unnatural disaster of Hurricane Katrina. A $50 billion plan to "let the river loose" in Louisiana recognizes that the ⑤ controlled Mississippi is washing away twenty-four square miles of that state annually.

* geometry: 기하학 ** capacity: 수용능력

[31~34] 다음 빈칸에 들어갈 말로 가장 적절한 것을 고르시오.

31. In a culture where there is a belief that you can have anything you truly want, there is no problem in choosing. Many cultures, however, do not maintain this belief. In fact, many people do not believe that life is about getting what you want. Life is about doing what you are *supposed* to do. The reason they have trouble making choices is they believe that what they may want is not related to what they are supposed to do. The weight of outside considerations is greater than their _____. When this is an issue in a group, we discuss what makes for good decisions. If a person can be unburdened from their cares and duties and, just for a moment, consider what appeals to them, they get the chance to sort out what is important to them. Then they can consider and negotiate with their external pressures.

① desires   ② merits   ③ abilities
④ limitations   ⑤ worries

32. Research has confirmed that athletes are less likely to participate in unacceptable behavior than are non-athletes. However, moral reasoning and good sporting behavior seem to decline as athletes progress to higher competitive levels, in part because of the increased emphasis on winning. Thus winning can be _____ in teaching character development. Some athletes may want to win so much that they lie, cheat, and break team rules. They may develop undesirable character traits that can enhance their ability to win in the short term. However, when athletes resist the temptation to win in a dishonest way, they can develop positive character traits that last a lifetime. Character is a learned behavior, and a sense of fair play develops only if coaches plan to teach those lessons systematically.

* trait: 특성

① a piece of cake
② a one-way street
③ a bird in the hand
④ a fish out of water
⑤ a double-edged sword

33. Due to technological innovations, music can now be experienced by more people, for more of the time than ever before. Mass availability has given individuals unheard-of control over their own sound-environment. However, it has also confronted them with the simultaneous availability of countless genres of music, in which they have to orient themselves. People start filtering out and organizing their digital libraries like they used to do with their physical music collections. However, there is the difference that the choice lies in their own hands. Without being restricted to the limited collection of music-distributors, nor being guided by the local radio program as a 'preselector' of the latest hits, the individual actively has to _____.
The search for the right song is thus associated with considerable effort. [3점]

* simultaneous: 동시의

① choose and determine his or her musical preferences
② understand the technical aspects of recording sessions
③ share unique and inspiring playlists on social media
④ interpret lyrics with background knowledge of the songs
⑤ seek the advice of a voice specialist for better performances

34. It is common to assume that creativity concerns primarily the relation between actor(creator) and artifact(creation). However, from a sociocultural standpoint, the creative act is never "complete" in the absence of a second position — that of an audience. While the actor or creator him/herself is the first audience of the artifact being produced, this kind of distantiation can only be achieved by _____.
This means that, in order to be an audience to your own creation, a history of interaction with others is needed. We exist in a social world that constantly confronts us with the "view of the other." It is the view we include and blend into our own activity, including creative activity. This outside perspective is essential for creativity because it gives new meaning and value to the creative act and its product. [3점]

* artifact: 창작물

① exploring the absolute truth in existence
② following a series of precise and logical steps
③ looking outside and drawing inspiration from nature
④ internalizing the perspective of others on one's work
⑤ pushing the audience to the limits of its endurance

35. 다음 글에서 전체 흐름과 관계 <u>없는</u> 문장은? [3점]

Health and the spread of disease are very closely linked to how we live and how our cities operate. The good news is that cities are incredibly resilient. Many cities have experienced epidemics in the past and have not only survived, but advanced. ① The nineteenth and early-twentieth centuries saw destructive outbreaks of cholera, typhoid, and influenza in European cities. ② Doctors such as Jon Snow, from England, and Rudolf Virchow, of Germany, saw the connection between poor living conditions, overcrowding, sanitation, and disease. ③ A recognition of this connection led to the replanning and rebuilding of cities to stop the spread of epidemics. ④ In spite of reconstruction efforts, cities declined in many areas and many people started to leave. ⑤ In the mid-nineteenth century, London's pioneering sewer system, which still serves it today, was built as a result of understanding the importance of clean water in stopping the spread of cholera.

* resilient: 회복력이 있는　** sewer system: 하수 처리 시스템

[36~37] 주어진 글 다음에 이어질 글의 순서로 가장 적절한 것을 고르시오.

36.

Starting from birth, babies are immediately attracted to faces. Scientists were able to show this by having babies look at two simple images, one that looks more like a face than the other.

(A) These changes help the organisms to survive, making them alert to enemies. By being able to recognize faces from afar or in the dark, humans were able to know someone was coming and protect themselves from possible danger.

(B) One reason babies might like faces is because of something called evolution. Evolution involves changes to the structures of an organism(such as the brain) that occur over many generations.

(C) By measuring where the babies looked, scientists found that the babies looked at the face-like image more than they looked at the non-face image. Even though babies have poor eyesight, they prefer to look at faces. But why?

① (A) − (C) − (B)　　　② (B) − (A) − (C)
③ (B) − (C) − (A)　　　④ (C) − (A) − (B)
⑤ (C) − (B) − (A)

37.

> People spend much of their time interacting with media, but that does not mean that people have the critical skills to analyze and understand it.

(A) Research from New York University found that people over 65 shared seven times as much misinformation as their younger counterparts. All of this raises a question: What's the solution to the misinformation problem?

(B) One well-known study from Stanford University in 2016 demonstrated that youth are easily fooled by misinformation, especially when it comes through social media channels. This weakness is not found only in youth, however.

(C) Governments and tech platforms certainly have a role to play in blocking misinformation. However, every individual needs to take responsibility for combating this threat by becoming more information literate.

* counterpart: 상대방

① (A) − (C) − (B)　　② (B) − (A) − (C)
③ (B) − (C) − (A)　　④ (C) − (A) − (B)
⑤ (C) − (B) − (A)

[38~39] 글의 흐름으로 보아, 주어진 문장이 들어가기에 가장 적절한 곳을 고르시오.

38.

> As the sticks approach each other, the air immediately in front of them is compressed and energy builds up.

Sound and light travel in waves. An analogy often given for sound is that of throwing a small stone onto the surface of a still pond. Waves radiate outwards from the point of impact, just as sound waves radiate from the sound source. (①) This is due to a disturbance in the air around us. (②) If you bang two sticks together, you will get a sound. (③) When the point of impact occurs, this energy is released as sound waves. (④) If you try the same experiment with two heavy stones, exactly the same thing occurs, but you get a different sound due to the density and surface of the stones, and as they have likely displaced more air, a louder sound. (⑤) And so, a physical disturbance in the atmosphere around us will produce a sound.

* analogy: 비유 ** radiate: 사방으로 퍼지다

39.

> It has been observed that at each level of transfer, a large proportion, 80 − 90 percent, of the potential energy is lost as heat.

Food chain means the transfer of food energy from the source in plants through a series of organisms with the repeated process of eating and being eaten. (①) In a grassland, grass is eaten by rabbits while rabbits in turn are eaten by foxes. (②) This is an example of a simple food chain. (③) This food chain implies the sequence in which food energy is transferred from producer to consumer or higher trophic level. (④) Hence the number of steps or links in a sequence is restricted, usually to four or five. (⑤) The shorter the food chain or the nearer the organism is to the beginning of the chain, the greater the available energy intake is. [3점]

* trophic: 영양의

40. 다음 글의 내용을 한 문장으로 요약하고자 한다. 빈칸 (A), (B)에 들어갈 말로 가장 적절한 것은?

> A woman named Rhonda who attended the University of California at Berkeley had a problem. She was living near campus with several other people — none of whom knew one another. When the cleaning people came each weekend, they left several rolls of toilet paper in each of the two bathrooms. However, by Monday all the toilet paper would be gone. It was a classic tragedy-of-the-commons situation: because some people took more toilet paper than their fair share, the public resource was destroyed for everyone else. After reading a research paper about behavior change, Rhonda put a note in one of the bathrooms asking people not to remove the toilet paper, as it was a shared item. To her great satisfaction, one roll reappeared in a few hours, and another the next day. In the other note-free bathroom, however, there was no toilet paper until the following weekend, when the cleaning people returned.

↓

> A small ___(A)___ brought about a change in the behavior of the people who had taken more of the ___(B)___ goods than they needed.

　　(A)　　　　　(B)
① reminder ······ shared
② reminder ······ recycled
③ mistake ······ stored
④ mistake ······ borrowed
⑤ fortune ······ limited

[41~42] 다음 글을 읽고, 물음에 답하시오.

If you were afraid of standing on balconies, you would start on some lower floors and slowly work your way up to higher ones. It would be easy to face a fear of standing on high balconies in a way that's totally controlled. Socializing is (a) trickier. People aren't like inanimate features of a building that you just have to be around to get used to. You have to interact with them, and their responses can be unpredictable. Your feelings toward them are more complex too. Most people's self-esteem isn't going to be affected that much if they don't like balconies, but your confidence can (b) suffer if you can't socialize effectively.

It's also harder to design a tidy way to gradually face many social fears. The social situations you need to expose yourself to may not be (c) available when you want them, or they may not go well enough for you to sense that things are under control. The progression from one step to the next may not be clear, creating unavoidable large (d) decreases in difficulty from one to the next. People around you aren't robots that you can endlessly experiment with for your own purposes. This is not to say that facing your fears is pointless when socializing. The principles of gradual exposure are still very (e) useful. The process of applying them is just messier, and knowing that before you start is helpful.

41. 윗글의 제목으로 가장 적절한 것은?

① How to Improve Your Self-Esteem
② Socializing with Someone You Fear: Good or Bad?
③ Relaxation May Lead to Getting Over Social Fears
④ Are Social Exposures Related with Fear of Heights?
⑤ Overcoming Social Anxiety Is Difficult; Try Gradually!

42. 밑줄 친 (a)~(e) 중에서 문맥상 낱말의 쓰임이 적절하지 않은 것은?

① (a)   ② (b)   ③ (c)   ④ (d)   ⑤ (e)

[43~45] 다음 글을 읽고, 물음에 답하시오.

(A)

When I was 17, I discovered a wonderful thing. My father and I were sitting on the floor of his study. We were organizing his old papers. Across the carpet I saw a fat paper clip. Its rust dusted the cover sheet of a report of some kind. I picked it up. I started to read. Then I started to cry.

(B)

"Daddy," I said, handing him the pages, "this speech — how did you ever get permission to give it? And weren't you scared?" "Well, honey," he said, "I didn't ask for permission. I just asked myself, 'What is the most important challenge facing my generation?' I knew immediately. Then (a) I asked myself, 'And if I weren't afraid, what would I say about it in this speech?'"

(C)

It was a speech he had written in 1920, in Tennessee. Then only 17 himself and graduating from high school, he had called for equality for African Americans. (b) I marvelled, proud of him, and wondered how, in 1920, so young, so white, and in the deep South, where the law still separated black from white, (c) he had had the courage to deliver it. I asked him about it.

(D)

"I wrote it. And I delivered it. About half way through I looked out to see the entire audience of teachers, students, and parents stand up — and walk out. Left alone on the stage, (d) I thought to myself, 'Well, I guess I need to be sure to do only two things with my life: keep thinking for myself, and not get killed.'" He handed the speech back to me, and smiled. "(e) You seem to have done both," I said.

43. 주어진 글 (A)에 이어질 내용을 순서에 맞게 배열한 것으로 가장 적절한 것은?

① (B) − (D) − (C)   ② (C) − (B) − (D)
③ (C) − (D) − (B)   ④ (D) − (B) − (C)
⑤ (D) − (C) − (B)

44. 밑줄 친 (a)~(e) 중에서 가리키는 대상이 나머지 넷과 다른 것은?

① (a)   ② (b)   ③ (c)   ④ (d)   ⑤ (e)

45. 윗글에 관한 내용으로 적절하지 않은 것은?

① 아버지와 나는 서류를 정리하고 있었다.
② 나는 서재에서 발견한 것을 읽고 나서 울기 시작했다.
③ 아버지는 연설을 하기 위한 허락을 구하지 않았다.
④ 아버지가 연설문을 썼을 당시 17세였다.
⑤ 교사, 학생, 학부모 모두 아버지의 연설을 끝까지 들었다.

---

* 확인 사항
○ 답안지의 해당란에 필요한 내용을 정확히 기입(표기)했는지 확인하시오.

18

001 □ PR director 홍보부 이사
002 □ corporation ⓝ 기업, 회사
003 □ redesign ⓥ 다시 설계하다
004 □ identity ⓝ 정체성
005 □ launch ⓥ 시작하다, 런칭하다
006 □ logo ⓝ (회사·조직을 나타내는) 상징[로고]
007 □ celebrate ⓥ 기념하다
008 □ anniversary ⓝ 기념일
009 □ request ⓥ 요청하다
010 □ suit ⓥ ~에 적합하다
011 □ core ⓝ 핵심
012 □ inspire ⓥ 고무시키다
013 □ humanity ⓝ 인류애
014 □ convey ⓥ 전달하다
015 □ capture ⓥ (사진이나 글로 감정·분위기 등을) 정확히 담아내다

19

016 □ thrilled ⓐ 몹시 기쁜, 황홀해하는
017 □ in person 직접
018 □ draw ⓥ 그리다
019 □ awe ⓝ 경외심
020 □ reply ⓥ 대답하다
021 □ at a loss (무슨 말을 해야 할지) 모르는
022 □ rooted ⓐ (~에) 붙박인
023 □ indifferent ⓐ 무관심한
024 □ embarrassed ⓐ 당황한
025 □ surprised ⓐ 놀라는
026 □ disappointed ⓐ 실망한
027 □ satisfied ⓐ 만족하는
028 □ jealous ⓐ 질투하는
029 □ confident ⓐ 자신감 있는

20

030 □ avoid ⓥ 피하다
031 □ discomfort ⓝ 불편함
032 □ actively ⓐⓓ 적극적으로
033 □ shut out ~을 차단하다[가로막다]
034 □ uncomfortable ⓐ 불편한
035 □ therefore ⓐⓓ 따라서
036 □ overcome ⓥ 극복하다
037 □ instinct ⓝ 본능
038 □ essential ⓐ 필수적인, 본질적인
039 □ comfort zone 안전지대, 일을 적당히 하거나 요령을 피우는 상태
040 □ magical ⓐ 마법의
041 □ formula ⓝ 공식, 제조법

21

042 □ tendency ⓝ 경향
043 □ interpret ⓥ 해석하다
044 □ selectively ⓐⓓ 선택적으로
045 □ stack ⓥ 쌓다, 포개다
046 □ viewpoint ⓝ 관점
047 □ perception ⓝ 지각, 인식
048 □ be based on ~에 기초하다, 근거하다
049 □ stand out 두드러지다
050 □ be related to ~와 관련이 있다
051 □ interest ⓝ 관심, 관심사
052 □ expectation ⓝ 기대
053 □ demand ⓐⓥ 요구

054 □ hammer ⓝ 망치
055 □ nail ⓝ 못
056 □ quote ⓝ 인용구
057 □ highlight ⓥ 강조하다
058 □ phenomenon ⓝ 현상
059 □ unwilling ⓐ (~하기를) 꺼리는, 마지못해 하는
060 □ meaningless ⓐ 무의미한
061 □ intend ⓥ 의도하다, 하려고 하는

22

062 □ punish ⓥ 처벌하다
063 □ encourage ⓥ 격려하다, 용기를 주다
064 □ motivate ⓥ 동기를 부여하다
065 □ incomplete ⓐ 미완성된
066 □ additional ⓐ 추가적인
067 □ up to ~까지
068 □ acceptable ⓐ 수용 가능한
069 □ belief ⓝ 믿음
070 □ submit ⓥ 제출하다
071 □ in large part 대체로
072 □ reason ⓥ 추론하다, 생각하다
073 □ substandard ⓐ 수준 이하의, 열악한
074 □ appropriate ⓐ 적절한
075 □ satisfactory ⓐ 만족스러운

23

076 □ curiosity ⓝ 호기심
077 □ view ~ as ... ~을 …로 여기다
078 □ challenge ⓝ 도전
079 □ take on (책임이나 일을) 맡다, 지다
080 □ opportunity ⓝ 기회
081 □ threat ⓝ 위협
082 □ approach ⓝ 접근법
083 □ be associated with ~와 관련이 있다
084 □ defensive ⓐ 방어적인
085 □ aggression ⓝ 공격
086 □ irritation ⓝ 짜증
087 □ hidden ⓐ 숨은
088 □ cope with ~에 대처하다
089 □ potential ⓐ 잠재적인
090 □ reduce ⓥ 감소시키다

24

091 □ development ⓝ 발전
092 □ rarely ⓐⓓ 거의 ~하지 않는
093 □ critical ⓐ 중요한
094 □ vertical ⓐ 수직의
095 □ transportation ⓝ 운송, 수송
096 □ journey ⓝ 이동
097 □ efficient ⓐ 능률적인, 유능한; 효율적인
098 □ expand ⓥ 확장하다
099 □ skyscraper ⓝ 고층 건물
100 □ architecture ⓝ 건축
101 □ probably ⓐⓓ 아마도
102 □ under construction 건설 중인
103 □ ancient ⓐ 고대의
104 □ overpopulation ⓝ 인구 과잉

25

105 □ spending ⓝ (정부·조직체의) 지출
106 □ share ⓝ 점유율

107 □ selected ⓐ 선택된, 선발된
108 □ on average 평균적으로
109 □ estimate ⓥ 추정하다, 추산하다
110 □ difference ⓝ 차이

26

111 □ on account of ~ 때문에
112 □ rock-like ⓐ 바위 같은
113 □ appearance ⓝ 겉모습
114 □ native to ~이 원산지인
115 □ desert ⓝ 사막
116 □ commonly ⓐⓓ 일반적으로
117 □ garden center 식물원
118 □ nursery ⓝ 종묘원
119 □ compacted ⓐ 빽빽한, 탄탄한
120 □ extreme ⓐ 극도의
121 □ temperature ⓝ 온도
122 □ surface ⓝ 표면
123 □ gather ⓥ 모으다, 모이다
124 □ stem ⓝ 줄기
125 □ conserve ⓥ 보존하다
126 □ moisture ⓝ 습기

27

127 □ go green 친환경적이 되다
128 □ share ⓥ 나누다, 공유하다
129 □ category ⓝ 부문, 분야
130 □ requirement ⓝ 요구 사항
131 □ participant ⓝ 참가자
132 □ entry ⓝ 출품작
133 □ deadline ⓝ 기한, 마감 시간[일자]
134 □ announce ⓥ 공지하다, 발표하다

28

135 □ virtual ⓐ 가상의
136 □ real time 실시간
137 □ discussion ⓝ 토론
138 □ upcoming ⓐ 다가오는
139 □ access ⓝ 접속
140 □ text message 문자 메시지
141 □ type ⓥ (타자기·컴퓨터로) 타자 치다[입력하다]
142 □ chatroom ⓝ 채팅방, 대화방

29

143 □ occasion ⓝ 경우
144 □ observe ⓥ 목격하다, 관찰하다
145 □ sense ⓥ 이해하다
146 □ genuine ⓐ 진짜인
147 □ obvious ⓐ 명백한, 분명한
148 □ identify ⓥ 알아보다, 식별하다
149 □ insincere ⓐ 진실하지 않은
150 □ primarily ⓐⓓ 주로
151 □ affect ⓥ 영향을 미치다
152 □ lower ⓐ 아래쪽의
153 □ mainly ⓐⓓ 주로
154 □ involved ⓐ 관련이 있는
155 □ manufacture ⓥ 만들다
156 □ impact ⓥ 영향을 미치다
157 □ wrinkle ⓝ 주름
158 □ noticeably ⓐⓓ 눈에 띄게, 두드러지게
159 □ eyebrow ⓝ 눈썹
160 □ eyelid ⓝ 눈꺼풀

161 □ slightly ⓐⓓ 살짝, 약간
162 □ enjoyment ⓝ 즐거움
163 □ entire ⓐ 전체의

30

164 □ detailed ⓐ 자세한
165 □ decade ⓝ 10[십]년
166 □ functioning ⓝ 기능, 작용
167 □ attempt ⓝ 노력, 시도
168 □ straighten ⓥ 바로 펴다, 똑바르게 하다
169 □ regular ⓐ 규칙적인
170 □ cross-section ⓝ 횡단면
171 □ perhaps ⓐⓓ 아마, 어쩌면
172 □ disastrous ⓐ 처참한, 피해가 막심한
173 □ irregular ⓐ 불규칙한
174 □ curve ⓥ 굽이치다
175 □ spill ⓥ 흐르다, 쏟아지다
176 □ floodplain ⓝ 범람원
177 □ leak into ~에 새어 들어가다
178 □ wetland ⓝ 습지
179 □ incredibly ⓐⓓ 엄청나게, 믿을 수 없게
180 □ shoreline ⓝ 강가
181 □ prevent ⓥ 막다[예방/방지하다]
182 □ variation ⓝ 변이, 변화
183 □ destroy ⓥ 파괴하다
184 □ disaster ⓝ 재난, 재앙
185 □ controlled ⓐ 통제된
186 □ square mile 제곱마일
187 □ annually ⓐⓓ 매년, 연마다

31

188 □ maintain ⓥ 유지하다
189 □ be supposed to ~하기로 되어 있다
190 □ have trouble ~ing ~하는 데 어려움을 겪다
191 □ consideration ⓝ 고려 사항
192 □ decision ⓝ 결정, 판단
193 □ unburden ⓥ 벗어나게 하다
194 □ sort out ~을 가려내다
195 □ negotiate ⓥ 협상하다
196 □ external ⓐ 외부적인
197 □ desire ⓝ 욕망
198 □ merit ⓝ 장점
199 □ limitation ⓝ 한계

32

200 □ confirm ⓥ (맞다고) 확인하다
201 □ athlete ⓝ 운동선수
202 □ unacceptable ⓐ 받아들여지지 않는, 용인되지 않는
203 □ moral ⓐ 도덕적인
204 □ reasoning ⓝ 추론 (능력)
205 □ decline ⓥ 감소하다
206 □ progress ⓝ (앞으로무엇을 향해) 감[나아감]
207 □ competitive ⓐ 경쟁하는, 경쟁력 있는
208 □ emphasis ⓝ 강조
209 □ cheat ⓥ 속이다
210 □ undesirable ⓐ 바람직하지 않은
211 □ enhance ⓥ 강화하다
212 □ short term 단기의, 비교적 단기간의
213 □ resist ⓥ 저항하다
214 □ temptation ⓝ 유혹

215 ☐ dishonest ⓐ 부정직한
216 ☐ learned ⓐ 학습된, 후천적인
217 ☐ systematically ⓐⓓ 체계적으로
218 ☐ a piece of cake 식은 죽 먹기, 아주 쉬운 일
219 ☐ a one-way street 일방 통행로
220 ☐ a bird in the hand 수중에 든 새, 확실한 일
221 ☐ a fish out of water 물 밖에 나온 고기, 낯선 환경에서 불편해 하는 사람
222 ☐ a double-edged sword 양날의 검, 양면성을 가진 상황

33
223 ☐ innovation ⓝ 혁신
224 ☐ availability ⓝ 이용 가능성
225 ☐ individual ⓝ 개인
226 ☐ unheard-of ⓐ 전례 없는
227 ☐ confront A with B A를 B와 대면시키다
228 ☐ countless ⓐ 헤아릴 수 없는, 무수한
229 ☐ orient ⓥ 적응하다, 익숙해지다, 자기 위치를 알다
230 ☐ filter out ~을 걸러 내다
231 ☐ collection ⓝ 수집
232 ☐ lie ⓥ 있다, 존재하다
233 ☐ restrict ⓥ 국한시키다, 제한하다
234 ☐ distributor ⓝ 배급 업자
235 ☐ considerable ⓐ 상당한
236 ☐ determine ⓥ 결정하다
237 ☐ preferences ⓝ 선호
238 ☐ aspect ⓝ 측면
239 ☐ knowledge ⓝ 지식

34
240 ☐ common ⓐ 일반적인
241 ☐ assume ⓥ 가정하다, 추정하다
242 ☐ concern ⓥ 관련되다
243 ☐ relation ⓝ 관계
244 ☐ actor ⓝ 행위자
245 ☐ sociocultural ⓐ 사회문화적인
246 ☐ standpoint ⓝ 관점
247 ☐ in the absence of ~이 없을 때에
248 ☐ position ⓝ 입장
249 ☐ audience ⓝ 관객, 청중
250 ☐ distantiation ⓝ 거리두기
251 ☐ interaction ⓝ 상호 작용
252 ☐ constantly ⓐⓓ 지속적으로
253 ☐ confront ⓥ 직면하다, 맞서다
254 ☐ blend into ~에 뒤섞다
255 ☐ include ⓥ 포함하다
256 ☐ perspective ⓝ 관점
257 ☐ absolute ⓐ 절대적인
258 ☐ in existence 현존하는
259 ☐ precise ⓐ 정확한
260 ☐ logical ⓐ 논리적인
261 ☐ internalize ⓥ 내면화하다
262 ☐ endurance ⓝ 인내심, 참을성

35
263 ☐ spread ⓝ 확산 ⓥ 퍼지다
264 ☐ be linked to ~와 연관되다[관련이 있다]
265 ☐ operate ⓥ 작동되다
266 ☐ epidemic ⓝ 전염병

267 ☐ destructive ⓐ 파괴적인
268 ☐ outbreak ⓝ 발발, 창궐
269 ☐ typhoid ⓝ 장티푸스
270 ☐ overcrowding ⓝ 과밀 거주, 초만원
271 ☐ sanitation ⓝ 위생 (관리)
272 ☐ recognition ⓝ 인식
273 ☐ in spite of 불구하고
274 ☐ reconstruction ⓝ 재건
275 ☐ pioneering ⓐ 선구적인
276 ☐ as a result of ~의 결과로

36
277 ☐ be attracted to ~에 끌리다
278 ☐ immediately ⓐⓓ 즉시, 즉각
279 ☐ organism ⓝ 유기체
280 ☐ survive ⓥ 살아남다, 생존하다
281 ☐ alert ⓐ 경계하는
282 ☐ enemy ⓝ 적
283 ☐ recognize ⓥ 알아보다
284 ☐ afar ⓐⓓ 멀리
285 ☐ coming ⓐ 다가오는, 다음의
286 ☐ protect ⓥ 보호하다, 지키다
287 ☐ possible ⓐ 할 수 있는
288 ☐ danger ⓝ 위험
289 ☐ involve ⓥ 수반하다
290 ☐ structure ⓝ 구조
291 ☐ occur ⓥ 발생하다
292 ☐ measure ⓥ 측정하다, 유심히 바라보다
293 ☐ eyesight ⓝ 시력
294 ☐ prefer to B보다 A를 더 좋아하다

37
295 ☐ interact with ~와 상호 작용하다
296 ☐ analyze ⓥ 분석하다
297 ☐ misinformation ⓝ 오보, 잘못된 정보
298 ☐ raise a question 의문을 제기하다
299 ☐ well-known ⓐ 잘 알려진
300 ☐ demonstrate ⓥ 입증하다
301 ☐ fool ⓥ 속이다
302 ☐ especially ⓐⓓ 특히
303 ☐ weakness ⓝ 약점
304 ☐ youth ⓝ 젊은이
305 ☐ government ⓝ 정부
306 ☐ block ⓥ 막다, 차단하다
307 ☐ take responsibility for ~을 책임지다
308 ☐ combat ⓥ 싸우다
309 ☐ literate ⓐ ~을 다룰 줄 아는, 글을 읽고 쓸 줄 아는

38
310 ☐ approach ⓥ 다가가다[오다]
311 ☐ immediately ⓐⓓ 바로 옆에[가까이에]
312 ☐ compress ⓥ 압축하다
313 ☐ build up 축적되다
314 ☐ travel ⓥ 이동하다
315 ☐ wave ⓝ 파장
316 ☐ often ⓐⓓ 자주
317 ☐ onto prep (이동을 나타내는 동사와 함께 쓰여) 위에
318 ☐ pond ⓝ 연못
319 ☐ outward ⓐ (중심·특정 지점에서) 밖으로 향하는

320 ☐ impact ⓝ 충격, 여파
321 ☐ due to …때문에
322 ☐ disturbance ⓝ 교란, 방해
323 ☐ bang ⓥ 쾅 하고 치다
324 ☐ release ⓥ 방출하다
325 ☐ experiment ⓝ 실험 ⓥ 실험하다
326 ☐ density ⓝ 밀도
327 ☐ displace ⓥ 대체하다, (평소의 위치에서) 옮겨 놓다
328 ☐ atmosphere ⓝ (지구의) 대기
329 ☐ produce ⓥ 만들다

39
330 ☐ each ⓐ 각
331 ☐ transfer ⓝ 이동
332 ☐ proportion ⓝ 비율
333 ☐ potential ⓐ 잠재적
334 ☐ food chain 먹이 사슬
335 ☐ transfer ⓥ 이동하다
336 ☐ plant ⓝ 식물
337 ☐ a series of 일련의
338 ☐ repeated ⓐ 반복[되풀이]되는
339 ☐ process ⓝ 과정
340 ☐ grassland ⓝ 풀밭, 초원
341 ☐ in turn 이윽고, 차례로
342 ☐ imply ⓥ 암시하다
343 ☐ sequence ⓝ 연쇄, 사슬
344 ☐ consumer ⓝ 소비자
345 ☐ hence ⓐⓓ 이런 이유로
346 ☐ sequence ⓝ 배열
347 ☐ usually ⓐⓓ 보통
348 ☐ intake ⓝ 섭취량

40
349 ☐ attend ⓥ 다니다, 참석하다
350 ☐ problem ⓝ 문제
351 ☐ near ⓐⓓ 근처
352 ☐ several pron (몇)몇의
353 ☐ toilet paper 화장실 휴지
354 ☐ classic ⓐ 고전적인
355 ☐ tragedy of the commons 공유지의 비극
356 ☐ fair ⓐ 공평한
357 ☐ share ⓝ 몫
358 ☐ public ⓐ 공공의
359 ☐ resource ⓝ 자원, 재원
360 ☐ research paper 연구 논문
361 ☐ behavior change 행동 변화
362 ☐ note ⓝ 쪽지
363 ☐ remove ⓥ 없애다
364 ☐ satisfaction ⓝ 만족(감), 흡족; 만족(감을 주는 것)
365 ☐ reappear ⓥ 다시 나타나다
366 ☐ note-free 쪽지가 없는
367 ☐ following ⓐ (시간상으로) 그다음의
368 ☐ bring about ~을 야기하다
369 ☐ behavior ⓝ 행동
370 ☐ reminder ⓝ (잊고 있었던 것을) 상기시켜 주는 것
371 ☐ recycle ⓥ 재활용[재생]하다
372 ☐ mistake ⓝ 실수, 잘못
373 ☐ stored ⓐ 축적된
374 ☐ borrowed ⓐ 빌린, 빌려온

375 ☐ fortune ⓝ 행운
376 ☐ limited ⓐ 제한된

41~42
377 ☐ afraid ⓐ 두려워[무서워]하는
378 ☐ standing ⓐ 서 있는
379 ☐ face ⓥ 직면하다
380 ☐ socialize ⓥ (사람과) 사귀다, 사회화하다
381 ☐ tricky ⓐ 까다로운, 다루기 힘든
382 ☐ inanimate ⓐ 무생물의
383 ☐ get used to ~에 익숙해지다
384 ☐ interact ⓥ 상호 작용을 하다
385 ☐ response ⓝ 반응
386 ☐ unpredictable ⓐ 예측 불가한
387 ☐ complex ⓐ 복잡한
388 ☐ self-esteem ⓝ 자존감
389 ☐ affected ⓐ 영향받는
390 ☐ suffer ⓥ 고통을 받다
391 ☐ effectively ⓐⓓ 효과적으로
392 ☐ confidence ⓝ 자신감
393 ☐ tidy ⓐ 깔끔한
394 ☐ gradually ⓐⓓ 점차적으로
395 ☐ social fear 사회적 공포
396 ☐ social situation 사회적 상황
397 ☐ expose ⓥ 노출시키다
398 ☐ sense ⓥ 감지하다, 알아차리다
399 ☐ under control 통제되는
400 ☐ progression ⓝ 진전
401 ☐ clear ⓐ 분명한
402 ☐ unavoidable ⓐ 피할 수 없는
403 ☐ decrease ⓥ 줄다[감소하다]
404 ☐ difficulty ⓝ 어려움
405 ☐ endlessly ⓐⓓ 끝없이
406 ☐ purpose ⓝ 목적
407 ☐ pointless ⓐ 의미 없는
408 ☐ principle ⓝ 원칙, 원리
409 ☐ exposure ⓝ (유해한 환경 등에의) 노출
410 ☐ messy ⓐ 어수선한, 지저분한
411 ☐ improve ⓥ 높아지다
412 ☐ relaxation ⓝ 휴식
413 ☐ get over something ~을 극복[처리]하다
414 ☐ fear of heights 고소 공포증
415 ☐ anxiety ⓝ 불안(감), 염려

43~45
416 ☐ discover ⓥ 발견하다
417 ☐ wonderful ⓐ 놀라운
418 ☐ study ⓝ 서재
419 ☐ organize ⓥ 정리하다, 조직하다
420 ☐ paper ⓝ 서류
421 ☐ rust ⓝ 녹
422 ☐ dust ⓥ ~을 먼지투성이로 만들다
423 ☐ handing ⓥ 건네주다, 넘겨주다
424 ☐ permission ⓝ 허락
425 ☐ scared ⓐ 두려운, 무서운
426 ☐ graduate from ~을 졸업하다
427 ☐ call for ~을 요구하다, 필요로 하다
428 ☐ equality ⓝ 평등
429 ☐ marvel ⓥ 놀라다
430 ☐ separate ⓥ 분리시키다
431 ☐ courage ⓝ 용기
432 ☐ deliver ⓥ (연설이나 강연을) 하다

09회

● 채점 : 맞은 개수 _____ / 80

TEST A-B 각 단어의 뜻을 [A] 영어는 우리말로, [B] 우리말은 영어로 쓰시오.

A	English	Korean	B	Korean	English
01	gather		01	겉모습	
02	build up		02	유혹	
03	intake		03	진전	
04	spread		04	흐르다, 쏟아지다	
05	appropriate		05	본능	
06	limitation		06	허락	
07	decline		07	입증하다	
08	quote		08	호기심	
09	aggression		09	관점	
10	analyze		10	인류애	
11	pointless		11	강화하다	
12	equality		12	충격, 여파	
13	blend into		13	위생 (관리)	
14	occasion		14	추가적인	
15	awe		15	복잡한, 엉망진창인	
16	identity		16	다가가다[오다]	
17	considerable		17	고층 건물	
18	proportion		18	자존감	
19	reappear		19	협상하다	
20	vertical		20	유지하다	

▶ A-D 정답 : 해설편 090쪽

TEST C-D 각 단어의 뜻을 골라 기호를 쓰시오.

C	English		Korean	D	Korean		English
01	undesirable	( )	ⓐ 현존하는	01	파괴적인	( )	ⓐ upcoming
02	celebrate	( )	ⓑ 녹	02	내면화하다	( )	ⓑ acceptable
03	restrict	( )	ⓒ 해석하다	03	노력, 시도	( )	ⓒ attempt
04	classic	( )	ⓓ 처참한, 피해가 막심한	04	쌓다, 포개다	( )	ⓓ insincere
05	slightly	( )	ⓔ 처벌하다	05	다가오는	( )	ⓔ bring about
06	conserve	( )	ⓕ 위협	06	시력	( )	ⓕ cope with
07	in existence	( )	ⓖ 싸우다	07	절대적인	( )	ⓖ weight
08	interpret	( )	ⓗ 식은 죽 먹기	08	이윽고, 차례로	( )	ⓗ disastrous
09	thrilled	( )	ⓘ 살짝, 약간	09	이용 가능성	( )	ⓘ embarrassed
10	a piece of cake	( )	ⓙ 보존하다	10	~을 야기하다	( )	ⓙ eyesight
11	manufacture	( )	ⓚ 바람직하지 않은	11	당황한	( )	ⓚ absolute
12	inanimate	( )	ⓛ 무생물의	12	처참한, 피해가 막심한	( )	ⓛ indifferent
13	distantiation	( )	ⓜ 몹시 기쁜, 황홀해하는	13	~에 대처하다	( )	ⓜ availability
14	disastrous	( )	ⓝ 만들다	14	인구 과잉	( )	ⓝ internalize
15	phenomenon	( )	ⓞ 현상	15	피할 수 없는	( )	ⓞ noticeably
16	threat	( )	ⓟ 기념하다	16	비중, 무게	( )	ⓟ overpopulation
17	punish	( )	ⓠ 국한시키다, 제한하다	17	진실하지 않은	( )	ⓠ stack
18	alert	( )	ⓡ 고전적인	18	무관심한	( )	ⓡ unavoidable
19	rust	( )	ⓢ 경계하는	19	눈에 띄게, 두드러지게	( )	ⓢ in turn
20	combat	( )	ⓣ 거리두기	20	수용 가능한	( )	ⓣ destructive

※ 영어 [독해] 파트만 수록한 문제지이므로 18번부터 시작합니다.　　● 점수 표시가 없는 문항은 모두 2점　● 문항수 28개 | 배점 63점 | 제한 시간 45분

18. 다음 글의 목적으로 가장 적절한 것은?

Dear Mr. Anderson

On behalf of Jeperson High School, I am writing this letter to request permission to conduct an industrial field trip in your factory. We hope to give some practical education to our students in regard to industrial procedures. With this purpose in mind, we believe your firm is ideal to carry out such a project. But of course, we need your blessing and support. 35 students would be accompanied by two teachers. And we would just need a day for the trip. I would really appreciate your cooperation.

Sincerely,
Mr. Ray Feynman

① 공장 견학 허가를 요청하려고
② 단체 연수 계획을 공지하려고
③ 입사 방법을 문의하려고
④ 출장 신청 절차를 확인하려고
⑤ 공장 안전 점검 계획을 통지하려고

19. 다음 글에 드러난 Erda의 심경으로 가장 적절한 것은?

Erda lay on her back in a clearing, watching drops of sunlight slide through the mosaic of leaves above her. She joined them for a little, moving with the gentle breeze, feeling the warm sun feed her. A slight smile was spreading over her face. She slowly turned over and pushed her face into the grass, smelling the green pleasant scent from the fresh wild flowers. Free from her daily burden, she got to her feet and went on. Erda walked between the warm trunks of the trees. She felt all her concerns had gone away.

① relaxed ② puzzled ③ envious ④ startled ⑤ indifferent

20. 다음 글에서 필자가 주장하는 바로 가장 적절한 것은?

The dish you start with serves as an anchor food for your entire meal. Experiments show that people eat nearly 50 percent greater quantity of the food they eat first. If you start with a dinner roll, you will eat more starches, less protein, and fewer vegetables. Eat the healthiest food on your plate first. As age-old wisdom suggests, this usually means starting with your vegetables or salad. If you are going to eat something unhealthy, at least save it for last. This will give your body the opportunity to fill up on better options before you move on to starches or sugary desserts.

* anchor: 닻　** starch: 녹말

① 피해야 할 음식 목록을 만들어라.
② 다양한 음식들로 식단을 구성하라.
③ 음식을 조리하는 방식을 바꾸어라.
④ 자신의 입맛에 맞는 음식을 찾아라.
⑤ 건강에 좋은 음식으로 식사를 시작하라.

21. 밑줄 친 by reading a body language dictionary가 의미하는 바로 가장 적절한 것은? [3점]

Authentic, effective body language is more than the sum of individual signals. When people work from this rote-memory, dictionary approach, they stop seeing the bigger picture, all the diverse aspects of social perception. Instead, they see a person with crossed arms and think, "Reserved, angry." They see a smile and think, "Happy." They use a firm handshake to show other people "who is boss." Trying to use body language by reading a body language dictionary is like trying to speak French by reading a French dictionary. Things tend to fall apart in an inauthentic mess. Your actions seem robotic; your body language signals are disconnected from one another. You end up confusing the very people you're trying to attract because your body language just rings false.

① by learning body language within social context
② by comparing body language and French
③ with a body language expert's help
④ without understanding the social aspects
⑤ in a way people learn their native language

22. 다음 글의 요지로 가장 적절한 것은?

A goal-oriented mind-set can create a "yo-yo" effect. Many runners work hard for months, but as soon as they cross the finish line, they stop training. The race is no longer there to motivate them. When all of your hard work is focused on a particular goal, what is left to push you forward after you achieve it? This is why many people find themselves returning to their old habits after accomplishing a goal. The purpose of setting goals is to win the game. The purpose of building systems is to continue playing the game. True long-term thinking is goal-less thinking. It's not about any single accomplishment. It is about the cycle of endless refinement and continuous improvement. Ultimately, it is your commitment to the process that will determine your progress.

① 발전은 한 번의 목표 성취가 아닌 지속적인 개선 과정에 의해 결정된다.
② 결승선을 통과하기 위해 장시간 노력해야 원하는 바를 얻을 수 있다.
③ 성공을 위해서는 구체적인 목표를 설정하는 것이 중요하다.
④ 지난 과정을 끊임없이 반복하는 것이 성공의 지름길이다.
⑤ 목표 지향적 성향이 강할수록 발전이 빠르게 이루어진다.

23. 다음 글의 주제로 가장 적절한 것은?

Like anything else involving effort, compassion takes practice. We have to work at getting into the habit of standing with others in their time of need. Sometimes offering help is a simple matter that does not take us far out of our way — remembering to speak a kind word to someone who is down, or spending an occasional Saturday morning volunteering for a favorite cause. At other times, helping involves some real sacrifice. "A bone to the dog is not charity," Jack London observed. "Charity is the bone shared with the dog, when you are just as hungry as the dog." If we practice taking the many small opportunities to help others, we'll be in shape to act when those times requiring real, hard sacrifice come along.

① benefits of living with others in harmony
② effects of practice in speaking kindly
③ importance of practice to help others
④ means for helping people in trouble
⑤ difficulties with forming new habits

24. 다음 글의 제목으로 가장 적절한 것은?

Every event that causes you to smile makes you feel happy and produces feel-good chemicals in your brain. Force your face to smile even when you are stressed or feel unhappy. The facial muscular pattern produced by the smile is linked to all the "happy networks" in your brain and will in turn naturally calm you down and change your brain chemistry by releasing the same feel-good chemicals. Researchers studied the effects of a genuine and forced smile on individuals during a stressful event. The researchers had participants perform stressful tasks while not smiling, smiling, or holding chopsticks crossways in their mouths (to force the face to form a smile). The results of the study showed that smiling, forced or genuine, during stressful events reduced the intensity of the stress response in the body and lowered heart rate levels after recovering from the stress.

① Causes and Effects of Stressful Events
② Personal Signs and Patterns of Stress
③ How Body and Brain React to Stress
④ Stress: Necessary Evil for Happiness
⑤ Do Faked Smiles Also Help Reduce Stress?

25. 다음 도표의 내용과 일치하지 <u>않는</u> 것은?

Most Important Device for Internet Access:
2014 and 2016 in UK

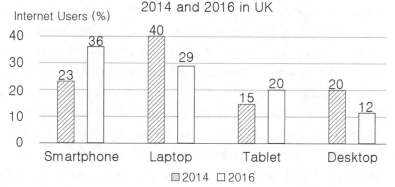

Internet Users (%)

☒2014 ☐2016

The above graph shows what devices British people considered the most important when connecting to the Internet in 2014 and 2016. ① More than a third of UK Internet users considered smartphones to be their most important device for accessing the Internet in 2016. ② In the same year, the smartphone overtook the laptop as the most important device for Internet access. ③ In 2014, UK Internet users were the least likely to select a tablet as their most important device for Internet access. ④ In contrast, they were the least likely to consider a desktop as their most important device for Internet access in 2016. ⑤ The proportion of UK Internet users who selected a desktop as their most important device for Internet access increased by half from 2014 to 2016.

* proportion: 비율

26. Sigrid Undset에 관한 다음 글의 내용과 일치하지 <u>않는</u> 것은?

Sigrid Undset was born on May 20, 1882, in Kalundborg, Denmark. She was the eldest of three daughters. She moved to Norway at the age of two. Her early life was strongly influenced by her father's historical knowledge. At the age of sixteen, she got a job at an engineering company to support her family. She read a lot, acquiring a good knowledge of Nordic as well as foreign literature, English in particular. She wrote thirty six books. None of her books leaves the reader unconcerned. She received the Nobel Prize for Literature in 1928. One of her novels has been translated into more than eighty languages. She escaped Norway during the German occupation, but she returned after the end of World War Ⅱ.

* Nordic: 북유럽 사람(의)

① 세 자매 중 첫째 딸로 태어났다.
② 어린 시절의 삶은 아버지의 역사적 지식에 큰 영향을 받았다.
③ 16세에 가족을 부양하기 위해 취업하였다.
④ 1928년에 노벨 문학상을 수상하였다.
⑤ 독일 점령 기간 중 노르웨이를 탈출한 후, 다시 돌아오지 않았다.

27. Swimming Summer Camp 2020에 관한 다음 안내문의 내용과 일치하지 <u>않는</u> 것은?

Swimming Summer Camp 2020

Great opportunity to learn basic swimming techniques with certified swimming coaches!

PARTICIPANTS & PERIOD
· Age 16 − 18 years
· July 27 − 31 (Monday − Friday)

DAILY SCHEDULE
11:00 a.m. − 12:00 p.m. Swimming Lesson
12:30 p.m. − 13:30 p.m. Lunch

PRICE
· $30 (lunch included)
※ A free swimming cap will be provided to all participants.

REGISTRATION
· Online only: www.friendlycoaches.ca

① 기본적인 수영 기법을 배울 수 있다.
② 오전 11시부터 수영 강습이 시작된다.
③ 요금에는 점심 식사비가 포함되어 있다.
④ 수영모가 모든 참가자에게 무료로 제공된다.
⑤ 등록을 위해 직접 방문해야 한다.

28. Rode Farmers Market에 관한 다음 안내문의 내용과 일치하는 것은?

Rode Farmers Market

This lively market is held every Saturday in July from 9:00 a.m. until 11:30 a.m.

Where	What to Do
Open Garden	Buy Local Organic Food
Picnic Area	Enjoy Fun Family Events and Local Music
Farmers' House	Learn Basic Farming Techniques

◈ In case of rain, some events may be cancelled.

Location
Village of Scholar Green on A34, Cheshire
◈ Free Parking

① 7월 매주 토요일 오후에 열린다.
② Open Garden에서 외국 음식을 구입할 수 있다.
③ Farmers' House에서 고급 농업 기술을 배울 수 있다.
④ 우천 시 몇몇 행사가 취소될 수 있다.
⑤ 주차 요금을 지불해야 한다.

29. 다음 글의 밑줄 친 부분 중, 어법상 <u>틀린</u> 것은? [3점]

　Positively or negatively, our parents and families are powerful influences on us. But even ① <u>stronger</u>, especially when we're young, are our friends. We often choose friends as a way of ② <u>expanding</u> our sense of identity beyond our families. As a result, the pressure to conform to the standards and expectations of friends and other social groups ③ <u>is likely</u> to be intense. Judith Rich Harris, who is a developmental psychologist, ④ <u>arguing</u> that three main forces shape our development: personal temperament, our parents, and our peers. The influence of peers, she argues, is much stronger than that of parents. "The world ⑤ <u>that</u> children share with their peers," she says, "is what shapes their behavior and modifies the characteristics they were born with, and hence determines the sort of people they will be when they grow up."

* temperament: 기질

30. (A), (B), (C)의 각 네모 안에서 문맥에 맞는 낱말로 가장 적절한 것은?

　The brain makes up just two percent of our body weight but uses 20 percent of our energy. In newborns, it's no less than 65 percent. That's partly why babies sleep all the time — their growing brains (A) warn / exhaust them — and have a lot of body fat, to use as an energy reserve when needed. Our muscles use even more of our energy, about a quarter of the total, but we have a lot of muscle. Actually, per unit of matter, the brain uses by far (B) more / less energy than our other organs. That means that the brain is the most expensive of our organs. But it is also marvelously (C) creative / efficient . Our brains require only about four hundred calories of energy a day — about the same as we get from a blueberry muffin. Try running your laptop for twenty-four hours on a muffin and see how far you get.

	(A)		(B)		(C)
①	warn	…	less	…	efficient
②	warn	…	more	…	efficient
③	exhaust	…	more	…	efficient
④	exhaust	…	more	…	creative
⑤	exhaust	…	less	…	creative

[31~34] 다음 빈칸에 들어갈 말로 가장 적절한 것을 고르시오.

31. When reading another scientist's findings, think critically about the experiment. Ask yourself: Were observations recorded during or after the experiment? Do the conclusions make sense? Can the results be repeated? Are the sources of information reliable? You should also ask if the scientist or group conducting the experiment was unbiased. Being unbiased means that you have no special interest in the outcome of the experiment. For example, if a drug company pays for an experiment to test how well one of its new products works, there is a special interest involved: The drug company profits if the experiment shows that its product is effective. Therefore, the experimenters aren't _____. They might ensure the conclusion is positive and benefits the drug company. When assessing results, think about any biases that may be present!

① inventive
② objective
③ untrustworthy
④ unreliable
⑤ decisive

32. Humans are champion long-distance runners. As soon as a person and a chimp start running they both get hot. Chimps quickly overheat; humans do not, because they are much better at shedding body heat. According to one leading theory, ancestral humans lost their hair over successive generations because less hair meant cooler, more effective long-distance running. That ability let our ancestors outmaneuver and outrun prey. Try wearing a couple of extra jackets — or better yet, fur coats — on a hot humid day and run a mile. Now, take those jackets off and try it again. You'll see what a difference _____ makes.

* shed: 떨어뜨리다　** outmaneuver: ~에게 이기다

① hot weather
② a lack of fur
③ muscle strength
④ excessive exercise
⑤ a diversity of species

33. Recently I was with a client who had spent almost five hours with me. As we were parting for the evening, we reflected on what we had covered that day. Even though our conversation was very collegial, I noticed that my client was holding one leg at a right angle to his body, seemingly wanting to take off on its own. At that point I said, "You really do have to leave now, don't you?" "Yes," he admitted. "I am so sorry. I didn't want to be rude but I have to call London and I only have five minutes!" Here was a case where my client's language and most of his body revealed nothing but positive feelings. His feet, however, were _____, and they clearly told me that as much as he wanted to stay, duty was calling. [3점]

* collegial: 평등하게 책임을 지는

① a signal of his politeness
② the subject of the conversation
③ expressing interest in my words
④ the most honest communicators
⑤ stepping excitedly onto the ground

34. One of the main reasons that students may think they know the material, even when they don't, is that they mistake familiarity for understanding. Here is how it works: You read the chapter once, perhaps highlighting as you go. Then later, you read the chapter again, perhaps focusing on the highlighted material. As you read it over, the material is familiar because you remember it from before, and this familiarity might lead you to think, "Okay, I know that." The problem is that this feeling of familiarity is not necessarily equivalent to knowing the material and may be of no help when you have to come up with an answer on the exam. In fact, familiarity can often lead to errors on multiple-choice exams because you might pick a choice that looks familiar, only to find later that it was something you had read, but _____. [3점]

* equivalent: 동등한

① you couldn't recall the parts you had highlighted
② it wasn't really the best answer to the question
③ that familiarity was based on your understanding
④ repetition enabled you to pick the correct answer
⑤ it indicated that familiarity was naturally built up

35. 다음 글에서 전체 흐름과 관계 없는 문장은?

Given the widespread use of emoticons in electronic communication, an important question is whether they help Internet users to understand emotions in online communication. ① Emoticons, particularly character-based ones, are much more ambiguous relative to face-to-face cues and may end up being interpreted very differently by different users. ② Nonetheless, research indicates that they are useful tools in online text-based communication. ③ One study of 137 instant messaging users revealed that emoticons allowed users to correctly understand the level and direction of emotion, attitude, and attention expression and that emoticons were a definite advantage in non-verbal communication. ④ In fact, there have been few studies on the relationships between verbal and nonverbal communication. ⑤ Similarly, another study showed that emoticons were useful in strengthening the intensity of a verbal message, as well as in the expression of sarcasm.

* ambiguous: 모호한 ** verbal: 언어적인 *** sarcasm: 풍자

[36~37] 주어진 글 다음에 이어질 글의 순서로 가장 적절한 것을 고르시오.

36.

Students work to get good grades even when they have no interest in their studies. People seek job advancement even when they are happy with the jobs they already have.

(A) It's like being in a crowded football stadium, watching the crucial play. A spectator several rows in front stands up to get a better view, and a chain reaction follows.

(B) And if someone refuses to stand, he might just as well not be at the game at all. When people pursue goods that are positional, they can't help being in the rat race. To choose not to run is to lose.

(C) Soon everyone is standing, just to be able to see as well as before. Everyone is on their feet rather than sitting, but no one's position has improved.

* rat race: 치열하고 무의미한 경쟁

① (A) − (C) − (B) ② (B) − (A) − (C)
③ (B) − (C) − (A) ④ (C) − (A) − (B)
⑤ (C) − (B) − (A)

37.

When we compare human and animal desire we find many extraordinary differences. Animals tend to eat with their stomachs, and humans with their brains.

(A) It is due, also, to the knowledge that, in an insecure world, pleasure is uncertain. Therefore, the immediate pleasure of eating must be exploited to the full, even though it does violence to the digestion.

(B) This is largely due to anxiety, to the knowledge that a constant supply of food is uncertain. Therefore, they eat as much as possible while they can.

(C) When animals' stomachs are full, they stop eating, but humans are never sure when to stop. When they have eaten as much as their bellies can take, they still feel empty, they still feel an urge for further gratification.

* gratification: 만족감

① (A) − (C) − (B)
② (B) − (A) − (C)
③ (B) − (C) − (A)
④ (C) − (A) − (B)
⑤ (C) − (B) − (A)

[38~39] 글의 흐름으로 보아, 주어진 문장이 들어가기에 가장 적절한 곳을 고르시오.

38.

Because of these obstacles, most research missions in space are accomplished through the use of spacecraft without crews aboard.

Currently, we cannot send humans to other planets. One obstacle is that such a trip would take years. (①) A spacecraft would need to carry enough air, water, and other supplies needed for survival on the long journey. (②) Another obstacle is the harsh conditions on other planets, such as extreme heat and cold. (③) Some planets do not even have surfaces to land on. (④) These explorations pose no risk to human life and are less expensive than ones involving astronauts. (⑤) The spacecraft carry instruments that test the compositions and characteristics of planets.

* composition: 구성 성분

39.

Grown-ups rarely explain the meaning of new words to children, let alone how grammatical rules work.

Our brains are constantly solving problems. (①) Every time we learn, or remember, or make sense of something, we solve a problem. (②) Some psychologists have characterized all infant language-learning as problem-solving, extending to children such scientific procedures as "learning by experiment," or "hypothesis-testing." (③) Instead they use the words or the rules in conversation and leave it to children to figure out what is going on. (④) In order to learn language, an infant must make sense of the contexts in which language occurs; problems must be solved. (⑤) We have all been solving problems of this kind since childhood, usually without awareness of what we are doing.

[3점]

40. 다음 글의 내용을 한 문장으로 요약하고자 한다. 빈칸 (A), (B)에 들어갈 말로 가장 적절한 것은? [3점]

Have you noticed that some coaches get the most out of their athletes while others don't? A poor coach will tell you what you did wrong and then tell you not to do it again: "Don't drop the ball!" What happens next? The images you see in your head are images of you dropping the ball! Naturally, your mind recreates what it just "saw" based on what it's been told. Not surprisingly, you walk on the court and drop the ball. What does the good coach do? He or she points out what could be improved, but will then tell you how you could or should perform: "I know you'll catch the ball perfectly this time." Sure enough, the next image in your mind is you *catching* the ball and *scoring* a goal. Once again, your mind makes your last thoughts part of reality — but this time, that "reality" is positive, not negative.

↓

Unlike ineffective coaches, who focus on players' ___(A)___, effective coaches help players improve by encouraging them to ___(B)___ successful plays.

	(A)		(B)
①	scores	⋯⋯	complete
②	scores	⋯⋯	remember
③	mistakes	⋯⋯	picture
④	mistakes	⋯⋯	ignore
⑤	strengths	⋯⋯	achieve

영어 영역(독해)

[41~42] 다음 글을 읽고, 물음에 답하시오.

Marketers have known for decades that you buy what you see first. You are far more likely to purchase items placed at eye level in the grocery store, for example, than items on the bottom shelf. There is an entire body of research about the way "product placement" in stores influences your buying behavior. This gives you a chance to use product placement to your advantage. Healthy items like produce are often the (a) least visible foods at home. You won't think to eat what you don't see. This may be part of the reason why 85 percent of Americans do not eat enough fruits and vegetables.

If produce is (b) hidden in a drawer at the bottom of your refrigerator, these good foods are out of sight and mind. The same holds true for your pantry. I used to have a shelf lined with salty crackers and chips at eye level. When these were the first things I noticed, they were my (c) primary snack foods. That same shelf is now filled with healthy snacks, which makes good decisions (d) easy. Foods that sit out on tables are even more critical. When you see food every time you walk by, you are likely to (e) avoid it. So to improve your choices, leave good foods like apples and pistachios sitting out instead of crackers and candy.

* produce: 농산물

41. 윗글의 제목으로 가장 적절한 것은?

① Why We Need to Consider Food Placement
② Pleasure Does Not Come from What You Buy
③ Which Do You Believe, Visible or Invisible?
④ A Secret for Health: Eat Less, Move More
⑤ Three Effective Ways to Tidy Things Up

42. 밑줄 친 (a)~(e) 중에서 문맥상 낱말의 쓰임이 적절하지 <u>않은</u> 것은? [3점]

① (a) ② (b) ③ (c) ④ (d) ⑤ (e)

[43~45] 다음 글을 읽고, 물음에 답하시오.

(A)

"Grandma," asked Amy, "are angels real?" "Some people say so," said Grandmother. Amy told Grandmother that she had seen them in pictures. But (a) she also wanted to know if her grandmother had ever actually seen an angel. Her grandmother said she had, but they looked different than in pictures. "Then, I am going to find one!" said Amy. "That's good! But I will go with you, because you're too little," said Grandmother. Amy complained, "But you walk so slowly." "I can walk faster than you think!" Grandmother replied, with a smile.

(B)

"That was not an angel!" said Amy. "No, in[…] Grandmother. So Amy walked ahead again. Then, (b)[…] beautiful woman who wore a dress as white as snow. "Y[…] be an angel!" cried Amy. "You dear little girl, do I really like an angel?" (c) she asked. "You are an angel!" replied An[…] But suddenly the woman's face changed when Amy stepped on[…] her dress by mistake. "Go away, and go back to your home!" she shouted.

(C)

So they started, Amy leaping and running. Then, she saw a horse coming towards them. On the horse sat a wonderful lady. When Amy saw her, the woman sparkled with jewels and gold, and her eyes were brighter than diamonds. "Are you an angel?" asked Amy. The lady gave no reply, but stared coldly at (d) her, leaving without saying a word.

(D)

As Amy stepped back from the woman, she stumbled and fell. (e) She lay in the dusty road and sobbed. "I am tired! Will you take me home, Grandma?" she asked. "Sure! That is what I came for," Grandmother said in a warm voice. They started to walk along the road. Suddenly Amy looked up and said, "Grandma, you are not an angel, are you?" "Oh, honey," said Grandmother, "I'm not an angel." "Well, Grandma, you are an angel to me because you always stay by my side," said Amy.

* stumble: 비틀거리다 ** sob: 흐느끼다

43. 주어진 글 (A)에 이어질 내용을 순서에 맞게 배열한 것으로 가장 적절한 것은?

① (B) − (D) − (C) ② (C) − (B) − (D)
③ (C) − (D) − (B) ④ (D) − (B) − (C)
⑤ (D) − (C) − (B)

44. 밑줄 친 (a)~(e) 중에서 가리키는 대상이 나머지 넷과 <u>다른</u> 것은?

① (a) ② (b) ③ (c) ④ (d) ⑤ (e)

45. 윗글의 Amy에 관한 내용으로 적절하지 <u>않은</u> 것은?

① 천사를 찾고 싶어했다.
② 한 여자의 드레스를 밟았다.
③ 말을 탄 여자로부터 친절한 대답을 들었다.
④ 할머니에게 집에 데려다 달라고 부탁했다.
⑤ 할머니를 천사라고 생각했다.

---

* 확인 사항

○ 답안지의 해당란에 필요한 내용을 정확히 기입(표기)했는지 확인하시오.

회차별 영단어 **QR 코드** ※ QR 코드를 스캔 후 모바일로 단어장처럼 학습할 수 있습니다. ● 고1 2020학년도 6월

001 ☐ **on behalf of** ~을 대표하여
002 ☐ **request** ⓥ 요청[요구/신청]하다
003 ☐ **permission** ⓝ 허가
004 ☐ **conduct** ⓥ 실시하다
005 ☐ **industrial** ⓐ 산업[공업]의
006 ☐ **field trip** 현장 견학
007 ☐ **practical** ⓐ 실제적인
008 ☐ **in regard to** ~에 관해
009 ☐ **procedure** ⓝ 절차
010 ☐ **ideal** ⓐ 이상적인
011 ☐ **carry out** 수행하다
012 ☐ **blessing** ⓝ 승인
013 ☐ **accompany** ⓥ ~와 동행하다
014 ☐ **appreciate** ⓥ 감사하다
015 ☐ **cooperation** ⓝ 협력, 협조

19
016 ☐ **clearing** ⓝ (숲 속의) 빈터
017 ☐ **sunlight** ⓝ 햇빛, 햇살
018 ☐ **mosaic** ⓐ 모자이크 모양의
019 ☐ **leaf** ⓝ (나뭇)잎
020 ☐ **above** prep (위치가) 위에
021 ☐ **gentle** ⓐ 부드러운
022 ☐ **breeze** ⓝ 산들바람
023 ☐ **feed** ⓝ 영양분, 먹이
024 ☐ **slight** ⓐ 약간의, 조금의
025 ☐ **spread** ⓥ 퍼지다
026 ☐ **scent** ⓝ 향기
027 ☐ **wild flowers** 야생화, 풀꽃
028 ☐ **free** ⓐ 벗어난
029 ☐ **burden** ⓝ 부담
030 ☐ **get to one's feet** 일어서다, 일어나다
031 ☐ **trunk** ⓝ (나무의) 기둥
032 ☐ **concern** ⓝ 걱정
033 ☐ **relaxed** ⓐ 여유로운
034 ☐ **puzzled** ⓐ 혼란스러운
035 ☐ **envious** ⓐ 부러워하는
036 ☐ **startled** ⓐ 놀란
037 ☐ **indifferent** ⓐ 무관심한

20
038 ☐ **dish** ⓝ 요리
039 ☐ **serve as** ~의 역할을 하다
040 ☐ **entire** ⓐ 전체의
041 ☐ **experiment** ⓝ 실험
042 ☐ **nearly** ad 거의
043 ☐ **quantity** ⓝ 양
044 ☐ **protein** ⓝ 단백질
045 ☐ **healthy** ⓐ 건강에 좋은
046 ☐ **plate** ⓝ 접시
047 ☐ **age-old** ⓐ 예로부터 전해 내려오는
048 ☐ **suggest** ⓥ 제안하다
049 ☐ **unhealthy** ⓐ 건강에 해로운
050 ☐ **opportunity** ⓝ 기회
051 ☐ **fill up** ~을 가득 채우다
052 ☐ **move on** ~로 넘어가다[이동하다]
053 ☐ **sugary** ⓐ 설탕이 든

21
054 ☐ **authentic** ⓐ 실효성 있는, 진짜의
055 ☐ **sum** ⓝ 합계

056 ☐ **individual** ⓐ 개별의
057 ☐ **signal** ⓝ 전달 신호
058 ☐ **rote-memory** ⓐ 기계적 암기의
059 ☐ **approach** ⓝ 접근법
060 ☐ **diverse** ⓐ 다양한
061 ☐ **aspect** ⓝ 측면
062 ☐ **perception** ⓝ 인식
063 ☐ **instead** ad 대신에
064 ☐ **reserved** ⓐ 과묵한
065 ☐ **fall apart** 분리되다
066 ☐ **inauthentic** ⓐ 진짜[진품/정통]가 아닌
067 ☐ **mess** ⓝ (많은 문제로) 엉망인 상황
068 ☐ **robotic** ⓐ (동작·표정 등이) 로봇같은
069 ☐ **disconnect** ⓥ 단절시키다
070 ☐ **end up** 결국 ~하게 되다
071 ☐ **attract** ⓥ (마음을) 끌다, 매혹시키다
072 ☐ **ring false** 잘못 전달되다
073 ☐ **context** ⓝ 맥락
074 ☐ **compare** ⓥ 비교하다
075 ☐ **expert** ⓝ 전문가의

22
076 ☐ **goal-oriented** ⓐ 목표 지향적인
077 ☐ **mind-set** ⓝ 사고방식
078 ☐ **work hard** 열심히 일하다
079 ☐ **as soon as** ~하자마자
080 ☐ **finish line** 결승선
081 ☐ **motivate** ⓥ 동기를 부여하다
082 ☐ **focus on** ~에 집중하다
083 ☐ **particular** ⓐ 특정한
084 ☐ **achieve** ⓥ 성취하다
085 ☐ **accomplish** ⓥ 성취하다
086 ☐ **long-term** ⓐ 장기적인
087 ☐ **endless** ⓐ 끝없는
088 ☐ **refinement** ⓝ 정제, 개선
089 ☐ **continuous** ⓐ 지속적인
090 ☐ **improvement** ⓝ 개선, 향상
091 ☐ **ultimately** ad 근본[본질]적으로
092 ☐ **commitment** ⓝ 몰두, 전념
093 ☐ **determine** ⓥ 결정하다
094 ☐ **progress** ⓝ 발전

23
095 ☐ **anything else** 무슨 다른 것
096 ☐ **involve** ⓥ (중요 요소로·필연적으로) 수반[포함]하다
097 ☐ **compassion** ⓝ 연민
098 ☐ **take practice** 연습하다
099 ☐ **get into a habit of** ~하는 습관을 들이다
100 ☐ **offering** ⓝ 제공된[내놓은] 것
101 ☐ **far** ad 멀리
102 ☐ **remembering** ⓝ 기억하기
103 ☐ **kind word** 선한 말
104 ☐ **occasional** ⓐ 가끔의
105 ☐ **cause** ⓝ 대의명분
106 ☐ **sacrifice** ⓝ 희생
107 ☐ **charity** ⓝ 자선
108 ☐ **just as** 꼭 ~처럼
109 ☐ **require** ⓥ 필요로 하다
110 ☐ **come along** 생기다, 발생하다
111 ☐ **benefit** ⓝ 혜택, 이득
112 ☐ **means** ⓝ 수단

24
113 ☐ **cause** ⓥ 원인 …을 야기하다
114 ☐ **produce** ⓥ 생산하다
115 ☐ **chemical** ⓝ 화학 물질
116 ☐ **force** ⓥ 억지[강제]로 …하다
117 ☐ **facial** ⓐ 얼굴의, 안면의
118 ☐ **muscular** ⓐ 근육의
119 ☐ **linked to** ~와 관계된, 연관된
120 ☐ **naturally** ad 자연스럽게
121 ☐ **calm down** 진정하다, ~을 진정시키다
122 ☐ **chemistry** ⓝ 화학 반응
123 ☐ **release** ⓥ 방출하다
124 ☐ **genuine** ⓐ 진정한
125 ☐ **during** prep (…하는 중에)
126 ☐ **participant** ⓝ 참가자
127 ☐ **perform** ⓥ 수행하다
128 ☐ **task** ⓝ 과업, 과제
129 ☐ **crossways** ad 옆으로, 가로로
130 ☐ **reduce** ⓥ 줄이다
131 ☐ **intensity** ⓝ 강도
132 ☐ **response** ⓝ 반응
133 ☐ **lower** ⓥ 낮추다
134 ☐ **heart rate** 심박동수
135 ☐ **recover from** ~에서 회복하다
136 ☐ **necessary evil** 필요악

25
137 ☐ **device** ⓝ 장치
138 ☐ **access** ⓝ 접속, 접근
       ⓥ ~에 접속하다, 접근하다
139 ☐ **consider** ⓥ 고려하다, 생각하다
140 ☐ **connect** ⓥ (인터넷이나 네트워크에) 접속하다
141 ☐ **overtake** ⓥ 추월하다
142 ☐ **proportion** ⓝ 비율
143 ☐ **increase** ⓥ 증가하다

26
144 ☐ **eldest** ⓐ 가장 나이가 많은 사람
145 ☐ **be influenced by** ~에 영향을 받다
146 ☐ **historical** ⓐ 역사적인
147 ☐ **knowledge** ⓝ 지식
148 ☐ **engineering** ⓝ 공학 기술
149 ☐ **support** ⓥ 지원하다, 뒷받침하다
150 ☐ **acquire** ⓥ 습득하다
151 ☐ **good** ⓐ 상당한
152 ☐ **literature** ⓝ 문학
153 ☐ **in particular** 특히
154 ☐ **unconcerned** ⓐ 무관심한, 흥미 없는
155 ☐ **translate A into B** A를 B로 번역하다
156 ☐ **escape** ⓥ 달아나다, 탈출하다
157 ☐ **occupation** ⓝ 점령

27
158 ☐ **learn** ⓥ 배우다
159 ☐ **basic** ⓐ 기초[기본]적인
160 ☐ **technique** ⓝ 기법
161 ☐ **certified** ⓐ 검증된, 보증된, 공인의
162 ☐ **period** ⓝ 기간, 시기
163 ☐ **included** ⓐ 포함된
164 ☐ **swimming cap** ⓝ 수영모
165 ☐ **registration** ⓝ 등록

28
166 ☐ **farmers market** 농산물 직판장
167 ☐ **lively** ⓐ 생동감 넘치는
168 ☐ **hold** ⓥ 열다, 거행[개최]하다
169 ☐ **farming technique** 농업기술
170 ☐ **in case of** ~의 경우에
171 ☐ **village** ⓝ (시골) 마을, 부락

29
172 ☐ **positively** ad 긍정적으로
173 ☐ **negatively** ad 부정적으로
174 ☐ **influence** ⓥ 영향을 미치다
175 ☐ **way** ⓝ 방법, 방식
176 ☐ **expand** ⓥ 확장하다
177 ☐ **sense of identity** 정체감
178 ☐ **beyond** prep ~을 넘어서서
179 ☐ **result** ⓝ 결과
180 ☐ **pressure** ⓝ 압박, 부담
181 ☐ **conform to** ~에 부합하다, 순응하다
182 ☐ **standard** ⓝ 기준
183 ☐ **expectation** ⓝ 기대
184 ☐ **social group** 사회 집단
185 ☐ **be likely to** 일어날 가능성이 있다
186 ☐ **intense** ⓐ 거센, 강렬한
187 ☐ **developmental** ⓐ 발달과 관련된
188 ☐ **argue** ⓥ 주장하다
189 ☐ **personal** ⓐ 개인적인
190 ☐ **peer** ⓝ 또래
191 ☐ **modify** ⓥ 수정하다
192 ☐ **characteristics** ⓝ 특성
193 ☐ **hence** ad 따라서, 이런 이유로

30
194 ☐ **make up** ~을 구성하다
195 ☐ **newborn** ⓝ 신생아
196 ☐ **no less than** 자그마치 ~이다
197 ☐ **partly** ad 부분적으로
198 ☐ **warn** ⓥ 주의를 주다
199 ☐ **exhaust** ⓥ 지치게 하다, 소진시키다
200 ☐ **reserve** ⓝ 보유량
201 ☐ **matter** ⓝ 물질
202 ☐ **organ** ⓝ (신체의) 기관
203 ☐ **marvelously** ad 놀랍도록
204 ☐ **creative** ⓐ 창의적인
205 ☐ **efficient** ⓐ 효율적인

31
206 ☐ **finding** ⓝ (조사, 연구 등의) 결과[결론]
207 ☐ **critically** ad 비판적으로
208 ☐ **observation** ⓝ 관찰
209 ☐ **conclusion** ⓝ 결론
210 ☐ **make sense** 합리적이다, 의미가 통하다
211 ☐ **source** ⓝ 출처
212 ☐ **reliable** ⓐ 신뢰성 있는, 믿을 만한
213 ☐ **unbiased** ⓐ 편파적이지 않은
214 ☐ **interest** ⓝ 이익
215 ☐ **outcome** ⓝ 결과
216 ☐ **profit** ⓥ 이득을 보다 ⓝ 이득
217 ☐ **experimenter** ⓝ 실험자
218 ☐ **ensure** ⓥ 보장하다
219 ☐ **assess** ⓥ 평가하다
220 ☐ **present** ⓐ 있는, 존재하는

221 ☐ inventive ⓐ 독창적인
222 ☐ objective ⓐ 객관적인
223 ☐ untrustworthy ⓐ 믿을 만하지 않은
224 ☐ decisive ⓐ 결정적인

32
225 ☐ champion ⓐ 최고의
226 ☐ long-distance runner 장거리 주자
227 ☐ overheat ⓥ 과열되다
228 ☐ according to (진술·기록 등에) 따르면
229 ☐ leading ⓐ 선도적인
230 ☐ theory ⓝ 이론
231 ☐ ancestral ⓐ 선조의, 조상의
232 ☐ successive ⓐ 잇따른, 연속적인
233 ☐ generation ⓝ 세대
234 ☐ outrun ⓥ ~보다 빨리 달리다
235 ☐ prey ⓝ 먹잇감
236 ☐ humid ⓐ 습한
237 ☐ excessive ⓐ 과도한
238 ☐ diversity ⓝ 다양성

33
239 ☐ client ⓝ 고객
240 ☐ part ⓥ 헤어지다
241 ☐ reflect on ~을 되새기다, 반추하다
242 ☐ cover ⓥ (기사 등에서) 다루다
243 ☐ notice ⓥ 알아채다
244 ☐ right angle 직각
245 ☐ seemingly ⓐⓓ 겉보기에는, 외견상
246 ☐ take off 떠나다
247 ☐ admit ⓥ 인정[시인]하다
248 ☐ rude ⓐ 무례한
249 ☐ case ⓝ 상황
250 ☐ reveal ⓥ 드러내 보이다
251 ☐ nothing but (단지) ~일 뿐인
252 ☐ clearly ⓐⓓ 분명히
253 ☐ duty ⓝ 맡은 일
254 ☐ subject ⓝ 주제
255 ☐ politeness ⓝ 공손함
256 ☐ communicator ⓝ 의사 전달자
257 ☐ excitedly ⓐⓓ 신나게, 들떠서

34
258 ☐ material ⓝ 자료
259 ☐ even ⓐⓓ (예상 밖이나 놀라운 일을 나타내어) …도[조차]
260 ☐ mistake ~ for ... ~를 …로 혼동하다
261 ☐ familiarity ⓝ 친숙함
262 ☐ understanding ⓝ (특정 주제·상황에 대한) 이해
263 ☐ chapter ⓝ (책의) 장
264 ☐ highlight ⓥ 강조 표시를 하다
265 ☐ later ⓐⓓ 나중에
266 ☐ not necessarily 반드시 ~한 것은 아니다
267 ☐ come up with ~을 떠올리다
268 ☐ multiple-choice ⓐ 선다형의, (시험 형태가) 객관식의
269 ☐ recall ⓥ 기억하다, 회상하다
270 ☐ repetition ⓝ 반복[되풀이]
271 ☐ enable ⓥ ~을 할 수 있게 하다
272 ☐ indicate ⓥ 나타내다[보여 주다]
273 ☐ build up 형성하다

35
274 ☐ given [prep] ~을 고려해 볼 때
275 ☐ widespread ⓐ 널리 퍼진
276 ☐ electronic ⓐ 전자상의
277 ☐ communication ⓝ 통신
278 ☐ emotion ⓝ 감정, 정서
279 ☐ particularly ⓐⓓ 특히
280 ☐ relative to ~에 비하여
281 ☐ face-to-face ⓐ 마주보는, 대면하는
282 ☐ cue ⓝ 신호
283 ☐ end up ~ing 결국 ~이 되다
284 ☐ interpret ⓥ 해석하다
285 ☐ different ⓐ 다른
286 ☐ nonetheless ⓐⓓ 그렇더라도
287 ☐ research ⓝ 연구
288 ☐ useful ⓐ 유용한
289 ☐ tool ⓝ 도구
290 ☐ allow ⓥ 허락하다
291 ☐ correct ⓐ 정확한
292 ☐ level and direction 정도와 방향
293 ☐ attitude ⓝ 태도
294 ☐ attention expression 주의력 표현
295 ☐ definite ⓐ 확실한
296 ☐ advantage ⓝ 장점
297 ☐ in fact 사실은
298 ☐ similarly ⓐⓓ 마찬가지로
299 ☐ expression ⓝ 표현
300 ☐ sarcasm ⓝ 풍자

36
301 ☐ interest ⓝ 관심
302 ☐ job advancement 승진
303 ☐ already ⓐⓓ 이미
304 ☐ crowded ⓐ 붐비는
305 ☐ stadium ⓝ 경기장
306 ☐ crucial ⓐ 중요한
307 ☐ spectator ⓝ (특히 스포츠 행사의) 관중
308 ☐ several ⓐ (몇)몇의
309 ☐ row ⓝ 열[줄]
310 ☐ in front 앞쪽에
311 ☐ view ⓥ 보다
312 ☐ chain reaction 연쇄 반응
313 ☐ refuse ⓥ 거절[거부]하다
314 ☐ pursue ⓥ 얻으려고 애쓰다, 추구하다
315 ☐ goods ⓝ 재화(이득)
316 ☐ positional ⓐ 위치상의
317 ☐ can't help ~ing ~하지 않을 수 없다
318 ☐ rat race 무의미한 경쟁
319 ☐ be on one's feet 일어서있다
320 ☐ position ⓝ 위치
321 ☐ improve ⓥ 나아지다, 개선되다

37
322 ☐ desire ⓝ 욕구, 욕망
323 ☐ extraordinary ⓐ 특별한
324 ☐ tend to (~하는) 경향이 있다
325 ☐ stomach ⓝ 위장
326 ☐ due ⓐ ~ 때문[덕분]에
327 ☐ insecure ⓐ 불안정한
328 ☐ uncertain ⓐ 불확실한
329 ☐ immediate ⓐ 즉각적인
330 ☐ pleasure ⓝ 즐거움

331 ☐ exploit ⓥ 이용하다
332 ☐ do violence ~을 해치다
333 ☐ digestion ⓝ 소화
334 ☐ largely ⓐⓓ 대체로, 주로
335 ☐ anxiety ⓝ 불안
336 ☐ constant ⓐ 지속적인
337 ☐ supply ⓝ 공급
338 ☐ possible ⓐ 가능한
339 ☐ belly ⓝ 배
340 ☐ empty ⓐ 공허한
341 ☐ urge ⓝ 충동
342 ☐ further ⓐ 더 이상의, 추가의

38
343 ☐ obstacle ⓝ 장애물
344 ☐ mission ⓝ 임무
345 ☐ space ⓝ 우주
346 ☐ spacecraft ⓝ 우주선
347 ☐ crew ⓝ 승무원
348 ☐ aboard ⓐⓓ 탑승하여
349 ☐ currently ⓐⓓ 현재, 지금
350 ☐ planet ⓝ 행성
351 ☐ send ⓥ 보내다
352 ☐ carry ⓥ 운반하다
353 ☐ survival ⓝ 생존
354 ☐ journey ⓝ (특히 멀리 가는) 여행
355 ☐ supplies ⓝ 물자, 보급품
356 ☐ harsh ⓐ 혹독한
357 ☐ condition ⓝ 조건
358 ☐ extreme ⓐ 극심한
359 ☐ land on ~에 착륙하다
360 ☐ exploration ⓝ 탐험, 탐사
361 ☐ pose a risk 위험을 끼치다
362 ☐ astronaut ⓝ 우주 비행사
363 ☐ instrument ⓝ 기구

39
364 ☐ grown-up ⓐ 다 큰, 어른이 된
365 ☐ rarely ⓐⓓ 거의 ~하지 않는
366 ☐ explain ⓥ 설명하다
367 ☐ meaning ⓝ 뜻[의미]
368 ☐ word ⓝ 단어
369 ☐ let alone ~은 말할 것도 없고, ~은 고사하고
370 ☐ grammatical ⓐ 문법적인
371 ☐ constantly ⓐⓓ 끊임없이
372 ☐ solve ⓥ 해결하다
373 ☐ make sense of ~을 이해하다
374 ☐ characterize ⓥ ~의 특징을 기술하다
375 ☐ infant ⓝ 유아
376 ☐ language-learning ⓝ 언어 학습
377 ☐ extend ⓥ 확장시키다
378 ☐ hypothesis ⓝ 가설
379 ☐ going on (일이) 일어나고 있는
380 ☐ in order to (목적) 위하여
381 ☐ awareness ⓝ 인식, 앎

40
382 ☐ coach ⓝ (스포츠 팀의) 코치
383 ☐ get the most out of ~을 최대한으로 활용하다
384 ☐ athlete ⓝ (운동) 선수

385 ☐ poor ⓐ 부족한
386 ☐ wrong ⓐ 틀린, 잘못된
387 ☐ drop ⓥ 떨어뜨리다
388 ☐ happen ⓥ 일어나다
389 ☐ naturally ⓐⓓ 당연히
390 ☐ recreate ⓥ 재현하다
391 ☐ surprisingly ⓐⓓ 놀랍게도
392 ☐ point out 지적하다
393 ☐ be improved 개선되다
394 ☐ perfectly ⓐⓓ 완벽하게
395 ☐ score ⓝ 득점 ⓥ 득점을 올리다
396 ☐ thought ⓝ 생각
397 ☐ negative ⓐ 부정적인
398 ☐ unlike [prep] ~와는 달리
399 ☐ ineffective ⓐ 무능한, 효과가 없는
400 ☐ encourage ⓥ 격려하다
401 ☐ successful ⓐ 성공적인
402 ☐ complete ⓥ 완수하다
403 ☐ picture ⓥ ~를 상상하다
404 ☐ ignore ⓥ 무시하다

41~42
405 ☐ decade ⓝ 수십년
406 ☐ item ⓝ 상품
407 ☐ grocery store 식료품점
408 ☐ bottom ⓝ 맨 아래
409 ☐ shelf ⓝ 선반
410 ☐ a body of 많은
411 ☐ placement ⓝ 배치
412 ☐ behavior ⓝ 행동
413 ☐ visible ⓐ 눈에 띄는
414 ☐ hide ⓥ 숨기다
415 ☐ refrigerator ⓝ 냉장고
416 ☐ to one's advantage ~에게 유리하게
417 ☐ pantry ⓝ 식료품 저장실
418 ☐ lined with ~이 줄지어 놓여있는
419 ☐ primary ⓐ 주된
420 ☐ filled with ~로 가득 찬
421 ☐ decision ⓝ 결정
422 ☐ sit ⓥ (어떤 곳에) 있다
423 ☐ critical ⓐ 중요한
424 ☐ avoid ⓥ 피하다
425 ☐ instead of … 대신에
426 ☐ tidy up ~을 정리하다

43~45
427 ☐ different than ~와는 다른
428 ☐ complain ⓥ 불평하다
429 ☐ reply ⓥ 대답하다 ⓝ 대답
430 ☐ indeed ⓐⓓ 정말[확실히]
431 ☐ ahead ⓐⓓ 앞으로, 앞에
432 ☐ suddenly ⓐⓓ 갑자기
433 ☐ step on ~을 밟다
434 ☐ by mistake 실수로
435 ☐ leap ⓥ 뛰어오르다
436 ☐ sparkle ⓥ 반짝이다
437 ☐ jewel ⓝ 보석
438 ☐ bright ⓐ 밝은
439 ☐ stare ⓥ 응시하다
440 ☐ coldly ⓐⓓ 차갑게
441 ☐ step back 뒤로 물러서다
442 ☐ dusty ⓐ 먼지투성이의

10회

TEST A-B 각 단어의 뜻을 [A] 영어는 우리말로, [B] 우리말은 영어로 쓰시오.

A	English	Korean	B	Korean	English
01	tidy up		01	지치게 하다, 소진시키다	
02	insecure		02	즉각적인	
03	excessive		03	물자, 보급품	
04	hypothesis		04	(기사 등에서) 다루다	
05	in case of		05	기억하다, 회상하다	
06	primary		06	점령	
07	refinement		07	관찰	
08	translate A into B		08	유아	
09	urge		09	추월하다	
10	quantity		10	평가하다	
11	conform to		11	대의명분	
12	reserve		12	허가	
13	anxiety		13	따라서, 이런 이유로	
14	scent		14	효율적인	
15	authentic		15	강도	
16	conduct		16	의사 전달자	
17	acquire		17	겉보기에는, 외견상	
18	leading		18	~하지 않을 수 없다	
19	row		19	이루다, 성취하다	
20	decisive		20	주의를 주다	

▶ A-D 정답 : 해설편 100쪽

TEST C-D 각 단어의 뜻을 골라 기호를 쓰시오.

C	English		Korean	D	Korean		English
01	let alone	( )	ⓐ ~와는 달리	01	이득을 보다; 이득	( )	ⓐ leap
02	developmental	( )	ⓑ 발달과 관련된	02	극심한	( )	ⓑ proportion
03	disconnect	( )	ⓒ 무관심한, 흥미 없는	03	결국 ~하게 되다	( )	ⓒ commitment
04	unlike	( )	ⓓ ~은 말할 것도 없고	04	습한	( )	ⓓ humid
05	unconcerned	( )	ⓔ 동기를 부여하다	05	붐비는	( )	ⓔ crowded
06	motivate	( )	ⓕ 이용하다	06	필요악	( )	ⓕ end up
07	a body of	( )	ⓖ 무례한	07	뛰어오르다	( )	ⓖ harsh
08	gentle	( )	ⓗ 수단	08	혹독한	( )	ⓗ profit
09	rude	( )	ⓘ ~을 대표하여	09	~와 동행하다	( )	ⓘ accompany
10	on behalf of	( )	ⓙ 많은	10	비율	( )	ⓙ certified
11	make sense of	( )	ⓚ ~을 이해하다	11	해석하다	( )	ⓚ necessary evil
12	compassion	( )	ⓛ 부드러운	12	검증된, 보증된, 공인의	( )	ⓛ interpret
13	reflect on	( )	ⓜ 연민	13	몰두, 전념	( )	ⓜ fall apart
14	means	( )	ⓝ 단절시키다	14	분리되다	( )	ⓝ extend
15	exploit	( )	ⓞ ~을 되새기다, 반추하다	15	확장시키다	( )	ⓞ extreme
16	grammatical	( )	ⓟ 확장하다	16	형성하다	( )	ⓟ build up
17	land on	( )	ⓠ ~에 착륙하다	17	보장하다	( )	ⓠ chemical
18	make up	( )	ⓡ ~을 구성하다	18	화학 물질	( )	ⓡ ensure
19	sum	( )	ⓢ 합계	19	영향을 미치다; 영향	( )	ⓢ influence
20	expand	( )	ⓣ 문법적인	20	중요한	( )	ⓣ critical

18. 다음 글의 목적으로 가장 적절한 것은?

To whom it may concern,

I am writing to express my deep concern about the recent change made by Pittsburgh Train Station. The station had traditional ticket offices with staff before, but these have been replaced with ticket vending machines. However, individuals who are unfamiliar with these machines are now experiencing difficulty accessing the railway services. Since these individuals heavily relied on the staff assistance to be able to travel, they are in great need of ticket offices with staff in the station. Therefore, I am urging you to consider reopening the ticket offices. With the staff back in their positions, many people would regain access to the railway services. I look forward to your prompt attention to this matter and a positive resolution.

Sincerely,
Sarah Roberts

① 승차권 발매기 수리를 의뢰하려고
② 기차표 단체 예매 방법을 문의하려고
③ 기차 출발 시간 지연에 대해 항의하려고
④ 기차역 직원의 친절한 도움에 감사하려고
⑤ 기차역 유인 매표소 재운영을 요구하려고

19. 다음 글에 드러난 Jeevan의 심경 변화로 가장 적절한 것은?

All the actors on the stage were focused on their acting. Then, suddenly, Arthur fell into the corner of the stage. Jeevan immediately approached Arthur and found his heart wasn't beating. Jeevan began CPR. Jeevan worked silently, glancing sometimes at Arthur's face. He thought, "Please, start breathing again, please." Arthur's eyes were closed. Moments later, an older man in a grey suit appeared, swiftly kneeling beside Arthur's chest. "I'm Walter Jacobi. I'm a doctor." He announced with a calm voice. Jeevan wiped the sweat off his forehead. With combined efforts, Jeevan and Dr. Jacobi successfully revived Arthur. Arthur's eyes slowly opened. Finally, Jeevan was able to hear Arthur's breath again, thinking to himself, "Thank goodness. You're back."

① thrilled → bored
② ashamed → confident
③ hopeful → helpless
④ surprised → indifferent
⑤ desperate → relieved

20. 다음 글에서 필자가 주장하는 바로 가장 적절한 것은?

As the parent of a gifted child, you need to be aware of a certain common parent trap. Of course you are a proud parent, and you should be. While it is very easy to talk nonstop about your little genius and his or her remarkable behavior, this can be very stressful on your child. It is extremely important to limit your bragging behavior to your very close friends, or your parents. Gifted children feel pressured when their parents show them off too much. This behavior creates expectations that they may not be able to live up to, and also creates a false sense of self for your child. You want your child to be who they are, not who they seem to be as defined by their incredible achievements. If not, you could end up with a driven perfectionist child or perhaps a drop-out, or worse.

① 부모는 자녀를 다른 아이와 비교하지 말아야 한다.
② 부모는 자녀의 영재성을 지나치게 자랑하지 말아야 한다.
③ 영재교육 프로그램에 대한 맹목적인 믿음을 삼가야 한다.
④ 과도한 영재교육보다 자녀와의 좋은 관계 유지에 힘써야 한다.
⑤ 자녀의 독립성을 기르기 위해 자기 일은 스스로 하게 해야 한다.

21. 밑줄 친 "hanging out with the winners"가 다음 글에서 의미하는 바로 가장 적절한 것은?

One valuable technique for getting out of helplessness, depression, and situations which are predominantly being run by the thought, "I can't," is to choose to be with other persons who have resolved the problem with which we struggle. This is one of the great powers of self-help groups. When we are in a negative state, we have given a lot of energy to negative thought forms, and the positive thought forms are weak. Those who are in a higher vibration are free of the energy from their negative thoughts and have energized positive thought forms. Merely to be in their presence is beneficial. In some self-help groups, this is called "hanging out with the winners." The benefit here is on the psychic level of consciousness, and there is a transfer of positive energy and relighting of one's own latent positive thought forms.

* latent: 잠재적인

① staying with those who sacrifice themselves for others
② learning from people who have succeeded in competition
③ keeping relationships with people in a higher social position
④ spending time with those who need social skill development
⑤ being with positive people who have overcome negative states

22. 다음 글의 요지로 가장 적절한 것은?

Our emotions are thought to exist because they have contributed to our survival as a species. Fear has helped us avoid dangers, expressing anger helps us scare off threats, and expressing positive emotions helps us bond with others. From an evolutionary perspective, an emotion is a kind of "program" that, when triggered, directs many of our activities (including attention, perception, memory, movement, expressions, etc.). For example, fear makes us very attentive, narrows our perceptual focus to threatening stimuli, will cause us either to face a situation (fight) or avoid it (flight), and may cause us to remember an experience more acutely (so that we avoid the threat in the future). Regardless of the specific ways in which they activate our systems, the specific emotions we possess are thought to exist because they have helped us (as a species) survive challenges within our environment long ago. If they had not helped us adapt and survive, they would not have evolved with us.

① 과거의 경험이 현재의 감정에 영향을 미친다.
② 문명의 발달에 따라 인간의 감정은 다양화되어 왔다.
③ 감정은 인간이 생존하도록 도와왔기 때문에 존재한다.
④ 부정적인 감정은 긍정적인 감정보다 더 오래 기억된다.
⑤ 두려움의 원인을 파악함으로써 두려움을 없앨 수 있다.

23. 다음 글의 주제로 가장 적절한 것은?

By improving accessibility of the workplace for workers that are typically at a disadvantage in the labour market, AI can improve inclusiveness in the workplace. AI-powered assistive devices to aid workers with visual, speech or hearing difficulties are becoming more widespread, improving the access to, and the quality of work for people with disabilities. For example, speech recognition solutions for people with dysarthric voices, or live captioning systems for deaf and hard of hearing people can facilitate communication with colleagues and access to jobs where inter-personal communication is necessary. AI can also enhance the capabilities of low-skilled workers, with potentially positive effects on their wages and career prospects. For example, AI's capacity to translate written and spoken word in real-time can improve the performance of non-native speakers in the workplace. Moreover, recent developments in AI-powered text generators can instantly improve the performance of lower-skilled individuals in domains such as writing, coding or customer service.

* dysarthric: (신경 장애로 인한) 구음(構音) 장애의

① jobs replaced by AI in the labour market
② ethical issues caused by using AI in the workplace
③ necessity of using AI technology for language learning
④ impacts of AI on supporting workers with disadvantages
⑤ new designs of AI technology to cure people with disabilities

24. 다음 글의 제목으로 가장 적절한 것은?

Whales are highly efficient at carbon storage. When they die, each whale sequesters an average of 30 tons of carbon dioxide, taking that carbon out of the atmosphere for centuries. For comparison, the average tree absorbs only 48 pounds of CO_2 a year. From a climate perspective, each whale is the marine equivalent of thousands of trees. Whales also help sequester carbon by fertilizing the ocean as they release nutrient-rich waste, in turn increasing phytoplankton populations, which also sequester carbon — leading some scientists to call them the "engineers of marine ecosystems." In 2019, economists from the International Monetary Fund (IMF) estimated the value of the ecosystem services provided by each whale at over $2 million USD. They called for a new global program of economic incentives to return whale populations to preindustrial whaling levels as one example of a "nature-based solution" to climate change. Calls are now being made for a global whale restoration program, to slow down climate change.

* sequester: 격리하다 ** phytoplankton: 식물성 플랑크톤

① Saving Whales Saves the Earth and Us
② What Makes Whales Go Extinct in the Ocean
③ Why Is Overpopulation of Whales Dangerous?
④ Black Money: Lies about the Whaling Industry
⑤ Climate Change and Its Effect on Whale Habitats

25. 다음 도표의 내용과 일치하지 <u>않는</u> 것은?

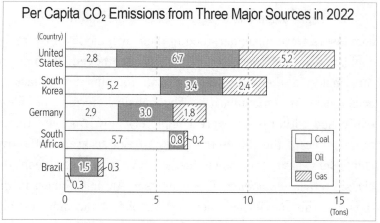

Per Capita CO₂ Emissions from Three Major Sources in 2022

The above graph shows per capita CO_2 emissions from coal, oil, and gas by countries in 2022. ① The United States had the highest total per capita CO_2 emissions, even though its emissions from coal were the second lowest among the five countries shown. ② South Korea's total per capita CO_2 emissions were over 10 tons, ranking it the second highest among the countries shown. ③ Germany had lower CO_2 emissions per capita than South Korea in all three major sources respectively. ④ The per capita CO_2 emissions from coal in South Africa were over three times higher than those in Germany. ⑤ In Brazil, oil was the largest source of CO_2 emissions per capita among its three major sources, just as it was in the United States and Germany.

* per capita: 1인당

26. Émilie du Châtelet에 관한 다음 글의 내용과 일치하지 <u>않는</u> 것은?

Émilie du Châtelet, a French mathematician and physicist, was born in Paris in 1706. During her childhood, with her father's support, she was able to get mathematical and scientific education that most women of her time did not receive. In 1737, she submitted her paper on the nature of fire to a contest sponsored by the French Academy of Sciences, and it was published a year later. In her book, *Institutions de Physique*, Émilie du Châtelet explained the ideas of space and time in a way that is closer to what we understand in modern relativity than what was common during her time. Her most significant achievement was translating Isaac Newton's *Principia* into French near the end of her life. Émilie du Châtelet's work was not recognized in her time, but she is now remembered as a symbol of the Enlightenment and the struggle for women's participation in science.

① 어린 시절에 수학과 과학 교육을 받았다.
② 불의 속성에 관한 그녀의 논문이 1737년에 출간되었다.
③ *Institutions de Physique*에서 공간과 시간의 개념을 설명했다.
④ 아이작 뉴턴의 *Principia*를 프랑스어로 번역했다.
⑤ 이룩한 업적은 당대에 인정받지 못했다.

27. 2024 Young Inventors Robot Competition에 관한 다음 안내문의 내용과 일치하지 <u>않는</u> 것은?

2024 Young Inventors Robot Competition

Join us for an exciting day of the Young Inventors Robot Competition!

☐ **Categories**
- Participants can compete in one of the following categories:
  · Robot Design · Robot Coding · Robot Remote Control

☐ **Date and Time**
- September 28, 2024, 10 a.m. to 3 p.m.

☐ **Location**
- Computer Lab, Oakwood University

☐ **Registration**
- From August 1 to August 10, 2024
- Open to high school students
- Online registration only (www.younginventors.edu)

☐ **Awards**
- In each competition category, three participants will be honored.
  · 1st place: $300 · 2nd place: $200 · 3rd place: $100

※ For more information, visit our website.

① 세 가지 분야 중 하나에 참가할 수 있다.
② 9월 28일에 5시간 동안 열린다.
③ 고등학생이 등록할 수 있다.
④ 등록은 온라인으로만 가능하다.
⑤ 수상자는 각 분야당 한 명이다.

28. Saintville Art Week Stamp Tour에 관한 다음 안내문의 내용과 일치하는 것은?

Saintville Art Week Stamp Tour

The 8th annual Saintville Art Week Stamp Tour is back this year! Anyone can participate in our event. Join us and enjoy exhibitions and new collections.

☐ **When:** The first week of October, 2024

☐ **Where:** Saintville Arts District

☐ **How:**
Step 1. Take a stamp tour map from the Saintville Arts Center.
Step 2. Get stamps from at least 3 out of 5 spots and receive your gift.
- You can choose either an umbrella or a mug with printed artwork on it for your gift.

※ For more information, please visit our website at www.SaintvilleArtsCenter.com.

① 참가 대상에 제한이 있다.
② 10월 둘째 주에 진행된다.
③ Saintville Arts Center에서 스탬프 투어 지도를 받는다.
④ 적어도 다섯 곳에서 도장을 받아야 선물을 받는다.
⑤ 선물로 가방과 머그잔 중 하나를 고를 수 있다.

29. 다음 글의 밑줄 친 부분 중, 어법상 <u>틀린</u> 것은?

From an organizational viewpoint, one of the most fascinating examples of how any organization may contain many different types of culture ① is to recognize the functional operations of different departments within the organization. The varying departments and divisions within an organization will inevitably view any given situation from their own biased and prejudiced perspective. A department and its members will acquire "tunnel vision" which disallows them to see things as others see ② them. The very structure of organizations can create conflict. The choice of ③ whether the structure is "mechanistic" or "organic" can have a profound influence on conflict management. A mechanistic structure has a vertical hierarchy with many rules, many procedures, and many levels of management ④ involved in decision making. Organic structures are more horizontal in nature, ⑤ which decision making is less centralized and spread across the plane of the organization.

* hierarchy: 위계

30. 다음 글의 밑줄 친 부분 중, 문맥상 낱말의 쓰임이 적절하지 <u>않은</u> 것은? [3점]

An excellent alternative to calming traffic is removing it. Some cities ① reserve an extensive network of lanes and streets for bikes, pedestrians, and the occasional service vehicle. This motivates people to travel by bike rather than by car, making streets safer for everyone. As bicycles become more ② popular in a city, planners can convert more automobile lanes and entire streets to accommodate more of them. Nevertheless, even the most bikeable cities still ③ require motor vehicle lanes for taxis, emergency vehicles, and delivery trucks. Delivery vehicles are frequently a target of animus, but they are actually an essential component to making cities greener. A tightly packed delivery truck is a far more ④ inefficient transporter of goods than several hybrids carrying a few shopping bags each. Distributing food and other goods to neighborhood vendors ⑤ allows them to operate smaller stores close to homes so that residents can walk, rather than drive, to get their groceries.

* animus: 반감, 미움

[31~34] 다음 빈칸에 들어갈 말로 가장 적절한 것을 고르시오.

31. You hear again and again that some of the greatest composers were misunderstood in their own day. Not everyone could understand the compositions of Beethoven, Brahms, or Stravinsky in their day. The reason for this initial lack of acceptance is unfamiliarity. The musical forms, or ideas expressed within them, were completely new. And yet, this is exactly one of the things that makes them so great. Effective composers have their own ideas. Have you ever seen the classic movie *Amadeus*? The composer Antonio Salieri is the "host" of this movie; he's depicted as one of the most famous non-great composers — he lived at the time of Mozart and was completely overshadowed by him. Now, Salieri wasn't a bad composer; in fact, he was a very good one. But he wasn't one of the world's great composers because his work wasn't _____. What he wrote sounded just like what everyone else was composing at the time.

① simple   ② original
③ familiar   ④ conventional
⑤ understandable

32. Every time a new medium comes along — whether it's the invention of the printed book, or TV, or SNS — and you start to use it, it's like you are putting on a new kind of goggles, with their own special colors and lenses. Each set of goggles you put on makes you see things differently. So when you start to watch television, before you absorb the message of any particular TV show — whether it's *Wheel of Fortune* or *The Wire* — you start to see the world as being shaped like television itself. That's why Marshall McLuhan said that every time a new medium comes along — a new way for humans to communicate — it has buried in it a message. It is gently guiding us to _____.
The way information gets to you, McLuhan argued, is more important than the information itself. TV teaches you that the world is fast; that it's about surfaces and appearances. [3점]

① see the world according to a new set of codes
② ignore unfamiliar messages from new media
③ maintain steady focus and clear understanding
④ interpret information through a traditional lens
⑤ enjoy various media contents with one platform

33. Concepts are vital to human survival, but we must also be careful with them because concepts open the door to essentialism. They _____. Stuart Firestein opens his book, *Ignorance*, with an old proverb, "It is very difficult to find a black cat in a dark room, especially when there is no cat." This statement beautifully sums up the search for essences. History has many examples of scientists who searched fruitlessly for an essence because they used the wrong concept to guide their hypotheses. Firestein gives the example of luminiferous ether, a mysterious substance that was thought to fill the universe so that light would have a medium to move through. The ether was a black cat, writes Firestein, and physicists had been theorizing in a dark room, and then experimenting in it, looking for evidence of a cat that did not exist. [3점]

① encourage us to see things that aren't present
② force scientists to simplify scientific theories
③ let us think science is essential and practical
④ drive physicists to explore philosophy
⑤ lead us to ignore the unknown

34. While social media attention is potentially an instrument to achieve ends like elite celebrity, some content creators desire ordinary fame as a social end in itself. Not unlike reality television stars, social media celebrities are often criticized for not having skills and talents associated with traditional, elite celebrity, such as acting or singing ability. This criticism highlights the fact that digital content creators face real barriers to crossing over to the sphere of elite celebrity. However, the criticism also misses the point that the phenomenon of ordinary celebrity _____. The elite celebrity is symbolized by the metaphor of the star, characterized by mystery and hierarchical distance and associated with naturalized qualities of talent and class. The ordinary celebrity attracts attention through regular and frequent interactions with other ordinary people. Achieving ordinary fame as a social media celebrity is like doing well at a game, because in this sphere, fame is nothing more nor less than relatively high scores on attention scales, the metrics of subscribers, followers, Likes, or clicks built into social media applications. [3점]

* sphere: 영역 ** metric: 측정 기준

① shifts to that of elite celebrity
② disappears gradually over time
③ focuses solely on talent and class
④ reconstructs the meaning of fame
⑤ restricts interactions with the public

35. 다음 글에서 전체 흐름과 관계 <u>없는</u> 문장은?

Why do we have the illusion that cramming for an exam is the best learning strategy? Because we are unable to differentiate between the various sections of our memory. Immediately after reading our textbook or our class notes, information is fully present in our mind. ① It sits in our conscious working memory, in an active form. ② We feel as if we know it, because it is present in our short-term storage space ... but this short-term section has nothing to do with the long-term memory that we will need in order to recall the same information a few days later. ③ After a few seconds or minutes, working memory already starts disappearing, and after a few days, the effect becomes enormous: unless you retest your knowledge, memory vanishes. ④ Focusing on exploring new topics rather than reviewing the same material over and over again can improve your academic performance. ⑤ To get information into long-term memory, it is essential to study the material, then test yourself, rather than spend all your time studying.

* cram: 벼락 공부를 하다

[36~37] 주어진 글 다음에 이어질 글의 순서로 가장 적절한 것을 고르시오.

36.

> The discovery of mirror neurons has profoundly changed the way we think of a fundamental human capacity, learning by observation.

(A) You may not see the tongue stick out each time you stick yours out at your newborn, but if you do it many times, the tongue will come out more often than if you do something different. Babies babble and later start to imitate the sounds their parents produce.

(B) As children we learn a lot by observing what our parents and friends do. Newborns, in the first week of life, have an inborn tendency to stick out their tongue if their parents stick out theirs. Such imitation is not perfect.

(C) Later still, they play with vacuum cleaners and hammers in imitation of their parents. Our modern cultures, in which we write, speak, read, build spaceships and go to school, can work only because we are not restricted to the behavior we are born with or learn by trial and error. We can learn a lot by simply watching others.

* babble: 옹알이하다

① (A) - (C) - (B)　　　② (B) - (A) - (C)
③ (B) - (C) - (A)　　　④ (C) - (A) - (B)
⑤ (C) - (B) - (A)

37.

Have you ever been surprised to hear a recording of your own voice? You might have thought, "Is that really what my voice sounds like?"

(A) There are two pathways through which we perceive our own voice when we speak. One is the route through which we perceive most external sounds, like waves that travel from the air through the outer, middle and inner ear.

(B) But because our vocal cords vibrate when we speak, there is a second internal path. Vibrations are conducted through our bones and stimulate our inner ears directly. Lower frequencies are emphasized along this pathway. That makes your voice sound deeper and richer to yourself than it may sound to other people.

(C) Maybe your accent is more pronounced in the recording than you realized, or your voice is higher than it seems to your own ears. This is of course quite a common experience. The explanation is actually fairly simple. [3점]

* vocal cords: 성대 ** frequency: 주파수

① (A) − (C) − (B)　　　② (B) − (A) − (C)
③ (B) − (C) − (A)　　　④ (C) − (A) − (B)
⑤ (C) − (B) − (A)

[38~39] 글의 흐름으로 보아, 주어진 문장이 들어가기에 가장 적절한 곳을 고르시오.

38.

"Homologous" traits, in contrast, may or may not have a common function, but they descended from a common ancestor and hence have some common structure that indicates their being "the same" organ.

Biologists distinguish two kinds of similarity. (①) "Analogous" traits are ones that have a common function but arose on different branches of the evolutionary tree and are in an important sense not "the same" organ. (②) The wings of birds and the wings of bees are both used for flight and are similar in some ways because anything used for flight has to be built in those ways, but they arose independently in evolution and have nothing in common beyond their use in flight. (③) The wing of a bat and the front leg of a horse have very different functions, but they are all modifications of the forelimb of the ancestor of all mammals. (④) As a result, they share nonfunctional traits like the number of bones and the ways they are connected. (⑤) To distinguish analogy from homology, biologists usually look at the overall architecture of the organs and focus on their most useless properties.

39.

Thus, as global warming raises the temperature of marine waters, it is self-evident that the amount of dissolved oxygen will decrease.

Seawater contains an abundance of dissolved oxygen that all marine animals breathe to stay alive. (①) It has long been established in physics that cold water holds more dissolved oxygen than warm water does — this is one reason that cold polar seas are full of life while tropical oceans are blue, clear, and relatively poorly populated with living creatures. (②) This is a worrisome and potentially disastrous consequence if allowed to continue to an ecosystem-threatening level. (③) Now scientists have analyzed data indicating that the amount of dissolved oxygen in the oceans has been declining for more than a half century. (④) The data show that the ocean oxygen level has been falling more rapidly than the corresponding rise in water temperature. (⑤) Falling oxygen levels in water have the potential to impact the habitat of marine organisms worldwide and in recent years this has led to more frequent anoxic events that killed or displaced populations of fish, crabs, and many other organisms. [3점]

* dissolved: 용해된 ** anoxic: 산소 결핍의

40. 다음 글의 내용을 한 문장으로 요약하고자 한다. 빈칸 (A), (B)에 들어갈 말로 가장 적절한 것은?

Capuchins — New World Monkeys that live in large social groups — will, in captivity, trade with people all day long, especially if food is involved. *I give you this rock and you give me a treat to eat.* If you put two monkeys in cages next to each other, and offer them both slices of cucumber for the rocks they already have, they will happily eat the cucumbers. If, however, you give one monkey grapes instead — grapes being universally preferred to cucumbers — the monkey that is still receiving cucumbers will begin to throw them back at the experimenter. Even though she is still getting "paid" the same amount for her effort of sourcing rocks, and so her particular situation has not changed, the comparison to another makes the situation unfair. Furthermore, she is now willing to abandon all gains — the cucumbers themselves — to communicate her displeasure to the experimenter.

↓

According to the passage, if the Capuchin monkey realizes the ___(A)___ in rewards compared to another monkey, she will ___(B)___ her rewards to express her feelings about the treatment, despite getting exactly the same rewards as before.

(A)　　　　　　(B)
① benefit　……　protect
② inequality　……　share
③ abundance　……　yield
④ inequality　……　reject
⑤ benefit　……　display

[41~42] 다음 글을 읽고, 물음에 답하시오.

Higher education has grown from an elite to a mass system across the world. In Europe and the USA, (a) <u>increased</u> rates of participation occurred in the decades after the Second World War. Between 2000 and 2014, rates of participation in higher education almost doubled from 19% to 34% across the world among the members of the population in the school-leaving age category (typically 18−23). The dramatic expansion of higher education has been marked by a wider range of institutions of higher learning and a more diverse demographic of students.

Changes from an elite system to a mass higher education system are associated with political needs to build a (b) <u>specialised</u> workforce for the economy. In theory, the expansion of higher education to develop a highly skilled workforce should diminish the role of examinations in the selection and control of students, initiating approaches to assessment which (c) <u>block</u> lifelong learning: assessment *for* learning and a focus on feedback for development. In reality, socio-political changes to expand higher education have set up a 'field of contradictions' for assessment in higher education. Mass higher education requires efficient approaches to assessment, such as examinations and multiple-choice quizzes, with minimalist, (d) <u>impersonal</u>, or standardised feedback, often causing students to focus more on grades than feedback. In contrast, the relatively small numbers of students in elite systems in the past (e) <u>allowed</u> for closer relationships between students and their teachers, with formative feedback shaping the minds, academic skills, and even the characters of students.

* demographic: 인구집단

41. 윗글의 제목으로 가장 적절한 것은?

① Is It Possible to Teach Without Assessment?
② Elite vs. Public: A History of Modern Class Society
③ Mass Higher Education and Its Reality in Assessment
④ Impacts of Mass Higher Education on Teachers' Status
⑤ Mass Higher Education Leads to Economic Development

42. 밑줄 친 (a)~(e) 중에서 문맥상 낱말의 쓰임이 적절하지 <u>않은</u> 것은? [3점]

① (a) ② (b) ③ (c) ④ (d) ⑤ (e)

[43~45] 다음 글을 읽고, 물음에 답하시오.

(A)

Once upon a time in the Iranian city of Shiraz, there lived the famous poet Sheikh Saadi. Like most other poets and philosophers, he led a very simple life. A rich merchant of Shiraz was preparing for his daughter's wedding and invited (a) <u>him</u> along with a lot of big businessmen of the town. The poet accepted the invitation and decided to attend.

(B)

The host personally led the poet to his seat and served out chicken soup to him. After a moment, the poet suddenly dipped the corner of his coat in the soup as if he fed it. All the guests were now staring at (b) <u>him</u> in surprise. The host said, "Sir, what are you doing?" The poet very calmly replied, "Now that I have put on expensive clothes, I see a world of difference here. All that I can say now is that this feast is meant for my clothes, not for me."

(C)

Seeing all this, the poet quietly left the party and went to a shop where he could rent clothes. There he chose a richly decorated coat, which made him look like a new person. With this coat, he entered the party and this time was welcomed with open arms. The host embraced him as (c) <u>he</u> would do to an old friend and complimented him on the clothes he was wearing. The poet did not say a word and allowed the host to lead (d) <u>him</u> to the dining room.

(D)

On the day of the wedding, the rich merchant, the host of the wedding, was receiving the guests at the gate. Many rich people of the town attended the wedding. They had come out in their best clothes. The poet wore simple clothes which were neither grand nor expensive. He waited for someone to approach him but no one gave (e) <u>him</u> as much as even a second glance. Even the host did not greet him and looked away.

43. 주어진 글 (A)에 이어질 내용을 순서에 맞게 배열한 것으로 가장 적절한 것은?

① (B) − (D) − (C) ② (C) − (B) − (D)
③ (C) − (D) − (B) ④ (D) − (B) − (C)
⑤ (D) − (C) − (B)

44. 밑줄 친 (a)~(e) 중에서 가리키는 대상이 나머지 넷과 <u>다른</u> 것은?

① (a) ② (b) ③ (c) ④ (d) ⑤ (e)

45. 윗글에 관한 내용으로 적절하지 <u>않은</u> 것은?

① 시인은 상인의 초대를 받아들였다.
② 상인은 시인의 외투 자락을 수프에 담갔다.
③ 시인은 옷을 빌릴 수 있는 가게로 갔다.
④ 결혼식 날 상인은 입구에서 손님을 맞이했다.
⑤ 마을의 많은 부유한 사람들이 결혼식에 참석했다.

* 확인 사항

◦ 답안지의 해당란에 필요한 내용을 정확히 기입(표기)했는지 확인하시오.

18

001	express	ⓥ 표현하다
002	concern	ⓝ 걱정
003	recent	ⓐ 최근의
004	station	ⓝ 역
005	traditional	ⓐ 전통의, 전통적인
006	ticket office	매표소
007	staff	ⓝ 직원
008	replace	ⓥ 대신하다
009	vending machine	자동판매기
010	unfamiliar	ⓐ 익숙하지 않은
011	experience	ⓥ 경험하다
012	railway	ⓝ 철도
013	rely	ⓥ 의지하다
014	assistance	ⓝ 도움
015	reopen	ⓥ 다시 열다
016	position	ⓝ 자리, 제자리
017	regain	ⓥ 되찾다, 회복하다
018	prompt	ⓐ 즉각적인, 지체 없는
019	resolution	ⓝ 해결책

19

020	actor	ⓝ 배우
021	stage	ⓝ 무대
022	focus	ⓥ 집중하다
023	acting	ⓝ (연극·영화에서의) 연기
024	corner	ⓝ 구석, 모서리, 모퉁이
025	immediately	ad 즉시
026	approach	ⓥ 접근하다
027	silently	ad 아무 말 없이, 잠자코, 조용히
028	glance	ⓥ 흘깃 보다
029	breathe	ⓥ 호흡하다, 숨을 쉬다
030	appear	ⓥ 나타나다
031	swiftly	ad 신속히, 빨리
032	kneel	ⓥ 무릎을 꿇다
033	chest	ⓝ 가슴, 흉부
034	announce	ⓥ 알리다
035	calm	ⓐ 침착한, 차분한
036	wipe	ⓥ 닦다
037	successfully	ad 성공적으로
038	revive	ⓥ 소생하다

20

039	gifted	ⓐ 재능이 있는
040	be aware of	알고 있다
041	trap	ⓝ 함정
042	proud	ⓐ 자랑스러워하는, 자랑스러운
043	nonstop	ad 중지 없이, 중단 없이
044	remarkable	ⓐ 눈에 띄는
045	behavior	ⓝ 행동, 행위, 처신
046	stressful	ⓐ 스트레스가 많은
047	extremely	ad 매우, 몹시
048	limit	ⓥ 한정하다
049	brag	ⓥ 자랑하다
050	expectation	ⓝ 기대
051	false	ⓐ 잘못된, 거짓된
052	incredible	ⓐ 놀라운
053	achievement	ⓝ 달성
054	perfectionist	ⓝ 완벽주의자

21

055	valuable	ⓐ 가치 있는

056	technique	ⓝ 기술
057	helplessness	ⓝ 무력감
058	depression	ⓝ 우울증
059	predominantly	ad 지배적인
060	resolve	ⓥ 해결하다
061	struggle	ⓥ 발버둥 치다, 몸부림치다, 싸우다
062	negative	ⓐ 부정적인
063	state	ⓝ 상태
064	positive	ⓐ 긍정적인
065	weak	ⓐ 약한, 힘이 없는
066	vibration	ⓝ 진동
067	beneficial	ⓐ 혜택의
068	consciousness	ⓝ 의식
069	latent	ⓐ 잠재적인

22

070	emotion	ⓝ 감정
071	contribute	ⓥ 기여하다
072	survival	ⓝ 생존
073	species	ⓝ 종(種)
074	avoid	ⓥ 피하다
075	danger	ⓝ 위험
076	scare off	겁을 줘 쫓아내다
077	threat	ⓝ 협박, 위협
078	bond	ⓥ 유대감을 형성하다
079	evolutionary	ⓐ 진화의, 진화적인
080	perspective	ⓝ 관점, 시각
081	trigger	ⓥ 야기하다
082	direct	ⓥ 지시하다
083	fear	ⓝ 공포, 두려움, 무서움
084	attentive	ⓐ 주의 깊은
085	perceptual	ⓐ 지각의
086	threatening	ⓐ 위협적인
087	stimulus	ⓝ 자극(pl. stimuli)
088	regardless	ad 상관하지 않고
089	specific	ⓐ 특정한
090	activate	ⓥ 활성화시키다
091	environment	ⓝ 환경
092	adapt	ⓥ 적응하다
093	evolve	ⓥ 진화하다

23

094	improve	ⓥ 향상시키다
095	accessibility	ⓝ 접근, 접근하기 쉬움
096	workplace	ⓝ 직장, 업무 현장
097	worker	ⓝ 노동자
098	typically	ad 보통, 일반적으로
099	disadvantage	ⓝ 불리한 점
100	inclusiveness	ⓝ 포괄성
101	assistive	ⓐ 도와주는
102	device	ⓝ 기기
103	aid	ⓥ 돕다
104	widespread	ⓐ 광범위한, 널리 퍼진
105	recognition	ⓝ 알아봄, 인식
106	dysarthric	ⓐ 구음 장애의
107	deaf	ⓐ 청각 장애가 있는
108	facilitate	ⓥ 용이하게 하다, 촉진하다
109	colleague	ⓝ 동료
110	necessary	ⓐ 필요한
111	enhance	ⓥ 향상시키다
112	capability	ⓝ 능력, 역량
113	wage	ⓝ 임금

114	prospect	ⓝ 전망
115	translate	ⓥ 번역하다
116	development	ⓝ 발달
117	instantly	ad 즉각, 즉시
118	individual	ⓝ 개인
119	domain	ⓝ 영역, 분야

24

120	whale	ⓝ 고래
121	efficient	ⓐ 효율적인
122	carbon	ⓝ 탄소
123	storage	ⓝ 저장
124	sequester	ⓥ 격리하다
125	average	ⓐ 평균의
126	carbon dioxide	이산화탄소
127	atmosphere	ⓝ 대기
128	comparison	ⓝ 대조
129	climate	ⓝ 기후
130	equivalent	ⓐ 상응하는, 상당하는
131	fertilize	ⓥ 비옥하게 하다
132	release	ⓥ 풀어 주다, 놓아 주다, 방출하다
133	increase	ⓥ 증가하다
134	phytoplankton	ⓝ 식물성 플랑크톤
135	population	ⓝ 개체군, 개체 수
136	ecosystem	ⓝ 생태계
137	economist	ⓝ 경제학자
138	estimate	ⓥ 추산하다
139	preindustrial	ⓐ 산업화 이전의, 산업 혁명 전의
140	solution	ⓝ 해결책
141	restoration	ⓝ 복원, 회복

25

142	per capita	1인당
143	emission	ⓝ 배출량
144	coal	ⓝ 석탄
145	rank	ⓥ 순위에 들다
146	major	ⓐ 주요한
147	source	ⓝ 원천

26

148	mathematician	ⓝ 수학자
149	physicist	ⓝ 물리학자
150	childhood	ⓝ 어린 시절
151	support	ⓝ 지원
152	scientific	ⓐ 과학의, 과학적인
153	receive	ⓥ 받다
154	submit	ⓥ 제출하다
155	paper	ⓝ 논문
156	nature	ⓝ 본질
157	publish	ⓥ 출간하다
158	explain	ⓥ 설명하다
159	relativity	ⓝ 상대성 이론
160	significant	ⓐ 중요한, 특별한 의미가 있는
161	recognize	ⓥ 인정하다
162	enlightenment	ⓝ (18세기의) 계몽주의 시대

27

163	inventor	ⓝ 발명가
164	competition	ⓝ 대회
165	category	ⓝ 분류

166	remote	ⓐ 원격의
167	registration	ⓝ 등록
168	participant	ⓝ 참여자

28

169	stamp	ⓝ 도장
170	annual	ⓐ 연간의
171	participate	ⓥ 참여하다
172	event	ⓝ 행사
173	join	ⓥ 참여하다
174	exhibition	ⓝ 전시회
175	collection	ⓝ 수집품
176	district	ⓝ 구역
177	spot	ⓝ (특정한) 곳
178	umbrella	ⓝ 우산, 양산

29

179	organizational	ⓐ 구조적인
180	viewpoint	ⓝ 시각
181	fascinate	ⓥ 멋지다
182	organization	ⓝ 조직, 단체, 기구
183	contain	ⓥ 포함하다
184	type	ⓝ 유형, 종류
185	functional	ⓐ 기능상의, 기능적인
186	operation	ⓝ 경영, 운용
187	department	ⓝ 부서
188	division	ⓝ (조직의) 분과
189	inevitably	ad 필연적으로, 부득이
190	biased	ⓐ 편향된, 선입견이 있는
191	prejudiced	ⓐ 편견이 있는
192	acquire	ⓥ 얻다
193	conflict	ⓝ 갈등
194	choice	ⓝ 선택
195	mechanistic	ⓐ 기계적인
196	organic	ⓐ 유기적인
197	profound	ⓐ 깊은
198	influence	ⓝ 영향
199	vertical	ⓐ 수직의
200	hierarchy	ⓝ 계급, 계층
201	procedure	ⓝ 절차
202	horizontal	ⓐ 수평의, 가로의
203	centralize	ⓥ 중앙화하다, 중앙 집권화하다

30

204	excellent	ⓐ 훌륭한
205	alternative	ⓝ 대체
206	traffic	ⓝ 교통
207	remove	ⓥ 제거하다
208	extensive	ⓐ 넓은, 광대한
209	lane	ⓝ 차선
210	pedestrian	ⓝ 보행자
211	occasional	ⓐ 가끔의
212	rather	ad 꽤, 약간, 상당히
213	popular	ⓐ 인기 있는
214	convert	ⓥ 바꾸다
215	automobile	ⓝ 자동차
216	entire	ⓐ 전체의, 온
217	accommodate	ⓥ 공간을 제공하다, 수용하다
218	require	ⓥ 필요하다, 필요로 하다
219	emergency	ⓝ 비상사태, 긴급, 응급
220	delivery	ⓝ 배송

221 ☐ frequently [ad] 자주, 흔히
222 ☐ target ⓝ 목표, 대상
223 ☐ animus ⓝ 반감, 적대감
224 ☐ actually [ad] 실제로, 정말로, 실지로
225 ☐ essential ⓐ 극히 중요한, 가장 중요한
226 ☐ component ⓝ 요소, 부품
227 ☐ tightly [ad] 단단히, 꽉

31
228 ☐ composer ⓝ 작곡가
229 ☐ misunderstand ⓥ 오해하다
230 ☐ composition ⓝ 구성
231 ☐ reason ⓝ 이유, 까닭, 사유
232 ☐ initial ⓐ 초기의
233 ☐ lack ⓝ 부족, 결핍
234 ☐ acceptance ⓝ 수락
235 ☐ unfamiliarity ⓝ 잘 모름, 익숙지 않음
236 ☐ completely [ad] 완전히
237 ☐ exactly [ad] 정확히, 꼭, 틀림없이
238 ☐ effective ⓐ 유능한
239 ☐ depict ⓥ 묘사하다
240 ☐ overshadow ⓥ 그늘지게 하다, 가리다

32
241 ☐ medium ⓝ 매체
242 ☐ come along 따라오다
243 ☐ invention ⓝ 발명
244 ☐ goggle ⓝ 고글
245 ☐ differently [ad] 다르게, 같지 않게
246 ☐ absorb ⓥ 흡수하다
247 ☐ particular ⓐ 특정한
248 ☐ communicate ⓥ 의사소통하다
249 ☐ bury ⓥ 묻다
250 ☐ gently [ad] 다정하게, 부드럽게
251 ☐ guide ⓥ 이끌다
252 ☐ argue ⓥ 주장하다
253 ☐ surface ⓝ 표면
254 ☐ appearance ⓝ 외모

33
255 ☐ concept ⓝ 개념
256 ☐ vital ⓐ 필수적인
257 ☐ careful ⓐ 조심스러운
258 ☐ essentialism ⓝ 본질주의
259 ☐ encourage ⓥ 부추기다
260 ☐ present ⓐ 있는, 존재하는
261 ☐ proverb ⓝ 속담
262 ☐ statement ⓝ 표현, 진술
263 ☐ sum up 요약하다
264 ☐ essence ⓝ 본질, 정수, 진수
265 ☐ fruitlessly [ad] 득 없이
266 ☐ hypothesis ⓝ 가설(pl. hypotheses)
267 ☐ luminiferous ⓐ 빛을 내는, 발광성의
268 ☐ mysterious ⓐ 신비한, 불가사의한
269 ☐ substance ⓝ 물질
270 ☐ medium ⓝ 도구
271 ☐ experiment ⓥ 실험하다
272 ☐ evidence ⓝ 증거
273 ☐ exist ⓥ 존재하다

34
274 ☐ attention ⓝ 관심

275 ☐ instrument ⓝ 도구
276 ☐ achieve ⓥ 달성하다
277 ☐ celebrity ⓝ 유명인
278 ☐ content ⓝ 콘텐츠
279 ☐ creator ⓝ 창작자
280 ☐ desire ⓥ 바라다, 원하다
281 ☐ ordinary ⓐ 평범한, 보통의, 일상적인
282 ☐ criticize ⓥ 비판하다
283 ☐ ability ⓝ 재능, 능력
284 ☐ highlight ⓥ 강조하다
285 ☐ barrier ⓝ 장벽
286 ☐ phenomenon ⓝ 현상
287 ☐ symbolize ⓥ 상징화되다
288 ☐ metaphor ⓝ 은유, 비유
289 ☐ characterize ⓥ 특징이 되다, 특징짓다
290 ☐ hierarchical ⓐ 계층제의, 계층에 따른
291 ☐ distance ⓝ 거리
292 ☐ attract attention 이목을 끌다
293 ☐ frequent ⓐ 잦은, 빈번한
294 ☐ interaction ⓝ 상호 작용
295 ☐ fame ⓝ 명성
296 ☐ sphere ⓝ 영역
297 ☐ relatively [ad] 상대적으로
298 ☐ subscriber ⓝ 구독자

35
299 ☐ illusion ⓝ 환각
300 ☐ cram ⓥ 벼락공부를 하다
301 ☐ strategy ⓝ 전략
302 ☐ differentiate ⓥ 차별화하다
303 ☐ section ⓝ 부분
304 ☐ memory ⓝ 기억
305 ☐ information ⓝ 정보
306 ☐ mind ⓝ 생각
307 ☐ conscious ⓐ 의식적인
308 ☐ disappear ⓥ 사라지다
309 ☐ effect ⓝ 효과
310 ☐ enormous ⓐ 막대한, 거대한
311 ☐ knowledge ⓝ 정보
312 ☐ vanish ⓥ 사라지다
313 ☐ performance ⓝ 실적, 성과

36
314 ☐ discovery ⓝ 발견
315 ☐ neuron ⓝ 뉴런
316 ☐ profoundly [ad] 풍부하게
317 ☐ fundamental ⓐ 기본적인
318 ☐ capacity ⓝ 능력
319 ☐ observation ⓝ 관찰
320 ☐ tongue ⓝ 혀
321 ☐ stick out ~을 내밀다
322 ☐ each time 언제나, 매번
323 ☐ newborn ⓝ 신생아
324 ☐ babble ⓥ 옹알이하다
325 ☐ observe ⓥ 관찰하다
326 ☐ imitation ⓝ 모방
327 ☐ vacuum cleaner 진공청소기
328 ☐ restrict ⓥ 제한하다
329 ☐ trial and error 시행착오

37
330 ☐ record ⓥ 녹음하다

331 ☐ pathway ⓝ 길
332 ☐ perceive ⓥ 인식하다
333 ☐ route ⓝ 경로, 길
334 ☐ external ⓐ 외부의
335 ☐ vocal cord ⓝ 성대
336 ☐ vibrate ⓥ 진동하다
337 ☐ internal ⓐ 내부의
338 ☐ path ⓝ 길, 경로
339 ☐ conduct ⓥ (열·전기·소리 등을) 전도하다
340 ☐ stimulate ⓥ 자극하다
341 ☐ directly [ad] 직접으로
342 ☐ frequency ⓝ 주파수
343 ☐ fairly [ad] 상당히, 꽤

38
344 ☐ biologist ⓝ 생물학자
345 ☐ similarity ⓝ 유사성
346 ☐ analogous ⓐ 유사한
347 ☐ arise ⓥ 생기다
348 ☐ branch ⓝ 나뭇가지
349 ☐ organ ⓝ 장기
350 ☐ independently [ad] 독립적으로
351 ☐ evolution ⓝ 진화
352 ☐ homologous ⓐ 상동의
353 ☐ trait ⓝ 특성
354 ☐ in contrast 그에 반해서, 그와 대조적으로
355 ☐ descend ⓥ 내려오다
356 ☐ common ⓐ 공통의
357 ☐ ancestor ⓝ 조상
358 ☐ hence [ad] 그러므로, 따라서
359 ☐ structure ⓝ 구조
360 ☐ indicate ⓥ 가리키다
361 ☐ modification ⓝ 변형
362 ☐ forelimb ⓝ (척추동물의) 앞다리
363 ☐ mammals ⓝ 포유류

39
364 ☐ abundance ⓝ 넘칠 만큼 많음, 다량
365 ☐ dissolved ⓐ 용해된
366 ☐ oxygen ⓝ 산소
367 ☐ establish ⓥ 확립하다, 수립하다
368 ☐ polar ⓐ 극지의
369 ☐ tropical ⓐ 열대 지방의, 열대의
370 ☐ poorly [ad] 부족하게
371 ☐ populate ⓥ 살다, 거주하다
372 ☐ creature ⓝ 생물
373 ☐ temperature ⓝ 온도
374 ☐ marine ⓐ 해양의
375 ☐ self-evident ⓐ 분명한
376 ☐ decrease ⓥ 감소하다
377 ☐ potentially [ad] 잠재적으로
378 ☐ disastrous ⓐ 재앙적인
379 ☐ consequence ⓝ 결과
380 ☐ analyze ⓥ 분석하다
381 ☐ rapidly [ad] 빨리, 급속히
382 ☐ correspond ⓥ 일치하다
383 ☐ anoxic ⓐ 산소 결핍의

40
384 ☐ large ⓐ 큰
385 ☐ social ⓐ 사회의
386 ☐ captivity ⓝ 감금, 억류, 포로

387 ☐ trade ⓥ 거래하다
388 ☐ involve ⓥ 포함하다
389 ☐ cage ⓝ 우리
390 ☐ cucumber ⓝ 오이
391 ☐ universally [ad] 공통적으로
392 ☐ prefer ⓥ 선호하다
393 ☐ experimenter ⓝ 실험자
394 ☐ effort ⓝ 노력
395 ☐ situation ⓝ 상황
396 ☐ unfair ⓐ 부당한
397 ☐ abandon ⓥ 버리다
398 ☐ displeasure ⓝ 불쾌감

41~42
399 ☐ elite ⓝ 엘리트
400 ☐ mass ⓝ 대량
401 ☐ participation ⓝ 참가
402 ☐ occur ⓥ 발생하다
403 ☐ education ⓝ 교육
404 ☐ population ⓝ 인구
405 ☐ diverse ⓐ 다양한
406 ☐ demographic ⓐ 인구학의
407 ☐ allow ⓥ 허락하다
408 ☐ relationship ⓝ 관계
409 ☐ formative ⓐ 형태적인
410 ☐ feedback ⓝ 평가

43~45
411 ☐ famous ⓐ 유명한
412 ☐ poet ⓝ 시인
413 ☐ philosopher ⓝ 철학가
414 ☐ prepare ⓥ 준비하다
415 ☐ invite ⓥ 초대하다
416 ☐ businessmen ⓝ 사업가
417 ☐ accept ⓥ 받아들이다
418 ☐ invitation ⓝ 초대장
419 ☐ attend ⓥ 참석하다

11회

● 채점 : 맞은 개수 _____ / 80

TEST A-B 각 단어의 뜻을 [A] 영어는 우리말로, [B] 우리말은 영어로 쓰시오.

A	English	Korean
01	express	
02	concern	
03	regain	
04	approach	
05	wipe	
06	revive	
07	remarkable	
08	incredible	
09	achievement	
10	predominantly	
11	state	
12	consciousness	
13	contribute	
14	perspective	
15	fear	
16	assistive	
17	device	
18	enhance	
19	efficient	
20	estimate	

B	Korean	English
01	기후	
02	배출량	
03	주요한	
04	원천	
05	물리학자	
06	지원	
07	제출하다	
08	발명가	
09	분류	
10	참여자	
11	연간의	
12	참여하다	
13	전시회	
14	시각	
15	기능상의, 기능적인	
16	얻다	
17	대체	
18	꽤, 약간, 상당히	
19	요소, 부품	
20	초기의	

▶ A-D 정답 : 해설편 111쪽

TEST C-D 각 단어의 뜻을 골라 기호를 쓰시오.

C	English		Korean
01	reason	( )	ⓐ 상호작용
02	depict	( )	ⓑ 모방
03	particular	( )	ⓒ 전략
04	communicate	( )	ⓓ 상징화되다
05	argue	( )	ⓔ 부분
06	vital	( )	ⓕ 능력
07	encourage	( )	ⓖ 자극하다
08	exist	( )	ⓗ 묘사하다
09	symbolize	( )	ⓘ 이유, 까닭, 사유
10	phenomenon	( )	ⓙ 현상
11	interaction	( )	ⓚ 부추기다
12	conscious	( )	ⓛ 관찰
13	strategy	( )	ⓜ 필수적인
14	section	( )	ⓝ 주장하다
15	observation	( )	ⓞ 존재하다
16	capacity	( )	ⓟ 내부의
17	imitation	( )	ⓠ 의사소통하다
18	pathway	( )	ⓡ 의식적인
19	internal	( )	ⓢ 길
20	stimulate	( )	ⓣ 특정한

D	Korean		English
01	공통의	( )	ⓐ involve
02	내려오다	( )	ⓑ descend
03	생기다	( )	ⓒ universally
04	일치하다	( )	ⓓ establish
05	확립하다, 수립하다	( )	ⓔ formative
06	온도	( )	ⓕ trade
07	다양한	( )	ⓖ mass
08	발생하다	( )	ⓗ arise
09	대량	( )	ⓘ temperature
10	받아들이다	( )	ⓙ situation
11	초대하다	( )	ⓚ effort
12	형태적인	( )	ⓛ occur
13	거래하다	( )	ⓜ diverse
14	상황	( )	ⓝ displeasure
15	버리다	( )	ⓞ unfair
16	불쾌감	( )	ⓟ invite
17	노력	( )	ⓠ accept
18	부당한	( )	ⓡ abandon
19	포함하다	( )	ⓢ common
20	공통적으로	( )	ⓣ correspond

※ 영어 [독해] 파트만 수록한 문제지이므로 18번부터 시작합니다. ● 점수 표시가 없는 문항은 모두 2점 ● 문항수 28개 | 배점 63점 | 제한 시간 45분

18. 다음 글의 목적으로 가장 적절한 것은?

Dear Professor Sanchez,

My name is Ellis Wight, and I'm the director of the Alexandria Science Museum. We are holding a Chemistry Fair for local middle school students on Saturday, October 28. The goal of the fair is to encourage them to be interested in science through guided experiments. We are looking for college students who can help with the experiments during the event. I am contacting you to ask you to recommend some students from the chemistry department at your college who you think are qualified for this job. With their help, I'm sure the participants will have a great experience. I look forward to hearing from you soon.

Sincerely,
Ellis Wight

① 과학 박물관 내 시설 이용 제한을 안내하려고
② 화학 박람회 일정이 변경된 이유를 설명하려고
③ 중학생을 위한 화학 실험 특별 강연을 부탁하려고
④ 중학교 과학 수업용 실험 교재 집필을 의뢰하려고
⑤ 화학 박람회에서 실험을 도울 대학생 추천을 요청하려고

19. 다음 글에 나타난 'I'의 심경 변화로 가장 적절한 것은?

Gregg and I had been rock climbing since sunrise and had had no problems. So we took a risk. "Look, the first bolt is right there. I can definitely climb out to it. Piece of cake," I persuaded Gregg, minutes before I found myself pinned. It wasn't a piece of cake. The rock was deceptively barren of handholds. I clumsily moved back and forth across the cliff face and ended up with nowhere to go...but down. The bolt that would save my life, if I could get to it, was about two feet above my reach. My arms trembled from exhaustion. I looked at Gregg. My body froze with fright from my neck down to my toes. Our rope was tied between us. If I fell, he would fall with me.

* barren of: ~이 없는

① joyful → bored
② confident → fearful
③ nervous → relieved
④ regretful → pleased
⑤ grateful → annoyed

20. 다음 글에서 필자가 주장하는 바로 가장 적절한 것은?

We are always teaching our children something by our words and our actions. They learn from seeing. They learn from hearing and from *overhearing*. Children share the values of their parents about the most important things in life. Our priorities and principles and our examples of good behavior can teach our children to take the high road when other roads look tempting. Remember that children do not learn the values that make up strong character simply by being *told* about them. They learn by seeing the people around them *act* on and *uphold* those values in their daily lives. Therefore show your child good examples of life by your action. In our daily lives, we can show our children that we respect others. We can show them our compassion and concern when others are suffering, and our own self-discipline, courage and honesty as we make difficult decisions.

① 자녀를 타인과 비교하는 말을 삼가야 한다.
② 자녀에게 행동으로 삶의 모범을 보여야 한다.
③ 칭찬을 통해 자녀의 바람직한 행동을 강화해야 한다.
④ 훈육을 하기 전에 자녀 스스로 생각할 시간을 주어야 한다.
⑤ 자녀가 새로운 것에 도전할 때 인내심을 가지고 지켜봐야 한다.

21. 밑줄 친 <u>fall silently in the woods</u>가 다음 글에서 의미하는 바로 가장 적절한 것은? [3점]

Most people have no doubt heard this question: If a tree falls in the forest and there is no one there to hear it fall, does it make a sound? The correct answer is no. Sound is more than pressure waves, and indeed there can be no sound without a hearer. And similarly, scientific communication is a two-way process. Just as a signal of any kind is useless unless it is perceived, a published scientific paper (signal) is useless unless it is both received *and* understood by its intended audience. Thus we can restate the axiom of science as follows: A scientific experiment is not complete until the results have been published *and understood*. Publication is no more than pressure waves unless the published paper is understood. Too many scientific papers <u>fall silently in the woods</u>.

* axiom: 자명한 이치

① fail to include the previous study
② end up being considered completely false
③ become useless because they are not published
④ focus on communication to meet public demands
⑤ are published yet readers don't understand them

22. 다음 글의 요지로 가장 적절한 것은?

We all negotiate every day, whether we realise it or not. Yet few people ever learn *how* to negotiate. Those who do usually learn the traditional, win-lose negotiating style rather than an approach that is likely to result in a win-win agreement. This old-school, adversarial approach may be useful in a one-off negotiation where you will probably not deal with that person again. However, such transactions are becoming increasingly rare, because most of us deal with the same people repeatedly — our spouses and children, our friends and colleagues, our customers and clients. In view of this, it's essential to achieve successful results for ourselves and maintain a healthy relationship with our negotiating partners at the same time. In today's interdependent world of business partnerships and long-term relationships, a win-win outcome is fast becoming the *only* acceptable result.

* adversarial: 적대적인

① 협상 상대의 단점뿐 아니라 장점을 철저히 분석해야 한다.
② 의사소통 과정에서 서로의 의도를 확인하는 것이 바람직하다.
③ 성공적인 협상을 위해 다양한 대안을 준비하는 것이 중요하다.
④ 양측에 유리한 협상을 통해 상대와 좋은 관계를 유지해야 한다.
⑤ 원만한 인간관계를 위해 상호독립성을 인정하는 것이 필요하다.

23. 다음 글의 주제로 가장 적절한 것은?

The interaction of workers from different cultural backgrounds with the host population might increase productivity due to positive externalities like knowledge spillovers. This is only an advantage up to a certain degree. When the variety of backgrounds is too large, fractionalization may cause excessive transaction costs for communication, which may lower productivity. Diversity not only impacts the labour market, but may also affect the quality of life in a location. A tolerant native population may value a multicultural city or region because of an increase in the range of available goods and services. On the other hand, diversity could be perceived as an unattractive feature if natives perceive it as a distortion of what they consider to be their national identity. They might even discriminate against other ethnic groups and they might fear that social conflicts between different foreign nationalities are imported into their own neighbourhood.

* externality: 외부 효과 ** fractionalization: 분열

① roles of culture in ethnic groups
② contrastive aspects of cultural diversity
③ negative perspectives of national identity
④ factors of productivity differences across countries
⑤ policies to protect minorities and prevent discrimination

24. 다음 글의 제목으로 가장 적절한 것은?

We think we are shaping our buildings. But really, our buildings and development are also shaping us. One of the best examples of this is the oldest-known construction: the ornately carved rings of standing stones at Göbekli Tepe in Turkey. Before these ancestors got the idea to erect standing stones some 12,000 years ago, they were hunter-gatherers. It appears that the erection of the multiple rings of megalithic stones took so long, and so many successive generations, that these innovators were forced to settle down to complete the construction works. In the process, they became the first farming society on Earth. This is an early example of a society constructing something that ends up radically remaking the society itself. Things are not so different in our own time.

* ornately: 화려하게 ** megalithic: 거석의

① Buildings Transform How We Live!
② Why Do We Build More Than We Need?
③ Copying Ancient Buildings for Creativity
④ Was Life Better in Hunter-gatherer Times?
⑤ Innovate Your Farm with New Constructions

25. 다음 도표의 내용과 일치하지 <u>않는</u> 것은?

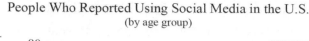

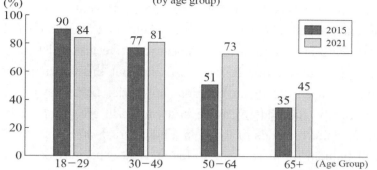

People Who Reported Using Social Media in the U.S. (by age group)

The graph above shows the percentages of people in different age groups who reported using social media in the United States in 2015 and 2021. ① In each of the given years, the 18-29 group had the highest percentage of people who said they used social media. ② In 2015, the percentage of people who reported using social media in the 30-49 group was more than twice that in the 65 and older group. ③ The percentage of people who said they used social media in the 50-64 group in 2021 was 22 percentage points higher than that in 2015. ④ In 2021, except for the 65 and older group, more than four-fifths of people in each age group reported using social media. ⑤ Among all the age groups, only the 18-29 group showed a decrease in the percentage of people who reported using social media from 2015 to 2021.

26. Bill Evans에 관한 다음 글의 내용과 일치하지 <u>않는</u> 것은?

American jazz pianist Bill Evans was born in New Jersey in 1929. His early training was in classical music. At the age of six, he began receiving piano lessons, later adding flute and violin. He earned bachelor's degrees in piano and music education from Southeastern Louisiana College in 1950. He went on to serve in the army from 1951 to 1954 and played flute in the Fifth Army Band. After serving in the military, he studied composition at the Mannes School of Music in New York. Composer George Russell admired his playing and hired Evans to record and perform his compositions. Evans became famous for recordings made from the late-1950s through the 1960s. He won his first Grammy Award in 1964 for his album *Conversations with Myself.* Evans' expressive piano works and his unique harmonic approach inspired a whole generation of musicians.

① 6세에 피아노 수업을 받기 시작했다.
② Southeastern Louisiana 대학에서 학위를 취득했다.
③ 군 복무 이후 뉴욕에서 작곡을 공부했다.
④ 작곡가 George Russell을 고용했다.
⑤ 1964년에 자신의 첫 번째 그래미상을 수상했다.

27. Silversmithing Class에 관한 다음 안내문의 내용과 일치하지 <u>않는</u> 것은?

Silversmithing Class

Kingston Club is offering a fine jewelry making class. Don't miss this great chance to make your own jewelry!

When & Where
· Saturday, October 21, 2023 (2 p.m. to 4 p.m.)
· Kingston Club studio

Registration
· Available only online
· Dates: October 1-14, 2023
· Fee: $40 (This includes all tools and materials.)
· Registration is limited to 6 people.

Note
· Participants must be at least 16 years old.
· No refund for cancellation on the day of the class

---

① 두 시간 동안 진행된다.
② 10월 1일부터 등록할 수 있다.
③ 등록 인원은 6명으로 제한된다.
④ 참가 연령에 제한이 없다.
⑤ 수업 당일 취소 시 환불이 불가하다.

28. 2023 Ocean Awareness Film Contest에 관한 다음 안내문의 내용과 일치하는 것은?

2023 Ocean Awareness Film Contest

Join our 7th annual film contest and show your knowledge of marine conservation.

☐ **Theme**
- Ocean Wildlife / Ocean Pollution
  (Choose one of the above.)

☐ **Guidelines**
- Participants: High school students
- Submission deadline: September 22, 2023
- The video must be between 10 and 15 minutes.
- All entries must be uploaded to our website.
- Only one entry per person

☐ **Prizes**
· 1st place: $100 · 2nd place: $70 · 3rd place: $50
  (Winners will be announced on our website.)

For more information, please visit www.oceanawareFC.com.

---

① 세 가지 주제 중 하나를 선택해야 한다.
② 중학생이 참가할 수 있다.
③ 영상은 10분을 넘길 수 없다.
④ 1인당 두 개까지 출품할 수 있다.
⑤ 수상자는 웹사이트에 공지될 것이다.

29. 다음 글의 밑줄 친 부분 중, 어법상 틀린 것은?

There is a reason the title "Monday Morning Quarterback" exists. Just read the comments on social media from fans discussing the weekend's games, and you quickly see how many people believe they could play, coach, and manage sport teams more ① successfully than those on the field. This goes for the boardroom as well. Students and professionals with years of training and specialized degrees in sport business may also find themselves ② being given advice on how to do their jobs from friends, family, or even total strangers without any expertise. Executives in sport management ③ have decades of knowledge and experience in their respective fields. However, many of them face criticism from fans and community members telling ④ themselves how to run their business. Very few people tell their doctor how to perform surgery or their accountant how to prepare their taxes, but many people provide feedback on ⑤ how sport organizations should be managed.

* boardroom: 이사회실

30. 다음 글의 밑줄 친 부분 중, 문맥상 낱말의 쓰임이 적절하지 않은 것은? [3점]

While moving is difficult for everyone, it is particularly stressful for children. They lose their sense of security and may feel disoriented when their routine is disrupted and all that is ① familiar is taken away. Young children, ages 3−6, are particularly affected by a move. Their understanding at this stage is quite literal, and it is ② easy for them to imagine beforehand a new home and their new room. Young children may have worries such as "Will I still be me in the new place?" and "Will my toys and bed come with us?" It is important to establish a balance between validating children's past experiences and focusing on helping them ③ adjust to the new place. Children need to have opportunities to share their backgrounds in a way that ④ respects their past as an important part of who they are. This contributes to building a sense of community, which is essential for all children, especially those in ⑤ transition.

[31~34] 다음 빈칸에 들어갈 말로 가장 적절한 것을 고르시오.

31. Many people are terrified to fly in airplanes. Often, this fear stems from a lack of control. The pilot is in control, not the passengers, and this lack of control instills fear. Many potential passengers are so afraid they choose to drive great distances to get to a destination instead of flying. But their decision to drive is based solely on emotion, not logic. Logic says that statistically, the odds of dying in a car crash are around 1 in 5,000, while the odds of dying in a plane crash are closer to 1 in 11 million. If you're going to take a risk, especially one that could possibly involve your well-being, wouldn't you want the odds in your favor? However, most people choose the option that will cause them the least amount of _____. Pay attention to the thoughts you have about taking the risk and make sure you're basing your decision on facts, not just feelings.

* instill: 스며들게 하다

① anxiety
② boredom
③ confidence
④ satisfaction
⑤ responsibility

32. The famous primatologist Frans de Waal, of Emory University, says humans downplay similarities between us and other animals as a way of maintaining our spot at the top of our imaginary ladder. Scientists, de Waal points out, can be some of the worst offenders — employing technical language to _____. They call "kissing" in chimps "mouth-to-mouth contact"; they call "friends" between primates "favorite affiliation partners"; they interpret evidence showing that crows and chimps can make tools as being somehow qualitatively different from the kind of toolmaking said to define humanity. If an animal can beat us at a cognitive task — like how certain bird species can remember the precise locations of thousands of seeds — they write it off as instinct, not intelligence. This and so many more tricks of language are what de Waal has termed "linguistic castration." The way we use our tongues to disempower animals, the way we invent words to maintain our spot at the top. [3점]

* primatologist: 영장류학자 ** affiliation: 제휴

① define human instincts
② overestimate chimps' intelligence
③ distance the other animals from us
④ identify animals' negative emotions
⑤ correct our misconceptions about nature

33. A key to engagement and achievement is providing students with _____. My scholarly work and my teaching have been deeply influenced by the work of Rosalie Fink. She interviewed twelve adults who were highly successful in their work, including a physicist, a biochemist, and a company CEO. All of them had dyslexia and had had significant problems with reading throughout their school years. While she expected to find that they had avoided reading and discovered ways to bypass it or compensate with other strategies for learning, she found the opposite. "To my surprise, I found that these dyslexics were enthusiastic readers...they rarely avoided reading. On the contrary, they sought out books." The pattern Fink discovered was that all of her subjects had been passionate in some personal interest. The areas of interest included religion, math, business, science, history, and biography. What mattered was that they read voraciously to find out more.

* dyslexia: 난독증 ** voraciously: 탐욕스럽게

① examples from official textbooks
② relevant texts they will be interested in
③ enough chances to exchange information
④ different genres for different age groups
⑤ early reading experience to develop logic skills

34. For many people, *ability* refers to intellectual competence, so they want everything they do to reflect how smart they are — writing a brilliant legal brief, getting the highest grade on a test, writing elegant computer code, saying something exceptionally wise or witty in a conversation. You could also define ability in terms of a particular skill or talent, such as how well one plays the piano, learns a language, or serves a tennis ball. Some people focus on their ability to be attractive, entertaining, up on the latest trends, or to have the newest gadgets. However ability may be defined, a problem occurs when _____.
The performance becomes the *only* measure of the person; nothing else is taken into account. An outstanding performance means an outstanding person; an average performance means an average person. Period. [3점]

① it is the sole determinant of one's self-worth
② you are distracted by others' achievements
③ there is too much competition in one field
④ you ignore feedback about a performance
⑤ it is not accompanied by effort

35. 다음 글에서 전체 흐름과 관계 <u>없는</u> 문장은? [3점]

Sensory nerves have specialized endings in the tissues that pick up a particular sensation. If, for example, you step on a sharp object such as a pin, nerve endings in the skin will transmit the pain sensation up your leg, up and along the spinal cord to the brain. ① While the pain itself is unpleasant, it is in fact acting as a protective mechanism for the foot. ② That is, you get used to the pain so the capacity with which you can avoid pain decreases. ③ Within the brain, nerves will connect to the area that controls speech, so that you may well shout 'ouch' or something rather less polite. ④ They will also connect to motor nerves that travel back down the spinal cord, and to the muscles in your leg that now contract quickly to lift your foot away from the painful object. ⑤ Sensory and motor nerves control almost all functions in the body — from the beating of the heart to the movement of the gut, sweating and just about everything else.

* spinal cord: 척수 ** gut: 장

[36~37] 주어진 글 다음에 이어질 글의 순서로 가장 적절한 것을 고르시오.

36.

Maybe you've heard this joke: "How do you eat an elephant?" The answer is "one bite at a time."

(A) Common crystal habits include squares, triangles, and six-sided hexagons. Usually crystals form when liquids cool, such as when you create ice cubes. Many times, crystals form in ways that do not allow for perfect shapes. If conditions are too cold, too hot, or there isn't enough source material, they can form strange, twisted shapes.

(B) So, how do you "build" the Earth? That's simple, too: one atom at a time. Atoms are the basic building blocks of crystals, and since all rocks are made up of crystals, the more you know about atoms, the better. Crystals come in a variety of shapes that scientists call *habits*.

(C) But when conditions are right, we see beautiful displays. Usually, this involves a slow, steady environment where the individual atoms have plenty of time to join and fit perfectly into what's known as the *crystal lattice*. This is the basic structure of atoms that is seen time after time. [3점]

① (A) — (C) — (B)   ② (B) — (A) — (C)
③ (B) — (C) — (A)   ④ (C) — (A) — (B)
⑤ (C) — (B) — (A)

37.

When you pluck a guitar string it moves back and forth hundreds of times every second.

(A) The vibration of the wood creates more powerful waves in the air pressure, which travel away from the guitar. When the waves reach your eardrums they flex in and out the same number of times a second as the original string.

(B) Naturally, this movement is so fast that you cannot see it — you just see the blurred outline of the moving string. Strings vibrating in this way on their own make hardly any noise because strings are very thin and don't push much air about.

(C) But if you attach a string to a big hollow box (like a guitar body), then the vibration is amplified and the note is heard loud and clear. The vibration of the string is passed on to the wooden panels of the guitar body, which vibrate back and forth at the same rate as the string.

* pluck: (현악기를) 뜯다 ** amplify: 증폭시키다

① (A) − (C) − (B) 　　② (B) − (A) − (C)
③ (B) − (C) − (A) 　　④ (C) − (A) − (B)
⑤ (C) − (B) − (A)

[38~39] 글의 흐름으로 보아, 주어진 문장이 들어가기에 가장 적절한 곳을 고르시오.

38.

Other individuals prefer integrating work and family roles all day long.

Boundaries between work and home are blurring as portable digital technology makes it increasingly possible to work anywhere, anytime. Individuals differ in how they like to manage their time to meet work and outside responsibilities. (①) Some people prefer to separate or segment roles so that boundary crossings are minimized. (②) For example, these people might keep separate email accounts for work and family and try to conduct work at the workplace and take care of family matters only during breaks and non-work time. (③) We've even noticed more of these "segmenters" carrying two phones — one for work and one for personal use. (④) Flexible schedules work well for these individuals because they enable greater distinction between time at work and time in other roles. (⑤) This might entail constantly trading text messages with children from the office, or monitoring emails at home and on vacation, rather than returning to work to find hundreds of messages in their inbox. [3점]

* entail: 수반하다

39.

However, do not assume that a product is perfectly complementary, as customers may not be completely locked in to the product.

A "complementary good" is a product that is often consumed alongside another product. (①) For example, popcorn is a complementary good to a movie, while a travel pillow is a complementary good for a long plane journey. (②) When the popularity of one product increases, the sales of its complementary good also increase. (③) By producing goods that complement other products that are already (or about to be) popular, you can ensure a steady stream of demand for your product. (④) Some products enjoy perfect complementary status — they *have* to be consumed together, such as a lamp and a lightbulb. (⑤) For example, although motorists may seem required to purchase gasoline to run their cars, they can switch to electric cars.

40. 다음 글의 내용을 한 문장으로 요약하고자 한다. 빈칸 (A), (B)에 들어갈 말로 가장 적절한 것은?

It's not news to anyone that we judge others based on their clothes. In general, studies that investigate these judgments find that people prefer clothing that matches expectations — surgeons in scrubs, little boys in blue — with one notable exception. A series of studies published in an article in June 2014 in the *Journal of Consumer Research* explored observers' reactions to people who broke established norms only slightly. In one scenario, a man at a black-tie affair was viewed as having higher status and competence when wearing a red bow tie. The researchers also found that valuing uniqueness increased audience members' ratings of the status and competence of a professor who wore red sneakers while giving a lecture. The results suggest that people judge these slight deviations from the norm as positive because they suggest that the individual is powerful enough to risk the social costs of such behaviors.

↓

A series of studies show that people view an individual   (A)   when the individual only slightly   (B)   the norm for what people should wear.

	(A)		(B)
①	positively	……	challenges
②	negatively	……	challenges
③	indifferently	……	neglects
④	negatively	……	meets
⑤	positively	……	meets

[41~42] 다음 글을 읽고, 물음에 답하시오.

Claims that local food production cut greenhouse gas emissions by reducing the burning of transportation fuel are usually not well founded. Transport is the source of only 11 percent of greenhouse gas emissions within the food sector, so reducing the distance that food travels after it leaves the farm is far (a) less important than reducing wasteful energy use on the farm. Food coming from a distance can actually be better for the (b) climate, depending on how it was grown. For example, field-grown tomatoes shipped from Mexico in the winter months will have a smaller carbon footprint than (c) local winter tomatoes grown in a greenhouse. In the United Kingdom, lamb meat that travels 11,000 miles from New Zealand generates only one-quarter the carbon emissions per pound compared to British lamb because farmers in the United Kingdom raise their animals on feed (which must be produced using fossil fuels) rather than on clover pastureland.

When food does travel, what matters most is not the (d) distance traveled but the travel mode (surface versus air), and most of all the load size. Bulk loads of food can travel halfway around the world by ocean freight with a smaller carbon footprint, per pound delivered, than foods traveling just a short distance but in much (e) larger loads. For example, 18-wheelers carry much larger loads than pickup trucks so they can move food 100 times as far while burning only one-third as much gas per pound of food delivered.

* freight: 화물 운송

41. 윗글의 제목으로 가장 적절한 것은?

① Shorten the Route, Cut the Cost
② Is Local Food Always Better for the Earth?
③ Why Mass Production Ruins the Environment
④ New Technologies: What Matters in Agriculture
⑤ Reduce Food Waste for a Smaller Carbon Footprint

42. 밑줄 친 (a)~(e) 중에서 문맥상 낱말의 쓰임이 적절하지 <u>않은</u> 것은?

① (a)　② (b)　③ (c)　④ (d)　⑤ (e)

[43~45] 다음 글을 읽고, 물음에 답하시오.

(A)

Long ago, an old man built a grand temple at the center of his village. People traveled to worship at the temple. So the old man made arrangements for food and accommodation inside the temple itself. He needed someone who could look after the temple, so (a) he put up a notice: Manager needed.

(B)

When that young man left the temple, the old man called him and asked, "Will you take care of this temple?" The young man was surprised by the offer and replied, "I have no experience caring for a temple. I'm not even educated." The old man smiled and said, "I don't want any educated man. I want a qualified person." Confused, the young man asked, "But why do (b) you consider me a qualified person?"

(C)

The old man replied, "I buried a brick on the path to the temple. I watched for many days as people tripped over that brick. No one thought to remove it. But you dug up that brick." The young man said, "I haven't done anything great. It's the duty of every human being to think about others. (c) I only did my duty." The old man smiled and said, "Only people who know their duty and perform it are qualified people."

(D)

Seeing the notice, many people went to the old man. But he returned all the applicants after interviews, telling them, "I need a qualified person for this work." The old man would sit on the roof of (d) his house every morning, watching people go through the temple doors. One day, (e) he saw a young man come to the temple.

43. 주어진 글 (A)에 이어질 내용을 순서에 맞게 배열한 것으로 가장 적절한 것은?

① (B) − (D) − (C)　② (C) − (B) − (D)
③ (C) − (D) − (B)　④ (D) − (B) − (C)
⑤ (D) − (C) − (B)

44. 밑줄 친 (a)~(e) 중에서 가리키는 대상이 나머지 넷과 <u>다른</u> 것은?

① (a)　② (b)　③ (c)　④ (d)　⑤ (e)

45. 윗글에 관한 내용으로 적절하지 <u>않은</u> 것은?

① 노인은 마을 중심부에 사원을 지었다.
② 젊은이가 사원을 나설 때 노인이 그를 불렀다.
③ 젊은이는 노인의 제안에 놀랐다.
④ 노인은 사원으로 통하는 길에 묻혀있던 벽돌을 파냈다.
⑤ 공고를 보고 많은 사람들이 노인을 찾아갔다.

* 확인 사항

○ 답안지의 해당란에 필요한 내용을 정확히 기입(표기)했는지 확인하시오.

18

001 □ hold ⓥ 개최하다
002 □ chemistry ⓝ 화학
003 □ fair ⓝ 박람회
004 □ local ⓐ 지역의, 지역의
005 □ experiment ⓝ 실험
006 □ college student 대학생
007 □ contact ⓥ 연락하다
008 □ recommend ⓥ 추천하다
009 □ department ⓝ 학과, 부서
010 □ qualified for ~에 적합한, 자격을 갖춘

19

011 □ rock climbing 암벽 등반
012 □ sunrise ⓝ 일출
013 □ take a risk 위험을 감수하다
014 □ bolt ⓝ 볼트, 나사못
015 □ definitely ⓐⓓ 확실히, 분명히
016 □ piece of cake 식은 죽 먹기, 몹시 쉬운 일
017 □ pinned ⓐ 고정된
018 □ deceptively ⓐⓓ 현혹될 정도로
019 □ handhold ⓝ (등반 도중) 손으로 잡을 수 있는 곳
020 □ clumsily ⓐⓓ 서툴게
021 □ back and forth 이리저리
022 □ cliff ⓝ 절벽
023 □ end up with 결국 ~에 처하다
024 □ get to ~에 도착하다
025 □ exhaustion ⓝ 피로
026 □ freeze ⓥ 얼어붙다
027 □ fright ⓝ 공포
028 □ toe ⓝ 발가락
029 □ rope ⓝ 밧줄
030 □ tie ⓥ 묶다
031 □ confident ⓐ 자신 있는
032 □ fearful ⓐ 겁에 질린
033 □ regretful ⓐ 유감스러운, 후회하는

20

034 □ learn from ~로부터 배우다
035 □ overhear ⓥ 엿듣다, 우연히 듣다
036 □ value ⓝ 가치 ⓥ 중시하다
037 □ priority ⓝ 우선순위
038 □ principle ⓝ 원칙
039 □ take the high road 확실한 길로 가다
040 □ tempting ⓐ 유혹적인, 솔깃한
041 □ make up ~을 구성하다
042 □ act on ~에 따라 행동하다
043 □ uphold ⓥ 유지하다, 떠받치다
044 □ compassion ⓝ 연민
045 □ concern ⓝ 걱정, 우려
046 □ suffer ⓥ 고통받다, 괴로워하다
047 □ self-discipline ⓝ 자제
048 □ honesty ⓝ 정직

21

049 □ no doubt 분명히, 틀림없이
050 □ fall ⓥ 쓰러지다, 넘어지다
051 □ pressure wave 압력파(압력 크기의 변화로 생성되는 파동)
052 □ hearer ⓝ 청자
053 □ similarly ⓐⓓ 비슷하게, 마찬가지로

054 □ scientific ⓐ 과학적인
055 □ signal ⓝ 신호 ⓥ 알리다
056 □ useless ⓐ 쓸모없는
057 □ publish ⓥ 출판하다, 게재하다
058 □ paper ⓝ 논문, 서류
059 □ intend ⓥ 목표로 하다, 의도하다
060 □ restate ⓥ (더 분명하게) 고쳐 말하다
061 □ as follows 다음과 같이
062 □ complete ⓐ 완성된
063 □ publication ⓝ 출판, 게재
064 □ no more than 단지 ~일 뿐인
065 □ previous ⓐ 이전의
066 □ false ⓐ 틀린
067 □ meet the demand 요구에 맞추다

22

068 □ negotiate ⓥ 협상하다
069 □ whether ~ or not ~이든 아니든
070 □ usually ⓐⓓ 보통
071 □ traditional ⓐ 전통적인
072 □ approach ⓝ 접근법 ⓥ 접근하다
073 □ result in 결과적으로 ~을 낳다
074 □ agreement ⓝ 합의, 동의
075 □ old-school ⓐ 구식의
076 □ adversarial ⓐ 적대적인
077 □ one-off ⓐ 단 한 번의
078 □ transaction ⓝ 거래
079 □ increasingly ⓐⓓ 점점 더
080 □ rare ⓐ 드문
081 □ repeatedly ⓐⓓ 반복해서
082 □ spouse ⓝ 배우자
083 □ in view of ~을 고려하면
084 □ essential ⓐ 필수적인, 아주 중요한
085 □ maintain ⓥ 유지하다
086 □ interdependent ⓐ 상호 의존적인
087 □ long-term ⓐ 장기의
088 □ outcome ⓝ 결과, 성과
089 □ acceptable ⓐ 수용 가능한

23

090 □ interaction ⓝ 상호 작용
091 □ cultural ⓐ 문화적인
092 □ background ⓝ 배경
093 □ population ⓝ 인구
094 □ productivity ⓝ 생산성
095 □ due to ~ 때문에
096 □ externality ⓝ 외부 효과(의도하지 않았지만 부수적으로 따르는 결과)
097 □ knowledge spillover 지식의 확산
098 □ variety ⓝ 다양성
099 □ fractionalization ⓝ 분열
100 □ excessive ⓐ 과도한
101 □ cost ⓝ 비용, 대가
102 □ lower ⓥ 떨어뜨리다
103 □ impact ⓝ 영향을 주다, 충격을 주다
104 □ labo(u)r market 노동 시장
105 □ quality of life 삶의 질
106 □ tolerant ⓐ 관용적인
107 □ multicultural ⓐ 다문화의
108 □ range ⓝ 범위
109 □ on the other hand 반면에
110 □ perceive A as B A를 B로 인식하다

111 □ distortion ⓝ 왜곡
112 □ identity ⓝ 정체성
113 □ discriminate against ~을 차별하다
114 □ ethnic ⓐ 민족의
115 □ conflict ⓝ 갈등
116 □ import ⓥ 유입하다, 수입하다
117 □ contrastive ⓐ 대비되는, 대립적인
118 □ factor ⓝ 요인
119 □ policy ⓝ 정책

24

120 □ shape ⓥ 형성하다
121 □ construction ⓝ 건설, 구성
122 □ ornately ⓐⓓ 화려하게
123 □ carve ⓥ 새기다
124 □ ancestor ⓝ 조상
125 □ erect ⓥ 세우다
126 □ hunter-gatherer ⓝ 수렵 채집인
127 □ multiple ⓐ 여럿의
128 □ megalithic ⓐ 거석의
129 □ successive ⓐ 연속된, 잇따른
130 □ innovator ⓝ 혁신가
131 □ be forced to 어쩔 수 없이 ~하다
132 □ settle down 정착하다
133 □ radically ⓐⓓ 근본적으로, 급진적으로
134 □ transform ⓥ 바꾸다, 변모시키다

25

135 □ age group 연령 집단
136 □ social media 소셜 미디어
137 □ each ⓐ 각각 ⓐ 각각의
138 □ given ⓐ 주어진 prep ~을 고려하면
139 □ more than ~ 이상
140 □ except for ~을 제외하고
141 □ among prep ~ 중에서
142 □ decrease ⓝ 감소

26

143 □ add ⓥ 추가하다
144 □ flute ⓝ 플루트
145 □ earn ⓥ 얻다, 취득하다, 벌다
146 □ bachelor's degree 학사 학위
147 □ serve in the army 군 복무하다
148 □ military ⓝ 군대 ⓐ 군사적인
149 □ composition ⓝ 작곡
150 □ admire ⓥ 감탄하다, 존경하다
151 □ perform ⓥ 연주하다
152 □ recording ⓝ 음반, 녹음
153 □ expressive ⓐ 표현이 풍부한
154 □ unique ⓐ 독특한
155 □ harmonic ⓐ (음악) 화성의

27

156 □ silversmith ⓝ 은세공하는 사람
157 □ fine ⓐ 정교한, 미세한
158 □ jewelry ⓝ 보석
159 □ miss a chance 기회를 놓치다
160 □ registration ⓝ 등록
161 □ material ⓝ 재료
162 □ refund ⓝ 환불
163 □ cancellation ⓝ 취소
164 □ on the day of ~의 당일에

28

165 □ awareness ⓝ 인식, 앎
166 □ annual ⓐ 매년의
167 □ marine ⓐ 해양의
168 □ conservation ⓝ 보존
169 □ wildlife ⓝ 야생 생물
170 □ pollution ⓝ 오염
171 □ guideline ⓝ 지침
172 □ submission ⓝ 제출
173 □ entry ⓝ 출품작, 참가, 입장

29

174 □ comment ⓝ 논평, 지적
175 □ discuss ⓥ 토론하다
176 □ field ⓝ 경기장, 분야
177 □ boardroom ⓝ 이사회실
178 □ professional ⓝ 전문가
179 □ specialized ⓐ 전문화된
180 □ total stranger 생판 남
181 □ expertise ⓝ 전문 지식
182 □ executive ⓝ 임원, 중역
183 □ respective ⓐ 각자의
184 □ face ⓥ 마주하다, 직면하다
185 □ criticism ⓝ 비평
186 □ run ⓥ (가게나 사업을) 운영하다
187 □ accountant ⓝ 회계사
188 □ tax ⓝ 세금
189 □ organization ⓝ 조직, 단체

30

190 □ particularly ⓐⓓ 특히
191 □ stressful ⓐ 스트레스가 되는
192 □ sense ⓝ 감각, 의식
193 □ security ⓝ 안정
194 □ disoriented ⓐ 혼란스러워 하는
195 □ routine ⓝ 일상, 루틴
196 □ disrupt ⓥ 무너뜨리다, 지장을 주다, 방해하다
197 □ familiar ⓐ 익숙한
198 □ take away 없애다, 빼앗다
199 □ understanding ⓝ 이해(력)
200 □ literal ⓐ 융통성 없는, 문자 그대로의
201 □ beforehand ⓐⓓ 미리
202 □ establish ⓥ 설정하다, 쌓다
203 □ balance ⓝ 균형 ⓥ 균형을 맞추다
204 □ validate ⓥ 인정하다, 승인하다, 입증하다
205 □ adjust to ~에 적응하다
206 □ share ⓥ 나누다, 공유하다
207 □ contribute to ~에 기여하다, ~의 원인이 되다
208 □ transition ⓝ 변화

31

209 □ terrified ⓐ 겁에 질린
210 □ stem from ~에서 기원하다
211 □ lack ⓝ 부족, 결여
212 □ instill ⓥ 스며들게 하다, 주입하다
213 □ potential ⓐ 잠재적인
214 □ destination ⓝ 목적지
215 □ solely ⓐⓓ 오로지
216 □ logic ⓝ 논리
217 □ statistically ⓐⓓ 통계적으로
218 □ odds ⓝ 공산, 가능성

219 □ in one's favor ~에 유리한
220 □ crash ⓝ (차나 비행기의) 사고, 충돌
221 □ close to ~에 근접한
222 □ involve ⓥ ~와 관련 있다
223 □ well-being ⓝ 안녕, 행복
224 □ make sure 반드시 ~하다
225 □ base ⓥ ~에 근거를 두다, 기반으로 하다
226 □ anxiety ⓝ 불안
227 □ boredom ⓝ 지루함

32

228 □ primatologist ⓝ 영장류학자
229 □ downplay ⓥ 경시하다
230 □ similarity ⓝ 유사성
231 □ spot ⓝ 위치 ⓥ 파악하다
232 □ imaginary ⓐ 상상의
233 □ ladder ⓝ 사다리
234 □ offender ⓝ 범죄자, 나쁜 짓을 하는 사람
235 □ employ ⓥ 이용하다, 고용하다
236 □ technical ⓐ 전문적인
237 □ language ⓝ 언어
238 □ chimp ⓝ 침팬지
239 □ primate ⓝ 영장류
240 □ affiliation ⓝ 제휴
241 □ interpret A as B A를 B로 해석하다
242 □ crow ⓝ 까마귀
243 □ somehow [ad] 왠지, 어떻게든
244 □ qualitatively [ad] 질적으로
245 □ toolmaking ⓝ 도구 제작
246 □ define ⓥ 정의하다
247 □ humanity ⓝ 인류
248 □ beat ⓥ 이기다
249 □ cognitive ⓐ 인지적인
250 □ certain ⓐ 특정한
251 □ precise ⓐ 정확한
252 □ write off as ~라고 치부하다
253 □ instinct ⓝ 본능
254 □ intelligence ⓝ 지능
255 □ trick ⓝ 수법, 트릭
256 □ term ⓥ (특정 용어로) 칭하다 ⓝ 용어
257 □ disempower ⓥ ~로부터 힘을 빼앗다
258 □ overestimate ⓥ 과대평가하다
259 □ distance A from B A와 B 사이에 거리를 두다
260 □ identify ⓥ 식별하다, 알아보다, 확인하다
261 □ misconception ⓝ 오해

33

262 □ engagement ⓝ 참여, 몰입
263 □ achievement ⓝ 성취
264 □ provide A with B A에게 B를 제공하다
265 □ highly [ad] 매우
266 □ physicist ⓝ 물리학자
267 □ biochemist ⓝ 생화학자
268 □ dyslexia ⓝ 난독증
269 □ significant ⓐ 상당한, 심각한
270 □ throughout [prep] ~ 내내
271 □ discover ⓥ 찾아내다, 발견하다
272 □ bypass ⓥ 우회하다
273 □ compensate for ~을 보완하다, 보상하다
274 □ opposite ⓝ 정반대
275 □ enthusiastic ⓐ 열정적인, 열성적인
276 □ seek out ~을 찾아내다
277 □ subject ⓝ 실험 대상자
278 □ personal ⓐ 개인적인
279 □ religion ⓝ 종교
280 □ biography ⓝ (인물의) 전기
281 □ voraciously [ad] 탐욕스럽게
282 □ official ⓐ 공식적인
283 □ relevant ⓐ 적절한

34

284 □ refer to ~을 일컫다
285 □ competence ⓝ 능력, 역량
286 □ reflect ⓥ 반영하다
287 □ brilliant ⓐ 뛰어난
288 □ brief ⓝ (법률) 취지서, 의견서, 보고서
289 □ elegant ⓐ 명쾌한, 멋들어진
290 □ exceptionally [ad] 탁월하게
291 □ witty ⓐ 재치 있는
292 □ in terms of ~의 면에서
293 □ serve a ball 서브를 넣다
294 □ attractive ⓐ 매력적인
295 □ entertaining ⓐ 재미있는, 즐거움을 주는
296 □ gadget ⓝ 장비, 기기
297 □ measure ⓝ 척도
298 □ take into account ~을 고려하다, 참작하다
299 □ outstanding ⓐ 뛰어난
300 □ sole ⓐ 유일한
301 □ determinant ⓝ 결정 요소
302 □ self-worth ⓝ 자존감, 자부심
303 □ distracted ⓐ 정신이 팔린

35

304 □ sensory ⓐ 감각의
305 □ nerve ⓝ 신경
306 □ tissue ⓝ (생체) 조직
307 □ sensation ⓝ 감각
308 □ step on ~을 밟다
309 □ sharp ⓐ 날카로운, 예리한
310 □ transmit ⓥ 전달하다
311 □ spinal cord 척수
312 □ unpleasant ⓐ 불쾌한
313 □ protective mechanism 보호 기제
314 □ capacity ⓝ 능력
315 □ speech ⓝ 발화
316 □ lift ⓥ 들어올리다
317 □ painful ⓐ 고통스러운
318 □ motor ⓐ 운동 신경의
319 □ gut ⓝ 내장, 소화관
320 □ sweating ⓝ 발한, 땀이 남

36

321 □ bite ⓝ 한 입 (베어문 조각) ⓥ 베어 물다
322 □ crystal ⓝ 결정
323 □ hexagon ⓝ 육각형
324 □ liquid ⓝ 액체
325 □ ice cube 얼음 조각
326 □ allow for ~을 허용하다
327 □ twisted ⓐ 뒤틀린
328 □ atom ⓝ 원자
329 □ be made up of ~로 구성되다
330 □ steady ⓐ 안정된, 꾸준한
331 □ plenty of 많은
332 □ fit into ~에 들어 맞다
333 □ lattice ⓝ 격자 (모양)
334 □ time after time 자주, 매번, 되풀이해서

37

335 □ pluck ⓥ (현악기를) 뜯다
336 □ string ⓝ 줄, 현악기
337 □ vibration ⓝ 진동
338 □ eardrum ⓝ 고막
339 □ flex ⓥ (근육을) 수축시키다, (관절을) 구부리다
340 □ naturally [ad] 당연히
341 □ blur ⓥ 흐리게 하다
342 □ outline ⓝ 윤곽, 개요
343 □ hardly any 거의 전혀 ~않다
344 □ thin ⓐ 얇은
345 □ attach A to B A를 B에 부착하다
346 □ hollow ⓐ (속이) 빈
347 □ amplify ⓥ 증폭시키다
348 □ panel ⓝ 판
349 □ rate ⓝ 속도, 비율

38

350 □ integrate ⓥ 통합하다
351 □ all day long 하루 종일
352 □ boundary ⓝ 경계
353 □ portable ⓐ 휴대용의
354 □ outside ⓐ 외부의
355 □ responsibility ⓝ 책무, 책임
356 □ separate ⓥ 분리하다 ⓐ 분리된, 개별의
357 □ segment ⓥ 분할하다, 나누다
358 □ minimize ⓥ 최소화하다
359 □ account ⓝ 계정
360 □ conduct ⓥ 수행하다
361 □ workplace ⓝ 직장
362 □ break ⓝ 쉬는 시간
363 □ carry ⓥ 들고 다니다
364 □ flexible schedule 유연근무제
365 □ distinction ⓝ 구별
366 □ role ⓝ 역할
367 □ entail ⓥ 수반하다
368 □ constantly [ad] 계속
369 □ trade ⓥ 교환하다
370 □ monitor ⓥ 확인하다, 감독하다, 점검하다
371 □ on vacation 휴가 중인
372 □ inbox ⓝ 수신함

39

373 □ assume ⓥ 가정하다
374 □ complementary ⓐ 보완하는
375 □ locked in 갇힌, 고정된
376 □ alongside [prep] ~와 함께
377 □ pillow ⓝ 베개
378 □ journey ⓝ 여정
379 □ complement ⓥ 보완하다, 보충하다
380 □ ensure ⓥ 확실히 하다, 보장하다
381 □ stream ⓝ 흐름
382 □ status ⓝ 지위, 입지
383 □ lightbulb ⓝ 전구
384 □ motorist ⓝ 운전자
385 □ gasoline ⓝ 휘발유
386 □ switch to ~로 바꾸다
387 □ electric ⓐ 전기의

40

388 □ in general 일반적으로
389 □ investigate ⓥ 연구하다, 조사하다
390 □ match ⓥ 일치하다, 맞다, 부합하다
391 □ surgeon ⓝ 외과 의사
392 □ scrubs ⓝ 수술복
393 □ notable ⓐ 눈에 띄는
394 □ exception ⓝ 예외
395 □ explore ⓥ 탐구하다
396 □ reaction ⓝ 반응
397 □ established ⓐ 확립된, 정해진
398 □ black-tie affair 격식을 차리는 모임
399 □ bow tie 나비 넥타이
400 □ uniqueness ⓝ 독특함, 고유함
401 □ deviation ⓝ 일탈
402 □ powerful ⓐ 영향력 있는, 강력한
403 □ risk ⓥ 위태롭게 하다
404 □ challenge ⓥ 반박하다, 도전하다
405 □ negatively [ad] 부정적으로
406 □ neglect ⓥ 등한시하다, 소홀히 하다

41~42

407 □ production ⓝ 생산
408 □ greenhouse gas 온실가스
409 □ emission ⓝ 배출(량)
410 □ well founded 근거가 충분한
411 □ sector ⓝ 부문
412 □ wasteful ⓐ 낭비하는
413 □ climate ⓝ 기후
414 □ depending on ~에 따라
415 □ ship ⓥ 운송하다, 수송하다
416 □ carbon footprint 탄소 발자국
417 □ lamb ⓝ 어린 양
418 □ generate ⓥ 발생시키다, 생성하다
419 □ raise ⓥ 기르다, 키우다
420 □ feed ⓝ 사료, 먹이
421 □ fossil fuel 화석 연료
422 □ pastureland ⓝ 목초지
423 □ travel mode 이동 수단
424 □ surface ⓝ 지면
425 □ load ⓝ 적재(량) ⓥ (짐을) 싣다
426 □ bulk ⓝ 대량 ⓐ 대량의
427 □ freight ⓝ 화물 운송
428 □ pickup truck 픽업트럭, 소형 오픈 트럭
429 □ shorten ⓥ 짧게 줄이다
430 □ ruin ⓥ 파괴하다, 망치다
431 □ agriculture ⓝ 농업

43~45

432 □ grand ⓐ 큰, 위대한
433 □ temple ⓝ 사원, 절
434 □ worship ⓥ 예배하다
435 □ make arrangements for ~을 준비하다
436 □ accommodation ⓝ 숙소
437 □ care for ~을 관리하다, 돌보다
438 □ bury ⓥ 묻다
439 □ brick ⓝ 벽돌
440 □ path ⓝ 길
441 □ trip over ~에 걸려 넘어지다
442 □ dig up 파내다
443 □ duty ⓝ 의무
444 □ applicant ⓝ 지원자

어휘 Review test 12

TEST A-B 각 단어의 뜻을 [A] 영어는 우리말로, [B] 우리말은 영어로 쓰시오.

A	English	Korean	B	Korean	English
01	fair		01	개최하다	
02	take a risk		02	완성된	
03	no doubt		03	자신 있는	
04	knowledge spillover		04	~이든 아니든	
05	negotiate		05	필수적인, 아주 중요한	
06	spouse		06	결과, 성과	
07	discriminate against		07	인구	
08	be forced to		08	건설, 구성	
09	given		09	보존	
10	awareness		10	목적지	
11	expertise		11	정확한	
12	adjust to		12	~을 보완하다, 보상하다	
13	enthusiastic		13	능력, 역량	
14	take into account		14	(생체) 조직	
15	be made up with		15	진동	
16	integrate		16	분리하다	
17	complementary		17	지위, 입지	
18	well founded		18	운송하다, 수송하다	
19	worship		19	의무	
20	uphold		20	확실히 하다, 보장하다	

▶ A-D 정답 : 해설편 122쪽

TEST C-D 각 단어의 뜻을 골라 기호를 쓰시오.

C	English		Korean	D	Korean		English
01	chemistry	( )	ⓐ 고정된	01	유혹적인, 솔깃한	( )	ⓐ regretful
02	pinned	( )	ⓑ 요구에 맞추다	02	~에 적합한, 자격을 갖춘	( )	ⓑ distortion
03	compassion	( )	ⓒ 상호 의존적인	03	~를 목표로 하다, 의도하다	( )	ⓒ factor
04	meet the demand	( )	ⓓ 연속된, 잇따른	04	적대적인	( )	ⓓ composition
05	transaction	( )	ⓔ 군 복무하다	05	배우자	( )	ⓔ switch to
06	interdependent	( )	ⓕ 제출	06	왜곡	( )	ⓕ adversarial
07	lower	( )	ⓖ 분할하다, 나누다	07	요인	( )	ⓖ intend
08	successive	( )	ⓗ 연민	08	정착하다	( )	ⓗ entail
09	submission	( )	ⓘ 화학	09	오염	( )	ⓘ tempting
10	serve in the army	( )	ⓙ ~에서 기원하다	10	작곡	( )	ⓙ respective
11	executive	( )	ⓚ 거래	11	유감스러운, 후회하는	( )	ⓚ spouse
12	stem from	( )	ⓛ 발한, 땀이 남	12	각자의	( )	ⓛ pollution
13	overestimate	( )	ⓜ 운전자	13	공산, 가능성	( )	ⓜ applicant
14	outstanding	( )	ⓝ 화물 운송	14	경시하다	( )	ⓝ notable
15	sweating	( )	ⓞ 외과 의사	15	난독증	( )	ⓞ assume
16	segment	( )	ⓟ 숙소	16	수반하다	( )	ⓟ odds
17	motorist	( )	ⓠ 뛰어난	17	~로 바꾸다	( )	ⓠ settle down
18	surgeon	( )	ⓡ 과대평가하다	18	눈에 띄는	( )	ⓡ qualified for
19	freight	( )	ⓢ 임원, 중역	19	지원자	( )	ⓢ dyslexia
20	accommodation	( )	ⓣ 떨어뜨리다	20	가정하다	( )	ⓣ downplay

※ 영어 [독해] 파트만 수록한 문제지이므로 18번부터 시작합니다.

● 점수 표시가 없는 문항은 모두 **2점** ● 문항수 **28개** | 배점 **63점** | 제한 시간 **45분**

18. 다음 글의 목적으로 가장 적절한 것은?

Dear Parents/Guardians,

Class parties will be held on the afternoon of Friday, December 16th, 2022. Children may bring in sweets, crisps, biscuits, cakes, and drinks. We are requesting that children do not bring in home-cooked or prepared food. All food should arrive in a sealed packet with the ingredients clearly listed. Fruit and vegetables are welcomed if they are pre-packed in a sealed packet from the shop. Please DO NOT send any food into school containing nuts as we have many children with severe nut allergies. Please check the ingredients of all food your children bring carefully. Thank you for your continued support and cooperation.

Yours sincerely,
Lisa Brown, Headteacher

① 학급 파티 일정 변경을 공지하려고
② 학교 식당의 새로운 메뉴를 소개하려고
③ 학생의 특정 음식 알레르기 여부를 조사하려고
④ 학부모의 적극적인 학급 파티 참여를 독려하려고
⑤ 학급 파티에 가져올 음식에 대한 유의 사항을 안내하려고

19. 다음 글에 나타난 'I'의 심경 변화로 가장 적절한 것은?

It was two hours before the submission deadline and I still hadn't finished my news article. I sat at the desk, but suddenly, the typewriter didn't work. No matter how hard I tapped the keys, the levers wouldn't move to strike the paper. I started to realize that I would not be able to finish the article on time. Desperately, I rested the typewriter on my lap and started hitting each key with as much force as I could manage. Nothing happened. Thinking something might have happened inside of it, I opened the cover, lifted up the keys, and found the problem — a paper clip. The keys had no room to move. After picking it out, I pressed and pulled some parts. The keys moved smoothly again. I breathed deeply and smiled. Now I knew that I could finish my article on time.

① confident → nervous
② frustrated → relieved
③ bored → amazed
④ indifferent → curious
⑤ excited → disappointed

20. 다음 글에서 필자가 주장하는 바로 가장 적절한 것은?

Experts on writing say, "Get rid of as many words as possible." Each word must do something important. If it doesn't, get rid of it. Well, this doesn't work for speaking. It takes more words to introduce, express, and adequately elaborate an idea in speech than it takes in writing. Why is this so? While the reader can reread, the listener cannot rehear. Speakers do not come equipped with a replay button. Because listeners are easily distracted, they will miss many pieces of what a speaker says. If they miss the crucial sentence, they may never catch up. This makes it necessary for speakers to talk *longer* about their points, using more words on them than would be used to express the same idea in writing.

① 연설 시 중요한 정보는 천천히 말해야 한다.
② 좋은 글을 쓰려면 간결한 문장을 사용해야 한다.
③ 말하기 전에 신중히 생각하는 습관을 길러야 한다.
④ 글을 쓸 때보다 말할 때 더 많은 단어를 사용해야 한다.
⑤ 청중의 이해를 돕기 위해 미리 연설문을 제공해야 한다.

21. 밑줄 친 fire a customer가 다음 글에서 의미하는 바로 가장 적절한 것은?

Is the customer *always* right? When customers return a broken product to a famous company, which makes kitchen and bathroom fixtures, the company nearly always offers a replacement to maintain good customer relations. Still, "there are times you've got to say 'no,'" explains the warranty expert of the company, such as when a product is undamaged or has been abused. Entrepreneur Lauren Thorp, who owns an e-commerce company, says, "While the customer is 'always' right, sometimes you just have to fire a customer." When Thorp has tried everything to resolve a complaint and realizes that the customer will be dissatisfied no matter what, she returns her attention to the rest of her customers, who she says are "the reason for my success."

① deal with a customer's emergency
② delete a customer's purchasing record
③ reject a customer's unreasonable demand
④ uncover the hidden intention of a customer
⑤ rely on the power of an influential customer

22. 다음 글의 요지로 가장 적절한 것은?

A recent study from Carnegie Mellon University in Pittsburgh, called "When Too Much of a Good Thing May Be Bad," indicates that classrooms with too much decoration are a source of distraction for young children and directly affect their cognitive performance. Being visually overstimulated, the children have a great deal of difficulty concentrating and end up with worse academic results. On the other hand, if there is not much decoration on the classroom walls, the children are less distracted, spend more time on their activities, and learn more. So it's our job, in order to support their attention, to find the right balance between excessive decoration and the complete absence of it.

① 아이들의 집중을 돕기 위해 과도한 교실 장식을 지양할 필요가 있다.
② 아이들의 인성과 인지 능력을 균형 있게 발달시키는 것이 중요하다.
③ 아이들이 직접 교실을 장식하는 것은 창의력 발달에 도움이 된다.
④ 다양한 교실 활동은 아이들의 수업 참여도를 증진시킨다.
⑤ 풍부한 시각 자료는 아이들의 학습 동기를 높인다.

23. 다음 글의 주제로 가장 적절한 것은?

For creatures like us, evolution smiled upon those with a strong need to belong. Survival and reproduction are the criteria of success by natural selection, and forming relationships with other people can be useful for both survival and reproduction. Groups can share resources, care for sick members, scare off predators, fight together against enemies, divide tasks so as to improve efficiency, and contribute to survival in many other ways. In particular, if an individual and a group want the same resource, the group will generally prevail, so competition for resources would especially favor a need to belong. Belongingness will likewise promote reproduction, such as by bringing potential mates into contact with each other, and in particular by keeping parents together to care for their children, who are much more likely to survive if they have more than one caregiver.

① skills for the weak to survive modern life
② usefulness of belonging for human evolution
③ ways to avoid competition among social groups
④ roles of social relationships in children's education
⑤ differences between two major evolutionary theories

24. 다음 글의 제목으로 가장 적절한 것은?

Many people make a mistake of only operating along the safe zones, and in the process they miss the opportunity to achieve greater things. They do so because of a fear of the unknown and a fear of treading the unknown paths of life. Those that are brave enough to take those roads less travelled are able to get great returns and derive major satisfaction out of their courageous moves. Being overcautious will mean that you will miss attaining the greatest levels of your potential. You must learn to take those chances that many people around you will not take, because your success will flow from those bold decisions that you will take along the way.

* tread: 밟다

① More Courage Brings More Opportunities
② Travel: The Best Way to Make Friends
③ How to Turn Mistakes into Success
④ Satisfying Life? Share with Others
⑤ Why Is Overcoming Fear So Hard?

25. 다음 도표의 내용과 일치하지 <u>않는</u> 것은?

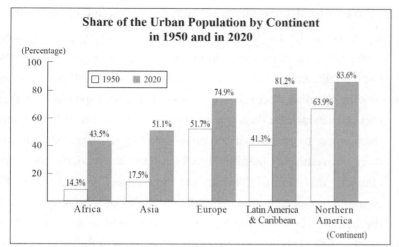

The graph above shows the share of the urban population by continent in 1950 and in 2020. ① For each continent, the share of the urban population in 2020 was larger than that in 1950. ② From 1950 to 2020, the share of the urban population in Africa increased from 14.3% to 43.5%. ③ The share of the urban population in Asia was the second lowest in 1950 but not in 2020. ④ In 1950, the share of the urban population in Europe was larger than that in Latin America and the Caribbean, whereas the reverse was true in 2020. ⑤ Among the five continents, Northern America was ranked in the first position for the share of the urban population in both 1950 and 2020.

26. Wilbur Smith에 관한 다음 글의 내용과 일치하지 <u>않는</u> 것은?

Wilbur Smith was a South African novelist specialising in historical fiction. Smith wanted to become a journalist, writing about social conditions in South Africa, but his father was never supportive of his writing and forced him to get a real job. Smith studied further and became a tax accountant, but he finally turned back to his love of writing. He wrote his first novel, *The Gods First Make Mad*, and had received 20 rejections by 1962. In 1964, Smith published another novel, *When the Lion Feeds*, and it went on to be successful, selling around the world. A famous actor and film producer bought the film rights for *When the Lion Feeds*, although no movie resulted. By the time of his death in 2021 he had published 49 novels, selling more than 140 million copies worldwide.

① 역사 소설을 전문으로 하는 소설가였다.
② 아버지는 그가 글 쓰는 것을 지지하지 않았다.
③ 첫 번째 소설은 1962년까지 20번 거절당했다.
④ 소설 *When the Lion Feeds*는 영화화되었다.
⑤ 죽기 전까지 49편의 소설을 출간했다.

27. 2022 Springfield Park Yoga Class에 관한 다음 안내문의 내용과 일치하지 <u>않는</u> 것은?

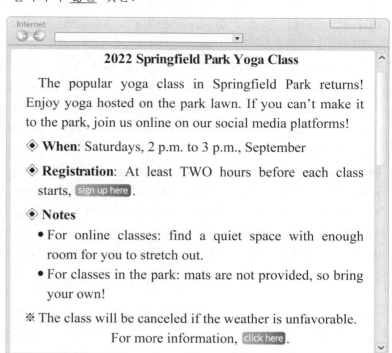

① 온라인으로도 참여할 수 있다.
② 9월 중 토요일마다 진행된다.
③ 수업 시작 2시간 전까지 등록해야 한다.
④ 매트가 제공된다.
⑤ 날씨가 좋지 않으면 취소될 것이다.

28. Kenner High School's Water Challenge에 관한 다음 안내문의 내용과 일치하는 것은?

Kenner High School's Water Challenge

Kenner High School's Water Challenge is a new contest to propose measures against water pollution. Please share your ideas for dealing with water pollution!

Submission
- **How**: Submit your proposal by email to admin@khswater.edu.
- **When**: September 5, 2022 to September 23, 2022

Details
- Participants must enter in teams of four and can only join one team.
- Submission is limited to one proposal per team.
- Participants must use the proposal form provided on the website.

Prizes
- 1 st: $50 gift certificate
- 2nd: $30 gift certificate
- 3rd: $10 gift certificate

Please visit www.khswater.edu to learn more about the challenge.

① 제안서는 직접 방문하여 제출해야 한다.
② 9월 23일부터 제안서를 제출할 수 있다.
③ 제안서는 한 팀당 4개까지 제출할 수 있다.
④ 제공된 제안서 양식을 사용해야 한다.
⑤ 2등은 10달러의 상품권을 받는다.

29. 다음 글의 밑줄 친 부분 중, 어법상 틀린 것은? [3점]

The human brain, it turns out, has shrunk in mass by about 10 percent since it ① <u>peaked</u> in size 15,000−30,000 years ago. One possible reason is that many thousands of years ago humans lived in a world of dangerous predators ② <u>where</u> they had to have their wits about them at all times to avoid being killed. Today, we have effectively domesticated ourselves and many of the tasks of survival — from avoiding immediate death to building shelters to obtaining food — ③ <u>has</u> been outsourced to the wider society. We are smaller than our ancestors too, and it is a characteristic of domestic animals ④ <u>that</u> they are generally smaller than their wild cousins. None of this may mean we are dumber — brain size is not necessarily an indicator of human intelligence — but it may mean that our brains today are wired up differently, and perhaps more efficiently, than ⑤ <u>those</u> of our ancestors.

30. 다음 글의 밑줄 친 부분 중, 문맥상 낱말의 쓰임이 적절하지 않은 것은? [3점]

It is widely believed that certain herbs somehow magically improve the work of certain organs, and "cure" specific diseases as a result. Such statements are unscientific and groundless. Sometimes herbs appear to work, since they tend to ① <u>increase</u> your blood circulation in an aggressive attempt by your body to eliminate them from your system. That can create a ② <u>temporary</u> feeling of a high, which makes it seem as if your health condition has improved. Also, herbs can have a placebo effect, just like any other method, thus helping you feel better. Whatever the case, it is your body that has the intelligence to ③ <u>regain</u> health, and not the herbs. How can herbs have the intelligence needed to direct your body into getting healthier? That is impossible. Try to imagine how herbs might come into your body and intelligently ④ <u>fix</u> your problems. If you try to do that, you will see how impossible it seems. Otherwise, it would mean that herbs are ⑤ <u>less</u> intelligent than the human body, which is truly hard to believe.

* placebo effect: 위약 효과

[31 ~ 34] 다음 빈칸에 들어갈 말로 가장 적절한 것을 고르시오.

31. We worry that the robots are taking our jobs, but just as common a problem is that the robots are taking our _____ . In the large warehouses so common behind the scenes of today's economy, human 'pickers' hurry around grabbing products off shelves and moving them to where they can be packed and dispatched. In their ears are headpieces: the voice of 'Jennifer', a piece of software, tells them where to go and what to do, controlling the smallest details of their movements. Jennifer breaks down instructions into tiny chunks, to minimise error and maximise productivity — for example, rather than picking eighteen copies of a book off a shelf, the human worker would be politely instructed to pick five. Then another five. Then yet another five. Then another three. Working in such conditions reduces people to machines made of flesh. Rather than asking us to think or adapt, the Jennifer unit takes over the thought process and treats workers as an inexpensive source of some visual processing and a pair of opposable thumbs. [3점]

* dispatch: 발송하다 ** chunk: 덩어리

① reliability   ② judgment
③ endurance   ④ sociability
⑤ cooperation

32. The prevailing view among developmental scientists is that people are active contributors to their own development. People are influenced by the physical and social contexts in which they live, but they also play a role in influencing their development by interacting with, and changing, those contexts. Even infants influence the world around them and construct their own development through their interactions. Consider an infant who smiles at each adult he sees; he influences his world because adults are likely to smile, use "baby talk," and play with him in response. The infant brings adults into close contact, making one-on-one interactions and creating opportunities for learning. By engaging the world around them, thinking, being curious, and interacting with people, objects, and the world around them, individuals of all ages are "_____."

① mirrors of their generation
② shields against social conflicts
③ explorers in their own career path
④ followers of their childhood dreams
⑤ manufacturers of their own development

33. The demand for freshness can _____.

While freshness is now being used as a term in food marketing as part of a return to nature, the demand for year-round supplies of fresh produce such as soft fruit and exotic vegetables has led to the widespread use of hot houses in cold climates and increasing reliance on total quality control — management by temperature control, use of pesticides and computer/satellite-based logistics. The demand for freshness has also contributed to concerns about food wastage. Use of 'best before', 'sell by' and 'eat by' labels has legally allowed institutional waste. Campaigners have exposed the scandal of over-production and waste. Tristram Stuart, one of the global band of anti-waste campaigners, argues that, with freshly made sandwiches, over-ordering is standard practice across the retail sector to avoid the appearance of empty shelf space, leading to high volumes of waste when supply regularly exceeds demand. [3점]

* pesticide: 살충제   ** logistics: 물류, 유통

① have hidden environmental costs
② worsen the global hunger problem
③ bring about technological advances
④ improve nutrition and quality of food
⑤ diversify the diet of a local community

34. In the studies of Colin Cherry at the Massachusetts Institute for Technology back in the 1950s, his participants listened to voices in one ear at a time and then through both ears in an effort to determine whether we can listen to two people talk at the same time. One ear always contained a message that the listener had to repeat back (called "shadowing") while the other ear included people speaking. The trick was to see if you could totally focus on the main message and also hear someone talking in your other ear. Cleverly, Cherry found it was impossible for his participants to know whether the message in the other ear was spoken by a man or woman, in English or another language, or was even comprised of real words at all! In other words, people could not _____. [3점]

① decide what they should do in the moment
② remember a message with too many words
③ analyze which information was more accurate
④ speak their own ideas while listening to others
⑤ process two pieces of information at the same time

35. 다음 글에서 전체 흐름과 관계 <u>없는</u> 문장은?

The fast-paced evolution of Information and Communication Technologies (ICTs) has radically transformed the dynamics and business models of the tourism and hospitality industry. ① This leads to new levels/forms of competitiveness among service providers and transforms the customer experience through new services. ② Creating unique experiences and providing convenient services to customers leads to satisfaction and, eventually, customer loyalty to the service provider or brand (i.e., hotels). ③ In particular, the most recent *technological* boost received by the tourism sector is represented by mobile applications. ④ Increasing competitiveness among service providers does not necessarily mean promoting quality of customer services. ⑤ Indeed, empowering tourists with mobile access to services such as hotel reservations, airline ticketing, and recommendations for local attractions generates strong interest and considerable profits.

* hospitality industry: 서비스업(호텔·식당업 등)

[36~37] 주어진 글 다음에 이어질 글의 순서로 가장 적절한 것을 고르시오.

36.

> With nearly a billion hungry people in the world, there is obviously no single cause.

(A) The reason people are hungry in those countries is that the products produced there can be sold on the world market for more than the local citizens can afford to pay for them. In the modern age you do not starve because you have no food, you starve because you have no money.

(B) However, far and away the biggest cause is poverty. Seventy-nine percent of the world's hungry live in nations that are net exporters of food. How can this be?

(C) So the problem really is that food is, in the grand scheme of things, too expensive and many people are too poor to buy it. The answer will be in continuing the trend of lowering the cost of food.

* net exporter: 순 수출국   ** scheme: 체계, 조직

① (A) − (C) − (B)   ② (B) − (A) − (C)
③ (B) − (C) − (A)   ④ (C) − (A) − (B)
⑤ (C) − (B) − (A)

37.

> Most people have a perfect time of day when they feel they are at their best, whether in the morning, evening, or afternoon.

(A) When your mind and body are less alert than at your "peak" hours, the muse of creativity awakens and is allowed to roam more freely. In other words, when your mental machinery is loose rather than standing at attention, the creativity flows.

(B) However, if the task you face demands creativity and novel ideas, it's best to tackle it at your "worst" time of day! So if you are an early bird, make sure to attack your creative task in the evening, and vice versa for night owls.

(C) Some of us are night owls, some early birds, and others in between may feel most active during the afternoon hours. If you are able to organize your day and divide your work, make it a point to deal with tasks that demand attention at your best time of the day. [3점]

* roam: (어슬렁어슬렁) 거닐다

① (A) − (C) − (B)   ② (B) − (A) − (C)
③ (B) − (C) − (A)   ④ (C) − (A) − (B)
⑤ (C) − (B) − (A)

[38 ~ 39] 글의 흐름으로 보아, 주어진 문장이 들어가기에 가장 적절한 곳을 고르시오.

38.

> Unfortunately, it is also likely to "crowd out" other activities that produce more sustainable social contributions to our social well-being.

Television is the number one leisure activity in the United States and Europe, consuming more than half of our free time. (①) We generally think of television as a way to relax, tune out, and escape from our troubles for a bit each day. (②) While this is true, there is increasing evidence that we are more motivated to tune in to our favorite shows and characters when we are feeling lonely or have a greater need for social connection. (③) Television watching does satisfy these social needs to some extent, at least in the short run. (④) The more television we watch, the less likely we are to volunteer our time or to spend time with people in our social networks. (⑤) In other words, the more time we make for *Friends*, the less time we have for friends in real life.

* *Friends*: 프렌즈(미국의 한 방송국에서 방영된 시트콤)

39.

> What we need is a reliable and reproducible method for measuring the relative hotness or coldness of objects rather than the rate of energy transfer.

We often associate the concept of temperature with how hot or cold an object feels when we touch it. In this way, our senses provide us with a qualitative indication of temperature. (①) Our senses, however, are unreliable and often mislead us. (②) For example, if you stand in bare feet with one foot on carpet and the other on a tile floor, the tile feels colder than the carpet *even though both are at the same temperature*. (③) The two objects feel different because tile transfers energy by heat at a higher rate than carpet does. (④) Your skin "measures" the rate of energy transfer by heat rather than the actual temperature. (⑤) Scientists have developed a variety of thermometers for making such quantitative measurements. [3점]

* thermometer: 온도계

40. 다음 글의 내용을 한 문장으로 요약하고자 한다. 빈칸 (A), (B)에 들어갈 말로 가장 적절한 것은?

> My colleagues and I ran an experiment testing two different messages meant to convince thousands of resistant alumni to make a donation. One message emphasized the opportunity to do good: donating would benefit students, faculty, and staff. The other emphasized the opportunity to feel good: donors would enjoy the warm glow of giving. The two messages were equally effective: in both cases, 6.5 percent of the unwilling alumni ended up donating. Then we combined them, because two reasons are better than one. Except they weren't. When we put the two reasons together, the giving rate dropped below 3 percent. Each reason alone was more than twice as effective as the two combined. The audience was already skeptical. When we gave them different kinds of reasons to donate, we triggered their awareness that someone was trying to persuade them — and they shielded themselves against it.
>
> * alumni: 졸업생 ** skeptical: 회의적인

↓

> In the experiment mentioned above, when the two different reasons to donate were given ____(A)____, the audience was less likely to be ____(B)____ because they could recognize the intention to persuade them.

     (A)   (B)
① simultaneously ⋯⋯ convinced
② separately ⋯⋯ confused
③ frequently ⋯⋯ annoyed
④ separately ⋯⋯ satisfied
⑤ simultaneously ⋯⋯ offended

[41 ~ 42] 다음 글을 읽고, 물음에 답하시오.

In a society that rejects the consumption of insects there are some individuals who overcome this rejection, but most will continue with this attitude. It may be very (a) difficult to convince an entire society that insects are totally suitable for consumption. However, there are examples in which this (b) reversal of attitudes about certain foods has happened to an entire society. Several examples in the past 120 years from European-American society are: considering lobster a luxury food instead of a food for servants and prisoners; considering sushi a safe and delicious food; and considering pizza not just a food for the rural poor of Sicily. In Latin American countries, where insects are already consumed, a portion of the population hates their consumption and (c) associates it with poverty. There are also examples of people who have had the habit of consuming them and (d) encouraged that habit due to shame, and because they do not want to be categorized as poor or uncivilized. According to Esther Katz, an anthropologist, if the consumption of insects as a food luxury is to be promoted, there would be more chances that some individuals who do not present this habit overcome ideas under which they were educated. And this could also help to (e) revalue the consumption of insects by those people who already eat them.

41. 윗글의 제목으로 가장 적절한 것은?

① The More Variety on the Table, The Healthier You Become
② Edible or Not? Change Your Perspectives on Insects
③ Insects: A Key to Solve the World Food Shortage
④ Don't Let Uniqueness in Food Culture Disappear
⑤ Experiencing Various Cultures by Food

42. 밑줄 친 (a)~(e) 중에서 문맥상 낱말의 쓰임이 적절하지 않은 것은?

① (a)   ② (b)   ③ (c)   ④ (d)   ⑤ (e)

[43 ~ 45] 다음 글을 읽고, 물음에 답하시오.

(A)

A boy had a place at the best school in town. In the morning, his granddad took him to the school. When (a) he went onto the playground with his grandson, the children surrounded them. "What a funny old man," one boy smirked. A girl with brown hair pointed at the pair and jumped up and down. Suddenly, the bell rang and the children ran off to their first lesson.

* smirk: 히죽히죽 웃다

(B)

In some schools the children completely ignored the old man and in others, they made fun of (b) him. When this happened, he would turn sadly and go home. Finally, he went onto the tiny playground of a very small school, and leant against the fence, exhausted. The bell rang, and the crowd of children ran out onto the playground. "Sir, are you all right? Shall I bring you a glass of water?" a voice said. "We've got a bench in the playground — come and sit down," another voice said. Soon a young teacher came out onto the playground.

(C)

The old man greeted (c) him and said: "Finally, I've found my grandson the best school in town." "You're mistaken, sir. Our school is not the best — it's small and cramped." The old man didn't argue with the teacher. Instead, he made arrangements for his grandson to join the school, and then the old man left. That evening, the boy's mom said to (d) him: "Dad, you can't even read. How do you know you've found the best teacher of all?" "Judge a teacher by his pupils," the old man replied.

* cramped: 비좁은

(D)

The old man took his grandson firmly by the hand, and led him out of the school gate. "Brilliant, I don't have to go to school!" the boy exclaimed. "You do, but not this one," his granddad replied. "I'll find you a school myself." Granddad took his grandson back to his own house, asked grandma to look after him, and went off to look for a teacher (e) himself. Every time he spotted a school, the old man went onto the playground, and waited for the children to come out at break time.

43. 주어진 글 (A)에 이어질 내용을 순서에 맞게 배열한 것으로 가장 적절한 것은?

① (B) − (D) − (C)   ② (C) − (B) − (D)
③ (C) − (D) − (B)   ④ (D) − (B) − (C)
⑤ (D) − (C) − (B)

44. 밑줄 친 (a)~(e) 중에서 가리키는 대상이 나머지 넷과 다른 것은?

① (a)   ② (b)   ③ (c)   ④ (d)   ⑤ (e)

45. 윗글에 관한 내용으로 적절하지 않은 것은?

① 갈색 머리 소녀가 노인과 소년을 향해 손가락질했다.
② 노인은 지쳐서 울타리에 기댔다.
③ 노인은 선생님과 논쟁을 벌였다.
④ 노인은 글을 읽을 줄 몰랐다.
⑤ 소년은 학교에 가지 않아도 된다고 소리쳤다.

★ 확인 사항
○ 답안지의 해당란에 필요한 내용을 정확히 기입(표기) 했는지 확인하시오.

13회

VOCA LIST 13

회차별 영단어 QR 코드 ※ QR 코드를 스캔 후 모바일로 단어장처럼 학습할 수 있습니다.

● 고1 2022학년도 9월

18

001 □ guardian ⓝ 보호자
002 □ hold ⓥ (행사를) 열다, 개최하다
003 □ bring in 가져오다
004 □ home-cooked ⓐ 집에서 요리한
005 □ sealed ⓐ 밀봉한
006 □ packet ⓝ 꾸러미
007 □ ingredient ⓝ 성분, 재료
008 □ clearly [ad] 명확하게
009 □ welcome ⓥ 환영하다
010 □ pre-packed ⓐ 사전 포장된
011 □ contain ⓥ 포함하다, 함유하다
012 □ severe ⓐ 심각한
013 □ carefully [ad] 주의 깊게
014 □ continued ⓐ 지속적인
015 □ cooperation ⓝ 협조, 협력
016 □ headteacher ⓝ (공립학교) 교장

19

017 □ submission ⓝ 제출
018 □ deadline ⓝ 마감
019 □ article ⓝ 기사
020 □ work ⓥ 작동하다
021 □ strike ⓥ 치다, 때리다, 두드리다
022 □ be able to ~할 수 있다
023 □ on time 제시간에
024 □ desperately [ad] 필사적으로
025 □ rest ⓥ 놓다
026 □ lap ⓝ 무릎
027 □ lift up 들어올리다
028 □ pick out 빼다, 뽑다
029 □ smoothly [ad] 부드럽게
030 □ deeply [ad] 깊이
031 □ frustrated ⓐ 좌절한

20

032 □ get rid of ~을 제거하다
033 □ as ~ as possible 최대한 ~한
034 □ work for ~에 효과가 있다
035 □ express ⓥ 표현하다
036 □ adequately [ad] 적절하게
037 □ elaborate ⓥ 부연 설명하다, 자세히 말하다
038 □ speech ⓝ 연설, 말하기
039 □ reread ⓥ 다시 읽다
040 □ distract ⓥ 주의를 분산시키다
041 □ crucial ⓐ 아주 중요한
042 □ catch up 따라잡다
043 □ necessary ⓐ 필수적인, 필연적인
044 □ point ⓝ 요점

21

045 □ broken ⓐ 고장 난
046 □ fixture ⓝ 설비, 살림, 세간
047 □ replacement ⓝ 대체(품)
048 □ maintain ⓥ 유지하다
049 □ relation ⓝ 관계
050 □ warranty ⓝ (상품 품질) 보증
051 □ undamaged ⓐ 멀쩡한, 손상되지 않은
052 □ abuse ⓥ 남용하다
053 □ entrepreneur ⓝ 기업가, 사업가
054 □ own ⓥ 소유하다
055 □ e-commerce ⓝ 전자 상거래
056 □ fire ⓥ 해고하다
057 □ resolve ⓥ 해결하다
058 □ complaint ⓝ 불만
059 □ dissatisfied ⓐ 불만족한
060 □ the rest of ~의 나머지
061 □ reason ⓝ 이유
062 □ emergency ⓝ 응급 상황, 비상 사태
063 □ delete ⓥ 지우다, 삭제하다
064 □ purchasing record 구매 기록
065 □ reject ⓥ 거절하다
066 □ unreasonable ⓐ 불합리한
067 □ uncover ⓥ 드러내다, 밝히다
068 □ intention ⓝ 의도, 목적
069 □ rely on ~에 의존하다
070 □ influential ⓐ 영향력 있는

22

071 □ indicate ⓥ 보여주다, 나타내다
072 □ distraction ⓝ 주의 산만, 집중을 방해하는 것
073 □ cognitive ⓐ 인지적인
074 □ visually [ad] 시각적으로
075 □ overstimulate ⓥ 과도하게 자극하다
076 □ a great deal of 상당한, 큰, 많은
077 □ concentrate ⓥ 집중하다
078 □ end up with 결국 ~하다
079 □ academic ⓐ 학업의
080 □ support ⓝ 지지 ⓥ 지지하다, 돕다
081 □ attention ⓝ 집중, 주의
082 □ balance ⓝ 균형
083 □ excessive ⓐ 과도한
084 □ complete ⓐ 완전한
085 □ absence ⓝ 부재

23

086 □ creature ⓝ 생명체, 피조물
087 □ evolution ⓝ 진화
088 □ reproduction ⓝ 번식, 재생
089 □ criterion ⓝ 기준
090 □ natural selection 자연 선택
091 □ form ⓝ 양식, 서류 ⓥ 형성하다
092 □ care for ~을 돌보다
093 □ scare off ~을 겁주어 쫓아버리다
094 □ predator ⓝ 포식자
095 □ fight against ~에 맞서 싸우다
096 □ divide ⓥ 나누다
097 □ prevail ⓥ 우세하다
098 □ favor ⓥ 선호하다
099 □ belongingness ⓝ 소속, 귀속, 친밀감
100 □ likewise [ad] 마찬가지로
101 □ caregiver ⓝ 양육자

24

102 □ make a mistake of ~의 실수를 범하다
103 □ operate ⓥ 작동하다, 기능하다
104 □ safe zone 안전 구역
105 □ opportunity ⓝ 기회
106 □ achieve ⓥ 성취하다
107 □ fear ⓝ 공포
108 □ unknown ⓐ 미지의, 알지 못하는
109 □ path ⓝ 길
110 □ brave ⓐ 용감한
111 □ return ⓝ 보상
112 □ derive ⓥ 끌어내다, 도출하다
113 □ courageous ⓐ 용감한
114 □ overcautious ⓐ 지나치게 조심하는
115 □ attain ⓥ 달성하다, 얻다
116 □ potential ⓝ 잠재력
117 □ make friends 친구를 사귀다
118 □ satisfying ⓐ 만족스러운

25

119 □ share ⓝ 점유율
120 □ urban ⓐ 도시의
121 □ population ⓝ 인구(수)
122 □ continent ⓝ 대륙
123 □ whereas [conj] ~한 반면에
124 □ reverse ⓝ 반대, 역전, 전환
125 □ among [prep] ~ 중에서
126 □ rank ⓥ ~의 순위를 매기다, (입지를) 차지하다

26

127 □ novelist ⓝ 소설가
128 □ specialize in ~을 전문으로 하다
129 □ historical ⓐ 역사적인
130 □ fiction ⓝ 소설, 허구
131 □ journalist ⓝ 언론인, 저널리스트
132 □ condition ⓝ 상황, 환경
133 □ be supportive of ~을 지지하다
134 □ force ⓥ 강요하다, 어쩔 수 없이 ~하게 만들다
135 □ tax accountant 세무사
136 □ turn back to ~로 돌아오다
137 □ publish ⓥ 출판하다
138 □ feed ⓥ 먹다, 먹이다
139 □ go on to 계속해서 ~하다
140 □ around the world 세계 곳곳에서
141 □ film rights 영화 판권, 상영권
142 □ by the time of ~할 무렵
143 □ worldwide [ad] 전 세계에

27

144 □ host ⓥ 열다, 개최하다
145 □ lawn ⓝ 잔디밭
146 □ make it 참석하다, 성공하다, 해내다
147 □ social media 소셜 미디어
148 □ registration ⓝ 등록
149 □ at least 적어도, 최소한
150 □ stretch out 몸을 뻗고 눕다
151 □ provide ⓥ 제공하다
152 □ bring ⓥ 가져오다, 지참하다
153 □ one's own 자기 자신의 (것)
154 □ unfavorable ⓐ (형편이) 나쁜, 우호적이지 않은

28

155 □ measure ⓝ 대책, 조치
156 □ against [prep] ~에 대항하여
157 □ water pollution 수질 오염
158 □ deal with ~을 다루다, ~에 대처하다
159 □ proposal ⓝ 제안서
160 □ be limited to ~로 제한되다
161 □ prize ⓝ 상(품)
162 □ gift certificate 상품권

29

163 □ turn out ~로 판명되다
164 □ shrink ⓥ 줄어들다
165 □ mass ⓝ 부피, 질량
166 □ about [ad] 대략, 약
167 □ peak ⓝ 정점 ⓥ 정점을 찍다
168 □ have one's wits about one ~의 기지를 발휘하다
169 □ at all times 항상, 늘
170 □ domesticate ⓥ 길들이다
171 □ immediate ⓐ 즉각적인, 임박한
172 □ shelter ⓝ 쉴 곳, 은신처
173 □ outsource ⓥ 외부에 위탁하다, 아웃소싱하다
174 □ ancestor ⓝ 조상
175 □ domestic ⓐ 가정의
176 □ dumb ⓐ 어리석은
177 □ not necessarily 반드시 ~하지는 않은
178 □ indicator ⓝ 지표
179 □ intelligence ⓝ 지능
180 □ wire ⓥ 연결하다, 장착하다
181 □ differently than ~와는 다르게

30

182 □ certain ⓐ 특정한, 어떤
183 □ somehow [ad] 왜인지는 몰라도, 어떻게든
184 □ magically [ad] 마법처럼
185 □ cure ⓥ (병을) 치유하다, 낫게 하다
186 □ statement ⓝ 진술
187 □ unscientific ⓐ 비과학적인
188 □ groundless ⓐ 근거가 없는
189 □ appear to ~처럼 보이다
190 □ blood circulation 혈액 순환
191 □ aggressive ⓐ 적극적인, 공격적인
192 □ attempt ⓝ 시도, 노력
193 □ eliminate ⓥ 제거하다, 없애다
194 □ temporary ⓐ 일시적인
195 □ high ⓝ 도취감
196 □ health condition 건강 상태
197 □ method ⓝ 방법
198 □ whatever the case 어떤 경우이든지
199 □ regain ⓥ 되찾다, 회복하다
200 □ impossible ⓐ 불가능한
201 □ intelligently [ad] 똑똑하게, 현명하게, 지적으로

31

202 □ warehouse ⓝ 창고
203 □ picker ⓝ 수확자, 집는 사람
204 □ headpiece ⓝ 헤드폰, 머리에 쓰는 것, 지성, 판단력
205 □ break down 쪼개다
206 □ instruction ⓝ 지시
207 □ tiny ⓐ 아주 작은
208 □ productivity ⓝ 생산성
209 □ shelf ⓝ 선반
210 □ politely [ad] 정중하게, 예의 바르게
211 □ reduce ⓥ 전락시키다, 격하시키다
212 □ flesh ⓝ (사람, 동물의) 살
213 □ adapt ⓥ 적응하다
214 □ take over 지배하다, 장악하다
215 □ inexpensive ⓐ 값싼

216 ☐ opposable ⓐ 마주볼 수 있는
217 ☐ reliability ⓝ 신뢰성
218 ☐ endurance ⓝ 인내
219 ☐ sociability ⓝ 사교성

32
220 ☐ prevailing ⓐ 지배적인, 만연한
221 ☐ developmental ⓐ 발달의
222 ☐ active ⓐ 적극적인, 능동적인
223 ☐ contributor ⓝ 기여자
224 ☐ influence ⓥ 영향을 주다
225 ☐ physical ⓐ 물리적인
226 ☐ context ⓝ 상황, 맥락
227 ☐ play a role in ~에서 역할을 하다
228 ☐ interact with ~와 상호작용하다
229 ☐ be likely to ~할 가능성이 높다
230 ☐ baby talk 아기 말(말을 배우는 유아나 어린 이에게 어른이 쓰는 말투)
231 ☐ in response (~에) 반응하여, 호응하여
232 ☐ close ⓐ 친밀한
233 ☐ contact ⓝ 접촉
234 ☐ one-on-one ⓐ 일대일의
235 ☐ generation ⓝ 세대
236 ☐ shield ⓝ 방패
237 ☐ conflict ⓝ 갈등
238 ☐ career path 진로
239 ☐ manufacturer ⓝ 생산자

33
240 ☐ demand ⓝ 요구, 수요
241 ☐ freshness ⓝ 신선함
242 ☐ term ⓝ 용어
243 ☐ as part of ~의 일환으로
244 ☐ nature ⓝ 자연, 천성
245 ☐ year-round ⓐ 연중 계속되는
246 ☐ produce ⓝ 농산물
247 ☐ exotic ⓐ 외국의, 이국적인
248 ☐ lead to ~을 낳다, ~로 이어지다
249 ☐ widespread ⓐ 광범위한
250 ☐ hot house 온실
251 ☐ reliance ⓝ 의존
252 ☐ quality control 품질 관리
253 ☐ temperature ⓝ 온도
254 ☐ satellite ⓝ 위성
255 ☐ contribute to ~의 원인이 되다
256 ☐ concern ⓝ 우려, 걱정
257 ☐ wastage ⓝ 낭비(되는 양)
258 ☐ institutional ⓐ 제도적인, 기관의
259 ☐ expose ⓥ 폭로하다, 드러내다, 노출시키다
260 ☐ over-production ⓝ 과잉 생산
261 ☐ retail ⓝ 소매
262 ☐ sector ⓝ 분야
263 ☐ appearance ⓝ 모습, 외관
264 ☐ worsen ⓥ 악화시키다
265 ☐ bring about ~을 가져오다, 야기하다
266 ☐ nutrition ⓝ 영양
267 ☐ diversify ⓥ 다양화하다

34
268 ☐ at a time 한 번에
269 ☐ in an effort to ~하기 위해서
270 ☐ determine ⓥ 판단하다

271 ☐ contain ⓥ 수용하다, 담다
272 ☐ shadowing ⓝ 섀도잉
273 ☐ trick ⓝ 속임수, 요령
274 ☐ totally ⓐ 완전히
275 ☐ comprise ⓥ ~을 구성하다
276 ☐ at all (부정문 끝에서) 전혀, 아예
277 ☐ analyze ⓥ 분석하다
278 ☐ accurate ⓐ 정확한
279 ☐ process ⓥ 처리하다

35
280 ☐ fast-paced ⓐ 빠른
281 ☐ radically ⓐ 급진적으로
282 ☐ transform ⓥ 변모시키다
283 ☐ dynamics ⓝ 역학, 역동성
284 ☐ competitiveness ⓝ 경쟁력, 경쟁적인 것
285 ☐ convenient ⓐ 편리한
286 ☐ satisfaction ⓝ 만족
287 ☐ loyalty ⓝ 충성도
288 ☐ in particular 특히
289 ☐ technological ⓐ 기술적인
290 ☐ boost ⓝ 부상, 상승
291 ☐ represent ⓥ 대표하다, 나타내다
292 ☐ application ⓝ (휴대폰, 컴퓨터 등의) 응용 프로그램, 애플리케이션
293 ☐ empower ⓥ 권한을 부여하다
294 ☐ access ⓝ 접근 (권한)
295 ☐ recommendation ⓝ 추천, 권장
296 ☐ attraction ⓝ (사람을 끄는) 명소, 명물, 매력
297 ☐ generate ⓥ 만들어내다
298 ☐ profit ⓝ 수익

36
299 ☐ billion ⓝ 10억
300 ☐ obviously ⓐ 분명히
301 ☐ cause ⓝ 원인
302 ☐ citizen ⓝ 시민
303 ☐ afford to ~할 여유가 되다
304 ☐ pay for ~을 지불하다, 대금을 치르다
305 ☐ modern ⓐ 현대의
306 ☐ starve ⓥ 굶주리다
307 ☐ far and away 단연코, 훨씬
308 ☐ poverty ⓝ 가난, 빈곤
309 ☐ grand ⓐ 거대한, 큰
310 ☐ continue ⓥ 지속하다
311 ☐ trend ⓝ 추세
312 ☐ lower ⓥ 낮추다, 줄이다

37
313 ☐ whether A or B A이든 B이든
314 ☐ alert ⓐ 초롱초롱한, 기민한
315 ☐ muse ⓝ 뮤즈, 영감
316 ☐ freely ⓐ 자유롭게
317 ☐ machinery ⓝ 조직, 기계
318 ☐ loose ⓐ 느슨한
319 ☐ stand at attention 차렷 자세를 취하다
320 ☐ demand ⓥ 요구하다
321 ☐ novel ⓐ 새로운, 신기한
322 ☐ tackle ⓥ 해결하다, 처리하다, 다루다
323 ☐ early bird 아침형 인간
324 ☐ make sure to 반드시 ~하다
325 ☐ vice versa 그 반대도 같다

326 ☐ night owl 저녁형 인간
327 ☐ make it a point to ~하기로 정하다, 으레 ~하다

38
328 ☐ unfortunately ⓐ 불행히도, 안타깝게도
329 ☐ crowd out 몰아내다
330 ☐ produce ⓥ 만들어내다
331 ☐ sustainable ⓐ 지속 가능한
332 ☐ contribution ⓝ 기여, 이바지
333 ☐ consume ⓥ 소비하다, 쓰다
334 ☐ free time 자유 시간, 여가 시간
335 ☐ think of A as B A를 B로 여기다, 간주하다, 취급하다
336 ☐ tune out 주의를 돌리다, 관심을 끄다
337 ☐ escape from ~로부터 도망치다
338 ☐ a bit 조금, 약간
339 ☐ tune in to ~에 채널을 맞추다
340 ☐ satisfy ⓥ 만족시키다, 충족하다
341 ☐ to some extent 어느 정도
342 ☐ in the short run 단기적으로

39
343 ☐ reliable ⓐ 신뢰할 수 있는
344 ☐ reproducible ⓐ 재현 가능한
345 ☐ measure ⓥ 측정하다
346 ☐ relative ⓐ 상대적인
347 ☐ object ⓝ 물체
348 ☐ rate ⓝ 비율, 속도
349 ☐ energy transfer 에너지 전도
350 ☐ associate A with B A를 B와 연관 짓다
351 ☐ provide A with B A에게 B를 제공하다
352 ☐ qualitative ⓐ 정성적인, 질적인
353 ☐ indication ⓝ 지표, 암시, 조짐
354 ☐ mislead ⓥ 잘못 이끌다
355 ☐ bare ⓐ 맨, 벌거벗은
356 ☐ actual ⓐ 실제의
357 ☐ a variety of 다양한
358 ☐ quantitative ⓐ 정량적인

40
359 ☐ colleague ⓝ 동료
360 ☐ mean to ~하기를 의도하다
361 ☐ resistant ⓐ 저항하는
362 ☐ make a donation 기부하다
363 ☐ emphasize ⓥ 강조하다
364 ☐ do good 선행을 하다
365 ☐ benefit ⓥ ~에게 이득이 되다
366 ☐ faculty ⓝ 교직원
367 ☐ donor ⓝ 기부자
368 ☐ glow ⓝ 빛, (기쁨이나 만족감을 동반한) 감정
369 ☐ end up ~ing 결국 ~하다
370 ☐ combine ⓥ 합치다, 결합하다
371 ☐ put together 합치다
372 ☐ more than ~ 이상
373 ☐ audience ⓝ 관객, 청중
374 ☐ trigger ⓥ 유발하다
375 ☐ awareness ⓝ 인식, 의식
376 ☐ persuade ⓥ 설득하다
377 ☐ shield ⓥ 보호하다
378 ☐ simultaneously ⓐ 동시에
379 ☐ separately ⓐ 따로, 별개로

380 ☐ frequently ⓐ 자주
381 ☐ satisfied ⓐ 만족한
382 ☐ offend ⓥ 공격하다, 기분 상하게 하다

41~42
383 ☐ consumption ⓝ 섭취, 소비
384 ☐ individual ⓝ 개인
385 ☐ overcome ⓥ 극복하다
386 ☐ continue with ~을 계속하다
387 ☐ attitude ⓝ 태도
388 ☐ convince ⓥ 납득시키다, 설득하다
389 ☐ entire ⓐ 온, 전체의
390 ☐ suitable for ~에 적합한
391 ☐ reversal ⓝ 역전
392 ☐ luxury ⓝ 호사, 사치
393 ☐ instead of ~ 대신에
394 ☐ servant ⓝ 하인
395 ☐ prisoner ⓝ 죄수
396 ☐ delicious ⓐ 맛있는
397 ☐ the poor 가난한 사람들
398 ☐ rural ⓐ 시골의
399 ☐ portion ⓝ 일부, 부분
400 ☐ encourage ⓥ 장려하다, 권장하다
401 ☐ due to ~ 때문에
402 ☐ shame ⓝ 수치심
403 ☐ categorize A as B A를 B라고 분류하다
404 ☐ anthropologist ⓝ 인류학자
405 ☐ promote ⓥ 장려하다, 촉진하다, 홍보하다, 증진하다
406 ☐ present ⓥ 내보이다, 제시하다
407 ☐ revalue ⓥ 재평가하다
408 ☐ variety ⓝ 종류, 다양성
409 ☐ edible ⓐ 먹을 수 있는
410 ☐ shortage ⓝ 부족
411 ☐ uniqueness ⓝ 고유성
412 ☐ disappear ⓥ 사라지다

43~45
413 ☐ take A to B A를 B로 데려다주다
414 ☐ playground ⓝ 운동장, 놀이터
415 ☐ grandson ⓝ 손자
416 ☐ surround ⓥ 둘러싸다, 에워싸다
417 ☐ point at ~을 가리키다, 손가락질하다
418 ☐ run off to ~로 뛰어가다, 달아나다
419 ☐ ignore ⓥ 무시하다
420 ☐ make fun of ~을 조롱하다
421 ☐ sadly ⓐ 슬프게
422 ☐ lean against ~에 기대다
423 ☐ fence ⓝ 울타리
424 ☐ exhausted ⓐ 지친, 소진된
425 ☐ crowd ⓝ 무리, 군중
426 ☐ greet ⓥ 인사하다
427 ☐ You are mistaken. 잘못 생각하고 계세요. 오해예요.
428 ☐ argue with ~와 논쟁하다
429 ☐ make arrangements for ~을 준비하다
430 ☐ pupil ⓝ 학생, 제자
431 ☐ firmly ⓐ 단단히, 꽉
432 ☐ gate ⓝ 문
433 ☐ exclaim ⓥ 소리치다, 외치다
434 ☐ look after ~을 돌보다
435 ☐ spot ⓥ 찾다, 발견하다

13회

● 채점 : 맞은 개수 _____ / 80

TEST A-B 각 단어의 뜻을 [A] 영어는 우리말로, [B] 우리말은 영어로 쓰시오.

A	English	Korean
01	guardian	
02	tune out	
03	fast-paced	
04	sealed	
05	domesticate	
06	elaborate	
07	wire	
08	reproduction	
09	derive	
10	criterion	
11	unfavorable	
12	indicator	
13	reliance	
14	starve	
15	loose	
16	institutional	
17	obviously	
18	sustainable	
19	trigger	
20	edible	

B	Korean	English
01	역학, 역동성	
02	일시적인	
03	부족	
04	친밀한	
05	부드럽게	
06	기업가, 사업가	
07	찾다, 발견하다	
08	불만족한	
09	~을 구성하다	
10	인내	
11	줄어들다	
12	미지의, 알지 못하는	
13	수용하다, 담다	
14	성분, 재료	
15	근거가 없는	
16	둘러싸다, 에워싸다	
17	섭취, 소비	
18	~에게 이득이 되다	
19	대책, 조치	
20	우세하다	

▶ A-D 정답 : 해설편 132쪽

TEST C-D 각 단어의 뜻을 골라 기호를 쓰시오.

C	English		Korean
01	pre-packed	( )	ⓐ 다양화하다
02	distract	( )	ⓑ 멀쩡한, 손상되지 않은
03	faculty	( )	ⓒ 재현 가능한
04	undamaged	( )	ⓓ 세무사
05	bare	( )	ⓔ 경쟁력, 경쟁적인 것
06	early bird	( )	ⓕ 사전 포장된
07	shame	( )	ⓖ 주의를 분산시키다
08	diversify	( )	ⓗ 설비, 살림, 세간
09	reproducible	( )	ⓘ 외국의, 이국적인
10	mass	( )	ⓙ 잘못 이끌다
11	tackle	( )	ⓚ 교직원
12	population	( )	ⓛ 새로운, 신기한
13	overcome	( )	ⓜ 맨, 벌거벗은
14	natural selection	( )	ⓝ 수치심
15	mislead	( )	ⓞ 부피, 질량
16	fixture	( )	ⓟ 해결하다, 처리하다, 다루다
17	competitiveness	( )	ⓠ 자연 선택
18	novel	( )	ⓡ 인구(수)
19	exotic	( )	ⓢ 극복하다
20	tax accountant	( )	ⓣ 아침형 인간

D	Korean		English
01	치다, 때리다, 두드리다	( )	ⓐ firmly
02	위성	( )	ⓑ night owl
03	남용하다	( )	ⓒ qualitative
04	지배적인, 만연한	( )	ⓓ frustrated
05	저녁형 인간	( )	ⓔ exhausted
06	죄수	( )	ⓕ tiny
07	장려하다, 촉진하다, 홍보하다	( )	ⓖ courageous
08	창고	( )	ⓗ strike
09	충성도	( )	ⓘ prevailing
10	좌절한	( )	ⓙ prisoner
11	단단히, 꽉	( )	ⓚ abuse
12	시골의	( )	ⓛ ignore
13	마주볼 수 있는	( )	ⓜ satellite
14	정성적인, 질적인	( )	ⓝ rural
15	아주 작은	( )	ⓞ opposable
16	속임수, 요령	( )	ⓟ trick
17	발달의	( )	ⓠ warehouse
18	용감한	( )	ⓡ loyalty
19	지친, 소진된	( )	ⓢ promote
20	무시하다	( )	ⓣ developmental

※ 영어 [독해] 파트만 수록한 문제지이므로 18번부터 시작합니다.　　　　● 점수 표시가 없는 문항은 모두 2점 ● 문항수 28개 | 배점 63점 | 제한 시간 45분

18. 다음 글의 목적으로 가장 적절한 것은?

Dear Mr. Dennis Brown,

We at G&D Restaurant are honored and delighted to invite you to our annual Fall Dinner. The annual event will be held on October 1st, 2021 at our restaurant. At the event, we will be introducing new wonderful dishes that our restaurant will be offering soon. These delicious dishes will showcase the amazing talents of our gifted chefs. Also, our chefs will be providing cooking tips, ideas on what to buy for your kitchen, and special recipes. We at G&D Restaurant would be more than grateful if you can make it to this special occasion and be part of our celebration. We look forward to seeing you. Thank you so much.

Regards,

Marcus Lee, Owner - G&D Restaurant

① 식당 개업을 홍보하려고
② 식당의 연례행사에 초대하려고
③ 신입 요리사 채용을 공고하려고
④ 매장 직원의 실수를 사과하려고
⑤ 식당 만족도 조사 참여를 부탁하려고

19. 다음 글의 상황에 나타난 분위기로 가장 적절한 것은?

　　In the middle of the night, Matt suddenly awakened. He glanced at his clock. It was 3:23. For just an instant he wondered what had wakened him. Then he remembered. He had heard someone come into his room. Matt sat up in bed, rubbed his eyes, and looked around the small room. "Mom?" he said quietly, hoping he would hear his mother's voice assuring him that everything was all right. But there was no answer. Matt tried to tell himself that he was just hearing things. But he knew he wasn't. There was someone in his room. He could hear rhythmic, scratchy breathing and it wasn't his own. He lay awake for the rest of the night.

① humorous and fun
② boring and dull
③ calm and peaceful
④ noisy and exciting
⑤ mysterious and frightening

20. 다음 글에서 필자가 주장하는 바로 가장 적절한 것은?

　　As you set about to write, it is worth reminding yourself that while you ought to have a point of view, you should avoid telling your readers what to think. Try to hang a question mark over it all. This way you allow your readers to think for themselves about the points and arguments you're making. As a result, they will feel more involved, finding themselves just as committed to the arguments you've made and the insights you've exposed as you are. You will have written an essay that not only avoids passivity in the reader, but is interesting and gets people to think.

① 저자의 독창적인 견해를 드러내야 한다.
② 다양한 표현으로 독자에게 감동을 주어야 한다.
③ 독자가 능동적으로 사고할 수 있도록 글을 써야 한다.
④ 독자에게 가치판단의 기준점을 명확히 제시해야 한다.
⑤ 주관적 관점을 배제하고 사실을 바탕으로 글을 써야 한다.

21. 밑줄 친 "matter out of place"가 다음 글에서 의미하는 바로 가장 적절한 것은?

Nothing is trash by nature. Anthropologist Mary Douglas brings back and analyzes the common saying that dirt is "matter out of place." Dirt is relative, she emphasizes. "Shoes are not dirty in themselves, but it is dirty to place them on the dining-table; food is not dirty in itself, but it is dirty to leave pots and pans in the bedroom, or food all over clothing; similarly, bathroom items in the living room; clothing lying on chairs; outdoor things placed indoors; upstairs things downstairs, and so on." Sorting the dirty from the clean — removing the shoes from the table, putting the dirty clothing in the washing machine — involves systematic ordering and classifying. Eliminating dirt is thus a positive process.

① something that is completely broken
② a tiny dust that nobody notices
③ a dirty but renewable material
④ what can be easily replaced
⑤ a thing that is not in order

22. 다음 글의 요지로 가장 적절한 것은?

It's important that you think independently and fight for what you believe in, but there comes a time when it's wiser to stop fighting for your view and move on to accepting what a trustworthy group of people think is best. This can be extremely difficult. But it's smarter, and ultimately better for you to be open-minded and have faith that the conclusions of a trustworthy group of people are better than whatever you think. If you can't understand their view, you're probably just blind to their way of thinking. If you continue doing what you think is best when all the evidence and trustworthy people are against you, you're being dangerously confident. The truth is that while most people can become incredibly open-minded, some can't, even after they have repeatedly encountered lots of pain from betting that they were right when they were not.

① 대부분의 사람들은 진리에 도달하지 못하고 고통을 받는다.
② 맹목적으로 다른 사람의 의견을 받아들이는 것은 위험하다.
③ 남을 설득하기 위해서는 타당한 증거로 주장을 뒷받침해야 한다.
④ 믿을만한 사람이 누구인지 판단하려면 열린 마음을 가져야 한다.
⑤ 자신의 의견이 최선이 아닐 수 있다는 것을 인정하는 것이 필요하다.

23. 다음 글의 주제로 가장 적절한 것은?

Vegetarian eating is moving into the mainstream as more and more young adults say no to meat, poultry, and fish. According to the American Dietetic Association, "approximately planned vegetarian diets are healthful, are nutritionally adequate, and provide health benefits in the prevention and treatment of certain diseases." But health concerns are not the only reason that young adults give for changing their diets. Some make the choice out of concern for animal rights. When faced with the statistics that show the majority of animals raised as food live in confinement, many teens give up meat to protest those conditions. Others turn to vegetarianism to support the environment. Meat production uses vast amounts of water, land, grain, and energy and creates problems with animal waste and resulting pollution.

* poultry: 가금류(닭·오리·거위 등)

① reasons why young people go for vegetarian diets
② ways to build healthy eating habits for teenagers
③ vegetables that help lower your risk of cancer
④ importance of maintaining a balanced diet
⑤ disadvantages of plant-based diets

24. 다음 글의 제목으로 가장 적절한 것은?

Diversity, challenge, and conflict help us maintain our imagination. Most people assume that conflict is bad and that being in one's "comfort zone" is good. That is not exactly true. Of course, we don't want to find ourselves without a job or medical insurance or in a fight with our partner, family, boss, or coworkers. One bad experience can be sufficient to last us a lifetime. But small disagreements with family and friends, trouble with technology or finances, or challenges at work and at home can help us think through our own capabilities. Problems that need solutions force us to use our brains in order to develop creative answers. Navigating landscapes that are varied, that offer trials and occasional conflicts, is more helpful to creativity than hanging out in landscapes that pose no challenge to our senses and our minds. Our two million-year history is packed with challenges and conflicts.

① Technology: A Lens to the Future
② Diversity: A Key to Social Unification
③ Simple Ways to Avoid Conflicts with Others
④ Creativity Doesn't Come from Playing It Safe
⑤ There Are No Challenges That Can't Be Overcome

25. 다음 도표의 내용과 일치하지 <u>않는</u> 것은?

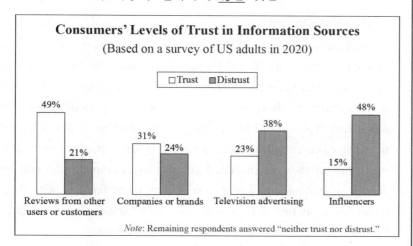

Consumers' Levels of Trust in Information Sources
(Based on a survey of US adults in 2020)

Note: Remaining respondents answered "neither trust nor distrust."

　The graph above shows the consumers' levels of trust in four different types of information sources, based on a survey of US adults in 2020. ① About half of US adults say they trust the information they receive from reviews from other users or customers. ② This is more than double those who say they hold distrust for reviews from other users or customers. ③ The smallest gap between the levels of trust and distrust among the four different types of information sources is shown in the companies or brands' graph. ④ Fewer than one-fifth of adults say they trust information from television advertising, outweighed by the share who distrust such information. ⑤ Only 15% of adults say they trust the information provided by influencers, while more than three times as many adults say they distrust the same source of information.

26. Paul Laurence Dunbar에 관한 다음 글의 내용과 일치하지 <u>않는</u> 것은?

　Paul Laurence Dunbar, an African-American poet, was born on June 27, 1872. By the age of fourteen, Dunbar had poems published in the *Dayton Herald*. While in high school he edited his high school newspaper. Despite being a fine student, Dunbar was financially unable to attend college and took a job as an elevator operator. In 1893, Dunbar published his first book, *Oak and Ivy*, at his own expense. In 1895, he published the second book, *Majors and Minors*, which brought him national and international recognition. The poems written in standard English were called "majors," and those in dialect were termed "minors." Although the "major" poems in standard English outnumber those written in dialect, it was the dialect poems that brought Dunbar the most attention.

① 14세쯤에 *Dayton Herald*에 시를 발표했다.
② 고등학교 재학 시 학교 신문을 편집했다.
③ 재정상의 이유로 대학에 진학하지 못했다.
④ 두 번째 출판한 책으로 국내외에서 인정받게 되었다.
⑤ 표준 영어로 쓴 시들로 가장 큰 주목을 받았다.

27. Premier Reading Challenge에 관한 다음 안내문의 내용과 일치하지 <u>않는</u> 것은?

Premier Reading Challenge
This is not a competition, but rather a challenge to inspire students with the love of reading.

- **Participants**
  − Students from 6th grade to 9th grade
- **Dates**
  − From June 1st to December 31st
- **Challenge**
  − Each student in 6th and 7th grade must read 15 books.
  − Each student in 8th and 9th grade must read 20 books.
- **Prize**
  − A bookmark for every participant
  − A Certificate of Achievement for students who complete the challenge
- **Registration**
  − Online only — www.edu.prc.com

※ For more information, see the school librarian or visit the website above.

---

① 6학년부터 9학년까지의 학생들을 대상으로 한다.
② 6월부터 5개월간 진행되는 행사이다.
③ 7학년의 도전과제는 15권의 책을 읽는 것이다.
④ 모든 참가자는 책갈피를 받는다.
⑤ 온라인으로만 등록할 수 있다.

28. Wolf Howls in Algonquin Park에 관한 다음 안내문의 내용과 일치하는 것은?

Wolf Howls in Algonquin Park
Wolf Howls in Algonquin Park is offering you a once-in-a-lifetime experience tonight! Don't miss the chance to hear the wolves communicate with our staff.

When & Where
- 8 p.m. Wednesday, August 25th, 2021
  (Only if the weather permits and a wolf pack is nearby.)
- Meet our staff at the outdoor theater and travel with them to the wolf howling location.

Fee
- $18.00 per person (Free for Ontario residents 65 and older)

Note
- Dress warmly for this special program which will last longer than three hours.
- No dogs are allowed during the event.
- If there are less than 5 people for the event, it will be cancelled.

※ Visit our website at www.algonquinpark.on for more information.

---

① 날씨에 상관없이 진행된다.
② Ontario 거주자 모두에게 무료이다.
③ 소요 시간은 3시간 미만이다.
④ 행사 내내 반려견을 동반할 수 있다.
⑤ 참가자 수에 따라 취소될 수 있다.

29. 다음 글의 밑줄 친 부분 중, 어법상 틀린 것은? [3점]

An economic theory of Say's Law holds that everything that's made will get sold. The money from anything that's produced is used to ① buy something else. There can never be a situation ② which a firm finds that it can't sell its goods and so has to dismiss workers and close its factories. Therefore, recessions and unemployment are impossible. Picture the level of spending like the level of water in a bath. Say's Law applies ③ because people use all their earnings to buy things. But what happens if people don't spend all their money, saving some of ④ it instead? Savings are a 'leakage' of spending from the economy. You're probably imagining the water level now falling, so there's less spending in the economy. That would mean firms producing less and ⑤ dismissing some of their workers.

* recession: 경기 후퇴

30. 다음 글의 밑줄 친 부분 중, 문맥상 낱말의 쓰임이 적절하지 않은 것은? [3점]

Hunting can explain how humans developed *reciprocal altruism* and *social exchange*. Humans seem to be unique among primates in showing extensive reciprocal relationships that can last years, decades, or a lifetime. Meat from a large game animal comes in quantities that ① exceed what a single hunter and his immediate family could possibly consume. Furthermore, hunting success is highly ② variable; a hunter who is successful one week might fail the next. These conditions ③ encourage food sharing from hunting. The costs to a hunter of giving away meat he cannot eat immediately are ④ high because he cannot consume all the meat himself and leftovers will soon spoil. The benefits can be large, however, when those who are given his food return the generous favor later on when he has failed to get food for himself. In essence, hunters can ⑤ store extra meat in the bodies of their friends and neighbors.

* reciprocal altruism: 상호 이타주의 ** primates: 영장류

[31~34] 다음 빈칸에 들어갈 말로 가장 적절한 것을 고르시오.

31. Sometimes it is the _____ that gives a business a competitive advantage. Until recently, bicycles had to have many gears, often 15 or 20, for them to be considered high-end. But fixed-gear bikes with minimal features have become more popular, as those who buy them are happy to pay more for much less. The overall profitability of these bikes is much higher than the more complex ones because they do a single thing really well without the cost of added complexity. Companies should be careful of getting into a war over adding more features with their competitors, as this will increase cost and almost certainly reduce profitability because of competitive pressure on price.

* high-end: 최고급의

① simpler product
② affordable price
③ consumer loyalty
④ customized design
⑤ eco-friendly technology

32. Many evolutionary biologists argue that humans _____. We needed to trade, and we needed to establish trust in order to trade. Language is very handy when you are trying to conduct business with someone. Two early humans could not only agree to trade three wooden bowls for six bunches of bananas but establish rules as well. What wood was used for the bowls? Where did you get the bananas? That business deal would have been nearly impossible using only gestures and confusing noises, and carrying it out according to terms agreed upon creates a bond of trust. Language allows us to be specific, and this is where conversation plays a key role.

① used body language to communicate
② instinctively knew who to depend on
③ often changed rules for their own needs
④ lived independently for their own survival
⑤ developed language for economic reasons

33. One big difference between science and stage magic is that while magicians hide their mistakes from the audience, in science you make your mistakes in public. You show them off so that everybody can learn from them. This way, you get the advantage of everybody else's experience, and not just your own idiosyncratic path through the space of mistakes. This, by the way, is another reason why we humans are so much smarter than every other species. It is not that our brains are bigger or more powerful, or even that we have the ability to reflect on our own past errors, but that we _____ that our individual brains have earned from their individual histories of trial and error.

* idiosyncratic: (개인에게) 특유한

① share the benefits
② overlook the insights
③ develop creative skills
④ exaggerate the achievements
⑤ underestimate the knowledge

34. The last two decades of research on the science of learning have shown conclusively that we remember things better, and longer, if _____.
This is the teaching method practiced by physics professor Eric Mazur. He doesn't lecture in his classes at Harvard. Instead, he asks students difficult questions, based on their homework reading, that require them to pull together sources of information to solve a problem. Mazur doesn't give them the answer; instead, he asks the students to break off into small groups and discuss the problem among themselves. Eventually, nearly everyone in the class gets the answer right, and the concepts stick with them because they had to find their own way to the answer. [3점]

① they are taught repeatedly in class
② we fully focus on them without any distractions
③ equal opportunities are given to complete tasks
④ there's no right or wrong way to learn about a topic
⑤ we discover them ourselves rather than being told them

35. 다음 글에서 전체 흐름과 관계 없는 문장은?

The Zeigarnik effect is commonly referred to as the tendency of the subconscious mind to remind you of a task that is incomplete until that task is complete. Bluma Zeigarnik was a Lithuanian psychologist who wrote in the 1920s about the effects of leaving tasks incomplete. ① She noticed the effect while watching waiters serve in a restaurant. ② The waiters would remember an order, however complicated, until the order was complete, but they would later find it difficult to remember the order. ③ Zeigarnik did further studies giving both adults and children puzzles to complete then interrupting them during some of the tasks. ④ They developed cooperation skills after finishing tasks by putting the puzzles together. ⑤ The results showed that both adults and children remembered the tasks that hadn't been completed because of the interruptions better than the ones that had been completed.

[36~37] 주어진 글 다음에 이어질 글의 순서로 가장 적절한 것을 고르시오.

36.

> Understanding how to develop respect for and a knowledge of other cultures begins with reexamining the golden rule: "I treat others in the way I want to be treated."

(A) It can also create a frustrating situation where we believe we are doing what is right, but what we are doing is not being interpreted in the way in which it was meant. This miscommunication can lead to problems.

(B) In a multicultural setting, however, where words, gestures, beliefs, and views may have different meanings, this rule has an unintended result; it can send a message that my culture is better than yours.

(C) This rule makes sense on some level; if we treat others as well as we want to be treated, we will be treated well in return. This rule works well in a monocultural setting, where everyone is working within the same cultural framework. [3점]

① (A) − (C) − (B)   ② (B) − (A) − (C)
③ (B) − (C) − (A)   ④ (C) − (A) − (B)
⑤ (C) − (B) − (A)

37.

In a study, a researcher pretending to be a volunteer surveyed a California neighborhood, asking residents if they would allow a large sign reading "Drive Carefully" to be displayed on their front lawns.

(A) The reason that they agreed was this: two weeks earlier, these residents had been asked by another volunteer to make a small commitment to display a tiny sign that read "Be a Safe Driver" in their windows.

(B) Since it was such a small and simple request, nearly all of them agreed. The astonishing result was that the initial small commitment deeply influenced their willingness to accept the much larger request two weeks later.

(C) To help them understand what it would look like, the volunteer showed his participants a picture of the large sign blocking the view of a beautiful house. Naturally, most people refused, but in one particular group, an incredible 76 percent actually approved. [3점]

① (A) − (C) − (B)　　② (B) − (A) − (C)
③ (B) − (C) − (A)　　④ (C) − (A) − (B)
⑤ (C) − (B) − (A)

[38~39] 글의 흐름으로 보아, 주어진 문장이 들어가기에 가장 적절한 곳을 고르시오.

38.

However, using caffeine to improve alertness and mental performance doesn't replace getting a good night's sleep.

Studies have consistently shown caffeine to be effective when used together with a pain reliever to treat headaches. (①) The positive correlation between caffeine intake and staying alert throughout the day has also been well established. (②) As little as 60mg (the amount typically in one cup of tea) can lead to a faster reaction time. (③) One study from 2018 showed that coffee improved reaction times in those with or without poor sleep, but caffeine seemed to increase errors in the group with little sleep. (④) Additionally, this study showed that even with caffeine, the group with little sleep did not score as well as those with adequate sleep. (⑤) It suggests that caffeine does not fully make up for inadequate sleep.

39.

The sales director kept an air horn outside his office and would come out and blow the horn every time a salesperson settled a deal.

Rewarding business success doesn't always have to be done in a material way. (①) A software company I once worked for had a great way of recognizing sales success. (②) The noise, of course, interrupted anything and everything happening in the office because it was unbelievably loud. (③) However, it had an amazingly positive impact on everyone. (④) Sometimes rewarding success can be as easy as that, especially when peer recognition is important. (⑤) You should have seen the way the rest of the sales team wanted the air horn blown for them.

* air horn: (압축 공기로 작동하는) 경적

40. 다음 글의 내용을 한 문장으로 요약하고자 한다. 빈칸 (A), (B)에 들어갈 말로 가장 적절한 것은? [3점]

Nancy Lowry and David Johnson conducted an experiment to study a teaching environment where fifth and sixth graders were assigned to interact on a topic. With one group, the discussion was led in a way that built an agreement. With the second group, the discussion was designed to produce disagreements about the right answer. Students who easily reached an agreement were less interested in the topic, studied less, and were less likely to visit the library to get additional information. The most noticeable difference, though, was revealed when teachers showed a special film about the discussion topic — during lunch time! Only 18 percent of the agreement group missed lunch time to see the film, but 45 percent of the students from the disagreement group stayed for the film. The thirst to fill a knowledge gap — to find out who was right within the group — can be more powerful than the thirst for slides and jungle gyms.

↓

According to the experiment above, students' interest in a topic _____(A)_____ when they are encouraged to _____(B)_____.

	(A)		(B)
①	increases	……	differ
②	increases	……	approve
③	increases	……	cooperate
④	decreases	……	participate
⑤	decreases	……	argue

[41~42] 다음 글을 읽고, 물음에 답하시오.

The market's way of telling a firm about its failures is harsh and brief. Not only are complaints less expensive to handle but they also can cause the seller to (a) improve. The seller may learn something as well. I remember a cosmetics company that received complaints about sticky sunblock lotion. At the time, all such lotions were more or less sticky, so the risk of having customers buy products from a rival company was not (b) great. But this was also an opportunity. The company managed to develop a product that was not sticky and captured 20 percent of the market in its first year. Another company had the (c) opposite problem. Its products were not sticky enough. The company was a Royal Post Office in Europe and the product was a stamp. The problem was that the stamp didn't stick to the envelope. Management contacted the stamp producer who made it clear that if people just moistened the stamps properly, they would stick to any piece of paper. What to do? Management didn't take long to come to the conclusion that it would be (d) less costly to try to educate its customers to wet each stamp rather than to add more glue. The stamp producer was told to add more glue and the problem didn't occur again.

Since it is better for the firm to have buyers complain rather than go elsewhere, it is important to make it (e) easier for dissatisfied customers to complain.

* stamp: 우표

41. 윗글의 제목으로 가장 적절한 것은?

① Designs That Matter the Most to Customers
② Complaints: Why Firms Should Welcome Them
③ Cheap Prices Don't Necessarily Mean Low Quality
④ More Sticky or Less Sticky: An Unsolved Problem
⑤ Treat Your Competitors Like Friends, Not Enemies

42. 밑줄 친 (a)~(e) 중에서 문맥상 낱말의 쓰임이 적절하지 <u>않은</u> 것은? [3점]

① (a)   ② (b)   ③ (c)   ④ (d)   ⑤ (e)

[43~45] 다음 글을 읽고, 물음에 답하시오.

(A)

A rich merchant lived alone in his house. Knowing that he was the only person living in the house, he was always prepared in case thieves came to his house. So, one day, when a thief entered his home, he remained calm and cool. Although he was awake, the merchant pretended to be in a deep sleep. He lay in bed and watched the thief in action. The thief had brought a new white sheet with (a) <u>him</u> to carry away the stolen goods.

(B)

(b) <u>He</u> then lay down and pretended to be asleep. When the thief had finished collecting as many valuables as he could, he hurriedly tied a knot in the white sheet which he thought was his. The merchant meanwhile ran out into the garden and yelled — "Thief! Thief!" with all the air in his lungs. The thief got nervous and quickly lifted the sheet. To (c) <u>his</u> surprise, the thin white sheet, filled with stolen goods, was torn apart.

(C)

All the stolen goods fell down on the floor creating a very loud and unpleasant noise. Seeing many people run towards him, the thief had to give up on all of the stolen goods. Leaving the goods behind in the house, he ran away in a hurry saying under his breath: "This man is such a skillful merchant; he is a businessman to the core. He has not only managed to save his valuables but has also taken away (d) <u>my</u> new sheet. He has stolen from a thief!" As he said that to himself, he ran away from the house.

(D)

He spread it out on the floor with the idea of putting all the stolen valuables into it, tying it, and carrying it away. While (e) <u>he</u> was busy gathering expensive-looking items from the merchant's luxurious house, the merchant quickly got out of the bed. Then he replaced the new white sheet with a similar looking white sheet, which was much weaker and much cheaper than the thief's one.

43. 주어진 글 (A)에 이어질 내용을 순서에 맞게 배열한 것으로 가장 적절한 것은?

① (B) − (D) − (C)   ② (C) − (B) − (D)
③ (C) − (D) − (B)   ④ (D) − (B) − (C)
⑤ (D) − (C) − (B)

44. 밑줄 친 (a)~(e) 중에서 가리키는 대상이 나머지 넷과 <u>다른</u> 것은?

① (a)   ② (b)   ③ (c)   ④ (d)   ⑤ (e)

45. 윗글에 관한 내용으로 적절하지 <u>않은</u> 것은?

① 상인은 도둑이 드는 상황에 항상 대비하고 있었다.
② 상인은 정원으로 뛰어나가 크게 소리쳤다.
③ 도둑이 훔친 물건들이 바닥에 떨어졌다.
④ 도둑은 상인의 물건들을 집밖으로 가지고 달아났다.
⑤ 상인의 보자기는 도둑의 보자기보다 값싼 것이었다.

* 확인 사항
○ 답안지의 해당란에 필요한 내용을 정확히 기입(표기)했는지 확인하시오.

18

001 ☐ honored ⓐ 명예로운, 영광으로 생각하여
002 ☐ delighted ⓐ 기쁜
003 ☐ annual ⓐ 연례의
004 ☐ dish ⓝ 요리
005 ☐ offer ⓥ 내놓다, 제공하다
006 ☐ showcase ⓥ 전시하다, 소개하다
007 ☐ talent ⓝ 재주, 재능
008 ☐ provide ⓥ 제공하다, 주다
009 ☐ tip ⓝ (실용적인, 작은) 조언
010 ☐ recipe ⓝ 조리법
011 ☐ grateful ⓐ 고마워하는
012 ☐ occasion ⓝ 행사
013 ☐ celebration ⓝ 기념, 축하
014 ☐ look forward to ~하기를 고대하다
015 ☐ owner ⓝ 주인, 소유주

19

016 ☐ awaken ⓥ 잠에서 깨다
017 ☐ glance at ~을 흘긋 보다
018 ☐ for an instant 잠시 동안
019 ☐ wonder ⓥ 궁금하다, 궁금해하다
020 ☐ rub ⓥ 비비다
021 ☐ assure ⓥ 확신시키다, 안심시키다
022 ☐ rhythmic ⓐ 리드미컬한, 규칙적으로 순환하는
023 ☐ scratchy ⓐ 긁는 듯한 소리가 나는
024 ☐ dull ⓐ 따분한, 재미없는
025 ☐ mysterious ⓐ 이해하기 힘든, 기이한
026 ☐ frightening ⓐ 무서운, 겁먹게 하는

20

027 ☐ be worth ~ing ~할 가치가 있다
028 ☐ remind ⓥ 상기시키다
029 ☐ ought to ~해야 하다
030 ☐ reader ⓝ 구독자
031 ☐ argument ⓝ 논점, 주장
032 ☐ involved ⓐ 열심인, 몰두(열중)하는
033 ☐ committed to ~에 몰입하는, 열중하는
034 ☐ insight ⓝ 통찰력
035 ☐ expose ⓥ 노출시키다
036 ☐ passivity ⓝ 수동성

21

037 ☐ trash ⓝ 쓰레기
038 ☐ by nature 본래, 천성적으로
039 ☐ anthropologist ⓝ 인류학자
040 ☐ bring back 소환하다
041 ☐ analyze ⓥ 분석하다
042 ☐ common ⓐ 흔한, 일반적인
043 ☐ out of place 제자리에 있지 않은
044 ☐ relative ⓐ 상대적인
045 ☐ emphasize ⓥ 강조하다
046 ☐ dining table 식탁
047 ☐ in oneself 그 자체로
048 ☐ indoors ⓐⓓ 실내에서
049 ☐ upstairs ⓝ 위층, 2층
050 ☐ downstairs ⓝ 아래층(특히 1층)
051 ☐ sort ⓥ 분류하다, 나누다
052 ☐ systematic ⓐ 체계적인
053 ☐ classify ⓥ 분류하다
054 ☐ eliminate ⓥ 제거하다, 없애다

055 ☐ process ⓝ 과정
056 ☐ completely ⓐⓓ 완전히, 전적으로
057 ☐ dust ⓝ 먼지, 티끌
058 ☐ renewable ⓐ 복구 가능한
059 ☐ replace ⓥ 대신[대체]하다
060 ☐ in order 정돈된, 적절한

22

061 ☐ independently ⓐⓓ 독자적으로
062 ☐ wiser ⓐ 지혜로운, 현명한
063 ☐ trustworthy ⓐ 믿을 만한
064 ☐ extremely ⓐⓓ 몹시, 극도로
065 ☐ ultimately ⓐⓓ 결국, 궁극적으로
066 ☐ open-minded ⓐ 마음이 열린
067 ☐ faith ⓝ 믿음
068 ☐ conclusion ⓝ 결론, (최종적인) 판단
069 ☐ whatever ⓟⓡⓞⓝ ~한 어떤 것
070 ☐ blind to ~을 보지 못하게 만들다
071 ☐ evidence ⓝ 증거, 단서
072 ☐ against ⓟⓡⓔⓟ ~에 반대하여
073 ☐ confident ⓐ 자신 있는
074 ☐ incredibly ⓐⓓ 놀랍도록, 엄청나게
075 ☐ repeatedly ⓐⓓ 반복해서, 되풀이하여
076 ☐ encounter ⓥ 접하다, 마주하다
077 ☐ bet ⓥ ~이 틀림없다, 분명하다(무엇에 대해 거의 확신함을 나타냄)

23

078 ☐ vegetarian ⓐ 채식의
079 ☐ mainstream ⓝ 주류
080 ☐ poultry ⓝ 가금류(닭·오리·거위 따위)
081 ☐ dietetic ⓐ 식이(성)의
082 ☐ approximately ⓐⓓ 대략적으로
083 ☐ healthful ⓐ 건강에 좋은
084 ☐ nutritionally ⓐⓓ 영양적으로
085 ☐ adequate ⓐ 적절한, 충분한
086 ☐ prevention ⓝ 예방
087 ☐ treatment ⓝ 치료
088 ☐ certain diseases 특정 질병
089 ☐ concern ⓝ 관심, 우려
090 ☐ statistics ⓝ 통계 자료, 통계학
091 ☐ majority ⓝ 가장 많은 수, 다수
092 ☐ raised ⓥ 키우다, 기르다
093 ☐ confinement ⓝ 가둠, 감금
094 ☐ teen ⓝ 십 대(= teenager)
095 ☐ protest ⓥ 항의하다
096 ☐ turn to ~로 바뀌다, ~에 의지하다
097 ☐ vegetarianism ⓝ 채식주의
098 ☐ vast ⓐ 방대한
099 ☐ land ⓝ 육지, 뭍, 땅
100 ☐ grain ⓝ 곡식
101 ☐ balanced diet 균형식(영양의 균형을 갖춘 식사)
102 ☐ disadvantage ⓝ 불리한 점, 단점
103 ☐ plant-based 채식 위주의

24

104 ☐ diversity ⓝ 다양성
105 ☐ conflict ⓝ 갈등
106 ☐ maintain ⓥ 유지하다
107 ☐ imagination ⓝ 상상력, 상상
108 ☐ assume ⓥ 가정하다, 추정하다

109 ☐ comfort ⓝ 안락, 편안
110 ☐ exactly ⓐⓓ 정확히, 꼭
111 ☐ ourselves ⓟⓡⓞⓝ 우리 자신
112 ☐ medical insurance 의료 보험
113 ☐ coworkers ⓝ 같이 일하는 사람, 동료
114 ☐ sufficient ⓐ 충분한
115 ☐ disagreement ⓝ 불화, 불일치
116 ☐ finance ⓝ 재정, 재무
117 ☐ think through ~에 대해 충분히 생각하다
118 ☐ capability ⓝ 능력
119 ☐ force ⓥ (~을 하도록) ~를 강요하다
120 ☐ navigate ⓥ 운전하다
121 ☐ landscape ⓝ 풍경, 지역
122 ☐ varied ⓐ 다양한
123 ☐ trial ⓝ 시련
124 ☐ occasional ⓐ 이따금씩 일어나는
125 ☐ pose a challenge to ~에 어려움을 주다
126 ☐ be packed with ~로 가득 차다
127 ☐ unification ⓝ 통일, 통합
128 ☐ play safe 위험을 피하다, 신중을 기하다
129 ☐ overcome ⓥ 극복하다

25

130 ☐ consumer ⓝ 소비자
131 ☐ sources ⓝ 자료[자료의 출처]
132 ☐ based on ~에 근거하여, 기반하여
133 ☐ survey ⓝ 설문조사
134 ☐ information ⓝ 정보
135 ☐ receive ⓥ 받다, 받아들이다
136 ☐ reviews ⓝ 비평, 평론
137 ☐ customer ⓝ 손님, 고객
138 ☐ distrust ⓝ 불신 ⓥ 불신하다
139 ☐ gap ⓝ 차이, 격차
140 ☐ among ⓟⓡⓔⓟ …에 둘러싸인, …의 가운데에
141 ☐ company ⓝ 회사
142 ☐ A be outweighed by B A가 B보다 덜 중요하다, B가 A보다 더 크다
143 ☐ share ⓝ 부분, 몫 ⓥ 함께 쓰다, 공유하다

26

144 ☐ poet ⓝ 시인
145 ☐ publish ⓥ 출판하다
146 ☐ edit ⓥ 편집하다
147 ☐ despite ⓟⓡⓔⓟ ~에도 불구하고
148 ☐ financially ⓐⓓ 재정적으로
149 ☐ operator ⓝ 기사, 운전자
150 ☐ at one's own expense 자비로, 사비로
151 ☐ bring ⓥ 가져다(제공해)주다 (과거형 : brought)
152 ☐ international ⓐ 국제적인
153 ☐ recognition ⓝ 인정
154 ☐ dialect ⓝ 방언
155 ☐ term ⓥ 이름짓다, 칭하다
156 ☐ A outnumber B A의 수가 B보다 많다

27

157 ☐ competition ⓝ 경쟁
158 ☐ rather ⓐⓓ 오히려, 차라리
159 ☐ inspire ⓥ 영감을 주다
160 ☐ participant ⓝ 참가자
161 ☐ bookmark ⓝ 책갈피
162 ☐ certificate ⓝ 수료증, 자격증

163 ☐ achievement ⓝ 성취, 달성
164 ☐ complete ⓥ 완료하다
165 ☐ librarian ⓝ (도서관) 사서

28

166 ☐ once-in-a-lifetime ⓐ (아주 특별하여) 평생에 한 번뿐인
167 ☐ permit ⓥ 허락하다
168 ☐ pack ⓝ 무리, 떼
169 ☐ nearby ⓐ 근처의, 인근의, 가까운 곳의
170 ☐ outdoor ⓐ 옥외(야외)의
171 ☐ howling ⓐ 울부짖는
172 ☐ last ⓥ 지속되다

29

173 ☐ economic ⓐ 경제적인
174 ☐ hold ⓥ 주장하다
175 ☐ theory ⓝ 이론
176 ☐ produce ⓥ 생산하다
177 ☐ situation ⓝ 상황, 처지, 환경
178 ☐ firm ⓝ 회사
179 ☐ dismiss ⓥ 해고하다, 내보내다
180 ☐ factory ⓝ 공장
181 ☐ recession ⓝ 경기 후퇴
182 ☐ unemployment ⓝ 실업
183 ☐ picture ⓥ ~를 상상하다
184 ☐ spending ⓝ 지출
185 ☐ apply ⓥ 적용하다
186 ☐ earnings ⓝ 수입, 소득
187 ☐ savings ⓝ 저축(액)
188 ☐ instead ⓐⓓ 대신에
189 ☐ leakage ⓝ 누수, 누출

30

190 ☐ develop ⓥ 발전시키다
191 ☐ reciprocal ⓐ 상호간의
192 ☐ altruism ⓝ 이타주의
193 ☐ unique ⓐ 특별한, 유일한
194 ☐ primates ⓝ 영장류
195 ☐ extensive ⓐ 광범위한, 폭넓은
196 ☐ game ⓝ 사냥감
197 ☐ quantity ⓝ 양
198 ☐ exceed ⓥ 넘어서다, 초과하다
199 ☐ immediate ⓐ (가족이) 직계인
200 ☐ consume ⓥ 먹다, 마시다
201 ☐ furthermore ⓐⓓ 게다가, 뿐만 아니라
202 ☐ variable ⓐ 변동이 심한, 가변적인
203 ☐ encourage ⓥ 장려하다
204 ☐ give away 나눠주다, 거저 주다
205 ☐ immediately ⓐⓓ 당장
206 ☐ leftover ⓝ (식사 후) 남은 음식
207 ☐ spoil ⓥ (음식이) 상하다
208 ☐ generous ⓐ 관대한
209 ☐ favor ⓝ 호의
210 ☐ in essence 결국, 본질적으로
211 ☐ extra ⓐ 여분의

31

212 ☐ competitive advantage 경쟁 우위
213 ☐ recently ⓐⓓ 최근에
214 ☐ high-end ⓐ 최고급의
215 ☐ fixed-gear ⓐ 고정식 기어의

216 ☐ bike ⓝ 자전거	270 ☐ discuss ⓥ 상의하다, 논하다	38	41~42
217 ☐ minimal ⓐ 최소의	271 ☐ eventually ⓐⓓ 결국	321 ☐ improve ⓥ 향상시키다, 개선하다	377 ☐ market ⓝ 시장
218 ☐ feature ⓝ (제품의) 기능, 특징	272 ☐ concept ⓝ 개념	322 ☐ alertness ⓝ 각성 상태, 기민함	378 ☐ failure ⓝ 실패
219 ☐ overall ⓐ 전반적인	273 ☐ stick with ~와 함께 머물다	323 ☐ mental ⓐ 정신의	379 ☐ harsh ⓐ 혹독한
220 ☐ profitability ⓝ 수익성	274 ☐ fully ⓐⓓ 완전히, 충분히	324 ☐ performance ⓝ 수행, 공연, 실적	380 ☐ brief ⓐ 간단한, 짧은
221 ☐ complexity ⓝ 복잡성	275 ☐ distraction ⓝ 정신을 산만하게 하는 것, 주의를 흩뜨리는 것	325 ☐ get a good night's sleep 숙면하다	381 ☐ complaint ⓝ 불평
222 ☐ competitor ⓝ 경쟁 업체	276 ☐ opportunity ⓝ 기회	326 ☐ consistently ⓐⓓ 지속적으로, 일관되게	382 ☐ less expensive 덜 비싼
223 ☐ certainly ⓐⓓ 틀림없이, 분명히, 확실히	277 ☐ topic ⓝ 화제, 주제	327 ☐ effective ⓐ 효과적인	383 ☐ handle ⓥ 다루다
224 ☐ reduce ⓥ 줄이다, 감소시키다		328 ☐ pain reliever 진통제	384 ☐ seller ⓝ 판매자
225 ☐ pressure ⓝ 압박	35	329 ☐ headaches ⓝ 두통, 골칫거리	385 ☐ cosmetics ⓝ 화장품
226 ☐ affordable ⓐ (가격 등이) 적당한, 감당 가능한	278 ☐ commonly ⓐⓓ 보통	330 ☐ correlation ⓝ 상관관계	386 ☐ sticky ⓐ 끈적거리는, 잘 달라붙는
227 ☐ loyalty ⓝ 충성도	279 ☐ refer to 나타내다	331 ☐ intake ⓝ 섭취	387 ☐ sunblock lotion 선크림 로션
228 ☐ customized ⓐ 맞춤 제작된	280 ☐ tendency ⓝ 경향	332 ☐ throughout the day 온종일, 하루 종일	388 ☐ rival ⓝ 경쟁자, 경쟁 상대
229 ☐ eco-friendly ⓐ 친환경적인	281 ☐ subconscious ⓐ 잠재의식의	333 ☐ established ⓐ 확립된	389 ☐ manage to 이럭저럭 ~하다
	282 ☐ remind A of B A에게 B를 상기시키다	334 ☐ typically ⓐⓓ 보통, 일반적으로	390 ☐ capture ⓥ 사로잡다
32	283 ☐ incomplete ⓐ 미완성된	335 ☐ reaction time 반응 시간	391 ☐ opposite ⓐ 정반대의
230 ☐ evolutionary ⓐ 진화의	284 ☐ notice ⓥ ~을 의식하다, (보거나 듣고) 알다	336 ☐ increase ⓥ 증가하다, 인상되다	392 ☐ stamp ⓝ 우표
231 ☐ biologist ⓝ 생물학자	285 ☐ complicated ⓐ 복잡한	337 ☐ additionally ⓐⓓ 게다가	393 ☐ stick to ~에 달라붙다
232 ☐ establish ⓥ 확립하다, 구축하다	286 ☐ interrupt ⓥ 방해하다, 끼어들다	338 ☐ suggest ⓥ 시사하다, 제안하다, 추천하다	394 ☐ envelope ⓝ 봉투
233 ☐ handy ⓐ 간편한	287 ☐ cooperation ⓝ 협동	339 ☐ make up for ~을 보상하다	395 ☐ management ⓝ 경영진
234 ☐ conduct ⓥ 수행하다	288 ☐ put together 조립하다, 만들다	340 ☐ inadequate ⓐ 불충분한	396 ☐ moisten ⓥ 적시다
235 ☐ early ⓐ (어떤 기간·사건 등의) 초창기의			397 ☐ properly ⓐⓓ 적절하게, 제대로
236 ☐ bunch ⓝ 다발, 송이, 묶음	36	39	398 ☐ come to the conclusion 결론에 이르다
237 ☐ as well (문미에서) 또한	289 ☐ respect ⓝ 존중	341 ☐ sales director 영업부장	399 ☐ costly ⓐ 많은 비용이 드는
238 ☐ confusing ⓐ 혼란스러운	290 ☐ reexamine ⓥ 재점검하다	342 ☐ blow ⓥ (입으로) 불다	400 ☐ educate ⓥ 교육하다, 가르치다
239 ☐ carry out 수행하다	291 ☐ golden rule 황금률	343 ☐ salesperson ⓝ 판매원, 영업사원	401 ☐ glue ⓝ 풀
240 ☐ terms ⓝ (합의, 계약 등의) 조건	292 ☐ treat ⓥ 대접하다	344 ☐ settle a deal 거래를 성사시키다	402 ☐ elsewhere ⓐⓓ 다른 곳으로
241 ☐ bond ⓝ 유대 (관계)	293 ☐ create ⓥ (어떤 느낌이나 인상을) 자아내다, 불러일으키다	345 ☐ deal ⓝ 거래	403 ☐ dissatisfied ⓐ 불만족한
242 ☐ specific ⓐ 구체적인	294 ☐ frustrating ⓐ 답답한, 좌절스러운	346 ☐ rewarding ⓐ 보람 있는	404 ☐ cheap ⓐ (값이) 싼, 돈이 적게 드는
243 ☐ key role 주요한 역할	295 ☐ interpret ⓥ 해석하다, 이해하다	347 ☐ material ⓐ 물질적인	405 ☐ unsolved ⓐ 해결되지 않은
244 ☐ instinctively ⓐⓓ 본능적으로	296 ☐ miscommunication ⓝ 의사소통 오류, 오해	348 ☐ recognize ⓥ 인정하다	406 ☐ competitor ⓝ 경쟁자, 경쟁 상대
	297 ☐ multicultural ⓐ 다문화의	349 ☐ anything and everything 무슨 일이든, 어떤 것이든지	407 ☐ enemy ⓝ 적
33	298 ☐ belief ⓝ 신념, 확신	350 ☐ unbelievably ⓐⓓ 믿을 수 없을 정도로	
245 ☐ magician ⓝ 마술사	299 ☐ unintended ⓐ 의도되지 않은	351 ☐ have an impact on ~에 영향을 미치다	43~45
246 ☐ audience ⓝ 청중[관중]	300 ☐ in return 보답으로, 반응으로	352 ☐ amazingly ⓐⓓ 놀랄 만큼	408 ☐ merchant ⓝ 상인
247 ☐ in public 공공연히	301 ☐ monocultural ⓐ 단일 문화의	353 ☐ especially ⓐⓓ 특히	409 ☐ prepare ⓥ 준비하다, 대비하다
248 ☐ advantage ⓝ 이점	302 ☐ framework ⓝ (판단·결정 등을 위한) 틀	354 ☐ peer ⓝ 동료, 또래, 동배	410 ☐ thief ⓝ 도둑, 절도범
249 ☐ idiosyncratic ⓐ 특이한, 특유의			411 ☐ remain ⓥ 계속(여전히) ~이다
250 ☐ species ⓝ (생물) 종	37	40	412 ☐ calm ⓐ 침착한, 차분한
251 ☐ ability ⓝ (~을) 할 수 있음, 능력	303 ☐ survey ⓥ 조사하다, 살피다, 점검하다	355 ☐ experiment ⓝ 실험	413 ☐ in action 활동을 하는
252 ☐ reflect on ~을 반추하다	304 ☐ resident ⓝ (특정 지역) 거주자, 주민	356 ☐ environment ⓝ 환경	414 ☐ sheet ⓝ 시트 (침대에 깔거나 위로 덮는 얇은 천)
253 ☐ past ⓝ 과거, 지난날	305 ☐ pretend ⓥ ~인 체하다	357 ☐ assign ⓥ (과업 등을) 할당하다	415 ☐ steal ⓥ 훔치다, 도둑질하다 (과거형 : stolen)
254 ☐ individual ⓐ 각각[개개]의	306 ☐ display ⓥ 전시하다	358 ☐ interact ⓥ 상호작용하다	416 ☐ valuable ⓝ 귀중품 ⓐ 귀한, 가치 있는
255 ☐ earn ⓥ (돈을) 벌다	307 ☐ lawn ⓝ 잔디	359 ☐ discussion ⓝ 논의, 상의	417 ☐ hurriedly ⓐⓓ 서둘러
256 ☐ history ⓝ 역사	308 ☐ make a commitment 약속하다	360 ☐ lead ⓥ 안내하다, 이끌다 (과거형 : led)	418 ☐ tie a knot 매듭을 묶다
257 ☐ trial and error 시행착오	309 ☐ tiny ⓐ 아주 작은	361 ☐ agreement ⓝ 합의	419 ☐ meanwhile ⓐⓓ 그 동안에
258 ☐ benefit ⓝ 혜택, 이득	310 ☐ request ⓝ 요구, 요청	362 ☐ design ⓥ (체제[방법] 등을) 설계하다	420 ☐ yell ⓥ 소리치다
259 ☐ overlook ⓥ 간과하다, 못 보고 넘어가다	311 ☐ astonishing ⓐ 놀라운	363 ☐ easily ⓐⓓ 쉽게, 수월하게	421 ☐ lung ⓝ 폐
260 ☐ exaggerate ⓥ 과장하다	312 ☐ initial ⓐ 처음의, 초기의	364 ☐ additional ⓐ 추가의	422 ☐ lift ⓥ 들어 올리다
261 ☐ underestimate ⓥ 과소평가하다, 경시하다	313 ☐ deeply ⓐⓓ (대단히·몹시의 뜻으로) 깊이, 크게	365 ☐ noticeable ⓐ 두드러지는, 눈에 띄는	423 ☐ to one's surprise ~로서는 놀랍게도
	314 ☐ willingness ⓝ 의향, ~하려는 마음, 기꺼이 하는 마음	366 ☐ difference ⓝ 차이	424 ☐ tear apart 찢다
34	315 ☐ block ⓥ 막다, 차단하다	367 ☐ reveal ⓥ 드러내다, 밝히다	425 ☐ floor ⓝ 바닥
262 ☐ conclusively ⓐⓓ 결론적으로	316 ☐ naturally ⓐⓓ 물론, 당연히	368 ☐ film ⓝ 영화	426 ☐ unpleasant ⓐ 불쾌한
263 ☐ teaching method 교수법	317 ☐ refuse ⓥ 거절하다, 거부하다	369 ☐ thirst ⓝ 갈망, 갈증	427 ☐ give up on ~을 포기하다, 단념하다
264 ☐ practice ⓥ 실천하다	318 ☐ particular ⓐ 특정한	370 ☐ fill a gap 격차를 메우다	428 ☐ under one's breath 낮은 목소리로
265 ☐ physics ⓝ 물리학	319 ☐ incredible ⓐ 믿을 수 없는, 놀라운	371 ☐ knowledge ⓝ 지식	429 ☐ skillful ⓐ 교묘한
266 ☐ lecture ⓥ (설명식) 강의를 하다	320 ☐ approve ⓥ 승인하다	372 ☐ slide ⓝ 미끄럼틀	430 ☐ to the core 속속들이, 완전히
267 ☐ pull together 모으다		373 ☐ according ⓐⓓ …에 따라서, 일치하여	431 ☐ spread out 펼치다
268 ☐ solve ⓥ 해결하다		374 ☐ differ ⓥ 다르다	432 ☐ gather ⓥ 모으다, 챙기다
269 ☐ break off ~을 분리시키다		375 ☐ cooperate ⓥ 협력하다	433 ☐ luxurious ⓐ 호화로운
		376 ☐ argue ⓥ 언쟁을 하다, 다투다	434 ☐ weak ⓐ 약한, 힘이 없는

14회

어휘 Review test 14

TEST A-B 각 단어의 뜻을 [A] 영어는 우리말로, [B] 우리말은 영어로 쓰시오.

A	English	Korean
01	overcome	
02	inadequate	
03	advantage	
04	recognition	
05	thirst	
06	extremely	
07	benefit	
08	relative	
09	grateful	
10	approximately	
11	initial	
12	sufficient	
13	moisten	
14	eventually	
15	savings	
16	exceed	
17	concern	
18	complexity	
19	display	
20	spread out	

B	Korean	English
01	확신시키다	
02	수행하다	
03	기쁜	
04	(과업 등을) 할당하다	
05	결론적으로	
06	영감을 주다	
07	제거하다, 없애다	
08	먹다, 마시다	
09	(제품의) 기능, 특징	
10	불만족한	
11	사로잡다	
12	간단한, 짧은	
13	해석하다, 이해하다	
14	가정하다, 추정하다	
15	충성도	
16	능력	
17	놀랍도록, 엄청나게	
18	불신, 불신하다	
19	확립하다, 구축하다	
20	게다가	

▶ A-D 정답 : 해설편 142쪽

TEST C-D 각 단어의 뜻을 골라 기호를 쓰시오.

C	English		Korean
01	material	( )	ⓐ ~하기를 고대하다
02	insight	( )	ⓑ 과장하다
03	exaggerate	( )	ⓒ 해결되지 않은
04	analyze	( )	ⓓ 권장[장려]하다
05	consumer	( )	ⓔ 드러내다, 밝히다
06	improve	( )	ⓕ 물질적인
07	complaint	( )	ⓖ 믿을 수 없는, 놀라운
08	extensive	( )	ⓗ 믿음
09	protest	( )	ⓘ 분석하다
10	unsolved	( )	ⓙ 지속적으로, 일
11	unintended	( )	ⓚ 불화, 불일치
12	incredible	( )	ⓛ 소비자
13	publish	( )	ⓜ 의도되지 않은
14	consistently	( )	ⓝ 광범위한, 폭넓은
15	encourage	( )	ⓞ 추가의
16	additional	( )	ⓟ 불평
17	reveal	( )	ⓠ 통찰력
18	faith	( )	ⓡ 항의하다
19	disagreement	( )	ⓢ 출판하다
20	look forward to	( )	ⓣ 향상시키다, 개선하다

D	Korean		English
01	본능적으로	( )	ⓐ vast
02	구체적인	( )	ⓑ approve
03	…에 둘러싸인	( )	ⓒ ultimately
04	완수하다	( )	ⓓ specific
05	결국, 궁극적으로	( )	ⓔ sort
06	혹독한	( )	ⓕ reflect on
07	동의하다, 승인하다	( )	ⓖ complicated
08	줄이다, 감소시키다	( )	ⓗ opposite
09	놀라운	( )	ⓘ instinctively
10	보답으로, 반응으로	( )	ⓙ unpleasant
11	복잡한	( )	ⓚ in essence
12	분류하다, 나누다	( )	ⓛ harsh
13	청중[관중]	( )	ⓜ frustrating
14	수행하다	( )	ⓝ conduct
15	답답한, 좌절스러운	( )	ⓞ reduce
16	결국, 본질적으로	( )	ⓟ complete
17	방대한	( )	ⓠ audience
18	불쾌한	( )	ⓡ astonishing
19	정반대의	( )	ⓢ in return
20	~을 반추하다	( )	ⓣ among

18. 다음 글의 목적으로 가장 적절한 것은?

Dear Wildwood residents,

Wildwood Academy is a local school that seeks to help children with disabilities and learning challenges. We currently have over 200 students enrolled. This year we'd like to add a music class in the hope that each of our students will have the opportunity to develop their musical abilities. To get the class started, we need more instruments than we have now. We are asking you to look around your house and donate any instruments that you may no longer use. Each one donated will be assigned to a student in need. Simply call us and we will be happy to drop by and pick up the instrument.

Sincerely,
Karen Hansen, Principal

① 고장 난 악기의 수리를 의뢰하려고
② 학부모 공개 수업 참석을 권장하려고
③ 음악 수업을 위한 악기 기부를 요청하려고
④ 추가로 개설된 음악 수업 신청을 독려하려고
⑤ 지역 주민을 위한 자선 음악 행사를 홍보하려고

19. 다음 글에 드러난 Salva의 심경 변화로 가장 적절한 것은?

Salva had to raise money for a project to help southern Sudan. It was the first time that Salva spoke in front of an audience. There were more than a hundred people. Salva's knees were shaking as he walked to the microphone. "H−h−hello," he said. His hands trembling, he looked out at the audience. Everyone was looking at him. At that moment, he noticed that every face looked interested in what he had to say. People were smiling and seemed friendly. That made him feel a little better, so he spoke into the microphone again. "Hello," he repeated. He smiled, feeling at ease, and went on. "I am here to talk to you about a project for southern Sudan."

① nervous → relieved
② indifferent → excited
③ worried → disappointed
④ satisfied → frustrated
⑤ confident → embarrassed

20. 다음 글에서 필자가 주장하는 바로 가장 적절한 것은?

Any goal you set is going to be difficult to achieve, and you will certainly be disappointed at some points along the way. So why not set your goals much higher than you consider worthy from the beginning? If they are going to require work, effort, and energy, then why not exert 10 times as much of each? What if you are underestimating your capabilities? You might be protesting, saying, "What of the disappointment that comes from setting unrealistic goals?" However, take just a few moments to look back over your life. Chances are that you have more often been disappointed by setting targets that are too low and achieving them — only to be shocked that you still didn't get what you wanted.

* exert: 발휘하다

① 매사에 최선을 다하는 태도를 가져야 한다.
② 목표는 자신의 생각보다 높게 설정해야 한다.
③ 변화하는 상황에 따라 목표를 수정해야 한다.
④ 과거의 실패를 되돌아보는 습관을 길러야 한다.
⑤ 목표 달성을 위해 계획을 구체적으로 세워야 한다.

21. 밑줄 친 <u>have that same scenario</u>가 다음 글에서 의미하는 바로 가장 적절한 것은? [3점]

There are more than 700 million cell phones used in the US today and at least 140 million of those cell phone users will abandon their current phone for a new phone every 14－18 months. I'm not one of those people who just "must" have the latest phone. Actually, I use my cell phone until the battery no longer holds a good charge. At that point, it's time. So I figure I'll just get a replacement battery. But I'm told that battery is no longer made and the phone is no longer manufactured because there's newer technology and better features in the latest phones. That's a typical justification. The phone wasn't even that old; maybe a little over one year? I'm just one example. Can you imagine how many countless other people <u>have that same scenario</u>? No wonder cell phones take the lead when it comes to "e-waste."

① have frequent trouble updating programs
② cannot afford new technology due to costs
③ spend a lot of money repairing their cell phones
④ are driven to change their still usable cell phones
⑤ are disappointed with newly launched phone models

22. 다음 글의 요지로 가장 적절한 것은?

Learners function within complex developmental, cognitive, physical, social, and cultural systems. Research and theory from diverse fields have contributed to an evolving understanding that all learners grow and learn in culturally defined ways in culturally defined contexts. While humans share basic brain structures and processes, as well as fundamental experiences such as relationships with family, age-related stages, and many more, each of these phenomena is shaped by an individual's precise experiences. Learning does not happen in the same way for all people because cultural influences are influential from the beginning of life. These ideas about the intertwining of learning and culture have been supported by research on many aspects of learning and development.

* intertwine: 뒤얽히다

① 문화 다양성에 대한 체계적 연구가 필요하다.
② 개인의 문화적 경험이 학습에 영향을 끼친다.
③ 인간의 뇌 구조는 학습을 통해 복잡하게 진화했다.
④ 원만한 대인관계 형성은 건강한 성장의 토대가 된다.
⑤ 학습 발달 단계에 적합한 자극을 제공하는 것이 좋다.

23. 다음 글의 주제로 가장 적절한 것은?

Animals as well as humans engage in play activities. In animals, play has long been seen as a way of learning and practicing skills and behaviors that are necessary for future survival. In children, too, play has important functions during development. From its earliest beginnings in infancy, play is a way in which children learn about the world and their place in it. Children's play serves as a training ground for developing physical abilities — skills like walking, running, and jumping that are necessary for everyday living. Play also allows children to try out and learn social behaviors and to acquire values and personality traits that will be important in adulthood. For example, they learn how to compete and cooperate with others, how to lead and follow, how to make decisions, and so on.

① necessity of trying out creative ideas
② roles of play in children's development
③ contrasts between human and animal play
④ effects of children's physical abilities on play
⑤ children's needs at various developmental stages

24. 다음 글의 제목으로 가장 적절한 것은?

The loss of many traditional jobs in everything from art to healthcare will partly be offset by the creation of new human jobs. Primary care doctors who focus on diagnosing known diseases and giving familiar treatments will probably be replaced by AI doctors. But precisely because of that, there will be much more money to pay human doctors and lab assistants to do groundbreaking research and develop new medicines or surgical procedures. AI might help create new human jobs in another way. Instead of humans competing with AI, they could focus on servicing and using AI. For example, the replacement of human pilots by drones has eliminated some jobs but created many new opportunities in maintenance, remote control, data analysis, and cyber security.

* offset: 상쇄하다

① What Makes Robots Smarter?
② Is AI Really a Threat to Your Job?
③ Watch Out! AI Can Read Your Mind
④ Future Jobs: Less Work, More Gains
⑤ Ongoing Challenges for AI Development

25. 다음 도표의 내용과 일치하지 <u>않는</u> 것은?

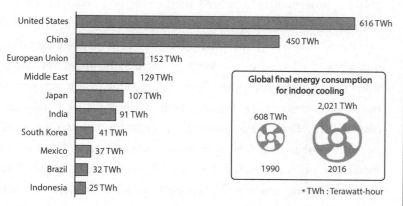

Final Energy Consumption for Indoor Cooling
by Country/Region in 2016

Country/Region	TWh
United States	616 TWh
China	450 TWh
European Union	152 TWh
Middle East	129 TWh
Japan	107 TWh
India	91 TWh
South Korea	41 TWh
Mexico	37 TWh
Brazil	32 TWh
Indonesia	25 TWh

Global final energy consumption
for indoor cooling

608 TWh — 1990
2,021 TWh — 2016

* TWh : Terawatt-hour

The graph above shows the final energy consumption for indoor cooling by country/region in 2016. ① The global final energy consumption for indoor cooling was over three times larger in 2016 than in 1990. ② It was the United States that had the largest final energy consumption, which amounted to 616 TWh. ③ The combined amount of the final energy consumption of the European Union, the Middle East, and Japan was less than the amount of China's final energy consumption. ④ The difference in amount between India's and South Korea's final energy consumption was more than 60 TWh. ⑤ Indonesia's final energy consumption was the smallest among the countries/regions above, totaling 25 TWh.

26. Jessie Redmon Fauset에 관한 다음 글의 내용과 일치하지 <u>않는</u> 것은?

Jessie Redmon Fauset was born in Snow Hill, New Jersey, in 1884. She was the first black woman to graduate from Cornell University. In addition to writing novels, poetry, short stories, and essays, Fauset taught French in public schools in Washington, D.C. and worked as a journal editor. While working as an editor, she encouraged many well-known writers of the Harlem Renaissance. Though she is more famous for being an editor than for being a fiction writer, many critics consider her novel *Plum Bun* Fauset's strongest work. In it, she tells the story of a black girl who could pass for white but ultimately claims her racial identity and pride. Fauset died of heart disease April 30, 1961, in Philadelphia.

* pass for: ~으로 여겨지다

① Cornell University를 졸업한 최초의 흑인 여성이었다.
② Washington, D.C.의 공립학교에서 프랑스어를 가르쳤다.
③ 편집자보다는 소설가로서 더 유명하다.
④ 흑인 소녀의 이야기를 다룬 소설을 썼다.
⑤ Philadelphia에서 심장병으로 사망했다.

27. Greenville Community Cleanup Day에 관한 다음 안내문의 내용과 일치하지 <u>않는</u> 것은?

Greenville Community Cleanup Day

The 6th annual Greenville Community Cleanup Day is just around the corner! Show your community you care.

■ **When:** Saturday, October 17, 2020
■ **Where:** North Strand Recreation Center
· Participants will be transported by bus to clean up litter.
■ **Who:**
· Any residents who want to join
· Children under 10 must be accompanied by an adult.
■ **Cleanup Schedule:**
· 9:00 a.m.: Registration
· 9:30 a.m. − 11:30 a.m.: Cleanup at various locations

✓ Safety vests and gloves will be provided.
✓ Don't forget to wear closed-toe shoes.
✓ All participants will get a free T-shirt and snack.

To sign up for the event, email your name and phone number to info@gvcommunity.org.

① 매년 열리는 청소 행사이다.
② 참가자들은 청소를 하기 위해 버스를 타고 이동할 것이다.
③ 10세 미만의 어린이는 성인과 동행해야 한다.
④ 안전 조끼와 장갑은 제공되지 않을 것이다.
⑤ 모든 참가자들은 티셔츠와 간식을 무료로 받을 것이다.

28. Springfield High School Book Fair에 관한 다음 안내문의 내용과 일치하는 것은?

Springfield High School Book Fair

For all book lovers! Come and enjoy the Springfield High School Book Fair.

Date & Time:
· November 9 − 13, 2020   · 9:00 a.m. − 3:00 p.m.

Place: School Library

Special Programs:
■ Book Cover Design Contest
· November 10, 11:00 a.m.
· Winners will get a gift certificate that can be used at the book fair.
■ Closing Ceremony
· November 13, 2:00 p.m.
· Don't miss the opportunity to meet Rosa Park, this year's best-selling author.

※ Anyone who wants to volunteer at the book fair must sign up online in advance.

① 행사 기간 동안 매일 4시간씩 진행된다.
② 학교 강당에서 개최된다.
③ 책 표지 디자인 대회 참가자 전원에게 상품권이 증정될 것이다.
④ 폐막식에서 올해의 베스트셀러 작가를 만날 기회가 제공된다.
⑤ 현장에서 자원봉사 등록이 가능하다.

29. 다음 글의 밑줄 친 부분 중, 어법상 틀린 것은? [3점]

Although it is obvious that part of our assessment of food is its visual appearance, it is perhaps surprising ① how visual input can override taste and smell. People find it very ② difficult to correctly identify fruit-flavoured drinks if the colour is wrong, for instance an orange drink that is coloured green. Perhaps even more striking ③ is the experience of wine tasters. One study of Bordeaux University students of wine and wine making revealed that they chose tasting notes appropriate for red wines, such as 'prune and chocolate', when they ④ gave white wine coloured with a red dye. Experienced New Zealand wine experts were similarly tricked into thinking ⑤ that the white wine Chardonnay was in fact a red wine, when it had been coloured with a red dye.

* override: ~에 우선하다　** prune: 자두

30. (A), (B), (C)의 각 네모 안에서 문맥에 맞는 낱말로 가장 적절한 것은? [3점]

Social connections are so essential for our survival and well-being that we not only cooperate with others to build relationships, we also compete with others for friends. And often we do both at the same time. Take gossip. Through gossip, we bond with our friends, sharing interesting details. But at the same time, we are (A) creating / forgiving potential enemies in the targets of our gossip. Or consider rival holiday parties where people compete to see who will attend *their* party. We can even see this (B) harmony / tension in social media as people compete for the most friends and followers. At the same time, competitive exclusion can also (C) generate / prevent cooperation. High school social clubs and country clubs use this formula to great effect: It is through selective inclusion *and exclusion* that they produce loyalty and lasting social bonds.

	(A)	(B)	(C)
①	creating	harmony	prevent
②	creating	tension	generate
③	creating	tension	prevent
④	forgiving	tension	prevent
⑤	forgiving	harmony	generate

[31~34] 다음 빈칸에 들어갈 말로 가장 적절한 것을 고르시오.

31. As the tenth anniversary of the terrorist attacks of September 11, 2001, approached, 9/11-related media stories peaked in the days immediately surrounding the anniversary date and then dropped off rapidly in the weeks thereafter. Surveys conducted during those times asked citizens to choose two "especially important" events from the past seventy years. Two weeks prior to the anniversary, before the media blitz began, about 30 percent of respondents named 9/11. But as the anniversary drew closer, and the media treatment intensified, survey respondents started identifying 9/11 in increasing numbers — to a high of 65 percent. Two weeks later, though, after reportage had decreased to earlier levels, once again only about 30 percent of the participants placed it among their two especially important events of the past seventy years. Clearly, the _____ of news coverage can make a big difference in the *perceived* significance of an issue among observers as they are exposed to the coverage.

* blitz: 대선전, 집중 공세

① accuracy　　② tone　　③ amount
④ source　　⑤ type

32. Here's the unpleasant truth: we are all biased. Every human being is affected by unconscious biases that lead us to make incorrect assumptions about other people. Everyone. To a certain extent, bias is a(n) _____. If you're an early human, perhaps *Homo Erectus*, walking around the jungles, you may see an animal approaching. You have to make very fast assumptions about whether that animal is safe or not, based solely on its appearance. The same is true of other humans. You make split-second decisions about threats in order to have plenty of time to escape, if necessary. This could be one root of our tendency to categorize and label others based on their looks and their clothes.

① necessary survival skill　　② origin of imagination
③ undesirable mental capacity　　④ barrier to relationships
⑤ challenge to moral judgment

33. In Dutch bicycle culture, it is common to have a passenger on the backseat. So as to follow the rider's movements, the person on the backseat needs to hold on tightly. Bicycles turn not just by steering but also by leaning, so the passenger needs to lean the same way as the rider. A passenger who would keep sitting up straight would literally be a pain in the behind. On motorcycles, this is even more critical. Their higher speed requires more leaning on turns, and lack of coordination can be disastrous. The passenger is a true partner in the ride, expected to _____. [3점]

① warn other people of danger
② stop the rider from speeding
③ mirror the rider's every move
④ relieve the rider's emotional anxiety
⑤ monitor the road conditions carefully

34. We're often told that newborns and infants are comforted by rocking because this motion is similar to what they experienced in the womb, and that they must take comfort in this familiar feeling. This may be true; however, to date there are no convincing data that demonstrate a significant relationship between the amount of time a mother moves during pregnancy and her newborn's response to rocking. Just as likely is the idea that newborns come to associate gentle rocking with being fed. Parents understand that rocking quiets a newborn, and they very often provide gentle, repetitive movement during feeding. Since the appearance of food is a primary reinforcer, newborns may _____ because they have been conditioned through a process of associative learning. [3점]

* womb: 자궁   ** reinforcer: 강화물

① acquire a fondness for motion
② want consistent feeding
③ dislike severe rocking
④ remember the tastes of food
⑤ form a bond with their mothers

35. 다음 글에서 전체 흐름과 관계 <u>없는</u> 문장은?

In a single week, the sun delivers more energy to our planet than humanity has used through the burning of coal, oil, and natural gas through *all of human history*. And the sun will keep shining on our planet for billions of years. ① Our challenge isn't that we're running out of energy. ② It's that we have been focused on the wrong source — the small, finite one that we're using up. ③ Indeed, all the coal, natural gas, and oil we use today is just solar energy from millions of years ago, a very tiny part of which was preserved deep underground. ④ Our efforts to develop technologies that use fossil fuels have shown meaningful results. ⑤ Our challenge, and our opportunity, is to learn to efficiently and cheaply use the *much more abundant* source that is the new energy striking our planet each day from the sun.

[36~37] 주어진 글 다음에 이어질 글의 순서로 가장 적절한 것을 고르시오.

36.

> We make decisions based on what we *think* we know. It wasn't too long ago that the majority of people believed the world was flat.

(A) It wasn't until that minor detail was revealed — the world is round — that behaviors changed on a massive scale. Upon this discovery, societies began to travel across the planet. Trade routes were established; spices were traded.

(B) This perceived truth impacted behavior. During this period, there was very little exploration. People feared that if they traveled too far they might fall off the edge of the earth. So for the most part they didn't dare to travel.

(C) New ideas, like mathematics, were shared between societies which allowed for all kinds of innovations and advancements. The correction of a simple false assumption moved the human race forward.

① (A) − (C) − (B)   ② (B) − (A) − (C)
③ (B) − (C) − (A)   ④ (C) − (A) − (B)
⑤ (C) − (B) − (A)

37.

Mirrors and other smooth, shiny surfaces reflect light. We see reflections from such surfaces because the rays of light form an image on the retina of our eyes.

(A) Keep your eyes on the reflected image while you are writing and not on your paper. After a little practice, it will be easier to write "backwards." When your friend receives such a message he will be able to read it by holding the paper up to a mirror.

(B) Stand a mirror upright on the table, so that a piece of paper on the table can be clearly seen in the mirror. Now write a message that looks right when you look in the mirror.

(C) Such images are always reversed. Look at yourself in a mirror, wink your right eye and your left eye seems to wink back at you. You can use a mirror to send a coded message to a friend.

* retina: (눈의) 망막

① (A) − (C) − (B) ② (B) − (A) − (C)
③ (B) − (C) − (A) ④ (C) − (A) − (B)
⑤ (C) − (B) − (A)

[38~39] 글의 흐름으로 보아, 주어진 문장이 들어가기에 가장 적절한 곳을 고르시오.

38.

The few times that they do occur, it is the possessor who tries to make someone leave the circle.

Reciprocity can be explored in captivity by handing one chimpanzee a large amount of food, such as a watermelon or leafy branch, and then observing what follows. (①) The owner will be center stage, with a group of others around him or her, soon to be followed by newly formed groups around those who obtained a sizable share, until all food has been distributed. (②) Beggars may complain and cry, but aggressive conflicts are rare. (③) She will hit them over their head with her branch or bark at them in a high-pitched voice until they leave her alone. (④) Whatever their rank, possessors control the food flow. (⑤) Once chimpanzees enter reciprocity mode, their social rank no longer matters. [3점]

* reciprocity: 호혜주의, 상호의 이익

39.

However, we live in a society where gender roles and boundaries are not as strict as in prior generations.

Gender research shows a complex relationship between gender and conflict styles. (①) Some research suggests that women from Western cultures tend to be more caring than men. (②) This tendency may result from socialization processes in which women are encouraged to care for their families and men are encouraged to be successful in competitive work environments. (③) There is significant variability in assertiveness and cooperation among women, as well as among men. (④) Although conflict resolution experts should be able to recognize cultural and gender differences, they should also be aware of within-group variations and the risks of stereotyping. (⑤) Culture and gender may affect the way people perceive, interpret, and respond to conflict; however, we must be careful to avoid overgeneralizations and to consider individual differences.

40. 다음 글의 내용을 한 문장으로 요약하고자 한다. 빈칸 (A), (B)에 들어갈 말로 가장 적절한 것은?

One way that music could express emotion is simply through a learned association. Perhaps there is nothing naturally sad about a piece of music in a minor key, or played slowly with low notes. Maybe we have just come to hear certain kinds of music as sad because we have learned to associate them in our culture with sad events like funerals. If this view is correct, we should have difficulty interpreting the emotions expressed in culturally unfamiliar music. Totally opposed to this view is the position that the link between music and emotion is one of resemblance. For example, when we feel sad we move slowly and speak slowly and in a low-pitched voice. Thus when we hear slow, low music, we hear it as sad. If this view is correct, we should have little difficulty understanding the emotion expressed in culturally unfamiliar music.

↓

It is believed that emotion expressed in music can be understood through a(n) _____(A)_____ learned association or it can be understood due to the _____(B)_____ between music and emotion.

　　　(A)　　　　　(B)
① culturally ······ similarity
② culturally ······ balance
③ socially ······ difference
④ incorrectly ······ connection
⑤ incorrectly ······ contrast

[41~42] 다음 글을 읽고, 물음에 답하시오.

A bedroom temperature of around 65 degrees Fahrenheit (18.3°C) is ideal for the sleep of most people, assuming standard bedding and clothing. This (a) surprises many, as it sounds just a little too cold for comfort. Of course, that specific temperature will vary depending on the individual in question and their gender and age. But like calorie recommendations, it's a good target for the average human being. Most of us set bedroom temperatures higher than are ideal for good sleep and this likely contributes to (b) lower quantity and quality of sleep than you are otherwise capable of getting. Lower than 55 degrees Fahrenheit can be harmful rather than helpful to sleep, unless warm bedding or nightclothes are used. However, most of us fall into the (c) opposite category of setting a controlled bedroom temperature that is too high: 70 or 72 degrees. Sleep clinicians treating patients who can't sleep at night will often ask about room temperature, and will advise patients to (d) raise their current thermostat set-point by 3 to 5 degrees from that which they currently use.

Anyone disbelieving of the influence of temperature on sleep can explore some related experiments on this topic. Scientists have, for example, gently warmed the feet or the body of rats to encourage blood to rise to the surface of the skin and release heat, thereby decreasing core body temperature. The rats fell asleep far (e) faster than was otherwise normal.

* thermostat: 온도 조절 장치

41. 윗글의 제목으로 가장 적절한 것은?

① Signs of Sleep Problems
② Stay Cool for Better Sleep
③ Turn Up the Heat in Your Room
④ How to Correct Bad Sleeping Posture
⑤ A Key to Quality Sleep: Clean Bedding

42. 밑줄 친 (a)~(e) 중에서 문맥상 낱말의 쓰임이 적절하지 않은 것은? [3점]

① (a)　　② (b)　　③ (c)　　④ (d)　　⑤ (e)

[43~45] 다음 글을 읽고, 물음에 답하시오.

(A)

A merchant in a small town had identical twin sons. The boys worked for their father in the store he owned and when he died, they took over the store. Everything went well until the day a twenty-dollar bill disappeared. One of the brothers had left the bill on the counter and walked outside with a friend. When he returned, the money was gone. (a) He asked his older brother, "Did you see that twenty-dollar bill on the counter?"

(B)

Then one day a man from another state stopped by the store. He walked in and asked the younger brother, "How long have you been here?" (b) He replied that he'd been there all his life. The customer said, "Twenty years ago I came into this town in a boxcar. I hadn't eaten for three days. I came into this store and saw a twenty-dollar bill on the counter. I put it in my pocket and walked out. All these years I haven't been able to forgive myself. So I had to come back to return it."

(C)

His older brother replied that he had not. But (c) the young man kept questioning him. "Twenty-dollar bills just don't get up and walk away! Surely you must have seen it!" There was subtle accusation in (d) his voice. Anger began to rise. Hatred set in. Before long, bitterness divided the twins. They refused to speak. They finally decided they could no longer work together and a dividing wall was built down the center of the store. For twenty years the hostility grew, spreading to their families and the community.

(D)

The customer was amazed to see tears well up in the eyes of the man. "Would you please go next door and tell that same story to (e) the man in the store?" the younger brother said. Then the customer was even more amazed to see the two middle-aged men hugging each other and weeping together in the front of the store. After twenty years, the brokenness was repaired. The wall of anger that divided them came down.

43. 주어진 글 (A)에 이어질 내용을 순서에 맞게 배열한 것으로 가장 적절한 것은?

① (B) − (D) − (C)　　② (C) − (B) − (D)
③ (C) − (D) − (B)　　④ (D) − (B) − (C)
⑤ (D) − (C) − (B)

44. 밑줄 친 (a)~(e) 중에서 가리키는 대상이 나머지 넷과 다른 것은?

① (a)　　② (b)　　③ (c)　　④ (d)　　⑤ (e)

45. 윗글에 관한 내용으로 적절하지 않은 것은?

① 쌍둥이 형제는 아버지의 가게를 물려받았다.
② 카운터 위에 놓여진 20달러 지폐가 없어졌다.
③ 손님은 20년 만에 가게에 다시 방문했다.
④ 쌍둥이 형제의 가게 중앙에 벽이 세워졌다.
⑤ 쌍둥이 형제는 끝까지 화해하지 못했다.

* 확인 사항
○ 답안지의 해당란에 필요한 내용을 정확히 기입(표기)했는지 확인하시오.

18
001 disability ⓝ 장애
002 challenge ⓝ 어려움, 도전
003 currently ⓐⓓ 현재
004 enroll ⓥ 등록하다
005 in the hope that ~을 바라고
006 opportunity ⓝ 기회
007 develop ⓥ 발전하다
008 instrument ⓝ 악기, 도구
009 donate ⓥ 기부하다, 기증하다
010 no longer 더 이상 ~하지 않는
011 assign ⓥ 배정하다
012 simply ⓐⓓ 그냥, 그저
013 drop by (~에) 들르다

19
014 raise money 모금하다
015 audience ⓝ 청중, 관중
016 knees ⓝ 무릎
017 shake ⓥ 흔들리다, 흔들다
018 microphone ⓝ 마이크
019 tremble ⓥ 떨다
020 at that moment 그때, 그 순간에
021 interested ⓐ 관심 있는
022 friendly ⓐ 친절한, 우호적인
023 repeat ⓥ 반복하다
024 at ease 편안한
025 relieved ⓐ 안도하는
026 indifferent ⓐ 무관심한
027 frustrated ⓐ 좌절한
028 embarrassed ⓐ 당황한

20
029 achieve ⓥ 달성하다, 성취하다
030 certainly ⓐⓓ 분명히
031 along the way 도중에
032 consider ⓥ (~을 ~로) 여기다
033 worthy ⓐ 가치 있는
034 from the beginning 애초부터
035 require ⓥ 요구하다, 필요로 하다
036 exert ⓥ 가하다, 있는 힘껏 노력하다
037 underestimate ⓥ 과소평가하다
038 capability ⓝ 능력
039 protest ⓥ 이의를 제기하다, 항의하다
040 disappointment ⓝ 실망
041 unrealistic ⓐ 비현실적인
042 look back 되돌아보다

21
043 user ⓝ 이용자, 사용자
044 abandon ⓥ 버리다
045 current ⓐ 현재의, 지금의
046 latest ⓐ (가장) 최근의, 최신의
047 until ⓟⓡⓔⓟ ~때 까지
048 battery ⓝ 건전지, 배터리
049 hold a charge 충전되다
050 figure ⓥ 생각하다
051 replacement ⓝ 교체
052 manufacture ⓥ 제조하다, 생산하다
053 feature ⓝ (제품 등의) 기능, 특징
054 typical ⓐ 전형적인
055 justification ⓝ 정당화, 합리화

056 countless ⓐ 수많은
057 scenario ⓝ 시나리오, 각본
058 no wonder ~하는 것도 당연하다
059 take the lead 선두에 있다
060 e-waste 전자 쓰레기, 폐전자제품
061 frequent ⓐ 잦은, 빈번한
062 afford ⓥ (~을 살·할) 여유[형편]가 되다
063 repair ⓥ 수리하다
064 usable ⓐ 사용할 수 있는
065 disappointed ⓐ 실망한
066 newly ⓐⓓ 새로, 최근에
067 launch ⓥ 출시하다, 시작하다

22
068 function ⓥ 기능하다
069 complex ⓐ 복잡한
070 developmental ⓐ 발달에 관련된
071 cognitive ⓐ 인지적인
072 physical ⓐ 육체의, 신체의
073 system ⓝ 제도, 체제, 체계
074 theory ⓝ 이론
075 diverse ⓐ 다양한
076 field ⓝ 분야
077 contribute to ~에 기여하다
078 evolving ⓐ 발전하는
079 define ⓥ 정의하다, 규정하다
080 context ⓝ 맥락, 상황
081 structure ⓝ 구조
082 fundamental ⓐ 기본적인
083 age-related ⓐ 나이와 관련된
084 phenomenon ⓝ 현상
085 shape ⓥ 형성하다
086 individual ⓝ 개인
087 precise ⓐ 정확한
088 influential ⓐ 영향력 있는
089 intertwining ⓥ 뒤얽히다
090 aspect ⓝ 측면, 면

23
091 engage in ~에 참여하다
092 activity ⓝ 활동
093 skill ⓝ 기술
094 behavior ⓝ 행동
095 necessary ⓐ 필요한
096 survival ⓝ 생존
097 function ⓝ 기능
098 development ⓝ 발달
099 earliest ⓐ 가장 빠른 때
100 beginning ⓝ 시작
101 infancy ⓝ 유아기
102 serve as ~의 역할을 하다
103 training ⓝ 교육, 훈련, 연수
104 try out 시도하다
105 acquire ⓥ 배우다, 습득하다
106 value ⓝ 가치
107 personality ⓝ 성격, 인격
108 trait ⓝ 특질, 특징
109 adulthood ⓝ 성인기
110 compete ⓥ 경쟁하다
111 cooperate ⓥ 협력하다
112 follow ⓥ 따르다
113 decision ⓝ 결정

114 necessity ⓝ 필요성
115 contrast ⓝ 차이, 대조

24
116 healthcare ⓝ 건강관리, 의료
117 partly ⓐⓓ 부분적으로
118 creation ⓝ 창조, 창작, 창출
119 primary care (동네 병원에서 주로 받는) 1차 진료
120 diagnose ⓥ 진단하다
121 disease ⓝ 질병, 질환
122 familiar ⓐ 익숙한, 친숙한
123 treatment ⓝ 처방, 치료
124 probably ⓐⓓ 아마
125 be replaced by ~에 의해 대체되다
126 precisely ⓐⓓ 바로, 정확히
127 assistant ⓝ 조수, 보조원
128 groundbreaking ⓐ 획기적인
129 medicine ⓝ 약, 의학, 의료
130 surgical ⓐ 수술의
131 procedure ⓝ 절차
132 drone ⓝ 드론
133 eliminate ⓥ 없애다, 제거하다
134 maintenance ⓝ 유지보수
135 analysis ⓝ 분석
136 security ⓝ 보안, 안보

25
137 consumption ⓝ 소비
138 indoor cooling 실내 냉방
139 region ⓝ 지역
140 amount to (양이) ~에 달하다
141 total ⓥ (합계가) ~에 이르다

26
142 graduate from ~을 졸업하다
143 in addition to 뿐만 아니라
144 poetry ⓝ 시
145 editor ⓝ 편집자
146 encourage ⓥ 격려[고무]하다, 용기를 북돋우다
147 well-known ⓐ 유명한
148 fiction writer 소설가
149 critic ⓝ 비평가, 평론가
150 ultimately ⓐⓓ 결국, 궁극적으로
151 claim ⓥ 주장하다
152 racial ⓐ 인종적인
153 identity ⓝ 정체성

27
154 annual ⓐ 해마다의, 연례의
155 be around the corner 코앞으로 다가오다, 목전에 닥치다
156 participant ⓝ 참가자
157 cleanup ⓝ 청소, 정화
158 transport ⓥ 이동하다, 수송하다
159 litter ⓝ 쓰레기
160 resident ⓝ 주민
161 accompany ⓥ ~와 동행하다
162 vest ⓝ 조끼
163 closed-toe shoes 발가락을 덮는 신발
164 sign up for ~을 신청하다

28
165 book fair 도서 박람회
166 cover ⓝ 표지
167 contest ⓝ 대회
168 winner ⓝ 우승자
169 gift certificate 상품권
170 miss ⓥ 놓치다
171 author ⓝ 작가, 저자
172 volunteer ⓥ 자원봉사하다
173 in advance 사전에, 미리

29
174 obvious ⓐ 분명한
175 assessment ⓝ 평가
176 visual ⓐ 시각의, 눈으로 보는
177 appearance ⓝ 외관, 겉모습
178 perhaps ⓐⓓ 아마, 어쩌면
179 input ⓝ 입력, 투입
180 override ⓥ ~보다 더 중요하다, 우선하다
181 identify ⓥ 식별하다, 알아보다
182 flavoured ⓐ ~ 맛이 나는
183 striking ⓐ 놀라운, 두드러진, 눈에 띄는
184 reveal ⓥ 드러내다, 밝히다
185 choose ⓥ 선택하다 (과거형 : chose)
186 tasting note 시음표
187 appropriate for ~에 적합한
188 prune ⓝ 자두
189 dye ⓝ 색소, 염료
190 expert ⓝ 전문가
191 trick A into B A를 속여 B하게 하다

30
192 social connection 사회적 관계
193 essential ⓐ 필수적인, 본질적인
194 survival ⓝ 생존
195 well-being ⓝ 행복, 안녕
196 gossip ⓝ 가십, 뒷담화, 험담 ⓥ 뒷담화하다, 험담을 하다
197 bond ⓝ 유대 ⓥ 유대를 형성하다
198 create ⓥ 만들어내다, 창조하다
199 forgive ⓥ 용서하다
200 potential ⓐ 잠재적인
201 tension ⓝ 긴장
202 competitive ⓐ 경쟁적인
203 exclusion ⓝ 배제
204 generate ⓥ 만들어내다
205 prevent ⓥ 막다, 예방하다, 방지하다
206 formula ⓝ 공식, 제조식
207 selective ⓐ 선택적인
208 inclusion ⓝ 포함
209 loyalty ⓝ 충성심

31
210 anniversary ⓝ 기념일
211 terrorist attack 테러리스트 공격
212 related ⓐ ~에 관련된
213 peak ⓥ 절정에 이르다
214 immediately ⓐⓓ 바로 옆에
215 surrounding ⓐ 인근의, 주위의
216 drop off 줄다
217 rapidly ⓐⓓ 급격하게
218 thereafter ⓐⓓ 그 후에

219 □ conduct ⓥ (특정한 활동을) 하다
220 □ prior to ~에 앞서
221 □ blitz ⓝ 대선전, 집중 공세
222 □ respondent ⓝ 응답자
223 □ drew closer 가까워지다
224 □ intensify ⓥ (정도, 빈도, 강도가) 심해지다, 격렬해지다
225 □ reportage ⓝ 보도
226 □ clearly ⓐ 명백하게, 또렷하게
227 □ coverage ⓝ 보도, 방송
228 □ perceive ⓥ 인지하다
229 □ significance ⓝ 중요성
230 □ observer ⓝ 관찰자
231 □ be exposed to ~에 노출되다
232 □ accuracy ⓝ 정확성
233 □ tone ⓝ 어조, 말투

32
234 □ unpleasant ⓐ 불쾌한
235 □ bias ⓝ 편견, 편향 ⓥ 편견을 갖게 하다
236 □ be affected by ~에 의해 영향을 받다
237 □ unconscious ⓐ 무의식적인
238 □ incorrect ⓐ 부정확한
239 □ assumption ⓝ 가정
240 □ to a certain extent 어느 정도
241 □ approach ⓥ 다가오다, 접근하다
242 □ solely ⓐ 단지, 오로지
243 □ the same is true of ~에도 해당하다
244 □ split-second ⓐ 찰나의, 순식간의
245 □ plenty ⓐ 풍부한, 충분한
246 □ escape ⓥ 탈출하다, 피하다
247 □ tendency ⓝ 성향, 기질, 경향
248 □ categorize ⓥ 범주화하다
249 □ label ⓥ 분류하다
250 □ undesirable ⓐ 바람직하지 않은, 달갑지 않은
251 □ capacity ⓝ 능력
252 □ barrier ⓝ 장애물
253 □ moral ⓐ 도덕적인

33
254 □ common ⓐ 흔한
255 □ passenger ⓝ 승객
256 □ backseat ⓝ 뒷좌석
257 □ rider ⓝ 운전자
258 □ movement ⓝ 움직임
259 □ tightly ⓐ 꽉, 단단히
260 □ steer ⓥ (핸들을) 조종하다
261 □ lean ⓥ (몸을) 기울이다
262 □ straight ⓐ 똑바로 (일직선으로)
263 □ literally ⓐ 말 그대로
264 □ pain ⓝ 골칫거리
265 □ motorcycle ⓝ 오토바이
266 □ critical ⓐ 중요한
267 □ lack ⓝ 부족, 결핍
268 □ coordination ⓝ (신체의) 협응(신체 기관이 서로 조화롭게 움직임)
269 □ disastrous ⓐ 재앙의
270 □ expect ⓥ 기대하다
271 □ warn A of B A에게 B를 경고하다
272 □ mirror ⓥ (거울처럼) 반영하다
273 □ emotional ⓐ 정서의, 감정의

274 □ anxiety ⓝ 불안
275 □ monitor ⓥ 추적 관찰하다, 감시하다
276 □ carefully ⓐ 꼼꼼히

34
277 □ newborn ⓝ 신생아
278 □ infant ⓝ 유아
279 □ comfort ⓝ 안락, 편안
280 □ rock ⓥ 흔들다
281 □ motion ⓝ 움직임
282 □ similar ⓐ 비슷한, 유사한
283 □ womb ⓝ 자궁
284 □ to date 지금까지
285 □ convincing ⓐ 설득력 있는
286 □ demonstrate ⓥ 입증하다
287 □ significant ⓐ 상당한, 유의미한
288 □ pregnancy ⓝ 임신 (기간)
289 □ associate A with B A와 B를 연관시키다
290 □ gentle ⓐ 부드러운
291 □ quiet ⓥ 진정시키다, 조용하게 하다
292 □ repetitive ⓐ 반복적인
293 □ appearance ⓝ 등장
294 □ primary ⓐ 일차적인, 주요한
295 □ reinforcer ⓝ 강화물
296 □ condition ⓥ 조건화하다
297 □ process ⓝ 과정, 절차
298 □ fondness ⓝ 좋아함
299 □ consistent ⓐ 계속되는
300 □ feed ⓝ (아기의) 우유
301 □ dislike ⓥ 싫어하다
302 □ severe ⓐ 심한, 가혹한

35
303 □ deliver ⓥ 전달하다
304 □ planet ⓝ 지구, 행성
305 □ humanity ⓝ 인류, 인간
306 □ burn ⓥ (연료가) 타다, 쓰이다
307 □ coal ⓝ 석탄
308 □ shine on ~을 비추다
309 □ billion ⓝ 10억
310 □ run out of ~이 고갈되다
311 □ finite ⓐ 한정적인, 유한한
312 □ use up 고갈시키다, 다 써 버리다
313 □ solar ⓐ 태양의
314 □ tiny ⓐ 아주 작은, 아주 적은
315 □ preserve ⓥ 보존하다
316 □ underground ⓐ 지하의
317 □ fossil fuel 화석 연료
318 □ meaningful ⓐ 의미 있는
319 □ efficiently ⓐ 효율적으로
320 □ cheaply ⓐ 싸게, 저렴하게
321 □ abundant ⓐ 풍부한
322 □ strike ⓥ (어떤 표면에) 부딪치다

36
323 □ majority ⓝ 다수, (특정 집단에서) 가장 많은 수
324 □ flat ⓐ 편평한
325 □ minor ⓐ 작은, 가벼운
326 □ massive ⓐ 대대적인, 거대한
327 □ discovery ⓝ 발견
328 □ trade route 무역로

329 □ establish ⓥ 만들다, 설립하다
330 □ spice ⓝ 향신료, 양념
331 □ impact ⓝ 영향 ⓥ 영향을 미치다
332 □ period ⓝ 시간, 시기
333 □ exploration ⓝ 탐험
334 □ fear ⓥ 두려워하다
335 □ fall off 떨어지다
336 □ edge ⓝ 모서리, 가장자리
337 □ for the most part 대체로
338 □ dare ⓥ 감히 ~하다
339 □ mathematic ⓝ 수학
340 □ innovation ⓝ 혁신
341 □ advancement ⓝ 발전
342 □ correction ⓝ 수정, 교정

37
343 □ smooth ⓐ 부드러운
344 □ surface ⓝ (사물의) 표면
345 □ reflection ⓝ (거울 등에) 반사된 것
346 □ ray ⓝ 광선, 선, 빛살
347 □ form ⓥ 형성하다
348 □ retina ⓝ (눈의) 망막
349 □ practice ⓥ 연습하다
350 □ backwards ⓐ 거꾸로, 뒤로
351 □ receive ⓥ 받다, 받아들이다
352 □ upright ⓐ 똑바로
353 □ reverse ⓥ 뒤집다
354 □ wink ⓥ 눈을 깜박거리다
355 □ coded ⓐ 암호화된, 부호화된

38
356 □ occur ⓥ 일어나다, 발생하다
357 □ possessor ⓝ 소유자
358 □ reciprocity ⓝ 호혜주의
359 □ explore ⓥ 탐구하다, 탐험하다
360 □ captivity ⓝ 포획, 감금
361 □ leafy ⓐ 잎이 많은
362 □ branch ⓝ 나뭇가지
363 □ observing ⓐ 관찰하는
364 □ obtain ⓥ 얻다
365 □ sizable ⓐ 상당한
366 □ share ⓝ 몫 ⓥ 나누다
367 □ distribute ⓥ 분배하다
368 □ beggar ⓝ 거지, 걸인
369 □ aggressive ⓐ 공격적인
370 □ conflict ⓝ 갈등, 충돌
371 □ rare ⓐ 드문, 희귀한
372 □ bark ⓥ 짖다
373 □ high-pitched ⓐ 고음의
374 □ leave ~ alone ~을 그대로 내버려 두다
375 □ rank ⓝ 서열, 지위, 계급
376 □ flow ⓝ 흐름
377 □ matter ⓥ 중요하다

39
378 □ gender role 성 역할
379 □ boundary ⓝ 경계
380 □ strict ⓐ 엄격한
381 □ generation ⓝ 세대
382 □ suggest ⓥ 시사하다
383 □ socialization ⓝ 사회화
384 □ variability ⓝ 가변성

385 □ assertiveness ⓝ 단호함, 자기 주장
386 □ resolution ⓝ 해결
387 □ within-group 그룹 내의
388 □ variation ⓝ 변화, 차이
389 □ stereotyping ⓝ (고정관념에 근거한) 유형화
390 □ affect ⓥ 영향을 끼치다
391 □ interpret ⓥ 해석하다
392 □ avoid ⓥ 피하다
393 □ overgeneralization ⓝ 과잉 일반화
394 □ individual ⓐ 개인의, 개별적인

40
395 □ association ⓝ 연관
396 □ minor key 단조
397 □ note ⓝ 음, 음색
398 □ funeral ⓝ 장례식
399 □ interpreting ⓝ 해석
400 □ unfamiliar ⓐ 친숙하지 않은
401 □ opposed to ~에 반대되는
402 □ resemblance ⓝ 유사성
403 □ low-pitched ⓐ 저음의
404 □ incorrectly ⓐ 부정확하게

41~42
405 □ assume ⓥ 가정하다
406 □ bedding ⓝ 침구
407 □ specific ⓐ 특정한, 구체적인
408 □ vary ⓥ 다르다
409 □ depending on ~에 따라
410 □ in question 문제의, 논의가 되고 있는
411 □ recommendation ⓝ 권장, 충고
412 □ ideal ⓐ 이상적인
413 □ quantity ⓝ 수
414 □ otherwise ⓐ 그렇지 않으면
415 □ nightclothes ⓝ 잠옷
416 □ category ⓝ 범주
417 □ clinician ⓝ 임상의
418 □ disbelieve of ~을 불신하다
419 □ surface ⓝ 표면
420 □ release ⓥ 방출하다
421 □ core body temperature 심부체온
422 □ posture ⓝ 자세
423 □ quality ⓝ 질 좋은

43~45
424 □ merchant ⓝ 상인
425 □ identical twin 일란성 쌍둥이
426 □ take over 인수하다, 물려받다
427 □ disappear ⓥ 사라지다
428 □ stop by 들르다
429 □ boxcar ⓝ (기차의) 유개화차
430 □ subtle ⓐ 미묘한
431 □ accusation ⓝ 비난, 기소
432 □ hatred ⓝ 증오
433 □ set in (특히 나쁜 일이 계속될 기세로) 시작되다
434 □ bitterness ⓝ 냉소, 쓰라림, (맛이) 씀
435 □ refuse ⓥ 거부하다
436 □ hostility ⓝ 적대감
437 □ spread ⓥ 퍼지다
438 □ weep ⓥ 울다
439 □ brokenness ⓝ 깨짐, 단절

어휘 Review test 15

TEST A-B 각 단어의 뜻을 [A] 영어는 우리말로, [B] 우리말은 영어로 쓰시오.

A	English	Korean
01	depending on	
02	consumption	
03	litter	
04	The same is true of	
05	severe	
06	infancy	
07	pregnancy	
08	surgical	
09	phenomenon	
10	cognitive	
11	clinician	
12	split-second	
13	warn A of B	
14	maintenance	
15	funeral	
16	currently	
17	generation	
18	drop by	
19	frustrated	
20	editor	

B	Korean	English
01	얻다	
02	정의하다, 규정하다	
03	입증하다	
04	적대감	
05	풍부한	
06	~에 앞서	
07	(몸을) 기울이다	
08	진단하다	
09	상당한, 유의미한	
10	무관심한	
11	없애다, 제거하다	
12	정확한	
13	범주화하다	
14	인종적인	
15	가변성	
16	뿐만 아니라	
17	작가, 저자	
18	외관, 겉모습	
19	A를 속여 B하게 하다	
20	불안	

▶ A-D 정답 : 해설편 152쪽

TEST C-D 각 단어의 뜻을 골라 기호를 쓰시오.

C	English		Korean
01	protest	( )	ⓐ 공식, 제조식
02	assumption	( )	ⓑ 가정
03	accusation	( )	ⓒ 엄격한
04	resemblance	( )	ⓓ 유사성
05	striking	( )	ⓔ 설득력 있는
06	to date	( )	ⓕ 지금까지
07	finite	( )	ⓖ 한정적인, 유한한
08	weep	( )	ⓗ 놀라운, 두드러진
09	formula	( )	ⓘ 이의를 제기하다, 항의하다
10	aggressive	( )	ⓙ 공격적인
11	steer	( )	ⓚ 경쟁적인
12	competitive	( )	ⓛ 울다
13	strict	( )	ⓜ 소유자
14	possessor	( )	ⓝ (핸들을) 조종하다
15	convincing	( )	ⓞ 비난, 기소
16	interpret	( )	ⓟ ~에 반대되는
17	opposed to	( )	ⓠ 권장, 충고
18	recommendation	( )	ⓡ 사라지다
19	disappear	( )	ⓢ 해석하다
20	spread	( )	ⓣ 퍼지다

D	Korean		English
01	선택적인	( )	ⓐ solely
02	포획, 감금	( )	ⓑ influential
03	증오	( )	ⓒ to a certain extent
04	나이와 관련된	( )	ⓓ age-related
05	상당한	( )	ⓔ hatred
06	영향력 있는	( )	ⓕ use up
07	다 써 버리다	( )	ⓖ captivity
08	단지, 오로지	( )	ⓗ assertiveness
09	(양이) ~에 달하다	( )	ⓘ amount to
10	배우다, 습득하다	( )	ⓙ sizable
11	어느 정도	( )	ⓚ acquire
12	발전하는	( )	ⓛ underestimate
13	단호함, 자기 주장	( )	ⓜ evolving
14	과소평가하다	( )	ⓝ selective
15	그렇지 않으면	( )	ⓞ otherwise
16	필요성	( )	ⓟ unpleasant
17	버리다	( )	ⓠ contrast
18	차이, 대조	( )	ⓡ abandon
19	불쾌한	( )	ⓢ massive
20	대대적인, 거대한	( )	ⓣ necessity

※ 영어 [독해] 파트만 수록한 문제지이므로 18번부터 시작합니다.

● 점수 표시가 없는 문항은 모두 2점 ● 문항수 28개 | 배점 63점 | 제한 시간 45분

18. 다음 글의 목적으로 가장 적절한 것은?

Dear Ms. MacAlpine,

I was so excited to hear that your brand is opening a new shop on Bruns Street next month. I have always appreciated the way your brand helps women to feel more stylish and confident. I am writing in response to your ad in the Bruns Journal. I graduated from the Meline School of Fashion and have worked as a sales assistant at LoganMart for the last five years. During that time, I've developed strong customer service and sales skills, and now I would like to apply for the sales position in your clothing store. I am available for an interview at your earliest convenience. I look forward to hearing from you. Thank you for reading my letter.

Yours sincerely,
Grace Braddock

① 영업 시작일을 문의하려고
② 인터뷰 일정을 변경하려고
③ 디자인 공모전에 참가하려고
④ 제품 관련 문의에 답변하려고
⑤ 의류 매장 판매직에 지원하려고

19. 다음 글에 드러난 'I'의 심경 변화로 가장 적절한 것은?

I had never seen a beach with such white sand or water that was such a beautiful shade of blue. Jane and I set up a blanket on the sand while looking forward to our ten days of honeymooning on an exotic island. "Look!" Jane waved her hand to point at the beautiful scene before us — and her gold wedding ring went flying off her hand. I tried to see where it went, but the sun hit my eyes and I lost track of it. I didn't want to lose her wedding ring, so I started looking in the area where I thought it had landed. However, the sand was so fine and I realized that anything heavy, like gold, would quickly sink and might never be found again.

① excited → frustrated
② pleased → jealous
③ nervous → confident
④ annoyed → grateful
⑤ relaxed → indifferent

20. 다음 글에서 필자가 주장하는 바로 가장 적절한 것은?

Unfortunately, many people don't take personal responsibility for their own growth. Instead, they simply run the race laid out for them. They do well enough in school to keep advancing. Maybe they manage to get a good job at a well-run company. But so many think and act as if their learning journey ends with college. They have checked all the boxes in the life that was laid out for them and now lack a road map describing the right ways to move forward and continue to grow. In truth, that's when the journey really begins. When school is finished, your growth becomes voluntary. Like healthy eating habits or a regular exercise program, you need to commit to it and devote thought, time, and energy to it. Otherwise, it simply won't happen — and your life and career are likely to stop progressing as a result.

① 성공 경험을 위해 달성 가능한 목표를 수립해야 한다.
② 체계적인 경력 관리를 위해 전문가의 도움을 받아야 한다.
③ 건강을 위해 꾸준한 운동과 식습관 관리를 병행해야 한다.
④ 졸업 이후 성장을 위해 자발적으로 배움을 실천해야 한다.
⑤ 적성에 맞는 직업을 찾기 위해 학교 교육에 충실해야 한다.

21. 밑줄 친 our brain and the universe meet가 다음 글에서 의미하는 바로 가장 적절한 것은? [3점]

Many people take the commonsense view that color is an objective property of things, or of the light that bounces off them. They say a tree's leaves are green because they reflect green light—a greenness that is just as real as the leaves. Others argue that color doesn't inhabit the physical world at all but exists only in the eye or mind of the viewer. They maintain that if a tree fell in a forest and no one was there to see it, its leaves would be colorless—and so would everything else. They say there is no such *thing* as color; there are only the people who see it. Both positions are, in a way, correct. Color is objective *and* subjective—"the place," as Paul Cézanne put it, "where our brain and the universe meet." Color is created when light from the world is registered by the eyes and interpreted by the brain.

① we see things beyond the range of perception
② objects appear different by the change of light
③ your perspectives and others' reach an agreement
④ our mind and physical reality interact with each other
⑤ structures of the human brain and the universe are similar

22. 다음 글의 요지로 가장 적절한 것은?

When writing a novel, research for information needs to be done. The thing is that some kinds of fiction demand a higher level of detail: crime fiction, for example, or scientific thrillers. The information is never hard to find; one website for authors even organizes trips to police stations, so that crime writers can get it right. Often, a polite letter will earn you permission to visit a particular location and record all the details that you need. But remember that you will drive your readers to boredom if you think that you need to pack everything you discover into your work. The details that matter are those that reveal the human experience. The crucial thing is telling a story, finding the characters, the tension, and the conflict—not the train timetable or the building blueprint.

① 작품의 완성도는 작가의 경험의 양에 비례한다.
② 작가의 상상력은 가장 훌륭한 이야기 재료이다.
③ 소설에서 사건 전개에 대한 묘사는 구체적일수록 좋다.
④ 소설을 쓸 때 독자의 관심사를 먼저 고려하는 것이 중요하다.
⑤ 소설에 포함될 세부 사항은 인간의 경험을 드러내는 것이어야 한다.

23. 다음 글의 주제로 가장 적절한 것은?

Nearly everything has to go through your mouth to get to the rest of you, from food and air to bacteria and viruses. A healthy mouth can help your body get what it needs and prevent it from harm — with adequate space for air to travel to your lungs, and healthy teeth and gums that prevent harmful microorganisms from entering your bloodstream. From the moment you are created, oral health affects every aspect of your life. What happens in the mouth is usually just the tip of the iceberg and a reflection of what is happening in other parts of the body. Poor oral health can be a cause of a disease that affects the entire body. The microorganisms in an unhealthy mouth can enter the bloodstream and travel anywhere in the body, posing serious health risks.

* microorganism: 미생물

① the way the immune system fights viruses
② the effect of unhealthy eating habits on the body
③ the difficulty in raising awareness about oral health
④ the importance of oral health and its impact on the body
⑤ the relationship between oral health and emotional well-being

24. 다음 글의 제목으로 가장 적절한 것은?

Kids tire of their toys, college students get sick of cafeteria food, and sooner or later most of us lose interest in our favorite TV shows. The bottom line is that we humans are easily bored. But why should this be true? The answer lies buried deep in our nerve cells, which are designed to reduce their initial excited response to stimuli each time they occur. At the same time, these neurons enhance their responses to things that change — especially things that change quickly. We probably evolved this way because our ancestors got more survival value, for example, from attending to what was moving in a tree (such as a puma) than to the tree itself. Boredom in reaction to an unchanging environment turns down the level of neural excitation so that new stimuli (like our ancestor's hypothetical puma threat) stand out more. It's the neural equivalent of turning off a front door light to see the fireflies.

* neural: 신경의 ** hypothetical: 가정(假定)의, 가설상의
*** equivalent: (~와) 같은 것, 대응물

① The Brain's Brilliant Trick to Overcome Fear
② Boredom: Neural Mechanism for Detecting Change
③ Humans' Endless Desire to Pursue Familiar Experiences
④ The Destruction of Nature in Exchange for Human Survival
⑤ How Humans Changed the Environment to Their Advantage

25. 다음 도표의 내용과 일치하지 <u>않는</u> 것은?

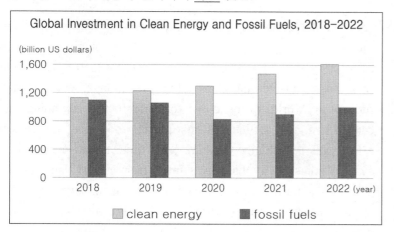

Global Investment in Clean Energy and Fossil Fuels, 2018-2022

(billion US dollars)

clean energy   fossil fuels

The above graph shows global energy investment in clean energy and in fossil fuels between 2018 and 2022. ① Since 2018 global energy investment in clean energy continued to rise, reaching its highest level in 2022. ② The investment gap between clean energy and fossil fuels in 2020 was larger than that in 2019. ③ Investment in fossil fuels was highest in 2018 and lowest in 2020. ④ In 2021, investment in clean energy exceeded 1,200 billion dollars, while investment in fossil fuels did not. ⑤ In 2022, the global investment in clean energy was more than double that of fossil fuels.

26. Frederick Douglass에 관한 다음 글의 내용과 일치하지 <u>않는</u> 것은?

Frederick Douglass was born into slavery at a farm in Maryland. His full name at birth was Frederick Augustus Washington Bailey. He changed his name to Frederick Douglass after he successfully escaped from slavery in 1838. He became a leader of the Underground Railroad — a network of people, places, and routes that helped enslaved people escape to the north. He assisted other runaway slaves until they could safely get to other areas in the north. As a slave, he had taught himself to read and write and he spread that knowledge to other slaves as well. Once free, he became a well-known abolitionist and strong believer in equality for all people including Blacks, Native Americans, women, and recent immigrants. He wrote several autobiographies describing his experiences as a slave. In addition to all this, he became the first African-American candidate for vice president of the United States.

* abolitionist: 노예제 폐지론자

① Maryland에서 노예로 태어났다.
② 노예들이 탈출하는 것을 돕는 조직의 리더가 되었다.
③ 다른 노예들로부터 읽고 쓰는 법을 배웠다.
④ 노예로서의 자신의 경험을 묘사한 자서전을 썼다.
⑤ 미국의 첫 아프리카계 미국인 부통령 후보가 되었다.

27. 2023 Australian Gateball Championships에 관한 다음 안내문의 내용과 일치하지 <u>않는</u> 것은?

2023 Australian Gateball Championships

The Diamond Coast is getting set to welcome the Australian Gateball Championships. Join this great outdoor competition and be the winner this year!

When & Where
‣ December 19 – 22, 2023
‣ Diamond Coast Performance Centre

Schedule of Matches
‣ Doubles matches (9 a.m. – 11 a.m.)
‣ Team matches (1 p.m. – 3 p.m.)

Prizes
‣ Every participant will receive a certificate for entry.
‣ Champions are awarded a medal.

Note
‣ Participation is free.
‣ Visit www.australiangateball.com for registration. (Registration on site is not available.)

---

① 4일 동안 진행된다.
② 복식 경기는 오전에 열린다.
③ 모든 참가자는 참가 증서를 받는다.
④ 참가비는 무료이다.
⑤ 현장에서 등록하는 것이 가능하다.

28. The Amazing Urban Adventure Quest에 관한 다음 안내문의 내용과 일치하는 것은?

The Amazing Urban Adventure Quest

Explore Central Park while solving clues and completing challenges! Guided by your smartphone, make your way among the well-known places in the park.

When & How
• Available 365 days a year (from sunrise to sunset)
• Start when you want.
• Get a stamp at each checkpoint.

Adventure Courses
• East Side: Starts at Twilight Gardens (no age limit)
• West Side: Starts at Strawberry Castle (over 15 years old)

Registration & Cost
• Sign up online at www.urbanquest.com.
• $40 for a team of 2-5 people
• Save 20% with discount code: CENTRALQUEST

---

① 참여하는 동안 스마트폰 사용은 금지된다.
② 일 년 내내 일몰 후 참여할 수 있다.
③ 서편 코스는 나이 제한이 없다.
④ 1인당 40달러의 요금이 든다.
⑤ 할인받을 수 있는 코드가 있다.

29. 다음 글의 밑줄 친 부분 중, 어법상 <u>틀린</u> 것은? [3점]

Some countries have proposed tougher guidelines for determining brain death when transplantation—transferring organs to others—is under consideration. In several European countries, there are legal requirements which specify ① <u>that</u> a whole team of doctors must agree over the diagnosis of death in the case of a potential donor. The reason for these strict regulations for diagnosing brain death in potential organ donors ② <u>is</u>, no doubt, to ease public fears of a premature diagnosis of brain death for the purpose of obtaining organs. But it is questionable whether these requirements reduce public suspicions as much as they create ③ <u>them</u>. They certainly maintain mistaken beliefs that diagnosing brain death is an unreliable process ④ <u>lack</u> precision. As a matter of consistency, at least, criteria for diagnosing the deaths of organ donors should be exactly the same as for those for ⑤ <u>whom</u> immediate burial or cremation is intended.

* diagnosis: 진단 ** donor: 기증자 *** cremation: 화장(火葬)

30. 다음 글의 밑줄 친 부분 중, 문맥상 낱말의 쓰임이 적절하지 <u>않은</u> 것은?

The term minimalism gives a negative impression to some people who think that it is all about sacrificing valuable possessions. This insecurity naturally stems from their ① <u>attachment</u> to their possessions. It is difficult to distance oneself from something that has been around for quite some time. Being an emotional animal, human beings give meaning to the things around them. So, the question arising here is that if minimalism will ② <u>hurt</u> one's emotions, why become a minimalist? The answer is very simple; the assumption of the question is fundamentally ③ <u>wrong</u>. Minimalism does not hurt emotions. You might feel a bit sad while getting rid of a useless item but sooner than later, this feeling will be ④ <u>maintained</u> by the joy of clarity. Minimalists never argue that you should leave every convenience of the modern era. They are of the view that you only need to ⑤ <u>eliminate</u> stuff that is unused or not going to be used in the near future.

[31~34] 다음 빈칸에 들어갈 말로 가장 적절한 것을 고르시오.

31. A remarkable characteristic of the visual system is that it has the ability of _____. Psychologist George M. Stratton made this clear in an impressive self-experiment. Stratton wore reversing glasses for several days, which literally turned the world upside down for him. In the beginning, this caused him great difficulties: just putting food in his mouth with a fork was a challenge for him. With time, however, his visual system adjusted to the new stimuli from reality, and he was able to act normally in his environment again, even seeing it upright when he concentrated. As he took off his reversing glasses, he was again confronted with problems: he used the wrong hand when he wanted to reach for something, for example. Fortunately, Stratton could reverse the perception, and he did not have to wear reversing glasses for the rest of his life. For him, everything returned to normal after one day.

* reverse: 뒤집다, 반전시키다

① adapting itself
② visualizing ideas
③ assessing distances
④ functioning irregularly
⑤ operating independently

32. Participants in a study were asked to answer questions like "Why does the moon have phases?" Half the participants were told to search for the answers on the internet, while the other half weren't allowed to do so. Then, in the second part of the study, all of the participants were presented with a new set of questions, such as "Why does Swiss cheese have holes?" These questions were unrelated to the ones asked during the first part of the study, so participants who used the internet had absolutely no advantage over those who hadn't. You would think that both sets of participants would be equally sure or unsure about how well they could answer the new questions. But those who used the internet in the first part of the study rated themselves as more knowledgeable than those who hadn't, even about questions they hadn't searched online for. The study suggests that having access to unrelated information was enough to _____.

* phase: (달의) 상(相)

① improve their judgment skills
② pump up their intellectual confidence
③ make them endure challenging situations
④ lead to a collaboration among the participants
⑤ motivate them to pursue in-depth knowledge

33. Anthropologist Gregory Bateson suggests that we tend to understand the world by _____.
Take platypuses. We might zoom in so closely to their fur that each hair appears different. We might also zoom out to the extent where it appears as a single, uniform object. We might take the platypus as an individual, or we might treat it as part of a larger unit such as a species or an ecosystem. It's possible to move between many of these perspectives, although we may need some additional tools and skills to zoom in on individual pieces of hair or zoom out to entire ecosystems. Crucially, however, we can only take up one perspective at a time. We can pay attention to the varied behavior of individual animals, look at what unites them into a single species, or look at them as part of bigger ecological patterns. Every possible perspective involves emphasizing certain aspects and ignoring others. [3점]

* anthropologist: 인류학자 ** platypus: 오리너구리

① using our experiences as a guide
② breaking the framework of old ideas
③ adding new information to what we know
④ focusing in on particular features within it
⑤ considering both bright and dark sides of it

34. Plato's realism includes all aspects of experience but is most easily explained by considering the nature of mathematical and geometrical objects such as circles. He asked the question, what is a circle? You might indicate a particular example carved into stone or drawn in the sand. However, Plato would point out that, if you looked closely enough, you would see that neither it, nor indeed any physical circle, was perfect. They all possessed flaws, and all were subject to change and decayed with time. So how can we talk about perfect circles if we cannot actually see or touch them? Plato's extraordinary answer was that the world we see is a poor reflection of a deeper unseen reality of *Forms*, or *universals*, where perfect cats chase perfect mice in perfect circles around perfect rocks. Plato believed that the *Forms* or *universals* are the true reality that exists in _____.

[3점]

① observable phenomena of the physical world
② our experiences shaped by external influences
③ an overlapping area between emotion and reason
④ an invisible but perfect world beyond our senses
⑤ our perception affected by stereotype or generalization

35. 다음 글에서 전체 흐름과 관계 <u>없는</u> 문장은?

In statistics, the law of large numbers describes a situation where having more data is better for making predictions. According to it, the more often an experiment is conducted, the closer the average of the results can be expected to match the true state of the world. ① For instance, on your first encounter with the game of roulette, you may have beginner's luck after betting on 7. ② But the more often you repeat this bet, the closer the relative frequency of wins and losses is expected to approach the true chance of winning, meaning that your luck will at some point fade away. ③ Each number's symbolic meanings can be interpreted in various ways and are promising in situations that may change unexpectedly. ④ Similarly, car insurers collect large amounts of data to figure out the chances that drivers will cause accidents, depending on their age, region, or car brand. ⑤ Both casinos and insurance industries rely on the law of large numbers to balance individual losses.

[36 ~ 37] 주어진 글 다음에 이어질 글의 순서로 가장 적절한 것을 고르시오.

36.

> The adolescent brain is not fully developed until its early twenties. This means the way the adolescents' decision-making circuits integrate and process information may put them at a disadvantage.

(A) On the other hand, the limbic system matures earlier, playing a central role in processing emotional responses. Because of its earlier development, it is more likely to influence decision-making. Decision-making in the adolescent brain is led by emotional factors more than the perception of consequences.

(B) Due to these differences, there is an imbalance between feeling-based decision-making ruled by the more mature limbic system and logical-based decision-making by the not-yet-mature prefrontal cortex. This may explain why some teens are more likely to make bad decisions.

(C) One of their brain regions that matures later is the prefrontal cortex, which is the control center, tasked with thinking ahead and evaluating consequences. It is the area of the brain responsible for preventing you from sending off an initial angry text and modifying it with kinder words. [3점]

* integrate: 통합하다 ** limbic system: 대뇌변연계
*** prefrontal cortex: 전전두엽 피질

① (A) - (C) - (B)   ② (B) - (A) - (C)
③ (B) - (C) - (A)   ④ (C) - (A) - (B)
⑤ (C) - (B) - (A)

37.

> Despite the remarkable progress in deep−learning based facial recognition approaches in recent years, in terms of identification performance, they still have limitations. These limitations relate to the database used in the learning stage.

(A) To counteract this problem, researchers have developed models for face aging or digital de−aging. It is used to compensate for the differences in facial characteristics, which appear over a given time period.

(B) If the selected database does not contain enough instances, the result may be systematically affected. For example, the performance of a facial biometric system may decrease if the person to be identified was enrolled over 10 years ago.

(C) The factor to consider is that this person may experience changes in the texture of the face, particularly with the appearance of wrinkles and sagging skin. These changes may be highlighted by weight gain or loss.

* biometric: 생체 측정의 ** sagging: 처진

① (A) − (C) − (B)　　　　② (B) − (A) − (C)
③ (B) − (C) − (A)　　　　④ (C) − (A) − (B)
⑤ (C) − (B) − (A)

[38 ~ 39] 글의 흐름으로 보아, 주어진 문장이 들어가기에 가장 적절한 곳을 고르시오.

38.

> Leaving the contribution of that strategy to one side, the danger of creating more uniform crops is that they are more at risk when it comes to disasters.

The decline in the diversity of our food is an entirely human−made process. The biggest loss of crop diversity came in the decades that followed the Second World War. (①) In an attempt to save millions from extreme hunger, crop scientists found ways to produce grains such as rice and wheat on an enormous scale. (②) And thousands of traditional varieties were replaced by a small number of new super−productive ones. (③) The strategy worked spectacularly well, at least to begin with. (④) Because of it, grain production tripled, and between 1970 and 2020 the human population more than doubled. (⑤) Specifically, a global food system that depends on just a narrow selection of plants has a greater chance of not being able to survive diseases, pests and climate extremes.

* pest: 해충

39.

> A few years ago, Cuba altered that uniform style, modernizing it and perhaps conforming to other countries' style; interestingly, the national team has declined since that time.

Between 1940 and 2000, Cuba ruled the world baseball scene. They won 25 of the first 28 World Cups and 3 of 5 Olympic Games. (①) The Cubans were known for wearing uniforms covered in red from head to toe, a strong contrast to the more conservative North American style featuring grey or white pants. (②) Not only were their athletic talents superior, the Cubans appeared even stronger from just the colour of their uniforms. (③) A game would not even start and the opposing team would already be scared. (④) The country that ruled international baseball for decades has not been on top since that uniform change. (⑤) Traditions are important for a team; while a team brand or image can adjust to keep up with present times, if it abandons or neglects its roots, negative effects can surface.

* conservative: 보수적인

40. 다음 글의 내용을 한 문장으로 요약하고자 한다. 빈칸 (A), (B)에 들어갈 말로 가장 적절한 것은? [3점]

> Many of the first models of cultural evolution drew noticeable connections between culture and genes by using concepts from theoretical population genetics and applying them to culture. Cultural patterns of transmission, innovation, and selection are conceptually likened to genetic processes of transmission, mutation, and selection. However, these approaches had to be modified to account for the differences between genetic and cultural transmission. For example, we do not expect the cultural transmission to follow the rules of genetic transmission strictly. If two biological parents have different forms of a cultural trait, their child is not necessarily equally likely to acquire the mother's or father's form of that trait. Further, a child can acquire cultural traits not only from its parents but also from nonparental adults and peers; thus, the frequency of a cultural trait in the population is relevant beyond just the probability that an individual's parents had that trait.

* mutation: 돌연변이 ** relevant: 유의미한

↓

> Early cultural evolution models used the ___(A)___ between culture and genes but had to be revised since cultural transmission allows for more ___(B)___ factors than genetic transmission.

	(A)		(B)
①	similarity	⋯	diverse
②	similarity	⋯	limited
③	difference	⋯	flexible
④	difference	⋯	complicated
⑤	interaction	⋯	credible

[해설편 p.160]

[41 ~ 42] 다음 글을 읽고, 물음에 답하시오.

A ball thrown into the air is acted upon by the initial force given it, persisting as inertia of movement and tending to carry it in the same straight line, and by the constant pull of gravity downward, as well as by the resistance of the air. It moves, accordingly, in a (a) curved path. Now the path does not represent the working of any particular force; there is simply the (b) combination of the three elementary forces mentioned; but in a real sense, there is something in the total action besides the isolated action of three forces, namely, their joint action. In the same way, when two or more human individuals are together, their mutual relationships and their arrangement into a group are things which would not be (c) concealed if we confined our attention to each individual separately. The significance of group behavior is greatly (d) increased in the case of human beings by the fact that some of the tendencies to action of the individual are related definitely to other persons, and could not be aroused except by other persons acting as stimuli. An individual in complete (e) isolation would not reveal their competitive tendencies, their tendencies towards the opposite sex, their protective tendencies towards children. This shows that the traits of human nature do not fully appear until the individual is brought into relationships with other individuals.

* inertia: 관성 ** arouse: 유발하다

41. 윗글의 제목으로 가장 적절한 것은?

① Common Misunderstandings in Physics
② Collaboration: A Key to Success in Relationships
③ Interpersonal Traits and Their Impact on Science
④ Unbalanced Forces Causing Objects to Accelerate
⑤ Human Traits Uncovered by Interpersonal Relationships

42. 밑줄 친 (a)~(e) 중에서 문맥상 낱말의 쓰임이 적절하지 않은 것은? [3점]

① (a)　　② (b)　　③ (c)　　④ (d)　　⑤ (e)

[43 ~ 45] 다음 글을 읽고, 물음에 답하시오.

(A)

There once lived a man in a village who was not happy with his life. He was always troubled by one problem or another. One day, a saint with his guards stopped by his village. Many people heard the news and started going to him with their problems. The man also decided to visit the saint. Even after reaching the saint's place in the morning, (a) he didn't get the opportunity to meet him till evening.

(B)

But the saint also asked if the man could do a small job for him. He told the man to take care of a hundred camels in his group that night, saying "When all hundred camels sit down, you can go to sleep." The man agreed. The next morning when the saint met that man, (b) he asked if the man had slept well. Tired and sad, the man replied that he couldn't sleep even for a moment.

(C)

In fact, the man tried very hard but couldn't make all the camels sit at the same time because every time (c) he made one camel sit, another would stand up. The saint told him, "You realized that no matter how hard you try, you can't make all the camels sit down. If one problem is solved, for some reason, another will arise like the camels did. So, humans should enjoy life despite these problems."

(D)

When the man got to meet the saint, (d) he confessed that he was very unhappy with life because problems always surrounded him, like workplace tension or worries about his health. (e) He said, "Please give me a solution so that all the problems in my life will end and I can live peacefully." The saint smiled and said that he would answer the request the next day.

43. 주어진 글 (A)에 이어질 내용을 순서에 맞게 배열한 것으로 가장 적절한 것은?

① (B) - (D) - (C)　　　　② (C) - (B) - (D)
③ (C) - (D) - (B)　　　　④ (D) - (B) - (C)
⑤ (D) - (C) - (B)

44. 밑줄 친 (a)~(e) 중에서 가리키는 대상이 나머지 넷과 다른 것은?

① (a)　　② (b)　　③ (c)　　④ (d)　　⑤ (e)

45. 윗글에 관한 내용으로 적절하지 않은 것은?

① 많은 사람들이 자신들의 문제를 가지고 성자에게 갔다.
② 성자는 자신을 위해 작은 일을 해 줄 수 있는지 남자에게 물었다.
③ 성자는 남자가 낙타를 모두 재우면 잠을 자러 가도 좋다고 했다.
④ 성자는 문제가 있어도 인생을 즐겨야 한다고 말했다.
⑤ 성자는 남자의 요청에 대한 답을 다음 날 말해 주기로 했다.

※ **확인 사항**

○ 답안지의 해당란에 필요한 내용을 정확히 기입(표기)했는지 확인하시오.

18

001 □ appreciate ⓥ 진가를 알아보다
002 □ stylish ⓐ 멋진, 우아한
003 □ confident ⓐ 자신 있는
004 □ response ⓝ 대답, 응답
005 □ ad ⓝ 광고(advertisement)
006 □ graduate ⓥ 졸업하다
007 □ sales assistant 판매 보조원
008 □ customer ⓝ 손님, 고객
009 □ convenience ⓝ 편의
010 □ forward to ~ing ~하기를 고대하다

19

011 □ shade ⓝ 색조, 그늘
012 □ blanket ⓝ 담요
013 □ honeymoon ⓝ 신혼여행
014 □ exotic ⓐ 이국적인
015 □ wave ⓥ 흔들다
016 □ wedding ring 결혼반지
017 □ track ⓝ 방향, 길
018 □ land ⓥ 떨어지다
019 □ realize ⓥ 깨닫다
020 □ sink ⓥ 가라앉다

20

021 □ unfortunately ⓪ 안타깝게도
022 □ personal ⓐ 개인적인
023 □ responsibility ⓝ 책임감
024 □ growth ⓝ 성장
025 □ instead ⓪ 대신에
026 □ race ⓝ 경주, 달리기
027 □ lay out 놓이다
028 □ manage ⓥ 관리하다
029 □ well-run ⓐ 운영이 잘 되는
030 □ journey ⓝ 여행, 여정
031 □ lay ⓥ 놓다, 눕히다 (과거형, 과거분사 laid)
032 □ lack ⓥ 부족하다 ⓝ 부족
033 □ road map 지침, 로드 맵
034 □ voluntary ⓐ 자발적인
035 □ healthy ⓐ 건강한
036 □ regular ⓐ 규칙적인
037 □ commit ⓥ 헌신하다, 전념하다
038 □ devote ⓥ 쏟다, 몰두하다
039 □ otherwise ⓪ 그렇지 않으면
040 □ progress ⓝ 전진, 진행, 진척
041 □ as a result 결과적으로

21

042 □ commonsense ⓐ 상식적인
043 □ objective ⓐ 객관적인
044 □ property ⓝ 속성, 재산
045 □ bounce off 반사하다
046 □ reflect ⓥ 반사하다
047 □ greenness ⓝ 녹색, 푸르름
048 □ argue ⓥ 주장하다, 논증하다
049 □ inhabit ⓥ ~에 존재하다
050 □ physical ⓐ 물리적인
051 □ mind ⓝ 마음, 정신
052 □ maintain ⓥ 주장하다
053 □ forest ⓝ 숲, 삼림
054 □ colorless ⓐ 무색의
055 □ position ⓝ 입장, 위치

056 □ in a way 어느 정도는, 어떤 면에서는
057 □ correct ⓐ 적절한, 옳은
058 □ subjective ⓐ 주관적인
059 □ register ⓥ 등록하다
060 □ interpret ⓥ 해석하다, 설명하다
061 □ range ⓝ 범위
062 □ perception ⓝ 인식
063 □ appear ⓥ 보이게 되다
064 □ perspective ⓝ 관점
065 □ interact ⓥ 상호 작용하다, 서로 영향을 끼치다
066 □ structure ⓝ 구조, 조직, 구성
067 □ similar ⓐ 비슷한, 유사한, 닮은

22

068 □ research ⓝ 연구, 조사
069 □ fiction ⓝ 소설
070 □ demand ⓥ 요구하다
071 □ detail ⓝ 세부 사항
072 □ scientific ⓐ 과학의
073 □ author ⓝ 작가
074 □ organize ⓥ 조직하다, 편성하다
075 □ police station 경찰서
076 □ crime ⓝ 범죄
077 □ often ⓪ 흔히, 종종, 자주
078 □ polite ⓐ 예의 바른, 공손한, 정중한
079 □ earn ⓥ 얻다
080 □ permission ⓝ 허락
081 □ record ⓥ 기록하다
082 □ drive ⓥ 만들다, 몰아가다
083 □ reader ⓝ 구독자
084 □ boredom ⓝ 지루함
085 □ crucial ⓐ 중대한, 결정적인
086 □ conflict ⓝ 갈등
087 □ blueprint ⓝ 계획, 청사진

23

088 □ nearly ⓪ 거의
089 □ rest ⓝ 나머지
090 □ prevent ⓥ 막다
091 □ harm ⓝ 해, 피해, 손해
092 □ adequate ⓐ 충분한
093 □ lung ⓝ 폐
094 □ tooth ⓝ 이, 치아, 이빨 (pl. teeth)
095 □ gum ⓝ 잇몸
096 □ microorganisms ⓝ 미생물
097 □ bloodstream ⓝ 피의 흐름, 혈류
098 □ oral ⓐ 입의, 구강의
099 □ affect ⓥ 영향을 미치다
100 □ iceberg ⓝ 빙산
101 □ reflection ⓝ 반영
102 □ poor ⓐ 좋지 못한
103 □ entire ⓐ 전체의
104 □ serious ⓐ 심각한
105 □ risk ⓝ 위험, 위험 요소
106 □ immune system 면역 체계
107 □ awareness ⓝ 인식
108 □ impact ⓥ 영향을 주다
109 □ relationship ⓝ 관계, 관련

24

110 □ sick of ~에 싫증나다

111 □ sooner or later 조만간, 머지않아
112 □ interest ⓝ 흥미
113 □ favorite ⓐ 마음에 드는, 매우 좋아하는
114 □ bottom line 요점
115 □ bury ⓥ 숨어있다
116 □ nerve cell 신경 세포
117 □ reduce ⓥ 줄이다, 감소시키다
118 □ initial ⓐ 처음의, 초기의
119 □ stimulus ⓝ 자극 (pl. stimuli)
120 □ occur ⓥ 일어나다, 발생하다
121 □ neuron ⓝ 뉴런(신경세포단위)
122 □ enhance ⓥ 강화하다
123 □ especially ⓪ 특히
124 □ probably ⓪ 아마도
125 □ evolve ⓥ 진화하다
126 □ ancestor ⓝ 조상
127 □ value ⓝ 가치
128 □ reaction ⓝ 반응, 반작용
129 □ environment ⓝ 환경
130 □ excitation ⓝ 자극
131 □ stimuli ⓝ 자극(stimulus)의 복수형
132 □ hypothetical ⓐ 가정의, 가상의
133 □ neural ⓐ 신경의
134 □ equivalent ⓝ 대응물
135 □ firefly ⓝ 반딧불이

25

136 □ investment ⓝ 투자, 투자액
137 □ fossil ⓝ 화석
138 □ fuel ⓝ 연료
139 □ reach ⓥ 도달하다
140 □ exceed ⓥ 초과하다
141 □ billion 10억

26

142 □ slavery ⓝ 노예
143 □ successfully ⓪ 성공적으로
144 □ escape ⓥ 달아나다, 탈출하다
145 □ route ⓝ 길
146 □ enslave ⓥ 노예로 만들다
147 □ assist ⓥ 돕다
148 □ runaway ⓐ 도망친, 탈주한
149 □ safely ⓪ 무사히, 안전하게
150 □ spread ⓥ 퍼뜨리다, 확산시키다
151 □ well-known 잘 알려진
152 □ abolitionist 노예제 폐지론자
153 □ believer ⓝ 믿는 사람, 신자, 신봉자
154 □ equality ⓝ 평등
155 □ Native American 아메리칸 원주민, 아메리칸 인디언
156 □ recent ⓐ 최근의
157 □ immigrant ⓝ 이민자, 이주민
158 □ several ⓐ 몇 개의
159 □ autobiography ⓝ 자서전
160 □ candidate ⓝ 후보자

27

161 □ get set 준비를 갖추다
162 □ outdoor ⓐ 집 밖의, 옥외의, 야외의
163 □ competition ⓝ 경기, 시합
164 □ participant ⓝ 참가자
165 □ receive ⓥ 받다

166 □ certificate ⓝ 증서, 증명서
167 □ entry ⓝ 참가
168 □ participation ⓝ 참가, 참여
169 □ registration ⓝ 등록

28

170 □ urban ⓐ 도시의, 도회지의
171 □ quest ⓝ 탐색, 탐구
172 □ explore ⓥ 탐험하다
173 □ solve ⓥ 해결하다
174 □ clue ⓝ 단서
175 □ complete ⓥ 완료하다
176 □ available ⓐ 이용할 수 있는
177 □ sunrise ⓝ 일출
178 □ sunset ⓝ 일몰
179 □ discount ⓝ 할인

29

180 □ propose ⓥ 제안하다
181 □ tough ⓐ 엄격한, 힘든
182 □ guideline ⓝ 지침
183 □ determine ⓥ 결정하다
184 □ brain death 뇌사
185 □ transplantation ⓝ 이식
186 □ transferring ⓝ 이동, 이송
187 □ organ ⓝ 장기
188 □ consideration ⓝ 고려, 숙고
189 □ legal ⓐ 법률의
190 □ requirement ⓝ 필요조건, 요건
191 □ specify ⓥ 구체화하다
192 □ diagnosis ⓝ 진단
193 □ potential ⓐ 잠재적인
194 □ donor ⓝ 기증자
195 □ strict ⓐ 엄격한
196 □ regulation ⓝ 규제
197 □ doubt ⓝ 의심, 의혹, 의문
198 □ ease ⓥ 완화시키다, 편하게 하다, 안심시키다
199 □ premature ⓐ 정상보다 이른
200 □ obtain ⓥ 얻다, 획득하다
201 □ questionable ⓐ 의심스러운, 미심쩍은
202 □ suspicion ⓝ 의심
203 □ certainly ⓪ 틀림없이, 분명히
204 □ belief ⓝ 생각, 신념
205 □ unreliable ⓐ 믿을 수 없는
206 □ consistency ⓝ 일관성
207 □ criteria ⓝ 기준
208 □ exactly ⓪ 정확히
209 □ immediate ⓐ 즉시
210 □ burial ⓝ 매장
211 □ cremation ⓝ 화장

30

212 □ term ⓝ 용어
213 □ impression ⓝ 인상
214 □ sacrifice ⓥ 희생하다
215 □ valuable ⓐ 가치 있는
216 □ possession ⓝ 소유
217 □ insecurity ⓝ 불안
218 □ stem ⓥ 비롯되다
219 □ attachment ⓝ 애착
220 □ distance ⓥ 거리를 두다
221 □ emotional ⓐ 정서의, 감정의

222 □ assumption ⓝ 가정
223 □ fundamentally ⓐⓓ 근본적으로
224 □ get rid of 버리다
225 □ sooner than later 머지않아
226 □ maintain ⓥ 유지하다
227 □ clarity ⓥ 명료하다
228 □ era ⓝ 시대
229 □ eliminate ⓥ 제거하다
230 □ unused ⓐ 사용하지 않는

31
231 □ remarkable ⓐ 두드러진, 놀라운, 주목할만한
232 □ characteristic ⓝ 특징, 특질
233 □ visual ⓐ 시각의
234 □ ability ⓝ 능력, 수완, 역량
235 □ psychologist ⓝ 심리학자
236 □ impressive ⓐ 인상적인
237 □ self-experiment 자가 실험
238 □ reverse ⓥ 뒤집다
239 □ literally ⓐⓓ 문자 그대로, 정말로
240 □ upside down 거꾸로, 전도되어, 뒤집혀
241 □ adjust to ~에 적응하다
242 □ upright ⓐ 똑바른
243 □ concentrate ⓥ 집중하다
244 □ confront ⓥ 직면하다

32
245 □ phase ⓝ 상
246 □ allow ⓥ 허락하다
247 □ present ⓥ 제시하다
248 □ unrelated ⓐ 관계없는
249 □ absolutely ⓐⓓ 전혀
250 □ advantage ⓝ 이점
251 □ equally ⓐⓓ 동등하게
252 □ rate ⓥ 평가하다
253 □ knowledgeable ⓐ 아는 것이 많은, 많이 아는
254 □ access ⓥ 접근하다
255 □ pump up 부풀리다
256 □ intellectual ⓐ 지적의
257 □ confidence ⓝ 자신감, 확신
258 □ endure ⓥ 견디다
259 □ pursue ⓥ 추구하다
260 □ in-depth ⓐ 깊은

33
261 □ anthropologist ⓝ 인류학자
262 □ feature ⓝ 특색, 특징, 특성
263 □ platypus ⓝ 오리너구리
264 □ zoom in 확대하다
265 □ fur ⓝ 털
266 □ zoom out 축소하다
267 □ extent ⓝ 정도, 한도
268 □ object ⓝ 사물
269 □ treat ⓥ 다루다, 취급하다
270 □ ecosystem ⓝ 생태계
271 □ additional ⓐ 추가의
272 □ crucially ⓐⓓ 결정적으로
273 □ take up 취하다
274 □ at a time 한 번에
275 □ attention ⓝ 주의 ,주목

276 □ varied ⓐ 다양한
277 □ unite ⓥ 합하다
278 □ ecological ⓐ 생태계의
279 □ emphasize ⓥ 강조하다

34
280 □ aspect ⓝ 측면
281 □ explain ⓥ 설명하다
282 □ nature ⓝ 특성, 본성
283 □ geometrical ⓐ 기하학의
284 □ indicate ⓥ 가리키다
285 □ particular ⓐ 특정한
286 □ carved ⓐ 곡선의
287 □ point out 가리키다, 지적하다
288 □ indeed ⓐⓓ 진정
289 □ possess ⓥ 소유하다
290 □ flaw ⓝ 결함
291 □ decay ⓥ 쇠하다, 부패하다
292 □ extraordinary ⓐ 비범한
293 □ form ⓝ 형상
294 □ universals ⓝ 보편자
295 □ chase ⓥ 쫓다
296 □ phenomena ⓝ 현상
297 □ overlapping ⓐ 중복된
298 □ stereotype ⓝ 고정관념
299 □ generalization ⓝ 일반화

35
300 □ statistics ⓝ 통계학
301 □ describe ⓥ 묘사하다, 말로 설명하다
302 □ situation ⓝ 상황, 처지, 환경
303 □ prediction ⓝ 예측
304 □ according to (진술·기록 등에) 따르면
305 □ experiment ⓝ 실험
306 □ conduct ⓥ 수행하다
307 □ average ⓝ 평균
308 □ encounter ⓥ 접하다, 만나다
309 □ beginner ⓝ 초보자
310 □ relativea. 비교상의, 상대적인
311 □ frequency ⓝ 빈도
312 □ symbolic ⓐ 상징적인
313 □ promise ⓥ 유망하다
314 □ unexpectedly ⓐⓓ 예상치 못하게
315 □ figure ⓝ 수치, 숫자
316 □ accident ⓝ 사고
317 □ insurance ⓝ 보험
318 □ rely on ~에 의존하다

36
319 □ adolescent ⓝ 청소년
320 □ decision-making ⓝ 의사 결정
321 □ circuit ⓝ 회로
322 □ integrate ⓥ 통합하다
323 □ disadvantage ⓝ 불리한 점, 약점
324 □ on the other hand 다른 한편으로는, 반면에
325 □ limbic system 대뇌변연계
326 □ mature ⓐ 성인의
327 □ be led by ~에 의해 이끌어지다
328 □ factor ⓝ 요인
329 □ consequence ⓝ 결과
330 □ imbalance ⓝ 불균형

331 □ prefrontal cortex 전전두엽 피질
332 □ region ⓝ 범위, 영역

37
333 □ facial ⓐ 얼굴의, 안면의
334 □ remarkable ⓐ 눈에 띄는
335 □ recognition ⓝ 식별
336 □ approach ⓥ 접근하다
337 □ in terms of ~에 관하여
338 □ identification ⓝ 인식
339 □ limitation ⓝ 한계
340 □ relate ⓥ 관련시키다
341 □ stage ⓝ 단계
342 □ counteract ⓥ 대응하다
343 □ de-aging ⓝ 노화 완화
344 □ compensate ⓥ 보완하다
345 □ biometric ⓐ 생물 측정의
346 □ decrease ⓥ 감소하다
347 □ identified ⓐ 확인된, 인정된, 식별된
348 □ enroll ⓥ 등록하다
349 □ texture ⓝ 감촉, 질감
350 □ appearance ⓝ 나타남, 출현
351 □ wrinkle ⓝ 주름
352 □ sagging ⓐ 처진

38
353 □ diversity ⓝ 다양성
354 □ decade ⓝ 수십 년의
355 □ attempt ⓝ 시도
356 □ wheat ⓝ 밀
357 □ scale ⓝ 규모
358 □ replace ⓥ 대체하다
359 □ super-productive ⓐ 초 생산적인
360 □ spectacularly ⓐⓓ 굉장히
361 □ triple ⓥ 세배가 되다
362 □ contribution ⓝ 기여
363 □ strategy ⓝ 전략
364 □ uniform ⓝ 유니폼
365 □ depend on ~에 의존하다
366 □ disease ⓝ 질병
367 □ pest ⓝ 해충
368 □ extreme ⓝ 위기

39
369 □ be known for ~로 잘 알려진
370 □ covered in ~로 뒤덮인
371 □ toe ⓝ 발끝
372 □ contrast ⓝ 대조
373 □ conservative ⓐ 보수적인
374 □ alter ⓥ 바꾸다
375 □ modernize ⓥ 현대화하다
376 □ decline ⓥ 쇠퇴하다
377 □ abandon ⓥ 버리다
378 □ neglect ⓥ 방치하다, 등한하다

40
379 □ evolution ⓝ 진화
380 □ noticeable ⓐ 주목할 만한
381 □ concept ⓝ 개념
382 □ theoretical ⓐ 이론적인
383 □ genetics ⓝ 유전학
384 □ transmission ⓝ 전이

385 □ innovation ⓝ 혁신
386 □ link to ~에 접근하다
387 □ mutation ⓝ 돌연변이
388 □ modify ⓥ 수정하다
389 □ trait ⓝ 특징
390 □ acquire ⓥ 얻다
391 □ peer ⓝ 동료
392 □ probability ⓝ 개연성
393 □ revise ⓥ 수정하다
394 □ similarity ⓝ 유사성
395 □ diverse ⓐ 다양한
396 □ limited ⓐ 제한적인
397 □ difference ⓝ 다름
398 □ flexible ⓐ 유연한
399 □ complicated ⓐ 복잡한
400 □ interaction ⓝ 상호작용
401 □ credible ⓐ 믿을 수 있는

41~42
402 □ persist ⓥ 저항하다
403 □ inertia ⓝ 관성
404 □ carry ⓥ 나아가다
405 □ constant ⓐ 끊임없는
406 □ gravity ⓝ 중력
407 □ downward ⓐ 아래의
408 □ resistance ⓝ 저항
409 □ combination ⓝ 결합
410 □ elementary ⓐ 기본의
411 □ isolated ⓐ 고립된
412 □ joint ⓐ 공동의
413 □ mutual ⓐ 상호의
414 □ arrangement ⓝ 배치
415 □ conceal ⓥ 감추다
416 □ confined ⓐ 좁은
417 □ significance ⓝ 중요성
418 □ behavior ⓝ 행동
419 □ increase ⓥ 증가하다
420 □ tendency ⓝ 경향
421 □ arouse ⓥ 유발하다
422 □ reveal ⓥ 드러내다
423 □ competitive ⓐ 경쟁적인
424 □ opposite ⓐ 정반대의
425 □ toward ⓟⓡⓔⓟ ~향하여
426 □ bring into 끌어들이다

43~45
427 □ saint ⓝ 성자
428 □ guard ⓝ 경호원
429 □ stop by ~에 들르다
430 □ decide ⓥ 결심하다
431 □ opportunity ⓝ 기회
432 □ confess ⓥ 고백하다
433 □ surrounded ⓐ 둘러싸인
434 □ tension ⓝ 긴장
435 □ take care of ~을 돌보다
436 □ camel ⓝ 낙타
437 □ arise ⓥ 발생하다
438 □ despite ~에도 불구하고

16회

● 채점 : 맞은 개수 _____ / 80

TEST A-B 각 단어의 뜻을 [A] 영어는 우리말로, [B] 우리말은 영어로 쓰시오.

A	English	Korean
01	confident	
02	convenience	
03	shade	
04	wave	
05	track	
06	growth	
07	devote	
08	responsibility	
09	commonsense	
10	objective	
11	reflect	
12	range	
13	demand	
14	drive	
15	prevent	
16	adequate	
17	awareness	
18	investment	
19	reach	
20	exceed	

B	Korean	English
01	평등	
02	증서, 증명서	
03	단서	
04	진단	
05	규제	
06	즉시	
07	구체화하다	
08	용어	
09	소유	
10	유지하다	
11	명료하다	
12	버리다	
13	시각의	
14	~에 적응하다	
15	똑바른	
16	뒤집다	
17	이점	
18	추구하다	
19	견디다	
20	관계없는	

▶ A-D 정답 : 해설편 163쪽

TEST C-D 각 단어의 뜻을 골라 기호를 쓰시오.

C	English		Korean
01	decrease	( )	ⓐ 동등하게
02	spectacularly	( )	ⓑ 결정적으로
03	equally	( )	ⓒ 합하다
04	indeed	( )	ⓓ 가리키다
05	alter	( )	ⓔ 쇠하다, 부패하다
06	modify	( )	ⓕ 진정
07	neglect	( )	ⓖ 중복된
08	compensate	( )	ⓗ 고정관념
09	overlapping	( )	ⓘ 빈도
10	encounter	( )	ⓙ 접하다, 만나다
11	decay	( )	ⓚ 수정하다
12	frequency	( )	ⓛ 식별
13	disease	( )	ⓜ 감소하다
14	counteract	( )	ⓝ 보완하다
15	integrate	( )	ⓞ 대응하다
16	unite	( )	ⓟ 굉장히
17	recognition	( )	ⓠ 질병
18	indicate	( )	ⓡ 바꾸다
19	stereotype	( )	ⓢ 무시하다
20	crucially	( )	ⓣ 통합하다

D	Korean		English
01	기본의	( )	ⓐ probability
02	조상	( )	ⓑ diverse
03	개연성	( )	ⓒ elementary
04	~향하여	( )	ⓓ reveal
05	이동, 이송	( )	ⓔ towards
06	고백하다	( )	ⓕ decide
07	다양한	( )	ⓖ confess
08	가정의, 가상의	( )	ⓗ surrounded
09	완료하다	( )	ⓘ opportunity
10	기회	( )	ⓙ fuel
11	둘러싸인	( )	ⓚ probably
12	자극	( )	ⓛ hypothetical
13	연료	( )	ⓜ excitation
14	아마도	( )	ⓝ ancestor
15	강화하다	( )	ⓞ enhance
16	시대	( )	ⓟ complete
17	두드러진, 놀라운, 주목할 만한	( )	ⓠ transferring
18	드러내다	( )	ⓡ era
19	결심하다	( )	ⓢ insecurity
20	불안	( )	ⓣ remarkable

※ 영어 [독해] 파트만 수록한 문제지이므로 18번부터 시작합니다.

● 점수 표시가 없는 문항은 모두 2점 ● 문항수 28개 | 배점 63점 | 제한 시간 45분

18. 다음 글의 목적으로 가장 적절한 것은?

Dear Mr. Krull,

I have greatly enjoyed working at Trincom Enterprises as a sales manager. Since I joined in 2015, I have been a loyal and essential member of this company, and have developed innovative ways to contribute to the company. Moreover, in the last year alone, I have brought in two new major clients to the company, increasing the company's total sales by 5%. Also, I have voluntarily trained 5 new members of staff, totaling 35 hours. I would therefore request your consideration in raising my salary, which I believe reflects my performance as well as the industry average. I look forward to speaking with you soon.

Kimberly Morss

① 부서 이동을 신청하려고
② 급여 인상을 요청하려고
③ 근무 시간 조정을 요구하려고
④ 기업 혁신 방안을 제안하려고
⑤ 신입 사원 연수에 대해 문의하려고

19. 다음 글에 드러난 'I'의 심경 변화로 가장 적절한 것은?

On one beautiful spring day, I was fully enjoying my day off. I arrived at the nail salon, and muted my cellphone so that I would be disconnected for the hour and feel calm and peaceful. I was so comfortable while I got a manicure. As I left the place, I checked my cellphone and saw four missed calls from a strange number. I knew immediately that something bad was coming, and I called back. A young woman answered and said that my father had fallen over a stone and was injured, now seated on a bench. I was really concerned since he had just recovered from his knee surgery. I rushed getting into my car to go see him.

① nervous → confident
② relaxed → worried
③ excited → indifferent
④ pleased → jealous
⑤ annoyed → grateful

20. 다음 글에서 필자가 주장하는 바로 가장 적절한 것은?

You already have a business and you're about to launch your blog so that you can sell your product. Unfortunately, here is where a 'business mind' can be a bad thing. Most people believe that to have a successful business blog promoting a product, they have to stay strictly 'on the topic.' If all you're doing is shamelessly promoting your product, then who is going to want to read the latest thing you're writing about? Instead, you need to give some useful or entertaining information away for free so that people have a reason to keep coming back. Only by doing this can you create an interested audience that you will then be able to sell to. So, the best way to be successful with a business blog is to write about things that your audience will be interested in.

① 인터넷 게시물에 대한 윤리적 기준을 세워야 한다.
② 블로그를 전문적으로 관리할 인력을 마련해야 한다.
③ 신제품 개발을 위해 상업용 블로그를 적극 활용해야 한다.
④ 상품에 대한 고객들의 반응을 정기적으로 분석할 필요가 있다.
⑤ 상업용 블로그는 사람들이 흥미 있어 할 정보를 제공해야 한다.

21. 밑줄 친 challenge this sacred cow가 다음 글에서 의미하는 바로 가장 적절한 것은? [3점]

Our language helps to reveal our deeper assumptions. Think of these revealing phrases: When we accomplish something important, we say it took "blood, sweat, and tears." We say important achievements are "hard-earned." We recommend a "hard day's work" when "day's work" would be enough. When we talk of "easy money," we are implying it was obtained through illegal or questionable means. We use the phrase "That's easy for you to say" as a criticism, usually when we are seeking to invalidate someone's opinion. It's like we all automatically accept that the "right" way is, inevitably, the harder one. In my experience this is hardly ever questioned. What would happen if you do challenge this sacred cow? We don't even pause to consider that something important and valuable could be made easy. What if the biggest thing keeping us from doing what matters is the false assumption that it has to take huge effort?

* invalidate: 틀렸음을 입증하다

① resist the tendency to avoid any hardship
② escape from the pressure of using formal language
③ doubt the solid belief that only hard work is worthy
④ abandon the old notion that money always comes first
⑤ break the superstition that holy animals bring good luck

22. 다음 글의 요지로 가장 적절한 것은?

The old saying is that "knowledge is power," but when it comes to scary, threatening news, research suggests the exact opposite. Frightening news can actually rob people of their inner sense of control, making them less likely to take care of themselves and other people. Public health research shows that when the news presents health-related information in a pessimistic way, people are actually less likely to take steps to protect themselves from illness as a result. A news article that's intended to warn people about increasing cancer rates, for example, can result in fewer people choosing to get screened for the disease because they're so terrified of what they might find. This is also true for issues such as climate change. When a news story is all doom and gloom, people feel depressed and become less interested in taking small, personal steps to fight ecological collapse.

① 두려움을 주는 뉴스는 사람들이 문제에 덜 대처하게 할 수 있다.
② 정보를 전달하는 시기에 따라 뉴스의 영향력이 달라질 수 있다.
③ 지속적인 환경 문제 보도가 사람들의 인식 변화를 가져온다.
④ 정보 제공의 지연은 정확한 문제 인식에 방해가 될 수 있다.
⑤ 출처가 불분명한 건강 정보는 사람들에게 유익하지 않다.

23. 다음 글의 주제로 가장 적절한 것은?

The most remarkable and unbelievable consequence of melting ice and rising seas is that together they are a kind of time machine, so real that they are altering the duration of our day. It works like this: As the glaciers melt and the seas rise, gravity forces more water toward the equator. This changes the shape of the Earth ever so slightly, making it fatter around the middle, which in turns slows the rotation of the planet similarly to the way a ballet dancer slows her spin by spreading out her arms. The slowdown isn't much, just a few thousandths of a second each year, but like the barely noticeable jump of rising seas every year, it adds up. When dinosaurs lived on the Earth, a day lasted only about twenty-three hours.

① cause of rising temperatures on the Earth
② principles of planets maintaining their shapes
③ implications of melting ice on marine biodiversity
④ way to keep track of time without using any device
⑤ impact of melting ice and rising seas on the length of a day

24. 다음 글의 제목으로 가장 적절한 것은?

Have you ever brought up an idea or suggestion to someone and heard them immediately say "No, that won't work."? You may have thought, "He/she didn't even give it a chance. How do they know it won't work?" When you are right about something, you close off the possibility of another viewpoint or opportunity. Being right about something means that "it is the way it is, period." You may be correct. Your particular way of seeing it may be true with the facts. However, considering the other option or the other person's point of view can be beneficial. If you see their side, you will see something new or, at worse, learn something about how the other person looks at life. Why would you think everyone sees and experiences life the way you do? Besides how boring that would be, it would eliminate all new opportunities, ideas, invention, and creativity.

① The Value of Being Honest
② Filter Out Negative Points of View
③ Keeping Your Word: A Road to Success
④ Being Right Can Block New Possibilities
⑤ Look Back When Everyone Looks Forward

25. 다음 도표의 내용과 일치하지 <u>않는</u> 것은?

Reasons for People Interested in Eating Less Meat and Non-meat Eaters in the UK (2018)

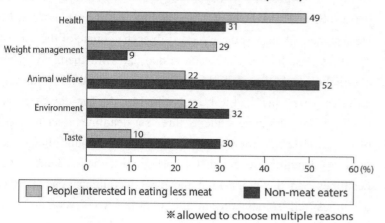

	People interested in eating less meat	Non-meat eaters
Health	49	31
Weight management	29	9
Animal welfare	22	52
Environment	22	32
Taste	10	30

※ allowed to choose multiple reasons

The graph above shows the survey results on reasons for people interested in eating less meat and those eating no meat in the UK in 2018. ① For the group of people who are interested in eating less meat, health is the strongest motivator for doing so. ② For the group of non-meat eaters, animal welfare accounts for the largest percentage among all reasons, followed by environment, health, and taste. ③ The largest percentage point difference between the two groups is in animal welfare, whereas the smallest difference is in environment. ④ The percentage of non-meat eaters citing taste is four times higher than that of people interested in reducing their meat consumption citing taste. ⑤ Weight management ranks the lowest for people who don't eat meat, with less than 10 percent.

26. Margaret Knight에 관한 다음 글의 내용과 일치하지 <u>않는</u> 것은?

Margaret Knight was an exceptionally prolific inventor in the late 19th century; journalists occasionally compared her to Thomas Edison by nicknaming her "a woman Edison." From a young age, she built toys for her older brothers. After her father died, Knight's family moved to Manchester. Knight left school in 1850, at age 12, to earn money for her family at a nearby textile factory, where she witnessed a fellow worker injured by faulty equipment. That led her to create her first invention, a safety device for textile equipment, but she never earned money from the invention. She also invented a machine that cut, folded and glued flat-bottomed paper bags and was awarded her first patent in 1871 for it. It eliminated the need for workers to assemble them slowly by hand. Knight received 27 patents in her lifetime and entered the National Inventors Hall of Fame in 2006.

*prolific: 다작(多作)의   ** patent: 특허

① 기자들이 '여자 Edison'이라는 별명을 지어 주었다.
② 가족을 위해 돈을 벌려고 학교를 그만두었다.
③ 직물 장비에 쓰이는 안전장치를 발명하여 많은 돈을 벌었다.
④ 밑이 평평한 종이 가방을 자르고 접고 붙이는 기계를 발명했다.
⑤ 2006년에 국립 발명가 명예의 전당에 입성했다.

27. E-Waste Recycling Day에 관한 다음 안내문의 내용과 일치하지 <u>않는</u> 것은?

E-Waste Recycling Day

E-Waste Recycling Day is an annual event in our city. Bring your used electronics such as cell phones, tablets, and laptops to recycle. Go green!

When
Saturday, December 17, 2022
8:00 a.m. – 11:00 a.m.

Where
Lincoln Sports Center

Notes
- Items NOT accepted: light bulbs, batteries, and microwaves
- All personal data on the devices must be wiped out in advance.
- This event is free but open only to local residents.

Please contact us at 986–571–0204 for more information.

① 3시간 동안 진행된다.
② Lincoln 스포츠 센터에서 열린다.
③ 전자레인지는 허용되지 않는 품목이다.
④ 기기 속 모든 개인 정보는 미리 삭제되어야 한다.
⑤ 거주 지역에 상관없이 참가할 수 있다.

28. Undersea Walking Activity에 관한 다음 안내문의 내용과 일치하는 것은?

Undersea Walking Activity

Enjoy a fascinating underwater walk on the ocean floor. Witness wonderful marine life on foot!

Age Requirement
10 years or older

Operating Hours
from Tuesday to Sunday
9:00 a.m. – 4:00 p.m.

Price
$30 (insurance fee included)

What to Bring
swim suit and towel

Notes
- Experienced lifeguards accompany you throughout the activity.
- With a special underwater helmet, you can wear glasses during the activity.
- Reservations can be made on-site or online at www.seawalkwonder.com.

① 연중무휴로 운영된다.
② 가격에 보험료는 포함되어 있지 않다.
③ 숙련된 안전 요원이 활동 내내 동행한다.
④ 특수 수중 헬멧 착용 시 안경을 쓸 수 없다.
⑤ 현장 예약은 불가능하다.

29. 다음 글의 밑줄 친 부분 중, 어법상 틀린 것은? [3점]

You may have seen headlines in the news about some of the things machines powered by artificial intelligence can do. However, if you were to consider all the tasks ① that AI-powered machines could actually perform, it would be quite mind-blowing! One of the key features of artificial intelligence ② is that it enables machines to learn new things, rather than requiring programming specific to new tasks. Therefore, the core difference between computers of the future and ③ those of the past is that future computers will be able to learn and self-improve. In the near future, smart virtual assistants will know more about you than your closest friends and family members ④ are. Can you imagine how that might change our lives? These kinds of changes are exactly why it is so important ⑤ to recognize the implications that new technologies will have for our world.

30. 다음 글의 밑줄 친 부분 중, 문맥상 낱말의 쓰임이 적절하지 않은 것은? [3점]

Plant growth is controlled by a group of hormones called auxins found at the tips of stems and roots of plants. Auxins produced at the tips of stems tend to accumulate on the side of the stem that is in the shade. Accordingly, the auxins ① stimulate growth on the shaded side of the plant. Therefore, the shaded side grows faster than the side facing the sunlight. This phenomenon causes the stem to bend and appear to be growing ② towards the light. Auxins have the ③ opposite effect on the roots of plants. Auxins in the tips of roots tend to limit growth. If a root is horizontal in the soil, the auxins will accumulate on the lower side and interfere with its development. Therefore, the lower side of the root will grow ④ faster than the upper side. This will, in turn, cause the root to bend ⑤ downwards, with the tip of the root growing in that direction.

[31~34] 다음 빈칸에 들어갈 말로 가장 적절한 것을 고르시오.

31. To demonstrate how best to defeat the habit of delaying, Dan Ariely, a professor of psychology and behavioral economics, performed an experiment on students in three of his classes at MIT. He assigned all classes three reports over the course of the semester. The first class had to choose three due dates for themselves, up to and including the last day of class. The second had no deadlines — all three papers just had to be submitted by the last day of class. In his third class, he gave students three set deadlines over the course of the semester. At the end of the semester, he found that students with set deadlines received the best grades, the students with no deadlines had the worst, and those who could choose their own deadlines fell somewhere in the middle. Ariely concludes that _____ — whether by the professor or by students who recognize their own tendencies to delay things — improves self-control and performance.

① offering rewards
② removing obstacles
③ restricting freedom
④ increasing assignments
⑤ encouraging competition

32. The best way in which innovation changes our lives is by _____. The main theme of human history is that we become steadily more specialized in what we produce, and steadily more diversified in what we consume: we move away from unstable self-sufficiency to safer mutual interdependence. By concentrating on serving other people's needs for forty hours a week — which we call a job — you can spend the other seventy-two hours (not counting fifty-six hours in bed) relying on the services provided to you by other people. Innovation has made it possible to work for a fraction of a second in order to be able to afford to turn on an electric lamp for an hour, providing the quantity of light that would have required a whole day's work if you had to make it yourself by collecting and refining sesame oil or lamb fat to burn in a simple lamp, as much of humanity did in the not so distant past. [3점]

* a fraction of a second: 아주 짧은 시간 ** refine: 정제하다

① respecting the values of the old days
② enabling people to work for each other
③ providing opportunities to think creatively
④ satisfying customers with personalized services
⑤ introducing and commercializing unusual products

33. If you've ever made a poor choice, you might be interested in learning how to break that habit. One great way to trick your brain into doing so is to sign a "Ulysses Contract." The name of this life tip comes from the Greek myth about Ulysses, a captain whose ship sailed past the island of the Sirens, a tribe of dangerous women who lured victims to their death with their irresistible songs. Knowing that he would otherwise be unable to resist, Ulysses instructed his crew to stuff their ears with cotton and tie him to the ship's mast to prevent him from turning their ship towards the Sirens. It worked for him and you can do the same thing by _____.
For example, if you want to stay off your cellphone and concentrate on your work, delete the apps that distract you or ask a friend to change your password!

* lure: 유혹하다 ** mast: 돛대

① letting go of all-or-nothing mindset
② finding reasons why you want to change
③ locking yourself out of your temptations
④ building a plan and tracking your progress
⑤ focusing on breaking one bad habit at a time

34. Our homes aren't just ecosystems, they're unique ones, hosting species that are adapted to indoor environments and pushing evolution in new directions. Indoor microbes, insects, and rats have all evolved the ability to survive our chemical attacks, developing resistance to antibacterials, insecticides, and poisons. German cockroaches are known to have developed a distaste for glucose, which is commonly used as bait in roach traps. Some indoor insects, which have fewer opportunities to feed than their outdoor counterparts, seem to have developed the ability to survive when food is limited. Dunn and other ecologists have suggested that as the planet becomes more developed and more urban, more species will _____. Over a long enough time period, indoor living could drive our evolution, too. Perhaps my indoorsy self represents the future of humanity.

[3점]

* glucose: 포도당 ** bait: 미끼

① produce chemicals to protect themselves
② become extinct with the destroyed habitats
③ evolve the traits they need to thrive indoors
④ compete with outside organisms to find their prey
⑤ break the boundaries between wildlife and humans

35. 다음 글에서 전체 흐름과 관계 없는 문장은?

Developing a personal engagement with poetry brings a number of benefits to you as an individual, in both a personal and a professional capacity. ① Writing poetry has been shown to have physical and mental benefits, with expressive writing found to improve immune system and lung function, diminish psychological distress, and enhance relationships. ② Poetry has long been used to aid different mental health needs, develop empathy, and reconsider our relationship with both natural and built environments. ③ Poetry is also an incredibly effective way of actively targeting the cognitive development period, improving your productivity and scientific creativity in the process. ④ Poetry is considered to be an easy and useful means of expressing emotions, but you fall into frustration when you realize its complexity. ⑤ In short, poetry has a lot to offer, if you give it the opportunity to do so.

* cognitive: 인지적인

[36~37] 주어진 글 다음에 이어질 글의 순서로 가장 적절한 것을 고르시오.

36.

Things are changing. It has been reported that 42 percent of jobs in Canada are at risk, and 62 percent of jobs in America will be in danger due to advances in automation.

(A) However, what's difficult to automate is the ability to creatively solve problems. Whereas workers in "doing" roles can be replaced by robots, the role of creatively solving problems is more dependent on an irreplaceable individual.

(B) You might say that the numbers seem a bit unrealistic, but the threat is real. One fast food franchise has a robot that can flip a burger in ten seconds. It is just a simple task but the robot could replace an entire crew.

(C) Highly skilled jobs are also at risk. A supercomputer, for instance, can suggest available treatments for specific illnesses in an automated way, drawing on the body of medical research and data on diseases.

① (A) − (C) − (B)　　② (B) − (A) − (C)
③ (B) − (C) − (A)　　④ (C) − (A) − (B)
⑤ (C) − (B) − (A)

17회

37.

Each beech tree grows in a particular location and soil conditions can vary greatly in just a few yards. The soil can have a great deal of water or almost no water. It can be full of nutrients or not.

(A) This is taking place underground through the roots. Whoever has an abundance of sugar hands some over; whoever is running short gets help. Their network acts as a system to make sure that no trees fall too far behind.

(B) However, the rate is the same. Whether they are thick or thin, all the trees of the same species are using light to produce the same amount of sugar per leaf. Some trees have plenty of sugar and some have less, but the trees equalize this difference between them by transferring sugar.

(C) Accordingly, each tree grows more quickly or more slowly and produces more or less sugar, and thus you would expect every tree to be photosynthesizing at a different rate. [3점]

* photosynthesize: 광합성하다

① (A) − (C) − (B)   ② (B) − (A) − (C)
③ (B) − (C) − (A)   ④ (C) − (A) − (B)
⑤ (C) − (B) − (A)

[38~39] 글의 흐름으로 보아, 주어진 문장이 들어가기에 가장 적절한 곳을 고르시오.

38.

Nevertheless, language is enormously important in human life and contributes largely to our ability to cooperate with each other in dealing with the world.

Should we use language to understand mind or mind to understand language? (①) Analytic philosophy historically assumes that language is basic and that mind would make sense if proper use of language was appreciated. (②) Modern cognitive science, however, rightly judges that language is just one aspect of mind of great importance in human beings but not fundamental to all kinds of thinking. (③) Countless species of animals manage to navigate the world, solve problems, and learn without using language, through brain mechanisms that are largely preserved in the minds of humans. (④) There is no reason to assume that language is fundamental to mental operations. (⑤) Our species *homo sapiens* has been astonishingly successful, which depended in part on language, first as an effective contributor to collaborative problem solving and much later, as collective memory through written records. [3점]

* appreciate: (제대로) 인식하다

39.

If we could magically remove the glasses, we would find the two water bodies would not mix well.

Take two glasses of water. Put a little bit of orange juice into one and a little bit of lemon juice into the other. (①)What you have are essentially two glasses of water but with a completely different chemical makeup. (②) If we take the glass containing orange juice and heat it, we will still have two different glasses of water with different chemical makeups, but now they will also have different temperatures. (③) Perhaps they would mix a little where they met; however, they would remain separate because of their different chemical makeups and temperatures. (④) The warmer water would float on the surface of the cold water because of its lighter weight. (⑤) In the ocean we have bodies of water that differ in temperature and salt content; for this reason, they do not mix.

40. 다음 글의 내용을 한 문장으로 요약하고자 한다. 빈칸 (A), (B)에 들어갈 말로 가장 적절한 것은?

One of the most powerful tools to find meaning in our lives is reflective journaling — thinking back on and writing about what has happened to us. In the 1990s, Stanford University researchers asked undergraduate students on spring break to journal about their most important personal values and their daily activities; others were asked to write about only the good things that happened to them in the day. Three weeks later, the students who had written about their values were happier, healthier, and more confident about their ability to handle stress than the ones who had only focused on the good stuff. By reflecting on how their daily activities supported their values, students had gained a new perspective on those activities and choices. Little stresses and hassles were now demonstrations of their values in action. Suddenly, their lives were full of meaningful activities. And all they had to do was reflect and write about it — positively reframing their experiences with their personal values.

* hassle: 귀찮은 일

↓

Journaling about daily activities based on what we believe to be ___(A)___ can make us feel that our life is meaningful by ___(B)___ our experiences in a new way.

    (A)   (B)   (A)   (B)
① factual   ······ rethinking   ② worthwhile ······ rethinking
③ outdated   ······ generalizing   ④ objective   ······ generalizing
⑤ demanding ······ describing

[41~42] 다음 글을 읽고, 물음에 답하시오.

Mike May lost his sight at the age of three. Because he had spent the majority of his life adapting to being blind — and even cultivating a skiing career in this state — his other senses compensated by growing (a) <u>stronger</u>. However, when his sight was restored through a surgery in his forties, his entire perception of reality was (b) <u>disrupted</u>. Instead of being thrilled that he could see now, as he'd expected, his brain was so overloaded with new visual stimuli that the world became a frightening and overwhelming place. After he'd learned to know his family through touch and smell, he found that he couldn't recognize his children with his eyes, and this left him puzzled. Skiing also became a lot harder as he struggled to adapt to the visual stimulation.

This (c) <u>confusion</u> occurred because his brain hadn't yet learned to see. Though we often tend to assume our eyes function as video cameras which relay information to our brain, advances in neuroscientific research have proven that this is actually not the case. Instead, sight is a collaborative effort between our eyes and our brains, and the way we process (d) <u>visual</u> reality depends on the way these two communicate. If communication between our eyes and our brains is disturbed, our perception of reality is altered accordingly. And because other areas of May's brain had adapted to process information primarily through his other senses, the process of learning how to see was (e) <u>easier</u> than he'd anticipated.

41. 윗글의 제목으로 가장 적절한 것은?

① Eyes and Brain Working Together for Sight
② Visualization: A Useful Tool for Learning
③ Collaboration Between Vision and Sound
④ How to Ignore New Visual Stimuli
⑤ You See What You Believe

42. 밑줄 친 (a)~(e) 중에서 문맥상 낱말의 쓰임이 적절하지 <u>않은</u> 것은?

① (a)   ② (b)   ③ (c)   ④ (d)   ⑤ (e)

[43~45] 다음 글을 읽고, 물음에 답하시오.

(A)

On my daughter Marie's 8th birthday, she received a bunch of presents from her friends at school. That evening, with her favorite present, a teddy bear, in her arms, we went to a restaurant to celebrate her birthday. Our server, a friendly woman, noticed my daughter holding the teddy bear and said, "My daughter loves teddy bears, too." Then, we started chatting about (a) <u>her</u> family.

(B)

When Marie came back out, I asked her what she had been doing. She said that she gave her teddy bear to our server so that she could give it to (b) <u>her</u> daughter. I was surprised at her sudden action because I could see how much she loved that bear already. (c) <u>She</u> must have seen the look on my face, because she said, "I can't imagine being stuck in a hospital bed. I just want her to get better soon."

(C)

I felt moved by Marie's words as we walked toward the car. Then, our server ran out to our car and thanked Marie for her generosity. The server said that (d) <u>she</u> had never had anyone doing anything like that for her family before. Later, Marie said it was her best birthday ever. I was so proud of her empathy and warmth, and this was an unforgettable experience for our family.

(D)

The server mentioned during the conversation that her daughter was in the hospital with a broken leg. (e) <u>She</u> also said that Marie looked about the same age as her daughter. She was so kind and attentive all evening, and even gave Marie cookies for free. After we finished our meal, we paid the bill and began to walk to our car when unexpectedly Marie asked me to wait and ran back into the restaurant.

43. 주어진 글 (A)에 이어질 내용을 순서에 맞게 배열한 것으로 가장 적절한 것은?

① (B) − (D) − (C)   ② (C) − (B) − (D)
③ (C) − (D) − (B)   ④ (D) − (B) − (C)
⑤ (D) − (C) − (B)

44. 밑줄 친 (a)~(e) 중에서 가리키는 대상이 나머지 넷과 <u>다른</u> 것은?

① (a)   ② (b)   ③ (c)   ④ (d)   ⑤ (e)

45. 윗글에 관한 내용으로 적절하지 <u>않은</u> 것은?

① Marie는 테디 베어를 팔에 안고 식당에 갔다.
② 'I'는 Marie의 갑작스러운 행동에 놀랐다.
③ 종업원은 Marie의 관대함에 고마워했다.
④ 종업원은 자신의 딸이 팔이 부러져서 병원에 있다고 말했다.
⑤ 종업원은 Marie에게 쿠키를 무료로 주었다.

* 확인 사항
o 답안지의 해당란에 필요한 내용을 정확히 기입(표기)했는지 확인하시오.

17회

18

001 enterprise ⓝ 기업
002 sales manager 영업 매니저
003 loyal ⓐ 충성스러운
004 essential ⓐ 핵심적인, 필수적인
005 innovative ⓐ 혁신적인
006 bring in ~을 데려오다
007 major ⓐ 주요한
008 increase ⓥ 증가시키다
009 voluntarily ⓐ 자원해서
010 request ⓥ 요청하다
011 raise ⓥ 올리다, 높이다
012 reflect ⓥ 반영하다

19

013 day off 휴가
014 naill salon 네일 숍
015 mute ⓥ 음소거하다
016 disconnected ⓐ 단절된
017 calm ⓐ 차분한
018 comfortable ⓐ 편안한
019 missed call 부재중 전화
020 immediately ⓐⓓ 즉시
021 call back 전화를 회신하다
022 fall over ~에 걸려 넘어지다
023 concerned ⓐ 걱정되는
024 recover from ~로부터 회복하다
025 surgery ⓝ 수술
026 rush ⓥ 서두르다
027 nervous ⓐ 긴장한
028 relaxed ⓐ 느긋한, 여유로운
029 indifferent ⓐ 무관심한
030 jealous ⓐ 질투하는
031 annoyed ⓐ 짜증 난
032 grateful ⓐ 고마워하는

20

033 be about to 막 ~하려는 참이다
034 launch ⓥ 시작하다, 출시하다
035 unfortunately ⓐⓓ 안타깝게도
036 promote ⓥ 홍보하다
037 strictly ⓐⓓ 엄격하게
038 shamelessly ⓐⓓ 뻔뻔하게
039 latest ⓐ 최신의
040 give away 공짜로 주다, 거저 주다
041 useful ⓐ 유용한
042 entertaining ⓐ 재미있는
043 interested ⓐ 흥미를 느끼는
044 audience ⓝ 청중, 독자
045 successful ⓐ 성공적인

21

046 reveal ⓥ 드러내다
047 assumption ⓝ 가정, 추정
048 phrase ⓝ 구절
049 sweat ⓝ 땀
050 achievement ⓝ 성취, 성과
051 hard-earned ⓐ 힘들게 얻은
052 recommend ⓥ 권하다, 추천하다
053 obtain ⓥ 얻다, 획득하다
054 imply ⓥ 암시하다
055 illegal ⓐ 불법적인

056 questionable ⓐ 의심스러운
057 means ⓝ 수단
058 criticism ⓝ 비판
059 seek to ~하려고 추구하다
060 invalidate ⓥ 틀렸음을 입증하다
061 automatically ⓐⓓ 저절로
062 inevitably ⓐⓓ 불가피하게, 필연적으로
063 hardly ⓐⓓ 거의 ~않다
064 challenge ⓥ 도전하다, 이의를 제기하다
065 sacred ⓐ 성스러운
066 pause ⓥ 잠시 멈추다
067 valuable ⓐ 가치로운
068 huge ⓐ 거대한
069 hardship ⓝ 고난, 난관, 어려움
070 formal ⓐ 공식적인
071 doubt ⓥ 의심하다
072 solid ⓐ 확고한
073 abandon ⓥ 버리다
074 notion ⓝ 관념
075 superstition ⓝ 미신

22

076 when it comes to ~에 관해서
077 threatening ⓐ 겁을 주는
078 exact opposite 정반대
079 rob A of B A에게서 B를 빼앗다
080 sense of control 통제력
081 public health 공공 보건
082 present ⓥ 제시하다
083 pessimistic ⓐ 염세적인, 비관적인
084 take steps to ~하기 위해 조치를 취하다
085 illness ⓝ 질병
086 as a result 결과적으로
087 article ⓝ 기사
088 be intended to ~할 의도이다
089 warn ⓥ 경고하다
090 cancer ⓝ 암
091 rate ⓝ 비율
092 screen ⓥ (어떤 질병이 있는지) 검진하다
093 terrified ⓐ 겁에 질린
094 doom ⓝ 불운, 파멸
095 gloom ⓝ 우울, 어둠
096 collapse ⓝ 붕괴 ⓥ 쓰러지다

23

097 remarkable ⓐ 현저한, 두드러지는
098 consequence ⓝ 결과, 영향
099 melt ⓥ 녹다
100 alter ⓥ 바꾸다
101 duration ⓝ 지속 시간
102 glacier ⓝ 빙하
103 gravity ⓝ 중력
104 force ⓥ 강제하다
105 equator ⓝ 적도
106 slightly ⓐⓓ 약간
107 rotation ⓝ 회전
108 spin ⓝ 회전
109 spread out 벌리다, 펴지다
110 slowdown ⓝ 둔화, 지연
111 barely ⓐⓓ 거의 ~않다, 가까스로
112 noticeable ⓐ 분명한, 뚜렷한
113 add up 쌓이다, 축적되다

114 last ⓥ 지속되다
115 principle ⓝ 원리
116 implication ⓝ 영향
117 biodiversity ⓝ 생물 다양성
118 keep track of ~을 추적하다

24

119 bring up (화제를) 꺼내다, (아이디어를) 내놓다
120 suggestion ⓝ 제안
121 give a chance 기회를 주다
122 close off 차단하다
123 possibility ⓝ 가능성
124 viewpoint ⓝ 관점, 견해
125 period ⓐⓓ (문장 끝에서) 끝, 이상이다, 더 말하지 마라
126 particular ⓐ 특정한
127 beneficial ⓐ 이로운
128 at worse 최소한, 적어도
129 besides ⓟⓡⓔⓟ ~을 제외하더라도, ~외에도 ⓐⓓ 게다가
130 eliminate ⓥ 제거하다
131 invention ⓝ 발명
132 filter out ~을 걸러내다, 여과하다
133 keep one's word 약속을 지키다
134 block ⓥ 차단하다
135 look back 뒤돌아보다

25

136 survey ⓝ 설문 조사
137 reason ⓝ 이유
138 meat ⓝ 고기
139 motivator ⓝ 동기 요인
140 welfare ⓝ 복지
141 account for ~을 차지하다
142 among ⓟⓡⓔⓟ ~ 중에서
143 followed by ~이 뒤를 잇다
144 environment ⓝ 환경
145 whereas ⓒⓞⓝⓙ ~한 반면에
146 cite ⓥ 언급하다, 인용하다
147 reduce ⓥ 줄이다
148 consumption ⓝ 소비
149 weight ⓝ 체중, 무게
150 rank ⓥ 순위가 ~이다

26

151 exceptionally ⓐⓓ 이례적으로, 특출나게
152 prolific ⓐ 다작의
153 inventor ⓝ 발명가
154 journalist ⓝ 기자
155 occasionally ⓐⓓ 가끔, 때때로
156 compare A to B A를 B와 비교하다, 견주다
157 nickname ⓥ 별명 짓다
158 leave school 학교를 그만두다
159 earn ⓥ 벌다
160 nearby ⓐ 근처의
161 witness ⓥ 목격하다
162 fellow ⓝ 동료
163 faulty ⓐ 결함이 있는
164 fold ⓥ 접다
165 glue ⓥ 접착하다

166 flat-bottomed ⓐ 밑이 평평한
167 award ⓥ 수여하다, 주다
168 patent ⓝ 특허
169 assemble ⓥ 조립하다
170 hall of fame 명예의 전당

27

171 e-waste ⓝ 전자 쓰레기
172 recycling ⓝ 재활용
173 laptop ⓝ 노트북 컴퓨터
174 green ⓐ 친환경적인
175 accept ⓥ 수용하다, 접수하다, 받다
176 microwave ⓝ 전자레인지
177 wipe out 지우다, 쓸어내다
178 in advance 미리
179 open to ~에게 개방되는
180 local resident 지역 주민

28

181 undersea ⓐ 해저의
182 fascinating ⓐ 매혹적인
183 ocean floor 해저
184 marine ⓐ 해양의
185 on foot 도보로
186 requirement ⓝ 필수 요건
187 operating hour 운영 시간
188 insurance fee 보험료
189 experienced ⓐ 숙련된
190 lifeguard ⓝ 안전 요원
191 accompany ⓥ 동행하다
192 throughout ⓟⓡⓔⓟ ~ 내내
193 on-site ⓐⓓ 현장에서 ⓐ 현장의

29

194 artificial intelligence 인공 지능
195 task ⓝ 과업, 일
196 perform ⓥ 수행하다
197 mind-blowing ⓐ 너무도 감동적인
198 feature ⓝ 특징
199 enable ⓥ ~이 …할 수 있게 하다
200 core ⓐ 핵심적인
201 self-improve ⓥ 자가 발전하다
202 virtual ⓐ 가상의
203 assistant ⓝ 조수, 비서
204 close ⓐ 친밀한, 가까운
205 exactly ⓐⓓ 바로, 정확히
206 recognize ⓥ 인식하다, 깨닫다

30

207 tip ⓝ 끝부분
208 stem ⓝ 줄기
209 accumulate ⓥ 축적되다, 쌓이다
210 accordingly ⓐⓓ 따라서
211 stimulate ⓥ 자극하다, 촉진하다
212 face ⓥ ~을 면하다, 마주보다
213 phenomenon ⓝ 현상
214 bend ⓥ 구부러지다
215 limit ⓥ 제한하다
216 horizontal ⓐ 수평적인
217 interfere with ~을 방해하다
218 in turn 한편, 결국, 차례로
219 downward(s) ⓐⓓ 아래로

31

220	demonstrate	ⓥ 입증하다
221	defeat	ⓥ 무너뜨리다, 패배시키다
222	behavioral	ⓐ 행동의
223	experiment	ⓝ 실험 ⓥ 실험하다
224	assign	ⓥ 할당하다
225	due date	마감일
226	for oneself	스스로
227	up to and including	~까지 포함해서
228	submit	ⓥ 제출하다
229	set	ⓐ 정해진
230	at the end of	~의 끝에
231	receive	ⓥ 받다
232	in the middle	중간에
233	tendency	ⓝ 경향, 성향
234	self-control	ⓝ 자기 통제
235	obstacle	ⓝ 장애물
236	restrict	ⓥ 제한하다

32

237	innovation	ⓝ 혁신
238	steadily	ⓐⓓ 꾸준히
239	specialize	ⓥ 전문화하다
240	diversify	ⓥ 다양화하다
241	consume	ⓥ 소비하다, 먹다, 마시다
242	unstable	ⓐ 불안정한
243	self-sufficiency	ⓝ 자급자족
244	mutual	ⓐ 상호의
245	interdependence	ⓝ 상호 의존성
246	concentrate on	~에 집중하다
247	serve one's needs	~의 필요를 충족하다, ~에게 도움이 되다
248	rely on	~에 의존하다
249	a fraction of a second	아주 짧은 시간
250	afford	ⓥ ~할 여유가 있다
251	turn on	~을 켜다
252	quantity	ⓝ 양
253	refine	ⓥ 정제하다
254	sesame oil	참기름
255	lamb	ⓝ (어린) 양
256	burn up	태우다
257	humanity	ⓝ 인류
258	distant	ⓐ 먼
259	satisfy	ⓥ 만족시키다, 충족하다
260	personalize	ⓥ 개인의 필요에 맞추다
261	commercialize	ⓥ 상업화하다

33

262	make a choice	선택하다
263	break a habit	습관을 깨다
264	trick A into B	A를 속여 B하게 하다
265	sign a contract	계약서에 서명하다
266	come from	~에서 기원하다
267	myth	ⓝ 신화
268	sail	ⓥ 항해하다
269	lure	ⓥ 유혹하다
270	irresistible	ⓐ 저항할 수 없는
271	resist	ⓥ 저항하다
272	instruct	ⓥ 지시하다, 가르치다
273	stuff	ⓥ (속을) 채우다, 막다
274	tie	ⓥ 묶다
275	mast	ⓝ 돛대

276	prevent	ⓥ 예방하다, 막다
277	distract	ⓥ 주의를 분산시키다, 산만하게 하다
278	let go of	~을 놔주다, 내려놓다
279	all-or-nothing	ⓐ 양자택일의, 이것 아니면 저것인
280	temptation	ⓝ 유혹

34

281	ecosystem	ⓝ 생태계
282	host	ⓥ (손님을) 접대하다, 수용하다, (행사를) 주최하다
283	adapt	ⓥ 적응시키다
284	indoor	ⓐ 실내의
285	microbe	ⓝ 미생물
286	resistance	ⓝ 내성, 저항력
287	antibacterial	ⓐ 항균성의 ⓝ 항균제
288	insecticide	ⓝ 살충제
289	cockroach	ⓝ 바퀴벌레
290	distaste	ⓝ 혐오
291	glucose	ⓝ 포도당
292	bait	ⓝ 미끼
293	counterpart	ⓝ 상대방, 대응물
294	ecologist	ⓝ 생태학자
295	urban	ⓐ 도시의, 도시적인
296	represent	ⓥ 표현하다, 나타내다
297	extinct	ⓐ 멸종한
298	habitat	ⓝ 서식지
299	prey	ⓝ 먹잇감

35

300	engagement	ⓝ 관계, 참여
301	poetry	ⓝ 시
302	individual	ⓝ 개인 ⓐ 개인의
303	capacity	ⓝ 능력, 역량
304	expressive	ⓐ 표현적인
305	immune system	면역 체계
306	lung	ⓝ 폐
307	diminish	ⓥ 줄이다, 감소시키다
308	distress	ⓝ 고통
309	enhance	ⓥ 향상시키다
310	aid	ⓥ 돕다, 원조하다
311	empathy	ⓝ 공감, 감정 이입
312	incredibly	ⓐⓓ 믿을 수 없을 정도로, 놀랍도록
313	cognitive	ⓐ 인지적인
314	productivity	ⓝ 생산성
315	frustration	ⓝ 좌절
316	complexity	ⓝ 복잡성

36

317	at risk	위험에 처한
318	due to	~로 인해
319	automation	ⓝ 자동화
320	automate	ⓥ 자동화하다
321	replace	ⓥ 대체하다
322	dependent on	~에 의존하는
323	irreplaceable	ⓐ 대체할 수 없는
324	unrealistic	ⓐ 비현실적인
325	threat	ⓝ 위협
326	flip	ⓥ 뒤집다
327	entire	ⓐ 전체의
328	crew	ⓝ (전체) 직원, 승무원

329	highly	ⓐⓓ 고도로, 매우
330	skilled	ⓐ 숙련된
331	available	ⓐ 이용 가능한
332	specific	ⓐ 특정한, 구체적인
333	draw on	~을 이용하다

37

334	beech tree	너도밤나무
335	vary	ⓥ 다르다
336	a great deal of	많은
337	nutrient	ⓝ 영양소
338	underground	ⓐⓓ 지하에서
339	abundance	ⓝ 풍부함
340	hand over	건네주다
341	run short	부족해지다
342	act as	~의 역할을 하다
343	fall behind	뒤처지다
344	leaf	ⓝ 이파리
345	plenty of	많은
346	equalize	ⓥ 동등하게 하다
347	transfer	ⓥ 전달하다
348	photosynthesize	ⓥ 광합성하다

38

349	enormously	ⓐⓓ 대단히, 거대하게
350	contribute to	~에 기여하다
351	cooperate with	~와 협력하다
352	deal with	~을 다루다, ~에 대처하다
353	analytic	ⓐ 분석적인
354	philosophy	ⓝ 철학
355	historically	ⓐⓓ 역사적으로
356	make sense	이치에 맞다
357	appreciate	ⓥ 제대로 인식하다
358	rightly	ⓐⓓ 마땅히
359	aspect	ⓝ 측면
360	fundamental	ⓐ 근본적인
361	countless	ⓐ 무수히 많은
362	navigate	ⓥ 항해하다
363	preserve	ⓥ 보존하다
364	operation	ⓝ 작용
365	astonishingly	ⓐⓓ 놀랍도록
366	in part	부분적으로
367	collaborative	ⓐ 협력적인
368	collective	ⓐ 집단적인

39

369	magically	ⓐⓓ 희한하게, 마법처럼
370	remove	ⓥ 제거하다
371	essentially	ⓐⓓ 본질적으로
372	completely	ⓐⓓ 완전히
373	makeup	ⓝ 구성
374	contain	ⓥ 포함하다
375	temperature	ⓝ 온도
376	separate	ⓐ 분리된
377	because of	~로 인해
378	float	ⓥ 뜨다
379	surface	ⓝ 표면
380	content	ⓝ 함량

40

381	reflective	ⓐ 성찰적인
382	journaling	ⓝ 일기 쓰기

383	think back on	~에 대해 되돌아보다
384	undergraduate	ⓐ 학부의
385	spring break	봄방학
386	daily activity	하루 활동, 일과
387	handle	ⓥ 대처하다, 다루다
388	focus on	~에 집중하다
389	support	ⓥ 뒷받침하다
390	perspective	ⓝ 관점, 시각
391	hassle	ⓝ 귀찮은 일
392	demonstration	ⓝ 입증, 시연
393	in action	활동 중인, 작용 중인
394	be full of	~로 가득하다
395	meaningful	ⓐ 유의미한
396	reframe	ⓥ 재구성하다
397	based on	~에 근거해
398	factual	ⓐ 사실적인
399	worthwhile	ⓐ 가치 있는
400	outdated	ⓐ 구식의
401	demanding	ⓐ 까다로운, 힘든

41~42

402	lose one's sight	시력을 잃다
403	majority	ⓝ 대다수, 대부분
404	cultivate	ⓥ 갈고 닦다, 배양하다
405	state	ⓝ 상태
406	compensate	ⓥ 보충하다, 보상하다
407	restore	ⓥ 회복하다, 복구하다
408	perception	ⓝ 인식, 지각
409	disrupt	ⓥ 지장을 주다, 방해하다
410	thrilled	ⓐ 황홀한, 전율을 느끼는
411	overloaded	ⓐ 과부하된
412	stimulus (pl. stimuli)	ⓝ 자극
413	frightening	ⓐ 겁을 주는, 두렵게 하는
414	overwhelming	ⓐ 버거운, 압도적인
415	puzzled	ⓐ 혼란스러운
416	struggle to	~하느라 고생하다
417	confusion	ⓝ 혼란
418	relay	ⓥ 전달하다
419	be not the case	사실이 아니다
420	primarily	ⓐⓓ 주로
421	anticipate	ⓥ 예상하다
422	visualization	ⓝ 시각화
423	ignore	ⓥ 무시하다

43~45

424	a bunch of	많은
425	present	ⓝ 선물
426	server	ⓝ 종업원
427	notice	ⓥ 알아차리다
428	chat about	~에 관해 이야기하다
429	so that	~하도록, ~하기 위해
430	surprised	ⓐ 놀란
431	sudden	ⓐ 갑작스러운
432	get well	(병 등이) 낫다
433	moved	ⓐ 감동한
434	walk toward	~ 쪽으로 걷다
435	generosity	ⓝ 관대함
436	unforgettable	ⓐ 잊을 수 없는
437	conversation	ⓝ 대화
438	attentive	ⓐ 주의 깊은, 세심한
439	pay the bill	값을 치르다
440	unexpectedly	ⓐⓓ 예기치 못하게

17회

TEST A-B 각 단어의 뜻을 [A] 영어는 우리말로, [B] 우리말은 영어로 쓰시오.

A	English	Korean
01	grateful	
02	launch	
03	witness	
04	accompany	
05	bend	
06	unstable	
07	beneficial	
08	irresistible	
09	prey	
10	empathy	
11	replace	
12	contribute to	
13	reflective	
14	get well	
15	barely	
16	criticism	
17	pessimistic	
18	in advance	
19	demonstrate	
20	equalize	

B	Korean	English
01	핵심적인, 필수적인	
02	~로부터 회복하다	
03	빙하	
04	~외에도, 게다가	
05	소비	
06	~할 여유가 있다	
07	생산성	
08	능력, 역량	
09	자극하다, 촉진하다	
10	이치에 맞다	
11	불법의	
12	홍보하다	
13	질투하는	
14	조립하다	
15	공짜로 주다, 거저 주다	
16	매혹적인	
17	할당하다	
18	신화	
19	대다수, 대부분	
20	서식지	

▶ A-D 정답 : 해설편 173쪽

TEST C-D 각 단어의 뜻을 골라 기호를 쓰시오.

C	English		Korean
01	voluntarily	( )	ⓐ 수술
02	inevitably	( )	ⓑ 최소한, 적어도
03	rob A of B	( )	ⓒ 인공지능
04	duration	( )	ⓓ 수평적인
05	at worse	( )	ⓔ 장애물
06	account for	( )	ⓕ 상호의
07	prolific	( )	ⓖ 주의를 분산시키다, 산만하게 하다
08	artificial intelligence	( )	ⓗ 멸종한
09	obstacle	( )	ⓘ 면역 체계
10	surgery	( )	ⓙ 보충하다, 보상하다
11	horizontal	( )	ⓚ ~을 차지하다
12	distract	( )	ⓛ 지속 시간
13	extinct	( )	ⓜ 다작한
14	immune system	( )	ⓝ 자원해서
15	abundance	( )	ⓞ 광합성하다
16	photosynthesize	( )	ⓟ 불가피하게, 필연적으로
17	makeup	( )	ⓠ A에게서 B를 빼앗다
18	compensate	( )	ⓡ ~를 다루다, ~에 대처하다
19	deal with	( )	ⓢ 풍부함
20	mutual	( )	ⓣ 구성

D	Korean		English
01	기업	( )	ⓐ take steps to
02	엄격하게	( )	ⓑ keep one's word
03	~하기 위해 조치를 취하다	( )	ⓒ virtual
04	생물 다양성	( )	ⓓ interfere with
05	언급하다, 인용하다	( )	ⓔ tendency
06	~을 방해하다	( )	ⓕ personalize
07	경향, 성향	( )	ⓖ resistance
08	주의 깊은, 세심한	( )	ⓗ cultivate
09	약속을 지키다	( )	ⓘ enterprise
10	개인의 필요에 맞추다	( )	ⓙ let go of
11	~을 놔주다, 내려놓다	( )	ⓚ enhance
12	내성, 저항력	( )	ⓛ run short
13	가상의	( )	ⓜ content
14	향상시키다	( )	ⓝ outdated
15	부족해지다	( )	ⓞ attentive
16	함량	( )	ⓟ perspective
17	구식의	( )	ⓠ biodiversity
18	갈고 닦다, 배양하다	( )	ⓡ strictly
19	관점, 시각	( )	ⓢ worthwhile
20	가치 있는	( )	ⓣ cite

※ 영어 [독해] 파트만 수록한 문제지이므로 18번부터 시작합니다.

● 점수 표시가 없는 문항은 모두 2점   ● 문항수 28개 | 배점 63점 | 제한 시간 45분

18. 다음 글의 목적으로 가장 적절한 것은?

> To the school librarian,
>
> I am Kyle Thomas, the president of the school's English writing club. I have planned activities that will increase the writing skills of our club members. One of the aims of these activities is to make us aware of various types of news media and the language used in printed newspaper articles. However, some old newspapers are not easy to access online. It is, therefore, my humble request to you to allow us to use old newspapers that have been stored in the school library. I would really appreciate it if you grant us permission.
>
> Yours truly,
> Kyle Thomas

① 도서관 이용 시간 연장을 건의하려고
② 신청한 도서의 대출 가능 여부를 문의하려고
③ 도서관에 보관 중인 자료 현황을 조사하려고
④ 글쓰기 동아리 신문의 도서관 비치를 부탁하려고
⑤ 도서관에 있는 오래된 신문의 사용 허락을 요청하려고

19. 다음 글에 드러난 "I"의 심경 변화로 가장 적절한 것은?

When my mom came home from the mall with a special present for me I was pretty sure I knew what it was. I was absolutely thrilled because I would soon communicate with a new cell phone! I was daydreaming about all of the cool apps and games I was going to download. But my mom smiled really big and handed me a book. I flipped through the pages, figuring that maybe she had hidden my new phone inside. But I slowly realized that my mom had not got me a phone and my present was just a little book, which was so different from what I had wanted.

① worried → furious
② surprised → relieved
③ ashamed → confident
④ anticipating → satisfied
⑤ excited → disappointed

20. 다음 글에서 필자가 주장하는 바로 가장 적절한 것은?

Some experts estimate that as much as half of what we communicate is done through the way we move our bodies. Paying attention to the nonverbal messages you send can make a significant difference in your relationship with students. In general, most students are often closely tuned in to their teacher's body language. For example, when your students first enter the classroom, their initial action is to look for their teacher. Think about how encouraging and empowering it is for a student when that teacher has a friendly greeting and a welcoming smile. Smiling at students — to let them know that you are glad to see them — does not require a great deal of time or effort, but it can make a significant difference in the classroom climate right from the start of class.

① 교사는 학생 간의 상호 작용을 주의 깊게 관찰해야 한다.
② 수업 시 교사는 학생의 수준에 맞는 언어를 사용해야 한다.
③ 학생과의 관계에서 교사는 비언어적 표현에 유의해야 한다.
④ 학교는 학생에게 다양한 역할 경험의 기회를 제공해야 한다.
⑤ 교사는 학생 안전을 위해 교실의 물리적 환경을 개선해야 한다.

21. 밑줄 친 a slap in our own face가 다음 글에서 의미하는 바로 가장 적절한 것은? [3점]

When it comes to climate change, many blame the fossil fuel industry for pumping greenhouse gases, the agricultural sector for burning rainforests, or the fashion industry for producing excessive clothes. But wait, what drives these industrial activities? Our consumption. Climate change is a summed product of each person's behavior. For example, the fossil fuel industry is a popular scapegoat in the climate crisis. But why do they drill and burn fossil fuels? We provide them strong financial incentives: some people regularly travel on airplanes and cars that burn fossil fuels. Some people waste electricity generated by burning fuel in power plants. Some people use and throw away plastic products derived from crude oil every day. Blaming the fossil fuel industry while engaging in these behaviors is a slap in our own face.

* scapegoat: 희생양

① giving the future generation room for change
② warning ourselves about the lack of natural resources
③ refusing to admit the benefits of fossil fuel production
④ failing to recognize our responsibility for climate change
⑤ starting to deal with environmental problems individually

22. 다음 글의 요지로 가장 적절한 것은?

Information is worthless if you never actually use it. Far too often, companies collect valuable customer information that ends up buried and never used. They must ensure their data is accessible for use at the appropriate times. For a hotel, one appropriate time for data usage is check-in at the front desk. I often check in at a hotel I've visited frequently, only for the people at the front desk to give no indication that they recognize me as a customer. The hotel must have stored a record of my visits, but they don't make that information accessible to the front desk clerks. They are missing a prime opportunity to utilize data to create a better experience focused on customer loyalty. Whether they have ten customers, ten thousand, or even ten million, the goal is the same: create a delightful customer experience that encourages loyalty.

① 기업 정보의 투명한 공개는 고객 만족도를 향상시킨다.
② 목표 고객층에 대한 분석은 기업의 이익 창출로 이어진다.
③ 고객 충성도를 높이기 위해 고객 정보가 활용될 필요가 있다.
④ 일관성 있는 호텔 서비스 제공을 통해 단골 고객을 확보할 수 있다.
⑤ 사생활 침해에 대한 우려로 고객 정보를 보관하는 데 어려움이 있다.

23. 다음 글의 주제로 가장 적절한 것은?

We used to think that the brain never changed, but according to the neuroscientist Richard Davidson, we now know that this is not true — specific brain circuits grow stronger through regular practice. He explains, "Well-being is fundamentally no different than learning to play the cello. If one practices the skills of well-being, one will get better at it." What this means is that you can actually train your brain to become more grateful, relaxed, or confident, by repeating experiences that evoke gratitude, relaxation, or confidence. Your brain is shaped by the thoughts you repeat. The more neurons fire as they are activated by repeated thoughts and activities, the faster they develop into neural pathways, which cause lasting changes in the brain. Or in the words of Donald Hebb, "Neurons that fire together wire together." This is such an encouraging premise: bottom line — we can intentionally create the habits for the brain to be happier.

* evoke: (감정을) 불러일으키다 ** premise: 전제

① possibility of forming brain habits for well-being
② role of brain circuits in improving body movements
③ importance of practice in playing musical instruments
④ effect of taking a break on enhancing memory capacity
⑤ difficulty of discovering how neurons in the brain work

24. 다음 글의 제목으로 가장 적절한 것은?

In modern times, society became more dynamic. Social mobility increased, and people began to exercise a higher degree of choice regarding, for instance, their profession, their marriage, or their religion. This posed a challenge to traditional roles in society. It was less evident that one needed to commit to the roles one was born into when alternatives could be realized. Increasing control over one's life choices became not only possible but desired. Identity then became a problem. It was no longer almost ready-made at birth but something to be discovered. Traditional role identities prescribed by society began to appear as masks imposed on people whose real self was to be found somewhere underneath.

* impose: 부여하다

① What Makes Our Modern Society So Competitive?
② How Modern Society Drives Us to Discover Our Identities
③ Social Masks: A Means to Build Trustworthy Relationships
④ The More Social Roles We Have, the Less Choice We Have
⑤ Increasing Social Mobility Leads Us to a More Equal Society

25. 다음 도표의 내용과 일치하지 <u>않는</u> 것은?

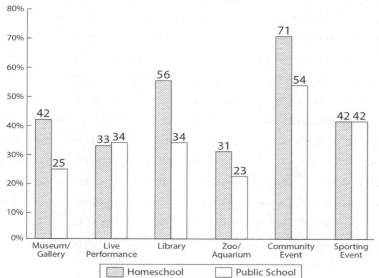

Percentage of U.S. Students Participating in Cultural Activities (2016)

Homeschool / Public School

- Museum/Gallery: 42 / 25
- Live Performance: 33 / 34
- Library: 56 / 34
- Zoo/Aquarium: 31 / 23
- Community Event: 71 / 54
- Sporting Event: 42 / 42

The graph above shows the percentage of U.S. homeschooled and public school students participating in cultural activities in 2016. ① With the exception of live performances and sporting events, the percentage of homeschooled students participating in cultural activities was higher than that of public school students. ② For each group of students, community events accounted for the largest percentage among all cultural activities. ③ The percentage point difference between homeschooled students and their public school peers was largest in visiting libraries. ④ The percentage of homeschooled students visiting museums or galleries was more than twice that of public school students. ⑤ Going to zoos or aquariums ranked the lowest for both groups of students, with 31 and 23 percent respectively.

26. Bessie Coleman에 관한 다음 글의 내용과 일치하지 <u>않는</u> 것은?

Bessie Coleman was born in Texas in 1892. When she was eleven, she was told that the Wright brothers had flown their first plane. Since that moment, she dreamed about the day she would soar through the sky. At the age of 23, Coleman moved to Chicago, where she worked at a restaurant to save money for flying lessons. However, she had to travel to Paris to take flying lessons because American flight schools at the time admitted neither women nor Black people. In 1921, she finally became the first Black woman to earn an international pilot's license. She also studied flying acrobatics in Europe and made her first appearance in an airshow in New York in 1922. As a female pioneer of flight, she inspired the next generation to pursue their dreams of flying.

*flying acrobatics: 곡예 비행

① 11살 때 Wright 형제의 첫 비행 소식을 들었다.
② 비행 수업을 듣기 위해 파리로 가야 했다.
③ 국제 조종사 면허를 딴 최초의 흑인 여성이 되었다.
④ 유럽에서 에어쇼에 첫 출현을 했다.
⑤ 다음 세대가 비행의 꿈을 추구하도록 영감을 주었다.

27. 2021 Camptonville Nature Photo Contest에 관한 다음 안내문의 내용과 일치하지 <u>않는</u> 것은?

2021 Camptonville Nature Photo Contest

This is the fourth year of the annual Camptonville Nature Photo Contest. You can show the beauty of nature in Camptonville by sharing your most amazing photos!

Submission
- Upload a maximum of 20 photos onto our website www.camptonvillephotocontest.org.
- Deadline is December 1.

Prizes
- 1st Place: $500 • 2nd Place: $200 • 3rd Place: $100
(Winners will be posted on our website on December 31.)

Details
- All winning photos will be exhibited at City Hall.
- Please contact us at 122-861-3971 for further information.

---

① 매년 열리는 대회이며 올해가 네 번째이다.
② 최대 20장의 사진을 이메일로 제출해야 한다.
③ 제출 마감 기한은 12월 1일이다.
④ 수상자는 웹 사이트에 게시될 것이다.
⑤ 모든 수상작은 시청에 전시될 것이다.

28. Willow Valley Hot Air Balloon Ride에 관한 다음 안내문의 내용과 일치하는 것은?

Willow Valley Hot Air Balloon Ride

Enjoy the best views of Willow Valley from the sky with our hot air balloon ride!

- **Capacity**: up to 8 people including a pilot
- **Time Schedule**

Spring & Summer (from April to September)	5:00 a.m. – 7:00 a.m.
Autumn & Winter (from October to March)	6:00 a.m. – 8:00 a.m.

※ Duration of Flight: about 1 hour

- **Fee**: $150 per person (insurance not included)
- **Note**
- Reservations are required and must be made online.
- You can get a full refund up to 24 hours in advance.
- Visit www.willowvalleyballoon.com for more information.

---

① 조종사를 제외하고 8인까지 탈 수 있다.
② 여름에는 오전 6시에 시작한다.
③ 요금에 보험이 포함되어 있다.
④ 예약은 온라인으로 해야 한다.
⑤ 환불은 예외 없이 불가능하다.

29. 다음 글의 밑줄 친 부분 중, 어법상 틀린 것은? [3점]

The reduction of minerals in our food is the result of using pesticides and fertilizers ① that kill off beneficial bacteria, earthworms, and bugs in the soil that create many of the essential nutrients in the first place and prevent the uptake of nutrients into the plant. Fertilizing crops with nitrogen and potassium ② has led to declines in magnesium, zinc, iron and iodine. For example, there has been on average about a 30% decline in the magnesium content of wheat. This is partly due to potassium ③ being a blocker against magnesium absorption by plants. Lower magnesium levels in soil also ④ occurring with acidic soils and around 70% of the farmland on earth is now acidic. Thus, the overall characteristics of soil determine the accumulation of minerals in plants. Indeed, nowadays our soil is less healthy and so are the plants ⑤ grown on it.

* pesticide: 살충제

30. 다음 글의 밑줄 친 부분 중, 문맥상 낱말의 쓰임이 적절하지 않은 것은?

For species approaching extinction, zoos can act as a last chance for survival. ① Recovery programs are established to coordinate the efforts of field conservationists and wildlife authorities. As populations of those species ② diminish it is not unusual for zoos to start captive breeding programs. Captive breeding acts to protect against extinction. In some cases captive-bred individuals may be released back into the wild, supplementing wild populations. This is most successful in situations where individuals are at greatest threat during a ③ particular life stage. For example, turtle eggs may be removed from high-risk locations until after they hatch. This may ④ increase the number of turtles that survive to adulthood. Crocodile programs have also been successful in protecting eggs and hatchlings, ⑤ capturing hatchlings once they are better equipped to protect themselves.

* captive breeding: 포획 사육 ** hatch: 부화하다

[31~34] 다음 빈칸에 들어갈 말로 가장 적절한 것을 고르시오.

31. We don't send telegraphs to communicate anymore, but it's a great metaphor for giving advance notice. Sometimes, you must inform those close to you of upcoming change by conveying important information well in advance. There's a huge difference between saying, "From now on, we will do things differently," which doesn't give people enough time to understand and accept the change, and saying something like, "Starting next month, we're going to approach things differently." Telegraphing empowers people to _____. Telegraphing involves the art of seeing an upcoming event or circumstance and giving others enough time to process and accept the change. Telegraph anything that will take people out of what is familiar and comfortable to them. This will allow processing time for them to accept the circumstances and make the most of what's happening.

① unite   ② adapt   ③ object
④ compete   ⑤ recover

32. Not only does memory underlie our ability to think at all, it defines the content of our experiences and how we preserve them for years to come. Memory _____. If I were to suffer from heart failure and depend upon an artificial heart, I would be no less myself. If I lost an arm in an accident and had it replaced with an artificial arm, I would still be essentially *me*. As long as my mind and memories remain intact, I will continue to be the same person, no matter which part of my body (other than the brain) is replaced. On the other hand, when someone suffers from advanced Alzheimer's disease and his memories fade, people often say that he "is not himself anymore," or that it is as if the person "is no longer there," though his body remains unchanged.

* intact: 손상되지 않은

① makes us who we are
② has to do with our body
③ reflects what we expect
④ lets us understand others
⑤ helps us learn from the past

33. Over time, babies construct expectations about what sounds they will hear when. They hold in memory the sound patterns that occur on a regular basis. They make hypotheses like, "If I hear *this* sound first, it probably will be followed by *that* sound." Scientists conclude that much of babies' skill in learning language is due to their _____. For babies, this means that they appear to pay close attention to the patterns that repeat in language. They remember, in a systematic way, how often sounds occur, in what order, with what intervals, and with what changes of pitch. This memory store allows them to track, within the neural circuits of their brains, the frequency of sound patterns and to use this knowledge to make predictions about the meaning in patterns of sounds. [3점]

① lack of social pressures
② ability to calculate statistics
③ desire to interact with others
④ preference for simpler sounds
⑤ tendency to imitate caregivers

34. Some deep-sea organisms are known to use bioluminescence as a lure, to attract prey with a little glow imitating the movements of their favorite fish, or like fireflies, as a sexual attractant to find mates. While there are many possible evolutionary theories for the survival value of bioluminescence, one of the most fascinating is to _____. The color of almost all bioluminescent molecules is blue-green, the same color as the ocean above. By self-glowing blue-green, the creatures no longer cast a shadow or create a silhouette, especially when viewed from below against the brighter waters above. Rather, by glowing themselves, they can blend into the sparkles, reflections, and scattered blue-green glow of sunlight or moonlight. Thus, they are most likely making their own light not to see, but to be un-seen. [3점]

* bioluminescence: 생물 발광 ** lure: 가짜 미끼

① send a signal for help
② threaten enemies nearby
③ lift the veil of hidden prey
④ create a cloak of invisibility
⑤ serve as a navigation system

35. 다음 글에서 전체 흐름과 관계 <u>없는</u> 문장은?

Internet activist Eli Pariser noticed how online search algorithms encourage our human tendency to grab hold of everything that confirms the beliefs we already hold, while quietly ignoring information that doesn't match those beliefs. ① We set up a so-called "filter-bubble" around ourselves, where we are constantly exposed only to that material that we agree with. ② We are never challenged, never giving ourselves the opportunity to acknowledge the existence of diversity and difference. ③ Creating a difference that others don't have is a way to succeed in your field, leading to the creation of innovations. ④ In the best case, we become naive and sheltered, and in the worst, we become radicalized with extreme views, unable to imagine life outside our particular bubble. ⑤ The results are disastrous: intellectual isolation and the real distortion that comes with believing that the little world we create for ourselves is *the* world.

* naive: 세상을 모르는 ** radicalize: 과격하게 만들다
*** distortion: 왜곡

[36~37] 주어진 글 다음에 이어질 글의 순서로 가장 적절한 것을 고르시오.

36.

Roughly twenty years ago, brick-and-mortar stores began to give way to electronic commerce. For good or bad, the shift fundamentally changed consumers' perception of the shopping experience.

(A) Before long, the e-commerce book market naturally expanded to include additional categories, like CDs and DVDs. E-commerce soon snowballed into the enormous industry it is today, where you can buy everything from toilet paper to cars online.

(B) Nowhere was the shift more obvious than with book sales, which is how online bookstores got their start. Physical bookstores simply could not stock as many titles as a virtual bookstore could. There is only so much space available on a shelf.

(C) In addition to greater variety, online bookstores were also able to offer aggressive discounts thanks to their lower operating costs. The combination of lower prices and greater selection led to the slow, steady rise of online bookstores.

* brick-and-mortar: 오프라인 거래의

① (A) – (C) – (B)　　② (B) – (A) – (C)
③ (B) – (C) – (A)　　④ (C) – (A) – (B)
⑤ (C) – (B) – (A)

37.

> Literary works, by their nature, suggest rather than explain; they imply rather than state their claims boldly and directly.

(A) What a text implies is often of great interest to us. And our work of figuring out a text's implications tests our analytical powers. In considering what a text suggests, we gain practice in making sense of texts.

(B) But whatever the proportion of a work's showing to telling, there is always something for readers to interpret. Thus we ask the question "What does the text suggest?" as a way to approach literary interpretation, as a way to begin thinking about a text's implications.

(C) This broad generalization, however, does not mean that works of literature do not include direct statements. Depending on when they were written and by whom, literary works may contain large amounts of direct telling and lesser amounts of suggestion and implication. [3점]

① (A) − (C) − (B)　　② (B) − (A) − (C)
③ (B) − (C) − (A)　　④ (C) − (A) − (B)
⑤ (C) − (B) − (A)

[38~39] 글의 흐름으로 보아, 주어진 문장이 들어가기에 가장 적절한 곳을 고르시오.

38.

> Worse, some are contaminated with other substances and contain ingredients not listed on the label.

According to top nutrition experts, most nutrients are better absorbed and used by the body when consumed from a whole food instead of a supplement. (①) However, many people feel the need to take pills, powders, and supplements in an attempt to obtain nutrients and fill the gaps in their diets. (②) We hope these will give us more energy, prevent us from catching a cold in the winter, or improve our skin and hair. (③) But in reality, the large majority of supplements are artificial and may not even be completely absorbed by your body. (④) For example, a recent investigative report found heavy metals in 40 percent of 134 brands of protein powders on the market. (⑤) With little control and regulation, taking supplements is a gamble and often costly.

* contaminate: 오염시키다 ** supplement: 보충제

39.

> But after this brief moment of rest, the pendulum swings back again and therefore part of the total energy is then given in the form of kinetic energy.

In general, kinetic energy is the energy associated with motion, while potential energy represents the energy which is "stored" in a physical system. Moreover, the total energy is always conserved. (①) But while the total energy remains unchanged, the kinetic and potential parts of the total energy can change all the time. (②) Imagine, for example, a pendulum which swings back and forth. (③) When it swings, it sweeps out an arc and then slows down as it comes closer to its highest point, where the pendulum does not move at all. (④) So at this point, the energy is completely given in terms of potential energy. (⑤) So as the pendulum swings, kinetic and potential energy constantly change into each other. [3점]

* pendulum: 추(錘)　** arc: 호(弧)

40. 다음 글의 내용을 한 문장으로 요약하고자 한다. 빈칸 (A), (B)에 들어갈 말로 가장 적절한 것은?

> There is often a lot of uncertainty in the realm of science, which the general public finds uncomfortable. They don't want "informed guesses," they want certainties that make their lives easier, and science is often unequipped to meet these demands. In particular, the human body is fantastically complex, and some scientific answers can never be provided in black-or-white terms. All this is why the media tends to oversimplify scientific research when presenting it to the public. In their eyes, they're just "giving people what they want" as opposed to offering more accurate but complex information that very few people will read or understand. A perfect example of this is how people want definitive answers as to which foods are "good" and "bad." Scientifically speaking, there are no "good" and "bad" foods; rather, food quality exists on a continuum, meaning that some foods are *better* than others when it comes to general health and well-being.

* continuum: 연속(체)

↓

> With regard to general health, science, by its nature, does not ___(A)___ the public's demands for certainty, which leads to the media giving less ___(B)___ answers to the public.

(A)	(B)	(A)	(B)
① satisfy	⋯⋯ simple	② satisfy	⋯⋯ complicated
③ ignore	⋯⋯ difficult	④ ignore	⋯⋯ simple
⑤ reject	⋯⋯ complicated		

[41~42] 다음 글을 읽고, 물음에 답하시오.

Since the turn of the twentieth century we've believed in genetic causes of diagnoses — a theory called genetic determinism. Under this model, our genes (and subsequent health) are determined at birth. We are "destined" to inherit certain diseases based on the misfortune of our DNA. Genetic determinism doesn't (a) consider the role of family backgrounds, traumas, habits, or anything else within the environment. In this dynamic we are not (b) active participants in our own health and wellness. Why would we be? If something is predetermined, it's not (c) necessary to look at anything beyond our DNA. But the more science has learned about the body and its interaction with the environment around it (in its various forms, from our nutrition to our relationships to our racially oppressive systems), the more (d) simplistic the story becomes. We are not merely expressions of coding but products of a remarkable variety of interactions that are both within and outside of our control. Once we see beyond the narrative that genetics are (e) destiny, we can take ownership of our health. This allows us to see how "choiceless" we once were and empowers us with the ability to create real and lasting change.

* oppressive: 억압적인

41. 윗글의 제목으로 가장 적절한 것은?

① Health Is in Our Hands, Not Only in Our Genes
② Genetics: A Solution to Enhance Human Wellness
③ How Did DNA Dominate Over Environment in Biology?
④ Never Be Confident in Your Health, but Keep Checking!
⑤ Why Scientific Innovation Affects Our Social Interactions

42. 밑줄 친 (a)~(e) 중에서 문맥상 낱말의 쓰임이 적절하지 않은 것은? [3점]

① (a)   ② (b)   ③ (c)   ④ (d)   ⑤ (e)

[43~45] 다음 글을 읽고, 물음에 답하시오.

(A)

One day a poor man brought a bunch of grapes to a prince as a gift. He was very excited to be able to bring a gift for (a) him because he was too poor to afford more. He placed the grapes beside the prince and said, "Oh, Prince, please accept this small gift from me." His face beamed with happiness as he offered his small gift.

(B)

If the prince had offered the grapes to them, they might have made funny faces and shown their distaste for the grapes. That would have hurt the feelings of that poor man. He thought to himself that it would be better to eat all of them cheerfully and please (b) him. He did not want to hurt the feelings of that poor man. Everyone around him was moved by his thoughtfulness.

(C)

The prince thanked him politely. As the man looked at him expectantly, the prince ate one grape. Then (c) he ate another one. Slowly the prince finished the whole bunch of grapes by himself. He did not offer grapes to anyone near him. The man who brought those grapes to (d) him was very pleased and left. The close friends of the prince who were around him were very surprised.

(D)

Usually the prince shared whatever he had with others. He would offer them whatever he was given and they would eat it together. This time was different. Without offering it to anyone, (e) he finished the bunch of grapes by himself. One of the friends asked, "Prince! How come you ate all the grapes by yourself and did not offer them to any one of us?" He smiled and said that he ate all the grapes by himself because the grapes were too sour.

43. 주어진 글 (A)에 이어질 내용을 순서에 맞게 배열한 것으로 가장 적절한 것은?

① (B) − (D) − (C)   ② (C) − (B) − (D)
③ (C) − (D) − (B)   ④ (D) − (B) − (C)
⑤ (D) − (C) − (B)

44. 밑줄 친 (a)~(e) 중에서 가리키는 대상이 나머지 넷과 다른 것은?

① (a)   ② (b)   ③ (c)   ④ (d)   ⑤ (e)

45. 윗글의 왕자에 관한 내용으로 적절하지 않은 것은?

① 가난한 남자에게 포도 한 송이를 선물로 받았다.
② 가난한 남자의 감정을 상하게 하고 싶지 않았다.
③ 곁에 있던 어떤 이에게도 포도를 권하지 않았다.
④ 가지고 있는 어떤 것이든 평소에 다른 사람들과 나눴다.
⑤ 포도가 너무 시어서 혼자 다 먹지 못했다.

* 확인 사항
◦ 답안지의 해당란에 필요한 내용을 정확히 기입(표기)했는지 확인하시오.

18

001 librarian ⓝ (도서관의) 사서
002 increase ~를 강화하다, 증진시키다
003 aim ⓝ 목표, 목적
004 various ⓐ 다양한
005 news media 뉴스미디어, 뉴스 매체
006 newspaper ⓝ 신문
007 article ⓝ (신문·잡지의) 글, 기사
008 access ⓥ 접속하다, 접근하다
009 humble ⓐ 겸손한
010 allow ⓥ 허락하다, 허용하다
011 store ⓥ 보관하다
012 grant ⓥ (공식적으로) 주다

19

013 pretty ⓐⓓ 꽤, 매우
014 absolutely ⓐⓓ 완전히, 절대적으로
015 thrilled ⓐ 아주 신이 난, 황홀한
016 soon ⓐⓓ 곧, 머지않아
017 communicate ⓥ 의사소통을 하다
018 daydream ⓥ 공상하다
019 hand ⓥ 건네주다, 넘겨주다
020 flip through (책장을) 휙휙 넘기다, 훑어보다
021 figure ⓥ 생각하다
022 hide ⓥ 감추다, 숨기다
023 realize ⓥ 깨닫다
024 furious ⓐ 몹시 화가 난
025 confident ⓐ 자신감 있는
026 anticipate ⓥ 기대하다

20

027 expert ⓝ 전문가
028 estimate ⓥ 추정하다
029 as much as ~ 정도
030 way ⓝ 방법, 방식
031 attention ⓝ 주의, 주목
032 nonverbal ⓐ 비언어적인
033 significant ⓐ 상당한, 유의미한, 중요한
034 difference ⓝ 차이
035 in general 보통, 대개, 일반적으로
036 often ⓐⓓ 자주, 종종
037 closely ⓐⓓ 면밀하게, 밀접하게
038 tune in to ~에 맞추다
039 body language 몸짓 언어, 보디랭귀지
040 enter ⓥ 들어가다
041 initial ⓐ 초기의
042 action ⓝ 행동
043 look for 찾다
044 encourage ⓥ 격려하다
045 empower ⓥ 능력을 주다, 힘을 주다
046 friendly ⓐ 친근한, 다정한
047 greeting ⓝ 인사
048 require ⓥ 요구하다
049 a great deal of (양이) 많은
050 effort ⓝ 노력
051 climate ⓝ 분위기

21

052 climate change 기후 변화
053 blame A for B B에 대해 A를 탓하다
054 fossil fuel 화석 연료

22

055 industry ⓝ 산업
056 greenhouse gas 온실 가스
057 agricultural ⓐ 농업의
058 sector ⓝ 부분, 분야
059 burn ⓥ 태우다
060 rainforest ⓝ 열대 우림
061 excessive ⓐ 과다한
062 behavior ⓝ 행동, 행위
063 popular ⓐ 일반적인
064 scapegoat ⓝ 희생양
065 crisis ⓝ 위기
066 drill ⓥ (자원, 연료 등을) 시추하다, 구멍을 뚫다
067 provide ⓥ 제공하다
068 financial ⓐ 재정상의, 금융의
069 incentive ⓝ 동기
070 waste ⓥ 낭비하다
071 electricity ⓝ 전기 ⓥ 발생시키다, 만들어 내다
072 power plant 발전소
073 derive ⓥ 유래하다, 파생하다
074 crude oil 원유
075 slap ⓥ 철썩 때리기
076 generation ⓝ 세대
077 room ⓝ 여지, 기회
078 natural resources 천연 자원
079 recognize ⓥ 인식하다, 알아보다
080 responsibility ⓝ 책임, 책무
081 environmental problems 환경 문제
082 individually ⓐⓓ 개별적으로

22

083 worthless ⓐ 무가치한
084 company ⓝ 기업
085 valuable ⓐ 소중한, 귀중한
086 customer ⓝ 고객, 손님
087 end up 결국 ~이 되다
088 bury ⓥ 묻다
089 ensure ⓥ 보장하다
090 accessible ⓐ 접근 가능한, 이용 가능한
091 appropriate ⓐ 적절한
092 usage ⓝ 사용
093 frequently ⓐⓓ 자주
094 store ⓥ 저장하다, 보관하다
095 record ⓝ 기록
096 clerk ⓝ 직원
097 prime ⓐ 가장 적합한, 최적의
098 opportunity ⓝ 기회
099 indication ⓝ 표시, 징후
100 utilize ⓥ 이용하다
101 loyalty ⓝ 충성도
102 delightful ⓐ 즐거운, 기쁜

23

103 neuroscientist ⓝ 신경과학자
104 specific ⓐ 특정한
105 circuit ⓝ 회로
106 explain ⓥ 설명하다
107 fundamentally ⓐⓓ 기본적으로
108 train ⓥ 훈련하다
109 grateful ⓐ 감사하는
110 relaxed ⓐ 편안한

24

111 repeat ⓥ 반복하다
112 shape ⓥ 형성하다
113 fire ⓥ 발화[점화]되다
114 activate ⓥ 활성화하다
115 neural ⓐ 신경의
116 wire ⓥ 연결하다
117 premise ⓝ (주장의) 전제
118 bottom line 핵심, 요점, 결론
119 intentionally ⓐⓓ 의도적으로
120 possibility ⓝ 가능성
121 musical instrument 악기
122 enhance ⓥ 향상시키다
123 capacity ⓝ 용량

24

124 modern times 현대
125 society ⓝ 사회
126 dynamic ⓐ 역동적인
127 mobility ⓝ 유동성
128 degree ⓝ 정도
129 regarding ⓟⓡⓔⓟ ~에 관하여
130 for instance 예를 들어
131 profession ⓝ 직업
132 marriage ⓝ 결혼
133 religion ⓝ 종교
134 pose a challenge 도전하다, 이의를 제기하다
135 traditional ⓐ 전통의, 전통적인
136 evident ⓐ 명백한
137 commit to ~에 전념하다
138 alternative ⓝ 대안
139 control ⓝ 통제력
140 ready-made ⓐ 이미 주어진, 기성품의
141 prescribe ⓥ 규정하다, 처방하다
142 appear ⓥ 보이기 시작하다
143 underneath ⓝ 아래
144 competitive ⓐ 경쟁적인
145 trustworthy ⓐ 신뢰할 수 있는

25

146 public school 공립학교
147 participate ⓥ 참여하다
148 with the exception of ~을 제외하고
149 account for ~을 차지하다
150 peer ⓝ 또래
151 gallery ⓝ 미술관
152 respectively ⓐⓓ 각각

26

153 moment ⓝ 때, 순간
154 dream ⓥ 꿈을 꾸다
155 soar ⓥ 솟아오르다
156 save money 돈을 모으다
157 admit ⓥ 입장[입학]을 허락하다
158 earn ⓥ 얻다, 획득하다
159 license ⓝ 면허증
160 also ⓐⓓ 또한
161 acrobatics ⓝ 곡예
162 appearance ⓝ 출현, 모습
163 pioneer ⓝ 선구자
164 inspire ⓥ 영감을 주다
165 pursue ⓥ 추구하다

27

166 annual ⓐ 매년 열리는
167 nature ⓝ 자연
168 submission ⓝ 제출
169 maximum ⓝ 최대
170 post ⓥ 게시하다
171 exhibit ⓥ 전시하다

28

172 pilot ⓝ 조종사
173 duration ⓝ (지속되는) 시간, 기간
174 flight ⓝ 비행
175 get a refund 환불을 받다
176 in advance 미리, 사전에

29

177 reduction ⓝ 감소
178 result ⓝ 결과
179 pesticide ⓝ 살충제, 농약
180 fertilizer ⓝ 비료
181 beneficial ⓐ 유익한, 이로운
182 earthworm ⓝ 지렁이
183 soil ⓝ 토양
184 essential ⓐ 필수적인, 본질적인
185 nutrient ⓝ 영양소, 영양분
186 in the first place 애초에, 우선
187 uptake ⓝ 흡수, 활용
188 fertilize ⓥ 비옥하게 하다, 비료를 주다
189 nitrogen ⓝ 질소
190 potassium ⓝ 칼륨
191 decline ⓝ 감소 ⓥ 감소하다
192 zinc ⓝ 아연
193 average ⓝ 평균
194 wheat ⓝ 밀
195 partly ⓐⓓ 부분적으로
196 blocker ⓝ 방해물, 차단제
197 absorption ⓝ 흡수
198 acidic ⓐ 산성의
199 farmland ⓝ 농지
200 characteristic ⓝ 특징, 특성
201 determine ⓥ 결정하다
202 accumulation ⓝ 축적

30

203 species ⓝ 종(種)
204 approach ⓥ ~에 이르다, ~에 가까워지다
205 extinction ⓝ 멸종
206 survival ⓝ 생존
207 recovery ⓝ 회복
208 establish ⓥ 수립하다
209 coordinate ⓥ 조직화하다, 통합하다
210 field ⓝ 현장
211 conservationist ⓝ 환경 보호 활동가
212 wildlife ⓝ 야생동물
213 authority ⓝ 당국
214 population ⓝ 개체수
215 diminish ⓥ 감소하다, 줄어들다
216 unusual ⓐ 드문
217 breeding ⓝ 사육, 번식
218 protect ⓥ 보호하다
219 release ⓥ 풀어 주다, 방생하다
220 supplement ⓥ 보충하다

221 ☐ threat ⓝ 위협
222 ☐ particular ⓐ 특정한
223 ☐ high-risk ⓐ 위험성이 높은
224 ☐ location ⓝ 위치, 장소
225 ☐ adulthood ⓝ 성체, 성인
226 ☐ hatchling ⓝ (갓 부화한) 유생
227 ☐ be equipped to ~할 준비를 갖추다

31
228 ☐ telegraph ⓝ 전보
229 ☐ anymore ⓐd 더 이상
230 ☐ metaphor ⓝ 은유
231 ☐ advance ⓐ 사전의
232 ☐ notice ⓝ 통지, 통보
233 ☐ upcoming ⓐ 다가오는
234 ☐ convey ⓥ 전달하다
235 ☐ from now on 이제부터, 지금부터
236 ☐ accept ⓥ 받아들이다
237 ☐ involve ⓥ 포함하다
238 ☐ circumstance ⓝ 상황
239 ☐ familiar ⓐ 익숙한
240 ☐ comfortable ⓐ 편안한
241 ☐ make the most of ~을 최대한 활용하다
242 ☐ happen ⓥ (일, 사건 등이) 일어나다

32
243 ☐ underlie ⓥ (~의) 기반을 이루다
244 ☐ ability ⓝ 능력
245 ☐ define ⓥ 규정하다
246 ☐ preserve ⓥ 보존하다
247 ☐ for years 수년간, 몇 해 동안
248 ☐ suffer ⓥ 앓다, 병들다
249 ☐ heart failure 심부전, 심장 부전
250 ☐ artificial heart 인공 심장
251 ☐ accident ⓝ 사고
252 ☐ replace ⓥ 교체하다
253 ☐ essentially ⓐd 본질적으로
254 ☐ intact ⓐ 손상되지 않은
255 ☐ continue ⓥ 계속되다
256 ☐ fade ⓥ 흐려지다, (빛이) 바래다
257 ☐ past ⓝ 과거

33
258 ☐ construct ⓥ 형성하다, 구성하다
259 ☐ expectation ⓝ 기대
260 ☐ occur ⓥ 일어나다, 발생하다
261 ☐ on a regular basis 규칙적으로
262 ☐ hypothesis ⓝ 가설
263 ☐ probably ⓐd 아마도
264 ☐ follow ⓥ 따라가다[오다]
265 ☐ conclude ⓥ 결론을 내리다
266 ☐ close attention 세심한 주의
267 ☐ systematic ⓐ 체계적인
268 ☐ order ⓝ 순서
269 ☐ interval ⓝ 간격
270 ☐ track ⓥ 추적하다
271 ☐ frequency ⓝ 빈도
272 ☐ make a prediction 예측하다
273 ☐ calculate ⓥ 계산하다
274 ☐ statistics ⓝ 통계
275 ☐ interact ⓥ 소통하다
276 ☐ tendency ⓝ 성향, 경향

277 ☐ imitate ⓥ 모방하다, 흉내내다
278 ☐ caregiver ⓝ 간병인

34
279 ☐ deep-sea ⓐ 심해의
280 ☐ organism ⓝ 유기체, 생물
281 ☐ bioluminescence ⓝ 생물[생체] 발광
282 ☐ lure ⓝ 미끼
283 ☐ attractant ⓝ 유인 물질
284 ☐ prey ⓝ 먹이
285 ☐ firefly ⓝ 반딧불이
286 ☐ mate ⓝ 짝
287 ☐ evolutionary ⓐ 진화의
288 ☐ theory ⓝ 이론
289 ☐ survival value 생존가(생체의 특질이 생존·번식에 기여하는 유용성)
290 ☐ fascinating ⓐ 매력적인, 흥미로운
291 ☐ almost all 거의 모든, 거의 전부의
292 ☐ molecule ⓝ 분자
293 ☐ cast ⓥ 드리우다, 던지다
294 ☐ shadow ⓝ 그림자
295 ☐ silhouette ⓝ 실루엣, 윤곽
296 ☐ blend into ~에 섞이다
297 ☐ sparkle ⓝ 반짝거림, 광채
298 ☐ scatter ⓥ 흩뜨리다, 분산하다
299 ☐ threaten ⓥ 위협하다
300 ☐ cloak ⓝ 망토
301 ☐ invisibility ⓝ 보이지 않음

35
302 ☐ activist ⓝ 활동가
303 ☐ algorithm ⓝ 알고리즘, 연산
304 ☐ grab hold of ~을 (갑자기) 움켜잡다
305 ☐ confirm ⓥ 확인하다
306 ☐ belief ⓝ 신념, 확신
307 ☐ quietly ⓐd 조용히
308 ☐ ignore ⓥ 무시하다
309 ☐ filter-bubble ⓝ 필터 버블(사용자가 인터넷 알고리즘에 의해 관심사에 맞는 정보만 제공받으며 왜곡된 인지 속에 갇히게 되는 것)
310 ☐ constantly ⓐd 끊임없이, 지속적으로
311 ☐ expose ⓥ 노출시키다
312 ☐ agree ⓥ 동의하다
313 ☐ acknowledge ⓥ 인정하다
314 ☐ existence ⓝ 존재
315 ☐ diversity ⓝ 다양성
316 ☐ field ⓝ 분야
317 ☐ innovation ⓝ 혁신
318 ☐ shelter ⓥ 보호하다
319 ☐ radicalize ⓥ 과격하게 하다
320 ☐ extreme ⓐ 극단적인
321 ☐ view ⓝ 시각
322 ☐ disastrous ⓐ 참담한
323 ☐ intellectual ⓐ 지적인
324 ☐ isolation ⓝ 고립
325 ☐ distortion ⓝ 왜곡

36
326 ☐ roughly ⓐd 약, 대략
327 ☐ brick-and-mortar ⓐ 소매(小賣)의, 오프라인 거래의
328 ☐ shift ⓥ 바꾸다

329 ☐ give way to ~로 바뀌다
330 ☐ electronic commerce 전자 상거래
331 ☐ perception ⓝ 인식
332 ☐ experience ⓝ 경험
333 ☐ before long 머지않아, 오래지 않아
334 ☐ e-commerce ⓝ 전자 상거래
335 ☐ naturally ⓐd 자연스럽게
336 ☐ expand ⓥ 확장되다
337 ☐ additional ⓐ 추가의
338 ☐ snowball ⓥ 눈덩이처럼 커지다
339 ☐ enormous ⓐ 거대한
340 ☐ toilet paper (화장실용) 화장지
341 ☐ obvious ⓐ 분명한
342 ☐ title ⓝ 서적, 출판물
343 ☐ shelf ⓝ 책꽂이
344 ☐ offer ⓥ 제공하다
345 ☐ aggressive ⓐ 공격적인, (대단히) 적극적인
346 ☐ operating cost 운영비
347 ☐ combination ⓝ 결합
348 ☐ steady ⓐ 꾸준한

37
349 ☐ literary ⓐ 문학의
350 ☐ literary works 문학 작품
351 ☐ nature ⓝ 본질, 본성
352 ☐ suggest ⓥ 암시하다
353 ☐ imply ⓥ 함축하다
354 ☐ boldly ⓐd 뚜렷하게, 대담하게
355 ☐ implication ⓝ 함축, 암시
356 ☐ analytical ⓐ 분석적인
357 ☐ consider ⓥ 고려하다
358 ☐ gain ⓥ 얻다
359 ☐ proportion ⓝ 비율
360 ☐ interpret ⓥ 해석하다
361 ☐ generalization ⓝ 일반화
362 ☐ direct ⓐ 직접적인
363 ☐ statement ⓝ 진술

38
364 ☐ contaminate ⓥ 오염시키다
365 ☐ substance ⓝ 물질
366 ☐ contain ⓥ ~이 들어있다
367 ☐ ingredient ⓝ 성분
368 ☐ nutrition ⓝ 영양
369 ☐ absorb ⓥ 흡수하다
370 ☐ whole food 자연식품
371 ☐ instead ⓐd 대신에
372 ☐ supplement ⓝ 보충제
373 ☐ pill ⓝ 알약
374 ☐ powder ⓝ 분말, 가루
375 ☐ obtain ⓥ 얻다
376 ☐ fill the gap 부족한 부분을 채우다, 간격을 메우다
377 ☐ prevent ⓥ 막다, 예방하다
378 ☐ improve ⓥ 개선하다
379 ☐ artificial ⓐ 인위적인
380 ☐ completely ⓐd 완전히
381 ☐ recent ⓐ 최근의
382 ☐ investigative ⓐ 조사의
383 ☐ heavy metal 중금속
384 ☐ protein ⓝ 단백질

385 ☐ regulation ⓝ 규제
386 ☐ gamble ⓝ 도박
387 ☐ costly ⓐ 대가가 큰, 많은 돈이 드는

39
388 ☐ brief ⓐ 짧은
389 ☐ pendulum ⓝ (시계의) 추
390 ☐ kinetic energy 운동 에너지
391 ☐ potential energy 위치 에너지
392 ☐ conserve ⓥ 보존하다
393 ☐ swing back and forth 앞뒤로 흔들리다
394 ☐ sweep out 쓸어내리다
395 ☐ arc ⓝ 호(弧)

40
396 ☐ uncertainty ⓝ 불확실성
397 ☐ realm ⓝ 영역
398 ☐ uncomfortable ⓐ 불편한
399 ☐ informed ⓐ 정보에 입각한
400 ☐ certainty ⓝ 확실성
401 ☐ demand ⓝ 요구
402 ☐ fantastically ⓐd 환상적으로, 엄청나게
403 ☐ complex ⓐ 복잡한
404 ☐ black-or-white ⓐ 흑백논리의, 양자택일의
405 ☐ term ⓝ 말, 용어
406 ☐ tend ⓥ 경향이 있다
407 ☐ oversimplify ⓥ 지나치게 단순화하다
408 ☐ as opposed to ~와는 반대로, ~이 아니라
409 ☐ accurate ⓐ 정확한
410 ☐ definitive ⓐ 확정적인
411 ☐ continuum ⓝ 연속체
412 ☐ with regard to ~에 관하여

41~42
413 ☐ genetic ⓐ 유전적인
414 ☐ genetic determinism 유전자 결정론
415 ☐ gene ⓝ 유전자
416 ☐ diagnosis ⓝ 진단, 진찰
417 ☐ subsequent ⓐ 차후의, 그다음의
418 ☐ inherit ⓥ 물려받다
419 ☐ environment ⓝ 환경
420 ☐ predetermined ⓐ 미리 결정된
421 ☐ interaction ⓝ 상호 작용
422 ☐ racially ⓐd 인종적으로
423 ☐ oppressive ⓐ 억압적인
424 ☐ simplistic ⓐ 단순한
425 ☐ merely ⓐd 단지
426 ☐ expression ⓝ 표현
427 ☐ remarkable ⓐ 놀랄 만한
428 ☐ narrative ⓝ 이야기
429 ☐ take ownership of ~을 갖다, 소유하다

43~45
430 ☐ bunch ⓝ (포도 등의) 송이
431 ☐ place ⓥ 놓다, 두다
432 ☐ beside prep 옆에
433 ☐ beam with ~으로 환히 웃다
434 ☐ politely ⓐd 정중하게
435 ☐ distaste ⓝ 불쾌감
436 ☐ thoughtfulness ⓝ 사려 깊음
437 ☐ expectantly ⓐd 기대하여

18회

● 채점 : 맞은 개수 _____ / 80

TEST A-B 각 단어의 뜻을 [A] 영어는 우리말로, [B] 우리말은 영어로 쓰시오.

A	English	Korean	B	Korean	English
01	drill		01	초기의	
02	anticipate		02	추정하다	
03	profession		03	상황	
04	ready-made		04	선구자	
05	extinction		05	표시, 징후	
06	daydream		06	면밀하게, 밀접하게	
07	enormous		07	전달하다	
08	uncertainty		08	기본적으로, 근본적으로	
09	fascinating		09	혁신	
10	bottom line		10	향상시키다	
11	empower		11	공격적인, (대단히) 적극적인	
12	annual		12	감소	
13	analytical		13	영감을 주다	
14	interval		14	본질, 본성	
15	accessible		15	각각	
16	excessive		16	부분, 분야	
17	essentially		17	보충하다	
18	regulation		18	물질	
19	sweep out		19	놀랄 만한	
20	systematic		20	필수적인, 본질적인	

▶ A-D 정답 : 해설편 183쪽

TEST C-D 각 단어의 뜻을 골라 기호를 쓰시오.

C	English		Korean	D	Korean		English
01	disastrous	( )	ⓐ 이용하다	01	(공식적으로) 주다	( )	ⓐ constantly
02	intentionally	( )	ⓑ 참담한	02	목표, 목적	( )	ⓑ worthless
03	thrilled	( )	ⓒ 해석하다	03	기대하여	( )	ⓒ characteristic
04	diagnosis	( )	ⓓ 불쾌감	04	운영비	( )	ⓓ crude oil
05	hypothesis	( )	ⓔ 흑백논리의, 양자택일의	05	흡수, 활용	( )	ⓔ fade
06	humble	( )	ⓕ 완전히, 절대적으로	06	드리우다, 던지다	( )	ⓕ uptake
07	underlie	( )	ⓖ 명백한	07	통계	( )	ⓖ expectantly
08	appropriate	( )	ⓗ 일반화	08	뚜렷하게, 대담하게	( )	ⓗ acknowledge
09	absolutely	( )	ⓘ 겸손한	09	보장하다	( )	ⓘ grant
10	prescribe	( )	ⓙ 의도적으로	10	지속적으로, 끊임없이	( )	ⓙ invisibility
11	distaste	( )	ⓚ 은유	11	특징, 특성	( )	ⓚ aim
12	utilize	( )	ⓛ 축적	12	농업의	( )	ⓛ ensure
13	evident	( )	ⓜ ~의 기반을 이루다	13	유전적인	( )	ⓜ operating cost
14	diminish	( )	ⓝ 아주 신이 난, 황홀한	14	인정하다	( )	ⓝ statistics
15	interpret	( )	ⓞ 적절한	15	보이지 않음	( )	ⓞ crisis
16	black-or-white	( )	ⓟ 단순한	16	원유	( )	ⓟ telegraph
17	metaphor	( )	ⓠ 진단, 진찰	17	무가치한	( )	ⓠ agricultural
18	simplistic	( )	ⓡ 가설	18	위기	( )	ⓡ boldly
19	generalization	( )	ⓢ 감소하다, 줄어들다	19	흐려지다, (빛이) 바래다	( )	ⓢ genetic
20	accumulation	( )	ⓣ 규정하다, 처방하다	20	전보	( )	ⓣ cast

※ 영어 [독해] 파트만 수록한 문제지이므로 18번부터 시작합니다.

● 점수 표시가 없는 문항은 모두 2점 ● 문항수 28개 | 배점 63점 | 제한 시간 45분

18. 다음 글의 목적으로 가장 적절한 것은?

> To whom it may concern:
>
> I was born and raised in the city of Boulder and have enjoyed our scenic natural spaces for my whole life. The land through which the proposed Pine Hill walking trail would cut is home to a variety of species. Wildlife faces pressure from development, and these animals need space where they can hide from human activity. Although trails serve as a wonderful source for us to access the natural world and appreciate the wildlife within it, if we continue to destroy habitats with excess trails, the wildlife will stop using these areas. Please reconsider whether the proposed trail is absolutely necessary.
>
> Sincerely,
> Tyler Stuart

① 환경 보호 캠페인 참여를 부탁하려고
② 지역 관광 프로그램에 대해 문의하려고
③ 산책로 조성 계획의 재고를 요청하려고
④ 보행자 안전을 위해 인도 설치를 건의하려고
⑤ 야생 동물 보호구역 관리의 문제점을 지적하려고

19. 다음 글에 드러난 'I'의 심경 변화로 가장 적절한 것은?

On my seventh birthday, my mom surprised me with a puppy waiting on a leash. It had beautiful golden fur and an adorable tail. It was exactly what I had always dreamed of. I took the dog everywhere and slept with it every night. A few months later, the dog got out of the backyard and was lost. I sat on my bed and cried for hours while my mother watched me silently from the doorway of my room. I finally fell asleep, exhausted from my grief. My mother never said a word to me about my loss, but I knew she felt the same as I did.

① delighted → sorrowful
② relaxed → annoyed
③ embarrassed → worried
④ excited → horrified
⑤ disappointed → satisfied

20. 다음 글에서 필자가 주장하는 바로 가장 적절한 것은?

When I was in high school, we had students who could study in the coffee shop and not get distracted by the noise or everything happening around them. We also had students who could not study if the library was not super quiet. The latter students suffered because even in the library, it was impossible to get the type of complete silence they sought. These students were victims of distractions who found it very difficult to study anywhere except in their private bedrooms. In today's world, it is impossible to run away from distractions. Distractions are everywhere, but if you want to achieve your goals, you must learn how to tackle distractions. You cannot eliminate distractions, but you can learn to live with them in a way that ensures they do not limit you.

① 자신에게 적합한 시간 관리법을 찾아야 한다.
② 집중을 방해하는 요인에 대처할 줄 알아야 한다.
③ 학습 공간과 휴식 공간을 명확하게 분리해야 한다.
④ 집중력 향상을 위해 정돈된 학습환경을 유지해야 한다.
⑤ 공공장소에서 타인에게 피해를 주는 행동을 삼가야 한다.

21. 밑줄 친 popped out of the box가 다음 글에서 의미하는 바로 가장 적절한 것은?

With the Internet, everything changed. Product problems, overpromises, the lack of customer support, differential pricing — all of the issues that customers actually experienced from a marketing organization suddenly popped out of the box. No longer were there any controlled communications or even business systems. Consumers could generally learn through the Web whatever they wanted to know about a company, its products, its competitors, its distribution systems, and, most of all, its truthfulness when talking about its products and services. Just as important, the Internet opened up a forum for customers to compare products, experiences, and values with other customers easily and quickly. Now the customer had a way to talk back to the marketer and to do so through public forums instantly.

* differential pricing: 가격 차등

① could not be kept secret anymore
② might disappear from public attention
③ were no longer available to marketers
④ became too complicated to understand
⑤ began to improve companies' reputations

22. 다음 글의 요지로 가장 적절한 것은?

FOBO, or Fear of a Better Option, is the anxiety that something better will come along, which makes it undesirable to commit to existing choices when making a decision. It's an affliction of abundance that drives you to keep all of your options open and to avoid risks. Rather than assessing your options, choosing one, and moving on with your day, you delay the inevitable. It's not unlike hitting the snooze button on your alarm clock only to pull the covers over your head and fall back asleep. As you probably found out the hard way, if you hit snooze enough times, you'll end up being late and racing for the office, your day and mood ruined. While pressing snooze feels so good at the moment, it ultimately demands a price.

* affliction: 고통

① 적당한 수준의 불안감은 업무 수행에 도움이 된다.
② 성급한 의사 결정은 의도하지 않은 결과를 초래한다.
③ 반복되는 실수를 줄이기 위해서는 신중함이 요구된다.
④ 더 나은 선택을 위해 결정을 미루는 것은 결국 해가 된다.
⑤ 규칙적인 생활 습관은 직장에서의 성공 가능성을 높인다.

23. 다음 글의 주제로 가장 적절한 것은?

The use of renewable sources of energy to produce electricity has increasingly been encouraged as a way to harmonize the need to secure electricity supply with environmental protection objectives. But the use of renewable sources also comes with its own consequences, which require consideration. Renewable sources of energy include a variety of sources such as hydropower and ocean-based technologies. Additionally, solar, wind, geothermal and biomass renewable sources also have their own impact on the environment. Hydropower dams, for example, have an impact on aquatic ecosystems and, more recently, have been identified as significant sources of greenhouse emissions. Wind, solar, and biomass also cause negative environmental impacts, such as visual pollution, intensive land occupation and negative effects on bird populations.

* geothermal: 지열의 ** biomass: 에너지로 사용 가능한 생물체

① environmental side effects of using renewable energy sources
② practical methods to meet increasing demand for electricity
③ negative impacts of the use of traditional energy sources
④ numerous ways to obtain renewable sources of energy
⑤ effective procedures to reduce greenhouse emissions

24. 다음 글의 제목으로 가장 적절한 것은?

Chewing leads to smaller particles for swallowing, and more exposed surface area for digestive enzymes to act on. In other words, it means the extraction of more fuel and raw materials from a mouthful of food. This is especially important for mammals because they heat their bodies from within. Chewing gives mammals the energy needed to be active not only during the day but also the cool night, and to live in colder climates or places with changing temperatures. It allows them to sustain higher levels of activity and travel speeds to cover larger distances, avoid predators, capture prey, and make and care for their young. Mammals are able to live in an incredible variety of habitats, from Arctic tundra to Antarctic pack ice, deep open waters to high-altitude mountaintops, and rainforests to deserts, in no small measure because of their teeth.

* enzyme: 효소

① Chewing: A Way to Ease Indigestion
② Boost Your Energy by Chewing More!
③ How Chewing Helps Mammals Survive
④ Different Types and Functions of Teeth
⑤ A Harsh Climate Makes Mammals Stronger

25. 다음 표의 내용과 일치하지 <u>않는</u> 것은?

Age Children Quit Regularly Playing a Sport

Sport	Average Age of Last Regular Participation	Average Length in Years of Participation
Soccer	9.1	3.0
Ice Hockey	10.9	3.1
Tennis	10.9	1.9
Basketball	11.2	3.2
Field Hockey	11.4	5.1
Golf	11.8	2.8
Skateboarding	12.0	2.8
Track and Field	13.0	2.0

The above table shows the average age of last regular participation of children in a sport and the average length of participation based on a 2019 survey. ① Among the eight sports above, soccer was the only sport that children quit at an average age of younger than 10. ② Children quit playing ice hockey and tennis at the same age on average, but the average length of participation in tennis was shorter than that in ice hockey. ③ Basketball, field hockey, and golf were sports which children quit playing on average before they turned 12, but golf had the shortest average participation length among the three sports. ④ Skateboarding was a sport children quit at the average age of 12, and the average length of participation was the same as golf. ⑤ Meanwhile, children quit participating in track and field at the average age of 13, but the average length of participation was the shortest among the eight sports.

26. Sarah Breedlove에 관한 다음 글의 내용과 일치하지 <u>않는</u> 것은?

Born in 1867, Sarah Breedlove was an American businesswoman and social activist. Orphaned at the age of seven, her early life was marked by hardship. In 1888, she moved to St. Louis, where she worked as a washerwoman for more than a decade, earning barely more than a dollar a day. During this time, long hours of backbreaking labor and a poor diet caused her hair to fall out. She tried everything that was available but had no success. After working as a maid for a chemist, she invented a successful hair care product and sold it across the country. Not only did she sell, she also recruited and trained lots of women as sales agents for a share of the profits. In the process she became America's first self-made female millionaire and she gave Black women everywhere an opportunity for financial independence.

① 미국인 사업가이자 사회 운동가였다.
② St. Louis에서 10년 넘게 세탁부로 일했다.
③ 장시간의 노동과 열악한 식사로 머리카락이 빠졌다.
④ 모발 관리 제품을 수입하여 전국에 판매했다.
⑤ 흑인 여성들에게 재정적 독립의 기회를 주었다.

27. 2020 Student Building Block Competition에 관한 다음 안내문의 내용과 일치하지 <u>않는</u> 것은?

2020 Student Building Block Competition

Students in every grade will compete to build the most creative and livable structure made out of blocks!

When & Where
• 2 p.m. − 4 p.m. Saturday, November 21
• Green Valley Elementary School Gym

Rules
• All building projects must be completed on site with supplied blocks only.
• Participants are not allowed to receive outside assistance.

Gifts & Prizes
• All the participants receive a T-shirt.
• One winner from each grade group wins $100 and a medal.

Sign up
• Participation is FREE!
• Email jeremywilson@greenvalley.org by November 15. (Registration on site is not available.)

① 초등학교 체육관에서 열린다.
② 제공되는 블록을 사용해야 한다.
③ 외부의 도움 없이 작품을 완성해야 한다.
④ 우승자에게 상금과 메달을 준다.
⑤ 현장에서 등록하는 것이 가능하다.

28. Crystal Castle Fireworks에 관한 다음 안내문의 내용과 일치하는 것은?

Crystal Castle Fireworks

Come and enjoy the biggest fireworks display in the South West of England!

Dates: 5th & 6th December, 2020

Location: Crystal Castle, 132 Oak Street

Time: 15:00 − 16:00 Live Music Show
16:30 − 17:30 Maze Garden
18:00 − 18:30 Fireworks Display

Parking: Free car park opens at 13:00.

Note:
Any child aged 12 or under must be accompanied by an adult.
All tickets must be reserved beforehand on our website www.crystalcastle.com.

① 영국의 북부 지역에서 가장 큰 불꽃놀이이다.
② 라이브 음악 쇼가 불꽃놀이 이후에 진행된다.
③ 불꽃놀이는 1시간 동안 진행된다.
④ 주차장은 오후 1시부터 유료로 이용 가능하다.
⑤ 12세 이하의 아동은 성인과 동행해야 한다.

29. 다음 글의 밑줄 친 부분 중, 어법상 틀린 것은? [3점]

Each species of animals can detect a different range of odours. No species can detect all the molecules that are present in the environment ① in which it lives — there are some things that we cannot smell but which some other animals can, and vice versa. There are also differences between individuals, relating to the ability to smell an odour, or how ② pleasantly it seems. For example, some people like the taste of coriander — known as cilantro in the USA — while others find ③ it soapy and unpleasant. This effect has an underlying genetic component due to differences in the genes ④ controlling our sense of smell. Ultimately, the selection of scents detected by a given species, and how that odour is perceived, will depend upon the animal's ecology. The response profile of each species will enable it ⑤ to locate sources of smell that are relevant to it and to respond accordingly.

* coriander: 고수

30. (A), (B), (C)의 각 네모 안에서 문맥에 맞는 낱말로 가장 적절한 것은? [3점]

Recent research suggests that evolving humans' relationship with dogs changed the structure of both species' brains. One of the various (A) physical / psychological changes caused by domestication is a reduction in the size of the brain: 16 percent for horses, 34 percent for pigs, and 10 to 30 percent for dogs. This is because once humans started to take care of these animals, they no longer needed various brain functions in order to survive. Animals who were fed and protected by humans did not need many of the skills required by their wild ancestors and (B) developed / lost the parts of the brain related to those capacities. A similar process occurred for humans, who seem to have been domesticated by wolves. About 10,000 years ago, when the role of dogs was firmly established in most human societies, the human brain also (C) expanded / shrank by about 10 percent.

	(A)	(B)	(C)
①	physical	developed	expanded
②	physical	lost	expanded
③	physical	lost	shrank
④	psychological	developed	shrank
⑤	psychological	lost	shrank

[31~34] 다음 빈칸에 들어갈 말로 가장 적절한 것을 고르시오.

31. There is nothing more fundamental to the human spirit than the need to be _____. It is the intuitive force that sparks our imaginations and opens pathways to life-changing opportunities. It is the catalyst for progress and personal freedom. Public transportation has been vital to that progress and freedom for more than two centuries. The transportation industry has always done more than carry travelers from one destination to another. It connects people, places, and possibilities. It provides access to what people need, what they love, and what they aspire to become. In so doing, it grows communities, creates jobs, strengthens the economy, expands social and commercial networks, saves time and energy, and helps millions of people achieve a better life.

* catalyst: 촉매, 기폭제

① secure
② mobile
③ exceptional
④ competitive
⑤ independent

32. Business consultant Frans Johansson describes the *Medici effect* as the emergence of new ideas and creative solutions when different backgrounds and disciplines come together. The term is derived from the 15th-century Medici family, who helped usher in the Renaissance by bringing together artists, writers, and other creatives from all over the world. Arguably, the Renaissance was a result of the exchange of ideas between these different groups in close contact with each other. Sound familiar? If you are unable to diversify your own talent and skill, then _____ might very well just do the trick. Believing that all new ideas come from combining existing notions in creative ways, Johansson recommends utilizing a mix of backgrounds, experiences, and expertise in staffing to bring about the best possible solutions, perspectives, and innovations in business. [3점]

* usher in: ~이 시작되게 하다

① having others around you to compensate
② taking some time to reflect on yourself
③ correcting the mistakes of the past
④ maximizing your own strength
⑤ setting a specific objective

33. As much as we can learn by examining fossils, it is important to remember that they seldom _____. Things only fossilize under certain sets of conditions. Modern insect communities are highly diverse in tropical forests, but the recent fossil record captures little of that diversity. Many creatures are consumed entirely or decompose rapidly when they die, so there may be no fossil record at all for important groups. It's a bit similar to a family photo album. Maybe when you were born your parents took lots of pictures, but over the years they took photographs occasionally, and sometimes they got busy and forgot to take pictures at all. Very few of us have a complete photo record of our life. Fossils are just like that. Sometimes you get very clear pictures of the past, while at other times there are big gaps, and you need to notice what they are. [3점]

* decompose: 부패하다

① tell the entire story
② require further study
③ teach us a wrong lesson
④ change their original traits
⑤ make room for imagination

34. Back in 1996, an American airline was faced with an interesting problem. At a time when most other airlines were losing money or going under, over 100 cities were begging the company to service their locations. However, that's not the interesting part. What's interesting is that the company turned down over 95 percent of those offers and began serving only four new locations. It turned down tremendous growth because _____. Sure, its executives wanted to grow each year, but they didn't want to grow too much. Unlike other famous companies, they wanted to set their own pace, one that could be sustained in the long term. By doing this, they established a safety margin for growth that helped them continue to thrive at a time when the other airlines were flailing. [3점]

* flail: 마구 흔들리다

① it was being faced with serious financial crises
② there was no specific long-term plan on marketing
③ company leadership had set an upper limit for growth
④ its executives worried about the competing airlines' future
⑤ the company had emphasized moral duties more than profits

35. 다음 글에서 전체 흐름과 관계 <u>없는</u> 문장은?

The Barnum Effect is the phenomenon where someone reads or hears something very general but believes that it applies to them. ① These statements appear to be very personal on the surface but in fact, they are true for many. ② Human psychology allows us to want to believe things that we can identify with on a personal level and even seek information where it doesn't necessarily exist, filling in the blanks with our imagination for the rest. ③ This is the principle that horoscopes rely on, offering data that appears to be personal but probably makes sense to countless people. ④ Reading daily horoscopes in the morning is beneficial as they provide predictions about the rest of the day. ⑤ Since the people reading them want to believe the information so badly, they will search for meaning in their lives that make it true.

* horoscope: 별자리 운세

[36~37] 주어진 글 다음에 이어질 글의 순서로 가장 적절한 것을 고르시오.

36.

> Imagine yourself at a party. It is dark and a group of friends ask you to take a picture of them. You grab your camera, point, and shoot your friends.

(A) This is a common problem called the *red-eye effect*. It is caused because the light from the flash penetrates the eyes through the pupils, and then gets reflected to the camera from the back of the eyes where a large amount of blood is present.

(B) The camera automatically turns on the flash as there is not enough light available to produce a correct exposure. The result is half of your friends appear in the picture with two bright red circles instead of their eyes.

(C) This blood is the reason why the eyes look red in the photograph. This effect is more noticeable when there is not much light in the environment. This is because pupils dilate when it is dark, allowing more light to get inside the eye and producing a larger red-eye effect.

* penetrate: 통과하다 ** pupil: 동공 *** dilate: 확장(팽창)하다

① (A) − (C) − (B)   ② (B) − (A) − (C)
③ (B) − (C) − (A)   ④ (C) − (A) − (B)
⑤ (C) − (B) − (A)

37.

> Even though two variables seem to be related, there may not be a causal relationship.

(A) Does this mean that the size of one's feet (independent variable) causes an improvement in reading skills (dependent variable)? Certainly not. This false relationship is caused by a third factor, age, that is related to shoe size as well as reading ability.

(B) Hence, when researchers attempt to make causal claims about the relationship between an independent and a dependent variable, they must control for — or rule out — other variables that may be creating a spurious relationship.

(C) In fact, the two variables may merely seem to be associated with each other due to the effect of some third variable. Sociologists call such misleading relationships spurious. A classic example is the apparent association between children's shoe size and reading ability. It seems that as shoe size increases, reading ability improves.

* variable: 변인 ** spurious: 허위의, 가짜의

① (A) − (C) − (B)   ② (B) − (A) − (C)
③ (B) − (C) − (A)   ④ (C) − (A) − (B)
⑤ (C) − (B) − (A)

[38~39] 글의 흐름으로 보아, 주어진 문장이 들어가기에 가장 적절한 곳을 고르시오.

38.

> It is the reason that individuals with certain forms of blindness do not entirely lose their circadian rhythm.

Daylight isn't the only signal that the brain can use for the purpose of biological clock resetting, though it is the principal and preferential signal, when present. (①) So long as they are reliably repeating, the brain can also use other external cues, such as food, exercise, and even regularly timed social interaction. (②) All of these events have the ability to reset the biological clock, allowing it to strike a precise twenty-four-hour note. (③) Despite not receiving light cues due to their blindness, other phenomena act as their resetting triggers. (④) Any signal that the brain uses for the purpose of clock resetting is termed a zeitgeber, from the German "time giver" or "synchronizer." (⑤) Thus, while light is the most reliable and thus the primary zeitgeber, there are many factors that can be used in addition to, or in the absence of, daylight.

* circadian rhythm: 24시간 주기 리듬

39.

> More recently, agriculture has in many places lost its local character, and has become incorporated into the global economy.

Earlier agricultural systems were integrated with and co-evolved with technologies, beliefs, myths and traditions as part of an integrated social system. (①) Generally, people planted a variety of crops in different areas, in the hope of obtaining a reasonably stable food supply. (②) These systems could only be maintained at low population levels, and were relatively non-destructive (but not always). (③) This has led to increased pressure on agricultural land for exchange commodities and export goods. (④) More land is being diverted from local food production to "cash crops" for export and exchange; fewer types of crops are raised, and each crop is raised in much greater quantities than before. (⑤) Thus, ever more land is converted from forest (and other natural systems) for agriculture for export, rather than using land for subsistence crops. [3점]

* subsistence crop: 자급자족용 작물

40. 다음 글의 내용을 한 문장으로 요약하고자 한다. 빈칸 (A), (B)에 들어갈 말로 가장 적절한 것은?

> In their study in 2007 Katherine Kinzler and her colleagues at Harvard showed that our tendency to identify with an in-group to a large degree begins in infancy and may be innate. Kinzler and her team took a bunch of five-month-olds whose families only spoke English and showed the babies two videos. In one video, a woman was speaking English. In the other, a woman was speaking Spanish. Then they were shown a screen with both women side by side, not speaking. In infant psychology research, the standard measure for affinity or interest is attention — babies will apparently stare longer at the things they like more. In Kinzler's study, the babies stared at the English speakers longer. In other studies, researchers have found that infants are more likely to take a toy offered by someone who speaks the same language as them. Psychologists routinely cite these and other experiments as evidence of our built-in evolutionary preference for "our own kind."

* affinity: 애착

↓

> Infants' more favorable responses to those who use a ___(A)___ language show that there can be a(n) ___(B)___ tendency to prefer in-group members.

	(A)	(B)		(A)	(B)
①	familiar	inborn	②	familiar	acquired
③	foreign	cultural	④	foreign	learned
⑤	formal	innate			

[41~42] 다음 글을 읽고, 물음에 답하시오.

Like all humans, the first *Homo* species to begin the long difficult process of constructing a language from scratch almost certainly never said entirely what was on their minds. At the same time, these primitive hominins would not have simply made (a) random sounds or gestures. Instead, they would have used means to communicate that they believed others would understand. And they also thought their hearers could "fill in the gaps", and connect their knowledge of their culture and the world to interpret what was uttered.

These are some of the reasons why the (b) origins of human language cannot be effectively discussed unless conversation is placed at the top of the list of things to understand. Every aspect of human language has evolved, as have components of the human brain and body, to (c) engage in conversation and social life. Language did not fully begin when the first hominid uttered the first word or sentence. It began in earnest only with the first conversation, which is both the source and the (d) goal of language. Indeed, language changes lives. It builds society and expresses our highest aspirations, our basest thoughts, our emotions and our philosophies of life. But all language is ultimately at the service of human interaction. Other components of language — things like grammar and stories — are (e) crucial to conversation.

* hominin: 인간의 조상으로 분류되는 종족
** hominid: 사람과(科)의 동물

41. 윗글의 제목으로 가장 적절한 것은?

① Various Communication Strategies of Our Ancestors
② Conversation: The Core of Language Development
③ Ending Conversation Without Offending Others
④ How Language Shapes the Way You Think
⑤ What Makes You a Good Communicator?

42. 밑줄 친 (a)~(e) 중에서 문맥상 낱말의 쓰임이 적절하지 않은 것은? [3점]

① (a)　② (b)　③ (c)　④ (d)　⑤ (e)

[43~45] 다음 글을 읽고, 물음에 답하시오.

(A)

James Walker was a renowned wrestler and he made his living through wrestling. In his town, there was a tradition in which the leader of the town chose a day when James demonstrated his skills. The leader announced one day that James would exhibit his skills as a wrestler and asked the people if there was anyone to challenge (a) him for the prize money.

(B)

When James saw the old man, he was speechless. Like everyone else, he thought that the old man had a death wish. The old man asked James to come closer since (b) he wanted to say something to him. James moved closer and the old man whispered, "I know it is impossible for me to win but my children are starving at home. Can you lose this competition to me so I can feed them with the prize money?"

(C)

Everyone was looking around in the crowd when an old man stood up and said with a shaking voice, "I will enter the contest against (c) him." Everyone burst out laughing thinking that it was a joke. James would crush him in a minute. According to the law, the leader could not stop someone who of his own free will entered the competition, so he allowed the old man to challenge the wrestler.

(D)

James thought he had an excellent opportunity to help a man in distress. (d) He did a couple of moves so that no one would suspect that the competition was fixed. However, he did not use his full strength and allowed the old man to win. The old man was overjoyed when he received the prize money. That night James felt the most victorious (e) he had ever felt.

43. 주어진 글 (A)에 이어질 내용을 순서에 맞게 배열한 것으로 가장 적절한 것은?

① (B) - (D) - (C)　② (C) - (B) - (D)
③ (C) - (D) - (B)　④ (D) - (B) - (C)
⑤ (D) - (C) - (B)

44. 밑줄 친 (a)~(e) 중에서 가리키는 대상이 나머지 넷과 다른 것은?

① (a)　② (b)　③ (c)　④ (d)　⑤ (e)

45. 윗글에 관한 내용으로 적절하지 않은 것은?

① James는 레슬링으로 생계를 유지했다.
② James는 노인을 보고 말문이 막혔다.
③ 노인의 아이들은 집에서 굶주리고 있었다.
④ 지도자는 노인이 James와 겨루는 것을 말렸다.
⑤ James는 노인과의 시합에서 전력을 다하지 않았다.

* 확인 사항
○ 답안지의 해당란에 필요한 내용을 정확히 기입(표기)했는지 확인하시오.

18

001 scenic ⓐ 경치 좋은
002 propose ⓥ 제안하다
003 walking trail 산책로
004 a variety of 여러 가지의
005 wildlife ⓝ 야생 동물
006 pressure ⓝ 압력
007 development ⓝ 개발, 발달
008 hide ⓥ 숨다
009 serve as ~의 역할을 하다
010 source ⓝ 원천
011 access ⓥ 접근하다
012 appreciate ⓥ 감상하다, 제대로 이해하다
013 continue ⓥ 계속하다
014 habitat ⓝ 서식지
015 excess ⓐ 과도한
016 reconsider ⓥ 재고하다
017 trail ⓝ 오솔길, 시골길, 산길
018 absolutely ⓐ 정말로, 전적으로

19

019 leash ⓝ (동물을 매어 두는) 줄, 사슬
020 fur ⓝ 털, 모피
021 adorable ⓐ 사랑스러운
022 backyard ⓝ 뒷마당
023 silently ⓐ 조용히
024 doorway ⓝ 출입구
025 exhausted ⓐ 기진맥진한
026 grief ⓝ 슬픔
027 loss ⓝ 상실
028 sorrowful ⓐ 슬픈

20

029 distract ⓥ 집중이 안 되게 하다
030 latter ⓐ (둘 중에서) 후자의
031 suffer ⓥ 시달리다, 고통받다, 겪다
032 complete ⓐ 완벽한
033 seek ⓥ 추구하다
034 victim ⓝ 희생자
035 private ⓐ 개인 소유의
036 run away from ~로부터 도망치다
037 distraction ⓝ 집중을 방해하는 것, 주의 산만
038 achieve ⓥ 달성하다
039 tackle ⓥ (힘든 문제상황과) 씨름하다, 맞붙다
040 eliminate ⓥ 제거하다
041 ensure ⓥ 반드시 ~하게 하다
042 limit ⓥ 제한하다

21

043 product ⓝ 상품
044 overpromise ⓝ 지나친 약속
045 lack ⓝ 부족
046 differential ⓝ 차이, 격차 ⓐ 차등을 두는
047 organization ⓝ 조직
048 pop out of ~ 밖으로 튀어나오다
049 generally ⓐ 일반적으로
050 competitor ⓝ 경쟁자
051 distribution ⓝ 유통, 분배
052 truthfulness ⓝ 진정성
053 forum ⓝ (토론의) 장, 토론회

054 compare ⓥ (A와 B를) 비교하다
055 talk back to ~에 대응하다, 말대답하다
056 instantly ⓐ 즉시
057 disappear ⓥ 사라지다
058 attention ⓝ 주목
059 complicated ⓐ 복잡한
060 reputation ⓝ 명성

22

061 anxiety ⓝ 불안
062 come along 생기다
063 undesirable ⓐ 탐탁지 않은, 원하지 않는
064 commit to ~에 전념하다
065 existing ⓐ 현존하는, 현재의
066 affliction ⓝ 고통
067 abundance ⓝ 풍족함
068 assess ⓥ 평가하다
069 delay ⓥ 미루다, 지연시키다
070 inevitable ⓐ 피할 수 없는, 반드시 있는
071 snooze button 스누즈 버튼(아침에 잠이 깬 뒤 조금 더 자기 위해 누르는 타이머 버튼)
072 end up 결국 ~하게 되다
073 ruin ⓥ 망치다
074 ultimately ⓐ 결국, 궁극적으로
075 demand ⓥ 요구하다

23

076 renewable ⓐ 재생 가능한
077 increasingly ⓐ 점점 더
078 encourage ⓥ 장려하다
079 harmonize A with B A와 B를 점점 더 조화시키다, 일치시키다
080 secure ⓥ 확보하다
081 environmental ⓐ 환경의
082 objective ⓝ 목적, 목표
083 consequence ⓝ 결과, 영향
084 consideration ⓝ 고려
085 hydropower ⓝ 수력
086 ocean-based ⓐ 해양 기반의
087 geothermal ⓐ 지열의
088 biomass ⓝ 에너지로 사용 가능한 생물체
089 have an impact on ~에 영향을 주다
090 aquatic ⓐ 수생의
091 identify ⓥ 확인하다
092 significant ⓐ 중요한, 유의미한
093 emission ⓝ 배출
094 intensive ⓐ 집약적인, 집중적인
095 occupation ⓝ 점유, 차지
096 population ⓝ 개체 수
097 practical ⓐ 현실적인, 실제적인
098 demand ⓝ 수요
099 numerous ⓐ 무수히 많은
100 effective ⓐ 효과적인
101 procedure ⓝ 절차

24

102 particle ⓝ 작은 조각
103 swallow ⓥ 삼키다
104 expose ⓥ 노출하다
105 digestive ⓐ 소화의
106 enzyme ⓝ 효소
107 act on ~에 작용하다

108 extraction ⓝ 추출
109 fuel ⓝ 연료
110 raw material 원료
111 mouthful ⓝ 한 입
112 mammal ⓝ 포유류
113 temperature ⓝ 온도
114 sustain ⓥ 유지하다
115 predator ⓝ 포식자
116 capture ⓥ 포획하다
117 prey ⓝ 먹이
118 arctic ⓐ 북극의
119 antarctic ⓐ 남극의
120 pack ice 총빙(叢氷), 유빙
121 high-altitude ⓐ 고도가 높은
122 mountaintop ⓝ 산꼭대기
123 rainforest ⓝ (열대) 우림
124 in no small measure 어느 정도는, 적잖이
125 ease ⓥ 완화시키다
126 indigestion ⓝ 소화불량
127 harsh ⓐ 가혹한

25

128 average ⓝ 평균 ⓐ 평균의
129 regular ⓐ 정기적인
130 participation ⓝ 참여
131 based on ~에 근거하여
132 among prep ~중에
133 above ⓐ (글에서) 위에(서), 앞에(서)
134 length ⓝ 길이
135 track and field 육상 (경기)

26

136 activist ⓝ 운동가, 활동가
137 orphan ⓝ 고아 ⓥ 고아로 만들다
138 mark ⓥ 특징짓다
139 hardship ⓝ 고난, 어려움
140 washerwoman ⓝ 세탁부
141 decade ⓝ 10년
142 barely ⓐ 간신히, 가까스로
143 backbreaking ⓐ 대단히 힘든
144 labor ⓝ 노동
145 fall out (머리 등이) 빠지다, 헐거워지다
146 maid ⓝ 가정부, 하녀
147 chemist ⓝ 화학자
148 recruit ⓥ 모집하다
149 sales agent 판매 대리인
150 share ⓝ 몫, 할당
151 profit ⓝ 이익, 수익
152 self-made ⓐ 자수성가한
153 female ⓐ 여성의
154 financial ⓐ 재정적인
155 independence ⓝ 독립

27

156 competition ⓝ (경연) 대회
157 compete ⓥ 경쟁하다
158 livable ⓐ 살만한, 살기 적합한
159 structure ⓝ 구조물
160 made out of ~로 만든
161 on site 현장에서
162 supply ⓥ 공급하다, 제공하다

163 assistance ⓝ 도움, 원조
164 registration ⓝ 등록

28

165 fireworks ⓝ 불꽃놀이
166 display ⓝ 전시
167 maze ⓝ 미로
168 accompany ⓥ 동반하다
169 reserve ⓥ 예약하다
170 beforehand ⓐ 사전에

29

171 detect ⓥ 감지하다, 알아차리다
172 range ⓝ 범주, 범위
173 odour ⓝ 냄새, 악취
174 molecule ⓝ 분자
175 present ⓐ 있는, 존재하는
176 vice versa 그 반대도 마찬가지다
177 relate to ~와 관련되다
178 pleasantly ⓐ 쾌적하게, 기분 좋게
179 cilantro ⓝ 고수
180 soapy ⓐ 비누 같은
181 unpleasant ⓐ 불쾌한
182 underlying ⓐ 내재된, 근본적인
183 genetic ⓐ 유전적인
184 component ⓝ 구성 요소
185 selection ⓝ 선발, (선택 가능한 것들의) 집합
186 scent ⓝ 냄새
187 perceive ⓥ 인지하다
188 ecology ⓝ 생태
189 response profile 반응 도표(네 가지 기본적인 맛감각에 대한 신경 세포의 반응을 보여주는 그래프)
190 profile ⓝ 프로필, 도표
191 locate ⓥ 찾아내다
192 relevant ⓐ 관련 있는, 적절한
193 accordingly ⓐ 그에 따라

30

194 evolve ⓥ 진화하다
195 physical ⓐ 신체적인
196 psychological ⓐ 심리적인
197 domestication ⓝ 사육, 길들이기
198 reduction ⓝ 감소
199 feed ⓥ 먹이를 주다
200 wild ⓐ 야생의
201 ancestor ⓝ 조상
202 capacity ⓝ 능력
203 occur ⓥ 일어나다, 발생하다
204 firmly ⓐ 확실히, 단호히
205 established ⓐ 자리를 잡은
206 expand ⓥ 커지다, 확장하다
207 shrink ⓥ 줄어들다

31

208 fundamental ⓐ 근본적인
209 intuitive ⓐ 직관적인
210 spark ⓥ 자극하다, 촉발시키다
211 pathway ⓝ 통로
212 catalyst ⓝ 촉매, 기폭제
213 progress ⓝ 진보, 진전

214 public transportation 대중교통
215 vital ⓐ 없어서는 안 되는, 필수적인
216 destination ⓝ 목적지
217 possibility ⓝ 가능성
218 aspire ⓥ 열망하다
219 strengthen ⓥ 강화하다
220 economy ⓝ 경제
221 commercial ⓐ 상업적
222 secure ⓐ 안정된
223 mobile ⓐ 이동하는, 기동성 있는
224 exceptional ⓐ 특출난, 이례적인

32
225 consultant ⓝ 자문 위원
226 describe ⓥ 말하다, 서술하다
227 emergence ⓝ 출현, 등장
228 background ⓝ 배경, 배후 사정
229 discipline ⓝ 분야
230 term ⓝ 용어, 말
231 derive A from B A를 B로부터 끌어내다
232 bring together 합치다, 묶다
233 arguably ⓐd 거의 틀림없이
234 in contact with ~와 접촉하는
235 diversify ⓥ 다양화하다
236 do the trick 성공하다, 효과가 있다
237 combine ⓥ 결합하다
238 notion ⓝ 개념, 생각
239 recommend ⓥ 추천하다
240 utilize ⓥ 활용[이용]하다
241 expertise ⓝ 전문 지식
242 staffing ⓝ 직원 채용
243 bring about ~을 유발[초래]하다
244 perspective ⓝ 관점
245 innovation ⓝ 혁신
246 compensate ⓥ 보완하다, 보상하다
247 reflect on ~을 돌아보다, 성찰하다
248 specific ⓐ 구체적인

33
249 examine ⓥ 조사하다
250 seldom ⓐd 좀처럼 ~않는
251 fossilize ⓥ 화석화하다
252 insect ⓝ 곤충
253 community ⓝ (생물의) 군집
254 diverse ⓐ 다양한
255 tropical ⓐ 열대 지방의, 열대의
256 diversity ⓝ 다양성
257 creature ⓝ 생물, 동물
258 consume ⓥ 먹다, 소비하다
259 entirely ⓐd 완전히
260 decompose ⓥ 부패하다
261 occasionally ⓐd 가끔, 때때로
262 notice ⓥ 알아채다, 인지하다
263 entire ⓐ 전체의, 완전한
264 lesson ⓝ 교훈, 수업
265 trait ⓝ 특성
266 make room for ~의 여지를 남기다, ~을 위해 (자리를) 양보하다

34
267 face ⓥ 직면하다
268 go under 파산하다

269 beg ⓥ 바라다, 부탁하다
270 service ⓥ (서비스를) 제공하다
271 location ⓝ 위치, 장소
272 turn down ~을 거절하다
273 tremendous ⓐ 엄청난
274 pace ⓝ 속도
275 term ⓝ 기간
276 establish ⓥ 설정하다, 확립하다
277 margin ⓝ 여유, 여지
278 thrive ⓥ 번창하다
279 flail ⓥ 마구 움직이다, 마구 흔들다
280 crisis ⓝ 위기
281 specific ⓐ 특정한
282 upper ⓐ 위쪽의
283 emphasize ⓥ 강조하다
284 moral ⓐ 도덕적인
285 duty ⓝ 의무

35
286 effect ⓝ 효과, 영향
287 phenomenon ⓝ 현상
288 apply to ~에 적용되다
289 statement ⓝ 진술
290 on the surface 표면적으로
291 identify with ~와 동일시하다
292 fill in the blank 공백을 메우다, 나머지를 상상하다
293 rest ⓝ 나머지
294 principle ⓝ 원리
295 rely on ~에 의존하다
296 offer ⓥ 제공하다
297 make sense 타당하다, 말이 되다
298 countless ⓐ 수많은
299 beneficial ⓐ 이로운
300 prediction ⓝ 예측

36
301 grab ⓥ 잡다
302 point ⓥ 향하게 하다
303 shoot ⓥ 촬영하다
304 red-eye effect 적목 현상
305 penetrate ⓥ 통과하다, 관통하다
306 reflect ⓥ 반사하다
307 automatically ⓐd 자동으로
308 available ⓐ 이용 가능한
309 exposure ⓝ 노출
310 half ⓝ 절반
311 noticeable ⓐ 두드러지는
312 environment ⓝ 환경
313 dilate ⓥ 확장하다, 팽창하다

37
314 causal relationship 인과 관계
315 independent ⓐ 독립적인
316 improvement ⓝ 향상, 개선
317 dependent ⓐ 의존적인
318 factor ⓝ 요인, 요소
319 researcher ⓝ 연구자
320 attempt ⓥ 시도하다
321 claim ⓥ 주장
322 rule out 배제하다
323 merely ⓐd 단지

324 associated with ~와 연관된
325 sociologist ⓝ 사회학자
326 misleading ⓐ 잘못된, 오도하는
327 classic ⓐ 전형적인
328 apparent ⓐ 명백한
329 association ⓝ 연관성

38
330 individual ⓝ 개인
331 certain ⓐ 특정한
332 blindness ⓝ 실명, 맹목
333 daylight ⓝ 햇빛, 일광
334 purpose ⓝ 목적
335 biological ⓐ 생물학적인
336 reset ⓥ 재설정하다
337 principal ⓐ 주요한, 주된
338 preferential ⓐ 우선시되는, 특혜의
339 reliably ⓐd 확실하게, 믿을 수 있게
340 external ⓐ 외부적인
341 cue ⓝ 신호
342 interaction ⓝ 상호 작용
343 strike ⓥ 치다, 부딪히다
344 precise ⓐ 정확한
345 note ⓝ (음악의) 음
346 trigger ⓝ 계기, 유인
347 term ⓥ 칭하다, 일컫다
348 synchronizer ⓝ 동기화 장치
349 reliable ⓐ 믿음직한
350 primary ⓐ 주된, 주요한
351 in addition to ~에 더하여
352 in the absence of ~의 부재 시에

39
353 agriculture ⓝ 농업
354 local ⓐ 지역의
355 incorporate A into B A를 B에 통합시키다
356 integrate ⓥ 통합하다
357 co-evolve ⓥ 함께 진화하다
358 myth ⓝ 신화
359 plant ⓥ 심다
360 crop ⓝ 농작물, 수확물
361 in the hope of ~라는 희망으로
362 obtain ⓥ 획득하다
363 reasonably ⓐd 합리적으로
364 stable ⓐ 안정적인
365 maintain ⓥ 유지하다
366 relatively ⓐd 상대적으로
367 non-destructive ⓐ 파괴적이지 않은
368 exchange ⓝ 교환
369 commodity ⓝ 상품
370 goods ⓝ 상품
371 divert ⓥ 전환시키다, 다른 데로 돌리다
372 production ⓝ 생산
373 raise ⓥ 기르다
374 quantity ⓝ 양(量)
375 convert ⓥ 전환하다, 개조하다

40
376 colleague ⓝ 동료
377 tendency ⓝ 경향
378 in-group ⓝ 내(內)집단

379 infancy ⓝ 유아기
380 innate ⓐ 타고난, 선천적인
381 psychology ⓝ 심리학
382 measure ⓝ 척도, 기준
383 interest ⓝ 관심
384 apparently ⓐd 분명히, 명백히
385 stare at ~을 쳐다보다, 응시하다
386 infant ⓝ 유아
387 routinely ⓐd 판에 박힌 듯, 관례대로
388 cite ⓥ 인용하다
389 evolutionary ⓐ 진화의
390 preference ⓝ 선호
391 favorable ⓐ 호의적인
392 inborn ⓐ 타고난
393 acquired ⓐ 후천적인, 습득된

41~42
394 species ⓝ 종(種)
395 construct ⓥ 구성하다
396 from scratch 맨 처음부터, 아무것도 없이
397 mind ⓝ 마음
398 primitive ⓐ 원시의
399 means ⓝ 수단
400 connect ⓥ 연결하다
401 interpret ⓥ 해석하다, 이해하다
402 utter ⓥ 발화하다
403 origin ⓝ 기원
404 effectively ⓐd 효과적으로
405 place ⓥ 두다
406 aspect ⓝ 측면, 양상
407 engage in ~에 관여하다, 참여하다
408 in earnest 본격적으로
409 aspiration ⓝ 열망
410 emotion ⓝ 감정
411 philosophy ⓝ 철학
412 crucial ⓐ 매우 중요한
413 various ⓐ 다양한
414 strategy ⓝ 전략
415 core ⓝ 핵심
416 offend ⓥ 마음을 상하게 하다
417 shape ⓥ 형성하다
418 communicator ⓝ 의사 전달자

43~45
419 renowned ⓐ 유명한
420 demonstrate ⓥ (시범을) 보이다
421 announce ⓥ 알리다
422 exhibit ⓥ 보여주다, 전시하다
423 challenge ⓥ 도전하다
424 speechless ⓐ 말문이 막힌
425 death wish 죽음에 대한 동경
426 whisper ⓥ 속삭이다
427 starve ⓥ 굶주리다
428 burst out ~을 터뜨리다
429 crush ⓥ 뭉개다, 진압하다, 눌러 부수다
430 of one's own free will 자유 의지로, 자발적으로
431 opportunity ⓝ 기회
432 distress ⓝ 곤경, 괴로움
433 suspect ⓥ 의심하다
434 overjoy ⓥ 매우 기쁘게 하다
435 victorious ⓐ 승리를 거둔

19회

TEST A-B 각 단어의 뜻을 [A] 영어는 우리말로, [B] 우리말은 영어로 쓰시오.

A	English	Korean
01	grief	
02	vital	
03	phenomenon	
04	on site	
05	disappear	
06	labor	
07	arguably	
08	construct	
09	margin	
10	molecule	
11	delay	
12	increasingly	
13	factor	
14	physical	
15	prediction	
16	crucial	
17	aspiration	
18	ecology	
19	convert	
20	consume	

B	Korean	English
01	진술	
02	예약하다	
03	살만한, 살기 적합한	
04	풍족함	
05	구체적인	
06	타고난, 선천적인	
07	상품	
08	전문 지식	
09	서식지	
10	특출난, 이례적인	
11	계기, 유인	
12	명백한	
13	소화의	
14	제안하다	
15	온도	
16	농업	
17	특성	
18	안정적인	
19	심리적인	
20	목적, 목표	

▶ A-D 정답 : 해설편 194쪽

TEST C-D 각 단어의 뜻을 골라 기호를 쓰시오.

C	English		Korean
01	strengthen	( )	ⓐ 현실적인, 실제적인
02	predator	( )	ⓑ 향상, 개선
03	serve as	( )	ⓒ 포식자
04	misleading	( )	ⓓ 평균
05	average	( )	ⓔ 측면, 양상
06	eliminate	( )	ⓕ 철학
07	detect	( )	ⓖ 중요한, 유의미한
08	unpleasant	( )	ⓗ 잘못된, 오도하는
09	consideration	( )	ⓘ 자리를 잡은
10	established	( )	ⓙ 설정하다, 확립하다
11	significant	( )	ⓚ 불쾌한
12	improvement	( )	ⓛ 동반하다
13	aspect	( )	ⓜ 노출
14	practical	( )	ⓝ 고려
15	exposure	( )	ⓞ 경쟁자
16	whisper	( )	ⓟ 강화하다
17	philosophy	( )	ⓠ 감지하다, 알아차리다
18	establish	( )	ⓡ ~의 역할을 하다
19	competitor	( )	ⓢ 제거하다
20	accompany	( )	ⓣ 속삭이다

D	Korean		English
01	엄청난	( )	ⓐ victim
02	~와 관련되다	( )	ⓑ tremendous
03	간신히, 가까스로	( )	ⓒ ruin
04	유통, 분배	( )	ⓓ reputation
05	~을 돌아보다, 성찰하다	( )	ⓔ relate to
06	평가하다	( )	ⓕ reflect on
07	통합하다	( )	ⓖ reduction
08	직관적인	( )	ⓗ intuitive
09	분야	( )	ⓘ absolutely
10	감소	( )	ⓙ assess
11	집약적인, 집중적인	( )	ⓚ barely
12	망치다	( )	ⓛ discipline
13	본격적으로	( )	ⓜ intensive
14	해석하다, 이해하다	( )	ⓝ diversify
15	외부적인	( )	ⓞ external
16	열망하다	( )	ⓟ in earnest
17	희생자	( )	ⓠ integrate
18	다양화하다	( )	ⓡ aspire
19	정말로, 전적으로	( )	ⓢ interpret
20	명성	( )	ⓣ distribution

※ 영어 [독해] 파트만 수록한 문제지이므로 18번부터 시작합니다.   ● 점수 표시가 없는 문항은 모두 2점   ● 문항수 28개 | 배점 63점 | 제한 시간 45분

18. 다음 글의 목적으로 가장 적절한 것은?

To the Principal of Alamda High School,

On behalf of the Youth Soccer Tournament Series, I would like to remind you of the 2019 Series next week. Surely, we understand the importance of a player's education. Regrettably, however, the Series will result in players missing two days of school for the competition. The games will be attended by many college coaches scouting prospective student athletes. Therefore, the Series can be a great opportunity for young soccer players to demonstrate their capabilities as athletes. I would like to request your permission for the absence of the players from your school during this event. Thank you for your understanding.

Best regards,
Jack D'Adamo, Director of the Youth Soccer Tournament Series

① 선수들의 학력 향상 프로그램을 홍보하려고
② 대학 진학 상담의 활성화 방안을 제안하려고
③ 선수들의 훈련 장비 추가 구입을 건의하려고
④ 선수들의 대회 참가를 위한 결석 허락을 요청하려고
⑤ 대회 개최를 위한 운동장 대여 가능 여부를 문의하려고

19. 다음 글에 드러난 Norm의 심경으로 가장 적절한 것은?

Norm and his friend Jason went on a winter camping trip. In the middle of the night, Norm suddenly woke up sensing something was terribly wrong. To his surprise, the stove was glowing red! Norm shook Jason awake and told him to look at the stove. Jason said he had filled it with every piece of wood he could fit into it. Norm thought the cabin was going to catch fire. He started swearing at Jason. He pulled Jason out of his bed, opened the front door and threw him out into the snow. Norm yelled out in anger, "Don't come back in until I get this stove cooled off!"

① alarmed and upset   ② thrilled and joyful
③ touched and grateful   ④ ashamed and guilty
⑤ encouraged and satisfied

20. 다음 글에서 필자가 주장하는 바로 가장 적절한 것은?

We tend to go long periods of time without reaching out to the people we know. Then, we suddenly take notice of the distance that has formed and we scramble to make repairs. We call people we haven't spoken to in ages, hoping that one small effort will erase the months and years of distance we've created. However, this rarely works: relationships aren't kept up with big one-time fixes. They're kept up with regular maintenance, like a car. In our relationships, we have to make sure that not too much time goes by between oil changes, so to speak. This isn't to say that you shouldn't bother calling someone just because it's been a while since you've spoken; just that it's more ideal not to let yourself fall out of touch in the first place. Consistency always brings better results.

① 가까운 사이일수록 적당한 거리를 유지해야 한다.
② 사교성을 기르려면 개방적인 태도를 가져야 한다.
③ 대화를 할 때 상대방의 의견을 먼저 경청해야 한다.
④ 인간관계를 지속하려면 일관된 노력을 기울여야 한다.
⑤ 원활한 의사소통을 위해 솔직하게 감정을 표현해야 한다.

21. 밑줄 친 "learn and live"가 다음 글에서 의미하는 바로 가장 적절한 것은? [3점]

There is a critical factor that determines whether your choice will influence that of others: the visible consequences of the choice. Take the case of the Adélie penguins. They are often found strolling in large groups toward the edge of the water in search of food. Yet danger awaits in the icy-cold water. There is the leopard seal, for one, which likes to have penguins for a meal. What is an Adélie to do? The penguins' solution is to play the waiting game. They wait and wait and wait by the edge of the water until one of them gives up and jumps in. The moment that occurs, the rest of the penguins watch with anticipation to see what happens next. If the pioneer survives, everyone else will follow suit. If it perishes, they'll turn away. One penguin's destiny alters the fate of all the others. Their strategy, you could say, is "learn and live."

* perish: 죽다

① occupy a rival's territory for safety
② discover who the enemy is and attack first
③ share survival skills with the next generation
④ support the leader's decisions for the best results
⑤ follow another's action only when it is proven safe

22. 다음 글의 요지로 가장 적절한 것은?

How many of you have a hard time saying no? No matter what anyone asks of you, no matter how much of an inconvenience it poses for you, you do what they request. This is not a healthy way of living because by saying yes all the time you are building up emotions of inconvenience. You know what will happen in time? You will resent the person who you feel you cannot say no to because you no longer have control of your life and of what makes you happy. You are allowing someone else to have control over your life. When you are suppressed emotionally and constantly do things against your own will, your stress will eat you up faster than you can count to three.

① 거절하지 못하고 삶의 통제권을 잃으면 스트레스가 생긴다.
② 상대방의 거절을 감정적으로 해석하지 않는 것이 바람직하다.
③ 대부분의 스트레스는 상대에 대한 지나친 요구에서 비롯된다.
④ 일에 우선순위를 정해서 자신의 삶을 통제하는 것이 필요하다.
⑤ 사람마다 생각이 다를 수 있다는 점을 인정하는 것이 중요하다.

23. 다음 글의 주제로 가장 적절한 것은?

You can say that information sits in one brain until it is communicated to another, unchanged in the conversation. That's true of *sheer* information, like your phone number or the place you left your keys. But it's not true of knowledge. Knowledge relies on judgements, which you discover and polish in conversation with other people or with yourself. Therefore you don't learn the details of your thinking until speaking or writing it out in detail and looking back critically at the result. "Is what I just said foolish, or is what I just wrote a deep truth?" In the speaking or writing, you uncover your bad ideas, often embarrassing ones, and good ideas too, sometimes fame-making ones. Thinking requires its expression.

① critical roles of speaking or writing in refining thoughts
② persuasive ways to communicate what you think to people
③ important tips to select the right information for your writing
④ positive effects of logical thinking on reading comprehension
⑤ enormous gaps between spoken language and written language

24. 다음 글의 제목으로 가장 적절한 것은?

It is said that among the Bantu peoples of Central Africa, when an individual from one tribe meets someone from a different group, they ask, "What do you dance?" Throughout time, communities have forged their identities through dance rituals that mark major events in the life of individuals, including birth, marriage, and death — as well as religious festivals and important points in the seasons. The social structure of many communities, from African tribes to Spanish gypsies, and to Scottish clans, gains much cohesion from the group activity of dancing. Historically, dance has been a strong, binding influence on community life, a means of expressing the social identity of the group, and participation allows individuals to demonstrate a belonging. As a consequence, in many regions of the world there are as many types of dances as there are communities with distinct identities.

* forge: 구축하다 ** cohesion: 결속

① What Makes Traditional Dance Hard to Learn?
② Dance: A Distinct Sign of Social Identity
③ The More Varieties, the Better Dances
④ Feeling Down? Enjoy Dancing!
⑤ The Origin of Tribal Dances

25. 다음 표의 내용과 일치하지 <u>않는</u> 것은?

Wellness Tourism Trips and Expenditures by Region in 2015 and 2017

Destination	Number of Trips (millions)		Expenditures ($ billions)	
	2015	2017	2015	2017
North America	186.5	204.1	$215.7	$241.7
Europe	249.9	291.8	$193.4	$210.8
Asia-Pacific	193.9	257.6	$111.2	$136.7
Latin America-The Caribbean	46.8	59.1	$30.4	$34.8
The Middle East-North Africa	8.5	11.0	$8.3	$10.7
Africa	5.4	6.5	$4.2	$4.8
Total	**691.0**	**830.0**	**$563.2**	**$639.4**

• Note: Figures may not sum to total due to rounding.

The table above shows the number of trips and expenditures for wellness tourism, travel for health and well-being, in 2015 and 2017. ① Both the total number of trips and the total expenditures were higher in 2017 compared to those in 2015. ② Of the six listed regions, Europe was the most visited place for wellness tourism in both 2015 and 2017, followed by Asia-Pacific. ③ In 2017, the number of trips to Latin America-The Caribbean was more than five times higher than that to The Middle East-North Africa. ④ While North America was the only region where more than 200 billion dollars was spent in 2015, it was joined by Europe in 2017. ⑤ Meanwhile, expenditures in The Middle East-North Africa and Africa were each less than 10 billion dollars in both 2015 and 2017.

26. George Boole에 관한 다음 글의 내용과 일치하지 <u>않는</u> 것은?

George Boole was born in Lincoln, England in 1815. Boole was forced to leave school at the age of sixteen after his father's business collapsed. He taught himself mathematics, natural philosophy and various languages. He began to produce original mathematical research and made important contributions to areas of mathematics. For those contributions, in 1844, he was awarded a gold medal for mathematics by the Royal Society. Boole was deeply interested in expressing the workings of the human mind in symbolic form, and his two books on this subject, *The Mathematical Analysis of Logic* and *An Investigation of the Laws of Thought* form the basis of today's computer science. In 1849, he was appointed the first professor of mathematics at Queen's College in Cork, Ireland and taught there until his death in 1864.

① 아버지의 사업 실패 후 학교를 그만두게 되었다.
② 수학, 자연 철학, 여러 언어를 독학했다.
③ Royal Society에서 화학으로 금메달을 받았다.
④ 오늘날 컴퓨터 과학의 기초를 형성한 책들을 저술했다.
⑤ Queen's College의 교수로 임명되었다.

27. Sustainable Mobility Week 2019에 관한 다음 안내문의 내용과 일치하지 <u>않는</u> 것은?

Sustainable Mobility Week 2019

This annual event for clean and sustainable transport runs from Nov 25 to Dec 1. The slogan for the event changes every year, and this year it is *Walk with Us!* You can participate in the activities below.

Walking Challenge:
Try to walk over 20,000 steps during the weekend of the event to promote a clean environment.

Selecting Sustainable Mobility:
Use public transport or a bicycle instead of your own car.

• Participants who complete both activities are qualified to apply for the Sustainable Mobility Week Awards.
• Participants must register online.

www.sustainablemobilityweek.org

---

① 슬로건이 매년 바뀐다.
② 주말 동안 2만보 넘게 걷는 것에 도전할 수 있다.
③ 대중교통이나 자전거를 이용하는 활동이 있다.
④ 한 가지 활동을 완료한 참가자는 수상 자격이 있다.
⑤ 참가자는 온라인으로 등록해야 한다.

28. Introduction to Furniture Making에 관한 다음 안내문의 내용과 일치하는 것은?

Introduction to Furniture Making

Throughout this four-week workshop, students will build a solid foundation for their new venture into woodworking.

• Age Requirement: 16 and older
• Location: Hoboken Community Center
• Dates: Dec 7 − Dec 28 (Every Saturday)
• Time: 1:00 p.m. − 5:00 p.m.
• Price: $399
• Note:
  − Previous woodworking experience is not necessary.
  − We offer full refunds if you cancel at least 10 days in advance.

With the guidance of an instructor, each student will leave with a hand-crafted side table.

For more information or to register, contact Dave Malka (davemalka@woodfurniture.org).

---

① 연령에 제한이 없다.
② 토요일에 5시간씩 진행된다.
③ 목공 경험이 없는 사람도 참여할 수 있다.
④ 적어도 일주일 전에 취소하면 전액을 환불해 준다.
⑤ 수강생들은 수작업으로 만든 의자를 가지고 가게 된다.

29. 다음 글의 밑줄 친 부분 중, 어법상 <u>틀린</u> 것은? [3점]

Non-verbal communication is not a substitute for verbal communication. Rather, it should function as a supplement, ① serving to enhance the richness of the content of the message that is being passed across. Non-verbal communication can be useful in situations ② where speaking may be impossible or inappropriate. Imagine you are in an uncomfortable position while talking to an individual. Non-verbal communication will help you ③ get the message across to him or her to give you some time off the conversation to be comfortable again. Another advantage of non-verbal communication is ④ what it offers you the opportunity to express emotions and attitudes properly. Without the aid of non-verbal communication, there are several aspects of your nature and personality that will not be adequately expressed. So, again, it does not substitute verbal communication but rather ⑤ complements it.

* supplement: 보충

30. (A), (B), (C)의 각 네모 안에서 문맥에 맞는 낱말로 가장 적절한 것은?

Intellectual humility is admitting you are human and there are limits to the knowledge you have. It involves (A) neglecting / recognizing that you possess cognitive and personal biases, and that your brain tends to see things in such a way that your opinions and viewpoints are favored above others. It is being willing to work to overcome those biases in order to be more objective and make informed decisions. People who display intellectual humility are more likely to be (B) receptive / resistant to learning from others who think differently than they do. They tend to be well-liked and respected by others because they make it clear that they (C) value / undervalue what other people bring to the table. Intellectually humble people want to learn more and are open to finding information from a variety of sources. They are not interested in trying to appear or feel superior to others.

	(A)	(B)	(C)
①	recognizing	······	receptive	······	value
②	recognizing	······	resistant	······	undervalue
③	recognizing	······	receptive	······	undervalue
④	neglecting	······	resistant	······	undervalue
⑤	neglecting	······	receptive	······	value

[31 ~ 34] 다음 빈칸에 들어갈 말로 가장 적절한 것을 고르시오.

31. People engage in typical patterns of interaction based on the relationship between their roles and the roles of others. Employers are expected to interact with employees in a certain way, as are doctors with patients. In each case, actions are restricted by the role responsibilities and obligations associated with individuals' positions within society. For instance, parents and children are linked by certain rights, privileges, and obligations. Parents are responsible for providing their children with the basic necessities of life — food, clothing, shelter, and so forth. These expectations are so powerful that not meeting them may make the parents vulnerable to charges of negligence or abuse. Children, in turn, are expected to do as their parents say. Thus, interactions within a relationship are functions not only of the individual personalities of the people involved but also of the role requirements associated with the _____ they have.

* vulnerable: 비난받기 쉬운 ** negligence: 태만

① careers
② statuses
③ abilities
④ motivations
⑤ perspectives

32. The title of Thomas Friedman's 2005 book, *The World Is Flat*, was based on the belief that globalization would inevitably bring us closer together. It has done that, but it has also inspired us _____. When faced with perceived threats — the financial crisis, terrorism, violent conflict, refugees and immigration, the increasing gap between rich and poor — people cling more tightly to their groups. One founder of a famous social media company believed social media would unite us. In some respects it has, but it has simultaneously given voice and organizational ability to new cyber tribes, some of whom spend their time spreading blame and division across the World Wide Web. There seem now to be as many tribes, and as much conflict between them, as there have ever been. Is it possible for these tribes to coexist in a world where the concept of "us and them" remains?

[3점]

① to build barriers
② to achieve equality
③ to abandon traditions
④ to value individualism
⑤ to develop technologies

[해설편 p.198]

33. Focusing on the differences among societies conceals a deeper reality: their similarities are greater and more profound than their dissimilarities. Imagine studying two hills while standing on a ten-thousand-foot-high plateau. Seen from your perspective, one hill appears to be three hundred feet high, and the other appears to be nine hundred feet. This difference may seem large, and you might focus your attention on what local forces, such as erosion, account for the difference in size. But this narrow perspective misses the opportunity to study the other, more significant geological forces that created what are actually two very similar mountains, one 10,300 feet high and the other 10,900 feet. And when it comes to human societies, people have been standing on a ten-thousand-foot plateau, letting the differences among societies _____. [3점]

* erosion: 침식

① prove the uniqueness of each society
② prevent cross-cultural understanding
③ mask the more overwhelming similarities
④ change their perspective on what diversity is
⑤ encourage them to step out of their mental frame

34. There is a famous Spanish proverb that says, "The belly rules the mind." This is a clinically proven fact. Food is the original mind-controlling drug. Every time we eat, we bombard our brains with a feast of chemicals, triggering an explosive hormonal chain reaction that directly influences the way we think. Countless studies have shown that the positive emotional state induced by a good meal _____. It triggers an instinctive desire to repay the provider. This is why executives regularly combine business meetings with meals, why lobbyists invite politicians to attend receptions, lunches, and dinners, and why major state occasions almost always involve an impressive banquet. Churchill called this "dining diplomacy," and sociologists have confirmed that this principle is a strong motivator across all human cultures. [3점]

* banquet: 연회

① leads us to make a fair judgement
② interferes with cooperation with others
③ does harm to serious diplomatic occasions
④ plays a critical role in improving our health
⑤ enhances our receptiveness to be persuaded

35. 다음 글에서 전체 흐름과 관계 없는 문장은?

Training and conditioning for baseball focuses on developing strength, power, speed, quickness and flexibility. ① Before the 1980s, strength training was not an important part of conditioning for a baseball player. ② People viewed baseball as a game of skill and technique rather than strength, and most managers and coaches saw strength training as something for bodybuilders, not baseball players. ③ Unlike more isolated bodybuilding exercises, athletic exercises train as many muscle groups and functions as possible at the same time. ④ They feared that weight lifting and building large muscles would cause players to lose flexibility and interfere with quickness and proper technique. ⑤ Today, though, experts understand the importance of strength training and have made it part of the game.

[36 ~ 37] 주어진 글 다음에 이어질 글의 순서로 가장 적절한 것을 고르시오.

36.

> Making a small request that people will accept will naturally increase the chances of their accepting a bigger request afterwards.

(A) After this, the salesperson asks you if you are interested in buying any cruelty-free cosmetics from their store. Given the fact that most people agree to the prior request to sign the petition, they will be more likely to purchase the cosmetics.

(B) For instance, a salesperson might request you to sign a petition to prevent cruelty against animals. This is a very small request, and most people will do what the salesperson asks.

(C) They make such purchases because the salesperson takes advantage of a human tendency to be consistent in their words and actions. People want to be consistent and will keep saying yes if they have already said it once.

* petition: 청원서

① (A) − (C) − (B)   ② (B) − (A) − (C)
③ (B) − (C) − (A)   ④ (C) − (A) − (B)
⑤ (C) − (B) − (A)

37.

> Many studies have shown that people's health and subjective well-being are affected by ethnic relations. Members of minority groups in general have poorer health outcomes than the majority group.

(A) One possible answer is stress. From multiple physiological studies, we know that encounters with members of other ethnic-racial categories, even in the relatively safe environment of laboratories, trigger stress responses.

(B) But that difference remains even when obvious factors, such as social class and access to medical services are controlled for. This suggests that dominance relations have their own effect on people's health. How could that be the case?

(C) Minority individuals have many encounters with majority individuals, each of which may trigger such responses. However minimal these effects may be, their frequency may increase total stress, which would account for part of the health disadvantage of minority individuals. [3점]

① (A) − (C) − (B)   ② (B) − (A) − (C)
③ (B) − (C) − (A)   ④ (C) − (A) − (B)
⑤ (C) − (B) − (A)

[38 ~ 39] 글의 흐름으로 보아, 주어진 문장이 들어가기에 가장 적절한 곳을 고르시오.

38.

> The stage director must gain the audience's attention and direct their eyes to a particular spot or actor.

Achieving focus in a movie is easy. Directors can simply point the camera at whatever they want the audience to look at. (①) Close-ups and slow camera shots can emphasize a killer's hand or a character's brief glance of guilt. (②) On stage, focus is much more difficult because the audience is free to look wherever they like. (③) This can be done through lighting, costumes, scenery, voice, and movements. (④) Focus can be gained by simply putting a spotlight on one actor, by having one actor in red and everyone else in gray, or by having one actor move while the others remain still. (⑤) All these techniques will quickly draw the audience's attention to the actor whom the director wants to be in focus.

39.

> In this way, quick judgements are not only relevant in employment matters; they are equally applicable in love and relationship matters too.

You've probably heard the expression, "first impressions matter a lot". (①) Life really doesn't give many people a second chance to make a good first impression. (②) It has been determined that it takes only a few seconds for anyone to assess another individual. (③) This is very noticeable in recruitment processes, where top recruiters can predict the direction of their eventual decision on any candidate within a few seconds of introducing themselves. (④) So, a candidate's CV may 'speak' knowledge and competence, but their appearance and introduction may tell of a lack of coordination, fear, and poor interpersonal skills. (⑤) On a date with a wonderful somebody who you've painstakingly tracked down for months, subtle things like bad breath or wrinkled clothes may spoil your noble efforts.

* CV: 이력서(curriculum vitae)

40. 다음 글의 내용을 한 문장으로 요약하고자 한다. 빈칸 (A), (B)에 들어갈 말로 가장 적절한 것은?

> The perception of the same amount of discount on a product depends on its relation to the initial price. In one study, respondents were presented with a purchase situation. The persons put in the situation of buying a calculator that cost $15 found out from the vendor that the same product was available in a different store 20 minutes away and at a promotional price of $10. In this case, 68% of respondents decided to make their way down to the store in order to save $5. In the second condition, which involved buying a jacket for $125, the respondents were also told that the same product was available in a store 20 minutes away and cost $120 there. This time, only 29% of the persons said that they would get the cheaper jacket. In both cases, the product was $5 cheaper, but in the first case, the amount was 1/3 of the price, and in the second, it was 1/25 of the price. What differed in both of these situations was the price context of the purchase.

↓

> When the same amount of discount is given in a purchasing situation, the _____(A)_____ value of the discount affects how people _____(B)_____ its value.

	(A)	(B)		(A)	(B)
①	absolute	⋯⋯ modify	②	absolute	⋯⋯ express
③	identical	⋯⋯ produce	④	relative	⋯⋯ perceive
⑤	relative	⋯⋯ advertise			

[41 ~ 42] 다음 글을 읽고, 물음에 답하시오.

Behavioral ecologists have observed clever copying behavior among many of our close animal relatives. One example was uncovered by behavioral ecologists studying the behavior of a small Australian animal called the quoll. Its survival was being (a) threatened by the cane toad, an invasive species introduced to Australia in the 1930s. To a quoll, these toads look as tasty as they are (b) poisonous, and the quolls who ate them suffered fatal consequences at a speedy rate. Behavioral ecologists identified a clever solution by using quolls' instincts to imitate. Scientists fed small groups of quolls toad sausages containing harmless but nausea-inducing chemicals, conditioning them to (c) avoid the toads. Groups of these 'toad-smart' quolls were then released back into the wild: they taught their own offspring what they'd learned. Other quolls copied these (d) constructive behaviors through a process of social learning. As each baby quoll learned to keep away from the hazardous toads, the chances of the survival of the whole quoll species — and not just that of each individual quoll — were (e) reduced. The quolls were saved via minimal human interference because ecologists were able to take advantage of quolls' natural imitative instincts.

* nausea: 메스꺼움

41. 윗글의 제목으로 가장 적절한 것은?

① Imitative Instinct as a Key to Survival for Animals
② Copy Quickly and Precisely to Be Productive
③ How to Stop the Spread of Invasive Species
④ The Role of Threats in Animal Cooperation
⑤ Ideal Habitats for Diverse Wildlife

42. 밑줄 친 (a) ~ (e) 중에서 문맥상 낱말의 쓰임이 적절하지 않은 것은? [3점]

① (a)　　② (b)　　③ (c)　　④ (d)　　⑤ (e)

[43 ~ 45] 다음 글을 읽고, 물음에 답하시오.

(A)

A long time ago, a farmer in a small town had a neighbor who was a hunter. The hunter owned a few fierce and poorly-trained hunting dogs. They jumped the fence frequently and chased the farmer's lambs. The farmer asked his neighbor to keep (a) his dogs in check, but his words fell on deaf ears. One day when the dogs jumped the fence, they attacked and severely injured several of the lambs.

(B)

To protect his sons' newly acquired playmates, the hunter built a strong doghouse for his dogs. The dogs never bothered the farmer's lambs again. Out of gratitude for the farmer's generosity toward (b) his children, the hunter often invited the farmer for feasts. In turn, the farmer offered him lamb meat and cheese he had made. The farmer quickly developed a strong friendship with (c) him.

(C)

"All right, I will offer you a solution that keeps your lambs safe and will also turn your neighbor into a good friend." Having heard the judge's solution, the farmer agreed. As soon as the farmer reached home, he immediately put the judge's suggestions to the test. (d) He selected three of the cutest lambs from his farm. He then presented them to his neighbor's three small sons. The children accepted with joy and began to play with them.

(D)

The farmer had had enough by this point. He went to the nearest city to consult a judge. After listening carefully to his story, the judge said, "I could punish the hunter and instruct (e) him to keep his dogs chained or lock them up. But you would lose a friend and gain an enemy. Which would you rather have for a neighbor, a friend or an enemy?" The farmer replied that he preferred a friend.

43. 주어진 글 (A)에 이어질 내용을 순서에 맞게 배열한 것으로 가장 적절한 것은?

① (B) − (D) − (C)　　　　② (C) − (B) − (D)
③ (C) − (D) − (B)　　　　④ (D) − (B) − (C)
⑤ (D) − (C) − (B)

44. 밑줄 친 (a) ~ (e) 중에서 가리키는 대상이 나머지 넷과 다른 것은?

① (a)　　② (b)　　③ (c)　　④ (d)　　⑤ (e)

45. 윗글의 농부에 관한 내용으로 적절하지 않은 것은?

① 그의 양이 사냥개의 공격을 받았다.
② 사냥꾼에게 양고기와 치즈를 받았다.
③ 재판관의 해결책에 동의했다.
④ 세 명의 아들을 둔 이웃이 있었다.
⑤ 도시로 조언을 구하러 갔다.

> ※ 확인 사항
> 답안지의 해당란에 필요한 내용을 정확히 기입(표기)했는지 확인하시오.

18

001 □ on behalf of ~을 대표하여, 대신하여
002 □ remind A of B A에게 B를 상기시키다
003 □ surely ad 물론, 확실히, 분명히
004 □ regrettably ad 유감스럽게
005 □ result in ~을 야기하다
006 □ competition ⓝ 대회, 시합
007 □ prospective ⓐ 유망한
008 □ athlete ⓝ 운동선수
009 □ demonstrate ⓥ 보여주다, 입증하다
010 □ capability ⓝ 역량, 능력
011 □ permission ⓝ 허락, 허가
012 □ absence ⓝ 결석

19

013 □ in the middle of ~의 도중에
014 □ suddenly ad 갑자기
015 □ sense ⓥ 감지하다
016 □ terribly ad 대단히, 지독하게
017 □ stove ⓝ 난로
018 □ glow ⓥ 타다, 빨개지다
019 □ fill ⓥ 채우다, 메우다
020 □ fit A into B A를 B에 끼워 넣다
021 □ cabin ⓝ 오두막
022 □ catch fire 불이 나다
023 □ swear at ~에게 욕하다
024 □ front door 현관문, 정문
025 □ yell out 소리치다
026 □ in anger 화가 나서, 노하여
027 □ cool off 식다, 식히다
028 □ alarmed ⓐ 불안한
029 □ thrilled ⓐ 신이 난, 황홀하게 하는
030 □ touched ⓐ 감동한, 감정적이 된
031 □ guilty ⓐ 죄책감이 드는

20

032 □ period ⓝ 기간
033 □ reach out 연락을 취하려 하다
034 □ take notice of ~을 알아차리다
035 □ distance ⓝ 거리감
036 □ form ⓥ 형성되다
037 □ make a repair 수리하다
038 □ scramble ⓥ 앞 다투다, 서로 밀치다
039 □ in ages 오랫동안
040 □ effort ⓝ 노력, 수고
041 □ erase ⓥ 지우다
042 □ relationship ⓝ 관계
043 □ fix ⓝ 해결책
044 □ regular ⓐ 정기적인, 규칙적인
045 □ maintenance ⓝ 유지, 보수
046 □ make sure 확실하게 하다
047 □ so to speak 말하자면
048 □ bother ⓥ 신경 쓰다, 애를 쓰다
049 □ ideal ⓐ 이상적인
050 □ fall out of touch 연락이 끊기다
051 □ touch ⓝ 접촉, 연락
052 □ in the first place 애초에
053 □ consistency ⓝ 일관성
054 □ result ⓝ 결과, 결실

21

055 □ critical ⓐ 중요한
056 □ determine ⓥ 결정하다
057 □ influence ⓝ 영향 ⓥ 영향을 미치다
058 □ visible ⓐ 가시적인, 눈에 보이는
059 □ consequence ⓝ 결과
060 □ stroll ⓥ 다니다, 거닐다
061 □ edge ⓝ 끝, 가장자리
062 □ await ⓥ ~을 기다리다
063 □ icy-cold ⓐ 차디찬
064 □ leopard seal 표범물개
065 □ play the waiting game 대기 전술을 펼치다, 기회를 기다리다
066 □ anticipation ⓝ 기대
067 □ pioneer ⓝ 개척자, 선구자
068 □ survive ⓥ 살아남다
069 □ follow suit 방금 남이 한 대로 따라하다
070 □ perish ⓥ (특히 끔찍하게) 죽다
071 □ destiny ⓝ 운명
072 □ alter ⓥ 바꾸다
073 □ fate ⓝ 운명
074 □ territory ⓝ 영토

22

075 □ inconvenience ⓝ 불편, 애로
076 □ pose ⓥ 놓다, 주다, (의문 등을) 제기하다
077 □ request ⓝ 요구[신청] (사항)
078 □ build up 쌓아 올리다
079 □ emotion ⓝ 감정
080 □ in time 즉시
081 □ resent ⓥ 분개하다
082 □ have control of ~을 통제하다
083 □ suppress ⓥ 억누르다, 참다
084 □ emotionally ad 감정적으로, 정서적으로
085 □ constantly ad 끊임없이
086 □ will ⓝ 의지

23

087 □ communicate ⓥ 전달하다
088 □ conversation ⓝ 대화, 회화
089 □ true of ~에 관해 사실인, ~에 해당되는
090 □ sheer ⓐ 순전한
091 □ knowledge ⓝ 지식
092 □ rely on ~에 의존하다
093 □ judgement ⓝ 판단
094 □ discover ⓥ 발견하다
095 □ polish ⓥ 다듬다
096 □ critically ad 비판적으로
097 □ foolish ⓐ 어리석은, 바보 같은
098 □ uncover ⓥ 발견하다
099 □ embarrassing ⓐ 당황스러운
100 □ fame ⓝ 명성
101 □ refine ⓥ 정제하다, 다듬다
102 □ persuasive ⓐ 설득력 있는
103 □ enormous ⓐ 엄청난

24

104 □ individual ⓝ 개인
105 □ tribe ⓝ 부족
106 □ community ⓝ 공동체
107 □ forge ⓥ 구축하다
108 □ identity ⓝ 정체성
109 □ ritual ⓝ 의식
110 □ mark ⓥ (중요 사건을) 기념[축하]하다

25

111 □ major ⓐ 중요한, 주요한
112 □ marriage ⓝ 결혼
113 □ religious ⓐ 종교적인
114 □ structure ⓝ 구조
115 □ cohesion ⓝ 결속, 화합, 결합
116 □ historically ad 역사적으로
117 □ bind ⓥ 단결시키다, 결속시키다
118 □ participation ⓝ 참여
119 □ belonging ⓝ 소속감, 친숙함
120 □ as a consequence 그 결과
121 □ distinct ⓐ 독특한, 뚜렷한

25

122 □ wellness ⓝ 건강
123 □ expenditure ⓝ 경비, 지출
124 □ total ⓐ 총, 전체의
125 □ rounding ⓝ 반올림
126 □ meanwhile ad 그 동안에, 한편

26

127 □ force ⓝ 힘 ⓥ (어쩔 수 없이) ~하게 만들다
128 □ collapse ⓥ (갑자기 또는 완전히) 실패하다
129 □ teach oneself 독학하다
130 □ mathematics ⓝ 수학
131 □ philosophy ⓝ 철학
132 □ mathematical ⓐ 수학의
133 □ make a contribution to ~에 공헌하다
134 □ area ⓝ 분야, 영역
135 □ award ⓥ 수여하다
136 □ deeply ad 깊이, 몹시
137 □ symbolic ⓐ 상징적인
138 □ subject ⓝ 주제
139 □ analysis ⓝ 분석
140 □ investigation ⓝ 수사, 조사, 연구
141 □ form the basis of ~의 기초를 쌓다
142 □ appoint A B A를 B로 지명하다

27

143 □ sustainable ⓐ 지속 가능한
144 □ mobility ⓝ 이동(성), 운동성
145 □ annual ⓐ 연례의
146 □ transport ⓝ 운송 (수단)
147 □ run ⓥ 진행하다
148 □ participate in ~에 참가하다
149 □ promote ⓥ 증진하다, 촉진하다
150 □ public transport 대중 교통
151 □ instead ad 대신에
152 □ complete ⓥ 완료하다, 끝마치다
153 □ be qualified to ~할 자격이 되다

28

154 □ throughout prep ~동안 쭉, 내내
155 □ solid ⓐ 탄탄한
156 □ foundation ⓝ 기초
157 □ venture ⓝ 도전, 모험
158 □ woodworking ⓝ 목공, 목공예
159 □ requirement ⓝ 필요조건, 요건
160 □ full refund 전액 환불
161 □ in advance 미리, 사전에
162 □ guidance ⓝ 지도, 안내
163 □ instructor ⓝ 강사, 교사
164 □ hand-crafted ⓐ 수작업의, 손으로 만든

29

165 □ non-verbal ⓐ 비언어적인
166 □ substitute ⓝ 대체물 ⓥ 대체하다
167 □ verbal ⓐ 언어의
168 □ function ⓝ 기능, 작용 ⓥ 기능하다
169 □ serve ⓥ 도움이 되다
170 □ enhance ⓥ 강화하다
171 □ richness ⓝ 풍부함, 풍요로움
172 □ content ⓝ 내용
173 □ pass across 전달하다
174 □ inappropriate ⓐ 부적절한
175 □ uncomfortable ⓐ 불편한
176 □ position ⓝ 위치, 처지, 입장
177 □ get A across to B A를 B에게 전하다, 이해시키다
178 □ properly ad 적절히
179 □ aid ⓝ 도움
180 □ adequately ad 적절하게
181 □ complement ⓥ 보완하다

30

182 □ intellectual ⓐ 지적인
183 □ humility ⓝ 겸손
184 □ admit ⓥ 인정하다
185 □ neglect ⓥ 무시하다, 소홀히 하다
186 □ recognize ⓥ 인식하다, 깨닫다
187 □ possess ⓥ 지니다, 가지다
188 □ cognitive ⓐ 인지적인
189 □ bias ⓝ 편견
190 □ favor ⓥ 선호하다
191 □ objective ⓐ 객관적인
192 □ informed decision 정보에 근거한 결정, 잘 알고 내린 결정
193 □ receptive ⓐ 수용적인
194 □ resistant ⓐ ~에 저항하는
195 □ respect ⓥ 존경하다
196 □ undervalue ⓥ 경시하다
197 □ bring to the table ~을 제시하다
198 □ humble ⓐ 겸손한
199 □ superior ⓐ 우월한

31

200 □ engage in ~에 참여하다, 관여하다
201 □ interaction ⓝ 상호 작용
202 □ employer ⓝ 고용주
203 □ interact with ~와 상호작용을 하다
204 □ employee ⓝ 종업원
205 □ restrict ⓥ 제한하다
206 □ responsibility ⓝ 책임
207 □ obligation ⓝ 의무
208 □ associated with ~와 관련된
209 □ link ⓥ 연결하다, 관련하다
210 □ privilege ⓝ 특권
211 □ necessity ⓝ 필수품
212 □ shelter ⓝ 주거지
213 □ expectation ⓝ 기대
214 □ vulnerable ⓐ 비난받기 쉬운, ~에 취약한
215 □ charge ⓝ 혐의, 비난
216 □ negligence ⓝ 태만, 부주의
217 □ abuse ⓝ 학대, 남용
218 □ career ⓝ 직업
219 □ status ⓝ 지위

220 motivation ⓝ 동기	275 politician ⓝ 정치인, 정치가	329 attention ⓝ 관심	383 clever ⓐ 영리한, 똑똑한
221 perspective ⓝ 관점	276 reception ⓝ 환영회	330 emphasize ⓥ 강조하다	384 copy ⓥ 모방하다, 베끼다
	277 occasion ⓝ 행사	331 glance ⓝ 흘긋 봄	385 relative ⓝ 친척
32	278 impressive ⓐ 인상적인	332 guilt ⓝ 죄책감	386 quoll ⓝ 주머니고양이
222 globalization ⓝ 세계화	279 banquet ⓝ 연회, 만찬	333 lighting ⓝ 조명	387 threaten ⓥ 위협하다
223 inevitably ⓐⓓ 필연적으로, 불가피하게	280 diplomacy ⓝ 외교	334 costume ⓝ 의상[분장/변장]	388 cane toad 수수두꺼비
224 inspire ⓥ 고무[격려]하다	281 sociologist ⓝ 사회학자	335 scenery ⓝ 경치, 풍경	389 invasive ⓐ 침입의
225 perceive ⓥ 인지하다	282 confirm ⓥ 사실임을 보여주다, 확인해 주다	336 movement ⓝ 움직임	390 poisonous ⓐ 독성이 있는
226 threat ⓝ 위협	283 principle ⓝ 원리	337 still ⓐ 가만히 있는	391 suffer ⓥ 겪다, 당하다
227 crisis ⓝ 위기	284 interfere with ~을 방해하다	338 technique ⓝ 기법, 기술	392 fatal ⓐ 치명적인
228 violent ⓐ 폭력적인	285 do harm to ~에 해를 끼치다	339 draw A's attention to B A의 관심을	393 speedy ⓐ 빠른
229 conflict ⓝ 갈등, 분쟁	286 diplomatic ⓐ 외교의	B로 돌리다	394 rate ⓝ 속도
230 refugee ⓝ 난민	287 receptiveness ⓝ 수용성		395 identify ⓥ 찾아내다, 확인하다
231 immigration ⓝ 이민자	288 persuade ⓥ 설득하다	**39**	396 instinct ⓝ 본능
232 gap between rich and poor 빈부격차		340 relevant ⓐ 관련 있는, 적절한	397 imitate ⓥ 모방하다
233 cling to ~에 달라붙다	**35**	341 employment ⓝ 채용	398 feed ⓥ 먹이를 주다 (과거형 : fed)
234 founder ⓝ 설립자	289 conditioning ⓝ 훈련, 조절	342 matter ⓝ 문제, 일, 사안	399 sausage ⓝ 소시지
235 unite ⓥ 결합시키다	290 quickness ⓝ 신속함	343 equally ⓐⓓ 똑같이	400 contain ⓥ ~이 함유되어 있다
236 simultaneously ⓐⓓ 동시에	291 flexibility ⓝ 유연성	344 applicable ⓐ 적용 가능한	401 harmless ⓐ 해가 없는, 무해한
237 organizational ⓐ 조직(상)의	292 unlike ⓟⓡⓔⓟ ~와는 달리	345 first impression 첫인상	402 release ⓥ 방출하다
238 blame ⓝ 책임, 탓, 비난	293 isolated ⓐ 분리된, 고립된	346 assess ⓥ 평가하다	403 offspring ⓝ 자손
239 division ⓝ 분열	294 athletic ⓐ 운동선수의	347 noticeable ⓐ 두드러지는, 눈에 띄는	404 constructive ⓐ 건설적인
240 coexist ⓥ 공존하다	295 muscle ⓝ 근육	348 recruitment ⓝ 채용, 모집	405 hazardous ⓐ 위험한
241 barrier ⓝ 장벽	296 fear ⓥ (~을) 두려워하다	349 predict ⓥ 예측하다	406 interference ⓝ 개입, 간섭
242 achieve ⓥ 성취하다	297 weight lifting 역도	350 eventual ⓐ 최종의, 궁극적인	407 precisely ⓐⓓ 정확히
243 equality ⓝ 평등	298 proper ⓐ 적절한	351 candidate ⓝ 지원자, 후보자	408 diverse ⓐ 다양한
244 abandon ⓥ 버리다		352 competence ⓝ 능력, 역량	409 wildlife ⓝ 야생 동물
245 individualism ⓝ 개인주의	**36**	353 appearance ⓝ 겉모습, 외모	
	299 naturally ⓐⓓ 자연스럽게	354 coordination ⓝ (신체 동작의) 조정력	**43~45**
33	300 afterwards ⓐⓓ 나중에, 이후에	355 interpersonal ⓐ 대인 관계의	410 farmer ⓝ 농부, 농장주
246 conceal ⓥ 숨기다	301 salesperson ⓝ 판매원	356 painstakingly ⓐⓓ 공들여, 힘들여	411 neighbor ⓝ 이웃
247 similarity ⓝ 유사점	302 cruelty ⓝ 잔인함	357 track down ~을 찾아내다	412 hunter ⓝ 사냥꾼
248 profound ⓐ 심오한	303 prior ⓐ (특정 시간보다) 사전의, ~전의	358 subtle ⓐ 미묘한, 감지하기 힘든	413 fierce ⓐ 사나운
249 dissimilarity ⓝ 차이점	304 petition ⓝ 진정서, 청원서	359 breath ⓝ 입김, 숨	414 poorly-trained 훈련이 잘되지 않은
250 plateau ⓝ 고원	305 purchase ⓝ 구매	360 wrinkle ⓥ 구겨지다, 주름이 지다	415 fence ⓝ 울타리, 장애물
251 erosion ⓝ 부식, 침식	306 take advantage of ~을 이용하다	361 spoil ⓥ 망치다	416 frequently ⓐⓓ 자주
252 narrow ⓐ 좁은	307 tendency ⓝ 경향	362 noble ⓐ 고귀한, 숭고한	417 chase ⓥ 쫓다
253 opportunity ⓝ 기회	308 consistent ⓐ 일관적인		418 lamb ⓝ 새끼 양
254 significant ⓐ 중대한, 유의미한		**40**	419 keep in check 제지하다, 감독하다
255 geological ⓐ 지질학적인	**37**	363 perception ⓝ 인식	420 fall on deaf ears 무시되다.
256 when it comes to ~에 관한 한	309 subjective ⓐ 주관적인	364 amount ⓝ 총액, 액수	남의 귀에 들어가지 않다
257 uniqueness ⓝ 고유성	310 ethnic ⓐ 민족적인	365 discount ⓝ 할인	421 severely ⓐⓓ 심하게
258 cross-cultural ⓐ 여러 문화가 섞인,	311 relation ⓝ 관계	366 depend on ~에 달려있다	422 injured ⓐ 부상을 입은, 다친
다문화적인	312 minority ⓝ 소수	367 initial ⓐ 최초의	423 acquire ⓥ 얻다
259 mask ⓥ 가리다, 감추다	313 poorer ⓐ 더 좋지 못한, 더 부족한	368 respondent ⓝ (특히 실태 조사에서) 응답	424 playmate ⓝ 놀이 친구
260 overwhelming ⓐ 압도적인	314 majority ⓝ 다수	자, 답변자	425 bother ⓥ 괴롭히다
261 diversity ⓝ 다양성	315 multiple ⓐ 다수의	369 present ⓥ 제시하다	426 gratitude ⓝ 감사
262 step out of ~에서 나오다	316 physiological ⓐ 생리학적인	370 calculator ⓝ 계산기	427 generosity ⓝ 관대함
	317 encounter ⓝ 마주침	371 find out 찾아내다, 알아내다	428 invite ⓥ 초대하다
34	318 category ⓝ 범주	372 vendor ⓝ (거리의) 행상인	429 feast ⓝ 진수성찬
263 proverb ⓝ 속담	319 relatively ⓐⓓ 비교적	373 promotional ⓐ 판촉의, 홍보의	430 develop ⓥ 키우다, 발전시키다
264 clinically ⓐⓓ 임상적으로	320 laboratory ⓝ 실험실	374 differ ⓥ 다르다	431 judge ⓝ 재판관
265 drug ⓝ 약, 마약	321 response ⓝ 반응, 대답, 응답	375 context ⓝ (어떤 일의) 맥락, 전후 사정	432 solution ⓝ 해결책
266 bombard A with B A에 B를 퍼붓다	322 obvious ⓐ 명백한	376 absolute ⓐ 절대적인	433 immediately ⓐⓓ 즉시
267 trigger ⓥ 유발하다	323 dominance ⓝ 우세	377 modify ⓥ 수정하다	434 suggestion ⓝ 제안
268 explosive ⓐ 폭발적인	324 frequency ⓝ 빈도	378 identical ⓐ 동일한	435 select ⓥ 고르다, 선택하다
269 countless ⓐ 수많은	325 account for ~을 설명하다	379 advertise ⓥ 광고하다	436 cutest ⓐ 가장 귀여운
270 induce ⓥ 유도하다	326 disadvantage ⓝ 불이익		437 nearest ⓐ 가장 가까운
271 instinctive ⓐ 본능적인		**41~42**	438 consult ⓥ 조언을 구하다
272 desire ⓝ 욕구, 갈망	**38**	380 behavioral ⓐ 행동의, 행동에 관한	439 punish ⓥ 벌하다
273 repay ⓥ 갚다, 보답하다	327 director ⓝ 감독	381 ecologist ⓝ 생태학자	440 instruct ⓥ 지시하다
274 executive ⓝ 경영진	328 audience ⓝ 관객	382 observe ⓥ 관찰하다	441 reply ⓥ 대답하다, 대응하다

20회

● 채점 : 맞은 개수 _____ / 80

TEST A-B   각 단어의 뜻을 [A] 영어는 우리말로, [B] 우리말은 영어로 쓰시오.

A	English	Korean
01	instinctive	
02	recruitment	
03	collapse	
04	step out of	
05	coexist	
06	precisely	
07	rely on	
08	punish	
09	restrict	
10	differ	
11	prospective	
12	substitute	
13	flexibility	
14	as a consequence	
15	diplomacy	
16	enormous	
17	emphasize	
18	subjective	
19	charge	
20	guilty	

B	Korean	English
01	운명	
02	정제하다, 다듬다	
03	학대, 남용	
04	의식	
05	가시적인, 눈에 보이는	
06	반올림	
07	분개하다	
08	겸손	
09	다듬다	
10	좁은	
11	명성	
12	상징적인	
13	지우다	
14	유발하다	
15	타다, 빨개지다	
16	평등	
17	평가하다	
18	절대적인	
19	도전, 모험	
20	다니다, 거닐다	

▶ A-D 정답 : 해설편 204쪽

TEST C-D   각 단어의 뜻을 골라 기호를 쓰시오.

C	English			Korean
01	mobility	(	)	ⓐ ~에 참여하다, 관여하다
02	refugee	(	)	ⓑ 난민
03	solid	(	)	ⓒ 미리, 사전에
04	feast	(	)	ⓓ 향연
05	possess	(	)	ⓔ 의무
06	bind	(	)	ⓕ 단결시키다, 결속시키다
07	complement	(	)	ⓖ 독특한, 뚜렷한
08	distinct	(	)	ⓗ 강화하다
09	judgement	(	)	ⓘ 결합시키다
10	unite	(	)	ⓙ 탄탄한
11	engage in	(	)	ⓚ 보완하다
12	enhance	(	)	ⓛ 중대한, 유의미한
13	in advance	(	)	ⓜ 지니다, 가지다
14	obligation	(	)	ⓝ 이동(성), 운동성
15	significant	(	)	ⓞ 판단
16	fatal	(	)	ⓟ 흘긋 봄
17	promotional	(	)	ⓠ 건강
18	competence	(	)	ⓡ 능력, 역량
19	wellness	(	)	ⓢ 판촉의, 홍보의
20	glance	(	)	ⓣ 치명적인

D	Korean			English
01	~을 대신하여	(	)	ⓐ foundation
02	우월한	(	)	ⓑ tribe
03	분리된, 고립된	(	)	ⓒ subtle
04	미묘한, 감지하기 힘든	(	)	ⓓ demonstrate
05	억누르다, 참다	(	)	ⓔ superior
06	~을 설명하다	(	)	ⓕ spoil
07	숨기다	(	)	ⓖ conceal
08	~을 알아차리다	(	)	ⓗ suppress
09	위협	(	)	ⓘ threat
10	부족	(	)	ⓙ on behalf of
11	말하자면	(	)	ⓚ so to speak
12	보여주다, 입증하다	(	)	ⓛ isolated
13	망치다	(	)	ⓜ account for
14	기초	(	)	ⓝ absence
15	결석	(	)	ⓞ take notice of
16	전달하다	(	)	ⓟ constructive
17	~을 기다리다	(	)	ⓠ physiological
18	심하게	(	)	ⓡ communicate
19	건설적인	(	)	ⓢ await
20	생리학적인	(	)	ⓣ severely

REAL
O R I G I N A L

전국연합학력평가
5개년 기출 문제집

고1 영어 독해 [해설편]

Contents

REAL
ORIGINAL

※ 수록된 정답률은 실제와 차이가 있을 수 있습니다.
문제 난도를 파악하는데 참고용으로 활용하시기
바랍니다.

· 정답 ·

18 ③ 19 ① 20 ② 21 ① 22 ③ 23 ① 24 ⑤ 25 ③ 26 ④ 27 ④ 28 ④ 29 ② 30 ③ 31 ① 32 ③
33 ③ 34 ⑤ 35 ④ 36 ④ 37 ③ 38 ① 39 ② 40 ① 41 ① 42 ④ 43 ⑤ 44 ④ 45 ②

★ 표기된 문항은 [등급을 가르는 문제]에 해당하는 문항입니다.

---

18 특별 강연 초청 편지 　　　　　　　　　　정답률 94% | 정답 ③

다음 글의 목적으로 가장 적절한 것은?

① 환경 보호의 중요성을 강조하려고
② 글쓰기에서 주의할 점을 알려 주려고
☑ 특강 강사로 작가의 방문을 요청하려고
④ 작가의 팬 사인회 일정 변경을 공지하려고
⑤ 작가가 쓴 책의 내용에 관하여 문의하려고

Dear Ms. Jane Watson,
친애하는 Jane Watson 씨,
I am John Austin, a science teacher / at Crestville High School.
저는 John Austin입니다. / Crestville 고등학교의
Recently, / I was impressed / by the latest book / you wrote about the environment.
최근에, / 저는 감명 받았습니다. / 최신 도서에 / 당신이 환경에 관해 쓴
Also, / my students read your book / and had a class discussion about it.
또한, / 저의 학생들은 당신의 책을 읽었고 / 그것에 대해 토론 수업을 하였습니다.
They are big fans of your book, / so I'd like to ask you / to visit our school / and give a special lecture.
그들은 당신의 책을 아주 좋아합니다. / 그래서 저는 당신에게 요청합니다. / 우리 학교에 방문하여 / 특별 강연을 해 주시기를
We can set the date and time / to suit your schedule.
우리는 날짜와 시간을 정할 수 있습니다. / 당신의 일정에 맞춰
Having you at our school / would be a fantastic experience for the students.
당신이 우리 학교에 와주신다면 / 학생들에게 멋진 경험이 될 것 같습니다.
We would be very grateful / if you could come.
우리는 정말 감사하겠습니다. / 당신이 와 주신다면
Best regards, // John Austin
안부를 전하며, // John Austin

친애하는 Jane Watson 씨, 저는 Crestville 고등학교의 과학 교사 John Austin입니다. 최근에, 저는 환경에 관해 당신이 쓴 최신 도서에 감명받았습니다. 또한 저의 학생들은 당신의 책을 읽었고 그것에 대해 토론 수업을 하였습니다. 그들은 당신의 책을 아주 좋아하고, 그래서 저는 당신이 우리 학교에 방문하여 특별 강연을 해 주시기를 요청드리고 싶습니다. 우리는 당신의 일정에 맞춰 날짜와 시간을 정하겠습니다. 당신이 우리 학교에 와 주신다면 학생들에게 멋진 경험이 될 것 같습니다. 우리는 당신이 와 주신다면 정말 감사하겠습니다. 안부를 전하며, John Austin

Why? 왜 정답일까?

Jane Watson에게 Crestville 고등학교에 방문하여 특별 강연을 해 주기를 요청하고 있기 때문에(I'd like to ask you to visit our school and give a special lecture.), 글의 목적으로 가장 적절한 것은 ③ '특강 강사로 작가의 방문을 요청하려고'이다.

● science ⑥ 과학
● impressed ⓐ 감명을 받은
● discussion ⑥ 토론
● suit ⓥ 맞추다
● recently ⓐⓓ 최근에
● environment ⑥ 환경
● lecture ⑥ 강의
● grateful ⓐ 감사한

구문 풀이

3행 Recently I was impressed by the latest book (that) you wrote about the environment.
　　　　　　　수동태 by 행위자　　최상급, 선행사　목적격 관계대명사 생략

---

19 모래성 만들기의 의의 　　　　　　　　　정답률 92% | 정답 ①

다음 글에 드러난 Sarah의 심경 변화로 가장 적절한 것은?

☑ sad → excited
슬픈　　신난
② envious → anxious
부러운　　불안한
③ bored → joyful
지루한　　즐거운
④ relaxed → regretful
안정된　　후회하는
⑤ nervous → surprised
긴장한　　놀란

Marilyn and her three-year-old daughter, Sarah, took a trip to the beach, / where Sarah built her first sandcastle.
Marilyn과 세 살 된 딸 Sarah는 해변으로 여행을 떠났고, / 그곳에서 Sarah는 처음으로 모래성을 쌓았다.
Moments later, / an enormous wave destroyed Sarah's castle.
잠시 후, / 거대한 파도가 Sarah의 성을 무너뜨렸다.
In response to the loss of her sandcastle, / tears streamed down Sarah's cheeks / and her heart was broken.
모래성을 잃은 것에 반응하여 / 눈물이 Sarah의 뺨을 타고 흘러내렸고, / 그녀의 마음은 무너졌다.
She ran to Marilyn, / saying she would never build a sandcastle again.
그녀는 Marilyn에게 달려갔다. / 그녀가 다시는 모래성을 쌓지 않겠다고 말하며
Marilyn said, / "Part of the joy of building a sandcastle / is that, in the end, / we give it as a gift / to the ocean."
Marilyn은 말했다. / "모래성을 쌓는 즐거움 중 일부는 / 결국에는 / 우리가 그것을 선물로 주는 것이란다. / 바다에게" 라고
Sarah loved this idea / and responded with enthusiasm / to the idea of building another castle / — this time, even closer to the water / so the ocean would get its gift sooner!
Sarah는 이 생각이 마음에 들었고 / 열정적으로 반응했다. / 다른 모래성을 만들 생각에 / 이번에는 바다와 훨씬 더 가까운 곳에 / 바다가 그 선물을 더 빨리 받을 수 있도록

Marilyn과 세 살 된 딸 Sarah는 해변으로 여행을 떠났고, 그곳에서 Sarah는 처음으로 모래성을 쌓았다. 잠시 후, 거대한 파도가 Sarah의 성을 무너뜨렸다. 모래성을 잃은 것에 반응하여 눈물이 Sarah의 뺨을 타고 흘러내렸고, 그녀의 마음은 무너졌다. 그녀는 다시는 모래성을 쌓지 않겠다고 말하며 Marilyn에게 달려갔다. Marilyn은 "모래성을 쌓는 즐거움 중 일부는 결국에는 우리가 그것을 바다에게 선물로 주는 것이란다."라고 말했다. Sarah는 이 생각이 마음에 들었고 또 다른 모래성을 만들 생각에 이번에는 바다와 훨씬 더 가까운 곳에서 바다가 그 선물을 더 빨리 받을 수 있도록 하겠다며 열정적으로 반응했다.

Why? 왜 정답일까?

Sarah가 해변에서 처음으로 쌓은 모래성을 파도가 무너뜨리자 울었다. 그러자 Marilyn은 Sarah에게 모래성을 바다에게 선물로 준 것이라 말한다. 이에 Sarah는 Marilyn의 말에 열정적으로 반응했다. 따라서 Sarah의 심정 변화로 적절한 것은 ① 'sad(슬픈) → excited(신난)'이다.

● sandcastle ⑥ 모래성
● destroy ⓥ 부수다
● ocean ⑥ 바다
● enthusiasm ⑥ 열정
● enormous ⓐ 거대한
● stream ⓥ 흐르다
● respond ⓥ 반응하다

구문 풀이

　　　　　　　　　　　　　　　　조동사＋동사원형◀
5행 She ran to Marilyn, saying she would never build a sandcastle again.
　　　　　　　　　　　　현재분사(~하면서)　　부정어

---

20 긍정적인 진술의 마법 　　　　　　　　　정답률 73% | 정답 ②

다음 글에서 필자가 주장하는 바로 가장 적절한 것은?

① 목표한 바를 꼭 이루려면 생각을 곧바로 행동으로 옮겨라.
☑ 자신감을 얻으려면 어려움을 긍정적인 진술로 바꿔 써라.
③ 어려운 일을 해결하려면 주변 사람에게 도움을 청하라.
④ 일상에서 자신감을 향상하려면 틈틈이 마술을 배워라.
⑤ 실생활에서 마주하는 도전을 피하지 말고 견뎌 내라.

Magic is what we all wish for / to happen in our life.
마법은 우리 모두가 바라는 것이다. / 자신의 삶에서 일어나기를
Do you love the movie *Cinderella* / like me?
여러분은 *신데렐라* 영화를 사랑하는가? / 나처럼
Well, / in real life, / you can also create magic.
그러면, / 실제 삶에서, / 여러분도 마법을 만들 수 있다.
Here's the trick.
여기 그 요령이 있다.
Write down / all the real-time challenges / that you face and deal with.
적어라. / 모든 실시간의 어려움을 / 여러분이 직면하고 처리하는
Just change the challenge statement / into positive statements.
어려움에 관한 진술을 바꾸기만 해라. / 긍정적인 진술로
Let me give you / an example here.
여러분에게 제시하겠다. / 예시를 여기에
If you struggle with / getting up early in the morning, / then write a positive statement / such as "I get up early in the morning / at 5:00 am every day."
만약 여러분이 어려움을 겪는다면 / 아침 일찍 일어나는 것에 / 그러면 긍정적인 진술을 작성해라. / 나는 일찍 일어난다. / 매일 아침 5시에
Once you write these statements, / get ready to witness magic and confidence.
이러한 진술들을 작성하고 나면, / 마법과 자신감을 목격할 준비를 해라.
You will be surprised / that just by writing these statements, / there is a shift / in the way you think and act.
당신은 놀랄 것이다. / 단지 이러한 진술들을 작성함으로써 / 변화가 있다는 것에 / 당신이 생각하고 행동하는 방식에
Suddenly / you feel more powerful and positive.
어느 순간 / 여러분은 더 강력하고 긍정적이라고 느끼게 된다.

마법은 우리 모두 자신의 삶에서 일어나기를 바라는 바이다. 여러분도 나처럼 *신데렐라* 영화를 사랑하는가? 그러면, 실제 삶에서, 여러분도 마법을 만들 수 있다. 여기 그 요령이 있다. 여러분이 직면하고 처리하는 모든 실시간의 어려움을 적어라. 그 어려움에 관한 진술을 긍정적인 진술로 바꾸어라. 여기서 여러분에게 한 예시를 제시하겠다. 만약 여러분이 아침 일찍 일어나는 것에 어려움을 겪는다면, 그러면 '나는 매일 일찍 아침 5시에 일어난다.'와 같은 긍정적인 진술을 써라. 일단 여러분이 이러한 진술을 적는다면, 마법과 자신감을 목격할 준비를 하라. 여러분은 단지 이러한 진술을 적음으로써 여러분이 생각하고 행동하는 방식에 변화가 있다는 것에 놀랄 것이다. 어느 순간 여러분은 더 강력하고 긍정적이라고 느끼게 된다.

Why? 왜 정답일까?

일상생활에서 마법을 이루는 방법으로 긍정적인 진술 작성을 제시하고 있기 때문에(Just change the challenge statement into positive statements.), 필자가 주장하는 바로 가장 적절한 것은 ② '자신감을 얻으려면 어려움을 긍정적인 진술로 바꿔 써라.'이다.

● magic ⑥ 마법, 마술
● statement ⑥ 진술
● struggle ⓥ 어려움을 겪다
● confidence ⑥ 자신감
● shift ⑥ 변화
● challenge ⑥ 어려움, 도전
● positive ⓐ 긍정적인
● witness ⓥ 목격하다
● surprise ⓥ 놀라게 하다
● powerful ⓐ 강력한

구문 풀이

　　　　　　　　　　　　　　　　　　조동사＋동사원형 수동태　┌종속접속사
10행 You will be surprised that just by writing these statements, there is a shift in the way you think and act.
　　　　　관계부사 the way(＝how)

---

21 Aristotle이 정의한 감각 　　　　　　　　정답률 49% | 정답 ①

밑줄 친 push animal senses into Aristotelian buckets가 다음 글에서 의미하는 바로 가장 적절한 것은? [3점]

☑ sort various animal senses into fixed categories
동물의 감각을 고정된 체계로 분류하다

② keep a balanced view to understand real senses
진짜 감각을 이해하기 위해서 균형잡힌 시각을 유지하다
③ doubt the traditional way of dividing all senses
모든 감각을 나누는 전통적인 방법을 의심하다
④ ignore the lessons on senses from Aristotle
Aristotle의 감각에 대한 지식을 무시하다
⑤ analyze more animals to find real senses
진짜 감각을 찾기 위해서 더 많은 동물을 분석하다

Consider the seemingly simple question / "*How many senses are there?*"
겉으로 보기에 단순한 질문을 고려해 보아라. / '얼마나 많은 감각이 존재하는가?'

Around 2,370 years ago, / Aristotle wrote / that there are five, in both humans and animals / — sight, hearing, smell, taste, and touch.
약 2,370년 전 / Aristotle은 썼다. / 인간과 동물 둘 다에게 다섯(감각)이 있다고 / 시각, 청각, 후각, 미각, 그리고 촉각의

However, / according to the philosopher Fiona Macpherson, / there are reasons to doubt it.
그러나 / 철학자 Fiona Macpherson에 따르면, / 그것을 의심할 이유가 존재한다.

For a start, / Aristotle missed a few in humans: / the perception of your own body / which is different from touch / and the sense of balance / which has links to both touch and vision.
우선, / Aristotle은 인간에게서 몇 가지를 빠뜨렸는데, / 그것은 자신의 신체에 대한 인식과, / 촉각과는 다른, / 그리고 균형의 감각 이었다. / 촉각과 시각 모두에 관련되어 있는

Other animals have senses / that are even harder to categorize.
다른 동물들도 감각을 가지고 있다. / 범주화하기 더욱 어려운

Many vertebrates have a different sense system / for detecting odors.
많은 척추동물들은 다른 감각 체계를 가지고 있다. / 냄새를 탐지하기 위한

Some snakes can detect the body heat / of their prey.
어떤 뱀들은 체열을 감지할 수 있다. / 그들의 먹잇감의

These examples tell us / that "senses cannot be clearly divided / into a limited number of specific kinds," / Macpherson wrote in *The Senses*.
이러한 예시들은 우리에게 알려 준다. / '감각은 명확하게 나누어지지 않을 수 있다. / 제한된 수의 특정한 종류로' / Macpherson이 'The Senses'에서 쓰기를

Instead of trying to push animal senses into Aristotelian buckets, / we should study them / for what they are.
동물의 감각을 Aristotle의 양동이로 밀어 넣는 대신, / 우리는 그것들을 연구해야 한다. / 존재하는 그대로

'얼마나 많은 감각이 존재하는가?'라는 겉으로 보기에 단순한 질문을 고려해 봐라. 약 2,370년 전 Aristotle은 인간과 동물 둘 다에게 시각, 청각, 후각, 미각, 그리고 촉각의 다섯(감각)이 있다고 썼다. 그러나, 철학자 Fiona Macpherson에 따르면, 그것을 의심할 이유가 존재한다. 우선, Aristotle은 인간에게서 몇 가지를 빠뜨렸는데, 그것은 촉각과는 다른 여러분 자신의 신체에 대한 인식과, 촉각과 시각 모두에 관련되어 있는 균형 감각이었다. 다른 동물들은 훨씬 더 범주화하기 어려운 감각을 가지고 있다. 많은 척추동물은 냄새를 탐지하기 위한 다른 감각 체계를 가지고 있다. 어떤 뱀은 그들의 먹잇감의 체열을 감지할 수 있다. Macpherson이 'The Senses'에서 쓰기를, 이러한 사례는 우리에게 '감각은 제한된 수의 특정한 종류로 명확하게 나누어지지 않을 수 있다.'라는 것을 알려 준다. 동물의 감각을 Aristotle의 양동이로 밀어 넣는 대신, 우리는 그것들을 존재하는 그대로 연구해야 한다.

Why? 왜 정답일까?

Aristotelian buckets가 의미하는 바는 Aristotle이 주장한 바이므로 다섯 개의 감각이 존재하는 것이다. Aristotelian bucket으로 밀어 넣는 것은 Aristotle의 주장을 받아들이는 것이므로, ① 'sort various animal senses into fixed categories'가 가장 적절하다.

- consider ⓥ 고려하다
- philosopher ⓝ 철학자
- perception ⓝ 인식
- link ⓝ 연결
- detect ⓥ 감지하다
- divide ⓥ 나누다
- bucket ⓝ 양동이
- sight ⓝ 시각
- doubt ⓥ 의심하다
- balance ⓝ 균형
- categorize ⓥ 분류하다
- prey ⓝ 먹잇감
- specific ⓐ 특정한

구문 풀이

12행 These examples tell us that "senses cannot be clearly divided into a limited number of specific kinds," Macpherson wrote in *The Senses*.
(주어 / 동사 / 직접목적어절 / ~으로 나누어지다. / 간접목적어)

22 리더로써의 잠재력 정답률 80% | 정답 ③

다음 글의 요지로 가장 적절한 것은?

① 훌륭한 리더는 고귀한 목표를 위해 희생적인 삶을 산다.
② 위대한 인물은 위기의 순간에 뛰어난 결단력을 발휘한다.
☑ 공동체를 위한 아이디어를 발전시키는 누구나 리더가 될 수 있다.
④ 다른 사람의 의견을 경청하는 자세는 목표 달성에 가장 중요하다.
⑤ 근면하고 경험이 풍부한 사람들은 경제적으로 성공할 수 있다.

When we think of leaders, / we may think of people / such as Abraham Lincoln or Martin Luther King, Jr.
우리가 리더에 대해서 생각할 때, / 우리는 사람들을 생각할지도 모른다. / Abraham Lincoln이나 Martin Luther King Jr.와 같은

If you consider / the historical importance and far-reaching influence / of these individuals, / leadership might seem like a noble and high goal.
만약 여러분이 고려한다면 / 역사적 중요성과 광범위한 영향력을 / 이러한 인물들의 / 리더십은 고귀하고 높은 목표처럼 보일지도 모른다.

But like all of us, / these people started out / as students, workers, and citizens / who possessed ideas / about how some aspect of daily life could be improved / on a larger scale.
그러나 우리 모두와 마찬가지로, / 이러한 인물들은 시작했다. / 학생, 근로자, 그리고 시민으로 / 생각을 가진 / 일상생활의 어느 측면이 어떻게 개선될 수 있는지에 대한 / 더 큰 규모로

Through diligence and experience, / they improved upon their ideas / by sharing them with others, / seeking their opinions and feedback / and constantly looking for the best way / to accomplish goals for a group.
근면함과 경험을 통해, / 그들은 생각을 발전시켰다. / 자신의 생각을 다른 사람들과 공유하고, / 그들의 의견과 반응을 구하며 / 끊임없이 가장 좋은 방법을 찾음으로써 / 집단의 목표를 성취할 수 있는

Thus we all have the potential to be leaders / at school, in our communities, and at work, / regardless of age or experience.
그러므로 우리는 모두 리더가 될 잠재력을 가지고 있다. / 학교, 공동체, 그리고 일터에서 / 나이나 경험에 관계 없이

우리가 리더에 대해 생각할 때, 우리는 Abraham Lincoln 혹은 Martin Luther King, Jr.와 같은 사람들에 대해 생각할지 모른다. 만약 여러분이 이러한 인물들의 역사적 중요성과 광범위한 영향력을 고려한다면, 리더십은 고귀하고 높은 목표처럼 보일지도 모른다. 그러나 우리 모두와 마찬가지로, 이러한 인물들은 일상생활의 어느 측면이 더 큰 규모로 어떻게 개선될 수 있는지에 대한 생각을 가졌던 학생, 근로자, 그리고 시민으로 시작했다. 근면함과 경험을 통해, 그들은 자신의 생각을 다른 사람과 공유하고, 그들의 의견과 반응을 구하며, 끊임없이 집단의 목표를 성취할 수 있는 가장 좋은 방법을 찾음으로써 자신의 생각을 발전시켰다. 그러므로 우리는 모두, 나이나 경험에 관계없이, 학교, 공동체, 그리고 일터에서 리더가 될 수 있는 잠재력을 가지고 있다.

Why? 왜 정답일까?

우리 모두 리더가 될 잠재력을 가지고 있다고 말하기 때문에(Thus we all have the potential to be leaders at school, in our communities, and at work, regardless of age or experience.), 글의 요지로 가장 적절한 것은 ③ '공동체를 위한 아이디어를 발전시키는 누구나 리더가 될 수 있다.'이다.

- historical ⓐ 역사적인
- influence ⓝ 영향력
- possess ⓥ 가지다, 소유하다
- improve ⓥ 개선하다
- feedback ⓝ 피드백
- accomplish ⓥ 성취하다
- community ⓝ 공동체
- far-reaching ⓐ 광범위한
- noble ⓐ 고귀한
- aspect ⓝ 측면
- diligence ⓝ 근면
- constantly ⓐⓓ 끊임없이
- potential ⓝ 잠재력
- regardless of ~와 관계없이

구문 풀이

8행 Through diligence and experience, they improved upon their ideas by sharing them with others, seeking their opinions and feedback and constantly looking for the best way to accomplish goals for a group.
(접속사(~을 통해서) / 동명사구1 / 동명사구2 / 동명사구3 / to 부정사 부사적 용법(목적 달성하기 위해서))

23 윤작의 방법과 특징 정답률 84% | 정답 ①

다음 글의 주제로 가장 적절한 것은?

☑ advantage of crop rotation in maintaining soil health
토지 건강을 유지하는 것에 있어서 윤작의 이점
② influence of purchasing organic food on farmers
농부들에게 유기농 음식을 사는 것의 영향
③ ways to choose three important crops for rich soil
비옥한 토양을 위해 세 가지 중요한 곡물을 고르는 방법
④ danger of growing diverse crops in small spaces
작은 공간에 다양한 곡물을 기르는 것의 위험성
⑤ negative impact of crop rotation on the environment
환경에 윤작의 부정적인 영향

Crop rotation is the process / in which farmers change the crops / they grow in their fields / in a special order.
윤작은 과정이다. / 농부가 작물을 바꾸는 / 그들이 자신의 밭에서 재배하는 / 특별한 순서로

For example, / if a farmer has three fields, / he or she may grow / carrots in the first field, / green beans in the second, / and tomatoes in the third.
예를 들어서, / 만약 한 농부가 세 개의 밭을 가지고 있다면, / 그들은 재배할 수 있다. / 첫 번째 밭에는 당근을, / 두 번째 밭에는 녹색 콩을, / 세 번째 밭에는 토마토를

The next year, / green beans will be in the first field, / tomatoes in the second field, / and carrots will be in the third.
그 다음 해에 / 첫 번째 밭에는 녹색 콩을 재배할 것이고, / 두 번째 밭에는 토마토를 재배하며, / 세 번째 밭에는 당근을 재배할 것이다.

In year three, / the crops will rotate again.
3년 차에 / 작물은 다시 순환할 것이다.

By the fourth year, / the crops will go back / to their original order.
4년째에 이르면 / 작물은 되돌아 갈 것이다. / 원래의 순서로

Each crop enriches the soil / for the next crop.
각각의 작물은 토양을 비옥하게 한다. / 다음 작물을 위해

This type of farming is sustainable / because the soil stays healthy.
이 유형의 농업은 지속 가능하다. / 토양이 건강하게 유지되기 때문에

윤작은 농부가 자신의 밭에서 재배하는 작물을 특별한 순서로 바꾸는 과정이다. 예를 들면, 만약 한 농부가 세 개의 밭을 가지고 있다면, 그들은 첫 번째 밭에는 당근을, 두 번째 밭에는 녹색 콩을, 세 번째 밭에는 토마토를 재배할 수 있다. 그 다음 해에 첫 번째 밭에는 녹색 콩을, 두 번째 밭에는 토마토를, 세 번째 밭에는 당근을 재배할 것이다. 3년 차에 작물은 다시 순환할 것이다. 4년째에 이르면 작물은 원래의 순서로 되돌아 갈 것이다. 각각의 작물은 다음 작물을 위한 토양을 비옥하게 한다. 이 유형의 농업은 토양이 건강하게 유지되기 때문에 지속 가능하다.

Why? 왜 정답일까?

윤작의 정의, 예시에 이어 윤작을 통해 토양이 건강하게 유지된다고(This type of farming is sustainable because the soil stays healthy.) 말하기 때문에, 글의 주제로 가장 적절한 것은 ① 'advantage of crop rotation in maintaining soil health'이다.

- crop rotation ⓝ 윤작
- rotate ⓥ 순환하다
- enrich ⓥ 비옥하게 하다
- field ⓝ 밭
- original ⓐ 원래의
- soil ⓝ 토양

구문 풀이

1행 Crop rotation is the process in which farmers change the crops (that) they grow in their fields in a special order.
(관계부사(=where) / 선행사 / 목적격 관계대명사 생략)

24 그림의 완성을 결정하기 정답률 67% | 정답 ⑤

다음 글의 제목으로 가장 적절한 것은?

① Drawing Inspiration from Diverse Artists
다양한 예술가로부터의 그림 영감

② Don't Spoil Your Painting by Leaving It Incomplete
덜 완성된 채로 둠으로써 당신의 그림을 망치지 마세요
③ Art Interpretation: Discover Meanings in a Painting
예술 해석: 그림에서 의미를 발견하기
④ Do Not Put Down Your Brush: The More, the Better
붓을 내려놓지 마세요: 더 많이 할수록, 더 낫습니다
✔ Avoid Overwork and Find the Right Moment to Finish
과한 작업을 피하고 끝낼 적절한 순간을 찾으세요

Working around the whole painting, / rather than concentrating on one area at a time, / will mean / you can stop at any point / and the painting can be considered "finished."
전체 그림에 대해서 작업하는 것은 / 한 번에 한 영역에만 집중하기보다 / 의미할 것이다. / 여러분이 어떤 지점에서도 멈출 수 있고 / 그림이 '완성'된 것으로 간주될 수 있다는 것을

Artists often find it difficult / to know when to stop painting, / and it can be tempting / to keep on adding more to your work.
화가들은 종종 어렵다는 것을 발견한다. / 그림을 언제 멈춰야 할지 알기가 / 그리고 유혹을 느낄 수 있다. / 자신의 그림에 계속해서 더 추가하고 싶은

It is important to take a few steps back from the painting / from time to time / to assess your progress.
그림에서 몇 걸음 뒤로 물러나는 것이 중요하다. / 때때로 / 자신의 진행 상황을 평가하기 위해

Putting too much into a painting / can spoil its impact / and leave it looking overworked.
한 그림에 너무 많은 것을 넣는 것은 / 영향력을 망칠 수 있고 / 그리고 그것이 과하게 작업된 것처럼 보이게 둘 수 있다.

If you find yourself struggling / to decide whether you have finished, / take a break and come back to it later with fresh eyes.
만약 여러분이 어려움을 겪고 있음을 알게 된다면 / 여러분이 끝냈는지를 결정하는 데에 / 잠시 휴식을 취하고 나중에 새로운 눈으로 그림으로 다시 돌아와라.

Then you can decide / whether any areas of your painting would benefit / from further refinement.
그러면 여러분은 결정할 수 있다. / 자신의 그림 어느 부분이 득을 볼지를 / 더 정교하게 꾸며서

한 번에 한 영역에만 집중하기보다 전체 그림에 대해서 작업하는 것은 여러분이 어떤 지점에서도 멈출 수 있고 그림이 '완성'된 것으로 간주될 수 있다는 것을 의미할 것이다. 화가인 여러분은 종종 언제 그림을 멈춰야 할지 알기 어렵다는 것을 발견하고, 자신의 그림에 계속해서 더 추가하고 싶은 유혹을 느낄 수도 있다. 때때로 자신의 진행 상황을 평가하기 위해 그림에서 몇 걸음 뒤로 물러나는 것이 중요하다. 한 그림에 너무 많은 것을 넣으면 그것의 영향력을 망칠 수 있고 그것이 과하게 작업된 것처럼 보이게 둘 수 있다. 만약 여러분이 끝냈는지를 결정하는 데 자신이 어려움을 겪고 있음을 알게 된다면, 잠시 휴식을 취하고 나중에 새로운 눈으로 그것(그림)으로 다시 돌아와라. 그러면 여러분은 더 정교하게 꾸며서 자신의 그림 어느 부분이 득을 볼지를 결정할 수 있다.

Why? 왜 정답일까?
그림을 그리며 어떤 지점에서 멈춰야 할지 알기가 어렵기 때문에 과하게 작업하기가 쉬우므로, 잠시 휴식을 취하라며 과한 작업을 피해야 할 필요성을 강조하고 있다. 따라서 ⑤ 'Avoid Overwork and Find the Right Moment to Finish'가 제목으로 가장 적절하다.

● concentrate ⓥ 집중하다
● spoil ⓥ 망쳐 놓다
● overwork ⓥ 과하게 작업하다
● assess ⓥ 평가하다
● impact ⓝ 영향(력)
● benefit ⓥ 득을 보다

구문 풀이

5행 It is important to take a few steps back from the painting from time to time to assess your progress.
가주어 it / 진주어 / 때때로, 이따금, 가끔 / to부정사 형용사적 용법(평가할)

---

25 2021년 기후 변화를 두려워하는 6개국 16-25세 인구의 순위   정답률 81% | 정답 ③

다음 도표의 내용과 일치하지 않는 것은?

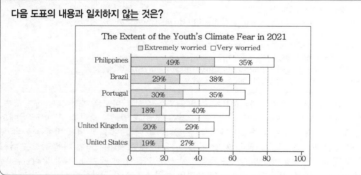

The Extent of the Youth's Climate Fear in 2021
☐ Extremely worried ☐ Very worried

	Extremely worried	Very worried
Philippines	49%	35%
Brazil	29%	38%
Portugal	30%	35%
France	18%	40%
United Kingdom	20%	29%
United States	19%	27%

The above graph shows the extent / to which young people aged 16 − 25 in six countries had fear / about climate change in 2021.
위의 그래프는 정도를 보여 준다. / 6개국의 16세에서 25세 사이 젊은 사람들이 두려움을 갖는 / 2021년 기후 변화에 대해

① The Philippines had the highest percentage of young people / who said they were extremely or very worried, / at 84 percent, / followed by 67 percent in Brazil.
필리핀은 젊은 사람들의 가장 높은 비율을 보여 준다. / 극도로 혹은 매우 걱정한다고 말한 / 84퍼센트로, / 67퍼센트로 브라질이 그 뒤를 잇고

② More than 60 percent of young people in Portugal said / they were extremely worried or very worried.
포르투갈은 60퍼센트 이상의 젊은 사람들이 말했다. / 극도로 혹은 매우 걱정하고 있다고

✔ In France, the percentage of young people who were extremely worried / was higher than that of young people / who were very worried.
프랑스는 극도로 걱정하는 젊은 사람들의 비율이 / 젊은 사람들의 비율보다 높았다. / 매우 걱정하는

④ In the United Kingdom, the percentage of young generation who said / that they were very worried / was 29 percent.
영국은 젊은 세대의 비율이 / 매우 걱정된다고 말하는 / 29퍼센트였다.

⑤ In the United States, the total percentage of extremely worried and very worried youth / was the smallest / among the six countries.
미국은 극도로 걱정하거나 걱정하는 젊은 사람들의 총비율이 / 가장 작았다. / 6개국 중에서

위 그래프는 2021년 6개국의 16세에서 25세 사이 젊은 사람들이 기후 변화에 대해 두려움을 갖는 정도를 보여 준다. ① 필리핀은 극도로 혹은 매우 걱정한다고 말한 젊은 사람들의 비율

이 84퍼센트로 가장 높았으며, 브라질이 67퍼센트로 그 뒤를 이었다. ② 포르투갈은 60퍼센트 이상의 젊은 사람들이 극도로 혹은 매우 걱정하고 있다고 말했다. ③ 프랑스는 극도로 걱정하는 젊은 사람들의 비율이 매우 걱정하는 젊은 사람들의 비율보다 높았다. ④ 영국은 매우 걱정한다고 말하는 젊은 세대의 비율이 29퍼센트였다. ⑤ 미국은 극도로 걱정하거나 매우 걱정하는 젊은 사람들의 총비율이 6개국 중에서 가장 작았다.

Why? 왜 정답일까?
프랑스는 극도로 걱정하는 젊은 사람들의 비율이 **18%**로 매우 걱정하는 젊은 사람들의 비율인 **40%**보다 낮기 때문에 도표의 내용과 일치하지 않는 것은 ③이다.

● extent ⓝ 정도
● extremely ⓐⓓ 극도로
● climate ⓝ 기후
● generation ⓝ 세대

구문 풀이

7행 In France, the percentage of young people who were extremely worried was higher than that of young people who were very worried.
선행사 / 주격관계대명사 / 동사 / 비교급 / 지시대명사 the percentage / 주격관계대명사

---

26 Jaroslav Heyrovsky의 일생   정답률 86% | 정답 ④

Jaroslav Heyrovsky에 관한 다음 글의 내용과 일치하지 않는 것은?
① 라틴어와 그리스어보다 자연 과학에 강한 흥미를 보였다.
② Czech University에서 화학, 물리학 및 수학을 공부했다.
③ 1910년부터 1914년까지 런던에서 학업을 이어 나갔다.
✔ 제1차 세계 대전이 끝난 후 군 병원에 복무했다.
⑤ 1959년에 노벨 화학상을 수상했다.

Jaroslav Heyrovsky was born in Prague / on December 20, 1890, / as the fifth child of Leopold Heyrovsky.
Jaroslav Heyrovsky는 Prague에서 태어났다. / 1890년 12월 20일에 / Leopold Heyrovsky의 다섯째 자녀로

In 1901 / Jaroslav went to a secondary school / called the Akademicke Gymnasium.
1901년에 / Jaroslav는 중등학교에 다녔다. / Akademicke Gymnasium이라는

『Rather than Latin and Greek, / he showed a strong interest in the natural sciences.』
라틴어와 그리스어보다, / 그는 자연 과학에 강한 흥미를 보였다.   ①의근거 일치

『At Czech University in Prague / he studied chemistry, physics, and mathematics.』
Prague에 있는 Czech University에서 / 그는 화학, 물리학, 그리고 수학을 공부했다.   ②의근거 일치

『From 1910 to 1914 / he continued his studies / at University College, London.』
1910년부터 1914년까지 / 그는 그의 학업을 이어 나갔다. / London의 University College에서   ③의근거 일치

『Throughout the First World War, / Jaroslav served in a military hospital.』   ④의근거 불일치
제1차 세계 대전 내내, / Jaroslav는 군 병원에 복무했다.

In 1926, / Jaroslav became the first Professor of Physical Chemistry / at Charles University in Prague.
1926년에, / Jaroslav는 최초의 물리화학 교수가 되었다. / Prague의 Charles University에서

『He won the Nobel Prize in chemistry / in 1959.』   ⑤의근거 일치
그는 노벨 화학상을 수상했다. / 1959년에

Jaroslav Heyrovsky는 1890년 12월 20일 Prague에서 Leopold Heyrovsky의 다섯째 자녀로 태어났다. 1901년 Jaroslav는 Akademicke Gymnasium이라고 불리는 중등학교에 다녔다. 그는 라틴어와 그리스어보다는 자연 과학에 강한 흥미를 보였다. Prague에 있는 Czech University에서 그는 화학, 물리학 및 수학을 공부했다. 1910년부터 1914년까지 그는 런던의 University College에서 학업을 이어 나갔다. 제1차 세계 대전 내내 Jaroslav는 군 병원에 복무했다. 1926년에 Jaroslav는 Prague에 있는 Charles University 최초의 물리화학 교수가 되었다. 그는 1959년에 노벨 화학상을 수상했다.

Why? 왜 정답일까?
'Throughout the First World War, Jaroslav served in a military hospital.'에서 Jaroslav Heyrovsky는 제1차 세계 대전 내내 군 병원에서 복무했다고 했으므로 글의 내용과 일치하지 않는 것은 ④ '제1차 세계 대전이 끝난 후 군 병원에 복무했다.'이다.

Why? 왜 오답일까?
① '~he showed a strong interest in the natural sciences.'의 내용과 일치한다.
② 'At Czech University in Prague he studied chemistry, physics, and mathematics.'의 내용과 일치한다.
③ 'From 1910 to 1914 he continued his studies at University College, London.'의 내용과 일치한다.
⑤ 'He won the Nobel Prize in chemistry in 1959.'의 내용과 일치한다.

● secondary school ⓝ 중등학교
● physics ⓝ 물리학
● throughout ⓟⓡⓔⓟ 내내
● chemistry ⓝ 화학
● mathematics ⓝ 수학
● military ⓝ 군대의

구문 풀이

1행 Jaroslav Heyrovsky was born in Prague on December 20, 1890, as the fifth child of Leopold Heyrovsky.
수동태 / 전치사(~로써)

---

27 청소년을 위한 봄철 차 교실 안내문   정답률 96% | 정답 ④

Spring Tea Class for Young People에 관한 다음 안내문의 내용과 일치하지 않는 것은?
① 수강생은 전 세계 다양한 문화권의 차를 경험할 수 있다.
② 금요일 수업은 오후에 1시간 30분 동안 진행된다.
③ 수강생에게 차와 간식을 제공한다.
✔ 15세 이하의 수강생은 30달러의 참가비를 내야 한다.
⑤ 음식 알레르기가 있는 수강생은 이메일을 미리 보내야 한다.

Spring Tea Class for Young People
청소년을 위한 봄철 차 교실

『Join us / for a delightful Spring Tea Class for young people, / where you'll experience the taste of tea / from various cultures around the world.』①의근거 일치
참여하세요. / 즐거운 봄철 차 교실에 / 여러분이 차를 맛보는 경험을 할 / 전 세계 다양한 문화권의

Class Schedule
수업 일정
『Friday, April 5 (4:30 p.m. − 6:00 p.m.)』②의근거 일치
4월 5일 금요일 (오후 4:30 ~ 오후 6:00)
Saturday, April 6 (9:30 a.m. − 11:00 a.m.)
4월 6일 토요일 (오전 9:30 ~ 오전 11:00)
Details
세부 내용
『We will give you tea and snacks.』③의근거 일치
우리는 여러분에게 차와 간식을 드리겠습니다.
We offer special tips / for hosting a tea party.
우리는 특별한 조언을 제공합니다. / 차 모임 주최를 위한
Participation Fee
참가비
『Age 13 − 15: $25 per person』④의근거 불일치
13 ~ 15세: 1인당 25달러
Age 16 − 18: $30 per person
16 ~ 18세: 1인당 30달러
Note
주의 사항
『If you have any food allergy, / you should email us in advance / at youth@seasonteaclass. com.』⑤의근거 일치
만약 여러분이 음식 알레르기가 있다면, / 저희에게 미리 이메일을 보내야 합니다. / youth@seasonteaclass.com으로

청소년을 위한 봄철 차 교실

청소년을 위한 즐거운 봄철 차 교실에 참여하세요.
그곳에서 여러분은 전 세계 다양한 문화권의 차를 맛보는 경험을 할 것입니다.

수업 일정
• 4월 5일 금요일 (오후 4:30 ~ 오후 6:00)
• 4월 6일 토요일 (오전 9:30 ~ 오전 11:00)

세부 내용
• 우리는 여러분에게 차와 간식을 드리겠습니다.
• 우리는 차 모임 주최를 위한 특별한 조언을 제공합니다.

참가비
• 13 ~ 15세: 1인당 25달러
• 16 ~ 18세: 1인당 30달러

주의 사항
만약 여러분이 음식 알레르기가 있다면 저희에게 미리 youth@seasonteaclass.com으로 이메일을 보내야 합니다.

Why? 왜 정답일까?
참가비 항목에 13 ~ 15세는 1인당 25달러의 참가비를 내야하므로 안내문의 내용과 일치하지 않는 것은 ④ '15세 이하의 수강생은 30달러의 참가비를 내야 한다.'이다.

Why? 왜 오답일까?
① '~you'll experience the taste of tea from various cultures around the world.'의 내용과 일치한다.
② 'Friday, April 5 (4:30 p.m. − 6:00 p.m.)'의 내용과 일치한다.
③ 'We will give you tea and snacks.'의 내용과 일치한다.
⑤ 'If you have any food allergy, you should email us in advance at youth@seasonteaclass.com.'의 내용과 일치한다.

• **delightful** ⓐ 즐거운
• **various** ⓐ 다양한
• **in advance** 미리
• **experience** ⓥ 경험하다
• **host** ⓥ (파티 등을) 주최하다

---

28 2024 의류 업사이클링 대회 안내문 　정답률 88% | 정답 ④

Clothes Upcycling Contest 2024에 관한 다음 안내문의 내용과 일치하는 것은?
① Lakewood에 사는 사람이면 누구든지 참가할 수 있다.
② 참가자는 출품 사진을 직접 방문하여 제출해야 한다.
③ 참가자는 5월 14일까지 출품 사진을 제출할 수 있다.
✔ 우승 상품은 지역 상점에서 쓸 수 있는 기프트 카드이다.
⑤ 지역 신문을 통해 우승자를 발표한다.

Clothes Upcycling Contest 2024
2024 의류 업사이클링 대회
Are you passionate / about fashion and the environment?
여러분은 열정이 있으신가요? / 패션과 환경에 대한
Then we have a contest for you!
그렇다면 우리가 여러분을 위한 대회를 개최합니다!
Participants
참가자
『Anyone living in Lakewood, aged 11 to 18』①의근거 불일치
Lakewood에 거주하는 11세에서 18세까지이면 누구나
How to participate
참여 방법
Take before and after photos / of your upcycled clothes.
전, 후 사진을 찍으세요. / 여러분의 업사이클된 옷의
『Email the photos at lovelw@lwplus.com.』②의근거 불일치
사진은 lovelw@lwplus.com으로 이메일을 보내세요.
『Send in the photos from April 14 to May 12.』
사진은 4월 14일부터 5월 12일까지 보내세요.
Winning Prize
우승 상품

『A $100 gift card to use at local shops』④의근거 일치
지역 상점에서 쓸 수 있는 100달러 기프트 카드 한 장
『The winner will be announced on our website on May 30.』⑤의근거 불일치
우승자를 우리 웹사이트에서 5월 30일에 발표할 것입니다.
For more details, visit our website www.lovelwplus.com.
더 많은 정보를 위해서는 우리 웹사이트(www.lovelwplus.com)를 방문하세요.

2024 의류 업사이클링 대회

여러분은 패션과 환경에 대한 열정이 있으신가요?
그렇다면 우리가 여러분을 위한 대회를 개최합니다!

• **참가자**
 − Lakewood에 거주하는 11세에서 18세까지이면 누구나

• **참여 방법**
 − 여러분의 업사이클된 옷의 전, 후 사진을 찍으세요.
 − 사진은 lovelw@lwplus.com으로 이메일을 보내세요.
 − 사진은 4월 14일부터 5월 12일까지 보내세요.

• **우승 상품**
 − 지역 상점에서 쓸 수 있는 100달러 기프트 카드 한 장
 − 우승자를 우리 웹사이트에서 5월 30일에 발표할 것입니다.

더 많은 정보를 위해서는 우리 웹사이트(www.lovelwplus.com)를 방문하세요.

Why? 왜 정답일까?
우승 상품이 'A $100 gift card to use at local shops'라고 했으므로 내용과 일치하는 것은 ④ '우승 상품은 지역 상점에서 쓸 수 있는 기프트 카드이다.'이다.

Why? 왜 오답일까?
① 'Anyone living in Lakewood, aged 11 to 18'에서 Lakewood에 사는 11세에서 18세만 참가할 수 있다고 하였다.
② 'Email the photos at lovelw@lwplus.com.'에서 출품 사진을 이메일로 제출하라 하였다.
③ 'Send in the photos from April 14 to May 12.'에서 5월 12일까지 출품 사진을 제출할 수 있다고 하였다.
⑤ 'The winner will be announced on our website on May 30.'에서 우승자는 웹사이트에서 발표된다고 하였다.

• **upcycled** ⓐ 업사이클된
• **passionate** ⓐ 열정적인
• **contest** ⓝ 대회
• **local** ⓐ 지역의
• **environment** ⓝ 환경
• **fashion** ⓝ 패션, 의류
• **announce** ⓥ 발표하다

---

29 의미 있는 일의 중요성 　정답률 68% | 정답 ②

다음 글의 밑줄 친 부분 중, 어법상 틀린 것은? [3점]

It would be hard to overstate / how important meaningful work is to human beings / — work ① that provides a sense of fulfillment and empowerment.
과장해서 말하기는 힘들 것이다. / 인간에게 의미 있는 일이 얼마나 중요한지를 / 성취감과 권한을 제공하는
Those who have found deeper meaning in their careers / find their days much more energizing and satisfying, / and ✔ count their employment as one of their greatest sources of joy and pride.
자신의 직업에서 더 깊은 의미를 찾은 사람은 / 자신의 하루하루가 훨씬 더 활기차고 만족감을 준다는 것을 발견하고, / 자신의 직업을 기쁨과 자부심의 가장 큰 원천 중 하나로 꼽는다.
Sonya Lyubomirsky, professor of psychology at the University of California, / has conducted numerous workplace studies ③ showing / that when people are more fulfilled on the job, / they not only produce higher quality work and a greater output, / but also generally earn higher incomes.
University of California의 심리학 교수인 Sonya Lyubomirsky는 / 보여 주는 수많은 업무 현장 연구를 수행했다. / 사람이 직업에 더 많은 성취감을 느낄 때 / 그들은 더 질 높은 업무와 더 큰 성과를 만들어 낼 뿐만 아니라 / 일반적으로 더 높은 수입을 거둔다는 것
Those most satisfied with their work / ④ are also much more likely to be happier with their lives overall.
자신의 일에 가장 만족하는 사람은 / 또한 전반적으로 자신의 삶에 더 행복해 할 가능성이 훨씬 더 크다.
For her book *Happiness at Work*, / researcher Jessica Pryce-Jones conducted a study of 3,000 workers in seventy-nine countries, / ⑤ finding that those who took greater satisfaction from their work / were 150 percent more likely to have a happier life overall.
자신의 저서 'Happiness at Work'를 위해 / 연구자 Jessica Pryce-Jones는 79개 국가의 3,000명의 근로자에 대한 연구를 수행했고, / 자신의 일로부터 더 큰 만족감을 갖는 사람이 / 전반적으로 더 행복한 삶을 살 가능성이 150퍼센트 더 크다는 것을 알아냈다.

인간에게 의미 있는 일, 즉 성취감과 권한을 제공하는 일이 얼마나 중요한지를 과장해서 말한다는 것은 어려울 것이다. 자신의 직업에서 더 깊은 의미를 찾은 사람은 자신의 하루하루가 훨씬 더 활기차고 만족감을 준다는 것을 발견하고, 자신의 직업을 기쁨과 자부심의 가장 큰 원천 중 하나로 꼽는다. University of California의 심리학 교수인 Sonya Lyubomirsky는 사람이 직업에 더 많은 성취감을 느낄 때 그들은 더 질 높은 업무와 더 큰 성과를 만들어 낼 뿐만 아니라 일반적으로 더 높은 수입을 거둔다는 것을 보여 주는 수많은 업무 현장 연구를 수행했다. 자신의 일에 가장 만족하는 사람은 또한 전반적으로 자신의 삶에 더 행복해 할 가능성이 훨씬 더 크다. 자신의 저서 'Happiness at Work'를 위해 연구자 Jessica Pryce-Jones는 79개 국가의 3,000명의 근로자에 대한 연구를 수행했고, 자신의 일로부터 더 큰 만족감을 갖는 사람이 전반적으로 더 행복한 삶을 살 가능성이 150퍼센트 더 크다는 것을 알아냈다.

Why? 왜 정답일까?
주어구가 'Those who have found deeper meaning in their careers'이기 때문에 등위접속사인 'and' 뒤에는 'find'와 동급인 동사 형태의 'count'가 와야 하기 때문에 ② 'to count'가 어법상 틀렸다.

Why? 왜 오답일까?
① 선행사로 work가 왔고, 뒷문장에 주어가 없으므로 주격관계대명사인 'that'이 쓰였다.

③ 앞 문장 전체를 수식하는 현재분사 형태인 'showing'이 쓰였다. "사람들이 더 직장에서 더 만족할 때 나타나는 결과"를 설명하고 있어 문법적으로 옳다.
④ 주어가 'Those most satisfied with their work'으로 복수이므로 be동사의 복수형태인 'are'이 쓰였다.
⑤ 앞의 문장 전체를 수식하는 현재분사로, 'study'의 결과를 보충 설명하며 덧붙이고 있어 문법적으로 옳다.

- overstate ⓥ 과장해서 말하다
- empowerment ⓝ 권한
- satisfying ⓐ 만족감을 주는
- source ⓝ 원천
- numerous ⓐ 수많은
- workplace ⓝ 업무 현장, 직장
- output ⓝ 성과
- income ⓝ 수입
- fulfillment ⓝ 성취감
- energizing ⓐ 활기찬
- employment ⓝ 직업, 고용
- conduct ⓥ 수행하다
- psychology ⓝ 심리
- quality ⓝ 질
- generally ⓐ𝓭 일반적으로
- overall ⓐ 전반적으로

구문 풀이

11행　Those (who are) most satisfied with their work are also much more likely
지시대명사　주격관계대명사 + be동사 생략　최상급　「be likely to: ~할 것 같은, ~할 확률이 높은」
to be happier with their lives overall.

★★★ 등급을 가르는 문제!

30　사람의 이동속도와 처리 능력　정답률 47% | 정답 ③

다음 글의 밑줄 친 부분 중, 문맥상 낱말의 쓰임이 적절하지 않은 것은? [3점]

The rate of speed at which one is traveling / will greatly determine the ability / to process detail in the environment.
사람이 이동하는 속도의 빠르기는 / 능력을 크게 결정할 것이다. / 환경 속 세세한 것을 처리하는
In evolutionary terms, / human senses are adapted to the ① speed / at which humans move through space / under their own power while walking.
진화론적 관점에서, / 인간의 감각은 속도에 적응되어 있다 / 공간을 이동하는 / 그 자신의 힘으로 걷는
Our ability to distinguish detail in the environment is / therefore ideally ② suited to movement at speeds / of perhaps five miles per hour and under.
환경 속에서 세세한 것을 구별하는 우리의 능력은 / 그래서 속도의 이동에 이상적으로 맞추어져 있다. / 대략 시속 5마일 또는 그 속도 이하의
The fastest users of the street, motorists, / therefore have a much more limited ability / to process details along the street / — a motorist simply has ✔less time or ability / to appreciate design details.
도로의 가장 빠른 사용자인 운전자는 / 그러므로 더 제한된 능력을 가지고 있고 / 도로를 따라서 (이동하며) 세세한 것을 처리하는 / 그래서 운전자는 적은 시간이나 능력이 있다. / 디자인의 세세한 것을 감상할 수 있는
On the other hand, / pedestrian travel, being much slower, / allows for the ④ appreciation of environmental detail.
반면에, / 보행자 이동은 훨씬 더 느려서, / 환경의 세세한 것을 감상할 수 있도록 허용해 준다.
Joggers and bicyclists fall somewhere in between these polar opposites; / while they travel faster than pedestrians, / their rate of speed is ordinarily much ⑤ slower / than that of the typical motorist.
조깅하는 사람과 자전거를 타는 사람은 이러한 극과 극 사이의 어딘가에 해당한다. / 그들은 보행자보다 더 빨리 이동하지만, / 속도의 빠르기는 훨씬 더 느리다. / 보통 전형적인 운전자의 그것보다

사람이 이동하는 속도의 빠르기는 환경 속 세세한 것을 처리하는 능력을 크게 결정할 것이다. 진화론적 관점에서, 인간의 감각은 그 자신의 힘으로 걸으며 공간을 이동하는 ① 속도에 적응되어 있다. 환경 속에서 세세한 것을 구별하는 우리의 능력은 그래서 대략 시속 5마일 또는 그 속도 이하의 이동에 이상적으로 ② 맞추어져 있다. 그러므로 도로의 가장 빠른 사용자인 운전자는 도로를 따라서 (이동하며) 세세한 것을 처리하는 훨씬 더 제한된 능력을 가지고 있고, 그래서 운전자는 단지 디자인의 세세한 것을 감상할 수 있는 ③ 충분한(→ 적은) 시간이나 능력이 있다. 반면에 보행자 이동은 훨씬 더 느려서, 환경의 세세한 것을 ④ 감상할 수 있도록 허용해 준다. 조깅하는 사람과 자전거를 타는 사람은 이러한 극과 극 사이의 어딘가에 해당한다. 그들은 보행자보다 더 빨리 이동하지만, 속도의 빠르기는 보통 전형적인 운전자의 그것보다 훨씬 ⑤ 더 느리다.

Why? 왜 정답일까?

인간의 감각은 보행 속도에 적응되어 있기 때문에, 도로의 가장 빠른 사용자인 운전자는 도로를 따라서 이동하며 세세한 것을 처리하는 능력이 비교적 제한되어 있다. 따라서 운전자는 디자인의 세세한 것을 감상할 수 있는 시간이 적기 때문에, ③ enough → less로 수정해야 한다.

- rate ⓝ 빠르기
- ability ⓝ 능력
- ideally ⓐ𝓭 이상적으로
- motorist ⓝ 운전자
- appreciate ⓥ 감상하다, 제대로 인식하다
- allow for 가능하게 하다, 허락하다
- opposite ⓝ 반대의 것
- typical ⓐ 전형적인
- determine ⓥ 결정하다
- adapted ⓐ 맞추어진, 적응된
- suited ⓐ 적합한
- limited ⓐ 제한된
- on the other hand 반면에
- polar ⓐ 극과 극의
- ordinarily ⓐ𝓭 보통

구문 풀이

2행　In evolutionary terms, human senses are adapted to the speed at which
전치사 + 관계대명사
humans move through space under their own power while walking.
「be adapted to : ~에 적응되었다, ~에 익숙해졌다」
~하는 동안에

★★ 문제 해결 꿀~팁 ★★

▶ 많이 틀린 이유는?
글은 이동 속도에 따라 변화하는 주변 감상 능력에 대해서 이야기하고 있다. 'Our ability to distinguish detail in the environment is therefore ideally suited to movement at speeds of perhaps five miles per hour and under.'에서 이동 속도가 걷는 속도, 즉 시간 당 5 마일 이상일 때 주변 감상 능력과의 관계는 반비례함을 알 수 있다. 보행자(pedestrian), 조깅하는 사람(jogger), 자전거를 타는 사람(bicyclist), 자동차를 타는 사람(motorist) 순으로 속도가 빨라지므로 주변 감상

능력 역시 감소한다. 따라서 도로에서 이동 속도가 가장 빠른 사람으로 제시된 자동차를 타는 사람은 주변을 감상할 시간과 능력이 가장 적기 때문에, 자동차를 타는 사람이 주변을 감상할 충분한 시간과 능력이 있다는 선지는 적절하지 않다.

▶ 문제 해결 방법은?
글의 요지를 파악한 후, 요지에 어긋나는 선지를 고른다. 해당 문제의 경우 글에 제시된 다른 이동 속도를 가진 사람들을 주변 감상 능력의 정도에 따라 줄 세우면 더욱 쉽게 풀 수 있다.

31　기후 변화와 종의 변화　정답률 51% | 정답 ②

다음 빈칸에 들어갈 말로 가장 적절한 것을 고르시오.
① endurance – 인내
③ development – 발달
⑤ communication – 의사소통
✔ movement – 이동
④ transformation – 변화

Every species has certain climatic requirements / — what degree of heat or cold it can endure, for example.
모든 종은 특정 기후 요건을 가지고 있다. / 예를 들자면 어느 정도의 더위나 추위를 견딜 수 있는지와 같은,
When the climate changes, / the places that satisfy those requirements change, too.
기후가 변할 때, / 그러한 요건을 충족시키는 장소도 역시 변한다.
Species are forced to follow.
종은 따르도록 강요받는다.
All creatures are capable of some degree of movement.
모든 생명체는 어느 정도의 이동이 가능하다.
Even creatures that appear immobile, / like trees and barnacles, / are capable of dispersal at some stage of their life / — as a seed, in the case of the tree, / or as a larva, in the case of the barnacle.
심지어 나무나 따개비처럼 움직이지 않는 것처럼 보이는 생명체도, / 그들 일생의 어느 단계에서 분산할 수 있다. / 나무의 경우는 씨앗으로, / 따개비의 경우는 유충으로,
A creature must get from the place it is born / — often occupied by its parent / — to a place where it can survive, grow, and reproduce.
생명체는 종종 자신이 태어난 장소로부터 / — 종종 자신의 부모에 의해 점유된 / — 생존하고 성장하며 번식할 수 있는 장소로 이동해야 한다.
From fossils, scientists know / that even creatures like trees / moved with surprising speed / during past periods of climate change.
화석으로부터, 과학자들은 / 심지어 나무와 같은 생명체도 / 기후 변화의 과거 시기 동안 / 놀라운 속도로 이동했다는 것을 알고 있다.

모든 종은, 예를 들자면 어느 정도의 더위나 추위를 견딜 수 있는지와 같은, 특정 기후 요건을 가지고 있다. 기후가 변할 때, 그러한 요건을 충족시키는 장소도 역시 변한다. 종은 따르도록 강요받는다. 모든 생명체는 어느 정도의 이동이 가능하다. 심지어 나무나 따개비처럼 움직이지 않는 것처럼 보이는 생명체도, 나무의 경우는 씨앗으로, 따개비의 경우는 유충으로, 그들 일생의 어느 단계에서 분산할 수 있다. 생명체는 종종 자신의 부모에 의해서 점유된, 그래서 자신이 태어난 장소로부터 생존하고 성장하며 번식할 수 있는 장소로 이동해야 한다. 화석으로부터, 과학자들은 심지어 나무와 같은 생명체도 기후 변화의 과거 시기 동안 놀라운 속도로 이동했다는 것을 알고 있다.

Why? 왜 정답일까?

종이 견딜 수 있는 특정한 기후 요건이 있고, 기후가 변화하면 종이 이동해야 한다고 설명하고 있기 때문에 빈칸에 적절한 표현은 ② 'movement'이다.

- climatic ⓐ 기후의
- endure ⓥ 견디다
- force ⓥ 강요하다
- immobile ⓐ 움직이지 않는
- seed ⓝ 씨앗
- occupy ⓥ 점유하다
- reproduce ⓥ 번식하다
- requirement ⓝ 요건
- satisfy ⓥ 충족시키다
- creature ⓝ 생명체
- capable ⓐ ~할 수 있는
- larva ⓝ 유충
- survive ⓥ 생존하다

구문 풀이

2행　When the climate changes, the places that satisfy those requirements
관계부사　선행사　주격관계대명사
change, too.

★★★ 등급을 가르는 문제!

32　반대 의견의 장점　정답률 26% | 정답 ③

다음 빈칸에 들어갈 말로 가장 적절한 것을 고르시오. [3점]
① unconditional loyalty – 무조건적인 충성
② positive attitude – 긍정적인 태도
✔ internal protest – 내부적인 저항
④ competitive atmosphere – 경쟁적인 분위기
⑤ outstanding performance – 눈에 띄는 수행

No respectable boss would say, / "I make it a point to discourage my staff from speaking up, / and I maintain a culture that prevents disagreeing viewpoints from ever getting aired."
존경할 만한 상사라면 누구라도 말하지는 않을 것이다. / '나는 반드시 내 직원이 자유롭게 의견을 내지 못하도록 하고, / 동의하지 않는 관점이 언제든 공공연히 알려지는 것을 가로막는 문화를 유지한다.'라고
If anything, / most bosses even say that they are pro-dissent.
오히려, / 대부분의 상사는 심지어 자신은 반대에 찬성한다고 말한다.
This idea can be found throughout the series of conversations / with corporate, university, and nonprofit leaders, / published weekly in the business sections of newspapers.
이러한 생각은 일련의 대담을 통해서 발견될 수 있다. / 기업, 대학, 그리고 비영리 (단체의) 리더와의 / 매주 발행되는 신문의 경제란에
In the interviews, / the featured leaders are asked about their management techniques, / and regularly claim to continually encourage internal protest from more junior staffers.
인터뷰에서, / (기사에) 다루어진 리더는 자신의 경영 기법에 대해 질문을 받고, / 내부적 저항이 더 많은 부하 직원에게서 (나오기를) 계속해서 장려하고 있다고 어김없이 주장한다.

As Bot Pittman remarked in one of these conversations: / "I want us to listen to these dissenters / because they may intend to tell you why we can't do something, / but if you listen hard, / what they're really telling you is what you must do to get something done."
Bot Pittman은 이러한 대담 중 하나에서 말했다. / "저는 우리가 이러한 반대자에게 귀 기울이기를 원합니다. / 왜냐하면 그들은 여러분에게 우리가 무엇인가를 할 수 없는 이유를 말하려고 의도할 수 있겠지만, / 그러나 만약에 여러분이 열심히 귀 기울이면, / 그들이 정말로 여러분에게 말하고 있는 것은 어떤 일이 이루어지도록 하기 위해서 여러분이 무엇을 해야만 하는가이기 때문입니다." 라고

존경할 만한 상사라면 누구라도 '나는 반드시 내 직원이 자유롭게 의견을 내지 못하도록 하고, 동의하지 않는 관점이 언제든 공공연히 알려지는 것을 가로막는 문화를 유지한다.'라고 말하지는 않을 것이다. 오히려, 대부분의 상사는 심지어 자신은 반대에 찬성한다고 말한다. 이러한 생각은 매주 발행되는 신문의 경제란에 기업, 대학, 그리고 비영리 (단체의) 리더와의 일련의 대담을 통해서 발견될 수 있다. 인터뷰에서, (기사에) 다루어진 리더는 자신의 경영 기법에 대해 질문을 받고, 내부적인 저항이 더 많은 부하 직원에게서 (나오기를) 계속해서 장려하고 있다고 어김없이 주장한다. Bot Pittman은 이러한 대담 중 하나에서 "저는 우리가 이러한 반대자에게 귀 기울이기를 원합니다. 왜냐하면 그들은 여러분에게 우리가 무엇인가를 할 수 없는 이유를 말하려고 의도할 수 있겠지만, 그러나 만약에 여러분이 열심히 귀 기울이면, 그들이 정말로 여러분에게 말하고 있는 것은 어떤 일이 이루어지도록 하기 위해서 여러분이 무엇을 해야만 하는가이기 때문입니다."라고 말했다.

Why? 왜 정답일까?

대부분의 상사들이 반대자의 의견을 좋아함을 언급하고(most bosses even say that they are pro-dissent), 반대자의 의견의 중요성에 대해서 얘기하고 있기 때문에 반대 의견을 독려함이 적절하다. 따라서 ③ 'internal protest'(내부적인 저항)이 정답이다.

- **respectable** ⓐ 존경할 만한
- **discourage** ⓥ 못하게 하다
- **maintain** ⓥ 유지하다
- **if anything** 오히려
- **corporate** ⓝ 기업
- **publish** ⓥ 발행하다, 출판하다
- **management** ⓝ 경영
- **regularly** ⓐ 어김없이, 규칙적으로
- **remark** ⓥ 말하다
- **make it a point** 반드시 ~하도록 하다
- **speak up** 자유롭게 의견을 내다
- **get aired** 공공연히 알려지다
- **conversation** ⓝ 대담, 대화
- **nonprofit** ⓐ 비영리인
- **feature** ⓥ (기사로) 다루다
- **techniques** ⓝ 기법
- **claim** ⓥ 주장하다

구문 풀이

4행 If anything, most bosses even say that they are pro-dissent.
오히려, 그러기는커녕 · 접속사

★★ 문제 해결 꿀~팁 ★★

▶ 많이 틀린 이유는?
글에 따르면 좋은 상사는 반대 의견에서 해결책을 찾아내기도 하기 때문에 부하 직원들이 반대 의견을 내는 것에 찬성한다. 반대 의견의 중요성에 대해 서술하고 있다. 따라서 인터뷰를 진행한 리더들에게 경영 기술을 물었을 때 꾸준히 반대 의견을 내는 것을 장려한다는 말이 자연스럽다.

▶ 문제 해결 방법은?
빈칸 문제는 본문의 주제를 파악하고, 선지를 올바르게 해석하는 것이 중요하다. 글의 서두와 말미의 문장에서 주제를 파악한 후, 빈칸에 들어갈 답을 고른다.

---

33 잠 자는 동안의 지각 이탈 · 정답률 55% | 정답 ③

다음 빈칸에 들어갈 말로 가장 적절한 것을 고르시오. [3점]
① get recovered easily – 빠르게 회복된다
② will see much better – 더 선명하게 볼 것이다
✔③ are functionally blind – 기능적으로는 실명 상태이다
④ are completely activated – 완전히 활성화되어 있다
⑤ process visual information – 시각 정보를 처리한다

One of the most striking characteristics / of a sleeping animal or person / is that they do not respond normally to environmental stimuli.
가장 두드러진 특징 중 하나는 / 잠을 자고 있는 동물이나 사람의 / 그들이 환경의 자극에 정상적으로 반응하지 않는다는 것이다.
If you open the eyelids of a sleeping mammal / the eyes will not see normally — they are functionally blind.
만약 당신이 잠을 자고 있는 포유류의 눈꺼풀을 열면, / 그 눈은 정상적으로 볼 수 없을 것인데, / 즉 그 눈은 기능적으로는 실명 상태이다.
Some visual information apparently gets in, / but it is not normally processed / as it is shortened or weakened; / same with the other sensing systems.
어떤 시각적 정보는 명백히 눈으로 들어오지만, / 그것은 짧아지거나 약화되어서 정상적으로 처리되지 않는데, / 이는 다른 감각 체계도 마찬가지다.
Stimuli are registered but not processed normally / and they fail to wake the individual.
자극은 등록되지만 정상적으로 처리되지 않고 / 사람을 깨우는 데 실패한다.
Perceptual disengagement probably serves the function of protecting sleep, / so some authors do not count it / as part of the definition of sleep itself.
지각 이탈은 추측건대 수면을 보호하는 기능을 제공해서 / 어떤 저자는 그것을 여기지 않는다. / 수면 자체의 정의의 일부로
But as sleep would be impossible without it, / it seems essential to its definition.
그러나 수면이 그것 없이는 불가능하기 때문에 / 그것(지각 이탈)은 그것(수면)의 정의에 필수적인 것으로 보여진다.
Nevertheless, / many animals (including humans) use the intermediate state of drowsiness / to derive some benefits of sleep / without total perceptual disengagement.
그럼에도 불구하고, / (인간을 포함한) 많은 동물은 졸음이라는 중간 상태를 이용한다. / 수면의 일부 이득을 끌어내기 위해서 / 완전한 지각 이탈 없이

잠을 자고 있는 동물이나 사람의 가장 두드러진 특징 중 하나는 그들이 환경의 자극에 정상적으로 반응하지 않는다는 것이다. 만약 당신이 잠을 자고 있는 포유류의 눈꺼풀을 열면, 그 눈은 정상적으로 볼 수 없을 것인데, 즉 그 눈은 기능적으로는 실명 상태이다. 어떤 시각적 정보는 명백히 눈으로 들어오지만, 그것은 짧아지거나 약화되어서 정상적으로 처리되지 않는데, 이는 다른 감각 체계도 마찬가지다. 자극은 등록되지만 정상적으로 처리되지 않고 사람을 깨우는 데 실패한다. 지각 이탈은 추측건대 수면을 보호하는 기능을 제공해서 어떤 저자는 그것을 수면 자체의 정의의 일부로 여기지 않는다. 그러나 수면이 그것 없이는 불가

능하기 때문에 그것(지각 이탈)은 그것(수면)의 정의에 필수적인 것으로 보여진다. 그럼에도 (인간을 포함한) 많은 동물은 완전한 지각 이탈 없이 수면의 일부 이득을 끌어내기 위해서 졸음이라는 중간 상태를 이용한다.

Why? 왜 정답일까?

잠을 잘 때 눈을 뜨면 시각 정보가 입력되기는 하지만 정보가 약해되거나 짧아져서 정상적으로 처리되지 않는다고 하였으므로 본래의 시기능을 하지 못한다는 ③ 'are functionally blind'가 적절하다.

- **striking** ⓐ 두드러진
- **eyelid** ⓝ 눈꺼풀
- **apparently** ⓐ 분명히
- **shorten** ⓥ 짧아지다
- **register** ⓥ 등록하다
- **definition** ⓝ 정의
- **derive** ⓥ 얻다
- **characteristics** ⓝ 특징
- **mammal** ⓝ 포유류
- **process** ⓥ 처리하다
- **weaken** ⓥ 약해지다
- **function** ⓝ 기능
- **essential** ⓐ 필수적인
- **perceptual** ⓐ 지각의

구문 풀이

13행 Nevertheless(그럼에도) many animals (including humans) use the intermediate
접속부사(그럼에도 불구하고)
state of drowsiness to derive some benefits of sleep without total perceptual
to부정사 부사적 용법(끌어내기 위해서) · 전치사(~없이)
disengagement.

---

34 지식의 저주 · 정답률 50% | 정답 ⑤

다음 빈칸에 들어갈 말로 가장 적절한 것을 고르시오. [3점]
① focus on the new functions of digital devices
디지털 기기의 새로운 기능에 집중하기
② apply new learning theories recently released
최근에 알려진 새로운 학습 이론을 적용하기
③ develop varieties of methods to test students
학생을 시험할 방법의 다양성 개발하기
④ forget the difficulties that we have had as students
학생으로서 우리가 가졌던 어려움 잊기
✔⑤ look at the learning process through students' eyes
학생들의 눈을 통해 학습 과정을 보기

A number of research studies have shown / how experts in a field often experience difficulties / when introducing newcomers to that field.
많은 조사 연구는 보여 준다. / 한 분야의 전문가가 어떻게 어려움을 종종 겪는지를 / 그 분야로 초보자를 입문시킬 때
For example, in a genuine training situation, / Dr.Pamela Hinds found that people expert in using mobile phones / were remarkably less accurate than novice phone users / in judging how long it takes people to learn to use the phones.
예를 들어, 실제 교육 상황에서, / Pamela Hinds 박사는 휴대 전화기를 사용하는 데 능숙한 사람들이 / 초보 휴대 전화기 사용자보다 놀랍도록 덜 정확하다는 것을 알아냈다. / 휴대 전화기 사용법을 배우는 것에 얼마나 오랜 시간이 걸리는지를 판단하는 데 있어서,
Experts can become insensitive / to how hard a task is for the beginner, / an effect referred to as the 'curse of knowledge'.
전문가는 무감각해질 수 있는데, / 한 과업이 초보자에게 얼마나 어려운지에 대해 / 이는 '지식의 저주'로 칭해지는 효과이다.
Dr.Hinds was able to show / that as people acquired the skill, / they then began to underestimate the level of difficulty of that skill.
Hinds 박사는 보여 줄 수 있었다. / 사람이 기술을 습득했을 때 / 그 이후에 그 기술의 어려움의 정도를 과소평가하기 시작했다는 것을
Her participants even underestimated / how long it had taken themselves / to acquire that skill in an earlier session.
그녀의 참가자는 심지어 과소평가했다. / 자신들이 얼마나 오래 걸렸는지를 / 이전 기간에 그 기술을 습득하는 데
Knowing that experts forget / how hard it was for them to learn, / we can understand the need to look at the learning process / through students' eyes, / rather than making assumptions / about how students 'should be' learning.
전문가가 잊어버린다는 것을 안다면, / 자신이 학습하는 것이 얼마나 어려웠는지를 / 우리는 학습 과정을 볼 필요성을 이해할 수 있을 것이다. / 학생들의 눈을 통해, / (근거 없는) 추정을 하기보다 / 학생이 어떻게 학습을 '해야 하는지'에 대한

많은 조사 연구는 한 분야의 전문가가 그 분야로 초보자를 입문시킬 때 어떻게 어려움을 종종 겪는지를 보여 주었다. 예를 들어, 실제 교육 상황에서 Pamela Hinds 박사는 휴대 전화기를 사용하는 데 능숙한 사람들이 휴대 전화기 사용법을 배우는 것에 얼마나 오랜 시간이 걸리는지를 판단하는 데 있어서, 초보 휴대 전화기 사용자보다 놀랍도록 덜 정확하다는 것을 알아냈다. 전문가는 한 과업이 초보자에게 얼마나 어려운지에 대해 무감각해질 수 있는데, 즉 '지식의 저주'로 칭해지는 효과이다. Hinds 박사는 사람이 기술을 습득했을 때 그 이후에 그 기술의 어려움의 정도를 과소평가하기 시작했다는 것을 보여 줄 수 있었다. 그녀의 참가자는 심지어 자신들이 이전 기간에 그 기술을 습득하는 데 얼마나 오래 걸렸는지를 과소평가했다. 전문가가 자신이 학습하는 것이 얼마나 어려웠는지를 잊어버리는 것을 안다면, 우리는 학생이 어떻게 학습을 '해야 하는지'에 대한 (근거 없는) 추정을 하기보다 학생들의 눈을 통해 학습 과정을 바라봐야 할 필요성을 이해할 수 있을 것이다.

Why? 왜 정답일까?

기술을 습득한 후 기술의 어려움을 과소평가하는 '지식의 저주'에 대한 글이고, 학생의 학습 방법에 대한 근거 없는 추정이 학습하려는 기술의 어려움을 과소평가하고 있는 것일 수도 있음을 시사한다. 따라서 학생들의 입장에서 학습 과정을 바라봐야 한다는 ⑤ 'look at the learning process through students' eyes'가 적절하다.

- **research** ⓝ 연구
- **difficulty** ⓝ 어려움
- **genuine** ⓐ 실제
- **accurate** ⓐ 정확한
- **insensitive** ⓐ 무감각한
- **underestimate** ⓥ 과소평가하다
- **assumption** ⓝ 추정, 가정
- **expert** ⓝ 전문가
- **newcomer** ⓝ 초보
- **remarkably** ⓐ 놀랍게
- **judge** ⓥ 판단하다
- **acquire** ⓥ 습득하다
- **session** ⓝ 기간, 시간

구문 풀이

11행 Her participants even underestimated how long it had taken themselves
to부정사 부사적 용법(얻기 위해서) · 비인칭 주어(시간)
to acquire that skill in an earlier session.
지시대명사 · 비교급

다음 글에서 전체 흐름과 관계 없는 문장은?

A group of psychologists studied / individuals with severe mental illness / who experienced weekly group music therapy, / including singing familiar songs and composing original songs.
한 심리학자 그룹이 연구했다. / 심각한 정신 질환이 있는 사람들을 / 집단 음악 치료를 매주 경험한 / 친숙한 노래 부르기와 독창적인 작곡하기를 포함한

① The results showed / that the group music therapy / improved the quality of participants' life, / with those participating in a greater number of sessions / experiencing the greatest benefits.
그 연구 결과는 보여 주었다. / 집단 음악 치료가 / 참여자의 삶의 질을 개선하였음을 / 참여자가 치료 활동에 참여한 횟수가 많을수록 / 가장 큰 효과를 경험하며

② Focusing on singing, / another group of psychologists reviewed articles / on the efficacy of group singing / as a mental health treatment / for individuals living with a mental health condition in a community setting.
노래 부르기에 초점을 두고, / 또 다른 그룹의 심리학자는 논문을 검토했다. / 집단 가창의 효능에 대한 / 정신 건강 치료로써의 / 집단 생활의 환경에서 정신적 건강 문제를 가지고 살고 있는 개인들에게 미치는

③ The findings showed that, / when people with mental health conditions participated in a choir, / their mental health and wellbeing significantly improved.
발견된 결과는, / 정신적인 건강 문제를 가진 사람이 합창단에 참여했을 때, / 정신 건강과 행복이 상당히 개선되었음을 보여 주었다.

✔ The negative effects of music / were greater than the psychologists expected.
음악의 부정적인 효과는 / 심리학자가 예상했던 것보다 더 컸다.

⑤ Group singing provided enjoyment, / improved emotional states, / developed a sense of belonging and enhanced self-confidence.
집단 가창은 즐거움을 제공했고, / 감정 상태를 개선하였으며, / 소속감을 키웠고, / 자신감을 강화했다.

한 심리학자 그룹이 친숙한 노래 부르기와 독창적인 작곡하기를 포함한 집단 음악 치료를 매주 경험한 심각한 정신 질환이 있는 사람들을 연구했다. ① 그 연구 결과는 참여자가 (치료) 활동에 참여한 횟수가 많을수록 가장 큰 효과를 경험했기에, 집단 음악 치료가 참여자의 삶의 질을 개선하였음을 보여 주었다. ② 노래 부르기에 초점을 두고, 또 다른 그룹의 심리학자는 집단생활의 환경에서 정신적인 건강 문제를 가지고 살고 있는 이들에게 미치는 집단 가창의 효능에 대한 논문을 검토했다. ③ 발견된 결과는, 정신적인 건강 문제를 가진 사람이 합창단에 참여했을 때, 정신 건강과 행복이 상당히 개선되었음을 보여 주었다. ④ 음악의 부정적인 효과는 심리학자가 예상했던 것보다 더 컸다. ⑤ 집단 가창은 즐거움을 제공했고 감정 상태를 개선하였으며 소속감을 키웠고 자신감을 강화하였다.

Why? 왜 정답일까?

정신 질환 환자들에게 있어서의 집단 음악 치료의 장점에 대해서 이야기하고 있기 때문에, '음악의 부정적인 효과는 심리학자가 예상했던 것보다 더 컸다.'라는 ④ 'The negative effects of music were greater than the psychologists expected.'는 글의 전체 흐름과 관계가 없다.

- psychologist ⓝ 심리학자
- mental ⓐ 정신적
- improve ⓥ 개선하다
- review ⓥ 검토하다
- finding ⓝ 결과
- wellbeing ⓝ 행복
- enhance ⓥ 강화하다
- severe ⓐ 심각한
- compose ⓥ 작곡하다
- session ⓝ 활동, 기간
- treatment ⓝ 치료
- choir ⓝ 합창단
- significantly ⓐⓓ 상당히

구문 풀이

> **14행** Group singing provided enjoyment, improved emotional states, developed
> 　　　　　　　　주어　　　　　동사1　　　　　　　　동사2
> a sense of belonging and enhanced self-confidence.
> 　　　　　　　　　　　　　　　동사4
（동사3）

주어진 글 다음에 이어질 글의 순서로 가장 적절한 것을 고르시오.

① (A) – (C) – (B)　　　② (B) – (A) – (C)
③ (B) – (C) – (A)　　　✔ (C) – (A) – (B)
⑤ (C) – (B) – (A)

In many sports, / people realized the difficulties / and even impossibilities / of young children participating fully / in many adult sport environments.
많은 스포츠에서, / 사람들은 어려움과 심지어 불가능하다는 것을 깨달았다. / 어린아이들이 완전히 참여하는 것의 / 여러 성인 스포츠 환경에

(C) They found / the road to success for young children / is unlikely / if they play on adult fields, / courts or arenas / with equipment that is too large, too heavy or too fast / for them to handle / while trying to compete / in adult-style competition.
그들은 발견했다. / 어린아이들이 성공으로 가는 길이 있을 것 같지 않다는 것을 / 만약 그들이 성인용 운동장에서, / 코트 또는 경기장에서 / 너무 크거나, 너무 무겁고 또는 너무 빠른 장비를 가지고 / 그들이 다룰 수 없는 / 성인 스타일의 시합에서 경쟁하려고 할 때

Common sense has prevailed: / different sports have made adaptations/ for children.
상식이 널리 퍼졌다: / 여러 스포츠는 조정을 했다. / 어린아이들을 위해

(A) As examples, / baseball has T ball, / football has flag football and junior soccer uses / a smaller and lighter ball / and (sometimes) a smaller field.
예를 들자면, / 야구에는 티볼이 있고, / 풋볼에는 플래그 풋볼이 있고 유소년 축구는 사용한다. / 더 작고 더 가벼운 공과 (가끔은) 더 작은 경기장을

All have junior competitive structures / where children play for shorter time periods / and often in smaller teams.
모두가 유소년 시합의 구조를 가진다. / 어린아이들이 더 짧은 시간 동안 경기하고 / 종종 더 작은 팀으로 경기하는

(B) In a similar way, / tennis has adapted the court areas, / balls and rackets / to make them more appropriate for children under 10.
비슷한 방식으로, / 테니스는 코트 면적, 공, 라켓을 조정했다. / 10세 미만의 어린아이에게 더 적합하도록 만들기 위해

The adaptations are progressive / and relate to the age of the child.
이러한 조정은 점진적이고 / 어린아이의 연령과 관련이 있다.

많은 스포츠에서 사람들은 어린아이들이 여러 성인 스포츠 환경에 완전히 참여하기란 어렵고 심지어 불가능하다는 것을 깨달았다.

(C) 어린아이들이 너무 크거나 너무 무겁고 또는 너무 빨라서 그들(어린아이들)이 다룰 수 없는 장비를 가지고 성인 스타일의 시합에서 경쟁하려고 하면서 성인용 운동장, 코트 또는 경기장에서 운동한다면 그들(어린아이들)이 성공으로 가는 길이 있을 것 같지 않다는 것을 그들은 발견했다. 이러한 공통된 견해가 널리 퍼졌기에 여러 스포츠는 어린아이들을 위한 조정을 했다.

(A) 예를 들자면, 야구에는 티볼이 있고, 풋볼에는 플래그 풋볼이 있고, 유소년 축구는 더 작고 더 가벼운 공과 (가끔은) 더 작은 경기장을 사용한다. 모두가 어린아이들이 더 짧아진 경기 시간 동안 그리고 종종 더 작은 팀으로 경기하는 유소년 시합의 구조를 가진다.

(B) 비슷한 방식으로, 테니스는 코트 면적, 공, 라켓을 10세 미만의 어린아이에게 더 적합하도록 만들기 위해 조정했다. 이러한 조정은 점진적이고 어린아이의 연령과 관련이 있다.

Why? 왜 정답일까?

어린아이들이 스포츠에 참여하는 데에 갖는 어려움을 언급하는 주어진 글 뒤로, 어린아이들이 스포츠에 참여하기가 어려운 이유를 제시하는 (C)가 연결된다. (C)의 후반부는 여러 스포츠가 어린아이들을 위한 조정을 했다고 밝히고, (A) 초반부에서 조정의 예시를 언급하기 때문에 (A)가 오는 것이 자연스럽다. (B) 역시 어린아이들을 위해 스포츠가 한 조정의 예시를 들고 있지만 비슷한 방식으로의 'In a similar way,'로 이전에 유사한 내용이 필요하다. 따라서 (A) 뒤에 (B)가 오는 것이 적절하다. 따라서 적절한 순서는 ④ (C) – (A) – (B)이다.

- realize ⓥ 깨닫다
- competitive ⓐ 경쟁적인
- period ⓝ 기간
- appropriate ⓐ 적절한
- relate to ~와 관련되다
- equipment ⓝ 장비
- adaptation ⓝ 조정
- impossibility ⓝ 불가능
- structure ⓝ 구조
- racket ⓝ 라켓
- progressive ⓐ 점진적인
- arena ⓝ 경기장
- common sense ⓝ (일반인들의) 공통된 견해, 상식

구문 풀이

> **9행** In a similar way, tennis has adapted the court areas, balls and rackets
> 　　　　　　　　　　　　　　　　　현재완료
> → to부정사 부사적 용법(만들기 위해서)
> to make them more appropriate for children under 10.
> 　　　　　　　　비교급

주어진 글 다음에 이어질 글의 순서로 가장 적절한 것을 고르시오. [3점]

① (A) – (C) – (B)　　　② (B) – (A) – (C)
✔ (B) – (C) – (A)　　　④ (C) – (A) – (B)
⑤ (C) – (B) – (A)

With no horses available, / the Inca empire excelled / at delivering messages on foot.
구할 수 있는 말이 없어서, / Inca 제국은 탁월했다. / 걸어서 메시지를 전달하는 데

(B) The messengers were stationed on the royal roads / to deliver the Inca king's orders and reports / coming from his lands.
전령들은 왕의 길에 배치되었다. / Inca 왕의 명령과 보고를 전달하기 위해 / 그의 영토에서 오는

Called Chasquis, / they lived in groups of four to six in huts, / placed from one to two miles apart along the roads.
Chasquis라고 불리는, / 그들은 네 명에서 여섯 명의 집단을 이루어 오두막에서 생활을 했다. / 길을 따라 1마일에서 2마일 간격으로 떨어져 배치된

(C) They were all young men / and especially good runners / who watched the road in both directions.
그들은 모두 젊은 남자였고, / 특히 잘 달리는 이들이었다. / 양방향으로 길을 주시하는

If they caught sight of another messenger coming, / they hurried out to meet them.
그들은 다른 전령이 오는 것을 발견하면, / 그들을 맞이하기 위해 서둘러 나갔다.

The Inca built the huts on high ground, / in sight of one another.
Inca 사람들은 오두막을 지었다. / 서로 볼 수 있는 높은 지대에

(A) When a messenger neared the next hut, / he began to call out / and repeated the message three or four times / to the one who was running out to meet him.
전령은 다음 오두막에 다가갈 때, / 소리치기 시작했고 / 메시지를 서너 번 반복했다. / 자신을 만나러 달려 나오는 전령에게

The Inca empire could relay messages 1,000 miles (1,610 km) / in three or four days under good conditions.
Inca 제국은 1,000마일(1,610km) 정도 메시지를 이어 갈 수 있었다. / 사정이 좋으면 사나흘 만에

구할 수 있는 말이 없어서, Inca 제국은 걸어서 메시지를 전달하는 데 탁월했다.

(B) 전령들은 Inca 왕의 명령과 그의 영토에서 오는 보고를 전달하기 위해 왕의 길에 배치되었다. Chasquis라고 불리는, 그들은 네 명에서 여섯 명의 집단을 이루어 길을 따라 1마일에서 2마일 간격으로 떨어져 배치된 오두막에서 생활했다.

(C) 그들은 모두 젊은 남자였고, 양방향으로 길을 주시하는 특히 잘 달리는 이들이었다. 그들은 다른 전령이 오는 것을 발견하면 그들을 맞이하기 위해 서둘러 나갔다. Inca 사람들은 서로를 볼 수 있는 높은 지대에 오두막을 지었다.

(A) 전령은 다음 오두막에 다가갈 때, 자신을 만나러 달려 나오고 있는 전령에게 소리치기 시작했고 메시지를 서너 번 반복했다. Inca 제국은 사정이 좋으면 사나흘 만에 1,000마일 (1,610km) 정도 메시지를 이어 갈 수 있었다.

Why? 왜 정답일까?

Inca 제국에서 말 없이 걸어서 메시지를 전달하는 전령과 Chasquis가 있음을 소개하는 (B)가 가장 먼저 오고, 전령과 Chasquis의 간단한 정보를 전달하는 (C)가 이어지는 것이 자연스럽다. (C)에서 다른 전령이 오는 것을 발견하면 그들을 맞이하기 위해 서둘러 나갔기 때문에, (A)의 자신을 만나러 달려 나오고 있는 전령에게 소리치기 시작했다는 내용이 이어져야 한다. 따라서 ③ (B) – (C) – (A)가 정답이다.

- available ⓐ 구할 수 있는
- excel ⓥ 빼어나다, 탁월하다
- deliver ⓥ 전달하다
- repeat ⓥ 반복하다
- condition ⓝ 사정, 상황
- royal ⓐ 왕의, 왕실의
- apart ⓐⓓ 떨어진
- empire ⓝ 제국
- on foot 걸어서, 도보로
- near ⓥ 다가가다
- relay ⓥ 이어가다
- station ⓥ 배치하다
- hut ⓝ 오두막
- especially ⓐⓓ 특히

- direction [n] 방향
- hurry out 서둘러 나오다

구문 풀이

3행 When a messenger neared the next hut, he began to call out and repeated the message three or four times to the one who was running out to meet him.
(전치사 / 주격관계대명사 / 동사1 / to부정사 명사적 용법(부르기를) / 동사2 / 부정대명사 / 과거 진행형 / to부정사 부사적 용법(만나기 위해서))

★★★ 등급을 가르는 문제!

38 잘못된 혀 지도

정답률 47% | 정답 ①

글의 흐름으로 보아, 주어진 문장이 들어가기에 가장 적절한 곳을 고르시오.

The tongue was mapped into separate areas / where certain tastes were registered: / sweetness at the tip, / sourness on the sides, / and bitterness at the back of the mouth.
혀는 개별적인 영역으로 구획화되었다. / 특정 맛이 등록되는 / 끝에는 단맛, / 측면에는 신맛, / 그리고 입의 뒤쪽에는 쓴맛이 등록된다.
✓ Research in the 1980s and 1990s, / however, / demonstrated that the "tongue map" explanation of how we taste was, / in fact, totally wrong.
1980년대와 1990년대의 연구는 / 그러나 / 우리가 맛을 느끼는 방식에 대한 '혀 지도' 설명이 ~것을 증명했다. / 사실은 완전히 틀렸다는
② As it turns out, / the map was a misinterpretation and mistranslation / of research conducted in Germany / at the turn of the twentieth century.
밝혀진 바와 같이, 그 지도는 오해하고 오역한 것이었다. / 독일에서 수행된 연구를 / 20세기 초입에
Today, / leading taste researchers believe / that taste buds are not grouped / according to specialty.
오늘날, / 선도적인 미각 연구자는 믿는다. / 미뢰가 분류되지 않는다고 / 맛을 느끼는 특화된 분야에 따라
③ Sweetness, saltiness, bitterness, and sourness / can be tasted / everywhere in the mouth, / although they may be perceived / at a little different intensities at different sites.
단맛, 짠맛, 쓴맛 그리고 신맛은 / 느껴질 수 있다. / 입안 어디에서나 / 비록 그것들이 지각될지라도 / 여러 위치에서 조금씩 다른 강도로
④ Moreover, / the mechanism at work is not place, / but time.
게다가, / 작동중인 기제는 위치가 아니라, / 시간이다.
⑤ It's not that you taste sweetness / at the tip of your tongue, / but rather that you register that perception *first*.
여러분이 단맛을 느끼는 것이 아니라 / 여러분의 혀 끝에서, / 오히려 그 지각(단맛)을 *'가장 먼저'* 등록하는 것이다.

혀는 특정 맛이 등록되는 개별적인 영역으로 구획되었는데, 즉, 끝에는 단맛, 측면에는 신맛, 그리고 입의 뒤쪽에는 쓴맛이 있었다. ① 그러나 1980년대와 1990년대의 연구는 우리가 맛을 느끼는 방식에 대한 '혀 지도' 설명이 사실은 완전히 틀렸다는 것을 보여 주었다. 밝혀진 바와 같이, 그 지도는 20세기 초입 독일에서 수행된 연구를 오해하고 오역한 것이었다. ② 오늘날, 선도적인 미각 연구자는 미뢰가 맛을 느끼는 특화된 분야에 따라 분류되지 않는다고 믿는다. ③ 비록 그것들이 여러 위치에서 조금씩 다른 강도로 지각될지도 모르겠지만, 단맛, 짠맛, 쓴맛 그리고 신맛은 입안 어디에서나 느낄 수 있다. ④ 게다가, 작동 중인 기제는 위치가 아니라 시간이다. ⑤ 여러분은 혀끝에서 단맛을 느낀다기보다 오히려 그 지각(단맛)을 '가장 먼저' 등록하는 것이다.

Why? 왜 정답일까?

특정 맛이 등록되는 개별적인 영역으로 구획된 혀 지도가 있음을 소개하고, 혀 지도가 잘못되었음을 시사하는 **As it turns out, the map was a misinterpretation and mistranslation of research conducted in Germany at the turn of the twentieth century.**(밝혀진 바와 같이, 그 지도는 20세기 초입 독일에서 수행된 연구를 오해하고 오역한 것이었다.) 문장 사이에 주어진 문장이 오는 것이 자연스럽다. 또한 'As it turns out,'(밝혀진 바와 같이)와 같은 전치사구 역시 앞뒤 문장을 적절하게 이어준다.

- demonstrate [v] 보여 주다
- explanation [n] 설명
- map [v] (지도에) 구획하다
- certain [a] 특정한
- tip [n] 끝
- bitterness [n] 쓴맛
- mistranslation [n] 오역
- leading [a] 선두적인
- specialty [n] 특화된 분야
- intensity [n] 강도
- mechanism [n] 기제
- tongue [n] 혀
- taste [n] 맛
- separate [a] 개별적인
- register [v] 등록하다
- sourness [n] 신맛
- misinterpretation [n] 오해
- conduct [v] 수행하다
- taste bud 미뢰
- perceive [v] 지각하다
- site [n] 위치

구문 풀이

14행 It's not that you taste sweetness at the tip of your tongue, but rather that you register that perception first.
(가주어 / 진주어 / 오히려 / 지시대명사)

★★ 문제 해결 꿀~팁 ★★

▶ 많이 틀린 이유는?
혀 지도에 대한 글이며, 글의 서두에서는 혀 지도에 대해 소개하고 있다. 그러나 글의 중반부부터는 서두에 제시한 혀 지도의 개념이 잘못 되었다고 이야기하고 있기 때문에 혀 지도에 대한 입장이 바뀌는 서두와 중반부 사이 ①에 주어진 문장이 오는 것이 자연스럽다.
▶ 문제 해결 방법은?
주어진 문장을 넣는 문제는 글의 흐름을 파악하는 것이 중요하다. 해당 문제에서는 'however'를 기점으로 제시하는 바가 달라진다. 주장하는 바가 달라지는 부분이나 새로운 개념이 나오는 부분을 잘 체크하여 어울리는 선지를 선택하자.

★★★ 등급을 가르는 문제!

39 동물마다 다른 치료법 적용의 필요성

정답률 45% | 정답 ②

글의 흐름으로 보아, 주어진 문장이 들어가기에 가장 적절한 곳을 고르시오.

No two animals are alike.
어떤 두 동물도 똑같지 않다.
① Animals from the same litter / will display some of the same features, / but will not be exactly the same as each other; / therefore, they may not respond in entirely the same way / during a healing session.
한 배에서 태어난 동물들은 / 똑같은 몇몇 특성을 보여 줄 수 있겠지만, / 서로 정확히 같지는 않을 것이다. / 그런 까닭에, 그들은 완전히 똑같은 방식으로 반응하지 않을지도 모른다. / 치료 활동 중에
✓ Environmental factors / can also determine how the animal will respond / during the treatment.
또한 환경적 요인은 / 동물이 어떻게 반응할지를 결정할 수 있다. / 치료 중에
For instance, / a cat in a rescue center / will respond very differently / than a cat within a domestic home environment.
예를 들어, / 구조 센터에 있는 고양이는 / 매우 다르게 반응할 것이다. / 가정집 환경 내에 있는 고양이와는
③ In addition, / animals that experience healing for physical illness / will react differently / than those accepting healing / for emotional confusion.
게다가, / 신체적 질병의 치료를 받는 동물은 / 다르게 반응할 것이다. / 감정적 동요의 치료를 받는 동물과는
④ With this in mind, / every healing session needs to be explored differently, / and each healing treatment / should be adjusted / to suit the specific needs / of the animal.
이를 염두에 두어, / 모든 치료 활동은 다르게 탐구되어야 하고, / 각각의 치료법은 / 조정되어야 한다. / 특정한 필요에 맞도록 / 동물의
⑤ You will learn / as you go; / healing is a constant learning process.
여러분은 배우게 될 것이다. / 직접 겪으며 / 치료가 끊임없는 학습의 과정인 것을

어떤 두 동물도 똑같지 않다. ① 한 배에서 태어난 동물들은 똑같은 몇몇 특성을 보여 줄 수 있겠지만, 서로 정확히 같지는 않을 것이다. 그런 까닭에, 그들은 치료 활동 중에 완전히 똑같은 방식으로 반응하지 않을지도 모른다. ② 또한 환경적 요인은 치료 중에 동물이 어떻게 반응할지를 결정할 수 있다. 예를 들어, 구조 센터에 있는 고양이는 가정집 환경 내에 있는 고양이와는 매우 다르게 반응할 것이다. ③ 게다가, 신체적 질병의 치료를 받는 동물은 감정적 동요의 치료를 받는 동물과는 다르게 반응할 것이다. ④ 이를 염두에 두어, 모든 치료 활동은 다르게 탐구되어야 하고, 각각의 치료법은 동물의 특정한 필요에 맞도록 조정되어야 한다. ⑤ 여러분은 치료가 끊임없는 학습의 과정인 것을 직접 겪으면서 배우게 될 것이다.

Why? 왜 정답일까?

환경적인 요소 또한 동물들이 치료에서 반응하는 것을 결정할 수 있다는 문장이 제시되었기 때문에, 환경적인 요소 외 동물들이 치료에서 반응하는 것을 결정하는 요소가 이전에 제시되어야 하고, 이후에는 환경적인 요소로 동물들이 다르게 반응하는 예시가 제시되어야 할 것이다. 따라서 동물들이 다르기 때문에 치료 활동 중에 동물들이 완전히 똑같이 반응하지 않을 것이라는 문장과 보호소의 고양이와 가정의 고양이가 다르게 반응할 것이라는 문장 사이인 ②에 오는 것이 자연스럽다.

- determine [v] 결정하다
- therefore [ad] 그런 까닭에
- rescue [v] 구조하다
- illness [n] 질병
- explore [v] 탐구하다
- constant [a] 끊임없는
- display [v] 보이다
- session [n] 활동
- domestic [a] 가정의
- confusion [n] 동요, 혼란
- specific [a] 특정한, 구체적인
- process [n] 과정

구문 풀이

11행 With this in mind, every healing session needs to be explored differently, and each healing treatment should be adjusted to suit the specific needs of the animal.
(주어구 / 동사 / 수동태 / 조동사+동사원형 / to부정사 부사적 용법(알맞기 위해서))

★★ 문제 해결 꿀~팁 ★★

▶ 많이 틀린 이유는?
동물이 치료를 받을 때 다르게 반응할 수 있고, 이에 영향을 미치는 요소들을 이야기하고 있다. 주어진 문장은 환경적인 요소가 영향을 끼칠 수 있다는 문장이며, 'also'를 보았을 때 이전에 다른 요소가 언급되어야 하며 이후에는 환경적인 요소의 영향에 대해 설명해야 자연스럽다.
▶ 문제 해결 방법은?
주어진 문장을 글에 넣는 문제는 글의 흐름 파악이 최우선이다. 흐름이 바뀌는 부분과 새로운 개념이 제시되는 부분에 표시를 하여 직관적으로 파악할 수 있게 하자.

40 의식적 마음과 잠재의식적 마음의 두려움 형성

정답률 55% | 정답 ①

다음 글의 내용을 한 문장으로 요약하고자 한다. 빈칸 (A), (B)에 들어갈 말로 가장 적절한 것은?

	(A)		(B)
✓	emotions 감정	……	forming 형성하는
②	actions 행동	……	overcoming 극복하는
③	emotions 감정	……	overcoming 극복하는
④	actions 행동	……	avoiding 피하는
⑤	moralities 도덕	……	forming 형성하는

The mind has parts / that are known as the conscious mind / and the subconscious mind.
마음은 부분을 갖고 있다. / 의식적 마음이라고 알려진 부분과 / 잠재의식적 마음이라고
The subconscious mind / is very fast to act / and doesn't deal with emotions.
잠재의식적 마음은 / 매우 빠르게 작동하고 / 감정을 다루지 않는다.
It deals with memories / of your responses to life, your memories and recognition.
그것은 기억을 다룬다. / 여러분의 삶에 대한 반응의 기억, 기억 및 인식을
However, / the conscious mind is the one / that you have more control over.
그러나, / 의식적 마음은 부분이다. / 여러분이 더 많은 통제력을 갖고 있는
You think.
여러분은 생각한다.
You can choose / whether to carry on a thought / or to add emotion to it / and this is the part of your mind / that lets you down frequently / because — fueled by emotions — you make the wrong decisions / time and time again.
여러분은 선택할 수 있다. / 생각을 계속할지를 / 또는 그 생각에 감정을 더할지를 / 그리고 이것은 마음의 부분이기도 하다. / 여러분을 빈번하게 낙담시키는 / 왜냐면 — 감정에 북받쳐 — 잘못된 결정을 내리게 만들기 때문에 / 반복해서
When your judgment is clouded by emotions, / this puts in / biases and all kinds of other negativities / that hold you back.
감정에 의해 여러분의 판단력이 흐려질 때, / 이것은 자리잡게 만든다. / 편견과 그 밖의 모든 종류의 부정성을 / 여러분을 억제하는

Scared of spiders? // Scared of the dark?
거미를 무서워하는가? // 어둠을 무서워하는가?

There are reasons for all of these fears, / but they originate in the conscious mind.
이러한 두려움 전부 이유가 있지만, / 그것들은 의식적 마음에서 비롯된다.

They only become real fears / when the subconscious mind records your reactions.
그것들은 오직 실제 두려움이 된다. / 잠재의식적 마음이 여러분의 반응을 기록할 때

➡ While the controllable conscious mind / deals with thoughts and (A) emotions, / the fast-acting subconscious mind / stores your responses, / (B) forming real fears.
통제할 수 있는 의식적 마음은 / 생각과 감정을 다루지만, / 빠르게 작동하는 잠재의식적 마음이 / 여러분의 반응을 저장하고, / 이는 실제 두려움을 형성한다.

마음은 의식적 마음과 잠재의식적 마음이라고 알려진 부분을 갖고 있다. 잠재의식적 마음은 매우 빠르게 작동하며 감정을 다루지 않는다. 그것은 여러분의 삶에 대한 반응의 기억, 기억 및 인식을 다룬다. 그러나 의식적 마음은 여러분이 더 많은 통제력을 갖고 있는 부분이다. 여러분은 생각한다. 의식적 마음은 생각을 계속할지 또는 그 생각에 감정을 더할지를 선택할 수 있다. 그리고 이것은 감정에 복받쳐 잘못된 결정을 반복해서 내리게 만들기 때문에 여러분을 빈번하게 낙담시키는 마음의 부분이기도 하다. 감정에 의해 여러분의 판단력이 흐려질 때 이것은 편견과 그 밖의 여러분을 억제하는 모든 종류의 부정성을 자리 잡게 만든다. 거미를 무서워하는가? 어둠을 무서워하는가? 이러한 두려움 전부 이유가 있지만 그것들은 의식적 마음에서 비롯된다. 그것들은 오직 잠재의식적 마음이 여러분의 반응을 기록할 때 실제 두려움이 된다.

➡ 통제할 수 있는 의식적 마음은 생각과 (A) 감정을 다루지만, 빠르게 작동하는 잠재의식적 마음이 여러분의 반응을 저장하고, 이는 실제 두려움을 (B) 형성한다.

Why? 왜 정답일까?

글에서 통제할 수 있는 의식적 마음과 통제가 어려운 잠재의식적 마음을 설명한다. 'However, the conscious mind is the one that you have more control over. ~ You can choose whether to carry on a thought or to add emotion to it ~.' 부분에서 의식적 마음이 생각과 감정을 다루는 것을 알 수 있고, 'They only become real fears when the subconscious mind records your reactions.'에서 잠재의식적 마음이 반응을 저장할 때 실제 두려움을 형성함을 알 수 있다.

- **conscious** ⓐ 의식적
- **recognition** ⓝ 인식
- **judgment** ⓝ 판단(력)
- **bias** ⓝ 편견
- **originate** ⓥ 비롯되다
- **subconscious** ⓐ 잠재의식(적)
- **frequently** [ad] 자주, 빈번히
- **cloud** ⓥ (기억력, 판단력 등을) 흐리게 하다
- **negativity** ⓝ 부정성
- **fear** ⓝ 두려움

구문 풀이

2행 The subconscious mind is very fast to act and doesn't deal with emotions.
동사1 to부정사 부사적 용법(행동하기에) └ 동사2

41-42 문화마다 다른 규범

「Norms are everywhere, / defining what is "normal" / and guiding our interpretations of social life at every turn.」 **41번의 근거**
규범은 어디에나 존재한다. / 무엇이 '정상적'인지를 규정하고 / 모든 순간 사회적 생활에 대한 우리의 해석을 안내해 주며

As a simple example, / there is a norm in Anglo society / to say *Thank you* to strangers / who have just done something to (a) help, / such as open a door for you, / point out that you've just dropped something, / or give you directions.
간단한 예로, / 규범이 Anglo 사회에 있다. / 낯선 사람에게 '감사합니다'라고 말하는 / 도움을 줄 수 있는 무언가를 이제 막 해준 / 문을 열어 주거나, / 여러분이 물건을 방금 떨어뜨렸다는 것을 짚어 주거나, / 길을 알려 주는 것과 같이

There is no law / that forces you to say *Thank you*.
법은 없다. / 여러분에게 '감사합니다'라고 말하도록 강요하는

But if people don't say *Thank you* / in these cases / it is marked.
하지만 사람들이 '감사합니다'라고 말하지 않으면 / 이런 상황에서 / 그것은 눈에 띄게 된다.

People expect / that you will say it.
사람들은 기대한다. / 여러분이 그렇게 말하기를

You become responsible.
여러분은 책임을 지게 되는 것이다.

(b) Failing to say it / will be both surprising and worthy of criticism.
그렇게 말하지 못하는 것은 / (주변을) 놀라게 하기도 하고 비판을 받을 만하다.

「Not knowing the norms of another community / is the (c) central problem of cross-cultural communication.」 **41번의 근거**
다른 집단의 규범을 모른다는 것은 / 문화 간 의사소통에서 중심적인 문제이다.

To continue the *Thank you* example, / even though another culture may have an expression / that appears translatable (many don't), / 「there may be (d) different norms for its usage,」 / for example, / such that you should say *Thank you* / only when the cost someone has caused is considerable. **42번의 근거**
'감사합니다'의 예를 이어 보자면, / 비록 또 다른 문화권이 표현을 가지고 있다 할지라도, / 번역할 수 있는 것처럼 보이는 (다수는 그렇지 못하지만) / 다른 규범이 있을 수 있다. / 예를 들어, / '감사합니다'라고 말해야 한다는 것처럼 / 누군가가 초래한 대가가 상당할 때만

「In such a case / it would sound ridiculous (i.e., unexpected, surprising, and worthy of criticism) / if you were to thank someone / for something so (e) minor / as holding a door open for you.」 **42번의 근거**
그 같은 상황에서 / 우스꽝스럽게(즉, 예상치 못하게, 놀랍게, 비판을 받을 만하게) 들릴 수 있을 것이다. / 만약 여러분이 누군가에게 감사해한다면 / 아주 사소한 일에 대해 / 여러분을 위해 문을 잡아주는 것과 같이

규범은 무엇이 '정상적'인지를 규정하고 모든 순간 사회적 생활에 대한 우리의 해석을 안내해 주며 어디에나 존재한다. 간단한 예로, 문을 열어 주거나, 여러분이 물건을 방금 떨어뜨렸다는 것을 짚어 주거나, 길을 알려주는 것과 같이 (a) 도움을 줄 수 있는 무언가를 이제 막 해준 낯선 사람에게 '감사합니다'라고 말하는 규범이 Anglo 사회에 있다. 여러분이 '감사합니다'라고 말하도록 강요하는 법은 없다. 하지만 이런 상황에서 사람들이 '감사합니다'라고 말하지 않으면 그것은 눈에 띄게 된다. 사람들은 여러분이 그렇게 말하기를 기대한다. 여러분은 책임을 지게 되는 것이다. 그렇게 (b) 말하지 못하는 것은 (주변을) 놀라게 하기도 하고 비판을 받을 만하다. 다른 집단의 규범을 모른다는 것은 문화 간 의사소통에서 (c) 중심적인 문제이다. '감사합니다'의 예를 이어 보자면, 비록 또 다른 문화권이 번역할 수 있는 것처럼 보이는 어떤 표현(다수는 그렇지 못하지만)을 가지고 있다 할지라도, 그것의 사용법에 대해, 예를 들어, 누군가가 초래한 대가가 상당할 때만 '감사합니다'라고 말해야 한다는 것처럼 (d) 유사한

(→ 다른) 규범이 있을 수 있다. 그 같은 상황에서 만약 여러분이 혹시라도, 여러분을 위해 문을 잡아주는 것과 같이 아주 (e) 사소한 일에 대해 누군가에게 감사해한다면, 그것은 우스꽝스럽게(즉, 예상치 못하게, 놀랍게, 비판을 받을 만하게) 들릴 수 있을 것이다.

- **norm** ⓝ 규범
- **interpretation** ⓝ 해석
- **marked** ⓐ 눈에 띄는
- **worthy** ⓐ 받을 만한
- **central** ⓐ 중심적인
- **cost** ⓝ 대가, 비용
- **ridiculous** ⓐ 우스꽝스러운
- **minor** ⓐ 사소한
- **define** ⓥ 규정하다
- **stranger** ⓝ 낯선 사람
- **responsible** ⓐ 책임이 있는
- **criticism** ⓝ 비난
- **translatable** ⓐ 번역할 수 있는
- **considerable** ⓐ 상당한
- **unexpected** ⓐ 예상치 못한

구문 풀이

18행 In such a case it would sound ridiculous (i.e., unexpected, surprising,
가주어← 조동사+동사원형 예를 들어서(= for example)
and worthy of criticism) if you were to thank someone for something so minor as
진주어 전치사(~처럼)←
holding a door open for you.
동명사

---

41 제목 파악 정답률 59% | 정답 ①

윗글의 제목으로 가장 적절한 것은?

✔ ① Norms: For Social Life and Cultural Communication – 규범: 사회적 삶과 문화적 의사소통
② Don't Forget to Say "Thank you" at Any Time – 언제든 '고맙습니다' 말하기를 잊지마라
③ How to Be Responsible for Your Behaviors – 당신의 행동에 책임지는 방법
④ Accept Criticism Without Hurting Yourself – 상처받지 않고 비판을 받아들이기
⑤ How Did Diverse Languages Develop? – 어떻게 다양한 언어가 발달되었는가?

Why? 왜 정답일까?

문화마다 다른 규범에 대해 '감사합니다'를 예로 들어 설명하는 글이다. 사회가 구성원에게 갖는 규범적 기대(People expect that you will say it. You become responsible.)에 이어 같은 말이라도 문화마다 다른 사용 규범이 있다는 것(there may be different norms for its usage)을 언급한다. 따라서 글의 제목으로 가장 적절한 것은 ① '규범: 사회적 삶과 문화적 의사소통'이다.

★★★ 등급을 가르는 문제!

42 어휘 추론 정답률 38% | 정답 ④

밑줄 친 (a) ~ (e) 중에서 문맥상 낱말의 쓰임이 적절하지 않은 것은?

① (a) ② (b) ③ (c) ✔ ④ (d) ⑤ (e)

Why? 왜 정답일까?

문화권마다 규범이 다르고, 한 문화권에서는 가벼운 일이라도 감사 인사를 해야하는 반면, 다른 문화권에서는 중대한 일에만 감사 인사를 하기도 함을 설명했다. "Thank you" 예시를 들며, 번역될 수 있는 것처럼 보이는 표현이라도 사용 규범이 다르다는 의미가 되어야 자연스러우므로, similar 대신 different를 쓰는 것이 적절하다. 따라서 낱말의 쓰임이 문맥상 적절하지 않은 것은 ④ (d)다.

★★ 문제 해결 꿀~팁 ★★

▶ 많이 틀린 이유는?
문화마다 다른 규범에 대해서 이야기하는 글이다. "감사합니다"를 예시로 전개하며 같은 말이라도 문화마다 갖는 무게가 다르기 때문에 다르게 사용해야 함을 강조한다. 이 글에서 중요하게 이야기하는 것은 문화 간의 규범의 차이이기 때문에, similar norms는 적절하지 않다.

▶ 문제 해결 방법은?
글이 길 때에는 글의 서두와 말미에서 주제를 정확히 파악하여 주제와 어색한 문장을 찾는다. 헷갈릴 때에는 반대의 뜻으로 바꾸어서 해석해 보며 대조해 보는 것도 좋다.

43-45 드림캐처의 기원

(A)

「Long ago, / when the world was young, / an old Native American spiritual leader Odawa / had a dream on a high mountain.」 **45번 ①의 근거** 일치
오래전, / 세상이 생겨난지 오래지 않을 무렵, / 아메리카 원주민의 늙은 영적 지도자인 Odawa는 / 높은 산에서 꿈을 꾸었다.

In his dream, / Iktomi, the great spirit and searcher of wisdom, / appeared to (a) him in the form of a spider.
자신의 꿈속에서, / 위대한 신령이자 지혜의 구도자인 Iktomi가 / 거미의 형태로 그에게 나타났다.

Iktomi spoke to him / in a holy language.
Iktomi는 그에게 말했다. / 성스러운 언어로

(D)

「Iktomi told Odawa / about the cycles of life.」 **45번 ⑤의 근거** 일치
Iktomi는 Odawa에게 말했다. / 삶의 순환에 관해서

(d) He said, / "We all begin our lives as babies, / move on to childhood, / and then to adulthood.
그는 ~라고 말했다. / 우리는 모두 아기로 삶을 출발하고, / 유년기를 거쳐 / 그 다음 성년기에 이르게 된다.

Finally, we come to old age, / where we must be taken care of / as babies again."
결국 우리는 노년기에 도달하며, / 거기서 우리는 보살핌을 받아야 한다." / 다시 아기처럼

Iktomi also told (e) him / that there are good and bad forces / in each stage of life.
또한 Iktomi는 그에게 말했다. / 좋고 나쁜 힘이 있다고 / 삶의 각 단계에는

"If we listen to the good forces, / they will guide us / in the right direction.
우리가 좋은 힘에 귀를 기울이면 / 그들은 우리를 올바른 방향으로 이끌 것이다.

But if we listen to the bad forces, / they will lead us the wrong way / and may harm us," / Iktomi said.
하지만 만약 나쁜 힘에 귀를 기울이면 / 그들은 우리를 잘못된 길로 이끌고 / 우리를 해칠 수도 있다." / 라고 Iktomi는 말했다.

(C)

「When Iktomi finished speaking, / he spun a web / and gave it to Odawa.」 **45번 ③의 근거** 일치
Iktomi가 말을 끝냈을 때, / 그는 거미집을 짜서 / Odawa에게 주었다.

He said to Odawa, / "The web is a perfect circle with a hole in the center.
그가 Odawa에게 말하기를, / "그 거미집은 가운데 구멍이 뚫린 완벽한 원이다.

Use the web / to help your people reach their goals.
거미집을 사용해라. / 너의 마을 사람들이 자신들의 목표에 도달할 수 있도록

Make good use of / their ideas, dreams, and visions.
잘 활용해라. / 그들의 생각, 꿈, 비전을

If (c) you believe in the great spirit, / the web will catch your good ideas / and the bad ones / will go through the hole.
만약 네가 위대한 신령을 믿는다면, / 그 거미집이 네 좋은 생각을 붙잡아 줄 것이고 / 나쁜 생각은 / 구멍을 통해 빠져나갈 것이다."

『Right after Odawa woke up, / he went back to his village.』 ◀ **45번 ④의 근거** 일치
Odawa는 잠에서 깨자마자 / 자기 마을로 되돌아갔다.

(B)

Odawa shared Iktomi's lesson / with (b) his people.
Odawa는 Iktomi의 교훈을 나누었다. / 그의 마을 사람들과

『Today, many Native Americans / have dream catchers / hanging above their beds.』
오늘날 많은 미국 원주민은 / 드림캐처를 가지고 있다. / 그들 침대 위에 건 ◀ **45번 ②의 근거** 불일치

Dream catchers are believed / to filter out bad dreams.
드림캐처는 믿어진다. / 나쁜 꿈을 걸러 준다고

The good dreams / are captured in the web of life / and carried with the people.
좋은 꿈은 / 인생이라는 거미집에 걸리고 / 사람들과 동반하게 된다.

The bad dreams / pass through the hole in the web / and are no longer a part of their lives.
나쁜 꿈은 / 거미집의 구멍 사이로 빠져나가고 / 더 이상 그들의 삶의 한 부분이 되지 못한다.

(A)

오래전, 세상이 생겨난지 오래지 않을 무렵, 아메리카 원주민의 늙은 영적 지도자인 Odawa는 높은 산에서 꿈을 꾸었다. 자신의 꿈속에서 위대한 신령이자 지혜의 구도자인 Iktomi가 거미의 형태로 (a) 그에게 나타났다. Iktomi는 성스러운 언어로 그에게 말했다.

(D)

Iktomi는 Odawa에게 삶의 순환에 관해서 말했다. (d) 그는 "우리는 모두 아기로 삶을 출발하고, 유년기를 거쳐 그다음 성년기에 이르게 된다. 결국 우리는 노년기에 도달하고, 거기서 우리는 다시 아기처럼 보살핌을 받아야 한다."라고 말했다. 또한 Iktomi는 삶의 각 단계에는 좋고 나쁜 힘이 있다고 (e) 그에게 말했다. "우리가 좋은 힘에 귀를 기울이면 그들은 우리를 올바른 방향으로 인도할 것이다. 하지만 만약 나쁜 힘에 귀를 기울이면 그들은 우리를 잘못된 길로 이끌고 우리를 해칠 수도 있다."라고 Iktomi는 말했다.

(C)

Iktomi가 말을 끝냈을 때, 그는 거미집을 짜서 Odawa에게 주었다. 그가 Odawa에게 말하기를, "그 거미집은 가운데 구멍이 뚫린 완벽한 원이다. 너의 마을 사람들이 자신들의 목표에 도달할 수 있도록 거미집을 사용해라. 그들의 생각, 꿈, 비전을 잘 활용해라. 만약 (c) 네가 위대한 신령을 믿는다면 그 거미집이 네 좋은 생각을 붙잡아 줄 것이고 나쁜 생각은 구멍을 통해 빠져나갈 것이다." Odawa는 잠에서 깨자마자 자기 마을로 되돌아갔다.

(B)

Odawa는 Iktomi의 교훈을 (b) 그의 마을 사람들과 나누었다. 오늘날 많은 미국 원주민은 침대 위에 드림캐처를 건다. 드림캐처는 나쁜 꿈을 걸러 준다고 믿어진다. 좋은 꿈은 인생이라는 거미집에 걸리고 사람들과 동반하게 된다. 나쁜 꿈은 거미집의 구멍 사이로 빠져나가고 더 이상 그들의 삶의 한 부분이 되지 못한다.

- **Native American** ⓝ 미국 원주민
- **holy** ⓐ 성스러운
- **cycle** ⓝ 순환
- **spiritual** ⓐ 영적인
- **spin** ⓥ 짜다(과거형 spun)

구문 풀이

(C) 1행 When Iktomi finished speaking, he spun a web and gave it to Odawa.
부사절의 접속사(~때) / 동명사 / 동사1 / 동사2

---

43 글의 순서 파악 정답률 70% | 정답 ⑤

주어진 글 (A)에 이어질 내용을 순서에 맞게 배열한 것으로 가장 적절한 것은?

① (B) − (D) − (C)　　② (C) − (B) − (D)
③ (C) − (D) − (B)　　④ (D) − (B) − (C)
☑ (D) − (C) − (B)

Why? 왜 정답일까?

Odawa가 꿈에서 Iktomi를 거미 형태로 만났다는 내용의 **(A)** 뒤로, Iktomi가 Odawa에게 삶의 순환에 대해 얘기했다는 내용의 **(D)**, Iktomi가 Odawa에게 거미집을 주며 Odawa와 마을 사람들에게 이롭게 거미집을 사용하라고 말하는 내용의 **(C)**, Odawa가 꿈에서 깨 마을 사람들과 거미집을 나눈 내용의 **(B)**가 순서대로 이어져야 자연스럽다. 따라서 글의 순서로 가장 적절한 것은 ⑤ **(D) − (C) − (B)**이다.

---

44 지칭 추론 정답률 71% | 정답 ④

밑줄 친 (a) ~ (e) 중에서 가리키는 대상이 나머지 넷과 다른 것은?

① (a)　　② (b)　　③ (c)　　☑ (d)　　⑤ (e)

Why? 왜 정답일까?

(a), (b), (c), (e)는 모두 Odawa를 가리키므로, (a) ~ (e) 중에서 가리키는 대상이 다른 하나는 ④ (d)이다.

---

45 세부 내용 파악 정답률 74% | 정답 ②

윗글에 관한 내용으로 적절하지 <u>않은</u> 것은?

① Odawa는 높은 산에서 꿈을 꾸었다.
☑ 많은 미국 원주민은 드림캐처를 현관 위에 건다.
③ Iktomi는 Odawa에게 거미집을 짜서 주었다.

---

④ Odawa는 잠에서 깨자마자 자신의 마을로 돌아갔다.
⑤ Iktomi는 Odawa에게 삶의 순환에 대해 알려 주었다.

Why? 왜 정답일까?

(B)의 'Today, many Native Americans have dream catchers hanging above their beds.'에서 많은 미국 원주민들은 드림캐처를 그들의 침대 위에 둔다고 하였기 때문에, 내용과 일치하지 않는 것은 ② '많은 미국 원주민은 드림캐처를 현관 위에 건다.'이다.

Why? 왜 오답일까?

① (A) 'Long ago, ~, Odawa had a dream on a high mountain'의 내용과 일치한다.
③ (C) 'When Iktomi finished speaking, he spun a web and gave it to Odawa.'의 내용과 일치한다.
④ (C) 'Right after Odawa woke up, he went back to his village'의 내용과 일치한다.
⑤ (D) 'Iktomi told Odawa about the cycles of life.'의 내용과 일치한다.

어휘 Review Test 01　　문제편 010쪽

A		B		C	D
01 맞추다		01 rescue		01 ⓔ	01 ①
02 가지다, 소유하다		02 certain		02 ⓑ	02 ⓙ
03 요건		03 lecture		03 ⓖ	03 ⓓ
04 해석		04 define		04 ⓠ	04 ⓠ
05 감지하다		05 extremely		05 ①	05 ⓚ
06 정의		06 structure		06 ⓓ	06 ⓔ
07 강도		07 acquire		07 ①	07 ①
08 열정		08 income		08 ①	08 ①
09 과하게 작업하다		09 station		09 ⓞ	09 ①
10 초보		10 insensitive		10 ⓜ	10 ⓐ
11 견디다		11 divide		11 ⓢ	11 ⓗ
12 편견		12 assess		12 ⓚ	12 ⓡ
13 지각하다		13 prey		13 ①	13 ⓟ
14 등록하다		14 norm		14 ⓝ	14 ⓝ
15 고귀한		15 arena		15 ⓟ	15 ⓒ
16 장비		16 output		16 ⓕ	16 ⓢ
17 작곡하다		17 treatment		17 ⓗ	17 ⓖ
18 군대의		18 rotate		18 ⓒ	18 ⓑ
19 자주, 빈번히		19 destroy		19 ⓗ	19 ⓞ
20 진술		20 illness		20 ⓐ	20 ⓜ

18　아파트 놀이터 시설 수리 요청　정답률 93% | 정답 ③

다음 글의 목적으로 가장 적절한 것은?

① 아파트의 첨단 보안 설비를 홍보하려고
② 아파트 놀이터의 임시 폐쇄를 공지하려고
✓ ③ 아파트 놀이터 시설의 수리를 요청하려고
④ 아파트 놀이터 사고의 피해 보상을 촉구하려고
⑤ 아파트 공용 시설 사용 시 유의 사항을 안내하려고

To whom it may concern,
관계자분께
I am a resident of the Blue Sky Apartment.
저는 Blue Sky 아파트의 거주자입니다.
Recently I observed / that the kid zone is in need of repairs.
최근에 저는 알게 되었습니다. / 아이들을 위한 구역이 수리가 필요하다는 것을
I want you to pay attention / to the poor condition of the playground equipment in the zone.
저는 귀하께서 관심을 기울여 주시기를 바랍니다. / 그 구역 놀이터 설비의 열악한 상태에
The swings are damaged, / the paint is falling off, / and some of the bolts on the slide are missing.
그네가 손상되었고, / 페인트가 떨어져 나가고 있고, / 미끄럼틀의 볼트 몇 개가 빠져 있습니다.
The facilities have been in this terrible condition / since we moved here.
시설들은 이렇게 형편없는 상태였습니다. / 우리가 이곳으로 이사 온 이후로
They are dangerous / to the children playing there.
이것들은 위험합니다. / 거기서 노는 아이들에게
Would you please have them repaired?
이것들을 수리해 주시겠습니까?
I would appreciate your immediate attention / to solve this matter.
즉각적인 관심을 보여주시면 감사하겠습니다. / 이 문제를 해결하기 위해
Yours sincerely, / Nina Davis
Nina Davis 드림

관계자분께
저는 Blue Sky 아파트의 거주자입니다. 최근에 저는 아이들을 위한 구역이 수리가 필요하다는 것을 알게 되었습니다. 저는 귀하께서 그 구역 놀이터 설비의 열악한 상태에 관심을 기울여 주시기를 바랍니다. 그네가 손상되었고, 페인트가 떨어져 나가고 있고, 미끄럼틀의 볼트 몇 개가 빠져 있습니다. 시설들은 우리가 이곳으로 이사 온 이후로 이렇게 형편없는 상태였습니다. 이것들은 거기서 노는 아이들에게 위험합니다. 이것들을 수리해 주시겠습니까? 이 문제를 해결하기 위한 즉각적인 관심을 보여주시면 감사하겠습니다.

Nina Davis 드림

Why? 왜 정답일까?

'I want you to pay attention to the poor condition of the playground equipment in the zone.'와 'Would you please have them repaired?'에 놀이터 시설 수리를 요청하는 필자의 목적이 잘 드러나 있다. 따라서 글의 목적으로 가장 적절한 것은 ③ '아파트 놀이터 시설의 수리를 요청하려고'이다.

● to whom it may concern 담당자 귀하, 관계자 귀하
● in need of ~이 필요한
● equipment ⓝ 장비
● fall off 벗겨지다, 떨어져 나가다
● immediate ⓐ 즉각적인
● pay attention to ~에 주의를 기울이다
● damaged ⓐ 손상된
● facility ⓝ 시설

구문 풀이

6행 The facilities have been in this terrible condition since we moved here.
현재완료　접속사(~ 이후로)　과거

19　야생에서 회색곰을 만난 필자　정답률 82% | 정답 ②

다음 글에 드러난 'I'의 심경 변화로 가장 적절한 것은?

① sad → angry
　슬픈　화난
✓ ② delighted → scared
　기쁜　겁에 질린
③ satisfied → jealous
　만족한　질투하는
④ worried → relieved
　걱정하는　안도한
⑤ frustrated → excited
　좌절한　신난

On a two-week trip in the Rocky Mountains, / I saw a grizzly bear in its native habitat.
로키산맥에서 2주간의 여행 중, / 나는 자연 서식지에서 회색곰 한 마리를 보았다.
At first, / I felt joy / as I watched the bear walk across the land.
처음에 / 나는 기분이 좋았다. / 내가 그 곰이 땅을 가로질러 걸어가는 모습을 보았을 때
He stopped every once in a while to turn his head about, / sniffing deeply.
그것은 이따금 멈춰 서서 고개를 돌려 / 깊게 코를 킁킁거렸다.
He was following the scent of something, / and slowly I began to realize / that this giant animal was smelling me!
그것은 무언가의 냄새를 따라가고 있었고, / 나는 서서히 깨닫기 시작했다! / 거대한 이 동물이 내 냄새를 맡고 있다는 것을

I froze.
나는 얼어붙었다.
This was no longer a wonderful experience; / it was now an issue of survival.
이것은 더는 멋진 경험이 아니었고, / 이제 그것은 생존의 문제였다.
The bear's motivation was to find meat to eat, / and I was clearly on his menu.
그 곰의 동기는 먹을 고기를 찾는 것이었고, / 나는 분명히 그의 메뉴에 올라 있었다.

로키산맥에서 2주간의 여행 중, 나는 자연 서식지에서 회색곰 한 마리를 보았다. 처음에 나는 그 곰이 땅을 가로질러 걸어가는 모습을 보았을 때 기분이 좋았다. 그것은 이따금 멈춰 서서 고개를 돌려 깊게 코를 킁킁거렸다. 그것은 무언가의 냄새를 따라가고 있었고, 나는 서서히 거대한 이 동물이 내 냄새를 맡고 있다는 것을 깨닫기 시작했다! 나는 얼어붙었다. 이것은 더는 멋진 경험이 아니었고, 이제 생존의 문제였다. 그 곰의 동기는 먹을 고기를 찾는 것이었고, 나는 분명히 그의 메뉴에 올라 있었다.

Why? 왜 정답일까?

처음에 회색곰을 발견하고 기분이 좋았던(At first, I felt joy as I watched the bear walk across the land.) 필자가 곰이 자신을 노린다는 것을 알고 겁에 질렸다(I froze.)는 내용이다. 따라서 'I'의 심경 변화로 가장 적절한 것은 ② '기쁜 → 겁에 질린'이다.

● grizzly bear (북미·러시아 일부 지역에 사는) 회색곰
● walk across ~을 횡단하다
● turn about 뒤돌아보다, 방향을 바꾸다
● scent ⓝ 냄새
● no longer 더 이상 ~않다
● jealous ⓐ 질투하는
● habitat ⓝ 서식지
● every once in a while 이따금
● sniff ⓥ 킁킁거리다
● freeze ⓥ 얼어붙다
● motivation ⓝ (행동의) 이유, 동기 (부여)
● frustrated ⓐ 좌절한

구문 풀이

3행 He stopped every once in a while to turn his head about, sniffing deeply.
목적(~하려고)　분사구문(~하면서)

20　신체 리듬이 정점일 때를 파악해 활용하기　정답률 81% | 정답 ⑤

다음 글에서 필자가 주장하는 바로 가장 적절한 것은?

① 부정적인 감정에 에너지를 낭비하지 말라.
② 자신의 신체 능력에 맞게 운동량을 조절하라.
③ 자기 성찰을 위한 아침 명상 시간을 확보하라.
④ 생산적인 하루를 보내려면 일을 균등하게 배분하라.
✓ ⑤ 자신의 에너지가 가장 높은 시간을 파악하여 활용하라.

It is difficult for any of us / to maintain a constant level of attention / throughout our working day.
우리 중 누구라도 어렵다. / 일정한 수준의 주의 집중을 유지하기는 / 근무일 내내
We all have body rhythms / characterised by peaks and valleys of energy and alertness.
우리 모두 신체 리듬을 가지고 있다. / 에너지와 기민함의 정점과 저점을 특징으로 하는
You will achieve more, / and feel confident as a benefit, / if you schedule your most demanding tasks / at times when you are best able to cope with them.
여러분은 더 많은 것을 이루고, / 이득으로 자신감을 느낄 것이다. / 여러분이 가장 힘든 작업을 하도록 계획을 잡으면 / 가장 잘 처리할 수 있는 시간에
If you haven't thought about energy peaks before, / take a few days to observe yourself.
만약 여러분이 전에 에너지 정점에 관해 생각해 본 적이 없다면, / 며칠 자신을 관찰할 시간을 가져라.
Try to note the times / when you are at your best.
때를 알아차리도록 노력하라. / 여러분이 상태가 제일 좋을
We are all different.
우리는 모두 다르다.
For some, / the peak will come first thing in the morning, / but for others / it may take a while to warm up.
어떤 사람에게는 / 정점이 아침에 제일 먼저 오지만, / 다른 사람에게는 / 준비되는 데 얼마간의 시간이 걸릴 수도 있다.

우리 중 누구라도 근무일 내내 일정한 수준의 주의 집중을 유지하기는 어렵다. 우리 모두 에너지와 기민함의 정점과 저점을 특징으로 하는 신체 리듬을 가지고 있다. 가장 힘든 작업을 가장 잘 처리할 수 있는 시간에 하도록 계획을 잡으면, 더 많은 것을 이루고, 이득으로 자신감을 느낄 것이다. 만약 전에 에너지 정점에 관해 생각해 본 적이 없다면, 며칠 동안 자신을 관찰하라. 상태가 제일 좋을 때를 알아차리도록 노력하라. 우리는 모두 다르다. 어떤 사람에게는 정점이 아침에 제일 먼저 오지만, 다른 사람에게는 준비되는 데 얼마간의 시간이 걸릴 수도 있다.

Why? 왜 정답일까?

힘든 작업을 분배할 수 있도록 하루 중 신체 리듬이 가장 좋은 시간을 찾아보라(Try to note the times when you are at your best.)고 조언하는 글이므로, 필자의 주장으로 가장 적절한 것은 ⑤ '자신의 에너지가 가장 높은 시간을 파악하여 활용하라.'이다.

● maintain ⓥ 유지하다
● throughout prep ~내내
● peaks and valleys 정점과 저점, 부침, 성쇠
● achieve ⓥ 성취하다
● benefit ⓝ 이득
● cope with ~을 처리하다
● constant ⓐ 지속적인
● characterise ⓥ ~을 특징으로 하다
● alertness ⓝ 기민함
● confident ⓐ 자신감 있는
● demanding ⓐ 까다로운, 힘든
● warm up 준비가 되다, 몸을 풀다

구문 풀이

7행 Try to note the times when you are at your best.
선행사(시간)　관계부사

21　더 많은 기술을 받아들인 대가　정답률 55% | 정답 ⑤

밑줄 친 The divorce of the hands from the head가 다음 글에서 의미하는 바로 가장 적절한 것은? [3점]

① ignorance of modern technology
　현대 기술에 대한 무지

② endless competition in the labor market
노동 시장에서의 끝없는 경쟁
③ not getting along well with our coworkers
동료와 잘 지내지 않는 것
④ working without any realistic goals for our career
경력을 위한 아무 현실적 목표도 없이 일하는 것
✓ our increasing use of high technology in the workplace
우리가 직장에서 고도의 기술을 점점 더 많이 사용하는 것

If we adopt technology, / we need to pay its costs.
만약 우리가 기술을 받아들이면, / 우리는 그것의 비용을 치러야 한다.
Thousands of traditional livelihoods / have been pushed aside by progress, / and the lifestyles around those jobs / removed.
수천 개의 전통적인 생계 수단이 / 발전 때문에 밀려났으며, / 그 직업과 관련된 생활 방식이 / 없어졌다.
Hundreds of millions of humans today / work at jobs they hate, / producing things they have no love for.
오늘날 수억 명의 사람들이 / 자기가 싫어하는 일자리에서 일한다 / 그들이 아무런 애정을 느끼지 못하는 것들을 생산하면서
Sometimes / these jobs cause physical pain, disability, or chronic disease.
때로 / 이러한 일자리는 육체적 고통, 장애 또는 만성 질환을 유발한다.
Technology creates many new jobs / that are certainly dangerous.
기술은 많은 새로운 일자리를 창출한다 / 확실히 위험한
At the same time, / mass education and media train humans / to avoid low-tech physical work, / to seek jobs working in the digital world.
동시에, / 대중 교육과 대중 매체는 인간을 훈련시킨다 / 낮은 기술의 육체노동을 피하고 / 디지털 세계에서 일하는 직업을 찾도록
The divorce of the hands from the head / puts a stress on the human mind.
손이 머리로부터 단절돼 있는 것은 / 인간의 정신에 부담을 준다.
Indeed, / the sedentary nature of the best-paying jobs / is a health risk / — for body and mind.
실제로, / 가장 보수가 좋은 직업이 주로 앉아서 하는 특성을 지녔다는 것은 / 건강상 위험 요소이다. / 신체와 정신에

만약 우리가 기술을 받아들이면, 우리는 그것의 비용을 치러야 한다. 수천 개의 전통적인 생계 수단이 발전 때문에 밀려났으며, 그 직업과 관련된 생활 방식이 없어졌다. 오늘날 수억 명의 사람들이 자기가 싫어하는 일자리에서 일하면서 아무런 애정을 느끼지 못하는 것들을 생산한다. 때로 이러한 일자리는 육체적 고통, 장애 또는 만성 질환을 유발한다. 기술은 확실히 위험한 많은 새로운 일자리를 창출한다. 동시에, 대중 교육과 대중 매체는 인간이 낮은 기술의 육체노동을 피하고 디지털 세계에서 일하는 직업을 찾도록 훈련시킨다. 손이 머리로부터 단절돼 있는 것은 인간의 정신에 부담을 준다. 실제로, 가장 보수가 좋은 직업이 주로 앉아서 하는 특성을 지녔다는 것은 신체 및 정신 건강의 위험 요소이다.

Why? 왜 정답일까?

첫 두 문장에서 우리는 더 많은 기술을 받아들이면서 더 많은 전통적 방식을 포기하게 되었다고 말한다. 특히 밑줄이 포함된 문장 앞뒤에서는 현대 인간이 육체노동을 덜 찾고 앉아서 하는 일을 찾도록(to avoid low-tech physical work, to seek jobs working in the digital world) 훈련되면서 더 많은 건강 위험에 노출되었다고 설명한다. 이러한 흐름으로 보아, 밑줄 부분은 결국 '인간이 기술을 더 많이 받아들인 대가로' 육체와 정신의 건강을 잃게 되었다는 뜻으로 볼 수 있다. 따라서 밑줄 친 부분의 의미로 가장 적절한 것은 ⑤ '우리가 직장에서 고도의 기술을 점점 더 많이 사용하는 것'이다.

- adopt ⓥ 수용하다, 받아들이다
- livelihood ⓝ 생계
- progress ⓝ 진보
- million ⓝ 100만
- have love for ~에 애정을 갖다
- disability ⓝ 장애
- certainly ⓐⓓ 분명히, 확실히
- seek ⓥ 찾다, 추구하다
- divorce A from B A와 B의 분리, A를 B로부터 분리시키다
- put a stress on ~에 스트레스[부담]를 주다
- nature ⓝ 본성, 특성
- ignorance ⓝ 무지
- competition ⓝ 경쟁
- get along (well) with ~와 잘 지내다
- cost ⓝ 비용 ⓥ (~의 비용을) 치르게 하다
- push aside 밀어치우다
- remove ⓥ 제거하다
- produce ⓥ 만들어내다
- physical ⓐ 신체적인
- chronic ⓐ 만성의
- mass ⓝ (일반) 대중 ⓐ 대중의, 대량의
- sedentary ⓐ 주로 앉아서 하는
- health risk 건강상 위험
- endless ⓐ 끝없는
- labor market 노동 시장
- realistic ⓐ 현실적인

구문 풀이

> **3행** Hundreds of millions of humans today work at jobs (that) they hate,
> 수억의 (목적격 관계대명사) producing things [they have no love for.]
> 선행사

22 숙련된 학습자의 융통성 정답률 83% | 정답 ①

다음 글의 요지로 가장 적절한 것은?

✓ 숙련된 학습자는 상황에 맞는 학습 전략을 사용할 줄 안다.
② 선다형 시험과 논술 시험은 평가의 형태와 목적이 다르다.
③ 문화마다 특정 행사와 상황에 맞는 복장 규정이 있다.
④ 학습의 양보다는 학습의 질이 학업 성과를 좌우한다.
⑤ 학습 목표가 명확할수록 성취 수준이 높아진다.

When students are starting their college life, / they may approach every course, test, or learning task the same way, / using what we like to call "the rubber-stamp approach."
학생들이 대학 생활을 시작할 때 / 그들은 모든 과목, 시험, 또는 학습 과제를 똑같은 방식으로 접근할지도 모른다 / 우리가 '고무도장 방식'이라고 부르고자 하는 방법을 이용하여
Think about it this way: / Would you wear a tuxedo to a baseball game? / A colorful dress to a funeral? / A bathing suit to religious services?
그것을 이렇게 생각해 보라. / 여러분은 야구 경기에 턱시도를 입고 가겠는가? / 장례식에 화려한 드레스를 입고 가겠는가? / 종교 예식에 수영복을 입고 가겠는가?
Probably not.
아마 아닐 것이다.
You know / there's appropriate dress for different occasions and settings.
여러분은 알고 있다. / 다양한 행사와 상황마다 적합한 옷이 있음을
Skillful learners know / that "putting on the same clothes" / won't work for every class.
숙련된 학습자는 알고 있다. / '같은 옷을 입는 것'이 / 모든 수업에 효과가 있지 않을 거라는 걸
They are flexible learners.
그들은 유연한 학습자이다.

They have different strategies / and know when to use them.
그들은 다양한 전략을 갖고 있으며 / 그것을 언제 사용해야 하는지 안다.
They know / that you study for multiple-choice tests differently / than you study for essay tests.
그들은 안다. / 여러분이 선다형 시험은 다르게 학습한다는 것을 / 여러분이 논술 시험을 위해 학습하는 것과는
And they not only know what to do, / but they also know how to do it.
그리고 그들은 무엇을 해야 하는지 알고 있을 뿐만 아니라, / 그것을 어떻게 해야 하는지도 알고 있다.

대학 생활을 시작할 때 학생들은 우리가 '고무도장 방식(잘 살펴보지도 않고 무조건 승인 또는 처리하는 방식)'이라고 부르고자 하는 방법을 이용하여 모든 과목, 시험, 또는 학습 과제를 똑같은 방식으로 접근할지도 모른다. 그것을 이렇게 생각해 보라. 여러분은 야구 경기에 턱시도를 입고 가겠는가? 장례식에 화려한 드레스를 입고 가겠는가? 종교 예식에 수영복을 입고 가겠는가? 아마 아닐 것이다. 다양한 행사와 상황마다 적합한 옷이 있음을 여러분은 알고 있다. 숙련된 학습자는 '같은 옷을 입는 것'이 모든 수업에 효과가 있지 않을 것이라는 걸 알고 있다. 그들은 유연한 학습자이다. 그들은 다양한 전략을 갖고 있으며 그것을 언제 사용해야 하는지 안다. 그들은 선다형 시험은 논술 시험을 위해 학습하는 것과는 다르게 학습한다는 것을 안다. 그리고 그들은 무엇을 해야 하는지 알고 있을 뿐만 아니라, 그것을 어떻게 해야 하는지도 알고 있다.

Why? 왜 정답일까?

숙련된 학습자는 상황마다 적절한 학습 전략이 있음을 알고 이를 융통성 있게 사용한다(Skillful learners know that "putting on the same clothes" won't work for every class. They are flexible learners. They have different strategies and know when to use them.)는 내용이다. 따라서 글의 요지로 가장 적절한 것은 ① '숙련된 학습자는 상황에 맞는 학습 전략을 사용할 줄 안다.'이다.

- course ⓝ 수업, 강좌
- rubber-stamp ⓝ 고무도장, 잘 살펴보지 않고 무조건 허가하는 사람
- colorful ⓐ 화려한, 색색의
- bathing suit 수영복
- appropriate ⓐ 적절한
- skillful ⓐ 숙련된
- strategy ⓝ 전략
- funeral ⓝ 장례식
- religious service 종교 의식
- occasion ⓝ 상황, 경우
- flexible ⓐ 융통성 있는
- multiple-choice test 객관식 시험, 선다형 시험

구문 풀이

> **1행** When students are starting their college life, they may approach every course, test, or learning task the same way, using what we like to call "the
> 분사구문 관계 (▶불완전한 문장)
> rubber-stamp approach." 대명사 (to call의 목적어가 없음)
> to call의 보어

★★★ 등급을 가르는 문제!

23 관광 산업이 성장한 배경 정답률 39% | 정답 ①

다음 글의 주제로 가장 적절한 것은?

✓ factors that caused tourism expansion – 관광 산업의 확장을 일으킨 요인
② discomfort at a popular tourist destination – 유명한 여행지에서의 불편
③ importance of tourism in society and economy – 사회와 경제에서 관광 산업이 갖는 중요성
④ negative impacts of tourism on the environment – 관광 산업이 환경에 미치는 부정적 영향
⑤ various types of tourism and their characteristics – 다양한 유형의 관광 산업과 그 특징

As the social and economic situation of countries got better, / wage levels and working conditions improved.
국가들의 사회적 및 경제적 상황이 더 나아지면서, / 임금 수준과 근로 여건이 개선되었다.
Gradually / people were given more time off.
점차 / 사람들은 더 많은 휴가를 받게 되었다.
At the same time, / forms of transport improved / and it became faster and cheaper / to get to places.
동시에, / 운송 형태가 개선되었고 / 더 빠르고 더 저렴해졌다. / 장소를 이동하는 것이
England's industrial revolution / led to many of these changes.
영국의 산업 혁명이 / 이러한 변화 중 많은 것을 일으켰다.
Railways, / in the nineteenth century, / opened up now famous seaside resorts / such as Blackpool and Brighton.
철도는 / 19세기에, / 현재 유명한 해안가 리조트를 개업시켰다. / Blackpool과 Brighton 같은
With the railways / came many large hotels.
철도가 생기면서 / 많은 대형 호텔이 생겨났다.
In Canada, for example, / the new coast-to-coast railway system made possible / the building of such famous hotels / as Banff Springs and Chateau Lake Louise in the Rockies.
예를 들어, 캐나다에서는 / 새로운 대륙 횡단 철도 시스템이 가능하게 했다. / 그런 유명한 호텔 건설을 / 로키산맥의 Banff Springs와 Chateau Lake Louise 같은
Later, / the arrival of air transport / opened up more of the world / and led to tourism growth.
이후에 / 항공 운송의 출현은 / 세계의 더 많은 곳을 열어 주었고 / 관광 산업의 성장을 이끌었다.

국가들의 사회적 및 경제적 상황이 더 나아지면서, 임금 수준과 근로 여건이 개선되었다. 점차 사람들은 더 많은 휴가를 받게 되었다. 동시에, 운송 형태가 개선되었고 장소를 이동하는 것이 더 빠르고 더 저렴해졌다. 영국의 산업 혁명이 이러한 변화 중 많은 것을 일으켰다. 19세기에, 철도로 인해 Blackpool과 Brighton 같은 현재 유명한 해안가 리조트가 들어서게 되었다. 철도가 생기면서 많은 대형 호텔이 생겨났다. 예를 들어, 캐나다에서는 새로운 대륙 횡단 철도 시스템이 로키산맥의 Banff Springs와 Chateau Lake Louise 같은 유명한 호텔 건설을 가능하게 했다. 이후에 항공 운송의 출현은 세계의 더 많은 곳(으로 가는 길)을 열어 주었고 관광 산업의 성장을 이끌었다.

Why? 왜 정답일까?

관광 산업의 성장(tourism growth)을 이끈 원인을 흐름에 따라 열거하는 글이다. 가장 먼저 사회경제적 상황이 개선되면서 임금 수준과 근로 조건이 개선되고, 이에 따라 여가가 늘어나고, 운송 사업이 발달하여 이동을 편하게 했다는 것이다. 따라서 글의 주제로 가장 적절한 것은 ① '관광 산업의 확장을 일으킨 요인'이다.

- wage ⓝ 임금
- improve ⓥ 향상되다
- time off 휴가
- industrial revolution 산업 혁명
- tourism ⓝ 관광(업)
- expansion ⓝ 확장
- tourist destination 관광지

- working condition 근무 조건
- gradually 🇦🇩 점차, 점점
- transport ⓝ 운송, 이동
- lead to ~을 초래하다
- factor ⓝ 요인
- discomfort ⓝ 불편
- characteristic ⓝ 특징

구문 풀이

7행 In Canada, for example, the new coast-to-coast railway system made
possible the building of such famous hotels as Banff Springs and Chateau Lake
Louise in the Rockies.
목적보어 / 목적어(길어서 뒤로 빠짐) / 동사

★★ 문제 해결 꿀~팁 ★★

▶ 많이 틀린 이유는?
사회경제적 변화 상황이 결국 '관광업의 성장'을 이끌었다는 결론이 글의 핵심이다. 따라서 첫 문장에 언급된 '사회와 경제'만 다소 두루뭉술하게 언급하는 ③은 답으로 부적합하다.

▶ 문제 해결 방법은?
시간 흐름에 따라 관광업의 성장을 이끈 배경 요인을 열거하는 글로, '그래서 결론이 무엇인지'를 파악하는 것이 중요하다.

---

24 성공적인 직업의 함정 정답률 67% | 정답 ②

다음 글의 제목으로 가장 적절한 것은?
① Don't Compete with Yourself – 자기 자신과 경쟁하지 말라
✓② A Trap of a Successful Career – 성공적인 직업의 함정
③ Create More Jobs for Young People – 젊은이들을 위해 더 많은 일자리를 창출하라
④ What Difficult Jobs Have in Common – 어려운 직업에는 어떤 공통점이 있는가
⑤ A Road Map for an Influential Employer – 영향력이 큰 고용주를 위한 지침

Success can lead you / off your intended path / and into a comfortable rut.
성공은 여러분을 이끌 수 있다. / 의도한 길에서 벗어나 / 틀에 박힌 편안한 생활로 들어가도록

If you are good at something / and are well rewarded for doing it, / you may want to keep doing it / even if you stop enjoying it.
여러분이 어떤 일을 잘하고 / 그 일을 하는 데 대한 보상을 잘 받는다면, / 여러분은 그걸 계속하고 싶을 수도 있다. / 여러분이 그것을 즐기지 않게 되더라도

The danger is / that one day you look around and realize / you're so deep in this comfortable rut / that you can no longer see the sun or breathe fresh air; / the sides of the rut have become so slippery / that it would take a superhuman effort / to climb out; / and, effectively, you're stuck.
위험한 점은 ~이다. / 어느 날 여러분이 주변을 둘러보고 깨닫게 되는 것 / 여러분이 틀에 박힌 이 편안한 생활에 너무나 깊이 빠져 있어서 / 더는 태양을 보거나 신선한 공기를 호흡할 수 없다고 / 그 틀에 박힌 생활의 양쪽 면이 너무나 미끄럽게 되어 / 초인적인 노력이 필요할 것이라고 / 기어올라 나오려면 / 그리고 사실상 여러분이 꼼짝할 수 없다는 것을

And it's a situation / that many working people worry / they're in now.
그리고 이는 상황이다. / 많은 근로자가 걱정하는 / 현재 자신이 처해 있다고

The poor employment market / has left them feeling locked / in what may be a secure, or even well-paying — but ultimately unsatisfying — job.
열악한 고용 시장은 / 이들이 갇혀 있다고 느끼게 했다. / 안정적이거나 심지어 보수가 좋을 수도 있지만 궁극적으로는 만족스럽지 못한 일자리에

성공은 여러분이 의도한 길에서 벗어나 틀에 박힌 편안한 생활로 들어가도록 이끌 수 있다. 여러분이 어떤 일을 잘하고 그 일을 하는 데 대한 보상을 잘 받는다면, 그것을 즐기지 않게 되더라도 계속하고 싶을 수도 있다. 위험한 점은 어느 날 여러분이 주변을 둘러보고, 자신이 틀에 박힌 이 편안한 생활에 너무나 깊이 빠져 있어서 더는 태양을 보거나 신선한 공기를 호흡할 수 없으며, 그 틀에 박힌 생활의 양쪽 면이 너무나 미끄럽게 되어 기어올라 나오려면 초인적인 노력이 필요할 것이고, 사실상 자신이 꼼짝할 수 없다는 것을 깨닫게 된다는 것이다. 그리고 이는 많은 근로자가 현재 자신이 처해 있다고 걱정하는 상황이다. 열악한 고용 시장은 이들이 안정적이거나 심지어 보수가 좋을 수도 있지만 궁극적으로는 만족스럽지 못한 일자리에 갇혀 있다고 느끼게 했다.

Why? 왜 정답일까?
첫 두 문장을 통해, 직업에서 성공하고 높은 보상을 누리게 된다면 그 일을 즐기지 않게 되거나 일에서의 만족을 느끼지 못하게 되더라도 그 일을 고수하게 된다(If you are good at something and are well rewarded for doing it, you may want to keep doing it even if you stop enjoying it.)는 주제를 파악할 수 있다. 따라서 글의 제목으로 가장 적절한 것은 ② '성공적인 직업의 함정'이다.

- intended ⓐ 의도된
- be rewarded for ~에 대해 보상받다
- slippery ⓐ 미끄러운
- superhuman ⓐ 초인적인
- be stuck 꼼짝 못하다
- well-paying ⓐ 보수가 좋은
- unsatisfying ⓐ 불만족스러운
- have ~ in common ~을 공통적으로 지니다

- rut ⓝ 틀에 박힌 생활
- breathe ⓥ 호흡하다
- take effort to ~하는 데 (···한) 노력이 들다
- effectively 🇦🇩 실질적으로, 사실상
- employment ⓝ 고용
- ultimately 🇦🇩 궁극적으로
- compete with ~와 경쟁하다
- influential ⓐ 영향력 있는

구문 풀이

8행 The poor employment market has left them feeling locked in [what may be a secure, or even well-paying — but ultimately unsatisfying — job].
동사 목적어 목적격 보어(현재분사) [ ]: in의 목적절 / may be의 주격 보어

---

25 국내 출생자 수와 사망자 수의 변화 추이 정답률 74% | 정답 ⑤

다음 도표의 내용과 일치하지 않는 것은?

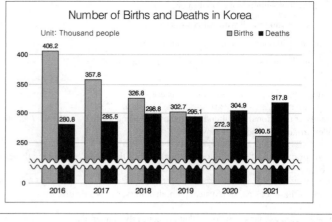

The above graph shows the number of births and deaths in Korea / from 2016 to 2021.
위 그래프는 한국에서의 출생자 수와 사망자 수를 보여 준다. / 2016년부터 2021년까지

① The number of births / continued to decrease / throughout the whole period.
출생자 수는 / 계속 감소했다 / 전체 기간 내내

② The gap between the number of births and deaths / was the largest in 2016.
출생자 수와 사망자 수 사이의 차이는 / 2016년에 가장 컸다.

③ In 2019, / the gap between the number of births and deaths / was the smallest, / with the number of births slightly larger than that of deaths.
2019년에는 / 출생자 수와 사망자 수 사이의 차이가 / 가장 작았는데, / 출생자 수가 사망자 수보다 약간 더 컸다.

④ The number of deaths / increased steadily during the whole period, / except the period from 2018 to 2019.
사망자 수는 / 전체 기간 동안 꾸준히 증가했다. / 2018년과 2019년까지의 기간을 제외하고

✓⑤ In 2021, / the number of deaths / was larger than that of births / for the first time.
2021년에는 / 사망자 수가 / 출생자 수보다 더 컸다. / 처음으로

위 그래프는 2016년부터 2021년까지 한국에서의 출생자 수와 사망자 수를 보여 준다. ① 출생자 수는 전체 기간 내내 계속 감소했다. ② 출생자 수와 사망자 수 사이의 차이는 2016년에 가장 컸다. ③ 2019년에는 출생자 수와 사망자 수 사이의 차이가 가장 작았는데, 출생자 수가 사망자 수보다 약간 더 컸다. ④ 사망자 수는 2018년과 2019년까지의 기간을 제외하고 전체 기간 동안 꾸준히 증가했다. ⑤ 2021년에는 처음으로 사망자 수가 출생자 수보다 더 컸다.

Why? 왜 정답일까?
도표에 따르면 한국의 사망자 수는 2020년에 이미 출생자 수를 추월했다. 따라서 도표와 일치하지 않는 것은 2021년에 사망자 수가 처음으로 출생자 수를 넘어섰다고 언급한 ⑤이다.

- decrease ⓥ 감소하다
- slightly 🇦🇩 약간

- gap between A and B A와 B 사이의 격차
- steadily 🇦🇩 꾸준히

구문 풀이

8행 In 2021, the number of deaths was larger than that of births for the first time.
「비교급 + than : ~보다 더 ···한」 = the number

---

26 Lilian Bland의 생애 정답률 91% | 정답 ⑤

Lilian Bland에 관한 다음 글의 내용과 일치하지 않는 것은?
① 승마와 사냥 같은 모험적인 활동을 즐겼다.
② 스포츠와 야생 동물 사진작가로 경력을 시작했다.
③ 자신의 비행기를 설계하고 제작했다.
④ 자동차 판매원으로 일하기도 했다.
✓⑤ 캐나다에서 생의 마지막 기간을 보냈다.

Lilian Bland was born in Kent, England in 1878.
Lilian Bland는 1878년 잉글랜드 Kent에서 태어났다.

「Unlike most other girls at the time / she wore trousers / and spent her time enjoying adventurous activities / like horse riding and hunting.」 ①의 근거 일치
당시 대부분의 다른 여자아이와 달리 / 그녀는 바지를 입었고, / 모험적인 활동을 즐기며 시간을 보냈다. / 승마와 사냥 같은

「Lilian began her career / as a sports and wildlife photographer for British newspapers.」 ②의 근거 일치
Lilian은 경력을 시작했다. / 영국 신문사의 스포츠와 야생 동물 사진작가로

「In 1910 / she became the first woman / to design, build, and fly her own airplane.」 ③의 근거 일치
1910년에 / 그녀는 최초의 여성이 되었다. / 자신의 비행기를 설계하고 제작하고 비행한

In order to persuade her / to try a slightly safer activity, / Lilian's dad bought her a car.
그녀가 ~하도록 설득하고자 / 약간 더 안전한 활동을 하도록 / Lilian의 아버지는 그녀에게 자동차를 사주었다.

「Soon Lilian was a master driver / and ended up working as a car dealer.」 ④의 근거 일치
곧 Lilian은 뛰어난 운전자가 되었고 / 결국 자동차 판매원으로 일하게 되었다.

She never went back to flying / but lived a long and exciting life nonetheless.
그녀는 비행에 결코 다시 복귀하지 않았지만, / 그렇기는 해도 오랫동안 흥미진진한 삶을 살았다.

She married, moved to Canada, and had a kid.
그녀는 결혼하여 캐나다로 이주했고, 아이를 낳았다.

「Eventually, / she moved back to England, / and lived there for the rest of her life.」 ⑤의 근거 불일치
결국 / 그녀는 잉글랜드로 돌아와 / 거기서 생의 마지막 기간을 보냈다.

Lilian Bland는 1878년 잉글랜드 Kent에서 태어났다. 당시 대부분의 다른 여자아이와 달리 그녀는 바지를 입었고, 승마와 사냥 같은 모험적인 활동을 즐기며 시간을 보냈다. Lilian은 영국 신문사의 스포츠와 야생 동물 사진작가로 경력을 시작했다. 1910년에 그녀는 자신의 비행기를 설계하고 제작하고 비행한 최초의 여성이 되었다. 그녀가 약간 더 안전한 활동을 하도록 설득하고자, Lilian의 아버지는 그녀에게 자동차를 사주었다. 곧 Lilian은 뛰어난 운전자가 되었고 결국 자동차 판매원으로 일하게 되었다. 그녀는 비행에 결코 다시 복귀하지 않았지만, 그렇기는 해도 오랫동안 흥미진진한 삶을 살았다. 그녀는 결혼하여 캐나다로 이주했고, 아이를 낳았다. 결국 그녀는 잉글랜드로 돌아와 거기서 생의 마지막 기간을 보냈다.

Why? 왜 정답일까?
'Eventually, she moved back to England, and lived there for the rest of her life.'에

따르면 Lilian Bland는 캐나다에서 살다가 잉글랜드로 돌아와 잉글랜드에서 생의 말년을 보냈다고 하므로, 내용과 일치하지 않는 것은 ⑤ '캐나다에서 생의 마지막 기간을 보냈다.'이다.

Why? 왜 오답일까?

① '~ spent her time enjoying adventurous activities like horse riding and hunting.'의 내용과 일치한다.
② 'Lilian began her career as a sports and wildlife photographer for British newspapers.'의 내용과 일치한다.
③ 'In 1910 she became the first woman to design, build, and fly her own airplane.'의 내용과 일치한다.
④ 'Soon Lilian ~ ended up working as a car dealer.'의 내용과 일치한다.

● unlike `prep` ~와 달리
● wildlife `n` 야생 동물
● persuade `v` 설득하다
● car dealer 자동차 판매상
● have a kid 자식을 낳다
● adventurous `a` 모험적인
● photographer `n` 사진 작가
● end up -ing 결국 ~하다
● nonetheless `ad` 그럼에도 불구하고
● the rest of ~의 나머지

구문 풀이

6행 In order to persuade her to try a slightly safer activity, Lilian's dad bought
└ 간접목적어 ┘ 목적(~하기 위해서) 동사
her a car.
└ 직접목적어 ┘

---

27 잡지 기사 공모 정답률 93% | 정답 ③

Call for Articles에 관한 다음 안내문의 내용과 일치하지 않는 것은?

① 13세에서 18세까지의 누구나 참여할 수 있다.
② 기사는 고화질 컬러 사진을 포함해야 한다.
☑ 사진 한 장에 5센트씩 지급한다.
④ 전화번호를 원고와 함께 보내야 한다.
⑤ 원고를 이메일로 제출해야 한다.

Call for Articles
기사 모집
Do you want to get your stories published?
여러분의 이야기가 출간되기를 원하시나요?
New Dream Magazine is looking for future writers!
New Dream Magazine은 미래의 작가를 찾고 있습니다!
「This event is open to anyone aged 13 to 18.」 ①의 근거 일치
이 행사는 13세에서 18세까지 누구나 참여할 수 있습니다.
Articles
기사
Length of writing: 300 – 325 words
원고 길이: 300 ~ 325단어
「Articles should also include high-quality color photos.」 ②의 근거 일치
기사에는 또한 고화질 컬러 사진이 포함되어야 합니다.
Rewards
사례금
Five cents per word
단어당 5센트
「Five dollars per photo」 ③의 근거 불일치
사진당 5달러
Notes
주의 사항
「You should send us your phone number / together with your writing.」 ④의 근거 일치
여러분의 전화번호를 보내주셔야 합니다. / 원고와 함께
「Please email your writing to us / at article@ndmag.com.」 ⑤의 근거 일치
여러분의 원고를 저희에게 보내세요. / 이메일 article@ndmag.com으로

기사 모집

여러분의 이야기가 출간되기를 원하시나요? *New Dream Magazine*은 미래의 작가를 찾고 있습니다! 이 행사는 13세에서 18세까지 누구나 참여할 수 있습니다.

기사
● 원고 길이: 300 ~ 325단어
● 기사에는 또한 고화질 컬러 사진이 포함되어야 합니다.

사례금
● 단어당 5센트
● 사진당 5달러

주의 사항
● 여러분의 전화번호를 원고와 함께 보내주셔야 합니다.
● 원고를 이메일 article@ndmag.com으로 보내주세요.

Why? 왜 정답일까?

'Five dollars per photo'에서 사진당 5달러가 지급된다고 하므로, 안내문의 내용과 일치하지 않는 것은 ③ '사진 한 장에 5센트씩 지급한다.'이다. 5센트는 단어당 정산되는 비용이다.

Why? 왜 오답일까?

① 'This event is open to anyone aged 13 to 18.'의 내용과 일치한다.
② 'Articles should also include high-quality color photos.'의 내용과 일치한다.
④ 'You should send us your phone number together with your writing.'의 내용과 일치한다.
⑤ 'Please email your writing to us at article@ndmag.com.'의 내용과 일치한다.

● publish `v` 출간하다
● high-quality `a` 고품질의
● article `n` 기사

---

28 롤러스케이팅장 이용 안내 정답률 90% | 정답 ④

Greenhill Roller Skating에 관한 다음 안내문의 내용과 일치하는 것은?

① 오전 9시부터 오후 9시까지 운영한다.
② 이용료는 시간 제한 없이 1인당 8달러이다.
③ 입장하려면 예약이 필요하다.
☑ 10세 미만 어린이는 어른과 동행해야 한다.
⑤ 추가 요금을 내면 롤러스케이트를 빌려준다.

Greenhill Roller Skating
Greenhill 롤러스케이팅
Join us for your chance / to enjoy roller skating!
기회를 함께 해요! / 롤러스케이팅을 즐길
Place: Greenhill Park, 351 Cypress Avenue
장소: Cypress Avenue 351번지 Greenhill Park
Dates: Friday, April 7 – Sunday, April 9
일자: 4월 7일 금요일 ~ 4월 9일 일요일
「Time: 9 a.m. – 6 p.m.」 ①의 근거 불일치
시간: 오전 9시 ~ 오후 6시
「Fee: $8 per person for a 50-minute session」 ②의 근거 불일치
요금: 50분간 1인당 8달러
Details
세부 사항
「Admission will be on a first-come, first-served basis / with no reservations.」 ③의 근거 불일치
입장은 선착순입니다. / 예약 없이
「Children under the age of 10 / must be accompanied by an adult.」 ④의 근거 일치
10세 미만의 어린이는 / 어른과 동행해야 합니다.
「We will lend you our roller skates for free.」 ⑤의 근거 불일치
롤러스케이트는 무료로 빌려드립니다.
Contact the Community Center for more information at 013-234-6114.
더 많은 정보를 위해서 주민센터 013-234-6114로 연락하세요.

Greenhill 롤러스케이팅

롤러스케이팅을 즐길 기회를 함께 해요!

● 장소: Cypress Avenue 351번지 Greenhill Park
● 일자: 4월 7일 금요일 ~ 4월 9일 일요일
● 시간: 오전 9시 ~ 오후 6시
● 요금: 50분간 1인당 8달러

세부 사항
– 입장은 예약 없이 선착순입니다.
– 10세 미만의 어린이는 어른과 동행해야 합니다.
– 롤러스케이트는 무료로 빌려드립니다.

더 많은 정보를 위해서 주민센터 013-234-6114로 연락하세요.

Why? 왜 정답일까?

'Children under the age of 10 must be accompanied by an adult.'에서 10세 미만 어린이는 성인 동반이 필수라고 하므로, 안내문의 내용과 일치하는 것은 ④ '10세 미만 어린이는 어른과 동행해야 한다.'이다.

Why? 왜 오답일까?

① 'Time: 9 a.m. – 6 p.m.'에서 운영 시간은 오전 9시부터 오후 6시라고 하였다.
② 'Fee: $8 per person for a 50-minute session'에서 이용료 8달러에 스케이트장 이용은 50분으로 제한돼 있음을 알 수 있다.
③ 'Admission will be on a first-come, first-served basis with no reservations.'에서 입장은 예약이 필요 없이 선착순으로 이뤄진다고 하였다.
⑤ 'We will lend you our roller skates for free.'에서 롤러스케이트는 무료로 대여해준다고 하였다.

● first-come, first-served 선착순
● for free 공짜로
● accompany `v` 동반하다

---

29 동물에게 투영된 인간의 특징 정답률 62% | 정답 ⑤

다음 글의 밑줄 친 부분 중, 어법상 틀린 것은? [3점]

The most noticeable human characteristic / projected onto animals / is ① that they can talk in human language.
가장 눈에 띄는 인간의 특징은 / 동물에게 투영된 / 동물이 인간의 언어로 대화할 수 있다는 점이다.
Physically, / animal cartoon characters and toys ② made after animals / are also most often deformed / in such a way as to resemble humans.
신체적으로도, / 동물 만화 캐릭터와 동물을 본떠 만든 장난감은 / 또한 변형되는 경우가 아주 많다. / 인간을 닮는 그런 방식으로
This is achieved / by ③ showing them / with humanlike facial features / and deformed front legs to resemble human hands.
이것은 이뤄진다 / 그들을 보여줌으로써 / 인간과 같은 얼굴 특징을 갖고 있는 / 그리고 사람의 손을 닮게 변형된 앞다리를
In more recent animated movies / the trend has been / to show the animals in a more "natural" way.
더 최근의 만화 영화에서 / 추세는 ~였다. / 동물을 더 '자연스러운' 방식으로 묘사하는 것
However, / they still use their front legs / ④ like human hands / (for example, lions can pick up and lift small objects with one paw), / and they still talk with an appropriate facial expression.
그러나 / 이 동물들은 여전히 앞다리를 사용하고, / 사람 손처럼 / (가령 사자가 한 발로 작은 물체를 집어들 수 있는 것처럼) / 그리고 그들은 여전히 적절한 표정을 지으며 이야기한다.
A general strategy / that is used to make the animal characters more emotionally appealing, / both to children and adults, / ☑ is to give them enlarged and deformed childlike features.
일반적인 전략은 / 동물 캐릭터를 더 감정적으로 매력적으로 만들기 위해 이용하는 / 아이와 어른 모두에게 / 그것들에 확대되고 변형된 어린이 같은 특징을 부여하는 것이다.

동물에게 투영된 가장 눈에 띄는 인간의 특징은 동물이 인간의 언어로 대화할 수 있다는 점이다. 신체적으로도, 동물 만화 캐릭터와 동물을 본떠 만든 장난감은 또한 인간을 닮도록 변형되는 경우가 아주 많다. 이것은 그들이 인간과 같은 얼굴 특징과 사람의 손을 닮게 변형된 앞다리를 갖고 있는 모습을 보여줌으로써 이뤄진다. 더 최근의 만화 영화에서 추세는 동물을 더 '자연스러운' 방식으로 묘사하는 것이었다. 그러나 이 동물들은 여전히 사람 손처럼 (가령 사자가 한 발로 작은 물체를 집어들 수 있는 것처럼) 앞다리를 사용하고, 여전히 적절한 표정을 지으며 이야기한다. 동물 캐릭터를 아이와 어른 모두에게 더 감정적으로 매력적이게 만들기 위해 이용하는 일반적인 전략은 그것들에 확대되고 변형된 어린이 같은 특징을 부여하는 것이다.

Why? 왜 정답일까?

핵심 주어가 단수 명사인 A general strategy이므로, 동사 또한 복수형인 are 대신 단수형인 is를 쓰는 것이 적합하다. 따라서 어법상 틀린 것은 ⑤이다.

Why? 왜 오답일까?

① 주격 보어 역할의 명사절을 이끌기 위해 접속사 that을 썼다.
② animal cartoon characters and toys가 '만들어지는' 대상이므로 과거분사 made를 사용해 꾸몄다.
③ 전치사 by 뒤에 목적어로 동명사 showing을 썼다.
④ 뒤에 명사구인 human hands가 나오는 것으로 보아 전치사 like(~처럼)가 적절히 쓰였다.

- noticeable ⓐ 눈에 띄는, 두드러지는
- project onto ~에게 투영시키다
- deform ⓥ 변형하다
- resemble ⓥ ~와 닮다
- natural ⓐ 자연스러운
- emotionally ⓐd 정서적으로
- enlarge ⓥ 확대하다
- characteristic ⓝ 특징
- cartoon character 만화 캐릭터
- in such a way as to ~한 방식으로
- humanlike ⓐ 인간 같은
- paw ⓝ (동물의) 발
- appealing ⓐ 매력적인
- feature ⓝ 특징, 이목구비

구문 풀이

2행 Physically, animal cartoon characters and toys made after animals
                     주어   과거분사구
are also most often deformed in such a way as to resemble humans.
        동사구(수동태)   ~하는 (그런) 식으로

★★★ 등급을 가르는 문제!

30 생산이 곧 수요 창출과 이득으로 이어지지 않는 시대 정답률 39% | 정답 ④

다음 글의 밑줄 친 부분 중, 문맥상 낱말의 쓰임이 적절하지 않은 것은? [3점]

The major philosophical shift in the idea of selling / came / when industrial societies became more affluent, / more competitive, / and more geographically spread out / during the 1940s and 1950s.
판매 개념에서의 주요한 철학적 변화가 / 일어났다. / 산업 사회가 더 부유해지고, / 더 경쟁적이 되고, / 지리적으로 더 확산되면서 / 1940년대와 1950년대 동안

This forced business / to develop ① closer relations with buyers and clients, / which in turn made business realize / that it was not enough / to produce a quality product at a reasonable price.
이로 인해 기업은 ~해야 했고 / 구매자 및 고객과 더 긴밀한 관계를 발전시켜야 / 이것은 결과적으로 기업이 깨닫게 했다. / 충분하지 않다는 것 / 합리적인 가격에 양질의 제품을 생산하는 것으로는

In fact, / it was equally ② essential / to deliver products / that customers actually wanted.
사실, / 마찬가지로 매우 중요했다. / 제품을 내놓는 것 / 고객이 실제로 원하는

Henry Ford produced his best-selling T-model Ford / in one color only (black) / in 1908, / but in modern societies / this was no longer ③ possible.
Henry Ford는 가장 많이 팔렸던 T-모델 Ford를 생산했지만, / 한 가지 색상(검은색)으로만 / 1908년에 / 현대 사회에서는 / 이것이 더 이상 가능하지 않았다.

The modernization of society / led to a marketing revolution / that ☑ destroyed the view / that production would create its own demand.
사회의 현대화는 / 마케팅 혁명으로 이어졌다. / 견해를 파괴한 / 생산이 그 자체의 수요를 창출할 것이라는

Customers, / and the desire to ⑤ meet their diverse and often complex needs, / became the focus of business.
고객 / 그리고 이들의 다양하고 흔히 복잡한 욕구를 충족하고자 하는 욕망이 / 기업의 초점이 되었다.

―――

산업 사회가 1940년대와 1950년대 동안 더 부유해지고, 더 경쟁적이 되고, 지리적으로 더 확산되면서 판매 개념에 주요한 철학적 변화가 일어났다. 이로 인해 기업은 구매자 및 고객과 ① 더 긴밀한 관계를 발전시켜야 했고, 이것은 결과적으로 기업이 합리적인 가격에 양질의 제품을 생산하는 것으로는 충분하지 않다는 것을 깨닫게 했다. 사실, 고객이 실제로 원하는 제품을 내놓는 것이 마찬가지로 ② 매우 중요했다. 1908년에 Henry Ford는 가장 많이 팔렸던 T-모델 Ford를 한 가지 색상(검은색)으로만 생산했지만, 현대 사회에서는 이것이 더 이상 ③ 가능하지 않았다. 사회의 현대화는 생산이 그 자체의 수요를 창출할 것이라는 견해를 ④ 강화한(→ 파괴한) 마케팅 혁명으로 이어졌다. 고객과 이들의 다양하고 흔히 복잡한 욕구를 ⑤ 충족하고자 하는 욕망이 기업의 초점이 되었다.

Why? 왜 정답일까?

현대 사회에 이르러 사람들이 전체적으로 풍족해지고 기업 간 경쟁이 치열해지면서, 합리적인 비용의 대량 생산으로 이득을 보던 시대는 지나고 고객마다의 다양한 수요에 부응할 필요성이 커졌다는 내용이다. ④가 포함된 문장 앞에서, 과거에는 Ford 사처럼 한 가지 색상만으로 제품을 생산해도 괜찮았지만 현대 사회에서는 이것이 '가능하지' 않다고 한다. 이 뒤에는 생산만으로 수요가 창출되리라는 기대가 '무너졌다'가 설명이 이어져야 적절하므로, ④의 strengthened를 destroyed로 고쳐야 한다. 따라서 문맥상 낱말의 쓰임이 적절하지 않은 것은 ④이다.

- philosophical ⓐ 철학적인
- industrial ⓐ 산업의
- geographically ⓐd 지리적으로
- in turn 결과적으로
- best-selling ⓐ 가장 많이 팔리는, 베스트셀러인
- revolution ⓝ 혁명
- complex ⓐ 복잡한
- shift ⓝ 변화, 전환 ⓥ 바뀌다
- affluent ⓐ 부유한
- spread ⓥ 퍼지다
- essential ⓐ 매우 중요한
- modernization ⓝ 현대화
- strengthen ⓥ 강화하다

구문 풀이

3행 [This forced business to develop closer relations with buyers and clients],   [ ]: 선행사
which in turn made business realize that it was not enough to produce a quality
계속적 용법   사역동사   원형부정사 가주어   진주어
product at a reasonable price.

★★ 문제 해결 꿀~팁 ★★

▶ 많이 틀린 이유는?
T-model Ford가 한 가지 색상으로 출시된 것이 어떤 예시인지 파악해야 한다. 색상을 한 가지로만 출시해도 차가 잘 팔렸다는 것은, 과거에는 '그저 질 좋은 제품을 합리적인 가격에 제공하는 것으로 족했다'는 의미와 같다. 하지만 지금은 상황이 달라져서, 이러한 전략이 더 이상(no longer) '가능하지' 않다는 의미로 ③은 자연스럽다.

▶ 문제 해결 방법은?
Ford 차의 예시를 일반화한 표현이 바로 'production would create its own demand'이다. 즉 '생산만으로 수요가 만들어지고 제품이 팔리는' 상황을 가리키는 것이다. 오늘날에는 이런 상황이나 견해가 '강화되는' 것이 아니라 점점 '깨지고' 있다는 것이 글의 주제이다.

31 비행 방향에 따른 시차 피로 차이 정답률 55% | 정답 ①

다음 빈칸에 들어갈 말로 가장 적절한 것을 고르시오.

☑ ① direction - 방향
② purpose - 목적
③ season - 계절
④ length - 길이
⑤ cost - 비용

People differ / in how quickly they can reset their biological clocks / to overcome jet lag, / and the speed of recovery depends on the direction of travel.
사람마다 서로 다르며, / 체내 시계를 얼마나 빨리 재설정할 수 있는지에 있어서 / 시차로 인한 피로감을 극복하기 위해서 / 그 회복 속도는 이동의 방향에 달려 있다.

Generally, / it's easier / to fly westward and lengthen your day / than it is to fly eastward and shorten it.
일반적으로 / 더 쉽다. / 서쪽으로 비행하여 여러분의 하루를 연장하는 것이 / 동쪽으로 비행하여 하루를 단축하는 것보다

This east-west difference in jet lag / is sizable enough / to have an impact on the performance of sports teams.
시차로 인한 피로감에 있어 이러한 동서의 차이는 / 충분히 크다. / 스포츠 팀의 경기력에 영향을 미칠 만큼

Studies have found / that teams flying westward perform significantly better / than teams flying eastward / in professional baseball and college football.
연구는 밝혔다. / 서쪽으로 비행하는 팀이 상당히 더 잘한다고 / 동쪽으로 비행하는 팀보다 / 프로 야구와 대학 미식 축구에서

A more recent study of more than 46,000 Major League Baseball games / found additional evidence / that eastward travel is tougher than westward travel.
46,000건 이상의 메이저 리그 야구 경기에 관한 더 최근의 연구에서는 / 추가적인 증거를 발견했다. / 동쪽으로 이동하는 것이 서쪽으로 이동하는 것보다 더 힘들다는

―――

시차로 인한 피로감을 극복하기 위해서 체내 시계를 얼마나 빨리 재설정할 수 있는지는 사람마다 서로 다르며, 그 회복 속도는 이동의 방향에 달려 있다. 일반적으로 동쪽으로 비행하여 하루를 단축하는 것보다 서쪽으로 비행해 하루를 연장하는 것이 더 쉽다. 시차로 인한 피로감에서 이러한 동서의 차이는 스포츠 팀의 경기력에 영향을 미칠 만큼 충분히 크다. 연구에 따르면 서쪽으로 비행하는 팀이 동쪽으로 비행하는 팀보다 프로 야구와 대학 미식 축구에서 상당히 더 잘한다. 46,000건 이상의 메이저 리그 야구 경기에 관한 더 최근의 연구에서는 동쪽으로 이동하는 것이 서쪽으로 이동하는 것보다 더 힘들다는 추가적인 증거를 발견했다.

Why? 왜 정답일까?

빈칸 뒤에서 동쪽으로 이동해 하루를 줄이게 되는 경우보다 서쪽으로 이동해 하루를 연장하게 되는 경우 시차 회복이 더 쉽다고 한다(Generally, it's easier to fly westward and lengthen your day than it is to fly eastward and shorten it.). 즉, 이동의 '방향'이 중요하다는 글이므로, 빈칸에 들어갈 말로 가장 적절한 것은 ① '방향'이다.

- biological clock 체내 시계
- jet lag 시차로 인한 피로감
- lengthen ⓥ 연장하다
- sizable ⓐ 꽤 큰, 상당한
- performance ⓝ (선수의) 경기력, 수행, 성과
- additional ⓐ 추가적인
- overcome ⓥ 극복하다
- depend on ~에 좌우되다
- shorten ⓥ 단축하다
- have an impact on ~에 영향을 주다
- significantly ⓐd 상당히, 현저히

구문 풀이

4행 This east-west difference in jet lag is sizable enough to have an impact on the performance of sports teams.
「형/부+enough+to부정사: ~할 만큼 충분히 …한」

32 일 처리에 걸리는 시간 제대로 파악하기 정답률 54% | 정답 ③

다음 빈칸에 들어갈 말로 가장 적절한 것을 고르시오.

① what benefits you can get - 여러분이 어떤 이득을 얻을 수 있는지
② how practical your tasks are - 여러분의 과업이 얼마나 현실성 있는지
☑ ③ how long things are going to take - 일에 시간이 얼마나 오래 걸릴지
④ why failures are meaningful in life - 실패가 왜 인생에서 의미가 있는지
⑤ why your leisure time should come first - 왜 여러분의 여가 시간이 가장 우선이어야 하는지

If you want the confidence / that comes from achieving / what you set out to do each day, / then it's important / to understand how long things are going to take.
만약 여러분이 자신감을 원한다면 / 성취해 얻어지는 / 매일 여러분이 하고자 착수하는 일을 / 그러면 중요하다. / 일에 시간이 얼마나 오래 걸릴지 이해하는 것이

Over-optimism about what can be achieved / within a certain time frame / is a problem.
성취될 수 있는 것에 대한 지나친 낙관주의는 / 어떤 특정 기간 내에 / 문제다.

So work on it. // Make a practice of estimating the amount of time needed / alongside items on your 'things to do' list, / and learn by experience / when tasks take a greater or lesser time than expected.

그러므로 그것을 개선하려고 노력하라. // 필요한 시간의 양을 추산하는 것을 습관화하고, '해야 할 일' 목록에 있는 항목과 함께, / 경험을 통해 배우라. / 언제 과제가 예상보다 더 많은 시간 또는 더 적은 시간을 필요로 하는지
Give attention / also to fitting the task to the available time.
주의를 기울여라. / 그 이용 가능한 시간에 과제를 맞추는 것에도 또한
There are some tasks / that you can only set about / if you have a significant amount of time available.
몇몇 과제가 있다. / 여러분이 비로소 시작할 수 있는 / 여러분이 이용할 시간이 상당히 많아야만
There is no point / in trying to gear up for such a task / when you only have a short period available.
무의미하다. / 그런 과제를 위해 준비하려 애쓰는 것은 / 여러분에게 이용 가능한 시간이 얼마 없을 때
So schedule the time / you need for the longer tasks / and put the short tasks into the spare moments in between.
그러므로 시간을 계획하라, / 여러분이 시간이 더 오래 걸리는 과제에 필요로 하는 / 그리고 그 사이 남는 시간에 시간이 짧게 걸리는 과제를 배치하라.

만약 매일 하고자 착수하는 일을 성취해 얻어지는 자신감을 원한다면 일에 시간이 얼마나 오래 걸릴지 아는 것이 중요하다. 어떤 특정 기간 내에 성취될 수 있는 것에 대한 지나친 낙관주의는 문제다. 그러므로 그것을 개선하려고 노력하라, '해야 할 일' 목록에 있는 항목과 함께, 필요한 시간의 양을 추산하는 것을 습관화하고, 언제 과제에 예상보다 더 많고 또 더 적은 시간이 걸리는지 경험을 통해 배우라. 그 이용 가능한 시간에 과제를 맞추는 것에도 또한 주의를 기울여라. 이용할 시간이 상당히 많아야만 시작할 수 있는 몇몇 과제가 있다. 여러분에게 이용 가능한 시간이 얼마 없을 때 그런 과제를 위해 준비하려 애쓰는 것은 무의미하다. 그러므로 시간이 더 오래 걸리는 과제에 필요한 시간을 계획하고, 그 사이 남는 시간에 시간이 짧게 걸리는 과제를 배치하라.

Why? 왜 정답일까?

과업을 끝내는 데 걸리는 시간을 정확히 추산하고 계획할 줄 알아야 한다(Make a practice of estimating the amount of time needed ~)는 내용의 글이므로, 빈칸에 들어갈 말로 가장 적절한 것은 ③ '일에 시간이 얼마나 오래 걸릴지'이다.

- **confidence** ⓝ 자신감
- **time frame** (어떤 일에 쓸 수 있는) 시간(대)
- **make a practice of** ~을 습관으로 하다
- **learn by experience** 경험을 통해 배우다
- **set about** ~을 시작하다
- **gear up** 준비를 갖추다, 대비하다
- **set out** 착수하다
- **work on** ~에 공을 들이다
- **estimate** ⓥ 추산하다
- **fit** ⓥ ~에 맞추다
- **there is no point in** ~하는 것은 의미가 없다
- **practical** ⓐ 현실성 있는, 타당한

구문 풀이

10행 There is no point in trying to gear up for such a task when you only have a short period available.
「there is no point in+동명사 : ~해봐야 의미가 없다」

★★★ 등급을 가르는 문제! ★★★

33 진화가 거듭되어도 상황이 변하지 않는 까닭   정답률 47% | 정답 ①

다음 빈칸에 들어갈 말로 가장 적절한 것을 고르시오. [3점]

✓① just stay in place – 제자리에 머무를 뿐이다
② end up walking slowly – 결국 느리게 걷게 된다
③ never run into each other – 결코 서로 마주치지 않는다
④ won't be able to adapt to changes – 변화에 적응할 수 없을 것이다
⑤ cannot run faster than their parents – 자기 부모보다 더 빨리 달릴 수 없다

In Lewis Carroll's *Through the Looking-Glass*, / the Red Queen takes Alice / on a race through the countryside.
Lewis Carroll의 *Through the Looking-Glass*에서 / 붉은 여왕은 Alice를 데리고 간다. / 시골을 통과하는 한 경주에
They run and they run, / but then Alice discovers / that they're still under the same tree / that they started from.
그들은 달리고 또 달리는데, / 그러다 Alice는 발견한다. / 그들이 나무 아래에 여전히 있음을 / 자신들이 출발했던
The Red Queen explains to Alice: / "*here*, you see, / it takes all the running you can do, / to keep in the same place."
붉은 여왕은 Alice에게 설명한다. / "*여기서는* 네가 보다시피 / 네가 할 수 있는 모든 뜀박질을 해야 한단다. / 같은 장소에 머물러 있으려면"이라고
Biologists sometimes use this Red Queen Effect / to explain an evolutionary principle.
생물학자들은 때때로 이 '붉은 여왕 효과'를 사용한다. / 진화의 원리를 설명하기 위해.
If foxes evolve to run faster / so they can catch more rabbits, / then only the fastest rabbits will live long enough / to make a new generation of bunnies / that run even faster / — in which case, of course, / only the fastest foxes will catch enough rabbits / to thrive and pass on their genes.
만약 여우가 더 빨리 달리게 진화한다면, / 그들이 더 많은 토끼를 잡기 위해 / 그러면 가장 빠른 토끼만이 충분히 오래 살아 / 새로운 세대의 토끼를 낳을 텐데 / 훨씬 더 빨리 달리는 / 이 경우 당연히도 / 가장 빠른 여우만이 충분한 토끼를 잡을 것이다 / 번성하여 자신들의 유전자를 물려줄 만큼.
Even though they might run, / the two species just stay in place.
그들이 달린다 해도 / 그 두 종은 제자리에 머무를 뿐이다.

Lewis Carroll의 *Through the Looking-Glass*에서, 붉은 여왕은 Alice를 데리고 시골을 통과하는 한 경주에 간다. 그들은 달리고 또 달리는데, 그러다 Alice는 자신들이 출발했던 나무 아래에 여전히 있음을 발견한다. 붉은 여왕은 Alice에게 "*여기서는* 보다시피 같은 장소에 머물러 있으려면 네가 할 수 있는 모든 뜀박질을 해야 한단다."라고 설명한다. 생물학자들은 때때로 이 '붉은 여왕 효과'를 사용해 진화의 원리를 설명한다. 만약 여우가 더 많은 토끼를 잡기 위해 더 빨리 달리게 진화한다면, 가장 빠른 토끼만이 충분히 오래 살아 훨씬 더 빨리 달리는 새로운 세대의 토끼를 낳을 텐데, 이 경우 당연히도 가장 빠른 여우만이 충분한 토끼를 잡아 번성하여 자신들의 유전자를 물려줄 것이다. 그 두 종은 달린다 해도 제자리에 머무를 뿐이다.

Why? 왜 정답일까?

원래 있던 자리를 유지하기 위해 전력 질주해야 하는(~ it takes all the running you can do, to keep in the same place.) 소설 속 상황에 빗대어 진화의 원리를 설명하는 글이다. 마지막 문장 앞에 제시된 여우와 토끼의 예시에 따르면, 여우가 토끼를 더 많이 잡기 위해 달리기가 빨라지도록 진화하면, 그 여우보다도 빠른 토끼만이 살아남아 번식하게 되므로 토끼 또한 더 빨라지도록 진화하게 된다. 이것은 다시 여우의 달리기가 더 빨라지게 하는 원인으로 작용하므로, 결과적으로 두 종의 상황은 시간이 지나도

차이가 없다. 따라서 빈칸에 들어갈 말로 가장 적절한 것은 ① '제자리에 머무를 뿐이다'이다.

- **discover** ⓥ 발견하다
- **evolutionary** ⓐ 진화적인
- **generation** ⓝ 세대
- **pass on** 물려주다
- **species** ⓝ (생물) 종
- **adapt to** ~에 적응하다
- **biologist** ⓝ 생물학자
- **principle** ⓝ 원리
- **thrive** ⓥ 번성하다
- **gene** ⓝ 유전자
- **run into** ~을 우연히 만나다

구문 풀이

2행 They run and they run, but then Alice discovers that they're still under the same tree that they started from.
접속사
선행사(the same+명) ↳ 목적격 관계대명사

★★ 문제 해결 꿀~팁 ★★

▶ 많이 틀린 이유는?
여우가 토끼를 더 많이 잡기 위해 더 빨리 뛰도록 진화해도, 토끼 또한 똑같이 진화하기 때문에 결국 둘 다 '제자리에 있는' 셈이라는 것이 글의 결론이다. ③은 두 동물이 '서로 절대 우연히 만나지 않는다'는 의미로, run이 있어 혼동될 수 있지만 의미상 연관이 없다.
▶ 문제 해결 방법은?
글에 인용구가 나오면 주제와 연관되는 경우가 많다. 여기서도 인용구 안의 to keep in the same place가 주제를 가리키는 핵심 표현이다.

34 머릿속 아이디어일 때 이미 완성된 미래   정답률 53% | 정답 ②

다음 빈칸에 들어갈 말로 가장 적절한 것을 고르시오. [3점]

① didn't even have the potential to accomplish – 성취할 잠재력조차 지니고 있지 않았던
✓② have mentally concluded about the future – 미래에 대해 머릿속에서 완성한
③ haven't been able to picture in our mind – (전에는) 머릿속에 그릴 수 없었던
④ considered careless and irresponsible – 조심성 없고 무책임하다고 여겼던
⑤ have observed in some professionals – 몇몇 전문가에게서 관찰해 낸

Everything in the world around us / was finished in the mind of its creator / before it was started.
우리 주변 세상의 모든 것은 / 그것을 만들어 낸 사람의 마음속에서 완성되었다. / 그것이 시작되기 전에
The houses we live in, / the cars we drive, / and our clothing / — all of these began with an idea.
우리가 사는 집, / 우리가 운전하는 자동차, / 우리 옷, / 이 모든 것이 아이디어에 시작했다.
Each idea was then studied, refined and perfected / before the first nail was driven / or the first piece of cloth was cut.
각각의 아이디어는 그런 다음 연구되고, 다듬어지고, 완성되었다. / 첫 번째 못이 박히거나 / 첫 번째 천 조각이 재단되기에 앞서
Long before the idea was turned into a physical reality, / the mind had clearly pictured the finished product.
그 아이디어가 물리적 실체로 바뀌기 훨씬 전에 / 마음은 완제품을 분명하게 그렸다.
The human being designs his or her own future / through much the same process.
인간은 자신의 미래를 설계한다. / 거의 똑같은 과정을 통해
We begin with an idea / about how the future will be.
우리는 아이디어로 시작한다. / 미래가 어떨지에 대한
Over a period of time / we refine and perfect the vision.
일정 기간에 걸쳐서 / 우리는 그 비전을 다듬어 완성한다.
Before long, / our every thought, decision and activity / are all working in harmony / to bring into existence / what we have mentally concluded about the future.
머지않아, / 우리의 모든 생각, 결정, 활동은 / 모두 조화롭게 작용하게 된다 / 생겨나게 하려고 / 우리가 미래에 대해 머릿속에서 완성한 것을

우리 주변 세상의 모든 것은 시작되기 전에 그것을 만들어 낸 사람의 마음속에서 완성되었다. 우리가 사는 집, 우리가 운전하는 자동차, 우리 옷, 이 모든 것이 아이디어에서 시작했다. 각각의 아이디어는 그런 다음 첫 번째 못이 박히거나 첫 번째 천 조각이 재단되기에 앞서 연구되고, 다듬어지고, 완성되었다. 그 아이디어가 물리적 실체로 바뀌기 훨씬 전에 마음은 완제품을 분명하게 그렸다. 인간은 거의 똑같은 과정을 통해 자신의 미래를 설계한다. 우리는 미래가 어떨지에 대한 아이디어로 시작한다. 일정 기간에 걸쳐서 우리는 그 비전을 다듬어 완성한다. 머지않아, 우리의 모든 생각, 결정, 활동은 우리가 미래에 대해 머릿속에서 완성한 것을 생겨나게 하려고 모두 조화롭게 작용하게 된다.

Why? 왜 정답일까?

첫 문장에서 세상 모든 것은 실체가 이전에 머릿속에서 이미 완성된 아이디어(finished in the mind of its creator)였다고 설명하는데, 글 중반부에서 우리 미래 역시 같은 식으로 설계된다고 말한다. 즉, 처음에 '이미 머릿속에서 만들어진' 아이디어가 다듬어지고 구현되는 과정이 똑같이 진행된다는 의미로, 빈칸에 들어갈 말로 가장 적절한 것은 ② '미래에 대해 머릿속에서 완성한'이다.

- **clothing** ⓝ 옷, 의복
- **perfect** ⓥ 완성하다, 완벽하게 하다
- **turn A into B** A를 B로 바꾸다
- **process** ⓝ 과정
- **before long** 머지않아
- **bring into existence** ~을 생겨나게 하다
- **careless** ⓐ 조심성 없는
- **professional** ⓝ 전문가 ⓐ 전문적인
- **refine** ⓥ 다듬다
- **nail** ⓝ 못
- **picture** ⓥ 상상하다, 그리다
- **over a period of time** 일정 기간에 걸쳐서
- **in harmony** 조화롭게
- **mentally** ⓐⓓ 머릿속에, 마음속으로
- **irresponsible** ⓐ 무책임한

구문 풀이

1행 Everything in the world around us was finished in the mind of its creator before it was started.
주어(every-)   동사(단수)

35 서술자에 따라 다르게 이해되는 이야기   정답률 61% | 정답 ④

다음 글에서 전체 흐름과 관계 없는 문장은?

Whose story it is / affects *what* the story is.
누구의 이야기인지가 / 무슨 이야기인지에 영향을 미친다.

Change the main character, / and the focus of the story must also change.
주인공을 바꿔보라, / 그러면 이야기의 초점도 틀림없이 바뀐다.

If we look at the events through another character's eyes, / we will interpret them differently.
만약 우리가 다른 등장인물의 눈을 통해 사건을 본다면, / 우리는 그것을 다르게 해석할 것이다.

① We'll place our sympathies with someone new.
우리는 새로운 누군가에게 공감할 것이다.

② When the conflict arises / that is the heart of the story, / we will be praying for a different outcome.
갈등이 발생할 때, / 이야기의 핵심인 / 우리는 다른 결과를 간절히 바랄 것이다.

③ Consider, for example, / how the tale of Cinderella would shift / if told from the viewpoint of an evil stepsister.
예컨대, 생각해 보라. / 신데렐라 이야기가 어떻게 바뀔지 / 사악한 의붓자매의 관점에서 이야기된다면

☑ We know / Cinderella's kingdom does not exist, / but we willingly go there anyway.
우리는 알지만, / 신데렐라의 왕국이 존재하지 않는다는 것을 / 어쨌든 우리는 기꺼이 그곳에 간다.

⑤ *Gone with the Wind* is Scarlett O'Hara's story, / but what if we were shown the same events / from the viewpoint of Rhett Butler or Melanie Wilkes?
*Gone with the Wind*는 Scarlett O'Hara의 이야기이지만, / 만약 같은 사건이 우리에게 제시된다면 어떠할 것인가? / Rhett Butler나 Melanie Wilkes의 관점에서

누구의 이야기인지가 무슨 이야기인지에 영향을 미친다. 주인공을 바꾸면, 이야기의 초점도 틀림없이 바뀐다. 만약 우리가 다른 등장인물의 눈을 통해 사건을 본다면, 우리는 그것을 다르게 해석할 것이다. ① 우리는 새로운 누군가에게 공감할 것이다. ② 이야기의 핵심인 갈등이 발생할 때, 우리는 다른 결과를 간절히 바랄 것이다. ③ 예컨대, 신데렐라 이야기가 사악한 의붓자매의 관점에서 이야기된다면 어떻게 바뀔지 생각해 보라. ④ 우리는 신데렐라의 왕국이 존재하지 않는다는 것을 알지만, 어쨌든 기꺼이 그곳에 간다. ⑤ *Gone with the Wind*는 Scarlett O'Hara의 이야기이지만, 만약 같은 사건이 Rhett Butler나 Melanie Wilkes의 관점에서 우리에게 제시된다면 어떠할 것인가?

Why? 왜 정답일까?

이야기의 주인공이 누구인가에 따라 이야기 내용이 다르게 받아들여진다는 내용인데, ④는 Cinderella의 왕국에 관해서만 지엽적으로 언급하고 있다. 따라서 전체 흐름과 관계 없는 문장은 ④이다.

- **affect** ⓥ 영향을 미치다
- **sympathy** ⓝ 공감
- **arise** ⓥ 발생하다
- **outcome** ⓝ 결과
- **shift** ⓥ 바꾸다
- **evil** ⓐ 사악한 ⓝ 악
- **kingdom** ⓝ 왕국
- **interpret** ⓥ 해석하다, 이해하다
- **conflict** ⓝ 갈등
- **pray for** ~을 위해 기도하다
- **tale** ⓝ 이야기
- **viewpoint** ⓝ 관점
- **stepsister** ⓝ 의붓자매
- **willingly** ⓐ 기꺼이

구문 풀이

6행 Consider, for example, [how the tale of Cinderella would shift if told from
명령문(~하라)   [ ]: 목적어   접속사 + 과거분사(~한다면)
the viewpoint of an evil stepsister].

★★★ 등급을 가르는 문제!

36 농경 생활로 인한 인간 사회의 변화   정답률 36% | 정답 ④

주어진 글 다음에 이어질 글의 순서로 가장 적절한 것을 고르시오.
① (A) – (C) – (B)   ② (B) – (A) – (C)
③ (B) – (C) – (A)   ☑ (C) – (A) – (B)
⑤ (C) – (B) – (A)

In the Old Stone Age, / small bands of 20 to 60 people / wandered from place to place / in search of food.
구석기 시대에는 / 20 ~ 60명의 작은 무리가 / 여기저기 돌아다녔다 / 먹을 것을 찾아

Once people began farming, / they could settle down near their farms.
일단 사람들이 농사를 짓기 시작하면서, / 그들은 자신의 농경지 근처에 정착할 수 있었다.

(C) As a result, / towns and villages grew larger.
그 결과, / 도시와 마을이 더 커졌다.

Living in communities / allowed people / to organize themselves more efficiently.
공동체 생활은 / 사람들이 / ~하게 했다 / 더 효율적으로 조직되게

They could divide up the work / of producing food and other things they needed.
그들은 일을 나눌 수 있었다 / 식량과 자신들에게 필요한 다른 것들을 생산하는

(A) While some workers grew crops, / others built new houses and made tools.
어떤 노동자들은 농작물을 재배하는 한편, / 다른 노동자들은 새로운 집을 짓고 도구를 만들었다.

Village dwellers also learned to work together / to do a task faster.
마을 거주자들은 또한 함께 일하는 법을 익혔다. / 일을 더 빨리 하려고

(B) For example, / toolmakers could share the work / of making stone axes and knives.
예를 들어, / 도구 제작자들은 작업을 함께 할 수 있었다 / 돌도끼와 돌칼을 만드는

By working together, / they could make more tools / in the same amount of time.
함께 일하여 / 그들은 더 많은 도구를 만들 수 있었다. / 같은 시간 안에

구석기 시대에는 20 ~ 60명의 작은 무리가 먹을 것을 찾아 여기저기 돌아다녔다. 일단 농사를 짓기 시작하면서, 사람들은 자신의 농경지 근처에 정착할 수 있었다.

(C) 그 결과, 도시와 마을이 더 커졌다. 공동체 생활을 통해 사람들은 더 효율적으로 조직될 수 있었다. 그들은 식량과 자신들에게 필요한 다른 것들을 생산하는 일을 나눌 수 있었다.

(A) 어떤 노동자들은 농작물을 재배하는 한편, 다른 노동자들은 새로운 집을 짓고 도구를 만들었다. 마을 거주자들은 또한 일을 더 빨리 하려고 함께 일하는 법도 익혔다.

(B) 예를 들어, 도구 제작자들은 돌도끼와 돌칼을 만드는 작업을 함께 할 수 있었다. 그들은 함께 일하여 같은 시간 안에 더 많은 도구를 만들 수 있었다.

Why? 왜 정답일까?

농경이 시작되면서 사람들이 정착할 수 있었다는 내용의 주어진 글 뒤로, '그 결과' 도시와 마을이 생기고 사람들이 일을 분배할 수 있게 되었다고 설명하는 (C)가 먼저 연결된다. 이어서 (A)는 (C)에서 언급된 '분업'이 어떻게 이루어졌는지 언급하며, 사람들이 함께 일하는 법 또한 배우게 되었다고 이야기한다. (B)에

서는 '함께 작업'하는 상황의 예를 제시하며 (A)를 보충 설명한다. 따라서 글의 순서로 가장 적절한 것은 ④ '(C) – (A) – (B)'이다.

- **Old Stone Age** 구석기 시대
- **wander** ⓥ 돌아다니다, 배회하다
- **settle down** 정착하다
- **dweller** ⓝ 거주자
- **community** ⓝ 공동체, 지역사회
- **efficiently** ⓐ 효율적으로
- **band** ⓝ (소규모) 무리
- **in search of** ~을 찾아서
- **crop** ⓝ 작물
- **axe** ⓝ 도끼
- **organize** ⓥ 조직하다, 정리하다
- **divide up** ~을 나누다

구문 풀이

2행 Once people began farming, they could settle down near their farms.
접속사(일단 ~한다면)

★★ 문제 해결 꿀~팁 ★★

▶ 많이 틀린 이유는?
글을 자세히 읽지 않고 연결어 중심으로만 보면, (B)가 주어진 글의 예시(For example)이고 (C)가 전체 글의 결론(As a result)일 것이라고 잘못 추론할 수 있다. 하지만, 내용적 단서가 중요하다. 주어진 글은 사람들이 농경을 시작하며 정착했다는 내용인데, (B)는 갑자기 '도구 제작자'를 언급하며, 이들이 업무를 분업해 담당했다는 설명을 제시하고 있다. 서로 전혀 다른 키워드로 보아 (B)가 주어진 글에 대한 예시라고 보기 어렵기 때문에 ②를 답으로 고르는 것은 적절하지 않다.

▶ 문제 해결 방법은?
사람들이 농경지 근처에 정착하여 살게 되면서, 마을이 성장하고 분업화가 일어나(C), 누구는 농사를 짓고 누구는 도구를 만드는 한편 공동 작업도 활성화되었으며(A), 공동 작업으로 더 쉽고 빠른 작업이 가능해졌다(B)는 흐름이다.

★★★ 등급을 가르는 문제!

37 광물의 형성   정답률 42% | 정답 ②

주어진 글 다음에 이어질 글의 순서로 가장 적절한 것을 고르시오. [3점]
① (A) – (C) – (B)   ☑ (B) – (A) – (C)
③ (B) – (C) – (A)   ④ (C) – (A) – (B)
⑤ (C) – (B) – (A)

Natural processes form minerals in many ways.
자연 과정은 많은 방법으로 광물을 형성한다.

For example, / hot melted rock material, / called magma, / cools / when it reaches the Earth's surface, / or even if it's trapped below the surface.
예를 들어, / 뜨거운 용암 물질은 / 마그마라고 불리는 / 식는다. / 그것이 지구의 표면에 도달할 때, / 또는 그것이 심지어 표면 아래에 갇혔을 때도

As magma cools, / its atoms lose heat energy, / move closer together, / and begin to combine into compounds.
마그마가 식으면서, / 마그마의 원자는 열에너지를 잃고, / 서로 더 가까이 이동해 / 화합물로 결합하기 시작한다.

(B) During this process, / atoms of the different compounds / arrange themselves into orderly, repeating patterns.
이 과정 동안, / 서로 다른 화합물의 원자가 / 질서 있고 반복적인 패턴으로 배열된다.

The type and amount of elements / present in a magma / partly determine / which minerals will form.
원소의 종류와 양이 / 마그마에 존재하는 / 부분적으로 결정한다. / 어떤 광물이 형성될지를

(A) Also, / the size of the crystals that form / depends partly / on how rapidly the magma cools.
또한, / 형성되는 결정의 크기는 / 부분적으로는 달려 있다. / 마그마가 얼마나 빨리 식냐에

When magma cools slowly, / the crystals that form / are generally large enough / to see with the unaided eye.
마그마가 천천히 식으면, / 형성되는 결정은 / 대개 충분히 크다. / 육안으로 볼 수 있을 만큼

(C) This is because the atoms have enough time / to move together and form into larger crystals.
이것은 원자가 충분한 시간을 가지기 때문이다. / 함께 이동해 더 큰 결정을 형성할

When magma cools rapidly, / the crystals that form / will be small.
마그마가 빠르게 식으면, / 형성되는 결정은 / 작을 것이다.

In such cases, / you can't easily see individual mineral crystals.
이런 경우에는 / 여러분은 개별 광물 결정을 쉽게 볼 수 없다.

자연 과정은 많은 방법으로 광물을 형성한다. 예를 들어, 마그마라고 불리는 뜨거운 용암 물질은 지구의 표면에 도달할 때, 또는 심지어 표면 아래에 갇혔을 때도 식는다. 마그마가 식으면서 마그마의 원자는 열에너지를 잃고, 서로 더 가까이 이동해 화합물로 결합하기 시작한다.

(B) 이 과정 동안, 서로 다른 화합물의 원자가 질서 있고 반복적인 패턴으로 배열된다. 마그마에 존재하는 원소의 종류와 양이 어떤 광물이 형성될지를 부분적으로 결정한다.

(A) 또한, 형성되는 결정의 크기는 부분적으로는 마그마가 얼마나 빨리 식냐에 달려 있다. 마그마가 천천히 식으면, 형성되는 결정은 대개 육안으로 볼 수 있을 만큼 충분히 크다.

(C) 이것은 원자가 함께 이동해 더 큰 결정을 형성할 충분한 시간을 가지기 때문이다. 마그마가 빠르게 식으면, 형성되는 결정은 작을 것이다. 이런 경우에는 개별 광물 결정을 쉽게 볼 수 없다.

Why? 왜 정답일까?

마그마가 식을 때 광물이 형성될 수 있다는 내용의 주어진 글 뒤로, '이 식어가는 과정' 동안 마그마 속 원소의 종류나 양에 따라 어떤 종류의 광물이 형성될지 결정된다고 설명하는 (B)가 먼저 연결된다. 이어서 Also로 시작하는 (A)는 추가로 마그마가 식는 속도에 따라 광물의 크기가 결정된다고 언급한다. 마지막으로 (C)는 (A) 후반부에서 언급되었듯이 마그마가 천천히 식을 때 광물의 크기가 커지는 이유에 관해 보충 설명한다. 따라서 글의 순서로 가장 적절한 것은 ② '(B) – (A) – (C)'이다.

- **form** ⓥ 형성하다
- **melt** ⓥ 녹이다, 녹다
- **trap** ⓥ 가두다
- **combine into** ~로 결합되다
- **partly** ⓐ 부분적으로
- **mineral** ⓝ 광물
- **surface** ⓝ 표면
- **atom** ⓝ 원자
- **compound** ⓝ 화합물
- **rapidly** ⓐ 빠르게

- **with the unaided eye** 육안으로
- **orderly** @ 질서 있는
- **in such cases** 이런 경우에
- **arrange** ⓥ 배열하다
- **element** ⓝ 원소, 구성요소

6행 Also, the size of the crystals that form depends partly on how rapidly the magma cools.
「how + 형/부 + 주어 + 동사 : 얼마나 ~한지」

★★ 문제 해결 꿀~팁 ★★

▶ 많이 틀린 이유는?
(B)는 마그마가 식는 속도에 따라 그로 인해 만들어지는 결정의 종류가 달라질 수 있다는 내용으로 끝나는데, (C)를 보면 갑자기 결정의 '크기'가 커지는 이유를 언급한다. (C)에 앞서 '크기'를 처음 언급하는 단락은 Also로 시작하는 (A)이다. (A)에서 먼저 size를 언급해줘야 크기가 커지는 '이유'를 설명하는 (C)가 자연스럽게 연결된다.

▶ 문제 해결 방법은?
(A)와 (C)가 둘 다 '크기'를 언급하고 있지만, (B)에는 '크기'에 관한 언급이 없다. 따라서 Also가 있는 (A)를 먼저 연결해 '크기'에 관한 내용을 추가한다는 뜻을 밝히고, 뒤이어 (C)를 연결해야 논리적 흐름이 자연스러워진다.

---

38 탄수화물의 종류 정답률 57% | 정답 ④

글의 흐름으로 보아, 주어진 문장이 들어가기에 가장 적절한 곳을 고르시오.

All carbohydrates are basically sugars.
모든 탄수화물은 기본적으로 당이다.
① Complex carbohydrates are the good carbohydrates for your body.
복합 탄수화물은 몸에 좋은 탄수화물이다.
② These complex sugar compounds / are very difficult to break down / and can trap other nutrients / like vitamins and minerals / in their chains.
이러한 복당류 화합물은 / 분해하기 매우 어렵고 / 다른 영양소를 가두어 둘 수 있다. / 비타민과 미네랄 같은 / 그것의 사슬 안에
③ As they slowly break down, / the other nutrients are also released into your body, / and can provide you with fuel for a number of hours.
그것들이 천천히 분해되면서, / 다른 영양소도 여러분의 몸으로 방출되고, / 많은 시간 동안 여러분에게 연료를 공급할 수 있다.
✔ Bad carbohydrates, / on the other hand, / are simple sugars.
나쁜 탄수화물은 / 반면에 / 단당류이다.
Because their structure is not complex, / they are easy to break down / and hold few nutrients for your body / other than the sugars from which they are made.
그것의 구조는 복잡하지 않기 때문에 / 그것은 분해되기 쉬우며, / 몸을 위한 영양소를 거의 가지고 있지 않다. / 그것을 구성하는 당 말고는
⑤ Your body breaks down these carbohydrates rather quickly / and what it cannot use / is converted to fat and stored in the body.
여러분의 몸은 이러한 탄수화물을 상당히 빨리 분해하며, / 몸이 사용하지 못하는 것은 / 지방으로 바뀌어 몸에 저장된다.

모든 탄수화물은 기본적으로 당이다. ① 복합 탄수화물은 몸에 좋은 탄수화물이다. ② 이러한 복당류 화합물은 분해하기 매우 어렵고, 비타민과 미네랄 같은 다른 영양소를 그것의 사슬 안에 가두어 둘 수 있다. ③ 그것들이 천천히 분해되면서, 다른 영양소도 여러분의 몸으로 방출되고, 많은 시간 동안 여러분에게 연료를 공급할 수 있다. ④ 반면에 나쁜 탄수화물은 단당류이다. 그것의 구조는 복잡하지 않기 때문에 분해되기 쉬우며, 그것을 구성하는 당 말고는 몸을 위한 영양소를 거의 가지고 있지 않다. ⑤ 여러분의 몸은 이러한 탄수화물을 상당히 빨리 분해하며, 몸이 사용하지 못하는 것은 지방으로 바뀌어 몸에 저장된다.

Why? 왜 정답일까?
복합 탄수화물과 단당류의 차이점을 설명하는 글이다. ④ 앞의 복합당의 경우 구조가 복잡하기 때문에 분해 시간이 느리고 오랜 시간 몸에 연료를 공급한다는 내용이다. 한편 주어진 문장은 '나쁜 탄수화물'인 단당류를 언급하고, ④ 뒤에서는 이 단당류를 they로 받아 이것이 분해되기 쉽고 당 외에는 다른 영양소를 가지고 있지도 않아 몸에서 다 쓰지 못하면 지방이 되어 쌓인다는 설명을 이어 간다. 따라서 주어진 문장이 들어가기에 가장 적절한 곳은 ④이다.

- **carbohydrate** ⓝ 탄수화물
- **break down** 분해하다
- **release** ⓥ 방출하다
- **a number of** 많은
- **be made from** ~로 구성되다
- **basically** @ 기본적으로
- **nutrient** ⓝ 영양소
- **provide A with B** A에게 B를 공급하다
- **structure** ⓝ 구조
- **convert** ⓥ 바꾸다

4행 These complex sugar compounds are very difficult to break down and can trap other nutrients like vitamins and minerals in their chains.
보어(형용사구) / 부사적 용법(~하기에)

---

39 초기 정보와 기대의 영향 정답률 48% | 정답 ⑤

글의 흐름으로 보아, 주어진 문장이 들어가기에 가장 적절한 곳을 고르시오. [3점]

People commonly make the mistaken assumption / that because a person has one type of characteristic, / then they automatically have other characteristics / which go with it.
흔히 사람들은 잘못된 가정을 한다. / 어떤 사람이 어떤 특성 하나를 가지고 있으므로 / 그러면 그들은 자동으로 다른 특성을 지니고 있다 / 그것과 어울리는
① In one study, / university students were given descriptions of a guest lecturer / before he spoke to the group.
한 연구에서, / 대학생들은 어떤 초청 강사에 대한 설명을 들었다. / 그가 그들 집단 앞에서 강연하기 전
② Half the students received a description / containing the word 'warm', / the other half were told / the speaker was 'cold'.
학생들 절반은 설명을 들었고 / '따뜻하다'라는 단어가 포함된 / 나머지 절반은 들었다. / 그 강사가 '차갑다'는 말을
③ The guest lecturer then led a discussion, / after which the students were asked / to give their impressions of him.
그리고 나서 그 초청 강사가 토론을 이끌었고, / 이후 학생들은 요청받았다. / 강사에 대한 인상을 말해 달라고
④ As expected, / there were large differences / between the impressions formed by the students, / depending upon their original information of the lecturer.
예상한 대로, / 큰 차이가 있었다. / 학생들에 의해 형성된 인상 간에는 / 그 강사에 대한 학생들의 최초 정보에 따라
✔ It was also found / that those students / who expected the lecturer to be warm / tended to interact with him more.
또한 밝혀졌다. / 그런 학생들은 / 그 강사가 따뜻할 거라고 기대했던 / 그와 더 많이 소통하는 경향이 있었다는 것이
This shows / that different expectations / not only affect the impressions we form / but also our behaviour and the relationship which is formed.
이것은 보여준다. / 서로 다른 기대가 / 우리가 형성하는 인상뿐만 아니라 (~에도) 영향을 미친다는 것을 / 우리의 행동 및 형성되는 관계에도

흔히 사람들은 어떤 사람이 어떤 특성 하나를 가지고 있으면 자동으로 그것과 어울리는 다른 특성을 지니고 있다는 잘못된 가정을 한다. ① 한 연구에서, 대학생들은 어떤 초청 강사가 그들 집단 앞에서 강연하기 전 그 강사에 대한 설명을 들었다. ② 학생들 절반은 '따뜻하다'라는 단어가 포함된 설명을 들었고, 나머지 절반은 그 강사가 '차갑다'는 말을 들었다. ③ 그리고 나서 그 초청 강사가 토론을 이끌었고, 이후 학생들은 강사에 대한 인상을 말해 달라고 요청받았다. ④ 예상한 대로, 학생들에 의해 형성된 인상 간에는 그 강사에 대한 학생들의 최초 정보에 따라 큰 차이가 있었다. ⑤ 또한, 그 강사가 따뜻할 거라고 기대했던 학생들은 그와 더 많이 소통하는 경향이 있었다는 것이 밝혀졌다. 이것은 서로 다른 기대가 우리가 형성하는 인상뿐만 아니라 우리의 행동 및 형성되는 관계에도 영향을 미친다는 것을 보여준다.

Why? 왜 정답일까?
대학생을 집단을 대상으로 초기 정보의 영향력을 연구한 실험을 소개하는 글이다. ① 이후로 ⑤ 앞까지 대학생들 두 집단이 똑같은 강사에 관해 상반된 정보를 들었고, 이에 따라 동일한 사람에 대해 서로 다른 인상을 갖게 되었다는 실험 내용이 소개된다. 이어서 주어진 문장은 추가적인 결과(was also found)로 각 집단이 강사와 소통하는 정도에도 영향이 있었다는 내용을 제시한다. 마지막으로 ⑤ 뒤에서는 서로 다른 초기 정보와 기대로 인해 강사에 대한 인상뿐 아니라 관계 맺음에도 차이가 생겼다는 최종적 결론을 제시한다. 따라서 주어진 문장이 들어가기에 가장 적절한 곳은 ⑤이다.

- **lecturer** ⓝ 강사, 강연자
- **commonly** @ 흔히
- **assumption** ⓝ 가정, 추정
- **description** ⓝ 설명
- **be told** ~을 듣다
- **impression** ⓝ 인상
- **original** @ 최초의, 원래의
- **relationship** ⓝ 관계
- **interact with** ~와 상호작용하다
- **mistaken** @ 잘못된, 틀린
- **automatically** @ 자동으로, 저절로
- **contain** ⓥ 포함하다, (~이) 들어 있다
- **discussion** ⓝ 토론, 논의
- **as expected** 예상된 대로
- **expectation** ⓝ 기대, 예상

---

40 사회적 증거의 위력 정답률 49% | 정답 ①

다음 글의 내용을 한 문장으로 요약하고자 한다. 빈칸 (A), (B)에 들어갈 말로 가장 적절한 것은?

	(A)		(B)
✔①	numbers 숫자	……	uncertain 불확실한
②	numbers 숫자	……	unrealistic 비현실적인
③	experiences 경험	……	unrealistic 비현실적인
④	rules 규칙	……	uncertain 불확실한
⑤	rules 규칙	……	unpleasant 불쾌한

To help decide what's risky and what's safe, / who's trustworthy and who's not, / we look for *social evidence*.
무엇이 위험하고 무엇이 안전한지 결정하는 것을 돕고자 / 누구를 신뢰할 수 있고 없는지를 / 우리는 *사회적 증거*를 찾는다.
From an evolutionary view, / following the group is almost always positive / for our prospects of survival.
진화의 관점에서 볼 때, / 집단을 따르는 것은 거의 항상 긍정적이다. / 우리의 생존 전망에
"If everyone's doing it, / it must be a sensible thing to do," / explains / famous psychologist and best-selling writer of *Influence*, / Robert Cialdini.
"모든 사람이 그것을 하고 있다면, / 그것은 분별 있는 행동임에 틀림없다."라고 / 설명한다. / 저명한 심리학자이자 *Influence*를 쓴 베스트셀러 작가 / Robert Cialdini는
While we can frequently see this today in product reviews, / even subtler cues within the environment / can signal trustworthiness.
오늘날 우리가 이를 자주 볼 수 있지만, / 환경 내의 훨씬 더 미묘한 신호가 / 신뢰성을 나타낼 수 있다.
Consider this: / when you visit a local restaurant, / are they busy?
다음을 생각해보라. / 여러분이 어느 현지 음식점을 방문할 때, / 그들이 바쁜가?
Is there a line outside / or is it easy to find a seat?
밖에 줄이 있는가, / 아니면 자리를 찾기 쉬운가?
It is a hassle to wait, / but a line can be a powerful cue / that the food's tasty, / and these seats are in demand.
기다리기는 성가시지만, / 줄이라는 것은 강력한 신호일 수 있다. / 음식이 맛있다는 / 그리고 이곳의 좌석이 수요가 많다
More often than not, / it's good / to adopt the practices of those around you.
대개는 / 좋다. / 주변 사람들의 행동을 따르는 것이
⇒ We tend to feel safe and secure in (A) numbers / when we decide how to act, / particularly when faced with (B) uncertain conditions.
우리는 숫자에서 안전함과 안도감을 느끼는 경향이 있다. / 어떻게 행동할지 결정할 때 / 특히 불확실한 상황에 직면해 있다면

무엇이 위험하고 무엇이 안전하며, 누구를 신뢰할 수 있고 없는지를 결정하는 것을 돕고자, 우리는 *사회적 증거*를 찾는다. 진화의 관점에서 볼 때, 집단을 따르는 것은 거의 항상 우리의 생존 전망에 긍정적이다. "모든 사람이 그것을 하고 있다면, 그것은 분별 있는 행동임에 틀림 없다."라고 저명한 심리학자이자 *Influence*를 쓴 베스트셀러 작가인 Robert Cialdini는 설명한다. 오늘날 상품평에서 이를 자주 볼 수 있지만, 환경 내의 훨씬 더 미묘한 신호가 신뢰성을 나타낼 수 있다. 다음을 생각해보라. 여러분이 어느 현지 음식점을 방문할 때, 그들(식당 사람들)이 바쁜가? 밖에 줄이 있는가, 아니면 (사람이 없어서) 자리를 찾기 쉬운가? 기다리기는 성가시지만, 줄이라는 것은 음식이 맛있고 이곳의 좌석이 수요가 많다는 강력한 신호일 수 있다. 대개는 주변 사람들의 행동을 따르는 것이 좋다.

⇒ 우리는 어떻게 행동할지 결정할 때 특히 (B) 불확실한 상황에 직면해 있다면 (A) 숫자에서 안전함과 안도감을 느끼는 경향이 있다.

Why? 왜 정답일까?
불확실한 상황에서 결정을 내려야 할 때 우리는 주변 집단의 행동을 따라 안전하게 선택하려 한다(~ following the group is almost always positive for our prospects of survival. / More often than not, it's good to adopt the practices of those around you.)는 내용

의 글이다. 따라서 요약문의 빈칸 (A), (B)에 들어갈 말로 가장 적절한 것은 ① '(A) numbers(숫자), (B) uncertain(불확실한)'이다.

- **risky** ⓐ 위험한
- **evidence** ⓝ 근거, 증거
- **sensible** ⓐ 분별 있는, 현명한
- **subtle** ⓐ 미묘한
- **tasty** ⓐ 맛있는
- **more often than not** 대개
- **faced with** ~와 직면한
- **unrealistic** ⓐ 비현실적인
- **unpleasant** ⓐ 불쾌한
- **trustworthy** ⓐ 신뢰할 만한
- **prospect** ⓝ 예상, 가망성
- **frequently** ⓐⓓ 자주, 빈번히
- **hassle** ⓝ 성가신 일
- **in demand** 수요가 많은
- **practice** ⓝ 관례, 실행
- **uncertain** ⓐ 불확실한
- **rule** ⓝ 규칙 ⓥ 지배하다

구문 풀이

1행 To help decide what's risky and what's safe, who's trustworthy and who's
목적(~하려면) 원형부정사 · · · 의문사절1 · · · · · 의문사절2
not, we look for *social evidence*.

41-42 익숙한 정보에 대한 전문가의 유리함

Chess masters shown a chess board / in the middle of a game for 5 seconds / with 20 to 30 pieces still in play / can immediately reproduce the position of the pieces from memory.
체스판을 본 체스의 달인들은 / 게임 중간에 5초 동안 / 20~30개의 말들이 아직 놓여 있는 상태로 / 그 말들의 위치를 외워서 즉시 재현할 수 있다.

Beginners, / of course, / are able to place only a few.
초보자들은 / 물론 / 겨우 몇 개만 기억해 낼 수 있다.

Now take the same pieces / and place them on the board randomly / and the (a) difference is much reduced.
이제 똑같은 말들을 가져다가 / 체스판에 무작위로 놓으라 / 그러면 그 차이는 크게 줄어든다.

『The expert's advantage is only for familiar patterns / — those previously stored in memory.』 42번의 근거
전문가의 유리함은 익숙한 패턴에 대해서만 있다. / 즉 이전에 기억에 저장된 패턴

Faced with unfamiliar patterns, / even when it involves the same familiar domain, / the expert's advantage (b) disappears.
익숙하지 않은 패턴에 직면하면, / 그것이 같은 익숙한 분야와 관련 있는 경우라도 / 전문가의 유리함은 사라진다.

『The beneficial effects of familiar structure on memory』 / have been observed for many types of expertise, / including music. 41번의 근거
익숙한 구조가 기억에 미치는 유익한 효과는 / 여러 전문 지식 유형에서 관찰되어 왔다 / 음악을 포함해

People with musical training / can reproduce short sequences of musical notation more accurately / than those with no musical training / when notes follow (c) conventional sequences, / but the advantage is much reduced / when the notes are ordered randomly.
음악 훈련을 받은 사람이 / 연속된 짧은 악보를 더 정확하게 재현할 수 있다 / 음악 훈련을 안 받은 사람보다 / 음표가 전형적인 순서를 따를 때는 / 하지만 그 유리함이 훨씬 줄어든다. / 음표가 무작위로 배열되면

Expertise also improves memory for sequences of (d) movements.
전문 지식은 또한 연속 동작에 대한 기억을 향상시킨다.

Experienced ballet dancers are able to repeat longer sequences of steps / than less experienced dancers, / and they can repeat a sequence of steps making up a routine better / than steps ordered randomly.
숙련된 발레 무용수가 경험이 적은 무용수보다 / 더 긴 연속 스텝을 반복할 수 있다 / 그리고 그들은 정해진 춤 동작을 이루는 연속 스텝을 더 잘 반복할 수 있다 / 무작위로 배열된 스텝보다

In each case, / memory range is (e) increased / by the ability to recognize familiar sequences and patterns.
각각의 경우, / 기억의 범위는 늘어난다. / 익숙한 순서와 패턴을 인식하는 능력에 의해

체스판을 게임 중간에 20~30개의 말들이 아직 놓여 있는 상태로 5초 동안 본 체스의 달인들은 그 말들의 위치를 외워서 즉시 재현할 수 있다. 물론 초보자들은 겨우 몇 개만 기억해 낼 수 있다. 이제 똑같은 말들을 가져다가 체스판에 무작위로 놓으면 그 (a) 차이는 크게 줄어든다. 전문가의 유리함은 익숙한 패턴, 즉 이전에 기억에 저장된 패턴에 대해서만 있다. 익숙하지 않은 패턴에 직면하면, 같은 익숙한 분야와 관련 있는 경우라도 전문가의 유리함은 (b) 사라진다. 익숙한 구조가 기억에 미치는 유익한 효과는 음악을 포함해 여러 전문 지식 유형에서 관찰되어 왔다. 음표가 (c) 특이한(→ 전형적인) 순서를 따를 때는 음악 훈련을 받은 사람이 음악 훈련을 안 받은 사람보다 연속된 짧은 악보를 더 정확하게 재현할 수 있지만, 음표가 무작위로 배열되면 그 유리함이 훨씬 줄어든다. 전문 지식은 또한 연속 (d) 동작에 대한 기억을 향상시킨다. 숙련된 발레 무용수가 경험이 적은 무용수보다 더 긴 연속 스텝을 반복할 수 있고, 무작위로 배열된 스텝보다 정해진 춤 동작을 이루는 연속 스텝을 더 잘 반복할 수 있다. 각각의 경우, 기억의 범위는 익숙한 순서와 패턴을 인식하는 능력에 의해 (e) 늘어난다.

- **in the middle of** ~의 한가운데에
- **reproduce** ⓥ 재현하다
- **beginner** ⓝ 초심자
- **randomly** ⓐⓓ 무작위로
- **advantage** ⓝ 유리함, 이점
- **previously** ⓐⓓ 이전에, 사전에
- **domain** ⓝ 영역, 분야
- **beneficial** ⓐ 유익한, 이로운
- **sequence** ⓝ 연속, 순서
- **accurately** ⓐⓓ 정확하게
- **experienced** ⓐ 숙련된, 경험 많은
- **guarantee** ⓥ 보장하다
- **in play** 시합 중인
- **from memory** 외워서, 기억하여
- **only a few** 몇 안 되는 (것)
- **reduce** ⓥ 줄이다, 감소시키다
- **familiar** ⓐ 익숙한, 친숙한
- **unfamiliar** ⓐ 익숙지 않은, 낯선
- **disappear** ⓥ 사라지다
- **expertise** ⓝ 전문 지식
- **musical notation** 악보
- **unusual** ⓐ 특이한
- **routine** ⓝ 습관, (정해진) 춤 동작, 루틴

구문 풀이

1행 Chess masters shown a chess board in the middle of a game for 5
주어 · · 과거분사 shown의 직접목적어
seconds with 20 to 30 pieces still in play can immediately reproduce the position
· · · · · · · 동사구
of the pieces from memory.

---

41 제목 파악   정답률 64% | 정답 ②

윗글의 제목으로 가장 적절한 것은?

---

① How Can We Build Good Routines? – 어떻게 하면 좋은 습관을 들일 수 있을까?
☑ Familiar Structures Help Us Remember – 익숙한 구조는 우리가 기억하는 것을 돕는다
③ Intelligence Does Not Guarantee Expertise – 지능이 전문 지식을 보장하지는 않는다
④ Does Playing Chess Improve Your Memory? – 체스를 하는 것이 기억력을 향상시킬까?
⑤ Creative Art Performance Starts from Practice – 창의적인 예술 공연은 연습에서 시작된다

Why? 왜 정답일까?

익숙한 정보가 기억력에 미치는 좋은 영향(The beneficial effects of familiar structure on memory)을 설명하는 글로, 전문가들의 경우 익숙하고 패턴화된 정보는 더 잘 기억하지만 무작위적인 정보는 전문 분야라고 하더라도 기억력 면에서 초심자와 큰 차이를 보이지 못한다는 예시를 다루고 있다. 따라서 글의 제목으로 가장 적절한 것은 ② '익숙한 구조는 우리가 기억하는 것을 돕는다'이다.

42 어휘 추론   정답률 48% | 정답 ③

밑줄 친 (a)~(e) 중에서 문맥상 낱말의 쓰임이 적절하지 <u>않은</u> 것은?
① (a)   ② (b)   ☑ (c)   ④ (d)   ⑤ (e)

Why? 왜 정답일까?

'The expert's advantage is only for familiar patterns ~'에서 전문가의 유리함, 즉 전문가들이 자기 분야의 정보를 더 잘 기억할 수 있는 까닭은 바로 정보의 '익숙한 구조'에 있다고 한다. 이를 음악 전문가들의 사례에 적용하면, 음표에 대한 음악 전문가들의 기억이 비전문가들을 넘어설 수 있는 경우는 음표가 '익숙한' 패턴으로 배열된 때일 것이므로, (c)에는 unusual 대신 conventional을 써야 한다. 따라서 문맥상 낱말의 쓰임이 적절하지 않은 것은 ③ '(c)'이다.

43-45 친절로 없어진 괴물

(A)

Once upon a time, / there was a king / who lived in a beautiful palace.
옛날 옛적에, / 한 왕이 있었다. / 아름다운 궁전에 사는

『While the king was away, / a monster approached the gates of the palace.』 45번 ①의 근거 일치
왕이 없는 동안, / 한 괴물이 궁전 문으로 접근했다.

The monster was so ugly and smelly / that the guards froze in shock.
그 괴물이 너무 추하고 냄새가 나서 / 경비병들은 충격으로 얼어붙었다.

He passed the guards / and sat on the king's throne.
괴물은 경비병들을 지나 / 왕의 왕좌에 앉았다.

The guards soon came to their senses, / went in, / and shouted at the monster, / demanding that (a) he get off the throne.
경비병들은 곧 정신을 차리고 / 안으로 들어가 / 괴물을 향해 소리치며 / 그에게 왕좌에서 내려올 것을 요구했다.

(D)

With each bad word the guards used, / the monster grew more ugly and smelly.
경비병들이 나쁜 말을 사용할 때마다, / 그 괴물은 더 추해졌고, 더 냄새가 났다.

『The guards got even angrier — / they began to brandish their swords / to scare the monster away from the palace.』 45번 ⑤의 근거 일치
경비병들은 한층 더 화가 났다. / 그들은 칼을 휘두르기 시작했다. / 그 괴물을 겁주어 궁전에서 쫓아내려고

But (e) he just grew bigger and bigger, / eventually taking up the whole room.
하지만 그는 그저 점점 더 커져서 / 결국 방 전체를 차지했다.

He grew more ugly and smelly than ever.
그는 그 어느 때보다 더 추해졌고, 더 냄새가 났다.

(B)

Eventually the king returned.
마침내 왕이 돌아왔다.

He was wise and kind / and saw what was happening.
그는 현명하고 친절했으며, / 무슨 일이 일어나고 있는지 알았다.

He knew what to do.
그는 어떻게 해야 할지 알고 있었다.

『He smiled and said to the monster, / "Welcome to my palace!"』 45번 ②의 근거 일치
그는 미소를 지으며 그 괴물에게 말했다, / "나의 궁전에 온 것을 환영하오!"라고

He asked the monster / if (b) he wanted a cup of coffee.
왕은 그 괴물에게 물었다. / 그가 커피 한 잔을 원하는지

The monster began to grow smaller / as he drank the coffee.
괴물은 더 작아지기 시작했다. / 그가 커피를 마시면서

(C)

The king offered (c) him some take-out pizza and fries.
왕은 그에게 약간의 테이크아웃 피자와 감자튀김을 제안했다.

The guards immediately called for pizza.
경비병들은 즉시 피자를 시켰다.

『The monster continued to get smaller / with the king's kind gestures.』 45번 ③의 근거 일치
그 괴물은 몸이 계속 더 작아졌다. / 왕의 친절한 행동으로

(d) He then offered the monster a full body massage.
그러고 나서 그는 괴물에게 전신 마사지를 제공해 주었다.

『As the guards helped with the relaxing massage, / the monster became tiny.』 45번 ④의 근거 불일치
경비병들이 편안한 마사지를 도와주자 / 그 괴물은 매우 작아졌다.

With another act of kindness to the monster, / he just disappeared.
그 괴물에게 또 한 번의 친절한 행동을 베풀자, / 그는 바로 사라졌다.

(A)

옛날 옛적에, 아름다운 궁전에 사는 한 왕이 있었다. 왕이 없는 동안, 한 괴물이 궁전 문으로 접근했다. 그 괴물이 너무 추하고 냄새가 나서 경비병들은 충격으로 얼어붙었다. 괴물은 경비병들을 지나 왕의 왕좌에 앉았다. 경비병들은 곧 정신을 차리고 안으로 들어가 괴물을 향해 소리치며 (a) 그에게 왕좌에서 내려올 것을 요구했다.

(D)

경비병들이 나쁜 말을 사용할 때마다, 그 괴물은 더 추해졌고, 더 냄새가 났다. 경비병들은 한층 더 화가 났다. 그들은 그 괴물을 겁주어 궁전에서 쫓아내려고 칼을 휘두르기 시작했다. 하지만 (e) 그는 그저 점점 더 커져서 결국 방 전체를 차지했다. 그는 그 어느 때보다 더 추해졌고, 더 냄새가 났다.

(B)
마침내 왕이 돌아왔다. 그는 현명하고 친절했으며, 무슨 일이 일어나고 있는지 알았다. 그는 어떻게 해야 할지 알고 있었다. 그는 미소를 지으며 그 괴물에게 "나의 궁전에 온 것을 환영하오!"라고 말했다. 왕은 그 괴물에게 (b) 그가 커피 한 잔을 원하는지 물었다. 괴물은 그 커피를 마시면서 더 작아지기 시작했다.

(C)
왕은 (c) 그에게 약간의 테이크아웃 피자와 감자튀김을 제안했다. 경비병들은 즉시 피자를 시켰다. 그 괴물은 왕의 친절한 행동에 몸이 계속 더 작아졌다. 그리고 나서 (d) 그는 괴물에게 전신 마사지를 제공해 주었다. 경비병들이 편안한 마사지를 도와주자 그 괴물은 매우 작아졌다. 그 괴물에게 또 한 번의 친절한 행동을 베풀자, 그는 바로 사라졌다.

- approach ⓥ 다가오다, 접근하다
- ugly ⓐ 추한
- in shock 충격을 받아
- come to one's senses 정신을 차리다
- get off ~을 떠나다
- take-out ⓐ 사서 가지고 가는
- gesture ⓝ 몸짓, (감정의) 표시, 표현
- brandish ⓥ 휘두르다
- take up ~을 차지하다
- gate ⓝ 문
- smelly ⓐ 냄새 나는, 악취가 나는
- throne ⓝ 왕좌
- shout at ~을 향해 소리치다
- wise ⓐ 현명한
- call for ~을 시키다, ~을 요구하다
- tiny ⓐ 아주 작은
- scare away ~을 겁주어 쫓아버리다
- than ever 그 어느 때보다

구문 풀이

(A) 5행 The guards soon came to their senses, went in, and shouted at the monster, demanding that he (should) get off the throne.
요구 동사 / 생략 / 동사원형

(D) 4행 But he just grew bigger and bigger, eventually taking up the whole room.
「비교급＋and＋비교급 : 점점 더 ~한」 / 분사구문(그리고 ~하다)

---

43 글의 순서 파악 정답률 77% | 정답 ④

주어진 글 (A)에 이어질 내용을 순서에 맞게 배열한 것으로 가장 적절한 것은?
① (B) − (D) − (C)
② (C) − (B) − (D)
③ (C) − (D) − (B)
✔④ (D) − (B) − (C)
⑤ (D) − (C) − (B)

Why? 왜 정답일까?

왕이 없을 때 어느 괴물이 왕좌에 대신 앉아버렸다는 내용의 (A) 뒤에는, 경비병들이 괴물을 위협하며 쫓아내려 했으나 오히려 괴물의 몸집이 점점 커질 뿐이었다는 내용의 (D), 왕이 돌아와서는 사태를 파악하고 괴물에게 친절을 베풀기 시작했다는 내용의 (B), 왕이 음식과 마사지 등 친절한 행동을 보탤 때마다 괴물이 점점 작아져서 마침내는 없어졌다는 내용의 (C)가 차례로 연결되어야 한다. 따라서 글의 순서로 가장 적절한 것은 ④ '(D) − (B) − (C)'이다.

---

44 지칭 추론 정답률 75% | 정답 ④

밑줄 친 (a) ~ (e) 중에서 가리키는 대상이 나머지 넷과 다른 것은?
① (a) ② (b) ③ (c) ✔④ (d) ⑤ (e)

Why? 왜 정답일까?

(a), (b), (c), (e)는 the monster, (d)는 the king을 가리키므로, (a) ~ (e) 중에서 가리키는 대상이 다른 하나는 ④ '(d)'이다.

---

45 세부 내용 파악 정답률 83% | 정답 ④

윗글에 관한 내용으로 적절하지 않은 것은?
① 왕이 없는 동안 괴물이 궁전 문으로 접근했다.
② 왕은 미소를 지으며 괴물에게 환영한다고 말했다.
③ 왕의 친절한 행동에 괴물의 몸이 계속 더 작아졌다.
✔④ 경비병들은 괴물을 마사지해 주기를 거부했다.
⑤ 경비병들은 겁을 주어 괴물을 쫓아내려 했다.

Why? 왜 정답일까?

(C) 'As the guards helped with the relaxing massage, ~'에서 경비병들은 괴물을 마사지해주기를 거부하지 않고, 오히려 마사지를 도와줬음을 알 수 있다. 따라서 내용과 일치하지 않는 것은 ④ '경비병들은 괴물을 마사지해 주기를 거부했다.'이다.

Why? 왜 오답일까?

① (A) 'While the king was away, a monster approached the gates of the palace.'의 내용과 일치한다.
② (B) 'He smiled and said to the monster, "Welcome to my palace!"'의 내용과 일치한다.
③ (C) 'The monster continued to get smaller with the king's kind gestures.'의 내용과 일치한다.
⑤ (D) 'The guards ~ began to brandish their swords to scare the monster away from the palace.'의 내용과 일치한다.

A	B	C	D
01 갈등	01 settle down	01 ⓒ	01 ⓗ
02 광물	02 efficiently	02 ⓗ	02 ⓢ
03 탄수화물	03 contain	03 ⓑ	03 ⓔ
04 토론	04 scare away	04 ⓜ	04 ⓜ
05 불쾌한	05 discover	05 ⓘ	05 ⓕ
06 다가오다, 접근하다	06 gene	06 ⓐ	06 ⓘ
07 보장하다	07 randomly	07 ⓙ	07 ⓞ
08 ~을 차지하다	08 constant	08 ⓕ	08 ⓕ
09 기꺼이	09 species	09 ⓙ	09 ⓚ
10 방출하다	10 organize	10 ⓞ	10 ⓑ
11 냄새	11 jealous	11 ⓠ	11 ⓐ
12 좌절한	12 motivation	12 ⓓ	12 ⓒ
13 자신감 있는	13 estimate	13 ⓚ	13 ⓓ
14 발생하다	14 wander	14 ⓟ	14 ⓘ
15 ~로 결합되다	15 principle	15 ⓔ	15 ⓖ
16 ~을 처리하다	16 impression	16 ⓕ	16 ⓙ
17 수용하다, 받아들이다	17 empathy	17 ⓝ	17 ⓘ
18 ~에 적응하다	18 habitat	18 ⓢ	18 ⓟ
19 유지하다	19 expectation	19 ⓖ	19 ⓠ
20 ~을 시키다, 요구하다	20 structure	20 ⓘ	20 ⓝ

• 정답 •

18 ② 19 ③ 20 ⑤ 21 ⑤ 22 ① 23 ④ 24 ② 25 ⑤ 26 ③ 27 ④ 28 ⑤ 29 ③ 30 ⑤ 31 ② 32 ③
33 ① 34 ① 35 ④ 36 ③ 37 ② 38 ④ 39 ② 40 ① 41 ⑤ 42 ⑤ 43 ② 44 ④ 45 ⑤

★ 표기된 문항은 [등급을 가르는 문제]에 해당하는 문항입니다.

---

18 모금 음악회 참석 요청   정답률 87% | 정답 ②

다음 글의 목적으로 가장 적절한 것은?

① 합창 대회 결과를 공지하려고
✔ 모금 음악회 참석을 요청하려고
③ 음악회 개최 장소를 예약하려고
④ 합창곡 선정에 조언을 구하려고
⑤ 기부금 사용 내역을 보고하려고

Dear Ms. Robinson,
Robinson 씨께,
The Warblers Choir is happy to announce / that we are invited to compete in the International Young Choir Competition.
Warblers 합창단은 알려드리게 되어 기쁩니다. / 저희가 국제 청년 합창 대회에서 실력을 겨루도록 초청받은 사실을
The competition takes place in London on May 20.
대회는 5월 20일 런던에서 열립니다.
Though we wish to participate in the event, / we do not have the necessary funds to travel to London.
비록 저희는 대회에 참가하고 싶지만, / 저희에게는 런던에 가는 데 필요한 자금이 없습니다.
So we are kindly asking you to support us / by coming to our fundraising concert.
그래서 귀하께서 저희를 후원해 주시기를 정중하게 부탁드립니다. / 저희 모금 음악회에 참석하셔서
It will be held on March 26.
음악회는 3월 26일에 개최될 것입니다.
In this concert, / we shall be able to show you / how big our passion for music is.
이 음악회에서 / 저희는 귀하께 보여드릴 수 있을 것입니다. / 음악에 대한 저희의 열정이 얼마나 큰지
Thank you in advance / for your kind support and help.
미리 감사드립니다. / 귀하의 친절한 후원과 도움에 대해
Sincerely, // Arnold Reynolds
Arnold Reynolds 드림

Robinson 씨께,
저희 Warblers 합창단이 국제 청년 합창 대회에서 실력을 겨루도록 초청받은 사실을 알려드리게 되어 기쁩니다. 대회는 5월 20일 런던에서 열립니다. 비록 저희는 대회에 참가하고 싶지만, 런던에 가는 데 필요한 자금이 없습니다. 그래서 귀하께서 저희 모금 음악회에 참석하셔서 저희를 후원해 주시기를 정중하게 부탁드립니다. 음악회는 3월 26일에 개최될 것입니다. 이 음악회에서 음악에 대한 저희의 열정이 얼마나 큰지 귀하께 보여드릴 수 있을 것입니다. 귀하의 친절한 후원과 도움에 대해 미리 감사드립니다.
Arnold Reynolds 드림

Why? 왜 정답일까?

'So we are kindly asking you to support us by coming to our fundraising concert.' 에서 모금 음악회에 참석하여 후원을 해주기를 바란다는 내용이 제시되므로, 글의 목적으로 가장 적절한 것은 ② '모금 음악회 참석을 요청하려고'이다.

● compete in ~에서 경쟁하다
● support ⓥ 후원하다 ⓝ 지지, 후원
● passion ⓝ 열정
● take place (행사 등이) 열리다
● fundraising ⓝ 모금
● in advance 미리

구문 풀이

8행 In this concert, we shall be able to show you how big our passion for music is.
　　　　　　　　　　　　　　　　4형식　간접　　　직접목적어(간접의문문)
　　　　　　　　　　　　　　　　동사　목적어

---

19 학업 최우수상을 받게 되어 기뻐하는 Zoe   정답률 80% | 정답 ③

다음 글에 드러난 Zoe의 심경 변화로 가장 적절한 것은?

① hopeful → disappointed
　기대하는　　실망한
② guilty → confident
　죄책감을 느끼는　자신 있는
✔ nervous → delighted
　긴장한　　　기쁜
④ angry → calm
　화난　　평온한
⑤ relaxed → proud
　느긋한　　자랑스러운

The principal stepped on stage.
교장 선생님이 무대 위로 올라갔다.
"Now, I present this year's top academic award / to the student who has achieved the highest placing."
"이제, 저는 올해의 학업 최우수상을 수여합니다. / 최고 등수를 차지한 학생에게"
He smiled at the row of seats / where twelve finalists had gathered.
그는 좌석 열을 향해 미소를 지었다. / 열두 명의 최종 입상 후보자가 모여 있는
Zoe wiped a sweaty hand on her handkerchief / and glanced at the other finalists.
Zoe는 땀에 젖은 손을 손수건에 문질러 닦고는 / 나머지 다른 최종 입상 후보자들을 힐끗 보았다.
They all looked as pale and uneasy as herself.
그들은 모두 그녀만큼 창백하고 불안해 보였다.
Zoe and one of the other finalists / had won first placing in four subjects / so it came down / to how teachers ranked their hard work and confidence.

Zoe와 나머지 다른 최종 입상 후보자 중 한 명이 / 네 개 과목에서 1위를 차지했으므로, / 이제 그것은 좁혀졌다. / 그들의 노력과 자신감을 선생님들이 어떻게 평가하는가로
"The Trophy for General Excellence / is awarded to Miss Zoe Perry," / the principal declared.
"전체 최우수상을 위한 트로피는 / Zoe Perry 양에게 수여됩니다."라고 / 교장 선생님이 공표했다.
"Could Zoe step this way, please?"
"Zoe는 이리로 나와 주시겠습니까?"
Zoe felt as if she were in heaven.
Zoe는 마치 천국에 있는 기분이었다.
She walked into the thunder of applause with a big smile.
그녀는 활짝 웃음을 지으며 우레와 같은 박수갈채를 받으며 걸어갔다.

교장 선생님이 무대 위로 올라갔다. "이제, 저는 최고 등수를 차지한 학생에게 올해의 학업 최우수상을 수여하겠습니다." 그는 열두 명의 최종 입상 후보자가 모여 있는 좌석 열을 향해 미소를 지었다. Zoe는 땀에 젖은 손을 손수건에 문질러 닦고는 나머지 다른 최종 입상 후보자들을 힐끗 보았다. 그들은 모두 그녀만큼 창백하고 불안해 보였다. Zoe와 나머지 다른 최종 입상 후보자 중 한 명이 네 개 과목에서 1위를 차지했으므로, 선생님들이 그들의 노력과 자신감을 어떻게 평가하는가로 좁혀졌다. "전체 최우수상 트로피는 Zoe Perry 양에게 수여됩니다."라고 교장 선생님이 공표했다. "Zoe는 이리로 나와 주시겠습니까?" Zoe는 마치 천국에 있는 기분이었다. 그녀는 활짝 웃음을 지으며 우레와 같은 박수갈채를 받으며 걸어갔다.

Why? 왜 정답일까?

학업 최우수상 수상자 발표를 앞두고 긴장했던(Zoe wiped a sweaty hand ~. ~ pale and uneasy as herself.) Zoe가 수상자로 호명된 뒤 기뻐했다(Zoe felt as if she were in heaven. She ~ with a big smile.)는 내용의 글이므로, Zoe의 심경 변화로 가장 적절한 것은 ③ '긴장한 → 기쁜'이다.

● row ⓝ 줄, 열
● gather ⓥ 모이다
● sweaty ⓐ 땀에 젖은
● pale ⓐ 창백한
● confidence ⓝ 자신감
● finalist ⓝ 최종 후보자, 결승 진출자
● wipe ⓥ 닦다
● glance at ~을 흘긋 보다
● uneasy ⓐ 불안한
● applause ⓝ 박수 갈채

구문 풀이

10행 Zoe felt as if she were in heaven.
「as if + 주어 + 과거 동사 : (실제로 ~이지 않지만) 마치 ~인 것처럼」

---

20 작은 일부터 잘 처리하기   정답률 87% | 정답 ⑤

다음 글에서 필자가 주장하는 바로 가장 적절한 것은?

① 숙면을 위해서는 침대를 깔끔하게 관리해야 한다.
② 일의 효율성을 높이려면 협동심을 발휘해야 한다.
③ 올바른 습관을 기르려면 정해진 규칙을 따라야 한다.
④ 건강을 유지하기 위해서는 기상 시간이 일정해야 한다.
✔ 큰일을 잘 이루려면 작은 일부터 제대로 수행해야 한다.

When I was in the army, / my instructors would show up in my barracks room, / and the first thing they would inspect / was our bed.
내가 군대에 있을 때, / 교관들이 나의 병영 생활관에 모습을 드러내곤 했었는데, / 그들이 맨 먼저 검사하곤 했던 것은 / 우리의 침대였다.
It was a simple task, / but every morning / we were required / to make our bed to perfection.
단순한 일이었지만, / 매일 아침 / 우리는 요구받았다. / 침대를 완벽하게 정돈하도록
It seemed a little ridiculous at the time, / but the wisdom of this simple act / has been proven to me many times over.
그것은 그 당시에는 약간 우스꽝스럽게 보였지만, / 이 단순한 행위의 지혜는 / 여러 차례 거듭하여 나에게 증명되었다.
If you make your bed every morning, / you will have accomplished the first task of the day.
그것은 여러분이 매일 아침 침대를 정돈한다면, / 여러분은 하루의 첫 번째 과업을 성취한 것이 된다.
It will give you a small sense of pride / and it will encourage you to do another task and another.
그것은 여러분에게 작은 자존감을 주고, / 그것은 또 다른 과업을 잇따라 이어가도록 용기를 줄 것이다.
By the end of the day, / that one task completed / will have turned into many tasks completed.
하루가 끝날 때쯤에는, / 완수된 그 하나의 과업이 / 여러 개의 완수된 과업으로 변해 있을 것이다.
If you can't do little things right, / you will never do the big things right.
여러분이 작은 일들을 제대로 할 수 없으면, / 여러분은 결코 큰일들을 제대로 할 수 없을 것이다.

내가 군대에 있을 때, 교관들이 나의 병영 생활관에 모습을 드러내곤 했었는데, 그들이 맨 먼저 검사하곤 했던 것은 우리의 침대였다. 단순한 일이었지만, 매일 아침 우리는 침대를 완벽하게 정돈하도록 요구받았다. 그 당시에는 약간 우스꽝스럽게 보였지만, 이 단순한 행위의 지혜는 여러 차례 거듭하여 나에게 증명되었다. 여러분이 매일 아침 침대를 정돈한다면, 여러분은 하루의 첫 번째 과업을 성취한 것이 된다. 그것은 여러분에게 작은 자존감을 주고, 또 다른 과업을 잇따라 이어가도록 용기를 줄 것이다. 하루가 끝날 때쯤에는, 완수된 그 하나의 과업이 여러 개의 완수된 과업으로 변해 있을 것이다. 작은 일들을 제대로 할 수 없으면, 여러분은 결코 큰일들을 제대로 할 수 없을 것이다.

Why? 왜 정답일까?

매일 잠자리 정돈부터 잘해야 했던 군대 시절 이야기를 토대로 작은 일부터 잘 해내야 큰일을 처리할 수 있다(If you can't do little things right, you will never do the big things right.)는 결론을 이끌어내는 글이다. 따라서 필자의 주장으로 가장 적절한 것은 ⑤ '큰일을 잘 이루려면 작은 일부터 제대로 수행해야 한다.'이다.

● inspect ⓥ 조사하다
● make the bed 잠자리를 정돈하다
● wisdom ⓝ 지혜
● turn into ~로 바뀌다
● task ⓝ 일, 과업, 과제
● ridiculous ⓐ 우스꽝스러운
● complete ⓥ 완수하다

구문 풀이

6행 If you make your bed every morning, you will have accomplished the first
　　　접속사(조건)　동사(현재)　　　　　　　　　　　　　　　동사(미래완료)
task of the day.

21 적극적으로 구직 활동하기

정답률 58% | 정답 ⑤

밑줄 친 Leave those activities to the rest of the sheep이 다음 글에서 의미하는 바로 가장 적절한 것은? [3점]

① Try to understand other job-seekers' feelings.
  다른 구직자들의 심정을 이해하려고 노력해보라.
② Keep calm and stick to your present position.
  평정심을 유지하고 현재 입장을 지키라.
③ Don't be scared of the job-seeking competition.
  구직 경쟁을 두려워하지 말라.
④ Send occasional emails to your future employers.
  미래 고용주들에게 가끔 이메일을 보내라.
✔ Be more active to stand out from other job-seekers.
  다른 구직자들보다 두드러지기 위해 더 적극적으로 하라.

A job search is not a passive task.
구직 활동은 수동적인 일이 아니다.

When you are searching, / you are not browsing, / nor are you "just looking".
여러분이 구직 활동을 할 때, / 여러분은 이것저것 훑어보고 다니지 않으며 / '그냥 구경만 하지'도 않는다.

Browsing is not an effective way / to reach a goal / you claim to want to reach.
훑어보고 다니는 것은 효과적인 방법이 아니다. / 목표에 도달할 수 있는 / 여러분이 도달하기를 원한다고 주장하는

If you are acting with purpose, / if you are serious about anything you chose to do, / then you need to be direct, / focused / and whenever possible, / clever.
만약 여러분이 목적을 가지고 행동한다면, / 만약 여러분이 하고자 선택한 어떤 것에 대해 진지하다면, / 여러분은 직접적이고, / 집중해야 하며, / 가능한 모든 경우에, / 영리해야 한다.

Everyone else searching for a job / has the same goal, / competing for the same jobs.
일자리를 찾는 다른 모든 사람이 / 같은 목표를 지니고 있으며, / 같은 일자리를 얻기 위해 경쟁한다.

You must do more than the rest of the herd.
여러분은 그 무리의 나머지 사람들보다 더 많은 것을 해야 한다.

Regardless of how long it may take you / to find and get the job you want, / being proactive will logically get you results faster / than if you rely only on browsing online job boards / and emailing an occasional resume.
여러분에게 얼마나 오랜 시간이 걸리든 간에, / 원하는 직업을 찾아서 얻는 데 / 진취적인 것이 논리적으로 여러분에게 더 빨리 결과를 가져다줄 것이다. / 여러분이 온라인 취업 게시판을 검색하는 것에만 의존하는 것보다는 / 그리고 가끔 이력서를 이메일로 보내는 것

Leave those activities to the rest of the sheep.
그런 활동들은 나머지 양들이 하도록 남겨 두라.

구직 활동은 수동적인 일이 아니다. 구직 활동을 할 때, 여러분은 이것저것 훑어보고 다니지 않으며 '그냥 구경만 하지'도 않는다. 훑어보고 다니는 것은 여러분이 도달하기를 원한다고 주장하는 목표에 도달할 수 있는 효과적인 방법이 아니다. 만약 여러분이 목적을 가지고 행동한다면, 하고자 선택한 어떤 것에 대해 진지하다면, 여러분은 직접적이고, 집중해야 하며, 가능한 한 영리해야 한다. 일자리를 찾는 다른 모든 사람이 같은 목표를 지니고 있으며, 같은 일자리를 얻기 위해 경쟁한다. 여러분은 그 무리의 나머지 사람들보다 더 많은 것을 해야 한다. 원하는 직업을 찾아서 얻는 데 얼마나 오랜 시간이 걸리든 간에, 온라인 취업 게시판을 검색하고 가끔 이력서를 이메일로 보내는 것에만 의존하는 것보다는 진취적인 것이 논리적으로 여러분이 더 빨리 결과를 얻도록 해줄 것이다. 그런 활동들은 나머지 양들이 하도록 남겨 두라.

Why? 왜 정답일까?

마지막 문장 바로 앞에서 온라인 취업 게시판을 검색하고 가끔 이메일을 보내는 것보다 더 적극적인 행동을 해야 한다(being proactive will ~ get you results faster)고 언급한 뒤, 마지막 문장에서 비교적 소극적인 행동은 남들더러 하게 두라고 말하며 적극적인 행동의 필요성을 다시금 주장한다. 따라서 밑줄 친 부분의 의미로 가장 적절한 것은 ⑤ '다른 구직자들보다 두드러지기 위해 더 적극적으로 하라.'이다.

- passive ⓐ 수동적인
- herd ⓝ 무리
- proactive ⓐ 상황을 앞서서 주도하는
- occasional ⓐ 가끔씩의
- stand out from ~에서 두드러지다
- claim ⓥ 주장하다
- regardless of ~와 상관없이
- logically ⓐ 논리적으로
- resume ⓝ 이력서

구문 풀이

1행 When you are searching, you are not browsing, nor are you "just looking".
「nor+동사+주어 : ~도 않다(도치 구문)」

---

22 수면의 중요한 기능

정답률 92% | 정답 ①

다음 글의 요지로 가장 적절한 것은?

✔ 수면은 건강 유지와 최상의 기능 발휘에 도움이 된다.
② 업무량이 증가하면 필요한 수면 시간도 증가한다.
③ 균형 잡힌 식단을 유지하면 뇌 기능이 향상된다.
④ 불면증은 주위 사람들에게 부정적인 영향을 미친다.
⑤ 꿈의 내용은 깨어 있는 시간 동안의 경험을 반영한다.

Many people view sleep as merely a "down time" / when their brain shuts off and their body rests.
많은 사람이 수면을 그저 '가동되지 않는 시간'으로 본다. / 그들의 뇌는 멈추고 신체는 쉬는

In a rush to meet work, school, family, or household responsibilities, / people cut back on their sleep, / thinking it won't be a problem, / because all of these other activities seem much more important.
일, 학교, 가족, 또는 가정의 책임을 다하기 위해 서두르는 와중에, / 사람들은 수면 시간을 줄이고, / 그것이 문제가 되지 않을 것으로 생각하는데, / 왜냐하면 이러한 모든 다른 활동들이 훨씬 더 중요해 보이기 때문이다.

But research reveals / that a number of vital tasks carried out during sleep / help to maintain good health / and enable people to function at their best.
하지만 연구는 밝히고 있다. / 수면 중에 수행되는 많은 매우 중요한 과업이 / 건강을 유지하는 데 도움이 되고 / 사람들이 최상의 수준으로 기능할 수 있게 해 준다는 것을

While you sleep, / your brain is hard at work / forming the pathways / necessary for learning and creating memories and new insights.
여러분이 잠을 자는 동안, / 여러분의 뇌는 열심히 일하고 있다. / 경로를 형성하느라 / 학습하고 기억과 새로운 통찰을 만드는 데 필요한

Without enough sleep, / you can't focus and pay attention / or respond quickly.
충분한 수면이 없다면, / 여러분은 정신을 집중하고 주의를 기울이거나 / 빠르게 반응할 수 없다.

A lack of sleep may even cause mood problems.
수면 부족은 심지어 감정 문제를 일으킬 수도 있다.

In addition, / growing evidence shows / that a continuous lack of sleep / increases the risk for developing serious diseases.
게다가, / 점점 더 많은 증거가 보여 준다. / 계속된 수면 부족이 / 심각한 질병의 발생 위험을 증가시킨다는 것을

많은 사람이 수면을 그저 뇌는 멈추고 신체는 쉬는 '가동되지 않는 시간'으로 본다. 일, 학교, 가족, 또는 가정의 책임을 다하기 위해 서두르는 와중에, 사람들은 수면 시간을 줄이고, 그것이 문제가 되지 않을 것으로 생각하는데, 왜냐하면 이러한 모든 다른 활동들이 훨씬 더 중요해 보이기 때문이다. 하지만 연구는 수면 중에 수행되는 매우 중요한 여러 과업이 건강을 유지하는 데 도움이 되고 사람들이 최상의 수준으로 기능할 수 있게 해 준다는 것을 밝히고 있다. 잠을 자는 동안, 여러분의 뇌는 학습하고 기억과 새로운 통찰을 만드는 데 필요한 경로를 형성하느라 열심히 일하고 있다. 충분한 수면이 없다면, 여러분은 정신을 집중하고 주의를 기울이거나 빠르게 반응할 수 없다. 수면이 부족하면 심지어 감정 (조절) 문제를 일으킬 수도 있다. 게다가, 계속된 수면 부족이 심각한 질병의 발생 위험을 증가시킨다는 것을 점점 더 많은 증거가 보여 준다.

Why? 왜 정답일까?

주제를 제시하는 'But ~ a number of vital tasks carried out during sleep help to maintain good health and enable people to function at their best.'에서 수면 중 이루어지는 많은 일이 건강 및 기능 유지에 도움이 된다고 하므로, 글의 요지로 가장 적절한 것은 ① '수면은 건강 유지와 최상의 기능 발휘에 도움이 된다.'이다.

- view A as B A를 B로 보다
- down time 정지 시간, 휴식 시간
- carry out ~을 수행하다
- develop a disease 병을 키우다
- merely ⓐ 그저, 단순히
- cut back on ~을 줄이다
- insight ⓝ 통찰력

구문 풀이

5행 But research reveals that a number of vital tasks carried out during sleep
접속사(~것) | 주어(a number of + 복수 명사 : 많은 ~) | 과거분사구
help to maintain good health and enable people to function at their best.
동사1 | 목적어 | 동사2 | 목적어 | 목적격 보어

---

23 미래 날씨 예측에 영향을 받는 인간의 생활

정답률 63% | 정답 ④

다음 글의 주제로 가장 적절한 것은? [3점]

① new technologies dealing with climate change
  기후 변화에 대처하는 신기술
② difficulties in predicting the weather correctly
  정확한 날씨 예측의 어려움
③ weather patterns influenced by rising temperatures
  온도 상승에 영향을 받는 날씨 패턴
✔ knowledge of the climate widely affecting our lives
  우리 삶에 광범위하게 영향을 미치는 기후에 관한 지식
⑤ traditional wisdom helping our survival in harsh climates
  혹독한 기후에서 우리의 생존을 돕는 전통적 지혜

The whole of human society / operates on knowing the future weather.
전체 인간 사회는 / 미래의 날씨를 아는 것을 기반으로 운영된다.

For example, / farmers in India know / when the monsoon rains will come next year / and so they know when to plant the crops.
예를 들어, / 인도의 농부들은 알고, / 내년에 몬순 장마가 올 시기를 / 그래서 그들은 작물을 심을 시기를 안다.

Farmers in Indonesia know / there are two monsoon rains each year, / so next year they can have two harvests.
인도네시아의 농부들은 알고, / 매년 몬순 장마가 두 번 있다는 것을 / 그래서 이듬해에 그들은 수확을 두 번 할 수 있다.

This is based on their knowledge of the past, / as the monsoons have always come / at about the same time each year in living memory.
이것은 과거에 대한 그들의 지식에 기반을 두고 있는데, / 몬순은 항상 왔기 때문이다. / 살아 있는 기억 속에서 매년 거의 같은 시기에

But the need to predict goes deeper than this; / it influences every part of our lives.
그러나 예측할 필요는 이것보다 더욱더 깊어지는데 / 그것은 우리 생활의 모든 부분에 영향을 미치기 때문이다.

Our houses, roads, railways, airports, offices, and so on / are all designed for the local climate.
우리의 집, 도로, 철도, 공항, 사무실 등은 / 모두 지역의 기후에 맞추어 설계된다.

For example, / in England all the houses have central heating, / as the outside temperature is usually below 20°C, / but no air-conditioning / as temperatures rarely go beyond 26°C, / while in Australia the opposite is true: / most houses have air-conditioning but rarely central heating.
예를 들어, / 영국에서는 모든 집은 중앙 난방을 갖추고 있지만, / 외부의 기온이 대체로 섭씨 20도 미만이기 때문에 / 냉방기는 없다. / 기온이 섭씨 26도 위로 올라가는 일은 거의 없어서 / 호주에서는 그 정반대가 사실인 반면에 / 대부분의 집은 냉방기를 갖추었지만 중앙 난방은 거의 없다.

전체 인간 사회는 미래의 날씨를 아는 것을 기반으로 운영된다. 예를 들어, 인도의 농부들은 내년에 몬순 장마가 올 시기를 알고, 그래서 그들은 작물을 심을 시기를 안다. 인도네시아의 농부들은 매년 몬순 장마가 두 번 있다는 것을 알고, 그래서 이듬해에 그들은 수확을 두 번 할 수 있다. 이것은 과거에 대한 그들의 지식에 기반을 두고 있는데, 살아 있는 기억 속에서 몬순은 매년 항상 거의 같은 시기에 왔기 때문이다. 그러나 예측할 필요는 이것보다 더욱더 깊어지는데, 그것은 우리 생활의 모든 부분에 영향을 미치기 때문이다. 우리의 집, 도로, 철도, 공항, 사무실 등은 모두 지역의 기후에 맞추어 설계된다. 예를 들어, 영국에서는 외부의 기온이 대체로 섭씨 20도 미만이기 때문에 모든 집은 중앙 난방을 갖추고 있지만, 기온이 섭씨 26도 위로 올라가는 일은 거의 없어서 냉방기는 없는 반면, 호주에서는 그 정반대이어서, 대부분의 집은 냉방기를 갖추었지만 중앙 난방은 거의 없다.

Why? 왜 정답일까?

첫 문장에서 인간 사회는 미래 날씨 예측에 기반하여 운영된다(The whole of human society operates on knowing the future weather.)는 중심 내용을 제시하는 것으로 보아, 글의 주제로 가장 적절한 것은 ④ '우리 삶에 광범위하게 영향을 미치는 기후에 관한 지식'이다.

- monsoon ⓝ (동남아 여름철의) 몬순, 우기, 장마
- predict ⓥ 예측하다
- harsh ⓐ 혹독한
- harvest ⓝ 수확
- influence ⓥ 영향을 미치다

구문 풀이

2행 For example, farmers in India know when the monsoon rains will come
　　　　　주어1　　　　　　　　동사1　　　　　　　목적어1(간접의문문)
next year and so they know when to plant the crops.
　　　　　　　주어2　　동사2　　목적어2(의문사 + to부정사)

---

24 감정을 인식하고 명명할 수 있는 능력　　　　　정답률 64% | 정답 ②

다음 글의 제목으로 가장 적절한 것은?

① True Friendship Endures Emotional Arguments – 진정한 우정은 감정적인 다툼을 견뎌낸다
✓② Detailed Labeling of Emotions Is Beneficial – 감정에 상세하게 이름을 붙이는 것은 이롭다
③ Labeling Emotions: Easier Said Than Done – 감정에 이름 붙이기: 말하기는 쉬워도 행하기는 어렵다
④ Categorize and Label Tasks for Efficiency – 효율성을 위해 작업을 분류하고 이름 붙이라
⑤ Be Brave and Communicate Your Needs – 용기를 갖고 여러분의 요구를 전달하라

Our ability to accurately recognize and label emotions / is often referred to as *emotional granularity*.
감정을 정확하게 인식하고 그것에 이름을 붙일 수 있는 우리의 능력은 / 흔히 *감정 입자도*라고 불린다.
In the words of Harvard psychologist Susan David, / "Learning to label emotions / with a more nuanced vocabulary / can be absolutely transformative."
Harvard 대학의 심리학자인 Susan David의 말에 의하면, / "이름을 붙이는 법을 배우는 것은 / 감정에 더 미묘한 차이가 있는 어휘로 / 절대적으로 변화시킬 수 있다."
David explains / that if we don't have a rich emotional vocabulary, / it is difficult / to communicate our needs / and to get the support that we need from others.
David는 설명한다. / 우리가 풍부한 감정적인 어휘를 갖고 있지 않으면, / 어렵다고 / 우리의 욕구를 전달하는 것이 / 그리고 우리가 필요로 하는 지지를 다른 사람들로부터 얻는 것이
But those / who are able to distinguish between a range of various emotions / "do much, much better / at managing the ups and downs of ordinary existence / than those who see everything in black and white."
그러나 사람들은 / 광범위한 다양한 감정을 구별할 수 있는 / "훨씬, 훨씬 더 잘한다. / 평범한 존재로 사는 중에 겪는 좋은 일들과 궂은 일들을 다스리는 일을 / 모든 것을 흑백 논리로 보는 사람들보다"
In fact, / research shows / that the process of labeling emotional experience / is related to greater emotion regulation and psychosocial well-being.
사실, / 연구 결과가 보여 준다. / 감정적인 경험에 이름을 붙이는 과정은 / 더 큰 감정 통제 및 심리 사회적인 행복과 관련되어 있다는 것을

감정을 정확하게 인식하고 그것에 이름을 붙일 수 있는 우리의 능력은 흔히 *감정 입자도*라고 불린다. Harvard 대학의 심리학자인 Susan David의 말에 의하면, "감정에 더 미묘한 차이가 있는 어휘로 이름을 붙이는 법을 배우는 것은 절대적으로 (사람을) 변화시킬 수 있다." David는 우리가 풍부한 감정적인 어휘를 갖고 있지 않으면, 우리의 욕구를 전달하고 다른 사람들로부터 우리가 필요로 하는 지지를 얻는 것이 어렵다고 설명한다. 그러나 광범위한 다양한 감정을 구별할 수 있는 사람들은 "모든 것을 흑백 논리로 보는 사람들보다 평범한 존재로 사는 중에 겪는 좋은 일들과 궂은 일들을 다스리는 일을 훨씬, 훨씬 더 잘한다." 사실, 감정적인 경험에 이름을 붙이는 과정은 더 큰 감정 통제 및 심리 사회적인 행복과 관련되어 있다는 것을 연구 결과가 보여 준다.

Why? 왜 정답일까?

마지막 문장에 따르면 감정적인 경험에 이름을 붙이는 것은 감정을 더 잘 통제하고 심리 사회적으로 더 큰 행복감을 느끼는 것과 관련되어 있다(~ the process of labeling emotional experience is related to greater emotion regulation and psychosocial well-being.)고 하므로, 글의 제목으로 가장 적절한 것은 ② '감정에 상세하게 이름을 붙이는 것은 이롭다'이다.

● accurately [ad] 정확하게　　● refer to A as B A를 B라고 부르다
● absolutely [ad] 절대적으로　　● transformative [a] 변화시키는
● communicate [v] 전달하다　　● distinguish [v] 구별하다
● ups and downs 좋은 일과 궂은 일, 오르락내리락　　● existence [n] 존재
● regulation [n] 통제　　● psychosocial [a] 심리사회적인

구문 풀이

1행 Our ability to accurately recognize and label emotions is often referred to
　　　주어　　　　　　　형용사적 용법　　　　　　　　　동사(refer to A as B의 수동태)
as *emotional granularity*.

---

25 온라인 강의와 학습 자료를 이용한 영국인들의 비율　　　정답률 68% | 정답 ⑤

다음 도표의 내용과 일치하지 않는 것은?

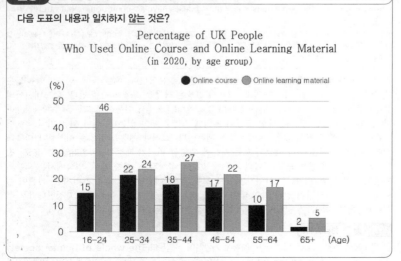

Percentage of UK People
Who Used Online Course and Online Learning Material
(in 2020, by age group)

● Online course ● Online learning material

Age	16-24	25-34	35-44	45-54	55-64	65+
Online course	15	22	18	17	10	2
Online learning material	46	24	27	22	17	5

The above graph shows the percentage of people in the UK / who used online courses and online learning materials, / by age group / in 2020.
위 도표는 영국 사람들의 비율을 보여 준다. / 온라인 강의와 온라인 학습 자료를 이용한 / 연령 집단별로 / 2020년도에
① In each age group, / the percentage of people / who used online learning materials / was higher than that of people / who used online courses.

각 연령 집단에서 / 사람들의 비율이 / 온라인 학습 자료를 이용한 / 사람들의 비율보다 더 높았다. / 온라인 강의를 이용한
② The 25 – 34 age group / had the highest percentage of people / who used online courses / in all the age groups.
25세에서 34세 연령 집단에서, / 차이는 /사람들의 비율과 / 온라인 강의를 이용한 / 모든 연령 집단 중
③ Those aged 65 and older / were the least likely to use online courses / among the six age groups.
65세 이상인 사람들이 / 온라인 강의를 이용할 가능성이 가장 낮았다. / 여섯 개의 연령 집단 가운데서
④ Among the six age groups, / the gap / between the percentage of people / who used online courses / and that of people who used online learning materials / was the greatest in the 16 – 24 age group.
여섯 개의 연령 집단 가운데서, / 차이는 / 사람들의 비율과 / 온라인 강의를 이용한 / 그리고 온라인 학습 자료를 이용한 사람들의 비율 사이의 /16에서 24세 연령 집단에서 가장 컸다.
✓⑤ In each of the 35 – 44, 45 – 54, and 55 – 64 age groups, / more than one in five people / used online learning materials.
35세에서 44세, 45세에서 54세, 55세에서 64세의 각 연령 집단에서 / 다섯 명 중 한 명이 넘는 비율의 사람들이 / 온라인 학습 자료를 이용했다.

위 도표는 2020년도에 온라인 강의와 온라인 학습 자료를 이용한 영국 사람들의 비율을 연령 집단별로 보여 준다. ① 각 연령 집단에서 온라인 학습 자료를 이용한 사람들의 비율이 온라인 강의를 이용한 사람들의 비율보다 더 높았다. ② 모든 연령 집단 중, 25세에서 34세 연령 집단에서 온라인 강의를 이용한 사람들의 비율이 가장 높았다. ③ 여섯 개의 연령 집단 가운데서, 65세 이상인 사람들이 온라인 강의를 이용할 가능성이 가장 낮았다. ④ 여섯 개의 연령 집단 가운데서, 온라인 강의를 이용한 사람들의 비율과 온라인 학습 자료를 이용한 사람들의 비율 차이는 16세에서 24세 연령 집단에서 가장 컸다. ⑤ 35세에서 44세, 45세에서 54세, 55세에서 64세의 각 연령 집단에서 다섯 명 중 한 명이 넘는 비율로 온라인 학습 자료를 이용했다.

Why? 왜 정답일까?

도표에 따르면 55 ~ 64세 집단에서 온라인 학습 자료를 이용한 비율은 17%로, 전체의 5분의 1에 미치지 못했다. 따라서 도표와 일치하지 않는 것은 ⑤이다.

● learning material 학습 자료　　● be the least likely to ~할 가능성이 가장 낮다

---

26 Antonie van Leeuwenhoek의 생애　　　정답률 91% | 정답 ③

Antonie van Leeuwenhoek에 관한 다음 글의 내용과 일치하지 않는 것은?

① 세포 연구로 잘 알려진 과학자였다.　　② 22살에 Delft로 돌아왔다.
✓③ 여러 개의 언어를 알았다.　　④ 유리로 물건을 만드는 방법을 알고 있었다.
⑤ 화가를 고용하여 설명하는 것을 그리게 했다.

「Antonie van Leeuwenhoek was a scientist / well known for his cell research.」 **①의 근거** 일치
Antonie van Leeuwenhoek은 과학자였다. / 세포 연구로 잘 알려진
He was born in Delft, the Netherlands, / on October 24, 1632.
그는 네덜란드 Delft에서 태어났다. / 1632년 10월 24일에
At the age of 16, / he began to learn job skills in Amsterdam.
16살에 / 그는 Amsterdam에서 직업 기술을 배우기 시작했다.
「At the age of 22, / Leeuwenhoek returned to Delft.」 **②의 근거** 일치
22살에 / Leeuwenhoek은 Delft로 돌아왔다.
It wasn't easy for Leeuwenhoek to become a scientist.
Leeuwenhoek이 과학자가 되기는 쉽지 않았다.
「He knew only one language — Dutch —.」 / which was quite unusual for scientists of his time. **③의 근거** 불일치
그는 오직 한 가지 언어, 즉 네덜란드어만을 알고 있었는데, / 그것은 그 당시 과학자들에게는 상당히 드문 것이었다.
But his curiosity was endless, / and he worked hard.
하지만 그의 호기심은 끝이 없었고, / 그는 열심히 노력했다.
He had an important skill.
그에게는 중요한 기술이 있었다.
「He knew how to make things out of glass.」 **④의 근거** 일치
그는 유리로 물건을 만드는 법을 알고 있었다.
This skill came in handy / when he made lenses for his simple microscope.
이 기술은 도움이 되었다. / 그가 자신의 간단한 현미경에 쓰일 렌즈를 만들 때
He saw tiny veins / with blood flowing through them.
그는 미세한 혈관을 보았다. / 그 속에 피가 흐르고 있는
He also saw living bacteria in pond water.
그는 또한 연못 물속에서 살아 있는 박테리아를 보았다.
He paid close attention to the things he saw / and wrote down his observations.
그는 자신이 본 것들에 세심한 주의를 기울였고 / 그가 관찰한 것을 기록했다.
「Since he couldn't draw well, / he hired an artist / to draw pictures of what he described.」 **⑤의 근거** 일치
그가 그림을 잘 그릴 수 없었기 때문에, / 그는 화가를 고용하여 / 자신이 설명하는 것을 그림으로 그리게 했다.

Antonie van Leeuwenhoek은 세포 연구로 잘 알려진 과학자였다. 그는 1632년 10월 24일 네덜란드 Delft에서 태어났다. 그는 16살에 Amsterdam에서 직업 기술을 배우기 시작했다. Leeuwenhoek은 22살에 Delft로 돌아왔다. Leeuwenhoek이 과학자가 되기는 쉽지 않았다. 그는 오직 한 가지 언어, 즉 네덜란드어만을 알고 있었는데, 그것은 그 당시 과학자들에게는 상당히 드문 것이었다. 하지만 그의 호기심은 끝이 없었고, 그는 열심히 노력했다. 그에게는 중요한 기술이 있었다. 그는 유리로 물건을 만드는 법을 알고 있었다. 이 기술은 그가 자신의 간단한 현미경에 쓰일 렌즈를 만들 때 도움이 되었다. 그는 피가 흐르고 있는 미세한 혈관을 보았다. 그는 또한 연못 물속에서 살아 있는 박테리아를 보았다. 그는 자신이 본 것들에 세심한 주의를 기울였고 관찰한 것을 기록했다. 그는 그림을 잘 그릴 수 없었기 때문에, 화가를 고용하여 자신이 설명하는 것을 그림으로 그리게 했다.

Why? 왜 정답일까?

'He knew only one language—Dutch ~'에서 Antonie van Leeuwenhoek는 오직 네덜란드어만 알았다고 하므로, 내용과 일치하지 않는 것은 ③ '여러 개의 언어를 알았다.'이다.

Why? 왜 오답일까?

① 'Antonie van Leeuwenhoek was a scientist well known for his cell research.'의 내용과 일치한다.
② 'At the age of 22, Leeuwenhoek returned to Delft.'의 내용과 일치한다.
④ 'He knew how to make things out of glass.'의 내용과 일치한다.
⑤ '~ he hired an artist to draw pictures of what he described.'의 내용과 일치한다.

- curiosity ⑩ 호기심
- make A out of B B로 A를 만들다
- pond ⑩ 연못
- endless ⓐ 끝없는
- microscope ⑩ 현미경
- observation ⑩ 관찰

구문 풀이

5행 He knew only one language — Dutch — which was quite unusual for
선행사(문장)   계속적 용법
scientists of his time.

---

27 꽃 교실 안내   정답률 95% | 정답 ④

Rachel's Flower Class에 관한 다음 안내문의 내용과 일치하지 않는 것은?
① 플라워 박스 만들기 수업은 오후 1시에 시작된다.
② 수강료에 꽃값과 다른 재료비가 포함된다.
③ 수강생은 가위와 가방을 가져와야 한다.
✓④ 수업 등록은 전화로만 할 수 있다.
⑤ 수업 당일 취소 시 환불을 받을 수 없다.

Rachel's Flower Class
Rachel의 꽃 교실
Make Your Life More Beautiful!
인생을 더 아름답게 만드세요!
Class Schedule (Every Monday to Friday)
수업 일정 (매주 월요일부터 금요일까지)

Flower Arrangement 꽃꽂이	11 a.m. – 12 p.m. 오전 11시 ~ 정오
『Flower Box Making 플라워 박스 만들기	1 p.m. – 2 p.m.』 ①의근거 일치 오후 1시 ~ 오후 2시

Price
가격
『$50 for each class (flowers and other materials included)』 ②의근거 일치
각 수업당 $50 (꽃값과 다른 재료비 포함)
『Bring your own scissors and a bag.』 ③의근거 일치
본인의 가위와 가방을 가져오세요.
Other Info.
다른 정보
『You can sign up for classes / either online or by phone.』 ④의근거 불일치
수업 등록을 할 수 있습니다. / 온라인이나 전화로
『No refund for cancellations on the day of your class』 ⑤의근거 일치
수업 당일 취소 시 환불 불가
To contact, / visit www.rfclass.com or call 03-221-2131.
연락하시려면, / www.rfclass.com을 방문하시거나 03-221-2131로 전화주세요.

Rachel의 꽃 교실

인생을 더 아름답게 만드세요!

수업 일정 (매주 월요일부터 금요일까지)

꽃꽂이	오전 11시 ~ 정오
플라워 박스 만들기	오후 1시 ~ 오후 2시

가격
• 각 수업당 $50 (꽃값과 다른 재료비 포함)
• 본인의 가위와 가방을 가져오세요.

다른 정보
• 온라인이나 전화로 수업 등록을 할 수 있습니다.
• 수업 당일 취소 시 환불 불가

연락하시려면, www.rfclass.com을 방문하시거나 03-221-2131로 전화주세요.

Why? 왜 정답일까?

'You can sign up for classes either online or by phone.'에서 수업 등록은 전화뿐 아니라 온라인으로도 가능하다고 하므로, 안내문의 내용과 일치하지 않는 것은 ④ '수업 등록은 전화로만 할 수 있다.'이다.

Why? 왜 오답일까?

① 'Flower Box Making / 01 p.m. – 02 p.m.'의 내용과 일치한다.
② '$50 for each class (flowers and other materials included)'의 내용과 일치한다.
③ 'Bring your own scissors and a bag.'의 내용과 일치한다.
⑤ 'No refund for cancellations on the day of your class'의 내용과 일치한다.

- flower arrangement 꽃꽂이
- sign up for ~에 등록하다

---

28 야간 궁궐 투어 안내   정답률 91% | 정답 ⑤

Nighttime Palace Tour에 관한 다음 안내문의 내용과 일치하는 것은?
① 금요일에는 하루에 두 번 투어가 운영된다.
② 8세 미만 어린이의 티켓은 5달러이다.
③ 예약은 투어 하루 전까지만 가능하다.
④ 투어 가이드의 안내 없이 궁궐을 둘러본다.
✓⑤ 추가 비용 없이 전통 의상을 입어 볼 수 있다.

Nighttime Palace Tour
야간 궁궐 투어
Date: Friday, April 29 – Sunday, May 15
날짜: 4월 29일 금요일 ~ 5월 15일 일요일

Time
시간

『Friday 금요일	7 p.m. – 8:30 p.m.』 ①의근거 불일치 오후 7시 ~ 오후 8시 30분
Saturday & Sunday 토요일과 일요일	6 p.m. – 7:30 p.m. 오후 6시 ~ 오후 7시 30분
	8 p.m. – 9:30 p.m. 오후 8시 ~ 오후 9시 30분

Tickets & Booking
티켓과 예약
$15 per person 『free for kids under 8』 ②의근거 불일치
1인당 15달러 (8세 미만 어린이는 무료)
『Bookings will be accepted / up to 2 hours before the tour starts.』 ③의근거 불일치
예약은 가능합니다. / 투어가 시작되기 2시간 전까지
Program Activities
프로그램 활동
『Group tour with a tour guide (1 hour)』 ④의근거 불일치
투어 가이드와 단체 투어 (1시간)
Trying traditional foods and drinks (30 minutes)
전통 음식 시식 및 음료 시음 (30분)
『You can try on traditional clothes / with no extra charge.』 ⑤의근거 일치
전통 의상을 입어 볼 수 있습니다. / 추가 비용 없이
For more information, / please visit our website, www.palacenighttour.com.
더 많은 정보를 원하시면, / 저희 웹 사이트 www.palacenighttour.com에 방문하세요.

야간 궁궐 투어

날짜: 4월 29일 금요일 ~ 5월 15일 일요일

시간

금요일	오후 7시 ~ 오후 8시 30분
토요일과 일요일	오후 6시 ~ 오후 7시 30분
	오후 8시 ~ 오후 9시 30분

티켓과 예약
• 1인당 15달러 (8세 미만 어린이는 무료)
• 예약은 투어 시작 2시간 전까지 가능합니다.

프로그램 활동
• 투어 가이드와 단체 투어 (1시간)
• 전통 음식 시식 및 음료 시음 (30분)

※ 추가 비용 없이 전통 의상을 입어 볼 수 있습니다.
※ 더 많은 정보를 원하시면, 저희 웹 사이트 www.palacenighttour.com에 방문하세요.

Why? 왜 정답일까?

'You can try on traditional clothes with no extra charge.'에서 전통 의상 착용은 추가 비용 없이도 가능하다고 하므로, 안내문의 내용과 일치하는 것은 ⑤ '추가 비용 없이 전통 의상을 입어 볼 수 있다.'이다.

Why? 왜 오답일까?

① 'Friday / 7 p.m. – 8:30 p.m.'에서 금요일 투어는 한 번만 열린다고 하였다.
② '(free for kids under 8)'에서 8세 미만 어린이는 무료 입장이라고 하였다.
③ 'Bookings will be accepted up to 2 hours before the tour starts.'에서 투어 예약은 투어 시작 2시간 전까지 가능하다고 하였다.
④ 'Group tour with a tour guide (1 hour)'에서 투어 가이드와 함께 1시간 동안 그룹 투어를 하게 된다고 하였다.

- palace ⑩ 궁전
- accept ⓥ 접수하다, 수용하다

---

29 비슷한 대상과 어울리기를 선호하는 경향   정답률 63% | 정답 ③

다음 글의 밑줄 친 부분 중, 어법상 틀린 것은?

We usually get along best with people / who we think are like us.
우리는 보통 사람들과 가장 잘 지낸다. / 우리가 같다고 생각하는
In fact, we seek them out.
사실, 우리는 그들을 찾아낸다.
It's why places like Little Italy, Chinatown, and Koreatown ① exist.
이 이유로 리틀 이탈리아, 차이나타운, 코리아타운과 같은 장소들이 존재한다.
But I'm not just talking about race, skin color, or religion.
하지만 나는 인종, 피부색, 또는 종교만을 말하는 것이 아니다.
I'm talking about people / who share our values / and look at the world / the same way we ② do.
나는 사람들을 말하는 것이다. / 우리의 가치관을 공유하고 / 세상을 바라보는 / 우리와 같은 방식으로
As the saying goes, / birds of a feather flock together.
속담에서처럼, / 같은 깃털을 가진 새가 함께 무리 짓는다.
This is a very common human tendency / ✓that is rooted in how our species developed.
이것은 매우 흔한 인간의 경향이다. / 우리 종이 발전한 방식에 깊게 뿌리박히 있는
Imagine you are walking out in a forest.
여러분이 숲에 나가 걷는다고 상상해 보라.
You would be conditioned / to avoid something unfamiliar or foreign / because there is a high likelihood / that ④ it would be interested in killing you.
여러분은 조건화되어 있을 것이다. / 친숙하지 않거나 낯선 것을 피하도록 / 가능성이 커서 / 그런 것이 여러분을 죽이는 데 관심이 있을
Similarities make us ⑤ relate better to other people / because we think / they'll understand us on a deeper level than other people.
유사점은 우리가 다른 사람들과 마음이 더 잘 통하도록 하는데, / 우리가 생각하기 때문이다. / 그들이 우리를 다른 사람들보다 더 깊이 있는 수준으로 이해할 것이라고

우리는 보통 우리와 같다고 생각하는 사람들과 가장 잘 지낸다. 사실, 우리는 그들을 찾아낸다. 이 이유로 리틀 이탈리아, 차이나타운, 코리아타운과 같은 장소들이 존재한다. 하지만 나

는 인종, 피부색, 또는 종교만을 말하는 것이 아니다. 우리의 가치관을 공유하고 우리와 같은 방식으로 세상을 바라보는 사람들을 말하는 것이다. 속담에서처럼, 같은 깃털을 가진 새가 함께 무리 짓는다(유유상종이다). 이것은 우리 종이 발전한 방식에 깊게 뿌리박혀 있는 매우 흔한 인간의 경향이다. 여러분이 숲에 나가 걷는다고 상상해 보라. 친숙하지 않거나 낯선 것은 여러분을 죽이는 데 관심이 있을 가능성이 커 여러분은 그런 것을 피하도록 조건화되어 있을 것이다. 유사점(을 갖고 있는 것)은 우리가 다른 사람들과 마음이 더 잘 통합될 수 있도록 하는데, 그들이 우리를 다른 사람들보다 더 깊이 있는 수준으로 이해할 것으로 생각하기 때문이다.

Why? 왜 정답일까?

관계대명사 what은 선행사를 포함하고 있는데, ③ 앞에는 선행사 a very common human tendency가 있으므로 what을 that 또는 which로 고쳐야 한다. 따라서 어법상 틀린 것은 ③이다.

Why? 왜 오답일까?

① 주어가 복수 명사인 places이므로 복수 동사 exist가 바르게 쓰였다. like Little Italy, Chinatown, and Koreatown은 주어 places를 꾸미는 전명구이다.
② 앞의 일반동사구 look at을 가리키는 대동사 do가 바르게 쓰였다.
④ something unfamiliar or foreign을 받는 단수 대명사 it이 바르게 쓰였다.
⑤ 사역동사 make의 목적격 보어로 원형부정사 relate가 바르게 쓰였다.

- get along with ~와 잘 지내다, 어울리다
- race ⓝ 인종
- be rooted in ~에 뿌리박고 있다, ~에 원인이 있다
- relate to ~을 이해하다, ~에 공감하다
- seek out (오랫동안 공들여) 찾아다니다
- as the saying goes 속담에서 말하듯이, 옛말처럼
- condition ⓥ 조건화하다

구문 풀이

1행 We usually get along best with people [who (we think) are like us].
선행사 주격 관·대 ( ): 삽입절

★★★ 등급을 가르는 문제!

30 거절에 대한 두려움 극복하기 　정답률 45% | 정답 ⑤

다음 글의 밑줄 친 부분 중, 문맥상 낱말의 쓰임이 적절하지 않은 것은? [3점]

Rejection is an everyday part of our lives, / yet most people can't handle it well.
거절은 우리 삶의 일상적인 부분이지만, / 대부분의 사람은 그것을 잘 감당하지 못한다.
For many, / it's so painful / that they'd rather not ask for something at all / than ask and ① risk rejection.
많은 사람에게 / 거절이 너무 고통스러워서, / 그들은 아예 무언가를 요청하지 않으려 한다. / 요청하고 거절의 위험을 감수하기보다는
Yet, as the old saying goes, / if you don't ask, / the answer is always no.
하지만 옛말처럼, / 여러분이 요청하지 않으면 / 대답은 항상 '아니오'이다.
Avoiding rejection / ② negatively affects many aspects of your life.
거절을 피하는 것은 / 여러분의 삶의 많은 측면에 부정적으로 영향을 준다.
All of that happens / only because you're not ③ tough enough to handle it.
이 모든 것은 일어난다. / 단지 여러분이 거절을 감당할 만큼 강하지 않기 때문에
For this reason, / consider rejection therapy.
이러한 이유로 / 거절 요법을 고려해 보라.
Come up with a ④ request or an activity / that usually results in a rejection.
요청이나 활동을 생각해 내라. / 일반적으로 거절당할 만한
Working in sales is one such example.
판매 분야에서 일하는 것이 그러한 사례 중 하나이다.
Asking for discounts at the stores / will also work.
매장에서 할인을 요청하는 것은 / 또한 효과가 있을 것이다.
By deliberately getting yourself ⑤ rejected / you'll grow a thicker skin / that will allow you to take on much more in life, / thus making you more successful / at dealing with unfavorable circumstances.
의도적으로 스스로를 거절당할 상황에 놓이게 함으로써 / 여러분은 더한 둔감함을 키우게 될 것이다. / 여러분이 인생에서 훨씬 더 많은 것을 떠맡을 수 있게 해주는, / 그리하여 여러분을 더 성공적이 될 / 호의적이지 않은 상황에 대처하는 것에

거절은 우리 삶의 일상적인 부분이지만, 대부분의 사람은 그것을 잘 감당하지 못한다. 많은 사람에게 거절이 너무 고통스러워서, 그들은 아예 무언가를 요청하지 않으려 아예 무언가를 요청하지 않으려 한다. 하지만 옛말처럼, 여러분이 요청하지 않으면 대답은 항상 '아니오'이다. 거절을 피하는 것은 여러분의 삶의 많은 측면에 ② 부정적으로 영향을 준다. 이 모든 것은 단지 여러분이 거절을 감당할 만큼 ③ 강하지 않기 때문에 일어난다. 이러한 이유로 거절 요법 (시도하는 것을) 고려해 보라. 일반적으로 거절당할 만한 ④ 요청이나 활동을 생각해 내라. 판매 분야에서 일하는 것이 그러한 사례 중 하나이다. 매장에서 할인을 요청하는 것 또한 효과가 있을 것이다. 의도적으로 스스로를 ⑤ 환영받을(→ 거절당할) 상황에 놓이게 함으로써 여러분은 더 둔감해지고, 인생에서 훨씬 더 많은 것을 떠맡을 수 있게 되며, 그리하여 호의적이지 않은 상황에 더 성공적으로 대처하게 될 것이다.

Why? 왜 정답일까?

⑤ 앞에서 판매 분야에서 일하는 등 거절을 경험할 법한 요청이나 활동에 참여해보라고 언급하는데, 이는 거절을 부르는 상황의 예시이므로 ⑤의 welcomed는 rejected로 바뀌어야 적절하다. 따라서 문맥상 낱말의 쓰임이 적절하지 않은 것은 ⑤이다.

- rejection ⓝ 거절
- grow a thick skin 무덤덤해지다, 둔감해지다
- circumstance ⓝ 상황, 환경
- come up with ~을 생각해내다, 떠올리다
- unfavorable ⓐ 호의적이지 않은

구문 풀이

2행 For many, it's so painful that they'd rather not ask for something at all than ask and risk rejection.
「so ~ that ··· : 너무 ~해서 ···하다」　차라리 ~않다　동사원형1
동사원형2

★★ 문제 해결 꿀~팁 ★★

▶ 많이 틀린 이유는?
오답 중 ③이 포함된 문장은 우리가 거절을 왜 피하려 하는지 그 이유를 설명하는 문장이다. 우리가

거절에 잘 대처할 만큼 '충분히 강하지' 않기 때문이라는 것이다. 그렇기에 훈련이 필요하다는 결론까지 자연스럽게 연결되므로, ③은 문맥상 어색하지 않다.

▶ 문제 해결 방법은?
정답인 ⑤가 포함된 문장은 예시 앞의 'Come up with a request or an activity that usually results in a rejection.'과 같은 의미이다. '일부러 거절이라는 결과를 초래할' 수 있는 상황은 '환영받는' 상황이 아니라 그야말로 '거부당하는' 상황이다.

★★★ 등급을 가르는 문제!

31 세밀한 묘사의 필요성 　정답률 46% | 정답 ②

다음 빈칸에 들어갈 말로 가장 적절한 것을 고르시오.
① similarities - 유사점　　✓ particulars - 세부 사항　　③ fantasies - 환상
④ boredom - 지루함　　⑤ wisdom - 지혜

Generalization without specific examples / that humanize writing / is boring to the listener and to the reader.
구체적인 사례가 없는 일반화 / 글을 인간미 있게 하는 / 듣는 사람과 읽는 사람에게 지루하다.
Who wants to read platitudes all day?
누가 상투적인 말을 온종일 읽고 싶어 하겠는가?
Who wants to hear the words / great, greater, best, smartest, finest, humanitarian, on and on and on / without specific examples?
누가 듣고 싶어 하겠는가? / 위대한, 더 위대한, 최고의, 제일 똑똑한, 가장 훌륭한, 인도주의적인, 이런 말들을 계속해서 끊임없이 / 구체적인 사례가 없이
Instead of using these 'nothing words,' / leave them out completely / and just describe the particulars.
이런 '공허한 말들'을 사용하는 대신에, / 그것들을 완전히 빼고 / 세부 사항만을 서술하라.
There is nothing worse than reading a scene in a novel / in which a main character is described up front / as heroic or brave or tragic or funny, / while thereafter, the writer quickly moves on to something else.
소설 속 장면을 읽는 것보다 더 끔찍한 것은 없다. / 주인공이 대놓고 묘사되는 / 영웅적이다, 용감하다, 비극적이다, 혹은 웃긴다고 / 한편 그 후 작가가 다른 것으로 빠르게 넘어가는
That's no good, no good at all.
그건 좋지 않으며, 전혀 좋지 않다.
You have to use less one word descriptions / and more detailed, engaging descriptions / if you want to make something real.
여러분은 한 단어 묘사는 덜 사용하고, / 세밀하고 마음을 끄는 묘사를 더 많이 사용해야 한다. / 여러분이 어떤 것을 실감 나는 것으로 만들고 싶다면

글을 인간미 있게 하는 구체적인 사례가 없는 일반화는 듣는 사람에게도 읽는 사람에게도 지루하다. 누가 상투적인 말을 온종일 읽고 싶어 하겠는가? 구체적인 사례가 없이 위대한, 더 위대한, 최고의, 제일 똑똑한, 가장 훌륭한, 인도주의적인, 이런 말들을 계속해서 끊임없이 듣고 싶어 하겠는가? 이런 '공허한 말들'을 사용하는 대신에, 그것들을 완전히 빼고 세부 사항만을 서술하라. 주인공을 대놓고 영웅적이다, 용감하다, 비극적이다, 혹은 웃긴다고 묘사한 후 작가가 다른 것으로 빠르게 넘어가는 소설 속 장면을 읽는 것보다 더 끔찍한 것은 없다. 그건 좋지 않으며, 전혀 좋지 않다. 어떤 것을 실감 나는 것으로 만들고 싶다면, 한 단어 짜리 묘사는 덜 사용하고, 세밀하고 마음을 끄는 묘사를 더 많이 사용해야 한다.

Why? 왜 정답일까?

마지막 문장에서 장면을 실감 나게 만들려면 세밀하고 마음을 끄는 묘사를 사용해야 한다(You have to use less one word descriptions and more detailed, engaging descriptions if you want to make something real.)고 언급하는 것으로 보아, 빈칸에 들어갈 말로 가장 적절한 것은 ② '세부 사항'이다. 이는 빈칸 앞의 specific examples을 재진술한 말이기도 하다.

- specific ⓐ 구체적인
- humanitarian ⓐ 인도주의적인
- engaging ⓐ 마음을 끄는, 몰입시키는
- humanize ⓥ 인간적으로 만들다
- leave out ~을 빼다

구문 풀이

6행 There is nothing worse than reading a scene in a novel [in which a main
「nothing + 비교급 + than : ~보다 더 ···한 것은 없다(최상급 의미)」　선행사 　=where
character is described up front as heroic or brave or tragic or funny, while thereafter, the writer quickly moves on to something else].

★★ 문제 해결 꿀~팁 ★★

▶ 많이 틀린 이유는?
첫 문장의 Generalization만 보고 ①을 고르면 안 된다. '특별한' 사례의 공통점을 찾아 '일반화'하라는 내용은 글 어디에도 없기 때문이다.

▶ 문제 해결 방법은?
빈칸이 주제문인 명령문에 있으므로, 마찬가지로 '~해야 한다'라는 당위의 의미를 나타내는 마지막 문장을 잘 읽어야 한다. more detailed, engaging와 같은 의미의 단어를 빈칸에 넣으면 된다.

★★★ 등급을 가르는 문제!

32 정보 공유에 있어 대면 상호작용의 중요성 　정답률 49% | 정답 ③

다음 빈칸에 들어갈 말로 가장 적절한 것을 고르시오.
① natural talent - 천부적 재능　　② regular practice - 규칙적인 연습
✓ personal contact - 개인적인 접촉　　④ complex knowledge - 복잡한 지식
⑤ powerful motivation - 강력한 동기

Face-to-face interaction / is a uniquely powerful — and sometimes the only — way / to share many kinds of knowledge, / from the simplest to the most complex.
대면 상호작용은 / 유례 없이 강력한 — 때로는 유일한 — 방법이다. / 많은 종류의 지식을 공유하는 / 가장 간단한 것부터 가장 복잡한 것까지
It is one of the best ways / to stimulate new thinking and ideas, / too.
그것은 가장 좋은 방법의 한 가지이다. / 새로운 생각과 아이디어를 자극하는 / 또한

Most of us would have had difficulty learning / how to tie a shoelace only from pictures, / or how to do arithmetic from a book.
우리 대부분이 배웠더면 어려움을 겪었을 것이다. / 그림만으로 신발 끈 묶는 법 / 또는 책으로부터 계산하는 방법을
Psychologist Mihàly Csikszentmihàlyi found, / while studying high achievers, / that a large number of Nobel Prize winners / were the students of previous winners: / they had access to the same literature as everyone else, / but personal contact made a crucial difference / to their creativity.
심리학자 Mihàly Csikszentmihàlyi는 발견했다. / 높은 성취도를 보이는 사람들을 연구하면서 / 다수의 노벨상 수상자가 / 이전 수상자들의 학생이라는 것을 / 그들은 다른 모든 사람들과 똑같은 문헌에 접근할 수 있었지만, / 개인적인 접촉이 결정적인 차이를 만들었다. / 이들의 창의성에
Within organisations / this makes conversation / both a crucial factor for high-level professional skills / and the most important way of sharing everyday information.
조직 내에서 / 이것은 대화를 만든다. / 고급 전문 기술을 위한 매우 중요한 요소이자 / 일상 정보를 공유하는 가장 중요한 방식으로

대면 상호 작용은 가장 간단한 것부터 가장 복잡한 것까지 많은 종류의 지식을 공유하는 유례 없이 강력한 —때로는 유일한— 방법이다. 그것은 새로운 생각과 아이디어를 자극하는 최고의 방법 중 하나이기도 하다. 우리 대부분이 그림으로만 신발 끈 묶는 법을 배웠거나, 책으로 셈법을 배웠다면 어려움을 겪었을 것이다. 심리학자 Mihàly Csikszentmihàlyi는 높은 성취도를 보이는 사람들을 연구하면서 다수의 노벨상 수상자가 이전 (노벨상) 수상자들의 학생이라는 것을 발견했다. 그들은 다른 모든 사람들과 똑같은 (연구) 문헌에 접근할 수 있었지만, 개인적인 접촉이 이들의 창의성에 결정적인 차이를 만들었다. 이로 인해 조직 내에서 대화는 고급 전문 기술을 위한 매우 중요한 요소이자 일상 정보를 공유하는 가장 중요한 방식이 된다.

Why? 왜 정답일까?

첫 문장과 마지막 문장에서 정보를 공유하는 가장 중요한 방법으로 대면 상호 작용(Face-to-face interaction) 또는 대화(conversation)를 언급하고 있다. 따라서 빈칸에 들어갈 말로 가장 적절한 것은 ③ '개인적인 접촉'이다.

● stimulate ⓥ 자극하다　　　　● crucial ⓐ 아주 중요한

구문 풀이

4행 Most of us would have had difficulty learning {how to tie a shoelace} only
「have difficulty + 동명사」 ~하는 데 어려움을 겪다」
from pictures, or {how to do arithmetic} from a book.
{ } : 명사구(how + to부정사: ~하는 방법)

★★ 문제 해결 꿀~팁 ★★

▶ 많이 틀린 이유는?
글 처음과 마지막에 many kinds of knowledge, from the simplest to the most complex 또는 high-level professional skills와 같은 표현이 등장하므로 얼핏 보면 ④가 적절해 보인다. 하지만 빈칸은 이러한 정보 공유나 전문 능력 개발에 '무엇이 영향을 미치는지' 그 요인을 밝히는 것이므로 ④를 빈칸에 넣기는 부적절하다.
▶ 문제 해결 방법은?
첫 문장의 Face-to-face interaction과 마지막 문장의 conversation이 키워드이다. 이 둘을 일반화할 수 있는 표현이 바로 '빈칸'이다.

---

33 영화 속 외국어 대화에 자막이 없을 때의 효과　정답률 59% | 정답 ①

다음 빈칸에 들어갈 말로 가장 적절한 것을 고르시오. [3점]
✓① seeing the film from her viewpoint – 그녀의 시각에서 영화를 보고 있게
② impressed by her language skills – 그녀의 언어 능력에 감명받게
③ attracted to her beautiful voice – 그녀의 아름다운 목소리에 이끌리게
④ participating in a heated debate – 열띤 토론에 참여하게
⑤ learning the language used in the film – 영화에서 사용된 언어를 배우고 있게

Most times a foreign language is spoken in film, / subtitles are used / to translate the dialogue for the viewer.
영화에서 외국어가 사용되는 대부분의 경우 / 자막이 사용된다. / 관객을 위해 대화를 통역하려고
However, / there are occasions / when foreign dialogue is left unsubtitled / (and thus incomprehensible to most of the target audience).
하지만 / 경우가 있다. / 외국어 대화가 자막 없이 처리되는 / (그리하여 대부분의 주요 대상 관객이 이해하지 못하게)
This is often done / if the movie is seen / mainly from the viewpoint of a particular character / who does not speak the language.
흔히 이렇게 처리된다. / 영화가 보여지는 경우에 / 주로 특정한 등장인물의 관점에서 / 그 언어를 할 줄 모르는
Such absence of subtitles / allows the audience / to feel a similar sense of incomprehension and alienation / that the character feels.
그러한 자막의 부재는 / 관객이 ~하게 한다. / 비슷한 몰이해와 소외의 감정을 / 그 등장인물이 느끼는
An example of this / is seen in *Not Without My Daughter*.
이것의 한 예는 / *Not Without My Daughter*에서 볼 수 있다.
The Persian language dialogue / spoken by the Iranian characters / is not subtitled / because the main character Betty Mahmoody does not speak Persian / and the audience is seeing the film from her viewpoint.
페르시아어 대화는 / 이란인 등장인물들이 하는 / 자막 없이 처리되며 / 왜냐하면 주인공 Betty Mahmoody가 페르시아어를 하지 못하기 때문에 / 관객은 그녀의 시각에서 영화를 보고 있게 된다.

영화에서 외국어가 사용되는 대부분의 경우 관객을 위해 대화를 통역하려고 자막이 사용된다. 하지만 외국어 대화가 자막 없이 (그리하여 대부분의 주요 대상 관객이 이해하지 못하게) 처리되는 경우가 있다. 영화가 그 언어를 할 줄 모르는 특정한 등장인물의 관점에서 주로 보여지는 경우에 흔히 이렇게 처리된다. 그러한 자막의 부재는 관객이 그 등장인물이 느끼는 것과 비슷한 몰이해와 소외의 감정을 느끼게 한다. 이것의 한 예를 *Not Without My Daughter*에서 볼 수 있다. 주인공 Betty Mahmoody가 페르시아어를 하지 못하기 때문에 이란인 등장인물들이 하는 페르시아어 대화에는 자막이 없으며, 관객은 그녀의 시각에서 영화를 보고 있게 된다.

Why? 왜 정답일까?

외국어 대화가 자막 없이 사용되는 경우는 그 언어를 할 줄 모르는 특정 등장인물의 시점에서 사건을 보게 만든다(~ if the movie is seen mainly from the viewpoint of a particular character

---

who does not speak the language.)는 설명으로 보아, 빈칸에 들어갈 말로 가장 적절한 것은 ① '그녀의 시각에서 영화를 보고 있게'이다.

● translate ⓥ 번역하다, 통역하다　　● occasion ⓝ 경우, 때
● viewpoint ⓝ 관점, 시점　　　　　　● absence ⓝ 부재

구문 풀이

2행 However, there are occasions [when foreign dialogue is left unsubtitled
선행사(경우)　관계부사　　　5형식 수동태　보어1(과거분사)
(and thus incomprehensible to most of the target audience)].
보어2(형용사)

★★★ 등급을 가르는 문제! ★★★

34 홈 이점이 발휘되지 못하는 경우　정답률 19% | 정답 ①

다음 빈칸에 들어갈 말로 가장 적절한 것을 고르시오. [3점]
✓① often welcome a road trip – 길을 떠나는 것을 흔히 반길
② avoid international matches – 국제적 경기를 피할
③ focus on increasing ticket sales – 티켓 매출을 높이는 데 집중할
④ want to have an eco-friendly stadium – 친환경적인 경기장을 갖기를 원할
⑤ try to advertise their upcoming games – 다가오는 경기를 광고하려 애쓸

One dynamic that can change dramatically in sport / is the concept of the home-field advantage, / in which perceived demands and resources seem to play a role.
스포츠에서 극적으로 바뀔 수 있는 한 가지 역학은 / 홈 이점이라는 개념으로, / 여기에는 인식된 부담과 자원이 역할을 하는 것처럼 보인다.
Under normal circumstances, / the home ground would appear / to provide greater perceived resources / (fans, home field, and so on).
일반적인 상황에서, / 홈그라운드는 보일 것이다. / 인식된 자원을 더 많이 제공하는 것처럼 / (팬, 홈 경기장 등)
However, / researchers Roy Baumeister and Andrew Steinhilber / were among the first / to point out / that these competitive factors can change; / for example, / the success percentage for home teams / in the final games of a playoff or World Series / seems to drop.
하지만, / 연구원 Roy Baumeister와 Andrew Steinhilber는 / 최초의 사람들 중 하나였다. / 지적한 / 이러한 경쟁력이 있는 요소들이 바뀔 수도 있다고 / 예를 들어, / 홈 팀들의 성공률은 / 우승 결정전이나 미국 프로 야구 선수권의 마지막 경기에서 / 떨어지는 것처럼 보인다.
Fans can become part of the perceived demands / rather than resources / under those circumstances.
팬들은 인식된 부담의 일부가 될 수 있다. / 자원보다는 / 이러한 상황에서
This change in perception can also explain / why a team that's struggling at the start of the year / will often welcome a road trip / to reduce perceived demands and pressures.
이러한 인식의 변화는 또한 설명할 수 있다. / 왜 연초에 고전하는 팀이 / 길을 떠나는 것을 흔히 반길 것인지 / 인식된 부담과 압박을 줄이기 위해

스포츠에서 극적으로 바뀔 수 있는 한 가지 역학은 홈 이점이라는 개념으로, 여기에는 인식되는 부담과 자원이 일조하는 것처럼 보인다. 일반적인 상황에서, 홈그라운드는 인식되는 자원(팬, 홈 경기장 등)을 더 많이 제공하는 것처럼 보일 것이다. 하지만, 연구원 Roy Baumeister와 Andrew Steinhilber는 이러한 경쟁력이 있는 요소들이 바뀔 수도 있다고 처음으로 지적한 사람 중 하나였다. 예를 들어, 우승 결정전이나 미국 프로 야구 선수권의 마지막 경기에서 홈 팀들의 성공률은 떨어지는 것처럼 보인다. 이러한 상황에서 팬들은 자원보다는 인식되는 부담의 일부가 될 수 있다. 이러한 인식의 변화는 왜 연초에 고전하는 팀이 인식되는 부담과 압박을 줄이기 위해 길을 떠나는 것(원정 경기를 가는 것)을 흔히 반길 것인지 또한 설명할 수 있다.

Why? 왜 정답일까?

홈그라운드의 이점은 부담에 대한 인식이나 자원에 의해 뒤집힐 수 있다(~ the concept of the home-field advantage, in which perceived demands and resources seem to play a role.)는 내용의 글이다. for example 뒤로 결승전 등 중요한 경기에서 팬들은 선수들에게 자원이 아닌 부담일 수 있기에 도리어 홈 팀의 성적이 부진해질 수 있다고 한다. 이를 근거로 볼 때, 마지막 문장은 부진하는 팀이 도리어 부담을 피하고자 '홈그라운드에서의 경기를 피한다'는 내용일 것이다. 따라서 빈칸에 들어갈 말로 가장 적절한 것은 ① '길을 떠나는 것을 흔히 반길'이다.

● play a role in ~에 역할을 하다, 일조하다　● competitive ⓐ 경쟁력 있는
● perception ⓝ 인식　　　　　　　　　　　● struggle ⓥ 고전하다, 분투하다

구문 풀이

1행 One dynamic [that can change dramatically in sport] is the concept of
주어(선행사)　주격 관계대명사　　　　동사(단수)　보어(선행사)
the home-field advantage, in which perceived demands and resources seem to
「전치사 + 관계대명사」
play a role.

★★ 문제 해결 꿀~팁 ★★

▶ 많이 틀린 이유는?
home-field advantage만 보면 정답과 정반대되는 의미의 ②를 고르기 쉽다. 하지만 사실 이 글은 '홈 구장의 이점'을 긍정하는 글이 아니라 이 이점이 '없을 수도 있는' 경우에 대한 글이다.
▶ 문제 해결 방법은?
for example 뒤에서, 홈 팀의 결승전 승률이 '떨어지는' 것처럼 보인다는 예를 제시한다. 이 점이 어떤 결과를 불러올까 생각해보면, 연초에 고전 중인 팀은 오히려 홈 팀에서 경기하기를 꺼릴 수도 있다는 추론이 가능하다.

---

35 커피의 부정적 영향 주의하기　정답률 60% | 정답 ④

다음 글에서 전체 흐름과 관계 없는 문장은?

Who hasn't used a cup of coffee / to help themselves stay awake while studying?
커피 한 잔을 이용해 보지 않은 사람이 있을까? / 공부하는 동안 깨어 있는 것을 돕기 위해
Mild stimulants / commonly found in tea, coffee, or sodas / possibly make you more

attentive / and, thus, better able to remember.
가벼운 자극제는 / 차, 커피 또는 탄산음료에서 흔히 발견되는 / 아마도 여러분을 더 주의 깊게 만들고, / 따라서 더 잘 기억할 수 있게 한다.

① However, / you should know / that stimulants are as likely / to have negative effects on memory / as they are to be beneficial.
하지만, / 여러분은 알아야 한다. / 자극제가 ~할 수도 있다는 것을 / 기억력에 부정적인 영향을 미칠 / 그것들이 이로울 수 있는 만큼

② Even if they could improve performance at some level, / the ideal doses are currently unknown.
비록 그것이 특정 수준에서 수행을 향상할 수 있다고 할지라도, / 이상적인 복용량은 현재 알려지지 않았다.

③ If you are wide awake and well-rested, / mild stimulation from caffeine can do little / to further improve your memory performance.
만약 여러분이 완전히 깨어 있고 잘 쉬었다면, / 카페인으로부터의 가벼운 자극은 거의 영향을 주지 못할 수 있다. / 여러분의 기억력을 더욱 향상하는 데

✔ In contrast, / many studies have shown / that drinking tea is healthier than drinking coffee.
반면에, / 많은 연구에서 밝혀졌다. / 커피를 마시는 것보다 차를 마시는 것이 건강에 더 좋다는 것이

⑤ Indeed, / if you have too much of a stimulant, / you will become nervous, / find it difficult to sleep, / and your memory performance will suffer.
실제로, / 만약 여러분이 자극제를 너무 많이 섭취하면, / 여러분은 신경이 과민해지고, / 잠을 자기 어려워지며, / 기억력도 저하될 것이다.

공부하는 동안 깨어 있는 것을 돕기 위해 커피 한 잔을 이용해 보지 않은 사람이 있을까? 차, 커피 또는 탄산음료에서 흔히 발견되는 가벼운 자극제는 아마도 여러분을 더 주의 깊게 만들고, 따라서 더 잘 기억할 수 있게 한다. ① 하지만, 자극제가 기억력에 이로울 수 있는 만큼 부정적인 영향을 미칠 수도 있다는 것을 알아야 한다. ② 비록 그것이 특정 수준에서 수행을 향상할 수 있다고 할지라도, (자극제의) 이상적인 복용량은 현재 알려지지 않았다. ③ 만약 여러분이 완전히 깨어 있고 잘 쉬었다면, 카페인으로부터의 가벼운 자극은 여러분의 기억력을 더욱 향상하는 데 거의 영향을 주지 못할 수 있다. ④ 반면에, 많은 연구에서 커피를 마시는 것보다 차를 마시는 것이 건강에 더 좋다는 것이 밝혀졌다. ⑤ 실제로 만약 여러분이 자극제를 너무 많이 섭취하면, 신경이 과민해지고, 잠을 자기 어려워지며, 기억력도 저하될 것이다.

Why? 왜 정답일까?
커피를 지나치게 많이 마시면 부정적 영향이 나타날 수 있다는 내용의 글인데, ④는 커피보다 차가 몸에 좋다는 무관한 설명을 제시하고 있다. 따라서 전체 흐름과 관계 없는 문장은 ④이다.

● attentive ⓐ 주의 깊은
● ideal ⓐ 이상적인
● have an effect on ~에 영향을 미치다
● suffer ⓥ 악화되다

구문 풀이

[4행] However, you should know that stimulants are as likely to have negative
접속사(~것) 「as + 원급 + as : ~만큼 …한」
effects on memory as they are to be beneficial.
be to 용법(~할 수 있다)

---

36 과거 시골 건축업자들의 건축 양식 정답률 58% | 정답 ③

주어진 글 다음에 이어질 글의 순서로 가장 적절한 것을 고르시오.
① (A) – (C) – (B)
② (B) – (A) – (C)
✔ (B) – (C) – (A)
④ (C) – (A) – (B)
⑤ (C) – (B) – (A)

Toward the end of the 19th century, / a new architectural attitude emerged.
19세기 말이 되면서, / 새로운 건축학적 사고방식이 나타났다.

Industrial architecture, / the argument went, / was ugly and inhuman; / past styles had more to do with pretension / than what people needed in their homes.
산업 건축은 / 그 주장에 따르면, / 추하고 비인간적이었다. / 과거의 스타일은 허세와 더욱 관련이 있었다. / 사람들이 자기 집에서 필요로 했던 것보다는

(B) Instead of these approaches, / why not look at the way / ordinary country builders worked in the past?
이러한 접근 대신에, / 방식을 살펴보는 것은 어떠한가? / 평범한 시골 건축업자들이 과거에 일했던

They developed their craft skills over generations, / demonstrating mastery of both tools and materials.
그들은 세대를 거쳐 공예 기술을 발전시켰다. / 도구와 재료 둘 다에 숙달한 기술을 보이며

(C) Those materials were local, / and used with simplicity — / houses built this way / had plain wooden floors and whitewashed walls inside.
그 재료는 지역적이고, / 단순하게 사용되었는데, / 이러한 방식으로 건축된 집들은 / 실내가 평범한 나무 바닥과 회반죽을 칠한 벽으로 되어 있었다.

(A) But they supplied people's needs perfectly / and, at their best, had a beauty / that came from the craftsman's skill / and the rootedness of the house in its locality.
그러나 그것들은 사람들의 필요를 완벽하게 충족시켰고, / 가장 좋은 경우 아름다움을 갖추고 있었다. / 장인의 솜씨에서 비롯된 / 그리고 그 집이 그 지역에 뿌리내림으로써 비롯된

19세기 말이 되면서, 새로운 건축학적 사고방식이 나타났다. 그 주장에 따르면, 산업 건축은 추하고 비인간적이었다. 과거의 스타일은 사람들이 자기 집에서 필요로 했던 것보다는 허세와 더욱 관련이 있었다.

(B) 이러한 접근 대신에, 평범한 시골 건축업자들이 과거에 일했던 방식을 살펴보는 것은 어떠한가? 그들은 도구와 재료 둘 다에 숙달한 기술을 보이며, 세대를 거쳐 공예 기술을 발전시켰다.

(C) 그 재료는 지역적이고, 단순하게 사용되었는데, 이러한 방식으로 건축된 집들은 실내가 평범한 나무 바닥과 회반죽을 칠한 벽으로 되어 있었다.

(A) 그러나 그것들은 사람들의 필요를 완벽하게 충족시켰고, 가장 좋은 경우 장인의 솜씨와 집이 그 지역에 뿌리내리며 비롯된 아름다움을 갖추고 있었다.

Why? 왜 정답일까?
산업 건축 양식을 언급하는 주어진 글 뒤로, '이 접근법' 대신 평범한 시골 건축업자들의 작업 방식을 살펴보자고 언급하는 (B), (B)에서 언급된 재료를 Those materials로 받으며 이것들이 단순하게 사용되었다고 설명하는 (C), '그래도' 이렇게 건축된 집들은 사람들의 필요만큼은 완벽하게 충족시켰다는 내용의 (A)가 차례로 연결된다. 따라서 글의 순서로 가장 적절한 것은 ③ '(B) – (C) – (A)'이다.

● architectural ⓐ 건축의
● emerge ⓥ 나타나다, 출현하다

● inhuman ⓐ 비인간적인
● rootedness ⓝ 뿌리내림, 고착, 정착
● demonstrate ⓥ 입증하다
● plain ⓐ 평범한, 단순한
● craftsman ⓝ 장인
● locality ⓝ (~이 존재하는) 지역, 곳
● mastery ⓝ 숙달한 기술

구문 풀이

[2행] Industrial architecture, (the argument went), was ugly and inhuman;
주어1 ( ): 삽입절 동사1
past styles had more to do with pretension than {what people needed in their
주어2 동사2(~와 더 관련이 있었다) 관계대명사(~것)
homes}.

---

37 좋은 음악과 나쁜 음악 정답률 61% | 정답 ②

주어진 글 다음에 이어질 글의 순서로 가장 적절한 것을 고르시오. [3점]
① (A) – (C) – (B)
✔ (B) – (A) – (C)
③ (B) – (C) – (A)
④ (C) – (A) – (B)
⑤ (C) – (B) – (A)

Robert Schumann once said, / "The laws of morals are those of art."
Robert Schumann은 언젠가 말했다. / "도덕의 법칙은 예술의 법칙이다."라고

What the great man is saying here / is that there is good music and bad music.
여기서 이 위인이 말하고 있는 것은 / 좋은 음악과 나쁜 음악이 있다는 것이다.

(B) The greatest music, / even if it's tragic in nature, / takes us to a world higher than ours; / somehow the beauty uplifts us.
가장 위대한 음악은, / 심지어 그것이 사실상 비극적일지라도, / 우리의 세상보다 더 높은 세상으로 우리를 데려간다. / 어떻게든지 아름다움은 우리를 고양시킨다.

Bad music, on the other hand, degrades us.
반면에 나쁜 음악은 우리를 격하시킨다.

(A) It's the same with performances: / a bad performance isn't necessarily the result of incompetence.
연주도 마찬가지다. / 나쁜 연주가 반드시 무능의 결과는 아니다.

Some of the worst performances occur / when the performers, / no matter how accomplished, / are thinking more of themselves / than of the music they're playing.
최악의 연주 중 일부는 발생한다. / 연주자들이 ~할 때 / 아무리 숙달되었더라도 / 자기 자신을 더 생각하고 있을 / 연주하고 있는 곡보다

(C) These doubtful characters aren't really listening / to what the composer is saying / — they're just showing off, / hoping that they'll have a great 'success' with the public.
이 미덥지 못한 사람들은 정말로 듣고 있는 것이 아니다. / 작곡가가 말하는 것을 / 그들은 그저 뽐내고 있을 뿐이다. / 그들이 대중적으로 큰 '성공'을 거두기를 바라며

The performer's basic task / is to try to understand the meaning of the music, / and then to communicate it honestly to others.
연주자의 기본 임무는 / 음악의 의미를 이해하려고 노력하고서, / 그것을 다른 사람들에게 정직하게 전달하는 것이다.

Robert Schumann은 "도덕의 법칙은 예술의 법칙이다."라고 말한 적이 있다. 여기서 이 위인이 말하고 있는 것은 좋은 음악과 나쁜 음악이 있다는 것이다.

(B) 가장 위대한 음악은, 심지어 그것이 사실상 비극적일지라도, 우리의 세상보다 더 높은 세상으로 우리를 데려가며, 아름다움은 어떻게든지 우리를 고양시킨다. 반면에 나쁜 음악은 우리를 격하시킨다.

(A) 연주도 마찬가지다. 나쁜 연주가 반드시 무능의 결과는 아니다. 최악의 연주 중 일부는 연주자들이 아무리 숙달되었더라도 연주하고 있는 곡보다 자기 자신을 더 생각하고 있을 때 발생한다.

(C) 이 미덥지 못한 사람들은 작곡가가 말하는 것을 정말로 듣고 있는 것이 아니다. 그들은 대중적으로 큰 '성공'을 거두기를 바라며 그저 뽐내고 있을 뿐이다. 연주자의 기본 임무는 음악의 의미를 이해하려고 노력하고서, 그것을 다른 사람들에게 정직하게 전달하는 것이다.

Why? 왜 정답일까?
음악에 좋은 음악과 나쁜 음악이 있음을 언급하는 주어진 글 뒤로, 두 음악의 특징을 풀어 설명하는 (B), 연주에도 나쁜 연주와 좋은 연주가 있음을 덧붙이는 (A), (A)에서 언급된 최악의 연주자를 These doubtful characters로 가리키는 (C)가 차례로 연결된다. 따라서 글의 순서로 가장 적절한 것은 ② '(B) – (A) – (C)'이다.

● accomplished ⓐ 숙달된, 기량이 뛰어난
● doubtful ⓐ 미심쩍은
● show off 과시하다, 뽐내다
● uplift ⓥ 고양시키다, 들어올리다
● composer ⓝ 작곡가

구문 풀이

[5행] Some of the worst performances occur when the performers, no matter
주어 동사(복수)
how accomplished (they are), are thinking more of themselves than of the music
「no matter how + 형/부 + 주어 + 동사 : 아무리 ~할지라도」
they're playing.

---

38 생물 다양성으로 인한 이득 정답률 52% | 정답 ④

글의 흐름으로 보아, 주어진 문장이 들어가기에 가장 적절한 곳을 고르시오. [3점]

When an ecosystem is biodiverse, / wildlife have more opportunities / to obtain food and shelter.
생태계에 생물 종이 다양할 때, / 야생 생물들은 더 많은 기회를 얻는다. / 먹이와 서식지를 얻을

Different species react and respond / to changes in their environment / differently.
다양한 종들은 작용하고 반응한다. / 그들의 환경 변화에 / 다르게

① For example, / imagine a forest with only one type of plant in it, / which is the only source of food and habitat / for the entire forest food web.
예를 들어, / 단 한 종류의 식물만 있는 숲을 상상해 보라 / 그 식물은 유일한 먹이원이자 서식지이다. / 숲의 먹이 그물 전체에 있어

② Now, / there is a sudden dry season / and this plant dies.
이제, / 갑작스러운 건기가 오고 / 이 식물이 죽는다.

③ Plant-eating animals / completely lose their food source and die out, / and so do the animals / that prey upon them.
초식 동물은 / 그들의 먹이원을 완전히 잃고 죽게 되고, / 동물들도 그렇게 된다. / 그들을 먹이로 삼는

✔ But, when there is biodiversity, / the effects of a sudden change / are not so dramatic.
하지만 종 다양성이 있을 때, / 갑작스러운 변화의 영향은 / 그렇게 극적이지 않다.

Different species of plants / respond to the drought differently, / and many can survive a dry season.
다양한 종의 식물들이 / 가뭄에 다르게 반응하고, / 많은 식물이 건기에 살아남을 수 있다.

⑤ Many animals have a variety of food sources / and don't just rely on one plant; / now our forest ecosystem is no longer at the death!
많은 동물은 다양한 먹이원을 가지고 있으며 / 그저 한 식물에 의존하지는 않는다; / 그래서 이제 우리의 숲 생태계는 더는 종말에 처해 있지 않다!

생태계에 생물 종이 다양할 때, 야생 생물들은 먹이와 서식지를 얻을 더 많은 기회를 얻는다. 다양한 종들은 그들의 환경 변화에 다르게 작용하고 반응한다. ① 예를 들어, 단 한 종류의 식물만 있는 숲을 상상해 보면, 그 식물은 숲의 먹이 그물 전체의 유일한 먹이원이자 서식지이다. ② 이제, 갑작스러운 건기가 오고 이 식물이 죽는다. ③ 초식 동물은 그들의 먹이원을 완전히 잃고 죽게 되고, 그들을 먹이로 삼는 동물들도 그렇게 된다. ④ 하지만 종 다양성이 있을 때, 갑작스러운 변화의 영향은 그렇게 극적이지 않다. 다양한 종의 식물들이 가뭄에 다르게 반응할 수 있으며 한 식물에만 의존하지 않기에, 이제 우리의 숲 생태계는 더는 종말에 처해 있지 않다!

Why? 왜 정답일까?

생물 다양성이 보장되면 환경 변화에 대처하기가 더 좋다는 내용의 글로, ④ 앞에서는 식물이 한 종류만 있는 숲의 예를 들어 이 경우 갑작스러운 건기라도 찾아와 식물이 죽으면 숲 전체 생태계가 망가진다는 내용을 제시한다. 한편 주어진 문장은 But으로 흐름을 반전시키며 생물 다양성이 있으면 상황이 다르다는 것을 언급한다. ④ 뒤에서는 '다양한 식물 종'을 언급하며, 이것들이 건기에 대처하는 방식이 모두 다르기에 많은 수가 살아남아 생태계가 유지될 수 있음을 설명한다. 따라서 주어진 문장이 들어가기에 가장 적절한 곳은 ④이다.

● ecosystem ⓝ 생태계
● die out 멸종되다, 자취를 감추다
● food web 먹이 그물, 먹이 사슬 체계
● prey upon ~을 잡아먹다, 괴롭히다

구문 풀이

5행 For example, imagine a forest with only one type of plant in it, which is
선행사 / 계속적 용법
the only source of food and habitat for the entire forest food web.

★★★ 등급을 가르는 문제!

39 우리 생활의 다방면에 연관된 밤하늘 　정답률 34% | 정답 ②

글의 흐름으로 보아, 주어진 문장이 들어가기에 가장 적절한 곳을 고르시오.

We are connected to the night sky in many ways.
우리는 많은 방식으로 밤하늘과 연결되어 있다.

① It has always inspired people / to wonder and to imagine.
그것은 항상 사람들에게 영감을 주었다 / 궁금해하고 상상하도록

✔ Since the dawn of civilization, / our ancestors created myths / and told legendary stories / about the night sky.
문명의 시작부터, / 우리 선조들은 신화를 만들었고 / 전설적 이야기를 했다 / 밤하늘에 대해

Elements of those narratives became embedded / in the social and cultural identities of many generations.
그러한 이야기들의 요소들은 깊이 새겨졌다 / 여러 세대의 사회·문화적 정체성에

③ On a practical level, / the night sky helped past generations / to keep track of time and create calendars / — essential to developing societies / as aids to farming and seasonal gathering.
실용적인 수준에서, / 밤하늘은 과거 세대들이 ~하도록 도왔고 / 시간을 기록하고 달력을 만들도록 / 이는 사회를 발전시키는 데 필수적이었다 / 농업과 계절에 따른 수확의 보조 도구로서

④ For many centuries, / it also provided a useful navigation tool, / vital for commerce and for exploring new worlds.
수 세기 동안, / 그것은 또한 유용한 항해 도구를 제공하였다 / 무역과 새로운 세계를 탐험하는 데 필수적인

⑤ Even in modern times, / many people in remote areas of the planet / observe the night sky / for such practical purposes.
심지어 현대에도, / 지구의 외딴 지역에 있는 많은 사람 / 밤하늘을 관찰한다 / 그러한 실용적인 목적을 위해

우리는 많은 방식으로 밤하늘과 연결되어 있다. ① 그것은 항상 사람들이 궁금해하고 상상하도록 영감을 주었다. 문명의 시작부터, 우리 선조들은 밤하늘에 대해 신화를 만들었고 전설적 이야기를 했다. 그러한 이야기들의 요소들은 여러 세대의 사회·문화적 정체성에 깊이 새겨졌다. ③ 실용적인 수준에서, 밤하늘은 과거 세대들이 시간을 기록하고 달력을 만들도록 도왔고 이는 농업과 계절에 따른 수확의 보조 도구로서 사회를 발전시키는 데 필수적이었다. ④ 수 세기 동안, 그것은 또한 무역과 새로운 세계를 탐험하는 데 필수적인 유용한 항해 도구를 제공하였다. ⑤ 심지어 현대에도, 지구의 외딴 지역에 있는 많은 사람이 그러한 실용적인 목적을 위해 밤하늘을 관찰한다.

Why? 왜 정답일까?

② 앞에서 인류는 밤하늘을 궁금해했다고 언급한 후, 주어진 문장은 인류가 거의 문명이 시작되던 시기부터 밤하늘에 대한 다양한 전설과 신화를 만들어냈다고 설명한다. 그리고 ② 뒤의 문장은 주어진 문장의 myths and legendary stories를 those narratives로 가리킨다. 따라서 주어진 문장이 들어가기에 가장 적절한 곳은 ②이다.

● keep track of ~을 기록하다
● vital ⓐ 필수적인, 매우 중요한
● gathering ⓝ 수집, 수확
● remote ⓐ 멀리 떨어진

구문 풀이

6행 On a practical level, the night sky helped past generations to keep track of
동사 / 목적어 / 목적격 보어1
time and (to) create calendars — (which are) essential to developing societies as
목적격 보어1 / 선행사 / 생략
aids to farming and seasonal gathering.

★★ 문제 해결 꿀~팁 ★★

▶ 많이 틀린 이유는?
③ 앞에서 밤하늘에 대한 이야기는 '사회문화적 정체성에 깊이 새겨졌다'고 하는데, ③ 뒤에서는 '실용

적으로 살펴보면' 밤하늘 연구가 달력 제작 등에 영향을 미쳤다고 한다. 즉 On a practical level 앞뒤로 일반적 논의에서 더 구체적 논의로 나아가는 내용이 자연스럽게 연결된다.

▶ 문제 해결 방법은?
② 앞에서는 '이야기'로 볼 만한 내용이 없는데, ② 뒤에서는 갑자기 those narratives를 언급하므로 논리적 공백이 발생한다. 이때 주어진 문장을 보면 myths와 legendary stories가 있으므로, 이것을 ② 뒤에서 those narratives로 연결했다는 것을 알 수 있다.

40 경쟁자 제거에 망가니즈를 활용하는 식물 　정답률 55% | 정답 ①

다음 글의 내용을 한 문장으로 요약하고자 한다. 빈칸 (A), (B)에 들어갈 말로 가장 적절한 것은?

	(A)	(B)		(A)	(B)
✔	increase 증가시키다	deadly 치명적인	②	increase 증가시키다	advantageous 이로운
③	indicate 보여주다	nutritious 영양가 있는	④	reduce 줄이다	dry 건조한
⑤	reduce 줄이다	warm 따뜻한			

The common blackberry (*Rubus allegheniensis*) / has an amazing ability / to move manganese from one layer of soil to another / using its roots.
common blackberry(*Rubus allegheniensis*)는 / 놀라운 능력이 있다 / 토양의 망가니즈를 한 층에서 다른 층으로 옮기는 / 뿌리를 이용하여

This may seem like a funny talent / for a plant to have, / but it all becomes clear / when you realize the effect / it has on nearby plants.
이것은 기이한 재능처럼 보일 수도 있지만, / 식물이 가지기에는 / 전부 명확해진다, / 여러분이 영향을 깨닫고 나면 / 그것이 근처의 식물에 미치는

Manganese can be very harmful to plants, / especially at high concentrations.
망가니즈는 식물에 매우 해로울 수 있으며, / 특히 고농도일 때 그렇다.

Common blackberry is unaffected by damaging effects of this metal / and has evolved two different ways of using manganese to its advantage.
common blackberry는 이 금속 원소의 해로운 효과에 영향을 받지 않으며, / 망가니즈를 자신에게 유리하게 사용하는 두 가지 다른 방법을 발달시켰다.

First, / it redistributes manganese / from deeper soil layers to shallow soil layers / using its roots as a small pipe.
첫째로, / 그것은 망가니즈를 재분배한다 / 깊은 토양층으로부터 얕은 토양층으로 / 그것의 뿌리를 작은 관으로 사용하여

Second, / it absorbs manganese as it grows, / concentrating the metal in its leaves.
둘째로, / 그것은 성장하면서 망가니즈를 흡수하여 / 그 금속 원소를 잎에 농축한다.

When the leaves drop and decay, / their concentrated manganese deposits / further poison the soil around the plant.
잎이 떨어지고 부패할 때, / 그것의 농축된 망가니즈 축적물은 / 그 식물 주변의 토양을 독성 물질로 더욱 오염시킨다.

For plants / that are not immune to the toxic effects of manganese, / this is very bad news.
식물에게 / 망가니즈의 유독한 영향에 면역이 없는 / 이것은 매우 나쁜 소식이다.

Essentially, / the common blackberry eliminates competition / by poisoning its neighbors with heavy metals.
본질적으로, / common blackberry는 경쟁자를 제거한다 / 중금속으로 그것의 이웃을 중독시켜

➡ The common blackberry has an ability / to (A) increase the amount of manganese / in the surrounding upper soil, / which makes the nearby soil / quite (B) deadly for other plants.
common blackberry는 능력이 있는데, / 망가니즈의 양을 증가시키는 / 주변의 위쪽 토양의 / 그것은 근처의 토양을 ~하게 만든다 / 다른 식물에게 상당히 치명적으로

common blackberry(*Rubus allegheniensis*)는 뿌리를 이용하여 토양의 한 층에서 다른 층으로 망가니즈를 옮기는 놀라운 능력이 있다. 이것은 식물이 가지기에는 기이한 재능처럼 보일 수도 있지만, 그것이 근처의 식물에 미치는 영향을 깨닫고 나면 전부 명확해진다. 망가니즈는 식물에 매우 해로울 수 있으며, 특히 고농도일 때 그렇다. common blackberry는 이 금속 원소의 해로운 효과에 영향을 받지 않으며, 망가니즈를 자신에게 유리하게 사용하는 두 가지 다른 방법을 발달시켰다. 첫째로, 그것은 뿌리를 작은 관으로 사용하여 망가니즈를 깊은 토양층으로부터 얕은 토양층으로 재분배한다. 둘째로, 그것은 성장하면서 망가니즈를 흡수하여 그 금속 원소를 잎에 농축한다. 잎이 떨어지고 부패할 때, 그것의 농축된 망가니즈 축적물은 그 식물 주변의 토양을 독성 물질로 더욱 오염시킨다. 망가니즈의 유독한 영향에 면역이 없는 식물에게 이것은 매우 나쁜 소식이다. 본질적으로, common blackberry는 중금속으로 그것의 이웃을 중독시켜 경쟁자를 제거한다.

➡ common blackberry는 주변 위쪽 토양에 있는 망가니즈의 양을 (A) 증가시키는 능력이 있는데, 그것은 근처의 토양이 다른 식물에게 상당히 (B) 치명적이게 만든다.

Why? 왜 정답일까?

첫 문장과 마지막 세 문장에 따르면 common blackberry는 뿌리를 이용해 망가니즈를 끌어올리거나 이동시킬 수 있어서 주변 토양에 망가니즈가 더 많아지게 할 수 있는데, 이것은 경쟁자 제거에 도움이 된다고 한다. 따라서 요약문의 빈칸 (A), (B)에 들어갈 말로 가장 적절한 것은 ① 'A) increase(증가시키다), (B) deadly(치명적인)'이다.

● concentration ⓝ 농도, 농축
● absorb ⓥ 흡수하다
● eliminate ⓥ 제거하다
● shallow ⓐ 얕은
● be immune to ~에 면역이 있다

구문 풀이

3행 This may seem like a funny talent for a plant to have, but it all becomes
주어1 / 동사1 / 주격 보어 / 의미상 주어 / 형용사적 용법 / 주어2 / 동사2
clear when you realize the effect [it has on nearby plants].
주격 보어2 / 선행사

41-42 우리를 가로막는 이들을 이해하기

The longest journey we will make / is the eighteen inches between our head and heart.
우리가 갈 가장 긴 여정은 / 우리의 머리에서 가슴까지의 18인치이다.

「If we take this journey, / it can shorten our (a) misery in the world.」 ◀41번의 근거
우리가 이 여정을 한다면, / 그것은 세상에서 우리의 비참함을 줄일 수 있다.

Impatience, judgment, frustration, and anger / reside in our heads.
조급함, 비난, 좌절, 그리고 분노가 / 우리 머릿속에 있다.

When we live in that place too long, / it makes us (b) unhappy.
우리가 그곳에서 너무 오래 살 때, / 그것은 우리를 불행하게 만든다.

우리가 그 장소에서 너무 오래 살면, / 그것은 우리를 불행하게 만든다.
But when we take the journey from our heads to our hearts, / something shifts (c) inside.
그러나 우리가 머리부터 가슴까지의 여행을 하면, / 내면에서 무엇인가 바뀐다.
What if we were able to love everything / that gets in our way?
만일 모든 것을 우리가 사랑할 수 있다면 어떻게 될까? / 우리를 가로막는
What if we tried loving the shopper / who unknowingly steps in front of us in line, / the driver who cuts us off in traffic, / the swimmer who splashes us with water during a belly dive, / or the reader who pens a bad online review of our writing?
만일 우리가 그 쇼핑객을 사랑하려고 노력한다면 어떨까? / 줄을 서 있는 우리 앞에 무심코 들어온 / 차량 흐름에서 우리 앞에 끼어든 그 운전자를, / 배 쪽으로 다이빙하면서 우리에게 물을 튀긴 수영하는 그 사람을, / 우리의 글에 대해 나쁜 온라인 후기를 쓴 그 독자를
「Every person who makes us miserable / is (d) like us」 — / a human being, / most likely doing the best they can, / deeply loved by their parents, a child, or a friend.
우리를 비참하게 만드는 모든 사람은 / 우리와 같다. / 인간, / 아마도 분명히 최선을 다하고 있으며, / 부모, 자녀, 또는 친구로부터 깊이 사랑받는
And how many times have we unknowingly stepped / in front of someone in line?
그리고 우리는 몇 번이나 무심코 들어갔을까? / 줄을 서 있는 누군가의 앞에
Cut someone off in traffic?
차량 흐름에서 누군가에게 끼어든 적은?
Splashed someone in a pool?
수영장에서 누군가에게 물을 튀긴 적은?
Or made a negative statement / about something we've read?
혹은 부정적인 진술을 한 적은 몇 번이었을까? / 우리가 읽은 것에 대해
It helps to (e) remember / that a piece of us resides in every person we meet.
기억하는 것은 도움이 된다. / 우리가 만나는 모든 사람 속에 우리의 일부가 있다는 것을

우리가 갈 가장 긴 여정은 우리의 머리에서 가슴까지의 18인치이다. 우리가 이 여행을 한다면, 그것은 세상에서 우리의 (a) 비참함을 줄일 수 있다. 조급함, 비난, 좌절, 그리고 분노가 우리 머릿속에 있다. 우리가 그 장소에서 너무 오래 살면, 그것은 우리를 (b) 불행하게 만든다. 그러나 우리가 머리부터 가슴까지의 여행을 하면, (c) 내면에서 무엇인가 바뀐다. 만일 우리를 가로막는 모든 것을 우리가 사랑할 수 있다면 어떻게 될까? 만일 줄을 서 있는 우리 앞에 무심코 들어온 그 쇼핑객을, 차량 흐름에서 우리 앞에 끼어든 그 운전자를, 배 쪽으로 다이빙하면서 우리에게 물을 튀긴 수영하는 그 사람을, 우리의 글에 대해 나쁜 온라인 후기를 쓴 그 독자를 우리가 사랑하려고 노력한다면 어떨까?
우리를 비참하게 만드는 모든 사람은 우리와 (d) 같다. 그들은 아마도 분명히 최선을 다하고 있으며, 부모, 자녀, 또는 친구로부터 깊이 사랑받는 인간일 것이다. 그리고 우리는 몇 번이나 무심코 줄을 서 있는 누군가의 앞에 끼어 들어갔을까? 차량 흐름에서 누군가에게 끼어든 적은? 수영장에서 누군가에게 물을 튀긴 적은? 혹은 우리가 읽은 것에 대해 부정적인 진술을 한 적은 몇 번이었을까? 우리가 만나는 모든 사람 속에 우리의 일부가 있다는 것을 (e) 부정하는(→기억하는) 것은 도움이 된다.

- misery ⑩ 불행, 비참함
- frustration ⑩ 좌절
- cut off ~을 가로막다
- deny ♡ 부인하다
- impatience ⑩ 조급함
- get in one's way ~을 방해하다
- splash ♡ (물을) 튀기다, 끼얹다

구문 풀이

6행 What if we were able to love everything [that gets in our way]?
「what if + 주어 + 과거 동사 ~? : 가정법 과거(실제로 ~하지 않지만 만일 ~한다면 어떨까?)」

41 제목 파악   정답률 52% | 정답 ⑤

윗글의 제목으로 가장 적절한 것은?
① Why It Is So Difficult to Forgive Others – 다른 사람을 용서하기는 왜 그토록 어려울까
② Even Acts of Kindness Can Hurt Somebody – 친절한 행동조차도 누군가를 상처 입힐 수 있다
③ Time Is the Best Healer for a Broken Heart – 실연에는 시간이 가장 좋은 약이다
④ Celebrate the Happy Moments in Your Everyday Life – 매일의 일상에서 행복한 순간을 축복하라
✔ Understand Others to Save Yourself from Unhappiness – 타인을 이해하여 스스로를 불행에서 구하라

Why? 왜 정답일까?

첫 두 문장인 'The longest journey we will make is the eighteen inches between our head and heart. If we take this journey, it can shorten our misery in the world.'에서 남을 이해하는 과정을 '머리부터 가슴까지의 여행'에 빗대어, 이 여행은 우리에게 가장 멀게 느껴지지만 잘 이뤄지면 우리를 불행에서 구해줄 수 있다고 한다. 따라서 글의 제목으로 가장 적절한 것은 ⑤ '타인을 이해하여 스스로를 불행에서 구하라'이다.

42 어휘 추론   정답률 54% | 정답 ⑤

밑줄 친 (a) ~ (e) 중에서 문맥상 낱말의 쓰임이 적절하지 않은 것은?
① (a)   ② (b)   ③ (c)   ④ (d)   ✔ (e)

Why? 왜 정답일까?

'Every person who makes us miserable is like us ~'에서 우리를 비참하게 하는 사람들에게도 우리 자신의 모습이 있다고 설명하는 것으로 보아, 이 점을 우리가 '기억하고' 있을 때 우리 마음속의 불행이 걷어진다는 결론이 적절하다. 즉 (e)의 deny를 remember로 고쳐야 한다. 따라서 문맥상 낱말의 쓰임이 적절하지 않은 것은 ⑤ '(e)'이다.

43-45 여행자들과 수도승의 대화

(A)
One day / a young man was walking along a road on his journey / from one village to another.
어느 날, / 한 젊은이가 한 마을로부터 다른 마을로
「As he walked / he noticed a monk working in the fields.」 45번 ①의 근거 일치
그가 걸어갈 때 / 그는 들판에서 일하는 한 수도승을 보게 되었다.
The young man turned to the monk and said, / "Excuse me.
그 젊은이는 그 수도승을 향해 돌아보며 말했다. / "실례합니다.

Do you mind if I ask (a) you a question?"
제가 스님께 질문을 하나 드려도 되겠습니까?"라고
"Not at all," replied the monk.
"물론입니다."라고 그 수도승은 대답했다.

(C)
"I am traveling / from the village in the mountains / to the village in the valley / and I was wondering / if (c) you knew what it is like in the village in the valley."
"저는 가고 있는데 / 산속의 마을로부터 / 골짜기의 마을로 / 저는 궁금합니다. / 스님께서 골짜기의 마을은 어떤지 아시는지"
"Tell me," / said the monk, / "what was your experience of the village in the mountains?"
"저에게 말해 보십시오." / 수도승은 말했다. / "산속의 마을에서의 경험은 어땠습니까?"라고
"Terrible," replied the young man.
그 젊은이는 "끔찍했습니다."라고 대답했다.
"I am glad to be away from there.
"그곳을 벗어나게 되어 기쁩니다.
I found the people most unwelcoming.
저는 그곳 사람들이 정말로 불친절하다고 생각했습니다.
So tell (d) me, / what can I expect in the village in the valley?"
그러니 저에게 말씀해 주십시오. / 제가 골짜기의 마을에서 무엇을 기대할 수 있을까요?"
"I am sorry to tell you," / said the monk, / "but I think / your experience will be much the same."
"말씀드리기에 유감이지만," / 수도승은 말했다. / "제 생각에 / 선생님의 경험은 그곳에서도 거의 같을 것 같다고 생각합니다."
「The young man lowered his head helplessly / and walked on.」 45번 ④의 근거 일치
그 젊은이는 힘없이 고개를 숙이고 / 계속 걸어갔다.

(B)
A while later / a middle-aged man journeyed down the same road / and came upon the monk.
잠시 후 / 한 중년 남자가 같은 길을 걸어와서 / 그 수도승을 만났다.
「"I am going to the village in the valley,"」 / said the man. 45번 ②의 근거 일치
"저는 골짜기의 마을로 가고 있습니다." / 그 남자는 말했다.
「"Do you know what it is like?"」 45번 ③의 근거 일치
"그곳이 어떤지 아십니까?"라고
"I do," / replied the monk, / "but first tell (b) me about the village where you came from."
"알고 있습니다." / 그 수도승은 대답했다. / "먼저 저에게 선생님께서 떠나오신 마을에 관해 말해 주십시오."라고
"I've come from the village in the mountains," / said the man.
"저는 산속의 마을로부터 왔습니다." / 그 남자는 말했다.
"It was a wonderful experience.
"그것은 멋진 경험이었습니다.
I felt / as though I was a member of the family in the village."
저는 느꼈습니다. / 마치 제가 그 마을의 가족의 일원인 것처럼

(D)
"Why did you feel like that?" asked the monk.
그 수도승은 "왜 그렇게 느끼셨습니까?"라고 물었다.
"The elders gave me much advice, / and people were kind and generous.
"어르신들은 저에게 많은 조언을 해 주셨고, / 사람들은 친절하고 너그러웠습니다.
「I am sad to have left there.」 45번 ⑤의 근거 불일치
저는 그곳을 떠나서 슬픕니다.
And what is the village in the valley like?" / he asked again.
그런데 골짜기의 마을은 어떻습니까?"라고 / 그는 다시 물었다.
"(e) I think you will find it much the same," / replied the monk.
"저는 선생님은 그곳이 거의 같다고 여기실 거로 생각합니다."라고 / 수도승은 대답했다.
"I'm glad to hear that," / the middle-aged man said smiling and journeyed on.
"그 말씀을 들으니 기쁩니다." / 그 중년 남자는 미소를 지으며 말하고서 여행을 계속했다.

(A)
어느 날 한 젊은이가 한 마을로부터 다른 마을로 여행하며 길을 따라 걷고 있었다. 그는 걷다가 들판에서 일하는 한 수도승을 보게 되었다. 그 젊은이는 그 수도승을 향해 돌아보며 "실례합니다. 제가 (a) 스님께 질문을 하나 드려도 되겠습니까?"라고 말했다. "물론입니다."라고 그 수도승은 대답했다.

(C)
"저는 산속의 마을로부터 골짜기의 마을로 가고 있는데 (c) 스님께서 골짜기의 마을은 어떤지 아시는지 궁금합니다." 수도승은 "저에게 말해 보십시오. 산속의 마을에서의 경험은 어땠습니까?"라고 말했다. 그 젊은이는 "끔찍했습니다."라고 대답했다. "그곳을 벗어나게 되어 기쁩니다. 그곳 사람들이 정말로 불친절하다고 생각했습니다. 그러니 (d) 저에게 말씀해 주십시오, 제가 골짜기의 마을에서 무엇을 기대할 수 있을까요?" "말씀드리기에 유감이지만, 제 생각에 선생님의 경험은 그곳에서도 거의 같을 것 같다고 생각합니다." 수도승이 말했다. 그 젊은이는 힘없이 고개를 숙이고 계속 걸어갔다.

(B)
잠시 후 한 중년 남자가 같은 길을 걸어와서 그 수도승을 만났다. 그 남자는 "저는 골짜기의 마을로 가고 있습니다. 그곳이 어떤지 아십니까?"라고 말했다. "알고 있습니다만, 먼저 (b) 저에게 선생님께서 떠나오신 마을에 관해 말해 주십시오."라고 그 수도승은 대답했다. 그 남자는 "저는 산속의 마을로부터 왔습니다. 그것은 멋진 경험이었습니다. 저는 마치 그 마을의 가족의 일원인 것처럼 느꼈습니다."라고 말했다.

(D)
그 수도승은 "왜 그렇게 느끼셨습니까?"라고 물었다. "어르신들은 저에게 많은 조언을 해 주셨고, 사람들은 친절하고 너그러웠습니다. 저는 그곳을 떠나서 슬픕니다. 그런데 골짜기의 마을은 어떻습니까?"라고 그는 다시 물었다. "(e) 저는 선생님은 그곳이 (산속 마을과) 거의 같다고 여기실 거로 생각합니다."라고 수도승은 대답했다. "그 말씀을 들으니 기쁩니다."라고 그 중년 남자는 미소를 지으며 말하고서 여행을 계속했다.

- come upon ~을 우연히 만나다
- unwelcoming ⑧ 불친절한, 환영하지 않는
- generous ⑧ 관대한
- valley ⑩ 골짜기
- helplessly [ad] 힘없이, 무기력하게

구문 풀이

(B) 6행 I felt as though I was a member of the family in the village.
접속사(마치 ~인 것처럼)

(C) 6행 I found the people most unwelcoming.
5형식 동사   목적어   목적격 보어(형용사)

(D) 2행 I am sad to have left there.
완료부정사(am보다 과거에 일어난 일 묘사)

43 글의 순서 파악　정답률 66% | 정답 ②

주어진 글 (A)에 이어질 내용을 순서에 맞게 배열한 것으로 가장 적절한 것은?

① (B) - (D) - (C)　　✓ (C) - (B) - (D)
③ (C) - (D) - (B)　　④ (D) - (B) - (C)
⑤ (D) - (C) - (B)

Why? 왜 정답일까?

여행 중이던 젊은이가 수도승을 만나 물어볼 것이 있다고 말했다는 (A) 뒤에는, 젊은이가 산속 마을에 대한 자신의 부정적 감상을 말하며 골짜기의 마을이 어떠한지 묻자 수도승이 산속 마을과 차이가 없을 것이라고 답했다는 내용의 (C)가 연결된다. 이어 (B)에서는 똑같이 산속 마을에서 출발한 중년 남자가 수도승과 비슷한 대화를 나누며 산속 마을에 관해 좋은 감상을 이야기했다는 내용이 나오고, (D)에서는 수도승이 그렇다면 골짜기 마을도 좋게 느껴질 것이라 답해주었다고 한다. 따라서 글의 순서로 가장 적절한 것은 ② '(C) - (B) - (D)'이다.

44 지칭 추론　정답률 64% | 정답 ④

밑줄 친 (a) ~ (e) 중에서 가리키는 대상이 나머지 넷과 다른 것은?

① (a)　② (b)　③ (c)　✓ (d)　⑤ (e)

Why? 왜 정답일까?

(a), (b), (c), (e)는 the monk, (d)는 the young man이므로, (a) ~ (e) 중에서 가리키는 대상이 다른 하나는 ④ '(d)'이다.

45 세부 내용 파악　정답률 72% | 정답 ⑤

윗글에 관한 내용으로 적절하지 않은 것은?

① 한 수도승이 들판에서 일하고 있었다.
② 중년 남자는 골짜기에 있는 마을로 가는 중이었다.
③ 수도승은 골짜기에 있는 마을에 대해 질문받았다.
④ 수도승의 말을 듣고 젊은이는 고개를 숙였다.
✓ 중년 남자는 산속에 있는 마을을 떠나서 기쁘다고 말했다.

Why? 왜 정답일까?

(D) 'I am sad to have left there.'에 따르면 중년 남자는 산속 마을을 떠나서 슬펐다고 말했으므로, 내용과 일치하지 않는 것은 ⑤ '중년 남자는 산속에 있는 마을을 떠나서 기쁘다고 말했다.'이다.

Why? 왜 오답일까?

① (A) 'As he walked he noticed a monk working in the fields.'의 내용과 일치한다.
② (B) '"I am going to the village in the valley," said the man.'의 내용과 일치한다.
③ (B) '"Do you know what it is like?"'의 내용과 일치한다.
④ (C) 'The young man lowered his head helplessly and walked on.'의 내용과 일치한다.

어휘 Review Test 03　문제편 030쪽

A	B	C	D
01 발표하다, 알리다	01 maintain	01 ⓕ	01 ⓟ
02 책임	02 communicate	02 ⓟ	02 ⓙ
03 열정	03 regulation	03 ⓚ	03 ⓘ
04 모이다	04 flow	04 ⓡ	04 ⓗ
05 일, 과업, 과제	05 foreign	05 ⓛ	05 ⓕ
06 완수하다	06 engaging	06 ⓜ	06 ⓘ
07 진지한	07 competitive	07 ⓞ	07 ⓣ
08 통찰력	08 necessarily	08 ⓔ	08 ⓔ
09 기온	09 material	09 ⓐ	09 ⓝ
10 인식하다	10 influence	10 ⓝ	10 ⓠ
11 호기심	11 traditional	11 ⓙ	11 ⓢ
12 감당하다	12 reply	12 ⓘ	12 ⓕ
13 구체적인	13 indeed	13 ⓒ	13 ⓐ
14 이전의	14 observe	14 ⓓ	14 ⓒ
15 관점, 시점	15 civilization	15 ⓘ	15 ⓚ
16 줄이다	16 currently	16 ⓖ	16 ⓓ
17 나타나다, 출현하다	17 claim	17 ⓢ	17 ⓖ
18 생태계	18 factor	18 ⓑ	18 ⓑ
19 살아남다	19 plain	19 ⓗ	19 ⓞ
20 제거하다	20 mainly	20 ⓠ	20 ⓜ

04회 | 2021학년도 3월 학력평가　고1

· 정답 ·

18 ④ 19 ① 20 ③ 21 ② 22 ⑤　23 ① 24 ⑤ 25 ③ 26 ⑤ 27 ⑤　28 ④ 29 ③ 30 ③ 31 ⑤ 32 ④
33 ① 34 ⑤ 35 ③ 36 ② 37 ③　38 ② 39 ④ 40 ② 41 ① 42 ⑤　43 ② 44 ⑤ 45 ②

★ 표기된 문항은 [등급을 가르는 문제]에 해당하는 문항입니다.

18 도서관 공사 자원봉사 모집　정답률 90% | 정답 ④

다음 글의 목적으로 가장 적절한 것은?

① 도서관 임시 휴관의 이유를 설명하려고
② 도서관 자원봉사자 교육 일정을 안내하려고
③ 도서관 보수를 위한 모금 행사를 제안하려고
✓ 도서관 공사에 참여할 자원봉사자를 모집하려고
⑤ 도서관에서 개최하는 글쓰기 대회를 홍보하려고

Dear members of Eastwood Library,
Eastwood 도서관 회원께,
Thanks to the Friends of Literature group, / we've successfully raised enough money / to remodel the library building.
Friends of Literature 모임 덕분에, / 우리는 충분한 돈을 성공적으로 모았습니다. / 도서관 건물을 리모델링하기 위한
John Baker, our local builder, / has volunteered to help us with the remodelling / but he needs assistance.
우리 지역의 건축업자인 John Baker 씨가 / 우리의 리모델링을 돕기로 자원했지만, / 그는 도움이 필요합니다.
By grabbing a hammer or a paint brush / and donating your time, / you can help with the construction.
망치나 페인트 붓을 쥐고 / 시간을 기부함으로써, / 여러분은 공사를 도울 수 있습니다.
Join Mr. Baker in his volunteering team / and become a part of making Eastwood Library a better place!
Baker 씨의 자원봉사 팀에 동참하여 / Eastwood 도서관을 더 좋은 곳으로 만드는 데 참여하십시오!
Please call 541-567-1234 for more information.
더 많은 정보를 원하시면 541-567-1234로 전화해 주십시오.
Sincerely, // Mark Anderson
Mark Anderson 드림

Eastwood 도서관 회원들께,

Friends of Literature 모임 덕분에, 우리는 도서관 건물을 리모델링하기 위한 충분한 돈을 성공적으로 모았습니다. 우리 지역의 건축업자인 John Baker 씨가 우리의 리모델링을 돕기로 자원했지만, 그는 도움이 필요합니다. 망치나 페인트 붓을 쥐고 시간을 기부함으로써, 여러분은 공사를 도울 수 있습니다. Baker 씨의 자원봉사 팀에 동참하여 Eastwood 도서관을 더 좋은 곳으로 만드는 데 참여하십시오! 더 많은 정보를 원하시면 541-567-1234로 전화해 주십시오.

Mark Anderson 드림

Why? 왜 정답일까?

'By grabbing a hammer or a paint brush and donating your time, you can help with the construction. Join Mr. Baker in his volunteering team ~'에서 자원봉사 팀에 참여하여 도서관 공사에 도움이 되어 달라고 언급하는 것으로 볼 때, 글의 목적으로 가장 적절한 것은 ④ '도서관 공사에 참여할 자원봉사자를 모집하려고'이다.

● raise ⓥ (돈을) 모으다
● assistance ⓝ 도움
● construction ⓝ 공사, 건설
● volunteer ⓥ 자원하다
● grab ⓥ 쥐다

구문 풀이

5행 By grabbing a hammer or a paint brush and donating your time, you can help with the construction.
「by + 동명사1 + / 동명사2 : ~하고 …함으로써」

19 새 친구가 생길 것이라는 기대감에 들뜬 Shirley　정답률 93% | 정답 ①

다음 글에 드러난 Shirley의 심경으로 가장 적절한 것은?

✓ curious and excited - 궁금하고 신난
② sorry and upset - 미안하고 언짢은
③ jealous and annoyed - 질투 나고 짜증 난
④ calm and relaxed - 평온하고 여유로운
⑤ disappointed and unhappy - 실망하고 불행한

On the way home, / Shirley noticed a truck parked / in front of the house across the street.
집에 오는 길에, / Shirley는 트럭 한 대가 주차된 것을 알아차렸다. / 길 건너편 집 앞에
New neighbors!
새 이웃이었다!
Shirley was dying to know about them.
Shirley는 그들에 대해 알고 싶어 죽을 지경이었다.
"Do you know anything about the new neighbors?" / she asked Pa at dinner.
"새 이웃에 대해 뭔가 알고 계셔요?"라고 / 저녁 식사 시간에 그녀는 아빠에게 물었다.
He said, / "Yes, and there's one thing / that may be interesting to you."
그는 말했다. / "그럼, 그리고 한 가지 있지, / 네 흥미를 끌 만한 것이"라고
Shirley had a billion more questions.
Shirley는 더 묻고 싶은 게 엄청나게 많았다.
Pa said joyfully, / "They have a girl just your age.
아빠는 기쁘게 말했다. / "딱 네 나이의 여자아이가 한 명 있어.
Maybe she wants to be your playmate."
아마 그 애가 네 놀이 친구가 되고 싶어 할 수도 있어."라고

Shirley nearly dropped her fork on the floor.
Shirley는 포크를 바닥에 떨어뜨릴 뻔했다.
How many times had she prayed for a friend?
그녀가 친구를 달라고 얼마나 많이 기도했던가?
Finally, her prayers were answered!
마침내 그녀의 기도가 응답받았다!
She and the new girl could go to school together, / play together, / and become best friends.
그녀와 새로 온 여자아이는 함께 학교에 가고, / 함께 놀고, / 그리고 제일 친한 친구가 될 수 있을지도 모른다.

집에 오는 길에, Shirley는 트럭 한 대가 길 건너편 집 앞에 주차된 것을 알아차렸다. 새 이웃이었다! Shirley는 그들에 대해 알고 싶어 죽을 지경이었다. 저녁 식사 시간에 그녀는 "새 이웃에 대해 뭔가 알고 계세요?"라고 아빠에게 물었다. 그는 "그럼. 그리고 네 흥미를 끌 만한 것이 한 가지 있지."라고 말했다. Shirley는 더 묻고 싶은 게 엄청나게 많았다. 아빠는 "딱 네 나이의 여자아이가 한 명 있어. 아마 그 애가 네 놀이 친구가 되고 싶어 할 수도 있어."라고 기쁘게 말했다. Shirley는 포크를 바닥에 떨어뜨릴 뻔했다. 그녀가 친구를 달라고 얼마나 많이 기도했던가? 마침내 그녀의 기도가 응답받았다! 그녀와 새로 온 여자아이는 함께 학교에 가고, 함께 놀고, 그리고 제일 친한 친구가 될 수 있을지도 모른다.

Why? 왜 정답일까?
새 이웃이 이사온 것을 본 Shirley가 새 친구에 대한 호기심과 설렘으로 기뻐하는 모습(Shirley was dying to know about them. / How many times had she prayed for a friend? Finally, her prayers were answered!)을 주로 묘사한 글이다. 따라서 Shirley의 심경으로 가장 적절한 것은 ① '궁금하고 신난'이다.

- notice ⓥ 알아차리다
- be dying to 간절히 ~하고 싶어 하다
- curious ⓐ 호기심이 많은
- disappointed ⓐ 실망한
- across the street 길 건너에
- joyfully ⓐⓓ 즐겁게
- jealous ⓐ 질투 나는

구문 풀이

1행 On the way home, Shirley noticed a truck parked in front of the house
across the street.
지각 동사 / 목적어 / 목적격 보어 (과거분사)

---

20 이메일을 보내기 전 꼭 최종 검토하기 정답률 91% | 정답 ③

다음 글에서 필자가 주장하는 바로 가장 적절한 것은?
① 중요한 이메일은 출력하여 보관해야 한다.
② 글을 쓸 때에는 개요 작성부터 시작해야 한다.
☑ 이메일을 전송하기 전에 반드시 검토해야 한다.
④ 업무와 관련된 컴퓨터 기능을 우선 익혀야 한다.
⑤ 업무상 중요한 내용은 이메일보다는 직접 전달해야 한다.

At a publishing house and at a newspaper / you learn the following:
출판사와 신문사에서 / 다음과 같이 알게 된다:
It's not a mistake / if it doesn't end up in print.
그것은 실수가 아니다. / 결국 인쇄물로 나오지 않으면
It's the same for email.
그것은 이메일에서도 마찬가지다.
Nothing bad can happen / if you haven't hit the Send key.
어떤 나쁜 일도 일어날 수 없다. / 여러분이 전송 버튼을 눌러 버리기 전까지는
What you've written / can have misspellings, errors of fact, rude comments, obvious lies, / but it doesn't matter.
여러분이 쓴 글에는 / 잘못 쓴 철자, 사실의 오류, 무례한 말, 명백한 거짓말이 있을 수 있지만, / 그것은 문제가 되지 않는다.
If you haven't sent it, / you still have time to fix it.
여러분이 그것을 전송하지 않았다면, / 여러분에게는 아직 그것을 고칠 시간이 있다.
You can correct any mistake / and nobody will ever know the difference.
여러분은 어떤 실수라도 수정할 수 있고 / 누구도 결코 그 변화를 모를 것이다.
This is easier said than done, of course.
물론, 이것은 말은 쉽지만 행하기는 어렵다.
Send is your computer's most attractive command.
전송은 여러분 컴퓨터의 가장 매력적인 명령어이다.
But before you hit the Send key, / make sure that you read your document carefully one last time.
그러나 여러분이 그 전송 버튼을 누르기 전에, / 반드시 문서를 마지막으로 한 번 주의 깊게 읽어 보라.

출판사와 신문사에서 다음과 같이 알게 된다. 결국 인쇄물로 나오지 않으면 그것은 실수가 아니다. 그것은 이메일에서도 마찬가지다. 전송 버튼을 눌러 버리기 전까지는 어떤 나쁜 일도 일어날 수 없다. 여러분이 쓴 글에는 잘못 쓴 철자, 사실의 오류, 무례한 말, 명백한 거짓말이 있을 수 있지만, 그것은 문제가 되지 않는다. 그것을 전송하지 않았다면, 아직 그것을 고칠 시간이 있다. 어떤 실수라도 수정할 수 있고 누구도 결코 그 변화를 모를 것이다. 물론, 이것은 말은 쉽지만 행하기는 어렵다. 전송은 여러분 컴퓨터의 가장 매력적인 명령어이다. 그러나 그 전송 버튼을 누르기 전에, 반드시 문서를 마지막으로 한 번 주의 깊게 읽어 보라.

Why? 왜 정답일까?
마지막 문장인 '~ before you hit the Send key, make sure that you read your document carefully one last time.'에서 이메일의 전송 버튼을 누르기 전 꼭 마지막에 주의 깊게 읽어보라고 언급하는 것으로 볼 때, 필자가 주장하는 바로 가장 적절한 것은 ③ '이메일을 전송하기 전에 반드시 검토해야 한다.'이다.

- in print 출간되는, 발표되는
- rude ⓐ 무례한
- fix ⓥ 고치다
- command ⓝ 명령(어) ⓥ 명령하다
- misspelling ⓝ 오탈자
- obvious ⓐ 명백한
- easier said than done 행동보다 말이 쉽다

구문 풀이

9행 But before you hit the Send key, make sure that you read your document
접속사(~ 전에) / 명령문(~하라) / 접속사
carefully one last time.
(~것을)

---

21 과거의 후회를 극복하고 미래를 기약하기 정답률 73% | 정답 ②

밑줄 친 translate it from the past tense to the future tense가 다음 글에서 의미하는 바로 가장 적절한 것은? [3점]
① look for a job linked to your interest – 흥미와 관련된 일을 찾을
☑ get over regrets and plan for next time – 후회를 극복하고 다음을 계획할
③ surround yourself with supportive people – 힘을 주는 사람들로 주변을 채울
④ study grammar and write clear sentences – 문법을 공부하여 명확한 문장을 쓸
⑤ examine your way of speaking and apologize – 말하는 방법을 돌아보고 사과할

Get past the 'I wish I hadn't done that!' reaction.
'내가 그것을 하지 말았어야 했는데'라는 반응을 넘어서라.
If the disappointment you're feeling / is linked to an exam you didn't pass / because you didn't study for it, / or a job you didn't get / because you said silly things at the interview, / or a person you didn't impress / because you took entirely the wrong approach, / accept that it's happened now.
만일 여러분이 느끼는 실망이 / 통과하지 못한 시험과 연관되어 있다면, / 여러분이 시험공부를 하지 않았기 때문에 / 또는 여러분이 얻지 못한 일자리 / 여러분이 면접에서 바보 같은 말을 했기 때문에 / 또는 여러분이 좋은 인상을 주지 못한 사람과 / 여러분이 완전히 잘못된 접근 방법을 택했기 때문에 / 이제는 그 일이 일어나 버렸다는 것을 받아들여라.
The only value of 'I wish I hadn't done that!' / is that you'll know better what to do next time.
'내가 그것을 하지 말았어야 했는데'의 유일한 가치는 / 여러분이 다음에 무엇을 할지 더 잘 알게 되리라는 점이다.
The learning pay-off is useful and significant.
배움으로 얻게 되는 이득은 유용하고 의미가 있다.
This 'if only I ...' agenda is virtual.
이러한 '내가 …하기만 했다면'이라는 의제는 가상의 것이다.
Once you have worked that out, / it's time to translate it / from the past tense to the future tense:
여러분이 그것을 파악했다면, / 이제 그것을 바꿀 때이다. / 과거 시제에서 미래 시제로
'Next time I'm in this situation, I'm going to try to ...'.
'다음에 내가 이 상황일 때 나는 …하려고 할 것이다.'

'내가 그것을 하지 말았어야 했는데!'라는 반응을 넘어서라. 만일 여러분이 느끼는 실망이 시험공부를 하지 않았기 때문에 통과하지 못한 시험, 면접에서 바보 같은 말을 해서 얻지 못한 일자리, 또는 완전히 잘못된 접근 방법을 택하는 바람에 좋은 인상을 주지 못한 사람과 연관되어 있다면, 이제는 그 일이 일어나 버렸다는 것을 받아들여라. '내가 그것을 하지 말았어야 했는데!'의 유일한 가치는 다음에 무엇을 할지 더 잘 알게 되리라는 점이다. 배움으로 얻게 되는 이득은 유용하고 의미가 있다. 이러한 '내가 …하기만 했다면'이라는 의제는 가상의 것이다. 여러분이 그것을 파악했다면, 이제 그것을 과거 시제에서 미래 시제로 바꿀 때이다. '다음에 내가 이 상황일 때 나는 …하려고 할 것이다.'

Why? 왜 정답일까?
'The only value of 'I wish I hadn't done that!' is that you'll know better what to do next time.'에서 과거에 이미 해버린 일을 하지 말았어야 한다는 후회는 다음에 할 일을 더 잘 알게 된다는 점에서만 의의가 있다고 한다. 이를 근거로 볼 때, '과거 시제 대신 미래 시제를 쓰라'는 뜻의 밑줄 친 부분은 후회되는 상황을 거울로 삼아 앞으로 같은 상황이 벌어졌을 때 할 일에 대한 대책을 세우라는 의미로 이해할 수 있다. 따라서 밑줄 친 부분이 의미하는 바로 가장 적절한 것은 ② '후회를 극복하고 다음을 계획할'이다.

- get past 지나가다, 추월하다
- impress ⓥ 인상을 주다
- pay-off ⓝ 이득, 보상
- translate ⓥ 바꾸다, 번역하다
- supportive ⓐ 힘이 되는, 지지를 주는
- disappointment ⓝ 실망
- entirely ⓐⓓ 완전히, 전적으로
- virtual ⓐ 가상의
- get over ~을 극복하다
- examine ⓥ 검토하다, 조사하다

구문 풀이

1행 If the disappointment [you're feeling] is linked to an exam [you didn't
접속사(~한다면) / 주어 / 동사구 / to의 목적어1
pass because you didn't study for it], or a job [you didn't get because you said
to의 목적어2
silly things at the interview], or a person [you didn't impress because you took
to의 목적어3
entirely the wrong approach], accept that it's happened now.
명령문(~하라) / 접속사 / =has

---

22 스트레스와 괴로움의 원천인 자기 의심 정답률 67% | 정답 ⑤

다음 글의 요지로 가장 적절한 것은?
① 비판적인 시각은 객관적인 문제 분석에 도움이 된다.
② 성취 욕구는 스트레스를 이겨 낼 원동력이 될 수 있다.
③ 적절한 수준의 스트레스는 과제 수행의 효율을 높인다.
④ 실패의 경험은 자존감을 낮추고, 타인에 의존하게 한다.
☑ 자기 의심은 스트레스를 유발하고, 객관적 판단을 흐린다.

If you care deeply about something, / you may place greater value on your ability / to succeed in that area of concern.
여러분이 무언가에 깊이 관심을 두면, / 여러분은 여러분의 능력에 더 큰 가치를 둘지도 모른다. / 그 관심 영역에서 성공하기 위한
The internal pressure / you place on yourself / to achieve or do well socially / is normal and useful, / but when you doubt your ability / to succeed in areas / that are important to you, / your self-worth suffers.
내적인 압박은 / 여러분이 스스로에게 가하는 / 성취하거나 사회적으로 성공하기 위해 / 정상적이고 유용하지만, / 여러분이 여러분의 능력을 의심하면, / 영역에서 성공하기 위한 / 자신에게 중요한 / 여러분의 자아 존중감은 상처를 입는다.
Situations are uniquely stressful for each of us / based on whether or not they activate our doubt.
상황은 우리 각각에게 저마다 다른 방식으로 스트레스를 준다. / 그것이 우리의 의심을 활성화하는지 여부에 따라
It's not the pressure to perform / that creates your stress.
결코 수행에 대한 압박이 아니다. / 여러분의 스트레스를 일으키는 것은
Rather, it's the self-doubt / that bothers you.
오히려, 바로 자기 의심이다. / 여러분을 괴롭히는 것은
Doubt causes you / to see positive, neutral, and even genuinely negative experiences / more negatively / and as a reflection of your own shortcomings.
의심은 여러분이 ~하게 한다. / 긍정적인 경험, 중립적인 경험, 그리고 심지어 진짜로 부정적인 경험을 보게 / 더 부정적으로 / 그리

고 여러분 자신의 단점을 반영한 것으로

When you see situations and your strengths more objectively, / you are less likely to have doubt / as the source of your distress.
여러분이 상황과 여러분의 강점을 더 객관적으로 바라볼 때, / 여러분은 의심을 덜 가질 것이다. / 괴로움의 원천인

무언가에 깊이 관심을 두면, 그 관심 영역에서 성공하기 위한 여러분의 능력에 더 큰 가치를 둘지도 모른다. 성취하거나 사회적으로 성공하기 위해 스스로에게 가하는 내적인 압박은 정상적이고 유용하지만, 자신에게 중요한 영역에서 성공하기 위한 여러분의 능력을 의심하면, 여러분의 자아 존중감은 상처를 입는다. 상황이 우리의 의심을 활성화하는지 여부에 따라 그것은 우리 각각에게 저마다 다른 방식으로 스트레스를 준다. 여러분의 스트레스를 일으키는 것은 결코 수행에 대한 압박이 아니다. 오히려, 여러분을 괴롭히는 것은 바로 자기 의심이다. 의심은 긍정적인 경험, 중립적인 경험, 그리고 심지어 진짜로 부정적인 경험을 더 부정적으로 보게 하고, 여러분 자신의 단점을 반영한 것으로 (그것들을) 보게 한다. 상황과 여러분의 강점을 더 객관적으로 바라볼 때, 여러분은 괴로움의 원천인 의심을 덜 가질 것이다.

Why? 왜 정답일까?

'Rather, it's the self-doubt that bothers you.' 이후로 수행에 대한 압박이 아닌 자기 의심이야말로 우리에게 스트레스를 주며 우리가 스스로를 실제보다 더 부정적으로 바라보도록 만든다는 내용이 제시된다. 따라서 글의 요지로 가장 적절한 것은 ⑤ '자기 의심은 스트레스를 유발하고, 객관적 판단을 흐린다.'이다.

- concern ⓝ 관심, 걱정
- doubt ⓝ 의심 ⓥ 의심하다
- uniquely ⓐⓓ 특유의 방법으로, 독특하게
- neutral ⓐ 중립적인
- reflection ⓝ 반영
- objectively ⓐⓓ 객관적으로
- internal ⓐ 내적인
- self-worth ⓝ 자아 존중감, 자기 가치감
- activate ⓥ 활성화하다
- genuinely ⓐⓓ 진정으로
- shortcoming ⓝ 단점

구문 풀이

2행 The internal pressure [(that) you place on yourself to achieve or do well
주어1(선행사)   목적격 관계대명사   부사적 용법(~하기 위해)
socially] is normal and useful, but when you doubt your ability to succeed in areas
동사(단수)   접속사(~할 때)   형용사적 용법   선행사
[that are important to you] your self-worth suffers.
주격 관계대명사   주어2   동사2

23 대화 중 거짓말을 할 때의 특징 정답률 68% | 정답 ①

다음 글의 주제로 가장 적절한 것은?

✓① delayed responses as a sign of lying – 거짓말의 징후로 늦어지는 대답
② ways listeners encourage the speaker – 청자가 화자를 격려하는 방식
③ difficulties in finding useful information – 유용한 정보를 찾는 데 있어서의 어려움
④ necessity of white lies in social settings – 사회적 상황에서 선의의 거짓말의 필요성
⑤ shared experiences as conversation topics – 대화 주제로서의 공유된 경험

When two people are involved in an honest and open conversation, / there is a back and forth flow of information.
두 사람이 솔직하고 진술한 대화에 참여하면 / 정보가 왔다 갔다 하며 흐른다.
It is a smooth exchange.
그것은 순조로운 대화이다.
Since each one is drawing on their past personal experiences, / the pace of the exchange is as fast as memory.
각자가 자신의 개인적인 과거 경험에 의존하고 있기 때문에, / 주고받는 속도가 기억만큼 빠르다.
When one person lies, / their responses will come more slowly / because the brain needs more time / to process the details of a new invention / than to recall stored facts.
한 사람이 거짓말하면, / 그 사람의 반응이 더 느리게 나올 텐데, / 뇌는 더 많은 시간이 필요하기 때문이다. / 새로 꾸며 낸 이야기의 세부 사항을 처리하는 데에 / 저장된 사실을 기억해 내는 데 비해
As they say, "Timing is everything."
사람들이 말하듯 "타이밍이 가장 중요하다."
You will notice the time lag / when you are having a conversation with someone / who is making things up as they go.
여러분은 시간의 지연을 알아차릴 것이다. / 여러분이 누군가와 이야기를 하고 있으면, / 말을 하면서 이야기를 꾸며 내고 있는
Don't forget / that the other person may be reading your body language as well, / and if you seem to be disbelieving their story, / they will have to pause / to process that information, too.
잊지 말라. / 상대가 여러분의 몸짓 언어 역시 읽고 있을지도 모른다는 것과 / 만약 여러분이 그 사람의 이야기를 믿지 않고 있는 것처럼 보이면, / 그 사람은 잠시 멈춰야 할 것임을 / 그 정보 또한 처리하기 위해

두 사람이 솔직하고 진술한 대화에 참여하면 정보가 왔다 갔다 하며 흐른다. 그것은 순조로운 대화이다. 각자가 자신의 개인적인 과거 경험에 의존하고 있기 때문에, 주고받는 속도가 기억만큼 빠르다. 한 사람이 거짓말하면, 그 사람의 반응이 더 느리게 나올 텐데, 뇌는 저장된 사실을 기억해 내는 데 비해 새로 꾸며 낸 이야기의 세부 사항을 처리하는 데에 더 많은 시간이 필요하기 때문이다. 사람들이 말하듯 "타이밍이 가장 중요하다." 말을 하면서 이야기를 꾸며 내고 있는 누군가와 이야기를 하고 있으면, 여러분은 시간의 지연을 알아차릴 것이다. 상대가 여러분의 몸짓 언어 역시 읽고 있을지도 모른다는 것과, 만약 여러분이 그 사람의 이야기를 믿지 않고 있는 것처럼 보이면 그 사람은 그 정보 또한 처리하기 위해 잠시 멈춰야 할 것임을 잊지 말아야 한다.

Why? 왜 정답일까?

'When one person lies, their responses will come more slowly ~'와 'You will notice the time lag when you are having a conversation with someone who is making things up as they go.'에서 두 사람이 모두 솔직하게 임하는 대화와는 달리 한 사람이 거짓말을 하고 있는 대화에서는 거짓말을 하고 있는 사람의 반응이 느려진다고 한다. 따라서 글의 주제로 가장 적절한 것은 ① '거짓말의 징후인 늦어지는 대답'이다.

- exchange ⓝ 대화, 주고받음, 교환
- process ⓥ 처리하다
- make up 만들어내다, 꾸며내다
- necessity ⓝ 필요성
- draw on ~에 의존하다, ~을 이용하다
- recall ⓥ 회상하다
- disbelieve ⓥ 불신하다, 믿지 않다

구문 풀이

5행 When one person lies, their responses will come more slowly because
시간 접속사   현재시제   미래시제   접속사(~ 때문에)
the brain needs more time to process the details of a new invention than to recall
부사적 용법1   부사적 용법2(than 앞뒤 병렬)
stored facts.

24 산 이후 사용하지 않아 낭비가 되어버리는 물건들 정답률 77% | 정답 ⑤

다음 글의 제목으로 가장 적절한 것은?

① Spending Enables the Economy – 소비가 경제를 가능하게 한다
② Money Management: Dos and Don'ts – 돈 관리: 해야 할 일과 하지 말아야 할 일
③ Too Much Shopping: A Sign of Loneliness – 너무 많은 쇼핑: 외로움의 신호
④ 3R's of Waste: Reduce, Reuse, and Recycle – 쓰레기의 3R: 줄이고, 다시 쓰고, 재활용하자
✓⑤ What You Buy Is Waste Unless You Use It – 당신이 사는 것은 당신이 그것을 이용하지 않는 한 낭비이다

Think, for a moment, / about something you bought / that you never ended up using.
잠시 생각해 봐. / 여러분이 산 물건에 대해 / 여러분이 결국 한 번도 사용하지 않았던
An item of clothing / you never ended up wearing?
옷 한 벌? / 여러분이 결국 한 번도 입지 않은
A book you never read?
여러분이 한 번도 읽지 않은 책 한 권?
Some piece of electronic equipment / that never even made it out of the box?
어떤 전자 기기? / 심지어 상자에서 꺼내 보지도 않은
It is estimated / that Australians alone / spend on average $10.8 billion AUD (approximately $9.99 billion USD) every year / on goods they do not use / — more than the total government spending on universities and roads.
추산되는데, / 호주인들만 봐도 / 매년 평균 108억 호주 달러(약 99억 9천 미국 달러)를 쓰는 것으로 / 그들이 사용하지 않는 물건에 / 이는 대학과 도로에 사용하는 정부 지출 총액을 넘는 금액이다
That is an average of $1,250 AUD (approximately $1,156 USD) / for each household.
그 금액은 평균 1,250 호주 달러(약 1,156 미국 달러)이다. / 각 가구당
All the things we buy / that then just sit there gathering dust / are waste / — a waste of money, a waste of time, / and waste in the sense of pure rubbish.
우리가 산 모든 물건은 / 그러고 나서 제자리에서 먼지를 뒤집어쓰고 있는 / 낭비인데, / 돈 낭비, / 시간 낭비, / 그리고 순전히 쓸모없는 물건이라는 의미에서 낭비이다.
As the author Clive Hamilton observes, / 'The difference / between the stuff we buy and what we use / is waste.'
작가인 Clive Hamilton이 말하는 것처럼, / "뺀 것은 / 우리가 사는 물건에서 우리가 사용하는 것을 / 낭비이다".

여러분이 사 놓고 결국 한 번도 사용하지 않았던 물건에 대해 잠시 생각해 봐라. 결국 한 번도 입지 않은 옷 한 벌? 한 번도 읽지 않은 책 한 권? 심지어 상자에서 꺼내 보지도 않은 어떤 전자 기기? 호주인들만 봐도 사용하지 않는 물건에 매년 평균 108억 호주 달러(약 99억 9천 미국 달러)를 쓰는 것으로 추산되는데, 이는 대학과 도로에 사용하는 정부 지출 총액을 넘는 금액이다. 그 금액은 각 가구당 평균 1,250 호주 달러(약 1,156 미국 달러)이다. 우리가 사고 나서 제자리에서 먼지를 뒤집어쓰고 있는 모든 물건은 낭비인데, 돈 낭비, 시간 낭비, 그리고 순전히 쓸모없는 물건이라는 의미에서 낭비이다. 작가인 Clive Hamilton이 말하는 것처럼 "우리가 사는 물건에서 우리가 사용하는 것을 뺀 것은 낭비이다".

Why? 왜 정답일까?

사고 나서 한 번도 사용하지 않아 먼지만 쌓이고 있는 물건은 모두 낭비라는 내용의 글로, 마지막 두 문장이 주제를 잘 제시한다(All the things we buy that then just sit there gathering dust are waste ~. ~ 'The difference between the stuff we buy and what we use is waste.') 따라서 글의 제목으로 가장 적절한 것은 ⑤ '당신이 사는 것은 당신이 그것을 이용하지 않는 한 낭비이다'이다.

- end up 결국 ~하다
- equipment ⓝ 기기, 장비
- gather ⓥ 모으다
- rubbish ⓝ 쓰레기
- difference ⓝ 뺀 것, (양의) 차이
- electronic ⓐ 전자의
- approximately ⓐⓓ 대략
- waste ⓝ 낭비, 쓰레기
- observe ⓥ 말하다, 관찰하다

구문 풀이

9행 All the things [(that) we buy] [that then just sit there gathering dust] are
주어(선행사)   목적격 관계대명사   주격 관계대명사   분사구문(~하면서)   동사(복수)
waste — a waste of money, a waste of time, and waste in the sense of pure rubbish.
보어   동격(보어 보충 설명)

25 교육용 콘텐츠를 이용하기 위해 기기를 사용한 학생들의 비율 정답률 80% | 정답 ③

다음 도표의 내용과 일치하지 않는 것은?

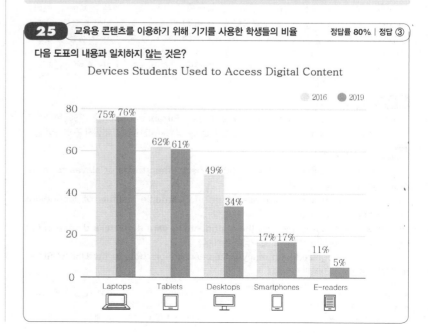

Devices Students Used to Access Digital Content

	Laptops	Tablets	Desktops	Smartphones	E-readers
2016	75%	62%	49%	17%	11%
2019	76%	61%	34%	17%	5%

The above graph shows / the percentage of students from kindergarten to 12th grade / who used devices / to access digital educational content / in 2016 and in 2019.
위 그래프는 보여 준다. / 유치원에서 12학년까지의 학생들의 비율을 / 기기를 사용한, / 교육용 디지털 콘텐츠를 이용하기 위해 / 2016년과 2019년에

① Laptops were the most used device / for students to access digital content / in both years.
노트북은 가장 많이 사용한 기기였다. / 학생들이 디지털 콘텐츠를 이용하기 위해 / 두 해 모두

② Both in 2016 and in 2019, / more than 6 out of 10 students used tablets.
2016년과 2019년 모두 / 10명 중 6명이 넘는 학생들이 태블릿을 사용했다.

✔ More than half the students used desktops / to access digital content / in 2016, / and more than a third used desktops in 2019.
절반이 넘는 학생들이 데스크톱을 사용하여 / 디지털 콘텐츠를 이용했고, / 2016년에는 / 2019년에는 3분의 1이 넘는 학생들이 데스크톱을 사용했다.

④ The percentage of smartphones in 2016 / was the same as that in 2019.
2016년 스마트폰의 비율은 / 2019년 스마트폰의 비율과 같았다.

⑤ E-readers ranked the lowest in both years, / with 11 percent in 2016 and 5 percent in 2019.
전자책 단말기는 두 해 모두 가장 낮은 순위를 차지했는데, / 2016년에는 11퍼센트였고 2019년에는 5퍼센트였다.

위 그래프는 2016년과 2019년에 교육용 디지털 콘텐츠를 이용하기 위해 기기를 사용한, 유치원에서 12학년까지의 학생들의 비율을 보여 준다. ① 두 해 모두 노트북은 학생들이 디지털 콘텐츠를 이용하기 위해 가장 많이 사용한 기기였다. ② 2016년과 2019년 모두 10명 중 6명이 넘는 학생들이 태블릿을 사용했다. ③ 2016년에는 절반이 넘는 학생들이 데스크톱을 사용하여 디지털 콘텐츠를 이용했고, 2019년에는 3분의 1이 넘는 학생들이 데스크톱을 사용했다. ④ 2016년 스마트폰의 비율은 2019년 스마트폰의 비율과 같았다. ⑤ 전자책 단말기는 두 해 모두 가장 낮은 순위를 차지했는데, 2016년에는 11퍼센트였고 2019년에는 5퍼센트였다.

Why? 왜 정답일까?
도표에 따르면 2016년 교육용 디지털 콘텐츠 이용 목적으로 데스크톱을 사용했던 학생들의 비율은 49%로 절반을 넘지 못했다. 따라서 도표와 일치하지 않는 것은 ③이다.

● kindergarten ⓝ 유치원
● educational ⓐ 교육의
● access ⓥ 이용하다, 접근하다, 접속하다

---

26 Elizabeth Catlett의 생애　　정답률 91% | 정답 ⑤

Elizabeth Catlett에 관한 다음 글의 내용과 일치하지 않는 것은?
① 할머니로부터 노예 이야기를 들었다.
② Carnegie Institute of Technology로부터 입학을 거절당했다.
③ University of Iowa에서 석사 학위를 취득했다.
④ 미국과 멕시코에서 많은 상을 받았다.
✔ 멕시코 시민권을 결국 받지 못했다.

Elizabeth Catlett was born in Washington, D.C. in 1915.
Elizabeth Catlett은 1915년 Washington, D.C.에서 태어났다.
『As a granddaughter of slaves, / Catlett heard the stories of slaves from her grandmother.』 ①의 근거 일치
노예의 손녀로서 / Catlett은 할머니로부터 노예 이야기를 들었다.
『After being disallowed entrance / from the Carnegie Institute of Technology / because she was black, / Catlett studied design and drawing at Howard University.』 ②의 근거 일치
입학을 거절당한 이후, / Carnegie Institute of Technology로부터 / 그녀가 흑인이라는 이유로 / Catlett은 Howard 대학에서 디자인과 소묘를 공부했다.
『She became one of the first three students / to earn a master's degree in fine arts / at the University of Iowa.』 ③의 근거 일치
그녀는 첫 세 명의 학생들 중 한 명이 되었다. / 순수 미술 석사 학위를 취득한 / Iowa 대학에서
Throughout her life, / she created art / representing the voices of people / suffering from social injustice.
평생 동안 / 그녀는 예술 작품을 창작했다. / 사람들의 목소리를 대변하는 / 사회적 불평등으로 고통받는
『She was recognized with many prizes and honors / both in the United States and in Mexico.』 ④의 근거 일치
그녀는 많은 상과 표창으로 인정받았다. / 미국과 멕시코 모두에서
『She spent over fifty years in Mexico, / and she took Mexican citizenship in 1962.』 ⑤의 근거 불일치
그녀는 멕시코에서 50년이 넘는 세월을 보냈고, / 1962년에 멕시코 시민권을 받았다.
Catlett died in 2012 at her home in Mexico.
Catlett은 2012년에 멕시코에 있는 자신의 집에서 생을 마쳤다.

Elizabeth Catlett은 1915년 Washington, D.C.에서 태어났다. 노예의 손녀로서 Catlett은 할머니로부터 노예 이야기를 들었다. 흑인이라는 이유로 Carnegie Institute of Technology로부터 입학을 거절당한 이후, Catlett은 Howard 대학에서 디자인과 소묘를 공부했다. 그녀는 Iowa 대학에서 순수 미술 석사 학위를 취득한 첫 세 명의 학생들 중 한 명이 되었다. 평생 동안 그녀는 사회적 불평등으로 고통받는 사람들의 목소리를 대변하는 예술 작품을 창작했다. 그녀는 미국과 멕시코 모두에서 많은 상과 표창으로 인정받았다. 그녀는 멕시코에서 50년이 넘는 세월을 보냈고, 1962년에 멕시코 시민권을 받았다. Catlett은 2012년에 멕시코에 있는 자신의 집에서 생을 마쳤다.

Why? 왜 정답일까?
'~ she took Mexican citizenship in 1962.'에 따르면 Elizabeth Catlett은 1962년에 멕시코 시민권을 취득하였다. 따라서 내용과 일치하지 않는 것은 ⑤ '멕시코 시민권을 결국 받지 못했다.'이다.

Why? 왜 오답일까?
① 'As a granddaughter of slaves, Catlett heard the stories of slaves from her grandmother.'의 내용과 일치한다.
② 'After being disallowed entrance from the Carnegie Institute of Technology because she was black, ~'의 내용과 일치한다.
③ 'She became one of the first three students to earn a master's degree in fine arts at the University of Iowa.'의 내용과 일치한다.
④ 'She was recognized with many prizes and honors both in the United States and in Mexico.'의 내용과 일치한다.

● slave ⓝ 노예
● entrance ⓝ 입학, 입장
● fine arts 순수 미술
● disallow ⓥ (공식적으로) 거절하다, 인정하지 않다
● earn ⓥ 얻다, 취득하다
● represent ⓥ 대표하다, 나타내다

● injustice ⓝ 불평등, 부당함
● citizenship ⓝ 시민권
● recognize ⓥ 인정하다

구문 풀이

3행 After being disallowed entrance from the Carnegie Institute of Technology
전치사(~ 후에)　수동동명사
because she was black, Catlett studied design and drawing at Howard University.
접속사(~ 때문에)　　　　주어　　동사

---

27 봄 농장 캠프 안내　　정답률 95% | 정답 ⑤

Spring Farm Camp에 관한 다음 안내문의 내용과 일치하지 않는 것은?
① 6세 ~ 10세 어린이가 참가할 수 있다.
② 참가비에 점심과 간식이 포함되어 있다.
③ 염소젖으로 치즈를 만드는 활동을 한다.
④ 딸기잼을 만들어 집으로 가져갈 수 있다.
✔ 비가 오면 운영하지 않는다.

Spring Farm Camp
봄 농장 캠프
Our one-day spring farm camp / gives your kids true, hands-on farm experience.
우리의 일일 봄 농장 캠프는 / 여러분의 자녀에게 진정한 농장 체험을 제공합니다.
When: Monday, April 19 – Friday, May 14
기간: 4월 19일 월요일 ~ 5월 14일 금요일
Time: 9 a.m. – 4 p.m.
시간: 오전 9시 ~ 오후 4시
『Ages: 6 – 10』 ①의 근거 일치
나이: 6세 ~ 10세
『Participation Fee: $70 per person (lunch and snacks included)』 ②의 근거 일치
참가비: 개인당 70달러 (점심과 간식 포함)
Activities:
활동:
『making cheese from goat's milk』 ③의 근거 일치
염소젖으로 치즈 만들기
picking strawberries
딸기 따기
『making strawberry jam to take home』 ④의 근거 일치
집으로 가져갈 딸기잼 만들기
『We are open rain or shine.』 ⑤의 근거 불일치
날씨에 상관없이 운영합니다.
For more information, / go to www.b_orchard.com.
더 많은 정보를 원하시면 / www.b_orchard.com에 접속하세요.

봄 농장 캠프

우리의 일일 봄 농장 캠프는 여러분의 자녀에게 진정한 농장 체험을 제공합니다.

기간: 4월 19일 월요일 ~ 5월 14일 금요일
시간: 오전 9시 ~ 오후 4시
나이: 6세 ~ 10세
참가비: 개인당 70달러 (점심과 간식 포함)

활동:
• 염소젖으로 치즈 만들기
• 딸기 따기
• 집으로 가져갈 딸기잼 만들기

날씨에 상관없이 운영합니다.
더 많은 정보를 원하시면 www.b_orchard.com에 접속하세요.

Why? 왜 정답일까?
'We are open rain or shine.'에서 농장 체험 행사는 날씨에 상관없이 열린다고 하므로, 안내문의 내용과 일치하지 않는 것은 ⑤ '비가 오면 운영하지 않는다.'이다.

Why? 왜 오답일까?
① 'Ages: 6 – 10'의 내용과 일치한다.
② 'Participation Fee: $70 per person / (lunch and snacks included)'의 내용과 일치한다.
③ 'making cheese from goat's milk'의 내용과 일치한다.
④ 'making strawberry jam to take home'의 내용과 일치한다.

● hands-on ⓐ 직접 해 보는, 체험의
● rain or shine 날씨에 상관없이

---

28 수족관 이용 안내　　정답률 92% | 정답 ④

Great Aquarium에 관한 다음 안내문의 내용과 일치하는 것은?
① 마지막 입장 시간은 오후 6시이다.
② 물고기 먹이 주기는 오후 1시에 시작한다.
③ 60세 이상의 티켓 가격은 33달러이다.
✔ 티켓 소지자는 무료 음료 쿠폰을 받는다.
⑤ 예약은 입장 30분 전까지 가능하다.

Great Aquarium
Great 수족관
Opening Hours: 10 a.m. – 6 p.m., daily
개장 시간: 매일 오전 10시 ~ 오후 6시
『Last entry is at 5 p.m.』 ①의 근거 불일치
마지막 입장은 오후 5시입니다.
Events
행사

| Fish Feeding
물고기 먹이 주기 | 『10 a.m. – 11 a.m.』 ②의 근거 불일치
오전 10시 ~ 오전 11시 |

Penguin Feeding 펭귄 먹이 주기	1 p.m. – 2 p.m. 오후 1시 ~ 오후 2시

Ticket Prices
티켓 가격

Age 나이	Price 가격
Kids (12 and under) 어린이(12세 이하)	$25 25달러
Adults (20 – 59) 성인(20세~59세)	$33 33달러
Teens (13 – 19) 십 대(13세~19세) 『Seniors (60 and above) 노인(60세 이상)	$30』 ③의 근거 불일치 30달러

『Ticket holders will receive a free drink coupon.』 ④의 근거 일치
티켓 소지자는 무료 음료 쿠폰을 받습니다.

Booking Tickets
티켓 예약

ALL visitors are required to book online.
'모든' 방문객은 온라인으로 예약해야 합니다.

『Booking will be accepted up to 1 hour before entry.』 ⑥의 근거 불일치
예약은 입장 1시간 전까지 받습니다.

Great 수족관

개장 시간: 매일 오전 10시 ~ 오후 6시
마지막 입장은 오후 5시입니다.

행사

물고기 먹이 주기	오전 10시 ~ 오전 11시
펭귄 먹이 주기	오후 1시 ~ 오후 2시

티켓 가격

나이	가격
어린이(12세 이하)	25달러
성인(20세 ~ 59세)	33달러
십 대(13세 ~ 19세) 노인(60세 이상)	30달러

* 티켓 소지자는 무료 음료 쿠폰을 받습니다.

티켓 예약

• '모든' 방문객은 온라인으로 예약해야 합니다.
• 예약은 입장 1시간 전까지 받습니다.

Why? 왜 정답일까?

'Ticket holders will receive a free drink coupon.'에서 티켓 소지자는 무료 음료 쿠폰을 받게 된다고 하므로, 안내문의 내용과 일치하는 것은 ④ '티켓 소지자는 무료 음료 쿠폰을 받는다.'이다.

Why? 왜 오답일까?

① 'Last entry is at 5 p.m.'에서 마지막 입장 시간은 오후 5시라고 하였다.
② 'Fish Feeding / 10 a.m. – 11 a.m.'에서 물고기 먹이 주기는 오전 10시에 시작한다고 하였다.
③ 'Seniors (60 and above) / $30'에서 60세 이상 노인의 티켓 가격은 십 대와 마찬가지로 30달러라고 하였다.
⑤ 'Booking will be accepted up to 1 hour before entry.'에서 예약은 입장 1시간 전까지 가능하다고 하였다.

● entry ⓝ 입장
● accept ⓥ 수용하다, 허용하다
● book ⓥ 예약하다
● up to ~까지

29 악기 연주를 배우기 전 악기를 탐구할 시간 주기   정답률 61% | 정답 ③

다음 글의 밑줄 친 부분 중, 어법상 틀린 것은? [3점]

Although there is usually a correct way / of holding and playing musical instruments, / the most important instruction to begin with / is ① that they are not toys / and that they must be looked after.
비록 정확한 방법이 대체로 있다고 해도 / 악기를 잡고 연주하는 / 우선적으로 가장 중요한 가르침은 / 악기가 장난감이 아니라는 것과 / 악기를 관리해야 한다는 것이다.

② Allow children time / to explore ways of handling and playing the instruments for themselves / before showing them.
아이들에게 시간을 주어라 / 악기를 직접 다루고 연주하는 방법을 탐구할 / 그것을 알려 주기 전에

Finding different ways to produce sounds / ✔is an important stage of musical exploration.
소리를 만들어 내는 여러 가지 방법을 찾는 것은 / 음악적 탐구의 중요한 단계이다.

Correct playing comes from the desire / ④ to find the most appropriate sound quality / and find the most comfortable playing position / so that one can play with control over time.
정확한 연주는 욕구에서 나온다 / 가장 알맞은 음질을 찾고 / 가장 편안한 연주 자세를 찾으려는 / 오랜 시간 동안 잘 다루면서 연주할 수 있도록

As instruments and music become more complex, / learning appropriate playing techniques / becomes ⑤ increasingly relevant.
악기와 음악이 더 복잡해짐에 따라 / 알맞은 연주 기술을 알게 되는 것 / 점점 더 유의미해진다.

비록 악기를 잡고 연주하는 정확한 방법이 대체로 있다고 해도 우선적으로 가장 중요한 가르침은 악기가 장난감이 아니라는 것과 악기를 관리해야 한다는 것이다. 아이들에게 (악기를 다루고 연주하는) 방법을 알려 주기 전에 직접 악기를 다루고 연주하는 방법을 탐구할 시간을 주어라. 소리를 만들어 내는 여러 가지 방법을 찾는 것은 음악적 탐구의 중요한 단계이다.

정확한 연주는 가장 알맞은 음질을 찾고 오랜 시간 동안 잘 다루면서 연주할 수 있도록 가장 편안한 연주 자세를 찾으려는 욕구에서 나온다. 악기와 음악이 더 복잡해짐에 따라, 알맞은 연주 기술을 알게 되는 것은 점점 더 유의미해진다.

Why? 왜 정답일까?

'Finding different ways ~'는 동명사구 주어이므로 단수 취급한다. 따라서 are 대신 is를 써야 한다. 어법상 틀린 것은 ③이다.

Why? 왜 오답일까?

① 뒤에 'they are not toys'라는 완전한 2형식 문장이 나오므로 앞에 접속사 that을 쓴 것은 적절하다. 참고로 that절은 동사 is의 주격 보어이다.
② 앞에 주어 You가 생략된 명령문으로 동사 Allow가 원형으로 바르게 쓰였다.
④ the desire를 꾸미는 말로 to부정사가 바르게 쓰였다. ability, attempt, chance, desire, opportunity 등은 to부정사의 꾸밈을 받는 명사임을 기억해 둔다.
⑤ 2형식 동사 becomes의 보어인 형용사 relevant를 꾸미기 위해 앞에 부사인 increasingly가 적절하게 쓰였다.

● instrument ⓝ 악기, 도구
● look after ~을 관리하다, 돌보다
● appropriate ⓐ 적절한
● increasingly ⓐⓓ 점점 더
● instruction ⓝ 지침, 가르침
● explore ⓥ 탐구하다
● complex ⓐ 복잡한
● relevant ⓐ 유의미한, 적절한, 관련 있는

구문 풀이

1행 Although there is usually a correct way of holding and playing musical
접속사(~에도 불구하고) 동사(단수) 주어
instruments, the most important instruction to begin with is {that they are not toys}
주어 동사 접속사1
and {that they must be looked after}.
접속사2 [ ] : is의 보어

30 인공 조명의 가격 하락에 따른 결과   정답률 59% | 정답 ③

다음 글의 밑줄 친 부분 중, 문맥상 낱말의 쓰임이 적절하지 않은 것은? [3점]

When the price of something fundamental / drops greatly, / the whole world can change.
기본적인 어떤 것의 가격이 / 크게 하락할 때, / 온 세상이 바뀔 수 있다.

Consider light.
조명을 생각해 보자.

Chances are / you are reading this sentence / under some kind of artificial light.
아마 ~일 것이다. / 여러분은 이 문장을 읽고 있을 / 어떤 유형의 인공조명 아래에서

Moreover, / you probably never thought about / whether using artificial light for reading was worth it.
또한, / 여러분은 ~에 대해 아마 생각해 본 적이 없을 것이다. / 독서를 위해 인공조명을 이용하는 것이 그럴 만한 가치가 있는지

Light is so ① cheap / that you use it without thinking.
조명이 너무 싸서 / 여러분은 생각 없이 그것을 이용한다.

But in the early 1800s, / it would have cost you four hundred times / what you are paying now / for the same amount of light.
하지만 1800년대 초반에는, / 여러분에게 400배만큼의 비용이 들었을 것이다. / 여러분이 오늘날 지불하고 있는 것의 / 같은 양의 조명에 대해

At that price, / you would ② notice the cost / and would think twice / before using artificial light to read a book.
그 가격이면, / 여러분은 비용을 의식할 것이고 / 다시 한 번 생각할 것이다. / 책을 읽기 위해 인공조명을 이용하기 전에

The ✔drop in the price of light / lit up the world.
조명 가격의 하락은 / 세상을 밝혔다.

Not only did it turn night into day, / but it allowed us to live and work in big buildings / that ④ natural light could not enter.
그것은 밤을 낮으로 바꾸었을 뿐 아니라, / 그것은 큰 건물에서 우리가 살고 일할 수 있게 해 주었다. / 자연의 빛이 들어올 수 있는

Nearly nothing we have today / would be ⑤ possible / if the cost of artificial light had not dropped to almost nothing.
우리가 오늘날 누리는 것 중에 거의 아무것도 없다. / 가능한 것은 / 만약 인공조명의 비용이 거의 공짜 수준으로 하락하지 않았더라면

기본적인 어떤 것의 가격이 크게 하락할 때, 온 세상이 바뀔 수 있다. 조명을 생각해 보자. 아마 여러분은 어떤 유형의 인공조명 아래에서 이 문장을 읽고 있을 것이다. 또한, 여러분은 독서를 위해 인공조명을 이용하는 것이 그럴 만한 가치가 있는지에 대해 아마 생각해 본 적이 없을 것이다. 조명이 너무 ① 싸서 여러분은 생각 없이 그것을 이용한다. 하지만 1800년대 초반에는, 같은 양의 조명에 대해 오늘날 지불하고 있는 것의 400배만큼의 비용이 들었을 것이다. 그 가격이면, 여러분은 비용을 ② 의식할 것이고 책을 읽기 위해 인공조명을 이용하기 전에 다시 한 번 생각할 것이다. 조명 가격의 ③ 증가(→ 하락)는 세상을 밝혔다. 그것은 밤을 낮으로 바꾸었을 뿐 아니라, ④ 자연의 빛(자연광)이 들어올 수 없는 큰 건물에서 우리가 살고 일할 수 있게 해 주었다. 만약 인공조명의 비용이 거의 공짜 수준으로 하락하지 않았더라면 우리가 오늘날 누리는 것 중에 ⑤ 가능한 것은 거의 아무것도 없을 것이다.

Why? 왜 정답일까?

마지막 두 문장에서 인공조명의 비용이 거의 공짜 수준으로 떨어졌기 때문에 오늘날 우리는 자연광이 들어올 수 없는 건물에서도 살고 일하며 많은 것들을 누릴 수 있게 되었다고 언급하고 있다. 이를 근거로 볼 때, ③이 포함된 문장은 한때는 몹시 높았던 인공조명의 가격이 '떨어지면서' 세상이 밝아졌다는 의미가 되어야 한다. 따라서 increase를 drop으로 고쳐야 한다. 문맥상 낱말의 쓰임이 적절하지 않은 것은 ③이다.

● fundamental ⓐ 기본적인
● artificial ⓐ 인공의
● cost ⓥ (~에게 …의 비용을) 요하다, 치르게 하다 ⓝ 비용
● drop ⓥ 하락하다, 떨어지다 ⓝ 하락
● worth ⓐ ~의 가치가 있는

구문 풀이

11행 Not only did it turn night into day, but it allowed us to live and work in
「조동사+주어+동사원형 : 도치 구문」 「allow+목적어+to부정사 : ~이 …하게 해 주다」
big buildings [that natural light could not enter].
선행사 「not only+A+but (also)+B : A뿐 아니라 B도(A, B 자리에 문장)」

31 동물을 보살필 때 일관적이고 예측 가능한 환경을 만들어줄 필요성　정답률 51% | 정답 ⑤

다음 빈칸에 들어갈 말로 가장 적절한 것을 고르시오.

① silent - 고요하도록
② natural - 자연스럽도록
③ isolated - 고립되도록
④ dynamic - 역동적이도록
✓ ⑤ predictable - 예측 가능하도록

One of the most important aspects of providing good care / is making sure / that an animal's needs are being met consistently and predictably.
좋은 보살핌을 제공하는 것의 가장 중요한 측면 중에 한 가지는 / 반드시 ~하는 것이다. / 동물의 욕구가 일관되고도 예측 가능하게 충족되도록

Like humans, / animals need a sense of control.
사람과 마찬가지로, / 동물은 통제감이 필요하다.

So an animal / who may get enough food / but doesn't know when the food will appear / and can see no consistent schedule / may experience distress.
그러므로 동물은 / 충분한 음식을 제공받고 있을지라도 / 음식이 언제 눈에 보일지 모르고 / 일관된 일정을 알 수 없는 / 괴로움을 겪을지도 모른다.

We can provide a sense of control / by ensuring that our animal's environment is predictable: / there is always water available / and always in the same place.
우리는 통제감을 줄 수 있다. / 우리 동물의 환경이 예측 가능하도록 보장함으로써 / 즉, 마실 수 있는 물이 늘 있고, / 늘 같은 곳에 있다.

There is always food / when we get up in the morning / and after our evening walk.
늘 음식이 있다. / 우리가 아침에 일어날 때 / 그리고 저녁 산책을 한 후에

There will always be a time and place to eliminate, / without having to hold things in to the point of discomfort.
변을 배설할 수 있는 시간과 장소가 늘 있을 것이다. / 불편할 정도로 참을 필요 없이

Human companions can display consistent emotional support, / rather than providing love one moment / and withholding love the next.
사람 친구는 일관된 정서적 지지를 보이는 것이 좋다. / 한순간에는 애정을 주다가 / 그다음에는 애정을 주지 않기보다는

When animals know what to expect, / they can feel more confident and calm.
동물이 기대할 수 있는 것이 무엇인지 알고 있을 때, / 그들은 자신감과 차분함을 더 많이 느낄 수 있다.

좋은 보살핌을 제공하는 것의 가장 중요한 측면 중에 한 가지는 반드시 동물의 욕구가 일관되고도 예측 가능하게 충족되도록 하는 것이다. 사람과 마찬가지로, 동물은 통제감이 필요하다. 그러므로 충분한 음식을 제공받고 있을지라도 음식이 언제 눈에 보일지 모르고 일관된 일정을 알 수 없는 동물은 괴로움을 겪지도 모른다. 우리 동물의 환경이 예측 가능하도록 보장함으로써 우리는 통제감을 줄 수 있다. 즉, 마실 수 있는 물이 늘 있고, 늘 같은 곳에 있다. 아침에 일어날 때 그리고 저녁 산책을 한 후에 늘 음식이 있다. 불편할 정도로 참을 필요 없이 변을 배설할 수 있는 시간과 장소가 늘 있을 것이다. 사람 친구는 한순간에는 애정을 주다가 그다음에는 애정을 주지 않기보다는 일관된 정서적 지지를 보이는 것이 좋다. 기대할 수 있는 것이 무엇인지 알고 있을 때, 동물은 자신감과 차분함을 더 많이 느낄 수 있다.

Why? 왜 정답일까?
첫 문장인 'One of the most important aspects of providing good care is making sure that an animal's needs are being met consistently and predictably.'에서 동물을 잘 보살피기 위해서는 동물의 욕구가 일관적이고도 예측 가능한 방식으로 충족되게 해줄 필요가 있다고 언급하고 있다. 따라서 빈칸에 들어갈 말로 가장 적절한 것은 동물의 환경을 '예측 가능하게' 만들어 주어야 한다는 의미를 완성하는 ⑤ '예측 가능하도록'이다.

- aspect ⓝ 측면
- consistently [ad] 일관적으로
- sense of control 통제감
- ensure ⓥ ~하다, 보장하다
- discomfort ⓝ 불편함
- confident ⓐ 자신감 있는
- make sure 반드시 ~하다
- predictably [ad] 예측 가능하게
- distress ⓝ 괴로움
- to the point of ~할 수 있을 정도로
- withhold ⓥ 주지 않다
- isolated ⓐ 고립된

구문 풀이
4행 So an animal [who may get enough food but doesn't know when the food will appear and can see no consistent schedule] may experience distress.

★★ 문제 해결 꿀~팁 ★★
▶ 많이 틀린 이유는?
빈칸 뒤에서 반려동물에게 정해진 장소와 시간에 따라 어떤 것을 기대할 수 있는 안정적인 환경을 제공할 필요가 있다는 내용이 주를 이룬다. 이 안정된 환경이 꼭 '자연스러운' 것이라고 볼 수는 없으므로 ②는 답으로 부적절하다.

▶ 문제 해결 방법은?
첫 문장에서 '일관되고 예측 가능한' 환경의 중요성을 언급한 데 이어, 마지막 문장에서도 동물에게 '무엇을 기대할 수 있는지'가 분명한 환경을 주는 것이 좋다는 내용을 제시하고 있으므로 ⑤가 답으로 가장 적절하다.

32 음식으로 아이의 기분을 달래주는 것의 장단기적 영향　정답률 74% | 정답 ④

다음 빈칸에 들어갈 말로 가장 적절한 것을 고르시오.

① make friends - 친구를 사귀는
② learn etiquettes - 예절을 배우는
③ improve memory - 기억을 향상시키는
✓ ④ manage emotions - 감정을 다스리는
⑤ celebrate achievements - 성취를 축하하는

When a child is upset, / the easiest and quickest way to calm them down / is to give them food.
아이가 화를 낼 때, / 아이를 진정시키는 가장 쉽고 가장 빠른 방법은 / 아이에게 음식을 주는 것이다.

This acts as a distraction / from the feelings they are having, / gives them something to do with their hands and mouth / and shifts their attention / from whatever was upsetting them.
이것은 주의를 돌리는 것으로 작용하고, / 아이가 가지고 있는 감정으로부터 / 손과 입으로 할 수 있는 무언가를 아이에게 제공하며, / 아이의 주의를 옮겨 가게 한다. / 화나게 하고 있는 것이 무엇이든 그것으로부터

If the food chosen is also seen as a treat / such as sweets or a biscuit, / then the child will feel 'treated' and happier.
또한 선택된 음식이 특별한 먹거리로 여겨지면, / 사탕이나 비스킷 같은 / 그 아이는 '특별한 대접을 받았다고' 느끼고 기분이 더 좋을 것이다.

In the shorter term / using food like this is effective.
단기적으로는 / 이처럼 음식을 이용하는 것은 효과적이다.

But in the longer term / it can be harmful / as we quickly learn / that food is a good way to manage emotions.
하지만 장기적으로는 / 그것은 해로울 수 있다. / 우리가 곧 알게 되기 때문에 / 음식이 감정을 다스리는 좋은 방법이라는 것을

Then as we go through life, / whenever we feel annoyed, anxious or even just bored, / we turn to food to make ourselves feel better.
그러면 우리가 삶을 살아가면서, / 짜증이 나거나, 불안하거나, 심지어 그저 지루함을 느낄 때마다, / 우리 자신의 기분을 더 좋게 만들기 위해 우리는 음식에 의존한다.

아이가 화를 낼 때, 아이를 진정시키는 가장 쉽고 가장 빠른 방법은 음식을 주는 것이다. 이것은 아이가 가지고 있는 감정으로부터 주의를 돌리는 것으로 작용하고, 손과 입으로 할 수 있는 무언가를 아이에게 제공하며, 화나게 하고 있는 것이 무엇이든 그것으로부터 아이의 주의를 옮겨 가게 한다. 또한 선택된 음식이 사탕이나 비스킷 같은 특별한 먹거리로 여겨지면, 그 아이는 '특별한 대접을 받았다고' 느끼고 기분이 더 좋을 것이다. 이처럼 음식을 이용하는 것은 단기적으로는 효과적이다. 하지만 음식이 감정을 다스리는 좋은 방법이라는 것을 우리가 곧 알게 되기 때문에 그것은 장기적으로는 해로울 수 있다. 그러면 우리가 삶을 살아가면서, 짜증이 나거나, 불안하거나, 심지어 그저 지루함을 느낄 때마다, 우리 자신의 기분을 더 좋게 만들기 위해 우리는 음식에 의존한다.

Why? 왜 정답일까?
화난 아이의 기분을 음식으로 달래주는 것이 단기적으로는 효과가 있지만 장기적으로는 아이가 기분이 좋지 않을 때 음식에 의존하게 하는 결과를 낳기 때문에 좋지 않을 수 있다는 내용을 다룬 글이다. 두 번째 문장과 세 번째 문장에서, 음식은 아이가 기분이 나쁠 때 주의를 돌려주는 효과가 있으며, 특히 그 음식이 특별한 먹거리로 여겨지는 경우 아이를 특히 더 기분 좋게 한다고 설명하고 있다. 또한 마지막 문장에서는 그리하여 우리가 장기적으로 '기분을 나아지게' 하고자 할 때 음식에 의존하는 결과가 나타날 수 있다고 한다. 따라서 빈칸에 들어갈 말로 가장 적절한 것은 ④ '감정을 다스리는'이다.

- distraction ⓝ 정신을 분산시키는 것, 주의를 돌리는 것
- shift ⓥ 돌리다, 바꾸다
- treat ⓝ 간식 ⓥ 대접하다
- anxious ⓐ 불안한
- celebrate ⓥ 축하하다
- see A as B A를 B로 간주하다
- harmful ⓐ 해로운
- turn to ~에 의지하다
- achievement ⓝ 성취

구문 풀이
10행 Then as we go through life, whenever we feel annoyed, anxious or even just bored, we turn to food to make ourselves feel better.

33 수생 생물의 특성을 유지하며 발달한 개구리　정답률 60% | 정답 ①

다음 빈칸에 들어갈 말로 가장 적절한 것을 고르시오. [3점]

✓ ① still kept many ties to the water - 여전히 물과의 여러 인연을 유지했다
② had almost all the necessary organs - 필요한 신체 기관을 거의 모두 갖추고 있었다
③ had to develop an appetite for new foods - 새로운 음식에 대한 식욕을 발달시켜야 했다
④ often competed with land-dwelling species - 땅에 사는 생물 종들과 종종 경쟁했다
⑤ suffered from rapid changes in temperature - 기온의 급격한 변화로 고생했다

Scientists believe / that the frogs' ancestors were water-dwelling, fishlike animals.
과학자들은 믿는다. / 개구리의 조상이 물에 사는, 물고기 같은 동물이었다고

The first frogs and their relatives / gained the ability / to come out on land / and enjoy the opportunities for food and shelter there.
최초의 개구리와 그들의 친척은 / 능력을 얻었다. / 육지로 나와 / 그곳에서 먹을 것과 살 곳에 대한 기회를 누릴 수 있는

But they still kept many ties to the water.
하지만 개구리는 여전히 물과의 여러 인연을 유지했다.

A frog's lungs do not work very well, / and it gets part of its oxygen / by breathing through its skin.
개구리의 폐는 그다지 기능을 잘하지 않고, / 개구리는 산소를 일부 얻는다. / 피부를 통해 호흡함으로써

But for this kind of "breathing" to work properly, / the frog's skin must stay moist.
하지만 이런 종류의 '호흡'이 제대로 이뤄지기 위해서는, / 개구리의 피부가 촉촉하게 유지되어야 한다.

And so the frog must remain near the water / where it can take a dip every now and then / to keep from drying out.
그래서 개구리는 물의 근처에 있어야 한다. / 이따금 몸을 잠깐 담글 수 있는 / 건조해지는 것을 막기 위해

Frogs must also lay their eggs in water, / as their fishlike ancestors did.
개구리 역시 물속에 알을 낳아야 한다. / 물고기 같은 조상들이 그랬던 것처럼

And eggs laid in the water / must develop into water creatures, / if they are to survive.
그리고 물속에 낳은 알은 / 물에 사는 생물로 발달해야 한다. / 그것들이 살아남으려면

For frogs, / metamorphosis thus provides the bridge / between the water-dwelling young forms and the land-dwelling adults.
개구리에게 있어서 / 따라서 탈바꿈은 다리를 제공한다. / 물에 사는 어린 형체와 육지에 사는 성체를 이어주는

과학자들은 개구리의 조상이 물에 사는, 물고기 같은 동물이었다고 믿는다. 최초의 개구리와 그들의 친척은 육지로 나와 그곳에서 먹을 것과 살 곳에 대한 기회를 누릴 수 있는 능력을 얻었다. 하지만 개구리는 여전히 물과의 여러 인연을 유지했다. 개구리의 폐는 그다지 기능을 잘하지 않고, 개구리는 피부를 통해 호흡함으로써 산소를 일부 얻는다. 하지만 이런 종류의 '호흡'이 제대로 이뤄지기 위해서는, 개구리의 피부가 촉촉하게 유지되어야 한다. 그래서 개구리는 건조해지는 것을 막기 위해 이따금 몸을 잠깐 담글 수 있는 물의 근처에 있어야 한다. 물고기 같은 조상들이 그랬던 것처럼, 개구리 역시 물속에 알을 낳아야 한다. 그리고 물속에 낳은 알이 살아남으려면, 물에 사는 생물로 발달해야 한다. 따라서, 개구리에게 있어서 탈바꿈은 물에 사는 어린 형체와 육지에 사는 성체를 이어주는 다리를 제공한다.

Why? 왜 정답일까?

개구리는 당초 물고기 같은 동물로 기원하여 육지에서 생활하도록 진화했지만 여전히 '물에 사는' 생물로서의 특징을 지니고 있다는 내용의 글이다. 빈칸 뒤에서 개구리는 폐가 그다지 발달해 있지 않아 피부를 이용해 호흡하는데, 호흡이 원활하기 위해서는 피부가 늘 젖어 있어야 하고, 따라서 물을 가까이 해야 하며, 알 또한 물속에 넣어 번식해야 하기에 '물에 살기 적합한' 생물로 발달할 수밖에 없는 운명임을 설명하고 있다. 이러한 흐름을 근거로 볼 때, 빈칸에 들어갈 말로 가장 적절한 것은 개구리가 '물고기다운' 특성을 완전히 포기하지 않았다는 의미의 ① '여전히 물과의 여러 인연을 유지했다'이다.

- ancestor ⓝ 조상
- relative ⓝ 친척
- moist ⓐ 촉촉한
- dry out 건조하다, 바짝 마르다
- tie ⓝ 관계, 연결
- appetite ⓝ 식욕
- dwell ⓥ 거주하다, 살다
- properly ⓐ 적절히
- take a dip 잠깐 수영을 하다
- lay ⓥ (알을) 낳다
- organ ⓝ (신체) 기관
- compete with ~와 경쟁하다

구문 풀이

7행 But for this kind of "breathing" to work properly, the frog's skin must stay moist.

★★★ 등급을 가르는 문제!

34 실질적 자유에 영향을 주는 요소 정답률 34% | 정답 ⑤

다음 빈칸에 들어갈 말로 가장 적절한 것을 고르시오. [3점]

① respecting others' rights to freedom
다른 사람들의 자유권을 존중하는가
② protecting and providing for the needy
궁핍한 사람들을 보호하고 돕는가
③ learning what socially acceptable behaviors are
사회적으로 수용 가능한 행동이 무엇인지 아는가
④ determining how much they can expect from others
다른 사람들에게 얼마나 많은 것을 기대할 수 있는지를 정하는가
✓⑤ having the means and ability to do what they choose
그들이 선택하는 것을 할 수 있는 수단과 능력을 갖추고 있는가

It is important / to distinguish between being legally allowed to do something, / and actually being able to go and do it.
중요하다. / 어떤 일을 할 수 있도록 법적으로 허용되는 것을 구별하는 것은 / 실제로 그것을 해 버릴 수 있는 것과
A law could be passed / allowing everyone, / if they so wish, / to run a mile in two minutes.
법이 통과될 수도 있다. / 모든 사람에게 허용하는 / 그들이 그러기를 원한다면, / 2분 안에 1마일을 달릴 수 있도록
That would not, however, increase their effective freedom, / because, although allowed to do so, / they are physically incapable of it.
그러나 그것이 그들의 실질적 자유를 증가시키지는 않을 것이다. / 그렇게 하는 것이 허용되더라도, / 그들이 물리적으로 그렇게 할 수 없기 때문에
Having a minimum of restrictions and a maximum of possibilities / is fine.
최소한의 제약과 최대한의 가능성을 두는 것은 / 괜찮다.
But in the real world / most people will never have the opportunity / either to become all that they are allowed to become, / or to need to be restrained from doing everything / that is possible for them to do.
하지만 현실 세계에서, / 대부분의 사람에게는 가능성이 없다. / 그들이 되어도 된다는 모든 것이 될 / 혹은 모든 것을 하지 못하게 저지당해야 할 / 그들이 하는 것이 가능한
Their effective freedom depends on / actually having the means and ability / to do what they choose.
그들의 실질적 자유는 달려 있다. / 실제로 수단과 능력을 갖추고 있는가에 / 그들이 선택하는 것을 할 수 있는

어떤 일을 할 수 있도록 법적으로 허용되는 것과 실제로 그것을 해 버릴 수 있는 것을 구별하는 것은 중요하다. 원한다면, 모든 사람이 2분 안에 1마일을 달릴 수 있도록 허용하는 법이 통과될 수도 있다. 그러나 그렇게 하는 것이 허용되더라도, 물리적으로 그렇게 할 수 없기 때문에, 그것이 그들의 실질적 자유를 증가시키지는 않을 것이다. 최소한의 제약과 최대한의 가능성을 두는 것은 괜찮다. 하지만 현실 세계에서, 대부분의 사람에게는 그들이 되어도 된다는 모든 것이 될 가능성이 없고, 할 수 있는 모든 것을 하지 못하게 저지당해야 할 가능성도 없을 것이다. 그들의 실질적 자유는 실제로 그들이 선택하는 것을 할 수 있는 수단과 능력을 갖추고 있는가에 달려 있다.

Why? 왜 정답일까?

첫 문장에서 어떤 것을 법적으로 해도 되는 상태와 실제로 그것을 행할 수 있는지를 구별하는 것이 중요하다고 언급한 데 이어, 2분 안에 1마일을 달리도록 허용하는 법이 통과되는 경우가 예시로 나온다. 예시에 따르면 2분 안에 1마일을 뛰는 것이 법적으로 가능해질지라도 '실제로 그렇게 할 수 있는' 사람들이 없기에 사람들의 실질적 자유가 증가되지 않는다고 한다. 이를 근거로 볼 때, 사람들의 '실질적' 자유란 '법으로 허용되는 행위를 실제 행할 능력이 있는지'에 따라 좌우된다는 결론을 도출할 수 있다. 따라서 빈칸에 들어갈 말로 가장 적절한 것은 ⑤ '그들이 선택하는 것을 할 수 있는 수단과 능력을 갖추고 있는가'이다.

- distinguish ⓥ 구별하다
- allowed ⓐ 허가받은, 허용된
- be incapable of ~을 할 수 없다
- physically ⓐ 신체적으로, 물리적으로
- needy ⓐ (경제적으로) 어려운, 궁핍한
- means ⓝ 수단
- legally ⓐ 법적으로
- effective ⓐ 실질적인, 효과적인
- restrain ⓥ 저지[제지]하다
- depend on ~에 좌우되다
- acceptable ⓐ 허용 가능한, 수용 가능한

구문 풀이

4행 That would not, however, increase their *effective* freedom, because, (although (they are) allowed to do so), they are physically incapable of it.

★★ 문제 해결 꿀~팁 ★★

▶ 많이 틀린 이유는?
실제로 행할 수 있는 행동이 법적으로 허용될 때 실질적 자유가 커질 수 있다는 내용의 글이다. 타인의 자유권을 존중하는 것에 관한 내용은 언급되지 않으므로 ①은 답으로 부적절하다.

▶ 문제 해결 방법은?
첫 문장에서 어떤 일이 법적으로 허용되는 것과 그 일을 실제 할 수 있는가는 다른 개념이라고 언급한다. 이어서 법적으로 허용되더라도 실제로는 할 수 없는 일일 때 사람들의 실질적 자유는 증가하지 않는다는 것을 뒷받침하는 예시가 나온다. 이를 토대로 볼 때, 자유에 있어 중요한 것은 어떤 일이 법적으로 허용되는 것을 넘어서 '그 일을 실제로 할 수 있는지' 여부임을 알 수 있다.

35 뮤지션들이 홀로 많은 것을 할 수 있게 된 오늘날의 음악 시장 정답률 65% | 정답 ③

다음 글에서 전체 흐름과 관계 없는 문장은?

Today's music business / has allowed musicians / to take matters into their own hands.
오늘날의 음악 사업은 / 뮤지션들이 ~하게 해 주었다. / 스스로 일을 처리할 수 있게
① Gone are the days of musicians / waiting for a gatekeeper / (someone / who holds power / and prevents you from being let in) / at a label or TV show / to say they are worthy of the spotlight.
뮤지션들의 시대는 지났다. / 문지기를 기다리던 / (사람 / 권력을 쥔 / 그리고 여러분이 들어가는 것을 막는) / 음반사나 TV 프로그램에서 / 그들이 스포트라이트를 받을 만하다고 말해주기를
② In today's music business, / you don't need to ask for permission / to build a fanbase / and you no longer need to pay thousands of dollars to a company / to do it.
오늘날의 음악 사업에서는, / 여러분은 허락을 요청할 필요가 없으며, / 팬층을 만들기 위해 / 여러분은 회사에 수천 달러를 지불할 필요도 더 이상 없다. / 그렇게 하려고
✓③ There are rising concerns / over the marketing of child musicians / using TV auditions.
우려가 증가하고 있다. / 나이 어린 뮤지션들을 마케팅하는 데에 대한 / TV 오디션을 이용하여
④ Every day, / musicians are getting their music out / to thousands of listeners / without any outside help.
매일, / 뮤지션들은 자신들의 음악을 내놓고 있다. / 수천 명의 청취자에게 / 어떤 외부의 도움 없이
⑤ They simply deliver it to the fans directly, / without asking for permission or outside help / to receive exposure or connect with thousands of listeners.
그들은 그저 그것을 팬들에게 직접 전달한다. / 허락이나 외부의 도움을 요청하지 않고, / 노출을 얻거나 수천 명의 청취자와 관계를 형성하기 위해

오늘날의 음악 사업은 뮤지션들이 스스로 일을 처리할 수 있게 해 주었다. ① 뮤지션들이 음반사나 TV 프로그램의 문지기(권력을 쥐고 사람들이 들어가는 것을 막는 사람)가 그들이 스포트라이트를 받을 만하다고 말해주기를 기다리던 시대는 지났다. ② 오늘날의 음악 사업에서는 팬층을 만들기 위해 허락을 요청할 필요가 없으며, 그렇게 하려고 회사에 수천 달러를 지불할 필요도 더 이상 없다. ③ TV 오디션을 이용하여 나이 어린 뮤지션들을 마케팅하는 데에 대한 우려가 증가하고 있다. ④ 매일 뮤지션들은 어떤 외부의 도움 없이 수천 명의 청취자에게 자신들의 음악을 내놓고 있다. ⑤ 그들은 노출을 얻거나 수천 명의 청취자와 관계를 형성하기 위해 허락이나 외부의 도움을 요청하지 않고, 그저 자신들의 음악을 팬들에게 직접 전달한다.

Why? 왜 정답일까?

오늘날 뮤지션들은 음반사 등에 크게 의지할 필요 없이 직접 대중에게 음악을 전달하고 스스로 마케팅할 수 있는 시장 환경에서 활동한다는 내용을 다룬 글이다. ①, ②, ④, ⑤는 주제에 부합하지만, ③은 TV 오디션을 통한 어린 뮤지션들의 마케팅에 관해 언급하고 있어 흐름에서 벗어난다. 따라서 전체 흐름과 관계 없는 문장은 ③이다.

- take matters into one's own hands 스스로 일을 추진하다, 일을 독자적으로 하다
- gatekeeper ⓝ 문지기, 수위
- permission ⓝ 허락
- deliver ⓥ 전달하다
- be worthy of ~을 받을 만하다, ~의 가치가 있다
- concern ⓝ 우려

구문 풀이

2행 Gone are the days of musicians waiting for a gatekeeper (someone [who holds power and prevents you from being let in]) at a label or TV show to say they are worthy of the spotlight.

36 스포츠에 활용되는 공의 특징 정답률 56% | 정답 ②

주어진 글 다음에 이어질 글의 순서로 가장 적절한 것을 고르시오.

① (A) - (C) - (B)
✓② (B) - (A) - (C)
③ (B) - (C) - (A)
④ (C) - (A) - (B)
⑤ (C) - (B) - (A)

Almost all major sporting activities / are played with a ball.
거의 모든 주요 스포츠 활동은 / 공을 갖고 행해진다.
(B) The rules of the game / always include rules / about the type of ball that is allowed, / starting with the size and weight of the ball.
경기의 규칙은 / 규칙을 늘 포함하고 있다. / 허용되는 공의 유형에 관한 / 공의 크기와 무게부터 시작해서
The ball must also have a certain stiffness.
공은 또한 특정 정도의 단단함을 갖추어야 한다.
(A) A ball might have the correct size and weight / but if it is made as a hollow ball of steel / it will be too stiff / and if it is made from light foam rubber with a heavy center / it will be too soft.
공이 적절한 크기와 무게를 갖출 수 있으나 / 그것이 속이 빈 강철 공으로 만들어지면 / 그것은 너무 단단할 것이고, / 그것이 무거운 중심부를 가진 가벼운 발포 고무로 만들어지면 / 그 공은 너무 물렁할 것이다.
(C) Similarly, along with stiffness, / a ball needs to bounce properly.
마찬가지로, 단단함과 더불어, / 공은 적절히 튈 필요가 있다.
A solid rubber ball / would be too bouncy for most sports, / and a solid ball made of clay / would not bounce at all.
순전히 고무로만 된 공은 / 대부분의 스포츠에 지나치게 잘 튈 것이고, / 순전히 점토로만 만든 공은 / 전혀 튀지 않을 것이다.

거의 모든 주요 스포츠 활동은 공을 갖고 행해진다.

(B) 경기의 규칙들은 공의 크기와 무게부터 시작해서 허용되는 공의 유형에 관한 규칙들을 늘 포함하고 있다. 공은 또한 특정 정도의 단단함을 갖추어야 한다.

(A) 공이 적절한 크기와 무게를 갖출 수 있으나 속이 빈 강철 공으로 만들어지면 그것은 너무 단단할 것이고, 무거운 중심부를 가진 가벼운 발포 고무로 만들어지면 그 공은 너무 물렁할 것이다.

(C) 마찬가지로, 공은 단단함과 더불어 적절히 뛸 필요가 있다. 순전히 고무로만 된 공은 대부분의 스포츠에 지나치게 잘 뛸 것이고, 순전히 점토로만 만든 공은 전혀 튀지 않을 것이다.

Why? 왜 정답일까?

스포츠에 활용되는 공이 갖추어야 할 특징에 관해 설명한 글이다. 먼저 주어진 글에서 공이 스포츠에서 널리 쓰인다는 내용을 제시한 데 이어, (B)에서는 경기 규칙을 보면 어떤 공이 사용되어야 하는지를 명시하고 있다는 내용과 함께 공이 단단함을 갖추어야 한다는 점을 언급한다. 이어서 (A)는 공이 적절한 크기나 무게를 갖추더라도 강철로 되어 있다면 지나치게 단단할 것이고, 역으로 (매트리스에 주로 활용되는) 발포 고무로 만들어진다면 너무 물렁할 것이라는 보충 설명을 제시한다. 이러한 (A)의 내용에 **Similarly**로 연결되는 (C)는 단단함과 더불어 필요한 특징으로서 잘 튀어오르는 속성을 언급하고 있다. 따라서 글의 순서로 가장 적절한 것은 ② '(B) – (A) – (C)'이다.

- **major** ⓐ 주요한
- **steel** ⓝ 강철
- **rubber** ⓝ 고무
- **bounce** ⓥ 튀어오르다
- **solid** ⓐ 순수한(다른 물질이 섞이지 않은)
- **hollow** ⓐ (속이) 빈
- **stiff** ⓐ 단단한
- **certain** ⓐ 확실한, 틀림없는
- **properly** [ad] 적절히
- **clay** ⓝ 점토

구문 풀이

3행 A ball might have the correct size and weight but if it is made as a hollow ball of steel it will be too stiff and if it is made from light foam rubber with a heavy center it will be too soft.

---

37 수학과 화학에서의 기호 사용   정답률 61% | 정답 ③

주어진 글 다음에 이어질 글의 순서로 가장 적절한 것을 고르시오. [3점]

① (A) – (C) – (B)　　　　② (B) – (A) – (C)
③ (B) – (C) – (A)　　　　④ (C) – (A) – (B)
⑤ (C) – (B) – (A)

If you had to write a math equation, / you probably wouldn't write, / "Twenty-eight plus fourteen equals forty-two."
만일 여러분이 수학 등식을 써야 한다면, / 여러분은 아마 쓰지 않을 것이다. / '스물여덟 더하기 열넷은 마흔둘과 같다.'라고

It would take too long to write / and it would be hard to read quickly.
그것은 쓰는 데 너무 오래 걸리고 / 빨리 읽기가 어려울 것이다.

(B) You would write, "28 + 14 = 42."
여러분은 '28 + 14 = 42'라고 쓸 것이다.

Chemistry is the same way.
화학도 마찬가지이다.

Chemists have to write chemical equations all the time, / and it would take too long to write and read / if they had to spell everything out.
화학자들은 항상 화학 방정식을 써야 하고, / 쓰고 읽는 데 너무 오래 걸릴 것이다. / 만약 그들이 모든 것을 상세히 다 써야 한다면

(C) So chemists use symbols, / just like we do in math.
그래서 화학자들은 기호를 사용한다. / 우리가 수학에서 하는 것처럼

A chemical formula lists all the elements / that form each molecule / and uses a small number / to the bottom right of an element's symbol / to stand for the number of atoms of that element.
화학식은 모든 원소를 나열하고 / 각 분자를 구성하는 / 작은 숫자를 사용한다. / 원소 기호의 오른쪽 아래에 / 그 원소의 원자 수를 나타내기 위해

(A) For example, / the chemical formula for water is H_2O.
예를 들어, / 물의 화학식은 H_2O이다.

That tells us / that a water molecule is made up / of two hydrogen ("H" and "2") atoms / and one oxygen ("O") atom.
그것은 우리에게 말해 준다. / 하나의 물 분자는 이루어져 있다는 것을 / 두 개의 수소 원자('H'와 '2')와 / 하나의 산소 원자('O')로

만일 여러분이 수학 등식을 써야 한다면, 여러분은 아마 '스물여덟 더하기 열넷은 마흔둘과 같다.'라고 쓰지 않을 것이다. 그것은 쓰는 데 너무 오래 걸리고 빨리 읽기가 어려울 것이다. (B) 여러분은 '28 + 14 = 42'라고 쓸 것이다. 화학도 마찬가지이다. 화학자들은 항상 화학 방정식을 써야 하고, 만약 그들이 모든 것을 상세히 다 써야 한다면 쓰고 읽는 데 너무 오래 걸릴 것이다. (C) 그래서 화학자들은 우리가 수학에서 하는 것처럼 기호를 사용한다. 화학식은 각 분자를 구성하는 모든 원소를 나열하고 그 원소의 원자 수를 나타내기 위해 원소 기호의 오른쪽 아래에 작은 숫자를 사용한다. (A) 예를 들어, 물의 화학식은 H_2O이다. 그것은 우리에게 하나의 물 분자는 두 개의 수소 원자('H'와 '2')와 하나의 산소 원자('O')로 이루어져 있다는 것을 말해 준다.

Why? 왜 정답일까?

주어진 글에서 우리가 수학 등식을 쓸 때 말로 풀어쓰지 않을 것이라 언급한 데 이어, (B)에서는 우리가 '28 + 14 = 42'와 같이 '기호'를 사용할 것이라고 설명한다. 이어서 (C)는 (B)의 후반부에 이어 화학에도 기호 사용이 필요하다고 언급하며, 특히 화학식의 경우 원소 기호 아래 작은 숫자를 사용하여 원자 수를 나타낸다는 내용을 덧붙인다. For example로 시작하는 (A)는 (C)에서 언급한 아래 첨자 사용을 보여줄 수 있는 예로 H_2O를 제시한다. 따라서 글의 순서로 가장 적절한 것은 ③ '(B) – (C) – (A)'이다.

- **equation** ⓝ 방정식, 등식
- **hydrogen** ⓝ 수소
- **spell out** 상세히 말하다
- **element** ⓝ 원소, 요소
- **be made up of** ~으로 구성되다, 이루어지다
- **atom** ⓝ 원자
- **symbol** ⓝ 기호
- **stand for** ~을 나타내다[대표하다]

구문 풀이

1행 If you had to write a math equation, you probably wouldn't write, "Twenty-eight plus fourteen equals forty-two."
「if + 주어 + 과거 동사 ~」 주어 + 조동사 과거형 + 동사원형 : 가정법 과거(현재 사실의 반대 가정),

★★★ 등급을 가르는 문제!

38 작은 발전으로 이루는 큰 변화   정답률 36% | 정답 ②

글의 흐름으로 보아, 주어진 문장이 들어가기에 가장 적절한 곳을 고르시오.

It is so easy / to overestimate the importance of one defining moment / and underestimate the value of making small improvements on a daily basis.
매우 쉽다. / 결정적인 한순간의 중요성을 과대평가하고 매일 작은 발전을 이루는 것의 가치를 과소평가하기는

Too often, / we convince ourselves / that massive success requires massive action.
너무 자주 / 우리는 스스로를 납득시킨다. / 거대한 성공에는 거대한 행동이

① Whether it is losing weight, / winning a championship, / or achieving any other goal, / we put pressure on ourselves / to make some earthshaking improvement / that everyone will talk about.
그것이 체중을 줄이는 것이든, / 결승전에서 이기는 것이든, / 혹은 어떤 다른 목표를 달성하는 것이든 간에, / 우리는 우리 스스로에게 압력을 가한다. / 지축을 흔들 만한 발전을 이루도록 / 모두가 이야기하게 될

☑ Meanwhile, / improving by 1 percent isn't particularly notable, / but it can be far more meaningful in the long run.
한편, / 1퍼센트 발전하는 것은 특별히 눈에 띄지는 않지만, / 그것은 장기적으로는 훨씬 더 의미가 있을 수 있다.

The difference / this tiny improvement can make over time / is surprising.
변화는 / 시간이 지남에 따라 이 작은 발전이 이룰 수 있는 / 놀랍다.

③ Here's how the math works out: / if you can get 1 percent better each day for one year, / you'll end up thirty-seven times better / by the time you're done.
다음과 같이 계산이 이루어지는데, / 만일 여러분이 1년 동안 매일 1퍼센트씩 더 나아질 수 있다면, / 여러분은 결국 37배 더 나아질 것이다. / 여러분이 끝마칠 때 즈음

④ Conversely, / if you get 1 percent worse each day for one year, / you'll decline nearly down to zero.
역으로, / 여러분이 1년 동안 매일 1퍼센트씩 나빠지면 / 여러분은 거의 0까지 떨어질 것이다.

⑤ What starts as a small win or a minor failure / adds up to something much more.
작은 승리나 사소한 패배로 시작한 것은 / 쌓여서 훨씬 더 큰 무언가가 된다.

결정적인 한순간의 중요성을 과대평가하고 매일 작은 발전을 이루는 것의 가치를 과소평가하기는 매우 쉽다. 너무 자주 우리는 거대한 성공에는 거대한 행동이 필요하다고 스스로를 납득시킨다. ① 체중을 줄이는 것이든, 결승전에서 이기는 것이든, 혹은 어떤 다른 목표를 달성하는 것이든 간에, 우리는 모두가 이야기하게 될 지축을 흔들 만한 발전을 이루도록 우리 스스로에게 압력을 가한다. ② 한편, 1퍼센트 발전하는 것은 특별히 눈에 띄지는 않지만, 장기적으로는 훨씬 더 의미가 있을 수 있다. 시간이 지남에 따라 이 작은 발전이 이룰 수 있는 변화는 놀랍다. ③ 다음과 같이 계산이 이루어지는데, 만일 여러분이 1년 동안 매일 1퍼센트씩 더 나아질 수 있다면, 끝마칠 때 즈음 여러분은 결국 37배 더 나아질 것이다. ④ 역으로, 1년 동안 매일 1퍼센트씩 나빠지면 여러분은 거의 0까지 떨어질 것이다. ⑤ 작은 승리나 사소한 패배로 시작한 것은 쌓여서 훨씬 더 큰 무언가가 된다.

Why? 왜 정답일까?

② 앞에서는 우리가 작은 변화의 가치를 과소평가하고 거대한 발전에 맞는 거대한 행동을 해나가도록 스스로를 압박한다는 내용이 주를 이룬다. 이에 이어 주어진 문장은 Meanwhile로 흐름을 전환하며 '1퍼센트만큼' 작게 발전하는 것이 당장은 눈에 띄지 않아도 장기적으로는 큰 의미를 가질 수 있다고 설명한다. ② 뒤의 문장은 주어진 문장에서 언급한 '1퍼센트의 발전'을 this tiny improvement라는 말로 바꾸며 '작은 발전'으로 인한 변화가 시간이 지난 후에는 놀라울 수 있음을 환기시킨다. 따라서 주어진 문장이 들어가기에 가장 적절한 곳은 ②이다.

- **meanwhile** [ad] 한편
- **in the long run** 장기적으로
- **underestimate** ⓥ 과소평가하다
- **convince** ⓥ 납득시키다, 설득하다
- **put pressure on** ~에 압박을 가하다
- **tiny** ⓐ 극히 작은
- **decline** ⓥ 떨어지다, 감소하다
- **notable** ⓐ 눈에 띄는, 두드러지는
- **overestimate** ⓥ 과대평가하다
- **on a daily basis** 매일
- **massive** ⓐ 거대한
- **earthshaking** ⓐ 극히 중대한, 세상을 떠들썩하게 하는
- **conversely** [ad] 역으로

구문 풀이

7행 (Whether it is losing weight, winning a championship, or achieving any other goal), we put pressure on ourselves to make some earthshaking improvement [that everyone will talk about].

★★ 문제 해결 꿀~팁 ★★

▶ 많이 틀린 이유는?

최다 오답인 ④ 앞뒤는 Conversely를 기점으로 매일 조금씩 1년 동안 발전하는 경우와 나빠지는 경우가 적절히 대비를 이루는 맥락이다. 따라서 ④에 주어진 문장을 넣기에는 부적절하다.

▶ 문제 해결 방법은?

② 앞에서는 거창한 결과를 이룩하려면 거창한 행동이 필요하다고 생각한다는 내용이 주를 이루는데, ② 뒤에서는 '이 작은 발전(this tiny improvement)'에 관해 언급한다. 즉 ② 앞뒤 내용이 서로 상충하므로 Meanwhile(한편)으로 시작하며 흐름을 반전하는 주어진 문장이 ②에 들어가야 한다.

★★★ 등급을 가르는 문제!

39 현지 환경을 미리 조사하고 대비하기   정답률 54% | 정답 ④

글의 흐름으로 보아, 주어진 문장이 들어가기에 가장 적절한 곳을 고르시오. [3점]

The continued survival of the human race / can be explained / by our ability to adapt to our environment.

[문제편 p.036]

인류의 지속적인 생존은 / 설명될 수 있을 것이다. / 환경에 적응하는 우리의 능력으로
① While we may have lost some of our ancient ancestors' survival skills, / we have learned new skills / as they have become necessary.
우리가 고대 조상들의 생존 기술 중 일부를 잃어버렸을지도 모르지만, / 우리는 새로운 기술을 배웠다. / 새로운 기술이 필요해지면서
② Today, / the gap / between the skills we once had / and the skills we now have / grows ever wider / as we rely more heavily on modern technology.
오늘날 / 간격이 / 한때 우리가 가졌던 기술과 현재 우리가 가진 기술 사이의 / 어느 때보다 더 커졌다. / 우리가 현대 기술에 더 크게 의존함에 따라
③ Therefore, / when you head off into the wilderness, / it is important / to fully prepare for the environment.
그러므로, / 여러분이 미지의 땅으로 향할 때에는 / 중요하다. / 그 환경에 대해 충분히 준비하는 것이
✓ Before a trip, / research / how the native inhabitants dress, work, and eat.
떠나기 전에, / 조사하라. / 토착 주민들이 어떻게 옷을 입고 일하고 먹는지를
How they have adapted to their way of life / will help you to understand the environment / and allow you to select the best gear / and learn the correct skills.
그들이 어떻게 자신들의 생활 방식에 적응하는가는 / 여러분이 그 환경을 이해하도록 도울 것이고, / 여러분이 최선의 장비를 선별하도록 해 줄 것이다 / 그리고 적절한 기술을 배우도록
⑤ This is crucial / because most survival situations arise / as a result of a series of events / that could have been avoided.
이것은 중요하다. / 생존이 걸린 대부분의 상황이 발생하기 때문에 / 일련의 사건의 결과로 / 피할 수도 있었던

인류의 지속적인 생존은 환경에 적응하는 우리의 능력으로 설명될 수 있을 것이다. ① 우리가 고대 조상들의 생존 기술 중 일부를 잃어버렸을지도 모르지만, 새로운 기술이 필요해지면서 우리는 새로운 기술을 배웠다. ② 오늘날 우리가 현대 기술에 더 크게 의존함에 따라 한때 우리가 가졌던 기술과 현재 우리가 가진 기술 사이의 간극이 어느 때보다 더 커졌다. ③ 그러므로, 미지의 땅으로 향할 때에는 그 환경에 대해 충분히 준비하는 것이 중요하다. ④ 떠나기 전에, 토착 주민들이 어떻게 옷을 입고 일하고 먹는지를 조사하라. 그들이 어떻게 자신들의 생활 방식에 적응했는가는 여러분이 그 환경을 이해하도록 도울 것이고, 여러분이 최선의 장비를 선별하고 적절한 기술을 배우도록 해 줄 것이다. ⑤ 생존이 걸린 대부분의 상황이 피할 수도 있었던 일련의 사건의 결과로 발생하기 때문에 이것은 중요하다.

Why? 왜 정답일까?

④ 앞의 두 문장에서 현대 기술에 대한 우리의 의존도가 높아짐에 따라 과거의 기술과 오늘날의 기술 간에 격차가 더 벌어졌으므로 잘 모르는 곳에 갈 때에는 그 환경에 대한 충분한 준비가 필요하다고 언급한다. 이에 대한 구체적인 조언으로서 주어진 문장은 떠나기 전 '토착 주민'의 옷, 음식, 일하는 문화 등을 조사하라고 언급한다. ④ 뒤의 문장은 주어진 문장의 '토착 주민'을 they로 언급하며 이들이 나름의 삶의 방식에 어떻게 적응해 있는지를 파악하면 그 환경을 이해하는 데 도움이 될 것이라고 설명한다. 따라서 주어진 문장이 들어가기에 가장 적절한 곳은 ④이다.

- **adapt to** ~에 적응하다
- **rely on** ~에 의존하다
- **wilderness** ⓝ 황무지
- **arise** ⓥ 발생하다, 일어나다
- **ancestor** ⓝ 조상
- **heavily** ⓐⓓ 심하게, 많이
- **crucial** ⓐ 매우 중요한
- **as a result of** ~의 결과로

구문 풀이

11행 How they have adapted to their way of life will help you to understand the environment and allow you to select the best gear and (to) learn the correct skills.
주어(간접의문문: 어떻게 ~하는지) 「help + 목적어 + to부정사: ~이 …하는 데 도움이 되다」 「allow + 목적어 + to부정사: ~이 …하게 하다」

★★ 문제 해결 꿀~팁 ★★

▶ 많이 틀린 이유는?
인간은 환경에 맞추어 계속 적응하고 변하는데, 오늘날 인간은 기술에 대한 의존도가 커서 과거와의 간극이 더욱 벌어졌기에 미지의 땅으로 나아갈 때에는 항상 환경에 대한 대비와 조사가 필요하다는 내용의 글이다. 특히 최다 오답인 ③ 앞뒤로 '과거 기술과 현대 기술의 간극이 커져서 → 새로운 땅으로 갈 때 환경을 잘 알아봐야 한다'라는 내용이 적절한 인과 관계로 연결되어 있다. 따라서 주어진 문장을 ③에 넣는 것은 부적절하다.

▶ 문제 해결 방법은?
④ 뒤의 문장에 they가 나오므로 앞에서 they로 받을 만한 복수 명사가 언급되어야 한다. ④ 앞의 문장에는 적절한 복수 명사가 없는 반면, 주어진 문장에는 the native inhabitants가 있다. 따라서 이 they에 '토착 주민'을 넣어서 읽어 보고 맥락이 자연스러운지 확인해 보면 답을 찾을 수 있다.

★★★ 등급을 가르는 문제!

40 존재만으로 관계를 상하게 하는 휴대폰 정답률 52% | 정답 ②

다음 글의 내용을 한 문장으로 요약하고자 한다. 빈칸 (A), (B)에 들어갈 말로 가장 적절한 것은?

(A)	(B)	(A)	(B)
① weakens 약화시킨다	answered 응대되고	✓② weakens 약화시킨다	ignored 무시되고
③ renews 새롭게 한다	answered 응대되고	④ maintains 유지시킨다	ignored 무시되고
⑤ maintains 유지시킨다	updated 업데이트되고		

In one study, / researchers asked pairs of strangers / to sit down in a room and chat.
한 연구에서, / 연구자들은 서로 모르는 사람끼리 짝을 지어 ~하게 했다. / 한 방에 앉아서 이야기하도록
In half of the rooms, / a cell phone was placed on a nearby table; / in the other half, / no phone was present.
절반의 방에는 / 근처 탁자 위에 휴대폰이 놓여 있었고, / 나머지 절반에는 / 휴대폰이 없었다.
After the conversations had ended, / the researchers asked the participants / what they thought of each other.
대화가 끝난 후, / 연구자들은 참가자들에게 물었다. / 그들이 서로에 대해 어떻게 생각하는지를
Here's what they learned: / when a cell phone was present in the room, / the participants reported / the quality of their relationship was worse / than those who'd talked in a cell phone-free room.
여기에 그들이 알게 된 것이 있다. / 방에 휴대폰이 있을 때 / 참가자들은 말했다. / 자신들의 관계의 질이 더 나빴다고 / 휴대폰이 없는 방에서 대화했던 참가자들에 비해
The pairs who talked in the rooms with cell phones / thought / their partners showed less empathy.

휴대폰이 있는 방에서 대화한 짝은 / 생각했다. / 자신의 상대가 공감을 덜 보여 주었다고
Think of all the times / you've sat down / to have lunch with a friend / and set your phone on the table.
모든 순간을 떠올려 보라. / 여러분이 자리에 앉아 / 친구와 점심을 먹기 위해 / 탁자 위에 휴대폰을 놓았던
You might have felt good about yourself / because you didn't pick it up / to check your messages, / but your unchecked messages / were still hurting your connection / with the person sitting across from you.
여러분은 잘했다고 느꼈을지 모르지만, / 여러분이 휴대폰을 집어 들지 않았으므로 / 메시지를 확인하려고 / 여러분의 확인하지 않은 메시지는 / 여전히 관계를 상하게 하고 있었다. / 맞은편에 앉아 있는 사람과의
➡ The presence of a cell phone / (A) weakens the connection / between people involved in conversations, / even when the phone is being (B) ignored.
휴대폰의 존재는 / 관계를 약화시킨다. / 대화에 참여하는 사람들 간의 / 심지어 휴대폰이 무시되고 있을 때조차

한 연구에서, 연구자들은 서로 모르는 사람들끼리 짝을 지어 한 방에 앉아서 이야기하도록 했다. 절반의 방에는 근처 탁자 위에 휴대폰이 놓여 있었고, 나머지 절반에는 휴대폰이 없었다. 대화가 끝난 후, 연구자들은 참가자들에게 서로에 대해 어떻게 생각하는지를 물었다. 여기에 그들이 알게 된 것이 있다. 방에 휴대폰이 있을 때 참가자들은 휴대폰이 없는 방에서 대화했던 참가자들에 비해 자신들의 관계의 질이 더 나빴다고 말했다. 휴대폰이 있는 방에서 대화한 짝은 자신의 상대가 공감을 덜 보여 주었다고 생각했다. 친구와 점심을 먹기 위해 자리에 앉아 탁자 위에 휴대폰을 놓았던 모든 순간을 떠올려 보라. 메시지를 확인하려고 휴대폰을 집어 들지 않았으므로 잘했다고 느꼈을지 모르지만, 여러분의 확인하지 않은 메시지는 여전히 맞은편에 앉아 있는 사람과의 관계를 상하게 하고 있었다.

➡ 휴대폰의 존재는 심지어 휴대폰이 (B) 무시되고 있을 때조차 대화에 참여하는 사람들 간의 관계를 (A) 약화시킨다.

Why? 왜 정답일까?

'~ when a cell phone was present in the room, the participants reported the quality of their relationship was worse than those who'd talked in a cell phone-free room.'과 '~ your unchecked messages were still hurting your connection with the person sitting across from you.'에서 우리가 휴대폰을 확인하지 않고 내버려두는 상황일지라도 휴대폰이 '있다'는 사실 자체로 상대방과의 관계가 약해질 수 있다는 연구 결과가 제시된다. 이를 근거로 볼 때, 요약문의 빈칸에 들어갈 말로 가장 적절한 것은 ② '(A) weakens(약화시킨다). (B) ignored(무시되고)'이다.

- **present** ⓐ 존재하는
- **unchecked** ⓐ 확인되지 않은
- **weaken** ⓥ 약화시키다
- **renew** ⓥ 새롭게 하다, 갱신하다, 재개하다
- **participant** ⓝ 참가자
- **hurt** ⓥ 손상시키다, 다치게 하다
- **ignore** ⓥ 무시하다
- **maintain** ⓥ 유지하다

구문 풀이

13행 You might have felt good about yourself because you didn't pick it up to
「might have + p.p. : ~했을지도 모른다」 접속사(~ 때문에)
check your messages, but your unchecked messages were still hurting your
주어 동사(과거진행)
connection with the person sitting across from you.
현재분사

★★ 문제 해결 꿀~팁 ★★

▶ 많이 틀린 이유는?
마지막 문장에서 '확인하지 않은(unchecked)' 휴대폰 메시지가 관계에 악영향을 미치고 있었다는 결론이 제시된다. 즉 요약문의 (B)에는 휴대전화에 '응답하고 있지 않은' 상황에조차 관계가 악화되고 있었다는 의미를 완성하는 말이 들어가야 한다. ①의 answered는 휴대전화에 '응답하는' 상황에조차 관계가 나빠지고 있었다는 의미를 나타내므로 부적절하다.

▶ 문제 해결 방법은?
요약문에서 '실험 - 결과' 구조의 글이 나오면 바로 결과가 제시되는 문장을 찾아 요약문을 그 문장과 일치시킨다는 느낌으로 문제를 풀면 된다. 이 문제에서도 실험의 결론을 제시하는 마지막 문장과 요약문의 내용이 서로 같아야 한다.

41-42 반복의 중요성

As kids, / we worked hard at learning to ride a bike; / when we fell off, / we got back on again, / until it became second nature to us.
아이였을 때, / 우리는 열심히 자전거 타기를 배웠고, / 우리가 넘어지면 / 우리는 다시 올라탔는데, / 그것이 우리에게 제2의 천성이 될 때까지 그러했다.
But when we try something new in our adult lives / we'll usually make just one attempt / before judging whether it's (a) worked.
그러나 우리가 어른으로 살면서 새로운 것을 시도할 때 / 우리는 대체로 단 한 번만 시도해 본다. / 그것이 잘되었는지 판단하기 전에
If we don't succeed the first time, / or if it feels a little awkward, / we'll tell ourselves / it wasn't a success / rather than giving it (b) another shot.
만일 우리가 처음에 성공하지 못하거나 / 혹은 그것이 약간 어색하게 느껴지면, / 우리는 스스로에게 말할 것이다. / 그것이 성공이 아니었다고 / 또 한번 시도해 보기보다는
「That's a shame, / because repetition is central / to the process of rewiring our brains.」
그것은 애석한 일인데, / 반복이 핵심적이기 때문이다. / 우리 뇌를 재연결하는 과정에서 **41번의 근거**
Consider the idea / that your brain has a network of neurons.
개념을 생각해 보라. / 여러분의 뇌가 뉴런의 연결망을 가지고 있다는
They will (c) connect with each other / whenever you remember to use a brain-friendly feedback technique.
그것들은 서로 연결될 것이다. / 여러분이 뇌 친화적인 피드백 기술을 잊지 않고 사용할 때마다
Those connections aren't very (d) reliable at first, / which may make your first efforts a little hit-and-miss.
그 연결은 처음에는 그리 신뢰할 만하지 않고, / 여러분의 첫 번째 시도가 다소 마구잡이가 되도록 할 수도 있다.
You might remember one of the steps involved, / and not the others.
여러분은 관련된 단계 중 하나를 기억하고, / 다른 것들을 기억하지 못할 수도 있다. **42번의 근거**
「But humans have a saying: / "neurons that fire together, wire together."」
그러나 과학자들은 말한다. / "함께 활성화되는 뉴런들은 함께 연결된다."라고
In other words, / repetition of an action / (e) strengthens the connections / between the neurons involved in that action.
다시 말하자면, / 어떤 행동의 반복은 / 연결을 강화한다. / 그 행동에 연관된 뉴런들 사이의

「That means / the more times you try using that new feedback technique, / the more easily it will come to you / when you need it.」 41번의 근거
그것은 의미한다. / 여러분이 새 새로운 피드백 기술을 더 여러 차례 사용해 볼수록, / 그것이 더 쉽게 여러분에게 다가올 것을 / 여러분이 그것을 필요로 할 때

아이였을 때, 우리는 열심히 자전거 타기를 배웠고, 넘어지면 다시 올라탔는데, 그것이 우리에게 제2의 천성이 될 때까지 그렇게 했다. 그러나 어른으로 살면서 새로운 것을 시도해 볼 때 우리는 대체로 단 한 번만 시도해 보고 나서 그것이 (a) 잘되었는지 판단하려 한다. 만일 우리가 처음에 성공하지 못하거나 혹은 약간 어색한 느낌이 들면, (b) 또 한번 시도해 보기보다는 그것이 성공이 아니었다고 스스로에게 말할 것이다.

그것은 애석한 일인데, 우리 뇌를 재연결하는 과정에서 반복이 핵심적이기 때문이다. 여러분의 뇌가 뉴런의 연결망을 가지고 있다는 개념을 생각해 보라. 여러분이 뇌 친화적인 피드백 기술을 잊지 않고 사용할 때마다 그것들은 서로 (c) 연결될 것이다. 그 연결은 처음에는 그리 (d) 신뢰할 만하지 않고, 여러분의 첫 번째 시도가 다소 마구잡이가 되도록 할 수도 있다. 여러분은 연관된 단계 중 하나를 기억하고, 다른 것들을 기억하지 못할 수도 있다. 그러나 과학자들은 "함께 활성화되는 뉴런들은 함께 연결된다."라고 말한다. 다시 말하자면, 어떤 행동의 반복은 그 행동에 연관된 뉴런들 사이의 연결을 (e) 차단한다(→ 강화한다). 그것은 여러분이 그 새로운 피드백 기술을 더 여러 차례 사용해 볼수록, 필요할 때 그것이 더 쉽게 여러분에게 다가올 것을 의미한다.

- work hard at ~을 들이파다, 열심히 하다
- nature ⓝ 본성, 천성
- awkward ⓐ (기분이) 어색한, 불편한
- shame ⓝ 애석한 일, 딱한 일
- central ⓐ 핵심적인
- hit-and-miss ⓐ 되는 대로 하는, 마구잡이로 하는
- curious ⓐ 호기심이 많은
- fall off 넘어지다
- make an attempt 시도하다
- give it a shot 시도해 보다
- repetition ⓝ 반복
- reliable ⓐ 신뢰할 만한
- block ⓥ 차단하다

구문 풀이

10행 They will connect with each other whenever you remember to use a brain-friendly feedback technique.
복합관계부사「remember + to부정사 : ~할 것을 기억하다」 (~할 때마다)

18행 That means the more times you try using that new feedback technique, the more easily it will come to you when you need it.
「the + 비교급 ~, the + 비교급 … : ~할수록 더 …하다」

---

41 제목 파악   정답률 72% | 정답 ①

윗글의 제목으로 가장 적절한 것은?

✔ ① Repeat and You Will Succeed - 반복하면 성공할 것이다
② Be More Curious, Be Smarter - 더 호기심을 가지고, 더 똑똑해져라
③ Play Is What Makes Us Human - 놀이는 우리를 인간답게 만드는 것이다
④ Stop and Think Before You Act - 행동하기 전에 가만히 생각하라
⑤ Growth Is All About Keeping Balance - 성장은 전적으로 균형 유지에 관한 것이다

Why? 왜 정답일까?

두 번째 단락의 첫 문장과 마지막 문장인 '~ repetition is central to the process of rewiring our brains.', '~ the more times you try using that new feedback technique, the more easily it will come to you when you need it.'에서 어떤 것을 반복할수록 다음에 그것이 필요할 때 더 쉽게 되살아날 가능성이 높아진다고 언급하는 것으로 볼 때, 글의 제목으로 가장 적절한 것은 기술 습득에 있어 '반복'이 중요하다는 의미의 ① '반복하면 성공할 것이다'이다.

---

42 어휘 추론   정답률 60% | 정답 ⑤

밑줄 친 (a)~(e) 중에서 문맥상 낱말의 쓰임이 적절하지 않은 것은?

① (a)   ② (b)   ③ (c)   ④ (d)   ✔ ⑤ (e)

Why? 왜 정답일까?

'But scientists have a saying: "neurons that fire together, wire together."'에서 함께 활성화되는 뉴런은 함께 연결된다고 언급하는 것으로 볼 때, (e)가 포함된 문장은 어떠한 행동을 반복할 때 그 행동과 연관된 뉴런들 사이의 연결이 '강화된다'는 의미여야 한다. 따라서 (e)는 blocks 대신 strengthens로 고쳐야 한다. 문맥상 낱말의 쓰임이 적절하지 않은 것은 ⑤ '(e)'이다.

43-45   동물도 상실의 고통을 느낀다는 것을 깨달은 사냥꾼 왕

(A)

Once upon a time, / there lived a young king / who had a great passion for hunting.
옛날 옛적에 / 젊은 왕이 살았다. / 사냥에 대해 엄청난 열정을 가진
His kingdom was located at the foot of the Himalayas.
그의 왕국은 히말라야 산기슭에 위치해 있었다.
「Once every year, / he would go hunting in the nearby forests.」 45번의 근거 일치
매년 한 번씩, / 그는 근처의 숲으로 사냥하러 가고는 했다.
(a) He would make all the necessary preparations, / and then set out for his hunting trip.
그는 모든 필요한 준비를 하고 / 자신의 사냥 여행을 떠나고는 했다.

(C)

Like all other years, / the hunting season had arrived.
여느 해처럼, / 사냥철이 왔다.
Preparations began in the palace / and the king got ready for (c) his hunting trip.
궁궐에서 준비가 시작되었고 / 왕은 자신의 사냥 여행을 갈 준비를 했다.
Deep in the forest, / he spotted a beautiful wild deer.
숲속 깊은 곳에서 / 그는 아름다운 야생 사슴을 발견했다.
It was a large stag.
그것은 큰 수사슴이었다.

His aim was perfect.
그의 겨냥은 완벽했다.
「When he killed the deer with just one shot of his arrow, / the king was filled with pride.」 45번 ③의 근거 일치
단 한 발의 화살로 그 사슴을 잡고서 / 왕은 의기양양했다.
(d) The proud hunter ordered a hunting drum / to be made out of the skin of the deer.
그 의기양양한 사냥꾼은 사냥용 북이 ~되도록 명령했다. / 그 사슴의 가죽으로 만들어지도록

(B)

Seasons changed.
계절이 바뀌었다.
A year passed by.
1년이 지나갔다.
And it was time to go hunting once again.
그리고 또 다시 사냥하러 갈 때가 되었다.
The king went to the same forest as the previous year.
왕은 작년과 같은 숲으로 갔다.
(b) He used his beautiful deerskin drum / to round up animals.
그는 아름다운 사슴 가죽으로 만든 북을 사용하여 / 동물을 몰았다.
But none came.
그러나 아무도 오지 않았다.
All the animals ran for safety, / except one doe.
모든 동물이 안전한 곳으로 도망쳤는데, / 암사슴 한 마리는 예외였다.
「She came closer and closer to the drummer.」 45번 ②의 근거 불일치
암사슴은 북 치는 사람에게 점점 더 가까이 다가왔다.
Suddenly, / she started fearlessly licking the deerskin drum.
갑자기, / 암사슴은 두려움 없이 사슴 가죽으로 만든 북을 핥기 시작했다.

(D)

The king was surprised by this sight.
이 광경을 보고 왕은 놀랐다.
「An old servant had an answer / to this strange behavior.」 45번 ④의 근거 일치
한 나이 든 신하가 답을 알고 있었다. / 이 이상한 행동에 대한
"The deerskin used to make this drum / belonged to her mate, / the deer who we hunted last year.
"이 북을 만드는 데 사용된 사슴 가죽은 / 암사슴의 짝의 것인데, / 우리가 작년에 사냥한 그 사슴입니다.
This doe is mourning the death of her mate," / (e) the man said.
이 암사슴은 짝의 죽음을 애도하고 있는 것입니다."라고 / (e) 그 남자는 말했다.
Upon hearing this, / the king had a change of heart.
이 말을 듣자마자, / 왕의 마음이 바뀌었다.
He had never realized / that an animal, too, felt the pain of loss.
그는 전혀 몰랐다. / 동물도 역시 상실의 고통을 느낀다는 것을
「He made a promise, / from that day on, / to never again hunt wild animals.」 45번 ⑤의 근거 일치
그는 약속했다. / 그날 이후 / 다시는 결코 야생 동물을 사냥하지 않겠다고

(A)

옛날 옛적에 사냥에 대해 엄청난 열정을 가진 젊은 왕이 살았다. 그의 왕국은 히말라야 산기슭에 위치해 있었다. 매년 한 번씩, 그는 근처의 숲으로 사냥하러 가고는 했다. (a) 그는 모든 필요한 준비를 하고 자신의 사냥 여행을 떠나고는 했다.

(C)

여느 해처럼, 사냥철이 왔다. 궁궐에서 준비가 시작되었고 왕은 (c) 자신의 사냥 여행을 갈 준비를 했다. 숲속 깊은 곳에서 그는 아름다운 야생 사슴을 발견했다. 그것은 큰 수사슴이었다. 그의 겨냥은 완벽했다. 단 한 발의 화살로 그 사슴을 잡고서 왕은 의기양양했다. (d) 그 의기양양한 사냥꾼은 그 사슴의 가죽으로 사냥용 북을 만들도록 명령했다.

(B)

계절이 바뀌었다. 1년이 지나갔다. 그리고 또 다시 사냥하러 갈 때가 되었다. 왕은 작년과 같은 숲으로 갔다. (b) 그는 아름다운 사슴 가죽으로 만든 북을 사용하여 동물을 몰았다. 그러나 아무도 오지 않았다. 모든 동물이 안전한 곳으로 도망쳤는데, 암사슴 한 마리는 예외였다. 암사슴은 북 치는 사람에게 점점 더 가까이 다가왔다. 갑자기, 암사슴은 두려움 없이 사슴 가죽으로 만든 북을 핥기 시작했다.

(D)

이 광경을 보고 왕은 놀랐다. 한 나이 든 신하가 이 이상한 행동의 이유를 알고 있었다. "이 북을 만드는 데 사용된 사슴 가죽은 암사슴의 짝의 것인데, 우리가 작년에 사냥한 그 사슴입니다. 이 암사슴은 짝의 죽음을 애도하고 있는 것입니다."라고 (e) 그 남자는 말했다. 이 말을 듣자마자, 왕의 마음이 바뀌었다. 그는 동물도 역시 상실의 고통을 느낀다는 것을 전혀 몰랐었다. 그는 그날 이후 다시는 결코 야생 동물을 사냥하지 않겠다고 약속했다.

- passion ⓝ 열정
- preparation ⓝ 준비, 채비
- previous ⓐ 이전의
- lick ⓥ 핥다
- aim ⓝ 겨냥, 목표 ⓥ 겨누다
- have a change of heart 마음을 바꾸다, 심경의 변화가 생기다
- loss ⓝ 상실
- at the foot of ~의 기슭에, 하단부에
- set out for ~을 향해 나서다
- fearlessly ⓐⓓ 겁 없이, 대담하게
- spot ⓥ 알아채다, 발견하다

구문 풀이

(A) 1행 Once upon a time, there lived a young king [who had a great passion for hunting].
(동사 / 주어 / 주격 관계대명사)

(C) 6행 The proud hunter ordered a hunting drum to be made out of the skin of the deer.
「order + 목적어 + to부정사 : ~이 …하게 명령하다」

(D) 2행 The deerskin used to make this drum belonged to her mate, the deer [who(m) we hunted last year].
(주어 / 과거분사 부사적 용법(목적) / 동사 / 동격(= her mate))

(D) 7행 He made a promise, from that day on, to never again hunt wild animals.
「to + 부사 + 동사원형 : 분리부정사(부정사를 수식하는 부사 to와 동사원형 사이에 삽입된 형태」

---

43 글의 순서 파악   정답률 82% | 정답 ②

주어진 글 (A)에 이어질 내용을 순서에 맞게 배열한 것으로 가장 적절한 것은?

① (B) - (D) - (C)   ✔ ② (C) - (B) - (D)

③ (C) − (D) − (B)　　　　　　④ (D) − (B) − (C)
⑤ (D) − (C) − (B)

Why? 왜 정답일까?

시간적 단서를 잘 활용해야 하는 순서 문제이다. 옛날에 어느 한 왕이 사냥에 대한 열정이 있어 매년 사냥 여행을 떠났다는 내용의 **(A)** 뒤에는, 다른 모든 해처럼 사냥철이 와서 왕이 사냥을 떠났고 아름다운 야생 사슴 한 마리를 잡아 그 기념으로 북을 만들었다는 내용의 **(C)**가 이어져야 한다. 이어서 **(B)**에서는 '1년 후' 다시 사냥하러 갈 때가 되어 길을 떠난 왕이 북소리에 피하지 않고 도리어 가까이 오는 암사슴 한 마리를 발견했다는 내용이 전개된다. 마지막으로 **(D)**는 '이 광경'에 왕이 놀라자, 한 신하가 상황을 설명해 주었다는 내용으로 마무리된다. 따라서 글의 순서로 가장 적절한 것은 ② '(C) − (B) − (D)'이다.

44 지칭 추론　　　　　　정답률 81% | 정답 ⑤

밑줄 친 (a) ~ (e) 중에서 가리키는 대상이 나머지 넷과 다른 것은?

① (a)　　② (b)　　③ (c)　　④ (d)　　✓(e)

Why? 왜 정답일까?

(a), (b), (c), (d)는 the king, (e)는 An old servant를 가리키므로, (a) ~ (e) 중에서 가리키는 대상이 다른 하나는 ⑤ '(e)'이다.

45 세부 내용 파악　　　　　　정답률 80% | 정답 ②

윗글에 관한 내용으로 적절하지 않은 것은?

① 왕은 매년 근처의 숲으로 사냥 여행을 갔다.
✓암사슴은 북 치는 사람으로부터 도망갔다.
③ 왕은 화살로 단번에 수사슴을 맞혔다.
④ 한 나이 든 신하가 암사슴의 행동의 이유를 알고 있었다.
⑤ 왕은 다시는 야생 동물을 사냥하지 않겠다고 약속했다.

Why? 왜 정답일까?

(B) 'She came closer and closer to the drummer.'에서 모든 동물들이 북소리를 듣는 안전한 곳으로 피신하는 가운데 암사슴 한 마리는 북 치는 사람에게 가까이 다가왔다고 하므로, 내용과 일치하지 않는 것은 ② '암사슴은 북 치는 사람으로부터 도망갔다.'이다.

Why? 왜 오답일까?

① **(A)** 'Once every year, he would go hunting in the nearby forests.'의 내용과 일치한다.
③ **(C)** 'When he killed the deer with just one shot of his arrow, ~'의 내용과 일치한다.
④ **(D)** 'An old servant had an answer to this strange behavior.'의 내용과 일치한다.
⑤ **(D)** 'He made a promise, from that day on, to never again hunt wild animals.'의 내용과 일치한다.

어휘 Review Test 04　　　　　　문제편 040쪽

A	B	C	D
01 해로운	01 disappointed	01 ⓗ	01 ①
02 거대한	02 appetite	02 ⓔ	02 ⓠ
03 무례한	03 accept	03 ⓒ	03 ⓐ
04 바꾸다, 번역하다	04 achievement	04 ①	04 ①
05 측면	05 convince	05 ①	05 ⓜ
06 자신감 있는	06 deliver	06 ⓑ	06 ⓚ
07 모으다	07 process	07 ⓖ	07 ①
08 대략	08 distress	08 ⓚ	08 ①
09 한편	09 equation	09 ①	09 ⓗ
10 ~의 가치가 있는	10 previous	10 ⓠ	10 ⓖ
11 고치다	11 discomfort	11 ⓜ	11 ⓝ
12 적절히	12 include	12 ①	12 ⓓ
13 발생하다, 일어나다	13 notable	13 ⓞ	13 ⓔ
14 즐겁게	14 central	14 ⓟ	14 ⓑ
15 악기, 도구	15 maintain	15 ⓐ	15 ①
16 복잡한	16 acceptable	16 ①	16 ⓟ
17 점점 더	17 dwell	17 ⓢ	17 ⓒ
18 입장	18 entrance	18 ⓝ	18 ⓢ
19 (신체) 기관	19 legally	19 ⓓ	19 ⓞ
20 ~에 적응하다	20 get past	20 ①	20 ⓡ

05 회 | 2020학년도 3월 학력평가 　　고1

• 정답 •

| 18 ④ | 19 ⑤ | 20 ② | 21 ③ | 22 ① | 23 ② | 24 ② | 25 ④ | 26 ④ | 27 ③ | 28 ④ | 29 ② | 30 ③ | 31 ③ | 32 ① |
| 33 ① | 34 ① | 35 ② | 36 ⑤ | 37 ④ | 38 ⑤ | 39 ④ | 40 ① | 41 ② | 42 ③ | 43 ③ | 44 ④ | 45 ⑤ |

★ 표기된 문항은 [등급을 가르는 문제]에 해당하는 문항입니다.

18 토스터기 교환 요청 대응　　　　　　정답률 83% | 정답 ④

다음 글의 목적으로 가장 적절한 것은?

① 새로 출시한 제품을 홍보하려고
② 흔히 생기는 고장 사례를 알려주려고
③ 품질 보증서 보관의 중요성을 강조하려고
✓고장 난 제품을 교환하는 방법을 안내하려고
⑤ 제품 만족도 조사에 참여해줄 것을 요청하려고

Dear Ms. Spadler,
Spadler씨께,
You've written to our company / complaining / that your toaster, which you bought only three weeks earlier, / doesn't work.
귀하는 저희 회사에 편지를 쓰셨습니다. / 불평하는 / 불과 3주 전에 구입한 귀하의 토스터가 / 작동하지 않는다고
You were asking for a new toaster or a refund.
귀하는 새 토스터나 환불을 요구하셨습니다.
Since the toaster has a year's warranty, / our company is happy / to replace your faulty toaster with a new toaster.
그 토스터는 1년의 품질 보증 기간이 있기 때문에, / 저희 회사는 기쁩니다. / 귀하의 고장 난 토스터를 새 토스터로 교환해 드리게 되어
To get your new toaster, / simply take your receipt and the faulty toaster / to the dealer from whom you bought it.
새 토스터를 받으시려면, / 귀하의 영수증과 고장 난 토스터를 가져가시기만 하면 됩니다. / 귀하가 그것을 구매했던 판매인에게
The dealer will give you a new toaster on the spot.
그 판매인이 그 자리에서 바로 새 토스터를 드릴 것입니다.
Nothing is more important to us / than the satisfaction of our customers.
저희에게 더 중요한 것은 없습니다. / 저희 고객의 만족보다
If there is anything else we can do for you, / please do not hesitate to ask.
만약 저희가 귀하를 위해 할 수 있는 기타 어떤 일이라면, / 주저하지 말고 요청하십시오.
Yours sincerely, // Betty Swan
Betty Swan 드림

Spadler씨께,

귀하는 불과 3주 전에 구입한 토스터가 작동하지 않는다고 저희 회사에 불평하는 편지를 쓰셨습니다. 귀하는 새 토스터나 환불을 요구하셨습니다. 그 토스터는 1년의 품질 보증 기간이 있기 때문에, 저희 회사는 귀하의 고장 난 토스터를 새 토스터로 기꺼이 교환해 드리겠습니다. 새 토스터를 받으시려면, 귀하의 영수증과 고장 난 토스터를 구매했던 판매인에게 가져가시기만 하면 됩니다. 그 판매인이 그 자리에서 바로 새 토스터를 드릴 것입니다. 저희에게 고객의 만족보다 더 중요한 것은 없습니다. 만약 저희가 귀하를 위해 할 수 있는 기타 어떤 일이 있다면, 주저하지 말고 요청하십시오.

Betty Swan 드림

Why? 왜 정답일까?

글 중간에서 필자는 편지를 받는 고객이 불만을 제기했던 토스터를 기꺼이 교환해주겠다면서, 영수증을 함께 챙겨 구매처로 찾아가면 교환이 가능할 것(To get your new toaster, simply take your receipt and the faulty toaster to the dealer from whom you bought it.)임을 알려주고 있다. 따라서 글의 목적으로 가장 적절한 것은 ④ '고장 난 제품을 교환하는 방법을 안내하려고'이다.

● complain ⓥ 불평하다　　　● refund ⓝ 환불
● warranty ⓝ 보증기간　　　● faulty ⓐ 결함이 있는
● dealer ⓝ 판매자　　　● on the spot 현장에서
● satisfaction ⓝ 만족　　　● hesitate ⓥ 망설이다

구문 풀이

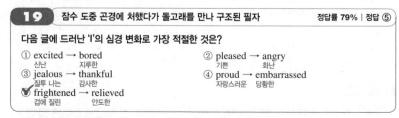

6행 To get your new toaster, simply take your receipt and the faulty toaster to the dealer [from whom you bought it].
부사적 용법(~하기 위해, 하려면)　　명령문　　목적어
선행사　　「전치사 + 관계대명사」

9행 Nothing is more important to us than the satisfaction of our customers.
「부정 주어 + 비교급 + than : 최상급 대용(~보다 ⋯한 것은 없다)」

19 잠수 도중 곤경에 처했다가 돌고래를 만나 구조된 필자　　　　　　정답률 79% | 정답 ⑤

다음 글에 드러난 'I'의 심경 변화로 가장 적절한 것은?

① excited → bored
　신난　　지루한
② pleased → angry
　기쁜　　화난
③ jealous → thankful
　질투 나는　감사한
④ proud → embarrassed
　자랑스러운　당황한
✓frightened → relieved
　겁에 질린　　안도한

I was diving alone in about 40 feet of water / when I got a terrible stomachache.
나는 40피트 정도의 물속에서 혼자 잠수하고 있었다. / 내가 배가 몹시 아팠을 때
I was sinking and hardly able to move.
나는 가라앉고 있었고 거의 움직일 수가 없었다.
I could see my watch / and knew there was only a little more time on the tank / before I would be out of air.
나는 시계를 볼 수 있었고 / (공기) 탱크 잔여 시간이 조금밖에 없다는 것을 알았다. / 내가 공기가 떨어지기 전까지
It was hard for me to remove my weight belt.
나는 웨이트 벨트를 벗기가 힘들었다.

Suddenly I felt a prodding from behind me / under the armpit.
갑자기 나는 뒤에서 쿡 찌르는 것을 느꼈다. / 겨드랑이 밑으로

My arm was being lifted forcibly.
내 팔이 강제로 들어 올려지고 있었다.

Around into my field of vision / came an eye.
내 시야 안으로 / 눈이 하나 들어왔다.

It seemed to be smiling.
그것은 웃고 있는 것 같았다.

It was the eye of a big dolphin.
그것은 큰 돌고래의 눈이었다.

Looking into that eye, / I knew I was safe.
그 눈을 들여다보니, / 나는 안전하다는 것을 알았다.

I felt / that the animal was protecting me, / lifting me toward the surface.
나는 느꼈다. / 그 동물이 나를 보호해 주고 있다고 / 나를 수면으로 들어 올려

40피트 정도의 물속에서 혼자 잠수하고 있었을 때, 나는 배가 몹시 아팠다. 나는 가라앉고 있었고 거의 움직일 수가 없었다. 나는 시계를 볼 수 있었고 공기가 떨어지기 전까지 (공기) 탱크 잔여 시간이 조금밖에 없다는 것을 알았다. 웨이트 벨트를 벗기가 힘들었다. 갑자기 나는 뒤에서 겨드랑이 밑으로 쿡 찌르는 것을 느꼈다. 내 팔이 강제로 들어 올려지고 있었다. 내 시야 안으로 눈이 하나 들어왔다. 그것은 웃고 있는 것 같았다. 그것은 큰 돌고래의 눈이었다. 그 눈을 들여다보니, 나는 안전하다는 것을 알았다. 나는 그 동물이 수면으로 나를 들어 올려 보호해 주고 있다고 느꼈다.

Why? 왜 정답일까?

'I was diving alone in about 40 feet of water when I got a terrible stomachache. I was sinking and hardly able to move.'에서 잠수하던 중 배가 아팠던 필자가 생명이 위험할 수도 있는 상황에 놓였음을 알 수 있고, 'Looking into that eye, I knew I was safe. I felt that the animal was protecting me, lifting me toward the surface.'에서 돌고래의 구조를 받게 된 필자가 위기를 벗어났음을 알 수 있다. 따라서 이를 통해 유추할 수 있는 'I'의 심경 변화로 가장 적절한 것은 ⑤ '겁에 질린 → 안도한'이다.

- **armpit** ⓝ 겨드랑이
- **field of vision** ⓝ 시야, 가시 범위
- **embarrassed** ⓐ 당황한
- **forcibly** ⓐ 강제로, 강력히
- **surface** ⓝ 표면

구문 풀이

> **6행** Around into my field of vision came an eye.
> 「장소 부사구 + 동사 + 주어 : 도치 구문」

---

20 하고 싶은 일을 적어보기 정답률 80% | 정답 ②

다음 글에서 필자가 주장하는 바로 가장 적절한 것은?

① 친구의 꿈을 응원하라. ☑ 하고 싶은 일을 적으라.
③ 신중히 생각한 후 행동하라. ④ 효과적인 기억법을 개발하라.
⑤ 실현 가능한 목표에 집중하라.

Keeping good ideas floating around in your head / is a great way / to ensure that they won't happen.
좋은 생각을 머릿속에서만 떠돌게 하는 것은 / 좋은 방법이다. / 반드시 그것이 이루어지지 않게 하는

Take a tip from writers, / who know / that the only good ideas that come to life / are the ones that get written down.
작가들로부터 조언을 얻으라, / 이들은 안다. / 생명력을 얻게 되는 좋은 생각은 / 오로지 종이에 적어둔 것들뿐임을

Take out a piece of paper / and record everything you'd love to do someday / — aim to hit one hundred dreams.
종이 한 장을 꺼내 / 언젠가 여러분이 하고 싶은 모든 것을 기록하고, / 꿈이 100개에 이르는 것을 목표로 해라.

You'll have a reminder and motivator / to get going on those things that are calling you, / and you also won't have the burden / of remembering all of them.
여러분은 상기시키고 동기를 부여해주는 것을 갖게 될 테고, / 자신을 부르고 있는 것들을 시작하도록 / 또한 여러분은 부담을 갖지 않을 것이다. / 그 모든 것을 기억해야 한다는

When you put your dreams into words / you begin putting them into action.
여러분이 꿈을 글로 적을 때 / 여러분은 그것을 실행하기 시작하는 것이다.

좋은 생각을 머릿속에서만 떠돌게 하는 것은 그것이 이루어지지 않게 하는 확실한 방법이다. 작가들로부터 조언을 얻어야 하는데, 이들은 생명력을 얻게 되는 좋은 생각은 오로지 종이에 적어둔 것들뿐임을 안다. 종이 한 장을 꺼내 언젠가 하고 싶은 모든 것을 기록하고, 꿈이 100개에 이르는 것을 목표로 해라. 여러분은 자신을 부르고 있는 것들을 시작하도록 (스스로에게) 상기시키고 동기를 부여해주는 것을 갖게 될 테고, 또한 그 모든 것을 기억해야 한다는 부담을 갖지 않을 것이다. 꿈을 글로 적을 때 여러분은 그것을 실행하기 시작하는 것이다.

Why? 왜 정답일까?

'When you put your dreams into words you begin putting them into action.'에서 필자는 꿈을 글로 적는 것이 실행의 첫걸음임을 언급하며 꿈을 써 나가는 것의 중요성을 상기시키고 있다. 따라서 필자의 주장으로 가장 적절한 것은 ② '하고 싶은 일을 적으라.'이다.

- **float** ⓥ 뜨다
- **aim** ⓥ 반드시 ~하다, 목표로 하다
- **motivator** ⓝ 동기 요인, 동기를 부여하는 것
- **put into action** ⓥ 실행에 옮기다
- **ensure** ⓥ 보장하다
- **reminder** ⓝ 상기시키는 것
- **burden** ⓝ 부담

구문 풀이

> **1행** Keeping good ideas floating around in your head is a great way to ensure
> 동명사구 주어   동사 주격 보어 형용사적 용법
> (단수)
> {that they won't happen}.
> { } : 명사절(~것)

---

21 논쟁에서 화내지 않기 정답률 61% | 정답 ③

밑줄 친 "rise to the bait"가 다음 글에서 의미하는 바로 가장 적절한 것은? [3점]
① stay calm – 침착함을 유지하다

---

② blame yourself – 스스로를 비난하다
☑ lose your temper – 화를 내다
④ listen to the audience – 청중의 말을 듣다
⑤ apologize for your behavior – 자신의 행동에 대해 사과하다

We all know / that tempers are one of the first things / lost in many arguments.
우리 모두 안다. / 화는 첫 번째 것들 중 하나임을 / 많은 논쟁에서 내게 되는

It's easy to say one should keep cool, / but how do you do it?
침착함을 유지해야 한다고 말하는 것은 쉽지만, / 그러나 어떻게 그렇게 하는가?

The point to remember is / that sometimes in arguments the other person / is trying to get you to be angry.
기억해야 할 점은 / 때로는 논쟁에서 상대방은 / 여러분을 화나게 하려고 한다는 것이다.

They may be saying things / that are intentionally designed to annoy you.
그들은 말을 하고 있을지도 모른다. / 여러분을 화나게 하기 위해 의도적으로 고안한

They know / that if they get you to lose your cool / you'll say something that sounds foolish; / you'll simply get angry / and then it will be impossible for you to win the argument.
그들은 안다. / 만약 그들이 여러분의 침착함을 잃게 한다면 / 여러분이 바보 같은 말을 할 것이고 / 여러분이 그저 화를 낼 것이고 / 그러면 여러분이 그 논쟁에서 이기기란 불가능할 것임을

So don't fall for it.
그러니 속아넘어가지 마라.

A remark may be made to cause your anger, / but responding with a cool answer / that focuses on the issue raised / is likely to be most effective.
어떤 말이 여러분의 화를 불러일으키기 위해 언급될지도 모르지만, / 침착한 답변으로 대응하는 것이 / 제기된 문제에 초점을 맞춘 / 가장 효과적인 것 같다.

Indeed, any attentive listener will admire the fact / that you didn't "rise to the bait."
정말로, 주의 깊은 청자라면 누구라도 사실에 감탄할 것이다. / 여러분이 '미끼를 물지' 않았다는

많은 논쟁에서 첫 번째로 저지르는 것 중에 하나가 화를 내는 것임을 우리 모두 안다. 침착함을 유지하라고 말하는 것은 쉽지만, 어떻게 침착함을 유지하는가? 기억해야 할 점은 때로는 논쟁에서 상대방은 여러분을 화나게 하려고 한다는 것이다. 그들은 여러분을 화나게 하기 위해 의도적으로 고안한 말을 하고 있을지도 모른다. 그들은 만약 자신들이 여러분의 침착함을 잃게 한다면 여러분은 바보 같은 말을 하고 그저 화를 낼 것이고 그러면 여러분이 그 논쟁에서 이기기란 불가능할 것임을 안다. 그러니 속아넘어가지 마라. 어떤 말이 여러분의 화를 불러일으키기 위해 언급될지도 모르지만, 제기된 문제에 초점을 맞춘 침착한 답변으로 대응하는 것이 가장 효과적인 것 같다. 정말로, 주의 깊은 청자라면 누구라도 여러분이 '미끼를 물지' 않았다는 사실에 감탄할 것이다.

Why? 왜 정답일까?

글에 따르면 논쟁에서 화가 나려 할 때 기억해야 할 점은 상대방이 우리를 화나게 하기 위해 일부러 어떤 말을 했을 수도 있다는 것이다(The point to remember is that sometimes in arguments the other person is trying to get you to be angry.). 마지막 두 문장에서는 그리하여 쉽게 화를 내지 않고 침착함을 유지하며 문제에만 초점을 맞춘 답변을 하면 상대방은 우리가 '화를 내지' 않았다는 바로 그 점에 감탄할 것이라는 결론을 도출하고 있다. 따라서 밑줄 친 부분이 의미하는 바로 가장 적절한 것은 ③ '화를 내다'이다.

- **lose one's temper** ⓥ 화를 내다
- **intentionally** ⓐ 일부러, 의도적으로
- **lose one's cool** ⓥ 침착함을 잃다
- **remark** ⓝ 말, 언급
- **admire** ⓥ 감탄하다
- **apologize for** ⓥ ~에 대해 사과하다
- **argument** ⓝ 논쟁
- **design** ⓥ 고안하다
- **fall for** ⓥ ~에 속아넘어가다
- **raise** ⓥ (문제 등을) 제기하다
- **rise to the bait** ⓥ 미끼를 물다

구문 풀이

> **8행** A remark may be made to cause your anger, but responding with a cool
> 주어1   동사1(조동사 수동태) ~하기 위해   주어2(동명사구) 선행사
> answer [that focuses on the issue raised] is likely to be most effective.
> └ 주격 관계대명사 └ 과거분사 동사2(~할 것 같다)

---

22 위험을 감수할 필요성 정답률 89% | 정답 ①

다음 글의 요지로 가장 적절한 것은?

☑ 위험을 무릅쓰지 않으면 아무 것도 얻지 못한다.
② 자신이 잘하는 일에 집중하는 것이 효율적이다.
③ 잦은 실패 경험은 도전할 의지를 잃게 한다.
④ 위험 요소가 있으면 미리 피하는 것이 좋다.
⑤ 부탁을 자주 거절하면 신뢰를 잃는다.

Practically anything of value requires / that we take a risk of failure or being rejected.
사실상 어떤 가치 있는 것이든 요구한다. / 우리가 실패나 거절당할 위험을 무릅쓸 것을

This is the price / we all must pay / for achieving the greater rewards lying ahead of us.
이것은 대가이다. / 우리 모두가 지불해야 하는 / 우리 앞에 놓인 더 큰 보상을 성취하기 위해

To take risks / means you will succeed sometime / but never to take a risk / means that you will never succeed.
위험을 무릅쓰는 것은 / 여러분이 언젠가 성공할 것이라는 것을 의미하지만 / 위험을 전혀 무릅쓰지 않는 것은 / 여러분이 결코 성공하지 못할 것임을 의미한다.

Life is filled with a lot of risks and challenges / and if you want to get away from all these, / you will be left behind in the race of life.
인생은 많은 위험과 도전으로 가득 차 있으며, / 여러분이 이 모든 것에서 벗어나기를 원하면 / 인생이라는 경주에서 뒤처지게 될 것이다.

A person who can never take a risk / can't learn anything.
결코 위험을 무릅쓰지 못하는 사람은 / 아무것도 배울 수 없다.

For example, if you never take the risk to drive a car, / you can never learn to drive.
예를 들어, 만약 여러분이 차를 운전하기 위해 위험을 무릅쓰지 않는다면, / 여러분은 결코 운전을 배울 수 없다.

If you never take the risk of being rejected, / you can never have a friend or partner.
여러분이 거절당할 위험을 무릅쓰지 않는다면 / 여러분은 친구나 파트너를 절대 얻을 수 없다.

Similarly, by not taking the risk of attending an interview, / you will never get a job.
마찬가지로 면접에 참석하는 위험을 무릅쓰지 않음으로써, / 여러분은 결코 일자리를 얻지 못할 것이다.

사실상 모든 가치 있는 것은 우리가 실패나 거절당할 위험을 무릅쓸 것을 요구한다. 이것은 우리 앞에 놓인 더 큰 보상을 성취하기 위해 우리 모두가 지불해야 하는 대가이다. 위험을 무

릅쓴다는 것은 언젠가 성공할 것이라는 것을 의미하지만 위험을 전혀 무릅쓰지 않는 것은 결코 성공하지 못할 것임을 의미한다. 인생은 많은 위험과 도전으로 가득 차 있으며, 이 모든 것에서 벗어나기를 원하면 인생이라는 경주에서 뒤처지게 될 것이다. 결코 위험을 무릅쓰지 못하는 사람은 아무것도 배울 수 없다. 예를 들어, 만약 차를 운전하기 위해 위험을 무릅쓰지 않는다면, 여러분은 결코 운전을 배울 수 없다. 거절당할 위험을 무릅쓰지 않는다면 친구나 파트너를 절대 얻을 수 없다. 마찬가지로 면접에 참석하는 위험을 무릅쓰지 않음으로써, 여러분은 결코 일자리를 얻지 못할 것이다.

Why? 왜 정답일까?

예시 앞에 나와 주제를 제시하는 'A person who can never take a risk can't learn anything.'에서 위험을 감수하지 않는 사람은 그 어떤 것도 배울 수 없다는 논지를 말하고 있다. 따라서 글의 요지로 가장 적절한 것은 ① '위험을 무릅쓰지 않으면 아무 것도 얻지 못한다.'이다.

- practically [ad] 사실상, 거의
- reject [v] 거절하다
- filled with ~로 가득 찬
- take a risk 위험을 무릅쓰다
- reward [n] 보상
- be left behind 뒤처지다

구문 풀이

1행 Practically anything of value requires that we (should) take a risk of failure or being rejected.
주어 =valuable 동사(요구) 생략 전치사← 목적어1
목적어2(수동 동명사)

---

23 소비자에게 중요한 요소인 촉감 정답률 77% | 정답 ②

다음 글의 주제로 가장 적절한 것은?
① benefits of using online shopping malls – 온라인 쇼핑몰 이용의 이점
✓② touch as an important factor for consumers – 소비자에게 중요한 요소인 촉감
③ importance of sharing information among consumers – 소비자 간 정보 공유의 중요성
④ necessity of getting feedback from consumers – 소비자 피드백을 수렴할 필요성
⑤ popularity of products in the latest styles – 최신 스타일 제품의 인기

Although individual preferences vary, / touch / (both what we touch with our fingers / and the way things feel as they come in contact with our skin) / is an important aspect of many products.
개인의 선호는 다양하지만, / 촉감은 / (우리가 손가락으로 만지는 것과 / 물건이 우리의 피부에 접촉될 때 느껴지는 방식 모두) / 많은 제품의 중요한 측면이다.
Consumers like some products / because of their feel.
소비자들은 어떤 제품을 좋아한다. / 그것들의 그 감촉 때문에
Some consumers buy skin creams and baby products / for their soothing effect on the skin.
일부 소비자들은 피부용 크림과 유아용품을 구입한다. / 피부를 진정시키는 그것들의 효과 때문에
In fact, consumers who have a high need for touch / tend to like products / that provide this opportunity.
실제로, 촉감에 대한 욕구가 많은 소비자는 / 제품을 좋아하는 경향이 있다. / 이런 기회를 제공하는
When considering products with material properties, / such as clothing or carpeting, / consumers like goods they can touch in stores more / than products they only see and read about online or in catalogs.
재료 속성과 함께 제품을 고려할 때, / 의류나 카펫과 같은 / 소비자들은 상점에서 만져볼 수 있는 제품을 더 좋아한다. / 그들이 온라인이나 카탈로그에서 보고 읽기만 하는 제품보다

개인의 선호는 다양하지만, 촉감(우리가 손가락으로 만지는 것과 물건이 우리의 피부에 접촉될 때 느껴지는 방식 모두)은 많은 제품의 중요한 측면이다. 소비자들은 어떤 제품을 그 감촉 때문에 좋아한다. 일부 소비자들은 피부 진정 효과 때문에 피부용 크림과 유아용품을 구입한다. 실제로, 촉감에 대한 욕구가 많은 소비자는 이런 기회를 제공하는 제품을 좋아하는 경향이 있다. 의류나 카펫과 같은 제품을 재료의 속성과 함께 고려할 때, 소비자들은 온라인이나 카탈로그에서 보고 읽기만 하는 제품보다 상점에서 만져볼 수 있는 제품을 더 좋아한다.

Why? 왜 정답일까?

'Although individual preferences vary, touch ~ is an important aspect of many products.'에서 소비자의 개인적 선호가 비록 다양하지만 촉감이 많은 제품에 있어 중요한 측면임을 언급하므로, 글의 주제로 가장 적절한 것은 ② '소비자에게 중요한 요소인 촉감'이다.

- preference [n] 선호
- aspect [n] 측면
- opportunity [n] 기회
- factor [n] 요인
- come in contact with [v] ~와 접촉하다
- soothing [a] 진정시키는
- material [n] 재료, 직물
- necessity [n] 필요성

구문 풀이

1행 Although individual preferences vary, touch (both what we touch with our
양보 접속사(비록 ~이지만) 자동사 주어 「both+A+and+B : A와 B 둘 다」
fingers and the way [things feel] as they come in contact with our skin) is an
동사(단수)
important aspect of many products.

---

24 아무리 많이 해도 지나침이 없는 교육 정답률 73% | 정답 ②

다음 글의 제목으로 가장 적절한 것은?
① All Play and No Work Makes Jack a Smart Boy
놀기만 하고 일하지 않는 것은 Jack(일반 사람을 나타냄)을 똑똑한 아이로 만든다
✓② Too Much Education Won't Hurt You
너무 많은 정보라고 해도 당신을 해하지 않을 것이다
③ Too Heads Are Worse than One
너무 (많은) 두뇌는 하나만 못하다
④ Don't Think Twice Before You Act
행동하기 전에 두 번 생각하지 마라
⑤ Learn from the Future, Not from the Past
과거가 아닌 미래로부터 배우라

In life, they say / that too much of anything is not good for you.
삶에서는 사람들이 말하기를 / 어떤 것이든 과하면 이롭지 않다고 한다.
In fact, too much of certain things in life / can kill you.
실제로, 삶에서 과하게 많은 어떤 것들은 / 당신을 죽일 수 있다.

For example, they say / that water has no enemy, / because water is essential to all life.
예를 들어, 사람들은 말하기를 / 물은 적이 없다고 한다. / 물은 모든 생물에게 필수적이기 때문에
But if you take in too much water, / like one who is drowning, / it could kill you.
그러나 당신이 만일 너무 많은 물을 마시면, / 물에 빠진 사람처럼 / 그것은 당신을 죽게 할 수 있다.
Education is the exception to this rule.
교육은 이 규칙에서 예외다.
You can never have too much education or knowledge.
당신은 교육이나 지식을 결코 지나치게 많이 지닐 수 없다.
The reality is / that most people will never have enough education in their lifetime.
실상은 / 대부분의 사람은 평생 충분한 교육을 받지 못하리라는 것이다.
I am yet to find that one person / who has been hurt in life by too much education.
나는 그런 사람을 아직 본 적이 없다. / 교육을 너무 받아서 삶에서 피해를 본
Rather, we see lots of casualties every day, worldwide, / resulting from the lack of education.
오히려 우리는 매일, 전 세계에서 수많은 피해자들을 본다. / 교육의 부족으로 인해 생긴
You must keep in mind / that education is a long-term investment / of time, money, and effort into humans.
당신은 명심해야 한다. / 교육이 장기 투자임을 / 인간에 대한 시간, 돈, 그리고 노력의

삶에서는 어떤 것이든 과하면 이롭지 않다고 한다. 실제로, 삶에서 어떤 것은 과하면 위험할 수 있다. 예를 들어, 물은 모든 생물에게 필수적이기 때문에 적이 없다고 한다. 그러나 만일 물에 빠진 사람처럼 너무 많은 물을 마시면, 이는 당신을 죽게 할 수 있다. 교육은 이 규칙에서 예외다. 교육이나 지식은 아무리 많이 있어도 지나치지 않는다. 실상은 대부분의 사람은 평생 충분한 교육을 받지 못하리라는 것이다. 나는 교육을 너무 받아서 삶에서 피해를 본 사람을 아직 본 적이 없다. 오히려 우리는 매일, 전 세계에서 교육의 부족으로 인해 생긴 수많은 피해자들을 본다. 교육이 인간에게 시간, 돈, 그리고 노력을 장기 투자하는 것임을 명심해야 한다.

Why? 왜 정답일까?

'Education is the exception to this rule.' 앞뒤로 인생에서 무엇이든 과하면 좋지 않다는 내용과, 교육은 이 규칙에서 예외라는 내용이 상반되고 있다. 특히 'You can never have too much education or knowledge.'에서 교육이나 정보는 아무리 많이 주어지더라도 지나침이 없다고 언급하는 것으로 볼 때, 글의 제목으로 가장 적절한 것은 ② '너무 많은 정보라고 해도 당신을 해하지 않을 것이다'이다.

- essential [a] 필수적인
- drown [v] 물에 빠지다, 익사하다
- lack [n] 부족, 결여
- investment [n] 투자
- take in [v] ~을 섭취하다
- exception [n] 예외
- keep in mind [v] ~을 명심하다, 염두에 두다

구문 풀이

8행 I am yet to find that one person [who has been hurt in life by too much
아직 ~하지 못하다 선행사 주격 관·대 현재완료 수동태
education].

---

25 세계에서 가장 많이 사용된 언어의 총 사용자 및 원어민 수 정답률 84% | 정답 ④

다음 도표의 내용과 일치하지 않는 것은?

The Most Spoken Languages Worldwide in 2015

• Note: Total Speakers = Native Speakers + Non-native Speakers

The above graph / shows the numbers of total speakers and native speakers / of the five most spoken languages worldwide in 2015.
위 그래프는 / 총 사용자 수와 원어민 수를 보여 준다. / 2015년에 전 세계에서 가장 많이 사용된 다섯 개 언어의
① English is the most spoken language worldwide, / with 1,500 million total speakers.
영어는 전 세계에서 가장 많이 사용되는 언어로, / 15억 명의 총 사용자가 있다.
② Chinese is second on the list / with 1,100 million total speakers.
중국어는 목록에서 2위로 / 11억 명의 총 사용자가 있다.
③ In terms of the number of native speakers, however, / Chinese is the most spoken language worldwide, / followed by Hindi.
하지만 원어민 수라는 면에서는, / 중국어가 전 세계에서 가장 많이 사용되는 언어이며, / 힌디어가 그 뒤를 잇는다.
✓④ The number of native speakers of English / is smaller than that of Spanish.
영어의 원어민 수는 / 스페인어의 원어민 수보다 더 적다.
⑤ French is the least spoken language among the five / in terms of the number of native speakers.
프랑스어는 다섯 개 언어 중 가장 적게 사용되는 언어이다. / 원어민 수라는 면에서

위 그래프는 2015년에 전 세계에서 가장 많이 사용된 다섯 개 언어의 총 사용자 수와 원어민 수를 보여 준다. ① 영어는 전 세계에서 가장 많이 사용되는 언어로, 15억 명의 총 사용자가 있다. ② 중국어는 목록에서 2위로 11억 명의 총 사용자가 있다. ③ 하지만 원어민 수라는 면에서는, 중국어가 전 세계에서 가장 많이 사용되는 언어이며, 힌디어가 그 뒤를 잇는다. ④ 영어의 원어민 수는 스페인어의 원어민 수보다 더 적다. ⑤ 프랑스어는 원어민 수라는 면에서 다섯 개 언어 중 가장 적게 사용되는 언어이다.

Why? 왜 정답일까?

도표에 따르면 영어 원어민의 수는 3억 7천 5백만 명으로 스페인어 원어민의 수인 3억 3천 3백만 명보다 많다. 따라서 도표와 일치하지 않는 것은 ④이다.

- native speaker ⓝ 원어민
- follow ⓥ ~의 뒤를 잇다
- in terms of ~의 면에서
- term ⓝ 용어, 말

---

26 Ellen Church의 생애 정답률 84% | 정답 ④

Ellen Church에 관한 다음 글의 내용과 일치하지 <u>않는</u> 것은?

① San Francisco에서 간호사로 일했다.
② 간호사가 비행 중에 승객을 돌봐야 한다고 제안했다.
③ 미국 최초의 여성 비행기 승무원이 되었다.
✓④ 자동차 사고로 다쳤지만 비행기 승무원 생활을 계속했다.
⑤ 고향인 Cresco에 그녀의 이름을 따서 붙인 공항이 있다.

Ellen Church was born in Iowa in 1904.
Ellen Church는 1904년에 Iowa에서 태어났다.
「After graduating from Cresco High School, / she studied nursing and worked as a nurse in San Francisco.」 ①의근거 일치
Cresco 고등학교를 졸업한 후, / 그녀는 간호학을 공부했고 San Francisco에서 간호사로 일했다.
「She suggested to Boeing Air Transport / that nurses should take care of passengers during flights / because most people were frightened of flying.」 ②의근거 일치
그녀는 Boeing Air Transport에 제안했다. / 간호사가 비행 중에 승객을 돌봐야 한다고 / 대부분의 사람이 비행을 무서워했기 때문에
「In 1930, she became the first female flight attendant in the U.S. / and worked on a Boeing 80A from Oakland, California to Chicago, Illinois.」 ③의근거 일치
1930년에 그녀는 미국 최초의 여성 비행기 승무원이 되었고 / California 주 Oakland에서 Illinois 주 Chicago까지 가는 Boeing 80A에서 근무했다.
「Unfortunately, a car accident injury / forced her to end her career after only eighteen months.」
불행하게도, 자동차 사고 부상은 / 그녀가 겨우 18개월 후에 어쩔 수 없이 일을 그만두게 만들었다. ④의근거 불일치
Church started nursing again at Milwaukee County Hospital / after she graduated from the University of Minnesota / with a degree in nursing education.
Church는 Milwaukee County 병원에서 다시 간호사 일을 시작했다. / 그녀가 Minnesota 대학을 졸업한 후 / 간호 교육학 학위와 함께
During World War Ⅱ, / she served as a captain in the Army Nurse Corps / and received an Air Medal.
제2차 세계대전 중 / 그녀는 육군 간호 부대에서 대위로 복무했고 / 항공 훈장을 받았다.
「Ellen Church Field Airport in her hometown, Cresco, / was named after her.」 ⑤의근거 일치
그녀의 고향인 Cresco에 있는 Ellen Church Field 공항은 / 그녀의 이름을 따서 붙여졌다.

Ellen Church는 1904년에 Iowa에서 태어났다. Cresco 고등학교를 졸업한 후, 그녀는 간호학을 공부했고 San Francisco에서 간호사로 일했다. 그녀는 대부분의 사람이 비행을 무서워하기 때문에 간호사가 비행 중에 승객을 돌봐야 한다고 Boeing Air Transport에 제안했다. 1930년에 그녀는 미국 최초의 여성 비행기 승무원이 되어 California 주 Oakland에서 Illinois 주 Chicago까지 가는 Boeing 80A에서 근무했다. 불행하게도, 자동차 사고 부상으로 그녀는 겨우 18개월 후에 일을 그만두어야 했다. Church는 간호 교육학 학위를 받으며 Minnesota 대학을 졸업한 후 Milwaukee County 병원에서 다시 간호사 일을 시작했다. 제2차 세계대전 중 그녀는 육군 간호 부대에서 대위로 복무했고 항공 훈장을 받았다. 그녀의 고향인 Cresco에 있는 Ellen Church Field 공항은 그녀의 이름을 따서 붙여졌다.

Why? 왜 정답일까?
'Unfortunately, a car accident injury forced her to end her career after only eighteen months.'에서 자동차 사고 부상으로 인해 Ellen Church는 18개월 만에 승무원 일을 그만두어야 했다고 하므로, 내용과 일치하지 않는 것은 ④ '자동차 사고로 다쳤지만 비행기 승무원 생활을 계속했다.'이다.

Why? 왜 오답일까?
① '~ she studied nursing and worked as a nurse in San Francisco.'의 내용과 일치한다.
② 'She suggested to Boeing Air Transport that nurses should take care of passengers during flights ~'의 내용과 일치한다.
③ 'In 1930, she became the first female flight attendant in the U.S. ~'의 내용과 일치한다.
⑤ 'Ellen Church Field Airport in her hometown, Cresco, was named after her.'의 내용과 일치한다.

- graduate from ⓥ ~을 졸업하다
- passenger ⓝ 승객
- flight attendant ⓝ 항공 승무원
- force ⓥ 어쩔 수 없이 ~하게 하다, 강요하다
- name after ⓥ ~의 이름을 따서 짓다
- take care of ⓥ ~을 돌보다
- frightened ⓐ 무서워하는, 겁에 질린
- injury ⓝ 부상
- serve as ⓥ ~로 복무하다, ~의 역할을 하다

구문 풀이

3행 She suggested to Boeing Air Transport that nurses should take care of
　　　　　　　　　제안 동사 +　　　　　　　　　　　that + 주어 + (should) 동사원형 : ~해야 한다고 제안하다
passengers during flights because most people were frightened of flying.
　　　　　　　　　　　　이유 접속사

---

27 과학 셀카 사진 대회 정답률 88% | 정답 ③

Science Selfie Competition에 관한 다음 안내문의 내용과 일치하지 <u>않는</u> 것은?

① 학교 밖에서 과학을 즐기는 셀카 사진을 출품한다.
② 셀카 사진에 관한 하나의 짧은 문장을 써야 한다.
✓③ 1인당 사진 여러 장을 출품할 수 있다.
④ 셀카 사진을 이름 및 소속 학급과 함께 이메일로 보내야 한다.
⑤ 수상자는 2020년 3월 27일에 발표될 것이다.

Science Selfie Competition
과학 셀카 사진 대회
For a chance to win science goodies, / 「just submit a selfie of yourself enjoying science outside of school!」 ①의근거 일치
상으로 좋은 과학 용품을 받을 기회를 얻으려면, / 학교 밖에서 과학을 즐기는 자신의 셀카 사진을 출품하기만 하면 됩니다!
Deadline: Friday, March 20, 2020, 6 p.m.
마감 기한: 2020년 3월 20일 금요일 오후 6시

Details:
세부 사항:
Your selfie / should include a visit to any science museum / or a science activity at home.
여러분의 셀카 사진은 / 아무 과학 박물관 방문을 포함해야 합니다. / 혹은 집에서 하는 과학 활동을
Be as creative as you like, / 「and write one short sentence about the selfie.」 ②의근거 일치
마음껏 창의력을 발휘하고, / 셀카 사진에 관한 하나의 짧은 문장을 쓰세요.
「Only one entry per person!」 ③의근거 불일치
1인당 한 장의 출품작만!
「Email your selfie with your name and class to mclara@oldfold.edu.」 ④의근거 일치
셀카 사진을 이름 및 소속 학급과 함께 mclara@oldfold.edu로 이메일로 보내세요.
「Winners will be announced on March 27, 2020.」 ⑤의근거 일치
수상자는 2020년 3월 27일에 발표될 것입니다.
Please visit www.oldfold.edu / to learn more about the competition.
www.oldfold.edu를 방문하세요. / 대회에 대해 더 자세히 알아보려면

과학 셀카 사진 대회

상으로 좋은 과학 용품을 받을 기회를 얻으려면, 학교 밖에서 과학을 즐기는 셀카 사진을 출품하기만 하면 됩니다!

마감 기한: 2020년 3월 20일 금요일 오후 6시

세부 사항:
• 셀카 사진에는 과학 박물관 방문이나 집에서 하는 과학 활동이 포함되어야 합니다.
• 마음껏 창의력을 발휘하고, 셀카 사진에 관한 하나의 짧은 문장을 쓰세요.
• 1인당 한 장의 출품작만!
• 셀카 사진을 이름 및 소속 학급과 함께 mclara@oldfold.edu로 이메일로 보내세요.

수상자는 2020년 3월 27일에 발표될 것입니다.

대회에 대해 더 자세히 알아보려면 www.oldfold.edu를 방문하세요.

Why? 왜 정답일까?
'Only one entry per person!'에서 출품작은 1인당 한 장만 낼 수 있다고 하므로, 안내문의 내용과 일치하지 않는 것은 ③ '1인당 사진 여러 장을 출품할 수 있다.'이다.

Why? 왜 오답일까?
① '~, just submit a selfie of yourself enjoying science outside of school!'의 내용과 일치한다.
② '~ write one short sentence about the selfie.'의 내용과 일치한다.
④ 'Email your selfie with your name and class to mclara@oldfold.edu.'의 내용과 일치한다.
⑤ 'Winners will be announced on March 27, 2020.'의 내용과 일치한다.

- selfie ⓝ 셀카 사진
- entry ⓝ 출품작
- goody ⓝ 매력적인 것, 갖고 싶은 것
- announce ⓥ 발표하다, 안내하다

---

28 장난감 창고 세일 정답률 89% | 정답 ④

Toy & Gift Warehouse Sale에 관한 다음 안내문의 내용과 일치하는 것은?

① 4월 16일부터 시작된다.
② 십 대를 위한 장난감은 판매하지 않는다.
③ 스무 개의 장난감 회사가 참여한다.
✓④ 월요일과 화요일에는 운영되지 않는다.
⑤ 반품은 구입 후 2주간 가능하다.

Toy & Gift Warehouse Sale
장난감과 선물 창고 세일
at Wilson Square
Wilson Square에서
「from April 3 to April 16」 ①의근거 불일치
4월 3일부터 4월 16일까지
We carry items / that are in stock at bigger retailers / for a cheaper price.
우리는 품목들을 취급합니다. / 더 큰 소매상에 재고로 있는 / 더 싼 가격에
「You can expect to find toys / for children from birth to teens.」 ②의근거 불일치
여러분은 장난감을 찾아볼 수 있습니다. / 신생아부터 십 대까지의 아이들을 위한
「Ten toy companies will participate in the sale.」 ③의근거 불일치
열 개의 장난감 회사가 이 판매에 참여할 것입니다.
Wednesday – Friday: 10 a.m. – 6 p.m.
수요일 ~ 금요일: 오전 10시 ~ 오후 6시
Saturday & Sunday: 11 a.m. – 5 p.m.
토요일과 일요일: 오전 11시 ~ 오후 5시
「Closed on Monday & Tuesday」 ④의근거 일치
월요일과 화요일에는 운영되지 않음
「Returns must be made within one week of purchase.」 ⑤의근거 불일치
반품은 구입 후 1주일 이내에 하셔야 합니다.
For more information, / please visit us at www.poptoy.com.
더 많은 정보를 원하시면, / www.poptoy.com을 방문하십시오.

장난감과 선물 창고 세일

Wilson Square에서
4월 3일부터 4월 16일까지

우리는 더 큰 소매상에 재고로 있는 품목들을 더 싼 가격에 취급합니다. 여러분은 신생아부터 십 대까지의 아이들을 위한 장난감을 찾아볼 수 있습니다. 열 개의 장난감 회사가 이 판매에 참여할 것입니다.

수요일 ~ 금요일: 오전 10시 ~ 오후 6시
토요일과 일요일: 오전 11시 ~ 오후 5시
월요일과 화요일에는 운영되지 않음

반품은 구입 후 1주일 이내에 하셔야 합니다.
더 많은 정보를 원하시면, www.poptoy.com을 방문하십시오.

Why? 왜 정답일까?

'Closed on Monday & Tuesday'에서 월요일과 화요일에는 문을 닫는다고 하므로, 안내문의 내용과 일치하는 것은 ④ '월요일과 화요일에는 운영되지 않는다.'이다.

Why? 왜 오답일까?

① 'from April 3 to April 16'에서 4월 3일이 시작일이고, 4월 16일이 종료일이라고 하였다.
② 'You can expect to find toys for children from birth to teens.'에서 신생아부터 십 대를 위한 장난감이 있다고 하였다.
③ 'Ten toy companies will participate in the sale.'에서 열 개의 장난감 회사가 세일에 참여한다고 하였다.
⑤ 'Returns must be made within one week of purchase.'에서 반품은 구입 후 1주일 안에 가능하다고 하였다.

- **warehouse** ⓝ 창고
- **in stock** 재고가 있는
- **return** ⓝ 반품
- **carry** ⓥ (상점이 상품을) 취급하다
- **retailer** ⓝ 소매상
- **purchase** ⓝ 구입

★★★ 등급을 가르는 문제!

29 식품 라벨을 통한 식품 정보 습득　　　정답률 51% | 정답 ②

다음 글의 밑줄 친 부분 중, 어법상 틀린 것은? [3점]

"You are what you eat."
'당신이 먹는 것이 바로 당신이다.'
That phrase is often used to ① show the relationship / between the foods you eat and your physical health.
그 구절은 흔히 관계를 보여주기 위해 사용된다. / 여러분이 먹는 음식과 여러분의 신체적 건강 사이의
But do you really know what you are eating / when you buy processed foods, canned foods, and packaged goods?
하지만 여러분은 자신이 무엇을 먹고 있는지 정말 아는가? / 가공식품, 통조림 식품, 포장 판매 식품을 살 때
Many of the manufactured products made today / contain so many chemicals and artificial ingredients / ✓that it is sometimes difficult / to know exactly what is inside them.
오늘날 만들어진 제조 식품 중 다수가 / 너무 많은 화학물질과 인공적인 재료를 함유하고 있어서 / 때로는 어렵다. / 정확히 그 안에 무엇이 들어 있는지 알기가
Fortunately, now there are food labels.
다행히도, 이제는 식품 라벨이 있다.
Food labels are a good way / ③ to find the information about the foods you eat.
식품 라벨은 좋은 방법이다. / 여러분이 먹는 식품에 관한 정보를 알아내는
Labels on food are ④ like the table of contents / found in books.
식품 라벨은 목차와 같다. / 책에서 볼 수 있는
The main purpose of food labels / ⑤ is to inform you / what is inside the food you are purchasing.
식품 라벨의 주된 목적 / 여러분에게 알려주는 것이다. / 여러분이 구입하고 있는 식품 안에 무엇이 들어 있는지

'당신이 먹는 것이 바로 당신이다(사람은 먹는 대로 이루어진다).' 그 구절은 흔히 여러분이 먹는 음식과 여러분의 신체적 건강 사이의 관계를 보여주기 위해 사용된다. 하지만 여러분은 가공식품, 통조림 식품, 포장 판매 식품을 살 때 자신이 무엇을 먹고 있는지 정말 아는가? 오늘날 만들어진 제조 식품 중 다수가 너무 많은 화학물질과 인공적인 재료를 함유하고 있어서 때로는 정확히 그 안에 무엇이 들어 있는지 알기가 어렵다. 다행히도, 이제는 식품 라벨이 있다. 식품 라벨은 여러분이 먹는 식품에 관한 정보를 알아내는 좋은 방법이다. 식품 라벨은 책에서 볼 수 있는 목차와 같다. 식품 라벨의 주된 목적은 여러분이 구입하고 있는 식품 안에 무엇이 들어 있는지 여러분에게 알려주는 것이다.

Why? 왜 정답일까?

'~ it is sometimes difficult ~'가 완전한 문장이므로 뒤에 불완전한 절이 나올 때 쓰는 관계대명사 which는 ② 자리에 나올 수 없다. 앞에 so many가 나오는 것으로 볼 때, 전체 문장은 'so ~ that …(너무 ~해서 …하다)' 구문임을 알 수 있다. 따라서 which를 결과의 부사절을 이끄는 접속사 that으로 고쳐야 한다. 어법상 틀린 것은 ②이다.

Why? 왜 오답일까?

① 'be used + to부정사(~하기 위해 사용되다)' 구문이 바르게 쓰였다.
③ a good way를 꾸미는 형용사적 용법의 to부정사구인 to find가 바르게 쓰였다.
④ be동사 뒤에서 보어 역할을 하는 전명구를 이루기 위해 전치사 like(~처럼)가 바르게 쓰였다.
⑤ 주어가 The main purpose라는 단수 명사이므로 단수 동사 is가 바르게 쓰였다.

- **phrase** ⓝ 구절
- **processed** ⓐ 가공된
- **packaged** ⓐ 포장된
- **artificial** ⓐ 인공의
- **purpose** ⓝ 목적
- **physical** ⓐ 신체적인, 물리적인
- **canned** ⓐ 통조림으로 된
- **contain** ⓥ 함유하다
- **ingredient** ⓝ 재료

구문 풀이

4행 Many of the manufactured products made today contain so many chemicals and artificial ingredients that it is sometimes difficult to know exactly what is inside them.
　주어　　과거분사　동사(복수) 「so ~ that … : 너무 ~해서 …하다」

★★ 문제 해결 꿀~팁 ★★

▶ 많이 틀린 이유는?
④의 like는 동사뿐 아니라 '~처럼'이라는 의미의 전치사로 쓰여 뒤에 명사구를 수반할 수 있다는 점을 기억해 둔다. 또한 ⑤는 주어와 동사의 수 일치를 묻는 경우로 핵심 주어와 수식어구를 구별하는 것이 풀이의 관건이다.
▶ 문제 해결 방법은?
② 'which vs. that'은 빈출되는 어법 사항이다. 둘 다 관계대명사로서 뒤에 불완전한 절을 수반할 수 있지만, that의 경우 접속사로도 쓰일 수 있기 때문에 뒤에 완전한 문장이 나오면 which가 아닌 that을 쓴다는 데 주의한다.

---

30 작은 변화를 무시하기 쉬운 이유　　　정답률 61% | 정답 ③

다음 글의 밑줄 친 부분 중, 문맥상 낱말의 쓰임이 적절하지 않은 것은? [3점]

We often ignore small changes / because they don't seem to ① matter very much in the moment.
우리는 흔히 작은 변화들을 무시한다. / 그것들이 당장은 크게 중요한 것 같지 않아서
If you save a little money now, / you're still not a millionaire.
여러분이 지금 돈을 약간 모아도, / 여러분은 여전히 백만장자가 아니다.
If you study Spanish for an hour tonight, / you still haven't learned the language.
여러분이 오늘 밤에 스페인어를 한 시간 동안 공부해도, / 여러분은 여전히 그 언어를 익힌 것은 아니다.
We make a few changes, / but the results never seem to come ② quickly / and so we slide back into our previous routines.
우리는 약간의 변화를 만들어 보지만, / 그러나 그 결과는 결코 빨리 오지 않는 것 같고 / 그래서 우리는 이전의 일상으로 다시 빠져든다.
The slow pace of transformation / also makes it ✓ difficult to break a bad habit.
변화의 느린 속도는 / 또한 나쁜 습관을 버리기 어렵게 만든다.
If you eat an unhealthy meal today, / the scale doesn't move much.
여러분이 오늘 몸에 좋지 않은 음식을 먹어도 / 체중계는 크게 움직이지 않는다.
A single decision is easy to ignore.
하나의 결정은 무시하기 쉽다.
But when we ④ repeat small errors, / day after day, / by following poor decisions again and again, / our small choices add up to bad results.
하지만 우리가 작은 오류를 반복한다면, / 날마다 / 잘못된 결정을 반복적으로 따르면서 / 우리의 작은 선택들이 모여 좋지 않은 결과를 만들어낸다.
Many missteps eventually lead to a ⑤ problem.
많은 실수는 결국 문제로 이어진다.

우리는 흔히 작은 변화들이 당장은 크게 ① 중요한 것 같지 않아서 그것들을 무시한다. 지금 돈을 약간 모아도, 여러분은 여전히 백만장자가 아니다. 오늘 밤에 스페인어를 한 시간 동안 공부해도, 여러분은 여전히 그 언어를 익힌 것은 아니다. 우리는 약간의 변화를 만들어 보지만, 그 결과는 결코 ② 빨리 오지 않는 것 같고 그래서 우리는 이전의 일상으로 다시 빠져든다. 변화의 느린 속도는 또한 나쁜 습관을 버리기 ③ 쉽게(→ 어렵게) 만든다. 오늘 몸에 좋지 않은 음식을 먹어도 체중계는 크게 움직이지 않는다. 하나의 결정은 무시하기 쉽다. 하지만 우리가 잘못된 결정을 반복적으로 따라 작은 오류를 날마다 ④ 반복한다면, 우리의 작은 선택들이 모여 좋지 않은 결과를 만들어낸다. 많은 실수는 결국 ⑤ 문제로 이어진다.

Why? 왜 정답일까?

'We make a few changes, but the results never seem to come quickly and so we slide back into our previous routines.'에서 우리가 변화를 시도하더라도 바로 변화가 나타나는 것이 아니기에 우리는 다시 변화 이전의 일상으로 돌아가게 된다고 설명한다. 이에 비추어 볼 때, 변화가 느리게 찾아온다는 점은 나쁜 습관을 버리기 '어렵게' 만든다는 의미가 되도록 ③의 easy를 difficult로 바꾸어야 한다. 문맥상 낱말의 쓰임이 적절하지 않은 것은 ③이다.

- **ignore** ⓥ 무시하다
- **in the moment** 당장, 지금
- **slide back into** ⓥ ~로 돌아가다, 복귀하다
- **routine** ⓝ 일상
- **break a bad habit** ⓥ 나쁜 습관을 버리다
- **scale** ⓝ 체중계, 저울
- **misstep** ⓝ 실수, 잘못된 조치
- **matter** ⓥ 중요하다
- **millionaire** ⓝ 백만장자
- **previous** ⓐ 이전의
- **transformation** ⓝ 변화
- **unhealthy** ⓐ 몸에 좋지 않은, 건강하지 않은
- **add up to** ⓥ (합이) 결국 ~이 되다
- **eventually** ⓐⓓ 결국

구문 풀이

6행 The slow pace of transformation also makes it easy to break a bad habit.
　　　　　　　　　　　　　5형식 동사　목적격 보어　진목적어
　　　　　　　　　　　　　　　　↳가목적어

---

31 상처 받은 상대방에게 시간을 주며 기다려주기　　　정답률 56% | 정답 ③

다음 빈칸에 들어갈 말로 가장 적절한 것을 고르시오.
① curiosity - 호기심
② independence - 자립
✓ patience - 인내
④ creativity - 창의성
⑤ honesty - 정직

Remember that patience is always of the essence.
인내가 항상 가장 중요하다는 것을 기억해라.
If an apology is not accepted, / thank the individual for hearing you out / and leave the door open / for if and when he wishes to reconcile.
사과가 받아들여지지 않으면, / 그 사람이 여러분의 말을 끝까지 들어줬다는 것에 감사하고, / 문(가능성)을 열어 두어라. / 그 사람이 화해하고 싶을 경우와 시기를 위해
Be conscious of the fact / that just because someone accepts your apology / does not mean she has fully forgiven you.
사실을 알고 있어라. / 단지 누군가가 여러분의 사과를 받아들인다고 해서 / 그 사람이 여러분을 온전히 용서했다는 뜻이 아니라는
It can take time, maybe a long time, / before the injured party can completely let go / and fully trust you again.
시간이 걸릴 수 있고, 어쩌면 오래 걸릴 수 있다. / 상처받은 당사자가 완전히 떨쳐 버리기까지 / 그리고 여러분을 온전히 다시 믿기까지
There is little you can do / to speed this process up.
여러분이 할 수 있는 것은 거의 없다. / 이 과정을 빨라지게 하기 위해
If the person is truly important to you, / it is worthwhile / to give him or her the time and space needed to heal.
그 사람이 여러분에게 진정으로 중요하다면, / 가치가 있다. / 그 사람에게 치유되는 데 필요한 시간과 공간을 주는 것이
Do not expect the person / to go right back to acting normally immediately.
그 사람에게 기대하지 마라. / 즉시 평상시처럼 행동하는 것으로 바로 돌아갈 것이라고

인내가 항상 가장 중요하다는 것을 기억해라. 사과가 받아들여지지 않으면, 그 사람이 여러분의 말을 끝까지 들어줬다는 것에 감사하고, 그 사람이 화해하고 싶을 경우와 시기를 위해 문(가능성)을 열어 두어라. 단지 누군가가 여러분의 사과를 받아들인다고 해서 그 사람이 여러분을 온전히 용서했다는 뜻이 아니라는 사실을 알고 있어라. 상처받은 당사자가 완전히 떨쳐 버리고 여러분을 온전히 다시 믿기까지 시간이 걸릴 수 있고, 어쩌면 오래 걸릴 수 있다. 이 과정을 빨라지게 하기 위해 여러분이 할 수 있는 것은 거의 없다. 그 사람이 여러분에게 진정으로 중요하다면, 그 사람에게 치유되는 데 필요한 시간과 공간을 주는 것이 가치가 있다. 그 사람이 즉시 평상시의 행동으로 바로 돌아갈 것이라고 기대하지 마라.

마지막 세 문장에서 용서의 과정을 빨라지게 할 방법은 없고, 상대방에게 시간을 줄 필요가 있으므로 상대방이 곧바로 평상시대로 돌아갈 것이라는 기대를 하지 말라(~ it is worthwhile to give him or her the time and space needed to heal. Do not expect the person to go right back to acting normally immediately.)고 조언하고 있다. 이는 상대방을 기다려주며 인내심을 발휘하라는 내용으로 요약할 수 있으므로, 빈칸에 들어갈 말로 가장 적절한 것은 ③ '인내'이다.

- essence ⓝ 본질
- hear ~ out ⓥ ~의 말을 끝까지 들어주다
- injured ⓐ 상처받은, 부상 당한
- worthwhile ⓐ 가치 있는
- independence ⓝ 자립, 독립
- apology ⓝ 사과
- conscious ⓐ 알고 있는, 의식하는
- speed up ⓥ 빨라지게 하다
- normally ⓐⓓ 정상적으로
- patience ⓝ 인내

구문 풀이

3행 Be conscious of the fact that just because someone accepts your apology
동격 접속사 / 주어(부사절이 명사절처럼 쓰임)
does not mean she has fully forgiven you.
동사 / 목적어

32 광고 교환 정답률 58% | 정답 ①

다음 빈칸에 들어갈 말로 가장 적절한 것을 고르시오.

☑ trading space – 공간을 교환함
② getting funded – 자금을 지원받음
③ sharing reviews – 상품평을 공유함
④ renting factory facilities – 공장 시설을 빌림
⑤ increasing TV commercials – TV 광고를 늘림

Although many small businesses have excellent websites, / they typically can't afford aggressive online campaigns.
비록 많은 작은 사업체들이 훌륭한 웹 사이트를 가지고 있지만, / 보통 그들은 매우 적극적인 온라인 캠페인을 할 여유가 없다.
One way to get the word out / is through an advertising exchange, / in which advertisers place banners on each other's websites for free.
소문나게 하는 한 가지 방법은 / 광고 교환을 통해서이다. / 광고주들이 서로의 웹 사이트에 무료로 배너를 게시하는
For example, / a company selling beauty products / could place its banner on a site that sells women's shoes, / and in turn, / the shoe company could put a banner on the beauty product site.
예를 들어, / 미용 제품을 판매하는 회사는 / 여성 신발을 판매하는 사이트에 자신의 배너를 게시할 수 있고, / 그다음에는 / 그 신발 회사가 미용 제품 사이트에 배너를 게시할 수 있다.
Neither company charges the other; / they simply exchange ad space.
두 회사 모두 상대에게 비용을 청구하지 않는데, / 그들은 그저 광고 공간을 교환하는 것이다.
Advertising exchanges are gaining in popularity, / especially among marketers / who do not have much money / and who don't have a large sales team.
광고 교환은 인기를 얻고 있다. / 특히 마케팅 담당자들 사이에서 / 돈이 많지 않거나 / 대규모 영업팀이 없는
By trading space, / advertisers find new outlets / that reach their target audiences / that they would not otherwise be able to afford.
공간을 교환함으로써, / 광고주들은 새로운 (광고의) 출구를 찾는다. / 자신의 목표 고객과 접촉할 수 있는 / 그러지 않으면 그들이 접촉할 여유가 없는

비록 많은 작은 사업체들이 훌륭한 웹 사이트를 가지고 있지만, 그들은 보통 매우 적극적인 온라인 캠페인을 할 여유가 없다. 소문나게 하는 한 가지 방법은 광고주들이 서로의 웹 사이트에 무료로 배너를 게시하는 광고 교환을 통해서이다. 예를 들어, 미용 제품을 판매하는 회사는 여성 신발을 판매하는 사이트에 자신의 배너를 게시할 수 있고, 그다음에는 그 신발 회사가 미용 제품 사이트에 배너를 게시할 수 있다. 두 회사 모두 상대에게 비용을 청구하지 않는데, 그들은 그저 광고 공간을 교환하는 것이다. 광고 교환은 특히 돈이 많지 않거나 대규모 영업팀이 없는 마케팅 담당자들 사이에서 인기를 얻고 있다. 공간을 교환함으로써, 광고주들은 그러지 않으면 접촉할 여유가 없는 자신의 목표 고객과 접촉할 수 있는 새로운 (광고의) 출구를 찾는다.

예시 앞의 주제문 'One way to get the word out is through an advertising exchange, in which advertisers place banners on each other's websites for free.'에서 작은 사업체들은 서로 웹 사이트에 무료로 배너를 게시하는 광고 교환을 통해 사업체를 홍보한다는 내용을 제시하므로, 빈칸에 들어갈 말로 가장 적절한 것은 ① '공간을 교환함'이다.

- typically ⓐⓓ 보통, 전형적으로
- get the word out ⓥ 말을 퍼뜨리다
- charge ⓥ (요금을) 청구하다, 부과하다
- fund ⓥ 기금을 지원하다 ⓝ 기금
- commercial ⓝ 광고 ⓐ 상업적인
- afford ⓥ ~할 여유가 있다
- in turn 차례로, 결국
- gain in popularity ⓥ 인기를 얻다
- facility ⓝ 시설

구문 풀이

2행 One way to get the word out is through an advertising exchange, in which
주어 / 형용사적 용법 / 동사 / 보어(전명구) / 계속적 용법
advertisers place banners on each other's websites for free.

33 관심의 표현을 통한 동기 부여 정답률 59% | 정답 ①

다음 빈칸에 들어갈 말로 가장 적절한 것을 고르시오.

☑ care about them – 그들에 대해 신경 쓴다
② keep your words – 약속을 지킨다
③ differ from them – 그들과 다르다
④ evaluate their performance – 그들의 수행을 평가한다
⑤ communicate with their parents – 그들의 부모와 소통한다

Motivation may come from several sources.
동기 부여는 여러 원천에서 올 수 있다.

It may be the respect / I give every student, / the daily greeting I give at my classroom door, / the undivided attention when I listen to a student, / a pat on the shoulder whether the job was done well or not, / an accepting smile, / or simply "I love you" when it is most needed.
그것은 존중일 수 있다. / 내가 모든 학생에게 하는 / 내가 우리반 교실 문에서 매일 하는 인사, / 내가 학생의 말을 들을 때의 완전한 집중, / 일을 잘했든 못했든 어깨를 토닥여주는 것, / 포용적인 미소, / 혹은 "사랑해"라는 말이 가장 필요할 때 그저 그 말을 해주는 것일 수도 있다.)
It may simply be asking how things are at home.
그것은 그저 집에 별일이 없는지를 물어보는 것일지도 모른다.
For one student considering dropping out of school, / it was a note from me after one of his frequent absences / saying that he made my day when I saw him in school.
학교를 중퇴하는 것을 고려하던 한 학생에게, / 그것은 그 학생의 잦은 결석 중 어느 한 결석 후에 쓴 나의 짧은 편지였다. / 내가 그 학생을 학교에서 보았을 때 그가 나를 매우 기쁘게 해주었다는 내용의
He came to me with the note with tears in his eyes / and thanked me.
그 학생은 눈물을 글썽이며 그 편지를 들고 내게 와서 / 고맙다고 했다.
He will graduate this year.
그 학생은 올해 졸업할 것이다.
Whatever technique is used, / the students must know that you care about them.
어떤 기법이 사용되든, / 학생들은 여러분이 그들에 대해 신경 쓴다는 것을 틀림없이 알 것이다.
But the concern must be genuine / — the students can't be fooled.
그런데 그 관심은 진심이어야 하는데 / 학생들이 속을 리가 없기 때문이다.

동기 부여는 여러 원천에서 올 수 있다. 그것은 내가 모든 학생에게 하는 존중, 교실 문에서 매일 하는 인사, 학생의 말을 들을 때의 완전한 집중, 일을 잘했든 못했든 어깨를 토닥여주는 것, 포용적인 미소, 혹은 "사랑해"라는 말이 가장 필요할 때 그저 그 말을 해주는 것일 수도 있다. 그것은 그저 집에 별일이 없는지를 물어보는 것일지도 모른다. 학교를 중퇴하는 것을 고려하던 한 학생에게, 그것은 그 학생의 잦은 결석 중 어느 한 결석 후에 그 학생을 학교에서 보니 매우 기뻤다고 쓴 나의 짧은 편지였다. 그 학생은 눈물을 글썽이며 그 편지를 들고 내게 와서 고맙다고 했다. 그 학생은 올해 졸업할 것이다. 어떤 기법이 사용되든, 학생들은 여러분이 그들에 대해 신경 쓴다는 것을 틀림없이 알 것이다. 그런데 그 관심은 진심이어야 하는데 학생들이 속을 리가 없기 때문이다.

학생들에게 동기를 부여하는 방식은 여러 가지가 있으며, 어떤 행위이든 학생에 대한 관심(concern)을 진실로 보여줄 수 있어야 한다는 내용을 다룬 글이다. 따라서 빈칸에 들어갈 말로 가장 적절한 것은 ① '그들에 대해 신경 쓴다'이다.

- undivided ⓐ 완전한, 전적인
- a pat on the shoulder (격려의 의미로) 어깨를 토닥임
- accepting ⓐ 포용적인, 수용적인
- frequent ⓐ 잦은, 빈번한
- concern ⓝ 관심, 걱정
- fool ⓥ 속이다
- evaluate ⓥ 평가하다
- attention ⓝ 집중, 주의
- drop out of school ⓥ 학교를 중퇴하다
- make one's day ⓥ ~을 행복하게 만들다
- genuine ⓐ 진실한, 진짜의
- keep one's words ⓥ 약속을 지키다

구문 풀이

1행 It may be the respect [I give every student], the daily greeting [I give at
보어1 / 보어2
my classroom door], the undivided attention when I listen to a student, a pat on
보어3 / 보어4
the shoulder whether the job was done well or not, an accepting smile, or simply
~이든 아니든
"I love you" when it is most needed.
보어6 / 보어5

★★★ 등급을 가르는 문제!
34 삶에 다양함을 주기 정답률 54% | 정답 ①

다음 빈칸에 들어갈 말로 가장 적절한 것을 고르시오. [3점]

☑ variety is the spice of life – 다양성이 인생의 묘미이다
② fantasy is the mirror of reality – 공상은 현실의 거울이다
③ failure teaches more than success – 실패는 성공보다 더 많은 것을 가르쳐준다
④ laziness is the mother of invention – 게으름은 발명의 어머니이다
⑤ conflict strengthens the relationship – 갈등은 관계를 강화시킨다

Say you normally go to a park to walk or work out.
여러분이 보통 어떤 공원에 산책이나 운동을 하러 간다고 하자.
Maybe today you should choose a different park.
어쩌면 오늘 여러분은 다른 공원을 선택해야겠다.
Why?
왜?
Well, who knows?
글쎄, 누가 알겠는가?
Maybe it's because you need the connection to the different energy / in the other park.
어쩌면 여러분이 다른 기운과 연결되는 것이 필요하기 때문일 것이다. / 다른 공원에서
Maybe you'll run into people there / that you've never met before.
어쩌면 여러분은 거기서 사람들을 만나게 될 것이다. / 여러분이 전에 만난 적이 없는
You could make a new best friend / simply by visiting a different park.
여러분은 새로운 가장 친한 친구를 사귈 수 있다. / 그저 다른 공원을 방문함으로써
You never know what great things will happen to you / until you step outside the zone where you feel comfortable.
여러분은 결코 자신에게 어떤 대단한 일이 일어날지 알지 못한다. / 여러분이 편안함을 느끼는 지대 밖으로 나가기 전까지
If you're staying in your comfort zone / and you're not pushing yourself past that same old energy, / then you're not going to move forward on your path.
여러분이 안락 지대에 머무르고 있다면, / 그리고 자신을 밀어붙여 늘 똑같은 기운에서 벗어나도록 하지 않는다면, / 그러면 여러분은 자신의 진로에서 앞으로 나아가지 못할 것이다.
By forcing yourself to do something different, / you're awakening yourself on a spiritual level / and you're forcing yourself to do something / that will benefit you in the long run.
자신에게 다른 어떤 것을 하게 만듦으로써, / 여러분은 영적인 차원에서 자신을 깨우치고, / 여러분은 스스로가 어떤 일을 하게 만들고 있다. / 결국에는 자신을 이롭게 할
As they say, variety is the spice of life.
사람들이 말하듯이, 다양성은 인생의 묘미이다.

보통 어떤 공원에 산책이나 운동을 하러 간다고 하자. 어쩌면 오늘 여러분은 다른 공원을 선택해야겠다. 왜? 글쎄, 누가 알겠는가? 어쩌면 여러분이 다른 공원에서 다른 기운과 연결되는 것이 필요하기 때문일 것이다. 어쩌면 여러분은 거기서 전에 만난 적이 없는 사람들을 만나게 될 것이다. 여러분은 그저 다른 공원을 방문함으로써 새로운 가장 친한 친구를 사귈 수 있다. 여러분은 편안함을 느끼는 지대 밖으로 나가고 나서야 비로소 자신에게 어떤 대단한 일이 벗어나도록 하지 않는다면, 자신의 진로에서 앞으로 나아가지 못할 것이다. 자신에게 다른 어떤 것을 하게 만듦으로써, 여러분은 영적인 차원에서 자신을 깨우치고, 결국에는 자신을 이롭게 할 어떤 일을 할 수 밖에 없다. 사람들이 말하듯이, <u>다양성은 인생의 묘미이다.</u>

Why? 왜 정답일까?

항상 익숙하고 편안한 안락 지대를 벗어나 새로운 무언가를 시도할 때 깨달음이 일어나고 스스로를 이롭게 할 수 있다(By forcing yourself to do something different, you're awakening yourself on a spiritual level and you're forcing yourself to do something that will benefit you in the long run.)는 내용의 글이다. 따라서 빈칸에 들어갈 말로 가장 적절한 것은 '새롭고 다양한 것을 시도해보면 좋다'는 의미를 담은 ① '다양성은 인생의 묘미이다'이다.

- **run into** ⓥ ~을 우연히 만나다
- **spiritual** ⓐ 영적인, 정신적인
- **spice** ⓝ 묘미, 향신료
- **invention** ⓝ 발명
- **strengthen** ⓥ 강화하다
- **force** ⓥ (어쩔 수 없이) ~하게 하다
- **in the long run** 결국에는, 장기적으로
- **laziness** ⓝ 게으름
- **conflict** ⓝ 갈등

구문 풀이

6행 You never know what great things will happen to you until you step outside
「not[never] + A + ... until + B : B하고 나서야 비로소 A하다」
the zone [where you feel comfortable].
선행사　관계부사

★★ 문제 해결 꿀~팁 ★★

▶ 많이 틀린 이유는?
글 마지막 문장에 빈칸이 나오면 보통 주제를 요약하므로, 글에서 언급되지 않은 내용은 답으로 고르지 않도록 주의한다. ②의 fantasy와 reality는 본문에서 언급된 바 없고, ③의 failure과 success는 글의 중심 소재가 아니다.

▶ 문제 해결 방법은?
이 글에서는 different라는 형용사가 곳곳에 등장하며 '다양한 것'을 시도하라는 주장을 펼치고 있으므로 이 형용사를 variety라는 명사로 바꾼 ①이 답으로 적절하다.

---

35 정보 공개에 관한 문화별 견해 차이　정답률 65% | 정답 ②

주어진 글 다음에 이어질 글의 순서로 가장 적절한 것을 고르시오. [3점]
① (A) – (C) – (B)　　✔ (B) – (A) – (C)
③ (B) – (C) – (A)　　④ (C) – (A) – (B)
⑤ (C) – (B) – (A)

Ideas about how much disclosure is appropriate / vary among cultures.
얼마나 많은 정보를 공개하는 것이 적절한지에 관한 생각은 / 문화마다 다르다.
(B) Those born in the United States / tend to be high disclosers, / even showing a willingness / to disclose information about themselves to strangers.
미국에서 태어난 사람들은 / 정보를 많이 공개하려는 경향이 있고, / 기꺼이 의향을 보이기까지 한다. / 자기 자신에 관한 정보를 낯선 이에게 공개하려는
This may explain / why Americans seem particularly easy to meet / and are good at cocktail-party conversation.
이것은 설명할 수 있다. / 왜 미국인들이 특히 만나기 편해 보이고 / 칵테일 파티에서 대화하는 것에 능숙한지를
(A) On the other hand, / Japanese tend to do little disclosing about themselves to others / except the few people with whom they are very close.
반면에, / 일본인들은 타인에게 자신에 관한 정보를 거의 공개하지 않는 경향이 있다. / 자신과 매우 친한 소수의 사람들을 제외하고는
In general, Asians do not reach out to strangers.
일반적으로 아시아인들은 낯선 이에게 관심을 내보이지 않는다.
(C) They do, however, show great care for each other, / since they view harmony as essential to relationship improvement.
그러나 그들은 서로를 매우 배려하는 모습을 보인다. / 그들이 조화를 관계 발전에 필수적이라고 간주하기 때문에
They work hard / to prevent those they view as outsiders / from getting information they believe to be unfavorable.
그들은 열심히 노력한다. / 그들이 외부인이라고 간주하는 사람들이 (~하지) 못하려 하려고 / 자신이 불리하다고 생각하는 정보를 얻는 것을

얼마나 많은 정보를 공개하는 것이 적절한지에 관한 생각은 문화마다 다르다.
(B) 미국에서 태어난 사람들은 정보를 많이 공개하려는 경향이 있고, 자기 자신에 관한 정보를 낯선 이에게 기꺼이 공개하려는 의향을 보이기까지 한다. 이것은 왜 미국인들이 특히 만나기 편해 보이고 칵테일 파티에서 대화하는 것에 능숙한지를 설명할 수 있다.
(A) 반면에, 일본인들은 자신과 매우 친한 소수의 사람들을 제외하고는 타인에게 자신에 관한 정보를 거의 공개하지 않는 경향이 있다. 일반적으로 아시아인들은 낯선 이에게 관심을 내보이지 않는다.
(C) 그러나 그들은 조화를 관계 발전에 필수적이라고 간주하기 때문에 서로를 매우 배려하는 모습을 보인다. 그들은 자신이 불리하다고 생각하는 정보를 외부인이라고 간주되는 사람들이 얻지 못하게 하려고 열심히 노력한다.

Why? 왜 정답일까?

정보 공개에 대한 생각이 문화마다 다르다고 언급한 주어진 글 뒤에는, 미국인들의 예를 들기 시작한 (B), 일본인의 예를 대조하는 (A), 일본인들이 자신에 대한 정보를 공개하려 하지는 않지만 조화를 중시하기 때문에 서로 배려를 하기 위해 애쓴다는 내용을 덧붙이는 (C)가 차례로 이어져야 한다. 따라서 글의 순서로 가장 적절한 것은 ② '(B) – (A) – (C)'이다.

- **appropriate** ⓐ 적절한
- **close** ⓐ 친한, 가까운
- **vary** ⓥ 다르다
- **reach out to** ⓥ ~에게 관심을 보이다

- **willingness** ⓝ 기꺼이 ~하려는 마음
- **unfavorable** ⓐ 불리한, 호의적이 아닌
- **essential** ⓐ 필수적인, 본질적인

구문 풀이

13행 They work hard to prevent those [they view as outsiders] from getting
「prevent + A + ... from + 동명사 : A가 ~하지 못하게 하다」
information [they believe to be unfavorable].
선행사

---

36 인간 창조에 관한 신화　정답률 60% | 정답 ⑤

주어진 글 다음에 이어질 글의 순서로 가장 적절한 것을 고르시오.
① (A) – (C) – (B)　　② (B) – (A) – (C)
③ (B) – (C) – (A)　　④ (C) – (A) – (B)
✔ (C) – (B) – (A)

A god called Moinee was defeated / by a rival god called Dromerdeener / in a terrible battle up in the stars.
Moinee라는 신이 패배했다. / Dromerdeener이라는 이름의 라이벌 신에게 / 하늘 위 별에서 벌어진 끔찍한 전투에서
Moinee fell out of the stars down to Tasmania to die.
Moinee는 별에서 Tasmania로 떨어져 죽었다.
(C) Before he died, / he wanted to give a last blessing to his final resting place, / so he decided to create humans.
그가 죽기 전에 / 그는 최후의 안식처에 마지막 축복을 해주고 싶어서 / 인간을 창조하기로 결심했다.
But he was in such a hurry, / knowing he was dying, / that he forgot to give them knees; / and he absent-mindedly gave them big tails like kangaroos, / which meant they couldn't sit down.
그러나 그는 매우 서둘렀기에 / 자신이 죽어가고 있다는 것을 알고 / 그들에게 무릎을 만들어 주는 것을 잊었고, / 그는 아무 생각 없이 캥거루처럼 큰 꼬리를 만들어 주었는데, / 그것은 그들이 앉을 수 없다는 것을 의미했다.
(B) Then he died.
그러고 나서 그는 죽었다.
The people hated having kangaroo tails and no knees, / and they cried out to the heavens for help.
사람들은 캥거루 같은 꼬리가 있고 무릎이 없는 것을 싫어했고, / 그들은 도움을 얻고자 하늘에 외쳤다.
Dromerdeener heard their cry / and came down to Tasmania to see what the matter was.
Dromerdeener는 그들의 외침을 듣고 / 무엇이 문제인지 보려고 Tasmania로 내려왔다.
(A) He took pity on the people, / gave them bendable knees / and cut off their inconvenient kangaroo tails / so they could all sit down at last.
그는 사람들을 불쌍히 여겨서 / 그들에게 구부러지는 무릎을 만들어 주고, / 그들의 불편한 캥거루 꼬리를 잘라냈다. / 마침내 그들이 모두 앉을 수 있도록
Then they lived happily ever after.
그 후 사람들은 영원히 행복하게 살았다.

Moinee라는 신이 하늘 위 별에서 벌어진 끔찍한 전투에서 Dromerdeener이라는 이름의 라이벌 신에게 패배했다. Moinee는 별에서 Tasmania로 떨어져 죽었다.
(C) 죽기 전에 그는 최후의 안식처에 마지막 축복을 해주고 싶어서 인간을 창조하기로 결심했다. 그러나 그는 자신이 죽어가고 있다는 것을 알고 매우 서둘렀기에 그들에게 무릎을 만들어 주는 것을 잊고, 아무 생각 없이 캥거루처럼 큰 꼬리를 만들어 주었는데, 그것은 그들이 앉을 수 없다는 것을 의미했다.
(B) 그러고 나서 그는 죽었다. 사람들은 캥거루 같은 꼬리가 있고 무릎이 없는 것을 싫어했고, 도움을 얻고자 하늘에 외쳤다. Dromerdeener는 그들의 외침을 듣고 무엇이 문제인지 보려고 Tasmania로 내려왔다.
(A) 그는 사람들을 불쌍히 여겨서 그들에게 구부러지는 무릎을 만들어 주고, 마침내 그들이 모두 앉을 수 있도록 불편한 캥거루 꼬리를 잘라냈다. 그 후 사람들은 영원히 행복하게 살았다.

Why? 왜 정답일까?

Moinee라는 신이 Dromerdeener와의 싸움에서 패배해서 죽게 되었다는 내용의 주어진 글 뒤에는, Moinee가 죽기 전에 서둘러 인간을 만들었는데 무릎이 없고 대신에 꼬리가 달린 형태였다는 내용의 (C), 그의 사후 사람들이 불편함을 해결하고자 하늘에 도움을 요청했다는 내용의 (B), Dromerdeener가 이 외침을 듣고 내려와 꼬리를 없애고 무릎을 만들어 주었다는 내용의 (A)가 차례로 이어져야 한다. 따라서 글의 순서로 가장 적절한 것은 ⑤ '(C) – (B) – (A)'이다.

- **defeat** ⓥ 패배시키다
- **fall out of** ⓥ ~에서 떨어지다
- **bendable** ⓐ 구부릴 수 있는
- **blessing** ⓝ 축복
- **absent-mindedly** ⓐ 아무 생각 없이, 멍하니
- **take pity on** ⓥ ~을 불쌍히 여기다
- **inconvenient** ⓐ 불편한
- **resting place** ⓝ 안식처

구문 풀이

12행 But he was in such a hurry, knowing he was dying, that he forgot to give
「such ~ that … : 너무 ~해서 하다」　　할 정도를 잇다
them knees; and he absent-mindedly gave them big tails like kangaroos, which
선행사　계속 용법
meant they couldn't sit down.

★★★ 등급을 가르는 문제!

37 Amondawa 부족의 독특한 시간 관념　정답률 38% | 정답 ④

글의 흐름으로 보아, 주어진 문장이 들어가기에 가장 적절한 곳을 고르시오. [3점]

There are some cultures / that can be referred to as "people who live outside of time."
어떤 문화가 있다. / '시간 밖에서 사는 사람들'이라고 부를 수 있는
The Amondawa tribe, living in Brazil, / does not have a concept of time / that can be measured or counted.
브라질에 사는 Amondawa 부족에게는 / 시간이라는 개념이 없다. / 측정되거나 셀 수 있는
① Rather they live in a world of serial events, / rather than seeing events as being rooted in time.
오히려 그들은 연속되는 사건의 세상에서 산다. / 사건이 시간에 뿌리를 두고 있다고 간주하기보다는
② Researchers also found that no one had an age.

연구자들은 또한 나이가 있는 사람이 아무도 없다는 것을 알아냈다.

③ Instead, they change their names / to reflect their stage of life and position within their society, / so a little child will give up their name to a newborn sibling / and take on a new one.
대신에 그들은 이름을 바꾼다. / 자신들의 생애 단계와 사회 내 위치를 반영하기 위해 / 그래서 어린아이는 자신의 이름을 갓 태어난 형제자매에게 넘겨주고 / 새로운 이름을 갖는다.

☑ In the U.S. we have so many metaphors for time and its passing / that we think of time as "a thing," / that is "the weekend is almost gone," or "I haven't got the time."
미국에는 시간과 시간의 흐름에 관한 매우 많은 은유가 있어서 / 우리는 시간을 '물건'으로 간주하는데, / 즉 "주말이 거의 다 지나갔다."라거나 "나는 시간이 없다."라는 식이다.

We think such statements are objective, / but they aren't.
우리는 그러한 말들이 객관적이라고 생각하지만, / 그것들은 그렇지 않다.

⑤ We create these metaphors, / but the Amondawa don't talk or think in metaphors for time.
우리는 이런 은유를 만들어 내지만, / Amondawa 사람들은 시간을 은유적으로 말하거나 생각하지 않는다.

'시간 밖에서 사는 사람들'이라고 부를 수 있는 어떤 문화가 있다. 브라질에 사는 Amondawa 부족에게는 측정되거나 셀 수 있는 시간이라는 개념이 없다. ① 오히려 그들은 사건이 시간에 뿌리를 두고 있다고 간주하기보다는 연속되는 사건의 세상에서 산다. ② 연구자들은 또한 나이가 있는 사람이 아무도 없다는 것을 알아냈다. ③ 대신에 그들은 자신들의 생애 단계와 사회 내 위치를 반영하기 위해 이름을 바꾸어서 어린아이는 자신의 이름을 갓 태어난 형제자매에게 넘겨주고 새로운 이름을 갖는다. ④ 미국에는 시간과 시간의 흐름에 관한 매우 많은 은유가 있어서 우리는 시간을 '물건'으로 간주하는데, 즉 "주말이 거의 다 지나갔다."라거나 "나는 시간이 없다."라는 식이다. 우리는 그러한 말들이 객관적이라고 생각하지만, 그렇지 않다. ⑤ 우리는 이런 은유를 만들어 내지만, Amondawa 사람들은 시간을 은유적으로 말하거나 생각하지 않는다.

Why? 왜 정답일까?

Amondawa 부족의 독특한 시간 관념을 소개한 글이다. ④ 앞에서는 이들이 사건을 시간별로 파악하기보다는 그저 연속된 사건 속에 살며 나이도 세지 않는다는 내용을 제시한다. 반면 주어진 문장은 미국의 예를 들어 시간과 시간의 흐름을 물건처럼 느끼게 하는 많은 은유가 있다고 언급하는데, ④ 뒤에서는 '이러한 은유적인 말들'이 객관적으로 보이더라도 Amondawa 부족의 관점에는 적용될 수 없다는 이야기임을 덧붙이고 있다. 따라서 주어진 문장이 들어가기에 가장 적절한 곳은 ④이다.

- passing ⓝ (시간의) 흐름, 경과
- refer to A as B ⓥ A를 B라고 부르다, 언급하다
- measure ⓥ 측정하다
- reflect ⓥ 반영하다
- objective ⓐ 객관적인
- think of A as B ⓥ A를 B라고 간주하다
- tribe ⓝ 부족
- rooted in ~에 뿌리를 둔
- statement ⓝ 말, 진술

구문 풀이

1행 In the U.S. we have so many metaphors for time and its passing that we
「so ~ that … : 너무 ~해서 …하다」
think of time as "a thing," that is "the weekend is almost gone," or "I haven't got
「think of + A + as + B : A를 B라고 간주하다」└→ 즉, 다시 말해
the time."

★★ 문제 해결 꿀~팁 ★★

▶ 많이 틀린 이유는?
⑤의 these metaphors가 주어진 문장의 따옴표 구절과 이어진다고 보면 ⑤를 답으로 고르기 쉽지만, 앞에 나오는 such statements 또한 가리키는 바가 불분명함을 염두에 두어야 한다.
▶ 문제 해결 방법은?
④ 뒤의 such statements가 가리키는 바에 주목해야 한다. 앞에 '진술'로 받을만한 말이 따로 나오지 않았는데 바로 '이러한 진술'이라는 언급을 이어가기는 부적절하며, 마침 주어진 문장이 따옴표로 다양한 구절을 제시하고 있는 것으로 볼 때, such statement 앞에 주어진 문장이 나와야 함을 알 수 있다.

★★★ 등급을 가르는 문제!

38 각종 동식물에 대한 태도 차이   정답률 39% | 정답 ⑤

글의 흐름으로 보아, 주어진 문장이 들어가기에 가장 적절한 곳을 고르시오.

The natural world provides a rich source of symbols / used in art and literature.
자연계는 상징의 풍부한 원천을 제공한다. / 예술과 문학에 사용되는

① Plants and animals are central / to mythology, dance, song, poetry, rituals, festivals, and holidays around the world.
식물과 동물은 중심에 있다. / 전 세계의 신화, 춤, 노래, 시, 의식, 축제 그리고 기념일의

② Different cultures can exhibit opposite attitudes / toward a given species.
각기 다른 문화는 상반되는 태도를 보일 수 있다. / 주어진 종에 대해

③ Snakes, for example, / are honored by some cultures / and hated by others.
예를 들어, 뱀은 일부 문화에서는 존경의 대상이고 / 다른 문화에서는 증오를 받는다.

④ Rats are considered pests in much of Europe and North America / and greatly respected in some parts of India.
쥐는 유럽과 북아메리카의 많은 지역에서 유해 동물로 여겨지고, / 인도의 일부 지역에서는 매우 중시된다.

☑ Of course, within cultures / individual attitudes can vary dramatically.
물론 (같은) 문화 내에서 / 개인의 태도는 극적으로 다를 수 있다.

For instance, in Britain many people dislike rodents, / and yet there are several associations / devoted to breeding them, / including the National Mouse Club and the National Fancy Rat Club.
예를 들어, 영국에서는 많은 사람들이 설치류를 싫어하지만, / 여러 협회들이 있다. / 그들을 기르는 데 전념하는 / National Mouse Club과 National Fancy Rat Club을 포함해서

자연계는 예술과 문학에서 사용되는 상징의 풍부한 원천을 제공한다. ① 식물과 동물은 전 세계의 신화, 춤, 노래, 시, 의식, 축제 그리고 기념일의 중심에 있다. ② 각기 다른 문화는 주어진 종에 대해 상반되는 태도를 보일 수 있다. ③ 예를 들어, 뱀은 일부 문화에서는 존경의 대상이고 다른 문화에서는 증오를 받는다. ④ 쥐는 유럽과 북아메리카의 많은 지역에서 유해 동물로 여겨지고, 인도의 일부 지역에서는 매우 중시된다. ⑤ 물론 (같은) 문화 내에서 개인의 태도는 극적으로 다를 수 있다. 예를 들어, 영국에서는 많은 사람들이 설치류를 싫어하지만, National Mouse Club과 National Fancy Rat Club을 포함해서 설치류를 기르는 데 전념하는 여러 협회들이 있다.

Why? 왜 정답일까?

각종 자연물에 대한 태도 차이를 설명한 글로, ⑤ 앞의 문장에서는 쥐가 유럽과 북미 등지에서는 유해한 동물로, 인도 일부 지역에서는 매우 귀중한 동물로 여겨진다는 점을 대조하여 설명하고 있다. 주어진 문장은 이에 추가적으로 같은 문화권 내에서 개인의 태도 또한 다를 수 있다는 점을 언급하고, ⑤ 뒤에서는 영국의 예를 들어 많은 사람들이 설치류를 싫어하지만 설치류를 기르기 위해 전념하는 여러 협회들이 또한 있다는 내용을 부연한다. 따라서 주어진 문장이 들어가기에 가장 적절한 곳은 ⑤이다.

- dramatically ⓐⓓ 극적으로
- mythology ⓝ 신화
- exhibit ⓥ 보여주다, 전시하다
- given ⓐ (이미)정해진; 특정한
- association ⓝ 협회, 연관
- literature ⓝ 문학
- ritual ⓝ 의식
- opposite ⓐ 정반대의
- honor ⓥ 존경하다
- breed ⓥ 기르다, 낳다

구문 풀이

8행 Rats are considered pests in much of Europe and North America and (are)
「A + be considered + B : A가 B로 간주되다」   생략
greatly respected in some parts of India.

★★ 문제 해결 꿀~팁 ★★

▶ 많이 틀린 이유는?
② 앞의 두 문장은 자연계의 대상들이 세계 각지의 예술과 문학에 핵심적인 역할을 했다는 넓은 내용을, ② 뒤의 문장은 특히 한 자연물에 대해서도 문화권마다 시각이 다르다는 좁은 내용을 제시한다. ③ 뒤의 문장은 이 좁혀진 내용에 대한 예를 제시하므로, ②와 ③ 앞뒤의 흐름이 자연스럽게 이어진다.
▶ 문제 해결 방법은?
Of course로 시작하는 주어진 문장은 '물론 한 문화권 내에서도' 사람따라 반응이 다르다는 내용을 이어 가고 있다. 따라서 앞에서 각 문화권의 시각 차이에 대한 언급이 마무리되고, 한 나라 안에서도 같은 대상에 대한 서로 다른 입장이 존재한다는 예로 넘어가는 ⑤에 주어진 문장이 들어가야 한다.

---

39 관계 맺음의 수적 한계   정답률 66% | 정답 ③

다음 글에서 전체 흐름과 관계 없는 문장은?

Paying attention to some people and not others / doesn't mean / you're being dismissive or arrogant.
일부 사람들에게 주의를 기울이고 다른 사람들에게 그렇게 하지 않는 것이 / 의미하지는 않는다. / 여러분이 남을 무시하고 있다거나 거만하게 굴고 있다는 것을

① It just reflects a hard fact: / there are limits on the number of people / we can possibly pay attention to or develop a relationship with.
그것은 단지 명백한 사실을 반영할 뿐인데, / 사람의 수에 한계가 있다는 것이다. / 우리가 아마 주의를 기울이거나 관계를 발전시킬 수 있는

② Some scientists even believe / that the number of people with / whom we can continue stable social relationships / might be limited naturally by our brains.
일부 과학자는 심지어 믿는다. / 사람의 수가 / 우리가 안정된 사회적 관계를 지속할 수 있는 / 우리의 뇌에 의해 자연스럽게 제한되는 것일지도 모른다고

☑ The more people you know of different backgrounds, / the more colorful your life becomes.
여러분이 다른 배경의 사람들을 더 많이 알수록, / 여러분의 삶은 더 다채로워진다.

④ Professor Robin Dunbar has explained / that our minds are only really capable of forming meaningful relationships / with a maximum of about a hundred and fifty people.
Robin Dunbar 교수는 설명했다. / 우리의 마음은 의미 있는 관계를 진정 형성할 수 있을 뿐이라고 / 최대 약 150명의 사람과

⑤ Whether that's true or not, / it's safe to assume / that we can't be real friends with everyone.
그것이 사실이든 아니든, / 가정하는 것이 안전하다. / 우리가 모든 사람과 진정한 친구가 될 수 있는 것은 아니라고

일부 사람들에게 주의를 기울이고 다른 사람들에게 그렇게 하지 않는 것이 여러분이 남을 무시하고 있다거나 거만하게 굴고 있다는 것을 의미하지는 않는다. ① 그것은 단지 명백한 사실을 반영할 뿐인데, 우리가 아마 주의를 기울이거나 관계를 발전시킬 수 있는 사람의 수에 한계가 있다는 것이다. ② 일부 과학자는 우리가 안정된 사회적 관계를 지속할 수 있는 사람의 수가 우리의 뇌에 의해 자연스럽게 제한되는 것일지도 모른다고까지 믿는다. ③ 여러분이 다른 배경의 사람들을 더 많이 알수록, 여러분의 삶은 더 다채로워진다. ④ Robin Dunbar 교수는 우리의 마음은 최대 약 150명의 사람과 의미 있는 관계를 진정 형성할 수 있을 뿐이라고 설명했다. ⑤ 그것이 사실이든 아니든, 우리가 모든 사람과 진정한 친구가 될 수 있는 것은 아니라고 가정하는 것이 안전하다.

Why? 왜 정답일까?

사람은 타인과 무한정 관계를 맺어갈 수 있는 것이 아니며, 유의미한 관계를 맺을 수 있는 수에 제한이 있다는 내용을 다룬 글이다. 하지만 ③은 우리가 다양한 배경을 지닌 사람들과 더 많이 관계를 맺을수록 좋다는 내용을 언급하고 있어 주제에서 벗어나 있다. 따라서 전체 흐름과 관계 없는 문장은 ③이다.

- pay attention to ⓥ ~에 주의를 기울이다
- hard fact 명백한 사실
- social relationship 사회적 관계
- background ⓝ 배경
- maximum ⓝ 최대
- reflect ⓥ 반영하다
- stable ⓐ 안정적인
- limited ⓐ 제한된
- meaningful ⓐ 유의미한
- assume ⓥ 가정하다

구문 풀이

4행 Some scientists even believe that the number of people [with whom we
접속사(~것)   주어   「전치사 + 관·대」
can continue stable social relationships] might be limited naturally by our brains.
조동사 수동태

---

40 사람들이 운전하는 동안 비협조적인 이유   정답률 59% | 정답 ①

다음 글의 내용을 한 문장으로 요약하고자 한다. 빈칸 (A), (B)에 들어갈 말로 가장 적절한 것은?

	(A)	(B)		(A)	(B)
☑①	uncooperative 비협조적인	little 거의 없는	②	careful 주의하는	direct 직접적인
③	confident 자신 있는	regular 정기적인	④	uncooperative 비협조적인	direct 직접적인
⑤	careful 주의하는	little 거의 없는			

While there are many evolutionary or cultural reasons for cooperation, / the eyes are one of the most important means of cooperation, / and eye contact may be the most powerful human force / we lose in traffic.
협동을 하는 진화적이거나 문화적인 많은 이유가 있지만, / 눈은 가장 중요한 협동 수단 중 하나이고, / 눈 맞춤은 가장 강력한 인간의 힘일지도 모른다. / 우리가 차량 운행 중에 잃고 마는

It is, arguably, the reason / why humans, normally a quite cooperative species, / can become so noncooperative on the road.
그것은 이유라고 주장할 수 있다. / 보통은 꽤 협동적인 종인 인간이 / 도로에서 그렇게 비협조적이 될 수 있는

Most of the time we are moving too fast / — we begin to lose the ability / to keep eye contact around 20 miles per hour — / or it is not safe to look.
대부분의 시간에 우리는 너무 빨리 움직이고 있어서, / 우리는 능력을 잃기 시작하거나, / 시속 20마일 정도에서 시선을 마주치는 / 혹은 (서로를) 보는 것이 안전하지 않다.

Maybe our view is blocked.
어쩌면 우리의 시야가 차단되어 있을 수도 있다.

Often other drivers are wearing sunglasses, / or their car may have tinted windows.
흔히 다른 운전자들이 선글라스를 끼고 있기도 하고, / 혹은 그들의 차에는 색이 옅게 들어간 창문이 있을 수 있다.

(And do you really want to make eye contact with those drivers?)
(그리고 당신은 정말로 그러한 운전자들과 시선을 마주치고 싶은가?)

Sometimes we make eye contact through the rearview mirror, / but it feels weak, not quite believable at first, / as it is not "face-to-face."
때로는 우리는 백미러를 통해 시선을 마주치지만, / 이것은 약하게, 처음에는 별로 믿을 수 없게 느껴진다. / 이것은 '얼굴을 마주하고 있는 것'이 아니기 때문에

➡ While driving, / people become (A) uncooperative, / because they make (B) little eye contact.
운전하는 동안, / 사람들은 비협조적이 되는데 / 왜냐하면 그들이 시선을 거의 마주치지 않기 때문이다.

협동을 하는 진화적이거나 문화적인 많은 이유가 있지만, 눈은 가장 중요한 협동 수단 중 하나이고, 눈 맞춤은 우리가 차량 운행 중에 잃고 마는 가장 강력한 인간의 힘일지도 모른다. 그것은 보통은 꽤 협동적인 종인 인간이 도로에서 그렇게 비협조적이 될 수 있는 이유라고 주장할 수 있다. 대부분의 시간에 우리는 너무 빨리 움직이고 있어서, 시속 20마일 정도에서 시선을 마주치는 능력을 잃기 시작하거나, 혹은 (서로를) 보는 것이 안전하지 않다. 어쩌면 우리의 시야가 차단되어 있을 수도 있다. 흔히 다른 운전자들이 선글라스를 끼고 있기도 하고, 혹은 그들의 차 창문 색깔이 옅게 들어가 있을 수도 있다. (그리고 당신은 정말로 그러한 운전자들과 시선을 마주치고 싶은가?) 때로는 우리는 백미러를 통해 시선을 마주치지만, '얼굴을 마주하고 있는 것'이 아니기 때문에 약하게, 처음에는 별로 믿을 수 없게 느껴진다.

➡ 운전하는 동안, 사람들은 (A) 비협조적이 되는데, 왜냐하면 그들이 (B) 거의 시선을 마주치지 않기 때문이다.

Why? 왜 정답일까?

첫 두 문장에서 눈은 사람이 협동하게 하는 가장 강력한 수단 중 하나인데, 운전하는 동안 우리는 상대방과 눈을 맞추지 못하므로 더 비협조적이 되고 만다(~ eye contact may be the most powerful human force we lose in traffic. It is, arguably, the reason why humans, normally a quite cooperative species, can become so noncooperative on the road.)는 주제를 소개하고 있다. 따라서 요약문의 빈칸 (A), (B)에 들어갈 말로 가장 적절한 것은 ① '(A) uncooperative (비협조적인), (B) little(거의 없는)'이다.

- evolutionary ⓐ 진화적인
- force ⓝ 힘
- quite ⓐⓓ 꽤, 상당히
- noncooperative ⓐ 비협조적인
- rearview mirror ⓝ 백미러
- believable ⓐ 믿을 수 있는
- eye contact ⓝ 눈 맞춤
- arguably ⓐⓓ 주장컨대
- normally ⓐⓓ 보통
- block ⓥ 차단하다
- weak ⓐ 약한
- confident ⓐ 자신감 있는

구문 풀이

4행 It is, arguably, the reason [why humans, (normally a quite cooperative]
　　　　　　　　　　　　　　선행사　관계부사　주어　( ): 삽입구
species), can become so noncooperative on the road].
　　　　　　동사　　　　　　　　보어

41-42 배경 소음이 공부에 미치는 영향에 대한 논란

Many high school students study and learn inefficiently / because they insist on doing their homework / while watching TV or listening to loud music.
많은 고등학생은 비효율적으로 공부하고 학습한다. / 그들이 숙제를 하겠다고 고집하기 때문에 / TV를 보거나 시끄러운 음악을 들으면서

These same students also typically (a) interrupt their studying / with repeated phone calls, trips to the kitchen, video games, and Internet surfing.
이 학생들은 또한 보통 자신의 공부를 방해한다. / 반복적인 전화 통화, 부엌에 들르기, 비디오 게임, 인터넷 서핑으로

Ironically, / students with the greatest need to concentrate when studying / are often the ones / who surround themselves with the most distractions.
모순적이게도, / 공부할 때 집중할 필요가 가장 큰 학생들은 / 흔히 학생들이다. / 주의를 산만하게 하는 것들로 가장 많이 자신을 에워싸는

「These teenagers argue / that they can study *better* with the TV or radio (b) playing.」 41번의 근거
이런 십 대들은 주장한다. / 그들이 TV나 라디오를 켜 둔 채로 공부를 더 잘 할 수 있다고

Some professionals actually (c) support their position.
일부 전문가는 실제로 그들의 견해를 지지한다.

「They argue / that many teenagers can actually study productively under less-than-ideal conditions / because they've been exposed repeatedly to "background noise" / since early childhood.」 42번의 근거
그들은 주장할 수 있다. / 많은 십 대들이 전혀 이상적이지 않은 상황에서 실제로 생산적으로 공부할 수 있다고 / 그들이 '배경 소음'에 반복적으로 노출되어 왔기 때문에 / 어린 시절부터

These educators argue / that children have become (d) used / to the sounds of the TV, video games, and loud music.
이 교육 전문가들은 주장한다. / 아이들이 익숙해졌다고 / TV, 비디오 게임, 그리고 시끄러운 음악 소리에

They also argue / that insisting students turn off the TV or radio / when doing homework / will not necessarily improve their academic performance.
그들은 또한 주장한다. / 학생들이 TV나 라디오를 꺼야 한다고 주장하는 것이 / 숙제를 할 때 / 반드시 그들의 학업 성적을 높이는 것은 아니라고

This position is certainly not generally shared, however.
그러나 이 견해는 분명히 일반적으로 공유되는 것은 아니다.

「Many teachers and learning experts / are (e) convinced by their own experiences / that students who study in a noisy environment / often learn inefficiently.」 41번의 근거
많은 교사와 학습 전문가는 / 스스로의 경험으로 확신한다. / 시끄러운 환경에서 공부하는 학생들이 / 흔히 비효율적으로 학습한다는 것을

많은 고등학생은 TV를 보거나 시끄러운 음악을 들으면서 숙제를 하겠다고 고집하기 때문에 비효율적으로 공부하고 학습한다. 이 학생들은 또한 반복적인 전화 통화, 부엌에 들르기, 비디오 게임, 인터넷 서핑으로 보통 자신의 공부를 (a) 방해한다. 모순적이게도, 공부할 때 집중할 필요가 가장 큰 학생들은 흔히 주의를 산만하게 하는 것들로 가장 많이 자신을 에워싸는 학생들이다. 이런 십 대들은 TV나 라디오를 (b) 켜 둔 채로 공부를 더 잘 할 수 있다고 주장한다. 일부 전문가는 실제로 그들의 견해에 (c) 반대한다(→ 지지한다). 그들은 많은 십 대들이 어린 시절부터 '배경 소음'에 반복적으로 노출되어 왔기 때문에 전혀 이상적이지 않은 상황에서 실제로 생산적으로 공부할 수 있다고 주장한다. 이 교육 전문가들은 아이들이 TV, 비디오 게임, 그리고 시끄러운 음악 소리에 (d) 익숙해졌다고 주장한다. 그들은 또한 숙제를 할 때 학생들이 TV나 라디오를 꺼야 한다고 주장하는 것이 반드시 그들의 학업 성적을 높이는 것은 아니라고 주장한다. 그러나 이 견해는 분명히 일반적으로 공유되는 것은 아니다. 많은 교사와 학습 전문가는 시끄러운 환경에서 공부하는 학생들이 흔히 비효율적으로 학습한다는 것을 스스로의 경험으로 (e) 확신한다.

- inefficiently ⓐⓓ 비효율적으로
- interrupt ⓥ 방해하다
- concentrate ⓥ 집중하다
- distraction ⓝ 주의를 산만하게 하는 것
- productively ⓐⓓ 생산적으로
- repeatedly ⓐⓓ 반복적으로
- improve ⓥ 높이다, 향상시키다
- convinced ⓐ 확신하는
- insist on ⓥ ~을 고집하다, 주장하다
- ironically ⓐⓓ 모순적이게도
- surround ⓥ 에워싸다
- professional ⓝ 전문가 ⓐ 전문적인
- less-than-ideal ⓐ 결코 이상적이지 않은
- not necessarily 반드시 ~인 것은 아니다
- generally ⓐⓓ 일반적으로

구문 풀이

19행 Many teachers and learning experts are convinced by their own
　　　　　　　　주어　　　　　　　　　　　　　　동사
experiences that students [who study in a noisy environment] often learn
접속사(~것)　　　주어(선행사)　　　　　　　　　　　　　동사
inefficiently.

41 제목 파악　　　　　　정답률 70% | 정답 ②

윗글의 제목으로 가장 적절한 것은?
① Successful Students Plan Ahead - 성공하는 학생은 미리 계획한다
✓② Studying with Distractions: Is It Okay? - 주의를 산만하게 만드는 것과 함께 공부하기: 괜찮을까?
③ Smart Devices as Good Learning Tools - 좋은 학습 도구로서의 스마트 기기
④ Parents & Teachers: Partners in Education - 부모와 교사: 교육에서의 파트너
⑤ Good Habits: Hard to Form, Easy to Break - 좋은 습관: 형성하기는 어렵고 버리기는 쉽다

Why? 왜 정답일까?

학생들은 음악, TV 소리 등 각종 배경 소음이나 공부에 방해가 되는 활동들이 학습에 별 방해가 되지 않는다고 주장하지만, 실상 많은 교사들과 학습 전문가들의 경험에 따르면 이 주장은 반박될 수 있다(~ students who study in a noisy environment often learn inefficiently.)는 내용을 다룬 글이다. 따라서 글의 제목으로 가장 적절한 것은 ② '주의를 산만하게 만드는 것과 함께 공부하기: 괜찮을까?'이다.

★★★ 등급을 가르는 문제!

42 어휘 추론　　　　　　정답률 44% | 정답 ③

밑줄 친 (a) ~ (e) 중에서 문맥상 낱말의 쓰임이 적절하지 않은 것은? [3점]
① (a) ② (b) ✓③ (c) ④ (d) ⑤ (e)

Why? 왜 정답일까?

③이 포함된 문장 뒤에서 일부 전문가들은 십 대들이 어렸을 때부터 배경 소음이 있는 환경에 익숙해져 왔기 때문에 소음이 있어도 능률적으로 공부할 수 있다(They argue that many teenagers can actually study productively under less-than-ideal conditions because they've been exposed repeatedly to "background noise" since early childhood.)고 주장한다는 내용이 나온다. 이는 전문가들이 TV나 라디오를 켜 놓고 공부를 더 잘 할 수 있다고 주장하는 십 대들을 지지 또는 옹호한 것으로 볼 수 있으므로, ③의 oppose는 support로 고쳐야 한다. 따라서 문맥상 낱말의 쓰임이 적절하지 않은 것은 ③ '(c)'이다.

★★ 문제 해결 꿀~팁 ★★

▶ 많이 틀린 이유는?
(b)의 playing은 TV나 라디오가 자동사인 play의 행위 주체임을 나타내는 현재분사로 '재생되고 있는, 켜져 있는'이라는 의미를 나타낸다. 한편 (d)의 used는 become used to(~에 익숙해지다)라는 의미의 관용 표현으로 바르게 쓰였다.

▶ 문제 해결 방법은?
상식이나 배경지식에 기초해서 풀면 (c)의 oppose가 적절해 보이지만, 바로 뒤의 'They argue ~'를 근거로 보면 Some professionals가 '배경 소음이 있어도 공부를 잘 할 수 있다'는 입장을 옹호하는 이들임을 알 수 있다.

43-45 집안에 불을 낼 뻔했던 Dorothy가 부모님의 반응을 보고 배운 교훈

(A)
Dorothy was home alone.
Dorothy는 집에 혼자 있었다.

「She was busy with a school project, / and suddenly wanted to eat French fries.

그녀는 학교 프로젝트로 바빴고, / 갑자기 프렌치프라이가 먹고 싶었다.

「She peeled two potatoes, / sliced them up / and put a pot with cooking oil on the stove.」
그녀는 감자 두 개를 깎아 / 그것들을 얇게 썰고 / 식용유를 넣은 냄비를 스토브에 올렸다. [45번 ①의 근거 일치]

Then the telephone rang.
그때 전화벨이 울렸다.

It was her best friend Samantha.
그녀의 가장 친한 친구 Samantha였다.

While chatting away on the phone, / Dorothy noticed a strange light shining from the kitchen, / and then (a) she remembered about the pot of oil on the stove!
전화로 수다를 떨다가 / Dorothy는 부엌에서 비치는 이상한 불빛을 알아차렸고 / 그때 그녀는 기름을 넣은 냄비를 스토브에 올려 둔 것이 기억났다!

(C)

Dorothy dropped the phone and rushed to the kitchen.
Dorothy는 전화기를 떨어뜨리고 부엌으로 달려 갔다.

The oil was on fire.
기름에 불이 붙어 있었다.

"Chill! Take a deep breath," (c) she said to herself.
"진정해! 심호흡해."라고 그녀는 혼잣말을 했다.

What did they teach us not to do in a situation like this?
이런 상황에서 하지 말라고 배운 것은 뭐였지?

「*Don't try to put it out by throwing water on it, / because it will cause an explosion, /* she remembered.」
물을 끼얹어서 불을 끄려고 하지 마라, / 왜냐하면 그렇게 하면 폭발이 일어날 테니까 / 그녀는 기억했다. [45번 ③의 근거 일치]

「She picked up the pot's lid / and covered the pot with it / to put out the flames.
그녀는 냄비 뚜껑을 집어 들었고 / 그것으로 냄비를 덮어 / 불을 껐다.

In the process she burned her hands.」
그 과정에서 그녀는 손을 데었다. [45번 ④의 근거 일치]

Dorothy felt dizzy and sat down at the kitchen table.
Dorothy는 머리가 어질어질해서 부엌 식탁에 앉았다.

(D)

A couple of minutes later, / her parents came rushing into the house.
몇 분 후 / 그녀의 부모님이 집에 급히 들어왔다.

Samantha had suspected / that something might be wrong / after Dorothy dropped the phone just like that, / and (d) she had phoned Dorothy's parents.
Samantha는 의심했다 / 뭔가 잘못된 것이 아닌가 하고 / Dorothy가 그렇게 전화를 떨어뜨린 후에 / 그리고 그녀는 Dorothy의 부모님께 전화를 걸었다.

Dorothy started to cry.
Dorothy는 울기 시작했다.

Her mother hugged her tightly and looked at the wound.
그녀의 어머니는 그녀를 꼭 껴안고 상처를 봤다.

"Tell me what happened," she said.
"무슨 일이 있었는지 말해봐."라고 어머니가 말했다.

Dorothy told her, sobbing and sniffing.
Dorothy는 흐느껴 울면서 코를 훌쩍거리며 어머니에게 말했다.

"Aren't you going to yell at me?" / (e) she asked them through the tears.
"저한테 고함치지 않으실 거에요?" / 그녀는 눈물을 흘리며 그들에게 물었다.

「Her father answered with a smile, / "I also put my lid on to keep me from exploding."
그녀의 아버지는 미소를 지으면서 대답했다. / "나도 (감정이) 폭발하지 않게 내 뚜껑을 덮었어."

Dorothy looked at him, relieved.」
Dorothy는 안심한 채 그를 바라보았다. [45번 ⑤의 근거 불일치]

"But be careful not to be so irresponsible again."
"하지만 다시는 그렇게 무책임하게 행동하지 않도록 조심해라."

(B)

A while later, after the wound had been treated, / the family sat around the kitchen table and talked.
잠시 후 그 상처가 치료된 뒤에, / 가족들은 부엌 식탁에 둘러앉아 이야기를 나누었다.

"I learned a big lesson today," Dorothy said.
"저는 오늘 큰 교훈을 배웠어요."라고 Dorothy는 말했다.

Her parents expected (b) her to say something about the fire.
그녀의 부모님은 그녀가 불에 대해 뭐라고 말할 것이라고 예상했다.

But she talked about something different.
하지만 그녀는 다른 것에 관해 말했다.

「"I have decided to use kind words more just like you."」
"저도 딱 엄마와 아빠처럼 친절한 말을 더 많이 쓰기로 했어요." [45번 ②의 근거 일치]

Her parents were very grateful, / because Dorothy had quite a temper.
그녀의 부모님은 매우 감사함을 느꼈다. / Dorothy는 꽤나 욱하는 성질이 있었기 때문에

(B)

잠시 후 그 상처를 치료한 뒤에, 가족들은 부엌 식탁에 둘러앉아 이야기를 나누었다. "저는 오늘 큰 교훈을 배웠어요."라고 Dorothy는 말했다. 그녀의 부모님은 (b) 그녀가 불이 난 것에 대해 뭐라고 말할 것이라고 예상했다. 하지만 그녀는 다른 것에 관해 말했다. "저도 딱 엄마와 아빠처럼 친절한 말을 더 많이 쓰기로 했어요." Dorothy는 꽤나 욱하는 성질이 있었기 때문에 그녀의 부모님은 매우 감사함을 느꼈다.

- busy with ~로 바쁜
- chat away ⓥ 수다 떨다
- treat 치료하다
- have quite a temper ⓥ 성질이 보통이 아니다
- rush to ~로 달려가다
- explosion ⓝ 폭발
- flame ⓝ 불꽃
- suspect ⓥ 의심하다
- yell at ~에게 고함지르다
- slice up ⓥ ~을 얇게 자르다
- wound ⓝ 상처
- grateful ⓐ 감사해하는
- drop ⓥ 떨어뜨리다
- put out ⓥ 불을 끄다
- lid ⓝ 뚜껑
- dizzy ⓐ 어지러운
- tightly [ad] 꼭, 단단히
- irresponsible ⓐ 무책임한

구문 풀이

(A) 5행 While chatting away on the phone, Dorothy noticed a strange light shining from the kitchen, and then she remembered about the pot of oil on the stove!
분사구문(~하는 동안) / 지각 동사 / 목적어 / 목적격 보어(현재분사)

(D) 2행 Samantha had suspected that something might be wrong after Dorothy dropped the phone just like that, and she had phoned Dorothy's parents.
주어1 / 동사1 / 접속사(~것) / 시간 접속사(~한 후에) / 주어2 / 동사2

---

43 글의 순서 파악   정답률 75% | 정답 ③

주어진 글 (A)에 이어질 내용을 순서에 맞게 배열한 것으로 가장 적절한 것은?

① (B) – (D) – (C)
② (C) – (B) – (D)
③ ✔(C) – (D) – (B)
④ (D) – (B) – (C)
⑤ (D) – (C) – (B)

Why? 왜 정답일까?

Dorothy가 프렌치프라이를 해 먹으려고 냄비를 올렸다가 깜빡 잊고 불을 낼 위기에 처했다는 내용의 (A) 뒤에는, Dorothy가 냄비를 뚜껑으로 덮어 불을 끄다가 손이 다쳤다는 내용의 (C), 친구의 전화를 받고 달려온 Dorothy의 부모님이 Dorothy를 나무라는 대신 잘 타일렀다는 내용의 (D), 상처를 치료한 뒤 Dorothy가 앞으로 부모님처럼 친절한 말을 많이 써야겠다는 각오를 언급했다는 내용의 (B)가 차례로 이어져야 한다. 따라서 글의 순서로 가장 적절한 것은 ③ '(C) – (D) – (B)'이다.

---

44 지칭 추론   정답률 69% | 정답 ④

밑줄 친 (a) ~ (e) 중에서 가리키는 대상이 나머지 넷과 다른 것은?

① (a) ② (b) ③ (c) ④ ✔(d) ⑤ (e)

Why? 왜 정답일까?

(a), (b), (c), (e)는 Dorothy를, (d)는 같은 문장의 주어 Samantha를 가리키므로, (a) ~ (e) 중에서 가리키는 대상이 다른 하나는 ④ '(d)'이다.

---

45 세부 내용 파악   정답률 77% | 정답 ⑤

윗글의 Dorothy에 관한 내용으로 적절하지 않은 것은?

① 프렌치프라이를 만들려고 감자 두 개를 깎았다.
② 친절한 말을 더 많이 쓰겠다고 다짐했다.
③ 불붙은 기름에 물을 끼얹지 말아야 한다는 것을 기억했다.
④ 뚜껑으로 냄비를 덮어 불을 끄다가 손을 데었다.
⑤ ✔아버지의 말을 듣고 화를 냈다.

Why? 왜 정답일까?

(D) 'Her father answered with a smile, "I also put my lid on to keep me from exploding." Dorothy looked at him, relieved.'에서 Dorothy는 '감정이 터지지 않게 뚜껑을 닫았다'는 아버지의 말을 듣고 안도했음을 알 수 있다. 따라서 내용과 일치하지 않는 것은 ⑤ '아버지의 말을 듣고 화를 냈다.'이다.

Why? 왜 오답일까?

① (A) 'She ~ suddenly wanted to eat French fries. She peeled two potatoes, ~'의 내용과 일치한다.
② (B) '"I have decided to use kind words more just like you."'의 내용과 일치한다.
③ (C) '~ *Don't try to put it out by throwing water on it, because it will cause an explosion,* she remembered.'의 내용과 일치한다.
④ (C) 'She picked up the pot's lid and covered the pot with it to put out the flames. In the process she burned her hands.'의 내용과 일치한다.

(A)

Dorothy는 집에 혼자 있었다. 그녀는 학교 프로젝트로 바빴고, 갑자기 프렌치프라이가 먹고 싶었다. 그녀는 감자 두 개를 깎아 얇게 썰고 식용유를 넣은 냄비를 스토브에 올렸다. 그때 전화벨이 울렸다. 그녀의 가장 친한 친구 Samantha였다. 전화로 수다를 떨다가 Dorothy는 부엌에서 비치는 이상한 불빛을 알아차렸고 그때 (a) 그녀는 기름을 넣은 냄비를 스토브에 올려 둔 것이 기억났다!

(C)

Dorothy는 전화기를 떨어뜨리고 부엌으로 달려 갔다. 기름에 불이 붙어 있었다. "진정해! 심호흡해."라고 (c) 그녀는 혼잣말을 했다. 이런 상황에서 하지 말라고 배운 것은 뭐였지? 물을 끼얹어서 불을 끄려고 하지 마라, 왜냐하면 그렇게 하면 폭발이 일어날 테니까.라고 그녀는 기억했다. 그녀는 냄비 뚜껑을 집어 들었고 그것으로 냄비를 덮어 불을 껐다. 그 과정에서 그녀는 손을 데었다. Dorothy는 머리가 어질어질해서 부엌 식탁에 앉았다.

(D)

몇 분 후 그녀의 부모님이 집으로 급히 들어왔다. Samantha는 Dorothy가 그렇게 전화를 떨어뜨린 후에 뭔가 잘못된 것이 아닌가 하고 의심하여 (d) 그녀는 Dorothy의 부모님께 전화를 걸었다. Dorothy는 울기 시작했다. 그녀의 어머니는 그녀를 꼭 껴안고 상처를 봤다. "무슨 일이 있었는지 말해봐."라고 어머니가 말했다. Dorothy는 흐느껴 울면서 코를 훌쩍거리며 어머니에게 말했다. "저한테 고함치지 않으실 거에요?"라고 (e) 그녀는 눈물을 흘리며 부모님에게 물었다. 그녀의 아버지는 미소를 지으면서 "나도 (감정이) 폭발하지 않게 내 뚜껑을 덮었어."라고 대답했다. Dorothy는 안심한 채 그를 바라보았다. "하지만 다시는 그렇게 무책임하게 행동하지 않도록 조심하렴."

A	B	C	D
01 화를 내다	01 faulty	01 ⓒ	01 ⑨
02 진정시키는	02 artificial	02 ⓐ	02 ⓑ
03 ~을 명심하다, 염두에 두다	03 raise	03 ⓗ	03 ①
04 겨드랑이	04 matter	04 ⓓ	04 ①
05 체중계, 저울	05 defeat	05 ⓚ	05 ⓔ
06 진실한, 진짜의	06 factor	06 ⓞ	06 ⓕ
07 기르다, 낳다	07 patience	07 ①	07 ①
08 자립, 독립	08 phrase	08 ①	08 ⓜ
09 비효율적으로	09 reject	09 ⓔ	09 ⓚ
10 ~의 면에서	10 frequent	10 ⑨	10 ⓝ
11 ~을 우연히 만나다	11 injury	11 ⓜ	11 ⓒ
12 감사해하는	12 stable	12 ①	12 ⓗ
13 구부릴 수 있는	13 strengthen	13 ①	13 ⓐ
14 다르다	14 ritual	14 ⓝ	14 ⓓ
15 확신하는	15 evaluate	15 ⓑ	15 ⓞ
16 동기 요인, 동기를 부여 하는 것	16 physical	16 ⓢ	16 ⓕ
17 일상	17 concern	17 ⓟ	17 ⓟ
18 갈등	18 undivided	18 ⓡ	18 ⓢ
19 협회, 연관	19 in the long run	19 ⓠ	19 ①
20 가정하다	20 inform	20 ①	20 ⓠ

· 정답 ·

18 ② 19 ② 20 ① 21 ② 22 ① 23 ⑤ 24 ① 25 ③ 26 ⑤ 27 ④ 28 ⑤ 29 ③ 30★⑤ 31 ② 32 ② 33 ⑤ 34★① 35 ③ 36 ③ 37 ② 38★③ 39 ④ 40 ① 41 ① 42★④ 43 ⑤ 44 ② 45 ④

★ 표기된 문항은 [등급을 가르는 문제]에 해당하는 문항입니다.

---

18 온라인 회원 전환 홍보　　　정답률 95% | 정답 ②

다음 글의 목적으로 가장 적절한 것은?
① 여행 일정 지연에 대해 사과하려고
✔ 잡지 온라인 구독을 권유하려고
③ 무료 잡지 신청을 홍보하려고
④ 여행 후기 모집을 안내하려고
⑤ 기사에 대한 독자 의견에 답변하려고

Dear Reader,
독자 여러분께,
We always appreciate / your support.
저희는 항상 감사드립니다. / 여러분의 지지에
As you know, / our service is now available / through an app.
아시다시피, / 저희의 서비스는 이제 가능합니다. / 앱을 통해서도
There has never been a better time / to switch to an online membership / of *TourTide Magazine*.
더 나은 때는 없었습니다. / 온라인 멤버십으로 바꾸기에 / *TourTide Magazine*의
At a 50% discount off your current print subscription, / you can access / a full year of online reading.
현재 여러분의 지간 구독물에서 50% 할인 된 가격으로, / 여러분은 접근할 수 있습니다. / 1년 온라인 읽기에
Get new issues and daily web pieces / at TourTide.com, / read or listen to *TourTide Magazine* / via the app, / and get our members-only newsletter.
새로운 소식과 일간 웹 이야기를 얻으세요. / TourTide.com에서 / *TourTide Magazine*에서 읽거나 들으세요. / 앱을 통해서, / 그리고 저희의 구독자 전용 뉴스레터를 얻으세요.
You'll also gain access / to our editors' selections / of the best articles.
여러분은 또한 접근 권한을 얻을 것입니다. / 저희의 편집자 선택에 / 최고 기사의
Join today!
오늘 가입하세요!
Yours,
여러분의,
TourTide Team
TourTide Team 드림

독자분께,

보내주신 성원에 항상 감사드립니다. 아시다시피, 이제앱을 통해서도 저희 서비스를 이용하실 수 있습니다. *TourTide Magazine*의 온라인 회원으로 전환하기에 이보다 더 좋은 시기는 없습니다. 당신의 현재 인쇄본 구독료에서 50% 할인된 가격으로 1년 치를 온라인으로 구독할 수 있습니다. TourTide.com에서 신간호와 일일 웹 기사를 받아보고, 앱을 통해 *TourTide Magazine*을 읽거나 청취해 보고, 회원 전용 뉴스레터도 받아보세요. 편집자들이 선정한 최고의 기사도 받아볼 수 있습니다. 오늘 가입하세요!

TourTide 팀 드림

Why? 왜 정답일까?

오프라인 서비스에서 온라인 회원으로 전환하기에 더욱 좋은 때는 없다(**There has never been a better time to switch to an online membership of** *TourTide Magazine*.)고 말하고 있기 때문에, 글의 목적으로 가장 적절한 것은 ② '잡지 온라인 구독을 권유하려고'이다.

● **appreciate** ⓥ 감사하다　　　● **support** ⓝ 지원
● **available** ⓐ 가능한　　　● **switch** ⓥ 전환하다
● **discount** ⓝ 할인　　　● **article** ⓝ 기사

구문 풀이

3행 There has never been a better time to switch to an online membership of
현재완료시제　　　 to부정사(형용사적 용법)◀　　　▶전치사(~로)
TourTide Magazine.

---

19 대학교 합격 편지 열기　　　정답률 83% | 정답 ②

다음 글에 드러난 'I'의 심경 변화로 가장 적절한 것은?
① relaxed → upset
　안심한　　화난
✔ anxious → delighted
　불안한　　기쁜
③ guilty → confident
　죄책감이 드는　자신감 있는
④ angry → grateful
　화난　　감사한
⑤ hopeful → disappointed
　희망찬　　실망한

As I walked from the mailbox, / my heart was beating rapidly.
우편함에서 걸어오면서, / 내 심장은 빠르게 뛰었다.
In my hands, / I held the letter / from the university / I had applied to.
내 손에는, / 편지를 쥐었다. / 대학에서부터 온 / 내가 지원한
I thought / my grades were good enough / to cross the line / and my application letter / was well-written, / but was it enough?
난 생각했다. / 내 성적도 충분했고 / 기준을 넘기기에 / 그리고 내 자기소개서도 / 잘 써졌다고 / 근데 그게 충분했나?
I hadn't slept a wink / for days.
난 한 숨도 못 잤다. / 며칠 째
As I carefully tore into the paper of the envelope, / the letter slowly emerged / with the opening phrase, / "It is our great pleasure..."
내가 조심스럽게 봉투의 종이를 뜯자, / 편지가 천천히 나타났다. / 첫줄과 함께 / "저희는 기쁘게..."라는

I shouted with joy, / "I am in!"
나는 기뻐서 소리쳤다. / "합격이다!"
As I held the letter, / I began to make a fantasy / about my college life / in a faraway city.
편지를 쥐며, / 환상을 만들기 시작했다. / 나의 대학교 생활에 대해서 / 먼 도시에서의

우체통에서 걸어올 때 내 심장은 빠르게 뛰고 있었다. 내 손에는 지원했던 대학에서 보낸 편지가 들려 있었다. 내 생각에는 합격할 만큼 성적이 좋았고 지원서도 잘 썼지만, 그것으로 충분했을까? 며칠 동안 한숨도 잘 수 없었다. 봉투의 종이를 조심스럽게 찢자 "매우 기쁘게도..."라는 첫 문구와 함께 편지가 천천히 모습을 드러냈다. 나는 기뻐서 소리 질렀다. "합격이야!" 나는 편지를 손에 쥐고 집에서 멀리 떨어진 도시에서의 대학 생활에 대해 상상하기 시작했다.

Why? 왜 정답일까?
우체통에서 편지를 꺼내어 걸어올 때 심장이 빠르게 뛰고 있었고(As I walked from the mailbox, my heart was beating rapidly.), 편지를 열어 합격임을 알고 기뻐서 소리 질렀다고 하였으니 (I shouted with joy, "I am in!") 'I'의 심경 변화로 가장 적절한 것은 ② 'anxious → delighted' 이다.

- **mailbox** ⓝ 우편함
- **rapidly** ⓐⓓ 빠르게
- **apply** ⓥ 지원하다
- **beat** ⓥ 뛰다
- **university** ⓝ 대학교
- **application** ⓝ 지원서

구문 풀이

8행 As I held the letter, I began to make a fantasy about my college life in a
~하면서   begin to부정사(= begin ~ing) : ~하는 것을 시작하다.
faraway city.

20 깨끗한 방의 힘   정답률 95% | 정답 ①

다음 글에서 필자가 주장하는 바로 가장 적절한 것은?
✓ 자신의 공간을 정돈하여 긍정적 변화를 도모하라.
② 오랜 시간 고민하기보다는 일단 행동으로 옮겨라.
③ 무질서한 환경에서 창의적인 생각을 시도하라.
④ 장기 목표를 위해 단기 목표를 먼저 설정하라.
⑤ 반복되는 일상을 새로운 관점으로 관찰하라.

Having a messy room / can add up to / negative feelings and destructive thinking.
어지러운 방은 / 결과로 이어질 수 있다. / 부정적인 감정과 파괴적인 생각의
Psychologists say / that having a disorderly room / can indicate a disorganized mental state.
심리학자들은 말한다. / 엉망인 방은 / 정리하지 않은 정신 상태를 가리킨다고
One of the professional tidying experts says / that the moment you start cleaning your room, / you also start changing your life / and gaining new perspective.
전문 정리 정돈 전문가 중 한 명이 말한다. / 당신이 당신의 방을 청소하는 순간, / 당신은 또한 당신의 삶을 바꾸기를 시작한다고 / 그리고 새 관점을 갖기를
When you clean your surroundings, / positive and good atmosphere / follows.
여러분 주변을 청소할 때, / 긍정적이고 좋은 분위기가 / 따라온다.
You can do more things / efficiently and neatly.
여러분은 더 많은 것을 할 수 있다. / 효과적으로 그리고 깔끔하게
So, clean up your closets, / organize your drawers, / and arrange your things first, / then peace of mind / will follow.
그러니, 옷장을 치우고, / 서랍을 정리하고, / 물건을 먼저 배열해라. / 그러면 마음의 평화가 / 따라올 것이다.

방이 지저분한 것은 결국 부정적인 감정과 파괴적인 사고로 이어질 수 있다. 심리학자들은 방이 무질서하다는 것은 정신 상태가 혼란스럽다는 것을 나타낼 수 있다고 말한다. 정리 전문가 중 한 명은 방 청소를 시작하는 순간 당신은 인생을 변화시키고 새로운 관점을 얻기 시작한다고 말한다. 주변을 청소하면 긍정적이고 좋은 분위기가 따라온다. 당신은 더 많은 일을 효율적이고 깔끔하게 할 수 있다. 그러니 먼저 옷장을 청소하고, 서랍을 정리하고, 물건을 정돈한다면 마음의 평화가 따라올 것이다.

Why? 왜 정답일까?
깨끗하지 않은 방에서는 부정적인 감정과 파괴적인 사고가 들지만(Having a messy room can add up to negative feelings and destructive thinking.), 주변을 청소하면 긍정적이고 좋은 분위기가 따라온다(When you clean your surroundings, positive and good atmosphere follows.)고 하였으므로 글에서 필자가 주장하는 바로 가장 적절한 것은 ① '자신의 공간을 정돈하여 긍정적 변화를 도모하라.'이다.

- **messy** ⓐ 지저분한
- **feeling** ⓝ 감정
- **expert** ⓝ 전문가
- **efficiently** ⓐⓓ 효과적인
- **negative** ⓐ 부정적인
- **destructive** ⓐ 파괴적인
- **surrounding** ⓝ 주변
- **atmosphere** ⓝ 분위기

구문 풀이

3행 One of the professional tidying experts says that the moment you
one of the 복수명사(~들 중에 하나(단수취급))   접속사
start cleaning your room, you also start changing your life and gaining new
start 동명사(= start to부정사) : ~하는 것을 시작하다.   동명사1   동명사2
perspective.

21 작물을 위한 완벽한 토양   정답률 54% | 정답 ②

밑줄 친 luxury real estate가 다음 글에서 의미하는 바로 가장 적절한 것은? [3점]
① a farm where a scientist's aid is highly required – 과학자의 도움이 매우 필요한 농장
✓ a field abundant with necessities for plants – 식물에게 필요한 것이 충분한 땅
③ a district accessible only for the rich – 부자들만 접근할 수 있는 구역
④ a place that is conserved for ecology – 생태계를 보존하는 장소
⑤ a region with higher economic value – 높은 경제적인 가치를 가진 지역

The soil of a farm field / is forced to be the perfect environment / for monoculture growth.
농장 땅의 흙은 / 완벽한 환경이 되도록 만들어진다. / 한 가지 작물의 성장을 위해
This is achieved by / adding nutrients in the form of fertilizer / and water by way of irrigation.
이것은 이루어진다. / 비료의 형태로 영양분을 추가하고 / 관개를 통해 물을 더함으로써
During the last fifty years, / engineers and crop scientists have helped farmers / become much more efficient / at supplying exactly the right amount of both.
지난 50년 동안, / 엔지니어들과 작물 과학자들은 농부들이 / 훨씬 더 효율적으로 되도록 도왔다. / 둘 다 정확한 양을 공급하는 데
World usage of fertilizer has tripled / since 1969, / and the global capacity for irrigation has almost doubled.
세계 비료 사용량은 세 배로 증가했다. / 1969년 이후로, / 그리고 전 세계 관개 능력은 거의 두 배로 늘었다.
We are feeding and watering our fields / more than ever, / and our crops are loving it.
우리는 우리의 농장에 비료와 물을 공급하고 있다. / 그 어느 때보다 많이, / 그리고 작물들은 그것을 좋아하고 있다.
Unfortunately, / these luxurious conditions / have also excited the attention / of certain agricultural undesirables.
불행히도, / 이러한 풍족한 조건들은 / 또한 관심을 끌었다. / 특정 농업에 바람직하지 않은 것들의
Because farm fields are loaded with nutrients and water / relative to the natural land that surrounds them, / they are desired as luxury real estate / by every random weed in the area.
농장 땅은 영양분과 물이 가득 차 있기 때문에 / 그것을 둘러싼 자연 땅에 비해, / 그곳은 고급 부동산으로 여겨진다. / 주변의 모든 잡초들에 의해

농지의 토양은 단일 작물 재배를 위한 완벽한 환경이어야 한다. 이것은 비료 형태로 양분을 더하고 관개로 물을 댐으로써 이루어진다. 지난 50년 동안 기술자와 농작물 연구자들은 농부들이 양쪽 모두의 정확한 적정량을 공급하는 데 훨씬 더 효율적일 수 있도록 도움을 주었다. 전 세계 비료 사용량은 1969년 이래로 세 배가 되었고, 전체 관개 능력은 거의 두 배가 되었다. 우리는 그 어느 때보다 들판을 기름지게 하고 물을 대고 있으며, 우리의 농작물은 이를 좋아한다. 불행히도, 이러한 호사스러운 상황은 농업에서는 달갑지 않은 것들의 관심도 끌어들였다. 농지는 주위를 둘러싼 자연 지대에 비해 영양분과 물이 풍족히 채워져 있기 때문에 그 지역의 어떤 잡초라도 원하는 고급 부동산이 된다.

Why? 왜 정답일까?
농작물 연구자들의 노력으로 작물을 위한 완벽한 토양을 만들어냈다(The soil of a farm field is forced to be the perfect environment for monoculture growth.)고 하였으므로, luxury real estate의 luxury는 물과 영양분이 충분함을 뜻하고, real estate는 땅을 뜻한다고 해석하는 것이 가장 적절하다. 따라서 답은 ② 'a field abundant with necessities for plants'이다.

- **monoculture** ⓝ 단일 작물 재배
- **efficient** ⓐ 효과적인
- **capacity** ⓝ 능력
- **achieve** ⓥ 달성하다
- **supply** ⓥ 제공하다
- **attention** ⓝ 관심

구문 풀이

4행 During the last fifty years, engineers and crop scientists have helped
~동안   현재완료시제
farmers become much more efficient at supplying exactly the right amount of both.
준사역동사(help) + 동사원형   동명사

22 사소한 관심의 영향   정답률 89% | 정답 ①

다음 글의 요지로 가장 적절한 것은?
✓ 사소한 관심이 타인에게 도움이 될 수 있다.
② 사람마다 행복의 기준이 제각기 다르다.
③ 선행을 통해 자신을 되돌아볼 수 있다.
④ 원만한 대인 관계는 경청에서 비롯된다.
⑤ 현재에 대한 만족이 행복의 필수조건이다.

When it comes to helping out, / you don't have to do much.
도움을 주는 일에 있어서, / 많은 것을 할 필요는 없다.
All you have to do / is come around / and show that you care.
네가 해야 할 일은 / 다가가서 / 네가 신경 쓰고 있음을 보여주는 것뿐이다.
If you notice someone who is lonely, / you could go and sit with them.
누군가 외로워 보인다면, / 그들과 함께 가서 앉아 있을 수 있다.
If you work with someone / who eats lunch all by themselves, / and you go and sit down with them, / they will begin to be more social after a while, / and they will owe it all to you.
만약 너와 함께 일하는 사람이 있다면 / 혼자서 점심을 먹는, / 네가 가서 그들과 앉아 있으면, / 시간이 지나면 그들은 더 사교적이게 될 것이고, / 그 모든 것을 너에게 고마워할 것이다.
A person's happiness / comes from attention.
사람의 행복은 / 관심에서 온다.
There are too many people / out in the world / who feel like everyone has forgotten them or ignored them.
너무 많은 사람들이 있다. / 세상 속에 / 모두가 자신을 잊었거나 무시했다고 느끼는
Even if you say hi / to someone passing by, / they will begin to feel better about themselves, / like someone cares.
심지어 네가 인사만 해도 / 지나가는 사람에게, / 그들은 스스로에 대해 더 나은 기분을 느끼기 시작할 것이다. / 마치 누군가가 자신을 신경 쓰는 것처럼

도움을 주는 것에 관해서 당신은 많은 것을 할 필요는 없다. 그저 다가가서 관심을 갖고 있다는 것을 보여주기만 하면 된다. 외로운 사람을 발견하면 가서 함께 앉아 있으면 된다. 혼자서 점심을 먹는 사람과 함께 일한다면, 그리고 그 사람에게 다가가서 함께 앉는다면 얼마 지나지 않아 그 사람은 더 사교적으로 변하기 시작할 것이고, 이 모든 것을 당신 덕분이라고 할 것이다. 한 사람의 행복은 관심에서 비롯된다. 세상에는 모든 이가 자신을 잊었거나 무시한다고 느끼는 사람이 너무 많다. 지나가는 사람들에게 인사만 건네도, 누군가가 (그들에게) 관심을 가져주는 것처럼, 그들은 자기 자신에 대해 기분이 좋아지기 시작할 것이다.

Why? 왜 정답일까?
도움은 많은 것을 해줄 필요가 없고, 관심을 갖고 있다는 것을 보여주기만 하면 된다(When it comes to helping out, you don't have to do much.)고 말하고 있기 때문에, 글의 요지로 가장 적절한 것은 ① '사소한 관심이 타인에게 도움이 될 수 있다.'이다.

- **notice** ⓥ 알아차리다
- **social** ⓐ 사회적인
- **attention** ⓝ 관심
- **lonely** ⓐ 외로운
- **owe** ⓥ 빚지다
- **pass by** 지나가다

구문 풀이

4행 If you work with someone who eats lunch all by themselves, and you
(가정법) *(주격관계대명사)*
go and sit down with them, they will begin to be more social after a while, and
(동사1) *(동사2)* *(곧(= soon))*
they will owe it all to you.

---

23 고난의 교훈
정답률 77% | 정답 ⑤

다음 글의 주제로 가장 적절한 것은?

① characteristics of well-equipped athletes – 잘 정비된 운동선수의 특징
② difficulties in overcoming life's sudden challenges – 삶의 급작스런 도전을 극복하는 어려움
③ relationship between personal habit and competence – 개인적인 습관과 경쟁 사이의 관계
④ risks of enduring hardship without any preparation – 준비 없이 고난을 겪는 것의 위험
☑ importance of confronting hardship in one's life – 삶에서 고난을 마주하는 중요성

We often try / to make cuts / in our challenges / and take the easy route.
우리는 종종 시도한다. / 지름길을 내려고 / 우리의 도전에서 / 그리고 쉬운 길을 선택하려고
When taking the quick exit, / we fail / to acquire the strength / to compete.
빠른 출구를 선택할 때, / 우리는 실패한다. / 힘을 얻는 데 / 경쟁할 수 있는
We often take / the easy route / to improve our skills.
우리는 종종 선택한다. / 쉬운 길을 / 우리의 기술을 향상시키기 위해
Many of us / never really work / to achieve mastery / in the key areas of life.
우리 중 많은 사람들은 / 결코 열심히 일하지 않는다. / 숙달을 이루기 위해 / 인생의 중요한 영역에서
These skills / are key tools / that can be useful / to our career, health, and prosperity.
이러한 기술은 / 중요한 도구들이다. / 유용할 수 있는 / 우리의 경력, 건강, 그리고 번영에
Highly successful athletes / don't win / because of better equipment; / they win / by facing hardship / to gain strength and skill.
매우 성공적인 운동선수들은 / 승리하지 않는다. / 더 좋은 장비 때문에; / 그들은 승리한다. / 어려움을 마주하면서 / 힘과 기술을 얻기 위해
They win / through preparation.
그들은 승리한다. / 준비를 통해
It's the mental preparation, / winning mindset, / strategy, and skill / that set them apart.
그것은 정신적 준비, / 승리하는 마음가짐, / 전략, 그리고 기술이다. / 그들을 구별하는
Strength comes / from struggle, / not from taking the path / of least resistance.
힘은 온다. / 투쟁에서, / 길을 선택하는 것에서가 아니라 / 최소한의 저항의
Hardship / is not just a lesson / for the next time / in front of us.
어려움은 / 단지 교훈이 아니다. / 다음을 위한 / 우리 앞에 있는
Hardship / will be / the greatest teacher / we will ever have / in life.
어려움은 / 될 것이다. / 가장 위대한 스승 / 우리가 인생에서 가질 / 존재 중에

우리는 종종 우리의 도전을 멈추고, 쉬운 길을 택하려고 한다. 쉬운 길을 택하면 경쟁할 수 있는 힘을 얻지 못한다. 우리는 종종 실력을 향상하기 위해 쉬운 길을 택한다. 우리 중 다수가 인생의 핵심이 되는 영역에서 숙달을 위한 노력을 하지 않는다. 이러한 기술은 경력, 건강, 번영에 도움이 될 수 있는 핵심 도구이다. 성공한 운동선수들은 더 좋은 장비 때문에 승리하는 것이 아니다. 그들은 힘과 실력을 얻기 위해 고난에 맞섬으로써 승리한다. 그들은 준비를 통해 승리한다. 그들을 돋보이게 하는 것은 바로 정신적 준비, 승리하는 마음가짐, 전략, 그리고 기술이다. 힘은 저항이 가장 적은 길을 택하는 것이 아니라 맞서 싸우는 데서 나온다. 고난은 단지 우리 앞에 놓인 다음을 위한 교훈만은 아니다. 고난은 우리 인생에서 가장 위대한 스승이 될 것이다.

Why? 왜 정답일까?

고난이 우리 인생에서 가장 위대한 스승이 될 것(Hardship will be the greatest teacher we will ever have in life.)이라 하였으므로, 글의 주제로 가장 적절한 것은 ⑤ 'importance of confronting hardship in one's life'이다.

- cut ⓝ 지름길
- route ⓝ 길
- mastery ⓝ 숙달
- hardship ⓝ 고난
- challenge ⓝ 도전
- acquire ⓥ 얻다, 획득하다
- prosperity ⓝ 번영
- preparation ⓝ 준비

구문 풀이

13행 Hardship will be the greatest teacher (which/that) we will ever have in life.
(the 형용사 최상급) *(목적격 관계대명사 생략)*

---

24 행동과 정체성의 관계
정답률 68% | 정답 ①

다음 글의 제목으로 가장 적절한 것은?

☑ Action Comes from Who You Think You Are – 당신이 누구인지 생각하는 데에서 기인하는 행동
② The Best Practices for Gaining More Voters – 더 많은 유권자들을 모으는 최고의 실행
③ Stop Pursuing Undesirable Behavior Change! – 바람직하지 않은 행동 변화 추구를 그만하라!
④ What to Do When Your Exercise Bores You – 운동이 당신을 지루하게 할 때 할 것
⑤ Your Actions Speak Louder than Your Words – 말보다 행동이 우선이다

Your behaviors / are usually / a reflection / of your identity.
당신의 행동은 / 대개 / 반영이다. / 당신의 정체성의
What you do / is an indication / of the type of person / you believe that you are — / either consciously or nonconsciously.
당신이 하는 것은 / 암시이다. / 당신이 믿는 / 사람의 유형에 대한 / 의식적으로든 무의식적으로든
Research has shown / that once a person believes in a particular aspect / of their identity, / they are more likely / to act according to that belief.
연구는 보여 주었다. / 한 사람이 특정 측면을 믿으면 / 그들의 정체성의, / 그들이 더 가능성이 높다는 것을 / 그 믿음에 따라 행동할
For example, / people who identified / as "being a voter" / were more likely / to vote / than those who simply claimed / "voting" was an action / they wanted to perform.
예를 들어, / 스스로를 규정한 사람들은 / "유권자"라고 / 더 가능성이 높았다. / 투표할 / 단순히 주장한 사람들보다 / "투표"는 그들 / 이 하고 싶었던 행동이라고
Similarly, / the person who accepts exercise / as the part of their identity / doesn't have to convince themselves / to train.
비슷하게, / 운동을 받아들이는 사람은 / 그들의 정체성의 일부로 / 스스로를 설득할 필요가 없다. / 훈련하기 위해

Doing the right thing / is easy.
올바른 일을 하는 것은 / 쉽다.
After all, / when your behavior and your identity / perfectly match, / you are no longer / pursuing behavior change.
결국, / 당신의 행동과 정체성이 / 완벽히 일치할 때, / 더 이상 / 행동 변화를 추구하지 않는다.
You are simply / acting like the type of person / you already believe yourself to be.
당신은 단순히 / 행동하고 있는 것이다. / 이미 스스로 믿고 있는 그 사람처럼

당신의 행동은 대개 당신의 정체성을 반영한다. 당신이 하는 행동은 의식적으로든 무의식적으로든 당신이 스스로를 어떤 사람이라고 믿고 있는지를 나타낸다. 연구에 따르면 자신의 정체성의 특정 측면을 믿는 사람은 그 믿음에 따라 행동할 가능성이 더 높다. 예를 들어, 자신을 "유권자"라고 느끼는 사람은 단순히 "투표"가 자신이 하고 싶은 행동이라고 주장하는 사람보다 투표할 가능성이 더 높았다. 마찬가지로, 운동을 자신의 정체성의 일부로 받아들이는 사람은 훈련하라고 스스로를 설득할 필요가 없다. 옳은 일을 하는 것은 쉽다. 결국, 자신의 행동과 정체성이 완벽하게 일치하면 더 이상 행동 변화를 추구하지 않아도 된다. 당신은 그저 당신 스스로가 그렇다고 이미 믿고 있는 유형의 사람처럼 행동하고 있을 뿐이다.

Why? 왜 정답일까?

투표를 예로 들며 생각하는 대로 행동한다(Your behaviors are usually a reflection of your identity.)는 얘기를 하고 있다. 따라서 제목으로 가장 적절한 것은 ① 'Action Comes from Who You Think You Are'이다.

- reflection ⓝ 반영
- indication ⓝ 지시
- accept ⓥ 받아들이다
- identity ⓝ 정체성
- similarly 🄰 비슷하게
- behavior ⓝ 행동

구문 풀이

6행 For example, people who identified as "being a voter" were more likely to
(주격관계대명사) *(be likely to : ~할 것 같다)*
vote than those who simply claimed "voting" was an action (which/that) they
(지시대명사) *(주격관계대명사)* *(목적격관계대명사)*
wanted to perform.

---

25 2016년과 2019년의 지역별 전자 폐기물 수거율 및 재활용률
정답률 84% | 정답 ③

다음 도표의 내용과 일치하지 않는 것은?

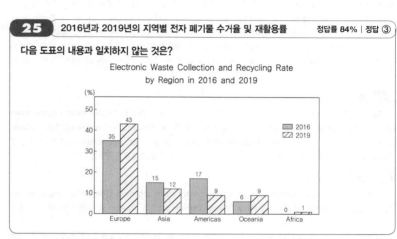

Electronic Waste Collection and Recycling Rate by Region in 2016 and 2019

The above graph shows / the electronic waste collection and recycling rate / by region / in 2016 and 2019.
위의 표는 보여준다. / 전자 쓰레기 수거와 재활용률을 / 지역마다의 / 2016년과 2019년의
① In both years, / Europe showed / the highest electronic waste collection and recycling rates.
두 해 모두, / 유럽은 보여 주었다. / 가장 높은 전자 쓰레기 수거와 재활용률을
② The electronic waste collection and recycling rate / of Asia / in 2019 / was lower than in 2016.
전자 쓰레기 수거와 재활용률은 / 아시아의 / 2019년의 / 2019년보다 낮았다.
☑ The Americas ranked third / both in 2016 and in 2019, / with 17 percent and 9 percent / respectively.
아메리카는 3위를 차지했다. / 2016과 2019년 모두 / 17퍼센트와 9퍼센트로 / 각각
④ In both years, / the electronic waste collection and recycling rate / in Oceania / remained under 10 percent.
두 해 모두, / 전자 쓰레기 수거와 재활용률은 / 오세아니아의 / 10퍼센트 미만을 유지했다.
⑤ Africa had / the lowest electronic waste collection and recycling rates / in both 2016 and 2019, / showing the smallest gap / between 2016 and 2019.
아프리카는 가졌다. / 가장 낮은 전자 쓰레기 수거와 재활용률을 / 2016년과 2019년 모두 / 가장 작은 차이를 보여 주며 / 2016년과 2019년의

위 도표는 2016년과 2019년의 지역별 전자 폐기물 수거율 및 재활용률을 보여 준다. 두 해 모두 유럽이 가장 높은 전자 폐기물 수거율 및 재활용률을 보였다. 2019년 아시아의 전자 폐기물 수거율 및 재활용률은 2016년보다 낮았다. (남·북·중앙)아메리카는 2016년과 2019년 모두 3위를 기록했으며, 그 비율은 각각 17퍼센트와 9퍼센트였다. 오세아니아의 전자 폐기물 수거율 및 재활용률은 두 해 모두 10퍼센트 아래에 머물렀다. 아프리카는 2016년과 2019년 모두 가장 낮은 전자 폐기물 수거율 및 재활용률을 기록했으며, 두 해 사이의 비율 격차가 가장 적었다.

Why? 왜 정답일까?

아메리카는 2016년에는 2위, 2019년에는 3위를 차지했기 때문에 도표의 내용과 일치하지 않는 것은 ③이다.

- recycling ⓝ 재활용
- electronic 🄰 전자의
- remain ⓥ 남다
- region ⓝ 지역
- respectively 🄰 각각
- collection ⓝ 수집

구문 풀이

9행 Africa had the lowest electronic waste collection and recycling rates in
(최상급)
both 2016 and 2019, showing the smallest gap between 2016 and 2019.
(현재분사) *(최상급)*

26 Fritz Zwicky의 일생

정답률 81% | 정답 ⑤

Fritz Zwicky에 관한 다음 글의 내용과 일치하지 <u>않는</u> 것은?

① 불가리아의 Varna에서 태어났다.
② 스위스에서 수학과 물리학 교육을 받았다.
③ 미국으로 이주하여 연구를 이어갔다.
④ 우주 이해에 영향을 미친 수많은 이론을 발전시켰다.
✔ 초창기 제트 엔진을 개발한 후 교수로 임용되었다.

『Fritz Zwicky, / a memorable astrophysicist / who coined the term 'supernova', / was born in Varna, Bulgaria, / to a Swiss father and a Czech mother.』 ①의근거 일치
Fritz Zwicky는 / 기억할만한 천체물리학자인 / '초신성'이라는 단어를 만든 / 불가리아의 Varna에서 태어났다. / 스위스인 아버지와 체코인 어머니에게서

At the age of six, / he was sent to his grandparents / who looked after him / for most of his childhood in Switzerland.
6살에, / 그는 그의 조부모님께 보내졌다. / 그를 돌봐준 / 그의 유아기 대부분을 / 스위스에서

『There, / he received an advanced education / in mathematics and physics.』 ②의근거 일치
그곳에서, / 그는 고등 교육을 받았다. / 수학과 물리학의

『In 1925, / he emigrated to the United States / and continued his physics research / at California Institute of Technology (Caltech).』 ③의근거 일치
1925년에, / 그는 미국으로 이주했다. / 그리고 그의 물리학 연구를 이어나갔다. / California Institute of Technoloy(Caltech)에서

『He developed / numerous theories / that have had a profound influence / on the understanding of our universe / in the early 21st century.』 ④의근거 일치
그는 발전시켰다. / 수많은 이론들을 / 풍부한 영향을 끼친 / 우리의 우주를 이해하는 데에 / 초기 21세기에

⑤의근거 불일치
『After being appointed / as a professor of astronomy / at Caltech in 1942, / he developed / some of the earliest jet engines / and holds more than 50 patents, / many in jet propulsion.』
임용된 후 / 천문학의 교수로써 / 1942년에 Caltech에서 / 그는 발전시켰다. / 초창기 제트 엔진을 / 그리고 50개 이상의 저작권을 가지고 있었다. / 제트 추진 분야에서

'초신성'이라는 용어를 만든 유명한 천체 물리학자 Fritz Zwicky는 불가리아의 Varna에서 스위스인 아버지와 체코인 어머니 사이에서 태어났다. 여섯 살이 되던 해, 그는 스위스에서 보낸 어린 시절의 대부분 동안 그를 돌봐준 조부모에게 보내졌다. 그곳에서, 그는 수학과 물리학에 대한 고급 교육을 받았다. 1925년 미국으로 이주하여 California Institute of Technology (Caltech)에서 물리학 연구를 이어갔다. 그는 21세기 초 우주에 대한 이해에 지대한 영향을 미친 수많은 이론을 발전시켰다. 1942년 Caltech의 천문학 교수로 임용된 후 그는 초창기 제트 엔진을 개발했고, 50개 이상의 특허를 보유하고 있으며, 이 중 많은 부분이 제트 추진 분야의 특허이다.

Why? 왜 정답일까?

1942년 Caltech의 천문학 교수로 임용된 후 초창기 제트 엔진을 개발했다(After being appointed as a professor of astronomy at Caltech in 1942, he developed some of the earliest jet engines and holds more than 50 patents, many in jet propulsion)고 했기 때문에, 글의 내용과 일치하지 않는 것은 ⑤ '초창기 제트 엔진을 개발한 후 교수로 임용되었다.'이다.

Why? 왜 오답일까?

① 'Fritz Zwicky, a memorable astrophysicist who coined the term 'supernova', was born in Varna, Bulgaria to a Swiss father and a Czech mother.'의 내용과 일치한다.
② 'There, he received an advanced education in mathematics and physics.'의 내용과 일치한다.
③ 'In 1925, he emigrated to the United States and continued his physics research at California Institute of Technology (Caltech).'의 내용과 일치한다.
④ 'He developed numerous theories that have had a profound influence on the understanding of our universe in the early 21st century.'의 내용과 일치한다.

● memorable ⓐ 기억할만한
● coin ⓥ (단어를) 발명하다
● patent ⓝ 특허권
● astrophysicist ⓝ 천제물리학자
● develop ⓥ 발달시키다
● propulsion ⓝ 추진력

구문 풀이

8행 He developed numerous theories that have had a profound influence on
주격관계대명사 현재완료시제
the understanding of our universe in the early 21st century.
동명사

27 미식 베이킹 대회

정답률 91% | 정답 ④

Gourmet Baking Competition에 관한 다음 안내문의 내용과 일치하지 <u>않는</u> 것은?

① 8월 3일 토요일에 개최된다.
② 온라인으로 참가 신청이 가능하다.
③ 누구나 참가할 수 있다.
✔ 참가자 한 명이 여러 부문에 참여할 수 있다.
⑤ 모든 참가자에게 기념품이 제공될 것이다.

Gourmet Baking Competition
미식가 베이킹 대회
Get out your cookbooks / and dust off / your greatest baking recipes.
당신의 요리책을 꺼내세요. / 그리고 먼지를 털어내세요. / 당신의 최고의 베이킹 레시피의
When & Where
시간 & 장소
『5 p.m. – 7 p.m. Saturday, August 3rd』 ①의근거 일치
8월 3일 토요일 오후 5시부터 7시까지
Gourmet Baking Studio
미식가 베이킹 스튜디오
Registration
등록
『Register online / at www.bakeoff.org by July 25th.』 ②의근거 일치
등록은 온라인으로 진행됩니다. / 7월 25일까지 www.bakeoff.org에서

『Anyone can participate / in the competition.』 ③의근거 일치
누구든 참여할 수 있습니다. / 대회에
Categories
분류
Pies, Cakes, and Cookies
파이, 케이크, 쿠키
『Each person can only enter / one category.』 ④의근거 불일치
한 사람은 참여할 수 있습니다. / 한 분류에만
Prizes & Gifts
상 & 선물
Prizes will be given / to the top three in each category.
상은 지급됩니다. / 각 분류의 상위 3등에게
『Souvenirs will be given / to every participant.』 ⑤의근거 일치
기념품은 주어집니다. / 모든 참가자들에게

미식 베이킹 대회

요리책을 꺼내 최고의 베이킹 레시피의 먼지를 털어내세요.

일시 및 장소
• 8월 3일 토요일 오후 5시 – 오후 7시
• Gourmet Baking Studio

참가 신청
• 7월 25일까지 www.bakeoff.org에서 온라인으로 신청하세요.
• 누구나 대회에 참가할 수 있습니다.

부문
• 파이, 케이크, 쿠키
• 참가자 한 명당 하나의 부문만 참가할 수 있습니다.

상 및 선물
• 각 부문별 최상위 3명에게는 상이 수여됩니다.
• 모든 참가자에게 기념품이 주어집니다.

Why? 왜 정답일까?

'Categories' 항목의 'Each person can only enter one category.'의 문장을 보았을 때, 참가자 한 명은 한 부문에 참여할 수 있기 때문에, 일치하지 않는 것은 ④ '참가자 한 명이 여러 부문에 참여할 수 있다.'이다.

Why? 왜 오답일까?

① 'When & Where'의 '5 p.m. – 7 p.m. Saturday, August 3rd'의 내용과 일치한다.
② 'Register online at www.bakeoff.org by July 25th.'의 내용과 일치한다.
③ 'Anyone can participate in the competition.'의 내용과 일치한다.
⑤ 'Souvenirs will be given to every participant.'의 내용과 일치한다.

● competition ⓝ 경쟁
● gourmet ⓝ 미식가
● souvenir ⓝ 기념품
● cookbook ⓝ 요리책
● category ⓝ 분류

28 겨울 스포츠 프로그램

정답률 95% | 정답 ⑤

Winter Sports Program에 관한 다음 안내문의 내용과 일치하는 것은?

① 오후 2시에서 4시 사이에 실시된다.
② 네 종목의 강좌가 개설된다.
③ 참가 연령에 제한은 없다.
④ 모든 종목 강좌의 수강료는 같다.
✔ 장갑은 각자 가져와야 한다.

Winter Sports Program
겨울 스포츠 프로그램
Winter is coming! // Let's have some fun together!
겨울이 다가오고 있습니다! / 같이 즐깁시다!
Time & Location
시간 & 장소
『Every Sunday in December / from 1 p.m. to 3 p.m.』 ①의근거 불일치
12월 매주 일요일 / 오후 1시부터 3시까지
Grand Blue Ice Rink
Grand Blue 아이스 링크장에서
Lesson Details
수업 설명
『Ice Hockey, Speed Skating, and Figure Skating』 ②의근거 불일치
아이스하키, 스피드 스케이팅, 피겨 스케이팅
『Participants must be 8 years of age or older.』 ③의근거 불일치
참가자들은 8세 이상이어야 합니다.
Fee
수업료
『Ice Hockey: $200
아이스하키: 200달러
Speed Skating / Figure Skating: $150』 ④의근거 불일치
스피드 스케이팅 / 피겨 스케이팅: 150달러
Notice
알림
Skates and helmets will be provided / for free.
스케이터 헬멧은 제공될 것입니다. / 무료로
『You should bring / your own gloves.』 ⑤의근거 일치
가지고 오세요. / 여러분의 장갑을
For more information, / visit www.wintersports.com.
더 많은 정보는 / www.wintersports.com를 방문하세요.

겨울 스포츠 프로그램

겨울이 옵니다! 같이 즐겨요!

시간 및 장소
- 12월 매주 일요일 오후 1시부터 오후 3시까지
- Grand Blue Ice Rink

강좌 세부 정보
- 아이스하키, 스피드 스케이팅, 피겨 스케이팅
- 참가자는 8세 이상이어야 합니다.

수강료
- 아이스하키: $200
- 스피드 스케이팅 / 피겨 스케이팅: $150

주의 사항
- 스케이트와 헬멧이 무료로 제공됩니다.
- 장갑은 각자 가져와야 합니다.

※ 더 많은 정보를 얻고자 한다면, www.wintersports.com에 방문하세요.

Why? 왜 정답일까?
'You should bring your own gloves.'에서 얘기하듯, 장갑은 각자 가져와야하기 때문에 안내문의 내용과 일치하는 것은 ⑤이다.

Why? 왜 오답일까?
① 'Every Sunday in December from 1 p.m. to 3 p.m.'라고 하였기 때문에 오후 1시에서 3시 사이에 실시된다.
② 'Ice Hockey, Speed Skating, and Figure Skating'에서 세 종목의 강좌가 개설됨을 알 수 있다.
③ 'Participants must be 8 years of age or older.'에서 참가 연령이 8세 이상임을 알 수 있다.
④ 'Ice Hockey: $200, Speed Skating / Figure Skating:$150'에서 종목 강좌의 수강료가 다름을 알 수 있다.

- provide ⓥ 제공하다
- gloves ⓝ 장갑
- bring ⓥ 가져오다
- information ⓝ 정보

29 문명의 탄생 정답률 69% | 정답 ③
다음 글의 밑줄 친 부분 중, 어법상 틀린 것은? [3점]

The hunter-gatherer lifestyle, / which ① be described as "natural" to human beings, / appears to have had much to recommend it.
수렵 채집 생활 방식은, / "인간에게 자연스러운" 것으로 묘사될 수 있는, / 추천할 만한 점이 많이 있었던 것으로 보인다.
Examination of human remains / from early hunter-gatherer societies ② has suggested / that our ancestors enjoyed abundant food, / obtainable without excessive effort, / and suffered very few diseases.
인간 유해의 연구는 시사했다. / 초기 수렵 채집 사회에서 나온 / 우리의 조상들이 풍부한 음식을 누렸다는 것, / 과도한 노력 없이 얻을 수 있었고, / 매우 적은 질병만 겪었다는 것
If this is true, / it is not clear / why so many humans settled in permanent villages / and developed agriculture, / growing crops and domesticating animals: cultivating fields / was hard work, / and it was in farming villages ✓ that epidemic diseases first took root.
만약 이것이 사실이라면, / 분명하지 않다. / 왜 그렇게 많은 사람들이 영구적인 마을에 정착했는지 / 그리고 농업을 발전시켰는지, / 작물을 재배하고 동물을 길렀는지 / 경작하는 것은 / 힘든 일이었고, / 전염병이 처음으로 뿌리내린 곳은 농촌 마을이었다.
Whatever its immediate effect / on the lives of humans, / the development of settlements and agriculture / ④ undoubtedly led to a high increase in population density.
즉각적인 영향이 어떻든 간에, / 그것이 인간 삶에 미친 / 정착지와 농업의 발전은 / 틀림없이 인구 밀도의 큰 증가를 이끌었다.
This period, / known as the New Stone Age, / was a major turning point in human development, / ⑤ opening the way / to the growth of the first towns and cities, / and eventually leading to settled "civilizations."
이 시기는, / 신석기 시대로 알려진, / 인간 발전의 중요한 전환점이었다. / 길을 열며 / 첫 번째 마을과 도시의 성장을 향해, / 결국 정착된 "문명"으로 이어졌다.

수렵 채집 생활 방식은 인류에게 "자연스러운" 것으로 묘사될 수 있으며, 그것을 추천할 만한 많은 것(장점)이 있는 것으로 보인다. 초기 수렵 채집 사회의 유적 조사는 인류의 조상들이 과도한 노력 없이도 구할 수 있는 풍족한 식량을 누릴 수 있었고 질병에 걸리는 일도 거의 없었다는 것을 알려준다. 이것이 사실이라면, 왜 그렇게 많은 인류가 영구적으로 마을에 정착하여 농작물을 재배하고 동물을 기르면서 농업을 발달시켰는지는 분명하지 않다. 밭을 경작하는 것은 힘든 일이었고, 전염병이 처음 뿌리를 내린 곳은 농경 마을이었다. 인간의 삶에 미치는 즉각적인 영향이 무엇이든, 정착지와 농업의 발전은 의심의 여지없이 인구 밀도의 높은 증가로 이어졌다. 신석기 시대로 알려진 이 시기는 인류 발전의 중요한 전환점으로, 최초의 마을과 도시가 성장하는 길을 열었고, 결국 정착된 "문명"으로 이어졌다.

Why? 왜 정답일까?
뒷 문장이 완전하므로 관계대명사 'what' 대신 'that'이 쓰이는 것이 알맞다. 따라서 어법상 틀린 것은 ③이다.

Why? 왜 오답일까?
① 주어가 'The hunter-gather lifestyle'이기 때문에 수동태가 오는 것이 알맞다.
② 주어가 'Examination'이기 때문에 단수인 'has'가 오는 것이 알맞다.
④ 뒷문장이 불완전하고 선행사가 없으므로 선행사가 없는 관계대명사인 'what'은 적절하다.
⑤ '열면서'라는 해석이 자연스러우므로 현재분사 'opening'은 적절하다.

- describe ⓥ 묘사하다
- recommend ⓥ 추천하다
- epidemic ⓐ 전염병의
- natural ⓐ 자연적인
- remains ⓝ 유적, 유해
- permanent ⓐ 영구적인

구문 풀이
13행 This period, (which is) known as the New Stone Age, was a major turning [주격관계대명사+be동사 생략] [동사]
point in human development, opening the way to the growth of the first towns [현재분사1]
and cities, and eventually leading to settled "civilizations." [현재분사2]

★★★ 등급을 가르는 문제!

30 즐거움에 대한 유혹과 저축의 사용 정답률 36% | 정답 ⑤
다음 글의 밑줄 친 부분 중, 문맥상 낱말의 쓰임이 적절하지 않은 것은? [3점]

Many human and non-human animals / save commodities or money / for future consumption.
많은 인간과 비인간 동물들은 / 재화나 돈을 저축한다. / 미래 소비를 위해
This behavior / seems to reveal a preference / of a ① delayed reward / over an immediate one:
이 행동은 / 선호를 나타내는 것 같다. / 지연된 보상을 / 즉각적인 보상보다
the agent / gives up some immediate pleasure / in exchange for a future one.
행위자는 / 즉각적인 쾌락을 일부 포기한다. / 미래의 쾌락을 얻기 위해
Thus / the discounted value / of the future reward / should be ② greater than / the un-discounted value of the present one.
따라서 / 할인된 가치가 / 미래 보상의 / 더 커야 한다. / 현재 보상의 할인되지 않은 가치보다
However / in some cases the agent does not wait / for the envisioned occasion / but uses their savings ③ prematurely.
그러나 / 일부 경우에는 / 행위자가 기다리지 않고 / 예상된 기회를 / 저축을 미리 사용해 버린다.
For example, / early in the year / an employee might set aside money / to buy Christmas presents / but then spend it / on a summer vacation instead.
예를 들어, / 연초에 / 직원이 돈을 따로 모아둘 수 있다. / 크리스마스 선물을 사기 위해 / 그러나 그것을 써버린다. / 대신 여름휴가에
Such cases / could be examples of ④ weakness of will.
이런 경우는 / 의지력의 약함의 예시가 될 수 있다.
That is, / the agents may judge or resolve / to spend their savings / in a certain way for the greatest benefit / but then act differently / when temptation for immediate pleasure ✓ appears.
즉, / 행위자가 판단하거나 결심할 수 있다. / 그들의 저축을 쓰기로 / 최대의 이익을 위해 특정 방식으로 / 그러나 다르게 행동한다. / 즉각적인 쾌락의 유혹이 나타날 때

많은 인간과 인간이 아닌 동물은 물건이나 돈을 미래의 소비를 위해 저축한다. 이러한 행동은 즉각적인 보상보다 ① 지연된 보상을 선호하는 것을 드러내는 듯하다. 즉, 행위자는 미래의 보상을 위해 당장의 쾌락을 포기하는 것이다. 그러므로 미래 보상의 하락된 가치는 하락되지 않은 현재의 가치보다 ② 더 커야만 한다. 그러나, 어떤 경우 행위자가 계획한 일을 기다리지 않고 그들의 저축을 ③ 조기에 사용하는 경우도 있다. 예를 들어, 연초에 한 직원이 자기 돈을 크리스마스 선물을 사기 위해 모아두었지만 대신 여름휴가에 사용할 수 있다. 이러한 사례는 의지의 ④ 약함의 예시가 될 수 있다. 즉, 행위자는 그들의 저축을 가장 큰 이익을 위해 특정 방식으로 사용하기로 판단하거나 결심했으나 즉각적인 즐거움에 대한 유혹이 ⑤ 사라지면(→ 생기면) 다르게 행동할 수도 있다.

Why? 왜 정답일까?
미래의 즐거움을 위해 현재의 소비를 미루고 저축을 하지만, 즉각적인 즐거움에 대한 유혹이 생기면 소비를 한다(For example, early in the year an employee might set aside money to buy Christmas presents but then spend it on a summer vacation instead.)는 예를 들었으므로 ⑤ 'disappears'를 'appears'로 바꾸는 것이 문맥상 적절하다.

- commodity ⓝ 상품
- behavior ⓝ 행동
- preference ⓝ 선호
- envision ⓥ 계획하다
- consumption ⓝ 소비
- reveal ⓥ 드러내다
- immediate ⓐ 즉각적인
- resolve ⓥ 결심하다

구문 풀이
7행 However, in some cases the agent does not wait for the envisioned [동사1] [과거분사]
occasion but uses their savings prematurely. [동사2]

★★ 문제 해결 꿀~팁 ★★

▶ 많이 틀린 이유는?
글은 문제의 지문은 사람들이 미래의 소비를 위해 저축하지만, 때로는 그 돈을 너무 일찍 써버리는 상황을 설명하고 있다. 문맥은 미래의 보상과 즉각적인 보상 사이의 선택을 다루고 있다. 문맥상 유혹은 사라지는 것이 아니라 존재하는 상황에서 즉각적인 보상에 넘어가게 되는 것이므로 "disappears(사라지다)"는 부적절하다. "appears(나타나다)"가 되어야 문맥에 맞다. 따라서 ⑤가 어색하다.
▶ 문제 해결 방법은?
문맥상 단어의 의미와 논리적 흐름을 파악하면 된다. 특히, 밑줄 친 부분의 단어가 문맥과 맞지 않는지 판단할 때 문장의 앞뒤 의미와 흐름을 충분히 고려하지 않으면 실수를 할 수 있기 때문에 정확한 해석이 필수적이다.

31 방해의 영향 정답률 52% | 정답 ②
다음 빈칸에 들어갈 말로 가장 적절한 것을 고르시오.
① misunderstandings – 오해
② interruptions – 방해 ✓
③ inequalities – 불평등
④ regulations – 규칙
⑤ arguments – 주장

The costs of interruptions / are well-documented.
방해의 비용은 / 잘 기록되어 있다.
Martin Luther King Jr. / lamented them / when he described / "that lovely poem / that didn't get written / because someone knocked on the door."
Martin Luther King Jr.는 / 그것들을 한탄했다. / 그가 묘사할 때 / "아름다운 시 / 쓰이지 못한 / 누군가 문을 두드렸기 때문에"
Perhaps / the most famous literary example / happened in 1797 / when Samuel Taylor Coleridge / started writing his poem *Kubla Khan* / from a dream he had / but then was visited / by an unexpected guest.
아마도 / 가장 유명한 문학적 예시는 / 1797년에 일어났다. / Samuel Taylor Coleridge / 그의 시 *Kubla Khan*을 쓰기 시작했을 때 / 그가 꿈에서 얻은 / 그러나 그 후 예기치 않은 손님이 찾아왔다.
For Coleridge, / by coincidence, / the untimely visitor / came at a particularly bad time.
Coleridge에게 / 우연히도 / 제때 오지 않은 손님이 / 특히 좋지 않은 시기에 왔다.
He forgot his inspiration / and left the work unfinished.
그는 영감을 잊어버렸고 / 작품을 미완성으로 남겼다.
While there are many documented cases / of sudden disruptions / that have had significant

[06회] 2024학년도 6월 **055**

consequences / for professionals in critical roles / such as doctors, nurses, control room operators, stock traders, and pilots, / they also impact most of us / in our everyday lives, / slowing down work productivity / and generally increasing stress levels.
여러 기록된 사례들이 있는 반면 / 갑작스러운 방해로 인해 / 중요한 직업을 가진 전문가들에게 / 심각한 결과를 초래한 / 예를 들어 의사, 간호사, 제어실 운영자, 주식 거래자, 그리고 조종사들이 / 그것들은 또한 우리 대부분에게 영향을 미친다. / 우리의 일상생활에서 / 업무 생산성을 저하시킴으로써 / 그리고 전반적으로 스트레스 수준을 높이며

방해로 인한 대가는 잘 기록되어 있다. Martin Luther King Jr.는 "누군가 문을 두드리는 바람에 쓰여지지 못한 사랑스러운 시"를 묘사하며 이를 슬퍼했다. 아마도 가장 유명한 문학적 사례는 1797년 Samuel Taylor Coleridge가 꿈을 꾸고 Kubla Khan이라는 시를 쓰기 시작했는데 뜻밖의 손님이 찾아왔을 때 일어났던 일일 것이다. 공교롭게도 Coleridge에게 이 불청객은 특히 좋지 않은 시기에 찾아왔다. 그는 영감을 잊고 작품을 미완성으로 남겼다. 의사, 간호사, 관제실 운영자, 주식 거래자, 조종사와 같은 중요한 역할을 담당하는 전문가들에게 심각한 결과를 초래한 갑작스러운 방해의 사례가 많이 기록되어 있지만, 갑작스러운 방해는 일상생활에서 대부분의 사람들에게도 영향을 미쳐 업무 생산성을 떨어뜨리며 일반적으로 스트레스 수준을 높인다.

Why? 왜 정답일까?

갑작스러운 방해로 영감을 잊고 작품을 완성하지 못한 예시(He forgot his inspiration and left the work unfinished.)와 같이, 집중의 흐름이 끊긴 예시를 제시한다. 따라서 빈칸에 들어갈 말로 가장 적절한 것은 ② 'interruptions'이다.

- well-documented 잘 기록된
- lament ⓥ 슬퍼하다
- describe ⓥ 묘사하다
- inspiration ⑩ 영감
- untimely ⓐ 때가 안 맞는
- interruption ⑩ 방해
- literary ⓐ 문학의
- productivity ⑩ 생산성

구문 풀이

[4행] Perhaps the most famous literary example happened in 1797 when Samuel Taylor Coleridge started writing his poem Kubla Khan from a dream (which/that) he had but then was visited by an unexpected guest.
(최상급 / 동사 / ~때 / start 동명사(= start to부정사) / 목적격관계대명사 생략)

---

32 뇌를 재구조화하는 집중　　　　　정답률 59% | 정답 ②

다음 빈칸에 들어갈 말로 가장 적절한 것을 고르시오.
① improved decision making – 향상된 의사결정
✓ the reshaping of the brain – 뇌의 재구조화
③ longterm mental tiredness – 장기적 정신 피곤
④ the development of hand skills – 손기술의 발달
⑤ increased levels of self-control – 자기통제의 향상된 정도

There's a lot of scientific evidence / demonstrating that / focused attention / leads to the reshaping of the brain.
많은 과학적 증거가 있다. / 증명하는 / 집중된 주의가 / 뇌의 재구조화로 이끔을
In animals / rewarded for noticing sound / (to hunt or to avoid being hunted for example), we find / much larger auditory centers / in the brain.
동물에서 / 소리를 인지한 것에 대해 보상받는 / (예를 들어 사냥을 하거나 사냥당하지 않기 위해). / 우리는 발견한다. / 훨씬 더 큰 청각 중심을 / 그들의 뇌에서
In animals / rewarded for sharp eyesight, / the visual areas are larger.
동물에서는 / 날카로운 시력을 보상받는, / 시각 영역이 더 크다.
Brain scans of violinists / provide more evidence, / showing dramatic growth and expansion / in regions of the cortex / that represent the left hand, / which has to finger the strings precisely, / often at very high speed.
바이올리니스트의 뇌 스캔은 / 더 많은 증거를 제공한다. / 극적인 성장과 확장을 보여주며 / 대뇌 피질 영역에서 / 왼손을 담당하는 / 현을 정확하게 짚어야 하는 / 종종 매우 빠른 속도로
Other studies / have shown that the hippocampus, / which is vital for spatial memory, / is enlarged in taxi drivers.
다른 연구들은 / 해마를 보여준다. / 공간 기억에 중요한 / 택시 운전사들에게 확대되었다는 것을
The point is / that the physical architecture of the brain / changes according to / where we direct our attention / and what we practice doing.
핵심은 / 뇌의 물리적 구조가 / 변화한다는 것이다. / 우리가 어디에 주의를 기울이는지 / 그리고 우리가 무엇을 연습하는지에 따라

주의 집중이 뇌의 재구조화로 이어진다는 과학적 증거는 많이 있다. (예를 들어 사냥하거나 사냥감이 되는 것을 피하기 위해), 소리를 알아채는 것에 대한 보상을 받은 동물에서 우리는 뇌의 청각 중추가 훨씬 더 큰 것을 발견한다. 예리한 시력에 대한 보상을 받은 동물에서는 시각 영역이 더 크다. 바이올린 연주자의 뇌 스캔 결과는 더 많은 증거를 제공해서 종종 매우 빠른 속도로 현을 정확하게 켜야 하는 왼손을 나타내는 피질 영역의 극적인 성장과 확장을 보여준다. 다른 연구는 공간 기억에 필수적인 해마가 택시 운전사에게서 확대되는 것을 보여준다. 요점은 우리가 어디에 주의를 기울이고 무엇을 연습하느냐에 따라 뇌의 물리적 구조가 달라진다는 것이다.

Why? 왜 정답일까?

시력과 청력이 중요한 동물들과 바이올린 연주자, 택시 운전사를 예로 들며 어느 부분에 집중하느냐에 따라 뇌가 발달하는 부분이 다르다는 글이다. 따라서 집중이 뇌를 재구조화한다는 ② 'the reshaping of the brain'이 빈칸에 적절하다.

- scientific ⓐ 과학적인
- demonstrate ⓥ 입증하다
- auditory ⓐ 청각의
- expansion ⑩ 확장
- hippocampus ⑩ 해마
- evidence ⑩ 증거
- attention ⑩ 집중
- dramatic ⓐ 극적인
- cortex ⑩ 대뇌피질
- enlarge ⓥ 확대되다

구문 풀이

[6행] Brain scans of violinists provide more evidence, showing dramatic growth and expansion in regions of the cortex that represent the left hand, which has to finger the strings precisely, often at very high speed.
(동사 / 현재분사 / 주격관계대명사 / 주격관계대명사)

---

33 인간 생각 진화　　　　　정답률 51% | 정답 ⑤

다음 빈칸에 들어갈 말로 가장 적절한 것을 고르시오. [3점]
① physical power to easily hunt prey – 사냥감을 쉽게 사냥하기 위한 물리적 힘
② individual responsibility in one's inner circle – 내부 원에서의 개인적 책임
③ instinctive tendency to avoid natural disasters – 자연 재해를 피하는 본능적인 경향
④ superiority in the number of one's descendants – 후손의 수의 우위
✓ competition and conflicts with other human tribes – 다른 인간 부족과의 경쟁과 갈등

How did the human mind evolve?
인간의 정신은 어떻게 진화했을까?
One possibility / is that competition and conflicts with other human tribes / caused our brains to evolve the way they did.
한 가지 가능성은 / 다른 인간 부족들과의 경쟁과 갈등이 / 우리의 뇌가 지금과 같은 방식으로 진화하게 만들었다는 것이다.
A human tribe / that could out-think its enemies, / even slightly, / possessed a vital advantage.
인간 부족은 / 적들보다 더 생각할 수 있다면, / 조금이라도, / 중요한 이점을 가졌다.
The ability of your tribe / to imagine and predict / where and when a hostile enemy tribe might strike, / and plan accordingly, / gives your tribe a significant military advantage.
당신의 부족이 가진 능력은 / 상상하고 예측하는 / 적대적인 부족이 어디에서 언제 공격할지를 / 그리고 그에 맞춰 계획하는 능력은 / 당신의 부족에게 중요한 군사적 이점을 준다.
The human mind became a weapon / in the struggle for survival, / a weapon far more decisive than any before it.
인간의 정신은 무기가 되었다. / 생존을 위한 투쟁에서 / 이전의 어떤 무기보다 훨씬 더 결정적인 무기로
And this mental advantage / was applied, / over and over, / within each succeeding generation.
그리고 이 정신적 이점은 / 적용되었다. / 반복해서, / 각 후속 세대에서
The tribe that could out-think its opponents / was more likely to succeed in battle / and would then / pass on the genes / responsible for this mental advantage / to its offspring.
상대보다 더 잘 생각할 수 있는 부족은 / 전투에서 성공할 가능성이 더 높았고 / 그 후 / 유전자를 물려주었다. / 이 정신적 이점을 책임지는 / 자손에게
You and I / are the descendants of the winners.
너와 나는 승자들의 후손이다.

인간의 생각은 어떻게 진화했을까? 한 가지 가능성은 다른 인간 부족과의 경쟁과 갈등이 우리 두뇌가 그렇게 진화하도록 했다는 것이다. 적보다 조금이라도 더 우수한 생각을 할 수 있는 인간 부족은 중요한 우위를 점했다. 적대적인 적 부족이 언제 어디서 공격할지 상상하고 예측하며 그에 따라 계획을 세울 수 있는 능력은 부족에게 상당한 군사적 우위를 가져다준다. 인간의 생각은 생존을 위한 투쟁에서 그 이전의 어떤 무기보다 훨씬 더 결정적인 무기가 되었다. 그리고 이러한 정신적 우위는 다음 세대에 걸쳐 계속해서 적용되었다. 상대보다 더 우수한 생각을 할 수 있는 부족은 전투에서 승리할 확률이 높았고, 이러한 정신적 우위를 담당하는 유전자를 자손에게 물려주었다. 당신과 나는 승자의 후손이다.

Why? 왜 정답일까?

적 부족과 경쟁을 예측하고 계획을 세울 수 있는 부족이 상당한 군사적 우위를 가졌다(The ability of your tribe to imagine and predict where and when a hostile enemy tribe might strike, and plan accordingly, gives your tribe a significant military advantage.)고 하며 조심스러운 부족이 후손을 가질 가능성이 높았다고 얘기한다. 따라서 빈칸에 들어갈 알맞은 말은 ⑤ 'competition and conflicts with other human tribes'이다.

- evolve ⓥ 진화하다
- tribe ⑩ 부족
- apply ⓥ 적용되다
- weapon ⑩ 무기
- gene ⑩ 유전자
- possibility ⑩ 가능성
- advantage ⑩ 장점
- hostile ⓐ 적대적인
- opponent ⑩ 상대
- descendant ⑩ 후손

구문 풀이

[5행] The ability of your tribe to imagine and predict where and when a hostile enemy tribe might strike, and plan accordingly, gives your tribe a significant military advantage.
(to부정사1 / to부정사2 / to부정사3 / 동사)

★★★ 등급을 가르는 문제!

34 브레인라이팅　　　　　정답률 41% | 정답 ①

다음 빈칸에 들어갈 말로 가장 적절한 것을 고르시오. [3점]
✓ developing and assessing ideas individually – 개별적으로 아이디어를 전개하고 평가하기
② presenting and discussing ideas out loud – 아이디어를 크게 발표하고 논의하기
③ assigning different roles to each member – 각각의 구성원에게 다른 역할을 할당하기
④ coming to an agreement on these options – 선택사항에 동의에 다다르기
⑤ skipping the step of judging these options – 이 선택사항을 판단하는 단계를 건너뛰기

To find / the hidden potential in teams, / instead of brainstorming, / we're better off shifting / to a process called brainwriting.
찾기 위해서 / 팀의 숨겨진 잠재력을 / 브레인스토밍 대신 / 우리는 바꾸는 것이 낫다. / 브레인라이팅이라고 불리는 과정으로
The initial steps are solo.
첫 단계는 단독이다.
You start / by asking everyone / to generate ideas / separately.
당신은 시작한다. / 모두에게 부탁하며 / 아이디어를 만들라고 / 개별적으로
Next, / you pool them / and share them / anonymously among the group.
그다음, / 당신은 아이디어를 모은다. / 그리고 팀원과 공유한다. / 팀에서 익명으로
To preserve independent judgment, / each member evaluates them / on their own.
독립적인 판단을 보전하기 위해서, / 각각의 팀원은 아이디어를 평가한다. / 그들 스스로
Only then / does the team come together / to select and refine / the most promising options.
그런 다음에야 / 팀은 모두 모여서 / 고르고 정제한다. / 가장 유망한 아이디어를
By developing and assessing ideas individually / before choosing and elaborating them, / teams can surface and advance possibilities / that might not get attention otherwise.
아이디어를 개별적으로 발달시키고 평가하므로써, / 아이디어를 선택하고 다듬기 전에 / 팀은 가능성을 마주하고 향상시킬 수 있다. / 그렇지 않으면 관심을 받지 못했을 아이디어의

This brainwriting process / makes sure / that all ideas are brought to the table / and all voices are brought into the conversation.
브레인라이팅 과정은 / 확실하게 한다. / 모든 아이디어가 관심을 받고 / 모든 목소리가 대화에 참여하도록
It is especially effective in groups / that struggle to achieve / collective intelligence.
이것은 특히 팀에 효과적이다. / 달성하기 위해 고군분투하는 / 집단지성을

팀의 숨겨진 잠재력을 찾으려면 브레인스토밍 대신 브레인라이팅이라는 과정으로 전환하는 것이 좋다. 초기 단계는 혼자서 진행한다. 먼저 모든 사람에게 개별적으로 아이디어를 내도록 요청한다. 그런 다음, 아이디어를 모아 익명으로 그룹에 공유한다. 독립적인 판단을 유지하기 위해 각 구성원이 스스로 그 아이디어를 평가한다. 그러고 나서야 팀이 함께 모여 가장 유망한 옵션을 선택하고 다듬는다. 아이디어를 선택하고 구체화하기 전에 개별적으로 아이디어를 전개하고 평가함으로써 팀은 다른 방법으로는 주목받지 못했을 가능성을 드러내고 발전시킬 수 있다. 이 브레인라이팅 과정은 모든 아이디어를 테이블에 올려놓고 모든 의견을 대화에 반영할 수 있도록 한다. 특히 집단 지성을 달성하는 데 어려움을 겪는 그룹에서 효과적이다.

Why? 왜 정답일까?
기존의 'brainstorming'과는 차이가 있는 'brainwriting'의 개념을 제시하며, 'To preserve independent judgment, each member evaluates them on their own.'이라며 개인적으로 모든 의견을 고려해야함을 얘기한다. 따라서 빈칸에 들어갈 알맞은 말은 ① 'developing and assessing ideas individually'이다.

- potential ⓝ 가능성
- separately ⓐⓓ 개별적으로
- surface ⓥ 드러내다
- shift ⓥ 바꾸다
- anonymously ⓐⓓ 익명으로
- struggle ⓥ 다투다

구문 풀이
7행 Only then does the team come together to select and refine the most
도치   동사1   to부정사(부사적 용법)   동사2   최상급
promising options.

★★ 문제 해결 꿀~팁 ★★
▶ 많이 틀린 이유는?
빈칸이 포함된 문장을 제대로 해석하지 못했거나, 앞뒤 문맥을 통해 논리적인 연결을 찾는 데 어려움을 겪었기 때문이다. 특히, 빈칸에 들어갈 적절한 표현을 찾기 위해서는 문장의 흐름과 글의 전반적인 논리를 정확하게 파악해야 하는데, 이 부분에서 실수하는 경우가 많다. 'brainstorming'과 다른 'brainwriting'의 특징을 파악하는 것이 이 문제를 풀기 위해 중요하다.
▶ 문제 해결 방법은?
빈칸 문제는 글의 흐름, 문맥 파악이 중요하다. 해당 글에서는 'brainwriting'의 절차를 설명하므로, 번호를 매기며 읽는 것이 직관적인 문제 풀이에 도움이 될 수 있다.

---

35 주인의식의 힘   정답률 53% | 정답 ③

다음 글에서 전체 흐름과 관계 없는 문장은?

Simply giving employees a sense of agency / — a feeling that they are in control, that they have genuine decision-making authority — / can radically increase how much energy and focus they bring to their jobs.
단순히 직원들에게 주권을 주는 것은 / —그들이 통제하고 있고, 진정한 의사 결정 권한을 가지고 있다는 느낌— / 그들이 직무에 투입하는 에너지와 집중력을 급격히 증가시킬 수 있다.
① One 2010 study / at a manufacturing plant in Ohio, / for instance, / carefully examined assembly-line workers / who were empowered / to make small decisions about their schedules and work environment.
2010년의 한 연구에서 / 오하이오의 한 제조 공장에서 / 예를 들어, / 조립 라인 노동자들을 면밀히 조사했다. / 권한을 부여받은 / 그들은 자신의 일정과 작업 환경에 대해 소규모 결정을 내릴
② They designed their own uniforms / and had authority over shifts / while all the manufacturing processes and pay scales stayed the same.
그들은 자신의 유니폼을 디자인했고 / 교대 근무에 대한 권한을 가졌으며 / 모든 제조 과정 및 급여 체계는 그대로 유지되었다.
☑ It led to decreased efficiency / because their decisions / were not uniform / or focused on / meeting organizational goals.
그것은 효율성 저하로 이끌었다. / 왜냐하면 그들의 결정이 / 통일되지 않았고 / 또는 집중하지 않았기 때문이다. / 조직의 목표달성에
④ Within two months, / productivity at the plant increased by 20 percent, / with workers taking shorter breaks and making fewer mistakes.
두 달 안에, / 공장의 생산성은 20% 증가했고, / 노동자들이 더 짧은 휴식을 취하고 실수를 덜 하게 되었다.
⑤ Giving employees a sense of control / improved how much self-discipline they brought to their jobs.
직원들에게 통제감을 주는 것은 / 그들이 직무에 가져오는 자기 규율의 수준을 향상시켰다.

단순히 직원들에게 주인의식(그들이 통제하고 있다는 느낌, 진정한 의사 결정 권한이 있다는 느낌)을 주는 것만으로도 그들이 자신의 업무에 쓰는 에너지와 집중력을 급격하게 높일 수 있다. ① 예를 들어, 오하이오 주의 한 제조 공장에서 진행된 2010년의 한 연구는 그들의 일정과 작업 환경에 대한 작은 결정 권한을 부여받은 조립 라인 근로자를 주의 깊게 살펴보았다. ② 그들은 그들 자신의 유니폼을 디자인했고, 근무 교대에 대한 권한을 가진 반면에, 모든 생산 과정과 임금 규모는 동일하게 유지되었다. ③ 결정이 합치되거나 조직의 목표 달성에 초점이 맞춰지지 않았기 때문에 그것은 효율성을 낮추는 결과를 낳았다. ④ 두 달 만에 직원들은 휴식 시간을 더 짧게 가졌고, 실수를 더 적게 하였으며, 그 공장의 생산성은 20퍼센트 증가했다. ⑤ 자신들이 통제권을 쥐고 있다는 느낌을 직원들에게 부여한 것이 그들이 업무에 끌어들이는 자기 통제력을 향상시켰다.

Why? 왜 정답일까?
직원들에게 주인의식을 주기만 함으로써 일의 효율이 높아짐을 얘기한다. 따라서 결정이 합치되거나 조직의 목표 달성에 초점이 맞춰져있지 않기 때문에 효율성을 낮춘다는 ③은 전체 흐름과 관계없다.

- employee ⓝ 직원
- genuine ⓐ 진짜의
- examine ⓥ 검사하다
- agency ⓝ 주인
- authority ⓝ 권한
- decision ⓝ 결정

구문 풀이
1행 Simply giving employees a sense of agency — a feeling that they are in
                  동명사   접속사
control, that they have genuine decision-making authority — can radically increase
           접속사
how much energy and focus (which/that) they bring to their jobs.
                         목적격관계대명사 생략

36 디지털 비즈니스 활동의 환경오염   정답률 56% | 정답 ③

주어진 글 다음에 이어질 글의 순서로 가장 적절한 것을 고르시오. [3점]
① (A) – (C) – (B)
② (B) – (A) – (C)
☑ (B) – (C) – (A)
④ (C) – (A) – (B)
⑤ (C) – (B) – (A)

As businesses shift some core business activities to digital, / such as sales, marketing, or archiving, / it is assumed that the impact on the environment will be less negative.
기업들이 일부 핵심 비즈니스 활동을 디지털로 전환하면서 / 판매, 마케팅 또는 기록 보관과 같은 / 환경에 미치는 영향이 덜 부정적일 것이라고 가정된다.
(B) However, / digital business activities / can still threaten the environment. /
그러나 / 디지털 비즈니스 활동은 / 여전히 환경을 위협할 수 있다.
In some cases, / the harm of digital businesses / can be even more hazardous.
어떤 경우에는 / 디지털 비즈니스가 주는 피해가 / 훨씬 더 해로울 수 있다.
A few decades ago, / offices used to have much more paper waste / since all documents were paper based.
몇 십 년 전만 해도 / 사무실은 훨씬 더 많은 종이 폐기물을 발생시켰다. / 모든 문서가 종이 기반이었기 때문에
(C) When workplaces / shifted from paper to digital documents, invoices, and emails, / it was a promising step to save trees.
직장이 / 종이에서 디지털 문서, 청구서와 이메일로 전환되었을 때, / 나무를 구할 수 있는 유망한 조치였다.
However, / the cost of the Internet and electricity for the environment / is neglected.
그러나 / 인터넷과 전기에 드는 환경 비용은 / 간과되고 있다.
A recent *Wired* report declared / that most data centers' energy source / is fossil fuels.
최근 *Wired* 보고서는 밝혔다. / 대부분의 데이터 센터의 에너지원이 / 화석 연료라고
(A) When we store bigger data on clouds, / increased carbon emissions / make our green clouds gray.
우리가 클라우드에 더 많은 데이터를 저장할 때, / 증가한 탄소 배출이 / 우리의 '녹색 클라우드'를 '회색 클라우드'로 만든다.
The carbon footprint of an email / is smaller than mail sent via a post office, / but still, / it causes four grams of CO_2, / and it can be as much as 50 grams if the attachment is big.
이메일의 탄소 발자국은 / 우편으로 보내는 편지보다 적지만, / 여전히 / 이로 인해 4g의 이산화탄소가 발생하고, / 첨부 파일이 크면 50g까지 될 수 있다.

기업이 영업, 마케팅, 파일 보관 등 일부 핵심 비즈니스 활동을 디지털로 전환함에 따라 환경에 미치는 영향이 덜 부정적일 것으로 예상된다.
(B) 그러나 디지털 비즈니스 활동은 여전히 환경을 위협할 수 있다. 경우에 따라서는 디지털 비즈니스가 끼치는 해악이 훨씬 더 위험할 수 있다. 수십 년 전만 해도 사무실에서는 모든 문서가 종이로 작성되었기 때문에 종이 폐기물이 훨씬 더 많았다.
(C) 직장에서 종이를 디지털 문서, (디지털) 송장, 이메일로 전환한 것은 나무를 보호할 수 있는 유망한 조치였다. 하지만 인터넷과 전기가 환경에 입히는 손실은 간과되고 있다. 최근 Wired의 보고서에 따르면 대부분의 데이터 센터의 에너지원은 화석 연료이다.
(A) 클라우드에 더 많은 데이터를 저장할수록 탄소 배출량이 증가하여 녹색 구름을 회색으로 변하게 만든다. 이메일의 탄소 발자국은 우체국을 통해 보내는 우편물보다 적지만 여전히 4g의 이산화탄소를 유발하며 첨부 파일이 크면 50g에 달할 수 있다.

Why? 왜 정답일까?
주어진 글은 비즈니스 활동을 디지털로 옮기며 환경에 미치는 영향이 부정적일 것이라고 한다. (B)에서는 디지털 비즈니스 활동이 환경에 여전히 위험할 수 있음을 언급하고, (C)는 인터넷과 전기가 환경에 입히는 손실이 간과된다며 자세히 심화 설명하고 있다. 따라서 (B)와 (A)가 이어져야 하고, 그 이후에도 가장 세부적인 예시인 클라우드를 설명하는 (C)가 마지막에 오는 순서가 알맞다. 따라서 답은 ③ '(B) – (C) – (A)'이다.

- core ⓐ 핵심적인, 가장 중요한
- environment ⓝ 환경
- hazardous ⓐ 위험한
- document ⓝ 자료
- electricity ⓝ 전기
- emission ⓝ 배출
- carbon footprint 탄소 발자국
- waste ⓝ 쓰레기
- workplace ⓝ 직장
- declare ⓥ 발표하다, 밝히다

구문 풀이
12행 A few decades ago, offices used to have much more paper waste since
       a few + 가산명사   used to 동사원형: ~하곤 했다.   때문에
all documents were paper based.

---

37 붉은 다람쥐와 회색 다람쥐   정답률 64% | 정답 ②

주어진 글 다음에 이어질 글의 순서로 가장 적절한 것을 고르시오.
① (A) – (C) – (B)
☑ (B) – (A) – (C)
③ (B) – (C) – (A)
④ (C) – (A) – (B)
⑤ (C) – (B) – (A)

Problems often arise / if an exotic species / is suddenly introduced to an ecosystem.
문제는 종종 발생한다. / 외래종이 / 갑자기 생태계에 도입되면
(B) Britain's red and grey squirrels / provide a clear example.
영국의 붉은 다람쥐와 회색 다람쥐는 / 명확한 예를 제공한다.
When the grey arrived from America in the 1870s, / both squirrel species competed for the same food and habitat, / which put the native red squirrel populations / under pressure.
회색 다람쥐가 1870년대에 미국에서 도착했을 때, / 두 다람쥐 종은 같은 먹이와 서식지를 두고 경쟁했다. / 이는 토종 붉은 다람쥐 개체군에게 / 큰 압박을 주었다.
(A) The grey had the edge / because it can adapt its diet; / it is able, for instance, / to eat green acorns, / while the red can only digest mature acorns.

회색 다람쥐는 우위를 가졌다. / 먹이를 적응할 수 있었기 때문에 / 예를 들어, 회색 다람쥐는 / 푸른 도토리를 먹을 수 있는 반면, / 붉은 다람쥐는 성숙한 도토리만 소화할 수 있었다.

Within the same area of forest, / grey squirrels can destroy the food supply / before red squirrels even have a bite.
같은 숲 지역에서 / 회색 다람쥐는 먹이 공급을 파괴할 수 있었다. / 붉은 다람쥐가 먹이를 먹기 전에

(C) Greys can also live / more densely and in varied habitats, / so have survived more easily when woodland has been destroyed.
회색 다람쥐는 또한 살 수 있어, / 더 밀집되고 다양한 서식지에서 / 숲이 파괴되었을 때 더 쉽게 생존했다.

As a result, / the red squirrel has come close to extinction / in England.
그 결과, / 붉은 다람쥐는 멸종 위기에 처하게 되었다. / 영국에서

외래종이 갑자기 생태계에 유입되면 문제가 종종 발생한다.

(B) 영국의 붉은색 다람쥐와 회색 다람쥐가 명확한 예를 제공한다. 1870년대 미국에서 회색 다람쥐가 왔을 때, 두 다람쥐 종은 동일한 먹이와 서식지를 놓고 경쟁했고, 이것이 토종의 붉은 다람쥐 개체군을 압박했다.

(A) 회색 다람쥐는 먹이를 조절할 수 있기 때문에 우위를 점했다. 예를 들어 회색 다람쥐는 설익은 도토리를 먹을 수 있는 반면, 붉은 다람쥐는 다 익은 도토리만 소화할 수 있다. 숲의 같은 지역 내에서 회색 다람쥐는 붉은 다람쥐가 한 입 먹기도 전에 식량 공급을 파괴할 수 있다.

(C) 회색 다람쥐는 또한 더 밀집하며 다양한 서식지에서 살 수 있어서 삼림이 파괴되었을 때 더 쉽게 살아남았다. 그 결과, 붉은 다람쥐는 영국에서 거의 멸종 위기에 이르렀다.

Why? 왜 정답일까?
외래종이 생태계에 미치는 위험성에 대해 얘기하고 있다. (B)에서는 회색 다람쥐가 외래종으로 붉은색 다람쥐의 서식지에 온 것을 언급하고, (A)는 외래종인 회색 다람쥐가 왜 붉은색 다람쥐보다 우위에 있었는지 설명하고 있다. 따라서 (B)와 (A)가 이어져야 하고, 그 이후의 결과가 나오는 (C)가 마지막에 오는 순서가 알맞다. 따라서 답은 ② '(B) - (A) - (C)'이다.

- exotic species 외래종
- introduce ⓥ 소개하다
- ecosystem ⓝ 생태계
- digest ⓥ 소화하다, 소화시키다
- bite ⓥ 베어 물다
- suddenly [ad] 갑자기
- edge ⓝ 우위
- acorn ⓝ 도토리
- destroy ⓥ 파괴하다, 말살하다
- survive ⓥ 살아남다

구문 풀이
13행 Greys can also live more densely and in varied habitats, so have survived
　　　동사1　　　　　수식어구1　　　　　수식어구2　　　　동사2
more easily when woodland has been destroyed.
　　　　　　　　　　　현재완료시제

★★★ 등급을 가르는 문제!
38 농작물 재배와 인구 증가의 관계　정답률 43% | 정답 ③
글의 흐름으로 보아, 주어진 문장이 들어가기에 가장 적절한 곳을 고르시오.

Growing crops forced people / to stay in one place.
농작물을 재배하는 것은 사람들을 / 한 곳에 머물게 했다.

Hunter-gatherers typically moved around frequently, / and they had to be able to carry / all their possessions with them / every time they moved.
수렵-채집인들은 주로 자주 이동했고, / 그들은 가지고 다닐 수 있어야 했다. / 그들의 모든 소지품을 / 그들이 이동할 때마다

① In particular, mothers / had to carry their young children.
특히 어머니들은 / 어린 자녀들을 데리고 다녀야 했다.

② As a result, hunter-gatherer mothers / could have only one baby / every four years or so, / spacing their births / so that they never had to carry more than one child at a time.
그 결과, 수렵-채집 사회의 어머니들은 / 아이를 하나만 낳을 수 있었다. / 대략 4년마다 / 출산 간격을 두어 / 한 번에 한 명 이상의 아이를 들고 다니지 않도록

✓ Farmers, on the other hand, / could live in the same place year after year / and did not have to worry about transporting young children long distances.
반면에 농부들은 / 매년 같은 장소에서 살 수 있었고 / 어린아이들을 먼 거리로 이동시키는 것에 대해 걱정할 필요가 없었다.

Societies that settled down in one place / were able to shorten their birth intervals / from four years to about two.
한 곳에 정착한 사회는 / 출산 간격을 단축할 수 있었다. / 4년에서 약 2년으로

④ This meant that each woman / could have more children / than her hunter-gatherer counterpart, / which in turn resulted in rapid population growth / among farming communities.
이는 각 여성이 / 더 많은 아이를 낳을 수 있다는 것을 의미했다. / 수렵-채집 사회의 여성보다 / 그 결과 인구가 급격하게 증가하게 되며 / 농경 사회에서

⑤ An increased population was actually an advantage / to agricultural societies, / because farming required large amounts of human labor.
증가한 인구는 실제로 장점이었다. / 농경 사회에 / 왜냐하면 농업은 많은 인간 노동을 필요로 했기 때문이다.

농작물 재배는 사람들이 한곳에 머무르게 했다. 수렵 채집인들은 일반적으로 자주 이동해야 했고, 이동할 때마다 모든 소유물을 가지고 다닐 수 있어야 했다. ① 특히, 어머니들은 어린 아이를 업고 이동해야 했다. ② 그 결과, 수렵 채집인 어머니들은 대략 4년마다 한 명의 아이만 낳을 수 있었고, 한 번에 한 명 이상의 아이를 업고 다닐 필요가 없도록 출산 간격을 두었다. ③ 반면, 농부들은 매년 같은 장소에서 살 수 있었고 어린아이를 장거리 이동시켜야 하는 걱정을 하지 않아도 되었다. 한곳에 정착하게 된 사회는 출산 간격을 4년에서 약 2년으로 단축할 수 있었다. ④ 이는 여성 한 명이 수렵 채집인인 상대보다 더 많은 아이를 낳을 수 있다는 것을 의미했고, 그 결과 그것은 농경 사회에서 급격한 인구 증가를 야기했다. ⑤ 인구 증가는 실제로 농경 사회에 유리했는데, 왜냐하면 농사는 많은 인간의 노동력을 필요로 했기 때문이다.

Why? 왜 정답일까?
글에서는 수렵 채집인들과 농작물 재배인을 비교하며 수렵 채집인들은 이동이 잦기 때문에 아이를 많이 낳을 수 없었지만, 농작물 재배인들은 이동이 거의 없었기 때문에 아이를 많이 낳을 수 있었다는 설명이다. 농작물 재배인들이 아이를 옮기지 않아도 된다는 내용은 따라서 ③에 오는 것이 가장 적절하다.

- transport ⓥ 이송하다
- possession ⓝ 소유물, 소지품
- frequently [ad] 자주
- settled ⓐ 정착한

- interval ⓝ 간격
- rapid ⓐ 빠른
- agricultural society 농경 사회, 농업사회
- counterpart ⓝ 상대
- population ⓝ 인구
- labor ⓝ 노동

구문 풀이
1행 Farmers, on the other hand, could live in the same place year after year
　　　　　　　　　　　　　　　　　동사1
and did not have to worry about transporting young children long distances.
　　　동사2　　　　　　　　　　　　동명사

★★ 문제 해결 꿀~팁 ★★
▶ 많이 틀린 이유는?
문단 내 문장들의 논리적 흐름을 잘못 이해했기 때문이다. 글의 전개가 사냥-채집 사회와 농경 사회의 차이점에 대한 비교로 이어진다. 수렵 채집인과 농경인의 상황을 비교하며 아이를 낳기가 불리하거나 유리하다는 결론으로 이끈다.
▶ 문제 해결 방법은?
문장 간의 인과관계와 논리적 연결을 파악해야 한다. ②번 문장은 사냥-채집 사회의 출산 간격을 설명하며, 여러 아이를 동시에 돌볼 수 없는 이유를 명시한다. ③번 문장은 농경 사회로 넘어가면서 출산 간격이 줄어든 이유를 설명한다. 이처럼 각 문장은 원인과 결과로 연결되어 있기 때문에, ②번 문장이 사냥-채집 사회의 설명을 마무리 짓고, ③번 문장에서 농경 사회로 자연스럽게 넘어가야 한다.

★★★ 등급을 가르는 문제!
39 유년기의 길이에 따른 적응의 차이　정답률 35% | 정답 ④
글의 흐름으로 보아, 주어진 문장이 들어가기에 가장 적절한 곳을 고르시오. [3점]

Spending time as children allows animals / to learn about their environment.
어린 시절을 보내는 것은 동물들이 / 환경에 대해 배우게 해준다.

Without childhood, / animals must rely more fully on hardware, / and therefore be less flexible.
어린 시절이 없으면, / 동물들은 더 완전히 하드웨어에 의존해야 하고, / 따라서 덜 유연해진다.

① Among migratory bird species, / those that are born knowing how, when, and where to migrate / — those that are migrating / entirely with instructions they were born with — / sometimes have very inefficient migration routes.
철새들 중에서 / 태어날 때부터 언제, 어디로, 어떻게 이동할지를 알고 태어난 종들은 / — 이주하는 종들 / 태어날 때 받은 지시만으로 — / 때때로 매우 비효율적인 이동 경로를 가진다.

② These birds, born knowing how to migrate, / don't adapt easily.
이주하는 방법을 알고 태어난 이 새들은 / 쉽게 적응하지 못한다.

③ So when lakes dry up, / forest becomes farmland, / or climate change pushes breeding grounds farther north, / those birds that are born knowing how to migrate / keep flying by the old rules and maps.
그래서 호수가 마르거나 / 숲이 농지로 바뀌거나 / 기후 변화로 인해 번식지가 더 북쪽으로 밀려나면 / 이주 방법을 알고 태어난 새들은 / 여전히 오래된 규칙과 지도를 따라 비행한다.

✓ By comparison, / birds with the longest childhoods, / and those that migrate with their parents, / tend to have the most efficient migration routes.
반면에, / 가장 긴 어린 시절을 가진 새들과 / 부모와 함께 이주하는 새들은 / 가장 효율적인 이동 경로를 가지는 경향이 있다.

Childhood facilitates / the passing on of cultural information, / and culture can evolve faster than genes.
어린 시절은 돕는다. / 문화적 정보를 전달하는 것을 / 문화는 유전자보다 더 빠르게 진화할 수 있다.

⑤ Childhood / gives flexibility / in a changing world.
어린 시절은 / 유연성을 준다. / 변화하는 세상에서

동물은 유년기를 보내면서 환경에 대해 배울 수 있다. 유년기가 없으면, 동물은 하드웨어에 더 많이 의존해야 하므로 유연성이 떨어질 수밖에 없다. ① 철새 중에서도 언제, 어디로, 어떻게 이동해야 하는지를 알고 태어나는 새들, 즉 전적으로 태어날 때부터 주어진 지침에 따라 이동하는 새들은 때때로 매우 비효율적인 이동 경로를 가지고 있다. ② 이동 방법을 알고 태어난 새들은 쉽게 적응하지 못한다. ③ 따라서 호수가 마르거나 숲이 농지로 바뀌거나 기후 변화로 번식지가 더 북쪽으로 밀려났을 때, 이동하는 방법을 알고 태어난 새들은 기존의 규칙과 지도를 따라 계속 날아간다. ④ 이에 비해 유년기가 가장 길고 부모와 함께 이동하는 새는 가장 효율적인 이동 경로를 가지고 있는 경향이 있다. 유년기는 문화적 정보의 전달을 촉진하며, 문화는 유전자보다 더 빠르게 진화할 수 있다. ⑤ 유년기는 변화하는 세상에서 유연성을 제공한다.

Why? 왜 정답일까?
유년기가 긴 동물과 유년기가 짧은 동물의 적응의 차이에 대한 글이다. 바뀐 환경에 적응하려면 유년기가 긴 것이 유리하기 때문에 유년기의 문화적 정보가 제공하는 이점의 앞부분이며 유년기가 짧은 동물들의 행동을 설명하는 문장 뒤인 ④에 주어진 문장이 오는 것이 가장 적절하다.

- comparison ⓝ 비교
- migrate ⓥ 이주하다
- flexible ⓐ 유연한
- entirely [ad] 전적으로
- inefficient ⓐ 비효율적인
- dry up (강·호수 등이) 바짝 마르다
- facilitate ⓥ 촉진하다
- childhood ⓝ 유년기
- migration ⓝ 이주
- migratory bird 철새
- instruction ⓝ 지시, 명령
- adapt ⓥ 적응하다
- breeding ground (야생 동물의) 번식지
- flexibility ⓝ 유연성

구문 풀이
5행 Without childhood, animals must rely more fully on hardware, and therefore
　　　~없이　　　　　　　　동사1
be less flexible.
동사2

★★ 문제 해결 꿀~팁 ★★
▶ 많이 틀린 이유는?
주어진 글은 "어린 시절이 긴 새들이 가장 효율적인 이동 경로를 가지고 있다"는 내용을 설명하고 있다. 이어지는 내용도 어린 시절을 통한 학습과 유전적 지식에만 의존하는 새들에 대한 비교를 다루고 있음을 알 수 있다. 따라서 어린 시절이 길지 않은 새들과의 비교하는 부분에 들어가야 가장 알맞다.

▶ 문제 해결 방법은?
문장 간 논리적 연결과 핵심 아이디어를 파악하는 것이 중요하다. 특히 'By comparison'과 같이 반대 의미를 담고 구를 주의해서 보자. 글을 읽으며 자신만의 기호로 글의 흐름의 변화를 표시하는 것도 도움이 된다.

40 | 장애를 가진 사람들의 디지털 프로젝트 | 정답률 49% | 정답 ①

다음 글의 내용을 한 문장으로 요약하고자 한다. 빈칸 (A), (B)에 들어갈 말로 가장 적절한 것은?

	(A)		(B)		(A)		(B)
✓	overlooked 간과하다	⋯⋯	inclusive 포함하는	②	accepted 받아들이다	⋯⋯	practical 실용적인
③	considered 고려하다	⋯⋯	inclusive 포함하는	④	accepted 받아들이다	⋯⋯	abstract 추상적인
⑤	overlooked 간과하다	⋯⋯	abstract 추상적인				

Over the last several decades, / scholars have developed / standards for how best to create, organize, present, and preserve digital information / for future generations.
지난 수십 년 동안, / 학자들은 개발해 왔다. / 디지털 정보를 가장 잘 창조하고, 조직하고, 제공하고, 보존하는 방법에 대한 기준들을 / 미래 세대를 위해

What has remained neglected for the most part, / however, are the needs of people with disabilities.
그러나 대체로 무시되어 온 것은 / 장애를 가진 사람들의 필요이다.

As a result, / many of the otherwise most valuable digital resources / are useless / for people who are deaf or hard of hearing, / as well as for people who are blind, have low vision, or have difficulty / distinguishing particular colors.
그 결과, / 가장 가치 있는 디지털 자원들 중 많은 것이 / 쓸모가 없다. / 귀가 들리지 않거나 난청인 사람들에게는 / 또한 시각 장애가 있거나, 저시력이거나, 어려운 사람에게도 / 특정 색을 구별하기가

While professionals / working in educational technology and commercial web design / have made significant progress / in meeting the needs of such users, / some scholars creating digital projects / all too often fail / to take these needs into account.
전문가들이 / 교육 기술과 상업용 웹 디자인에서 일하는 / 상당한 진전을 이루었음에도, / 그러한 사용자들의 필요를 충족시키는 데 있어 / 일부 디지털 프로젝트를 만드는 학자들은 / 너무 자주 실패한다. / 이러한 필요를 고려하는 데

This situation / would be much improved / if more projects embraced the idea / that we should always keep / the largest possible audience in mind / as we make design decisions, / ensuring that our final product / serves the needs / of those with disabilities as well as those without.
이 상황은 / 크게 개선될 수 있을 것이다. / 더 많은 프로젝트가 생각을 수용한다면, / 우리가 염두에 둬야 한다는 / 가능한 가장 큰 청중을 / 우리가 디자인 결정을 내릴 때, / 최종 제품이 / 필요를 모두 충족하도록 보장하면서 / 장애를 가진 사람들과 그렇지 않은 사람들의

➡ The needs of people with disabilities / have often been (A) overlooked / in digital projects, / which could be changed / by adopting a(n) (B) inclusive design.
장애를 가진 사람들의 필요는 / 간과되어 왔다. / 디지털 프로젝트에서 / 이것은 바뀔 수 있다. / 포함적인 디자인을 받아들임으로써

지난 수십 년 동안 학자들은 미래 세대를 위해 디지털 정보를 가장 잘 만들고, 정리하고, 제시하고, 보존하는 방법에 대한 표준을 개발해 왔다. 그러나 대부분의 경우 장애가 있는 사람들의 요구는 여전히 무시되어 왔다. 그 결과, 청각 장애가 있거나 듣는 것이 힘든 사람, 시각 장애가 있거나 시력이 낮거나 특정 색상을 구분하기 어려운 사람에게는 그렇지 않은 경우라면 가장 가치 있었던 디지털 자원 중 상당수가 무용지물이 되고 있다. 교육 기술 및 상업용 웹 디자인에 종사하는 전문가들은 이러한 사용자의 요구를 충족시키는 데 상당한 진전을 이루었지만, 디지털 프로젝트를 만드는 일부 학자들은 이러한 요구를 고려하지 못하는 경우가 너무 많다. 더 많은 프로젝트에서 디자인을 결정할 때 최대한 많은 사용자를 항상 염두에 두고 최종 제품이 장애가 있는 사람들과 그렇지 않은 사람들 모두의 요구를 충족시킬 수 있도록 해야 한다는 생각을 받아들인다면 이러한 상황은 훨씬 개선될 것이다.

➡ 장애가 있는 사람들의 요구는 디지털 프로젝트에서 종종 (A) 간과되어 왔으며, 이것은 (B) 포괄(포용)적인 디자인을 채택함으로써 변화될 수 있다.

Why? 왜 정답일까?

'What has remained neglected for the most part, however, are the needs of people with disabilities.'와 'This situation would be much improved if more projects embraced the idea that we should always keep the largest possible audience in mind as we make design decisions, ensuring that our final product serves the needs of those with disabilities as well as those without.'의 문장을 보았을 때 미래 세대를 위해 만든 디지털 정보에 장애가 있는 사람들의 접근이 어려움을 언급하고 있다. 따라서 'overlooked'와 'inclusive'가 들어가는 것이 가장 알맞다.

● scholar ⓝ 학자
● organize ⓥ 정리하다
● preserve ⓥ 보존하다
● valuable ⓐ 가치가 큰, 소중한
● distinguish ⓥ 구별하다
● develop ⓥ 발전시키다
● present ⓥ 제공하다
● disability ⓝ 장애
● resource ⓝ 원천
● situation ⓝ 상황

구문 풀이

14행 This situation would be much improved if more projects embraced the [가정법] idea that we should always keep the largest possible audience in mind as we [최상급] [~하면서] make design decisions, ensuring that our final product serves the needs of those [현재분사] [접속사] [지시대명사] with disabilities as well as those without. [마찬가지로] [지시대명사]

41-42 | 안전한 위험이 주는 쾌락

All humans, to an extent, seek activities / that cause a degree of pain in order to experience pleasure, / whether this is found in spicy food, strong massages, / or stepping into a too-cold or too-hot bath.
모든 인간은 어느 정도, 활동을 찾는다. / 쾌락을 경험하기 위해 어느 정도의 고통을 유발하는 / 이것이 매운 음식, 강한 마사지에서든, / 너무 차갑거나 너무 뜨거운 욕조에 들어가는 것에서든 상관없이

『The key / is that it is a 'safe threat'.』 42번의 근거
핵심은 / 이것이 '안전한 위험'이라는 것이다.

The brain perceives the stimulus to be painful / but ultimately (a) non-threatening.
뇌는 그 자극을 고통스럽게 인식하지만, / 궁극적으로는 위협적이지 않다고 여긴다.

Interestingly, / this could be similar to the way humor works: / a 'safe threat' that causes pleasure by playfully violating norms.
흥미롭게도, / 이것은 유머가 작동하는 방식과 유사할 수 있다: / 규범을 장난스럽게 위반하여 쾌락을 유발하는 '안전한 위험'

We feel uncomfortable, / but safe.
우리는 불편함을 느끼지만, / 안전함도 느낀다.

In this context, where (b) survival is clearly not in danger, / the desire for pain is actually the desire for a reward, / not suffering or punishment.
생존이 분명히 위협받지 않는 이 상황에서, / 고통에 대한 욕구는 사실 보상을 향한 욕구이다. / 고통이나 처벌을 향한 것이 아니라.

This reward-like effect / comes from the feeling / of mastery over the pain.
이 보상 같은 효과는 / 느낌에서 온다. / 고통에 대한 통제감이라는

The closer you look at your chilli-eating habit, / the more remarkable it seems.
매운 고추를 먹는 습관을 더 자세히 들여다볼수록, / 그것이 더욱 놀랍게 보인다.

When the active ingredient of chillies — capsaicin — touches the tongue, / it stimulates exactly the same receptor / that is activated when any of these tissues are burned.
고추의 활성 성분인 캡사이신이 혀에 닿으면, / 그것은 정확히 같은 수용체를 자극한다. / 우리가 조직을 태울 때 활성화되는

『Knowing that our body is firing off danger signals, / but that we are actually completely safe, / (c) produces pleasure.』 41번의 근거
우리의 몸이 위험 신호를 보내고 있는 것을 알지만, / 실제로는 완전히 안전하다는 것을 알 때, / 쾌락이 생긴다.

All children start off hating chilli, / but many learn to derive pleasure from it through repeated exposure / and knowing that they will never experience any real (d) threat.
모든 아이들은 처음에 고추를 싫어하지만, / 많은 이들이 반복된 노출을 통해 쾌락을 얻는 법을 배운다. / 그리고 그들이 결코 진정한 해를 경험하지 않을 것임을 알면서

Interestingly, seeking pain for the pain itself / appears to be (e) uniquely human.
흥미롭게도, 고통 그 자체를 위해 고통을 찾는 행위는 / 독특하게 인간만의 특징인 것 같다.

The only way / scientists have trained animals / to have a preference for chilli or to self-harm / is to have the pain / always directly associated / with a pleasurable reward.
유일한 방법은 / 동물에게 훈련시킨 / 과학자들이 고추를 선호하거나 자해하도록 / 고통이 / 직접적으로 연관되도록 하는 것이다. / 항상 쾌락적인 보상과

모든 인간은 어느 정도는 쾌락을 경험하기 위해 약간의 고통을 유발하는 활동을 추구한다. 이것이 매운 음식 또는 강한 마사지, 너무 차갑거나 뜨거운 욕조에 들어가기 중 어디에서 발견되든지 간에 말이다. 핵심은 그것이 '안전한 위험'이라는 점이다. 뇌는 자극이 고통스럽지만 궁극적으로 (a) 위협적이지 않은 것으로 인식한다. 흥미롭게도 이것은 유머가 작동하는 방식, 즉 규범을 장난스럽게 위반함으로써 쾌락을 유발하는 '안전한 위험'과 유사할 수 있다. 우리는 불편하지만 안전하다고 느낀다. (b) 생존이 위험하지 않은 이런 상황에서 고통에 대한 욕구는 실제로는 고통이나 처벌이 아닌 보상에 대한 욕구이다. 이러한 보상과 같은 효과는 고통에 대한 숙달된 느낌에서 비롯된다. 칠리를 먹는 습관을 자세히 들여다볼수록 이는 더욱 분명하게 드러난다. 칠리의 활성 성분인 캡사이신이 혀에 닿으면 피부 조직이 화상을 입었을 때 활성화되는 것과 똑같은 수용체를 자극한다. 우리 몸이 위험 신호를 보내고 있지만 실제로는 완전히 안전하다는 것을 알면 쾌감이 (c) 생긴다. 모든 아이들은 처음에는 칠리를 싫어하지만, 반복적인 노출과 실질적인 (d) 기쁨(→ 해)을 경험하지 않는다는 것을 알게 됨을 통해 그것에서 쾌락을 얻는 방법을 배우게 된다. 흥미롭게도 고통 그 자체를 위해 고통을 추구하는 것은 (e) 인간만이 할 수 있는 행동으로 보인다. 동물이 칠리를 선호하게 하거나 스스로에게 해를 가하도록 과학자들이 훈련시키는 유일한 방법은 고통을 항상 즐거운 보상과 직접적으로 연관시키는 것이다.

● seek ⓥ 찾다
● threat ⓝ 협박, 위협
● norm ⓝ 규범
● receptor ⓝ 수용체
● completely ⓐⓓ 완전히
● pleasure ⓝ 즐거움
● painful ⓐ 고통스러운, 아픈
● punishment ⓝ 처벌, 형벌
● tissue ⓝ 조직
● preference ⓝ 선호

구문 풀이

14행 When the active ingredient of chillies — capsaicin — touches the tongue, [때] it stimulates exactly the same receptor that is activated when any of these [주격관계대명사] [수동태] [때] tissues are burned.

41 | 제목 파악 | 정답률 54% | 정답 ①

윗글의 제목으로 가장 적절한 것은?
✓ The Secret Behind Painful Pleasures – 고통스러운 즐거움 뒤의 비밀
② How 'Safe Threat' Changes into Real Pain – '안전한 위험'이 진짜 고통으로 어떻게 바뀌는가
③ What Makes You Stronger, Pleasure or Pain? – 무엇이 당신을 강하게 만드는가, 즐거움인가 고통인가?
④ How Does Your Body Detect Danger Signals? – 당신의 몸이 어떻게 위험 신호를 감지하는가?
⑤ Recipes to Change Picky Children's Eating Habits – 까다로운 아이들의 식습관을 바꿀 레시피

Why? 왜 정답일까?

실질적으로 위협이 되지 않는다는 것을 알 때 보상의 원리로 고통 뒤에 쾌락이 온다고 설명하고 있다. 따라서 윗글의 제목으로 가장 적절한 것은 ① 'The Secret Behind Painful Pleasures'이다.

★★★ 등급을 가르는 문제!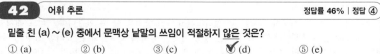

42 | 어휘 추론 | 정답률 46% | 정답 ④

밑줄 친 (a)~(e) 중에서 문맥상 낱말의 쓰임이 적절하지 않은 것은?
① (a) ② (b) ③ (c) ✓ (d) ⑤ (e)

Why? 왜 정답일까?

글에 따르면 많은 아이들이 칠리를 싫어하지만, 반복된 노출을 통해 이끌어진 쾌락을 배운다. 즉, 위협적이지 않은 고통인 칠리 뒤에 쾌락이 오는 것을 깨달았다고 하니 그들이 진짜 위험을 경험하지 않았다고 하는 것이 자연스럽다. 따라서 ④ (d)의 'joy'를 'threat'로 바꾸는 것이 문맥상 자연스럽다.

43-45 파일럿 교육생의 비행

(A)

An airplane flew high above / the deep blue seas / far from any land.
비행기가 위로 높이 날아가고 있었다. / 깊고 푸른 바다 / 육지에서 멀리 떨어진 곳에서

『Flying the small plane / was a student pilot / who was sitting alongside / an experienced flight instructor.』 45번 ①의 근거 일치
작은 비행기를 조종하고 있는 사람은 / 학생 조종사였고, / 그 옆에 앉아 있었다. / 경험 많은 비행 교관이

As the student looked out the window, / (a) she was filled with wonder and appreciation / for the beauty of the world.
학생이 창밖을 바라보자, / 그녀는 경이로움과 감사함으로 가득 차게 되었다. / 세상의 아름다움에 대한

Her instructor, meanwhile, / waited patiently / for the right time / to start a surprise flight emergency training exercise.
그녀의 교관은, 그동안, / 인내심 있게 기다리고 있었다. / 적절한 순간을 / 갑작스러운 비행 비상 훈련을 시작할

(D)

When the plane hit a bit of turbulence, / the instructor pushed a hidden button.
비행기가 약간의 난기류에 부딪혔을 때, / 교관이 숨겨진 버튼을 눌렀다.

『Suddenly, / all the monitors inside the plane / flashed several times / then went out completely!』 45번 ④의 근거 불일치
갑자기, / 비행기 안의 모든 모니터가 / 여러 번 깜빡이더니 / 완전히 꺼져 버렸다!

Now the student was in control of an airplane that was flying well, / but (e) she had no indication of where she was / or where she should go.
이제 학생은 잘 날고 있는 비행기를 조종하고 있었지만, / 그녀는 자신이 어디에 있는지, / 어디로 가야 할지 알 수 없었다.

『She did have a map, / but no other instruments.』 45번 ⑤의 근거 일치
그녀에게는 지도는 있었지만, / 다른 계기는 없었다.

She was at a loss / and then the plane shook again.
그녀는 당황했고, / 비행기는 다시 흔들렸다.

(C)

When the student began to panic, / the instructor said, / "Stay calm and steady. / (c) You can do it."
학생이 당황하기 시작했을 때, / 교관이 말했다. / "침착하고 안정적으로 해. / 너는 할 수 있어."

Calm as ever, / the instructor told her student, / "Difficult times always happen during flight.
언제나처럼 침착하게, / 교관은 학생에게 말했다. / "비행 중에는 언제나 어려운 순간이 찾아온단다.

『The most important thing / is to focus on your flight in those situations."』 45번 ③의 근거 일치
가장 중요한 것은 / 그러한 상황에서 비행에 집중하는 거야."

Those words encouraged the student / to focus on flying the aircraft first.
그 말은 학생을 격려했고, / 학생이 먼저 비행에 집중하게 되었다.

"Thank you, / I think (d) I can make it," / she said, / "As I've been trained, / I should search for visual markers."
"고맙습니다. / 저 해낼 수 있을 것 같아요." / 그녀는 말했다. / "제가 훈련받았던 것처럼, / 시각적 표식을 찾아봐야겠어요."

(B)

Then, the student carefully flew low enough / to see if she could find any ships / making their way across the surface of the ocean.
그 후, 학생은 조심스럽게 낮게 비행했다. / 배를 찾을 수 있는지 보기 위해 / 바다 위를 지나가고 있는

Now the instructor and the student / could see some ships.
이제 교관과 학생은 / 몇몇 배를 볼 수 있었다.

『Although the ships were far apart, / they were all sailing in a line.』 45번 ②의 근거 일치
배들이 서로 멀리 떨어져 있었지만, / 모두 한 줄로 항해하고 있었다.

With the line of ships in view, / the student could see the way / to home and safety.
배들의 줄이 보이자, / 학생은 길을 볼 수 있었다. / 집과 안전으로 가는

The student looked at (b) her in relief, / who smiled proudly back at her student.
학생은 그녀를 안도하며 바라보았고, / 교관은 자랑스러운 미소로 학생을 바라보았다.

(A)
비행기가 육지에서 멀리 떨어진 깊고 푸른 바다 위를 높이 날고 있었다. 소형 비행기를 조종하고 있는 것은 노련한 비행 교관과 나란히 앉아 있는 한 파일럿 교육생이었다. 교육생이 창문 밖을 바라볼 때, (a) 그녀는 세상의 아름다움에 대한 경이로움과 감탄으로 가득 찼다. 한편, 비행 교관은 비행 중 돌발 비상 상황 대처 훈련을 시작할 적절한 때를 인내심을 가지고 기다리고 있었다.

(D)
비행기가 약간의 난기류를 만났을 때, 교관은 숨겨진 버튼을 눌렀다. 갑자기, 비행기 안의 모든 모니터가 여러 번 깜빡이다가 완전히 꺼졌다! 이제 교육생은 잘 날고 있는 비행기를 조종하고 있었지만, (e) 그녀는 자신이 어디에 있는지, 어디로 가야 하는지 알 방도가 없었다. 교육생은 지도는 가지고 있었지만, 다른 도구는 가지고 있지 않았다. 그녀는 어쩔 줄 몰라 했고 그때 비행기가 다시 흔들렸다.

(C)
교육생이 당황하기 시작하자 교관은 "침착하세요. (c) 당신은 할 수 있습니다." 여느 때처럼 침착한 교관은 교육생에게 "비행 중에는 항상 어려운 상황이 발생합니다. 그러한 상황에서는 비행에 집중하는 것이 가장 중요합니다."라고 말했다. 그 말이 교육생이 먼저 비행에 집중할 수 있게끔 용기를 주었다. "감사합니다. (d) 제가 해낼 수 있을 것 같아요."라고 그녀는 말했다. "훈련받은 대로, 저는 시각 표식을 찾아야겠어요."

(B)
그런 다음 교육생은 바다 표면을 가로지르는 배가 보이는지 확인할 수 있을 정도로 충분히 낮게 조심히 비행하였다. 이제 교관과 교육생은 배 몇 척을 볼 수 있었다. 배들은 멀리 떨어

져 있었지만 모두 한 줄을 이루고 항해하고 있었다. 배들이 줄을 지어있는 것이 보이자, 교육생은 안전하게 복귀하는 길을 알 수 있었다. 교육생은 안도하며 (b) 그녀를 바라봤고, 그녀도 교육생을 향해 자랑스럽게 웃어보였다.

- instructor ⓝ 교관
- appreciation ⓝ 감사
- emergency ⓝ 긴급 상황
- aircraft ⓝ 비행기
- wonder ⓝ 궁금증
- patiently ⓐⓓ 침착하게
- relief ⓝ 안도
- turbulence ⓝ 난기류

구문 풀이

(B) 1행 Then, the student carefully flew low enough to see if she could find any
　　　　　　　　　　　　　　　　　　　　　　　　　　　　to부정사(부사적 용법) ↵　가정법
ships (that were) making their way across the surface of the ocean.
　　　현재분사 주격관계대명사＋be동사 생략

43 글의 순서 파악　　　정답률 69% | 정답 ⑤

주어진 글 (A)에 이어질 내용을 순서에 맞게 배열한 것으로 가장 적절한 것은?

① (B) − (D) − (C)　　　　　　② (C) − (B) − (D)
③ (C) − (D) − (B)　　　　　　④ (D) − (B) − (C)
✓⑤ (D) − (C) − (B)

Why? 왜 정답일까?

주어진 글은 파일럿 교육생과 비행 교관이 함께 비행을 하며 시작한다. 비행기가 난기류를 만난 장면을 묘사하는 (D)가, 비행 교관이 격려하는 (C), 마지막으로 힌트를 얻어 난기류를 잘 해결한 (B)의 순서가 자연스럽다. 따라서 알맞은 순서는 ⑤ (D) − (C) − (B)이다.

44 지칭 추론　　　정답률 65% | 정답 ②

밑줄 친 (a) ~ (e) 중에서 가리키는 대상이 나머지 넷과 다른 것은?

① (a)　　✓② (b)　　③ (c)　　④ (d)　　⑤ (e)

Why? 왜 정답일까?

(a), (c), (d), (e) 모두 비행 교육생을 가리키기 때문에, 비행 교관을 뜻하는 (b)는 가리키는 대상이 나머지 넷과 다르다. 따라서 답은 ② '(b)'이다.

45 세부 내용 파악　　　정답률 67% | 정답 ④

윗글에 관한 내용으로 적절하지 <u>않은</u> 것은?

① 교관과 교육생이 소형 비행기에 타고 있었다.
② 배들은 서로 떨어져 있었지만 한 줄을 이루고 있었다.
③ 교관은 어려운 상황에서는 집중이 가장 중요하다고 말했다.
✓④ 비행기 내부의 모니터가 깜박이다가 다시 정상 작동했다.
⑤ 교육생은 지도 이외의 다른 도구는 가지고 있지 않았다.

Why? 왜 정답일까?

(D)의 'Suddenly, all the monitors inside the plane flashed several times then went out completely!'에서 알 수 있듯이, 비행기의 내부 모니터는 깜박이더니 완전히 나가버렸다. 윗글에 대한 내용으로 적절하지 않은 것은 '④ 비행기 내부의 모니터가 깜박이다가 다시 정상 작동했다.'이다.

Why? 왜 오답일까?

① (A) 'Flying the small plane was a student pilot who was sitting alongside an experienced flight instructor'의 내용과 일치한다.
② (B) 'Although the ships were far apart, they were all sailing in a line.'의 내용과 일치한다.
③ (C) 'The most important thing is to focus on your flight in those situations.'의 내용과 일치한다.
⑤ (D) 'She did have a map, but no other instruments.'의 내용과 일치한다.

A	B	C	D
01 계획하다	01 tribe	01 ⓜ	01 ①
02 기사	02 switch	02 ①	02 ⓞ
03 지시	03 evidence	03 ⓚ	03 ⓔ
04 배출	04 relief	04 ⓓ	04 ⓗ
05 특허권	05 interval	05 ⓖ	05 ①
06 발표하다, 밝히다	06 apply	06 ⓟ	06 ①
07 분위기	07 comparison	07 ①	07 ⓐ
08 뛰다	08 capacity	08 ⓔ	08 ⓢ
09 구별하다	09 migrate	09 ⓗ	09 ⓖ
10 청각의	10 struggle	10 ①	10 ⓟ
11 영감	11 rapid	11 ①	11 ①
12 묘사하다	12 labor	12 ⓢ	12 ①
13 드러내다	13 ecosystem	13 ⓞ	13 ①
14 길	14 destructive	14 ⓒ	14 ①
15 긴급 상황	15 punishment	15 ⓑ	15 ⓚ
16 빠르게	16 document	16 ①	16 ①
17 선호	17 preserve	17 ①	17 ⓑ
18 감사하다	18 souvenir	18 ⓐ	18 ⓜ
19 주변	19 supply	19 ⓠ	19 ①
20 검사하다	20 hardship	20 ⓝ	20 ⓒ

07회 | 2023학년도 6월 학력평가　　고1

| 정답과 해설 |

• 정답 •

18 ② 19 ① 20 ⑤ 21 ① 22 ③ **23 ②** **24 ①** **25 ④** **26 ③** **27 ⑤** 28 ⑤ 29 ④ 30 ② **31 ④** 32 ①
33 ② 34 ③ 35 ④ 36 ② 37 ⑤ **38 ②** **39 ⑤** **40 ②** 41 ① 42 ③ 43 ④ 44 ② 45 ③

★ 표기된 문항은 [등급을 가르는 문제]에 해당하는 문제입니다.

07회

18　여름 휴가 패키지 홍보　　　　정답률 93% | 정답 ②

다음 글의 목적으로 가장 적절한 것은?

① 여행 일정 변경을 안내하려고
☑ 패키지 여행 상품을 홍보하려고
③ 여행 상품 불만족에 대해 사과하려고
④ 여행 만족도 조사 참여를 부탁하려고
⑤ 패키지 여행 업무 담당자를 모집하려고

ACC Travel Agency Customers:
ACC 여행사 고객님께
Have you ever wanted / to enjoy a holiday in nature?
당신은 원한 적이 있습니까? / 자연 속에서 휴가를 즐기기를
This summer is the best time / to turn your dream into reality.
이번 여름이 최고의 시간입니다. / 당신의 꿈을 현실로 바꿀
We have a perfect travel package for you.
우리에게는 당신을 위한 완벽한 패키지 여행 상품이 있습니다.
This travel package / includes special trips to Lake Madison / as well as massage and meditation to help you relax.
이 패키지 여행 상품은 / Lake Madison으로의 특별한 여행을 포함합니다. / 당신이 편히 쉴 수 있도록 돕는 마사지와 명상뿐만 아니라
Also, / we provide yoga lessons / taught by experienced instructors.
또한, / 우리는 요가 강의도 제공합니다. / 숙련된 강사에 의해 지도되는
If you book this package, / you will enjoy all this at a reasonable price.
만약 당신이 이 패키지를 예약한다면, / 당신은 이 모든 것을 합리적인 가격으로 즐길 것입니다.
We are sure / that it will be an unforgettable experience for you.
우리는 확신합니다. / 그것이 당신에게 잊지 못할 경험이 될 것이라고
If you call us, / we will be happy to give you more details.
당신이 우리에게 전화하시면, / 우리는 당신에게 더 많은 세부 사항을 기꺼이 알려드리겠습니다.

ACC 여행사 고객님께

자연 속에서 휴가를 즐기는 것을 원한 적이 있습니까? 이번 여름이 당신의 꿈을 현실로 바꿀 최고의 시간입니다. 우리에게는 당신을 위한 완벽한 패키지 여행 상품이 있습니다. 이 패키지 여행 상품은 당신이 편히 쉴 수 있도록 돕는 마사지와 명상뿐만 아니라 Lake Madison으로의 특별한 여행을 포함합니다. 또한, 우리는 숙련된 강사의 요가 강의도 제공합니다. 만약 당신이 이 패키지를 예약한다면, 당신은 이 모든 것을 합리적인 가격으로 즐길 것입니다. 우리는 그것이 당신에게 잊지 못할 경험이 될 것이라고 확신합니다. 우리에게 전화하시면, 우리는 당신에게 더 많은 세부 사항을 기꺼이 알려드리겠습니다.

Why? 왜 정답일까?

여름 휴가에 적합한 패키지 여행 상품이 있음을 홍보하는 글(We have a perfect travel package for you.)이므로, 글의 목적으로 가장 적절한 것은 ② '패키지 여행 상품을 홍보하려고'이다.

● travel agency 여행사
● experienced ⓐ 경험 많은, 숙련된
● unforgettable ⓐ 잊지 못할
● meditation ⓝ 명상
● instructor ⓝ 강사

구문 풀이

4행　This travel package includes special trips to Lake Madison as well as massage and meditation to help you relax.
「A + as well as + B : B뿐 아니라 A도」
「help + 목적어 + 원형부정사 : ~이 …하는 데 도움이 되다」

19　남편과 딸이 없어진 줄 알았다가 다시 찾고는 안도한 필자　정답률 88% | 정답 ①

다음 글에 드러난 'I'의 심경 변화로 가장 적절한 것은?

☑ anxious → relieved
　불안한　　안도한
② delighted → unhappy
　기쁜　　　불행한
③ indifferent → excited
　무관심한　　신난
④ relaxed → upset
　안도한　　언짢은
⑤ embarrassed → proud
　당황한　　자랑스러운

When I woke up in our hotel room, / it was almost midnight.
내가 호텔 방에서 깨어났을 때는 / 거의 자정이었다.
I didn't see my husband nor daughter.
남편과 딸이 보이지 않았다.
I called them, / but I heard their phones ringing in the room.
나는 그들에게 전화를 걸었지만, / 나는 그들의 전화가 방에서 울리는 것을 들었다.
Feeling worried, / I went outside and walked down the street, / but they were nowhere to be found.
걱정이 되어, / 나는 밖으로 나가 거리를 걸어 내려갔지만, / 그들을 어디에서도 찾을 수 없었다.
When I decided / I should ask someone for help, / a crowd nearby caught my attention.
내가 마음 먹었을 때 / 내가 누군가에게 도움을 요청해야겠다고 / 근처에 있던 군중이 내 주의를 끌었다.
I approached, / hoping to find my husband and daughter, / and suddenly I saw two familiar faces.
나는 다가갔고, / 남편과 딸을 찾으려는 희망을 안고 / 갑자기 낯익은 두 얼굴이 보였다.
I smiled, feeling calm.
나는 안도하며 웃었다.

Just then, / my daughter saw me and called, / "Mom!"
바로 그때, / 딸이 나를 보고 외쳤다. / "엄마!"라고
They were watching the magic show.
그들은 마술 쇼를 보고 있는 중이었다.
Finally, / I felt all my worries disappear.
마침내, / 나는 내 모든 걱정이 사라지는 것을 느꼈다.

내가 호텔 방에서 깨어났을 때는 거의 자정이었다. 남편과 딸이 보이지 않았다. 나는 그들에게 전화를 걸었지만, 나는 그들의 전화가 방에서 울리는 것을 들었다. 걱정이 되어, 나는 밖으로 나가 거리를 걸어 내려갔지만, 그들을 어디에서도 찾을 수 없었다. 내가 누군가에게 도움을 요청하려고 했을 때, 근처에 있던 군중이 내 주의를 끌었다. 나는 남편과 딸을 찾으려는 희망을 안고 다가갔고, 갑자기 낯익은 두 얼굴이 보였다. 나는 안도하며 웃었다. 바로 그때, 딸이 나를 보고 "엄마!"라고 외쳤다. 그들은 마술 쇼를 보고 있는 중이었다. 마침내, 나는 내 모든 걱정이 사라지는 것을 느꼈다.

Why? 왜 정답일까?

호텔 방에서 잠을 자다가 깬 필자가 남편과 딸이 없어서 걱정했다가(Feeling worried, ~) 둘이 마술 쇼를 보고 있었다는 것을 알고 안도했다는(I smiled, feeling calm. / Finally, I felt all my worries disappear.)는 글이다. 따라서 'I'의 심경 변화로 가장 적절한 것은 ① '불안한 → 안도한'이다.

- worried ⓐ 걱정한
- ask for help 도움을 요청하다
- approach ⓥ 다가가다
- disappear ⓥ 사라지다
- delighted ⓐ 기쁜
- decide ⓥ 결심하다, 정하다
- catch one's attention 관심을 끌다
- familiar ⓐ 익숙한
- anxious ⓐ 불안한
- embarrassed ⓐ 당황한

구문 풀이

3행 Feeling worried, I went outside and walked down the street, but they
분사구문(~하면서)
were nowhere to be found.
수동 부정사(they 보충 설명)

---

20 업무와 개인 용무를 한 곳에 정리하기 | 정답률 78% | 정답 ⑤

다음 글에서 필자가 주장하는 바로 가장 적절한 것은?
① 결정한 것은 반드시 실행하도록 노력하라.
② 자신이 담당한 업무에 관한 전문성을 확보하라.
③ 업무 집중도를 높이기 위해 책상 위를 정돈하라.
④ 좋은 아이디어를 메모하는 습관을 길러라.
✓ 업무와 개인 용무를 한 곳에 정리하라.

Research shows / that people who work have two calendars: / one for work and one for their personal lives.
연구는 보여준다. / 일하는 사람들이 두 개의 달력을 가지고 있다는 것을 / 업무를 위한 달력 하나와 개인적인 삶을 위한 달력 하나
Although it may seem sensible, / having two separate calendars for work and personal life / can lead to distractions.
비록 이것이 현명해 보일지 모르지만, / 업무와 개인적인 삶을 위한 두 개의 별도의 달력을 갖는 것은 / 주의를 산만하게 할 수 있다.
To check if something is missing, / you will find yourself / checking your to-do lists multiple times.
누락된 것이 있는지를 확인하고자 / 당신은 자신이 ~한다는 것을 깨닫게 될 것이다. / 당신의 할 일 목록을 여러 번 확인하고 있는 것을
Instead, / organize all of your tasks in one place.
그렇게 하는 대신에, / 당신의 모든 일들을 한 곳에 정리하라.
It doesn't matter / if you use digital or paper media.
중요하지 않다. / 당신이 디지털 매체를 사용하든 종이 매체를 사용하든
It's okay / to keep your professional and personal tasks in one place.
괜찮다. / 당신의 업무와 개인 용무를 한 곳에 둬도
This will give you / a good idea of how time is divided between work and home.
이것은 당신에게 줄 것이다. / 일과 가정 사이에 시간이 어떻게 나눠지는지에 관한 좋은 생각을
This will allow you / to make informed decisions / about which tasks are most important.
이것은 당신이 ~하게 할 것이다. / 잘 알고 결정하게 / 어떤 일이 가장 중요한지에 대해

연구는 일하는 사람들이 두 개의 달력을 가지고 있다는 것을 보여준다. 하나는 업무를 위한 달력이고 하나는 개인적인 삶을 위한 달력이다. 비록 이것이 현명해 보일지도 모르지만, 업무와 개인적인 삶을 위한 두 개의 별도의 달력을 갖는 것은 주의를 산만하게 할 수 있다. 누락된 것이 있는지를 확인하고자 당신은 자신이 할 일 목록을 여러 번 확인하고 있다는 것을 깨닫게 될 것이다. 그렇게 하는 대신에, 당신의 모든 일들을 한 곳에 정리하라. 당신이 디지털 매체를 사용하든 종이 매체를 사용하든 중요하지 않다. 당신의 업무와 개인 용무를 한 곳에 둬도 괜찮다. 이것은 당신에게 일과 가정 사이에 시간이 어떻게 나눠지는지에 대해 잘 알게 해줄 것이다. 이것은 어떤 일이 가장 중요한지에 대해 잘 알고 결정하게 할 것이다.

Why? 왜 정답일까?

개인 용무와 일을 한 곳에 정리하라고(~ keep your professional and personal tasks in one place.) 조언하는 글이므로, 필자가 주장하는 바로 가장 적절한 것은 ⑤ '업무와 개인 용무를 한 곳에 정리하라.'이다.

- sensible ⓐ 분별 있는, 현명한
- distraction ⓝ 주의 분산, 정신을 흩뜨리는 것
- organize ⓥ 정리하다
- make an informed decision 잘 알고 결정하다
- separate ⓐ 별개의
- multiple ⓐ 여럿의, 다수의
- divide ⓥ 나누다, 분배하다

구문 풀이

4행 To check if something is missing, you will find yourself checking your
목적(~하려면) 접속사(~인지 아닌지) 동사 목적어 목적격 보어
to-do lists multiple times.

---

21 고객의 구매 후 행동을 관찰할 필요성 | 정답률 56% | 정답 ①

밑줄 친 become unpaid ambassadors가 다음 글에서 의미하는 바로 가장 적절한 것은?

✓① recommend products to others for no gain – 대가 없이 다른 사람들에게 제품을 추천할
② offer manufacturers feedback on products – 제조업자들에게 제품에 대한 피드백을 제공할
③ become people who don't trust others' words – 다른 사람들의 말을 믿지 않는 사람이 될
④ get rewards for advertising products overseas – 해외에 광고를 해줘서 보상을 받을
⑤ buy products without worrying about the price – 가격에 대해 걱정하지 않고 제품을 살

Why do you care / how a customer reacts to a purchase?
왜 당신은 신경 쓰는가? / 고객이 구매품에 어떻게 반응하는지
Good question.
좋은 질문이다.
By understanding post-purchase behavior, / you can understand the influence / and the likelihood of whether a buyer will repurchase the product / (and whether she will keep it or return it).
구매 후 행동을 이해함으로써, / 당신은 그 영향력을 이해할 수 있다. / 그리고 구매자가 제품을 재구매할지 하는 가능성을 / (그리고 그 사람이 제품을 계속 가질지 반품할지)
You'll also determine / whether the buyer will encourage others / to purchase the product from you.
또한 당신은 알아낼 것이다. / 구매자가 다른 사람들에게 권할지 아닐지를 / 당신으로부터 제품을 구매하도록
Satisfied customers can become unpaid ambassadors for your business, / so customer satisfaction should be on the top of your to-do list.
만족한 고객은 당신의 사업을 위한 무급 대사가 될 수 있으므로, / 고객 만족이 할 일 목록의 최상단에 있어야 한다.
People tend to believe the opinions of people they know.
사람들은 자기가 아는 사람들의 의견을 믿는 경향이 있다.
People trust friends over advertisements any day.
사람들은 언제든 광고보다 친구를 더 신뢰한다.
They know / that advertisements are paid to tell the "good side" / and that they're used / to persuade them to purchase products and services.
그들은 알고 있다. / 광고는 '좋은 면'을 말하도록 돈을 지불받고, / 그것은 이용된다는 것을 / 그들더러 제품과 서비스를 구매하게 설득하려고
By continually monitoring your customer's satisfaction after the sale, / you have the ability / to avoid negative word-of-mouth advertising.
판매 후 고객의 만족을 지속적으로 관찰하여 / 당신은 능력을 얻는다. / 부정적인 입소문 광고를 피할 수 있는

왜 당신은 고객이 구매품에 어떻게 반응하는지 신경 쓰는가? 좋은 질문이다. 구매 후 행동을 이해함으로써, 당신은 그 영향력과 구매자가 제품을 재구매할지(그리고 그 사람이 제품을 계속 가질지 반품할지) 하는 가능성을 이해할 수 있다. 또한 당신은 구매자가 다른 사람들에게 당신으로부터 제품을 구매하도록 권할지 아닐지도 알아낼 것이다. 만족한 고객은 당신의 사업을 위한 무급 대사가 될 수 있으므로, 고객 만족이 할 일 목록의 최상단에 있어야 한다. 사람들은 아는 사람들의 의견을 믿는 경향이 있다. 사람들은 언제든 광고보다 친구를 더 신뢰한다. 그들은 광고는 '좋은 면'을 말하도록 돈을 지불받고, 그것은 그들더러 제품과 서비스를 구매하게 설득하려고 이용된다는 것을 알고 있다. 판매 후 고객의 만족을 지속적으로 관찰하여 당신은 부정적인 입소문 광고를 피할 수 있는 능력을 얻는다.

Why? 왜 정답일까?

구매 후 행동을 관찰하면 구매자들이 다른 사람들에게 제품을 권해줄지(~ whether the buyer will encourage others to purchase the product from you.) 알 수 있다는 내용으로 보아, 밑줄 친 부분의 의미로 가장 적절한 것은 ① '대가 없이 다른 사람들에게 제품을 추천할'이다.

- purchase ⓝ 구매 ⓥ 사다
- return ⓥ 반품하다
- unpaid ⓐ 무급의
- advertisement ⓝ 광고
- word-of-mouth ⓐ 구전의
- likelihood ⓝ 가능성, 확률
- satisfied ⓐ 만족한
- ambassador ⓝ (외교 시 나라를 대표하는) 대사, 사절
- continually ⓐⓓ 지속적으로
- overseas ⓐⓓ 해외에

구문 풀이

10행 They know {that advertisements are paid to tell the "good side"} and {that they're used to persuade them to purchase products and services}.
「be used to + 동사원형」: ~하기 위해 사용되다 { }: know의 목적어

---

22 컴퓨터화된 사회에서 오히려 일이 늘어난 소비자들 | 정답률 54% | 정답 ③

다음 글의 요지로 가장 적절한 것은?
① 컴퓨터 기반 사회에서는 여가 시간이 더 늘어난다.
② 회사 업무의 전산화는 업무 능률을 향상시킨다.
✓③ 컴퓨터화된 사회에서 소비자는 더 많은 일을 하게 된다.
④ 온라인 거래가 모든 소비자들을 만족시키기에는 한계가 있다.
⑤ 산업의 발전으로 인해 기계가 인간의 일자리를 대신하고 있다.

The promise of a computerized society, / we were told, / was that it would pass to machines all of the repetitive drudgery of work, / allowing us humans / to pursue higher purposes / and to have more leisure time.
컴퓨터화된 사회의 약속은 / 우리가 듣기로, / ~이었다. / 그것이 모든 반복적인 고된 일을 기계에 넘겨 / 우리 인간들이 ~하게 해준다는 것 / 더 높은 목적을 추구하고 / 더 많은 여가 시간을 가질 수 있게
It didn't work out this way.
일은 이런 식으로 되지는 않았다.
Instead of more time, / most of us have less.
더 많은 시간 대신에, / 우리 대부분은 더 적은 시간을 가지고 있다.
Companies large and small / have off-loaded work onto the backs of consumers.
크고 작은 회사들은 / 일을 소비자들의 등에 떠넘겼다.
Things that used to be done for us, / as part of the value-added service of working with a company, / we are now expected to do ourselves.
우리를 위해 행해지던 일들을 / 회사에 맡겨 행해지던 부가적 서비스의 일환으로, / 우리는 이제 스스로 하도록 기대받는다.
With air travel, / we're now expected / to complete our own reservations and check-in, / jobs that used to be done by airline employees or travel agents.
항공 여행의 경우, / 이제는 우리는 기대된다 / 예약과 체크인을 직접 완수하도록 / 항공사 직원이나 여행사 직원이 하던 일인
At the grocery store, / we're expected to bag our own groceries / and, in some supermarkets, / to scan our own purchases.
식료품점에서는, / 우리가 우리 자신의 식료품을 직접 봉지에 넣도록 기대받는다. / 그리고 일부 슈퍼마켓에서는 / 우리가 직접 구매한 물건을 스캔하도록

우리가 듣기로, 컴퓨터화된 사회의 약속은 그것이 모든 반복적인 고된 일을 기계에 넘겨 우리 인간들이 더 높은 목적을 추구하고 더 많은 여가 시간을 가질 수 있게 해준다는 것이었다. 일은 이런 식으로 되지는 않았다. 더 많은 시간 대신에, 우리 대부분은 더 적은 시간을 가지고 있다. 크고 작은 회사들은 일을 소비자들의 등에 떠넘겼다. 우리는 회사에 맡겨 해결하던 부가가치 서비스의 일환으로 우리를 위해 행해지던 일들을 이제 스스로 하도록 기대받는다. 항공 여행의 경우, 항공사 직원이나 여행사 직원들이 하던 일인 예약과 체크인을 이제는 우리가 직접 완수하도록 기대된다. 식료품점에서는, 우리가 우리 자신의 식료품을 직접 봉지에 넣도록, 그리고 일부 슈퍼마켓에서는 우리가 직접 구매한 물건을 스캔하도록 기대받는다.

Why? 왜 정답일까?

컴퓨터화된 사회가 도래하면 개인은 더 많은 여가 시간을 누릴 것으로 기대되었지만, 실상은 반대로 더 많은 일을 하게 되었다(Instead of more time, most of us have less. Companies large and small have off-loaded work onto the backs of consumers.)는 내용이다. 따라서 글의 요지로 가장 적절한 것은 ③ '컴퓨터화된 사회에서 소비자는 더 많은 일을 하게 된다.'이다.

- repetitive ⓐ 반복되는
- pursue ⓥ 추구하다
- as part of ~의 일환으로
- drudgery ⓝ 고된 일
- off-load ⓥ 짐을 내리다, 떠넘기다
- grocery store 슈퍼, 식료품 가게

구문 풀이

6행 Things [that used to be done for us], (as part of the value-added service
to do의 목적어 / ~하곤 했다 / ( ): 삽입구
of working with a company), we are now expected to do ourselves.
주어 / 「be expected + to부정사: ~하도록 기대되다」

---

23 자신을 평균 이상으로 보는 경향
정답률 66% | 정답 ②

다음 글의 주제로 가장 적절한 것은?

① importance of having a positive self-image as a leader
리더로서 긍정적인 자아상을 갖는 것의 중요성
✓② our common belief that we are better than average
우리가 평균보다 낫다는 일반적인 믿음
③ our tendency to think others are superior to us
남들이 우리보다 낫다고 생각하는 우리의 경향
④ reasons why we always try to be above average
우리가 늘 평균보다 나아지려고 노력하는 이유
⑤ danger of prejudice in building healthy social networks
건전한 사회적 네트워크를 구축할 때 편견의 위험성

We tend to believe / that we possess a host of socially desirable characteristics, / and that we are free of most of those / that are socially undesirable.
우리는 믿는 경향이 있다. / 우리가 사회적으로 바람직한 특성들을 많이 지니고 있고, / 우리가 특성을 대부분은 지니고 있지 않다고 / 사회적으로 바람직하지 않은

For example, / a large majority of the general public thinks / that they are more intelligent, / more fair-minded, / less prejudiced, / and more skilled behind the wheel of an automobile / than the average person.
예를 들어, / 대다수의 일반 대중들은 생각한다. / 자신이 더 지적이고, / 더 공정하고, / 편견을 덜 가지고, / 자동차를 운전할 때 더 능숙하다고 / 보통 사람보다

This phenomenon is so reliable and ubiquitous / that it has come to be known as the "Lake Wobegon effect," / after Garrison Keillor's fictional community / where "the women are strong, / the men are good-looking, / and all the children are above average."
이 현상은 너무 신뢰할 수 있고 어디서나 볼 수 있기 때문에 / 그것은 'Lake Wobegon effect'라고 알려지게 되었다. / Garrison Keillor의 허구적인 공동체의 이름을 따서 / '여성들은 강하고, / 남성들은 잘생겼으며, / 모든 아이들은 평균 이상'인

A survey of one million high school seniors found / that 70% thought they were above average in leadership ability, / and only 2% thought they were below average.
고등학교 졸업반 학생 100만 명을 대상으로 한 설문조사는 밝혔다. / 70%는 자신이 리더십 능력에 있어 평균 이상이라고 생각했고, / 2%만이 자신이 평균 이하라고 생각했다는 것을

In terms of ability to get along with others, / all students thought they were above average, / 60% thought they were in the top 10%, / and 25% thought they were in the top 1%!
다른 사람들과 잘 지내는 능력에 있어서, / 모든 학생들은 자신이 평균 이상이라고 생각했고, / 60%는 자신이 상위 10%에 속한다고 생각했고, / 25%는 자신이 상위 1%에 속한다고 생각했다!

우리는 우리가 사회적으로 바람직한 특성들을 많이 지니고 있고, 사회적으로 바람직하지 않은 특성들 대부분은 지니고 있지 않다고 믿는 경향이 있다. 예를 들어, 대다수의 일반 대중들은 자신이 보통 사람보다 더 지적이고, 더 공정하고, 편견을 덜 가지고, 자동차를 운전할 때 더 능숙하다고 생각한다. 이 현상은 너무 신뢰할 수 있고 어디서나 볼 수 있기 때문에 '여성들은 강하고, 남성들은 잘생겼으며, 모든 아이들은 평균 이상'인 Garrison Keillor의 허구적인 공동체의 이름을 따서 'Lake Wobegon effect'라고 알려지게 되었다. 고등학교 졸업반 학생 100만 명을 대상으로 한 설문조사에서, (학생들의) 70%는 자신이 리더십 능력에 있어 평균 이상이라고 생각했고, 2%만이 자신이 평균 이하라고 생각했다는 것을 발견했다. 다른 사람들과 잘 지내는 능력에 있어서, 모든 학생들은 자신이 평균 이상이라고 생각했고, 60%는 자신이 상위 10%에 속한다고 생각했고, 25%는 자신이 상위 1%에 속한다고 생각했다!

Why? 왜 정답일까?

사람들은 스스로 바람직한 특성은 더 많이 가지고 있고, 바람직하지 않은 특성은 덜 가지고 있다고 믿는 경향이 있음(We tend to believe that we possess a host of socially desirable characteristics, and that we are free of most of those that are socially undesirable.)을 설명하는 글이다. 뒤에 이어지는 여러 예시에도 사람들이 스스로를 특정 항목에서 '평균 이상'이라고 생각한다는 내용이 주를 이룬다. 따라서 글의 주제로 가장 적절한 것은 ② '우리가 평균보다 낫다는 일반적인 믿음'이다.

- possess ⓥ 지니다, 소유하다
- desirable ⓐ 바람직한
- fair-minded ⓐ 공정한
- skilled ⓐ 능숙한
- automobile ⓝ 자동차
- reliable ⓐ 믿을 만한
- fictional ⓐ 허구의
- million ⓝ 100만
- self-image ⓝ 자아상(사람이 자기 자신에 대해 가진 이미지)
- superior to ~보다 우월한
- a host of 여러, 다수의
- characteristic ⓝ 특성
- prejudiced ⓐ 고정 관념이 있는
- behind the wheel 운전할 때, 핸들을 잡은
- phenomenon ⓝ 현상
- ubiquitous ⓐ 도처에 있는
- good-looking ⓐ 잘생긴

구문 풀이

1행 We tend to believe {that we possess a host of socially desirable
( ): to believe의 목적절
characteristics}, and {that we are free of most of those that are socially
대명사(= characteristics)
undesirable}.

---

24 부유한 국가의 스트레스 요소
정답률 64% | 정답 ①

다음 글의 제목으로 가장 적절한 것은?

✓① Why Are Even Wealthy Countries Not Free from Stress?
왜 심지어 부유한 국가들도 스트레스에서 자유롭지 못한 걸까?
② In Search of the Path to Escaping the Poverty Trap
가난의 덫을 벗어나기 위한 길을 찾아서
③ Time Management: Everything You Need to Know
시간 관리: 당신이 알아야 할 모든 것
④ How Does Stress Affect Human Bodies?
스트레스는 우리 몸에 어떤 영향을 미칠까?
⑤ Sound Mind Wins the Game of Life!
건전한 정신이 인생이란 게임에서 이긴다!

Few people will be surprised / to hear that poverty tends to create stress: / a 2006 study / published in the American journal *Psychosomatic Medicine*, / for example, / noted / that a lower socioeconomic status / was associated with higher levels of stress hormones in the body.
놀랄 사람은 거의 없을 것이다. / 가난이 스트레스를 유발하는 경향이 있다는 것을 듣고 / 2006년 연구는 / 미국의 저널 *Psychosomatic Medicine*에 발표된 / 예를 들어, / 언급했다. / 더 낮은 사회 경제적 지위가 / 체내의 더 높은 수치의 스트레스 호르몬과 관련이 있다

However, / richer economies have their own distinct stresses.
하지만, / 더 부유한 국가는 그들만의 독특한 스트레스를 가지고 있다.

The key issue is time pressure.
핵심 쟁점은 시간 압박이다.

A 1999 study of 31 countries / by American psychologist Robert Levine and Canadian psychologist Ara Norenzayan / found / that wealthier, more industrialized nations had a faster pace of life / — which led to a higher standard of living, / but at the same time / left the population feeling a constant sense of urgency, / as well as being more prone to heart disease.
31개국을 대상으로 한 1999년 연구는 / 미국 심리학자 Robert Levine과 캐나다 심리학자 Ara Norenzayan에 의한 / 알아냈다. / 더 부유하고 더 산업화된 국가들이 더 빠른 삶의 속도를 가지고 있다는 것, / 그리고 이것이 더 높은 생활 수준으로 이어졌지만, / 동시에 / 사람들에게 지속적인 촉박함을 느끼게 했다는 것 / 심장병에 걸리기 더 쉽게 했을 뿐 아니라

In effect, / fast-paced productivity creates wealth, / but it also leads people to feel time-poor / when they lack the time / to relax and enjoy themselves.
사실, / 빠른 속도의 생산력은 부를 창출하지만, / 이는 또한 사람들이 시간이 부족하다고 느끼게 한다. / 그들이 시간이 부족할 때 / 긴장을 풀고 즐겁게 지낼

가난이 스트레스를 유발하는 경향이 있다는 것을 듣고 놀랄 사람은 거의 없을 것이다. 예를 들어, 미국의 저널 *Psychosomatic Medicine*에 발표된 2006년 연구는 더 낮은 사회 경제적 지위가 체내의 더 높은 수치의 스트레스 호르몬과 관련이 있다고 언급했다. 하지만, 더 부유한 국가는 그들 특유의 스트레스를 가지고 있다. 핵심 쟁점은 시간 압박이다. 미국 심리학자 Robert Levine과 캐나다 심리학자 Ara Norenzayan이 31개국을 대상으로 한 1999년 연구는 더 부유하고 더 산업화된 국가들이 더 빠른 삶의 속도를 가지고 있다는 것, 그리고 이것이 더 높은 생활 수준으로 이어졌지만, 동시에 사람들이 심장병에 걸리기 더 쉽게 했을 뿐 아니라 지속적인 촉박함을 느끼게 했다는 것을 알아냈다. 사실, 빠른 속도의 생산력은 부를 창출하지만, 이는 또한 사람들이 긴장을 풀고 즐겁게 지낼 시간이 없을 때 시간이 부족하다고 느끼게 한다.

Why? 왜 정답일까?

부유한 국가에 사는 사람들이 시간 압박이라는 스트레스에 시달린다(However, richer economies have their own distinct stresses. The key issue is time pressure.)는 내용이므로, 글의 제목으로 가장 적절한 것은 ① '왜 심지어 부유한 국가들도 스트레스에서 자유롭지 못한 걸까?'이다.

- poverty ⓝ 가난
- status ⓝ 지위
- psychologist ⓝ 심리학자
- industrialize ⓥ 산업화하다
- urgency ⓝ 다급함
- productivity ⓝ 생산성
- socioeconomic ⓐ 사회경제적인
- distinct ⓐ 특유의, 독특한, 뚜렷한
- wealthy ⓐ 부유한
- constant ⓐ 지속적인
- prone to ~에 걸리기 쉬운

구문 풀이

1행 Few people will be surprised to hear that poverty tends to create stress: ~
감정 형용사 / 원인(~해서)

---

25 지역별 산림 면적 점유율 비교
정답률 80% | 정답 ④

다음 도표의 내용과 일치하지 않는 것은?

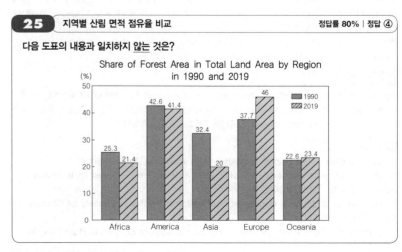

Share of Forest Area in Total Land Area by Region in 1990 and 2019

The above graph shows / the share of forest area / in total land area by region / in 1990 and 2019.

위 도표는 보여준다. / 산림 면적의 점유율을 / 지역별 총 토지 면적에서 / 1990년과 2019년의
① Africa's share of forest area in total land area / was over 20% in both 1990 and 2019.
아프리카의 전체 토지 면적에서 산림 면적의 점유율이 / 1990년과 2019년 둘 다 20%를 넘었다.
② The share of forest area in America / was 42.6% in 1990, / which was larger than that in 2019.
아메리카의 산림 면적 점유율은 / 1990년에 42.6%였고, / 이는 2019년보다 더 컸다.
③ The share of forest area in Asia / declined from 1990 to 2019 / by more than 10 percentage points.
아시아의 산림 면적 점유율은 / 1990년부터 2019년까지 감소했다. / 10퍼센트포인트 이상만큼
☑ In 2019, / the share of forest area in Europe / was the largest among the five regions, / more than three times that in Asia in the same year.
2019년 / 유럽의 산 면적 점유율은 / 다섯 개 지역 중 가장 컸고, / 같은 해 아시아의 세 배가 넘었다.
⑤ Oceania showed the smallest gap between 1990 and 2019 / in terms of the share of forest area in total land area.
오세아니아는 1990년과 2019년 사이에 가장 작은 차이를 보였다. / 총 토지 면적에서 산림 면적의 점유율에 있어

위 도표는 1990년과 2019년의 지역별 총 토지 면적에서 산림 면적의 점유율을 보여준다. ① 아프리카의 전체 토지 면적에서 산림 면적의 점유율이 1990년과 2019년 둘 다 20%를 넘었다. ② 1990년 아메리카의 산림 면적 점유율은 42.6%였고, 이는 2019년보다 더 컸다. ③ 아시아의 산림 면적 점유율은 1990년부터 2019년까지, 10퍼센트포인트 이상 감소했다. ④ 2019년 유럽의 산 면적 점유율은 다섯 개 지역 중 가장 컸고, 같은 해 아시아의 세 배가 넘었다. ⑤ 오세아니아는 1990년과 2019년 사이에 총 토지 면적에서 산림 면적의 점유율에 있어 가장 작은 차이를 보였다.

Why? 왜 정답일까?

도표에 따르면 2019년 아시아의 산림 면적 점유율은 20%인데, 유럽의 점유율은 46%이므로 두 비율은 3배 이상 차이 나지 않는다. 따라서 도표와 일치하지 않는 것은 ④이다.

● region ⓝ 지역 ● decline ⓥ 감소하다, 줄어들다

---

26 Gary Becker의 생애 정답률 86% | 정답 ③

Gary Becker에 관한 다음 글의 내용과 일치하지 <u>않는</u> 것은?
① New York City의 Brooklyn에서 자랐다.
② 아버지는 금융과 정치 문제에 깊은 관심이 있었다.
☑ Princeton University에서의 경제학 교육에 만족했다.
④ 1955년에 경제학 박사 학위를 취득했다.
⑤ Business Week에 경제학 칼럼을 기고했다.

「Gary Becker was born in Pottsville, Pennsylvania in 1930 / and grew up in Brooklyn, New York City.」 ①의 근거 일치
Gary Becker는 1930년 Pennsylvania 주 Pottsville에서 태어났고 / New York City의 Brooklyn에서 자랐다.
「His father, / who was not well educated, / had a deep interest in financial and political issues.」 ②의 근거 일치
그의 아버지는 / 교육을 제대로 받지 못했는데 / 금융과 정치 문제에 깊은 관심이 있었다.
After graduating from high school, / Becker went to Princeton University, / where he majored in economics.
고등학교를 졸업한 후, / Becker는 Princeton University로 진학했고, / 거기서 그는 경제학을 전공했다.
「He was dissatisfied / with his economic education at Princeton University / because "it didn't seem to be handling real problems."」 ③의 근거 불일치
그는 불만족했다. / Princeton University에서의 경제학 교육에 / '그것이 현실적인 문제를 다루고 있는 것처럼 보이지 않기' 때문에
「He earned a doctor's degree in economics / from the University of Chicago / in 1955.」 ④의 근거 일치
그는 경제학 박사 학위를 취득했다. / University of Chicago에서 / 1955년에
His doctoral paper on the economics of discrimination / was mentioned by the Nobel Prize Committee / as an important contribution to economics.
차별의 경제학에 대한 그의 박사 논문은 / 노벨상 위원회에 의해 언급되었다. / 경제학에 대한 중요한 기여로
「Since 1985, / Becker had written a regular economics column in Business Week, / explaining economic analysis and ideas to the general public.」 ⑤의 근거 일치
1985년부터, / Becker는 Business Week에 경제학 칼럼을 정기적으로 기고했다. / 경제학적 분석과 아이디어를 일반 대중에게 설명하는
In 1992, / he was awarded / the Nobel Prize in economic science.
1992년에, / 그는 수상했다. / 노벨 경제학상을

Gary Becker는 1930년 Pennsylvania 주 Pottsville에서 태어났고 New York City의 Brooklyn에서 자랐다. 교육을 제대로 받지 못한 그의 아버지는 금융과 정치 문제에 깊은 관심이 있었다. 고등학교를 졸업한 후, Becker는 Princeton University로 진학했고, 거기서 그는 경제학을 전공했다. 'Princeton University에서의 경제학 교육이 현실적인 문제를 다루고 있는 것처럼 보이지 않았기' 때문에 그는 그것에 불만족했다. 그는 1955년에 University of Chicago에서 경제학 박사 학위를 취득했다. 차별의 경제학에 대한 그의 박사 논문은 노벨상 위원회에 의해 경제학에 대한 중요한 기여로 언급되었다. 1985년부터, Becker는 Business Week에 경제학적 분석과 아이디어를 일반 대중에게 설명하는 경제학 칼럼을 정기적으로 기고했다. 1992년에, 그는 노벨 경제학상을 수상했다.

Why? 왜 정답일까?

'He was dissatisfied with his economic education at Princeton University ~'에서 Gary Becker는 Princeton University에서의 경제학 교육에 불만족했다고 하므로, 내용과 일치하지 않는 것은 ③ 'Princeton University에서의 경제학 교육에 만족했다.'이다.

Why? 왜 오답일까?

① 'Gary Becker ~ grew up in Brooklyn, New York City.'의 내용과 일치한다.
② 'His father, who was not well educated, had a deep interest in financial and political issues.'의 내용과 일치한다.
④ 'He earned a doctor's degree in economics from the University of Chicago in 1955.'의 내용과 일치한다.
⑤ 'Since 1985, Becker had written a regular economics column in Business Week, ~'의 내용과 일치한다.

● financial ⓐ 재정적인 ● handle ⓥ 다루다, 대처하다

● doctoral paper 박사 논문 ● discrimination ⓝ 차별
● mention ⓥ 언급하다 ● contribution ⓝ 기여, 이바지
● analysis ⓝ 분석 ● award ⓥ 상을 주다, 수여하다

구문 풀이

13행 In 1992, he was awarded the Nobel Prize in economic science.
4형식 수동태 ／ 직접목적어

---

27 드론 레이싱 선수권 정답률 94% | 정답 ⑤

2023 Drone Racing Championship에 관한 다음 안내문의 내용과 일치하지 <u>않는</u> 것은?
① 7월 9일 일요일에 개최된다.
② 고등학생만 참가할 수 있다.
③ 자신의 드론을 가져와야 한다.
④ 상금과 메달이 우승자에게 수여될 것이다.
☑ 20명의 참가자가 기념품을 받을 것이다.

2023 Drone Racing Championship
2023 드론 레이싱 선수권
Are you the best drone racer?
여러분은 최고의 드론 레이서인가요?
Then take the opportunity / to prove you are the one!
그렇다면 기회를 잡으세요! / 여러분이 바로 그 사람이라는 것을 증명할
When & Where
일시 & 장소
「6 p.m. – 8 p.m., Sunday, July 9」 ①의 근거 일치
7월 9일 일요일 오후 6시부터 오후 8시까지
Lakeside Community Center
Lakeside 주민센터
Requirements
필수 조건
「Participants: High school students only」 ②의 근거 일치
참가자: 고등학생만
「Bring your own drone for the race.」 ③의 근거 일치
레이스를 위해 당신의 드론을 가져 오세요.
Prize
부상
「$500 and a medal will be awarded to the winner.」 ④의 근거 일치
500달러와 메달이 우승자에게 수여될 것입니다.
Note
참고 사항
「The first 10 participants will get souvenirs.」 ⑤의 근거 불일치
선착순 10명의 참가자들은 기념품을 받게 될 것입니다.
For more details, / please visit www.droneracing.com / or call 313-6745-1189.
더 많은 세부 정보를 원하시면, / www.droneracing.com을 방문하거나 / 313-6745-1189로 전화하세요.

2023 Drone Racing Championship(2023 드론 레이싱 선수권)

여러분은 최고의 드론 레이서인가요? 그렇다면 여러분이 바로 그 사람이라는 것을 증명할 기회를 잡으세요!

일시 & 장소
• 7월 9일 일요일 오후 6시부터 오후 8시까지
• Lakeside 주민센터

필수 조건
• 참가자: 고등학생만
• 레이스를 위해 당신의 드론을 가져 오세요.

부상
• 500달러와 메달이 우승자에게 수여될 것입니다.

참고 사항
• 선착순 10명의 참가자들은 기념품을 받게 될 것입니다.

더 많은 세부 정보를 원하시면, www.droneracing.com을 방문하거나 313-6745-1189로 전화하세요.

Why? 왜 정답일까?

'The first 10 participants will get souvenirs.'에서 선착순 10명의 참가자에게 기념품을 준다고 하므로, 안내문의 내용과 일치하지 않는 것은 ⑤ '20명의 참가자가 기념품을 받을 것이다.'이다.

Why? 왜 오답일까?

① '6 p.m. – 8 p.m., Sunday, July 9'의 내용과 일치한다.
② 'Participants: High school students only'의 내용과 일치한다.
③ 'Bring your own drone for the race.'의 내용과 일치한다.
④ '$500 and a medal will be awarded to the winner.'의 내용과 일치한다.

● drone ⓝ 드론, 무인 항공기 ● championship ⓝ 선수권
● take an opportunity 기회를 잡다 ● prove ⓥ 증명하다
● requirement ⓝ 필수 요건 ● bring ⓥ 가져오다, 지참하다
● souvenir ⓝ 기념품

---

28 스쿠버 다이빙 일일 수업 광고 정답률 86% | 정답 ⑤

Summer Scuba Diving One-day Class에 관한 다음 안내문의 내용과 일치하는 것은?
① 오후 시간에 바다에서 다이빙 기술을 연습한다.
② 그룹 수업의 최대 정원은 4명이다.
③ 다이빙 장비를 유료로 대여할 수 있다.
④ 연령에 관계없이 참가할 수 있다.
☑ 적어도 수업 시작 5일 전까지 등록해야 한다.

Summer Scuba Diving One-day Class
여름 스쿠버 다이빙 일일 수업
Join our summer scuba diving lesson for beginners, / and become an underwater explorer!
초보자용 여름 스쿠버 다이빙 수업에 참여하여 / 수중 탐험가가 되세요!
Schedule
일정
10:00 – 12:00 Learning the basics
10시 – 12시 기초 배우기
「13:00 – 16:00 Practicing diving skills in a pool」 [①의 근거] 불일치
13시 – 16시 수영장에서 다이빙 기술 연습하기
Price
가격
Private lesson: $150
개인 수업: $150
「Group lesson (up to 3 people): $100 per person」 [②의 근거] 불일치
그룹 수업 (최대 3명): 1인당 $100
「Participants can rent our diving equipment for free.」 [③의 근거] 불일치
참가자는 다이빙 장비를 무료로 대여할 수 있습니다.
Notice
알림
「Participants must be 10 years old or over.」 [④의 근거] 불일치
참가자는 10세 이상이어야 합니다.
「Participants must register / at least 5 days before the class begins.」 [⑤의 근거] 일치
참가자는 등록해야 합니다. / 적어도 수업 시작 5일 전까지
For more information, / please go to www.ssdiver.com.
더 많은 정보를 원하시면, / www.ssdiver.com을 방문하세요.

Summer Scuba Diving One-day Class(여름 스쿠버 다이빙 일일 수업)

초보자용 여름 스쿠버 다이빙 수업에 참여하여 수중 탐험가가 되세요!

일정
- 10시 – 12시 기초 배우기
- 13시 – 16시 수영장에서 다이빙 기술 연습하기

가격
- 개인 수업: $150
- 그룹 수업 (최대 3명): 1인당 $100
- 참가자는 다이빙 장비를 무료로 대여할 수 있습니다.

알림
- 참가자는 10세 이상이어야 합니다.
- 참가자는 적어도 수업 시작 5일 전까지 등록해야 합니다.

더 많은 정보를 원하시면, www.ssdiver.com을 방문하세요.

Why? 왜 정답일까?

'Participants must register at least 5 days before the class begins.'에서 참가를 원하면 적어도 수업 시작 5일 전까지 등록하라고 하므로, 안내문의 내용과 일치하는 것은 ⑤ '적어도 수업 시작 5일 전까지 등록해야 한다.'이다.

Why? 왜 오답일까?

① '13:00 – 16:00 Practicing diving skills in a pool'에서 다이빙 기술을 연습하는 장소는 바다가 아니라 수영장이라고 하였다.
② 'Group lesson (up to 3 people): ~'에서 그룹 수업은 최대 3명까지라고 하였다.
③ 'Participants can rent our diving equipment for free.'에서 다이빙 장비는 무료로 대여할 수 있다고 하였다.
④ 'Participants must be 10 years old or over.'에서 참가 가능 연령은 10세 이상이라고 하였다.

- one-day class 일일 수업
- explorer [n] 탐험가
- private lesson 개인 레슨
- underwater [a] 물속의, 수중의
- basics [n] 기본, 필수적인 것들
- equipment [n] 장비

29 칭찬이 아이들의 자존감에 미치는 효과 정답률 55% | 정답 ④

다음 글의 밑줄 친 부분 중, 어법상 틀린 것은? [3점]

Although praise is one of the most powerful tools / available for improving young children's behavior, / it is equally powerful / for improving your child's self-esteem.
칭찬은 가장 강력한 도구 중 하나이지만, / 어린 아이들의 행동을 개선하는 데 사용할 수 있는 / 그것은 똑같이 강력하다. / 아이의 자존감을 향상시키는 데에도
Preschoolers believe / what their parents tell ① them / in a very profound way.
미취학 아동들은 여긴다. / 그들의 부모가 그들에게 하는 말을 / 매우 뜻 깊게
They do not yet have the cognitive sophistication / to reason ② analytically and reject false information.
그들은 인지적 정교함을 아직 가지고 있지 않다. / 분석적으로 추론하고 잘못된 정보를 거부할 수 있는
If a preschool boy consistently hears from his mother / ③ that he is smart and a good helper, / he is likely to incorporate that information into his self-image.
만약 미취학 소년이 그의 어머니로부터 계속 듣는다면, / 그가 똑똑하고 좋은 조력자라는 것을 / 그는 그 정보를 자기 자아상으로 통합시킬 가능성이 높다.
Thinking of himself as a boy / who is smart and knows how to do things / ✔④ is likely to make him endure longer in problem-solving efforts / and increase his confidence in trying new and difficult tasks.
스스로를 소년으로 생각하는 것은 / 똑똑하고 일을 어떻게 하는지 아는 / 그가 문제 해결 노력에 있어 더 오래 지속하게 만들 가능성이 높다. / 그리고 새롭고 어려운 일을 시도할 때 그의 자신감을 높일
Similarly, / thinking of himself as the kind of boy / who is a good helper / will make him more likely / to volunteer ⑤ to help with tasks at home and at preschool.
마찬가지로, / 자신을 그런 부류의 소년으로 생각하는 것은 / 좋은 조력자인 / 그가 ~할 가능성이 더 커지게 할 것이다. / 집과 유치원에서 일을 자발적으로 도울

칭찬은 어린 아이들의 행동을 개선하는 데 사용할 수 있는 가장 강력한 도구 중 하나이지만, 그것은 아이의 자존감을 향상시키는 데에도 똑같이 강력하다. 미취학 아동들은 그들의 부모가 그들에게 하는 말을 매우 뜻 깊게 여긴다. 그들은 분석적으로 추론하고 잘못된 정보를 거부할 수 있는 인지적 정교함을 아직 가지고 있지 않다. 만약 미취학 소년이 그의 어머니로부터 그가 똑똑하고 좋은 조력자라는 것을 계속 듣는다면, 그는 그 정보를 자기 자아상으로 통합시킬 가능성이 높다. 스스로를 똑똑하고 일을 어떻게 하는지 아는 소년으로 생각하는 것은 그가 문제 해결 노력에 있어 더 오래 지속하게 하고, 새롭고 어려운 일을 시도할 때 그의 자신감을 높일 가능성이 높다. 마찬가지로, 자신을 좋은 조력자인 그런 부류의 소년으로 생각하는 것은 그가 집과 유치원에서 일을 자발적으로 도울 가능성이 더 커지게 할 것이다.

Why? 왜 정답일까?

주어인 동명사구(Thinking of himself as a boy ~) 뒤에 동사가 있어야 하므로, being을 is로 고쳐야 한다. 따라서 어법상 틀린 것은 ④이다.

Why? 왜 오답일까?

① tell의 주어는 their parents인데, 목적어는 문맥상 문장의 주어인 Preschoolers이다. 따라서 재귀대명사를 쓰지 않고, 인칭대명사 them을 썼다.
② to부정사구 to reason을 수식하는 부사 analytically이다.
③ hears의 목적절을 이끄는 접속사로 that이 알맞다. from his mother가 동사 앞으로 들어간 구조이다.
⑤ volunteer는 to부정사를 목적어로 취하므로 to help가 알맞다.

- self-esteem [n] 자존감
- profound [a] 뜻 깊은
- sophistication [n] 정교화(함)
- analytically [ad] 분석적으로
- incorporate A into B A를 B로 통합시키다
- preschooler [n] 미취학 아동
- cognitive [a] 인지적인
- reason [v] 추론하다
- consistently [ad] 지속적으로
- endure [v] 지속하다, 참다

구문 풀이

6행 If a preschool boy consistently hears(동사) from his mother(부사구) {that he is smart and a good helper}({ }: hears의 목적어), he is likely to incorporate that information into his self-image.

30 광고주의 메시지 조절 정답률 55% | 정답 ②

다음 글의 밑줄 친 부분 중, 문맥상 낱말의 쓰임이 적절하지 않은 것은?

Advertisers often displayed considerable facility / in ① adapting their claims / to the market status of the goods they promoted.
광고주들은 상당한 능력을 자주 보여주었다. / 그들의 주장을 맞추는 데 있어 / 그들이 홍보하는 상품의 시장 지위에
Fleischmann's yeast, / for instance, / was used / as an ingredient for cooking homemade bread.
Fleischmann의 효모는 / 예를 들어, / 사용되었다. / 집에서 만든 빵을 요리하는 재료로
Yet / more and more people in the early 20th century / were buying their bread from stores or bakeries, / so consumer demand for yeast ✔② declined.
하지만 / 20세기 초의 점점 더 많은 사람들이 / 가게나 빵집에서 빵을 사고 있었고, / 그래서 효모에 대한 소비자 수요는 감소했다.
The producer of Fleischmann's yeast / hired the J. Walter Thompson advertising agency / to come up with a different marketing strategy / to ③ boost sales.
Fleischmann의 효모의 생산자는 / J. Walter Thompson 광고 대행사를 고용했다. / 다른 마케팅 전략을 고안하려고 / 판매를 촉진하기 위해서
No longer the "Soul of Bread," / the Thompson agency first turned yeast / into an important source of vitamins / with significant health ④ benefits.
더 이상 "Soul of Bread"를 쓰지 않고, / Thompson 광고 대행사는 먼저 효모를 바꾸었다. / 중요한 비타민 공급원으로 / 상당한 건강상의 이점이 있는
Shortly thereafter, / the advertising agency transformed yeast into a natural laxative.
그 이후 얼마 안 되어, / 광고 대행사는 효모를 천연 완하제로 바꾸었다.
⑤ Repositioning yeast / helped increase sales.
효모의 이미지 전환은 / 매출을 증가시키는 것을 도왔다.

광고주들은 그들이 홍보하는 상품의 시장 지위에 주장을 ① 맞추는 상당한 능력을 자주 보여주었다. 예를 들어, Fleischmann의 효모는 집에서 만든 빵을 요리하는 재료로 사용되었다. 하지만 20세기 초에 점점 더 많은 사람들이 가게나 빵집에서 빵을 사고 있었고, 그래서 효모에 대한 소비자 수요는 ② 증가했다(→ 감소했다). Fleischmann의 효모의 생산자는 판매를 ③ 촉진하기 위해서 다른 마케팅 전략을 고안하려고 J. Walter Thompson 광고 대행사를 고용했다. 더 이상 "Soul of Bread"를 쓰지 않고, Thompson 광고 대행사는 먼저 효모를 상당한 건강상의 ④ 이점이 있는 중요한 비타민 공급원으로 바꾸었다. 그 이후 얼마 안 되어, 광고 대행사는 효모를 천연 완하제로 바꾸었다. 효모의 ⑤ 이미지 전환은 매출을 증가시키는 것을 도왔다.

Why? 왜 정답일까?

과거 효모는 집에서 굽는 빵의 재료로 쓰였지만, 20세기에 접어들어 사람들이 점점 가게에서 구운 빵을 사면서 효모에 대한 수요가 '떨어졌다'는 설명이 되도록 increased를 declined로 고쳐야 한다. 따라서 문맥상 낱말의 쓰임이 적절하지 않은 것은 ②이다.

- considerable [a] 상당한
- ingredient [n] 재료
- come up with 떠올리다, 고안하다
- significant [a] 상당한, 중요한
- laxative [n] 완하제(배변을 쉽게 하는 약·음식·음료)
- facility [n] 능력, 재능
- hire [v] 고용하다
- strategy [n] 전략
- transform [v] 변모시키다
- reposition [v] (제품의) 이미지를 바꾸다

구문 풀이

1행 Advertisers often displayed considerable facility in adapting their claims(~하는 데 있어, ~할 때) to the market status of the goods(선행사) [(that) they promoted](생략).

★★★ 등급을 가르는 문제!

31 탁월함과 타인의 신뢰 정답률 50% | 정답 ④

다음 빈칸에 들어갈 말로 가장 적절한 것을 고르시오.

① Patience – 인내심 ② Sacrifice – 희생 ③ Honesty – 정직함
✔④ Excellence – 탁월함 ⑤ Creativity – 창의력

Individuals / who perform at a high level in their profession / often have instant credibility with others.
사람들은 / 자기 직업에서 높은 수준으로 수행하는 / 흔히 다른 사람들에게 즉각적인 신뢰를 얻는다.

People admire them, / they want to be like them, / and they feel connected to them.
사람들은 그들을 존경하고, / 그들처럼 되고 싶어 하고, / 그들과 연결되어 있다고 느낀다.

When they speak, / others listen / — even if the area of their skill / has nothing to do with the advice they give.
그들이 말할 때, / 다른 사람들은 경청한다. / 비록 그들의 기술 분야가 / 그들이 주는 조언과 전혀 관련이 없을지라도

Think about a world-famous basketball player.
세계적으로 유명한 농구 선수에 대해 생각해 보라.

He has made more money from endorsements / than he ever did playing basketball.
그는 광고로부터 더 많은 돈을 벌었다. / 그가 농구를 하면서 그간 벌었던 것보다

Is it because of / his knowledge of the products he endorses?
그것이 ~ 때문일까? / 그가 광고하는 제품에 대한 그의 지식

No.
아니다.

It's because of / what he can do with a basketball.
그것은 ~ 때문이다. / 그가 농구로 할 수 있는 것

The same can be said of an Olympic medalist swimmer.
올림픽 메달리스트 수영 선수도 마찬가지이다.

People listen to him / because of what he can do in the pool.
사람들은 그의 말을 경청한다. / 그가 수영장에서 할 수 있는 것 때문에

And when an actor tells us / we should drive a certain car, / we don't listen / because of his expertise on engines.
그리고 어떤 배우가 우리에게 말할 때, / 우리가 특정 자동차를 운전해야 한다고 / 우리는 경청하는 것은 아니다. / 엔진에 대한 그의 전문 지식 때문에

We listen / because we admire his talent.
우리는 경청한다. / 그의 재능을 존경하기 때문에

Excellence connects.
탁월함이 연결된다.

If you possess a high level of ability in an area, / others may desire to connect with you / because of it.
만약 당신이 어떤 분야에서 높은 수준의 능력을 갖고 있다면, / 다른 사람들은 당신과 연결되기를 원할 수도 있다. / 그것 때문에

자기 직업에서 높은 수준으로 수행하는 사람들은 흔히 다른 사람들에게 즉각적인 신뢰를 얻는다. 사람들은 그들을 존경하고, 그들처럼 되고 싶어 하고, 그들과 연결되어 있다고 느낀다. 그들이 말할 때, 다른 사람들은 비록 그들의 기술 분야가 그들이 주는 조언과 전혀 관련이 없을지라도 경청한다. 세계적으로 유명한 농구 선수에 대해 생각해 보라. 그는 그가 농구를 하면서 그간 벌었던 것보다 광고로부터 더 많은 돈을 벌었다. 그것이 그가 광고하는 제품에 대한 그의 지식 때문일까? 아니다. 그것은 그가 농구로 할 수 있는 것 때문이다. 올림픽 메달리스트 수영 선수도 마찬가지이다. 사람들은 그가 수영장에서 할 수 있는 것 때문에 그의 말을 경청한다. 그리고 어떤 배우가 우리에게 특정 자동차를 운전해야 한다고 말할 때, 우리는 엔진에 대한 그의 전문 지식 때문에 경청하는 것은 아니다. 우리는 그의 재능을 존경하기 때문에 경청한다. 탁월함이 연결된다. 만약 당신이 어떤 분야에서 높은 수준의 능력을 갖고 있다면, 다른 사람들은 그것 때문에 당신과 연결되기를 원할 수도 있다.

Why? 왜 정답일까?

처음(Individuals who perform at a high level in their profession often have instant credibility with others.)과 마지막(If you possess a high level of ability in an area, others may desire to connect with you because of it.)에서 자기 분야에서 '높은 수준의 능력'을 가진 사람들은 다른 이들의 신뢰를 사기 쉽다고 언급하는 것으로 보아, 빈칸에 들어갈 말로 가장 적절한 것은 ④ '탁월함'이다.

- profession ⓝ 직업
- credibility ⓝ 신뢰
- have nothing to do with ~와 관련이 없다
- endorsement ⓝ (유명인의 텔레비전 등에서의 상품) 보증 선전
- endorse ⓥ (유명인이 광고에 나와 특정 상품을) 보증하다, 홍보하다
- medalist ⓝ 메달리스트
- patience ⓝ 인내심
- instant ⓐ 즉각적인
- admire ⓥ 존경하다
- world-famous ⓐ 세계적으로 유명한
- expertise ⓝ 전문 지식
- sacrifice ⓝ 희생

구문 풀이

6행 He has made more money from endorsements than he ever did playing basketball.
대동사(= made money)

★★ 문제 해결 꿀~팁 ★★

▶ 많이 틀린 이유는?
빈칸 바로 앞에서 '전문 지식' 때문이 아니라 '재능' 때문에 유명인들의 말을 듣게 된다고 하는데, 이것을 ② '희생'이나 ③ '정직함'의 사례로 볼 수는 없다.
▶ 문제 해결 방법은?
글 처음과 마지막에 요지가 반복 제시된다. 즉 주제문인 첫 문장을 보고 빈칸을 완성하면 간단하다.

★★★ 등급을 가르는 문제! ★★★

32 도시처럼 상호작용으로 작동하는 뇌   정답률 43% | 정답 ①

다음 빈칸에 들어갈 말로 가장 적절한 것을 고르시오. [3점]

✔ operates in isolation – 독립적으로 작동하지
② suffers from rapid changes – 급속한 변화로 고생하지
③ resembles economic elements – 경제적 요소를 닮지
④ works in a systematic way – 체계적으로 작동하지
⑤ interacts with another – 서로 상호작용하지

Think of the brain as a city.
뇌를 도시라고 생각해보라.

If you were to look out over a city / and ask "where is the economy located?" / you'd see / there's no good answer to the question.
만약 당신이 도시를 내다보며 / "경제는 어디에 위치해 있나요?"라고 묻는다면 / 당신은 알게 될 것이다. / 그 질문에 좋은 답이 없다는 것을

Instead, / the economy emerges / from the interaction of all the elements / — from the stores and the banks / to the merchants and the customers.
대신, / 경제는 나타난다. / 모든 요소의 상호 작용으로부터 / 상점과 은행에서 / 상인과 고객에 이르기까지

And so it is with the brain's operation: / it doesn't happen in one spot.
뇌의 작용도 그렇다. / 즉 그것은 한 곳에서 일어나지 않는다.

Just as in a city, / no neighborhood of the brain / operates in isolation.
도시에서처럼, / 뇌의 어떤 지역도 ~않는다. / 독립적으로 작동하지

In brains and in cities, / everything emerges / from the interaction between residents, / at all scales, / locally and distantly.
뇌와 도시 안에서, / 모든 것은 나타난다. / 거주자들 간의 상호 작용으로부터 / 모든 규모로, / 근거리든 원거리든

Just as trains bring materials and textiles into a city, / which become processed into the economy, / so the raw electrochemical signals from sensory organs / are transported along superhighways of neurons.
기차가 자재와 직물을 도시로 들여오고, / 그것이 경제 속으로 처리되는 것처럼, / 감각 기관으로부터의 가공되지 않은 전기화학적 신호는 / 뉴런의 초고속도로를 따라서 전해진다.

There / the signals undergo processing / and transformation into our conscious reality.
거기서 / 신호는 처리를 겪는다. / 그리고 우리의 의식적인 현실로의 변형을

뇌를 도시라고 생각해보라. 만약 당신이 도시를 내다보며 "경제는 어디에 위치해 있나요?"라고 묻는다면 그 질문에 좋은 답이 없다는 것을 알게 될 것이다. 대신, 경제는 상점과 은행에서 상인과 고객에 이르기까지 모든 요소의 상호 작용으로부터 나타난다. 뇌의 작용도 그렇다. 즉 그것은 한 곳에서 일어나지 않는다. 도시에서처럼, 뇌의 어떤 지역도 독립적으로 작동하지 않는다. 뇌와 도시 안에서, 모든 것은 모든 규모로, 근거리든 원거리든, 거주자들 간의 상호 작용으로부터 나타난다. 기차가 자재와 직물을 도시로 들여오고, 그것이 경제 속으로 처리되는 것처럼, 감각 기관으로부터의 가공되지 않은 전기화학적 신호는 뉴런의 초고속도로를 따라서 전해진다. 거기서 신호는 처리와 우리의 의식적인 현실로의 변형을 겪는다.

Why? 왜 정답일까?

경제가 모든 요소의 상호 작용으로 작동하는 것처럼 뇌 또한 그렇다(And so it is with the brain's operation: it doesn't happen in one spot. / ~ everything emerges from the interaction ~)는 내용이므로, 빈칸에 들어갈 말로 가장 적절한 것은 ① '독립적으로 작동하지'이다.

- think of A as B A를 B로 여기다
- element ⓝ 요소
- operation ⓝ 작동, 작용
- distantly ⓐ 멀리, 원거리로
- process ⓥ 가공하다, 처리하다
- electrochemical ⓐ 전기화학의
- transport ⓥ 수송하다, 실어 나르다
- transformation ⓝ 변화, 변모
- in isolation 고립되어
- emerge ⓥ 나타나다, 생겨나다
- merchant ⓝ 상인
- locally ⓐ 국지적으로
- textile ⓝ 직물
- raw ⓐ 원재료의, 날것의
- sensory organ 감각 기관
- undergo ⓥ 거치다, 겪다
- conscious ⓐ 의식적인

구문 풀이

1행 If you were to look out over a city and ask "where is the economy
「if + 주어 + were to + 동사원형 + ~   동사원형2 ~
located?" you'd see there's no good answer to the question.
주어 + 조동사 과거형 + 동사원형 : 가정법 미래(거의 불가능한 상황에 대한 가정)

★★ 문제 해결 꿀~팁 ★★

▶ 많이 틀린 이유는?
도시가 많은 경제 주체의 상호 작용을 통해 돌아가듯이 뇌 또한 수많은 요소의 상호 작용으로 돌아간다는 내용이다. 주어가 「no + 명사」 형태이므로, 빈칸에는 주제와 반대되는 말을 넣어야 문장 전체가 주제를 나타내게 된다. 하지만 ③은 '경제 주체와 비슷하다'는 주제를 직접 제시하므로, 이를 빈칸에 넣어서 읽으면 '뇌의 그 어느 구역도 경제 주체와 비슷하지 않다'는 의미가 되어버린다. 즉 ③은 주제와 정반대되는 의미를 완성한다.
▶ 문제 해결 방법은?
'뇌 = 도시'라는 비유를 확인하고, 둘의 공통점이 무엇인지 파악한 후, 선택지를 하나씩 대입하며 빈칸 문장의 의미를 주의 깊게 이해해 보자.

33 신체로부터 발생하는 감정   정답률 57% | 정답 ②

다음 빈칸에 들어갈 말로 가장 적절한 것을 고르시오. [3점]

① language guides our actions – 언어가 우리 행동을 이끈다
✔ emotions arise from our bodies – 감정이 우리 신체에 발생한다
③ body language hides our feelings – 신체 언어는 우리 감정을 숨긴다
④ what others say affects our mood – 다른 사람들의 말이 우리 감정에 영향을 미친다
⑤ negative emotions easily disappear – 부정적 감정은 쉽게 사라진다

Someone else's body language affects our own body, / which then creates an emotional echo / that makes us feel accordingly.
다른 사람의 신체 언어는 우리 자신의 신체에 영향을 미치며, / 그것은 그 후 감정적인 메아리를 만들어낸다. / 우리가 그에 맞춰 느끼게 하는

As Louis Armstrong sang, / "When you're smiling, / the whole world smiles with you."
Louis Armstrong이 노래했듯이, / "당신이 미소 지을 때, / 전 세계가 당신과 함께 미소 짓는다."

If copying another's smile / makes us feel happy, / the emotion of the smiler / has been transmitted via our body.
만약 다른 사람의 미소를 따라 하는 것이 / 우리를 행복하게 한다면, / 그 미소 짓는 사람의 감정은 / 우리의 신체를 통해 전달된 것이다.

Strange as it may sound, / this theory states / that emotions arise from our bodies.
이상하게 들릴지 모르지만, / 이 이론은 말한다. / 감정이 우리 신체에서 발생한다고

For example, / our mood can be improved / by simply lifting up the corners of our mouth.
예를 들어, / 우리의 기분은 좋아질 수 있다. / 단순히 입꼬리를 올리는 것으로

If people are asked / to bite down on a pencil lengthwise, / taking care not to let the pencil touch their lips / (thus forcing the mouth into a smile-like shape), / they judge cartoons funnier / than if they have been asked to frown.
만약 사람들이 요구받으면, / 연필을 긴 방향으로 꽉 물라고 / 연필이 입술에 닿지 않도록 조심하면서 / (그래서 억지로 입을 미소 짓는 것과 같은 모양이 되도록), / 그들은 만화를 더 재미있다고 판단한다. / 그들이 인상을 찌푸리라고 요구받은 경우보다

The primacy of the body / is sometimes summarized in the phrase / "I must be afraid, / because I'm running."

신체가 우선한다는 것은 / 때로로 구절로 요약된다. / "나는 분명 두려운가보다. / 왜냐하면 나는 도망치고 있기 때문이다."라는

다른 사람의 신체 언어는 우리 자신의 신체에 영향을 미치며, 그것은 그 후 우리가 그에 맞춰 (감정을) 느끼게 하는 감정적인 메아리를 만들어낸다. Louis Armstrong이 노래했듯이, "당신이 미소 지을 때, 전 세계가 당신과 함께 미소 짓는다." 만약 다른 사람의 미소를 따라 하는 것이 우리를 행복하게 한다면, 그 미소 짓는 사람의 감정은 우리의 신체를 통해 전달된 것이다. 이상하게 들릴지 모르지만, 이 이론은 감정이 우리 신체에서 발생한다고 말한다. 예를 들어, 우리의 기분은 단순히 입꼬리를 올리는 것으로 좋아질 수 있다. 만약 사람들이 연필을 긴 방향으로 꽉 물라고 요구받으면, 연필이 입술에 닿지 않도록 조심하면서 (그래서 억지로 입을 미소 짓는 것과 같은 모양이 되도록), 그들은 인상을 찌푸리라고 요구받은 경우보다 만화를 더 재미있다고 판단한다. 신체가 (감정에) 우선한다는 것은 "나는 분명 두려운가보다, 왜냐하면 나는 도망치고 있기 때문이다."라는 구절로 때로로 요약된다.

Why? 왜 정답일까?

빈칸 뒤의 실험에서 우리가 입꼬리를 올리고 있다 보면 더 기분이 좋아질 수 있다(~ our mood can be improved by simply lifting up the corners of our mouth.)고 설명하고, 이를 마지막 문장에서는 '(감정에 대한) 신체의 우선(The primacy of the body)'이라고 요약했다. 따라서 빈칸에 들어갈 말로 가장 적절한 것은 ② '감정이 우리 신체에서 발생한다'이다.

- emotional ⓐ 정서적인
- transmit ⓥ 전달하다
- theory ⓝ 이론
- lift up ~을 들어올리다
- bite down on ~을 깨물다
- frown ⓥ 얼굴을 찡그리다
- summarize ⓥ 요약하다
- hide ⓥ 숨기다
- accordingly ⓐⓓ 그에 따라
- via prep ~을 통해서
- state ⓥ 진술하다
- be asked to ~하도록 요청받다
- lengthwise ⓐⓓ 길게
- primacy ⓝ 우선함
- arise from ~에서 생겨나다

구문 풀이

5행 Strange as it may sound, this theory states that emotions arise from our bodies.
「보어+as+주어+동사 : 비록 ~일지라도(양보 구문)」

---

34 구매를 이끄는 희소성 · 정답률 59% | 정답 ③

다음 빈칸에 들어갈 말로 가장 적절한 것을 고르시오. [3점]
① Promoting products through social media
소셜 미디어를 통해 제품을 홍보하는 것
② Reducing the risk of producing poor quality items
질이 좋지 않은 제품을 생산할 위험을 낮추는 것
③ Restricting the number of items customers can buy
고객이 구입할 수 있는 품목의 개수를 제한하는 것
④ Offering several options that customers find attractive
고객들이 매력적이라고 생각하는 몇 가지 선택 사항을 제시하는 것
⑤ Emphasizing the safety of products with research data
연구 데이터로 제품의 안전성을 강조하는 것

Restricting the number of items customers can buy / boosts sales.
고객이 구입할 수 있는 품목의 개수를 제한하는 것은 / 매출을 증가시킨다.
Brian Wansink, / Professor of Marketing at Cornell University, / investigated the effectiveness of this tactic in 1998.
Brian Wansink는 / Cornell University의 마케팅 교수인 / 1998년에 이 전략의 효과를 조사했다.
He persuaded three supermarkets in Sioux City, Iowa, / to offer Campbell's soup at a small discount: / 79 cents rather than 89 cents.
그는 Iowa 주 Sioux City에 있는 세 개의 슈퍼마켓을 설득했다. / Campbell의 수프를 약간 할인하여 제공하도록 / 즉 89센트가 아닌 79센트로
The discounted soup was sold in one of three conditions: / a control, / where there was no limit on the volume of purchases, / or two tests, / where customers were limited to either four or twelve cans.
할인된 수프는 세 가지 조건 중 하나의 조건으로 판매되었다. / 즉 하나의 통제 집단, / 구매량에 제한이 없는 / 또는 두 개의 실험 집단 / 고객이 4개 아니면 12개의 캔으로 제한되는
In the unlimited condition / shoppers bought 3.3 cans on average, / whereas in the scarce condition, / when there was a limit, / they bought 5.3 on average.
무제한 조건에서 / 구매자들은 평균 3.3캔을 구입했고, / 반면 희소 조건에서는 / 제한이 있던 / 그들은 평균 5.3캔을 구입했다.
This suggests / scarcity encourages sales.
이것은 보여준다. / 희소성이 판매를 장려한다는 것을
The findings are particularly strong / because the test took place / in a supermarket with genuine shoppers.
그 결과는 특히 타당하다. / 이 실험이 진행되었기 때문에 / 진짜 구매자들이 있는 슈퍼마켓에서
It didn't rely on claimed data, / nor was it held in a laboratory / where consumers might behave differently.
그것은 주장된 데이터에 의존하지 않았고, / 그것은 실험실에서 이루어진 것도 아니었다. / 소비자들이 다르게 행동할지도 모르는

고객이 구입할 수 있는 품목의 개수를 제한하는 것은 매출을 증가시킨다. Cornell University의 마케팅 교수인 Brian Wansink는 1998년에 이 전략의 효과를 조사했다. 그는 Iowa 주 Sioux City에 있는 세 개의 슈퍼마켓이 Campbell의 수프를 약간 할인하여 89센트가 아닌 79센트로 제공하도록 설득했다. 할인된 수프는 세 가지 조건 중 하나의 조건으로 판매되었다. 구매량에 제한이 없는 하나의 통제 집단, 또는 고객이 4개 아니면 12개의 캔으로 제한되는 두 개의 실험 집단이었다. 무제한 조건에서 구매자들은 평균 3.3캔을 구입했던 반면, 제한이 있던 희소 조건에서는 평균 5.3캔을 구입했다. 이것은 희소성이 판매를 장려한다는 것을 보여준다. 이 실험은 진짜 구매자들이 있는 슈퍼마켓에서 진행되었기 때문에 그 결과는 특히 타당하다. 그것은 주장된 데이터에 의존하지 않았고, 소비자들이 다르게 행동할지도 모르는 실험실에서 이루어진 것도 아니었다.

Why? 왜 정답일까?

빈칸 뒤로 소개된 연구에서, 구매 개수에 제한이 있었던 실험군이 제품을 가장 많이 구입했다고 설명하며, 희소성이 판매를 장려한다는 결론을 정리하고 있다(~ scarcity encourages sales.). 따라서 빈칸에 들어갈 말로 가장 적절한 것은 ③ '고객이 구입할 수 있는 품목의 개수를 제한하는 것'이다.

- investigate ⓥ 조사하다
- tactic ⓝ 전략
- rather than ~ 대신에
- effectiveness ⓝ 유효성, 효과 있음
- persuade ⓥ 설득하다
- condition ⓝ 조건

07회 (side tab)

- control ⓝ 통제 집단(실험에서 처치를 가하지 않고 둔 집단)
- unlimited ⓐ 제한되지 않은, 무제한의
- genuine ⓐ 진짜의
- laboratory ⓝ 실험실
- differently ⓐⓓ 다르게
- emphasize ⓥ 강조하다
- scarcity ⓝ 희소성
- rely on ~에 의존하다
- behave ⓥ 행동하다
- attractive ⓐ 매력적인

구문 풀이

13행 It didn't rely on claimed data, nor was it held in a laboratory where
부정문 「부정어+be+주어+p.p. : 도치 구문(~도 않다)」
consumers might behave differently.

---

35 기술과 생산성의 관계 · 정답률 58% | 정답 ④

다음 글에서 전체 흐름과 관계 없는 문장은?

Although technology has the potential / to increase productivity, / it can also have a negative impact on productivity.
기술은 잠재력을 가지고 있지만, / 생산성을 높일 수 있는 / 그것은 또한 생산성에 부정적인 영향을 미칠 수 있다.
For example, / in many office environments / workers sit at desks with computers / and have access to the internet.
예를 들어, / 많은 사무실 환경에서 / 직원들은 컴퓨터가 있는 책상에 앉아 / 인터넷에 접속한다.
① They are able to check their personal e-mails / and use social media / whenever they want to.
그들은 개인 이메일을 확인하고 / 소셜 미디어를 사용할 수 있다. / 그들이 원할 때마다
② This can stop them from doing their work / and make them less productive.
이것은 그들이 일을 하는 것을 방해하고 / 생산성이 떨어지게 할 수 있다.
③ Introducing new technology / can also have a negative impact on production / when it causes a change to the production process / or requires workers to learn a new system.
새로운 기술을 도입하는 것은 / 또한 생산에 부정적인 영향을 미칠 수 있다. / 그것이 생산 공정에 변화를 야기하거나 / 직원들에게 새로운 시스템을 배우도록 요구할 때
④ Using technology / can enable businesses / to produce more goods / and to get more out of the other factors of production.
기술을 사용하는 것은 / 기업이 ~할 수 있게 한다. / 더 많은 제품을 생산하고 / 다른 생산 요소로부터 더 많은 것을 얻게
⑤ Learning to use new technology / can be time consuming and stressful for workers / and this can cause a decline in productivity.
새로운 기술 사용법을 배우는 것은 / 직원들에게 시간이 많이 드는 일이고 스트레스를 줄 수 있으며, / 이것은 생산성 저하를 야기할 수 있다.

기술은 생산성을 높일 수 있는 잠재력을 가지고 있지만, 또한 생산성에 부정적인 영향을 미칠 수 있다. 예를 들어, 많은 사무실 환경에서 직원들은 컴퓨터가 있는 책상에 앉아 인터넷에 접속한다. ① 그들은 원할 때마다 개인 이메일을 확인하고 소셜 미디어를 사용할 수 있다. ② 이것은 그들이 일을 하는 것을 방해하고 생산성이 떨어지게 할 수 있다. ③ 또한 새로운 기술을 도입하는 것은 생산 공정에 변화를 야기하거나 직원들에게 새로운 시스템을 배우도록 요구할 때 생산에 부정적인 영향을 미칠 수 있다. ④ 기술을 사용하는 것은 기업이 더 많은 제품을 생산하고 다른 생산 요소들로부터 더 많은 것을 얻게 할 수 있다. ⑤ 새로운 기술 사용법을 배우는 것은 직원들에게 시간이 많이 드는 일이고 스트레스를 줄 수 있으며, 이것은 생산성 저하를 야기할 수 있다.

Why? 왜 정답일까?

기술이 생산성을 떨어뜨릴 수 있다는 내용인데, ④는 기술 사용이 더 많은 제품 생산에 도움이 되고 생산 요소로부터 더 많은 것을 얻게 한다는 긍정적 내용이다. 따라서 전체 흐름과 관계 없는 문장은 ④이다.

- impact ⓝ 영향, 충격
- production ⓝ 생산, 제조
- require ⓥ 요구하다
- time-consuming ⓐ 시간이 많이 걸리는
- have access to ~에 접근하다, ~을 이용하다
- cause ⓥ 야기하다
- factor ⓝ 요인, 요소

구문 풀이

5행 This can stop them from doing their work and make them less productive.
「stop+A+from+B : A가 B하지 못하게 하다」 5형식 동사 목적어 형용사 보어

---

36 시계의 발명 · 정답률 78% | 정답 ②

주어진 글 다음에 이어질 글의 순서로 가장 적절한 것을 고르시오. [3점]
① (A) – (C) – (B)
② (B) – (A) – (C)
③ (B) – (C) – (A)
④ (C) – (A) – (B)
⑤ (C) – (B) – (A)

Up until about 6,000 years ago, / most people were farmers.
약 6,000년 전까지 / 대부분의 사람들은 농부였다.
Many lived in different places throughout the year, / hunting for food / or moving their livestock to areas with enough food.
많은 사람들은 일 년 내내 여러 장소에서 살았다, / 식량을 찾아다니거나 / 가축을 충분한 먹이가 있는 지역으로 옮겼다.
(B) There was no need to tell the time / because life depended on natural cycles, / such as the changing seasons or sunrise and sunset.
시간을 알 필요가 없었다. / 삶이 자연적인 주기에 달려 있었기 때문에 / 변화하는 계절이나 일출과 일몰 같은
Gradually more people started to live in larger settlements, / and some needed to tell the time.
점점 더 많은 사람들이 더 큰 정착지에서 살기 시작했고, / 어떤 사람들은 시간을 알 필요가 있었다.
(A) For example, / priests wanted to know / when to carry out religious ceremonies.
예를 들어, / 성직자들은 알고 싶었다. / 언제 종교적인 의식을 수행해야 하는지
This was when people first invented clocks / — devices that show, measure, and keep track of passing time.
이때 사람들이 처음으로 발명했다. / 시간을 보여주고, 측정하고, 흐르는 시간을 추적하는 장치인 시계를
(C) Clocks have been important ever since.
시계는 그 이후로도 중요했다.
Today, / clocks are used for important things / such as setting busy airport timetables / — if the time is incorrect, / aeroplanes might crash into each other / when taking off or landing!

오늘날, / 시계는 중요한 일에 사용된다. / 바쁜 공항 시간표를 설정하는 것과 같은 / 만약 시간이 부정확하다면, / 비행기는 서로 충돌할지도 모른다! / 이륙하거나 착륙할 때

약 6,000년 전까지 대부분의 사람들은 농부였다. 많은 사람들은 일 년 내내 여러 장소에서 살았고, 식량을 찾아다니거나 가축을 충분한 먹이가 있는 지역으로 옮겼다.

(B) 변화하는 계절이나 일출과 일몰 같은 자연적인 주기에 삶이 달려 있었기 때문에 시간을 알 필요가 없었다. 점점 더 많은 사람들이 더 큰 정착지에서 살기 시작했고, 어떤 사람들은 시간을 알 필요가 있었다.

(A) 예를 들어, 성직자들은 언제 종교적인 의식을 수행해야 하는지 알고 싶었다. 이때 사람들이 시간을 보여주고, 측정하고, 흐르는 시간을 추적하는 장치인 시계를 처음으로 발명했다.

(C) 시계는 그 이후로도 중요했다. 오늘날, 시계는 바쁜 공항 시간표를 설정하는 것과 같은 중요한 일에 사용된다. 만약 시간이 부정확하다면, 비행기는 이륙하거나 착륙할 때 서로 충돌할지도 모른다!

Why? 왜 정답일까?

사람들이 대부분 농부였던 시절을 언급하는 주어진 글 뒤로, 이때는 시계가 필요 없었다는 내용으로 시작하는 (B)가 연결된다. 한편, (B)의 후반부는 그러다 일부 사람들이 시계를 필요로 하기 시작했다는 내용이고, (A)는 그런 사람들의 예로 성직자를 언급한다. (C)는 시계가 처음 발명된 이후로 시계의 중요성이 높아졌고, 오늘날에도 시계가 중요한 역할을 담당하고 있음을 설명한다. 따라서 글의 순서로 가장 적절한 것은 ② '(B) – (A) – (C)'이다.

- hunt for ~을 사냥하다
- carry out 수행하다
- device ⓝ 장치
- keep track of ~을 추적하다, 기록하다
- gradually ⓐⓓ 점차
- tell the time 시간을 알다
- take off 이륙하다
- livestock ⓝ 가축
- religious ⓐ 종교적인
- measure ⓥ 측정하다
- natural cycle 자연적 주기
- settlement ⓝ 정착(지)
- crash into ~에 충돌하다
- land ⓥ 착륙하다

구문 풀이

12행 Today, clocks are used for important things such as setting busy airport timetables — if the time is incorrect, aeroplanes might crash into each other when taking off or landing!
접속사를 포함한 분사구문(= when they take off or land)

---

37 생산성과 노동 분업   정답률 58% | 정답 ⑤

주어진 글 다음에 이어질 글의 순서로 가장 적절한 것을 고르시오.
① (A) – (C) – (B)
② (B) – (A) – (C)
③ (B) – (C) – (A)
④ (C) – (A) – (B)
☑ ⑤ (C) – (B) – (A)

Managers are always looking for ways / to increase productivity, / which is the ratio of costs to output in production.
관리자들은 항상 방법을 찾고 있는데, / 생산성을 높일 수 있는 / 이것은 생산에서 비용 대비 생산량의 비율이다.

Adam Smith, / writing when the manufacturing industry was new, / described a way / that production could be made more efficient, / known as the "division of labor."
Adam Smith는 / 제조 산업이 새로 등장했을 때 저술한 / 방식을 설명했다 / 생산이 더 효율적으로 될 수 있는 / 이것은 '노동 분업'으로 알려져 있다.

(C) Making most manufactured goods / involves several different processes / using different skills.
대부분의 공산품을 만드는 것은 / 여러 가지 다른 과정을 포함한다 / 다른 기술을 사용하는

Smith's example was the manufacture of pins: / the wire is straightened, / sharpened, / a head is put on, / and then it is polished.
Smith의 예는 핀의 제조였다. / 철사가 곧게 펴지고, / 뾰족해지고, / 머리가 끼워지고, / 그러고 나서 그것은 다듬어진다.

(B) One worker could do all these tasks, / and make 20 pins in a day.
한 명의 노동자가 이 모든 작업들을 할 수 있고, / 하루에 20개의 핀을 만들 수도 있다.

But this work can be divided into its separate processes, / with a number of workers each performing one task.
그러나 이 일은 별개의 과정으로 분리될 수 있다. / 많은 노동자가 각각 한 가지 작업을 수행하며

(A) Because each worker specializes in one job, / he or she can work much faster / without changing from one task to another.
각 노동자는 한 가지 작업을 전문으로 하기 때문에, / 이 사람은 훨씬 더 빠르게 일할 수 있다. / 한 작업에서 다른 작업으로 옮겨가지 않으면서

Now 10 workers can produce thousands of pins in a day / — a huge increase in productivity / from the 200 / they would have produced before.
이제 10명의 노동자가 하루에 수천 개의 핀을 생산할 수 있다. / 이는 큰 증가이다 / 이는 생산성의 큰 증가이다. / 200개로부터 / 이전에 그들이 생산했던

관리자들은 항상 생산성을 높일 수 있는 방법을 찾고 있는데, 생산성은 생산에서 비용 대비 생산량의 비율이다. 제조 산업이 새로 등장했을 때 저술한 Adam Smith는 생산이 더 효율적으로 될 수 있는 방식을 설명했고, 이것은 '노동 분업'으로 알려져 있다. (C) 대부분의 공산품을 만드는 것은 다른 기술을 사용하는 여러 가지 다른 과정을 포함한다. Smith의 예는 핀의 제조였다. 철사를 곧게 펴고, 뾰족하게 만들고, 머리를 끼운 다음, 그것을 다듬는다. (B) 한 명의 노동자가 이 모든 작업들을 할 수 있고, 하루에 20개의 핀을 만들 수도 있다. 그러나 이 일은 많은 노동자가 각각 한 가지 작업을 수행하며 별개의 과정으로 분리될 수 있다. (A) 각 노동자는 한 가지 작업을 전문으로 하기 때문에, 이 사람은 한 작업에서 다른 작업으로 옮겨가지 않으면서 훨씬 더 빠르게 일할 수 있다. 이제 10명의 노동자가 하루에 수천 개의 핀을 생산할 수 있다. 이는 이전에 그들이 생산했던 200개로부터 생산성 측면에서 크게 증가한 것이다.

Why? 왜 정답일까?

'노동 분업'의 개념을 소개하는 주어진 글 뒤로, 핀 제조 과정을 예로 설명하는 (C), 이 제조 과정은 한 사

람에 의해 수행될 수도 있지만, 분업으로 진행될 수도 있다고 설명하는 (B), 분업 상황의 장점을 소개하는 (A)가 차례로 이어져야 자연스럽다. 따라서 글의 순서로 가장 적절한 것은 ⑤ '(C) – (B) – (A)'이다.

- ratio ⓝ 비율
- manufacturing industry 제조업
- efficient ⓐ 효율적인
- specialize in ~에 특화되다
- involve ⓥ 포함하다, 수반하다
- sharpen ⓥ 뾰족하게 하다
- output ⓝ 산출
- describe ⓥ 설명하다
- division of labor 분업
- a number of 많은
- straighten ⓥ 곧게 펴다
- polish ⓥ 다듬다

구문 풀이

12행 But this work can be divided into its separate processes, with a number of workers each performing one task.
「with + 명사 + 분사 : ~이 …한 채로(부대상황 분사구문)」

★★★ 등급을 가르는 문제!

38 느리게라도 계속 진행되는 변화   정답률 39% | 정답 ②

글의 흐름으로 보아, 주어진 문장이 들어가기에 가장 적절한 곳을 고르시오.

Sometimes the pace of change is far slower.
때때로 변화의 속도는 훨씬 더 느리다.

① The face you saw / reflected in your mirror this morning / probably appeared no different / from the face you saw the day before / — or a week or a month ago.
당신이 본 얼굴은 / 오늘 아침 거울에 비춰진 / 아마도 다르지 않게 보였을 것이다. / 당신이 그 전날에 본 얼굴과 / 또는 일주일이나 한 달 전에

☑ Yet we know / that the face that stares back at us from the glass / is not the same, / cannot be the same, / as it was 10 minutes ago.
그러나 우리는 안다. / 거울에서 우리를 마주보는 얼굴이 / 같지 않고, 같을 수 없다는 것을 / 10분 전과

The proof is in your photo album: / Look at a photograph / taken of yourself 5 or 10 years ago / and you see clear differences / between the face in the snapshot / and the face in your mirror.
증거는 당신의 사진 앨범에 있다. / 사진을 보라 / 5년 또는 10년 전에 당신을 찍은 / 그러면 당신은 명확한 차이를 보게 될 것이다 / 스냅사진 속의 얼굴과 / 거울 속 얼굴 사이의

③ If you lived in a world without mirrors for a year / and then saw your reflection, / you might be surprised by the change.
만약 당신이 일 년간 거울이 없는 세상에 살고 / 그 이후 (거울에) 비친 당신의 모습을 본다면, / 당신은 그 변화 때문에 깜짝 놀랄지도 모른다.

④ After an interval of 10 years / without seeing yourself, / you might not at first recognize the person / peering from the mirror.
10년의 기간이 지난 후, / 스스로를 보지 않고 / 당신은 그 사람을 처음에는 알아보지 못할지도 모른다. / 거울에서 쳐다보고 있는

⑤ Even something as basic as our own face / changes from moment to moment.
심지어 우리 자신의 얼굴같이 아주 기본적인 것조차도 / 순간순간 변한다.

때때로 변화의 속도는 훨씬 더 느리다. ① 오늘 아침 당신이 거울에 비춰진 것을 본 얼굴은 아마도 당신이 그 전날 또는 일주일이나 한 달 전에 본 얼굴과 다르지 않게 보였을 것이다. ② 그러나 우리는 거울에서 우리를 마주보는 얼굴이 10분 전과 같지 않고, 같을 수 없다는 것을 안다. 증거는 당신의 사진 앨범에 있다. 5년 또는 10년 전에 찍은 당신의 사진을 보면 당신은 스냅사진 속의 얼굴과 거울 속 얼굴 사이의 명확한 차이를 보게 될 것이다. ③ 만약 당신이 일 년간 거울이 없는 세상에 살고 그 이후 (거울에) 비친 당신의 모습을 본다면, 당신은 그 변화 때문에 깜짝 놀랄지도 모른다. ④ 스스로를 보지 않고 10년의 기간이 지난 후, 당신은 거울에서 쳐다보고 있는 사람을 처음에는 알아보지 못할지도 모른다. ⑤ 심지어 우리 자신의 얼굴같이 아주 기본적인 것조차도 순간순간 변한다.

Why? 왜 정답일까?

② 앞은 오늘 아침 거울로 본 얼굴이 전날, 일주일 전, 또는 한 달 전에 본 얼굴과 다르지 않았을 것이라는 내용인데, ② 뒤는 얼굴이 명확히 '달라졌다'는 것을 알 수 있는 증거에 관한 내용이다. 즉 ② 앞뒤로 상반된 내용이 제시되어 흐름이 어색하게 끊기므로, 주어진 문장이 들어가기에 가장 적절한 곳은 ②이다.

- reflect ⓥ 반사하다
- snapshot ⓝ 스냅사진, 짧은 묘사
- surprised ⓐ 놀란
- peer ⓥ 응시하다
- clear ⓐ 명확한
- reflection ⓝ (물이나 거울에 비친) 그림자
- interval ⓝ 간격
- from moment to moment 시시각각

구문 풀이

12행 Even something as basic as our own face changes from moment to moment.
「as + 원급 + as : ~만큼 …한」

★★ 문제 해결 꿀~팁 ★★

▶ 많이 틀린 이유는?
가장 헷갈리는 ③ 앞을 보면, 우리가 5~10년 전 찍은 사진을 보면 지금 거울로 보는 얼굴과 다르다는 것을 알 수 있다는 내용이며, 주어진 문장 또한 우리 얼굴이 단 10분 사이에도 '달라진다'는 내용이다. 하지만 주어진 문장은 Yet(그럼에도 불구하고)으로 시작하므로, 이 앞에는 '다르지 않다'라는 반대되는 내용이 나와야 한다. 따라서 주어진 문장 내용과 똑같은 내용이 앞에 나오는 ③ 자리에 주어진 문장을 넣을 수는 없다.

▶ 문제 해결 방법은?
② 앞뒤로 발생하는 논리적 공백에 주목하자. ②는 거울로 보는 우리 얼굴이 '별 차이가 없어보인다'는 내용인데, ②는 사진 앨범 속 우리 얼굴이 '명확한 차이'를 보인다는 내용이다. 즉 ② 앞뒤의 의미가 '다르지 않다 ↔ 다르다'로 상반되는 상황인데, 이 경우 반드시 역접 연결어(주어진 문장의 Yet)가 있어야만 한다.

★★★ 등급을 가르는 문제!

39 나이가 들면서 호기심이 줄어드는 까닭   정답률 31% | 정답 ⑤

글의 흐름으로 보아, 주어진 문장이 들어가기에 가장 적절한 곳을 고르시오. [3점]

According to educational psychologist Susan Engel, / curiosity begins to decrease / as young as four years old.
교육 심리학자 Susan Engel에 따르면, / 호기심은 줄어들기 시작한다. / 네 살 정도라는 어린 나이에

By the time we are adults, / we have fewer questions and more default settings.
우리가 어른이 될 무렵, / 질문은 더 적어지고 기본값은 더 많아진다.

As Henry James put it, / "Disinterested curiosity is past, / the mental grooves and channels set."
Henry James가 말했듯이, / '무관심한 호기심은 없어지고, / 정신의 고랑과 경로가 자리잡는다.'

① The decline in curiosity / can be traced / in the development of the brain through childhood.
호기심의 감소는 / 원인을 찾을 수 있다. / 유년 시절 동안의 뇌의 발달에서

② Though smaller than the adult brain, / the infant brain contains millions more neural connections.
비록 성인의 뇌보다 작지만, / 유아의 뇌는 수백만 개 더 많은 신경 연결을 가지고 있다.

③ The wiring, however, is a mess; / the lines of communication between infant neurons / are far less efficient / than between those in the adult brain.
그러나 연결 상태는 엉망인데, / 유아의 뉴런 간의 전달은 / 훨씬 덜 효율적이다. / 성인 뇌 속 뉴런끼리의 전달보다

④ The baby's perception of the world / is consequently both intensely rich and wildly disordered.
세상에 대한 아기의 인식은 / 결과적으로 매우 풍부하면서도 상당히 무질서하다.

☑ As children absorb more evidence / from the world around them, / certain possibilities become much more likely and more useful / and harden into knowledge or beliefs.
아이들이 더 많은 증거를 흡수함에 따라, / 그들 주변의 세상으로부터 / 특정한 가능성들이 훨씬 더 커지게 되고 더 유용하게 되며 / 지식이나 믿음으로 굳어진다.

The neural pathways / that enable those beliefs / become faster and more automatic, / while the ones / that the child doesn't use regularly / are pruned away.
신경 경로는 / 그러한 믿음을 가능하게 하는 / 더 빠르고 자동적으로 이루어지게 되고, / 반면에 경로는 / 아이가 주기적으로 사용하지 않는 / 제거된다.

교육 심리학자 Susan Engel에 따르면, 호기심은 네 살 정도라는 어린 나이에 줄어들기 시작한다. 우리가 어른이 될 무렵, 질문은 더 적어지고 기본값은 더 많아진다. Henry James가 말했듯이, '무관심한 호기심은 없어지고, 정신의 고랑과 경로가 자리잡는다.' ① 호기심의 감소는 유년 시절 동안의 뇌의 발달에서 원인을 찾을 수 있다. ② 비록 성인의 뇌보다 작지만, 유아의 뇌는 수백만 개 더 많은 신경 연결을 가지고 있다. ③ 그러나 연결 상태는 엉망인데, 유아의 뉴런 간의 전달은 성인 뇌 속 뉴런끼리의 전달보다 훨씬 덜 효율적이다. ④ 결과적으로 세상에 대한 아기의 인식은 매우 풍부하면서도 상당히 무질서하다. ⑤ 아이들이 그들 주변의 세상으로부터 더 많은 증거를 흡수함에 따라, 특정한 가능성들이 훨씬 더 커지게 되고 더 유용하게 되며 지식이나 믿음으로 굳어진다. 그러한 믿음을 가능하게 하는 신경 경로는 더 빠르고 자동적으로 이루어지게 되고, 반면에 아이가 주기적으로 사용하지 않는 경로는 제거된다.

Why? 왜 정답일까?

⑤ 앞은 아기의 인식이 성인에 비해 무질서하다는 내용인데, ⑤ 뒤에서는 갑자기 '믿음'을 언급하며, 신경 경로의 자동화와 제거를 설명한다. 이때 주어진 문장을 보면, 아이들이 주변 세상에서 더 많은 근거를 얻고 더 유용한 가능성을 취하면서 '믿음'이 굳어지기 시작한다고 한다. 이 '믿음'이 ⑤ 뒤와 연결되는 것이므로, 주어진 문장이 들어가기에 가장 적절한 곳은 ⑤이다.

- absorb ⓥ (정보를) 받아들이다
- educational ⓐ 교육의
- decrease ⓥ 감소하다
- disinterested ⓐ 무관심한
- channel ⓝ 경로
- childhood ⓝ 어린 시절
- neural ⓐ 신경의
- perception ⓝ 지각, 인식
- intensely ⓐⓓ 대단히, 강렬하게
- pathway ⓝ 경로
- prune ⓥ 가지치기하다
- harden ⓥ 굳어지다
- curiosity ⓝ 호기심
- default setting 기본값
- groove ⓝ 고랑
- development ⓝ 발달
- infant ⓝ 유아
- mess ⓝ 엉망
- consequently ⓐⓓ 그 결과
- disordered ⓐ 무질서한
- automatic ⓐ 자동적인

구문 풀이

1행 As children absorb more evidence from the world around them, certain
접속사(~함에 따라)   = children
possibilities become much more likely and more useful and harden into
동사1   주격 보어(비교급 형용사)   동사2
knowledge or beliefs.

★★ 문제 해결 꿀~팁 ★★

▶ 많이 틀린 이유는?
① 뒤의 문장 이후, ②~⑤ 사이의 내용은 모두 부연 설명이다. 호기심이 감소하는 까닭은 뇌 발달에 있다는 일반적인 내용 뒤로, 아이들의 뇌가 성인의 뇌보다 작지만 연결고리가 훨씬 더 많다는 설명, 그렇지만 그 연결고리가 엉망이라는 설명, 그렇기에 아이의 세상 인식은 어른보다 풍부할지언정 무질서하다는 설명이 모두 자연스럽게 이어지고 있다. 주어진 문장은 이 모든 설명이 마무리된 후 '어쩌다' 호기심이 떨어지는 것인지 마침내 언급하는 문장이다.

▶ 문제 해결 방법은?
연결어 힌트가 없어서 난해하게 느껴질 수 있지만, 지시어 힌트를 활용하면 아주 쉽다. ⑤ 뒤에는 '그러한 믿음(those beliefs)'이라는 표현이 나오는데, 이는 앞에서 '믿음'을 언급했어야만 쓸 수 있는 표현이다. 하지만 ⑤ 앞까지는 beliefs가 전혀 등장하지 않고, 오로지 주어진 문장에만 knowledge or beliefs가 등장한다.

★★★ 등급을 가르는 문제! ★★★

40 식단의 좋고 나쁨 · · · · · · · · · · · · · · · 정답률 53% | 정답 ②

다음 글의 내용을 한 문장으로 요약하고자 한다. 빈칸 (A), (B)에 들어갈 말로 가장 적절한 것은?

(A)		(B)
① incorrect 부정확한	······	limited to ~에 한정된
☑② appropriate 적절한	······	composed of ~로 구성되는
③ wrong 틀린	······	aimed at ~을 목표로 하는
④ appropriate 적절한	······	tested on ~에 시험된
⑤ incorrect 부정확한	······	adjusted to ~에 맞춰진

Nearly eight of ten U.S. adults believe / there are "good foods" and "bad foods."
미국 성인 10명 중 거의 8명이 믿는다. / '좋은 음식'과 '나쁜 음식'이 있다고

Unless we're talking / about spoiled stew, poison mushrooms, or something similar, / however, no foods can be labeled as either good or bad.
우리가 이야기하고 있지 않는 한, / 상한 스튜, 독버섯, 또는 이와 유사한 것에 관해 / 하지만 어떤 음식도 좋고 나쁘로 분류될 수 없다.

There are, / however, / combinations of foods / that add up to a healthful or unhealthful diet.
~이 있다. / 하지만 / 음식들의 조합 / 결국 건강에 좋은 식단이나 건강에 좋지 않은 식단이 되는

Consider the case of an adult / who eats only foods thought of as "good" / — for example, / raw broccoli, apples, orange juice, boiled tofu, and carrots.
성인의 경우를 생각해보자. / '좋은' 음식이라고 생각되는 음식만 먹는 / 가령 / 생브로콜리, 사과, 오렌지 주스, 삶은 두부와 당근과 같이

Although all these foods are nutrient-dense, / they do not add up to a healthy diet / because they don't supply / a wide enough variety of the nutrients we need.
비록 이 모든 음식들이 영양이 풍부하지만, / 그것들은 결국 건강한 식단이 되지 않는다. / 그것들이 공급하진 않기에 / 우리가 필요로 하는 충분히 다양한 영양소를

Or take the case of the teenager / who occasionally eats fried chicken, / but otherwise stays away from fried foods.
또는 십 대의 경우를 예로 들어보자. / 튀긴 치킨을 가끔 먹지만, / 다른 경우에는 튀긴 음식을 멀리하는

The occasional fried chicken / isn't going to knock his or her diet off track.
가끔 먹는 튀긴 치킨은 / 이 십 대의 식단을 궤도에서 벗어나게 하지 않을 것이다.

But the person / who eats fried foods every day, / with few vegetables or fruits, / and loads up on supersized soft drinks, candy, and chips for snacks / has a bad diet.
하지만 사람은 / 매일 튀긴 음식을 먹고, / 채소나 과일을 거의 먹지 않으면서 / 간식으로 초대형 탄산음료, 사탕, 그리고 감자 칩으로 배를 가득 채우는 / 식단이 나쁜 것이다.

➡ Unlike the common belief, / defining foods as good or bad / is not (A) appropriate; / in fact, / a healthy diet is determined / largely by what the diet is (B) composed of.
일반적인 믿음과 달리, / 음식을 좋고 나쁘로 정의하는 것은 / 적절하지 않고, / 사실 / 건강에 좋은 식단이란 결정된다. / 대체로 그 식단이 무엇으로 구성되는지에 의해

미국 성인 10명 중 거의 8명이 '좋은 음식'과 '나쁜 음식'이 있다고 믿는다. 하지만, 우리가 상한 스튜, 독버섯, 또는 이와 유사한 것에 관해 이야기하고 있지 않는 한, 어떤 음식도 좋고 나쁘로 분류될 수 없다. 하지만, 결국 건강에 좋은 식단이나 건강에 좋지 않은 식단이 되는 음식들의 조합이 있다. 가령 생브로콜리, 사과, 오렌지 주스, 삶은 두부와 당근과 같이 '좋은' 음식이라고 생각되는 음식만 먹는 성인의 경우를 생각해보라. 비록 이 모든 음식들이 영양이 풍부하지만, 그것들은 우리가 필요로 하는 충분히 다양한 영양소를 공급하진 않기에 결국 건강한 식단이 되지 않는다. 또는 튀긴 치킨을 가끔 먹지만, 다른 경우에는 튀긴 음식을 멀리하는 십 대의 경우를 예로 들어보자. 가끔 먹는 튀긴 치킨은 이 십 대의 식단을 궤도에서 벗어나게 하지 않을 것이다. 하지만 채소나 과일을 거의 먹지 않으면서 매일 튀긴 음식을 먹고, 간식으로 초대형 탄산음료, 사탕, 그리고 감자 칩으로 배를 가득 채우는 사람은 식단이 나쁜 것이다.

➡ 일반적인 믿음과 달리, 음식을 좋고 나쁘로 정의하는 것은 (A) 적절하지 않고, 사실 건강에 좋은 식단이란 대체로 그 식단이 무엇으로 (B) 구성되는지에 의해 결정된다.

Why? 왜 정답일까?

첫 세 문장에서 음식을 절대적으로 좋고 나쁘다고 분류할 수는 없고(~ no foods can be labeled as either good or bad.), 그 조합이 중요하다(There are, however, combinations of foods that add up to a healthful or unhealthful diet.)고 말한다. 따라서 요약문의 빈칸 (A), (B)에 들어갈 말로 가장 적절한 것은 ② '(A) appropriate(적절한), (B) composed of(~로 구성되는)'이다.

- nearly ⓐⓓ 거의
- spoiled ⓐ 상한
- label A as B A를 B라고 분류하다
- add up to 결국 ~이 되다
- broccoli ⓝ 브로콜리
- nutrient-dense ⓐ 영양이 풍부한
- nutrient ⓝ 영양분
- otherwise ⓐⓓ 그렇지 않으면, 다른 경우에는
- off track 제 길에서 벗어난
- composed of ~로 구성된
- unless ⓒⓞⓝⓙ ~하지 않는 한
- poison mushroom 독버섯
- combination ⓝ 조합
- healthful ⓐ 건강에 좋은
- tofu ⓝ 두부
- a wide variety of 매우 다양한
- occasionally ⓐⓓ 가끔
- stay away from ~을 멀리하다
- load up on ~로 배를 가득 채우다

구문 풀이

2행 Unless we're talking about spoiled stew, poison mushrooms, or something
접속사(~하지 않는 한)
similar, however, no foods can be labeled as either good or bad.
「A + be labeled as + B : A가 B라고 분류되다」

★★ 문제 해결 꿀~팁 ★★

▶ 많이 틀린 이유는?
두 번째 문장에서 음식을 절대적으로 좋고 나쁘다고 분류할 수 없다고 언급하는 것으로 보아, 음식의 분류가 '부정확하지' 않다, 즉 '정확하다'는 의미를 완성하는 ①과 ⑤의 incorrect를 (A)에 넣기는 부적절하다.

▶ 문제 해결 방법은?
글 초반에 however가 두 번 연속해 등장하여 주제를 강조한다. Consider 이하는 이 주제에 대한 사례이므로 결론만 가볍게 확인하며 읽어도 충분하다.

41-42 농업 발전과 생활 변화

Early hunter-gatherer societies had (a) minimal structure.
초기 수렵 채집인 사회는 최소한의 구조를 가지고 있었다.

A chief or group of elders / usually led the camp or village.
추장이나 장로 그룹이 / 주로 캠프나 마을을 이끌었다.

Most of these leaders / had to hunt and gather / along with the other members / because the

surpluses of food and other vital resources / were seldom (b) <u>sufficient</u> / to support a
full-time chief or village council.
대부분의 이러한 지도자들은 / 사냥과 채집을 해야 했다. / 다른 구성원들과 함께 / 왜냐하면 식량과 기타 필수 자원의 잉여분이 /
충분한 경우가 드물었기 때문에 / 전임 추장이나 마을 의회를 지원할 만큼
『The development of agriculture changed work patterns.』 41번의 근거
농업의 발전은 작업 패턴을 변화시켰다.
Early farmers could reap 3-10 kg of grain / from each 1 kg of seed planted.
초기 농부들은 / 3-10kg의 곡물을 수확할 수 있었다. / 심은 씨앗 1kg마다
Part of this food/energy surplus / was returned to the community / and (c) <u>provided</u> support
for nonfarmers / such as chieftains, village councils, men who practice medicine, priests,
and warriors.
이 식량/에너지 잉여분의 일부는 / 지역 사회에 환원되었고 / 비농민에 대한 지원을 제공했다. / 족장, 마을 의회, 의술가, 사제, 전사
와 같은
『In return, / the nonfarmers provided leadership and security / for the farming population, /
enabling it / to continue to increase food/energy yields / and provide ever larger surpluses.』 42번의 근거
그 대가로, / 비농민들은 리더십과 안보를 제공하여, / 농업 인구에게, / 그들이 ~할 수 있게 하였다. / 식량/에너지 생산량을 지속적
으로 늘리고 / 항상 더 많은 잉여를 제공할 수 있게
With improved technology and favorable conditions, / agriculture produced consistent
surpluses of the basic necessities, / and population groups grew in size.
개선된 기술과 유리한 조건으로, / 농업은 기본 생필품의 지속적인 흑자를 창출했고, / 인구 집단은 규모가 커졌다.
These groups concentrated in towns and cities, / and human tasks (d) <u>specialized</u> further.
이러한 집단은 마을과 도시에 집중되었고, / 인간의 업무는 더욱 전문화되었다.
Specialists / such as carpenters, blacksmiths, merchants, traders, and sailors / developed
their skills / and became more efficient / in their use of time and energy.
전문가들은 / 목수, 대장장이, 상인, 무역업자, 선원과 같은 / 기술을 계발하고 / 더 효율적이 되었다. / 자신의 시간과 에너지 사용 면
에서
『The goods and services they provided / brought about / an (e) <u>improved</u> quality of life, /
a higher standard of living, / and, for most societies, / increased stability.』 41번의 근거
그들이 제공한 재화와 서비스는 / 가져왔다. / 삶의 질 향상, / 생활 수준 개선, / 그리고 대부분의 사회에서 / 안정성의 향상

초기 수렵 채집인 사회는 (a) <u>최소한의</u> 구조만 가지고 있었다. 추장이나 장로 그룹이 주로
캠프나 마을을 이끌었다. 식량과 기타 필수 자원의 잉여분이 전임 추장이나 마을 의회를
지원할 만큼 (b) <u>충분한</u> 경우가 드물었기 때문에 대부분의 이러한 지도자들은 다른 구성원
들과 함께 사냥과 채집을 해야 했다. 농업의 발전은 작업 패턴을 변화시켰다. 초기 농부들
은 심은 씨앗 1kg마다 3-10kg의 곡물을 수확할 수 있었다. 이 식량/에너지 잉여분의 일부
는 지역 사회에 환원되었고 족장, 마을 의회, 의술가, 사제, 전사와 같은 비농민에 대한 지
원을 (c) <u>제한했다</u>(→ 제공했다). 그 대가로, 비농민들은 농업 인구에게 리더십과 안보를 제
공하여, 그들이 식량/에너지 생산량을 지속적으로 늘리고 항상 더 많은 잉여를 제공할 수
있게 하였다.
개선된 기술과 유리한 조건으로, 농업은 기본 생필품의 지속적인 흑자를 창출했고, 인구 집
단은 규모가 커졌다. 이러한 집단은 마을과 도시에 집중되었고, 인간의 업무는 더욱 (d) <u>전문
화되었다</u>. 목수, 대장장이, 상인, 무역업자, 선원과 같은 전문가들은 기술을 계발하고 자신의
시간과 에너지 사용을 더 효율적으로 하게 되었다. 그들이 제공한 재화와 서비스로 인해 삶
의 질 (e) <u>향상</u>, 생활 수준 개선, 그리고 대부분의 사회에서 안정성의 향상을 가져왔다.

- **hunter-gatherer** ⓝ 수렵 채집인
- **vital** ⓐ 필수적인, 매우 중요한
- **reap** ⓥ (농작물을) 베어들이다
- **practice medicine** 의사로 개업하다, 의술을 행하다
- **warrior** ⓝ 전사
- **yield** ⓝ 수확량
- **concentrate** ⓥ 집중되다
- **blacksmith** ⓝ 대장장이
- **bring about** ~을 야기하다, 초래하다, 가져오다
- **surplus** ⓝ 잉여, 흑자
- **sufficient** ⓐ 충분한
- **chieftain** ⓝ 수령, 두목
- **security** ⓝ 안보
- **basic necessity** 기본 필수품
- **carpenter** ⓝ 목수
- **sailor** ⓝ 선원
- **stability** ⓝ 안정성

구문 풀이

20행 The goods and services [they provided] brought about an improved quality
　　　 _{주어}　　　　　　　　　　　　　 _{동사}　　　　　　 _{목적어1}
of life, a higher standard of living, and, for most societies, increased stability.
　 _{목적어2}　　　　　　　　　　　　　　　　　　　　　 _{목적어3}

41 제목 파악　　　　　　　　　　　　　　　 정답률 61% | 정답 ①

윗글의 제목으로 가장 적절한 것은?
✓① How Agriculture Transformed Human Society
　 농업은 어떻게 인간 사회를 바꿨나
② The Dark Shadow of Agriculture: Repetition
　 농업의 어두운 그늘: 반복
③ How Can We Share Extra Food with the Poor?
　 우리는 가난한 사람들과 남은 음식을 어떻게 나눌 수 있을까?
④ Why Were Early Societies Destroyed by Agriculture?
　 왜 초기 사회는 농업으로 파괴되었나?
⑤ The Advantages of Large Groups Over Small Groups in Farming
　 농업에 있어 대규모 집단이 소규모 집단보다 유리한 점

Why? 왜 정답일까?
농업 이전 사회에서는 비교적 단순했던 사회 구조가 농업 이후로 어떻게 변화했는지 설명하는 내용이다.
우선 작업의 패턴이 변하고(The development of agriculture changed work patterns.), 잉
여 생산물이 늘어남에 따라 사회 규모도 바뀌면서 삶의 질도 향상되었다(~ an improved quality of
life, a higher standard of living, and, for most societies, increased stability.)는 설명이
주를 이룬다. 따라서 글의 제목으로 가장 적절한 것은 ① '농업은 어떻게 인간 사회를 바꿨나'이다.

42 어휘 추론　　　　　　　　　　　　　　　 정답률 58% | 정답 ③

밑줄 친 (a)~(e) 중에서 문맥상 낱말의 쓰임이 적절하지 않은 것은? [3점]
① (a)　　　② (b)　　　✓③ (c)　　　④ (d)　　　⑤ (e)

Why? 왜 정답일까?
In return 앞뒤는 농민이 비농민에게 무언가를 해준 '보답으로' 비농민 또한 비농민에게 안보를 제공하여
생산에 집중하게 했다는 내용이다. 즉 (c)는 농민의 잉여 생산물이 비농민에 대한 지원을 '제공하는 데'

쓰였다는 의미일 것이므로, limited 대신 provided를 써야 자연스럽다. 따라서 문맥상 낱말의 쓰임이
적절하지 않은 것은 ③ '(c)'이다.

43-45 모르는 노인의 임종을 지킨 군인

(A)
A nurse took a tired, anxious soldier to the bedside.
한 간호사가 피곤하고 불안해하는 군인을 침대 곁으로 데려갔다.
"Jack, your son is here," / the nurse said to an old man / lying on the bed.
"Jack, 당신 아들이 왔어요."라고 / 간호사가 노인에게 말했다. / 침대에 누워있는
She had to repeat the words several times / before the old man's eyes opened.
그녀는 그 말을 여러 번 반복해야 했다. / 그 노인이 눈을 뜨기 전에
『Suffering from the severe pain / because of heart disease, he barely saw the young
uniformed soldier / standing next to him.』 45번 ①의 근거 일치
극심한 고통을 겪고 있던 / 심장병 때문에 / 그는 제복을 입은 젊은 군인을 간신히 보았다. / 자기 옆에 서 있는
(a) <u>He</u> reached out his hand to the soldier.
그는 손을 그 군인에게 뻗었다.

(D)
The soldier gently wrapped his fingers / around the weak hand of the old man.
그 군인은 부드럽게 자기 손가락을 감쌌다. / 노인의 병약한 손 주위로
『The nurse brought a chair / so that the soldier could sit beside the bed.』 45번 ④의 근거 일치
간호사는 의자를 가져왔다. / 군인이 침대 옆에 앉을 수 있도록
All through the night / the young soldier sat there, / holding the old man's hand / and
offering (e) <u>him</u> words of support and comfort.
밤새 / 젊은 군인은 거기에 앉아, / 노인의 손을 잡고 / 그에게 지지와 위로의 말을 건넸다.
『Occasionally, / she suggested / that the soldier take a rest for a while.
가끔, / 그녀는 제안했다. / 군인에게 잠시 쉬라고
He politely said no.』 45번 ⑤의 근거 일치
그는 정중히 거절했다.

(B)
Whenever the nurse came into the room, / she heard the soldier say a few gentle words.
간호사가 병실에 들어올 때마다, / 그녀는 그 군인이 상냥한 말을 하는 것을 들었다.
The old man said nothing, / only held tightly to (b) <u>him</u> all through the night.
노인은 아무 말도 하지 않았다. / 밤새도록 그에게 손만 꼭 잡힌 채로
Just before dawn, / the old man died.
동트기 직전에, / 그 노인은 죽었다.
『The soldier released the old man's hand / and left the room to find the nurse.』 45번 ②의 근거 일치
그 군인은 노인의 손을 놓고 / 간호사를 찾기 위해 병실을 나갔다.
After she was told what happened, / she went back to the room with him.
그녀가 무슨 일이 있었는지 들은 후, / 그녀는 그와 함께 병실로 돌아갔다.
The soldier hesitated for a while and asked, / "Who was this man?"
군인은 잠시 머뭇거리고는 물었다. / "그분은 누구였나요?"라고

(C)
She was surprised and asked, / "Wasn't he your father?"
그녀는 깜짝 놀라서 물었다. / "그가 당신의 아버지가 아니었나요?"
『"No, he wasn't. / I've never met him before," / the soldier replied.』 45번 ③의 근거 불일치
"아니요. / 저는 그분을 이전에 만난 적이 없어요."라고 / 군인이 대답했다.
She asked, / "Then why didn't you say something / when I took you to (c) <u>him</u>?"
그녀는 물었다. / "그러면 당신은 왜 아무 말도 하지 않았나요? / 내가 당신을 그에게 안내했을 때"
He said, / "I knew there had been a mistake, / but when I realized / that he was too sick to
tell / whether or not I was his son, / I could see how much (d) <u>he</u> needed me. / So, I
stayed."
그가 말했다. / "저는 실수가 있었다는 것을 알았지만, / 제가 알게 되었을 때, / 그분이 너무도 위독해서 구별할 수 없다는 걸 / 제가
아들인지 아닌지 / 저는 그가 얼마나 저를 필요로 하는지 알 수 있었습니다. / 그래서 저는 머물렀습니다."

(A)
한 간호사가 피곤하고 불안해하는 군인을 침대 곁으로 데려갔다. "Jack, 당신 아들이 왔어
요."라고 간호사가 침대에 누워있는 노인에게 말했다. 그 노인이 눈을 뜨기 전에 그녀는 그
말을 여러 번 반복해야 했다. 심장병 때문에 극심한 고통을 겪고 있던 그는 제복을 입은 젊은
군인이 자기 옆에 선 것을 간신히 보았다. (a) <u>그는</u> 손을 그 군인에게 뻗었다.

(D)
그 군인은 노인의 병약한 손을 부드럽게 감쌌다. 간호사는 군인이 침대 옆에 앉을 수 있도록
의자를 가져왔다. 밤새 젊은 군인은 거기에 앉아, 노인의 손을 잡고 (e) <u>그에게</u> 지지와 위로
의 말을 건넸다. 가끔, 그녀는 군인에게 잠시 쉬라고 제안했다. 그는 정중하게 거절했다.

(B)
간호사가 병실에 들어올 때마다, 그녀는 그 군인이 상냥한 말을 하는 것을 들었다. 밤새도록
(b) <u>그에게</u> 손만 꼭 잡힌 채로 노인은 아무 말도 하지 않았다. 동트기 직전에, 그 노인은 죽었
다. 그 군인은 노인의 손을 놓고 간호사를 찾기 위해 병실을 나갔다. 그녀가 무슨 일이 있었
는지 들은 후, 그녀는 그와 함께 병실로 돌아갔다. 군인은 잠시 머뭇거리고는 "그분은 누구였
나요?"라고 물었다.

(C)
그녀는 깜짝 놀라서 물었다. "그가 당신의 아버지가 아니었나요?" "아니요. 저는 그분을 이전
에 만난 적이 없어요."라고 군인이 대답했다. 그녀는 물었다. "그러면 내가 당신을 (c) <u>그에게</u>
안내했을 때 왜 아무 말도 하지 않았나요?" 그가 말했다. "저는 실수가 있었다는 것을 알았
지만, 그분이 너무도 위독해서 제가 아들인지 아닌지 구별할 수 없다는 걸 알게 되었을 때, 저는
(d) <u>그가</u> 얼마나 저를 필요로 하는지 알 수 있었습니다. 그래서 저는 머물렀습니다."

- **severe** ⓐ 극심한
- **reach out one's hand** 손을 뻗다
- **hesitate** ⓥ 주저하다
- **barely** ⓓ 간신히 ~하다, 거의 못 ~하다
- **dawn** ⓝ 새벽

구문 풀이

(A) 4행 Suffering from the severe pain because of heart disease, he barely saw
　　　　　 _{분사구문}　　　　　　 _{전치사구} ~때문에　　　　　　　　 _{지각동사}
the young uniformed soldier standing next to him.
　 _{목적어}　　　　　　　　 _{현재분사}

(D) 2행 The nurse brought a chair so that the soldier could sit beside the bed.
　　　　　　　　　　　　　　　　 _{접속사(~하도록)}

43 글의 순서 파악 | 정답률 77% | 정답 ④

주어진 글 (A)에 이어질 내용을 순서에 맞게 배열한 것으로 가장 적절한 것은?
① (B) – (D) – (C)　　　　② (C) – (B) – (D)
③ (C) – (D) – (B)　　　　✔ (D) – (B) – (C)
⑤ (D) – (C) – (B)

Why? 왜 정답일까?

간호사가 한 군인을 임종이 임박한 노인에게 데려갔다는 내용의 (A) 뒤로, 군인이 노인 곁에 밤새 있었다는 내용의 (D), 마침내 노인이 임종한 뒤 군인이 그 노인이 누구였는지 물었다는 내용의 (B), 간호사가 놀라서 왜 노인 곁에 있었는지 묻고 군인이 답했다는 내용의 (C)가 순서대로 이어져야 자연스럽다. 따라서 글의 순서로 가장 적절한 것은 ④ '(D) – (B) – (C)'이다.

44 지칭 추론 | 정답률 64% | 정답 ②

밑줄 친 (a)~(e) 중에서 가리키는 대상이 나머지 넷과 <u>다른</u> 것은?
① (a)　　✔ (b)　　③ (c)　　④ (d)　　⑤ (e)

Why? 왜 정답일까?

(a), (c), (d), (e)는 the old man, (b)는 the soldier를 가리키므로, (a)~(e) 중에서 가리키는 대상이 다른 하나는 ② '(b)'이다.

45 세부 내용 파악 | 정답률 75% | 정답 ③

윗글에 관한 내용으로 적절하지 않은 것은?
① 노인은 심장병으로 극심한 고통을 겪고 있었다.
② 군인은 간호사를 찾기 위해 병실을 나갔다.
✔ 군인은 노인과 이전에 만난 적이 있다고 말했다.
④ 간호사는 군인이 앉을 수 있도록 의자를 가져왔다.
⑤ 군인은 잠시 쉬라는 간호사의 제안을 정중히 거절하였다.

Why? 왜 정답일까?

(C) "No, he wasn't. I've never met him before."에서 군인은 노인을 만난 적이 없다고 말하므로, 내용과 일치하지 않는 것은 ③ '군인은 노인과 이전에 만난 적이 있다고 말했다.'이다.

Why? 왜 오답일까?

① (A) 'Suffering from the severe pain because of heart disease, ~'의 내용과 일치한다.
② (B) 'The soldier ~ left the room to find the nurse.'의 내용과 일치한다.
④ (D) 'The nurse brought a chair so that the soldier could sit beside the bed.'의 내용과 일치한다.
⑤ (D) 'Occasionally, she suggested that the soldier take a rest for a while. He politely said no.'의 내용과 일치한다.

어휘 Review Test 07

문제편 070쪽

A	B	C	D
01 명상	01 familiar	01 ⓗ	01 ⑨
02 불안한	02 possess	02 ⓞ	02 ⓘ
03 가능성, 확률	03 productivity	03 ①	03 ①
04 ~보다 우월한	04 experienced	04 ⓢ	04 ⓕ
05 허구의	05 unpaid	05 ⓠ	05 ⓠ
06 지위	06 decline	06 ⓝ	06 ⓚ
07 지속적으로	07 award	07 ⓚ	07 ⓐ
08 도움을 요청하다	08 hire	08 ⓓ	08 ⓑ
09 능력, 재능	09 state	09 ⓔ	09 ⓟ
10 나타나다, 생겨나다	10 emphasize	10 ①	10 ⓜ
11 응시하다	11 curiosity	11 ⓟ	11 ⓢ
12 잉여, 흑자	12 barely	12 ①	12 ⓒ
13 주저하다	13 vital	13 ①	13 ⓓ
14 지속하다, 참다	14 stability	14 ⓜ	14 ⓞ
15 지역	15 contribution	15 ⓐ	15 ①
16 특유의, 독특한, 뚜렷한	16 embarrassed	16 ⓑ	16 ①
17 현상	17 considerable	17 ⓒ	17 ⓔ
18 바람직한	18 composed of	18 ⑨	18 ①
19 추구하다	19 unless	19 ⓕ	19 ⓝ
20 주의 산만, 정신을 흩뜨리는 것	20 reflect	20 ①	20 ⓗ

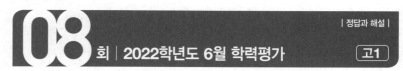

· 정답 ·

18 ② 19 ② 20 ⑤ 21 ③ 22 ① 23 ② 24 ① 25 ⑤ 26 ③ 27 ④ 28 ② 29 ④ 30 ② 31 ① 32 ②
33 ③ 34 ② 35 ④ 36 ③ 37 ⑤ 38 ④ 39 ⑤ 40 ③ 41 ① 42 ④ 43 ④ 44 ② 45 ④

★ 표기된 문항은 [등급을 가르는 문제]에 해당하는 문항입니다.

18 분실물 확인 요청 | 정답률 96% | 정답 ②

다음 글의 목적으로 가장 적절한 것은?
① 제품의 고장 원인을 문의하려고
✔ 분실물 발견 시 연락을 부탁하려고
③ 시설물의 철저한 관리를 당부하려고
④ 여행자 보험 가입 절차를 확인하려고
⑤ 분실물 센터 확장의 필요성을 건의하려고

Dear Boat Tour Manager,
보트투어 담당자께
On March 15, / my family was on one of your Glass Bottom Boat Tours.
3월 15일에 / 저희 가족은 귀사의 Glass Bottom Boat Tours 중 하나에 참여했습니다.
When we returned to our hotel, / I discovered that I left behind my cell phone case.
저희가 호텔에 돌아왔을 때, / 제가 휴대 전화 케이스를 놓고 왔다는 것을 발견했습니다.
The case must have fallen off my lap and onto the floor / when I took it off my phone to clean it.
제 무릎에서 케이스가 바닥으로 떨어졌던 것이 틀림없습니다. / 제가 케이스를 닦기 위해 휴대 전화에서 분리했을 때
I would like to ask you / to check if it is on your boat.
저는 당신에게 부탁드리고 싶습니다. / 그것이 보트에 있는지 확인해 주시길
Its color is black / and it has my name on the inside.
그것의 색깔은 검은색이며 / 안쪽에 제 이름이 있습니다.
If you find the case, / I would appreciate it if you would let me know.
만약 케이스가 발견된다면, / 저에게 알려주시면 감사하겠습니다.
Sincerely, // Sam Roberts
Sam Roberts 드림

보트 투어 담당자께

3월 15일에 저희 가족은 귀사의 Glass Bottom Boat Tours 중 하나에 참여했습니다. 호텔에 돌아왔을 때, 제가 휴대 전화 케이스를 놓고 왔다는 것을 발견했습니다. 케이스를 닦기 위해 휴대 전화에서 분리했을 때 제 무릎에서 케이스가 바닥으로 떨어졌던 것이 틀림없습니다. 그것이 보트에 있는지 확인해 주시길 부탁드립니다. 그것의 색깔은 검은색이며 안쪽에 제 이름이 있습니다. 만약 케이스가 발견된다면, 저에게 알려주시면 감사하겠습니다.

Sam Roberts 드림

Why? 왜 정답일까?

보트 투어 중 잃어버린 휴대 전화 케이스가 보트에 있는지 확인해줄 것을 부탁하는(I would like to ask you to check if it is on your boat.) 글이다. 따라서 글의 목적으로 가장 적절한 것은 ② '분실물 발견 시 연락을 부탁하려고'이다.

● leave behind ~을 남겨놓고 오다　　● fall ⓥ 떨어지다
● lap ⓝ 무릎　　● appreciate ⓥ 감사하다

구문 풀이

4행 The case must have fallen off my lap and onto the floor when I took it off
　　　　　　「must have + 과거분사 : ~했음에 틀림없다」
my phone to clean it.
　부사적 용법(~하기 위해)

19 공원에 놀러갔다가 얼마 못 놀고 돌아가게 된 Matthew | 정답률 93% | 정답 ②

다음 글에 드러난 Matthew의 심경 변화로 가장 적절한 것은?
① embarrassed → indifferent
　당황한　　　　　무관심한
✔ excited → disappointed
　신난　　　　실망한
③ cheerful → ashamed
　즐거운　　　수치스러운
④ nervous → touched
　긴장한　　　감동한
⑤ scared → relaxed
　겁에 질린　　느긋한

One Saturday morning, / Matthew's mother told Matthew / that she was going to take him to the park.
어느 토요일 아침, / Matthew의 어머니는 Matthew에게 말했다. / 자신이 그를 공원으로 데리고 가겠다고
A big smile came across his face.
그의 얼굴에 환한 미소가 드리워졌다.
As he loved to play outside, / he ate his breakfast and got dressed quickly / so they could go.
그는 밖에 나가서 노는 것을 좋아했기 때문에, / 그는 서둘러 아침을 먹고 옷을 입었다. / 그들이 나가기 위해
When they got to the park, / Matthew ran all the way over to the swing set.
그들이 공원에 도착했을 때, / Matthew는 그네를 향해 바로 뛰어갔다.
That was his favorite thing to do at the park.
그것은 그가 공원에서 가장 좋아하는 것이었다.
But the swings were all being used.
하지만 그네는 이미 모두 이용되고 있었다.
His mother explained / that he could use the slide / until a swing became available, / but it was broken.
그의 어머니는 말했지만, / 그가 미끄럼틀을 탈 수 있다고 / 그네를 이용할 수 있을 때까지 / 그것은 부서져 있었다.

Suddenly, his mother got a phone call / and she told Matthew they had to leave.
갑자기 그의 어머니는 전화를 받고 / 그녀는 Matthew에게 떠나야 한다고 말했다.
His heart sank.
그는 가슴이 내려앉았다.

어느 토요일 아침, Matthew의 어머니는 Matthew에게 공원으로 데리고 가겠다고 말했다. 그의 얼굴에 환한 미소가 드리워졌다. 그는 밖에 나가서 노는 것을 좋아했기 때문에, 나가기 위해 서둘러 아침을 먹고 옷을 입었다. 공원에 도착했을 때, Matthew는 그네를 향해 바로 뛰어갔다. 그것은 그가 공원에서 가장 좋아하는 것이었다. 하지만 그네는 이미 모두 이용되고 있었다. 그의 어머니는 그네를 이용할 수 있을 때까지 미끄럼틀을 탈 수 있다고 말했지만, 그것은 부서져 있었다. 갑자기 그의 어머니가 전화를 받고 Matthew에게 떠나야 한다고 말했다. 그는 가슴이 내려앉았다.

Why? 왜 정답일까?

아침에 어머니와 함께 공원으로 가게 되어 기뻐하던 Matthew가(A big smile came across his face.) 제대로 놀지도 못한 채 갑자기 떠나야 한다는 이야기를 듣고 실망했다(His heart sank.)는 내용의 글이다. 따라서 Matthew의 심경 변화로 가장 적절한 것은 ② '신난 → 실망한'이다.

- swing ⓝ 그네
- broken ⓐ 고장난, 부서진
- embarrassed ⓐ 당황한
- slide ⓝ 미끄럼틀
- sink ⓥ 가라앉다
- touched ⓐ 감동한

구문 풀이

3행 As he loved to play outside, he ate his breakfast and got dressed quickly
접속사(이유) / 동사1 / 동사2
so (that) they could go.
접속사(목적): ~하도록

---

20 회의 안건을 사전에 작성해 공유하기
정답률 88% | 정답 ⑤

다음 글에서 필자가 주장하는 바로 가장 적절한 것은?
① 회의 결과는 빠짐없이 작성해서 공개해야 한다.
② 중요한 정보는 공식 회의를 통해 전달해야 한다.
③ 생산성 향상을 위해 정기적인 평가회가 필요하다.
④ 모든 참석자의 동의를 받아서 회의를 열어야 한다.
✓ 회의에서 다룰 사항은 미리 작성해서 공유해야 한다.

Meetings encourage creative thinking / and can give you ideas / that you may never have thought of on your own.
회의는 창의적 사고를 촉진하며 / 아이디어들을 당신에게 제공할 수 있다. / 당신이 혼자서는 절대 떠올리지 못할 만한
However, on average, / meeting participants consider / about one third of meeting time / to be unproductive.
그러나, 평균적으로, / 회의 참석자들은 여긴다. / 회의 시간의 대략 3분의 1 정도를 / 비생산적으로
But you can make your meetings / more productive and more useful / by preparing well in advance.
하지만 당신은 회의를 만들 수 있다. / 더 생산적이고 유용하게 / 사전에 잘 준비함으로써
You should create a list of items to be discussed / and share your list with other participants / before a meeting.
당신은 논의하게 될 사항들의 목록을 만들고 / 다른 회의 참석자들에게 공유해야 한다. / 회의 전에
It allows them / to know what to expect in your meeting / and prepare to participate.
그것은 참석자들이 ~하도록 만들어 준다. / 회의에서 무엇을 기대하는지를 알고 / 회의 참석을 준비할 수 있도록

회의는 창의적 사고를 촉진하며, 당신이 혼자서는 절대 떠올리지 못했을 만한 아이디어들을 당신에게 제공할 수 있다. 그러나, 평균적으로, 회의 참석자들은 회의 시간의 대략 3분의 1 정도를 비생산적으로 여긴다. 하지만 당신은 사전에 잘 준비함으로써 회의를 더 생산적이고 유용하게 만들 수 있다. 당신은 논의하게 될 사항들의 목록을 만들어 그 목록을 회의 전에 다른 회의 참석자들에게 공유해야 한다. 그것은 참석자들이 회의에서 무엇을 기대할지를 알고 회의의 참석을 준비할 수 있도록 만들어 준다.

Why? 왜 정답일까?

'You should create a list of items to be discussed and share your list with other participants before a meeting.'에서 회의 전 논의 사항을 미리 작성해 공유하는 것이 좋다고 하므로, 필자가 주장하는 바로 가장 적절한 것은 ⑤ '회의에서 다룰 사항은 미리 작성해서 공유해야 한다.'이다.

- encourage ⓥ 촉진하다, 격려하다
- on average 평균적으로
- on one's own 혼자서, 스스로
- unproductive ⓐ 비생산적인

구문 풀이

7행 It allows them to know {what to expect in your meeting} and (to) prepare
동사 / 목적어 / 목적격 보어1 / { }: 명사구(무엇을 ~할지) / 목적격 보어2
to participate.

---

21 스트레스 관리의 원칙
정답률 80% | 정답 ③

밑줄 친 put the glass down이 다음 글에서 의미하는 바로 가장 적절한 것은? [3점]
① pour more water into the glass – 잔에 물을 더 부어야
② set a plan not to make mistakes – 실수하지 않기 위해 계획을 세워야
✓ let go of the stress in your mind – 마음속에서 스트레스를 떨쳐내야
④ think about the cause of your stress – 스트레스의 원인을 생각해 보아야
⑤ learn to accept the opinions of others – 다른 사람들의 의견을 받아들이는 법을 배워야

A psychology professor raised a glass of water / while teaching stress management principles to her students, / and asked them, / "How heavy is this glass of water I'm holding?"
한 심리학 교수가 물이 든 유리잔을 들어 올리고 / 학생들에게 스트레스 관리 원칙을 가르치던 중 / 그들에게 물었다. / "제가 들고 있는 이 물 잔의 무게는 얼마나 될까요?"라고
Students shouted out various answers.
학생들은 다양한 대답을 외쳤다.

The professor replied, / "The absolute weight of this glass doesn't matter. / It depends on how long I hold it. / If I hold it for a minute, / it's quite light.
그 교수가 답했다. / "이 잔의 절대 무게는 중요하지 않습니다. / 이는 제가 이 잔을 얼마나 오래 들고 있느냐에 달려 있죠. / 만약 제가 이것을 1분 동안 들고 있다면, / 꽤 가볍죠.
But, if I hold it for a day straight, / it will cause severe pain in my arm, / forcing me to drop the glass to the floor.
하지만, 만약 제가 이것을 하루종일 들고 있다면 / 이것은 제 팔에 심각한 고통을 야기하고 / 잔을 바닥에 떨어뜨리게 할 것입니다.
In each case, / the weight of the glass is the same, / but the longer I hold it, / the heavier it feels to me."
각 사례에서 / 잔의 무게는 같지만, / 제가 오래 들고 있을수록 / 그것은 저에게 더 무겁게 느껴지죠."
As the class nodded their heads in agreement, / she continued, / "Your stresses in life are like this glass of water. / If you still feel the weight of yesterday's stress, / it's a strong sign / that it's time to put the glass down."
학생들은 동의하며 고개를 끄덕였고, / 교수는 이어 말했다. / "여러분이 인생에서 느끼는 스트레스들도 이 물 잔과 같습니다. / 만약 아직도 어제 받은 스트레스의 무게를 느낀다면, / 그것은 강한 신호입니다. / 잔을 내려놓아야 할 때라는"

한 심리학 교수가 학생들에게 스트레스 관리 원칙을 가르치던 중 물이 든 유리잔을 들어 올리고 "제가 들고 있는 이 물 잔의 무게는 얼마나 될까요?"라고 물었다. 학생들은 다양한 대답을 외쳤다. 그 교수가 답했다. "이 잔의 절대 무게는 중요하지 않습니다. 이는 제가 이 잔을 얼마나 오래 들고 있느냐에 달려 있죠. 만약 제가 이것을 1분 동안 들고 있다면, 꽤 가볍죠. 하지만, 만약 제가 이것을 하루종일 들고 있다면 이것은 제 팔에 심각한 고통을 야기하고 잔을 바닥에 떨어뜨릴 수밖에 없게 할 것입니다. 각 사례에서 잔의 무게는 같지만, 제가 오래 들고 있을수록 그것은 저에게 더 무겁게 느껴지죠." 학생들은 동의하며 고개를 끄덕였고, 교수는 이어 말했다. "여러분이 인생에서 느끼는 스트레스들도 이 물 잔과 같습니다. 만약 아직도 어제 받은 스트레스의 무게를 느낀다면, 그것은 잔을 내려놓아야 할 때라는 강한 신호입니다."

Why? 왜 정답일까?

물 잔의 무게를 느낄 때 중요한 것은 잔의 절대적 무게가 아니라 얼마나 오래 들고 있는지(It depends on how long I hold it.)이며, 같은 잔이라고 할지라도 더 오래 들고 있을수록 더 무겁게 느껴진다(the longer I hold it, the heavier it feels to me.)고 한다. 이를 스트레스 상황에 적용하면, 스트레스의 무게가 더 무겁게 느껴질수록 그 스트레스를 오래 안고 있었다는 뜻이므로 '스트레스를 떨쳐내기' 위해 노력해야 한다는 것을 알 수 있다. 따라서 밑줄 친 부분이 의미하는 바로 가장 적절한 것은 ③ '마음속에서 스트레스를 떨쳐내야'이다.

- principle ⓝ 원칙, 원리
- nod ⓥ 끄덕이다
- put down ~을 내려놓다
- let go of ~을 내려놓다, 버리다, 포기하다
- severe ⓐ 심각한
- in agreement 동의하며
- pour ⓥ 쏟다, 붓다

구문 풀이

6행 But, if I hold it for a day straight, it will cause severe pain in my arm,
접속사(조건) / 동사(현재) / 동사(미래)
forcing me to drop the glass to the floor.
분사구문(= and will force ~)

---

22 상황을 오해하게 하는 감정
정답률 82% | 정답 ①

다음 글의 요지로 가장 적절한 것은?
✓ 자신의 감정으로 인해 상황을 오해할 수 있다.
② 자신의 생각을 타인에게 강요해서는 안 된다.
③ 인간관계가 우리의 감정에 영향을 미친다.
④ 타인의 감정에 공감하는 자세가 필요하다.
⑤ 공동체를 위한 선택에는 보상이 따른다.

Your emotions deserve attention / and give you important pieces of information.
당신의 감정은 주목할 만하고 / 당신에게 중요한 정보를 준다.
However, / they can also sometimes be / an unreliable, inaccurate source of information.
그러나, / 감정은 또한 될 수도 있다. / 가끔 신뢰할 수 없고, 부정확한 정보의 원천이
You may feel a certain way, / but that does not mean / those feelings are reflections of the truth.
당신이 분명하게 느낄지 모르지만, / 그것은 뜻하지는 않는다. / 그러한 감정들이 사실의 반영이라는 것을
You may feel sad / and conclude that your friend is angry with you / when her behavior simply reflects / that she's having a bad day.
당신은 슬플지도 모르고 / 그녀가 당신에게 화가 났다고 결론을 내릴지도 모른다. / 단지 친구의 행동이 나타낼 때에도, / 그 친구가 안 좋은 날을 보내고 있음을
You may feel depressed / and decide that you did poorly in an interview / when you did just fine.
당신은 기분이 우울할지도 모르고 / 자신이 면접에서 못했다고 판단할지도 모른다. / 당신이 잘했을 때도
Your feelings can mislead you into thinking things / that are not supported by facts.
당신의 감정은 당신을 속여 생각하게 할 수 있다. / 사실에 의해 뒷받침되지 않는 것들을

당신의 감정은 주목할 만하고 당신에게 중요한 정보를 준다. 그러나, 감정은 또한 가끔 신뢰할 수 없고, 부정확한 정보의 원천이 될 수도 있다. 당신이 특정하게 느낄지 모르지만, 그것은 그러한 감정들이 사실의 반영이라는 뜻은 아니다. 친구의 행동이 단지 그 친구가 안 좋은 날을 보내고 있음을 나타낼 때에도, 당신이 슬프기 때문에 그녀가 당신에게 화가 났다고 결론을 내릴지도 모른다. 당신은 기분이 우울해서 면접에서 잘했을 때도 못했다고 판단할지도 모른다. 당신의 감정은 당신을 속여 사실에 의해 뒷받침되지 않는 것들을 생각하게 할 수 있다.

Why? 왜 정답일까?

'However, they can also sometimes be an unreliable, inaccurate source of information.'와 'Your feelings can mislead you into thinking things that are not supported by facts.'를 통해, 감정이 상황을 오해하게 하는 경우가 생길 수 있다는 중심 내용을 파악할 수 있으므로, 글의 요지로 가장 적절한 것은 ① '자신의 감정으로 인해 상황을 오해할 수 있다.'이다.

- deserve ⓥ ~을 받을 만하다
- inaccurate ⓐ 부정확한
- reflection ⓝ 반영
- depressed ⓐ 우울한
- support ⓥ 뒷받침하다, 지지하다
- unreliable ⓐ 믿을 만하지 않은
- source of information 정보 출처
- conclude ⓥ 결론 짓다
- mislead A into B A를 속여 B하게 하다

구문 풀이

8행 Your feelings can mislead you into thinking things [that are not supported
「mislead + A + into + B : A를 잘못 인도해 B하게 하다」 선행사 주격 관·대
by facts].

---

23 아이들이 수학적 개념을 익혀 가는 방식
정답률 78% | 정답 ②

다음 글의 주제로 가장 적절한 것은?

① difficulties of children in learning how to count – 아이들이 수를 세는 법을 배우는 데 있어 어려움
✓ how children build mathematical understanding – 아이들은 수학적 이해를 어떻게 쌓아나가는가
③ why fingers are used in counting objects – 수를 셀 때 왜 손가락을 쓰는가
④ importance of early childhood education – 아동 조기 교육의 중요성
⑤ advantages of singing number songs – 숫자 노래 부르기의 이점

Every day, / children explore and construct relationships among objects.
매일, / 아이들은 사물 사이의 관계들을 탐구하고 구성한다.

Frequently, / these relationships focus on / how much or how many of something exists.
빈번히, / 이러한 관계들은 ~에 초점을 맞춘다. / 무언가가 얼마만큼 혹은 몇 개 존재하는지

Thus, / children count / — "One cookie, / two shoes, / three candles on the birthday cake, / four children in the sandbox."
따라서, / 아이들은 센다. / "쿠키 하나, / 신발 두 개, / 생일 케이크 위에 초 세 개, / 모래놀이 통에 아이 네 명."

Children compare / — "Which has more? Which has fewer? Will there be enough?"
아이들은 비교한다. / "무엇이 더 많지? 무엇이 더 적지? 충분할까?"

Children calculate / — "How many will fit? Now, I have five. I need one more."
아이들은 계산한다. / "몇 개가 알맞을까? 나는 지금 다섯 개가 있어, 하나 더 필요하네."

In all of these instances, / children are developing a notion of quantity.
이 모든 예시에서, / 아이들은 양의 개념을 발달시키는 중이다.

Children reveal and investigate mathematical concepts / through their own activities or experiences, / such as figuring out how many crackers to take at snack time / or sorting shells into piles.
아이들은 수학적 개념을 밝히고 연구한다. / 그들만의 활동이나 경험을 통해 / 간식 시간에 몇 개의 크래커를 가져갈지 알아내거나 / 조개껍질들을 더미로 분류하는 것과 같은

매일, 아이들은 사물 사이의 관계들을 탐구하고 구성한다. 빈번히, 이러한 관계들은 무언가가 얼마만큼 혹은 몇 개 존재하는지에 초점을 맞춘다. 따라서, 아이들은 센다. "쿠키 하나, 신발 두 개, 생일 케이크 위에 초 세 개, 모래놀이 통에 아이 네 명." 아이들은 비교한다. "무엇이 더 많지? 무엇이 더 적지? 충분할까?" 아이들은 계산한다. "몇 개가 알맞을까? 나는 지금 다섯 개가 있어. 하나 더 필요하네." 이 모든 예시에서, 아이들은 수량의 개념을 발달시키는 중이다. 아이들은 간식 시간에 몇 개의 크래커를 가져갈지 알아내거나 조개껍질들을 더미로 분류하는 것과 같은, 그들만의 활동이나 경험을 통해 수학적 개념을 밝히고 연구한다.

Why? 왜 정답일까?

아이들은 자기만의 활동이나 경험을 통해 수학적 개념을 익혀 간다(Children reveal and investigate mathematical concepts through their own activities or experiences ~)는 것이 핵심 내용이므로, 글의 주제로 가장 적절한 것은 ② '아이들은 수학적 이해를 어떻게 쌓아나가는가'이다.

● explore ⓥ 탐구하다
● sandbox ⓝ (어린이가 안에서 노는) 모래놀이 통
● fit ⓥ 맞다, 적합하다
● notion ⓝ 개념
● investigate ⓥ 연구하다, 조사하다
● shell ⓝ (조개 등의) 껍데기
● construct ⓥ 구성하다
● calculate ⓥ 계산하다
● instance ⓝ 예시, 사례
● quantity ⓝ (측정 가능한) 양, 수량
● sort A into B A를 B로 분류하다

구문 풀이

2행 Frequently, these relationships focus on {how much or how many of something exists}. { } : 「how + 형/부 + 주어 + 동사 : 얼마나 ~한지」

---

24 알고리듬의 시대
정답률 76% | 정답 ①

다음 글의 제목으로 가장 적절한 것은?

✓ We Live in an Age of Algorithms – 우리는 알고리듬의 시대에 산다
② Mysteries of Ancient Civilizations – 고대 문명의 미스터리
③ Dangers of Online Banking Algorithms – 온라인 뱅킹 알고리듬의 위험성
④ How Algorithms Decrease Human Creativity – 알고리듬은 어떻게 인간의 창의력을 떨어뜨리는가
⑤ Transportation: A Driving Force of Industry – 교통: 산업 발달의 원동력

Only a generation or two ago, / mentioning the word *algorithms* / would have drawn a blank from most people.
한두 세대 전만 해도, / *알고리듬*이라는 단어를 언급하는 것은 / 대부분의 사람들로부터 아무 반응을 얻지 못했을 것이다.

Today, algorithms appear in every part of civilization.
오늘날, 알고리듬은 문명의 모든 부분에서 나타난다.

They are connected to everyday life.
그것들은 일상에 연결되어 있다.

They're not just in your cell phone or your laptop / but in your car, your house, your appliances, and your toys.
그것들은 당신의 휴대 전화나 노트북 속뿐 아니라 / 당신의 자동차, 집, 가전과 장난감 안에도 있다.

Your bank is a huge web of algorithms, / with humans turning the switches here and there.
당신의 은행은 알고리듬의 거대한 망이다. / 인간들이 여기저기서 스위치를 돌리고 있는

Algorithms schedule flights / and then fly the airplanes.
알고리듬은 비행 일정을 잡고 / 비행기를 운항한다.

Algorithms run factories, / trade goods, / and keep records.
알고리듬은 공장을 운영하고, / 상품을 거래하며, / 기록 문서를 보관한다.

If every algorithm suddenly stopped working, / it would be the end of the world / as we know it.
만일 모든 알고리듬이 갑자기 작동을 멈춘다면, / 이는 세상의 끝이 될 것이다. / 우리가 알고 있는

한두 세대 전만 해도, *알고리듬*이라는 단어를 언급하는 것은 대부분의 사람들로부터 아무 반응을 얻지 못했을 것이다. 오늘날, 알고리듬은 문명의 모든 부분에서 나타난다. 그것들은 일상에 연결되어 있다. 그것들은 당신의 휴대 전화나 노트북 속뿐 아니라 당신의 자동차, 집, 가전과 장난감 안에도 있다. 당신의 은행은 인간들이 여기저기서 스위치를 돌리고 있는, 알고리듬의 거대한 망이다. 알고리듬은 비행 일정을 잡고 비행기를 운항한다. 알고리듬은 공장을 운영하고, 상품을 거래하며, 기록 문서를 보관한다. 만일 모든 알고리듬이 갑자기 작동을 멈춘다면, 이는 우리가 알고 있는 세상의 끝이 될 것이다.

Why? 왜 정답일까?

오늘날 문명의 모든 영역에서 알고리듬을 찾아볼 수 있다(Today, algorithms appear in every part of civilization.)는 것이 핵심 내용이므로, 글의 제목으로 가장 적절한 것은 ① '우리는 알고리듬의 시대에 산다'이다.

● generation ⓝ 세대
● civilization ⓝ 문명
● fly an airplane 비행기를 운항하다
● draw a blank 아무 반응을 얻지 못하다
● appliance ⓝ 가전 (제품)
● trade ⓥ 거래하다, 교역하다

구문 풀이

8행 If every algorithm suddenly stopped working, it would be the end of the
「if + 주어 + 과거시제 동사 ~, 주어 + 조동사 과거형 + 동사원형 : 가정법 과거(현재 사실 반대)」
world as we know it.

---

25 미국에서 반려동물을 키우는 가정의 비율
정답률 88% | 정답 ⑤

다음 도표의 내용과 일치하지 않는 것은?

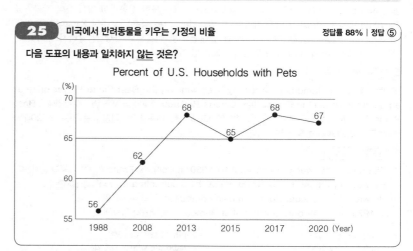

Percent of U.S. Households with Pets

The graph above shows the percent of households with pets / in the United States (U.S.) / from 1988 to 2020.
위 그래프는 반려동물을 기르는 가정의 비율을 보여준다. / 미국의 / 1988년부터 2020년까지

① In 1988, / more than half of U.S. households owned pets, / and more than 6 out of 10 U.S. households / owned pets from 2008 to 2020.
1988년에는 / 절반 이상의 미국 가정이 반려동물을 길렀고, / 10개 중 6개 이상의 미국 가정이 / 2008에서 2020년까지 반려동물을 길렀다.

② In the period between 1988 and 2008, / pet ownership increased among U.S. households / by 6 percentage points.
1988년과 2008년 사이, / 반려동물 보유는 미국 가정들에서 증가했다. / 6퍼센트포인트만큼

③ From 2008 to 2013, / pet ownership rose an additional 6 percentage points.
2008년과 2013년 사이, / 반려동물 보유는 6퍼센트포인트가 추가적으로 올랐다.

④ The percent of U.S. households with pets in 2013 / was the same as that in 2017, / which was 68 percent.
2013년의 반려동물을 기르는 미국 가정의 비율은 / 2017년의 비율과 같고, / 68퍼센트였다.

✓ In 2015, / the rate of U.S. households with pets / was 3 percentage points lower than in 2020.
2015년에는, / 반려동물을 기르는 미국 가정의 비율이 / 2020년보다 3퍼센트포인트 더 낮았다.

위 그래프는 1988년부터 2020년까지 반려동물을 기르는 미국 가정의 비율을 보여준다. ① 1988년에는 절반 이상의 미국 가정이 반려동물을 길렀고, 2008년에서 2020년까지 10개 중 6개 이상의 미국 가정이 반려동물을 길렀다. ② 1988년과 2008년 사이, 반려동물 보유는 미국 가정들에서 6퍼센트포인트 증가했다. ③ 2008년과 2013년 사이, 반려동물 보유는 6퍼센트포인트가 추가적으로 올랐다. ④ 2013년의 반려동물을 기르는 미국 가정의 비율은 2017년의 비율과 같고, 68퍼센트였다. ⑤ 2015년에는, 반려동물을 기르는 미국 가정의 비율이 2020년보다 3퍼센트포인트 더 낮았다.

Why? 왜 정답일까?

도표에 따르면 미국에서 반려동물을 기르는 가정의 비율은 2015년 65%, 2020년 67%로, 두 해 간 비율은 2퍼센트포인트의 격차를 보인다. 따라서 도표와 일치하지 않는 것은 ⑤이다.

● household ⓝ 가정, 가구
● rise ⓥ 오르다
● ownership ⓝ 보유, 소유

---

26 Claude Bolling의 생애
정답률 93% | 정답 ③

Claude Bolling에 관한 다음 글의 내용과 일치하지 않는 것은?

① 1930년에 프랑스에서 태어났다.
② 학교 친구를 통해 재즈를 소개받았다.
✓ 20대에 Best Piano Player 상을 받았다.
④ 성공적인 영화 음악 작곡가였다.
⑤ 1975년에 플루트 연주자와 협업했다.

「Pianist, composer, and big band leader, / Claude Bolling, was born on April 10, 1930, / in Cannes, France,」 / but spent most of his life in Paris. ①의 근거 일치
피아니스트, 작곡가, 그리고 빅 밴드 리더인 / Claude Bolling은 1930년 4월 10일 태어났지만, / 프랑스 칸에서 / 삶의 대부분을 파리에서 보냈다.

He began studying classical music as a youth.
그는 젊었을 때 클래식 음악을 공부하기 시작했다.

『He was introduced to the world of jazz / by a schoolmate.』②의근거 일치
그는 재즈의 세계를 소개받았다. / 학교 친구를 통해
Later, / Bolling became interested in the music of Fats Waller, / one of the most excellent jazz musicians.
후에 / Bolling은 Fats Waller의 음악에 관심을 가졌다. / 최고의 재즈 음악가들 중 한 명인
『Bolling became famous as a teenager / by winning the Best Piano Player prize / at an amateur contest in France.』③의근거 불일치
그는 10대 때 유명해졌다. / Best Piano Player 상을 수상하며 / 프랑스의 아마추어 대회에서
『He was also a successful film music composer, / writing the music for more than one hundred films.』④의근거 일치
그는 또한 성공적인 영화 음악 작곡가였고, / 100편이 넘는 영화의 음악을 작곡했다.
『In 1975, he collaborated with flutist Rampal / and published *Suite for Flute and Jazz Piano Trio*, / which he became most well-known for.』⑤의근거 일치
1975년에, 그는 플루트 연주자 Rampal과 협업했고, / *Suite for Flute and Jazz Piano Trio*를 발매했으며, / 이것으로 가장 잘 알려지게 되었다.
He died in 2020, / leaving two sons, David and Alexandre.
그는 2020년 사망했다. / 두 아들 David와 Alexandre를 남기고

피아니스트, 작곡가, 그리고 빅 밴드 리더인 Claude Bolling은 1930년 4월 10일 프랑스 칸에서 태어났지만, 삶의 대부분을 파리에서 보냈다. 그는 젊었을 때 클래식 음악을 공부하기 시작했다. 그는 학교 친구를 통해 재즈의 세계를 소개받았다. 후에 Bolling은 최고의 재즈 음악가들 중 한 명인 Fats Waller의 음악에 관심을 가졌다. 그는 10대 때 프랑스의 아마추어 대회에서 Best Piano Player 상을 수상하며 유명해졌다. 그는 또한 성공적인 영화 음악 작곡가였고, 100편이 넘는 영화의 음악을 작곡했다. 1975년에, 그는 플루트 연주자 Rampal과 협업했고, *Suite for Flute and Jazz Piano Trio*를 발매했으며, 이것으로 가장 잘 알려지게 되었다. 그는 두 아들 David와 Alexandre를 남기고 2020년 사망했다.

Why? 왜 정답일까?
'Bolling became famous as a teenager by winning the Best Piano Player prize at an amateur contest in France.'에서 Claude Bolling이 아마추어 재즈 연주자 대회에서 Best Piano Player 상을 받은 것은 10대 시절이었다고 하므로, 내용과 일치하지 않는 것은 ③ '20대에 Best Piano Player 상을 받았다.'이다.

Why? 왜 오답일까?
① 'Claude Bolling, was born on April 10, 1930, in Cannes, France, ~'의 내용과 일치한다.
② 'He was introduced to the world of jazz by a schoolmate.'의 내용과 일치한다.
④ 'He was also a successful film music composer, ~'의 내용과 일치한다.
⑤ 'In 1975, he collaborated with flutist Rampal ~'의 내용과 일치한다.

● composer ⓝ 작곡가 ● youth ⓝ 젊은 시절, 청춘
● introduce ⓥ 소개하다 ● collaborate with ~와 협업하다
● flutist ⓝ 플루티스트 ● publish ⓥ 발매하다, 출간하다
● well-known for ~로 유명한

구문 풀이
1행 Pianist, composer, and big band leader, Claude Bolling, was born on
주어 동격   주어   동사1
April 10, 1930, in Cannes, France, but spent most of his life in Paris.
동사2

---

27 여름방학 태권도 프로그램 정답률 94% | 정답 ④

Kids Taekwondo Program에 관한 다음 안내문의 내용과 일치 하지 <u>않는</u> 것은?
① 8월 8일부터 3일간 운영한다.
② 5세 이상의 어린이가 참가할 수 있다.
③ 자기 방어 훈련 활동을 한다.
☑ 참가비에 간식비는 포함되지 않는다.
⑤ 물병과 수건을 가져와야 한다.

Kids Taekwondo Program
Kids Taekwondo Program(어린이 태권도 프로그램)
Enjoy our taekwondo program this summer vacation.
이번 여름방학에 태권도 프로그램을 즐기세요.
Schedule
일정
『Dates: August 8th – August 10th』①의근거 일치
날짜: 8월 8일 ~ 8월 10일
Time: 9:00 a.m. – 11:00 a.m.
시간: 오전 9시 ~ 오전 11시
Participants
참가자
『Any child aged 5 and up』②의근거 일치
5세 이상 어린이가 누구나
Activities
활동
『Self-defense training』③의근거 일치
자기 방어 훈련
Team building games to develop social skills
사교성 발달을 위한 팀 빌딩 게임
Participation Fee
참가비
『$50 per child (includes snacks)』④의근거 불일치
1인당 $50 (간식 포함)
Notice
알림
『What to bring: water bottle, towel』⑤의근거 일치
가져올 것: 물병, 수건
What not to bring: chewing gum, expensive items
가져오지 말아야 할 것: 껌, 비싼 물건

Kids Taekwondo Program(어린이 태권도 프로그램)

이번 여름방학에 태권도 프로그램을 즐기세요.
□ 일정
• 날짜: 8월 8일 ~ 8월 10일
• 시간: 오전 9시 ~ 오전 11시
□ 참가자
• 5세 이상 어린이가 누구나
□ 활동
• 자기 방어 훈련
• 사교성 발달을 위한 팀 빌딩 게임
□ 참가비
• 1인당 $50 (간식 포함)
□ 알림
• 가져올 것: 물병, 수건
• 가져오지 말아야 할 것: 껌, 비싼 물건

Why? 왜 정답일까?
'$50 per child (includes snacks)'에서 참가비는 50달러인데, 간식이 포함된 금액이라고 한다. 따라서 안내문의 내용과 일치하지 않는 것은 ④ '참가비에 간식비는 포함되지 않는다.'이다.

Why? 왜 오답일까?
① 'Dates: August 8th – August 10th'의 내용과 일치한다.
② 'Participants / Any child aged 5 and up'의 내용과 일치한다.
③ 'Activities / Self-defense'의 내용과 일치한다.
⑤ 'What to bring: water bottle, towel'의 내용과 일치한다.

● self-defense ⓝ 자기 방어 ● social skill 사교성
● expensive ⓐ 비싼

---

28 초콜릿 공장 투어 정답률 93% | 정답 ②

Moonlight Chocolate Factory Tour에 관한 다음 안내문의 내용과 일치하는 것은?
① 주말 오후 시간에 운영한다. ☑ 초콜릿 제조 과정을 볼 수 있다.
③ 네 가지 종류의 초콜릿을 시식한다. ④ 마스크 착용은 참여자의 선택 사항이다.
⑤ 공장 내부에서 사진 촬영이 가능하다.

Moonlight Chocolate Factory Tour
Moonlight Chocolate Factory Tour(Moonlight 초콜릿 공장 투어)
Take this special tour / and have a chance to enjoy our most popular chocolate bars.
이 특별한 투어에 참여하여 / 우리의 가장 인기 있는 초콜릿 바를 즐길 기회를 가지세요.
Operating Hours
운영 시간
『Monday – Friday, 2:00 p.m. – 5:00 p.m.』①의근거 불일치
월요일~금요일, 오후 2시~오후 5시
Activities
활동
『Watching our chocolate-making process』②의근거 일치
초콜릿 제조 과정 견학
『Tasting 3 types of chocolate (dark, milk, and mint chocolate)』③의근거 불일치
초콜릿 3종 (다크, 밀크 및 민트 초콜릿) 시식
Notice
알림
Ticket price: $30
티켓 가격 : $30
『Wearing a face mask is required.』④의근거 불일치
마스크 착용은 필수입니다.
『Taking pictures is not allowed inside the factory.』⑤의근거 불일치
공장 내부에서 사진 촬영은 허용되지 않습니다.

Moonlight Chocolate Factory Tour (Moonlight 초콜릿 공장 투어)

이 특별한 투어에 참여하여 우리의 가장 인기 있는 초콜릿 바를 즐길 기회를 가지세요.
□ 운영 시간
• 월요일 ~ 금요일, 오후 2시 ~ 오후 5시
□ 활동
• 초콜릿 제조 과정 견학
• 초콜릿 3종 (다크, 밀크 및 민트 초콜릿) 시식
□ 알림
• 티켓 가격: $30
• 마스크 착용은 필수입니다.
• 공장 내부에서 사진 촬영은 허용되지 않습니다.

Why? 왜 정답일까?
'Activities / Watching our chocolate-making'에서 초콜릿 제조 과정을 견학할 수 있다고 하므로, 안내문의 내용과 일치하는 것은 ② '초콜릿 제조 과정을 볼 수 있다.'이다.

Why? 왜 오답일까?
① 'Monday – Friday, 2:00 p.m. – 5:00 p.m.'에서 운영 시간은 평일 오후라고 하였다.
③ 'Tasting 3 types of chocolate (dark, milk, and mint chocolate)'에서 시식할 수 있는 초콜릿은 세 종류라고 하였다.
④ 'Wearing a face mask is required.'에서 마스크 착용은 필수라고 하였다.
⑤ 'Taking pictures is not allowed inside the factory.'에서 공장 내부 사진 촬영은 불가하다고 하였다.

● have a chance to ~할 기회를 갖다 ● operating hour 운영 시간

29 더 많은 것을 소비하게 하는 첨단 생활방식

정답률 59% | 정답 ④

다음 글의 밑줄 친 부분 중, 어법상 틀린 것은?

Despite all the high-tech devices / that seem to deny the need for paper, / paper use in the United States / ① has nearly doubled recently.
모든 첨단 기기들에도 불구하고, / 종이의 필요성을 부정하는 것처럼 보이는 / 미국에서 종이 사용은 / 최근 거의 두 배로 증가했다.

We now consume more paper than ever: / 400 million tons globally and growing.
우리는 현재 그 어느 때보다도 더 많은 종이를 소비하고 있어서, / 전 세계에서 4억 톤을 쓰고 있으며 그 양은 증가하고 있다.

Paper is not the only resource / ② that we are using more of.
자원은 종이만이 아니다. / 우리가 더 많이 사용하고 있는

Technological advances often come / with the promise of ③ using fewer materials.
기술의 발전은 흔히 온다. / 더 적은 재료의 사용 가능성과 함께

However, / the reality is / that they have historically caused more materials use, / making us ☑ dependent on more natural resources.
그러나, / 현실은 ~이다. / 그것들이 역사적으로 더 많은 재료 사용을 야기해 / 우리가 더 많은 천연자원 사용에 의존하게 한다는 것

The world now consumes far more "stuff" / than it ever has.
세계는 이제 훨씬 더 많은 '것'을 소비한다. / 그것이 그래 왔던 것보다

We use twenty-seven times more industrial minerals, / such as gold, copper, and rare metals, / than we ⑤ did just over a century ago.
우리는 산업 광물을 27배 더 많이 사용한다. / 금, 구리, 희귀 금속과 같은 / 우리가 고작 1세기 이전에 그랬던 것보다

We also each individually use more resources.
우리는 또한 각자 더 많은 자원을 사용한다.

Much of that is due to our high-tech lifestyle.
그중 많은 부분은 우리의 첨단 생활방식 때문이다.

종이의 필요성을 부정하는 것처럼 보이는 모든 첨단 기기들에도 불구하고, 미국에서 종이 사용은 최근 거의 두 배로 증가했다. 우리는 현재 그 어느 때보다도 더 많은 종이를 소비하고 있어서, 전 세계에서 4억 톤을 쓰고 있으며 그 양은 증가하고 있다. 우리가 더 많이 사용하고 있는 자원은 종이만이 아니다. 기술의 발전은 흔히 더 적은 재료의 사용 가능성을 수반한다. 그러나, 현실은 그것들이 역사적으로 더 많은 재료 사용을 야기해 더 많은 천연자원에 의존하게 한다는 것이다. 세계는 이제 그 어느 때보다도 훨씬 더 많은 '재료'를 소비한다. 우리는 금, 구리, 희귀 금속과 같은 산업 광물을 고작 1세기 이전보다 27배 더 많이 사용한다. 우리는 또한 각자 더 많은 자원을 사용한다. 그중 많은 부분은 우리의 첨단 생활방식 때문이다.

Why? 왜 정답일까?

make는 형용사를 목적격 보어로 취하는 5형식 동사이므로, 부사 dependently를 형용사 dependent로 고쳐 making의 보어 자리를 채워야 한다. 따라서 어법상 틀린 것은 ④이다.

Why? 왜 오답일까?

① 주어 paper use가 불가산명사이므로 단수 동사 has가 어법상 적절하다.
② 선행사 the only resource 뒤로 목적어가 없는 불완전한 절을 이끌고자 관계대명사 that이 알맞게 쓰였다. 참고로 선행사에 the only가 있으면 관계대명사 that이 주로 쓰인다.
③ 전치사 of 뒤에 목적어인 동명사 using이 알맞게 쓰였다.
⑤ 앞에 나온 일반동사 use를 대신하는데 시제가 과거이므로(over a century ago) 대동사 did가 알맞게 쓰였다.

- **high-tech** ⓐ 첨단 기술의
- **material** ⓝ 물질, 자재, 재료
- **dependently** ⓐⓓ 의존적으로, 남에게 의지하여
- **rare** ⓐ 희귀한
- **consume** ⓥ 소비하다
- **historically** ⓐⓓ 역사적으로
- **industrial** ⓐ 산업의

구문 풀이

6행 However, the reality is {that they have historically caused more materials use, making us dependently on more natural resources}. 〔 〕: 명사절(주격 보어)
분사구문(= and they make ~)

30 삶을 사랑하는 법

정답률 61% | 정답 ②

다음 글의 밑줄 친 부분 중, 문맥상 낱말의 쓰임이 적절하지 않은 것은? [3점]

Do you sometimes feel like / you don't love your life?
당신은 가끔 느끼는가? / 당신이 삶을 사랑하지 않는다고

Like, deep inside, something is missing?
마치 마음 깊은 곳에 뭔가가 빠진 것처럼?

That's because we are living someone else's life.
왜냐하면 우리가 타인의 삶을 살고 있기 때문이다.

We allow other people to ① influence our choices.
우리는 타인이 우리의 선택에 영향을 주도록 허용한다.

We are trying to meet their expectations.
우리는 그들의 기대감을 만족시키기 위해 노력하고 있다.

Social pressure is deceiving / — we are all impacted without noticing it.
사회적 압력은 현혹시킨다. / 우리 모두는 그것을 눈치채지도 못한 채 영향을 받는다.

Before we realize / we are losing ownership of our lives, / we end up ☑ envying how other people live.
우리가 깨닫기도 전에, / 우리의 삶에 대한 소유권을 잃었다는 것을 / 우리는 결국 다른 사람들이 어떻게 사는지를 부러워하게 된다.

Then, we can only see the greener grass / — ours is never good enough.
그러면, 우리는 더 푸른 잔디만 볼 수 있게 된다. / 우리의 삶은 만족할 만큼 충분히 좋아질 수 없다.

To regain that passion for the life you want, / you must ③ recover control of your choices.
당신이 원하는 삶에 대한 열정을 되찾기 위해서는 / 당신의 선택에 대한 통제력을 회복해야 한다.

No one but yourself / can choose how you live.
당신 자신을 제외한 그 누구도 / 당신이 어떻게 살지를 선택할 수 없다.

But, how?
하지만 어떻게 해야 할까?

The first step to getting rid of expectations / is to treat yourself ④ kindly.
기대감을 버리는 첫 단계는 / 자신을 친절하게 대하는 것이다.

You can't truly love other people / if you don't love yourself first.
당신은 다른 사람을 진정으로 사랑할 수 없다. / 당신이 자신을 먼저 사랑하지 않으면

When we accept who we are, / there's no room for other's ⑤ expectations.
우리가 우리 있는 그대로를 받아들일 때, / 타인의 기대를 위한 여지는 남지 않는다.

당신은 가끔 삶을 사랑하지 않는다고 느끼는가? 마치 마음 깊은 곳에서 뭔가가 빠진 것처럼? 왜냐하면 우리가 타인의 삶을 살고 있기 때문이다. 우리는 타인이 우리의 선택에 ① 영향을 주도록 허용한다. 우리는 그들의 기대감을 만족시키기 위해 노력하고 있다. 사회적 압력은 (우리를) 현혹시켜서, 우리 모두는 그것을 눈치채지도 못한 채 영향을 받는다. 우리의 삶에 대한 소유권을 잃어가고 있다는 것을 깨닫기도 전에, 우리는 결국 다른 사람들이 어떻게 사는지를 ② 무시하게(→ 부러워하게) 된다. 그러면, 우리는 더 푸른 잔디(타인의 삶이 더 좋아 보이는 것)만 볼 수 있게 되어, 우리의 삶은 (만족할 만큼) 충분히 좋아질 수 없다. 당신이 원하는 삶에 대한 열정을 되찾기 위해서는 당신의 선택에 대한 통제력을 ③ 회복해야 한다. 당신 자신을 제외한 그 누구도 당신이 어떻게 살지를 선택할 수 없다. 하지만 어떻게 해야 할까? 기대감을 버리는 첫 단계는 자기 자신에게 ④ 친절하게 대하는 것이다. 자신을 먼저 사랑하지 않으면 다른 사람을 진정으로 사랑할 수 없다. 우리가 우리 있는 그대로를 받아들일 때, 타인의 ⑤ 기대를 위한 여지는 남지 않는다.

Why? 왜 정답일까?

타인의 기대를 만족시키는 삶을 살아갈 때에는 삶을 사랑할 수 없기에 자신을 친절하게 대하며 삶에 대한 주도권을 회복해 나가야 한다는 내용의 글이다. 흐름상 ② 앞뒤는 타인의 삶을 살다 보면 자신의 삶에 대한 통제력을 잃었음을 알기도 전에 이미 타인의 삶을 더 좋게 보고 '부러워하게' 된다는 문맥이므로, ignoring을 envying으로 고쳐야 한다. 따라서 문맥상 낱말의 쓰임이 적절하지 않은 것은 ②이다.

- **missing** ⓐ 빠진, 실종된
- **meet the expectation** 기대를 충족하다
- **impact** ⓥ 영향을 미치다
- **recover** ⓥ 회복하다
- **influence** ⓥ 영향을 미치다 ⓝ 영향
- **deceiving** ⓐ 현혹시키는, 속이는
- **ownership** ⓝ 소유권
- **get rid of** ~을 없애다

구문 풀이

9행 No one but yourself can choose {how you live}. 〔 〕: 간접의문문(어떻게 ~할지)
~을 제외하고(= except)

★★★ 등급을 가르는 문제!

31 혁신 지속에 도움이 되는 가상 환경의 특징

정답률 49% | 정답 ①

다음 빈칸에 들어갈 말로 가장 적절한 것을 고르시오.

☑ restrictions – 제한점
② responsibilities – 책임감
③ memories – 기억
④ coincidences – 우연의 일치
⑤ traditions – 전통

One of the big questions faced this past year / was how to keep innovation rolling / when people were working entirely virtually.
작년에 직면한 가장 큰 질문 중 하나는 / 어떻게 혁신을 지속할 것인가 하는 것이었다. / 사람들이 완전히 가상 공간에서 작업할 때

But experts say / that digital work didn't have a negative effect / on innovation and creativity.
그러나 전문가들은 말한다. / 디지털 작업이 부정적인 영향을 미치지 않았다고 / 혁신과 창의성에

Working within limits / pushes us to solve problems.
한계 내에서 일하는 것은 / 우리에게 문제를 해결하도록 독려한다.

Overall, / virtual meeting platforms put more constraints / on communication and collaboration / than face-to-face settings.
전반적으로, / 가상 미팅 플랫폼은 더 많은 제약들을 가한다. / 의사소통과 협업에 / 대면 설정보다

For instance, / with the press of a button, / virtual meeting hosts can control the size of breakout groups / and enforce time constraints; / only one person can speak at a time; / nonverbal signals, / particularly those below the shoulders, / are diminished; / "seating arrangements" are assigned by the platform, / not by individuals; / and visual access to others may be limited / by the size of each participant's screen.
예를 들어, / 버튼을 누르면, / 가상 회의 진행자는 소모임 그룹의 크기를 제어하고 시간 제한을 시행할 수 있다. / 한 번에 한 사람만이 말할 수 있다. / 비언어적 신호, / 특히 어깨 아래의 신호는 / 줄어든다. / '좌석 배치는 플랫폼에 의해 할당된다. / 개인이 아닌 / 그리고 다른 사람에 대한 시각적 접근은 제한될 수 있다. / 각 참가자의 화면 크기에 의해

Such restrictions are likely to stretch participants / beyond their usual ways of thinking, / boosting creativity.
이러한 제한점은 참가자들을 확장시킬 가능성이 높다. / 일반적인 사고방식 너머까지 / 그리고 창의력을 증진시킬

작년에 직면한 가장 큰 질문 중 하나는 사람들이 완전히 가상 공간에서 작업할 때 어떻게 혁신을 지속할 것인가 하는 것이었다. 그러나 전문가들은 디지털 작업이 혁신과 창의성에 부정적인 영향을 미치지 않았다고 말한다. 한계 내에서 일하는 것은 우리에게 문제를 해결하도록 독려한다. 전반적으로, 가상 미팅 플랫폼은 대면 환경보다 의사소통과 협업에 더 많은 제약들을 가한다. 예를 들어, 버튼을 누르면, 가상 회의 진행자는 소모임 그룹의 크기를 제어하고 시간 제한을 시행할 수 있다. 한 번에 한 사람만이 말할 수 있다. 비언어적 신호, 특히 어깨 아래의 신호는 줄어든다. '좌석 배치'는 개인이 아닌 플랫폼에 의해 할당된다. 그리고 다른 사람에 대한 시각적 접근은 각 참가자의 화면 크기에 따라 제한될 수 있다. 이러한 제한점은 참가자들을 일반적인 사고방식 너머까지 확장시켜 창의력을 증진시킬 가능성이 높다.

Why? 왜 정답일까?

'Working within limits pushes us to solve problems.'에서 한계 내에서 작업하는 것이 문제 해결을 독려한다고 언급하는 것으로 보아, 빈칸에 들어갈 말로 가장 적절한 것은 ① '제한점'이다.

- **virtually** ⓐⓓ (컴퓨터를 이용해) 가상으로
- **have a negative effect on** ~에 부정적 영향을 미치다
- **constraint** ⓝ 제한, 한계
- **enforce** ⓥ 시행하다
- **seating arrangement** 좌석 배치
- **stretch** ⓥ 늘이다, 확장하다
- **breakout group** (전체에서 나누어진) 소집단
- **diminish** ⓥ 줄이다
- **assign** ⓥ 배정하다, 할당하다
- **coincidence** ⓝ 우연의 일치, 동시 발생

구문 풀이

1행 One of the big questions faced this past year was {how to keep innovation
주어(one of the + 복수명사) 과거분사 동사(단수)
rolling when people were working entirely virtually}.
〔 〕: 주격 보어(how + to부정사: ~하는 방법)

★★★ 등급을 가르는 문제!

32 전통적 수요 법칙의 예외인 기펜재
정답률 56% | 정답 ②

다음 빈칸에 들어갈 말로 가장 적절한 것을 고르시오. [3점]

① order more meat – 더 많은 고기를 주문한다
✓② consume more rice – 더 많은 쌀을 소비한다
③ try to get new jobs – 새로운 일자리를 구하려 한다
④ increase their savings – 저축액을 늘린다
⑤ start to invest overseas – 해외에 투자하기 시작한다

The law of demand is / that the demand for goods and services increases / as prices fall, / and the demand falls / as prices increase.
수요의 법칙은 ~이다. / 상품과 서비스에 대한 수요가 증가하고, / 가격이 하락할수록 / 수요가 감소하는 것 / 가격이 상승할수록
Giffen goods are special types of products / for which the traditional law of demand does not apply.
기펜재는 특별한 유형의 상품이다. / 전통적인 수요 법칙이 적용되지 않는
Instead of switching to cheaper replacements, / consumers demand more of giffen goods / when the price increases / and less of them when the price decreases.
저렴한 대체품으로 바꾸는 대신 / 소비자들은 기펜재를 더 많이 필요로 한다. / 가격이 상승할 때 / 그리고 가격이 하락할 때 덜
Taking an example, / rice in China is a giffen good / because people tend to purchase less of it / when the price falls.
예를 들어, / 중국의 쌀은 기펜재이다. / 사람들이 그것을 덜 구매하는 경향이 있기 때문에 / 가격이 하락할 때
The reason for this is, / when the price of rice falls, / people have more money / to spend on other types of products / such as meat and dairy / and, therefore, change their spending pattern.
그 이유는 ~이다. / 쌀값이 하락하면, / 사람들이 돈이 많아지고, / 다른 종류의 상품에 쓸 / 고기나 유제품 같은 / 그 결과 소비 패턴을 바꾸기 때문에
On the other hand, / as rice prices increase, / people consume more rice.
반면에, / 쌀값이 상승하면, / 사람들은 더 많은 쌀을 소비한다.

수요의 법칙은 가격이 하락할수록 상품과 서비스에 대한 수요가 증가하고, 가격이 상승할수록 수요가 감소하는 것이다. *기펜재*는 전통적인 수요 법칙이 적용되지 않는 특별한 유형의 상품이다. 저렴한 대체품으로 바꾸는 대신 소비자들은 가격이 상승할 때 기펜재를 더 많이, 가격이 하락할 때 덜 필요로 한다. 예를 들어, 중국의 쌀은 가격이 하락할 때 사람들이 덜 구매하는 경향이 있기 때문에 기펜재이다. 그 이유는, 쌀값이 하락하면, 사람들이 고기나 유제품 같은 다른 종류의 상품에 쓸 돈이 많아지고, 그 결과 소비 패턴을 바꾸기 때문이다. 반면에, 쌀값이 상승하면, 사람들은 더 많은 쌀을 소비한다.

Why? 왜 정답일까?
전통적인 수요 법칙에 따르면 가격과 수요는 반비례하지만, 이 법칙의 예외에 있는 기펜재는 가격과 상승 및 하락 흐름을 같이한다(Instead of switching to cheaper replacements, consumers demand more of giffen goods when the price increases and less of them when the price decreases.)는 내용의 글이다. 중반 이후로 중국의 쌀이 기펜재의 예시로 언급되므로, 쌀 가격이 오를 때 오히려 사람들은 '쌀을 더 산다'는 내용이 결론이어야 한다. 따라서 빈칸에 들어갈 말로 가장 적절한 것은 ② '더 많은 쌀을 소비한다'이다.

● demand ⓝ 수요 ⓥ 필요로 하다, 요구하다　　● apply for ~에 적용되다
● switch to ~로 바꾸다　　　　　　　　　● replacement ⓝ 대체(품)
● dairy ⓝ 유제품　　　　　　　　　　　● overseas ⓐ 해외에

구문 풀이

3행 *Giffen goods* are special types of products [for which the traditional law of demand does not apply].
선행사 「전치사+관계대명사」

★★★ 등급을 가르는 문제!

33 지적 능력 발달에 있어 천성보다 중요한 양육
정답률 44% | 정답 ③

다음 빈칸에 들어갈 말로 가장 적절한 것을 고르시오. [3점]

① by themselves for survival – 생존을 위해 스스로
② free from social interaction – 사회적 상호작용 없이
✓③ based on what is around you – 여러분 주변에 있는 것에 따라
④ depending on genetic superiority – 유전적 우월성에 따라
⑤ so as to keep ourselves entertained – 우리 자신을 계속 즐겁게 하기 위해

In a study at Princeton University in 1992, / research scientists looked at two different groups of mice.
1992년 프린스턴 대학의 한 연구에서, / 연구 과학자들은 두 개의 다른 쥐 집단을 관찰했다.
One group was made intellectually superior / by modifying the gene for the glutamate receptor.
한 집단은 지적으로 우월하게 만들어졌다. / 글루타민산염 수용체에 대한 유전자를 변형함으로써
Glutamate is a brain chemical / that is necessary in learning.
글루타민산염은 뇌 화학 물질이다. / 학습에 필수적인
The other group was genetically manipulated / to be intellectually inferior, / also done by modifying the gene for the glutamate receptor.
다른 집단도 유전적으로 조작되었다. / 지적으로 열등하도록 / 역시 글루타민산염 수용체에 대한 유전자를 변형함으로써 이루어진
The smart mice were then raised in standard cages, / while the inferior mice were raised in large cages / with toys and exercise wheels / and with lots of social interaction.
그 후 똑똑한 쥐들은 표준 우리에서 길러졌다. / 열등한 쥐들은 큰 우리에서 길러진 반면 / 장난감과 운동용 쳇바퀴가 있고 / 사회적 상호작용이 많은
At the end of the study, / although the intellectually inferior mice were genetically handicapped, / they were able to perform just as well / as their genetic superiors.
연구가 끝날 무렵, / 비록 지적 능력이 떨어지는 쥐들이 유전적으로 장애가 있었지만, / 그들은 딱 그만큼 잘 수행할 수 있었다. / 그들의 유전적인 우월군들만큼
This was a real triumph for nurture over nature.
이것은 천성에 대한 양육의 진정한 승리였다.
Genes are turned on or off / based on what is around you.
유전자는 작동하거나 멈춘다. / 여러분 주변에 있는 것에 따라

1992년 프린스턴 대학의 한 연구에서, 연구 과학자들은 두 개의 다른 쥐 집단을 관찰했다. 한 집단은 글루타민산염 수용체에 대한 유전자를 변형함으로써 지적으로 우월하게 만들어졌다. 글루타민산염은 학습에 필수적인 뇌 화학 물질이다. 다른 집단도 역시 글루타민산염 수용체에 대한 유전자를 변형함으로써, 지적으로 열등하도록 유전적으로 조작되었다. 그 후 똑똑한 쥐들은 표준 우리에서 길러진 반면에 열등한 쥐들은 장난감과 운동용 쳇바퀴가 있고 사회적 상호작용이 많은 큰 우리에서 길러졌다. 연구가 끝날 무렵, 비록 지적 능력이 떨어지는 쥐들이 유전적으로 장애가 있었지만, 그들은 딱 유전적인 우월군들만큼 잘 수행할 수 있었다. 이것은 천성(선천적 성질)에 대한 양육(후천적 환경)의 진정한 승리였다. 유전자는 여러분 주변에 있는 것에 따라 작동하거나 멈춘다.

Why? 왜 정답일까?
빈칸이 있는 문장 바로 앞에서 양육, 즉 후천적 환경이 타고난 천성을 이겼다(a real triumph for nurture over nature)는 말로 연구 결과를 정리하고 있다. 따라서 빈칸에 들어갈 말로 가장 적절한 것은 '환경, 양육'과 같은 의미의 ③ '여러분 주변에 있는 것에 따라'이다.

● intellectually ⓐⓓ 지적으로　　　　● modify ⓥ 수정하다, 바꾸다
● receptor ⓝ 수용체　　　　　　　● genetically ⓐⓓ 유전적으로
● inferior ⓐ 열등한　　　　　　　　● handicapped ⓐ 장애가 있는, 불리한 입장인
● triumph ⓝ 승리　　　　　　　　　● nurture ⓝ 양육
● free from ~ 없이, ~을 면하여

구문 풀이

5행 The other group was genetically manipulated to be intellectually inferior,
선행사
(which was) also done by modifying the gene for the glutamate receptor.
생략(계속적 용법)　과거분사

★★★ 등급을 가르는 문제!

34 기후 변화에 대한 대처가 '현재' 이루어지지 않는 이유
정답률 45% | 정답 ②

다음 빈칸에 들어갈 말로 가장 적절한 것을 고르시오. [3점]

① it is not related to science – 그것이 과학과 관련이 없다
✓② it is far away in time and space – 그것이 시공간적으로 멀리 떨어져 있다
③ energy efficiency matters the most – 에너지 효율이 가장 중요하다
④ careful planning can fix the problem – 신중한 계획이 문제를 해결할 수 있다
⑤ it is too late to prevent it from happening – 그것이 일어나지 않도록 막기에는 너무 늦었다

Researchers are working on a project / that asks coastal towns / how they are preparing for rising sea levels.
연구원들은 프로젝트를 진행하고 있다. / 해안가 마을들에게 묻는 / 해수면 상승에 어떻게 대비하고 있는지
Some towns have risk assessments; / some towns even have a plan.
어떤 마을들은 위험 평가를 하고 / 어떤 마을들은 심지어 계획을 가지고 있다.
But it's a rare town / that is actually carrying out a plan.
하지만 마을은 드물다. / 실제로 계획을 실행하고 있는
One reason we've failed to act on climate change / is the common belief / that it is far away in time and space.
우리가 기후 변화에 대처하는 데 실패한 한 가지 이유는 / 일반적인 믿음 때문이다. / 그것이 시공간적으로 멀리 떨어져 있다는
For decades, / climate change was a prediction about the future, / so scientists talked about it in the future tense.
수십 년 동안, / 기후 변화는 미래에 대한 예측이었기 때문에 / 과학자들은 미래 시제로 기후 변화에 대해 이야기했다.

This became a habit / — so that even today / many scientists still use the future tense, / even though we know / that a climate crisis is ongoing.
이것이 습관이 되어 / 그 결과 오늘날에도 / 많은 과학자들이 여전히 미래 시제를 사용하고 있다. / 우리가 알고 있음에도, / 기후 위기가 진행중이라는 것을

Scientists also often focus on regions / most affected by the crisis, / such as Bangladesh or the West Antarctic Ice Sheet, / which for most Americans are physically remote.
과학자들은 또한 지역에 초점을 맞추고 있으며, / 위기의 영향을 가장 많이 받는 / 방글라데시나 서남극 빙상처럼 / 그 지역은 대부분의 미국인들에게는 물리적으로 멀리 떨어져 있다.

연구원들은 해안가 마을들이 해수면 상승에 어떻게 대비하고 있는지 묻는 프로젝트를 진행하고 있다. 어떤 마을들은 위험 평가를 하고 어떤 마을들은 심지어 계획을 가지고 있다. 하지만 실제로 계획을 실행하고 있는 마을은 드물다. 우리가 기후 변화에 대처하는 데 실패한 한 가지 이유는 <u>그것이 시공간적으로 멀리 떨어져 있다</u>는 일반적인 믿음 때문이다. 수십 년 동안, 기후 변화는 미래에 대한 예측이었기 때문에 과학자들은 미래 시제로 기후 변화에 대해 이야기했다. 이것이 습관이 되어, 비록 우리가 기후 위기가 진행중이라는 것을 알고 있음에도, 많은 과학자들이 오늘날에도 여전히 미래 시제를 사용하고 있다. 과학자들은 또한 방글라데시나 서남극 빙상처럼 위기의 영향을 가장 많이 받는 지역에 초점을 맞추고 있으며, 그 지역은 대부분의 미국인들에게는 물리적으로 멀리 떨어져 있다.

Why? 왜 정답일까?

빈칸 뒤에 따르면, 기후 변화는 현재가 아닌 미래의 사건으로 여겨져 늘 미래 시제로 묘사되며(use the future tense), 기후 위기에 취약한 지역 또한 과학자들에게는 물리적으로 멀리 떨어진(physically remote) 곳이다. 다시 말해 기후 변화와 그로 인한 여파는 늘 '지금 여기'와는 동떨어진' 사건으로 취급되고 있다는 것이 글의 핵심 내용이므로, 빈칸에 들어갈 말로 가장 적절한 것은 ② '그것이 시공간적으로 멀리 떨어져 있다'이다.

- **sea level** 해수면
- **prediction** ⓝ 예측
- **crisis** ⓝ 위기
- **Antarctic** ⓐ 남극의
- **remote** ⓐ 멀리 떨어진
- **assessment** ⓝ 평가
- **tense** ⓝ (문법) 시제
- **ongoing** ⓐ 진행 중인
- **physically** ⓐ 물리적으로, 신체적으로

구문 풀이

4행 One reason [we've failed to act on climate change] is the common belief {that it is far away in time and space}.
주어 [ ] : 관계부사절 동사(단수) 주격 보어 [ ] : 동격절(=the common belief)

★★ 문제 해결 꿀~팁 ★★

▶ 많이 틀린 이유는?
⑤는 일반적으로 많이 언급되는 내용이지만 글에서 보면 기후 변화를 막기에 '시간적으로 너무 늦었다'는 내용은 글에서 다루어지지 않았다.

▶ 문제 해결 방법은?
빈칸이 글 중간에 있으면 주로 뒤에 답에 대한 힌트가 있다. 여기서도 빈칸 뒤를 보면, 과학자들은 기후 변화에 관해 아직도 미래 시제로 말하며, 지리적으로도 멀리 떨어진 곳을 연구하는 데 집중한다는 점을 지적하고 있다. 이는 기후 변화를 '시간 · 공간적으로 동떨어진' 일로 여기는 경향을 비판하는 것이다.

---

35 패션의 의미 정답률 66% | 정답 ④

다음 글에서 전체 흐름과 관계 없는 문장은?

According to Marguerite La Caze, / fashion contributes to our lives / and provides a medium for us / to develop and exhibit important social virtues.
Marguerite La Caze에 따르면, / 패션은 우리의 삶에 기여하고 / 우리에게 수단을 제공한다 / 중요한 사회적 가치를 개발하고 나타낼

① Fashion may be beautiful, innovative, and useful; / we can display creativity and good taste in our fashion choices.
패션은 아름다울 수 있고, 혁신적일 수 있으며, 유용할 수 있다. / 우리는 패션을 선택하는 데 있어서 창의성과 좋은 취향을 드러낼 수 있다.

② And in dressing with taste and care, / we represent / both self-respect and a concern for the pleasure of others.
그리고 취향과 관심에 따라 옷을 입을 때, / 우리는 보여준다. / 자아존중과 타인의 즐거움에 대한 관심 모두를

③ There is no doubt / that fashion can be a source of interest and pleasure / which links us to each other.
의심의 여지가 없다. / 패션은 흥미와 즐거움의 원천이 될 수 있다는 것은 / 우리와 타인을 연결해 주는

④ Although the fashion industry / developed first in Europe and America, / today it is an international and highly globalized industry.
비록 패션 산업은 / 유럽과 미국에서 처음 발달했지만, / 오늘날에는 국제적이고 매우 세계화된 산업이 되었다.

⑤ That is, / fashion provides a sociable aspect / along with opportunities to imagine oneself differently / — to try on different identities.
다시 말해, / 패션은 친교적인 측면을 제공한다. / 자신을 다르게 상상하는 기회와 더불어 / 즉, 다른 정체성을 시도하는

Marguerite La Caze에 따르면, 패션은 우리의 삶에 기여하고, 우리가 중요한 사회적 가치를 개발하고 나타낼 수단을 제공한다. ① 패션은 어쩌면 아름다울 수 있고, 혁신적일 수 있으며, 유용할 수 있다. 우리는 패션을 선택하는 데 있어서 창의성과 좋은 취향을 드러낼 수 있다. ② 그리고 취향과 관심에 따라 옷을 입을 때, 우리는 자아존중과 타인의 즐거움에 대한 관심 모두를 보여준다. ③ 의심의 여지없이, 패션은 우리를 서로 연결해 주는 흥미와 즐거움의 원천이 될 수 있다. ④ 패션 산업은 유럽과 미국에서 처음 발달했지만, 오늘날에는 국제적이고 매우 세계화된 산업이 되었다. ⑤ 다시 말해, 패션은 자신을 다르게 상상하는, 즉 다른 정체성을 시도하는 기회와 더불어 친교적인 측면을 제공한다.

Why? 왜 정답일까?

패션이 삶에서 갖는 의미를 설명한 글로, 개인의 삶과 타인과의 상호작용에서 어떤 의미를 갖는지 주로 언급된다. 하지만 ④는 패션 사업의 발달에 관해 언급하며 글의 흐름에서 벗어나므로, 전체 흐름과 관계 없는 문장은 ④이다.

- **contribute to** ~에 기여하다, ~의 원인이 되다
- **exhibit** ⓥ 보여주다, 드러내다
- **medium** ⓝ 수단, 매체
- **taste** ⓝ 취향

- **represent** ⓥ 나타내다, 표현하다
- **link A to B** A와 B를 연결하다
- **sociable** ⓐ 사교적인, 사람들과 어울리기 좋아하는
- **concern** ⓝ 관심, 우려
- **highly** ⓐ 매우
- **along with** ~와 더불어

구문 풀이

6행 There is no doubt {that fashion can be a source of interest and pleasure [which links us to each other]}.
부정 주어 { } : doubt의 동격절 선행사 [ ] 주격 관·대

---

36 선생님에게 그림으로 감사를 표현한 Douglas 정답률 79% | 정답 ③

주어진 글 다음에 이어질 글의 순서로 가장 적절한 것을 고르시오.
① (A) – (C) – (B) ② (B) – (A) – (C)
③ (B) – (C) – (A) ④ (C) – (A) – (B)
⑤ (C) – (B) – (A)

Mrs. Klein told her first graders / to draw a picture of something to be thankful for.
Klein 선생님은 1학년 학생들에게 말했다. / 감사히 여기는 것을 그려보라고

She thought / that most of the class would draw turkeys or Thanksgiving tables.
그녀는 생각했다. / 반 아이들 대부분이 칠면조나 추수감사절 식탁을 그릴 것으로

But Douglas drew something different.
하지만 Douglas는 색다른 것을 그렸다.

(B) Douglas was a boy / who usually spent time alone and stayed around her / while his classmates went outside together during break time.
Douglas는 소년이었다. / 보통 혼자 시간을 보내고 그녀 주변에 머무르는 / 그의 반 친구들이 쉬는 시간에 함께 밖으로 나가 있는 동안

What the boy drew was a hand.
그 소년이 그린 것은 손이었다.

But whose hand?
그런데 누구의 손일까?

His image immediately attracted the other students' interest.
그의 그림은 즉시 다른 학생들의 관심을 끌었다.

(C) So, / everyone rushed to talk / about whose hand it was.
그래서, / 모두가 앞다투어 말하려 했다. / 그것이 누구의 손인지에 관해

"It must be the hand of God / that brings us food," / said one student.
"그것은 신의 손이 틀림없어. / 우리에게 음식을 가져다주는" / 한 학생이 말했다.

"A farmer's," / said a second student, / "because they raise the turkeys."
"농부의 손이야," / 두 번째 학생이 말했다. / "왜냐하면 그들은 칠면조를 기르거든."이라고

"It looks more like a police officer's," / added another, / "they protect us."
"경찰관의 손과 더 비슷해 보여," / 또 다른 학생이 덧붙였다. / "그들은 우리를 보호해 줘."라고

(A) The class was so responsive / that Mrs. Klein had almost forgotten about Douglas.
반 아이들이 몹시 호응해서 / Klein 선생님은 Douglas에 대해 하마터면 잊어버릴 뻔했다.

After she had the others at work on another project, / she asked Douglas whose hand it was.
그녀가 나머지 아이들에게 다른 과제를 하도록 지도한 후, / 그녀는 Douglas에게 그 손이 누구인지 물었다.

He answered softly, / "It's yours. Thank you, Mrs. Klein."
그는 조용히 대답했다. / "선생님 손이에요. 고마워요, Klein 선생님."이라고

Klein 선생님은 1학년 학생들에게 감사히 여기는 것을 그려보라고 말했다. 그녀는 반 아이들 대부분이 칠면조나 추수감사절 식탁을 그릴 것으로 생각했다. 하지만 Douglas는 색다른 것을 그렸다.

(B) Douglas는 그의 반 친구들이 쉬는 시간에 함께 밖으로 나가 있는 동안, 보통 혼자 시간을 보내고 그녀 주변에 머무르는 소년이었다. 그 소년이 그린 것은 손이었다. 그런데 누구의 손일까? 그의 그림은 즉시 다른 학생들의 관심을 끌었다.

(C) 그래서, 모두가 그것이 누구의 손인지에 관해 앞다투어 말하려 했다. "그것은 우리에게 음식을 가져다주는 신의 손이 틀림없어."라고 한 학생이 말했다. "농부의 손이야, 왜냐하면 그들은 칠면조를 기르거든."이라고 두 번째 학생이 말했다. "경찰관의 손과 더 비슷해 보여, 그들은 우리를 보호해 줘."라고 또 다른 학생이 덧붙였다.

(A) 반 아이들의 호응에 Klein 선생님은 Douglas에 대해 하마터면 잊어버릴 뻔했다. 그녀는 나머지 아이들에게 다른 과제를 하도록 지도한 후, Douglas에게 그 손이 누구 손인지 물었다. "선생님 손이에요. 고마워요, Klein 선생님."이라고 그는 조용히 대답했다.

Why? 왜 정답일까?

고마운 것을 그려보는 시간에 Douglas가 무언가 색다른 것을 그렸다는 내용의 주어진 글 뒤에는, Douglas가 그린 것이 손이었다는 내용의 (B), 아이들이 누구의 손인지 맞춰보려 했다는 내용의 (C), 나중에 Douglas가 그것이 선생님의 손임을 말했다는 내용의 (A)가 차례로 이어져야 자연스럽다. 따라서 글의 순서로 가장 적절한 것은 ③ '(B) – (C) – (A)'이다.

- **turkey** ⓝ 칠면조
- **immediately** ⓐ 즉시
- **raise** ⓥ 기르다, 키우다
- **responsive** ⓐ 즉각 반응하는, 관심을 보이는
- **attract one's interest** ~의 관심을 끌다

구문 풀이

1행 Mrs. Klein told her first graders to draw a picture of something to be thankful for.
동사 목적어 목적격 보어 대명사(-thing) 형용사적 용법

---

37 흡혈귀가 존재했을 수 없는 이유 정답률 62% | 정답 ⑤

주어진 글 다음에 이어질 글의 순서로 가장 적절한 것을 고르시오. [3점]
① (A) – (C) – (B) ② (B) – (A) – (C)
③ (B) – (C) – (A) ④ (C) – (A) – (B)
⑤ (C) – (B) – (A)

According to legend, / once a vampire bites a person, / that person turns into a vampire / who seeks the blood of others.

전설에 따르면, / 흡혈귀가 사람을 물면 / 그 사람은 흡혈귀로 변한다. / 다른 사람의 피를 갈구하는
A researcher came up with some simple math, / which proves that these highly popular creatures can't exist.
한 연구자는 간단한 계산법을 생각해냈다. / 이 잘 알려진 존재가 실존할 수 없다는 것을 증명하는
(C) University of Central Florida physics professor / Costas Efthimiou's work breaks down the myth.
University of Central Florida의 물리학과 교수인 / Costas Efthimiou의 연구가 그 미신을 무너뜨렸다.
Suppose / that on January 1st, 1600, / the human population was just over five hundred million.
가정해 보자. / 1600년 1월 1일에 / 인구가 5억 명이 넘는다고
(B) If the first vampire came into existence / that day and bit one person a month, / there would have been two vampires by February 1st, 1600.
그날 최초의 흡혈귀가 생겨나서 / 한 달에 한 명을 물었다면, / 1600년 2월 1일까지 흡혈귀가 둘 있었을 것이다.
A month later there would have been four, / the next month eight, / then sixteen, / and so on.
한 달 뒤면 넷이 되었을 것이고 / 그다음 달은 여덟, / 그리고 열여섯 / 등등이 되었을 것이다.
(A) In just two-and-a-half years, / the original human population / would all have become vampires / with no humans left.
불과 2년 반 만에, / 원래의 인류는 / 모두 흡혈귀가 되었을 것이다. / 인간이 하나도 남지 않은 채로
But look around you.
하지만 주위를 둘러보라.
Have vampires taken over the world?
흡혈귀가 세상을 정복하였는가?
No, because there's no such thing.
아니다. 왜냐하면 흡혈귀는 존재하지 않으니까.

전설에 따르면, 흡혈귀가 사람을 물면 그 사람은 다른 사람의 피를 갈구하는 흡혈귀로 변한다. 한 연구자는 이 대단히 잘 알려진 존재가 실존할 수 없다는 것을 증명하는 간단한 계산법을 생각해냈다.

(C) University of Central Florida의 물리학과 교수 Costas Efthimiou의 연구가 그 미신을 무너뜨렸다. 1600년 1월 1일에 인구가 막 5억 명을 넘겼다고 가정해 보자.

(B) 그날 최초의 흡혈귀가 생겨나서 한 달에 한 명을 물었다면, 1600년 2월 1일까지 흡혈귀가 둘 있었을 것이다. 한 달 뒤면 넷, 그다음 달은 여덟, 그리고 열여섯 등등으로 계속 늘어났을 것이다.

(A) 불과 2년 반 만에, 원래의 인류는 모두 흡혈귀가 되어 더 이상 남아 있지 않았을 것이다. 하지만 주위를 둘러보라. 흡혈귀가 세상을 정복하였는가? 아니다. 왜냐하면 흡혈귀는 존재하지 않으니까.

Why? 왜 정답일까?

흡혈귀가 존재했음을 부정하는 계산식을 생각해낸 사람이 있다는 내용의 주어진 글 뒤에는, 먼저 **1600년 1월 1일**에 인구가 5억 명이 넘었다고 가정해 보자며 계산식에 관해 설명하기 시작한 **(C)**가 연결된다. 이어서 **(B)**는 (C)에서 언급한 날짜를 **that day**로 가리키며, 흡혈귀가 달마다 두 배씩 늘어가는 상황을 가정해 보자고 설명한다. 마지막으로 **(A)**는 (C) – (B)의 상황이 성립한다면 5억 명의 사람들이 불과 2년 반 만에 모두 흡혈귀로 변했을 것인데, 인류는 현재까지 지속되고 있으므로 흡혈귀가 존재했을 수 없다는 결론을 제시하고 있다. 따라서 글의 순서로 가장 적절한 것은 ⑤ '(C) – (B) – (A)'이다.

- **legend** ⓝ 전설
- **come into existence** 생기다, 나타나다
- **myth** ⓝ 미신, (잘못된) 통념
- **take over** ~을 지배하다, 장악하다
- **break down** 무너뜨리다

구문 풀이

5행 In just two-and-a-half years, the original human population would all have become vampires with no humans left.
「would have + 과거분사 : ~했을 것이다(가정법 과거완료 주절)」 「with + 명사 + 과거분사 : ~이 …된 채로」

---

38 마찰력의 특징 정답률 73% | 정답 ④

글의 흐름으로 보아, 주어진 문장이 들어가기에 가장 적절한 곳을 고르시오.

Friction is a force / between two surfaces / that are sliding, or trying to slide, / across each other.
마찰력은 힘이다. / 두 표면 사이에 작용하는 / 미끄러지거나 미끄러지려고 하는 / 서로 엇갈리게
For example, / when you try to push a book along the floor, / friction makes this difficult.
예를 들어, / 당신이 바닥 위 책을 밀려고 할 때, / 마찰이 이를 어렵게 만든다.
Friction always works in the direction / opposite to the direction / in which the object is moving, or trying to move.
마찰은 항상 방향으로 작용한다. / 방향과 반대인 / 물체가 움직이거나 움직이려고 하는
So, friction always slows a moving object down.
그래서 마찰은 항상 움직이는 물체를 느리게 만든다.
① The amount of friction depends on the surface materials.
마찰의 양은 표면 물질에 따라 달라진다.
② The rougher the surface is, / the more friction is produced.
표면이 거칠수록 / 더 많은 마찰력이 발생한다.
③ Friction also produces heat.
마찰은 또한 열을 발생시킨다.
☑ For example, / if you rub your hands together quickly, / they will get warmer.
예를 들어, / 만약 당신이 손을 빠르게 비비면, / 손이 더 따뜻해질 것이다.
Friction can be a useful force / because it prevents our shoes slipping on the floor / when we walk / and stops car tires skidding on the road.
마찰력은 유용한 힘으로 작용할 수 있다. / 그것이 신발이 바닥에 미끄러지는 것을 방지하며 / 우리가 걸을 때 / 자동차 타이어가 도로에서 미끄러지는 것을 막아주므로
⑤ When you walk, / friction is caused / between the tread on your shoes and the ground, / acting to grip the ground and prevent sliding.
당신이 걸을 때, / 마찰은 발생하며, / 당신의 신발 접지면과 바닥 사이에 / 땅을 붙잡아 미끄러지는 것을 방지하는 역할을 한다.

마찰력은 서로 엇갈리게 미끄러지거나 미끄러지려고 하는 두 표면 사이에 작용하는 힘이다. 예를 들어, 당신이 바닥 위 책을 밀려고 할 때, 마찰이 이를 어렵게 만든다. 마찰은 항상 물체가 움직이거나 움직이려고 하는 방향과 반대 방향으로 작용한다. 그래서 마찰은 항상 움직이는 물체를 느려지게 만든다. ① 마찰의 양은 표면 물질에 따라 달라진다. ② 표면이 거칠수록 더 많은 마찰력이 발생한다. ③ 마찰은 또한 열을 발생시킨다. ④ 예를 들어, 만약 당신이 손을 빠르게 비비면, 손이 더 따뜻해질 것이다. 마찰력은 우리가 걸을 때 신발이 바닥에서 미끄러지는 것을 방지하고 자동차 타이어가 도로에서 미끄러지는 것을 막아주므로 유용한 힘이 될 수 있다. ⑤ 걸을 때, 마찰은 당신의 신발 접지면과 바닥 사이에 발생하여 땅을 붙잡아 미끄러지는 것을 방지하는 역할을 한다.

Why? 왜 정답일까?

주어진 문장은 마찰과 열을 관련지어 설명하고 있으므로, 앞에 열에 관한 내용이 언급된 후 예시(For example)로 이어질 수 있다. 글에서 열에 관해 언급하는 문장은 ④ 앞의 문장이므로, 주어진 문장이 들어가기에 가장 적절한 곳은 ④이다.

- **rub** ⓥ 문지르다
- **surface** ⓝ 표면
- **slow down** ~을 느려지게 하다
- **slip** ⓥ (넘어지거나 넘어질 뻔하게) 미끄러지다
- **friction** ⓝ 마찰
- **opposite** ⓐ 반대의
- **rough** ⓐ 거친
- **grip** ⓥ 붙잡다

구문 풀이

9행 The rougher the surface is, the more friction is produced.
「the + 비교급 ~, the + 비교급 … : ~할수록 더 …하다」

★★★ 등급을 가르는 문제!
39 선천적 시각장애인의 세상 이해 정답률 46% | 정답 ⑤

글의 흐름으로 보아, 주어진 문장이 들어가기에 가장 적절한 곳을 고르시오.

Humans born without sight / are not able to collect visual experiences, / so they understand the world / entirely through their other senses.
선천적으로 시각장애가 있는 사람은 / 시각적 경험을 수집할 수 없어서, / 그들은 세상을 이해한다. / 전적으로 다른 감각을 통해
① As a result, / people with blindness at birth / develop an amazing ability / to understand the world / through the collection of experiences and memories / that come from these non-visual senses.
그 결과, / 선천적으로 시각장애가 있는 사람들은 / 놀라운 능력을 발달시킨다. / 세상을 이해하는 / 경험과 기억의 수집을 통해 / 이러한 비시각적 감각에서 오는
② The dreams of a person / who has been without sight since birth / can be just as vivid and imaginative / as those of someone with normal vision.
사람이 꾸는 꿈은 / 선천적으로 시각장애가 있는 / 생생하고 상상력이 풍부할 수 있다. / 정상 시력을 가진 사람의 꿈처럼
③ They are unique, however, / because their dreams are constructed / from the non-visual experiences and memories / they have collected.
그러나 그들은 특별하다. / 그들의 꿈은 구성되기 때문에 / 비시각적 경험과 기억으로부터 / 그들이 수집한
④ A person with normal vision / will dream about a familiar friend / using visual memories of shape, lighting, and colour.
정상적인 시력을 가진 사람들은 / 친숙한 친구에 대해 꿈을 꿀 것이다. / 형태, 빛 그리고 색의 시각적 기억을 사용하여
☑ But, / a blind person will associate the same friend / with a unique combination of experiences / from their non-visual senses / that act to represent that friend.
하지만, / 시각장애인은 그 친구를 연상할 것이다. / 독특한 조합의 경험으로 / 비시각적 감각에서 나온 / 그 친구를 구현하는 데 작용하는
In other words, / people blind at birth / have similar overall dreaming experiences / even though they do not dream in pictures.
다시 말해, / 선천적 시각장애인들은 / 전반적으로 비슷한 꿈을 경험한다. / 그들이 시각적인 꿈을 꾸지는 않지만

선천적으로 시각장애가 있는 사람은 시각적 경험을 수집할 수 없어서, 전적으로 다른 감각을 통해 세상을 이해한다. ① 그 결과, 선천적으로 시각장애가 있는 사람들은 이러한 비시각적 감각에서 오는 경험과 기억의 수집을 통해 세상을 이해하는 놀라운 능력을 발달시킨다. ② 선천적으로 시각장애가 있는 사람이 꾸는 꿈은 정상 시력을 가진 사람의 꿈처럼 생생하고 상상력이 풍부할 수 있다. ③ 그러나 그들의 꿈은 그들이 수집한 비시각적 경험과 기억으로부터 구성되기 때문에 특별하다. ④ 정상적인 시력을 가진 사람들은 형태, 빛 그리고 색의 시각적 기억을 사용하여 친숙한 친구에 대해 꿈을 꿀 것이다. ⑤ 하지만, 시각장애인은 그 친구를 구현하는 데 작용하는 자신의 비시각적 감각에서 나온 독특한 조합의 경험으로 바로 그 친구를 연상할 것이다. 다시 말해, 선천적 시각장애인들은 시각적인 꿈을 꾸지는 않지만, 전반적으로 비슷한 꿈을 경험한다.

Why? 왜 정답일까?

선천적 시각장애인은 시각적 경험이 없지만 비시각적 경험과 기억을 통해 세상을 이해하는 특별한 방법을 구성해 나간다는 내용의 글로, ⑤ 이후로 시각장애인이 꿈꾸는 방식을 예로 들고 있다. ⑤ 앞의 문장에서 비시각장애인은 시각적 경험을 이용해 친구에 관한 꿈을 꾼다고 언급하는데, 주어진 문장은 But으로 흐름을 뒤집으며 선천적 시각장애인은 비시각적 감각 경험을 토대로 친구를 연상한다고 설명한다. In other words로 시작하는 ⑤ 뒤의 문장은 주어진 문장의 의미를 풀어볼 때 시각장애인도 결국 꿈을 비슷하게 경험한다는 것을 알 수 있다고 결론 짓는다. 따라서 주어진 문장이 들어가기에 가장 적절한 곳은 ⑤이다.

- **associate A with B** A와 B를 연결 짓다, 연상하다
- **combination** ⓝ 조합
- **vivid** ⓐ 생생한
- **sight** ⓝ 시력
- **imaginative** ⓐ 상상력이 풍부한

구문 풀이

9행 The dreams of a person [who has been without sight since birth] can be
주어(복수) / 주격 관·대(a person 수식) / 전치사(~ 이후로) / 동사
just as vivid and imaginative as those of someone with normal vision.
「as + 원급 + as : ~만큼 …한」 / 대명사(= the dreams)

★★ 문제 해결 꿀~팁 ★★

▶ 많이 틀린 이유는?
가장 헷갈리는 ③ 앞을 보면, 선천적 시각 장애인의 꿈도 비장애인의 꿈과 마찬가지로 생생하고 상상력이 풍부하다는 내용이다. 이어서 ③ 뒤에서는 however와 함께, '그런데' 이들의 꿈은 비시각적 경험과 기억에 바탕을 두기 때문에 '특별하다'는 내용을 추가하고 있다. 즉, ③ 앞뒤는 역접어 however를 기점으로 '우리와 다르지 않다 → 특별하다'로 자연스럽게 전환되는 흐름인 것이다.

---

40 권위가 있는 부모 밑에서 자란 자녀들의 학업 성취 　정답률 65% | 정답 ③

다음 글의 내용을 한 문장으로 요약하고자 한다. 빈칸 (A), (B)에 들어갈 말로 가장 적절한 것은? [3점]

(A)	(B)	(A)	(B)
① likely 가능성이 크며	random 무작위적인	② willing 자발적이며	minimal 최소한의
✓ willing 자발적이며	active 적극적인	④ hesitant 망설이며	unwanted 원치 않는
⑤ hesitant 망설이며	constant 지속적인		

According to a study of Swedish adolescents, / an important factor of adolescents' academic success / is how they respond to challenges.
스웨덴 청소년들에 대한 연구에 따르면, / 청소년들의 학업 성공의 중요한 요인은 / 그들이 어려움에 반응하는 방식이다.

The study reports / that when facing difficulties, / adolescents exposed to an authoritative parenting style / are less likely to be passive, helpless, and afraid to fail.
이 연구는 보고하고 있다. / 어려움에 직면했을 때 / 권위가 있는 양육 방식에 노출된 청소년들은 / 덜 수동적이고, 덜 무기력하며, 실패를 덜 두려워한다고

Another study of nine high schools / in Wisconsin and northern California / indicates / that children of authoritative parents do well in school, / because these parents put a lot of effort / into getting involved in their children's school activities.
9개 고교에서 진행된 또 다른 연구는 / Wisconsin과 northern California의 / 밝히고 있다. / 권위가 있는 부모들의 아이들이 학습을 잘하는데, / 그 이유는 이러한 부모들이 많은 노력을 기울이기 때문이라고 / 아이들의 학교 활동에 관여하고자

That is, / authoritative parents are significantly more likely / to help their children with homework, / to attend school programs, / to watch their children in sports, / and to help students select courses.
즉, / 권위가 있는 부모들은 ~할 가능성이 훨씬 더 크다. / 아이들의 숙제를 도와주고, / 학교 프로그램에 참여하며, / 스포츠에 참여하는 아이들을 지켜보고, / 아이들의 과목 선택을 도와줄

Moreover, / these parents are more aware / of what their children do and how they perform in school.
게다가, / 이러한 부모들은 더 잘 인지하고 있다. / 아이들이 학교에서 하고 있는 일과 수행하는 방식에 대해

Finally, / authoritative parents / praise academic excellence and the importance of working hard more / than other parents do.
마지막으로, / 권위가 있는 부모들은 / 학문적 탁월함과 근면함의 중요성을 더 많이 칭찬한다. / 다른 부모들에 비해

➡ The studies above show / that the children of authoritative parents / often succeed academically, / since they are more (A) willing to deal with their difficulties / and are affected by their parents' (B) active involvement.
위 연구는 보여준다. / 권위가 있는 부모의 아이들이 / 학업 성취가 좋다는 것을 / 그들이 어려움에 대처하는 데 더 자발적이며, / 그 부모들의 적극적인 관여에 영향을 받기 때문에

스웨덴 청소년들에 대한 연구에 따르면, 청소년들의 학업 성공의 중요한 요인은 그들이 어려움에 반응하는 방식이다. 이 연구는 어려움에 직면했을 때 권위가 있는 양육 방식에 노출된 청소년들은 덜 수동적이고, 덜 무기력하며, 실패를 덜 두려워한다고 보고하고 있다. Wisconsin과 northern California의 9개 고교에서 진행된 또 다른 연구는 권위가 있는 부모들의 아이들이 학습을 잘하는데, 그 이유는 이러한 부모들이 아이들의 학교 활동에 관여하고자 많은 노력을 기울이기 때문이라고 밝히고 있다. 즉, 권위가 있는 부모들은 아이들의 숙제를 도와주고, 학교 프로그램에 참여하며, 스포츠에 참여하는 아이들을 지켜보고, 아이들의 과목 선택을 도와줄 가능성이 훨씬 더 크다. 게다가, 이러한 부모들은 아이들이 학교에서 무엇을 하는지, 어떤 성과를 내는지 더 잘 인지하고 있다. 마지막으로, 권위가 있는 부모들은 다른 부모에 비해 학문적 탁월함과 근면함의 중요성을 더 많이 칭찬한다.

➡ 위 연구는 권위가 있는 부모의 아이들이 어려움에 대처하는 데 더 (A) 자발적이며, 그 부모들의 (B) 적극적인 관여에 영향을 받기 때문에 학업 성취가 좋다는 것을 보여준다.

Why? 왜 정답일까?

두 번째 문장인 '~ when facing difficulties, adolescents exposed to an authoritative parenting style are less likely to be passive ~'에서 권위적인 양육 방식에 노출된 자녀는 어려움 앞에서 덜 수동적이라고 한다. 이어서 '~ children of authoritative parents do well in school, because these parents put a lot of effort into getting involved in their children's school activities.'에서 권위가 있는 부모는 자녀의 학습에 더 적극 관여하기 때문에, 이들 자녀의 학업 성취가 실제로 더 좋다는 연구 결과를 언급하고 있다. 따라서 요약문의 빈칸 (A), (B)에 들어갈 말로 가장 적절한 것은 ③ '(A) willing(자발적이며), (B) active(적극적인)'이다.

- adolescent ⓝ 청소년
- authoritative ⓐ 권위적인
- put effort into ~에 노력을 쏟다
- hesitant ⓐ 망설이는
- factor ⓝ 요인
- helpless ⓐ 무기력한
- significantly ⓐⓓ 상당히

구문 풀이

3행 The study reports that when facing difficulties, adolescents exposed to
분사구문(~할 때)　　　주어　　과거분사
an authoritative parenting style are less likely to be passive, helpless, and
동사구(~할 가능성이 적다) 주격 보어1 주격 보어2
afraid to fail.
주격 보어3

41-42 취침 시간과 심장 건강의 연관관계

『U.K. researchers say / a bedtime of between 10 p.m. and 11 p.m. is best.
영국 연구원들은 이야기한다. / 밤 10시와 밤 11시 사이의 취침 시간이 가장 좋다고

They say / people who go to sleep between these times / have a (a) lower risk of heart disease.』 41번의 근거
그들은 이야기한다. / 이 시간대 사이에 잠드는 사람들이 / 더 낮은 심장 질환의 위험성을 가지고 있다고

Six years ago, / the researchers collected data / on the sleep patterns of 80,000 volunteers.
6년 전, / 그 연구원들은 데이터를 수집했다. / 8만 명의 자원자들의 수면 패턴에 관해

The volunteers had to wear a special watch for seven days / so the researchers could collect data / on their sleeping and waking times.
그 자원자들은 7일간 특별한 시계를 착용해야만 했고, / 그래서 그 연구원은 데이터를 수집할 수 있었다. / 그들의 수면과 기상 시간에 대한

The scientists then monitored the health of the volunteers.
그러고 나서 연구원들은 그 자원자들의 건강을 관찰했다.

Around 3,000 volunteers later showed heart problems.
약 3천 명의 자원자들이 이후에 심장 문제를 보였다.

『They went to bed earlier or later / than the (b) ideal 10 p.m. to 11 p.m. timeframe.』
그들은 더 이르거나 더 늦게 잠자리에 들었다. / 밤 10시와 밤 11시 사이라는 이상적인 시간대보다　42번의 근거

One of the authors of the study, Dr. David Plans, / commented on his research / and the (c) effects of bedtimes on the health of our heart.
그 연구 저자 중 한 명인 Dr. David Plans는 / 자신의 연구에 대해 언급했다. / 그리고 취침 시간이 우리의 심장 건강에 끼치는 영향에 대해

He said / the study could not give a certain cause for their results, / but it suggests / that early or late bedtimes may be more likely / to disrupt the body clock, / with (d) negative consequences for cardiovascular health.
그는 이야기했다. / 그 연구가 결과에 특정한 원인을 시사하지는 못하지만, / 그것은 제시한다. / 이르거나 늦은 취침 시간이 ~할 가능성이 더 높을 수 있다는 것을 / 체내 시계를 혼란케 할 / 심혈관 건강에 부정적인 결과와 함께

He said / that it was important for our body / to wake up to the morning light, / and that the worst time to go to bed / was after midnight / because it may (e) reduce the likelihood of seeing morning light / which resets the body clock.
그는 말했다. / 우리의 몸에 중요하고, / 아침 빛에 맞추어 일어나는 것이 / 잠자리에 드는 가장 나쁜 시간이 / 자정 이후인데, / 그것이 아침 빛을 볼 가능성을 낮출 수도 있기 때문이라고 / 우리의 체내 시계를 재설정하는

He added / that we risk cardiovascular disease / if our body clock is not reset properly.
그는 덧붙였다. / 우리가 심혈관 질환의 위험을 안게 된다고 / 만약 우리의 체내 시계가 적절하게 재설정되지 않으면

영국 연구원들은 밤 10시와 밤 11시 사이의 취침 시간이 가장 좋다고 이야기한다. 그들은 이 시간대 사이에 잠드는 사람들이 (a) 더 낮은 심장 질환의 위험성을 가지고 있다고 이야기한다. 6년 전, 그 연구원들은 8만 명의 자원자들의 수면 패턴 데이터를 수집했다. 그 자원자들은 연구원들이 그들의 수면과 기상 시간에 대한 데이터를 수집할 수 있도록 7일간 특별한 시계를 착용해야 했다. 그러고 나서 연구원들은 그 자원자들의 건강을 관찰했다. 약 3천 명의 자원자들이 이후에 심장 문제를 보였다. 그들은 밤 10시에서 밤 11시 사이라는 (b) 이상적인 시간대보다 더 이르거나 더 늦게 잠자리에 들었다. 그 연구 저자 중 한 명인 Dr. David Plans는 자신의 연구와 취침 시간이 우리의 심장 건강에 끼치는 (c) 영향에 대해 언급했다. 그는 그 연구가 결과의 특정한 원인을 시사하지는 못하지만, 이르거나 늦은 취침 시간이 심혈관 건강에 (d) 긍정적인(→ 부정적인) 결과와 함께 체내 시계를 혼란케 할 가능성이 더 높을 수 있다는 것을 제시한다고 이야기했다. 그는 우리의 몸이 아침 빛에 맞추어 일어나는 것이 중요하고, 잠자리에 드는 가장 나쁜 시간이 자정 이후인데, 우리의 체내 시계를 재설정하는 아침 빛을 볼 가능성을 (e) 낮출 수도 있기 때문이라고 말했다. 그는 만약 우리의 체내 시계가 적절하게 재설정되지 않으면 우리가 심혈관 질환의 위험을 안게 된다고 덧붙였다.

- author ⓝ 저자
- consequence ⓝ 결과, 영향
- likelihood ⓝ 가능성, 공산
- sound ⓐ 좋은, 건전한
- body clock 생체 시계
- reduce ⓥ 낮추다, 줄이다
- properly ⓐⓓ 적절하게

구문 풀이

15행 He said {that it was important for our body to wake up to the morning
가주어　　동사1　　　　의미상 주어　　진주어(주어)
light,} and {that the worst time to go to bed was after midnight because it may
주어2　　　형용사적 용법　동사2　　　접속새(이유)
reduce the likelihood of seeing morning light [which resets the body clock]}.
선행사　　　주격 관·대

---

41 제목 파악 　정답률 67% | 정답 ①

윗글의 제목으로 가장 적절한 것은?

✓ The Best Bedtime for Your Heart – 당신의 심장을 위한 최적의 취침 시간
② Late Bedtimes Are a Matter of Age – 늦은 취침 시간은 나이 문제이다
③ For Sound Sleep: Turn Off the Light – 숙면을 위해: 불을 끄세요
④ Sleeping Patterns Reflect Personalities – 수면 패턴은 성격을 반영한다
⑤ Regular Exercise: A Miracle for Good Sleep – 규칙적인 운동: 숙면을 위한 기적

Why? 왜 정답일까?

취침 시간이 심혈관 건강에 미치는 영향에 관한 연구 내용을 들어 적절한 취침 시간의 중요성을 설명하는 글로, 첫 두 문장에 화제가 잘 제시된다(~ a bedtime of between 10 p.m. and 11 p.m. is best. ~ people who go to sleep between these times have a lower risk of heart disease.)이다. 따라서 글의 제목으로 가장 적절한 것은 ① '당신의 심장을 위한 최적의 취침 시간'이다.

---

42 어휘 추론 　정답률 68% | 정답 ④

밑줄 친 (a) ~ (e) 중에서 문맥상 낱말의 쓰임이 적절하지 않은 것은?
① (a)　② (b)　③ (c)　✓ (d)　⑤ (e)

Why? 왜 정답일까?

연구 결과를 언급하는 첫 문단의 마지막 두 문장에 따르면, 이상적인 취침 시간보다 이르거나 늦게 잠드는 사람들은 이후 심장 문제가 생길 가능성이 높다(Around 3,000 volunteers later showed heart problems. They went to bed earlier or later than the ideal 10 p.m. to 11 p.m. timeframe.)고 한다. 즉 이상적인 취침시간보다 빨리 자든 늦게 자든, 그로 인해 '부정적인' 영향을 입을 수 있다는 것이므로, (d)의 positive를 negative로 고쳐야 한다. 따라서 문맥상 낱말의 쓰임이 적절하지 않은 것은 ④ '(d)'이다.

08회

(A)

Once, / a farmer lost his precious watch / while working in his barn.
어느 날, / 한 농부가 그의 귀중한 시계를 잃어버렸다. / 헛간에서 일하는 동안

It may have appeared to be an ordinary watch to others, / but 「it brought a lot of happy childhood memories to him.」 45번 ①의 근거 일치
그것은 다른 이들에게는 평범한 시계로 보일 수도 있었지만 / 그것은 그에게 어린 시절의 많은 행복한 기억을 불러왔다.

It was one of the most important things to (a) him.
그것은 그에게 가장 중요한 것들 중 하나였다.

After searching for it for along time, / the old farmer became exhausted.
오랜 시간 동안 그것을 찾아본 뒤에 / 그 나이 든 농부는 지쳐버렸다.

(D)

However, / the tired farmer did not want to give up / on the search for his watch / and asked a group of children playing outside to help him.
그러나, / 그 지친 농부는 포기하고 싶지 않았기에 / 자기 시계를 찾는 것을 / 밖에서 놀던 한 무리의 아이들에게 도와 달라고 요청했다.

(e) He promised an attractive reward / for the person who could find it.
그는 매력적인 보상을 약속했다. / 자기 시계를 찾는 사람에게

「After hearing about the reward, / the children hurried inside the barn / and went through and round the entire pile of hay / looking for the watch.」 45번 ④의 근거 불일치
보상에 대해 듣고 난 뒤, / 그 아이들은 헛간 안으로 서둘러 들어갔고 / 전체 건초 더미 사이와 주변으로 걸어갔다. / 시계를 찾으러

「After a long time searching for it, / some of the children got tired and gave up.」 45번 ⑤의 근거 일치
시계를 찾느라 오랜 시간을 보낸 후, / 아이들 중 일부는 지쳐서 포기했다.

(B)

The number of children looking for the watch / slowly decreased / and only a few tired children were left.
시계를 찾는 아이들의 숫자가, / 천천히 줄어들었고 / 지친 아이들 몇 명만이 남았다.

The farmer gave up all hope of finding it / and called off the search.
그 농부는 시계를 찾을 거라는 모든 희망을 포기하고 / 찾는 것을 멈추었다.

「Just when the farmer was closing the barn door, / a little boy came up to him / and asked the farmer to give him another chance.」 45번 ②의 근거 일치
농부가 막 헛간 문을 닫고 있었을 때 / 한 어린 소년이 그에게 다가와서 / 자신에게 또 한 번의 기회를 달라고 요청했다.

The farmer did not want / to lose out on any chance of finding the watch / so let (b) him in the barn.
농부는 원하지 않아서 / 시계를 찾을 어떤 가능성도 놓치는 것을 / 그를 헛간 안으로 들어오게 해주었다.

(C)

「After a little while / the boy came out with the farmer's watch in his hand.」 45번 ③의 근거 일치
잠시 후 / 그 소년이 한 손에 농부의 시계를 들고 나왔다.

(c) He was happily surprised / and asked how he had succeeded to find the watch / while everyone else had failed.
그는 행복에 겨워 놀랐고 / 소년이 어떻게 시계를 찾는 데 성공했는지를 물었다. / 다른 모두가 실패했던 반면

He replied / "I just sat there and tried listening for the sound of the watch. / In silence, / it was much easier / to hear it and follow the direction of the sound."
그는 답했다. / "저는 거기에 앉아서 시계의 소리를 들으려고 했어요. / 침묵 속에서, / 훨씬 쉬웠어요. / 그것을 듣고 소리의 방향을 따라가는 것이"

(d) He was delighted to get his watch back / and rewarded the little boy as promised.
그는 시계를 되찾아 기뻤고 / 그 어린 소년에게 약속했던 대로 보상해 주었다.

(A)

어느 날, 한 농부가 헛간에서 일하는 동안 그의 귀중한 시계를 잃어버렸다. 그것은 다른 이들에게는 평범한 시계로 보일 수도 있었지만 그것은 그에게 어린 시절의 많은 행복한 기억을 불러일으켰다. 그것은 (a) 그에게 가장 중요한 것들 중 하나였다. 오랜 시간 동안 그것을 찾아본 뒤에 그 나이 든 농부는 지쳐버렸다.

(D)

그러나, 그 지친 농부는 자기 시계를 찾는 것을 포기하고 싶지 않았기에 밖에서 놀던 한 무리의 아이들에게 도와 달라고 요청했다. (e) 그는 자기 시계를 찾는 사람에게 매력적인 보상을 약속했다. 보상에 대해 듣고 난 뒤, 그 아이들은 헛간 안으로 서둘러 들어갔고 시계를 찾으러 전체 건초 더미 사이와 주변을 다녔다. 시계를 찾느라 오랜 시간을 보낸 후, 아이들 중 일부는 지쳐서 포기했다.

(B)

시계를 찾는 아이들의 숫자가 천천히 줄어들었고 지친 아이들 몇 명만이 남았다. 그 농부는 시계를 찾을 거라는 모든 희망을 포기하고 찾는 것을 멈추었다. 농부가 막 헛간 문을 닫고 있었을 때 한 어린 소년이 그에게 다가와서 자신에게 또 한 번의 기회를 달라고 요청했다. 농부는 시계를 찾을 어떤 가능성도 놓치고 싶지 않아서 (b) 그를 헛간 안으로 들어오게 해주었다.

(C)

잠시 후 그 소년이 한 손에 농부의 시계를 들고 나왔다. (c) 그는 행복에 겨워 놀랐고 다른 모두가 실패했던 반면 소년이 어떻게 시계를 찾는 데 성공했는지를 물었다. 그는 "저는 거기에 앉아서 시계의 소리를 들으려고 했어요. 침묵 속에서, 그것을 듣고 소리의 방향을 따라가는 것이 훨씬 쉬웠어요."라고 답했다. (d) 그는 시계를 되찾아 기뻤고 그 어린 소년에게 약속했던 대로 보상해 주었다.

- **precious** ⓐ 소중한, 귀중한
- **lose out on** ~을 놓치다, ~에게 지다
- **pile** ⓝ 더미
- **hay** ⓝ 건초
- **call off** ~을 중단하다, 멈추다
- **attractive** ⓐ 매력적인

구문 풀이

[(B) 1행] The number of children looking for the watch slowly decreased and
주어1(the number of+복수명사 : ~의 수) 현재분사 동사1

only a few tired children were left.
주어2 동사2

[(C) 5행] In silence, it was much easier to hear it and follow the direction of the sound.
가주어 비교급 강조(훨씬) 진주어

---

43   글의 순서 파악   정답률 77% | 정답 ④

주어진 글 (A)에 이어질 내용을 순서에 맞게 배열한 것으로 가장 적절한 것은?

① (B) – (D) – (C)   ② (C) – (B) – (D)
③ (C) – (D) – (B)   ✔ (D) – (B) – (C)
⑤ (D) – (C) – (B)

Why? 왜 정답일까?

아끼던 시계를 잃어버린 농부를 소개하는 (A) 뒤로, 농부가 아이들에게 시계 찾기를 맡겼다는 내용의 (D), 모두가 실패한 가운데 한 소년이 다시 자원했다는 내용의 (B), 소년이 시계를 찾아냈다는 내용의 (C)가 차례로 이어져야 자연스럽다. 따라서 글의 순서로 가장 적절한 것은 ④ '(D) – (B) – (C)'이다.

44   지칭 추론   정답률 73% | 정답 ②

밑줄 친 (a) ~ (e) 중에서 가리키는 대상이 나머지 넷과 다른 것은?

① (a)   ✔ (b)   ③ (c)   ④ (d)   ⑤ (e)

Why? 왜 정답일까?

(a), (c), (d), (e)는 the farmer, (b)는 a little boy이므로, (a) ~ (e) 중에서 가리키는 대상이 다른 하나는 ② '(b)'이다.

45   세부 내용 파악   정답률 76% | 정답 ④

윗글에 관한 내용으로 적절하지 않은 것은?

① 농부의 시계는 어린 시절의 행복한 기억을 불러일으켰다.
② 한 어린 소년이 농부에게 또 한 번의 기회를 달라고 요청했다.
③ 소년이 한 손에 농부의 시계를 들고 나왔다.
✔ 아이들은 시계를 찾기 위해 헛간을 뛰쳐나왔다.
⑤ 아이들 중 일부는 지쳐서 시계 찾기를 포기했다.

Why? 왜 정답일까?

(D) 'After hearing about the reward, the children hurried inside the barn ~'에서 아이들이 농부가 잃어버린 시계를 찾기 위해 헛간을 나온 것이 아니라 들어갔다고 하므로, 내용과 일치하지 않는 것은 ④ '아이들은 시계를 찾기 위해 헛간을 뛰쳐나왔다.'이다.

Why? 왜 오답일까?

① (A) '~ it brought a lot of happy childhood memories to him.'의 내용과 일치한다.
② (B) 'a little boy came up to him and asked the farmer to give him another chance.'의 내용과 일치한다.
③ (C) 'After a little while the boy came out with the farmer's watch in his hand.'의 내용과 일치한다.
⑤ (D) 'After a long time searching for it, some of the children got tired and gave up.'의 내용과 일치한다.

어휘 Review Test 08   문제편 080쪽

A	B	C	D
01 현혹시키는, 속이는	01 process	01 ①	01 ⓓ
02 매력적인	02 overseas	02 ⓝ	02 ①
03 원칙, 원리	03 consume	03 ①	03 ⓞ
04 자기 방어	04 participant	04 ⓐ	04 ①
05 논의하다	05 surface	05 ⓜ	05 ⓝ
06 탐구하다	06 modify	06 ⓟ	06 ⓙ
07 물리적으로, 신체적으로	07 raise	07 ①	07 ⓢ
08 붙잡다	08 superior	08 ⓖ	08 ①
09 반영	09 household	09 ⓔ	09 ①
10 믿을 만하지 않은	10 construct	10 ⓓ	10 ⓑ
11 우연의 일치, 동시 발생	11 recover	11 ①	11 ④
12 예측	12 inaccurate	12 ⓑ	12 ⓗ
13 유전적으로	13 assessment	13 ⓢ	13 ①
14 독특한	14 sink	14 ⓓ	14 ⓚ
15 보유, 소유	15 historically	15 ⓗ	15 ⓔ
16 양, 수량	16 introduce	16 ⓚ	16 ⓐ
17 결과, 영향	17 precious	17 ①	17 ①
18 양육	18 constraint	18 ⓞ	18 ⓜ
19 감동한	19 comment	19 ⓒ	19 ⓟ
20 발매하다, 출간하다	20 concern	20 ①	20 ⓒ

09회 | 2021학년도 6월 학력평가 고1

• 정답 •
18 ① 19 ③ 20 ① 21 ③ 22 ⑤ 23 ② 24 ① 25 ⑤ 26 ③ 27 ⑤ 28 ④ 29 ⑤ 30 ③ 31 ① 32 ⑤
33 ① 34 ④ 35 ④ 36 ⑤ 37 ② 38 ③ 39 ④ 40 ① 41 ⑤ 42 ④ 43 ② 44 ② 45 ⑤

★ 표기된 문항은 [등급을 가르는 문제]에 해당하는 문항입니다.

---

18 | 브랜드 로고 제작 요청 | 정답률 89% | 정답 ①

다음 글의 목적으로 가장 적절한 것은?

✓① 회사 로고 제작을 의뢰하려고
② 변경된 회사 로고를 홍보하려고
③ 회사 비전에 대한 컨설팅을 요청하려고
④ 회사 창립 10주년 기념품을 주문하려고
⑤ 회사 로고 제작 일정 변경을 공지하려고

Dear Mr. Jones,
Jones씨에게.
I am James Arkady, PR Director of KHJ Corporation.
저는 KHJ Corporation의 홍보부 이사 James Arkady입니다.
We are planning / to redesign our brand identity / and launch a new logo / to celebrate our 10th anniversary.
저희는 계획하고 있습니다. / 저희 회사 브랜드 정체성을 다시 설계하고 / 새로운 로고를 선보이려고 / 회사의 창립 10주년을 기념하기 위해서
We request you to create a logo / that best suits our company's core vision, / 'To inspire humanity.'
저희는 당신께 로고를 제작해 주시기를 요청합니다. / 저희 회사의 핵심 비전을 가장 잘 반영한 / '인류애를 고양하자'
I hope / the new logo will convey our brand message / and capture the values of KHJ.
저는 바랍니다. / 새로운 로고가 저희 회사 브랜드 메시지를 전달하고 / KHJ의 가치를 담아내기를
Please send us your logo design proposal / once you are done with it.
로고 디자인 제안서를 보내 주십시오. / 당신이 완성하는 대로
Thank you.
감사합니다.
Best regards, // James Arkady
James Arkady 드림

Jones씨에게,

저는 KHJ Corporation의 홍보부 이사 James Arkady입니다. 저희 회사의 창립 10주년을 기념하기 위해서 저희 회사 브랜드 정체성을 다시 설계하고 새로운 로고를 선보일 계획입니다. 저희 회사의 핵심 비전 '인류애를 고양하자'를 가장 잘 반영한 로고를 제작해 주시기를 요청합니다. 새로운 로고가 저희 회사 브랜드 메시지를 전달하고 KHJ의 가치를 담아내기를 바랍니다. 로고 디자인 제안서를 완성하는 대로 보내 주십시오. 감사합니다.

James Arkady 드림

Why? 왜 정답일까?

'We request you to create a logo that best suits our company's core vision, ~'에서 회사 핵심 비전을 잘 반영한 로고를 제작해줄 것을 요청한다고 하므로, 글의 목적으로 가장 적절한 것은 ① '회사 로고 제작을 의뢰하려고'이다.

● identity ⓝ 정체성
● celebrate ⓥ 기념하다
● suit ⓥ ~에 적합하다
● humanity ⓝ 인류애
● launch ⓥ 시작하다, 런칭하다
● anniversary ⓝ 기념일
● inspire ⓥ 고무시키다

구문 풀이

4행 We request you to create a logo [that best suits our company's core vision, 'To inspire humanity.']
5형식 동사 목적어 목적격 보어 선행사 ↳주격 관계대명사

---

19 | 카페에서 우연히 유명한 화가를 마주친 Cindy | 정답률 79% | 정답 ③

다음 글에 드러난 Cindy의 심경 변화로 가장 적절한 것은?

① relieved → worried
   안도한   걱정하는
② indifferent → embarrassed
   무관심한   당황한
✓③ excited → surprised
   들뜬   놀란
④ disappointed → satisfied
   실망한   만족한
⑤ jealous → confident
   질투하는   자신 있는

One day, / Cindy happened to sit next to a famous artist in a café, / and she was thrilled to see him in person.
어느 날, / Cindy는 카페에서 우연히 유명한 화가 옆에 앉게 되었고, / 그녀는 그를 직접 만나게 되어 몹시 기뻤다.
He was drawing on a used napkin over coffee.
그는 커피를 마시면서 사용하던 냅킨에 그림을 그리고 있었다.
She was looking on in awe.
그녀는 경외심을 가지고 지켜보았다.
After a few moments, / the man finished his coffee / and was about to throw away the napkin / as he left.
잠시 후에, / 그 남자는 커피를 다 마시고 / 그 냅킨을 버리려고 했다. / 그가 자리를 뜨면서
Cindy stopped him.
Cindy는 그를 멈춰 세웠다.
"Can I have that napkin you drew on?", she asked.
"당신이 그림을 그렸던 냅킨을 가져도 될까요?"라고 그녀가 물었다.

"Sure," he replied.
"물론이죠,"라고 그가 대답했다.
"Twenty thousand dollars."
"2만 달러입니다."
She said, with her eyes wide-open, / "What? It took you like two minutes to draw that."
그녀는 눈을 동그랗게 뜨고 말했다. / "뭐라고요? 그리는 데 2분밖에 안 걸렸잖아요."
"No," he said.
"아니요," 라고 그가 말했다.
"It took me over sixty years to draw this."
"나는 이것을 그리는 데 60년 넘게 걸렸어요."
Being at a loss, / she stood still rooted to the ground.
어쩔 줄 몰라 / 그녀는 여전히 꼼짝 못한 채 서 있었다.

어느 날, Cindy는 카페에서 우연히 유명한 화가 옆에 앉게 되었고, 그를 직접 만나게 되어 몹시 기뻤다. 그는 커피를 마시면서 사용하던 냅킨에 그림을 그리고 있었다. 그녀는 경외심을 가지고 지켜보았다. 잠시 후에, 그 남자는 커피를 다 마시고 자리를 뜨면서 그 냅킨을 버리려고 했다. Cindy는 그를 멈춰 세웠다. "당신이 그림을 그렸던 냅킨을 가져도 될까요?"라고 그녀가 물었다. "물론이죠,"라고 그가 대답했다. "2만 달러입니다." 그녀는 눈을 동그랗게 뜨고 말했다. "뭐라고요? 그리는 데 2분밖에 안 걸렸잖아요." "아니요,"라고 그가 말했다. "나는 이것을 그리는 데 60년 넘게 걸렸어요." 그녀는 어쩔 줄 몰라 여전히 꼼짝 못한 채 서 있었다.

Why? 왜 정답일까?

첫 문장에서 우연히 유명한 화가를 카페에서 만난 Cindy가 몹시 기뻐했다(~ she was thrilled to see him in person.)는 것을 알 수 있고, 마지막 문장에서 그가 냅킨에 그린 그림을 가지려다가 너무 비싼 값을 들은 Cindy가 말문이 막힐 정도로 놀랐다(Being at a loss, she stood still rooted to the ground.)는 것을 알 수 있다. 따라서 Cindy의 심경 변화로 가장 적절한 것은 ③ '들뜬 → 놀란'이다.

● thrilled ⓐ 몹시 기쁜, 황홀해하는
● awe ⓝ 경외심
● rooted ⓐ (~에) 붙박인
● embarrassed ⓐ 당황한
● jealous ⓐ 질투하는
● in person 직접
● at a loss (무슨 말을 해야 할지) 모르는
● indifferent ⓐ 무관심한
● disappointed ⓐ 실망한

구문 풀이

1행 One day, Cindy happened to sit next to a famous artist in a café, and she
      우연히 ~하다
was thrilled to see him in person.
감정 형용사 ↳부사적 용법(~해서)

---

20 | 성공을 위해 변화를 시도하기 | 정답률 90% | 정답 ①

다음 글에서 필자가 주장하는 바로 가장 적절한 것은?

✓① 불편할지라도 성공하기 위해서는 새로운 것을 시도해야 한다.
② 일과 생활의 균형을 맞추는 성공적인 삶을 추구해야 한다.
③ 갈등 해소를 위해 불편함의 원인을 찾아 개선해야 한다.
④ 단계별 목표를 설정하여 익숙한 것부터 도전해야 한다.
⑤ 변화에 적응하기 위해 직관적으로 문제를 해결해야 한다.

Sometimes, / you feel the need to avoid something / that will lead to success / out of discomfort.
가끔씩은 / 당신은 무언가를 피할 필요가 있다고 느낀다. / 성공으로 이끌어 줄 / 불편함을 벗어나
Maybe you are avoiding extra work / because you are tired.
아마도 당신은 추가적인 일을 피하고 있다. / 당신이 피곤하기 때문에
You are actively shutting out success / because you want to avoid being uncomfortable.
당신은 적극적으로 성공을 차단하고 있다. / 당신이 불편한 것을 피하고 싶어서
Therefore, / overcoming your instinct / to avoid uncomfortable things at first / is essential.
따라서 / 당신의 본능을 극복하는 것이 / 처음에 불편한 것을 피하려는 / 필요하다.
Try doing new things outside of your comfort zone.
편안함을 주는 곳을 벗어나서 새로운 일을 시도하라.
Change is always uncomfortable, / but it is key to doing things differently / in order to find that magical formula for success.
변화는 항상 불편하지만, / 일을 색다르게 하는 데 있어서는 핵심이다. / 성공을 위한 마법의 공식을 찾기 위해

가끔씩은 당신은 불편함을 벗어나서 성공으로 이끌어 줄 무언가를 피할 필요가 있다고 느낀다. 아마도 당신은 피곤하기 때문에 추가적인 일을 피하고 있다. 당신은 불편한 것을 피하고 싶어서 적극적으로 성공을 차단하고 있다. 따라서 처음에는 불편한 것을 피하려는 당신의 본능을 극복하는 것이 필요하다. 편안함을 주는 곳을 벗어나서 새로운 일을 시도하라. 변화는 항상 불편하지만, 성공을 위한 마법의 공식을 찾기 위해 일을 색다르게 하는 데 있어서는 핵심이다.

Why? 왜 정답일까?

마지막 두 문장에서 성공하기 위해서는 변화가 핵심이므로 불편하더라도 이를 감수하고 새로운 것을 시도할 필요가 있다(Try doing new things ~. Change is always uncomfortable, but it is key to doing things differently in order to find that magical formula for success.)고 조언하고 있다. 따라서 필자가 주장하는 바로 가장 적절한 것은 ① '불편할지라도 성공하기 위해서는 새로운 것을 시도해야 한다.'이다.

● discomfort ⓝ 불편함
● instinct ⓝ 본능
● comfort zone 안전지대, 일을 적당히 하거나 요령을 피우는 상태
● formula ⓝ 공식, 제조법
● overcome ⓥ 극복하다
● essential ⓐ 필수적인, 본질적인

구문 풀이

4행 Therefore, overcoming your instinct to avoid uncomfortable things at first
            동명사구 주어   형용사적 용법
is essential.
동사(단수)

밑줄 친 want to use a hammer가 다음 글에서 의미하는 바로 가장 적절한 것은? [3점]

① are unwilling to stand out
두드러지기를 꺼리면
② make our effort meaningless
우리의 노력을 무의미하게 만들면
✓③ intend to do something in a certain way
무언가를 특정한 방식으로 하려고 하면
④ hope others have a viewpoint similar to ours
다른 사람들이 우리와 비슷한 관점을 지니기를 바라면
⑤ have a way of thinking that is accepted by others
다른 사람들에게 받아들여지는 사고 방식을 갖고 있다면

We have a tendency / to interpret events selectively.
우리는 경향이 있다. / 사건을 선택적으로 해석하는
If we want things to be "this way" or "that way" / we can most certainly select, stack, or arrange evidence / in a way that supports such a viewpoint.
만약 우리가 일이 '이렇게' 혹은 '저렇게' 되기를 원한다면, / 우리는 틀림없이 증거를 선택하거나 쌓거나 배열할 수 있다. / 그러한 관점을 뒷받침하는 방식으로
Selective perception is based / on what seems to us to stand out.
선택적인 지각은 기반을 둔다. / 우리에게 두드러져 보이는 것에
However, / what seems to us to be standing out / may very well be related / to our goals, interests, expectations, past experiences, or current demands of the situation / — "with a hammer in hand, / everything looks like a nail."
그러나 / 우리에게 두드러져 보이는 것은 / 매우 관련 있을지도 모른다 / 우리의 목표, 관심사, 기대, 과거의 경험 또는 상황에 대한 현재의 요구와 / "망치를 손에 들고 있으면, / 모든 것은 못처럼 보인다."
This quote highlights the phenomenon of selective perception.
이 인용문은 선택적 지각의 현상을 강조한다.
If we want to use a hammer, / then the world around us / may begin to look / as though it is full of nails!
만약 우리가 망치를 사용하기를 원하면, / 우리 주변의 세상은 / 보이기 시작할지도 모른다! / 못으로 가득 찬 것처럼

우리는 사건을 선택적으로 해석하는 경향이 있다. 만약 우리가 일이 '이렇게' 혹은 '저렇게' 되기를 원한다면, 우리는 틀림없이 그러한 관점을 뒷받침하는 방식으로 증거를 선택하거나 쌓거나 배열할 수 있다. 선택적인 지각은 우리에게 두드러져 보이는 것에 기반을 둔다. 그러나 우리에게 두드러져 보이는 것은 우리의 목표, 관심사, 기대, 과거의 경험 또는 상황에 대한 현재의 요구와 매우 관련 있을지도 모른다 — "망치를 손에 들고 있으면, 모든 것은 못처럼 보인다." 이 인용문은 선택적 지각의 현상을 강조한다. 만약 우리가 망치를 사용하기를 원하면, 우리 주변의 세상은 못으로 가득 찬 것처럼 보이기 시작할지도 모른다!

Why? 왜 정답일까?

우리의 지각은 우리 눈에 두드러져 보이는 것에 초점이 맞추어져 있다는 내용 뒤로, 사실 이 눈에 띄는 것들은 우리의 목표나 기대 등과 관련되어 있다는 내용이 제시된다(However, what seems to us to be standing out may very well be related to our goals, ~). 특히 망치를 손에 들고 있으면 모두 못처럼 보인다는 직접 인용구의 내용으로 미루어볼 때, 밑줄이 포함된 문장은 우리가 특정한 목표나 기대를 갖고 상황을 바라볼 때 그 목표나 기대를 적용하기 유리한 대로 상황을 해석할 가능성이 크다는 의미여야 한다. 따라서 밑줄 친 부분이 의미하는 바로 가장 적절한 것은 ③ '무언가를 특정한 방식으로 하려고 하면'이다.

- interpret ⓥ 해석하다
- stack ⓥ 쌓다, 포개다
- quote ⓝ 인용구
- phenomenon ⓝ 현상
- selectively ⓐⓓ 선택적으로
- stand out 두드러지다
- highlight ⓥ 강조하다
- unwilling ⓐ (~하기를) 꺼리는, 마지못해 하는

구문 풀이

9행   If we want to use a hammer, then the world around us may begin to look
접속사(만일 ~라면)   주어   동사
as though it is full of nails!
접속사(마치 ~처럼)

다음 글의 요지로 가장 적절한 것은?

① 학생에게 평가 결과를 공개하는 것은 학습 동기를 떨어뜨린다.
② 학생에게 추가 과제를 부여하는 것은 학업 부담을 가중시킨다.
③ 지속적인 보상은 학업 성취도에 장기적으로 부정적인 영향을 준다.
④ 학생의 자기주도적 학습 능력은 정서적으로 안정된 학습 환경에서 향상된다.
✓⑤ 학생의 과제가 일정 수준에 도달하도록 개선 기회를 주면 동기 부여에 도움이 된다.

Rather than attempting to punish students / with a low grade or mark / in the hope / it will encourage them to give greater effort in the future, / teachers can better motivate students / by considering their work as incomplete / and then requiring additional effort.
학생에게 벌을 주는 대신, / 낮은 성적이나 점수로 / 희망하며 / 그것이 학생으로 하여금 미래에 더 노력을 기울이도록 독려할 것이라 / 교사는 학생들에게 동기 부여를 더 잘할 수 있다. / 그들의 과제를 미완성으로 보고 / 추가적인 노력을 요구함으로써
Teachers at Beachwood Middle School in Beachwood, Ohio, / record students' grades as A, B, C, or I (Incomplete).
오하이오 주 Beachwood의 Beachwood 중학교 교사는 / 학생의 성적을 A, B, C 또는 I(미완성)로 기록한다.
Students who receive an I grade / are required to do additional work / in order to bring their performance / up to an acceptable level.
I 성적을 받은 학생은 / 추가적인 과제를 하도록 요구받는다. / 자신의 과제 수행을 끌어올리기 위해서 / 수용 가능한 수준까지
This policy is based on the belief / that students perform at a failure level / or submit failing work / in large part because teachers accept it.
이런 방침은 믿음에 근거한다. / 학생이 낙제 수준으로 수행하거나 / 낙제 과제를 제출하는 것이 / 대체로 교사가 그것을 받아들이기 때문이라는
The Beachwood teachers reason / that if they no longer accept substandard work, / students will not submit it.
Beachwood의 교사는 생각한다. / 만약 그들이 더 이상 기준 이하의 과제를 받아들이지 않는다면, / 학생이 그것을 제출하지 않을 것이라고
And with appropriate support, / they believe / students will continue to work / until their performance is satisfactory.
그리고 적절한 도움을 받아서 / 그들은 믿는다. / 학생들이 계속 노력할 것이라고 / 자신의 과제 수행이 만족스러울 때까지

낮은 성적이나 점수가 학생으로 하여금 미래에 더 노력을 기울이도록 독려할 것이라 희망하며 학생에게 그것으로 벌을 주는 대신, 교사는 그들의 과제를 미완성으로 보고 추가적인 노력을 요구함으로써 학생들에게 동기 부여를 더 잘할 수 있다. 오하이오 주 Beachwood의 Beachwood 중학교 교사는 학생의 성적을 A, B, C 또는 I(미완성)로 기록한다. I 성적을 받은 학생은 자신의 과제 수행을 수용 가능한 수준까지 끌어올리기 위해서 추가적인 과제를 하도록 요구받는다. 이런 방침은 학생이 낙제 수준으로 수행하거나 낙제 과제를 제출하는 것이 대체로 교사가 그것을 받아들이기 때문이라는 믿음에 근거한다. Beachwood의 교사는 만약 그들이 더 이상 기준 이하의 과제를 받아들이지 않는다면, 학생이 그것을 제출하지 않을 것이라고 생각한다. 그리고 그들은 학생들이 적절한 도움을 받아서 자신의 과제 수행이 만족스러울 때까지 계속 노력할 것이라고 믿는다.

Why? 왜 정답일까?

첫 문장에서 학생들의 과제가 일정 수준 미만일 때 그저 점수를 낮게 주기보다는 '미완성된' 과제로 보고 더 노력을 들이도록 요구하는 것이 동기 부여에 좋다(~ teachers can better motivate students by considering their work as incomplete and then requiring additional effort.)고 하므로, 글의 요지로 가장 적절한 것은 ⑤ '학생의 과제가 일정 수준에 도달하도록 개선 기회를 주면 동기 부여에 도움이 된다.'이다.

- punish ⓥ 처벌하다
- additional ⓐ 추가적인
- substandard ⓐ 수준 이하의, 열악한
- satisfactory ⓐ 만족스러운
- incomplete ⓐ 미완성된
- acceptable ⓐ 수용 가능한
- appropriate ⓐ 적절한

구문 풀이

1행   Rather than attempting to punish students with a low grade or mark in
~라는 희망으로   'encourage + 목적어 + to부정사 : ~에 …하도록 독려하다'
the hope (that) it will encourage them to give greater effort in the future, teachers   주어
can better motivate students by considering their work as incomplete and then
동사구   전치사   동명사1
requiring additional effort.
동명사2

다음 글의 주제로 가장 적절한 것은?

① importance of defensive reactions in a tough situation – 힘든 상황에서 방어적인 반응의 중요성
✓② curiosity as the hidden force of positive reframes – 긍정적인 재구성의 숨은 동력인 호기심
③ difficulties of coping with stress at work – 직장에서의 스트레스에 대처하는 것의 어려움
④ potential threats caused by curiosity – 호기심으로 인한 잠재적 위험
⑤ factors that reduce human curiosity – 인간의 호기심을 떨어뜨리는 요인

Curiosity makes us / much more likely to view a tough problem / as an interesting challenge to take on.
호기심은 우리를 만든다. / 어려운 문제를 더 여기게 / 맡아야 할 흥미로운 도전으로
A stressful meeting with our boss / becomes an opportunity to learn.
상사와의 스트레스를 받는 회의는 / 배울 수 있는 기회가 된다.
A nervous first date / becomes an exciting night out with a new person.
긴장이 되는 첫 데이트는 / 새로운 사람과의 멋진 밤이 된다.
A colander becomes a hat.
주방용 체는 모자가 된다.
In general, / curiosity motivates us / to view stressful situations as challenges / rather than threats, / to talk about difficulties more openly, / and to try new approaches to solving problems.
일반적으로, / 호기심은 우리에게 동기를 부여해 준다. / 스트레스를 받는 상황을 도전으로 여기게 하고, / 위험보다는 / 어려움을 더 터놓고 말하게 하고, / 문제 해결에 있어 새로운 접근을 시도하도록
In fact, / curiosity is associated / with a less defensive reaction to stress / and, as a result, less aggression / when we respond to irritation.
실제로 / 호기심은 관련이 있다. / 스트레스에 대한 방어적인 반응이 줄어드는 것과 / 그리고 그 결과 공격성이 줄어드는 것과 / 우리가 짜증에 반응할 때

호기심은 우리가 어려운 문제를 맡아야 할 흥미로운 도전으로 더 여기게 한다. 상사와의 스트레스를 받는 회의는 배울 수 있는 기회가 된다. 긴장이 되는 첫 데이트는 새로운 사람과의 멋진 밤이 된다. 주방용 체는 모자가 된다. 일반적으로, 호기심은 우리가 스트레스를 받는 상황을 위험보다는 도전으로 여기게 하고, 어려움을 더 터놓고 말하게 하고, 문제 해결에 있어 새로운 접근을 시도하도록 동기를 부여해 준다. 실제로 호기심은 스트레스에 대한 방어적인 반응이 줄어들고, 그 결과 짜증에 반응할 때 공격성이 줄어드는 것과 관련이 있다.

Why? 왜 정답일까?

'Curiosity makes us much more likely to view a tough problem as an interesting challenge to take on.'에서 호기심은 우리가 어려운 문제를 흥미로운 도전처럼 여길 수 있게 해준다고 언급한 데 이어, 'In general, curiosity motivates us to view stressful situations as challenges ~'에서도 같은 내용을 제시한다. 따라서 글의 주제로 가장 적절한 것은 ② '긍정적인 재구성의 숨은 동력인 호기심'이다.

- curiosity ⓝ 호기심
- threat ⓝ 위협
- aggression ⓝ 공격
- cope with ~에 대처하다
- take on (책임이나 일을) 맡다, 지다
- defensive ⓐ 방어적인
- irritation ⓝ 짜증

구문 풀이

1행   Curiosity makes us much more likely to view a tough problem as an
5형식 동사↑   목적어   목적격 보어   'view + A + as + B : A를 B로 여기다'
interesting challenge to take on.

다음 글의 제목으로 가장 적절한 것은?

✓① Elevators Bring Buildings Closer to the Sky
엘리베이터는 빌딩이 하늘에 더 가까워지게 만든다

② The Higher You Climb, the Better the View
더 높이 오를수록 경치가 더 좋다
③ How to Construct an Elevator Cheap and Fast
엘리베이터를 싸고 빠르게 짓는 방법
④ The Function of the Ancient and the Modern City
고대 및 현대 도시의 기능
⑤ The Evolution of Architecture: Solutions for Overpopulation
건축의 진화 : 인구 과잉의 해결책

When people think about the development of cities, / rarely do they consider / the critical role of vertical transportation.
사람들이 도시 발전에 대해 생각할 때, / 그들은 거의 고려하지 않는다. / 수직 운송 수단의 중요한 역할을
In fact, each day, / more than 7 billion elevator journeys / are taken in tall buildings all over the world.
실제로 매일 / 70억 회 이상의 엘리베이터 이동이 / 전 세계 높은 빌딩에서 이루어진다.
Efficient vertical transportation / can expand our ability / to build taller and taller skyscrapers.
효율적인 수직 운송 수단은 / 우리의 능력을 확장시킬 수 있다. / 점점 더 높은 고층 건물을 만들 수 있는
Antony Wood, / a Professor of Architecture at the Illinois Institute of Technology, / explains / that advances in elevators over the past 20 years / are probably the greatest advances / we have seen in tall buildings.
Antony Wood는 / Illinois 공과대학의 건축학과 교수인 / 설명한다. / 지난 20년 간 엘리베이터의 발전은 / 아마도 가장 큰 발전이라고 / 우리가 높은 건물에서 봐 왔던
For example, / elevators in the Jeddah Tower in Jeddah, Saudi Arabia, / under construction, / will reach a height record of 660m.
예를 들어, / 사우디아라비아 Jeddah의 Jeddah Tower에 있는 엘리베이터는 / 건설 중인 / 660미터라는 기록적인 높이에 이를 것이다.

사람들은 도시 발전에 대해 생각할 때, 수직 운송 수단의 중요한 역할을 거의 고려하지 않는다. 실제로 매일 70억 회 이상의 엘리베이터 이동이 전 세계 높은 빌딩에서 이루어진다. 효율적인 수직 운송 수단은 점점 더 높은 고층 건물을 만들 수 있는 우리의 능력을 확장시킬 수 있다. Illinois 공과대학의 건축학과 교수인 Antony Wood는 지난 20년 간 엘리베이터의 발전은 아마도 우리가 높은 건물에서 봐 왔던 가장 큰 발전이라고 설명한다. 예를 들어, 건설 중인 사우디아라비아 Jeddah의 Jeddah Tower에 있는 엘리베이터는 660미터라는 기록적인 높이에 이를 것이다.

Why? 왜 정답일까?

'Efficient vertical transportation can expand our ability to build taller and taller skyscrapers.'에서 수직 운송 수단, 즉 엘리베이터가 더 높은 고층 건물을 짓도록 도와준다고 언급하는 것으로 보아, 글의 제목으로 가장 적절한 것은 ① '엘리베이터는 빌딩이 하늘에 더 가까워지게 만든다'이다.

- critical ⓐ 중요한
- transportation ⓝ 운송, 수송
- skyscraper ⓝ 고층 건물
- overpopulation ⓝ 인구 과잉
- vertical ⓐ 수직의
- expand ⓥ 확장하다
- under construction 건설 중인

구문 풀이

1행 When people think about the development of cities, rarely do they consider the critical role of vertical transportation.
「부정어구 + 조동사 + 주어 + 동사원형 : 도치 구문」

---

25 국가별 GDP 대비 의료 지출 정답률 81% | 정답 ⑤

다음 도표의 내용과 일치하지 않는 것은?

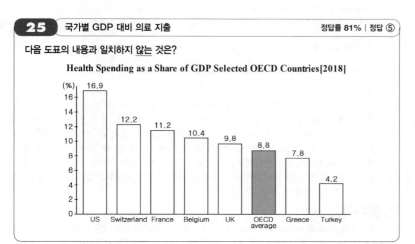

Health Spending as a Share of GDP Selected OECD Countries[2018]

The above graph shows health spending / as a share of GDP / for selected OECD countries / in 2018.
위 그래프는 의료 지출을 보여준다. / GDP 점유율로 / 선택된 OECD 국가들의 / 2018년에
① On average, / OECD countries were estimated / to have spent 8.8 percent of their GDP on health care.
평균적으로, / OECD 국가들은 추정되었다. / GDP의 8.8%를 의료에 지출한 것으로
② Among the given countries above, / the US had the highest share, / with 16.9 percent, / followed by Switzerland at 12.2 percent.
위 국가들 중 / 미국은 가장 높은 점유율을 보였고, / 16.9%로 / 이어 스위스는 12.2%를 보였다.
③ France spent more than 11 percent of its GDP, / while Turkey spent less than 5 percent of its GDP on health care.
프랑스는 GDP의 11% 이상을 지출했던 반면, / 터키는 GDP의 5% 이하를 의료에 지출했다.
④ Belgium's health spending as a share of GDP / sat between that of France and the UK.
GDP 점유율로서 벨기에의 의료 지출은 / 프랑스와 영국 사이였다.
☑ There was a 3 percentage point difference / in the share of GDP / spent on health care / between the UK and Greece.
3%p의 차이가 있었다. / GDP의 점유율에 있어 / 의료에 지출된 / 영국과 그리스 사이에

위 그래프는 2018년 선택된 OECD 국가들의 의료 지출을 GDP 점유율로 보여준다. ① 평균적으로, OECD 국가들은 GDP의 8.8%를 의료에 지출한 것으로 추정되었다. ② 위 국가들 중 미국은 GDP의 16.9%로 가장 높은 점유율을 보였고, 이어 스위스는 12.2%를 보였다. ③ 프랑스는 GDP의 11% 이상을 지출했던 반면, 터키는 GDP의 5% 이하를 의료에 지출했다. ④ GDP 점유율로서 벨기에의 의료 지출은 프랑스와 영국 사이였다. ⑤ 영국과 그리스 사이에는 의료에 지출된 GDP의 점유율에 있어 3%p의 차이가 있었다.

Why? 왜 정답일까?

도표에 따르면 GDP를 기준으로 영국의 의료 지출은 9.8%, 그리스의 의료 지출은 7.8%였다. 즉 두 국가 간 비율의 차이는 2%p이므로, 도표와 일치하지 않는 것은 ⑤이다.

- on average 평균적으로
- estimate ⓥ 추정하다, 추산하다

---

26 Lithops의 특징 정답률 63% | 정답 ③

Lithops에 관한 다음 글의 내용과 일치하지 않는 것은?

① 살아있는 돌로 불리는 식물이다.
② 원산지는 남아프리카 사막 지역이다.
☑ 토양의 표면 위로 대개 1인치 이상 자란다.
④ 줄기가 없으며 땅속에 대부분 묻혀 있다.
⑤ 겉모양은 수분 보존 효과를 갖고 있다.

『Lithops are plants / that are often called 'living stones' / on account of their unique rock-like appearance.』 ①의근거 일치
Lithops는 식물이다. / 종종 '살아있는 돌'로 불리는 / 독특한 바위 같은 겉모양 때문에
『They are native to the deserts of South Africa / but commonly sold in garden centers and nurseries.』 ②의근거 일치
이것은 원산지가 남아프리카 사막이지만, / 식물원과 종묘원에서 흔히 팔린다.
Lithops grow well / in compacted, sandy soil with little water / and extreme hot temperatures.
Lithops는 잘 자란다. / 수분이 거의 없는 빡빡한 모래 토양과 / 극히 높은 온도에서
『Lithops are small plants, / rarely getting more than an inch above the soil surface / and usually with only two leaves.』 ③의근거 불일치
Lithops는 작은 식물로, / 토양의 표면 위로 1인치 이상 거의 자라지 않고 / 보통 단 두 개의 잎을 가지고 있다.
The thick leaves resemble the cleft in an animal's foot / or just a pair of grayish brown stones gathered together.
두꺼운 잎은 동물 발의 갈라진 틈과 닮았다 / 혹은 함께 모여있는 한 쌍의 회갈색 빛을 띠는 돌과
『The plants have no true stem / and much of the plant is underground.』 ④의근거 일치
이 식물은 실제 줄기는 없고 / 식물의 대부분이 땅속에 묻혀 있다.
『Their appearance has the effect of conserving moisture.』 ⑤의근거 일치
겉모양은 수분을 보존하는 효과를 가지고 있다.

Lithops는 독특한 바위 같은 겉모양 때문에 종종 '살아있는 돌'로 불리는 식물이다. 이것은 원산지가 남아프리카 사막이지만, 식물원과 종묘원에서 흔히 팔린다. Lithops는 수분이 거의 없는 빡빡한 모래 토양과 극히 높은 온도에서 잘 자란다. Lithops는 작은 식물로, 토양의 표면 위로 1인치 이상 거의 자라지 않고 보통 단 두 개의 잎을 가지고 있다. 두꺼운 잎은 동물 발의 갈라진 틈이나 함께 모여있는 한 쌍의 회갈색 빛을 띠는 돌과 닮았다. 이 식물은 실제 줄기는 없고 식물의 대부분이 땅속에 묻혀 있다. 겉모양은 수분을 보존하는 효과를 가지고 있다.

Why? 왜 정답일까?

'Lithops are small plants, rarely getting more than an inch above the soil surface ~'에서 Lithops는 토양 표면 위로 1인치 이상 자라는 일이 거의 없다고 하므로, 내용과 일치하지 않는 것은 ③ '토양의 표면 위로 대개 1인치 이상 자란다.'이다.

Why? 왜 오답일까?

① 'Lithops are plants that are often called 'living stones' ~'의 내용과 일치한다.
② 'They are native to the deserts of South Africa ~'의 내용과 일치한다.
④ 'The plants have no true stem and much of the plant is underground.'의 내용과 일치한다.
⑤ 'Their appearance has the effect of conserving moisture.'의 내용과 일치한다.

- on account of ~ 때문에
- native to ~이 원산지인
- compacted ⓐ 빡빡한, 탄탄한
- gather ⓥ 모으다, 모이다
- conserve ⓥ 보존하다
- appearance ⓝ 겉모습
- desert ⓝ 사막
- extreme ⓐ 극도의
- stem ⓝ 줄기

구문 풀이

1행 Lithops are plants [that are often called 'living stones' on account of their unique rock-like appearance].
선행사 / 주격 관·대 / 5형식 수동태 / 보어

---

27 친환경 글짓기 대회 정답률 92% | 정답 ⑤

"Go Green" Writing Contest에 관한 다음 안내문의 내용과 일치하지 않는 것은?

① 대회 주제는 환경 보호이다.
② 참가자는 한 부문에만 참가해야 한다.
③ 마감 기한은 7월 5일이다.
④ 작품은 이메일로 제출해야 한다.
☑ 수상자는 개별적으로 연락받는다.

"Go Green" Writing Contest
"Go Green" Writing Contest
Share your talents & conserve the environment
여러분의 재능을 나누세요 & 환경을 보존하세요
Main Topic: 『Save the Environment』 ①의근거 일치
주제: 환경을 보호하자
Writing Categories
글쓰기 부문
Slogan // Poem // Essay
표어 // 시 // 에세이
Requirements:
요구 사항:
Participants: High school students
참가자: 고등학생
『Participate in one of the above categories』 ②의근거 일치

위 글쓰기 부문 중 하나에 참가하세요.
(only one entry per participant)
(참가자 1인당 한 작품만)
「Deadline: July 5th, 2021」③의 근거 일치
마감 기한: 2021년 7월 5일
「Email your work to apply@gogreen.com.」④의 근거 일치
apply@gogreen.com으로 작품을 이메일로 보내세요.
Prize for Each Category
부문별 상금
1st place: $80
1등: 80달러
2nd place: $60
2등: 60달러
3rd place: $40
3등: 40달러
「The winners will be announced / only on the website on July 15th, 2021」⑤의 근거 불일치
수상자는 공지될 예정입니다. / 2021년 7월 15일에 웹 사이트에서만
No personal contact will be made.
개별 연락은 없을 것입니다.
For more information, visit www.gogreen.com.
추가 정보를 원한다면, www.gogreen.com을 방문하시오.

"Go Green" Writing Contest
여러분의 재능을 나누세요 & 환경을 보존하세요

□ 주제 : 환경을 보호하자
□ 글쓰기 부문
 • 표어 • 시 • 에세이
□ 요구 사항:
 • 참가자 : 고등학생
 • 위 글쓰기 부문 중 하나에 참가하세요.
  (참가자 1인당 한 작품만)
□ 마감 기한 : 2021년 7월 5일
 • apply@gogreen.com으로 작품을 이메일로 보내세요.
□ 부문별 상금
 • 1등 : 80달러 • 2등 : 60달러 • 3등 : 40달러
□ 수상자는 2021년 7월 15일에 웹 사이트에서만 공지될 예정입니다. 개별 연락은 없습니다.
□ 추가 정보를 원한다면, www.gogreen.com을 방문하시오.

Why? 왜 정답일까?
'The winners will be announced only on the website on July 15th, 2021. No personal contact will be made.'에서 수상자는 웹 사이트에만 공지되며, 개별 연락은 없을 예정이라고 하였다. 따라서 안내문의 내용과 일치하지 않는 것은 ⑤ '수상자는 개별적으로 연락받는다.'이다.

Why? 왜 오답일까?
① 'Main Topic : Save the Environment'의 내용과 일치한다.
② 'Participate in one of the above categories'의 내용과 일치한다.
③ 'Deadline : July 5th, 2021'의 내용과 일치한다.
④ 'Email your work to apply@gogreen.com.'의 내용과 일치한다.

● go green 친환경적이 되다 ● conserve ⓥ 보존하다
● entry ⓝ 출품작

---

28 학교 축제 관련 온라인 회의   정답률 83% | 정답 ④

Virtual Idea Exchange에 관한 다음 안내문의 내용과 일치하는 것은?
① 동아리 회원이라면 누구나 참여 가능하다.
② 티켓 판매는 논의 대상에서 제외된다.
③ 회의는 3시간 동안 열린다.
✓ 접속 링크를 문자로 받는다.
⑤ 채팅방 입장 시 동아리명으로 참여해야 한다.

Virtual Idea Exchange
Virtual Idea Exchange
Connect in real time / and have discussions about the upcoming school festival.
실시간으로 접속하여 / 다가오는 학교 축제에 관해 토론하세요.
Goal
목표
Plan the school festival and share ideas for it.
학교 축제를 계획하고 아이디어를 공유하세요.
「Participants: Club leaders only」①의 근거 불일치
참가자: 동아리장만
What to Discuss
토론 내용
Themes // 「Ticket sales」 // Budget
주제 // 티켓 판매 // 예산 ②의 근거 불일치
「Date & Time: 5 to 7 p.m. on Friday, June 25th, 2021」③의 근거 불일치
날짜 & 시간: 2021년 6월 25일 금요일 오후 5시 ~ 7시
Notes
참고사항
「Get the access link by text message / 10 minutes before the meeting / and click it.」
문자 메시지로 전송되는 접속 링크를 받아서 / 회의 10분 전에 / 클릭하세요. ④의 근거 일치
「Type your real name / when you enter the chatroom.」⑤의 근거 불일치
실명을 입력하세요. / 당신이 대화방에 들어올 때

Virtual Idea Exchange
실시간으로 접속하여 다가오는 학교 축제에 관해 토론하세요.

□ 목표
 • 학교 축제를 계획하고 아이디어를 공유하세요.
□ 참가자 : 동아리장만
□ 토론 내용
 • 주제 • 티켓 판매 • 예산
□ 날짜 & 시간 : 2021년 6월 25일 금요일 오후 5시 ~ 7시
□ 참고사항
 • 회의 10분 전에 문자 메시지로 전송되는 접속 링크를 받아서 클릭하세요.
 • 대화방에 들어올 때 실명을 입력하세요.

Why? 왜 정답일까?
'Get the access link by text message 10 minutes before the meeting and click it.'에서 회의 10분 전에 회의 접속 링크가 문자 메시지로 전송된다고 하므로, 안내문의 내용과 일치하는 것은 ④ '접속 링크를 문자로 받는다.'이다.

Why? 왜 오답일까?
① 'Participants: Club leaders only'에서 동아리장들만 참여 가능하다고 하였다.
② 'What to Discuss / Ticket sales'에서 티켓 판매가 논의 대상에 포함된다고 하였다.
③ 'Date & Time: 5 to 7 p.m. on Friday, June 25th, 2021'에서 회의는 오후 5시부터 7시까지 2시간 동안 열린다고 하였다.
⑤ 'Type your real name when you enter the chatroom.'에서 채팅방에 들어올 때 실명을 입력해야 한다고 하였다.

● virtual ⓐ (컴퓨터를 이용한) 가상의 ● real time 실시간
● upcoming ⓐ 다가오는 ● budget ⓝ 예산

---

29 진짜 미소와 가짜 미소의 차이   정답률 61% | 정답 ⑤

다음 글의 밑줄 친 부분 중, 어법상 틀린 것은? [3점]

There have been occasions / ① in which you have observed a smile / and you could sense it was not genuine.
경우가 있었다. / 당신이 미소를 관찰했는데 / 당신이 그것이 진짜가 아니라고 느낄 수 있는
The most obvious way / of identifying a genuine smile from an insincere ② one / is / that a fake smile / primarily only affects the lower half of the face, / mainly with the mouth alone.
가장 명확한 방법은 / 진짜 미소와 진실하지 못한 미소를 알아보는 / ~이다. / 가짜 미소는 / 주로 얼굴의 아랫부분에만 영향을 미친다는 것 / 주로 입에만
The eyes don't really get involved.
눈은 별로 관련이 없다.
Take the opportunity to look in the mirror / and manufacture a smile / ③ using the lower half your face only.
거울을 볼 기회를 잡아서 / 미소를 지어보라. / 당신의 얼굴 아랫부분만을 사용하여
When you do this, / judge ④ how happy your face really looks / — is it genuine?
당신이 이렇게 할 때, / 당신의 얼굴이 실제로 얼마나 행복해 보이는지를 판단해 보라. / 그것은 진짜인가?
A genuine smile will impact / on the muscles and wrinkles around the eyes / and less noticeably, / the skin between the eyebrow and upper eyelid / ✓ is lowered slightly with true enjoyment.
진짜 미소는 영향을 주며, / 눈가 근육과 주름에 / 티가 좀 덜 나게 / 눈썹과 윗눈꺼풀 사이의 피부는 / 진정한 즐거움으로 살짝 내려온다.
The genuine smile can impact on the entire face.
진짜 미소는 얼굴 전체에 영향을 줄 수 있다.

당신이 미소를 관찰했는데 그것이 진짜가 아니라고 느낄 수 있는 경우가 있었다. 진짜 미소와 진실하지 못한 미소를 알아보는 가장 명확한 방법은 가짜 미소는 주로 얼굴의 아랫부분, 주로 입에만 영향을 미친다는 것이다. 눈은 별로 관련이 없다. 거울을 볼 기회를 잡아서 당신의 얼굴 아랫부분만을 사용하여 미소를 지어보라. 당신이 이렇게 할 때, 당신의 얼굴이 실제로 얼마나 행복해 보이는지를 판단해 보라. 그것은 진짜인가? 진짜 미소는 눈가 근육과 주름에 영향을 주며, 티가 좀 덜 나게 눈썹과 윗눈꺼풀 사이의 피부는 진정한 즐거움으로 살짝 내려온다. 진짜 미소는 얼굴 전체에 영향을 줄 수 있다.

Why? 왜 정답일까?
and 앞에 'A genuine smile will impact ~'라는 '주어+동사' 한 쌍이 나온 뒤 and 뒤로 새로운 '주어+동사'가 이어지고 있다. 이때 단수 명사 주어인 the skin에 맞추어 동사인 are를 is로 고쳐야 한다. 따라서 어법상 틀린 것은 ⑤이다.

Why? 왜 오답일까?
① 뒤에 and로 연결된 두 문장 'you have observed a smile and you could sense ~'가 모두 완전한 3형식 구조이다. 따라서 '전치사+관계대명사' 형태의 in which가 바르게 쓰였다.
② 앞에 나온 smile을 지칭하기 위해 단수 부정대명사 one이 바르게 쓰였다.
③ 분사 뒤에 목적어 the lower half your face only가 나오는 것으로 보아 현재분사 using이 바르게 쓰였다.
④ 뒤에 '형용사+주어+동사'가 이어지는 것으로 보아 의문부사 how가 바르게 쓰였다. 의문부사 how가 '얼마나'라는 뜻이면 주로 'how+형/부+주어+동사' 어순으로 쓰인다.

● occasion ⓝ 경우 ● genuine ⓐ 진짜인
● obvious ⓐ 명백한, 분명한 ● identify ⓥ 알아보다, 식별하다
● insincere ⓐ 진실하지 않은 ● primarily ⓐⓓ 주로
● manufacture ⓥ 만들다 ● impact ⓥ 영향을 미치다
● noticeably ⓐⓓ 눈에 띄게, 두드러지게 ● slightly ⓐⓓ 살짝, 약간
● entire ⓐ 전체의

구문 풀이

2행 The most obvious way of identifying a genuine smile from an insincere
                                                              주어
one is that a fake smile primarily only affects the lower half of the face, mainly
동사(단수)   주어   동사   목적어
with the mouth alone.

30 자연계의 복잡한 형태
정답률 34% | 정답 ③

다음 글의 밑줄 친 부분 중, 문맥상 낱말의 쓰임이 적절하지 않은 것은? [3점]

Detailed study over the past two or three decades / is showing / that the complex forms of natural systems / are essential to their functioning.
지난 20년 혹은 30년 동안의 상세한 연구는 / 보여주고 있다. / 자연계의 복잡한 형태가 / 그 기능에 필수적이라는 것을

The attempt / to ① straighten rivers / and give them regular cross-sections / is perhaps the most disastrous example / of this form-and-function relationship.
시도는 / 강을 직선화하고 / 규칙적인 횡단면으로 만들고자 하는 / 아마도 가장 피해 막심한 사례가 될 수 있다. / 이러한 형태-기능 관계의

The natural river has a very ② irregular form: / it curves a lot, / spills across floodplains, / and leaks into wetlands, / giving it an ever-changing and incredibly complex shoreline.
자연 발생적인 강은 매우 불규칙한 형태를 가지고 있다. / 그것은 많이 굽이치고, / 범람원을 가로질러 넘쳐 흐르고, / 습지로 스며 들어가서 / 끊임없이 바뀌고 엄청나게 복잡한 강가를 만든다.

This allows the river / to ✓③accommodate variations in water level and speed.
이것은 강이 ~하게 한다. / 강의 수위와 속도 변화를 조절할 수 있게

Pushing the river into tidy geometry / ④ destroys functional capacity / and results in disasters / like the Mississippi floods of 1927 and 1993 / and, more recently, the unnatural disaster of Hurricane Katrina.
강을 질서정연한 기하학적 형태에 맞춰 넣는 것은 / 기능적 수용 능력을 파괴하고 / 재난을 초래한다. / 1927년과 1993년의 미시시피 강의 홍수와 같은 / 그리고 더 최근에 허리케인 Katrina라는 비정상적인 재난을

A \$50 billion plan to "let the river loose" in Louisiana / recognizes / that the ⑤ controlled Mississippi / is washing away / twenty-four square miles of that state annually.
루이지애나에서 "강이 자유롭게 흐르도록 두라(let the river loose)"라는 500억 달러 계획은 / 인정한 것이다. / 통제된 미시시피 강이 / 유실시키고 있다는 것을 / 매년 그 주의 24제곱마일을

지난 20년 혹은 30년 동안의 상세한 연구는 자연계의 복잡한 형태가 그 기능에 필수적이라는 것을 보여주고 있다. 강을 ① 직선화하고 규칙적인 횡단면으로 만들고자 하는 시도는 아마도 이러한 형태 — 기능 관계의 가장 피해 막심한 사례가 될 수 있다. 자연 발생적인 강은 매우 ② 불규칙한 형태를 가지고 있다. 그것은 많이 굽이치고, 범람원을 가로질러 넘쳐 흐르고, 습지로 스며 들어가서 끊임없이 바뀌고 엄청나게 복잡한 강가를 만든다. 이것은 강의 수위와 속도 변화를 ③ 막을(→ 조절할) 수 있게 한다. 강을 질서정연한 기하학적 형태에 맞춰 넣는 것은 기능적 수용 능력을 ④ 파괴하고 1927년과 1993년의 미시시피 강의 홍수와 더 최근인 허리케인 Katrina와 같은 비정상적인 재난을 초래한다. 루이지애나에서 "강이 자유롭게 흐르도록 두라(let the river loose)"라는 500억 달러 계획은 ⑤ 통제된 미시시피 강이 매년 그 주의 24제곱마일을 유실시키고 있다는 것을 인정한 것이다.

Why? 왜 정답일까?

첫 문장에서 자연계의 복잡한 형태는 자연계가 기능하는 데 필수적이라는 주제를 제시하고 있다. 'The natural river ~'에서 자연 발생적인 강이 예시로 나오는데, 이러한 강이 매우 복잡한 형태를 띠고 있지만 바로 그 형태로 인해 물의 수위 변화와 속도를 조절할 수 있다는 내용이 이어져야 하므로 ③의 prevent를 accommodate로 고쳐야 한다. 따라서 문맥상 낱말의 쓰임이 적절하지 않은 것은 ③이다.

- essential ⓐ 필수적인
- straighten ⓥ 바로 펴다, 똑바르게 하다
- irregular ⓐ 불규칙한
- spill ⓥ 흐르다, 쏟아지다
- incredibly [ad] 엄청나게, 믿을 수 없게
- attempt ⓝ 노력, 시도
- disastrous ⓐ 처참한, 피해가 막심한
- curve ⓥ 굽이치다
- leak into ~에 새어 들어가다
- annually [ad] 매년, 연마다

구문 풀이

3행 The attempt to straighten rivers and give them regular cross-sections is
주어 / 형용사적 용법1 / 형용사적 용법2 / 동사(단수)
perhaps the most disastrous example of this form-and-function relationship.
주격 보어

★★ 문제 해결 꿀~팁 ★★

▶ 많이 틀린 이유는?
자연의 복잡한 형태가 자연의 기능 수행에 도움이 된다는 다소 생소한 내용의 지문이다. 특히 글의 마지막 부분에서 강의 모양을 인위적으로 변형시키려 하다가는 이례적인 재난이 야기될 수 있어서 루이지애나 주 등에서 강의 모양을 '통제하려는' 시도를 그만두고 있다는 내용이 제시된다. 이러한 맥락으로 보아 최다 오답인 ⑤ 'controlled'는 적절하게 쓰였다.

▶ 문제 해결 방법은?
③이 포함된 문장에서 주어인 This는 앞 문장 내용, 즉 자연 발생적인 강이 복잡한 형태를 띤다는 내용을 받는다. 이러한 복잡한 형태가 자연의 기능 수행에 도움이 되는 요소임을 고려하면, 복잡한 형태가 강의 수위나 속도 변화를 '막아버린다'는 설명은 흐름상 어색하다.

31 원하는 것과 해야 할 것
정답률 41% | 정답 ①

다음 빈칸에 들어갈 말로 가장 적절한 것을 고르시오.

✓① desires - 욕망
② merits - 장점
③ abilities - 능력
④ limitations - 한계
⑤ worries - 걱정

In a culture / where there is a belief / that you can have anything you truly want, / there is no problem in choosing.
문화에서는 / 믿음이 있는 / 당신이 진정으로 원하는 것은 무엇이든지 가질 수 있다는 / 선택이 문제가 안 된다.

Many cultures, however, / do not maintain this belief.
그러나 많은 문화들은 / 이러한 믿음을 유지하지 못한다.

In fact, / many people do not believe / that life is about getting what you want.
사실, / 많은 사람들은 믿지 않는다. / 삶이란 당신이 원하는 것을 얻는 것이라고

Life is about doing what you are *supposed* to do.
인생은 당신이 *해야* 할 것을 하는 것이다.

The reason they have trouble making choices / is / they believe / that what they may want is not related / to what they are supposed to do.
그들이 선택을 하는 데 있어 어려움을 겪는 이유는 / ~이다. / 그들이 믿기 때문에 / 그들이 원하는 것이 관련이 없다고 / 그들이 해야 할 일과

The weight of outside considerations / is greater than their desires.
외적으로 고려할 문제의 비중은 / 그들의 욕망보다 더 크다.

When this is an issue in a group, / we discuss what makes for good decisions.
이것이 어떤 집단에서 논의 대상이 될 때, / 우리는 어떤 것이 좋은 결정인지 의논을 한다.

If a person can be unburdened from their cares and duties / and, just for a moment, / consider what appeals to them, / they get the chance / to sort out what is important to them.
만약 어떤 사람이 걱정과 의무로부터 벗어나 / 잠시 동안 / 자신에게 호소하는 것이 무엇인지를 생각해 볼 수 있다면, / 그들은 기회를 얻게 된다. / 자신에게 무엇이 중요한지를 가려낼

Then they can consider and negotiate / with their external pressures.
그러고 나서 그들은 고려하고 협상할 수 있다. / 외적인 부담에 대해

당신이 진정으로 원하는 것은 무엇이든지 가질 수 있다고 믿는 문화에서는 선택이 문제가 안 된다. 그러나 많은 문화들은 이러한 믿음을 유지하지 못한다. 사실, 많은 사람들은 삶이란 당신이 원하는 것을 얻는 것이라고 믿지 않는다. 인생은 당신이 *해야* 할 것을 하는 것이다. 그들이 선택을 하는 데 있어 어려움을 겪는 이유는 그들이 원하는 것이 그들이 해야 할 일과 관련이 없다고 믿기 때문이다. 외적으로 고려할 문제의 비중이 그들의 욕망보다 더 크다. 이것이 어떤 집단에서 논의 대상이 될 때, 우리는 어떤 것이 좋은 결정인지 의논을 한다. 만약 어떤 사람이 걱정과 의무로부터 벗어나 자신에게 호소하는 것이 무엇인지를 잠시 동안 생각해 볼 수 있다면, 그들은 자신에게 무엇이 중요한지를 가려낼 기회를 얻게 된다. 그러고 나서 그들은 외적인 부담에 대해 고려하고 협상할 수 있다.

Why? 왜 정답일까?

첫 두 문장에 따르면 많은 문화권에서 원하는 것을 다 가질 수 있다는 믿음이 유지되지 못한다고 한다. 이를 근거로 할 때, 빈칸이 포함된 문장은 '원하는 것' 이외에 고려할 문제가 더 많다는 의미여야 한다. 따라서 빈칸에 들어갈 말로 가장 적절한 것은 ① '욕망'이다.

- maintain ⓥ 유지하다
- weight ⓝ 비중, 무게
- negotiate ⓥ 협상하다
- desire ⓝ 욕망
- limitation ⓝ 한계
- have trouble ~ing ~하는 데 어려움을 겪다
- consideration ⓝ 고려 사항
- external ⓐ 외부적인
- merit ⓝ 장점

구문 풀이

1행 In a culture [where there is a belief {that you can have anything you truly
선행사 / 관계부사 / { } : 동격(= a belief)
want}], there is no problem in choosing.
동사 / 주어

★★ 문제 해결 꿀~팁 ★★

▶ 많이 틀린 이유는?
이 글은 우리가 원하는 바를 모두 성취하지 못하고 해야 하는 일 등 외부적 요소를 고려하여 선택을 하는 경우가 대부분이라는 내용을 다루고 있다. '능력'에 관해서는 중요하게 언급되지 않으므로 ③은 빈칸에 부적절하다.

▶ 문제 해결 방법은?
'what you want'와 'what you are *supposed* to do'가 두 가지 핵심 소재인데, 빈칸 문장의 outside consideration은 이중 'what you are *supposed* to do'와 같은 말이다. 따라서 빈칸에는 'what you want'를 달리 표현하는 말이 들어가야 한다.

32 선수의 인성 및 도덕성 함양에 양면적으로 작용하는 승리
정답률 43% | 정답 ⑤

다음 빈칸에 들어갈 말로 가장 적절한 것을 고르시오.

① a piece of cake - 식은 죽 먹기
② a one-way street - 일방통행로
③ a bird in the hand - 수중에 든 새
④ a fish out of water - 물 밖에 나온 고기
✓⑤ a double-edged sword - 양날의 검

Research has confirmed / that athletes are less likely to participate in unacceptable behavior / than are non-athletes.
연구는 확인해준다. / 운동선수는 받아들여지지 않는 행동을 덜 할 것이라고 / 선수가 아닌 사람들보다

However, / moral reasoning and good sporting behavior / seem to decline / as athletes progress to higher competitive levels, / in part because of the increased emphasis on winning.
그러나 / 도덕적 분별력과 바람직한 스포츠 행위가 / 감소하는 것 같다. / 운동선수가 더 높은 경쟁적 수준까지 올라감에 따라 / 부분적으로 승리에 대한 강조가 커지기 때문에

Thus winning can be a double-edged sword / in teaching character development.
그래서 승리라는 것은 양날의 검이 될 수 있다. / 인성 함양을 가르치는 데 있어서

Some athletes may want to win so much / that they lie, cheat, and break team rules.
어떤 선수는 너무나 이기려고 하다 보니 / 그 결과 거짓말하고 속이고 팀 규칙을 위반한다.

They may develop undesirable character traits / that can enhance their ability to win in the short term.
그들은 바람직하지 못한 인격 특성을 계발할지 모른다. / 단기간에 이길 수 있는 자신의 능력을 강화할 수 있는

However, / when athletes resist the temptation / to win in a dishonest way, / they can develop positive character traits / that last a lifetime.
그러나 / 선수가 유혹에 저항할 때 / 부정직한 방법으로 이기고자 하는 / 그들은 긍정적인 인격 특성을 계발할 수 있다. / 일생동안 지속되는

Character is a learned behavior, / and a sense of fair play develops / only if coaches plan to teach those lessons systematically.
인성이라는 것은 학습되는 행동이며 / 페어플레이 정신이 발달한다. / 코치가 그러한 교훈을 체계적으로 가르치고자 계획할 때 비로소

연구에 따르면 운동선수는 선수가 아닌 사람들보다 (사회적으로) 받아들여지지 않는 행동을 덜 할 것이라고 한다. 그러나 운동선수가 더 높은 경쟁적 수준까지 올라감에 따라 부분적으로 승리에 대한 강조가 커지기 때문에 도덕적 분별력과 바람직한 스포츠 행위가 감소하는 것 같다. 그래서 승리라는 것은 인성 함양을 가르치는 데 있어서 양날의 검이 될 수 있다. 어떤 선수는 너무나 이기려고 하다 보니 그 결과 거짓말하고 속이고 팀 규칙을 위반한다. 그들은 단시간에 이길 수 있는 자신의 능력을 강화할 수 있는 바람직하지 못한 인격 특성을 계발할지 모른다. 그러나 선수가 부정직한 방법으로 이기고자 하는 유혹에 저항할 때 그들은 일생 동안 지속되는 긍정적인 인격 특성을 계발할 수 있다. 인성이라는 것은 학습되는 행동이며 코치가 그러한 교훈을 체계적으로 가르치고자 계획할 때 비로소 페어플레이 정신이 발달한다.

첫 두 문장에 따르면 운동선수는 선수가 아닌 사람들에 비할 때 사회적으로 용인되지 않는 행동을 덜 하는 경향이 있지만, 승리가 강조되는 환경에 살기 때문에 경쟁이 심해질수록 도덕적 분별력이 떨어질 수 있다고 한다(~ athletes are less likely to participate in unacceptable behavior ~. However, moral reasoning and good sporting behavior seem to decline ~.). 따라서 빈칸에 들어갈 말로 가장 적절한 것은 승리라는 것이 선수의 인격 또는 도덕성 함양에 양면적으로 작용할 수 있다는 의미의 ⑤ '양날의 검'이다.

- confirm ⓥ (맞다고) 확인하다
- reasoning ⓝ 추론 (능력)
- competitive ⓐ 경쟁하는, 경쟁력 있는
- undesirable ⓐ 바람직하지 않은
- resist ⓥ 저항하다
- dishonest ⓐ 부정직한
- systematically 〔ad〕 체계적으로
- a bird in the hand 수중에 든 새, 확실한 일
- a fish out of water 물 밖에 나온 고기, 낯선 환경에서 불편해하는 사람
- a double-edged sword 양날의 검, 양면성을 가진 상황
- unacceptable ⓐ 받아들여지지 않는, 용인되지 않는
- decline ⓥ 감소하다
- emphasis ⓝ 강조
- enhance ⓥ 강화하다
- temptation ⓝ 유혹
- learned ⓐ 학습된, 후천적인
- a piece of cake 식은 죽 먹기, 아주 쉬운 일

구문 풀이

1행 Research has confirmed that athletes are less likely to participate in
접속사(~것) 「be less likely + to부정사 : 덜 ~하는 경향이 있다」
unacceptable behavior than are non-athletes.
「than + 동사 + 주어 : 도치 구문」

★★ 문제 해결 꿀~팁 ★★

▶ 많이 틀린 이유는?
빈칸 뒤에 따르면 선수들은 승리를 위해 부도덕한 행동을 저지르면서 바람직하지 못한 인격 특성을 키우게 될 수 있지만, 한편으로 부정직한 승리의 유혹에 저항하는 과정에서 좋은 인격 특성을 함양하게 될 수도 있다고 한다. 이는 결국 승리가 선수에게 좋은 쪽과 나쁜 쪽 둘 다로 작용할 수 있다는 의미이므로, ② 'a one-way street(일방통행로)'은 빈칸에 적합하지 않다. 또한 ① 'a piece of cake(식은 죽 먹기)'는 글의 내용과 전혀 관련이 없다.

▶ 문제 해결 방법은?
빈칸 뒤의 세부 진술을 읽고 일반적인 결론을 도출한 뒤, 이를 다시 비유적으로 잘 나타낸 선택지를 찾아야 하는 문제이다. 핵심은 승리의 '양면성'에 있음을 염두에 둔다.

★★★ 등급을 가르는 문제!

33 개인에게 넘어간 음악 선택권 정답률 38% | 정답 ①

다음 빈칸에 들어갈 말로 가장 적절한 것을 고르시오. [3점]

✓① choose and determine his or her musical preferences
자신이 선호하는 음악을 선택하고 결정해야
② understand the technical aspects of recording sessions
녹음 세션의 기술적 측면을 이해해야
③ share unique and inspiring playlists on social media
독특하고 영감을 주는 재생 목록을 소셜 미디어에 공유해야
④ interpret lyrics with background knowledge of the songs
노래에 대한 배경지식을 가지고 가사를 해석해야
⑤ seek the advice of a voice specialist for better performances
더 나은 공연을 위해 음성 전문가의 조언을 구해야

Due to technological innovations, / music can now be experienced by more people, / for more of the time than ever before.
기술 혁신으로 인해, / 음악은 이제 더 많은 사람에 의해 경험될 수 있다. / 이전보다 더 많은 시간 동안
Mass availability has given individuals unheard-of control / over their own sound-environment.
대중 이용 가능성은 개인들에게 전례 없는 통제권을 주었다. / 각자의 음향 환경에 대한
However, / it has also confronted them / with the simultaneous availability of countless genres of music, / in which they have to orient themselves.
하지만 / 그것은 그들을 맞닥뜨리게 했고 / 무수한 장르의 음악을 동시에 이용할 수 있는 상황에 / 그들이 그 상황에 적응해야만 한다.
People start filtering out and organizing their digital libraries / like they used to do with their physical music collections.
사람들은 자신들의 디지털 라이브러리를 걸러 내고 정리하기 시작한다. / 이전에 그들이 물리적 형태를 지닌 음악을 수집했던 것처럼
However, / there is the difference / that the choice lies in their own hands.
하지만 / 차이가 있다. / 선택권은 자신이 가진다는
Without being restricted to the limited collection of music-distributors, / nor being guided by the local radio program / as a 'preselector' of the latest hits, / the individual actively has to choose and determine his or her musical preferences.
음악 배급자의 제한된 컬렉션에 국한되지 않고, / 또한 지역 라디오 프로그램의 안내를 받지 않고, / 최신 히트곡의 '사전 선택자'인 / 개인은 적극적으로 자신이 선호하는 음악을 선택하고 결정해야 한다.
The search for the right song / is thus associated with considerable effort.
적절한 노래를 찾는 것은 / 따라서 상당한 노력과 관련이 있다.

기술 혁신으로 인해, 음악은 이제 이전보다 더 많은 시간 동안 더 많은 사람에 의해 경험될 수 있다. 대중 이용 가능성은 개인들에게 각자의 음향 환경에 대한 전례 없는 통제권을 주었다. 하지만 그들은 무수한 장르의 음악을 동시에 이용할 수 있는 상황에 맞닥뜨리게 되었고 그 상황에 적응해야만 한다. 사람들은 이전에 물리적 형태를 지닌 음악을 수집했던 것처럼 자신들의 디지털 라이브러리를 걸러 내고 정리하기 시작한다. 하지만 선택권은 자신이 가진다는 차이가 있다. 음악 배급자의 제한된 컬렉션에 국한되지 않고, 또한 최신 히트곡의 '사전 선택자'인 지역 라디오 프로그램의 안내를 받지 않고, 개인은 적극적으로 자신이 선호하는 음악을 선택하고 결정해야 한다. 따라서 적절한 노래를 찾는 것은 상당한 노력과 관련이 있다.

Why? 왜 정답일까?
첫 두 문장에서 기술 혁신으로 인해 개인이 자신의 음향 환경을 통제할 수 있는 권한을 갖게 되었다고 한다. 특히 'However, there is the difference that the choice lies in their own hands.'에서는 무수한 장르의 음악 속에서 자신의 디지털 라이브러리를 어떻게 구성할 것인지에 대한 선택권이 개인 자신에게 있다고 언급한다. 따라서 빈칸에 들어갈 말로 가장 적절한 것은 ① '자신이 선호하는 음악을 선택하고 결정해야'이다.

- availability ⓝ 이용 가능성
- confront A with B A를 B와 대면시키다
- orient ⓥ (새로운 상황에) 적응하다, 익숙해지다, 자기 위치를 알다
- restrict ⓥ 국한시키다, 제한하다
- considerable ⓐ 상당한
- unheard-of ⓐ 전례 없는

- distributor ⓝ 배급 업자
- interpret ⓥ 해석하다

구문 풀이

4행 However, it has also confronted them with the simultaneous availability
「confront + A + with + B : A를 B와 대면시키다」
of countless genres of music, in which they have to orient themselves.
계속적 용법(= where)

★★ 문제 해결 꿀~팁 ★★

▶ 많이 틀린 이유는?
기술 혁신으로 개인이 음악 선택권을 갖게 되었다는 내용의 글이다. 최다 오답인 ③은 개인이 소셜 미디어에 플레이리스트를 공유해야 한다는 의미인데, 개인이 직접 만든 플레이리스트를 공유해야 하는지는 글에서 언급되지 않았다. 특히 '소셜 미디어'라는 소재 자체가 글에서 아예 언급되지 않았다.

▶ 문제 해결 방법은?
주제가 드러나는 'However ~.' 문장을 잘 읽으면 쉽다. 'the choice lies in their own hands'가 문제 해결에 핵심적인 표현이다.

---

34 관객과의 상호 작용을 요하는 창작 행위 정답률 49% | 정답 ④

다음 빈칸에 들어갈 말로 가장 적절한 것을 고르시오. [3점]

① exploring the absolute truth in existence
현존하는 절대적 진리를 탐구하는 것
② following a series of precise and logical steps
정확하고 논리적인 일련의 단계를 따르는 것
③ looking outside and drawing inspiration from nature
밖을 보고 자연으로부터 영감을 얻는 것
✓④ internalizing the perspective of others on one's work
다른 사람의 관점을 자신의 작품 속에 내면화하는 것
⑤ pushing the audience to the limits of its endurance
관객을 인내심의 한계까지 밀어붙이는 것

It is common to assume / that creativity concerns primarily the relation / between actor(creator) and artifact(creation).
가정하는 것이 일반적이다. / 창조성은 주로 관계와 연관되어 있다고 / 행위자(창작자)와 창작물(창작) 간의
However, from a sociocultural standpoint, / the creative act is never "complete" / in the absence of a second position / — that of an audience.
그러나 사회 문화적 관점에서 볼 때, / 창작 행위는 결코 '완전'하지 않다. / 제2의 입장이 부재한 상황에서는 / 다시 말해 관객의 부재
While the actor or creator him/herself / is the first audience of the artifact being produced, / this kind of distantiation can only be achieved / by internalizing the perspective of others on one's work.
행위자나 창작자 자신은 / 만들어지고 있는 창작물의 첫 번째 관객이지만, / 이런 거리두기는 오로지 이루어진다. / 다른 사람의 관점을 자신의 작품 속에 내면화하는 것으로서만
This means / that, in order to be an audience to your own creation, / a history of interaction with others is needed.
이것은 의미한다. / 자신의 창작 활동에 관객이 되기 위해서는 / 다른 사람들과 상호 작용하는 역사가 필요하다는 것을
We exist in a social world / that constantly confronts us with the "view of the other."
우리는 사회적인 세상에 살고 있다. / 끊임없이 '상대방의 관점'에 마주하는
It is the view / we include and blend into our own activity, / including creative activity.
그것은 관점이다. / 우리가 우리 자신의 활동에 통합시키고 뒤섞게 되는 / 창조적인 행위를 포함해서
This outside perspective is essential for creativity / because it gives new meaning and value / to the creative act and its product.
이러한 외부 관점은 창조성에는 필수적이다. / 그것이 새로운 의미와 가치를 부여하기 때문에 / 창작 행위와 그 결과물에

창조성은 주로 행위자(창작자)와 창작물(창작) 간의 관계와 연관되어 있다고 가정하는 것이 일반적이다. 그러나 사회 문화적 관점에서 볼 때, 창작 행위는 관객의 부재, 다시 말해 제2의 입장이 부재한 상황에서는 결코 '완전'하지 않다. 행위자나 창작자 자신은 만들어지고 있는 창작물의 첫 번째 관객이지만, 이런 거리두기는 다른 사람의 관점을 자신의 작품 속에 내면화하는 것으로서만 이루어진다. 이것은 자신의 창작 활동에 관객이 되기 위해서는 다른 사람들과 상호 작용하는 역사가 필요하다는 것을 의미한다. 우리는 끊임없이 '상대방의 관점'에 마주하는 사회적인 세상에 살고 있다. 그것은 창조적인 행위를 포함해서 우리가 우리 자신의 활동에 통합시키고 뒤섞게 되는 관점이다. 이러한 외부 관점은 창작 행위와 그 결과물에 새로운 의미와 가치를 부여하기 때문에 창조성에는 필수적이다.

Why? 왜 정답일까?
두 번째 문장에서 사회 문화적 관점에 따르면 창작 행위는 제2의 관점, 즉 관객의 시각이 빠진 상태에서는 결코 완전할 수 없다고 한다. 이어서 'This means that, ~' 이하로 창작 활동에는 다른 사람과 상호 작용하는, 즉 '상대방의 관점'이 창조적 활동에 통합되는 과정이 꼭 필요하다는 내용이 이어진다. 따라서 빈칸에 들어갈 말로 가장 적절한 것은 ④ '다른 사람의 관점을 자신의 작품 속에 내면화하는 것'이다.

- primarily 〔ad〕 주로
- in the absence of ~이 없을 때에
- distantiation ⓝ 거리두기
- blend into ~에 뒤섞다
- absolute ⓐ 절대적인
- precise ⓐ 정확한
- endurance ⓝ 인내심, 참을성

- standpoint ⓝ 관점
- audience ⓝ 관객, 청중
- constantly 〔ad〕 지속적으로
- essential ⓐ 필수적인, 본질적인
- in existence 현존하는
- internalize ⓥ 내면화하다

구문 풀이

8행 This means that, in order to be an audience to your own creation, a history
접속사(~것) 부사적 용법(~하기 위해) 주어
of interaction with others is needed.
동사(단수)

---

35 전염병의 확산과 이에 대한 도시 환경의 대응력 정답률 58% | 정답 ④

다음 글에서 전체 흐름과 관계 없는 문장은? [3점]

Health and the spread of disease / are very closely linked / to how we live and how our cities operate.
건강과 질병의 확산은 / 매우 밀접하게 연관되어 있다. / 우리가 어떻게 살고 우리의 도시가 어떻게 작동하느냐와
The good news is / that cities are incredibly resilient.
좋은 소식은 ~이다. / 도시가 믿을 수 없을 정도로 회복력이 있다는 것
Many cities have experienced epidemics in the past / and have not only survived, but advanced.
많은 도시는 과거에 전염병을 경험했고 / 살아남았을 뿐만 아니라 발전했다.
① The nineteenth and early-twentieth centuries / saw destructive outbreaks of cholera, typhoid, and influenza / in European cities.
19세기와 20세기 초 / 콜레라, 장티푸스, 독감의 파괴적인 창궐을 목격했다. / 유럽의 도시에서
② Doctors such as Jon Snow, from England, / and Rudolf Virchow, of Germany, / saw the connection / between poor living conditions, overcrowding, sanitation, and disease.
영국 출신의 Jon Snow와 같은 의사들은 / 그리고 독일의 Rudolf Virchow와 같은 / 연관성을 알게 되었다. / 열악한 주거 환경, 인구 과밀, 위생과 질병의
③ A recognition of this connection / led to the replanning and rebuilding of cities / to stop the spread of epidemics.
이 연관성에 대한 인식은 / 도시 재계획과 재건축으로 이어졌다. / 전염병의 확산을 막기 위한
☑ In spite of reconstruction efforts, / cities declined in many areas / and many people started to leave.
재건 노력에도 불구하고 / 많은 지역에서 도시는 쇠퇴했고 / 많은 사람이 떠나기 시작했다.
⑤ In the mid-nineteenth century, / London's pioneering sewer system, / which still serves it today, / was built / as a result of understanding the importance of clean water / in stopping the spread of cholera.
19세기 중반에, / 런던의 선구적인 하수 처리 시스템은 / 오늘날까지도 사용되고 있는 / 만들어졌다. / 깨끗한 물의 중요성에 대한 이해의 결과로 / 콜레라의 확산을 막는 데 있어

건강과 질병의 확산은 우리가 어떻게 살고 우리의 도시가 어떻게 작동하느냐와 매우 밀접하게 연관되어 있다. 좋은 소식은 도시가 믿을 수 없을 정도로 회복력이 있다는 것이다. 많은 도시는 과거에 전염병을 경험했고 살아남았을 뿐만 아니라 발전했다. ① 19세기와 20세기 초 유럽의 도시들은 콜레라, 장티푸스, 독감의 파괴적인 창궐을 목격했다. ② 영국 출신의 Jon Snow와 독일의 Rudolf Virchow와 같은 의사들은 열악한 주거 환경, 인구 과밀, 위생과 질병의 연관성을 알게 되었다. ③ 이 연관성에 대한 인식은 전염병의 확산을 막기 위한 도시 재계획과 재건축으로 이어졌다. ④ 재건 노력에도 불구하고 많은 지역에서 도시는 쇠퇴했고 많은 사람이 떠나기 시작했다. ⑤ 19세기 중반에 지어진, 오늘날까지도 사용되고 있는 런던의 선구적인 하수 처리 시스템은 깨끗한 물이 콜레라의 확산을 막는 데 중요하다는 이해의 결과로 만들어졌다.

Why? 왜 정답일까?
첫 문장에서 전염병의 확산은 우리의 생활방식 및 도시 환경과 밀접하게 연관되어 있다는 주제를 제시한 뒤, ①, ②, ③, ⑤는 19~20세기 초 각종 전염병의 창궐을 경험한 유럽 도시들이 도시 환경의 개선을 통해 전염병을 극복했던 예시를 든다. 하지만 ④는 도시가 재건 노력에도 불구하고 쇠퇴했다는 무관한 내용을 제시한다. 따라서 전체 흐름과 관계 없는 문장은 ④이다.

- spread ⓝ 확산, 퍼지다
- epidemic ⓝ 전염병
- outbreak ⓝ 발발, 창궐
- sanitation ⓝ 위생 (관리)
- incredibly [ad] 놀라울 정도로
- destructive ⓐ 파괴적인
- overcrowding ⓝ 과밀 거주, 초만원
- reconstruction ⓝ 재건

구문 풀이
1행 Health and the spread of disease are very closely linked to how we live
주어 / 동사구(복수) / 간접의문문1
and how our cities operate.
간접의문문2

---

36 아기가 사람 얼굴을 선호하는 이유   정답률 69% | 정답 ⑤

주어진 글 다음에 이어질 글의 순서로 가장 적절한 것을 고르시오.
① (A) − (C) − (B)   ② (B) − (A) − (C)
③ (B) − (C) − (A)   ④ (C) − (A) − (B)
☑ (C) − (B) − (A)

Starting from birth, / babies are immediately attracted to faces.
태어나면서부터, / 아기는 즉각적으로 사람 얼굴에 끌린다.
Scientists were able to show this / by having babies look at two simple images, / one that looks more like a face than the other.
과학자들은 이것을 보여줄 수 있었다. / 아기에게 간단한 두 개의 이미지를 보여줌으로써 / 하나가 다른 것에 비해 더 사람 얼굴처럼 보이는 이미지
(C) By measuring where the babies looked, / scientists found / that the babies looked at the face-like image more / than they looked at the non-face image.
아기가 바라보는 곳을 유심히 살펴보면서, / 과학자들은 발견하게 되었다. / 아기가 얼굴처럼 보이는 이미지를 더 바라본다는 것을 / 그들이 얼굴처럼 보이지 않는 이미지를 보는 것보다
Even though babies have poor eyesight, / they prefer to look at faces.
아기는 시력이 좋지 않음에도 불구하고 / 그들은 얼굴을 보는 것을 더 좋아한다.
But why?
그런데 왜 그럴까?
(B) One reason babies might like faces / is because of something called evolution.
아기가 얼굴을 좋아하는 것 같은 하나의 이유는 / 진화라고 불리는 것 때문이다.
Evolution involves changes / to the structures of an organism(such as the brain) / that occur over many generations.
진화는 변화를 수반한다. / 유기체 구조(뇌와 같은 것)에 있어서의 / 여러 세대를 거쳐 발생하는
(A) These changes help the organisms to survive, / making them alert to enemies.
이런 변화들은 유기체가 생존하도록 도와준다. / 적들을 경계하게 해서
By being able to recognize faces / from afar or in the dark, / humans were able to know / someone was coming / and protect themselves from possible danger.
얼굴을 알아볼 수 있음으로써, / 멀리서 또는 어둠 속에서 / 인간은 알 수 있었고 / 누군가가 다가오는지 / 있을 법한 위험으로부터 자신을 보호할 수 있었다.

태어나면서부터, 아기는 즉각적으로 사람 얼굴에 끌린다. 과학자들은 아기에게 간단한 두 개의 이미지, 하나가 다른 것에 비해 더 사람 얼굴처럼 보이는 이미지를 보여줌으로써 이것을 보여줄 수 있었다.

(C) 과학자들은 아기가 바라보는 곳을 유심히 살펴보면서, 아기가 얼굴처럼 보이지 않는 이미지보다는 얼굴처럼 보이는 이미지를 더 바라본다는 것을 발견하게 되었다. 아기는 시력이 좋지 않음에도 불구하고 얼굴을 보는 것을 더 좋아한다. 그런데 왜 그럴까?

(B) 아기가 얼굴을 좋아하는 것 같은 하나의 이유는 진화라고 불리는 것 때문이다. 진화는 여러 세대를 거쳐 발생하는 유기체 구조(뇌와 같은 것)의 변화를 수반한다.

(A) 이런 변화들은 적들을 경계하게 해서 유기체가 생존하도록 도와준다. 멀리서 또는 어둠 속에서 얼굴을 알아볼 수 있음으로써, 인간은 누군가가 다가오는지 알 수 있었고 있을 법한 위험으로부터 자신을 보호할 수 있었다.

Why? 왜 정답일까?
주어진 글에서 아기들은 태어나면서부터 사람 얼굴에 끌리고, 이를 뒷받침하는 실험이 있다고 언급한다. (C)는 주어진 글의 실험에 따르면 아기들이 시력이 좋지 않은데도 불구하고 얼굴 이미지를 선호하는데 '왜 그런 것인지' 의문을 던진다. (B)는 (C)에서 제시된 질문에 '진화' 때문이라는 답을 제시한다. (A)는 (B)에서 언급된 '진화'를 보충 설명하는 내용이다. 따라서 글의 순서로 가장 적절한 것은 ⑤ '(C) − (B) − (A)'이다.

- alert ⓐ 경계하는
- structure ⓝ 구조
- evolution ⓝ 진화
- eyesight ⓝ 시력

구문 풀이
8행 One reason [babies might like faces] is because of something called evolution.
주어 / 동사(단수) / 전치사 / 명사 / 과거분사

---

37 미디어상의 잘못된 정보 공유 문제   정답률 65% | 정답 ②

주어진 글 다음에 이어질 글의 순서로 가장 적절한 것을 고르시오.
① (A) − (C) − (B)   ☑ (B) − (A) − (C)
③ (B) − (C) − (A)   ④ (C) − (A) − (B)
⑤ (C) − (B) − (A)

People spend much of their time / interacting with media, / but that does not mean / that people have the critical skills / to analyze and understand it.
사람들은 많은 시간을 소비하지만, / 미디어를 이용해 상호작용하는 데 / 그렇다고 해서 뜻하지는 않는다. / 사람들이 중요한 기술을 가지고 있다고 / 미디어를 분석하고 이해하는 데
(B) One well-known study from Stanford University in 2016 / demonstrated / that youth are easily fooled by misinformation, / especially when it comes through social media channels.
2016년 Stanford 대학의 잘 알려진 한 연구는 / 보여주었다. / 젊은이들이 잘못된 정보에 쉽게 속는다는 것을 / 특히 그것이 소셜 미디어 채널을 통해 올 때
This weakness is not found only in youth, however.
그러나 이러한 약점은 젊은이에게서만 발견되는 것은 아니다.
(A) Research from New York University found / that people over 65 / shared seven times as much misinformation / as their younger counterparts.
New York 대학의 조사에서 밝혔다. / 65세 이상의 사람들이 / 7배나 더 많은 잘못된 정보를 공유한다고 / 젊은이들보다
All of this raises a question:
이 모든 것이 의문을 제기한다.
What's the solution to the misinformation problem?
잘못된 정보 문제에 대한 해결책은 무엇인가?
(C) Governments and tech platforms / certainly have a role / to play in blocking misinformation.
정부와 기술 플랫폼은 / 분명 해야 할 역할을 가지고 있다. / 잘못된 정보를 막아내는 데 있어
However, / every individual needs to take responsibility / for combating this threat / by becoming more information literate.
그러나 / 모든 개인은 책임을 지닐 필요가 있다. / 이러한 위협에 맞서 싸울 / 정보를 더 잘 분별함으로써

사람들은 미디어를 이용해 상호작용하는 데 많은 시간을 소비하지만, 그렇다고 해서 사람들이 미디어를 분석하고 이해하는 데 중요한 기술을 가지고 있는 것은 아니다.

(B) 2016년 Stanford 대학의 잘 알려진 한 연구는 특히 정보가 소셜 미디어 채널을 통해 올 때 젊은이들이 잘못된 정보에 쉽게 속는다는 것을 보여주었다. 그러나 이러한 약점은 젊은이에게서만 발견되는 것은 아니다.

(A) New York 대학의 조사에서 65세 이상의 사람들이 젊은이들보다 7배나 더 많은 잘못된 정보를 공유한다고 밝혔다. 이 모든 것이 (다음의) 의문을 제기한다. 잘못된 정보 문제에 대한 해결책은 무엇인가?

(C) 정부와 기술 플랫폼은 분명 잘못된 정보를 막아내는 데 있어 해야 할 역할을 가지고 있다. 그러나 모든 개인은 정보를 더 잘 분별함으로써 이러한 위협에 맞서 싸울 책임을 지닐 필요가 있다.

Why? 왜 정답일까?
주어진 글에서 오늘날 사람들은 미디어를 많이 쓰고 있음에도 미디어를 분석하고 이해하는 데 필요한 능력을 갖추고 있지는 못하다고 지적한다. 이어서 (B)는 한 연구를 사례로 들며, 특히 젊은이들이 잘못된 정보에 쉽게 속는다는 점을 언급한다. (A)에서는 (B)의 말미에서 언급된 대로 '젊은 사람들뿐 아니라' 65세 이상의 연령대에서도 잘못된 정보 공유 문제가 발생한다고 언급한다. 이어서 (C)는 (A)의 마지막에 제시된, 정보 공유 문제에 대한 해결책을 묻는 질문에 대해 정부와 개인의 역할을 나누어 답하고 있다. 따라서 글의 순서로 가장 적절한 것은 ② '(B) − (A) − (C)'이다.

- critical ⓐ 중요한
- misinformation ⓝ 오보, 잘못된 정보
- demonstrate ⓥ 입증하다
- combat ⓥ 싸우다
- literate ⓐ ~을 다룰 줄 아는, 정통한, 글을 읽고 쓸 줄 아는
- analyze ⓥ 분석하다
- raise a question 의문을 제기하다
- take responsibility for ~을 책임지다

구문 풀이
1행 People spend much of their time interacting with media, but that does
「spend + 시간 + 동명사」: ~하는 데 …을 소비하다 / 지시대명사(but 앞 문장)
not mean that people have the critical skills to analyze and understand it.
접속사(~것) / 형용사적 용법1 / 형용사적 용법2

38 소리가 들리는 원리
정답률 59% | 정답 ③

글의 흐름으로 보아, 주어진 문장이 들어가기에 가장 적절한 곳을 고르시오.

Sound and light travel in waves.
소리와 빛은 파장으로 이동한다.
An analogy often given for sound / is that of throwing a small stone / onto the surface of a still pond.
소리 현상에 대해 자주 언급되는 비유는 / 작은 돌멩이를 던지는 것이다. / 고요한 연못 표면에
Waves radiate outwards from the point of impact, / just as sound waves radiate from the sound source.
파장이 충격 지점으로부터 바깥으로 퍼져나간다. / 음파가 음원으로부터 사방으로 퍼지는 것처럼
① This is due to a disturbance / in the air around us.
이것은 교란 작용 때문이다. / 우리 주변 공기 중의
② If you bang two sticks together, / you will get a sound.
만약에 당신이 막대기 두 개를 함께 꽝 친다면 / 당신은 소리를 듣게 될 것이다.
☑ As the sticks approach each other, / the air immediately in front of them / is compressed / and energy builds up.
막대기들이 서로 가까워질 때, / 막대들 바로 앞에 있는 공기가 / 압축되고 / 에너지는 축적된다.
When the point of impact occurs, / this energy is released as sound waves.
충돌점이 발생하면 / 이 에너지는 음파로 퍼져나간다.
④ If you try the same experiment with two heavy stones, / exactly the same thing occurs, / but you get a different sound / due to the density and surface of the stones, / and as they have likely displaced more air, / a louder sound.
당신이 두 개의 무거운 돌을 가지고 같은 실험을 해보면 / 똑같은 일이 일어나지만, / 당신은 다른 소리를 듣게 된다. / 돌의 밀도와 표면 때문에 / 그리고 그 돌이 아마 더 많은 공기를 바꿔 놓았기 때문에 / 더 큰 소리
⑤ And so, / a physical disturbance in the atmosphere around us / will produce a sound.
따라서 / 우리 주변의 대기 중에서 일어나는 물리적 교란 작용이 / 소리를 만든다.

소리와 빛은 파장으로 이동한다. 소리 현상에 대해 자주 언급되는 비유는 작은 돌멩이를 고요한 연못 표면에 던지는 것이다. 음파가 음원으로부터 사방으로 퍼지는 것처럼 파장이 충격 지점으로부터 바깥으로 퍼져나간다. ① 이것은 우리 주변 공기 중의 교란 작용 때문이다. ② 만약에 당신이 막대기 두 개를 함께 꽝 친다면 소리를 듣게 될 것이다. ③ 막대기들이 서로 가까워질 때, 막대들 바로 앞에 있는 공기가 압축되고 에너지는 축적된다. 충돌점이 발생하면 이 에너지는 음파로 퍼져나간다. ④ 두 개의 무거운 돌을 가지고 같은 실험을 해보면 똑같은 일이 일어나지만, 돌의 밀도와 표면 때문에 당신은 다른 소리를 듣게 되고, 그 돌이 아마 더 많은 공기를 바꿔 놓았기 때문에 당신은 더 큰 소리를 듣게 된다. ⑤ 따라서 우리 주변의 대기 중에서 일어나는 물리적 교란 작용이 소리를 만든다.

Why? 왜 정답일까?

소리를 듣게 되는 원리를 설명한 글로, ③ 앞의 문장에서 막대기 두 개를 함께 쳐서 소리를 듣는 상황을 예로 들고 있다. 주어진 문장은 두 막대기(the sticks)가 서로 가까워질 때 막대 바로 앞의 공기가 압축되고 에너지가 모인다고 설명한다. ③ 뒤의 문장은 그러다 충돌점이 발생하면 모였던 에너지(this energy)가 음파 형태로 퍼져나간다고 언급한다. 따라서 주어진 문장이 들어가기에 가장 적절한 곳은 ③이다.

- compress ⓥ 압축하다
- surface ⓝ 표면
- disturbance ⓝ 교란, 방해
- density ⓝ 밀도
- build up 축적되다
- impact ⓝ 충격, 여파
- release ⓥ 방출하다
- displace ⓥ 대체하다, (평소의 위치에서) 옮겨 놓다

구문 풀이

3행 An analogy often given for sound is that of throwing a small stone onto the surface of a still pond.
주어 / 과거분사 / 동사 / └지시대명사(= analogy)

39 먹이 사슬의 특징
정답률 58% | 정답 ④

글의 흐름으로 보아, 주어진 문장이 들어가기에 가장 적절한 곳을 고르시오. [3점]

Food chain means the transfer of food energy / from the source in plants / through a series of organisms / with the repeated process of eating and being eaten.
먹이 사슬은 식품 에너지가 이동하는 것을 의미한다. / 식물 안에 있는 에너지원으로부터 / 일련의 유기체를 통해 / 먹고 먹히는 반복되는 과정 속에서
① In a grassland, / grass is eaten by rabbits / while rabbits in turn are eaten by foxes.
초원에서 / 풀은 토끼에게 먹히지만 / 토끼는 이윽고 여우에게 먹힌다.
② This is an example of a simple food chain.
이것은 단순한 먹이 사슬의 예이다.
③ This food chain implies the sequence / in which food energy is transferred / from producer to consumer or higher trophic level.
이 먹이 사슬은 연쇄를 의미한다. / 식품 에너지가 전달되는 / 생산자로부터 소비자 또는 더 높은 영양 수준으로
☑ It has been observed / that at each level of transfer, / a large proportion, 80 − 90 percent, of the potential energy / is lost as heat.
관찰되어 왔다. / 각 이동 단계에서 / 잠재적 에너지의 상당한 부분인 80 ~ 90%가 / 열로 손실되는 것으로
Hence / the number of steps or links in a sequence / is restricted, / usually to four or five.
그래서 / 하나의 사슬 안에 있는 단계나 연결의 수는 / 제한된다. / 보통 4 ~ 5개로
⑤ The shorter the food chain / or the nearer the organism is to the beginning of the chain, / the greater the available energy intake is.
먹이 사슬이 짧을수록 / 또는 유기체가 사슬의 시작 단계에 가까울수록 / 이용 가능한 에너지 섭취량이 더 커진다.

먹이 사슬은 식물 안에 있는 에너지원으로부터 먹고 먹히는 반복되는 과정 속에서 일련의 유기체를 통해 식품 에너지가 이동하는 것을 의미한다. ① 초원에서 풀은 토끼에게 먹히지만 토끼는 이윽고 여우에게 먹힌다. ② 이것은 단순한 먹이 사슬의 예이다. ③ 이 먹이 사슬은 식품 에너지가 생산자로부터 소비자 또는 더 높은 영양 수준으로 전달되는 연쇄를 의미한다. ④ 각 이동 단계에서 잠재적 에너지의 상당한 부분인 80 ~ 90%가 열로 손실되는 것으로 관찰되어 왔다. 그래서 하나의 사슬 안에 있는 단계나 연결의 수는 보통 4 ~ 5개로 제한된다. ⑤ 먹이 사슬이 짧을수록 또는 유기체가 사슬의 시작 단계(하위 영양 단계)에 가까울수록 이용 가능한 에너지 섭취량이 더 커진다.

Why? 왜 정답일까?

④ 앞의 문장에서 먹이 사슬은 식품 에너지가 생산자에서 소비자로, 즉 더 높은 영양 수준으로 이동하는

연쇄적 과정을 의미하는 것이라고 한다. 이어서 주어진 문장은 먹이 사슬의 각 이동 단계(each level of transfer)에서 에너지의 80 ~ 90%가 열로 손실되어 버린다는 사실을 언급한다. ④ 뒤의 문장은 주어진 문장에서 언급된 이유로(Hence) 한 먹이 사슬 안의 단계 수가 4 ~ 5개로 제한된다고 설명한다. 따라서 주어진 문장이 들어가기에 가장 적절한 곳은 ④이다.

- transfer ⓝ 이동
- in turn 이윽고, 차례로
- restrict ⓥ 제한하다
- proportion ⓝ 비율
- imply ⓥ 암시하다
- intake ⓝ 섭취량

구문 풀이

11행 The shorter the food chain or the nearer the organism is to the beginning
「the + 비교급1 ~ / the + 비교급2 ~,
of the chain, the greater the available energy intake is.
the + 비교급 … : ~하거나 ~할수록 더 …하다

40 공공재의 비극을 막을 방법
정답률 63% | 정답 ①

다음 글의 내용을 한 문장으로 요약하고자 한다. 빈칸 (A), (B)에 들어갈 말로 가장 적절한 것은?

	(A)	(B)		(A)	(B)
☑①	reminder 상기물	shared 공유	②	reminder 상기물	recycled 재활용된
③	mistake 실수	stored 저장된	④	mistake 실수	borrowed 빌려온
⑤	fortune 행운	limited 제한된			

A woman named Rhonda / who attended the University of California at Berkeley / had a problem.
Rhonda라는 여자에게는 / Berkeley에 있는 California 대학에 다니는 / 한 가지 문제 상황이 있었다.
She was living near campus with several other people / — none of whom knew one another.
그녀는 여러 사람들과 함께 캠퍼스 근처에 살고 있었는데 / 그들 중 누구도 서로를 알지 못했다.
When the cleaning people came each weekend, / they left several rolls of toilet paper / in each of the two bathrooms.
청소부가 주말마다 왔을 때 / 그들은 몇 개의 두루마리 화장지를 두고 갔다. / 화장실 두 칸 각각에
However, / by Monday all the toilet paper would be gone.
그러나 / 월요일 즈음 모든 화장지가 없어지곤 했다.
It was a classic tragedy-of-the-commons situation: / because some people took more toilet paper / than their fair share, / the public resource was destroyed for everyone else.
그것은 전형적인 공유지의 비극 상황이었다. / 일부 사람들이 더 많은 휴지를 가져갔기 때문에 / 자신이 사용할 수 있는 몫보다 / 그 외 모두를 위한 공공재가 파괴됐다.
After reading a research paper about behavior change, / Rhonda put a note in one of the bathrooms / asking people not to remove the toilet paper, / as it was a shared item.
행동 변화에 대한 한 연구논문을 읽고 나서, / Rhonda는 쪽지를 화장실 한 곳에 두었다. / 사람들에게 화장실 화장지를 가져가지 말라고 요청하는 / 그것이 공유재이므로
To her great satisfaction, / one roll reappeared in a few hours, / and another the next day.
아주 만족스럽게도, / 몇 시간 후에 화장지 한 개가 다시 나타났고 / 그다음 날에는 또 하나가 다시 나타났다.
In the other note-free bathroom, however, / there was no toilet paper until the following weekend, / when the cleaning people returned.
하지만 쪽지가 없는 화장실에서는 / 그다음 주말까지 화장지가 없었다. / 청소부가 돌아오는
➡ A small (A) reminder brought about a change / in the behavior of the people / who had taken more of the (B) shared goods / than they needed.
자그마한 상기물은 변화를 일으켰다. / 사람의 행동에 / 더 많은 공유 재화를 가져갔던 / 그들이 필요한 것보다

Berkeley에 있는 California 대학에 다니는 Rhonda라는 여자에게는 한 가지 문제 상황이 있었다. 그녀는 여러 사람들과 함께 캠퍼스 근처에 살고 있었는데 그들 중 누구도 서로를 알지 못했다. 청소부가 주말마다 왔을 때 화장실 두 칸 각각에 몇 개의 두루마리 화장지를 두고 갔다. 그러나 월요일 즈음 모든 화장지가 없어지곤 했다. 그것은 전형적인 공유지의 비극 상황이었다. 일부 사람들이 자신들이 사용할 수 있는 몫보다 더 많은 휴지를 가져갔기 때문에 그외 모두를 위한 공공재가 파괴됐다. 행동 변화에 대한 한 연구논문을 읽고 나서, Rhonda는 화장실 화장지는 공유재이므로 사람들에게 가져가지 말라고 요청하는 쪽지를 화장실 한 곳에 두었다. 아주 만족스럽게도, 몇 시간 후에 화장지 한 개가 다시 나타났고 그다음 날에는 또 하나가 다시 나타났다. 하지만 쪽지가 없는 화장실에서는 청소부가 돌아오는 그다음 주말까지 화장지가 없었다.

➡ 자그마한 (A) 상기물은 필요한 것보다 더 많은 (B) 공유 재화를 가져갔던 사람의 행동에 변화를 일으켰다.

Why? 왜 정답일까?

실험을 소개한 글이므로 결과 부분에 주목한다. 마지막 세 문장에 따르면, 화장실 휴지가 공유재임을 상기시키는 쪽지를 붙인 화장실에는 없어졌던 휴지가 다시 돌아온 반면, 쪽지를 붙이지 않은 화장실에는 휴지가 돌아오지 않았다고 한다. 이를 토대로, 어떤 것이 공유재임을 '환기시켜 주는' 장치가 있을 때 '공유재'를 가져갔던 이들의 행동에 변화가 일어날 수 있다는 결론을 도출할 수 있다. 따라서 요약문의 빈칸 (A), (B)에 들어갈 말로 가장 적절한 것은 ① 'A) reminder(상기물), (B) shared(공유)'이다.

- classic ⓐ 고전적인
- destroy ⓥ 파괴하다
- bring about ~을 야기하다
- tragedy of the commons 공유지의 비극
- reappear ⓥ 다시 나타나다
- reminder ⓝ (잊고 있었던 것을) 상기시켜주는 것

구문 풀이

2행 She was living near campus with several other people — none of whom
선행사(사람) / 계속적 용법
knew one another.

41-42 사회적 두려움을 극복하는 방법

If you were afraid of standing on balconies, / you would start on some lower floors / and slowly work your way up to higher ones.
당신이 발코니에 서 있는 것을 두려워한다면, / 당신은 더 낮은 층에서 시작해서 / 천천히 더 높은 층으로 올라갈 것이다.
It would be easy / to face a fear of standing on high balconies / in a way that's totally controlled.

쉬울 것이다. / 높은 발코니에 서 있는 두려움을 직면하기는 / 완전히 통제된 방식으로

Socializing is (a) trickier.
사람을 사귄다는 것은 더 까다롭다.

People aren't like inanimate features of a building / that you just have to be around to get used to.
사람은 건물과 같은 무생물이 아니다. / 그저 주변에 있어서 여러분이 익숙해지는

You have to interact with them, / and their responses can be unpredictable.
당신은 그들과 상호 작용을 해야 하며 / 그들의 반응을 예측하기가 힘들 수 있다.

Your feelings toward them / are more complex too.
그들에 대한 당신의 느낌도 / 역시 더 복잡하다.

Most people's self-esteem / isn't going to be affected that much / if they don't like balconies, / but your confidence can (b) suffer / if you can't socialize effectively.
대부분의 사람들의 자존감은 / 그렇게 많이 영향을 받지 않을 것이지만, / 그들이 발코니를 좋아하지 않는다고 해도 / 당신의 자신감은 상처받을 수 있다. / 당신이 효과적으로 사람들을 사귈 수 없다면

It's also harder / to design a tidy way / to gradually face many social fears.
또한 더 어렵다. / 깔끔한 방법을 설계하는 것 / 점진적으로 마주할 여러 사교적 두려움을

「The social situations / you need to expose yourself to / may not be (c) available / when you want them, or they may not go well enough / for you to sense / that things are under control.」
사교적 상황이 / 당신을 드러낼 필요가 있는 / 형성되지 않을 수 있고, / 당신이 원할 때 / 또는 그것들은 충분히 잘 진행되지 않을지도 모른다. / 당신이 감지할 만큼 / 상황이 통제 가능하다고 42번의 근거

The progression from one step to the next / may not be clear, / creating unavoidable large (d) increases in difficulty / from one to the next.
한 단계에서 다음 단계로의 진행은 / 분명하지 않을 수 있으며, / 피할 수 없이 어려움이 크게 늘어나게 된다. / 한 단계에서 다음 단계로 진행할 때

People around you aren't robots / that you can endlessly experiment with / for your own purposes.
당신 주변의 사람들은 로봇이 아니다. / 당신이 끊임없이 실험해 볼 수 있는 / 당신 자신의 목적을 위해서

This is not to say / that facing your fears is pointless / when socializing.
이것은 말하는 것이 아니다. / 당신의 두려움을 직면하는 것이 의미가 없고 / 사람을 사귈 때

「The principles of gradual exposure / are still very (e) useful.」
점진적인 노출의 원칙은 / 여전히 매우 유용하다.

The process of applying them / is just messier, / and knowing that before you start / is helpful.」 41번의 근거
그것들을 적용하는 과정은 / 더 복잡하지만, / 시작하기 전에 그것을 아는 것은 / 도움이 된다.

발코니에 서 있는 것을 두려워한다면, 당신은 더 낮은 층에서 시작해서 천천히 더 높은 층으로 올라갈 것이다. 완전히 통제된 방식으로 높은 발코니에 서 있는 두려움을 직면하기는 쉬울 것이다. 사람을 사귄다는 것은 (a) 더 까다롭다. 사람은 그저 주변에 있어서 익숙해지는 건물과 같은 무생물이 아니다. 당신은 그들과 상호 작용을 해야 하며 그들의 반응을 예측하기가 힘들 수 있다. 그들에 대한 당신의 느낌도 역시 더 복잡하다. 대부분의 사람들의 자존감은 그들이 발코니를 좋아하지 않는다고 해도 그렇게 많이 영향을 받지 않을 것이지만, 당신이 효과적으로 사람들을 사귈 수 없다면 당신의 자신감은 (b) 상처받을 수 있다. 점차적으로 마주할 여러 사교적 두려움을 깔끔한 방법을 설계하는 것 또한 더 어렵다. 당신을 드러낼 필요가 있는 사교적 상황이 당신이 원할 때 (c) 형성되지 않을 수 있고, 또는 그것들은 상황이 통제 가능하다고 감지할 만큼 충분히 잘 진행되지 않을지도 모른다. 한 단계에서 다음 단계로의 진행은 분명하지 않을 수 있으며, 한 단계에서 다음 단계로 진행할 때 피할 수 없이 어려움이 크게 (d) 줄어들게(→ 늘어나게) 된다. 당신 주변의 사람들은 당신 자신의 목적을 위해서 끊임없이 실험해 볼 수 있는 로봇이 아니다. 이것은 사람을 사귈 때 당신의 두려움을 직면하는 것이 의미가 없다는 말이 아니다. 점진적인 노출의 원칙은 여전히 매우 (e) 유용하다. 그것들을 적용하는 과정은 더 복잡하지만, 시작하기 전에 그것을 아는 것은 도움이 된다.

- socialize ⓥ (사람과) 사귀다, 사회화하다
- inanimate ⓐ 무생물의
- unpredictable ⓐ 예측 불가한
- confidence ⓝ 자신감
- under control 통제되는
- unavoidable ⓐ 피할 수 없는
- pointless ⓐ 의미 없는
- tricky ⓐ 까다로운, 다루기 힘든
- get used to ~에 익숙해지다
- self-esteem ⓝ 자존감
- gradually ⓐⓓ 점차적으로
- progression ⓝ 진전
- endlessly ⓐⓓ 끝없이
- principle ⓝ 원칙, 원리

구문 풀이

1행 If you were afraid of standing on balconies, you would start on some
「if+주어+과거 동사 ~, 주어+조동사 과거형+동사원형1 +
lower floors and slowly work your way up to higher ones.
동사원형2」: 가정법 과거

★★★ 등급을 가르는 문제!

41 제목 파악 정답률 39% | 정답 ⑤

윗글의 제목으로 가장 적절한 것은?
① How to Improve Your Self-Esteem
자존감을 높이는 방법
② Socializing with Someone You Fear: Good or Bad?
당신이 두려워하는 사람과 어울리는 것: 좋을까, 나쁠까?
③ Relaxation May Lead to Getting Over Social Fears
휴식은 사회적 두려움을 극복하게 해줄 수 있다
④ Are Social Exposures Related with Fear of Heights?
사회적 노출은 고소공포증과 연관이 있을까?
⑤ Overcoming Social Anxiety Is Difficult; Try Gradually!
사회적 불안을 극복하는 것은 어렵지만, 점진적으로 시도하라!

Why? 왜 정답일까?

마지막 두 문장에 따르면 사교적으로 불안을 느끼는 상황에 점진적 노출 기법을 적용하기는 어렵지만 그래도 여전히 이 기법은 유용하다고 한다. 따라서 글의 제목으로 가장 적절한 것은 ⑤ '사회적 불안을 극복하는 것은 어렵지만, 점진적으로 시도하라!'이다.

★★ 문제 해결 꿀~팁 ★★

▶ 많이 틀린 이유는?
사교에 대한 두려움을 고소공포증 극복처럼 점진적 노출 기법, 즉 두려운 상황의 강도를 조금씩 높여

가며 노출되는 방식으로 극복해나갈 수 있는지 논한 글이다. 무서워하는 사람과 상호작용을 하는 것이 좋은지 나쁜지 판단하는 내용은 없으므로 ②는 답으로 부적절하다.

▶ 문제 해결 방법은?
명확한 주제문 없이 '사교적 두려움 극복'이라는 소재에 관해 설명하고 마지막 부분에서 결론을 내리는 구조의 글이므로, 전체적으로 글을 다 읽되 필자의 의견이 가장 잘 드러난 부분을 찾아 답으로 연결시켜야 한다.

42 어휘 추론 정답률 57% | 정답 ④

밑줄 친 (a)~(e) 중에서 문맥상 낱말의 쓰임이 적절하지 않은 것은?
① (a) ② (b) ③ (c) ④ (d) ⑤ (e)

Why? 왜 정답일까?

두 번째 단락의 첫 두 문장에서 사회적 불안을 점진적으로 직면할 수 있는 상황을 형성하거나 통제하는 것은 어렵다고 설명하고 있다. 이를 근거로 볼 때, (d)가 포함된 문장은 상황의 단계가 진행될수록 어려움이 '커진다'는 내용이어야 하므로, (d)의 decreases를 increases로 고쳐야 한다. 따라서 문맥상 낱말의 쓰임이 적절하지 않은 것은 ④ '(d)'이다.

43-45 아버지의 연설문을 보고 감동한 필자

(A)
When I was 17, / I discovered a wonderful thing.
내가 17살 때 / 나는 놀라운 물건을 발견했다.
My father and I were sitting on the floor of his study.
아버지와 나는 서재 바닥에 앉아 있었다.
「We were organizing his old papers.」 45번 ①의 근거 일치
우리는 아버지의 오래된 서류들을 정리하고 있었다.
Across the carpet I saw a fat paper clip.
나는 카펫 너머에 있는 두꺼운 종이 클립을 보았다.
Its rust dusted the cover sheet of a report of some kind.
그것의 녹이 어떤 보고서의 표지를 더럽혔다.
I picked it up.
나는 그것을 집어 들었다.
「I started to read.
나는 읽기 시작했다.
Then I started to cry.」 45번 ②의 근거 일치
그리고 나서 나는 울기 시작했다.

(C)
「It was a speech / he had written in 1920, in Tennessee.
그것은 연설문이었다. / 1920년 Tennessee 주에서 아버지가 썼던
Then only 17 himself and graduating from high school, / he had called for equality for African Americans.」 45번 ④의 근거 일치
당시 단지 17살에 고등학교를 졸업했을 뿐이더 / 아버지는 아프리카계 미국인들을 위한 평등을 요구했다.
(b) I marvelled, / proud of him, / and wondered / how, in 1920, / so young, so white, / and in the deep South, / where the law still separated black from white, / (c) he had had the courage to deliver it.
나는 놀라웠고, / 아버지를 자랑스럽게 여기면서 / 궁금했다. / 어떻게 1920년에 / 그렇게 어리고 백인이었던 / 그리고 최남부 지역에서 / 법으로 백인과 흑인을 여전히 분리시키고 있었던 / 그가 그 연설을 할 용기를 가지고 있었는지
I asked him about it.
나는 그에게 그것에 관해 물었다.

(B)
"Daddy," I said, / handing him the pages, / "this speech — how did you ever get permission to give it?
"아빠," 나는 말했다. / 아빠에게 서류를 건네 드리며 / "이 연설, 어떻게 이렇게 하도록 허락을 받으셨어요?
And weren't you scared?"
두렵지 않으셨어요?"
"Well, honey," he said, / "I didn't ask for permission.」 45번 ③의 근거 일치
"아들아," 그가 말했다. / "난 허락을 구하지 않았단다.
I just asked myself, / 'What is the most important challenge / facing my generation?'
단지 나 자신에게 물었지. / '가장 중요한 도전 과제는 무엇인가? / 우리 세대가 직면하고 있는'
I knew immediately.
난 즉시 알았어.
Then (a) I asked myself, / 'And if I weren't afraid, / what would I say about it in this speech?'"
그 뒤 나는 스스로에게 물었어. / '내가 두려워하지 않는다면, / 이 연설에서 이것에 대해 무엇을 말할까?'"라고

(D)
"I wrote it.
"난 글을 썼어.
And I delivered it.
그리고 연설을 했지.
「About half way through / I looked out to see / the entire audience of teachers, students, and parents / stand up — and walk out.」 45번 ⑤의 근거 불일치
대략 반쯤 연설을 했을 때 / 나는 바라보았어. / 교사, 학생, 학부모로 이루어진 전체 청중이 / 일어나더니 나가 버리는 것을
Left alone on the stage, / (d) I thought to myself, / 'Well, I guess I need to be sure / to do only two things with my life: / keep thinking for myself, and not get killed.'"
무대에 홀로 남겨진 채 / 나는 마음속으로 생각했어. / '그래, 나는 확실히 하면 되겠구나. / 내 인생에서 두 가지만 해내는 것을 / 계속 스스로 생각하는 것과 죽임을 당하지 않는 것'이라고
He handed the speech back to me, and smiled.
아버지는 연설문을 나에게 돌려주며 미소 지었다.
"(e) You seem to have done both," I said.
"아빠는 그 두 가지 모두를 해내신 것 같네요."라고 나는 말했다.

(A)
17살 때 나는 놀라운 물건을 발견했다. 아버지와 나는 서재 바닥에 앉아 있었다. 우리는 아버지의 오래된 서류들을 정리하고 있었다. 나는 카펫 너머에 있는 두꺼운 종이 클립을 보았다. 그것의 녹이 어떤 보고서의 표지를 더럽혔다. 나는 그것을 집어 들었다. 나는 읽기 시작했다. 그리고 나서 나는 울기 시작했다.

(C)

그것은 1920년 Tennessee 주에서 아버지가 썼던 연설문이었다. 아버지는 당시 단지 17살에 고등학교를 졸업했을 뿐인데 아프리카계 미국인들을 위한 평등을 요구했다. 아버지를 자랑스럽게 여기면서 (b) 나는 놀라워했고, 1920년에 법으로 백인과 흑인을 여전히 분리시키고 있었던 최남부 지역에서 그렇게 어리고 백인이었던 (c) 그가 어떻게 그 연설을 할 용기를 가지고 있었는지 궁금했다. 나는 그에게 그것에 관해 물었다.

(B)

아빠에게 서류를 건네 드리며 "아빠, 이 연설, 어떻게 이렇게 하도록 허락을 받으셨나요? 두렵지 않으셨나요?"라고 말했다. "아들아," 그가 말했다. "난 허락을 구하지 않았단다. 단지 '우리 세대가 직면하고 있는 가장 중요한 도전 과제는 무엇인가?'라고 나 자신에게 물었지. 난 즉시 알았어. 그 뒤 '내가 두려워하지 않는다면, 이 연설에서 이것에 대해 무엇을 말할까?'라고 (a) 나는 스스로에게 물었어."

(D)

"난 글을 썼어. 그리고 연설을 했지. 대략 반쯤 연설을 했을 때 교사, 학생, 학부모로 이루어진 전체 청중이 일어나더니 나가 버리는 것을 바라보았어. 무대에 홀로 남겨진 채 '그래, 내 인생에서 두 가지만 확실히 해내면 되겠구나. 계속 스스로 생각하는 것과 죽임을 당하지 않는 것.'이라고 (d) 나는 마음속으로 생각했어." 아버지는 연설문을 나에게 돌려주며 미소 지으셨다. "(e) 아빠는 그 두 가지 모두를 해내신 것 같네요."라고 나는 말했다.

- study ⓝ 서재
- permission ⓝ 허락
- call for ~을 요구하다, 필요로 하다
- marvel ⓥ 놀라다
- courage ⓝ 용기
- entire ⓐ 전체의
- rust ⓝ 녹
- generation ⓝ 세대
- equality ⓝ 평등
- separate ⓥ 분리시키다
- deliver ⓥ (연설이나 강연을) 하다

구문 풀이

(B) 5행 And if I weren't afraid, what would I say about it in this speech?
「if + 주어 + 과거 동사 ~, 조동사 과거형 + 주어 + 동사원형」: 가정법 과거 의문문

(C) 3행 I marvelled, (being) proud of him, and wondered {how, in 1920, (being) so
동사1 / 생략(분사구문) / 동사2 / 의문사
young, so white, and in the deep South, where the law still separated black from
선행사 / 관계부사 / 생략(분사구문): he 보충 설명
white, he had had the courage to deliver it}. (} : 목적어(간접의문문)
주어 / 동사

(D) 3행 Left alone on the stage, I thought to myself, 'Well, I guess (that) I need to
분사구문 / 생략(접속사)
be sure to do only two things with my life: keep thinking for myself, and not get
동격(= two things)
killed.'

---

43 글의 순서 파악 　　　정답률 68% | 정답 ②

주어진 글 (A)에 이어질 내용을 순서에 맞게 배열한 것으로 가장 적절한 것은?

① (B) − (D) − (C)　　　✔ (C) − (B) − (D)
③ (C) − (D) − (B)　　　④ (D) − (B) − (C)
⑤ (D) − (C) − (B)

Why? 왜 정답일까?

필자가 아버지와 서재를 정리하다가 아버지가 17살 때 썼던 연설문을 발견했다는 내용의 (A) 뒤에는, 연설문을 읽은 필자가 아버지에게 어떻게 그런 연설을 할 용기를 냈는지 물었다는 내용의 (C)가 연결된다. 이어서 (B)에서 아버지는 아들인 필자의 물음에 답하기 시작하고, (D)에서는 답을 마무리한다. 따라서 글의 순서로 가장 적절한 것은 ② '(C) − (B) − (D)'이다.

---

44 지칭 추론 　　　정답률 44% | 정답 ②

밑줄 친 (a)~(e) 중에서 가리키는 대상이 나머지 넷과 <u>다른</u> 것은?

① (a)　　✔ (b)　　③ (c)　　④ (d)　　⑤ (e)

Why? 왜 정답일까?

(a), (c), (d), (e)는 My father, (b)는 필자인 'I'를 가리키므로, (a) ~ (e) 중에서 가리키는 대상이 다른 하나는 ② '(b)'이다.

---

45 세부 내용 파악 　　　정답률 68% | 정답 ⑤

윗글에 관한 내용으로 적절하지 않은 것은?

① 아버지와 나는 서류를 정리하고 있었다.
② 나는 서재에서 발견한 것을 읽고 나서 울기 시작했다.
③ 아버지는 연설을 하기 위한 허락을 구하지 않았다.
④ 아버지가 연설문을 썼을 당시 17세였다.
✔ 교사, 학생, 학부모 모두 아버지의 연설을 끝까지 들었다.

Why? 왜 정답일까?

(D) 'About half way through I looked out to see the entire audience of teachers, students, and parents stand up — and walk out.'에 따르면 필자의 아버지가 절반쯤 연설을 진행했을 때 교사, 학생, 학부모 등 전체 관중이 모두 일어나 나갔다고 하므로, 내용과 일치하지 않는 것은 ⑤ '교사, 학생, 학부모 모두 아버지의 연설을 끝까지 들었다.'이다.

Why? 왜 오답일까?

① (A) 'We were organizing his old papers.'의 내용과 일치한다.
② (A) 'I started to read. Then I started to cry.'의 내용과 일치한다.
③ (B) 'I didn't ask for permission.'의 내용과 일치한다.
④ (C) 'It was a speech he had written in 1920, in Tennessee. Then only 17 himself and graduating from high school, ~'의 내용과 일치한다.

A	B	C	D
01 모으다, 모이다	01 appearance	01 ⓚ	01 ⓛ
02 축적되다	02 temptation	02 ⓟ	02 ⓝ
03 섭취량	03 progression	03 ⓠ	03 ⓒ
04 확산, 퍼지다	04 spill	04 ⓡ	04 ⓠ
05 적절한	05 instinct	05 ⓘ	05 ⓐ
06 한계	06 permission	06 ⓘ	06 ⓙ
07 감소하다	07 demonstrate	07 ⓐ	07 ⓚ
08 인용구	08 curiosity	08 ⓒ	08 ⓢ
09 공격	09 standpoint	09 ⓜ	09 ⓜ
10 분석하다	10 humanity	10 ⓗ	10 ⓔ
11 의미 없는	11 enhance	11 ⓝ	11 ⓘ
12 평등	12 impact	12 ⓘ	12 ⓗ
13 ~에 뒤섞다	13 sanitation	13 ⓙ	13 ⓘ
14 경우	14 additional	14 ⓓ	14 ⓟ
15 경외심	15 messy	15 ⓞ	15 ⓡ
16 정체성	16 approach	16 ⓕ	16 ⓖ
17 상당한	17 skyscraper	17 ⓔ	17 ⓓ
18 비율	18 self-esteem	18 ⓢ	18 ⓕ
19 다시 나타나다	19 negotiate	19 ⓑ	19 ⓞ
20 수직의	20 maintain	20 ⓖ	20 ⓑ

• 정답 •

18 ① 19 ① 20 ⑤ 21 ④ 22 ① 23 ③ 24 ⑤ 25 ⑤ 26 ⑤ 27 ⑤ 28 ④ 29 ④ 30 ③ 31 ② 32 ②
33 ④ 34 ② 35 ④ 36 ① 37 ⑤ 38 ④ 39 ③ 40 ③ 41 ① 42 ⑤ 43 ② 44 ⑤ 45 ③

★ 표기된 문항은 [등급을 가르는 문제]에 해당하는 문항입니다.

---

18 공장에 산업 견학 요청하기   정답률 92% | 정답 ①

다음 글의 목적으로 가장 적절한 것은?

✓① 공장 견학 허가를 요청하려고
② 단체 연수 계획을 공지하려고
③ 입사 방법을 문의하려고
④ 출장 신청 절차를 확인하려고
⑤ 공장 안전 점검 계획을 통지하려고

Dear Mr. Anderson,
Anderson 씨에게,
On behalf of Jeperson High School, / I am writing this letter to request permission / to conduct an industrial field trip in your factory.
Jeperson 고등학교를 대표해서, / 저는 허가를 요청하기 위해 이 편지를 쓰고 있습니다. / 귀하의 공장에서 산업 현장견학을 할 수 있도록
We hope to give some practical education to our students / in regard to industrial procedures.
저희는 학생들에게 몇 가지 실제적인 교육을 하기를 희망합니다. / 산업 절차와 관련해
With this purpose in mind, / we believe / your firm is ideal to carry out such a project.
이러한 목적을 생각할 때, / 저희는 믿습니다. / 귀사가 그러한 프로젝트를 진행하는 데 이상적이라고
But of course, we need your blessing and support.
물론, 저희는 귀사의 승인과 협조가 필요합니다.
35 students would be accompanied by two teachers.
두 명의 선생님이 35명의 학생들과 동행할 것입니다.
And we would just need a day for the trip.
저희는 이 현장 견학을 위해 하루만 있으면 됩니다.
I would really appreciate your cooperation.
협조해주시면 정말 감사하겠습니다.
Sincerely, // Mr. Ray Feynman
Ray Feynman 드림

Anderson 씨에게,

Jeperson 고등학교를 대표해서, 저는 귀하의 공장에서 산업 현장견학을 할 수 있도록 허가를 요청하기 위해 이 편지를 쓰고 있습니다. 저희는 학생들에게 산업 절차와 관련해 몇 가지 실제적인 교육을 하기를 희망합니다. 이러한 목적을 생각할 때, 저희는 귀사가 그러한 프로젝트를 진행하는 데 이상적이라고 믿습니다. 물론, 저희는 귀사의 승인과 협조가 필요합니다. 두 명의 선생님이 35명의 학생들과 동행할 것입니다. 저희는 이 현장 견학을 위해 하루만 있으면 됩니다. 협조해주시면 정말 감사하겠습니다.

Ray Feynman 드림

Why? 왜 정답일까?

'On behalf of Jeperson High School, I am writing this letter to request permission to conduct an industrial field trip in your factory.'와 마지막 두 문장에서 공장 견학을 할 수 있도록 허가를 해 달라고 요청하는 내용이 나오므로, 글의 목적으로 가장 적절한 것은 ① '공장 견학 허가를 요청하려고'이다.

● on behalf of ~을 대표하여
● conduct ⓥ 실시하다
● in regard to ~에 관해
● accompany ⓥ ~와 동행하다
● permission ⓝ 허가
● practical ⓐ 실제적인
● ideal ⓐ 이상적인

구문 풀이

2행 On behalf of Jeperson High School, I am writing this letter to request
~을 대표하여 ┘   목적(~하기 위해)
permission to conduct an industrial field trip in your factory.
  └ 형용사적 용법

---

19 자연에서 여유를 즐기는 Erda   정답률 80% | 정답 ①

다음 글에 드러난 Erda의 심경으로 가장 적절한 것은?

✓① relaxed – 여유로운
② puzzled – 혼란스러운
③ envious – 부러워하는
④ startled – 놀란
⑤ indifferent – 무관심한

Erda lay on her back in a clearing, / watching drops of sunlight slide / through the mosaic of leaves above her.
Erda는 빈터에 드러누워 / 부서진 햇살이 스며드는 것을 지켜보았다. / 그녀 위쪽의 나뭇잎 점점 사이로
She joined them for a little, / moving with the gentle breeze, / feeling the warm sun feed her.
그녀는 그것들과 잠시 함께 했다. / 미풍을 따라 움직이면서 / 따뜻한 태양이 자신에게 자양분을 주는 것을 느끼며
A slight smile was spreading over her face.
그녀의 얼굴에 옅은 미소가 번지고 있었다.
She slowly turned over / and pushed her face into the grass, / smelling the green pleasant scent from the fresh wild flowers.
그녀는 몸을 천천히 돌려 / 풀밭으로 얼굴을 내밀었다. / 신선한 야생화로부터 풍겨오는 푸르고 상쾌한 향기를 맡으며
Free from her daily burden, / she got to her feet and went on.
일상의 부담에서 벗어나 / 그녀는 일어서서 나아갔다.
Erda walked between the warm trunks of the trees.
Erda는 나무들의 따뜻한 기둥 사이를 걸었다.
She felt all her concerns had gone away.
그녀는 모든 걱정이 사라졌음을 느꼈다.

Erda는 빈터에 드러누워 그녀 위쪽의 나뭇잎 점점 사이로 부서진 햇살이 스며드는 것을 지켜보았다. 그녀는 따뜻한 태양이 자신에게 자양분을 주는 것을 느끼며, 미풍을 따라 움직이면서 그것들과 잠시 함께 했다. 그녀의 얼굴에 옅은 미소가 번지고 있었다. 그녀는 몸을 천천히 돌려 신선한 야생화로부터 풍겨오는 푸르고 상쾌한 향기를 맡으며 풀밭으로 얼굴을 내밀었다. 일상의 부담에서 벗어나 그녀는 일어서서 나아갔다. Erda는 나무들의 따뜻한 기둥 사이를 걸었다. 그녀는 모든 걱정이 사라졌음을 느꼈다.

Why? 왜 정답일까?

'A slight smile was spreading over her face.', 'Free from her daily burden, she got to her feet and went on.', 'She felt all her concerns had gone away.'을 통해 Erda가 일상의 스트레스에서 벗어나 자연과 함께 휴식을 만끽하며 여유로운 기분을 느끼고 있음을 파악할 수 있다. 따라서 Erda의 심경으로 가장 적절한 것은 ① '여유로운'이다.

● clearing ⓝ (숲 속의) 빈터
● spread ⓥ 퍼지다
● get to one's feet ⓥ 일어서다. 일어나다
● trunk ⓝ (나무의) 기둥
● gentle ⓐ 부드러운
● scent ⓝ 향기

구문 풀이

6행 (Being) Free from her daily burden, she got to her feet and went on.
생략(분사구문) └ 형용사   동사구1   동사구2

---

20 몸에 좋은 음식부터 먹기   정답률 90% | 정답 ⑤

다음 글에서 필자가 주장하는 바로 가장 적절한 것은?

① 피해야 할 음식 목록을 만들어라.
② 다양한 음식들로 식단을 구성하라.
③ 음식을 조리하는 방식을 바꾸어라.
④ 자신의 입맛에 맞는 음식을 찾아라.
✓⑤ 건강에 좋은 음식으로 식사를 시작하라.

The dish you start with / serves as an anchor food for your entire meal.
당신이 먼저 먹는 요리가 / 당신의 전체 식사에 닻을 내리는 음식의 역할을 한다.
Experiments show / that people eat nearly 50 percent greater quantity of the food / they eat first.
실험은 보여준다. / 사람들이 음식을 거의 50% 더 많이 먹는다는 것을 / 그들이 먼저 먹는
If you start with a dinner roll, / you will eat more starches, less protein, and fewer vegetables.
만약 당신이 디너 롤로 시작하면, / 당신은 더 많은 녹말과 더 적은 단백질, 그리고 더 적은 채소를 먹을 것이다.
Eat the healthiest food on your plate first.
접시에 있는 가장 건강에 좋은 음식을 먼저 먹어라.
As age-old wisdom suggests, / this usually means starting with your vegetables or salad.
오래된 지혜가 시사하듯이, / 이것은 보통 채소나 샐러드를 먼저 먹는 것을 의미한다.
If you are going to eat something unhealthy, / at least save it for last.
만약 당신이 건강에 좋지 않은 음식을 먹을 것이라면, / 적어도 그것을 마지막 순서로 남겨둬라.
This will give your body the opportunity / to fill up on better options / before you move on to starches or sugary desserts.
이것은 당신의 몸에 기회를 줄 것이다. / 더 나은 선택 사항들로 채울 / 여러분이 녹말이나 설탕이 든 디저트로 이동하기 전에

당신이 먼저 먹는 요리가 당신의 전체 식사에 닻을 내리는(전체 식사를 결정짓는) 음식의 역할을 한다. 실험은 사람들이 먼저 먹는 음식을 거의 50% 더 많이 먹는다는 것을 보여준다. 만약 당신이 디너 롤로 시작하면, 당신은 더 많은 녹말과 더 적은 단백질, 그리고 더 적은 채소를 먹을 것이다. 접시에 있는 가장 건강에 좋은 음식을 먼저 먹어라. 오래된 지혜에서 알 수 있듯이, 이것은 보통 채소나 샐러드를 먼저 먹는 것을 의미한다. 만약 당신이 건강에 좋지 않은 음식을 먹을 것이라면, 적어도 그것을 마지막 순서로 남겨둬라. 이것은 여러분이 녹말이나 설탕이 든 디저트로 이동하기 전에 당신의 몸을 더 나은 선택 사항들로 채울 기회를 줄 것이다.

Why? 왜 정답일까?

글 중간의 명령문 'Eat the healthiest food on your plate first.'에서 가장 건강에 좋은 음식부터 먹으라고 조언하는 것으로 볼 때, 필자가 주장하는 바로 가장 적절한 것은 ⑤ '건강에 좋은 음식으로 식사를 시작하라.'이다.

● serve as ⓥ ~의 역할을 하다
● fill up ⓥ ~을 가득 채우다
● quantity ⓝ 양
● sugary ⓐ 설탕이 든

구문 풀이

8행 This will give your body the opportunity to fill up on better options before
미래시제   └ 형용사적 용법   시간 접속사
you move on to starches or sugary desserts.
현재시제

★★★ 등급을 가르는 문제!
21 몸짓 언어의 이해   정답률 27% | 정답 ④

밑줄 친 by reading a body language dictionary가 의미하는 바로 가장 적절한 것은? [3점]

① by learning body language within social context – 사회적 맥락 안에서 언어를 배움으로써
② by comparing body language and French – 몸짓 언어와 프랑스어를 비교함으로써
③ with a body language expert's help – 몸짓 언어 전문가의 도움을 받아
✓④ without understanding the social aspects – 사회적 측면을 이해하지 못한 채로
⑤ in a way people learn their native language – 사람들이 자기 모국어를 배우는 방식으로

Authentic, effective body language / is more than the sum of individual signals.
실제성 있고 효과적인 몸짓 언어는 / 개별 전달 신호의 합계 이상이다.
When people work from this rote-memory, dictionary approach, / they stop seeing the bigger picture, / all the diverse aspects of social perception.
사람들이 이러한 암기식의 사전식 접근법으로부터 시작할 때, / 그들은 더 큰 그림을 보지 못하게 된다. / 즉 사회적 인식의 모든 다양한 측면을
Instead, they see a person with crossed arms / and think, "Reserved, angry."
대신, 그들은 팔짱을 낀 사람을 보고 / '과묵하고 화가 난' 것으로 생각한다.
They see a smile and think, "Happy."
그들은 미소를 보고 '행복한' 것으로 생각한다.

They use a firm handshake / to show other people "who is boss."
그들은 세게 악수를 한다. / 다른 사람들에게 '누가 윗사람인가'를 보여 주기 위해
Trying to use body language / by reading a body language dictionary / is like trying to speak French / by reading a French dictionary.
몸짓 언어를 사용하려고 하는 것은 / 몸짓 언어 사전을 읽어서 / 프랑스어를 말하려고 하는 것과 같다. / 프랑스어 사전을 읽어서
Things tend to fall apart in an inauthentic mess.
요소들은 실효성 없는 상태로 분리되어 버리는 경향이 있다.
Your actions seem robotic; / your body language signals are disconnected from one another.
당신의 행동은 로봇처럼 어색해 보이고, / 당신의 몸짓 언어 신호는 서로 단절된다.
You end up confusing the very people / you're trying to attract / because your body language just rings false.
당신은 결국에는 바로 그 사람들을 혼란스럽게 하고 만다. / 당신이 마음을 끌려고 하는 / 당신의 몸짓 언어가 그야말로 잘못 전달되었기 때문에

실효성 있고 효과적인 몸짓 언어는 개별 전달 신호의 합계 이상이다. 사람들이 이러한 암기식의 사전식 접근법으로부터 의사전달을 할 때, 그들은 더 큰 그림, 즉 사회적 인식의 모든 다양한 측면을 보지 못하게 된다. 대신, 그들은 팔짱을 낀 사람을 보고 '과묵하고 화가 난' 것으로 생각한다. 그들은 미소를 보고 '행복한' 것으로 생각한다. 그들은 다른 사람들에게 '누가 윗사람인가'를 보여 주기 위해 세게 악수를 한다. 몸짓 언어 사전을 읽어서 몸짓 언어를 사용하려고 하는 것은 프랑스어 사전을 읽어서 프랑스어를 말하려고 하는 것과 같다. (의미 구성의) 요소들은 실효성 없는 상태로 분리되어 버리는 경향이 있다. 당신의 행동은 로봇처럼 어색해 보이고, 당신의 몸짓 언어 신호는 서로 단절된다. 당신의 몸짓 언어가 그야말로 잘못 전달되었기 때문에 결국에는 당신이 마음을 끌려고 하는 바로 그 사람들을 혼란스럽게 하고 만다.

Why? 왜 정답일까?

'When people work from this rote-memory, dictionary approach, they stop seeing the bigger picture, all the diverse aspects of social perception.'에서 사전식으로 몸짓 언어를 바라보면 사회적 인식의 다양한 면을 보지 못한다고 하므로, 다시금 몸짓 언어 사전을 언급하는 밑줄 친 부분의 의미로 가장 적절한 것은 ④ '사회적 측면을 이해하지 못한 채로'이다.

- authentic ⓐ 실효성 있는, 진짜의
- rote-memory ⓐ 기계적 암기의
- disconnect ⓥ 단절시키다
- attract ⓥ (마음을) 끌다, 매혹시키다
- sum ⓝ 합계
- fall apart ⓥ 분리되다
- end up ⓥ 결국 ~하게 되다

구문 풀이

11행 You end up confusing the very people [you're trying to attract] because your body language just rings false.
(end up: 결국 ~하게 되다 / the very: 바로 그 / people: 선행사 / because: 이유 접속사)

★★ 문제 해결 꿀~팁 ★★

▶ 많이 틀린 이유는?
서두에서 사전식으로 몸짓 언어에 접근하면 큰 그림, 즉 사회적 맥락에 관한 정보를 놓치게 된다고 언급한다. 이를 근거로 볼 때, '몸짓 언어 사전을 읽으려는' 행위가 '맥락 속에서 몸짓 언어를 배우려는' 행위라고 설명한 ①은 아예 틀린 진술이다.
▶ 문제 해결 방법은?
a body language dictionary라는 비유적 표현을 이해하려면 **dictionary approach**라는 표현이 포함된 두 번째 문장을 주의 깊게 읽어야 한다. 여기서 말하는 '사전식 접근'이란 '사회적 인식의 면면을 파악하는 것과 동떨어진 것'임을 이해한 후 답을 찾도록 한다.

22 진정한 발전을 이끄는 사고방식

정답률 66% | 정답 ①

다음 글의 요지로 가장 적절한 것은?

✔ 발전은 한 번의 목표 성취가 아닌 지속적인 개선 과정에 의해 결정된다.
② 결승선을 통과하기 위해 장시간 노력해야 원하는 바를 얻을 수 있다.
③ 성공을 위해서는 구체적인 목표를 설정하는 것이 중요하다.
④ 지난 과정을 끊임없이 반복하는 것이 성공의 지름길이다.
⑤ 목표 지향적 성향이 강할수록 발전이 빠르게 이루어진다.

A goal-oriented mind-set can create a "yo-yo" effect.
목표 지향적인 사고방식은 "요요" 효과를 낼 수 있다.
Many runners work hard for months, / but as soon as they cross the finish line, / they stop training.
많은 달리기 선수들이 몇 달 동안 열심히 연습하지만, / 그들이 결승선을 통과하는 순간 / 그들은 훈련을 중단한다.
The race is no longer there to motivate them.
그 경기는 더 이상 그들에게 동기를 주지 않는다.
When all of your hard work is focused on a particular goal, / what is left to push you forward / after you achieve it?
당신의 모든 노력이 특정한 목표에 집중될 때, / 당신을 앞으로 밀고 나가도록 하는 것 중에 무엇이 남았는가? / 당신이 그것을 성취한 후에
This is why many people find themselves / returning to their old habits after accomplishing a goal.
이것이 많은 사람들이 자신을 발견하는 이유다. / 목표를 성취한 후 옛 습관으로 되돌아가는
The purpose of setting goals / is to win the game.
목표를 설정하는 목적은 / 경기에서 이기기 위함이다.
The purpose of building systems / is to continue playing the game.
시스템을 구축하는 목적은 / 게임을 계속하기 위한 것이다.
True long-term thinking is goal-less thinking.
진정한 장기적 사고는 목표가 없는 사고이다.
It's not about any single accomplishment.
그것은 어떤 하나의 성취에 관한 것이 아니다.
It is about the cycle / of endless refinement and continuous improvement.
그것은 순환에 관한 것이다. / 끝없는 정제와 지속적인 개선의
Ultimately, it is your commitment to the process / that will determine your progress.
궁극적으로, 그 과정에 당신이 몰두하는 것이다. / 당신의 발전을 결정짓는 것은

목표 지향적인 사고방식은 "요요" 효과를 낼 수 있다. 많은 달리기 선수들이 몇 달 동안 열심히 연습하지만, 결승선을 통과하는 순간 훈련을 중단한다. 그 경기는 더 이상 그들에게 동기를 주지 않는다. 당신의 모든 노력이 특정한 목표에 집중될 때, 당신이 그것을 성취한 후에 당신을 앞으로 밀고 나갈 수 있는 것 중에 무엇이 남았는가? 이것이 많은 사람들이 목표를 성취한 후 옛 습관으로 되돌아가는 자신을 발견하는 이유다. 목표를 설정하는 목적은 경기에서 이기기 위함이다. 시스템을 구축하는 목적은 게임을 계속하기 위한 것이다. 진정한 장기적 사고는 목표가 없는 사고이다. 그것은 어떤 하나의 성취에 관한 것이 아니다. 그것은 끝없는 정제와 지속적인 개선의 순환에 관한 것이다. 궁극적으로, 당신의 발전을 결정짓는 것은 그 과정에 당신이 몰두하는 것이다.

Why? 왜 정답일까?

마지막 세 문장인 'It's not about any single accomplishment. It is about the cycle of endless refinement and continuous improvement. Ultimately, it is your commitment to the process ~'에서 발전을 결정 짓는 것은 목표 또는 목표의 성취가 아니고 개선의 순환을 유지시키는 것, 즉 과정에 몰두하는 것임을 서술하고 있다. 따라서 글의 요지로 가장 적절한 것은 ① '발전은 한 번의 목표 성취가 아닌 지속적인 개선 과정에 의해 결정된다.'이다.

- goal-oriented ⓐ 목표 지향적인
- accomplish ⓥ 성취하다
- improvement ⓝ 개선, 향상
- motivate ⓥ 동기를 부여하다
- refinement ⓝ 정제, 개선
- commitment ⓝ 몰두, 전념

구문 풀이

11행 Ultimately, it is your commitment to the process that will determine your progress.
(「it is + 강조하는 말 + that + 나머지 문장: 강조구문(~한 것은 바로 …이다)」)

23 타인에게 도움을 주는 연습하기

정답률 69% | 정답 ③

다음 글의 주제로 가장 적절한 것은?

① benefits of living with others in harmony – 타인과 조화롭게 살아가는 것의 이점
② effects of practice in speaking kindly – 친절하게 말하는 데 있어서의 연습의 효과
✔ importance of practice to help others – 타인을 돕기 위한 연습의 중요성
④ means for helping people in trouble – 곤경에 처한 사람들을 돕기 위한 수단
⑤ difficulties with forming new habits – 새로운 습관을 형성하는 데 있어서의 어려움

Like anything else involving effort, / compassion takes practice.
노력과 관련된 다른 어떤 것과 마찬가지로, / 연민은 연습이 필요하다.
We have to work at getting into the habit / of standing with others in their time of need.
우리는 습관을 기르는 데 매진해야 한다. / 곤경에 빠진 다른 사람들과 함께 하는
Sometimes offering help is a simple matter / that does not take us far out of our way / — remembering to speak a kind word to someone who is down, / or spending an occasional Saturday morning volunteering for a favorite cause.
때때로 도움을 주는 것은 단순한 일이다. / 우리의 일상에서 멀리 벗어나지 않는 / 낙담한 사람에게 친절한 말을 해 줄 것을 기억하거나 / 가끔 토요일 아침에 가장 좋아하는 명분의 자원 봉사를 하는 것
At other times, helping involves some real sacrifice.
다른 때에는, 남을 돕는 것은 진정한 희생을 수반한다.
"A bone to the dog is not charity," / Jack London observed.
"개에게 뼈를 주는 것은 자선이 아니다." / Jack London은 말했다.
"Charity is the bone shared with the dog, / when you are just as hungry as the dog."
"개와 함께 나누는 그 뼈가 자선이다. / 당신이 딱 그 개만큼 배가 고플 때"
If we practice taking the many small opportunities to help others, / we'll be in shape to act / when those times requiring real, hard sacrifice come along.
만약 우리가 다른 사람들을 돕기 위해 많은 작은 기회를 갖는 연습을 하면, / 우리는 행동할 준비가 될 것이다. / 진정한 힘든 희생이 필요한 시기가 올 때

노력과 관련된 다른 어떤 것과 마찬가지로, 연민은 연습이 필요하다. 우리는 곤경에 빠진 다른 사람들과 함께 하는 습관을 기르는 데 매진해야 한다. 때때로 도움을 주는 것은 우리의 일상에서 멀리 벗어나지 않는 단순한 일 — 낙담한 사람에게 친절한 말을 해 줄 것을 기억하거나 가끔 토요일 아침에 가장 좋아하는 명분의 자원 봉사를 하는 것이다. 다른 때에는, 남을 돕는 것은 진정한 희생을 수반한다. Jack London은 "개에게 뼈를 주는 것은 자선이 아니다. 당신이 딱 그 개만큼 배가 고플 때 개와 함께 나누는 그 뼈가 자선이다."라고 했다. 만약 우리가 다른 사람들을 돕기 위해 많은 작은 기회를 갖는 연습을 하면, 우리는 진정한 힘든 희생이 필요한 시기가 올 때 행동할 준비가 될 것이다.

Why? 왜 정답일까?

'We have to work at getting into the habit of standing with others in their time of need.'와 'If we practice taking the many small opportunities to help others, we'll be in shape to act when those times requiring real, hard sacrifice come along.'에서 남에 대한 연민을 베풀기 위해서는 곤경에 빠진 다른 사람과 함께 하는 습관을 들이고 타인을 돕기 위한 작은 기회를 많이 가져야 한다고 언급하고 있다. 따라서 글의 주제로 가장 적절한 것은 ③ '타인을 돕기 위한 연습의 중요성'이다.

- compassion ⓝ 연민
- occasional ⓐ 가끔의
- sacrifice ⓝ 희생
- means ⓝ 수단
- get into a habit of ~하는 습관을 들이다
- cause ⓝ 대의명분
- come along ⓥ 생기다, 발생하다

구문 풀이

3행 Sometimes offering help is a simple matter [that does not take us far out of our way] — remembering to speak a kind word to someone [who is down], or spending an occasional Saturday morning volunteering for a favorite cause.
(offering help: 동명사구 주어 / is: 동사(단수) / a simple matter: 주격 보어(선행사) / that: 주격 관계대명사 / remembering: 동명사1 / spending: 동명사2(a simple matter의 예시))

24 스트레스를 줄이는 데 도움이 되는 미소 짓기

정답률 62% | 정답 ⑤

다음 글의 제목으로 가장 적절한 것은?

① Causes and Effects of Stressful Events – 스트레스가 많은 사건의 원인과 결과

② Personal Signs and Patterns of Stress - 스트레스의 개인적 징후와 유형
③ How Body and Brain React to Stress - 신체와 뇌는 스트레스에 어떻게 반응하는가
④ Stress: Necessary Evil for Happiness - 스트레스: 행복을 위한 필요악
☑ Do Faked Smiles Also Help Reduce Stress? - 가짜 미소도 스트레스를 줄이는 데 도움이 될까?

Every event that causes you to smile / makes you feel happy / and produces feel-good chemicals in your brain.
여러분을 미소 짓게 만드는 온갖 사건들은 / 여러분이 행복감을 느끼게 하고, / 여러분의 뇌에서 기분을 좋게 만들어주는 화학물질을 생산해낸다.

Force your face to smile / even when you are stressed or feel unhappy.
억지로 미소를 지어보자. / 심지어 스트레스를 받거나 불행하다고 느낄 때조차

The facial muscular pattern produced by the smile / is linked to all the "happy networks" in your brain / and will in turn naturally calm you down / and change your brain chemistry / by releasing the same feel-good chemicals.
미소에 의해 만들어지는 안면 근육의 형태는 / 뇌의 모든 "행복 연결망"과 연결되어 있어 / 결국 자연스럽게 여러분을 안정시키고 / 뇌의 화학 작용을 변화시킬 것이다. / 기분을 좋게 만들어주는 바로 그 화학물질들을 배출하여

Researchers studied the effects / of a genuine and forced smile on individuals / during a stressful event.
연구자들은 영향을 연구하였다. / 진정한 미소와 억지 미소가 개개인들에게 미치는 / 스트레스가 상당한 상황에서

The researchers had participants perform stressful tasks / while not smiling, smiling, / or holding chopsticks crossways in their mouths / (to force the face to form a smile).
연구자들은 참가자들이 스트레스를 수반한 과업을 수행하도록 했다. / 미소 짓지 않거나, 미소 짓거나, / 입에 젓가락을 옆으로 물고서 / (억지 미소를 짓게 하기 위해)

The results of the study showed / that smiling, forced or genuine, during stressful events / reduced the intensity of the stress response in the body / and lowered heart rate levels / after recovering from the stress.
연구 결과는 보여주었다. / 스트레스가 상당한 상황에서 미소는 억지이든 진짜이든 / 신체의 스트레스 반응의 강도를 줄였고, / 심장 박동률의 수준도 낮추었다는 것을 / 스트레스로부터 회복한 후의

여러분을 미소 짓게 만드는 온갖 사건들은 여러분이 행복감을 느끼게 하고, 여러분의 뇌에서 기분을 좋게 만들어주는 화학물질을 생산해 낸다. 심지어 스트레스를 받거나 불행하다고 느낄 때조차 미소를 지어보자. 미소에 의해 만들어지는 안면 근육의 형태는 뇌의 모든 "행복 연결망"과 연결되어 있어 결국 자연스럽게 여러분을 안정시키고 기분을 좋게 만들어주는 바로 그 화학물질들을 배출하여 뇌의 화학 작용을 변화시킬 것이다. 연구자들은 스트레스가 상당한 상황에서 진정한 미소와 억지 미소가 개개인들에게 미치는 영향을 연구하였다. 연구자들은 참가자들이 미소 짓지 않거나, 미소 짓거나, (억지 미소를 짓게 하기 위해) 입에 젓가락을 옆으로 물고서 스트레스를 수반한 과업을 수행하도록 했다. 연구 결과는 스트레스가 상당한 상황에서 미소는 억지이든 진짜이든 신체의 스트레스 반응의 강도를 줄였고, 스트레스로부터 회복한 후의 심장 박동률의 수준도 낮추었다는 것을 보여주었다.

Why? 왜 정답일까?
예시 앞의 'The facial muscular pattern produced by the smile is linked to all the "happy networks" in your brain and will in turn naturally calm you down and change your brain chemistry by releasing the same feel-good chemicals.'에서 스트레스를 받거나 불행하다고 느낄 때조차 미소를 지으면 자연스럽게 안정되고 기분이 좋아질 수 있다고 언급한 데 이어, 예시 뒤의 결론 또한 억지 미소이든 진짜 미소이든 인체의 스트레스 반응 강도를 낮추는 데 기여할 수 있다는 내용을 소개한다. 따라서 글의 제목으로 가장 적절한 것은 위와 같은 내용을 이끌어내기 적합한 질문 형태인 ⑤ '가짜 미소도 스트레스를 줄이는 데 도움이 될까?'이다.

- muscular ⓐ 근육의
- crossways ⓐ 옆으로, 가로로
- recover from ~에서 회복하다
- genuine ⓐ 진정한
- intensity ⓝ 강도
- necessary evil ⓝ 필요악

구문 풀이

3행 The facial muscular pattern produced by the smile is linked to all the "happy networks" in your brain and will in turn naturally calm you down and change your brain chemistry by releasing the same feel-good chemicals.

---

25 영국인들이 인터넷에 접속할 때 가장 중요하게 생각한 기기 정답률 64% | 정답 ⑤

다음 도표의 내용과 일치하지 않는 것은?

Most Important Device for Internet Access: 2014 and 2016 in UK

(막대그래프: Internet Users (%))
- Smartphone: 23 (2014), 36 (2016)
- Laptop: 40 (2014), 29 (2016)
- Tablet: 15 (2014), 20 (2016)
- Desktop: 20 (2014), 12 (2016)
□ 2014 □ 2016

The above graph shows / what devices British people considered the most important / when connecting to the Internet / in 2014 and 2016.
위 도표는 보여 준다. / 영국인들이 어떤 기기들이 가장 중요하다고 생각했는지를 / 인터넷에 접속을 할 때 / 2014년과 2016년에

① More than a third of UK Internet users / considered smartphones to be their most important device / for accessing the Internet / in 2016.
3분의 1이 넘는 영국 인터넷 사용자들은 / 스마트폰을 가장 중요한 기기로 생각했다. / 인터넷에 접속하기 위한 / 2016년도에

② In the same year, / the smartphone overtook the laptop / as the most important device for Internet access.
같은 해에, / 스마트폰이 노트북을 추월하였다. / 인터넷 접속을 위해 가장 중요한 기기로서

③ In 2014, UK Internet users were the least likely to select a tablet / as their most important device for Internet access.
2014년에, 영국 인터넷 사용자들은 태블릿을 가장 적게 선택하는 경향이 있었다. / 인터넷 접속을 위한 가장 중요한 기기로

④ In contrast, / they were the least likely to consider a desktop / as their most important

device for Internet access. / in 2016.
대조적으로, / 그들은 데스크탑을 가장 적게 선택하는 경향이 있었다. / 인터넷 접속을 위한 가장 중요한 기기로 / 2016년에는

☑ The proportion of UK Internet users / who selected a desktop as their most important device for Internet access / increased by half from 2014 to 2016.
영국 인터넷 사용자들의 비율은 / 인터넷 접속을 위한 가장 중요한 기기로 데스크탑을 선택한 / 2016년도에 2014년도 비율의 절반만큼 증가하였다.

위 도표는 2014년과 2016년에 영국인들이 인터넷에 접속을 할 때 어떤 기기들이 가장 중요하다고 생각했는지를 보여 준다. ① 2016년도에 3분의 1이 넘는 영국 인터넷 사용자들은 스마트폰을 가장 중요한 인터넷 접속 기기로 생각했다. ② 같은 해에, 스마트폰이 인터넷 접속을 위해 가장 중요한 기기로서 노트북을 추월하였다. ③ 2014년에, 영국 인터넷 사용자들은 인터넷 접속을 위한 가장 중요한 기기로 태블릿을 가장 적게 선택하는 경향이 있었다. ④ 대조적으로, 2016년에는 인터넷 접속을 위한 가장 중요한 기기로 데스크탑을 가장 적게 선택하는 경향이 있었다. ⑤ 인터넷 접속을 위한 가장 중요한 기기로 데스크탑을 선택한 영국 인터넷 사용자들의 비율은 2016년도에 2014년도 비율의 절반만큼 증가하였다.

Why? 왜 정답일까?
도표에 따르면 2014년에 인터넷 접속 기기로 데스크탑을 가장 중요하게 여긴 영국인 인터넷 사용자 비율은 20%인데, 2016년에는 동일한 항목의 비율이 12%로 감소했다. 따라서 도표와 일치하지 않는 것은 ⑤이다.

- access ⓥ ~에 접속하다, 접근하다 ⓝ 접속, 접근
- proportion ⓝ 비율
- overtake ⓥ 추월하다

---

26 Sigrid Undset의 생애 정답률 85% | 정답 ⑤

Sigrid Undset에 관한 다음 글의 내용과 일치하지 않는 것은?
① 세 자매 중 첫째 딸로 태어났다.
② 어린 시절의 삶은 아버지의 역사적 지식에 큰 영향을 받았다.
③ 16세에 가족을 부양하기 위해 취업하였다.
④ 1928년에 노벨 문학상을 수상하였다.
☑ 독일 점령 기간 중 노르웨이를 탈출한 후, 다시 돌아오지 않았다.

Sigrid Undset was born / on May 20, 1882, in Kalundborg, Denmark.
Sigrid Undset은 태어났다. / 1882년 5월 20일 덴마크의 Kalundborg에서

「She was the eldest of three daughters.」 ①의근거 일치
그녀는 세 자매 중 첫째 딸이었다.

She moved to Norway at the age of two.
그녀는 2살에 노르웨이로 이주하였다.

「Her early life was strongly influenced / by her father's historical knowledge.」 ②의근거 일치
그녀의 어린 시절은 크게 영향을 받았다. / 아버지의 역사적 지식에

「At the age of sixteen, / she got a job at an engineering company / to support her family.」
16세에 / 그녀는 기술 회사에 취업을 하였다. / 가족을 부양하기 위해 ③의근거 일치

She read a lot, / acquiring a good knowledge of Nordic / as well as foreign literature, English in particular.
그녀는 책을 많이 읽었고, / 북유럽 (문학)에 관한 상당한 지식을 습득하였다. / 외국 문학, 특히 영국 문학 뿐만 아니라

She wrote thirty six books.
그녀는 36권의 책을 집필하였다.

None of her books leaves the reader unconcerned.
독자의 관심을 끌지 못한 그녀의 책은 없다.

「She received the Nobel Prize for Literature in 1928.」 ④의근거 일치
1928년에 그녀는 노벨 문학상을 수상하였다.

One of her novels / has been translated into more than eighty languages.
그녀의 소설 중 한 권은 / 80개 이상의 언어로 번역되었다.

「She escaped Norway during the German occupation, / but she returned after the end of World War Ⅱ.」 ⑤의근거 불일치
그녀는 독일 점령 기간 중 노르웨이를 떠났으나, / 2차 세계대전이 종료된 후 돌아왔다.

Sigrid Undset은 1882년 5월 20일 덴마크의 Kalundborg에서 태어났다. 그녀는 세 자매 중 첫째 딸이었다. 그녀는 2살에 노르웨이로 이주하였다. 그녀의 어린 시절은 아버지의 역사적 지식에 크게 영향을 받았다. 그녀는 16세에 가족을 부양하기 위해 기술 회사에 취업을 하였다. 그녀는 책을 많이 읽었고, 외국 문학, 특히 영국 문학 뿐만 아니라, 북유럽 문학에 관한 상당한 지식을 습득하였다. 그녀는 36권의 책을 집필하였다. 독자의 관심을 끌지 못한 책은 없다. 1928년에 그녀는 노벨 문학상을 수상하였다. 그녀의 소설 중 한 권은 80개 이상의 언어로 번역되었다. 그녀는 독일 점령 기간 중 노르웨이를 떠났으나, 2차 세계대전이 종료된 후 돌아왔다.

Why? 왜 정답일까?
'She escaped Norway during the German occupation, but she returned after the end of World War Ⅱ.'에서 Sigrid Undset는 독일 점령 기간 중 노르웨이를 떠났지만 종전 이후 다시 돌아왔다고 하므로, 내용과 일치하지 않는 것은 ⑤ '독일 점령 기간 중 노르웨이를 탈출한 후, 다시 돌아오지 않았다.'이다.

Why? 왜 오답일까?
① 'She was the eldest of three daughters.'의 내용과 일치한다.
② 'Her early life was strongly influenced by her father's historical knowledge.'의 내용과 일치한다.
③ 'At the age of sixteen, she got a job at an engineering company to support her family.'의 내용과 일치한다.
④ 'She received the Nobel Prize for Literature in 1928.'의 내용과 일치한다.

- strongly ⓐ 강하게
- engineering ⓝ 공학 기술
- in particular 특히
- translate A into B ⓥ A를 B로 번역하다
- historical ⓐ 역사적인
- acquire ⓥ 습득하다
- unconcerned ⓐ 무관심한, 흥미 없는
- occupation ⓝ 점령

구문 풀이

5행 She read a lot, acquiring a good knowledge of Nordic as well as foreign literature, English in particular.

Swimming Summer Camp 2020에 관한 다음 안내문의 내용과 일치하지 <u>않는</u> 것은?

① 기본적인 수영 기법을 배울 수 있다.
② 오전 11시부터 수영 강습이 시작된다.
③ 요금에는 점심 식사비가 포함되어 있다.
④ 수영모가 모든 참가자에게 무료로 제공된다.
☑ 등록을 위해 직접 방문해야 한다.

Swimming Summer Camp 2020
Swimming Summer Camp 2020(2020 여름 수영 캠프)
『Great opportunity to learn basic swimming techniques / with certified swimming coaches!』 ①의 근거 일치
기본적인 수영 기법들을 배울 수 있는 절호의 기회! / 검증된 수영 코치들과 함께
PARTICIPANTS & PERIOD
참가자와 시기
Age 16 – 18 years
16세에서 18세까지
July 27 – 31 (Monday – Friday)
7월 27일부터 31일까지 (월요일부터 금요일까지)
DAILY SCHEDULE
일정
『11:00 a.m. – 12:00 p.m. Swimming Lesson』 ②의 근거 일치
오전 11:00 – 오후 12:00 수영 강습
12:30 p.m. – 13:30 p.m. Lunch
오후 12:30 – 오후 13:30 점심 식사
PRICE
가격
『$30 (lunch included)』 ③의 근거 일치
30달러 (점심 식사 포함)
『A free swimming cap will be provided to all participants.』 ④의 근거 일치
수영모가 모든 참가자들에게 무료로 제공될 것입니다.
REGISTRATION
등록
『Online only: www.friendlycoaches.ca』 ⑤의 근거 불일치
온라인으로만 가능: www.friendlycoaches.ca

Swimming Summer Camp 2020
(2020 여름 수영 캠프)

검증된 수영 코치들과 함께
기본적인 수영 기법들을 배울 수 있는 절호의 기회!

참가자와 시기
• 16세에서 18세까지
• 7월 27일부터 31일까지 (월요일부터 금요일까지)

일정
오전 11:00 – 오후 12:00 수영 강습
오후 12:30 – 오후 13:30 점심 식사

가격
• 30달러 (점심 식사 포함)
※ 무료 수영모가 모든 참가자들에게 무료로 제공될 것입니다.

등록
• 온라인으로만 가능: www.friendlycoaches.ca

Why? 왜 정답일까?

'Online only: www.friendlycoaches.ca'에서 등록은 온라인으로만 가능하다고 하므로, 안내문의 내용과 일치하지 않는 것은 ⑤ '등록을 위해 직접 방문해야 한다.'이다.

Why? 왜 오답일까?

① 'Great opportunity to learn basic swimming techniques ~'의 내용과 일치한다.
② '11:00 a.m. – 12:00 p.m. Swimming Lesson'의 내용과 일치한다.
③ '$30 (lunch included)'의 내용과 일치한다.
④ 'A free swimming cap will be provided to all participants.'의 내용과 일치한다.

● certified ⓐ 검증된, 보증된, 공인의   ● participant ⓝ 참가자
● swimming cap ⓝ 수영모   ● registration ⓝ 등록

---

28 주말 농산물 직판장 운영 안내   정답률 86% | 정답 ④

Rode Farmers Market에 관한 다음 안내문의 내용과 일치하는 것은?

① 7월 매주 토요일 오후에 열린다.
② Open Garden에서 외국 음식을 구입할 수 있다.
③ Farmers' House에서 고급 농업 기술을 배울 수 있다.
☑ 우천 시 몇몇 행사가 취소될 수 있다.
⑤ 주차 요금을 지불해야 한다.

Rode Farmers Market
Rode Farmers Market(Rode 농산물 직판장)
『This lively market is held / every Saturday in July from 9:00 a.m. until 11:30 a.m.』 ①의 근거 불일치
이 생동감 넘치는 시장은 열립니다. / 7월 매주 토요일 오전 9시부터 11시 30분까지

Where 장소	What to Do 할 일
『Open Garden Open Garden	Buy Local Organic Food』 ②의 근거 불일치 지역 유기농 음식을 구입하세요
Picnic Area Picnic Area	Enjoy Fun Family Events and Local Music 즐거운 가족 행사와 지역 음악을 즐기세요
『Farmers' House Farmers' House	Learn Basic Farming Techniques』 ③의 근거 불일치 기초적인 농사 기법을 배우세요

『In case of rain, some events may be cancelled.』 ④의 근거 일치
우천 시 몇몇 행사가 취소될 수 있습니다.
Location
위치
Village of Scholar Green on A34, Cheshire
Village of Scholar Green on A34, Cheshire
『Free Parking』 ⑤의 근거 불일치
무료 주차

Rode Farmers Market(Rode 농산물 직판장)

이 생동감 넘치는 시장은 7월 매주 토요일 오전 9시부터 11시 30분까지 열립니다.

장소	할 일
Open Garden	지역 유기농 음식을 구입하세요
Picnic Area	즐거운 가족 행사와 지역 음악을 즐기세요
Farmers' House	기초적인 농사 기법을 배우세요

◈ 우천 시 몇몇 행사가 취소될 수 있습니다.

위치
Village of Scholar Green on A34, Cheshire
◈ 무료 주차

Why? 왜 정답일까?

'In case of rain, some events may be cancelled.'에서 우천 시에는 몇 가지 행사가 취소될 수 있다고 하므로, 안내문의 내용과 일치하는 것은 ④ '우천 시 몇몇 행사가 취소될 수 있다.'이다.

Why? 왜 오답일까?

① 'This lively market is held every Saturday in July from 9:00 a.m. until 11:30 a.m.'에서 농산물 직판장은 7월 매주 토요일 오전에 열린다고 하였다.
② 'Open Garden / Buy Local Organic Food'에서 지역 유기농 음식을 살 수 있다고 하였다.
③ 'Farmers' House / Learn Basic Farming Techniques'에서 기초적인 농업 기술을 배울 수 있다고 하였다.
⑤ 'Free Parking'에서 주차는 무료라고 하였다.

● farmers market ⓝ 농산물 직판장   ● lively ⓐ 생동감 넘치는
● in case of ~의 경우에

---

29 또래 친구들이 우리에게 끼치는 영향   정답률 49% | 정답 ④

다음 글의 밑줄 친 부분 중, 어법상 틀린 것은? [3점]

Positively or negatively, / our parents and families are powerful influences on us.
긍정적이든 부정적이든, / 우리의 부모님과 가족은 우리에게 강력한 영향을 미친다.
But even ① stronger, especially when we're young, / are our friends.
하지만 특히 우리가 어렸을 때, / 훨씬 더 강한 영향을 주는 것은 / 우리의 친구들이다.
We often choose friends / as a way of ② expanding our sense of identity beyond our families.
우리는 흔히 친구들을 선택한다. / 가족의 범위를 넘어서 우리의 (자아) 정체감을 확장하는 방법으로
As a result, / the pressure to conform / to the standards and expectations of friends and other social groups / ③ is likely to be intense.
그 결과, / 부합해야 한다는 압박감이 / 친구와 다른 사회 집단의 기준과 기대에 / 거세질 가능성이 있다.
Judith Rich Harris, who is a developmental psychologist, / ☑ argues that three main forces shape our development: / personal temperament, our parents, and our peers.
발달 심리학자 Judith Rich Harris는 / 세 가지 주요한 힘이 우리의 발달을 형성한다고 주장한다. / 개인적인 기질, 우리의 부모님, 우리의 또래들
The influence of peers, / she argues, / is much stronger than that of parents.
또래들의 영향은 / 그녀는 주장한다, / 부모의 영향보다 훨씬 더 강하다고
"The world ⑤ that children share with their peers," / she says, / "is what shapes their behavior / and modifies the characteristics they were born with, / and hence determines the sort of people they will be when they grow up."
"아이들이 그들의 또래들과 공유하는 세상은" / 그녀는 말한다, / "그들의 행동을 형성하는 것이고, / 그들이 가지고 태어난 특성을 수정하는 것이며, / 따라서 그들이 자라서 어떤 부류의 사람이 될지를 결정하는 것이다."라고

긍정적이든 부정적이든, 우리의 부모님과 가족은 우리에게 강력한 영향을 미친다. 하지만 특히 우리가 어렸을 때, 훨씬 더 강한 영향을 주는 것은 우리의 친구들이다. 가족의 범위를 넘어서 우리의 (자아) 정체감을 확장하는 방법으로 우리는 흔히 친구들을 선택한다. 그 결과, 친구와 다른 사회 집단의 기준과 기대에 부합해야 한다는 압박감이 거세질 가능성이 있다. 발달 심리학자 Judith Rich Harris는 세 가지 주요한 힘이 우리의 발달을 형성한다고 주장하는데, 바로 개인적인 기질, 우리의 부모님, 우리의 또래들이다. 또래들의 영향은 부모의 영향보다 훨씬 더 강하다고 그녀는 주장한다. "아이들이 그들의 또래들과 공유하는 세상은 그들의 행동을 형성하는 것이고, 그들이 가지고 태어난 특성을 수정하는 것이며, 따라서 그들이 자라서 어떤 사람이 될지를 결정하는 것이다."라고 그녀는 말한다.

Why? 왜 정답일까?

주어인 Judith Rich Harris 뒤로 주어를 부연하는 관계절이 잇따른 후, 주어에 이어지는 동사가 나와야 하므로 arguing을 argues로 고쳐야 한다. 따라서 어법상 틀린 것은 ④이다.

Why? 왜 오답일까?

① 형용사 보어가 앞에 나와 주어와 동사가 도치된 구조이다. 즉 주어 our friends, 동사 are와 연결되어 보어 역할을 하는 비교급 형용사 stronger가 바르게 쓰였다.
② a way of(~할 방법으로)에 연결되는 동명사 expanding이 바르게 쓰였다.
③ 주어가 the pressure라는 단수 명사이므로 단수 동사 is가 알맞게 쓰였다. 'to conform ~'은 주어를 보충 설명한다.

⑤ 뒤에 나오는 관계절 'children share ~'가 목적어가 없는 불완전한 구조인 것으로 보아 **that**은 목적격 관계대명사로 알맞게 쓰였다.

- **positively** ad 긍정적으로
- **expand** ⓥ 확장하다
- **conform to** ⓥ ~에 부합하다, 순응하다
- **developmental** ⓐ 발달과 관련된
- **hence** ad 따라서, 이런 이유로
- **negatively** ad 부정적으로
- **sense of identity** ⓝ 정체감
- **intense** ⓐ 거센, 강렬한
- **modify** ⓥ 수정하다

구문 풀이

2행 But even stronger, (especially when we're young), are our friends.
보어(도치)　　( ): 삽입절　　　동사　주어(복수)

---

30 뇌의 에너지 소모　　　　정답률 67% | 정답 ③

(A), (B), (C)의 각 네모 안에서 문맥에 맞는 낱말로 가장 적절한 것은?

	(A)	(B)	(C)
①	warn 경고하다	less 더 적은	efficient 효율적인
②	warn 경고하다	more 더 많은	efficient 효율적인
✓③	exhaust 지치게 하다	more 더 많은	efficient 효율적인
④	exhaust 지치게 하다	more 더 많은	creative 창의적인
⑤	exhaust 지치게 하다	less 더 적은	creative 창의적인

The brain makes up just two percent of our body weight / but uses 20 percent of our energy.
뇌는 몸무게의 2퍼센트만을 차지하지만 / 우리 에너지의 20퍼센트를 사용한다.
In newborns, it's no less than 65 percent.
갓 태어난 아기의 경우, 그 비율은 자그마치 65퍼센트이다.
That's partly why babies sleep all the time / — their growing brains (A) exhaust them — / and have a lot of body fat, / to use as an energy reserve when needed.
그것은 부분적으로 아기들이 항상 잠을 자고 / 그들의 성장 중인 뇌가 그들을 지치게 하고 / 많은 체지방을 보유하는 이유인데, / 필요할 때 보유한 에너지를 사용하려는 것이다.
Our muscles use even more of our energy, about a quarter of the total, / but we have a lot of muscle.
근육은 약 4분의 1 정도로 훨씬 더 많은 에너지를 사용하지만, / 우리에게는 근육이 많다.
Actually, per unit of matter, / the brain uses by far (B) more energy than our other organs.
실제로, 물질 단위당, / 뇌는 다른 기관보다 훨씬 더 많은 에너지를 사용한다.
That means / that the brain is the most expensive of our organs.
그것은 의미한다. / 우리 장기 중 뇌가 단연 가장 비용 소모가 많다는 것을
But it is also marvelously (C) efficient.
하지만 그것은 또한 놀랍도록 효율적이다.
Our brains require only about four hundred calories of energy a day / — about the same as we get from a blueberry muffin.
뇌는 하루에 약 400칼로리의 에너지만 필요로 하는데, / 우리가 블루베리 머핀에서 얻는 것과 거의 같다.
Try running your laptop for twenty-four hours on a muffin / and see how far you get.
머핀으로 24시간 동안 노트북을 작동시켜서 / 얼마나 가는지 보라.

뇌는 몸무게의 2퍼센트만을 차지하지만 우리 에너지의 20퍼센트를 사용한다. 갓 태어난 아기의 경우, 그 비율은 자그마치 65퍼센트이다. 그것은 부분적으로 아기들이 항상 잠을 자고 — 뇌의 성장이 그들을 (A) 지치게 하고 — 많은 체지방을 보유하는 이유인데, 필요할 때 보유한 에너지를 사용하려는 것이다. 근육은 약 4분의 1 정도로 훨씬 더 많은 에너지를 사용하지만, 우리에게는 (워낙) 근육이 많다. 실제로, 물질 단위당, 뇌는 다른 기관보다 훨씬 (B) 더 많은 에너지를 사용한다. 그것은 우리 장기 중 뇌가 단연 가장 비용(에너지) 소모가 많다는 것을 의미한다. 하지만 그것은 또한 놀랍도록 (C) 효율적이다. 뇌는 하루에 약 400칼로리의 에너지만 필요로 하는데, 블루베리 머핀에서 얻는 것과 거의 같다. 머핀으로 24시간 동안 노트북을 작동시켜서 얼마나 가는지 보라.

Why? 왜 정답일까?
(A) 두 번째 문장에서 갓 태어난 아기들은 에너지의 65퍼센트를 뇌에서 소비한다고 언급하는 것으로 보아, 아이들의 뇌가 에너지를 '소모시켜서' 아기들이 항상 잠을 자는 것이라는 설명이 뒤따라야 한다. 따라서 (A)에는 exhaust가 들어가야 한다.
(B) 뒤따르는 문장 '~ the brain is the most expensive of our organs.'에서 우리 몸에서 가장 에너지 소모가 많은 기관은 뇌라고 언급하는 것으로 보아, (B)에는 more가 들어가야 한다.
(C) 바로 앞 문장에서 뇌는 우리 몸에서 단연 가장 많은 에너지를 쓰는 기관임을 언급한 후, But으로 흐름이 반전되고 있다. 뒤에 나온 설명을 함께 읽어볼 때, 뇌는 블루베리 머핀 하나에서 얻는 에너지만 있으면 우리 몸을 위해 그 모든 기능을 수행할 만큼 '효율적'이라는 사실을 상기시키는 맥락임을 알 수 있다. 따라서 (C)에는 efficient가 들어가야 한다. 따라서 각 네모 안에서 문맥에 맞는 낱말로 가장 적절한 것은 ③ '(A) 지치게 하다 – (B) 더 많은 – (C) 효율적인'이다.

- **make up** ⓥ ~을 구성하다
- **no less than** 자그마치 ~이다
- **reserve** ⓝ 보유량
- **marvelously** ad 놀랍도록
- **efficient** ⓐ 효율적인
- **newborn** ⓝ 신생아
- **exhaust** ⓥ 지치게 하다, 소진시키다
- **organ** ⓝ (신체의) 기관
- **creative** ⓐ 창의적인

구문 풀이

3행 That's partly why babies sleep all the time — their growing brains exhaust
관계부사　주어　동사1　　삽입절(babies sleep 부연 설명)
them — and have a lot of body fat, to use as an energy reserve when needed.
동사2　　　　~하기 위해　　「접속사 + 분사구문 : ~할 때」

★★★ 등급을 가르는 문제!
31 실험을 비판적으로 바라보기　　　　정답률 39% | 정답 ②

다음 빈칸에 들어갈 말로 가장 적절한 것을 고르시오.
① inventive – 독창적이지
✓② objective – 객관적이지

---

③ untrustworthy – 믿을 수 없는지
④ unreliable – 신뢰성이 없는지
⑤ decisive – 결정적이지

When reading another scientist's findings, / think critically about the experiment.
다른 과학자의 실험 결과물을 읽을 때, / 그 실험에 대해 비판적으로 생각하라.
Ask yourself: / Were observations recorded / during or after the experiment?
당신 자신에게 물어라. / 관찰들이 기록되었나? / 실험 도중에 혹은 후에
Do the conclusions make sense?
결론이 합리적인가?
Can the results be repeated?
그 결과들은 반복될 수 있는가?
Are the sources of information reliable?
정보의 출처는 신뢰할만한가?
You should also ask / if the scientist or group conducting the experiment / was unbiased.
당신은 또한 물어야 한다. / 실험을 수행한 그 과학자나 그룹이 / 한쪽으로 치우치지 않았는지
Being unbiased means / that you have no special interest / in the outcome of the experiment.
한쪽으로 치우치지 않음은 의미한다. / 당신이 특별한 이익을 얻지 않는다는 것을 / 실험의 결과로
For example, if a drug company pays for an experiment / to test how well one of its new products works, / there is a special interest involved:
예를 들면, 만약 한 제약 회사가 실험 비용을 지불한다면, / 그 회사의 새로운 제품 중 하나가 얼마나 잘 작용하는지 시험해보기 위한 / 특별한 이익이 관련된 것이다.
The drug company profits / if the experiment shows that its product is effective.
그 제약 회사는 이익을 본다. / 만약 실험이 그 제품이 효과 있음을 보여준다면
Therefore, the experimenters aren't objective.
따라서, 그 실험자들은 객관적이지 않다.
They might ensure / the conclusion is positive and benefits the drug company.
그들은 보장할지도 모른다. / 결론이 긍정적이며 제약 회사에 이익을 주도록
When assessing results, / think about any biases that may be present!
결과들을 평가할 때, / 있을 수 있는 어떤 치우침에 대해 생각하라!

다른 과학자의 실험 결과물을 읽을 때, 그 실험에 대해 비판적으로 생각하라. 당신 자신에게 물어라. 관찰들이 실험 도중에 혹은 후에 기록되었나? 결론이 합리적인가? 그 결과들은 반복될 수 있는가? 정보의 출처는 신뢰할만한가? 당신은 실험을 수행한 그 과학자나 그룹이 한쪽으로 치우치지 않았는지도 물어야 한다. 한쪽으로 치우치지 않음은 당신이 실험의 결과로 특별한 이익을 얻지 않는다는 것을 의미한다. 예를 들면, 만약 한 제약 회사가 그 회사의 새로운 제품 중 하나가 얼마나 잘 작용하는지 시험해보기 위한 실험 비용을 지불한다면, 특별한 이익이 관련된 것이다. 즉 만약 실험이 그 제품이 효과 있음을 보여준다면, 그 제약 회사는 이익을 본다. 따라서, 그 실험자들은 객관적이지 않다. 그들은 결론이 긍정적이며 제약 회사에 이익을 주도록 보장할지도 모른다. 결과들을 평가할 때, 있을 수 있는 어떤 치우침에 대해 생각하라!

Why? 왜 정답일까?
첫 문장에서 실험을 비판적으로 바라보라고 조언한 후 'You should also ask if the scientist or group conducting the experiment was unbiased.', 'When assessing results, think about any biases that may be present!'에서 특히 실험이 어느 한쪽으로 편향되지 않는지 확인해야 한다는 조언을 보태고 있다. 따라서 빈칸에 들어갈 말로 가장 적절한 것은 실험이 '객관적이지' 않을 수 있으므로 주의가 필요함을 상기시키는 ② '객관적이지'이다.

- **critically** ad 비판적으로
- **make sense** 합리적이다, 의미가 통하다
- **conduct** ⓥ 수행하다
- **interest** ⓝ 이익
- **profit** ⓥ 이득을 보다 ⓝ 이득
- **ensure** ⓥ 보장하다
- **inventive** ⓐ 독창적인
- **untrustworthy** ⓐ 믿을 만하지 않은
- **observation** ⓝ 관찰
- **reliable** ⓐ 신뢰성 있는, 믿을 만한
- **unbiased** ⓐ 편파적이지 않은
- **outcome** ⓝ 결과
- **experimenter** ⓝ 실험자
- **assess** ⓥ 평가하다
- **objective** ⓐ 객관적인
- **decisive** ⓐ 결정적인

구문 풀이

5행 You should also ask if the scientist or group conducting the experiment
접속사(~인지 아닌지)↲　　　주어　　　　　현재분사구
was unbiased.
동사

★★ **문제 해결 꿀~팁** ★★

▶ 많이 틀린 이유는?
빈칸 앞에 aren't라는 부정 표현이 나오므로 빈칸에 주제와 반대되는 말이 들어가야 하는데, ③의 untrustworthy와 ④의 unreliable은 모두 '신뢰성이 없다'는 의미로 그 자체로 주제를 나타낸다.
▶ 문제 해결 방법은?
앞 문장의 내용을 충실히 이해하면 쉽게 답을 고를 수 있다. 앞에서 제약 회사가 연구에 돈을 대는 경우 '특별한 이익이 관련된다'고 언급하는데, 이는 바꾸어 말하면 연구의 '객관성'이 떨어진다는 뜻이다.

★★★ 등급을 가르는 문제!
32 인간이 쉽게 과열되지 않는 이유　　　　정답률 44% | 정답 ②

다음 빈칸에 들어갈 말로 가장 적절한 것을 고르시오.
① hot weather – 더운 날씨
✓② a lack of fur – 털의 부족
③ muscle strength – 근력
④ excessive exercise – 과도한 운동
⑤ a diversity of species – 다양한 종들

Humans are champion long-distance runners.
인간들은 최고의 장거리 달리기 선수들이다.
As soon as a person and a chimp start running / they both get hot.
한 사람과 침팬지가 달리기를 시작하자마자 / 그들은 둘 다 더위를 느낀다.
Chimps quickly overheat; humans do not, / because they are much better at shedding body heat.

침팬지는 빠르게 체온이 오르지만, 인간들은 그렇지 않은데, / 그들은 신체 열을 떨어뜨리는 것을 훨씬 잘하기 때문이다.
According to one leading theory, / ancestral humans lost their hair over successive generations / because less hair meant cooler, more effective long-distance running.
유력한 한 이론에 따르면, / 선조들은 잇따른 세대에 걸쳐서 털을 잃었다. / 적은 털이 더 시원하고 장거리 달리기에 더 효과적인 것을 의미하기 때문에

That ability let our ancestors outmaneuver and outrun prey.
그런 능력은 우리 조상들이 먹잇감을 이기고 앞질러서 달리게 했다.
Try wearing a couple of extra jackets / — or better yet, fur coats — / on a hot humid day / and run a mile.
여분의 재킷 두 개를 입는 것을 시도하고 / 혹은 더 좋게는, 털 코트를 / 덥고 습한 날에 / 1마일을 뛰어라.
Now, take those jackets off and try it again.
이제, 그 재킷을 벗고 다시 시도하라.
You'll see what a difference a lack of fur makes.
당신은 털의 부족이 만드는 차이점이 무엇인지 알 것이다.

인간들은 최고의 장거리 달리기 선수들이다. 한 사람과 침팬지가 달리기를 시작하자마자 그들은 둘 다 더위를 느낀다. 침팬지는 빠르게 체온이 오르지만, 인간들은 그렇지 않은데, 그들은 신체 열을 떨어뜨리는 것을 훨씬 잘하기 때문이다. 유력한 한 이론에 따르면, 털이 더 적으면 더 시원하고 장거리 달리기에 더 효과적인 것을 의미하기 때문에 선조들은 잇따른 세대에 걸쳐서 털을 잃었다. 그런 능력은 우리 조상들이 먹잇감을 이기고 앞질러서 달리게 했다. 덥고 습한 날에 여분의 재킷 두 개 — 혹은 더 좋게는, 털 코트 — 입는 것을 시도하고 1마일을 뛰어라. 이제, 그 재킷을 벗고 다시 시도하라. 당신은 털의 부족이 만드는 차이점이 무엇인지 알 것이다.

Why? 왜 정답일까?

'According to one leading theory, ancestral humans lost their hair over successive generations because less hair meant cooler, more effective long-distance running.'에서 털이 더 적으면 더 시원해지고 장거리 달리기를 더 잘하게 되므로 인간은 연이은 세대에 걸쳐 계속 털이 적어지게 되었다고 설명하고 있다. 따라서 빈칸에 들어갈 말로 가장 적절한 것은 ② '털의 부족'이다.

- overheat ⓥ 과열되다
- ancestral ⓐ 선조의, 조상의
- generation ⓝ 세대
- outrun ⓥ ~보다 빨리 달리다
- lack ⓝ 부족, 결여
- leading ⓐ 선도적인
- successive ⓐ 잇따른, 연속적인
- effective ⓐ 효과적인
- humid ⓐ 습한
- excessive ⓐ 과도한

구문 풀이

2행 Chimps quickly overheat; humans do not, because they are much better at shedding body heat.
주어1 / 동사1 / 주어2 / 동사2(= do not overheat) / 이유 접속사
「be good at + 동명사 : ~을 잘하다」

★★ 문제 해결 꿀~팁 ★★

▶ 많이 틀린 이유는?
인간이 침팬지와 다르게 장시간을 달려도 크게 과열되지 않는 근본적인 이유를 파악해야 한다. ①의 '더운 날씨'는 원인으로 지적되지 않았고, ④의 '과도한 운동' 또한 '장거리 달리기'를 비약시킨 표현에 불과하다.

▶ 문제 해결 방법은?
글 중간에서 조상들이 '털을 잃어왔다'는 내용이 등장한 이유를 생각해 본다. 이는 인간이 다른 동물에 비해 '털이 적기 때문에' 체온 조절에 능하다는 내용을 보충하기 위한 것이다.

★★★ 등급을 가르는 문제!

33 의뢰인의 속마음을 드러내준 의뢰인의 발 | 정답률 40% | 정답 ④

다음 빈칸에 들어갈 말로 가장 적절한 것을 고르시오. [3점]
① a signal of his politeness – 그의 공손함의 표시
② the subject of the conversation – 대화의 주제
③ expressing interest in my words – 내 말에 관심을 나타내고 있는
✓④ the most honest communicators – 가장 정직한 의사 전달자
⑤ stepping excitedly onto the ground – 발을 경쾌하게 내딛고 있는

Recently I was with a client / who had spent almost five hours with me.
최근에 나는 고객과 함께 있었다. / 나와 거의 5시간을 보낸
As we were parting for the evening, / we reflected on what we had covered that day.
저녁을 위해 헤어지면서, / 우리는 그날 다룬 내용을 되새겼다.
Even though our conversation was very collegial, / I noticed / that my client was holding one leg at a right angle to his body, / seemingly wanting to take off on its own.
비록 우리의 대화가 매우 평등했음에도 불구하고, / 나는 알아챘는데, / 나의 고객이 한쪽 다리를 몸과 직각으로 두고 있다는 것을 / 외견상 (한쪽 다리가) 혼자서 떠나고 싶어 하는 것 같았다.
At that point I said, / "You really do have to leave now, don't you?"
그때 나는 말했다. / "지금 정말 가셔야 하죠, 그렇지 않나요?"라고
"Yes," he admitted.
"네."라고 그는 인정했다.
"I am so sorry. / I didn't want to be rude / but I have to call London and I only have five minutes!"
"정말 미안합니다. / 무례하게 굴고 싶지는 않았지만 / 전 런던에 전화해야 하는데 시간이 5분밖에 없어요!"
Here was a case / where my client's language and most of his body / revealed nothing but positive feelings.
이것은 상황이었다. / 내 의뢰인의 언어와 그의 몸의 대부분이 / 긍정적인 감정만을 드러냈
His feet, however, were the most honest communicators, / and they clearly told me / that as much as he wanted to stay, duty was calling.
그러나 그의 발은 가장 정직한 의사 전달자였고 / 그것들은 내게 분명히 나타냈다 / 그가 남아있고 싶어 하지만 일이 그를 부르고 있다는 것

최근에 나는 나와 거의 5시간을 보낸 고객과 함께 있었다. 저녁을 위해 헤어지면서, 우리는 그날 다룬 내용을 되새겼다. 비록 우리의 대화가 매우 평등했음에도 불구하고, 나는 나의 고객이 한쪽 다리를 몸과 직각으로 두고 있다는 것을 알아챘는데, 외견상 (한쪽 다리가) 혼자서

떠나고 싶어 하는 것 같았다. 그때 나는 "지금 정말 가셔야 하죠, 그렇지 않나요?"라고 말했다. "네."라고 그는 인정했다. "정말 미안합니다. 무례하게 굴고 싶지는 않았지만 런던에 전화해야 하는데 시간이 5분밖에 없어요!" 여기서 내 의뢰인의 언어와 그의 몸의 대부분은 긍정적인 감정만을 드러내고 있었다. 그러나 그의 발은 가장 정직한 의사 전달자였고 그것들은 그가 남아있고 싶어 하지만 해야 할 일이 있다는 것을 분명히 나타냈다.

Why? 왜 정답일까?

'~ I noticed that my client was holding one leg at a right angle to his body, seemingly wanting to take off on its own.'에서 필자는 의뢰인이 한쪽 발을 몸과 직각으로 위치하게 빼둔 것을 보고 의뢰인이 빨리 가야 한다고 생각하고 있음을 눈치챘다고 하므로, 빈칸에 들어갈 말로 가장 적절한 것은 ④ '가장 정직한 의사 전달자'이다.

- reflect on ⓥ ~을 되새기다, 반추하다
- right angle ⓝ 직각
- rude ⓐ 무례한
- communicator ⓝ 의사 전달자
- cover ⓥ (기사 등에서) 다루다
- take off ⓥ 떠나다
- politeness ⓝ 공손함
- excitedly ⓐⓓ 신나게, 들떠서

구문 풀이

10행 His feet, however, were the most honest communicators, and they clearly told me that as much as he wanted to stay, duty was calling.
주어1 / 동사1 / 주어2 / 동사2 / 「(문두의) as + 원급 + as : ~하기는 하지만」 / 접속사(~것) / 주어 / 동사

★★ 문제 해결 꿀~팁 ★★

▶ 많이 틀린 이유는?
일화가 나오면 부분적인 표현에 집중하기보다 이야기의 전체적인 흐름을 파악해야 한다. ①은 본문의 'I didn't want to be rude'만, ⑤는 '~ seemingly wanting to take off on its own.'만 보았을 때 각각 고르기 쉬운 오답이다.

▶ 문제 해결 방법은?
이 일화의 핵심은 필자의 고객이 말이나 몸 자세로 대체로 긍정적인 신호를 나타내고 있었음에도 불구하고 유일하게 '몸과 직각을 이루며 떠나고 싶어 하는 것처럼 보였던' 그의 발이 그의 진심을 대변해주고 있었다는 것이다. 이렇듯 이야기 흐름의 큰 줄기를 파악한 후 이를 토대로 추론할 수 있는 논리적인 결론을 선택지에서 찾도록 한다.

★★★ 등급을 가르는 문제!

34 친숙함이 빚는 오해 | 정답률 41% | 정답 ②

다음 빈칸에 들어갈 말로 가장 적절한 것을 고르시오. [3점]
① you couldn't recall the parts you had highlighted
당신은 강조 표시한 부분을 기억하지 못했다
✓② it wasn't really the best answer to the question
사실 그 질문에 대한 가장 좋은 해답은 아니었다
③ that familiarity was based on your understanding
익숙함은 이해에 기초를 둔 것이었다
④ repetition enabled you to pick the correct answer
반복은 당신이 정답을 고를 수 있게 해주었다
⑤ it indicated that familiarity was naturally built up
그것은 친숙함이 자연스럽게 쌓이는 것임을 나타냈다

One of the main reasons / that students may think they know the material, / even when they don't, / is that they mistake familiarity for understanding.
주된 이유 중 하나는 / 학생들이 자료의 내용을 알고 있다고 생각할 수도 있는 / 그들이 알지 못할 때조차도, / 친숙함을 이해로 착각하기 때문이다.
Here is how it works:
그것이 작동하는 방식이 여기 있다.
You read the chapter once, / perhaps highlighting as you go.
당신은 그 장을 한 번 읽는다. / 읽을 때 아마도 강조 표시를 하면서
Then later, you read the chapter again, / perhaps focusing on the highlighted material.
그러고 나서 나중에, 당신은 그 장을 다시 읽는다. / 아마도 강조 표시된 자료에 집중하면서
As you read it over, / the material is familiar / because you remember it from before, / and this familiarity might lead you to think, / "Okay, I know that."
당신은 그것을 거듭 읽어서, / 자료가 친숙하고, / 이전에 읽은 것으로부터 그것을 기억하기 때문에 / 이러한 친숙함은 당신이 생각하게 할지도 모른다 / "좋아, 그것을 알겠어."라고
The problem is / that this feeling of familiarity / is not necessarily equivalent to knowing the material / and may be of no help / when you have to come up with an answer on the exam.
문제는 / 이런 친숙한 느낌이 / 반드시 자료를 아는 것과 같은 것은 아니며 / 아무런 도움이 되지 않을 수도 있다는 점이다. / 시험에서 답을 생각해내야 할 때
In fact, familiarity can often lead to errors on multiple-choice exams / because you might pick a choice that looks familiar, / only to find later / that it was something you had read, / but it wasn't really the best answer to the question.
사실, 친숙함은 종종 선다형 시험에서 오류를 일으킬 수 있는데, / 당신이 익숙해 보이는 선택지를 선택할 수 있기 때문에 / 결국 나중에 알게 되는 것은 / 그것은 당신이 읽었던 것인데, / 하지만 사실 그 질문에 대한 가장 좋은 해답은 아니었다는 것이다.

자료의 내용을 알지 못할 때조차도 학생들이 알고 있다고 생각할 수도 있는 주된 이유 중 하나는 친숙함을 이해로 착각하기 때문이다. 그것이 작동하는 방식이 여기 있다. 당신은 읽을 때 아마도 강조 표시를 하면서, 그 장을 한 번 읽는다. 그러고 나서 나중에, 아마도 강조 표시된 자료에 집중하면서, 그 장을 다시 읽는다. 그것을 거듭 읽어서, 이전에 읽은 것으로부터 그것을 기억하기 때문에 자료가 친숙하고, 이러한 친숙함으로 인해 "좋아, 그것을 알겠어."라고 생각하게 될지도 모른다. 문제는 이런 친숙한 느낌이 반드시 자료를 아는 것과 같은 것은 아니며 시험에서 답을 생각해내야 할 때 아무런 도움이 되지 않을 수도 있다는 점이다. 사실, 당신이 익숙해 보이는 선택지를 선택할 수 있기 때문에 친숙함은 종종 선다형 시험에서 오류를 일으킬 수 있는데, 결국 나중에 알게 되는 것은 그 선택지가 당신이 읽었던 것이지만 사실 그 질문에 대한 가장 좋은 해답은 아니었다는 것이다.

Why? 왜 정답일까?

첫 문장인 'One of the main reasons that students may think they know the material, even when they don't, is that they mistake familiarity for understanding.'에서 학생들은 종종 어떤 것이 친숙할 때 그것을 알고 있다고 착각한다는 주제를 제시한다. 이어서 빈칸 문장은 학생

[문제편 p.095]

들이 시험에서 익숙해 보이는 선택지를 답으로 골라서 오류를 빚는다고 하므로, 익숙한 것이 '답은 아니기' 때문이라는 설명이 빈칸에 들어가야 할 것이다. 따라서 답으로 가장 적절한 것은 ② '사실 그 질문에 대한 가장 좋은 해답은 아니었다'이다.

- **familiarity** ⓝ 친숙함
- **not necessarily** 반드시 ~한 것은 아니다
- **multiple-choice** ⓐ 선다형의, (시험 형태가) 객관식의
- **recall** ⓥ 기억하다, 회상하다
- **highlight** ⓥ 강조 표시를 하다
- **come up with** ⓥ ~을 떠올리다

구문 풀이

11행 In fact, familiarity can often lead to errors on multiple-choice exams
~로 이어지다
because you might pick a choice [that looks familiar], only to find later that it was
이유 접속사 / 선행사 / 주격 관·대 2형식 동사 / 부사적 용법(결국 ~하다) 접속사(~것)
something [you had read], but it wasn't really the best answer to the question.
형용사 보어

★★ 문제 해결 꿀~팁 ★★

▶ 많이 틀린 이유는?
첫 문장에서 사람들은 익숙한 것을 아는 것으로 착각한다는 핵심 내용을 제시하는데, ③은 '익숙함이 이해에 기초를 둔다'는 뜻으로 주제와 정반대되는 의미를 나타낸다.

▶ 문제 해결 방법은?
'어떤 내용이 익숙하다고 해서 그 내용을 이해하고 있는 것은 아니'라는 것이 글의 주된 내용임을 고려할 때, 시험에서 익숙해보이는 선택지를 골랐어도 그것이 '정답이 아닐 수 있다'는 결론이 빈칸에 들어가야 한다.

---

35 이모티콘의 유용성
정답률 58% | 정답 ④

다음 글에서 전체 흐름과 관계 없는 문장은?

Given the widespread use of emoticons in electronic communication, / an important question is / whether they help Internet users / to understand emotions in online communication.
전자 통신에서 이모티콘이 널리 사용되고 있다는 점을 고려할 때, / 중요한 문제는 / 그것들이 인터넷 사용자들에게 도움을 주는가의 여부이다. / 온라인상의 의사소통에서 감정을 이해하는 데

① Emoticons, particularly character-based ones, / are much more ambiguous / relative to face-to-face cues / and may end up being interpreted very differently / by different users.
이모티콘, 특히 문자를 기반으로 한 것들은, / 훨씬 더 모호하며 / 면대면을 통한 단서에 비해 / 결국 매우 다르게 해석될 수 있다. / 다른 사용자들에 의해

② Nonetheless, research indicates / that they are useful tools in online text-based communication.
그럼에도 불구하고, 연구는 보여준다. / 그것들이 온라인상의 텍스트 기반 의사소통에서 유용한 도구라는 것을

③ One study of 137 instant messaging users revealed / that emoticons allowed users / to correctly understand the level and direction of emotion, attitude, and attention expression / and that emoticons were a definite advantage in non-verbal communication.
137명의 즉석 메시지 사용자들을 대상으로 한 연구는 밝혀냈다. / 이모티콘이 사용자들로 하여금 허락해주고 / 감정, 태도, 관심 표현의 정도와 방향을 정확하게 이해할 수 있게 / 이모티콘이 비언어적 의사소통에서 확실한 장점이라는 것을

☑ In fact, / there have been few studies / on the relationships between verbal and nonverbal communication.
사실, / 연구는 거의 없었다. / 언어적 의사소통과 비언어적 의사소통 간의 관계에 관한

⑤ Similarly, another study showed / that emoticons were useful / in strengthening the intensity of a verbal message, / as well as in the expression of sarcasm.
마찬가지로, 또 다른 연구는 보여주었다. / 이모티콘이 유용하다는 것을 / 언어적 메시지의 강도를 강화하는 데 / 풍자의 표현에서 뿐만 아니라

전자 통신에서 이모티콘이 널리 사용되고 있다는 점을 고려할 때, 중요한 문제는 인터넷 사용자들이 온라인상의 의사소통에서 감정을 이해하는 데 그것들이 도움을 주는가의 여부이다. ① 이모티콘, 특히 문자를 기반으로 한 것들은, 면대면을 통한 단서에 비해 훨씬 더 모호하며 결국 다른 사용자들에 의해 매우 다르게 해석될 수 있다. ② 그럼에도 불구하고, 연구는 그것들이 온라인상의 텍스트 기반 의사소통에서 유용한 도구라는 것을 보여준다. ③ 137명의 즉석 메시지 사용자들을 대상으로 한 연구는 이모티콘이 사용자들로 하여금 감정, 태도, 관심 표현의 정도와 방향을 정확하게 이해할 수 있게 해주고 이모티콘이 비언어적 의사소통에서 확실한 장점이라는 것을 밝혀냈다. ④ 사실, 언어적 의사소통과 비언어적 의사소통 간의 관계에 관한 연구는 거의 없었다. ⑤ 마찬가지로, 또 다른 연구는 이모티콘이 풍자의 표현에서 뿐만 아니라, 언어적 메시지의 강도를 강화하는 데 유용하다는 것을 보여주었다.

Why? 왜 정답일까?

이모티콘이 텍스트를 기반으로 하는 인터넷상의 의사소통에서 유용하다는 내용을 다룬 글로, ④는 언어적 의사소통과 비언어적 의사소통의 관계만을 언급하여 흐름에서 벗어난다. 따라서 무관한 문장은 ④이다.

- **widespread** ⓐ 널리 퍼진
- **relative to** ~에 비하여
- **interpret** ⓥ 해석하다
- **strengthen** ⓥ 강화하다
- **electronic** ⓐ 전자상의
- **face-to-face** ⓐ 면대면의
- **definite** ⓐ 확실한
- **intensity** ⓝ 강도

구문 풀이

1행 Given the widespread use of emoticons in electronic communication,
~을 고려할 때(= Considering)
an important question is whether they help Internet users to understand emotions
주어 / 동사 / 접속사(~인지 아닌지) / 목적어 / 목적 보어
in online communication.
준사역동사

---

36 더 나은 것을 위한 지속된 추구
정답률 50% | 정답 ①

주어진 글 다음에 이어질 글의 순서로 가장 적절한 것을 고르시오.

☑ (A) – (C) – (B)
② (B) – (A) – (C)
③ (B) – (C) – (A)
④ (C) – (A) – (B)
⑤ (C) – (B) – (A)

Students work to get good grades / even when they have no interest in their studies.
학생들은 좋은 성적을 얻기 위해 공부한다. / 그들이 공부에 관심이 없을 때에도

People seek job advancement / even when they are happy with the jobs / they already have.
사람들은 승진을 추구한다. / 심지어 그들이 직업에 만족할 때에도 / 그들이 이미 가지고 있는

(A) It's like being in a crowded football stadium, / watching the crucial play.
그것은 마치 사람들로 붐비는 축구 경기장에 있는 것과 같다. / 중요한 경기를 관람하면서

A spectator several rows in front / stands up to get a better view, / and a chain reaction follows.
몇 줄 앞에 있는 한 관중이 / 더 잘 보기 위해 일어서고, / 뒤이어 연쇄 반응이 일어난다.

(C) Soon everyone is standing, / just to be able to see as well as before.
곧 모든 사람들이 일어서게 된다. / 단지 이전처럼 잘 보기 위해

Everyone is on their feet rather than sitting, / but no one's position has improved.
모두가 앉기보다는 일어서지만, / 그 누구의 위치도 나아지지 않았다.

(B) And if someone refuses to stand, / he might just as well not be at the game at all.
그리고 만약 누군가가 일어서기를 거부한다면, / 그는 경기에 있지 않는 편이 나을 것이다.

When people pursue goods that are positional, / they can't help being in the rat race.
사람들이 위치상의 이익을 추구할 때, / 그들은 치열하고 무의미한 경쟁을 하지 않을 수 없다.

To choose not to run is to lose.
뛰지 않기로 선택하는 것은 지는 것이다.

학생들은 심지어 공부에 관심이 없을 때에도 좋은 성적을 얻기 위해 공부한다. 사람들은 심지어 이미 가지고 있는 직업에 만족할 때에도 승진을 추구한다.

(A) 그것은 마치 사람들로 붐비는 축구 경기장에서 중요한 경기를 관람하는 것과 같다. 몇 줄 앞에 있는 한 관중이 더 잘 보기 위해 일어서고, 뒤이어 연쇄 반응이 일어난다.

(C) 단지 이전처럼 잘 보기 위해 곧 모든 사람들이 일어서게 된다. 모두가 앉기보다는 일어서지만, 그 누구의 위치도 나아지지 않았다.

(B) 그리고 만약 누군가가 일어서기를 거부한다면, 그는 경기에 있지 않는 편이 나을 것이다. 사람들이 위치상의 이익을 추구할 때, 그들은 치열하고 무의미한 경쟁을 하지 않을 수 없다. 뛰지 않기로 선택하는 것은 지는 것이다.

Why? 왜 정답일까?

주어진 글에서 학생들과 직장인들의 예를 들어 사람들은 계속 더 나은 것을 추구한다는 점을 언급한 데 이어, (A)는 축구 경기장의 비유를 소개하고 있다. (A)의 마지막 부분은 한 사람이 더 잘 보려고 일어서면 연쇄 반응이 일어난다는 내용으로 끝나고, (C)는 결국 모든 사람이 일어서게 된다고 설명한다. (B)는 일어서기를 거부하는 누군가가 있다면 그 사람은 경기장에 없는 편이 나을 것임을 언급하며 비유를 마무리한다. 따라서 글의 순서로 가장 적절한 것은 ① '(A) – (C) – (B)'이다.

- **job advancement** ⓝ 승진
- **crucial** ⓐ 중요한
- **improve** ⓥ 나아지다, 개선되다
- **crowded** ⓐ 붐비는
- **positional** ⓐ 위치상의

구문 풀이

7행 And if someone refuses to stand, he might just as well not be at the
조건 접속사 / 「refuse + to부정사 : ~하기를 거부하다」 / 「might as well not + 동사원형 : ~하지 않는 것이 낫다」
game at all.

---

37 인간이 배가 불러도 음식을 계속 먹는 이유
정답률 50% | 정답 ⑤

주어진 글 다음에 이어질 글의 순서로 가장 적절한 것을 고르시오.

① (A) – (C) – (B)
② (B) – (A) – (C)
③ (B) – (C) – (A)
④ (C) – (A) – (B)
☑ (C) – (B) – (A)

When we compare human and animal desire / we find many extraordinary differences.
우리가 인간과 동물의 욕망을 비교할 때 / 우리는 많은 특별한 차이점을 발견한다.

Animals tend to eat with their stomachs, / and humans with their brains.
동물은 위장으로 먹는 경향이 있고, / 인간은 뇌로 먹는 경향이 있다.

(C) When animals' stomachs are full, they stop eating, / but humans are never sure when to stop.
동물은 배가 부르면 먹는 것을 멈추지만, / 인간은 언제 멈춰야 할지 결코 확신하지 못한다.

When they have eaten as much as their bellies can take, / they still feel empty, / they still feel an urge for further gratification.
인간은 배에 담을 수 있는 만큼 먹었을 때, / 그들은 여전히 허전함을 느끼고 / 여전히 추가적인 만족감에 대한 충동을 느낀다.

(B) This is largely due to anxiety, / to the knowledge that a constant supply of food is uncertain.
이것은 주로 불안감 때문이다. / 지속적인 식량 공급이 불확실하다는 인식에 따른

Therefore, they eat as much as possible / while they can.
그러므로 그들은 가능한 한 많이 먹는다. / 그들이 먹을 수 있을 때

(A) It is due, also, to the knowledge / that, in an insecure world, pleasure is uncertain.
또한, 그것은 인식 때문이다. / 불안정한 세상에서 즐거움이 불확실하다는

Therefore, the immediate pleasure of eating / must be exploited to the full, / even though it does violence to the digestion.
따라서 즉각적인 먹는 즐거움은 / 충분히 이용되어야 한다. / 그것이 소화에 무리가 되더라도

인간과 동물의 욕망을 비교할 때 우리는 많은 특별한 차이점을 발견한다. 동물은 위장으로, 인간은 뇌로 먹는 경향이 있다.

(C) 동물은 배가 부르면 먹는 것을 멈추지만, 인간은 언제 멈춰야 할지 결코 확신하지 못한다. 인간은 배에 담을 수 있는 만큼 먹었을 때, 그들은 여전히 허전함을 느끼고 여전히 추가적인 만족감에 대한 충동을 느낀다.

(B) 이것은 주로 지속적인 식량 공급이 불확실하다는 인식에 따른 불안감 때문이다. 그러므로 그들은 먹을 수 있을 때 가능한 한 많이 먹는다.

(A) 또한, 그것은 불안정한 세상에서 즐거움이 불확실하다는 인식 때문이다. 따라서 즉각적인 먹는 즐거움을 소화에 무리가 되더라도 충분히 이용하여야 한다.

Why? 왜 정답일까?

동물과 인간의 욕망에는 차이가 있음을 언급하며 식욕의 예를 들기 시작하는 주어진 글 뒤에는, 동물의 경우 배가 부르면 먹는 것을 멈추지만 인간은 그렇지 않다고 설명하는 (C), 인간이 배가 불러도 계속 먹

는 이유를 설명하는 (B), 이유를 추가하는 (A)가 차례로 이어져야 한다. 따라서 글의 순서로 가장 적절한 것은 ⑤ '(C) – (B) – (A)'이다.

- extraordinary ⓐ 특별한
- uncertain ⓐ 불확실한
- exploit ⓥ 이용하다
- digestion ⓝ 소화
- constant ⓐ 지속적인
- insecure ⓐ 불안정한
- immediate ⓐ 즉각적인
- do violence ⓥ ~을 해치다
- anxiety ⓝ 불안
- urge ⓝ 충동

구문 풀이

4행 It is due, also, to the knowledge that, in an insecure world, pleasure is
「due to+명사: ~ 때문에」 　동격 접속사　　　　　　　　주어　동사
uncertain.
보어

---

38 우주 연구가 무인선에 의해 이루어지는 이유　　정답률 45% | 정답 ④

글의 흐름으로 보아, 주어진 문장이 들어가기에 가장 적절한 곳을 고르시오.

Currently, we cannot send humans to other planets.
현재, 우리는 인간을 다른 행성으로 보낼 수 없다.
One obstacle is / that such a trip would take years.
한 가지 장애물은 / 그러한 여행이 수 년이 걸릴 것이라는 점이다.
① A spacecraft would need to carry enough air, water, and other supplies / needed for survival on the long journey.
우주선은 충분한 공기, 물, 그리고 다른 물자를 운반할 필요가 있을 것이다. / 긴 여행 중 생존에 필요한
② Another obstacle is the harsh conditions on other planets, / such as extreme heat and cold.
또 다른 장애물은 다른 행성들의 혹독한 기상 조건이다. / 극심한 열과 추위 같은
③ Some planets do not even have surfaces to land on.
어떤 행성들은 착륙할 표면조차 가지고 있지 않다.
✓ Because of these obstacles, / most research missions in space / are accomplished through the use of spacecraft / without crews aboard.
이러한 장애물들 때문에, / 우주에서의 대부분의 연구 임무는 / 우주선을 사용해서 이루어진다. / 승무원이 탑승하지 않은
These explorations pose no risk to human life / and are less expensive than ones involving astronauts.
이런 탐험들은 인간의 생명에 아무런 위험도 주지 않으며 / 우주 비행사들을 포함하는 탐험보다 비용이 덜 든다.
⑤ The spacecraft carry instruments / that test the compositions and characteristics of planets.
이 우주선은 기구들을 운반한다. / 행성의 구성 성분과 특성을 실험하는

현재, 우리는 인간을 다른 행성으로 보낼 수 없다. 한 가지 장애물은 그러한 여행이 수 년이 걸릴 것이라는 점이다. ① 우주선은 긴 여행 중 생존에 필요한 충분한 공기, 물, 그리고 다른 물자를 운반할 필요가 있을 것이다. ② 또 다른 장애물은 극심한 열과 추위 같은, 다른 행성들의 혹독한 기상 조건이다. ③ 어떤 행성들은 착륙할 표면조차 가지고 있지 않다. ④ 이러한 장애물들 때문에, 우주에서의 대부분의 연구 임무는 승무원이 탑승하지 않은 우주선을 사용해서 이루어진다. 이런 탐험들은 인간의 생명에 아무런 위험도 주지 않으며 우주 비행사들을 포함하는 탐험보다 비용이 덜 든다. ⑤ 이 우주선은 행성의 구성 성분과 특성을 실험하는 기구들을 운반한다.

Why? 왜 정답일까?

우주 탐사가 주로 무인 우주선에 의해 이루어지는 이유를 설명한 글이다. ④ 앞에서는 우주 여행이 너무 오래 걸리고, 다른 행성이 착륙이나 생존에 적합한 조건을 갖추고 있는 것도 아니라는 이유를 제시한다. 주어진 문장은 앞에 열거된 이유를 these obstacles로 나타내며 '그리하여' 우주 연구에 무인 우주선이 동원된다는 점을 언급한다. ④ 뒤의 문장은 무인 우주선에 의한 탐사를 These explorations로 지칭한다. 따라서 주어진 문장이 들어가기에 가장 적절한 곳은 ④이다.

- obstacle ⓝ 장애물
- crew ⓝ 승무원
- harsh ⓐ 혹독한
- land on ⓥ ~에 착륙하다
- astronaut ⓝ 우주 비행사
- accomplish ⓥ 이루다, 성취하다
- supplies ⓝ 물자, 보급품
- extreme ⓐ 극심한
- pose a risk ⓥ 위험을 끼치다
- characteristic ⓝ 특성

구문 풀이

10행 These explorations pose no risk to human life and are less expensive
동사1　　　　　　　　　　　　동사2 「less+원급: 덜 ~한」
than ones involving astronauts.
= explorations

---

39 문제 해결로서의 언어 학습　　정답률 51% | 정답 ③

글의 흐름으로 보아, 주어진 문장이 들어가기에 가장 적절한 곳을 고르시오. [3점]

Our brains are constantly solving problems.
우리의 뇌는 끊임없이 문제를 해결하고 있다.
① Every time we learn, or remember, or make sense of something, / we solve a problem.
우리가 무언가를 배우거나, 기억하거나, 이해할 때마다, / 우리는 문제를 해결한다.
② Some psychologists / have characterized all infant language-learning as problem-solving, / extending to children / such scientific procedures as "learning by experiment," or "hypothesis-testing."
일부 심리학자들은 / 모든 유아 언어 학습을 문제 해결이라고 특정지었고, / 이를 어린이에게 확장하여 / 그러한 과학적 절차들을 '실험을 통한 학습' 혹은 '가설 검증'으로 보았다.
✓ Grown-ups rarely explain the meaning of new words to children, / let alone how grammatical rules work.
어른들은 아이들에게 새로운 단어의 의미를 거의 설명하지 않는다. / 문법적인 규칙이 어떻게 작용하는지는 말할 것도 없고
Instead they use the words or the rules in conversation / and leave it to children / to figure out what is going on.
대신에 그들은 대화에서 단어나 규칙을 사용하고, / 아이들에게 맡긴다. / 무슨 일이 일어나고 있는지 알아내는 일을
④ In order to learn language, / an infant must make sense of the contexts / in which language occurs; / problems must be solved.

언어를 배우기 위해서는, / 유아는 맥락을 파악해야 하는데, / 언어를 사용하는 / 즉 문제는 반드시 해결돼야 한다는 것이다.
⑤ We have all been solving problems of this kind since childhood, / usually without awareness of what we are doing.
우리 모두는 어린 시절부터 이런 종류의 문제들을 해결해왔다. / 우리가 무엇을 하고 있는지 대체로 인식하지 못한 채

우리의 뇌는 끊임없이 문제를 해결하고 있다. ① 우리가 무언가를 배우거나, 기억하거나, 이해할 때마다, 우리는 문제를 해결한다. ② 일부 심리학자들은 모든 유아 언어 학습을 문제 해결이라고 특정지었고, 이를 어린이에게 확장하여 그러한 과학적 절차들을 '실험을 통한 학습' 혹은 '가설 검증'으로 보았다. ③ 어른들은 아이들에게 문법적인 규칙이 어떻게 작용하는지 말할 것도 없고, 새로운 단어의 의미를 거의 설명하지 않는다. 대신에 그들은 대화에서 단어나 규칙을 사용하고, 무슨 상황인지 알아내는 일을 아이들에게 맡긴다. ④ 언어를 배우기 위해서는, 유아는 언어를 사용하는 맥락을 파악해야 하는데, 즉 문제는 반드시 해결돼야 한다는 것이다. ⑤ 우리 모두는 우리가 무엇을 하고 있는지 인식하지 못한 채 이 어린 시절부터 이런 종류의 문제들을 해결해왔다.

Why? 왜 정답일까?

③ 앞에서 일부 심리학자들은 유아 언어 학습을 문제 해결로 규정하였다고 언급한 후, ③ 뒤의 문장에 they가 나오는데, 이 they는 앞에 이어서 Some psychologists를 가리키지 않는다. 즉 심리학자들이 언어 학습을 문제 해결의 과정으로 보았다는 내용 뒤로, 실제로 어른들이 언어를 배우는 아이들에게 문법 규칙이나 단어에 관해 설명하는 경우는 드물다는 주어진 문장이 연결된 후, '대신에' 이 어른들은 아이들이 스스로 파악하고 해결할 수 있도록 내버려둔다는 설명이 이어지는 맥락인 것이다. 따라서 주어진 문장이 들어가기에 가장 적절한 곳은 ③이다.

- let alone ~은 말할 것도 없고, ~은 고사하고
- constantly ⓐⓓ 끊임없이
- characterize ⓥ ~의 특징을 기술하다
- extend ⓥ 확장시키다
- hypothesis ⓝ 가설
- grammatical ⓐ 문법적인
- make sense of ⓥ ~을 이해하다
- infant ⓝ 유아
- procedure ⓝ 절차
- awareness ⓝ 인식, 앎

구문 풀이

10행 In order to learn language, an infant must make sense of the contexts
목적(~하기 위해) 　　　　　　　　　　　　　　　선행사
[in which language occurs]; problems must be solved.
= where　　　　　　　　　　조동사 수동태

---

40 유능한 코치와 그렇지 않은 코치의 차이　　정답률 52% | 정답 ③

다음 글의 내용을 한 문장으로 요약하고자 한다. 빈칸 (A), (B)에 들어갈 말로 가장 적절한 것은? [3점]

	(A)		(B)
①	scores 점수	……	complete 완수하다
②	scores 점수	……	remember 기억하다
✓③	mistakes 실수	……	picture 상상하다
④	mistakes 실수	……	ignore 무시하다
⑤	strengths 강점	……	achieve 성취하다

Have you noticed / that some coaches get the most out of their athletes / while others don't?
당신은 알아챘는가? / 어떤 코치들은 선수들에게서 최상의 결과를 이끌어 내는 것을 / 다른 코치들은 그렇지 않은 반면
A poor coach will tell you what you did wrong / and then tell you not to do it again:
서투른 코치는 당신이 무엇을 잘못했는지 알려주고 나서 / 다시는 그러지 말라고 말할 것이다.
"Don't drop the ball!"
"공을 떨어뜨리지 마라!"
What happens next?
그다음 무슨 일이 일어날까?
The images you see in your head / are images of you dropping the ball!
당신이 머릿속에서 보게 되는 이미지는 / 당신이 공을 떨어뜨리는 이미지이다!
Naturally, your mind recreates what it just "saw" / based on what it's been told.
당연히, 당신의 마음은 방금 '본' 것을 재현한다. / 그것이 들은 것을 바탕으로
Not surprisingly, / you walk on the court and drop the ball.
놀랄 것도 없이, / 당신은 코트에 걸어가서 공을 떨어뜨린다.
What does the good coach do?
좋은 코치는 무엇을 하는가?
He or she points out what could be improved, / but will then tell you how you could or should perform: / "I know you'll catch the ball perfectly this time."
그 사람은 개선될 수 있는 것을 지적하지만, / 그 후에 어떻게 할 수 있는지 또는 어떻게 해야 하는지에 대해 말할 것이다. / "이번에는 네가 공을 완벽하게 잡을 거라는 걸 알아."
Sure enough, / the next image in your mind / is you *catching* the ball and *scoring* a goal.
아니나 다를까, / 다음으로 당신의 마음속에 떠오르는 이미지는 / 당신이 공을 잡고 골을 넣는 것이다.
Once again, your mind makes your last thoughts part of reality / — but this time, that "reality" is positive, not negative.
다시 한 번, 당신의 마음은 당신의 마지막 생각을 현실의 일부로 만들지만, / 이번에는, 그 '현실'이 부정적이지 않고, 긍정적이다.
➡ Unlike ineffective coaches, / who focus on players' (A) mistakes, / effective coaches help players improve / by encouraging them to (B) picture successful plays.
유능하지 않은 코치와 달리, / 선수의 실수에 초점을 맞추는 / 유능한 코치는 선수들이 향상되도록 돕는다. / 그들이 성공적인 경기를 상상하도록 격려함으로써

어떤 코치들은 선수들에게서 최상의 결과를 이끌어 내는 반면 다른 코치들은 그렇지 않다는 것을 알아챘는가? 서투른 코치는 당신이 무엇을 잘못했는지 알려주고 나서 다시는 그러지 말라고 말할 것이다. "공을 떨어뜨리지 마라!" 그다음 무슨 일이 일어날까? 당신이 머릿속에서 보게 되는 이미지는 당신이 공을 떨어뜨리는 이미지이다! 당연히, 당신의 마음은 그것이 들은 것을 바탕으로 방금 '본' 것을 재현한다. 놀랄 것도 없이, 당신은 코트에 걸어가서 공을 떨어뜨린다. 좋은 코치는 무엇을 하는가? 그 사람은 개선될 수 있는 것을 지적하지만, 그 후에 어떻게 할 수 있는지 또는 어떻게 해야 하는지에 대해 말할 것이다. "이번에는 네가 공을 완벽하게 잡을 거라는 걸 알아." 아나나 다를까, 다음으로 당신의 마음속에 떠오르는 이미지는 당신이 공을 잡고 골을 넣는 것이다. 다시 한 번, 당신의 마음은 당신의 마지막 생각을 현실의 일부로 만들지만, 이번에는, 그 '현실'이 부정적이지 않고, 긍정적이다.

➡ 선수의 (A) 실수에 초점을 맞추는 유능하지 않은 코치와 달리, 유능한 코치는 선수들이 성공적인 경기를 (B) 상상하도록 격려함으로써 그들이 향상되도록 돕는다.

유능한 코치와 서투른 코치의 특성을 대조한 글이다. 본문에 따르면 서투른 코치는 선수가 무엇을 잘못했는가에 집중하지만(A poor coach will tell you what you did wrong and then tell you not to do it again: ~) 유능한 코치는 선수가 보완해야 할 점을 지적하면서도 선수로 하여금 성공적인 모습을 상상하게 만들어 실제로 선수의 경기력이 향상되도록 돕는다(He or she ~ will then tell you how you could or should perform: ~)고 한다. 이를 근거로 할 때, 요약문의 빈칸 (A), (B)에 들어갈 말로 가장 적절한 것은 ③ '(A) mistakes(실수), (B) picture(상상하다)'이다.

● get the most out of ⓥ ~을 최대한으로 활용하다
● recreate ⓥ 재현하다
● unlike prep ~와는 달리
● encourage ⓥ 격려하다
● perfectly ad 완벽하게
● ineffective ⓐ 무능한, 효과가 없는

4행 The images [you see in your head] are images of you dropping the ball!
　　　　주어　　　　　　　　　　동사　보어 전치사 　동명사 →의미상 주어

41-42 식단 개선을 위한 조언

Marketers have known for decades / that you buy what you see first.
마케팅 담당자들은 수십 년 동안 알고 있었다. / 당신이 먼저 보는 것을 산다는 것을

You are far more likely to purchase items / placed at eye level in the grocery store, / for example, / than items on the bottom shelf.
당신은 상품을 구매할 가능성이 훨씬 더 높다. / 식료품점의 눈높이에 놓여져 있는 / 예를 들어, / 아래쪽 선반에 있는 상품보다

There is an entire body of research about the way / "product placement" in stores influences your buying behavior.
방식에 대한 매우 많은 연구가 있다. / 매장에서의 '제품 배치'가 당신의 구매 행동에 영향을 미치는

This gives you a chance / to use product placement to your advantage.
이것은 당신에게 기회를 준다. / 유리하게 제품 배치를 사용할

Healthy items like produce / are often the (a) least visible foods at home.
농산물과 같은 건강한 식품은 / 종종 집에서 가장 덜 눈에 띄는 음식이다.

「You won't think to eat what you don't see.」 42번의 근거
당신은 보이지 않는 것을 먹으려고 생각하지 않을 것이다.

This may be part of the reason / why 85 percent of Americans do not eat enough fruits and vegetables.
이것이 이유 중 일부일지도 모른다. / 85%의 미국인이 과일과 채소를 충분히 먹지 않는

If produce is (b) hidden in a drawer / at the bottom of your refrigerator, / these good foods are out of sight and mind.
만약 농산물이 서랍에 숨겨져 있으면, / 냉장고 아래쪽에 있는 / 이 좋은 음식들은 시야와 마음에서 벗어나 있다.

The same holds true for your pantry.
식료품 저장실에도 마찬가지다.

I used to have a shelf / lined with salty crackers and chips at eye level.
나는 선반을 가지고 있었다. / 눈높이에 짠 크래커와 칩이 줄지어 놓여 있는

When these were the first things I noticed, / they were my (c) primary snack foods.
이것들이 내게 먼저 눈에 띄는 것이었을 때, / 그것들이 나의 주된 간식이었다.

That same shelf is now filled with healthy snacks, / which makes good decisions (d) easy.
그 동일한 선반은 이제 건강에 좋은 간식으로 가득 차 있어, / 좋은 결정을 내리기 쉽게 해준다.

Foods that sit out on tables / are even more critical.
식탁에 나와 있는 음식들은 / 훨씬 더 중요하다.

When you see food every time you walk by, / you are likely to (e) eat it.
당신이 지나갈 때마다 음식을 보면, / 당신은 그것을 먹기 쉽다.

「So to improve your choices, / leave good foods like apples and pistachios sitting out / instead of crackers and candy.」 41번의 근거
따라서 당신의 선택을 개선하기 위해, / 사과와 피스타치오 같은 좋은 음식이 나와 있게 해라. / 크래커와 사탕 대신

마케팅 담당자들은 당신이 먼저 보는 것을 산다는 것을 수십 년 동안 알고 있었다. 예를 들어, 아래쪽 선반에 있는 상품보다 식료품점의 눈높이에 놓여져 있는 상품을 구매할 가능성이 훨씬 더 높다. 매장에서의 '제품 배치'가 구매 행동에 영향을 미치는 방식에 대한 매우 많은 연구가 있다. 이것은 당신에게 유리하게 제품 배치를 사용할 기회를 준다. 농산물과 같은 건강한 식품은 종종 집에서 (a) 가장 덜 눈에 띄는 음식이다. 당신은 보이지 않는 것을 먹으려고 생각하지 않을 것이다. 이것이 85%의 미국인들이 과일과 채소를 충분히 먹지 않는 이유 중 일부일지도 모른다. 만약 농산물이 냉장고 아래쪽에 있는 서랍에 (b) 숨겨져 있으면, 이 좋은 음식들은 시야와 마음에서 벗어나 있다. 식료품 저장실에도 마찬가지다. 나는 눈높이에 짠 크래커와 칩이 줄지어 놓여 있는 선반을 가지고 있었다. 이것들이 내게 먼저 눈에 띄는 것이었을 때, 그것들이 나의 (c) 주된 간식이었다. 그 동일한 선반은 이제 건강에 좋은 간식으로 가득 차 있어, 좋은 결정을 내리기 (d) 쉽게 해준다. 식탁에 나와 있는 음식들은 훨씬 더 중요하다. 당신이 지나갈 때마다 음식을 보면, 당신은 그것을 (e) 피하기(→ 먹기) 쉽다. 따라서 당신의 선택을 개선하기 위해, 크래커와 사탕 대신 사과와 피스타치오 같은 좋은 음식이 나와 있게 해라.

● grocery store 식료품점
● placement ⓝ 배치
● to one's advantage ~에게 유리하게
● primary ⓐ 주된
● critical ⓐ 중요한
● a body of 많은
● influence ⓥ 영향을 미치다 ⓝ 영향
● pantry ⓝ 식료품 저장실
● filled with ~로 가득 찬
● tidy up ⓥ ~을 정리하다

19행 So to improve your choices, leave good foods like apples and pistachios
　　　목적(~하기 위해)　　　　　　　5형식 동사　　　목적어
sitting out instead of crackers and candy.
목적격 보어(현재분사) └전치사(~ 대신에)

41 제목 파악
정답률 72% | 정답 ①

윗글의 제목으로 가장 적절한 것은?

✓① Why We Need to Consider Food Placement – 왜 우리는 식품 배치를 고려할 필요가 있는가
② Pleasure Does Not Come from What You Buy – 기쁨은 당신이 사는 것에서 오지 않는다
③ Which Do You Believe, Visible or Invisible? – 보이는 것과 보이지 않는 것 중 무엇을 믿는가?
④ A Secret for Health: Eat Less, Move More – 건강을 위한 비결: 더 적게 먹고, 더 많이 움직여라
⑤ Three Effective Ways to Tidy Things Up – 물건을 깔끔하게 정리하는 세 가지 효과적인 방법

첫 단락에서 제품 배치가 소비자의 구매 행위에 미치는 영향을 언급한 후, 이를 음식 선택에 적용시킬 수 있다는 조언을 담은 글이다. 마지막 문장인 'So to improve your choices, leave good foods like apples and pistachios sitting out instead of crackers and candy.'에서 더 건강한 음식을 먹는 식단으로 나아가기 위해서는 크래커나 사탕 대신에 사과와 피스타치오 등 건강에 좋은 음식을 눈 앞에 보이도록 꺼내두어야 한다고 언급하고 있으므로, 글의 제목으로 가장 적절한 것은 ① '왜 우리는 식품 배치를 고려할 필요가 있는가'이다.

42 어휘 추론
정답률 50% | 정답 ⑤

밑줄 친 (a) ~ (e) 중에서 문맥상 낱말의 쓰임이 적절하지 않은 것은? [3점]
① (a)　　　② (b)　　　③ (c)　　　④ (d)　　　✓⑤ (e)

'You won't think to eat what you don't see.'에서 눈에 보이지 않는 음식은 먹지 않는다고 언급하는 것으로 보아, 역으로 식탁에 나와 있는 음식은 우리가 '먹기' 좋다는 내용이 이어져야 한다. 따라서 (e)의 avoid를 eat으로 고쳐야 한다. 문맥상 낱말의 쓰임이 적절하지 않은 것은 ⑤ '(e)'이다.

43-45 천사를 찾기 위한 Amy의 여정

(A)

"Grandma," asked Amy, "are angels real?"
"할머니, 천사는 정말 있어요?" Amy가 물었다.

"Some people say so," said Grandmother.
"몇몇 사람들은 그렇다고 하지," 할머니가 말했다.

Amy told Grandmother / that she had seen them in pictures.
Amy는 할머니에게 말했다. / 그녀가 그림에서 천사를 본 적이 있다고

But (a) she also wanted to know / if her grandmother had ever actually seen an angel.
하지만 그녀는 또한 알고 싶어 했다. / 그녀의 할머니가 실제로 천사를 본 적이 있는지

Her grandmother said she had, / but they looked different than in pictures.
할머니는 천사를 본 적이 있다고 하였으나 / 그림에서 본 것과는 다르다고 말했다.

「"Then, I am going to find one!" said Amy.」 45번 ①의 근거 일치
"그럼, 천사를 찾으러 가볼래요!" Amy가 말했다.

"That's good! / But I will go with you, because you're too little," / said Grandmother.
"그거 좋네! / 하지만 나는 너와 함께 가야겠어. 너는 너무 어리잖니." / 할머니가 말했다.

Amy complained, "But you walk so slowly."
"하지만 할머니는 너무 천천히 걷잖아요." Amy가 불평했다.

"I can walk faster than you think!"
"할머니는 네가 생각하는 것보다 더 빨리 걸을 수 있어."

Grandmother replied, with a smile.
할머니가 미소를 지으며 대답했다.

(C)

So they started, / Amy leaping and running.
그래서 그들은 길을 나섰고 / Amy는 뛰어나갔다.

Then, she saw a horse coming towards them.
그때, 그녀가 그들 쪽으로 다가오는 말을 보았다.

On the horse sat a wonderful lady.
그 말에는 멋진 여자가 타고 있었다.

When Amy saw her, / the woman sparkled with jewels and gold, / and her eyes were brighter than diamonds.
Amy가 그녀를 보았을 때 / 그녀는 보석과 황금으로 반짝이고 있었고, / 그녀의 눈은 다이아몬드보다 더욱 밝게 빛났다.

"Are you an angel?" asked Amy.
"당신은 천사인가요?" Amy가 물었다.

「The lady gave no reply, but stared coldly at (d) her, / leaving without saying a word.」 45번 ③의 근거 불일치
그 여자는 대답하지 않고 그녀를 차갑게 바라보며 / 아무 말도 없이 자리를 떠났다.

(B)

"That was not an angel!" said Amy.
"저 사람은 천사가 아니야!" Amy가 말했다.

"No, indeed!" said Grandmother.
"아니고 말고!" 할머니가 말했다.

So Amy walked ahead again.
그래서 Amy는 다시 앞장서서 길을 걷기 시작했다.

Then, (b) she met a beautiful woman / who wore a dress as white as snow.
그때, 그녀는 한 아름다운 여자를 만났다. / 눈처럼 하얀 드레스를 입은

"You must be an angel!" cried Amy.
"당신은 천사가 틀림없어요!" Amy가 외쳤다.

"You dear little girl, do I really look like an angel?" / (c) she asked.
"귀여운 아가씨, 내가 정말 천사처럼 보여?" / 그녀가 물었다.

"You are an angel!" replied Amy.
"당신은 천사예요!" Amy가 말했다.

「But suddenly the woman's face changed / when Amy stepped on her dress by mistake.」 45번 ②의 근거 일치
하지만 갑자기 그녀의 얼굴이 돌변했다. / Amy가 실수로 그녀의 드레스를 밟았을 때

"Go away, and go back to your home!" she shouted.
"저리 비켜, 집에나 가!" 그녀가 외쳤다.

(D)

As Amy stepped back from the woman, / she stumbled and fell.
Amy가 그녀로부터 뒤로 물러나며 / 비틀거리다 바닥에 넘어졌다.

(e) She lay in the dusty road and sobbed.
그녀는 더러운 길에 넘어졌고 울음을 터뜨렸다.

「"I am tired! Will you take me home, Grandma?" / she asked.」 45번 ④의 근거 일치
"저 피곤해요! 할머니, 저를 집에 데려다 주실래요? / 그녀는 부탁했다.

"Sure! That is what I came for," / Grandmother said in a warm voice.
"물론이지! 그래서 내가 여기 있는 거잖니." / 할머니가 따뜻한 목소리로 말했다.

They started to walk along the road.
그들은 길을 따라 걷기 시작했다.

Suddenly Amy looked up and said, / "Grandma, you are not an angel, are you?"
갑자기 그녀가 고개를 들어 말했다. / "할머니, 할머닌 천사가 아니죠, 그렇죠?"

"Oh, honey," said Grandmother, "I'm not an angel."
"오, 아가, 난 천사가 아니야."라고 할머니가 말했다.

『"Well, Grandma, you are an angel to me / because you always stay by my side," / said Amy.』 45번 ⑤의 근거 일치
"음, 할머니, 할머니는 저에게 천사가 맞아요. / 왜냐면 항상 제 곁에 있어 주시니까요."라고 / Amy가 말했다.

(A)
"할머니, 천사는 정말 있어요?" Amy가 물었다. "몇몇 사람들은 그렇다고 하지." 할머니가 말했다. Amy는 할머니에게 그녀가 그림에서 천사들을 본 적이 있다고 말했다. 하지만 (a) 그녀는 또한 그녀의 할머니도 실제로 천사를 본 적이 있는지 알고 싶어 했다. 할머니는 천사를 본 적이 있다고 하였으나 그림에서 본 것과는 다르다고 말했다. "그럼, 천사를 찾으러 가볼래요!" Amy가 말했다. "그거 좋네! 하지만 나는 너와 함께 가야겠어. 네가 너무 어리잖니." 할머니가 말했다. "하지만 할머니는 너무 천천히 걷잖아요." Amy가 불평했다. "할머니는 네가 생각하는 것보다 더 빨리 걸을 수 있어." 할머니가 미소를 지으며 대답했다.

(C)
그래서 그들은 길을 나섰고 Amy는 뛰어나갔다. 그때, 그녀가 그들 쪽으로 다가오는 말을 보았다. 그 말에는 멋진 여자가 타고 있었다. Amy가 그녀를 보았을 때 그녀는 보석과 황금으로 반짝이고 있었고, 그녀의 눈은 다이아몬드보다 더욱더 밝게 빛났다. "당신은 천사인가요?" Amy가 물었다. 그 여자는 대답하지 않고 (d) 그녀를 차갑게 바라보며 아무 말도 없이 자리를 떠났다.

(B)
"저 사람은 천사가 아니야!" Amy가 말했다. "아니고 말고!" 할머니가 말했다. 그래서 Amy는 다시 앞장서서 길을 걷기 시작했다. 그때, (b) 그녀는 눈처럼 하얀 드레스를 입은 한 아름다운 여자를 만났다. "당신은 천사가 틀림없어요!" Amy가 외쳤다. "귀여운 아가씨, 내가 정말 천사처럼 보여?" (c) 그녀가 물었다. "당신은 천사예요!" Amy가 말했다. 하지만 Amy가 실수로 그녀의 드레스를 밟았을 때 갑자기 그녀의 얼굴이 돌변했다. "저리 비켜, 집에나 가!" 그녀가 외쳤다.

(D)
Amy가 그녀로부터 뒤로 물러나며 비틀거리다 바닥으로 넘어졌다. (e) 그녀는 더러운 길가에 넘어졌고 울음을 터뜨렸다. "저 피곤해요! 할머니, 저를 집으로 좀 데려다 주세요." 그녀는 부탁했다. "물론이지! 그래서 내가 여기 있는 거잖니." 할머니가 따뜻한 목소리로 말했다. 그들은 길을 따라 걷기 시작했다. 갑자기 그녀가 고개를 들어 말했다. "할머니, 할머닌 천사가 아니죠, 그렇죠?" "오, 아가, 난 천사가 아니야." "음, 할머니, 할머니는 저에게 천사가 맞아요. 왜냐면 항상 제 곁에 있어 주시니까요."라고 Amy가 말했다.

- different than ~와는 다른
- by mistake 실수로
- dusty ⓐ 먼지투성이의
- step on ⓥ ~을 밟다
- leap ⓥ 뛰어오르다

구문 풀이

(A) 4행 Her grandmother said she had, but they looked different than in pictures.
= had seen an angel(앞 문장 동사) 2형식 동사 형용사 보어

(B) 2행 Then, she met a beautiful woman [who wore a dress as white as snow].
선행사 주격 관·대 「as+원급+as : ~만큼 …한」

(C) 1행 So they started, Amy leaping and running.
주어 동사 의미상 주어 분사구문

---

43 글의 순서 파악   정답률 73% | 정답 ②

주어진 글 (A)에 이어질 내용을 순서에 맞게 배열한 것으로 가장 적절한 것은?
① (B) - (D) - (C)   ✔ (C) - (B) - (D)
③ (C) - (D) - (B)   ④ (D) - (B) - (C)
⑤ (D) - (C) - (B)

Why? 왜 정답일까?
Amy가 천사에 관해 할머니와 대화를 나누다가 직접 천사를 찾으러 가겠다고 결심했다는 내용의 (A) 뒤에는, Amy가 길을 나서서 말을 탄 여자를 보고 말을 걸었지만 답을 듣지 못했다는 내용의 (C), Amy가 천사처럼 보이는 다른 여자를 만났지만 여자의 드레스를 밟아 여자가 화를 냈다는 내용의 (B), Amy가 여자로부터 물러나다가 바닥에 넘어졌고 할머니와 다시 집으로 돌아가다가 문득 할머니가 천사라고 생각하게 되었다는 내용의 (D)가 차례로 이어져야 한다. 따라서 글의 순서로 가장 적절한 것은 ② '(C) - (B) - (D)'이다.

44 지칭 추론   정답률 68% | 정답 ③

밑줄 친 (a)~(e) 중에서 가리키는 대상이 나머지 넷과 다른 것은?
① (a)   ② (b)   ✔ (c)   ④ (d)   ⑤ (e)

Why? 왜 정답일까?
(a), (b), (d), (e)는 Amy를, (c)는 'a beautiful woman who wore a dress ~'를 가리키므로, (a)~(e) 중에서 가리키는 대상이 다른 하나는 ③ '(c)'이다.

45 세부 내용 파악   정답률 75% | 정답 ③

윗글의 Amy에 관한 내용으로 적절하지 <u>않은</u> 것은?
① 천사를 찾고 싶어 했다.
② 한 여자의 드레스를 밟았다.

☑ 말을 탄 여자로부터 친절한 대답을 들었다.
④ 할머니에게 집에 데려다 달라고 부탁했다.
⑤ 할머니를 천사라고 생각했다.

Why? 왜 정답일까?
(C) 'The lady gave no reply, but stared coldly at her, leaving without saying a word.'에서 Amy는 말을 탄 여자에게 천사인지 물었지만 여자로부터 아무런 대답도 듣지 못했다고 하므로, 내용과 일치하지 않는 것은 ③ '말을 탄 여자로부터 친절한 대답을 들었다.'이다.

Why? 왜 오답일까?
① (A) '"Then, I am going to find one!" said Amy.'의 내용과 일치한다.
② (B) '~ Amy stepped on her dress by mistake.'의 내용과 일치한다.
④ (D) '"I am tired! Will you take me home, Grandma?" she asked.'의 내용과 일치한다.
⑤ (D) '"Well, Grandma, you are an angel to me because you always stay by my side," said Amy.'의 내용과 일치한다.

어휘 Review Test 10   문제편 100쪽

A	B	C	D
01 ~을 정리하다	01 exhaust	01 ⓓ	01 ⓗ
02 불안정한	02 immediate	02 ⓑ	02 ⓞ
03 과도한	03 supplies	03 ⓝ	03 ⓕ
04 가설	04 cover	04 ⓐ	04 ⓓ
05 ~의 경우에	05 recall	05 ⓒ	05 ⓔ
06 주된	06 occupation	06 ⓔ	06 ⓚ
07 정제, 개선	07 observation	07 ⓛ	07 ⓐ
08 A를 B로 번역하다	08 infant	08 ⓘ	08 ⓖ
09 충동	09 overtake	09 ⓖ	09 ⓙ
10 양	10 assess	10 ⓙ	10 ⓑ
11 ~에 부합하다, 순응하다	11 cause	11 ⓚ	11 ⓛ
12 보유량	12 permission	12 ⓜ	12 ⓙ
13 불안	13 hence	13 ⓞ	13 ⓒ
14 향기	14 efficient	14 ⓗ	14 ⓜ
15 실효성 있는, 진짜의	15 intensity	15 ⓕ	15 ⓝ
16 실시하다	16 communicator	16 ⓘ	16 ⓟ
17 습득하다	17 seemingly	17 ⓠ	17 ⓡ
18 선도적인	18 can't help ~ing	18 ⓡ	18 ⓠ
19 열[줄]	19 accomplish	19 ⓢ	19 ⓢ
20 결정적인	20 warn	20 ⓟ	20 ⓣ

• 정답 •

18 ⑤ 19 ⑤ 20 ② 21 ⑤ 22 ③ 23 ④ 24 ① 25 ④ 26 ② 27 ⑤ 28 ③ 29 ⑤ 30 ④ 31 ② 32 ①
33 ① 34 ④ 35 ④ 36 ② 37 ④ 38 ③ 39 ② 40 ④ 41 ③ 42 ③ 43 ⑤ 44 ③ 45 ②

★ 표기된 문항은 [등급을 가르는 문제]에 해당하는 문항입니다.

---

18 유인 매표소 재운영 요구 글 | 정답률 88% | 정답 ⑤

다음 글의 목적으로 가장 적절한 것은?

① 승차권 발매기 수리를 의뢰하려고
② 기차표 단체 예매 방법을 문의하려고
③ 기차 출발 시간 지연에 대해 항의하려고
④ 기차역 직원의 친절한 도움에 감사하려고
☑ 기차역 유인 매표소 재운영을 요구하려고

To whom it may concern,
관계자분께,
I am writing to express my deep concern / about the recent change made by Pittsburgh
Train Station.
저는 깊은 우려를 표하고자 이 글을 씁니다. / Pittsburgh Train Station에서 최근에 이루어진 변화에 대해
The station had traditional ticket offices with staff before, / but these have been replaced
with ticket vending machines.
기차역에는 예전에는 직원이 있는 전통적인 매표소가 있었으나, / 이제는 자동발권기로 대체되었습니다.
However, individuals who are unfamiliar with these machines / are now experiencing
difficulty accessing the railway services.
그러나, 이 기계에 익숙하지 않은 사람들은 / 지금 철도 서비스를 이용하는 데 어려움을 겪고 있습니다.
Since these individuals heavily relied on the staff assistance to be able to travel, / they are
in great need of ticket offices with staff in the station.
이들은 여행하기 위해 직원의 도움에 크게 의존해 왔기 때문에, / 역에 직원이 있는 매표소가 절실히 필요합니다.
Therefore, I am urging you to consider reopening the ticket offices.
그러므로, 저는 매표소 재운영을 고려해 주시기를 촉구합니다.
With the staff back in their positions, / many people would regain access to the railway services.
직원이 다시 그들의 자리로 돌아오면, / 많은 사람들이 철도 서비스를 다시 이용할 수 있을 것입니다.
I look forward to your prompt attention to this matter and a positive resolution.
저는 이 문제에 대해 신속한 관심과 긍정적인 해결을 기대합니다.
Sincerely, / Sarah Roberts
진심을 담아, / 사라 로버츠

관계자분께,

저는 Pittsburgh Train Station에 의한 최근의 변경에 대해 저의 깊은 우려를 표하기 위해 글을 쓰고 있습니다. 이전에는 역에 직원이 있는 전통적인 매표소가 있었지만, 이것들은 승차권 발매기로 대체되었습니다. 그러나 이러한 기계에 익숙하지 않은 사람들은 현재 철도 서비스에 접근하는 데 어려움을 겪고 있습니다. 이 사람들은 이동할 수 있기 위해 직원의 도움에 크게 의존했기 때문에, 그들은 역 내에 직원이 있는 매표소를 매우 필요로 합니다. 그러므로 저는 당신에게 매표소 재운영을 고려할 것을 촉구합니다. 직원이 그들의 자리로 돌아오면 많은 사람이 철도 서비스에 대한 접근을 다시 얻을 것입니다. 저는 이 문제에 대한 당신의 신속한 관심과 긍정적인 해결을 기대합니다.

진심을 담아,
Sarah Roberts

Why? 왜 정답일까?

Pittsburgh Train Station에 전통적인 매표소를 키오스크가 대체하자 기계에 익숙하지 않은 사람들이 현재 철도 서비스에 접근하는 데에 어려움을 겪고 있다고 하였으므로('However, individuals who are unfamiliar with these machines are now experiencing difficulty accessing the railway services.'), 글의 목적으로 가장 적절한 것은 ⑤ '기차역 유인 매표소 재운영을 요구하려고'이다.

● express ⓥ 표현하다
● traditional ⓐ 전통의, 전통적인
● unfamiliar ⓐ 익숙하지 않은
● station ⓝ 역
● reopen ⓥ 다시 열다
● prompt ⓐ 즉각적인, 지체 없는

● concern ⓝ 걱정
● vending machine 자동판매기
● experience ⓥ 경험하다
● assistance ⓝ 도움
● regain ⓥ 되찾다, 회복하다
● resolution ⓝ 해결책

구문 풀이

8행 Since these individuals heavily relied on the staff assistance to be able to
   (때문에)   (의존하다(= depend))   (to부정사 부사적 용법(위해서))
travel, they are in great need of ticket offices with staff in the station.

---

19 Arthur 살리기 | 정답률 82% | 정답 ⑤

다음 글에 드러난 Jeevan의 심경 변화로 가장 적절한 것은?

① thrilled → bored
   긴장한   지루한
② ashamed → confident
   부끄러운 자신감 있는
③ hopeful → helpless
   희망에 찬 어찌할 수 없는
④ surprised → indifferent
   놀란   무관심한
☑ desperate → relieved
   절망한   안심한

All the actors on the stage were focused on their acting.
무대에 있던 모든 배우들은 연기에 집중하고 있었다.
Then, suddenly, Arthur fell into the corner of the stage.
그러다, 갑자기 Arthur가 무대 구석에 쓰러졌다.
Jeevan immediately approached Arthur / and found his heart wasn't beating.
Jeevan은 즉시 Arthur에게 다가갔고 / 그의 심장이 뛰지 않음을 발견했다.

Jeevan began CPR.
Jeevan은 심폐소생술을 시작했다.
Jeevan worked silently, / glancing sometimes at Arthur's face.
Jeevan은 침묵 속에서, / 가끔 Arthur의 얼굴을 힐긋 보았다.
He thought, / "Please, start breathing again, please."
그는 생각했다, / "제발 다시 숨 쉬어 줘, 제발."
Arthur's eyes were closed.
Arthur의 눈은 감겨 있었다.
Moments later, / an older man in a grey suit appeared, / swiftly kneeling beside Arthur's chest.
잠시 후, / 회색 정장을 입은 나이 든 남자가 나타나서 / 빠르게 Arthur의 가슴 옆에 무릎을 꿇었다.
"I'm Walter Jacobi. I'm a doctor." / He announced with a calm voice.
"나는 Walter Jacobi다. 나는 의사다." / 그는 침착한 목소리로 말했다.
Jeevan wiped the sweat off his forehead.
Jeevan은 이마의 땀을 닦았다.
With combined efforts, / Jeevan and Dr. Jacobi successfully revived Arthur.
Jeevan과 Jacobi 박사는 힘을 합쳐 / Arthur를 성공적으로 소생시켰다.
Arthur's eyes slowly opened.
Arthur의 눈이 천천히 떠졌다.
Finally, Jeevan was able to hear Arthur's breath again, / thinking to himself, / "Thank
goodness. You're back."
마침내, Jeevan은 다시 Arthur의 숨소리를 들을 수 있었고, / 속으로 생각했다, / "다행이야. 네가 돌아왔구나."

무대 위의 모든 배우가 그들의 연기에 집중하고 있었다. 그 때 갑자기 Arthur가 무대의 한쪽 구석에 쓰러졌다. Jeevan이 즉각 Arthur에게 다가갔고 그의 심장이 뛰지 않는 것을 알아차렸다. Jeevan은 CPR을 시작했다. Jeevan은 때때로 Arthur의 얼굴을 힐긋 보며 조용히 작업했다. 그는 '제발, 다시 숨쉬기를 시작해요, 제발.'이라고 생각했다. Arthur의 눈은 감겨 있었다. 잠시 뒤, 회색 정장 차림의 한 노인이 나타났고, Arthur의 가슴 옆에 재빠르게 무릎을 꿇었다. "저는 Walter Jacobi입니다. 저는 의사입니다." 그는 차분한 목소리로 전했다. Jeevan은 그의 이마에서 땀을 닦아냈다. 협력하여, Jeevan과 Dr. Jacobi는 Arthur를 성공적으로 소생시켰다. Arthur의 눈이 천천히 떠졌다. 마침내 Jeevan은 Arthur의 숨을 다시 들을 수 있었고, '다행이다. 깨어났다.'라고 자신에게 되뇌었다.

Why? 왜 정답일까?

Arthur가 쓰러졌고, Jeevan은 Arthur에게 심폐소생술을 진행하며 제발 다시 숨을 쉬라고 생각했으며(He thought, "Please, start breathing again, please."), Jeevan과 Dr. Jacobi의 노력으로 Arthur가 다시 눈을 뜨자 다시 숨을 쉬어서 너무 다행이라고 생각했기 때문에(Finally, Jeevan was able to hear Arthur's breath again, thinking to himself, "Thank goodness. You're back."), Jeevan의 심경 변화로 가장 적절한 것은 ⑤ 'desperate → relieved'이다.

● stage ⓝ 무대
● immediately ⓐⓓ 즉시
● kneel ⓥ 무릎을 꿇다
● successfully ⓐⓓ 성공적으로

● focus ⓥ 집중하다
● approach ⓥ 접근하다
● wipe ⓥ 닦다
● revive ⓥ 소생하다

구문 풀이

12행 Finally, Jeevan was able to hear Arthur's breath again, thinking to himself,
          (be able to 할 수 있다↵)   (감각동사)   (재귀대명사(목적어))
"Thank goodness. You're back."

---

20 영재 부모의 자랑 | 정답률 75% | 정답 ②

다음 글에서 필자가 주장하는 바로 가장 적절한 것은?

① 부모는 자녀를 다른 아이와 비교하지 말아야 한다.
☑ 부모는 자녀의 영재성을 지나치게 자랑하지 말아야 한다.
③ 영재교육 프로그램에 대한 맹목적인 믿음을 삼가야 한다.
④ 과도한 영재교육보다 자녀와의 좋은 관계 유지에 힘써야 한다.
⑤ 자녀의 독립성을 기르기 위해 자기 일은 스스로 하게 해야 한다.

As the parent of a gifted child, / you need to be aware of / a certain common parent trap.
재능 있는 아이의 부모로서, / 인식해야 한다. / 흔히 빠지기 쉬운 부모의 함정에 대해
Of course you are a proud parent, / and you should be.
물론 당신은 자랑스러운 부모일 것이며, / 그래야 마땅하다.
While it is very easy / to talk nonstop about your little genius / and his or her remarkable
behavior, / this can be very stressful on your child.
매우 쉬운 일이지만, / 당신의 작은 천재에 대해 끊임없이 이야기하는 것은 / 그리고 그들의 놀라운 행동에 / 이것은 아이에게 매우 스트레스를 줄 수 있다.
It is extremely important / to limit your bragging behavior / to your very close friends, or
your parents.
매우 중요하다. / 당신의 자랑을 제한하는 것이 / 매우 가까운 친구들이나 부모에게만
Gifted children / feel pressured / when their parents show them off too much.
재능 있는 아이들은 / 부담을 느낀다. / 부모가 자신을 너무 과시하면
This behavior creates expectations / that they may not be able to live up to, / and also
creates a false sense of self for your child.
이런 행동은 기대를 만들어낸다. / 아이가 충족할 수 없을지도 모르는 / 또한 아이에게 잘못된 자아 인식을 심어줄 수 있다.
You want your child to be who they are, / not who they seem to be as defined / by their
incredible achievements.
당신은 아이가 있는 그대로의 사람이 되길 원할 것이다. / 정의된 사람이 아니라, / 그들의 놀라운 성과로
If not, / you could end up with a driven perfectionist child / or perhaps a drop-out, or worse.
그렇지 않으면, / 당신은 완벽주의에 집착하는 아이나 학교를 그만두는 아이, / 혹은 더 나쁜 결과를 마주할 수 있다.

영재의 부모로서, 당신은 어떤 흔한 부모의 덫을 주의할 필요가 있다. 물론, 당신은 자랑스러워하는 부모이고, 그리고 그래야 한다. 당신의 작은 천재와 그 또는 그녀의 놀라운 행동에 대해서 쉬지 않고 말하는 것은 매우 쉬우나, 이것은 당신의 아이에게 매우 스트레스가 될 수 있다. 당신의 자랑하는 행동을 당신의 아주 가까운 친구나, 당신의 부모에게로 제한하는 것이 매우 중요하다. 영재는 그들의 부모가 지나치게 그들을 자랑할 때 부담을 느낀다. 이러한 행동은 그들이 부응할 수 없을지도 모르는 기대를 만들고, 또한 당신의 자녀에게 있어 잘못된 자의식을 만든다. 당신은 당신의 자녀가 그들의 엄청난 업적에 의해서 규정지어진 대로 보이는 누군가가 아니라 있는 그대로의 그들이기를 바란다. 그렇지 않으면, 당신은 결국 지나친 완벽주의자 아이 또는 아마도 학업 중단자이거나 그보다 더 안 좋은 것을 마주하게 될 것이다.

영재 부모가 아이에 대한 자랑을 과도하게 하면 아이가 부담을 느껴 문제를 일으킬 수도 있다고 하였으므로(This behavior creates expectations that they may not be able to live up to, and also creates a false sense of self for your child.), 필자가 주장하는 바로 가장 적절한 것은 ② '부모는 자녀의 영재성을 지나치게 자랑하지 말아야 한다.'이다.

- **gifted** ⓐ 재능이 있는
- **remarkable** ⓐ 눈에 띄는
- **brag** ⓥ 자랑하다
- **incredible** ⓐ 놀라운
- **be aware of** 알고 있다
- **limit** ⓥ 한정하다
- **expectation** ⓝ 기대
- **achievement** ⓝ 달성

구문 풀이

10행 You want your child to be who they are, not who they seem to
　　　　　　　　　　　　주격관계대명사　　　　　　주격관계대명사
be as defined by their incredible achievements.
　수동태 + 행위자

---

21 자조 집단의 힘 　　　　　　　　　정답률 74% | 정답 ⑤

밑줄 친 "hanging out with the winners"가 다음 글에서 의미하는 바로 가장 적절한 것은?

① staying with those who sacrifice themselves for others
　타인을 위해 스스로를 희생한 사람들과 지내기
② learning from people who have succeeded in competition
　경쟁에서 이긴 사람들로부터 배우기
③ keeping relationships with people in a higher social position
　높은 사회적 지위에 있는 사람들과의 관계를 유지하기
④ spending time with those who need social skill development
　사회적 기술 발달을 필요로 하는 사람들과 시간을 보내기
✓⑤ being with positive people who have overcome negative states
　부정적인 상태를 극복한 긍정적인 사람들과 함께 있기

One valuable technique / for getting out of helplessness, depression, and situations / which are predominantly being run by the thought, / "I can't," / is to choose to be with other persons / who have resolved the problem / with which we struggle.
하나의 유용한 기법은 / 무력감, 우울증, 상황에서 벗어나는 / 그리고 생각이 주로 지배하는 / "나는 할 수 없어."라는 / 사람들과 함께하는 것을 선택하는 것이다. / 문제를 해결했던 / 우리가 겪고 있는
This is one of the great powers / of self-help groups.
이것이 큰 힘 중 하나이다. / 자기계발 그룹의
When we are in a negative state, / we have given a lot of energy to negative thought forms, / and the positive thought forms are weak.
우리가 부정적인 상태에 있을 때, / 우리는 많은 에너지를 부정적인 사고 형태에 주며, / 긍정적인 사고 형태는 약해진다.
Those who are in a higher vibration / are free of the energy / from their negative thoughts / and have energized positive thought forms.
더 높은 진동 상태에 있는 사람들은 / 에너지로부터 자유롭다. / 그들의 부정적인 생각에서부터의 / 그리고 긍정적인 사고 형태에 에너지를 불어넣는다.
Merely to be in their presence / is beneficial.
그들 곁에 있는 것만으로도 / 유익하다.
In some self-help groups, / this is called "hanging out with the winners."
일부 자기계발 그룹에서는 / 이것을 "승자들과 함께 어울리기"라고 부른다.
The benefit here / is on the psychic level of consciousness, / and there is a transfer / of positive energy / and relighting of one's own latent positive thought forms.
여기서의 이점은 / 의식의 심리적 차원에서 발생하며, / 전이가 있다. / 긍정적인 에너지의 / 그리고 자신의 잠재적 긍정적 사고 형태가 다시 붙는 것이

'무력함, 우울감, 그리고 '나는 할 수 없다'는 생각에 의해 현저히 지배당하는 상황에서 벗어나기 위한 한 가지 유용한 기술은 우리가 분투하고 있는 문제를 해결해 본 타인과 함께 있기로 선택하는 것이다. 이것은 자조 집단의 큰 힘 중 하나이다. 우리가 부정적인 상태에 있을 때, 우리는 부정적인 사고 형태에 많은 에너지를 투입해 왔고 긍정적인 사고 형태는 약하다. 더 높은 진동에 있는 사람들은 그들의 부정적인 사고에서 나오는 에너지가 없고, 긍정적인 사고 형태를 활기 띠게 했다. 단지 그들이 있는 자리에 있기만 하는 것도 유익하다. 일부 자조 집단에서 이것은 '승자들과 어울리기'라고 불린다. 여기에서의 이점은 의식의 정신적 수준에 있으며, 긍정적인 에너지의 전달과 자신의 잠재적인 긍정적인 사고 형태의 재점화가 있다.

자조 집단의 장점은 겪고 있는 어려움을 극복한 누군가의 에너지를 받는 것이라 얘기하고 있으므로(The benefit here is on the psychic level of consciousness, and there is a transfer of positive energy and relighting of one's own latent positive thought forms), "hanging out with the winners"가 글에서 의미하는 바는 ⑤ 'being with positive people who have overcome negative states'이다.

- **valuable** ⓐ 가치있는
- **predominantly** [ad] 지배적인
- **state** ⓝ 상태
- **beneficial** ⓐ 혜택의
- **latent** ⓐ 잠재적인
- **technique** ⓝ 기술
- **negative** ⓐ 부정적인
- **vibration** ⓝ 진동
- **consciousness** ⓝ 의식

구문 풀이

7행 Those who are in a higher vibration are free of the energy from their
　　　지시대명사 주격관계대명사　　　　　　　　　동사1
negative thoughts and have energized positive thought forms.
　　　　　　　　　동사2

---

22 감정 존재의 의미 　　　　　　　　정답률 87% | 정답 ③

다음 글의 요지로 가장 적절한 것은?

① 과거의 경험이 현재의 감정에 영향을 미친다.
② 문명의 발달에 따라 인간의 감정은 다양화되어 왔다.
✓③ 감정은 인간이 생존하도록 도와왔기 때문에 존재한다.
④ 부정적인 감정은 긍정적인 감정보다 더 오래 기억된다.
⑤ 두려움의 원인을 파악함으로써 두려움을 없앨 수 있다.

Our emotions are thought to exist / because they have contributed to / our survival as a species.

우리의 감정은 존재한다고 여겨진다. / 왜냐하면 그것들이 기여했기 때문이다. / 우리 종의 생존에
Fear has helped us avoid dangers, / expressing anger helps us scare off threats, / and expressing positive emotions helps us bond with others.
두려움은 우리가 위험을 피하도록 도와주었고, / 분노를 표현하는 것은 위협을 몰아내는 데 도움을 주며, / 긍정적인 감정을 표현하는 것은 우리가 다른 사람들과 유대감을 형성하도록 돕는다.
From an evolutionary perspective, / an emotion is a kind of "program" that, / when triggered, directs many of our activities.
진화적인 관점에서, / 감정은 일종의 '프로그램'이다. / 그것이 촉발될 때, 우리의 많은 활동을 지시하는
For example, / fear makes us very attentive, / narrows our perceptual focus to threatening stimuli, / will cause us either to face a situation (fight) or avoid it (flight), / and may cause us to remember an experience more acutely.
예를 들어, / 두려움은 우리를 매우 주의 깊게 만들고, / 우리의 지각 초점을 위협적인 자극으로 좁히며, / 상황에 맞서거나 (싸우거나) 피하도록 하고 (달아나도록), / 더 날카롭게 경험을 기억하게 만들 수 있다.
So that we avoid the threat in the future.
그리하여 우리가 미래에 그 위협을 피할 수 있게 된다.
Regardless of the specific ways / in which they activate our systems, / the specific emotions we possess / are thought to exist / because they have helped us (as a species) survive challenges within our environment long ago.
특정 방식과 상관없이, / 그것들이 우리의 시스템을 활성화하는 / 우리가 가진 특정 감정들은 / 존재한다고 여겨진다. / 우리가 (종족으로서) 도전에 맞서도록 도왔기 때문에 / 오래 전 우리의 환경에서
If they had not helped us adapt and survive, / they would not have evolved with us.
만약 그것들이 우리가 적응하고 생존하는 것을 돕지 않았다면, / 그것들은 우리와 함께 진화하지 않았을 것이다.

우리의 감정은 그것들이 종으로서 우리의 생존에 기여해 왔기 때문에 존재한다고 여겨진다. 두려움은 우리가 위험을 피하는 데 도움을 주어 왔고, 분노를 표현하는 것은 우리가 위협을 쫓아내도록 돕고, 긍정적인 감정을 표현하는 것은 우리가 다른 사람과 유대감을 형성하도록 돕는다. 진화적 관점에서, 감정은 유발될 때 (주의, 지각, 기억, 움직임, 표현 등을 포함하는) 우리의 많은 활동을 지시하는 일종의 '프로그램'이다. 예를 들어, 두려움은 우리를 매우 주의 깊게 만들고, 우리의 지각의 초점을 위협적인 자극으로 좁히고, 우리로 하여금 상황을 정면으로 대하거나 (싸우거나) 그것을 피하도록 (도피하도록) 하며, 우리로 하여금 경험을 더 강렬하게 기억하도록 (그래서 우리가 미래에 위험을 피하도록) 할 수도 있다. 그것들이 우리의 시스템을 활성화하는 구체적인 방식과는 관계없이, 우리가 소유한 특정한 감정은 그것들이 오래전에 우리의 환경 내에서 우리가 (종으로서) 힘든 상황에서 생존하도록 도움을 주어 왔기 때문에 존재한다고 여겨진다. 만약 그것들이 우리가 적응하고 생존하도록 도움을 주지 않았었더라면 그것들은 우리와 함께 진화해 오지 않았을 것이다.

감정은 인간의 생존에 이롭기 때문에 존재했다고 얘기하고 있기 때문에(Regardless of the specific ways in which they activate our systems, the specific emotions we possess are thought to exist because they have helped us (as a species) survive challenges within our environment long ago.), 글의 요지로 가장 적절한 것은 ③ '감정은 인간이 생존하도록 도와왔기 때문에 존재한다.'이다.

- **contribute** ⓥ 기여하다
- **avoid** ⓥ 피하다
- **perspective** ⓝ 관점, 시각
- **fear** ⓝ 공포, 두려움, 무서움
- **environment** ⓝ 환경
- **survival** ⓝ 생존
- **scare off** 겁을 줘 쫓아내다
- **trigger** ⓥ 야기하다
- **perceptual** ⓐ 지각의
- **evolve** ⓥ 진화하다

구문 풀이

1행 Our emotions are thought to exist because they have contributed to our
　　　　　　　　　수동태　　　to부정사 (명사적 용법)　　　　　현재완료
survival as a species.

---

23 노동 시장에서 AI의 역할 　　　　　정답률 68% | 정답 ④

다음 글의 주제로 가장 적절한 것은?

① jobs replaced by AI in the labour market
　노동 시장에서 AI에 의해 대체된 직업들
② ethical issues caused by using AI in the workplace
　AI를 직장에서 사용하며 발생하는 도덕적 문제들
③ necessity of using AI technology for language learning
　언어 학습을 위해 AI를 사용하는 것의 필요성
✓④ impacts of AI on supporting workers with disadvantages
　장애가 있는 노동자들을 지원하는 AI의 영향
⑤ new designs of AI technology to cure people with disabilities
　장애를 가진 사람들을 치료하기 위한 AI 기술의 새로운 디자인

By improving accessibility of the workplace / for workers / that are typically at a disadvantage / in the labour market, / AI can improve / inclusiveness in the workplace.
직장에서의 접근성을 향상시키므로써 / 노동자를 위해 / 일반적으로 노동시장에서 불리한 / AI가 향상시킬 수 있다. / 직장에서 포용성을
AI-powered assistive devices / to aid workers / with visual, speech or hearing difficulties / are becoming more widespread, / improving the access to, / and the quality of work for people with disabilities.
AI 기반의 보조적 기구는 / 노동자를 돕기 위한 / 시각, 말하기 또는 청각적 불편함이 있는 / 더 널리 퍼지고 있다. / 접근성을 높이며 / 그리고 장애가 있는 사람들의 일의 질을
For example, / speech recognition solutions for people with dysarthric voices, / or live captioning systems / for deaf and hard of hearing people / can facilitate communication with colleagues / and access to jobs where inter-personal communication is necessary.
예를 들어, / 음성 인식 솔루션이나 / 발음이 부정확한 사람들을 위한 / 실시간 자막 시스템은 / 청각 장애인들을 위한 / 동료들과의 의사소통을 돕고 / 대인관계 소통이 필요한 직업에 대한 접근을 가능하게 한다.
AI can also enhance the capabilities of low-skilled workers, / with potentially positive effects / on their wages and career prospects.
AI는 또한 저숙련 근로자의 능력을 향상시킬 수 있으며, / 이는 긍정적인 영향을 미칠 수 있다. / 그들의 임금과 경력 전망에
For example, / AI's capacity to translate written and spoken word in real-time / can improve the performance of non-native speakers in the workplace.
예를 들어, / AI의 실시간 번역 능력은 / 비원어민 근로자의 직장 내 성과를 향상시킬 수 있다.
Moreover, recent developments in AI-powered text generators / can instantly improve the performance of lower-skilled individuals / in domains such as writing, coding or customer service.
또한, 최근 AI 기반 텍스트 생성기의 발전은 / 저숙련 근로자들의 성과를 즉시 향상시킬 수 있다. / 글쓰기, 코딩, 고객 서비스와 같은 분야에서

노동 시장에서 일반적으로 불리한 위치에 있는 노동자를 위한 일터로의 접근성을 향상시킴으로써, AI는 일터에서 포괄성을 향상시킬 수 있다. 시각, 발화 또는 청각 장애가 있는 노동자들을 돕기 위한 AI 동력의 보조 장치들이 더 널리 보급되어, 장애를 지닌 사람들의 업무 접근성과 업무의 질을 향상시키고 있다. 예를 들어, 구음 장애가 있는 사람들을 위한 발화 인식 솔루션이나 청각 장애인과 난청인을 위한 실시간 자막 시스템은 동료와의 의사소통과 대인 의사소통이 필요한 일에 대한 접근을 용이하게 할 수 있다. AI는 또한 그들의 임금과 경력 전망에 잠재적으로 긍정적인 영향과 함께 저숙련 노동자들의 능력을 향상시킬 수 있다. 예를 들어, 문자 언어와 음성 언어를 실시간으로 번역하는 AI의 능력은 일터에서 비원어민의 수행을 향상시킬 수 있다. 게다가, 최근의 AI 동력의 텍스트 생성기의 발전은 글쓰기, 코딩, 고객 서비스와 같은 영역에서 저숙련된 개인의 수행을 즉시 향상시킬 수 있다.

Why? 왜 정답일까?

AI가 노동 시장에서 미칠 수 있는 긍정적인 영향을 언급하고 있기 때문에(By improving accessibility of the workplace for workers that are typically at a disadvantage in the labour market, AI can improve inclusiveness in the workplace.), 글의 주제로 가장 적절한 것은 ④ 'impacts of AI on supporting workers with disadvantages'이다.

- accessibility ⓝ 접근, 접근하기 쉬움
- workplace ⓝ 직장
- device ⓝ 기기
- dysarthric ⓐ 구음 장애의
- enhance ⓥ 향상시키다
- development ⓝ 발달
- disadvantage ⓝ 불리한 점
- assistive ⓐ 도와주는
- aid ⓥ 돕다
- colleague ⓝ 동료
- wage ⓝ 임금
- individiaul ⓝ 개인

구문 풀이

3행 AI-powered assistive devices to aid workers with visual, speech or

to부정사(부사적 용법)

hearing difficulties are becoming more widespread, improving the access to, and

동사 / 현재분사(향상시키며)

the quality of work for people with disabilities.

---

24 고래가 환경에 미치는 긍정적 영향   정답률 73% | 정답 ①

다음 글의 제목으로 가장 적절한 것은?

☑ Saving Whales Saves the Earth and Us – 고래를 살리는 것이 지구와 우리를 살린다
② What Makes Whales Go Extinct in the Ocean – 바다에서 고래를 멸종하게 하는 것
③ Why Is Overpopulation of Whales Dangerous? – 왜 과도한 개체수의 고래가 위험할까?
④ Black Money: Lies about the Whaling Industry – 검은 돈: 고래 산업에 대한 거짓말
⑤ Climate Change and Its Effect on Whale Habitats – 기후 변화와 고래 거주지에 끼치는 영향

Whales are highly efficient at carbon storage.
고래는 탄소 저장에 매우 효율적이다.
When they die, / each whale sequesters an average of 30 tons of carbon dioxide, / taking that carbon out of the atmosphere for centuries.
고래가 죽을 때, / 각각의 고래는 평균적으로 30톤의 이산화 탄소를 격리하며, / 이 탄소를 수세기 동안 대기에서 제거한다.
For comparison, / the average tree absorbs only 48 pounds of CO_2 a year.
비교하자면, / 평균적인 나무는 매년 48파운드의 CO_2만을 흡수한다.
From a climate perspective, / each whale is the marine equivalent of thousands of trees.
기후 관점에서, / 각각의 고래는 수천 그루의 나무에 해당하는 해양 생물이다.
Whales also help sequester carbon / by fertilizing the ocean as they release nutrient-rich waste, / in turn increasing phytoplankton populations, / which also sequester carbon — / leading some scientists to call them the "engineers of marine ecosystems."
고래는 또한 탄소 격리에 도움을 주는데 / 영양이 풍부한 배설물을 방출하여 바다를 비옥하게 만들고, / 그 결과 식물성 플랑크톤의 개체 수를 증가시키며, / 이는 또한 탄소를 격리한다 — / 이로 인해 일부 과학자들은 고래를 "해양 생태계의 엔지니어"라고 부른다.
In 2019, economists from the International Monetary Fund (IMF) / estimated the value of the ecosystem services provided by each whale at over $2 million USD.
2019년에, 국제통화기금(IMF)의 경제학자들은 / 각각의 고래가 제공하는 생태계 서비스의 가치를 200만 달러 이상으로 추산했다.
They called for a new global program of economic incentives / to return whale populations to preindustrial whaling levels / as one example of a "nature-based solution" to climate change.
그들은 새로운 글로벌 경제적 인센티브 프로그램을 촉구했다. / 고래 개체 수를 산업화 이전의 포경 수준으로 되돌리기 위해 / 기후 변화에 대한 '자연 기반 해결책'의 한 예로서
Calls are now being made / for a global whale restoration program, / to slow down climate change.
현재 / 글로벌 고래 복원 프로그램에 대한 요청이 이루어지고 있다. / 기후 변화를 늦추기 위해

고래는 탄소 저장에 매우 효율적이다. 그들이 죽을 때, 각각의 고래는 평균 30톤의 이산화 탄소를 격리하며, 수 세기 동안 대기로부터 그 탄소를 빼내어 둔다. 비교하자면, 평균적인 나무는 연간 48파운드의 이산화 탄소만을 흡수한다. 기후의 관점에서 각각의 고래는 수천 그루의 나무에 상응하는 바다에 사는 것이다. 고래는 또한 영양이 풍부한 배설물을 내보내면서 바다를 비옥하게 함으로써 탄소를 격리하는 데 도움을 주는데, 결과적으로 식물성 플랑크톤 개체를 증가시키고 이는 또한 탄소를 격리한다. 그리하여 몇몇 과학자들은 그들을 '해양 생태계의 기술자'라고 부르게 되었다. 2019년 국제 통화 기금(IMF)의 경제학자들은 각각의 고래에 의해서 제공되는 생태계 서비스의 가치를 미화 200만 달러가 넘게 추정했다. 그들은 기후 변화에 대한 '자연 기반 해결책의 한 예로서 고래 개체수를 산업화 이전의 고래잡이 수준으로 되돌리기 위한 새로운 글로벌 경제적 인센티브 프로그램을 요구했다. 기후 변화를 늦추기 위해 세계적인 고래 복원 프로그램에 대한 요구가 현재 제기되고 있다.

Why? 왜 정답일까?

고래가 탄소를 저장하고, 바다를 비옥하게 하여 환경에 긍정적인 영향을 끼치며, 국제 통화 기금은 고래 개체수를 늘려야 한다고 주장하고 있기 때문에(They called for a new global program of economic incentives to return whale populations to preindustrial whaling levels as one example of a "nature-based solution" to climate change.), 제목으로 가장 적절한 것은 ① 'Saving Whales Saves the Earth and Us'이다.

- efficient ⓐ 효율적인
- atmosphere ⓝ 대기
- equivalent ⓐ 상응하는, 상당하는
- increase ⓥ 증가하다
- sequester ⓥ 격리하다
- comparison ⓝ 대조
- absorb ⓥ 흡수하다
- population ⓝ 개체군, 개체 수

- economist ⓝ 경제학자
- solution ⓝ 해결책
- estimate ⓥ 추산하다
- climate ⓝ 기후

구문 풀이

1행 When they die, each whale sequesters an average of 30 tons of carbon

~할 때 / 각각의, 단수취급

dioxide, taking that carbon out of the atmosphere for centuries.

현재분사

---

25 2022년 국가별 1인당 이산화 탄소 배출량   정답률 79% | 정답 ④

다음 도표의 내용과 일치하지 않는 것은?

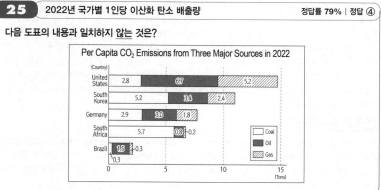

Per Capita CO₂ Emissions from Three Major Sources in 2022

The above graph shows per capita CO_2 emissions / from coal, oil, and gas by countries in 2022.
위 그래프는 각국의 1인당 CO_2 배출량을 보여준다. / 2022년의 석탄, 석유, 가스에 의한
① The United States had the highest total per capita CO_2 emissions, / even though its emissions from coal were the second lowest among the five countries shown.
미국은 총 1인당 CO_2 배출량이 가장 높았으나, / 석탄에 의한 배출량은 다섯 나라 중 두 번째로 낮았다.
② South Korea's total per capita CO_2 emissions were over 10 tons, / ranking it the second highest among the countries shown.
한국의 총 1인당 CO_2 배출량은 10톤을 넘었으며, / 표시된 국가들 중 두 번째로 높았다.
③ Germany had lower CO_2 emissions per capita than South Korea / in all three major sources respectively.
독일은 세 주요 원천에서 / 각각 한국보다 1인당 CO_2 배출량이 더 낮았다.
☑ The per capita CO_2 emissions from coal in South Africa / were over three times higher than those in Germany.
남아프리카의 석탄에 의한 1인당 CO_2 배출량은 / 독일보다 세 배 이상 높았다.
⑤ In Brazil, oil was the largest source of CO_2 emissions per capita / among its three major sources, / just as it was in the United States and Germany.
브라질에서는 석유가 1인당 CO_2 배출의 가장 큰 원천이었으며, / 이는 미국과 독일에서도 마찬가지였다.

위 그래프는 2022년의 국가별 석탄, 석유, 천연가스에서 나온 1인당 이산화 탄소 배출량을 보여 준다. ① 석탄에서 나온 배출량은 보여진 다섯 개의 국가 중 두 번째로 낮았음에도 불구하고, 미국은 가장 높은 1인당 이산화 탄소 총배출량을 가졌다. ② 한국의 1인당 이산화 탄소 총배출량은 10톤이 넘고, 보여진 국가 중 두 번째로 높은 순위를 차지했다. ③ 독일은 한국보다 각각의 모든 세 가지 주요한 원천에서 더 낮은 1인당 이산화 탄소 배출량을 가졌다. ④ 남아프리카 공화국의 석탄으로부터의 1인당 이산화 탄소 배출량은 독일의 그것보다 세 배보다 더 높았다. ⑤ 브라질에서 석유는 브라질의 세 가지 주요한 원천 중에서 1인당 이산화 탄소 배출량의 가장 큰 원천이었고, 그것은 미국과 독일에서도 마찬가지였다.

Why? 왜 정답일까?

남아프리카 공화국의 석탄으로부터의 1인당 이산화 탄소 배출량은 5.7톤이고, 독일의 석탄으로부터의 1인당 이산화 탄소 배출량은 2.9톤이기 때문에 도표의 내용과 일치하지 않는 것은 ④이다.

- emission ⓝ 배출량
- rank ⓥ 순위에 들다
- source ⓝ 원천
- per capita 1인당
- major ⓐ 주요한

구문 풀이

2행 The United States had the highest total per capita CO₂ emissions,

최상급

even though its emissions from coal were the second lowest among the five

비록 / 주어

countries shown.

---

26 Émilie du Châtelet의 일생   정답률 70% | 정답 ②

Émilie du Châtelet에 관한 다음 글의 내용과 일치하지 않는 것은?

① 어린 시절에 수학과 과학 교육을 받았다.
☑ 불의 속성에 관한 그녀의 논문이 1737년에 출간되었다.
③ Institutions de Physique에서 공간과 시간의 개념을 설명했다.
④ 아이작 뉴턴의 Principia를 프랑스어로 번역했다.
⑤ 이룩한 업적은 당대에 인정받지 못했다.

Émilie du Châtelet, a French mathematician and physicist, / was born in Paris in 1706.
프랑스의 수학자이자 물리학자인 Émilie du Châtele는 / 1706년에 파리에서 태어났다.
「During her childhood, / with her father's support, / she was able to get mathematical and scientific education / that most women of her time did not receive.」 ①의 근거 일치
어린 시절에, / 아버지의 지원으로 / 그녀는 수학과 과학 교육을 받을 수 있었다. / 당시 대부분의 여성들이 받지 못했던
「In 1737, / she submitted her paper on the nature of fire / to a contest sponsored by the French Academy of Sciences, / and it was published a year later.」 ②의 근거 불일치
1737년에, / 그녀는 불의 본질에 관한 논문을 제출했다. / French Academy of Sciences가 주최한 경연에 / 그리고 그것은 1년 후에 출판되었다.
「In her book, Institutions de Physique, / Émilie du Châtelet explained the ideas of space and time / in a way that is closer to what we understand in modern relativity / than what was common during her time.」 ③의 근거 일치
그녀의 책 Institutions de Physique에서, / Émilie du Châtele는 공간과 시간에 대한 개념을 설명했다. / 우리가 현대의 상대성 이론에서 이해하는 방식에 더 가까운 / 그녀 시대의 일반적인 이해보다

「Her most significant achievement / was translating Isaac Newton's *Principia* into French / near the end of her life.」 ④의근거 일치
그녀의 가장 중요한 업적은 / 아이작 뉴턴의 *Principia*를 프랑스어로 번역한 것이다. / 그녀 생애 말년에   ⑤의근거 일치

「Émilie du Châtelet's work was not recognized in her time, / but she is now remembered / as a symbol of the Enlightenment and the struggle for women's participation in science.」
Émilie du Châtele의 업적은 그녀 생애 동안 인정받지 못했지만, / 현재 그녀는 기억되고 있다. / 계몽주의와 여성의 과학 참여 투쟁의 상징으로서

프랑스 수학자이자 물리학자인 Émilie du Châtelet은 1706년에 파리에서 태어났다. 어린 시절에 아버지의 도움으로 그녀는 당대 대부분의 여성들은 받지 못했던 수학과 과학 교육을 받을 수 있었다. 1737년에 그녀는 불의 속성에 관한 논문을 French Academy of Sciences에 의해 후원되는 대회에 제출했으며, 그것은 1년 후에 출간되었다. 그녀의 책 *Institutions de Physique*에서 Émilie du Châtelet는 당대에 일반적이었던 것보다 현대의 상대성 이론에서 우리가 이해하는 것에 더 가까운 방식으로 공간과 시간의 개념을 설명했다. 그녀의 가장 주요한 성과는 그녀의 말년 무렵 아이작 뉴턴의 *Principia*를 프랑스어로 번역한 것이었다. Émilie du Châtelet의 업적은 당대에 인정받지 못했지만, 현재 그녀는 계몽주의와 여성의 과학 분야 참여를 위한 투쟁의 상징으로 기억된다.

Why? 왜 정답일까?

'In 1737, she submitted her paper on the nature of fire to a contest sponsored by the French Academy of Sciences, and it was published a year later.'에서 논문이 출간된 것은 **1738년**임을 알 수 있기 때문에, 글의 내용과 일치하지 않는 것은 ② '불의 속성에 관한 그녀의 논문이 **1737년**에 출간되었다.'이다.

Why? 왜 오답일까?

① 'During her childhood, ~ she was able to get mathematical and scientific education ~ did not receive.'의 내용과 일치한다.
③ 'In her book, Institutions de Physique, Émilie du Châtelet explained the ideas of space and time ~ during her time'의 내용과 일치한다.
④ 'Her most significant achievement was translating Isaac Newton's Principia into French near the end of her life.'의 내용과 일치한다.
⑤ 'Émilie du Châtelet's work was not recognized in her time, ~ participatio in science.'의 내용과 일치한다.

- mathematician ⓝ 수학자
- childhood ⓝ 어린 시절
- receive ⓥ 받다
- publish ⓥ 출간하다
- relativity ⓝ 상대성 이론
- enlightenment ⓝ (18세기의) 계몽주의 시대
- physicist ⓝ 물리학자
- support ⓝ 지원
- submit ⓥ 제출하다
- explain ⓥ 설명하다
- significant ⓐ 중요한, 특별한 의미가 있는

구문 풀이

7행 In her book, Institutions de Physique, Émilie du Châtelet explained the
ideas of space and time in a way that is closer to what we understand in modern
주격관계대명사   관계대명사1(the thing that)
relativity than what was common during her time.
관계대명사2(the thing that)

---

27 2024 청소년 발명가 로봇 대회 안내문   정답률 90% | 정답 ⑤

2024 Young Inventors Robot Competition에 관한 다음 안내문의 내용과 일치하지 <u>않는</u> 것은?

① 세 가지 분야 중 하나에 참가할 수 있다.
② 9월 28일에 5시간 동안 열린다.
③ 고등학생이 등록할 수 있다.
④ 등록은 온라인으로만 가능하다.
☑ 수상자는 각 분야당 한 명이다.

2024 Young Inventors Robot Competition
2024년 청소년 발명가 로봇 대회
Join us for an exciting day of the Young Inventors Robot Competition!
청소년 발명가 로봇 대회의 신나는 날에 참여하세요!
Categories
분류
「Participants can compete in one of the following categories:」 ①의근거 일치
참가자들은 아래의 분류 중 한 개의 대회에 참여할 수 있습니다:
Robot Design
로봇 디자인
Robot Coding
로봇 코딩
Robot Remote Control
로봇 원격 조종
Date and Time
날짜와 시간
「September 28, 2024, 10 a.m. to 3 p.m.」 ②의근거 일치
2024년 9월 28일, 오전 10시부터 오후 3시까지
Location
장소
Computer Lab, Oakwood University
Oakwood 대학교의 컴퓨터실
Registration
등록
From August 1 to August 10, 2024
2024년 8월 1일부터 8월 10일까지
「Open to high school students」 ③의근거 일치
고등학생이 등록 가능
「Online registration only (www.younginventors.edu)」 ④의근거 일치
온라인 등록만 받습니다 (www.younginventors.edu)
Awards

상품
「In each competition category, three participants will be honored.」 ⑤의근거 불일치
각각의 분류 대회에서 세 명의 참가자들이 수상합니다.
1st place: $300
1등: 300 달러
2nd place: $200
2등: 200 달러
3rd place: $100
3등: 100달러
For more information, visit our website.
더 많은 정보는 웹사이트를 방문해주세요.

2024 Young Inventors Robot Competition

Young Inventors Robot Competition의 신나는 날에 우리와 함께하세요!

□ 분야
 – 참가자들은 다음 분야 중 하나에 참가할 수 있습니다.
 • 로봇 디자인 • 로봇 코딩 • 로봇 원격 조종

□ 날짜와 시간
 – 2024년 9월 28일, 오전 10시부터 오후 3시까지

□ 장소
 – Oakwood University 컴퓨터실

□ 등록
 – 2024년 8월 1일부터 8월 10일까지
 – 고등학생이 등록 가능
 – 온라인 등록만 가능 (www.younginventors.edu)

□ 시상
 – 각 경쟁 분야에서 세 명의 참가자가 수상할 것입니다.
 • 1등: 300달러 • 2등: 200달러 • 3등: 100달러

※ 더 많은 정보를 원하시면, 저희 웹사이트를 방문하세요

Why? 왜 정답일까?

'Awards' 항목의 'In each competition category, three participants will be honored.'의 문장을 보았을 때, 각 분야당 수상자는 세 명이므로 안내문과 일치하지 않는 것은 ⑤ '수상자는 각 분야당 한 명이다.'이다.

Why? 왜 오답일까?

① 'Categories' 아래의 내용에서 참가자들은 주어진 세 가지 분야 중 하나에 참가할 수 있다고 제시한다.
② 'September 28, 2024, 10 a.m. to 3 p.m.'의 내용과 일치한다.
③ 'Registration'의 'Open to high school students'의 내용과 일치한다.
④ 'Online registration only'의 내용과 일치한다.

- inventor ⓝ 발명가
- category ⓝ 분류
- registration ⓝ 등록
- competition ⓝ 대회
- participant ⓝ 참여자

---

28 제8회 Saintville Art Week 스탬프 투어 안내   정답률 90% | 정답 ③

Saintville Art Week Stamp Tour에 관한 다음 안내문의 내용과 일치하는 것은?
① 참가 대상에 제한이 있다.
② 10월 둘째 주에 진행된다.
☑ Saintville Arts Center에서 스탬프 투어 지도를 받는다.
④ 적어도 다섯 곳에서 도장을 받아야 선물을 받는다.
⑤ 선물로 가방과 머그잔 중 하나를 고를 수 있다.

Saintville Art Week Stamp Tour
Saintville Art 주 스탬프 투어
The 8th annual Saintville Art Week Stamp Tour is back this year!
올해 연례 Saintville Art 주 8회 스탬프 투어가 돌아왔습니다!
「Anyone can participate in our event.」 ①의근거 불일치
누구나 행사에 참여 가능합니다.
Join us and enjoy exhibitions and new collections.
참여하시고 전시회와 새 수집품을 즐기세요.
When: 「The first week of October, 2024」 ②의근거 불일치
언제: 2024년 10월 첫째 주
Where: Saintville Arts District
어디서: Saintville Arts 구역
How:
어떻게:
Step 1. 「Take a stamp tour map from the Saintville Arts Center.」 ③의근거 일치
1단계. Saintville Arts Center에서 스탬프 투어 지도를 가져가세요.
Step 2. 「Get stamps from at least 3 out of 5 spots and receive your gift.」 ④의근거 불일치
2단계. 5곳 중 최소 3곳에서 스탬프를 찍고 선물을 받으세요.
「You can choose either an umbrella or a mug with printed artwork on it for your gift.」 ⑤의근거 불일치
선물로 우산 또는 예술품이 그려진 머그컵을 고를 수 있습니다.
For more information, please visit our website at www.SaintvilleArtsCenter.com.
더 많은 정보는 우리의 웹사이트 www.SaintvilleArtsCenter.com를 방문하세요.

Saintville Art Week Stamp Tour

해마다 열리는 8번째 Saintville Art Week Stamp Tour가 올해도 돌아왔습니다! 누구나 우리의 행사에 참가할 수 있습니다. 우리와 함께하여 전시와 새로운 컬렉션을 즐겨 보세요.

□ 언제: 2024년 10월 첫째 주
□ 어디서: Saintville Arts District
□ 어떻게:
 1단계: Saintville Arts Center에서 스탬프 투어 지도를 받으세요.
 2단계: 다섯 곳 중 적어도 세 곳에서 도장을 받고 선물을 받으세요.

– 예술 작품이 인쇄된 우산이나 머그잔 중 하나를 선물로 선택할 수 있습니다.

※ 더 많은 정보를 원하시면, 저희 웹사이트 www.SaintvilleArtsCenter.com을 방문해 주세요.

Why? 왜 정답일까?

'Take a stamp tour map from the Saintville Arts Center.'에서 Saintville Arts Center에서 스탬프 투어 지도를 받는다고 안내하기 때문에 안내문의 내용과 일치하는 것은 ③이다.

Why? 왜 오답일까?

① 'Anyone can participate in our event.'라고 하였기 때문에 참가 대상에는 제한이 없다.
② 'The first week of October, 2024'에서 대회는 10월 첫째 주에 진행됨을 알 수 있다.
④ 'Get stamps from at least 3 out of 5 spots and receive your gift.'에서 선물을 받기 위해서는 세 곳에서만 도장을 받아도 된다고 알린다.
⑤ 'You can choose either an umbrella or a mug with printed artwork on it for your gift.'에서 선물로 우산과 머그잔 중 하나를 고를 수 있다고 안내한다.

- stamp ⓝ 도장
- participate ⓥ 참여하다
- join ⓥ 참여하다
- collectin ⓝ 수집품
- annual ⓐ 연간의
- event ⓝ 행사
- exhibition ⓝ 전시회

★★★ 등급을 가르는 문제!

29 터널 시야 현상　　　　정답률 41% | 정답 ⑤

다음 글의 밑줄 친 부분 중, 어법상 틀린 것은?

From an organizational viewpoint, / one of the most fascinating examples / of how any organization may contain many different types of culture / ① is to recognize / the functional operations of different departments within the organization.
조직적 관점에서, / 가장 흥미로운 예 중 하나는 / 조직 내에 다양한 유형의 문화가 존재할 수 있다는 / 인식하는 것이다. / 조직 내 각 부서의 기능적 운영을

The varying departments / and divisions within an organization / will inevitably view any given situation / from their own biased and prejudiced perspective.
다양한 부서와 / 조직 내의 부문은 / 필연적으로 주어진 상황을 바라볼 것이다. / 자신들의 편향되고 선입견이 있는 시각에서

A department and its members / will acquire "tunnel vision" / which disallows them / to see things as others see ② them.
부서와 그 구성원은 / "터널 비전"을 가지게 되어, / 못하게 될 것이다. / 다른 사람들이 보는 방식으로 상황을 보지

The very structure of organizations / can create conflict.
조직의 구조 자체가 / 갈등을 일으킬 수 있다.

The choice of ③ whether the structure / is "mechanistic" or "organic" / can have a profound influence on conflict management.
구조를 선택하는 것은 / "기계적"인지 "유기적"인지를 / 갈등 관리에 깊은 영향을 미칠 수 있다.

A mechanistic structure has / a vertical hierarchy with many rules, / many procedures, / and many levels of management ④ involved in decision making.
기계적 구조는 가지고 있다. / 의사 결정에 관여하는 많은 규칙, 절차, / 그리고 여러 관리 계층을 가진 수직적 위계 구조를

Organic structures are more horizontal in nature, / ✔ where decision making is less centralized / and spread across the plane of the organization.
유기적 구조는 더 수평적인 성격을 가지며, / 의사 결정이 덜 중앙 집중화되고 / 조직 내 여러 곳에 분산된다.

조직의 관점에서, 어떤 조직이 어떻게 많은 다른 문화 유형들을 포함할 수 있는지에 대한 가장 매력적인 예시 중 하나는 조직 내 다른 부서들의 기능적 운영을 인식하는 것이다. 조직 내 다양한 부서와 과는 필연적으로 어떤 주어진 상황이라도 그들 자신만의 편향적이고 편파적인 관점에서 볼 것이다. 한 부서와 그 구성원들은 그들을 다른 이들이 그것들을 보는 대로 볼 수 없게 하는 '터널 시야 현상'을 갖게 될 것이다. 조직의 구조 자체가 갈등을 만들어낼 수 있다. 구조가 '기계적'인지 또는 '유기적'인지의 선택은 갈등 관리에 깊은 영향을 미칠 수 있다. 기계적 구조는 많은 규칙, 많은 절차 그리고 의사결정에 포함된 많은 수준의 관리를 가진 수직적 위계를 갖는다. 유기적 구조는 본래 더 수평적이고, 여기서는 의사결정이 덜 중앙 집중화되고, 조직 전반에 걸쳐 펼쳐진다.

Why? 왜 정답일까?

뒤 문장이 완전하므로 관계대명사 'which' 대신 관계부사 'where'이 쓰이는 것이 알맞다. 따라서 어법상 틀린 것은 ⑤이다.

Why? 왜 오답일까?

① 'is'의 주어가 'one of the most fascinationg examples'이므로 단수 be 동사 'is'가 적절히 쓰였다.
② 'tunnel vision'이 그들이 타인이 그들을 보듯이 스스로를 보는 것을 방해한다고 하였기 때문에 목적어 형태인 'them'이 알맞다.
③ 'whether A or B'는 A든지 B든지라는 숙어로, 적절하다.
④ '포함한'이라고 해석되어야 자연스러우므로 과거분사 'involved'는 적절하다.

- organizational ⓐ 구조적인
- fascinate ⓥ 멋지다
- functional ⓐ 기능상의, 기능적인
- acquire ⓥ 얻다
- influence ⓝ 영향
- viewpoint ⓝ 시각
- contain ⓥ 포함하다
- biased ⓐ 편향된, 선입견이 있는
- choice ⓝ 선택
- hierarchy ⓝ 계급, 계층

구문 풀이

1행 From an organizational viewpoint, one of the most fascinating examples
　　　　　　　　　　　　　　　　　one of the 복수명사 (단수취급)
of how any organization may contain many different types of culture is to recognize
　　　　　　　　　　　　　　　　　　조동사+동사원형　　　　　동사 to부정사(부사적 용법)
the functional operations of different departments within the organization.

★★ 문제 해결 꿀~팁 ★★

▶ 많이 틀린 이유는?
관계대명사와 관계부사의 차이와 관계대명사의 쓰임을 알아야 풀 수 있는 문제이다. 관계대명사는 뒤 문장이 불완전하며, 선행사를 필요로 한다. 해당 문장에서는 뒤 문장이 완전하기 때문에 관계대명사가 아닌 관계부사가 쓰이는 것이 적절하다.

▶ 문제 해결 방법은?
관계부사와 관계대명사의 개념을 확실히 하자. 관계부사는 뒤 문장이 완전하고, 장소, 시간, 방법 등의 정해진 단어들로 교체가 가능하다. 관계대명사는 뒤 문장이 불완전하며, 선행사를 필요로 한다. 헷갈리는 문법적 개념은 나올 때마다 정리해두자.

30 친환경적인 도로 만들기　　　　정답률 67% | 정답 ④

다음 글의 밑줄 친 부분 중, 문맥상 낱말의 쓰임이 적절하지 않은 것은? [3점]

An excellent alternative to calming traffic / is removing it.
교통을 진정시키는 훌륭한 대안은 / 그것을 제거하는 것이다.

Some cities ① reserve / an extensive network of lanes and streets / for bikes, pedestrians, and the occasional service vehicle.
일부 도시는 예약해 둔다. / 넓은 도로와 차선을 / 자전거, 보행자, 그리고 가끔 다니는 서비스 차량을 위해 /

This motivates people to travel by bike rather than by car, / making streets safer for everyone.
이것은 사람들이 자동차 대신 자전거로 이동하게 하며, / 모두에게 더 안전한 거리를 만든다.

As bicycles become more ② popular in a city, / planners can convert more automobile lanes and entire streets / to accommodate more of them.
자전거가 도시에 점점 더 인기를 얻게 되면서, / 도시 계획자들은 더 많은 자동차 차선과 전체 도로를 전환할 수 있다. / 자전거를 수용할 수 있도록

Nevertheless, / even the most bikeable cities still ③ require motor vehicle lanes / for taxis, emergency vehicles, and delivery trucks.
그럼에도 불구하고, / 자전거 친화적인 도시들도 여전히 자동차 차선이 필요하다. / 택시, 응급 차량, 그리고 배달 트럭을 위해

Delivery vehicles are frequently a target of animus, / but they are actually an essential component to making cities greener.
배달 차량은 자주 반감의 대상이 되지만, / 사실 그것들은 도시를 더 친환경적으로 만드는 데 중요한 요소이다.

A tightly packed delivery truck / is a far more ✔ efficient transporter of goods / than several hybrids carrying a few shopping bags each.
가득 실린 배달 트럭은 / 몇 개의 쇼핑 가방을 나르는 여러 대의 하이브리드 자동차보다 / 훨씬 더 효율적인 화물 운송 수단이다.

Distributing food and other goods to neighborhood vendors / ⑤ allows them to operate smaller stores close to homes / so that residents can walk, rather than drive, to get their groceries.
음식과 기타 물품을 인근 상점에 배달함으로써 / 그들이 집 근처에서 더 작은 가게를 운영할 수 있도록 허용하며, / 주민들이 장을 보기 위해 차 대신 걸을 수 있게 한다.

교통을 진정시키는 훌륭한 대안은 그것을 제거하는 것이다. 몇몇 도시는 자전거, 보행자, 그리고 수시 서비스 차량을 위한 광범위한 망의 도로와 거리를 ① 마련해 둔다. 이것은 사람들이 자동차보다 자전거로 이동을 하도록 동기를 부여하여 거리를 모두에게 더 안전하게 만든다. 자전거가 도시에서 더 ② 대중적이 되면, 계획자들은 더 많은 자동차 도로와 전체 거리를 더 많은 자전거를 수용할 수 있도록 전환할 수 있다. 그럼에도 불구하고, 가장 자전거를 타기 좋은 도시들조차도 여전히 택시, 긴급 차량, 그리고 배달 트럭을 위한 자동차 도로를 ③ 필요로 한다. 배달 차량은 자주 반감의 대상이지만, 그것들은 실제로 도시를 더 친환경적으로 만드는 필수 구성요소이다. 짐이 빽빽하게 들어찬 배달 트럭은 각각 몇 개의 쇼핑백을 실은 여러 하이브리드 차량보다 훨씬 더 ④ 비효율적인(→ 효율적인) 상품 운송 수단이다. 음식과 다른 상품을 동네 상인에게 배포하는 것은 그들이 집에 가까운 더 작은 상점을 ⑤ 운영할 수 있게 하고 그 결과 주민들은 식료품을 사기 위해 운전하기보다는 걸어갈 수 있다.

Why? 왜 정답일까?

배달 차량이 반감을 사지만 실제로는 이점이 더 많기 때문에 여러 하이브리드 차량보다 효율적인 상품 운송 수단이라고 바꾸는 것이 자연스럽다. 따라서 정답은 ④ 'inefficient'이다.

- excellent ⓐ 훌륭한
- traffic ⓝ 교통
- pedestrian ⓝ 보행자
- popular ⓐ 인기있는
- accommodate ⓥ 공간을 제공하다. 수용하다
- animus ⓝ 반감, 적대감
- component ⓝ 요소, 부품
- alternative ⓝ 대체
- remove ⓥ 제거하다
- rather ⓐ 꽤, 약간, 상당히
- convert ⓥ 바꾸다
- delivery ⓝ 배송
- essential ⓐ 극히 중요한, 가장 중요한
- tightly ⓐ 단단히, 꽉

구문 풀이

14행 Distributing food and other goods to neighborhood vendors allows them
　　　　동명사　　　　　　　　　　　　　neighborhood ←　　　동사
to operate smaller stores close to homes so that residents can walk, rather than
to부정사(부사적 용법)　←비교급　　　　　　　그래서　　　　　　동사1
drive, to get their groceries.
동사2　 to부정사(부사적 용법)

★★★ 등급을 가르는 문제!

31 창작의 매력　　　　정답률 31% | 정답 ②

다음 빈칸에 들어갈 말로 가장 적절한 것을 고르시오.

① simple – 단순한
✔ original – 독창적인
③ familiar – 익숙한
④ conventional – 전통적인
⑤ understandable – 이해할 수 있는

You hear again and again / that some of the greatest composers were misunderstood / in their own day.
당신은 계속해서 듣는다. / 가장 위대한 작곡가들 중 일부가 오해받았다는 이야기를 / 그들의 시대에는

Not everyone could understand the compositions / of Beethoven, Brahms, or Stravinsky / in their day.
모두가 이해할 수 있었던 것은 아니었다. / 베토벤, 브람스, 또는 스트라빈스키의 작품을 / 그들의 시대에

The reason for this initial lack of acceptance / is unfamiliarity.
이러한 초기의 받아들임 부족의 이유는 / 익숙하지 않음이다.

The musical forms, or ideas expressed within them, / were completely new.
그 음악 형식, 혹은 그 안에 표현된 아이디어들은 / 완전히 새로웠다.

And yet, this is exactly one of the things / that makes them so great.
그리고 이 점이 바로 / 그들을 위대하게 만드는 것들 중 하나다.

Effective composers have their own ideas.

유능한 작곡가들은 자신만의 아이디어를 가지고 있다.
Have you ever seen the classic movie *Amadeus?*
당신은 고전 영화 *Amadeus*를 본 적이 있는가?
The composer Antonio Salieri is the "host" of this movie; / he's depicted as one of the most famous non-great composers.
작곡가 Antonio Salieri는 이 영화의 "주최자"이다; / 그는 가장 유명한 비위대한 작곡가 중 한 명으로 묘사된다.
He lived at the time of Mozart / and was completely overshadowed by him.
그는 모차르트와 같은 시대에 살았으며 / 완전히 그에 의해 가려졌다.
Now, Salieri wasn't a bad composer; / in fact, he was a very good one.
Salieri는 나쁜 작곡가가 아니었다; / 사실 그는 매우 훌륭한 작곡가였다.
But he wasn't one of the world's great composers / because his work wasn't <u>original</u>.
그러나 그는 세계의 위대한 작곡가 중 한 명이 아니었다. / 그의 작품이 독창적이지 않았기 때문에.
What he wrote / sounded just like what everyone else was composing / at the time.
그가 쓴 음악은 / 다른 모든 사람들이 작곡한 것과 비슷하게 들렸다. / 그 당시에

여러분은 몇몇 가장 위대한 작곡가들이 그들의 시대에 진가를 인정받지 못했다고 몇 번이고 듣는다. 그들의 시대에 베토벤, 브람스, 스트라빈스키의 곡들을 모든 사람이 이해할 수 있었던 것은 아니었다. 이러한 초기의 수용 부족의 이유는 낯섦이다. 음악적 형식, 또는 그 안에 표현된 생각은 완전히 새로운 것이었다. 그럼에도 불구하고 이것이 바로 그들을 그토록 위대하게 만드는 것들 중 하나이다. 유능한 작곡가는 그들 자신만의 생각을 갖는다. 당신은 고전 영화 *Amadeus*를 본 적이 있는가? 작곡가 Antonio Salieri가 이 영화의 '주인공'이다. 그는 가장 유명한 위대하지 않은 작곡가 중 한 명으로 묘사된다. 그는 모차르트 시대에 살았고 그에 의해 완전히 가려졌다. 인제 보니 Salieri는 형편없는 작곡가가 아니었다. 사실, 그는 매우 훌륭한 작곡가였다. 하지만 그의 작품이 독창적이지 않았기 때문에 그는 세계의 위대한 작곡가들 중 한 명은 아니었다. 그가 쓴 곡은 마치 그 당시 모든 다른 사람들이 작곡했던 것처럼 들렸다.

Why? 왜 정답일까?

'What he wrote / sounded just like what everyone else was composing at the time. (그가 쓴 곡은 마치 그 당시 모든 다른 사람들이 작곡했던 것처럼 들렸다.)'를 미루어 보아 작곡의 독창성이 중요하다고 얘기하고 있으므로 ② 'original'이 빈칸에 들어갈 말로 적절하다.

- **composer** ⓝ 작곡가
- **composition** ⓝ 구성
- **initial** ⓐ 초기의
- **acceptance** ⓝ 수락
- **effective** ⓐ 유능한
- **misunderstand** ⓥ 오해하다
- **reason** ⓝ 이유, 까닭, 사유
- **lack** ⓝ 부족, 결핍
- **completely** ⓐⓓ 완전히
- **depict** ⓥ 묘사하다

구문 풀이

1행 You hear ┌─again and again 계속해서─┐
　　　 　　　　　　　　 again and again that some of the greatest composers were
　　　　지각동사　　　　　　　　　 접속사　　　 some of the 복수명사(복수취급)
misunderstood in their own day.

★★ 문제 해결 꿀~팁 ★★

▶ 많이 틀린 이유는?
Salieri가 위대한 작곡가가 아니었던 이유가 다른 사람들의 것과 차별성이 없었기 때문이라고 설명하는 글이다. 빈칸 문장의 다음 문장 'What he wrote sounded just like what everyone else was composing at the time.'이 가장 분명한 힌트다. 가장 많이 고른 ③ 'familiar' (익숙한)는 ② 'original' (독창적인)과 반대의 뜻으로, 'Now, Salieri wasn't a bad composer; in fact, he was a very good one.'의 문장 때문에 헷갈릴 수 있다.
▶ 문제 해결 방법은?
주어진 빈칸의 문장이 접속사 'But'으로 시작하므로 앞의 내용과 반대되어야 자연스럽다. 빈칸 문제는 본문의 주제와 글의 흐름을 파악해야 풀 수 있는데, 주로 접속사에 큰 힌트를 얻을 수 있다.

---

32 메시지에 매체가 끼치는 영향　　　정답률 49% | 정답 ①

다음 빈칸에 들어갈 말로 가장 적절한 것을 고르시오. [3점]

✔ see the world according to a new set of codes – 새로운 코드에 따라 세상을 바라보다.
② ignore unfamiliar messages from new media – 새로운 매체에서의 낯선 메시지를 무시하다.
③ maintain steady focus and clear understanding – 꾸준한 집중과 명료한 이해를 유지하다.
④ interpret information through a traditional lens – 전통적인 렌즈를 통해 정보를 해석하다.
⑤ enjoy various media contents with one platform – 한가지 매체에서 다양한 미디어 콘텐츠를 즐기다.

Every time a new medium comes along / — whether it's the invention of the printed book, or TV, or SNS — / and you start to use it, / it's like you are putting on a new kind of goggles, / with their own special colors and lenses.
새로운 매체가 등장할 때마다 / — 그것이 인쇄된 책, TV, 또는 SNS의 발명이든 간에 — / 그것을 사용하기 시작하면, / 마치 새로운 종류의 고글을 쓰는 것과 같다. / 그만의 특별한 색과 렌즈를 가진
Each set of goggles you put on / makes you see things differently.
다른 고글을 쓸 때마다 / 세상을 다르게 보게 된다.
So when you start to watch television, / before you absorb the message of any particular TV show / — whether it's *Wheel of Fortune* or *The Wire* — / you start to see the world / as being shaped like television itself.
그래서 TV를 보기 시작하면 / 특정 TV 프로그램의 메시지를 받아들이기 전에 / — 그것이 *Wheel of Fortune*이든 *The Wire*이든 — / 세상이 보이기 시작한다. / TV 자체처럼 형성된 것처럼
That's why Marshall McLuhan said / that every time a new medium comes along / — a new way for humans to communicate — / it has buried in it a message.
이것이 Marshall McLuhan이 말한 이유이다. / 새로운 매체가 등장할 때마다 / — 인간이 소통하는 새로운 방식이 — / 그 안에 메시지가 담겨져 있다고
It is gently guiding us / to see the world according to a new set of codes.
그것은 우리를 부드럽게 이끌어 / 새로운 코드 세트에 따라 세상을 보게 한다.
The way information gets to you, McLuhan argued, / is more important than the information itself.
McLuhan은 주장했다, / 정보가 전달되는 방식이 정보 자체보다 더 중요하다고
TV teaches you that the world is fast; / that it's about surfaces and appearances.
TV는 세상이 빠르다고 가르친다.; / 그것은 표면과 외양에 관한 것이라고

인쇄된 책의 발명이든 텔레비전의 발명이든 SNS의 발명이든, 새로운 매체가 나타나 여러분이 그것을 쓰기 시작할 때마다 여러분은 고유의 색깔과 렌즈를 가진 새 고글을 쓰는 것과 같다.

여러분이 쓰는 각각의 고글은 세상을 다른 방식으로 바라보게 한다. 그러므로 여러분이 텔레비전을 보기 시작하면, 그것이 *Wheel of Fortune*이든 *The Wire*든, 특정 텔레비전 프로그램의 메시지를 흡수하기 이전에 이미 세상을 텔레비전 그 자체처럼 형성된 것으로 바라보게 된다. 이러한 이유로 Marshall McLuhan이 새로운 매체, 즉, 인간이 의사소통하는 새로운 방식이 나타날 때마다 그 안에 메시지가 담겨 있다고 말한 것이다. 새로운 매체는 자연스럽게 우리가 새로운 일련의 방식에 따라 세상을 바라보게 한다. McLuhan은 정보가 여러분에게 도달하는 방식이 정보 자체보다 더 중요하다고 주장했다. 텔레비전은 우리에게 세상은 빠르고, 중요한 것은 표면과 겉모습이라고 가르친다.

Why? 왜 정답일까?

인쇄된 책, 텔레비전, SNS 등의 새로운 매체가 나타날 때마다 새 고글을 쓰는 것과 같다고 하였으니 (Every time a new medium comes along — whether it's the invention of the printed book, or TV, or SNS — and you start to use it, it's like you are putting on a new kind of goggles, with their own special colors and lenses.) 매체마다 메시지가 다르게 전달된다는 것이 주제임을 알 수 있다. 따라서 빈칸에는 ① 'see the world according to a new set of codes'가 적절하다.

- **medium** ⓝ 매체
- **invention** ⓝ 발명
- **absorb** ⓥ 흡수하다
- **particular** ⓐ 특정한
- **bury** ⓥ 묻다
- **guide** ⓥ 이끌다
- **appearance** ⓝ 외모
- **come along** 따라오다
- **goggle** ⓝ 고글
- **differently** ⓐⓓ 다르게, 같지 않게
- **communicate** ⓥ 의사소통하다
- **gently** ⓐⓓ 다정하게, 부드럽게
- **argue** ⓥ 주장하다

구문 풀이

13행 The way information gets to you, McLuhan argued, is more important
　　　　　　 관계부사 how　　　　　　　　　　　　　　　　　　　　　　 비교급
than the information itself.
　　　　　　　재귀대명사(그 자체)

---

33 개념에 대한 집착의 위험성　　　정답률 47% | 정답 ①

다음 빈칸에 들어갈 말로 가장 적절한 것을 고르시오. [3점]

✔ encourage us to see things that aren't present – 존재하지 않는 것을 보도록 부추긴다.
② force scientists to simplify scientific theories – 과학적 이론을 단순화하기 위해서 과학자들을 강제한다.
③ let us think science is essential and practical – 과학이 필수적이고 실용적이라고 생각하게 만든다.
④ drive physicists to explore philosophy – 물리학자들이 철학을 탐구하게 이끈다.
⑤ lead us to ignore the unknown – 우리를 미지를 무시하도록 이끈다.

Concepts are vital to human survival, / but we must also be careful with them / because concepts open the door to essentialism.
개념은 인간의 생존에 필수적이지만, / 우리는 그것들을 주의 깊게 다뤄야 한다. / 왜냐하면 개념은 본질주의로 이어질 수 있기 때문에
They encourage us to see things that aren't present.
그것들은 우리가 존재하지 않는 것을 보도록 부추긴다.
Stuart Firestein opens his book, *Ignorance*, / with an old proverb, / "It is very difficult to find a black cat in a dark room, / especially when there is no cat."
Stuart Firestein은 그의 책 *Ignorance*을 / 오래된 속담으로 시작한다, / "어두운 방에서 검은 고양이를 찾는 것은 매우 어렵다. / 특히 고양이가 없을 때는 더더욱"
This statement / beautifully sums up / the search for essences.
이 문장은 / 아름답게 요약한다. / 본질을 찾는 과정
History has many examples of scientists / who searched fruitlessly for an essence / because they used the wrong concept to guide their hypotheses.
역사는 많은 예가 있다. / 잘못된 개념을 사용하여 가설을 세운 결과 / 본질을 헛되이 찾은 과학자들의
Firestein gives the example of luminiferous ether, / a mysterious substance that was thought to fill the universe / so that light would have a medium to move through.
Firestein은 발광성 에테르의 예를 든다. / 우주를 채우고 있다고 여겨진 신비로운 물질로서 / 빛이 이동할 수 있는 매체로서
The ether was a black cat, / writes Firestein, / and physicists had been theorizing in a dark room, / and then experimenting in it, / looking for evidence of a cat that did not exist.
에테르는 검은 고양이였고, / Firestein은 쓴다. / 물리학자들은 어두운 방에서 이론을 세우고 / 실험하며, / 존재하지 않는 고양이의 증거를 찾고 있었다고

개념은 인간의 생존에 필수적이지만, 개념이 본질주의로 향하는 문을 열기 때문에 우리는 또한 그것들을 주의해야 한다. 그것들은 존재하지 않는 것들을 보도록 우리를 부추긴다. Stuart Firestein은 "어두운 방에서 검은 고양이를 찾는 것은 특히 고양이가 없을 때 매우 어렵다."라는 옛 속담으로 그의 책, *Ignorance*를 시작한다. 이 말은 본질에 대한 탐구를 훌륭하게 요약한다. 역사는 가설을 이끄는 잘못된 개념을 사용했기 때문에 헛되이 본질을 탐색했던 과학자들의 많은 예를 가지고 있다. Firestein은 빛이 통과할 수 있는 매개체를 갖도록 우주를 가득 채워줄 것이라 여겨진 신비한 물질인 발광 에테르의 예를 제시한다. Firestein이 쓰기를, 에테르는 검은 고양이였고, 물리학자들은 어두운 방에서 이론을 세우고, 그리고 나서 존재하지 않았던 고양이라는 증거를 찾으며, 그 안에서 실험을 하고 있었던 것이었다.

Why? 왜 정답일까?

개념에 과도하게 집중하게 되면 본질주의로 빠질 우려가 있다며 우주를 채우고 있다는 에테르라는 성분을 예로 들며 설명한다. 어두운 방에서 검은 고양이를 찾는 비유를 하며 검은 고양이가 실제로는 존재하지 않고, 따라서 개념에 과도하게 집착하는 것은 존재하지 않는 것들을 보도록 만들기 때문에 ① 'encourage us to see things that aren't present'가 자연스럽다.

- **concept** ⓝ 개념
- **careful** ⓐ 조심스러운
- **encourage** ⓥ 부추기다
- **fruitlessly** ⓐⓓ 득없이
- **medium** ⓝ 도구
- **evidence** ⓝ 증거
- **vital** ⓐ 필수적인
- **essentialism** ⓝ 본질주의
- **statement** ⓝ 표현, 진술
- **luminiferous** ⓐ 빛을 내는, 발광성의
- **experiment** ⓥ 실험하다
- **exist** ⓥ 존재하다

구문 풀이

12행 The ether was a black cat, writes Firestein, and physicists had been
　　　　　　　　　　　　　　　　　　　　　　　　　　　 과거완료진행1

theorizing in a dark room, and then experimenting in it, looking for evidence of a
과거완료진행2　　　　　　　　　현재분사
cat that did not exist.
주격관계대명사

★★★ 등급을 가르는 문제!

34　새로운 명성의 개념　　　　정답률 35% | 정답 ④

다음 빈칸에 들어갈 말로 가장 적절한 것을 고르시오. [3점]

① shifts to that of elite celebrity – 엘리트 유명인의 것으로 변화한다.
② disappears gradually over time – 시간이 지남에 따라 점차적으로 사라진다.
③ focuses solely on talent and class – 재능과 계층에만 집중한다.
④ reconstructs the meaning of fame – 명성의 의미를 재구성한다.
⑤ restricts interactions with the public – 대중과의 상호작용을 제한한다.

While social media attention is potentially an instrument / to achieve ends like elite celebrity, / some content creators desire ordinary fame / as a social end in itself.
소셜 미디어 주목은 수단이 될 수 있지만, / 엘리트 연예인과 같은 목적을 달성하는 / 일부 콘텐츠 제작자들은 평범한 명성을 원한다. / 그것 자체로서 사회적 목표로서의
Not unlike reality television stars, / social media celebrities are often criticized / for not having skills and talents / associated with traditional, elite celebrity, / such as acting or singing ability.
리얼리티 TV 스타들과 마찬가지로, / 소셜 미디어 유명인들은 종종 비판을 받는다. / 전통적인 엘리트 유명인들이 가진 / 연기나 노래와 같은 / 기술이나 재능이 없다는
This criticism highlights the fact / that digital content creators face / real barriers to crossing over / to the sphere of elite celebrity.
이 비판은 사실을 강조한다. / 디지털 콘텐츠 제작자들이 마주함이 / 실제 장벽을 넘어가는 데에 / 엘리트 유명인의 영역으로
However, the criticism also misses the point / that the phenomenon of ordinary celebrity / reconstructs the meaning of fame.
그러나, 이 비판은 또한 중요한 점을 놓치는데, / 평범한 명성의 현상이 / 명성의 의미를 재구성한다는 점이다.
The elite celebrity is symbolized by the metaphor of the star, / characterized by mystery and hierarchical distance / and associated with naturalized qualities of talent and class.
엘리트 유명인은 별의 은유로 상징되며, / 신비와 계층적 거리를 특징으로 하며 / 타고난 재능과 계급의 속성과 연결된다.
The ordinary celebrity attracts attention / through regular and frequent interactions / with other ordinary people.
평범한 유명인은 주목을 끈다. / 정기적이고 빈번한 상호작용을 통해 / 다른 일반인들과의
Achieving ordinary fame as a social media celebrity / is like doing well at a game, / because in this sphere, fame is nothing more nor less / than relatively high scores on / attention scales, the metrics of subscribers, followers, Likes, or clicks built into social media applications.
소셜 미디어 유명인으로서 평범한 명성을 얻는 것은 / 게임을 잘하는 것과 같다. / 왜냐하면 이 영역에서 명성은 그 이상도 이하도 아니고 / 상대적으로 높은 점수일 뿐이다. / 소셜 미디어 애플리케이션에 내장된 구독자, 팔로워, 좋아요, 또는 클릭 수와 같은 관심의 척도인

소셜 미디어 관심은 잠재적으로 엘리트 명성과 같은 목적을 달성하기 위한 도구인 반면, 일부 콘텐츠 제작자들은 사회적 목적 그 자체로서 평범한 명성을 원한다. 리얼리티 텔레비전 스타들과 다르지 않게, 소셜 미디어 유명인들은 연기나 가창력과 같은 전통적인 엘리트 명성과 관련된 기술과 재능을 가지고 있지 않다는 이유로 종종 비판을 받는다. 이러한 비판은 디지털 콘텐츠 제작자들이 엘리트 명성의 영역으로 넘어가는 데 있어 실질적인 장벽에 직면하고 있다는 사실을 강조한다. 그러나 이 비판은 또한 평범한 명성 현상이 명성의 의미를 재구성한다는 점을 놓친다. 엘리트 유명인은 스타라는 은유로 상징되고, 신비로움과 계층적 거리로 특징지어지며, 타고난 자질의 재능과 계층에 연관되어 있다. 평범한 유명인은 다른 평범한 사람들과의 정기적이고 빈번한 상호작용을 통해 관심을 끈다. 소셜 미디어 유명인으로서 평범한 명성을 얻는 것은 게임에서 잘하는 것과 같은데, 왜냐하면 이 영역에서 명성은 관심 척도, 즉, 소셜 미디어 애플리케이션에 내장된 구독자, 팔로워, 좋아요 또는 클릭의 측정 기준에서 상대적으로 높은 점수 그 이상도 그 이하도 아니기 때문이다.

Why? 왜 정답일까?

기존의 'elite celebrity'와 대조되는 'ordinary celebrity'의 개념을 제시하며, 'elite celebrity'는 비밀스럽고 고귀한 모습을 보이는 반면 'ordinary celebrity'는 대중과 친숙하고 소통을 잘 하는 특징을 가지고 있다고 설명한다. 따라서 'ordinary celebrity'는 명성의 의미를 재구성한다는 ④ 'reconstructs the meaning of fame'가 빈칸에 적절하다.

- celebrity ⑩ 유명인
- instrument ⑩ 도구
- content ⑩ 컨텐츠
- phenomenon ⑩ 현상
- hierarchical ⓐ 계층제의, 계층에 따른
- attention ⑩ 관심
- achieve ⓥ 달성하다
- creator ⑩ 창작자
- symbolize ⓥ 상징화되다
- interaction ⑩ 상호 작용

구문 풀이

15행 Achieving ordinary fame as a social media celebrity is like doing well at a
　　　　동명사　　　　　　　　　　　　　　　　　　　동명사
game, because in this sphere, fame is nothing more nor less than relatively high
　　　　　　　　　　　　　　　　그 이상도 그 이하도 아니다
scores on attention scales, the metrics of subscribers, followers, Likes, or clicks
(that are) built into social media applications.
주격관계대명사＋be 동사 생략

★★ 문제 해결 꿀~팁 ★★

▶ 많이 틀린 이유는?
글에서 핵심적으로 강조하는 것은 'ordinary celebrity'와 'elite celebrity' 간의 차이점이다. 소셜 미디어에서의 유명세는 기존의 엘리트적 명성과 기준이 다르다는 것이다. 가장 많이 고른 ① 'shifts to that of elite celebrity'는 그럴듯해 보이지만, 전환은 언급되지 않았다. 'ordinary celebrity'와 'elite celebrity'의 명성에 대한 기준은 다르고, 새로운 'ordinary celebrity'의 명성의 기준이 생겼다고 이해하는 것이 맞다.
▶ 문제 해결 방법은?
빈칸 문제는 글의 흐름, 문맥 파악이 중요하다. 해당 글에서는 'ordinary celebrity'와 'elite celebrity'

를 비교하고 있으므로 'ordinary celebrity'에 해당하는 단어와 'elite celebrity'에 해당하는 단어를 각각 다른 표시로 체크해가며 읽는 것이 직관적인 문제 풀이에 도움이 될 수 있다.

35　장기기억으로 기억을 넘기기　　　　정답률 75% | 정답 ④

다음 글에서 전체 흐름과 관계 <u>없는</u> 문장은?

Why do we have the illusion / that cramming for an exam / is the best learning strategy?
왜 우리는 착각을 할까? / 시험에 벼락치기가 / 가장 좋은 학습 방법이라는
Because we are unable to differentiate / between the various sections of our memory.
그것은 우리가 구별하지 못하기 때문이다 / 기억의 다양한 부분을
Immediately after reading our textbook or our class notes, / information is fully present in our mind.
교과서나 강의 노트를 읽고 난 직후, / 정보는 완전히 우리의 마음속에 있다.
① It sits in our conscious working memory, / in an active form.
그것은 의식적인 작업 기억에 자리 잡고 있다. / 활성화된 형태로
② We feel as if we know it, / because it is present / in our short-term storage space ... / but this short-term section has nothing to do with the long-term memory / that we will need in order to recall / the same information a few days later.
우리는 그것을 알고 있는 것처럼 느낀다. / 우리의 단기 기억 공간에 ... / 그러나 이 단기 기억 부분은 장기 기억과는 아무런 관련이 없다. / 기억을 위해 필요한 / 며칠 후에 같은 정보를
③ After a few seconds or minutes, / working memory already starts disappearing, / and after a few days, the effect becomes enormous: / unless you retest your knowledge, / memory vanishes.
몇 초 또는 몇 분 후에, / 작업 기억은 이미 사라지기 시작하며, / 며칠이 지나면 그 효과는 더욱 커진다: / 지식을 다시 테스트하지 않으면, / 기억은 사라진다.
④ Focusing on exploring new topics / rather than reviewing the same material over and over again / can improve your academic performance.
같은 자료를 반복해서 복습하는 대신 / 새로운 주제를 탐구하는 데 집중하는 것이 / 학업 성과를 향상시킬 수 있다.
⑤ To get information into long-term memory, / it is essential to study the material, then test yourself, / rather than spend all your time studying.
정보를 장기 기억에 저장하려면, / 자료를 공부한 다음 스스로 테스트하는 것이 필수적이다. / 시간을 모두 공부에만 할애하는 대신

왜 우리는 시험을 위해 벼락 공부를 하는 것이 최고의 학습 전략이라는 착각을 하는 것일까? 우리가 우리의 기억의 다양한 구획을 구별할 수 없기 때문이다. 우리의 교과서나 수업 노트를 읽은 직후에는 정보가 우리 머릿속에 완전히 존재한다. ① 그것은 우리의 의식적인 작업 기억에 활동적인 형태로 자리한다. ② 그것은 우리의 단기 저장 공간에 존재하기 때문에 우리는 마치 우리가 그것을 알고 있는 것처럼 느끼지만, 이 단기 구획은 며칠 후 같은 정보를 기억하기 위해 우리가 필요로 할 장기 기억과는 아무런 관련이 없다. ③ 몇 초 또는 몇 분 후, 작업 기억은 이미 사라지기 시작하고, 며칠 후 그 영향은 엄청나게 되어, 여러분이 자신의 지식을 다시 테스트하지 않으면 기억은 사라진다. ④ 같은 자료를 반복해서 다시 복습하는 것보다 새로운 주제를 탐구하는 데 집중하는 것이 여러분의 학업 성취를 향상시킬 수 있다. ⑤ 정보를 장기 기억에 넣으려면, 여러분의 모든 시간을 공부하는 데에 쓰기보다는 자료를 공부하고 나서 스스로를 테스트하는 것이 필수적이다.

Why? 왜 정답일까?

단기 기억을 장기 기억으로 옮기는 방법에 대해 얘기하고 있다. 이전 지식을 다시 테스트해야 기억에 남아있는다고 하기 때문에(After a few seconds or minutes, working memory already starts disappearing, and after a few days, the effect becomes enormous: unless you retest your knowledge, memory vanishes.) 전체 흐름과 관계 없는 문장은 ④이다.

- illusion ⑩ 환각
- strategy ⑩ 전략
- section ⑩ 부분
- information ⑩ 정보
- conscious ⓐ 의식적인
- effect ⑩ 효과
- knowledge ⑩ 정보
- cram ⓥ 벼락 공부를 하다
- differentiate ⓥ 차별화하다
- memory ⑩ 기억
- mind ⑩ 생각
- disappear ⓥ 사라지다
- enormous ⓐ 막대한, 거대한
- vanish ⓥ 사라지다

구문 풀이

13행 Focusing on exploring new topics rather than reviewing the same material
　　　　동명사　　　동명사1　　　　　~보다　　　동명사2
over and over again can improve your academic performance.
계속하여

36　관찰에 의한 모방　　　　정답률 72% | 정답 ②

주어진 글 다음에 이어질 글의 순서로 가장 적절한 것을 고르시오.

① (A) – (C) – (B)
② (B) – (A) – (C)
③ (B) – (C) – (A)
④ (C) – (A) – (B)
⑤ (C) – (B) – (A)

The discovery of mirror neurons has profoundly changed / the way we think of a fundamental human capacity, / learning by observation.
거울 뉴런의 발견은 크게 바꿨다. / 우리가 인간의 근본적인 능력에 대해 생각하는 방식을, / 관찰을 통한 학습을
(B) As children / we learn a lot / by observing what our parents and friends do.
어린 시절 / 우리는 많은 것을 배운다. / 부모님과 친구들이 하는 것을 관찰함으로써
Newborns, in the first week of life, / have an inborn tendency / to stick out their tongue / if their parents stick out theirs.
신생아는, 후후 첫 주에, / 타고난 경향을 가지고 있다. / 그들도 혀를 내미는 / 부모가 혀를 내밀면
Such imitation is not perfect.
그러한 모방은 완벽하지 않다.
(A) You may not see the tongue stick out each time / you stick yours out at your newborn, / but if you do it many times, / the tongue will come out more often / than if you do something different.
매번 혀를 내밀 때마다 보지 못할 수도 있다. / 신생아가 혀를 내미는 것을, / 그러나 여러 번 하면, / 혀를 더 자주 내밀게 될 것이다. / 다른 행동을 할 때보다
Babies babble / and later start to imitate / the sounds their parents produce.

아기들은 옹알이를 하고 / 이후에는 흉내 내기 시작한다. / 부모가 내는 소리를
(C) Later still, / they play with vacuum cleaners and hammers / in imitation of their parents.
그 후에는, / 진공청소기나 망치로 놀기도 한다. / 부모를 흉내 내어
Our modern cultures, / in which we write, speak, read, build spaceships / and go to school, / can work only because we are not restricted to the behavior / we are born with or learn by trial and error.
우리 현대 문화는, / 우리가 글을 쓰고, 말하고, 읽고, 우주선을 만들고 / 학교에 다니는, / 행동에만 제한되지 않기 때문에 가능한 것이다. / 태어날 때부터 가지고 있거나 시행착오로 배우는
We can learn a lot / by simply watching others.
우리는 많은 것을 배울 수 있다. / 단순히 다른 사람들을 관찰함으로써

거울 뉴런의 발견은 관찰에 의한 학습이라는 근본적인 인간의 능력에 대해 우리가 생각하는 방식을 완전히 바꾸어 놓았다.
(B) 어린이일 때 우리는 우리의 부모와 친구들이 하는 것을 관찰하면서 많이 배운다. 갓난아기들은 생의 첫 주에 그들의 부모가 그들의 것(혀)을 내밀면 자신의 혀를 내미는 선천적인 성향을 갖고 있다. 그러한 모방은 완벽하지 않다.
(A) 당신은 당신의 갓난아기에게 당신의 것(혀)을 내밀 때마다 (아기의) 혀가 내밀어 나오는 것을 보지 못할 수도 있지만, 만약 당신이 그것을 여러 번 한다면 당신이 다른 것을 할 때보다 (아기의) 혀가 더 자주 나올 것이다. 아기들은 옹알이하고 이후에 그들의 부모가 내는 소리를 모방하기 시작한다.
(C) 이후에도 여전히, 그들은 부모들을 흉내 내어 진공청소기와 망치를 갖고 논다. 쓰고 말하고 읽고 우주선을 만들고 학교에 가는 우리의 현대 문화는 단지 우리가 가지고 태어나는 또는 시행착오를 통해 배우는 행동에 국한되지 않기 때문에 작동할 수 있다. 우리는 그저 다른 사람들을 관찰하는 것을 통해 많이 배울 수 있다.

Why? 왜 정답일까?

주어진 글은 거울 뉴런을 발견하며 관찰에 의한 학습이라는 생각이 바뀐다고 한다. (B)에서는 혀를 내미는 행동의 관찰에 대한 얘기를 하고 있고, (A)는 혀를 내미는 것을 너머 옹알이와 소리를 모방한다고 한다. 따라서 (B)와 (A)가 이어져야 하고, 그 이후에도 모방으로 학습한다는 (C)가 마지막에 오는 순서가 알맞다. 따라서 답은 ② '(B) – (A) – (C)'이다.

- **discovery** ⓝ 발견
- **profoundly** ⓐⓓ 풍부하게
- **capacity** ⓝ 능력
- **babble** ⓥ 옹알이하다
- **imitation** ⓝ 모방
- **neuron** ⓝ 뉴런
- **fundamental** ⓐ 기본적인
- **observation** ⓝ 관찰
- **tongue** ⓝ 혀

구문 풀이

4행 You may not see the tongue stick out each time you stick yours out at [지각동사] [동사원형] your newborn, but if you do it many times, the tongue will come out more often [가정법] [조동사+동사원형] than if you do something different.

---

37 녹음된 목소리가 다르게 들리는 이유 정답률 73% | 정답 ④

주어진 글 다음에 이어질 글의 순서로 가장 적절한 것을 고르시오. [3점]
① (A) – (C) – (B)   ② (B) – (A) – (C)
③ (B) – (C) – (A)   ✓④ (C) – (A) – (B)
⑤ (C) – (B) – (A)

Have you ever been surprised / to hear a recording of your own voice?
당신은 자신의 목소리가 녹음된 것을 듣고 / 놀란 적이 있는가?
You might have thought, / "Is that really what my voice sounds like?"
당신은 아마 생각했을 것이다. / "저게 정말 내 목소리야?"
(C) Maybe your accent is more pronounced in the recording / than you realized, / or your voice is higher than it seems to your own ears.
아마도 당신의 억양이 녹음에서 더 두드러지게 들릴 것이다. / 당신이 인지한 것보다, / 또는 당신의 목소리가 당신이 듣기에는 생각보다 더 높게
This is of course quite a common experience.
이것은 물론 매우 흔한 경험이다.
The explanation is actually fairly simple.
그 설명은 사실 꽤 간단하다.
(A) There are two pathways / through which we perceive our own voice / when we speak.
두 가지 경로가 있다. / 자신의 목소리를 인지하는 / 우리가 말을 할 때
One is the route / through which we perceive most external sounds, / like waves that travel from the air through the outer, middle and inner ear.
하나는 경로인데, / 우리가 대부분의 외부 소리를 인지하는 / 공기 중의 파동이 외이, 중이, 내이를 통해 전달되는 것처럼
(B) But because our vocal cords vibrate when we speak, / there is a second internal path.
그러나 우리가 말을 할 때 성대가 진동하기 때문에, / 두 번째 내부 경로가 있다.
Vibrations are conducted through our bones / and stimulate our inner ears directly.
진동이 우리의 뼈를 통해 전달되어 / 내이를 직접 자극한다.
Lower frequencies are emphasized along this pathway.
이 경로에서는 저주파가 강조된다.
That makes your voice sound deeper and richer to yourself / than it may sound to other people.
그 때문에 당신 자신의 목소리가 더 깊고 풍부하게 들린다. / 다른 사람들이 듣는 것보다

당신은 당신의 음성 녹음을 듣고 놀랐던 적이 있는가? 당신은 '내 목소리가 정말 이렇게 들리는가?'라고 생각했을지도 모른다.
(C) 어쩌면 녹음에서는 당신이 인식한 것보다 당신의 억양이 더 강조되거나, 당신의 목소리가 당신의 귀에 들리는 것 같은 것보다 더 높다. 이것은 당연히 꽤 흔한 경험이다. 이 설명은 사실 꽤 간단하다.
(A) 우리가 말할 때 우리 자신의 목소리를 인지하는 데는 두 가지 경로가 있다. 하나는 외이, 중이, 내이를 통하는 공기로부터 이동하는 파동처럼 우리가 대부분의 외부의 소리를 인지하는 경로이다.
(B) 그러나 우리가 말할 때 우리의 성대가 진동하기 때문에 두 번째 내부의 경로가 있다. 진동은 뼈를 통해 전해지고, 우리의 내이를 직접 자극한다. 낮은 주파수는 이 경로를 따라

두드러진다. 그것은 당신의 목소리가 다른 사람에게 들릴 수 있는 것보다 당신 자신에게 더 깊고 풍부하게 들리게 한다.

Why? 왜 정답일까?

스스로의 목소리가 생각했던 것과 다르게 들리는 경험을 얘기하고 있다. 따라서 스스로의 목소리가 생각했던 것과 다르게 들리는 예시를 제시하는 (C)가 주어진 글 뒤에 오고, 이것의 이유를 설명하는 (A), 마지막으로 (A)의 구조적 설명을 자세히 하는 (B)가 오는 것이 자연스럽다. 따라서 ④ (C) – (A) – (B)가 정답이다.

- **record** ⓥ 녹음하다
- **perceive** ⓥ 인식하다
- **external** ⓐ 외부의
- **vibrate** ⓥ 진동하다
- **conduct** ⓥ (열·전기·소리 등을) 전도하다
- **stimulate** ⓥ 자극하다
- **frequency** ⓝ 주파수
- **pathway** ⓝ 길
- **route** ⓝ 경로, 길
- **vocal cord** ⓝ 성대
- **internal** ⓐ 내부의
- **frequency** ⓝ 주파수
- **directly** ⓐⓓ 직접으로
- **fairly** ⓐⓓ 상당히, 꽤

구문 풀이

9행 Vibrations are conducted through our bones and stimulate our inner ears [수동태1] [전치사(~을 통해서)] [수동태2] directly.

---

38 상사형질과 상동형질의 차이점 정답률 57% | 정답 ③

글의 흐름으로 보아, 주어진 문장이 들어가기에 가장 적절한 곳을 고르시오.

Biologists distinguish two kinds of similarity.
생물학자는 두 가지의 유사함을 구분한다.
① "Analogous" traits / are ones that have a common function / but arose on different branches of the evolutionary tree / and are in an important sense not "the same" organ.
"유사한" 특징은 / 공통된 기능을 가지고 있는 것이다. / 하지만 다른 진화적 나무의 가지에서 나는 것이다. / 그리고 "같지 않은" 장기라는 중요한 감각이 있다.
② The wings of birds / and the wings of bees / are both used for flight and are similar in some ways / because anything used for flight / has to be built in those ways, / but they arose independently in evolution / and have nothing in common / beyond their use in flight.
새들의 날개와 / 벌들의 날개는 / 모두 비행을 위해 사용되고 어떤 방법에서는 비슷하다. / 왜냐하면 비행을 위해 사용되는 어느 것이든 / 그러한 방법으로 만들어져야 하기 때문이다. / 하지만 그들은 진화에서 독립적으로 자라난다. / 그리고 공통점이 없다. / 비행이라는 그들의 사용 외에는
✓③ "Homologous" traits, / in contrast, / may or may not have a common function, / but they descended from a common ancestor / and hence have some common structure / that indicates their being "the same" organ.
"동종의" 특징은, / 반대로, / 공통된 기능을 가지고 있거나 가지고 있지 않을 수 있다. / 하지만 공통 조상으로부터 내려온 것이다. / 그리고 따라서 약간의 공통 구조를 가진다. / 그들을 "같은" 장기라고 규정하는
The wing of a bat and the front leg of a horse / have very different functions, / but they are all modifications of the forelimb / of the ancestor of all mammals.
박쥐의 날개와 말의 앞다리는 / 아주 다른 기능을 가지고 있다. / 하지만 그들 모두는 앞다리의 변형이다. / 모든 포유류의 조상의
④ As a result, / they share nonfunctional traits / like the number of bones and the ways they are connected.
결과적으로, / 그들은 비기능적인 특징을 공유한다. / 뼈의 개수 그리고 그들이 연결되어 있는 방식과 같은
⑤ To distinguish analogy from homology, / biologists usually look at the overall architecture of the organs / and focus on their most useless properties.
유사성과 동종성을 구별하기 위해서, / 생물학자들은 주로 장기의 전체적인 구조를 본다. / 그리고 그들의 가장 쓸모없는 자질에 집중한다.

생물학자들은 두 종류의 유사성을 구별한다. ① '상사' 형질은 공통된 기능을 가지는 것들이지만, 진화 계보의 다른 가지에서 생겨났고 중요한 면에서 '동일한' 기관이 아닌 형질이다. ② 새의 날개들과 벌의 날개들은 둘 다 비행에 쓰이고 비행에 쓰이는 것은 어떤 것이든 그러한 방식으로 만들어져야 하기 때문에 일부 방식에서 유사하지만, 그것들은 진화상에 별개로 생겨났고, 비행에서 그것들의 쓰임 외에는 공통점이 없다. ③ 대조적으로, '상동' 형질은 공통된 기능이 있을 수도 없을 수도 있으나 그것들은 공통의 조상으로부터 내려왔으므로 그들이 '동일한' 기관임을 보여주는 어떤 공통된 구조를 가진다. 박쥐의 날개와 말의 앞다리는 매우 다른 기능들을 가지나, 그것들은 모든 포유류의 조상의 앞다리가 모두 변형된 것들이다. ④ 그 결과, 그들은 뼈의 개수와 그것들이 연결된 방식과 같은 비기능적 형질을 공유한다. ⑤ 상사성과 상동성을 구별하기 위해, 생물학자들은 주로 그 기관의 전체적인 구성을 살펴보고 그들의 가장 쓰임이 없는 특성에 집중한다.

Why? 왜 정답일까?

상사 형질은 공통된 기능이지만 진화 계보가 다른 가지인 형질을, 상동 형질은 기능은 공통되지 않을 수 있지만 진화 계보의 가지가 같은 형질임을 설명한다. ③을 기준으로 위에는 상사 형질의 특징을, 상사 형질의 특징과 다른 특징을 설명하고 있기 때문에 상동 형질에 대해 설명하는 주어진 문장은 ③에 들어가는 것이 알맞다.

- **biologist** ⓝ 생물학자
- **analogous** ⓐ 유사한
- **organ** ⓝ 장기
- **evolution** ⓝ 진화
- **common** ⓐ 공통의
- **structure** ⓝ 구조
- **forelimb** ⓝ (척추동물의) 앞다리
- **similarity** ⓝ 유사성
- **arise** ⓥ 생기다
- **independently** ⓐⓓ 독립적으로
- **descend** ⓥ 내려오다
- **ancestor** ⓝ 조상
- **indicate** ⓥ 가리키다
- **mammals** ⓝ 포유류

구문 풀이

1행 "Homologous" traits, in contrast, may or may not have a common [조동사+동사원형] function, but they descended from a common ancestor and hence have some [homologous traits] common structure that indicates their being "the same" organ. [선행사] [주격관계대명사]

★★★ 등급을 가르는 문제!

39 용존 산소의 중요성 정답률 30% | 정답 ②

글의 흐름으로 보아, 주어진 문장이 들어가기에 가장 적절한 곳을 고르시오. [3점]

Seawater contains an abundance of dissolved oxygen / that all marine animals breathe to stay alive.
해수는 많은 용해된 산소를 포함한다. /모든 해양 생물들이 살기 위해서 호흡해야하는
① It has long been established in physics / that cold water holds more dissolved oxygen / than warm water does / — this is one reason / that cold polar seas are full of life / while tropical oceans are blue, clear, and relatively poorly populated with living creatures.
물리학에서 오랫동안 정립되었다. / 차가운 물이 더 많은 용해된 산소를 포함한다고 / 따뜻한 물보다 / — 이것이 한 가지 이유이다. / 차가운 극지방의 바다가 생명으로 가득한 / 열대 바다는 파랗고, 맑고, 생명체가 덜 살지만
☑ Thus, as global warming raises the temperature of marine waters, / it is self-evident / that the amount of dissolved oxygen will decrease.
따라서, 지구 온난화가 해수의 온도를 올리면 / 분명하다. / 용해된 산소의 양이 감소한다는 것이
This is a worrisome / and potentially disastrous consequence / if allowed to continue to an ecosystem-threatening level.
이것은 걱정할만하고, / 그리고 파멸적인 결과를 불러올 수 있다. / 만약 생태계가 위협받는 상태까지 계속된다면
③ Now scientists have analyzed data / indicating that the amount of dissolved oxygen in the oceans / has been declining for more than a half century.
지금 과학자들은 정보를 분석했다. / 바다의 용해된 산소의 양을 가리키며 / 지난 반 세기 넘게 감소한
④ The data show that the ocean oxygen level / has been falling more rapidly than the corresponding rise in water temperature.
정보는 바다 산소 레벨을 보여준다. / 맞는 해수 온도로 더 빠르게 떨어짐을
⑤ Falling oxygen levels in water / have the potential to impact the habitat of marine organisms worldwide / and in recent years this has led to more frequent anoxic events / that killed or displaced populations / of fish, crabs, and many other organisms.
감소하는 물의 산소 레벨은 / 전세계의 해양 유기체의 거주지에 영향을 끼칠 가능성이 있다. / 그리고 최근 몇 년 간 이것은 자주 산소 결핍의 사건으로 이끌었다. / 죽이거나 개체수가 도망가도록 / 물고기, 게, 그리고 많은 다른 유기체들을

해수는 모든 해양 동물이 살아있기 위해 호흡하는 다량의 용존 산소를 포함한다. ① 따뜻한 물이 보유하고 있는 것보다 차가운 물이 더 많은 용존 산소를 보유하고 있다는 사실은 물리학에서 오랫동안 확립되어 왔으며, 이는 열대 해양은 푸르고 맑고 생물이 상대적으로 적게 서식하는 반면 차가운 극지의 바다는 생명으로 가득한 하나의 이유이다. ② 따라서 지구 온난화가 해양 수온을 높임에 따라 용존 산소의 양이 감소할 것은 자명하다. 만약 생태계를 위협하는 수준까지 계속되도록 허용된다면 이는 걱정스럽고 잠재적으로 파괴적인 결과이다. ③ 현재 과학자들은 해양에서 용존 산소의 양이 반세기가 넘는 기간 동안 감소해 왔다는 것을 가리키는 데이터를 분석해 왔다. ④ 이 데이터는 해양 산소 농도가 상응하는 수온 상승보다 더 빠르게 감소해 오고 있음을 보여 준다. ⑤ 감소하는 수중 산소 농도는 세계적으로 해양 생물의 서식지에 영향을 끼칠 가능성을 갖고 있으며 최근에 이것은 물고기, 게, 그리고 많은 다른 생물의 개체군을 죽이거나 쫓아낸 더 빈번한 산소 결핍 사건을 초래해 왔다.

Why? 왜 정답일까?
해수에 용해된 산소, 즉 용존 산소가 해양 생물이 물에서 숨을 쉴 수 있게 해주어 해양 생태계에 필수적인 요소임을 말하고 있다. 용존 산소가 풍부한 극지방의 바다와 용존 산소가 부족한 열대 바다를 비교하고, 용존 산소가 생태계를 위협할 만큼 부족해지면 재앙적인 결과가 나올 것이라 얘기한다. 따라서 지구 온난화가 해수의 온도를 올리면 용존 산소가 부족해질 것이라는 주어진 문장은 ②에 오는 것이 알맞다.

- abundance ⓝ 넘칠 만큼 많음, 다량
- oxygen ⓝ 산소
- polar ⓐ 극지의
- populate ⓥ 살다, 거주하다
- temperature ⓝ 온도
- self-evident ⓐ 분명한
- potentially ⓐⓓ 잠재적으로
- consequence ⓝ 결과
- correspond ⓥ 일치하다
- dissolved ⓐ 용해된
- establish ⓥ 확립하다, 수립하다
- poorly ⓐⓓ 부족하게
- creature ⓝ 생물
- marine ⓐ 해양의
- decrease ⓥ 감소하다
- disastrous ⓐ 재앙적인
- analyze ⓥ 분석하다
- anoxic ⓐ 산소 결핍의

구문 풀이

1행 Thus, as global warming raises the temperature of marine waters, it is
　　　　 ~하면서　　　　　　　　　　　　　　　　　　　　　　　　　　　　 가주어
self-evident that the amount of dissolved oxygen will decrease.
　　　　　　　　 진주어

★★ 문제 해결 꿀~팁 ★★

▶ 많이 틀린 이유는?
글은 용존 산소의 중요성에 대해 얘기하고 있다. 'It has long been established in physics that cold water holds more dissolved oxygen than warm water does — this is one reason that cold polar seas are full of life while tropical oceans are blue, clear, and relatively poorly populated with living creatures.' → 여기서는 차가운 물이 따뜻한 물보다 더 많은 산소를 포함하고 있으며, 이것이 왜 극지방의 바다가 생명으로 가득한 반면, 열대 바다는 상대적으로 생명체가 적은지를 설명한다. 이 부분에서 주어진 문장을 넣으면 자연스럽게 이어진다. 차가운 물이 더 많은 산소를 포함한다는 사실을 바탕으로, 지구 온난화가 물의 온도를 상승시키면서 산소량을 감소시킨다는 논리가 연결된다. 따라서 ② 위치가 가장 적절하다.

▶ 문제 해결 방법은?
글의 흐름과 논리적 연관성을 파악하는 것이 우선이다. 주어진 문장은 지구 온난화로 인한 해양 온도 상승과 산소량 감소를 결과로 설명하고 있으므로, 온도와 용존 산소 간의 관계를 설명하는 ② 위치가 가장 적절하다.

40 카푸친 원숭이 실험　　　　　　　정답률 53% | 정답 ④

다음 글의 내용을 한 문장으로 요약하고자 한다. 빈칸 (A), (B)에 들어갈 말로 가장 적절한 것은?

	(A)		(B)			(A)		(B)
①	benefit 혜택	·····	protect 보호하다		②	inequality 불평등	·····	share 공유하다
③	abundance 충분함	·····	yield 양보하다		✓④	inequality 불평등	·····	reject 거절하다
⑤	benefit 혜택	·····	display 보여주다					

Capuchins / — New World Monkeys that live in large social groups — / will, in captivity, trade with people all day long, / especially if food is involved.

카푸친은 / — 큰 사회적 집단으로 사는 새로운 세계의 원숭이 — / 포로로써, 사람들과 하루 종일 거래할 것이다. / 특히 음식이 걸려 있다면
I give you this rock / and you give me a treat to eat.
내가 이 돌을 너에게 주면 / 너는 나에게 먹을 간식을 준다.
If you put two monkeys in cages next to each other, / and offer them both slices of cucumber / for the rocks they already have, / they will happily eat the cucumbers.
만약 케이지에 있는 두 원숭이들을 옆에 두고, / 모두에게 오이 조각을 주면 / 그들이 이미 가지고 있는 돌과 바꿔서 / 그들은 행복하게 오이를 먹을 것이다.
If, however, you give one monkey grapes instead / — grapes being universally preferred to cucumbers — / the monkey that is still receiving cucumbers / will begin to throw them back at the experimenter.
하지만 만약 당신이 한 원숭이에게는 오이 대신 포도를 준다면 / — 포도를 오이보다 전체적으로 좋아한다 — / 아직 오이를 받는 원숭이는 / 실험자에게 오이를 다시 던지기 시작할 것이다.
Even though she is still getting "paid" the same amount / for her effort of sourcing rocks, / and so her particular situation has not changed, / the comparison to another makes the situation unfair.
비록 원숭이가 여전히 같은 양으로 "보상받고 있지만" / 돌을 주는 노력으로 / 그리고 특정한 상황이 바뀌지는 않았지만, / 다른 원숭이와의 비교는 상황을 불공평하게 만든다.
Furthermore, / she is now willing to abandon all gains — the cucumbers themselves — / to communicate her displeasure to the experimenter.
게다가, / 원숭이는 얻은 모든 것을 이제 기꺼이 버린다. / —오이를— / 실험자에게 불만을 토로하기 위해서
➡ According to the passage, / if the Capuchin monkey realizes the (A) inequality in rewards / compared to another monkey, / she will (B) reject her rewards / to express her feelings about the treatment, / despite getting exactly the same rewards as before.
글에 따르면, / 만약 카푸친 원숭이가 보상에서의 불공평함을 알아차리면 / 다른 원숭이와 비교했을 때, / 원숭이는 보상을 거절할 것이다. / 보상에 대한 감정을 표현하기 위해서 / 비록 전과 같은 보상을 받지만

대규모의 사회 집단으로 서식하는 New World Monkey인 Capuchin은 간힌 상태에서 온종일 사람들과 거래를 할 것인데 특히 먹이가 연관된다면 그럴 것이다. '내가 너에게 이 돌을 주고 너는 나에게 먹을 간식을 준다.' 만약 당신이 두 마리의 원숭이들을 나란히 있는 우리에 넣고 그들이 이미 가지고 있는 돌의 대가로 오이 조각을 둘 모두에게 주었을 때 그들은 그 오이를 기쁘게 먹을 것이다. 하지만 만약 당신이 한 원숭이에게는 포도를 대신 준다면, 일반적으로 포도는 오이보다 더 선호되는데, 여전히 오이를 받은 원숭이는 그것들을 실험자에게 던지기 시작할 것이다. 비록 그녀가 돌을 모은 그녀의 수고에 대한 대가로 같은 양을 여전히 '받고', 그래서 그녀의 특정한 상황이 변화가 없더라도, 다른 원숭이와의 비교는 그 상황을 부당하게 만든다. 게다가, 그녀는 실험자에게 그녀의 불쾌함을 전달하기 위해 모든 얻은 것들을, 즉, 오이 자체를 이제 기꺼이 포기한다.

➡ 이 글에 따르면, 만약 Capuchin 원숭이가 다른 원숭이와 비교하여 보상에서의 (A) 불평등을 알아차린다면, 그녀는 이전과 정확히 똑같은 보상을 받더라도 대우에 대한 그녀의 감정을 표현하기 위해 그녀의 보상을 (B) 거부할 것이다.

Why? 왜 정답일까?
카푸친 원숭이 실험을 설명한다. 돌을 주면 간식을 주는 거래이고, 두 원숭이가 돌을 주면 오이를 주었다. 다시 두 원숭이가 돌을 주었을 때 한 원숭이에게는 그대로 오이를 주고 한 원숭이에게는 포도를 주면 오이를 받은 원숭이가 부당하다고 느껴 오이도 먹지 않는다는 실험이었다. 따라서 보상에서의 'inequality'를 느끼면 전과 같은 보상이라도 'reject' 한다는 ④가 알맞다.

- large ⓐ 큰
- captivity ⓝ 감금, 억류, 포로
- involve ⓥ 포함하다
- cucumber ⓝ 오이
- prefer ⓥ 선호하다
- effort ⓝ 노력
- unfair ⓐ 부당한
- displeasure ⓝ 불쾌감
- social ⓐ 사회의
- trade ⓥ 거래하다
- cage ⓝ 우리
- universally ⓐⓓ 공통적으로
- experimenter ⓝ 실험자
- situation ⓝ 상황
- abandon ⓥ 버리다

구문 풀이

4행 If you put two monkeys in cages next to each other, and offer them both
　　　　　가정법　　동사1　　　　　　　　　　　　　　　　 동사2 two monkeys
slices of cucumber for the rocks (that/which) they already have, they will happily
　　　　　　　　　　　　　　　 목적격 관계대명사 생략　　　　　　　 조동사+동사원형
eat the cucumbers.

41-42 고등 교육의 변화

Higher education has grown / from an elite to a mass system / across the world.
고등교육은 성장해왔다. / 엘리트 시스템으로 대중 시스템으로 / 전 세계적으로
In Europe and the USA, / (a) increased rates of participation / occurred in the decades / after the Second World War.
유럽과 미국에서는, / 참여율이 증가했고 / 수십 년간 일어났다. / 제2차 세계대전 이후
Between 2000 and 2014, / rates of participation in higher education / almost doubled / from 19% to 34% / across the world / among the members of the population / in the school-leaving age category / (typically 18 – 23).
2000년과 2014년 사이에, / 고등교육 참여율이 거의 두 배로 증가했다. / 19%에서 34%로 / 전 세계적으로 / 학교를 떠나는 연령대의 인구들 사이에서 / (보통 18세에서 23세)
The dramatic expansion of higher education / has been marked by / a wider range of institutions of higher learning / and a more diverse demographic of students.
고등교육의 극적인 확장은 / 특징지어진다. / 더 넓은 범위의 고등 교육 기관들로 / 그리고 더 다양한 학생 인구 통계로
Changes from an elite system / to a mass higher education system / are associated with / political needs / to build a (b) specialised workforce / for the economy.
엘리트 시스템에서의 변화는 / 대중 고등교육 시스템으로의 변화와 / 연관되어 있다. / 정치적 필요성과 / 경제를 위한 전문화된 노동력을 구축하기 위한
In theory, / the expansion of higher education / to develop a highly skilled workforce / should diminish / the role of examinations / in the selection and control of students, / initiating approaches to assessment / which (c) enable lifelong learning: / assessment *for* learning / and a focus on feedback for development.
이론적으로, / 고등교육의 확장은 / 고숙련 노동력을 개발하기 위해 / 줄여야 한다. / 시험의 역할을 / 학생 선발과 통제에서 / 평가 방식을 도입하면서 / 평생 학습을 촉진하는: / 학습을 *위한* 평가 / 그리고 성장을 위한 피드백에 중점을 둔
「In reality, / socio-political changes / to expand higher education / have set up / a 'field of contradictions' / for assessment in higher education.」 [41번의 근거]
현실적으로, / 사회정치적 변화가 / 고등교육을 확장하려는 / 세워 놓았다. / '모순의 장'을 / 고등교육 평가에서

「Mass higher education / requires efficient approaches to assessment, / such as examinations / and multiple-choice quizzes, with minimalist, / (d) impersonal, / or standardised feedback, / often causing students / to focus more on grades / than feedback.」 42번의 근거
대중 고등교육은 / 효율적인 평가 방식을 요구한다, / 예를 들어 시험 / 그리고 객관식 퀴즈 같은 최소한의, / 비인격적인, / 또는 표준화된 피드백을 통해, / 종종 학생들로 하여금 / 성적에 더 집중하게 만든다. / 피드백보다

In contrast, / the relatively small numbers of students / in elite systems in the past / (e) allowed for closer relationships / between students and their teachers, / with formative feedback / shaping the minds, / academic skills, / and even the characters of students.
대조적으로, / 상대적으로 적은 수의 학생들이 / 과거의 엘리트 시스템에서 / 더 밀접한 관계를 허용했다. / 학생들과 그들의 교사들 간에 / 형성적 피드백을 통해 / 사고를 형성하고, / 학업 능력과, / 심지어 학생들의 성격까지도

고등 교육은 전 세계에 걸쳐 엘리트에서 대중 체제로 성장해 왔다. 유럽과 미국에서는 2차 세계 대전 이후 수십 년 동안 (a) 증가된 참여율이 나타났다. 2000년과 2014년 사이에 졸업 연령 범주(대체로 18세에서 23세) 내 집단 구성원 사이에서의 고등 교육 참여율은 전 세계에 걸쳐 19%에서 34%로 거의 두 배가 되었다. 고등 교육의 극적인 확대는 더 광범위한 고등 학습 기관과 더 다양한 학생 인구 집단으로 특징지어져 왔다. 엘리트 체제에서 대중 고등 교육의 변화는 경제를 위한 (b) 전문화된 노동력을 구축하려는 정치적 필요성과 관련이 있다. 이론적으로, 고도로 숙련된 노동력을 개발하기 위한 고등 교육의 확대는 평생학습을 (c) 막는(→ 가능하게 하는) 평가로의 접근 방법, 즉, 학습을 '위한' 평가와 발달을 위한 피드백에 집중을 시작하면서, 학생의 선발과 통제에 있어 시험의 역할을 감소시킬 것이다. 실제로는 고등 교육을 확대하기 위한 사회 정치적 변화는 고등 교육에서의 평가에 있어 '모순의 장'을 조성해 왔다. 대중 고등 교육은 최소한이거나 (d) 비개인적이거나 표준화된 피드백을 갖춘, 시험과 선다형 퀴즈와 같은, 평가로의 효율적인 접근 방법을 필요로 하며, 이는 종종 학생이 피드백보다 성적에 더 집중하게 만든다. 대조적으로, 과거에 엘리트 체제의 상대적으로 적은 학생의 수는 형성적 피드백이 학생의 마음, 학업 기술, 그리고 심지어 학생의 성격을 형성하면서, 학생과 그들의 선생님 사이의 더 긴밀한 관계를 (e) 허용했다.

- elite ⓝ 엘리트
- increase ⓥ 증가하다
- occur ⓥ 발생하다
- population ⓝ 인구
- diverse ⓐ 다양한
- allow ⓥ 허락하다
- formative ⓐ 형태적인
- mass ⓝ 대량
- participation ⓝ 참가
- education ⓝ 교육
- category ⓝ 분류
- demographic ⓐ 인구학의
- relationship ⓝ 관계
- feedback ⓝ 평가

11행 Changes from an elite system to a mass higher education system are
from A to B : A에서 B까지   동사
associated with political needs to build a specialised workforce for the economy.
to부정사(부사적 용법)   과거분사

41 제목 파악   정답률 58% | 정답 ③

윗글의 제목으로 가장 적절한 것은?
① Is It Possible to Teach Without Assessment? – 평가 없이 가르치는 것이 가능한가?
② Elite vs. Public: A History of Modern Class Society – 엘리트 대 대중: 현대 계급 사회의 역사
☑ Mass Higher Education and Its Reality in Assessment – 대중 고등 교육과 평가의 현실
④ Impacts of Mass Higher Education on Teachers' Status – 교사의 지위에 대중 고등 교육의 영향
⑤ Mass Higher Education Leads to Economic Development – 대중 고등 교육이 경제 발달로 이끈다

Why? 왜 정답일까?
고등 교육이 엘리트 집단에서 대중 체제로 이동하는 과정에서 겪는 평가의 문제에 대해 다룬 글이다. 학습을 위한 평가와 발달을 위한 피드백에 집중하며 시험의 역할이 감소하고, 이것을 '모순의 장'이라고 일컫는다. 왜냐하면 발달을 위한 피드백이 종종 학생들이 피드백보다 성적에 더 집중하게 만들기 때문이라고 설명한다. 과거 엘리트 체제의 형성적 피드백이 학생의 발달에 더 효과적이었다고 글을 마치기 때문에, 제목으로 가장 적절한 것은 ③ 'Mass Higher Education and Its Reality in Assessment'이다.

★★★ 등급을 가르는 문제!

42 어휘 추론   정답률 38% | 정답 ③

밑줄 친 (a) ~ (e) 중에서 문맥상 낱말의 쓰임이 적절하지 않은 것은? [3점]
① (a)   ② (b)   ☑ (c)   ④ (d)   ⑤ (e)

Why? 왜 정답일까?
고등 교육이 대중을 대상으로 행해졌을 때 엘리트를 대상으로 행해졌을 때보다 평가의 측면에서 본래 목적인 학생들의 발달에 집중하지 못한다는 글이다. 따라서 'In theory, the expansion of higher education to develop a highly skilled workforce should diminish the role of examinations in the selection and control of students, initiating approaches to assessment which block lifelong learning: assessment for learning and a focus on feedback for development,'(이론적으로, 고도로 숙련된 노동력을 개발하기 위한 고등 교육의 확대는 평생학습을 막는 평가로의 접근 방법, 즉, 학습을 '위한' 평가와 발달을 위한 피드백에 집중을 시작하면서, 학생의 선발과 통제에 있어 시험의 역할을 감소시킬 것이다.)는 문장은 어색하다. 따라서 답은 ③ '(c)'이다.

★★ 문제 해결 꿀~팁 ★★
▶ 많이 틀린 이유는?
고등 교육이 대중을 대상으로 행해졌을 때와 엘리트를 대상으로 행해졌을 때의 차이를 이해해야 풀 수 있다. 고숙련 노동력 개발을 위해 고등 교육이 대중화된 것이라면, 평생 학습을 지향해야 논리적이므로 'diminish'는 'enable'로 바꿔야 자연스럽다.
▶ 문제 해결 방법은?
개념이 두 개 이상 나오는 지문일 경우, 개념마다 해당되는 개념을 분리해서 이해해야한다. 자신만의 기호를 사용하여 표시하는 것도 직관적인 문제 풀이에 도움이 되니 활용해보자.

43-45 시인의 옷차림 바꾸기

(A)
Once upon a time / in the Iranian city of Shiraz, / there lived / the famous poet Sheikh Saadi.
옛날 옛적 / 이란의 시라즈라는 도시에, / 살고 있었다 / 유명한 시인 세이크 사디가
Like most other poets and philosophers, / he led / a very simple life.
다른 대부분의 시인과 철학자들처럼, / 그는 살았다. / 매우 소박한 삶을
A rich merchant of Shiraz / was preparing / for his daughter's wedding / and invited (a) him / along with a lot of big businessmen / of the town.
시라즈의 부유한 상인이 / 준비하고 있었다. / 딸의 결혼식을 / 그리고 그를 초대했다 / 많은 부유한 상인들과 함께 / 그 마을의
「The poet accepted the invitation / and decided / to attend.」 45번 ①의 근거 일치
시인은 그 초대를 수락했고 / 결정했다. / 참석하기로

(D)
「On the day of the wedding, / the rich merchant, / the host of the wedding, / was receiving the guests / at the gate.」 45번 ④의 근거 일치
결혼식 날, / 부유한 상인인, / 결혼식의 주최자인, / 손님들을 맞이하고 있었다. / 문 앞에서
「Many rich people of the town / attended the wedding.」 45번 ⑤의 근거 일치
그 마을의 많은 부유한 사람들이 / 그 결혼식에 참석했다.
They had come out / in their best clothes.
그들은 나왔다. / 최고의 옷을 입고
The poet wore simple clothes / which were neither grand / nor expensive.
시인은 간단한 옷을 입었다. / 그것은 화려하지도 / 비싸지도 않았다.
He waited / for someone to approach him / but no one gave (e) him / as much as even a second glance.
그는 기다렸다. / 누군가가 그에게 다가오기를 / 하지만 아무도 그에게 주지 않았다. / 두 번째 눈길조차도
Even the host / did not greet him / and looked away.
심지어 주최자조차도 / 그를 맞이하지 않았고 / 외면했다.

(C)
「Seeing all this, / the poet quietly left the party / and went / to a shop / where he could rent clothes.」 45번 ③의 근거 일치
이 모든 것을 보고, / 시인은 조용히 파티를 떠났고 / 가게로 갔다. / 그가 옷을 빌릴 수 있는
There he chose / a richly decorated coat, / which made him / look like a new person.
그곳에서 그는 골랐다. / 화려하게 장식된 코트를, / 그것은 그를 만들었다. / 새로운 사람처럼 보이게
With this coat, / he entered the party / and this time was welcomed / with open arms.
이 코트를 입고, / 그는 파티에 들어갔고 / 이번에는 환영받았다. / 따뜻하게
The host / embraced him / as (c) he would do / to an old friend / and complimented him / on the clothes / he was wearing.
주최자는 / 그를 포옹했다 / 그가 할 법한 것처럼 / 오랜 친구에게 / 그리고 칭찬했다 그를 / 그가 입고 있는 옷을
The poet / did not say a word / and allowed the host / to lead (d) him / to the dining room.
시인은 / 한 마디도 하지 않았고 / 주최자가 이끌도록 했다. / 그를 / 식당으로

(B)
The host personally led the poet / to his seat / and served out / chicken soup / to him.
주최자는 직접 시인을 이끌어 / 그의 자리로 / 그리고 대접했다. / 치킨 수프를 / 그에게
「After a moment, the poet suddenly dipped / the corner of his coat in the soup / as if he fed it.」 45번 ②의 근거 불일치
잠시 후, 시인은 갑자기 담갔다. / 그의 코트의 자락을 수프에 / 마치 그것을 먹이는 것처럼
All the guests / were now staring / at (b) him / in surprise.
모든 손님들이 / 이제 쳐다보고 있었다. / 그를 / 놀란 표정으로
The host said, / "Sir, what are you doing?"
주최자가 말했다. / "선생님, 무엇을 하고 계신 겁니까?"
The poet very calmly replied, / "Now that I have put on / expensive clothes, / I see / a world of difference / here.
시인은 매우 침착하게 대답했다. / "이제 내가 입었으니 / 비싼 옷을, / 나는 본다. / 여기에 엄청난 차이가 있음을
All that I can say now is that / this feast / is meant for my clothes, / not for me."
내가 이제 할 수 있는 말은 / 이 잔치는 / 내 옷을 위한 것이고, / 나를 위한 것이 아니라는 것이다."

(A)
옛날 옛적에 이란의 도시 Shiraz에 유명한 시인 Sheikh Saadi가 살았다. 대부분의 다른 시인들과 철학자들처럼 그는 매우 검소한 생활을 했다. Shiraz의 부유한 상인이 그의 딸의 결혼식을 준비하고 있었고 (a) 그를 그 마을의 많은 큰 사업가들과 함께 초대했다. 그 시인은 초대를 수락했고 참석하기로 결정했다.

(D)
결혼식 날, 결혼식의 혼주인 부유한 상인은 입구에서 손님을 맞이하고 있었다. 마을의 많은 부유한 사람들이 결혼식에 참석했다. 그들은 자신의 가장 좋은 옷차림으로 나왔다. 시인은 거창하지도 비싸지도 않은 소박한 옷을 입었다. 그는 누군가가 자신에게 다가오기를 기다렸지만 아무도 (e) 그에게 단 일 초의 눈길도 주지 않았다. 혼주조차도 그에게 인사하지 않고 눈길을 돌렸다.

이 모든 것을 보고 시인은 조용히 파티를 떠나 그가 옷을 빌릴 수 있는 가게로 갔다. 그곳에서 그는 화려하게 장식된 외투를 골랐고, 그것은 그를 새로운 사람처럼 보이게 만들었다. 이 외투를 입고, 그는 파티에 들어갔고 이번에는 두 팔 벌려 환영을 받았다. 혼주는 (c) 그가 오랜 친구에게 하듯이 그를 껴안았고, 그가 입고 있는 옷에 대해 그에게 칭찬했다. 시인은 한마디도 하지 않고 혼주가 (d) 그를 식당으로 안내하도록 허락했다.

(B)
혼주는 직접 시인을 그의 자리로 안내했고 그에게 닭고기 수프를 내주었다. 잠시 후에 시인은 마치 음식을 먹이듯 그의 외투 자락을 수프에 갑자기 담갔다. 모든 손님들이 바로 (b) 그를 놀라서 바라보고 있었다. 혼주가 말했다. "선생님, 뭐 하는 겁니까?" 시인은 매우 침착하게 대답했다. "내가 비싼 옷을 입으니, 이곳에서 엄청난 차이를 봅니다. 내가 지금 할 수 있는 모든 말은 이 진수성찬이 내 옷을 위한 것이지, 나를 위한 것이 아니라는 것뿐입니다."

- famous ⓐ 유명한
- poet ⓝ 시인
- invite ⓥ 초대하다
- accept ⓥ 받아들이다
- attend ⓥ 참석하다
- philosopher ⓝ 철학자
- prepare ⓥ 준비하다
- businessmen ⓝ 사업가
- ivitation ⓝ 초대장

(C) 1행 Seeing all this, the poet quietly left the party and went to a shop where
분사구문(= After he saw)   동사1   동사2   관계부사
he could rent clothes.

43 글의 순서 파악

정답률 61% | 정답 ⑤

주어진 글 (A)에 이어질 내용을 순서에 맞게 배열한 것으로 가장 적절한 것은?

① (B) – (D) – (C)
② (C) – (B) – (D)
③ (C) – (D) – (B)
④ (D) – (B) – (C)
✔ (D) – (C) – (B)

Why? 왜 정답일까?

주어진 글은 **Shiraz**의 부유한 상인이 결혼식을 준비하며 사업가들을 초대했다고 한다. 시인이 파티 초대를 받아들인 후 파티를 하는 결혼식 날 시작을 묘사하는 **(D)**가, 아무도 반겨주지 않아 시인이 파티를 떠나는 **(C)**, 시인이 기존에 입었던 옷보다 화려한 옷을 입은 **(C)**, 마지막으로 옷차림에 따라 대우가 달라진다는 **(B)**의 순서가 자연스럽다. 따라서 알맞은 순서는 ⑤ **(D) – (C) – (B)**이다.

44 지칭 추론

정답률 65% | 정답 ③

밑줄 친 (a) ~ (e) 중에서 가리키는 대상이 나머지 넷과 다른 것은?

① (a) ② (b) ✔ (c) ④ (d) ⑤ (e)

Why? 왜 정답일까?

(a), **(b)**, **(d)**, **(e)** 모두 시인을 가리키기 때문에, 파티 주최자를 뜻하는 **(c)**는 가리키는 대상이 나머지 넷과 다르다. 따라서 답은 ③ **'(c)'**이다.

45 세부 내용 파악

정답률 69% | 정답 ②

윗글에 관한 내용으로 적절하지 않은 것은?

① 시인은 상인의 초대를 받아들였다.
✔ 상인은 시인의 외투 자락을 수프에 담갔다.
③ 시인은 옷을 빌릴 수 있는 가게로 갔다.
④ 결혼식 날 상인은 입구에서 손님을 맞이했다.
⑤ 마을의 많은 부유한 사람들이 결혼식에 참석했다.

Why? 왜 정답일까?

(B)의 **'After a moment, the poet suddenly dipped the corner of his coat in the soup as if he fed it'**에서 **'he'**는 시인을 가리키기 때문에 시인이 외투 자락을 수프에 담근 것이므로 윗글에 대한 내용으로 적절하지 않은 것은 '② 상인은 시인의 외투 자락을 수프에 담갔다.'이다.

Why? 왜 오답일까?

① **(A)** **'The poet accepted the invitation and decided to attend.'**의 내용과 일치한다.
③ **(C)** **'Seeing all this, the poet quietly left the party and went to a shop where he could rent clothes.'**의 내용과 일치한다.
④ **(D)** **'On the day of the wedding, the rich merchant, the host of the wedding, was receiving the guests at the gate.'**의 내용과 일치한다.
⑤ **(D)** **'Many rich people of the town attended the wedding.'**의 내용과 일치한다.

어휘 Review Test 11

문제편 110쪽

A	B	C	D
01 표현하다	01 climate	01 ⓘ	01 ⓢ
02 걱정	02 emission	02 ⓗ	02 ⓑ
03 되찾다, 회복하다	03 major	03 ⓣ	03 ⓗ
04 접근하다	04 source	04 ⓠ	04 ⓣ
05 닦다	05 physicist	05 ⓝ	05 ⓓ
06 소생하다	06 support	06 ⓜ	06 ⓘ
07 눈에 띄는	07 submit	07 ⓚ	07 ⓜ
08 놀라운	08 inventor	08 ⓞ	08 ⓛ
09 달성	09 category	09 ⓓ	09 ⓖ
10 지배적인	10 participant	10 ⓙ	10 ⓠ
11 상태	11 annual	11 ⓐ	11 ⓟ
12 의식	12 participate	12 ⓡ	12 ⓔ
13 기여하다	13 exhibition	13 ⓒ	13 ⓕ
14 관점, 시각	14 viewpoint	14 ⓔ	14 ⓙ
15 공포, 두려움, 무서움	15 functional	15 ⓛ	15 ⓡ
16 도와주는	16 acquire	16 ⓕ	16 ⓝ
17 기기	17 alternative	17 ⓑ	17 ⓚ
18 향상시키다	18 rather	18 ⓢ	18 ⓞ
19 효율적인	19 component	19 ⓟ	19 ⓐ
20 추산하다	20 initial	20 ⓖ	20 ⓒ

12회 | 2023학년도 9월 학력평가 [고1]

• 정답 •

18 ⑤ 19 ② 20 ② 21 ⑤ 22 ④ 23 ② 24 ① 25 ④ 26 ④ 27 ④ 28 ⑤ ★29 ④ 30 ② 31 ① 32 ③
33 ② ★34 ① ★35 ② 36 ② 37 ③ ★38 ⑤ 39 ⑤ 40 ① 41 ② ★42 ⑤ 43 ④ 44 ③ 45 ④

★ 표기된 문항은 **[등급을 가르는 문제]**에 해당하는 문항입니다.

18 학생 인력 추천 요청

정답률 86% | 정답 ⑤

다음 글의 목적으로 가장 적절한 것은?

① 과학 박물관 내 시설 이용 제한을 안내하려고
② 화학 박람회 일정이 변경된 이유를 설명하려고
③ 중학생을 위한 화학 실험 특별 강연을 부탁하려고
④ 중학교 과학 수업용 실험 교재 집필을 의뢰하려고
✔ 화학 박람회에서 실험을 도울 대학생 추천을 요청하려고

Dear Professor Sanchez,
Sanchez 교수님께
My name is Ellis Wight, / and I'm the director of the Alexandria Science Museum.
제 이름은 Ellis Wight이고 / 저는 Alexandria 과학 박물관의 관장입니다.
We are holding a Chemistry Fair / for local middle school students / on Saturday, October 28.
저희는 화학 박람회를 개최합니다. / 지역 중학교 학생을 위한 / 10월 28일 토요일에
The goal of the fair is / to encourage them to be interested in science / through guided experiments.
이 박람회의 목적은 ~입니다. / 학생들이 과학에 관한 관심을 갖도록 장려하는 것 / 안내자가 있는 실험을 통해
We are looking for college students / who can help with the experiments during the event.
저희는 대학생을 모집하고자 합니다. / 행사 기간 동안 실험을 도와줄 수 있는
I am contacting you / to ask you to recommend some students / from the chemistry department at your college / who you think are qualified for this job.
저는 당신께 연락드렸습니다. / 학생 몇 명을 추천해 달라는 요청을 드리고자 / 귀교의 화학과 소속인 / 당신이 이 일에 적합하다고 생각하는
With their help, / I'm sure / the participants will have a great experience.
그 학생들의 도움으로 / 저는 확신합니다. / 참가자들이 훌륭한 경험을 하게 될 것이라고
I look forward to hearing from you soon.
빠른 시일 내에 귀하로부터 연락 받기를 기대하겠습니다.
Sincerely, // Ellis Wight
Ellis Wight 드림

Sanchez 교수님께

제 이름은 Ellis Wight이고 Alexandria 과학 박물관의 관장입니다. 저희는 10월 28일 토요일에 지역 중학교 학생을 위한 화학 박람회를 개최합니다. 이 박람회의 목적은 안내자가 있는 실험을 통해 학생들이 과학에 관한 관심을 갖도록 장려하는 것입니다. 저희는 행사 기간 동안 실험을 도와줄 수 있는 대학생을 모집하고자 합니다. 저는 이 일에 적합하다고 생각되는 귀교의 화학과 학생 몇 명을 추천해 달라는 요청을 드리고자 연락드렸습니다. 그 학생들의 도움으로 참가자들이 훌륭한 경험을 하게 될 것이라 확신합니다. 빠른 시일 내에 귀하로부터 연락 받기를 기대하겠습니다.

Ellis Wight 드림

Why? 왜 정답일까?

박람회에서 진행할 실험을 도와줄 화학과 학생을 추천해달라는(**I am contacting you to ask you to recommend some students from the chemistry department at your college who you think are qualified for this job.**) 내용이므로, 글의 목적으로 가장 적절한 것은 ⑤ '화학 박람회에서 실험을 도울 대학생 추천을 요청하려고'이다.

- **hold** [v] 개최하다
- **fair** [n] 박람회
- **experiment** [n] 실험
- **department** [n] 학과, 부서
- **chemistry** [n] 화학
- **local** [a] 지역의, 지역의
- **recommend** [v] 추천하다
- **qualified for** ~에 적합한, 자격을 갖춘

구문 풀이

7행 **I am contacting you to ask you to recommend some students from the chemistry department at your college [who (you think) are qualified for this job].**
「ask + 목적어 + to부정사 : ~이 …하기를 요청하다」 / 선행사 / 주격 관·대 / 삽입절 / 동사

19 암벽 등반 중 위기를 맞이한 필자 일행

정답률 69% | 정답 ②

다음 글에 나타난 'I'의 심경 변화로 가장 적절한 것은?

① joyful → bored (즐거운 → 지루한)
✔ confident → fearful (자신 있는 → 겁에 질린)
③ nervous → relieved (긴장한 → 안도한)
④ regretful → pleased (후회하는 → 즐거운)
⑤ grateful → annoyed (고마운 → 짜증 난)

Gregg and I had been rock climbing since sunrise / and had had no problems.
Gregg와 나는 일출 이후에 암벽 등반을 하고 있었고, / 아무런 문제가 없었다.
So we took a risk.
그래서 우리는 위험을 감수했다.
"Look, the first bolt is right there. / I can definitely climb out to it. / Piece of cake," / I persuaded Gregg, / minutes before I found myself pinned.
"봐, 첫 번째 볼트가 바로 저기야. / 난 분명히 거기까지 올라갈 수 있어. / 식은 죽 먹기야."라고 / 나는 Gregg를 설득했고, / 얼마 지나지 않아 나는 내가 꼼짝 못하게 되었다는 것을 알게 되었다.
It wasn't a piece of cake.
그것은 식은 죽 먹기가 아니었다.
The rock was deceptively barren of handholds.
그 바위는 믿을 수 없게도 손으로 잡을 곳이 없었다.

I clumsily moved back and forth across the cliff face / and ended up with nowhere to go...but down.
나는 서툴게 절벽 면을 이리저리 가로질러 보았지만 / 갈 곳이… 결국 아래쪽밖에는 없었다.
The bolt that would save my life, / if I could get to it, / was about two feet above my reach.
내 목숨을 구해줄 볼트는 / 만약 내가 거기까지 갈 수 있다면 / 내 손이 닿을 수 있는 곳에서 약 2피트 위에 있었다.
My arms trembled from exhaustion.
내 팔은 극도의 피로로 떨렸다.
I looked at Gregg.
나는 Gregg를 쳐다보았다.
My body froze with fright / from my neck down to my toes.
내 몸은 공포로 얼어붙었다. / 목에서부터 발끝까지
Our rope was tied between us.
우리 사이에 밧줄이 묶여 있었다.
If I fell, / he would fall with me.
내가 떨어지면, / 그도 나와 함께 떨어질 것이었다.

Gregg와 나는 일출 이후에 암벽 등반을 하고 있었고, 아무런 문제가 없었다. 그래서 우리는 위험을 감수했다. "봐, 첫 번째 볼트가 바로 저기야. 난 분명히 거기까지 올라갈 수 있어. 식은 죽 먹기야."라고 나는 Gregg를 설득했고, 얼마 지나지 않아 나는 내가 꼼짝 못하게 되었다는 것을 알게 되었다. 그것은 식은 죽 먹기가 아니었다. 그 바위는 믿을 수 없게도 손으로 잡을 곳이 없었다. 나는 서툴게 절벽 면을 이리저리 가로질러 보았지만 갈 곳이… 결국 아래쪽밖에는 없었다. 만약 내가 거기까지 갈 수 있다면, 내 목숨을 구해줄 볼트는 내 손이 닿을 수 있는 곳에서 약 2피트 위에 있었다. 내 팔은 극도의 피로로 떨렸다. 나는 Gregg를 쳐다보았다. 내 몸은 목에서부터 발끝까지 공포로 얼어붙었다. 우리 사이에 밧줄이 묶여 있었다. 내가 떨어지면, 그도 나와 함께 떨어질 것이었다.

Why? 왜 정답일까?

첫 번째 볼트까지 쉽게 오를 수 있다며 자신했던(I can definitely climb out to it. Piece of cake. ~) 필자가 생각과 다른 현실에 공포감에 휩싸였다(My body froze with fright ~)는 내용이다. 따라서 'I'의 심경 변화로 가장 적절한 것은 ② '자신 있는 → 겁에 질린'이다.

- sunrise ⓝ 일출
- bolt ⓝ 볼트, 나사못
- piece of cake 식은 죽 먹기, 몹시 쉬운 일
- deceptively 〔ad〕 현혹될 정도로
- clumsily 〔ad〕 서툴게
- cliff ⓝ 절벽
- exhaustion ⓝ 피로
- fright ⓝ 공포
- fearful @ 겁에 질린
- take a risk 위험을 감수하다
- definitely 〔ad〕 확실히, 분명히
- pinned @ 고정된
- handhold ⓝ (등반 도중) 손으로 잡을 수 있는 곳
- back and forth 이리저리
- end up with 결국 ~에 처하다
- freeze ⓥ 얼어붙다
- confident @ 자신 있는
- regretful @ 유감스러운, 후회하는

구문 풀이

7행 The bolt [that would save my life], (if I could get to it), was about two feet
주어 / 주격 관·대 / 삽입절 / 동사(단수) / 대략, 약
above my reach.

20 자녀에게 행동으로 모범을 보이기 정답률 93% | 정답 ②

다음 글에서 필자가 주장하는 바로 가장 적절한 것은?
① 자녀를 타인과 비교하는 말을 삼가야 한다.
✓ 자녀에게 행동으로 삶의 모범을 보여야 한다.
③ 칭찬을 통해 자녀의 바람직한 행동을 강화해야 한다.
④ 훈육을 하기 전에 자녀 스스로 생각할 시간을 주어야 한다.
⑤ 자녀가 새로운 것에 도전할 때 인내심을 가지고 지켜봐야 한다.

We are always teaching our children something / by our words and our actions.
우리는 항상 우리 자녀에게 무언가를 가르치고 있다. / 우리의 말과 행동으로
They learn from seeing.
그들은 보는 것으로부터 배운다.
They learn from hearing and from *overhearing*.
그들은 듣거나 우연히 들은 것으로부터 배운다.
Children share the values of their parents / about the most important things in life.
아이들은 부모의 가치관을 공유한다. / 인생에서 가장 중요한 것에 관한
Our priorities and principles and our examples of good behavior / can teach our children to take the high road / when other roads look tempting.
우리의 우선순위와 원칙, 그리고 훌륭한 행동에 대한 본보기는 / 우리 자녀에게 올바른 길로 가도록 가르칠 수 있다. / 다른 길이 유혹적으로 보일 때
Remember / that children do not learn the values / that make up strong character / simply by being *told* about them.
기억하라. / 아이들은 가치를 배우지 않는다는 것을 / 확고한 인격을 구성하는 / 단순히 그것에 관해 들어서
They learn / by seeing the people around them / *act* on and *uphold* those values in their daily lives.
그들은 배운다. / 주변 사람들을 보면서 / 일상생활에서 그러한 가치를 좇아 행동하고 유지하는 것을
Therefore / show your child good examples of life / by your action.
그러므로 / 여러분의 자녀에게 삶의 모범을 보이라. / 행동으로
In our daily lives, / we can show our children / that we respect others.
우리 일상생활에서, / 우리는 자녀에게 보여줄 수 있다. / 우리가 타인을 존중하는 것을
We can show them our compassion and concern / when others are suffering, / and our own self-discipline, courage and honesty / as we make difficult decisions.
우리는 그들에게 우리의 연민과 걱정을 보여줄 수 있다. / 타인이 괴로워할 때 / 그리고 우리 자신의 자제력과 용기와 정직을 / 우리가 어려운 결정을 할 때

우리는 항상 우리 자녀에게 말과 행동으로 무언가를 가르치고 있다. 그들은 보는 것으로부터 배운다. 그들은 듣거나 우연히 들은 것으로부터 배운다. 아이들은 인생에서 가장 중요한 것에 관한 부모의 가치관을 공유한다. 우리의 우선순위와 원칙, 그리고 훌륭한 행동에 대한 본보기는 우리 자녀가 다른 길이 유혹적으로 보일 때 올바른 길로 가도록 가르칠 수 있다. 아이들은 확고한 인격을 구성하는 가치를 단순히 그것에 관해 들어서 배우지 않는다는 것을 기억하라. 그들은 주변 사람들이 일상생활에서 그러한 가치를 좇아 행동하고 유지하는 것을 보면서 배운다. 그러므로 여러분의 자녀에게 행동으로 삶의 모범을 보이라. 우리 일상생활에서, 우리는 자녀에게 우리가 타인을 존중하는 것을 보여줄 수 있다. 우리는 타인이 괴로워할 때

우리의 연민과 걱정을, 어려운 결정을 할 때 우리 자신의 자제력과 용기와 정직을 그들에게 보여줄 수 있다.

Why? 왜 정답일까?

글 중반부에서 행동을 통해 자녀에게 삶의 본보기를 보여주라고(Therefore show your child good examples of life by your action.) 조언하는 것으로 볼 때, 필자가 주장하는 바로 가장 적절한 것은 ② '자녀에게 행동으로 삶의 모범을 보여야 한다.'이다.

- overhear ⓥ 엿듣다, 우연히 듣다
- priority ⓝ 우선순위
- take the high road 확실한 길로 가다
- make up ~을 구성하다
- uphold ⓥ 유지하다, 떠받치다
- concern ⓝ 걱정, 우려
- self-discipline ⓝ 자제
- value ⓝ 가치 ⓥ 중시하다
- principle ⓝ 원칙
- tempting @ 유혹적인, 솔깃한
- act on ~에 따라 행동하다
- compassion ⓝ 연민
- suffer ⓥ 고통받다, 괴로워하다

구문 풀이

7행 Remember that children do not learn the values [that make up strong
접속사 / 선행사 / 주격 관·대
character] simply by being *told* about them.
동명사의 수동태(~되는 것)

21 출판을 넘어 독자에게 이해되어야 비로소 완성되는 과학 연구 정답률 45% | 정답 ⑤

밑줄 친 fall silently in the woods가 다음 글에서 의미하는 바로 가장 적절한 것은? [3점]
① fail to include the previous study
이전 연구를 포함하지 못한다
② end up being considered completely false
결국 완전히 틀렸다고 간주된다
③ become useless because they are not published
출판되지 않아서 쓸모없게 되어버린다
④ focus on communication to meet public demands
대중의 요구를 맞추기 위해 커뮤니케이션에 집중한다
✓ are published yet readers don't understand them
출판되지만 독자가 그것을 이해하지 못한다

Most people have no doubt heard this question: / If a tree falls in the forest / and there is no one there to hear it fall, / does it make a sound?
대부분의 사람들은 틀림없이 이 질문을 들어 봤을 것이다. / 만약 숲에서 나무가 쓰러지고 / 그것이 쓰러지는 것을 들을 사람 거기 없다면 / 그것은 소리를 낼까?
The correct answer is no.
정답은 '아니요'이다.
Sound is more than pressure waves, / and indeed there can be no sound without a hearer.
소리는 압력파 이상이며, / 정말로 듣는 사람 없이는 소리가 있을 수 없다.
And similarly, / scientific communication is a two-way process.
마찬가지로, / 과학적 커뮤니케이션은 양방향 프로세스이다.
Just as a signal of any kind is useless / unless it is perceived, / a published scientific paper (signal) is useless / unless it is both received *and* understood / by its intended audience.
어떠한 종류의 신호든 쓸모가 없는 것처럼, / 그것이 감지되지 않으면 / 출판된 과학 논문(신호)은 쓸모가 없다. / 그것이 수신되고 *나아가* 이해되지 않으면 / 목표 독자에 의해
Thus we can restate the axiom of science as follows: / A scientific experiment is not complete / until the results have been published *and understood*.
따라서 우리는 과학의 자명한 이치를 다음과 같이 풀어 말할 수 있다. / 과학 실험은 완성된 것이 아니다. / 결과가 출판되고 *나아가 이해될* 때까지
Publication is no more than pressure waves / unless the published paper is understood.
출판은 압력파에 지나지 않는다. / 출판된 논문이 이해되지 않으면
Too many scientific papers / fall silently in the woods.
너무 많은 과학 논문이 / 소리 없이 숲속에 쓰러진다.

대부분의 사람들은 틀림없이 이 질문을 들어 봤을 것이다. 만약 숲에서 나무가 쓰러지고 그것이 쓰러지는 것을 들을 사람이 거기 없다면, 그것은 소리를 낼까? 정답은 '아니요'이다. 소리는 압력파 이상이며, 정말로 듣는 사람 없이는 소리가 있을 수 없다. 마찬가지로, 과학적 커뮤니케이션은 양방향 프로세스이다. 어떠한 종류의 신호든 감지되지 않으면 쓸모가 없는 것처럼, 출판된 과학 논문(신호)은 그것이 목표 독자에게 수신되고 *나아가* 이해까지 되지 않으면 쓸모가 없다. 따라서 우리는 과학의 자명한 이치를 다음과 같이 풀어 말할 수 있다. 과학 실험은 결과가 출판되고 *나아가* 이해될 때 비로소 완성된다. 출판된 논문이 이해되지 않으면 출판은 압력파에 지나지 않는다. 너무 많은 과학 논문이 소리 없이 숲속에서 쓰러진다.

Why? 왜 정답일까?

글에 따르면, 소리가 청자가 있을 때 비로소 만들어지듯이, 과학 논문 또한 출판되고 독자에게 '이해될' 때 비로소 완성된다고 한다. 밑줄 부분 또한 독자의 이해를 강조하는 비유로, 독자에게 '이해되지' 않으면 논문은 '진정한 소리'가 되어 나오지 못하고 그저 사라져버린다는 뜻이다. 따라서 밑줄 친 부분의 의미로 가장 적절한 것은 ⑤ '출판되지만 독자가 그것을 이해하지 못한다'이다.

- no doubt 분명히, 틀림없이
- pressure wave 압력파(압력 크기의 변화로 생성되는 파동)
- similarly 〔ad〕 비슷하게, 마찬가지로
- signal ⓝ 신호 ⓥ 알리다
- publish ⓥ 출판하다, 게재하다
- intend ⓥ 목표로 하다, 의도하다
- as follows 다음과 같이
- publication ⓝ 출판, 게재
- previous @ 이전의
- meet the demand 요구에 맞추다
- scientific @ 과학적인
- useless @ 쓸모없는
- paper ⓝ 논문, 서류
- restate ⓥ (더 분명하게) 고쳐 말하다
- complete @ 완성된
- no more than 단지 ~일 뿐인
- false @ 틀린

구문 풀이

8행 Thus we can restate the axiom of science as follows: A scientific experiment is not complete until the results have been published *and understood*.
「not + A + until + B : B하고 나서야 비로소 A하다」

22 원윈을 추구하여 협상 상대와 건전한 관계를 유지하기 정답률 83% | 정답 ④

다음 글의 요지로 가장 적절한 것은?

① 협상 상대의 단점뿐 아니라 장점을 철저히 분석해야 한다.
② 의사소통 과정에서 서로의 의도를 확인하는 것이 바람직하다.
③ 성공적인 협상을 위해 다양한 대안을 준비하는 것이 중요하다.
✓④ 양측에 유리한 협상을 통해 상대와 좋은 관계를 유지해야 한다.
⑤ 원만한 인간관계를 위해 상호독립성을 인정하는 것이 필요하다.

We all negotiate every day, / whether we realise it or not.
우리 모두는 매일 협상한다. / 우리가 알든 모르든
Yet few people ever learn *how* to negotiate.
하지만 이제까지 *어떻게* 협상하는지를 배운 사람은 거의 없다.
Those who do / usually learn the traditional, win-lose negotiating style / rather than an approach / that is likely to result in a win-win agreement.
그렇게 하는 사람들은 / 대개 이기고 지는 쪽이 생기는 전통적인 협상 방식을 배운다. / 접근법보다는 / 양쪽 모두에 유리한 합의를 도출할 가능성이 있는
This old-school, adversarial approach / may be useful in a one-off negotiation / where you will probably not deal with that person again.
이런 구식의 적대적인 접근법은 / 일회성 협상에서는 유용할지도 모른다. / 아마도 여러분이 그 사람을 다시 상대하지 않을
However, / such transactions are becoming increasingly rare, / because most of us deal with the same people repeatedly / — our spouses and children, our friends and colleagues, our customers and clients.
하지만 / 이런 식의 거래는 점점 더 드물어지고 있다. / 우리 대부분은 동일한 사람들을 반복적으로 상대하기 때문에, / 배우자와 자녀, 친구와 동료, 고객과 의뢰인같이
In view of this, / it's essential / to achieve successful results for ourselves / and maintain a healthy relationship with our negotiating partners at the same time.
이러한 관점에서, / 중요하다. / 우리 자신을 위해 성공적인 결과를 얻어내는 것이 / 그리고 동시에 협상 파트너들과 건전한 관계를 유지하는 것이
In today's interdependent world of business partnerships and long-term relationships, / a win-win outcome is fast becoming the *only* acceptable result.
오늘날 비즈니스 파트너십과 장기적 관계의 상호 의존적인 세계에서, / 양측에 유리한 성과는 수용 가능한 유일한 결과로 빠른 속도로 자리잡고 있다.

우리 모두는 우리가 알든 모르든 매일 협상한다. 하지만 이제까지 *어떻게* 협상하는지를 배운 사람은 거의 없다. (협상 방식을) 배우는 사람들은 대개 양쪽 모두에 유리한 합의를 도출할 가능성이 있는 접근법보다는, 이기고 지는 쪽이 생기는 전통적인 협상 방식을 배운다. 이런 구식의 적대적인 접근법은 아마도 여러분이 그 사람을 다시 상대하지 않을 일회성 협상에서는 유용할지도 모른다. 하지만 우리 대부분은 배우자와 자녀, 친구와 동료, 고객과 의뢰인같이 동일한 사람들을 반복적으로 상대하기 때문에, 이런 식의 거래는 점점 더 드물어지고 있다. 이러한 관점에서, 우리 자신을 위해 성공적인 결과를 얻어내는 동시에 협상 파트너들과 건전한 관계를 유지하는 것이 중요하다. 오늘날 비즈니스 파트너십과 장기적 관계의 상호 의존적인 세계에서, 양측에 유리한 성과는 수용 가능한 유일한 결과로 빠른 속도로 자리잡고 있다.

Why? 왜 정답일까?
협상 시 서로에게 모두 유리한 성과를 도출하면서 상대와 건전한 관계를 유지해야 한다(~ it's essential to achieve successful results for ourselves and maintain a healthy relationship with our negotiating partners at the same time.)고 조언하는 글이다. 따라서 글의 요지로 가장 적절한 것은 ④ '양측에 유리한 협상을 통해 상대와 좋은 관계를 유지해야 한다.'이다.

- **negotiate** ⓥ 협상하다
- **usually** ⓐⓓ 보통
- **agreement** ⓝ 합의, 동의
- **adversarial** ⓐ 적대적인
- **transaction** ⓝ 거래
- **rare** ⓐ 드문
- **spouse** ⓝ 배우자
- **essential** ⓐ 필수적인, 아주 중요한
- **interdependent** ⓐ 상호 의존적인
- **outcome** ⓝ 결과, 성과
- **whether ~ or not** ~이든 아니든
- **traditional** ⓐ 전통적인
- **old-school** ⓐ 구식의
- **one-off** ⓐ 단 한 번의
- **increasingly** ⓐⓓ 점점 더
- **repeatedly** ⓐⓓ 반복해서
- **in view of** ~을 고려하면
- **maintain** ⓥ 유지하다
- **long-term** ⓐ 장기의
- **acceptable** ⓐ 수용 가능한

구문 풀이

4행 This old-school, adversarial approach may be useful in a one-off negotiation [where you will probably not deal with that person again].
선행사(상황) / 관계부사

23 문화적 다양성이 너무 클 때의 문제점   정답률 58% | 정답 ②

다음 글의 주제로 가장 적절한 것은?
① roles of culture in ethnic groups
민족 집단에서 문화의 역할
✓② contrastive aspects of cultural diversity
문화적 다양성의 대립적 양상
③ negative perspectives of national identity
국가 정체성에 대한 부정적인 시각
④ factors of productivity differences across countries
국가 간 생산성 차이의 요인
⑤ policies to protect minorities and prevent discrimination
소수자를 보호하며 차별을 방지하려는 정책들

The interaction of workers from different cultural backgrounds with the host population / might increase productivity / due to positive externalities like knowledge spillovers.
다른 문화적 배경을 가진 노동자들과 현지 주민의 상호 작용은 / 생산성을 증가시킬 수 있다. / 지식의 확산과 같은 긍정적인 외부 효과로 인해
This is only an advantage / up to a certain degree.
이것은 오로지 장점이다 / 어느 정도까지만
When the variety of backgrounds is too large, / fractionalization may cause excessive transaction costs for communication, / which may lower productivity.
배경의 다양성이 너무 크면, / 분열은 의사소통에 대한 과도한 거래 비용을 초래하고, / 이는 생산성을 저하시킬 수 있다.
Diversity not only impacts the labour market, / but may also affect the quality of life in a location.
다양성은 노동 시장에 영향을 줄 뿐만 아니라 / 한 지역의 삶의 질에도 영향을 미칠 수 있다.
A tolerant native population / may value a multicultural city or region / because of an increase in the range of available goods and services.
관용적인 원주민은 / 다문화 도시나 지역을 가치 있게 여길 수 있다. / 이용 가능한 재화와 용역 범위의 증가로 인해
On the other hand, / diversity could be perceived as an unattractive feature / if natives

perceive it / as a distortion of what they consider to be their national identity.
반면에, / 다양성은 매력적이지 않은 특징으로 인지될 수 있다. / 원주민들이 그것을 왜곡으로 인식한다면 / 그들이 국가 정체성이라고 여기는 것에 대한
They might even discriminate against other ethnic groups / and they might fear / that social conflicts between different foreign nationalities / are imported into their own neighbourhood.
그들은 심지어 다른 민족 집단을 차별할 수도 있고, / 그들은 두려워할 수도 있다. / 다양한 외국 국적들 간의 사회적 갈등이 / 그들 인근으로 유입되는 것을

다른 문화적 배경을 가진 노동자들과 현지 주민의 상호 작용은 지식의 확산과 같은 긍정적인 외부 효과로 인해 생산성을 증가시킬 수 있다. 이것은 어느 정도까지만 장점이다. 배경의 다양성이 너무 크면, 분열은 의사소통에 대한 과도한 거래 비용을 초래하고, 이는 생산성을 저하시킬 수 있다. 다양성은 노동 시장에 영향을 줄 뿐만 아니라 한 지역의 삶의 질에도 영향을 미칠 수 있다. 관용적인 원주민은 이용 가능한 재화와 용역 범위의 증가로 인해 다문화 도시나 지역을 가치 있게 여길 수 있다. 반면에, 원주민들이 다양성을 국가 정체성이라고 여겨지는 것에 대한 왜곡으로 인식한다면 그것(다양성)은 매력적이지 않은 특징으로 인지될 수 있다. 그들은 심지어 다른 민족 집단을 차별할 수도 있고, 다양한 외국 국적들 간의 사회적 갈등이 그들 인근으로 유입되는 것을 두려워할 수도 있다.

Why? 왜 정답일까?
한 지역 사회 내에서 외지 출신 노동자들의 문화적 다양성이 일정 수준을 넘어가면 생산성 또는 삶의 질 저하나 갈등을 겪게 될 수 있다는 내용이다. 따라서 글의 주제로 가장 적절한 것은 ② '문화적 다양성의 대립적 양상'이다.

- **cultural** ⓐ 문화적인
- **population** ⓝ 인구
- **externality** ⓝ 외부 효과(의도하지 않았지만 부수적으로 따르는 결과)
- **knowledge spillover** 지식의 확산
- **fractionalization** ⓝ 분열
- **cost** ⓝ 비용, 대가
- **impact** ⓥ 영향을 주다, 충격을 주다
- **quality of life** 삶의 질
- **multicultural** ⓐ 다문화의
- **perceive A as B** A를 B로 인식하다
- **identity** ⓝ 정체성
- **ethnic** ⓐ 민족의
- **import** ⓥ 유입하다, 수입하다
- **factor** ⓝ 요인
- **background** ⓝ 배경
- **productivity** ⓝ 생산성
- **variety** ⓝ 다양성
- **excessive** ⓐ 과도한
- **lower** ⓥ 떨어뜨리다
- **labo(u)r market** 노동 시장
- **tolerant** ⓐ 관용적인
- **on the other hand** 반면에
- **distortion** ⓝ 왜곡
- **discriminate against** ~을 차별하다
- **conflict** ⓝ 갈등
- **contrastive** ⓐ 대비되는, 대립적인
- **policy** ⓝ 정책

구문 풀이

10행 On the other hand, diversity could be perceived as an unattractive
~로 인식되다
feature if natives perceive it as a distortion of [what they consider to be their
전치사 관계대명사(~것)
national identity].

24 인간의 생활방식에 깊은 영향을 주는 건물과 개발   정답률 60% | 정답 ①

다음 글의 제목으로 가장 적절한 것은?
✓① Buildings Transform How We Live! – 건물이 우리의 삶의 방식을 바꾼다!
② Why Do We Build More Than We Need? – 우리는 왜 필요 이상으로 건물을 지을까?
③ Copying Ancient Buildings for Creativity – 창의성을 위해 고대 건물을 베끼기
④ Was Life Better in Hunter-gatherer Times? – 수렵 채집인 시대에는 삶이 더 괜찮았을까?
⑤ Innovate Your Farm with New Constructions – 새로운 건축물로 농장을 혁신하라

We think we are shaping our buildings.
우리는 우리가 건물을 형성하고 있다고 생각한다.
But really, / our buildings and development are also shaping us.
그러나 실제로, / 우리의 건물과 개발도 또한 우리를 형성하고 있다.
One of the best examples of this / is the oldest-known construction: / the ornately carved rings of standing stones at Göbekli Tepe in Turkey.
이것의 가장 좋은 예 중 하나는 / 가장 오래된 것으로 알려진 건축물이다. / 튀르키예의 Göbekli Tepe에 있는, 화려하게 조각된 입석의 고리
Before these ancestors got the idea / to erect standing stones / some 12,000 years ago, / they were hunter-gatherers.
이 조상들이 아이디어를 얻기 전에, / 입석을 세우는 / 약 12,000년 전에 / 그들은 수렵 채집인이었다.
It appears / that the erection of the multiple rings of megalithic stones / took so long, / and so many successive generations, / that these innovators were forced to settle down / to complete the construction works.
~인 것으로 보인다. / 거석으로 된 여러 개의 고리를 세우는 것은 / 오랜 시간을 필요로 하고 / 그리고 많은 잇따른 세대를 / 이 혁신가들은 정착해야만 했던 것으로 보인다. / 건설 작업을 완료하기 위해
In the process, / they became the first farming society on Earth.
그 과정에서, / 그들은 지구상 최초의 농업 사회가 되었다.
This is an early example of a society constructing something / that ends up radically remaking the society itself.
이것은 무언가를 건설하는 사회의 초기 예이다. / 결국 사회 자체를 근본적으로 재구성하는
Things are not so different in our own time.
우리 시대에도 상황이 그렇게 다르지 않다.

우리는 우리가 건물을 형성하고 있다고 생각한다. 그러나 실제로 우리의 건물과 개발도 또한 우리를 형성하고 있다. 이것의 가장 좋은 예 중 하나는 가장 오래된 것으로 알려진 건축물인, 튀르키예의 Göbekli Tepe에 있는 화려하게 조각된 입석의 고리이다. 이 조상들이 약 12,000년 전에 입석을 세우는 아이디어를 얻기 전에, 그들은 수렵 채집인이었다. 거석으로 된 여러 개의 고리를 세우는 데 오랜 시간이 걸리고 많은 잇따른 세대를 거쳤어야 했기에, 이 혁신가들은 건설 작업을 완료하기 위해 정착해야만 했던 것으로 보인다. 그 과정에서, 그들은 지구상 최초의 농업 사회가 되었다. 이것은 결국 사회 자체를 근본적으로 재구성하는 무언가를 건설하는 사회의 초기 예이다. 우리 시대에도 상황이 그렇게 다르지 않다.

Why? 왜 정답일까?
튀르키예의 초기 인류가 입석을 건설하며 수렵 채집인에서 농경인으로 정착하게 된 예시를 들어, 건물이

나 개발이 인간 (사회)를 형성한다(~ our buildings and development are also shaping us.) 는 점을 설명하는 글이다. 따라서 글의 제목으로 가장 적절한 것은 ① '건물이 우리의 삶의 방식을 바꾼다'이다.

- **shape** ⓥ 형성하다
- **ornately** [ad] 화려하게
- **erect** ⓥ 세우다
- **multiple** ⓐ 여럿의
- **successive** ⓐ 연속된, 잇따른
- **settle down** 정착하다
- **transform** ⓥ 바꾸다, 변모시키다
- **construction** ⓝ 건설, 구성
- **carve** ⓥ 새기다
- **hunter-gatherer** ⓝ 수렵 채집인
- **megalithic** ⓐ 거석의
- **be forced to** 어쩔 수 없이 ~하다
- **radically** [ad] 근본적으로, 급진적으로

구문 풀이

6행 It appears that the erection of the multiple rings of megalithic stones
~한 것으로 보인다
took so long, and so many successive generations, that these innovators
「so ~ that … : 너무 ~해서 …하다」
were forced to settle down to complete the construction works.
어쩔 수 없이 ~했다

---

25 미국 내의 연령대별 소셜 미디어 사용자 비율   정답률 77% | 정답 ④

다음 도표의 내용과 일치하지 않는 것은?

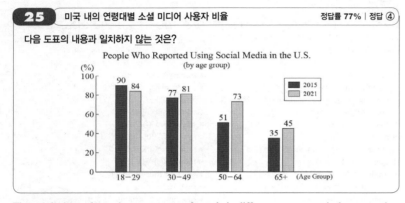

The graph above shows the percentages of people in different age groups / who reported using social media / in the United States / in 2015 and 2021.
위 그래프는 다양한 연령 집단 내 사람들의 비율을 보여 준다. / 소셜 미디어를 사용한다고 보고한 / 미국에서 / 2015년과 2021년에
① In each of the given years, / the 18-29 group had the highest percentage of people / who said they used social media.
주어진 각각의 해에, / 18~29세 집단에서 사람들의 비율이 제일 높았다. / 소셜 미디어를 사용한다고 말한
② In 2015, / the percentage of people / who reported using social media in the 30-49 group / was more than twice that in the 65 and older group.
2015년에 / 사람들의 비율은 / 소셜 미디어를 사용한다고 보고한 / 30~49세 집단에서 / 65세 이상 집단의 두 배 이상이었다.
③ The percentage of people / who said they used social media / in the 50-64 group in 2021 / was 22 percentage points higher / than that in 2015.
사람들의 비율은 / 소셜 미디어를 사용한다고 말한 / 2021년에 50~64세 집단에서 / 22퍼센트포인트 더 높았다. / 2015년의 비율보다
☑ In 2021, / except for the 65 and older group, / more than four-fifths of people in each age group / reported using social media.
2021년에 / 65세 이상 집단을 제외하고 / 각 연령 집단에서 5분의 4가 넘는 사람들이 / 소셜 미디어를 사용한다고 보고했다.
⑤ Among all the age groups, / only the 18-29 group showed a decrease / in the percentage of people / who reported using social media / from 2015 to 2021.
모든 연령 집단 중에서 / 18~29세 집단만이 감소를 보였다. / 사람들의 비율에서 / 소셜 미디어를 사용한다고 보고한 / 2015년에서 2021년까지

위 그래프는 2015년과 2021년에 미국에서 소셜 미디어를 사용한다고 보고한 다양한 연령 집단 내 사람들의 비율을 보여 준다. ① 주어진 각각의 해에, 18~29세 집단에서 소셜 미디어를 사용한다고 말한 사람들의 비율이 제일 높았다. ② 2015년에 30~49세 집단에서 소셜 미디어를 사용한다고 보고한 사람들의 비율은 65세 이상 집단의 두 배 이상이었다. ③ 2021년에 50~64세 집단에서 소셜 미디어를 사용한다고 말한 사람들의 비율은 2015년보다 22퍼센트포인트 더 높았다. ④ 2021년에 65세 이상 집단을 제외한 각 연령 집단에서 5분의 4가 넘는 사람들이 소셜 미디어를 사용한다고 보고했다. ⑤ 모든 연령 집단 중에서 18~29세 집단만이 2015년에서 2021년까지 소셜 미디어를 사용한다고 보고한 사람들의 비율에서 감소를 보였다.

Why? 왜 정답일까?
도표에 따르면 2021년에 미국에서 소셜 미디어를 사용하고 있다고 보고한 50~64세 인구는 73%인데, 이는 5분의 4인 80%에 미치지 못하는 수치이다. 따라서 도표와 일치하지 않는 것은 ④이다.

- **social media** 소셜 미디어
- **more than** ~ 이상
- **decrease** ⓝ 감소
- **given** ⓐ 주어진 [prep] ~을 고려하면
- **except for** ~을 제외하고

---

26 Bill Evans의 생애   정답률 80% | 정답 ④

Bill Evans에 관한 다음 글의 내용과 일치하지 않는 것은?
① 6세에 피아노 수업을 받기 시작했다.
② Southeastern Louisiana 대학에서 학위를 취득했다.
③ 군 복무 이후 뉴욕에서 작곡을 공부했다.
☑ 작곡가 George Russell을 고용했다.
⑤ 1964년에 자신의 첫 번째 그래미상을 수상했다.

American jazz pianist Bill Evans / was born in New Jersey in 1929.
미국인 재즈 피아니스트 Bill Evans는 / 뉴저지에서 1929년에 태어났다.
His early training was in classical music.
그의 초기 교육은 클래식 음악이었다.
「At the age of six, / he began receiving piano lessons, / later adding flute and violin.」
6세에 / 그는 피아노 수업을 받기 시작해서, / 나중에 플루트와 바이올린도 추가했다.   ①의 근거 일치
「He earned bachelor's degrees in piano and music education / from Southeastern Louisiana College / in 1950.」   ②의 근거 일치
그는 피아노와 음악 교육에서 학사 학위를 취득했다. / Southeastern Louisiana 대학에서 / 1950년에

He went on to serve in the army from 1951 to 1954 / and played flute in the Fifth Army Band.
그는 1951에서 1954년까지 군 복무를 하며 / 제5군악대에서 플루트를 연주했다.
「After serving in the military, / he studied composition / at the Mannes School of Music in New York.」   ③의 근거 일치
군 복무 이후 / 그는 작곡을 공부했다. / 뉴욕에 있는 Mannes School of Music에서
「Composer George Russell admired his playing / and hired Evans / to record and perform his compositions.」   ④의 근거 불일치
작곡가 George Russell은 그의 연주에 감탄하여 / Evans를 고용했다. / 자신의 곡을 녹음하고 연주하게 하려
Evans became famous for recordings / made from the late-1950s through the 1960s.
Evans는 음반으로 유명해졌다. / 1950년대 후반부터 1960년대 동안 만들어진
「He won his first Grammy Award in 1964 / for his album *Conversations with Myself*.」
그는 1964년에 자신의 첫 번째 그래미상을 수상했다. / 자신의 앨범 *Conversations with Myself*로   ⑤의 근거 일치
Evans' expressive piano works and his unique harmonic approach / inspired a whole generation of musicians.
Evans의 표현이 풍부한 피아노 작품과 그의 독특한 화성적 접근은 / 전 세대의 음악가들에게 영감을 주었다.

미국인 재즈 피아니스트 Bill Evans는 뉴저지에서 1929년에 태어났다. 그의 초기 교육은 클래식 음악이었다. 그는 6세에 피아노 수업을 받기 시작해서, 나중에 플루트와 바이올린도 추가했다. 그는 1950년에 Southeastern Louisiana 대학에서 피아노와 음악 교육에서 학사 학위를 취득했다. 그는 1951에서 1954년까지 군 복무를 하며 제5군악대에서 플루트를 연주했다. 군 복무 이후 그는 뉴욕에 있는 Mannes School of Music에서 작곡을 공부했다. 작곡가 George Russell은 그의 연주에 감탄하여 Evans를 고용해 자신의 곡을 녹음하고 연주하게 했다. Evans는 1950년대 후반부터 1960년대 동안 만들어진 음반으로 유명해졌다. 그는 자신의 앨범 *Conversations with Myself*로 1964년에 자신의 첫 번째 그래미상을 수상했다. Evans의 표현이 풍부한 피아노 작품과 그의 독특한 화성적 접근은 전 세대의 음악가들에게 영감을 주었다.

Why? 왜 정답일까?
'Composer George Russell admired his playing and hired Evans to record and perform his compositions.'에서 Evans는 작곡가 George Russell을 고용한 것이 아니고, 그에게 고용되어 그의 음악을 녹음하고 연주했다고 한다. 따라서 내용과 일치하지 않는 것은 ④ '작곡가 George Russell을 고용했다.'이다.

Why? 왜 오답일까?
① 'At the age of six, he began receiving piano lessons, ~'의 내용과 일치한다.
② 'He earned bachelor's degrees in piano and music education from Southeastern Louisiana College in 1950.'의 내용과 일치한다.
③ 'After serving in the military, he studied composition at the Mannes School of Music in New York.'의 내용과 일치한다.
⑤ 'He won his first Grammy Award in 1964 ~'의 내용과 일치한다.

- **add** ⓥ 추가하다
- **bachelor's degree** 학사 학위
- **military** ⓝ 군대 ⓐ 군사적인
- **admire** ⓥ 감탄하다, 존경하다
- **expressive** ⓐ 표현이 풍부한
- **harmonic** ⓐ (음악) 화성의
- **earn** ⓥ 얻다, 취득하다, 벌다
- **serve in the army** 군 복무하다
- **composition** ⓝ 작곡
- **recording** ⓝ 음반, 녹음
- **unique** ⓐ 독특한

구문 풀이

9행 Composer George Russell admired his playing and hired Evans to record
동사1   동사2   목적(~하기 위해)
and perform his compositions.

---

27 보석 만들기 수업   정답률 95% | 정답 ④

Silversmithing Class에 관한 다음 안내문의 내용과 일치하지 않는 것은?
① 두 시간 동안 진행된다.
② 10월 1일부터 등록할 수 있다.
③ 등록 인원은 6명으로 제한된다.
☑ 참가 연령에 제한이 없다.
⑤ 수업 당일 취소 시 환불이 불가하다.

Silversmithing Class
Silversmithing Class(은세공 수업)
Kingston Club is offering a fine jewelry making class.
Kingston Club은 정교한 보석 만들기 수업을 제공합니다.
Don't miss this great chance / to make your own jewelry!
이런 좋은 기회를 놓치지 마세요! / 여러분만의 보석을 만들어볼
When & Where
시간 & 장소
「Saturday, October 21, 2023 (2 p.m. to 4 p.m.)」   ①의 근거 일치
2023년 10월 21일 토요일(오후 2시부터 오후 4시까지)
Kingston Club studio
Kingston Club 스튜디오
Registration
등록
Available only online
온라인으로만 가능
「Dates: October 1 – 14, 2023」   ②의 근거 일치
일자: 2023년 10월 1일 ~ 14일
Fee: $40 (This includes all tools and materials.)
비용: 40달러(이것은 모든 도구와 재료를 포함합니다.)
「Registration is limited to 6 people.」   ③의 근거 일치
등록은 6명으로 제한됩니다.
Note
유의 사항
「Participants must be at least 16 years old.」   ④의 근거 불일치
참가자는 16세 이상이어야 합니다.
「No refund for cancellation on the day of the class」   ⑤의 근거 일치
수업 당일 취소 시 환불 불가

Silversmithing Class(은세공 수업)

Kingston Club은 정교한 보석 만들기 수업을 제공합니다. 여러분만의 보석을 만들어볼 이런 좋은 기회를 놓치지 마세요!

시간 & 장소
- 2023년 10월 21일 토요일(오후 2시부터 오후 4시까지)
- Kingston Club 스튜디오

등록
- 온라인으로만 가능
- 일자: 2023년 10월 1 ~ 14일
- 비용: 40달러(이것은 모든 도구와 재료를 포함합니다.)
- 등록은 6명으로 제한됩니다.

유의 사항
- 참가자는 16세 이상이어야 합니다.
- 수업 당일 취소 시 환불 불가

Why? 왜 정답일까?

'Participants must be at least 16 years old.'에서 참가자는 16세 이상이어야 한다고 하므로, 안내문의 내용과 일치하지 않는 것은 ④ '참가 연령에 제한이 없다.'이다.

Why? 왜 오답일까?

① 'Saturday, October 21, 2023 (2 p.m. to 4 p.m.)'의 내용과 일치한다.
② 'Dates: October 1~14, 2023'의 내용과 일치한다.
③ 'Registration is limited to 6 people.'의 내용과 일치한다.
⑤ 'No refund for cancellation on the day of the class'의 내용과 일치한다.

- **silversmith** ⓝ 은세공하는 사람
- **jewelry** ⓝ 보석
- **cancellation** ⓝ 취소
- **fine** ⓐ 정교한, 미세한
- **miss a chance** 기회를 놓치다

---

28 해양 인식 관련 영상 대회   정답률 93% | 정답 ⑤

2023 Ocean Awareness Film Contest에 관한 다음 안내문의 내용과 일치하는 것은?
① 세 가지 주제 중 하나를 선택해야 한다. ② 중학생이 참가할 수 있다.
③ 영상은 10분을 넘길 수 없다. ④ 1인당 두 개까지 출품할 수 있다.
✔ 수상자는 웹사이트에 공지될 것이다.

2023 Ocean Awareness Film Contest
2023 Ocean Awareness Film Contest(2023 해양 보존 인식 영상 대회)
Join our 7th annual film contest / and show your knowledge of marine conservation.
우리 일곱 번째 연례 영상 대회에 참여해서 / 해양 보존에 관한 여러분의 지식을 보여 주세요.
Theme
주제
『Ocean Wildlife / Ocean Pollution
해양 야생 생물 / 해양 오염
(Choose one of the above.)』 ①의 근거 불일치
(위에서 하나를 선택하세요.)
Guidelines
지침
『Participants: High school students』 ②의 근거 불일치
참가자: 고등학생
Submission deadline: September 22, 2023
제출 기한: 2023년 9월 22일
『The video must be between 10 and 15 minutes.』 ③의 근거 불일치
영상은 10분에서 15분 사이여야 합니다.
All entries must be uploaded to our website.
모든 출품작은 우리 웹사이트에 업로드되어야 합니다.
『Only one entry per person』 ④의 근거 불일치
1인당 출품작 하나만 가능
Prizes
상금
1st place: $100 / 2nd place: $70 / 3rd place: $50
1등: 100달러 / 2등: 70달러 / 3등: 50달러
『(Winners will be announced on our website.)』 ⑤의 근거 일치
(수상자는 우리 웹사이트에 공지될 것입니다.)
For more information, / please visit www.oceanawareFC.com.
더 많은 정보를 위해 / www.oceanawareFC.com을 방문하세요.

2023 Ocean Awareness Film Contest
(2023 해양 보존 인식 영상 대회)

우리 일곱 번째 연례 영상 대회에 참여해서 해양 보존에 관한 여러분의 지식을 보여 주세요.
□ 주제
 – 해양 야생 생물 / 해양 오염
  (위에서 하나를 선택하세요.)
□ 지침
 – 참가자: 고등학생
 – 제출 기한: 2023년 9월 22일
 – 영상은 10분에서 15분 사이여야 합니다.
 – 모든 출품작은 우리 웹사이트에 업로드되어야 합니다.
 – 1인당 출품작 하나만 가능
□ 상금
 • 1등: 100달러 • 2등: 70달러 • 3등: 50달러
  (수상자는 우리 웹사이트에 공지될 것입니다.)
    더 많은 정보를 위해 www.oceanawareFC.com을 방문하세요.

Why? 왜 정답일까?

'(Winners will be announced on our website.)'에서 수상자는 웹사이트에서 알려준다고 하므로, 안내문의 내용과 일치하는 것은 ⑤ '수상자는 웹사이트에 공지될 것이다.'이다.

Why? 왜 오답일까?

① 'Ocean Wildlife / Ocean Pollution / (Choose one of the above.)'에서 주제는 2개 중 하나를 선택하는 것이라고 하였다.
② 'Participants: High school students'에서 참가자는 고등학생으로 명시되었다.
③ 'The video must be between 10 and 15 minutes.'에서 영상 길이는 10~15분 사이면 된다고 하였다.
④ 'Only one entry per person'에서 출품은 1인당 하나의 영상만 가능하다고 하였다.

- **awareness** ⓝ 인식, 앎
- **conservation** ⓝ 보존
- **pollution** ⓝ 오염
- **entry** ⓝ 출품작, 참가, 입장
- **annual** ⓐ 매년의
- **wildlife** ⓝ 야생 생물
- **submission** ⓝ 제출

★★★ 등급을 가르는 문제!
29 다른 사람들의 사후 비판을 유독 많이 듣는 스포츠 업계 사람들   정답률 33% | 정답 ④

다음 글의 밑줄 친 부분 중, 어법상 틀린 것은?

There is a reason / the title "Monday Morning Quarterback" exists.
이유가 있다. / 'Monday Morning Quarterback'이라는 명칭이 존재하는
Just read the comments on social media from fans / discussing the weekend's games, / and you quickly see / how many people believe / they could play, coach, and manage sport teams more ① successfully / than those on the field.
팬들의 소셜 미디어의 댓글을 읽어보기만 하라 / 주말 경기에 대해 토론하는 / 그러면 여러분은 금방 알 수 있다. / 얼마나 많은 사람들이 믿는지 / 자기가 더 성공적으로 경기를 뛰고, 감독하고, 스포츠팀을 관리할 수 있다고 / 경기장에 있는 이들보다
This goes for the boardroom as well.
이것은 이사회실에서도 마찬가지이다.
Students and professionals / with years of training and specialized degrees in sport business / may also find themselves ② being given advice / on how to do their jobs / from friends, family, or even total strangers without any expertise.
학생들과 전문가들 / 스포츠 사업에서 수년간의 훈련을 받고 전문 학위를 가진 / 또한 충고를 듣고 있는 자신을 발견할지도 모른다. / 어떻게 일해야 할지에 관해 / 전문 지식이 전혀 없는 친구나 가족이나 혹은 심지어 생판 남으로부터
Executives in sport management / ③ have decades of knowledge and experience / in their respective fields.
스포츠 경영 임원진들은 / 수십 년의 지식과 경험을 가지고 있다. / 각자 자기 분야에서
However, / many of them face criticism / from fans and community members / telling ✔ them how to run their business.
하지만, / 그들 중 많은 사람들이 비난에 직면한다. / 팬들과 지역 사회 구성원들로부터의 / 그들에게 사업 운영 방식을 알려주는
Very few people tell / their doctor how to perform surgery / or their accountant how to prepare their taxes, / but many people provide feedback / on ⑤ how sport organizations should be managed.
알려주는 사람은 거의 없지만, / 의사에게 수술하는 방법을 알려주거나 / 회계사에게 세금을 준비하는 방법을 / 많은 이들이 피드백을 제공한다. / 스포츠 조직이 어떻게 관리되어야 하는지에 대한

'Monday Morning Quarterback(월요일 아침 쿼터백: 일이 이미 있고 난 뒤 이러쿵저러쿵하는 사람)'이라는 명칭이 존재하는 이유가 있다. 주말 경기에 대해 토론하는 팬들의 소셜 미디어의 댓글만 읽어봐도, 여러분은 얼마나 많은 사람들이 경기장에 있는 이들보다 자기가 더 성공적으로 경기를 뛰고, 감독하고, 스포츠팀을 관리할 수 있다고 믿는지 금방 알 수 있다. 이것은 이사회실에서도 마찬가지이다. 스포츠 사업에서 수년간의 훈련을 받고 전문 학위를 가진 학생들과 전문가들 또한, 전문 지식이 전혀 없는 친구나 가족이나 혹은 심지어 생판 남으로부터 어떻게 일해야 할지에 관해 충고를 듣고 있는 자신을 발견할지도 모른다. 스포츠 경영 임원진들은 각자 자기 분야에서 수십 년의 지식과 경험을 가지고 있다. 하지만, 그들 중 많은 사람들이 자신에게 사업 운영 방식을 알려주는 팬들과 지역 사회 구성원들의 비난에 직면한다. 의사에게 수술하는 방법을 알려주거나, 회계사에게 세금을 준비하는 방법을 알려주는 사람은 거의 없지만, 스포츠 조직이 어떻게 관리되어야 하는지에 대한 피드백은 많은 이들이 제공한다.

Why? 왜 정답일까?

telling의 의미상 주어가 fans and community members인데, 목적어는 many of them(= executives)이므로, 둘은 서로 다른 대상을 지칭한다. 재귀대명사는 주어와 목적어가 일치할 때만 쓰므로, themselves 대신 them을 써야 어법상 맞다. 따라서 어법상 틀린 것은 ④이다.

Why? 왜 오답일까?

① 동사구인 could play, coach, and manage를 꾸미기 위해 부사 more successfully를 쓴 것이다.
② may also find의 목적어인 themselves가 '충고를 듣는' 입장이므로, 수동을 나타내는 「being + 과거분사」 형태를 적절하게 썼다.
③ 복수 명사 주어인 Executives에 맞춰 복수 동사 have를 쓴 것은 어법상 맞다.
⑤ 완전한 문장인 sport organizations should be managed를 이끌기 위해 의문부사 how(어떻게)를 쓴 것은 어법상 맞다.

- **boardroom** ⓝ 이사회실
- **specialized** ⓐ 전문화된
- **expertise** ⓝ 전문 지식
- **respective** ⓐ 각자의
- **criticism** ⓝ 비평
- **accountant** ⓝ 회계사
- **organization** ⓝ 조직, 단체
- **professional** ⓝ 전문가
- **total stranger** 생판 남
- **executive** ⓝ 임원, 중역
- **face** ⓥ 마주하다, 직면하다
- **run** ⓥ (가게나 사업을) 운영하다
- **tax** ⓝ 세금

구문 풀이

14행 Very few people tell their doctor how to perform surgery or their accountant how to prepare their taxes, but many people provide feedback on how sport organizations should be managed.
(→4형식 동사 / ~하는 사람은 거의 없다 / 간접목적어1 / 직접목적어1 / 간접목적어2 / 직접목적어2)

▶ 많이 틀린 이유는?
themselves가 사람이므로 '충고를 주는' 주체처럼 보여서 ②를 고르기 쉽다. 하지만 문맥을 보면, 이들은 일을 어떻게 할지에 대한 충고를 남에게 '받는' 입장이 맞다.

▶ 문제 해결 방법은?
재귀대명사를 쓰려면, 행위를 나타내는 동사 또는 준동사를 기준으로 (의미상) 주어와 목적어가 같아야 한다. 여기서는 현재분사 telling을 중심으로 판단해야 하는데, 현재분사의 의미상 주어는 분사가 꾸미는 명사이고, 목적어는 분사 뒤에 나오는 명사이므로, 두 대상이 같은지 다른지 비교하면 된다.

---

30 새로운 환경을 상상하기 어려워하는 어린 아이들   정답률 58% | 정답 ②

다음 글의 밑줄 친 부분 중, 문맥상 낱말의 쓰임이 적절하지 <u>않은</u> 것은? [3점]

While moving is difficult for everyone, / it is particularly stressful for children.
이사는 모두에게 힘들지만, / 아이들에게 특히 스트레스가 된다.
They lose their sense of security / and may feel disoriented / when their routine is disrupted / and all that is ① familiar is taken away.
그들은 안정감을 잃고, / 혼란스러움을 느낄 수도 있다. / 그들의 일상이 무너지고 / 익숙한 모든 것이 사라질 때
Young children, ages 3-6, / are particularly affected by a move.
3세에서 6세 사이의 어린아이들은 / 이사에 특히 영향을 받는다.
Their understanding at this stage / is quite literal, / and it is ☑ hard for them / to imagine beforehand a new home and their new room.
이 시기 그들의 이해력은 / 꽤 융통성이 없어서, / 그들로서는 어렵다. / 새로운 집과 자신의 새로운 방을 미리 상상하기가
Young children may have worries / such as "Will I still be me in the new place?" / and "Will my toys and bed come with us?"
어린아이들은 걱정들을 가질지도 모른다. / "내가 새로운 곳에서도 여전히 나야?"와 / "내 장난감과 침대는 우리랑 같이 가?"와 같은
It is important / to establish a balance / between validating children's past experiences / and focusing on helping them ③ adjust to the new place.
중요하다. / 균형을 잡는 것이 / 아이들의 과거 경험을 인정하는 것 / 그리고 그들이 새로운 곳에 적응하도록 돕는 데 집중하는 것 사이에
Children need to have opportunities / to share their backgrounds / in a way that ④ respects their past / as an important part of who they are.
아이들은 기회를 가져봐야 한다. / 자신의 배경을 나눌 / 자기 과거를 존중하는 방식으로 / 자신의 존재에 대한 중요한 부분으로서
This contributes to building a sense of community, / which is essential for all children, / especially those in ⑤ transition.
이것은 공동체 의식을 형성하는 데 기여하고, / 이는 모든 아이들에게 몹시 중요하다. / 특히 변화를 겪는 아이들

이사는 모두에게 힘들지만, 아이들에게 특히 스트레스가 된다. 그들은 안정감을 잃고, 그들의 일상이 무너지고 ① 익숙한 모든 것이 사라질 때 혼란스러움을 느낄 수도 있다. 3세에서 6세 사이의 어린아이들은 이사에 특히 영향을 받는다. 이 시기에 그들의 이해력은 꽤 융통성이 없어서, 그들이 새로운 집과 자신의 새로운 방을 미리 상상하기란 ② 쉽다(→ 어렵다). 어린아이들은 "내가 새로운 곳에서도 여전히 나야?"와 "내 장난감과 침대는 우리랑 같이 가?"와 같은 걱정들을 가질지도 모른다. 아이들의 과거 경험을 인정하는 것, 그리고 그들이 새로운 곳에 ③ 적응하도록 돕는 데 집중하는 것 사이에 균형을 잡는 것이 중요하다. 아이들은 자신의 존재에 대한 중요한 부분으로서 자기 과거를 ④ 존중하는 방식으로 자신의 배경을 나눌 기회를 가져봐야 한다. 이것은 공동체 의식을 형성하는 데 기여하고, 이는 모든 아이들, 특히 ⑤ 변화를 겪는 아이들에게 몹시 중요하다.

Why? 왜 정답일까?
② 뒤로 아이들은 새로운 곳에 가도 자기 존재가 그대로일지, 물건도 그대로 있을지 잘 상상하지 못한다는 예시가 나오는 것으로 보아, 아이들은 새로운 환경에 처하기 전에 미리 그 환경을 상상해보는 것을 '어려워한다'는 설명이 적합하다. 즉 easy를 hard로 바꾸어야 하므로, 문맥상 쓰임이 적절하지 않은 단어는 ②이다.

- **particularly** [ad] 특히
- **disoriented** [a] 혼란스러워 하는
- **disrupt** [v] 무너뜨리다, 지장을 주다, 방해하다
- **take away** 빼앗다, 빼앗다
- **literal** [a] 융통성 없는, 문자 그대로의
- **establish** [v] 설정하다, 쌓다
- **validate** [v] 인정하다, 승인하다, 입증하다
- **share** [v] 나누다, 공유하다
- **transition** [n] 변화
- **security** [n] 안정
- **routine** [n] 일상, 루틴
- **familiar** [a] 익숙한
- **understanding** [n] 이해(력)
- **beforehand** [ad] 미리
- **balance** [n] 균형 [v] 균형을 맞추다
- **adjust to** ~에 적응하다
- **contribute to** ~에 기여하다, ~의 원인이 되다

구문 풀이

14행 This contributes to building a sense of community, **which** is essential for
　　　　　　　　　　　　　　　　　　　　선행사　　　　계속적 용법
all children, especially **those** in transition.
　　　　　　　　= children

---

31 사실보다 감정에 기반한 우리의 선택   정답률 54% | 정답 ①

다음 빈칸에 들어갈 말로 가장 적절한 것을 고르시오.

☑ anxiety - 불안감   ② boredom - 지루함   ③ confidence - 자신감
④ satisfaction - 만족감   ⑤ responsibility - 책임감

Many people are terrified to fly in airplanes.
많은 사람들은 비행기를 타는 것을 두려워한다.
Often, / this fear stems from a lack of control.
종종, / 이 두려움은 통제력의 부족에서 비롯된다.
The pilot is in control, / not the passengers, / and this lack of control instills fear.
조종사는 통제를 하지만 / 승객은 그렇지 않으며, / 이러한 통제력의 부족은 두려움을 스며들게 한다.
Many potential passengers are so afraid / they choose to drive great distances / to get to a destination / instead of flying.
많은 잠재적인 승객들은 너무 두려운 나머지 / 그들은 먼 거리를 운전하는 것을 선택한다. / 목적지에 도착하기 위해 / 비행기를 타는 대신
But / their decision to drive / is based solely on emotion, / not logic.
그러나 / 운전을 하기로 한 그들의 결정은 / 오직 감정에 근거한다. / 논리가 아닌

Logic says / that statistically, / the odds of dying in a car crash / are around 1 in 5,000, / while the odds of dying in a plane crash / are closer to 1 in 11 million.
논리에 따르면, / 통계적으로 / 자동차 사고로 사망할 확률은 / 약 5,000분의 1이다. / 비행기 사고로 사망할 확률은 / 1,100만분의 1에 가까운 반면
If you're going to take a risk, / especially one that could possibly involve your well-being, / wouldn't you want the odds in your favor?
만약 여러분이 위험을 감수할 것이라면, / 특히 여러분의 안녕을 혹시 포함할 수 있는 위험을 / 여러분에게 유리한 확률을 원하지 않겠는가?
However, / most people choose the option / that will cause them the least amount of anxiety.
그러나 / 사람들 대부분은 선택을 한다. / 그들에게 최소한의 불안감을 야기할
Pay attention to the thoughts / you have about taking the risk / and make sure you're basing your decision on facts, / not just feelings.
생각에 주의를 기울여보고 / 여러분이 위험을 감수하는 데 관해 하고 있는 / 여러분이 사실에 기반하여 결정을 내리고 있는지 확인하라. / 단지 감정이 아니고

많은 사람들은 비행기를 타는 것을 두려워한다. 종종, 이 두려움은 통제력의 부족에서 비롯된다. 조종사는 통제를 하지만 승객은 그렇지 않으며, 이러한 통제력의 부족은 두려움을 스며들게 한다. 많은 잠재적인 승객들은 너무 두려운 나머지 비행기를 타는 대신 먼 거리를 운전해 목적지에 도착하기를 선택한다. 그러나 운전을 하기로 한 그들의 결정은 논리가 아닌 오직 감정에 근거한다. 논리에 따르면, 통계적으로 자동차 사고로 사망할 확률은 약 5,000분의 1인 반면, 비행기 사고로 사망할 확률은 1,100만분의 1에 가깝다고 한다. 만약 여러분이 위험을 감수할 것이라면, 특히 여러분의 안녕을 혹시 포함할 수 있는 위험을 감수할 것이라면, 여러분에게 유리한 확률을 원하지 않겠는가? 그러나 사람들 대부분은 그들에게 최소한의 불안감을 야기할 선택을 한다. 여러분이 위험을 감수하는 데 관해 하고 있는 생각에 주의를 기울여보고, 단지 감정이 아니고 사실에 기반하여 결정을 내리고 있는지 확인하라.

Why? 왜 정답일까?
글에서 사람들이 비행기를 타는 대신 장거리 운전을 하기로 결심하는 것은 사실상 사고의 실질적 확률을 고려하지 않은, 감정 중심의 선택(their decision to drive is based solely on emotion)이라고 지적하고 있다. 즉, 사람들은 실제 통계적으로 교통사고 확률이 비행기 사고 확률보다 높은데도 오로지 '불안'을 피하려고 운전을 선택한다는 것이므로, 빈칸에 들어갈 말로 가장 적절한 것은 ① '불안감'이다.

- **terrified** [a] 겁에 질린
- **lack** [n] 부족, 결여
- **potential** [a] 잠재적인
- **solely** [ad] 오로지
- **statistically** [ad] 통계적으로
- **in one's favor** ~에 유리한
- **well-being** [n] 안녕, 행복
- **base** [v] ~에 근거를 두다, 기반으로 하다
- **boredom** [n] 지루함
- **stem from** ~에서 기원하다
- **instill** [v] 스며들게 하다, 주입하다
- **destination** [n] 목적지
- **logic** [n] 논리
- **odds** [n] 공산, 가능성
- **crash** [n] (차나 비행기) 사고, 충돌
- **make sure** 반드시 ~하다
- **anxiety** [n] 불안

구문 풀이

3행 Many potential passengers are **so** afraid (that) they choose to drive great
　　　　　　　　　　　　　　　　「so ~ that : 너무 ~해서 …하다」　　목적어(~것)
distances **to get** to a destination instead of flying.
　　　　　부사적 용법(~하기 위해)

---

32 언어적 수법으로 다른 동물과 거리를 두는 인간   정답률 43% | 정답 ③

다음 빈칸에 들어갈 말로 가장 적절한 것을 고르시오. [3점]
① define human instincts - 인간의 본능을 정의하는
② overestimate chimps' intelligence - 침팬지의 지능을 과대평가하는
☑ distance the other animals from us - 우리와 다른 동물들 사이에 거리를 두는
④ identify animals' negative emotions - 동물의 부정적 감정을 식별하는
⑤ correct our misconceptions about nature - 자연에 대한 우리의 오해를 정정하는

The famous primatologist Frans de Waal, of Emory University, / says / humans downplay similarities / between us and other animals / as a way of maintaining our spot / at the top of our imaginary ladder.
Emory 대학의 유명한 영장류학자 Frans de Waal은 / 말한다. / 인간은 유사성을 경시한다고 / 우리와 다른 동물들 사이의 / 우리 위치를 유지할 방법으로 / 상상 속 사다리의 꼭대기에 있는
Scientists, / de Waal points out, / can be some of the worst offenders / — employing technical language / to distance the other animals from us.
과학자들은 / de Waal은 지적한다. / 최악의 죄를 범하는 자들 중 일부일 수 있다고 / 전문 언어를 사용하는 / 우리와 다른 동물들 사이에 거리를 두기 위해
They call "kissing" in chimps "mouth-to-mouth contact"; / they call "friends" between primates "favorite affiliation partners"; / they interpret evidence / showing that crows and chimps can make tools / as being somehow qualitatively different / from the kind of toolmaking said to define humanity.
그들은 침팬지의 '키스'를 '입과 입의 접촉'이라고 부르고, / 그들은 영장류 사이의 '친구'를 '좋아하는 제휴 파트너'라고 부르며, / 그들은 증거를 해석한다. / 까마귀와 침팬지가 도구를 만들 수 있다는 것을 보여주는 / 아무래도 질적으로 다르다고 / 인류를 정의한다고 하는 도구 제작과는
If an animal can beat us at a cognitive task / — like how certain bird species can remember the precise locations of thousands of seeds — / they write it off as instinct, / not intelligence.
만약 동물이 인지적인 과업에서 우리를 이길 수 있다면, / 특정 종의 새들이 수천 개의 씨앗의 정확한 위치를 기억할 수 있듯이 / 그들은 그것을 본능으로 치부한다. / 지능이 아니라
This and so many more tricks of language / are what de Waal has termed "linguistic castration."
이것과 더 많은 언어적 수법은 / de Waal이 '언어적 거세'라고 명명한 것이다.
The way we use our tongues / to disempower animals, / the way we invent words / to maintain our spot at the top.
우리의 언어를 사용하는 방식이며, / 우리가 동물로부터 힘을 빼앗기 위해 / 우리가 단어들을 만들어내는 방식이다. / 우리의 꼭대기 위치를 지키려고

Emory 대학의 유명한 영장류학자 Frans de Waal은 인간은 상상 속 사다리의 꼭대기에 있는 우리 위치를 유지할 방법으로 우리와 다른 동물들 사이의 유사성을 경시한다고 말한다. de Waal은 과학자들이 전문 언어를 사용해 우리와 다른 동물들 사이에 거리를 두는 최악의 죄

를 범하는 자들 중 일부일 수 있다고 지적한다. 그들은 침팬지의 '키스'를 '입과 입의 접촉'이라고 부르고, 영장류 사이의 '친구'를 '좋아하는 제휴 파트너'라고 부르며, 그들은 까마귀와 침팬지가 도구를 만들 수 있다는 것을 보여주는 증거가 인류를 정의한다고 하는 종류의 도구 제작과는 아무래도 질적으로 다르다고 해석한다. 만약 특정 종의 새들이 수천 개의 씨앗의 정확한 위치를 기억할 수 있는 경우처럼, 동물이 인지적인 과업에서 우리를 이길 수 있다면, 그들은 그것을 지능이 아니라 본능으로 치부한다. 이것과 더 많은 언어적 수법은 de Waal이 '언어적 거세'라고 명명한 것이다. 우리가 동물로부터 힘을 빼앗기 위해 우리의 언어를 사용하는 방식이며, 우리의 꼭대기 위치를 지키려고 단어들을 만들어내는 방식이다.

우리가 인간과 동물이 서로 다름을 강조하는(humans downplay similarities between us and other animals) 언어 사용으로 교묘하게 우월한 입지를 지키려고 한다는 것을 지적하는 내용이므로, 빈칸에 들어갈 말로 가장 적절한 것은 ③ '우리와 다른 동물들 사이에 거리를 두는'이다.

- **primatologist** ⓝ 영장류학자
- **similarity** ⓝ 유사성
- **imaginary** ⓐ 상상의
- **offender** ⓝ 범죄자, 나쁜 짓을 하는 사람
- **technical** ⓐ 전문적인
- **chimp** ⓝ 침팬지
- **affiliation** ⓝ 제휴
- **crow** ⓝ 까마귀
- **toolmaking** ⓝ 도구 제작
- **humanity** ⓝ 인류
- **cognitive** ⓐ 인지적인
- **write off as** ~라고 치부하다
- **intelligence** ⓝ 지능
- **term** ⓝ (특정 용어로) 칭하다 ⓝ 용어
- **overestimate** ⓥ 과대평가하다
- **identify** ⓥ 식별하다, 알아보다, 확인하다
- **downplay** ⓥ 경시하다
- **spot** ⓝ 위치 ⓥ 파악하다
- **ladder** ⓝ 사다리
- **employ** ⓥ 이용하다, 고용하다
- **language** ⓝ 언어
- **primate** ⓝ 영장류
- **interpret A as B** A를 B로 해석하다
- **qualitatively** ⓐⓓ 질적으로
- **define** ⓥ 정의하다
- **beat** ⓥ 이기다
- **precise** ⓐ 정확한
- **instinct** ⓝ 본능
- **trick** ⓝ 수법, 트릭
- **disempower** ⓥ ~로부터 힘을 빼앗다
- **distance A from B** A와 B 사이에 거리를 두다
- **misconception** ⓝ 오해

6행 ~ they interpret evidence (showing that crows and chimps can make tools)
「interpret + A +
as being somehow qualitatively different from the kind of toolmaking [(that is)
as + B : A를 B로 해석하다」   생략
said to define humanity].

33 학습자의 관심사에 맞는 읽기 자료 제공   정답률 56% | 정답 ②

다음 빈칸에 들어갈 말로 가장 적절한 것을 고르시오.
① examples from official textbooks – 공식 교과서에서 뽑은 예시
✔ relevant texts they will be interested in – 학생들이 관심 있어 할 적절한 글
③ enough chances to exchange information – 정보를 교환할 충분한 기회
④ different genres for different age groups – 각 연령대마다 다른 장르
⑤ early reading experience to develop logic skills – 논리력을 키우기 위한 조기 읽기 경험

A key to engagement and achievement / is providing students with relevant texts / they will be interested in.
참여와 성취의 핵심은 / 적절한 글을 학생들에게 제공하는 것이다. / 그들이 관심 있어 할
My scholarly work and my teaching / have been deeply influenced / by the work of Rosalie Fink.
내 학문적인 연구와 수업은 / 깊이 영향을 받아왔다. / Rosalie Fink의 연구에 의해
She interviewed twelve adults / who were highly successful in their work, / including a physicist, a biochemist, and a company CEO.
그녀는 열두 명의 성인들과 면담했다. / 자기 직업에서 매우 성공한 / 물리학자, 생화학자, 회사의 최고 경영자를 포함해
All of them had dyslexia / and had had significant problems with reading / throughout their school years.
그들 모두가 난독증이 있었고, / 읽기에 상당한 문제를 겪었다. / 학령기 내내
While she expected to find / that they had avoided reading / and discovered ways / to bypass it or compensate with other strategies for learning, / she found the opposite.
그녀는 알게 되리라고 예상했다 / 그들이 학습할 때 읽기를 피하고, / 방법을 찾아냈다는 것을 / 그것을 우회하거나 다른 전략으로 학습을 보완할 / 하지만 그녀는 정반대를 알아냈다.
"To my surprise, / I found / that these dyslexics were enthusiastic readers... / they rarely avoided reading. / On the contrary, / they sought out books."
"놀랍게도, / 나는 알아냈다. / 난독증이 있는 이런 사람들이 열성적인 독자인 것을… / 이들이 좀처럼 읽기를 피하지 않는 것을 / 거꾸로, 그들은 책을 찾았다."
The pattern Fink discovered / was / that all of her subjects had been passionate / in some personal interest.
Fink가 발견한 패턴은 / ~이었다. / 그녀의 실험 대상자 모두가 열정적이었다는 것 / 어떤 개인적인 관심사에
The areas of interest included / religion, math, business, science, history, and biography.
관심 분야는 포함했다. / 종교, 수학, 상업, 과학, 역사 그리고 생물학을
What mattered was / that they read voraciously to find out more.
중요한 것은 ~이었다. / 그들이 더 많이 알아내기 위해 탐욕스럽게 읽었다는 것

참여와 성취의 핵심은 학생들이 관심 있어 할 적절한 글을 그들에게 제공하는 것이다. 내 학문적인 연구와 수업은 Rosalie Fink의 연구에 깊이 영향을 받아왔다. 그녀는 물리학자, 생화학자, 회사의 최고 경영자를 포함해 자기 직업에서 매우 성공한 열두 명의 성인들과 면담했다. 그들 모두가 난독증이 있었고, 학령기 내내 읽기에 상당한 문제를 겪었다. 그녀는 그들이 학습할 때 읽기를 피하고, 그것을 우회하거나 다른 전략으로 학습을 보완할 방법을 찾아냈다는 것을 알게 되리라고 예상했으나, 정반대를 알아냈다. "놀랍게도, 나는 난독증이 있는 이런 사람들이 열성적인 독자인 것을… 이들이 좀처럼 읽기를 피하지 않는 것을 알아냈다. 거꾸로, 그들은 책을 찾았다." Fink가 발견한 패턴은 그녀의 실험 대상자 모두가 어떤 개인적인 관심사에 열정적이었다는 것이었다. 관심 분야는 종교, 수학, 상업, 과학, 역사 그리고 생물학을 포함했다. 중요한 것은 그들이 더 많이 알아내기 위해 탐욕스럽게 읽었다는 것이었다.

마지막 두 문장에서 어린 시절 난독증을 겪었으나 성공한 사람들을 연구한 결과, 자신이 관심을 두었던 분야에 대해 열정을 갖고 있었으며(passionate in some personal interest) 더 많은 것을 알기 위

해 닥치는 대로 글을 읽었다는 것을 알아냈다고 한다. 이를 통해 결국 학생을 좋은 학습자로 만들려면 '흥미를 가질 만한 글을 제시하라는 결론을 도출할 수 있다. 따라서 빈칸에 들어갈 말로 가장 적절한 것은 ② '학생들이 관심 있어 할 적절한 글'이다.

- **engagement** ⓝ 참여, 몰입
- **provide A with B** A에게 B를 제공하다
- **biochemist** ⓝ 생화학자
- **significant** ⓐ 상당한, 심각한
- **bypass** ⓥ 우회하다
- **opposite** ⓝ 정반대
- **seek out** ~을 찾아내다
- **personal** ⓐ 개인적인
- **biography** ⓝ (인물의) 전기
- **official** ⓐ 공식적인
- **achievement** ⓝ 성취
- **physicist** ⓝ 물리학자
- **dyslexia** ⓝ 난독증
- **discover** ⓥ 찾아내다, 발견하다
- **compensate for** ~을 보완하다, 보상하다
- **enthusiastic** ⓐ 열정적인, 열성적인
- **subject** ⓝ 실험 대상자
- **religion** ⓝ 종교
- **voraciously** ⓐⓓ 탐욕스럽게
- **relevant** ⓐ 적절한

8행 While she expected to find [that they had avoided reading and
「expect + to부정사 : ~하기를 기대하다」   동사1
discovered ways to bypass it or compensate with other strategies for learning],
동사2   수식(형용사적 용법)
she found the opposite.

★★★ 등급을 가르는 문제!
34 수행으로 자기 자신의 가치를 매길 때   정답률 37% | 정답 ①

다음 빈칸에 들어갈 말로 가장 적절한 것을 고르시오. [3점]
✔ it is the sole determinant of one's self-worth – 그것이 자신의 가치를 결정하는 유일한 요소일
② you are distracted by others' achievements – 다른 사람의 성취에 의해 주의가 분산될
③ there is too much competition in one field – 한 분야의 경쟁이 너무 심할
④ you ignore feedback about a performance – 수행에 관한 피드백을 무시할
⑤ it is not accompanied by effort – 그것에 노력이 따르지 않을

For many people, / *ability* refers to intellectual competence, / so they want everything they do / to reflect how smart they are / — writing a brilliant legal brief, / getting the highest grade on a test, / writing elegant computer code, / saying something exceptionally wise or witty in a conversation.
많은 사람들에게 / 능력은 지적 능력을 의미하기 때문에, / 그들은 자신이 하는 모든 것이 ~하기를 원한다. / 자신이 얼마나 똑똑한지를 보여주기를 / 훌륭한 소송 의견서를 작성하는 것, / 시험에서 최고의 성적을 받는 것, / 명쾌한 컴퓨터 코드를 작성하는 것, / 대화 도중 탁월하게 현명하거나 재치 있는 말을 하는 것
You could also define ability / in terms of a particular skill or talent, / such as how well one plays the piano, / learns a language, / or serves a tennis ball.
여러분은 또한 능력을 정의할 수도 있다. / 특정 기술이나 재능의 관점에서 / 피아노를 얼마나 잘 치는지, / 언어를 얼마나 잘 배우는지, / 테니스공을 얼마나 잘 서브하는지와 같은
Some people focus on their ability / to be attractive, entertaining, up on the latest trends, / or to have the newest gadgets.
어떤 사람들은 능력에 초점을 맞춘다. / 매력적이고, 재미있고, 최신 유행에 맞출 수 있는 / 혹은 최신 기기를 가질 수 있는
However ability may be defined, / a problem occurs / when it is the sole determinant of one's self-worth.
능력이 어떻게 정의되든지, / 문제가 발생한다. / 그것이 자신의 가치를 결정하는 유일한 요소일 때
The performance becomes the *only* measure of the person; / nothing else is taken into account.
수행이 그 사람의 유일한 척도가 되며, / 다른 것은 고려되지 않는다.
An outstanding performance means an outstanding person; / an average performance means an average person. // Period.
뛰어난 수행은 뛰어난 사람을 의미하고, / 평범한 수행은 평범한 사람을 의미한다. // 끝.

많은 사람들에게 능력은 지적 능력을 의미하기 때문에, 그들은 자신이 하는 모든 것이 자신이 얼마나 똑똑한지를 보여주기를 원한다. 예컨대, 훌륭한 소송 의견서를 작성하는 것, 시험에서 최고의 성적을 받는 것, 명쾌한 컴퓨터 코드를 작성하는 것, 대화 도중 탁월하게 현명하거나 재치 있는 말을 하는 것이다. 여러분은 또한 피아노를 얼마나 잘 치는지, 언어를 얼마나 잘 배우는지, 테니스공을 얼마나 잘 서브하는지와 같은 특정한 기술이나 재능의 관점에서 능력을 정의할 수도 있다. 어떤 사람들은 매력적이고, 재미있고, 최신 유행에 맞추거나, 최신 기기를 가질 수 있는 능력에 초점을 맞춘다. 능력이 어떻게 정의되든지, 그것이 자신의 가치를 결정하는 유일한 요소일 때 문제가 발생한다. 수행이 그 사람의 유일한 척도가 되며, 다른 것은 고려되지 않는다. 뛰어난 수행은 뛰어난 사람을 의미하고, 평범한 수행은 평범한 사람을 의미한다. 끝.

빈칸 뒤에서 수행을 자신의 가치에 대한 유일한 평가 척도로 삼는 경우(The performance becomes the *only* measure of the person; nothing else is taken into account.)의 부작용을 언급하는 것으로 보아, 빈칸에 들어갈 말로 가장 적절한 것은 ① '그것이 자신의 가치를 결정하는 유일한 요소일'이다.

- **competence** ⓝ 능력, 역량
- **brilliant** ⓐ 뛰어난
- **elegant** ⓐ 명쾌한, 멋들어진
- **witty** ⓐ 재치 있는
- **serve a ball** 서브를 넣다
- **entertaining** ⓐ 재미있는, 즐거움을 주는
- **measure** ⓝ 척도
- **outstanding** ⓐ 뛰어난
- **determinant** ⓝ 결정 요소
- **distracted** ⓐ 정신이 팔린
- **reflect** ⓥ 반영하다
- **brief** ⓝ (법률) 취지서, 의견서, 보고서
- **exceptionally** ⓐⓓ 탁월하게
- **in terms of** ~의 면에서
- **attractive** ⓐ 매력적인
- **gadget** ⓝ 장비, 기기
- **take into account** ~을 고려하다, 참작하다
- **sole** ⓐ 유일한
- **self-worth** ⓝ 자존감, 자부심

10행 However ability may be defined, a problem occurs when it is the sole
복합관계부사(어떻게 ~하든 간에 = no matter how)
determinant of one's self-worth.

▶ 많이 틀린 이유는?
특정 분야의 재능이나 역량을 보여주려 한다는 내용 때문에, 빈칸 뒤를 제대로 읽지 않으면 남과의 비교를 언급하는 ②나 수행에 대한 피드백을 언급하는 ④가 빈칸에 적절해 보인다. 하지만 빈칸 문제를 풀 때는 해당 지문 자체의 내용에 충실해야 한다.

▶ 문제 해결 방법은?
빈칸 뒤에서 수행이 '한 사람을 평가하는 유일한 척도(the *only* measure of the person)'가 될 때를 언급하는데, 이 표현이 거의 그대로 ①에서 재진술되었다(the sole determinant of one's self-worth).

★★★ 등급을 가르는 문제!
35 감각 신경의 작용　　　　　　　　정답률 38% | 정답 ②

다음 글에서 전체 흐름과 관계 없는 문장은? [3점]

Sensory nerves have specialized endings in the tissues / that pick up a particular sensation.
감각 신경은 특화된 말단을 조직에 가지고 있다. / 특정 감각을 포착하는
If, for example, / you step on a sharp object such as a pin, / nerve endings in the skin / will transmit the pain sensation up your leg, / up and along the spinal cord to the brain.
만약 예를 들어, / 여러분이 핀과 같이 날카로운 물체를 밟는다면, / 피부의 신경 말단이 / 통증 감각을 여러분의 다리 위로 전달할 것이다. / 그리고 척수를 타고 위로 뇌까지
① While the pain itself is unpleasant, / it is in fact acting as a protective mechanism for the foot.
통증 자체는 불쾌하지만, / 이것은 사실 발을 보호하는 메커니즘으로 작용하고 있다.
✔ That is, / you get used to the pain / so the capacity with which you can avoid pain decreases.
즉, / 여러분은 그 통증에 익숙해진다 / 그래서 통증을 피할 수 있는 능력이 감소한다.
③ Within the brain, / nerves will connect to the area / that controls speech, / so that you may well shout 'ouch' / or something rather less polite.
뇌 안에서, / 신경은 부분에 연결될 것이고, / 언어를 통제하는 / 그래서 여러분은 '아야'를 외칠 것이다. / 또는 다소 덜 공손한 무언가를
④ They will also connect to motor nerves / that travel back down the spinal cord, / and to the muscles in your leg / that now contract quickly / to lift your foot away from the painful object.
그것들은 또한 운동 신경에 연결될 것이다. / 척수를 타고 다시 내려오는 / 그리고 여러분의 다리 근육에 / 이제 재빨리 수축하여 / 고통을 주는 물체로부터 발을 떼서 들어 올리는
⑤ Sensory and motor nerves / control almost all functions in the body / — from the beating of the heart / to the movement of the gut, sweating and just about everything else.
감각 신경과 운동 신경은 / 신체의 거의 모든 기능을 통제한다. / 심장의 박동에서부터 / 장 운동, 발한과 그 밖에 모든 것에 이르기까지

감각 신경은 특정 감각을 포착하는 특화된 말단을 조직에 가지고 있다. 예를 들어, 만약 여러분이 핀과 같이 날카로운 물체를 밟는다면, 피부의 신경 말단이 통증 감각을 여러분의 다리 위로, 그리고 척수를 따라 위로 뇌까지 전달할 것이다. ① 통증 자체는 불쾌하지만, 이것은 사실 발을 보호하는 메커니즘으로 작용하고 있다. ② 즉, 여러분은 그 통증에 익숙해져 통증을 피할 수 있는 능력이 감소한다. ③ 뇌 안에서, 신경은 언어를 통제하는 부분에 연결될 것이고, 그래서 여러분은 '아야' 또는 다소 덜 공손한 무언가를 외칠 것이다. ④ 그것들은 또한 척수를 타고 다시 내려오는 운동 신경에 연결될 것이고, 그리고 이제 재빨리 수축하여 고통을 주는 물체로부터 발을 떼서 들어 올리게 하는 여러분의 다리 근육에 연결될 것이다. ⑤ 감각 신경과 운동 신경은 심장의 박동에서부터 장 운동, 발한과 그 밖에 모든 것에 이르기까지 신체의 거의 모든 기능을 통제한다.

Why? 왜 정답일까?
통증이 위험을 피하는 보호 기제 역할을 한다는 예시를 들어 감각 신경의 작용을 설명하는 글인데, ②는 통증에 익숙해져 둔감해진다는 내용이다. 따라서 전체 흐름과 관계 없는 문장은 ②이다.

- sensory ⓐ 감각의
- tissue ⓝ (생체) 조직
- transmit ⓥ 전달하다
- unpleasant ⓐ 불쾌한
- capacity ⓝ 능력
- painful ⓐ 고통스러운
- gut ⓝ 내장, 소화관
- nerve ⓝ 신경
- sensation ⓝ 감각
- spinal cord 척수
- protective mechanism 보호 기제
- lift ⓥ 들어올리다
- motor ⓐ 운동 신경의
- sweating ⓝ 발한, 땀이 남

구문 풀이

6행 That is, you get used to the pain so the capacity [with which you can
　　　주어1 동사1(~에 익숙해지다)　　　　　주어2　　「전치사 + 목적격 관·대」
avoid pain] decreases.
　　　　　　 동사2

★★ 문제 해결 꿀~팁 ★★

▶ 많이 틀린 이유는?
③에서 갑자기 '언어(speech)'가 언급되어 글과 무관해 보이지만, '아야'라는 말이 결국에는 고통에서 비롯된 반응의 예시이므로 전체 흐름상 어색하지 않다.
▶ 문제 해결 방법은?
정답인 ②에도 핵심 소재(pain)가 그대로 등장하므로 자연스러워 보일 수 있지만, 큰 소재만 대충 읽지 말고 주제와 문장별 핵심 내용을 더 세부적으로 파악해야 한다.

36 결정의 형성　　　　　　　　정답률 72% | 정답 ②

주어진 글 다음에 이어질 글의 순서로 가장 적절한 것을 고르시오. [3점]
① (A) - (C) - (B)　　　　　　✔ (B) - (A) - (C)
③ (B) - (C) - (A)　　　　　　④ (C) - (A) - (B)
⑤ (C) - (B) - (A)

Maybe you've heard this joke: / "How do you eat an elephant?"
아마 여러분은 이 농담을 들어본 적이 있을 것이다. / "코끼리를 어떻게 먹지?"

The answer is "one bite at a time."
정답은 '한 번에 한 입'이다.
(B) So, how do you "build" the Earth?
그렇다면, 여러분은 어떻게 지구를 '건설'하는가?
That's simple, too: / one atom at a time.
이것도 간단하다. / 한 번에 하나의 원자다.
Atoms are the basic building blocks of crystals, / and since all rocks are made up of crystals, / the more you know about atoms, / the better.
원자는 결정의 기본 구성 요소이고, / 모든 암석은 결정으로 이루어져 있기 때문에, / 여러분이 원자에 대해 더 많이 알수록 / 더 좋다.
Crystals come in a variety of shapes / that scientists call *habits*.
결정은 다양한 모양으로 나온다. / 과학자들이 습성이라고 부르는
(A) Common crystal habits / include squares, triangles, and six-sided hexagons.
일반적인 결정 습성은 / 사각형, 삼각형, 육면의 육각형을 포함한다.
Usually crystals form / when liquids cool, / such as when you create ice cubes.
보통 결정이 형성된다. / 액체가 차가워질 때 / 여러분이 얼음을 만들 때와 같이
Many times, / crystals form in ways / that do not allow for perfect shapes.
많은 경우, / 결정은 방식으로 형성된다. / 완벽한 모양을 허용하지 않는
If conditions are too cold, too hot, / or there isn't enough source material, / they can form strange, twisted shapes.
조건이 너무 차갑거나, / 너무 뜨겁거나, / 혹은 원천 물질이 충분하지 않으면 / 그것들은 이상하고 뒤틀린 모양을 형성할 수 있다.
(C) But when conditions are right, / we see beautiful displays.
하지만 조건이 맞을 때, / 우리는 아름다운 배열을 본다.
Usually, / this involves a slow, steady environment / where the individual atoms have plenty of time to join / and fit perfectly into what's known as the *crystal lattice*.
보통, / 이것은 느리고 안정적인 환경을 수반한다. / 개별적인 원자들이 충분한 시간을 들여 결합해서 / *결정격자*라고 알려진 것에 완벽하게 들어맞게 되는
This is the basic structure of atoms / that is seen time after time.
이것은 원자의 기본적인 구조이다. / 반복하여 보이는

아마 여러분은 이 농담을 들어본 적이 있을 것이다. "코끼리를 어떻게 먹지?" 정답은 '한 번에 한 입'이다.

(B) 그렇다면, 여러분은 어떻게 지구를 '건설'하는가? 이것도 간단하다. 한 번에 하나의 원자이다. 원자는 결정의 기본 구성 요소이고, 모든 암석은 결정으로 이루어져 있기 때문에, 여러분은 원자에 대해 더 많이 알수록 더 좋다. 결정은 과학자들이 습성이라고 부르는 다양한 모양으로 나온다.

(A) 일반적인 결정 습성은 사각형, 삼각형, 육면의 육각형을 포함한다. 보통 여러분이 얼음을 만들 때와 같이 액체가 차가워질 때 결정이 형성된다. 많은 경우, 결정은 완벽한 모양을 허용하지 않는 방식으로 형성된다. 조건이 너무 차갑거나, 너무 뜨겁거나, 혹은 원천 물질이 충분하지 않으면 이상하고 뒤틀린 모양을 형성할 수 있다.

(C) 하지만 조건이 맞을 때, 우리는 아름다운 배열을 본다. 보통, 이것은 개별적인 원자들이 충분한 시간을 들여 결합해서 *결정격자*라고 알려진 것에 완벽하게 들어맞게 되는 느리고 안정적인 환경을 수반한다. 이것은 반복하여 보이는 원자의 기본적인 구조이다.

Why? 왜 정답일까?
주어진 글에서 '코끼리를 어떻게 먹나'라는 물음에 '한 번에 한 입씩' 먹으면 된다는 농담이 있다고 하는데, (B)는 이것이 지구가 만들어진 과정에도 적용될 수 있다면서 결정의 습성을 언급한다. (A)는 이 결정의 습성을 설명하면서, 많은 경우 결정이 뒤틀린 모양으로 형성된다고 언급하는데, (C)는 But으로 흐름을 반전시켜 아름다운 배열을 지닌 결정도 만들어진다고 설명한다. 따라서 글의 순서로 가장 적절한 것은 ② '(B) - (A) - (C)'이다.

- bite ⓝ 한 입 (베어문 조각) ⓥ 베어 물다
- hexagon ⓝ 육각형
- ice cube 얼음 조각
- twisted 뒤틀린
- plenty of 많은
- lattice ⓝ 격자 (모양)
- crystal ⓝ 결정
- liquid ⓝ 액체
- allow for ~을 허용하다
- atom ⓝ 원자
- steady ⓐ 안정된, 꾸준한
- fit into ~에 들어 맞다
- time after time 자주, 매번, 되풀이해서

구문 풀이

15행 Usually, this involves a slow, steady environment [where the individual
　　　　　　　　　　　　　　　선행사(상황)　　　　　관계부사
atoms have plenty of time to join and fit perfectly into {what's known as the
　　　　　　　　　　　　형용사적 용법　　　　　전치사　　　명사절
crystal lattice}].

37 기타가 소리를 내는 과정　　　　　　　정답률 63% | 정답 ③

주어진 글 다음에 이어질 글의 순서로 가장 적절한 것을 고르시오.
① (A) - (C) - (B)　　　　　　② (B) - (A) - (C)
✔ (B) - (C) - (A)　　　　　　④ (C) - (A) - (B)
⑤ (C) - (B) - (A)

When you pluck a guitar string / it moves back and forth hundreds of times every second.
여러분이 기타 줄을 뜯을 때 / 그것은 매초 수백 번 이리저리 움직인다.
(B) Naturally, / this movement is so fast / that you cannot see it / — you just see the blurred outline of the moving string.
당연히, / 이 움직임은 너무 빨라서 / 여러분은 볼 수 없다. / 여러분은 그저 움직이는 줄의 흐릿한 윤곽만 본다.
Strings vibrating in this way on their own / make hardly any noise / because strings are very thin / and don't push much air about.
이렇게 스스로 진동하는 줄들은 / 거의 소리가 나지 않는데, / 이는 줄이 매우 가늘고 / 많은 공기를 밀어내지 못하기 때문이다.
(C) But if you attach a string to a big hollow box / (like a guitar body), / then the vibration is amplified / and the note is heard loud and clear.
하지만 여러분이 속이 빈 커다란 상자에 줄을 달면, / (기타 몸통 같이) / 그 진동은 증폭되어 / 그 음이 크고 선명하게 들린다.
The vibration of the string is passed on / to the wooden panels of the guitar body, / which vibrate back and forth / at the same rate as the string.
그 줄의 진동은 전달된다 / 기타 몸통의 나무판으로 / 그리고 그것은 이리저리 떨린다. / 줄과 같은 정도로
(A) The vibration of the wood / creates more powerful waves in the air pressure, / which travel away from the guitar.
그 나무의 진동은 / 공기의 압력에 더 강력한 파동을 만들어 내고 / 그것은 기타로부터 멀리 퍼진다.

When the waves reach your eardrums / they flex in and out / the same number of times a second / as the original string.
그 파동이 여러분의 고막에 도달할 때 / 그것은 굽이쳐 들어가고 나온다. / 초당 동일한 횟수로 / 원래의 줄과

여러분이 기타 줄을 뜯을 때 그것은 매초 수백 번 이리저리 움직인다.

(B) 당연히, 이 움직임은 너무 빨라서 여러분은 볼 수 없다. 여러분은 그저 움직이는 줄의 흐릿한 윤곽만 본다. 이렇게 스스로 진동하는 줄들은 거의 소리가 나지 않는데, 이는 줄이 매우 가늘어 많은 공기를 밀어내지 못하기 때문이다.

(C) 하지만 여러분이 (기타 몸통 같이) 속이 빈 커다란 상자에 줄을 달면, 그 진동은 증폭되어 그 음이 크고 선명하게 들린다. 그 줄의 진동은 기타 몸통의 나무판으로 전달되어 줄과 같은 정도로 이리저리 떨린다.

(A) 그 나무의 진동은 공기의 압력에 더 강력한 파동을 만들어 내어 기타로부터 멀리 퍼진다. 그 파동이 여러분의 고막에 도달할 때 원래의 줄과 초당 동일한 횟수로 굽이쳐 들어가고 나온다.

Why? 왜 정답일까?

기타 줄을 뜯으면 줄이 떨린다는 주어진 글에 이어, (B)는 우리가 이 움직임을 평소에는 볼 수 없으며, 혼자서 진동하는 줄은 공기를 충분히 밀어내지 못해 소리도 내지 못한다고 언급한다. (C)는 But으로 흐름을 반전시키며, 줄을 기타 몸통 같은 상자에 달아서 진동을 증폭시키는 상황을 제시하고, (A)는 이 진동이 소리로 나오게 된다는 내용으로 글을 맺는다. 따라서 글의 순서로 가장 적절한 것은 ③ '(B) - (C) - (A)'이다.

- pluck ⓥ (현악기를) 뜯다
- vibration ⓝ 진동
- flex ⓥ (근육을) 수축시키다, (관절을) 구부리다
- thin ⓐ 얇은
- hollow ⓐ (속이) 빈
- panel ⓝ 판
- string ⓝ 줄, 현악기
- eardrum ⓝ 고막
- blur ⓥ 흐리게 하다
- attach A to B A를 B에 부착하다
- amplify ⓥ 증폭시키다
- rate ⓝ 속도, 비율

구문 풀이

9행 Strings (vibrating in this way on their own) make hardly any noise
(주어 / 현재분사 / 동사(복수) / 거의 전혀 ~않다)
because strings are very thin and don't push much air about.

★★★ 등급을 가르는 문제! ★★★

38 일과 가정의 경계 　　정답률 26% | 정답 ⑤

글의 흐름으로 보아, 주어진 문장이 들어가기에 가장 적절한 곳을 고르시오. [3점]

Boundaries between work and home / are blurring / as portable digital technology makes it increasingly possible / to work anywhere, anytime.
직장과 가정의 경계가 / 흐릿해지고 있다. / 휴대용 디지털 기술이 점차 가능하게 하면서, / 언제 어디서든 작업하는 것을

Individuals differ / in how they like to manage their time / to meet work and outside responsibilities.
사람들은 서로 다르다. / 자기 시간을 관리하기를 바라는 방식에 있어서 / 직장과 외부의 책임을 수행하기 위해

① Some people prefer to separate or segment roles / so that boundary crossings are minimized.
어떤 사람들은 역할을 분리하거나 분할하기를 선호한다. / 경계 교차 지점이 최소화되도록

② For example, / these people might keep separate email accounts / for work and family / and try to conduct work at the workplace / and take care of family matters / only during breaks and non-work time.
예를 들어, / 이러한 사람들은 별개의 이메일 계정을 유지하고 / 직장과 가정을 위한 / 직장에서 일하려고 하며, / 집안일을 처리하려고 할지도 모른다. / 쉴 때나 일하지 않는 시간 중에만

③ We've even noticed / more of these "segmenters" / carrying two phones — one for work and one for personal use.
우리는 심지어 알게 되었다. / 더 많은 이러한 '분할자들'이 / 전화기 두 대를 가지고 다니고 있음을 / 하나는 업무용이고 다른 하나는 개인용인

④ Flexible schedules work well for these individuals / because they enable greater distinction / between time at work and time in other roles.
유연근무제는 이런 사람들에게 잘 적용되는데, / 이것은 더 큰 구별을 가능하게 하기 때문이다. / 직장에서의 시간과 다른 역할에서의 시간 간에

☑ Other individuals prefer / integrating work and family roles all day long.
다른 사람들은 선호한다. / 하루 종일 직장과 가정의 역할을 통합하기를

This might entail / constantly trading text messsages with children from the office, / or monitoring emails at home and on vacation, / rather than returning to work to find hundreds of messages in their inbox.
이것은 수반할 수도 있다. / 사무실에서 아이들과 문자 메시지를 계속 주고받는 것을 / 혹은 집에 있을 때나 휴가 중에 이메일을 체크하는 것을 / 직장으로 돌아가서 받은 편지함에서 수백 개의 메시지를 발견하는 대신

휴대용 디지털 기술이 언제 어디서든 작업하는 것을 점차 가능하게 하면서, 직장과 가정의 경계가 흐릿해지고 있다. 사람들은 직장과 외부의 책임을 수행하기 위해 자기 시간을 관리하기를 바라는 방식이 서로 다르다. ① 어떤 사람들은 경계 교차 지점이 최소화되도록 역할을 분리하거나 분할하기를 선호한다. ② 예를 들어, 이러한 사람들은 직장과 가정을 위한 별개의 이메일 계정을 유지하고 직장에서 일하려고 하며, 쉴 때나 일하지 않는 시간 중에만 집안일을 처리하려고 할지도 모른다. ③ 우리는 더 많은 이러한 '분할자들'이 하나는 업무용이고 다른 하나는 개인용인 전화기 두 대를 가지고 다니고 있음을 심지어 알게 되었다. ④ 유연근무제는 이런 사람들에게 잘 적용되는데, 직장에서의 시간과 다른 역할에서의 시간 간에 더 큰 구별을 가능하게 하기 때문이다. ⑤ 다른 사람들은 하루 종일 직장과 가정의 역할을 통합하기를 선호한다. 이것은 직장으로 돌아가서 받은 편지함에서 수백 개의 메시지를 발견하는 대신, 사무실에서 아이들과 문자 메시지를 계속 주고받거나, 집에 있을 때나 휴가 중에 이메일을 체크하는 것을 수반할 수도 있다.

Why? 왜 정답일까?

⑤ 앞까지 일과 가정을 '분리하는' 사람들을 언급하는데, ⑤ 뒤에는 직장에서도 가족과 연락하고, 집에 있을 때도 업무 처리를 하는 등 둘을 '통합하는' 사람들을 언급하고 있다. 따라서 '통합자들'에 관한 화제로 처음 넘어가는 주어진 문장이 들어가기에 가장 적절한 곳은 ⑤이다.

- integrate ⓥ 통합하다
- all day long 하루 종일

- boundary ⓝ 경계
- outside ⓐ 외부의
- segment ⓥ 분할하다, 나누다
- account ⓝ 계정
- carry ⓥ 들고 다니다
- distinction ⓝ 구별
- constantly ⓐⓓ 계속
- monitor ⓥ 확인하다, 감독하다, 점검하다
- inbox ⓝ 수신함
- portable ⓐ 휴대용의
- separate ⓥ 분리하다 ⓐ 분리된, 개별의
- minimize ⓥ 최소화하다
- conduct ⓥ 수행하다
- flexible schedule 유연근무제
- entail ⓥ 수반하다
- trade ⓥ 교환하다
- on vacation 휴가 중인

구문 풀이

3행 Boundaries between work and home are blurring as portable digital
(　　　　　　　　　　　가목적어 / 접속사(~ 때문에))
technology makes it increasingly possible to work anywhere, anytime.
(5형식 동사 / 목적격 보어 / 진목적어)

★★ 문제 해결 꿀~팁 ★★

▶ 많이 틀린 이유는?
주어진 문장이 Other로 시작하므로, 앞에 Some이 있는 ②를 고르기 쉽다. 「Some ~ Other …」의 대구가 자연스러워 보이기 때문이다. 하지만 ② 뒤의 these people이 문맥상 ② 앞의 Some people이므로, 주어진 문장을 ②에 넣어 대명사의 흐름을 끊으면 안 된다. 또한 뒤에 갑자기 '유연근무제'라는 새로운 소재가 등장하는 ④도 정답처럼 보이기 쉽지만, ④ 앞뒤가 여전히 '일과 가정을 분리하는' 사람들에 대해서 설명하고 있어서 흐름이 끊기지 않기 때문에 다른 문장이 필요하지 않다.

▶ 문제 해결 방법은?
⑤ 뒤의 'trading ~ or monitoring ~'이 주어진 문장의 'integrating ~'에 대한 예시임을 파악해야 한다.

39 보완재의 개념 　　정답률 50% | 정답 ⑤

글의 흐름으로 보아, 주어진 문장이 들어가기에 가장 적절한 곳을 고르시오.

A "complementary good" is a product / that is often consumed alongside another product.
'보완재'는 제품이다. / 종종 또 다른 제품과 함께 소비되는

① For example, / popcorn is a complementary good to a movie, / while a travel pillow is a complementary good / for a long plane journey.
예를 들어, / 팝콘은 영화에 대한 보완재인 한편, / 여행 베개는 보완재이다. / 긴 비행기 여행에 대한

② When the popularity of one product increases, / the sales of its complementary good / also increase.
한 제품의 인기가 높아지면 / 그것의 보완재 판매량도 / 또한 늘어난다.

③ By producing goods / that complement other products / that are already (or about to be) popular, / you can ensure a steady stream of demand for your product.
제품을 생산해서 / 다른 제품을 보완하는 / 이미 인기가 있는 (또는 곧 있을) / 여러분은 여러분의 제품에 대한 꾸준한 수요 흐름을 보장할 수 있다.

④ Some products enjoy perfect complementary status / — they *have* to be consumed together, / such as a lamp and a lightbulb.
일부 제품들은 완벽한 보완적 상태를 누리고 있고, / 그것들은 함께 소비되어야 한다. / 램프와 전구와 같이

☑ However, / do not assume / that a product is perfectly complementary, / as customers may not be completely locked in to the product.
그러나 / 가정하지 말라. / 어떤 제품이 완벽하게 보완적이라고 / 고객들이 그 제품에 완전히 고정되어 있지 않을 수 있으므로

For example, / although motorists may seem required to purchase gasoline / to run their cars, / they can switch to electric cars.
예를 들어, / 비록 운전자들이 휘발유를 구매할 필요가 있는 것처럼 보이기는 해도, / 차를 운전하기 위해 / 이들이 전기 자동차로 바꿀 수도 있다.

'보완재'는 종종 또 다른 제품과 함께 소비되는 제품이다. ① 예를 들어, 팝콘은 영화에 대한 보완재인 한편, 여행 베개는 긴 비행기 여행에 대한 보완재이다. ② 한 제품의 인기가 높아지면 그것의 보완재 판매량도 늘어난다. ③ 여러분은 이미 인기가 있는 (또는 곧 있을) 다른 제품을 보완하는 제품을 생산해서 여러분의 제품에 대한 꾸준한 수요 흐름을 보장할 수 있다. ④ 일부 제품들은 완벽한 보완적 상태를 누리고 있고, 그것들은 램프와 전구와 같이 함께 소비되어야 한다. ⑤ 그러나 고객들이 그 제품에 완전히 고정되어 있지 않을 수 있으므로, 어떤 제품이 완벽하게 보완적이라고 가정하지 말라. 예를 들어, 비록 운전자들이 차를 운전하기 위해 휘발유를 구매할 필요가 있는 것처럼 보이기는 해도, 이들이 전기 자동차로 바꿀 수도 있다.

Why? 왜 정답일까?

보완재에 관해 설명하는 글이다. ⑤ 앞에서 일부 제품은 램프 – 전구의 예시처럼 완벽히 서로 보완 관계에 있다고 하는데, ⑤ 뒤에서는 자동차 – 기름의 예시로, 운전자들이 전기 차로 넘어갈 수도 있기 때문에 둘을 완벽한 보완 관계로 볼 수 없다고 한다. 즉, ⑤ 앞뒤로 내용이 서로 반대된다. 이때 주어진 문장은 '보완재인 두 재화가 항상 보완 관계에 있을 거라고 가정하지 말라'는 내용으로, However가 있어 흐름 전환을 적절히 유도한다. 따라서 주어진 문장이 들어가기에 가장 적절한 곳은 ⑤이다.

- assume ⓥ 가정하다
- locked in 갇힌, 고정된
- complement ⓥ 보완하다, 보충하다
- stream ⓝ 흐름
- motorist ⓝ 운전자
- switch to ~로 바꾸다
- complementary ⓐ 보완하는
- alongside prep ~와 함께
- ensure ⓥ 확실히 하다, 보장하다
- status ⓝ 지위, 입지
- gasoline ⓝ 휘발유
- electric ⓐ 전기의

구문 풀이

14행 For example, although motorists may seem required to purchase gasoline
(접속사(~에도 불구하고) / 2형식 동사 / 주격 보어)
to run their cars, they can switch to electric cars.
(~하기 위해)

40 규범에서 약간 벗어나는 옷차림을 좋게 보는 우리들 　　정답률 50% | 정답 ①

다음 글의 내용을 한 문장으로 요약하고자 한다. 빈칸 (A), (B)에 들어갈 말로 가장 적절한 것은?

	(A)	(B)		(A)	(B)
✓	positively 긍정적으로	·····	challenges 도전할	②	negatively 부정적으로	·····	challenges 도전할
③	indifferently 무심하게	·····	neglects 등한시할	④	negatively 부정적으로	·····	meets 일치할
⑤	positively 긍정적으로	·····	meets 일치할			

It's not news to anyone / that we judge others based on their clothes.
누구에게도 새로운 일이 아니다. / 우리가 남들을 옷으로 판단한다는 것은

In general, / studies that investigate these judgments / find / that people prefer clothing that matches expectations — surgeons in scrubs, little boys in blue — / with one notable exception.
일반적으로, / 이러한 판단을 조사하는 연구는 / 발견한다. / 사람들이 예상에 맞는 의복을 선호한다는 것을 / 수술복을 입은 외과 의사, 파란 옷을 입은 남자아이와 같이 (그러면서) / 눈에 띄는 예외가 하나 있는

A series of studies / published in an article in June 2014 / in the *Journal of Consumer Research* / explored observers' reactions to people / who broke established norms only slightly.
일련의 연구는 / 2014년 6월 논문에 실린 / *Journal of Consumer Research*의 / 사람들에 대한 관찰자들의 반응을 탐구했다. / 확립된 규범을 아주 약간 어긴

In one scenario, / a man at a black-tie affair / was viewed as having higher status and competence / when wearing a red bow tie.
한 시나리오에서는, / 정장 차림의 행사에 있는 한 남자가 / 더 높은 지위와 능력을 지녔다고 여겨졌다. / 빨간 나비 넥타이를 맸을 때

The researchers also found / that valuing uniqueness / increased audience members' ratings of the status and competence of a professor / who wore red sneakers while giving a lecture.
연구자들은 또한 발견했다. / 독특함을 중시하는 것이 / 교수의 지위와 역량에 대한 청중들의 평가를 높였다는 것을 / 강의 중에 빨간 운동화를 신은

The results suggest / that people judge these slight deviations from the norm as positive / because they suggest / that the individual is powerful enough / to risk the social costs of such behaviors.
그 결과들은 시사하는데, / 사람들이 이런 식으로 규범을 약간 어긴 것을 긍정적으로 판단한다는 것을 / 왜냐하면 그것들은 암시하기 때문이다. / 그 사람이 충분히 강하다는 것을 / 그러한 행동으로 인한 사회적 비용을 감수할 만큼

➡ A series of studies show / that people view an individual (A) positively / when the individual only slightly (B) challenges the norm / for what people should wear.
일련의 연구는 나타낸다. / 사람들이 어떤 개인을 긍정적으로 본다는 것을 / 그 사람이 규범에 아주 약간 도전할 때 / 사람들이 무엇을 입을지에 대한

우리가 남들을 옷으로 판단한다는 것은 누구에게도 새로운 일이 아니다. 일반적으로, 이러한 판단을 조사하는 연구는 사람들이 수술복을 입은 외과 의사, 파란 옷을 입은 남자아이와 같이 예상에 맞는 의복이되 눈에 띄는 예외가 하나 있는 것을 선호한다는 것을 발견한다. *Journal of Consumer Research*의 2014년 6월 논문에 실린 일련의 연구는 확립된 규범을 아주 약간 어긴 사람들에 대한 관찰자들의 반응을 탐구했다. 한 시나리오에서는, 정장 차림의 행사에 있는 한 남자가 빨간 나비 넥타이를 맸을 때 더 높은 지위와 능력을 지녔다고 여겨졌다. 연구자들은 또한, 독특함을 중시하는 것이 강의 중에 빨간 운동화를 신은 교수의 지위와 역량에 대한 청중들의 평가를 높였다는 것을 발견했다. 그 결과들은 사람들이 이런 식으로 규범을 약간 어긴 것을 긍정적으로 판단한다는 것을 시사하는데, 왜냐하면 그것들은 그 사람이 그러한 행동으로 인한 사회적 비용을 감수할 만큼 충분히 강하다는 것을 암시하기 때문이다.

➡ 일련의 연구는 사람들이 무엇을 입을지에 대한 규범에 개인이 아주 약간 (B) 도전할 때 사람들이 그 사람을 (A) 긍정적으로 본다는 것을 나타낸다.

Why? 왜 정답일까?

의복에 대한 규범을 살짝 어기는 사람이 더 긍정적으로 여겨진다(people judge these slight deviations from the norm as positive)는 연구를 소개하는 글이다. 따라서 요약문의 빈칸 (A), (B)에 들어갈 말로 가장 적절한 것은 ① '(A) positively(긍정적으로), (B) challenges(도전할)'이다.

- in general 일반적으로
- match ⓥ 일치하다, 맞다, 부합하다
- scrubs ⓝ 수술복
- exception ⓝ 예외
- reaction ⓝ 반응
- black-tie affair 격식을 차리는 모임
- uniqueness ⓝ 독특함, 고유함
- powerful ⓐ 영향력 있는, 강력한
- challenge ⓥ 반박하다, 도전하다
- neglect ⓥ 등한시하다, 소홀히 하다
- investigate ⓥ 연구하다, 조사하다
- surgeon ⓝ 외과 의사
- notable ⓐ 눈에 띄는
- explore ⓥ 탐구하다
- established ⓐ 확립된, 정해진
- bow tie 나비 넥타이
- deviation ⓝ 일탈
- risk ⓥ 위태롭게 하다
- negatively ⓐⓓ 부정적으로

구문 풀이

10행 The researchers also found that valuing uniqueness increased audience
접속사 ↑ 동명사구 주어 ↑ 동사
members' ratings of the status and competence of a professor [who wore red
↑주격 관·대
sneakers while giving a lecture].
분사구문(= while he or she gave ~)

41-42 식품 수송의 탄소 발자국을 줄이기 위해 거리보다 더 중요한 요소들

「Claims / that local food production cut greenhouse gas emissions / by reducing the burning of transportation fuel / are usually not well founded.」 41번의 근거
주장은 / 로컬푸드 생산이 온실가스 배출을 줄였다는 / 운송 연료의 연소를 줄여서 / 대개 근거가 충분하지 않다.

Transport is the source / of only 11 percent of greenhouse gas emissions / within the food sector, / so reducing the distance / that food travels after it leaves the farm / is far (a) less important / than reducing wasteful energy use on the farm.
운송은 원천이 / 온실가스 배출의 11퍼센트만을 차지하는 / 식품 부문 내에서 / 그래서 거리를 줄이는 것은 / 식품이 농장을 떠난 후 이동하는 / 훨씬 덜 중요하다. / 농장에서 낭비되는 에너지 사용을 줄이는 것보다

Food coming from a distance / can actually be better for the (b) climate, / depending on how it was grown.
먼 곳에서 오는 식품은 / 실제로 기후에 더 좋을 수 있다. / 그것이 어떻게 재배되었느냐에 따라

For example, / field-grown tomatoes / shipped from Mexico in the winter months / will have a smaller carbon footprint / than (c) local winter tomatoes / grown in a greenhouse.
예를 들어, / 밭에서 재배된 토마토는 / 겨울에 멕시코로부터 수송된 / 탄소 발자국이 더 적을 것이다. / 현지의 겨울 토마토보다 / 온실에서 재배된

In the United Kingdom, / lamb meat that travels 11,000 miles from New Zealand / generates only one-quarter the carbon emissions per pound / compared to British lamb / because farmers in the United Kingdom / raise their animals on feed / (which must be produced using fossil fuels) / rather than on clover pastureland.
영국에서는, / 뉴질랜드에서 11,000마일을 이동하는 양고기는 / 파운드당 탄소 배출량의 4분의 1만 발생시키는데, / 영국의 양고기에 비해 / 영국의 농부들은 / 사료로 자신의 동물들을 기르기 때문이다. / (화석 연료를 사용하여 생산되어야 하는) / 클로버 목초지에서가 아닌

When food does travel, / what matters most is not the (d) distance traveled / but the travel mode (surface versus air), / and most of all the load size.
식품이 이동할 때, / 가장 중요한 것은 이동 거리가 아니고, / 이동 방식(지상 대 공중) / 그리고 무엇보다도 적재량의 규모이다.

Bulk loads of food can travel halfway around the world by ocean freight / with a smaller carbon footprint, per pound delivered, / than foods traveling just a short distance but in much (e) smaller loads.
대량의 적재된 식품은 해상 화물 운송으로 세계 절반을 이동할 수 있다. / 배달된 파운드당 탄소 발자국이 더 적게 / 단거리만 이동하지만 적재량이 훨씬 더 적은 식품에 비해

「For example, / 18-wheelers carry much larger loads than pickup trucks / so they can move food 100 times as far / while burning only one-third as much gas / per pound of food delivered.」 42번의 근거
예를 들어, / 18륜 대형트럭은 픽업트럭보다 훨씬 더 많은 적재량을 운반하므로, / 그것들은 100배 멀리 식품을 이동시킬 수 있다. / 3분의 1의 연료만 연소하면서 / 배달된 식품 파운드당

로컬푸드 생산이 운송 연료의 연소를 줄여서 온실가스 배출을 줄였다는 주장들은 대개 근거가 충분하지 않다. 운송은 식품 부문 내에서 온실가스 배출의 11퍼센트만을 차지하는 원천이기에, 식품이 농장을 떠난 후 이동하는 거리를 줄이는 것은 농장에서 낭비되는 에너지 사용을 줄이는 것보다 훨씬 (a) 덜 중요하다. 먼 곳에서 오는 식품은 그것이 어떻게 재배되었느냐에 따라 실제로 (b) 기후에 더 좋을 수 있다. 예를 들어, 겨울에 멕시코로부터 수송된 밭에서 재배된 토마토는 온실에서 재배된 (c) 현지의 겨울 토마토보다 탄소 발자국이 더 적을 것이다. 영국에서는, 뉴질랜드에서 11,000마일을 이동하는 양고기는 영국의 양고기에 비해 파운드당 탄소 배출량의 4분의 1만 발생시키는데, 영국의 농부들은 클로버 목초지에서가 아닌 (화석 연료를 사용하여 생산되어야 하는) 사료로 자신의 동물들을 기르기 때문이다. 식품이 이동할 때, 가장 중요한 것은 이동 (d) 거리가 아니고, 이동 방식(지상 대 공중)과 무엇보다도 적재량의 규모이다. 대량의 적재된 식품은 단거리만 이동하지만 적재량이 훨씬 (e) 더 많은(→ 더 적은) 식품에 비해, 해상 화물 운송으로 배달된 파운드당 탄소 발자국을 더 적게 들여 세계 절반을 이동할 수 있다. 예를 들어, 18륜 대형트럭은 픽업트럭보다 훨씬 더 많은 적재량을 운반하므로, 배달된 식품 파운드당 3분의 1의 연료만 연소하면서 100배 멀리 식품을 이동시킬 수 있다.

- greenhouse gas 온실가스
- well founded 근거가 충분한
- wasteful ⓐ 낭비하는
- ship ⓥ 운송하다, 수송하다
- lamb ⓝ 어린 양
- raise ⓥ 기르다, 키우다
- fossil fuel 화석 연료
- travel mode 이동 수단
- load ⓝ 적재량 ⓥ (짐을) 싣다
- freight ⓝ 화물 운송
- shorten ⓥ 짧게 줄이다
- agriculture ⓝ 농업
- emission ⓝ 배출(량)
- sector ⓝ 부문
- depending on ~에 따라
- carbon footprint 탄소 발자국
- generate ⓥ 발생시키다, 생성하다
- feed ⓝ 사료, 먹이
- pastureland ⓝ 목초지
- surface ⓝ 지면
- bulk ⓝ 대량 ⓐ 대량의
- pickup truck 픽업트럭, 소형 오픈 트럭
- ruin ⓥ 파괴하다, 망치다

구문 풀이

17행 When food does travel, what matters most is not {the distance traveled}
동사 강조 ↑ not + (A) +
but {the travel mode (surface versus air), and most of all the load size}.
but + (B) : A가 아니라 B인

41 제목 파악 · 정답률 56% | 정답 ②

윗글의 제목으로 가장 적절한 것은?
① Shorten the Route, Cut the Cost
거리를 줄여서 비용을 줄여라
✓ Is Local Food Always Better for the Earth?
로컬푸드가 지구를 위해 항상 더 좋을까?
③ Why Mass Production Ruins the Environment
왜 대량 생산이 환경을 망치나
④ New Technologies: What Matters in Agriculture
신기술: 농업에서 중요한 것
⑤ Reduce Food Waste for a Smaller Carbon Footprint
더 적은 탄소 발자국을 위해 음식물 쓰레기를 줄여라

Why? 왜 정답일까?

로컬푸드로 식품 수송의 거리를 줄여 탄소 발자국을 줄일 수 있다는 주장에 대한 반박으로, 거리보다는 수송 수단이나 적재량 등 다른 요소가 더 중요하다(When food does travel, what matters most is not the distance traveled but the travel mode ~ and most of all the load size.)고 주장하는 글이다. 따라서 글의 제목으로 가장 적절한 것은 ② '로컬푸드가 지구를 위해 항상 더 좋을까?'이다.

★★★ 등급을 가르는 문제!

42 어휘 추론 · 정답률 38% | 정답 ⑤

밑줄 친 (a) ~ (e) 중에서 문맥상 낱말의 쓰임이 적절하지 않은 것은?
① (a) ② (b) ③ (c) ④ (d) ✓ (e)

Why? 왜 정답일까?

마지막 문장에서 적재량이 더 많을 때 탄소 발자국을 훨씬 줄여 이동할 수 있다(~ 18-wheelers carry much larger loads than pickup trucks so they can move food 100 times as far while burning only one-third as much gas per pound of food delivered.)는 예를 드는 것으로 보아, 적재량이 '더 적을' 때보다 많을 때가 낫다는 설명이 적합하다. 즉 (e)의 larger를 smaller로 고쳐야 하므로, 문맥상 낱말의 쓰임이 적절하지 않은 것은 ⑤ '(e)'이다.

▶ 많이 틀린 이유는?
첫 문장 내용을 잘 이해하지 못하면 ①이 어색해 보일 수 있다. 하지만 식품 수송 거리를 줄인다고 해서 탄소 발자국을 줄일 수 있다는 주장에 '근거가 부족하다'는 말은 결국 거리 단축이 비교적 '덜 중요하다'는 뜻이 맞다.
▶ 문제 해결 방법은?
마지막 문장의 예시는 더 가까운 거리를 가더라도 적재량이 '더 적은' 경우보다, 더 먼 거리를 가도 양이 많은 편이 더 낫다는 핵심 내용으로 귀결된다. (e)가 than 뒤에 나온다는 점에 주의해야 한다.

43-45　사원에 묻어둔 벽돌을 파낸 젊은이를 사원 관리자로 채용한 노인

(A)

「Long ago, / an old man built a grand temple / at the center of his village.」 45번①의 근거 일치
옛날, / 한 노인이 큰 사원을 지었다. / 마을 중심부에

People traveled to worship at the temple.
사람들이 사원에서 예배를 드리기 위해 멀리서 왔다.

So the old man made arrangements for food and accommodation / inside the temple itself.
그래서 노인은 음식과 숙소를 준비했다. / 사원 안에

He needed someone / who could look after the temple, / so (a) he put up a notice: / Manager needed.
그는 사람이 필요했고, / 사원을 관리할 수 있는 / 그래서 그는 공고를 붙였다. / '관리자 구함'이라는

(D)

「Seeing the notice, / many people went to the old man.」 45번⑤의 근거 일치
공고를 보고, / 많은 사람들이 노인을 찾아갔다.

But he returned all the applicants after interviews, / telling them, / "I need a qualified person for this work."
그러나 그는 면접 후 모든 지원자들을 돌려보냈다. / 그들에게 말하면서 / "이 일에는 자격을 갖춘 사람이 필요합니다."라고

The old man would sit on the roof of (d) his house every morning, / watching people go through the temple doors.
노인은 매일 아침 자기 집 지붕에 앉아 있곤 했다. / 사람들이 사원의 문을 통과하는 것을 지켜보며

One day, / (e) he saw a young man come to the temple.
어느 날 / 그는 한 젊은이가 사원으로 오는 것을 보았다.

(B)

「When that young man left the temple, / the old man called him and asked, / "Will you take care of this temple?"」 45번②의 근거 일치
젊은이가 사원을 나설 때, / 노인이 그를 불러 질문했다. / "이 사원의 관리를 맡아 주겠소?"라고

「The young man was surprised by the offer / and replied, / "I have no experience caring for a temple. / I'm not even educated."」 45번③의 근거 일치
젊은이는 그 제안에 놀라서 / 대답했다. / "저는 사원을 관리한 경험이 없습니다. / 저는 심지어 교육도 받지 못했습니다."라고

The old man smiled and said, / "I don't want any educated man. / I want a qualified person."
노인은 웃으며 말했다. / "나는 교육을 받은 사람이 필요한 게 아니오. / 나는 자격 있는 사람을 원하오."라고

Confused, / the young man asked, / "But why do (b) you consider me a qualified person?"
혼란스러워하며, / 젊은이는 물었다. / "그런데 당신은 왜 제가 자격이 있는 사람이라고 여기시나요?"라고

(C)

「The old man replied, / "I buried a brick on the path to the temple. / I watched for many days / as people tripped over that brick. / No one thought to remove it. / But you dug up that brick."」 45번④의 근거 불일치
노인은 대답했다. / "나는 사원으로 통하는 길에 벽돌 한 개를 묻었소. / 나는 여러 날 동안 지켜보았소. / 사람들이 그 벽돌에 발이 걸려 넘어질 때 / 아무도 그것을 치울 생각을 하지 않았소. / 하지만 당신은 그 벽돌을 파냈소."

The young man said, / "I haven't done anything great. / It's the duty of every human being / to think about others. / (c) I only did my duty."
젊은이는 말했다. / "저는 대단한 일을 한 것이 아닙니다. / 모든 사람의 의무인 걸요. / 타인을 생각하는 것은 / 저는 제 의무를 다했을 뿐입니다."라고

The old man smiled and said, / "Only people who know their duty and perform it / are qualified people."
노인은 미소를 지으며 말했다. / "자신의 의무를 알고 그 의무를 수행하는 사람만이 / 자격이 있는 사람이오."라고

(A)
옛날, 한 노인이 마을 중심부에 큰 사원을 지었다. 사람들이 사원에서 예배를 드리기 위해 멀리서 왔다. 그래서 노인은 사원 안에 음식과 숙소를 준비했다. 그는 사원을 관리할 수 있는 사람이 필요했고, 그래서 (a) 그는 '관리자 구함'이라는 공고를 붙였다.

(D)
공고를 보고, 많은 사람들이 노인을 찾아갔다. 그러나 그는 "이 일에는 자격을 갖춘 사람이 필요합니다."라고 말하며 면접 후 모든 지원자들을 돌려보냈다. 노인은 사람들이 사원의 문을 통과하는 것을 지켜보며 매일 아침 (d) 자기 집 지붕에 앉아 있곤 했다. 어느 날 (e) 그는 한 젊은이가 사원으로 오는 것을 보았다.

(B)
젊은이가 사원을 나설 때, 노인이 그를 불러 "이 사원의 관리를 맡아 주겠소?"라고 질문했다. 젊은이는 그 제안에 놀라서 "저는 사원을 관리한 경험이 없고, 심지어 교육도 받지 못했습니다."라고 대답했다. 노인은 웃으며 "나는 교육을 받은 사람이 필요한 게 아니오. 나는 자격 있는 사람을 원하오."라고 말했다. 혼란스러워하며, 젊은이는 "그런데 (b) 당신은 왜 제가 자격이 있는 사람이라고 여기시나요?"라고 물었다.

(C)
노인은 대답했다. "나는 사원으로 통하는 길에 벽돌 한 개를 묻었소. 나는 여러 날 동안 사람들이 그 벽돌에 발이 걸려 넘어지는 것을 지켜보았소. 아무도 그것을 치울 생각을 하지 않았소. 하지만 당신은 그 벽돌을 파냈소." 젊은이는 "저는 대단한 일을 한 것이 아닙니다. 타인을 생각하는 것은 모든 사람의 의무인 걸요. (c) 전 제 의무를 다했을 뿐입니다."라고 말했다. 노인은 미소를 지으며 "자신의 의무를 알고 그 의무를 수행하는 사람만이 자격이 있는 사람이오."라고 말했다.

- **grand** ⓐ 큰, 위대한
- **worship** ⓥ 예배하다
- **accommodation** ⓝ 숙소
- **bury** ⓥ 묻다
- **temple** ⓝ 사원, 절
- **make arrangements for** ~을 준비하다
- **care for** ~을 관리하다, 돌보다
- **brick** ⓝ 벽돌

- **trip over** ~에 걸려 넘어지다
- **duty** ⓝ 의무
- **dig up** 파내다
- **applicant** ⓝ 지원자

구문 풀이

(B) 6행 Confused, the young man asked, "But why do you consider me a qualified person?"
분사구문(Being 생략)　5형식 동사　목적어 / 목적격 보어

(D) 3행 The old man would sit on the roof of his house every morning, watching
조동사과거 습관　　　　지각동사
people go through the temple doors.
목적어　원형부정사

43　글의 순서 파악　정답률 83% | 정답 ④

주어진 글 (A)에 이어질 내용을 순서에 맞게 배열한 것으로 가장 적절한 것은?
① (B) – (D) – (C)　② (C) – (B) – (D)
③ (C) – (D) – (B)　✓④ (D) – (B) – (C)
⑤ (D) – (C) – (B)

Why? 왜 정답일까?
한 노인이 사원을 짓고 관리자 모집에 나섰다는 (A) 뒤로, 지원자들이 몰려들었지만 노인은 계속 자격 있는 사람을 기다렸다는 (D), 어떤 젊은이가 다녀가는 것을 보고 노인이 관리자 직을 제안했다는 (B), 왜 자신을 채용하려 하는지 묻는 젊은이에게 노인이 답을 주었다는 (C)가 차례로 연결된다. 따라서 글의 순서로 가장 적절한 것은 ④ '(D) – (B) – (C)'이다.

44　지칭 추론　정답률 84% | 정답 ③

밑줄 친 (a)~(e) 중에서 가리키는 대상이 나머지 넷과 다른 것은?
① (a)　② (b)　✓③ (c)　④ (d)　⑤ (e)

Why? 왜 정답일까?
(a), (b), (d), (e)는 the old man을, (c)는 the young man을 가리키므로, (a)~(e) 중에서 가리키는 대상이 다른 하나는 ③ '(c)'이다.

45　세부 내용 파악　정답률 79% | 정답 ④

윗글에 관한 내용으로 적절하지 않은 것은?
① 노인은 마을 중심부에 사원을 지었다.
② 젊은이가 사원을 나설 때 노인이 그를 불렀다.
③ 젊은이는 노인의 제안에 놀랐다.
✓④ 노인은 사원으로 통하는 길에 묻혀있던 벽돌을 파냈다.
⑤ 공고를 보고 많은 사람들이 노인을 찾아갔다.

Why? 왜 정답일까?
(C) "I buried a brick on the path to the temple. I watched for many days as people tripped over that brick. No one thought to remove it. But you dug up that brick."에서 노인은 자신이 묻어뒀던 벽돌을 파낸 사람이 젊은이라고 말하고 있으므로, 내용과 일치하지 않는 것은 ④ '노인은 사원으로 통하는 길에 묻혀있던 벽돌을 파냈다.'이다.

Why? 왜 오답일까?
① (A) 'Long ago, an old man built a grand temple at the center of his village.'의 내용과 일치한다.
② (B) 'When that young man left the temple, the old man called him ~'의 내용과 일치한다.
③ (B) 'The young man was surprised by the offer ~'의 내용과 일치한다.
⑤ (D) 'Seeing the notice, many people went to the old man.'의 내용과 일치한다.

A	B	C	D
01 박람회	01 hold	01 ①	01 ①
02 위험을 감수하다	02 complete	02 ⓐ	02 ⓕ
03 분명히, 틀림없이	03 confident	03 ⓗ	03 ⓖ
04 지식의 확산	04 whether ~ or not	04 ⓑ	04 ①
05 협상하다	05 essential	05 ⓚ	05 ⓚ
06 배우자	06 outcome	06 ⓒ	06 ⓗ
07 ~을 차별하다	07 population	07 ①	07 ⓒ
08 어쩔 수 없이 ~하다	08 construction	08 ⓓ	08 ⓠ
09 주어진, ~을 고려하면	09 conservation	09 ①	09 ①
10 인식, 앎	10 destination	10 ⓔ	10 ⓓ
11 전문 지식	11 precise	11 ⓢ	11 ⓐ
12 ~에 적응하다	12 compensate for	12 ①	12 ①
13 열정적인	13 competence	13 ⓕ	13 ⓟ
14 ~을 고려하다, 참작하다	14 tissue	14 ⓠ	14 ①
15 ~로 구성되다	15 vibration	15 ①	15 ⓢ
16 통합하다	16 separate	16 ⓖ	16 ⓗ
17 보완하는	17 status	17 ⓜ	17 ⓔ
18 근거가 충분한	18 ship	18 ⓞ	18 ⓞ
19 예배하다	19 duty	19 ⓝ	19 ⓜ
20 유지하다, 떠받치다	20 ensure	20 ⓟ	20 ⓞ

---

13 회 | 2022학년도 9월 학력평가

| 정답과 해설 |

고1

18 ⑤ 19 ② 20 ④ 21 ③ 22 ① 23 ② 24 ① 25 ③ 26 ④ 27 ④ 28 ④ 29 ③ 30 ⑤ 31 ② 32 ⑤
33 ① 34 ⑤ 35 ④ 36 ② 37 ⑤ 38 ④ 39 ⑤ 40 ① 41 ② 42 ④ 43 ④ 44 ③ 45 ③

★ 표기된 문항은 [등급을 가르는 문제]에 해당하는 문항입니다.

---

18   학급 파티에 가져올 음식에 관한 유의 사항   정답률 93% | 정답 ⑤

다음 글의 목적으로 가장 적절한 것은?

① 학급 파티 일정 변경을 공지하려고
② 학교 식당의 새로운 메뉴를 소개하려고
③ 학생의 특정 음식 알레르기 여부를 조사하려고
④ 학부모의 적극적인 학급 파티 참여를 독려하려고
☑ 학급 파티에 가져올 음식에 대한 유의 사항을 안내하려고

Dear Parents/Guardians,
부모님들 / 보호자들께,
Class parties will be held / on the afternoon of Friday, December 16th, 2022.
학급 파티가 열릴 것입니다. / 2022년 12월 16일 금요일 오후에
Children may bring in / sweets, crisps, biscuits, cakes, and drinks.
아이들은 가져올 수 있습니다. / 사탕류, 포테이토 칩, 비스킷, 케이크, 그리고 음료를
We are requesting / that children do not bring in home-cooked or prepared food.
우리는 요청합니다. / 아이들이 집에서 만들거나 준비한 음식을 가져오지 않기를
All food should arrive in a sealed packet / with the ingredients clearly listed.
모든 음식은 밀봉된 꾸러미로 가져와야 합니다. / 성분이 명확하게 목록으로 작성되어
Fruit and vegetables are welcomed / if they are pre-packed in a sealed packet from the shop.
과일과 채소는 환영합니다. / 그것이 가게에서 밀봉된 꾸러미로 사전 포장된 것이라면
Please DO NOT send any food into school / containing nuts / as we have many children with severe nut allergies.
음식은 어떤 것도 학교에 보내지 '마십시오'. / 견과류가 포함된 / 심각한 견과류 알레르기가 있는 학생들이 많이 있기 때문에
Please check the ingredients of all food / your children bring / carefully.
모든 음식의 성분을 확인해 주십시오. / 아이들이 가져오는 / 주의 깊게
Thank you for your continued support and cooperation.
여러분의 지속적인 지원과 협조에 감사드립니다.
Yours sincerely, // Lisa Brown, Headteacher
교장 Lisa Brown 드림

부모님들 / 보호자들께,

학급 파티가 2022년 12월 16일 금요일 오후에 열릴 것입니다. 아이들은 사탕류, 포테이토 칩, 비스킷, 케이크, 그리고 음료를 가져올 수 있습니다. 우리는 아이들이 집에서 만들거나 준비한 음식을 가져오지 않기를 요청합니다. 모든 음식은 성분을 명확하게 목록으로 작성하여 밀봉된 꾸러미로 가져와야 합니다. 과일과 채소는 가게에서 밀봉된 꾸러미로 사전 포장된 것이라면 환영합니다. 심각한 견과류 알레르기가 있는 학생들이 많이 있기 때문에 견과류가 포함된 음식은 어떤 것도 학교에 보내지 마십시오. 아이들이 가져오는 모든 음식의 성분을 주의 깊게 확인해 주십시오. 여러분의 지속적인 지원과 협조에 감사드립니다.

교장 Lisa Brown 드림

Why? 왜 정답일까?

두 번째 문장부터 학급 파티에 어떤 음식을 가져올 수 있는지 열거한 뒤, 음식의 성분을 꼭 확인해달라고 요청하고 있다(Please check the ingredients of all food ~). 따라서 글의 목적으로 가장 적절한 것은 ⑤ '학급 파티에 가져올 음식에 대한 유의 사항을 안내하려고'이다.

- **guardian** ⓝ 보호자
- **sealed** ⓐ 밀봉한
- **pre-packed** ⓐ 사전 포장된
- **headteacher** ⓝ (공립학교) 교장
- **home-cooked** ⓐ 집에서 요리한
- **ingredient** ⓝ 성분, 재료
- **severe** ⓐ 심각한

구문 풀이

4행 We are requesting that children do not bring in homecooked or prepared food.
　　　　　　 현재진행 　　 접속사(~것)

---

19   뉴스 마감 전 고장 난 타자기를 고치고 안도한 필자   정답률 90% | 정답 ②

다음 글에 나타난 'I'의 심경 변화로 가장 적절한 것은?

① confident → nervous
　자신 있는　　긴장한
② frustrated → relieved
　절망한　　　안도한
③ bored → amazed
　지루한　 놀란
④ indifferent → curious
　무관심한　　 호기심 많은
⑤ excited → disappointed
　신난　　 실망한

It was two hours before the submission deadline / and I still hadn't finished my news article.
제출 마감 시간 두 시간 전이었고 / 나는 여전히 나의 뉴스 기사를 끝내지 못했다.
I sat at the desk, / but suddenly, the typewriter didn't work.
나는 책상에 앉았는데, / 갑자기 타자기가 작동하지 않았다.
No matter how hard I tapped the keys, / the levers wouldn't move to strike the paper.
내가 아무리 세게 키를 두드려도, / 레버는 종이를 두드리려 움직이지 않았다.
I started to realize / that I would not be able to finish the article on time.
나는 깨닫기 시작했다. / 내가 제시간에 그 기사를 끝낼 수 없으리라는 것을
Desperately, / I rested the typewriter on my lap / and started hitting each key / with as much force as I could manage.
필사적으로, / 나는 타자기를 내 무릎 위에 올려놓고 / 각각의 키를 누르기 시작했다. / 내가 감당할 수 있는 최대한 센 힘으로
Nothing happened.

아무 일도 일어나지 않았다.

Thinking something might have happened inside of it, / I opened the cover, / lifted up the keys, / and found the problem — a paper clip.
타자기 내부에 무슨 일이 일어났을지도 모르겠다고 생각하면서, / 나는 그 덮개를 열고, / 키들을 들어 올리고, / 문제를 발견했다 — 종이 집게였다.

The keys had no room to move.
키들이 움직일 공간이 없었다.

After picking it out, / I pressed and pulled some parts.
그것을 집어서 꺼낸 후에, / 나는 몇 개의 부품들을 누르고 당겼다.

The keys moved smoothly again.
키들이 매끄럽게 다시 움직였다.

I breathed deeply and smiled.
나는 깊게 숨을 내쉬고 미소 지었다.

Now I knew / that I could finish my article on time.
이제는 나는 알았다. / 내가 제시간에 기사를 끝낼 수 있음을

제출 마감 시간 두 시간 전이었고 나는 여전히 나의 뉴스 기사를 끝내지 못했다. 나는 책상에 앉았는데, 갑자기 타자기가 작동하지 않았다. 내가 아무리 세게 키를 두드려도, 레버는 종이를 두드리려 움직이지 않았다. 나는 내가 제시간에 그 기사를 끝낼 수 없으리라는 것을 깨닫기 시작했다. 필사적으로, 나는 타자기를 내 무릎 위에 올려놓고 각각의 키를 최대한 센 힘으로 누르기 시작했다. 아무 일도 일어나지 않았다. 타자기 내부에 무슨 일이 일어났을지도 모르겠다고 생각하면서, 나는 그 덮개를 열고, 키들을 들어 올리고, 문제를 발견했다 — 종이 집게였다. 키들이 움직일 공간이 없었다. 그것을 집어서 꺼낸 후에, 나는 몇 개의 부품들을 누르고 당겼다. 키들이 매끄럽게 다시 움직였다. 나는 깊게 숨을 내쉬고 미소 지었다. 이제는 내가 제시간에 기사를 끝낼 수 있음을 알았다.

Why? 왜 정답일까?

뉴스 마감을 앞두고 타자기가 작동하지 않아 기사를 끝내지 못할까봐 절망했던(~ I would not be able to finish the article on time.) 필자가 무사히 타자기를 고치고 안도의 미소를 지었다(I breathed deeply and smiled.)는 내용의 글이다. 따라서 'I'의 심경 변화로 가장 적절한 것은 ② '절망한 → 안도한'이다.

- strike ⓥ 치다, 때리다, 두드리다
- lift up 들어올리다
- frustrated ⓐ 좌절한
- desperately [ad] 필사적으로
- smoothly [ad] 부드럽게

구문 풀이

5행 Desperately, I rested the typewriter on my lap and started hitting each 부사문장 수식
key with as much force as I could manage.
「as+원급+as+주어+can[could] : ~할 수 있는 한 최대로」

---

20 글보다 많은 단어를 필요로 하는 말하기 　정답률 70% | 정답 ④

다음 글에서 필자가 주장하는 바로 가장 적절한 것은?
① 연설 시 중요한 정보는 천천히 말해야 한다.
② 좋은 글을 쓰려면 간결한 문장을 사용해야 한다.
③ 말하기 전에 신중히 생각하는 습관을 길러야 한다.
④ 글을 쓸 때보다 말할 때 더 많은 단어를 사용해야 한다.
⑤ 청중의 이해를 돕기 위해 미리 연설문을 제공해야 한다.

Experts on writing say, / "Get rid of as many words as possible."
글쓰기 전문가들은 말한다. / '가능한 많은 단어를 삭제하라'고

Each word must do something important.
각 단어는 무언가 중요한 일을 해야 한다.

If it doesn't, / get rid of it.
만일 그렇지 않다면 / 그것을 삭제하라.

Well, this doesn't work for speaking.
자, 이 방법은 말하기에서는 통하지 않는다.

It takes more words / to introduce, express, and adequately elaborate an idea in speech / than it takes in writing.
더 많은 단어가 필요하다. / 말로 아이디어를 소개하고, 표현하며, 적절히 부연 설명하는 데 / 글을 쓸 때보다

Why is this so?
이것은 왜 그러한가?

While the reader can reread, / the listener cannot rehear.
독자는 글을 다시 읽을 수 있으나 / 청자는 다시 들을 수 없다.

Speakers do not come equipped with a replay button.
화자는 반복 재생 버튼을 갖추고 있지 않다.

Because listeners are easily distracted, / they will miss many pieces of what a speaker says.
청자들은 쉽게 주의력이 흐려지기 때문에 / 그들은 화자가 말하는 것 중 많은 부분을 놓칠 것이다.

If they miss the crucial sentence, / they may never catch up.
그들이 중요한 문장을 놓친다면, / 그들은 절대로 따라잡을 수 없을 것이다.

This makes it necessary / for speakers to talk *longer* about their points, / using more words on them / than would be used to express the same idea in writing.
이것은 필요가 있게 한다. / 화자들이 요점을 *더 길게 말할* / 그것에 관해 더 많은 단어를 사용하여 / 글을 쓸 때 같은 아이디어를 표현하기 위해 사용할 것보다

글쓰기 전문가들은 '가능한 한 많은 단어를 삭제하라'고 말한다. 각 단어는 무언가 중요한 일을 해야 한다. 만일 그렇지 않다면 그것을 삭제하라. 자, 이 방법은 말하기에서는 통하지 않는다. 말을 할 때는 아이디어를 소개하고, 표현하며, 적절히 부연 설명하는 데 글을 쓸 때보다 더 많은 단어가 필요하다. 이것은 왜 그러한가? 독자는 글을 다시 읽을 수 있으나 청자는 다시 들을 수 없다. 화자는 반복 재생 버튼을 갖추고 있지 않다. 청자들은 쉽게 주의력이 흐려지기 때문에 화자가 말하는 것 중 많은 부분을 놓칠 것이다. 그들이 중요한 문장을 놓친다면, 절대로 따라잡을 수 없을 것이다. 이것은 화자들이 글을 쓸 때 같은 아이디어를 표현하기 위해 사용할 단어 수보다 더 많은 단어를 사용하여 요점을 *더 길게 말할* 필요가 있게 한다.

Why? 왜 정답일까?

'It takes more words to introduce, express, and adequately elaborate an idea in speech than it takes in writing.'에서 글보다 말에서 더 많은 단어가 필요하다고 언급하고, 그 이

유를 부연 설명한 뒤 다시 논지를 반복하고 있다. 따라서 필자가 주장하는 바로 가장 적절한 것은 ④ '글을 쓸 때보다 말할 때 더 많은 단어를 사용해야 한다.'이다.

- get rid of ~을 제거하다
- elaborate ⓥ 부연 설명하다, 자세히 말하다
- crucial ⓐ 아주 중요한
- adequately [ad] 적절하게
- distract ⓥ 주의를 분산시키다
- catch up 따라잡다

구문 풀이

8행 This makes it necessary for speakers to talk longer about their points,
　　　　가목적어　목적격 보어　의미상 주어　진목적어
using more words on them than would be used to express the same idea in
분사구문　선행사　유사관계대명사(비교급 선행사 뒤에 불완전한 절 연결)
writing.

---

21 고객에게 아니라고 말해야 할 순간 　정답률 71% | 정답 ③

밑줄 친 fire a customer가 다음 글에서 의미하는 바로 가장 적절한 것은?
① deal with a customer's emergency – 고객의 응급 상황을 해결해야
② delete a customer's purchasing record – 고객의 구매 기록을 지워야
③ reject a customer's unreasonable demand – 고객의 불합리한 요구를 거절해야
④ uncover the hidden intention of a customer – 고객의 숨은 의도를 밝혀야
⑤ rely on the power of an influential customer – 영향력 있는 고객의 힘에 의존해야

Is the customer *always* right?
고객은 항상 옳은가?

When customers return a broken product to a famous company, / which makes kitchen and bathroom fixtures, / the company nearly always offers a replacement / to maintain good customer relations.
한 유명한 회사에 고객들이 고장 난 제품을 반품할 때 / 주방과 욕실 설비를 만드는 / 그 회사는 거의 항상 대체품을 제공한다. / 좋은 고객 관계를 유지하기 위해

Still, / "there are times you've got to say 'no,'" / explains the warranty expert of the company, / such as when a product is undamaged or has been abused.
그럼에도, / "'안 돼요.'라고 말을 해야 할 때가 있다."고 / 그 회사의 상품 보증 전문가는 설명한다. / 상품이 멀쩡하거나 남용되었을 때와 같이

Entrepreneur Lauren Thorp, / who owns an e-commerce company, / says, / "While the customer is 'always' right, / sometimes you just have to fire a customer."
기업가 Lauren Thorp는 / 전자 상거래 회사를 소유한 / 말한다. / "고객이 '항상' 옳지만, 때로는 고객을 해고해야만 한다."고

When Thorp has tried everything to resolve a complaint / and realizes that the customer will be dissatisfied no matter what, / she returns her attention to the rest of her customers, / who she says are "the reason for my success."
Thorp가 고객의 불만을 해결하기 위해 최선을 다했는데 / 그 고객이 어떠한 경우에도 만족하지 않을 것이라 사실을 깨달을 때, / 그녀는 나머지 다른 고객들에게로 관심을 돌리는데, / 그 고객들이 "내 성공의 이유"라고 그녀는 말한다.

고객은 항상 옳은가? 주방과 욕실 설비를 만드는 한 유명한 회사에 고객들이 고장 난 제품을 반품할 때 그 회사는 좋은 고객 관계를 유지하기 위해 거의 항상 대체품을 제공한다. 그럼에도, 그 회사의 상품 보증 전문가는 상품이 멀쩡하거나 남용되었을 때와 같이, "'안 돼요.'라고 말을 해야 할 때가 있다."고 설명한다. 전자 상거래 회사를 소유한 기업가 Lauren Thorp는 "고객이 '항상' 옳지만, 때로는 고객을 해고해야만 한다."고 말한다. Thorp가 고객의 불만을 해결하기 위해 최선을 다했는데 그 고객이 어떠한 경우에도 만족하지 않을 것이란 사실을 깨달을 때, 그녀는 나머지 다른 고객들에게로 관심을 돌리는데, 그 고객들이 "내 성공의 이유"라고 그녀는 말한다.

Why? 왜 정답일까?

고객에게 '안 된다'고 말하는 순간이 필요하다(there are times you've got to say 'no,' ~)는 내용의 글로, 마지막 두 문장에서 불만 해결에 최선을 다했는데도 결코 만족하지 않을 고객에 대해서는 과감히 '신경을 끄고' 다른 고객들에 집중하는 사업가의 사례를 언급하고 있다. 따라서 밑줄 친 부분이 의미하는 바로 가장 적절한 것은 ③ '고객의 불합리한 요구를 거절해야'이다.

- fixture ⓝ 설비, 살림, 세간
- undamaged ⓐ 멀쩡한, 손상되지 않은
- entrepreneur ⓝ 기업가, 사업가
- replacement ⓝ 대체(품)
- abuse ⓥ 남용하다
- dissatisfied ⓐ 불만족한

구문 풀이

8행 When Thorp has tried everything to resolve a complaint and realizes that
　　　　　　　　동사1　　　　부사적 용법(목적)　　　　　　동사2
the customer will be dissatisfied no matter what, she returns her attention to the
　　　　　　　　　　　　무엇을 하든 간에
rest of her customers, who (she says) are "the reason for my success."
　　　　선행사　　주격 관·대 삽입절 동사

---

22 교실 장식이 적당할 필요성 　정답률 82% | 정답 ①

다음 글의 요지로 가장 적절한 것은?
① 아이들의 집중을 돕기 위해 과도한 교실 장식을 지양할 필요가 있다.
② 아이들의 인성과 인지 능력을 균형 있게 발달시키는 것이 중요하다.
③ 아이들이 직접 교실을 장식하는 것은 창의력 발달에 도움이 된다.
④ 다양한 교실 활동은 아이들의 수업 참여도를 증진시킨다.
⑤ 풍부한 시각 자료는 아이들의 학습 동기를 높인다.

A recent study from Carnegie Mellon University in Pittsburgh, / called "When Too Much of a Good Thing May Be Bad," / indicates / that classrooms with too much decoration / are a source of distraction for young children / and directly affect their cognitive performance.
피츠버그 Carnegie Mellon University에서 이루어진 최근 연구가 / '너무 많은 좋은 것이 나쁠 수도 있을 때'라고 불리는 / 나타낸다. / 너무 많은 장식이 있는 교실은 / 어린이들의 주의 산만의 원인이고 / 그들의 인지적인 수행에 직접적으로 영향을 미친다고

Being visually overstimulated, / the children have a great deal of difficulty concentrating / and end up with worse academic results.
시각적으로 지나치게 자극되었을 때, / 아이들은 집중하는 데 많이 어려워하고 / 결국 학습 결과가 더 나빠진다.

On the other hand, / if there is not much decoration on the classroom walls, / the children

are less distracted, / spend more time on their activities, / and learn more.
반면에, / 교실 벽에 장식이 많지 않으면, / 아이들은 덜 산만해지고, / 수업 활동에 더 많은 시간을 사용하고, / 더 많이 배운다.
So it's our job, / in order to support their attention, / to find the right balance / between excessive decoration and the complete absence of it.
그래서 우리가 할 일이다. / 이들의 집중을 도우려면 / 적절한 균형을 찾는 것이 / 지나친 장식과 장식이 전혀 없는 것 사이의

피츠버그시 Carnegie Mellon University에서 이루어진, '너무 많은 좋은 것이 나쁠 수도 있을 때'라고 불리는 최근 한 연구에 따르면, 너무 많은 장식이 있는 교실은 어린이들의 주의 산만의 원인이고 그들의 인지적 수행에 직접적으로 영향을 미친다. 시각적으로 지나치게 자극되었을 때, 아이들은 집중하는 데 많이 어려워하고 결국 학습 결과가 더 나빠진다. 반면에, 교실 벽에 장식이 많지 않으면, 아이들은 덜 산만해지고, 수업 활동에 더 많은 시간을 사용하고, 더 많이 배운다. 그래서 이들의 집중을 도우려면 지나친 장식과 장식이 전혀 없는 것 사이의 적절한 균형을 찾는 것이 우리가 할 일이다.

Why? 왜 정답일까?

교실 장식이 과하면 아이들의 집중력이 떨어진다는 연구 내용을 토대로, 아이들의 집중력을 높여주려면 적당한 교실 장식의 균형을 찾아야 한다(~ **in order to support their attention, to find the right balance between excessive decoration and the complete absence of it.**)는 결론을 이끌어내고 있다. 따라서 글의 요지로 가장 적절한 것은 ⑤ '아이들의 집중을 돕기 위해 과도한 교실 장식을 지양할 필요가 있다.'이다.

- **decoration** ⓝ 장식
- **a great deal of** 상당한, 큰, 많은
- **excessive** ⓐ 과도한
- **overstimulate** ⓥ 과도하게 자극하다
- **end up with** 결국 ~하다
- **absence** ⓝ 부재

구문 풀이

5행 Being visually overstimulated, the children have a great deal of difficulty
분사구문 「have difficulty + 동명사 : ~하는 데 어려움을 겪다」
concentrating and end up with worse academic results.

---

23 인간 진화와 소속 욕구 　　정답률 59% | 정답 ②

다음 글의 주제로 가장 적절한 것은?

① skills for the weak to survive modern life – 약자가 현대 생활에서 생존하는 기술
✓ usefulness of belonging for human evolution – 인간 진화에 있어 소속의 유용성
③ ways to avoid competition among social groups – 사회적 집단 간의 경쟁을 피하는 방법
④ roles of social relationships in children's education – 아이들의 교육에 있어 사회적 관계의 역할
⑤ differences between two major evolutionary theories – 두 가지 주요 진화론의 차이

For creatures like us, / evolution smiled upon those / with a strong need to belong.
우리와 같은 창조물에 있어, / 진화는 이들에게 미소지어 주었다 / 강한 소속 욕구를 가진
Survival and reproduction / are the criteria of success by natural selection, / and forming relationships with other people / can be useful for both survival and reproduction.
생존과 번식은 / 자연 선택에 의한 성공의 기준이고, / 다른 사람들과 관계를 형성하는 것은 / 생존과 번식 모두에 유용할 수 있다.
Groups can share resources, / care for sick members, / scare off predators, / fight together against enemies, / divide tasks so as to improve efficiency, / and contribute to survival in many other ways.
집단은 자원을 공유하고, / 아픈 구성원을 돌보고, / 포식자를 쫓아버리고, / 적에 맞서서 함께 싸우고, / 효율성을 향상시키기 위해 일을 나누고, / 많은 다른 방식으로 생존에 기여한다.
In particular, / if an individual and a group want the same resource, / the group will generally prevail, / so competition for resources / would especially favor a need to belong.
특히, / 한 개인과 한 집단이 같은 자원을 원하면, / 집단이 일반적으로 우세하고, / 그래서 자원에 대한 경쟁은 / 소속하려는 욕구를 특별히 좋아할 것이다.
Belongingness will likewise promote reproduction, / such as by bringing potential mates into contact with each other, / and in particular by keeping parents together / to care for their children, / who are much more likely to survive / if they have more than one caregiver.
마찬가지로 소속되어 있다는 것은 번식을 촉진시키는데, / 이를테면 잠재적인 짝을 서로 만나게 해주거나, / 특히 부모가 함께 있도록 하면서 / 자녀를 돌보기 위해 / 자녀들은 훨씬 더 생존하기 쉬울 것이다. / 한 명 이상의 돌보는 이가 있으면

우리(인간)와 같은 창조물에게 있어, 진화는 강한 소속 욕구를 가진 이들에게 미소지어 주었다. 생존과 번식은 자연 선택에 의한 성공의 기준이고, 다른 사람들과 관계를 형성하는 것은 생존과 번식 모두에 유용할 수 있다. 집단은 자원을 공유하고, 아픈 구성원을 돌보고, 포식자를 쫓아버리고, 적에 맞서서 함께 싸우고, 효율성을 향상시키기 위해 일을 나누고, 많은 다른 방식으로 생존에 기여한다. 특히, 한 개인과 한 집단이 같은 자원을 원하면, 집단이 일반적으로 우세하고, 그래서 자원에 대한 경쟁은 소속하려는 욕구를 특별히 좋아할 것이다. 마찬가지로 소속되어 있다는 것은 이를테면 잠재적인 짝을 서로 만나게 해주거나, 특히 부모가 자녀를 돌보기 위해 함께 있도록 하면서 번식을 촉진시키는데, 자녀들은 한 명 이상의 돌보는 이가 있으면 훨씬 더 생존하기 쉬울 것이다.

Why? 왜 정답일까?

첫 문장인 'For creatures like us, evolution smiled upon those with a strong need to belong.'에서 진화의 과정은 강한 소속 욕구를 지닌 이들을 선호했다는 주제를 제시한 후, 소속 욕구가 진화에 어떤 식으로 도움이 되었는지 구체적으로 부연하고 있다. 따라서 글의 주제로 가장 적절한 것은 ② '인간 진화에 있어 소속의 유용성'이다.

- **reproduction** ⓝ 번식, 재생
- **natural selection** 자연 선택
- **fight against** ~에 맞서 싸우다
- **belongingness** ⓝ 소속, 귀속, 친밀감
- **criterion** ⓝ 기준
- **scare off** ~을 겁주어 쫓아버리다
- **prevail** ⓥ 우세하다
- **caregiver** ⓝ 양육자

구문 풀이

4행 Groups can share resources, care for sick members, scare off predators,
동사1　　　　　　　 동사2　　　　　　 동사3
fight together against enemies, divide tasks so as to improve efficiency, and
동사4　　　　　　 동사5　　　　 목적(~하기 위해)
contribute to survival in many other ways.
동사6

---

24 용기가 불러오는 기회 　　정답률 65% | 정답 ①

다음 글의 제목으로 가장 적절한 것은?

✓ More Courage Brings More Opportunities – 더 큰 용기가 더 많은 기회를 부른다
② Travel: The Best Way to Make Friends – 여행: 친구를 사귀는 가장 좋은 방법
③ How to Turn Mistakes into Success – 실수를 성공으로 바꾸는 방법
④ Satisfying Life? Share with Others – 만족스러운 삶? 남들과 나누라
⑤ Why Is Overcoming Fear So Hard? – 공포를 극복하는 것은 왜 이리 어려울까?

Many people make a mistake / of only operating along the safe zones, / and in the process / they miss the opportunity / to achieve greater things.
많은 사람들이 실수를 저지르고, / 안전 구역에서만 움직이는 / 그 과정에서 / 그들은 기회를 놓친다. / 더 위대한 일들을 달성할
They do so / because of a fear of the unknown / and a fear of treading the unknown paths of life.
그들은 그렇게 한다. / 미지의 세계에 대한 두려움 때문에 / 그리고 알려지지 않은 삶의 경로를 밟는 것에 대한 두려움
Those / that are brave enough / to take those roads less travelled / are able to get great returns / and derive major satisfaction out of their courageous moves.
사람들은 / 충분히 용감한 / 사람들이 잘 다니지 않는 길을 택할 만큼 / 엄청난 보상을 받을 수 있고 / 용감한 행동으로부터 큰 만족감을 끌어낼 수 있다
Being overcautious will mean / that you will miss / attaining the greatest levels of your potential.
지나치게 조심하는 것은 의미할 것이다. / 여러분이 놓친다는 것을 / 잠재력의 최고 수준을 달성하는 것을
You must learn to take those chances / that many people around you will not take, / because your success will flow from those bold decisions / that you will take along the way.
여러분은 기회를 택하는 법을 배워야 하는데, / 주변에 있는 많은 사람들이 선택하지 않을 / 왜냐하면 여러분의 성공은 용감한 결정으로부터 나올 것이기 때문이다. / 삶의 과정에서 여러분이 내릴

많은 사람들이 안전 구역에서만 움직이는 실수를 저지르고, 그 과정에서 더 위대한 일들을 달성할 기회를 놓친다. 그들은 미지의 세계에 대한 두려움과 알려지지 않은 삶의 경로를 밟는 것에 대한 두려움 때문에 그렇게 한다. 사람들이 잘 다니지 않는 길을 택할 만큼 충분히 용감한 사람들은 엄청난 보상을 받을 수 있고 용감한 행동으로부터 큰 만족감을 끌어낼 수 있다. 지나치게 조심하는 것은 잠재력의 최고 수준을 달성하는 것을 놓친다는 의미일 것이다. 여러분은 주변에 있는 많은 사람들이 선택하지 않을 기회를 택하는 법을 배워야 하는데, 왜냐하면 여러분의 성공은 삶의 과정에서 여러분이 내릴 용감한 결정으로부터 나올 것이기 때문이다.

Why? 왜 정답일까?

결론을 제시하는 마지막 문장에서 많은 기회와 성공은 용기에서 파생되므로 더 과감해질 필요가 있다고 조언하므로(**You must learn to take those chances that many people around you will not take, because your success will flow from those bold decisions that you will take along the way.**), 글의 제목으로 가장 적절한 것은 ① '더 큰 용기가 더 많은 기회를 부른다'이다.

- **safe zone** 안전 구역
- **derive** ⓥ 끌어내다, 도출하다
- **overcautious** ⓐ 지나치게 조심하는
- **unknown** ⓐ 미지의, 알지 못하는
- **courageous** ⓐ 용감한

구문 풀이

4행 Those that are brave enough to take those roads less travelled are able
「형/부 + enough + to부정사 : ~할 만큼 충분히 ···한」 　　과거분사
to get great returns and derive major satisfaction out of their courageous moves.

---

25 대륙별 도시 인구 점유율 비교 　　정답률 86% | 정답 ③

다음 도표의 내용과 일치하지 않는 것은?

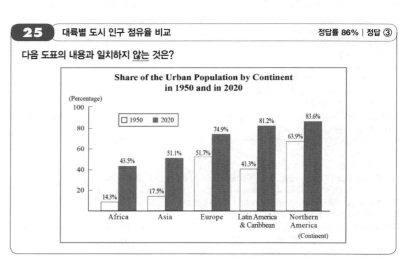

Share of the Urban Population by Continent in 1950 and in 2020

(Percentage)
□ 1950　■ 2020

Continent	1950	2020
Africa	14.3%	43.5%
Asia	17.5%	51.1%
Europe	51.7%	74.9%
Latin America & Caribbean	41.3%	81.2%
Northern America	63.9%	83.6%

The graph above shows / the share of the urban population by continent / in 1950 and in 2020.
위 그래프는 보여준다. / 대륙별 도시 인구 점유율을 / 1950년과 2020년의
① For each continent, / the share of the urban population in 2020 / was larger than that in 1950.
각 대륙에서, / 2020년의 도시 인구 점유율이 / 1950년에 비해 더 컸다.
② From 1950 to 2020, / the share of the urban population in Africa / increased from 14.3% to 43.5%.
1950년부터 2020년까지 / 아프리카의 도시 인구 점유율은 / 14.3%에서 43.5%로 증가했다.
✓ The share of the urban population in Asia / was the second lowest in 1950 / but not in 2020.
아시아의 도시 인구 점유율은 / 1950년에는 두 번째로 낮았지만, / 2020년에는 그렇지 않았다.
④ In 1950, / the share of the urban population in Europe / was larger than that in Latin America and the Caribbean, / whereas the reverse was true in 2020.
1950년에는 / 유럽의 도시 인구 점유율이 / 라틴 아메리카 및 카리브해 지역보다 더 컸지만, / 2020년에는 그 반대가 사실이었다.
⑤ Among the five continents, / Northern America was ranked in the first position / for the share of the urban population / in both 1950 and 2020.
다섯 개 대륙 중, / 북아메리카는 1위를 차지했다. / 도시 인구 점유율에서 / 1950년과 2020년 모두

위 그래프는 1950년과 2020년의 대륙별 도시 인구 점유율을 보여준다. ① 각 대륙에서, 2020년의 도시 인구 점유율이 1950년에 비해 더 컸다. ② 1950년부터 2020년까지 아프리카의 도시 인구 점유율은 14.3%에서 43.5%로 증가했다. ③ 아시아의 도시 인구 점유율은 두 번째로 낮았나 1950년에는, 2020년에는 그렇지 않았다. ④ 1950년에는 유럽의 도시 인구 점유율이 라틴 아메리카 및 카리브해 지역보다 더 컸지만, 2020년에는 역전이 일어났다. ⑤ 다섯 개 대륙 중, 북아메리카는 도시 인구 점유율에서 1950년과 2020년 모두 1위를 차지했다.

Why? 왜 정답일까?

도표에 따르면 2020년 아시아 대륙에서의 도시 인구 점유율은 **51.1%**로 전체에서 두 번째로 낮았는데, 이는 **1950년**과 동일한 순위이다. 따라서 도표와 일치하지 않는 것은 ③이다.

- urban ⓐ 도시의
- reverse ⓝ 반대, 역전, 전환
- population ⓝ 인구(수)

구문 풀이

5행 The share of the urban population in Asia was the second lowest in 1950
「서수 + 최상급: 몇 번째로 ~한」
but not in 2020.

---

26 Wilbur Smith의 생애　　　정답률 82% | 정답 ④

Wilbur Smith에 관한 다음 글의 내용과 일치하지 <u>않는</u> 것은?
① 역사 소설을 전문으로 하는 소설가였다.
② 아버지는 그가 글 쓰는 것을 지지하지 않았다.
③ 첫 번째 소설은 1962년까지 20번 거절당했다.
✓ 소설 *When the Lion Feeds*는 영화화되었다.
⑤ 죽기 전까지 49편의 소설을 출간했다.

「Wilbur Smith was a South African novelist / specialising in historical fiction.」 ①의 근거 일치
Wilbur Smith는 남아프리카 소설가였다. / 역사 소설을 전문으로 하는
Smith wanted to become a journalist, / writing about social conditions in South Africa, / but 「his father was never supportive of his writing / and forced him to get a real job.」 ②의 근거 일치
Smith는 언론인이 되고 싶었으나, / 남아프리카의 사회 환경에 관해 글을 쓰는 / 그의 아버지는 그가 글을 쓰는 것을 절대로 지지하지 않았고 / 그가 현실적인 직업을 갖도록 강요했다.
Smith studied further / and became a tax accountant, / but he finally turned back to his love of writing.
Smith는 더 공부하여 / 세금 회계사가 되었으나 / 결국에는 그가 사랑하는 글 쓰는 일로 돌아왔다.
「He wrote his first novel, *The Gods First Make Mad*, / and had received 20 rejections by 1962.」 ③의 근거 일치
그는 첫 번째 소설, *The Gods First Make Mad*를 썼고 / 1962년까지 20번의 거절을 당했다.
In 1964, / Smith published another novel, *When the Lion Feeds*, / and it went on to be successful, / selling around the world.
1964년에 / Smith는 또 다른 소설, *When the Lion Feeds*를 출간했고, / 그것은 성공을 거두었다. / 전 세계에 팔리면서
「A famous actor and film producer / bought the film rights for *When the Lion Feeds*, / although no movie resulted.」 ④의 근거 불일치
한 유명한 배우이자 영화 제작자가 / *When the Lion Feeds*에 대한 영화 판권을 샀다. / 비록 영화화되지는 않았지만
「By the time of his death in 2021 / he had published 49 novels, / selling more than 140 million copies worldwide.」 ⑤의 근거 일치
2021년 죽기 전까지 / 그는 49편의 소설을 출간했으며 / 전 세계적으로 1억 4천만 부 이상을 판매했다.

Wilbur Smith는 역사 소설을 전문으로 하는 남아프리카 소설가였다. Smith는 남아프리카의 사회 환경에 관해 글을 쓰는 언론인이 되고 싶었으나, 그의 아버지는 그가 글을 쓰는 것을 절대로 지지하지 않았고 그가 현실적인 직업을 갖도록 강요했다. Smith는 더 공부하여 세금 회계사가 되었으나 결국에는 그가 사랑하는 글 쓰는 일로 돌아왔다. 그는 첫 번째 소설, *The Gods First Make Mad*를 썼고 1962년까지 20번의 거절을 당했다. 1964년에 Smith는 또 다른 소설, *When the Lion Feeds*를 출간했고, 그것이 전 세계에 팔리면서 성공을 거두었다. 비록 영화화되지는 않았지만, 한 유명한 배우이자 영화 제작자가 *When the Lion Feeds*에 대한 영화 판권을 샀다. 2021년 죽기 전까지 그는 49편의 소설을 출간했으며 전 세계적으로 1억 4천만 부 이상을 판매했다.

Why? 왜 정답일까?

'A famous actor and film producer bought the film rights for *When the Lion Feeds*, although no movie resulted.'에서 소설 *When the Lion Feeds*의 영화 판권은 팔렸지만, 실제로 이것이 영화화되지는 않았다고 하므로, 내용과 일치하지 않는 것은 ④ '소설 *When the Lion Feeds*는 영화화되었다.'이다.

Why? 왜 오답일까?

① 'Wilbur Smith was a South African novelist specialising in historical fiction.'의 내용과 일치한다.
② '~ his father was never supportive of his writing ~'의 내용과 일치한다.
③ 'He wrote his first novel, *The Gods First Make Mad*, and had received 20 rejections by 1962.'의 내용과 일치한다.
⑤ 'By the time of his death in 2021 he had published 49 novels, ~'의 내용과 일치한다.

- novelist ⓝ 소설가
- fiction ⓝ 소설, 허구
- tax accountant 세무사
- rejection ⓝ 거절
- historical ⓐ 역사적인
- be supportive of ~을 지지하다
- turn back to ~로 돌아오다

구문 풀이

11행 By the time of his death in 2021 he had published 49 novels, selling more
　　　　~할 무렵　　　　　　　　　　　　과거완료　　　　　　분사구문(그리고 ~하다)
than 140 million copies worldwide.

---

27 야외 요가 수업 광고　　　정답률 95% | 정답 ④

2022 Springfield Park Yoga Class에 관한 다음 안내문의 내용과 일치하지 <u>않는</u> 것은?

---

① 온라인으로도 참여할 수 있다.　　② 9월 중 토요일마다 진행된다.
③ 수업 시작 2시간 전까지 등록해야 한다.　✓ 매트가 제공된다.
⑤ 날씨가 좋지 않으면 취소될 것이다.

2022 Springfield Park Yoga Class
2022 Springfield Park Yoga Class(2022 Springfield Park 요가 수업)
The popular yoga class in Springfield Park / returns!
Springfield Park에서의 인기 있는 요가 수업이 / 돌아옵니다!
Enjoy yoga hosted on the park lawn.
공원 잔디밭에서 열리는 요가를 즐겨보세요.
「If you can't make it to the park, / join us online on our social media platforms!」 ①의 근거 일치
만약 여러분이 공원에 오지 못한다면, / 저희의 소셜미디어 플랫폼에서 온라인으로 저희와 함께하세요!
When: 「Saturdays, 2 p.m. to 3 p.m., September」 ②의 근거 일치
일시: 9월 매주 토요일 오후 2시부터 3시까지
Registration: / 「At least TWO hours before each class starts, / sign up here.」 ③의 근거 일치
등록: 매 수업이 시작 적어도 2시간 전까지, / 여기서 등록하세요.
Notes
주의 사항
For online classes: / find a quiet space with enough room / for you to stretch out.
온라인 수업 / 충분한 공간을 가진 조용한 장소를 찾으세요 / 여러분이 스트레칭을 할 만큼
For classes in the park: 「mats are not provided, / so bring your own!」 ④의 근거 불일치
공원 수업: / 매트는 제공되지 않으니, / 본인 것을 가져오세요!
「The class will be canceled / if the weather is unfavorable.」 ⑤의 근거 일치
수업은 취소될 것입니다. / 만약 날씨가 좋지 않으면
For more information, / click here.
더 많은 정보를 위해서는, / 여기를 클릭하세요.

2022 Springfield Park Yoga Class
(2022 Springfield Park 요가 수업)

Springfield Park에서의 인기 있는 요가 수업이 돌아옵니다! 공원 잔디밭에서 열리는 요가를 즐겨보세요. 만약 여러분이 공원에 오지 못한다면, 저희의 소셜미디어 플랫폼에서 온라인으로 저희와 함께하세요!

◈ 일시: 9월 매주 토요일 오후 2시부터 3시까지
◈ 등록: 매 수업이 시작하기 적어도 2시간 전까지, 여기서 등록하세요.
◈ 주의 사항
 • 온라인 수업: 여러분이 스트레칭을 할 만큼 충분한 공간을 가진 조용한 장소를 찾으세요.
 • 공원 수업: 매트는 제공되지 않으니, 본인 것을 가져오세요!

※ 만약 날씨가 좋지 않으면 수업은 취소될 것입니다.

더 많은 정보를 위해서는, 여기를 클릭하세요.

Why? 왜 정답일까?

'For classes in the park: mats are not provided, so bring your own!'에서 매트는 제공되지 않아서 수업을 듣는 사람이 직접 지참해야 한다고 했으므로, 안내문의 내용과 일치하지 않는 것은 ④ '매트가 제공된다.'이다.

Why? 왜 오답일까?

① '~ join us online on our social media platforms!'의 내용과 일치한다.
② 'Saturdays, 2 p.m. to 3 p.m., September'의 내용과 일치한다.
③ 'At least TWO hours before each class starts'의 내용과 일치한다.
⑤ 'The class will be canceled if the weather is unfavorable.'의 내용과 일치한다.

- lawn ⓝ 잔디밭
- stretch out 몸을 쭉 뻗고 눕다
- make it 참석하다, 성공하다, 해내다
- unfavorable ⓐ (형편이) 나쁜, 우호적이지 않은

구문 풀이

9행 ~ find a quiet space with enough room for you to stretch out.
「enough + 명사 + 의미상 주어 + to부정사 : ~가 … 할 만큼 충분한 (명사)」

---

28 수질 오염 대책 아이디어 공모전　　　정답률 86% | 정답 ④

Kenner High School's Water Challenge에 관한 다음 안내문의 내용과 일치하는 것은?
① 제안서는 직접 방문하여 제출해야 한다.
② 9월 23일부터 제안서를 제출할 수 있다.
③ 제안서는 한 팀당 4개까지 제출할 수 있다.
✓ 제공된 제안서 양식을 사용해야 한다.
⑤ 2등은 10달러의 상품권을 받는다.

Kenner High School's Water Challenge
Kenner High School's Water Challenge(Kenner 고등학교 물 챌린지)
Kenner High School's Water Challenge is a new contest / to propose measures against water pollution.
Kenner High School's 고등학교 물 챌린지는 새로운 대회입니다. / 수질 오염에 대한 대책을 제안하는
Please share your ideas / for dealing with water pollution!
여러분의 아이디어를 공유해 주세요! / 수질 오염에 대처하기 위한
Submission
제출
「How: / Submit your proposal by email / to admin@khswater.edu.」 ①의 근거 불일치
방법: / 여러분의 제안서를 이메일로 제출해 주세요. / admin@khswater.edu로
「When: September 5, 2022 to September 23, 2022.」 ②의 근거 불일치
일시: 2022년 9월 5일부터 2022년 9월 23일까지
Details
세부 사항
Participants must enter in teams of four / and can only join one team.
참가자들은 반드시 4인으로 구성된 팀으로 참가해야 하며, / 오직 한 팀에만 참여할 수 있습니다.
「Submission is limited to one proposal per team.」 ③의 근거 불일치
한 팀당 한 개의 제안서만 제출할 수 있습니다.
「Participants must use the proposal form / provided on the website.」 ④의 근거 일치

참가자들은 제안서 양식을 사용해야 합니다. / 웹사이트에 제공된

Prizes
상품
1st: $50 gift certificate
1등: 50달러 상품권
『2nd: $30 gift certificate』 ⑤의 근거 불일치
2등: 30달러 상품권
3rd: $10 gift certificate
3등: 10달러 상품권
Please visit www.khswater.edu / to learn more about the challenge.
www.khswater.edu를 방문해 주세요. / 대회에 대해 더 알고 싶으면

Kenner High School's Water Challenge
(Kenner 고등학교 물 챌린지)

Kenner 고등학교 물 챌린지는 수질 오염에 대한 대책을 제안하는 새로운 대회입니다. 수질 오염에 대처하기 위한 여러분의 아이디어를 공유해 주세요!

제출
– **방법**: 여러분의 제안서를 이메일 admin@khswater.edu로 제출해 주세요.
– **일시**: 2022년 9월 5일부터 2022년 9월 23일까지

세부 사항
– 참가자들은 반드시 4인으로 구성된 팀으로 참가해야 하며, 오직 한 팀에만 참여할 수 있습니다.
– 한 팀당 한 개의 제안서만 제출할 수 있습니다.
– 참가자들은 웹사이트에 제공된 제안서 양식을 사용해야 합니다.

상품
– 1등: 50달러 상품권
– 2등: 30달러 상품권
– 3등: 10달러 상품권

대회에 대해 더 알고 싶으면, www.khswater.edu를 방문해 주세요.

Why? 왜 정답일까?

'Participants must use the proposal form provided on the website.'에서 제안서는 제공된 양식을 사용해 작성되어야 한다고 공지하므로, 안내문의 내용과 일치하는 것은 ④ '제공된 제안서 양식을 사용해야 한다.'이다.

Why? 왜 오답일까?

① 'Submit your proposal by email to admin@khswater.edu.'에서 제안서는 이메일로 제출하면 된다고 하였다.
② 'When: September 5, 2022 to September 23, 2022'에서 9월 23일은 제출 시작일이 아니라 마감일이라고 하였다.
③ 'Submission is limited to one proposal per team.'에서 팀별로 제안서는 하나만 제출할 수 있다고 하였다.
⑤ '2nd: $30 gift certificate'에서 2등은 30달러짜리 상품권을 받는다고 하였다.

● measure ⓝ 대책, 조치
● gift certificate 상품권
● water pollution 수질 오염

---

29 인간의 뇌 크기 감소　　　　정답률 67% | 정답 ③

다음 글의 밑줄 친 부분 중, 어법상 틀린 것은? [3점]

The human brain, / it turns out, / has shrunk in mass by about 10 percent / since it ① peaked in size 15,000-30,000 years ago.
인간의 뇌는 / 밝혀졌다. / 부피가 약 10퍼센트 줄어들었다는 것이 / 그것이 15,000년에서 30,000년 전 정점에 도달한 이래
One possible reason is / that many thousands of years ago / humans lived in a world of dangerous predators / ② where they had to have their wits about them at all times / to avoid being killed.
한 가지 가능한 이유는 ~이다. / 수천 년 전에 / 인간은 위험한 포식자의 세계에서 살았다는 것 / 그들이 늘 기지를 발휘해야 했던 / 죽임을 당하는 것을 피하기 위해
Today, / we have effectively domesticated ourselves / and many of the tasks of survival / — from avoiding immediate death / to building shelters / to obtaining food — / ☑ have been outsourced to the wider society.
오늘날, / 우리는 우리 자신을 효율적으로 길들여 왔고 / 생존의 많은 과업이 / 즉각적인 죽음을 피하는 것부터 / 쉴 곳을 짓고 / 음식을 얻어 내는 일까지 / 더 넓은 사회로 위탁되어 왔다.
We are smaller than our ancestors too, / and it is a characteristic of domestic animals / ④ that they are generally smaller than their wild cousins.
우리는 우리의 조상보다 더 작기도 한데, / 가축의 특징 중 하나다. / 이들이 그들의 야생 사촌보다 일반적으로 더 작다는 것은
None of this may mean we are dumber / — brain size is not necessarily an indicator of human intelligence — / but it may mean / that our brains today are wired up differently, / and perhaps more efficiently, / than ⑤ those of our ancestors.
이중 어떤 것도 우리가 더 어리석다는 뜻은 아니지만 / 뇌 크기가 반드시 인간의 지능의 지표는 아니다 / 그것은 뜻할 수도 있다. / 오늘날 우리의 뇌가 다른 식으로 장착되어 있음을 / 그리고 아마도 더 효율적으로 / 우리 조상들의 뇌보다

인간의 뇌는 15,000년에서 30,000년 전 크기가 정점에 도달한 이래 부피가 약 10퍼센트 줄어들었다는 것이 밝혀졌다. 한 가지 가능한 이유는 수천 년 전에 인간은 죽임을 당하는 것을 피하기 위해 그들이 늘 기지를 발휘해야 했던 위험한 포식자의 세계에서 살았다는 것이다. 오늘날, 우리는 우리 자신을 효율적으로 길들여 왔고 생존의 많은 과업이 — 즉각적인 죽음을 피하는 것부터 쉴 곳을 짓고 음식을 얻어 내는 일까지 — 더 넓은 사회로 위탁되어 왔다. 우리는 우리의 조상보다 더 작기도 한데, 가축이 그들의 야생 사촌보다 일반적으로 더 작다는 것은 이들의 특징 중 하나다. 이중 어떤 것도 우리가 더 어리석다는 뜻은 아니지만 — 뇌 크기가 반드시 인간의 지능의 지표는 아니다 — 그것은 오늘날 우리의 뇌가 다른 식으로, 그리고 우리 조상보다 아마도 더 효율적으로 장착되어 있음을 뜻할 수도 있다.

Why? 왜 정답일까?

and 뒤에 새로 나온 주어가 many of the tasks of survival이라는 복수 명사구이므로, 단수형 has를 복수형 have로 고쳐야 한다. 따라서 어법상 틀린 것은 ③이다.

Why? 왜 오답일까?

① '주어 + 현재완료 동사 ~, since + 주어 + 과거 동사 ~' 형태가 알맞게 쓰였다.
② 선행사가 바로 앞의 predators가 아닌 a world이므로, 장소의 관계부사 where가 알맞게 쓰였다.
④ it이 가주어이고, 'they are generally smaller ~'가 진주어이므로 명사절을 이끄는 접속사 that을 알맞게 썼다.
⑤ than 앞의 복수 명사 brains를 가리키기 위해 복수 대명사 those를 썼다.

● shrink ⓥ 줄어들다
● have one's wits about one ~의 기지를 발휘하다
● domesticate ⓥ 길들이다
● wire ⓥ 연결하다, 장착하다
● mass ⓝ 부피, 질량
● indicator ⓝ 지표

구문 풀이

[3행] One possible reason is that many thousands of years ago humans lived in a world of dangerous predators where they had to have their wits about them (장소 선행사) (관계부사) (= predators) at all times to avoid being killed. (수동 동명사(~되는 것))

---

30 허브의 건강상 효과　　　　정답률 58% | 정답 ⑤

다음 글의 밑줄 친 부분 중, 문맥상 낱말의 쓰임이 적절하지 않은 것은? [3점]

It is widely believed / that certain herbs somehow magically improve the work of certain organs, / and "cure" specific diseases as a result.
널리 알려져 있다. / 어떤 허브는 왜인지는 몰라도 마법처럼 특정 장기의 기능을 향상시키고, / 그 결과 특정한 질병을 '치유한다'고
Such statements are unscientific and groundless.
그러한 진술은 비과학적이고 근거가 없다.
Sometimes herbs appear to work, / since they tend to ① increase your blood circulation / in an aggressive attempt by your body / to eliminate them from your system.
때때로 허브는 효과가 있는 것처럼 보이는데, / 그것이 혈액 순환을 증가시키는 경향이 있기 때문이다. / 당신 몸이 적극 시도하는 과정에서 / 신체로부터 그것을 제거하려고
That can create a ② temporary feeling of a high, / which makes it seem / as if your health condition has improved.
이는 일시적으로 좋은 기분을 만들어 줄 수 있고, / 마치 보이게 만든다. / 당신의 건강 상태가 향상된 것처럼
Also, / herbs can have a placebo effect, / just like any other method, / thus helping you feel better.
또한, / 허브는 위약 효과를 가지고 있다 / 여느 다른 방법과 마찬가지로, / 그래서 당신이 더 나아졌다고 느끼도록 도와준다.
Whatever the case, / it is your body / that has the intelligence to ③ regain health, / and not the herbs.
어떠한 경우든, / 바로 당신의 몸이다. / 건강을 되찾게 하는 지성을 가진 것은 / 허브가 아니라
How can herbs have the intelligence / needed to direct your body into getting healthier?
어떻게 허브가 지성을 가질 수 있겠는가? / 당신의 몸을 더 건강해지는 방향으로 인도하는 데 필요한
That is impossible.
그것은 불가능하다.
Try to imagine / how herbs might come into your body / and intelligently ④ fix your problems.
상상해 보라. / 어떻게 허브가 당신의 몸 안으로 들어가 / 영리하게 당신의 문제를 해결할 수 있는지
If you try to do that, / you will see how impossible it seems.
만약 당신이 그렇게 해 본다면 / 당신은 그것이 얼마나 불가능하게 보이는지를 알게 될 것이다.
Otherwise, / it would mean / that herbs are ☑ more intelligent than the human body, / which is truly hard to believe.
그렇지 않다면, / 그것은 의미할 텐데, / 허브가 인간의 몸보다 더 지적이라는 것을 / 이는 정말로 믿기 어렵다.

어떤 허브는 왜인지는 몰라도 마법처럼 특정 장기의 기능을 향상시키고, 그 결과 특정한 질병을 '치유한다'고 널리 알려져 있다. 그러한 진술은 비과학적이고 근거가 없다. 때때로 허브는 효과가 있는 것처럼 보이는데, 이는 당신 몸이 신체로부터 그것을 제거하려고 적극 시도하는 과정에서 그것이 혈액 순환을 ① 증가시키는 경향이 있기 때문이다. 이는 ② 일시적으로 좋은 기분을 만들어 줄 수 있고, 마치 당신의 건강 상태가 향상된 것처럼 보이게 만든다. 또한 여느 다른 방법과 마찬가지로, 허브는 위약 효과를 가지고 있어서, 당신이 더 나아졌다고 느끼도록 도와준다. 어떠한 경우든, 건강을 ③ 되찾게 하는 지성을 가진 것은 허브가 아니라 바로 당신의 몸이다. 허브가 어떻게 당신의 몸을 더 건강해지는 방향으로 인도하는 데 필요한 지성을 가질 수 있겠는가? 그것은 불가능하다. 어떻게 허브가 당신의 몸 안으로 들어가 영리하게 당신의 문제를 ④ 해결할 수 있는지 상상해 보라. 만약 그렇게 해 본다면 당신은 그것이 얼마나 불가능하게 보이는지를 알게 될 것이다. 그렇지 않다면, 그것은 허브가 인간의 몸보다 ⑤ 덜(→더) 지적이라는 것을 의미할 텐데, 이는 정말로 믿기 어렵다.

Why? 왜 정답일까?

허브가 몸 안에서 어떻게 건강 문제를 해결해줄 수 있는지 상상해보면 얼마나 어려운지 깨닫게 될 것이라는 내용 뒤에는 허브가 인간의 몸보다 '더 똑똑하다' 생각은 믿기 어렵다는 결론이 이어져야 하므로, ⑤의 less를 more로 고쳐야 한다. 따라서 문맥상 낱말의 쓰임이 적절하지 않은 것은 ⑤이다.

● groundless ⓐ 근거가 없는
● eliminate ⓥ 제거하다, 없애다
● high ⓝ 도취감
● aggressive ⓐ 적극적인, 공격적인
● temporary ⓐ 일시적인
● whatever the case 어떤 경우이든지

구문 풀이

[9행] Whatever the case, it is your body that has the intelligence to regain (어느 경우이든 간에) (「it is ~ that … : …한 것은 바로 …이다」) health, and not the herbs.

★★★ 등급을 가르는 문제!
31 우리의 판단력을 앗아가는 로봇　　　　정답률 46% | 정답 ②

다음 빈칸에 들어갈 말로 가장 적절한 것을 고르시오. [3점]
① reliability – 신뢰성　　　☑ judgment – 판단력　　　③ endurance – 인내
④ sociability – 사교성　　　⑤ cooperation – 협력

We worry that the robots are taking our jobs, / but just as common a problem is / that the robots are taking our judgment.
우리는 로봇이 우리의 직업을 빼앗고 있다고 걱정하지만, / 그만큼 흔한 문제는 ~이다. / 로봇이 우리의 판단력을 빼앗고 있다는 것

In the large warehouses / so common behind the scenes of today's economy, / human 'pickers' hurry around / grabbing products off shelves / and moving them to where they can be packed and dispatched.
거대한 창고에서, / 오늘날의 경제 배후에 있는 아주 흔한 / 인간 '집게'는 서둘러서 / 선반에서 상품을 집어내고, / 그것들이 포장되고 발송될 수 있는 곳으로 이동시킨다.

In their ears are headpieces: / the voice of 'Jennifer', / a piece of software, / tells them where to go and what to do, / controlling the smallest details of their movements.
그들의 귀에는 헤드폰이 있는데, / 'Jennifer'의 목소리가 / 한 소프트웨어 프로그램인 / 이들에게 어디로 가고 무엇을 할지 말해준다. / 이들 움직임의 가장 작은 세부 사항들을 조종하면서

Jennifer breaks down instructions into tiny chunks, / to minimise error and maximise productivity / — for example, / rather than picking eighteen copies of a book off a shelf, / the human worker would be politely instructed to pick five.
Jennifer는 지시 사항을 아주 작은 덩어리로 쪼개는데, / 실수를 줄이고 생산성을 최대화하기 위해 / 가령 / 선반에서 책 18권을 집어내기보다는, / 인간 작업자는 5권을 집어내라고 정중하게 지시받을 것이다.

Then another five. // Then yet another five. // Then another three.
그다음 또 5권. // 그다음 또 5권. // 그다음 또 3권.

Working in such conditions / reduces people to machines / made of flesh.
그러한 조건에서 일하는 것은 / 사람을 기계로 격하시킨다. / 살로 만들어진

Rather than asking us to think or adapt, / the Jennifer unit takes over the thought process / and treats workers as an inexpensive source / of some visual processing and a pair of opposable thumbs.
우리에게 생각하거나 적응하라고 요구하기보다는, / Jennifer라는 장치는 사고 과정을 지배하고, / 작업자들을 값싼 자원으로 다룬다. / 약간의 시각적 처리 과정과 마주 볼 수 있는 엄지 한 쌍이 있는

우리는 로봇이 우리의 직업을 빼앗고 있다고 걱정하지만, 그만큼 흔한 문제는 로봇이 우리의 판단력을 빼앗고 있다는 것이다. 오늘날의 경제 배후에 있는 아주 흔한 거대한 창고에서, 인간 '집게'는 서둘러서 선반에서 상품을 집어내고, 그것들이 포장되고 발송될 수 있는 곳으로 이동시킨다. 그들의 귀에는 헤드폰이 있는데, 한 소프트웨어 프로그램인 'Jennifer'의 목소리가 이들 움직임의 가장 작은 세부 사항을 조종하면서, 이들에게 어디로 가고 무엇을 할지 말해준다. Jennifer는 실수를 줄이고 생산성을 최대화하기 위해 지시 사항을 아주 작은 덩어리로 쪼개는데, 가령 인간 작업자는 선반에서 책 18권을 집어내기보다는, 5권을 집어내라고 정중하게 지시받을 것이다. 그다음 또 5권, 그다음 또 5권. 그다음 또 3권을 집으라는 지시를 받을 것이다. 그러한 조건에서 일하는 것은 사람을 살로 만들어진 기계로 격하시킨다. Jennifer라는 장치는 우리에게 생각하거나 적응하라고 요구하기보다는, 사고 과정을 지배하고, 작업자들을 약간의 시각적 처리 과정과 마주 볼 수 있는 엄지 한 쌍이 있는 값싼 자원으로 다룬다.

Why? 왜 정답일까?

창고 노동자들이 기계에게 아주 작은 행동까지 지시받으며 일한다(~ tells them where to go and what to do, controlling the smallest details of their movements.)는 예시를 통해, 인간이 기계로 격하되고 사고 과정을 박탈당하는 상황에 놓여 있음을 설명하는 글이다. 따라서 빈칸에 들어갈 말로 가장 적절한 것은 로봇에 지배당한 사고 과정(thought process)을 다르게 표현한 말인 ② '판단력'이다.

- warehouse ⓝ 창고
- headpiece ⓝ 헤드폰, 머리에 쓰는 것, 지성, 판단력
- break down 쪼개다
- take over 지배하다, 장악하다
- endurance ⓝ 인내
- grab ⓥ 집어내다
- flesh ⓝ (사람, 동물의) 살
- opposable ⓐ 마주볼 수 있는

구문 풀이

12행 Working in such conditions reduces people to machines made of flesh.
동명사구 주어 / 동사(단수) / 과거분사구

★★ 문제 해결 꿀~팁 ★★

▶ 많이 틀린 이유는?
로봇 때문에 인간의 신뢰성이나 사교성이 떨어진다는 내용은 아니므로 ①이나 ④는 답으로 적절하지 않다.

▶ 문제 해결 방법은?
예시의 결론을 정리하는 'Rather than asking us to think or adapt, the Jennifer unit takes over the thought process ~'가 핵심이다. 이 thought process와 통하는 단어를 골라야 한다.

32 자신의 발달 환경을 주도적으로 만드는 인간　　정답률 53% | 정답 ⑤

다음 빈칸에 들어갈 말로 가장 적절한 것을 고르시오.
① mirrors of their generation – 자기 세대의 거울
② shields against social conflicts – 사회적 갈등을 막는 방패
③ explorers in their own career path – 자기 진로의 탐색가
④ followers of their childhood dreams – 어린 시절의 꿈을 좇는 사람
☑ manufacturers of their own development – 자신의 발달을 생산하는 사람

The prevailing view among developmental scientists / is / that people are active contributors to their own development.
발달 과학자들 사이에서 지배적인 견해는 / ~이다. / 사람들이 자신의 발달에 능동적인 기여자라는 것

People are influenced by the physical and social contexts / in which they live, / but they also play a role / in influencing their development / by interacting with, and changing, those contexts.
사람들은 물리적 및 사회적 환경의 영향을 받지만, / 자신이 사는 / 그들은 또한 역할을 한다. / 자신의 발달에 영향을 주는 데 있어 / 그 환경들과 상호작용을 하고 그것을 변화시켜

Even infants influence the world around them / and construct their own development / through their interactions.
심지어 유아도 자기 주변의 세상에 영향을 주고, / 자신의 발달을 구성한다. / 상호작용을 통해

Consider an infant / who smiles at each adult he sees; / he influences his world / because

adults are likely to smile, / use "baby talk," / and play with him / in response.
유아를 생각해 보라. / 그가 바라보는 어른마다 미소 짓는 / 그는 자신의 세상에 영향을 준다. / 어른들은 미소 짓고, / '아기 말'을 사용하고, / 그와 함께 놀아줄 것이기 때문에 / 이에 반응하여

The infant brings adults into close contact, / making one-on-one interactions / and creating opportunities for learning.
그 유아는 어른들을 친밀한 연결로 끌어들여서, / 일대일 상호작용을 하고 / 학습의 기회를 만든다.

By engaging the world around them, / thinking, / being curious, / and interacting with people, objects, and the world around them, / individuals of all ages / are manufacturers of their own development.
주변 세상의 관심을 끌고, / 생각하고, / 호기심을 가지고, / 주변 사람, 사물, 세상과 상호작용함으로써, / 모든 연령대의 개인들은 / '자신의 발달을 생산하는 사람'이다.

발달 과학자들 사이에서 지배적인 견해는 사람들이 자신의 발달에 능동적인 기여자라는 것이다. 사람들은 자신이 사는 물리적 및 사회적 환경의 영향을 받지만, 그들은 또한 그 환경들과 상호작용하고 그것을 변화시켜 자신의 발달에 영향을 주는 역할을 한다. 심지어 유아들도 자기 주변의 세상에 영향을 주고, 상호작용을 통해 자신의 발달을 구성한다. 그가 바라보는 어른마다 미소 짓는 유아를 생각해 보라. 어른들은 이에 반응하여 미소 짓고, '아기 말'을 사용하고, 그와 함께 놀아줄 것이기 때문에 그는 자신의 세상에 영향을 준다. 그 유아는 어른들을 친밀한 연결로 끌어들여서, 일대일 상호작용을 하고 학습의 기회를 만든다. 주변 세상의 관심을 끌고, 생각하고, 호기심을 가지고, 주변 사람, 사물, 세상과 상호작용함으로써, 모든 연령대의 개인들은 '자신의 발달을 생산하는 사람'이다.

Why? 왜 정답일까?

주제문인 첫 문장에서 인간은 자신의 발달에 능동적으로 기여하는 주체(~ people are active contributors to their own development.)라고 언급하므로, 빈칸에 들어갈 말로 가장 적절한 것은 ⑤ '자신의 발달을 생산하는 사람'이다.

- prevailing ⓐ 지배적인, 만연한
- baby talk 아기 말(말을 배우는 유아나 어린이에게 어른이 쓰는 말투)
- close ⓐ 친밀한
- conflict ⓝ 갈등
- developmental ⓐ 발달의
- one-on-one ⓐ 일대일의

구문 풀이

7행 Consider an infant [he sees]; he influences his
명령문(~하라) / 목적어 / 주격 관계대명사
world because adults are likely to smile, use "baby talk," and play with him in
~할 것이다 / 동사원형1 / 동사원형2 / 동사원형3
response. [ ]: 목적격 관계대명사절

33 신선함의 환경적 대가　　정답률 48% | 정답 ①

다음 빈칸에 들어갈 말로 가장 적절한 것을 고르시오. [3점]
☑ have hidden environmental costs – 숨겨진 환경적인 대가를 지니고 있을
② worsen the global hunger problem – 세계 기아 문제를 악화시킬
③ bring about technological advances – 기술 진보를 가져올
④ improve nutrition and quality of food – 영양과 음식 품질을 개선할
⑤ diversify the diet of a local community – 지역 사회의 식단을 다양화할

The demand for freshness / can have hidden environmental costs.
신선함에 대한 요구는 / 숨겨진 환경적인 대가를 지니고 있을 수 있다.

While freshness is now being used / as a term in food marketing / as part of a return to nature, / the demand for year-round supplies of fresh produce / such as soft fruit and exotic vegetables / has led to / the widespread use of hot houses in cold climates / and increasing reliance on total quality control — / management by temperature control, use of pesticides and computer/satellite-based logistics.
현재 신선함이 사용되고 있는 한편, / 식품 마케팅에서 하나의 용어로 / 자연으로 돌아가는 것의 일환으로 / 신선한 식품의 연중 공급에 대한 요구는 / 부드러운 과일이나 외국산 채소와 같은 / ~로 이어져 왔다. / 추운 기후에서의 광범위한 온실 사용과 / 총체적인 품질 관리에 대한 의존성의 증가로 / 즉 온도 조절에 의한 관리, 살충제 사용, 그리고 컴퓨터/위성 기반물류

The demand for freshness / has also contributed to concerns about food wastage.
신선함에 대한 요구는 / 또한 식량 낭비에 대한 우려의 원인이 되었다.

Use of 'best before', 'sell by' and 'eat by' labels / has legally allowed institutional waste.
'유통 기한', '판매 시한', '섭취 시한' 등의 라벨 사용은 / 제도적인 폐기물 생산을 법적으로 허용해 왔다.

Campaigners have exposed the scandal of over-production and waste.
운동가들은 과잉 생산이나 폐기물에 대한 추문을 폭로해 왔다.

Tristram Stuart, / one of the global band of anti-waste campaigners, / argues / that, with freshly made sandwiches, / over-ordering is standard practice across the retail sector / to avoid the appearance of empty shelf space, / leading to high volumes of waste / when supply regularly exceeds demand.
Tristram Stuart는 / 폐기물 반대 세계 연대 소속 운동 중 한 명인 / 주장한다. / 신선하게 만들어진 샌드위치와 함께, / 초과 주문이 소매 산업 분야 전반에서 이루어지는 일반적인 행태이며, / 판매대가 비어 보이는 것을 막기 위한 / 이것은 엄청난 양의 폐기물로 이어진다고 / 공급이 정기적으로 수요를 초과하면

신선함에 대한 요구는 숨겨진 환경적인 대가를 지니고 있을 수 있다. 자연으로 돌아가는 것의 일환으로 현재 신선함이 식품 마케팅에서 하나의 용어로 사용되고 있는 한편, 부드러운 과일이나 외국산 채소와 같은 신선한 식품의 연중 공급에 대한 요구는 추운 기후에서의 광범위한 온실 사용과 총체적인 품질 관리—온도 조절에 의한 관리, 살충제 사용, 그리고 컴퓨터/위성 기반 물류—에 대한 의존성의 증가로 이어져 왔다. 신선함에 대한 요구는 또한 식량 낭비에 대한 우려의 원인이 되었다. '유통 기한', '판매 시한', '섭취 시한' 등의 라벨 사용은 제도적인 폐기물 생산을 법적으로 허용해 왔다. (환경) 운동가들은 과잉 생산이나 폐기물에 대한 추문을 폭로해 왔다. 폐기물 반대 세계 연대 소속 운동가 중 한 명인 Tristram Stuart는 신선하게 만들어진 샌드위치와 함께, 판매대가 비어 보이는 것을 막기 위한 초과 주문이 소매 산업 분야 전반에서 이루어지는 일반적인 행태이며, 이것은 공급이 정기적으로 수요를 초과하면 엄청난 양의 폐기물로 이어진다고 주장한다.

Why? 왜 정답일까?

빈칸 뒤에서 '신선한' 식품 공급에 대한 요구가 커지면서 환경적 비용을 많이 야기하는 온실 또는 품질 관리 기법에 대한 의존성이 증가했으며, 폐기물 또한 더 많이 용인되는 사태가 일어났다고 한다. 따라서 빈칸에 들어갈 말로 가장 적절한 것은 ① '숨겨진 환경적인 대가를 지니고 있을'이다.

- **year-round** ⓐ 연중 계속되는
- **reliance** ⓝ 의존
- **institutional** ⓐ 제도적인, 기관의
- **diversify** ⓥ 다양화하다
- **exotic** ⓐ 외국의, 이국적인
- **satellite** ⓝ 위성
- **bring about** ~을 가져오다, 야기하다

구문 풀이

2행 While freshness is now being used as a term in food marketing as part of
a return to nature, the demand (for year-round supplies of fresh produce) (such
as soft fruit and exotic vegetables) has led to the widespread use of hot houses
in cold climates and increasing reliance on total quality control — {management
by temperature control, use of pesticides and computer/satellite-based logistics}.

[ ] : total quality control 보충 설명

---

34 두 가지 다른 정보를 동시에 처리할 수 없는 인간 　　　정답률 51% | 정답 ⑤

다음 빈칸에 들어갈 말로 가장 적절한 것을 고르시오. [3점]

① decide what they should do in the moment - 그들이 그 순간 뭘 해야 하는지를 판단할
② remember a message with too many words - 너무 긴 메시지를 기억할
③ analyze which information was more accurate - 어떤 정보가 더 정확한지 분석할
④ speak their own ideas while listening to others - 다른 사람들의 말을 들으면서 자기 생각을 말할
✓ process two pieces of information at the same time - 두 개의 정보를 동시에 처리할

In the studies of Colin Cherry / at the Massachusetts Institute for Technology / back in the
1950s, / his participants listened to voices in one ear at a time / and then through both ears
/ in an effort to determine / whether we can listen to two people talk at the same time.
Colin Cherry의 연구에서, / 메사추세츠 공과대학 소속이었던 / 1950년대 / 참가자들은 한 번은 한쪽 귀로만 목소리를 듣고, /
그다음에는 양쪽 귀로 들었다 / 판단하기 위해 / 우리가 두 사람이 이야기하는 것을 동시에 들을 수 있는지

One ear always contained a message / that the listener had to repeat back / (called
"shadowing") / while the other ear included people speaking.
한쪽 귀로는 메시지를 계속 들려주었고 / 듣는 사람이 다시 반복해야 하는 / ('섀도잉'이라 불림) / 다른 한쪽 귀로는 사람들이 말하는
것을 들려주었다.

The trick was to see / if you could totally focus on the main message / and also hear
someone talking in your other ear.
속임수는 알아보기 위한 것이었다. / 사람들이 주된 메시지에 완전히 집중하면서 / 다른 귀로는 다른 사람이 말하는 것 또한 들을 수
있는지를

Cleverly, / Cherry found / it was impossible / for his participants to know / whether the
message in the other ear / was spoken by a man or woman, / in English or another
language, / or was even comprised of real words at all!
영리하게도, / Cherry는 발견했다 / 불가능했다는 것을 / 참가자들이 알아차리는 것이 / 다른 한쪽 귀로 들리는 메시지가 / 남자가
말한 것인지 혹은 여자가 말한 것인지, / 영어인지 다른 외국어인지, / 심지어 실제 단어로 구성된 것인지조차 전혀

In other words, / people could not process two pieces of information at the same time.
다시 말해서, / 사람들은 두 개의 정보를 동시에 처리할 수 없었다.

1950년대 메사추세츠 공과대학 소속이었던 Colin Cherry의 연구에서, 우리가 두 사람이 이야기하는 것을 동시에 들을 수 있는지 판단하기 위해 참가자들은 한 번은 한쪽 귀로만 목소리를 듣고, 그다음에는 양쪽 귀로 들었다. 한쪽 귀로는 듣는 사람이 다시 반복해야 하는('섀도잉'이라 불림) 메시지를 계속 들려주었고 다른 한쪽 귀로는 사람들이 말하는 것을 들려주었다. 속임수는 사람들이 주된 메시지에 완전히 집중하면서 다른 귀로는 다른 사람이 말하는 것 또한 들을 수 있는지를 알아보기 위한 것이었다. 영리하게도, Cherry는 참가자들이 다른 한쪽 귀로 들리는 메시지가 남자가 말한 것인지 혹은 여자가 말한 것인지, 영어인지 다른 외국어인지, 심지어 실제 단어로 구성된 것인지조차 전혀 알아차리지 못했다는 것을 발견했다! 다시 말해서, 사람들은 두 개의 정보를 동시에 처리할 수 없었다.

Why? 왜 정답일까?

실험 결과를 제시하는 '~ it was impossible for his participants to know whether the message in the other ear was spoken by a man or woman, in English or another language, or was even comprised of real words at all!'에서 사람들은 양쪽 귀에 각기 다른 정보가 들어올 때 이를 동시에 처리하지 못하여, 화자가 남자였는지 여자였는지, 사용된 언어가 영어였는지 다른 언어였는지 등등을 제대로 판별하지 못했다고 한다. 따라서 빈칸에 들어갈 말로 가장 적절한 것은 ⑤ '두 개의 정보를 동시에 처리할'이다.

- **at a time** 한 번에
- **contain** ⓥ 수용하다, 담다
- **shadowing** ⓝ 섀도잉(남의 말을 듣는 동시에 따라서 하는 것)
- **trick** ⓝ 속임수, 요령
- **accurate** ⓐ 정확한
- **in an effort to** ~하기 위해서
- **comprise** ⓥ ~을 구성하다

구문 풀이

7행 The trick was to see if you could totally focus on the main message and
also hear someone talking in your other ear.

---

35 기술 진보로 가능해진 새로운 서비스 제공 　　　정답률 49% | 정답 ④

다음 글에서 전체 흐름과 관계 <u>없는</u> 문장은?

The fast-paced evolution of Information and Communication Technologies (ICTs) / has
radically transformed / the dynamics and business models of the tourism and hospitality
industry.
정보와 의사소통 기술(ICTs)의 빠른 진화는 / 급격하게 변화시켰다. / 관광업과 서비스업의 역학과 비즈니스 모델을

① This leads to new levels/forms of competitiveness among service providers / and
transforms the customer experience through new services.
이것은 서비스 제공자 간 새로운 수준/형식의 경쟁으로 이어지고, / 새로운 서비스를 통해 고객 경험을 변화시킨다.

② Creating unique experiences / and providing convenient services to customers / leads to
satisfaction / and, eventually, customer loyalty / to the service provider or brand (i.e.,
hotels).

독특한 경험을 만드는 것과 / 고객에게 편리한 서비스를 제공하는 것은 / 만족감을 낳고, / 종국에는 고객 충성도로 이어진다. / 서비스 제공자나 브랜드(즉, 호텔)에 대한

③ In particular, / the most recent *technological* boost / received by the tourism sector / is
represented by mobile applications.
특히, / 가장 최근의 *기술적* 부상은 / 관광업 분야에서 받아들여진 / 모바일 애플리케이션으로 대표된다.

✓ Increasing competitiveness among service providers / does not necessarily mean /
promoting quality of customer services.
서비스 제공자 간의 경쟁을 증가시키는 것이 / 반드시 의미하지는 않는다. / 고객 서비스의 질을 증진시키는 것을

⑤ Indeed, / empowering tourists with mobile access to services / such as hotel
reservations, airline ticketing, and recommendations for local attractions / generates strong
interest and considerable profits.
사실, / 서비스에 대한 모바일 접근 권한을 관광객에게 주는 것은 / 호텔 예약, 항공권 발권, 그리고 지역 관광지 추천과 같은 / 강력한 흥미와 상당한 수익을 만들어 낸다.

정보와 의사소통 기술(ICTs)의 빠른 진화는 관광업과 서비스업의 역학과 비즈니스 모델을 급격하게 변화시켰다. ① 이것은 서비스 제공자 간 새로운 수준/형식의 경쟁으로 이어지고, 새로운 서비스를 통해 고객 경험을 변화시킨다. ② 독특한 경험을 만드는 것과 고객에게 편리한 서비스를 제공하는 것은 만족감을 낳고, 종국에는 서비스 제공자나 브랜드(즉, 호텔)에 대한 고객 충성도로 이어진다. ③ 특히, 관광업 분야에서 받아들여진 가장 최근의 *기술적* 부상은 모바일 애플리케이션으로 대표된다. ④ 서비스 제공자 간의 경쟁을 증가시키는 것이 반드시 고객 서비스의 질을 증진시키는 것을 의미하지는 않는다. ⑤ 사실, 관광객에게 호텔 예약, 항공권 발권, 그리고 지역 관광지 추천과 같은 서비스에 대한 모바일 접근 권한을 주는 것은 강력한 흥미와 상당한 수익을 만들어 낸다.

Why? 왜 정답일까?

빠른 기술적 진보로 소비자에게 새로운 경험과 서비스를 제공하는 것이 가능해졌고, 이것이 고객 만족도나 충성도, 수익 면에서 모두 좋은 결과를 이끌어낼 수 있다는 내용. ③과 ⑤는 특히 관광업의 모바일 애플리케이션을 예로 들고 있다. 한편 ④는 서비스 제공자 간 경쟁의 증가가 고객 서비스 질을 반드시 높이지는 않는다는 내용이어서 흐름상 무관하다. 따라서 전체 흐름과 관계 없는 문장은 ④이다.

- **fast-paced** ⓐ 빠른
- **dynamics** ⓝ 역학, 역동성
- **loyalty** ⓝ 충성도
- **profit** ⓝ 수익
- **radically** ⓐⓓ 급진적으로
- **competitiveness** ⓝ 경쟁력, 경쟁적인 것
- **empower** ⓥ 권한을 부여하다

구문 풀이

8행 In particular, the most recent technological boost received by the tourism
sector is represented by mobile applications.

---

36 식량 문제와 그 해결 　　　정답률 64% | 정답 ②

주어진 글 다음에 이어질 글의 순서로 가장 적절한 것을 고르시오.

① (A) – (C) – (B)
② (B) – (A) – (C)
③ (B) – (C) – (A)
④ (C) – (A) – (B)
⑤ (C) – (B) – (A)

With nearly a billion hungry people in the world, / there is obviously no single cause.
전 세계에 거의 10억 명의 굶주리는 사람들이 있는데, / 분명 원인이 단 하나만 있는 것은 아니다.

(B) However, / far and away the biggest cause is poverty.
그렇지만, / 가장 큰 원인은 단연 빈곤이다.

Seventy-nine percent of the world's hungry / live in nations / that are net exporters of food.
세계의 굶주리는 사람들의 79퍼센트가 / 나라에 살고 있다. / 식량 순 수출국인

How can this be?
어떻게 이럴 수가 있을까?

(A) The reason people are hungry in those countries / is / that the products produced there
/ can be sold on the world market for more / than the local citizens can afford to pay for
them.
그러한 국가에서 사람들이 굶주리는 이유는 / ~이다. / 그곳에서 생산된 산물들이 / 세계 시장에서 더 비싸게 팔릴 수 있기 때문이
다. / 현지 시민들이 그것들에 지불할 수 있는 것보다

In the modern age / you do not starve because you have no food, / you starve because you
have no money.
현대에는 / 여러분이 식량이 없어서 굶주리는 것이 아니라, / 여러분은 돈이 없어서 굶주리는 것이다.

(C) So the problem really is / that food is, in the grand scheme of things, too expensive /
and many people are too poor to buy it.
그래서 진짜 문제는 ~이다. / 식량이 거대한 체계로 볼 때 너무 비싸고 / 많은 사람들은 너무 가난하여 그것을 구매할 수 없다는 것

The answer will be / in continuing the trend of lowering the cost of food.
해답은 있을 것이다. / 식량의 가격을 낮추는 추세를 지속하는 데

전 세계에 거의 10억 명의 굶주리는 사람들이 있는데, 분명 원인이 단 하나만 있는 것은 아니다.

(B) 그렇지만, 가장 큰 원인은 단연 빈곤이다. 세계의 굶주리는 사람들의 79퍼센트가 식량 순 수출국에 살고 있다. 어떻게 이럴 수가 있을까?

(A) 그러한 국가에서 사람들이 굶주리는 이유는 그곳에서 생산된 산물들이 현지 시민들이 그것들에 지불할 수 있는 것보다 더 비싸게 세계 시장에서 팔릴 수 있기 때문이다. 현대에는 여러분이 식량이 없어서 굶주리는 것이 아니라, 돈이 없어서 굶주리는 것이다.

(C) 그래서 진짜 문제는 거대한 체계로 볼 때 식량이 너무 비싸고 많은 사람들은 너무 가난하여 그것을 구매할 수 없다는 것이다. 해답은 식량의 가격을 낮추는 추세를 지속하는 데 있을 것이다.

Why? 왜 정답일까?

식량 문제의 원인이 다양함을 언급하는 주어진 글 뒤로, 빈곤이 가장 큰 원인임을 제시하는 (B), 빈곤한 국가의 굶주리는 사람들은 말 그대로 돈이 없어서 굶주린다는 설명을 이어 가는 (A), 해결책을 언급하며 글을 맺는 (C)가 차례로 이어져야 한다. 따라서 글의 순서로 가장 적절한 것은 ② '(B) – (A) – (C)'이다.

- **billion** ⓝ 10억
- **afford to** ~할 여유가 되다
- **poverty** ⓝ 가난, 빈곤
- **obviously** ⓐⓓ 분명히
- **starve** ⓥ 굶주리다

3행 The reason (that) people are hungry in those countries is that the
주어 / 생략 / 동사(단수)← / 접속사(~것)
products produced there can be sold on the world market for more than the local
조동사 수동태(조동사+be p.p.)
citizens can afford to pay for them.

★★★ 등급을 가르는 문제!

37 생산성이 최악인 시간에 오히려 더 발휘되는 창의성 　정답률 44% | 정답 ⑤

주어진 글 다음에 이어질 글의 순서로 가장 적절한 것을 고르시오. [3점]

① (A) - (C) - (B)　　　　② (B) - (A) - (C)
③ (B) - (C) - (A)　　　　④ (C) - (A) - (B)
⑤ (C) - (B) - (A)

Most people have a perfect time of day / when they feel they are at their best, / whether in the morning, evening, or afternoon.
대부분의 사람들은 완벽한 시간을 갖는다. / 하루 중 그들이 최고의 상태에 있다고 느끼는 / 아침이든 저녁이든 혹은 오후든

(C) Some of us are night owls, / some early birds, / and others in between / may feel most active during the afternoon hours.
우리 중 몇몇은 저녁형 인간이고, / 몇몇은 아침형 인간이며, / 그 사이에 있는 누군가는 / 오후의 시간 동안 가장 활력을 느낄지도 모른다.

If you are able to organize your day / and divide your work, / make it a point / to deal with tasks that demand attention / at your best time of the day.
여러분이 하루를 계획할 수 있다면 / 그리고 업무를 분배할 / ~하기로 정하라. / 집중을 요구하는 과업을 처리하기로 / 하루 중 최적의 시간에

(B) However, / if the task you face demands creativity and novel ideas, / it's best to tackle it / at your "worst" time of day!
그러나, / 만약 여러분이 직면한 과업이 창의성과 새로운 아이디어를 요구한다면, / 처리하는 것이 최선이다! / 하루 중 '최악의' 시간에

So if you are an early bird, / make sure to attack your creative task in the evening, / and vice versa for night owls.
그래서 만약 여러분이 아침형 인간이라면 / 반드시 저녁에 창의적인 작업에 착수하고, / 저녁형 인간이라면 반대로 하라.

(A) When your mind and body / are less alert at your "peak" hours, / the muse of creativity awakens / and is allowed to roam more freely.
여러분의 정신과 신체가 / '정점' 시간보다 주의력이 덜할 때, / 창의성의 영감이 깨어나 / 더 자유롭게 거니는 것이 허용된다.

In other words, / when your mental machinery is loose / rather than standing at attention, / the creativity flows.
다시 말해서, / 여러분의 정신 기제가 느슨하게 풀려있을 때 / 차렷 자세로 있을 때보다 / 창의성이 샘솟는다.

대부분의 사람들은 아침이든 저녁이든 혹은 오후든, 하루 중 그들이 최고의 상태에 있다고 느끼는 완벽한 시간을 갖는다.

(C) 우리 중 몇몇은 저녁형 인간이고, 몇몇은 아침형 인간이며, 그 사이에 있는 누군가는 오후의 시간 동안 가장 활력을 느낄지도 모른다. 여러분이 하루를 계획하고 업무를 분배할 수 있다면, 집중을 요구하는 과업을 하루 중 최적의 시간에 처리하기로 정하라.

(B) 그러나, 만약 여러분이 직면한 과업이 창의성과 새로운 아이디어를 요구한다면, 하루 중 '최악의' 시간에 처리하는 것이 최선이다! 그래서 만약 여러분이 아침형 인간이라면 반드시 저녁에 창의적인 작업에 착수하고, 저녁형 인간이라면 반대로 하라.

(A) 여러분의 정신과 신체가 '정점' 시간보다 주의력이 덜할 때, 창의성의 영감이 깨어나 더 자유롭게 거니는 것이 허용된다. 다시 말해서, 여러분의 정신 기제가 차렷 자세로 있을 때보다(힘과 긴장이 바짝 들어가 있을 때보다) 느슨하게 풀려있을 때 창의성이 샘솟는다.

Why? 왜 정답일까?
사람들에게는 자기 신체와 잘 맞는 시간이 있다고 언급하는 주어진 글 뒤로, 집중력이 필요한 과업은 최적의 시간대에 처리해야 한다는 (C), '반면에' 창의성이 필요한 과업은 최악의 시간대에 처리하는 것이 좋다는 (B), 그 이유를 보충 설명하는 (A)가 연결되어야 자연스럽다. 따라서 글의 순서로 가장 적절한 것은 ⑤ 'C) - (B) - (A)'이다.

● **whether A or B** A이든 B이든
● **stand at attention** 차렷 자세를 취하다
● **tackle** ⓥ 해결하다, 처리하다, 다루다
● **vice versa** 그 반대도 같다
● **make it a point to** ~하기로 정하다, 으레 ~하다
● **loose** ⓐ 느슨한
● **novel** ⓐ 새로운, 신기한
● **early bird** 아침형 인간
● **night owl** 저녁형 인간

11행 Some of us are night owls, some (are) early birds, and others in between
주어1 / 주어2(여럿 중 일부) / 생략(중복) / 주어3(또 다른 일부)
may feel most active during the afternoon hours.

★★ 문제 해결 꿀~팁 ★★

▶ 많이 틀린 이유는?
(C) - (A)를 잘못 연결하기 쉽지만, (C)는 '정점' 시간에 수행할 과업(= 집중력이 필요한 일)을 언급하는 반면 (A)는 정점 시간이 '아닐' 때 수행할 과업(= 창의력이 필요한 일)을 언급한다. 즉 두 단락은 다루는 소재가 다르므로 적절한 흐름 전환의 연결어가 없으면 연결될 수 없다.

▶ 문제 해결 방법은?
하루 중 최적의 시간대가 개인마다 다르다는 주어진 글 뒤로, 누구는 아침이 좋고, 또 누구는 밤이 좋으니 각자 정점의 시간마다 집중력이 필요한 일을 처리하는 것이 좋다는 (C)가 먼저 연결된다. 즉 주어진 글과 (C)는 '일반적 내용 - 구체적 사례'의 흐름으로 자연스럽게 연결된다. 이어서 (A), (B)는 모두 (C)와는 달리 '창의력 과업을 수행하기 좋은 시간대'에 관한 내용인데, 이렇듯 흐름이나 소재가 달라질 때는 역접어가 있는 단락을 먼저 연결해야 한다. 따라서 (B) - (A)의 순서가 적합하다.

★★★ 등급을 가르는 문제!

38 사회적 활동 시간을 줄이는 텔레비전 　정답률 47% | 정답 ④

글의 흐름으로 보아, 주어진 문장이 들어가기에 가장 적절한 곳을 고르시오.

Television is the number one leisure activity / in the United States and Europe, / consuming more than half of our free time.
텔레비전은 제1의 여가활동으로, / 미국과 유럽에서, / 우리의 자유 시간 중 절반 이상을 소비한다.

① We generally think of television / as a way to relax, tune out, and escape from our troubles / for a bit each day.
일반적으로 우리는 텔레비전을 취급한다. / 휴식하고, 관심을 끄고, 우리의 문제로부터 탈출하는 한 가지 방법으로서 / 매일 잠시나마

② While this is true, / there is increasing evidence / that we are more motivated / to tune in to our favorite shows and characters / when we are feeling lonely / or have a greater need for social connection.
이것이 사실이긴 하지만, / 증거가 늘어나고 있다. / 우리가 동기가 더 부여된다는 / 우리가 좋아하는 쇼들과 등장인물들을 보려는 / 우리가 외롭다고 느끼고 있거나 / 사회적 관계를 위한 더 큰 욕구를 가질 때

③ Television watching does satisfy these social needs / to some extent, / at least in the short run.
텔레비전을 보는 것이 이러한 사회적인 욕구를 정말로 만족시킨다. / 어느 정도까지는 / 적어도 단기적으로는

✓ Unfortunately, / it is also likely to "crowd out" other activities / that produce more sustainable social contributions to our social well-being.
불행히도, / 그것은 또한 다른 활동들을 '몰아내기' 쉽다. / 우리의 사회적 행복에 더 지속적인 사회적 기여를 만들어 내는

The more television we watch, / the less likely we are / to volunteer our time / or to spend time with / in our social networks.
텔레비전을 더 많이 볼수록, / 우리는 가능성이 더 적다. / 우리의 시간을 기꺼이 할애하거나 / 사람들과 함께 시간을 보낼 / 사회적 관계망 속에서

⑤ In other words, / the more time we make for *Friends*, / the less time we have for friends in real life.
다시 말해서, / 우리가 *Friends*를 위해 더 많은 시간을 낼수록, / 우리는 실제 친구들을 위한 시간을 덜 갖게 된다.

텔레비전은 미국과 유럽에서 제1의 여가활동으로, 우리의 자유시간 중 절반 이상을 소비한다. ① 일반적으로 우리는 휴식하고, 관심을 끄고, 매일 잠시나마 우리의 문제로부터 탈출하는 한 가지 방법으로서 텔레비전을 취급한다. ② 이것이 사실이긴 하지만, 우리가 외롭다고 느끼고 있거나 사회적 관계를 위한 더 큰 욕구를 가질 때 우리가 좋아하는 쇼들과 등장인물들을 보려는 동기가 더 부여된다는 증거가 늘어나고 있다. ③ 적어도 단기적으로는, 텔레비전을 보는 것이 이러한 사회적인 욕구를 어느 정도까지는 정말로 만족시킨다. ④ 불행히도, 그것은 또한 우리의 사회적 행복에 더 지속적인 사회적 기여를 만들어 내는 다른 활동들을 '몰아내기' 쉽다. 텔레비전을 더 많이 볼수록, 우리는 사회적 관계망 속에서 우리의 시간을 기꺼이 할애하거나 사람들과 함께 시간을 보낼 가능성이 더 적다. ⑤ 다시 말해서, 우리가 *Friends*를 위해 더 많은 시간을 낼수록, 실제 친구들을 위한 시간은 덜 갖게 된다.

Why? 왜 정답일까?
주어진 문장에 역접어인 Unfortunately가 있으므로, 글의 흐름이 갑자기 반전되는 지점에 주어진 문장이 들어갈 것이다. ④ 앞에서 텔레비전은 어느 정도 사회적 욕구 충족에 도움이 된다고 하는데, ④ 뒤에서는 갑자기 텔레비전을 볼수록 사회적 활동 시간이 줄어든다고 한다. 즉 ④ 앞뒤로 글의 논리적 흐름이 단절되는 것으로 보아, 주어진 문장이 들어가기에 가장 적절한 곳은 ④이다.

● **crowd out** 몰아내다
● **leisure** ⓝ 여가, 레저
● **tune in to** ~에 채널을 맞추다
● **sustainable** ⓐ 지속 가능한
● **tune out** 주의를 돌리다, 관심을 끄다
● **in the short run** 단기적으로

5행 We generally think of television as a way to relax, tune out, and escape
「think of + A + as + B : A를 B로 여기다」 / 형용사적 용법(a way 수식)
from our troubles for a bit each day.

★★ 문제 해결 꿀~팁 ★★

▶ 많이 틀린 이유는?
가장 헷갈리는 ③ 앞뒤를 보면, 먼저 ③ 앞에서 우리가 사회적 욕구를 충족하고 싶을 때 TV를 보고 싶어 한다고 언급한 후, ③ 뒤는 실제로 TV 시청이 '어느 정도는' 사회적 욕구 충족에 도움이 된다고 설명하고 있다. 즉 ③ 앞에 제시된 내용을 ③ 뒤에서 일부 긍정하는 흐름이므로, '일반적 사실-보충 설명'의 흐름이 적절하게 연결된다.

▶ 문제 해결 방법은?
정답인 ④ 앞은 TV가 사회적 욕구 충족에 적어도 단기적으로 도움을 준다는 내용인데, ④ 뒤의 두 문장은 모두 TV 시청을 하다 보면 실생활에서 친구를 사귀려는 노력이 덜해진다는 내용이다. 즉 ④ 앞뒤로 서로 반대되는 내용이 제시되지만 역접어가 등장하지 않는데, 주어진 문장을 보면 이 논리적 공백을 메꿔줄 역접어(Unfortunately)가 있다.

★★★ 등급을 가르는 문제!

39 정확한 온도 측정 　정답률 42% | 정답 ⑤

글의 흐름으로 보아, 주어진 문장이 들어가기에 가장 적절한 곳을 고르시오. [3점]

We often associate the concept of temperature / with how hot or cold an object feels / when we touch it.
우리는 흔히 온도 개념을 연관 짓는다. / 얼마나 뜨겁게 또는 차갑게 느껴지는지와 / 우리가 물건을 만졌을 때

In this way, / our senses provide us / with a qualitative indication of temperature.
이런 식으로, / 우리의 감각은 우리에게 제공한다. / 온도의 정성적 지표를

① Our senses, / however, / are unreliable / and often mislead us.
우리의 감각은 / 그러나, / 신뢰할 수 없으며 / 종종 우리를 잘못 인도한다.

② For example, / if you stand in bare feet / with one foot on carpet / and the other on a tile floor, / the tile feels colder than the carpet / *even though both are at the same temperature.*
예를 들어, / 여러분이 맨발로 서서 / 한쪽 발은 카펫 위에, / 다른 한쪽 발은 타일 바닥 위에 놓고, / 카펫보다 타일이 더 차갑게 느껴질 것이다. / 둘 다 같은 온도임에도 불구하고

③ The two objects feel different / because tile transfers energy by heat / at a higher rate than carpet does.
그 두 물체는 다르게 느껴진다. / 타일이 에너지를 열의 형태로 전달하기 때문에 / 카펫보다 더 높은 비율로

④ Your skin "measures" the rate of energy transfer by heat / rather than the actual temperature.
여러분의 피부는 열에너지 전도율을 '측정'한다. / 실제 온도보다는

✓ What we need / is a reliable and reproducible method / for measuring the relative hotness or coldness of objects / rather than the rate of energy transfer.

우리가 필요로 하는 것은 / 신뢰할 수 있고 재현 가능한 수단이다. / 물체의 상대적인 뜨거움과 차가움을 측정하기 위한 / 에너지 전도율보다는

Scientists have developed a variety of thermometers / for making such quantitative measurements.
과학자들은 다양한 온도계를 개발해 왔다. / 그런 정량적인 측정을 하기 위해

우리는 흔히 물건을 만졌을 때 얼마나 뜨겁게 또는 차갑게 느껴지는지를 온도 개념과 연관 짓는다. 이런 식으로, 우리의 감각은 우리에게 온도의 정성적 지표를 제공한다. ① 그러나, 우리의 감각은 신뢰할 수 없으며 종종 우리를 잘못 인도한다. ② 예를 들어, 여러분이 맨발로 한쪽 발은 카펫 위에, 다른 한쪽 발은 타일 바닥 위에 놓고 서 있다면, 둘 다 같은 온도임에도 불구하고 타일이 더 차갑게 느껴질 것이다. ③ 타일이 카펫보다 더 높은 비율로 에너지를 열의 형태로 전달하기 때문에 그 두 물체는 다르게 느껴진다. ④ 여러분의 피부는 실제 온도보다는 열에너지 전도율을 '측정한다'. ⑤ 우리가 필요로 하는 것은 에너지 전도율보다는 물체의 상대적인 뜨거움과 차가움을 측정하기 위한 신뢰할 수 있고 재현 가능한 수단이다. 과학자들은 그런 정량적인 측정을 하기 위해 다양한 온도계를 개발해 왔다.

Why? 왜 정답일까?

우리의 감각이 온도에 대한 정성적 지표를 제공하기는 하지만 완전히 정확한 정보를 주지는 못한다는 내용의 글로, ⑤ 앞의 문장은 이것이 피부가 실제 온도보다는 열에너지 전도율을 측정하기 때문이라고 설명한다. 한편 주어진 문장에서는 이 상황에서 우리에게 필요한 것이 상대적 온도를 신뢰 높게 측정할 수 있는 도구라고 언급하고, ⑤ 뒤에서는 이 도구가 바로 정량적 측정이 가능한 온도계라고 밝힌다. 따라서 주어진 문장이 들어가기에 가장 적절한 곳은 ⑤이다.

- reproducible ⓐ 재현 가능한
- qualitative ⓐ 정성적인, 질적인
- bare ⓐ 맨, 벌거벗은
- energy transfer 에너지 전도
- mislead ⓥ 잘못 이끌다
- quantitative ⓐ 정량적인

구문 풀이

10행 The two objects feel different because tile transfers energy by heat at a
　　　　　　　감각동사↙　　　　형용사 보어
higher rate than carpet does.
　　　　　대동사(= transfers)

★★ 문제 해결 꿀~팁 ★★

▶ 많이 틀린 이유는?
③, ④가 헷갈리므로 하나씩 살펴보자. 먼저 ③ 앞은 서로 온도가 같은 타일과 카펫이 '다르게' 느껴진다는 예를 드는데, ③ 뒤는 그것이 '열에너지 전도율의 차이' 때문이라고 설명한다. 이어서 ④ 뒤도 우리 피부가 실제 온도보다는 '열에너지 전도율'에 집중한다고 한다. 즉, ③~④ 앞뒤 문장들은 지시어나 연결어의 공백 없이 모두 자연스럽게 연결된다.

▶ 문제 해결 방법은?
⑤ 앞에서 우리가 측정하는 것이 '열에너지 전도율'이라고 언급한 데 이어, 주어진 문장은 '이것 말고 우리에게 실제 필요한 것'이 무엇인지 언급하고 있다. 그것이 바로 주어진 문장에서 언급한, '물체의 상대적 온도를 신뢰성 있게 측정할 수 있는 수단'인데, ⑤ 뒤에서는 '그래서' 온도계가 개발되었다는 결론을 제시하고 있다.

★★★ 등급을 가르는 문제!

40 기부하도록 설득하기　　　　　　정답률 43% | 정답 ①

다음 글의 내용을 한 문장으로 요약하고자 한다. 빈칸 (A), (B)에 들어갈 말로 가장 적절한 것은?

	(A)		(B)		(A)		(B)
✓①	simultaneously 동시에	……	convinced 설득될	②	separately 따로	……	confused 혼란을 느낄
③	frequently 자주	……	annoyed 짜증을 낼	④	separately 따로	……	satisfied 만족할
⑤	simultaneously 동시에	……	offended 기분 상할				

My colleagues and I ran an experiment / testing two different messages / meant to convince thousands of resistant alumni to make a donation.
내 동료들과 나는 한 연구를 진행했다. / 두 개의 다른 메시지들을 실험하는 / 저항하는 졸업생 수천 명에게 기부하도록 설득할 의도로 작성된

One message emphasized the opportunity to do good: / donating would benefit students, faculty, and staff.
하나의 메시지는 좋은 일을 할 기회를 강조했다. / '기부하는 것은 학생들, 교직원, 그리고 직원들에게 이익을 줄 것이다.'

The other emphasized the opportunity to feel good: / donors would enjoy the warm glow of giving.
다른 하나는 좋은 기분을 느끼는 기회를 강조했다. / '기부자들은 기부의 따뜻한 온기를 즐길 것이다.'

The two messages were equally effective: / in both cases, / 6.5 percent of the unwilling alumni ended up donating.
두 메시지들은 똑같이 효과적이었다. / 두 경우 모두, / 마음 내키지 않았던 졸업생 6.5%가 결국에는 기부했다.

Then we combined them, / because two reasons are better than one. // Except they weren't.
그러고 나서 우리는 그것들을 결합했는데, / 두 개 이유가 한 개보다 더 낫기 때문이었다. // 안 그럴 경우를 제외한다면 말이다.

When we put the two reasons together, / the giving rate dropped below 3 percent.
우리가 두 이유를 합쳤을 때, / 기부율은 3% 아래로 떨어졌다.

Each reason alone / was more than twice as effective / as the two combined.
각각의 이유를 따로 봤을 때 / 두 배 이상 효과적이었다 / 둘을 합친 것보다

The audience was already skeptical.
청중은 이미 회의적이었다.

When we gave them different kinds of reasons to donate, / we triggered their awareness / that someone was trying to persuade them / — and they shielded themselves against it.
우리가 그들에게 기부해야 할 다양한 이유를 주었을 때, / 우리는 그들이 인식하게 했고 / 누군가가 그들을 설득하려고 하는 중이라고 / 그리고 그들은 그것에 맞서 스스로를 보호했다.

➡ In the experiment mentioned above, / when the two different reasons to donate / were given (A) simultaneously, / the audience was less likely to be (B) convinced / because they could recognize the intention / to persuade them.
위에 언급된 실험에서, / 기부할 이유 두 가지가 / 동시에 주어졌을 때, / 청중들은 설득될 가능성이 더 적었는데, / 그들이 의도를 인식했기 때문이었다. / 그들을 설득하려는

내 동료들과 나는 (기부에) 저항하는 졸업생 수천 명이 기부하도록 설득할 의도로 작성된 두 개의 다른 메시지들을 실험하는 한 연구를 진행했다. 하나의 메시지는 좋은 일을 할 기회를

강조했다. '기부하는 것은 학생들, 교직원, 그리고 직원들에게 이익을 줄 것이다.' 다른 하나는 좋은 기분을 느끼는 기회를 강조했다. '기부자들은 기부의 따뜻한 온기를 즐길 것이다.' 두 메시지들은 똑같이 효과적이었다. 두 경우 모두에서, 마음 내키지 않았던 졸업생 6.5%가 결국에는 기부했다. 그러고 나서 우리는 그것들을 결합했는데, 두 개 이유가 한 개보다 더 낫기 때문이었다. 안 그럴 경우를 제외한다면 말이다. 우리가 두 이유를 합쳤을 때, 기부율은 3% 아래로 떨어졌다. 각각의 이유를 따로 봤을 때 둘을 합친 것보다 두 배 이상 효과적이었다. 청중은 이미 회의적이었다. 우리가 그들에게 기부해야 할 다양한 이유를 주었을 때, 우리는 그들이 누군가가 그들을 설득하려고 하는 중이라고 인식하게 했고 — 그리고 그들은 그것에 맞서 스스로를 보호했다.

➡ 위에 언급된 실험에서, 기부할 이유 두 가지가 (A) 동시에 주어졌을 때, 청중들은 (B) 설득될 가능성이 더 적었는데, 그들을 설득하려는 의도를 인식했기 때문이었다.

Why? 왜 정답일까?

실험 결과를 제시하는 마지막 문장에서, 기부해야 할 여러 이유를 한꺼번에 주면 청중들은 이미 기부를 해달라고 설득하려는 화자의 의도를 알아차리기 때문에 더 방어적이 된다고 한다. 따라서 요약문의 빈칸 (A), (B)에 들어갈 말로 가장 적절한 것은 ① 'A) simultaneously(동시에), (B) convinced(설득될)'이다.

- make a donation 기부하다
- faculty ⓝ 교직원
- end up ~ing 결국 ~하다
- trigger ⓥ 유발하다
- benefit ⓥ ~에게 이득이 되다
- glow ⓝ 빛, (기쁨이나 만족감을 동반한) 감정
- put together 합치다
- simultaneously ⓐⓓ 동시에

구문 풀이

11행 Each reason alone was more than twice as effective as the two combined.
「배수사 + as + 원급 + as : 몇 배 더 ~한」

★★ 문제 해결 꿀~팁 ★★

▶ 많이 틀린 이유는?
마지막 문장에서 두 가지 다른 이유를 '한꺼번에' 주었을 때 사람들은 기부를 권유하는 이면의 의도를 더 잘 읽었기 때문에 오히려 기부에 더 회의적인 태도를 보였다고 한다. ②와 ④는 공통적으로 (A)에 separately가 있는데, 이는 이유를 '따로' 주었다는 의미를 완성하므로, 실험의 핵심 결과와 모순된다.

▶ 문제 해결 방법은?
①의 (A)는 본문의 combined와 together를, (B)는 마지막 문장의 persuade를 재진술한 표현이다.

41-42 곤충 섭취에 대한 태도 바꾸기

In a society / that rejects the consumption of insects / there are some individuals / who overcome this rejection, / but most will continue with this attitude.
사회에서는 / 곤충 섭취를 거부하는 / 몇몇 개인들이 있지만, / 이러한 거부를 극복한 / 대부분 이러한 태도를 지속할 것이다.

It may be very (a) difficult / to convince an entire society / that insects are totally suitable for consumption.
매우 어려울지도 모른다. / 전체 사회에 납득시키기는 / 곤충이 섭취에 완전히 적합하다는 것을

However, / there are examples / in which this (b) reversal of attitudes about certain foods / has happened to an entire society.
하지만, / 사례들이 있다. / 특정 음식에 대한 이러한 태도의 역전이 / 전체 사회에 발생한

Several examples in the past 120 years from European-American society / are: / considering lobster a luxury food / instead of a food for servants and prisoners; / considering sushi a safe and delicious food; / and considering pizza / not just a food for the rural poor of Sicily.
지난 120년 간 유럽-아메리카 사회로부터의 몇몇 사례는 / ~이다. / 로브스터를 고급진 음식으로 여기는 것, / 하인과 죄수용 음식 대신에 / 초밥을 안전하고 맛있는 음식으로 여기는 것, / 그리고 피자를 여기는 것이다. / 단지 시칠리아 시골의 가난한 사람들이 먹는 음식이 아니라고

In Latin American countries, / where insects are already consumed, / a portion of the population hates their consumption / and (c) associates it with poverty.
라틴 아메리카 국가들에서는 / 곤충이 이미 섭취되는 / 일부 인구는 곤충 섭취를 싫어하며, / 이를 빈곤과 연관 짓는다.

There are also examples of people / who have had the habit of consuming them / and (d) abandoned that habit due to shame, / and 「because they do not want to be categorized / as poor or uncivilized.」 42번의 근거
또한 사람들의 사례들도 있다. / 그것을 섭취하는 습관이 있었으나 / 수치심 때문에 그 습관을 버린 / 그리고 분류되고 싶지 않아서 / 가난하거나 미개하다고

「According to Esther Katz, an anthropologist, / if the consumption of insects as a food luxury / is to be promoted, / there would be more chances / that some individuals who do not present this habit / overcome ideas / under which they were educated.」
인류학자인 Esther Katz에 따르면, / 만약 호사스러운 음식으로서의 곤충 섭취가 / 장려된다면, / 가능성이 더 커질 것이다. / 이러한 습관을 보이지 않는 몇몇 개인들이 / 생각을 극복할 / 자신이 교육받았던

And this could also help / to (e) revalue the consumption of insects / by those people who already eat them.」 41번의 근거
그리고 이것은 또한 도움을 줄 수 있다. / 곤충 섭취를 재평가하는 데에도 / 이미 곤충을 먹고 있는 사람들에 의한

곤충 섭취를 거부하는 사회에서는 이러한 거부를 극복한 몇몇 개인들이 있지만, 대부분은 이러한 태도를 지속할 것이다. 곤충이 섭취에 완전히 적합하다는 것을 전체 사회에 납득시키기는 매우 (a) 어려울지도 모른다. 하지만, 특정 음식에 대한 이러한 태도의 (b) 역전이 전체 사회에 발생한 사례들이 있다. 지난 120년 간 유럽-아메리카 사회로부터의 몇몇 사례는 로브스터를 하인과 죄수용 음식 대신에 고급진 음식으로 여기는 것, 초밥을 안전하고 맛있는 음식으로 여기는 것, 그리고 피자를 단지 시칠리아 시골의 가난한 사람들이 먹는 음식으로 여기지 않는 것이다. 곤충이 이미 섭취되는 라틴 아메리카 국가들에서는 일부 인구는 곤충 섭취를 싫어하며, 이를 빈곤과 (c) 연관 짓는다. 또한 그것을 섭취하는 습관이 있었으나 수치심 때문에, 그리고 가난하거나 미개하다고 분류되고 싶지 않아서 그 습관을 (d) 권장한(→ 버린) 사람들의 사례들도 있다. 인류학자인 Esther Katz에 따르면, 만약 호사스러운 음식으로서의 곤충 섭취가 장려된다면, 이러한 습관을 보이지 않는 몇몇 개인들이 자신이 교육받았던 생각을 극복할 가능성이 더 커질 것이다. 그리고 이것은 또한 이미 곤충을 먹고 있는 사람들에 의한 곤충 섭취를 (e) 재평가하는 데에도 도움을 줄 수 있다.

- consumption ⓝ 섭취, 소비
- convince ⓥ 납득시키다, 설득하다
- prisoner ⓝ 죄수
- associate A with B A와 B를 연관 짓다
- categorize A as B A를 B라고 분류하다
- promote ⓥ 장려하다, 촉진하다, 홍보하다
- shortage ⓝ 부족
- overcome ⓥ 극복하다
- suitable for ~에 적합한
- rural ⓐ 시골의
- shame ⓝ 수치심
- anthropologist ⓝ 인류학자
- edible ⓐ 먹을 수 있는

---

41 제목 파악　　　　　　　　　　　　　정답률 56% | 정답 ②

윗글의 제목으로 가장 적절한 것은?
① The More Variety on the Table, The Healthier You Become
　식탁에 놓인 음식 종류가 다양할수록, 더 건강해진다
✓ Edible or Not? Change Your Perspectives on Insects
　먹을 수 있는가, 없는가? 곤충에 대한 당신의 관점을 바꾸라
③ Insects: A Key to Solve the World Food Shortage
　곤충: 세계 식량 부족을 해결하는 열쇠
④ Don't Let Uniqueness in Food Culture Disappear
　식문화의 고유성이 사라지게 내버려두지 말라
⑤ Experiencing Various Cultures by Food
　음식으로 다양한 문화 경험하기

Why? 왜 정답일까?

곤충 섭취에 대한 부정적 태도가 바뀐 사례나, 반대로 부정적 인식 때문에 곤충 섭취 습관을 포기했던 사례를 언급한 후, 이 부정적 태도를 전환할 방법을 제시하는 글이다. 따라서 글의 제목으로 가장 적절한 것은 ② '먹을 수 있는가, 없는가? 곤충에 대한 당신의 관점을 바꾸라'이다.

---

42 어휘 추론　　　　　　　　　　　　　정답률 56% | 정답 ④

밑줄 친 (a) ~ (e) 중에서 문맥상 낱말의 쓰임이 적절하지 않은 것은?
① (a)　　② (b)　　③ (c)　　✓ (d)　　⑤ (e)

Why? 왜 정답일까?

(d) 뒤의 '~ due to shame, and because they do not want to be categorized as poor or uncivilized.'는 곤충을 섭취하던 사람들이 수치심이나, 가난 또는 미개한 사람들로 분류되고 싶지 않은 마음 때문에 이 습관을 '포기했음'을 설명하는 것이므로, (d)의 encouraged를 abandoned로 고쳐야 한다. 따라서 문맥상 낱말의 쓰임이 적절하지 않은 것은 ④ '(d)'이다.

43-45 손자에게 최고의 학교를 찾아주려 한 할아버지

(A)

A boy had a place at the best school in town.
한 소년이 마을에 있는 가장 좋은 학교에 한 자리를 얻었다.
In the morning, / his granddad took him to the school.
아침에 / 그의 할아버지는 그를 학교에 데리고 갔다.
When (a) he went onto the playground with his grandson, / the children surrounded them.
그가 손자와 함께 운동장으로 들어갔을 때, / 아이들이 그들을 둘러쌌다.
"What a funny old man," / one boy smirked.
"진짜 우스꽝스러운 할아버지."라며 / 한 소년이 히죽히죽 웃었다.
『A girl with brown hair / pointed at the pair / and jumped up and down.』 45번 ①의 근거 일치
갈색 머리 소녀가 / 그 둘에게 손가락질하며 / 위아래로 뛰었다.
Suddenly, / the bell rang / and the children ran off to their first lesson.
갑자기 / 종이 울렸고, / 아이들이 첫 수업에 급히 뛰어갔다.

(D)

The old man took his grandson firmly by the hand, / and led him out of the school gate.
노인은 손자의 손을 꽉 잡고, / 그를 교문 밖으로 데리고 나갔다.
『"Brilliant, I don't have to go to school!" / the boy exclaimed.』 45번 ⑤의 근거 일치
"굉장한걸, 나 학교에 가지 않아도 되네!"라고 / 소년이 소리쳤다.
"You do, but not this one," / his granddad replied. / "I'll find you a school myself."
"가긴 가야지, 그렇지만 이 학교는 아니야."라고 / 할아버지가 대답했다. / "내가 직접 네게 학교를 찾아주마."
Granddad took his grandson back to his own house, / asked grandma to look after him, / and went off to look for a teacher (e) himself.
할아버지는 손자를 집으로 데리고 돌아가 / 할머니에게 그를 돌봐달라고 하고 나서, / 자신이 선생님을 찾아 나섰다.
Every time he spotted a school, / the old man went onto the playground, / and waited for the children to come out at break time.
그가 학교를 발견할 때마다, / 노인은 운동장으로 들어가서 / 아이들이 쉬는 시간에 나오기를 기다렸다.

(B)

In some schools / the children completely ignored the old man / and in others, / they made fun of (b) him.
몇몇 학교에서는 / 아이들이 노인을 완전히 무시했고, / 다른 학교들에서는 / 아이들이 그를 놀렸다.
When this happened, / he would turn sadly and go home.
이런 일이 일어났을 때, / 그는 슬프게 돌아서서 집으로 가곤 했다.
『Finally, / he went onto the tiny playground of a very small school, / and leant against the fence, / exhausted.』 45번 ②의 근거 일치
마침내, / 그는 매우 작은 한 학교의 아주 작은 운동장으로 들어섰고, / 울타리에 기댔다, / 지쳐서
The bell rang, / and the crowd of children ran out onto the playground.
종이 울렸고, / 아이들 무리가 운동장으로 달려 나왔다.
"Sir, are you all right? / Shall I bring you a glass of water?" / a voice said.
"할아버지, 괜찮으세요? / 물 한 잔 가져다드릴까요?" / 누군가가 말했다.
"We've got a bench in the playground / — come and sit down," / another voice said.
"우리 운동장에 벤치가 있어요, / 오셔서 앉으세요." / 또 다른 누군가가 말했다.
Soon a young teacher came out onto the playground.
곧 한 젊은 선생님이 운동장으로 나왔다.

(C)

The old man greeted (c) him and said: / "Finally, I've found my grandson the best school in town."
노인은 그에게 인사하면서 이렇게 말했다. / "마침내, 제가 손자에게 마을 최고의 학교를 찾아주었어요."
"You're mistaken, sir. / Our school is not the best / — it's small and cramped."
"잘못 아신 겁니다, 어르신. / 우리 학교는 최고가 아니에요. / 작고 비좁은걸요."
『The old man didn't argue with the teacher.』 45번 ③의 근거 불일치
노인은 선생님과 논쟁을 벌이지 않았다.
Instead, / he made arrangements / for his grandson to join the school, / and then the old man left.
대신, / 노인은 준비해주고, / 손자가 그 학교에 다닐 수 있도록 / 그런 다음 그 노인은 떠났다.
That evening, / the boy's mom said to (d) him: / "Dad, you can't even read. / How do you know / you've found the best teacher of all?" 45번 ④의 근거 일치
그날 저녁, / 소년의 어머니는 그에게 말했다. / "아버지, 글을 읽을 줄도 모르시잖아요. / 아버지는 어떻게 아세요? / 최고의 선생님을 찾았다는 것을"
"Judge a teacher by his pupils," / the old man replied.
"선생님은 그 제자를 보고 판단해야 해."라고 / 노인이 대답했다.

(A)

한 소년이 마을에 있는 가장 좋은 학교에 한 자리를 얻었다. 아침에 그의 할아버지는 그를 학교에 데리고 갔다. (a) 그가 손자와 함께 운동장으로 들어갔을 때, 아이들이 그들을 둘러쌌다. "진짜 우스꽝스러운 할아버지."라며 한 소년이 히죽히죽 웃었다. 갈색 머리 소녀가 그 둘에게 손가락질하며 위아래로 뛰었다. 갑자기 종이 울렸고, 아이들이 첫 수업에 급히 뛰어갔다.

(D)

노인은 손자의 손을 꽉 잡고, 그를 교문 밖으로 데리고 나갔다. "굉장한걸, 나 학교에 가지 않아도 되네!"라고 소년이 소리쳤다. "가긴 가야지, 그렇지만 이 학교는 아니야."라고 할아버지가 대답했다. "내가 직접 네게 학교를 찾아주마." 할아버지는 손자를 집으로 데리고 돌아가 할머니에게 그를 돌봐달라고 하고 나서, (e) 자신이 선생님을 찾아 나섰다. 학교를 발견할 때마다, 노인은 운동장으로 들어가서 아이들이 쉬는 시간에 나오기를 기다렸다.

(B)

몇몇 학교에서는 아이들이 노인을 완전히 무시했고, 다른 학교들에서는 아이들이 (b) 그를 놀렸다. 이런 일이 일어났을 때, 그는 슬프게 돌아서서 집으로 가곤 했다. 마침내, 그는 매우 작은 한 학교의 아주 작은 운동장으로 들어섰고, 지쳐서 울타리에 기댔다. 종이 울렸고, 아이들 무리가 운동장으로 달려 나왔다. "할아버지, 괜찮으세요? 물 한 잔 가져다드릴까요?" 누군가가 말했다. "우리 운동장에 벤치가 있어요, 오셔서 앉으세요." 또 다른 누군가가 말했다. 곧 한 젊은 선생님이 운동장으로 나왔다.

(C)

노인은 (c) 그에게 인사하면서 이렇게 말했다. "마침내, 제가 손자에게 마을 최고의 학교를 찾아주었네요." "잘못 아신 겁니다, 어르신. 우리 학교는 최고가 아니에요. 작고 비좁은걸요." 노인은 선생님과 논쟁을 벌이지 않았다. 대신, 노인은 손자가 그 학교에 다닐 수 있도록 준비해주고, 그런 다음 떠났다. 그날 저녁, 소년의 어머니는 (d) 그에게 말했다. "아버지, 글을 읽을 줄도 모르시잖아요. 최고의 선생님을 찾았다는 것을 어떻게 아세요?" "선생님은 그 제자를 보고 판단해야 해."라고 노인이 대답했다.

- grandson ⓝ 손자
- run off to ~로 뛰어가다, 달아나다
- make fun of ~을 조롱하다
- lean against ~에 기대다
- You are mistaken. 잘못 생각하고 계세요, 오해예요.
- make arrangements for ~을 준비하다
- firmly ⓐⓓ 단단히, 꽉
- look after ~을 돌보다
- surround ⓥ 둘러싸다, 에워싸다
- ignore ⓥ 무시하다
- tiny ⓐ 아주 작은
- exhausted ⓐ 지친, 소진된
- pupil ⓝ 학생, 제자
- exclaim ⓥ 소리치다, 외치다
- spot ⓥ 찾다, 발견하다

---

43 글의 순서 파악　　　　　　　　　　　정답률 69% | 정답 ④

주어진 글 (A)에 이어질 내용을 순서에 맞게 배열한 것으로 가장 적절한 것은?
① (B) – (D) – (C)　　　　　　② (C) – (B) – (D)
③ (C) – (D) – (B)　　　　　　✓ (D) – (B) – (C)
⑤ (D) – (C) – (B)

Why? 왜 정답일까?

한 할아버지가 손자를 데리고 마을 최고의 학교로 갔다가 아이들에게 놀림을 받았다는 내용의 (A) 뒤에는, 할아버지가 손자를 집에 데려다 놓고 직접 다른 학교를 찾아나섰다는 내용의 (D), 할아버지가 어느 예의 바른 아이들 무리와 선생님을 만나게 되었다는 내용의 (B), 할아버지가 학교를 결정했고, 그 결정이 어떻게 내려진 것인지 결론 짓는 내용의 (C)가 차례로 연결되어야 한다. 따라서 글의 순서로 가장 적절한 것은 ④ '(D) – (B) – (C)'이다.

---

44 지칭 추론　　　　　　　　　　　　　정답률 69% | 정답 ③

밑줄 친 (a) ~ (e) 중에서 가리키는 대상이 나머지 넷과 다른 것은?
① (a)　　② (b)　　✓ (c)　　④ (d)　　⑤ (e)

Why? 왜 정답일까?

(a), (b), (d), (e)는 the old man[grandad], (c)는 a young teacher를 가리키므로, (a) ~ (e) 중에서 가리키는 대상이 다른 하나는 ③ '(c)'이다.

윗글에 관한 내용으로 적절하지 않은 것은?

① 갈색 머리 소녀가 노인과 소년을 향해 손가락질했다.
② 노인은 지쳐서 울타리에 기댔다.
✓③ 노인은 선생님과 논쟁을 벌였다.
④ 노인은 글을 읽을 줄 몰랐다.
⑤ 소년은 학교에 가지 않아도 된다고 소리쳤다.

Why? 왜 정답일까?

(C) 'The old man didn't argue with the teacher.'에서 노인은 선생님과 논쟁을 벌이지 않았다고 하므로, 내용과 일치하지 않는 것은 ③ '노인은 선생님과 논쟁을 벌였다.'이다.

Why? 왜 오답일까?

① (A) 'A girl with brown hair pointed at the pair and jumped up and down.'의 내용과 일치한다.
② (B) '~ leant against the fence, exhausted.'의 내용과 일치한다.
④ (C) 'Dad, you can't even read.'의 내용과 일치한다.
⑤ (D) '"Brilliant, I don't have to go to school!" the boy exclaimed.'의 내용과 일치한다.

어휘 Review Test 13　　　　　　　　　　　문제편 130쪽

A		B		C	D
01	보호자	01	dynamics	01 ①	01 ⓗ
02	주의를 돌리다, 관심을 끄다	02	temporary	02 ⑨	02 ⓜ
03	빠른	03	shortage	03 ⓚ	03 ⓚ
04	밀봉한	04	close	04 ⓑ	04 ①
05	길들이다	05	smoothly	05 ⓜ	05 ⓑ
06	부연 설명하다, 자세히 말하다	06	entrepreneur	06 ①	06 ①
07	연결하다, 장착하다	07	spot	07 ⓝ	07 ⓢ
08	번식, 재생	08	dissatisfied	08 ⓐ	08 ⓠ
09	끌어내다, 도출하다	09	comprise	09 ⓒ	09 ⓡ
10	기준	10	endurance	10 ⓞ	10 ⓓ
11	(형편이) 나쁜, 우호적이지 않은	11	shrink	11 ⓟ	11 ⓐ
12	지표	12	unknown	12 ⓡ	12 ⓝ
13	의존	13	contain	13 ⓢ	13 ⓞ
14	굶주리다	14	ingredient	14 ⓠ	14 ⓒ
15	느슨한	15	groundless	15 ①	15 ①
16	제도적인, 기관의	16	surround	16 ⓗ	16 ⓟ
17	분명히	17	consumption	17 ⓔ	17 ①
18	지속 가능한	18	benefit	18 ①	18 ⑨
19	유발하다	19	measure	19 ①	19 ⓔ
20	먹을 수 있는	20	prevail	20 ⓓ	20 ①

14회 | 2021학년도 9월 학력평가　　고1

| 정답과 해설 |

· 정답 ·

18 ② 19 ⑤ 20 ③ 21 ⑤ 22 ⑤ 23 ① 24 ④ 25 ④ 26 ⑤ 27 ② 28 ⑤ 29 ② 30 ④ 31 ① 32 ⑤
33 ① 34 ⑤ 35 ④ 36 ⑤ 37 ④ 38 ③ 39 ② 40 ① 41 ② 42 ④ 43 ④ 44 ② 45 ④

★ 표기된 문항은 [등급을 가르는 문제]에 해당하는 문항입니다.

18　식당 연례행사 초대　　　　　　　　정답률 90% | 정답 ②

다음 글의 목적으로 가장 적절한 것은?

① 식당 개업을 홍보하려고
✓② 식당의 연례행사에 초대하려고
③ 신입 요리사 채용을 공고하려고
④ 매장 직원의 실수를 사과하려고
⑤ 식당 만족도 조사 참여를 부탁하려고

Dear Mr. Dennis Brown,
Dennis Brown씨께,
We at G&D Restaurant are honored and delighted / to invite you to our annual Fall Dinner.
우리 G&D 식당은 영광이고 기쁩니다. / 우리의 연례행사인 Fall Dinner에 당신을 초대하게 되어
The annual event will be held / on October 1st, 2021 at our restaurant.
그 연례행사는 열릴 것입니다. / 2021년 10월 1일에 우리 식당에서
At the event, / we will be introducing new wonderful dishes / that our restaurant will be offering soon.
그 행사에서, / 우리는 새로운 멋진 음식들을 소개할 것입니다. / 우리 식당이 곧 제공할
These delicious dishes will showcase / the amazing talents of our gifted chefs.
이 맛있는 음식들은 보여줄 것입니다. / 우리의 뛰어난 요리사들의 멋진 재능을
Also, our chefs will be providing cooking tips, / ideas on what to buy for your kitchen, / and special recipes.
또한, 우리의 요리사들은 요리 비법들을 제공할 것입니다. / 당신의 주방을 위해 무엇을 사야 할지에 대한 생각들, / 그리고 특별한 요리법을
We at G&D Restaurant would be more than grateful / if you can make it to this special occasion / and be part of our celebration.
우리 G&D 식당은 매우 감사할 것입니다. / 만약에 당신이 이 특별한 행사에 와서 / 축하의 일원이 되어준다면
We look forward to seeing you.
우리는 당신을 곧 뵙기를 고대합니다.
Thank you so much.
매우 감사합니다.
Regards, // Marcus Lee, Owner - G&D Restaurant
G&D 식당 주인, Marcus Lee 드림

Dennis Brown씨께,

우리 G&D 식당은 우리의 연례행사인 Fall Dinner에 당신을 초대하게 되어 영광이고 기쁩니다. 그 연례행사는 2021년 10월 1일에 우리 식당에서 열릴 것입니다. 그 행사에서, 우리는 우리 식당이 곧 제공할 새로운 멋진 음식들을 소개합니다. 이 맛있는 음식들은 우리의 뛰어난 요리사들의 멋진 재능을 보여줄 것입니다. 또한, 우리의 요리사들은 요리 비법들과 당신의 주방을 위해 무엇을 사야 할지에 대한 생각들, 그리고 특별한 요리법을 제공할 것입니다. 우리 G&D 식당은 만약에 당신이 이 특별한 행사에 와서 축하의 일원이 되어준다면 매우 감사할 것입니다. 우리는 당신을 곧 뵙기를 고대합니다. 매우 감사합니다.

G&D 식당 주인, Marcus Lee 드림

Why? 왜 정답일까?

'We at G&D Restaurant are honored and delighted to invite you to our annual Fall Dinner.'에서 식당 연례행사에 초대하게 되어 영광이라고 언급한 뒤, 후반부에서 행사의 일원이 되어주기를 거듭 당부하고 있다. 따라서 글의 목적으로 가장 적절한 것은 ② '식당의 연례행사에 초대하려고'이다.

● delighted ⓐ 기쁜　　　　　　　● annual ⓐ 연례의
● gifted ⓐ 재능 있는　　　　　　● grateful ⓐ 고마워하는
● celebration ⓝ 기념, 축하　　　● look forward to ~하기를 고대하다

구문 풀이

7행　Also, our chefs will be providing cooking tips, ideas on what to buy for your kitchen, and special recipes.
동사(미래진행) / 목적어1 / 목적어2 / 「what+to부정사 : 무엇을 ~할지」 / 목적어3

19　누군가 방에 들어와서 겁 먹은 Matt　　　정답률 89% | 정답 ⑤

다음 글의 상황에 나타난 분위기로 가장 적절한 것은?

① humorous and fun – 웃기고 재미있는
② boring and dull – 지루하고 따분한
③ calm and peaceful – 평온하고 평화로운
④ noisy and exciting – 시끄럽고 신나는
✓⑤ mysterious and frightening – 수상하고 무서운

In the middle of the night, / Matt suddenly awakened.
한밤중에, / Matt는 갑자기 잠에서 깼다.
He glanced at his clock.
그는 그의 시계를 흘긋 보았다.
It was 3:23.
3시 23분이었다.
For just an instant / he wondered what had wakened him.
잠시 동안 / 그는 무엇이 그를 깨웠는지 궁금했다.
Then he remembered.
그때 그는 기억했다.
He had heard someone come into his room.
그는 누군가 그의 방에 들어오는 것을 들었다.

누군가가 자기 방에 들어오는 소리를 들었다는 것을.

Matt sat up in bed, / rubbed his eyes, / and looked around the small room.
Matt은 침대에 꼿꼿이 앉아 / 그의 눈을 비비고 / 작은 방을 둘러보았다.

"Mom?" he said quietly, / hoping he would hear his mother's voice / assuring him that everything was all right.
"엄마?" 그는 조용히 말했다. / 그가 엄마의 목소리를 듣기를 바라면서 / 모든 것이 괜찮다고 그에게 확신을 주는

But there was no answer.
그런데 답이 없었다.

Matt tried to tell himself / that he was just hearing things.
Matt은 스스로에게 말하려 했다. / 자신이 방금 물건 소리를 들은 것이라고

But he knew he wasn't.
그런데 그는 그렇지 않았다는 것을 알았다.

There was someone in his room.
그의 방에는 누군가가 있었다.

He could hear rhythmic, scratchy breathing / and it wasn't his own.
그는 규칙적으로 긁는 듯한 숨소리를 들을 수 있었고, / 그것은 자신의 것이 아니었다.

He lay awake for the rest of the night.
그는 남은 밤 동안 깬 상태로 누워있었다.

한밤중에 Matt는 갑자기 잠에서 깼다. 그는 시계를 흘긋 보았다. 3시 23분이었다. 잠시 동안 그는 무엇이 그를 깨웠는지 궁금했다. 그때 그는 기억했다. 누군가가 자기 방에 들어오는 소리를 들었다는 것을. Matt는 침대에 꼿꼿이 앉아 눈을 비비고 작은 방을 둘러보았다. "엄마?" 그는 모든 것이 괜찮다고 그에게 확신을 주는 엄마의 목소리가 들리기를 바라면서 조용히 말했다. 그런데 답이 없었다. Matt는 자신이 방금 물건 소리를 들은 것이라고 스스로에게 말하려 했다. 그런데 그는 그렇지 않았다는 것을 알았다. 그의 방에는 누군가가 있었다. 그는 규칙적으로 긁는 듯한 숨소리를 들을 수 있었고, 그것은 자신의 것이 아니었다. 그는 남은 밤 동안 깬 상태로 누워있었다.

Why? 왜 정답일까?

한밤중에 누군가 방으로 들어오는 소리를 듣고 잠에서 깬 Matt가 다시 누군가의 숨소리를 듣고 겁에 질려 남은 밤 동안 잠을 이루지 못했다는 내용의 글이다. 따라서 글의 분위기로 가장 적절한 것은 ⑤ '수상하고 무서운'이다.

- glance at ~을 흘긋 보다
- assure ⓥ 확신시키다
- frightening ⓐ 무서운, 겁먹게 하는
- rub ⓥ 비비다
- scratchy ⓐ 긁는 듯한 소리가 나는

구문 풀이

5행 "Mom?" he said quietly, hoping he would hear his mother's voice
　　　　　　　　　　　　　분사구문
assuring him that everything was all right.
「assure + A + B : A에게 B를 확신시키다」

---

20 독자들을 능동적으로 생각하게 하며 글쓰기 　　 정답률 81% | 정답 ③

다음 글에서 필자가 주장하는 바로 가장 적절한 것은?
① 저자의 독창적인 견해를 드러내야 한다.
② 다양한 표현으로 독자에게 감동을 주어야 한다.
✓ 독자가 능동적으로 사고할 수 있도록 글을 써야 한다.
④ 독자에게 가치판단의 기준점을 명확히 제시해야 한다.
⑤ 주관적 관점을 배제하고 사실을 바탕으로 글을 써야 한다.

As you set about to write, / it is worth reminding yourself / that while you ought to have a point of view, / you should avoid telling your readers what to think.
당신이 글을 쓰려고 할 때, / 스스로 상기할 가치가 있다. / 당신은 관점을 가져야 하는 한편, / 당신은 독자에게 무엇을 생각할지 말하는 것을 피해야 한다고

Try to hang a question mark over it all.
그것 전체에 물음표를 달기 위해 노력해라.

This way you allow your readers / to think for themselves / about the points and arguments you're making.
이런 방식으로 당신은 독자들이 ~할 수 있게 만든다. / 스스로 생각하게 / 당신의 요점과 주장들에 대해

As a result, / they will feel more involved, / finding themselves just as committed / to the arguments you've made / and the insights you've exposed / as you are.
결과적으로 / 독자들은 좀 더 열중하는 느낌을 받게 될 것이다. / 딱 그렇게 몰입되는 자신을 발견하면서, / 당신이 한 주장과 / 당신이 드러내는 통찰력에 / 당신만큼이나

You will have written an essay / that not only avoids passivity in the reader, / but is interesting and gets people to think.
당신은 글을 쓰게 될 것이다. / 독자들의 수동성을 피하면서도 / 흥미롭고 사람들을 생각하게 만드는

당신이 글을 쓰려고 할 때, 당신의 관점을 가져야 하는 한편, 독자에게 무엇을 생각할지 말하는 것을 피해야 한다고 스스로 상기할 가치가 있다. (논점) 전체에 물음표를 달기 위해 노력해라. 이런 방식으로 당신은 독자들이 당신의 요점과 주장들에 대해 스스로 생각할 수 있게 만든다. 결과적으로 독자들은 당신만큼이나 당신이 한 주장과 당신이 드러내는 통찰력에 몰입되는 자신을 발견하면서, 좀 더 열중하는 느낌을 받게 될 것이다. 당신은 독자들의 수동성을 피하면서도 흥미롭고 사람들을 생각하게 만드는 글을 쓰게 될 것이다.

Why? 왜 정답일까?

명령문인 'Try to hang a question mark over it all.' 이후로 논점을 물음 형태로 제시하면 독자들이 필자의 견해에 관해 스스로 생각해 보게 유도할 수 있다고 한다. 따라서 필자가 주장하는 바로 가장 적절한 것은 ③ '독자가 능동적으로 사고할 수 있도록 글을 써야 한다.'이다.

- be worth ~ing ~할 가치가 있다
- insight ⓝ 통찰력
- committed to ~에 몰입하는, 열중하는
- passivity ⓝ 수동성

구문 풀이

1행 As you set about to write, it is worth reminding yourself {that (while you
　　　　　　　　　　　　　　　　　　　「be worth + 동명사 : ~할 가치가 있다」
ought to have a point of view), you should avoid telling your readers what to
　　　　　　　　　　　　　　　( ) : 부사절
think}.[ ] : 명사절

★★★ 등급을 가르는 문제!

21 더러움의 정의 　　 정답률 40% | 정답 ⑤

밑줄 친 "matter out of place"가 다음 글에서 의미하는 바로 가장 적절한 것은?
① something that is completely broken – 완전히 부서진 물건
② a tiny dust that nobody notices – 아무도 눈치채지 못하는 아주 작은 먼지
③ a dirty but renewable material – 더럽지만 복구할 수 있는 물체
④ what can be easily replaced – 쉽게 대체될 수 있는 것
✓ a thing that is not in order – 정돈되지 않은 것

Nothing is trash by nature.
어떤 것도 본래부터 쓰레기인 것은 없다.

Anthropologist Mary Douglas / brings back and analyzes the common saying / that dirt is "matter out of place."
인류학자 Mary Douglas는 / 흔히 하는 말을 다시 가져와 해석했다. / 더러운 것은 "제자리에 놓여있지 않은 물체"라는

Dirt is relative, / she emphasizes.
더러운 것은 상대적이다. / 그녀가 강조하기로

"Shoes are not dirty in themselves, / but it is dirty to place them on the dining-table; / food is not dirty in itself, / but it is dirty to leave pots and pans in the bedroom, / or food all over clothing; / similarly, / bathroom items in the living room; / clothing lying on chairs; / outdoor things placed indoors; / upstairs things downstairs, and so on."
"신발은 그 자체로는 더럽지 않지만, / 그러나 식탁 위에 놓여 있을 때 더러운 것이며, / 음식은 그 자체로는 더럽지 않지만, / 그러나 침실에 냄비와 팬을 놓아둔다면 더럽다. / 혹은 음식이 옷에 다 묻어 있을 때 / 마찬가지로, / 거실에 있는 욕실 용품, / 의자 위에 놓여 있는 옷, / 실내에 있는 실외 물품들, / 아래층에 있는 위층 물건들 등등."

Sorting the dirty from the clean — / removing the shoes from the table, / putting the dirty clothing in the washing machine — / involves systematic ordering and classifying.
깨끗한 것과 더러운 것을 분류하는 것은 / 식탁에서 신발을 치우는 것, / 세탁기에 더러운 옷을 넣는 것 / 체계적인 정리와 분류를 포함하는 것이다.

Eliminating dirt is thus a positive process.
그러므로 더러운 것을 제거하는 것은 긍정적인 과정이다.

어떤 것도 본래부터 쓰레기인 것은 없다. 인류학자 Mary Douglas는 더러운 것은 "제자리에 놓여있지 않은 물체"라는 흔히 하는 말을 다시 가져와 해석했다. 그녀가 강조하기로, 더러운 것은 상대적이다. "신발은 그 자체로는 더럽지 않지만, 식탁 위에 놓여 있을 때 더러운 것이며, 음식은 그 자체로는 더럽지 않지만, 침실에 냄비와 팬을 놓아둔다면, 혹은 음식이 옷에 다 묻어 있을 때 더럽다. 마찬가지로 거실에 있는 욕실 용품, 의자 위에 놓여 있는 옷, 실내에 있는 실외 물품들, 아래층에 있는 위층 물건들 등등이 더럽다." 깨끗한 것과 더러운 것을 분류하는 것, 즉 식탁에서 신발을 치우는 것, 세탁기에 더러운 옷을 넣는 것은 체계적인 정리와 분류를 포함하는 것이다. 그러므로 더러운 것을 제거하는 것은 긍정적인 과정이다.

Why? 왜 정답일까?

세 번째 문장에서 더러운 것은 상대적(Dirt is relative, ~)이라고 언급한 후, 이어지는 예시를 통해 식탁 위에 놓여있는 신발, 침실에 놓여 있거나 옷에 묻어 있는 음식, 거실에 있는 욕실 용품 등 있어야 할 자리에 있지 않은 물건들이 더러운 것이라고 설명하고 있다. 따라서 밑줄 친 부분의 의미로 가장 적절한 것은 ⑤ '정돈되지 않은 것'이다.

- by nature 본래, 천성적으로
- analyze ⓥ 분석하다
- relative ⓐ 상대적인
- in oneself 그 자체로
- eliminate ⓥ 제거하다, 없애다
- in order 정돈된, 적절한
- anthropologist ⓝ 인류학자
- out of place 제자리에 있지 않은
- emphasize ⓥ 강조하다
- sort ⓥ 분류하다, 나누다
- renewable ⓐ 복구 가능한

구문 풀이

3행 Dirt is relative, she emphasizes.
　　　목적어(강조를 위해 도치)　주어　　동사

★★ 문제 해결 꿀~팁 ★★

▶ 많이 틀린 이유는?
'더러운' 것이 무엇인지 정의하는 내용이므로 dirty를 포함한 ③이 오답으로 많이 나왔다. 하지만 글에서 더러움의 복구 가능성(renewable)에 관해서는 언급되지 않는다.

▶ 문제 해결 방법은?
직접인용구의 예시에서 엉뚱한 자리에 있는 물건을 열거하고 있고, out of place와 not in order가 둘 다 '제자리에 있지 않은, 정돈되지 않은' 등의 의미를 나타내므로 ⑤가 답으로 가장 적절하다.

---

22 자신의 의견을 때때로 내려놓기 　　 정답률 60% | 정답 ⑤

다음 글의 요지로 가장 적절한 것은?
① 대부분의 사람들은 진리에 도달하지 못하고 고통을 받는다.
② 맹목적으로 다른 사람의 의견을 받아들이는 것은 위험하다.
③ 남을 설득하기 위해서는 타당한 증거로 주장을 뒷받침해야 한다.
④ 믿을만한 사람이 누구인지 판단하려면 열린 마음을 가져야 한다.
✓ 자신의 의견이 최선이 아닐 수 있다는 것을 인정하는 것이 필요하다.

It's important / that you think independently / and fight for what you believe in, / but there comes a time / when it's wiser / to stop fighting for your view / and move on to accepting / what a trustworthy group of people think is best.
중요하지만, / 여러분이 독자적으로 생각하는 / 그리고 자신이 믿는 것을 위해 싸우는 것도 / 그러나 때가 온다. / 더 현명한 / 자신의 생각을 위해 싸우기를 중단하고 / 받아들이는 쪽으로 나아 가는 것이 / 신뢰할 수 있는 집단이 가장 좋다고 생각하는 것을

This can be extremely difficult.
이것은 매우 어려울 수 있다.

But it's smarter, and ultimately better / for you to be open-minded and have faith / that the conclusions of a trustworthy group of people / are better than whatever you think.
하지만 더 영리하고 그리고 궁극적으로 더 좋다. / 여러분이 마음을 열고 믿음을 갖는 것이 / 신뢰할 수 있는 집단의 결론이 / 여러분이 생각하는 어떤 것보다 낫다는

If you can't understand their view, / you're probably just blind to their way of thinking.
만약 여러분이 그들의 생각을 이해할 수 없다면, / 여러분은 아마도 단지 그들이 생각하는 방식을 보지 못하는 것이다.

14회

[문제편 p.131]

[14회] 2021학년도 9월　133

If you continue doing what you think is best / when all the evidence and trustworthy people are against you, / you're being dangerously confident.
당신이 최선이라고 생각하는 것을 계속한다면, / 모든 증거와 신뢰할 수 있는 사람들이 당신에게 반대할 때 / 당신은 위험할 정도로 자신감에 차 있는 것이다.

The truth is / that while most people can become incredibly open-minded, / some can't, / even after they have repeatedly encountered lots of pain / from betting that they were right / when they were not.
사실은 / 대부분의 사람들은 놀랍도록 마음을 열게 되는 반면에, / 어떤 사람들은 그러지 못한다. / 그들이 여러 차례 많은 고통을 겪고 난 후에도 / 자신이 옳았다고 확신하는 것으로부터 / 자신이 옳지 않았을 때

독자적으로 생각하고 자신이 믿는 것을 위해 싸우는 것도 중요하지만, 자신의 생각을 위해 싸우기를 중단하고 신뢰할 수 있는 집단이 가장 좋다고 생각하는 것을 받아들이는 쪽으로 나아 가는 것이 더 현명한 때가 온다. 이것은 매우 어려울 수 있다. 하지만 여러분이 마음을 열고 신뢰할 수 있는 집단의 결론이 여러분이 생각하는 어떤 것보다 낫다는 믿음을 갖는 것이 더 영리하고 궁극적으로 더 좋다. 만약 여러분이 그들의 생각을 이해할 수 없다면, 여러분은 아마도 단지 그들이 생각하는 방식을 보지 못하는 것이다. 모든 증거와 신뢰할 수 있는 사람 들이 당신에게 반대할 때 당신이 최선이라고 생각하는 것을 계속한다면, 당신은 위험할 정도 로 자신감에 차 있는 것이다. 사실 대부분의 사람들은 놀랍도록 마음을 열게 되는 반면에, 어 떤 사람들은 자신이 옳지 않았을 때 옳았다고 확신하는 것으로부터 여러 차례 많은 고통을 겪고 난 후에도 그러지 못한다.

첫 문장과 세 번째 문장에서 때로는 자신의 의견보다 다른 의견이 더 낫다는 것을 받아들이는 것이 좋다 (~ it's wiser to ~ move on to accepting what a trustworthy group of people think is best.)고 언급하는 것으로 볼 때, 글의 요지로 가장 적절한 것은 ⑤ '자신의 의견이 최선이 아닐 수 있 다는 것을 인정하는 것이 필요하다.'이다.

- independently [ad] 독자적으로
- trustworthy [a] 믿을 만한
- ultimately [ad] 결국, 궁극적으로
- faith [n] 믿음
- whatever [pron] ~한 어떤 것
- evidence [n] 증거, 단서
- confident [a] 자신 있는
- repeatedly [ad] 반복해서, 되풀이하여
- bet [v] ~이 틀림없다, 분명하다(무엇에 대해 거의 확신함을 나타냄)
- wiser [a] 지혜로운, 현명한
- extremely [ad] 몹시, 극도로
- open-minded [a] 마음이 열린
- conclusion [n] 결론, (최종적인) 판단
- blind to ~을 보지 못하게 만들다
- against [prep] ~에 반대하여
- incredibly [ad] 놀랍도록, 엄청나게
- encounter [v] 접하다, 마주하다

5행 But it's smarter, and ultimately better for you to be open-minded and
(가주어 / 의미상 주어 / 진주어구)
have faith {that the conclusions of a trustworthy group of people are better than
(주어(복수) / 동사)
whatever you think}. { } : 동격절(= faith)
(복합관계대명사(~하는 무엇이든))

23 젊은이들이 채식을 선택하는 이유
정답률 74% | 정답 ①

다음 글의 주제로 가장 적절한 것은?
✓① reasons why young people go for vegetarian diets – 젊은 사람들이 채식주의 식단을 선택하는 이유
② ways to build healthy eating habits for teenagers – 십 대들이 건강한 식습관을 기르는 방법
③ vegetables that help lower your risk of cancer – 암 위험을 낮추는 데 도움이 되는 채소
④ importance of maintaining a balanced diet – 균형 잡힌 식습관 유지의 중요성
⑤ disadvantages of plant-based diets – 식물 중심 식단의 단점

Vegetarian eating is moving into the mainstream / as more and more young adults say no to meat, poultry, and fish.
채식은 주류가 되어가고 있다. / 점점 더 많은 젊은이들이 고기, 가금류, 생선에 반대함에 따라

According to the American Dietetic Association, / "approximately planned vegetarian diets / are healthful, / are nutritionally adequate, / and provide health benefits / in the prevention and treatment of certain diseases."
American Dietetic Association에 따르면, / '대략적으로 계획된 채식 식단이 / 건강에 좋고, / 영양학적으로도 적당하고, / 건강상의 이점을 제공한다. / 특정한 질병을 예방하고 치료하는 데'

But health concerns are not the only reason / that young adults give for changing their diets.
그러나 건강에 대한 염려만이 유일한 이유는 아니다. / 젊은이들이 식단을 바꾸려고 하는

Some make the choice / out of concern for animal rights.
몇몇은 선택한다. / 동물의 권리에 대한 관심 때문에

When faced with the statistics / that show / the majority of animals / raised as food / live in confinement, / many teens give up meat / to protest those conditions.
통계자료를 볼 때, / 보여주는 / 대다수의 동물들이 / 음식으로 길러지는 / 갇혀서 산다는 것을 / 많은 십 대들은 고기를 포기한다. / 그러한 상황에 저항하기 위해

Others turn to vegetarianism / to support the environment.
다른 사람들은 채식주의자가 된다. / 환경을 지지하기 위해

Meat production uses vast amounts of water, land, grain, and energy / and creates problems / with animal waste and resulting pollution.
고기를 생산하는 것은 거대한 양의 물, 땅, 곡식과 에너지를 사용하고 / 문제들을 만들어낸다. / 가축에서 나오는 쓰레기와 그에 따른 오염과 같은

채식은 점점 더 많은 젊은이들이 고기, 가금류, 생선에 반대함에 따라 주류가 되어가고 있다. American Dietetic Association에 따르면, '대략적으로 계획된 채식 식단이 건강에 좋고, 영양 학적으로도 적당하고, 특정한 질병을 예방하고 치료하는 데 건강상의 이점을 제공한다.' 그 러나 건강에 대한 염려만이 젊은이들이 식단을 바꾸려고 하는 유일한 이유는 아니다. 몇몇은 동물의 권리에 관심 때문에 선택한다. 음식으로 길러지는 대다수의 동물들이 갇혀서 산 다는 것을 보여주는 통계자료를 볼 때, 많은 십 대들은 그러한 상황에 저항하기 위해 고기를 포기한다. 다른 사람들은 환경을 지지하기 위해 채식주의자가 된다. 고기를 생산하는 것은 거대한 양의 물, 땅, 곡식과 에너지를 사용하고 가축에서 나오는 쓰레기와 그에 따른 오염과 같은 문제들을 만들어낸다.

글 초반부에서 젊은이들은 건강상의 이유로 채식주의 식단을 선택한다는 내용이 제시된 후, 'But

---

health concerns are not the only reason ~'부터는 환경적인 이유 또한 이러한 선택의 근거라 는 내용이 제시된다. 따라서 글의 주제로 가장 적절한 것은 ① '젊은 사람들이 채식주의 식단을 선택하는 이유'이다.

- vegetarian [a] 채식의
- healthful [a] 건강에 좋은
- adequate [a] 적절한, 충분한
- treatment [n] 치료
- statistics [n] 통계 자료, 통계학
- protest [v] 항의하다
- vast [a] 방대한
- approximately [ad] 대략적으로
- nutritionally [ad] 영양적으로
- prevention [n] 예방
- concern [n] 관심, 우려
- confinement [n] 가둠, 감금
- turn to ~로 바뀌다, ~에 의지하다
- disadvantage [n] 불리한 점, 단점

8행 When faced with the statistics [that show (that) the majority of animals
(접속사 / 분사구문 / 선행사 / 주격 관·대 / (생략) / 주어)
(raised as food) live in confinement], many teens give up meat to protest those
(과거분사 / 동사 / 주어 / 동사 / 부사적 용법(목적))
conditions.

24 문제와 갈등에서 나오는 창의성
정답률 50% | 정답 ④

다음 글의 제목으로 가장 적절한 것은?
① Technology: A Lens to the Future – 기술: 미래를 보는 렌즈
② Diversity: A Key to Social Unification – 다양성: 사회적 통합의 핵심
③ Simple Ways to Avoid Conflicts with Others – 다른 사람들과의 갈등을 피하는 간단한 방법
✓④ Creativity Doesn't Come from Playing It Safe – 창의성은 위험을 피하는 것에서 근원하지 않는다
⑤ There Are No Challenges That Can't Be Overcome – 극복되지 못할 어려움은 없다

Diversity, challenge, and conflict / help us maintain our imagination.
다양성, 어려움, 그리고 갈등은 / 우리의 상상력을 유지하게 도와준다.

Most people assume / that conflict is bad / and that being in one's "comfort zone" is good.
대부분의 사람들은 생각한다. / 갈등은 나쁜 것이고 / '편안한 구역'에 머무는 것이 좋은 것이라고

That is not exactly true.
그것은 정확히는 사실이 아니다.

Of course, / we don't want to find ourselves / without a job or medical insurance / or in a fight with our partner, family, boss, or coworkers.
물론, / 우리는 자신의 모습을 보고 싶어 하지 않는다. / 직장 또는 의료보험이 없거나, / 배우자, 가족, 직장 상사, 직장 동료들과의 다툼에 빠진

One bad experience can be sufficient / to last us a lifetime.
하나의 나쁜 경험이 충분할 수 있다. / 우리에게 평생 지속되는 데

But small disagreements with family and friends, / trouble with technology or finances, / or challenges at work and at home / can help us think through our own capabilities.
하지만 가족과 친구들과의 작은 의견 충돌, / 기술적 또는 재정적 문제, / 직장과 가정에서의 어려움이 / 우리의 능력에 대해 충분히 생각해보는 데 도움이 된다.

Problems that need solutions / force us to use our brains / in order to develop creative answers.
해결책이 필요한 문제들은 / 우리의 뇌를 사용하도록 강요한다. / 창의적인 해답을 개발하기 위해

Navigating landscapes / that are varied, / that offer trials and occasional conflicts, / is more helpful to creativity / than hanging out in landscapes / that pose no challenge to our senses and our minds.
지역을 걸어가는 것은 / 변화무쌍한 / 시련과 갈등을 주는, / 창의성에 더 도움을 준다. / 지역을 다니는 것보다 / 우리 감각과 마음에 아무런 어려움을 주지 않는

Our two million-year history is packed / with challenges and conflicts.
우리의 2백만년 역사는 가득 차 있다. / 어려움과 갈등으로

다양성, 어려움, 그리고 갈등은 우리의 상상력을 유지하게 도와준다. 대부분의 사람들은 갈 등은 나쁜 것이고 '편안한 구역'에 머무는 것이 좋은 것이라고 생각한다. 그것은 정확히는 사 실이 아니다. 물론, 우리는 직장 또는 의료보험이 없거나, 배우자, 가족, 직장 상사, 직장 동 료들과의 다툼에 빠진 자신의 모습을 보고 싶어 하지 않는다. 하나의 나쁜 경험이 우리에게 평생 지속되는 데 충분할 수 있다. 하지만 가족과 친구들과의 작은 의견 충돌, 기술적 또는 재정적 문제, 직장과 가정에서의 어려움이 우리의 능력에 대해 충분히 생각해보는 데 도움이 된다. 해결책이 필요한 문제들은 창의적인 해답들을 개발하기 위해 우리의 뇌를 사용하도록 강요한다. 시련과 갈등을 주는, 변화무쌍한 지역을 걸어가는 것은 우리 감각과 마음에 아무 런 어려움을 주지 않는 지역을 다니는 것보다 창의성에 더 도움을 준다. 우리의 2백만년 역 사는 어려움과 갈등으로 가득 차 있다.

첫 문장에 이어 But 뒤로 우리가 문제를 해결하고 창의성을 발현하도록 돕는 것은 우리 삶의 시련과 각종 문제(But small disagreements ~, trouble ~, or challenges ~ can help us think through our own capabilities.)라는 내용이 제시된다. 따라서 글의 제목으로 가장 적절한 것은 ④ '창의성은 위험을 피하는 것에서 근원하지 않는다'이다.

- conflict [n] 갈등
- medical insurance 의료 보험
- disagreement [n] 불화, 불일치
- capability [n] 능력
- varied [a] 다양한
- pose a challenge to ~에 어려움을 주다
- play safe 위험을 피하다, 신중을 기하다
- assume [v] 가정하다, 추정하다
- sufficient [a] 충분한
- think through ~에 대해 충분히 생각하다
- landscape [n] 풍경, 지역
- occasional [a] 이따금씩 일어나는
- be packed with ~로 가득 차다
- overcome [v] 극복하다

12행 Navigating landscapes [that are varied], [that offer trials and occasional
(주어(동명사구) / 주격 관·대1 / 주격 관·대2)
conflicts], is more helpful to creativity than hanging out in landscapes [that pose
(동사(단수) / 선행사 / 주격 관·대)
no challenge to our senses and our minds].

25 정보 출처별 소비자 신뢰도
정답률 76% | 정답 ④

다음 도표의 내용과 일치하지 않는 것은?

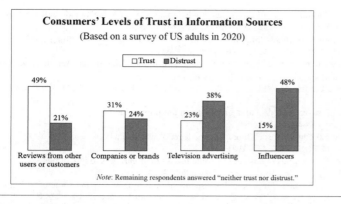

Consumers' Levels of Trust in Information Sources
(Based on a survey of US adults in 2020)

□Trust ■Distrust

- Reviews from other users or customers: 49% / 21%
- Companies or brands: 31% / 24%
- Television advertising: 23% / 38%
- Influencers: 15% / 48%

Note: Remaining respondents answered "neither trust nor distrust."

The graph above shows the consumers' levels of trust / in four different types of information sources, / based on a survey of US adults in 2020.
위 그래프는 소비자의 신뢰 정도를 보여준다. / 네 가지 다른 종류의 정보 출처들에 대한 / 2020년 미국 성인들을 대상으로 한 설문조사에 기반하여

① About half of US adults say / they trust the information / they receive from reviews from other users or customers.
미국 성인의 절반 정도가 말한다 / 그들이 정보를 믿는다고 / 그들이 다른 사용자들이나 고객들의 상품평에서 얻은

② This is more than double / those who say / they hold distrust for reviews from other users or customers.
이것은 두 배 이상이다 / 말하는 미국 성인들의 / 그들이 다른 사용자들이나 고객들의 상품평에 대해 불신을 갖는다고

③ The smallest gap / between the levels of trust and distrust / among the four different types of information sources / is shown in the companies or brands' graph.
가장 적은 차이는 / 신뢰와 불신 정도 사이의 / 네 가지 다른 종류의 정보 출처들 중에서 / 회사나 상표에서 보인다.

✔ Fewer than one-fifth of adults say / they trust information from television advertising, / outweighed by the share who distrust such information.
미국 성인의 1/5 미만이 말하는데 / 그들이 텔레비전 광고의 정보를 신뢰한다고 / 이는 그러한 정보를 불신하는 쪽의 수치에 의해 능가되었다

⑤ Only 15% of adults say / they trust the information provided by influencers, / while more than three times as many adults say / they distrust the same source of information.
미국 성인의 15%만 말하는데 / 그들이 인플루언서가 제공하는 정보를 신뢰한다고 / 반면에 이보다 세 배 이상 많은 수치의 미국 성인이 말한다 / 그들은 같은 정보 출처를 불신한다고

위 그래프는 2020년 미국 성인들을 대상으로 한 설문조사에 기반하여 네 가지 다른 종류의 정보 출처들에 대한 소비자의 신뢰 정도를 보여준다. ① 미국 성인의 절반 정도가 다른 사용자들이나 고객들의 상품평에서 얻은 정보를 믿는다고 말한다. ② 이것은 다른 사용자들이나 고객들의 상품평에 대해 불신을 갖는다고 말하는 미국 성인들의 두 배 이상이다. ③ 네 가지 다른 종류의 정보 출처들 중에서 신뢰와 불신 정도 사이의 가장 적은 차이는 회사나 상표에서 보인다. ④ 미국 성인의 1/5 미만이 텔레비전 광고의 정보를 신뢰한다고 말하는데, 그러한 정보를 불신하는 쪽의 수치가 이를 능가했다. ⑤ 미국 성인의 15%만 인플루언서가 제공하는 정보를 신뢰한다고 말하는데, 반면에 이보다 세 배 이상 많은 수치의 미국 성인이 같은 정보 출처를 불신한다고 말한다.

Why? 왜 정답일까?

도표에 따르면 텔레비전 광고로부터 얻는 정보를 신뢰한다고 답한 미국 성인은 23%로, 전체의 1/5을 넘는다. 따라서 도표와 일치하지 않는 것은 ④이다.

- distrust ⓝ 불신 ⓥ 불신하다
- A be outweighed by B A가 B보다 덜 중요하다, B가 A보다 더 크다

---

26 Paul Laurence Dunbar의 생애 정답률 63% | 정답 ⑤

Paul Laurence Dunbar에 관한 다음 글의 내용과 일치하지 <u>않는</u> 것은?
① 14세쯤에 *Dayton Herald*에 시를 발표했다.
② 고등학교 재학 시 학교 신문을 편집했다.
③ 재정상의 이유로 대학에 진학하지 못했다.
④ 두 번째 출판한 책으로 국내외에서 인정받게 되었다.
✔ 표준 영어로 쓴 시들로 가장 큰 주목을 받았다.

Paul Laurence Dunbar, an African-American poet, / was born on June 27, 1872.
아프리카계 미국인 시인인 Paul Laurence Dunbar는 / 1872년 6월 27일에 태어났다.

『By the age of fourteen, / Dunbar had poems published in the *Dayton Herald*.』 ①의근거 일치
14세 무렵 / Dunbar는 *Dayton Herald*에 시를 발표했다.

『While in high school / he edited his high school newspaper.』 ②의근거 일치
고등학교에 다닐 때 / 그는 학교 신문을 편집했다.

『Despite being a fine student, / Dunbar was financially unable to attend college / and took a job as an elevator operator.』 ③의근거 일치
훌륭한 학생이었음에도 / Dunbar는 재정상 대학에 갈 수 없었고 / 엘리베이터 운전자라는 직업을 가졌다.

In 1893, / Dunbar published his first book, *Oak and Ivy*, / at his own expense.
1893년 / Dunbar는 자신의 첫 번째 책인 *Oak and Ivy*를 출판했다. / 자비로

『In 1895, / he published the second book, *Majors and Minors*, / which brought him national and international recognition.』 ④의근거 일치
1895년, / 그는 두 번째 책인 *Majors and Minors*를 출판했고, / 이것은 그에게 국내외의 인정을 가져다주었다.

The poems written in standard English / were called "majors," / and those in dialect were termed "minors."
표준 영어로 쓴 시들은 / 'majors'라 불렸고, / 방언으로 쓴 시는 'minors'라 불렸다.

『Although the "major" poems in standard English / outnumber those written in dialect, / it was the dialect poems / that brought Dunbar the most attention.』 ⑤의근거 불일치
표준 영어로 쓴 'majors' 시들이 / 방언으로 쓴 시들보다 많지만, / 방언으로 쓴 시들이었다 / Dunbar가 가장 큰 주목을 받게 해준 것은

아프리카계 미국인 시인인 Paul Laurence Dunbar는 1872년 6월 27일에 태어났다. 14세 무렵 Dunbar는 *Dayton Herald*에 시를 발표했다. 그는 고등학교에 다닐 때 학교 신문을 편집했다. 훌륭한 학생이었음에도 Dunbar는 재정상 대학에 갈 수 없었고 엘리베이터 운전자라는 직업을 가졌다. 1893년 Dunbar는 자신의 첫 번째 책인 *Oak and Ivy*를 자비로 출판했다. 1895년, 그는 두 번째 책인 *Majors and Minors*를 출판했고, 이것은 그에게 국내외의 인정을

가져다주었다. 표준 영어로 쓴 시들은 'majors'라 불렸고, 방언으로 쓴 시는 'minors'라 불렸다. 표준 영어로 쓴 'majors' 시들이 방언으로 쓴 시들보다 많지만, Dunbar가 가장 큰 주목을 받게 해준 것은 방언으로 쓴 시들이었다.

Why? 왜 정답일까?

'~ it was the dialect poems that brought Dunbar the most attention.'에서 Dunbar는 표준 영어로 된 시(majors)보다 방언으로 된 시(minors)를 통해 가장 큰 주목을 받았다고 한다. 따라서 내용과 일치하지 않는 것은 ⑤ '표준 영어로 쓴 시들로 가장 큰 주목을 받았다.'이다.

Why? 왜 오답일까?

① 'By the age of fourteen, Dunbar had poems published in the *Dayton Herald*.'의 내용과 일치한다.
② 'While in high school he edited his high school newspaper.'의 내용과 일치한다.
③ 'Despite being a fine student, Dunbar was financially unable to attend college ~'의 내용과 일치한다.
④ 'In 1895, he published the second book, *Majors and Minors*, which brought him national and international recognition.'의 내용과 일치한다.

- publish ⓥ 출판하다
- financially ⓐⓓ 재정적으로
- recognition ⓝ 인정
- A outnumber B A의 수가 B보다 많다
- edit ⓥ 편집하다
- at one's own expense 자비로, 사비로
- dialect ⓝ 방언

구문 풀이

3행 While (he was) in high school he edited his high school newspaper.
접속사 생략 전명구

---

27 독서 도전과제 정답률 91% | 정답 ②

Premier Reading Challenge에 관한 다음 안내문의 내용과 일치하지 <u>않는</u> 것은?
① 6학년부터 9학년까지의 학생들을 대상으로 한다.
✔ 6월부터 5개월간 진행되는 행사이다.
③ 7학년의 도전과제는 15권의 책을 읽는 것이다.
④ 모든 참가자는 책갈피를 받는다.
⑤ 온라인으로만 등록할 수 있다.

Premier Reading Challenge
Premier Reading Challenge

This is not a competition, / but rather a challenge to inspire students / with the love of reading.
이 행사는 경쟁하는 대회가 아니고, / 오히려 학생들에게 영감을 주기 위한 도전과제입니다. / 독서에 대한 사랑으로

Participants
참가자들

『Students from 6th grade to 9th grade』 ①의근거 일치
6학년부터 9학년까지의 학생들

Dates
날짜

『From June 1st to December 31st』 ②의근거 불일치
6월 1일 ~ 12월 31일

Challenge
도전과제

『Each student in 6th and 7th grade must read 15 books.』 ③의근거 일치
6학년과 7학년 각 학생은 15권의 책을 읽어야 합니다.

Each student in 8th and 9th grade must read 20 books.
8학년과 9학년 각 학생은 20권의 책을 읽어야 합니다.

Prize
상품

『A bookmark for every participant』 ④의근거 일치
모든 참가자들에게 책갈피

A Certificate of Achievement / for students who complete the challenge
수료증 / 도전과제를 완수한 학생들에게

Registration
등록

『Online only — www.edu.prc.com』 ⑤의근거 일치
온라인만 가능 — www.edu.prc.com

※ For more information, / see the school librarian or visit the website above.
더 많은 정보를 얻으려면, / 학교 도서관 사서를 찾아가거나 위에 있는 웹 사이트를 방문하세요.

Premier Reading Challenge

이 행사는 경쟁하는 대회가 아니라 오히려 학생들이 독서에 대한 사랑을 가지도록 영감을 주기 위한 도전과제입니다.

• **참가자들**
 − 6학년부터 9학년까지의 학생들

• **날짜**
 − 6월 1일 ~ 12월 31일

• **도전과제**
 − 6학년과 7학년 각 학생은 15권의 책을 읽어야 합니다.
 − 8학년과 9학년 각 학생은 20권의 책을 읽어야 합니다.

• **상품**
 − 모든 참가자들에게 책갈피
 − 도전과제를 완수한 학생들에게 수료증

• **등록**
 − 온라인만 가능 — www.edu.prc.com

※ 더 많은 정보를 얻으려면, 학교 도서관 사서를 찾아가거나 위에 있는 웹 사이트를 방문하세요.

14회

'From June 1st to December 31st'에서 도전과제 기간은 6월 1일부터 12월 31일, 즉 7개월간이라고 하였다. 따라서 안내문의 내용과 일치하지 않는 것은 ② '6월부터 5개월간 진행되는 행사이다.'이다.

Why? 왜 오답일까?

① 'Students from 6th grade to 9th grade'의 내용과 일치한다.
③ 'Each student in 6th and 7th grade must read 15 books.'의 내용과 일치한다.
④ 'A bookmark for every participant'의 내용과 일치한다.
⑤ 'Online only — www.edu.prc.com'의 내용과 일치한다.

- rather ad 오히려, 차라리
- certificate ⓝ 수료증, 자격증
- inspire ⓥ 영감을 주다
- librarian ⓝ (도서관) 사서

---

28 늑대 울음소리를 들을 수 있는 공원 프로그램　정답률 83% | 정답 ⑤

Wolf Howls in Algonquin Park에 관한 다음 안내문의 내용과 일치하는 것은?

① 날씨에 상관없이 진행된다.
② Ontario 거주자 모두에게 무료이다.
③ 소요 시간은 3시간 미만이다.
④ 행사 내내 반려견을 동반할 수 있다.
☑ 참가자 수에 따라 취소될 수 있다.

Wolf Howls in Algonquin Park
늑대 울음소리를 들을 수 있는 공원 프로그램
Wolf Howls in Algonquin Park is offering you / a once-in-a-lifetime experience tonight!
*Wolf Howls in Algonquin Park*는 당신에게 선사합니다! / 오늘밤 평생 한 번뿐인 경험을
Don't miss the chance / to hear the wolves communicate with our staff.
기회를 놓치지 마세요. / 늑대들이 우리 직원과 나누는 대화를 들을
When & Where
일시 & 장소
8 p.m. Wednesday, August 25th, 2021
2021년 8월 25일 수요일 오후 8시
「(Only if the weather permits / and a wolf pack is nearby.)」 ①의 근거 불일치
(날씨가 허락하고 / 늑대 무리가 근처에 있을 때만 가능)
Meet our staff at the outdoor theater / and travel with them to the wolf howling location.
야외극장에서 직원을 만나서 / 늑대가 우는 장소까지 함께 오세요.
Fee
이용 요금
$18.00 per person / 「(Free for Ontario residents 65 and older)」 ②의 근거 불일치
1인당 18달러 / (65세 이상 Ontario 거주자는 무료)
Note
공지
「Dress warmly for this special program / which will last longer than three hours.」 ③의 근거 불일치
이 특별 프로그램을 위해 옷을 따뜻하게 입으세요. / 3시간 이상 진행되는
「No dogs are allowed during the event.」 ④의 근거 불일치
행사 중 반려견을 동반할 수 없습니다.
「If there are less than 5 people for the event, / it will be cancelled.」 ⑤의 근거 일치
행사에 5인 미만 신청 시 / 취소됩니다.
Visit our website at www.algonquinpark.on / for more information.
우리 웹 사이트 www.algonquinpark.on에 방문하세요. / 더 많은 정보를 원하시면

Wolf Howls in Algonquin Park

*Wolf Howls in Algonquin Park*는 오늘밤 당신에게 평생 한 번뿐일 경험을 선사합니다!
늑대들이 우리 직원과 나누는 대화를 들을 기회를 놓치지 마세요.

일시 & 장소
• 2021년 8월 25일 수요일 오후 8시
 (날씨가 허락하고 늑대 무리가 근처에 있을 때만 가능)
• 야외극장에서 직원을 만나서 늑대가 우는 장소까지 함께 오세요.

이용 요금
• 1인당 18달러(65세 이상 Ontario 거주자는 무료)

공지
• 3시간 이상 진행되는 이 특별 프로그램을 위해 옷을 따뜻하게 입으세요.
• 행사 중 반려견을 동반할 수 없습니다.
• 행사에 5인 미만 신청 시 취소됩니다.

※ 더 많은 정보를 원하시면, 우리 웹 사이트 www.algonquinpark.on에 방문하세요.

Why? 왜 정답일까?

'If there are less than 5 people for the event, it will be cancelled.'에서 신청 인원이 5인 미만이면 취소될 수 있다고 하므로, 안내문의 내용과 일치하는 것은 ⑤ '참가자 수에 따라 취소될 수 있다.'이다.

Why? 왜 오답일까?

① 'Only if the weather permits ~'에서 날씨가 허락할 때만 진행된다고 하였다.
② 'Free for Ontario residents 65 and older'에서 Ontario 거주자 중 65세 이상만이 무료로 입장 가능하다고 하였다.
③ '~ this special program which will last longer than three hours.'에서 프로그램은 3시간 이상 진행된다고 하였다.
④ 'No dogs are allowed during the event.'에서 행사 중 반려견을 동반할 수 없다고 하였다.

- once-in-a-lifetime ⓐ 평생에 한 번뿐인
- last ⓥ 지속되다
- pack ⓝ 무리, 떼

---

29 Say의 법칙　정답률 48% | 정답 ②

다음 글의 밑줄 친 부분 중, 어법상 틀린 것은? [3점]

An economic theory of Say's Law holds / that everything that's made will get sold.
경제이론인 Say의 법칙은 주장한다. / 만들어진 모든 물품이 팔리기 마련이라고
The money from anything that's produced / is used to ① buy something else.
모든 생산된 물품으로부터 나오는 돈은 / 다른 물품을 사는 데 사용된다.
There can never be a situation / ☑ where a firm finds / that it can't sell its goods / and so has to dismiss workers and close its factories.
상황은 절대 있을 수 없다. / 한 회사가 알게 되는 / 그것이 물품을 팔 수 없게 되어서 / 직원들을 해고하고 공장의 문을 닫아야 한다는 것을
Therefore, recessions and unemployment are impossible.
따라서, 경기 후퇴와 실업은 불가능하다.
Picture the level of spending / like the level of water in a bath.
지출의 정도를 상상해 보아라. / 욕조 안의 물 높이로
Say's Law applies / ③ because people use all their earnings to buy things.
Say의 법칙이 적용된다. / 사람들이 그들의 모든 수입을 물품을 사는 데 사용하기 때문에
But what happens / if people don't spend all their money, / saving some of ④ it instead?
하지만 무슨 일이 일어날까? / 만약 사람들이 그들의 돈을 전부 사용하지 않고 / 대신에 돈의 일부를 모은다면
Savings are a 'leakage' of spending from the economy.
저축은 경제로부터 지출이 '누수'되는 것이다.
You're probably imagining the water level now falling, / so there's less spending in the economy.
당신은 아마 물의 높이가 지금 낮아지고 있는 것을 상상하고 있을 것이다. / 그래서 경제에서 지출이 적어지는 것을
That would mean / firms producing less / and ⑤ dismissing some of their workers.
그것은 의미할 것이다. / 회사들이 더 적게 생산하고 / 일부 직원들을 해고한다는

경제이론인 Say의 법칙은 만들어진 모든 물품이 팔리기 마련이라고 주장한다. 모든 생산된 물품으로부터 나오는 돈은 다른 물품을 사는 데 사용된다. 한 회사가 물품을 팔 수 없게 되어서 직원들을 해고하고 공장의 문을 닫아야 하는 상황은 절대 있을 수 없다. 따라서, 경기 후퇴와 실업은 불가능하다. 지출의 정도를 욕조 안의 물 높이로 상상해 보아라. 사람들이 그들의 모든 수입을 물품을 사는 데 사용하기 때문에 Say의 법칙이 적용된다. 하지만 만약 사람들이 그들의 돈을 전부 사용하는 대신, 돈의 일부를 모은다면 무슨 일이 일어날까? 저축은 경제로부터 지출이 '누수'되는 것이다. 당신은 아마 물의 높이가 지금 낮아져서 경제에서 지출이 적어지는 것을 상상하고 있을 것이다. 그것은 회사들이 더 적게 생산하고 일부 직원들을 해고한다는 의미일 것이다.

Why? 왜 정답일까?

뒤에 'a firm finds that ~'과 같이 주어, 동사, 목적어를 모두 갖춘 완전한 문장이 연결되고 있다. 이 경우 관계대명사가 아닌 관계부사를 써야 하므로, which를 where로 바꾸어야 한다. 따라서 어법상 틀린 것은 ②이다.

Why? 왜 오답일까?

① 「be used to + 동사원형(~하기 위해 사용되다)」의 buy가 적절히 쓰였다.
③ 뒤에 'people use ~'라는 절이 나오므로, 접속사 because가 적절히 쓰였다.
④ 앞에 나온 money는 불가산명사로, 대명사로 받을 경우 단수 취급하므로 it이 적절히 쓰였다.
⑤ and 앞에 producing이라는 동명사가 있으므로 and 뒤에 dismissing이 적절히 쓰였다. 「mean + 동명사(~하는 것을 뜻하다)」를 기억해 둔다.

- hold ⓥ (주로 뒤에 that절과 함께 나와) 주장하다
- unemployment ⓝ 실업
- savings ⓝ 저축(액)
- spending ⓝ 지출
- dismiss ⓥ 해고하다, 내보내다
- earnings ⓝ 수입, 소득
- leakage ⓝ 누수, 누출

구문 풀이

3행　There can never be a situation [where a firm finds {that it can't sell its
　　　　　　　　　　　　　　선행사　　관계부사　주어　　동사
goods and so has to dismiss workers and close its factories}]. [ ] : 목적어

---

30 사냥에서 기원한 인간의 상호 이타주의　정답률 51% | 정답 ④

다음 글의 밑줄 친 부분 중, 문맥상 낱말의 쓰임이 적절하지 않은 것은? [3점]

Hunting can explain / how humans developed *reciprocal altruism* and *social exchange*.
사냥은 설명할 수 있다. / 인간이 어떻게 상호 이타주의와 사회적 교류를 발전시켰는지
Humans seem to be unique among primates / in showing extensive reciprocal relationships / that can last years, decades, or a lifetime.
인간은 영장류 중에서 특별한 것 같다. / 광범위한 상호 관계를 보여준다는 점에서 / 몇 년, 수십 년, 혹은 평생 지속될 수 있는
Meat from a large game animal / comes in quantities / that ① exceed / what a single hunter and his immediate family could possibly consume.
큰 사냥감의 고기는 / 양으로 나온다. / 초과하는 / 사냥꾼 한 명과 그의 직계가족이 소비할 수 있을 만한 양을
Furthermore, hunting success is highly ② variable; / a hunter who is successful one week / might fail the next.
게다가, 사냥의 성공은 매우 변동이 심하다. / 어떤 주에는 성공한 사냥꾼이 / 다음 주에는 실패할 수도 있다.
These conditions ③ encourage food sharing from hunting.
이러한 조건들은 사냥으로 인한 음식 공유를 장려한다.
The costs to a hunter of giving away meat / he cannot eat immediately / are ☑ low / because he cannot consume all the meat himself / and leftovers will soon spoil.
사냥꾼이 고기를 나눠 주는 데 드는 비용은 / 그가 당장 먹을 수 없는 / 적게 든다. / 왜냐하면 그가 혼자서 고기를 다 먹을 수 없고 / 남은 고기는 곧 상하기 때문에
The benefits can be large, however, / when those who are given his food / return the generous favor later on / when he has failed to get food for himself.
그러나 이 혜택은 클 수 있다. / 그 사람의 음식을 받은 다른 사람들이 / 나중에 관대한 호의에 보답할 때 / 그 사람이 스스로 음식을 얻지 못했을 때
In essence, hunters can ⑤ store extra meat / in the bodies of their friends and neighbors.
결국 사냥꾼들은 여분의 고기를 저장할 수 있다. / 자신의 친구와 이웃의 몸에

사냥은 인간이 어떻게 상호 이타주의와 사회적 교류를 발전시켰는지를 설명할 수 있다. 인간은 영장류 중에서 몇 년, 수십 년, 혹은 평생 지속될 수 있는 광범위한 상호 관계를 보여준다는 점에서 특별한 것 같다. 큰 사냥감의 고기는 사냥꾼 한 명과 그의 직계가족이 소비할 수 있을 만한 양을 ① 초과한다. 게다가, 사냥의 성공은 매우 ② 변동이 심하다. 어떤 주에는 성공한 사냥꾼이 다음 주에는 실패할 수도 있다. 이러한 조건들은 사냥으로 인한 음식 공유를 ③ 장려한다. 사냥꾼이 당장 먹을 수 없는 고기를 나눠 주는 데 드는 비용은 혼자서 고기를 다 먹을 수 없고 남은 고기는 곧 상하기 때문에 ④ 많이(→ 적게) 든다. 그러나 그 사람이 나

중에 스스로 음식을 얻지 못했을 때 그 사람의 음식을 받은 다른 사람들이 관대한 호의에 보답한다면 그 혜택은 클 수 있다. 결국 사냥꾼들은 자신의 친구와 이웃의 몸에 여분의 고기를 ⑤ 저장할 수 있다.

Why? 왜 정답일까?

④ 뒤의 because가 이끄는 절에서, 사냥꾼이 나누어주는 고기는 당장은 자신이 다 먹을 수 없고 놔두면 곧 상할 고기라고 하였다. 즉 어차피 자신에게 남는 고기를 나누어준다는 뜻이므로, 이로 인해 치르는 비용이 크다고 볼 수 없기에 ④의 high를 low로 고쳐야 한다. 따라서 문맥상 낱말의 쓰임이 적절하지 않은 것은 ④이다.

- **extensive** ⓐ 광범위한, 폭넓은
- **quantity** ⓝ 양
- **immediate** ⓐ (가족이) 직계인
- **variable** ⓐ 변동이 심한, 가변적인
- **leftover** ⓝ (식사 후) 남은 음식
- **game** ⓝ 사냥감
- **exceed** ⓥ 넘어서다, 초과하다
- **consume** ⓥ 먹다, 마시다
- **give away** 나눠주다, 거저 주다
- **in essence** 결국, 본질적으로

구문 풀이

10행 The costs (to a hunter of giving away meat) [he cannot eat immediately]
주어 선행사
are low because he cannot consume all the meat himself and leftovers will soon
동사(복수) 접속사(이유) 재귀대명사(he 강조)
spoil.

---

31 더 단순한 제품의 이점   정답률 53% | 정답 ①

다음 빈칸에 들어갈 말로 가장 적절한 것을 고르시오.
- ☑ simpler product – 더 단순한 제품
- ② affordable price – 적당한 가격
- ③ consumer loyalty – 고객 충성도
- ④ customized design – 맞춤화된 디자인
- ⑤ eco-friendly technology – 친환경 기술

Sometimes it is the simpler product / that gives a business a competitive advantage.
때때로 더 단순한 제품이다. / 기업에게 경쟁 우위를 주는 것은
Until recently, / bicycles had to have many gears, / often 15 or 20, / for them to be considered high-end.
최근까지, / 자전거는 많은 기어가 있어야 했다. / 흔히 15개 혹은 20개의 / 최고급이라고 여겨지기 위해서는
But fixed-gear bikes with minimal features / have become more popular, / as those who buy them / are happy to pay more for much less.
그러나 최소한의 기능을 가지고 있는 고정식 기어 자전거은 / 점점 더 인기를 얻게 되었다. / 이를 사는 사람들이 ~함에 따라 / 훨씬 적은 것에 기꺼이 더 지불함에
The overall profitability of these bikes / is much higher than the more complex ones / because they do a single thing really well / without the cost of added complexity.
이런 자전거들의 전반적인 수익성은 / 더 복잡한 것들보다 훨씬 더 큰데 / 그것들이 한 가지를 정말 잘하기 때문이다 / 추가되는 복잡성에 대한 비용 없이
Companies should be careful of getting into a war / over adding more features with their competitors, / as this will increase cost / and almost certainly reduce profitability / because of competitive pressure on price.
기업들은 전쟁을 하는 것을 조심해야 하는데, / 경쟁 업체와 더 많은 기능을 추가하는 것에 관한 / 이것이 비용을 증가시키고 / 수익성을 거의 확실히 감소시킬 것이기 때문이다. / 가격에 대한 경쟁적인 압박 때문에

때때로 기업에게 경쟁 우위를 주는 것은 더 단순한 제품이다. 최근까지, 자전거는 최고급이라고 여겨지기 위해서는 흔히 15개 혹은 20개의 많은 기어가 있어야 했다. 그러나 최소한의 기능을 가지고 있는 고정식 기어 자전거는 이를 사는 사람들이 훨씬 적은 것에 기꺼이 더 지불함에 따라 점점 더 인기를 얻게 되었다. 이런 자전거들의 전반적인 수익성은 더 복잡한 것들보다 훨씬 더 큰데 그것들이 추가되는 복잡성에 대한 비용 없이 한 가지를 정말 잘하기 때문이다. 기업들은 경쟁 업체와 더 많은 기능을 추가하는 전쟁을 하는 것을 조심해야 하는데, 이것이 가격에 대한 경쟁적인 압박 때문에 비용을 증가시키고 수익성을 거의 확실히 감소시킬 것이기 때문이다.

Why? 왜 정답일까?

글 중반 이후 단순한 제품은 생산 비용의 증가 없이 확실한 강점을 가져 전반적인 수익성이 더 높다(The overall profitability of these bikes is much higher than the more complex ones ~)는 내용이 제시되므로, 빈칸에 들어갈 말로 가장 적절한 것은 ① '더 단순한 제품'이다.

- **competitive advantage** 경쟁 우위
- **feature** ⓝ (제품의) 기능, 특징
- **profitability** ⓝ 수익성
- **reduce** ⓥ 줄이다, 감소시키다
- **loyalty** ⓝ 충성도
- **minimal** ⓐ 최소의
- **overall** ⓐ 전반적인
- **complexity** ⓝ 복잡성
- **affordable** ⓐ (가격이) 적당한, 감당 가능한
- **customized** ⓐ 맞춤 제작된

구문 풀이

2행 Until recently, bicycles had to have many gears, (often 15 or 20), for them
( ): 삽입구(many gears 부연) 의미상 주어
to be considered high-end.
부사적 용법(목적)

---

32 언어 발달의 이유   정답률 63% | 정답 ⑤

다음 빈칸에 들어갈 말로 가장 적절한 것을 고르시오.
- ① used body language to communicate – 의사소통하기 위해 몸짓 언어를 사용했다
- ② instinctively knew who to depend on – 누구에게 의지할지 본능적으로 알았다
- ③ often changed rules for their own needs – 자신의 필요를 위해 종종 규칙을 바꾸었다
- ④ lived independently for their own survival – 생존을 위해 독립적으로 살았다
- ☑ developed language for economic reasons – 경제적인 이유로 언어를 발달시켰다

Many evolutionary biologists argue / that humans developed language for economic reasons.
많은 진화 생물학자들은 주장한다. / 인간이 경제적인 이유로 언어를 발달시켰다고
We needed to trade, / and we needed to establish trust / in order to trade.

우리는 거래해야 했고, / 우리는 신뢰를 확립해야 했다. / 거래하기 위해서는
Language is very handy / when you are trying to conduct business with someone.
언어는 매우 편리하다. / 당신이 누군가와 거래할 때
Two early humans could not only agree / to trade three wooden bowls for six bunches of bananas / but establish rules as well.
초창기의 두 인간은 동의할 수 있었을 뿐만 아니라 / 3개의 나무 그릇을 6다발의 바나나와 거래하기로 / 규칙을 정할 수도 있었다.
What wood was used for the bowls?
그 그릇들을 만드는 데 무슨 나무를 사용했나?
Where did you get the bananas?
어디서 그 바나나를 얻게 되었나?
That business deal would have been nearly impossible / using only gestures and confusing noises, / and carrying it out / according to terms agreed upon / creates a bond of trust.
그 상업 거래는 거의 불가능했을 것이고, / 단지 제스처와 혼란스런 소음만을 사용해서는 / 그것을 실행하는 것이 / 합의된 조항에 따라서 / 신뢰라는 결속을 만든다.
Language allows us to be specific, / and this is where conversation plays a key role.
언어는 우리가 구체적이도록 해주고, / 여기서 대화가 중요한 역할을 한다.

많은 진화 생물학자들은 인간이 경제적인 이유로 언어를 발달시켰다고 주장한다. 우리는 거래해야 했고, 거래하기 위해서는 신뢰를 확립해야 했다. 언어는 당신이 누군가와 거래할 때 매우 편리하다. 초창기의 두 인간은 3개의 나무 그릇을 6다발의 바나나와 거래하기로 동의할 수 있었을 뿐만 아니라 규칙을 정할 수도 있었다. 그 그릇들을 만드는 데 무슨 나무를 사용했나? 어디서 그 바나나를 얻게 되었나? 단지 제스처와 혼란스런 소음만을 사용해서는 그 상업 거래는 거의 불가능했을 것이고, 합의된 조항에 따라서 그것을 실행하는 것이 신뢰라는 결속을 만든다. 언어는 우리가 구체적이도록 해주고, 여기서 대화가 중요한 역할을 한다.

Why? 왜 정답일까?

예시를 마무리하는 마지막 두 문장에서 초기 인간은 제스처와 소음만을 사용해서 상업 거래를 수행할 수 없었을 것이므로 언어를 발달시켜 대화를 수행했다고 한다. 따라서 빈칸에 들어갈 말로 가장 적절한 것은 ⑤ '경제적인 이유로 언어를 발달시켰다'이다.

- **evolutionary** ⓐ 진화의
- **conduct** ⓥ 수행하다
- **carry out** 수행하다
- **bond** ⓝ 유대 (관계)
- **instinctively** ⓐ 본능적으로
- **establish** ⓥ 확립하다, 구축하다
- **as well** (문미에서) 또한
- **terms** ⓝ (합의, 계약 등의) 조건
- **specific** ⓐ 구체적인

구문 풀이

8행 That business deal would have been nearly impossible using only
주어1 동사1(과거에 대한 추측) 분사구문(~하면서)
gestures and confusing noises, and carrying it out according to terms agreed upon
주어2(동명사구) 과거분사구
creates a bond of trust.
동사2(단수)

★★★ 등급을 가르는 문제!

33 실수를 통한 이익   정답률 36% | 정답 ①

다음 빈칸에 들어갈 말로 가장 적절한 것을 고르시오.
- ☑ share the benefits – 이익을 공유해서
- ② overlook the insights – 통찰력을 간과해서
- ③ develop creative skills – 창의력을 발달시켜서
- ④ exaggerate the achievements – 성취를 과장해서
- ⑤ underestimate the knowledge – 지식을 과소평가해서

One big difference between science and stage magic / is / that while magicians hide their mistakes from the audience, / in science / you make your mistakes in public.
과학과 무대 마술 사이의 한 가지 큰 차이점은 / ~이다. / 마술사들이 실수를 관중에게 숨기는 반면, / 과학에서는 / 공공연히 실수를 한다는 것
You show them off / so that everybody can learn from them.
당신은 실수를 드러내 보여준다. / 모두가 실수로부터 배울 수 있도록
This way, / you get the advantage of everybody else's experience, / and not just your own idiosyncratic path / through the space of mistakes.
이런 식으로, / 당신은 다른 모든 사람들의 경험이라는 이익을 얻는다. / 당신 자신만의 특유한 길뿐만 아니라, / 실수라는 영역을 거쳐 온
This, by the way, is another reason / why we humans are so much smarter / than every other species.
한편, 이는 또 다른 이유이다. / 왜 우리 인간이 훨씬 더 영리한지에 대한 / 다른 모든 종보다
It is not that our brains are bigger or more powerful, / or even that we have the ability / to reflect on our own past errors, / but that we share the benefits / that our individual brains have earned / from their individual histories of trial and error.
그것은 우리의 뇌가 더 크거나 더 강력해서, / 혹은 심지어 우리 능력을 가져서가 아니라, / 우리 자신의 과거 실수들을 반추하는 / 우리가 이익들을 공유해서이다. / 우리 개개인들의 뇌가 얻어낸 / 각자 자신의 시행착오의 역사로부터

과학과 무대 마술 사이의 한 가지 큰 차이점은 마술사들이 실수를 관중에게 숨기는 반면, 과학에서는 공공연히 실수를 한다는 것이다. 당신은 모두가 실수로부터 배울 수 있도록 실수를 드러내 보여준다. 이런 식으로, 당신은 실수라는 영역을 거쳐 온 당신 자신만의 특유한 길(에서 얻은 이익)뿐만 아니라, 다른 모든 사람들의 경험이라는 이익을 얻는다. 한편, 이는 왜 우리 인간이 다른 모든 종보다 훨씬 더 영리한지에 대한 또 다른 이유이다. 그것은 우리의 뇌가 더 크거나 더 강력해서, 혹은 심지어 우리가 우리 자신의 과거 실수들을 반추하는 능력을 가져서가 아니라, 우리 개개인들의 뇌가 각자 자신의 시행착오의 역사로부터 얻어낸 이익들을 공유해서이다.

Why? 왜 정답일까?

'You show them off so that everybody can learn from them. This way, you get the advantage of everybody else's experience, ~'에서 서로 실수를 드러내 보여주면 실수를 통해 얻은 경험과 이익을 공유할 수 있다고 했다. 이를 근거로 볼 때, 인간이 똑똑한 이유를 설명하는 마지막 문장은 '실수로 인한 이익이 공유되기' 때문이라는 의미가 되어야 하므로, 빈칸에 들어갈 말로 가장 적절한 것은 ① '이익들을 공유해서'이다.

- **advantage** ⓝ 이점
- **species** ⓝ (생물) 종

- **reflect on** ~을 반추하다
- **overlook** ⓥ 간과하다, 못 보고 넘어가다
- **underestimate** ⓥ 과소평가하다
- **trial and error** 시행착오
- **exaggerate** ⓥ 과장하다

8행 It is not {that our brains are bigger or more powerful}, or even {that we
not + A · or A' +
have the ability to reflect on our own past errors}, but {that we share the benefits
but + B : A나 A'가 아니라 B인 (A, A', B 자리에 모두 that절) · · · · · · · · · 선행사
[that our individual brains have earned from their individual histories of trial and
목적격 관·대
error]}.

★★ 문제 해결 꿀~팁 ★★

▶ 많이 틀린 이유는?
첫 두 문장에서 모두가 배울 수 있도록 실수를 드러내 보이는 것을 글의 주된 소재로 언급하고 있다.
창의력 발달에 관해서는 언급되지 않으므로 ③은 답으로 적절하지 않다.
▶ 문제 해결 방법은?
'You show them[your mistakes] off so that everybody can learn from them. This
way, you get the advantage of everybody else's experience. ~'에서 show off가
①의 share로, advantage가 ①의 benefits로 재진술되었다.

34 직접 찾아내면 더 오래 남는 지식　　정답률 52% | 정답 ⑤

다음 빈칸에 들어갈 말로 가장 적절한 것을 고르시오. [3점]
① they are taught repeatedly in class
　그들이 수업에서 반복해서 배운다면
② we fully focus on them without any distractions
　우리가 어떤 방해도 받지 않고 그들에게 완전히 집중한다면
③ equal opportunities are given to complete tasks
　과업을 완수할 기회가 똑같이 부여된다면
④ there's no right or wrong way to learn about a topic
　어떤 주제에 대해 배우는 옳은 방식도 틀린 방식도 없다면
✔ we discover them ourselves rather than being told them
　우리가 무언가에 관해서 듣기보다 스스로 발견한다면

The last two decades of research / on the science of learning / have shown conclusively /
that we remember things better, and longer, / if we discover them ourselves rather than
being told them.
지난 20년간의 연구는 / 학습과학에 관한 / 결론적으로 보여주었다. / 우리는 무언가를 더 잘 기억하고, 더 오래 기억한다는 것을 /
만약 우리가 그것들에 관해서 듣기보다 스스로 발견한다면

This is the teaching method / practiced by physics professor Eric Mazur.
이것은 실천되는 교수법이다. / 물리학 교수 Eric Mazur에 의해

He doesn't lecture in his classes at Harvard.
그는 하버드 수업에서 강의를 하지 않는다.

Instead, he asks students difficult questions, / based on their homework reading, / that
require them to pull together sources of information / to solve a problem.
대신에, 그는 학생들에게 어려운 질문을 던진다. / 독서 활동 과제에 기반하여 / 그들이 정보 자료를 모으도록 요구하는 / 문제를 해결하기 위해

Mazur doesn't give them the answer; / instead, he asks the students / to break off into small
groups / and discuss the problem among themselves.
Mazur는 그들에게 답을 주지 않는다. / 대신에, 그는 학생들에게 요구한다. / 소그룹으로 나누어 / 그들 스스로 문제를 토론하도록

Eventually, / nearly everyone in the class gets the answer right, / and the concepts stick
with them / because they had to find their own way to the answer.
결국, / 강좌의 거의 모든 사람들이 정답을 맞히고, / 이러한 개념들은 그들에게 오래 남는다 / 그들이 정답으로 가는 길을 스스로 찾았기 때문에

학습과학에 관한 지난 20년간의 연구는 만약 우리가 무언가에 관해서 듣기보다 스스로 발견한다면 우리는 그것들을 더 잘 기억하고, 더 오래 기억한다는 것을 결론적으로 보여주었다. 이것은 물리학 교수 Eric Mazur에 의해 실천되는 교수법이다. 그는 하버드 수업에서 (설명식) 강의를 하지 않는다. 대신에, 그는 독서 활동 과제에 기반하여 학생들이 문제를 해결하기 위해 정보 자료를 모으도록 요구하는 어려운 질문을 던진다. Mazur는 그들에게 답을 주지 않는다. 대신에, 그는 학생들을 소그룹으로 나누어 그들 스스로 문제를 토론하도록 요구한다. 결국, 강좌의 거의 모든 사람들이 정답을 맞히고, 그들이 정답으로 가는 길을 스스로 찾았기 때문에 이러한 개념들은 그들에게 오래 남는다.

Why? 왜 정답일까?
마지막 두 문장에서 Eric Mazur 교수는 학생들에게 질문을 던진 후 직접 토론해 답을 도출하게 하여 머릿속에 더 오래 남는 지식을 알려준다는 내용을 제시한다. 따라서 빈칸에 들어갈 말로 가장 적절한 것은 우리가 어떤 것을 더 오래 기억하려면 직접 알아내보는 것이 낫다는 의미를 완성하는 ⑤ '우리가 무언가에 관해서 듣기보다 스스로 발견한다면'이다.

- **conclusively** ⓐⓓ 결론적으로
- **break off** ~을 분리시키다
- **stick with** ~와 함께 머물다
- **distraction** ⓝ 정신을 산만하게 하는 것, 주의를 흩뜨리는 것
- **complete** ⓥ 완수하다
- **physics** ⓝ 물리학
- **eventually** ⓐⓓ 결국
- **repeatedly** ⓐⓓ 반복해서

6행 Instead, he asks students difficult questions, (based on their homework
4형식 동사　간접목적어　직접목적어　　　( ) : 삽입구
reading), [that require them to pull together sources of information to solve a
주격 관·대
problem.] [ ] : 직접목적어 수식

35 Zeigarnik 효과　　정답률 65% | 정답 ④

다음 글에서 전체 흐름과 관계 없는 문장은?

The Zeigarnik effect is commonly referred to / as the tendency of the subconscious mind /
to remind you of a task / that is incomplete / until that task is complete.
Zeigarnik 효과는 보통 일컫는다. / 잠재의식의 경향을 / 당신에게 과업을 상기시켜주는 / 끝나지 않은 / 그 과업이 끝날 때까지

Bluma Zeigarnik was a Lithuanian psychologist / who wrote in the 1920s / about the
effects of leaving tasks incomplete.
Bluma Zeigarnik는 리투아니아 심리학자이다. / 1920년대에 쓴 / 과업을 완성하지 못한 채로 남겨두는 것의 효과에 대해

① She noticed the effect / while watching waiters serve in a restaurant.
그녀는 그 효과를 알아차렸다. / 한 식당에서 웨이터들이 서빙하는 것을 보던 중

② The waiters would remember an order, / however complicated, / until the order was
complete, / but they would later find it difficult / to remember the order.
웨이터들은 주문을 기억했는데, / 아무리 복잡하더라도 / 그 주문이 끝날 때까지 / 나중에는 어렵다는 것을 알았다. / 그 주문을 기억하는 것을

③ Zeigarnik did further studies / giving both adults and children puzzles to complete /
then interrupting them / during some of the tasks.
Zeigarnik는 후속 연구를 했다. / 어른들과 아이들 둘 다에게 완성할 퍼즐을 주고 / 그러고 나서 그들을 방해하는 / 그 과업들 중 몇몇을 하는 도중에

✔ They developed cooperation skills / after finishing tasks / by putting the puzzles together.
그들은 협동 기술을 발달시켰다. / 과업들을 마친 후에 / 퍼즐을 같이 맞춤으로써

⑤ The results showed / that both adults and children remembered the tasks / that hadn't
been completed because of the interruptions / better than the ones that had been completed.
결과는 보여주었다. / 어른들과 아이들 둘 다 과업들을 기억했다. / 방해로 인해 완성되지 못한 / 완성된 것들보다 더 잘

Zeigarnik 효과는 보통 당신에게 끝나지 않은 과업이 끝날 때까지 그 과업을 상기시켜주는 잠재의식의 경향을 일컫는다. Bluma Zeigarnik는 1920년대에 과업을 완성하지 못한 채로 남겨두는 것이 주는 효과에 대해 쓴 리투아니아 심리학자이다. ① 그녀는 한 식당에서 웨이터들이 서빙하는 것을 보던 중 그 효과를 알아차렸다. ② 웨이터들은 아무리 복잡하더라도 주문이 끝날 때까지 주문을 기억했는데, 나중에는 그 주문을 기억하는 것이 어렵다는 것을 알았다. ③ Zeigarnik는 어른들과 아이들 둘 다에게 완성할 퍼즐을 주고 나서 그 과업들 중 몇몇을 하는 도중 그들을 방해하는 후속 연구를 했다. ④ 그들은 퍼즐을 같이 맞춤으로써 과업들을 마친 후에 협동 기술을 발달시켰다. ⑤ 결과에 따르면 어른들과 아이들 둘 다 방해로 인해 완성되지 못한 과업들을 완성된 것들보다 더 잘 기억했다.

Why? 왜 정답일까?
과업이 미완성 상태로 남겨져 있다면 오래 기억된다는 심리적 효과에 관한 글이다. ①과 ②는 식당 웨이터를 대상으로 한 관찰 내용을 언급하고, ③과 ⑤는 어른들과 아이들에게 퍼즐 과업을 주었던 후속 연구를 언급하고 있다. 하지만 ④는 퍼즐 과업과 협동 기술을 연관지어 설명하므로 흐름에서 벗어난다. 따라서 전체 흐름과 관계 없는 문장은 ④이다.

- **subconscious** ⓐ 잠재의식의
- **incomplete** ⓐ 미완성된
- **interrupt** ⓥ 방해하다, 끼어들다
- **remind A of B** A에게 B를 상기시키다
- **complicated** ⓐ 복잡한
- **put together** 조립하다, 만들다

6행 The waiters would remember an order, (however complicated), until the
( ) : 삽입절
order was complete, but they would later find it difficult to remember the order.
5형식 동사 │목적격 보어 │ 진목적어
└ 가목적어

36 '내가 대접받고 싶은 대로 상대를 대접한다'라는 규칙의 맹점　　정답률 58% | 정답 ⑤

주어진 글 다음에 이어질 글의 순서로 가장 적절한 것을 고르시오. [3점]
① (A) - (C) - (B)　　② (B) - (A) - (C)　　③ (B) - (C) - (A)
④ (C) - (A) - (B)　　✔ (C) - (B) - (A)

Understanding how to develop / respect for and a knowledge of other cultures / begins
with reexamining the golden rule: / "I treat others / in the way I want to be treated."
발달시키는 방법을 이해하는 것은 / 다른 문화에 대한 존중과 지식을 / 다음의 황금률을 재점검해보는 일에서 시작된다. / "나는 상대를 대접한다. / 내가 대접받고 싶은 대로"

(C) This rule makes sense on some level; / if we treat others as well as we want to be
treated, / we will be treated well in return.
이 법칙은 어느 수준에서는 일리가 있다. / 만약 우리가 다른 사람들을 우리가 대접받고 싶은 만큼 대접한다면 / 우리는 보답으로 잘 대접받게 될 것이다.

This rule works well in a monocultural setting, / where everyone is working within the
same cultural framework.
이 법칙은 단일 문화 환경에서는 잘 통한다. / 모든 사람이 같은 문화적 틀 안에서 일하는

(B) In a multicultural setting, however, / where words, gestures, beliefs, and views / may
have different meanings, / this rule has an unintended result; / it can send a message / that
my culture is better than yours.
그러나 다문화 환경에서는 / 단어, 제스처, 신념과 관점이 / 다른 의미를 지닐지도 모르는 / 이 법칙은 의도치 않은 결과를 낳는다. / 그것은 메시지를 줄 수 있다. / 나의 문화가 상대의 것보다 낫다는

(A) It can also create a frustrating situation / where we believe we are doing what is right, /
but what we are doing is not being interpreted / in the way in which it was meant.
그것은 또한 답답한 상황을 낳을 수도 있다. / 우리가 자신이 하는 것이 옳다고 믿지만, / 그러나 우리가 하는 일이 해석되지 않는 / 그것이 의도된 방식으로

This miscommunication can lead to problems.
이러한 의사소통 오류는 문제를 야기할 수 있다.

다른 문화에 대한 존중과 지식을 발달시키는 방법을 이해하는 것은 다음의 황금률을 재점검해보는 일에서 시작된다. "나는 상대를 내가 대접받고 싶은 대로 대접한다."

(C) 이 법칙은 어느 수준에서는 일리가 있다. 만약 다른 사람들을 우리가 대접받고 싶은 만큼 대접한다면 우리는 보답으로 잘 대접받게 될 것이다. 이 법칙은 모든 사람이 같은 문화적 틀 안에서 일하는 단일 문화 환경에서는 잘 통한다.

(B) 그러나 단어, 제스처, 신념과 관점이 다른 의미를 지닐지도 모르는 다문화 환경에서는 이 법칙이 의도치 않은 결과를 낳는다. 그것은 나의 문화가 상대의 것보다 낫다는 메시지를 줄 수 있다.

(A) 그것은 또한 우리가 하는 것이 옳다고 믿지만, 그것이 의도된 방식으로 해석되지 않는 답답한 상황을 낳을 수도 있다. 이러한 의사소통 오류는 문제를 야기할 수 있다.

Why? 왜 정답일까?
자신이 대접받기를 원하는 대로 상대를 대접한다는 황금률을 다시 살펴봐야 한다는 주어진 글 뒤로, 이 법칙(This rule)이 단일 문화 환경에서는 잘 통한다는 내용의 (C), 하지만(however) 다문화 환경에서

는 잘 안 통할 수 있다는 내용의 **(B)**, 안 통할 때 생기는 문제에 관해 부연하는 **(A)**가 차례로 이어져야 자연스럽다. 따라서 글의 순서로 가장 적절한 것은 ⑤ **'(C) – (B) – (A)'**이다.

- reexamine ⓥ 재점검하다
- frustrating ⓐ 답답한, 좌절스러운
- miscommunication ⓝ 의사소통 오류, 오해
- unintended ⓐ 의도되지 않은
- in return 보답으로, 반응으로
- golden rule 황금률
- interpret ⓥ 해석하다, 이해하다
- multicultural ⓐ 다문화의
- make sense 일리가 있다, 의미가 통하다
- monocultural ⓐ 단일 문화의

구문 풀이

4행 It can also create a frustrating situation [where we believe (that) we
　　　　　　　　　　　　　　　　　　　선행사　　　　관계부사　　　생략 주어1
are doing what is right, but what we are doing is not being interpreted in the way
동사1　　　　　　　　주어2(관계대명사절 : ~것)　　　동사2(현재진행 수동태)　　　선행사
[in which it was meant]].

★★★ 등급을 가르는 문제!

37 큰 요청을 하기 앞서 작은 요청을 하는 것의 효과　　　　정답률 37% | 정답 ④

주어진 글 다음에 이어질 글의 순서로 가장 적절한 것을 고르시오. [3점]

① (A) – (C) – (B)
② (B) – (A) – (C)
③ (B) – (C) – (A)
✓④ (C) – (A) – (B)
⑤ (C) – (B) – (A)

In a study, / a researcher pretending to be a volunteer / surveyed a California neighborhood, / asking residents / if they would allow a large sign / reading "Drive Carefully" / to be displayed on their front lawns.
한 연구에서, / 자원봉사자로 가장한 연구자가 / 한 캘리포니아 동네에 설문조사했다. / 주민들에게 물으면서 / 그들이 큰 표지판을 허락할지를 / '운전 조심'이라고 쓰인 / 그들의 앞마당에 세워 두는 것을

(C) To help them understand what it would look like, / the volunteer showed his participants / a picture of the large sign / blocking the view of a beautiful house.
그것이 어떻게 보일지에 대한 이해를 돕기 위해, / 그 자원봉사자는 참여자들에게 보여주었다. / 큰 표지판 사진을 / 아름다운 집의 전망을 막는

Naturally, most people refused, / but in one particular group, / an incredible 76 percent actually approved.
당연하게도 대부분의 사람들은 거절했지만, / 어떤 특정 그룹에서 / 놀랍게도 76퍼센트가 실제로 승낙했다.

(A) The reason that they agreed was this: / two weeks earlier, / these residents had been asked by another volunteer / to make a small commitment / to display a tiny sign / that read "Be a Safe Driver" / in their windows.
그들이 동의한 이유는 이것이다. / 2주 전에, / 이 주민들은 다른 자원봉사자로부터 요청받은 적이 있었다. / 작은 약속을 하도록 / 아주 작은 표지판을 붙인다는 / '안전운전자가 되세요'라고 쓰인 / 그들의 창문에

(B) Since it was such a small and simple request, / nearly all of them agreed.
그것이 아주 작고 간단한 요청이었기 때문에, / 그들 거의 모두가 동의했다.

The astonishing result was / that the initial small commitment / deeply influenced their willingness / to accept the much larger request two weeks later.
놀라운 결과는 / 처음의 작은 약속이 그들의 의향에 깊은 영향을 끼쳤다는 것이다. / 2주 후의 훨씬 더 큰 요청을 받아들이려는

한 연구에서, 자원봉사자로 가장한 연구자가 한 캘리포니아 동네에서 주민들에게 그들의 앞마당에 '운전 조심'이라고 쓰인 큰 표지판을 세워 두는 것을 허락할지를 설문조사했다. (C) 그것이 어떻게 보일지에 대한 이해를 돕기 위해, 그 자원봉사자는 참여자들에게 아름다운 집의 전망을 막는 큰 표지판 사진을 보여주었다. 당연하게도 대부분의 사람들은 거절했지만, 어떤 특정 그룹에서 놀랍게도 76퍼센트가 실제로 승낙했다. (A) 그들이 동의한 이유는 이것이다. 2주 전에, 이 주민들은 다른 자원봉사자로부터 '안전운전자가 되세요'라고 쓰인 아주 작은 표지판을 창문에 붙인다는 작은 약속을 하도록 요청받은 적이 있었다. (B) 그것이 아주 작고 간단한 요청이었기 때문에, 그들 거의 모두가 동의했다. 놀라운 결과는, 처음의 작은 약속이 그들이 2주 후의 훨씬 더 큰 요청을 기꺼이 받아들이는 데 깊은 영향을 끼쳤다는 것이다.

Why? 왜 정답일까?
주어진 글에서 자원봉사자로 가장한 연구자가 동네 주민들에게 '운전 조심'이라고 쓰인 큰 표지판을 세우는 것에 동의해줄지를 물어보았다고 언급한 데 이어, **(C)**는 이 연구자(the volunteer)가 대체로 거절의 답변을 얻은 가운데 한 집단에서 다수의 승낙을 받아냈다는 결과를 소개한다. **(A)**는 **(C)**에서 언급된 '동의해준 사람들'을 they로 지칭하며, 이들은 실험 2주 전 아주 작은 표지판을 창문에 붙여달라는 요청을 받은 적이 있었다고 설명한다. **(B)**는 '작은 표지판을 창문에 붙이는 것'을 it으로 가리키며, 이렇듯 작은 요청을 먼저 받은 후 큰 요청을 받았기에 주민들의 선택이 다른 집단과 달라졌다는 최종적 해석을 제시한다. 따라서 글의 순서로 가장 적절한 것은 ④ **'(C) – (A) – (B)'**이다.

- pretend ⓥ ~인 체하다
- make a commitment 약속하다
- astonishing ⓐ 놀라운
- willingness ⓝ 의향, (기꺼이) ~하려는 마음
- block ⓥ 막다, 차단하다
- display ⓥ 전시하다
- tiny ⓐ 아주 작은
- initial ⓐ 처음의, 초기의
- incredible ⓐ 믿을 수 없는, 놀라운
- approve ⓥ 승인하다

구문 풀이

1행 In a study, a researcher (pretending to be a volunteer) surveyed a California
　　　　　　　　　　주어　　　　　　　　　　　　　　　　　동사
neighborhood, asking residents {if they would allow a large sign (reading "Drive
　　　　　　　　분사구문　간접목적어　　　5형식 동사　　　목적어
Carefully") to be displayed on their front lawns}.
　　　　　　　목적격 보어　　　　　[ ] : 직접목적어

★★ 문제 해결 꿀~팁 ★★

▶ 많이 틀린 이유는?
(B)와 (C)의 첫 문장에 모두 it이 나오므로 it이 가리키는 바를 잘 찾아야 한다.
(B)의 it은 '작고 간단한 요청'이고, (C)의 it은 '아름다운 집 정경을 모두 가릴 만큼 큰 표지판'이다. 주

어진 글에 등장하는 **a large sign**은 둘 중 **(C)**의 **it**과 연결되므로, 선택지 중 **(B)**로 시작하는 ②와 ③은 답에서 제외된다.

▶ 문제 해결 방법은?
대명사 힌트에 주목하면 답을 쉽게 고를 수 있다.
주어진 글의 **a large sign**이 **(C)**의 it, **(C)**의 **an incredible 76 percent**가 **(A)**의 they, **(A)**의 'to display a tiny sign ~'이 **(B)**의 it으로 연결되고 있다.

38 수면을 대체할 수 없는 카페인　　　　정답률 66% | 정답 ③

글의 흐름으로 보아, 주어진 문장이 들어가기에 가장 적절한 곳을 고르시오.

Studies have consistently shown / caffeine to be effective / when used together with a pain reliever / to treat headaches.
연구는 지속적으로 밝혀왔다. / 카페인이 효과가 있다는 것을 / 진통제와 함께 사용할 때 / 두통 치료 목적으로

① The positive correlation / between caffeine intake / and staying alert throughout the day / has also been well established.
양의 상관관계가 / 카페인 섭취와 / 하루 종일 각성 상태를 유지하는 것 사이에는 / 또한 잘 확립되어 있다.

② As little as 60 mg / (the amount typically in one cup of tea) / can lead to a faster reaction time.
60mg만큼의 적은 양으로도 / (일반적으로 차 한 잔에 들어 있는 양) / 반응 시간이 빨라질 수 있다.

✓ However, / using caffeine to improve alertness and mental performance / doesn't replace getting a good night's sleep.
하지만, / 각성과 정신적 수행능력을 향상시키기 위해 카페인을 사용하는 것은 / 숙면을 취하는 것을 대체하지 못한다.

One study from 2018 showed / that coffee improved reaction times / in those with or without poor sleep, / but caffeine seemed to increase errors / in the group with little sleep.
2018년 한 연구는 보여주었다. / 커피는 반응 시간은 개선시켰지만, / 수면이 부족한 사람이나 부족하지 않은 사람에게나 / 카페인은 오류를 증가시키는 듯 하다는 것을 / 수면이 부족한 집단 내에서는

④ Additionally, / this study showed / that even with caffeine, / the group with little sleep did not score as well / as those with adequate sleep.
게다가, / 이 연구는 보여주었다. / 카페인을 섭취하더라도, / 수면이 부족한 그룹은 점수를 잘 받지 못했다는 것을 / 충분한 수면을 취한 집단만큼

⑤ It suggests / that caffeine does not fully make up for inadequate sleep.
이는 보여준다. / 카페인이 불충분한 수면을 충분히 보충하지 못한다는 것을

연구에서 지속적으로 밝히기로는 카페인을 두통 치료 목적으로 진통제와 함께 사용할 때 효과가 있다. ① 또한 카페인 섭취와 하루 종일 각성 상태를 유지하는 것 사이에는 양의 상관관계가 잘 확립되어 있다. ② 60mg(일반적으로 차 한 잔에 들어 있는 양)만큼의 적은 양으로도 반응 시간이 빨라질 수 있다. ③ 하지만, 각성과 정신적 수행능력을 향상시키기 위해 카페인을 사용하는 것은 숙면을 취하는 것을 대체하지 못한다. 2018년 한 연구가 밝히기로 커피는 수면이 부족한 사람이나 부족하지 않은 사람에게나 반응 시간은 개선시켰지만, 카페인은 수면이 부족한 집단 내에서는 오류를 증가시키는 듯 하다. ④ 게다가, 이 연구는 카페인을 섭취하더라도, 수면이 부족한 그룹은 충분한 수면을 취한 집단만큼 점수를 잘 받지 못했다는 것을 보여주었다. ⑤ 이는 카페인이 불충분한 수면을 충분히 보충하지 못한다는 것을 보여준다.

Why? 왜 정답일까?
③ 앞뒤로 글의 흐름이 반전되고 있다. ③ 앞에서 카페인 섭취와 각성 상태 사이에는 양의 상관관계가 있으며, 차 한 잔에 들어있는 양만큼만 마셔도 우리의 반응 시간이 빨라진다는 내용이 제시된다. 하지만 ③ 뒤에는 수면이 부족한 집단에 카페인을 주었을 때 오류가 증가되는 것 같다고 한다. 이러한 맥락으로 보아, **However**로 시작하여 흐름을 반전시킬 수 있는 주어진 문장이 들어가기에 가장 적절한 곳은 ③이다.

- improve ⓥ 향상시키다, 개선하다
- get a good night's sleep 숙면하다
- pain reliever 진통제
- additionally ⓐ 게다가
- inadequate ⓐ 불충분한
- alertness ⓝ 각성 상태, 기민함
- consistently ⓐ 지속적으로, 일관되게
- established ⓐ 확립된
- make up for ~을 보상하다

구문 풀이

3행 Studies have consistently shown caffeine to be effective when (it is) used
　　　　　　　　　　　동사　　　　　　목적어　　목적격 보어　　접속사 생략 과거분사
together with a pain reliever to treat headaches.
　　　　　　　　　　　　부사적 용법(목적)

39 업무에 대한 비금전적 보상과 그 영향　　　　정답률 53% | 정답 ②

글의 흐름으로 보아, 주어진 문장이 들어가기에 가장 적절한 곳을 고르시오.

Rewarding business success / doesn't always have to be done in a material way.
일의 성공을 보상하는 것은 / 항상 물질적인 방식으로 되어야 하는 것은 아니다.

① A software company I once worked for / had a great way of recognizing sales success.
내가 예전에 근무했던 한 소프트웨어 회사는 / 판매 성공을 인정해주는 멋진 방법을 가지고 있었다.

✓ The sales director kept an air horn outside his office / and would come out and blow the horn / every time a salesperson settled a deal.
영업부장은 자기 사무실 밖에 경적을 두었고 / 나와서 경적을 불곤 했다. / 영업직원이 거래를 성사할 때마다

The noise, of course, / interrupted anything and everything / happening in the office / because it was unbelievably loud.
물론, 그 소리는 / 무슨 일이든 방해했다. / 사무실에서 생기는 / 그것이 믿을 수 없이 시끄러웠기 때문에

③ However, / it had an amazingly positive impact on everyone.
그러나 / 그것은 모두에게 놀랄 만큼 긍정적인 영향을 주었다.

④ Sometimes rewarding success can be as easy as that, / especially when peer recognition is important.
때때로 성공을 보상하는 것은 그처럼 쉬울 수 있는데, / 특히 동료의 인정이 중요할 때 그렇다.

⑤ You should have seen the way / the rest of the sales team wanted / the air horn blown for them.
당신은 그 방식을 봤어야 했다. / 그 영업부서의 나머지 사람들이 바라는 / 자신을 위해 경적이 불리기를

일의 성공을 보상하는 것은 항상 물질적인 방식으로 되어야 하는 것은 아니다. ① 내가 예전에 근무했던 한 소프트웨어 회사는 판매 성공을 인정해주는 멋진 방법을 가지고 있었다.

② 영업부장은 자기 사무실 밖에 경적을 두었고 영업직원이 거래를 성사할 때마다 나와서 경적을 불곤 했다. 물론, 그 소리는 믿을 수 없이 시끄러웠기 때문에 사무실에서 생기는 무슨 일이든 방해했다. ③ 그러나 그것은 모두에게 놀랄 만큼 긍정적인 영향을 주었다. ④ 때때로 성공을 보상하는 것은 그처럼 쉬울 수 있는데, 특히 동료의 인정이 중요할 때 그렇다. ⑤ 당신은 그 영업부서의 나머지 사람들이 자신을 위해 경적이 불리기를 바라는 그 방식을 봤어야 했다.

Why? 왜 정답일까?

② 앞에서 필자는 자신이 다녔던 소프트웨어 회사에 업무 성과를 보상해주는 멋진 방법이 있었다고 언급하는데, 주어진 문장은 그 방법의 구체적 내용을 제시한다. 즉 영업부장이 자기 사무실 밖에 경적을 두고 거래가 성사될 때마다 그 경적을 불어주었다는 것인데, ② 뒤의 문장은 그 경적 소리(The noise)에 관해 언급한다. 따라서 주어진 문장이 들어가기에 가장 적절한 곳은 ②이다.

- sales director 영업부장
- material ⓐ 물질적인
- anything and everything 무슨 일이든, 어떤 것이든지
- unbelievably ⓐⓓ 믿을 수 없을 정도로
- amazingly ⓐⓓ 놀랄 만큼
- settle a deal 거래를 성사시키다
- interrupt ⓥ 방해하다
- have an impact on ~에 영향을 미치다

구문 풀이

11행 You should have seen the way [the rest of the sales team wanted the air
「should have p.p. : ~했어야 했다」　선행사　　　　동사　　목적어
horn blown for them].
목적격 보어

★★★ 등급을 가르는 문제!

40 의견 불일치가 학생들에게 미치는 영향　　정답률 38% | 정답 ①

다음 글의 내용을 한 문장으로 요약하고자 한다. 빈칸 (A), (B)에 들어갈 말로 가장 적절한 것은?　[3점]

	(A)		(B)
✓①	increases 증가한다	……	differ 의견을 달리하도록
②	increases 증가한다	……	approve 동의하도록
③	increases 증가한다	……	cooperate 협력하도록
④	decreases 감소한다	……	participate 참여하도록
⑤	decreases 감소한다	……	argue 논쟁하도록

Nancy Lowry and David Johnson conducted an experiment / to study a teaching environment / where fifth and sixth graders were assigned to interact on a topic.
Nancy Lowry와 David Johnson은 실험을 진행했다. / 교수환경을 연구하고자 / 5학년과 6학년 학생들이 한 주제에 대해 상호 작용을 하게 지정받은

With one group, / the discussion was led in a way / that built an agreement.
한 집단에서는, / 토론이 방식으로 유도되었다. / 합의를 도출하는

With the second group, / the discussion was designed / to produce disagreements about the right answer.
두 번째 집단에서는, / 토론이 설계되었다. / 옳은 정답에 대해 불일치를 낳도록

Students who easily reached an agreement / were less interested in the topic, / studied less, / and were less likely to visit the library / to get additional information.
쉽게 합의에 도달한 학생들은 / 주제에 흥미를 덜 보이고 / 더 적게 공부했으며 / 도서관에 가는 경향이 더 적었다. / 부가적인 정보를 얻기 위해

The most noticeable difference, though, / was revealed / when teachers showed a special film about the discussion topic / — during lunch time!
그러나 가장 눈에 띄는 차이는 / 나타났다 / 교사가 학생들에게 토론 주제와 관련된 특별한 영화를 보여주었을 때 / 점심시간 동안

Only 18 percent of the agreement group / missed lunch time to see the film, / but 45 percent of the students from the disagreement group / stayed for the film.
동의한 집단의 18퍼센트만이 / 영화를 보기 위해 점심시간을 놓쳤으나 / 동의하지 않은 집단의 45퍼센트는 / 그 영화를 보기 위해 남았다.

The thirst to fill a knowledge gap / — to find out who was right within the group — / can be more powerful / than the thirst for slides and jungle gyms.
지식 격차를 메우려는 열망은 / 집단 내에서 누가 옳았는지 알기 위해 / 더 강했던 것이다. / 미끄럼틀과 정글짐을 향한 열망보다

➡ According to the experiment above, / students' interest in a topic (A) increases / when they are encouraged to (B) differ.
위 연구에 따르면, / 주제에 대한 학생들의 흥미는 증가한다. / 학생들이 의견을 달리하도록 장려될 때

Nancy Lowry와 David Johnson은 교수환경을 연구하고자 5학년과 6학년 학생들이 한 주제에 대해 상호작용을 하게 하는 실험을 진행했다. 한 집단에서는 토론이 합의를 도출하는 방식으로 유도되었다. 두 번째 집단에서는 토론이 옳은 정답에 대해 불일치를 낳도록 설계되었다. 쉽게 합의에 도달한 학생들은 주제에 흥미를 덜 보이고 더 적게 공부했으며 부가적인 정보를 얻기 위해 도서관에 가는 경향이 더 적었다. 그러나 가장 눈에 띄는 차이는 교사가 학생들에게 점심시간 동안 토론 주제와 관련된 특별한 영화를 보여주었을 때 나타났다! 동의한 집단의 18퍼센트만이 영화를 보기 위해 점심시간을 놓쳤으나 동의하지 않은 집단의 45퍼센트는 그 영화를 보기 위해 남았다. 집단 내에서 누가 옳았는지 알기 위해 지식 격차를 메우려는 열망은 미끄럼틀과 정글짐을 향한 열망보다 더 강했던 것이다.

➡ 위 연구에 따르면 주제에 대한 학생들의 흥미는 학생들이 (B) 의견을 달리하도록 장려될 때 (A) 증가한다.

Why? 왜 정답일까?

실험 결과를 제시한 마지막 두 문장에서 토론 중 의견 불일치를 경험한 학생들은 점심시간에 토론 주제와 관련된 영화를 보여주었을 때 거의 절반 가까이 남아서 볼 정도로 그 주제에 대한 관심이 크게 증가해 있었다고 한다. 따라서 요약문의 빈칸 (A), (B)에 들어갈 말로 가장 적절한 것은 ① '(A) increases(증가한다), (B) differ(의견을 달리하도록)'이다.

- assign ⓥ (과업 등을) 할당하다
- noticeable ⓐ 두드러지는, 눈에 띄는
- thirst ⓝ 갈망, 갈증
- approve ⓥ 동의하다, 승인하다
- disagreement ⓝ 불일치, 불화
- reveal ⓥ 드러내다, 밝히다
- fill a gap 격차를 메우다

구문 풀이

15행 The thirst (to fill a knowledge gap) — (to find out who was right within the
주어　　형용사적 용법　　　( ): 삽입구('to fill ~' 보충 설명)
group) — can be more powerful than the thirst for slides and jungle gyms.
동사

★★ 문제 해결 꿀~팁 ★★

▶ 많이 틀린 이유는?
'The most noticeable difference, ~' 이후로 제시되는 실험 결과를 잘 이해해야 한다. 결과에 따르면 토론 중 합의에 도달했던 그룹보다 합의에 이르지 못하고 의견이 서로 불일치했던 그룹에서 더 많은 수가 토론 주제와 관련된 영화를 추가로 보러 남았다고 한다. ②, ③은 서로의 의견에 '동의하거나' '협력할' 때 학생들의 흥미가 커질 수 있다는 내용을 완성하는데, 이는 주제와 반대된다.

▶ 문제 해결 방법은?
글의 disagreement가 ①의 differ로 재진술된 것임에 유의한다.

41-42 회사에 기회를 열어줄 수 있는 소비자 불평

The market's way of telling a firm about its failures / is harsh and brief.
회사에게 실패에 대해 말해주는 시장의 방식은 / 가혹하면서 간단하다.

『Not only are complaints less expensive to handle / but they also can cause the seller to (a) improve.』 41번의 근거
불평은 다루기에 비용이 덜 들뿐 아니라 / 판매자가 향상되도록 만들 수도 있다.

The seller may learn something as well.
판매자는 또한 뭔가를 배울지도 모른다.

I remember a cosmetics company / that received complaints about sticky sunblock lotion.
나는 화장품 회사를 기억한다. / 끈적거리는 선크림 로션에 대한 불평을 받은

At the time, all such lotions were more or less sticky, / so the risk of having customers / buy products from a rival company / was not (b) great.
그 당시에, 그러한 로션은 모두 다소 끈적거렸기에 / 고객들이 ~하게 하는 위험은 / 경쟁사의 제품을 사게 / 크지 않았다.

But this was also an opportunity.
하지만 이것은 또한 기회였다.

The company managed to develop a product / that was not sticky / and captured 20 percent of the market in its first year.
그 회사는 제품을 개발했고 / 끈적거리지 않는 / 첫 해에 시장의 20퍼센트를 점유했다.

Another company had the (c) opposite problem.
또 다른 회사는 반대되는 문제를 가졌다.

Its products were not sticky enough.
그 회사의 상품은 충분히 끈적거리지 않았다.

The company was a Royal Post Office in Europe / and the product was a stamp.
그 회사는 유럽에 있는 Royal Post Office였고 / 상품은 우표였다.

The problem was / that the stamp didn't stick to the envelope.
문제는 / 우표가 편지 봉투에 붙지 않았다는 것이다.

Management contacted the stamp producer / who made it clear / that if people just moistened the stamps properly, / they would stick to any piece of paper.
경영진은 우표 제작자에게 연락했는데, / 그는 명확히 밝혔다. / 만약 사람들이 우표를 적절히 적시기만 한다면, / 우표가 어떤 종이에든 달라붙을 것이라는 점을

What to do?
어떻게 할까?

Management didn't take long to come to the conclusion / that it would be (d) more costly / to try to educate its customers to wet each stamp / rather than to add more glue.
경영진은 오래지 않아 결론에 이르렀다. / 비용이 더 들 것이라는 / 고객에 우표를 적시도록 교육하려 애쓰는 데 / 더 많은 풀을 첨가하는 것보다

『The stamp producer was told to add more glue / and the problem didn't occur again.』 42번의 근거
우표 제작자는 더 많은 풀을 첨가하라고 지시받았고 / 그 문제는 더 이상 일어나지 않았다.

Since it is better for the firm / to have buyers complain / rather than go elsewhere, / it is important to make it (e) easier / for dissatisfied customers to complain.
회사에게는 더 나은 일이기 때문에, / 구매자가 불평하게 하는 것이 / 다른 곳으로 가게 하는 것보다는 / 더 쉽게 만드는 것이 중요하다. / 불만족한 고객들이 불평하는 것을

회사에게 실패에 대해 말해주는 시장의 방식은 가혹하면서 간단하다. 불평은 다루기에 비용이 덜 들뿐 아니라 판매자가 (a) 향상되도록 만들 수도 있다. 판매자는 또한 뭔가를 배울지도 모른다. 나는 끈적거리는 선크림 로션에 대한 불평을 받은 한 화장품 회사를 기억한다. 그 당시에, 그러한 로션은 모두 다소 끈적거렸기에 고객들이 경쟁사의 제품을 사게 하는 위험은 (b) 크지 않았다. 하지만 이것은 또한 기회였다. 그 회사는 끈적거리지 않는 제품을 개발해냈고 첫 해에 시장의 20퍼센트를 점유했다. 또 다른 회사는 (c) 반대되는 문제를 가졌다. 그 회사의 상품은 충분히 끈적거리지 않았다. 그 회사는 유럽에 있는 Royal Post Office였고 상품은 우표였다. 문제는 우표가 편지 봉투에 붙지 않았다는 것이다. 경영진은 우표 제작자에게 연락했는데, 그는 만약 사람들이 우표를 적절히 적시기만 한다면, 우표가 어떤 종이에든 달라붙을 것이라는 점을 명확히 밝혔다. 어떻게 할까? 경영진은 오래지 않아 (우표에) 더 많은 풀을 첨가하는 것보다 고객에게 우표를 적시도록 교육하려 애쓰는 데 비용이 (d) 덜(→ 더)들 것이라는 결론에 이르렀다. 우표 제작자는 더 많은 풀을 첨가하라고 지시받았고 그 문제는 더 이상 일어나지 않았다.
구매자가 다른 곳으로 가게 하는 것보다는 불평하게 하는 것이 회사에게는 더 나은 일이기 때문에, 불만족한 고객들이 불평하는 것을 (e) 더 쉽게 만드는 것이 중요하다.

- market ⓝ 시장
- harsh ⓐ 혹독한
- complaint ⓝ 불평
- handle ⓥ 다루다
- cosmetics ⓝ 화장품
- sunblock lotion 선크림 로션
- manage to 이럭저럭 ~하다
- opposite ⓐ 정반대의
- stick to ~에 달라붙다
- management ⓝ 경영진
- properly ⓐⓓ 적절하게, 제대로
- costly ⓐ 많은 비용이 드는
- failure ⓝ 실패
- brief ⓐ 간단한, 짧은
- less expensive 덜 비싼
- seller ⓝ 판매자
- sticky ⓐ 끈적거리는, 잘 달라붙는
- rival ⓝ 경쟁자, 경쟁 상대
- capture ⓥ 사로잡다
- stamp ⓝ 우표
- envelope ⓝ 봉투
- moisten ⓥ 적시다
- come to the conclusion 결론에 이르다
- educate ⓥ 교육하다, 가르치다

- glue ⓝ 풀
- dissatisfied ⓐ 불만족한
- unsolved ⓐ 해결되지 않은
- enemy ⓝ 적
- elsewhere [ad] 다른 곳으로
- cheap ⓐ (값이) 싼, 돈이 적게 드는
- competitor ⓝ 경쟁자, 경쟁 상대

구문 풀이

2행 Not only **are** **complaints** less expensive to handle but they also can
　　　「부정어구+be동사+주어 : 도치 구문」　　　「not only + A + but also + B : A뿐만 아니라 B도」
cause the seller to improve.
「cause + 목적어 + to부정사 : ~이 …하도록 야기하다」

---

41 제목 파악　　　　정답률 55% | 정답 ②

윗글의 제목으로 가장 적절한 것은?

① Designs That Matter the Most to Customers
　소비자들에게 가장 중요한 디자인
✔② Complaints: Why Firms Should Welcome Them
　불평: 왜 회사들은 이것을 환영해야 하는가
③ Cheap Prices Don't Necessarily Mean Low Quality
　싼 가격이 꼭 저품질을 뜻하는 것은 아니다
④ More Sticky or Less Sticky: An Unsolved Problem
　더 끈적거릴 것인가, 덜 끈적거릴 것인가: 해결되지 않은 문제
⑤ Treat Your Competitors Like Friends, Not Enemies
　경쟁자를 적이 아닌 친구처럼 대하라

Why? 왜 정답일까?

'Not only are complaints less expensive to handle but they also can cause the seller to improve.'에서 언급하듯이 소비자의 불평은 처리하는 데 돈도 덜 비싸게 들거니와 판매자에게 나아질 기회를 제공해 주기에 의미가 있다는 내용의 글이다. 따라서 글의 제목으로 가장 적절한 것은 ② '불평: 왜 회사들은 이것을 환영해야 하는가'이다.

★★★ 등급을 가르는 문제!

42 어휘 추론　　　　정답률 42% | 정답 ④

밑줄 친 (a) ~ (e) 중에서 문맥상 낱말의 쓰임이 적절하지 <u>않은</u> 것은? [3점]

① (a)　② (b)　③ (c)　✔④ (d)　⑤ (e)

Why? 왜 정답일까?

우표 제작에 관한 두 번째 예시를 마무리하는 'The stamp producer was told to add more glue and the problem didn't occur again.'에서, 우표 제작자는 결국 잘 달라붙지 않는 우표에 풀을 더 첨가할 것을 요청받았고 더 이상 같은 문제는 발생하지 않게 되었다고 한다. 이는 경영진에서 소비자에게 우표 사용법을 교육하는 것보다 제작 때 풀을 더 넣는 것이 비용상 이득이라고 판단했기에 이행된 대처로 볼 수 있다. 다시 말해, 소비자를 교육하는 것이 제작 과정을 수정하는 것보다 비용이 '더' 드는 일이었다는 의미가 되도록 (d)의 less를 more로 고쳐야 한다. 따라서 문맥상 낱말의 쓰임이 적절하지 않은 것은 ④ '(d)'이다.

★★ 문제 해결 꿀~팁 ★★

▶ 많이 틀린 이유는?
최다 오답인 ③의 (c) 앞에서 끈적거리는 선크림(sticky sunblock lotion)에 관해 불평을 받았던 화장품 회사를 언급한 후, (c) 뒤에서는 충분히 끈적거리지 않는(not sticky enough) 우표 때문에 문제가 있었던 회사를 언급하고 있다. 즉 (c) 앞뒤로 '반대되는' 예가 제시되므로 (c)에 opposite를 쓴 것은 맥락상 맞다.

▶ 문제 해결 방법은?
(d)의 구문이 다소 복잡하므로 (d) 뒤의 'The stamp producer was told ~' 문장을 먼저 잘 이해한 뒤 (d)가 포함된 문장을 다시 읽도록 한다. (d) 뒤에 따르면 우표 제작자가 결국 우표에 풀을 더 첨가하라는 지시를 받았다고 하는데, 이는 '소비자들에게 우표를 적시라고 교육하는 것'과 '우표에 풀을 더 발라 제작하는 것' 사이에서 경영진이 후자를 선택했기 때문이다. (d)는 경영진이 이와 같은 결정을 내린 까닭으로 제작 과정을 수정하는 것보다 소비자를 교육하는 데 돈이 오히려 '더 들기' 때문임을 설명하는 것이다. 따라서 less 대신 more를 쓸 때 문맥이 자연스럽다.

43-45 도둑을 솜씨 좋게 골탕먹인 상인

(A)

A rich merchant lived alone in his house.
부유한 상인이 자신의 집에 혼자 살았다.
Knowing that he was the only person living in the house, /「he was always prepared / in case thieves came to his house.」 45번 ①의 근거 일치
그 집에 사는 사람이 자기밖에 없다는 것을 알았기 때문에, / 그는 항상 대비하고 있었다. / 자신의 집에 도둑이 드는 상황에
So, one day, when a thief entered his home, / he remained calm and cool.
그래서 어느 날, 도둑이 집에 들어왔을 때, / 그는 차분하고 침착했다.
Although he was awake, / the merchant pretended to be in a deep sleep.
비록 그가 깨어 있었지만, / 상인은 깊이 잠든 척했다.
He lay in bed and watched the thief in action.
그는 침대에 누워서 도둑이 움직이는 것을 지켜보았다.
The thief had brought a new white sheet with (a) him / to carry away the stolen goods.
도둑은 흰 새 보자기를 가지고 왔다. / 훔친 물건들을 운반하기 위해

(D)

He spread it out on the floor / with the idea of putting all the stolen valuables into it, / tying it, / and carrying it away.
그는 그것을 바닥에 펼쳐놓았다. / 훔친 귀중품들을 모두 넣을 생각으로 / 그것을 묶고 / 그리고 그것을 운반할
While (e) he was busy gathering expensive-looking items / from the merchant's luxurious house, / the merchant quickly got out of the bed.
그가 비싸게 보이는 물건을 모으느라 분주한 사이, / 상인의 호화로운 집에서 / 상인은 재빨리 침대에서 일어났다.
「Then he replaced the new white sheet / with a similar looking white sheet, / which was much weaker and much cheaper than the thief's one.」 45번 ⑤의 근거 일치
그러고 나서 그는 도둑의 흰 새 보자기를 바꾸었는데, / 비슷하게 생긴 흰 보자기로 / 이것은 도둑의 것보다 훨씬 약하고 값쌌다.

(B)

(b) He then lay down and pretended to be asleep.
그러고 나서 그는 누워서 자는 척했다.
When the thief had finished / collecting as many valuables as he could, / he hurriedly tied a knot in the white sheet / which he thought was his.
도둑이 마쳤을 때, / 가능한 한 많은 귀중품들을 훔치는 것을 / 그는 흰 보자기의 매듭을 서둘러 묶었다. / 그가 자신의 것이라고 생각했던
「The merchant meanwhile ran out into the garden / and yelled — "Thief! Thief!" / with all the air in his lungs.」 45번 ②의 근거 일치
그 동안에 상인은 정원으로 뛰어나가 / "도둑이야 도둑!"이라고 소리쳤다. / 있는 힘껏
The thief got nervous and quickly lifted the sheet.
도둑은 초조해져서 서둘러 보자기를 들어올렸다.
To (c) his surprise, / the thin white sheet, / filled with stolen goods, / was torn apart.
그가 놀랍게도 / 얇은 흰 보자기가 / 훔친 물건들로 가득 찬 / 찢어졌다.

(C)

「All the stolen goods fell down on the floor / creating a very loud and unpleasant noise.」 45번 ③의 근거 일치
훔친 모든 물건들이 바닥에 떨어져 / 아주 크고 불쾌한 소리를 냈다.
Seeing many people run towards him, / the thief had to give up on all of the stolen goods.
많은 사람들이 자신에게 달려드는 것을 보고 / 도둑은 훔친 모든 물건들을 포기해야만 했다.
「Leaving the goods behind in the house, / he ran away in a hurry saying under his breath:」 / "This man is such a skillful merchant; he is a businessman to the core. 45번 ④의 근거 불일치
그 물건들을 집에 남겨두고 떠나면서, / 그는 서둘러 도망치며 작은 목소리로 말했다. / "이 사람은 교묘한 상인이야. / 그는 뼛속까지 장사꾼이야.
He has not only managed to save his valuables / but has also taken away (d) my new sheet.
그는 그의 귀중품들을 지켜냈을 뿐 아니라, / 내 새 보자기도 빼앗았다고.
He has stolen from a thief!"
그는 도둑한테서 훔쳤어!"
As he said that to himself, / he ran away from the house.
그가 이렇게 혼잣말을 하면서 / 그는 집밖으로 뛰쳐나갔다.

(A)
부유한 상인이 자신의 집에 혼자 살았다. 그 집에 사는 사람이 자기밖에 없다는 것을 알았기 때문에, 그는 자신의 집에 도둑이 드는 상황에 항상 대비하고 있었다. 그래서 어느 날, 도둑이 집에 들어왔을 때, 그는 차분하고 침착했다. 비록 상인은 깨어 있었지만, 깊이 잠든 척했다. 그는 침대에 누워서 도둑이 움직이는 것을 지켜보았다. 도둑은 훔친 물건들을 운반하기 위해 흰 새 보자기를 (a) 그와 함께 가지고 왔다.

(D)
그는 훔친 귀중품들을 모두 넣어 묶은 뒤 운반할 생각으로 그것을 바닥에 펼쳐놓았다. (e) 그가 상인의 호화로운 집에서 비싸게 보이는 물건을 모으느라 분주한 사이, 상인은 재빨리 침대에서 일어났다. 그러고 나서 그는 도둑의 흰 새 보자기를 비슷하게 생긴 흰 보자기로 바꾸었는데, 이것은 도둑의 것보다 훨씬 약하고 값싼 것이었다.

(B)
그러고 나서 (b) 그(상인)는 누워서 자는 척했다. 도둑이 가능한 한 많은 귀중품들을 훔치는 것을 마쳤을 때, 그는 자신의 것이라고 생각했던 흰 보자기의 매듭을 서둘러 묶었다. 그 동안에 상인은 정원으로 뛰어나가 있는 힘껏 소리쳤다. ― "도둑이야! 도둑!" 도둑은 초조해져서 서둘러서 보자기를 들어올렸다. (c) 그가 놀랍게도 훔친 물건들로 가득 찬 얇은 흰 보자기가 찢어졌다.

(C)
훔친 모든 물건들이 바닥에 떨어져 아주 크고 불쾌한 소리를 냈다. 많은 사람들이 자신에게 달려드는 것을 보고 도둑은 훔친 모든 물건들을 포기해야만 했다. 그 물건들을 집에 남겨두고 떠나면서, 그는 서둘러 도망치며 작은 목소리로 말했다. "이 사람은 교묘한 상인이야. 그는 뼛속까지 장사꾼이야. 그는 그의 귀중품들을 지켜냈을 뿐 아니라, (d) 내 새 보자기도 빼앗았다고. 그는 도둑한테서 훔쳤어!" 이렇게 혼잣말을 하면서 그는 집밖으로 뛰쳐나갔다.

- merchant ⓝ 상인
- in action 활동을 하는
- tie a knot 매듭을 묶다
- to one's surprise ~로서는 놀랍게도
- unpleasant ⓐ 불쾌한
- under one's breath 낮은 목소리로
- spread out 펼치다
- pretend ⓥ ~인 체하다
- valuable ⓝ 귀중품 ⓐ 귀한, 가치 있는
- yell ⓥ 소리치다
- tear apart 찢다
- give up on ~을 포기하다, 단념하다
- to the core 속속들이, 완전히

구문 풀이

(B) 1행 When the thief had finished collecting as many valuables as he could, he
　　　　접속사(~할 때)　　　　　　동사(과거완료)
hurriedly tied a knot in the white sheet [which (he thought) was his].
동사(과거)　　　　　　　　　　선행사 ↰　　( ) : 삽입절

(D) 3행 While he was busy gathering expensive-looking items from the
　　　　　　　「be busy + 동명사 : ~하느라 바쁘다」
merchant's luxurious house, the merchant quickly got out of the bed.

---

43 글의 순서 파악　　　　정답률 66% | 정답 ④

주어진 글 (A)에 이어질 내용을 순서에 맞게 배열한 것으로 가장 적절한 것은?

① (B) - (D) - (C)　　　② (C) - (B) - (D)
③ (C) - (D) - (B)　✔④ (D) - (B) - (C)
⑤ (D) - (C) - (B)

Why? 왜 정답일까?

혼자 살아서 도둑이 드는 상황에 늘 대비하고 있던 상인이 어느 날 정말 집에 도둑이 든 것을 알았다는 내용의 (A) 뒤로, 도둑이 귀한 물건을 찾느라 분주한 사이 상인이 도둑의 흰 보자기를 다른 것으로 바꾸어 놓았다는 (D)가 연결된다. 이어서 (B)에서는 도둑이 갈 채비를 하자 상인이 밖으로 나가 도둑이 들었다며 소리를 질렀고 이에 도둑이 바삐 움직이다 보자기가 찢어졌다는 내용이 전개된다. 마지막으로 (C)는 보자기가 찢어지는 바람에 물건이 모두 떨어졌고, 도둑은 모든 것을 포기한 채 상인이 한 수 위임을 인정하고 떠났다는 결말을 제시한다. 따라서 글의 순서로 가장 적절한 것은 ④ '(D) - (B) - (C)'이다.

44 지칭 추론 정답률 47% | 정답 ②

밑줄 친 (a)~(e) 중에서 가리키는 대상이 나머지 넷과 <u>다른</u> 것은?

① (a)　　②✔ (b)　　③ (c)　　④ (d)　　⑤ (e)

Why? 왜 정답일까?

(a), (c), (d), (e)는 the thief, (b)는 the merchant를 가리키므로, (a)~(e) 중에서 가리키는 대상이 다른 하나는 ② '(b)'이다.

---

45 세부 내용 파악 정답률 68% | 정답 ④

윗글에 관한 내용으로 적절하지 <u>않은</u> 것은?

① 상인은 도둑이 드는 상황에 항상 대비하고 있었다.
② 상인은 정원으로 뛰어나가 크게 소리쳤다.
③ 도둑이 훔친 물건들이 바닥에 떨어졌다.
④✔ 도둑은 상인의 물건들을 집밖으로 가지고 달아났다.
⑤ 상인의 보자기는 도둑의 보자기보다 값쌌던 것이었다.

Why? 왜 정답일까?

(C) 'Leaving the goods behind in the house, he ran away in a hurry ~'에서 도둑은 훔치려던 물건을 모두 집에 두고 황급히 달아났다고 하므로, 내용과 일치하지 않는 것은 ④ '도둑은 상인의 물건들을 집밖으로 가지고 달아났다.'이다.

Why? 왜 오답일까?

① (A) '~ he was always prepared in case thieves came to his house.'의 내용과 일치한다.
② (B) 'The merchant meanwhile ran out into the garden and yelled ~'의 내용과 일치한다.
③ (C) 'All the stolen goods fell down on the floor ~'의 내용과 일치한다.
⑤ (D) '~ a similar looking white sheet, which was much weaker and much cheaper than the thief's one.'의 내용과 일치한다.

어휘 Review Test 14

문제편 140쪽

A	B	C	D
01 극복하다	01 assure	01 ⓕ	01 ①
02 불충분한	02 carry out	02 ⓠ	02 ⓓ
03 이점	03 delighted	03 ⓑ	03 ①
04 인정	04 assign	04 ⓝ	04 ⓟ
05 갈망, 갈증	05 conclusively	05 ①	05 ⓒ
06 몹시, 극도로	06 inspire	06 ①	06 ①
07 혜택, 이득	07 eliminate	07 ⓟ	07 ⓑ
08 상대적인	08 consume	08 ⓝ	08 ⓞ
09 고마워하는	09 feature	09 ⓡ	09 ⓡ
10 대략적으로	10 dissatisfied	10 ⓒ	10 ⓢ
11 처음의, 초기의	11 capture	11 ⓜ	11 ⓖ
12 충분한	12 brief	12 ⓖ	12 ⓔ
13 적시다	13 interpret	13 ⓢ	13 ⓠ
14 결국	14 assume	14 ①	14 ⓝ
15 저축(액)	15 loyalty	15 ⓓ	15 ⓜ
16 넘어서다, 초과하다	16 capability	16 ⓞ	16 ⓚ
17 관심, 우려	17 incredibly	17 ⓔ	17 ⓐ
18 복잡성	18 distrust	18 ⓗ	18 ①
19 전시하다	19 establish	19 ⓚ	19 ⓗ
20 펼치다	20 additionally	20 ⓐ	20 ①

15회 | 2020학년도 9월 학력평가 [고1]

| 정답과 해설 |

· 정답 ·

18 ③ 19 ① 20 ② 21 ④ 22 ② 23 ② 24 ② 25 ④ 26 ③ 27 ④ 28 ④ 29 ④ 30 ② 31 ③ 32 ①
33 ③ 34 ① 35 ④ 36 ② 37 ⑤ 38 ③ 39 ③ 40 ① 41 ② 42 ④ 43 ② 44 ⑤ 45 ⑤

★ 표기된 문항은 [등급을 가르는 문제]에 해당하는 문항입니다.

---

18 악기 기부 요청 정답률 90% | 정답 ③

다음 글의 목적으로 가장 적절한 것은?

① 고장 난 악기의 수리를 의뢰하려고
② 학부모 공개 수업 참석을 권장하려고
③✔ 음악 수업을 위한 악기 기부를 요청하려고
④ 추가로 개설된 음악 수업 신청을 독려하려고
⑤ 지역 주민을 위한 자선 음악 행사를 홍보하려고

Dear Wildwood residents,
Wildwood 지역 주민들께,

Wildwood Academy is a local school / that seeks to help children with disabilities and learning challenges.
Wildwood Academy는 지역 학교입니다. / 장애와 학습의 어려움을 가진 아이들을 돕고자 하는

We currently have over 200 students enrolled.
현재 200명이 넘는 학생들이 등록되어 있습니다.

This year we'd like to add a music class / in the hope that each of our students will have the opportunity / to develop their musical abilities.
올해 저희는 음악 수업을 추가 개설하고자 합니다. / 학생들 각각이 기회를 얻기를 바라며 / 그들의 음악적 능력을 발전시킬

To get the class started, / we need more instruments / than we have now.
이 수업을 시작하기 위해, / 저희는 더 많은 악기가 필요합니다. / 지금 저희가 가지고 있는 것보다

We are asking you / to look around your house and donate any instruments / that you may no longer use.
저희는 여러분께 요청합니다. / 집을 둘러보고 어떠한 악기든지 기부해 주시기를 / 여러분이 더 이상 사용하지 않을지도 모르는

Each one donated will be assigned to a student in need.
기부된 각 악기는 필요로 하는 학생에게 배정될 것입니다.

Simply call us / and we will be happy to drop by and pick up the instrument.
그저 전화만 주세요 / 그러면 저희가 기꺼이 방문하여 악기를 가져가겠습니다.

Sincerely, // Karen Hansen, Principal
교장 Karen Hansen 드림

Wildwood 지역 주민들께,

Wildwood Academy는 장애와 학습의 어려움을 가진 아이들을 돕고자 하는 지역 학교입니다. 현재 200명이 넘는 학생들이 등록되어 있습니다. 올해 저희는 학생들 각각이 그들의 음악적 능력을 발전시킬 기회를 얻기를 바라며 음악 수업을 추가 개설하고자 합니다. 이 수업을 시작하기 위해, 저희는 지금 저희가 가지고 있는 것보다 더 많은 악기가 필요합니다. 저희는 여러분이 집을 둘러보고 더 이상 사용하지 않을지도 모르는 악기를 기부해 주시기를 요청합니다. 기부된 각 악기는 필요로 하는 학생에게 배정될 것입니다. 전화만 주시면 저희가 기꺼이 방문하여 악기를 가져가겠습니다.

교장 Karen Hansen 드림

Why? 왜 정답일까?

'We are asking you to look around your house and donate any instruments that you may no longer use.'에서 집에 사용하지 않는 악기가 있으면 학교에 기부해달라고 요청하고 있으므로, 글의 목적으로 가장 적절한 것은 ③ '음악 수업을 위한 악기 기부를 요청하려고'이다.

● disability ⓝ 장애
● enroll ⓥ 등록하다
● assign 배정하다
● currently ⓐⓓ 현재
● instrument ⓝ 악기, 도구
● drop by ⓥ (~에) 들르다

구문 풀이

7행 We are asking you to look around your house and donate any instruments
　　　　　　　　5형식 동사　목적어　　　목적격 보어1　　　　　　　목적격 보어2
[that you may no longer use].
목적격 관계대명사

---

19 모금 프로젝트를 위해 연설에 나선 Salva 정답률 88% | 정답 ①

다음 글에 드러난 Salva의 심경 변화로 가장 적절한 것은?

①✔ nervous → relieved
　긴장한 → 안도한
② indifferent → excited
　무관심한 → 신난
③ worried → disappointed
　걱정한 → 실망한
④ satisfied → frustrated
　만족한 → 좌절한
⑤ confident → embarrassed
　자신 있는 → 당황한

Salva had to raise money / for a project to help southern Sudan.
Salva는 모금을 해야 했다. / 남부 수단을 돕기 위한 프로젝트를 위해서

It was the first time / that Salva spoke in front of an audience.
처음이었다. / Salva가 관중 앞에서 말하는 것은

There were more than a hundred people.
백 명이 넘는 사람들이 있었다.

Salva's knees were shaking / as he walked to the microphone.
Salva의 무릎이 후들거리고 있었다. / 그가 마이크로 걸어갈 때

"H-h-hello," he said.
"아-아-안녕하세요," 그가 말했다.

His hands trembling, / he looked out at the audience.
그는 손을 떨면서 / 그는 관중을 바라보았다.

Everyone was looking at him.

모든 사람들이 그를 보고 있었다.

At that moment, / he noticed that every face looked interested / in what he had to say.
그때, / 그는 모든 얼굴이 관심이 있어 보임을 알아차렸다. / 그가 할 말에

People were smiling and seemed friendly.
사람들은 미소 짓고 있었고 우호적으로 보였다.

That made him feel a little better, / so he spoke into the microphone again.
그것이 그의 기분을 좀 더 나아지게 해서, / 그는 다시 마이크에 대고 말했다.

"Hello," he repeated.
"안녕하세요." 그는 반복했다.

He smiled, / feeling at ease, / and went on.
그는 미소를 지었고 / 안도한 기분으로 / 말을 이어갔다.

"I am here to talk to you / about a project for southern Sudan."
저는 여러분께 말씀드리려고 이 자리에 섰습니다. / 남부 수단을 위한 프로젝트에 관해

Salva는 남부 수단을 돕기 위한 프로젝트를 위해서 모금을 해야 했다. Salva가 관중 앞에서 말하는 것은 처음이었다. 백 명이 넘는 사람들이 있었다. Salva가 마이크로 걸어갈 때 그의 무릎이 후들거리고 있었다. "아-아-안녕하세요," 그가 말했다. 그는 손을 떨면서 관중을 바라보았다. 모든 사람들이 그를 보고 있었다. 그때, 그는 모든 얼굴이 그가 할 말에 관심이 있어 보임을 알아차렸다. 사람들은 미소 짓고 있었고 우호적으로 보였다. 그것이 그의 기분을 좀 더 나아지게 해서 그는 다시 마이크에 대고 말했다. "안녕하세요." 그는 반복했다. 그는 미소를 지었고 안도한 기분으로 말을 이어갔다. "저는 남부 수단을 위한 프로젝트에 관해 여러분께 말씀드리려고 이 자리에 섰습니다."

Why? 왜 정답일까?

'Salva's knees were shaking as he walked to the microphone.', 'His hands trembling, he looked out at the audience.'에서 Salva가 연설을 시작하며 몹시 긴장해 있었음을, 'He smiled, feeling at ease, and went on.'에서 사람들이 자신의 말에 관심이 있어 보이는 상황임을 알고 Salva가 안도했음을 알 수 있다. 따라서 Salva의 심경 변화로 가장 적절한 것은 ① '긴장한 → 안도한'이다.

- raise money ⓥ 모금하다
- at ease 편안한
- frustrated ⓐ 좌절한
- tremble ⓥ 떨다
- indifferent ⓐ 무관심한
- embarrassed ⓐ 당황한

구문 풀이

6행 At that moment, he noticed that every face looked interested in what he had to say.
접속사 / 2형식 동사 / 형용사 보어 / 전치사 / 관계대명사(~것)

---

20 더 높은 목표 설정하기 정답률 76% | 정답 ②

다음 글에서 필자가 주장하는 바로 가장 적절한 것은?

① 매사에 최선을 다하는 태도를 가져야 한다.
② 목표는 자신의 생각보다 높게 설정해야 한다. ✔
③ 변화하는 상황에 따라 목표를 수정해야 한다.
④ 과거의 실패를 되돌아보는 습관을 길러야 한다.
⑤ 목표 달성을 위해 계획을 구체적으로 세워야 한다.

Any goal you set / is going to be difficult to achieve, / and you will certainly be disappointed / at some points along the way.
여러분이 세우는 어떤 목표든 / 달성하기 어려울 것이고, / 여러분은 분명히 실망하게 될 것이다. / 도중에 어느 시점에서

So why not set your goals much higher / than you consider worthy from the beginning?
그러니 여러분의 목표들을 훨씬 더 높게 세우는 것은 어떤가? / 애초부터 여러분이 가치 있다고 여기는 것보다

If they are going to require work, effort, and energy, / then why not exert 10 times as much of each?
만약에 그것들이 일, 노력, 그리고 에너지를 요구한다면, / 각각을 10배 더 많이 발휘하는 것은 어떤가?

What if you are underestimating your capabilities?
만약 여러분이 자신의 능력을 과소평가하고 있는 것이라면 어떻겠는가?

You might be protesting, saying, / "What of the disappointment that comes from setting unrealistic goals?"
~라고 말하며, 여러분은 이의를 제기할지도 모른다. / "비현실적 목표를 세우는 것으로부터 오는 실망은 어떻게 합니까?"

However, / take just a few moments / to look back over your life.
그러나, / 그저 잠깐의 시간을 가져보라. / 여러분의 삶을 되돌아보기 위해

Chances are / that you have more often been disappointed / by setting targets that are too low / and achieving them / — only to be shocked that you still didn't get what you wanted.
아마 ~것이다. / 여러분은 더욱 자주 실망했을 / 너무 낮은 목표들을 세우고 / 그것들을 달성은 했으나, / 결국 자신이 원했던 것을 여전히 얻지 못했음에 깜짝 놀라며

여러분이 세우는 어떤 목표든 달성하기 어려울 것이고, 여러분은 분명히 도중에 어느 시점에서 실망하게 될 것이다. 그러나 여러분의 목표들을 애초부터 여러분이 가치 있다고 여기는 것보다 훨씬 더 높게 세우는 것은 어떤가? 만약에 그것들이 일, 노력, 그리고 에너지를 요구한다면, 각각을 10배 더 많이 발휘하는 것은 어떤가? 만약 여러분이 자신의 능력을 과소평가하고 있는 것이라면 어떻겠는가? "비현실적 목표를 세우는 것으로부터 오는 실망은 어떻게 합니까?"라는 말로 여러분은 이의를 제기할지도 모른다. 그러나 그저 잠깐 시간을 갖고 여러분의 삶을 되돌아보라. 아마 여러분은 너무 낮은 목표들을 세우고 그것들을 달성은 했으나, 결국 자신이 원했던 것을 여전히 얻지 못했음에 깜짝 놀라며 더욱 자주 실망했을 것이다.

Why? 왜 정답일까?

'So why not set your goals much higher than you consider worthy from the beginning?'에서 생각보다 훨씬 더 높은 목표를 세울 것을 제안한 데 이어, 마지막 두 문장에서는 너무 낮은 목표를 세워 버릇하면 목표를 달성하더라도 진정 원하는 것은 여전히 얻지 못해 반복적으로 실망하게 된다고 언급하고 있다. 따라서 필자가 주장하는 바로 가장 적절한 것은 ② '목표는 자신의 생각보다 높게 설정해야 한다.'이다.

- worthy ⓐ 가치 있는
- underestimate ⓥ 과소평가하다
- protest ⓥ 이의를 제기하다, 항의하다
- look back ⓥ 되돌아보다
- from the beginning 애초부터
- capability ⓝ 능력
- unrealistic ⓐ 비현실적인

구문 풀이

2행 So why not set your goals much higher than you consider worthy from the beginning?
비교급 수식(훨씬) / 5형식 동사 / 목적격 보어
「비교급+than : ~보다 더 …한/하게」

21 휴대전화 교체 주기가 짧은 이유 정답률 70% | 정답 ④

밑줄 친 have that same scenario가 다음 글에서 의미하는 바로 가장 적절한 것은? [3점]

① have frequent trouble updating programs
   프로그램 업데이트에 잦은 어려움을 겪는다
② cannot afford new technology due to costs
   비용 때문에 신기술을 구입하지 못한다
③ spend a lot of money repairing their cell phones
   그들의 휴대전화를 고치는 데 많은 돈을 쓴다
④ are driven to change their still usable cell phones ✔
   아직 쓸만한 그들의 휴대전화를 바꾸도록 유도된다
⑤ are disappointed with newly launched phone models
   새로 출시된 휴대전화 모델에 실망한다

There are more than 700 million cell phones used in the US today / and at least 140 million of those cell phone users / will abandon their current phone for a new phone / every 14-18 months.
오늘날 미국에서 사용되는 휴대전화가 7억 개가 넘고 / 그 휴대전화 사용자들 중 적어도 1억 4천만 명은 / 새 휴대전화를 위해 그들의 현재 휴대전화를 버릴 것이다. / 14~18개월마다

I'm not one of those people / who just "must" have the latest phone.
나는 그런 사람들 중 한 명은 아니다. / 최신 휴대전화를 그냥 '반드시' 가져야 하는

Actually, / I use my cell phone / until the battery no longer holds a good charge.
사실 / 나는 내 휴대전화를 사용한다. / 배터리가 더 이상 충전이 잘 되지 않을 때까지

At that point, / it's time.
그때라면 / 때가 된 것이다.

So I figure / I'll just get a replacement battery.
그래서 나는 생각한다. / 그저 교체용 배터리를 사야겠다고

But I'm told / that battery is no longer made / and the phone is no longer manufactured / because there's newer technology and better features / in the latest phones.
그러나 나는 듣게 된다. / 그 배터리가 더 이상 만들어지지 않고, / 그 휴대전화는 더 이상 제조되지 않는다고 / 더 새로운 기술과 더 나은 기능들이 있기 때문에 / 최신 휴대전화에

That's a typical justification.
그것이 전형적인 정당화이다.

The phone wasn't even that old; / maybe a little over one year?
그 휴대전화는 심지어 그렇게 오래되지도 않았다. / 아마도 1년이 좀 넘었을까?

I'm just one example.
나는 단지 한 사례일 뿐이다.

Can you imagine / how many countless other people have that same scenario?
당신은 상상할 수 있는가? / 얼마나 수많은 다른 사람들이 이와 똑같은 시나리오를 갖는지

No wonder / cell phones take the lead / when it comes to "e-waste."
놀랍지 않다. / 휴대전화가 선두에 있다는 것은 / '전자 쓰레기'에 대해서

오늘날 미국에서 사용되는 휴대전화가 7억 개가 넘고 이 휴대전화 사용자들 중 적어도 1억 4천만 명은 새 휴대전화를 위해 14~18개월마다 그들의 현재 휴대전화를 버릴 것이다. 나는 최신 휴대전화를 그냥 '반드시' 가져야 하는 그런 사람들 중 한 명은 아니다. 사실 나는 배터리가 더 이상 충전이 잘되지 않을 때까지 내 휴대전화를 사용한다. 그때라면 때가 된 것이다. 그래서 나는 그저 교체용 배터리를 사야겠다고 생각한다. 그러나 나는 그 배터리가 더 이상 만들어지지 않고, 최신 휴대전화에 더 새로운 기술과 더 나은 기능들이 있기 때문에 그 휴대전화는 더 이상 제조되지 않는다고 듣게 된다. 그것이 전형적인 정당화이다. 그 휴대전화는 심지어 그렇게 오래되지도 않았다. 아마도 1년이 좀 넘었을까? 나는 단지 한 사례일 뿐이다. 얼마나 수많은 다른 사람들이 이와 똑같은 시나리오를 갖는지 당신은 상상할 수 있는가? '전자 쓰레기'에 대해서 휴대전화가 선두에 있다는 것은 놀랍지 않다.

Why? 왜 정답일까?

글에 따르면 필자는 그저 배터리만 교체하고 더 쓰려던 휴대전화인데도 기능이 더 우수한 신형 전화들이 출시됨에 따라 그 배터리나 전화 자체가 더 이상 제조되지 않아서 휴대전화를 바꿔야만 한다. 이에 근거할 때, 많은 사람들이 '이와 동일한 시나리오를 갖는다'라고 해석되는 밑줄 친 부분은 결국 사람들이 '휴대전화가 아직 쓸 만한 데도 교체해야 하는 상황에 처한다'는 의미를 나타낸다. 따라서 밑줄 친 부분이 의미하는 바로 가장 적절한 것은 ④ '아직 쓸만한 그들의 휴대전화를 바꾸도록 유도된다'이다.

- abandon ⓥ 버리다
- manufacture ⓥ 제조하다, 생산하다
- justification ⓝ 정당화, 합리화
- no wonder ~하는 것도 당연하다
- launch ⓥ 출시하다, 시작하다
- hold a charge ⓥ 충전되다
- feature ⓝ (제품 등의) 기능, 특징
- countless ⓐ 수많은
- usable ⓐ 사용할 수 있는

구문 풀이

7행 But I'm told {that battery is no longer made and the phone is no longer
동사(4형식 수동태) / 접속사(~것) / 주어1 / 동사구1 / 주어2 / 동사구2
manufactured because there's newer technology and better features in the latest
이유 접속사 / 동사 / 주어
phones}. 〔 〕: 문장의 목적어

22 개인의 문화적 경험에 영향을 받는 학습 정답률 76% | 정답 ②

다음 글의 요지로 가장 적절한 것은?

① 문화 다양성에 대한 체계적 연구가 필요하다.
② 개인의 문화적 경험이 학습에 영향을 끼친다. ✔
③ 인간의 뇌 구조는 학습을 통해 복잡하게 진화했다.
④ 원만한 대인관계 형성은 건강한 성장의 토대가 된다.
⑤ 학습 발달 단계에 적합한 자극을 제공하는 것이 좋다.

Learners function / within complex developmental, cognitive, physical, social, and cultural systems.
학습자들은 기능한다. / 복잡한 발달적, 인지적, 신체적, 사회적, 그리고 문화적 체계 안에서

Research and theory from diverse fields / have contributed to an evolving understanding / that all learners grow and learn / in culturally defined ways / in culturally defined contexts.

다양한 분야에서의 연구와 이론은 / 이해의 발전에 기여해 왔다. / 모든 학습자들이 성장하고 배운다는 / 문화적으로 정의된 방식으로 / 문화적으로 정의된 맥락 안에서

While humans share basic brain structures and processes, / as well as fundamental experiences / such as relationships with family, age-related stages, and many more, / each of these phenomena is shaped / by an individual's precise experiences.
인간은 기본적인 뇌 구조와 처리 과정을 공유하지만, / 기본적인 경험뿐만 아니라 / 가족 관계, 연령대별 단계, 기타 등등 / 각각의 이러한 현상은 형성된다. / 개인의 정확한 경험에 의해

Learning does not happen in the same way for all people / because cultural influences are influential / from the beginning of life.
학습은 모든 사람들에게 똑같은 방식으로 일어나지는 않는다. / 문화적 영향이 영향력이 있기 때문에 / 인생의 시작부터

These ideas about the intertwining of learning and culture / have been supported by research / on many aspects of learning and development.
학습과 문화의 뒤얽힘에 관한 이러한 생각은 / 연구에 의해 지지되어 왔다. / 학습과 발달의 많은 측면에 대한

학습자들은 복잡한 발달적, 인지적, 신체적, 사회적, 그리고 문화적 체계 안에서 기능한다. 다양한 분야에서의 연구와 이론은 모든 학습자들이 문화적으로 정의된 맥락 안에서 문화적으로 정의된 방식으로 성장하고 배운다는 이해의 발전에 기여해 왔다. 인간은 가족 관계, 연령대별 단계, 기타 등등 기본적인 경험뿐만 아니라 기본적인 뇌 구조와 처리 과정을 공유하지만, 각각의 이러한 현상은 개인의 정확한 경험에 의해 형성된다. 문화적 영향은 인생의 시작부터 영향력이 있기 때문에 학습은 모든 사람들에게 똑같은 방식으로 일어나지는 않는다. 학습과 문화의 뒤얽힘에 관한 이러한 생각은 학습과 발달의 많은 측면에 대한 연구에 의해 지지되어 왔다.

Why? 왜 정답일까?

'Learning does not happen in the same way for all people because cultural influences are influential from the beginning of life.'에서 문화적 영향이 인생의 처음부터 영향을 미치기 때문에 학습은 개인마다 다르게 일어나게 된다는 핵심 내용을 제시한다. 따라서 글의 요지로 가장 적절한 것은 ② '개인의 문화적 경험이 학습에 영향을 끼친다.'이다.

- developmental ⓐ 발달에 관련된
- evolving ⓐ 발전하는
- age-related ⓐ 나이와 관련된
- precise ⓐ 정확한
- cognitive ⓐ 인지적인
- define ⓥ 정의하다, 규정하다
- phenomenon ⓝ 현상
- influential ⓐ 영향력 있는

구문 풀이

[5행] While humans share basic brain structures and processes, as well as
~한 반면 「A + as well as + B : B뿐만 아니라 A도」
fundamental experiences such as relationships with family, age-related stages,
and many more, each of these phenomena is shaped by an individual's precise
주어(each of + 복수명사)   동사(단수)
experiences.

---

23 아이들의 발달 과정에서 놀이가 행하는 역할   정답률 60% | 정답 ②

다음 글의 주제로 가장 적절한 것은?

① necessity of trying out creative ideas – 새로운 아이디어를 시도해보는 것의 필요성
② roles of play in children's development – 아이들의 발달 과정에서 놀이의 역할
③ contrasts between human and animal play – 인간의 놀이와 동물의 놀이의 차이점
④ effects of children's physical abilities on play – 아이들의 신체 능력이 놀이에 미치는 영향
⑤ children's needs at various developmental stages – 다양한 발달 단계에서의 아이들의 욕구

Animals as well as humans / engage in play activities.
인간뿐만 아니라 동물도 / 놀이 활동에 참여한다.

In animals, / play has long been seen as a way / of learning and practicing skills and behaviors / that are necessary for future survival.
동물에 있어, / 놀이는 오랫동안 방식으로 여겨져 왔다. / 기술과 행동을 학습하고 연마하는 / 미래 생존에 필요한

In children, too, / play has important functions during development.
아이들에게 있어서도 / 놀이는 발달하는 동안 중요한 기능을 한다.

From its earliest beginnings in infancy, / play is a way / in which children learn about the world and their place in it.
유아기의 가장 초기부터, / 놀이는 방식이다. / 아이들이 세상과 그 안에서의 자신의 위치에 대해 배우는

Children's play serves as a training ground / for developing physical abilities / — skills like walking, running, and jumping / that are necessary for everyday living.
아이들의 놀이는 훈련의 토대 역할을 한다. / 신체 능력을 발달시키기 위한 / — 걷기, 달리기, 그리고 점프하기 등의 능력을 / 매일의 삶에 필요한

Play also allows children / to try out and learn social behaviors / and to acquire values and personality traits / that will be important in adulthood.
놀이는 또한 아이들이 ~하도록 한다. / 사회적 행동을 시도하며 배우고, / 가치관과 성격적 특성을 습득하도록 / 성인기에 중요할

For example, / they learn / how to compete and cooperate with others, / how to lead and follow, / how to make decisions, and so on.
예를 들어, / 그들은 배운다. / 다른 사람들과 경쟁하고 협력하는 방식, / 이끌고 따르는 방식, / 결정하는 방식 등을

인간뿐만 아니라 동물도 놀이 활동에 참여한다. 동물에게 있어 놀이는 오랫동안 미래 생존에 필요한 기술과 행동을 학습하고 연마하는 방식으로 여겨져 왔다. 아이들에게 있어서도 놀이는 발달하는 동안 중요한 기능을 한다. 유아기의 가장 초기부터, 놀이는 아이들이 세상과 그 안에서의 자신의 위치에 대해 배우는 방식이다. 아이들의 놀이는 신체 능력, 즉 매일의 삶에 필요한 걷기, 달리기, 그리고 점프하기 등의 능력을 발달시키기 위한 훈련의 토대 역할을 한다. 놀이는 또한 아이들이 사회적 행동을 시도하며 배우고, 성인기에 중요할 가치관과 성격적 특성을 습득하도록 한다. 예를 들어, 그들은 다른 사람들과 경쟁하고 협력하는 방식, 이끌고 따르는 방식, 결정하는 방식 등을 배운다.

Why? 왜 정답일까?

'In children, too, play has important functions during development.'에서 동물과 마찬가지로 아이들에게 있어서도 놀이가 발달 과정에서 중요한 역할을 담당한다고 하므로, 글의 주제로 가장 적절한 것은 ② '아이들의 발달 과정에서 놀이의 역할'이다.

- engage in ⓥ ~에 참여하다
- serve as ⓥ ~의 역할을 하다
- acquire ⓥ 배우다, 습득하다
- necessity ⓝ 필요성
- infancy ⓝ 유아기
- try out ⓥ 시도하다
- adulthood ⓝ 성인기
- contrast ⓝ 차이, 대조

구문 풀이

[4행] From its earliest beginnings in infancy, play is a way [in which children
선행사   「전치사 + 관계대명사」
learn about the world and their place in it].

---

24 AI 기술 발달과 인간의 일자리 변화   정답률 76% | 정답 ②

다음 글의 제목으로 가장 적절한 것은?

① What Makes Robots Smarter? – 무엇이 로봇을 더 똑똑하게 할까?
② Is AI Really a Threat to Your Job? – AI가 당신의 일자리에 정말 위험이 될까?
③ Watch Out! AI Can Read Your Mind – 조심하세요! AI는 당신의 마음을 읽을 수 있습니다
④ Future Jobs: Less Work, More Gains – 미래의 직업: 일은 더 적고 수익은 더 많다
⑤ Ongoing Challenges for AI Development – AI 발달에 대한 현재의 도전 과제들

The loss of many traditional jobs / in everything from art to healthcare / will partly be offset / by the creation of new human jobs.
많은 전통적인 직업의 소실은 / 예술부터 건강관리에 이르는 모든 것에서 / 부분적으로 상쇄될 것이다. / 인간의 새로운 직업의 생성에 의해

Primary care doctors / who focus on diagnosing known diseases and giving familiar treatments / will probably be replaced by AI doctors.
1차 진료 의사들은 / 밝혀진 질병을 진단하고 일반적인 처방을 내리는 일을 주로 하는 / 아마도 AI 의사에 의해 대체될 것이다.

But precisely because of that, / there will be much more money / to pay human doctors and lab assistants / to do groundbreaking research / and develop new medicines or surgical procedures.
그러나 바로 그것 때문에, / 돈이 훨씬 더 많을 것이다. / 인간 의사와 실험실 조교에게 지급할 / 획기적인 연구를 하고 / 새로운 약이나 수술 절차를 개발하도록

AI might help create new human jobs / in another way.
AI는 인간의 새로운 직업을 만드는 것을 도울지도 모른다. / 또 다른 방식으로

Instead of humans competing with AI, / they could focus on servicing and using AI.
인간은 AI와 경쟁하는 대신에, / 그들은 AI를 정비하고 활용하는 것에 집중할 수 있다.

For example, / the replacement of human pilots by drones / has eliminated some jobs / but created many new opportunities / in maintenance, remote control, data analysis, and cyber security.
예를 들어, / 인간 조종사를 드론으로 대체한 것은 / 몇몇 직업을 없애 버렸지만, / 많은 새로운 기회를 만들어 냈다. / 정비, 원격조종, 데이터 분석, 그리고 사이버 보안에 있어서

예술부터 건강관리에 이르는 모든 것에서 많은 전통적인 직업의 소실은 인간의 새로운 직업의 생성으로 일부 상쇄될 것이다. 밝혀진 질병을 진단하고 일반적인 처방을 내리는 일을 주로 하는 1차 진료 의사들은 아마도 AI 의사에 의해 대체될 것이다. 그러나 바로 그것 때문에, 획기적인 연구를 하고 새로운 약이나 수술 절차를 개발하도록 인간 의사와 실험실 조교에게 지급할 돈이 훨씬 더 많을 것이다. AI는 또 다른 방식으로 인간의 새로운 직업을 만드는 것을 도울지도 모른다. 인간은 AI와 경쟁하는 대신에, AI를 정비하고 활용하는 것에 집중할 수 있다. 예를 들어, 인간 조종사를 드론으로 대체한 것은 몇몇 직업을 없애 버렸지만, 정비, 원격조종, 데이터 분석, 그리고 사이버 보안에 있어서 많은 새로운 기회를 만들어 냈다.

Why? 왜 정답일까?

첫 문장에서 AI 기술의 발달로 전통적인 직업이 소실되더라도 결국 인간이 할 수 있는 새로운 직업이 생겨나 이를 상쇄할 것이라는(The loss of many traditional jobs ~ will partly be offset by the creation of new human jobs.) 주제를 제시하고 있다. 따라서 글의 제목으로 가장 적절한 것은 ② 'AI가 당신의 일자리에 정말 위협이 될까?'이다.

- primary care ⓝ (동네 병원에서 주로 받는) 1차 진료
- diagnose ⓥ 진단하다
- groundbreaking ⓐ 획기적인
- procedure ⓝ 절차
- maintenance ⓝ 유지보수
- precisely ⓐⓓ 바로, 정확히
- surgical ⓐ 수술의
- eliminate ⓥ 없애다, 제거하다
- analysis ⓝ 분석

구문 풀이

[1행] The loss of many traditional jobs in everything (from art to healthcare)
주어   「from + A + to + B : A부터 B에 이르는」
will partly be offset by the creation of new human jobs.
동사(조동사 수동태)

---

25 2016 실내 냉방 에너지 소비량   정답률 89% | 정답 ④

다음 도표의 내용과 일치하지 않는 것은?

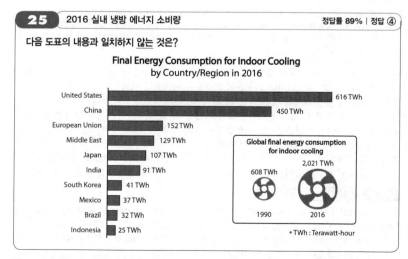

Final Energy Consumption for Indoor Cooling
by Country/Region in 2016

United States — 616 TWh
China — 450 TWh
European Union — 152 TWh
Middle East — 129 TWh
Japan — 107 TWh
India — 91 TWh
South Korea — 41 TWh
Mexico — 37 TWh
Brazil — 32 TWh
Indonesia — 25 TWh

Global final energy consumption for indoor cooling
608 TWh (1990)   2,021 TWh (2016)

* TWh : Terawatt-hour

The graph above shows / the final energy consumption for indoor cooling / by country / region in 2016.
위 그래프는 보여 준다. / 실내 냉방을 위한 최종 에너지 소비를 / 2016년 국가/지역별

① The global final energy consumption for indoor cooling / was over three times larger in 2016 than in 1990.
실내 냉방을 위한 전 세계의 최종 에너지 소비는 / 2016년에 1990년보다 3배 넘게 많았다.

② It was the United States / that had the largest final energy consumption, / which amounted to 616 TWh.
미국이었고, / 최종 에너지를 가장 많이 소비한 곳은 / 그 양은 616 TWh에 달했다.

③ The combined amount of the final energy consumption / of the European Union, the Middle East, and Japan / was less than the amount of China's final energy consumption.
최종 에너지 소비량의 총합은 / 유럽 연합, 중동, 일본의 / 중국의 최종 에너지 소비량보다 적었다.

✓ The difference in amount between India's and South Korea's final energy consumption / was more than 60 TWh.
인도와 한국의 최종 에너지 소비량의 차이는 / 60 TWh보다 많았다.

⑤ Indonesia's final energy consumption was the smallest / among the countries / regions above, / totaling 25 TWh.
인도네시아의 최종 에너지 소비는 가장 적었고, / 위의 국가들 / 지역들 중에 / 총 25 TWh이었다.

위 그래프는 2016년 실내 냉방을 위한 국가/지역별 최종 에너지 소비를 보여준다. ① 2016년 실내 냉방을 위한 전 세계의 최종 에너지 소비는 1990년보다 3배 넘게 많았다. ② 최종 에너지를 가장 많이 소비한 곳은 미국이었고, 그 양은 616 TWh에 달했다. ③ 유럽 연합, 중동, 일본의 최종 에너지 소비량의 총합은 중국의 최종 에너지 소비량보다 적었다. ④ 인도와 한국의 최종 에너지 소비량의 차이는 60 TWh보다 많았다. ⑤ 인도네시아의 최종 에너지 소비는 위의 국가들/지역들 중에 가장 적었고, 총 25 TWh이었다.

Why? 왜 정답일까?
도표에 따르면 인도의 최종 냉방 에너지 소비량은 **91 TWh**, 한국의 최종 냉방 에너지 소비량은 **41 TWh**로, 둘의 차이는 **50 TWh**이다. 따라서 도표와 일치하지 않는 것은 ④이다.

● consumption ⓝ 소비   ● amount to ⓥ (양이) ~에 달하다
● total ⓥ (합계가) ~에 이르다

---

26 Jessie Redmon Fauset의 생애   정답률 81% | 정답 ③

Jessie Redmon Fauset에 관한 다음 글의 내용과 일치하지 않는 것은?
① Cornell University를 졸업한 최초의 흑인 여성이었다.
② Washington, D.C.의 공립학교에서 프랑스어를 가르쳤다.
✓ 편집자보다는 소설가로서 더 유명하다.
④ 흑인 소녀의 이야기를 다룬 소설을 썼다.
⑤ Philadelphia에서 심장병으로 사망했다.

Jessie Redmon Fauset was born / in Snow Hill, New Jersey, in 1884.
Jessie Redmon Fauset은 태어났다. / 1884년 New Jersey의 Snow Hill에서

『She was the first black woman / to graduate from Cornell University.』 ①의 근거 일치
그녀는 최초의 흑인 여성이었다. / Cornell University를 졸업한

『In addition to writing novels, poetry, short stories, and essays, / Fauset taught French in public schools in Washington, D.C.』 ②의 근거 일치 / and worked as a journal editor.
소설, 시, 단편 소설, 수필을 쓰는 것 외에도, / Fauset은 Washington, D.C.의 공립학교에서 프랑스어를 가르쳤고, / 저널 편집자로서 일했다.

While working as an editor, / she encouraged many well-known writers of the Harlem Renaissance.
편집자로 일하는 동안, / 그녀는 Harlem Renaissance(흑인 예술 문화 부흥 운동)의 많은 유명한 작가들을 고무시켰다.

『Though she is more famous for being an editor』 / than for being a fiction writer, / many critics consider her novel *Plum Bun* Fauset's strongest work. ③의 근거 불일치
비록 그녀는 편집자로서 더 유명하지만, / 소설보다 / 많은 비평가들은 Fauset의 소설 *Plum Bun*을 그녀의 가장 뛰어난 작품으로 간주한다.

『In it, / she tells the story of a black girl / who could pass for white / but ultimately claims her racial identity and pride.』 ④의 근거 일치
그 작품에서, / 그녀는 흑인 소녀의 이야기를 다룬다. / 백인으로 여겨질 수 있지만 / 결국에는 자신의 인종적 정체성과 자부심을 주장하는

『Fauset died of heart disease April 30, 1961, in Philadelphia.』 ⑤의 근거 일치
Fauset은 1961년 4월 30일에 Philadelphia에서 심장병으로 사망했다.

Jessie Redmon Fauset은 1884년 New Jersey의 Snow Hill에서 태어났다. 그녀는 Cornell University를 졸업한 최초의 흑인 여성이었다. Fauset은 소설, 시, 단편 소설, 수필을 쓰는 것 외에도, Washington, D.C.의 공립학교에서 프랑스어를 가르쳤고, 저널 편집자로서 일했다. 편집자로 일하는 동안, 그녀는 Harlem Renaissance(흑인 예술 문화 부흥 운동)의 많은 유명한 작가들을 고무시켰다. 비록 그녀는 소설가보다 편집자로서 더 유명하지만, 많은 비평가들은 Fauset의 소설 *Plum Bun*을 그녀의 가장 뛰어난 작품으로 간주한다. 그 작품에서, 그녀는 백인으로 여겨질 수 있지만 결국에는 자신의 인종적 정체성과 자부심을 주장하는 흑인 소녀의 이야기를 다룬다. Fauset은 1961년 4월 30일에 Philadelphia에서 심장병으로 사망했다.

Why? 왜 정답일까?
'Though she is more famous for being an editor than for being a fiction writer, ~'에서 Jessie Redmon Fauset은 소설가보다는 편집자로서 더 유명하다고 하므로, 내용과 일치하지 않는 것은 ③ '편집자보다는 소설가로서 더 유명하다.'이다.

Why? 왜 오답일까?
① 'She was the first black woman to graduate from Cornell University.'의 내용과 일치한다.
② '~ Fauset taught French in public schools in Washington, D.C. ~'의 내용과 일치한다.
④ 'In it, she tells the story of a black girl ~'의 내용과 일치한다.
⑤ 'Fauset died of heart disease April 30, 1961, in Philadelphia.'의 내용과 일치한다.

● in addition to 뿐만 아니라   ● editor ⓝ 편집자
● well-known ⓐ 유명한   ● ultimately ⓐⓓ 결국, 궁극적으로
● racial ⓐ 인종적인   ● identity ⓝ 정체성

구문 풀이

> **7행** Though she is more famous for being an editor than for being a fiction
> 『비교급 + than / ~보다 더 ~한(than 앞뒤로 전명구 병렬구조)』
> writer, many critics consider her novel *Plum Bun* Fauset's strongest work.
> 『consider + A + B : A를 B라고 간주하다』

---

27 마을 청소 행사 안내   정답률 93% | 정답 ④

Greenville Community Cleanup Day에 관한 다음 안내문의 내용과 일치하지 않는 것은?
① 매년 열리는 청소 행사이다.
② 참가자들은 청소를 하기 위해 버스를 타고 이동할 것이다.
③ 10세 미만의 어린이는 성인과 동행해야 한다.
✓ 안전 조끼와 장갑은 제공되지 않을 것이다.
⑤ 모든 참가자들은 티셔츠와 간식을 무료로 받을 것이다.

Greenville Community Cleanup Day
Greenville 마을 청소의 날

『The 6th annual Greenville Community Cleanup Day is just around the corner!』 ①의 근거 일치
제6회 연례 Greenville 마을 청소의 날이 다가옵니다!

Show your community you care.
여러분이 마을에 관심이 있다는 것을 보여 주세요.

When: Saturday, October 17, 2020
언제: 2020년 10월 17일 토요일

Where: North Strand Recreation Center
어디서: North Strand Recreation Center

『Participants will be transported by bus / to clean up litter.』 ②의 근거 일치
참가자들은 버스를 타고 이동할 것입니다. / 쓰레기를 치우기 위해

Who:
누가:

Any residents who want to join
참가를 원하는 주민 누구나

『Children under 10 / must be accompanied by an adult.』 ③의 근거 일치
10세 미만의 어린이는 / 성인과 동행해야 합니다.

Cleanup Schedule:
청소 일정:

9:00 a.m.: Registration
오전 9시: 등록

9:30 a.m. − 11:30 a.m.: Cleanup at various locations
오전 9시 30분 ~ 오전 11시 30분: 다양한 장소에서 청소

『Safety vests and gloves will be provided.』 ④의 근거 불일치
안전 조끼와 장갑은 제공될 것입니다.

Don't forget to wear closed-toe shoes.
앞이 막힌 신발을 신고 오는 것을 잊지 마세요.

『All participants will get a free T-shirt and snack.』 ⑤의 근거 일치
모든 참가자들은 티셔츠와 간식을 무료로 받을 것입니다.

To sign up for the event, / email your name and phone number to info@gvcommunity.org.
행사에 등록하기 위해서는 / 이름과 전화번호를 info@gvcommunity.org로 보내 주세요.

Greenville Community Cleanup Day
(Greenville 마을 청소의 날)

제6회 연례 Greenville Community Cleanup Day가 다가옵니다! 여러분이 마을에 관심이 있다는 것을 보여주세요.

■ **일시**: 2020년 10월 17일 토요일

■ **장소**: North Strand Recreation Center
• 참가자들은 쓰레기를 치우기 위해 버스를 타고 이동할 것입니다.

■ **참가자**:
• 참가를 원하는 주민 누구나
• 10세 미만의 어린이는 성인과 동행해야 합니다.

■ **청소 일정**:
• 오전 9시: 등록
• 오전 9시 30분 ~ 오전 11시 30분: 다양한 장소에서 청소

✓ 안전 조끼와 장갑은 제공될 것입니다.
✓ 앞이 막힌 신발을 신고 오는 것을 잊지 마세요.
✓ 모든 참가자들은 티셔츠와 간식을 무료로 받을 것입니다.

행사에 등록하기 위해서는 이름과 전화번호를 info@gvcommunity.org로 보내 주세요.

Why? 왜 정답일까?
'Safety vests and gloves will be provided.'에서 안전 조끼와 장갑은 제공된다고 하므로, 안내문의 내용과 일치하지 않는 것은 ④ '안전 조끼와 장갑은 제공되지 않을 것이다.'이다.

Why? 왜 오답일까?
① 'The 6th annual Greenville Community Cleanup Day is just around the corner!'의 내용과 일치한다.
② 'Participants will be transported by bus to clean up litter.'의 내용과 일치한다.
③ 'Children under 10 must be accompanied by an adult.'의 내용과 일치한다.
⑤ 'All participants will get a free T-shirt and snack.'의 내용과 일치한다.

● cleanup ⓝ 청소, 정화   ● transport ⓥ 이동하다, 수송하다
● litter ⓝ 쓰레기   ● accompany ⓥ ~와 동행하다

---

28 책 박람회 안내   정답률 90% | 정답 ④

Springfield High School Book Fair에 관한 다음 안내문의 내용과 일치하는 것은?
① 행사 기간 동안 매일 4시간씩 진행된다.
② 학교 강당에서 개최된다.
③ 책 표지 디자인 대회 참가자 전원에게 상품권이 증정될 것이다.
✓ 폐막식에서 올해의 베스트셀러 작가를 만날 기회가 제공된다.
⑤ 현장에서 자원봉사 등록이 가능하다.

Springfield High School Book Fair
Springfield 고등학교 책 박람회

For all book lovers!
책을 사랑하는 모든 분들!
Come and enjoy the Springfield High School Book Fair.
Springfield 고등학교 책 박람회에 와서 즐기세요.
Date & Time:
날짜 & 시간:
November 9 – 13, 2020
2020년 11월 9일~13일
「9:00 a.m. – 3:00 p.m.」 ①의 근거 불일치
오전 9시 ~ 오후 3시
「Place: School Library」 ②의 근거 불일치
장소: 학교 도서관
Special Programs:
특별 프로그램:
Book Cover Design Contest
책 표지 디자인 대회
November 10, 11:00 a.m.
11월 10일, 오전 11시
「Winners will get a gift certificate / that can be used at the book fair.」 ③의 근거 불일치
수상자들은 상품권을 받을 것입니다. / 책 박람회에서 사용 가능
Closing Ceremony
폐막식
November 13, 2:00 p.m.
11월 13일, 오후 2시
「Don't miss the opportunity / to meet Rosa Park, this year's best-selling author.」 ④의 근거 일치
기회를 놓치지 마세요. / 올해의 베스트셀러 작가인 Rosa Park를 만날
「Anyone who wants to volunteer at the book fair / must sign up online in advance.」 ⑤의 근거 불일치
책 박람회에서 자원봉사하기를 원하는 사람은 누구나 / 사전에 온라인 등록을 해야 합니다.

Springfield High School Book Fair
(Springfield 고등학교 책 박람회)

책을 사랑하는 모든 분들! Springfield High School Book Fair에 와서 즐기세요.

날짜 & 시간:
• 2020년 11월 9일 ~ 13일   • 오전 9시 ~ 오후 3시

장소: 학교 도서관

특별 프로그램:
■ 책 표지 디자인 대회
• 11월 10일, 오전 11시
• 수상자들은 책 박람회에서 사용 가능한 상품권을 받을 것입니다.

■ 폐막식
• 11월 13일, 오후 2시
• 올해의 베스트셀러 작가인 Rosa Park를 만날 기회를 놓치지 마세요.

※ 책 박람회에서 자원봉사하기를 원하는 사람은 누구나 사전에 온라인 등록을 해야 합니다.

Why? 왜 정답일까?

'Don't miss the opportunity to meet Rosa Park, this year's best-selling author.'에서 폐막식에서 올해의 베스트셀러 작가인 Rosa Park를 만날 수 있다고 하므로, 안내문의 내용과 일치하는 것은 ④ '폐막식에서 올해의 베스트셀러 작가를 만날 기회가 제공된다.'이다.

Why? 왜 오답일까?

① '9:00 a.m. – 3:00 p.m.'에서 매일 6시간씩 진행된다고 하였다.
② 'Place: School Library'에서 개최 장소는 학교 도서관이라고 하였다.
③ 'Winners will get a gift certificate that can be used at the book fair.'에서 표지 디자인 대회의 수상자들에 한해 상품권이 증정된다고 하였다.
⑤ 'Anyone who wants to volunteer at the book fair must sign up online in advance.'에서 책 박람회에서 자원봉사하기를 원하는 사람들은 사전에 온라인상에서 신청해야 한다고 하였다.

● gift certificate ⓝ 상품권
● volunteer ⓥ 자원봉사하다
● author ⓝ 작가, 저자
● in advance 사전에, 미리

★★★ 등급을 가르는 문제!

29 음식에 대한 평가에 지대한 영향을 끼치는 시각적 정보   정답률 42% | 정답 ④

다음 글의 밑줄 친 부분 중, 어법상 틀린 것은? [3점]

Although it is obvious / that part of our assessment of food is its visual appearance, / it is perhaps surprising / ① how visual input can override taste and smell.
비록 분명하지만 / 우리 평가의 일부가 음식의 시각적 외관인 것은 / 아마 놀라울 것이다. / 어떻게 시각적인 입력 정보가 맛과 냄새에 우선할 수 있는가는

People find it very ② difficult / to correctly identify fruit-flavoured drinks / if the colour is wrong, / for instance an orange drink that is coloured green.
사람들은 매우 어렵다는 것을 알게 된다. / 과일 맛이 나는 음료를 정확하게 식별하는 것이 / 만약 색깔이 잘못되어 있다면, / 예를 들어 초록색인 오렌지 음료와 같이

Perhaps even more striking ③ is the experience of wine tasters.
포도주 맛을 감정하는 사람들의 경험은 어쩌면 훨씬 더 놀랍다.

One study of Bordeaux University students of wine and wine making / revealed / that they chose tasting notes appropriate for red wines, / such as 'prune and chocolate', / when they ✓ were given white wine coloured with a red dye.
포도주와 포도주 제조에 관해 공부하는 Bordeaux University 학생들을 대상으로 한 연구는 / 보여주었다 / 그들이 적포도주에 적합한 시음표를 선택했다는 것을 / '자두와 초콜릿'과 같은 / 그들이 붉은색 색소로 물들인 백포도주를 받았을 때

Experienced New Zealand wine experts / were similarly tricked into thinking / ⑤ that the white wine Chardonnay was in fact a red wine, / when it had been coloured with a red dye.
숙련된 뉴질랜드 포도주 전문가들도 / 마찬가지로 속아서 생각하게 되었다. / 백포도주 Chardonnay가 실제로 적포도주라고 / 그것을 붉은색 색소로 물들였을 때

비록 음식에 대한 우리 평가의 일부가 음식의 시각적 외관인 것은 분명하지만, 어떻게 시각적인 입력 정보가 맛과 냄새에 우선할 수 있는가는 놀라울 것이다. 만약 예를 들어 색이 초록

색인 오렌지 음료의 경우처럼 색깔이 잘못되어 있다면, 사람들은 과일 맛이 나는 음료를 정확하게 식별하기가 매우 어렵다는 것을 알게 된다. 포도주 맛을 감정하는 사람들의 경험은 어쩌면 훨씬 더 놀랍다. 포도주와 포도주 제조에 관해 공부하는 Bordeaux University 학생들을 대상으로 한 연구는 그들이 붉은색 색소로 물들인 백포도주를 받았을 때, '자두와 초콜릿'과 같은 적포도주에 적합한 시음표를 선택했다는 것을 보여주었다. 숙련된 뉴질랜드 포도주 전문가들도 마찬가지로 백포도주 Chardonnay를 붉은색 색소로 물들였을 때 속아서 그것이 실제로 적포도주라고 생각하게 되었다.

Why? 왜 정답일까?

4형식 동사 give는 능동태로 쓰일 때 목적어를 2개 취하며, 이 중 주로 사람에 해당하는 간접 목적어를 주어로 삼아 수동태를 쓰더라도 뒤에 '~을'에 해당하는 목적어 1개가 남는다. 여기서도 '~을'에 해당하는 목적어 white wine이 뒤에 나오고, 주어인 they가 이것을 '받는' 입장임을 고려할 때, gave를 were given으로 고쳐야 한다. 어법상 틀린 것은 ④이다.

Why? 왜 오답일까?

① 뒤에 주어, 동사, 목적어를 모두 갖춘 완전한 문장이 나오는 것으로 보아 how(어떻게)의 쓰임은 적절하다.
② find 동사를 포함한 5형식 가목적어 구문이므로, 가목적어 it과 진목적어인 to부정사 사이에 보어 역할을 하는 형용사 difficult가 적절하게 쓰였다.
③ 형용사 보어가 문장 맨 앞에 나오고 주어와 동사가 서로 위치를 바꾼 도치 구문이다. 즉 뒤에 나오는 단수 명사 the experience가 주어이므로 is가 앞에 바르게 쓰였다.
⑤ 'trick A into B(A를 속여 B하게 하다)'의 수동태인 'A be tricked into B(A가 속아서 B하다)' 구문에서, B에 해당하는 동명사 thinking 뒤로 목적어인 완전한 명사절이 이어지고 있다. 따라서 접속사 that이 바르게 쓰였다.

● assessment ⓝ 평가
● appearance ⓝ 외관, 겉모습
● striking ⓐ 놀라운, 두드러진, 눈에 띄는
● dye ⓝ 색소, 염료
● visual ⓐ 시각의, 눈으로 보는
● identify ⓥ 식별하다, 알아보다
● appropriate for ~에 적합한
● trick A into B ⓥ A를 속여 B하게 하다

구문 풀이

[1행] Although it is obvious {that part of our assessment of food is its visual appearance}, it is perhaps surprising {how visual input can override taste and smell}.
양보 접속사(~일지라도) ┗→ 가주어   접속사(~것)
가주어   의문부사(어떻게) ┗ 주어   동사   목적어
{ }: 진주어

★★ 문제 해결 꿀~팁 ★★

▶ 많이 틀린 이유는?
최다 오답인 ③은 도치 구문의 수 일치를 묻고 있다. 주어 역할을 할 수 있는 것은 명사(구)뿐인데 is 앞의 even more striking은 형용사이다. 이는 강조되기 위해 앞에 나온 보어일 수밖에 없고, 뒤에는 '동사+주어'의 어순이 이어지므로 the experience를 근거로 is가 적절한지를 판단해야 한다.

▶ 문제 해결 방법은?
④의 '능동 vs. 수동' 문제를 해결하기 위해서는 원칙적으로 주어를 잘 살펴야 한다. 주어가 '행하는' 주체이면 능동태를, 주어가 '당하는' 대상이면 수동태를 쓴다는 점을 명심하자.

30 경쟁과 협력 둘 다를 통해 형성되는 사회적 유대   정답률 56% | 정답 ②

(A), (B), (C)의 각 네모 안에서 문맥에 맞는 낱말로 가장 적절한 것은? [3점]

	(A)	(B)	(C)
①	creating 만들어내는	harmony 조화	prevent 막다
✓②	creating 만들어내는	tension 긴장	generate 만들어내다
③	creating 만들어내는	tension 긴장	prevent 막다
④	forgiving 용서하는	tension 긴장	prevent 막다
⑤	forgiving 용서하는	harmony 조화	generate 만들어내다

Social connections are so essential for our survival and well-being / that we not only cooperate with others to build relationships, / we also compete with others for friends.
사회적 관계는 우리의 생존과 행복을 위해 매우 필수적이어서 / 우리는 관계를 형성하기 위해 다른 사람과 협력할 뿐만 아니라, / 친구를 얻기 위해 다른 사람과 경쟁하기도 한다.

And often we do both at the same time.
그리고 우리는 흔히 둘 다를 동시에 한다.

Take gossip.
가십을 생각해보자.

Through gossip, / we bond with our friends, / sharing interesting details.
가십을 통해 / 우리는 친구들과 유대를 형성한다, / 흥미로운 세부사항을 공유하면서

But at the same time, / we are (A) creating potential enemies / in the targets of our gossip.
그러나 동시에, / 우리는 잠재적인 적을 만들어내고 있다. / 가십의 대상들 중에서

Or consider rival holiday parties / where people compete to see who will attend *their* party.
또는 라이벌 관계의 휴일 파티를 생각해 보라. / 누가 그들의 파티에 참석할 것인지를 알아보기 위해 경쟁하는

We can even see this (B) tension in social media / as people compete for the most friends and followers.
우리는 심지어 소셜 미디어에서도 이러한 긴장을 볼 수 있다. / 사람들이 가장 많은 친구들과 팔로워들을 얻기 위해 경쟁할 때

At the same time, / competitive exclusion can also (C) generate cooperation.
동시에, / 경쟁적 배제는 또한 협력도 만들어낼 수 있다.

High school social clubs and country clubs / use this formula to great effect:
고등학교 친목 동아리와 컨트리클럽은 / 이러한 공식을 사용하여 큰 효과를 발휘한다:

It is through selective inclusion *and* exclusion / that they produce loyalty and lasting social bonds.
바로 선택적인 포함 그리고 배제를 통해서이다. / 그들이 충성심과 지속적인 사회적 유대를 형성하는 것은

사회적 관계는 우리의 생존과 행복을 위해 매우 필수적이어서 우리는 관계를 형성하기 위해 다른 사람과 협력할 뿐만 아니라, 친구를 얻기 위해 다른 사람과 경쟁하기도 한다. 그리고 우리는 흔히 둘 다를 동시에 한다. 가십을 생각해 보자. 가십을 통해 우리는 친구들과 흥미로운

세부사항을 공유하면서 유대를 형성한다. 그러나 동시에 우리는 가십의 대상들 중에서 잠재적인 적을 (A) 만들어내고 있다. 또는 누가 *그들의* 파티에 참석할 것인지를 알아보기 위해 경쟁하는 라이벌 관계의 휴일 파티를 생각해 보라. 우리는 심지어 소셜 미디어에서도 사람들이 가장 많은 친구들과 팔로워들을 얻기 위해 경쟁할 때 이러한 (B) 긴장을 볼 수 있다. 동시에 경쟁적 배제는 또한 협력도 (C) 만들어낼 수 있다. 고등학교 친목 동아리와 컨트리클럽(전원 생활을 즐기려는 도시 사람을 위하여 테니스장, 수영장 등의 시설을 교외에 갖춰둔 단체)은 이러한 공식을 사용하여 큰 효과를 발휘한다. 그들이 충성심과 지속적인 사회적 유대를 형성하는 것은 바로 선택적인 포함과 *배제*를 통해서이다.

Why? 왜 정답일까?

(A) But 앞에서 우리는 가십을 통해 친구들과 유대를 형성할 수 있다고 하므로, But 뒤에는 이와 상반된 내용이 이어져야 한다. 따라서 (A)에는 가십을 하는 도중에 적도 '만들어질 수 있다'는 의미를 완성하는 creating이 들어가야 한다.
(B) 앞 문장에서 누가 서로의 파티에 참석할지 의식하는 라이벌 관계의 파티를 예로 들고 있다. 이와 같은 맥락에서 (B)가 포함된 문장은 사람들이 소셜 미디어에서도 서로 더 많은 친구나 팔로워를 얻기 위해 경쟁한다는 의미를 나타내야 한다. 따라서 (B)에는 tension이 들어가야 적절하다.
(C) 마지막 두 문장에서 고등학교 친목 동아리와 컨트리클럽을 예로 들어 이들은 선택적인 포함뿐 아니라 배제를 통해 지속적인 유대감과 충성심을 만들어낸다고 한다. 따라서 (C)에는 협력을 '만들어낸다'는 의미를 완성하는 generate가 들어가야 한다. (A), (B), (C)의 각 네모 안에서 문맥에 맞는 낱말로 가장 적절한 것은 ② '(A) 만들어내는 – (B) 긴장 – (C) 만들어내다'이다.

- **essential** ⓐ 필수적인, 본질적인
- **gossip** ⓝ 가십, 뒷담화, 험담 ⓥ 뒷담화하다
- **forgive** ⓥ 용서하다
- **exclusion** ⓝ 배제
- **prevent** ⓥ 막다, 예방하다, 방지하다
- **selective** ⓐ 선택적인
- **loyalty** ⓝ 충성심
- **well-being** ⓝ 행복, 안녕
- **create** ⓥ 만들어내다, 창조하다
- **tension** ⓝ 긴장
- **generate** ⓥ 만들어내다
- **formula** ⓝ 공식, 제조식
- **inclusion** ⓝ 포함

구문 풀이

7행 Or consider rival holiday parties [where people compete to see who will attend *their* party].
(선행사(공간) / 관계부사 / ~하기 위해 / 의문사(누가))

★★★ 등급을 가르는 둘째!

31 사건의 중요성 인식에 영향을 미치는 뉴스 보도의 양 정답률 44% | 정답 ③

다음 빈칸에 들어갈 말로 가장 적절한 것을 고르시오.
① accuracy – 정확성
② tone – 어조
✔ amount – 양
④ source – 근원
⑤ type – 유형

As the tenth anniversary of the terrorist attacks of September 11, 2001, approached, / 9/11-related media stories peaked / in the days immediately surrounding the anniversary date / and then dropped off rapidly in the weeks thereafter.
2001년 9월 11일 테러리스트 공격의 10주년 추모일이 다가오면서, / 9/11 관련 언론 기사(의 양)가 정점에 이르렀고, / 추모일 바로 전후로 / 그 후 몇 주 동안 급격히 줄어들었다.

Surveys conducted during those times / asked citizens to choose two "especially important" events / from the past seventy years.
그 시기 동안 실시된 조사는 / 시민들에게 '특히 중요한' 두 가지 사건을 선택하도록 요청했다. / 지난 70년 동안 있었던

Two weeks prior to the anniversary, / before the media blitz began, / about 30 percent of respondents named 9/11.
추모일 2주 전, / 미디어 대선전이 시작되기 전인 / 응답자의 약 30퍼센트가 9/11을 언급했다.

But as the anniversary drew closer, / and the media treatment intensified, / survey respondents started identifying 9/11 in increasing numbers / — to a high of 65 percent.
그러나 추모일이 더 가까워지고, / 미디어 보도가 증가함에 따라, / 더 많은 응답자들이 9/11을 선택하기 시작했고, / 그 수가 65퍼센트까지 올랐다.

Two weeks later, though, / after reportage had decreased to earlier levels, / once again only about 30 percent of the participants / placed it among their two especially important events / of the past seventy years.
그러나 2주 후에 / 보도가 이전 수준으로 줄어들자, / 다시 한 번 참가자의 약 30퍼센트만이 / 그것을 특히 중요한 두 가지 사건으로 선택했다. / 지난 70년 동안의

Clearly, / the amount of news coverage can make a big difference / in the *perceived* significance of an issue among observers / as they are exposed to the coverage.
명백하게, / 뉴스 보도의 양은 큰 차이를 만들 수 있다. / 관찰자들 사이에서 *인지된* 문제의 중요성에 있어 / 그들이 그 보도에 노출될 때

2001년 9월 11일 테러리스트 공격의 10주년 추모일이 다가오면서, 9/11 관련 언론 기사(의 양)가 추모일 바로 전후로 정점에 이르렀고, 그 후 몇 주 동안 급격히 줄어들었다. 그 시기 동안 실시된 조사는 시민들에게 지난 70년 동안 있었던 '특히 중요한' 두 가지 사건을 선택하도록 요청했다. 미디어 대선전이 시작되기 전인 추모일 2주 전, 응답자의 약 30퍼센트가 9/11을 언급했다. 그러나 추모일이 더 가까워지고, 미디어 보도가 증가함에 따라, 더 많은 응답자들이 9/11을 선택하기 시작했고, 그 수가 65퍼센트까지 올랐다. 그러나 보도가 2주 후에 이전 수준으로 줄어들자, 다시 한 번 참가자의 약 30퍼센트만이 그것을 지난 70년 동안의 특히 중요한 두 가지 사건으로 선택했다. 명백하게, 뉴스 보도의 양은 관찰자들이 그 보도에 노출될 때 그들 사이에서 *인지된* 문제의 중요성에 있어 큰 차이를 만들 수 있다.

Why? 왜 정답일까?

빈칸 앞의 두 문장에서 9/11 추모일이 가까워지면서 미디어 보도가 증가하자 사람들은 9/11을 '특히 중요한' 사건으로 더 많이 언급했지만, 미디어 보도가 다시 이전 수준으로 감소하자 9/11 보도를 중요한 사건으로 꼽는 사람들이 줄어들었다고 설명한다. 즉 어떤 사건에 대해 뉴스 보도가 '얼마나 많이' 이루어지는가에 따라 사건에 대한 사람들의 인식이 달라질 수 있다는 내용의 글이므로, 빈칸에 들어갈 말로 가장 적절한 것은 ③ '양'이다.

- **immediately** ⓐⓓ 바로 옆에
- **drop off** 줄다
- **intensify** ⓥ (정도, 빈도, 강도가) 심해지다, 격렬해지다
- **reportage** ⓝ 보도
- **significance** ⓝ 중요성
- **anniversary** ⓝ 기념일
- **prior to** ~에 앞서
- **perceive** ⓥ 인지하다
- **accuracy** ⓝ 정확성

구문 풀이

10행 Two weeks later, though, after reportage had decreased to earlier levels,
(부사(하지만) / 시간 접속사(~한 후에) / 과거완료)
once again only about 30 percent of the participants placed it among their two
(주어 / 동사)
especially important events of the past seventy years.

★★ 문제 해결 꿀~팁 ★★

▶ 많이 틀린 이유는?
예시 내용을 일반화하여 빈칸에 들어갈 말을 찾아야 하는데, 글에서 9/11 테러 사건이 '얼마나 많이' 보도되었는지만 언급하고 있을 뿐, 보도의 구체적인 유형을 나누고 있지는 않으므로 ⑤는 답으로 부적합하다.

▶ 문제 해결 방법은?
'the media treatment intensified ~', 'after reportage had decreased to earlier levels ~' 등을 참고하면 보도의 '양'이 곧 사건에 대한 사람들의 인식에 영향을 주는 요인임을 알 수 있다.

---

32 생존 기술의 일종인 편향 정답률 65% | 정답 ①

다음 빈칸에 들어갈 말로 가장 적절한 것을 고르시오.
✔ necessary survival skill – 필수적인 생존 기술
② origin of imagination – 상상력의 근원
③ undesirable mental capacity – 바람직하지 않은 정신적 능력
④ barrier to relationships – 관계에 대한 장애물
⑤ challenge to moral judgment – 도덕적 판단에 대한 도전 과제

Here's the unpleasant truth: / we are all biased.
여기 불편한 진실이 있다. / 우리는 모두 편향되어 있다.

Every human being is affected by unconscious biases / that lead us to make incorrect assumptions about other people.
모든 인간은 무의식적인 편견에 영향을 받는다. / 우리가 다른 사람들에 대해 부정확한 추측을 하도록 이끄는

Everyone.
모두 그렇다.

To a certain extent, / bias is an necessary survival skill.
어느 정도, / 편견은 필수적인 생존 기술이다.

If you're an early human, perhaps *Homo Erectus*, / walking around the jungles, / you may see an animal approaching.
만약에 당신이, 가령 호모 에렉투스처럼, 초기 인류라면, / 정글을 돌아다니는 / 당신은 어떤 동물이 다가오는 것을 볼지 모른다.

You have to make very fast assumptions / about whether that animal is safe or not, / based solely on its appearance.
당신은 매우 빨리 추측해야 한다. / 그 동물이 안전한지 아닌지에 대해서 / 그 동물의 외양에만 기초하여

The same is true of other humans.
이것은 다른 인류에게도 똑같이 적용된다.

You make split-second decisions about threats / in order to have plenty of time to escape, / if necessary.
당신은 위협에 대해서 순간적인 결정을 내려야 한다. / 도망갈 시간이 충분하도록 / 만약 필요하다면

This could be one root of our tendency / to categorize and label others / based on their looks and their clothes.
이것은 우리의 성향의 한 근간일 수도 있다. / 타인을 범주화하고 분류하려는 / 그들의 외모와 옷으로

여기 불편한 진실이 있는데, 우리는 모두 편향되어 있다. 모든 인간은 다른 사람들에 대해 부정확한 추측을 하도록 이끄는 무의식적인 편견에 영향을 받는다. 모두가 그렇다. 어느 정도, 편견은 필수적인 생존 기술이다. 만약에 당신이, 가령 호모 에렉투스처럼, 정글을 돌아다니는 초기 인류라면, 당신은 어떤 동물이 다가오는 것을 볼지 모른다. 당신은 그 동물의 외양에만 기초하여 그 동물이 안전한지 아닌지에 대해서 매우 빨리 추측해야 한다. 이것은 다른 인류에게도 똑같이 적용된다. 당신은 만약 필요하다면 도망갈 시간이 충분하도록 위협에 대해서 순간적인 결정을 내려야 한다. 이것은 타인의 외모와 옷으로 그들을 범주화하고 분류하려는 성향의 한 근간일 수도 있다.

Why? 왜 정답일까?

빈칸 뒤를 통해 우리는 초기 인류 시절 동물을 보고 위험한지 아닌지를 빨리 판단해야 도망갈 시간을 벌 수 있었기에 편향을 발달시켜 왔고, 이것을 오늘날까지 유지해온 것임을 알 수 있다. 따라서 빈칸에 들어갈 말로 가장 적절한 것은 편향이 우리의 '생존'을 위해 발달되어 온 것이라는 의미를 완성하는 ① '필수적인 생존 기술'이다.

- **unpleasant** ⓐ 불쾌한
- **unconscious** ⓐ 무의식적인
- **assumption** ⓝ 가정
- **approach** ⓥ 다가오다, 접근하다
- **The same is true of** ~에도 해당하다
- **categorize** ⓥ 범주화하다
- **bias** ⓥ 편견을 갖게 하다 ⓝ 편견, 편향
- **incorrect** ⓐ 부정확한
- **to a certain extent** 어느 정도
- **solely** ⓐⓓ 단지, 오로지
- **split-second** ⓐ 찰나의, 순식간의
- **undesirable** ⓐ 바람직하지 않은, 달갑지 않은

구문 풀이

8행 You make split-second decisions about threats in order to have plenty of
(~하기 위해)
time to escape, if (it is) necessary.
(접속사 / 형용사적 용법 / 생략 / 보어(형용사))

---

33 자전거 또는 오토바이를 탈 때 운전자와 움직임을 맞춰야 하는 동승자들 정답률 48% | 정답 ③

다음 빈칸에 들어갈 말로 가장 적절한 것을 고르시오. [3점]
① warn other people of danger – 다른 사람들에게 위험을 경고하도록
② stop the rider from speeding – 운전자가 과속하지 못하게 막도록
✔ mirror the rider's every move – 운전자의 모든 움직임을 따라하도록

④ relieve the rider's emotional anxiety – 운전자의 정서 불안을 완화해 주도록
⑤ monitor the road conditions carefully – 도로 상황을 면밀히 주시하도록

In Dutch bicycle culture, / it is common / to have a passenger on the backseat.
네덜란드의 자전거 문화에서, / 흔하다. / 뒷좌석에 동승자를 앉히는 것은

So as to follow the rider's movements, / the person on the backseat needs to hold on tightly.
자전거 운전자의 움직임을 따르기 위해서, / 뒷좌석에 앉은 사람은 꽉 잡을 필요가 있다.

Bicycles turn / not just by steering but also by leaning, / so the passenger needs to lean / the same way as the rider.
자전거는 방향을 바꾸는데 / 핸들을 조종하는 것뿐만 아니라 몸을 기울임으로써, / 동승자는 몸을 기울일 필요가 있다. / 자전거 운전자와 같은 방향으로

A passenger who would keep sitting up straight / would literally be a pain in the behind.
뒷좌석에서 계속해서 똑바로 앉아 있는 동승자는 / 말 그대로 뒷좌석의 골칫거리가 될 것이다.

On motorcycles, / this is even more critical.
오토바이를 탈 때는, / 이것이 훨씬 더 중요하다.

Their higher speed requires more leaning on turns, / and lack of coordination can be disastrous.
오토바이의 더 높은 속도는 방향을 바꿀 때 몸을 더 많이 기울일 것을 요구하고, / 협응의 부족은 재앙이 될 수 있다.

The passenger is a true partner in the ride, / expected to mirror the rider's every move.
동승자는 주행 시 진정한 동반자이다. / 운전자의 모든 움직임을 따라하도록 기대되기 때문에

네덜란드의 자전거 문화에서, 뒷좌석에 동승자를 앉히는 것은 흔하다. 자전거 운전자의 움직임을 따르기 위해서, 뒷좌석에 앉은 사람은 꽉 잡을 필요가 있다. 자전거는 핸들을 조종하는 것뿐만 아니라 몸을 기울여서 방향을 바꾸기에 동승자는 자전거 운전자와 같은 방향으로 몸을 기울일 필요가 있다. 뒷좌석에서 계속해서 똑바로 앉아 있는 동승자는 말 그대로 뒷좌석의 골칫거리가 될 것이다. 오토바이를 탈 때는 이것이 훨씬 더 중요하다. 오토바이의 더 높은 속도는 방향을 바꿀 때 몸을 더 많이 기울일 것을 요구하고, 협응의 부족은 재앙이 될 수 있다. 동승자는 운전자의 모든 움직임을 따라하도록 기대되기 때문에 주행 시 진정한 동반자이다.

Why? 왜 정답일까?
자전거와 오토바이에서 동승자는 운전자의 움직임에 맞추어 같은 방향으로 몸을 기울이는 등 '협응'할 필요성이 있다는 내용의 글이다. 따라서 예시를 일반화하여 결론을 내리는 빈칸에 들어갈 말로 가장 적절한 것은 ③ '운전자의 모든 움직임을 따라하도록'이다.

- **tightly** ⓐⓓ 꽉, 단단히
- **lean** ⓥ (몸을) 기울이다
- **critical** ⓐ 중요한
- **coordination** ⓝ (신체의) 협응(신체 기관이 서로 조화롭게 움직임)
- **disastrous** ⓐ 재앙의
- **anxiety** ⓝ 불안
- **steer** ⓥ (핸들을) 조종하다
- **literally** ⓐⓓ 말 그대로
- **warn A of B** ⓥ A에게 B를 경고하다

구문 풀이

2행 So as to follow the rider's movements, the person on the backseat
~하기 위해서(= in order to ~)   주어
needs to hold on tightly.
동사(~할 필요가 있다)

★★★ 등급을 가르는 문제!
34 신생아가 부드러운 흔들림을 좋아하는 이유   정답률 27% | 정답 ①

다음 빈칸에 들어갈 말로 가장 적절한 것을 고르시오. [3점]
✓ ① acquire a fondness for motion – 움직임을 좋아하게 되고
② want consistent feeding – 계속 젖을 먹고 싶어 하고
③ dislike severe rocking – 너무 심한 흔들림을 싫어하고
④ remember the tastes of food – 음식의 맛을 기억하고
⑤ form a bond with their mothers – 엄마와 유대감을 형성하고

We're often told / that newborns and infants are comforted by rocking / because this motion is similar / to what they experienced in the womb, / and that they must take comfort in this familiar feeling.
우리는 ~라는 말을 자주 듣는다. / 신생아와 유아가 흔들림에 의해 편안해지는데, / 이것은 이런 움직임이 유사하기 때문이고, / 자궁 안에서 그들이 경험했던 것과 / 그들이 이런 친숙한 느낌에서 편안해지는 것이 틀림없다는

This may be true; / however, to date there are no convincing data / that demonstrate a significant relationship / between the amount of time a mother moves during pregnancy / and her newborn's response to rocking.
이것은 사실일 수 있다. / 하지만, 현재까지 설득력 있는 데이터는 없다. / 상당한 관계가 있음을 입증하는 / 임신 기간에 엄마가 움직이는 시간의 양과 / 흔들림에 대한 신생아의 반응 사이에

Just as likely is the idea / that newborns come to associate gentle rocking with being fed.
~라는 생각도 그만큼 가능할 법하다. / 신생아가 부드러운 흔들림을 젖 먹는 것과 연관시키게 된다는

Parents understand that rocking quiets a newborn, / and they very often provide gentle, repetitive movement during feeding.
부모는 흔들어 주는 것이 신생아를 달래 준다는 것을 알고 있어서, / 그들은 젖을 주는 동안 부드럽고, 반복적인 움직임을 매우 자주 제공한다.

Since the appearance of food is a primary reinforcer, / newborns may acquire a fondness for motion / because they have been conditioned / through a process of associative learning.
음식의 등장은 일차 강화물이기 때문에, / 신생아는 움직임을 좋아하게 되었을지 모른다. / 그들이 조건화되어 왔기 때문에 / 연관 학습의 과정을 통해

신생아와 유아는 흔들림에 의해 편안해지는데, 이것은 이런 움직임이 자궁 안에서 그들이 경험했던 것과 유사하기 때문이고, 그들이 이런 친숙한 느낌에서 편안해지는 것이 틀림없다는 말을 자주 듣는다. 이것은 사실일 수 있지만, 현재까지 임신 기간에 엄마가 움직이는 시간의 양과 흔들림에 대한 신생아의 반응 사이에 상당한 관계가 있음을 입증하는 설득력 있는 데이터는 없다. 신생아가 부드러운 흔들림을 젖을 먹는 것과 연관시키게 된다는 생각도 그만큼 가능할 법하다. 부모는 흔들어 주는 것이 신생아를 달래 준다는 것을 알고 있어서, 그들은 젖을 주는 동안 부드럽고 반복적인 움직임을 매우 자주 제공한다. 음식의 등장은 일차 강화물이기 때문에, 신생아는 움직임을 좋아하게 되고, 그 이유는 그들이 연관 학습의 과정을 통해 조건화되어 왔기 때문이다.

Why? 왜 정답일까?
신생아가 부드러운 흔들림을 좋아하는 이유에 관해 다룬 글로, 'Just as likely is the idea ~'에서 아이들은 흔들림을 젖 먹는 것과 연관 짓게 되면서 흔들림을 좋아하게 될 수도 있다는 견해를 제시한다. 이어서 엄마가 아이에게 젖을 먹이는 동안 보통 아이를 편안하게 해주기 위해서 아이를 흔들어 주는 과정에서 젖, 즉 음식이 흔들림을 '좋아하게' 되는 강화물로 기능하게 된다는 설명이 나온다. 따라서 빈칸에 들어갈 말로 가장 적절한 것은 ① '움직임을 좋아하게 되고'이다.

- **infant** ⓝ 유아
- **to date** 지금까지
- **demonstrate** ⓥ 입증하다
- **pregnancy** ⓝ 임신 (기간)
- **appearance** ⓝ 등장
- **acquire** ⓥ 얻다, 습득하다
- **consistent** ⓐ 계속되는
- **rock** ⓥ 흔들다
- **convincing** ⓐ 설득력 있는
- **significant** ⓐ 상당한, 유의미한
- **associate A with B** ⓥ A와 B를 연관시키다
- **condition** ⓥ 조건화하다
- **fondness** ⓝ 좋아함
- **severe** ⓐ 심한, 가혹한

구문 풀이

1행 We're often told {that newborns and infants are comforted by rocking
동사구(~을 듣다) 접속사1   주어   동사(수동태)
because this motion is similar to what they experienced in the womb}, and {that
접속사(~때문에)   ~와 비슷한 관계대명사(~것)   접속사2
they must take comfort in this familiar feeling}. [ ]: 문장의 목적어
주어   동사

★★ 문제 해결 꿀~팁 ★★
▶ 많이 틀린 이유는?
첫 문장에서 'newborns and infants are comforted by rocking'을 통해 신생아나 유아는 흔들림을 좋아한다는 전제를 제시했다. 이후 'because this motion is similar to ~'와 '~ associate gentle rocking with being fed.'에서 신생아가 흔들림을 좋아하는 이유를 밝히고 있다. 따라서 결론에 해당하는 빈칸에는 전제이자 요지인 ①이 들어가야 한다. ②와 ④는 둘 다 '움직임을 좋아하는' 특성에 관한 언급 없이 '먹는 것'과 관련된 내용만을 제시하므로 오답이다.
▶ 문제 해결 방법은?
더 자세히 살펴보면, 이 글은 신생아들이 흔들림을 좋아하는 이유에 관한 통념을 반박하고 새로운 견해를 제시하는 글로, however가 흐름의 전환을 이끈다. 글을 꼼꼼히 읽기 전에 이런 연결사 중심으로 구조를 파악해 두면 핵심 내용을 쉽게 이해하는 데 도움이 된다.

35 방대한 태양에너지를 효율적으로 활용할 방법을 찾아낼 필요성   정답률 61% | 정답 ④

다음 글에서 전체 흐름과 관계 없는 문장은?

In a single week, / the sun delivers more energy to our planet / than humanity has used through the burning of coal, oil, and natural gas / through *all of human history*.
단 한 주 만에, / 태양은 더 많은 에너지를 지구에 전달한다. / 인간이 석탄, 석유, 그리고 천연가스의 연소를 통해 사용해 온 것보다 / *모든 인간의 역사에 걸쳐*

And the sun will keep shining on our planet for billions of years.
그리고 태양은 수십억 년 동안 계속하여 지구를 비출 것이다.

① Our challenge isn't / that we're running out of energy.
우리의 당면 과제는 아니다. / 에너지가 고갈되고 있다는 것이

② It's that we have been focused on the wrong source / — the small, finite one that we're using up.
그것은 우리가 잘못된 원천에 집중하고 있다는 것이다. / 우리가 고갈시키고 있는 (양이) 적고 한정적인 것

③ Indeed, / all the coal, natural gas, and oil / we use today / is just solar energy from millions of years ago, / a very tiny part of which was preserved deep underground.
사실, / 모든 석탄, 천연가스, 그리고 석유는 / 우리가 오늘날 사용하고 있는 / 수백만 년 전에 온 태양에너지일 뿐이며, / 그것의 극히 일부분만이 지하 깊은 곳에 보존되어 있었다.

✓ ④ Our efforts to develop technologies / that use fossil fuels / have shown meaningful results.
기술을 개발하기 위한 우리의 노력은 / 화석 연료를 사용하는 / 의미 있는 결과를 거둬왔다.

⑤ Our challenge, and our opportunity, / is to learn to efficiently and cheaply use the *much more abundant* source / that is the new energy striking our planet each day from the sun.
우리의 당면 과제이자 기회는 / *훨씬 더 풍부한* 원천을 효율적으로 그리고 저비용으로 사용하는 것을 배우는 것이다. / 태양으로부터 매일 지구에 도달하는 새로운 에너지인

단 한 주 만에, 태양은 모든 인간의 역사에 걸쳐 인간이 석탄, 석유, 그리고 천연가스의 연소를 통해 사용해 온 것보다 더 많은 에너지를 지구에 전달한다. 그리고 태양은 수십억 년 동안 계속하여 지구를 비출 것이다. ① 우리의 당면 과제는 에너지가 고갈되고 있다는 것이 아니다. ② 그것은 우리가 잘못된 원천 — 우리가 고갈시키고 있는 (양이) 적고 한정적인 것 — 에 집중하고 있다는 것이다. ③ 사실, 우리가 오늘날 사용하고 있는 모든 석탄, 천연가스, 그리고 석유는 수백만 년 전에 온 태양에너지일 뿐이며, 그것의 극히 일부분만이 지하 깊은 곳에 보존되어 있었다. ④ 화석 연료를 사용하는 기술을 개발하기 위한 우리의 노력은 의미 있는 결과를 거둬왔다. ⑤ 우리의 당면 과제이자 기회는 태양으로부터 매일 지구에 도달하는 새로운 에너지인 훨씬 더 풍부한 원천을 효율적이고도 저비용으로 사용하는 것을 배우는 것이다.

Why? 왜 정답일까?
에너지 분야에서의 과제는 화석 연료가 고갈되어 가고 있다는 사실이 아니라, 모든 인류 역사상 가장 방대한 에너지원으로 기능해 왔던 태양에너지를 어떻게 효율적으로 사용할지 알아내는 것이라는 내용의 글이다. ①, ②, ③, ⑤는 모두 주제를 적절히 보충 설명하지만, ④는 화석 연료 사용 기술에 관해 논하고 있어 흐름에서 벗어난다. 따라서 전체 흐름과 관계 없는 문장은 ④이다.

- **billion** ⓝ 10억
- **use up** ⓥ 고갈시키다. 다 써 버리다
- **efficiently** ⓐⓓ 효율적으로
- **finite** ⓐ 한정적인, 유한한
- **preserve** ⓥ 보존하다
- **abundant** ⓐ 풍부한

구문 풀이

10행 Our challenge, and our opportunity, is to learn to efficiently and cheaply
주어   동사 주격 보어 명사적 용법(to + 부사 + 동사원형 : 분리부정사)
use the *much more abundant* source [that is the new energy striking our planet
                선행사   주격 관계대명사   현재분사
each day from the sun].

36 행동의 변화를 이끌어내는 것 정답률 57% | 정답 ②

주어진 글 다음에 이어질 글의 순서로 가장 적절한 것을 고르시오.

① (A) - (C) - (B)　　　　✓② (B) - (A) - (C)
③ (B) - (C) - (A)　　　　④ (C) - (A) - (B)
⑤ (C) - (B) - (A)

We make decisions / based on what we *think* we know.
우리는 결정을 한다. / 우리가 안다고 *생각하는* 것을 기반으로
It wasn't too long ago / that the majority of people believed / the world was flat.
그다지 오래되지 않았다. / 대다수의 사람들이 믿었던 것은 / 세상이 편평하다고
(B) This perceived truth impacted behavior.
이렇게 인지된 사실은 행동에 영향을 미쳤다.
During this period, / there was very little exploration.
이 기간에는 / 탐험이 거의 없었다.
People feared / that if they traveled too far / they might fall off the edge of the earth.
사람들은 두려워했다. / 만약 그들이 너무 멀리 가면 / 그들이 지구의 가장자리에서 떨어질까 봐
So for the most part / they didn't dare to travel.
그래서 대체로 / 그들은 감히 이동하지 않았다.
(A) It wasn't until that minor detail was revealed / — the world is round — / that behaviors changed on a massive scale.
그런 사소한 사항이 드러나고 나서였다. / 세상은 둥글다 / 비로소 대대적으로 행동이 변화한 것은
Upon this discovery, / societies began to travel across the planet.
이것이 발견된 후 곧, / 사람들은 세상을 돌아다니기 시작했다.
Trade routes were established; / spices were traded.
무역 경로가 만들어졌으며, / 향신료가 거래되었다.
(C) New ideas, like mathematics, / were shared / between societies / which allowed for all kinds of innovations and advancements.
수학 같은 새로운 개념이 / 공유되었다. / 사회들 사이에 / 모든 종류의 혁신과 진보를 고려했던
The correction of a simple false assumption / moved the human race forward.
단순한 잘못된 가정의 수정이 / 인류를 앞으로 나아가게 했다.

우리는 우리가 안다고 *생각하는* 것을 기반으로 결정을 한다. 대다수의 사람들이 세상이 편평하다고 믿었던 것은 그다지 오래되지 않았다.
(B) 이렇게 인지된 사실은 행동에 영향을 미쳤다. 이 기간에는 탐험이 거의 없었다. 사람들은 만약 너무 멀리 가면 지구의 가장자리에서 떨어질까 봐 두려워했다. 그래서 대체로 그들은 감히 이동하지 않았다.
(A) 대대적으로 행동이 변화한 것은 비로소 그런 사소한 사항 — 세상은 둥글다 — 이 드러나고 나서였다. 이것이 발견된 후 곧, 사람들은 세상을 돌아다니기 시작했다. 무역 경로가 만들어졌으며, 향신료가 거래되었다.
(C) 모든 종류의 혁신과 진보를 고려했던 사회들 사이에 수학 같은 새로운 개념이 공유되었다. 단순한 잘못된 가정의 수정이 인류를 앞으로 나아가게 했다.

Why? 왜 정답일까?
인간은 본래 세상이 편평하다고 믿었음을 언급하는 주어진 글 뒤에는, 사람들의 이러한 믿음이 행동에도 영향을 미쳤기에 옛날에는 탐험이 잘 이루어지지 않았다고 설명하는 (B), 지구는 둥글다는 믿음이 퍼지면서 인간은 탐험과 무역을 시작했다고 언급하는 (A), 앞의 내용을 토대로 잘못된 가정의 수정이 인류를 진보시켰다는 결론을 내리는 (C)가 차례로 이어져야 한다. 따라서 글의 순서로 가장 적절한 것은 ② '(B) - (A) - (C)'이다.

- **majority** ⓝ 다수, (특정 집단에서) 가장 많은 수
- **massive** ⓐ 대대적인, 거대한
- **impact** ⓥ 영향을 미치다 ⓝ 영향
- **for the most part** 대체로
- **innovation** ⓝ 혁신
- **assumption** ⓝ 가정
- **flat** ⓐ 편평한
- **establish** ⓥ 만들다, 설립하다
- **exploration** ⓝ 탐험
- **dare** ⓥ 감히 ~하다
- **correction** ⓝ 수정, 교정

구문 풀이
4행 It wasn't until that minor detail was revealed — (the world is round) — that behaviors changed on a massive scale.
'it is[was] not until + A + ' ( ): 동격(= that minor detail)
'that + B : A하고 나서야 B하다[했다]'

★★★ 등급을 가르는 문제!
37 반사면을 활용하여 암호 메시지 작성하기 정답률 40% | 정답 ⑤

주어진 글 다음에 이어질 글의 순서로 가장 적절한 것을 고르시오.

① (A) - (C) - (B)　　　　② (B) - (A) - (C)
③ (B) - (C) - (A)　　　　④ (C) - (A) - (B)
✓⑤ (C) - (B) - (A)

Mirrors and other smooth, shiny surfaces / reflect light.
거울과 부드럽고, 광택이 나는 다른 표면들은 / 빛을 반사한다.
We see reflections from such surfaces / because the rays of light form an image on the retina of our eyes.
우리는 그런 표면들로부터 반사된 것을 본다. / 광선이 우리 눈의 망막에 이미지를 형성하기 때문에
(C) Such images are always reversed.
그런 이미지들은 항상 거꾸로 되어 있다.
Look at yourself in a mirror, / wink your right eye / and your left eye seems to wink back at you.
거울에 비친 여러분의 모습을 보며 / 오른쪽 눈을 깜박여 보아라, / 그러면 왼쪽 눈이 여러분에게 눈을 깜박이는 것처럼 보일 것이다.
You can use a mirror / to send a coded message to a friend.
여러분은 거울을 사용하여 / 친구에게 암호로 된 메시지를 보낼 수 있다.
(B) Stand a mirror upright on the table, / so that a piece of paper on the table can be clearly seen in the mirror.
거울을 탁자 위에 수직으로 세워라. / 탁자 위에 놓인 한 장의 종이가 거울 속에 명확하게 보일 수 있도록
Now write a message that looks right / when you look in the mirror.
이제 정상적으로 보이는 메시지를 적어라. / 거울을 볼 때

(A) Keep your eyes on the reflected image / while you are writing / and not on your paper.
반사되는 이미지를 계속 보아라. / 여러분이 쓰는 동안 / 종이가 아니라
After a little practice, / it will be easier to write "backwards."
조금 연습을 하고 나면, / '거꾸로' 쓰는 것이 더 쉬울 것이다.
When your friend receives such a message / he will be able to read it / by holding the paper up to a mirror.
여러분의 친구가 그런 메시지를 받으면, / 그는 그것을 읽을 수 있을 것이다. / 그 종이를 거울에 비춰 봄으로써

거울과 부드럽고 광택이 나는 다른 표면들은 빛을 반사한다. 광선이 우리 눈의 망막에 이미지를 형성하기 때문에 우리는 그런 표면들로부터 반사된 것을 본다.
(C) 그런 이미지들은 항상 거꾸로 되어 있다. 거울에 비친 여러분의 모습을 보며 오른쪽 눈을 깜박여 보아라. 그러면 왼쪽 눈이 여러분에게 눈을 깜박이는 것처럼 보일 것이다. 여러분은 거울을 사용하여 친구에게 암호로 된 메시지를 보낼 수 있다.
(B) 탁자 위에 놓인 한 장의 종이가 거울 속에 명확하게 보일 수 있도록 거울을 탁자 위에 수직으로 세워라. 이제 거울을 볼 때 정상적으로 보이는 메시지를 적어라.
(A) 쓰는 동안 종이가 아니라 반사되는 이미지를 계속 보아라. 조금 연습을 하고 나면, '거꾸로' 쓰는 것이 더 쉬울 것이다. 여러분의 친구가 그런 메시지를 받으면, 그는 그 종이를 거울에 비춰 봄으로써 그것을 읽을 수 있을 것이다.

Why? 왜 정답일까?
거울 등 반짝이는 표면은 빛을 반사한다는 것을 언급하는 주어진 글 뒤에는, 반사된 이미지는 늘 거꾸로 되어 있기에 이를 활용하면 친구에게 암호 메시지를 보낼 수 있다는 내용의 (C), 거울을 이용하여 암호 메시지를 쓰는 방법을 설명하는 내용의 (B), 쓰는 동안 주의할 점을 언급한 후 몇 번의 연습을 거치면 친구에게 메시지를 잘 전달할 수 있다는 결론으로 이어지는 (A)가 차례로 이어져야 한다. 따라서 글의 순서로 가장 적절한 것은 ⑤ '(C) - (B) - (A)'이다.

- **reflection** ⓝ (거울 등에) 반사된 것
- **reverse** ⓥ 뒤집다
- **upright** ⓐ 똑바로
- **coded** ⓐ 암호화된, 부호화된

구문 풀이
6행 When your friend receives such a message he will be able to read it
접속사(~할 때)　　'such a + (형) + 명 : 그러한 (~한) …'
by holding the paper up to a mirror.
~함으로써

★★ 문제 해결 꿀~팁 ★★
▶ 많이 틀린 이유는?
주어진 글의 Mirrors만 보고 기계적으로 (B)를 연결해서는 안 된다. 주어진 글에 '메시지'에 관한 언급이 없는데 (B)에서는 갑자기 거울을 세워놓고 종이를 꺼내 '메시지'를 써 볼 것을 지시하고 있다. 더구나 주어진 글의 특정 표현이나 어구가 (B)에서 재진술되거나 반복되지 않는 것으로 보아, 주어진 글 뒤에 (B)가 나올 수 없다.
▶ 문제 해결 방법은?
주어진 글 후반부의 an image를 (C)의 Such images와 대응시킨 후, 나머지 두 단락은 전체적으로 가볍게 훑으며 논리적인 흐름에 맞게 순서를 연결시키도록 한다.

★★★ 등급을 가르는 문제!
38 호혜주의에 기반한 침팬지 무리 속에서 주도권을 쥐는 먹이 소유자 정답률 28% | 정답 ③

글의 흐름으로 보아, 주어진 문장이 들어가기에 가장 적절한 곳을 고르시오. [3점]

Reciprocity can be explored in captivity / by handing one chimpanzee a large amount of food, / such as a watermelon or leafy branch, / and then observing what follows.
호혜주의는 포획된 상황에서 탐구될 수 있다. / 침팬지 한 마리에게 많은 양의 먹이를 건네주고 / 수박이나 잎이 많은 나뭇가지처럼 / 뒤이어 일어나는 것을 관찰함으로써
① The owner will be center stage, / with a group of others around him or her, / soon to be followed by newly formed groups / around those who obtained a sizable share, / until all food has been distributed.
먹이 소유자가 중심에 있게 되고, / 자기 주위의 다른 침팬지들에 둘러싸여 / 새로이 형성된 무리들이 곧 뒤따르게 된다. / 꽤 큰 몫을 얻은 침팬지들 주변으로 / 모든 먹이가 다 분배될 때까지
② Beggars may complain and cry, / but aggressive conflicts are rare.
먹이를 구걸하는 침팬지들은 불평하고 울부짖을 수도 있지만 / 호전적인 충돌은 드물다.
✓③ The few times that they do occur, / it is the possessor / who tries to make someone leave the circle.
간혹 그러한 일이 정말 일어날 때, / 먹이 소유자다. / 누군가를 무리에서 떠나게 하려는 것은
She will hit them over their head with her branch / or bark at them in a high-pitched voice / until they leave her alone.
먹이 소유자는 그들의 머리를 나뭇가지로 때리거나 / 그들에게 고음으로 울부짖는다. / 그들이 자신을 귀찮게 하지 않을 때까지
④ Whatever their rank, / possessors control the food flow.
그들의 서열이 무엇이든 간에, / 먹이 소유자가 먹이의 흐름을 제어한다.
⑤ Once chimpanzees enter reciprocity mode, / their social rank no longer matters.
침팬지들이 호혜주의 상태에 접어들게 되면, / 사회적 서열은 더 이상 중요한 것이 아니다.

호혜주의는 포획된 상황에서 침팬지 한 마리에게 수박이나 잎이 많은 가지처럼 많은 양의 먹이를 건네주고 뒤이어 일어나는 것을 관찰함으로써 탐구될 수 있다. ① 먹이 소유자가 주위의 다른 침팬지들에 둘러싸여 중심에 있게 되고, 모든 먹이가 다 분배될 때까지 꽤 큰 몫을 얻은 침팬지들 주변으로 새로이 형성된 무리들이 곧 뒤따르게 된다. ② 먹이를 구걸하는 침팬지들은 불평하고 울부짖을 수도 있지만 호전적인 충돌은 드물다. ③ 간혹 그러한 일이 정말 일어날 때, 누군가를 무리에서 떠나게 하려는 것은 먹이 소유자다. 먹이 소유자는 그들이 자신을 귀찮게 하지 않을 때까지 그들의 머리를 나뭇가지로 때리거나 그들에게 고음으로 울부짖는다. ④ 그들의 서열이 무엇이든 간에, 먹이 소유자가 먹이의 흐름을 제어한다. ⑤ 침팬지들이 호혜주의 상태에 접어들게 되면, 사회적 서열은 더 이상 중요한 것이 아니다.

Why? 왜 정답일까?
침팬지들이 호혜주의에 접어들면 서열보다도 먹이 소유자인지 아닌지가 중요해진다는 내용의 글이다. ③ 앞의 문장은 먹이 소유자에게 먹이를 구걸하는 침팬지들이 불평은 할 수 있지만 충돌은 피한다는 내용

을 제시하는데, 주어진 문장은 '그런 상황', 즉 충돌의 상황이 빚어질 때 이를 통제하는 것이 먹이 소유자임을 언급한다. ③ 뒤의 문장은 먹이 소유자가 갈등 상황에서 취하는 행동을 열거한다. 따라서 주어진 문장이 들어가기에 가장 적절한 곳은 ③이다.

- possessor ⑩ 소유자
- leafy ⓐ 잎이 많은
- sizable ⓐ 상당한
- distribute ⓥ 분배하다
- high-pitched ⓐ 고음의
- captivity ⑩ 포획, 감금
- obtain ⓥ 얻다
- share ⓥ 몫, 나누다
- aggressive ⓐ 공격적인
- leave ~ alone ~을 그대로 내버려 두다

구문 풀이

1행 The few times [that they do occur], it is the possessor who tries to make
선행사 동사 강조 「it is ~ who[that] … : 강조 구문(…한 것은 바로 ~이다)」
someone leave the circle.

★★ 문제 해결 꿀~팁 ★★

▶ 많이 틀린 이유는?
④ 앞의 문장에서 먹이 소유자가 다른 구성원들을 '때리며' 상황에 대한 자신의 의사를 표현할 수 있다고 언급한 것을 근거로, ④ 뒤에서는 서열보다도 먹이 소유자인지 아닌지가 먹이 흐름을 제어할 권한을 준다는 결론을 정리하고 있다. 따라서 ④ 앞에는 논리적 공백이 없다.
▶ 문제 해결 방법은?
③ 앞뒤의 논리적 공백에 주목한다. ③ 앞에서 갈등은 '드물다'고 언급했는데 ③ 뒤에서는 갑자기 She, 즉 먹이 소유자가 구성원들을 때리며 불편함을 나타내는 상황이 제시된다. 이는 '드물게도 갈등이 일어났을 때' 먹이 소유자가 취할 행동으로 볼 수 있으므로, '갈등이 일어났을 때'라는 말로 시작하는 주어진 문장이 ③에 들어가야 한다.

---

39 성별에 관한 연구에서 개인차를 고려할 필요성 | 정답률 46% | 정답 ③

글의 흐름으로 보아, 주어진 문장이 들어가기에 가장 적절한 곳을 고르시오.

Gender research shows / a complex relationship between gender and conflict styles.
성별에 관한 연구는 보여준다. / 성별과 갈등 유형 사이의 복잡한 관계를
① Some research suggests / that women from Western cultures tend to be more caring than men.
몇몇 연구는 시사한다. / 서양 문화권에서 여성이 남성보다 더 주변을 돌보는 경향이 있다는 것을
② This tendency may result from socialization processes / in which women are encouraged to care for their families / and men are encouraged to be successful / in competitive work environments.
이런 경향은 사회화 과정의 결과물일지 모른다. / 여성은 가족을 돌보도록 권장 받고, / 남성은 성공하도록 권장 받는 / 경쟁적인 직업 환경에서
✔ However, / we live in a society / where gender roles and boundaries / are not as strict as in prior generations.
그러나, / 우리는 사회에 살고 있다. / 성 역할과 경계가 / 이전 세대만큼 엄격하지 않은
There is significant variability / in assertiveness and cooperation among women, / as well as among men.
상당한 정도의 차이가 있다. / 여들 사이에서도 단호함과 협동에는 / 남성들 사이에서뿐 아니라
④ Although conflict resolution experts should be able to recognize cultural and gender differences, / they should also be aware / of within-group variations and the risks of stereotyping.
갈등 해결 전문가는 문화적 차이와 성별의 차이를 인지할 수 있어야 하지만, / 그들은 또한 알고 있어야 한다. / 그룹 내의 차이와 유형화의 위험성도
⑤ Culture and gender may affect the way / people perceive, interpret, and respond to conflict; / however, / we must be careful / to avoid overgeneralizations / and to consider individual differences.
문화와 성별은 방식에 영향을 미칠 수도 있다. / 사람들이 갈등을 인식하고 해석하고 갈등에 반응하는 / 하지만, / 우리는 주의해야 한다. / 과잉일반화를 피하고 / 개인적인 차이를 고려하도록

성별에 관한 연구는 성별과 갈등 유형 사이의 복잡한 관계를 보여준다. ① 몇몇 연구는 서양 문화권에서 여성이 남성보다 더 주변을 돌보는 경향이 있다고 시사한다. ② 이런 경향은 여성은 가족을 돌보도록 권장 받고, 남성은 경쟁적인 직업 환경에서 성공하도록 권장 받는 사회화 과정의 결과물일지 모른다. ③ 그러나 우리는 성 역할과 경계가 이전 세대만큼 엄격하지 않은 사회에 살고 있다. 남성들 사이에서뿐 아니라 여성들 사이에서도 단호함과 협동에는 상당한 정도의 차이가 있다. ④ 갈등 해결 전문가는 문화적 차이와 성별의 차이를 인지할 수 있어야 하지만, 그들은 또한 그룹 내의 차이와 유형화의 위험성도 알고 있어야 한다. ⑤ 문화와 성별은 사람들이 갈등을 인식하고 해석하고 갈등에 반응하는 방식에 영향을 미칠 수도 있지만, 우리는 과잉 일반화를 피하고 개인적인 차이를 고려하도록 주의해야 한다.

Why? 왜 정답일까?

③ 앞에서 성별과 갈등 유형을 서로 연관시켜 분석하는 것은 남성과 여성이 전통적으로 서로 다른 역할을 맡는다고 여겨져 온 것의 결과물일 수 있다고 언급한 데 이어, 주어진 문장은 However로 흐름을 반전시키며 오늘날에는 성 역할에 대한 경계가 무너져 가고 있음을 지적한다. ③ 뒤에서는 그리하여 남녀 각 집단에서도 개인에 따라 단호함과 협동이 나타나는 정도가 다르다는 내용을 제시하며 개인차의 중요성을 환기하고 있다. 따라서 주어진 문장이 들어가기에 가장 적절한 곳은 ③이다.

- strict ⓐ 엄격한
- socialization ⑩ 사회화
- significant ⓐ 상당한, 유의미한
- assertiveness ⑩ 단호함, 자기 주장
- stereotyping ⑩ (고정관념에 근거한) 유형화
- overgeneralization ⑩ 과잉 일반화
- generation ⑩ 세대
- competitive ⓐ 경쟁적인
- variability ⑩ 가변성
- resolution ⑩ 해결
- interpret ⓥ 해석하다

구문 풀이

5행 This tendency may result from socialization processes [in which women
~에서 기인하다 선행사 「전치사 + 관·대」 주어1
are encouraged to care for their families and men are encouraged to be successful
동사1 보어1 주어2 동사2 보어2
in competitive work environments].

---

40 음악과 감정 표현에 관한 두 가지 견해 | 정답률 63% | 정답 ①

다음 글의 내용을 한 문장으로 요약하고자 한다. 빈칸 (A), (B)에 들어갈 말로 가장 적절한 것은?

	(A)		(B)		(A)		(B)
✔	culturally 문화적으로	……	similarity 유사성	②	culturally 문화적으로	……	balance 균형
③	socially 사회적으로	……	difference 차이	④	incorrectly 부정확하게	……	connection 연결성
⑤	incorrectly 부정확하게	……	contrast 대조				

One way that music could express emotion / is simply through a learned association.
음악이 감정을 표현할 수 있는 한 방법은 / 단지 학습된 연관을 통해서이다.
Perhaps there is nothing naturally sad / about a piece of music in a minor key, or played slowly with low notes.
본질적으로 슬픈 무언가가 있는 것은 아마 아닐 것이다. / 단조나 낮은 음으로 느리게 연주된 악곡에 대해
Maybe we have just come to hear certain kinds of music as sad / because we have learned / to associate them in our culture with sad events like funerals.
어쩌면 우리는 어떤 종류의 음악을 슬프게 듣게 되는데 / 우리가 학습해 왔기 때문에 / 우리의 문화 속에서 그것들을 장례식과 같은 슬픈 일과 연관시키는 것을
If this view is correct, / we should have difficulty interpreting the emotions / expressed in culturally unfamiliar music.
만약 이 관점이 옳다면, / 우리는 감정을 이해하는 데 분명 어려움이 있을 것이다. / 문화적으로 친숙하지 않은 음악에 표현된
Totally opposed to this view / is the position / that the link between music and emotion is one of resemblance.
이 관점과 완전히 반대되는 입장은 / 입장이다. / 음악과 감정 사이의 연결고리는 유사함이라는
For example, / when we feel sad / we move slowly / and speak slowly and in a low-pitched voice.
예컨대, / 슬프다고 느낄 때 / 우리는 느리게 움직이고 / 낮은 음의 목소리로 느리게 말한다.
Thus when we hear slow, low music, / we hear it as sad.
따라서 우리가 느리고 낮은 음의 음악을 들을 때, / 우리는 그것을 슬프게 듣는다.
If this view is correct, / we should have little difficulty understanding the emotion / expressed in culturally unfamiliar music.
만약 이 관점이 옳다면, / 우리는 감정을 이해하는 데 분명 어려움이 거의 없을 것이다. / 문화적으로 친숙하지 않은 음악에 표현된
➡ It is believed / that emotion expressed in music / can be understood / through a(n) (A) culturally learned association / or it can be understood / due to the (B) similarity between music and emotion.
믿어진다. / 음악에 표현된 감정은 / 이해될 수 있다거나 / 문화적으로 학습된 연관을 통해서 / 혹은 이해될 수 있다고 / 음악과 감정 사이의 유사성 때문에

음악이 감정을 표현할 수 있는 한 방법은 단지 학습된 연관을 통해서이다. 단조나 낮은 음으로 느리게 연주된 악곡에 대해 본질적으로 슬픈 무언가가 있는 것은 아마 아닐 것이다. 어쩌면 우리는 우리의 문화 속에서 어떤 종류의 음악을 장례식과 같은 슬픈 일과 연관시키는 것을 학습해 왔기 때문에 그것을 슬프게 듣게 된다. 만약 이 관점이 옳다면, 우리는 문화적으로 친숙하지 않은 음악에 표현된 감정을 이해하는 데 분명 어려움이 있을 것이다. 이 관점과 완전히 반대되는 입장은 음악과 감정 사이의 연결고리는 유사함이라는 것이다. 예컨대, 슬프다고 느낄 때 우리는 느리게 움직이고 낮은 음의 목소리로 느리게 말한다. 따라서 우리가 느리고 낮은 음의 음악을 들을 때, 우리는 그것을 슬프게 듣는다. 만약 이 관점이 옳다면, 우리는 문화적으로 친숙하지 않은 음악에 표현된 감정을 이해하는 데 분명 어려움이 거의 없을 것이다.

➡ 음악에 표현된 감정은 (A) 문화적으로 학습된 연관을 통해서 이해될 수 있다고 믿어지거나, 혹은 음악과 감정 사이의 (B) 유사성 때문에 이해될 수 있다고 믿어진다.

Why? 왜 정답일까?

음악을 통한 감정 표현에 대한 두 가지 상반된 시각이 존재한다는 내용의 글이다. 첫 문장에서는 음악이 특정 감정과 연관지어 이해되는 까닭이 문화적인 학습(a learned association)에 기인한다고 설명한다. 즉, 단조로 된 음악을 우리가 슬프게 듣는 까닭은 단조가 본질적으로 슬픈 까닭이 아니라 우리가 단조를 슬픔과 연관시켜 듣도록 학습해 왔기 때문이라는 것이다. 이와는 반대로 'Totally opposed to this view ~'에서는 특정한 음악 형식이 특정한 감정과 본질적으로 유사한 까닭에 그 감정을 나타낼 수 있다고 보는 견해를 소개한다. 따라서 요약문의 빈칸 (A), (B)에 들어갈 말로 가장 적절한 것은 각 견해의 핵심어를 반영한 ① 'A) culturally(문화적으로), similarity(유사성)'이다.

- association ⑩ 연관
- culturally ⓐⓓ 문화적으로
- opposed to ~에 반대되는
- low-pitched ⓐ 저음의
- funeral ⑩ 장례식
- unfamiliar ⓐ 친숙하지 않은
- resemblance ⑩ 유사성

구문 풀이

8행 Totally opposed to this view is the position that the link between music
「주격 보어 + 동사 + 주어 : 도치 구문」 동격(= 주어)
and emotion is one of resemblance.

41-42 양질의 수면을 위한 적정한 침실 온도

A bedroom temperature of around 65 degrees Fahrenheit (18.3°C) / is ideal for the sleep of most people, / assuming standard bedding and clothing.
대략 화씨 65도(섭씨 18.3도)의 침실 온도가 / 대부분의 사람들의 수면에 이상적이다. / 표준적인 침구와 복장을 가정할 때
This (a) surprises many, / as it sounds just a little too cold for comfort.
이것은 많은 사람을 놀라게 한다. / 안락함을 위해서는 다소 너무 추운 것처럼 들리기 때문에
Of course, / that specific temperature will vary / depending on the individual in question and their gender and age.
물론, / 그 특정 온도는 다를 것이다. / 해당하는 사람과 그들의 성별 그리고 나이에 따라
But like calorie recommendations, / it's a good target for the average human being.
하지만, 권장 칼로리처럼, / 그것은 평균적인 사람에게 좋은 목표다.
Most of us set bedroom temperatures higher / than are ideal for good sleep / and this likely contributes to (b) lower quantity and quality of sleep / than you are otherwise capable of getting. 41번의 근거
우리 대부분은 침실 온도를 높게 설정하는데, / 좋은 수면을 위해 이상적인 것보다 / 이는 더 낮은 수면의 양과 질을 초래할 것이다. / 그렇게 하지 않는다면 당신이 얻을 수 있는 것보다
Lower than 55 degrees Fahrenheit / can be harmful rather than helpful to sleep, / unless warm bedding or nightclothes are used.

화씨 55도보다 더 낮은 온도는 / 잠을 자는데 도움이 되기보다 오히려 해로울 수 있다. / 따뜻한 침구와 잠옷이 사용되지 않는다면

『However, / most of us fall into the (c) opposite category / of setting a controlled bedroom temperature / that is too high: 70 or 72 degrees.』 42번의 근거

하지만, / 우리 대부분은 정반대의 범주에 속한다. / 침실 온도를 설정하는 / 70도 또는 72도라는 너무 높은

Sleep clinicians treating patients / who can't sleep at night / will often ask about room temperature, / and will advise patients to (d) drop their current thermostat set-point / by 3 to 5 degrees / from that which they currently use.

환자를 치료하는 수면 임상의는 / 밤에 잠을 못자는 / 종종 침실 온도를 묻고, / 환자들에게 온도 조절 장치의 현재 설정값을 낮추라고 조언할 것이다. / 3도에서 5도 가량 / 그들이 지금 사용하는 설정값보다

Anyone disbelieving of the influence of temperature on sleep / can explore some related experiments on this topic.

온도가 수면에 미치는 영향에 대해 불신하는 사람은 누구든지 / 이 주제에 관한 몇몇 관련 실험들을 살펴볼 수 있다.

Scientists have, for example, gently warmed the feet or the body of rats / to encourage blood to rise to the surface of the skin / and release heat, / thereby decreasing core body temperature.

예를 들어, 과학자들은 쥐의 발이나 몸을 서서히 따뜻하게 했고, / 혈액을 피부의 표면으로 올라가게 하고 / 열을 방출시키기 위해 / 그럼으로써 심부 체온을 낮추었다.

The rats fell asleep far (e) faster / than was otherwise normal.

쥐들은 훨씬 더 빨리 잠들었다. / 그렇지 않았던 평상시보다

표준적인 침구와 복장을 가정할 때 대략 화씨 65도(섭씨 18.3도)의 침실 온도가 대부분의 사람들의 수면에 이상적이다. 이것은 안락함을 위해서는 다소 너무 추운 것처럼 들리기 때문에 많은 사람을 (a) 놀라게 한다. 물론, 이 특정 온도는 해당하는 사람과 그들의 성별 그리고 나이에 따라 다를 것이다. 하지만, 권장 칼로리처럼, 그것은 평균적인 사람에게 좋은 목표이다. 우리 대부분은 좋은 수면을 위해 침실 온도를 이상적인 것보다 높게 설정하는데, 이는 그렇게 하지 않는다면 당신이 얻을 수 있는 것보다 (b) 더 낮은 수면의 양과 질을 초래할 것이다. 따뜻한 침구와 잠옷이 사용되지 않는다면 화씨 55도보다 더 낮은 온도는 잠을 자는 데 도움이 되기보다 오히려 해로울 수 있다. 하지만, 우리 대부분은 70도 또는 72도라는 너무 높은 침실 온도를 설정하는 (c) 정반대의 범주에 속한다. 밤에 잠을 못 자는 환자를 치료하는 수면 임상의는 종종 침실 온도를 묻고, 환자들에게 온도 조절 장치의 현재 설정값을 그들이 지금 사용하는 설정값보다 3도에서 5도 가량 (d) 올리라고(→ 낮추라고) 조언할 것이다. 온도가 수면에 미치는 영향에 대해 불신하는 사람은 누구든지 주제에 관한 몇몇 관련 실험들을 살펴볼 수 있다. 예를 들어, 과학자들은 혈액을 피부의 표면으로 올라가게 하고 열을 방출시키기 위해 쥐의 발이나 몸을 서서히 따뜻하게 했고, 그럼으로써 심부 체온을 낮추었다. 그 쥐들은 그렇지 않았던 평상시보다 훨씬 (e) 더 빨리 잠들었다.

- specific ⓐ 특정한, 구체적인
- depending on prep ~에 따라
- ideal ⓐ 이상적인
- otherwise ad 그렇지 않으면
- disbelieve of ⓥ ~을 불신하다
- vary ⓥ 다르다
- recommendation ⓝ 권장, 충고
- quantity ⓝ 수
- clinician ⓝ 임상의
- surface ⓝ 표면

구문 풀이

7행 Most of us set bedroom temperatures higher than are ideal for good
　　　 주어1　　　 동사1
sleep and this likely contributes to lower quantity and quality of sleep than you
　주어2　　 동사2(~의 원인이 되다)　　 명사구(to의 목적어)
are otherwise capable of getting.

---

41 제목 파악
정답률 66% | 정답 ②

윗글의 제목으로 가장 적절한 것은?

① Signs of Sleep Problems – 수면 문제의 징후
✓② Stay Cool for Better Sleep – 더 좋은 수면을 위해 시원하게 유지해라
③ Turn Up the Heat in Your Room – 당신의 방 온도를 높여라
④ How to Correct Bad Sleeping Posture – 나쁜 수면 자세를 고치는 방법
⑤ A Key to Quality Sleep: Clean Bedding – 양질의 수면을 위한 비결: 깨끗한 침구

Why? 왜 정답일까?

첫 두 문장에 따르면 일반 사람들에게 적합한 침실 온도는 얼핏 '춥다'고 느껴질 수 있는 섭씨 18.3도 정도이지만, 'Most of us set bedroom temperatures higher than are ideal for good sleep and this likely contributes to lower quantity and quality of sleep than you are otherwise capable of getting.'에서 언급하듯이 대부분의 사람들은 이상적인 수준보다 높게 침실 온도를 설정하므로 이에 따라 수면의 양과 질이 저하되는 문제를 겪을 수 있다. 따라서 글의 제목으로 가장 적절한 것은 ② '더 좋은 수면을 위해 시원하게 유지해라'이다.

---

42 어휘 추론
정답률 51% | 정답 ④

밑줄 친 (a) ~ (e) 중에서 문맥상 낱말의 쓰임이 적절하지 않은 것은? [3점]

① (a)　　② (b)　　③ (c)　　✓④ (d)　　⑤ (e)

Why? 왜 정답일까?

'However, most of us fall into the opposite category of setting a controlled bedroom temperature that is too high: ~'에서 너무 낮은 온도도 수면에 방해가 되지만, 대부분의 사람들은 이와 반대로 너무 높은 온도를 설정해 둔다고 언급한다. 이에 이어지는 (d)가 포함된 문장은 그리하여 수면 임상의들이 환자들을 볼 때면 종종 침실 온도를 물어보고 온도를 '낮추도록' 권유한다는 의미를 나타내야 한다. 따라서 (d)의 raise를 반의어인 drop으로 고쳐야 한다. 밑줄 친 (a) ~ (e) 중 문맥상 낱말의 쓰임이 적절하지 않은 것은 ④ '(d)'이다.

43-45 지폐가 부른 오해로 20년간 단절된 채 지냈던 쌍둥이 형제

(A)

A merchant in a small town had identical twin sons.
어느 작은 마을의 한 상인에게 일란성 쌍둥이 아들이 있었다.

『The boys worked for their father in the store he owned / and when he died, / they took over the store.』 45번 ①의 근거 일치
그 아들들은 아버지가 소유했던 가게에서 일했고 / 아버지가 죽었을 때, / 그들은 그 가게를 물려받았다.

『Everything went well / until the day a twenty-dollar bill disappeared.』
모든 일이 잘 풀렸다. / 20달러 지폐가 사라졌던 날까지

One of the brothers had left the bill on the counter / and walked outside with a friend.
형제 중 한 명이 카운터에 지폐를 두고 / 친구와 밖으로 나갔다.

When he returned, / the money was gone.』 45번 ②의 근거 일치
그가 돌아왔을 때, / 돈은 사라졌다.

(a) He asked his older brother, / "Did you see that twenty-dollar bill on the counter?"
그가 그의 형에게 물었다. / "카운터에 있던 그 20달러 지폐 봤어?"라고

(C)

His older brother replied that he had not.
그의 형은 보지 못했다고 대답했다.

But (c) the young man kept questioning him.
그러나 그 동생은 계속해서 그에게 물었다.

"Twenty-dollar bills just don't get up and walk away!
"20달러 지폐가 일어나서 걸어 나갈 리 없잖아!

Surely you must have seen it!"
분명히 형은 그것을 봤을 거야!"

There was subtle accusation in (d) his voice.
그의 목소리에는 미묘한 비난이 담겨 있었다.

Anger began to rise.
화가 나기 시작했다.

Hatred set in.
증오가 자리 잡았다.

Before long, / bitterness divided the twins.
머지않아 / 적대감이 쌍둥이 형제를 갈라놓았다.

They refused to speak.
그들은 말하는 것을 거부했다.

『They finally decided / they could no longer work together / and a dividing wall was built down the center of the store.』 45번 ④의 근거 일치
그들은 마침내 결심했고 / 그들이 더 이상 함께 일하지 않기로 / 가게를 나누는 벽이 가게 중앙에 세워졌다.

For twenty years the hostility grew, / spreading to their families and the community.
20년 동안 증오심이 자랐고, / 그들의 가족과 지역사회에 전해졌다.

(B)

Then one day / a man from another state stopped by the store.
그러던 어느 날 / 다른 주의 한 남자가 가게에 들렀다.

He walked in and asked the younger brother, / "How long have you been here?"
그가 들어와 동생에게 물었다. / "당신은 얼마나 여기에 있었나요?"라고

(b) He replied that he'd been there all his life.
그는 평생 그곳에 있었다고 대답했다.

『The customer said, / "Twenty years ago / I came into this town in a boxcar.
손님은 말했다. / "20년 전에 / 저는 이 마을에 유개화차를 타고 왔어요.

I hadn't eaten for three days.
3일 동안 음식을 먹지 못했죠.

I came into this store / and saw a twenty-dollar bill on the counter.
저는 이 가게에 들어와 / 카운터 위의 20달러 지폐 한 장을 봤어요.

I put it in my pocket and walked out.
저는 그것을 주머니에 넣고 나갔죠.

All these years / I haven't been able to forgive myself.
지금까지 / 저는 제 자신을 용서할 수 없었어요.

So I had to come back to return it."』 45번 ③의 근거 일치
그래서 저는 그것을 돌려주러 돌아와야 했어요."라고

(D)

The customer was amazed / to see tears well up in the eyes of the man.
손님은 놀랐다. / 그 남자의 눈에 눈물이 샘솟는 것을 보고

"Would you please go next door / and tell that same story to (e) the man in the store?" / the younger brother said.
"당신은 옆 가게로 가서 / 가게에 있는 남자에게 똑같은 이야기를 해줄 수 있나요?"라고 / 동생은 말했다.

Then the customer was even more amazed / to see the two middle-aged men hugging each other / and weeping together in the front of the store.
그런 다음 손님은 훨씬 더 놀랐다. / 두 중년의 남자가 서로 안고 / 가게 앞에서 흐느껴 우는 것을 보고

『After twenty years, / the brokenness was repaired.』 45번 ⑤의 근거 불일치
20년 후에, / 단절된 관계가 회복되었다.

The wall of anger that divided them came down.
그들을 갈라놓았던 분노의 벽은 무너졌다.

(A)

어느 작은 마을의 한 상인에게 일란성 쌍둥이 아들들이 있었다. 그 아들들은 아버지가 소유했던 가게에서 일했고 아버지가 죽었을 때, 그들은 그 가게를 물려받았다. 20달러 지폐가 사라졌던 날까지는 모든 일이 잘 풀렸다. 형제 중 한 명이 카운터에 지폐를 두고 친구와 밖으로 나갔다. 그가 돌아왔을 때, 돈은 사라졌다. (a) 그가 그의 형에게 "카운터에 있던 그 20달러 지폐 봤어?"라고 물었다.

(C)

그의 형은 보지 못했다고 대답했다. 그러나 (c) 그 동생은 계속해서 그에게 물었다. "20달러 지폐가 일어나서 걸어 나갈 리 없잖아! 분명히 형은 그것을 봤을 거야!" (d) 그의 목소리에는 미묘한 비난이 담겨 있었다. 화가 나기 시작했다. 증오가 자리 잡았다. 머지않아 적대감이 쌍둥이 형제를 갈라놓았다. 그들은 말하는 것을 거부했다. 그들은 마침내 더 이상 함께 일하지 않기로 결심했고 가게를 나누는 벽이 가게 중앙에 세워졌다. 20년 동안 증오심이 자랐고, 그들의 가족과 지역사회에 전해졌다.

(B)

그러던 어느 날 다른 주의 한 남자가 가게에 들렀다. 그가 들어와서 동생에게 "당신은 얼마나 여기에 있었나요?"라고 물었다. (b) 그는 평생 그곳에 있었다고 대답했다. 손님은 "20년 전에 저는 이 마을에 유개화차를 타고 왔어요. 3일 동안 음식을 먹지 못했죠. 저는 이 가게에 들어와 카운터 위의 20달러 지폐 한 장을 봤어요. 저는 그것을 주머니에 넣고 나갔죠. 지금까지 저는 제 자신을 용서할 수 없었어요. 그래서 저는 그것을 돌려주러 돌아와야 했어요."라고 말했다.

(D)

손님은 그 남자의 눈에 눈물이 샘솟는 것을 보고 놀랐다. 동생은 "당신은 옆 가게로 가서 안

에 있는 (e) 남자에게 똑같은 이야기를 해줄 수 있나요?"라고 말했다. 그런 다음 손님은 두 중년의 남자가 가게 앞에서 서로 안고 흐느껴 우는 것을 보고 훨씬 더 놀랐다. 20년 후에, 단절된 관계가 회복되었다. 그들을 갈라놓았던 분노의 벽은 무너졌다.

- merchant ⓝ 상인
- disappear ⓥ 사라지다
- subtle ⓐ 미묘한
- hatred ⓝ 증오
- bitterness ⓝ 냉소, 쓰라림, (맛이) 씀
- spread ⓥ 퍼지다
- brokenness ⓝ 깨짐, 단절

- identical twin ⓝ 일란성 쌍둥이
- boxcar ⓝ (기차의) 유개화차
- accusation ⓝ 비난, 기소
- set in ⓥ (특히 나쁜 일이 계속될 기세로) 시작되다
- hostility ⓝ 적대감
- weep ⓥ 울다

구문 풀이

(A) 4행 One of the brothers had left the bill on the counter and walked outside with a friend.
주어 / 동사1(과거완료) / 동사2(과거)

(C) 2행 "Twenty-dollar bills just don't get up and walk away! Surely you must have seen it!"
문장 수식 부사 / 「must have + 과거분사 : ~했음에 틀림없다」

(D) 3행 Then the customer was even more amazed to see the two middle-aged men hugging each other and weeping together in the front of the store.
비교급 수식 부사 / 감정 형용사 / 부사적 용법(~해서) / to see의 목적어 / to see의 목·보1 / to see의 목·보2

---

43 글의 순서 파악   정답률 77% | 정답 ②

주어진 글 (A)에 이어질 내용을 순서에 맞게 배열한 것으로 가장 적절한 것은?
① (B) − (D) − (C)   ✔②(C) − (B) − (D)
③ (C) − (D) − (B)   ④ (D) − (B) − (C)
⑤ (D) − (C) − (B)

Why? 왜 정답일까?

사이가 좋았던 쌍둥이 형제의 가게에서 어느 날 20달러짜리 지폐가 없어졌다는 내용의 (A) 뒤에는, 20달러를 보았냐는 동생의 물음에 형이 모른다고 답하자 동생이 비난조로 응수했고 형제가 서로 미워하게 된 채로 20년을 보내게 되었다는 내용의 (C)가 먼저 연결된다. 이어서 (B)는 '그러던 어느 날' 한 남자가 동생의 가게로 찾아와 20달러짜리 지폐를 자신이 가져갔었다고 고백하는 내용을, (D)는 오해를 푼 형제가 서로 화해했다는 내용을 제시한다. 따라서 글의 순서로 가장 적절한 것은 ② '(C) − (B) − (D)'이다.

---

44 지칭 추론   정답률 71% | 정답 ⑤

밑줄 친 (a) ~ (e) 중에서 가리키는 대상이 나머지 넷과 다른 것은?
① (a)   ② (b)   ③ (c)   ④ (d)   ✔⑤(e)

Why? 왜 정답일까?

(a), (b), (c), (d)는 모두 쌍둥이 동생을, (e)는 쌍둥이 형을 가리키므로, (a) ~ (e) 중에서 가리키는 대상이 다른 하나는 ⑤ '(e)'이다.

---

45 세부 내용 파악   정답률 85% | 정답 ⑤

윗글에 관한 내용으로 적절하지 <u>않은</u> 것은?
① 쌍둥이 형제는 아버지의 가게를 물려받았다.
② 카운터 위에 놓여진 20달러 지폐가 없어졌다.
③ 손님은 20년 만에 가게에 다시 방문했다.
④ 쌍둥이 형제의 가게 중앙에 벽이 세워졌다.
✔⑤ 쌍둥이 형제는 끝까지 화해하지 못했다.

Why? 왜 정답일까?

(D) 'After twenty years, the brokenness was repaired.'에 따르면 지폐의 행방에 관해 20년 만에 밝혀진 진실 덕분에 쌍둥이 형제는 마침내 관계를 회복했다. 따라서 내용과 일치하지 않는 것은 ⑤ '쌍둥이 형제는 끝까지 화해하지 못했다.'이다.

Why? 왜 오답일까?

① (A) 'The boys worked for their father in the store he owned and when he died, they took over the store.'의 내용과 일치한다.
② (A) 'One of the brothers had left the bill on the counter ~. When he returned, the money was gone.'의 내용과 일치한다.
③ (B) 'The customer said, "Twenty years ago ~ I came into this store and saw a twenty-dollar bill on the counter. I put it in my pocket and walked out. ~ I had to come back to return it."'의 내용과 일치한다.
④ (C) '~ a dividing wall was built down the center of the store.'의 내용과 일치한다.

A	B	C	D
01 ~에 따라	01 obtain	01 ⓘ	01 ⓝ
02 소비	02 define	02 ⓑ	02 ⓖ
03 쓰레기	03 demonstrate	03 ⓞ	03 ⓔ
04 ~에도 해당하다	04 hostility	04 ⓓ	04 ⓓ
05 심한, 가혹한	05 abundant	05 ⓗ	05 ⓙ
06 유아기	06 prior to	06 ⓕ	06 ⓥ
07 임신 (기간)	07 lean	07 ⓖ	07 ⓕ
08 수술의	08 diagnose	08 ⓛ	08 ⓐ
09 현상	09 significant	09 ⓐ	09 ⓘ
10 인지적인	10 indifferent	10 ⓙ	10 ⓚ
11 임상의	11 eliminate	11 ⓝ	11 ⓒ
12 찰나의, 순식간의	12 precise	12 ⓚ	12 ⓜ
13 A에게 B를 경고하다	13 categorize	13 ⓒ	13 ⓗ
14 유지보수	14 racial	14 ⓜ	14 ⓛ
15 장례식	15 variability	15 ⓔ	15 ⓞ
16 현재	16 in addition to	16 ⓢ	16 ⓣ
17 세대	17 author	17 ⓟ	17 ⓡ
18 (~에) 들르다	18 appearance	18 ⓗ	18 ⓠ
19 좌절한	19 trick A into B	19 ⓡ	19 ⓟ
20 편집자	20 anxiety	20 ⓘ	20 ⓢ

• 정답 •

18 ⑤ 19 ① 20 ④ 21 ④ 22 ⑤ 23 ④ 24 ② 25 ⑤ 26 ③ 27 ⑤ 28 ⑤ 29★ 30 ④ 31 ①★ 32 ②
33 ④ 34 ④ 35 ③ 36 ④ 37 ③ 38 ⑤★ 39 ④ 40 ① 41 ⑤ 42 ④★ 43 ④ 44 ② 45 ③

★ 표기된 문항은 [등급을 가르는 문제]에 해당하는 문항입니다.

---

18 구직을 위해 담당자에게 보내는 편지 　　　　　정답률 89% | 정답 ⑤

다음 글의 목적으로 가장 적절한 것은?
① 영업 시작일을 문의하려고
② 인터뷰 일정을 변경하려고
③ 디자인 공모전에 참가하려고
④ 제품 관련 문의에 답변하려고
✔ 의류 매장 판매직에 지원하려고

Dear Ms. MacAlpine,
친애하는 MacAlpine씨에게,
I was so excited to hear / that your brand is opening a new shop / on Bruns Street next month.
저는 듣고 매우 들떴습니다. / 당신의 브랜드가 새 매장을 연다는 것을 / 다음 달에 Bruns 거리에
I have always appreciated the way / your brand helps women to feel more stylish and confident.
저는 항상 높이 평가해 왔습니다. / 당신의 브랜드가 여성들이 더 멋지고 자신감 있게 느끼도록 도와주는 방식을
I am writing in response to your ad / in the Bruns Journal.
저는 당신의 광고에 대한 응답으로 편지를 쓰고 있습니다. / Bruns Jornal에 있는
I graduated from the Meline School of Fashion / and have worked as a sales assistant / at LoganMart for the last five years.
저는 Meline 패션 학교를 졸업했습니다. / 그리고 판매 보조원으로 일해 왔습니다. / 지난 5년간 LoganMart에서
During that time, / I've developed strong customer service and sales skills, / and now I would like to apply for the sales position / in your clothing store.
그 기간 동안, / 저는 뛰어난 고객 서비스 및 판매 기술을 발달시켜 왔습니다. / 그리고 이제 판매직에 지원하고 싶습니다. / 당신의 의류 매장의
I am available for an interview / at your earliest convenience.
저는 인터뷰가 가능합니다. / 당신이 편한 가장 빠른 시간에
I look forward to hearing from you.
당신으로부터 대답을 듣게 되기를 기대합니다.
Thank you for reading my letter.
저의 편지를 읽어 주셔서 감사합니다.
Yours sincerely, // Grace Braddock
Grace Braddock 드림

친애하는 MacAlpine씨에게,

저는 당신의 브랜드가 다음 달에 Bruns 거리에 새 매장을 연다는 것을 듣고 매우 들떴습니다. 저는 당신의 브랜드가 여성들이 더 멋지고 자신감 있게 느끼도록 도와주는 방식을 항상 높이 평가해 왔습니다. 저는 Bruns Journal에 있는 당신의 광고에 대한 응답으로 편지를 쓰고 있습니다. 저는 Meline 패션 학교를 졸업했고 지난 5년간 LoganMart에서 판매 보조원으로 일해 왔습니다. 그 기간 동안, 저는 뛰어난 고객 서비스 및 판매 기술을 발달시켜 왔고, 이제 당신의 의류 매장의 판매직에 지원하고 싶습니다. 저는 당신이 편한 가장 빠른 시간에 인터뷰가 가능합니다. 당신으로부터 대답을 듣게 되기를 기대합니다. 저의 편지를 읽어 주셔서 감사드립니다.

Grace Braddock 드림

Why? 왜 정답일까?
광고를 보고 구직을 위해 담당자에게 보내는 글(During that time, I've developed strong customer service and sales skills, and now I would like to apply for the sales position in your clothing store.)이므로, 글의 목적으로 가장 적절한 것은 ⑤ '의류 매장 판매직에 지원하려고'이다.

● confident ⓐ 자신 있는　　● ad ⓝ 광고(advertisement)
● sales assistant 판매 보조원　● convenience ⓝ 편의

구문 풀이

1행 「주어+동사 so 형용사/부사(원인) that 주어+동사(결과)」
I was **so** excited to hear **that** your brand is opening a new shop on Bruns
　　　　　　to 부정사(부사적용법)
Street next month.

---

19 신혼여행에서 생긴 에피소드 　　　　　정답률 86% | 정답 ①

다음 글에 드러난 'I'의 심경 변화로 가장 적절한 것은?
✔ excited → frustrated　　　② pleased → jealous
　흥분한　　좌절한　　　　　　기쁜　　질투난
③ nervous → confident　　　④ annoyed → grateful
　긴장한　　자신 있는　　　　　짜증난　　감사한
⑤ relaxed → indifferent
　안도한　　무관심한

I had never seen a beach / with such white sand or water / that was such a beautiful shade of blue.
나는 해변을 한 번도 본 적이 없었다. / 그렇게 하얀 모래나 물을 가진 / 그렇게 아름다운 푸른 색조의 바다를
Jane and I set up a blanket / on the sand / while looking forward to our ten days of honeymooning / on an exotic island.
Jane과 나는 담요를 깔았다. / 모래 위에 / 열흘간의 신혼여행을 기대하면서 / 이국적인 섬에서의
"Look!" / Jane waved her hand / to point at the beautiful scene / before us — and her gold wedding ring went flying / off her hand.
"저기 좀 봐!" / Jane이 그녀의 손을 흔들었다. / 아름다운 풍경을 가리키기 위해서 / 우리 앞의 / 그러자 그녀의 금으로 된 결혼반지가 날아갔다. / 그녀의 손에서 빠져

I tried to see / where it went, / but the sun hit my eyes / and I lost track of it.
나는 보기 위해 노력했다. / 그것이 날아간 곳을 / 그러나 햇빛이 눈에 들어왔다 / 그리고 나는 그것의 가던 방향을 놓쳤다.
I didn't want to lose her wedding ring, / so I started looking in the area / where I thought it had landed.
나는 그녀의 결혼 반지를 잃어버리고 싶지 않았다. / 그래서 나는 장소를 들여다보기 시작했다. / 내가 생각하기에 그것이 떨어졌을
However, / the sand was so fine / and I realized / that anything heavy, like gold, / would quickly sink / and might never be found again.
하지만 / 모래가 너무 고왔다. / 그리고 나는 깨달았다. / 금처럼 무거운 것은 / 빨리 가라앉는다는 것을 / 그리고 다시는 발견되지 않을 수도 있겠다는 것을

나는 그렇게 하얀 모래나 그렇게 아름다운 푸른 색조의 바다를 가진 해변을 한 번도 본 적이 없었다. 이국적인 섬에서의 열흘간의 신혼여행을 기대하면서 Jane과 나는 모래 위에 담요를 깔았다. "저기 좀 봐!" Jane이 아름다운 풍경을 가리키기 위해서 그녀의 손을 흔들었다. 그러자 그녀의 금으로 된 결혼반지가 그녀의 손에서 빠져 날아갔다. 나는 그것이 날아간 곳을 보기 위해 노력했지만, 햇빛이 눈에 들어와 그것의 가던 방향을 놓쳤다. 나는 그녀의 결혼 반지를 잃어버리고 싶지 않아서 내가 생각하기에 그것이 떨어졌을 장소를 들여다보기 시작했다. 하지만 모래가 너무 고왔고 나는 금처럼 무거운 것은 빨리 가라앉아 다시는 발견되지 않을 수도 있겠다는 것을 깨달았다.

Why? 왜 정답일까?
신혼여행에서 아름다운 풍경을 보다 결혼반지를 잃어버리게 되었다("Look!" Jane waved her hand to point at the beautiful scene before us — and her gold wedding ring went flying off her hand.)는 글이다. 따라서 'I'의 심경 변화로 가장 적절한 것은 ① '흥분한 → 좌절한'이다.

● shade ⓝ 색조, 그늘　　● blanket ⓝ 담요
● exotic ⓐ 이국적인　　　● wave ⓥ 흔들다
● track ⓝ 방향, 길　　　　● land ⓥ 떨어지다
● realize ⓥ 깨닫다　　　　● sink ⓥ 가라앉다

구문 풀이

1행 I had never seen a beach with such white sand or water that was such a
　　　　　과거분사(경험)　　　　　　　선행사　　　　　　　관계대명사(주격)
beautiful shade of blue.

---

20 대학 졸업 이후 자발적 배움의 중요성 　　　　정답률 81% | 정답 ④

다음 글에서 필자가 주장하는 바로 가장 적절한 것은?
① 성공 경험을 위해 달성 가능한 목표를 수립해야 한다.
② 체계적인 경력 관리를 위해 전문가의 도움을 받아야 한다.
③ 건강을 위해 꾸준한 운동과 식습관 관리를 병행해야 한다.
✔ 졸업 이후 성장을 위해 자발적으로 배움을 실천해야 한다.
⑤ 적성에 맞는 직업을 찾기 위해 학교 교육에 충실해야 한다.

Unfortunately, / many people don't take personal responsibility / for their own growth.
안타깝게도 / 많은 사람들이 개인적인 책임을 지지 않는다. / 그들 자신의 성장에 대해
Instead, / they simply run the race / laid out for them.
대신 / 그들은 단지 경주를 한다. / 그들에게 놓인
They do well enough in school / to keep advancing.
그들은 학교에서 제법 잘한다. / 계속 발전할 만큼
Maybe / they manage to get a good job / at a well-run company.
아마도 / 그들은 좋은 일자리를 얻는 것을 해낸다. / 잘 운영되는 회사에서
But / so many think and act / as if their learning journey ends with college.
하지만 / 아주 많은 사람들이 생각하고 행동한다. / 마치 그들의 배움의 여정이 대학으로 끝나는 것처럼
They have checked all the boxes in the life / that was laid out for them / and now lack a road map / describing the right ways / to move forward and continue to grow.
그들은 삶의 모든 사항을 체크했다. / 그들에게 놓인 / 그리고 이제는 로드맵이 없다. / 올바른 방법을 설명해 주는 / 앞으로 나아가고 계속 성장할 수 있는
In truth, / that's when the journey really begins.
사실 / 그때가 여정이 진정으로 시작되는 때이다.
When school is finished, / your growth becomes voluntary.
학교 교육이 끝나면 / 여러분의 성장은 자발적이게 된다.
Like healthy eating habits or a regular exercise program, / you need to commit to it / and devote thought, time, and energy to it.
건강한 식습관이나 규칙적인 운동 프로그램처럼 / 여러분은 그것에 전념할 필요가 있다. / 그리고 그것에 생각, 시간, 그리고 에너지를 쏟을
Otherwise, / it simply won't happen / — and your life and career are likely to stop progressing / as a result.
그렇지 않으면 / 그것은 그냥 일어나지 않을 것이다. / 그리고 여러분의 삶과 경력이 진전을 멈출 가능성이 있다. / 결과적으로

안타깝게도 많은 사람들이 그들 자신의 성장에 대해 개인적인 책임을 지지 않는다. 대신, 그들은 단지 그들에게 놓인 경주를 한다. 그들은 학교에서 계속 발전할 만큼 제법 잘한다. 아마도 그들은 잘 운영되는 회사에서 좋은 일자리를 얻는 것을 해낸다. 하지만 아주 많은 사람들이 마치 그들의 배움의 여정이 대학으로 끝나는 것처럼 생각하고 행동한다. 그들은 그들에게 놓인 삶의 모든 사항을 체크했고 이제는 앞으로 나아가고 계속 성장할 수 있는 올바른 방법을 설명해 주는 로드맵이 없다. 사실, 그때가 여정이 진정으로 시작되는 때이다. 학교 교육이 끝나면, 여러분의 성장은 자발적이게 된다. 건강한 식습관이나 규칙적인 운동 프로그램처럼 여러분은 그것에 전념하고 그것에 생각, 시간, 그리고 에너지를 쏟을 필요가 있다. 그렇지 않으면 그것은 그냥 일어나지 않을 것이고, 결과적으로 여러분의 삶과 경력이 진전을 멈출 가능성이 있다.

Why? 왜 정답일까?
대학이 끝이 아니라, 졸업 이후에도 자발적인 배움으로 계속 성장하기 위해 노력해야 한다(In truth, that's when the journey really begins. When school is finished, your growth becomes voluntary.)고 조언하는 글이므로, 필자가 주장하는 바로 가장 적절한 것은 ④ '졸업 이후 성장을 위해 자발적으로 배움을 실천해야 한다.'이다.

● unfortunately ⓐⓓ 안타깝게도　● personal ⓐ 개인적인
● responsibility ⓝ 책임감　　　● growth ⓝ 성장
● lay out 놓이다　　　　　　　　● manage ⓥ 관리하다

- **lack** ⓥ 부족하다 ⓝ 부족
- **voluntary** ⓐ 자발적인
- **progress** ⓝ 전진, 진행, 진척
- **journey** ⓝ 여정, 여행
- **devote** ⓥ 쏟다, 몰두하다

구문 풀이

5행 But so many think and act as if their learning journey ends with college.
주어(대명사) 동사 부사절 접속사

---

21 객관적이자 주관적으로 바라보는 색   정답률 52% | 정답 ④

밑줄 친 **our brain and the universe meet**가 다음 글에서 의미하는 바로 가장 적절한 것은? [3점]

① we see things beyond the range of perception – 우리는 인식의 범위를 넘어 사물을 본다
② objects appear different by the change of light – 사물은 빛의 변화에 따라 다르게 나타난다
③ your perspectives and others' reach an agreement – 나와 타인의 관점이 합의에 도달한다
✔ our mind and physical reality interact with each other – 정신과 물리적 현실은 서로 상호작용한다
⑤ structures of the human brain and the universe are similar – 인간 뇌의 구조와 우주는 닮았다

Many people take the commonsense view / that color is an objective property / of things, / or of the light that bounces off them.
많은 사람들이 상식적인 견해를 취한다. / 색은 객관적인 속성이다 / 사물의 / 또는 사물로부터 튕겨 나오는 빛의

They say a tree's leaves are green / because they reflect green light / — a greenness that is just as real as the leaves.
그들은 나뭇잎이 녹색이라고 말한다. / 그들이 녹색 빛을 반사하기 때문에 / 나뭇잎만큼 진짜인 녹색

Others argue / that color doesn't inhabit the physical world at all / but exists only / in the eye or mind of the viewer.
다른 사람들은 주장한다. / 색이 물리적인 세계에 전혀 존재하지 않는다고 / 보는 사람의 눈이나 정신 안에만 존재한다고

They maintain / that if a tree fell in a forest / and no one was there to see it, / its leaves would be colorless / — and so would everything else.
그들은 주장한다. / 만약 나무가 숲에서 쓰러진다면 / 그리고 그것을 볼 사람이 아무도 거기에 없다면 / 그것의 잎은 색이 없을 것이다. / 그리고 다른 모든 것들도 그럴 것이라고

They say there is no such *thing* as color; / there are only the people who see it.
그들은 색 같은 '것'은 없다고 말한다 / 다시 말하면 그것을 보는 사람들만 있다

Both positions are, in a way, correct.
두 가지 입장 모두 어떤 면에서는 옳다.

Color is objective *and* subjective / — "the place," as Paul Cézanne put it, / "where our brain and the universe meet."
색은 객관적이고 '동시에' 주관적이다. / 즉 Paul Cézanne이 말했듯이 ~이다. / '우리의 뇌와 우주가 만나는 곳'

Color is created / when light from the world is registered by the eyes / and interpreted by the brain.
색은 만들어진다. / 세상으로부터의 빛이 눈에 의해 등록될 때 / 그리고 뇌에 의해 해석될 때

많은 사람들이 색은 사물 또는 사물로부터 튕겨 나오는 빛의 객관적인 속성이라는 상식적인 견해를 취한다. 그들은 나뭇잎이 녹색 빛(정확히 나뭇잎만큼 진짜인 녹색)을 반사하기 때문에 녹색이라고 말한다. 다른 사람들은 색이 물리적인 세계에 전혀 존재하지 않고 보는 사람의 눈이나 정신 안에만 존재한다고 주장한다. 그들은 만약 나무가 숲에서 쓰러지고 그것을 볼 사람이 아무도 거기에 없다면, 다른 모든 것들도 그럴 것이라고 주장한다. 두 가지 입장 모두 어떤 면에서는 옳다. 색은 객관적이고 '동시에' 주관적이며, Paul Cézanne이 말했듯이 '우리의 뇌와 우주가 만나는 곳'이다. 색은 세상으로부터의 빛이 눈에 의해 등록되고 뇌에 의해 해석될 때 만들어진다.

Why? 왜 정답일까?

색은 사물로부터 튕겨 나오는 빛인 동시에 사람이 인식하면서 만들어진다(**Color is created when light from the world is registered by the eyes and interpreted by the brain.**)고 말하는 것으로 보아, 밑줄 친 부분의 의미로 가장 적절한 것은 ④ '정신과 물리적 현실은 서로 상호작용한다'이다.

- **commonsense** ⓐ 상식적인
- **property** ⓝ 속성, 재산
- **reflect** ⓥ 반사하다
- **physical** ⓐ 물리적인
- **subjective** ⓐ 주관적인
- **perception** ⓝ 인식
- **objective** ⓐ 객관적인
- **bounce off** 반사하다
- **greenness** 녹색, 푸르름
- **position** ⓝ 입장, 위치
- **range** ⓝ 범위
- **perspective** ⓝ 관점

구문 풀이

5행 Others argue that color doesn't inhabit the physical world at all but exists
관계대명사(목적격)
only in the eye or mind of the viewer.
'not A but B : A가 아니라 B다'

---

22 소설을 쓸 때 중요한 것   정답률 66% | 정답 ⑤

다음 글의 요지로 가장 적절한 것은?

① 작품의 완성도는 작가의 경험의 양에 비례한다.
② 작가의 상상력은 가장 훌륭한 이야기 재료이다.
③ 소설에서 사건 전개에 대한 묘사는 구체적일수록 좋다.
④ 소설을 쓸 때 독자의 관심사를 먼저 고려하는 것이 중요하다.
✔ 소설에 포함될 세부 사항은 인간의 경험을 드러내는 것이어야 한다.

When writing a novel, / research for information needs to be done.
소설을 쓸 때 / 정보를 위한 조사가 행해질 필요가 있다.

The thing is / that some kinds of fiction demand a higher level of detail: / crime fiction, for example, or scientific thrillers.
문제는 ~는 것이다. / 어떤 종류의 소설은 더 높은 수준의 세부 사항을 요구한다. / 예를 들어 범죄 소설이나 과학 스릴러와 같은

The information is never hard to find; / one website for authors even organizes trips to police stations, / so that crime writers can get it right.
정보는 찾기에 결코 어렵지 않다. / 작가들을 위한 한 웹사이트는 심지어 경찰서로의 탐방을 조직하기도 한다. / 범죄물 작가들이 정보를 제대로 얻을 수 있도록

Often, / a polite letter will earn you permission / to visit a particular location / and record all the details / that you need.
종종 / 정중한 편지는 여러분에게 허가를 얻어 줄 것이다. / 특정한 장소를 방문할 수 있는 / 그리고 모든 세부 사항을 기록할 수 있는 / 여러분이 필요한

But remember / that you will drive your readers to boredom / if you think / that you need to pack everything you discover / into your work.
하지만 기억하라. / 여러분은 독자들을 지루하게 만들 것 이라는 것을 / 만약 여러분이 생각할 경우 / 여러분이 발견한 모든 것을 담아야 한다고 / 여러분의 작품에

The details that matter / are those that reveal the human experience.
중요한 세부 사항은 / 인간의 경험을 드러내는 것이다.

The crucial thing is telling a story, / finding the characters, the tension, and the conflict / — not the train timetable or the building blueprint.
중요한 것은 이야기를 말하는 것이다. / 인물, 긴장, 그리고 갈등을 찾아가며 / 기차 시간표나 건물 청사진이 아니라

소설을 쓸 때 정보를 위한 조사가 행해질 필요가 있다. 문제는 예를 들어 범죄 소설이나 과학 스릴러와 같은 어떤 종류의 소설은 더 높은 수준의 세부 사항을 요구한다는 것이다. 정보는 찾기에 결코 어렵지 않다. 작가들을 위한 한 웹사이트는 범죄물 작가들이 정보를 제대로 얻을 수 있도록 심지어 경찰서로의 탐방을 조직하기도 한다. 종종 정중한 편지는 여러분에게 특정한 장소를 방문하고 필요한 모든 세부 사항을 기록할 수 있는 허가를 얻어 줄 것이다. 하지만 만약 여러분이 발견한 모든 것을 작품에 담아야 한다고 생각할 경우 여러분은 독자들을 지루하게 만들 것 이라는 것을 기억하라. 중요한 세부 사항은 인간의 경험을 드러내는 것이다. 중요한 것은 기차 시간표나 건물 청사진이 아니라 인물, 긴장, 그리고 갈등을 찾아가며 이야기를 말하는 것이다.

Why? 왜 정답일까?

소설을 쓸 때 범죄 소설이나, 스릴러는 더 높은 수준의 세부 사항을 요구하는데 이때 세부 사항은 인간의 경험을 드러내야 한다(**The details that matter are those that reveal the human experience.**)는 내용이다. 따라서 글의 요지로 가장 적절한 것은 ⑤ '소설에 포함될 세부 사항은 인간의 경험을 드러내는 것이어야 한다.'이다.

- **demand** ⓥ 요구하다
- **author** ⓝ 작가
- **drive** ⓥ 만들다, 몰아가다
- **fiction** ⓝ 소설
- **permission** ⓝ 허락
- **boredom** ⓝ 지루함

구문 풀이

4행 The information is never hard to find; one website for authors even
to부정사(형용사적 용법)
organizes trips to police stations, so that crime writers can get it right.
접속사(~할 수 있도록)

---

23 구강 건강의 중요성   정답률 82% | 정답 ④

다음 글의 주제로 가장 적절한 것은?

① the way the immune system fights viruses
면역 체계가 바이러스와 싸우는 방법
② the effect of unhealthy eating habits on the body
건강하지 않은 식습관이 몸에 미치는 영향
③ the difficulty in raising awareness about oral health
구강 건강에 관한 인식이 증가하는 것에 대한 어려움
✔ the importance of oral health and its impact on the body
구강 건강의 중요성과 몸에 미치는 영향
⑤ the relationship between oral health and emotional well-being
구강건강과 정신적 웰빙 사이의 관계

Nearly everything has to go through your mouth / to get to the rest of you, / from food and air to bacteria and viruses.
거의 모든 것이 여러분의 구강을 거쳐야 한다. / 여러분의 나머지 부분에 도달하기 위해 / 음식과 공기에서부터 박테리아와 바이러스까지

A healthy mouth can help your body get / what it needs and prevent it from harm / — with adequate space for air to travel to your lungs, and healthy teeth and gums / that prevent harmful microorganisms from entering your bloodstream.
건강한 구강은 당신의 몸이 얻는 것을 도와줄 수 있다. / 몸이 필요한 것을 얻고, 피해로부터 몸을 지키도록 / 공기가 폐로 이동할 수 있는 적당한 공간, 그리고 건강한 치아와 잇몸으로부터 / 해로운 미생물이 혈류로 들어가는 것을 막는

From the moment you are created, / oral health affects every aspect of your life.
여러분이 생겨난 순간부터 / 구강 건강은 여러분의 삶의 모든 측면에 영향을 미친다.

What happens in the mouth / is usually just the tip of the iceberg / and a reflection / of what is happening in other parts of the body.
구강 안에서 일어나는 일은 / 대개 빙산의 일각일 뿐이다. / 그리고 반영이다. / 신체의 다른 부분에서 일어나고 있는 일의

Poor oral health can be a cause of a disease / that affects the entire body.
나쁜 구강 건강은 질병의 원인일 수 있다. / 전체 몸에 영향을 끼치는

The microorganisms in an unhealthy mouth / can enter the bloodstream / and travel anywhere in the body, / posing serious health risks.
건강하지 않은 구강 안의 미생물은 / 혈류로 들어갈 수 있다. / 그리고 신체의 어느 곳이든 이동할 수 있다. / 그 결과 심각한 건강상의 위험을 초래할 수 있다.

음식과 공기에서부터 박테리아와 바이러스까지 거의 모든 것이 여러분의 나머지 부분에 도달하기 위해 여러분의 구강을 거쳐야 한다. 건강한 구강은 공기가 폐로 이동할 수 있는 적당한 공간, 그리고 해로운 미생물이 혈류로 들어가는 것을 막는 건강한 치아와 잇몸으로부터 여러분의 몸이 필요한 것을 얻고, 피해로부터 몸을 지키도록 도와줄 수 있다. 여러분이 생겨난 순간부터 구강 건강은 여러분의 삶의 모든 측면에 영향을 미친다. 구강 안에서 일어나는 일은 대개 빙산의 일각일 뿐이며 신체의 다른 부분에서 일어나고 있는 일의 반영이다. 나쁜 구강 건강은 전체 몸에 영향을 끼치는 질병의 원인일 수 있다. 건강하지 않은 구강 안의 미생물은 혈류로 들어가고 신체의 어느 곳이든 이동하여 그 결과 심각한 건강상의 위험을 초래할 수 있다.

Why? 왜 정답일까?

건강한 구강은 몸에 필요한 것들을 전달하고 해로운 것들을 막는 역할을 한다(**A healthy mouth can help your body get what it needs and prevent it from harm — with adequate space for air to travel to your lungs, and healthy teeth and gums that prevent harmful microorganisms from entering your bloodstream.**)는 내용이다. 구강 건강이 나빠지면 몸에 해로운 미생물이 혈류로 들어가 위험할 수 있다는 내용이 뒤따른다. 따라서 글의 주제로 가장 적절한 것은 ④ '구강 건강의 중요성과 몸에 미치는 영향'이다.

     [문제편 p.152]

- **prevent** ⓥ 막다
- **lung** ⓝ 폐
- **affect** ⓥ 영향을 미치다
- **iceberg** ⓝ 빙산
- **poor** ⓐ 좋지 못한
- **entire** ⓐ 전체의
- **immune system** 면역 체계
- **impact** ⓥ 영향을 주다
- **adequate** ⓐ 충분한
- **microorganism** ⓝ 미생물
- **aspect** ⓝ 측면
- **reflection** ⓝ 반영
- **disease** ⓝ 질병
- **serious** ⓐ 심각한
- **awareness** ⓝ 인식
- **emotional** ⓐ 감정적인

구문 풀이

2행 A healthy mouth can help your body get what it needs and prevent it
from harm — with adequate space for air to travel to your lungs, and healthy
teeth and gums that prevent harmful microorganisms from entering your
bloodstream.

---

24 신경 매커니즘에 따른 지루함 정답률 72% | 정답 ②

다음 글의 제목으로 가장 적절한 것은?
① The Brain's Brilliant Trick to Overcome Fear
   두려움 극복에 대한 뇌의 뛰어난 속임수
☑ Boredom: Neural Mechanism for Detecting Change
   지루함: 변화를 감지하는 신경 매커니즘
③ Humans' Endless Desire to Pursue Familiar Experiences
   친숙한 경험을 추구하는 것에 대한 인간의 끝없는 욕망
④ The Destruction of Nature in Exchange for Human Survival
   인간 생존의 대가로의 자연 파괴
⑤ How Humans Changed the Environment to Their Advantage
   인간이 어떻게 환경을 자신들에게 유리하게 변화시켰는가

Kids tire of their toys, / college students get sick of cafeteria food, / and sooner or later most of us lose interest / in our favorite TV shows.
아이들은 자기들의 장난감에 지루해 한다. / 대학생들은 카페테리아 음식에 싫증을 낸다. / 그리고 머지않아 우리 중 대부분은 흥미를 잃는다. / 우리가 가장 좋아하는 TV 쇼에
The bottom line is / that we humans are easily bored.
요점은 ~이다. / 우리 인간이 쉽게 지루해한다는 것
But why should this be true?
그런데 왜 이것이 사실이어야 할까?
The answer lies buried deep / in our nerve cells, / which are designed to reduce their initial excited response / to stimuli each time they occur.
답은 깊이 숨어있다. / 우리의 신경 세포 안에 / 그것에 대한 초기의 흥분된 반응을 약화하도록 설계된 / 자극이 일어날 때마다
At the same time, / these neurons enhance their responses to things that change / especially things that change quickly.
동시에 / 이 뉴런들은 변화하는 것들에 대한 반응을 강화한다. / 특히 빠르게 변화하는 것들
We probably evolved this way / because our ancestors got more survival value, / for example, / from attending to what was moving in a tree (such as a puma) / than to the tree itself.
우리는 아마도 이런 방식으로 진화했을 것이다. / 왜냐하면 우리의 조상이 더 많은 생존 가치를 얻었기 때문이다. / 예를 들어 / 나무에서 움직이는 것에 주의를 기울이는 것으로부터 (퓨마처럼) / 나무 그 자체보다
Boredom in reaction to an unchanging environment turns down / the level of neural excitation / so that new stimuli (like our ancestor's hypothetical puma threat) stand out more.
변지 않는 환경에 대한 반응으로의 지루함은 낮춘다 / 신경 흥분의 수준을 / 그래서 새로운 자극이 더 두드러지게 한다. (우리 조상이 가정한 퓨마의 위협과 같은)
It's the neural equivalent / of turning off a front door light / to see the fireflies.
이것은 신경적 대응물이다. / 앞문의 불을 끄는 것의 / 반딧불이를 보기 위해

아이들은 자기들의 장난감에 지루해하고, 대학생들은 카페테리아 음식에 싫증을 내고, 머지않아 우리 중 대부분은 우리가 가장 좋아하는 TV 쇼에 흥미를 잃는다. 요점은 우리 인간이 쉽게 지루해한다는 것이다. 그런데 왜 이것이 사실이어야 할까? 답은 자극이 일어날 때마다 그것에 대한 초기의 흥분된 반응을 약화하도록 설계된 우리의 신경 세포 안에 깊이 숨어있다. 동시에 이 뉴런들은 변화하는 것들, 특히 빠르게 변화하는 반응을 강화한다. 예를 들면 우리는 아마도 우리의 조상이 나무 그 자체보다 (퓨마처럼) 나무에서 움직이는 것에 주의를 기울이는 것으로부터 더 많은 생존 가치를 얻었기 때문에 이런 방식으로 진화했을 것이다. 변하지 않는 환경에 대한 반응으로의 지루함은 신경 흥분의 수준을 낮춰 (우리 조상이 가정한 퓨마의 위협과 같은) 새로운 자극이 더 두드러지게 한다. 이것은 반딧불이를 보기 위해 앞문의 불을 끄는 것의 신경적 대응물이다.

Why? 왜 정답일까?

인간은 쉽게 지루함을 느끼는데, 자극이 일어날 때마다 초기의 흥분된 반응을 약화하고 빠르게 변화하는 것에 대한 반응을 강화하도록 설계되었다(The answer lies buried deep in our nerve cells, which are designed to reduce their initial excited response to stimuli each time they occur. At the same time, these neurons enhance their responses to things that change especially things that change quickly.)는 내용이므로, 글의 제목으로 가장 적절한 것은 ② '지루함: 변화를 감지하는 신경 매커니즘'이다.

- **sick of** ~에 싫증나다
- **bottom line** 요점
- **neuron** ⓝ 뉴런(신경세포단위)
- **probably** ⓐⓓ 아마도
- **ancestor** ⓝ 조상
- **stimuli** ⓝ 자극(stimulus)의 복수형
- **neural** ⓐ 신경의
- **firefly** ⓝ 반딧불이
- **interest** ⓝ 흥미
- **bury** ⓥ 숨어있다
- **enhance** ⓥ 강화하다
- **evolve** ⓥ 진화하다
- **excitation** ⓝ 자극
- **hypothetical** ⓐ 가정의, 가상의
- **equivalent** ⓝ 대응물

구문 풀이

4행 The answer lies buried deep in our nerve cells, which are designed to
reduce their initial excited response to stimuli each time they occur.

---

25 청정에너지와 화석 연료에 대한 전세계 투자액 비교 정답률 84% | 정답 ⑤

다음 도표의 내용과 일치하지 <u>않는</u> 것은?

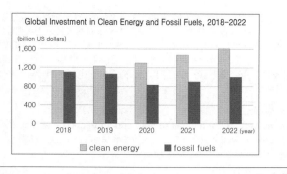

The above graph shows / global energy investment / in clean energy and in fossil fuels / between 2018 and 2022.
위의 그래프는 보여 준다. / 전 세계 에너지 투자액을 / 청정에너지와 화석 연료에 대한 / 2018년과 2022년 사이에
① Since 2018 / global energy investment in clean energy / continued to rise, / reaching its highest level in 2022.
2018년 이후로 / 청정에너지에 대한 전 세계 투자액은 / 계속해서 상승했다. / 그리고 2022년에 가장 높은 수준에 도달했다.
② The investment gap / between clean energy and fossil fuels in 2020 / was larger than that in 2019.
투자액 격차는 / 2020년 청정에너지와 화석 연료 사이의 / 2019년의 그것보다 컸다.
③ Investment in fossil fuels was highest in 2018 / and lowest in 2020.
화석 연료에 대한 투자액은 2018년에 가장 높았다. / 그리고 2020년에 가장 낮았다.
④ In 2021, / investment in clean energy exceeded 1,200 billion dollars, / while investment in fossil fuels did not.
2021년에는 / 청정에너지에 대한 투자액이 1조 2000억 달러를 넘었다. / 반면에 화석 연료에 대한 투자액은 그러지 않았다.
☑ In 2022, / the global investment in clean energy / was more than double / that of fossil fuels.
2022년에 / 청정에너지에 대한 전 세계 투자액이 / 두 배 이상이었다. / 화석 연료의 그것의

위의 그래프는 2018년과 2022년 사이에 청정에너지와 화석 연료에 대한 전 세계 에너지 투자액을 보여준다. ① 2018년 이후로 청정에너지에 대한 전 세계 투자액은 계속해서 상승했으며, 2022년에 가장 높은 수준에 도달했다. ② 2020년의 청정에너지와 화석 연료 사이 투자액 격차는 2019년의 그것보다 컸다. ③ 화석 연료에 대한 투자액은 2018년에 가장 높았고 2020년에 가장 낮았다. ④ 2021년에는 청정에너지에 대한 투자액이 1조 2000억 달러를 넘은 반면, 화석 연료에 대한 투자액은 그러지 않았다. ⑤ 2022년에는 청정에너지에 대한 전 세계 투자액이 화석 연료 그것의 두 배 이상이었다.

Why? 왜 정답일까?

도표에 따르면 2022년 청정에너지에 대한 전 세계 투자액은 화석 연료에 대한 투자액의 두 배 이하다. 따라서 도표와 일치하지 않는 것은 ⑤이다.

- **fossil** ⓝ 화석
- **investment** ⓝ 투자
- **exceed** ⓥ 초과하다
- **fuel** ⓝ 연료
- **reach** ⓥ 도달하다
- **billion** 10억

구문 풀이

2행 Since 2018 global energy investment in clean energy continued to rise,
reaching its highest level in 2022.

---

26 Frederick Douglass의 생애 정답률 91% | 정답 ③

Frederick Douglass에 관한 다음 글의 내용과 일치하지 <u>않는</u> 것은?
① Maryland에서 노예로 태어났다.
② 노예들이 탈출하는 것을 돕는 조직의 리더가 되었다.
☑ 다른 노예들로부터 읽고 쓰는 법을 배웠다.
④ 노예로서의 자신의 경험을 묘사한 자서전을 썼다.
⑤ 미국의 첫 아프리카계 미국인 부통령 후보가 되었다.

「Frederick Douglass was born into slavery / at a farm in Maryland.」①의근거 일치
Frederick Douglass는 노예로 태어났다. / Maryland의 한 농장에서
His full name / at birth / was Frederick Augustus Washington Bailey.
그의 성명은 / 태어났을 때 / Frederick Augustus Washington Bailey였다.
He changed his name to Frederick Douglass / after he successfully escaped from slavery in 1838.
그는 그의 이름을 Frederick Douglass로 바꿨다. / 1838에 노예 상태에서 성공적으로 탈출한 후
「He became a leader of the Underground Railroad / — a network of people, places, and routes / that helped enslaved people escape to the north.」②의근거 일치
그는 Underground Railroad의 리더가 되었다. / 사람, 장소, 경로의 조직인 / 노예가 된 사람들을 북쪽으로 탈출하도록 돕는
He assisted other runaway slaves / until they could safely get to other areas / in the north.
그는 다른 도망친 노예들을 도왔다. / 그들이 다른 지역에 안전하게 도착할 수 있을 때까지 / 북쪽에
「As a slave, / he had taught himself to read and write / and he spread / that knowledge to other slaves as well.」③의근거 불일치
노예로서 / 그는 읽고 쓰는 것을 독학했다. / 그리고 그는 전파했다. / 그 지식을 다른 노예들에게도
Once free, / he became a well-known abolitionist / and strong believer in equality for all people / including Blacks, Native Americans, women, and recent immigrants.
자유로워지고 난 뒤 / 그는 유명한 노예제 폐지론자가 되었다. / 그리고 모든 사람들을 위한 평등에 대한 강한 신봉자가 되었다. / 흑인, 아메리카 원주민, 여성, 그리고 최근 이민자들을 포함한
「He wrote several autobiographies / describing his experiences as a slave.」④의근거 일치
그는 몇 권의 자서전을 썼다. / 노예로서의 자신의 경험을 묘사한
「In addition to all this, / he became the first African-American candidate / for vice president of the United States.」⑤의근거 일치
이 모든 것에 더하여 / 그는 첫 아프리카계 미국인 후보가 되었다. / 미국의 부통령을 위한

Frederick Douglass는 Maryland의 한 농장에서 노예로 태어났다. 태어났을 때 그의 성명은 Frederick Augustus Washington Bailey였다. 그는 1838년에 노예 상태에서 성공적으로 탈출한 후 자신의 이름을 Frederick Douglass로 바꿨다. 그는 노예가 된 사람들을 북쪽으로 탈출하도록 돕는 사람, 장소, 경로의 조직인 Underground Railroad의 리더가 되었다. 그는 다른

16회

도망친 노예들이 북쪽의 다른 지역에 안전하게 도착할 수 있을 때까지 그들을 도왔다. 노예로서 그는 읽고 쓰는 것을 독학했고, 그 지식을 다른 노예들에게도 전파했다. 자유로워지고 난 뒤 그는 유명한 노예제 폐지론자이자 흑인, 아메리카 원주민, 여성, 그리고 최근 이민자들을 포함한 모든 사람들을 위한 평등에 대한 강한 신봉자가 되었다. 그는 노예로서의 자신의 경험을 묘사한 몇 권의 자서전을 썼다. 이 모든 것에 더하여 그는 미국의 첫 아프리카계 미국인 부통령 후보가 되었다.

Why? 왜 정답일까?

'As a slave, he had taught himself to read and write and he spread that knowledge to other slaves as well.'에서 스스로 읽고 쓰는 법을 배웠다고 하므로, 내용과 일치하지 않는 것은 ③ '다른 노예들로부터 읽고 쓰는 법을 배웠다.'이다.

Why? 왜 오답일까?

① 'Frederick Douglass was born into slavery at a farm in Maryland.'의 내용과 일치한다.
② 'He became a leader of the Underground Railroad — a network of people, places, and routes that helped enslaved people escape to the north.'의 내용과 일치한다.
④ 'He wrote several autobiographies describing his experiences as a slave.'의 내용과 일치한다.
⑤ 'In addition to all this, he became the first African–American candidate for vice president of the United States.'의 내용과 일치한다.

- slavery ⓝ 노예
- enslave ⓥ 노예로 만들다
- abolitionist 노예제 폐지론자
- recent ⓐ 최근의
- several ⓐ 몇 개의
- candidate ⓝ 후보자
- route ⓝ 길
- well-known 잘 알려진
- equality ⓝ 평등
- immigrant ⓝ 이민자, 이주민
- autobiography ⓝ 자서전

구문 풀이

4행 He became a leader of the Underground Railroad — a network of people,
선행사
places, and routes that helped enslaved people escape to the north.
관계대명사(주격)↵   동사   목적어   목적보어(동사원형)

27 게이트볼 챔피언십 · 정답률 89% | 정답 ⑤

2023 Australian Gateball Championships에 관한 다음 안내문의 내용과 일치하지 않는 것은?
① 4일 동안 진행된다.
② 복식 경기는 오전에 열린다.
③ 모든 참가자는 참가 증서를 받는다.
④ 참가비는 무료이다.
☑ 현장에서 등록하는 것이 가능하다.

2023 Australian Gateball Championships
2023 오스트레일리아 게이트볼 챔피언십
The Diamond Coast is getting set / to welcome the Australian Gateball Championships.
Diamond Coast는 준비를 하고 있다. / 오스트레일리아 게이트볼 챔피언십을 환영할
Join this great outdoor competition / and be the winner this year!
이 멋진 야외 대회에 참여하세요. / 그리고 올해 우승자가 되세요!
When & Where
언제 & 어디서
「December 19 − 22, 2023」 ①의근거 일치
2023년 1월 19일부터 22일까지
Diamond Coast Performance Centre
Diamond Coast 공연 센터
Schedule of Matches
경기 일정
「Doubles matches (9 a.m. − 11 a.m.)」 ②의근거 일치
복식 경기 (오전 9시부터 오전 11시까지)
Team matches (1 p.m. − 3 p.m.)
단체 경기 (오후 1시부터 오후 3시까지)
Prizes
상
「Every participant will receive a certificate for entry.」 ③의근거 일치
모든 참가자는 참가 증서를 받을 것입니다.
Champions are awarded a medal.
우승자들은 메달을 받습니다.
Note
참고
「Participation is free.」 ④의근거 일치
참가비는 무료입니다.
Visit www.australiangateball.com for registration.
등록을 위해 www.australiangateball.com을 방문하십시오.
「(Registration on site is not available.)」 ⑤의근거 불일치
(현장 등록은 불가합니다.)

2023 오스트레일리아 게이트볼 챔피언십

Diamond Coast는 오스트레일리아 게이트볼 챔피언십을 환영할 준비를 하고 있습니다. 이 멋진 야외 대회에 참여해서 올해 우승자가 되세요!

언제 & 어디서
▶ 2023년 12월 19일부터 22일까지
▶ Diamond Coast 공연 센터

경기 일정
▶ 복식 경기 (오전 9시부터 오전 11시까지)
▶ 단체 경기 (오후 1시부터 오후 3시까지)

상
▶ 모든 참가자는 참가 증서를 받을 것입니다.
▶ 우승자들은 메달을 받습니다.
참고
▶ 참가비는 무료입니다.
▶ 등록을 위해 www.australiangateball.com을 방문하십시오. (현장 등록은 불가합니다.)

Why? 왜 정답일까?

'Registration on site is not available.'에서 현장 등록이 불가능하다고 하므로, 안내문의 내용과 일치하지 않는 것은 ⑤ '현장에서 등록하는 것이 가능하다'이다.

Why? 왜 오답일까?

① 'December 19 − 22, 2023'의 내용과 일치한다.
② 'Doubles matches (9 a.m. − 11 a.m.)'의 내용과 일치한다.
③ 'Every participant will receive a certificate for entry.'의 내용과 일치한다.
④ 'Participation is free.'의 내용과 일치한다.

- get set 준비를 갖추다
- participant ⓝ 참가자
- entry ⓝ 참가
- competition ⓝ 경기, 시합
- certificate ⓝ 증서, 증명서

28 도시 어드벤처 탐험 광고 · 정답률 89% | 정답 ⑤

The Amazing Urban Adventure Quest에 관한 다음 안내문의 내용과 일치하는 것은?
① 참여하는 동안 스마트폰 사용은 금지된다.
② 일 년 내내 일몰 후 참여할 수 있다.
③ 서편 코스는 나이 제한이 없다.
④ 1인당 40달러의 요금이 든다.
☑ 할인받을 수 있는 코드가 있다.

The Amazing Urban Adventure Quest
놀라운 도시 어드벤처 탐험
Explore Central Park while solving clues / and completing challenges!
단서를 해결하면서 Central Park를 탐험하세요! / 그리고 도전을 완수하면서
「Guided by your smartphone, / make your way among the well-known places / in the park.」 ①의근거 불일치
스마트폰의 안내를 받으면서 / 명소들 속 자신의 길을 만들어 보세요. / 공원의
When & How
언제 & 어떻게
「Available 365 days a year // (from sunrise to sunset)」 ②의근거 불일치
1년 365일 이용 가능 // (일출부터 일몰까지)
Start when you want.
여러분이 원할 때 시작하세요.
Get a stamp at each checkpoint.
각 체크포인트에서 스탬프를 받으세요.
Adventure Courses
어드벤처 코스
East Side: Starts at Twilight Gardens (no age limit)
동편: Twilight Gardens에서 시작합니다. (나이 제한 없음)
「West Side: Starts at Strawberry Castle (over 15 years old)」 ③의근거 불일치
서편: Strawberry Castle에서 시작합니다. (15세 초과)
Registration & Cost
등록 & 비용
Sign up online at www.urbanquest.com.
www.urbanquest.com에서 온라인으로 등록하세요.
「$40 for a team of 2 − 5 people」 ④의근거 불일치
2−5명으로 구성된 팀 당 40달러
「Save 20% with discount code: CENTRALQUEST」 ⑤의근거 일치
할인 코드 CENTRALQUEST로 20%를 절약하세요.

놀라운 도시 어드벤처 탐험

단서를 해결하고 도전을 완수하면서 Central Park를 탐험하세요! 스마트폰의 안내를 받으면서 공원의 명소들 속 자신의 길을 만들어 보세요.

언제 & 어떻게
• 1년 365일 이용 가능 (일출부터 일몰까지)
• 여러분이 원할 때 시작하세요.
• 각 체크포인트에서 스탬프를 받으세요.

어드벤처 코스
• 동편: Twilight Gardens에서 시작합니다. (나이 제한 없음)
• 서편: Strawberry Castle에서 시작합니다. (15세 초과)

등록 & 비용
• www.urbanquest.com에서 온라인으로 등록하세요.
• 2−5명으로 구성된 팀 당 40달러
• 할인 코드 CENTRALQUEST로 20%를 절약하세요.

Why? 왜 정답일까?

'Save 20% with discount code: CENTRALQUEST'에서 20% 할인 코드를 안내하고 있으므로, 안내문의 내용과 일치하는 것은 ⑤ '할인받을 수 있는 코드가 있다.'이다.

Why? 왜 오답일까?

① 'Guided by your smartphone, make your way among the well-known places in the park.'에서 스마트폰의 안내를 받으라고 하며 이용을 권장하였다.
② 'Available 365 days a year (from sunrise to sunset)'에서 일출부터 일몰까지 참여할 수 있다고 하였다.
③ 'West Side: Starts at Strawberry Castle (over 15 years old)'에서 서편 코스는 15세 초과부터 참여 가능하다고 하였다.
④ '$40 for a team of 2 − 5 people'에서 2 − 5명의 팀 당 40달러의 요금이 든다고 하였다.

- **urban** ⓐ 도시의, 도회지의
- **explore** ⓥ 탐험하다
- **complete** ⓥ 완료하다
- **quest** ⓝ 탐색, 탐구
- **clue** ⓝ 단서
- **discount** ⓝ 할인

★★★ 등급을 가르는 문제!

29 뇌사 결정에 대한 엄격한 지침   정답률 47% | 정답 ④

다음 글의 밑줄 친 부분 중, 어법상 틀린 것은? [3점]

Some countries have proposed tougher guidelines / for determining brain death / when transplantation — transferring organs to others — is under consideration.
일부 국가는 더 엄격한 지침을 제안했다 / 뇌사를 결정하는 것에 대한 / 장기 이식, 즉 다른 사람에게 장기를 전달하는 것을 고려 중일 때
In several European countries, / there are legal requirements / which specify ① that a whole team of doctors must agree over the diagnosis of death / in the case of a potential donor.
몇몇 유럽 국가에는 / 법적 요건이 있다 / 의사 팀 전체가 사망 진단에 동의해야 한다고 명시하는 / 잠재적 기증자의 경우
The reason for these strict regulations / for diagnosing brain death / in potential organ donors / ② is, / no doubt, / to ease public fears of a premature diagnosis of brain death / for the purpose of obtaining organs.
이러한 엄격한 규정들의 이유는 / 뇌사 진단에 대한 / 잠재적인 장기 기증자의 / ~것 이다. / 의심할 바 없이 / 너무 이른 뇌사 진단에 대한 대중의 두려움을 완화하기 위한 / 장기 확보를 위한
But it is questionable / whether these requirements reduce public suspicions / as much as they create ③ them.
하지만 이것은 의문이다. / 이러한 요건들이 대중의 의심을 줄여 주는지 / 그것을 만들어내는 만큼
They certainly maintain mistaken beliefs / that diagnosing brain death is an unreliable process / ✔ lacking precision.
그것들은 잘못된 믿음을 확실히 유지시킨다. / 뇌사 진단이 신뢰하기 어려운 과정이라는 / 정확성이 결여된
As a matter of consistency, / at least, / criteria for diagnosing the deaths of organ donors should be exactly the same / as for those for ⑤ whom immediate burial / or cremation is intended.
일관성의 이유로 / 적어도 / 장기 기증자의 사망 진단 기준은 정확히 동일해야 한다. / 즉각적인 매장 또는 화장이 예정된 사람들에 대한 그것과

일부 국가는 장기 이식, 즉 다른 사람에게 장기를 전달하는 것을 고려 중일 때 뇌사를 결정하는 것에 대한 더 엄격한 지침을 제안했다. 몇몇 유럽 국가에는 잠재적 기증자의 경우 의사 팀 전체가 사망 진단에 동의해야 한다고 명시하는 법적 요건들이 있다. 잠재적인 장기 기증자의 뇌사 진단에 대한 이러한 엄격한 규정들의 이유는 의심할 바 없이 장기 확보를 위한 너무 이른 뇌사 진단에 대한 대중의 두려움을 완화하기 위한 것이다. 하지만 이러한 요건들이 대중의 의심을 만들어내는 만큼 그것을 줄여 주는지는 의문이다. 그것들은 뇌사 진단이 정확성이 결여된 신뢰하기 어려운 과정이라는 잘못된 믿음을 확실히 유지시킨다. 적어도 일관성의 이유로 장기 기증자의 사망 진단 기준은 즉각적인 매장 또는 화장이 예정된 사람들에 대한 그것과 정확히 동일해야 한다.

Why? 왜 정답일까?
접속사 that 절 안에 이미 동사(is)가 있으므로, process를 수식하는 분사 형태인 lacking이 와야 한다. 따라서 어법상 틀린 것은 ④이다.

Why? 왜 오답일까?
① specify의 목적어 역할을 하는 목적격 관계대명사 that이다.
② for these ~ organ donors는 주어 the reason의 수식어구 이므로 단수 동사인 is가 오는 것이 맞다.
③ them은 suspicions의 대명사 이므로 복수형이 맞다.
⑤ those를 선행사로 하는 목적격 관계대명사 자리으므로 whom이 오는 것이 맞다.

- **tough** ⓐ 엄격한, 힘든
- **transferring** ⓝ 이동, 이송
- **consideration** ⓝ 고려
- **diagnosis** ⓝ 진단
- **donor** ⓝ 기증자
- **regulation** ⓝ 규제
- **belief** ⓝ 생각, 신념
- **criteria** ⓝ 기준
- **burial** ⓝ 매장
- **transplantation** ⓝ 이식
- **organ** ⓝ 장기
- **specify** ⓥ 구체화하다
- **potential** ⓐ 잠재적인
- **strict** ⓐ 엄격한
- **premature** ⓐ 정상보다 이른
- **consistency** ⓝ 일관성
- **immediate** ⓐ 즉시
- **cremation** ⓝ 화장

구문 풀이

9행 But it is questionable whether these requirements reduce public suspicions
부사절(~인지 아닌지)
as much as they create them.
「as much as : ~만큼」

★★ 문제 해결 꿀~팁 ★★

▶ 많이 틀린 이유는?
④번의 경우 that은 관계대명사가 아니라 동격의 that이므로 뒤에 완전한 문장이 와야 하는데 이미 is가 본동사로 쓰였으므로 동사가 두 개 올 수 없다. 따라서 lack을 process를 수식하는 현재분사 형태인 lacking으로 바꿔야 한다. ⑤번은 for whom 이하의 문장이 those를 수식하고 있는 형태로, 전치사+관계대명사 뒤에는 완벽한 문장이 와야 한다. 이 문장에는 수동태가 쓰였는데, 수동태 또한 주어 동사를 갖춘 완전한 문장임을 알아야 한다.

▶ 문제 해결 방법은?
①번은 that명사절과 what명사절을 비교하는 문제임으로 뒤에 완전한 문장인지 불완전한 문장인지 확인하여 완전한 경우 that을 고르면 된다. ②번은 단수동사 is와 복수동사 are를 비교하는 문제임으로 주어를 찾아 단수인지 복수인지 확인하면 된다. ③번은 단수 대명사 it과 복수 대명사 them을 비교하는 문제로 문장 내에서 명사를 찾아서 확인하면 된다. ④번은 동격의 that 다음에 완전한 문장이 와야 하므로 문장 내에 주어와 동사가 제대로 있는지 확인하면 된다. ⑤번은 전치사+관계대명사 뒤에 완전한 문장이 나오는지 확인해야한다.

30 미니멀리즘에 대한 이해   정답률 62% | 정답 ④

다음 글의 밑줄 친 부분 중, 문맥상 낱말의 쓰임이 적절하지 않은 것은?

The term minimalism gives a negative impression / to some people who think / that it is all about sacrificing valuable possessions.
미니멀리즘이라는 용어는 부정적인 인상을 준다. / 생각하는 일부 사람들에게 / 그것을 소중한 소유물을 희생하는 것에 관한 것으로만
This insecurity naturally stems from their ① attachment / to their possessions.
이러한 불안은 그들의 애착에서 자연스럽게 비롯된다. / 자신의 소유물에 대한
It is difficult to distance oneself from something / that has been around for quite some time.
것으로부터 자신을 멀리 두는 것은 어렵다. / 꽤 오랫동안 곁에 있어 왔던
Being an emotional animal, / human beings give meaning to the things around them.
감정의 동물이기 때문에 / 인간은 그들의 곁에 있는 물건에 의미를 부여한다.
So, / the question arising here is that / if minimalism will ② hurt one's emotions, / why become a minimalist?
그래서 / 여기서 생기는 질문은 ~는 것이다. / 미니멀리즘이 사람의 감정을 상하게 한다면 / 왜 미니멀리스트가 되느냐
The answer is very simple; / the assumption of the question is fundamentally ③ wrong.
대답은 매우 간단하다. / 그 질문의 가정은 근본적으로 틀리다
Minimalism does not hurt emotions.
미니멀리즘은 감정을 상하게 하지 않는다.
You might feel a bit sad / while getting rid of a useless item / but sooner than later, / this feeling will be ✔ overcame / by the joy of clarity.
여러분은 조금 슬퍼할 수도 있다 / 쓸모없는 물건을 치우면서 / 그러나 머지않아 / 이 느낌은 명료함의 기쁨으로 극복될 것이다.
Minimalists never argue / that you should leave every convenience of the modern era.
미니멀리스트는 주장하지 않는다. / 여러분이 현대의 모든 편의를 버려야 한다고
They are of the view / that you only need to ⑤ eliminate stuff / that is unused or not going to be used / in the near future.
그들은 견해를 가지고 있다. / 여러분이 물건을 없애기만 하면 된다는 / 사용되지 않거나 사용되지 않을 / 가까운 미래에

미니멀리즘이라는 용어는 그것을 소중한 소유물을 희생하는 것에 관한 것으로만 생각하는 일부 사람들에게 부정적인 인상을 준다. 이러한 불안은 자신의 소유물에 대한 ① 애착에서 자연스럽게 비롯된다. 꽤 오랫동안 곁에 있어 왔던 것으로부터 자신을 멀리 두는 것은 어렵다. 감정의 동물이기 때문에, 인간은 그들의 곁에 있는 물건에 의미를 부여한다. 그래서 여기서 생기는 질문은 미니멀리즘이 사람의 감정을 ② 상하게 한다면 왜 미니멀리스트가 되느냐는 것이다. 대답은 매우 간단하다. 그 질문의 가정은 근본적으로 ③ 틀리다. 미니멀리즘은 감정을 상하게 하지 않는다. 여러분은 쓸모없는 물건을 치우면서 조금 슬퍼할 수도 있지만 머지않아 이 느낌은 명료함의 기쁨으로 ④ 유지될(→ 극복될) 것이다. 미니멀리스트는 여러분이 현대의 모든 편의를 버려야 한다고 주장하지 않는다. 그들은 여러분이 사용되지 않거나 가까운 미래에 사용되지 않을 물건을 ⑤ 없애기만 하면 된다는 견해를 가지고 있다.

Why? 왜 정답일까?
미니멀리즘은 소요물을 전부 버리는 것이 아니라 필요 없게 되어 사용하지 않는 물건을 없애는 것이므로 버리는 순간에는 슬플 수 있지만 곧 기쁨으로 '극복될' 것이라는 설명이 알맞다. 따라서 maintain을 overcame으로 고쳐야 한다.

- **term** ⓝ 용어
- **valuable** ⓐ 가치 있는
- **insecurity** ⓝ 불안
- **distance** ⓥ 거리를 두다
- **assumption** ⓝ 가정
- **get rid of** 버리다
- **maintain** ⓥ 유지하다
- **era** ⓝ 시대
- **unused** ⓐ 사용하지 않는
- **sacrifice** ⓥ 희생하다
- **possession** ⓝ 소유
- **stem** ⓥ 비롯되다
- **arise** ⓥ 발생하다
- **fundamentally** [ad] 근본적으로
- **sooner than later** 머지않아
- **clarity** ⓝ 명료하다
- **eliminate** ⓥ 제거하다

구문 풀이

4행 It is difficult to distance oneself from something that has been around for quite some time.
가주어 / 진주어 / 선행사 / 관계대명사(주격)

31 시각 체계의 특징   정답률 61% | 정답 ①

다음 빈칸에 들어갈 말로 가장 적절한 것을 고르시오.

✔ adapting itself   스스로 적응하는
② visualizing ideas   아이디어를 시각화하는
③ assessing distances   거리를 측정하는
④ functioning irregularly   불규칙적으로 기능하는
⑤ operating independently   독립적으로 작동하는

A remarkable characteristic of the visual system is / that it has the ability of adapting itself.
시각 체계의 두드러진 특징은 / 스스로 적응하는 능력이 있다는 것이다.
Psychologist George M. Stratton made this clear / in an impressive self-experiment.
심리학자 George M. Stratton은 이것을 분명히 했다. / 인상적인 자가 실험에서
Stratton wore reversing glasses for several days, / which literally turned the world upside down for him.
Stratton은 며칠 동안 반전 안경을 착용했다. / 그런데 그 안경은 말 그대로 그에게 세상을 뒤집어 놓았다.
In the beginning, / this caused him great difficulties: / just putting food in his mouth with a fork / was a challenge for him.
처음에 / 이것은 그에게 큰 어려움을 초래하였다. / 포크로 음식을 입에 넣는 것조차 / 그에게는 도전이었다.
With time, / however, / his visual system adjusted to the new stimuli from reality, / and he was able to act normally / in his environment again, / even seeing it upright / when he concentrated.
시간이 지나면서 / 그러나 / 그의 시각 체계는 현실의 새로운 자극에 적응했다. / 그리고 그는 정상적으로 행동할 수 있었다. / 다시 자신의 환경에서 / 심지어 똑바로 보면서 / 그가 집중했을 때
As he took off his reversing glasses, / he was again confronted with problems: / he used the wrong hand / when he wanted to reach for something, / for example.
반전 안경을 벗었을 때 / 그는 다시 문제에 직면했다. / 그는 반대 손을 사용했다. / 그가 무언가를 잡기를 원할 때 / 예를 들어
Fortunately, / Stratton could reverse the perception, / and he did not have to wear reversing glasses / for the rest of his life.
다행히 / Stratton은 지각을 뒤집을 수 있었다. / 그리고 그는 반전 안경을 착용하지 않아도 되었다. / 평생
For him, / everything returned to normal after one day.
그에게 / 하루 만에 모든 것이 정상으로 돌아왔다.

시각 체계의 두드러진 특징은 스스로 적응하는 능력이 있다는 것이다. 심리학자 George M. Stratton은 인상적인 자가 실험에서 이것을 분명히 했다. Stratton은 며칠 동안 반전 안경을

착용했는데 그 안경은 말 그대로 그에게 세상을 뒤집어 놓았다. 처음에 이것은 그에게 큰 어려움을 초래하였다. 포크로 음식을 입에 넣는 것조차 그에게는 도전이었다. 그러나 시간이 지나면서 그의 시각 체계는 현실의 새로운 자극에 적응했고, 그가 집중했을 때는 심지어 똑바로 보면서, 다시 자신의 환경에서 정상적으로 행동할 수 있었다. 반전 안경을 벗었을 때 그는 다시 문제에 직면했다. 예를 들어 그가 무언가를 잡기를 원할 때 그는 반대 손을 사용했다. 다행히 Stratton은 지각을 뒤집을 수 있었고 평생 반전 안경을 착용하지 않아도 되었다. 그에게 하루 만에 모든 것이 정상으로 돌아왔다.

Why? 왜 정답일까?

처음 반전 안경을 착용했을 때 어려움을 겪었지만 시간이 지나면서 금세 적응하였고(With time, however, his visual system adjusted to the new stimuli from reality, and he was able to act normally in his environment again, even seeing it upright when he concentrated.), 이후 안경을 벗었을 때도 다시 원상태에 적응했다고 얘기하고 있다. 따라서 빈칸에 들어갈 말로 가장 적절한 것은 ① '스스로 적응하는'이다.

- remarkable ⓐ 두드러진, 놀라운, 주목할 만한
- ability ⓝ 능력, 수완, 역량
- impressive ⓐ 인상적인
- literally ⓐⓓ 문자 그대로, 정말로
- adjust to ~에 적응하다
- concentrate ⓥ 집중하다
- visual ⓐ 시각의
- psychologist ⓝ 심리학자
- reverse ⓥ 뒤집다
- upside down 거꾸로, 전도되어, 뒤집혀
- upright ⓐ 똑바른
- confront ⓥ 직면하다

구문 풀이

4행 Stratton wore reversing glasses for several days, which literally turned the world upside down for him.
(선행사(앞문장 전체)) (주격 관계대명사(계속적))

★★★ 등급을 가르는 문제!

32 정보의 접근여부와 지적 자신감과의 관계 ｜ 정답률 46% ｜ 정답 ②

다음 빈칸에 들어갈 말로 가장 적절한 것을 고르시오.

① improve their judgment skills – 그들의 판단 능력을 증가시키기
✓ pump up their intellectual confidence – 그들의 지적 자신감을 부풀리기
③ make them endure challenging situations – 도전 상황에서 그들을 견디도록 시키기
④ lead to a collaboration among the participants – 참가자들 사이에서 협동을 이끌어 내기
⑤ motivate them to pursue in-depth knowledge – 깊은 지식을 추구하도록 동기를 부여하기

Participants in a study were asked to answer questions / like "Why does the moon have phases?"
한 연구의 참가자들이 질문에 답하도록 요청받았다. / '달은 왜 상을 가지고 있을까'와 같은

Half the participants were told / to search for the answers on the internet, / while the other half weren't allowed to do so.
참가자의 절반은 말을 들었다. / 인터넷에서 답을 검색하라는 / 반면 나머지 절반은 그렇게 하도록 허용되지 않았다.

Then, / in the second part of the study, / all of the participants were presented / with a new set of questions, / such as "Why does Swiss cheese have holes?"
그다음 / 연구의 두 번째 단계에서 / 모든 참가자는 제시받았다 / 일련의 새로운 질문들을 / '스위스 치즈에는 왜 구멍이 있을까'와 같은

These questions were unrelated to the ones asked / during the first part of the study, / so participants who used the internet had absolutely no advantage over those / who hadn't.
이 질문들은 질문받았던 것들과는 관련이 없었다 / 연구의 첫 번째 단계에서 / 그래서 인터넷을 사용한 참가자들은 이점이 전혀 없었다. / 그렇지 않은 참가자들보다

You would think / that both sets of participants would be equally sure or unsure / about how well they could answer the new questions.
여러분은 생각할 것이다. / 두 집단의 참가자들이 동일한 정도로 확신하거나 확신하지 못할 것으로 / 그들이 새로운 질문들에 얼마나 잘 대답할 수 있을지에 대해

But / those who used the internet / in the first part of the study / rated themselves as more knowledgeable / than those who hadn't, / even about questions / they hadn't searched online for.
그러나 / 인터넷을 사용했던 참가자들은 / 연구의 첫 번째 단계에서 / 스스로 더 많이 알고 있다고 평가했다. / 그러지 않았던 참가자들보다 / 질문에 대해서조차 / 자신이 온라인에서 검색하지 않았던

The study suggests / that having access to unrelated information / was enough to pump up their intellectual confidence.
이 연구는 시사한다. / 관련 없는 정보에 접근하는 것이 ~는 것을 / 그들의 지적 자신감을 부풀리기 충분했다

한 연구의 참가자들이 '달은 왜 상을 가지고 있을까'와 같은 질문들에 답하도록 요청받았다. 참가자의 절반은 인터넷에서 답을 검색하라는 말을 들었고 나머지 절반은 그렇게 하도록 허용되지 않았다. 그다음, 연구의 두 번째 단계에서 모든 참가자는 '스위스 치즈에는 왜 구멍이 있을까'와 같은 일련의 새로운 질문들을 제시받았다. 이 질문들은 연구의 첫 번째 단계에서 질문받았던 것들과는 관련이 없어서 인터넷을 사용한 참가자들은 그러지 않은 참가자들보다 이점이 전혀 없었다. 여러분은 두 집단의 참가자들이 새로운 질문들에 얼마나 잘 대답할 수 있을지에 대해 동일한 정도로 확신하거나 확신하지 못할 것으로 생각할 것이다. 그러나 연구의 첫 번째 단계에서 인터넷을 사용했던 참가자들은 자신이 온라인에서 검색하지 않았던 질문들에 대해서조차 그러지 않았던 참가자들보다 스스로가 더 많이 알고 있다고 평가했다. 이 연구는 관련 없는 정보에 접근하는 것이 그들의 지적 자신감을 부풀리기 충분했다는 것을 시사한다.

Why? 왜 정답일까?

첫 번째 질문에서 인터넷 접근을 허용받은 사람들이 두 번째 질문에서도 스스로 더 많이 알고 있다고 평가했다(But those who used the internet in the first part of the study rated themselves as more knowledgeable than those who hadn't, even about questions they hadn't searched online for.)는 내용이므로, 빈칸에 들어갈 말로 가장 적절한 것은 ② '그들의 지적 자신감을 부풀리기'이다.

- phase ⓝ 상
- unrelated ⓐ 관계없는
- equally ⓐⓓ 동등하게
- knowledgeable ⓐ 아는 것이 많은, 많이 아는
- intellectual ⓐ 지적인
- pursue ⓥ 추구하다
- present ⓥ 제시하다
- advantage ⓝ 이점
- rate ⓥ 평가하다
- pump up 부풀리다
- endure ⓥ 견디다
- in-depth ⓐ 깊은

구문 풀이

11행 But those who used the internet in the first part of the study rated
「those who : ~하는 사람들」 (동사)
themselves as more knowledgeable than those who hadn't, even about questions they hadn't searched online for.

★★ 문제 해결 꿀~팁 ★★

▶ 많이 틀린 이유는?
지문에서 연구가 등장하면 그 연구의 결과가 글의 주제와 밀접하게 연관되어 있다. ①번, ③번, ④번은 해당 내용에서 판단 능력, 도전 상황, 협동 등이 언급되지 않았으므로 답이 될 수 없다. ⑤번 또한 참가자들이 실제로 깊은 지식을 얻도록 동기가 부여된 내용이 나오지 않았기에 답이 될 수 없다.

▶ 문제 해결 방법은?
빈칸이 포함된 문장을 먼저 정확하게 해석하는 것이 중요하다. 연구를 통해서 '정보에 접근하는 것이 ~하기에 충분했다는 것을 시사한다'는 내용을 미리 머릿속에 생각해 둔 후 다시 처음부터 읽어보며 힌트를 찾으면 된다. 먼저 연구의 결과를 파악해야하는데, 첫 번째 단계에서 인터넷을 사용했던 참가자들이 후에 모르는 질문에 대해서도 알고 있다고 파악하는 경향이 많았다고 이야기하고 있다. 이는 실제로 지식을 얻은 것이 아님에도 알고 있다고 착각하는 것이므로 ⑤번은 답이 될 수 없다.

33 관점에 대한 고찰 ｜ 정답률 61% ｜ 정답 ④

다음 빈칸에 들어갈 말로 가장 적절한 것을 고르시오. [3점]

① using our experiences as a guide – 가이드로 우리의 경험을 이용함으로써
② breaking the framework of old ideas – 오래된 생각의 틀을 깸으로써
③ adding new information to what we know – 우리가 아는 것에 관한 새로운 정보를 추가함으로써
✓ focusing in on particular features within it – 세상 안의 특정한 특징에 초점을 맞춤으로써
⑤ considering both bright and dark sides of it – 밝은 면과 어두운 면을 모두 고려함으로써

Anthropologist Gregory Bateson suggests / that we tend to understand the world / by focusing in on particular features within it.
인류학자 Gregory Bateson은 제안한다. / 우리가 세상을 이해하는 경향이 있다고 / 세상 안의 특정한 특징에 초점을 맞춤으로써

Take platypuses. // We might zoom in so closely to their fur / that each hair appears different.
오리너구리를 예로 들어 보자. // 우리가 그들의 털을 매우 가까이 확대하면 / 각 가닥이 다르게 보인다.

We might also zoom out / to the extent / where it appears as a single, uniform object.
우리는 또한 축소할 수도 있다. / 정도까지 / 그것이 하나의 동일한 개체로 보이는

We might take the platypus / as an individual, / or we might treat it / as part of a larger unit / such as a species or an ecosystem.
우리는 오리너구리를 취급할 수도 있다. / 개체로 / 또는 취급할 수도 있다. / 더 큰 단위의 일부로 / 종 또는 생태계와 같이

It's possible to move / between many of these perspectives, / although we may need some additional tools and skills / to zoom in on individual pieces of hair / or zoom out to entire ecosystems.
이동하는 것은 가능하다. / 이러한 많은 관점 사이를 / 비록 몇 가지 추가 도구와 기술이 필요할지도 모르지만 / 개별 머리카락을 확대하기 위해서 / 또는 전체 생태계로 축소하기 위해

Crucially, / however, / we can only take up one perspective at a time.
결정적으로 / 그러나 / 우리는 한 번에 하나의 관점만 취할 수 있다.

We can pay attention to the varied behavior of individual animals, / look at / what unites them into a single species, / or look at them as part of bigger ecological patterns.
우리는 개별 동물의 다양한 행동에 주의를 기울일 수 있다. / 그리고 살펴볼 수 있다. / 그들을 단일 종으로 합하는 것을 / 또는 더 큰 생태학적 패턴의 일부로서 그들을 살펴볼 수도 있다.

Every possible perspective / involves emphasizing certain aspects / and ignoring others.
가능한 모든 관점은 / 포함한다. / 특정 측면을 강조하는 것을 / 그리고 다른 측면을 외면하는 것을

인류학자 Gregory Bateson은 우리가 세상 안의 특정한 특징에 초점을 맞춤으로써 세상을 이해하는 경향이 있다고 제안한다. 오리너구리를 예로 들어보자. 우리가 그들의 털을 매우 가까이 확대하면 각 가닥이 다르게 보인다. 우리는 또한 그것이 하나의 동일한 개체로 보이는 정도까지 축소할 수도 있다. 우리는 오리너구리를 개체로 취급할 수도 있고 종 또는 생태계와 같이 더 큰 단위의 일부로 취급할 수도 있다. 비록 개별 머리카락을 확대하거나 전체 생태계로 축소하기 위해 몇 가지 추가 도구와 기술이 필요할지도 모르지만, 이러한 많은 관점 사이를 이동하는 것은 가능하다. 그러나 결정적으로 우리는 한 번에 하나의 관점만 취할 수 있다. 우리는 개별 동물의 다양한 행동에 주의를 기울일 수 있고, 그들을 단일 종으로 합하는 것을 살펴볼 수도 있고, 더 큰 생태학적 패턴의 일부로서 그들을 살펴볼 수도 있다. 가능한 모든 관점은 특정 측면을 강조하고 다른 측면을 외면하는 것을 포함한다.

Why? 왜 정답일까?

오리너구리를 예로 들어 사람은 관점 사이를 이동하여 이를 개체로 취급할 수도 있지만 한 번에 하나의 관점으로만 바라볼 수 있다(Crucially, however, we can only take up one perspective at a time.)는 내용이므로, 빈칸에 들어갈 말로 가장 적절한 것은 ④ '세상 안의 특정한 특징에 초점을 맞춤으로써'이다.

- anthropologist ⓝ 인류학자
- zoom out 축소하다
- ecosystem ⓝ 생태계
- take up 취하다
- unite ⓥ 합하다
- zoom in 확대하다
- object ⓝ 사물
- crucially ⓐⓓ 결정적으로
- varied ⓐ 다양한
- ecological ⓐ 생태계의

구문 풀이

4행 We might also zoom out to the extent where it appears as a single, uniform object.
(관계부사)

34 플라톤의 실재론 ｜ 정답률 53% ｜ 정답 ④

다음 빈칸에 들어갈 말로 가장 적절한 것을 고르시오. [3점]

① observable phenomena of the physical world – 물리적 세계의 관찰 가능한 현상
② our experiences shaped by external influences – 외부 영향에 의해 만들어진 경험

[문제편 p.154]

③ an overlapping area between emotion and reason – 감정과 이성 사이의 겹친 영역
✔ an invisible but perfect world beyond our senses – 보이지 않지만 우리의 감각을 넘어선 완벽한 세계
⑤ our perception affected by stereotype or generalization – 고정관념과 일반화에 영향받은 인식

Plato's realism includes all aspects of experience / but is most easily explained / by considering the nature of mathematical and geometrical objects / such as circles.
플라톤의 실재론은 경험의 모든 측면을 포함한다. / 하지만 가장 쉽게 설명된다. / 수학적이고 기하학적인 대상의 특성을 고려함으로써 / 원과 같은

He asked the question, / what is a circle?
그는 질문을 했다. / 원이란 무엇인가?

You might indicate a particular example / carved into stone or drawn in the sand.
여러분은 특정한 예를 가리킬 수 있다. / 돌에 새겨져 있거나 모래에 그려진

However, / Plato would point out that, / if you looked closely enough, / you would see / that neither it, nor indeed any physical circle, was perfect.
그러나 / 플라톤은 지적할 것이다. / 만약 여러분이 충분히 면밀히 관찰한다면 / 여러분이 알게 될 것이다. / 그 어느 것도 진정 어떤 물리적인 원도 완벽하지 않다는 것을

They all possessed flaws, / and all were subject to change / and decayed with time.
그것들 모두는 결함을 가지고 있다. / 그리고 모두 변화의 영향을 받는다. / 그리고 시간이 지남에 따라 쇠하였다.

So how can we talk about perfect circles / if we cannot actually see or touch them?
그렇다면 우리가 어떻게 완벽한 원에 대해 이야기할 수 있을까? / 만약 우리가 그것을 실제로 보거나 만질 수 없다면

Plato's extraordinary answer was / that the world we see is a poor reflection / of a deeper unseen reality of *Forms*, or *universals*, / where perfect cats chase perfect mice / in perfect circles around perfect rocks.
플라톤의 비범한 대답은 ~이다. / 우리가 보는 세상이 불충분한 반영물이라는 것 / '형상' 또는 '보편자'라는 더 깊은 보이지 않는 실재의 / 완벽한 고양이가 완벽한 쥐를 쫓는 / 완벽한 암석 주변에서 완벽한 원을 그리며

Plato believed / that the *Forms* or *universals* are the true reality / that exists in an invisible but perfect world beyond our senses.
플라톤은 믿었다. / '형상' 또는 '보편자'가 진정한 실재라고 / 보이지 않지만 우리의 감각을 넘어선 완벽한 세계에 존재하는

플라톤의 실재론은 경험의 모든 측면을 포함하지만, 원과 같은 수학적이고 기하학적인 대상의 특성을 고려함으로써 가장 쉽게 설명된다. 그는 '원이란 무엇인가?'라는 질문을 했다. 여러분은 돌에 새겨져 있거나 모래에 그려진 특정한 예를 가리킬 수 있다. 그러나 플라톤은 여러분이 충분히 면밀히 관찰한다면, 여러분이 그 어느 것도, 진정 어떤 물리적인 원도 완벽하지 않다는 것을 알게 될 것이라고 지적할 것이다. 그것들 모두는 결함을 가지고 있었고, 모두 변화의 영향을 받고 시간이 지남에 따라 쇠하였다. 그렇다면, 우리가 완벽한 원을 실제로 보거나 만질 수 없다면, 그것에 대해 어떻게 이야기할 수 있을까? 플라톤의 비범한 대답은 우리가 보는 세상이 완벽한 고양이가 완벽한 암석 주변에서 완벽한 원을 그리며 완벽한 쥐를 쫓는 '형상' 또는 '보편자'라는 더 깊은 보이지 않는 실재의 불충분한 반영물이라는 것이다. 플라톤은 '형상' 또는 '보편자'가 보이지 않지만 우리의 감각을 넘어선 완벽한 세계에 존재하는 진정한 실재라고 믿었다.

Why? 왜 정답일까?

플라톤은 세상이 우리가 보이지 않는 실재의 불충분한 반영물(Plato's extraordinary answer was that the world we see is a poor reflection of a deeper unseen reality of *Forms*, or *universals*, where perfect cats chase perfect mice in perfect circles around perfect rocks.)이라고 말하고 있으므로 빈칸에 들어갈 말로 가장 적절한 것은 ④ '보이지 않지만 우리의 감각을 넘어선 완벽한 세계'이다.

- **nature** ⓝ 특성, 본성
- **indicate** ⓥ 가리키다
- **indeed** ⓐⓓ 진정
- **decay** ⓥ 썩다, 부패하다
- **form** ⓝ 형상
- **chase** ⓥ 쫓다
- **overlapping** ⓐ 중복된
- **generalization** ⓝ 일반화
- **geometrical** ⓐ 기하학의
- **carved** ⓐ 곡선의
- **possess** ⓥ 소유하다
- **extraordinary** ⓐ 비범한
- **universals** ⓝ 보편자
- **phenomena** ⓝ 현상
- **stereotype** ⓝ 고정관념

구문 풀이

10행 Plato's extraordinary answer was [주어] that [접속사(보어역할)] the world {we see} [선행사][{ }: 수식] is a poor [동사] reflection of a deeper unseen reality of *Forms*, or *universals*, where [관계부사] perfect cats chase perfect mice in perfect circles around perfect rocks.

---

35 대수의 법칙
정답률 64% | 정답 ③

다음 글에서 전체 흐름과 관계 <u>없는</u> 문장은?

In statistics, / the law of large numbers describes / a situation where having more data is better for making predictions.
통계학에서 / 대수의 법칙은 설명한다. / 더 많은 데이터를 갖는 것이 예측하는데 더 좋은 상황을

According to it, / the more often an experiment is conducted, / the closer the average of the results can be expected / to match the true state of the world.
그것에 따르면 / 실험이 더 자주 수행될수록 / 그 결과의 평균이 예상될 수 있다. / 세상의 실제 상태에 더 맞춰지는 것으로

① For instance, / on your first encounter with the game of roulette, / you may have beginner's luck / after betting on 7.
예를 들어 / 룰렛 게임을 처음 접했을 때 / 여러분은 초보자의 운이 있을 수 있다. / 7에 베팅한 후

② But / the more often you repeat this bet, / the closer the relative frequency of wins and losses is expected to approach / the true chance of winning, / meaning that your luck will at some point fade away.
하지만 / 당신이 이 베팅을 더 자주 반복할수록 / 승패의 상대적인 빈도가 더 가까워질 것으로 예상된다. / 진짜 승률에 / 이는 당신의 운이 어느 순간 사라진다는 것을 의미한다.

✔ Each number's symbolic meanings can be interpreted / in various ways / and are promising / in situations that may change unexpectedly.
각 숫자의 상징적인 의미는 해석될 수 있다. / 다양한 방식으로 / 그리고 유망하다. / 예상치 못하게 바뀔 수 있는 상황에서

④ Similarly, / car insurers collect large amounts of data / to figure out the chances / that drivers will cause accidents, / depending on their age, region, or car brand.
마찬가지로 / 자동차 보험사는 많은 양의 데이터를 수집한다. / 확률을 파악하기 위해 / 운전자가 사고를 일으킬 / 그들의 연령, 지역 또는 자동차 브랜드에 따라

⑤ Both casinos and insurance industries / rely on the law of large numbers / to balance individual losses.
카지노와 보험 산업 모두 / 대수의 법칙에 의존한다. / 개별 손실의 균형을 맞추기 위해

통계학에서 대수의 법칙은 더 많은 데이터를 갖는 것이 예측하는데 더 좋은 상황을 설명한다. 그것에 따르면 실험이 더 자주 수행될수록 그 결과의 평균이 세상의 실제 상태에 더 맞춰지는 것으로 예상될 수 있다. ① 예를 들어 룰렛 게임을 처음 접했을 때 7에 베팅한 후 여러분은 초보자의 운이 있을 수 있다. ② 하지만 당신이 이 베팅을 더 자주 반복할수록 승패의 상대적인 빈도가 진짜 승률에 더 가까워질 것으로 예상되는데 이는 당신의 운이 어느 순간 사라진다는 것을 의미한다. ③ 각 숫자의 상징적인 의미는 다양한 방식으로 해석될 수 있으며 예상치 못하게 바뀔 수 있는 상황에서 유망하다. ④ 마찬가지로 자동차 보험사는 운전자가 그들의 연령, 지역 또는 자동차 브랜드에 따라 사고를 일으킬 확률을 파악하기 위해 많은 양의 데이터를 수집한다. ⑤ 카지노와 보험 산업 모두 개별 손실의 균형을 맞추기 위해 대수의 법칙에 의존한다.

Why? 왜 정답일까?

대수의 법칙은 데이터가 많을수록 예측에 도움이 된다는 내용인데 ③은 룰렛 게임 내 숫자의 해석에 대해 얘기하고 있다. 따라서 전체 흐름과 관계 없는 문장은 ③이다.

- **statistics** ⓝ 통계학
- **experiment** ⓝ 실험
- **encounter** ⓥ 접하다, 만나다
- **symbolic** ⓐ 상징적인
- **unexpectedly** ⓐⓓ 예상치 못하게
- **prediction** ⓝ 예측
- **conduct** ⓥ 수행하다
- **frequency** ⓝ 빈도
- **promise** ⓥ 유망하다
- **rely on** ~에 의존하다

구문 풀이

3행 According to it, the more often an experiment is conducted, the closer
「the 비교급 S + V ~, the 비교급 S + V ~ : ~하면 할수록 ~하다」
the average of the results can be expected to match the true state of the world.

---

36 청소년기의 뇌
정답률 63% | 정답 ④

주어진 글 다음에 이어질 글의 순서로 가장 적절한 것을 고르시오. [3점]

① (A) – (C) – (B)
② (B) – (A) – (C)
③ (B) – (C) – (A)
✔ (C) – (A) – (B)
⑤ (C) – (B) – (A)

The adolescent brain is not fully developed / until its early twenties.
청소년기의 뇌는 완전히 발달하지 않는다. / 20대 초반까지는

This means / the way the adolescents' decision-making circuits integrate and process information / may put them at a disadvantage.
이것은 의미한다. / 청소년의 의사 결정 회로가 정보를 통합하고 처리하는 방식이 / 그들을 불리하게 만들 수 있음을

(C) One of their brain regions that matures later is the prefrontal cortex, / which is the control center, / tasked with thinking ahead and evaluating consequences.
나중에 성숙하는 뇌 영역 중 하나는 전전두엽 피질이다. / 통제 센터인 / 그리고 그것은 미리 생각하고 결과를 평가하는 임무를 맡고 있다.

It is the area of the brain / responsible for preventing you / from sending off an initial angry text / and modifying it with kinder words.
그것은 뇌의 영역이다. / 당신이 막는 역할을 하는 / 초기의 화가 난 문자를 보내는 것을 / 그리고 그것을 더 친절한 단어로 수정하는

(A) On the other hand, / the limbic system matures earlier, / playing a central role in processing emotional responses.
반면 / 대뇌변연계는 더 일찍 성숙한다. / 그래서 정서적 반응을 처리하는 데 중심적인 역할을 한다.

Because of its earlier development, / it is more likely to influence decision-making.
그것의 더 이른 발달로 인해 / 그것이 의사 결정에 영향을 미칠 가능성이 더 높다.

Decision-making in the adolescent brain is led / by emotional factors more than the perception of consequences.
청소년기의 뇌에서 의사 결정은 이끌어진다. / 결과의 인식보다 감정적인 요인에 의해

(B) Due to these differences, / there is an imbalance / between feeling-based decision-making / ruled by the more mature limbic system / and logical-based decision-making / by the not-yet-mature prefrontal cortex.
이러한 차이점 때문에 / 불균형이 존재한다. / 감정 기반의 의사 결정 사이에 / 더 성숙한 대뇌변연계에 의해 지배되는 / 논리 기반 의사 결정과 / 아직 성숙하지 않은 전전두엽 피질에 의한

This may explain / why some teens are more likely to make bad decisions.
이것은 설명해 줄 수 있다. / 왜 일부 십 대들이 그릇된 결정을 내릴 가능성이 더 높은지를

청소년기의 뇌는 20대 초반까지는 완전히 발달하지 않는다. 이것은 청소년의 의사 결정 회로가 정보를 통합하고 처리하는 방식이 그들을 불리하게 만들 수 있음을 의미한다.

(C) 나중에 성숙하는 뇌 영역 중 하나는 통제 센터인 전전두엽 피질이며, 그것은 미리 생각하고 결과를 평가하는 임무를 맡고 있다. 그것은 당신이 초기의 화가 난 문자를 보내는 것을 막고 그것을 더 친절한 단어로 수정하게 하는 역할을 하는 뇌의 영역이다.

(A) 반면 대뇌변연계는 더 일찍 성숙하여 정서적 반응을 처리하는 데 중심적인 역할을 한다. 그것의 더 이른 발달로 인해 그것이 의사 결정에 영향을 미칠 가능성이 더 높다. 청소년기의 뇌에서 의사 결정은 결과의 인식보다 감정적인 요인에 의해 이끌어진다.

(B) 이러한 차이점 때문에 더 성숙한 대뇌변연계에 의해 지배되는 감정 기반 의사 결정과 아직 성숙하지 않은 전전두엽 피질에 의한 논리 기반 의사 결정 사이에는 불균형이 존재한다. 이것은 왜 일부 십 대들이 그릇된 결정을 내릴 가능성이 더 높은지를 설명해 줄 수 있다.

Why? 왜 정답일까?

주어진 글에서는 청소년기의 뇌는 완전히 발달하지 않는다고 이야기하고 있다. 이후 (C)에서 뇌의 영역 중 전전두엽 피질이 나중에 성숙한다고 주장을 뒷받침 하고 있으며, (A)에서는 반대로 대뇌변연계는 일찍 성숙한다고 이야기하고 있다. (B)에서 언급된 이러한 차이점은 (C)와 (A) 사이의 차이점을 언급한 것이므로 글의 순서로 가장 적절한 것은 ④ '(C) – (A) – (B)'이다.

- **adolescent** ⓝ 청소년
- **disadvantage** ⓝ 불리한 점, 약점
- **limbic system** 대뇌변연계
- **be led by** ~에 의해 이끌어지다
- **imbalance** ⓝ 불균형
- **integrate** ⓥ 통합하다
- **modify** ⓥ 수정하다
- **mature** ⓐ 성인의
- **consequence** ⓝ 결과
- **prefrontal cortex** 전전두엽 피질

14행 **This may explain why some teens are more likely to make bad decisions.**
관계부사

---

37 딥 러닝을 기반으로 한 얼굴 인식 　　　　　　정답률 49% | 정답 ③

주어진 글 다음에 이어질 글의 순서로 가장 적절한 것을 고르시오.

① (A) – (C) – (B)　　　　　② (B) – (A) – (C)
✓③ (B) – (C) – (A)　　　　　④ (C) – (A) – (B)
⑤ (C) – (B) – (A)

Despite the remarkable progress / in deep-learning based facial recognition approaches / in recent years, / in terms of identification performance, / they still have limitations.
눈에 띄는 발전에도 불구하고 / 딥 러닝 기반의 얼굴 인식 접근법의 / 최근 몇 년 동안 / 식별 성능 측면에서 / 여전히 그것은 한계를 가지고 있다.

These limitations relate to the database / used in the learning stage.
이러한 한계는 데이터베이스와 관련이 있다. / 학습 단계에서 사용되는

(B) If the selected database does not contain enough instances, / the result may be systematically affected.
선택된 데이터베이스가 충분한 사례를 포함하지 않으면 / 그 결과가 시스템적으로 영향을 받을 수 있다.

For example, / the performance of a facial biometric system may decrease / if the person to be identified was enrolled / over 10 years ago.
예를 들어 / 안면 생체 측정 시스템의 성능이 저하될 수 있다. / 만약 식별된 사람이 등록된 경우 / 10년도 더 전에

(C) The factor to consider is / that this person may experience changes / in the texture of the face, / particularly with the appearance of wrinkles and sagging skin.
고려해야 할 요인은 ~이다. / 이 사람이 변화를 경험할 수 있다는 것 / 얼굴의 질감에서 / 특히 주름과 처진 피부가 나타나는 것을 동반한

These changes may be highlighted / by weight gain or loss.
이러한 변화는 두드러질 수 있다. / 체중 증가 또는 감소에 의해

(A) To counteract this problem, / researchers have developed models / for face aging or digital de-aging.
이 문제에 대응하기 위해 / 연구자들은 모델을 개발했다. / 얼굴 노화나 디지털 노화 완화의

It is used to compensate / for the differences in facial characteristics, / which appear over a given time period.
그것은 보완하는 데 사용된다. / 얼굴 특성의 차이를 / 주어진 기간 동안 나타나는

최근 몇 년 동안 딥 러닝 기반의 얼굴 인식 접근법의 눈에 띄는 발전에도 불구하고, 식별 성능 측면에서 여전히 그것은 한계를 가지고 있다. 이러한 한계는 학습 단계에서 사용되는 데이터베이스와 관련이 있다.

(B) 선택된 데이터베이스가 충분한 사례를 포함하지 않으면 그 결과가 시스템적으로 영향을 받을 수 있다. 예를 들어 만약 식별될 사람이 10년도 더 전에 등록된 경우 안면 생체 측정 시스템의 성능이 저하될 수 있다.

(C) 고려해야 할 요인은 이 사람이 특히 주름과 처진 피부가 나타나는 것을 동반한 얼굴의 질감에서 변화를 경험할 수 있다는 것이다. 이러한 변화는 체중 증가 또는 감소에 의해 두드러질 수 있다.

(A) 이 문제에 대응하기 위해 연구자들은 얼굴 노화나 디지털 노화 완화의 모델을 개발했다. 그것은 주어진 기간 동안 나타나는 얼굴 특성의 차이를 보완하는 데 사용된다.

Why? 왜 정답일까?

딥러닝 기반의 얼굴 인식에 한계가 있다는 주어진 글 뒤로, 데이터 베이스의 불충분한 사례를 설명하는 (B), 불충분한 사례의 원인인 성능 저하에 대해 이야기하는 (C), 그리고 대응 방법인 (A)가 차례로 이어져야 자연스럽다. 따라서 글의 순서로 가장 적절한 것은 ③ '(B) – (C) – (A)'이다.

- remarkable ⓐ 눈에 띄는
- approach ⓥ 접근하다
- identification ⓝ 인식
- biometric ⓐ 생물 측정의
- wrinkle ⓝ 주름
- counteract ⓥ 대응하다
- recognition ⓝ 식별
- in terms of ~에 관하여
- limitation ⓝ 한계
- decrease ⓥ 감소하다
- sagging ⓐ 처진
- compensate ⓥ 보완하다

구문 풀이

6행 **It is used to compensate for the differences in facial characteristics,**
「be used to : ~하는데 사용된다」
which appear over a given time period.
관계대명사(주격)

★★★ 등급을 가르는 문제!

38 음식 다양성의 감소 　　　　　　정답률 38% | 정답 ⑤

글의 흐름으로 보아, 주어진 문장이 들어가기에 가장 적절한 곳을 고르시오.

The decline in the diversity of our food / is an entirely human-made process.
우리 음식의 다양성의 감소는 / 전적으로 인간이 만든 과정이다.

The biggest loss of crop diversity came / in the decades / that followed the Second World War.
농작물 다양성의 가장 큰 손실은 / 수십 년 동안 / 제2차 세계 대전 이후 나타났다.

① In an attempt to save millions / from extreme hunger, / crop scientists found ways to produce grains / such as rice and wheat / on an enormous scale.
수백 만 명의 사람들을 구하고자 하는 시도에서 / 극도의 배고픔에서 / 작물 과학자들이 곡물을 생산하는 방법을 발견했다. / 쌀과 밀과 같은 / 엄청난 규모로

② And thousands of traditional varieties were replaced / by a small number of new super-productive ones.
그리고 수천 개의 전통적인 종들은 대체되었다. / 소수의 새로운 초생산적인 종들로

③ The strategy worked spectacularly well, / at least to begin with.
그 전략은 굉장히 잘 작동했다. / 적어도 처음에는

④ Because of it, / grain production tripled, / and between 1970 and 2020 / the human population more than doubled.
그것 때문에 / 곡물 생산량은 세 배가 되었다. / 그리고 1970년과 2020년 사이에 / 인구는 두 배 이상 증가했다.

✓Leaving the contribution of that strategy to one side, / the danger of creating more uniform crops is / that they are more at risk / when it comes to disasters.
그 전략의 기여를 차치하고 / 더 획일적인 작물을 만드는 것의 위험은 / 그것들이 더 큰 위험에 처한다는 것이다. / 재앙과 관련해

Specifically, / a global food system / that depends on just a narrow selection of plants / has a greater chance of / not being able to survive diseases, pests and climate extremes.
특히 / 세계적인 식량 시스템은 / 농작물의 좁은 선택에만 의존하는 / 더 높은 가능성을 가진다. / 질병, 해충, 및 기후 위기로부터 생존하지 못할

우리 음식의 다양성의 감소는 전적으로 인간이 만든 과정이다. 농작물 다양성의 가장 큰 손실은 제2차 세계 대전 이후 수십 년 동안 나타났다. ① 수백 만 명의 사람들을 극도의 배고픔에서 구하고자 하는 시도에서 작물 과학자들이 쌀과 밀과 같은 곡물을 엄청난 규모로 생산하는 방법을 발견했다. ② 그리고 수천 개의 전통적인 종들은 소수의 새로운 초(超)생산적인 종들로 대체되었다. ③ 그 전략은 적어도 처음에는 굉장히 잘 작동했다. ④ 그것 때문에 곡물 생산량은 세 배가 되었고 1970년과 2020년 사이에 인구는 두 배 이상 증가했다. ⑤ 그 전략의 기여를 차치하고, 더 획일적인 작물을 만드는 것의 위험은 그것들이 재앙과 관련해 더 큰 위험에 처한다는 것이다. 특히 농작물의 좁은 선택에만 의존하는 세계적인 식량 시스템은 질병, 해충 및 기후 위기로부터 생존하지 못할 더 높은 가능성을 가진다.

Why? 왜 정답일까?

⑤ 앞은 음식의 다양성이 감소한 이유는 전쟁 이후 대량 생산이 가능한 작물 위주로 농사를 지었기 때문이라고 설명하고 있으며, ⑤ 뒤에서는 좁은 선택에 의존하는 것은 생존하지 못할 가능성을 높인다고 얘기하고 있다. 주어진 문장에서는 획일적인 작물을 만드는 것에 대한 위험을 언급하고 있으므로, 주어진 문장이 들어가기에 가장 적절한 곳은 ⑤이다.

- diversity ⓝ 다양성
- attempt ⓝ 시도
- scale ⓝ 규모
- super-productive 초 생산적인
- triple ⓥ 세배가 되다
- strategy ⓝ 전략
- depend on ~에 의존하다
- pest ⓝ 해충
- decade ⓐ 수십 년의
- wheat ⓝ 밀
- replace ⓥ 대체하다
- spectacularly ⓐⓓ 굉장히
- contribution ⓝ 기여
- uniform ⓝ 유니폼
- disease ⓝ 질병
- extreme ⓝ 위기

구문 풀이

14행 **Specifically, a global food system {that depends on just a narrow selection**
주어　　관계대명사(주격)　　{ }: 수식
of plants} has a greater chance of not being able to survive diseases, pests and
동사
climate extremes.

★★ 문제 해결 꿀~팁 ★★

▶ 많이 틀린 이유는?
문장을 꼼꼼하게 해석해야 한다. 주어진 글에서 전략의 기여에 대해 이야기하고 있는데 그 기여가 주어진 글 보다 먼저 나와야 하므로 ④번은 답이 될 수 없다.

▶ 문제 해결 방법은?
먼저 주어진 문장을 정확하게 해석한 후, 주어진 문장에서 쓰인 대명사나 연결 접속사를 파악하여 전후 관계를 파악하면 된다. 먼저 글에서 언급된 'that strategy'와 'the danger'가 주어진 문장보다 앞에 등장해야한다. 따라서 ①번, ②번은 답이 될 수 없다. ③번 이후에 'the strategy'가 등장하는데 전략이 잘 작동했다고 말하고 있다. 주어진 글에서 전략의 기여를 차치한다고 하였으므로 전략에 대한 기여에 대한 내용 뒤인 ⑤번에 오는 것이 맞다.

---

39 쿠바의 야구 　　　　　　정답률 48% | 정답 ④

글의 흐름으로 보아, 주어진 문장이 들어가기에 가장 적절한 곳을 고르시오.

Between 1940 and 2000, / Cuba ruled the world baseball scene.
1940년과 2000년 사이에 / 쿠바는 세계 야구계를 지배했다.

They won 25 of the first 28 World Cups / and 3 of 5 Olympic Games.
그들은 첫 28회의 월드컵 중 25회를 이겼다. / 그리고 5회의 올림픽 게임 중 3회를 이겼다.

① The Cubans were known for wearing uniforms / covered in red from head to toe, / a strong contrast to the more conservative North American style / featuring grey or white pants.
쿠바인들은 유니폼을 입는 것으로 알려져 있다. / 머리부터 발끝까지 빨간색으로 뒤덮인 / 그런데 이것은 더 보수적인 북미 스타일과 강한 대조를 이룬다. / 회색이나 흰색 바지를 특징으로 하는

② Not only were their athletic talents superior, / the Cubans appeared even stronger from just the colour of their uniforms.
쿠바인들의 운동 재능이 뛰어났을 뿐만 아니라 / 그들은 그들의 유니폼의 색깔만으로도 훨씬 더 강하게 보였다.

③ A game would not even start / and the opposing team would already be scared.
심지어 경기가 시작되지 않았다. / 그리고 상대 팀은 이미 겁에 질리곤 했다.

✓④ A few years ago, / Cuba altered that uniform style, / modernizing it and perhaps conforming to other countries' style; / interestingly, / the national team has declined / since that time.
몇 년 전 쿠바는 그 유니폼 스타일을 바꿨다. / 유니폼을 현대화하고 아마도 다른 나라의 스타일에 맞추면서 / 흥미롭게도 / 국가 대표 팀은 쇠퇴해 왔다. / 그 시기부터

The country that ruled international baseball / for decades / has not been on top / since that uniform change.
국제 야구를 지배했던 그 나라는 / 수십 년 동안 / 정상에 오른 적이 없었다. / 그 유니폼 교체 이후로

⑤ Traditions are important for a team; / while a team brand or image can adjust to keep up with present times, / if it abandons or neglects its roots, / negative effects can surface.
전통은 팀에 중요하다. / 하지만 팀 브랜드나 이미지는 현대시대를 따르기 위해 조정될 수 있다 / 만약 팀이 그들의 뿌리를 버리거나 무시하면 / 부정적인 영향이 표면화될 수 있다.

1940년과 2000년 사이에 쿠바는 세계 야구계를 지배했다. 그들은 첫 28회의 월드컵 중 25회와 5회의 올림픽 게임 중 3회를 이겼다. ① 쿠바인들은 머리부터 발끝까지 빨간색으로 뒤덮인 유니폼을 입는 것으로 알려져 있었는데, 이것은 회색이나 흰색 바지를 특징으로 하는 더 보수적인 북미 스타일과 강한 대조를 이룬다. ② 쿠바인들의 운동 재능이 뛰어났을 뿐만 아니라 그들은 그들의 유니폼의 색깔만으로도 훨씬 더 강하게 보였다. ③ 심지어 경기가 시작하지 않았는데도 상대 팀은 이미 겁에 질리곤 했다. ④ 몇 년 전 쿠바는 유니폼을 현대화하고 아마도 다른 나라의 스타일에 맞추면서 그 유니폼 스타일을 바꿨다. 흥미롭게도 국가 대표 팀은 그 시기부터 쇠퇴해 왔다. 수십 년 동안 국제 야구를 지배했던 그 나라는 그 유니폼 교체 이후로

정상에 오른 적이 없었다. ⑤ 전통은 팀에게 중요하다. 팀 브랜드나 이미지는 현시대를 따르기 위해 조정될 수 있지만 만약 팀이 그들의 뿌리를 버리거나 무시하면 부정적인 영향이 표면화될 수 있다.

- **be known for** ~로 잘 알려진
- **toe** ⓝ 발끝
- **conservative** ⓐ 보수적인
- **modernize** ⓥ 현대화하다
- **abandon** ⓥ 버리다
- **covered in** ~로 뒤덮인
- **contrast** ⓝ 대조
- **alter** ⓥ 바꾸다
- **decline** ⓥ 쇠퇴하다
- **neglect** ⓥ 무시하다

구문 풀이

8행 Not only were their athletic talents superior, the Cubans appeared even
부정어   동사(도치)   주어
stronger from just the colour of their uniforms.

---

40 문화와 유전학의 관계
정답률 54% | 정답 ①

다음 글의 내용을 한 문장으로 요약하고자 한다. 빈칸 (A), (B)에 들어갈 말로 가장 적절한 것은? [3점]

(A)		(B)		(A)		(B)
✓ similarity 유사성	.....	diverse 다양한		② similarity 유사성	.....	limited 제한적인
③ difference 차이점	.....	flexible 유연한		④ difference 차이점	.....	complicated 복잡한
⑤ interaction 상호작용	.....	credible 믿을 수 있는				

Many of the first models of cultural evolution / drew noticeable connections / between culture and genes / by using concepts from theoretical population genetics / and applying them to culture.
문화 진화의 많은 초기 모델들은 / 주목할 만한 접점을 이끌어 냈다. / 문화와 유전자 사이의 / 이론 집단 유전학의 개념을 사용함으로써 / 그리고 그것들을 문화에 적용함으로써

Cultural patterns of transmission, innovation, and selection / are conceptually likened / to genetic processes of transmission, mutation, and selection.
전파, 혁신, 선택의 문화적 방식은 / 개념적으로 유사하다. / 전달, 돌연변이, 선택의 유전적 과정과

However, / these approaches had to be modified / to account for the differences / between genetic and cultural transmission.
그러나, / 이러한 접근법은 수정되어야만 했다. / 차이점을 설명하기 위해 / 유전자의 전달과 문화 전파 사이의

For example, / we do not expect / the cultural transmission to follow / the rules of genetic transmission / strictly.
예를 들어, / 우리는 예상하지 않는다. / 문화 전파가 따를 것이라고 / 유전자 전달의 규칙을 / 엄격하게

If two biological parents have different forms of a cultural trait, / their child is not necessarily equally likely to acquire / the mother's or father's form of that trait.
만약 두 명의 생물학적인 부모가 서로 다른 문화적인 특성의 형태를 가진다면 / 그들의 자녀는 반드시 동일하게 획득하지 않을 수 있다. / 엄마 혹은 아빠의 그 특성의 형태를

Further, / a child can acquire cultural traits / not only from its parents but also from nonparental adults and peers; / thus, / the frequency of a cultural trait / in the population / is relevant / beyond just the probability / that an individual's parents had that trait.
더욱이 / 아이는 문화적인 특성을 얻을 수 있다. / 부모로부터 뿐만 아니라 부모가 아닌 성인이나 또래로부터도 / 따라서 / 문화적인 특성의 빈도는 / 집단의 유의미하다. / 단지 확률을 넘어서 / 한 개인의 부모가 그 특성을 가졌던

➡ Early cultural evolution models used the (A) <u>similarity</u> / between culture and genes / but had to be revised / since cultural transmission allows for more (B) <u>diverse</u> factors / than genetic transmission.
초기의 문화 진화 모델들은 유사성을 사용했다. / 문화와 유전자 사이의 / 하지만 수정되어야만 했다. / 문화 전파가 더 다양한 요인을 허용하기 때문에 / 유전자의 전달보다

문화 진화의 많은 초기 모델들은 이론 집단 유전학의 개념을 사용함으로써 그리고 그것들을 문화에 적용함으로써 문화와 유전자 사이의 주목할 만한 접점을 이끌어 냈다. 전파, 혁신, 선택의 문화적 방식은 전달, 돌연변이, 선택의 유전적 과정과 개념적으로 유사하다. 그러나 이러한 접근법은 유전자의 전달과 문화 전파 사이의 차이점을 설명하기 위해 수정되어야만 했다. 예를 들어, 우리는 문화 전파가 유전자 전달의 규칙을 엄격하게 따를 것이라고 예상하지 않는다. 만약 두 명의 생물학적인 부모가 서로 다른 문화적인 특성의 형태를 가진다면, 그들의 자녀는 반드시 엄마 혹은 아빠의 그 특성의 형태를 동일하게 획득하지 않을 수 있다. 더욱이 아이는 문화적인 특성을 부모로부터 뿐만 아니라 부모가 아닌 성인이나 또래로부터도 얻을 수 있다. 따라서 집단의 문화적인 특성의 빈도는 단지 한 개인의 부모가 그 특성을 가졌던 확률을 넘어서 유의미하다.

➡ 초기의 문화 진화 모델들은 문화와 유전자 사이의 (A) <u>유사</u>성을 사용했지만, 문화 전파가 유전자의 전달보다 더 (B) <u>다양한</u> 요인을 허용하기 때문에 수정되어야만 했다.

- **evolution** ⓝ 진화
- **concept** ⓝ 개념
- **genetics** ⓝ 유전학
- **innovation** ⓝ 혁신
- **mutation** ⓝ 돌연변이
- **trait** ⓝ 특징
- **noticeable** ⓐ 주목할 만한
- **theoretical** ⓐ 이론적인
- **transmission** ⓝ 전이
- **link to** ~에 접근하다
- **modify** ⓥ 수정하다
- **acquire** ⓥ 얻다

- **peer** ⓝ 동료
- **revise** ⓥ 수정하다
- **diverse** ⓐ 다양한
- **difference** ⓝ 차이점
- **complicated** ⓐ 복잡한
- **credible** 믿을 수 있는
- **probability** ⓝ 개연성
- **similarity** ⓝ 유사성
- **limited** ⓐ 제한적인
- **flexible** ⓐ 유연한
- **interaction** ⓝ 상호작용

구문 풀이

13행 Further, a child can acquire cultural traits not only from its parents but also
「not only A, but also B : A뿐만 아니라 B도」
from nonparental adults and peers; thus, the frequency of a cultural trait in the population is relevant beyond just the probability that an individual's parents had that trait.

41-42 공동작용의 예시

A ball thrown into the air is acted / upon by the initial force given it, / persisting as inertia of movement / and tending to carry it / in the same straight line, / and by the constant pull of gravity downward, / as well as by the resistance of the air.
공중으로 던져진 공은 움직여진다. / 초기에 그것에 주어진 힘에 의해 / 운동의 관성으로 지속하며 / 그리고 나아가려는 경향을 보인다. / 같은 직선으로 / 그리고 아래로 지속적으로 당기는 중력에 의해서도 / 공기의 저항뿐만 아니라

It moves, / accordingly, / in a (a) curved path.
공은 움직인다. / 그에 맞춰 / 곡선의 경로로

「Now / the path does not represent / the working of any particular force; 」 / there is simply the (b) combination / of the three elementary forces mentioned; / 「but in a real sense, / there is something in the total action / besides the isolated action of three forces, / namely, / their joint action.」
이제 / 그 경로는 나타내지는 않는다 / 어떤 특정한 힘의 작용을/ 결합이 존재할 뿐이다. / 언급된 세 가지 기본적인 힘의 / 하지만 사실은 / 전체적인 작용에 무언가가 있다. / 세 가지 힘의 고립된 작용 외에 / 이름하여 그 공동 작용이다

In the same way, / when two or more human individuals are together, / their mutual relationships and their arrangement into a group are things / which would not be (c) uncovered / if we confined our attention to each individual separately.
같은 방식으로 / 두 명 혹은 그 이상의 인간 개인이 같이 있을 때 / 그들의 상호 관계와 그들의 집단으로의 배치는 것들이다 / 드러나지 않을 / 만약 우리가 관심을 개별적으로 각각의 개인에게 국한시킨다면

The significance of group behavior is greatly (d) increased / in the case of human beings / by the fact / that some of the tendencies to action of the individual / are related definitely to other persons, / and could not be aroused / except by other persons acting as stimuli.
그룹 행동의 중요성은 크게 증가된다. / 인간의 경우 / 사실로 의해 / 개인 행동의 몇몇 경향은 / 명백하게 다른 사람들과 관련이 있다 / 그리고 유발되지 않을 수 있다, / 자극으로 작동하는 다른 사람들 없이는

An individual in complete (e) isolation / would not reveal / their competitive tendencies, their tendencies towards the opposite sex, their protective tendencies towards children.
완전한 고립 속의 개인은 / 드러내지 않을 것이다. / 그들의 경쟁적인 성향, 이성에 대한 그들의 성향, 아이에 대한 그들의 보호적 성향을

This shows / that the traits of human nature do not fully appear / until the individual is brought into relationships / with other individuals.
이것은 보여준다. / 인간 본성의 특성이 완전히 나타나지 않는다는 것을 / 개인이 관계에 관여될 때까지는 / 다른 개인과의

공중으로 던져진 공은 초기에 그것에 주어진 힘에 의해 움직여지는데, 운동의 관성으로 지속하며 같은 직선으로 나아가려는 경향을 보이고, 공기의 저항뿐만 아니라 아래로 지속적으로 당기는 중력에 의해서도 움직여진다. 그에 맞춰 공은 (a) 곡선의 경로로 움직인다. 이제 그 경로는 어떤 특정한 힘의 작동을 나타내지는 않는다. 언급된 세 가지 기본적인 힘의 (b) 결합이 존재할 뿐이다. 하지만 사실은 세 가지 힘의 고립된 작용 외에 전체적인 작용에 무언가가 있다. 이름하여 그들의 공동 작용이다. 같은 방식으로, 두 명 혹은 그 이상의 인간 개인이 같이 있을 때 그들의 상호 관계와 그들의 집단으로의 배치는 만약 우리가 관심을 개별적으로 각각의 개인에게 국한시킨다면 (c) 감춰지지(→ 드러나지) 않을 것이다. 개인 행동의 몇몇 경향은 명백하게 다른 사람들과 관련이 있고 자극으로 작동하는 다른 사람들 없이는 유발되지 않을 수 있다는 사실로 인해 그룹 행동의 중요성이 인간의 경우 크게 (d) 증가된다. 완전한 (e) 고립 속의 개인은 그들의 경쟁적인 성향, 이성에 대한 그들의 성향, 아이에 대한 그들의 보호적 성향을 드러내지 않을 것이다. 이것은 개인이 다른 개인과의 관계에 관여될 때까지는 인간 본성의 특성이 완전히 나타나지 않는다는 것을 보여준다.

- **persist** ⓥ 저항하다
- **carry** ⓥ 나아가다
- **gravity** ⓝ 중력
- **resistance** ⓝ 저항
- **elementary** ⓐ 기본의
- **joint** ⓐ 공동의
- **arrangement** ⓝ 배치
- **confined** ⓐ 좁은
- **behavior** ⓝ 행동
- **tendency** ⓝ 경향
- **reveal** ⓥ 드러내다
- **opposite** ⓐ 정반대의
- **bring into** 끌어들이다
- **inertia** ⓝ 관성
- **constant** ⓐ 끊임없는
- **downward** ⓐ 아래의
- **combination** ⓝ 결합
- **isolated** ⓐ 고립된
- **mutual** ⓐ 상호의
- **conceal** ⓥ 감추다
- **significance** ⓝ 중요성
- **increase** ⓥ 증가하다
- **arouse** ⓥ 유발하다
- **competitive** ⓐ 경쟁적인
- **towards** prep ~향하여

구문 풀이

1행 A ball thrown into the air is acted upon by the initial force given it, persisting as inertia of movement and tending to carry it in the same straight line, and by the constant pull of gravity downward, as well as by the resistance of the air.
「A as well as B : B뿐만 아니라 A도」

---

41 제목 파악
정답률 48% | 정답 ⑤

윗글의 제목으로 가장 적절한 것은?
① Common Misunderstandings in Physics – 물리학에서 흔히 볼 수 있는 오해
② Collaboration: A Key to Success in Relationships – 협력: 관계에서 성공을 위한 열쇠
③ Interpersonal Traits and Their Impact on Science – 대인 관계의 특성과 그것이 과학에 미치는 영향
④ Unbalanced Forces Causing Objects to Accelerate – 개체를 가속시키는 불균형한 힘
✓ Human Traits Uncovered by Interpersonal Relationships – 대인 관계에 의해 드러난 인간의 특성

공을 공기 중으로 던질 때 작용하는 힘 외에도 눈에 보이지 않는 힘이 있는데 바로 이들의 공동작용이다 (but in a real sense, there is something in the total action besides the isolated action of three forces, namely, their joint action.). 사람의 관계에 적용했을 때를 예시로 들어 개인이 다른 개인과의 관계에 관여될 때까지는 인간 본성의 특성이 완전히 나타나지 않는다고 말하고 있으므로, 글의 제목으로 가장 적절한 것은 ⑤ '대인 관계에 의해 드러난 인간의 특성'이다.

★★★ 등급을 가르는 문제!

| 42 | 어휘 추론 | | 정답률 42% | 정답 ③ |

밑줄 친 (a)~(e) 중에서 문맥상 낱말의 쓰임이 적절하지 않은 것은? [3점]
① (a)　　② (b)　　☑ (c)　　④ (d)　　⑤ (e)

Why? 왜 정답일까?

'Now the path ~'에서 공이 곡선으로 움직이는 것은 어떤 특정한 힘의 작동을 나타내지 않는다고 설명하는 것으로 보아, 만약 개별에 관심을 국한시킨다면 감춰지는 것이 아니라 '드러난다'는 내용이 맞다. 따라서 concealed 대신 uncovered를 써야 자연스럽다. 낱말의 쓰임이 문맥상 적절하지 않은 것은 ③ '(c)'이다.

★★ 문제 해결 꿀~팁 ★★

▶ 많이 틀린 이유는?
공중으로 던져진 공은 초기에 주어진 힘들이 결합되어서 곡선으로 움직이게 된다고 이야기하고 있다. 이 결합된 힘은 공동 작용인데 각각의 고립된 힘은 따로 존재한다는 것을 기억해 두어야 한다. ③번에서는 인간이 집단으로 있을 때에 대입하여 주제를 이야기하고 있는데, 집단 내에서 발생하는 공동작용은 각 개인의 고립된 힘에 집중했을 때는 드러나지 않는 것이 주제와 일치한다. ④번에서는 인간은 다른 사람들과 상호작용하여 행동이 드러나기 때문에 그룹 행동의 중요성이 증가된다는 것이 주제와 일치한다.

▶ 문제 해결 방법은?
글의 큰 주제를 파악한 후에 논리적으로 주제와 일맥상통하는지 찾아보면 된다. 문장 내에서 문맥상 낱말의 쓰임이 적절한지를 파악할 때는 반의어를 염두에 두고 비교해보면 좋다.

| 43-45 | 행복에 대한 자세 |

(A)
There once lived a man in a village / who was not happy with his life.
옛날 어느 마을에 한 남자가 살았다. / 자신의 삶이 행복하지 않은
He was always troubled / by one problem or another.
그는 항상 어려움을 겪었다. / 하나 혹은 또 다른 문제로
One day, / a saint with his guards stopped by his village.
어느 날 / 한 성자가 그의 경호인들과 함께 그의 마을에 들렀다.
「Many people heard the news / and started going to him with their problems.」
많은 사람들이 그 소식을 들었다. / 그리고 그들의 문제를 가지고 그에게 가기 시작했다. 45번 ①의 근거 일치
The man also decided / to visit the saint.
그 남자 역시 결정했다. / 성자를 방문하기로
Even after reaching the saint's place in the morning, / (a) he didn't get the opportunity / to meet him till evening.
아침에 성자가 있는 곳에 도착하고 난 후에도 / 그는 기회를 얻지 못했다. / 저녁때까지 그를 만날

(D)
When the man got to meet the saint, / (d) he confessed / that he was very unhappy with life / because problems always surrounded him, / like workplace tension or worries about his health.
마침내 그가 성자를 만났을 때 / 그는 고백했다. / 삶이 매우 불행하다고 / 항상 문제가 자기를 둘러싸고 있어서 / 직장 내 긴장이나 건강에 대한 걱정과 같이
(e) He said, / "Please give me a solution / so that all the problems in my life will end / and I can live peacefully."
그는 말했다. / 제발 해결책을 주세요. / 나의 삶의 모든 문제가 끝나기 위해서 / 그리고 제가 평화롭게 살 수 있도록
「The saint smiled / and said / that he would answer the request the next day.」
성자는 미소지었다. / 그리고 말했다. / 그가 다음 날 그 요청에 답해주겠다고 45번 ⑤의 근거 일치

(B)
「But / the saint also asked / if the man could do a small job for him.」 45번 ②의 근거 일치
그런데 / 성자는 또한 물었다. / 그 남자가 그를 위해 작은 일을 해 줄 수 있는지
「He told the man to take care of a hundred camels / in his group that night, / saying "When all hundred camels sit down, you can go to sleep."」 45번 ③의 근거 불일치
그는 남자에게 백 마리 낙타를 돌봐 달라고 말했다. / 그날 밤에 그의 일행에 있는 / "백 마리 낙타 모두가 자리에 앉으면 당신은 자러 가도 좋습니다."라고 말하면서
The man agreed. // The next morning when the saint met that man, / (b) he asked / if the man had slept well.
그 남자는 동의했다. // 다음 날 아침에 성자가 그 남자를 만났을 때 / 그는 물어보았다. / 남자가 잠을 잘 잤는지
Tired and sad, / the man replied / that he couldn't sleep even for a moment.
피곤해 하고 슬퍼하면서 / 그 남자는 대답했다. / 한순간도 잠을 자지 못했다고

(C)
In fact, / the man tried very hard / but couldn't make all the camels sit at the same time / because every time (c) he made one camel sit, / another would stand up.
사실 / 그 남자는 열심히 노력했다. / 그러나 모든 낙타를 동시에 앉게 할 수 없었다. / 왜냐하면 그가 낙타 한 마리를 앉힐 때마다 / 다른 낙타 한 마리가 일어섰기 때문이다.
The saint told him, / "You realized that / no matter how hard you try, / you can't make all the camels sit down.
그 성자는 그에게 말했다. / 당신은 깨달았습니다. / 당신이 아무리 노력하더라도 / 당신은 모든 낙타를 앉게 할 수 없습니다.
If one problem is solved, / for some reason, / another will arise / like the camels did.
만약 한 가지 문제가 해결되면 / 어떤 이유로 / 또 다른 문제가 일어날 것입니다. / 낙타가 그런 것처럼
「So, / humans should enjoy life / despite these problems."」 45번 ④의 근거 일치
그래서 / 인간은 삶을 즐겨야 합니다. / 이러한 문제에도 불구하고

(A)
옛날 어느 마을에 자신의 삶이 행복하지 않은 한 남자가 살았다. 그는 항상 하나 혹은 또 다른 문제로 어려움을 겪었다. 어느 날 한 성자가 그의 경호인들과 함께 그의 마을에 들렀다. 많은

사람들이 그 소식을 듣고 그들의 문제를 가지고 그에게 가기 시작했다. 그 남자 역시 성자를 방문하기로 결정했다. 아침에 성자가 있는 곳에 도착하고 난 후에도 (a) 그는 저녁때까지 그를 만날 기회를 얻지 못했다.

(D)
마침내 그가 성자를 만났을 때 (d) 그는 직장 내 긴장이나 건강에 대한 걱정과 같이 항상 문제가 자기를 둘러싸고 있어서 삶이 매우 불행하다고 고백했다. (e) 그는 "나의 삶의 모든 문제가 끝나고 제가 평화롭게 살 수 있도록 제발 해결책을 주세요."라고 말했다. 성자는 미소 지으면서 그가 다음 날 그 요청에 답해주겠다고 말했다.

(B)
그런데 성자는 또한 그 남자가 그를 위해 작은 일을 해 줄 수 있는지 물었다. 성자는 그 남자에게 "백 마리 낙타 모두가 자리에 앉으면 당신은 자러 가도 좋습니다."라고 말하면서 그날 밤에 그의 일행에 있는 백 마리 낙타를 돌봐 달라고 말했다. 그 남자는 동의했다. 다음 날 아침에 성자가 그 남자를 만났을 때 (b) 그는 남자가 잠을 잘 잤는지 물어보았다. 피곤해하고 슬퍼하면서 남자는 한순간도 잠을 자지 못했다고 대답했다.

(C)
사실 그 남자는 아주 열심히 노력했지만 (c) 그가 낙타 한 마리를 앉힐 때마다 다른 낙타 한 마리가 일어섰기 때문에 모든 낙타를 동시에 앉게 할 수 없었다. 그 성자는 그에게 "당신이 아무리 열심히 노력하더라도 모든 낙타를 앉게 만들 수는 없다는 것을 깨달았습니다. 만약 한 가지 문제가 해결되면 낙타가 그런 것처럼 어떤 이유로 또 다른 문제가 일어날 것입니다. 그래서 인간은 이러한 문제에도 불구하고 삶을 즐겨야 합니다."라고 말했다.

● saint ⑥ 성자
● stop by ~에 들르다
● opportunity ⑥ 기회
● surrounded ⑥ 둘러싸인
● take care of ~을 돌보다
● arise ⑥ 발생하다
● guard ⑥ 경호원
● decide ⑥ 결심하다
● confess ⑥ 고백하다
● tension ⑥ 긴장
● camel ⑥ 낙타
● despite ~에도 불구하고

구문 풀이

(B) 1행 But the saint also asked if the man could do a small job for him.
부사절(~인지 아닌지)

| 43 | 글의 순서 파악 | | 정답률 82% | 정답 ④ |

주어진 글 (A)에 이어질 내용을 순서에 맞게 배열한 것으로 가장 적절한 것은?
① (B) – (D) – (C)　　② (C) – (B) – (D)
③ (C) – (D) – (B)　　☑ (D) – (B) – (C)
⑤ (D) – (C) – (B)

Why? 왜 정답일까?

성자가 마을에 들렀다는 내용의 (A)의 뒤로, 마침내 남자가 성자를 만났다는 내용의 (D), 성자가 백마리 낙타를 돌봐달라고 요청한 내용의 (B), 아무리 노력해도 모든 낙타를 앉게 할 수 없었다는 내용의 (C)가 순서대로 이어져야 자연스럽다. 따라서 글의 순서로 가장 적절한 것은 ④ '(D) – (B) – (C)'이다.

| 44 | 지칭 추론 | | 정답률 74% | 정답 ② |

밑줄 친 (a)~(e) 중에서 가리키는 대상이 나머지 넷과 다른 것은?
① (a)　　☑ (b)　　③ (c)　　④ (d)　　⑤ (e)

Why? 왜 정답일까?

(a), (c), (d), (e)는 the man, (b)는 the saint를 가리키므로, (a)~(e) 중에 가리키는 대상이 다른 하나는 ② '(b)'이다.

| 45 | 세부 내용 파악 | | 정답률 67% | 정답 ③ |

윗글에 관한 내용으로 적절하지 않은 것은?
① 많은 사람들이 자신들의 문제를 가지고 성자에게 갔다.
② 성자는 자신을 위해 작은 일을 해 줄 수 있는지 남자에게 물었다.
☑ 성자는 남자가 낙타를 모두 재우면 잠을 자러 가도 좋다고 했다.
④ 성자는 문제가 있어도 인생을 즐겨야 한다고 말했다.
⑤ 성자는 남자의 요청에 대한 답을 다음 날 말해 주기로 했다.

Why? 왜 정답일까?

(B) 'He told the man to take care of a hundred camels in his group that night, saying "When all hundred camels sit down, you can go to sleep."'에서 낙타를 모두 앉히면 잠을 자러 가도 좋다고 했으므로, 내용과 일치하지 않는 것은 ③ '성자는 남자가 낙타를 모두 재우면 잠을 자러 가도 좋다고 했다.'이다.

Why? 왜 오답일까?

① (A) 'Many people heard the news and started going to him with their problems.'의 내용과 일치한다.
② (B) 'But the saint also asked if the man could do a small job for him.'의 내용과 일치한다.
④ (C) 'So, humans should enjoy life despite these problems.'의 내용과 일치한다.
⑤ (D) 'The saint smiled / and said / that he would answer the request the next day.'의 내용과 일치한다.

A	B	C	D
01 자신 있는	01 equality	01 ⓜ	01 ⓒ
02 편의	02 certificate	02 ⓟ	02 ⓝ
03 색조, 그늘	03 clue	03 ⓐ	03 ⓐ
04 흔들다	04 diagnosis	04 ⓕ	04 ⓔ
05 방향, 길	05 regulation	05 ⓡ	05 ⓠ
06 성장	06 immediate	06 ⓚ	06 ⓖ
07 쏟다, 몰두하다	07 specify	07 ⓢ	07 ⓑ
08 책임감	08 term	08 ⓝ	08 ⓛ
09 상식적인	09 possession	09 ⓖ	09 ⓟ
10 객관적인	10 maintain	10 ⓙ	10 ⓘ
11 반사하다	11 clarity	11 ⓔ	11 ⓗ
12 범위	12 get rid of	12 ⓘ	12 ⓜ
13 요구하다	13 visual	13 ⓠ	13 ⓙ
14 만들다, 몰아가다	14 adjust to	14 ⓞ	14 ⓚ
15 막다	15 upright	15 ⓛ	15 ⓞ
16 충분한	16 reverse	16 ⓒ	16 ⓡ
17 인식	17 advantage	17 ⓣ	17 ⓣ
18 투자, 투자액	18 pursue	18 ⓓ	18 ⓓ
19 도달하다	19 endure	19 ⓗ	19 ⓕ
20 초과하다	20 unrelated	20 ⓑ	20 ⓢ

17회 | 2022학년도 11월 학력평가　　　고1

| 정답과 해설 |

• 정답 •
18 ② 19 ② 20 ⑤ 21 ③ 22 ① 23 ⑤ 24 ④ 25 ④ 26 ③ 27 ⑤ 28 ③ 29 ④ 30 ④ 31 ③ 32 ②
33 ③ 34 ③ 35 ④ 36 ③ 37 ⑤ 38 ⑤ 39 ④ 40 ② 41 ① 42 ⑤ 43 ④ 44 ④ 45 ④

★ 표기된 문항은 [등급을 가르는 문제]에 해당하는 문제입니다.

18　급여 인상 요청　　　정답률 79% | 정답 ②

다음 글의 목적으로 가장 적절한 것은?

① 부서 이동을 신청하려고
☑ 급여 인상을 요청하려고
③ 근무 시간 조정을 요구하려고
④ 기업 혁신 방안을 제안하려고
⑤ 신입 사원 연수에 대해 문의하려고

Dear Mr. Krull,
친애하는 Krull씨께
I have greatly enjoyed working at Trincom Enterprises / as a sales manager.
저는 Trincom Enterprises에서 일하는 것을 매우 즐겨 왔습니다. / 영업 매니저로
Since I joined in 2015, / I have been a loyal and essential member of this company, / and have developed innovative ways / to contribute to the company.
제가 2015년에 입사한 이후, / 저는 이 회사의 충성스럽고 필수적인 구성원이었고, / 혁신적인 방법들을 개발해 왔습니다. / 회사에 기여할
Moreover, in the last year alone, / I have brought in two new major clients to the company, / increasing the company's total sales by 5%.
게다가, 작년 한 해만 / 저는 두 개의 주요 고객사를 회사에 새로 유치하여 / 회사의 총매출을 5% 증가시켰습니다.
Also, / I have voluntarily trained 5 new members of staff, / totaling 35 hours.
또한, / 저는 신규 직원 5명을 자발적으로 교육해 왔고 / 그 합계가 35시간이 되었습니다.
I would therefore request your consideration / in raising my salary, / which I believe reflects my performance / as well as the industry average.
따라서 저는 고려를 요청드리며, / 제 급여를 인상하는 데 있어 / 이것이 제 성과도 반영한다고 믿습니다. / 업계 평균뿐만 아니라
I look forward to speaking with you soon.
저는 귀하와 곧 이야기하기를 기대합니다.
Kimberly Morss
Kimberly Morss 드림

친애하는 Krull씨께

저는 Trincom Enterprises에서 영업 매니저로 일하는 것을 매우 즐겨 왔습니다. 2015년에 입사한 이후, 저는 이 회사의 충성스럽고 필수적인 구성원이었고, 회사에 기여할 혁신적인 방법들을 개발해 왔습니다. 게다가, 저는 작년 한 해만 두 개의 주요 고객사를 회사에 새로 유치하여 회사의 총매출을 5% 증가시켰습니다. 또한 저는 신규 직원 5명을 자발적으로 교육해 왔고 그 합계가 35시간이 되었습니다. 따라서 저는 제 급여를 인상하는 것을 고려해 주시기를 요청드리며, 이것이 업계 평균뿐만 아니라 제 성과도 반영한다고 믿습니다. 귀하와 곧 이야기하기를 기대합니다.

Kimberly Morss 드림

Why? 왜 정답일까?

'I would therefore request your consideration in raising my salary, ~'에서 급여 인상을 고려해달라는 요청이 나오므로, 글의 목적으로 가장 적절한 것은 ② '급여 인상을 요청하려고'이다.

- enterprise ⓝ 기업
- loyal ⓐ 충성스러운
- voluntarily ⓐⓓ 자원해서
- sales manager 영업 매니저
- essential ⓐ 핵심적인, 필수적인
- raise ⓥ 올리다, 높이다

구문 풀이

9행　I would therefore request your consideration in raising my salary, which
　　　　　　　　　　　　　　　　　　　　　　선행사　　주격 관·대
(I believe) reflects my performance as well as the industry average.　( ): 삽입절
　동사

19　휴가 도중 아버지의 부상 소식을 들은 필자　　정답률 83% | 정답 ②

다음 글에 드러난 'I'의 심경 변화로 가장 적절한 것은?

① nervous → confident
　긴장한　　자신 있는
③ excited → indifferent
　신난　　무관심한
⑤ annoyed → grateful
　짜증 난　　고마워하는

☑ relaxed → worried
　여유로운　걱정하는
④ pleased → jealous
　즐거운　질투하는

On one beautiful spring day, / I was fully enjoying my day off.
어느 아름다운 봄날, / 나는 휴가를 충분히 즐기고 있었다.
I arrived at the nail salon, / and muted my cellphone / so that I would be disconnected for the hour / and feel calm and peaceful.
나는 네일 숍에 도착해서 / 내 휴대폰을 음소거했다. / 그 시간 동안 나는 단절되도록 / 그리고 차분하고 평화로운 기분을 느끼도록
I was so comfortable / while I got a manicure.
나는 아주 편안했다. / 내가 매니큐어를 받는 동안
As I left the place, / I checked my cellphone / and saw four missed calls from a strange number.
내가 그곳을 떠나면서, / 나는 나의 휴대폰을 확인했고 / 낯선 번호에서 걸려 온 네 통의 부재중 전화를 봤다.
I knew immediately / that something bad was coming, / and I called back.
나는 즉시 알고 / 뭔가 나쁜 일이 생겼다는 것을 / 나는 다시 전화했다.
A young woman answered and said / that my father had fallen over a stone and was injured, / now seated on a bench.
한 젊은 여성이 전화를 받아 말했다. / 우리 아버지가 돌에 걸려 넘어져 다쳤고 / 지금 벤치에 앉아 있다고

17회

I was really concerned / since he had just recovered from his knee surgery.
나는 정말 걱정되었다. / 아버지는 무릎 수술에서 회복한 직후라서
I rushed getting into my car / to go see him.
나는 급히 차에 올랐다. / 아버지를 보러 가기 위해

어느 아름다운 봄날, 나는 휴가를 충분히 즐기고 있었다. 나는 네일 숍에 도착해서 내 휴대폰을 음소거하고 그 시간 동안 단절되어 차분하고 평화로운 기분을 느끼고자 했다. 나는 매니큐어를 받는 동안 아주 편안했다. 그곳을 떠나면서, 나는 나의 휴대폰을 확인했고 낯선 번호에서 걸려 온 네 통의 부재중 전화를 봤다. 나는 뭔가 나쁜 일이 생겼다는 것을 즉시 알고 다시 전화했다. 한 젊은 여성이 전화를 받아 우리 아버지가 돌에 걸려 넘어져 다쳤고 지금 벤치에 앉아 있다고 말했다. 아버지는 무릎 수술에서 회복한 직후라서 나는 정말 걱정되었다. 나는 아버지를 보러 가기 위해 급히 차에 올랐다.

Why? 왜 정답일까?

네일숍에 들러 휴가를 여유롭게(feel calm and peaceful, comfortable) 즐기고 있던 필자가 아버지가 넘어져 다쳤다는 소식에 몹시 걱정했다(concerned)는 내용이다. 따라서 'I'의 심경 변화로 가장 적절한 것은 ② '여유로운 → 걱정하는'이다.

- mute ⓥ 음소거하다
- comfortable ⓐ 편안한
- fall over ~에 걸려 넘어지다
- recover from ~로부터 회복하다
- rush ⓥ 서두르다
- jealous ⓐ 질투하는
- disconnected ⓐ 단절된
- call back 전화를 회신하다
- concerned ⓐ 걱정되는
- surgery ⓝ 수술
- indifferent ⓐ 무관심한
- grateful ⓐ 고마워하는

구문 풀이

1행 I arrived at the nail salon, and muted my cellphone so that I would be
접속사(~하기 위해)┘   동사1
disconnected for the hour and (would) feel calm and peaceful.
동사2

---

20 상업용 블로그를 성공시킬 방법 정답률 89% | 정답 ⑤

다음 글에서 필자가 주장하는 바로 가장 적절한 것은?

① 인터넷 게시물에 대한 윤리적 기준을 세워야 한다.
② 블로그를 전문적으로 관리할 인력을 마련해야 한다.
③ 신제품 개발을 위해 상업용 블로그를 적극 활용해야 한다.
④ 상품에 대한 고객들의 반응을 정기적으로 분석할 필요가 있다.
✓ 상업용 블로그는 사람들이 흥미 있어 할 정보를 제공해야 한다.

You already have a business / and you're about to launch your blog / so that you can sell your product.
여러분은 이미 사업체를 가지고 있고 / 여러분은 블로그를 시작하려는 참이다. / 여러분의 제품을 팔 수 있도록
Unfortunately, / here is where a 'business mind' can be a bad thing.
유감스럽게도, / 이 지점에서 '비즈니스 정신'은 나쁜 것이 될 수 있다.
Most people believe / that to have a successful business blog / promoting a product, / they have to stay strictly 'on the topic.'
대부분의 사람들은 믿는다. / 성공적인 상업용 블로그를 가지기 위해서 / 제품을 홍보하는 / 엄격하게 '그 주제에' 머물러야 한다고
If all you're doing is shamelessly promoting your product, / then who is going to want to read the latest thing / you're writing about?
만일 여러분이 그저 뻔뻔스럽게 제품을 홍보하는 일만 하면, / 그렇다면 누가 최신 글을 읽고 싶어 할까? / 여러분이 쓰고 있는
Instead, / you need to give some useful or entertaining information away for free / so that people have a reason / to keep coming back.
대신에, / 여러분은 어떤 유용하거나 재미있는 정보를 무료로 줄 필요가 있다. / 사람들이 이유를 가지도록 / 계속해서 다시 방문할
Only by doing this / can you create an interested audience / that you will then be able to sell to.
이렇게 해야만 / 여러분은 관심 있는 독자를 만들 수 있다. / 여러분이 다음번에 판매할 수 있게 될
So, / the best way to be successful with a business blog / is to write about things / that your audience will be interested in.
따라서, / 상업용 블로그로 성공하기 위한 가장 좋은 방법은 / 대상들에 대해 글을 쓰는 것이다. / 여러분의 독자들이 관심을 가질 만한

여러분은 이미 사업체를 가지고 있고 여러분의 제품을 팔 수 있도록 블로그를 시작하려는 참이다. 유감스럽게도, 이 지점에서 '비즈니스 정신'은 나쁜 것이 될 수 있다. 대부분의 사람들은 제품을 홍보하는 성공적인 상업용 블로그를 가지기 위해서 엄격하게 '그 주제에' 머물러야 한다고 믿는다. 만일 여러분이 그저 뻔뻔스럽게 제품을 홍보하는 일만 하면, 그렇다면 누가 여러분이 쓰고 있는 최신 글을 읽고 싶어할까? 대신에, 사람들이 계속해서 다시 방문할 이유를 가지도록 여러분은 어떤 유용하거나 재미있는 정보를 무료로 줄 필요가 있다. 이렇게 해야만 여러분은 다음번에 판매할 수 있게 될 관심 있는 독자를 만들 수 있다. 따라서, 상업용 블로그로 성공하기 위한 가장 좋은 방법은 여러분의 독자들이 관심을 가질 만한 것들에 대해 글을 쓰는 것이다.

Why? 왜 정답일까?

'Instead, you need to give some useful or entertaining information ~.'과 'So, the best way to be successful with a business blog is to write about things that your audience will be interested in.'에서 상업용 블로그를 성공시키려면 제품이나 사업에 관한 홍보만 하지 말고 사람들이 관심을 보일 내용에 관해 글을 쓰라고 한다. 따라서 필자가 주장하는 바로 가장 적절한 것은 ⑤ '상업용 블로그는 사람들이 흥미 있어 할 정보를 제공해야 한다.'이다.

- launch ⓥ 시작하다, 출시하다
- strictly ⓐⓓ 엄격하게
- give away 공짜로 주다, 거저 주다
- audience ⓝ 청중, 독자
- promote ⓥ 홍보하다
- shamelessly ⓐⓓ 뻔뻔하게
- entertaining ⓐ 재미있는
- successful ⓐ 성공적인

구문 풀이

9행 Only by doing this can you create an interested audience that you will
준부정어(오로지 ~밖에)   조동사 주어 동사원형(도치)
then be able to sell to.

---

21 노력만이 가치 있다는 믿음에 대한 반박 정답률 45% | 정답 ③

밑줄 친 challenge this sacred cow가 다음 글에서 의미하는 바로 가장 적절한 것은? [3점]

① resist the tendency to avoid any hardship
그 어떤 난관이든 피하려는 경향에 저항한다
② escape from the pressure of using formal language
공식적인 언어를 사용해야 한다는 압박에서 벗어난다
✓ doubt the solid belief that only hard work is worthy
오로지 노력만이 가치 있다는 확고한 믿음을 의심한다
④ abandon the old notion that money always comes first
돈이 항상 먼저라는 오래된 관념을 버린다
⑤ break the superstition that holy animals bring good luck
신성한 동물은 행운을 가져다 준다는 미신을 깬다

Our language helps to reveal our deeper assumptions.
우리의 언어는 우리의 더 깊은 전제를 드러내는 것을 돕는다.
Think of these revealing phrases: / When we accomplish something important, / we say it took "blood, sweat, and tears."
이것을 잘 드러내는 다음과 같은 문구들을 생각해 보라. / 우리가 중요한 무언가를 성취할 때 / 우리는 그것이 '피, 땀, 그리고 눈물'을 필요로 했다고 말한다.
We say / important achievements are "hard-earned."
우리는 말한다. / 중요한 성과는 '힘들게 얻은' 것이라고
We recommend a "hard day's work" / when "day's work" would be enough.
우리는 '하루 동안의 고생'이라는 말을 권한다. / '하루 동안의 일'이라는 말로도 충분할 때
When we talk of "easy money," / we are implying / it was obtained through illegal or questionable means.
우리가 '쉬운 돈'이라는 말을 할 때, / 우리는 넌지시 드러낸다. / 그것이 불법적이거나 의심스러운 수단을 통해 얻어졌다는 것을
We use the phrase "That's easy for you to say" / as a criticism, / usually when we are seeking to invalidate someone's opinion.
우리는 '말은 쉽지'라는 문구를 사용한다. / 비판으로 / 우리가 보통 누군가의 의견이 틀렸음을 입증하려 할 때
It's like we all automatically accept / that the "right" way is, inevitably, the harder one.
이는 마치 우리 모두가 저절로 받아들이는 것과 같다. / '올바른' 방법은 반드시 더 어려운 방법이라는 것을
In my experience / this is hardly ever questioned.
나의 경험상 / 여기에는 거의 한 번도 의문이 제기되지 않는다.
What would happen / if you do challenge this sacred cow?
무슨 일이 일어날까? / 만약 여러분이 정말로 이 신성한 소에 맞선다면
We don't even pause to consider / that something important and valuable / could be made easy.
우리는 잠시 멈춰 생각해 보지도 않는다. / 중요하고 가치 있는 무언가가 / 쉬워질 수 있다고
What if the biggest thing / keeping us from doing what matters / is the false assumption / that it has to take huge effort?
만약 가장 큰 것이 / 우리가 중요한 일을 하지 못하게 하는 / 잘못된 전제라면 어떨까? / 그것은 엄청난 노력이 들어야 한다는

우리의 언어는 우리의 더 깊은 전제를 드러내는 것을 돕는다. 이것을 잘 드러내는 다음과 같은 문구들을 생각해 보라. 우리는 중요한 무언가를 성취할 때 그것이 '피, 땀, 그리고 눈물'을 필요로 했다고 말한다. 우리는 중요한 성과는 '힘들게 얻은' 것이라고 말한다. 우리는 '하루 동안의 일'이라는 말로도 충분할 때 '하루 동안의 고생'이라는 말을 권한다. 우리가 '쉬운 돈'이라는 말을 할 때, 우리는 그것이 불법적이거나 의심스러운 수단을 통해 얻어졌다는 것을 넌지시 드러낸다. 우리는 보통 누군가의 의견이 틀렸음을 입증하려 할 때, 우리는 '말은 쉽지'라는 문구를 비판으로 사용한다. 이는 마치 우리 모두가 '올바른' 방법은 반드시 더 어려운 방법이라는 것을 저절로 받아들이는 것과 같다. 나의 경험상 여기에는 거의 한 번도 의문이 제기되지 않는다. 만약 여러분이 정말로 이 신성한 소에 맞선다면 무슨 일이 일어날까? 우리는 중요하고 가치 있는 무언가가 쉬워질 수 있다고 잠시 멈춰 생각해 보지도 않는다. 만약 우리가 중요한 일을 하지 못하게 하는 가장 큰 것이 중요한 일은 엄청난 노력이 들어야 한다는 잘못된 전제라면 어떨까?

Why? 왜 정답일까?

밑줄 친 부분 앞까지 우리는 성과가 힘들게 얻어진다는 믿음을 우리 언어를 통해 드러내는 경향이 있다는 내용이 주를 이룬다. 이어서 밑줄 친 부분은 이러한 우리의 믿음을 '신성한 소'에 비유하며, 이 믿음에 '맞선다면' 무슨 일이 생길 것인지 묻고 있다. 즉, '노력과 수고만이 가치롭다'는 믿음에 '의문을 품는다'는 것이 밑줄 친 부분의 의미이므로, 답으로 가장 적절한 것은 ③ '오로지 노력만이 가치 있다는 확고한 믿음을 의심한다'이다.

- assumption ⓝ 가정, 추정
- achievement ⓝ 성취, 성과
- imply ⓥ 암시하다
- questionable ⓐ 의심스러운
- invalidate ⓥ 틀렸음을 입증하다
- inevitably ⓐⓓ 불가피하게, 필연적으로
- sacred ⓐ 성스러운
- hardship ⓝ 고난, 난관, 어려움
- solid ⓐ 확고한
- superstition ⓝ 미신
- sweat ⓝ 땀
- hard-earned ⓐ 힘들게 얻은
- illegal ⓐ 불법적인
- criticism ⓝ 비판
- automatically ⓐⓓ 저절로
- challenge ⓥ 도전하다, 이의를 제기하다
- huge ⓐ 거대한
- formal ⓐ 공식적인
- abandon ⓥ 버리다

구문 풀이

13행 What if the biggest thing (keeping us from doing what matters) is the
~라면 어떨까?   주어   ( ): 주어 수식(현재분사구)   동사(단수)
false assumption [that it has to take huge effort]? [ ]: 동격절(=the false assumption)

★★ 문제 해결 꿀~팁 ★★

▶ 많이 틀린 이유는?
첫 문장의 주어가 '언어'이므로 얼핏 보면 언어를 언급하는 ②가 정답일 것 같지만, '공식적인 언어' 사용은 전혀 글과 관련이 없다. 이 글은 쉬운 성공을 경시하고 힘든 노력을 가치 있게 말하는 언어 습관이 우리에게 어떤 영향을 미치는지에 관한 글이다.

▶ 문제 해결 방법은?
this sacred cow가 가리키는 것은 문맥상 the "right" way is, inevitably, the harder one 이다. 이는 '힘든 노력만을 옳게' 여기는 사고방식인데, 밑줄 부분은 여기에 '반박을 제기한다'는 의미다.

---

22 두려움을 주는 뉴스의 부작용 정답률 70% | 정답 ①

다음 글의 요지로 가장 적절한 것은?

☑ 두려움을 주는 뉴스는 사람들이 문제에 덜 대처하게 할 수 있다.
② 정보를 전달하는 시기에 따라 뉴스의 영향력이 달라질 수 있다.
③ 지속적인 환경 문제 보도가 사람들의 인식 변화를 가져온다.
④ 정보 제공의 지연은 정확한 문제 인식에 방해가 될 수 있다.
⑤ 출처가 불분명한 건강 정보는 사람들에게 유익하지 않다.

The old saying is / that "knowledge is power," / but when it comes to scary, threatening news, / research suggests the exact opposite.
오래된 격언은 / '아는 것이 힘이다'이지만, / 무섭고 위협적인 뉴스에 관해서는 / 연구에서 정반대를 시사한다.

Frightening news / can actually rob people of their inner sense of control, / making them less likely / to take care of themselves and other people.
두려움을 주는 뉴스는 / 실제로 사람들로부터 내면의 통제력을 빼앗을 수 있어서, / 가능성을 더 낮아지게 한다. / 그들이 스스로와 다른 사람들을 돌볼

Public health research shows / that when the news presents health-related information / in a pessimistic way, / people are actually less likely to take steps / to protect themselves from illness / as a result.
공중 보건 연구는 보여준다. / 뉴스가 건강과 관련된 정보를 제시할 때, / 비관적인 방식으로 / 사람들이 조치를 취할 가능성이 실제로 더 낮다는 것을 / 질병으로부터 자신을 보호하기 위한 / 결과적으로

A news article / that's intended to warn people about increasing cancer rates, / for example, / can result in fewer people / choosing to get screened for the disease / because they're so terrified of what they might find.
뉴스 기사는 / 증가하는 암 발생률에 대해 사람들에게 경고하려는 / 예를 들어, / 더 적은 사람이 하는 결과를 가져올 수 있다. / 병에 대해 검사받기로 선택하는 / 그들이 발견될지도 모르는 것을 너무 두려워하기 때문에

This is also true for issues / such as climate change.
이것은 문제에도 해당된다. / 기후 변화와 같은

When a news story is all doom and gloom, / people feel depressed and become less interested / in taking small, personal steps to fight ecological collapse.
뉴스가 온통 파멸과 암울한 상황일 때, / 사람들은 우울한 기분을 느끼고 흥미를 덜 느끼게 된다. / 생태학적 붕괴와 싸우기 위한 작고 개인적인 조치를 취하는 데

오래된 격언에 따르면 '아는 것이 힘이다'라고 하지만, 무섭고 위협적인 뉴스에 관해서는 연구에서 정반대를 시사한다. 두려움을 주는 뉴스는 실제로 사람들로부터 내면의 통제력을 빼앗을 수 있어서, 그들이 스스로와 다른 사람들을 돌볼 가능성을 더 낮아지게 한다. 공중 보건 연구는 뉴스가 건강과 관련된 정보를 비관적인 방식으로 제시할 때, 결과적으로 사람들이 질병으로부터 자신을 보호하기 위한 조치를 취할 가능성이 실제로 더 낮다는 것을 보여준다. 예를 들어, 증가하는 암 발생률에 대해 사람들에게 경고하려는 뉴스 기사는 사람들이 발견될지도 모르는 것을 너무 두려워하기 때문에 병에 대해 검사받기로 선택하는 이들이 더 적어지는 결과를 가져올 수 있다. 이것은 기후 변화와 같은 문제에도 해당된다. 뉴스가 온통 파멸과 암울한 상황일 때, 사람들은 우울한 기분을 느끼고 생태학적 붕괴와 싸우기 위한 작고 개인적인 조치를 취하는 데 흥미를 덜 느끼게 된다.

Why? 왜 정답일까?

두려움을 주는 뉴스는 사람들의 문제 대처 능력을 약화시킨다는 내용의 글로, 'Frightening news can actually rob people of their inner sense of control, making them less likely to take care of themselves and other people.'에 주제가 잘 제시된다. 따라서 글의 요지로 가장 적절한 것은 ① '두려움을 주는 뉴스는 사람들이 문제에 덜 대처하게 할 수 있다.'이다.

- threatening ⓐ 겁을 주는
- public health 공공 보건
- take steps to ~하기 위해 조치를 취하다
- article ⓝ 기사
- screen ⓥ (어떤 질병이 있는지) 검진하다
- doom ⓝ 불운, 파멸
- collapse ⓝ 붕괴, 쓰러지다
- rob A of B A에게서 B를 빼앗다
- pessimistic ⓐ 염세적인, 비관적인
- illness ⓝ 질병
- be intended to ~할 의도이다
- terrified ⓐ 겁에 질린
- gloom ⓝ 우울, 어둠

구문 풀이

8행 A news article [that's intended to warn people about increasing cancer rates], for example, can result in fewer people choosing to get screened for the disease because they're so terrified of what they might find.
(주어 / 동사구 / 의미상 주어 / 동명사(in의 목적어))

---

23 해수면 상승의 결과   정답률 70% | 정답 ⑤

다음 글의 주제로 가장 적절한 것은?

① cause of rising temperatures on the Earth
지구의 온도가 상승하는 원인
② principles of planets maintaining their shapes
행성이 모양을 유지하는 원리
③ implications of melting ice on marine biodiversity
녹는 얼음이 해양 생물 다양성에 미치는 영향
④ way to keep track of time without using any device
어떤 장치도 쓰지 않고 시간을 아는 방법
☑ impact of melting ice and rising seas on the length of a day
녹는 얼음과 해수면 상승이 하루의 시간 길이에 미치는 영향

The most remarkable and unbelievable consequence of melting ice and rising seas / is that together they are a kind of time machine, / so real / that they are altering the duration of our day.
녹는 얼음과 상승하는 바다의 가장 놀랍고 믿을 수 없는 결과는 / 그것들이 함께 일종의 타임머신이 된다는 것인데, / 이것은 너무도 현실적이어서 / 우리 하루의 지속시간을 바꾸고 있다.

It works like this: / As the glaciers melt and the seas rise, / gravity forces more water toward the equator.
그것은 다음과 같이 작동한다. / 빙하가 녹고 바다가 높아지면서 / 중력이 적도를 향해 더 많은 물을 밀어 넣는다.

This changes the shape of the Earth ever so slightly, / making it fatter around the middle, / which in turns slows the rotation of the planet / similarly to the way / a ballet dancer slows her spin / by spreading out her arms.
이것은 지구의 모양을 아주 약간 변화시켜 / 가운데 주변으로 더 불룩해지게 만들고, / 이것은 결과적으로 행성의 회전을 늦춘다. / 방식과 유사하게 / 발레 무용수가 양팔을 뻗어서 회전을 늦추는 / 양팔을 뻗어서

The slowdown isn't much, / just a few thousandths of a second each year, / but like the barely noticeable jump of rising seas every year, / it adds up.
이 감속이 크지는 않지만, / 매년 단지 몇천 분의 1초로 / 해마다 상승하는 바다의 거의 드러나지 않는 증가와 마찬가지로 / 그것은 쌓인다.

When dinosaurs lived on the Earth, / a day lasted only about twenty-three hours.
공룡들이 지구에 살았을 때, / 하루는 약 23시간만 지속되었다.

녹는 얼음과 상승하는 바다의 가장 놀랍고 믿을 수 없는 결과는 그것들이 함께 일종의 타임머신이 된다는 것인데, 이것은 너무도 현실적이어서 우리 하루의 지속시간을 바꾸고 있다. 그것은 다음과 같이 작동한다. 빙하가 녹고 바다가 높아지면서 중력이 적도를 향해 더 많은 물을 밀어 넣는다. 이것은 지구의 모양을 아주 약간 변화시켜 가운데 주변으로 더 불룩해지게 만들고, 이것은 결과적으로 발레 무용수가 양팔을 뻗어서 회전을 늦추는 방식과 유사하게 행성의 회전을 늦춘다. 이 감속이 매년 단지 몇천 분의 1초로 크지는 않지만, 해마다 상승하는 바다의 거의 드러나지 않는 증가와 마찬가지로 그것은 쌓인다. 공룡들이 지구에 살았을 때, 하루는 약 23시간만 지속되었다.

Why? 왜 정답일까?

지구 온난화로 인한 해수면 상승이 지구의 가운데를 더 불룩해지게 만들어 지구의 하루가 지속되는 시간을 연장할 수 있다(The most remarkable and unbelievable consequence of melting ice and rising seas ~ so real that they are altering the duration of our day.)는 내용의 글이다. 따라서 글의 주제로 가장 적절한 것은 ⑤ '녹는 얼음과 해수면 상승이 하루의 시간 길이에 미치는 영향'이다.

- remarkable ⓐ 현저한, 두드러지는
- alter ⓥ 바꾸다
- glacier ⓝ 빙하
- equator ⓝ 적도
- rotation ⓝ 회전
- spread out 벌리다, 펴지다
- barely ⓐⓓ 거의 ~않다, 가까스로
- last ⓥ 지속되다
- implication ⓝ 영향
- keep track of ~을 추적하다
- consequence ⓝ 결과, 영향
- duration ⓝ 지속 시간
- gravity ⓝ 중력
- slightly ⓐⓓ 약간
- spin ⓝ 회전
- slowdown ⓝ 둔화, 지연
- noticeable ⓐ 분명한, 뚜렷한
- principle ⓝ 원리
- biodiversity ⓝ 생물 다양성

구문 풀이

1행 The most remarkable and unbelievable consequence (of melting ice and rising seas) is that together they are a kind of time machine, so real that they are altering the duration of our day.
(주어(최상급) / 동사(단수) / 「so ~ that … : 너무 ~해서 …하다」)

---

24 새로운 관점에 마음 열기   정답률 50% | 정답 ④

다음 글의 제목으로 가장 적절한 것은?

① The Value of Being Honest – 정직의 가치
② Filter Out Negative Points of View – 부정적인 관점을 걸러라
③ Keeping Your Word: A Road to Success – 약속 지키기: 성공으로 향하는 길
☑ Being Right Can Block New Possibilities – 옳다는 것은 새로운 가능성을 차단할 수 있다
⑤ Look Back When Everyone Looks Forward – 모두가 앞을 볼 때 뒤를 봐라

Have you ever brought up an idea or suggestion to someone / and heard them immediately say / "No, that won't work."?
여러분이 누군가에게 아이디어나 제안을 내놨는데, / 그들이 즉시 말한 것을 들은 적이 있는가? / "아니, 그건 안 될 거야."라고

You may have thought, / "He/she didn't even give it a chance. / How do they know it won't work?"
여러분은 아마도 생각했을 것이다. / "그 사람은 기회조차 주지 않았는데. / 어떻게 그것이 안 될 것이라고 알지?"라고

When you are right about something, / you close off the possibility of another viewpoint or opportunity.
여러분이 어떤 일에 대해 옳다면, / 여러분은 다른 관점이나 기회의 가능성을 닫아 버린다.

Being right about something means / that "it is the way it is, period."
어떤 일에 대해 옳다는 것은 의미한다. / "그것은 원래 그런 거야, 끝."이라고 하는 것을

You may be correct.
여러분이 맞을 수도 있다.

Your particular way of seeing it / may be true with the facts.
여러분이 그것을 보는 특정한 방법이 / 사실에 부합할 수도 있다.

However, / considering the other option or the other person's point of view / can be beneficial.
하지만 / 다른 선택지나 다른 사람의 관점을 고려하는 것은 / 이로울 수 있다.

If you see their side, / you will see something new / or, at worse, learn something / about how the other person looks at life.
만약 여러분이 그들의 관점을 안다면, / 여러분은 새로운 것을 알게 되거나 / 적어도 무언가를 배울 것이다. / 다른 사람이 삶을 바라보는 방식에 대한

Why would you think / everyone sees and experiences life / the way you do?
왜 여러분은 생각하는가? / 모두가 삶을 보거나 경험할 거라고 / 여러분이 하는 방식대로

Besides how boring that would be, / it would eliminate all new opportunities, ideas, invention, and creativity.
그것이 얼마나 지루할지는 제외하고라도, / 그것은 모든 새로운 기회, 아이디어, 발명, 그리고 창의성을 없앨 것이다.

누군가에게 아이디어나 제안을 내놨는데, 그들이 즉시 "아니, 그건 안 될 거야."라고 말한 것을 들은 적이 있는가? 여러분은 아마도 "그 사람은 기회조차 주지 않았는데, 어떻게 그것이 안 될 것이라고 알지?"라고 생각했을 것이다. 여러분이 어떤 일에 대해 옳다면, 여러분은 다른 관점이나 기회의 가능성을 닫아 버린다. 어떤 일에 대해 옳다는 것은 "그것은 원래 그런 거야, 끝."이라고 하는 것을 의미한다. 여러분이 맞을 수도 있다. 여러분이 그것을 보는 특정한 방법이 사실에 부합할 수도 있다. 하지만 다른 선택지나 다른 사람의 관점을 고려하는 것은 이로울 수 있다. 만약 여러분이 그들의 관점을 안다면, 여러분은 새로운 것을 알게 되거나 적어도 다른 사람이 삶을 바라보는 방식에 대한 무언가를 배울 것이다. 왜 모두가 여러분이 하는 방식대로 삶을 보거나 경험할 거라고 생각하는가? 그것이 얼마나 지루할지는 제외하고라도, 그것은 모든 새로운 기회, 아이디어, 발명, 그리고 창의성을 없앨 것이다.

Why? 왜 정답일까?

어떤 것에 대해 옳다는 것은 새로운 가능성을 차단할 수 있다(When you are right about something, you close off the possibility of another viewpoint or opportunity.)고 지적한 뒤, 새로운 관점을 고려하려는 태도가 필요하다고 조언하는 글이다. 따라서 글의 제목으로 가장 적절한 것은 ④ '옳다는 것은 새로운 가능성을 차단할 수 있다'이다.

- bring up (화제를) 꺼내다, (아이디어를) 내놓다
- close off 차단하다
- period ad (문장 끝에서) 끝, 이상이다, 더 말하지 마라
- beneficial ⓐ 이로운
- besides prep ~을 제외하더라도, ~외에도 ad 게다가
- eliminate ⓥ 제거하다
- filter out ~을 걸러내다, 여과하다
- block ⓥ 차단하다
- suggestion ⓝ 제안
- viewpoint ⓝ 관점, 견해
- at worse 최소한, 적어도
- invention ⓝ 발명
- keep one's word 약속을 지키다

구문 풀이

1행 Have you ever brought up an idea or suggestion to someone and heard
→동사1←   동사2(지각동사)
them immediately say "No, that won't work."?
목적어   원형부정사

---

25 고기를 덜 먹거나 먹지 않는 사람들의 이유   정답률 74% | 정답 ④

다음 도표의 내용과 일치하지 않는 것은?

Reasons for People Interested in Eating Less Meat
and Non-meat Eaters in the UK (2018)

Health 49 / 31
Weight management 29 / 9
Animal welfare 22 / 52
Environment 22 / 32
Taste 10 / 30

☐ People interested in eating less meat   ■ Non-meat eaters
※ allowed to choose multiple reasons

The graph above shows the survey results on reasons / for people interested in eating less meat / and those eating no meat / in the UK in 2018.
위 그래프는 이유에 대한 조사 결과를 보여 준다. / 고기를 덜 먹는 것에 관심 있는 사람들과 / 고기를 먹지 않는 사람들의 / 2018년 영국에서의

① For the group of people / who are interested in eating less meat, / health is the strongest motivator / for doing so.
집단 사람들에게 / 고기를 덜 먹는 것에 관심 있는 / 가장 강력한 동기는 건강이다. / 그렇게 하려는

② For the group of non-meat eaters, / animal welfare accounts for the largest percentage among all reasons, / followed by environment, health, and taste.
고기를 먹지 않는 집단 사람들의 경우, / 모든 이유 중 동물 복지가 가장 큰 비율을 차지하고, / 환경, 건강, 그리고 맛이 그 뒤를 따른다.

③ The largest percentage point difference / between the two groups / is in animal welfare, / whereas the smallest difference is in environment.
퍼센트포인트 격차가 가장 큰 것은 / 두 집단 간 / 동물 복지에서이다. / 가장 작은 격차는 환경인 반면

✔ The percentage of non-meat eaters citing taste / is four times higher / than that of people / interested in reducing their meat consumption / citing taste.
고기를 먹지 않는 사람들 중 맛을 언급한 비율은 / 4배 높다. / 사람들의 비율보다 / 고기 섭취를 줄이는 데 관심이 있는 / 맛을 언급한

⑤ Weight management ranks the lowest for people / who don't eat meat, / with less than 10 percent.
체중 관리는 사람들에게 가장 낮은 순위를 차지한다. / 고기를 먹지 않는 / 10퍼센트 미만으로

위 그래프는 고기를 덜 먹는 것에 관심 있는 사람들과 고기를 먹지 않는 사람들의 이유에 대한 2018년 영국에서의 조사 결과를 보여 준다. ① 고기를 덜 먹는 것에 관심 있는 집단 사람들에게 그렇게 하려는 가장 강력한 동기는 건강이다. ② 고기를 먹지 않는 집단 사람들의 경우, 모든 이유 중 동물 복지가 가장 큰 비율을 차지하고, 환경, 건강, 그리고 맛이 그 뒤를 따른다. ③ 두 집단 간 퍼센트포인트 격차가 가장 큰 것은 동물 복지인 반면, 가장 작은 격차는 환경이다. ④ 고기를 먹지 않는 사람들 중 맛을 언급한 비율은 고기 섭취를 줄이는 데 관심이 있는 사람들 중 맛을 언급한 비율보다 4배 높다. ⑤ 체중 관리는 고기를 먹지 않는 사람들에게 10퍼센트 미만으로 가장 낮은 순위를 차지한다.

Why? 왜 정답일까?

도표에 따르면 고기를 먹지 않는 사람들 중 맛 때문이라고 언급한 사람은 **30%**인데, 이는 고기를 덜 먹으려는 사람들 중 맛을 이유로 언급한 비율(10%)의 3배이다. 따라서 도표와 일치하지 않는 것은 ④이다.

- survey ⓝ 설문 조사
- motivator ⓝ 동기 요인
- account for ~을 차지하다
- cite ⓥ 언급하다, 인용하다
- weight ⓝ 체중, 무게
- reason ⓝ 이유
- welfare ⓝ 복지
- followed by ~이 뒤를 잇다
- consumption ⓝ 소비

구문 풀이

9행 The percentage of non-meat eaters citing taste is four times higher than
「배수사 + 비교급 + than : ~보다 몇 배 더 …한」
that of people (interested in reducing their meat consumption) (citing taste).
= the percentage   ( ) : people 수식

---

26 Margaret Knight의 생애   정답률 84% | 정답 ③

Margaret Knight에 관한 다음 글의 내용과 일치하지 않는 것은?
① 기자들이 '여자 Edison'이라는 별명을 지어 주었다.
② 가족을 위해 돈을 벌려고 학교를 그만두었다.
✔ 직물 장비에 쓰이는 안전장치를 발명하여 많은 돈을 벌었다.
④ 밑이 평평한 종이 가방을 자르고 접고 붙이는 기계를 발명했다.
⑤ 2006년에 국립 발명가 명예의 전당에 입성했다.

「Margaret Knight was an exceptionally prolific inventor / in the late 19th century; / journalists occasionally compared her to Thomas Edison / by nicknaming her "a woman Edison."」 ①의 근거 일치
Margaret Knight는 특출나게 다작한 발명가였고, / 19세기 후반에 / 기자들은 가끔 그녀를 Thomas Edison과 비교했다. / 그녀에게 '여자 Edison'이라는 별명을 지어주며

From a young age, / she built toys for her older brothers.
어린 나이부터, / 그녀는 오빠들을 위해 장난감을 만들었다.

After her father died, / Knight's family moved to Manchester.
아버지가 돌아가신 후, / Knight의 가족은 Manchester로 이사했다.

「Knight left school in 1850, / at age 12, / to earn money for her family / at a nearby textile factory,」 / where she witnessed a fellow worker / injured by faulty equipment. ②의 근거 일치
Knight는 1850년에 학교를 그만두었는데, / 12세의 나이에, / 가족을 위해 돈을 벌기 위해 / 가까이에 있는 직물 공장에서 / 그곳에서 그녀는 동료 노동자를 목격했다. / 결함이 있는 장비에 부상 당하는 것을

「That led her to create her first invention, / a safety device for textile equipment, / but she never earned money from the invention.」 ③의 근거 일치
이로 인해 그녀는 첫 번째 발명품을 만들었지만, / 즉 직물 장비에 쓰이는 안전장치를 / 그녀는 결코 그 발명품으로 돈을 벌지 않았다.

「She also invented a machine / that cut, folded and glued flat-bottomed paper bags / and was awarded her first patent in 1871 for it.」 ④의 근거 일치
그녀는 또한 기계를 발명해 / 밑이 평평한 종이 가방을 자르고 접어 붙이는 / 1871년에 그것으로 첫 특허를 받았다.

It eliminated the need / for workers to assemble them slowly by hand.
그것은 필요가 없어지게 했다. / 작업자들이 손으로 그것들을 천천히 조립할

「Knight received 27 patents in her lifetime / and entered the National Inventors Hall of Fame in 2006.」 ⑤의 근거 일치
Knight는 일생 동안 27개의 특허를 받았고, / 2006년에 국립 발명가 명예의 전당에 입성했다.

Margaret Knight는 19세기 후반에 특출나게 다작한 발명가였고, 기자들은 가끔 '여자 Edison'이라는 별명을 지어주며 그녀를 Thomas Edison과 비교했다. 어린 나이부터, 그녀는 오빠들을 위해 장난감을 만들었다. 아버지가 돌아가신 후, Knight의 가족은 Manchester로 이사했다. Knight는 가족을 위해 가까이에 있는 직물 공장에서 돈을 벌기 위해 1850년에 12세의 나이에 학교를 그만두었는데, 그곳에서 그녀는 동료 노동자가 결함이 있는 장비에 부상 당하는 것을 목격했다. 이로 인해 그녀는 첫 번째 발명품, 즉 직물 장비에 쓰이는 안전장치를 만들었지만, 그녀는 결코 그 발명품으로 돈을 벌지 않았다. 그녀는 또한 밑이 평평한 종이 가방을 자르고 접어 붙이는 기계를 발명해 1871년에 그것으로 첫 특허를 받았다. 그것은 작업자들이 손으로 그것들을 천천히 조립할 필요가 없어지게 했다. Knight는 일생 동안 27개의 특허를 받았고, 2006년에 국립 발명가 명예의 전당에 입성했다.

Why? 왜 정답일까?

'~ a safety device for textile equipment, but she never earned money from the invention.'에서 Margaret Knight는 동료가 직물 장비에 부상당하는 것을 본 후 장비에 적용할 안전장치를 만들었지만 이것으로 돈을 벌지는 않았다고 한다. 따라서 내용과 일치하지 않는 것은 ③ '직물 장비에 쓰이는 안전장치를 발명하여 많은 돈을 벌었다.'이다.

Why? 왜 오답일까?

① '~ journalists occasionally compared her to Thomas Edison by nicknaming her "a woman Edison."'의 내용과 일치한다.
② 'Knight left school in 1850, at age 12, to earn money for her family ~'의 내용과 일치한다.
④ 'She also invented a machine that cut, folded and glued flat-bottomed paper bags ~'의 내용과 일치한다.
⑤ '~ entered the National Inventors Hall of Fame in 2006.'의 내용과 일치한다.

- exceptionally ad 이례적으로, 특출나게
- journalist ⓝ 기자
- witness ⓥ 목격하다
- faulty ⓐ 결함이 있는
- glue ⓥ 접착하다
- assemble ⓥ 조립하다
- prolific ⓐ 다작한
- occasionally ad 가끔, 때때로
- fellow ⓝ 동료
- fold ⓥ 접다
- flat-bottomed ⓐ 밑이 평평한
- hall of fame 명예의 전당

구문 풀이

1행 ~ journalists occasionally compared her to Thomas Edison by nicknaming
「by + 동명사 : ~함으로써」
her "a woman Edison."

---

27 전자 폐기물 재활용 행사 공지   정답률 88% | 정답 ⑤

E−Waste Recycling Day에 관한 다음 안내문의 내용과 일치하지 않는 것은?
① 3시간 동안 진행된다.
② Lincoln 스포츠 센터에서 열린다.
③ 전자레인지는 허용되지 않는 품목이다.
④ 기기 속 모든 개인 정보는 미리 삭제되어야 한다.
✔ 거주 지역에 상관없이 참가할 수 있다.

E-Waste Recycling Day
전자 폐기물 재활용의 날
E-Waste Recycling Day is an annual event in our city.
전자 폐기물 재활용의 날은 우리 시의 연례행사입니다.
Bring your used electronics / such as cell phones, tablets, and laptops / to recycle.
중고 전자 제품을 가져오세요. / 휴대폰, 태블릿, 노트북과 같이 / 재활용할
Go green!
친환경적이 되세요!
When
일시
Saturday, December 17, 2022
2022년 12월 17일 토요일
「8:00 a.m. − 11:00 a.m.」 ①의 근거 일치
오전 8시부터 오전 11시까지
Where
장소
「Lincoln Sports Center」 ②의 근거 일치
Lincoln 스포츠 센터

Notes
주의 사항
『Items NOT accepted: light bulbs, batteries, and microwaves』 ③의 근거 일치
허용되지 않는 품목들: 전구, 건전지, 전자레인지
『All personal data on the devices / must be wiped out in advance.』 ④의 근거 일치
기기 속 모든 개인 정보는 / 미리 삭제되어야 합니다.
『This event is free / but open only to local residents.』 ⑤의 근거 불일치
이 행사는 무료이나 / 지역 주민에게만 개방됩니다.
Please contact us at 986-571-0204 / for more information.
986-571-0204로 연락주세요. / 더 많은 정보를 원하시면

전자 폐기물 재활용의 날

전자 폐기물 재활용의 날은 우리 시의 연례행사입니다. 휴대폰, 태블릿, 노트북과 같이 재활용할 중고 전자 제품을 가져오세요. 친환경적이 되세요!

일시
2022년 12월 17일 토요일
오전 8시부터 오전 11시까지

장소
Lincoln 스포츠 센터

주의 사항
• 허용되지 않는 품목들: 전구, 건전지, 전자레인지
• 기기 속 모든 개인 정보는 미리 삭제되어야 합니다.
• 이 행사는 무료이나 지역 주민에게만 개방됩니다.

더 많은 정보를 원하시면 986-571-0204로 연락주세요.

Why? 왜 정답일까?
'This event is free but open only to local residents.'에서 거주민에게만 개방되는 행사라고 하므로, 안내문의 내용과 일치하지 않는 것은 ⑤ '거주 지역에 상관없이 참가할 수 있다.'이다.

Why? 왜 오답일까?
① '8:00 a.m. – 11:00 a.m.'의 내용과 일치한다.
② 'Lincoln Sports Center'의 내용과 일치한다.
③ 'Items NOT accepted: ~ microwaves'의 내용과 일치한다.
④ 'All personal data on the devices must be wiped out in advance.'의 내용과 일치한다.

● e-waste ⓝ 전자 쓰레기
● accept ⓥ 수용하다, 접수하다, 받다
● wipe out 지우다, 쓸어내다
● local resident 지역 주민
● recycling ⓝ 재활용
● microwave ⓝ 전자레인지
● in advance 미리

구문 풀이

3행 명령문(~하라)
Bring your used electronics such as cell phones, tablets, and laptops
          목적어
to recycle.
형용사적 용법(목적어 수식)

28 해저 걷기 활동 안내 정답률 83% | 정답 ③

Undersea Walking Activity에 관한 다음 안내문의 내용과 일치하는 것은?
① 연중무휴로 운영된다.
② 가격에 보험료는 포함되어 있지 않다.
✓③ 숙련된 안전 요원이 활동 내내 동행한다.
④ 특수 수중 헬멧 착용 시 안경을 쓸 수 없다.
⑤ 현장 예약은 불가능하다.

Undersea Walking Activity
해저 걷기 활동
Enjoy a fascinating underwater walk on the ocean floor.
해저에서 매력적인 수중 걷기를 즐기세요.
Witness wonderful marine life on foot!
걸어 다니며 멋진 바다 생물을 직접 보세요!
Age Requirement
연령 요건
10 years or older
10세 이상
Operating Hours
영업시간
『from Tuesday to Sunday』 ①의 근거 불일치
화요일부터 일요일까지
9:00 a.m. – 4:00 p.m.
오전 9시부터 오후 4시까지
Price
가격
『$30 (insurance fee included)』 ②의 근거 불일치
$30 (보험료 포함)
What to Bring
준비물
swim suit and towel
수영복과 수건
Notes
주의 사항
『Experienced lifeguards accompany you / throughout the activity.』 ③의 근거 일치
숙련된 안전 요원이 여러분과 동행합니다. / 활동 내내
『With a special underwater helmet, / you can wear glasses during the activity.』 ④의 근거 불일치
특수 수중 헬멧 착용 시 / 여러분은 활동 중에 안경을 쓸 수 있습니다.
『Reservations can be made on-site or online / at www.seawalkwonder.com.』 ⑤의 근거 불일치
예약은 현장 또는 온라인으로 가능합니다. / www.seawalkwonder.com에서

해저 걷기 활동

해저에서 매력적인 수중 걷기를 즐기세요. 걸어 다니며 멋진 바다 생물을 직접 보세요!

연령 요건
10세 이상

영업시간
화요일부터 일요일까지
오전 9시부터 오후 4시까지

가격
$30 (보험료 포함)

준비물
수영복과 수건

주의 사항
• 숙련된 안전 요원이 활동 내내 여러분과 동행합니다.
• 특수 수중 헬멧 착용 시 여러분은 활동 중에 안경을 쓸 수 있습니다.
• 예약은 현장 또는 www.seawalkwonder.com에서 온라인으로 가능합니다.

Why? 왜 정답일까?
'Experienced lifeguards accompany you throughout the activity.'에서 숙련된 안전 요원이 활동 내내 동행한다고 하므로, 안내문의 내용과 일치하는 것은 ③ '숙련된 안전 요원이 활동 내내 동행한다.'이다.

Why? 왜 오답일까?
① 'from Tuesday to Sunday'에서 월요일이 휴무일임을 알 수 있다.
② '$30 (insurance fee included)'에서 입장 가격에 보험료가 포함돼 있다고 하였다.
④ 'With a special underwater helmet, you can wear glasses during the activity.'에서 특수 헬멧을 쓰면 안경 착용이 가능하다고 하였다.
⑤ 'Reservations can be made on-site ~'에서 현장 예약도 가능하다고 하였다.

● fascinating ⓐ 매혹적인
● operating hour 운영 시간
● experienced ⓐ 숙련된
● accompany ⓥ 동행하다
● on-site ⓐⓓ 현장에서, ⓐ 현장의
● ocean floor 해저
● insurance fee 보험료
● lifeguard ⓝ 안전 요원
● throughout prep ~ 내내

★★★ 등급을 가르는 문제!

29 인공 지능의 핵심 특징 정답률 44% | 정답 ④

다음 글의 밑줄 친 부분 중, 어법상 틀린 것은? [3점]

You may have seen headlines in the news / about some of the things / machines powered by artificial intelligence can do.
여러분은 헤드라인들을 뉴스에서 본 적이 있을 것이다. / 몇 가지 일에 대한 / 인공 지능으로 구동되는 기계가 할 수 있는
However, / if you were to consider all the tasks / ① that AI-powered machines could actually perform, / it would be quite mind-blowing!
하지만, / 여러분이 모든 작업을 고려한다면 / AI로 구동되는 기계가 실제로 수행할 수 있는 / 꽤 놀라울 것이다!
One of the key features of artificial intelligence / ② is / that it enables machines to learn new things, / rather than requiring programming specific to new tasks.
인공 지능의 핵심 특징들 중 하나는 / ~이다. / 이것이 기계가 새로운 것을 학습할 수 있게 한다는 것 / 새로운 작업에 특화된 프로그래밍을 필요로 하기보다는
Therefore, / the core difference / between computers of the future and ③ those of the past / is / that future computers will be able to learn and self-improve.
그러므로, / 핵심 차이점은 / 미래 컴퓨터와 과거 컴퓨터 사이의 / ~이다. / 미래의 컴퓨터가 학습하고 스스로 개선할 수 있을 것이라는 점
In the near future, / smart virtual assistants will know more about you / than your closest friends and family members ✓ do.
가까운 미래에, / 스마트 가상 비서는 여러분에 관해 더 많이 알게 될 것이다. / 여러분의 가장 가까운 친구나 가족보다도
Can you imagine / how that might change our lives?
여러분은 상상할 수 있는가? / 그것이 우리의 삶을 어떻게 변화시킬지
These kinds of changes are / exactly why it is so important / ⑤ to recognize the implications / that new technologies will have for our world.
이러한 변화가 ~이다. / 아주 중요한 바로 그 이유 / 영향을 인식하는 것이 / 새로운 기술들이 우리 세계에 미칠

여러분은 인공 지능으로 구동되는 기계가 할 수 있는 몇 가지 일에 대한 헤드라인들을 뉴스에서 본 적이 있을 것이다. 하지만, AI로 구동되는 기계가 실제로 수행할 수 있는 모든 작업을 고려한다면 꽤 놀라울 것이다! 인공 지능의 핵심 특징들 중 하나는 이것에 새로운 작업에 특화된 프로그래밍이 필요하다기보다는, 이것(인공 지능)이 기계가 새로운 것을 학습할 수 있게 한다는 것이다. 그러므로, 미래 컴퓨터와 과거 컴퓨터 사이의 핵심 차이점은 미래의 컴퓨터가 학습하고 스스로 개선할 수 있을 것이라는 점이다. 가까운 미래에, 스마트 가상 비서는 여러분의 가장 가까운 친구나 가족보다도 여러분에 관해 더 많이 알게 될 것이다. 그것이 우리의 삶을 어떻게 변화시킬지 상상할 수 있는가? 이러한 변화가 바로 새로운 기술들이 우리 세계에 미칠 영향을 인식하는 것이 아주 중요한 이유이다.

Why? 왜 정답일까?
비교급 구문의 than 앞에 일반동사인 will know가 나오므로, than 뒤에 일반동사의 대동사인 do를 써야 한다. 따라서 어법상 틀린 것은 ④이다.

Why? 왜 오답일까?
① 앞에 나온 all the tasks를 꾸미면서 뒤에 목적어가 없는 문장(AI-powered machines could actually perform)을 연결하는 목적격 관계대명사 that의 쓰임이 알맞다.
② 'one of the + 복수 명사'가 주어이므로 단수동사 is는 알맞게 쓰였다.
③ 앞의 복수 명사 computers를 가리키는 복수 대명사 those가 알맞게 쓰였다.
⑤ 가주어 it에 대응되는 진주어 역할의 to부정사구 to recognize가 알맞게 쓰였다.

● artificial intelligence 인공 지능
● mind-blowing ⓐ 너무도 감동적인
● self-improve ⓥ 자가 발전하다
● perform ⓥ 수행하다
● feature ⓝ 특징
● virtual ⓐ 가상의

- **assistant** ⓝ 조수, 비서
- **recognize** ⓥ 인식하다, 깨닫다
- **exactly** ⓐ 바로, 정확히

구문 풀이

9행 In the near future, smart virtual assistants will know more about you than your closest friends and family members **do**.
대동사(= know about you)

★★ 문제 해결 꿀~팁 ★★

▶ 많이 틀린 이유는?
③이 포함된 문장을 보면, 문맥상 미래의 컴퓨터와 과거의 '컴퓨터(computers)'를 비교한다는 의미를 나타내면서 컴퓨터라는 명사의 중복을 피하기 위해 **those**를 알맞게 썼다. 이렇듯 대명사에 밑줄이 있으면 가장 기본적으로 대명사의 수 일치를 집중적으로 살펴봐야 한다.

▶ 문제 해결 방법은?
정답인 ④ **are**는 대동사의 쓰임을 묻는 선택지이다. 대동사는 간단한 듯 싶어도 문맥을 전체적으로 살펴야 하기에 어렵게 나오면 한없이 어려워진다. 여기서는 비교구문의 **than** 앞뒤는 병렬구조를 이루므로 **than** 앞의 동사와 **than** 뒤의 동사가 서로 같은 종류여야 한다는 점에 집중하면 된다.

---

30 옥신의 작용과 식물 생장 정답률 47% | 정답 ④

다음 글의 밑줄 친 부분 중, 문맥상 낱말의 쓰임이 적절하지 <u>않은</u> 것은? [3점]

Plant growth is controlled / by a group of hormones / called auxins / found at the tips of stems and roots of plants.
식물의 성장은 조절된다. / 호르몬 그룹에 의해 / 옥신이라고 불리는 / 식물의 줄기와 뿌리의 끝에서 발견되는

Auxins / produced at the tips of stems / tend to accumulate / on the side of the stem / that is in the shade.
옥신은 / 줄기의 끝에서 생산된 / 축적되는 경향이 있다. / 줄기 옆면에 / 그늘진 곳에 있는

Accordingly, / the auxins ① stimulate growth / on the shaded side of the plant.
따라서, / 옥신은 성장을 촉진한다. / 식물의 그늘진 면의

Therefore, / the shaded side grows faster / than the side facing the sunlight.
그러므로 / 그늘진 면은 더 빨리 자란다. / 햇빛을 마주하는 면보다

This phenomenon causes the stem / to bend and appear to be growing ② towards the light.
현상은 줄기가 ~하게 한다. / 휘어지고 빛을 향해 성장하는 것처럼 보이게

Auxins have the ③ opposite effect / on the roots of plants.
옥신은 반대 효과를 나타낸다. / 식물의 뿌리에서는

Auxins in the tips of roots / tend to limit growth.
뿌리 끝에 있는 옥신은 / 성장을 억제하는 경향이 있다.

If a root is horizontal in the soil, / the auxins will accumulate on the lower side / and interfere with its development.
만약 뿌리가 토양 속에서 수평이라면, / 옥신은 아래쪽에 축적되어 / 그것의 발달을 방해할 것이다.

Therefore, / the lower side of the root / will grow ✔ slower than the upper side.
그러므로 / 뿌리 아래쪽은 / 위쪽보다 더 느리게 자라게 된다.

This will, in turn, / cause the root to bend ⑤ downwards, / with the tip of the root growing in that direction.
이것은 결과적으로 / 뿌리가 아래로 휘어지게 하고, / 뿌리 끝부분은 그쪽으로 자라난다.

식물의 성장은 식물의 줄기와 뿌리의 끝에서 발견되는 옥신이라고 불리는 호르몬 그룹에 의해 조절된다. 줄기의 끝에서 생산된 옥신은 그늘진 곳에 있는 줄기 옆면에 축적되는 경향이 있다. 따라서, 옥신은 식물의 그늘진 면에서의 성장을 ① 촉진한다. 그러므로 그늘진 면은 햇빛을 마주하는 면보다 더 빨리 자란다. 이 현상은 줄기가 휘어지고 빛을 ② 향해 성장하는 것처럼 보이게 한다. 옥신은 식물의 뿌리에서는 ③ 반대 효과를 나타낸다. 뿌리 끝에 있는 옥신은 성장을 억제하는 경향이 있다. 만약 뿌리가 토양 속에서 수평이라면, 옥신은 아래쪽에 축적되어 그것의 발달을 방해할 것이다. 그러므로 뿌리 아래쪽은 위쪽보다 ④ 더 빠르게(→ 더 느리게) 자라게 된다. 이것은 결과적으로 뿌리가 ⑤ 아래로 휘어지게 하고, 뿌리 끝부분은 그쪽으로 자라난다.

Why? 왜 정답일까?

식물 생장에 있어 옥신의 작용 방식을 설명한 글이다. 줄기에 작용하는 옥신은 어두운 쪽의 성장을 자극하므로 식물은 마치 빛을 '향해' 작용하는 것처럼 보이게 되지만, 뿌리에서는 상황이 '반대'라고 한다. 즉, 뿌리 아래쪽에 축적된 옥신은 아래쪽의 성장을 오히려 '방해해서' 위쪽보다 '더 천천히' 자라게 만들 것이라는 내용을 추론할 수 있다. 따라서 문맥상 낱말의 쓰임이 적절하지 않은 것은 ④이며, **faster**를 **slower**로 바꿔야 한다.

- **tip** ⓝ 끝부분
- **accumulate** ⓥ 축적되다, 쌓이다
- **stimulate** ⓥ 자극하다, 촉진하다
- **bend** ⓥ 구부러지다
- **horizontal** ⓐ 수평적인
- **interfere with** ~을 방해하다
- **downward(s)** ⓐⓓ 아래로
- **stem** ⓝ 줄기
- **accordingly** ⓐⓓ 따라서
- **phenomenon** ⓝ 현상
- **limit** ⓥ 제한하다
- **soil** ⓝ 토양, 흙
- **in turn** 한편, 결국, 차례로

구문 풀이

12행 This will, in turn, cause the root to bend downwards, with the tip of the root growing in that direction.
「with + 명사 + 분사 : ~이 …한 채로」

---

31 정해진 마감일이 과업 성과에 미치는 영향 정답률 56% | 정답 ③

다음 빈칸에 들어갈 말로 가장 적절한 것을 고르시오.

① offering rewards – 보상을 제공하는 것
② removing obstacles – 장애물을 제거하는 것
✔ restricting freedom – 자유를 제한하는 것
④ increasing assignments – 과제를 늘리는 것
⑤ encouraging competition – 경쟁을 부추기는 것

To demonstrate how best to defeat the habit of delaying, / Dan Ariely, a professor of psychology and behavioral economics, / performed an experiment on students / in three of his classes at MIT.
미루는 습관을 가장 잘 무너뜨리는 방법을 설명하기 위해, / 심리학 및 행동경제학 교수인 Dan Ariely는 / 학생들을 대상으로 실험을 수행했다. / MIT에서의 수업 중 세 반에서

He assigned all classes three reports / over the course of the semester.
그는 모든 수업에 보고서 세 개를 과제로 부여했다. / 학기 과정 동안

The first class had to choose three due dates for themselves, / up to and including the last day of class.
첫 번째 수업의 학생들은 마감일 세 개를 스스로 선택해야 했다. / 종강일까지 포함해서

The second had no deadlines / — all three papers just had to be submitted / by the last day of class.
두 번째는 마감일이 없었고, / 세 개의 보고서 모두 제출되기만 하면 되었다. / 종강일까지

In his third class, / he gave students three set deadlines / over the course of the semester.
세 번째 수업에서, / 그는 학생들에게 세 개의 정해진 마감일을 주었다. / 학기 과정 동안

At the end of the semester, / he found / that students with set deadlines / received the best grades, / the students with no deadlines / had the worst, / and those who could choose their own deadlines / fell somewhere in the middle.
학기 말에, / 그는 발견했다. / 마감일이 정해진 학생들이 / 최고의 성적을 받았고, / 마감일이 없는 학생은 / 최하의 성적을 받았으며, / 마감일을 선택할 수 있었던 학생들은 / 그 중간 어딘가의 위치에 있었다는 것을

Ariely concludes / that restricting freedom / — whether by the professor / or by students who recognize their own tendencies to delay things — / improves self-control and performance.
Ariely는 결론짓는다. / 자유를 제한하는 것은 / 교수에 의해서든 / 혹은 일을 미루는 자기 성향을 인식하는 학생들에 의해서든, / 자기 통제와 성과를 향상시킨다는 것을

미루는 습관을 가장 잘 무너뜨리는 방법을 설명하기 위해, 심리학 및 행동경제학 교수인 Dan Ariely는 MIT에서의 수업 중 세 반에서 학생들을 대상으로 실험을 수행했다. 그는 학기 과정 동안 모든 수업에 보고서 세 개를 과제로 부여했다. 첫 번째 수업의 학생들은 종강일까지 포함해서 마감일 세 개를 스스로 선택해야 했다. 두 번째는 마감일이 없었고, 세 개의 보고서 모두 종강일까지 제출되기만 하면 되었다. 세 번째 수업에서, 그는 학기 과정 동안 학생들에게 세 개의 정해진 마감일을 주었다. 학기 말에, 그는 마감일이 정해진 학생들이 최고의 성적을 받았고, 마감일이 없는 학생들은 최하의 성적을 받았으며, 마감일을 선택할 수 있었던 학생들은 그 중간 어딘가의 위치에 있었다는 것을 알아냈다. Ariely가 결론짓기로, 교수에 의해서든 혹은 일을 미루는 자기 성향을 인식하는 학생들에 의해서든, 자유를 제한하는 것은 자기 통제와 성과를 향상시킨다.

Why? 왜 정답일까?

연구를 소개하는 글이므로 결과 부분인 '~ he found that students with set deadlines received the best grades, ~'이 중요하다. 이 내용에 따르면, 마감일이 '정해져' 있었던 학생들이 다른 두 집단에 비해 성적이 가장 높았다고 한다. 마감을 정해진다는 것은 결국 일정 부분 '자유를 제한한다'는 의미와 같으므로, 빈칸에 들어갈 말로 가장 적절한 것은 ③ '자유를 제한하는 것'이다.

- **demonstrate** ⓥ 입증하다
- **behavioral** ⓐ 행동의
- **for oneself** 스스로
- **set** ⓐ 정해진
- **tendency** ⓝ 경향, 성향
- **obstacle** ⓝ 장애물
- **defeat** ⓥ 무너뜨리다, 패배시키다
- **assign** ⓥ 할당하다
- **up to and including** ~까지 포함해서
- **receive** ⓥ 받다
- **self-control** ⓝ 자기 통제
- **restrict** ⓥ 제한하다

구문 풀이

12행 Ariely concludes that restricting freedom — whether by the professor or by students who recognize their own tendencies to delay things — improves self-control and performance.
주어(동명사) / 「whether+A or+B : A이든 B이든(부사절)」 / 동사(단수)

★★★ 등급을 가르는 문제! 32 혁신이 우리 삶을 바꾸는 방식 정답률 37% | 정답 ②

다음 빈칸에 들어갈 말로 가장 적절한 것을 고르시오. [3점]

① respecting the values of the old days – 과거의 가치관을 존중하는 것
✔ enabling people to work for each other – 사람들이 서로를 위해 일할 수 있게 하는 것
③ providing opportunities to think creatively – 창의적으로 사고할 기회를 주는 것
④ satisfying customers with personalized services – 개인에 맞춰진 서비스로 고객을 만족시키는 것
⑤ introducing and commercializing unusual products – 특이한 제품을 도입하고 상업화하는 것

The best way in which innovation changes our lives / is by enabling people to work for each other.
혁신이 우리 삶을 바꾸는 최고의 방법은 / 사람들이 서로를 위해 일할 수 있게 하는 것이다.

The main theme of human history / is that we become steadily more specialized / in what we produce, / and steadily more diversified / in what we consume: / we move away / from unstable self-sufficiency / to safer mutual interdependence.
인류 역사의 주요한 주제는 / 우리가 꾸준히 더 전문화되고 / 우리가 생산하는 것에 있어, / 꾸준히 더 다양화되는 것이다. / 우리가 소비하는 것에 있어 / 즉, 우리는 옮겨간다는 것이다. / 불안정한 자급자족에서 / 더 안전한 서로 간의 상호의존으로

By concentrating on serving other people's needs / for forty hours a week / — which we call a job — / you can spend the other seventy-two hours / (not counting fifty-six hours in bed) / relying on the services / provided to you by other people.
다른 사람들의 필요를 충족시키는 것에 집중하여 / 일주일에 40시간 동안 / 즉 우리가 직업이라고 부르는 것에 / 여러분은 나머지 72시간을 보낼 수 있다. / (잠자는 56시간은 빼고) / 서비스에 의지해 / 다른 사람에 의해 여러분에게 제공되는

Innovation has made it possible / to work for a fraction of a second / in order to be able to afford to turn on an electric lamp for an hour, / providing the quantity of light / that would have required a whole day's work / if you had to make it yourself / by collecting and refining sesame oil or lamb fat / to burn in a simple lamp, / as much of humanity did / in the not so distant past.
혁신은 가능하게 해주었는데 / 아주 짧은 시간 일하는 것을 / 전등을 한 시간 켤 수 있는 여유를 갖기 위해 / 이는 ~한 만큼의 빛을 제공해 준다. / 하루 종일의 노고가 들었을 / 여러분이 그 등을 스스로 만들어야 했다면 / 참기름이나 양의 지방을 모으고 정제해 / 그저 등 하나를 켜기 위해 / 많은 인류가 했던 것처럼 / 그리 멀지 않은 과거에

혁신이 우리의 삶을 바꾸는 최고의 방법은 <u>사람들이 서로를 위해 일할 수 있게 하는</u> 것이다. 인류 역사의 주요한 주제는 우리가 생산에 있어 꾸준히 더 전문화되고 소비에 있어 꾸준히 더 다양화되는 것이다. 즉, 우리는 불안정한 자급자족에서 더 안전한 서로 간의 상호의존으로 옮겨간다는 것이다. 일주일에 40시간 동안 다른 사람들의 필요를 충족시키는 것, 즉 우리가 직업이라고 부르는 것에 집중하여, 여러분은 (잠자는 56시간은 빼고) 나머지 72시간을 다른 사람들이 제공하는 서비스에 의지해 보낼 수 있다. 혁신은 아주 짧은 시간 일하고도 전등을 한 시간 켤 수 있는 여유를 갖게 해주었는데, 이는 그리 멀지 않은 과거에 많은 인류가 했던 것처럼 여러분이 그저 등 하나를 켜기 위해 참기름이나 양의 지방을 모으고 정제해 그 등을 스스로 만들어야 했다면 하루 종일의 노고가 들었을 만큼의 빛을 제공해 준다.

Why? 왜 정답일까?

생산이 꾸준히 전문화되고 소비가 꾸준히 다양해지는 과정에서 인간은 각자 맡은 일에 집중하는 동시에 타인의 서비스에도 의존해 살게 된다(By concentrating on serving other people's needs for forty hours a week ~ you can spend ~ relying on the services provided to you by other people.)고 한다. 즉 각자 세분화된 역할을 수행하는 사람들이 '서로 의존해가며' 삶이 변화되는 과정이 곧 혁신이라는 것이다. 따라서 빈칸에 들어갈 말로 가장 적절한 것은 ② '사람들이 서로를 위해 일할 수 있게 하는 것'이다.

- **innovation** ⓝ 혁신
- **specialize** ⓥ 전문화하다
- **unstable** ⓐ 불안정한
- **mutual** ⓐ 상호의
- **concentrate on** ~에 집중하다
- **serve one's needs** ~의 필요를 충족하다, ~에게 도움이 되다
- **rely on** ~에 의존하다
- **afford** ⓥ ~할 여유가 있다
- **refine** ⓥ 정제하다
- **burn up** 태우다
- **commercialize** ⓥ 상업화하다
- **steadily** ⓐ 꾸준히
- **diversify** ⓥ 다양화하다
- **self-sufficiency** ⓝ 자급자족
- **interdependence** ⓝ 상호 의존성
- **a fraction of a second** 아주 짧은 시간
- **quantity** ⓝ 양
- **lamb** ⓝ (어린) 양
- **personalize** ⓥ 개인의 필요에 맞추다

구문 풀이

9행 Innovation has made it possible to work for a fraction of a second in
가목적어 / 진목적어
order to be able to afford to turn on an electric lamp for an hour, providing the
분사구문
quantity of light [that would have required a whole day's work if you had to make
선행사 / ~했을 것이다
it yourself by collecting and refining sesame oil or lamb fat to burn in a simple
lamp, as much of humanity did in the not so distant past]. [ ]: 형용사절
대동사(=made it by themselves by collecting and refining ~)

★★ 문제 해결 꿀~팁 ★★

▶ 많이 틀린 이유는?
Innovation을 보고 creatively가 포함된 ③을 고른다거나, more specialized를 보고 personalized가 포함된 ④를 고를 수 있지만, 모두 글의 핵심 내용과 관련이 없다. 이 글의 주제는 사람들이 모든 일을 혼자 해결하던 시대에 비해 점점 각자 전문화된 일을 맡으며 각자 자기 분야가 아닌 일에 대해서는 '서로 의존할 수밖에 없게 된다'는 것이다.

▶ 문제 해결 방법은?
빈칸 뒤의 핵심어인 mutual interdependence를 재진술한 표현이 정답이다.

33 유혹을 극복하는 방법   정답률 51% | 정답 ③

다음 빈칸에 들어갈 말로 가장 적절한 것을 고르시오.
① letting go of all-or-nothing mindset – 양자택일의 사고방식을 버림
② finding reasons why you want to change – 왜 변하고 싶은지 이유를 찾음
✓③ locking yourself out of your temptations – 여러분 자신을 유혹으로부터 차단함
④ building a plan and tracking your progress – 계획을 세워 진행 상황을 추적함
⑤ focusing on breaking one bad habit at a time – 한 번에 하나의 나쁜 습관을 깨는 데 집중함

If you've ever made a poor choice, / you might be interested / in learning how to break that habit.
여러분이 한 번이라도 좋지 못한 선택을 한 적이 있다면, / 여러분은 관심이 있을지도 모른다. / 그런 습관을 깨는 방법을 배우는 데
One great way / to trick your brain into doing so / is to sign a "Ulysses Contract."
한 가지 좋은 방법은 / 여러분의 뇌를 속여 그렇게 하는 / 'Ulysses 계약'에 서명하는 것이다.
The name of this life tip / comes from the Greek myth about Ulysses, a captain / whose ship sailed past the island of the Sirens, / a tribe of dangerous women / who lured victims to their death with their irresistible songs.
이 인생에 대한 조언의 이름은 / Ulysses에 관한 그리스 신화에서 유래되었는데, / 그는 선장이었다. / 그의 배가 사이렌의 섬을 지나던 / 위험한 여성 부족인 / 저항할 수 없는 노래를 통해 희생자들을 죽음으로 유혹
Knowing that he would otherwise be unable to resist, / Ulysses instructed his crew / to stuff their ears with cotton / and tie him to the ship's mast / to prevent him from turning their ship towards the Sirens.
그렇게 하지 않으면 저항할 수 없다는 것을 알고, / Ulysses는 선원들에게 지시했다. / 귀를 솜으로 막고 / 자신을 배의 돛대에 묶으라고 / 그가 사이렌 쪽으로 배를 돌리지 못하게 막기 위해
It worked for him / and you can do the same thing / by locking yourself out of your temptations.
그것은 그에게 효과가 있었고, / 여러분은 똑같은 일을 할 수 있다. / 여러분 자신을 유혹으로부터 차단함으로써
For example, / if you want to stay off your cellphone / and concentrate on your work, / delete the apps that distract you / or ask a friend to change your password!
예를 들어, / 만약 여러분이 휴대폰을 멀리하고 / 일에 집중하고 싶다면, / 여러분의 주의를 산만하게 하는 앱들을 삭제하거나, / 친구에게 여러분의 비밀번호를 바꿔달라고 요청하라!

여러분이 한 번이라도 좋지 못한 선택을 한 적이 있다면, 그런 습관을 깨는 방법을 배우는 데 관심이 있을지도 모른다. 여러분의 뇌를 속여 그렇게 하는 한 가지 좋은 방법은 'Ulysses 계약'에 서명하는 것이다. 이 인생에 대한 조언의 이름은 Ulysses에 관한 그리스 신화에서 유래되었는데, 그는 저항할 수 없는 노래를 통해 희생자들을 죽음으로 유혹한 위험한 여성 부족인 사이렌의 섬을 지나던 배의 선장이었다. Ulysses는 그렇게 하지 않으면 저항할 수 없다는

것을 알고, 선원들에게 귀를 솜으로 막고 자신을 배의 돛대에 묶게 시켜 자신이 사이렌 쪽으로 배를 돌리지 못하게 했다. 그것은 그에게 효과가 있었고, 여러분은 여러분 자신을 유혹으로부터 차단함으로써 똑같은 일을 할 수 있다. 예를 들어, 만약 여러분이 휴대폰을 멀리하고 일에 집중하고 싶다면, 여러분의 주의를 산만하게 하는 앱들을 삭제하거나, 친구에게 여러분의 비밀번호를 바꿔달라고 요청하라!

Why? 왜 정답일까?

빈칸 앞에서 신화 속 인물 Ulysses는 선원들을 시켜 자기 몸을 돛대에 묶게 해서 사이렌의 노래에 유혹되려는 자기 자신을 막았다고 한다. 빈칸에는 이러한 Ulysses의 조치를 일반화할 수 있는 표현이 필요하므로, 답으로 가장 적절한 것은 ③ '여러분 자신을 유혹으로부터 차단함'이다. 일에 집중하기 위해 일에 도움이 안 되는 앱을 지우거나 친구를 통해 비밀번호를 바꾸라는 내용 또한 '유혹에 넘어가지 않기'를 위한 예시에 해당한다.

- **break a habit** 습관을 깨다
- **myth** ⓝ 신화
- **lure** ⓥ 유혹하다
- **instruct** ⓥ 지시하다, 가르치다
- **tie** ⓥ 묶다
- **distract** ⓥ 주의를 분산시키다, 산만하게 하다
- **all-or-nothing** ⓐ 양자택일의, 이것 아니면 저것인
- **trick A into B** A를 속여 B하게 하다
- **sail** ⓥ 항해하다
- **irresistible** ⓐ 저항할 수 없는
- **stuff** ⓥ (속을) 채우다, 막다
- **mast** ⓝ 돛대
- **let go of** ~을 놔주다, 내려놓다
- **temptation** ⓝ 유혹

구문 풀이

3행 The name of this life tip comes from the Greek myth about Ulysses, (a captain whose ship sailed past the island of the Sirens), {a tribe of dangerous women who lured victims to their death with their irresistible songs}.
( ): Ulysses와 동격
{ }: the Sirens와 동격

★★★ 등급을 가르는 문제!

34 생물의 진화 방향을 이끄는 실내 공간과 생활   정답률 46% | 정답 ③

다음 빈칸에 들어갈 말로 가장 적절한 것을 고르시오. [3점]
① produce chemicals to protect themselves
스스로를 보호하고자 화학 물질을 만들어낼
② become extinct with the destroyed habitats
파괴된 서식지와 함께 멸종할
✓③ evolve the traits they need to thrive indoors
실내에서 번성하기 위해 자신에게 필요한 특성들을 진화시킬
④ compete with outside organisms to find their prey
먹잇감을 찾고자 야외 생물들과 경쟁할
⑤ break the boundaries between wildlife and humans
야생 종과 인간 사이의 경계를 무너뜨릴

Our homes aren't just ecosystems, / they're unique ones, / hosting species / that are adapted to indoor environments / and pushing evolution in new directions.
우리의 집은 단순한 생태계가 아니라 / 그것은 독특한 곳이며, / 종들을 수용하고 / 실내 환경에 적응된 / 새로운 방향으로 진화를 밀어붙인다.
Indoor microbes, insects, and rats / have all evolved the ability / to survive our chemical attacks, / developing resistance to antibacterials, insecticides, and poisons.
실내 미생물, 곤충, 그리고 쥐들은 / 모두 능력을 진화시켰다. / 우리의 화학적 공격에서 살아남을 수 있는 / 항균제, 살충제, 독에 대한 내성을 키우면서
German cockroaches are known / to have developed a distaste for glucose, / which is commonly used as bait in roach traps.
독일 바퀴벌레는 알려져 있는데, / 포도당에 대한 혐오감을 발달시킨 것으로 / 이것은 바퀴벌레 덫에서 미끼로 흔히 사용된다.
Some indoor insects, / which have fewer opportunities to feed / than their outdoor counterparts, / seem to have developed the ability / to survive when food is limited.
일부 실내 곤충은 / 먹이를 잡아먹을 기회가 더 적은 / 야외에 있는 상대방에 비해 / 능력을 발달시킨 것으로 보인다. / 먹이가 제한적일 때 생존할 수 있는
Dunn and other ecologists have suggested / that as the planet becomes more developed and more urban, / more species will evolve the traits / they need to thrive indoors.
Dunn과 다른 생태학자들은 말했는데, / 지구가 점점 더 발전되고 도시화되면서, / 더 많은 종들이 특성들을 진화시킬 것이라고 / 실내에서 번성하기 위해 자신에게 필요한
Over a long enough time period, / indoor living could drive our evolution, too.
충분히 긴 시간에 걸쳐, / 실내 생활은 또한 우리의 진화를 이끌 수 있었다.
Perhaps my indoorsy self represents the future of humanity.
아마도 실내 생활을 좋아하는 나의 모습은 인류의 미래를 대변할 것이다.

우리의 집은 단순한 생태계가 아니라 독특한 곳이며, 실내 환경에 적응된 종들을 수용하고 새로운 방향으로 진화를 밀어붙인다. 실내 미생물, 곤충, 그리고 쥐들은 모두 항균제, 살충제, 독에 대한 내성을 키우면서 우리의 화학적 공격에서 살아남을 수 있는 능력을 진화시켰다. 독일 바퀴벌레는 바퀴벌레 덫에서 미끼로 흔히 사용되는 포도당에 대한 혐오감을 발달시킨 것으로 알려져 있다. 야외에 있는 상대방에 비해 먹이를 잡아먹을 기회가 더 적은 일부 실내 곤충은 먹이가 제한적일 때 생존할 수 있는 능력을 발달시킨 것으로 보인다. Dunn과 다른 생태학자들은 지구가 점점 더 발전되고 도시화되면서, 더 많은 종들이 실내에서 번성하기 위해 자신에게 필요한 특성들을 진화시킬 것이라고 말했다. 충분히 긴 시간에 걸쳐, 실내 생활은 또한 우리의 진화를 이끌 수 있었다. 아마도 실내 생활을 좋아하는 나의 모습은 인류의 미래를 대변할 것이다.

Why? 왜 정답일까?

첫 문장과 빈칸 뒤의 문장에서 집, 즉 실내 공간이 우리 진화를 이끌어 간다(indoor living could drive our evolution)는 주제를 반복하여 제시한다. 따라서 빈칸에 들어갈 말로 가장 적절한 것은 우리가 실내 생활에 필요한 방향으로 발전해 간다는 의미의 ③ '실내에서 번성하기 위해 자신에게 필요한 특성들을 진화시킬'이다.

- **host** ⓥ (손님을) 접대하다, 수용하다, (행사를) 주최하다
- **microbe** ⓝ 미생물
- **antibacterial** ⓐ 항균성의 ⓝ 항균제
- **cockroach** ⓝ 바퀴벌레
- **glucose** ⓝ 포도당
- **counterpart** ⓝ 상대방, 대응물
- **represent** ⓥ 표현하다, 나타내다
- **habitat** ⓝ 서식지
- **resistance** ⓝ 내성, 저항력
- **insecticide** ⓝ 살충제
- **distaste** ⓝ 혐오
- **bait** ⓝ 미끼
- **ecologist** ⓝ 생태학자
- **extinct** ⓐ 멸종한
- **prey** ⓝ 먹잇감

5행 German cockroaches are known to have developed a distaste for
(be known+to have p.p. : ~했다고 알려지다(완료부정사))
선행사
glucose, which is commonly used as bait in roach traps.
계속적 용법(보충 설명)

★★ 문제 해결 꿀~팁 ★★

▶ 많이 틀린 이유는?
chemical attacks 등 지엽적 소재만 보면 ①을 답으로 고르기 쉽다. 하지만 풀이의 핵심은 생태계의 생명체들이 '어떤 방향으로' 진화하도록 유도되어 왔는지를 파악하는 데 있다.
▶ 문제 해결 방법은?
빈칸 뒤를 보면 '실내 생활이 우리 진화를 이끌 수 있었다(indoor living could drive our evolution)'는 결론이 나온다. 이 결론과 동일한 말이 빈칸에도 들어갈 것이다.

---

35 시 쓰기의 이점   정답률 62% | 정답 ④

다음 글에서 전체 흐름과 관계 없는 문장은?

Developing a personal engagement with poetry / brings a number of benefits to you / as an individual, / in both a personal and a professional capacity.
시와의 개인적 관계를 발전시키는 것은 / 여러분에게 많은 이점을 가져다준다. / 한 개인으로서의 / 개인적인 능력과 전문적인 능력 모두에서
① Writing poetry has been shown / to have physical and mental benefits, / with expressive writing found to improve immune system and lung function, / diminish psychological distress, / and enhance relationships.
시 쓰기는 알려져 왔다. / 신체적, 정신적 이점을 지닌 것으로 / 표현적 글쓰기가 면역 체계와 폐 기능을 향상시킨다고 밝혀지면서 / 심리적 고통을 줄인다고 / 그리고 관계를 증진시킨다고
② Poetry has long been used / to aid different mental health needs, / develop empathy, / and reconsider our relationship with both natural and built environments.
시는 오랫동안 사용되었다. / 여러 정신 건강에 필요한 것들을 지원하고, / 공감 능력을 개발하고, / 자연 환경과 만들어진 환경 둘 다와의 관계를 재고하기 위해
③ Poetry is also / an incredibly effective way of actively targeting the cognitive development period, / improving your productivity and scientific creativity in the process.
시는 또한 / 인지 발달 시기를 적극적으로 겨냥하는 놀랍도록 효과적인 방법이며, / 그 과정에서 여러분의 생산성과 과학적 창의력을 향상시킨다.
✓ Poetry is considered / to be an easy and useful means of expressing emotions, / but you fall into frustration / when you realize its complexity.
시는 여겨지지만, / 감정을 표현하는 쉽고 유용한 수단이라고 / 여러분은 좌절에 빠진다. / 여러분이 그것의 복잡성을 알면
⑤ In short, / poetry has a lot to offer, / if you give it the opportunity to do so.
간단히 말해서, / 시는 많은 것을 제공해줄 수 있다. / 여러분이 시에게 그럴 기회를 준다면

시와의 개인적 관계를 발전시키는 것은 개인적인 능력과 전문적인 능력 모두에서 한 개인으로서의 여러분에게 많은 이점을 가져다준다. ① 표현적 글쓰기가 면역 체계와 폐 기능을 향상시키고, 심리적 고통을 줄이고, 관계를 증진시킨다고 밝혀지면서, 시 쓰기는 신체적, 정신적 이점을 지닌 것으로 알려져 왔다. ② 시는 여러 정신 건강에 필요한 것들을 지원하고, 공감 능력을 개발하고, 자연 환경과 만들어진 환경 둘 다와의 관계를 재고하기 위해 오랫동안 사용되었다. ③ 시는 또한 인지 발달 시기를 적극적으로 겨냥하는 놀랍도록 효과적인 방법이며, 그 과정에서 여러분의 생산성과 과학적 창의력을 향상시킨다. ④ 시는 감정을 표현하는 쉽고 유용한 수단으로 여겨지지만, 여러분은 그것의 복잡성을 알면 좌절에 빠진다. ⑤ 간단히 말해서, 여러분이 그럴 기회를 준다면 시는 많은 것을 제공해줄 수 있다.

Why? 왜 정답일까?

시 쓰기의 이점을 두루 열거하는 글인데, ④는 시의 복잡함을 알면 우리가 좌절에 빠질 수 있다는 내용이므로 흐름상 어색하다. 따라서 전체 흐름과 관계 없는 문장은 ④이다.

- engagement ⓝ 관계, 참여
- capacity ⓝ 능력, 역량
- lung ⓝ 폐
- distress ⓝ 고통
- empathy ⓝ 공감, 감정 이입
- cognitive ⓐ 인지적인
- frustration ⓝ 좌절
- poetry ⓝ 시
- immune system 면역 체계
- diminish ⓥ 줄이다, 감소시키다
- enhance ⓥ 향상시키다
- incredibly 젣 믿을 수 없을 정도로, 놀랍도록
- productivity ⓝ 생산성
- complexity ⓝ 복잡성

구문 풀이

1행 Developing a personal engagement with poetry brings a number of
동명사구 주어   동사(단수)
benefits to you as an individual, in both a personal and a professional capacity.
「a number of + 복수 명사 : 많은 ~」

---

36 노동의 자동화로 인한 일자리 위기   정답률 58% | 정답 ③

주어진 글 다음에 이어질 글의 순서로 가장 적절한 것을 고르시오.

① (A) - (C) - (B)   ② (B) - (A) - (C)
✓ (B) - (C) - (A)   ④ (C) - (A) - (B)
⑤ (C) - (B) - (A)

Things are changing.
상황이 변하고 있다.
It has been reported / that 42 percent of jobs in Canada / are at risk, / and 62 percent of jobs in America / will be in danger / due to advances in automation.
보도되었다. / 캐나다의 일자리 중 42퍼센트가 / 위기에 처했으며, / 미국의 일자리 중 62퍼센트가 / 위기에 처할 것이라고 / 자동화의 발전으로 인해
(B) You might say / that the numbers seem a bit unrealistic, / but the threat is real.
여러분은 말할지 모른다. / 그 숫자들이 약간 비현실적으로 보인다고 / 하지만 그 위험은 현실이다.
One fast food franchise has a robot / that can flip a burger in ten seconds.
한 패스트푸드 체인점은 로봇을 가지고 있다. / 10초 안에 버거 하나를 뒤집을 수 있는

It is just a simple task / but the robot could replace an entire crew.
그것은 단지 단순한 일일 뿐이지만, / 그 로봇은 전체 직원을 대체할 수도 있다.
(C) Highly skilled jobs are also at risk.
고도로 숙련된 직업들 또한 위기에 처해 있다.
A supercomputer, / for instance, / can suggest available treatments / for specific illnesses / in an automated way, / drawing on the body of medical research and data on diseases.
슈퍼컴퓨터는 / 예를 들면, / 이용 가능한 치료법을 제안할 수 있다. / 특정한 질병들에 대해 / 자동화된 방식으로 / 질병에 대한 방대한 양의 의학 연구와 데이터를 이용하여
(A) However, / what's difficult to automate / is the ability / to creatively solve problems.
하지만, / 자동화하기 어려운 것은 / 능력이다. / 문제를 창의적으로 해결하는
Whereas workers in "doing" roles / can be replaced by robots, / the role of creatively solving problems / is more dependent on an irreplaceable individual.
'하는' 역할의 노동자들은 / 로봇들에 의해 대체될 수 있는 반면에, / 창의적으로 문제를 해결하는 역할은 / 대체 불가능한 개인에 더 의존한다.

상황이 변하고 있다. 캐나다의 일자리 중 42퍼센트가 위기에 처했으며, 미국의 일자리 중 62퍼센트가 자동화의 발전으로 인해 위기에 처할 것이라고 보도되었다.

(B) 여러분은 그 숫자들이 약간 비현실적으로 보인다고 말할지 모르지만, 그 위험은 현실이다. 한 패스트푸드 체인점은 10초 안에 버거 하나를 뒤집을 수 있다. 그것은 단지 단순한 일일 뿐이지만, 로봇은 전체 직원을 대체할 수도 있다.

(C) 고도로 숙련된 직업들 또한 위기에 처해 있다. 예를 들면, 슈퍼컴퓨터는 질병에 대한 방대한 양의 의학 연구와 데이터를 이용하여 특정한 질병들에 대해 이용 가능한 치료법을 자동화된 방식으로 제안할 수 있다.

(A) 하지만, 자동화하기 어려운 것은 문제를 창의적으로 해결하는 능력이다. '(기계적인 일을) 하는' 역할의 노동자들은 로봇들에 의해 대체될 수 있는 반면에, 창의적으로 문제를 해결하는 역할은 대체 불가능한 개인에 더 의존한다.

Why? 왜 정답일까?

노동 시장의 상황이 변하고 있다며 경각심을 일깨우는 주어진 글 뒤로, 주어진 글에 언급된 수치들을 the numbers로 지칭하는 (B)가 연결된다. (B)에서는 '이 수치들'이 비현실적인 것 같아도 사실적임을 보충 설명하는데, (C)는 여기에 이어 고도로 숙련된 직군 또한(also) 위기에 처해 있다고 설명한다. 마지막으로 상황을 반전시키는(However) (A)는 자동화하기 어려운 대상으로 인간의 창의적 문제 해결 능력을 언급한다. 따라서 글의 순서로 가장 적절한 것은 ③ '(B) - (C) - (A)'이다.

- at risk 위험에 처한
- replace ⓥ 대체하다
- unrealistic ⓐ 비현실적인
- crew ⓝ (전체) 직원, 승무원
- automation ⓝ 자동화
- irreplaceable ⓐ 대체할 수 없는
- flip ⓥ 뒤집다
- draw on ~을 이용하다

구문 풀이

1행 It has been reported [that 42 percent of jobs in Canada are at risk, and
가주어
62 percent of jobs in America will be in danger due to advances in automation].
[ ] : 진주어

---

37 너도밤나무의 광합성   정답률 52% | 정답 ⑤

주어진 글 다음에 이어질 글의 순서로 가장 적절한 것을 고르시오. [3점]

① (A) - (C) - (B)   ② (B) - (A) - (C)
③ (B) - (C) - (A)   ④ (C) - (A) - (B)
✓ (C) - (B) - (A)

Each beech tree grows in a particular location / and soil conditions can vary greatly / in just a few yards.
각각의 너도밤나무는 고유한 장소에서 자라고 / 토양의 조건들은 크게 달라질 수 있다. / 단 몇 야드 안에서도
The soil can have a great deal of water / or almost no water.
토양은 물이 많거나 / 거의 없을 수도 있다.
It can be full of nutrients or not.
그것은 영양분이 가득할 수도 있고 아닐 수도 있다.
(C) Accordingly, / each tree grows more quickly or more slowly, / and produces more or less sugar, / and thus you would expect every tree / to be photosynthesizing at a different rate.
이에 따라, / 각 나무는 더 빨리 혹은 더 느리게 자라고 / 더 많거나 더 적은 당분을 생산하는데, / 그래서 여러분은 모든 나무가 ~할 거라고 기대할 것이다. / 다른 정도로 광합성을 할 거라고
(B) However, the rate is the same.
그러나 그 정도는 동일하다.
Whether they are thick or thin, / all the trees of the same species / are using light / to produce the same amount of sugar per leaf.
그것들이 굵든 가늘든 간에, / 같은 종의 모든 나무들은 / 빛을 사용하고 있다. / 이파리당 같은 양의 당을 생산하기 위해
Some trees have plenty of sugar / and some have less, / but the trees equalize this difference between them / by transferring sugar.
어떤 나무들은 충분한 당을 지니고 / 어떤 것들은 더 적게 지니지만, / 나무들은 그들 사이의 이 차이를 균등하게 한다. / 당을 전달하여
(A) This is taking place underground through the roots.
이것은 뿌리를 통해 지하에서 일어나고 있다.
Whoever has an abundance of sugar / hands some over; / whoever is running short / gets help.
풍부한 당을 가진 나무가 누구든 간에 / 일부를 건네주고, / 부족해지는 나무는 누구든 간에 / 도움을 받는다.
Their network acts as a system / to make sure that no trees fall too far behind.
그들의 연결망은 시스템 역할을 한다. / 그 어떤 나무도 너무 뒤처지지 않는 것을 확실히 하기 위한

각각의 너도밤나무는 고유한 장소에서 자라고 토양의 조건들은 단 몇 야드 안에서도 크게 달라질 수 있다. 토양은 물이 많거나 거의 없을 수도 있다. 영양분이 가득할 수도 있고 아닐 수도 있다.

(C) 이에 따라, 각 나무는 더 빨리 혹은 더 느리게 자라고 더 많거나 더 적은 당분을 생산하는데, 그래서 여러분은 모든 나무가 다른 정도로 광합성을 할 거라고 기대할 것이다.

(B) 그러나 그 정도는 동일하다. 굵든 가늘든 간에, 같은 종의 모든 나무들은 빛을 사용하여 이파리당 같은 양의 당을 생산하고 있다. 어떤 나무들은 충분한 당을 지니고 어떤 것들은 더 적게 지니지만, 나무들은 당을 전달하여 그들 사이의 이 차이를 균등하게 한다.

(A) 이것은 뿌리들을 통해 지하에서 일어나고 있다. 풍부한 당을 가진 나무가 누구든 간에 일부를 건네주고, 부족해지는 나무는 누구든 간에 도움을 받는다. 그들의 연결망은 그 어떤 나무도 너무 뒤쳐지지 않는 것을 확실히 하기 위한 시스템 역할을 한다.

Why? 왜 정답일까?

너도밤나무가 자라는 토양 조건이 상이할 수 있다는 내용의 주어진 글 뒤로, (C)는 그래서 (Accordingly) 광합성 정도가 나무마다 다를 것이라는 추측이 나올 수 있다고 한다. However로 시작하는 (B)는 사실은 그렇지 않다고 하며, 나무들끼리 서로 당을 주고받기 때문에 차이가 조절된다는 설명을 이어 간다. (A)는 이러한 '주고받음'이 뿌리를 통해 이뤄진다는 보충 설명과 함께, 나무끼리의 연결망이 각 나무에게 도움이 된다는 결론을 제시한다. 따라서 글의 순서로 가장 적절한 것은 ⑤ '(C) – (B) – (A)'이다.

- **beech tree** 너도밤나무
- **abundance** ⓝ 풍부함
- **run short** 부족해지다
- **equalize** ⓥ 동등하게 하다
- **photosynthesize** ⓥ 광합성하다
- **a great deal of** 많은
- **hand over** 건네주다
- **fall behind** 뒤처지다
- **transfer** ⓥ 전달하다

구문 풀이

5행 [Whoever has an abundance of sugar] hands some over; [whoever is running short] gets help.
주어1 / 동사1(단수) / 주어2 / 동사2(단수) / [ ]: 복합관계대명사절(~하는 누구든지)

★★★ 등급을 가르는 문제!

38 언어와 사고의 관계 정답률 42% | 정답 ⑤

글의 흐름으로 보아, 주어진 문장이 들어가기에 가장 적절한 곳을 고르시오. [3점]

Should we use language to understand mind / or mind to understand language?
우리는 사고를 이해하기 위해 언어를 사용해야 할까, / 아니면 언어를 이해하기 위해 사고를 사용해야 할까?

① Analytic philosophy historically assumes / that language is basic / and that mind would make sense / if proper use of language was appreciated.
분석 철학은 역사적으로 가정한다. / 언어가 기본이고 / 그 사고가 이치에 맞을 것이라고 / 적절한 언어 사용이 제대로 인식된다면

② Modern cognitive science, / however, / rightly judges / that language is just one aspect of mind / of great importance in human beings / but not fundamental to all kinds of thinking.
현대 인지 과학은 / 그러나 / 당연히 판단한다. / 언어가 사고의 한 측면일 뿐 / 인간에게 매우 중요한 / 하지만 모든 종류의 사고에 근본적이지는 않다고

③ Countless species of animals / manage to navigate the world, / solve problems, / and learn / without using language, / through brain mechanisms / that are largely preserved in the minds of humans.
수많은 종의 동물들이 / 세계를 향해하고, / 문제를 해결하고, / 학습해낸다. / 언어를 사용하지 않고 / 두뇌의 메커니즘을 통해 / 인간의 사고 속에 대체로 보존된

④ There is no reason to assume / that language is fundamental to mental operations.
가정할 이유는 없다. / 언어가 정신 작용의 기본이라고

☑ Nevertheless, / language is enormously important in human life / and contributes largely to our ability / to cooperate with each other / in dealing with the world.
그럼에도 불구하고, / 언어는 인간의 삶에서 매우 중요하며 / 우리의 능력에 상당히 기여한다. / 서로 협력하는 / 세계를 다루는 데 있어서

Our species *homo sapiens* / has been astonishingly successful, / which depended in part on language, / first as an effective contributor / to collaborative problem solving / and much later, as collective memory / through written records.
우리 종족인 호모 사피엔스는 / 놀라운 성공을 거두어 왔는데, / 이것은 언어에 부분적으로 의존했다. / 처음에는 효과적인 기여 요소로서, / 협력적인 문제 해결로 / 그리고 훨씬 나중에는 집단 기억으로서 / 글로 쓰인 기록을 통한

우리는 사고를 이해하기 위해 언어를 사용해야 할까, 아니면 언어를 이해하기 위해 사고를 사용해야 할까? ① 분석 철학은 언어가 기본이고 적절한 언어 사용이 제대로 인식된다면 그 사고가 이치에 맞을 것이라고 역사적으로 가정한다. ② 그러나 현대 인지 과학은 언어가 인간에게 매우 중요한 사고의 한 측면일 뿐 모든 종류의 사고에 근본적이지는 않다고 당연히 판단한다. ③ 수많은 종의 동물들이 인간의 사고 속에 대체로 보존된 두뇌의 메커니즘을 통해 언어를 사용하지 않고 세계를 향해하고, 문제를 해결하고, 학습해낸다. ④ 언어가 정신 작용의 기본이라고 가정할 이유는 없다. ⑤ 그럼에도 불구하고, 언어는 인간의 삶에서 매우 중요하며 세계를 다루는 데 있어서 서로 협력하는 우리의 능력에 상당히 기여한다. 우리 종족인 호모 사피엔스는 놀라운 성공을 거두어 왔는데, 이것은 처음에는 협력적인 문제 해결에 효과적인 기여 요소로서, 그리고 훨씬 나중에는 글로 쓰인 기록을 통한 집단 기억으로서 언어에 부분적으로 의존했다.

Why? 왜 정답일까?

언어가 먼저인지 사고가 먼저인지 논하는 글로, 분석 철학과 현대 인지 과학의 시각이 대비되고 있다. ⑤ 앞까지는 주로 현대 인지 과학의 관점에서 언어가 중요하기는 해도 근간은 사고력에 있다는 내용이 제시된다. 하지만 주어진 문장은 언어가 매우 중요함을 강조하며 특히 인간의 협동 능력에 크게 기여한다는 내용으로 흐름의 반전을 이끈다. 이어서 ⑤ 뒤의 문장은 주어진 문장에서 언급한 '협력'과 관련해 언어가 중요했다는 내용을 다시금 설명한다. 따라서 주어진 문장이 들어가기에 가장 적절한 곳은 ⑤이다.

- **enormously** ⓐⓓ 대단히, 거대하게
- **deal with** ~을 다루다, ~에 대처하다
- **philosophy** ⓝ 철학
- **make sense** 이치에 맞다
- **fundamental** ⓐ 근본적인
- **navigate** ⓥ 향해하다
- **contribute to** ~에 기여하다
- **analytic** ⓐ 분석적인
- **historically** ⓐⓓ 역사적으로
- **appreciate** ⓥ 제대로 인식하다
- **countless** ⓐ 무수히 많은
- **astonishingly** ⓐⓓ 놀랍도록

구문 풀이

13행 There is no reason to assume [that language is fundamental to mental operations]. [ ]: to assume의 목적어

★★ 문제 해결 꿀~팁 ★★

▶ 많이 틀린 이유는?
④ 앞뒤로 논리적 공백이 발생하는지 점검해 보면, 먼저 ④ 앞은 언어가 없는 동물도 세계를 향해하고

문제를 해결하는 데 문제가 없다는 내용이다. 한편 ④ 뒤는 그렇기에 언어가 정신 작용의 근간이라고 추정할 근거가 없다는 내용이다. 즉 ④ 앞을 근거로 ④ 뒤와 같은 결론을 내릴 수 있는 것이므로, ④의 위치에서 논리적 공백은 발생하지 않는다.

▶ 문제 해결 방법은?
⑤ 앞은 언어가 정신 작용에 근본적이라고 추정할 필요는 없다는 내용인데, ⑤ 뒤는 호모 사피엔스의 성공에 언어가 부분적으로 중요한 기여를 했다는 내용이다. 즉 ⑤ 앞뒤가 서로 반대되는 내용이므로, 사이에 적절한 역접어(Nevertheless)가 있어야 흐름이 자연스러워진다.

---

39 온도와 화학적 성질이 다른 물잔 섞기 정답률 48% | 정답 ③

글의 흐름으로 보아, 주어진 문장이 들어가기에 가장 적절한 곳을 고르시오.

Take two glasses of water.
물 두 잔을 가져오라.

Put a little bit of orange juice into one / and a little bit of lemon juice into the other.
하나의 잔에는 약간의 오렌지주스를 넣고, / 다른 잔에는 약간의 레몬주스를 넣으라.

① What you have / are essentially two glasses of water / but with a completely different chemical makeup.
여러분이 가지고 있는 것은 / 본질적으로 물 두 잔이다. / 완전히 다른 화학적 성질을 지닌

② If we take the glass containing orange juice / and heat it, / we will still have two different glasses of water / with different chemical makeups, / but now they will also have different temperatures.
만약 우리가 오렌지주스가 든 잔을 가져와서 / 그것을 가열한다면, / 우리는 여전히 서로 다른 물 두 잔을 가지고 있을 것이지만, / 다른 화학적 성질을 지닌 / 이제 그것들은 또한 다른 온도를 가질 것이다.

☑ If we could magically remove the glasses, / we would find / the two water bodies would not mix well.
만약 우리가 마법처럼 그 유리잔들을 없앨 수 있다면, / 우리는 알게 될 것이다. / 두 액체가 잘 섞이지 않는다는 것을

Perhaps they would mix a little / where they met; / however, / they would remain separate / because of their different chemical makeups and temperatures.
어쩌면 그것들은 조금 섞일 것이다. / 그것들이 접한 부분에서 / 하지만, / 이것들은 분리된 상태로 남아 있을 것이다. / 다른 화학적 성질과 온도로 인해

④ The warmer water would float / on the surface of the cold water / because of its lighter weight.
더 따뜻한 물은 떠 있을 것이다. / 찬물의 표면에 / 그것의 무게가 더 가볍기 때문에

⑤ In the ocean we have bodies of water / that differ in temperature and salt content; / for this reason, / they do not mix.
바다에는 수역(물줄기)들이 있다. / 온도와 염분 함량이 다른 / 이러한 이유로, / 그것들은 섞이지 않는다.

물 두 잔을 가져오라. 하나의 잔에는 약간의 오렌지주스를 넣고, 다른 잔에는 약간의 레몬주스를 넣으라. ① 여러분이 가지고 있는 것은 본질적으로 물 두 잔이지만 둘은 완전히 다른 화학적 성질을 지녔다. ② 만약 우리가 오렌지주스가 든 잔을 가져와서 가열한다면, 우리는 여전히 다른 화학적 성질을 지닌 서로 다른 물 두 잔을 가지고 있을 것이지만, 이제 그것들은 또한 다른 온도를 가질 것이다. ③ 만약 우리가 마법처럼 그 유리잔들을 없앨 수 있다면, 우리는 두 액체가 잘 섞이지 않는다는 것을 알게 될 것이다. 어쩌면 그것들은 서로 접한 부분에서 조금 섞일 것이다. 하지만, 이것들은 다른 화학적 성질과 온도로 인해 분리된 상태로 남아 있을 것이다. ④ 더 따뜻한 물은 무게가 더 가볍기 때문에 찬물의 표면에 떠 있을 것이다. ⑤ 바다에는 온도와 염분이 다른 수역(물줄기)들이 있다. 이러한 이유로, 그것들은 섞이지 않는다.

Why? 왜 정답일까?

③ 앞까지는 물 두 잔에 각각 오렌지주스와 레몬주스를 섞어 성질을 달리하고, 한쪽에만 약간의 열을 더해 온도 또한 달리하는 과정을 설명한다. 여기에 이어 주어진 문장은 만일 이 상황에서 유리잔을 제거해보면 두 액체가 서로 잘 섞이지 않는다는 사실을 알게 된다고 설명한다. ③ 뒤는 주어진 문장에 이어 두 액체가 서로 화학적 성질과 온도가 달라 섞이지 않는다고 설명한다. 따라서 주어진 문장이 들어가기에 가장 적절한 곳은 ③이다. 글은 원칙적으로 일반적 진술에서 구체적 진술로 나아가므로, ③에서 주어진 문장이 '두 액체가 안 섞인다'는 일반적 사실을 제시해야 ③ 뒤에서 '왜 안 섞이는지'에 대한 구체적 진술이 자연스럽게 이어질 수 있음을 유념해 둔다.

- **essentially** ⓐⓓ 본질적으로
- **separate** ⓐ 분리된
- **content** ⓝ 함량
- **makeup** ⓝ 구성
- **float** ⓥ 뜨다

구문 풀이

1행 If we could magically remove the glasses, we would find the two water bodies would not mix well.
「if + 주어 + 과거 동사 ~ / 주어 + 조동사 과거 + 동사원형: 가정법 과거」

---

40 성찰적 일기 쓰기의 긍정적 효과 정답률 52% | 정답 ②

다음 글의 내용을 한 문장으로 요약하고자 한다. 빈칸 (A), (B)에 들어갈 말로 가장 적절한 것은?

	(A)	(B)
①	factual 사실적인	rethinking 다시 생각하는 것
☑②	worthwhile 가치 있는	rethinking 다시 생각하는 것
③	outdated 구식인	generalizing 일반화하는 것
④	objective 객관적인	generalizing 일반화하는 것
⑤	demanding 까다로운	describing 기술하는 것

One of the most powerful tools / to find meaning in our lives / is reflective journaling / — thinking back on and writing about what has happened to us.
가장 강력한 도구 중 하나는 / 우리의 삶에서 의미를 찾기 위한 / 성찰적 일기 쓰기이다. / 즉 우리에게 일어난 일을 돌아보고 그것에 관해 쓰는

In the 1990s, / Stanford University researchers / asked undergraduate students on spring break / to journal about their most important personal values and their daily activities; / others were asked / to write about only the good things / that happened to them in the day.

1990년대에 / Stanford University 연구자들은 / 봄방학에 학부생들에게 요청했다. / 가장 중요한 개인적인 가치와 하루 활동에 대해 써보라고 / 다른 사람들은 요청받았다. / 좋은 일만 쓰도록 / 그날 있었던

Three weeks later, / the students who had written about their values / were happier, healthier, and more confident / about their ability to handle stress / than the ones who had only focused on the good stuff.
3주 후에, / 자신의 가치에 관해 썼던 학생들은 / 더 행복하고, 더 건강하고, 더 자신 있었다. / 스트레스에 대처할 수 있는 능력에 대해 / 좋은 것에만 초점을 맞췄던 학생보다

By reflecting on / how their daily activities supported their values, / students had gained a new perspective / on those activities and choices.
성찰하면서 / 어떻게 자신의 하루 일과가 자신의 가치관을 뒷받침하는지를 / 학생들은 새로운 관점을 얻었다. / 그 활동들과 선택들에 대해

Little stresses and hassles / were now demonstrations of their values in action.
작은 스트레스와 귀찮은 일들은 / 이제 그들의 가치가 행해지고 있음을 보여주는 것이었다.

Suddenly, / their lives were full of meaningful activities.
갑자기 / 그들의 삶은 의미 있는 활동으로 가득 찼다.

And all they had to do / was reflect and write about it / — positively reframing their experiences with their personal values.
그리고 그들이 해야 했던 일이라고는 / 그것에 대해 돌아보고 쓰는 것뿐이었다. / 그들의 경험을 개인적인 가치로 긍정적으로 재구성하면서

➡ Journaling about daily activities / based on what we believe to be (A) worthwhile / can make us feel / that our life is meaningful / by (B) rethinking our experiences in a new way.
일과에 관해 일기를 쓰는 것은 / 우리가 가치 있다고 믿는 것에 근거해 / 우리가 느끼게 만들 수 있다. / 우리 삶이 의미 있다고 / 새로운 방식으로 경험을 다시 생각하면서

우리의 삶에서 의미를 찾기 위한 가장 강력한 도구 중 하나는 성찰적 일기 쓰기, 즉 우리에게 일어난 일을 돌아보고 그것에 관해 쓰는 것이다. 1990년대에 Stanford University 연구자들은 봄방학에 학부생들에게 가장 중요한 개인적인 가치와 하루 활동에 대해 써보라고 요청했다. 다른 사람들은 그날 있었던 좋은 일만 쓰도록 요청받았다. 3주 후에, 자신의 가치에 관해 썼던 학생들은 좋은 것에만 초점을 맞췄던 학생들보다 더 행복하고, 더 건강하고, 스트레스에 대처할 수 있는 능력에 자신 있었다. 어떻게 자신의 하루 일과가 자신의 가치관을 뒷받침하는지를 성찰하면서, 학생들은 그 활동들과 선택들에 대해 새로운 관점을 얻었다. 작은 스트레스와 귀찮은 일들은 이제 그들의 가치가 행해지고 있음을 보여주는 것이었다. 갑자기 그들의 삶은 의미 있는 활동으로 가득 찼다. 그리고 그들이 해야 했던 일이라고는 그들의 경험을 개인적인 가치로 긍정적으로 재구성하면서 그것에 대해 돌아보고 쓰는 것뿐이었다.

➡ 우리가 (A) 가치 있다고 믿는 것에 근거해 일과에 관해 일기를 쓰는 것은 우리가 새로운 방식으로 경험을 (B) 다시 생각하면서 삶이 의미 있다고 느끼게 만들 수 있다.

Why? 왜 정답일까?

연구 결과를 정리하는 마지막 문장에서, 삶의 의미를 느끼기 위해 필요했던 일은 일과 중 있었던 경험을 가치관에 근거해 다시 생각해보고 정리하는 일뿐이었다(~ positively reframing their experiences with their personal values.)고 한다. 따라서 요약문의 빈칸 (A), (B)에 들어갈 말로 가장 적절한 것은 ② 'rethinking'(가치 있는), (B) rethinking(다시 생각하는)'이다.

- reflective ⓐ 성찰적인
- think back on ~에 대해 되돌아보다
- handle ⓥ 대처하다, 다루다
- perspective ⓝ 관점, 시각
- demonstration ⓝ 입증, 시연
- reframe ⓥ 재구성하다
- worthwhile ⓐ 가치 있는
- demanding ⓐ 까다로운, 힘든
- journaling ⓝ 일기 쓰기
- undergraduate ⓐ 학부의
- support ⓥ 뒷받침하다
- hassle ⓝ 귀찮은 일
- in action 활동 중인, 작용 중인
- factual ⓐ 사실적인
- outdated ⓐ 구식의

구문 풀이

14행 And all they had to do was reflect and write about it — positively
　　　　　　　　　주어　　　　　　동사　　　주격 보어(원형부정사)
reframing their experiences with their personal values.

41-42 눈과 뇌의 협응으로 가능해지는 시각적 정보 처리

Mike May lost his sight at the age of three.
Mike May는 세 살 때 시력을 잃었다.

Because he had spent the majority of his life / adapting to being blind / — and even cultivating a skiing career in this state — / his other senses compensated / by growing (a) stronger.
그는 인생 대부분을 보냈기 때문에, / 보이지 않는 데 적응하고, / 심지어 이 상태로 스키 경력을 쌓으면서 / 그의 다른 감각들은 보충되었다. / 더 강해지는 것으로

However, / when his sight was restored through a surgery in his forties, / his entire perception of reality / was (b) disrupted.
하지만 / 그의 시력이 40대에 수술로 회복되었을 때, / 현실에 대한 그의 전반적 인식은 / 지장을 받았다.

Instead of being thrilled / that he could see now, / as he'd expected, / his brain was so overloaded with new visual stimuli / that the world became a frightening and overwhelming place. 42번의 근거
감격하는 대신, / 그가 이제 볼 수 있다는 데 / 그가 예상했던 것처럼 / 그의 뇌는 새로운 시각적 자극으로 과부하된 나머지 / 세상은 두렵고 압도적인 장소가 되었다.

After he'd learned to know his family / through touch and smell, / he found / that he couldn't recognize his children with his eyes, / and this left him puzzled.
그가 가족을 알아보는 것을 배운 후에, / 만지는 것과 냄새를 통해 / 그는 알게 되었고, / 그가 자기 아이들을 눈으로는 알아볼 수 없다는 것을 / 그리고 이것은 그를 혼란스럽게 했다.

Skiing also became a lot harder / as he struggled to adapt to the visual stimulation.
스키 또한 훨씬 더 어려워졌다. / 그가 시각적인 자극에 적응하려고 힘쓰면서

This (c) confusion occurred / because his brain hadn't yet learned to see.
이 혼란은 생겼다. / 그의 뇌가 아직 보는 것을 배우지 못했기 때문에

Though we often tend to assume / that our eyes function as video cameras / which relay information to our brain, / advances in neuroscientific research have proven / that this is actually not the case.
비록 우리는 흔히 가정하는 경향이 있지만, / 우리 눈이 비디오카메라 역할을 한다고 / 뇌에 정보를 전달하는 / 신경 과학 연구의 발전은 증명했다. / 이것이 실제로 그렇지 않다는 것을

Instead, / sight is a collaborative effort / between our eyes and our brains, / and the way we process (d) visual reality / depends on the way these two communicate. 41번의 근거
대신, / 시각은 협력적인 노력이며, / 우리의 눈과 뇌 사이의 / 우리가 시각적 현실을 처리하는 방법은 / 이 두 가지가 소통하는 방식에 달려 있다.

If communication between our eyes and our brains / is disturbed, / our perception of reality / is altered accordingly.
만약 우리의 눈과 뇌 사이의 의사소통이 / 방해된다면, / 현실에 대한 우리의 인식은 / 그에 따라 바뀐다.

And because other areas of May's brain / had adapted to process information / primarily through his other senses, / the process of learning how to see / was (e) more difficult / than he'd anticipated.
그리고 May의 뇌의 다른 부분들은 / 정보를 처리하는 것에 적응했었기 때문에, / 주로 그의 다른 감각을 통해 / 보는 방법을 배우는 과정은 / 더 어려웠다. / 그가 예상했던 것보다

Mike May는 세 살 때 시력을 잃었다. 그는 보이지 않는 데 적응하고, 심지어 이 상태로 스키 경력을 쌓으면서 인생 대부분을 보냈기 때문에, 그의 다른 감각들은 (a) 더 강해지는 것으로 보충되었다. 하지만 그의 시력이 40대에 수술로 회복되었을 때, 현실에 대한 그의 전반적 인식은 (b) 지장을 받았다. 그가 예상했던 것처럼 이제 볼 수 있다는 데 감격하는 대신, 그의 뇌는 새로운 시각적 자극으로 과부하된 나머지 세상은 두렵고 압도적인 장소가 되었다. 그가 만지는 것과 냄새를 통해 가족을 알아보는 것을 배운 후에서, 그는 자기 아이들을 눈으로는 알아볼 수 없다는 것을 알게 되었고, 이것은 그를 혼란스럽게 했다. 스키 또한 그가 시각적인 자극에 적응하려고 힘쓰면서 훨씬 더 어려워졌다. 이 (c) 혼란은 그의 뇌가 아직 보는 것을 배우지 못했기 때문에 생겼다. 비록 우리는 흔히 우리 눈이 뇌에 정보를 전달하는 비디오카메라 역할을 한다고 가정하는 경향이 있지만, 신경 과학 연구의 발전은 이것이 실제로 그렇지 않다는 것을 증명했다. 대신, 시각은 우리의 눈과 뇌 사이의 협력적인 노력이며, 우리가 (d) 시각적 현실을 처리하는 방법은 이 두 가지가 소통하는 방식에 달려 있다. 만약 우리의 눈과 뇌 사이의 의사소통이 방해된다면, 현실에 대한 우리의 인식은 그에 따라 바뀐다. 그리고 May의 뇌의 다른 부분들은 주로 그의 다른 감각을 통해 정보를 처리하는 것에 적응했었기 때문에, 보는 방법을 배우는 과정은 그가 예상했던 것보다 (e) 더 쉬웠다(→ 더 어려웠다).

- lose one's sight 시력을 잃다
- cultivate ⓥ 갈고 닦다, 배양하다
- restore ⓥ 회복하다, 복구하다
- overloaded ⓐ 과부하된
- overwhelming ⓐ 버거운, 압도적인
- relay ⓥ 전달하다
- anticipate ⓥ 예상하다
- ignore ⓥ 무시하다
- majority ⓝ 대다수, 대부분
- compensate ⓥ 보충하다, 보상하다
- disrupt ⓥ 지장을 주다, 방해하다
- stimulus (pl. stimuli) ⓝ 자극
- struggle to ~하느라 고생하다
- primarily ⓐⓓ 주로
- visualization ⓝ 시각화

구문 풀이

1행 Because he had spent the majority of his life adapting to being
　　　　　　　　　┗spend┛　　 시각1┛ 　　　　동명사1┛
blind — and even cultivating a skiing career in this state — his other senses
　　　　　　　　┗동명사2 : ~하고 ~하면서 시간을 보내다┛
compensated by growing stronger.

41 제목 파악　　　　　　　　　　　　정답률 65% | 정답 ①

윗글의 제목으로 가장 적절한 것은?
✔ Eyes and Brain Working Together for Sight – 시각을 위해 함께 일하는 눈과 뇌
② Visualization: A Useful Tool for Learning – 시각화: 유용한 학습 도구
③ Collaboration Between Vision and Sound – 시각과 청각 사이의 협력
④ How to Ignore New Visual Stimuli – 새로운 시각적 자극을 어떻게 무시하는가
⑤ You See What You Believe – 여러분은 보이는 것을 믿는다

Why? 왜 정답일까?

어린 시절 시각을 잃어 다른 감각으로 사는 데 익숙했던 May가 시력을 회복하고서 더 어려움을 겪었던 사례를 통해, 시각적 정보 처리는 자연히 가능한 것이 아니고 눈과 뇌의 협력을 통해 가능하다(Instead, sight is a collaborative effort between our eyes and our brains, ~.)는 주제를 제시한 글이다. 따라서 글의 제목으로 가장 적절한 것은 ① '시각을 위해 함께 일하는 눈과 뇌'이다.

42 어휘 추론　　　　　　　　　　　　정답률 55% | 정답 ⑤

밑줄 친 (a)~(e) 중에서 문맥상 낱말의 쓰임이 적절하지 않은 것은?
① (a)　　② (b)　　③ (c)　　④ (d)　　✔ (e)

Why? 왜 정답일까?

글에 따르면 May는 시력 회복 수술 후 시각 정보로 인해 뇌가 과부하되어 일상에서 예상보다 더 큰 지장을 겪게 되었다(~ his brain was so overloaded with new visual stimuli that the world became a frightening and overwhelming place.)고 한다. 이를 근거로 볼 때, May가 '보는 법'을 익히는 것은 예상보다 더 '어려웠다'는 의미가 되도록 ⑤의 easier를 more difficult로 고쳐야 한다. 따라서 문맥상 낱말의 의미가 적절하지 않은 것은 ⑤이다.

43-45 생일 선물로 받은 곰 인형을 다시 선물한 Marie

(A)

On my daughter Marie's 8th birthday, / she received a bunch of presents / from her friends at school.
우리 딸 Marie의 8번째 생일에, / 그녀는 많은 선물을 받았다. / 학교 친구들에게

That evening, / with her favorite present, a teddy bear, in her arms, / we went to a restaurant / to celebrate her birthday. 45번의 근거 일치
그날 저녁, / 그녀가 가장 좋아한 선물인 테디 베어를 품에 안고 / 우리는 식당에 갔다. / 그녀의 생일을 축하하러

Our server, a friendly woman, / noticed my daughter holding the teddy bear / and said, / "My daughter loves teddy bears, too."
다정한 여성이었던 종업원은 / 우리 딸이 테디 베어를 안고 있다는 것을 알아차렸고, / 말했다. / "제 딸도 테디 베어를 좋아해요."라고

Then, / we started chatting about (a) her family.
그러고 나서 우리는 그녀의 가족에 대해 이야기를 나누기 시작했다.

(D)

『The server mentioned during the conversation / that her daughter was in the hospital with a broken leg.』 <mark>45번 ④의 근거</mark> 불일치
대화 도중 그 종업원은 말했다. / 자신의 딸이 다리가 부러져 병원에 있다고
(e) She also said / that Marie looked about the same age as her daughter.
또한 그녀는 말했다. / Marie가 자기 딸과 거의 또래 같아 보인다고
『She was so kind and attentive all evening, / and even gave Marie cookies for free.』 <mark>45번 ⑤의 근거</mark> 일치
그녀는 저녁 내내 매우 친절하고 세심했고 / 심지어 Marie에게 쿠키를 무료로 주었다.
After we finished our meal, / we paid the bill / and began to walk to our car / when unexpectedly Marie asked me to wait / and ran back into the restaurant.
우리가 식사를 마친 후 / 우리는 값을 지불하고 / 우리 차로 걸어가기 시작했는데 / 그때 갑자기 Marie가 내게 기다려 달라고 부탁하고 / 식당으로 다시 뛰어 들어갔다.

(B)

When Marie came back out, / I asked her what she had been doing.
Marie가 돌아왔을 때 / 나는 그녀에게 뭘 하고 왔는지 물었다.
She said / that she gave her teddy bear to our server / so that she could give it to (b) her daughter.
그녀는 말했다. / 자신의 테디 베어를 종업원에게 주어 / 그녀가 자기 딸에게 그것을 갖다 줄 수 있게 했다고
『I was surprised at her sudden action / because I could see / how much she loved that bear already.』 <mark>45번 ②의 근거</mark> 일치
나는 딸의 갑작스러운 행동에 놀랐다. / 내가 알 수 있었기에 / 딸아이가 이미 그 곰인형을 얼마나 좋아하는지
(c) She must have seen the look on my face, / because she said, / "I can't imagine being stuck in a hospital bed. / I just want her to get better soon."
딸은 내 얼굴 표정을 분명히 봤을 것인데, / 왜냐하면 그녀가 말했기 때문이다. / "저는 병원 침대에 갇혀 있는 것을 상상할 수 없어요. / 그저 그 애가 빨리 나았으면 좋겠어요."라고

(C)

I felt moved by Marie's words / as we walked toward the car.
나는 그녀의 말에 감동받았다. / 우리가 차를 향해 걸어가면서
『Then, / our server ran out to our car / and thanked Marie for her generosity.』 <mark>45번 ③의 근거</mark> 일치
그때 / 우리의 종업원이 우리 차로 달려 나와 / Marie의 관대함에 고마워했다.
The server said / that (d) she had never had anyone / doing anything like that for her family before.
종업원은 말했다. / 그녀에게 한 명도 없었다고 / 전에는 자기 가족을 위해 그런 일을 해준
Later, / Marie said / it was her best birthday ever.
후에 / Marie는 말했다. / 그날이 최고의 생일이었다고
I was so proud of her empathy and warmth, / and this was an unforgettable experience for our family.
나는 그녀의 공감과 따뜻함이 너무 자랑스러웠고, / 이것은 우리 가족에게 잊을 수 없는 경험이었다.

(A)

우리 딸 Marie의 8번째 생일에, 그녀는 학교에서 친구들에게 많은 선물을 받았다. 그날 저녁, 그녀가 가장 좋아한 선물인 테디 베어를 팔에 안고 우리는 그녀의 생일을 축하하러 식당에 갔다. 다정한 여성이었던 종업원은 우리 딸이 테디 베어를 안고 있다는 것을 알아차렸고, "제 딸도 테디 베어를 좋아해요."라고 말했다. 그러고 나서 우리는 (a) 그녀의 가족에 대해 이야기를 나누기 시작했다.

(D)

대화 도중 그 종업원은 자신의 딸이 다리가 부러져 병원에 있다고 말했다. 또한 (e) 그녀는 Marie가 자기 딸과 거의 또래 같아 보인다고 말했다. 그녀는 저녁 내내 매우 친절하고 세심했고 심지어 Marie에게 쿠키를 무료로 주었다. 우리는 식사를 마친 후 값을 지불하고 차로 걸어가기 시작했는데 그때 갑자기 Marie가 내게 기다려 달라고 부탁하고 식당으로 다시 뛰어 들어갔다.

(B)

Marie가 돌아왔을 때 나는 그녀에게 뭘 하고 왔는지 물었다. 그녀는 자신의 테디 베어를 종업원에게 주어 그녀가 (b) 자기 딸에게 그것을 갖다 줄 수 있게 했다고 말했다. 나는 딸아이가 이미 그 곰인형을 얼마나 좋아하는지 알 수 있었기에 딸의 갑작스러운 행동에 놀랐다. (c) 딸(Marie)은 내 얼굴 표정을 분명히 봤을 것인데, 왜냐하면 "저는 병원 침대에 갇혀 있는 것을 상상할 수 없어요. 그저 그 애가 빨리 나았으면 좋겠어요."라고 말했기 때문이다.

(C)

차를 향해 걸어가면서 나는 그녀의 말에 감동받았다. 그때 우리의 종업원이 우리 차로 달려 나와 Marie의 관대함에 고마워했다. 종업원은 전에는 (d) 그녀에게 그녀 가족을 위해 그런 일을 해준 사람이 한 명도 없었다고 했다. 후에 Marie는 그날이 최고의 생일이었다고 말했다. 나는 그녀의 공감과 따뜻함이 너무 자랑스러웠고, 이것은 우리 가족에게 잊을 수 없는 경험이었다.

- server ⓝ 종업원
- get well (병 등이) 낫다
- generosity ⓝ 관대함
- attentive ⓐ 주의 깊은, 세심한
- chat about ~에 관해 이야기하다
- moved ⓐ 감동한
- unforgettable ⓐ 잊을 수 없는

구문 풀이

(B) 5행 She must have seen the look on my face, because she said, "I can't
과거에 대한 강한 추측(~했음에 틀림없다)
imagine being stuck in a hospital bed. I just want her to get better soon."
목적어(수동 동명사)

---

43 글의 순서 파악 정답률 73% | 정답 ④

주어진 글 (A)에 이어질 내용을 순서에 맞게 배열한 것으로 가장 적절한 것은?
① (B) – (D) – (C)
② (C) – (B) – (D)
③ (C) – (D) – (B)
④ (D) – (B) – (C) ✔
⑤ (D) – (C) – (B)

Why? 왜 정답일까?

필자가 딸인 Marie의 생일을 기념해 가족끼리 저녁 식사를 하러 갔다가 식당 종업원과 이야기를 나누었다는 내용의 (A) 뒤로, 종업원이 병원에 입원해 있는 Marie 또래의 딸에 관해 이야기했다는 내용의 (D), Marie가 그 딸을 위해 자신이 선물받은 테디 베어를 전해주었다는 내용의 (B), 필자와 종업원이 모두 감

---

44 지칭 추론 정답률 62% | 정답 ③

밑줄 친 (a) ~ (e) 중에서 가리키는 대상이 나머지 넷과 다른 것은?
① (a) ② (b) ③ (c) ✔ ④ (d) ⑤ (e)

Why? 왜 정답일까?

(a), (b), (d), (e)는 the server, (c)는 Marie를 가리키므로, (a) ~ (e) 중에서 가리키는 대상이 다른 하나는 ③ '(c)'이다.

---

45 세부 내용 파악 정답률 69% | 정답 ④

윗글에 관한 내용으로 적절하지 않은 것은?
① Marie는 테디 베어를 팔에 안고 식당에 갔다.
② 'I'는 Marie의 갑작스러운 행동에 놀랐다.
③ 종업원은 Marie의 관대함에 고마워했다.
④ 종업원은 자신의 딸이 팔이 부러져서 병원에 있다고 말했다. ✔
⑤ 종업원은 Marie에게 쿠키를 무료로 주었다.

Why? 왜 정답일까?

(D) 'The server mentioned during the conversation that her daughter was in the hospital with a broken leg.'에서 종업원의 딸은 팔이 아니라 다리가 부러져서 병원에 입원했음을 알 수 있다. 따라서 내용과 일치하지 않는 것은 ④ '종업원은 자신의 딸이 팔이 부러져서 병원에 있다고 말했다.'이다.

Why? 왜 오답일까?

① (A) 'That evening, with her favorite present, a teddy bear, in her arms, we went to a restaurant ~'의 내용과 일치한다.
② (B) 'I was surprised at her sudden action ~'의 내용과 일치한다.
③ (C) 'Then, our server ~ thanked Marie for her generosity.'의 내용과 일치한다.
⑤ (D) 'She ~ even gave Marie cookies for free.'의 내용과 일치한다.

17회

어휘 Review Test 17 문제편 170쪽

A		B		C	D
01 고마워하는		01 essential		01 ⓝ	01 ⓘ
02 시작하다, 출시하다		02 recover from		02 ⓟ	02 ⓕ
03 목격하다		03 glacier		03 ⓠ	03 ⓐ
04 동행하다		04 besides		04 ⓙ	04 ⓖ
05 구부러지다		05 consumption		05 ⓑ	05 ⓣ
06 불안정한		06 afford		06 ⓚ	06 ⓓ
07 이로운		07 productivity		07 ⓜ	07 ⓔ
08 저항할 수 없는		08 capacity		08 ⓒ	08 ⓞ
09 먹잇감		09 stimulate		09 ⓔ	09 ⓑ
10 공감, 감정 이입		10 make sense		10 ⓐ	10 ⓕ
11 대체하다		11 illegal		11 ⓗ	11 ⓙ
12 ~에 기여하다		12 promote		12 ⓖ	12 ⓖ
13 성찰적인		13 jealous		13 ⓗ	13 ⓒ
14 (병 등이) 낫다		14 assemble		14 ⓘ	14 ⓚ
15 거의 ~ 않다		15 give away		15 ⓢ	15 ⓛ
16 비판		16 fascinating		16 ⓞ	16 ⓜ
17 염세적인, 비관적인		17 assign		17 ⓣ	17 ⓗ
18 미리		18 myth		18 ⓛ	18 ⓗ
19 입증하다		19 majority		19 ⓡ	19 ⓟ
20 동등하게 하다		20 habitat		20 ⓕ	20 ⓢ

18회 | 2021학년도 11월 학력평가 [고1]

· 정답 ·

18 ⑤ 19 ⑤ 20 ③ 21 ④ 22 ③ 23 ① 24 ② 25 ④ 26 ④ 27 ② 28 ④ 29 ④ 30 ⑤ 31 ② 32 ①
33 ② 34 ④ 35 ③ 36 ③ 37 ⑤ 38 ④ 39 ⑤ 40 ② 41 ① 42 ④ 43 ③ 44 ② 45 ⑤

★ 표기된 문항은 [등급을 가르는 문제]에 해당하는 문항입니다.

18 신문 이용에 관한 허락 구하기 | 정답률 93% | 정답 ⑤

다음 글의 목적으로 가장 적절한 것은?

① 도서관 이용 시간 연장을 건의하려고
② 신청한 도서의 대출 가능 여부를 문의하려고
③ 도서관에 보관 중인 자료 현황을 조사하려고
④ 글쓰기 동아리 신문의 도서관 비치를 부탁하려고
☑ 도서관에 있는 오래된 신문의 사용 허락을 요청하려고

To the school librarian,
학교 사서 선생님께,
I am Kyle Thomas, / the president of the school's English writing club.
저는 Kyle Thomas입니다. / 학교 영어 글쓰기 동아리 회장인
I have planned activities / that will increase the writing skills of our club members.
저는 활동들을 계획해 왔습니다. / 저희 동아리 회원들의 글쓰기 실력을 증진할
One of the aims of these activities / is / to make us aware of various types of news media /
and the language used in printed newspaper articles.
이러한 활동들의 목표 중 하나는 / ~입니다. / 저희가 뉴스 미디어의 다양한 유형을 인식하게 만드는 것 / 그리고 인쇄된 신문 기사에 사용된 언어
However, / some old newspapers are not easy to access online.
그러나 / 일부 오래된 신문은 온라인으로 접근하는 것이 쉽지 않습니다.
It is, therefore, my humble request to you / to allow us to use old newspapers / that have been stored in the school library.
그러므로 선생님께 드리는 저의 겸허한 요청입니다. / 저희가 오래된 신문을 사용할 수 있도록 허락해 달라는 것이 / 학교 도서관에 보관되어 온
I would really appreciate it / if you grant us permission.
정말 감사하겠습니다. / 만약 선생님께서 저희에게 허락해 주시면
Yours truly, // Kyle Thomas
Kyle Thomas 드림

학교 사서 선생님께,

저는 학교 영어 글쓰기 동아리 회장인 Kyle Thomas입니다. 저는 저희 동아리 회원들의 글쓰기 실력을 증진할 활동들을 계획해 왔습니다. 이러한 활동들의 목표 중 하나는 저희가 뉴스 미디어의 다양한 유형과 인쇄된 신문 기사에 사용된 언어를 인식하게 만드는 것입니다. 그러나 일부 오래된 신문은 온라인으로 접근하는 것이 쉽지 않습니다. 그러므로 학교 도서관에 보관되어 온 오래된 신문을 저희가 사용할 수 있도록 허락해 달라는 것이 선생님께 드리는 저의 겸허한 요청입니다. 만약 선생님께서 저희에게 허락해 주시면 정말 감사하겠습니다.

Kyle Thomas 드림

Why? 왜 정답일까?

'It is, therefore, my humble request to you to allow us to use old newspapers that have been stored in the school library.'에서 도서관에 보관된 오래된 신문을 이용할 수 있게 해 달라고 요청하므로, 글의 목적으로 가장 적절한 것은 ⑤ '도서관에 있는 오래된 신문의 사용 허락을 요청하려고'이다.

● aim ⓝ 목표, 목적
● appreciate ⓥ 감사하다
● humble ⓐ 겸손한
● grant ⓥ (공식적으로) 주다

구문 풀이

4행 주어(one of the + 복수명사 : ~ 중 하나)
One of the aims of these activities is to make us aware of various types
동사(단수) 보어(~것) of의 목적어1
of news media and the language used in printed newspaper articles.
of의 목적어2 과거분사

19 기대했던 선물을 받지 못해 실망한 필자 | 정답률 90% | 정답 ⑤

다음 글에 드러난 'I'의 심경 변화로 가장 적절한 것은?

① worried → furious
걱정한 → 분노한
② surprised → relieved
놀란 → 안도한
③ ashamed → confident
부끄러운 → 자신감에 찬
④ anticipating → satisfied
기대하는 → 만족한
☑ excited → disappointed
신난 → 실망한

When my mom came home from the mall / with a special present for me / I was pretty sure I knew what it was.
엄마가 상점에서 집에 왔을 때 / 나를 위한 특별한 선물을 가지고 / 나는 그것이 무엇인지 안다고 꽤 확신했다.
I was absolutely thrilled / because I would soon communicate with a new cell phone!
나는 완전히 들떴는데 / 왜냐하면 내가 곧 새로운 휴대폰으로 소통할 것이기 때문이었다!
I was daydreaming about all of the cool apps and games / I was going to download.
나는 모든 멋진 앱과 게임을 상상하고 있었다. / 내가 다운로드할
But my mom smiled really big / and handed me a book.
하지만 엄마는 함박웃음을 지으며 / 나에게 책 한 권을 건네주었다.
I flipped through the pages, / figuring that maybe she had hidden my new phone inside.
나는 책장을 획획 넘겨보았다. / 아마도 엄마가 나의 새로운 휴대폰을 책 속에 숨겨 두었을 것이라 생각하며
But I slowly realized / that my mom had not got me a phone / and my present was just a little book, / which was so different from what I had wanted.
그러나 나는 서서히 깨달았으며, / 엄마가 나에게 휴대폰을 사 주지 않았고 / 나의 선물이 겨우 작은 책이라는 것을 / 그것은 내가 원했던 것과는 너무 달랐다.

엄마가 나를 위한 특별한 선물을 가지고 상점에서 집에 왔을 때 나는 그것이 무엇인지 안다고 꽤 확신했다. 나는 완전히 들떴는데 왜냐하면 곧 새로운 휴대폰으로 소통할 것이기 때문이었다! 나는 내가 다운로드할 모든 멋진 앱과 게임을 상상하고 있었다. 하지만 엄마는 함박웃음을 지으며 나에게 책 한 권을 건네주었다. 나는 아마도 엄마가 나의 새로운 휴대폰을 책 속에 숨겨 두었을 것이라 생각하며 책장을 획획 넘겨보았다. 그러나 나는 엄마가 나에게 휴대폰을 사 주지 않았고 나의 선물이 겨우 작은 책이라는 것을 서서히 깨달았으며, 그것이 내가 원했던 것과는 너무 달랐다.

Why? 왜 정답일까?

어머니에게 핸드폰을 선물로 받을 것이라 예상한 필자가 기대감에 들떠 있었다가(I was absolutely thrilled ~), 선물이 작은 책이었음을 알고 실망했다는(~ my mom had not got me a phone and my present was just a little book, which was so different from what I had wanted.) 내용의 글이다. 따라서 'I'의 심경 변화로 가장 적절한 것은 ⑤ '신난 → 실망한'이다.

● absolutely ⓐⓓ 완전히, 절대적으로
● daydream ⓥ 공상하다
● anticipate ⓥ 기대하다
● thrilled ⓐ 아주 신이 난, 황홀한
● flip through (책장을) 획획 넘기다, 훑어보다

구문 풀이

7행 But I slowly realized {that my mom had not got me a phone and my
{ }: 명사절(realized의 목적어)
present was just a little book}, which was so different from what I had wanted.
선행사 계속적 용법 관계대명사(~것)

20 교사와 학생의 관계에서 비언어적 표현의 중요성 | 정답률 87% | 정답 ③

다음 글에서 필자가 주장하는 바로 가장 적절한 것은?

① 교사는 학생 간의 상호 작용을 주의 깊게 관찰해야 한다.
② 수업 시 교사는 학생의 수준에 맞는 언어를 사용해야 한다.
☑ 학생과의 관계에서 교사는 비언어적 표현에 유의해야 한다.
④ 학교는 학생에게 다양한 역할 경험의 기회를 제공해야 한다.
⑤ 교사는 학생 안전을 위해 교실의 물리적 환경을 개선해야 한다.

Some experts estimate / that as much as half of what we communicate / is done through the way we move our bodies.
일부 전문가들은 추정한다. / 우리가 전달하는 것의 절반 정도는 / 우리가 우리의 몸을 움직이는 방식을 통해 행해진다고
Paying attention to the nonverbal messages you send / can make a significant difference / in your relationship with students.
여러분이 보내는 비언어적인 메시지에 주의를 기울이는 것은 / 중요한 차이를 만들 수 있다. / 학생들과 여러분의 관계에
In general, / most students / are often closely tuned in to their teacher's body language.
일반적으로 / 대부분의 학생들은 / 자신의 선생님의 몸짓 언어에 종종 관심이 면밀하게 맞춰져 있다.
For example, / when your students first enter the classroom, / their initial action is to look for their teacher.
예를 들어 / 여러분의 학생들이 처음 교실에 들어갈 때 / 그들의 첫 행동은 선생님을 찾는 것이다.
Think about how encouraging and empowering it is for a student / when that teacher has a friendly greeting and a welcoming smile.
학생에게 얼마나 격려와 힘이 되는지 생각해 보자. / 그 선생님이 친근하게 인사를 하고 환영하는 미소를 지어줄 때
Smiling at students / — to let them know that you are glad to see them — / does not require a great deal of time or effort, / but it can make a significant difference in the classroom climate / right from the start of class.
학생들에게 미소 짓는 것, / 즉 그들에게 여러분이 그들을 알게 돼서 기쁘다는 것을 알려 주는 것이 / 많은 시간이나 노력을 요구하지는 않지만, / 그것은 교실 분위기에 중요한 차이를 만들 수 있다. / 수업의 바로 시작부터

일부 전문가들은 우리가 전달하는 것의 절반 정도는 우리가 몸을 움직이는 방식을 통해 행해진다고 추정한다. 여러분이 보내는 비언어적인 메시지에 주의를 기울이는 것은 학생들과 여러분의 관계에 중요한 차이를 만들 수 있다. 일반적으로 대부분의 학생들은 선생님의 몸짓 언어에 종종 관심이 면밀하게 맞춰져 있다. 예를 들어, 여러분의 학생들이 처음 교실에 들어갈 때 처음 하는 행동은 선생님을 찾는 것이다. 선생님이 친근하게 인사하고 환영하는 미소를 지어줄 때 학생에게 얼마나 격려와 힘이 되는지 생각해 보자. 학생들에게 미소 짓는 것, 즉 그들에게 여러분이 그들을 알게 돼서 기쁘다는 것을 알려 주는 것이 많은 시간이나 노력을 요구하지는 않지만, 그것은 수업의 바로 시작부터 교실 분위기를 크게 달라지게 할 수 있다.

Why? 왜 정답일까?

'Paying attention to the nonverbal messages you send can make a significant difference in your relationship with students.'에서 교사는 학생과의 관계에서 자신이 사용하는 비언어적 표현에 주의를 기울일 필요가 있음을 시사하는 것으로 보아, 필자의 주장으로 가장 적절한 것은 ③ '학생과의 관계에서 교사는 비언어적 표현에 유의해야 한다.'이다.

● estimate ⓥ 추정하다
● significant ⓐ 상당한, 유의미한
● tune in to ~에 맞추다
● empower ⓥ 권한을 주다, 힘을 주다
● nonverbal ⓐ 비언어적인
● closely ⓐⓓ 면밀하게, 밀접하게
● initial ⓐ 초기의
● a great deal of (양이) 많은

구문 풀이

1행 Some experts estimate that as much as half of what we communicate
접속사(~것) 주어(half of + 전체)
is done through the way [we move our bodies].
동사(단수) 선행사

21 기후 변화에 관한 우리 자신의 책임 인식하기 | 정답률 54% | 정답 ④

밑줄 친 a slap in our own face가 다음 글에서 의미하는 바로 가장 적절한 것은? [3점]

① giving the future generation room for change
미래 세대에 변화의 여지를 주는 것
② warning ourselves about the lack of natural resources
우리 자신에게 천연자원 부족을 경고하는 것
③ refusing to admit the benefits of fossil fuel production
화석 연료 생산의 이점을 인정하기를 거부하는 것

[문제편 p.171]

☑ failing to recognize our responsibility for climate change
기후 변화에 대한 우리의 책임을 인식하지 못하는 것
⑤ starting to deal with environmental problems individually
환경 문제를 따로 다루기 시작하는 것

When it comes to climate change, / many blame the fossil fuel industry for pumping greenhouse gases, / the agricultural sector for burning rainforests, / or the fashion industry for producing excessive clothes.
기후 변화에 관해 / 많은 사람들은 온실가스를 배출하는 것에 대해 화석 연료 산업을 탓한다. / 열대 우림을 태우는 것에 대해 농업 분야를, / 혹은 과다한 의복을 생산하는 것에 대해 패션 산업을

But wait, / what drives these industrial activities?
하지만 잠깐, / 무엇이 이러한 산업 활동들을 가동시키는가?

Our consumption.
우리의 소비이다.

Climate change is / a summed product of each person's behavior.
기후 변화는 / 각 개인 행위의 합쳐진 산물이다.

For example, / the fossil fuel industry / is a popular scapegoat in the climate crisis.
예를 들어, / 화석 연료 산업은 / 기후 위기에 있어서 일반적인 희생양이다.

But why do they drill and burn fossil fuels?
하지만 왜 그들은 화석 연료를 시추하고 태울까?

We provide them strong financial incentives: / some people regularly travel on airplanes and cars / that burn fossil fuels.
우리가 그들에게 강력한 금전적인 동기를 제공한다. / 어떤 사람들은 비행기와 차로 정기적으로 여행한다. / 화석 연료를 태우는

Some people waste electricity / generated by burning fuel in power plants.
어떤 사람들은 전기를 낭비한다. / 발전소에서 연료를 태워 생산된

Some people use and throw away plastic products / derived from crude oil / every day.
어떤 사람들은 플라스틱 제품을 사용하고 버린다. / 원유로부터 얻어진 / 매일

Blaming the fossil fuel industry / while engaging in these behaviors / is a slap in our own face.
화석 연료 산업을 탓하는 것은 / 이러한 행위들에 참여하면서 / 자기 얼굴 때리기이다.

기후 변화에 관해 많은 사람들은 온실가스를 배출하는 것에 대해 화석 연료 산업을, 열대 우림을 태우는 것에 대해 농업 분야를, 혹은 과다한 의복을 생산하는 것에 대해 패션 산업을 탓한다. 하지만 잠깐, 무엇이 이러한 산업 활동들을 가동시키는가? 우리의 소비이다. 기후 변화는 각 개인 행위의 합쳐진 산물이다. 예를 들어, 화석 연료 산업은 기후 위기에 있어서 일반적인 희생양이다. 하지만 왜 그들은 화석 연료를 시추하고 태울까? 우리가 그들에게 강력한 금전적인 동기를 제공한다. 예를 들어, 어떤 사람들은 화석 연료를 태우는 비행기와 차로 정기적으로 여행한다. 어떤 사람들은 발전소에서 연료를 태워 생산된 전기를 낭비한다. 어떤 사람들은 원유로부터 얻어진 플라스틱 제품을 매일 사용하고 버린다. 이러한 행위들에 참여하면서 화석 연료 산업을 탓하는 것은 자기 얼굴 때리기이다.

Why? 왜 정답일까?

For example 앞에서 기후 변화의 원인으로 지적되는 산업 활동을 촉발하는 것은 우리의 소비이고, 그러므로 기후 변화는 개인의 행위를 합친 산물로 볼 수 있다(Our consumption. Climate change is a summed product of each person's behavior.)고 언급한다. 이어서 'But why do they drill and burn fossil fuels? We provide them strong financial incentives: ~'에서도 애초에 화석 연료를 태우는 까닭이 우리가 그럴 동기를 제공하기 때문이라는 내용을 제시한다. 이러한 흐름으로 보아, 마지막 문장은 결국 기후 변화의 원인을 화석 연료 사용에 돌리는 것이 '자기 얼굴에 침 뱉기'와 같다는 뜻이다. 따라서 밑줄 친 부분이 의미하는 바로 가장 적절한 것은 ④ '기후 변화에 대한 우리의 책임을 인식하지 못하는 것'이다.

- blame A for B B에 대해 A를 탓하다
- excessive ⓐ 과다한
- crisis ⓝ 위기
- crude oil 원유
- agricultural ⓐ 농업의
- consumption ⓝ 소비
- drill ⓥ (자원, 연료 등을) 시추하다, 구멍을 뚫다
- slap ⓝ 철썩 때리기

구문 풀이

1행 When it comes to climate change, many blame {the fossil fuel industry}
~에 관하여   「blame + (A) + for + (B): B에 대해 A를 탓하다」
for {pumping greenhouse gases}, {the agricultural sector} for {burning rainforests},
or {the fashion industry} for {producing excessive clothes}.

---

22 고객 정보를 적절히 활용할 필요성　　정답률 74% | 정답 ③

다음 글의 요지로 가장 적절한 것은?

① 기업 정보의 투명한 공개는 고객 만족도를 향상시킨다.
② 목표 고객층에 대한 분석은 기업의 이익 창출로 이어진다.
☑ 고객 충성도를 높이기 위해 고객 정보가 활용될 필요가 있다.
④ 일관성 있는 호텔 서비스 제공을 통해 단골 고객을 확보할 수 있다.
⑤ 사생활 침해에 대한 우려로 고객 정보를 보관하는 데 어려움이 있다.

Information is worthless / if you never actually use it.
정보는 가치가 없다. / 만약 여러분이 결코 그것을 실제로 사용하지 않는다면

Far too often, / companies collect valuable customer information / that ends up buried and never used.
너무나 자주 / 기업들은 귀중한 고객 정보를 수집한다. / 결국에는 묻히고 절대로 사용되지 않는

They must ensure / their data is accessible for use at the appropriate times.
그들은 보장해야 한다. / 그들의 정보가 적절한 때의 사용을 위해 접근 가능하도록

For a hotel, / one appropriate time for data usage / is check-in at the front desk.
호텔의 경우 / 정보 사용을 위한 하나의 적절한 때는 / 프런트데스크에서 체크인할 때이다.

I often check in at a hotel / I've visited frequently, / only for the people at the front desk to give no indication / that they recognize me as a customer.
나는 호텔에 종종 체크인하는데 / 내가 자주 방문했던 / 프런트데스크에 있는 사람들은 결국 표시를 보여 주지 않는다. / 그들이 나를 고객으로 알아차린다는

The hotel must have stored a record of my visits, / but they don't make that information / accessible to the front desk clerks.
그 호텔은 내 방문 기록을 저장하고 있음이 분명하지만 / 그 정보가 ~하도록 해 주지 않는다. / 프런트데스크 직원들에게 접근 가능하도록

They are missing a prime opportunity to utilize data / to create a better experience / focused on customer loyalty.
그들은 정보를 활용할 최적의 기회를 놓치고 있다. / 더 나은 경험을 만들 수 있도록 / 고객 충성도에 초점을 맞춘

Whether they have ten customers, ten thousand, or even ten million, / the goal is the same: / create a delightful customer experience / that encourages loyalty.
그들이 열 명, 만 명 혹은 심지어 천만 명의 고객을 보유하든 / 목표는 동일하다. / 즐거운 고객 경험을 만드는 것 / 충성도를 높이는

만약 여러분이 결코 정보를 실제로 사용하지 않는다면 그것은 가치가 없다. 너무나 자주 기업들은 결국에는 묻히고 절대로 사용되지 않는 귀중한 고객 정보를 수집한다. 그들은 그들의 정보가 적절한 때의 사용을 위해 접근 가능하도록 보장해야 한다. 호텔의 경우 정보 사용을 위한 하나의 적절한 때는 프런트데스크에서 체크인할 때이다. 나는 내가 자주 방문했던 호텔에 종종 체크인하는데, 프런트데스크에 있는 사람들은 결국 나를 고객으로 알아차린다는 표시를 보여 주지 않는다. 그 호텔은 내 방문 기록을 저장하고 있음이 분명하지만 그 정보가 프런트데스크 직원들에게 접근 가능하도록 해 주지 않는다. 그들은 고객 충성도에 초점을 맞춘 더 나은 경험을 만들 수 있도록 정보를 활용할 최적의 기회를 놓치고 있다. 그들이 열 명, 만 명 혹은 심지어 천만 명의 고객을 보유하든 목표는 동일하다. 즉, 그것은 충성도를 높이는 즐거운 고객 경험을 만드는 것이다.

Why? 왜 정답일까?

첫 두 문장에서 고객 정보를 수집해 놓더라도 실제로 사용하지 않는다면 가치가 없다고 언급한 뒤, 세 번째 문장에서 고객 정보를 적절한 때 쓸 수 있도록 해 주어야 한다(They must ensure their data is accessible for use at the appropriate times.)고 주장하고 있다. 따라서 글의 요지로 가장 적절한 것은 ③ '고객 충성도를 높이기 위해 고객 정보가 활용될 필요가 있다.'이다.

- worthless ⓐ 무가치한
- ensure ⓥ 보장하다
- appropriate ⓐ 적절한
- utilize ⓥ 이용하다
- delightful ⓐ 즐거운, 기쁜
- end up 결국 ~이 되다
- accessible ⓐ 접근 가능한, 이용 가능한
- indication ⓝ 표시, 징후
- loyalty ⓝ 충성도

구문 풀이

5행 I often check in at a hotel [I've visited frequently], only for the people at
　　　　　　　　　　　　　　　　선행사　　　　　　「only + 의미상 주어 +
the front desk to give no indication {that they recognize me as a customer}.
　　　　　　to부정사: 결과(~가 결국 …하다)」　　( ): 동격절(= indication)

---

23 행복한 뇌를 위한 습관 만들기　　정답률 75% | 정답 ①

다음 글의 주제로 가장 적절한 것은?

☑ possibility of forming brain habits for well-being
행복한 뇌 습관을 만들어낼 수 있는 가능성
② role of brain circuits in improving body movements
신체 움직임을 향상하는 데 있어 뇌 회로의 역할
③ importance of practice in playing musical instruments
악기 연주에서 연습의 중요성
④ effect of taking a break on enhancing memory capacity
휴식이 기억력 향상에 미치는 영향
⑤ difficulty of discovering how neurons in the brain work
뇌 속 뉴런의 작동 방식을 발견하는 것의 어려움

We used to think / that the brain never changed, / but according to the neuroscientist Richard Davidson, / we now know that this is not true — specific brain circuits grow stronger through regular practice.
우리는 생각했었지만 / 뇌가 절대 변하지 않는다고 / 신경과학자 Richard Davidson에 따르면 / 우리는 이제 이것이 사실이 아님을 안다. / 특정한 뇌 회로가 규칙적인 연습을 통해 더 강해진다는 것

He explains, / "Well-being is fundamentally no different / than learning to play the cello. / If one practices the skills of well-being, / one will get better at it."
그는 설명한다. / "행복은 기본적으로 다르지 않다. / 첼로 연주하는 것을 배우는 것과 / 만약 어떤 이가 행복의 기술을 연습한다면 / 그 사람은 그것을 더 잘하게 된다."라고

What this means is / that you can actually train your brain / to become more grateful, relaxed, or confident, / by repeating experiences / that evoke gratitude, relaxation, or confidence.
이것이 의미하는 바는 ~이다. / 여러분이 여러분의 뇌를 실제로 훈련시킬 수 있다는 것 / 더 감사하고, 편안하고 또는 자신감을 갖도록 / 경험을 반복함으로써 / 감사, 휴식 또는 자신감을 불러일으키는

Your brain is shaped by the thoughts you repeat.
여러분의 뇌는 여러분이 반복하는 생각에 의해 형성된다.

The more neurons fire / as they are activated by repeated thoughts and activities, / the faster they develop into neural pathways, / which cause lasting changes in the brain.
뉴런은 더 많이 점화할수록 / 그것이 반복된 생각과 활동에 의해 활성화되면서 / 그것은 신경 경로로 더 빠르게 발달하게 되고 / 이는 뇌에 지속적인 변화를 야기한다.

Or in the words of Donald Hebb, / "Neurons that fire together wire together."
혹은 Donald Hebb의 말을 빌리면 / "함께 점화하는 뉴런은 함께 연결된다."

This is such an encouraging premise: / bottom line — we can intentionally create the habits / for the brain to be happier.
이는 대단히 고무적인 전제이다. / 결론은 / 즉, 우리가 습관을 의도적으로 만들 수 있다는 것이다. / 뇌가 더 행복해지도록

우리는 뇌가 절대 변하지 않는다고 생각했었지만, 신경과학자 Richard Davidson에 따르면 우리는 이제 이것이 사실이 아님을, 즉, 특정한 뇌 회로가 규칙적인 연습을 통해 더 강해진다는 것을 안다. 그는 "행복은 첼로 연주를 배우는 것과 기본적으로 다르지 않다. 만약 어떤 이가 행복의 기술을 연습한다면 그 사람은 그것을 더 잘하게 된다."라고 설명한다. 이것이 의미하는 바는 여러분이 감사, 휴식 또는 자신감을 불러일으키는 경험을 반복함으로써 더 감사하거나 편안하거나 자신감을 갖도록 여러분의 뇌를 실제로 훈련시킬 수 있다는 것이다. 뇌는 여러분이 반복하는 생각에 의해 형성된다. 뉴런은 반복된 생각과 활동에 의해 활성화되면서 더 많이 점화할수록 신경 경로로 더 빠르게 발달하게 되고, 이는 뇌에 지속적인 변화를 야기한다. 혹은 Donald Hebb의 말을 빌리면 "함께 점화하는 뉴런은 함께 연결된다." 이는 대단히 고무적인 전제이다. 즉, 결론은 뇌가 더 행복해지도록 우리가 습관을 의도적으로 만들 수 있다는 것이다.

Why? 왜 정답일까?

마지막 문장(~ we can intentionally create the habits for the brain to be happier.)에서 우리는 뇌를 더 행복하게 할 습관을 만들어 갈 수 있다는 결론을 제시하므로, 글의 주제로 가장 적절한 것은 ① '행복을 위한 뇌 습관을 만들어낼 수 있는 가능성'이다.

- neuroscientist ⓝ 신경과학자
- grateful ⓐ 감사하는
- bottom line 핵심, 요점, 결론
- enhance ⓥ 향상시키다
- fundamentally ⓐ 기본적으로
- activate ⓥ 활성화하다
- intentionally ⓐ 의도적으로

구문 풀이

9행 The more neurons fire as they are activated by repeated thoughts and
「the＋비교급 ～
activities, the faster they develop into neural pathways, which cause lasting
the＋비교급 … : ～할수록 더 …하다」　　　　　　　　계속적 용법(주절 보충)
changes in the brain.

24　현대 사회에서의 정체성　　　　　　　정답률 57% | 정답 ②

다음 글의 제목으로 가장 적절한 것은?

① What Makes Our Modern Society So Competitive?
　무엇이 우리 현대 사회를 이토록 경쟁적으로 만드는가?
✓ How Modern Society Drives Us to Discover Our Identities
　현대 사회는 어떻게 우리가 정체성을 발견하도록 부추기는가
③ Social Masks: A Means to Build Trustworthy Relationships
　사회적 가면: 믿을 만한 관계를 구축하는 수단
④ The More Social Roles We Have, the Less Choice We Have
　더 많은 사회적 역할을 가질수록, 선택권은 더 적어진다
⑤ Increasing Social Mobility Leads Us to a More Equal Society
　사회적 유동성의 증가가 더 평등한 사회로 이끈다

In modern times, / society became more dynamic.
현대에는 / 사회가 더욱 역동적이 되었다.
Social mobility increased, / and people began to exercise a higher degree of choice /
regarding, for instance, their profession, their marriage, or their religion.
사회적 유동성이 증가하였고 / 사람들은 더 높은 정도의 선택권을 행사하기 시작했다. / 예를 들어 자신의 직업, 결혼 혹은 종교와 관련하여
This posed a challenge to traditional roles in society.
이것은 사회의 전통적인 역할에 이의를 제기했다.
It was less evident / that one needed to commit to the roles / one was born into / when
alternatives could be realized.
덜 분명해졌다. / 개인이 역할에 전념할 필요가 있다는 것은 / 자신이 타고난 / 대안이 실현될 수 있을 때
Increasing control over one's life choices / became not only possible but desired.
자신의 삶의 선택에 대한 통제력을 늘리는 것이 / 가능해졌을 뿐만 아니라 바람직하게 되었다.
Identity then became a problem.
그러자 정체성이 문제가 되었다.
It was no longer almost ready-made at birth / but something to be discovered.
그것은 더 이상 태어날 때 대체로 주어진 것이 아닌, / 발견되어야 할 것이었다.
Traditional role identities prescribed by society / began to appear as masks imposed on
people / whose real self was to be found somewhere underneath.
사회에 의해 규정된 전통적인 역할 정체성은 / 사람들에게 부여된 가면처럼 보이기 시작했다. / 그 뒤 어딘가에서 진정한 자아가 발견되어야 하는

현대에는 사회가 더욱 역동적이 되었다. 사회적 유동성이 증가하였고, 사람들은 가령 자신의 직업, 결혼 혹은 종교와 관련하여 더 높은 정도의 선택권을 행사하기 시작했다. 이것은 사회의 전통적인 역할에 이의를 제기했다. 대안이 실현될 수 있을 때 개인이 타고난 역할에 전념할 필요가 있다는 것은 덜 분명해졌다. 자신의 삶의 선택에 대한 통제력을 늘리는 것이 가능해졌을 뿐만 아니라 바람직하게 되었다. 그러자 정체성이 문제가 되었다. 그것은 더 이상 태어날 때 대체로 주어진 것이 아닌, 발견되어야 할 것이었다. 사회에 의해 규정된 전통적인 역할 정체성은 사람들에게 부여된 가면처럼 보이기 시작해서, 진정한 자아는 그 뒤 어딘가에서 발견되어야 하는 것처럼 여겨지기 시작했다.

Why? 왜 정답일까?

역동적인 현대 사회에서 우리의 정체성은 태어날 때 주어진 것보다는 사회적으로 발견되어야 하는 것이 되었다(Identity then became a problem. It was no longer almost ready-made at birth but something to be discovered.)는 내용의 글이다. 따라서 글의 제목으로 가장 적절한 것은 ② '현대 사회는 어떻게 우리가 정체성을 발견하도록 부추기는가'이다.

● mobility ⓝ 유동성　　　　● profession ⓝ 직업
● pose a challenge 도전하다, 이의를 제기하다　● evident ⓐ 명백한
● commit to ～에 전념하다　　● ready-made ⓐ 이미 주어진, 기성품의
● prescribe ⓥ 규정하다, 처방하다

구문 풀이

9행 Traditional role identities prescribed by society began to appear as
　　　　주어　　　과거분사　　　　　　동사　전치사(～로서)
masks imposed on people [whose real self was to be found somewhere
명사　과거분사　　　　소유격 관·대　be to 용법: ～해야 한다(의무)
underneath].

25　문화 활동별 참여 비율　　　　　정답률 73% | 정답 ④

다음 도표의 내용과 일치하지 <u>않는</u> 것은?

Percentage of U.S. Students Participating in Cultural Activities (2016)

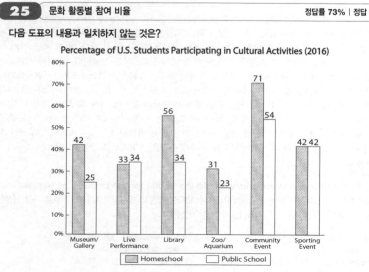

The graph above shows / the percentage of U.S. homeschooled and public school students
/ participating in cultural activities in 2016.
위 도표는 보여 준다. / 미국의 홈스쿨링 학생과 공립 학교 학생의 비율을 / 2016년에 문화 활동에 참여한
① With the exception of live performances and sporting events, / the percentage of
homeschooled students / participating in cultural activities / was higher than that of public
school students.
라이브 공연과 스포츠 행사를 제외하고 / 홈스쿨링 학생의 비율이 / 문화 활동에 참여하는 / 공립 학교 학생의 비율에 비해 높았다.
② For each group of students, / community events accounted for the largest percentage /
among all cultural activities.
각 집단의 학생에 있어 / 지역사회 행사는 가장 큰 비율을 차지했다. / 모든 문화 활동 중에서
③ The percentage point difference / between homeschooled students and their public
school peers / was largest in visiting libraries.
퍼센트포인트 차이는 / 홈스쿨링 학생과 공립 학교 또래 간의 / 도서관 방문에서 가장 컸다.
✓ The percentage of homeschooled students / visiting museums or galleries / was more
than twice that of public school students.
홈스쿨링 학생의 비율은 / 박물관이나 미술관에 방문하는 / 공립 학교 학생의 비율에 비해 두 배 이상이었다.
⑤ Going to zoos or aquariums / ranked the lowest for both groups of students, / with 31
and 23 percent respectively.
동물원이나 수족관에 가는 것이 / 두 학생 집단에서 가장 낮은 순위를 차지했는데, / 각각 31퍼센트와 23퍼센트였다.

위 도표는 미국에서 2016년에 문화 활동에 참여한 홈스쿨링 학생과 공립 학교 학생의 비율을 보여 준다. ① 라이브 공연과 스포츠 행사를 제외하고 문화 활동에 참여하는 홈스쿨링 학생의 비율이 공립 학교 학생에 비해 높았다. ② 각 집단의 학생에 있어 지역사회 행사는 모든 문화 활동 중에서 가장 큰 비율을 차지했다. ③ 홈스쿨링 학생과 공립 학교 또래 간의 퍼센트포인트 차이는 도서관 방문에서 가장 컸다. ④ 박물관이나 미술관에 방문하는 홈스쿨링 학생의 비율은 공립 학교 학생에 비해 두 배 이상이었다. ⑤ 동물원이나 수족관에 가는 것이 두 학생 집단에서 가장 낮은 순위를 차지했는데, 각각 31퍼센트와 23퍼센트였다.

Why? 왜 정답일까?

도표에 따르면 홈스쿨링 학생 중 박물관이나 미술관에 가는 비율(42%)은 공립 학교 학생의 비율(25%)의 두 배에 미치지 못한다. 따라서 도표와 일치하지 않는 것은 ④이다.

● with the exception of ～을 제외하고　● account for ～을 차지하다
● respectively ⓐⓓ 각각

구문 풀이

9행 The percentage of homeschooled students visiting museums or galleries
　　→동사(단수)　　　　　　　　주어　　　　　　　　현재분사
was more than twice that of public school students.
～ 이상인　　　지시대명사(= the percentage)

26　Bessie Coleman의 생애　　　　　정답률 85% | 정답 ④

Bessie Coleman에 관한 다음 글의 내용과 일치하지 <u>않는</u> 것은?

① 11살 때 Wright 형제의 첫 비행 소식을 들었다.
② 비행 수업을 듣기 위해 파리로 가야 했다.
③ 국제 조종사 면허를 딴 최초의 흑인 여성이 되었다.
✓ 유럽에서 에어쇼에 첫 출현을 했다.
⑤ 다음 세대가 비행의 꿈을 추구하도록 영감을 주었다.

Bessie Coleman was born in Texas in 1892.
Bessie Coleman은 1892년에 텍사스에서 태어났다.
「When she was eleven, / she was told / that the Wright brothers had flown their first plane.」
그녀가 11살이었을 때 / 그녀는 들었다. / Wright 형제가 첫 비행을 했다는 것을　　①의 근거 일치
Since that moment, / she dreamed about the day / she would soar through the sky.
그때부터 / 그녀는 그 날을 꿈꿨다. / 자신이 하늘을 높이 날아오르는
At the age of 23, / Coleman moved to Chicago, / where she worked at a restaurant / to save
money for flying lessons.
23살 때 / Coleman은 시카고로 이사했고 / 그곳에서 그녀는 식당 일을 했다. / 비행 수업을 위한 돈을 모으기 위해
「However, / she had to travel to Paris / to take flying lessons / because American flight
schools at the time admitted neither women nor Black people.」
그러나 / 그녀는 파리로 가야 했다. / 비행 수업을 듣기 위해 / 왜냐하면 그 당시 미국 비행 학교가 여성이나 흑인의 입학을 허가하지 않았기 때문에　②의 근거 일치
「In 1921, / she finally became the first Black woman / to earn an international pilot's
license.」
1921년에 / 그녀는 마침내 최초의 흑인 여성이 되었다. / 국제 조종사 면허를 딴　③의 근거 일치
「She also studied flying acrobatics in Europe / and made her first appearance / in an
airshow in New York in 1922.」　④의 근거 불일치
그녀는 또한 유럽에서 곡예 비행을 공부했고 / 첫 출현을 했다. / 1922년에 뉴욕의 에어쇼에
「As a female pioneer of flight, / she inspired the next generation / to pursue their dreams of
flying.」　⑤의 근거 일치
여성 비행 개척자로서 / 그녀는 다음 세대에게 영감을 주었다. / 비행의 꿈을 추구하도록

Bessie Coleman은 1892년에 텍사스에서 태어났다. 그녀가 11살이었을 때 그녀는 Wright 형제가 첫 비행을 했다는 것을 들었다. 그때부터 그녀는 자신이 하늘을 높이 날아오르는 그 날을 꿈꿨다. 23살 때 Coleman은 시카고로 이사했고 그곳에서 식당 일을 하여 비행 수업을 위한 돈을 모았다. 그러나 그 당시 미국 비행 학교가 여성이나 흑인의 입학을 허가하지 않았기 때문에 그녀는 비행 수업을 듣기 위해 파리로 가야 했다. 1921년에 그녀는 마침내 국제 조종사 면허를 딴 최초의 흑인 여성이 되었다. 그녀는 또한 유럽에서 곡예 비행을 공부했고 1922년에 뉴욕의 에어쇼에 첫 출현을 했다. 여성 비행 개척자로서 그녀는 다음 세대가 비행의 꿈을 추구하도록 영감을 주었다.

Why? 왜 정답일까?

'She also studied flying acrobatics in Europe and made her first appearance in an airshow in New York in 1922.'에 따르면 Coleman은 유럽에서 곡예 비행을 공부한 후 첫 에어쇼를 뉴욕에서 치렀다. 따라서 내용과 일치하지 않는 것은 ④ '유럽에서 에어쇼에 첫 출현을 했다.'이다.

Why? 왜 오답일까?

① 'When she was eleven, she was told that the Wright brothers had flown their first plane.'의 내용과 일치한다.

---

② 'However, she had to travel to Paris to take flying lessons ~'의 내용과 일치한다.
③ 'In 1921, she finally became the first Black woman to earn an international pilot's license.'의 내용과 일치한다.
⑤ '~ she inspired the next generation to pursue their dreams of flying.'의 내용과 일치한다.

● soar ⓥ 솟아오르다　　　　　　● pioneer ⓝ 선구자
● inspire ⓥ 영감을 주다

구문 풀이

1행　When she was eleven, she was told {that the Wright brothers had flown
　　　　　　　　　　　　　4형식 수동태(~을 듣다)　　　　　　　　　　　과거완료
their first plane}. [ ]: 목적어

---

27 자연 사진 대회 안내　　　　　　정답률 82% | 정답 ②

2021 Camptonville Nature Photo Contest에 관한 다음 안내문의 내용과 일치하지 않는 것은?

① 매년 열리는 대회이며 올해가 네 번째이다.
✔② 최대 20장의 사진을 이메일로 제출해야 한다.
③ 제출 마감 기한은 12월 1일이다.
④ 수상자는 웹 사이트에 게시될 것이다.
⑤ 모든 수상작은 시청에 전시될 것이다.

2021 Camptonville Nature Photo Contest
2021 Camptonville 자연 사진 대회
『This is the fourth year of the annual Camptonville Nature Photo Contest.』①의 근거 일치
올해는 매년 열리는 Camptonville 자연 사진 대회의 네 번째 해입니다.
You can show the beauty of nature in Camptonville / by sharing your most amazing photos!
여러분은 Camptonville의 자연미를 보여 줄 수 있습니다! / 자신의 가장 멋진 사진을 공유함으로써
Submission
제출
『Upload a maximum of 20 photos / onto our website www.camptonvillephotocontest.org.』
최대 20장의 사진을 올리세요. / 우리 웹 사이트 www.camptonvillephotocontest.org에　②의 근거 불일치
『Deadline is December 1.』③의 근거 일치
마감 기한은 12월 1일입니다.
Prizes
상
1st Place: $500
1위: 500달러
2nd Place: $200
2위: 200달러
3rd Place: $100
3위: 100달러
(『Winners will be posted on our website on December 31.』)④의 근거 일치
(수상자는 12월 31일에 우리 웹 사이트에 게시될 것입니다.)
Details
세부 사항
『All winning photos will be exhibited at City Hall.』⑤의 근거 일치
모든 수상작은 시청에 전시될 것입니다.
Please contact us at 122-861-3971 for further information.
더 많은 정보를 얻으시려면 122-861-3971로 연락 주세요.

2021 Camptonville 자연 사진 대회

올해는 매년 열리는 Camptonville 자연 사진 대회의 네 번째 해입니다. 여러분은 여러분이 찍은 가장 멋진 사진을 공유함으로써 Camptonville의 자연미를 보여 줄 수 있습니다!

제출
－ 최대 20장의 사진을 우리 웹 사이트 www.camptonvillephotocontest.org에 올리세요.
－ 마감 기한은 12월 1일입니다.

상
• 1위: 500달러　　• 2위: 200달러　　• 3위: 100달러
(수상자는 12월 31일에 우리 웹 사이트에 게시될 것입니다.)

세부 사항
－ 모든 수상작은 시청에 전시될 것입니다.
－ 더 많은 정보를 얻으시려면 122-861-3971로 연락 주세요.

Why? 왜 정답일까?

'Upload a maximum of 20 photos onto our website ~'에서 사진은 웹 사이트에 올려 출품하라고 하므로, 따라서 안내문의 내용과 일치하지 않는 것은 ② '최대 20장의 사진을 이메일로 제출해야 한다.'이다.

Why? 왜 오답일까?

① 'This is the fourth year of the annual Camptonville Nature Photo Contest.'의 내용과 일치한다.
③ 'Deadline is December 1.'의 내용과 일치한다.
④ '(Winners will be posted on our website on December 31.)'의 내용과 일치한다.
⑤ 'All winning photos will be exhibited at City Hall.'의 내용과 일치한다.

● annual ⓐ 매년 열리는

---

28 열기구 탑승 안내　　　　　　정답률 91% | 정답 ④

Willow Valley Hot Air Balloon Ride에 관한 다음 안내문의 내용과 일치하는 것은?

① 조종사를 제외하고 8인까지 탈 수 있다.

---

② 여름에는 오전 6시에 시작한다.
③ 요금에 보험이 포함되어 있다.
✔④ 예약은 온라인으로 해야 한다.
⑤ 환불은 예외 없이 불가능하다.

Willow Valley Hot Air Balloon Ride
Willow Valley 열기구 탑승
Enjoy the best views of Willow Valley from the sky / with our hot air balloon ride!
하늘에서 Willow Valley의 최고의 풍경을 즐겨보세요! / 우리의 열기구를 타고
『Capacity: up to 8 people including a pilot』①의 근거 불일치
정원: 조종사 포함 8인까지
Time Schedule
일정표

『Spring & Summer ②의 근거 불일치 (from April to September)』 봄과 여름 (4월부터 9월까지)	5:00 a.m. – 7:00 a.m.』 오전 5시 – 오전 7시
Autumn & Winter (from October to March) 가을과 겨울 (10월부터 3월까지)	6:00 a.m. – 8:00 a.m. 오전 6시 – 오전 8시

Duration of Flight: about 1 hour
비행 시간: 약 1시간
Fee: $150 per person / (『insurance not included』)③의 근거 불일치
요금: 인당 150달러 / (보험은 포함되지 않음)
Note
공지사항
『Reservations are required and must be made online.』④의 근거 일치
예약은 필수이며 온라인으로 해야 합니다.
『You can get a full refund up to 24 hours in advance.』⑤의 근거 불일치
24시간 전까지는 전액 환불을 받을 수 있습니다.
Visit www.willowvalleyballoon.com for more information.
더 많은 정보를 위해서 www.willowvalleyballoon.com을 방문해 주십시오.

Willow Valley 열기구 탑승

우리의 열기구를 타고 하늘에서 Willow Valley의 최고의 풍경을 즐겨보세요!

• 정원: 조종사 포함 8인까지

• 일정표

봄과 여름 (4월부터 9월까지)	오전 5시 – 오전 7시
가을과 겨울 (10월부터 3월까지)	오전 6시 – 오전 8시

※ 비행 시간: 약 1시간

• 요금: 인당 150달러 (보험은 포함되지 않음)

• 공지사항
－ 예약은 필수이며 온라인으로 해야 합니다.
－ 24시간 전까지는 전액 환불을 받을 수 있습니다.
－ 더 많은 정보를 위해서 www.willowvalleyballoon.com을 방문해 주십시오.

Why? 왜 정답일까?

'Reservations are required and must be made online.'에서 예약은 필수이며 온라인으로 해야 한다고 하므로, 안내문의 내용과 일치하는 것은 ④ '예약은 온라인으로 해야 한다.'이다.

Why? 왜 오답일까?

① 'Capacity: up to 8 people including a pilot'에서 8인이라는 정원에 조종사가 포함된다고 하였다.
② 'Spring & Summer / (from April to September) / 5:00 a.m.–7:00 a.m.'에서 봄과 여름에는 오전 5시부터 시작된다고 하였다.
③ '(insurance not included)'에서 보험은 요금에 포함되지 않는다고 하였다.
⑤ 'You can get a full refund up to 24 hours in advance.'에서 탑승 24시간 전까지는 전액 환불이 가능하다고 하였다.

● get a refund 환불을 받다　　● in advance 미리, 사전에

---

29 살충제와 비료의 사용으로 초래된 결과　　정답률 45% | 정답 ④

다음 글의 밑줄 친 부분 중, 어법상 틀린 것은? [3점]

The reduction of minerals in our food / is the result of using pesticides and fertilizers / ① that kill off beneficial bacteria, earthworms, and bugs in the soil / that create many of the essential nutrients / in the first place / and prevent the uptake of nutrients into the plant.
우리의 식품 속 미네랄의 감소는 / 살충제와 비료 사용의 결과이다. / 토양에 있는 이로운 박테리아, 지렁이 그리고 벌레를 죽이고 / 많은 필수 영양소를 만들어 내는 / 우선적으로 / 식물로 영양소를 흡수하는 것을 막는
Fertilizing crops with nitrogen and potassium / ② has led to declines in magnesium, zinc, iron and iodine.
농작물에 질소와 포타슘으로 비료를 주는 것은 / 마그네슘, 아연, 철 그리고 아이오딘의 감소로 이어져 왔다.
For example, / there has been on average about a 30% decline / in the magnesium content of wheat.
예를 들어, / 평균 약 30%의 감소가 있었다. / 밀의 마그네슘 함량에서
This is partly due to / potassium ③ being a blocker against magnesium absorption by plants.
이는 부분적으로 ~ 때문이다. / 식물이 마그네슘을 흡수하는 데 포타슘이 방해물이 되기
Lower magnesium levels in soil / also ✔④ occur with acidic soils / and around 70% of the farmland on earth / is now acidic.
토양의 더 낮은 마그네슘 수치는 / 산성 토양에서도 나타나는데 / 지구상에 있는 농지의 약 70%가 / 현재 산성이다.

Thus, / the overall characteristics of soil / determine the accumulation of minerals in plants.
따라서 / 토양의 전반적인 특성은 / 식물 속 미네랄의 축적을 결정한다.
Indeed, / nowadays our soil is less healthy / and so are the plants ⑤ grown on it.
실제로 / 오늘날 우리의 토양은 덜 건강하고 / 그 위에서 길러진 식물도 그러하다.

우리의 식품 속 미네랄의 감소는 우선적으로 많은 필수 영양소를 만들어 내는 토양에 있는 이로운 박테리아, 지렁이 그리고 벌레를 죽이고 식물이 영양소를 흡수하는 것을 막는 살충제와 비료를 사용한 결과이다. 농작물에 질소와 포타슘으로 비료를 주는 것은 마그네슘, 아연, 철 그리고 아이오딘의 감소로 이어져 왔다. 예를 들어 밀의 마그네슘 함량에서 평균적으로 약 30%의 감소가 있었다. 이는 부분적으로 식물이 마그네슘을 흡수하는 데 포타슘이 방해물이 되기 때문이다. 토양의 마그네슘 수치 감소는 산성 토양에서도 나타나는데, 지구상에 있는 농지의 약 70%가 현재 산성이다. 따라서 토양의 전반적인 특성은 식물 속 미네랄의 축적을 결정한다. 실제로 오늘날 우리의 토양은 덜 건강하고 그 위에서 길러진 식물도 그러하다.

Why? 왜 정답일까?

and 앞뒤로 2개의 절이 연결되는 구조로, 첫 번째 주어인 Lower magnesium levels 뒤로 동사가 필요하기 때문에 occurring을 occur로 고쳐야 한다. 따라서 어법상 틀린 것은 ④이다.

Why? 왜 오답일까?

① pesticides and fertilizers를 꾸미는 주격 관계대명사로 that을 썼다.
② 주어가 동명사구인 'Fertilizing crops ~'이므로 단수 취급하여 has를 썼다.
③ 전치사처럼 쓰이는 due to(~ 때문에) 뒤로 동명사 또는 명사를 써야 하므로 being을 썼다. potassium은 being의 의미상 주어이다.
⑤ the plants가 '키워지는' 대상이므로 수동의 의미를 나타내는 과거분사 grown을 썼다.

- reduction ⑩ 감소
- in the first place 애초에, 우선
- fertilize ⑨ 비옥하게 하다, 비료를 주다
- absorption ⑩ 흡수
- characteristic ⑩ 특징, 특성
- essential ⓐ 필수적인, 본질적인
- uptake ⑩ 흡수, 활용
- decline ⑩ 감소 ⑨ 감소하다
- acidic ⓐ 산성의
- accumulation ⑩ 축적

구문 풀이

12행 Indeed, nowadays our soil is less healthy and so are the plants grown on it.
「so+동사+주어: 동의 구문(~도 그렇다)」

★★★ 등급을 가르는 문제!

30 동물원의 포획 사육 프로그램 정답률 24% | 정답 ⑤

다음 글의 밑줄 친 부분 중, 문맥상 낱말의 쓰임이 적절하지 않은 것은?

For species approaching extinction, / zoos can act as a last chance for survival.
멸종에 이르고 있는 종에게 / 동물원은 생존을 위한 마지막 기회로 작용할 수 있다.
① Recovery programs are established / to coordinate the efforts of field conservationists and wildlife authorities.
회복 프로그램이 수립된다. / 현장 환경 보호 활동가와 야생 동물 당국의 노력을 통합하기 위해
As populations of those species ② diminish / it is not unusual for zoos / to start captive breeding programs.
그 종의 개체수가 ② 감소하면서 / 동물원으로서는 드물지 않다 / 포획 사육 프로그램을 시작하는 것이
Captive breeding acts to protect against extinction.
포획 사육은 멸종을 막기 위해 작용한다.
In some cases / captive-bred individuals may be released back into the wild, / supplementing wild populations.
어떤 경우에는 / 포획 사육된 개체가 다시 야생으로 방생되어 / 야생 개체수를 보충할 수도 있다.
This is most successful in situations / where individuals are at greatest threat / during a ③ particular life stage.
이는 상황에서 가장 성공적이다 / 개체가 가장 위협에 놓여 있는 / 특정한 생애 주기 동안에
For example, / turtle eggs may be removed from high-risk locations / until after they hatch.
예를 들어 / 거북이 알은 고위험 장소로부터 제거될 수도 있다. / 그들이 부화한 이후까지
This may ④ increase the number of turtles / that survive to adulthood.
이는 거북이 수를 증가시킬 수 있다. / 성체까지 생존하는
Crocodile programs have also been successful / in protecting eggs and hatchlings, / ✓ releasing hatchlings / once they are better equipped to protect themselves.
악어 프로그램 역시 성공적이었으며 / 알과 부화한 유생을 보호하는 데 있어서 / 부화한 유생을 방생한다 / 일단 그것이 스스로를 보호 준비를 더 잘 갖추면

멸종에 이르고 있는 종에게 동물원은 생존을 위한 마지막 기회로 작용할 수 있다. 현장 환경 보호 활동가와 야생 동물 당국의 노력을 통합하기 위해 ① 회복 프로그램이 수립된다. 그 종의 개체수가 ② 감소하면서 동물원이 포획 사육 프로그램을 시작하는 것은 드물지 않다. 포획 사육은 멸종을 막기 위해 작용한다. 어떤 경우에는 포획 사육된 개체가 다시 야생으로 방생되어 야생 개체수를 보충할 수도 있다. 이는 개체가 ③ 특정한 생애 주기 동안에 가장 큰 위협에 놓여 있는 상황에서 가장 성공적이다. 예를 들어 거북이 알은 부화 이후까지 고위험 장소로부터 제거될 수도 있다. 이는 성체까지 생존하는 거북이 수를 ④ 증가시킬 수 있다. 악어 프로그램 역시 알과 부화한 유생을 보호하는 데 있어서 성공적이었으며, 일단 그것이 스스로를 보호할 준비를 더 잘 갖추면 부화한 유생을 ⑤ 포획한다(→ 방생한다).

Why? 왜 정답일까?

멸종 위기 종의 개체수를 회복하는 데 동물원이 도움을 줄 수 있다는 내용의 글로, '~ it is not unusual for zoos to start captive breeding programs.' 뒤로 포획 사육 프로그램의 내용이 소개되고 있다. 이 포획 사육 프로그램에서는 멸종 위기 동물이나 그 알을 잡아두었다가 위험한 시기가 지나고 동물이 스스로를 보호할 준비가 되면 그 동물을 다시 야생에 '돌려보낸다'. 이러한 흐름으로 볼 때, ⑤의 capturing을 releasing으로 고쳐야 한다. 따라서 문맥상 낱말의 쓰임이 가장 적절하지 않은 것은 ⑤이다.

- extinction ⑩ 멸종
- authority ⑩ 당국
- supplement ⑨ 보충하다
- be equipped to ~할 준비를 갖추다
- conservationist ⑩ 환경 보호 활동가
- diminish ⑨ 감소하다, 줄어들다
- hatchling ⑩ (갓 부화한) 유생

구문 풀이

7행 This is most successful in situations [where individuals are at greatest threat during a particular life stage].
선행사(추상적 공간) ┘   관계부사

★★ 문제 해결 꿀~팁 ★★

▶ 많이 틀린 이유는?
동물원의 포획 사육이라는 생소한 소재를 다루어 이해하기 까다로운 지문이다. 가장 헷갈리는 ④ 주변의 문맥을 살펴보면, 포획 사육이 생존에 큰 위험이 있는 시기를 지나는 동물에게 도움이 된다는 일반적인 내용 뒤로 바다거북의 사례가 언급된다. 바다거북의 알은 부화하기 전까지 고위험 지역으로부터 다른 곳으로 옮겨진다고 했다. 이는 바다거북이 무사히 부화해 성체까지 생존할 수 있도록 돕는 절차이므로, 실제로 이 조치를 통해 살아남는 바다거북의 수가 '증가할' 수 있다는 뜻의 ④ increase는 문맥상 적절하다.
▶ 문제 해결 방법은?
정답인 ⑤의 capturing은 핵심 소재인 captive (breeding programs)와 비슷한 형태의 단어이지만, 문맥적 의미는 정반대이다. 포획 사육 기간에 악어가 스스로를 보호할 준비를 갖추고 나면 '계속 잡아두는' 것이 아니라 '방생해야' 야생 동물의 보호와 생존에 도움이 된다.

31 사전 통보로 변화에 적응할 시간을 주기 정답률 61% | 정답 ②

다음 빈칸에 들어갈 말로 가장 적절한 것을 고르시오.
① unite - 연합할 ✓ adapt - 적응할 ③ object - 반대할
④ compete - 경쟁할 ⑤ recover - 회복할

We don't send telegraphs to communicate anymore, / but it's a great metaphor for giving advance notice.
우리는 소통하기 위해 더 이상 전보를 보내지 않지만 / 이것은 사전 통보를 하는 것에 대한 훌륭한 비유이다.
Sometimes, / you must inform those close to you / of upcoming change / by conveying important information well in advance.
때때로 / 여러분은 자신에게 가까운 사람들에게 알려야 한다. / 다가오는 변화를 / 중요한 정보를 미리 잘 전달함으로써
There's a huge difference / between saying, "From now on, we will do things differently," / which doesn't give people enough time / to understand and accept the change, / and saying something like, "Starting next month, we're going to approach things differently."
큰 차이가 있다. / 말하는 것과 "지금부터 우리는 일을 다르게 할 겁니다."라고 / 사람들에게 충분한 시간을 주지 않는 / 그 변화를 이해하고 받아들일 / "다음 달부터 우리는 일에 다르게 접근할 겁니다." 같은 말을 하는 것 사이에는
Telegraphing empowers people to adapt.
전보를 보내는 것은 사람들이 적응할 수 있도록 해 준다.
Telegraphing involves the art / of seeing an upcoming event or circumstance / and giving others enough time / to process and accept the change.
전보를 보내는 것은 기술을 포함한다. / 다가오는 사건이나 상황을 보고 / 다른 사람들에게 충분한 시간을 주는 / 그 변화를 처리하고 받아들일
Telegraph anything / that will take people out of / what is familiar and comfortable to them.
무엇이든 전보로 보내라. / 사람들을 ~에서 벗어나게 할 / 그들에게 익숙하고 편안한 것
This will allow processing time / for them to accept the circumstances / and make the most of what's happening.
이것은 처리 시간을 허락할 것이다. / 그들이 그 상황을 받아들이고 / 일어나고 있는 일을 최대한으로 활용할 수 있는

우리는 소통하기 위해 더 이상 전보를 보내지 않지만 이것은 사전 통보를 하는 것에 대한 훌륭한 비유이다. 때때로 여러분은 중요한 정보를 미리 잘 전달함으로써 다가오는 변화를 자신에게 가까운 사람들에게 알려야 한다. 사람들에게 그 변화를 이해하고 받아들일 충분한 시간을 주지 않고 "지금부터 우리는 일을 다르게 할 겁니다."라고 말하는 것과 "다음 달부터 우리는 일에 다르게 접근할 겁니다." 같은 말을 하는 것 사이에는 큰 차이가 있다. 전보를 보내는 것은 사람들이 적응할 수 있도록 해 준다. 전보를 보내는 것은 다가오는 사건이나 상황을 보고 다른 사람들에게 그 변화를 처리하고 받아들일 충분한 시간을 주는 기술을 포함한다. 사람들을 익숙하고 편안한 것에서 벗어나게 할 무엇이든 전보로 보내라. 이것은 그들이 그 상황을 받아들이고 일어나고 있는 일을 최대한으로 활용할 수 있는 처리 시간을 허락할 것이다.

Why? 왜 정답일까?

빈칸이 포함된 문장 뒤에서 비유적 의미의 전보는 사람들이 다가오는 변화를 처리하고 받아들일 시간을 충분히 준다(Telegraphing involves the art of seeing an upcoming event or circumstance and giving others enough time to process and accept the change. / This will allow processing time for them to accept the circumstances and make the most of what's happening.)고 설명하므로, 빈칸에 들어갈 말로 가장 적절한 것은 ② '적응할' 이다.

- telegraph ⑩ 전보
- convey ⑨ 전달하다
- circumstance ⑩ 상황
- metaphor ⑩ 은유
- empower ⑨ 권한을 주다
- make the most of ~을 최대한 활용하다

구문 풀이

2행 Sometimes, you must inform those close to you of upcoming change by conveying important information well in advance.
「inform+A」 「of+B: A에게 B를 알리다」
「by+동명사: ~함으로써」

32 우리의 존재를 규정하는 기억 정답률 62% | 정답 ①

다음 빈칸에 들어갈 말로 가장 적절한 것을 고르시오.
✓ makes us who we are - 우리를 우리 모습으로 만들어 준다
② has to do with our body - 우리 신체와 관련이 있다
③ reflects what we expect - 우리의 예상을 반영한다
④ lets us understand others - 우리가 남을 이해하게 해준다
⑤ helps us learn from the past - 우리가 과거로부터 배우도록 도와준다

Not only does memory / underlie our ability to think at all, / it defines the content of our experiences / and how we preserve them for years to come.
기억은 ~할 뿐만 아니라 / 어쨌든 우리의 사고력의 기반이 될 / 그것은 우리의 경험의 내용을 규정한다. / 그리고 다가올 수년 간 우리가 그것을 보존하는 방식을

Memory makes us who we are.
기억은 우리를 우리 모습으로 만들어 준다.

If I were to suffer from heart failure / and depend upon an artificial heart, / I would be no less myself.
만약 내가 심부전을 앓고 / 인공 심장에 의존한다 해도 / 나는 역시 여느 때의 나일 것이다.

If I lost an arm in an accident / and had it replaced with an artificial arm, / I would still be essentially *me*.
만약 내가 사고로 한 팔을 잃고 / 그것을 인공 팔로 교체한다 해도 / 나는 여전히 본질적으로 *나*일 것이다.

As long as my mind and memories remain intact, / I will continue to be the same person, / no matter which part of my body (other than the brain) is replaced.
나의 정신과 기억이 손상되지 않은 한, / 나는 계속 같은 사람일 것이다. / (뇌를 제외하고) 내 신체의 어떤 부분이 교체될지라도

On the other hand, / when someone suffers from advanced Alzheimer's disease / and his memories fade, / people often say / that he "is not himself anymore," / or that it is as if the person "is no longer there," / though his body remains unchanged.
반면 / 누군가 후기 알츠하이머병을 앓고 / 그의 기억이 흐려진다면, / 사람들은 종종 말한다. / 그는 '더 이상 여느 때의 그가 아니다'라거나 / 마치 그 사람이 '더 이상 그곳에 없다'는 것 같다고 / 비록 그의 신체는 변하지 않은 채로 남아 있음에도 불구하고

기억은 어쨌든 우리의 사고력의 기반이 될 뿐만 아니라 우리의 경험의 내용과 다가올 수년 간 우리가 그것을 보존하는 방식을 규정한다. 기억은 <u>우리를 우리 모습으로 만들어 준다.</u> 만약 내가 심부전을 앓고 인공 심장에 의존한다 해도 나는 역시 여느 때의 나일 것이다. 만약 내가 사고로 한 팔을 잃고 인공 팔로 교체한다 해도 나는 여전히 본질적으로 *나*일 것이다. 나의 정신과 기억이 손상되지 않은 한, (뇌를 제외하고) 내 신체의 어떤 부분이 교체될지라도 나는 계속 같은 사람일 것이다. 반면 누군가 후기 알츠하이머병을 앓고 그의 기억이 흐려진다면, 비록 그의 신체는 변하지 않은 채로 남아 있음에도 불구하고 사람들은 종종 '더 이상 여느 때의 그가 아니'라거나 마치 그 사람이 '더 이상 그곳에 없'는 것 같다고 말한다.

Why? 왜 정답일까?

빈칸 뒤에서 예시를 통해 우리는 기억을 보존하는 한 같은 사람으로 여겨지지만 (As long as my mind and memories remain intact, I will continue to be the same person, ~) 기억을 잃는 경우에는 그렇지 않다는 내용을 제시하고 있다. 따라서 예시 내용을 요약하는 빈칸에 들어갈 말로 가장 적절한 것은 기억이 곧 우리 존재의 본질을 결정짓는다는 의미의 ① '우리를 우리 모습으로 만들어 준다'이다.

- **underlie** ⓥ (~의) 기반을 이루다
- **essentially** [ad] 본질적으로
- **fade** ⓥ 흐려지다, (빛이) 바래다

구문 풀이

3행 If I were to suffer from heart failure and depend upon an artificial heart, I would be no less myself.
┌ 'if + 주어 + were to + 동사원형 ~'┐
주어 + 조동사 과거형 + 동사원형 : 가정법 미래(가능성이 희박한 일)

★★★ 등급을 가르는 문제!

33 아기의 언어 습득에 바탕이 되는 통계 분석 능력   정답률 41% | 정답 ②

다음 빈칸에 들어갈 말로 가장 적절한 것을 고르시오. [3점]
① lack of social pressures – 사회적 압력의 부족
✓ ability to calculate statistics – 통계를 계산하는 능력
③ desire to interact with others – 타인과 상호작용하려는 욕구
④ preference for simpler sounds – 더 간단한 소리에 대한 선호
⑤ tendency to imitate caregivers – 양육자를 모방하려는 경향

Over time, / babies construct expectations / about what sounds they will hear when.
시간이 지나면서 / 아기는 기대를 형성한다. / 자신이 어떤 소리를 언제 들을지에 대한

They hold in memory the sound patterns / that occur on a regular basis.
그들은 소리 패턴을 기억한다. / 규칙적으로 발생하는

They make hypotheses / like, "If I hear *this* sound first, / it probably will be followed by *that* sound."
그들은 가설을 세운다. / '내가 *이* 소리를 먼저 들으면 / 그것에 아마도 *저* 소리가 따라올 것이다'와 같은

Scientists conclude / that much of babies' skill in learning language / is due to their <u>ability to calculate statistics.</u>
과학자들은 결론짓는다. / 아기의 언어 학습 능력의 상당 부분이 / 통계를 계산하는 능력 때문이라고

For babies, / this means / that they appear to pay close attention / to the patterns that repeat in language.
아기에게 있어 / 이것은 의미한다. / 그들이 세심한 주의를 기울이는 것처럼 보인다는 것을 / 언어에서 반복되는 패턴에

They remember, in a systematic way, / how often sounds occur, / in what order, / with what intervals, / and with what changes of pitch.
그들은 체계적인 방식으로 기억한다. / 소리가 얼마나 자주 발생하는지를 / 어떤 순서로, / 어떤 간격으로 / 그리고 어떤 음조의 변화로

This memory store allows them to track, / within the neural circuits of their brains, / the frequency of sound patterns / and to use this knowledge / to make predictions about the meaning in patterns of sounds.
이 기억 저장소는 그들이 추적하게 해 주고, / 자신의 뇌의 신경 회로 내에서 / 소리 패턴의 빈도를 / 이 지식을 사용하도록 해 준다. / 소리 패턴의 의미에 대한 예측을 하기 위해

시간이 지나면서 아기는 자신이 어떤 소리를 언제 들을지에 대한 기대를 형성한다. 그들은 규칙적으로 발생하는 소리 패턴을 기억한다. 그들은 '내가 *이* 소리를 먼저 들으면 아마도 *저* 소리가 따라올 것이다'와 같은 가설을 세운다. 과학자들은 아기의 언어 학습 능력의 상당 부분이 통계를 계산하는 능력 때문이라고 결론짓는다. 아기에게 있어 이것은 그들이 언어에서 반복되는 패턴에 세심한 주의를 기울이는 것처럼 보인다는 것을 의미한다. 그들은 소리가 얼마나 자주, 어떤 순서로, 어떤 간격으로, 어떤 음조의 변화로 발생하는지를 체계적인 방식으로 기억한다. 이 기억 저장소는 그들이 뇌의 신경 회로 내에서 소리 패턴의 빈도를 추적하고, 이 지식을 사용해 소리 패턴의 의미에 대해 예측하게 해준다.

Why? 왜 정답일까?

마지막 두 문장에서 아기들은 패턴이 어떻게 반복되는지에 관한 세부 사항을 기억하고, 패턴의 빈도를 추

적하여 후에 의미를 예측할 때 그러한 정보를 사용한다고 설명하고 있다. 빈칸에는 이러한 일련의 인지 작용을 일반화하는 말이 필요하므로, 빈칸에 들어갈 말로 가장 적절한 것은 ② '통계를 계산하는 능력'이다.

- **construct** ⓥ 형성하다, 구성하다
- **hypothesis** ⓝ 가설
- **interval** ⓝ 간격
- **calculate** ⓥ 계산하다
- **on a regular basis** 규칙적으로
- **systematic** ⓐ 체계적인
- **make a prediction** 예측하다
- **statistics** ⓝ 통계

구문 풀이

10행 This memory store allows them to track, (within the neural circuits of 5형식 동사 목적어 목적격 보어1
their brains), the frequency of sound patterns and to use this knowledge to make
( ): 삽입구   to track 목적어   목적격 보어2   부사적 용법(목적)
predictions about the meaning in patterns of sounds.

★★ 문제 해결 꿀~팁 ★★

▶ 많이 틀린 이유는?
아기들의 언어 소리 습관에 관한 글이다. 빈칸 뒤로, 아기들이 언어에서 반복되는 소리에 주의를 기울이고, 소리의 빈도나 순서, 고저를 분석하여 언어 패턴을 익혀 나간다는 설명이 이어지고 있다. '더 간단한' 소리를 선호한다는 내용은 언급되지 않기에 ④는 답으로 적절하지 않다.
▶ 문제 해결 방법은?
아기들이 주변에서 들은 소리 데이터를 바탕으로 그 패턴을 분석하여 추후 예측에 활용한다는 설명을 '통계 자료 계산(calculate statistics)'이라는 비유적 표현으로 일반화할 수 있어야 한다.

34 심해 생물이 자체 발광하는 이유   정답률 55% | 정답 ④

다음 빈칸에 들어갈 말로 가장 적절한 것을 고르시오. [3점]
① send a signal for help – 도움 요청의 신호를 보내는
② threaten enemies nearby – 주위의 적을 위협하는
③ lift the veil of hidden prey – 숨어 있는 먹이의 베일을 벗기는
✓ create a cloak of invisibility – 보이지 않는 망토를 만드는
⑤ serve as a navigation system – 네비게이션 시스템의 역할을 하는

Some deep-sea organisms / are known to use bioluminescence as a lure, / to attract prey with a little glow / imitating the movements of their favorite fish, / or like fireflies, / as a sexual attractant to find mates.
일부 심해 생물은 / 가짜 미끼로 생물 발광을 활용한다고 알려져 있다. / 작은 빛으로 먹이를 유혹하기 위해 / 그들이 좋아하는 물고기의 움직임을 모방하는 / 혹은 반딧불이처럼 / 짝을 찾기 위한 성적 유인 물질로

While there are many possible evolutionary theories / for the survival value of bioluminescence, / one of the most fascinating is / to create a cloak of invisibility.
많은 가능한 진화 이론이 있지만 / 생물 발광의 생존가에 대한 / 가장 흥미로운 것 중 하나는 ~이다. / 보이지 않는 망토를 만드는 것

The color of almost all bioluminescent molecules / is blue-green, / the same color as the ocean above.
거의 모든 생물 발광 분자의 색깔은 / 청록색이다. / 바다 위층과 같은 색인

By self-glowing blue-green, / the creatures no longer cast a shadow or create a silhouette, / especially when viewed from below / against the brighter waters above.
청록색으로 자체 발광함으로써 / 생물은 더 이상 그림자를 드리우거나 실루엣을 만들어 내지 않는다. / 특히 아래에서 보여질 때 / 위쪽의 더 밝은 물을 배경으로

Rather, / by glowing themselves, / they can blend into the sparkles, reflections, and scattered blue-green glow / of sunlight or moonlight.
오히려 / 스스로 발광함으로써 / 그들은 반짝임, 반사 그리고 분산된 청록색 빛에 섞일 수 있다. / 햇빛 혹은 달빛의

Thus, / they are most likely making their own light / not to see, but to be un-seen.
따라서 / 그들은 자신만의 빛을 분명 만들어 내고 있을 것이다. / 보기 위해서가 아니라 보이지 않기 위해서

일부 심해 생물은 그들이 좋아하는 물고기의 움직임을 모방하는 작은 빛으로 먹이를 유혹하기 위해 가짜 미끼로, 혹은 반딧불이처럼 짝을 찾기 위한 성적 유인 물질로 생물 발광을 활용한다고 알려져 있다. 생물 발광의 생존가에 대한 많은 가능한 진화 이론이 있지만, 가장 흥미로운 것 중 하나는 보이지 않는 망토를 만드는 것이다. 거의 모든 생물 발광 분자의 색깔은 바다 위층과 같은 색인 청록색이다. 청록색으로 자체 발광함으로써 생물은 특히 위쪽의 더 밝은 물을 배경으로 아래에서 볼 때 더 이상 그림자를 드리우거나 실루엣을 만들어 내지 않는다. 오히려 스스로 발광함으로써 그들은 햇빛 혹은 달빛의 반짝임, 반사 그리고 분산된 청록색 빛에 섞일 수 있다. 따라서 그들은 보기 위해서가 아니라 보이지 않기 위해서 분명 자신만의 빛을 만들어 내고 있을 것이다.

Why? 왜 정답일까?

마지막 문장에서 심해 생물들이 자체 발광하는 이유를 설명하는데, 이들은 바다 위층과 똑같은 색인 청록색으로 빛을 냄으로써 오히려 그 빛에 섞이고(~ by glowing themselves, they can blend into ~), 눈에 더 띄지 않게 될 수 있다(~ most likely making their own light not to see, but to be un-seen.)는 것이다. 따라서 빈칸에 들어갈 말로 가장 적절한 것은 ④ '보이지 않으려' 한다는 목적을 비유적으로 설명한 ④ '보이지 않는 망토를 만드는'이다.

- **attractant** ⓝ 유인 물질
- **cast** ⓥ 드리우다, 던지다
- **scatter** ⓥ 흩뜨리다, 분산하다
- **cloak** ⓝ 망토
- **fascinating** ⓐ 매력적인, 흥미로운
- **blend into** ~에 섞이다
- **threaten** ⓥ 위협하다
- **invisibility** ⓝ 보이지 않음

구문 풀이

1행 Some deep-sea organisms are known to use bioluminescence as a lure,
전치사1(~로서)
「be known + to부정사 : ~한다고 알려지다」
to attract prey with a little glow imitating the movements of their favorite fish, or
부사적 용법(~하기 위해)
like fireflies, as a sexual attractant to find mates.
전치사2(~로서)   형용사적 용법

35 인간의 편향을 강화하도록 작용하는 검색 알고리즘   정답률 62% | 정답 ③

다음 글에서 전체 흐름과 관계 <u>없는</u> 문장은?

Internet activist Eli Pariser noticed / how online search algorithms encourage our human tendency / to grab hold of everything / that confirms the beliefs we already hold, / while quietly ignoring information / that doesn't match those beliefs.
인터넷 활동가인 Eli Pariser는 주목했는데, / 온라인 검색 알고리즘이 인간의 경향을 어떻게 조장하는지에 / 모든 것을 움켜쥐고, / 우리가 이미 지닌 신념이 옳음을 확인해 주는 / 반면에 정보는 조용히 무시하는 / 그러한 신념과 맞지 않는

① We set up a so-called "filter-bubble" around ourselves, / where we are constantly exposed only to that material / that we agree with.
우리는 자신의 주변에 소위 '필터 버블'을 설치하는데 / 그곳에서 우리는 그런 자료에만 끊임없이 노출된다. / 자신이 동의하는

② We are never challenged, / never giving ourselves the opportunity / to acknowledge the existence of diversity and difference.
우리는 결코 이의를 제기 받지 않으며 / 결코 우리 자신에게 기회를 주지 않는다. / 다양성과 차이의 존재를 인정할

✓ Creating a difference that others don't have / is a way to succeed in your field, / leading to the creation of innovations.
다른 사람이 갖지 못한 차이를 만들어 내는 것이 / 자신의 분야에서 성공하는 방법이며 / 혁신의 창조를 이끈다.

④ In the best case, / we become naive and sheltered, / and in the worst, / we become radicalized with extreme views, / unable to imagine life outside our particular bubble.
최상의 경우, / 우리는 세상을 모르고 보호 받으며, / 최악의 경우 / 우리는 극단적인 시각으로 과격화되어 / 우리의 특정 버블 밖의 삶을 상상할 수 없게 된다.

⑤ The results are disastrous: / intellectual isolation and the real distortion / that comes with believing / that the little world we create for ourselves / is *the* world.
그 결과는 참담하다. / 지적 고립과 진정한 왜곡 / 믿게 되어 따라오는 / 우리가 스스로 만드는 작은 세계가 / *전* 세계라고

인터넷 활동가인 Eli Pariser는 온라인 검색 알고리즘이 우리가 이미 지닌 신념이 옳음을 확인해 주는 모든 것을 움켜쥐고, 반면에 그러한 신념과 맞지 않는 정보는 조용히 무시하는 인간의 경향을 어떻게 조장하는지에 주목했다. ① 우리는 자신의 주변에 소위 '필터 버블'을 설치하는데 그곳에서 우리는 자신이 동의하는 그런 자료에만 끊임없이 노출된다. ② 우리는 결코 이의를 제기 받지 않으며 스스로에게 다양성과 차이의 존재를 인정할 기회를 주지 않는다. ③ 다른 사람이 갖지 못한 차이를 만들어 내는 것이 자신의 분야에서 성공하는 방법이며 혁신의 창조를 이끈다. ④ 최상의 경우 우리는 세상을 모르고 보호 받으며, 최악의 경우 우리는 극단적인 시각으로 과격화되어 우리의 특정 버블 밖의 삶을 상상할 수 없게 된다. ⑤ 그 결과는 참담하여, 예를 들면 지적 고립과 우리가 스스로 만드는 작은 세계가 *전* 세계라고 믿게 되어 따라오는 진정한 왜곡이 있다.

Why? 왜 정답일까?
첫 문장에서 온라인 검색 알고리즘은 이미 믿고 있는 신념을 확인해주는 정보를 주로 보려 하는 인간의 편향을 강화한다고 언급한다. 이어서 ①과 ②는 우리가 '필터 버블' 안에 갇혀 다양성과 차이를 인정할 기회를 갖지 못한다고 설명하고, ④와 ⑤는 그로 인한 부정적 결과를 설명한다. 하지만 ③은 다른 사람이 갖지 못한 차이를 만들어낼 때 자기 분야에서 성공할 수 있다는 내용이므로 흐름에서 벗어난다. 따라서 전체 흐름과 관계 없는 문장은 ③이다.

- grab hold of ~을 (갑자기) 움켜잡다
- filter-bubble ⓝ 필터 버블(사용자가 인터넷 알고리즘에 의해 관심 있는 정보만 접하며 왜곡된 인지 속에 갇히는 것)
- acknowledge 인정하다
- existence ⓝ 존재
- innovation ⓝ 혁신
- disastrous ⓐ 참담한
- isolation ⓝ 고립

구문 풀이

4행 We set up a so-called "filter-bubble" around ourselves, where we are
장소 선행사 / 계속적 용법
constantly exposed only to that material [that we agree with].
선행사 / 목적격 관·대

★★★ 등급을 가르는 문제!
36 전자 상거래의 성장 정답률 42% | 정답 ③
주어진 글 다음에 이어질 글의 순서로 가장 적절한 것을 고르시오.
① (A) - (C) - (B) ② (B) - (A) - (C) ✓ (B) - (C) - (A)
④ (C) - (A) - (B) ⑤ (C) - (B) - (A)

Roughly twenty years ago, / brick-and-mortar stores began to give way to electronic commerce.
대략 20년 전 / 오프라인 거래 상점이 전자 상거래(온라인)로 바뀌기 시작했다.
For good or bad, / the shift fundamentally changed consumers' perception of the shopping experience.
좋든 나쁘든 간에 / 그 변화는 쇼핑 경험에 대한 소비자의 인식을 근본적으로 바꾸었다.
(B) Nowhere was the shift more obvious / than with book sales, / which is how online bookstores got their start.
그 변화가 더 분명한 곳은 없었는데 / 책 판매보다 / 그렇게 해서 온라인 서점이 시작되었다.
Physical bookstores simply could not stock / as many titles as a virtual bookstore could.
물리적인 서점은 그야말로 구비할 수 없었다 / 가상 서점이 할 수 있는 만큼 많은 서적을
There is only so much space available on a shelf.
딱 책꽂이 위의 공간만큼만 이용 가능했다.
(C) In addition to greater variety, / online bookstores were also able to offer aggressive discounts / thanks to their lower operating costs.
더 많은 다양성뿐만 아니라 / 온라인 서점은 또한 대단히 적극적으로 할인을 제공할 수 있었다. / 그들의 더 낮은 운영비 덕분에
The combination of lower prices and greater selection / led to the slow, steady rise of online bookstores.
더 낮은 가격과 더 많은 선택의 결합은 / 온라인 서점의 느리지만 꾸준한 상승으로 이어졌다.
(A) Before long, / the e-commerce book market / naturally expanded to include additional categories, / like CDs and DVDs.
머지않아 / 전자 상거래 책 시장은 / 추가적인 항목을 포함하도록 자연스럽게 확장되었다. / CD와 DVD 같은
E-commerce soon snowballed / into the enormous industry it is today, / where you can buy everything / from toilet paper to cars online.
전자 상거래는 곧 눈덩이처럼 불어났고, / 오늘날의 거대 산업으로 / 여기서 여러분은 모든 것을 온라인으로 살 수 있다. / 화장실 휴지에서 자동차까지

대략 20년 전 오프라인 거래 상점이 전자 상거래(온라인)로 바뀌기 시작했다. 좋든 나쁘든 간에 그 변화는 쇼핑 경험에 대한 소비자의 인식을 근본적으로 바꾸었다.
(B) 그 변화가 책 판매보다 더 분명한 곳은 없었는데, 그렇게 해서 온라인 서점이 시작되었다. 물리적인 서점은 가상 서점이 할 수 있는 만큼 많은 서적을 그야말로 구비할 수 없었다. 딱 책꽂이 위의 공간만큼만 이용 가능했다.

(C) 더 많은 다양성뿐만 아니라 온라인 서점은 또한 더 낮은 운영비 덕분에 대단히 적극적으로 할인을 제공할 수 있었다. 더 싼 가격과 더 많은 선택의 결합은 온라인 서점의 느리지만 꾸준한 상승으로 이어졌다.

(A) 머지않아 전자 상거래 책 시장은 CD와 DVD 같은 추가적인 항목을 포함하도록 자연스럽게 확장되었다. 전자 상거래는 곧 오늘날의 거대 산업으로 눈덩이처럼 불어났고, 여기서 여러분은 화장실 휴지에서 자동차까지 모든 것을 온라인으로 살 수 있다.

Why? 왜 정답일까?
주어진 글은 약 20년 전 전자 상거래가 시작되어 쇼핑에 대한 인식을 변화시켰다는 일반적인 내용을 제시한다. 이어서 (B)는 특히 온라인 서점의 사례를 언급하며, 물리적 서점에 비해 온라인 서점이 공간적 이점을 지녔다고 설명한다. (C)는 온라인 서점이 또한 가격 우위를 지녔음을 언급하고, (A)는 온라인 서점 분야가 CD, DVD 등으로 확장되었음을 설명한다. 따라서 글의 순서로 가장 적절한 것은 ③ '(B) - (C) - (A)'이다.

- roughly ⓐⓓ 약, 대략
- fundamentally ⓐⓓ 근본적으로
- aggressive ⓐ 공격적인, (대단히) 적극적인
- give way to ~로 바뀌다
- enormous ⓐ 거대한
- operating cost 운영비

구문 풀이

9행 Nowhere was the shift more obvious than with book sales, which is how
'장소 부사구 + 동사 + 주어 : 도치 구문' / 계속적 용법(선행사 : 앞 문장)
online bookstores got their start.

★★ 문제 해결 꿀~팁 ★★
▶ 많이 틀린 이유는?
(B) 이후 (A)와 (C)의 순서를 잘 잡는 것이 관건이다. (B)에서 온라인 서점이 오프라인 서점보다 책을 다양하게 구비했다는 장점을 소개한 후, (A)는 온라인 서점 시장이 다른 부문으로 확장되었다는 내용을, (C)는 온라인 서점의 추가적 장점을 언급한다. 흐름상 (C)에서 온라인 서점의 장점에 관한 설명을 마무리하고, (A)에서 이 장점을 바탕으로 다른 상품 분야로의 확장이 가능했다는 결론을 내리는 것이 자연스럽다. 따라서 ② '(B) - (A) - (C)'는 답으로 부적절하다.
▶ 문제 해결 방법은?
(B)의 as many titles as a virtual bookstore가 (C)의 greater variety로 연결된다. 이어서 (C)의 결론인 the slow, steady rise of online bookstores가 (A)의 the e-commerce book market naturally expanded to include additional categories로 연결되며, 온라인 서점 사업이 책을 넘어 CD, DVD 등 다양한 부문으로 확장되었다는 최종적 결론에 이르고 있다.

★★★ 등급을 가르는 문제!
37 문학 텍스트의 이해 정답률 43% | 정답 ⑤
주어진 글 다음에 이어질 글의 순서로 가장 적절한 것을 고르시오. [3점]
① (A) - (C) - (B) ② (B) - (A) - (C) ③ (B) - (C) - (A)
④ (C) - (A) - (B) ✓ (C) - (B) - (A)

Literary works, / by their nature, / suggest rather than explain; / they imply rather than state their claims boldly and directly.
문학 작품들은 / 그 본질상 / 설명하기보다는 암시하는데, / 그들은 그들의 주장을 뚜렷하고 직접적으로 진술하기보다는 함축한다.
(C) This broad generalization, / however, / does not mean / that works of literature do not include direct statements.
이 넓은 일반화는 / 그러나 / 뜻하지는 않는다. / 문학 작품들이 직접적인 진술을 포함하지 않는다는 것을
Depending on when they were written and by whom, / literary works may include large amounts of direct telling / and lesser amounts of suggestion and implication.
그들이 언제 그리고 누구에 의해 쓰였는지에 따라 / 문학 작품들은 많은 양의 직접적 말하기를 포함할 수도 있다. / 그리고 더 적은 양의 암시와 함축을
(B) But whatever the proportion of a work's showing to telling, / there is always something for readers to interpret.
하지만 작품에서 말하기 대 보여 주기의 비율이 어떻든 간에 / 독자가 해석해야 하는 무언가가 항상 존재한다.
Thus we ask the question / "What does the text suggest?" / as a way to approach literary interpretation, / as a way to begin thinking about a text's implications.
그러므로 우리는 질문을 한다. / "그 텍스트가 무엇을 암시하는가?"라는 / 문학적 해석에 접근하는 방법이자 / 텍스트의 함축에 대해 생각하기 시작하는 방법인
(A) What a text implies / is often of great interest to us.
텍스트가 무엇을 함축하는지는 / 종종 우리에게 매우 흥미롭다.
And our work of figuring out a text's implications / tests our analytical powers.
그리고 / 텍스트의 함축을 알아내는 우리의 작업은 / 우리의 분석적 능력을 시험한다.
In considering what a text suggests, / we gain practice in making sense of texts.
텍스트가 무엇을 암시하는지를 고려하는 과정에서 / 우리는 텍스트를 이해하는 기량을 얻게 된다.

문학 작품들은 그 본질상 설명하기보다는 암시하는데, 그들은 주장을 뚜렷하게 직접적으로 진술하기보다는 함축한다.
(C) 그러나 이 넓은 일반화는 문학 작품들이 직접적인 진술을 포함하지 않는다는 뜻은 아니다. 그들이 언제 누구에 의해 쓰였는지에 따라, 문학 작품들은 많은 양의 직접적 말하기와 더 적은 양의 암시와 함축을 포함할 수도 있다.
(B) 하지만 작품에서 말하기 대 보여 주기의 비율이 어떻든 간에 독자가 해석해야 하는 무언가가 항상 존재한다. 그러므로 우리는 문학적 해석에 접근하는 방법이자 텍스트의 함축에 대해 생각하기 시작하는 방법으로 "그 텍스트가 무엇을 암시하는가?"라는 질문을 한다.
(A) 텍스트가 무엇을 함축하는지는 종종 우리에게 매우 흥미롭다. 그리고 텍스트의 함축을 알아내는 작업은 우리의 분석적 능력을 시험한다. 텍스트가 무엇을 암시하는지를 고려하는 과정에서 우리는 텍스트를 이해하는 기량을 얻게 된다.

Why? 왜 정답일까?
주어진 글은 문학 작품의 특징으로 함축적 진술을 언급한다. 이어서 (C)는 however로 주의를 환기하며 문학 작품 안에 직접적 진술이 전혀 없지는 않다는 점을 상기시킨다. 한편 But으로 시작하는 (B)는 직접적 진술과 함축적 진술의 비율이 어떻든 간에 문학 텍스트에는 항상 독자가 해석해야 하는 부분이 있으며, 이 때문에 우리가 '그 텍스트가 무엇을 암시하는지' 자문하게 된다고 언급한다. (A)는 (B)의 "What does the text suggest?"를 What a text implies로 바꾸어 표현하며, 텍스트가 함축하는 바를

알아내는 과정에서 우리가 텍스트를 이해하는 능력을 기르게 된다고 설명한다. 따라서 글의 순서로 가장 적절한 것은 ⑤ '(C) − (B) − (A)'이다.

- literary ⓐ 문학의
- boldly ⓐ 뚜렷하게, 대담하게
- analytical ⓐ 분석적인
- generalization ⓝ 일반화
- nature ⓝ 본질, 본성
- implication ⓝ 함축, 암시
- interpret ⓥ 해석하다

구문 풀이
3행 What a text implies is often of great interest to us.
주어(명사절)　　　　　 동사(단수)　 보어(=greatly interesting)

★★ 문제 해결 꿀~팁 ★★

▶ 많이 틀린 이유는?
(B)와 (C)의 순서를 잘 파악하는 것이 관건이다. 얼핏 보면 주어진 글의 imply rather than state가 (B)의 showing과 telling으로 바로 연결되는 것 같지만, (B)의 핵심은 '독자의 해석과 이해에 관한 것이다. 이에 반해 (C)는 주어진 글과 마찬가지로 문학적인 글의 말하기 방식에 관해서 다루고 있으므로, 화제의 흐름상 (C)가 먼저 나온 뒤 (B)로 전환되는 것이 자연스럽다.

▶ 문제 해결 방법은?
주어진 글의 'Literary works ~ imply rather than state their claims boldly and directly.'가 (C)의 This broad generalization으로 이어지고, (C)의 literary works may contain large amounts of direct telling and lesser amounts of suggestion and implication이 (B)의 the proportion of a work's showing to telling으로 연결된다. 즉 (C)까지 문학 작품 속의 말하기와 보여주기(의 비중)에 관해 설명한 뒤, (B)에서 '그 비중에 상관없이' 독자가 해석할 부분이 있다는 내용으로 넘어가는 흐름임을 파악하도록 한다.

---

38 보충제를 통한 영양소 섭취
정답률 58% | 정답 ④

글의 흐름으로 보아, 주어진 문장이 들어가기에 가장 적절한 곳을 고르시오.

According to top nutrition experts, / most nutrients are better absorbed and used by the body / when consumed from a whole food / instead of a supplement.
최고의 영양 전문가들에 의하면 / 많은 영양소가 신체에 의해 더 잘 흡수되고 사용된다. / 자연식품으로부터 섭취되었을 때 / 보충제 대신에

① However, / many people feel the need / to take pills, powders, and supplements / in an attempt to obtain nutrients / and fill the gaps in their diets.
그러나 / 많은 사람들이 필요성을 느낀다. / 알약, 분말 그리고 보충제를 섭취할 / 영양소를 얻기 위한 시도로 / 그리고 자신의 식단에 있어 부족한 부분을 채우기 위한

② We hope / these will give us more energy, / prevent us from catching a cold in the winter, / or improve our skin and hair.
우리는 바란다. / 이것들이 우리에게 더 많은 에너지를 주고, / 우리가 겨울에 감기에 걸리는 것을 막아 주거나 / 혹은 우리의 피부와 모발을 개선해 주기를

③ But in reality, / the large majority of supplements are artificial / and may not even be completely absorbed by your body.
그러나 실제로는 / 대다수의 보충제가 인위적이고 / 여러분의 신체에 의해 완전히 흡수조차 되지 않을 수도 있다.

✔ Worse, / some are contaminated with other substances / and contain ingredients not listed on the label.
더 심각한 것은, / 어떤 것들은 다른 물질로 오염되어 있으며 / 라벨에 실려 있지 않은 성분을 포함한다.

For example, / a recent investigative report found heavy metals / in 40 percent of 134 brands of protein powders on the market.
예를 들어 / 최근 한 조사 보고는 중금속을 발견했다. / 시장에 있는 단백질 분말 134개 브랜드 중 40퍼센트에서

⑤ With little control and regulation, / taking supplements is a gamble and often costly.
단속과 규제가 거의 없다면 / 보충제를 섭취하는 것은 도박이며 종종 대가가 크다.

최고의 영양 전문가들에 의하면 많은 영양소가 보충제 대신에 자연식품으로부터 섭취되었을 때 신체에서 더 잘 흡수되고 사용된다. ① 그러나 많은 사람들이 영양소를 얻고 식단에 있어 부족한 부분을 채우기 위한 시도로 알약, 분말 그리고 보충제를 섭취할 필요성을 느낀다. ② 우리는 이것들이 우리에게 더 많은 에너지를 주거나, 겨울에 감기에 걸리는 것을 막아 주거나 우리의 피부와 모발을 개선해 주기를 바란다. ③ 그러나 실제로는 대다수의 보충제가 인위적이고 여러분의 신체에서 완전히 흡수조차 되지 않을 수도 있다. ④ 더 심각한 것은, 어떤 것들은 다른 물질로 오염되어 있으며 라벨에 실려 있지 않은 성분을 포함한다. 예를 들어 최근 한 조사 보고는 시장에 있는 단백질 분말 134개 브랜드 중 40퍼센트에서 중금속을 발견했다. ⑤ 단속과 규제가 거의 없다면 보충제를 섭취하는 것은 도박이며 종종 대가가 크다.

Why? 왜 정답일까?
보충제를 통해 영양소를 섭취하는 것은 생각보다 효과가 없거나 위험할 수 있다는 내용의 글이다. ④ 앞의 문장에서 대다수의 보충제가 실제로 우리 몸에서 잘 흡수되지 않는다고 설명한 후, 주어진 문장은 이것보다 더 심각한 문제(Worse)로 보충제가 다른 물질로 오염되어 있거나 라벨에 없는 성분을 포함하기도 한다고 지적한다. ④ 뒤의 문장은 주어진 문장에 대한 예시로 시중 단백질 분말 브랜드의 40%가 중금속으로 오염되어 있다는 내용을 언급한다. 따라서 주어진 문장이 들어가기에 가장 적절한 곳은 ④이다.

- whole food 자연식품
- nutrition ⓝ 영양
- fill the gap 부족한 부분을 채우다, 간격을 메우다
- regulation ⓝ 규제
- substance ⓝ 물질
- absorb ⓥ 흡수하다
- artificial ⓐ 인위적인

구문 풀이
7행 We hope (that) these will give us more energy, prevent us from catching
　　　　　생략　　　　　　 동사1　　　　 동사2(prevent + A + from + B : A가 B하지 못하게 막다)
a cold in the winter, or improve our skin and hair.
　　　　　　　　　　 동사3

★★★ 등급을 가르는 문제!

39 운동 에너지와 위치 에너지
정답률 35% | 정답 ⑤

글의 흐름으로 보아, 주어진 문장이 들어가기에 가장 적절한 곳을 고르시오. [3점]

[문제편 p.176]

In general, / kinetic energy is the energy associated with motion, / while potential energy represents the energy / which is "stored" in a physical system.
일반적으로 / 운동 에너지는 운동과 관련 있는 에너지이며 / 반면에 위치 에너지는 에너지를 나타낸다. / 물리계에 '저장되는'

Moreover, / the total energy is always conserved.
게다가 총 에너지는 항상 보존된다.

① But while the total energy remains unchanged, / the kinetic and potential parts of the total energy / can change all the time.
그러나 총 에너지가 변하지 않는 채로 있는 반면 / 총 에너지의 운동과 위치 에너지 비율은 / 항상 변할 수 있다.

② Imagine, for example, a pendulum / which swings back and forth.
예를 들어 추를 상상해 보자. / 앞뒤로 흔들리는

③ When it swings, / it sweeps out an arc / and then slows down / as it comes closer to its highest point, / where the pendulum does not move at all.
그것이 흔들릴 때 / 그것은 호 모양으로 쓸어내리듯 움직이다가 / 그리고 나서 속도가 줄어드는데, / 그것이 최고점에 가까워지면서 / 이 지점에서 추는 더 이상 움직이지 않는다.

④ So at this point, / the energy is completely given in terms of potential energy.
그래서 이 지점에서 / 에너지는 완전히 위치 에너지로 주어지게 된다.

✔ But after this brief moment of rest, / the pendulum swings back again / and therefore part of the total energy is then given / in the form of kinetic energy.
하지만 이 짧은 순간의 멈춤 이후에 / 그 추는 다시 뒤로 흔들리게 되며 / 따라서 총 에너지의 일부가 그때 주어진다. / 운동 에너지의 형태로

So as the pendulum swings, / kinetic and potential energy / constantly change into each other.
그래서 그 추가 흔들리면서 / 운동과 위치 에너지는 / 끊임없이 서로 바뀐다.

일반적으로 운동 에너지는 운동과 관련 있는 에너지인 반면에, 위치 에너지는 물리계에 '저장되는' 에너지를 나타낸다. 게다가 총 에너지는 항상 보존된다. ① 그러나 총 에너지가 변하지 않는 채로 있는 반면 총 에너지의 운동과 위치 에너지 비율은 항상 변할 수 있다. ② 예를 들어 앞뒤로 흔들리는 추를 상상해 보자. ③ 그것은 흔들릴 때 호 모양으로 쓸어내리듯 움직이다가, 그리고 나서 최고점에 가까워지면서 속도가 줄어드는데, 이 지점에서 추는 더 이상 움직이지 않는다. ④ 그래서 이 지점에서 에너지는 완전히 위치 에너지로 주어지게 된다. ⑤ 하지만 이 짧은 순간의 멈춤 이후에 그 추는 다시 뒤로 흔들리게 되며, 따라서 총 에너지의 일부가 그때 운동 에너지의 형태로 주어진다. 그래서 그 추가 흔들리면서 운동과 위치 에너지는 끊임없이 서로 바뀐다.

Why? 왜 정답일까?
위치 에너지와 운동 에너지는 같은 에너지 총량 안에서 계속 서로 바뀐다는 내용의 글로, ② 뒤의 문장부터 흔들리는 추를 예로 들어 이 변화를 설명하고 있다. ⑤ 앞의 두 문장에서 추의 높이가 최고점에 이르면 추는 더 이상 움직이지 않고, 모든 에너지가 위치 에너지로 바뀐다고 언급한다. 주어진 문장은 But으로 흐름을 전환하며, 이 짧은 멈춤(this brief moment of rest) 이후에 다시 추가 뒤로 흔들리면서 일부 에너지가 다시 운동 에너지로 바뀐다고 설명한다. ⑤ 뒤의 문장은 그리하여 운동 에너지와 위치 에너지는 서로 끊임없이 교환되는 관계라는 결론을 제시한다. 따라서 주어진 문장이 들어가기에 가장 적절한 곳은 ⑤이다.

- kinetic energy 운동 에너지
- swing back and forth 앞뒤로 흔들리다
- constantly ⓐ 지속적으로, 끊임없이
- potential energy 위치 에너지
- sweep out 쓸어내리다

구문 풀이
10행 When it swings, it sweeps out an arc and then slows down as it comes
　　　　　　　　　　　　　　동사1　　　　　　　　　　　 동사2
closer to its highest point, where the pendulum does not move at all.
　　　선행사　　　　　 관계부사(계속적 용법)　　 접속사(~하면서, ~함에 따라)

★★ 문제 해결 꿀~팁 ★★

▶ 많이 틀린 이유는?
④ 앞의 does not move가 바로 주어진 문장의 this brief moment of rest로 연결되는 것처럼 보일 수 있지만, 사실 이 does not move는 ④ 뒤의 at this point로 연결된다. 이 '움직이지 않는' 지점에서 에너지는 모두 위치에너지로 전환되었음을 알 수 있다는 것이다.

▶ 문제 해결 방법은?
⑤ 앞뒤 문장에 모두 결론의 So가 나오므로, 이 So가 어느 내용에 이어져야 하는지에 주목하며 읽는다.

---

40 건강에 관한 과학 연구가 단순하게 소개되는 이유
정답률 48% | 정답 ②

다음 글의 내용을 한 문장으로 요약하고자 한다. 빈칸 (A), (B)에 들어갈 말로 가장 적절한 것은?

	(A)		(B)
①	satisfy 만족시키지	‥‥‥	simple 간단한
✔②	satisfy 만족시키지	‥‥‥	complicated 복잡한
③	ignore 무시하지	‥‥‥	difficult 어려운
④	ignore 무시하지	‥‥‥	simple 간단한
⑤	reject 거부하지	‥‥‥	complicated 복잡한

There is often a lot of uncertainty / in the realm of science, / which the general public finds uncomfortable.
종종 많은 불확실성이 존재하며 / 과학의 영역에는 / 일반 대중은 그것을 불편하다고 느낀다.

They don't want "informed guesses," / they want certainties / that make their lives easier, / and science is often unequipped to meet these demands.
그들은 '정보에 근거한 추측'을 원하지 않고 / 그들은 확실성을 원하는데, / 자신의 삶을 더 편하게 만들어 주는 / 과학은 종종 이러한 요구를 만족시키도록 갖추어져 있지 않다.

In particular, / the human body is fantastically complex, / and some scientific answers can never be provided / in black-or-white terms.
특히 / 인간의 신체는 굉장히 복잡하며 / 어떤 과학적인 답변은 절대 제공될 수 없다. / 흑백 양자택일의 말로는

All this is why / the media tends to oversimplify scientific research / when presenting it to the public.
이 모든 것은 ~한 이유이다. / 미디어는 과학적 연구를 지나치게 단순화하는 경향이 있는 / 그것을 대중에게 제시할 때

In their eyes, / they're just "giving people what they want" / as opposed to offering more accurate but complex information / that very few people will read or understand.

그들의 시각에서는 / 그들은 단지 '사람들에게 그들이 원하는 것을 제공하고' 있는 것이다. / 더 정확하지만 복잡한 정보를 제공하는 것과는 반대로 / 극소수의 사람들만이 읽거나 이해할

A perfect example of this is / how people want definitive answers / as to which foods are "good" and "bad."
이것의 완벽한 하나의 예시는 ~이다. / 사람들이 확정적 답변을 원하는 방식 / 어떤 음식이 '좋은'지 '나쁜'지에 관해

Scientifically speaking, / there are no "good" and "bad" foods; / rather, food quality exists on a continuum, / meaning that some foods are *better* than others / when it comes to general health and well-being.
과학적으로 말하자면 / '좋고' '나쁜' 음식은 없으며, / 오히려 음식의 질은 연속체상에 존재하는데 / 이는 어떤 음식이 다른 것들보다 더 *낫다*는 것을 의미한다. / 일반 건강 및 웰빙 면에서

➡ With regard to general health, / science, by its nature, / does not (A) satisfy the public's demands for certainty, / which leads to the media giving less (B) complicated answers to the public.
일반 건강과 관련하여 / 과학은 본질적으로 / 확실성에 대한 대중의 요구를 만족시키지 않으며, / 이것은 미디어가 대중에게 덜 복잡한 답변을 제공하게 만든다.

과학의 영역에는 종종 많은 불확실성이 존재하며 일반 대중은 그것을 불편하다고 느낀다. 그들은 '정보에 근거한 추측'을 원하지 않으며 자신의 삶을 더 편하게 만들어 주는 확실성을 원하는데, 과학은 종종 이러한 요구를 만족시키도록 갖춰져 있지 않다. 특히 인간의 신체는 굉장히 복잡하며 어떤 과학적인 답변은 흑백 양자택일의 말로는 절대 제공될 수 없다. 이 모든 것 때문에 미디어가 과학적 연구를 대중에게 제시할 때 그것을 지나치게 단순화하는 경향이 있다. 그들의 시각에서는, 그들은 극소수의 사람들만이 읽거나 이해할 더 정확하지만 복잡한 정보를 제공하는 것과는 반대로, 단지 '사람들에게 그들이 원하는 것을 제공하고' 있는 것이다. 이것의 완벽한 하나의 예시는 어떤 음식이 '좋은'지 '나쁜'지에 관해 사람들이 확정적인 답변을 원하는 방식이다. 과학적으로 말하자면 '좋고' '나쁜' 음식은 없으며, 오히려 음식의 질은 연속체상에 존재하는데 이는 어떤 음식들이 다른 것들보다 일반 건강과 웰빙 면에서 더 낫다는 것을 의미한다.

➡ 일반 건강과 관련하여 과학은 본질적으로 확실성에 대한 대중의 요구를 (A) 만족시키지 않으며, 이것은 미디어가 대중에게 덜 (B) 복잡한 답변을 제공하게 만든다.

Why? 왜 정답일까?

첫 두 문장에서 대중은 과학에 확실성을 기대하지만 과학은 이러한 요구를 흔히 만족시키지 못한다(~ science is often unequipped to meet these demands.)고 언급하는데, 'All this is why the media tends to oversimplify scientific research ~'에서는 이 때문에 미디어가 연구 내용을 지나치게 단순화하여 대중이 원할 만한 답을 주려 하는 상황이 생긴다고 언급한다. 따라서 요약문의 빈칸 (A), (B)에 들어갈 말로 가장 적절한 것은 ② '(A) satisfy(만족시키지), (B) complicated (복잡한)'이다.

- uncertainty ⓝ 불확실성
- informed ⓐ 정보에 입각한
- black-or-white ⓐ 흑백논리의, 양자택일의
- with regard to ~에 관하여
- realm ⓝ 영역
- fantastically ⓐd 환상적으로, 엄청나게
- as opposed to ~와는 반대로, ~이 아니라

구문 풀이

1행 There is often a lot of uncertainty in the realm of science, which
선행사 / 계속적 용법(목적격 관·대)
the general public finds uncomfortable.
주어 / 동사 / 목적격 보어

41-42 단순히 유전자의 산물이 아닌 인간

Since the turn of the twentieth century / we've believed in genetic causes of diagnoses / — a theory called genetic determinism.
20세기로의 전환 이래로 / 우리는 진단의 유전적 원인을 믿어 왔다 / 유전자 결정론이라 불리는 이론

Under this model, / our genes (and subsequent health) are determined at birth.
이 모델 하에서 / 우리의 유전자(와 차후의 건강)은 태어날 때 결정된다.

We are "destined" to inherit certain diseases / based on the misfortune of our DNA.
우리는 특정 질병을 물려받을 '운명'이다. / 자신의 DNA의 불행을 바탕으로

Genetic determinism doesn't (a) consider the role / of family backgrounds, traumas, habits, / or anything else within the environment.
유전자 결정론은 역할을 고려하지 않는다. / 가정 환경, 정신적 충격, 습관, / 또는 환경 내의 다른 어떤 것의

In this dynamic / we are not (b) active participants / in our own health and wellness.
이 역학 관계에서 / 우리는 능동적인 참여자가 아니다. / 우리 자신의 건강과 안녕에 있어

Why would we be?
우리가 왜 그러겠는가?

If something is predetermined, / it's not (c) necessary / to look at anything beyond our DNA.
만약 무언가가 미리 결정되어 있다면 / 필요하지 않다. / 우리의 DNA를 넘어서 어떤 것을 보는 것이

But the more science has learned / about the body and its interaction with the environment around it / (in its various forms, / from our nutrition to our relationships / to our racially oppressive systems), / the more (d) complex the story becomes.
하지만 과학이 더 많이 알게 될수록, / 신체와 그 주변 환경과의 상호 작용에 대해 / (다양한 형태인 / 우리의 영양에서부터 관계, / 그리고 인종적으로 억압적인 시스템에 이르기까지) / 이야기는 더욱 복잡해진다.

『We are not merely expressions of coding / but products of a remarkable variety of interactions / that are both within and outside of our control.』 42번의 근거
우리는 단지 (유전적) 코딩의 표현이 아니라 / 놀랍도록 다양한 상호 작용의 산물이다. / 우리의 통제 내부와 외부 모두에 있는

『Once we see beyond the narrative / that genetics are (e) destiny, / we can take ownership of our health.』
일단 우리가 이야기를 넘어 보게 된다면 / 유전자가 운명이라는 / 우리는 자신의 건강에 대한 소유권을 가질 수 있다.

This allows us to see / how "choiceless" we once were / and empowers us with the ability / to create real and lasting change.』 41번의 근거
이것은 우리에게 알 수 있게 해 주며 / 자신이 한때 얼마나 '선택권이 없는' 상태였는지 / 우리에게 능력을 부여한다. / 실제적이고 지속적인 변화를 만들어 낼 수 있는

20세기로 전환된 이래로 우리는 진단의 유전적인 원인, 즉 유전자 결정론이라 불리는 이론을 믿어 왔다. 이 모델 하에서 우리의 유전자(와 차후의 건강)은 태어날 때 결정된다. 우리는 자신의 DNA의 불행을 바탕으로 특정 질병을 물려받을 '운명'이다. 유전자 결정론은 가정 환경, 정신적 충격, 습관 또는 환경 내의 다른 어떤 것의 역할을 (a) 고려하지 않는다. 이 역학 관계에서 우리는 우리 자신의 건강과 안녕에 있어 (b) 능동적인 참여자가 아니다. 우리가 왜 그러겠는가? 만약 무언가가 미리 결정되어 있다면 우리의 DNA를 넘어서 어떤 것을 보는 것이 (c) 필요하지 않다. 하지만 과학이 신체와 (우리의 영양에서부터 관계, 그리고 인종적으로 억

압적인 시스템에 이르기까지 다양한 형태인) 신체 주변 환경과의 상호 작용에 대해 더 많이 알게 될수록, 이야기는 더욱 (d) 단순해진다(→ 복잡해진다). 우리는 단지 (유전적) 코딩의 표현이 아니라 우리의 통제 내부와 외부 모두에 있는 놀랍도록 다양한 상호 작용의 산물이다. 일단 우리가 유전자가 (e) 운명이라는 이야기를 넘어서 보게 된다면 우리는 자신의 건강에 대한 소유권을 가질 수 있다. 이것은 우리가 한때 얼마나 '선택권이 없는' 상태였는지 알 수 있게 해 주며 우리에게 실제적이고 지속적인 변화를 만들어 낼 수 있는 능력을 부여한다.

- genetic ⓐ 유전적인
- subsequent ⓐ 차후의, 그다음의
- predetermined ⓐ 미리 결정된
- simplistic ⓐ 단순한
- take ownership of ~을 갖다, 소유하다
- diagnosis ⓝ 진단, 진찰
- inherit ⓥ 물려받다
- racially ⓐd 인종적으로
- remarkable ⓐ 놀랄 만한

구문 풀이

17행 This allows us to see how "choiceless" we once were and empowers us
├ 'allow+A+to부정사 : A가 ~하도록 하다'
├ '의문사+주어+동사 : 간접의문문'
with the ability to create real and lasting change.
'empowers A with B : A가 B할 능력을 부여하다'

41 제목 파악 정답률 50% | 정답 ①

윗글의 제목으로 가장 적절한 것은?
✔ ① Health Is in Our Hands, Not Only in Our Genes
건강은 유전자에만 있는 것이 아니라 우리 손 안에 있다
② Genetics: A Solution to Enhance Human Wellness
유전학: 인간 건강을 증진하는 데 있어 해결책
③ How Did DNA Dominate Over Environment in Biology?
어떻게 DNA가 생물학에서 환경을 지배했는가
④ Never Be Confident in Your Health, but Keep Checking!
건강을 과신하지 말고, 계속 점검하세요!
⑤ Why Scientific Innovation Affects Our Social Interactions
왜 과학적 혁신은 사회적 상호작용에 영향을 미치는가

Why? 왜 정답일까?

마지막 세 문장에서 인간은 단순히 유전자의 산물이 아니며, 자신의 건강을 직접 통제하고 관리할 수 있는 존재임을 설명하고 있다(Once we see beyond the narrative that genetics are destiny, we can take ownership of our health). 따라서 글의 제목으로 가장 적절한 것은 ① '건강은 유전자에만 있는 것이 아니라 우리 손 안에 있다'이다.

42 어휘 추론 정답률 57% | 정답 ④

밑줄 친 (a)~(e) 중에서 문맥상 낱말의 쓰임이 적절하지 않은 것은? [3점]
① (a)   ② (b)   ③ (c)   ✔ (d)   ⑤ (e)

Why? 왜 정답일까?

(d)가 포함된 'But the more science ~' 문장을 기점으로 글의 흐름이 반전되고 있다. 앞에서는 인간의 신체와 건강이 유전자에 의해 '운명적으로' 결정된다고 보는 유전자 결정론의 시각을 설명하는 반면, 뒤에서는 인간이 단순한 유전자의 발현이 아니라 건강을 위한 행동을 선택할 수 있는 존재라는 내용이 이어지고 있다. 이러한 흐름으로 볼 때, 유전자 외의 다른 요소를 고려하기 시작하면 건강에 대한 이해가 더 '복잡해진다'는 의미로 (d)의 simplistic을 complex로 고쳐야 한다. 따라서 문맥상 낱말의 쓰임이 적절하지 않은 것은 ④ '(d)'이다.

43-45 선물한 사람을 배려한 사려 깊은 왕자

(A)

『One day / a poor man / brought a bunch of grapes to a prince / as a gift.』 45번 ①의 근거 일치
어느 날 / 한 가난한 남자가 / 포도 한 송이를 왕자에게 가져왔다. / 선물로

He was very excited / to be able to bring a gift for (a) him / because he was too poor to afford more.
그는 매우 흥분했다. / 그를 위한 선물을 가져올 수 있어서 / 그가 너무 가난해서 그 이상의 여유가 없었기 때문에

He placed the grapes beside the prince and said, / "Oh, Prince, please accept this small gift from me."
그는 왕자의 옆에 포도를 놓고 말했다. / "오, 왕자님, 저의 이 작은 선물을 부디 받아주세요."라고

His face beamed with happiness / as he offered his small gift.
그의 얼굴은 행복으로 빛났다. / 그가 자신의 작은 선물을 바치면서

(C)

The prince thanked him politely.
왕자는 그에게 정중하게 감사를 표했다.

As the man looked at him expectantly, / the prince ate one grape.
그 남자가 기대에 부풀어 그를 바라보았을 때 / 왕자는 포도 한 알을 먹었다.

Then (c) he ate another one.
그러고 나서 그는 또 다른 하나를 먹었다.

Slowly the prince finished the whole bunch of grapes by himself.
천천히 왕자는 혼자서 포도 한 송이 전부를 다 먹었다.

『He did not offer grapes to anyone near him.』 45번 ③의 근거 일치
그는 자신의 곁에 있는 어떤 이에게도 포도를 권하지 않았다.

The man who brought those grapes to (d) him / was very pleased and left.
그 포도를 그에게 가져온 남자는 / 매우 기뻐하며 떠났다.

The close friends of the prince / who were around him / were very surprised.
왕자의 가까운 친구들은 / 그의 주변에 있던 / 매우 놀랐다.

(D)

『Usually / the prince shared whatever he had with others.』 45번 ④의 근거 일치
평소에 / 왕자는 자신이 가지고 있는 어떤 것이든 다른 사람들과 나눴다.

He would offer them whatever he was given / and they would eat it together.
그는 그들에게 자신이 받은 것은 무엇이든지 권하고 / 그들은 그것을 함께 먹곤 했다.

This time was different.
이번에는 달랐다.

Without offering it to anyone, / (e) he finished the bunch of grapes by himself.
아무에게도 그것을 권하지 않고 / 그는 포도 한 송이를 혼자 다 먹었다.
One of the friends asked, / "Prince! / How come you ate all the grapes by yourself / and did not offer them to any one of us?"
그 친구들 중 한 명이 물었다. / "왕자님! / 어찌하여 혼자서 포도를 다 드시고 / 우리 중 그 누구에게도 그것을 권하지 않으셨나요?"라고

「He smiled and said / that he ate all the grapes by himself / because the grapes were too sour.」 **45번 ⑤의 근거** 불일치
그는 웃으며 말했다. / 그가 혼자서 모든 포도를 다 먹었다고 / 그 포도가 너무 시어서

(B)

If the prince had offered the grapes to them, / they might have made funny faces / and shown their distaste for the grapes.
만약 왕자가 그들에게 그 포도를 권했다면 / 그들은 우스꽝스러운 표정을 지으며 / 포도에 대한 불쾌감을 드러냈을 것이다.
That would have hurt the feelings of that poor man.
그것은 그 가난한 남자의 감정을 상하게 했을 것이다.
He thought to himself / that it would be better / to eat all of them cheerfully and please (b) him.
그는 속으로 생각했다. / 더 낫다고 / 모든 포도를 기분 좋게 먹고 남자를 기쁘게 하는 것이
「He did not want to hurt the feelings of that poor man.」 **45번 ②의 근거** 일치
그는 그 가난한 남자의 감정을 상하게 하고 싶지 않았다.
Everyone around him / was moved by his thoughtfulness.
주위의 모든 사람들은 / 그의 사려 깊음에 감동 받았다.

(A)

어느 날 한 가난한 남자가 포도 한 송이를 왕자에게 선물로 가져왔다. 그는 너무 가난해서 그 이상의 여유가 없었기 때문에 (a) 그를 위한 선물을 가져올 수 있어서 매우 흥분했다. 그는 왕자의 옆에 포도를 놓고 "오, 왕자님, 저의 이 작은 선물을 부디 받아주세요."라고 말했다. 그의 얼굴은 작은 선물을 바치면서 행복으로 빛났다.

(C)

왕자는 그에게 정중하게 감사를 표했다. 그 남자가 기대에 부풀어 그를 바라보았을 때 왕자는 포도 한 알을 먹었다. 그러고 나서 (c) 그는 또 다른 하나를 먹었다. 천천히 왕자는 혼자서 포도 한 송이 전부를 다 먹었다. 그는 자신의 곁에 있는 어떤 이에게도 포도를 권하지 않았다. 그 포도를 (d) 그에게 가져온 남자는 매우 기뻐하고 떠났다. 왕자의 주변에 있던 그의 가까운 친구들은 매우 놀랐다.

(D)

평소에 왕자는 자신이 가지고 있는 어떤 것이든 다른 사람들과 나눴다. 그는 그들에게 자신이 받은 것은 무엇이든지 권하고 그들은 그것을 함께 먹곤 했다. 이번에는 달랐다. 아무에게도 그것을 권하지 않고 (e) 그는 포도 한 송이를 혼자 다 먹었다. 그 친구들 중 한 명이 "왕자님! 어찌하여 혼자서 포도를 다 드시고 우리 중 그 누구에게도 그것을 권하지 않으셨나요?"라고 물었다. 그는 웃으며 그 포도가 너무 시어서 혼자서 모든 포도를 다 먹었다고 말했다.

(B)

만약 왕자가 그들에게 그 포도를 권했다면 그들은 우스꽝스러운 표정을 지으며 포도에 대한 불쾌감을 드러냈을 것이다. 그것은 그 가난한 남자의 감정을 상하게 했을 것이다. 그는 모든 포도를 기분 좋게 먹고 (b) 남자를 기쁘게 하는 것이 더 낫다고 속으로 생각했다. 그는 그 가난한 남자의 감정을 상하게 하고 싶지 않았다. 주위의 모든 사람들은 그의 사려 깊음에 감동 받았다.

- beam with ~으로 환히 웃다
- thoughtfulness ⑩ 사려 깊음
- distaste ⑩ 불쾌감
- expectantly ⑳ 기대하여

구문 풀이

(A) 2행 He was very excited to be able to bring a gift for him because he was
감정 형용사 | 부사적 용법(~해서)
too poor to afford more.
「too ~ to … : 너무 ~해서 …하지 못하다」

(B) 1행 If the prince had offered the grapes to them, they might have made funny
「if + 주어 + had p.p. ~ | 주어 + 조동사 과거형 + have p.p. ~ : 가정법 과거완료(과거 사실의 반대)」
faces and shown their distaste for the grapes.

(D) 1행 Usually the prince shared whatever he had with others.
복합관계대명사(~하는 것은 무엇이든)

---

43 글의 순서 파악　　정답률 73% | 정답 ③

주어진 글 (A)에 이어질 내용을 순서에 맞게 배열한 것으로 가장 적절한 것은?
① (B) - (D) - (C)
② (C) - (B) - (D)
✔ (C) - (D) - (B)
④ (D) - (B) - (C)
⑤ (D) - (C) - (B)

Why? 왜 정답일까?

왕자가 가난한 남자로부터 포도를 선물 받았다는 내용의 (A) 뒤로, 왕자가 주변 사람에게 권하지 않고 그 포도를 다 먹었다는 내용의 (C), 평소 왕자는 가진 것은 다른 사람들과 다 나누는 성품이기에 주변 사람들이 의아해하며 이유를 물었다는 내용의 (D), 이유를 자세히 설명하는 (B)가 차례로 이어진다. 따라서 글의 순서로 가장 적절한 것은 ③ '(C) - (D) - (B)'이다.

---

44 지칭 추론　　정답률 71% | 정답 ②

밑줄 친 (a) ~ (e) 중에서 가리키는 대상이 나머지 넷과 다른 것은?
① (a)　✔ (b)　③ (c)　④ (d)　⑤ (e)

Why? 왜 정답일까?

(a), (c), (d), (e)는 the prince, (b)는 that poor man을 가리키므로, (a) ~ (e) 중에서 가리키는 대상이 다른 하나는 ② '(b)'이다.

---

45 세부 내용 파악　　정답률 80% | 정답 ⑤

윗글의 왕자에 관한 내용으로 적절하지 않은 것은?
① 가난한 남자에게 포도 한 송이를 선물로 받았다.
② 가난한 남자의 감정을 상하게 하고 싶지 않았다.
③ 곁에 있던 어떤 이에게도 포도를 권하지 않았다.
④ 가지고 있는 어떤 것이든 평소에 다른 사람들과 나눴다.
✔ 포도가 너무 시어서 혼자 다 먹지 못했다.

Why? 왜 정답일까?

(D) '~ he ate all the grapes by himself because the grapes were too sour.'에서 왕자는 가난한 남자가 가져온 포도가 너무 시어서 누구에게도 권하지 않고 혼자 다 먹었다고 하므로, 내용과 일치하지 않는 것은 ⑤ '포도가 너무 시어서 혼자 다 먹지 못했다.'이다.

Why? 왜 오답일까?

① (A) 'One day a poor man brought a bunch of grapes to a prince as a gift.'의 내용과 일치한다.
② (B) 'He did not want to hurt the feelings of that poor man.'의 내용과 일치한다.
③ (C) 'He did not offer grapes to anyone near him.'의 내용과 일치한다.
④ (D) 'Usually the prince shared whatever he had with others.'의 내용과 일치한다.

어휘 Review Test 18　　문제편 180쪽

A	B	C	D
01 시추하다, 구멍을 뚫다	01 initial	01 ⓑ	01 ①
02 기대하다	02 estimate	02 ①	02 ⓚ
03 직업	03 circumstance	03 ⓝ	03 ⑨
04 이미 주어진, 기성품의	04 pioneer	04 ⓠ	04 ⓜ
05 멸종	05 indication	05 ⓡ	05 ⓕ
06 공상하다	06 closely	06 ①	06 ①
07 거대한	07 convey	07 ⓜ	07 ⓝ
08 불확실성	08 fundamentally	08 ⓞ	08 ⓕ
09 매력적인, 흥미로운	09 innovation	09 ⓕ	09 ①
10 핵심, 요점, 결론	10 enhance	10 ①	10 ⓐ
11 권한을 주다	11 aggressive	11 ⓓ	11 ⓒ
12 매년 열리는	12 reduction	12 ⓐ	12 ⑨
13 분석적인	13 inspire	13 ⑨	13 ⓢ
14 간격	14 nature	14 ⓗ	14 ⓗ
15 접근 가능한, 이용 가능한	15 respectively	15 ⓒ	15 ①
16 과다한	16 sector	16 ⓞ	16 ⓓ
17 본질적으로	17 supplement	17 ⓚ	17 ⓑ
18 규제	18 substance	18 ⓟ	18 ⓞ
19 쓸어내리다	19 remarkable	19 ⓗ	19 ⓔ
20 체계적인	20 essential	20 ①	20 ⓟ

18회

정답

18 ③ 19 ① 20 ② 21 ① 22 ④ 23 ① 24 ③ 25 ⑤ 26 ④ 27 ⑤ 28 ⑤ 29 ② 30 ③ 31 ② 32 ①
33 ① 34 ③ 35 ④ 36 ② 37 ④ 38 ③ 39 ⑤ 40 ① 41 ② 42 ⑤ 43 ② 44 ① 45 ④

★ 표기된 문항은 [등급을 가르는 문제]에 해당하는 문항입니다.

---

18 산책로 조성 계획에 대한 재고 요청 정답률 65% | 정답 ③

다음 글의 목적으로 가장 적절한 것은?

① 환경 보호 캠페인 참여를 부탁하려고
② 지역 관광 프로그램에 대해 문의하려고
✓ ③ 산책로 조성 계획의 재고를 요청하려고
④ 보행자 안전을 위해 인도 설치를 건의하려고
⑤ 야생 동물 보호구역 관리의 문제점을 지적하려고

To whom it may concern:
담당자 귀하
I was born and raised in the city of Boulder / and have enjoyed our scenic natural spaces for my whole life.
저는 Boulder 시에서 태어나고 자랐으며 / 평생 동안 우리의 경치 좋은 자연 공간을 누려왔습니다.
The land / through which the proposed Pine Hill walking trail would cut / is home to a variety of species.
그 땅은 / 제안된 Pine Hill 산책로가 지나가게 될 / 다양한 종들의 서식지입니다.
Wildlife faces pressure from development, / and these animals need space / where they can hide from human activity.
야생 동물은 개발의 압력에 직면해 있고, / 이 동물들은 공간이 필요합니다. / 인간 활동으로부터 숨을 수 있는
Although trails serve as a wonderful source / for us to access the natural world and appreciate the wildlife within it, / if we continue to destroy habitats with excess trails, / the wildlife will stop using these areas.
비록 산책로는 훌륭한 원천의 역할을 하지만, / 우리가 자연 세계에 접근하고 그 안의 야생 동물을 감상할 수 있는 / 만약 우리가 계속해서 과도한 산책로들로 서식지를 파괴한다면 / 야생 동물은 이 지역들을 이용하는 것을 중단할 것입니다.
Please reconsider / whether the proposed trail is absolutely necessary.
재고해 주시기 바랍니다. / 제안된 산책로가 정말로 필요한지
Sincerely, // Tyler Stuart
Tyler Stuart 드림

담당자 귀하
저는 Boulder 시에서 태어나고 자랐으며 평생 동안 우리의 경치 좋은 자연 공간을 누려왔습니다. 제안된 Pine Hill 산책로가 지나가게 될 그 땅은 다양한 종들의 서식지입니다. 야생 동물은 개발의 압력에 직면해 있고, 이 동물들은 인간 활동으로부터 숨을 수 있는 공간이 필요합니다. 비록 산책로는 우리가 자연 세계에 접근하고 그 안의 야생 동물을 감상할 수 있는 훌륭한 원천의 역할을 하지만, 만약 우리가 계속해서 과도한 산책로들로 서식지를 파괴한다면 야생 동물은 이 지역들을 이용하는 것을 중단할 것입니다. 제안된 산책로가 정말로 필요한지 재고해 주시기 바랍니다.
Tyler Stuart 드림

Why? 왜 정답일까?

산책로가 지나갈 땅에 다양한 야생 동물 종이 서식하므로 산책로 조성 계획을 재고해줄 것을 요청하는 글이다(Please reconsider whether the proposed trail is absolutely necessary.). 따라서 글의 목적으로 가장 적절한 것은 ③ '산책로 조성 계획의 재고를 요청하려고'이다.

- scenic @ 경치 좋은
- wildlife ⓝ 야생 동물
- appreciate ⓥ 감상하다, 제대로 이해하다
- absolutely ⓐⓓ 정말로, 전적으로
- propose ⓥ 제안하다
- serve as ~의 역할을 하다
- habitat ⓝ 서식지

구문 풀이

7행 Although trails serve as a wonderful source for us to access the natural
양보 접속사 ／ 꾸밈 받는 명사 ／ 의미상 주어 / to부정사1
world and appreciate the wildlife within it, if we continue to destroy habitats with
to부정사2(형용사적 용법) ／ 조건 접속사 ／ 주어 ／ 동사(현재)
excess trails, the wildlife will stop using these areas.
주어 ／ 동사(미래) ／ 목적어

---

19 생일선물로 받은 강아지를 몇 달 뒤 잃어버린 필자 정답률 73% | 정답 ①

다음 글에 드러난 'I'의 심경 변화로 가장 적절한 것은?

✓ ① delighted → sorrowful
기쁜 → 슬픈
② relaxed → annoyed
느긋한 → 짜증이 난
③ embarrassed → worried
당황한 → 걱정하는
④ excited → horrified
신이 난 → 겁에 질린
⑤ disappointed → satisfied
실망한 → 만족한

On my seventh birthday, / my mom surprised me / with a puppy waiting on a leash.
나의 일곱 번째 생일에, / 엄마는 나를 놀라게 했다. / 목줄을 매고 기다리고 있는 강아지로
It had beautiful golden fur and an adorable tail.
그것은 아름다운 황금빛 털과 사랑스러운 꼬리를 가지고 있었다.
It was exactly what I had always dreamed of.
그것은 바로 내가 항상 꿈꿨던 것이었다.
I took the dog everywhere / and slept with it every night.
나는 그 강아지를 어디든 데리고 다녔고 / 매일 밤 같이 잤다.

A few months later, / the dog got out of the backyard and was lost.
몇 달 후, / 그 강아지는 뒷마당에서 빠져나가 사라졌다.
I sat on my bed and cried for hours / while my mother watched me silently from the doorway of my room.
나는 침대에 앉아 몇 시간 동안 울었다. / 엄마가 내 방 문간에서 조용히 나를 바라보는 동안
I finally fell asleep, / exhausted from my grief.
나는 마침내 잠이 들었다. / 슬픔에 지쳐
My mother never said a word to me about my loss, / but I knew she felt the same as I did.
엄마는 나의 상실에 대해 나에게 한마디도 하지 않았지만, / 나는 엄마도 나와 똑같이 느꼈다는 것을 알았다.

나의 일곱 번째 생일에, 목줄을 매고 기다리고 있는 강아지로 엄마는 나를 놀라게 했다. 그것은 아름다운 황금빛 털과 사랑스러운 꼬리를 가지고 있었다. 그것은 바로 내가 항상 꿈꿨던 것이었다. 나는 그 강아지를 어디든 데리고 다녔고 매일 밤 같이 잤다. 몇 달 후, 그 강아지는 뒷마당에서 빠져나가 사라졌다. 엄마가 내 방 문간에서 조용히 나를 바라보는 동안 나는 침대에 앉아 몇 시간 동안 울었다. 나는 슬픔에 지쳐 마침내 잠이 들었다. 엄마는 나의 상실에 대해 나에게 한마디도 하지 않았지만, 나는 엄마도 나와 똑같이 느꼈다는 것을 알았다.

Why? 왜 정답일까?

'A few months later, the dog got out of the backyard and was lost.' 앞뒤로 글의 흐름이 반전된다. 앞에서는 꿈꾸던 강아지를 선물 받은 필자가 어딘 강아지를 데리고 다니며 매일 밤 함께 잠을 정도로 좋아했다는(It was exactly what I had always dreamed of. I took the dog everywhere and slept with it every night.) 내용이 제시되는 한편, 뒤에서는 강아지가 집을 나간 뒤 필자가 몇 시간이고 울 만큼 슬퍼했다는(~ exhausted from my grief.) 내용이 주로 제시된다. 따라서 'I'의 심경 변화로 가장 적절한 것은 ① '기쁜 → 슬픈'이다.

- leash ⓝ (동물을 매어 두는) 줄, 사슬
- grief ⓝ 슬픔
- adorable @ 사랑스러운

구문 풀이

7행 I finally fell asleep, exhausted from my grief.
2형식 동사↲ 보어 분사구문(~하면서)

---

20 집중에 방해가 되는 요인을 모두 제거하려 하기보다 적절히 대처하는 법 배우기 정답률 82% | 정답 ②

다음 글에서 필자가 주장하는 바로 가장 적절한 것은?

① 자신에게 적합한 시간 관리법을 찾아야 한다.
✓ ② 집중을 방해하는 요인에 대처할 줄 알아야 한다.
③ 학습 공간과 휴식 공간을 명확하게 분리해야 한다.
④ 집중력 향상을 위해 정돈된 학습환경을 유지해야 한다.
⑤ 공공장소에서 타인에게 피해를 주는 행동을 삼가야 한다.

When I was in high school, / we had students / who could study in the coffee shop / and not get distracted by the noise or everything happening around them.
내가 고등학교에 다닐 때, / 학생들이 있었다. / 커피숍에서 공부할 수 있는 / 그리고 소음이나 그들 주변에서 일어나는 모든 것에 방해 받지 않을 수 있는
We also had students who could not study / if the library was not super quiet.
공부할 수 없는 학생들도 있었다. / 도서관이 아주 조용하지 않으면
The latter students suffered / because even in the library, / it was impossible to get the type of complete silence they sought.
후자의 학생들은 고통을 받았다. / 도서관에서조차 / 그들이 추구하는 유형의 완전한 고요함을 얻는 것이 불가능했기 때문에
These students were victims of distractions / who found it very difficult / to study anywhere except in their private bedrooms.
이 학생들은 집중에 방해가 되는 것들의 희생자였다. / 매우 어렵다는 것을 알게 된 / 개인 침실을 제외하고 어디에서나 공부하는 것이
In today's world, / it is impossible to run away from distractions.
요즘 세상에서 / 집중에 방해가 되는 것들로부터 도망치는 것은 불가능하다.
Distractions are everywhere, / but if you want to achieve your goals, / you must learn how to tackle distractions.
집중에 방해가 되는 것들은 어디에나 있지만, / 여러분이 목표를 달성하고 싶다면 / 여러분은 집중에 방해가 되는 것들에 대처하는 법을 배워야 한다.
You cannot eliminate distractions, / but you can learn to live with them / in a way that ensures they do not limit you.
여러분은 집중에 방해가 되는 것들을 제거할 수는 없지만, / 여러분은 그것들과 함께 살아가는 것을 배울 수 있다. / 그것들이 여러분을 제한하지 않도록 하는 방식으로

내가 고등학교에 다닐 때, 커피숍에서 공부하면서 소음이나 그들 주변에서 일어나는 모든 것에 방해를 받지 않을 수 있는 학생들이 있었다. 도서관이 아주 조용하지 않으면 공부할 수 없는 학생들도 있었다. 후자의 학생들은 도서관에서조차 그들이 추구하는 유형의 완전한 고요함을 얻는 것이 불가능했기 때문에 고통을 받았다. 이 학생들은 개인 침실을 제외하고 어디에서든 공부하는 것이 매우 어렵다는 것을 알게 된, 집중에 방해가 되는 것들의 희생자였다. 요즘 세상에서 집중에 방해가 되는 것들로부터 도망치는 것은 불가능하다. 집중에 방해가 되는 것들은 어디에나 있지만, 목표를 달성하고 싶다면 여러분은 집중에 방해가 되는 것들에 대처하는 법을 배워야 한다. 집중에 방해가 되는 것들을 제거할 수는 없지만, 그것들이 여러분을 제한하지 않도록 하는 방식으로 그것들과 함께 살아가는 것을 배울 수 있다.

Why? 왜 정답일까?

'~ if you want to achieve your goals, you must learn how to tackle distractions.'에서 목표를 달성하려면 집중에 방해가 되는 요인에 대처하는 방법을 알아야 한다고 언급하는 것으로 보아, 필자가 주장하는 바로 가장 적절한 것은 ② '집중을 방해하는 요인에 대처할 줄 알아야 한다.'이다.

- distract ⓥ 집중이 안 되게 하다
- victim ⓝ 희생자
- tackle ⓥ (문제 등에) 대처하다, 맞서다
- ensure ⓥ 반드시 ~하게 하다
- complete @ 완전한
- run away from ~로부터 도망치다
- eliminate ⓥ 제거하다

구문 풀이

6행 These students were victims of distractions [who found it very difficult
선행사 ／ 주격 관·대 ／ 5형식 동사 ／ 가목적어 / 목적격 보어
to study anywhere except in their private bedrooms].
진목적어

21 | 인터넷 시대가 도래한 이후 마케터들에 대응할 수단을 갖게 된 소비자들 | 정답률 41% | 정답 ①

밑줄 친 popped out of the box가 다음 글에서 의미하는 바로 가장 적절한 것은?

☑ ① could not be kept secret anymore – 더 이상 비밀로 지켜질 수 없었다
② might disappear from public attention – 대중의 관심에서 사라질 수도 있었다
③ were no longer available to marketers – 마케터들에게 더 이상 이용 가능하지 않았다
④ became too complicated to understand – 너무 복잡해서 이해할 수 없었다
⑤ began to improve companies' reputations – 회사의 명성을 높이기 시작했다

With the Internet, everything changed.
인터넷의 등장으로 모든 것이 변했다.

Product problems, overpromises, the lack of customer support, differential pricing — / all of the issues / that customers actually experienced from a marketing organization / suddenly popped out of the box.
제품 문제, 과잉 약속, 고객 지원 부족, 가격 차등 / 모든 문제가 / 소비자가 마케팅 조직으로부터 실제로 경험했던 / 갑자기 상자 밖으로 튀어나왔다.

No longer were there / any controlled communications or even business systems.
더는 존재하지 않았다 / 통제된 의사소통이나 사업 체계조차

Consumers could generally learn through the Web / whatever they wanted to know / about a company, its products, its competitors, its distribution systems, / and, most of all, its truthfulness / when talking about its products and services.
대개 소비자들은 인터넷을 통해 알 수 있었다 / 한 회사와 그곳의 제품, 경쟁사, 유통 체계에 대해 / 그리고 무엇보다도 진정성에 대해 / 그 회사의 제품과 서비스에 관해 이야기할 때의

Just as important, / the Internet opened up a forum / for customers to compare products, experiences, and values with other customers easily and quickly.
그만큼이나 중요하게도, / 인터넷은 장(場)을 열었다 / 소비자들이 제품, 경험 그리고 가치를 다른 소비자들과 쉽고 빠르게 비교할 수 있는

Now the customer had a way / to talk back to the marketer / and to do so through public forums instantly.
이제 소비자는 수단을 가졌다 / 마케터에게 대응하고 / 즉시 공론의 장을 통해 그렇게 할

인터넷의 등장으로 모든 것이 변했다. 제품 문제, 과잉 약속, 고객 지원 부족, 가격 차등과 같은, 소비자들이 마케팅 조직으로부터 실제로 경험했던 모든 문제가 갑자기 상자 밖으로 튀어나왔다. 통제된 의사소통이나 사업 체계조차 더는 존재하지 않았다. 소비자들은 한 회사와 그곳의 제품, 경쟁사, 유통 체계, 그리고 무엇보다도 그 회사의 제품과 서비스에 관해 이야기할 때의 진정성에 대해 그들이 알고 싶어 하는 것은 무엇이든 대개 인터넷을 통해 알 수 있었다. 그만큼이나 중요하게도, 인터넷은 소비자들이 제품, 경험 그리고 가치를 다른 소비자들과 쉽고 빠르게 비교할 수 있는 장(場)을 열었다. 이제 소비자는 마케터에게 대응하고, 즉시 공론의 장을 통해 그렇게 할 수단을 가졌다.

Why? 왜 정답일까?

'Just as important, ~' 이하에서 인터넷이 등장하면서 소비자들은 제품 정보나 사용 경험을 자유롭게 공유하고 비교할 뿐 아니라 마케터들에게도 대응할 수 있는 공론의 장을 갖게 되었다고 언급한다. 따라서 밑줄 친 부분의 의미로 가장 적절한 것은 소비자들이 마케팅 조직과의 관계에서 경험했던 문제가 '이전처럼 묻혀 있지 못하고' 겉으로 나타나기 시작했다는 뜻의 ① '더 이상 비밀로 지켜질 수 없었다'이다.

● pop out of ~ 밖으로 튀어나오다
● distribution ⓝ 유통, 분배
● talk back to ~에 대응하다, 말대답하다
● disappear ⓥ 사라지다
● reputation ⓝ 명성
● competitor ⓝ 경쟁자
● truthfulness ⓝ 진정성
● instantly ⓐⓓ 즉시
● complicated ⓐ 복잡한

구문 풀이

6행 Consumers could generally learn through the Web {whatever they wanted to know about a company, its products, its competitors, its distribution systems, and, most of all, its truthfulness when talking about its products and services}.
동사구 / 복합관계대명사(~하는 무엇이든지) / 전치사 / 목적어1 / 목적어2 / 목적어3 / 목적어4 / 목적어5 / 분사구문(~할 때)
{ }: 문장의 목적어

★★ 문제 해결 꿀~팁 ★★

▶ 많이 틀린 이유는?
인터넷 시대가 도래하면서 소비자들은 이전까지 서로 공유하지 못했던 제품 사용 경험이나 서비스에 대한 정보를 자유롭게 나눌 수 있게 되었다는 내용이다. ③은 인터넷 시대 이후 소비자들이 마케팅 회사와 겪는 문제를 마케터들이 접할 수 없게 되었다는 의미로, 글의 내용과 무관하다.

▶ 문제 해결 방법은?
소비자들이 그간 겪었던 문제가 '상자 밖으로 튀어나와' 인터넷에서 논의되기 시작했다는 것이 글의 핵심적인 내용이므로, 밑줄 부분은 문제가 '더 이상 비밀이 아니게 되었다'는 의미로 이해할 수 있다.

22 | 결정을 미루는 것에 수반되는 대가 | 정답률 61% | 정답 ④

다음 글의 요지로 가장 적절한 것은?

① 적당한 수준의 불안감은 업무 수행에 도움이 된다.
② 성급한 의사 결정은 의도하지 않은 결과를 초래한다.
③ 반복되는 실수를 줄이기 위해서는 신중함이 요구된다.
☑ ④ 더 나은 선택을 위해 결정을 미루는 것은 결국 해가 된다.
⑤ 규칙적인 생활 습관은 직장에서의 성공 가능성을 높인다.

FOBO, or Fear of a Better Option, is the anxiety / that something better will come along, / which makes it undesirable / to commit to existing choices when making a decision.
FOBO, 즉 더 나은 선택에 대한 두려움은 불안감인데, / 더 나은 어떤 것이 생길 것이라는 / 이것은 탐탁지 않게 한다. / 결정을 내릴 때 기존의 선택지에 전념하는 것을

It's an affliction of abundance / that drives you to keep all of your options open / and to avoid risks.
그것은 풍족함의 고통이다. / 여러분이 모든 선택지를 열어 두게 만드는 / 그리고 위험을 피하도록

Rather than assessing your options, choosing one, and moving on with your day, / you delay the inevitable.
여러분의 선택지들을 평가하고, 하나를 선택하고 여러분의 하루를 살아가기보다는, / 여러분은 꼭 해야 할 것을 미룬다.

It's not unlike hitting the snooze button on your alarm clock / only to pull the covers over your head and fall back asleep.
그것은 알람시계의 스누즈 버튼을 누르는 것과 다르지 않다. / 그리고 결국 이불을 머리 위로 뒤집어 쓰고 다시 잠들어 버리는 것과

As you probably found out the hard way, / if you hit snooze enough times, / you'll end up being late and racing for the office, / your day and mood ruined.
아마도 여러분이 고생하여 알게 되었듯이 / 여러분이 스누즈 버튼을 많이 누르면, / 여러분은 결국 늦어서 사무실로 달리게 되고, / 여러분의 하루와 기분을 망치게 된다.

While pressing snooze feels so good at the moment, / it ultimately demands a price.
스누즈 버튼을 누르는 것이 그때는 기분이 아주 좋겠지만, / 그것은 결국 대가를 요구한다.

FOBO, 즉 더 나은 선택에 대한 두려움은 더 나은 어떤 것이 생길 것이라는 불안감인데, 이것은 결정을 내릴 때 기존의 선택지에 전념하는 것을 탐탁지 않게 한다. 그것은 여러분이 모든 선택지를 열어 두고 위험을 피하도록 만드는 풍족함의 고통이다. 그것은 여러분의 선택지들을 평가하고, 하나를 선택하고 여러분의 하루를 살아가기보다는, 여러분은 꼭 해야 할 것을 미룬다. 그것은 알람시계의 스누즈 버튼을 누르고는 결국 이불을 머리 위로 뒤집어 쓰고 다시 잠들어 버리는 것과 다르지 않다. 아마도 여러분이 고생하여 알게 되었듯이 스누즈 버튼을 많이 누르면, 결국 늦어서 사무실로 달리게 되고, 여러분의 하루와 기분을 망치게 된다. 스누즈 버튼을 누르는 것이 그때는 기분이 아주 좋겠지만, 그것은 결국 대가를 요구한다.

Why? 왜 정답일까?

더 나은 선택이 생길지도 모른다는 생각으로 결정하기를 미루다 보면 결국 대가가 따를 수 있다(~ it ultimately demands a price.)는 내용의 글로, 특히 글 후반부에서 '결정을 미루는' 행위를 '아침 알람이 울릴 때 스누즈 버튼을 누르는' 행위에 비유하고 있다. 따라서 글의 요지로 가장 적절한 것은 ④ '더 나은 선택을 위해 결정을 미루는 것은 결국 해가 된다.'이다.

● anxiety ⓝ 불안
● commit to ~에 전념하다
● assess ⓥ 평가하다
● inevitable ⓐ 피할 수 없는, 반드시 있는
● snooze button 스누즈 버튼(아침에 잠이 깬 뒤 조금 더 자기 위해 누르는 타이머 버튼)
● end up 결국 ~하게 되다
● ultimately ⓐⓓ 결국, 궁극적으로
● undesirable ⓐ 탐탁지 않은, 원하지 않는
● abundance ⓝ 풍족함
● delay ⓥ 미루다, 지연시키다
● ruin ⓥ 망치다

구문 풀이

8행 As you probably found out the hard way, if you hit snooze enough times, you'll end up being late and racing for the office, your day and mood ruined.
접속사(~대로, ~듯이) / 조건 접속사 / 현재시제 / 분사구문(그리고 ~하다) / 미래시제 / 동명사1 / 동명사2 / 의미상 주어

23 | 재생 가능한 에너지원 이용에 따르는 환경적 부작용 | 정답률 74% | 정답 ①

다음 글의 주제로 가장 적절한 것은?

☑ ① environmental side effects of using renewable energy sources
재생 가능한 에너지원을 사용하는 것의 환경적 부작용
② practical methods to meet increasing demand for electricity
늘어나는 전기 수요를 맞추기 위한 현실적인 방법
③ negative impacts of the use of traditional energy sources
전통적 에너지원 사용의 부정적 영향
④ numerous ways to obtain renewable sources of energy
재생 가능한 에너지를 얻기 위한 무수히 많은 방법
⑤ effective procedures to reduce greenhouse emissions
온실가스 배출을 줄이기 위한 효과적 절차

The use of renewable sources of energy / to produce electricity / has increasingly been encouraged / as a way / to harmonize the need to secure electricity supply / with environmental protection objectives.
재생 가능한 에너지원의 사용은 / 전력 생산을 위한 / 점점 장려되어 왔다. / 방법으로 / 전력 공급 확보의 필요성을 일치시키기 위한 / 환경 보호 목적과

But / the use of renewable sources / also comes with its own consequences, / which require consideration.
그러나 / 재생 가능한 자원의 이용 / 또한 그 자체의 결과가 수반되는데, / 이는 고려할 필요가 있다.

Renewable sources of energy include a variety of sources / such as hydropower and ocean-based technologies.
재생 가능한 에너지원은 다양한 자원을 포함한다. / 수력 발전과 해양 기반 기술처럼

Additionally, / solar, wind, geothermal and biomass renewable sources / also have their own impact on the environment.
게다가, / 태양열, 풍력, 지열 그리고 바이오매스 재생 에너지원 / 또한 환경에 저마다의 영향을 미친다.

Hydropower dams, / for example, / have an impact on aquatic ecosystems / and, more recently, / have been identified as significant sources of greenhouse emissions.
수력 발전 댐은 / 예를 들어, / 수생 생태계에 영향을 미치고, / 더 최근에는 / 온실가스 배출의 중요한 원인으로 확인되었다.

Wind, solar, and biomass also cause negative environmental impacts, / such as visual pollution, intensive land occupation and negative effects on bird populations.
풍력, 태양열 그리고 바이오매스 또한 부정적인 환경 영향을 초래한다. / 시각 공해, 집약적인 토지 점유 그리고 조류 개체 수에 미치는 부정적인 영향과 같은

전력 생산을 위한 재생 가능한 에너지원의 사용은 전력 공급 확보의 필요성과 환경 보호 목적을 일치시키기 위한 방법으로 점점 장려되어 왔다. 그러나 재생 가능한 자원의 이용 또한 그 자체의 결과가 수반되는데, 이는 고려할 필요가 있다. 재생 가능한 에너지원은 수력 발전과 해양 기반 기술처럼 다양한 자원을 포함한다. 게다가, 태양열, 풍력, 지열 그리고 바이오매스(에너지로 사용 가능한 생물체) 재생 에너지원 또한 환경에 저마다의 영향을 미친다. 예를 들어, 수력 발전 댐은 수생 생태계에 영향을 미치고, 더 최근에는 온실가스 배출의 중요한 원인으로 확인되었다. 풍력, 태양열 그리고 바이오매스 또한 시각 공해, 집약적인 토지 점유 그리고 조류 개체 수에 미치는 부정적인 영향과 같은 부정적인 환경 영향을 초래한다.

Why? 왜 정답일까?

'But the use of renewable sources also comes with its own consequences, which require consideration.' 이후로 재생 가능한 에너지원을 쓰더라도 나름의 환경적 영향이 따르므로 이에 관한 고려가 필요하다는 내용이 이어지고 있다. 따라서 글의 주제로 가장 적절한 것은 ① '재생 가능한 에너지원을 사용하는 것의 환경적 부작용'이다.

● renewable ⓐ 재생 가능한
● harmonize A with B A와 B를 점점 더 조화시키다, 일치시키다
● increasingly ⓐⓓ 점점 더

- secure ⓥ 확보하다
- consequence ⓝ 결과, 영향
- hydropower ⓝ 수력
- identify ⓥ 확인하다
- intensive ⓐ 집약적인, 집중적인
- practical ⓐ 현실적인, 실제적인
- objective ⓝ 목적, 목표
- consideration ⓝ 고려
- have an impact on ~에 영향을 주다
- significant ⓐ 중요한, 유의미한
- occupation ⓝ 점유, 차지
- numerous ⓐ 무수히 많은

1행 The use of renewable sources of energy to produce electricity
주어 ←전치사(~로서) ←하기 위한
has increasingly been encouraged as a way to harmonize the need to secure
현재완료 수동태(~되어 왔다) 형용사적 용법 형용사적 용법
electricity supply with environmental protection objectives.

24 포유류의 생존에 도움이 되는 씹는 행위 정답률 74% | 정답 ③

다음 글의 제목으로 가장 적절한 것은?

① Chewing: A Way to Ease Indigestion – 씹기: 소화불량을 완화할 방법
② Boost Your Energy by Chewing More! – 더 많이 씹어서 에너지를 북돋워라!
③ How Chewing Helps Mammals Survive – 씹는 것은 포유류 생존에 어떻게 도움이 되는가
④ Different Types and Functions of Teeth – 치아의 다양한 유형과 기능
⑤ A Harsh Climate Makes Mammals Stronger – 혹독한 기후가 포유류들을 더 강하게 만든다

Chewing leads to smaller particles for swallowing, / and more exposed surface area / for digestive enzymes to act on.
씹는 삼키기 위한 더 작은 조각들로 이어진다. / 그리고 더 노출된 표면으로 / 소화 효소가 작용할
In other words, / it means the extraction of more fuel and raw materials / from a mouthful of food.
다시 말해서, / 그것은 더 많은 연료와 원료의 추출을 의미한다. / 한입의 음식으로부터
This is especially important for mammals / because they heat their bodies from within.
이것은 포유류에게 특히 중요하다. / 그들이 체내에서 자신의 몸을 따뜻하게 하기 때문에
Chewing gives mammals the energy / needed to be active not only during the day but also the cool night, / and to live in colder climates or places with changing temperatures.
씹기는 포유류에게 에너지를 준다. / 낮은 물론 서늘한 밤 동안에도 활동하는 데 필요한 / 그리고 더 추운 기후나 기온이 변하는 장소에서 사는 데
It allows them / to sustain higher levels of activity and travel speeds / to cover larger distances, / avoid predators, / capture prey, / and make and care for their young.
그것은 그들에게 ~하게 한다. / 더 높은 수준의 활동과 이동 속도를 유지하게 / 더 먼 거리를 가고, / 천적을 피하고, / 먹이를 포획하고 / 새끼를 낳고 돌볼 수 있도록
Mammals are able to live in an incredible variety of habitats, / from Arctic tundra to Antarctic pack ice, / deep open waters to high-altitude mountaintops, / and rainforests to deserts, / in no small measure because of their teeth.
포유류는 매우 다양한 서식지에서 살 수 있다. / 북극 툰드라부터 남극의 유빙까지, / 심해부터 고도가 높은 산꼭대기까지 / 그리고 열대 우림부터 사막까지 / 어느 정도는 그들의 이빨로 인해

씹기는 삼킬 조각이 더 작아지게 하고 소화 효소가 작용할 표면이 더 노출되게 한다. 다시 말해서, 한입의 음식으로부터 더 많은 연료와 원료를 추출하는 것을 의미한다. 이것은 포유류들이 체내에서 자신의 몸을 따뜻하게 하기 때문에 포유류에게 특히 중요하다. 씹기는 포유류에게 낮은 물론 서늘한 밤 동안에도 활동하고, 더 추운 기후나 기온이 변하는 장소에서 사는 데 필요한 에너지를 준다. 그것은 그들에게 더 먼 거리를 가고, 천적을 피하고, 먹이를 포획하고 새끼를 낳고 돌볼 수 있도록 더 높은 수준의 활동과 이동 속도를 유지하게 한다. 포유류는 어느 정도는 그들의 이빨로 인해 북극 툰드라부터 남극의 유빙까지, 심해부터 고도가 높은 산꼭대기까지 그리고 열대 우림부터 사막까지 매우 다양한 서식지에서 살 수 있다.

Why? 왜 정답일까?

'This is especially important for mammals because they heat their bodies from within.' 이후로 씹는 행위가 포유류가 생존하는 데 어떤 식으로 도움이 되는지 설명하는 글이다. 따라서 글의 제목으로 가장 적절한 것은 ③ '씹는 것은 포유류 생존에 어떻게 도움이 되는가'이다.

- digestive ⓐ 소화의
- extraction ⓝ 추출
- temperature ⓝ 온도
- predator ⓝ 포식자
- incredible ⓐ (너무 좋거나 커서) 믿을 수 없는
- in no small measure 어느 정도는, 적잖이
- indigestion ⓝ 소화불량
- act on ~에 작용하다
- mammal ⓝ 포유류
- sustain ⓥ 유지하다
- prey ⓝ 먹이
- habitat ⓝ 서식지
- ease ⓥ 완화시키다
- harsh ⓐ 혹독한, 가혹한

5행 Chewing gives mammals the energy needed to be active not only during
4형식 동사 간접목적어 직접목적어 과거분사 부사적 용법1 「not only A +
the day but also the cool night, and to live in colder climates or places with
but also B : A뿐만 아니라 B도」 부사적 용법2
changing temperatures.

25 어린이들의 스포츠 참여 연령 및 기간 조사 정답률 83% | 정답 ⑤

다음 표의 내용과 일치하지 않는 것은?

Age Children Quit Regularly Playing a Sport

Sport	Average Age of Last Regular Participation	Average Length in Years of Participation
Soccer	9.1	3.0
Ice Hockey	10.9	3.1
Tennis	10.9	1.9
Basketball	11.2	3.2
Field Hockey	11.4	5.1
Golf	11.8	2.8
Skateboarding	12.0	2.8
Track and Field	13.0	2.0

The above table / shows the average age of last regular participation of children in a sport / and the average length of participation / based on a 2019 survey.
위 표는 / 어린이들이 마지막으로 스포츠에 정기적으로 참여한 평균 연령을 보여 준다. / 그리고 평균 참여 기간을 / 2019년 조사를 바탕으로
① Among the eight sports above, / soccer was the only sport / that children quit at an average age of younger than 10.
위 여덟 개의 스포츠 중에서 / 축구는 유일한 스포츠였다. / 어린이들이 평균 10세보다 어린 나이에 중단한
② Children quit playing ice hockey and tennis / at the same age on average, / but the average length of participation in tennis was shorter / than that in ice hockey.
어린이들은 아이스하키와 테니스를 중단했지만, / 평균적으로 같은 연령에 / 테니스에 참여한 평균 기간은 아이스하키보다 더 짧았다.
③ Basketball, field hockey, and golf were sports / which children quit playing / on average before they turned 12, / but golf had the shortest average participation length / among the three sports.
농구, 필드하키 그리고 골프는 스포츠였지만, / 어린이들이 중단한 / 평균적으로 그들이 12세가 되기 전에 / 골프는 평균 참여 기간이 가장 짧았다. / 이 세 가지 스포츠 중에서
④ Skateboarding was a sport / children quit at the average age of 12, / and the average length of participation / was the same as golf.
스케이트보드는 스포츠였고, / 어린이들이 평균 12세에 중단한 / 그 평균 참여 기간은 / 골프와 같았다.
✓ Meanwhile, / children quit participating in track and field / at the average age of 13, / but the average length of participation / was the shortest among the eight sports.
한편, / 어린이들은 육상경기 참여를 중단했으나, / 평균 13세에 / 평균 참여 기간은 / 여덟 개의 스포츠 중에서 가장 짧았다.

위 표는 2019년 조사를 바탕으로 어린이들이 마지막으로 스포츠에 정기적으로 참여한 평균 연령과 평균 참여 기간을 보여 준다. ① 위 여덟 개의 스포츠 중에서 축구는 어린이들이 평균 10세보다 어린 나이에 중단한 유일한 스포츠였다. ② 어린이들은 아이스하키와 테니스를 평균적으로 같은 연령에 중단했지만, 테니스에 참여한 평균 기간은 아이스하키보다 더 짧았다. ③ 농구, 필드하키 그리고 골프는 어린이들이 평균적으로 그들이 12세가 되기 전에 중단한 스포츠였지만, 골프는 이 세 가지 스포츠 중에서 평균 참여 기간이 가장 짧았다. ④ 스케이트보드는 어린이들이 평균 12세에 중단한 스포츠였고, 그 평균 참여 기간은 골프와 같았다. ⑤ 한편, 어린이들은 육상경기 참여를 평균 13세에 중단했으나, 평균 참여 기간은 여덟 개의 스포츠 중에서 가장 짧았다.

Why? 왜 정답일까?

도표에 따르면 어린이들이 육상경기 참여를 평균 13세에 중단했다는 설명은 맞지만, 여덟 개 스포츠 중 평균 참여 기간이 가장 짧았던 종목은 테니스였다. 따라서 도표와 일치하지 않는 것은 ⑤이다.

- average ⓐ 평균의 ⓝ 평균
- track and field 육상 (경기)
- participation ⓝ 참여

26 Sarah Breedlove의 생애 정답률 78% | 정답 ④

Sarah Breedlove에 관한 다음 글의 내용과 일치하지 않는 것은?

① 미국인 사업가이자 사회 운동가였다.
② St. Louis에서 10년 넘게 세탁부로 일했다.
③ 장시간의 노동과 열악한 식사로 머리카락이 빠졌다.
✓ 모발 관리 제품을 수입하여 전국에 판매했다.
⑤ 흑인 여성들에게 재정적 독립의 기회를 주었다.

「Born in 1867, / Sarah Breedlove was an American businesswoman and social activist.」
1867년에 태어난 / Sarah Breedlove는 미국인 사업가이자 사회 운동가였다. ①의 근거 일치
Orphaned at the age of seven, / her early life was marked by hardship.
7살에 고아가 되고 / 그녀의 어린 시절은 고난으로 얼룩졌다.
「In 1888, she moved to St. Louis, / where she worked as a washerwoman for more than a decade, / earning barely more than a dollar a day.」
1888년에 그녀는 St. Louis로 이사했고, / 그곳에서 10년 넘게 세탁부로 일했다. / 하루에 겨우 1달러가 넘는 돈을 벌면서 ②의 근거 일치
「During this time, / long hours of backbreaking labor and a poor diet / caused her hair to fall out.」
이 시기 동안 / 장시간의 고된 노동과 열악한 식사 / 그녀의 머리카락을 빠지게 했다. ③의 근거 일치
She tried everything that was available / but had no success.
그녀는 할 수 있는 모든 것을 시도했지만 / 효과를 보지 못했다.
「After working as a maid for a chemist, / she invented a successful hair care product / and sold it across the country.」
한 화학자의 가정부로 일한 후 / 그녀는 성공적인 모발 관리 제품을 발명했고 / 그것을 전국에 판매했다. ④의 근거 불일치
Not only did she sell, / she also recruited and trained lots of women as sales agents / for a share of the profits.
그녀는 판매를 했을 뿐 아니라, / 그녀는 많은 여성을 판매 대리인으로 모집하여 교육하기도 했다. / 수익금의 할당을 위해
「In the process / she became America's first self-made female millionaire / and she gave Black women everywhere / an opportunity for financial independence.」 ⑤의 근거 일치
그 과정에서 / 그녀는 미국 최초의 자수성가한 여성 백만장자가 되었고 / 도처의 흑인 여성들에게 주었다. / 재정적 독립의 기회를

1867년에 태어난 Sarah Breedlove는 미국인 사업가이자 사회 운동가였다. 7살에 고아가 되고 그녀의 어린 시절은 고난으로 얼룩졌다. 1888년에 그녀는 St. Louis로 이사했고, 그곳에서 10년 넘게 세탁부로 일하면서 하루에 겨우 1달러가 넘는 돈을 벌었다. 이 시기 동안 장시간의 고된 노동과 열악한 식사로 인해 그녀의 머리카락이 빠졌다. 그녀는 할 수 있는 모든 것을 시도했지만 효과를 보지 못했다. 한 화학자의 가정부로 일한 후 그녀는 성공적인 모발 관리 제품을 발명했고 그것을 전국에 판매했다. 그녀는 판매를 했을 뿐 아니라, 수익금의 할당을 위해 많은 여성을 판매 대리인으로 모집하여 교육하기도 했다. 그 과정에서 그녀는 미국 최초의 자수성가한 여성 백만장자가 되었고 도처의 흑인 여성들에게 재정적 독립의 기회를 주었다.

Why? 왜 정답일까?

'~ she invented a successful hair care product and sold it across the country.'에 따르면 Sarah Breedlove는 모발 관리 제품을 수입한 것이 아니라 직접 발명하여 전국에 판매했음을 알 수 있다. 따라서 내용과 일치하지 않는 것은 ④ '모발 관리 제품을 수입하여 전국에 판매했다.'이다.

Why? 왜 오답일까?

① 'Born in 1867, Sarah Breedlove was an American businesswoman and social activist.'의 내용과 일치한다.
② 'In 1888, she moved to St. Louis, where she worked as a washerwoman for

more than a decade. ~'의 내용과 일치한다.
③ 'During this time, long hours of backbreaking labor and a poor diet caused her hair to fall out.'의 내용과 일치한다.
⑤ '~ she gave Black women everywhere an opportunity for financial independence.'의 내용과 일치한다.

- activist ⓝ 운동가, 활동가
- hardship ⓝ 고난, 어려움
- barely ⓐⓓ 간신히, 가까스로
- labor ⓝ 노동
- chemist ⓝ 화학자
- millionaire ⓝ 백만장자
- orphan ⓥ 고아로 만들다 ⓝ 고아
- washerwoman ⓝ 세탁부
- backbreaking ⓐ 매우 힘든, 소모시키는
- fall out (머리 등이) 빠지다, 헐거워지다
- self-made ⓐ 자수성가한

구문 풀이
9행 Not only did she sell, she also recruited and trained lots of women as sales agents for a share of the profits.
『부정어구+조동사+주어+동사원형 : 도치 구문』 동사1 동사2 전치사(~로서) 공통 목적어

2020 Student Building Block Competition에 관한 다음 안내문의 내용과 일치하지 <u>않는</u> 것은?
① 초등학교 체육관에서 열린다.
② 제공되는 블록을 사용해야 한다.
③ 외부의 도움 없이 작품을 완성해야 한다.
④ 우승자에게 상금과 메달을 준다.
☑ 현장에서 등록하는 것이 가능하다.

2020 Student Building Block Competition
2020 학생 블록 쌓기 대회
Students in every grade will compete / to build the most creative and livable structure / made out of blocks!
모든 학년의 학생들이 경쟁할 것입니다! / 가장 창의적이고 살기에 알맞은 건축물을 만들기 위해 / 블록으로 만든
When & Where
일시와 장소
2 p.m. – 4 p.m. Saturday, November 21
11월 21일, 토요일, 오후 2시~오후 4시
『Green Valley Elementary School Gym』 ①의근거 일치
Green Valley 초등학교 체육관
Rules
규칙
『All building projects must be completed on site / with supplied blocks only.』②의근거 일치
모든 건축 프로젝트는 현장에서 완성되어야 합니다. / 제공된 블록만으로
『Participants are not allowed / to receive outside assistance.』③의근거 일치
참가자들은 허용되지 않습니다. / 외부의 도움을 받는 것이
Gifts & Prizes
선물과 상
All the participants receive a T-shirt.
모든 참가자들은 티셔츠를 받습니다.
『One winner from each grade group / wins $100 and a medal.』④의근거 일치
각 학년 그룹별 우승자는 / 100달러와 메달을 받습니다.
Sign up
등록
Participation is FREE!
참가는 무료입니다!
Email jeremywilson@greenvalley.org by November 15.
11월 15일까지 jeremywilson@greenvalley.org로 이메일을 보내세요.
『(Registration on site is not available.)』⑤의근거 불일치
(현장에서 등록은 가능하지 않습니다.)

2020 학생 블록 쌓기 대회

각 학년의 학생들이 블록으로 만든 가장 창의적이고 살기에 알맞은 건축물을 만들기 위해 경쟁할 것입니다!

일시와 장소
• 11월 21일, 토요일, 오후 2시 ~ 오후 4시
• Green Valley 초등학교 체육관

규칙
• 모든 건축 프로젝트는 제공된 블록만으로 현장에서 완성되어야 합니다.
• 참가자들은 외부의 도움을 받는 것이 허용되지 않습니다.

선물과 상
• 모든 참가자들은 티셔츠를 받습니다.
• 각 학년 그룹별 우승자는 100달러와 메달을 받습니다.

등록
• 참가는 무료입니다!
• 11월 15일까지 jeremywilson@greenvalley.org로 이메일을 보내세요.
(현장에서 등록은 가능하지 않습니다.)

Why? 왜 정답일까?
'Registration on site is not available.'에서 현장 등록은 가능하지 않다고 하므로, 안내문의 내용과 일치하지 않는 것은 ⑤ '현장에서 등록하는 것이 가능하다.'이다.

Why? 왜 오답일까?
① 'Green Valley Elementary School Gym'의 내용과 일치한다.
② 'All building projects must be completed on site with supplied blocks only.'의 내용과 일치한다.
③ 'Participants are not allowed to receive outside assistance.'의 내용과 일치한다.

---

④ 'One winner from each grade group wins $100 and a medal.'의 내용과 일치한다.

- compete ⓥ 경쟁하다
- made out of ~로 만든
- assistance ⓝ 도움, 원조
- livable ⓐ 살만한, 살기 적합한
- on site 현장에서

Crystal Castle Fireworks에 관한 다음 안내문의 내용과 일치하는 것은?
① 영국의 북부 지역에서 가장 큰 불꽃놀이이다.
② 라이브 음악 쇼가 불꽃놀이 이후에 진행된다.
③ 불꽃놀이는 1시간 동안 진행된다.
④ 주차장은 오후 1시부터 유료로 이용 가능하다.
☑ 12세 이하의 아동은 성인과 동행해야 한다.

Crystal Castle Fireworks
Crystal Castle 불꽃놀이
『Come and enjoy the biggest fireworks display / in the South West of England!』①의근거 불일치
가장 큰 불꽃놀이에 와서 즐기세요! / 영국의 남서부 지역에서
Dates: 5th & 6th December, 2020
날짜: 2020년 12월 5일과 6일
Location: Crystal Castle, 132 Oak Street
장소: Oak 가 132 Crystal Castle
Time: 『15:00 – 16:00 Live Music Show』②의근거 불일치
시간: 15:00 ~ 16:00 라이브 음악 쇼
16:30 – 17:30 Maze Garden
16:30 ~ 17:30 미로 정원
『18:00 – 18:30 Fireworks Display』③의근거 불일치
18:00 ~ 18:30 불꽃놀이
Parking: 『Free car park opens at 13:00.』④의근거 불일치
주차: 무료 주차장이 13시에 개방됩니다.
Note:
주의 사항:
『Any child aged 12 or under / must be accompanied by an adult.』⑤의근거 일치
12세 이하의 모든 아동은 / 성인과 동행해야 합니다.
All tickets must be reserved beforehand / on our website www.crystalcastle.com.
모든 티켓은 미리 예매해야 합니다. / 저희 웹사이트 www.crystalcastle.com에서

Crystal Castle 불꽃놀이

영국의 남서부 지역에서 가장 큰 불꽃놀이에 와서 즐기세요!

날짜: 2020년 12월 5일과 6일

장소: Oak 가 132 Crystal Castle

시간: 15:00 ~ 16:00 라이브 음악 쇼
16:30 ~ 17:30 미로 정원
18:00 ~ 18:30 불꽃놀이

주차: 무료 주차장이 13시에 개방됩니다.

주의 사항:
12세 이하의 모든 아동은 성인과 동행해야 합니다.
모든 티켓은 저희 웹사이트 www.crystalcastle.com에서 미리 예매해야 합니다.

Why? 왜 정답일까?
'Any child aged 12 or under must be accompanied by an adult.'에서 12세 이하의 아동은 성인과 동행해야 한다고 하므로, 안내문의 내용과 일치하는 것은 ⑤ '12세 이하의 아동은 성인과 동행해야 한다.'이다.

Why? 왜 오답일까?
① 'Come and enjoy the biggest fireworks display in the South West of England!'에서 영국의 북부 지역이 아닌 남서부 지역에서 가장 큰 불꽃놀이라고 하였다.
② 'Time: 15:00 – 16:00 Live Music Show'에 따르면 15시에 라이브 음악 쇼가 먼저 열린 후 18시에 불꽃놀이가 열린다.
③ '18:00 – 18:30 Fireworks Display'에서 불꽃놀이는 30분 동안 진행된다고 하였다.
④ 'Parking: Free car park opens at 13:00.'에서 오후 1시부터 이용 가능한 주차장은 무료라고 하였다.

- firework ⓝ 불꽃놀이, 폭죽
- reserve ⓥ 예약하다
- accompany ⓥ 동반하다
- beforehand ⓐⓓ 사전에

다음 글의 밑줄 친 부분 중, 어법상 틀린 것은? [3점]

Each species of animals / can detect a different range of odours.
각 종의 동물들은 / 서로 다른 범주의 냄새를 감지할 수 있다.
No species can detect all the molecules / that are present in the environment / ① in which it lives / — there are some things / that we cannot smell / but which some other animals can, / and vice versa.
어떤 종도 모든 분자를 감지할 수는 없는데, / 환경에 존재하는 / 그것이 살고 있는 / 몇 가지 것들이 있고, / 우리는 냄새를 맡을 수 없지만 / 몇몇 다른 동물들은 냄새를 맡을 수 있는 / 그 반대의 경우도 있다.
There are also differences between individuals, / relating to the ability to smell an odour, / or how ② pleasant it seems.
개체들 사이의 차이 역시 존재한다. / 어떤 냄새를 맡을 수 있는 능력과 관련된 / 또는 그것이 얼마나 좋은 느낌을 주는지와
For example, / some people like the taste of coriander / — known as cilantro in the USA / — while others find ③ it soapy and unpleasant.
예를 들어, / 어떤 사람들은 고수(coriander)의 맛을 좋아한다. / 미국에서 고수(cilantro)라고 알려진 / 다른 사람들은 그것이 비누 맛이 나고 불쾌하다고 여기는 반면
This effect has an underlying genetic component / due to differences in the genes / ④ controlling our sense of smell.

이러한 결과에는 내재된 유전적 요소가 있다. / 유전자 차이로 인한 / 우리의 후각을 조절하는
Ultimately, / the selection of scents detected by a given species, / and how that odour is perceived, / will depend upon the animal's ecology.
궁극적으로, / 특정 종에 의해 감지된 냄새들의 집합 / 그리고 그 냄새가 어떻게 인식되는가는 / 그 동물의 생태에 달려 있을 것이다.
The response profile of each species / will enable it ⑤ to locate sources of smell / that are relevant to it / and to respond accordingly.
각 종의 반응 도표는 / 그 종이 냄새의 원천을 찾게 해 줄 것이다. / 자신과 관련된 / 그리고 그에 따라 반응할 수 있게

각 종의 동물들은 서로 다른 범주의 냄새를 감지할 수 있다. 어떤 종도 그것이 살고 있는 환경에 존재하는 모든 분자를 감지할 수는 없는데, 우리는 냄새를 맡을 수 없지만 몇몇 다른 동물들은 냄새를 맡을 수 있는 몇 가지 것들이 있고, 그 반대의 경우도 있다. 어떤 냄새를 맡을 수 있는 능력이나 그것이 얼마나 좋은 느낌을 주는지와 관련된 개체들 사이의 차이 역시 존재한다. 예를 들어, 어떤 사람들은 미국에서 고수(cilantro)라고 알려진 고수(coriander)의 맛을 좋아하는 반면, 다른 사람들은 그것이 비누 맛이 나고 불쾌하다고 여긴다. 이러한 결과에는 우리의 후각을 조절하는 유전자 차이로 인한 내재된 유전적 요소가 있다. 궁극적으로, 특정 종에 의해 감지된 냄새들의 집합 그리고 그 냄새가 어떻게 인식되는가는 그 동물의 생태에 달려 있을 것이다. 각 종의 반응 도표는 그 종이 자신과 관련된 냄새의 원천을 찾고 그에 따라 반응할 수 있게 해 줄 것이다.

Why? 왜 정답일까?

how가 이끄는 간접의문문의 어순은 'how + 형/부 + 주어 + 동사'인데, 이때 형용사나 부사 중 무엇을 쓸지는 동사에 따라 결정된다. 여기서는 뒤에 형용사 보어를 취하는 2형식 동사 seems가 나온 것으로 보아 부사 pleasantly 대신 형용사 pleasant를 써야 한다. 따라서 어법상 틀린 것은 ②이다.

Why? 왜 오답일까?

① 뒤에 나오는 'it lives'가 완전한 1형식 문장이므로 '전치사 + 관계대명사' 형태의 in which를 써서 관계절을 연결한 것은 적절하다. 앞에 나온 the environment가 장소의 선행사이므로 이때 in which는 where로 바꿀 수 있다.
③ 앞에 나온 단수명사 the taste of coriander를 받기 위해 단수대명사 it이 바르게 쓰였다.
④ 뒤에 our sense of smell이라는 목적어가 나오는 것으로 보아 능동을 나타내는 현재분사 controlling이 바르게 쓰였다. 이 'controlling ~'은 the genes를 꾸민다.
⑤ 'enable + 목적어 + to부정사(~이 …할 수 있게 하다)'의 5형식 구조를 완성하기 위해 to locate가 바르게 쓰였다.

- **detect** ⓥ 감지하다, 알아차리다
- **molecule** ⓝ 분자
- **relate to** ~와 관련되다
- **unpleasant** ⓐ 불쾌한
- **genetic** ⓐ 유전적인
- **ecology** ⓝ 생태
- **response profile** 반응 도표(네 가지 기본적인 맛감각에 대한 신경 세포의 반응을 보여주는 그래프)
- **accordingly** ⓐd 그에 따라
- **odour** ⓝ 냄새, 악취
- **vice versa** 그 반대도 마찬가지다
- **soapy** ⓐ 비누 같은
- **underlying** ⓐ 내재된, 근본적인
- **component** ⓝ 구성 요소

구문 풀이

10행 Ultimately, the selection of scents detected by a given species, and
　　　　　　　　　　주어1　　　　　　　과거분사
how that odour is perceived, will depend upon the animal's ecology.
　주어2(간접의문문)　　　　　　동사

---

30 인간과 개의 뇌 크기가 줄어든 이유　　　　정답률 49% | 정답 ③

(A), (B), (C)의 각 네모 안에서 문맥에 맞는 낱말로 가장 적절한 것은? [3점]

	(A)	(B)	(C)
①	physical 신체적인	developed 발달시켰다	expanded 커졌다
②	physical 신체적인	lost 잃어버렸다	expanded 커졌다
✓③	physical 신체적인	lost 잃어버렸다	shrank 줄어들었다
④	psychological 심리적인	developed 발달시켰다	shrank 줄어들었다
⑤	psychological 심리적인	lost 잃어버렸다	shrank 줄어들었다

Recent research suggests / that evolving humans' relationship with dogs / changed the structure of both species' brains.
최근의 연구는 시사한다. / 인간과 개의 관계 진화가 / 두 종 모두의 뇌 구조를 바꿨다는 것을
One of the various (A) physical changes / caused by domestication / is a reduction in the size of the brain: / 16 percent for horses, / 34 percent for pigs, / and 10 to 30 percent for dogs.
다양한 신체적 변화들 중 하나는 / 사육으로 인해 야기된 / 뇌 크기의 감소인데, / 말은 16%, / 돼지는 34%, / 그리고 개는 10에서 30% 감소했다.
This is because once humans started to take care of these animals, / they no longer needed various brain functions / in order to survive.
이는 일단 인간이 이 동물들을 돌보기 시작하면서 / 그것들이 다양한 뇌 기능을 더는 필요로 하지 않았기 때문이다. / 생존하기 위해
Animals who were fed and protected by humans / did not need many of the skills / required by their wild ancestors / and (B) lost the parts of the brain / related to those capacities.
인간이 먹이를 주고 보호해 주는 동물들은 / 기술 중 많은 것들을 필요로 하지 않았고 / 그것들의 야생 조상들에 의해 요구된 / 뇌의 부분을 잃어버렸다 / 그러한 능력들과 관련된
A similar process occurred for humans, / who seem to have been domesticated by wolves.
유사한 과정이 인간에게 나타났는데, / 이들은 늑대에 의해 길들여진 것으로 보인다.
About 10,000 years ago, / when the role of dogs was firmly established in most human societies, / the human brain also (C) shrank by about 10 percent.
약 1만 년 전, / 개의 역할이 대부분의 인간 사회에서 확실히 정해졌을 때, / 인간의 뇌도 약 10% 줄어들었다.

최근의 연구는 인간과 개의 관계 진화가 두 종 모두의 뇌 구조를 바꿨다는 것을 시사한다. 사육으로 인해 야기된 다양한 (A) 신체적 변화들 중 하나는 뇌 크기의 감소인데, 말은 16%, 돼지는 34%, 그리고 개는 10에서 30% 감소했다. 이는 일단 인간이 이 동물들을 돌보기 시작하면서 그것들이 생존하기 위해 다양한 뇌 기능을 더는 필요로 하지 않았기 때문이다. 인간이 먹이를 주고 보호해 주는 동물들은 야생 조상들에 의해 요구된 기술 중 많은 것들을 필요로 하지 않았고 그러한 능력들과 관련된 뇌의 부분을 (B) 잃어버렸다. 유사한 과정이 인간에

게 나타났는데, 이들은 늑대에 의해 길들여진 것으로 보인다. 약 1만 년 전, 개의 역할이 대부분의 인간 사회에서 확실히 정해졌을 때, 인간의 뇌도 약 10% (C) 줄어들었다.

Why? 왜 정답일까?

(A) 네모 뒤에서 신체적 변화로 볼 수 있는 뇌 크기 감소가 언급되므로, physical이 적절하다.
(B) 'This is because ~' 문장에서 개를 포함한 동물들의 뇌가 줄어든 까닭은 인간에 의해 길들여지면서 생존에 필요했던 기능이 더 이상 필요하지 않게 되었기 때문임을 언급한다. 이를 근거로 할 때, 한때 필요했으나 더는 필요 없어진 능력과 관련된 뇌 부분이 실제로 '손실되면서' 뇌 크기가 줄어들었을 것임을 추론할 수 있다. 따라서 (B)에는 lost가 적절하다.
(C) 'A similar process occurred for humans, ~'에서 인간 또한 한때는 위협적이었던 늑대를 개로 키우게 되면서 늑대에 '길들게' 되었고, 이로 인해 '유사한 과정', 즉 뇌 크기가 줄어드는 일을 겪게 되었음을 시사하고 있다. 따라서 (C)에는 shrank가 적절하다. (A), (B), (C)의 각 네모 안에서 문맥에 맞는 낱말로 가장 적절한 것은 ③ '(A) 신체적인 - (B) 잃어버렸다 - (C) 줄어들었다'이다.

- **physical** ⓐ 신체적인
- **domestication** ⓝ 사육, 길들이기
- **feed[-fed-fed]** ⓥ 먹이를 주다
- **capacity** ⓝ 능력
- **established** ⓐ 자리를 잡은
- **shrink** ⓥ 줄어들다
- **psychological** ⓐ 심리적인
- **reduction** ⓝ 감소
- **ancestor** ⓝ 조상
- **firmly** ⓐd 확실히, 단호히
- **expand** ⓥ 커지다, 확장하다

구문 풀이

7행 Animals [who were fed and protected by humans] did not need many of
　　　　　　　주어　　▲주격 관계대명사　　　　　　　　　　동사1　　　　목적어1
the skills required by their wild ancestors and lost the parts of the brain related
　　　　　　　　▲ 과거분사　　　　　　　　　　동사2　　목적어2
to those capacities.
　　　　　　　▲ 과거분사(the parts 수식)

---

31 이동을 통한 인간의 진보와 자유 실현　　　　정답률 45% | 정답 ②

다음 빈칸에 들어갈 말로 가장 적절한 것을 고르시오.

① secure - 안정되려는　　✓② mobile - 이동하려는　　③ exceptional - 특출나려는
④ competitive - 경쟁하려는　　⑤ independent - 독립하려는

There is nothing more fundamental to the human spirit / than the need to be mobile.
인간의 정신에는 더 근본적인 것은 없다. / 이동하려는 욕구보다
It is the intuitive force / that sparks our imaginations / and opens pathways to life-changing opportunities.
그것은 직관적인 힘이다. / 우리의 상상력을 자극하고 / 삶을 변화시킬 기회로 가는 길을 열어주는
It is the catalyst for progress and personal freedom.
그것은 진보와 개인의 자유의 촉매이다.
Public transportation has been vital / to that progress and freedom / for more than two centuries.
대중교통은 없어서는 안 될 것이었다. / 그 진보와 자유에 / 2세기 넘게
The transportation industry / has always done more / than carry travelers from one destination to another.
운송 산업은 / 항상 더 많은 일을 해 왔다. / 한 목적지에서 다른 목적지로 이동하는 사람들을 실어나르는 것보다
It connects people, places, and possibilities.
그것은 사람, 장소 그리고 가능성을 연결해 준다.
It provides access / to what people need, / what they love, / and what they aspire to become.
그것은 접근성을 제공해 준다. / 사람들이 필요로 하는 것과 / 그들이 좋아하는 것과 / 그들이 되고자 열망하는 것에 대한
In so doing, / it grows communities, / creates jobs, / strengthens the economy, / expands social and commercial networks, / saves time and energy, / and helps millions of people achieve a better life.
그렇게 하면서 / 그것은 공동체를 성장시키고, / 일자리를 창출하고, / 경제를 강화하고, / 사회와 상업 네트워크를 확장하고, / 시간과 에너지를 절약해 주며 / 수백만 명의 사람들이 더 나은 삶을 누릴 수 있도록 돕는다.

인간의 정신에는 이동하려는 욕구보다 더 근본적인 것은 없다. 그것은 우리의 상상력을 자극하고 삶을 변화시킬 기회로 가는 길을 열어주는 직관적인 힘이다. 그것은 진보와 개인의 자유의 촉매이다. 대중교통은 2세기 넘게 그 진보와 자유에 없어서는 안 될 것이었다. 운송 산업은 항상 한 목적지에서 다른 목적지로 이동하는 사람들을 실어 나르는 것 이상의 일을 해 왔다. 그것은 사람, 장소 그리고 가능성을 연결해 준다. 그것은 사람들이 필요로 하는 것과 좋아하는 것과 되고자 열망하는 것에 대한 접근성을 제공해 준다. 그렇게 하면서 그것은 공동체를 성장시키고, 일자리를 창출하고, 경제를 강화하고, 사회와 상업 네트워크를 확장하고, 시간과 에너지를 절약해 주며 수백만 명의 사람들이 더 나은 삶을 누릴 수 있도록 돕는다.

Why? 왜 정답일까?

'Public transportation has been vital ~' 이하로 인간의 이동을 가능케 하는 수단인 대중교통이 인간의 진보와 자유에 없어서는 안 될 것이었다는 설명이 제시되고 있다. 이를 근거로 볼 때, 빈칸이 포함된 문장 또한 인간의 '이동'이 매우 근본적이고 중요하다는 의미를 나타내야 한다. 따라서 빈칸에 들어갈 말로 가장 적절한 것은 ② '이동하려는'이다.

- **fundamental** ⓐ 근본적인
- **spark** ⓥ 자극하다, 유발하다
- **public transportation** 대중교통
- **aspire** ⓥ 열망하다
- **secure** ⓐ 안정된
- **exceptional** ⓐ 특출난, 이례적인
- **intuitive** ⓐ 직관적인
- **progress** ⓝ 진보, 진전
- **vital** ⓐ 없어서는 안 되는, 필수적인
- **strengthen** ⓥ 강화하다
- **mobile** ⓐ 이동하는, 기동성 있는

구문 풀이

2행 It is the intuitive force [that sparks our imaginations and opens pathways
　　　　　　대명사　　　선행사　　주격 관·대 동사1　　　　　　　　　동사2
to life-changing opportunities].

---

32 현대 기업 상황에 맞는 메디치 효과의 의미　　　　정답률 48% | 정답 ①

다음 빈칸에 들어갈 말로 가장 적절한 것을 고르시오. [3점]

✓ having others around you to compensate - 여러분 주위에 보완할 다른 사람들을 두는 것

② taking some time to reflect on yourself – 자신을 돌아볼 시간을 좀 갖는 것
③ correcting the mistakes of the past – 과거의 실수를 고치는 것
④ maximizing your own strength – 자신만의 강점을 극대화하는 것
⑤ setting a specific objective – 구체적인 목표를 세우는 것

Business consultant Frans Johansson / describes the *Medici effect* / as the emergence of new ideas and creative solutions / when different backgrounds and disciplines come together.
기업 자문가인 Frans Johansson은 / 메디치 효과를 기술한다. / 새로운 아이디어와 창의적인 해결책의 출현으로 / 다양한 배경과 학문 분야가 합쳐질 때

The term is derived from the 15th-century Medici family, / who helped usher in the Renaissance / by bringing together artists, writers, and other creatives / from all over the world.
그 용어는 15세기 메디치 가문에서 유래하는데, / 그들은 르네상스 시대가 시작되도록 도왔다. / 예술가, 작가 그리고 다른 창작자들을 함께 모아 / 전 세계로부터

Arguably, / the Renaissance was a result of the exchange of ideas / between these different groups / in close contact with each other.
거의 틀림없이, / 르네상스 시대는 아이디어가 교환된 결과였다. / 이 다양한 집단들 사이에서 / 서로 근접한

Sound familiar?
익숙하게 들리는가?

If you are unable to diversify your own talent and skill, / then having others around you to compensate / might very well just do the trick.
만약 여러분이 자신의 재능과 기술을 다양화할 수 없다면, / 그때는 여러분 주위에 보완할 다른 사람들을 두는 것이 / 효과가 있을 수 있다.

Believing / that all new ideas come from combining existing notions in creative ways, / Johansson recommends / utilizing a mix of backgrounds, experiences, and expertise in staffing / to bring about the best possible solutions, perspectives, and innovations in business.
믿으면서, / 모든 새로운 아이디어는 기존 개념들을 창의적인 방식으로 합치는 것에서 나온다고 / Johansson은 추천한다. / 인력 배치에서 배경과 경험과 전문 지식을 혼합하여 활용할 것을 / 기업에서 가능한 최고의 해결책, 전망 그리고 혁신을 유발하기 위해

기업 자문가인 Frans Johansson은 메디치 효과를 다양한 배경과 학문 분야가 합쳐질 때 새로운 아이디어와 창의적인 해결책이 출현하는 것이라고 기술한다. 그 용어는 15세기 메디치 가문에서 유래하는데, 그들은 전 세계의 예술가, 작가 그리고 다른 창작자들을 함께 모아 르네상스 시대가 시작되도록 도왔다. 거의 틀림없이, 르네상스 시대는 서로 근접한 이 다양한 집단들 사이에서 아이디어가 교환된 결과였다. 익숙하게 들리는가? 만약 여러분이 자신의 재능과 기술을 다양화할 수 없다면, 그때는 여러분 주위에 보완할 다른 사람들을 두는 것이 효과가 있을 수 있다. 모든 새로운 아이디어는 기존 개념들을 창의적인 방식으로 합치는 것에서 나온다고 믿으면서, Johansson은 기업에서 가능한 최고의 해결책, 전망 그리고 혁신을 유발하기 위해 인력 배치에서 배경과 경험과 전문 지식을 혼합하여 활용할 것을 추천한다.

Why? 왜 정답일까?

'메디치 효과'의 의미를 설명하는 '~ by bringing together artists, writers, and other creatives from all over the world. Arguably, the Renaissance was a result of the exchange of ideas between these different groups in close contact with each other.'에 따르면 르네상스 시대는 메디치 가문이 전 세계의 예술가, 작가 등 다양한 집단을 한데 모아 아이디어의 교환을 촉진했던 것에서 기원했다고 한다. 이를 오늘날의 기업 상황에 적용하면, '각기 다른 재능, 기술, 경험을 지닌 사람들이 함께할 때' 혁신이 이루어질 것이라는 결론을 도출할 수 있다. 따라서 빈칸에 들어갈 말로 가장 적절한 것은 ① '여러분 주위에 보완할 다른 사람들을 두는 것'이다.

- emergence ⓝ 출현, 등장
- derive A from B A를 B로부터 끌어내다
- in contact with ~와 접촉하다
- do the trick 성공하다, 효과가 있다
- compensate ⓥ 보완하다, 보상하다
- specific ⓐ 구체적인
- discipline ⓝ 분야
- arguably ⓐⓓ 거의 틀림없이
- diversify ⓥ 다양화하다
- expertise ⓝ 전문 지식
- reflect on ~을 돌아보다, 성찰하다
- objective ⓝ 목표

구문 풀이

8행 If you are unable to diversify your own talent and skill, then having others
「be unable + to부정사: ~할 수 없다」   동명사구 주어
around you to compensate might very well just do the trick.
                              아마 ~일 것이다   성공하다, 효과가 있다

---

33 화석으로 얻는 정보의 불완전성 정답률 49% | 정답 ①

다음 빈칸에 들어갈 말로 가장 적절한 것을 고르시오. [3점]

✓① tell the entire story – 완전한 이야기를 전달하지
② require further study – 더 깊은 연구를 필요로 하지
③ teach us a wrong lesson – 우리에게 잘못된 교훈을 가르쳐주지
④ change their original traits – 그것의 원래 특성을 바꾸지
⑤ make room for imagination – 상상의 여지를 남기지

As much as we can learn by examining fossils, / it is important to remember / that they seldom tell the entire story.
우리가 화석을 조사하며 많은 것을 배울 수 있기는 하지만, / 기억하는 것이 중요하다. / 그것들이 좀처럼 완전한 이야기를 전달하지 않는다는 것을

Things only fossilize under certain sets of conditions.
생물들은 일련의 특정 조건 하에서만 화석화된다.

Modern insect communities are highly diverse in tropical forests, / but the recent fossil record captures little of that diversity.
현대 곤충 군집들은 열대 우림 지역에서 매우 다양하지만, / 최근 화석 기록은 그 다양성을 거의 담아내지 않는다.

Many creatures are consumed entirely or decompose rapidly / when they die, / so there may be no fossil record at all / for important groups.
많은 생명체는 완전히 먹히거나 급속히 부패해서 / 그들이 죽을 때 / 화석 기록이 전혀 존재하지 않을 수도 있다. / 중요한 집단에 관한

It's a bit similar to a family photo album.
그것은 가족 사진첩과도 약간 비슷하다.

Maybe when you were born / your parents took lots of pictures, / but over the years / they took photographs occasionally, / and sometimes they got busy / and forgot to take pictures at all.

아마도 여러분이 태어났을 때 / 여러분의 부모님은 사진을 많이 찍었겠지만, / 시간이 흐르면서 / 그들은 가끔 사진을 찍었고, / 때로는 그들은 바빠져서 / 사진 찍는 것을 아예 잊어버렸을지도 모른다.

Very few of us have a complete photo record of our life.
우리 중 인생의 완전한 사진 기록을 가진 사람은 거의 없다.

Fossils are just like that.
화석이 바로 그것과 같다.

Sometimes you get very clear pictures of the past, / while at other times there are big gaps, / and you need to notice what they are.
때때로 여러분은 과거에 대한 매우 명확한 그림을 가지지만 / 다른 때에는 큰 공백들이 존재하고, / 여러분은 그것들이 무엇인지를 인지할 필요가 있다.

우리가 화석을 조사하며 많은 것을 배울 수 있기는 하지만, 그것들이 좀처럼 완전한 이야기를 전달하지 않는다는 것을 기억하는 것이 중요하다. 생물들은 일련의 특정 조건 하에서만 화석화된다. 현대 곤충 군집들은 열대 우림 지역에서 매우 다양하지만, 최근 화석 기록은 그 다양성을 거의 담아내지 않는다. 많은 생명체는 죽을 때 완전히 먹히거나 급속히 부패해서 중요한 집단에 관한 화석 기록이 전혀 존재하지 않을 수도 있다. 그것은 가족 사진첩과도 약간 비슷하다. 아마도 여러분이 태어났을 때 여러분의 부모님은 사진을 많이 찍었겠지만, 시간이 흐르면서 그들은 가끔 사진을 찍었고, 때로는 바빠져서 사진 찍는 것을 아예 잊어버렸을지도 모른다. 우리 중 인생의 완전한 사진 기록을 가진 사람은 거의 없다. 화석이 바로 그것과 같다. 때때로 여러분은 과거에 대한 매우 명확한 그림을 가지지만 다른 때에는 큰 공백들이 존재하고, 여러분은 그것들이 무엇인지를 인지할 필요가 있다.

Why? 왜 정답일까?

마지막 두 문장인 'Fossils are just like that. Sometimes you get very clear pictures of the past, while at other times there are big gaps, ~'에서 화석을 통해 과거에 대해 명확한 그림을 얻는 경우도 있지만 다른 경우 공백도 있을 수 있다고 언급하는 것으로 보아, 빈칸이 포함된 문장은 화석을 통해 '온전한 이야기를 얻지' 못할 수도 있다는 의미가 되어야 한다. 따라서 빈칸에 들어갈 말로 가장 적절한 것은 ① '완전한 이야기를 전달하지'이다.

- examine ⓥ 조사하다
- consume ⓥ 먹다, 소비하다
- occasionally ⓐⓓ 가끔, 때때로
- make room for ~의 여지를 남기다, ~을 위해 (자리를) 양보하다
- fossilize ⓥ 화석화하다
- entirely ⓐⓓ 완전히
- trait ⓝ 특성

구문 풀이

1행 「(문장 맨 앞의) as + 원급 + as : ~하기는 하지만, ~한 만큼이나」
As much as we can learn by examining fossils, it is important to remember
            ~함으로써   가주어   진주어
that they seldom tell the entire story.
접속사(~것) 준부정어(좀처럼 ~않다)

19회

★★★ 등급을 가르는 문제!

34 한 항공사가 어려운 시기에도 성장해갈 수 있었던 비결 정답률 34% | 정답 ③

다음 빈칸에 들어갈 말로 가장 적절한 것을 고르시오. [3점]

① it was being faced with serious financial crises
  그것이 심각한 재정 위기에 직면하고 있었다
② there was no specific long-term plan on marketing
  마케팅에 관한 구체적인 장기 계획이 없었다
✓③ company leadership had set an upper limit for growth
  회사 지도부가 성장의 상한치를 설정했다
④ its executives worried about the competing airlines' future
  회사 경영진이 경쟁 항공사의 미래를 걱정했다
⑤ the company had emphasized moral duties more than profits
  회사가 이익보다도 도덕적 의무를 강조했기

Back in 1996, / an American airline was faced with an interesting problem.
1996년에 / 한 미국 항공사가 흥미로운 문제에 직면했다.

At a time / when most other airlines were losing money or going under, / over 100 cities were begging the company to service their locations.
시기에, / 대부분의 다른 항공사들이 손해를 보거나 파산하던 / 100개가 넘는 도시가 그 회사에 그들의 지역에 취항할 것을 부탁하고 있었다.

However, that's not the interesting part.
하지만, 그것이 흥미로운 부분은 아니다.

What's interesting is / that the company turned down over 95 percent of those offers / and began serving only four new locations.
흥미로운 것은 / 회사는 그 제안 중 95퍼센트 넘게 거절했고 / 네 개의 새로운 지역만 취항을 시작했다는 점이다.

It turned down tremendous growth / because company leadership had set an upper limit for growth.
회사는 엄청난 성장을 거절했는데 / 회사 지도부가 성장의 상한치를 설정했기 때문이다.

Sure, its executives wanted to grow each year, / but they didn't want to grow too much.
물론, 그 경영진들은 매년 성장하기를 원했지만, / 그들은 너무 많이 성장하는 것을 원하지는 않았다.

Unlike other famous companies, / they wanted to set their own pace, / one that could be sustained in the long term.
다른 유명한 회사들과는 달리, / 그들은 자신만의 속도를 정하기를 원했다. / 즉 장기간 지속될 수 있는 것

By doing this, / they established a safety margin for growth / that helped them continue to thrive / at a time / when the other airlines were flailing.
이렇게 함으로써, / 그들은 성장의 안전이 보장되는 여유를 설정했다. / 그들이 계속 번창하는 데 도움이 됐던 / 시기에 / 다른 항공사들이 마구 흔들리던

1996년에 한 미국 항공사가 흥미로운 문제에 직면했다. 대부분의 다른 항공사들이 손해를 보거나 파산하던 시기에, 100개가 넘는 도시가 그 회사에 그들의 지역에 취항할 것을 부탁하고 있었다. 하지만, 그것이 흥미로운 부분은 아니다. 흥미로운 것은 회사는 그 제안 중 95퍼센트 넘게 거절했고 네 개의 새로운 지역만 취항을 시작했다는 점이다. 회사는 엄청난 성장을 거절했는데 회사 지도부가 성장의 상한치를 설정했기 때문이다. 물론, 그 경영진들은 매년 성장하기를 원했지만, 너무 많이 성장하는 것을 원하지는 않았다. 다른 유명한 회사들과는 달리, 그들은 장기간 지속될 수 있는 것, 즉 자신만의 속도를 정하기를 원했다. 이렇게 함으로써 그들은 다른 항공사들이 마구 흔들리던 시기에 그들이 계속 번창하는 데 도움이 됐던, 성장의 안전이 보장되는 여유를 설정했다.

Why? 왜 정답일까?

'Sure, its executives wanted to grow each year, but they didn't want to grow too much. Unlike other famous companies, they wanted to set their own pace, ~'에 따

르면 경쟁사가 고전하는 가운데 홀로 취항요청을 받았던 항공사의 경영진들은 과한 성장보다는 회사 나름의 속도대로 오래 지속되는 성장을 바랐다고 한다. 이를 근거로 할 때, 회사의 성장이 과해지지 않도록 조절하는 '상한치'가 있었을 것임을 추론할 수 있다. 따라서 빈칸에 들어갈 말로 가장 적절한 것은 ③ '회사 지도부가 성장의 상한치를 설정했기'이다.

- go under 파산하다
- tremendous ⓐ 엄청난
- establish ⓥ 설정하다, 확립하다
- thrive ⓥ 번창하다
- emphasize ⓥ 강조하다
- turn down ~을 거절하다
- executive ⓝ 경영진, 운영진, 간부
- margin ⓝ 여유, 여지
- crisis ⓝ 위기

구문 풀이

9행 Unlike other famous companies, they wanted to set their own pace, one [that could be sustained in the long term].

전치사(~와는 달리) / 주어 / 동사구 / 목적어 / 부정대명사(= pace) / 주격 관·대 / 조동사 수동태

★★ 문제 해결 꿀~팁 ★★

▶ 많이 틀린 이유는?
글에 따르면 미국의 한 항공사는 100개가 넘는 지역으로부터 취항 제의를 받았음에도 '회사 나름의 속도에 맞게' 성장하려는 원칙을 고수하고자 네 군데에서만 새로 취항을 시작했다. 경쟁 항공사를 신경 썼다는 내용은 언급되지 않으므로 ④는 답으로 적절하지 않다.

▶ 문제 해결 방법은?
'didn't want to grow too much', 'set their own pace' 등 핵심 표현을 재진술한 말이 빈칸에 들어가야 한다.

35 바넘 효과   정답률 62% | 정답 ④

다음 글에서 전체 흐름과 관계 없는 문장은?

The Barnum Effect is the phenomenon / where someone reads or hears something very general / but believes that it applies to them.
바넘 효과는 현상이다. / 누군가가 매우 일반적인 것을 읽거나 듣지만 / 그것이 자신에게 적용된다고 믿는

① These statements appear to be very personal on the surface / but in fact, they are true for many.
이러한 진술들은 표면적으로는 매우 개인적인 것처럼 보이지만 / 실제로는 많은 사람에게 적용된다.

② Human psychology allows us / to want to believe things / that we can identify with on a personal level / and even seek information / where it doesn't necessarily exist, / filling in the blanks with our imagination for the rest.
인간 심리는 우리가 ~하게 한다. / 것들을 믿고, / 우리가 개인적 차원에서 동일시할 수 있는 / 정보를 심지어 찾고 싶어 하게 / 정보가 반드시 존재하지는 않는 경우에도 / 나머지에 대해서는 우리의 상상으로 공백을 채우면서

③ This is the principle / that horoscopes rely on, / offering data / that appears to be personal / but probably makes sense to countless people.
이것은 원리이다. / 별자리 운세가 의존하는 / 정보를 제공하는 / 개인적인 것처럼 보이지만 / 수많은 사람에게 대개 들어맞는

✔ Reading daily horoscopes in the morning / is beneficial / as they provide predictions about the rest of the day.
아침에 매일 별자리 운세를 읽는 것은 / 유익하다. / 그것들이 남은 하루에 대한 예측을 제공하기 때문에

⑤ Since the people reading them / want to believe the information so badly, / they will search for meaning in their lives / that make it true.
그것들을 읽는 사람들이 ~ 때문에 / 그 정보를 너무나도 믿고 싶어 하기 / 그들은 삶에서 의미를 찾을 것이다. / 그것을 사실로 만드는

바넘 효과는 누군가가 매우 일반적인 것을 읽거나 듣지만 그것이 자신에게 적용된다고 믿는 현상이다. ① 이러한 진술들은 표면적으로는 매우 개인적인 것처럼 보이지만 실제로는 많은 사람에게 적용된다. ② 인간 심리는 우리가 개인적 차원에서 동일시할 수 있는 것들을 믿고, 정보가 반드시 존재하지는 않는 경우에도 나머지에 대해서는 우리의 상상으로 공백을 채우면서 정보를 심지어 찾고 싶어 하게 한다. ③ 이것은 개인적인 것처럼 보이지만 수많은 사람에게 대개 들어맞는 정보를 제공하는 별자리 운세가 의존하는 원리이다. ④ 아침에 매일 별자리 운세를 읽는 것은 그것들이 남은 하루에 대한 예측을 제공하기 때문에 유익하다. ⑤ 그것들을 읽는 사람들이 그 정보를 너무나도 믿고 싶어 하기 때문에 그들은 그것을 사실로 만드는 삶에서 의미를 찾을 것이다.

Why? 왜 정답일까?

일반적인 진술을 개인적인 것으로 믿고 받아들이게 하는 바넘 효과에 관해 설명한 글이다. ①, ②, ③, ⑤는 흐름에 적합하지만, ④는 ③에서 예로 언급된 별자리 운세에 초점을 맞추어 사람들이 아침마다 별자리 운세를 읽으면 좋은 이유에 관해 언급하므로 흐름상 적절하지 않다. 따라서 글의 흐름과 관계 없는 문장은 ④이다.

- phenomenon ⓝ 현상
- identify with ~와 동일시하다
- principle ⓝ 원리
- countless ⓐ 수많은
- prediction ⓝ 예측
- statement ⓝ 진술
- fill in the blank 공백을 메우다. 나머지를 상상하다
- make sense 일리가 있다
- beneficial ⓐ 이로운

구문 풀이

4행 Human psychology allows us to want to believe things [that we can identify with on a personal level] and even seek information where it doesn't necessarily exist, filling in the blanks with our imagination for the rest.

5형식 동사 / 목적어 / 목적격 보어1 / 선행사 / 목적격 관계대명사 / 목적격 보어2 / 접속사(~한 곳에서) / 분사구문

36 적목 현상이 일어나는 이유   정답률 81% | 정답 ②

주어진 글 다음에 이어질 글의 순서로 가장 적절한 것을 고르시오.
① (A) − (C) − (B)   ✔ (B) − (A) − (C)
③ (B) − (C) − (A)   ④ (C) − (A) − (B)
⑤ (C) − (B) − (A)

Imagine yourself at a party.
파티에 있는 자신을 상상해 보라.
It is dark / and a group of friends ask you to take a picture of them.
어두운데 / 친구들이 사진을 찍어 달라고 요청한다.
You grab your camera, point, and shoot your friends.
당신은 카메라를 잡고 친구들을 향해 사진을 찍는다.

(B) The camera automatically turns on the flash / as there is not enough light available / to produce a correct exposure.
카메라는 자동으로 플래시를 켠다. / 사용할 수 있는 빛이 충분하지 않기 때문에 / 정확한 노출을 만들어 내기 위해
The result is / half of your friends appear in the picture / with two bright red circles / instead of their eyes.
그 결과 / 친구 중 절반은 사진에 나온다. / 두 개의 밝은 빨간색 원과 함께 / 그들의 눈 대신

(A) This is a common problem / called the red-eye effect.
이것은 흔한 문제다. / 적목(赤目) 현상이라고 불리는
It is caused / because the light from the flash / penetrates the eyes through the pupils, / and then gets reflected to the camera / from the back of the eyes / where a large amount of blood is present.
그것은 발생한다. / 플래시에서 나오는 빛 때문에 / 동공을 통해 눈을 통과한 뒤, / 카메라로 반사되는 / 눈 뒤쪽으로부터 / 다량의 피가 있는

(C) This blood is the reason / why the eyes look red in the photograph.
이 피가 이유이다. / 사진에서 눈이 빨갛게 보이는
This effect is more noticeable / when there is not much light in the environment.
이 현상은 더욱 두드러진다. / 주위에 빛이 많지 않을 때
This is because pupils dilate when it is dark, / allowing more light to get inside the eye / and producing a larger red-eye effect.
이는 어두울 때 동공이 팽창하기 때문이다. / 더 많은 빛이 눈 안쪽으로 들어오게 하면서 / 더 큰 적목 현상을 일으키면서

파티에 있는 자신을 상상해 보라. 어두운데 친구들이 사진을 찍어 달라고 요청한다. 카메라를 잡고 친구들을 향해 사진을 찍는다.

(B) 정확한 노출을 만들어 내기 위해 사용할 수 있는 빛이 충분하지 않기 때문에 카메라는 자동으로 플래시를 켠다. 그 결과 친구 중 절반은 눈 대신 두 개의 밝은 빨간색 원과 함께 사진에 나온다.

(A) 이것은 적목(赤目) 현상이라고 불리는 흔한 문제다. 그것은 플래시에서 나오는 빛이 동공을 통해 눈을 통과한 뒤, 다량의 피가 있는 눈 뒤쪽으로부터 카메라로 반사되기 때문에 발생한다.

(C) 이 피 때문에 사진에서 눈이 빨갛게 보인다. 이 현상은 주위에 빛이 많지 않을 때 더욱 두드러진다. 이는 어두울 때 동공이 팽창하여, 더 많은 빛이 눈 안쪽으로 들어오게 하면서 더 큰 적목 현상을 일으키기 때문이다.

Why? 왜 정답일까?

적목 현상이 일어나는 이유를 설명한 글이다. 주어진 글에서 어두운 파티장에서 친구들의 사진을 찍어줄 때를 생각해 보라고 언급한 후, (B)는 이 경우 빛이 충분하지 않아 자동으로 카메라 플래시가 터지고, 이후 사진을 보면 눈 대신 붉은 원이 보이게 된다는 설명을 제시한다. (A)는 (B)에 소개된 현상을 This로 받으며 이를 '적목 현상'이라는 용어로 정리한다. 한편 (A)의 후반부에서는 카메라 플래시에서 나온 빛이 눈을 통과한 후 피가 몰려 있는 눈 뒤쪽으로부터 다시 반사되기 때문에 적목 현상이 일어난다고 설명하는데, (C)는 바로 이 피(This blood) 때문에 사진에서 눈이 붉게 나오는 것이라고 언급한다. 따라서 글의 순서로 가장 적절한 것은 ② '(B) − (A) − (C)'이다.

- grab ⓥ 붙잡다
- present ⓐ 존재하는
- reflect ⓥ 반사하다
- automatically ⓐⓓ 자동으로
- noticeable ⓐ 두드러지는

구문 풀이

4행 It is caused because the light from the flash penetrates the eyes through the pupils, and then gets reflected to the camera from the back of the eyes [where a large amount of blood is present].

접속사(~ 때문에) / 주어 / 동사1 / 동사2(수동태) / 장소 선행사 / 관계부사

37 두 변인 사이의 인과관계를 연구할 때 주의할 점   정답률 56% | 정답 ④

주어진 글 다음에 이어질 글의 순서로 가장 적절한 것을 고르시오.
① (A) − (C) − (B)   ② (B) − (A) − (C)
③ (B) − (C) − (A)   ✔ (C) − (A) − (B)
⑤ (C) − (B) − (A)

Even though two variables seem to be related, / there may not be a causal relationship.
비록 두 변인이 관련된 것처럼 보일지라도 / 인과 관계가 없을 수도 있다.
(C) In fact, / the two variables may merely seem to be associated with each other / due to the effect of some third variable.
사실, / 그 두 변인은 단지 서로 관련된 것처럼 보일지도 모른다. / 어떤 제3 변인의 영향으로
Sociologists call such misleading relationships spurious.
사회학자들은 이러한 오해의 소지가 있는 관계를 허위라고 부른다.
A classic example is the apparent association / between children's shoe size and reading ability.
전형적인 예는 명백한 연관성이다. / 아이들의 신발 크기와 읽기 능력 사이의
It seems / that as shoe size increases, / reading ability improves.
~한 것처럼 보인다. / 신발 크기가 커질수록, / 읽기 능력이 향상되는
(A) Does this mean / that the size of one's feet (independent variable) / causes an improvement in reading skills (dependent variable)?
이것이 의미하는가? / 사람의 발 크기(독립 변인)가 / 읽기 능력(종속 변인)의 향상을 유발한다는 것을
Certainly not.
물론 아니다.
This false relationship is caused by a third factor, age, / that is related to shoe size as well as reading ability.
이러한 허위 관계는 제3 변인인 연령에 의해 발생한다. / 읽기 능력은 물론 신발 크기와도 관련된 있는
(B) Hence, / when researchers attempt to make causal claims / about the relationship between an independent and a dependent variable, / they must control for — or rule

out — other variables / that may be creating a spurious relationship.
따라서, 연구자들이 인과 관계를 주장하려고 할 때 / 독립 변인과 종속 변인 사이의 관계에 대한 / 그들은 다른 변인들을 통제하거나 배제해야만 한다. / 허위 관계를 만들어 낼 수도 있는

비록 두 변인이 관련된 것처럼 보일지라도 인과 관계가 없을 수도 있다.

(C) 사실, 그 두 변인은 어떤 제3 변인의 영향으로 단지 서로 관련된 것처럼 보일지도 모른다. 사회학자들은 이러한 오해의 소지가 있는 관계를 허위라고 부른다. 전형적인 예는 아이들의 신발 크기와 읽기 능력 사이의 명백한 연관성이다. 신발 크기가 커질수록, 읽기 능력이 향상되는 것처럼 보인다.

(A) 이것이 사람의 발 크기(독립 변인)가 읽기 능력(종속 변인)의 향상을 유발한다는 것을 의미하는가? 물론 아니다. 이러한 허위 관계는 읽기 능력은 물론 신발 크기와도 관련이 있는 제3 변인인 연령에 의해 발생한다.

(B) 따라서, 연구자들이 독립 변인과 종속 변인 사이의 관계에 대한 인과 관계를 주장하려고 할 때 그들은 허위 관계를 만들어 낼 수도 있는 다른 변인들을 통제하거나 배제해야만 한다.

Why? 왜 정답일까?

어떤 두 변인의 인과 관계를 연구할 때 주의할 점에 관해 설명한 글이다. 주어진 글에서 언뜻 관련되어 보이는 두 요인 간에도 인과 관계가 없을 수 있다는 점을 언급한 뒤, (C)는 두 변인 사이에 제3의 변인이 관여되어서 두 변인이 표면적으로 관련되어 보일 수 있기 때문임을 설명한다. 이어서 (C)의 후반부에는 신발 크기와 읽기 능력이라는 두 가지 변인 사이 관계가 예로 제시되는데, (A)는 이 두 변인 사이에 연령이라는 제3의 변인이 영향을 미치고 있음을 지적한다. (B)는 (C)와 (A)의 내용을 토대로 두 변인 사이의 인과 관계를 연구할 때에는 영향을 미칠 수 있는 다른 변인들에 대한 통제가 필수적이라는 결론(Hence)을 이끌어 낸다. 따라서 글의 순서로 가장 적절한 것은 ④ '(C) – (A) – (B)'이다.

- causal relationship 인과 관계
- factor ⓝ 요인
- associated with ~와 연관된
- apparent ⓐ 명백한
- improvement ⓝ 향상, 개선
- rule out 배제하다
- misleading ⓐ 잘못된, 오도하는

구문 풀이

8행 Hence, when researchers attempt to make causal claims about the
접속사(~할 때) ~하려고 시도하다
relationship between an independent and a dependent variable, they must
주어 동사
control for — or rule out — other variables [that may be creating a spurious
삽입구(동사2) 목적어(선행사) 주격 관계대명사
relationship].

★★★ 등급을 가르는 문제!
38 생체 시계를 다시 설정하는 데 이용되는 신호들   정답률 40% | 정답 ③

글의 흐름으로 보아, 주어진 문장이 들어가기에 가장 적절한 곳을 고르시오.

Daylight isn't the only signal / that the brain can use / for the purpose of biological clock resetting, / though it is the principal and preferential signal, / when present.
햇빛은 유일한 신호는 아니다. / 뇌가 사용할 수 있는 / 생체 시계 재설정을 목적으로 / 비록 그것이 중요하고 우선시되는 신호지만, / 있을 때는

① So long as they are reliably repeating, / the brain can also use other external cues, / such as food, exercise, and even regularly timed social interaction.
그것들이 확실하게 반복되는 한, / 뇌는 다른 외부적인 신호들도 사용할 수 있다. / 음식과 운동과 심지어는 정기적인 사회적 상호 작용과 같은

② All of these events / have the ability to reset the biological clock, / allowing it to strike a precise twenty-four-hour note.
이 모든 경우는 / 생체 시계를 재설정하는 능력이 있어 / 정확한 24시간 음을 치도록 한다.

✓ It is the reason / that individuals with certain forms of blindness / do not entirely lose their circadian rhythm.
그것이 이유이다. / 어떤 유형의 시력 상실이 있는 개인도 / 24시간 주기의 리듬을 완전히 잃지 않는

Despite not receiving light cues / due to their blindness, / other phenomena act as their resetting triggers.
빛 신호를 받지 못함에도 불구하고, / 그들의 시력 상실 때문에 / 다른 현상들이 재설정의 유인 역할을 한다.

④ Any signal / that the brain uses for the purpose of clock resetting / is termed a zeitgeber, / from the German "time giver" or "synchronizer."
모든 신호는 / 뇌가 시계 재설정을 목적으로 이용하는 / 차이트게버(자연 시계)라고 불린다. / '시간 제공자' 또는 '동기화 장치'라는 독일어에서 유래

⑤ Thus, / while light is the most reliable and thus the primary zeitgeber, / there are many factors / that can be used in addition to, or in the absence of, daylight.
따라서, / 빛이 가장 신뢰할 수 있어서 주된 자연 시계인 반면, / 많은 요인이 있다. / 햇빛과 함께 혹은 햇빛이 없을 때 사용될 수 있는

햇빛은 비록 있을 때는 중요하고 우선시되는 신호지만 뇌가 생체 시계 재설정을 목적으로 사용할 수 있는 유일한 신호는 아니다. ① 확실하게 반복되는 한, 뇌는 음식과 운동과 심지어는 정기적인 사회적 상호 작용과 같은 다른 외부적인 신호들도 사용할 수 있다. ② 이 모든 경우는 생체 시계를 재설정하는 능력이 있어 정확한 24시간 음을 치도록 한다(24시간을 정확히 알게 한다). ③ 이러한 이유로 어떤 유형의 시력 상실도 개인도 24시간 주기의 리듬을 완전히 잃지 않는다. 그들의 시력 상실 때문에 빛 신호를 받지 않음에도 불구하고, 다른 현상들이 재설정의 유인 역할을 한다. ④ 뇌가 시계 재설정을 목적으로 이용하는 모든 신호는 '시간 제공자' 또는 '동기화 장치'라는 독일어에서 유래한 차이트게버(자연 시계)라고 불린다. ⑤ 따라서, 빛이 가장 신뢰할 수 있어서 주된 자연 시계인 반면, 햇빛과 함께 혹은 햇빛이 없을 때 사용될 수 있는 많은 요인이 있다.

Why? 왜 정답일까?

③ 앞의 두 문장에서 뇌는 햇빛뿐 아니라 음식, 운동, 정기적인 상호 작용 등 다양한 외부 신호를 이용하여 생체 시계를 재설정할 수 있으며 이에 우리 몸이 정확히 24시간의 주기를 알 수 있다고 설명하고 있다. 여기에 이어 주어진 문장은 '이러한 이유로' 시력 상실을 경험하고 있는 개인일지라도 생체 리듬을 잃지 않는다는 내용을 제시한다. ③ 뒤의 문장은 주어진 문장에서 언급한 'individuals with certain forms of blindness'을 'their blindness'로 다시 언급하며, 시력 상실을 겪고 있는 사람들은 비록 빛을 볼 수 없지만 다른 현상을 통해 생체 시계를 맞춰나갈 수 있다고 설명한다. 따라서 주어진 문장이 들어가기에 가장 적절한 곳은 ③이다.

- entirely ⓐⓓ 완전히, 전적으로
- reliably ⓐⓓ 확실하게, 믿을 수 있게
- strike ⓥ 치다, 부딪치다
- note ⓝ (음악의) 음
- trigger ⓝ 계기, 유인
- in the absence of ~의 부재 시에
- preferential ⓐ 우선시되는, 특혜의
- external ⓐ 외부적인
- precise ⓐ 정확한
- phenomenon ⓝ 현상 (pl. phenomena)
- synchronizer ⓝ 동기화 장치

구문 풀이

3행 Daylight isn't the only signal [that the brain can use for the purpose of
선행사 목적격 관계대명사
biological clock resetting], though it is the principal and preferential signal, when
접속사(~일지라도) 접속사
(it is) present.
생략 형용사 보어

★★ 문제 해결 꿀~팁 ★★

▶ 많이 틀린 이유는?
생체 시계 재설정이라는 생소한 소재에 관한 글이다. 최다 오답인 ④ 앞에서 햇빛 외에도 다른 현상들이 생체 시계를 다시 설정하도록 유인하는 역할을 할 수 있다고 설명한 데 이어, ④ 뒤의 문장에서는 이렇듯 시간 재설정에 기여할 수 있는 모든 신호를 '차이트게버'라는 용어로 부를 수 있다고 언급하고 있다. 즉 ④ 앞까지 다룬 내용을 ④ 뒤에서 용어와 함께 정리해주며 맥락이 자연스럽게 연결되므로 주어진 문장을 ④에 넣으면 안 된다.

▶ 문제 해결 방법은?
③ 뒤의 문장에서 '시력 상실을 경험하고 있는 사람'을 대명사인 their로 지칭하고 있다. 즉 이 문장 바로 앞에 시력 상실을 경험하고 있는 사람들(individuals with certain forms of blindness)에 관한 언급이 있어야 한다.

★★★ 등급을 가르는 문제!
39 농업 체제의 변화   정답률 43% | 정답 ③

글의 흐름으로 보아, 주어진 문장이 들어가기에 가장 적절한 곳을 고르시오. [3점]

Earlier agricultural systems / were integrated with and co-evolved with technologies, beliefs, myths and traditions / as part of an integrated social system.
초기의 농업 시스템은 / 기술, 신념, 신화 그리고 전통과 통합되고 함께 발전했다. / 통합된 사회 시스템의 일부로서

① Generally, / people planted a variety of crops in different areas, / in the hope of obtaining a reasonably stable food supply.
일반적으로 / 사람들은 여러 지역에 다양한 작물을 심었다. / 상당히 안정적인 식량 공급을 얻기를 기대하며

② These systems could only be maintained at low population levels, / and were relatively non-destructive (but not always).
이 시스템은 낮은 인구 수준에서만 유지될 수 있었고, / 비교적 파괴적이지 않았다(항상 그런 것은 아니지만).

✓ More recently, / agriculture has in many places lost its local character, / and has become incorporated into the global economy.
더 최근에는 / 농업이 많은 곳에서 그 지역적 특성을 잃고 세계 경제에 통합되어 왔다.

This has led to increased pressure on agricultural land / for exchange commodities and export goods.
이로 인해 농경지에 대한 압력이 증가하게 되었다. / 교환 상품과 수출 상품을 위한

④ More land is being diverted / from local food production / to "cash crops" / for export and exchange; / fewer types of crops are raised, / and each crop is raised in much greater quantities than before.
더 많은 땅이 전환되고 있는데, / 지역 식량 생산에서 / '환금 작물'로 / 수출과 교환을 위한 / 더 적은 종류의 작물이 재배되고, / 각 작물은 이전보다 훨씬 더 많은 양으로 재배된다.

⑤ Thus, / ever more land is converted from forest (and other natural systems) / for agriculture for export, / rather than using land for subsistence crops.
따라서 / 어느 때보다 더 많은 토지가 산림(그리고 다른 자연 시스템)으로부터 전환된다. / 수출을 위한 농업을 위해 / 자급자족용 작물을 위해 땅을 사용하기보다는

초기의 농업 시스템은 통합된 사회 시스템의 일부로서 기술, 신념, 신화 그리고 전통과 통합되고 함께 발전했다. ① 일반적으로 사람들은 상당히 안정적인 식량 공급을 얻기를 기대하며 여러 지역에 다양한 작물을 심었다. ② 이 시스템은 낮은 인구 수준에서만 유지될 수 있었고, 비교적 파괴적이지 않았다(항상 그런 것은 아니지만). ③ 더 최근에는 농업이 많은 곳에서 그 지역적 특성을 잃고 세계 경제에 통합되어 왔다. 이로 인해 교환 상품과 수출 상품을 위한 농경지에 대한 압력이 증가하게 되었다. ④ 더 많은 땅이 지역 식량 생산에서 수출과 교환을 위한 '환금 작물'로 전환되고 있는데, 더 적은 종류의 작물이 재배되고, 각 작물은 이전보다 훨씬 더 많은 양으로 재배된다. ⑤ 따라서 자급자족용 작물을 위해 땅을 사용하기보다는, 수출을 위한 농업을 위해 어느 때보다 더 많은 토지가 산림(그리고 다른 자연 시스템)으로부터 전환된다.

Why? 왜 정답일까?

③ 앞에서 초기의 농업 시스템은 사회 시스템의 일부로 여러 다른 체계와 통합되어 발전하면서 식량 공급을 주 목적으로 했고 파괴성이 덜했다고 설명한다. 이어서 More recently로 시작하는 주어진 문장은 '더 최근'의 시점으로 넘어와 농업은 지역적 특성을 잃고 세계 경제에 통합되어 왔다는 사실을 제시한다. ③ 뒤에서는 주어진 문장과 같은 상황이 되었기 때문에 교환 상품이나 수출 상품을 재배할 농경지가 더 많이 필요해졌고, 재배되는 작물의 종류는 줄어들었으며, 환금 작물 중심의 농업이 이루어지고 있다는 내용이 이어진다. 따라서 주어진 문장이 들어가기에 가장 적절한 곳은 ③이다.

- agriculture ⓝ 농업
- integrate ⓥ 통합하다
- stable ⓐ 안정적인
- commodity ⓝ 상품
- convert ⓥ 전환하다, 개조하다
- incorporate A into B A를 B에 통합시키다
- in the hope of ~라는 희망으로
- non-destructive ⓐ 파괴적이지 않은
- divert ⓥ 전환시키다, 다른 데로 돌리다

구문 풀이

11행 More land is being diverted from local food production to "cash crops"
주어 동사(현재진행 수동태) 'from + A + to + B : A에서 B로,
for export and exchange; fewer types of crops are raised, and each crop is raised
비급급 수식 부사 주어1 동사1 주어2 동사2
in much greater quantities than before.
비급급 형용사

▶ 많이 틀린 이유는?
농경 변천에 관한 글로, 흐름을 잘 파악해야 한다. 최다 오답인 ④ 앞에서 교환 및 수출 작물용 농경지에 대한 압박이 커졌다고 하는데, ④ 뒤에서는 이를 '환금 작물'이라는 용어로 바꾸며 식량보다는 무역 수익을 위한 농경이 많이 이루어지는 상황임을 설명하고 있다. 즉 ④ 앞뒤로 흐름 전환이나 논리적 공백이 발생하지 않으므로 ④에 주어진 문장을 넣을 필요가 없다.

▶ 문제 해결 방법은?
③ 앞에서 초기 농업은 안정적 식량 확보를 주된 목적으로 했다고 설명하는데, ③ 뒤에서는 '이로 인해' 교환 작물 또는 수출 작물을 키워야 한다는 압력이 커진다고 언급한다. 두 내용은 서로 상충하므로, ③에 '최근의 농업' 이야기로 흐름을 전환하는 문장이 들어가야 함을 알 수 있다.

---

40 내집단을 동일시하고 선호하는 인간의 선천적 경향 정답률 49% | 정답 ①

다음 글의 내용을 한 문장으로 요약하고자 한다. 빈칸 (A), (B)에 들어갈 말로 가장 적절한 것은?

	(A)		(B)		(A)		(B)
✓	familiar 친숙한	……	inborn 선천적인	②	familiar 친숙한	……	acquired 후천적인
③	foreign 이질적인	……	cultural 문화적인	④	foreign 이질적인	……	learned 학습된
⑤	formal 공식적인	……	innate 타고난				

In their study in 2007 / Katherine Kinzler and her colleagues at Harvard showed / that our tendency to identify with an in-group / to a large degree begins in infancy / and may be innate.
2007년에 있었던 연구에서 / Katherine Kinzler와 그녀의 하버드 동료들은 보여 주었다. / 내(內)집단과 동일시하려는 우리의 경향이 / 상당 부분 유아기에 시작되고 / 선천적일 수 있음을

Kinzler and her team took a bunch of five-month-olds / whose families only spoke English / and showed the babies two videos.
Kinzler와 그녀의 팀은 한 무리의 5개월 된 아이들을 골라 / 가족이 영어로만 말하는 / 아기들에게 두 개의 영상을 보여 주었다.

In one video, / a woman was speaking English.
한 영상에서 / 한 여성이 영어를 말하고 있었다.

In the other, / a woman was speaking Spanish.
다른 영상에서 / 한 여성이 스페인어로 말하고 있었다.

Then they were shown a screen / with both women side by side, not speaking.
그러고 나서 그들에게 화면을 보여 주었다. / 두 여성 모두 말없이 나란히 있는

In infant psychology research, / the standard measure for affinity or interest / is attention / — babies will apparently stare longer at the things / they like more.
유아 심리학 연구에서 / 애착이나 관심의 표준 척도는 / 주목인데, / 아기들은 분명 대상을 더 오래 쳐다볼 것이다 / 그들이 더 좋아하는

In Kinzler's study, / the babies stared at the English speakers longer.
Kinzler의 연구에서 / 아기들은 영어 사용자들을 더 오래 쳐다보았다.

In other studies, / researchers have found / that infants are more likely to take a toy / offered by someone / who speaks the same language as them.
다른 연구들에서 / 연구자들은 발견했다 / 유아들이 장난감을 받을 가능성이 더 높다는 점을 / 사람이 제공하는 / 자신들과 같은 언어를 사용하는

Psychologists routinely cite these and other experiments / as evidence of our built-in evolutionary preference for "our own kind."
심리학자들은 이것들과 다른 실험들을 판례대로 인용한다. / '우리와 같은 종류'에 대한 우리의 내재된 진화론적인 선호에 대한 증거로

➡ Infants' more favorable responses / to those who use a (A) familiar language / show / that there can be a(n) (B) inborn tendency / to prefer in-group members.
유아들의 더 호의적인 반응은 / 친숙한 언어를 사용하는 사람들에 대한 / 보여 준다. / 선천적인 경향이 있을 수 있음을 / 내집단 구성원을 선호하는

2007년에 있었던 연구에서 Katherine Kinzler와 그녀의 하버드 동료들은 내(內)집단과 동일시하려는 우리의 경향이 상당 부분 유아기에 시작되고 선천적일 수 있음을 보여 주었다. Kinzler와 그녀의 팀은 가족들이 영어로만 말하는 한 무리의 5개월 된 아이들을 골라 두 개의 영상을 보여 주었다. 한 영상에서 한 여성이 영어를 말하고 있었다. 다른 영상에서는 한 여성이 스페인어로 말하고 있었다. 그러고 나서 그들에게 두 여성 모두 말없이 나란히 있는 화면을 보여 주었다. 유아 심리학 연구에서 애착이나 관심의 표준 척도는 주목인데, 아기들은 분명 그들이 더 좋아하는 대상을 더 오래 쳐다볼 것이다. Kinzler의 연구에서 아기들은 영어 사용자들을 더 오래 쳐다보았다. 다른 연구들에서 연구자들은 유아들이 자신들과 같은 언어를 사용하는 사람이 제공하는 장난감을 받을 가능성이 더 높다는 점을 발견했다. 심리학자들은 '우리와 같은 종류'에 대한 우리의 내재된 진화론적인 선호에 대한 증거로 이것들과 다른 실험들을 반복해서 인용한다.

➡ (A) 친숙한 언어를 사용하는 사람들에 대한 유아들의 더 호의적인 반응은 내집단 구성원들을 선호하는 (B) 선천적인 경향이 있을 수 있음을 보여 준다.

Why? 왜 정답일까?

첫 문장과 마지막 문장(~ our tendency to identify with an in-group to a large degree begins in infancy and may be innate. / ~ our built-in evolutionary preference for "our own kind.")을 통해 인간은 내집단, 즉 친숙하고 비슷한 집단을 거의 선천적이라 볼 수 있을 정도로 아주 이른 시기부터 선호한다는 것을 알 수 있다. 따라서 요약문의 빈칸 (A), (B)에 들어갈 말로 가장 적절한 것은 ① '(A) familiar(친숙한), (B) inborn(선천적인)'이다.

- identify with ~와 동일시하다
- innate ⓐ 타고난, 선천적인
- stare at ~을 쳐다보다, 응시하다
- cite ⓥ 인용하다
- acquired ⓐ 후천적인, 습득된
- infancy ⓝ 유아기, 초창기
- apparently ad 분명히, 명백히
- routinely ad 판에 박힌 듯, 관례대로
- inborn ⓐ 타고난

구문 풀이

1행 In their study in 2007 Katherine Kinzler and her colleagues at Harvard showed that our tendency to identify with an in-group to a large degree begins in infancy and may be innate.

41-42 언어의 근원이자 목적인 대화

Like all humans, / the first Homo species / to begin the long difficult process of constructing a language from scratch / almost certainly never said entirely / what was on their minds.
모든 인간처럼, / 최초의 호모 종은 / 맨 처음부터 언어를 구성하는 길고 힘든 과정을 시작한 / 거의 틀림없이 온전히 말하지 않았다. / 자신의 마음에 있는 것을

At the same time, / these primitive hominins / would not have simply made (a) random sounds or gestures.
동시에, / 이 원시 호미닌들은 / 단순히 무작위적인 소리를 내거나 몸짓을 하지는 않았을 것이다.

Instead, / they would have used means to communicate / that they believed others would understand.
대신, / 그들은 의사소통 수단을 사용했을 것이다. / 남들이 이해할 것이라고 믿는

And they also thought / their hearers could "fill in the gaps", / and connect their knowledge of their culture and the world / to interpret what was uttered.
그리고 그들은 또한 생각했다. / 자신의 청자들이 '빈틈을 메울' 수 있고, / 그들의 문화와 세계에 대한 지식을 연결할 수 있다고 / 발화된 것을 해석하기 위해

These are some of the reasons / why the (b) origins of human language cannot be effectively discussed / unless conversation is placed / at the top of the list of things to understand.
이러한 것들이 몇 가지 이유이다. / 인간 언어의 기원이 효과적으로 논의될 수 없는 / 대화가 놓여지지 않는 한, / 이해해야 할 것들의 목록 중 맨 위에

『Every aspect of human language has evolved, / as have components of the human brain and body, / to (c) engage in conversation and social life.』 41번의 근거
인간 언어의 모든 측면은 진화해 왔다. / 인간의 뇌와 신체의 구성 요소들이 그래왔듯이, / 대화와 사회 생활에 관여하도록

Language did not fully begin / when the first hominid uttered the first word or sentence.
언어는 온전히 시작된 것은 아니었다. / 최초의 호미니드가 최초의 단어나 문장을 발화했을 때

It began in earnest only with the first conversation, / which is both the source and the (d) goal of language.
그것은 최초의 대화와 함께 본격적으로 시작되었는데, / 이는 언어의 근원이자 목적이다.

Indeed, language changes lives.
실제로, 언어는 삶을 변화시킨다.

It builds society / and expresses our highest aspirations, our basest thoughts, our emotions and our philosophies of life.
그것은 사회를 세우고, / 우리의 가장 높은 열망, 가장 기본적인 생각, 감정 그리고 삶의 철학을 표현한다.

『But all language is ultimately at the service of human interaction.』 42번의 근거
하지만 모든 언어는 궁극적으로 인간의 상호 작용을 위한 것이다.

Other components of language / — things like grammar and stories — / are (e) secondary to conversation.
언어의 다른 요소들, / 즉 문법과 이야기와 같은 것은 / 대화에 부차적인 것들이다.

모든 인간처럼, 맨 처음부터 언어를 구성하는 길고 힘든 과정을 시작한 최초의 호모 종은 거의 틀림없이 자신의 마음에 있는 것을 온전히 말하지 않았다. 동시에, 이 원시 호미닌(인간의 조상으로 분류되는 종족)들은 단순히 (a) 무작위적인 소리를 내거나 몸짓을 하지는 않았을 것이다. 대신, 그들은 남들이 이해할 것이라고 믿는 의사소통 수단을 사용했을 것이다. 그리고 그들은 또한 자신의 청자들이 '빈틈을 메울' 수 있고, 발화된 것을 해석하기 위해 그들의 문화와 세계에 대한 지식을 연결할 수 있다고 생각했다. 이러한 것들이 대화가 이해해야 할 것들의 목록 중 맨 위에 놓여지지 않는 한, 인간 언어의 (b) 기원이 효과적으로 논의될 수 없는 몇 가지 이유이다. 인간의 뇌와 신체의 구성 요소들이 그래왔듯이, 인간 언어의 모든 측면은 대화와 사회 생활에 (c) 관여하도록 진화해 왔다. 언어는 최초의 호미니드(사람과의 동물)가 최초의 단어나 문장을 발화했을 때 온전히 시작된 것은 아니었다. 그것은 최초의 대화와 함께 비로소 본격적으로 시작되었는데, 이는 언어의 근원이자 (d) 목적이다. 실제로, 언어는 삶을 변화시킨다. 그것은 사회를 세우고, 우리의 가장 높은 열망, 가장 기본적인 생각, 감정 그리고 삶의 철학을 표현한다. 하지만 모든 언어는 궁극적으로 인간의 상호 작용을 위한 것이다. 언어의 다른 요소들, 즉 문법과 이야기와 같은 것은 대화에 (e) 중요한(→ 부차적인) 것들이다.

- construct 구성하다
- primitive ⓐ 원시의
- utter ⓥ 발화하다
- aspect ⓝ 측면, 양상
- in earnest 본격적으로
- philosophy ⓝ 철학
- crucial ⓐ 매우 중요한
- from scratch 맨 처음부터, 아무것도 없이
- interpret ⓥ 해석하다, 이해하다
- effectively ad 효과적으로
- engage in ~에 관여하다, 참여하다
- aspiration ⓝ 열망
- ultimately ad 궁극적으로
- offend ⓥ 마음을 상하게 하다

구문 풀이

1행 Like all humans, the first Homo species to begin the long difficult process of constructing a language from scratch almost certainly never said entirely what was on their minds.

---

41 제목 파악 정답률 64% | 정답 ②

윗글의 제목으로 가장 적절한 것은?
① Various Communication Strategies of Our Ancestors – 조상들의 다양한 의사소통 전략
✓ Conversation: The Core of Language Development – 대화: 언어 발달의 핵심
③ Ending Conversation Without Offending Others – 타인을 기분 상하게 하지 않고 대화 끝내기
④ How Language Shapes the Way You Think – 언어는 어떻게 당신의 사고방식을 형성하는가
⑤ What Makes You a Good Communicator? – 무엇이 의사소통을 잘하게 만드는가?

Why? 왜 정답일까?

두 번째 단락의 'Every aspect of human language has evolved, ~ to engage in conversation and social life.'를 통해 인간은 대화와 사회 상호작용에 참여하기 위해 언어를 발달시켜 왔다는 내용을 파악할 수 있다. 따라서 글의 제목으로 가장 적절한 것은 ② '대화: 언어 발달의 핵심'이다.

★★★ 등급을 가르는 문제!
42 어휘 추론 정답률 44% | 정답 ⑤

밑줄 친 (a) ~ (e) 중에서 문맥상 낱말의 쓰임이 적절하지 <u>않은</u> 것은? [3점]

① (a)   ② (b)   ③ (c)   ④ (d)   ☑ (e)

Why? 왜 정답일까?

'But all language is ultimately at the service of human interaction.'에서 모든 언어는 궁극적으로 인간의 상호 작용을 목적으로 한다고 언급한 것으로 보아, 상호 작용 외의 요소, 즉 문법이나 이야기 등은 언어 발달 또는 대화의 '부수적' 요소임을 추론할 수 있다. 따라서 ⑤의 crucial은 secondary로 고쳐야 한다. 문맥상 낱말의 쓰임이 가장 적절하지 않은 것은 ⑤ '(e)'이다.

★★ 문제 해결 꿀~팁 ★★

▶ 많이 틀린 이유는?
최다 오답인 (d) goal이 포함된 문장 바로 앞에서 언어가 제대로 시작된 것은 말이 처음 이루어졌을 때가 아니라 '대화'가 처음 이루어졌을 때라고 한다. 이에 비추어 볼 때, 대화가 언어의 출발점이면서 '목적'이기도 했다는 의미의 goal은 맥락에 적합하다.

▶ 문제 해결 방법은?
두 번째 단락의 첫 문장에서 인간 언어의 기원을 효과적으로 논의하기 위해서는 대화를 가장 중요하게 고려해야 한다고 했다. 이를 근거로 볼 때, 문법 등 나머지 요소는 '아주 중요한' 요소라기보다는 '부차적인' 요소이다.

43-45   가난한 노인의 부탁에 따라 레슬링 시합에서 져 준 James

(A)

『James Walker was a renowned wrestler / and he made his living through wrestling.』
James Walker는 유명한 레슬링 선수였고 / 그는 레슬링으로 생계를 유지했다.   45번①의 근거 일치

In his town, / there was a tradition / in which the leader of the town chose a day / when James demonstrated his skills.
그의 마을에는 / 전통이 있었다. / 마을의 지도자가 하루를 정해 / James가 자신의 기술을 보여 주는

The leader announced one day / that James would exhibit his skills as a wrestler / and asked the people / if there was anyone / to challenge (a) him for the prize money.
지도자는 어느 날 알렸고, / James가 레슬링 선수로서 자신의 기술을 보여 줄 것임을 / 사람들에게 물었다. / 사람이 있는지 / 상금을 위해 그에게 도전할

(C)

Everyone was looking around in the crowd / when an old man stood up / and said with a shaking voice, / "I will enter the contest against (c) him."
모두가 군중 속에서 주위를 둘러보고 있었다 / 한 노인이 일어나서 / 떨리는 목소리로 말했을 때 / "내가 그와의 경기에 참가하겠소."라고

Everyone burst out laughing / thinking that it was a joke.
모두가 웃음을 터뜨렸다. / 그것이 농담이라고 여기며

James would crush him in a minute.
James는 그를 바로 뭉개버릴 것이었다.   45번④의 근거 불일치

『According to the law, the leader could not stop someone / who of his own free will entered the competition, / so he allowed the old man to challenge the wrestler.』
관례에 따라 / 지도자는 사람을 막을 수가 없었기에 / 본인의 자유 의지로 경기에 참여하려는 / 그는 그 노인이 그 레슬링 선수에게 도전하는 것을 허용했다.

(B)

『When James saw the old man, / he was speechless.』   45번②의 근거 일치
James가 그 노인을 봤을 때, / 그는 말문이 막혔다.

Like everyone else, / he thought that the old man had a death wish.
다른 모든 사람과 마찬가지로 / 그는 그 노인이 죽기를 바란다고 생각했다.

The old man asked James to come closer / since (b) he wanted to say something to him.
노인은 James에게 더 가까이 와줄 것을 청했다. / 그가 James에게 할 말이 있었기 때문에

James moved closer / and the old man whispered, / "I know it is impossible for me to win / but my children are starving at home.』   45번③의 근거
James가 더 가까이 가자 / 노인은 속삭였다. / "내가 이기는 게 불가능하다는 것은 알고 있지만 / 내 아이들이 집에서 굶주리고 있소.

Can you lose this competition to me / so I can feed them with the prize money?"
나에게 이 시합을 져줄 수 있소? / 내가 상금으로 아이들에게 밥을 먹일 수 있게"라고

(D)

James thought / he had an excellent opportunity / to help a man in distress.
James는 생각했다. / 아주 좋은 기회를 얻었다고 / 곤경에 처한 사람을 도울

(d) He did a couple of moves / so that no one would suspect / that the competition was fixed.
그는 몇 가지 동작을 했다. / 아무도 의심하지 못하도록 / 그 시합이 정해졌다고

『However, / he did not use his full strength / and allowed the old man to win.』   45번⑤의 근거 일치
그러나 / 그는 전력을 다하지 않았고 / 그 노인이 이기게 했다.

The old man was overjoyed / when he received the prize money.
노인은 매우 기뻐했다. / 그가 상금을 받았을 때

That night James felt the most victorious / (e) he had ever felt.
그날 밤 James는 가장 큰 승리감을 느꼈다. / 그가 이제껏 느껴보지 못한

(A)

James Walker는 유명한 레슬링 선수였고 레슬링으로 생계를 유지했다. 그의 마을에는 마을의 지도자가 하루를 정해 James가 자신의 기술을 보여 주는 전통이 있었다. 지도자는 어느 날 James가 레슬링 선수로서 기술을 보여 줄 것임을 알렸고, 사람들에게 상금을 위해 (a) 그에게 도전할 사람이 있는지 물었다.

(C)

모두가 군중 속에서 주위를 둘러보던 중 한 노인이 일어나서 떨리는 목소리로 "내가 (c) 그와의 경기에 참가하겠소."라고 말했다. 모두가 그것이 농담이라고 여기며 웃음을 터뜨렸다. James는 그를 바로 뭉개버릴 것이었다. 관례에 따라 지도자는 본인의 자유 의지로 경기에 참여하려는 사람을 막을 수가 없었기에 그 노인이 그 레슬링 선수에게 도전하는 것을 허용했다.

(B)

James가 그 노인을 봤을 때, 그는 말문이 막혔다. 다른 모든 사람과 마찬가지로 그는 그 노인이 죽기를 바란다고 생각했다. (b) 그(노인)가 James에게 할 말이 있었기 때문에 노인은 James에게 더 가까이 와줄 것을 청했다. James가 더 가까이 가자 노인은 "내가 이기는 게 불가능하다는 것은 알고는 있지만 내 아이들이 집에서 굶주리고 있소. 내가 상금으로 아이들에게 밥을 먹일 수 있게 나에게 이 시합을 져줄 수 있소?"라고 속삭였다.

(D)

James는 곤경에 처한 사람을 도울 아주 좋은 기회를 얻었다고 생각했다. (d) 그는 아무도 그 시합이 정해졌다고 의심하지 못하도록 몇 가지 동작을 했다. 그러나 그는 전력을 다하지 않았고 그 노인이 이기게 했다. 노인은 상금을 받고 매우 기뻐했다. 그날 밤 James는 (e) 그가 이제껏 느껴보지 못한 가장 큰 승리감을 느꼈다.

- ● renowned ⓐ 유명한
- ● exhibit ⓥ 보여주다, 전시하다
- ● whisper ⓥ 속삭이다
- ● competition ⓝ 대회, 경쟁
- ● of one's own free will 자유 의지로, 자발적으로
- ● suspect ⓥ 의심하다
- ● victorious ⓐ 승리한, 만족한
- ● demonstrate ⓥ (시범을) 보이다
- ● speechless ⓐ 말문이 막힌
- ● starve ⓥ 굶주리다
- ● crush ⓥ 뭉개다, 진압하다, 눌러 부수다
- ● distress ⓝ 곤경, 괴로움
- ● overjoyed ⓐ 매우 기뻐하는

구문 풀이

[A] 2행   In his town, there was a tradition [in which the leader of the town chose a day [when James demonstrated his skills]].
동사 / 주어(선행사) / = where / 선행사 / 관계부사

[B] 6행   Can you lose this competition to me so (that) I can feed them with the prize money?
~하기 위해, ~하도록

[C] 4행   According to the law, the leader could not stop someone [who of his own free will entered the competition], so he allowed the old man to challenge the wrestler.
선행사 / 주격 관계대명사 / 부사구 / 동사 / 「allow + 목적어 + to부정사」: ~이 …하게 허락하다

---

43   글의 순서 파악   정답률 74% | 정답 ②

주어진 글 (A)에 이어질 내용을 순서에 맞게 배열한 것으로 가장 적절한 것은?
① (B) – (D) – (C)
☑ (C) – (B) – (D)
③ (C) – (D) – (B)
④ (D) – (B) – (C)
⑤ (D) – (C) – (B)

Why? 왜 정답일까?

(A)에서 마을의 유명한 레슬링 선수였던 James가 레슬링 기술을 선보이는 날이 돌아왔고, 마을 지도자는 그에게 도전할 의사가 있는 사람이 있는지 물었다고 했다. 이어서 어떤 노인이 도전자로 나섰다는 내용의 (C)가 연결된다. 이 (C)는 지도자가 관례에 따라 노인의 도전을 허락해주었다는 내용으로 끝나는데, (B)는 James가 상대로 나선 노인을 보고 말문이 막혔다는 내용으로 시작한다. 이어서 (B)의 후반부는 노인이 James에게 자신의 궁핍한 사정을 설명하며 져줄 것을 부탁했다는 내용으로 마무리되고, (D)는 James가 이 부탁에 응하여 시합에서 전력을 다하지 않고 실제로 져 준 뒤 오히려 뿌듯해 했다는 결말을 제시한다. 따라서 글의 순서로 가장 적절한 것은 ② '(C) – (B) – (D)'이다.

---

44   지칭 추론   정답률 73% | 정답 ②

밑줄 친 (a)~(e) 중에서 가리키는 대상이 나머지 넷과 다른 것은?
① (a)   ☑ (b)   ③ (c)   ④ (d)   ⑤ (e)

Why? 왜 정답일까?

(a), (c), (d), (e)는 James를, (b)는 The old man을 가리키므로, (a)~(e) 중에서 가리키는 대상이 다른 하나는 ② '(b)'이다.

---

45   세부 내용 파악   정답률 79% | 정답 ④

윗글에 관한 내용으로 적절하지 않은 것은?
① James는 레슬링으로 생계를 유지했다.
② James는 노인을 보고 말문이 막혔다.
③ 노인의 아이들은 집에서 굶주리고 있었다.
☑ 지도자는 노인이 James와 겨루는 것을 말렸다.
⑤ James는 노인과의 시합에서 전력을 다하지 않았다.

Why? 왜 정답일까?

(C) 'According to the law, the leader could not stop someone who of his own free will entered the competition, so he allowed the old man to challenge the wrestler.'에서 관례상 지도자는 노인이 James와 겨루는 것을 말릴 수 없었기에 노인과 James의 겨루기를 허락했다고 하였다. 따라서 내용과 일치하지 않는 것은 ④ '지도자는 노인이 James와 겨루는 것을 말렸다.'이다.

Why? 왜 오답일까?

① (A) '~ he made his living through wrestling.'의 내용과 일치한다.
② (B) 'When James saw the old man, he was speechless.'의 내용과 일치한다.
③ (B) 'I know it is impossible for me to win but my children are starving at home.'의 내용과 일치한다.
⑤ (D) 'However, he did not use his full strength and allowed the old man to win.'의 내용과 일치한다.

19회

A	B	C	D
01 슬픔	01 statement	01 ⓟ	01 ⓑ
02 필수적인	02 reserve	02 ⓒ	02 ⓔ
03 현상	03 livable	03 ⓡ	03 ⓚ
04 현장에서	04 abundance	04 ⓗ	04 ⓘ
05 사라지다	05 specific	05 ⓓ	05 ⓕ
06 노동	06 innate	06 ⓢ	06 ⓙ
07 거의 틀림없이	07 commodity	07 ⓠ	07 ⓠ
08 구성하다	08 expertise	08 ⓚ	08 ⓗ
09 여유, 여지	09 habitat	09 ⓝ	09 ⓛ
10 분자	10 exceptional	10 ⓘ	10 ⓖ
11 미루다, 지연시키다	11 trigger	11 ⓖ	11 ⓜ
12 점점 더	12 apparent	12 ⓑ	12 ⓒ
13 요인	13 digestive	13 ⓔ	13 ⓟ
14 신체적인	14 propose	14 ⓐ	14 ⓢ
15 예측	15 temperature	15 ⓜ	15 ⓞ
16 매우 중요한	16 agriculture	16 ⓛ	16 ⓡ
17 열망	17 trait	17 ⓕ	17 ⓐ
18 생태	18 stable	18 ⓙ	18 ⓝ
19 전환하다, 개조하다	19 psychological	19 ⓞ	19 ⓘ
20 먹다, 소비하다	20 objective	20 ⓘ	20 ⓓ

20회 | 2019학년도 11월 학력평가 　고1

· 정답 ·

18 ④ 19 ① 20 ④ 21 ⑤ 22 ① 23 ① 24 ② 25 ⑤ 26 ③ 27 ④ 28 ③ 29 ④ 30 ③ 31 ② 32 ①
33 ③ 34 ⑤ 35 ③ 36 ② 37 ② 38 ③ 39 ⑤ 40 ④ 41 ① 42 ⑤ 43 ⑤ 44 ④ 45 ②

★ 표기된 문항은 [등급을 가르는 문제]에 해당하는 문항입니다.

18　축구 토너먼트 참여로 인한 결석 허가 요청　정답률 86% | 정답 ④

다음 글의 목적으로 가장 적절한 것은?

① 선수들의 학력 향상 프로그램을 홍보하려고
② 대학 진학 상담의 활성화 방안을 제안하려고
③ 선수들의 훈련 장비 추가 구입을 건의하려고
✔ 선수들의 대회 참가를 위한 결석 허락을 요청하려고
⑤ 대회 개최를 위한 운동장 대여 가능 여부를 문의하려고

To the Principal of Alamda High School,
Alamda 고등학교 교장 선생님께,
On behalf of the Youth Soccer Tournament Series, / I would like to remind you / of the 2019 Series next week.
청소년 축구 토너먼트 시리즈를 대표하여 / 저는 귀하에게 상기시켜 드리고 싶습니다. / 다음 주 2019 시리즈에 대해
Surely, we understand the importance of a player's education.
물론 저희는 선수 교육의 중요성을 알고 있습니다.
Regrettably, however, / the Series will result in / players missing two days of school / for the competition.
하지만, 유감스럽게도 / 시리즈는 야기할 것입니다. / 선수들이 이틀 동안 학교를 빠지는 일을 / 대회 때문에
The games will be attended / by many college coaches / scouting prospective student athletes.
이 경기들에 참석할 것입니다. / 많은 대학 코치들이 / 유망한 학생 선수들을 스카우트하는
Therefore, the Series can be a great opportunity / for young soccer players / to demonstrate their capabilities as athletes.
그러므로 이 시리즈는 엄청난 기회가 될 수 있습니다. / 어린 축구 선수들이 / 운동선수로서 자신의 역량을 보여줄 수 있는
I would like to request your permission / for the absence of the players from your school / during this event.
저는 귀하의 허락을 요청하고자 합니다. / 귀교 선수들의 학교 결석에 대한 / 이 대회 동안
Thank you for your understanding.
이해해 주셔서 감사합니다.
Best regards,
Jack D'Adamo, Director of the Youth Soccer Tournament Series
청소년 축구 토너먼트 시리즈 대표 Jack D'Adamo 드림

Alamda 고등학교 교장 선생님께,

청소년 축구 토너먼트 시리즈를 대표하여 귀하에게 다음 주 2019 시리즈에 대해 상기시켜 드리고 싶습니다. 물론 저희는 선수 교육의 중요성을 알고 있습니다. 하지만, 유감스럽게도 시리즈는 선수들이 대회 때문에 이틀 동안 학교를 빠지는 일을 야기할 것입니다. 이 경기들에 유망한 학생 선수들을 스카우트하는 많은 대학 코치들이 참석할 것입니다. 그러므로 이 시리즈는 어린 축구 선수들이 운동선수로서 자신의 역량을 보여줄 수 있는 엄청난 기회가 될 수 있습니다. 이 대회 동안 귀교 선수들의 학교 결석에 대한 귀하의 허락을 요청하고자 합니다. 이해해 주셔서 감사합니다.

청소년 축구 토너먼트 시리즈 대표 Jack D'Adamo 드림

Why?　왜 정답일까?

마지막 부분에서 대회 동안 선수들이 학교를 결석하는 것에 대한 허락을 구한다(I would like to request your permission for the absence of the players from your school during this event.)는 내용이 나오므로, 글의 목적으로 가장 적절한 것은 ④ '선수들의 대회 참가를 위한 결석 허락을 요청하려고'이다.

● **on behalf of** ~을 대표하여, 대신하여
● **importance** ⓝ 중요성
● **prospective** ⓐ 유망한
● **capability** ⓝ 역량, 능력
● **remind A of B** ⓥ A에게 B를 상기시키다
● **result in** ⓥ ~을 야기하다
● **demonstrate** ⓥ 보여주다, 입증하다
● **absence** ⓝ 결석

구문 풀이

4행 Regrettably, however, the Series will result in players missing two days of school for the competition.
~을 야기하다　의미상 주어　동명사

19　캠핑 도중 불타는 난로를 보고 당황한 Norm　정답률 78% | 정답 ①

다음 글에 드러난 Norm의 심경으로 가장 적절한 것은?

✔ alarmed and upset – 불안하고 화가 난
② thrilled and joyful – 신나고 즐거운
③ touched and grateful – 감동 받고 고마운
④ ashamed and guilty – 부끄럽고 죄책감이 드는
⑤ encouraged and satisfied – 고무되고 만족한

Norm and his friend Jason / went on a winter camping trip.
Norm과 그의 친구 Jason이 / 겨울 캠프 여행을 갔다.
In the middle of the night, / Norm suddenly woke up / sensing something was terribly wrong.
한밤중에 / Norm은 갑자기 깼다. / 뭔가 대단히 잘못된 것을 감지하고
To his surprise, the stove was glowing red!
놀랍게도 난로가 빨갛게 타고 있었다!

Norm shook Jason awake / and told him to look at the stove.
Norm이 Jason을 흔들어 깨워 / 그에게 난로를 보라고 말했다.

Jason said he had filled it / with every piece of wood / he could fit into it.
Jason은 자신이 난로에 채워 넣었다고 말했다. / 모든 나무 조각 / 자신이 거기에 집어 넣을 수 있는

Norm thought / the cabin was going to catch fire.
Norm은 생각했다. / 오두막에 불이 날 것이라고

He started swearing at Jason.
그가 Jason에게 욕하기 시작했다.

He pulled Jason out of his bed, / opened the front door / and threw him out into the snow.
그는 Jason을 그의 침대에서 끌어내려 / 앞문을 열고 / 그를 눈 속으로 내쫓았다.

Norm yelled out in anger, / "Don't come back in until I get this stove cooled off!"
Norm은 화가 나서 소리쳤다. / "내가 이 난로를 식힐 때까지 들어오지 마"라고

Norm과 그의 친구 Jason이 겨울 캠프 여행을 갔다. 한밤중에 Norm은 갑자기 뭔가 대단히 잘못된 것을 감지하고 깼다. 놀랍게도 난로는 빨갛게 타고 있었다! Norm이 Jason을 흔들어 깨워 그에게 난로를 보라고 말했다. Jason은 자신이 거기에 집어넣을 수 있는 모든 나무 조각을 난로에 채워 넣었다고 말했다. Norm은 오두막에 불이 날 것이라고 생각했다. 그가 Jason에게 욕하기 시작했다. 그는 Jason을 그의 침대에서 끌어내려 앞문을 열고 그를 눈 속으로 내쫓았다. Norm은 화가 나서 "내가 이 난로를 식힐 때까지 들어오지 마"라고 소리쳤다.

Why? 왜 정답일까?

'He started swearing at Jason.'와 'Norm yelled out in anger, ~'을 통해 난로가 심하게 타는 것을 보고 당황한 Norm이 Jason에게 화를 내고 있음을 알 수 있다. 따라서 Norm의 심경으로 가장 적절한 것은 ① '불안하고 화가 난'이다.

- **sense** ⓥ 감지하다
- **glow** ⓥ 타다, 빨개지다
- **cabin** ⓝ 오두막
- **swear at** ⓥ ~에게 욕하다
- **alarmed** ⓐ 불안한
- **guilty** ⓐ 죄책감이 드는
- **terribly** ⓐ 대단히, 지독하게
- **fit A into B** A를 B에 끼워 넣다
- **catch fire** 불이 나다
- **yell out** ⓥ 소리치다
- **grateful** ⓐ 고마워하는

구문 풀이

4행 Jason said (that) he had filled it with every piece of wood [(that) he could fit into it].
접속사(~것) / 과거완료 / 선행사 / 목적격 관계대명사

---

20 관계를 유지하기 위한 일관된 노력의 중요성 정답률 59% | 정답 ④

다음 글에서 필자가 주장하는 바로 가장 적절한 것은?
① 가까운 사이일수록 적당한 거리를 유지해야 한다.
② 사교성을 기르려면 개방적인 태도를 가져야 한다.
③ 대화를 할 때는 상대방의 의견을 먼저 경청해야 한다.
✓ 인간관계를 지속하려면 일관된 노력을 기울여야 한다.
⑤ 원활한 의사소통을 위해 솔직하게 감정을 표현해야 한다.

We tend to go long periods of time / without reaching out to the people we know.
우리는 오랜 기간의 시간을 보내는 경향이 있다. / 우리가 알고 있는 사람들에게 연락하지 않은 채

Then, we suddenly take notice / of the distance that has formed / and we scramble to make repairs.
그러다 우리는 갑자기 알아차리고 / 생겨 버린 거리감을 / 우리는 앞다퉈 수리를 한다.

We call people / we haven't spoken to in ages, / hoping that one small effort will erase / the months and years of distance / we've created.
우리는 사람들에게 전화하면서, / 우리가 오랫동안 이야기하지 못했던 / 작은 노력 하나가 지우길 바란다 / 몇 달과 몇 년의 거리를 / 우리가 만들어 낸

However, this rarely works: / relationships aren't kept up with big one-time fixes.
그러나 이것은 거의 효과가 없다. / 왜냐하면 관계들은 커다란 일회성의 해결책들로 지속되지 않기 때문이다.

They're kept up with regular maintenance, / like a car.
그것들은 정기적인 정비로 유지된다. / 자동차처럼

In our relationships, / we have to make sure / that not too much time goes by between oil changes, / so to speak.
우리의 관계들에서 / 우리가 확실히 해야 한다. / (엔진) 오일 교환 사이에 너무 많은 시간이 흘러가지 않도록 / 말하자면

This isn't to say / that you shouldn't bother calling someone / just because it's been a while / since you've spoken; / just that it's more ideal / not to let yourself fall out of touch in the first place.
이것은 말하는 것이 아니라, / 여러분이 누군가에게 애써 전화해서는 안 된다고 / 단지 오래되었기 때문에 / 여러분이 이야기한 지 / 단지 더 이상적이라고 말하는 것이다. / 스스로를 애초에 연락이 끊기지 않게 하는 것이

Consistency always brings better results.
일관성이 항상 더 나은 결과들을 가져온다.

우리는 우리가 알고 있는 사람들에게 연락하지 않은 채 오랜 기간의 시간을 보내는 경향이 있다. 그러다 우리는 생겨 버린 거리감을 갑자기 알아차리고 앞다퉈 수리를 한다. 우리는 우리가 오랫동안 이야기하지 못했던 사람들에게 전화하면서, 작은 노력 하나가 우리가 만들어 낸 몇 달과 몇 년의 거리를 지우길 바란다. 그러나 이것은 거의 효과가 없다. 왜냐하면 관계들은 커다란 일회성의 해결책들로 지속되지 않기 때문이다. 그것들은 자동차처럼 정기적인 정비로 유지된다. 말하자면, 우리의 관계들에서 우리가 (엔진) 오일 교환 사이에 너무 많은 시간이 흘러가지 않도록 확실히 해야 한다. 이것은 여러분이 단지 이야기한 지 오래되었기 때문에 누군가에게 애써 전화해서는 안 된다고 말하는 것이 아니라, 스스로를 애초에 연락이 끊기지 않게 하는 것이 더 이상적이라고 말하는 것이다. 일관성이 항상 더 나은 결과를 가져온다.

Why? 왜 정답일까?

마지막 세 문장에서 연락하지 않은 채로 시간이 오래 지난 뒤 사이를 회복하고자 애쓰는 것보다 애초에 연락이 끊기지 않고 유지되게 하는 것이 중요하다(~ it's more ideal not to let yourself fall out of touch in the first place. Consistency always brings better results.)는 주제를 나타내고 있다. 따라서 필자의 주장으로 가장 적절한 것은 ④ '인간관계를 지속하려면 일관된 노력을 기울여야 한다.'이다.

- **reach out to** ~에 손을 뻗다, 접촉하다
- **scramble** ⓥ 앞다투다, 서로 밀치다
- **take notice of** ~을 알아차리다
- **make a repair** ⓥ 수리하다

- **erase** ⓥ 지우다
- **so to speak** 말하자면
- **consistency** ⓝ 일관성
- **maintenance** ⓝ 유지, 보수
- **fall out of touch** ⓥ 연락이 끊기다

구문 풀이

9행 This isn't to say that you shouldn't bother calling someone just because
접속사1(~것) / 애써 ~하다
it's been a while since you've spoken; just that it's more ideal not to let yourself
현재완료 / ~ 이래로 / 접속사2(~것) / 가주어 / 진주어
fall out of touch in the first place. 「not + A + but(;) + B : A가 아니라 B인(A, B자리에 that절)」
원형부정사(to let의 목·보)

---

21 타인의 선택에 영향을 미치는 요인 정답률 58% | 정답 ⑤

밑줄 친 "learn and live"가 다음 글에서 의미하는 바로 가장 적절한 것은? [3점]
① occupy a rival's territory for safety
안전을 위해 경쟁자의 영토를 차지한다
② discover who the enemy is and attack first
누가 적인지 판단하고 먼저 공격한다
③ share survival skills with the next generation
다음 세대와 생존 기술을 공유한다
④ support the leader's decisions for the best results
최선의 결과를 위해 리더의 결정을 지지한다
✓⑤ follow another's action only when it is proven safe
다른 개체의 행동이 안전하다고 입증될 때에만 그 행동을 따른다

There is a critical factor that determines / whether your choice will influence that of others: / the visible consequences of the choice.
결정하는 중요한 한 가지 요인이 있는데, / 여러분의 선택이 다른 사람들의 선택에 영향을 미칠지를 / 바로 그 선택의 가시적 결과들

Take the case of the Adélie penguins.
Adélie 펭귄들의 사례를 들어보자.

They are often found strolling in large groups / toward the edge of the water / in search of food.
그들이 큰 무리를 지어 다니는 것이 종종 발견된다. / 물가를 향해 / 먹이를 찾아

Yet danger awaits in the icy-cold water.
하지만 얼음같이 차가운 물속에 위험이 기다리고 있다.

There is the leopard seal, for one, / which likes to have penguins for a meal.
한 예로, 표범물개가 있다. / 식사로 펭귄들을 먹는 것을 좋아하는

What is an Adélie to do?
Adélie 펭귄은 무엇을 할까?

The penguins' solution / is to play the waiting game.
펭귄의 해결책은 / 대기 전술을 펼치는 것이다.

They wait and wait and wait by the edge of the water / until one of them gives up and jumps in.
그들은 물가에서 기다리고 기다리고 또 기다린다. / 자기들 중 한 마리가 포기하고 뛰어들 때까지

The moment that occurs, / the rest of the penguins watch with anticipation / to see what happens next.
그것이 일어나는 순간, / 나머지 펭귄들은 기대감을 갖고 지켜본다. / 다음에 무슨 일이 일어날지를 보기 위해

If the pioneer survives, / everyone else will follow suit.
만약 그 선두 주자가 살아남으면, / 다른 모두가 방금 그 펭귄이 한 대로 따를 것이다.

If it perishes, / they'll turn away.
만약 그 펭귄이 죽는다면, / 그들은 돌아설 것이다.

One penguin's destiny / alters the fate of all the others.
한 펭귄의 운명이 / 모든 나머지 펭귄들의 운명을 바꾼다.

Their strategy, / you could say, / is "learn and live."
그들의 전략은 / 당신은 말할 수 있을 것이다. / '배워서 사는 것이다'라고

여러분의 선택이 다른 사람들의 선택에 영향을 미칠지를 결정하는 중요한 한 가지 요인이 있는데, 바로 그 선택의 가시적 결과들이다. Adélie 펭귄들의 사례를 들어보자. 그들이 먹이를 찾아 물가를 향해 큰 무리를 지어 다니는 것이 종종 발견된다. 하지만 얼음같이 차가운 물속에 위험이 기다리고 있다. 한 예로, 식사로 펭귄들을 먹는 것을 좋아하는 표범물개가 있다. Adélie 펭귄은 무엇을 할까? 펭귄의 해결책은 대기 전술을 펼치는 것이다. 그들은 자기들 중 한 마리가 포기하고 뛰어들 때까지 물가에서 기다리고 기다리고 또 기다린다. 그것이 일어나는 순간, 나머지 펭귄들은 다음에 무슨 일이 일어날지를 보기 위해 기대감을 갖고 지켜본다. 만약 그 선두 주자가 살아남으면, 다른 모두가 방금 그 펭귄이 한 대로 따를 것이다. 만약 그 펭귄이 죽는다면, 그들은 돌아설 것이다. 한 펭귄의 운명이 모든 나머지 펭귄들의 운명을 바꾼다. 그들의 전략은 '배워서 사는 것이다'라고 할 수 있을 것이다.

Why? 왜 정답일까?

예시의 결론 부분에서 먼저 물에 뛰어든 펭귄이 살아남는지 여부에 따라 다른 펭귄들도 뛰어드는 행동을 할지 말지를 결정한다(If the pioneer survives, everyone else will follow suit. If it perishes, they'll turn away.)는 내용이 나온다. 이를 근거로 할 때, 밑줄 친 부분이 의미하는 바로 가장 적절한 것은 ⑤ '다른 개체의 행동이 안전하다고 입증될 때에만 그 행동을 따른다'이다.

- **critical** ⓐ 중요한
- **visible** ⓐ 가시적인, 눈에 보이는
- **stroll** ⓥ 다니다, 거닐다
- **play the waiting game** 대기 전술을 펼치다, 기회를 기다리다
- **anticipation** ⓝ 기대
- **alter** ⓥ 바꾸다
- **territory** ⓝ 영토
- **influence** ⓥ 영향을 미치다 ⓝ 영향
- **consequence** ⓝ 결과
- **await** ⓥ ~을 기다리다
- **follow suit** ⓥ 방금 남이 한 대로 따라하다
- **fate** ⓝ 운명

구문 풀이

9행 The moment that occurs, the rest of the penguins watch with anticipation
~하는 순간 / 지시대명사 / 「the rest of + 복수 명사 + 복수 동사」
to see what happens next.
~하기 위해 / 의문사(무엇이 ~인지)

---

22 잘 거절하지 못할 때 생기는 결과 정답률 84% | 정답 ①

다음 글의 요지로 가장 적절한 것은?
✓① 거절하지 못하고 삶의 통제권을 잃으면 스트레스가 생긴다.
② 상대방의 거절을 감정적으로 해석하지 않는 것이 바람직하다.

③ 대부분의 스트레스는 상대에 대한 지나친 요구에서 비롯된다.
④ 일에 우선순위를 정해서 자신의 삶을 통제하는 것이 필요하다.
⑤ 사람마다 생각이 다를 수 있다는 점을 인정하는 것이 중요하다.

How many of you / have a hard time saying no?
여러분 중 얼마나 많은 사람이 / 거절하는 데 어려움을 겪고 있을까?
No matter what anyone asks of you, / no matter how much of an inconvenience it poses for you, / you do what they request.
어떤 사람이 여러분에게 무엇을 요청하더라도, / 그것이 여러분에게 아무리 많은 불편함을 주더라도 / 여러분은 그들이 요구하는 것을 한다.
This is not a healthy way of living / because by saying yes all the time / you are building up emotions of inconvenience.
이것은 건강한 삶의 방식이 아니다. / 항상 승낙함으로써 / 여러분이 불편함이라는 감정을 쌓아가고 있기 때문에
You know what will happen in time?
여러분은 조만간 무슨 일이 벌어질지 아는가?
You will resent the person / who you feel you cannot say no to / because you no longer have control of your life / and of what makes you happy.
여러분은 사람에 분개할 것이다. / 여러분이 거절하지 못할 것 같은 / 여러분이 자신의 삶에 대해 더 이상 통제권을 갖지 않기 때문에 / 그리고 자신을 행복하게 만드는 것에 대해
You are allowing someone else / to have control over your life.
여러분은 다른 사람에게 허락하고 있다 / 여러분의 삶에 대한 통제권을 갖도록
When you are suppressed emotionally / and constantly do things against your own will, / your stress will eat you up faster / than you can count to three.
여러분이 감정적으로 억눌리고 / 끊임없이 여러분 자신의 의지에 반하는 일들을 할 때, / 스트레스는 더 빠르게 여러분을 잡아먹을 것이다. / 여러분이 셋까지 셀 수 있는 것보다도

여러분 중 얼마나 많은 사람이 거절하는 데 어려움을 겪고 있을까? 어떤 사람이 여러분에게 무엇을 요청하더라도, 그것이 여러분에게 아무리 많은 불편함을 주더라도 여러분은 그들이 요구하는 것을 한다. 항상 승낙함으로써 여러분이 불편함이라는 감정을 쌓아가고 있기 때문에 이것은 건강한 삶의 방식이 아니다. 여러분은 조만간 무슨 일이 벌어질지 아는가? 여러분이 자신의 삶과 자신을 행복하게 만드는 것에 대해 더 이상 통제권을 갖지 않기 때문에, 여러분은 여러분이 거절하지 못할 것 같은 사람에게 분개할 것이다. 여러분은 다른 사람이 여러분의 삶에 대한 통제권을 갖도록 하고 있다. 여러분이 감정적으로 억눌리고 끊임없이 여러분 자신의 의지에 반하는 일들을 할 때, 스트레스는 여러분이 셋까지 셀 수 있는 것보다도 더 빠르게(셋까지 세기도 전에) 여러분을 잡아먹을 것이다.

Why? 왜 정답일까?

'You know what will happen in time?' 이후로 상대에게 거절을 잘 하지 못할 때 닥칠 결과를 말하고 있다. 즉 거절을 못 하면 타인에게 삶의 주도권을 넘겨주게 되어 스트레스가 빠르게 쌓인다(You are allowing someone else to have control over your life. When you are suppressed emotionally and constantly do things against your own will, your stress will eat you up faster than you can count to three.)는 것이다. 따라서 글의 요지로 가장 적절한 것은 ① '거절하지 못하고 삶의 통제권을 잃으면 스트레스가 생긴다.'이다.

- inconvenience ⓝ 불편함
- resent ⓥ 분개하다
- suppress ⓥ 억누르다, 참다
- will ⓝ 의지
- pose ⓥ 놓다, 주다, (의문 등을) 제기하다
- have control of ⓥ ~을 통제하다
- constantly ⓐⓓ 끊임없이

구문 풀이

1행 No matter what anyone asks of you, no matter how much of an
= whatever(무엇을 ~ 하든) 「no matter how + 형/부 + 주어 + 동사 : 아무리 ~이든」
inconvenience it poses for you, / you do what they request.
관계대명사(~것)

---

23 말이나 글을 통한 사고 표현의 필요성 정답률 51% | 정답 ①

다음 글의 주제로 가장 적절한 것은?

✓① critical roles of speaking or writing in refining thoughts
사고를 정제하는 데 있어 말 또는 글의 중대한 역할
② persuasive ways to communicate what you think to people
생각하는 바를 사람들에게 전달하는 설득력 있는 방법
③ important tips to select the right information for your writing
글에 적합한 정보를 선별하기 위한 중요한 조언
④ positive effects of logical thinking on reading comprehension
독해에 논리적 사고가 미치는 긍정적 영향
⑤ enormous gaps between spoken language and written language
구어와 문어 사이의 엄청난 격차

You can say / that information sits in one brain / until it is communicated to another, / unchanged in the conversation.
여러분은 말할 수 있다. / 정보는 한 뇌에 머물러 있으며 / 그것이 다른 뇌로 전달될 때까지 / 대화 속에서 변하지 않는다고
That's true of *sheer* information, / like your phone number / or the place you left your keys.
이것은 순전한 정보에 대해서는 사실이다. / 여러분의 전화번호 / 혹은 여러분이 열쇠를 놓아둔 장소와 같은
But it's not true of knowledge.
하지만 이것은 지식에 대해서는 사실이 아니다.
Knowledge relies on judgements, / which you discover and polish / in conversation with other people or with yourself.
지식은 판단에 의존하는데, / 여러분은 그 판단을 발견하고 다듬는다. / 다른 사람들 혹은 자신과의 대화 속에서
Therefore you don't learn the details of your thinking / until speaking or writing it out in detail / and looking back critically at the result.
그러므로 여러분은 자신의 사고의 세부 내용을 알지 못한다. / 그것을 상세하게 이야기하거나 글로 쓰고 / 그 결과를 비판적으로 되돌아볼 때까지
"Is what I just said foolish, / or is what I just wrote a deep truth?"
"내가 방금 이야기한 것이 바보 같은가, / 혹은 내가 방금 쓴 것이 깊은 진실인가?"
In the speaking or writing, / you uncover your bad ideas, often embarrassing ones, / and good ideas too, / sometimes fame-making ones.
말하거나 글을 쓸 때 / 여러분은 종종 당황스러운 자신의 형편없는 생각들을 발견하게 된다. / 그리고 좋은 생각들 또한, / 때로는 유명세를 만들어주는
Thinking requires its expression.
사고는 표현이 필요하다.

여러분은 정보가 다른 뇌로 전달될 때까지 한 뇌에 머물러 있으며 대화 속에서 변하지 않는

다고 말할 수 있다. 이것은 여러분의 전화번호 혹은 여러분이 열쇠를 놓아둔 장소와 같은 순전한 정보에 대해서는 사실이다. 하지만 이것은 지식에 대해서는 사실이 아니다. 지식은 판단에 의존하는데, 여러분은 다른 사람들 혹은 자신과의 대화 속에서 그 판단을 발견하고 다듬는다. 그러므로 여러분은 그것을 상세하게 이야기하거나 글로 쓰고 그 결과를 비판적으로 되돌아볼 때까지 자신의 사고의 세부 내용을 알지 못한다. "내가 방금 이야기한 것이 바보 같은가, 혹은 내가 방금 쓴 것이 깊은 진실인가?" 말하거나 글을 쓸 때 여러분은 종종 당황스러운 자신의 형편없는 생각들과, 때로는 유명세를 만들어주는 좋은 생각들을 또한 발견하게 된다. 사고는 표현이 필요하다.

Why? 왜 정답일까?

'Therefore you don't learn the details of your thinking until speaking or writing it out in detail and looking back critically at the result.'에서 사고는 상세하게 이야기되거나 글로 쓰이기 전까지는 그 세부 내용이 파악되지 않는다고 말한 데 이어, 마지막 문장에서는 사고가 그 표현을 필요로 한다(Thinking requires its expression.)는 결론을 제시하고 있다. 따라서 글의 주제로 가장 적절한 것은 ① '사고를 정제하는 데 있어 말 또는 글의 중대한 역할'이다.

- communicate ⓥ 전달하다
- sheer ⓐ 순전한
- judgement ⓝ 판단
- critically ⓐⓓ 비판적으로
- embarrassing ⓐ 당황스러운
- refine ⓥ 정제하다, 다듬다
- true of ~에 관해 사실인, ~에 해당되는
- rely on ⓥ ~에 의존하다
- polish ⓥ 다듬다
- uncover ⓥ 발견하다
- fame ⓝ 명성
- enormous ⓐ 엄청난

구문 풀이

4행 Knowledge relies on judgements, which you discover and polish in
선행사 계속적 용법 주어 타동사구
conversation with other people or with yourself.

---

24 사회적 정체성의 표시인 춤 정답률 81% | 정답 ②

다음 글의 제목으로 가장 적절한 것은?

① What Makes Traditional Dance Hard to Learn? – 무엇이 전통 춤을 배우기 어렵게 만드는가?
✓② Dance: A Distinct Sign of Social Identity – 춤: 사회적 정체성의 두드러진 표시
③ The More Varieties, the Better Dances – 종류가 더 많을수록, 춤은 더 좋아진다
④ Feeling Down? Enjoy Dancing! – 우울한가? 춤을 즐겨라!
⑤ The Origin of Tribal Dances – 부족 춤의 기원

It is said / that among the Bantu peoples of Central Africa, / when an individual from one tribe / meets someone from a different group, / they ask, "What do you dance?"
이야기된다. / 중앙아프리카 반투족들 사이에서는 / 한 부족의 사람이 / 다른 부족 사람을 만났을 때, / 그들은 "당신은 어떤 춤을 추나요?"라고 묻는다고
Throughout time, / communities have forged their identities / through dance rituals / that mark major events in the life of individuals, / including birth, marriage, and death / — as well as religious festivals and important points in the seasons.
오랫동안 / 공동체들은 자신들의 정체성을 구축해 왔다. / 춤 의식들을 통해 / 개인들의 삶에서 중요한 사건들을 기념하는 / 출생, 결혼, 죽음을 포함한 / 종교적인 축제들과 계절의 중요한 시점들뿐만 아니라
The social structure of many communities, / from African tribes to Spanish gypsies, and to Scottish clans, / gains much cohesion / from the group activity of dancing.
많은 공동체들의 사회적 구조는 / 아프리카 부족들부터 스페인의 집시들과 스코틀랜드의 씨족들까지 / 많은 결속을 얻게 된다. / 춤이라는 집단적 행동으로부터
Historically, / dance has been a strong, binding influence on community life, / a means of expressing the social identity of the group, / and participation allows individuals / to demonstrate a belonging.
역사적으로, / 춤은 (사람들을) 단결시켜 주는 강한 영향력을 공동체 삶에 미쳐 왔으며, / 그 집단의 사회적 정체성을 표현하는 수단으로서 / (춤에의) 참여는 개인들에게 허용한다 / 소속감을 보이도록
As a consequence, in many regions of the world / there are as many types of dances / as there are communities with distinct identities.
그 결과, 세계의 많은 지역에는 / 많은 종류의 춤들이 존재한다. / 각기 다른 정체성을 가진 공동체들이 존재하는 만큼

중앙아프리카 반투족들 사이에서는 한 부족의 사람이 다른 부족 사람을 만났을 때, 그들은 "당신은 어떤 춤을 추나요?"라고 묻는다고 한다. 오랫동안 공동체들은 종교적인 축제들과 계절의 중요한 시점들뿐만 아니라, 출생, 결혼, 죽음을 포함한 개인들의 삶에서 중요한 사건들을 기념하는 춤 의식들을 통해 자신들의 정체성을 구축해 왔다. 아프리카 부족들부터 스페인의 집시들과 스코틀랜드의 씨족들까지 많은 공동체들의 사회적 구조는 춤이라는 집단적 행동으로부터 많은 결속을 얻게 된다. 역사적으로, 춤은 그 집단의 사회적 정체성을 표현하는 수단으로서 (사람들을) 단결시켜 주는 강한 영향력을 공동체 삶에 미쳐 왔으며, (춤에의) 참여는 개인들이 소속감을 보이도록 해준다. 그 결과, 세계의 많은 지역에는 각기 다른 정체성을 가진 공동체들이 존재하는 만큼 많은 종류의 춤들이 존재한다.

Why? 왜 정답일까?

'Historically, dance has been a strong, binding influence on community life, a means of expressing the social identity of the group, and participation allows individuals to demonstrate a belonging.'에서 춤은 집단 정체성을 표현하는 수단으로 기능해 왔으며 개인은 춤에 참여함으로써 소속감을 드러낼 수 있다는 내용을 제시하고 있다. 따라서 글의 제목으로 가장 적절한 것은 ② '춤: 사회적 정체성의 두드러진 표시'이다.

- tribe ⓝ 부족
- ritual ⓝ 의식
- religious ⓐ 종교적인
- demonstrate ⓥ 보여주다, 입증하다
- distinct ⓐ 독특한, 뚜렷한
- identity ⓝ 정체성
- mark ⓥ 기념하다, 표시하다
- bind ⓥ 단결시키다, 결속시키다
- as a consequence 그 결과

구문 풀이

9행 Historically, dance has been a strong, binding influence on community
주어1 동사1
life, a means of expressing the social identity of the group, and participation
보어1(보어 보충설명)
allows individuals to demonstrate a belonging.
동사2 주어2
보어2 주어2
동사2 「allow + 목적어 + to부정사 : ~이 …하게 허락하다」

25. 지역별 건강 관광 여행 수 및 경비
정답률 75% | 정답 ⑤

다음 표의 내용과 일치하지 않는 것은?

Wellness Tourism Trips and Expenditures by Region in 2015 and 2017

Destination	Number of Trips (millions)		Expenditures ($ billions)	
	2015	2017	2015	2017
North America	186.5	204.1	$215.7	$241.7
Europe	249.9	291.8	$193.4	$210.8
Asia-Pacific	193.9	257.6	$111.2	$136.7
Latin America-The Caribbean	46.8	59.1	$30.4	$34.8
The Middle East-North Africa	8.5	11.0	$8.3	$10.7
Africa	5.4	6.5	$4.2	$4.8
Total	691.0	830.0	$563.2	$639.4

* Note: Figures may not sum to total due to rounding.

The table above shows / the number of trips and expenditures / for wellness tourism, / travel for health and well-being, / in 2015 and 2017.
위 표는 보여 준다. / 여행 수와 경비를 / 건강 관광의 / 건강과 웰빙을 위한 여행인 / 2015년과 2017년의

① Both the total number of trips and the total expenditures / were higher in 2017 / compared to those in 2015.
총 여행 수와 총 경비 둘 다 / 2017년에 더 높았다. / 2015년의 그것들에 비해서

② Of the six listed regions, / Europe was the most visited place for wellness tourism / in both 2015 and 2017, / followed by Asia-Pacific.
목록의 여섯 개 지역 중에서, / 유럽이 건강 관광을 위해 가장 많이 방문된 장소였으며, / 2015년과 2017년 두 해 모두 / 아시아-태평양이 그 뒤를 따랐다.

③ In 2017, / the number of trips to Latin America-The Caribbean / was more than five times higher / than that to The Middle East-North Africa.
2017년에 / 라틴 아메리카-카리브 해로의 여행 수가 / 5배 이상 더 많았다. / 중동-북아프리카로의 그것보다

④ While North America was the only region / where more than 200 billion dollars was spent in 2015, / it was joined by Europe in 2017.
북아메리카가 유일한 지역이었던 반면 / 2015년에 2천억 달러 이상이 소비된 / 2017년에는 유럽이 합류했다.

✓⑤ Meanwhile, / expenditures in The Middle East-North Africa and Africa / were each less than 10 billion dollars / in both 2015 and 2017.
한편 / 중동-북아프리카와 아프리카에서의 경비는 / 각각 100억 달러 미만이었다. / 2015년과 2017년 두 해 모두

위 표는 2015년과 2017년의 건강과 웰빙을 위한 여행인 건강 관광의 여행 수와 경비를 보여 준다. ① 총 여행 수와 총 경비 둘 다 2015년의 그것들에 비해서 2017년에 더 높았다. ② 목록의 여섯 개 지역 중에서, 유럽이 2015년과 2017년 두 해 모두 건강 관광을 위해 가장 많이 방문된 장소였으며, 아시아-태평양이 그 뒤를 따랐다. ③ 2017년에 라틴 아메리카-카리브 해로의 여행 수가 중동-북아프리카로의 그것보다 5배 이상 더 많았다. ④ 2015년에는 북아메리카가 2천억 달러 이상이 소비된 유일한 지역이었던 반면 2017년에는 유럽이 합류했다. ⑤ 한편 중동-북아프리카와 아프리카에서의 경비는 각각 2015년과 2017년 두 해 모두 100억 달러 미만이었다.

Why? 왜 정답일까?

도표에 따르면 중동-북아프리카 지역에서의 경비는 2017년에 100억 달러를 넘어 107억을 기록했다. 따라서 도표와 일치하지 않는 것은 ⑤이다.

- wellness ⓝ 건강
- rounding ⓝ 반올림
- expenditure ⓝ 경비, 지출

26. George Boole의 생애
정답률 84% | 정답 ③

George Boole에 관한 다음 글의 내용과 일치하지 않는 것은?
① 아버지의 사업 실패 후 학교를 그만두게 되었다.
② 수학, 자연 철학, 여러 언어를 독학했다.
✓③ Royal Society에서 화학으로 금메달을 받았다.
④ 오늘날 컴퓨터 과학의 기초를 형성한 책들을 저술했다.
⑤ Queen's College의 교수로 임명되었다.

George Boole was born / in Lincoln, England in 1815.
George Boole은 태어났다. / 1815년 영국 Lincoln에서

「Boole was forced to leave school / at the age of sixteen / after his father's business collapsed.」 ①의 근거 일치
Boole은 학교를 어쩔 수 없이 그만두게 되었다. / 16세의 나이에 / 아버지의 사업이 실패한 후

「He taught himself / mathematics, natural philosophy and various languages.」 ②의 근거 일치
그는 독학했다. / 수학, 자연 철학, 여러 언어를

He began to produce original mathematical research / and made important contributions / to areas of mathematics.
그는 독창적인 수학적 연구를 만들어 내기 시작했고 / 중요한 공헌을 했다. / 수학 분야에서

「For those contributions, / in 1844, he was awarded / a gold medal for mathematics / by the Royal Society.」 ③의 근거 불일치
그러한 공헌으로 / 1844년 그는 받았다. / 수학으로 금메달을 / Royal Society에서

Boole was deeply interested / in expressing the workings of the human mind in symbolic form, / and his two books on this subject, / 『The Mathematical Analysis of Logic and An Investigation of the Laws of Thought / form the basis of today's computer science.』 ④의 근거 일치
Boole은 매우 관심이 있었으며 / 기호 형태로 인간 사고방식의 작용을 표현하는 것에 / 이 주제에 대한 그의 책 두 권, / The Mathematical Analysis of Logic과 An Investigation of the Laws of Thought가 / 오늘날의 컴퓨터 과학의 기초를 형성한다.

「In 1849, he was appointed / the first professor of mathematics / at Queen's College in Cork, Ireland / and taught there until his death in 1864.」 ⑤의 근거 일치
1849년 그는 임명되어 / 최초 수학 교수로 / 아일랜드 Cork의 Queen's College의 / 1864년 생을 마감할 때까지 그곳에서 가르쳤다.

George Boole은 1815년 영국 Lincoln에서 태어났다. Boole은 아버지의 사업이 실패한 후 16

세의 나이에 학교를 어쩔 수 없이 그만두게 되었다. 그는 수학, 자연 철학, 여러 언어를 독학했다. 그는 독창적인 수학적 연구를 만들어 내기 시작했고 수학 분야에서 중요한 공헌을 했다. 그러한 공헌으로 1844년 그는 Royal Society에서 수학으로 금메달을 받았다. Boole은 기호 형태로 인간 사고방식의 작용을 표현하는 것에 매우 관심이 있었으며 이 주제에 대한 그의 책 두 권, The Mathematical Analysis of Logic과 An Investigation of the Laws of Thought가 오늘날의 컴퓨터 과학의 기초를 형성한다. 1849년 그는 아일랜드 Cork의 Queen's College의 최초 수학 교수로 임명되어 1864년 생을 마감할 때까지 그곳에서 가르쳤다.

Why? 왜 정답일까?

'For those contributions, in 1844, he was awarded a gold medal for mathematics by the Royal Society.'에서 George Boole이 금메달을 받은 과목은 수학이라고 하므로, 내용과 일치하지 않는 것은 ③ 'Royal Society에서 화학으로 금메달을 받았다.'이다.

Why? 왜 오답일까?

① 'Boole was forced to leave school at the age of sixteen after his father's business collapsed.'의 내용과 일치한다.
② 'He taught himself mathematics, natural philosophy and various languages.'의 내용과 일치한다.
④ '~ his two books on this subject, ~ form the basis of today's computer science.'의 내용과 일치한다.
⑤ 'In 1849, he was appointed the first professor of mathematics at Queen's College ~'의 내용과 일치한다.

- collapse ⓥ (갑자기 또는 완전히) 실패하다
- symbolic ⓐ 상징적인
- appoint A B ⓥ A를 B로 지명하다
- make a contribution to ⓥ ~에 공헌하다
- form the basis of ⓥ ~의 기초를 쌓다

구문 풀이

7행 Boole was deeply interested in expressing the workings of the human
(주어1) (동사1) (주격 보어)
mind in symbolic form, and his two books on this subject, *The Mathematical*
(주어2)
Analysis of Logic and An Investigation of the Laws of Thought form the basis of
(=his two books) (동사2)
today's computer science.

27. 지속 가능한 이동 주간 행사 안내
정답률 89% | 정답 ④

Sustainable Mobility Week 2019에 관한 다음 안내문의 내용과 일치하지 않는 것은?
① 슬로건이 매년 바뀐다.
② 주말 동안 2만보 넘게 걷는 것에 도전할 수 있다.
③ 대중교통이나 자전거를 이용하는 활동이 있다.
✓④ 한 가지 활동을 완료한 참가자는 수상 자격이 있다.
⑤ 참가자는 온라인으로 등록해야 한다.

Sustainable Mobility Week 2019
2019 지속 가능한 이동 주간
This annual event for clean and sustainable transport / runs from Nov 25 to Dec 1.
깨끗하고 지속 가능한 교통수단을 위한 이 연례 행사는 / 11월 25일부터 12월 1일까지 진행합니다.
「The slogan for the event changes every year, / and this year it is *Walk with Us!*」 ①의 근거 일치
이 행사의 슬로건은 매년 바뀌며 / 올해는 우리와 함께 걸어요!입니다.
You can participate in the activities below.
여러분은 아래의 활동들에 참여할 수 있습니다.
Walking Challenge:
걷기 도전:
「Try to walk over 20,000 steps / during the weekend of the event / to promote a clean environment.」 ②의 근거 일치
2만보 넘게 걷도록 노력하십시오. / 이 행사의 주말 동안 / 깨끗한 환경을 증진시키기 위해
Selecting Sustainable Mobility:
지속 가능한 이동 선택하기:
「Use public transport or a bicycle / instead of your own car.」 ③의 근거 일치
대중교통이나 자전거를 이용하십시오. / 자차 대신에
「Participants who complete both activities / are qualified to apply / for the Sustainable Mobility Week Awards.」 ④의 근거 불일치
두 가지 활동 모두를 완료한 참가자들은 / 지원 자격이 있습니다. / 지속 가능한 이동 주간 상에
「Participants must register online.」 ⑤의 근거 일치
참가자들은 온라인으로 등록해야 합니다.
www.sustainablemobilityweek.org

2019 지속 가능한 이동 주간

깨끗하고 지속 가능한 교통수단을 위한 이 연례행사는 11월 25일부터 12월 1일까지 진행합니다. 이 행사의 슬로건은 매년 바뀌며 올해는 *우리와 함께 걸어요!*입니다. 여러분은 아래의 활동들에 참여할 수 있습니다.

걷기 도전:
깨끗한 환경을 증진시키기 위해 이 행사의 주말 동안 2만보 넘게 걷도록 노력하십시오.

지속 가능한 이동 선택하기:
자차 대신에 대중교통이나 자전거를 이용하십시오.
• 두 가지 활동 모두를 완료한 참가자들은 지속 가능한 이동 주간 상에 지원할 자격이 있습니다.
• 참가자들은 온라인으로 등록해야 합니다.
www.sustainablemobilityweek.org

Why? 왜 정답일까?

'Participants who complete both activities are qualified to apply for the Sustainable Mobility Week Awards.'에서 두 가지 활동을 완료해야 수상 자격이 있다고 하므로, 안내문의 내용과 일치하지 않는 것은 ④ '한 가지 활동을 완료한 참가자는 수상 자격이 있다.'이다.

① 'The slogan for the event changes every year. ~'의 내용과 일치한다.

② 'Try to walk over 20,000 steps during the weekend of the event ~'의 내용과 일치한다.

③ 'Use public transport or a bicycle instead of your own car.'의 내용과 일치한다.

⑤ 'Participants must register online.'의 내용과 일치한다.

- **sustainable** ⓐ 지속 가능한
- **annual** ⓐ 연례의
- **promote** ⓥ 증진하다, 촉진하다
- **mobility** ⓝ 이동(성), 운동성
- **transport** ⓝ 운송 (수단)
- **be qualified to** ⓥ ~할 자격이 되다

---

28 | 목공 워크숍 안내 | 정답률 82% | 정답 ③

Introduction to Furniture Making에 관한 다음 안내문의 내용과 일치하는 것은?

① 연령에 제한이 없다.

② 토요일에 5시간씩 진행된다.

✔ 목공 경험이 없는 사람도 참여할 수 있다.

④ 적어도 일주일 전에 취소하면 전액을 환불해 준다.

⑤ 수강생들은 수작업으로 만든 의자를 가지고 가게 된다.

Introduction to Furniture Making
가구 제작 입문

Throughout this four-week workshop, / students will build a solid foundation / for their new venture into woodworking.
이 4주간의 워크숍 동안 / 학생들은 탄탄한 기초를 세울 것입니다. / 목공을 향한 그들의 새로운 도전에

『Age Requirement: 16 and older』 ①의근거 불일치
연령 요건: 16세 이상

Location: Hoboken Community Center
위치: Hoboken 주민 센터

『Dates: Dec 7 – Dec 28 (Every Saturday)』
날짜: 12월 7일부터 12월 28일까지(매주 토요일)

Time: 1:00 p.m. – 5:00 p.m. ②의근거 불일치
시간: 오후 1시부터 오후 5시까지

Price: $399
가격: 399달러

Note:
참고:

『Previous woodworking experience is not necessary.』 ③의근거 일치
이전 목공 경험은 필요하지 않습니다.

『We offer full refunds / if you cancel at least 10 days in advance.』 ④의근거 불일치
저희는 전액을 환불해 드립니다. / 여러분이 적어도 10일 전에 취소하면

『With the guidance of an instructor, / each student will leave with a hand-crafted side table.』 ⑤의근거 불일치
강사의 지도로 / 각각의 학생은 수작업으로 만든 보조 탁자를 가져가게 될 것입니다.

For more information or to register, / contact Dave Malka (davemalka@woodfurniture.org).
더 많은 정보나 등록을 위해서는 / Dave Malka(davemalka@woodfurniture.org)에게 연락하십시오.

가구 제작 입문

이 4주간의 워크숍 동안 학생들은 목공을 향한 새로운 도전에 탄탄한 기초를 세울 것입니다.

- 연령 요건: 16세 이상
- 위치: Hoboken 주민 센터
- 날짜: 12월 7일부터 12월 28일까지(매주 토요일)
- 시간: 오후 1시부터 오후 5시까지
- 가격: 399달러
- 참고:
  − 이전 목공 경험은 필요하지 않습니다.
  − 여러분이 적어도 10일 전에 취소하면 전액을 환불해 드립니다.

강사의 지도로 각각의 학생은 수작업으로 만든 보조 탁자를 가져가게 될 것입니다.

더 많은 정보나 등록을 위해서는 Dave Malka (davemalka @ woodfurniture.org)에게 연락하십시오.

Why? 왜 정답일까?

'Previous woodworking experience is not necessary.'에서 이전 목공 경험은 필요하지 않다고 하므로, 안내문의 내용과 일치하는 것은 ③ '목공 경험이 없는 사람도 참여할 수 있다.'이다.

Why? 왜 오답일까?

① 'Age Requirement: 16 and older'에서 참가자 연령은 16세 이상으로 제한된다고 하였다.

② 'Dates: Dec 7 – Dec 28 (Every Saturday) / Time: 1:00 p.m. – 5:00 p.m.'에서 4주 동안 매주 토요일에 4시간씩 진행된다고 하였다.

④ 'We offer full refunds if you cancel at least 10 days in advance.'에서 전액 환불을 받으려면 최소 10일 전에 취소해야 한다고 하였다.

⑤ 'With the guidance of an instructor, each student will leave with a hand-crafted side table.'에서 수강생들은 강사의 지도를 받아 보조 탁자를 제작하게 될 것이라고 하였다.

- **solid** ⓐ 탄탄한
- **venture** ⓝ 도전, 모험
- **in advance** 미리, 사전에
- **foundation** ⓝ 기초
- **woodworking** ⓝ 목공
- **hand-crafted** ⓐ 수작업의, 손으로 만든

---

29 | 비언어적 의사소통의 역할 | 정답률 52% | 정답 ④

다음 글의 밑줄 친 부분 중, 어법상 틀린 것은? [3점]

Non-verbal communication / is not a substitute for verbal communication.
비언어적 의사소통은 / 언어적 의사소통의 대체물이 아니다.

Rather, it should function as a supplement, / ① serving to enhance the richness of the content of the message / that is being passed across.
오히려 그것은 보충으로서 기능해야 한다. / 메시지 내용의 풍부함을 강화시키도록 도와주면서 / 전달되고 있는

Non-verbal communication / can be useful in situations / ② where speaking may be impossible or inappropriate.
비언어적 의사소통은 / 상황에서 유용할 수 있다. / 말하기가 불가능하거나 부적절할지도 모르는

Imagine you are in an uncomfortable position / while talking to an individual.
여러분이 불편한 입장에 있다고 상상해 보라. / 어떤 개인과 이야기하는 동안

Non-verbal communication will help you / ③ get the message across to him or her / to give you some time off the conversation / to be comfortable again.
비언어적 의사소통은 여러분을 도와줄 것이다. / 그 사람에게 메시지를 전하게 / 대화에서 잠깐 벗어날 시간을 달라는 / 다시 편안해지도록

Another advantage of non-verbal communication is / ✔ that it offers you the opportunity / to express emotions and attitudes properly.
비언어적 의사소통의 또 다른 장점은 / 여러분에게 기회를 제공한다는 것이다. / 감정과 태도를 적절하게 표현할

Without the aid of non-verbal communication, / there are several aspects of your nature and personality / that will not be adequately expressed.
비언어적 의사소통의 도움이 없다면 / 여러분의 본성과 성격의 여러 측면들이 있다. / 적절하게 표현되지 못할

So, again, / it does not substitute verbal communication / but rather ⑤ complements it.
따라서 다시 말하면, / 그것은 언어적 의사소통을 대체하는 것이 아니라 / 오히려 그것을 보완한다.

비언어적 의사소통은 언어적 의사소통의 대체물이 아니다. 오히려 그것은 전달되고 있는 메시지 내용의 풍부함을 강화시키도록 도와주면서 보충으로서 기능해야 한다. 비언어적 의사소통은 말하기가 불가능하거나 부적절할지도 모르는 상황에서 유용할 수 있다. 여러분이 어떤 개인과 이야기하는 동안 불편한 입장에 있다고 상상해 보라. 비언어적 의사소통은 여러분이 그 사람에게 다시 편안해지도록 대화에서 잠깐 벗어날 시간을 달라는 메시지를 전하게 도와줄 것이다. 비언어적 의사소통의 또 다른 장점은 그것이 여러분에게 감정과 태도를 적절하게 표현할 기회를 제공한다는 것이다. 비언어적 의사소통의 도움이 없다면 적절하게 표현되지 못할 여러분의 본성과 성격의 여러 측면들이 있다. 따라서 다시 말하면, 그것은 언어적 의사소통을 대체하는 것이 아니라 오히려 그것을 보완한다.

Why? 왜 정답일까?

뒤에 나오는 'it offers you the opportunity ~'가 완전한 4형식 구조임을 미루어볼 때, 뒤에 불완전한 문장을 수반하는 관계대명사 what을 쓰기에는 부적절하다. 따라서 what을 명사절 접속사인 that으로 고쳐야 한다. 어법상 틀린 것은 ④이다.

Why? 왜 오답일까?

① 완전한 주절 뒤로 '~하면서'라는 뜻의 분사구문이 적절히 연결되고 있다. 뒤에 나오는 to부정사는 serving의 목적어로, 'serve + to부정사(~하는 것을 돕다)'를 기억해 둔다.

② 앞에 추상적 공간의 선행사 situations가 나온 후 뒤에 may be가 동사인 완전한 2형식 구조가 나오는 것으로 보아 관계부사 where의 쓰임은 적절하다.

③ 준사역동사 help는 목적어와 목적격 보어가 능동 관계일 때 원형부정사 또는 to부정사를 목적격 보어로 취한다. 따라서 get의 쓰임이 적절하다.

⑤ 「not A but (rather) B(A가 아니라 B인)」 구문에서 A 자리에 주어 it에 연결되는 단수 동사 does not substitute가 나오므로, B 자리에도 단수 동사 complements가 적절하게 나왔다.

- **substitute** ⓝ 대체물 ⓥ 대체하다
- **pass across** ⓥ 전달하다
- **get A across to B** ⓥ A를 B에게 전하다, 이해시키다
- **properly** [ad] 적절하게
- **adequately** [ad] 적절하게
- **enhance** ⓥ 강화하다
- **inappropriate** ⓐ 부적절한
- **aid** ⓝ 도움
- **complement** ⓥ 보완하다

구문 풀이

2행 Rather, it should function as a supplement, serving to enhance the
　　　　　　　　　　　　자동사(기능하다)　　　　　　　　　분사구문(~하면서)
richness of the content of the message [that is being passed across].
　　　　　　　　　　　　　　　　　　선행사　　　　　　현재진행 수동태(~되고 있다)

---

30 | 지적 겸손의 개념 | 정답률 62% | 정답 ①

(A), (B), (C)의 각 네모 안에서 문맥에 맞는 낱말로 가장 적절한 것은?

	(A)	(B)	(C)
✔	recognizing 인식하는 것	receptive 수용적인	value 존중한다
②	recognizing 인식하는 것	resistant 저항하는	undervalue 경시하다
③	recognizing 인식하는 것	receptive 수용적인	undervalue 경시하다
④	neglecting 무시하는 것	resistant 저항하는	undervalue 경시하다
⑤	neglecting 무시하는 것	receptive 수용적인	value 존중한다

Intellectual humility is admitting / you are human / and there are limits to the knowledge you have.
지적 겸손이란 인정하는 것이다. / 여러분이 인간이고 / 여러분이 가진 지식에 한계가 있다는 것을

It involves (A) recognizing / that you possess cognitive and personal biases, / and that your brain tends to see things / in such a way / that your opinions and viewpoints are favored above others.
이것은 인식하는 것을 포함한다. / 여러분이 인지적이고 개인적인 편견을 가지고 있고, / 여러분의 두뇌가 사물을 바라보는 경향이 있다고 / 그런 방식으로 / 자신의 의견과 견해가 다른 것보다 선호되는

It is being willing to work to overcome those biases / in order to be more objective / and make informed decisions.
이것은 그러한 편견들을 극복하고 기꺼이 노력하는 것이다. / 더 객관적이 되고 / 정보에 근거한 결정들을 내리기 위해

People who display intellectual humility / are more likely to be (B) receptive to learning from others / who think differently than they do.
지적 겸손을 보이는 사람들은 / 다른 사람들에게 배우는 것에 더 수용적일 것이다. / 자신들이 생각하는 것과 다르게 생각하는

They tend to be well-liked and respected by others / because they make it clear / that they (C) value what other people bring to the table.
그들은 다른 사람들에게 호감을 사고 존경받는 경향이 있다. / 그들이 분명히 하기 때문에 / 그들이 다른 사람들이 제시하는 것을 존중한다는

Intellectually humble people want to learn more / and are open to finding information / from a variety of sources.
지적으로 겸손한 사람들은 더 많은 것을 배우고 싶어 하고 / 정보를 찾는 것에 개방적이다. / 다양한 출처로부터

They are not interested / in trying to appear or feel superior to others.
그들은 관심이 없다. / 다른 사람들보다 우월하게 보이거나 느끼려고 애쓰는 데

지적 겸손이란 여러분이 인간이고 여러분이 가진 지식에 한계가 있다는 것을 인정하는 것이다. 이것은 여러분이 인지적이고 개인적인 편견을 가지고 있고, 여러분의 두뇌가 자신의 의견과 견해를 다른 것보다 선호하는 방식으로 사물을 바라보는 경향이 있다고 (A) 인식하는 것을 포함한다. 이것은 더 객관적이 되고 정보에 근거한 결정들을 내리기 위해 그러한 편견들을 극복하고자 기꺼이 노력하는 것이다. 지적 겸손을 보이는 사람들은 자신들이 생각하는 것과 다르게 생각하는 다른 사람들에게 배우는 것에 더 (B) 수용적일 것이다. 그들은 다른 사람들이 제시하는 것을 (C) 존중한다는 것을 분명히 하기 때문에 다른 사람들에게 호감을 사고 존경받는 경향이 있다. 지적으로 겸손한 사람들은 더 많은 것을 배우고 싶어 하고 다양한 출처로부터 정보를 찾는 것에 개방적이다. 그들은 다른 사람들보다 우월하게 보이거나 느끼려고 애쓰는 데 관심이 없다.

Why? 왜 정답일까?

(A) 앞에서 자기 지식에 한계가 있음을 인정하는 것이 지적 겸손이라고 설명하는 것으로 보아, (A)에는 지적 겸손 안에 자신의 편견을 '인식한다'는 행동이 포함된다는 뜻의 **recognizing**이 들어가야 적절하다.
(B) 앞에서 지적 겸손을 보이는 이들은 자신의 편견을 극복하고자 기꺼이 노력한다는 내용이 나오는 것으로 보아, (B)에는 이들이 타인에게 배움을 얻는 데 '수용적'이라는 뜻의 **receptive**가 들어가야 적절하다.
(C) 마지막 두 문장에서 지적으로 겸손한 사람들은 더 많이 배우고 싶어 하며, 다양한 출처로부터 정보를 취하고자 하고, 타인보다 우월해 보이는 데 관심을 두지 않는다고 언급하는 것으로 보아, (C)에는 이들이 타인의 견해를 '존중한다'는 뜻의 **value**가 들어가야 적절하다. 따라서 각 네모 안에서 문맥에 맞는 낱말로 가장 적절한 것은 ① '(A) 인식하는 것 - (B) 수용적인 - (C) 존중한다'이다.

- humility ⓝ 겸손
- recognize ⓥ 인식하다, 깨닫다
- cognitive ⓐ 인지적인
- favor ⓥ 선호하다
- objective ⓐ 객관적인
- informed decision ⓝ 정보에 근거한 결정, 잘 알고 내린 결정
- receptive ⓐ 수용적인
- bring to the table 〜을 제시하다

- neglect ⓥ 무시하다, 소홀히 하다
- possess ⓥ 지니다, 가지다
- bias ⓝ 편견
- overcome ⓥ 극복하다

- resistant ⓐ 〜에 저항하는
- superior ⓐ 우월한

구문 풀이

7행 People [who display intellectual humility] are more likely to be receptive
주어 「be likely + to부정사 : 〜하는 경향이 있다」
to learning from others [who think differently than they do].
선행사 〜에 수용적인 = think

★★★ 등급을 가르는 문제!
31 역할의 상호 작용으로 이해할 수 있는 관계 내 상호 작용 정답률 32% | 정답 ②

다음 빈칸에 들어갈 말로 가장 적절한 것을 고르시오.
① careers - 직업   ✓ statuses - 지위   ③ abilities - 능력
④ motivations - 동기   ⑤ perspectives - 관점

People engage in typical patterns of interaction / based on the relationship / between their roles and the roles of others.
사람들은 전형적인 양식의 상호 작용에 참여한다. / 관계에 근거하여 / 자신의 역할과 다른 사람의 역할 사이의
Employers are expected / to interact with employees in a certain way, / as are doctors with patients.
고용주들은 기대된다. / 직원들과 특정한 방식으로 상호 작용하도록 / 의사가 환자들과 그러한 것처럼
In each case, actions are restricted / by the role responsibilities and obligations / associated with individuals' positions within society.
각각의 경우에 행동은 제한된다. / 역할 책임과 의무에 의해 / 개인의 사회 내 지위와 관련된
For instance, parents and children are linked / by certain rights, privileges, and obligations.
예를 들어 부모와 자식은 연결된다. / 특정한 권리, 특권, 의무에 의해
Parents are responsible / for providing their children with the basic necessities of life / — food, clothing, shelter, and so forth.
부모는 책임이 있다. / 자기 자녀에게 기본적인 생필품을 제공할 / 의식주 등
These expectations are so powerful / that not meeting them may make the parents vulnerable / to charges of negligence or abuse.
이러한 기대는 너무 강해서 / 그것을 충족시키지 못하는 것은 부모를 비난받기 쉽게 할지도 모른다. / 태만이나 학대 혐의로
Children, in turn, are expected / to do as their parents say.
역으로 아이들은 기대된다. / 자신의 부모가 말하는 대로 하도록
Thus, interactions within a relationship are functions / not only of the individual personalities of the people involved / but also of the role requirements associated with the statuses they have.
그러므로 관계 내의 상호 작용은 작용이다. / 연관된 사람들 개개의 성격뿐만 아니라 / 그들이 지닌 지위와 관련된 역할 요구의

사람들은 자신의 역할과 다른 사람의 역할 사이의 관계에 근거하여 전형적인 양식의 상호 작용에 참여한다. 의사들이 환자들과 그러한 것처럼 고용주들은 직원들과 특정한 방식으로 상호 작용하도록 기대된다. 각각의 경우에 행동은 개인의 사회 내 지위와 관련된 역할 책임과 의무에 의해 제한된다. 예를 들어 부모와 자식은 특정한 권리, 특권, 의무에 의해 연결된다. 부모는 자기 자녀에게 의식주 등 기본적인 생필품을 제공할 책임이 있다. 이러한 기대가 너무 강해서 그것을 충족시키지 못하는 것은 부모를 태만이나 학대 혐의로 비난받기 쉽게 할지도 모른다. 역으로 아이들은 자신의 부모가 말하는 대로 하도록 기대된다. 그러므로 관계 내의 상호 작용은 연관된 사람들 개개의 성격의 작용일 뿐만 아니라 그들이 지닌 지위와 관련된 역할 요구의 작용이다.

Why? 왜 정답일까?

첫 문장에서 사람들은 역할 간의 관계에 근거한 전형적인 상호 작용에 참여하게 된다고 언급한 후, 다양한 예시가 이어지고 있다. 특히 '〜 actions are restricted by the role responsibilities and obligations associated with individuals' positions within society.'에서 개인의 행동은 사회 내에서의 '지위'와 연관된 책임과 의무로 인해 제한을 받게 된다고 설명하는 것을 근거로 볼 때, 빈칸에 들어갈 말로 가장 적절한 것은 ② '지위'이다.

- engage in 〜에 참여하다, 관여하다
- restrict ⓥ 제한하다

- obligation ⓝ 의무
- privilege ⓝ 특권
- charge ⓝ 혐의, 비난
- status ⓝ 지위

- associated with 〜와 관련된
- necessity ⓝ 필수품
- abuse ⓝ 학대, 남용
- perspective ⓝ 관점

구문 풀이

9행 These expectations are so powerful that not meeting them may make
「so ~ that … : 너무 ~해서 …하다」 동명사구 주어   5형식 동사
the parents vulnerable to charges of negligence or abuse.
목적어   형용사 보어

★★ 문제 해결 꿀팁 ★★

▶ 많이 틀린 이유는?
글은 상호작용의 주체가 각자의 '지위'에 따라 역할이나 책임을 부여받는다는 내용을 다루고 있다. ③의 '능력'은 언급되지 않았다.

▶ 문제 해결 방법은?
예시 앞에는 대체로 주제가 나오므로, 여기서도 For instance 앞의 'In each case ~'에 답의 근거가 있음을 예상할 수 있다.

★★★ 등급을 가르는 문제!
32 세계화로 강화된 집단 간 장벽 정답률 34% | 정답 ①

다음 빈칸에 들어갈 말로 가장 적절한 것을 고르시오. [3점]
✓ to build barriers - 장벽을 쌓도록
② to achieve equality - 평등을 성취하도록
③ to abandon traditions - 전통을 버리도록
④ to value individualism - 개인주의를 중시하도록
⑤ to develop technologies - 기술을 발전시키도록

The title of Thomas Friedman's 2005 book, The World Is Flat, / was based on the belief / that globalization would inevitably bring us closer together.
Thomas Friedman의 2005년 저서의 제목인 The World Is Flat은 / 믿음에 근거하였다. / 세계화가 필연적으로 우리를 더 가깝게 만들 것이라는
It has done that, / but it has also inspired us to build barriers.
그것은 그렇게 해왔지만 / 또한 우리가 장벽을 쌓도록 해왔다.
When faced with perceived threats / — the financial crisis, terrorism, violent conflict, refugees and immigration, the increasing gap between rich and poor — / people cling more tightly to their groups.
인지된 위험들에 직면할 때, / 금융 위기, 테러 행위, 폭력적 분쟁, 난민과 이민자, 증가하는 빈부 격차 / 사람들은 자신의 집단에 더 단단히 달라붙는다.
One famous founder of a famous social media company / believed social media would unite us.
한 유명 소셜 미디어 회사 설립자는 / 소셜 미디어가 우리를 결합시킬 것이라고 믿었다.
In some respects it has, / but it has simultaneously given voice and organizational ability / to new cyber tribes, / some of whom spend their time / spreading blame and division across the World Wide Web.
어떤 면에서는 그것은 그래 왔지만 / 그것은 동시에 목소리와 조직력을 부여해 왔고, / 새로운 사이버 부족들에게 / 이들 중 일부는 / 그들의 시간을 보낸다. / 월드 와이드 웹(World Wide Web)에서 비난과 분열을 퍼뜨리는 데
There seem now to be as many tribes, / and as much conflict between them, / as there have ever been.
현재 많은 부족들이 존재하는 것처럼 보인다. / 그리고 그들 사이의 많은 분쟁이 / 지금까지 존재해 온 만큼이나
Is it possible for these tribes to coexist / in a world where the concept of "us and them" remains?
이러한 부족들이 공존하는 것이 가능할까? / '우리와 그들'이라는 개념이 남아 있는 세계에서

Thomas Friedman의 2005년 저서의 제목인 The World Is Flat은 세계화가 필연적으로 우리를 더 가깝게 만들 것이라는 믿음에 근거하였다. 그것(세계화)은 그렇게 해왔지만 또한 우리가 장벽을 쌓도록 해왔다. 금융 위기, 테러 행위, 폭력적 분쟁, 난민과 이민자, 증가하는 빈부 격차 같은 인지된 위험들에 직면할 때, 사람들은 자신의 집단에 더 단단히 달라붙는다. 한 유명 소셜 미디어 회사 설립자는 소셜 미디어가 우리를 결합시킬 것이라고 믿었다. 어떤 면에서는 그래 왔지만 그것은 동시에 새로운 사이버 부족들에게 목소리와 조직력을 부여해 왔고, 이들 중 일부는 월드 와이드 웹(World Wide Web)에서 비난과 분열을 퍼뜨리는 데 그들의 시간을 보낸다. 지금까지 그래 온 만큼이나 현재 많은 부족들, 그리고 그들 사이의 많은 분쟁이 존재하는 것처럼 보인다. '우리와 그들'이라는 개념이 남아 있는 세계에서 이러한 부족들이 공존하는 것이 가능할까?

Why? 왜 정답일까?

세계화로 인해 각 집단은 가까워질 것으로 기대되었지만 한편으로 서로 간 단절이 심화되었다는 점을 지적한 글이다. 특히 마지막 두 문장에서 사이버 상의 각 부족들 별로 아직도 많은 분쟁이 존재하고 있으며 '우리'와 '그들'이라는 구별이 여전히 남아 있음(There seem now to be as many tribes, and as much conflict between them, ~.)을 언급하므로, 빈칸에 들어갈 말로 가장 적절한 것은 ① '장벽을 쌓도록'이다.

- inevitably ⓐⓓ 필연적으로, 불가피하게
- threat ⓝ 위협
- conflict ⓝ 분쟁, 갈등
- gap between rich and poor ⓝ 빈부격차
- founder ⓝ 설립자
- simultaneously ⓐⓓ 동시에
- spread ⓥ 퍼뜨리다
- equality ⓝ 평등

- inspire ⓥ 고무하다, 자극하다
- crisis ⓝ 위기
- refugee ⓝ 난민
- cling to ⓥ 〜에 달라붙다
- unite ⓥ 결합시키다
- organizational ⓐ 조직(상)의
- coexist ⓥ 공존하다
- individualism ⓝ 개인주의

구문 풀이

8행 In some respects it has (united us), but it has simultaneously given voice
생략(앞 문장에 나옴)
and organizational ability to new cyber tribes, some of whom spend their time
선행사   목적격 관·대 「spend + 시간 + 동명사 :
spreading blame and division across the World Wide Web.
〜하는 데 …을 들이다」

★★★ 등급을 가르는 문제!

33 차이점에 집중할 때 가려지는 유사점   정답률 32% | 정답 ③

다음 빈칸에 들어갈 말로 가장 적절한 것을 고르시오. [3점]

① prove the uniqueness of each society – 각 사회의 고유함을 입증하게
② prevent cross-cultural understanding – 다문화적 이해를 막게
③ mask the more overwhelming similarities – 더 압도적인 유사점을 가리게
④ change their perspective on what diversity is – 다양성이 무엇인가에 대한 그들의 견해를 바꾸게
⑤ encourage them to step out of their mental frame – 그들이 정신적 틀을 벗어나도록 장려하게

Focusing on the differences among societies / conceals a deeper reality: / their similarities are greater and more profound / than their dissimilarities.
사회들 사이의 차이점에 집중하는 것은 / 더 깊은 실체를 숨기는데 / 그것들의 유사점은 더 크고 더 심오하다 / 차이점보다
Imagine studying two hills / while standing on a ten-thousand-foot-high plateau.
두 개의 언덕을 유심히 본다고 상상해 보라. / 1만 피트 높이의 고원에 서서
Seen from your perspective, / one hill appears to be three hundred feet high, / and the other appears to be nine hundred feet.
여러분의 관점에서 보면, / 한 언덕이 300피트 높이인 것처럼 보이고 / 다른 언덕이 900피트 높이인 것처럼 보인다.
This difference may seem large, / and you might focus your attention / on what local forces, such as erosion, / account for the difference in size.
이 차이가 커 보일 수 있고 / 여러분은 자신의 관심을 집중시킬지도 모른다. / 침식과 같은 어떤 국부적인 힘이 / 크기의 차이를 설명하는지에
But this narrow perspective misses the opportunity / to study the other, more significant geological forces / that created what are actually two very similar mountains, / one 10,300 feet high and the other 10,900 feet.
그러나 이 좁은 관점은 기회를 놓치고 있다. / 다른 관점을 연구할 / 더 중대한 지질학적 힘 / 사실상 아주 비슷한 두 개의 산을 만들어 낸 / 하나는 10,300피트 높이이고 다른 하나는 10,900피트 높이로
And when it comes to human societies, / people have been standing on a ten-thousand-foot plateau, / letting the differences among societies / <u>mask the more overwhelming similarities.</u>
그리고 인간 사회에 관한 한, / 사람들은 1만 피트의 고원에 서서 / 사회들 사이의 차이점으로 하여금 허락하고 있다. / 더 압도적인 유사점을 가리게

사회들 사이의 차이점에 집중하는 것은 더 깊은 실체를 숨기는데, 그것들의 유사점은 차이점보다 더 크고 더 심오하다. 1만 피트 높이의 고원에 서서 두 개의 언덕을 유심히 본다고 상상해 보라. 여러분의 관점에서 보면, 한 언덕이 300피트 높이인 것처럼 보이고 다른 언덕이 900피트 높이인 것처럼 보인다. 이 차이가 커 보일 수 있고 여러분은 침식과 같은 어떤 국부적인 힘이 크기의 차이를 설명하는지에 관심을 집중할지도 모른다. 그러나 이 좁은 관점은 다른 관점, 즉 하나는 10,300피트 높이이고 다른 하나는 10,900피트 높이로 사실상 아주 비슷한 두 개의 산을 만들어 낸 더 중대한 지질학적 힘을 연구할 기회를 놓치고 있다. 그리고 인간 사회에 관한 한, 사람들은 1만 피트의 고원에 서서 사회들 사이의 차이점이 더 압도적인 유사점을 가리게 두고 있다.

Why? 왜 정답일까?
첫 문장에서 사회들 사이의 차이점에 주목하면 그들간의 유사점이라는 더 깊은 실체를 놓치게 된다 (Focusing on the differences among societies conceals a deeper reality: their similarities are greater and more profound than their dissimilarities.)고 언급하고 있다. 따라서 빈칸에 들어갈 말로 가장 적절한 것은 ③ '더 압도적인 유사점을 가리게'이다.

- conceal ⓥ 숨기다
- dissimilarity ⓝ 차이점
- account for ⓥ ~을 설명하다
- significant ⓐ 중대한, 유의미한
- when it comes to ~에 관한 한
- overwhelming ⓐ 압도적인
- profound ⓐ 심오한
- plateau ⓝ 고원
- narrow ⓐ 좁은
- geological ⓐ 지질학적인
- uniqueness ⓝ 고유성
- step out of ⓥ ~에서 나오다

구문 풀이

6행   This difference may seem large, and you might focus your attention on
의문형용사(어떤)   2형식 동사   형용사 보어   「focus+A+on+B : A를 B에 집중시키다」
what local forces, such as erosion, account for the difference in size.
명사(주어)   삽입구   동사

★★★ 등급을 가르는 문제!

34 음식이 마음에 미치는 영향   정답률 37% | 정답 ⑤

다음 빈칸에 들어갈 말로 가장 적절한 것을 고르시오. [3점]

① leads us to make a fair judgement – 우리가 공정한 판단을 내리게 유도한다
② interferes with cooperation with others – 타인과의 협력을 방해한다
③ does harm to serious diplomatic occasions – 심각한 외교 상황에 해를 끼친다
④ plays a critical role in improving our health – 우리의 건강을 증진하는 데 중요한 역할을 한다
⑤ enhances our receptiveness to be persuaded – 설득되는 데 대한 우리의 수용성을 높인다

There is a famous Spanish proverb / that says, "The belly rules the mind."
유명한 스페인 속담이 있다. / '배가 마음을 다스린다'라고 하는
This is a clinically proven fact.
이것은 임상적으로 증명된 사실이다.
Food is the original mind-controlling drug.
음식은 원래 마음을 지배하는 약이다.
Every time we eat, / we bombard our brains with a feast of chemicals, / triggering an explosive hormonal chain reaction / that directly influences the way we think.
우리가 먹을 때마다 / 우리는 자신의 두뇌에 화학 물질의 향연을 퍼부어 / 폭발적인 호르몬 연쇄 반응을 유발하는 / 우리가 생각하는 방식에 직접적으로 영향을 미치는
Countless studies have shown / that the positive emotional state / induced by a good meal / enhances our receptiveness to be persuaded.
수많은 연구는 보여주었다. / 긍정적인 감정 상태가 / 근사한 식사로 유도된 / 설득되는 데 대한 우리의 수용성을 높인다는 것을
It triggers an instinctive desire / to repay the provider.
그것은 본능적인 욕구를 유발한다. / 그 제공자에게 보답하려는
This is why executives regularly combine business meetings with meals, / why lobbyists invite politicians / to attend receptions, lunches, and dinners, / and why major state occasions / almost always involve an impressive banquet.
이것이 경영진이 정기적으로 업무 회의와 식사를 결합하는 이유이고, / 로비스트들이 정치인들을 초대하는 이유이고, / 환영회, 점심 식사, 저녁 식사에 참석하도록 / 주요 국가 행사가 거의 항상 인상적인 연회를 포함하는 이유이다.
Churchill called this "dining diplomacy," / and sociologists have confirmed / that this principle is a strong motivator / across all human cultures.
Churchill은 이것을 '식사 외교'라고 불렀고, / 사회학자들은 확인해 왔다. / 이 원리가 강력한 동기 부여물이라는 것을 / 모든 인류 문화에 걸쳐

'배가 마음을 다스린다'라고 하는 유명한 스페인 속담이 있다. 이것은 임상적으로 증명된 사실이다. 음식은 원래 마음을 지배하는 약이다. 우리가 먹을 때마다 우리는 자신의 두뇌에 화학 물질의 향연을 퍼부어 우리가 생각하는 방식에 직접적으로 영향을 미치는 폭발적인 호르몬 연쇄 반응을 유발한다. 수많은 연구는 근사한 식사로 유도된 긍정적인 감정 상태가 설득되는 데 대한 우리의 수용성을 높인다는 것을 보여주었다. 그것은 그 제공자에게 보답하려는 본능적인 욕구를 유발한다. 이것이 경영진이 정기적으로 업무 회의와 식사를 결합하는 이유이고, 로비스트들이 정치인들을 환영회, 점심 식사, 저녁 식사에 참석하도록 초대하는 이유이고, 주요 국가 행사가 거의 항상 인상적인 연회를 포함하는 이유이다. Churchill은 이것을 '식사 외교'라고 불렀고, 사회학자들은 이 원리가 모든 인류 문화에 걸쳐 강력한 동기 부여물이라는 것을 확인해 왔다.

Why? 왜 정답일까?
첫 세 문장에서 스페인 속담을 예로 들며 음식이 마음을 지배한다(Food is the original mind-controlling drug.)는 것이 사실이라는 점을 언급하고, 빈칸 뒤에서는 이러한 이유로 각종 업무 상황에 연회와 식사가 포함된다고 설명한다. 따라서 빈칸에 들어갈 말로 가장 적절한 것은 근사한 식사로 긍정적인 감정 상태에 이르렀을 때의 결과를 적절히 유추한 ⑤ '설득되는 데 대한 우리의 수용성을 높인다'이다.

- clinically ⓐⓓ 임상적으로
- feast ⓝ 향연
- explosive ⓐ 폭발적인
- instinctive ⓐ 본능적인
- reception ⓝ 환영회
- diplomacy ⓝ 외교
- interfere with ~을 방해하다
- enhance ⓥ 높이다, 향상시키다
- bombard A with B ⓥ A에 B를 퍼붓다
- trigger ⓥ 유발하다
- induce ⓥ 유도하다
- executive ⓝ 경영진
- impressive ⓐ 인상적인
- principle ⓝ 원리
- do harm to ⓥ ~에 해를 끼치다
- receptiveness ⓝ 수용성, 감수성

구문 풀이

3행   Every time we eat, we bombard our brains with a feast of chemicals,
~할 때마다   「bombard +A + with + B : A에 B를 퍼붓다」
triggering an explosive hormonal chain reaction [that directly influences the way
분사구문(그리고 ~하다)   선행사   주격 관계대명사
we think].

35 야구 선수를 위한 운동의 일부로 자리하게 된 근력 운동   정답률 66% | 정답 ③

다음 글에서 전체 흐름과 관계 <u>없는</u> 문장은?

Training and conditioning for baseball / focuses on developing strength, power, speed, quickness and flexibility.
야구를 위한 훈련과 몸만들기는 / 체력, 힘, 속도, 신속함, 유연성을 발달시키는 데 초점을 둔다.
① Before the 1980s, / strength training was not an important part / of conditioning for a baseball player.
1980년대 이전에 / 근력 운동은 중요한 부분이 아니었다. / 야구 선수를 위한 몸만들기의
② People viewed baseball / as a game of skill and technique rather than strength, / and most managers and coaches saw strength training / as something for bodybuilders, not baseball players.

사람들은 야구를 보았고, / 근력보다는 기술과 테크닉의 경기로 / 대부분의 감독과 코치는 근력 운동을 여겼다. / 야구 선수가 아닌 보디빌더를 위한 것으로

☑ Unlike more isolated bodybuilding exercises, / athletic exercises train as many muscle groups and functions as possible / at the same time.
더 분리된 보디빌딩 운동과는 달리 / 운동선수용 운동은 가능한 한 많은 근육군과 기능을 훈련시킨다. / 동시에

④ They feared / that weight lifting and building large muscles / would cause players to lose flexibility / and interfere with quickness and proper technique.
그들은 두려워했다. / 역도와 큰 근육을 키우는 것이 / 선수로 하여금 유연성을 잃어버리게 하고 / 신속함과 적절한 테크닉을 방해할 것이라고

⑤ Today, though, / experts understand the importance of strength training / and have made it part of the game.
그렇지만 오늘날 / 전문가들은 근력 운동의 중요성을 이해하고 / 그것을 경기의 일부로 만들어 오고 있다.

야구를 위한 훈련과 몸만들기는 체력, 힘, 속도, 신속함, 유연성을 발달시키는 데 초점을 둔다. ① 1980년대 이전에 근력 운동은 야구 선수를 위한 몸만들기의 중요한 부분이 아니었다. ② 사람들은 야구를 근력보다는 기술과 테크닉의 경기로 보았고, 대부분의 감독과 코치는 근력 운동을 야구 선수가 아닌 보디빌더를 위한 것으로 여겼다. ③ 더 분리된 보디빌딩 운동과는 달리 운동선수용 운동은 가능한 한 많은 근육군과 기능을 동시에 훈련시킨다. ④ 그들은 역도와 큰 근육을 키우는 것이 선수들로 하여금 유연성을 잃어버리게 하고 신속함과 적절한 테크닉을 방해할 것이라고 두려워했다. ⑤ 그렇지만 오늘날 전문가들은 근력 운동의 중요성을 이해하고 그것을 경기의 일부로 만들어 오고 있다.

Why? 왜 정답일까?

근력 운동은 본디 야구 선수를 위한 운동으로 여겨지지 않았지만 시간이 지나며 야구 선수를 위한 운동의 일부로 자리하게 되었다는 내용을 다룬 글이다. 하지만 ③은 보디빌딩 운동과 운동선수용 운동의 차이를 설명하는 데 중점을 두고 있다. 따라서 전체 흐름과 관계없는 문장은 ③이다.

- conditioning ⑩ 훈련, 조절
- isolated ⓐ 분리된, 고립된
- weight lifting ⑩ 역도
- proper ⓐ 적절한
- flexibility ⑩ 유연성
- athletic ⓐ 운동선수의
- interfere with ⓥ ~을 방해하다

구문 풀이

9행 They feared that weight lifting and building large muscles would cause
players to lose flexibility and (would) interfere with quickness and proper technique.

---

36 작은 요구를 먼저 한 후 큰 요구를 제시하는 설득의 기술 | 정답률 64% | 정답 ②

주어진 글 다음에 이어질 글의 순서로 가장 적절한 것을 고르시오.

① (A) - (C) - (B)   ☑ (B) - (A) - (C)
③ (B) - (C) - (A)   ④ (C) - (A) - (B)
⑤ (C) - (B) - (A)

Making a small request / that people will accept / will naturally increase the chances / of their accepting a bigger request afterwards.
작은 요구를 하는 것은 / 사람들이 수락할 / 가능성을 자연스럽게 증가시킬 것이다. / 나중에 그들이 더 큰 요구를 수락할

(B) For instance, / a salesperson might request you to sign a petition / to prevent cruelty against animals.
예를 들어 / 한 판매원이 여러분에게 청원서에 서명하도록 요구할지도 모른다. / 동물에 대한 잔인함을 막기 위한

This is a very small request, / and most people will do what the salesperson asks.
이것은 아주 작은 요구이고 / 대부분의 사람들은 판매원이 요구하는 바를 할 것이다.

(A) After this, the salesperson asks you / if you are interested / in buying any cruelty-free cosmetics from their store.
그 이후에 판매원은 여러분에게 물어본다. / 여러분이 관심이 있는지를 / 잔인함을 가하지 않은 어떤 화장품을 자신의 매장에서 사는 것에

Given the fact / that most people agree to the prior request / to sign the petition, / they will be more likely to purchase the cosmetics.
사실을 고려하면 / 이전 요구에 사람들이 동의한다는 / 청원서에 서명해 달라는 / 그들이 화장품을 구매할 가능성이 더 높을 것이다.

(C) They make such purchases / because the salesperson takes advantage of a human tendency / to be consistent in their words and actions.
그들은 그러한 구매를 한다. / 그 판매원이 인간의 경향을 이용하기 때문에 / 자기 말과 행동에 있어 일관되고자 하는

People want to be consistent / and will keep saying yes / if they have already said it once.
사람들은 일관되기를 원하며 / 계속 예라고 말할 것이다. / 만약 자신이 이미 한번 그렇게 말했다면

사람들이 수락할 작은 요구를 하는 것은 나중에 그들이 더 큰 요구를 수락할 가능성을 자연스럽게 증가시킬 것이다.

(B) 예를 들어 한 판매원이 여러분에게 동물들에 대한 잔인함을 막기 위한 청원서에 서명하도록 요구할지도 모른다. 이것은 아주 작은 요구이고 대부분의 사람들은 판매원이 요구하는 바를 할 것이다.

(A) 그 이후에 판매원은 여러분에게 (동물들에게) 잔인함을 가하지 않은 어떤 화장품을 자신의 매장에서 사는 것에 관심이 있는지를 물어본다. 청원서에 서명해 달라는 이전 요구에 사람들이 동의한다는 사실을 고려하면 그들이 화장품을 구매할 가능성이 더 높을 것이다.

(C) 그 판매원이 자기 말과 행동에 있어 일관되고자 하는 인간의 경향을 이용하기 때문에 그들은 그러한 구매를 한다. 사람들은 일관되기를 원하며 만약 자신이 이미 한번 그렇게 말했다면 계속 예라고 말할 것이다.

Why? 왜 정답일까?

작은 요구를 먼저 한 후 큰 요구를 제시하면 사람들이 큰 요구를 수용할 가능성이 높아질 수 있다고 언급한 주어진 글 뒤에는, 판매원이 먼저 동물 학대에 반대하는 청원서를 작성해달라고 부탁하는 예를 제시하는 (B), 이후에 판매원이 동물에게 해를 가하지 않은 화장품 구매를 권유한다는 내용의 (A), 이 경우 사람들이 화장품 구매까지 하게 될 가능성이 높아지는 이유를 설명하는 (C)가 차례로 이어지는 것이 자연스럽다. 따라서 글의 순서로 가장 적절한 것은 ② '(B) - (A) - (C)'이다.

- cruelty ⑩ 잔인함
- consistent ⓐ 일관적인
- take advantage of ⓥ ~을 이용하다

구문 풀이

1행 Making a small request [that people will accept] will naturally increase the chances of their accepting a bigger request afterwards.

5행 Given the fact [that most people agree to the prior request to sign the petition], they will be more likely to purchase the cosmetics.

★★★ 등급을 가르는 문제!

37 소수 집단과 다수 집단의 건강 지표 차이 | 정답률 38% | 정답 ②

주어진 글 다음에 이어질 글의 순서로 가장 적절한 것을 고르시오. [3점]

① (A) - (C) - (B)   ☑ (B) - (A) - (C)   ③ (B) - (C) - (A)
④ (C) - (A) - (B)   ⑤ (C) - (B) - (A)

Many studies have shown / that people's health and subjective well-being / are affected by ethnic relations.
많은 연구들이 보여주었다. / 사람들의 건강과 주관적 웰빙이 / 민족 관계에 의해 영향을 받는다는 것

Members of minority groups in general / have poorer health outcomes / than the majority group.
소수 집단의 구성원들이 일반적으로 / 더 좋지 않은 건강 결과를 보인다. / 다수 집단보다

(B) But that difference remains / even when obvious factors, / such as social class and access to medical services / are controlled for.
그러나 그러한 차이가 남아 있다. / 명백한 요소들이 / 사회 계층과 의료 서비스에 대한 접근성 같은 / 통제될 때조차도

This suggests / that dominance relations have their own effect / on people's health.
이것은 보여 준다. / 우세 관계가 그 자체의 영향을 미친다는 것을 / 사람들의 건강에

How could that be the case?
어떻게 그럴 수 있을까?

(A) One possible answer is stress.
한 가지 가능한 답은 스트레스이다.

From multiple physiological studies, / we know / that encounters with members of other ethnic-racial categories, / even in the relatively safe environment of laboratories, / trigger stress responses.
다수의 생리학적 연구를 통해 / 우리는 안다. / 다른 민족적-인종적 범주의 구성원들과 마주치는 것이 / 비교적 안전한 실험실 환경에서조차도 / 스트레스 반응을 유발한다는 것을

(C) Minority individuals / have many encounters with majority individuals, / each of which may trigger such responses.
소수 집단의 개인들은 / 다수 집단의 개인들과 많은 마주침을 가지며, / 각각의 마주침은 이러한 반응을 유발할지도 모른다.

However minimal these effects may be, / their frequency may increase total stress, / which would account for / part of the health disadvantage of minority individuals.
이러한 영향이 아무리 작을지라도 / 그것의 빈번한 발생이 총체적 스트레스를 증가시킬지도 모르며 / 이는 설명할 것이다. / 소수 집단 개인들의 건강상 불이익의 일부

많은 연구들이 사람들의 건강과 주관적 웰빙이 민족 관계에 의해 영향을 받는다는 것을 보여주었다. 소수 집단의 구성원들이 일반적으로 다수 집단보다 더 좋지 않은 건강 결과를 보인다.

(B) 그러나 사회 계층과 의료 서비스에 대한 접근성 같은 명백한 요소들이 통제될 때조차도 그러한 차이가 남아 있다. 이것은 우세 관계가 사람들의 건강에 자체적인 영향을 미친다는 것을 보여 준다. 어떻게 그럴 수 있을까?

(A) 한 가지 가능한 답은 스트레스이다. 다수의 생리학적 연구를 통해 우리는 비교적 안전한 실험실 환경에서조차도 다른 민족적 - 인종적 범주의 구성원들과 마주치는 것이 스트레스 반응을 유발한다는 것을 안다.

(C) 소수 집단의 개인들은 다수 집단의 개인들과 많이 마주치며, 각각의 마주침은 이러한 반응을 유발할지도 모른다. 이러한 영향이 아무리 작을지라도 그것의 빈번한 발생이 총체적 스트레스를 증가시킬지도 모르며 이는 소수 집단 개인들의 건강상 불이익의 일부를 설명할 것이다.

Why? 왜 정답일까?

소수 집단의 구성원들이 대체로 다수 집단의 구성원보다 건강이 더 좋지 않다는 일반적인 내용을 제시하는 주어진 글 뒤에는, 심지어 사회 계층이나 의료 서비스에 대한 접근성 등 다른 요소가 통제되었을 때조차 왜 이러한 결과가 나타나는지 자문하는 (B), 그 답이 스트레스에 있음을 제시하는 (A), 답을 보충 설명하는 (C)가 차례로 이어지는 것이 자연스럽다. 따라서 글의 순서로 가장 적절한 것은 ② '(B) - (A) - (C)'이다.

- subjective ⓐ 주관적인
- physiological ⓐ 생리학적인
- trigger ⓥ 유발하다
- have an effect on ⓥ ~에 영향을 미치다
- account for ⓥ ~을 설명하다
- ethnic ⓐ 민족적인
- encounter ⑩ 마주침 ⓥ 마주치다
- dominance ⑩ 우세
- frequency ⑩ 빈도
- disadvantage ⑩ 불이익

구문 풀이

15행 However minimal these effects may be, / their frequency may increase total stress, which would account for part of the health disadvantage of minority individuals.

★★ 문제 해결 꿀~팁 ★★

▶ 많이 틀린 이유는?
주어진 글의 Members of minority groups만 보고 바로 (C)를 연결시켜서는 안 된다. 주어진 글의 마지막 문장은 전체적으로 볼 때 소수 집단 사람들과 다수 집단 사람들의 건강 지표상 차이를 언급하는 내용이어서, 이를 (B)에서 that difference로 요약하는 것이다.

▶ 문제 해결 방법은?
주어진 글의 마지막 문장이 (B)의 that difference로, (B)의 'How could that be the case?'라는 질문이 (A)의 One possible answer라는 답으로 연결된다는 것을 파악하면 쉽게 정답을 찾을 수 있다.

38 무대에서 관객을 집중시키는 방법
정답률 58% | 정답 ③

글의 흐름으로 보아, 주어진 문장이 들어가기에 가장 적절한 곳을 고르시오.

Achieving focus in a movie is easy.
영화에서 (관객의) 집중을 얻는 쉽다.

Directors can simply point the camera / at whatever they want the audience to look at.
감독은 단지 카메라를 향하게 하면 된다. / 자신이 관객으로 하여금 바라보기를 원하는 어떤 것에든

① Close-ups and slow camera shots / can emphasize a killer's hand / or a character's brief glance of guilt.
근접 촬영과 느린 카메라 촬영이 / 살인자의 손을 강조할 수 있다. / 또는 등장인물의 짧은 죄책감의 눈짓

② On stage, focus is much more difficult / because the audience is free to look / wherever they like.
무대 위에서는 (관객의) 집중이 훨씬 더 어려운 일이다. / 관객이 자유롭게 볼 수 있기 때문에 / 자신이 원하는 어느 곳이든

☑ The stage director must gain the audience's attention / and direct their eyes to a particular spot or actor.
무대 감독은 관객의 주의를 얻고 / 그들의 시선을 특정한 장소나 배우로 향하게 해야만 한다.

This can be done / through lighting, costumes, scenery, voice, and movements.
이것은 이루어질 수 있다. / 조명, 의상, 배경, 목소리, 움직임을 통해

④ Focus can be gained / by simply putting a spotlight on one actor, / by having one actor in red and everyone else in gray, / or by having one actor move / while the others remain still.
(관객의) 집중은 얻어질 수 있다. / 단지 한 명의 배우에게 스포트라이트를 비추거나, / 한 명의 배우는 빨간색으로 입히고 다른 모든 배우들은 회색으로 입히거나, / 한 명의 배우는 움직임으로써 / 다른 배우들이 가만히 있는 동안

⑤ All these techniques / will quickly draw the audience's attention to the actor / whom the director wants to be in focus.
이러한 모든 기법들은 / 관객의 주의를 배우 쪽으로 빠르게 끌 것이다. / 감독이 (관객의) 집중 안에 들기를 원하는

영화에서 (관객의) 집중을 얻기는 쉽다. 감독은 자신이 관객으로 하여금 바라보기를 원하는 어떤 것에든 단지 카메라를 향하게 하면 된다. ① 근접 촬영과 느린 카메라 촬영이 살인자의 손이나 등장인물의 짧은 죄책감의 눈짓을 강조할 수 있다. ② 무대 위에서는 관객이 자신이 원하는 어느 곳이든 자유롭게 볼 수 있기 때문에 (관객의) 집중이 훨씬 더 어려운 일이다. ③ 무대 감독은 관객의 주의를 얻고 그들의 시선을 특정한 장소나 배우로 향하게 해야만 한다. 이것은 조명, 의상, 배경, 목소리, 움직임을 통해 이루어질 수 있다. ④ (관객의) 집중은 단지 한 명의 배우에게 스포트라이트를 비추거나, 한 명의 배우는 빨간색으로 입히고 다른 모든 배우들은 회색으로 입히거나, 다른 배우들이 가만히 있는 동안 한 명의 배우는 움직이게 함으로써 얻어질 수 있다. ⑤ 이러한 모든 기법들은 감독이 (관객의) 집중 안에 들기를 원하는 배우 쪽으로 관객의 주의를 빠르게 끌 것이다.

Why? 왜 정답일까?

③ 앞에서 무대 위에서는 관객을 집중시키기가 더 어렵다고 언급한 데 이어, 주어진 문장은 '무대 감독'이 관객의 주의를 끌어 특정한 방향으로 시선을 향하게 해야 한다고 설명한다. ③ 뒤의 문장은 주어진 문장의 내용을 This로 가리키며, 관객의 주의를 얻기 위해서는 조명, 의상, 배경, 목소리, 움직임 등이 동원될 수 있다고 한다. 따라서 주어진 문장이 들어가기에 가장 적절한 곳은 ③이다.

● emphasize ⓥ 강조하다
● guilt ⓝ 죄책감
● glance ⓝ 흘긋 봄
● draw A's attention to B A의 관심을 B로 돌리다

구문 풀이

3행 Directors can simply point the camera at whatever they want the audience to look at.
복합관계대명사 「want + 목적어 + to부정사 : (= anything that) ~이 …하기를 원하다」

12행 All these techniques will quickly draw the audience's attention to the actor [whom the director wants to be in focus].
목적격 관계대명사 / 선행사 / 주어 / 동사 / 목적격 보어

39 첫인상의 중요성
정답률 39% | 정답 ⑤

글의 흐름으로 보아, 주어진 문장이 들어가기에 가장 적절한 곳을 고르시오.

You've probably heard the expression, / "first impressions matter a lot".
여러분은 아마도 표현을 들어본 적이 있을 것이다. / '첫인상이 매우 중요하다'라는

① Life really doesn't give many people a second chance / to make a good first impression.
삶은 실제로 많은 사람들에게 두 번째 기회를 주지 않는다. / 좋은 첫인상을 만들

② It has been determined / that it takes only a few seconds / for anyone to assess another individual.
밝혀져 왔다. / 단지 몇 초만 걸린다는 것이 / 누군가가 또 다른 개인을 평가하는 데

③ This is very noticeable in recruitment processes, / where top recruiters can predict the direction / of their eventual decision on any candidate / within a few seconds of introducing themselves.
이것은 채용 과정에서 매우 두드러지는데, / 최고의 모집자는 방향을 예측할 수 있다. / 어떤 지원자에 대한 자신의 최종 결정의 / 그들이 자신을 소개하는 몇 초 안에

④ So, a candidate's CV may 'speak' knowledge and competence, / but their appearance and introduction / may tell of a lack of coordination, fear, and poor interpersonal skills.
따라서 후보자의 이력서가 지식과 능력을 '진술'할지도 모르지만, / 그들의 외모와 소개는 / 신체 조정 능력의 부족, 불안, 그리고 형편없는 대인 관계 기술을 알려줄지도 모른다.

☑ In this way, / quick judgements are not only relevant in employment matters; / they are equally applicable / in love and relationship matters too.
이런 식으로, / 빠른 판단들이 단지 채용 문제에만 관련된 것은 아니며 / 이것들은 똑같이 적용된다. / 또한 사랑과 관계 문제에도

On a date with a wonderful somebody / who you've painstakingly tracked down for months, / subtle things like bad breath or wrinkled clothes / may spoil your noble efforts.
멋진 누군가와의 데이트에서, / 여러분이 몇 달간 공들여 쫓아다닌 / 입 냄새 또는 구겨진 옷과 같은 미묘한 것들이 / 여러분의 숭고한 노력을 망칠지도 모른다.

여러분은 아마도 '첫인상이 매우 중요하다'라는 표현을 들어본 적이 있을 것이다. ① 삶은 실제로 많은 사람들에게 좋은 첫인상을 만들 두 번째 기회를 주지 않는다. ② 누군가가 또 다른 개인을 평가하는 데 단지 몇 초만 걸린다는 것이 밝혀져 왔다. ③ 이것은 채용 과정에서 매우 두드러지는데, 채용 과정에서 최고의 모집자는 (지원자가) 자신을 소개하는 몇 초 안에 지원

자에 대한 자신의 최종 결정의 방향을 예측할 수 있다. ④ 따라서 후보자의 이력서가 지식과 능력을 '진술'할지도 모르지만, 그들의 외모와 소개는 신체 조정 능력의 부족, 불안, 그리고 형편없는 대인 관계 기술을 알려줄지도 모른다. ⑤ 이런 식으로 빠른 판단들은 단지 채용 문제에만 관련된 것은 아니며 또한 사랑과 관계 문제에도 똑같이 적용된다. 여러분이 몇 달간 공들여 쫓아다닌 멋진 누군가와의 데이트에서, 입 냄새 또는 구겨진 옷과 같은 미묘한 것들이 여러분의 숭고한 노력을 망칠지도 모른다.

Why? 왜 정답일까?

⑤ 앞에서 채용 과정을 예로 들어 첫인상의 중요성을 주로 설명한 데 이어, 주어진 문장은 첫인상의 문제가 사랑이나 관계 문제에도 마찬가지로 적용될 수 있다고 한다. ⑤ 뒤의 문장은 데이트 상황에서 첫인상을 망치게 되면 몇 달간의 노력이 허사가 될 수도 있다는 설명으로 주어진 문장의 내용을 보충한다. 따라서 주어진 문장이 들어가기에 가장 적절한 곳은 ⑤이다.

● relevant ⓐ 관련 있는, 적절한
● assess ⓥ 평가하다
● recruitment ⓝ 채용, 모집
● eventual ⓐ 최종의, 궁극적인
● competence ⓝ 능력, 역량
● coordination ⓝ (신체 동작의) 조정력
● painstakingly ⓐⓓ 공들여, 힘들여
● spoil ⓥ 망치다
● applicable ⓐ 적용 가능한
● noticeable ⓐ 두드러지는, 눈에 띄는
● predict ⓥ 예측하다
● candidate ⓝ 지원자, 후보자
● tell of ⓥ ~을 알려주다
● interpersonal ⓐ 대인 관계의
● subtle ⓐ 미묘한, 감지하기 힘든

구문 풀이

13행 On a date with a wonderful somebody [who(m) you've painstakingly
선행사 / 목적격 관계대명사
tracked down for months], subtle things like bad breath or wrinkled clothes may
주어 / 동사
spoil your noble efforts.

40 동일한 할인액에 대한 인식을 좌우하는 요인
정답률 51% | 정답 ④

다음 글의 내용을 한 문장으로 요약하고자 한다. 빈칸 (A), (B)에 들어갈 말로 가장 적절한 것은?

(A)	(B)
① absolute 절대적인	modify 수정하다
② absolute 절대적인	express 표현하다
③ identical 동일한	produce 만들어내다
☑④ relative 상대적인	perceive 인식하다
⑤ relative 상대적인	advertise 광고하다

The perception of the same amount of discount on a product / depends on its relation to the initial price.
상품의 똑같은 할인액에 대한 인식은 / 그것의 최초 가격과의 관계에 달려있다.

In one study, / respondents were presented with a purchase situation.
한 연구에서, / 응답자들은 어떤 구매 상황을 제시받았다.

The persons put in the situation of buying a calculator / that cost $15 / found out from the vendor / that the same product was available / in a different store 20 minutes away / and at a promotional price of $10.
계산기를 사는 상황에 놓인 사람들은 / 15달러 가격의 / 판매자로부터 알게 되었다. / 같은 제품이 이용 가능하다는 것을 / 20분 떨어진 다른 상점에서 / 10달러의 판촉가에

In this case, 68% of respondents / decided to make their way down to the store / in order to save $5.
이 경우 응답자의 68%가 / 그 가게까지 가기로 결심했다. / 5달러를 절약하기 위해

In the second condition, / which involved buying a jacket for $125, / the respondents were also told / that the same product was available / in a store 20 minutes away / and cost $120 there.
두 번째 상황에서, / 이는 125달러짜리 재킷을 사는 것과 관련 있었는데, / 응답자들은 또한 들었다. / 같은 제품이 이용 가능하고 / 20분 떨어진 상점에서 / 그곳에서는 120달러라고

This time, only 29% of the persons said / that they would get the cheaper jacket.
이번에는 단지 사람들의 29%만이 말했다. / 그들이 더 저렴한 재킷을 살 것이라고

In both cases, the product was $5 cheaper, / but in the first case, the amount was 1/3 of the price, / and in the second, it was 1/25 of the price.
두 경우 모두 제품은 5달러 더 저렴했으나, / 첫 번째의 경우 그 액수가 가격의 3분의 1이었고, / 두 번째의 경우 그것은 가격의 25분의 1이었다.

What differed in both of these situations / was the price context of the purchase.
이 두 상황 모두에서 달랐던 것은 / 구매의 가격 맥락이었다.

➡ When the same amount of discount is given / in a purchasing situation, / the (A) relative value of the discount / affects how people (B) perceive its value.
동일한 정도의 할인액이 주어질 때, / 구매 상황에서 / 그 할인의 상대적인 가치가 / 사람들이 그 가치를 어떻게 인식하는지에 영향을 미친다.

상품의 똑같은 할인액에 대한 인식은 그것의 최초 가격과의 관계에 달려있다. 한 연구에서, 응답자들은 어떤 구매 상황을 제시받았다. 15달러 가격의 계산기를 사는 상황에 놓인 사람들이 같은 제품을 20분 떨어진 다른 상점에서 10달러의 판촉가에 살 수 있다는 것을 판매자로부터 알게 되었다. 이 경우 응답자의 68%가 5달러를 절약하기 위해 그 가게까지 가기로 결심했다. 두 번째 상황에서, 이는 125달러짜리 재킷을 사는 것과 관련 있었는데, 응답자들은 또한 같은 제품을 20분 떨어진 상점에서 살 수 있고 그곳에서는 120달러라고 들었다. 이번에는 단지 사람들의 29%만이 더 저렴한 재킷을 살 것이라고 말했다. 두 경우 모두 제품은 5달러 더 저렴했으나, 첫 번째의 경우 그 액수가 가격의 3분의 1이었고, 두 번째의 경우 그것은 가격의 25분의 1이었다. 이 두 상황 모두에서 달랐던 것은 구매의 가격 맥락이었다.

➡ 구매 상황에서 동일한 정도의 할인액이 주어질 때, 그 할인의 (A) 상대적인 가치가 사람들이 그 가치를 어떻게 (B) 인식하는지에 영향을 미친다.

Why? 왜 정답일까?

첫 문장에서 똑같은 할인액에 대한 인식도 최초 가격에 따라 달라질 수 있다(The perception of the same amount of discount on a product depends on its relation to the initial price.)는 주제가 제시되는 것으로 보아, 요약문의 (A)와 (B)에 들어갈 말로 가장 적절한 것은 ④ '(A) relative(상대적인), (B) perceive(인식하다)'이다.

● perception ⓝ 인식
● be presented with ~을 제시받다
● initial ⓐ 최초의
● calculator ⓝ 계산기

- **promotional** ⓐ 판촉의, 홍보의
- **absolute** ⓐ 절대적인
- **differ** ⓥ 다르다
- **identical** ⓐ 동일한

구문 풀이

3행 The persons [put in the situation of buying a calculator {that cost $15}]
　　　　주어　　거품사　　　　　　　　　　　　　　　선행사　　주격 관계대명사
found out from the vendor {that the same product was available in a different
동사　　전명구(삽입)　　접속사(~것)
store 20 minutes away and at a promotional price of $10}. 〔 〕: 목적어

41-42 주머니고양이의 모방 본능

Behavioral ecologists have observed clever copying behavior / among many of our close animal relatives.
행동 생태학자들이 영리한 모방 행동을 관찰해 왔다. / 우리와 가까운 다수의 동류 동물에게서

One example was uncovered by behavioral ecologists / studying the behavior of a small Australian animal / called the quoll.
한 예가 행동 생태학자들에 의해 발견되었다. / 작은 호주 동물의 행동을 연구하는 / 주머니고양이라고 불리는

Its survival was being (a) <u>threatened</u> by the cane toad, / an invasive species / introduced to Australia in the 1930s.
이들의 생존은 수수두꺼비에 의해 위협받고 있었다. / 외래종인 / 1930년대에 호주에 도입된

To a quoll, these toads look as tasty / as they are (b) <u>poisonous</u>, / and the quolls who ate them / suffered fatal consequences at a speedy rate.
주머니고양이에게 이 두꺼비들은 먹음직스러워 보이는 / 독성이 있는 만큼이나 / 그들을 먹은 주머니고양이는 / 빠른 속도로 치명적인 결과를 겪었다.

Behavioral ecologists identified a clever solution / by using quolls' instincts to imitate.
행동 생태학자들은 영리한 해결책을 찾아냈다. / 주머니고양이의 모방하는 본능을 이용하여

Scientists fed small groups of quolls toad sausages, / containing harmless but nausea-inducing chemicals, / conditioning them to (c) <u>avoid</u> the toads.
과학자들은 주머니고양이 소집단에게 두꺼비 소시지를 먹여 / 무해하지만 메스꺼움을 유발하는 화학 물질을 함유한 / 그들이 두꺼비를 피하도록 조건화했다.

Groups of these 'toad-smart' quolls / were then released back into the wild: / they taught their own offspring what they'd learned.
이러한 '두꺼비에 대해 똑똑해진' 주머니고양이 집단은 / 그 후 야생으로 다시 방출되었고 그들은 자신이 배운 것을 자기 새끼들에게 가르쳤다.

Other quolls copied these (d) <u>constructive</u> behaviors / through a process of social learning.
다른 주머니고양이들은 이러한 건설적인 행동들을 모방했다. / 사회적 학습의 과정을 통해 〔42번의 근거〕

「As each baby quoll learned / to keep away from the hazardous toads,」 / the chances of the survival of the whole quoll species / — and not just that of each individual quoll — / were (e) <u>improved</u>.
각각의 새끼 주머니고양이가 배웠으므로, / 위험한 두꺼비를 피하는 법을 / 전체 주머니고양이 종의 생존 확률이 / 개별 주머니고양이 각각의 생존 확률 뿐만 아니라 / 높아졌다.

「The quolls were saved / via minimal human interference / because ecologists were able to take advantage of quolls' natural imitative instincts.」 〔41번의 근거〕
주머니고양이는 구해졌는데, / 최소한의 인간의 개입을 통해 / 왜냐하면 생태학자들이 주머니고양이의 타고난 모방 본능을 이용할 수 있었기 때문이었다.

행동 생태학자들이 우리와 가까운 다수의 동류 동물에게서 영리한 모방 행동을 관찰해 왔다. 한 예가 주머니고양이라고 불리는 작은 호주 동물의 행동을 연구하는 행동 생태학자들에 의해 발견되었다. 이들의 생존은 1930년대에 호주에 도입된 외래종인 수수두꺼비에 의해 (a) 위협받고 있었다. 주머니고양이에게 이 두꺼비들은 (b) 독성이 있는 만큼이나 먹음직스러워 보이며 그들을 먹은 주머니고양이는 빠른 속도로 치명적인 결과를 겪었다. 행동 생태학자들은 주머니고양이의 모방하는 본능을 이용하여 영리한 해결책을 찾아냈다. 과학자들은 주머니고양이 소집단에게 무해하지만 메스꺼움을 유발하는 화학 물질을 함유한 두꺼비 소시지를 먹여 그들이 두꺼비를 (c) 피하도록 조건화했다. 이러한 '두꺼비에 대해 똑똑해진' 주머니고양이 집단은 그 후 야생으로 다시 방출되었고 자신이 배운 것을 자기 새끼들에게 가르쳤다. 다른 주머니고양이들은 사회적 학습의 과정을 통해 이러한 (d) 건설적인 행동들을 모방했다. 각각의 새끼 주머니고양이가 위험한 두꺼비를 피하는 법을 배웠으므로, 개별 주머니고양이 각각의 생존 확률뿐만 아니라 전체 주머니고양이 종의 생존 확률이 (e) 줄어들었다(→ 높아졌다). 주머니고양이는 최소한의 인간의 개입을 통해 구해졌는데, 왜냐하면 생태학자들이 주머니고양이의 타고난 모방 본능을 이용할 수 있었기 때문이었다.

- **ecologist** ⓝ 생태학자
- **threaten** ⓥ 위협하다
- **introduce** ⓥ 도입하다
- **consequence** ⓝ 결과
- **instinct** ⓝ 본능
- **induce** ⓥ 유발하다
- **constructive** ⓐ 건설적인
- **interference** ⓝ 개입, 간섭
- **precisely** ⓐⓓ 정확히
- **uncover** ⓥ 밝히다
- **invasive** ⓐ 침입의
- **fatal** ⓐ 치명적인
- **identify** ⓥ 찾아내다, 확인하다
- **harmless** ⓐ 무해한
- **offspring** ⓝ 자손
- **hazardous** ⓐ 위험한
- **take advantage of** ⓥ ~을 이용하다

구문 풀이

6행 To a quoll, these toads look as tasty as they are poisonous, and the quolls
　　　　　　　　　　　　　　　「as + 원급 + as : ~만큼 ~한」　　　　주어(선행사)
[who ate them] suffered fatal consequences at a speedy rate.
= toads 타동사(~을 겪다)　　목적어

---

41 제목 파악 정답률 56% | 정답 ①

윗글의 제목으로 가장 적절한 것은?

✓ ① Imitative Instinct as a Key to Survival for Animals – 동물에게 있어 생존의 열쇠인 모방 본능
② Copy Quickly and Precisely to Be Productive – 생산적이 되려면 빠르고 정확하게 복제하라
③ How to Stop the Spread of Invasive Species – 침입종의 확산을 막는 방법
④ The Role of Threats in Animal Cooperation – 동물 협력에 있어 위협의 역할
⑤ Ideal Habitats for Diverse Wildlife – 다양한 야생동물에게 이상적인 서식지

Why? 왜 정답일까?

예시의 결론을 말하는 마지막 문장에서 주머니고양이들이 인간의 최소 개입으로도 살아남을 수 있었던

까닭은 특유의 모방 본능 덕분이었다고 언급하는 것으로 볼 때, 글의 제목으로 가장 적절한 것은 ① '동물에게 있어 생존의 열쇠인 모방 본능'이다.

42 어휘 추론 정답률 46% | 정답 ⑤

밑줄 친 (a) ~ (e) 중에서 문맥상 낱말의 쓰임이 적절하지 않은 것은? [3점]

① (a)　② (b)　③ (c)　④ (d)　✓ ⑤ (e)

Why? 왜 정답일까?

(e)가 포함된 문장의 As절에서 모방 본능을 통해 새끼 주머니고양이들이 위험한 두꺼비를 피하도록 학습했다는 내용이 나오는 것으로 보아, 각각의 주머니고양이뿐 아니라 종 전체의 생존 확률이 '올라갔다'는 결론이 뒤따라야 한다. 따라서 (e)의 reduced를 improved로 고쳐야 한다. 문맥상 낱말의 쓰임이 적절하지 않은 것은 ⑤ '(e)'이다.

43-45 적이 될 뻔한 사냥꾼 이웃과 친구가 된 농부

(A)

A long time ago, / a farmer in a small town had a neighbor / who was a hunter.
오래전 / 작은 마을의 한 농부가 이웃을 두었다. / 사냥꾼인

The hunter owned a few fierce and poorly-trained hunting dogs.
사냥꾼은 사납고 훈련이 잘되지 않은 사냥개 몇 마리를 소유하고 있었다.

They jumped the fence frequently / and chased the farmer's lambs.
그들은 울타리를 자주 뛰어넘어 / 농부의 새끼 양들을 쫓아 다녔다.

The farmer asked his neighbor / to keep (a) <u>his</u> dogs in check, / but his words fell on deaf ears.
농부는 그 이웃에게 요청했지만, / 그의 개들을 제지해 달라고 / 이 말은 무시되었다.

「One day when the dogs jumped the fence, / they attacked and severely injured several of the lambs.」 〔45번 ①의 근거〕 일치
그 개들이 울타리를 뛰어넘는 어느 날, / 그들은 새끼 양 중 몇 마리를 공격해서 심하게 다치게 했다.

(D)

The farmer had had enough by this point.
농부는 이쯤 되자 진절머리가 났다.

「He went to the nearest city / to consult a judge.」 〔45번 ⑤의 근거〕 일치
그는 가장 가까운 도시로 갔다. / 재판관에게 조언을 구하기 위해

After listening carefully to his story, / the judge said, / "I could punish the hunter / and instruct (e) <u>him</u> / to keep his dogs chained or lock them up.
그의 이야기를 주의 깊게 들은 후 / 그 재판관이 말했다. / "저는 사냥꾼을 벌하고 / 그에게 지시할 수 있습니다. / 개들을 사슬로 묶거나 가두라고

But you would lose a friend / and gain an enemy.
하지만 당신은 친구를 잃고 / 적을 얻게 될 것입니다.

Which would you rather have for a neighbor, / a friend or an enemy?"
당신은 이웃을 어느 쪽으로 두고 싶습니까? / 친구 아니면 적 중에"

The farmer replied that he preferred a friend.
농부는 친구가 더 좋다고 대답했다.

(C)

"All right, I will offer you a solution / that keeps your lambs safe / and will also turn your neighbor into a good friend."
"좋습니다. 저는 당신에게 해결책을 제안하겠습니다. / 당신의 새끼 양들을 안전하게 지키고 / 당신의 이웃 또한 좋은 친구로 바꿀 수 있는"

「Having heard the judge's solution, / the farmer agreed.」 〔45번 ③의 근거〕 일치
재판관의 해결책을 듣고, / 농부는 동의했다.

As soon as the farmer reached home, / he immediately put the judge's suggestions to the test.
농부가 집에 도착하자마자, / 그는 즉시 재판관의 제안을 시험해 보았다.

(d) He selected three of the cutest lambs from his farm.
그는 자신의 농장에서 가장 귀여운 새끼 양들 중 세 마리를 골랐다.

「He then presented them / to his neighbor's three small sons.」 〔45번 ④의 근거〕 일치
그리고 나서 그는 그것들을 선물했다. / 자기 이웃의 어린 세 아들들에게

The children accepted with joy / and began to play with them.
아이들은 기뻐하며 받고 / 새끼 양들과 함께 놀기 시작했다.

(B)

To protect his sons' newly acquired playmates, / the hunter built a strong doghouse for his dogs.
자기 아들들의 새로 얻은 놀이 친구를 보호하기 위해서, / 사냥꾼은 자기 개들을 위해 튼튼한 개집을 지었다.

The dogs never bothered the farmer's lambs again.
그 개들은 농부의 새끼 양들을 다시는 괴롭히지 않았다.

Out of gratitude / for the farmer's generosity toward (b) <u>his</u> children, / the hunter often invited the farmer for feasts.
감사한 마음에서, / 자기 아이들에 대한 농부의 관대함에 / 사냥꾼은 농부를 진수성찬에 자주 초대했다.

「In turn, the farmer offered him / lamb meat and cheese he had made.」 〔45번 ②의 근거〕 불일치
그 답례로 농부는 그에게 제공했다. / 양고기와 자신이 만든 치즈를

The farmer quickly developed a strong friendship with (c) <u>him</u>.
농부는 금세 그와 진한 우정을 키우게 되었다.

(A)

오래전 작은 마을의 한 농부가 사냥꾼인 이웃을 두었다. 사냥꾼은 사납고 훈련이 잘되지 않은 사냥개 몇 마리를 소유하고 있었다. 그들은 울타리를 자주 뛰어넘어 농부의 새끼 양들을 쫓아 다녔다. 농부는 그 이웃에게 (a) 그의 개들을 제지해 달라고 요청했지만, 이 말은 무시되었다. 그 개들이 울타리를 뛰어넘는 어느 날, 그들은 새끼 양 중 몇 마리를 공격해서 심하게 다치게 했다.

(D)

농부는 이쯤 되자 진절머리가 났다. 그는 재판관에게 조언을 구하기 위해 가장 가까운 도시로 갔다. 그의 이야기를 주의 깊게 들은 후 그 재판관이 말했다. "저는 사냥꾼을 벌하고 (e) 그에게 개들을 사슬로 묶거나 가두라고 지시할 수 있습니다. 하지만 당신은 친구를 잃고 적을 얻게 될 것입니다. 당신은 이웃을 친구 아니면 적, 어느 쪽으로 두고 싶습니까?" 농부는 친구가 더 좋다고 대답했다.

(C)

"좋습니다. 저는 당신에게 새끼 양들을 안전하게 지키고 당신의 이웃 또한 좋은 친구로 바꿀

수 있는 해결책을 제안하겠습니다." 재판관의 해결책을 듣고, 농부는 동의했다. 농부가 집에 도착하자마자, 그는 즉시 재판관의 제안을 시험해 보았다. (d) 그(the farmer)는 자신의 농장에서 가장 귀여운 새끼 양들 중 세 마리를 골랐다. 그러고 나서 그는 자기 이웃의 어린 세 아들들에게 그것들을 선물했다. 아이들은 기뻐하며 받고 새끼 양들과 함께 놀기 시작했다.

(B)

자기 아들들의 새로 얻은 놀이 친구들을 보호하기 위해서, 사냥꾼은 자기 개들을 위해 튼튼한 개집을 지었다. 그 개들은 농부의 새끼 양들을 다시는 괴롭히지 않았다. (b) 자기 아이들에 대한 농부의 관대함에 감사한 마음에서, 사냥꾼은 농부를 진수성찬에 자주 초대했다. 그 답례로 농부는 양고기와 자신이 만든 치즈를 제공했다. 농부는 금세 (c) 그와 진한 우정을 키우게 되었다.

- poorly-trained ⓐ 훈련이 잘되지 않은
- fall on deaf ears ⓥ 무시되다, 남의 귀에 들어가지 않다
- keep in check ⓥ 제지하다, 감독하다
- gratitude ⓝ 감사
- feast ⓝ 진수성찬, 연회
- suggestion ⓝ 제안
- frequently ⓐⓓ 자주
- severely ⓐⓓ 심하게
- generosity ⓝ 관대함
- put ~ to the test ⓥ ~을 시험해보다
- punish ⓥ 벌하다

구문 풀이

(A) 5행 One day [when the dogs jumped the fence], they attacked and severely
시간 선행사 관계부사   동사1
injured several of the lambs.
동사2
(C) 2행 Having heard the judge's solution, the farmer agreed.
완료분사구문(agreed보다 먼저 일어남)

43 글의 순서 파악 ······ 정답률 68% | 정답 ⑤

주어진 글 (A)에 이어질 내용을 순서에 맞게 배열한 것으로 가장 적절한 것은?

① (B) − (D) − (C)
② (C) − (B) − (D)
③ (C) − (D) − (B)
④ (D) − (B) − (C)
☑ (D) − (C) − (B)

Why? 왜 정답일까?

사냥개를 키우는 이웃 때문에 피해를 본 농부를 소개하는 (A) 뒤에는, 농부가 재판관에게 해결책을 구했다는 내용의 (D), 재판관이 준 해결책을 농부가 실천에 옮겼다는 내용의 (C), 해결책이 잘 통하여 사냥꾼 이웃과 농부가 친구가 되었다는 내용의 (B)가 차례로 이어져야 자연스럽다. 따라서 글의 순서로 가장 적절한 것은 ⑤ '(D) − (C) − (B)'이다.

44 지칭 추론 ······ 정답률 59% | 정답 ④

밑줄 친 (a) ~ (e) 중에서 가리키는 대상이 나머지 넷과 다른 것은?

① (a)   ② (b)   ③ (c)   ☑ (d)   ⑤ (e)

Why? 왜 정답일까?

(a), (b), (c), (e)는 the hunter를, (d)는 바로 앞 문장의 the farmer를 가리키므로, (a) ~ (e) 중에서 가리키는 대상이 다른 하나는 ④ '(d)'이다.

45 세부 내용 파악 ······ 정답률 60% | 정답 ②

윗글의 농부에 관한 내용으로 적절하지 <u>않은</u> 것은?

① 그의 양이 사냥개의 공격을 받았다.
☑ 사냥꾼에게 양고기와 치즈를 받았다.
③ 재판관의 해결책에 동의했다.
④ 세 명의 아들을 둔 이웃이 있었다.
⑤ 도시로 조언을 구하러 갔다.

Why? 왜 정답일까?

(B) 'In turn, the farmer offered him lamb meat and cheese he had made.'에서 농부는 친구가 된 사냥꾼에게 양고기와 치즈를 주었다고 하므로, 내용과 일치하지 않는 것은 ② '사냥꾼에게 양고기와 치즈를 받았다.'이다.

Why? 왜 오답일까?

① (A) 'One day when the dogs jumped the fence, they attacked and severely injured several of the lambs.'의 내용과 일치한다.
③ (C) 'Having heard the judge's solution, the farmer agreed.'의 내용과 일치한다.
④ (C) 'He then presented them to his neighbor's three small sons.'에서 이웃인 사냥꾼에게 세 명의 아들이 있었음을 알 수 있다.
⑤ (D) 'He went to the nearest city to consult a judge.'의 내용과 일치한다.

A	B	C	D
01 본능적인	01 fate	01 ⓝ	01 ⓙ
02 채용, 모집	02 refine	02 ⓑ	02 ⓔ
03 (갑자기 또는 완전히) 실패하다	03 abuse	03 ⓛ	03 ⓛ
04 ~에서 나오다	04 ritual	04 ⓓ	04 ⓒ
05 공존하다	05 visible	05 ⓜ	05 ⓗ
06 정확히	06 rounding	06 ⓕ	06 ⓜ
07 ~에 의존하다	07 resent	07 ⓚ	07 ⓖ
08 벌하다	08 humility	08 ⓖ	08 ⓞ
09 제한하다	09 polish	09 ⓞ	09 ⓕ
10 다르다	10 narrow	10 ⓙ	10 ⓑ
11 유망한	11 fame	11 ⓐ	11 ⓚ
12 대체물; 대체하다	12 symbolic	12 ⓗ	12 ⓓ
13 유연성	13 erase	13 ⓒ	13 ⓕ
14 그 결과	14 trigger	14 ⓔ	14 ⓐ
15 외교	15 glow	15 ⓘ	15 ⓝ
16 엄청난	16 equality	16 ⓘ	16 ⓘ
17 강조하다	17 assess	17 ⓢ	17 ⓢ
18 주관적인	18 absolute	18 ⓡ	18 ⓣ
19 혐의, 비난	19 venture	19 ⓠ	19 ⓟ
20 죄책감이 드는	20 stroll	20 ⓟ	20 ⓠ